OXFORD COMMENTARIES ON
INTERNATIONAL LAW

General Editors: *Professor Philip Alston*, Professor of International Law at New York University, and *Vaughan Lowe QC*, Essex Court Chambers, London; Emeritus Fellow, All Souls College, Oxford.

The UNCITRAL Arbitration Rules

The UNCITRAL Arbitration Rules

A Commentary

(With an Integrated and Comparative Discussion of the 2010 and 1976 UNCITRAL Arbitration Rules)

Second Edition

DAVID D. CARON
LEE M. CAPLAN

OXFORD
UNIVERSITY PRESS

Great Clarendon Street, Oxford, OX2 6DP,
United Kingdom

Oxford University Press is a department of the University of Oxford.
It furthers the University's objective of excellence in research, scholarship,
and education by publishing worldwide. Oxford is a registered trade mark of
Oxford University Press in the UK and in certain other countries

© David D. Caron and Lee M. Caplan, 2012

The moral rights of the authors have been asserted

First Edition published in 2013

All rights reserved. No part of this publication may be reproduced, stored in
a retrieval system, or transmitted, in any form or by any means, without the
prior permission in writing of Oxford University Press, or as expressly permitted
by law, by licence or under terms agreed with the appropriate reprographics
rights organization. Enquiries concerning reproduction outside the scope of the
above should be sent to the Rights Department, Oxford University Press, at the
address above

You must not circulate this work in any other form
and you must impose this same condition on any acquirer

Crown copyright material is reproduced under Class Licence
Number C01P0000148 with the permission of OPSI
and the Queen's Printer for Scotland

Published in the United States of America by Oxford University Press
198 Madison Avenue, New York, NY 10016, United States of America

British Library Cataloguing in Publication Data
Data available

Library of Congress Cataloging in Publication Data
Data available

ISBN 978–0–19–969630–7

Links to third party websites are provided by Oxford in good faith and
for information only. Oxford disclaims any responsibility for the materials
contained in any third party website referenced in this work.

To Susan, my partner in all things – DDC
To Christina, for all her love and support – LMC

Preface

This project arises out of our experiences, initially, as Legal Assistants at the Iran–US Claims Tribunal and, subsequently, as arbitration counsel, as scholars, as life-long students of international dispute resolution, and as a governmental representative to UNCITRAL. Our careers have witnessed the emergence of the 1976 UNCITRAL Rules through the work of the Iran–US Claims Tribunal's practice, its widespread designation as a basis for arbitration in bilateral investment treaties and its subsequent use in arbitrations brought under those treaties, and the global influence the Rules have played on the Rules adopted by Arbitration Centers in cities around the world and by global institutions offering arbitration services. For us, it has always been clear that the practice regarding the UNCITRAL Rules of Arbitral Procedure, if analyzed and accessible, would be very significant.

This commentary takes a unique approach. In addition to a commentary on the Rules based on their drafting history, the corpus of Iran–US Claims Tribunal practice, and the ever-growing practice of investor–state arbitrations constituted in accordance with the UNCITRAL Rules, this work reproduces the extracts from the procedural decisions of these various sources. Our experiences have repeatedly shown that new issues, issues of first impression, continue to arise in arbitration. For this reason, we believe access to the procedural decisions themselves is essential. Some of these decisions have been reprinted in various sources, but many have not. In preparing this study, thousands of procedural orders and decisions have been reviewed and many of those orders are easily available only in this volume. It is our hope that this study's dual function of analysis and access will lead to a more refined system of arbitral procedure, provide a sounding board for parties and arbitrators who seek to understand the issues before them, and promote further the arbitration regime we both feel is essential to more complex systems of order and interdependence.

The authors have greatly benefited from the assistance of many throughout their work on the second edition of this Commentary. We particularly wish to thank three research assistants for their outstanding and dedicated assistance in completing this revision: Preeti Khanna (LLM 2012 Berkeley), Rebecca Callaway (JD 2010 Berkeley) and Brittney Lovato (JD 2013 Berkeley). Many other students have assisted since the first edition of this Commentary: Anderson Berry, Hugh Carlson, Stephan Pages, Alexandra Widman, Luke Hagelberg, Shaina Johnson, Louise Balsan, Elliot Schackleford, Felix Mormann and Rodrigo Gil. Their interest and energy have been a constant source of inspiration.

David D. Caron, Berkeley
Lee M. Caplan,[1] Washington DC
March 2013

---

[1] The contributions to this book by Lee M. Caplan are a product of his own personal views and not those of the US Government.

Table of Contents

Table of Cases and Other Practice — xxvii
Table of Instruments — lix
List of Abbreviations — lxxxiii

Chapter 1: Introduction

1. Introduction — 1
2. The International Arbitral Process and the Work of UNCITRAL — 2
3. The Development of the UNCITRAL Rules of Procedure — 3
   A. The Drafting of the 1976 Rules — 3
   B. The UNCITRAL Rules and the Iran–US Claims Tribunal — 4
      (1) The Origins and Structure of the Iran–US Claims Tribunal — 4
      (2) The Tribunal's Use of the UNCITRAL Arbitration Rules — 5
   C. The UNCITRAL Rules and the 1985 UNCITRAL Model Law — 6
   D. Adoption of the UNCITRAL Rules in other Public and Private Institutions — 6
   E. Investor–State Arbitration and the UNCITRAL Rules — 7
   F. The 2010 UNCITRAL Rules — 8
   G. The Work of UNCITRAL on Rules for Transparency in Investor–State Arbitration — 9
4. How to Use this Commentary — 10
   A. Navigating the Text — 10
   B. The Interplay between the 1976 Rules and 2010 Rules in Application and Interpretation — 10
   C. The Extracts — 10
   D. Further Research — 11
5. Conclusion — 11

PART I: FUNDAMENTAL PRINCIPLES AND THE LEGAL FRAMEWORK WITHIN WHICH THE ARBITRAL TRIBUNAL OPERATES

Introduction — 13

Chapter 2: Scope of Application, General Provisions, and Place of Arbitration

1. Introduction — 16
2. Scope of Application—Article 1 — 16
   A. Text of the 2010 UNCITRAL Rule — 16
   B. Commentary — 17
      (1) General comments — 17
      (2) Scope of application — 18
      (3) No writing requirement for agreement to arbitration — 18
      (4) Party autonomy and modification of the Rules — 19
      (5) Presumptive scope of application — 20

	(6) Future transparency rules for investor–state arbitration	23
	(7) Model arbitration clause	24
	(8) Comparison to the 1976 UNCITRAL Rules	24
C.	Extracts from the Practice of Investment and other Tribunals	26
	(1) Article 1(1) (1976 Rules)—scope and modification	26
	(2) Article 1(2) (1976 Rules)—non-derogation from mandatory law	28

3. General Provisions—Article 17 29
   A. Text of the 2010 UNCITRAL Rule 29
   B. Commentary 30
      (1) Basic principles—Article 17(1) 30
         (a) Arbitral autonomy and its limits 30
         (b) Confidentiality in UNCITRAL arbitration 36
         (c) Non-disputing party (*amicus*) participation in UNCITRAL arbitration 39
         (d) The nature of the proceedings before the Iran–US Claims Tribunal 41
         (e) Concluding comments 45
      (2) Provisional timetable and modification of time periods—Article 17(2) 46
         (a) Provisional timetable 46
         (b) Modifications of time periods 47
         (c) Issues of general application 49
      (3) Right to a hearing—Article 17(3) 49
         (a) Scope of hearings 49
         (b) Timing of hearing requests 51
         (c) Preliminary meetings 52
      (4) Communication of documents—Article 17(4) 53
      (5) Joinder of third persons—Article 17(5) 54
      (6) Consolidation of claims 57
      (7) Comparison to the 1976 UNCITRAL Rules 58
   C. Extracts from the Practice of Investment and other Tribunals 59
      (1) Article 15(1) (1976 Rules)—general 59
      (2) Article 15(1) (1976 Rules)—*amicus* submissions 65
   D. Extracts from the Practice of the Iran–US Claims Tribunal 69
      (1) General and Tribunal Rules (1983), Article 15(1) 69
      (2) Tribunal Rules (1983), Article 15(2) 74

4. Place of Arbitration—Article 18 77
   A. Text of the 2010 UNCITRAL Rule 77
   B. Commentary 78
      (1) Meaning of "place of arbitration" 78
      (2) Selection of the place of arbitration—Article 18(1) 80
         (a) Considerations to be taken into account 80
            (1) Nature and suitability of the local law 81
            (2) Enforceability of the award 85
            (3) Neutrality 87
            (4) Practical considerations 89
         (b) Decision on place of arbitration not procedural: consultation with the parties 91
      (3) Where the award is "deemed to have been made" 92
      (4) The location of tribunal deliberations and meetings "for any other purpose, including hearings"—Article 18(2) 93
      (5) Comparison to the 1976 UNCITRAL Rules 95
   C. Extracts from the Practice of Investment Tribunals 96
   D. Extracts from the Practice of the Iran–US Claims Tribunal 109

Chapter 3: Applicable Law, *Amiable Compositeur*

1. Introduction — 111
2. Applicable Law—Article 35 — 112
   - A. Text of the 2010 UNCITRAL Rule — 112
   - B. Commentary — 112
     - (1) The primary rule—Article 35(1) — 112
       - (a) The principle of party autonomy and its application — 112
       - (b) Choice of applicable law where not designated by the parties — 118
     - (2) *Amiable compositeur* or *ex aequo et bono*—Article 35(2) — 119
     - (3) The significance of the contract and of trade usages—Article 35(3) — 121
     - (4) Comparison to the 1976 UNCITRAL Rules — 123
     - (5) A note on the Iran–US Claims Tribunal — 128
   - C. Extracts from the Practice of Investment Tribunals — 129
   - D. Extracts from the Practice of the Iran–US Claims Tribunal — 131
     - (1) Tribunal Rules (1983), Article 33(1) — 131
     - (2) Tribunal Rules (1983), Article 33(2) — 140
     - (3) Tribunal Rules (1983), Article 33(3) — 140
     - (4) Other practice of the Iran–US Claims Tribunal — 142

PART II: ARBITRAL PROCEDURES TO CONTROL THE SELECTION AND CONDUCT OF ARBITRATORS

Introduction — 145

Chapter 4: The Number and Selection of Arbitrators

1. Introduction — 148
2. Designating and Appointing Authorities—Article 6 — 148
   - A. Text of the 2010 UNCITRAL Rule — 148
   - B. Commentary — 149
     - (1) Opportunities for agreement on an appointing authority—Article 6(1) — 149
     - (2) The role of the designating authority—Article 6(2) and (4) — 151
     - (3) Suspension of time periods in the absence of an appointing authority—Article 6(3) — 153
     - (4) The role of the appointing authority—Article 6(5)–(7) — 153
   - C. Extracts from the Practice of the Iran–US Claims Tribunal — 155
3. The Number of Arbitrators—Article 7 — 157
   - A. Text of the 2010 UNCITRAL Rule — 157
   - B. Commentary — 157
     - (1) The default rule on the number of arbitrators—Article 7(1) — 157
     - (2) The exception to the default rule of three arbitrators—Article 7(2) — 160
     - (3) A number of arbitrators other than one or three — 161
4. Appointment of the Sole Arbitrator—Article 8 — 162
   - A. Text of the 2010 UNCITRAL Rule — 162
   - B. Commentary — 163
5. Appointment of a Three-Person Panel—Article 9 — 164
   - A. Text of the 2010 UNCITRAL Rule — 164
   - B. Commentary — 164
     - (1) The right of each party to appoint an arbitrator — 164
     - (2) The appointment of the presiding arbitrator — 165
   - C. Extracts from the Practice of Investment Tribunals — 166

6. Appointment in Multi-Party Arbitration—Article 10 — 169
   A. Text of the 2010 UNCITRAL Rule — 169
   B. Commentary — 169
      (1) The requirements for appointment—Article 10(1) and (2) — 169
      (2) The power of the appointing authority to appoint and reappoint—Article 10(3) — 170
7. Comparison to the 1976 UNCITRAL Rules — 172

Chapter 5: The Challenge of Arbitrators

1. Introduction — 177
   A. An Overview of Challenges before Investment and other Tribunals — 178
      (1) Challenge decision of April 15, 1993 — 178
      (2) Challenge decision of January 11, 1995 — 179
      (3) Challenge decision by a Division of the LCIA—October–December 2005 — 179
      (4) The US Government's challenge of Professor James Anaya in the *Grand River* arbitration—2007 — 180
      (5) The Argentine Government's challenge of Mr Judd L Kessler in the *National Grid* arbitration—2007 — 180
      (6) The Argentine Government's challenges of Professor Gabrielle Kaufmann-Kohler in the *AWG Group* arbitration—2007–2008 — 181
         (a) The Argentine Government's first challenge—2007 — 181
         (b) The Argentine Government's second challenge—2008 — 181
      (7) The Argentine Government's challenge of Mr Stanimir Alexandrov in the *ICS* arbitration—2009 — 182
      (8) The claimant's challenge to Mr J Christopher Thomas in the *Gallo* arbitration—2009 — 182
   B. An Overview of the Challenges before the Iran–US Claims Tribunal — 183
      (1) The Iranian Government challenge of Nils Mangård—1982 — 183
      (2) The US Government challenge of Judges Kashani and Shafeiei—1984 — 184
      (3) The first Iranian Government challenge of Judge Briner in Case No 55, *Amoco Iran* and *Islamic Republic of Iran*—1988 — 184
      (4) The second Iranian Government challenge of Judge Briner—1989 — 184
      (5) The third Iranian Government challenge of Judge Briner—1989 — 185
      (6) The US claimant's challenge of Judge Noori in Case No 248, *Carlson* and *Melli Industrial Group*—1990 — 186
      (7) The Iranian Government challenge of Judge Arangio-Ruiz—1991 — 186
      (8) The Iranian Government challenges of Judge Krzysztof Skubiszewski—1999 — 186
      (9) The US Government challenge of Judge Bengt Broms—2001 — 187
      (10) The US claimant's challenge of Judge Bengt Broms in connection with Case No 485, *Frederica Lincoln Riahi*—2004 — 187
      (11) The US Government challenge of Judges Assadollah Noori, Koorosh Ameli, and Mohsen Aghahosseini—2005–2006 — 188
      (12) The Iranian Government challenge of Judge Krzystof Skubiszewski and the US Government challenge of Judge Hamid Reza Oloumi Yazdi—2007 — 188
      (13) The Iranian Government challenge of Judge Krzystof Skubiszewski and Judge Gaetano Arangio-Ruiz—2009 — 189
      (14) The US Government challenge of Judge Seyed Jamal Seifi—2010 — 190
      (15) The Iranian Government challenge of Judge Charles Brower—2010 — 190
   C. The Exclusivity of the UNCITRAL Challenge Procedure — 191

2. The Duty to Disclose—Article 11 — 194
A. Text of the 2010 UNCITRAL Rule — 194
B. Commentary — 195
- (1) The duty to disclose — 195
- (2) Model statements of independence — 198
- (3) Disclosure guidelines of the Iran–US Claims Tribunal — 200
C. Extracts from the Practice of Investment Tribunals — 201
D. Extracts from the Practice of the Iran–US Claims Tribunal — 202
- (1) General — 202
- (2) Disclosure by the US Arbitrators — 205

3. The Grounds for Challenge—Article 12 — 207
A. Text of the 2010 UNCITRAL Rule — 207
B. Commentary — 208
- (1) Challenge on the ground of justifiable doubts as to impartiality or independence—general remarks on Article 12(1) — 208
  - (a) The standard for impartiality and independence is objective — 208
  - (b) The same standard applies to party-appointed and non-party appointed arbitrators — 209
  - (c) Criteria regarding and examples of justifiable doubts — 211
- (2) Challenge on the ground of justifiable doubts as to impartiality or independence — 212
  - (a) The meaning of "impartiality" and "independence" — 213
  - (b) When are doubts as to impartiality or independence justified? — 213
    - (1) An arbitrator's relationship with a witness — 215
    - (2) An arbitrator's financial relationship with a party (shareholding) — 216
    - (3) An arbitrator's financial relationship with a party (salary) — 217
    - (4) An arbitrator's previous employment by the parent corporation of a party — 217
    - (5) An arbitrator's representation in another forum that is adverse to a party — 218
    - (6) An arbitrator's previous advocacy on behalf of a country formerly adverse to a sovereign party — 218
    - (7) An arbitrator's representation of a third party with a right to intervene in the proceedings — 219
    - (8) An arbitrator's handling of the proceedings — 220
    - (9) An arbitrator's statement regarding a party or the dispute — 222
    - (10) An arbitrator's decision-making — 222
    - (11) An arbitrator's breach of the confidentiality of deliberations — 223
    - (12) An arbitrator's physical assault of a fellow arbitrator — 225
  - (c) The standard of independence and impartiality does not vary according to the stage of the proceedings — 225
  - (d) A failure to disclose under Article 11 may give rise to, but does not per se establish, justifiable doubts as to impartiality or independence — 226
  - (e) Are there any limitations on the circumstances which may be used as the basis for justifiable doubts? — 228
- (3) Article 12(1) as providing the exclusive grounds for challenge — 228
- (4) When may a party challenge the arbitrator it has appointed?—Article 12(2) — 230
C. Extracts from the Practice of Investment and other Tribunals — 231
D. Extracts From the Practice of the Iran–US Claims Tribunal — 235
- (1) Tribunal Rules (1983), Article 10(1) — 235
- (2) Tribunal Rules (1983), Article 10(2) — 240

4. The Initiation of the Challenge and the Potential for Agreement to the Challenge—Article 13 — 241
   A. Text of the 2010 UNCITRAL Rule — 241
   B. Commentary — 241
      (1) When notice of challenge must be made—Article 13(1) — 241
         (a) General comments on the *travaux préparatoires* — 241
         (b) When circumstances "became known" to the challenging party — 243
            (1) Burden of proof — 243
            (2) Actual prior knowledge — 245
      (2) To whom should notice be sent; what form should notice take; sufficiency of the notice; who may send notice—Article 13(2) — 248
      (3) Procedure if challenge is accepted by all parties or challenged arbitrator withdraws—Article 13(3) — 253
      (4) Timeline for seeking a decision on a challenge—Article 13(4) — 256
   C. Extracts from the Practice of Investment Tribunals — 256
   D. Extracts from the Practice of the Iran–US Claims Tribunal — 257
      (1) Tribunal Rules (1983), Article 11(1) — 257
      (2) Tribunal Rules (1983), Article 11(2) — 263
      (3) Tribunal Rules (1983), Article 11(3) — 267
5. The Resolution of the Challenge — 268
   A. Text of the 2010 UNCITRAL Rule — 268
   B. Commentary — 268
      (1) Which authority shall make the decision on the challenge if the other party does not agree to the challenge or the challenged arbitrator does not withdraw? — 268
      (2) When may a party seek the assistance of the PCA Secretary-General in designating an appointing authority? — 270
      (3) What procedures the appointing authority may follow in deciding the challenge — 271
      (4) Limitations on the powers of the appointing authority — 272
   C. Extracts from the Practice of Investment Tribunals — 272
   D. Extracts from the Practice of the Iran–US Claims Tribunal — 273
      (1) Tribunal Rules (1983), Article 12(1) — 273
      (2) Tribunal Rules (1983), Article 12(2) — 274
6. Comparison to the 1976 UNCITRAL Rules — 274

Chapter 6: Failure to Act, other Disruptions, and the Replacement of an Arbitrator

1. Introduction — 278
2. Failure to Act and other Disruptions—Article 12(3) — 278
   A. Text of the 2010 UNCITRAL Rule — 278
   B. Commentary — 278
      (1) Drafting history of the rule and general comments — 278
      (2) Iran—US Claims Tribunal practice with respect to an arbitrator's failure to act — 280
      (3) Iran—US Claims Tribunal practice with respect to other disruptions — 282
         (a) A note on substitute arbitrators — 282
         (b) A note on truncated proceedings — 283
            (1) The absence of Mr Sani, Fall 1983 — 284
            (2) The absence of Judge Mostafavi, Spring 1988 — 284
            (3) The practice of the Tribunal regarding absence from the hearing — 285

		(4)	The practice of the Tribunal regarding the rendering of awards despite a refusal to sign	286
		(5)	The practice of the Tribunal regarding the rendering of awards on agreed terms despite no participation by an arbitrator	286
		(6)	The practice of the Tribunal regarding the holding of pre-hearing conference despite the absence of an arbitrator	286
		(c)	A note on resignation of an arbitrator	286
	(4)	Comparison to the 1976 UNCITRAL Rules		289
	C.	Extracts from the Practice of Investment Tribunals		289
	D.	Extracts from the Practice of the Iran–US Claims Tribunal		290
		(1)	Tribunal Rules (1983), Article 13(1)—Resignation	290
		(2)	Tribunal Rules (1983), Article 13(2)—Failure to act	291
		(3)	Tribunal Rules (1983), Article 13(3)	302
		(4)	Tribunal Rules (1983), Article 13(4)	302
		(5)	Tribunal Rules (1983), Article 13(5)	302
3.	Replacement of an Arbitrator—Article 14			305
	A.	Text of the 2010 UNCITRAL Rule		305
	B.	Commentary		305
		(1)	Rationale for the revised approach: the problem of spurious resignations	305
		(2)	Procedures when an arbitrator "has to be replaced"—Article 14(1)	307
		(3)	Replacement of an arbitrator in "exceptional circumstances"—Article 14(2)	308
			(a) Depriving a party of its right to appoint	308
			(b) Procedural requirements	311
			(c) Exclusivity of the discretion of the appointing authority	312
			(d) Agreement between the parties	313
		(4)	Comparison to the 1976 UNCITRAL Rules	314
			(a) The express power to proceed	315
			(b) The inherent power to proceed	317
4.	Repetition of Hearings in the Event of Replacement of an Arbitrator—Article 15			318
	A.	Text of the 2010 UNCITRAL Rule		318
	B.	Commentary		318
		(1)	General comments	318
		(2)	Comparison to the 1976 UNCITRAL Rules	320
	C.	Extracts from the Practice of the Iran–US Claims Tribunal		322

Chapter 7: Exclusion of Liability for Arbitrators and other Participants

1.	Introduction		325
2.	Exclusion of Liability for Arbitrators and other Key Actors—Article 16		325
	A. Text of the 2010 UNCITRAL Rule		325
	B. Commentary		326
		(1) General	326
		(2) Practice of the Iran–US Claims Tribunal	330
		(3) Comparison to the 1976 UNCITRAL Rules	330
	C. Extracts from the Practice of Investment Tribunals		330
	D. Extracts from the Practice of the Iran–US Claims Tribunal		331

Chapter 8: The Institution of the Appointing Authority

1. Evolution of the UNCITRAL Approach? 337
2. The Appointing Authority and Composition Generally 338
3. Lessons from the Iran–US Claims Tribunal for the Office of the Appointing Authority 340

PART III: THE INITIATION OF THE ARBITRATION AND THE IDENTIFICATION AND CLARIFICATION OF THE ISSUES PRESENTED

Introduction 345

Chapter 9: Representation and Assistance

1. Introduction 347
2. Representation and Assistance—Article 5 347
   A. Text of the 2010 UNCITRAL Rule 347
   B. Commentary 348
      (1) The right to representation and assistance by persons chosen 348
      (2) Communicating the identity and role of representatives and advisers 351
      (3) Proof of a representative's authority 352
      (4) Practice of the Iran–US Claims Tribunal 353
      (5) Comparison to the 1976 UNCITRAL Rules 354
   C. Extracts from the Practice of Investment Tribunals 355
   D. Extracts from the Practice of the Iran–US Claims Tribunal 356

Chapter 10: The Notice Initiating Arbitration and the Response

1. Introduction 359
2. The Notice Initiating Arbitration—Article 3 360
   A. Text of the 2010 UNCITRAL Rule 360
   B. Commentary 361
      (1) The requirement to communicate a notice of arbitration—Article 3(1) 361
      (2) The date of commencement of arbitration proceedings—Article 3(2) 362
      (3) Mandatory information provided in the notice of arbitration—Article 3(3) 363
      (4) Additional information provided in the notice of arbitration—Article 3(4) 364
      (5) Insufficiency of the notice of arbitration—Article 3(5) 364
      (6) International investment agreements and the notice of arbitration 365
      (7) The notice of arbitration at the Iran–US Claims Tribunal 366
      (8) Comparison to the 1976 UNCITRAL Rules 368
   C. Extracts from the Practice of Investment Tribunals 369
3. The Response to the Notice of Arbitration—Article 4 370
   A. Text of the 2010 UNCITRAL Rule 370
   B. Commentary 370
      (1) The requirement to respond to the notice of arbitration—Article 4(1) 370
      (2) Mandatory contents of the response to the notice of arbitration—Article 4(1) 372
      (3) Optional contents of the response to the notice of arbitration—Article 4(2) 373

(4)	Absence, lateness, or insufficiency of the response to the notice of arbitration—Article 4(3)	373
(5)	Comparison to the 1976 UNCITRAL Rules	373

Chapter 11: The Choice of Language

1. Introduction	375
2. The Choice of Language—Article 19	376
A. Text of the 2010 UNCITRAL Rule	376
B. Commentary	376
(1) Determination of the language of arbitration—Article 19(1)	376
(2) Translation of documents and exhibits—Article 19(2)	382
(3) Comparison to the 1976 UNCITRAL Rules	384
C. Extracts from the Practice of Investment Tribunals	384
D. Extracts from the Practice of the Iran–US Claims Tribunal	385
(1) Tribunal Rules (1983), Article 17(1)	385
(2) Tribunal Rules (1983), Article 17(2)	387

Chapter 12: Notice and the Calculation of Periods of Time

1. Introduction	393
2. Notice and Calculation of Periods of Time—Article 2	394
A. Text of the 2010 UNCITRAL Rule	394
B. Commentary	395
(1) What form notice may take—Article 2(1)	395
(2) When notice becomes effective—Article 2(2)–(4)	397
(a) A notice is "deemed to have been received"	397
(b) Means of delivery, including by electronic communication	399
(1) Electronic communications	400
(c) Application of Article 2(1) of the 1976 UNCITRAL Rules by the Iran–US Claims Tribunal	401
(3) How to calculate periods of time under the Rules—Article 2(5)–(6)	402
(4) Comparison to the 1976 UNCITRAL Rules	403
C. Extracts from the Practice of Investment Tribunals	404
D. Extracts from the Practice of the Iran–United States Claims Tribunal	404
(1) Tribunal Rules (1983), Article 2(1)	404
(2) Tribunal Rules (1983), Article 2(2)	405
(3) Tribunal Rules (1983), Article 2(3)	405
(4) Tribunal Rules (1983), Article 2(4)	407
(5) Tribunal Rules (1983), Article 2(5)	407

Chapter 13: Statements of Claim and Defence

1. Introduction	409
2. The Statement of Claim—Article 20	410
A. Text of the 2010 UNCITRAL Rule	410
B. Commentary	411
(1) Submission of the statement of claim	411
(2) Contents of the statement of claim	412
(3) Sanctions for an inadequate statement of claim	414
(4) A note on the Iran–US Claims Tribunal	415
(5) Comparison to the 1976 UNCITRAL Rules	416
C. Extracts from the Practice of Investment Tribunals	417

	D. Extracts from the Practice of the Iran–US Claims Tribunal		419
	(1) Tribunal Rules (1983), Article 18(1)		419
	(2) Tribunal Rules (1983), Article 18(2)		419
3.	The Statement of Defence—Article 21		421
	A Text of the 2010 UNCITRAL Rule		422
	B Commentary		422
	(1) Submission of the statement of defence		422
	(2) Contents of the statement of defence		423
	(3) Submission of counterclaims and claims for the purpose of set-off		424
	(a) General issues		424
	(b) The counterclaim or the claim for a set-off must be within the jurisdiction of the arbitral tribunal		426
	(4) Supplementary provisions on counterclaims and claims for the purpose of set-off		428
	(5) Comparison to the 1976 UNCITRAL Rules		429
	C. Extracts from the Practice of Investment Tribunals		432
	D. Extracts from the Practice of the Iran–US Claims Tribunal		434
	(1) Tribunal Rules (1983), Article 19(1)		434
	(2) Tribunal Rules (1983), Article 19(2)		436
	(3) Tribunal Rules (1983), Article 19(3)		436
	(4) Tribunal Rules (1983), Article 19(4)		447

Chapter 14: Objections to the Jurisdiction of the Arbitral Tribunal

1.	Introduction		449
2.	Objections to Jurisdiction—Article 23		450
	A. Text of the 2010 UNCITRAL Rule		450
	B. Commentary		450
	(1) The power of the tribunal to determine its own jurisdiction—Article 23(1)		450
	(2) Objections to the existence or validity of the contract of which the arbitration agreement is a part and the doctrine of separability—Article 23(1)		453
	(3) When objections should be raised—Article 23(2)		455
	(4) When objections should be ruled upon—Article 23(3)		457
	(5) Comparison to the 1976 UNCITRAL Rules		458
	C. Extracts from the Practice of Investment Tribunals		459
	D. Extracts from the Practice of the Iran–US Claims Tribunal		463
	(1) Tribunal Rules (1983), Article 21(1)		463
	(2) Tribunal Rules (1983), Article 21(2)		463
	(3) Tribunal Rules (1983), Article 21(3)		464
	(4) Tribunal Rules (1983), Article 21(4)		464

Chapter 15: Amendments to the Claim or Defence

1.	Introduction		467
2.	Amendments to the Claim or Defence—Article 22		467
	A. Text of the 2010 UNCITRAL Rule		467
	B. Commentary		468
	(1) General		468
	(2) The amendment must not fall outside the jurisdiction of the arbitral tribunal		469

(3) Grounds for rejecting an amendment: delay, prejudice or other circumstances		471
(4) Procedural questions		474
(5) Comparison to the 1976 UNCITRAL Rules		475
C. Extracts from the Practice of Investment Tribunals		475
D. Extracts from the Practice of the Iran–US Claims Tribunal		479

Chapter 16: Further Written Statements and Time Limits on Submission

1. Introduction	491
2. Further Written Statements—Article 24	491
A. Text of the 2010 UNCITRAL Rule	491
B. Commentary	492
(1) General comments	492
(2) Comparison to the 1976 UNCITRAL Rules	496
C. Extracts from the Practice of Investment Tribunals	496
D. Extracts from the Practice of the Iran–US Claims Tribunal	498
3. Time Limits on Submission—Article 25	505
A. Text of the 2010 UNCITRAL Rule	505
B. Commentary	505
(1) General comments	505
(2) Comparison to the 1976 UNCITRAL Rules	508
C. Extracts from the Practice of Investment Tribunals	508
D. Extracts from the Practice of the Iran–US Claims Tribunal	508

Chapter 17: Interim Measures

1. Introduction	513
2. Interim Measures—Article 26	514
A. Text of the 2010 UNCITRAL Rule	514
B. Commentary	515
(1) The precondition of a request by a party—Article 26(1)	516
(2) Types of interim measures that may be granted—Article 26(2)	517
(a) Maintain or restore the *status quo*	518
(b) Prevent prejudice to the arbitral process itself	518
(c) Preserve assets for possible satisfaction of award	519
(d) Preserve evidence	519
(3) Conditions for the ordering of interim measures—Article 26(3)	520
(a) A likely harm not adequately reparable by an award of damages	521
(b) An appropriate balance of likely harms	522
(c) A reasonable possibility of success on the merits	522
(d) Further conditions imposed by the agreement of the parties	524
(4) Conditions relaxed for the preservation of evidence—Article 26(4)	524
(5) The form (award or order) in which interim measures are granted	524
(6) Tribunal's power to modify, suspend or terminate interim measures—Article 26(5)	525
(7) Security for the costs of interim measures—Article 26(6)	526
(8) Disclosure by any party of any material change—Article 26(7)	527
(9) Liability for costs and damages—Article 26(8)	528
(10) Relations between the arbitral tribunal and municipal courts in issuing interim measures—Article 26(9)	529
(11) Issuance of preliminary orders	530
(12) Comparison to the 1976 UNCITRAL Rules	532

C. Extracts from the Practice of Investment Tribunals	533
D. Extracts from the Practice of the Iran–US Claims Tribunal	543
(1) Tribunal Rules (1983), Article 26(1)	543
(2) Tribunal Rules (1983), Article 26(2)	550
(3) Tribunal Rules (1983), Article 26(3)	551

PART IV: THE PRESENTATION OF THE CASE: EVIDENCE AND HEARINGS

Introduction	553

Chapter 18: Evidence

1. Introduction	555
2. Evidence—Article 27	557
A. Text of the 2010 UNCITRAL Rule	557
B. Commentary	557
(1) Burden of proof—Article 27(1)	557
(2) Definition of "witnesses"—Article 27(2)	561
(a) General comments	561
(b) Practice of the Iran–US Claims Tribunal	563
(3) Written witness statements—Article 27(2)	564
(4) Production of documents—Article 27(3)	565
(a) General comments	565
(b) Production of documents at the request of a party	567
(c) "Enforcement" of production orders	570
(5) Admissibility, relevance, materiality, and weight of the evidence—Article 27(4)	571
(6) Comparison to the 1976 UNCITRAL Rules	574
C. Extracts from the Practice of Investment Tribunals	576
(1) Article 27(1) (1976 Rules)—Burden of proof	576
(2) Article 27(2) (1976 Rules)—Definition of "witnesses"	577
(3) Article 27(2) (1976 Rules)—Written witness statements	577
(4) Article 27(3) (1976 Rules)—Production of documents	577
(5) Article 27(4) (1976 Rules)—Admissibility, relevance, materiality, and weight of the evidence	579
D. Extracts from the Practice of the Iran–US Claims Tribunal	580
(1) Tribunal Rules (1983), Article 24(1)—Burden of proof	580
(2) Tribunal Rules (1983), Article 24(2)—Summary of evidence	587
(3) Tribunal Rules (1983), Article 24(3)—Document production	588
(4) Tribunal Rules (1983), Article 25(5)—Written witness statements	593
(5) Tribunal Rules (1983), Article 25(6)—Admissibility, relevance, materiality, and weight of the evidence	594

Chapter 19: The Hearings

1. Introduction	601
2. The Hearings—Article 28	602
A. Text of the 2010 UNCITRAL Rule	602
B. Commentary	602
(1) Notice of hearing—Article 28(1)	602
(2) The conduct of the hearing—Article 28(2)–(4)	604

	(a) The conditions for and manner of witness examination		604
	(1) Notice of hearing and witness testimony		605
	(2) Cross-examination		605
	(3) Declarations		606
	(b) Hearings normally held *in camera*		607
	(c) Retirement of witnesses		608
	(d) Examination without physical presence of witness		609
	(e) Translation of oral statements, record of the hearing		610
	(3) Comparison to the 1976 UNCITRAL Rules		611
	C. Extracts from the Practice of Investment Tribunals		613
	(1) The conditions for and manner of witness examination		613
	(2) Hearings held in camera		617
	D. Extracts from the Practice of the Iran–US Claims Tribunal		617
	(1) Tribunal Rules (1983), Article 25(1)		617
	(2) Tribunal Rules (1983), Article 25(2)		619
	(3) Tribunal Rules (1983), Article 25(3)		623
	(4) Tribunal Rules (1983), Article 25(4)		624
3.	Closure of the Hearing—Article 31		624
	A. Text of the 2010 UNCITRAL Rule		624
	B. Commentary		625
	(1) Closure of the hearing—Article 31(1)		625
	(2) Reopening of the hearing—Article 31(2)		626
	(3) Comparison to the 1976 UNCITRAL Rules		628
	C. Extracts from the Practice of Investment Tribunals		629
	D. Extracts from the Practice of the Iran–US Claims Tribunal		629
	(1) Tribunal Rules (1983), Article 29(1)		629
	(2) Tribunal Rules (1983), Article 29(2)		630

Chapter 20: Tribunal-Appointed Experts

1.	Introduction		635
2.	Tribunal-Appointed Experts—Article 29		636
	A. Text of the 2010 UNCITRAL Rule		636
	B. Commentary		637
	(1) General comments		637
	(2) Appointment by the tribunal and terms of reference—Article 29(1)–(2)		638
	(a) Appointment		638
	(b) Terms of reference		640
	(3) Objections to the qualifications or the impartiality and independence of the tribunal-appointed expert—Article 29(2)		642
	(4) The provision of relevant information to the tribunal-appointed expert—Article 29(3)		644
	(5) The tribunal-appointed expert's report—Article 29(4)		645
	(6) Expert hearings—Article 29(5)		646
	(7) Note on party-appointed "expert witnesses"		647
	(8) Comparison to the 1976 UNCITRAL Rules		648
	C. Extracts from the Practice of Investment Tribunals		648
	D. Extracts from the Practice of the Iran–US Claims Tribunal		650
	(1) Tribunal Rules (1983), Article 27(1)—appointment and terms of reference		650
	(a) The *Shahin Shaine Ebrahimi* case		650
	(b) The *Arco Exploration* case		653
	(c) The *Starrett Housing* case		655

	(d) The *Richard D Harza* case		656
	(e) The *Behring International* case		660
(2)	Tribunal Rules (1983), Article 27(2)—provision of relevant information		662
(3)	Tribunal Rules (1983), Article 27(3)—expert report		663
	(a) The *Shahin Shaine Ebrahimi* case		663
	(b) The *Arco Exploration* case		664
	(c) The *Behring International* case		665
	(d) The *Richard D Harza* case		665
	(e) The *Starrett Housing* case		665
(4)	Tribunal Rules (1983), Article 27(4)—expert hearing		667

PART V: DEFAULT AND WAIVER

Introduction   669

Chapter 21: Default

1. Introduction   671
2. Default—Article 30   671
   A. Text of the 2010 UNCITRAL Rule   671
   B. Commentary   672
      (1) General comments   672
      (2) Failure to file early written submissions—Article 30(1)   675
      (3) Failure to appear at a hearing—Article 30(2)   677
      (4) Failure to produce documentary evidence—Article 30(3)   677
      (5) Comparison to the 1976 UNCITRAL Rules   678
   C. Extracts from the Practice of Investment Tribunals   679
   D. Extracts from the Practice of the Iran–US Claims Tribunal   683
      (1) General and Tribunal Rules (1983), Article 28   683
      (2) Tribunal Rules (1983), Article 28(2)   685
      (3) Tribunal Rules (1983), Article 28(3)   687

Chapter 22: Waiver

1. Introduction   691
2. Waiver—Article 32   691
   A. Text of the 2010 UNCITRAL Rule   691
   B. Commentary   692
      (1) General comments   692
      (2) The level of knowledge required   693
      (3) Comparison to the 1976 UNCITRAL Rules   695
   C. Extracts from the Practice of Investment Tribunals   695
   D. Extracts from the Practice of the Iran–US Claims Tribunal   696

PART VI: THE AWARD

Introduction   697

Chapter 23: Deliberations and Decisions

1. Introduction   699
2. Decisions—Article 33   700

		A. Text of the 2010 UNCITRAL Rule	700
		B. Commentary	700
		(1) Awards and other Decisions by Majority Vote—Article 33(1)	700
		(a) General comments	700
		(b) Majority decision-making by the Iran–US Claims Tribunal	704
		(1) The dynamics of deliberations	704
		(2) The practice of deliberating and drafting awards	705
		(2) Decision-Making on Procedural Questions—Article 33(2)	706
		(a) The meaning of "questions of procedure"	709
		(b) Revision	710
		(3) Confidentiality of deliberations—Article 31, Note 2 of the 1983 Tribunal Rules	711
		(a) The scope of the rule of confidentiality	712
		(b) Enforcing the rule of confidentiality	715
		(1) Censure of written statements	715
		(2) Statements of disapproval by fellow arbitrators	716
		(3) Challenge proceedings	716
		(4) Comparison to the 1976 UNCITRAL Rules	716
		C. Extracts from the Practice of Investment and other Tribunals	717
		D. Extracts from the Practice of the Iran–US Claims Tribunal	719
		(1) Tribunal Rules (1983), Article 31(1)	719
		(2) Tribunal Rules (1983), Article 31(2)	722
		(3) Tribunal Rules (1983), Article 31, Note 2—Confidentiality of deliberations	723

Chapter 24: Form and Effect

1. Introduction	732
2. Form and Effect—Article 34	732
A. Text of the 2010 UNCITRAL Rule	732
B. Commentary	733
(1) Discretion to make separate awards—Article 34(1)	733
(2) The award is "final and binding" and the parties must "carry out the award without delay"—Article 34(2)	738
(a) General commentary on "final and binding"	738
(1) "Final"	738
(2) "Binding"	741
(b) Waiver of recourse against the award—optional provision	742
(3) Written award and designation of the date and place of the award's making—Article 34(2) and (4)	745
(4) Obligation to sign and failure to sign the award—Article 34(4)	746
(a) General comments on the travaux préparatoires	746
(b) Practical matters regarding the statement of reasons for the absence of an arbitrator's signature	749
(5) Statement of reasons for the award and dissenting opinions—Article 34(3)	750
(a) Statement of reasons for the award	750
(b) Dissenting and separate opinions	752
(6) Publication of the award—Article 34(5)	755
(7) Copies of the award to the parties—Article 34(6)	757
(8) Filing and registration of the award	759
(9) Comparison to the 1976 UNCITRAL Rules	759

C.	Extracts from the Practice of Investment and other Tribunals	761
	(1) Article 32(1) (1976 Rules)—Types of award	761
	(2) Article 32(2) (1976 Rules)—Final and binding	762
	(3) Article 32(2) and (4) (1976 Rules)—Date, place, and signature	763
	(4) Article 32(4) (1976 Rules)—Failure to sign the award	764
	(5) Article 32(7) (1976 Rules)—Filing and registration of an award	765
D.	Extracts from the Practice of the Iran–US Claims Tribunal	766
	(1) Tribunal Rules (1983), Article 32(1)—Types of award	766
	(2) Tribunal Rules (1983), Article 32(2)—Final and binding award	767
	(3) Tribunal Rules (1983), Article 32(3) and (4)—Date, place, and signature	767
	(4) Tribunal Rules (1983), Article 32(3)—Reasons for the award	768
	(5) Tribunal Rules (1983), Article 32(4)—Failure to sign the award	769
	(a) Statements of reasons for failure to sign the award	769
	(b) Improper statements of reasons and post-award exchanges	773
	(6) Tribunal Rules (1983), Article 32(5)—Publication of the award	776

Chapter 25: Settlement and other Grounds for Termination

1. Introduction — 781
2. Settlement and other Termination—Article 36 — 781
   A. Text of the 2010 UNCITRAL Rule — 781
   B. Commentary — 782
     (1) Settlement—Article 36(1) — 782
       (a) Types of settlement agreement and the practice of awards on agreed terms — 782
       (b) Discretion to record a settlement agreement — 784
       (c) Pre-settlement negotiations — 786
     (2) Other grounds for termination—Article 36(2) — 788
       (a) Continuation of the arbitration is "unnecessary" or "impossible" — 788
       (b) The existence of "remaining matters" — 790
     (3) Technical requirements for awards on agreed terms—Article 36(3) — 790
     (4) Comparison to the 1976 UNCITRAL Rules — 790
   C. Extracts from the Practice of Investment Tribunals — 792
   D. Extracts from the Practice of the Iran–US Claims Tribunal — 793
     (1) Tribunal Rules (1983), Article 34(1) — 793
     (2) Tribunal Rules (1983), Article 34(2) — 798

Chapter 26: Post-Award Proceedings

1. Introduction — 801
2. Interpretation of the Award—Article 37 — 802
   A. Text of the 2010 UNCITRAL Rule — 802
   B. Commentary — 802
     (1) General — 802
     (2) Comparison to the 1976 UNCITRAL Rules — 806
   C. Extracts from the Practice of Investment Tribunals — 806
   D. Extracts from the Practice of the Iran–US Claims Tribunal — 808
3. Correction of the Award—Article 38 — 811
   A. Text of the 2010 UNCITRAL Rule — 811
   B. Commentary — 811
     (1) General — 811
     (2) Comparison to the 1976 UNCITRAL Rules — 814
   C. Extracts from the Practice of Investment Tribunals — 815

D. Extracts from the Practice of the Iran–US Claims Tribunal		815
(1) Request for correction granted		815
(2) Request for correction denied		817
4. Additional Award—Article 39		821
A. Text of the 2010 UNCITRAL Rule		821
B. Commentary		821
(1) General		821
(2) Comparison to the 1976 UNCITRAL Rules		824
C. Extracts from the Practice of Investment Tribunals		825
D. Extracts from the Practice of the Iran–US Claims Tribunal		825
(1) Request for additional award granted		825
(2) Request for additional award denied		825
5. The Finality of Awards and the Inherent Power to Reconsider		827
A. Commentary		827
B. Extracts from the Practice of Investment Tribunals		831
C. Extracts from the Practice of the Iran–US Claims Tribunal		832
(1) Limited power of review		832
(2) Revision to address fraud or corruption		836

Chapter 27: The Costs of Arbitration

1. Introduction		840
2. The Costs of Arbitration—Article 40		841
A. Text of the 2010 UNCITRAL Rule		841
B. Commentary		841
(1) The duty to fix the costs of arbitration		841
(2) Costs defined		843
(a) Subparagraph (a)		843
(b) Subparagraphs (b) and (c)		844
(c) Subparagraph (d)		844
(d) Subparagraph (e)		845
(e) Subparagraph (f)		846
(3) The costs of interpretation, correction and completion of an award—Article 40(3)		847
(4) Note on the costs of the Iran–US Claims Tribunal		848
(5) Comparison to the 1976 UNCITRAL Rules		848
C. Extracts from the Practice of Investment and other Tribunals		849
3. Arbitrators' Fees—Article 41		852
A. Text of the 2010 UNCITRAL Rule		852
B. Commentary		853
(1) Regulation of the arbitrators' fees and expenses under the Rules—general background, Article 41(1) and (2)		853
(2) Determining the fees and expenses of the arbitral tribunal and potential review by a neutral arbiter—Article 41(3)–(6)		855
(a) The manner in which fees and expenses will be determined—Article 41(3) and (5)		856
(1) Transparency		857
(2) Neutral Mechanism		858
(3) Efficiency		859
(b) The computation of the arbitral tribunal's fees and expenses—Article 41(4)–(6)		860
(1) Transparency		860
(2) Neutral Mechanism		860
(3) Efficiency		861

		(3)	Comparison to the 1976 UNCITRAL Rules	862
	C.	Extracts from the Practice of Investment Tribunals		863
4.	Apportionment of Costs—Article 42			865
	A.	Text of the 2010 UNCITRAL Rule		865
	B.	Commentary		865
		(1)	Apportioning and awarding costs	865
		(2)	"The circumstances of the case"	870
			(a) The degree of success of the parties	870
			(b) The conduct of the parties	871
			(c) The nature of the parties	873
			(d) The nature of the dispute resolution mechanism	874
		(3)	Requirements for making a claim for costs	875
			(a) Documentation	875
			(b) Timing of requests	875
			(c) Proof of reasonable legal costs	876
		(4)	Comparison to the 1976 UNCITRAL Rules	877
	C.	Extracts from the Practice of Investment Tribunals		877
		(1)	Article 40(1) and (2) (1976 Rules)—General	877
		(2)	Article 40(1) and (2) (1976 Rules)—"Circumstances of the case"	879
			(a) The success of the parties	879
			(b) The conduct of the parties	882
			(c) The nature of the dispute resolution mechanism	887
	D.	Extracts from the Practice of the Iran–US Claims Tribunal		891
		(1)	Tribunal Rules (1983), Article 40(1) and (2)—General	891
		(2)	Tribunal Rules (1983), Article 40(1) and (2)—"Circumstances of the case"	892
			(a) The success of the parties	892
			(b) The conduct of the parties	894
5.	Deposit of Costs—Article 43			896
	A.	Text of the 2010 UNCITRAL Rule		896
	B.	Commentary		897
		(1)	The request for deposits	897
		(2)	Consultation with the appointing authority	899
		(3)	Failure to make requested deposits	899
		(4)	The right to an accounting and the return of unexpended deposits	900
		(5)	Comparison to the 1976 UNCITRAL Rules	901
	C.	Extracts from the Practice of Investment Tribunals		901
	D.	Extracts from the Practice of the Iran–US Claims Tribunal		903

Appendices

Appendix 1—UNCITRAL Arbitration Rules (as revised in 2010)	907
Appendix 2—UNCITRAL Arbitration Rules (1976)	925
Appendix 3—A Tabular Comparison of the 1976–2010 UNCITRAL Arbitration Rules	939
Appendix 4—UNCITRAL Notes on Organizing Arbitral Proceedings (May 28–June 14, 1996)	967
Appendix 5—The Tribunal Rules of Procedure Provisionally adopted May 3, 1983, as amended May 27, 1997	983
Appendix 6—Recommendations to Assist Arbitral Institutions and Other Interested Bodies with regard to Arbitration under the UNCITRAL Arbitration Rules as revised in 2010	1007

Select Bibliography 1021

Index 1033

Table of Cases and Other Practice

THE PRACTICE OF TRIBUNALS APPLYING THE UNCITRAL RULES

A. Iran–US Claims Tribunal

(1) Awards, decisions, and orders

(a) State-to-state claims

Case No A1	287, 594, 719, 769, 785–6, 788
Case No A2	368, 440, 873–4, 894
Case No A3	53, 76, 288–9, 304, 618–19, 734, 791, 827, 830, 834, 873
Case No A4	544
Case No A8	53, 76, 288–9, 304, 618–19, 734, 791, 827, 830, 834, 873
Case No A9	53, 76, 288–9, 304, 618–19, 734, 791, 827, 830, 834
Case No A11	704, 721
Case No A12	444
Case No A14	53, 76, 288–9, 304, 618–19, 734, 791, 827, 830, 834
Case No A15	68, 189–90, 292, 524, 544–5, 549 50, 738, 767
Case No A16	594, 624
Case No A17	40, 798, 817
Case No A18	464–6, 753
Case No A20	560, 596, 832
Case No A21	43, 292
Case No A24	521, 549–50
Case No A25	380
Case No A26(I, II and III)–FT	790
Case No A27	810, 821, 823, 827, 837
Case No A28	187, 223, 229, 421, 706, 712, 714–16, 727–8, 754, 767
Case No A30	591
Case No A33	506, 512, 710
Case No B1	223–4, 282, 302, 421, 424, 446, 458, 466, 549, 567, 709–10, 723, 738
Case No B9	141
Case No B12	141
Case No B16	53, 76
Case No B25	783
Case No B36	116, 140, 803, 813, 820, 836
Case No B61	189–90, 205, 211, 251, 266, 288–9, 304, 603, 618–19, 713, 734, 791, 823, 827, 830, 834

(b) Claims of Nationals

Abrahamian, Katrin Zohrabegian and Government of the Islamic Republic of Iran, Award No ITL 74–377–3 (1 December 1989), 23 Iran-US CTR 285 (1989–II) ... 678

Aeronutronic Overseas Services Inc and the Islamic Republic of Iran:
　Case No 158, Chamber One, Order of 9 March 1984 ....472, 482
　Interim Award No ITM 47–158–1 (14 March 1985) 546, 548
Aeronutronic Overseas Services Inc and Telecommunications Co of Iran:
　Order of 28 June 1985 510
　Order of 6 August 1986 ....508, 510
Agrostruct International Inc and Iran State Cereals Organization, Award No 358–195–1
　(15 April 1988), 18 Iran-US CTR 180, 187, 197 (1988–I)............. 494, 501, 871, 892
Ainsworth, Jonathan and the Islamic Republic of Iran, Case No 454, Order of
　7 November 1983, 4 Iran-US CTR 26 (1983–II).................................411, 414, 420
Allen, Juliette and the Islamic Republic of Iran:
　Case No 930, Order of 30 November 1990 689
　Case No 930, Order of 5 March 1991 689
　Case No 930, Order of 14 May 1991 ....678, 689
　Award No 541–930–3 (11 December 1992) 28 Iran-US
　　CTR 382, 382–83 (1992)...377, 384, 390
American Bell International Inc and the Islamic Republic of Iran:
　Interlocutory Award No ITL 41–48–3 (11 June 1984), 6 Iran-US CTR 74, 83–84,
　　95, 97–98, 100–103 (1984–II).......................... 112, 116, 131, 425–6, 431, 438–9
　Case No 48 (12 September 1985), 9 Iran-US CTR 409, 410, 412, 413
　　(1985–II) 289, 303, 707, 708, 722
　Award No 255–48–3 (19 September 1986), 12 Iran-US CTR 170, 172, 186-7, 225,
　　228 (1986–III) 120, 122, 140, 426, 441, 443, 494, 499, 639
　Decision No DEC 58–48–3 (19 March 1987), 14 Iran-US CTR 173, 174
　　(1987–I).. 803, 809, 813, 818
American International Group Inc and the Islamic Republic of Iran, Award No 93–2–3
　(19 December 1983), 4 Iran-US CTR 96–8, 111 (1983–II)... 322, 470, 721, 812, 815
Amman & Whitney and Ministry of Housing and Urban Development (Khuzestan
　Department of Housing and Urban Development):
　Case No 198, Chamber One, Order of 30 January 1984 ....42, 70
　Award No 248–198–1, pp. 8–9 (25 Aug 1986) 442
Amoco 227, 243, 257–8
Amoco International Finance Corp and the Islamic Republic of Iran:
　Case No 56, Chamber Three, Order of 8 October 1986................................875, 892
　Award No 310–56–3 (14 July 1987), 15 Iran–US
　　CTR 189, 236–41 (1987–II)... 128–9, 133, 144
Amoco International Finance Corp and National Iranian Oil Co, Case No 56, Chamber
　Three, Order of 22 February 1984..676, 684
Amoco Iran Oil Co and the Islamic Republic of Iran, Case No 55...............184, 414, 420
Anaconda-Iran Inc and the Islamic Republic of Iran:
　Order of 11 October 1984, Case No 167, Chamber Three..................425–6, 439, 507
　Award No ITL 65–167–3 (10 December 1986), 13 Iran–US
　　CTR 199, 232–33 (1986–III)..127–9, 143
Arco Exploration Inc and National Iranian Oil Co:
　Case No 20, Chamber One, Order of 17 December 1986 ....508, 510
　Case No 21, Chamber One, Order of 7 December 1989 ....641, 653, 664
　Case Nos 20 & 21, Chamber One, Order of 13 June 1990 .... 637, 644, 653, 663–4
　Case Nos 20 & 21, Chamber One, Order of 20 November 1990........................... 654

Case Nos 20 & 21, Chamber One, Order of 5 February 1991 665
Case Nos 20 & 21, Chamber One, Order of 2 June 1992 665
Case Nos 20 & 21, Chamber One Order of 17 July 1992 667
Arthur Young & Co and the Islamic Republic of Iran, Award No 338–484–1
  (30 November 1987), (1 December 1987) 17 Iran-US CTR 245, 253–54, 262–63
  (1987–IV) 412, 419, 471, 473, 484, 560, 584
Aryeh, Ouziel et al and the Islamic Republic of Iran:
  Case Nos 839 and 840, Chamber One, Order of 13 May 1994 .... 506, 512
  Case Nos 839 and 840, Chamber Three, Order of 18 January 1996 .... 566, 568, 591
  Award No 584–839/840–3 (25 September 1997), 33 Iran–US
    CTR 460, 477 (1997) 116, 140
Aryeh, Vera-Jo Miller et al and the Islamic Republic of Iran:
  Case Nos 842, 843 and 844, Chamber One, Order of 15 January 1992 .... 384, 390
  Case Nos 842, 843 and 844, Chamber One, Order of 6 March 1992 590
  Case Nos 842, 843 and 844, Chamber One, Order of 15 February 1993 .... 507, 511
  Award No 581–842/843/844–1 (22 May 1997), 33 Iran-US CTR 272, 278,
    282, 287 (1997) 31, 73, 383, 391, 494, 504, 559, 586, 625–7, 629, 896
Assistance in Developing Educational System Inc and the Islamic Republic of Iran, Case
  No 218 Chamber One, Order of 31 October 1983 .... 822, 825
Atlantic Richfield Co and the Islamic Republic of Iran, Award No ITM 50–396–1
  (8 May 1985), 8 Iran-US CTR 179, 181–182 (1985–I) 545
Austin Co and Machine Sazi Arak, Case No 295, Chamber Two, Order of
  30 July 1982 .... 30, 53, 74
Avco Corp and Iran Aircraft Industries:
  Case No 261, Chamber Three, Order of 27 January 1984 544
  Award No 377–261–3 (18 July 1988), 19 Iran-US CTR 200, 214, 231, 235, 238,
    253, 254–55 (1988–II) 34, 44, 672, 753–4, 812, 819
Bank Markazi Iran and Bank of Boston International, New York, Case No 733, Chamber
  Two, Order of 8 December 1983 .... 472, 479
Bank Markazi Iran and European American Banking Corp, Case No 679, Chamber Two,
  Order of 22 January 1986 .... 813, 817
Bank Markazi Iran and Federal Reserve Bank of New York, Award No 595–823–3
  (16 November 1999), Dissenting Opinion of Mohsen Aghahosseini
  (June 13, 2000) 458, 466
Bank Markazi Iran and Rainier National Bank, Case No 738, Chamber Two, Order of
  29 November 1985 .... 789, 798
Bank Melli and Chase Manhattan Bank, Cases Nos. 510, 534, 540, 541, 543, 548,
  and 556 443
Bank Mellat and United States of America (Case Nos 582 and 591),
  Award No 108-A-16/582/591-FT (25 January 1984), 5 Iran-US
  CTR 57, 59 (1984–I) 443, 624
Bank Tejarat, Case No 163 684
Bechtel Inc et al and Government of the Islamic Republic of Iran et al,
  Case No 181, Chamber One, Order of 17 February 1986 .... 900, 904
Behring International Inc and the Islamic Republic of Iran Air Force:
  Decision No DEC 27–382–3 (19 December 1983), 4 Iran-US CTR 89, 92–5
  (1983–III) 637, 639, 660, 661, 664, 897, 904

Amendment to Decision of 19 December 1983, 6 Iran-US
   CTR 30, 32 (1984–II) 645, 665
Amendment to Decision of 3 May 1984, 6 Iran-US CTR 30 (1984–II) 641
Award No ITM 46–382–3 (22 February 1985), 8 Iran-US
   CTR 44, 46, 47–48 (1985–I) 527, 536, 550, 737
Award No ITM/ITL 52–382–3 (21 June 1985), 8 Iran-US CTR 238, 265, 273,
   275–76, 280 (1985–I) 424, 439, 518, 530, 546, 551, 646
Award No 52–382–3 (29 Oct 1991), 27 Iran-US
   CTR 218, 245–46 (1991–II) 678, 689, 872, 895
Bendix Corp and the Islamic Republic of Iran:
   Case No 208, Chamber Two, Order of 24 August 1987 511
   Case No 208, Chamber Two, Order of 28 September 1987 ....508, 510
Bendone-Derossi International and the Islamic Republic of Iran, Award No ITM
   40–375–1 (7 June 1984), 6 Iran-US CTR 130, 131–132, 133 (1984–II) 523, 545
Birnbaum, Harold and the Islamic Republic of Iran:
   Award No 549–967–2 (6 July 1993) 29 Iran-US
      CTR 260, 265 (1993) 486, 816, 820
   Decision No DEC 124–967–2 (14 December 1995), 31 Iran-US
      CTR 286, 289–90 (1995) 811, 820, 833–4
Blount Brothers Corp and the Islamic Republic of Iran:
   Award No 74–62–3 (2 September 1983), 3 Iran-US CTR 225, 226, 237–38, 254–55,
      268–69, 276–77, 291–96 (1983–II) 427, 437, 770, 775
   Award No 216–53–1 (6 March 1986), 10 Iran-US
      CTR 95, 96, 102 (1986–I) 292, 875
Boeing Co. et al and Government of the Islamic Republic of Iran, Award No ITM
   34–222–1 (17 February 1984), 5 Iran US CTR 152.. 549
Boyle, Charles W (a claim of less than US $250,000 presented by the United States of
   America) and the Islamic Republic of Iran, Case No 12129, Chamber Three, Order of
   13 September 1990..788, 799
Brown & Root Inc and the Islamic Republic of Iran:
   Case No 432, Chamber One, Order of 31 May 1985 798
   Case No 432, Chamber One, Order of 4 December 1987 .... 495, 501, 575–6, 587
   Case No 50, Chamber One, Order of 4 January 1993 ....568–70, 590
Buckamier, W Jack and the Islamic Republic of Iran, Award No 528–941–3
   (6 March 1992) 28 Iran-US CTR 53, 60–2, 74–76 (1992) 471–2, 485,
   .... 508, 511, 560, 564, 574, 585, 587, 598, 789
Burton, Marks et al and the Islamic Republic of Iran, Award No ITL 53–458–3 (26 June
   1985), 8 Iran-US CTR 290 (1985–I) 738
Cabot International Capital Corp and Overseas Private Investment Corp and the Islamic
   Republic of Iran Case No 96, Chamber One, Order of 25 March 1983 ....495, 498
Cal-Maine Foods Inc and the Islamic Republic of Iran, Award No 133–340–3 (11 June
   1984), 6 Iran-US CTR 52, 59–60, 62–63 (1984–II).........................472–3, 481, 559
Carlson, RPM and the Islamic Republic of Iran, Case No 248, Chamber One,
   Order of 12 August 1986 ....568, 590
Carolina Brass Inc and Arya Shipping Lines, Award No 252–10035–2
   (12 September 1986), 12 Iran–US CTR 139, 144–145 (1986–III) 126, 133
CBS Inc and the Islamic Republic of Iran, Award No 486–197–2 (28 June 1990),
   25 Iran-US CTR 131, 149–50 (1990–II)...431, 445

Chamness, Ronald E and Government of the Islamic Republic of Iran et al,
  Award No 488–380–3 (9 August 1990), 25 Iran-US CTR
  172, 176 (1990–II) 872, 895
Chas T Main International Inc and Khusestan Water & Power Authority et al:
  Award No ITL 23–120–2 (27 July 1983), 3 Iran-US CTR
    156, 168 (1983–II) 637, 644–5, 770, 775, 897, 903
  Award No 70–185–3 (2 September 1983), 3 Iran-US CTR 237–38, 254–55,
    268–69, 276–77, 291–96 (1983–II) 770, 775
  Case No 120, Chamber Two, Order of 23 November 1983, 4 Iran-US
    CTR 60 (1983–III) 646
  Award No ITL 35–120–2 (16 March 1984), 5 Iran-US
    CTR 185, 185–6 (1984–I) 738, 898
  Award No 45–120–2 (8 February 1985), 11 Iran-US CTR 41 (1986–II) 738
  Case No 120, Chamber Two, Order of
    14 February 1986 .... 565, 572–3, 593, 595, 604, 617, 662, 667
Cherafat, Gloria Jean and the Islamic Republic of Iran, Decision No DEC 106–277–2
  (25 June 1992), 28 Iran-US CTR 216, 221–23 (1992) 30, 45, 71, 791–2
Chevron Research Co and National Iranian Oil Co:
  Case No 19, Chamber One, Order of 19 November 1982 .... 455, 464
  Award on Agreed Terms No 48–18–1 (1 June 1983), 2 Iran-US CTR
    364, 364–65 (1983–I) 776
Civil International Inc 128
CMI International Inc and Ministry of Roads and Transportation of the Islamic
  Republic of Iran, Award No 99–245–2 (27 December 1983), 4 Iran–US CTR
  263, 267–68 (1983–III) 128, 142, 560, 582
Collins Systems International Inc and Navy of the Islamic Republic of Iran, Case
  No 431, Chamber Two, Order of 23 September 1987 .... 425, 441
Commercial Development Centre and US State Dept (Ex US Embassy in Iran), Case
  No B65, Chamber Two, Order of 28 September 1987 .... 494, 501
Component Builders Inc et al and the Islamic Republic of Iran:
  Case No 395, Chamber Three, Order of 19 February 1985 .... 50, 75
  Award No ITM/ITL 51–395–3 (27 May 1985), 8 Iran-US
    CTR 216, 220, 225–26 (1985–I) 523, 546
  Case No 395, Chamber Three, Order of 22 November 1985 .... 678, 687
  Decision No DEC 40–395–3 (18 December 1985), 9 Iran-US
    CTR 404 (1985–II) 817
  Correction to Award No 431–395–3 (2 February 1990), 23 Iran-US
    CTR 122, 123, 125 (1989–III) 812, 816, 819
Computer Sciences Corp and the Islamic Republic of Iran:
  Award No ITL 49–65–1 (18 April 1985), 8 Iran-US CTR 99 (1985–I) 738
  Award No 221–65–1 (16 April 1986), 10 Iran-US CTR 269, 272–273, 309-11, 316
    (1986–I) 379, 386, 430, 440, 442, 508–9, 846
Continental Grain Export Corp and Government Trading Corp et al,
  Award No 75–112–1 (5 September 1983), 3 Iran-US CTR 319 (1983–II) 736
Control Data Corp and the Islamic Republic of Iran:
  Case No 88, Chamber Three, Order of 20 December 1985 .... 493, 495, 498
  Decision No DEC 86–88–3 (30 June 1989), 22 Iran-US
    CTR 151, 153 (1989–II) 812, 816

Cook Industries Inc and Foreign Transactions Co et al, Case No 393, Chamber Two,
  Order of 6 September 1985 ....694, 696
Craig, Alan and Ministry of Energy of Iran, Award No 71–346–3 (2 September 1983),
  3 Iran-US CTR 237–38, 254–55, 268–69, 276–77, 291–93, 294–96
  (1983–II) 720, 770, 775
Cummins, John Francis and the Islamic Republic of Iran (a claim of less than
  US $250, 000 presented by the United States of America):
  Case No 11723, Chamber One, Order of 7 November 1986 688
  Case No 11723, Chamber One, Order of 21 January 1987, 14 Iran-US
    CTR 21, 21 (1987–I) 678, 688
Cyrus Petroleum Ltd and the Islamic Republic of Iran:
  Case No 624, Chamber One Order of 30 May 1985 ....414, 420, 423, 436
  Award No 230–624–1 (2 May 1986), 11 Iran-US CTR 70, 71 (1986–II).......415, 436
Dadras International and the Islamic Republic of Iran:
  Case Nos 213, 214, 215, Chamber Three, Order of 13 January 1993...................... 621
  Case Nos 213, 214, 215, Chamber Three, Order of 22 January 1993..............612, 621
  Case Nos 213 and 215, Chamber Three, Letter from the Agent of the Islamic
    Republic of Iran, (27 May 1994) 628
  Case Nos 213 and 215, Order of 22 July 1994, 30 Iran-US CTR
    104, 105, 109–12 (1994)...626–7, 628, 630, 631
  Award No 567–213/215–3 (7 November 1995), 31 Iran-US CTR
    127, 135–36, 143-4, 204–5 (1995) 31, 72–3, 76, 494, 503, 559, 585–6, 607,
                                                                              622, 624, 628, 632, 895–6
Daley, Leonard and Mavis, a claim less than US $250,000 presented by United States of
  America and the Islamic Republic of Iran, Award No 360–10514–1 (20 April 1988)
  18 Iran-US CTR 232, 242 (1988–I) 560, 584
Dallal and the Islamic Republic of Iran, Bank Mellat:
  Award No 53–149–1 (10 June 1983) 3 Iran-US
    CTR 10, 11 (1983–II)... 44, 472, 480, 560, 582, 754
  Decision No DEC 30–149–1 (10 January 1984) 5 Iran-US
    CTR 74, 75 (1984–I) 71–2, 836
Dames & Moore and the Islamic Republic of Iran:
  Award No 97–54–3 322–3
  Decision No DEC 36–54–3 (23 April 1985), 5 Iran-US CTR 107, 117–18 (1984–I)
    and 8 Iran-US CTR 107, 115, 117 (1985–I).......... 30, 70, 71–2, 627, 829–30, 836
Davidson, George E (Homayounjah) and Government of the Islamic Republic of Iran:
  Case No 457, Chamber One, Order of 14 February 1995 ....384, 390
  Award No 585–457–1 (5 March 1998), 34 Iran-US CTR 4, 5–6 (1998) 380, 391
Development and Resources Corp and the Islamic Republic of Iran:
  Case No 60, Chamber Three, Order of 31 January 1985................................388, 507
  Award No 485–60–3 (25 June 1990), 25 Iran-US CTR 20, 109–10
    (1990–II) 627, 871, 893
  Decision No DEC 98–60–3 (30 May 1991), 26 Iran-US CTR 256,
    261 (1991–I).. 833
DIC of Delaware Inc and Tehran Redevelopment Corp, Award No 176–255–3
  (26 April 1985), 8 Iran–US CTR 144, 156–7, 160–162
  (1985–I)..122, 127, 132, 140

Donin de Rosiere, Paul and the Islamic Republic of Iran:
    Case No 498, Chamber One, Order of 6 September 1985 637
    Award No ITM 64–498–1 (4 December 1986), 13 Iran-US
        CTR 193, 194, 196–98 (1986–IV) 519, 548, 737
    Decision No DEC 57–498–1 (10 February 1987), 14 Iran-US
        CTR 100, 101 (1987–I) 803, 809, 812, 818
Dow Chemical Co, Judge Kashani's Reasons for Not Signing Award No 127–257–1
    (undated), 6 Iran-US CTR 39, 40 (1984–II) 775
Dresser Industries Inc and the Islamic Republic of Iran and SSK Magcobar Iran, Case
    Nos 107, 109 and 110, Chamber Three, Order of 27 January 1983 .... 567–8, 588
Drucker, George W Jr and Foreign Transaction Co:
    Case No 121, Chamber Two, Order of 8 May 1984 .... 561, 583
    Case No 121, Chamber Two, Order of 2 May 1986 .... 46, 70
E-Systems Inc and the Islamic Republic of Iran:
    Interim Award No ITM 13–388-FT (February 1983), 2 Iran-US
        CTR 51, 54, 57 .... 46, 49, 543–4, 546–8
    Award on Agreed Terms 94–388–1 (19 December 1983), 4 Iran-US
        CTR 197, 197–98 (1983–III) 777
Eastman Kodak Co and the Islamic Republic of Iran, Dec No DEC 102–227–3
    (30 December 1991), 27 Iran-US CTR 269, 269 (1991–II) 830
Ebrahimi, Shahin Shaine and Government of the Islamic Republic of Iran:
    Dr. Aghahosseini's Dissent to Order of 26 July 1991 in Cases Nos. 44, 46,
        47 and 146 294
    Case Nos 44, 46 & 47, Chamber Three, Order of 20 July 1992 .... 648, 650–3
    Case Nos 44, 46 & 47, Chamber Three, Order of 5 October 1992 .... 640–1, 651
    Case Nos 44, 46 & 47, Chamber Three, Order of
        14 December 1992 .... 640–1, 651, 897, 904
    Case Nos 44, 46 & 47, Chamber Three, Order of 4 February 1993, 30 Iran-US
        CTR 170 (1994) 637, 652, 663
    Award No 560–44/46/47–3 (12 October 1994), 30 Iran-US CTR
        170, 204, 236 (1994) 471, 487, 646, 648, 664, 721
Economy Forms Corp and the Islamic Republic of Iran, Award No 55–165–1
    (14 June 1983), 3 Iran–US CTR 42, 47–48, 55 (1983–II), 5 Iran-US CTR
    1, 23 (1984–I) 122, 126, 132, 563, 597, 619, 620, 705, 719
Electronic Systems International Inc and Ministry of Defence of the Islamic Republic
    of Iran et al, Award No 430–814–1 (28 July 1989), 22 Iran-US CTR 339, 335
    (1989–II) 871, 893
Elghanayan, Dora Sholeh et al and the Islamic Republic of Iran, Award on Agreed
    Terms No 576–800/801/802/803/804–3 (10 December 1996), 32 Iran-US
    CTR 221, 222 (1996) 779
Endo Laboratories Inc and the Islamic Republic of Iran, Decision No DEC 74–366–3
    (25 February 1988), 18 Iran-US CTR 113 (1988–I) 80, 809, 818–19
Esphanian, Judge Shafeiei's Reasons for Not Signing Award No 31–157–2
    (29 March 1983), 2 Iran-US CTR 170, 170 (1983–I) 769, 774
Etezadi, Catherine and Government of the Islamic Republic of Iran, Award
    No 554–319–1 (23 March 1994), Dissenting Opinion of Richard M Mosk
    (23 March 1994), 30 Iran–US CTR 45, 49–50 (1994) 139

Exxon Research and Engineering Co and the Islamic Republic of Iran, Decision No DEC
    63–155–3 (29 July 1987), 16 Iran-US CTR 110, 111 (1987–III)....................823, 826
Fedders Corp and Loristan Refrigeration Industries:
    Decision No DEC 51–250–3 (28 October 1986), 13 Iran-US CTR
        97, 98 (1986–IV) 469, 473, 483–4
    Case No 250, Chamber Three, Order of 5 January 1988......................................42, 71
Fereydoon Ghaffari and the Islamic Republic of Iran:
    Case No 10792, Chamber Two, Order of 15 September 1987, 18 Iran-US
        CTR 64 (1988–I) 472, 483
    Case No 968, Chamber Two, Order of 2 February 1988, Dissenting Opinion of
        Judge Khalilian (10 February 1988), 18 Iran-US CTR 79 (1988–I)............457, 464
    Case No 968, Communication to the Parties, (10 February 1988) 707
    Decision No DEC 123–968–2 (30 October 1995), 31 Iran-US
        CTR 124 (1995) 820
First National Bank of Boston and the Islamic Republic of Iran Decision No DEC
    83–202–2 (19 September 1988), Separate Opinion of Seyed Khalil Khalilian
    (23 September 1988), 19 Iran-US CTR 310, 311–12 (1988–II) 430, 445
Flexi-Van Leasing Inc and the Islamic Republic of Iran:
    Judge Holtzmann's Dissent from Order of 15 June 1982, 1 Iran-US CTR
        166, 167 (15 June 1982)..354, 356
    Order of 17 June 1982, 1 Iran-US CTR 166, 167 (1982)....................................... 355
    Case No 36, Chamber One, Order of 15 December 1982, 1 Iran-US CTR
        455 (1981–82) 580
    Case No 36, Chamber One, Order of 20 December 1982, 1 Iran-US CTR
        455 (1981–82) 594
    Award No 259–36–1 (13 October 1986), 12 Iran-US CTR 335, 346
        (1986–III) 472, 558, 560, 596
    Decision No DEC 54–36–1 (18 December 1986), 13 Iran-US CTR
        324, 324–27 (1986–IV) 610, 623, 823, 826
Fluor Corp and the Islamic Republic of Iran:
    Award No ITM 62–333–1 (6 August 1986), 11 Iran-US CTR 296 (1986–II) 737
    Case No 810, Chamber One, Order of 16 February 1987 ....383, 388, 493, 500
Ford Aerospace & Communications Corp et al and Air Force of the Islamic Republic of Iran:
    Award No ITM 16-93-2 (27 April 1983), 2 Iran-US CTR
        281, 282 (1983–I) 518, 543
    Case No 93, Dissenting Opinion of Mohsen Mostafavi to the Order of 28 February
        1986, 4 March 1986, 10 Iran-US CTR 108, 109 (1986–1) 33
    Decision No DEC 47–159–3 (2 October 1986), 12 Iran-US CTR
        304 (1986–III) 803, 806, 808
    Award No 289–93–1 (29 January 1987) 484
Foremost Tehran Inc and the Islamic Republic of Iran, Case Nos 37 and 231,
    Chamber One Order of 15 September 1983, 3 Iran-US CTR
    361, 362 (1983–II)...32–3, 70, 500
Forum Selection Clause Cases:
    Dissent of Judges Holtzmann, Aldrich, and Mosk from the Procedural Decisions
    in Nine Forum Selection Clause Cases, Case Nos 6, 51, 68, 121, 140, 159,
    254, 293 and 466 (6 July 1982), 1 Iran-US CTR 320, 320, 324
    (1981–82) 673, 684

Dissenting and Concurring Opinion of Richard M Mosk on the Issues of Jurisdiction
(5 November 1982), 1 Iran-US CTR 305, 308 (1981–82) 463
Concurring and Dissenting Opinions of Howard M Holtzmann with respect to
Interlocutory Awards on Jurisdiction in Nine Cases, (5 November 1982), 1 Iran-US
CTR 284, 294 (1981–82)..453, 463–4
Dissent by Judge Mosk from Orders Granting Further Extensions of Time to File
Statements of Defence (1983 Tribunal Rules) 673
Dissent of Howard M Holtzmann from Orders Granting Further Extensions of Time
to File Statements of Defence, Case Nos 452 and 926, Chamber One (20 June
1983), 3 Iran-US CTR 84, 85–86 (1983–II).. 684
Futura Trading Inc and Khuzestan Water and Power Authority, Award No 187–325–3
(19 August 1985), 9 Iran-US CTR 46 (1985–II).. 875
Gabay, Norman and the Islamic Republic of Iran:
   Case No 771, Chamber Two, Order of 5 December 1986..........................678, 688
   Decision No DEC 99–77–2 (24 September 1991), 27 Iran-US CTR
   194, 195 (1991–II)..803, 810
Gami Investments Inc and Government of The United Mexican States, Procedural Order
No 1 (31 January 2003) (Ad Hoc Proceeding)...494, 497, 505
General Dynamics Telephone Systems Center and the Islamic Republic of Iran, Award
No 192–285–2 (4 October 1985), 9 Iran-US CTR 153 444
General Electric Co and Government of the Islamic Republic of Iran:
   Case No 386 Chamber One, Order of 10 December 1987 .... 30, 33, 71, 493, 501
   Award No 507 386–1 (15 March 1991), 26 Iran-US CTR 1
   48, 183 (1991–I) 871, 876, 893
General Motors Corp et al and Government of the Islamic Republic of Iran et al:
   Partial Award on Agreed Terms No 147–94–1 (28 August 1984), 7 Iran-US CTR
   220, 221–22 (1984–III) 778
   Case No 94, Chamber One, Order of 18 January 1983, Iranian Assets Litigation
   Reporter 6247 (18 March 1983) 560
General Petrochemicals Corp and the Islamic Republic of Iran, Award No 522–828–1
(21 October 1991), 27 Iran-US CTR 196 (1991–II).. 627
George J Meyer Manufacturing Division of Figgie International Inc and Zamzam
Bottling Company:
   Case No 299, Chamber One, Order of 26 September 1983................................. 685
   Case No 299, Chamber One, Order of 22 March 1984 ....673, 677, 685
Gianoplus, Konstantine A and the Islamic Republic of Iran, Case No 314, Chamber
One, Order of 29 March 1984 687
Gibbs & Hill Inc and Iran Power Generation and Transmission Co et al, Award No ITL
1–6-FT (5 November 1982), 1 Iran-US CTR 236 (1981–82) 737
Golpira, Judge Shafeiei's Reasons for Not Signing Award No 32–211–2 (29 March 1983),
2 Iran-US CTR 177, 177 (1983–I) 769, 774
Golshani, Abraham Rahman and the Islamic Republic of Iran, Award No 546–812–3
(2 March 1993), 29 Iran-US CTR 78, 93, 116 (1993) 559, 585, 631
Gould Marketing Inc and Ministry of Defence of the Islamic Republic of Iran:
   Award No ITL 24–49–23 (27 July 1983), 3 Iran-US CTR 155
   (1983–II)...770, 775
   Award No 136–49/50 (29 June 1984), 6 Iran-US CTR 272 (1984–II)............43, 424

Government of the United States of America on behalf and for the benefit of Linen, Fortinberry and Associates Inc, and the Islamic Republic of Iran, Award No ITM 48–10513–2 (10 April 1985), 8 Iran-US CTR 85 (1985–I) 737
Government of the United States of America on behalf and for the benefit of Shipside Packing Co Inc and the Islamic Republic of Iran:
   Award No ITM 27–11875–1 (6 September 1983), 3 Iran-US CTR
     331 (1983–II) 737
   Award on Agreed Terms No 102–11875–1 (12 January 1984), 5 Iran-US CTR
     80, 80–81, 82, 84 (1984–I) 778
Granger Associates and the Islamic Republic of Iran et al, Award No 320–184–1
   (20 October 1987), 16 Iran-US CTR 317–34 (1987–III) 754
Granite State Machine Co Inc and the Islamic Republic of Iran et al:
   Partial Award No 9–30–3 (29 July 1982), 1 Iran-US CTR
     185, 187–88 (1981–82) 711, 736, 766
   Award No 18–30–3 (15 December 1982), 1 Iran-US CTR
     442, 447, 44 (1981–82)..723, 846
Gruen Associates Inc and Iran Housing Co, Award No 61–188–2 (27 July 1983)
   3 Iran-US CTR 97, 107, 108–09, 124, 124–25 (1983–II) 639, 769, 774, 775
Gruen Associates and the Islamic Republic of Iran, Award No 61–180–2 (27 July 1983),
   3 Iran-US CTR 97, 108 (1983–II).. 283
Gulf Associates, et al and the Islamic Republic of Iran et al, Case No 385, Chamber Two
   Order of 11 December 1997 ....844, 898–9, 905
H A Spalding Inc and Ministry of Roads and Transport of the Islamic Republic of Iran
   et al, Final Award of 24 February 1986, 10 Iran-US CTR 22, 25 (1986) 353–4
Harnischfeger Corp and Ministry of Roads and Transportation:
   Partial Award No 144–180–3 (13 July 1984), (31 July 1984) 7 Iran–US CTR
     90, 97–98, 99 (1984–III).. 128, 132, 289, 303, 736, 766
   Award No 175–180–3 (26 April 1985), 8 Iran-US CTR 119, 134 (1985–I) 406
Harris International Telecommunications Inc and the Islamic Republic of Iran:
   Order of 6 March 1986.. 500
   Award No 323–409–1 (2 November 1987), 17 Iran-US CTR 31, 45–52, 55–61, 62–3
     (1987–II) 72–3, 425–6, 442, 471, 473–4, 483, 485, 494, 500–1, 503,
                  504, 511,559, 563–5, 593, 597, 612, 620, 625, 629
   Decision No DEC 73–409–1 (26 January 1988), 18 Iran-US CTR
     76, 77 (1986–IV) 818, 823, 826
HAUS *see* Housing and Urban Services International Inc and The Government of the Islamic Republic of Iran et al
Herman Blum Consulting Engineers Inc and the Islamic Republic of Iran, Case
   No 138, Chamber One, Order of 20 September 1982 ....429, 447
Hoffman Export Corp (a division of Gould Inc) and Ministry of National Defence of
   Iran Case No 50, Chamber Two, Order of 8 December 1983................................ 508
Hood Corp and the Islamic Republic of Iran, Decision No DEC 34–100–3 (1 March
   1985), 8 Iran-US CTR 53–4 (1985–I).. 379–80, 386, 402, 405
Hooshang, Kahen and the Islamic Republic of Iran, Case No 315, Chamber Two, Order
   of 22 January 1986 ....381, 384, 388
Housing and Urban Services International Inc and the Islamic Republic of Iran et al:
   Case No 174, Chamber One, Order of 17 January 1984 ....127, 131
   Award No 201–174–1 (22 November 1985), 9 Iran-US CTR 313, 329 138–9

Houston Contracting Co and National Iranian Oil Co et al, Award No 378–173–3 (22 July 1988), 20 Iran-US CTR 3, 36–8, 128 (1988–III) 431, 444, 872, 895

Howard Needles Tammen & Bergendoff and the Islamic Republic of Iran, Award No 244–68–2 (8 August 1986), 11 Iran-US CTR 302, 327 (1986–II) 442, 560, 584

Hyatt International Corp et al and Government of the Islamic Republic of Iran et al, Award No ITL 54–134–1 (17 September 1985), 9 Iran-US CTR 72 (1985–II) 738

INA Corp and the Islamic Republic of Iran, Award No 184–61–1 (12 & 13 August 1985), 8 Iran-US CTR 373, 377, 382 (1985–I) 570, 573, 589, 595

Interfirst Bank Dallas, NA and the Islamic Republic of Iran, Decision No DEC 66–338–2 (9 October 1987), 16 Iran-US CTR 291 (1987–III) 424, 441

International Ore & Fertilizer Corp and Razi Chemical Co Ltd, Award No 351–468–3 (19 February 1988), Dissenting Opinion of Judge Brower (February 29, 1988), 18 Iran-US CTR 98, 102 et seq (1988–I) 559

International Schools Services Inc and the Islamic Republic of Iran et al:
  Award No ITL 37–111-FT (6 April 1984), 5 Iran-US CTR 338 (1984–I) 737
  Award No 194–111–1 (10 October 1985) 141
  Award No ITL 57–123–1 (30 January 1986), 10 Iran-US CTR 6 (1986–I) 469, 472, 474, 480, 484–5, 488, 738, 872
  Award No 290–123–1 (29 January 1987), 14 Iran-US CTR 65, 80 (1987–I) 832, 872, 894
  Decision No DEC 61–123–1 (28 April 1987), 14 Iran-US CTR 279 (1987–I) 823, 826

International Systems & Controls Corp and Industrial Development and Renovation Organization et al, Award No 256–439–2 (September 26, 1986), Dissenting Opinion of Judge Brower (26 September 1986), 12 Iran-US CTR 265, 268, note 9 (1986–III) 706, 708, 722

International Systems & Controls and National Iranian Gas Co, Case No 494, Chamber Three, Order of 24 December 1986 .... 569, 590

International Technical Products Corp et al and Government of the Islamic Republic of Iran, 9 Iran-US CTR 10, 15 (1985–II) 353, 354
  Partial Award No 186–302–3 (19 August 1985) (linguistics), 9 Iran-US CTR 10, 32–5 (1985–II) 637
  Award No 196–302–3 (24 & 28 October 1985), 9 Iran-US CTR 206, 226–27 (1985–II) 425, 440–1, 444, 875
  Decision No DEC 41–302–3 (16 June 1986) 11 Iran-US CTR 182, 183 (1986–II) 405, 805

Intrend International Inc and Imperial Iranian Air Force, Award No 59-220-2 (27 July 1982), 3 Iran-US CTR 110, 116, 117, 117–18, 124–5 (1983–II) 425, 436, 770, 774–5

Iran Chevron Oil Co and the Islamic Republic of Iran, Case No 73, Chamber Three, Order of 15 April 1986 .... 786, 793

Iran National Airlines Co and United States of America, Award No 337-B10–2 (30 November 1987), 17 Iran–US CTR 238, 239–40 (1987–III) 141

Isaiah, Benjamin R and Bank Mellat (as successor to International Bank of Iran), Award No 35–219–2 (30 March 1983), 2 Iran-US CTR 232, 237, 238–39 (1983–I) 128, 133, 141, 560, 581

ITEL International Corp and Social Security Organization of Iran et al, Award No ITL
  43–476–2 (22 June 1984), 7 Iran-US CTR 31 (1984–III) 737
ITT Industries Inc and the Islamic Republic of Iran et al, Award No 47–156–2 (26 May
  1983) 712
JL Case Co and the Islamic Republic of Iran, Award No 57–224–1 (15 June 1983),
  Dissenting Opinion of Judge Holtzmann (27 July 1983), 3 Iran-US CTR
  62, 66 et seq (1983–II) 559, 573
Karim-Panahi, Parviz and Government of the United States of America, Decision
  No DEC 108–182–2 (27 October 1992), 28 Iran-US CTR 318 (1992) 803, 810
Karubian, Rouhollah and the Islamic Republic of Iran, Case No 419, Chamber Two,
  Order of 17 March 1986 .... 383, 388
Kaysons International Corp and the Islamic Republic of Iran et al, Case No 367,
  Chamber Two, Order of 8 October 1992 .... 563, 599
Khoshravi, Thomas K and Government of the Islamic Republic of Iran:
  Case No 146, Chamber Three, Order of 2 March 1995 618
  Case No 146, Chamber Three, Order of 18 October 1985 .... 683, 685
Kianoosh Jafari and the Islamic Republic of Iran, Award No 349–420–3 (29 February
  1988), 18 Iran-US CTR 90 (1988–I) 678
Kimberly-Clark Corp and Bank Markazi Iran et al, Award No 46–57–2 (25 May 1983),
  2 Iran-US CTR 334, 344, 338, 343 (1983–I) 470, 480, 769
Ladjevardi (formerly Burgel), Ninni and the Islamic Republic of Iran:
  Case No 118, Chamber One, Order of 24 March 1993 .... 50, 76
  Award No 553–118–1 (8 December 1993), 29 Iran-US
    CTR 367, 377 (1993) 494, 502
Leach, Jimmie B and the Islamic Republic of Iran, Award No 440–12183–1 (6 October
  1989), 23 Iran-US CTR 233, 234 (1989–III) 289, 304
Lerner, Kay and the Islamic Republic of Iran, Case No 242, Chamber Three, Order of
  6 August 1982, 1 Iran-US CTR 215 (1981–82) 414–15, 419
Levitt, William J and the Islamic Republic of Iran, Award No 297–207–1 (22 April
  1987) 14 Iran-US CTR 91, 197–98 (1987–I) 612, 619–20
Litton Systems Inc and the Islamic Republic of Iran, Award No 249–769–1 (25 August
  1986), 12 Iran-US CTR 126, 131 (1986–III) 472, 483
McCollough & Co Inc and Ministry of Post, Telegraph and Telephone:
  Award No 225–89–3 (22 April 1986), 11 Iran-US CTR
    3, 17–18, 35, 44 (1986–II) 472–3, 482, 487, 639, 846, 871, 892
  Decision No DEC 44–89–3 (7 July 1986), 11 Iran-US CTR 287 (1986–II) 405
Malek, Reza Said and the Islamic Republic of Iran:
  Award No ITL 68–193–3 (23 June 1988), 19 Iran-US CTR
    48, 52–53 (1988–II) 472, 485, 678
  Award No 534–193–3 (11 August 1992), 28 Iran-US CTR
    246, 249–50, 287–88, 291–92 (1992) 73, 503, 558, 584
Malekzadeh, Joan Ward and the Islamic Republic of Iran, Case No 356, Chamber One,
  Order of 12 August 1993 .... 495, 502
Marine Midland Bank NA and Bank Tejarat, Case No 163, Chamber Two, Order of
  14 July 1983 .... 676, 684
MCA Inc and the Islamic Republic of Iran, Case No 768, Chamber Two, Order of
  6 October 1983 .... 567–8, 588

Mercantile Trust Co National Association and the Islamic Republic of Iran, Case No 351
 Chamber Two, Order of 23 April 1993 ....789, 800
Ministry of Defence of the Islamic Republic of Iran v Gould Inc:
 Order of 14 January 1988, (1988) Mealey's International Arb Rep 3....................... 43
 Decision of 23 October 1989, [1989] CDOS 7832, 7835, 7836 43–4
Ministry of National Defence of the Islamic Republic of Iran and United States of
 America and Bell Helicopter Textron Co, Decision No DEC 100-A3/A8-FT
 (22 November 1991), 27 Iran-US CTR 256 (1991–II) 791, 873, 874
Ministry of National Defence of the Islamic Republic of Iran and United States of
 America:
  Case No B1, Full Tribunal, Order of 18 November 1983, 4 Iran-US CTR
   57, 58 (1983–III) 588
  Award No 247-B59/B69–1 (15 August 1986) 12 Iran-US CTR
   33, 36 (1986–III) 872, 894
  Order of 2 July 1987, Dissenting Opinion of Mr Ameli (2 July 1987), 18 Iran-US
   CTR 47–48 (1988–I) 723
Mobil Oil Iran Inc et al and the Islamic Republic of Iran, Award No 311–74/
 76/81/150–3 (14 July 1987), 16 Iran-US CTR 3, 20-8, 55
 (1987–III) 114, 116, 129, 136, 788
Mohajer-Shojaee, Reza and Shahnaz and the Islamic Republic of Iran, Decision No DEC
 95–273–1 (26 December 1990), 25 Iran-US CTR 273, 274 (1990–II)......406, 823, 826
Morris, Henry and Government of the Islamic Republic of Iran et al, Decision No DEC
 26–200–1 (16 September 1983), 3 Iran-US CTR 364–5 (1983–II) 71–2, 829
Morrison-Knudsen Pacific Ltd and Ministry of Roads and Transportation,
 Award No 143–127–3 (13 July 1984), 7 Iran-US CTR
 54, 56, 82–84 (1984–III)... 289, 302, 322, 425, 431, 438
Movsessian, Mishik and the Islamic Republic of Iran, Case No 272, Chamber Three,
 Order of 9 July 1982..414, 419
National Airmotive Corp:
 Award No 58–449–3 (9 August 1983), 3 Iran-US CTR 124, 124–25 (1983–II).... 774
 Award No 61–188–2 (14 July 1983), 3 Iran-US CTR 92 (1983–II) 769
Nazari, Mohsen Asgari and the Islamic Republic of Iran:
 Decision No DEC 105–221–1 (16 June 1992), 28 Iran-US CTR 192................... 486
 Interlocutory Award No ITL 79-22-1 471
 Award No 559-221-1 (24 August 1994), 30 Iran-US CTR
  123, 126, 163, 168–69 (1994)..486, 752, 768
Near East Technological Services USA Inc and the Islamic Republic of Iran Air Force,
 Award No 406–845–1 (9 January 1988), 21 Iran-US CTR 13, 19 (1989–I)........873, 895
Nikpour, Rana and the Islamic Republic of Iran, Case No 336, Chamber One, Interlocu-
 tory Award No ITL 81–336–1 (18 February 1993), 29 Iran-US CTR
 67, 68 (1993) 495, 502
Nourafchan, Richard and the Islamic Republic of Iran, Award No 348–414–3
 (29 February 1988), 18 Iran-US CTR 88 (1988–I) 678
Nourafchan, Zaman Azar and the Islamic Republic of Iran, Award No 550–412/415–3
 (19 October 1993) 384
Offshore Co and National Iranian Oil Co, Case No 133, Chamber Two, Order of
 26 June 1986 ....565, 589

Oil Cases 675
    Case Nos 72–76, 78–81 and 150, Chamber Three, Order of 22 February 1984 685
Oil Field of Texas Inc and Iran:
    ITL 10–43-FT (9 December 1982), (Concurring Opinion of Richard M Mosk,
        10 December 1982) 131
    Award No 258–43–1 (8 October 1986), 12 Iran-US CTR
        308, 315 (1986–III) 559, 586
Otis Elevator Company and the Islamic Republic of Iran et al, Award No 304–284–2
    (29 April 1987) 14 Iran-US CTR 283, 284, 291 (1988–I) 563, 597, 621
Pan American World Airways Inc et al and the Islamic Republic of Iran et al, Award on
    Agreed Terms No 96–488–1 (19 December 1983), 4 Iran-US CTR
    205–06, 209 (1983–II) 379, 385, 777
Payne, Thomas Earl and the Islamic Republic of Iran:
    Case No 335, Chamber Two, Order of 12 December 1983 .... 565, 593
    Case No 335, Chamber Two, Order of 14 February 1986 .... 506, 509
    Award No 245–335–2 (8 August 1986) 11 Iran-US CTR 3, 6
        (1986–III) 472, 482, 484
Pepsico Inc and the Islamic Republic of Iran:
    Case No 18, Chamber One, Order of 30 June 1982, 1 Iran-US CTR 173
        (1981–82) 423, 434
    Howard M Holtzmann, Dissent from Decision Granting Second Extension of Time
        for Filing Statement of Defence (9 July 1982) 1 Iran-US CTR 174
        (1981–82) 423, 434
    Award No 260–18–1 (11 October 1986), 13 Iran-US CTR
        3, 17, 45, 54–5 (1986–IV) 472, 482, 484, 559
    Decision No DEC 55–18–1 (19 December 1986), 13 Iran-US CTR
        328, 329–30 (1986–IV) 808
Pereira Associates and the Islamic Republic of Iran, Award No 116–1–3 (19 March
    1984) 322
Petrolane Inc and the Islamic Republic of Iran, Decision No DEC 101–131–2
    (25 November 1991), 27 Iran-US CTR 264–65 (1991–II) 380–1, 389, 813, 819
Phelps Dodge Corp et al and the Islamic Republic of Iran:
    Case No 99, Chamber Two, Order of 8 May 1984 .... 52, 74
    Award No 217–99–2 (19 March 1986) 144
Phibro Corp and Ministry of War-Etka Co Ltd, Decision No DEC 97–474–3 (17 May
    1991), 26 Iran-US CTR 254–55 (1991–I) 803, 810
Phillips Petroleum Co Iran and the Islamic Republic of Iran 185
    Cases Nos 39 and 55, Chamber Two, Order of 27 April 1983, 2 Iran-US CTR
        283, 284 (1983–I) 423, 435
    Case No 39, Chamber Two, Order of 7 November 1986 508–9
    Award No 425–39–2 (19 June 1989), 21 Iran-US CTR
        79, 256, 258–59 (1989–I) 380, 389, 676, 683, 712, 715, 725, 773, 819
Picker International Corp and the Islamic Republic of Iran, Decision No DEC
    48–10173–3 (7 October 1986), 12 Iran-US CTR 306, 307
    (1986–II) 803, 808, 813, 818
Plicoflex Inc and the Islamic Republic of Iran, Award No 535–354–1 (16 October 1992)
    28 Iran-US CTR 309, 312 (1992) 604, 618, 677, 687

Pointon, Vernie Rodney and Government of the Islamic Republic of Iran, Award No
    516–322–1 (23 July 1991), 27 Iran-US CTR 49 (1991–II) 627
Pomeroy, RN and the Islamic Republic of Iran, Award No 50–40–3 (8 June 1983)
    2 Iran-US CTR 372, 382 (1983–I) 559, 582
Poura, Isaac and the Islamic Republic of Iran, Case No 323, Chamber One, Order of
    3 March 1993 .... 789, 799
Protiva, Edgar et al and Government of the Islamic Republic of Iran, Award No 566–316–2
    (14 July 1995), 31 Iran-US CTR 89, 102–03 .... 73, 503
Queens Office Tower Associates and Iran National Airlines Corp, Award No 37172–1
    (15 April 1983), 2 Iran-US CTR 247, 254 141
Questech Inc and Ministry of National Defence of the Islamic Republic of Iran:
    Award No ITM 15–59–1 (1 March 1983), 2 Iran-US CTR 96 (1983–I) 737
    Case No 59, Chamber One, Order of 2 March 1984 .... 527, 550
    Award No 191-59-1 (25 September 1985), 9 Iran-US CTR
        107, 134–36, 138 (1985–II) 414, 421, 431, 439, 444, 484, 501, 721
R J Reynolds Tobacco Co and the Islamic Republic of Iran:
    Case No 35, Chamber Three, Order of 21 December 1983 322
    Award No 145–35–3 (6 August 1984), 7 Iran–US CTR 181, 191–92 (1984–III),
        9 Iran-US CTR 181, 183 (1985–II) 128, 142, 323
RAM International Industries Inc and Air Force of the Islamic Republic of Iran,
    Decision No DEC 118–148–1 (28 December 1993), 29 Iran-US
    CTR 383, 390 (1993) 45, 834, 836
Rankin, Jack and the Islamic Republic of Iran, Award No 326—10913–2 (3 November
    1987), 17 Iran–US CTR 135, 142–43 (1987–III) 128, 144
Raygo Wagner Equipment Co and Star Line Iran Co:
    Award No 20–17–3 (15 December 1982), 1 Iran-US CTR 411, 415–7, 424–28, 441
        (1981–82) 711, 713, 714, 715, 723, 724, 769, 773
    (3 March 1983), 1 Iran-US CTR 425 (1981–82) 749
RCA Global Communications Inc and the Islamic Republic of Iran:
    Case No 160, Chamber One, Order of 2 June, 1983, 3 Iran-US CTR 8 (1983–II) 550
    Award No ITM 30–160–1 (31 October, 1983), 4 Iran-US CTR 9,
        11–12 (1983–III) 544, 547
Rexnord Inc and the Islamic Republic of Iran, Award No 21–132–3 (10 January 1983),
    2 Iran–US CTR 6, 12, 27–29 (1983–I) 122, 131, 712, 715, 724
Reynolds Metals Co, Award No 60–83–2, 3 Iran-US CTR 120, 124–25
    (1983–II) 770, 774
Riahi, Frederica Lincoln and the Islamic Republic of Iran:
    Case No 485, Chamber One, Order of 23 February 1993 .... 568, 591
    Partial Award on Agreed Terms No 568–A13/A15(I and IV:C) A26(I, II, and III)-FT,
        para 9 (22 February 1996), 32 Iran-US CTR 207 (1996) 790
    Case No 485, Chamber One, Order of 26 October 1998 618
    Partial Award on Agreed Terms No 596–485–1 (24 February 2000) 790
    Case No 485, Chamber One, Order of 4 May 2000 622
    Award No 600-485–1 (27 February 2003) 471, 488, 494, 504, 559, 570, 586,
                                                                                                            592, 603
    Decision No DEC 133–485–1 (17 November 2004), (2004) 19(12) Mealey's
        International Arb Rep C–1 .... 833, 837

Richard D Harza and the Islamic Republic of Iran:
   Order of June 1982 436
   Case No 97, Chamber Two, Order of 4 November 1982, 1 Iran-US CTR
      234, 235 (1981–82) 641, 656
   Case No 97, Chamber Two, Order of 9 November 1982, 1 Iran-US CTR
      234 (1981–82) 377, 383, 387
   Case No 97, Chamber Two, Order of 6 December 1982 656
   Award No ITL 14–97–2 (17 February 1983), 2 Iran-US CTR 68, 71–75
      (1983–I) 637, 645, 647, 656–7, 662, 665, 738, 897, 903
   Award No ITL 14–97–2 (23 February 1983), 2 Iran-US CTR 68, 71
      (1983–I) 426, 436
   Case No 97, Chamber Two, Order of 13 September 1983 ....644–5, 662
   Award No ITL 14–97–2 (21 November 1983), 4 Iran-US CTR 59
      (1983–III) 897, 900, 904
   Case No 97, Chamber Two, Order of 24 July 1985 ....647, 667
   Award No 232–97–2 (2 May 1986), 11 Iran-US CTR 76, 136
      (1986–II) 641, 869, 873
RJ Reynolds Tobacco Co and Iranian Tobacco Co, Award No 145–35–3 (31 July 1984)
   (6 August 1984), 7 Iran-US CTR 181, 183 (1984–III) 560, 583, 603, 736, 767
Rockwell International Systems Inc and the Islamic Republic of Iran:
   Award No ITM 20–430–1 (6 June 1983), 2 Iran-US CTR 369, 371 (1983–I) 543
   Case No 430, Chamber One, Order of 18 September 1986 618–19
   Award No 438–430–1, (5 September 1989), 23 Iran-US CTR
      150, 166, 217, 229 (1989–III) 487, 871, 893
Sabet, Aram et al and the Islamic Republic of Iran et al:
   Case No 816, Chamber Three, Order of 27 January 1987 688
   Case No 816, Chamber Three, Order of 20 February 1987 ....678, 688
   Case Nos 815, 816 and 817, Chamber Two, Order of 19 November 1996 ......611, 623
   Case Nos 815, 816 and 817, Chamber Two, Order of 10 September 1997 ......899, 905
   Partial Award No 593–815/816/817–2 (30 June 1999) 736, 767
Saboonchian, Esahak and the Islamic Republic of Iran, Decision No DEC 103–313–2
   (13 February 1992), 28 Iran-US CTR 51, 51–52 (1992) 823, 826
Saghi, James M et al and Government of the Islamic Republic of Iran, Award No ITL
   66–298–2 (12 January 1987), 14 Iran-US CTR 3, 8 (1987–I) 737, 775
Samrad, Parvin Mariam and the Islamic Republic of Iran, Case No 465, Chamber Two,
   Order of 28 July 1986 ....31, 75
Schering Corp and the Islamic Republic of Iran, Award No 122–38–3 (16 April 1984),
   5 Iran-US CTR 361, 374 (1984–I) 322, 559, 582, 583
Sea-Land Service Inc and the Islamic Republic of Iran, Case No 33, Chamber One,
   Order of 19 November 1982 464
Seaboard Flour Corp and the Islamic Republic of Iran, Case No 318, Chamber Three,
   Order of 9 April 1985 ....788, 798
Sedco Inc and the Islamic Republic of Iran:
   Case No 129, Chamber Three, Order of 17 May 1985 686
   Award No ITL 55–129–3 (28 October 1985), 9 Iran-US CTR
      248, 257 265–66 (1985–II) 481, 611, 622
   Case No 129, Order of 6 January 1986, Mealey's Litigation Rep: Iranian Claims
      3705 (7 February 1986) 471

Award No ITL 61–260–2 (20 June 1986), 11 Iran-US CTR 210 (1986–II) 737
Award No 309–129–3 (7 July 1987), 15 Iran-US CTR 23, 29, 49, 184, 185, 187–8
    (1987–II) 128, 133,563, 573, 596, 772, 776, 869, 872, 894
Decision No DEC 64–129–3 (18 September 1987) 16 Iran-US CTR
    282, 283–84 (1987–III) 289, 303, 832
Shannon and Wilson Inc and Atomic Energy Organization of Iran, Case No 217,
    Chamber Two, Order of 14 September 1983...384, 387
Starrett Housing Corp and the Islamic Republic of Iran:
    Order of 17 December 1982, 1 Iran US CTR 385, 388 (1982)......................... 353–4
    Award No ITL 32–24–1 (19 & 21 December 1983), 4 Iran-US
        CTR 122, 157–59, 176, 179–80 (1983–III), 7 Iran-US CTR 119, 135–36
        (1984–III) 442, 458, 464, 637, 641, 644, 655, 662, 720, 752, 768, 898, 904
    Case No 24, Chamber One, Order of 30 July 1986 667
    Case No 24, Chamber One, Order of 18 December 1986 ....844, 899, 904
    Award No 314–21–1 (14 August 1987), 16 Iran-US CTR 112, 192, 196–99, 237,
        238, 255, 255–56 (1987–III)... 644–7, 665, 721, 772, 776
Sterling Drug Inc and the Islamic Republic of Iran:
    Case No 491, Order of 21 September 1984... 499
    Case No 491, Chamber Three, Order of 11 January 1985...............................495, 499
Sun Co Inc and National Iranian Oil Co:
    Settlement Agreement (14 August 1992) 28 Iran-US CTR 396 (1992) 794
    Joint Request for Arbitral Award on Agreed Terms (28 September 1992), 28 Iran-US
        CTR 395 (1992) 784, 793
    Award on Agreed Terms No 537–21–1 (19 October 1992), 28 Iran-US CTR
        394 (1992) 796
Sylvania Technical Systems Inc and the Islamic Republic of Iran:
    Case No 64, Chamber One, Order of 10 May 1983 .... 52, 74, 472, 475, 479
    Award No 180–64–1 (27 June 1985), 8 Iran-US CTR 298, 300, 323–4, 329,
        331 (1985–I)..440, 444, 484, 500, 573, 595, 844, 845–6,
                                                                                         870–1, 875–6, 891, 893, 894, 896
Tai Inc and the Islamic Republic of Iran, Case No 421, Chamber One, Order of
    12 August 1986 ....30, 53, 75, 482
Tavakoli, Vivian Mai and the Islamic Republic of Iran:
    Order of 17 April 1996 503
    Award No 580–832–3 (23 April 1997), 33 Iran-US CTR
        206, 201, 211 (1997)..30, 73, 469, 488, 494, 503, 812, 816
Tchacosh Company Inc and Government of the Islamic Republic of Iran et al, Award
    No 540–192–1 (9 December 1992), 28 Iran-US CTR
    371, 376–7, 379–80.. 51–2, 75, 77, 632, 789
TCSB Inc and the Islamic Republic of Iran, Award No114–140–2 (16 March 1984),
    5 Iran-US CTR 160, 168, 173 (1984–I) 431, 437, 440, 444
Texaco Iran Ltd and National Iranian Oil Company and the Islamic Republic of Iran,
    Case No 72, Chamber Three, Order of 9 September 1983 506–8
Time Inc and the Islamic Republic of Iran, Award No 139–166–2 (22 June 1984)
    7 Iran-US CTR 8 (1984–III) 560, 583
Tippetts, Abbett, McCarthy, Stratton and the Islamic Republic of Iran, Award No 4
    1–7–2 (29 June 1984) 6 Iran-US CTR 229 (1984–II)...........................481, 772, 775

Touche Ross and Company and the Islamic Republic of Iran, Award No 197–480–1
(30 October 1985), 9 Iran-US CTR 284 (1985–II) 627
Uiterwyk Corp and the Islamic Republic of Iran:
Order of 4 December 1987, Chamber One 725
Award No 375–381–1 (6 July 1988), 19 Iran-US CTR 107,
116-17, 161, 167–9, 170–71 (1988–II), 26 Iran-US
CTR 5 .... 280, 284–5, 290, 292, 293, 572, 597, 612, 621, 772, 799
Decision No DEC 96–381–1 (22 November 1988), 19 Iran-US CTR
171, 172–74 (1988–II) 711, 803, 809, 812, 815
Ultrasystems Inc and the Islamic Republic of Iran:
Partial Award No 27–84–3 (4 March 1983), 2 Iran-US CTR 100, 101, 114, 123
(1983–I) 323, 628, 632, 704, 719, 736, 766, 872, 894
Award No 89–84–3, (7 December 1983), 4 Iran-US CTR 77, 80
(1983–III) 572, 595, 720
Unidyne Corp Inc and the Islamic Republic of Iran:
Award No 551–368–3 (10 November 1993), 29 Iran-US CTR 310, 313, 349,
355–56, 364–66 (1993) 508, 511, 726, 727
Decision No DEC 122–368–3 (9 March 1994), 30 Iran-US
CTR 19, 20 (1994) 714, 716, 833
Supplemental Opinion of Arangio-Ruiz and Allison 711
Union Special Corp Inc, a claim of less than US $250,000 presented by the United States
of America and the Islamic Republic of Iran, Case No 10863, Chamber One, Order of
29 August 1988 ....788, 798
United Painting Co Inc, a claim of less than US $250,000 presented by the United States
of America and the Islamic Republic of Iran, Award No 458–11286–3 (20 December
1989) 23 Iran-US CTR 351, 356–57 (1989–III) 128, 138
United States of America on behalf and for the benefit of Harrington & Associates Inc
and the Islamic Republic of Iran:
Case No 10712, Chamber Three, Order of 2 July 1986 ....494, 499
Case No 10712, Chamber Three, Order of 23 October 1986 499
United States of America on behalf and for the benefit of the New York Blower Co and
the Islamic Republic of Iran, Case No 10418, Chamber Two, Order of 1 September
1986 ....30, 75
United States of America on behalf and for the benefit of Tadjer-Cohen Associates Inc
and the Islamic Republic of Iran:
Award No ITM 50–12118–3 (11 November 1985), 9 Iran-US CTR
302, 304–05 (1985–II) 523, 546–7
Case No 12118, Chamber Three, Interim Award No ITM 56–12118–3 filed on
11 November 1985 551
Case No 12118, Chamber Three, Order of 4 August 1986 551
United States of America on behalf and for the benefit of Thomas A Todd and the
Islamic Republic of Iran, Case No 10856, Chamber One, Order of
9 January 1986 ....379–80, 386, 508–9
United Technologies International Inc et al and Iranian Air Force, Award on Agreed
Terms No 146–42–3 (8 August 1984), 7 Iran-US CTR 209, 210 (1984–III) 778
Varo International Corp and the Islamic Republic of Iran:
Case No 275, Chamber One, Order of 13 March 1986 ....493, 495, 499

Award No 482–275–1 (21 June 1990), 25 Iran-US CTR 3, 6 (1990–II).........694, 696
Warnecke & Associates, Award No 72–124–3, (2 September 1983), 3 Iran-US CTR
    237–38, 254–55, 268–69, 276–77, 291–93, 294–96 (1983–II) 770, 775
Watkins-Johnson Company and the Islamic Republic of Iran:
    Case No 370, Chamber One, Order of 3 December 1987 ....30, 33, 70
    Award No 429–370–1 (28 July 1989), 22 Iran-US CTR 257, 336 (1989–II) 868
Weatherford International Inc and the Islamic Republic of Iran, Case No 305, Chamber
    Two, Order of 15 February 1985..567–8, 589
Westinghouse Electric Corp and the Islamic Republic of Iran:
    Award No ITL 67–389–2, 14 Iran-US CTR 104, 105 (1987–I).....................431, 737
    Award No 579–389–2 (20 March 1997), 33 Iran-US CTR
        60, 75–76, 195, 198–200 (1997)...469, 471, 473, 487
    Decision No DEC 127–389–2 (April 23, 1997) 811, 821, 827
White Consolidated Industries Inc and Iran Compressor Manufacturing Co, Case No
    126, Chamber Two, Order of 7 December 1984 ....30, 74
Whittaker Corp (1983 Tribunal Rules), Dissenting Opinion of Judge Holtzmann
    (27 April 1987), 14 Iran-US CTR 271 (1987–I) 289–90
William L Pereira Associates Iran and the Islamic Republic of Iran, Case No 1, Chamber
    Three Order of 22 September 1982 ....425, 436
Williams, Gordon and the Islamic Republic of Iran:
    Case No 187, Chamber Three, Order of 5 October 1982...............................673, 685
    Award No 342–187–3 (18 December 1987), 17 Iran-US CTR
        269, 293 (1987–III) 45, 354, 830–1
Woodward-Clyde Consultants and the Islamic Republic of Iran:
    Award No 73–67–3, (2 September 1983), 3 Iran-US CTR 237–38, 239, 248–49,
        254–55, 268–69, 276–77, 291–93, 294, 294–296 (1983–II) 574, 594, 770, 775
    Case No 67, Chamber Three, Order of 30 December 1983 ....823, 825
World Farmers Trading Inc and Government Trading Corporation:
    Case No 764, Order of 4 August 1986, Chamber One 52, 75
    Award No 428–764–1 (7 July 1989), 22 Iran-US CTR 204 (1989–II) 76, 632
    Decision No DEC 93–764–1, para 3 (3 October 1990), 25 Iran-US CTR
        186, 187 (1990–II).. 71
Xtra Inc and Government of the Islamic Republic of Iran, Case No 500, Chamber One
    Order of 8 January 1991 ....788, 799

(2) Challenge cases

Judge Aghahosseini, US Government Challenge, 2005–2006............................188, 204,
    217, 239–40, 246–7, 263, 271
Judge Ameli, US Government Challenge, 2005–2006..............................188, 204, 217,
    239–40, 246–7, 263, 271
Judge Arangio-Ruiz, Challenge by Iran, 2009...........................186, 189, 211, 213, 222,
    249, 274, 280–1, 294, 299–301
Judge Briner:
    First Challenge by Iran, 1988, Case No 55, Amoco Iran Oil Co and the Islamic
        Republic of Iran...............................184, 214–15, 225, 240, 243–4, 249, 252, 254,
            257–9, 264–5, 267, 273, 712–13, 716, 726
    Challenge by Iran, 1989...223, 263

Second challenge by Iran, 1989, Case No 39 .... 184, 204, 214, 220, 228, 236–7,
247–9, 259, 261, 265, 282–3, 403, 405–6
Third Challenge by Iran, 1989 .... 185, 237–8, 245, 249, 260

Judge Broms:
  Challenge by the United States, 2001, Case No A/28 .... 187, 209,
  223, 229–30, 238–9, 244, 712–13, 716, 728
  US Claimant's Challenge, Case No 485, Frederica Lincoln Riahi 2004 .... 187, 195,
  203, 260
Judge Brower, Iranian Government Challenge, 2010 .... 190–1, 266–7
Judge Kashani, US Government Challenge, 17 September 1984 .... 184, 225, 228,
  230, 235, 249, 257, 264, 268, 273, 280–1
Judge Mangård, Challenge by Iran, 1982 .... 155, 183, 191, 193, 249,
  253, 263, 270–1, 273, 275, 341

Judge Noori:
  US Claimant's Challenge, Case No 248, Carlson and Melli Industrial Group
  1990 .... 186, 210, 217, 227, 238, 249, 262
  US Government Challenge, 2005–2006 .... 188, 204, 217, 239–40,
  246–7, 262–3, 271
Judge Seifi, US Government Challenge, 2010 .... 190, 195–6, 204–5, 251, 266
Judge Shafeiei, US Government Challenge, 17 September 1984 .... 184, 225,
  228–30, 235, 249, 257, 264, 268, 273, 280–1, 285

Judge Skubiszewski:
  Iranian Government Challenges, 1999 .... 186, 262
  Iranian Government Challenge, 2007 ..... 188, 224, 240, 251, 265, 711, 713, 715, 729
  Iranian Government Challenge, 2009 .... 189, 211, 213, 222
Judge Oloumi Yazdi, US Government Challenge, 2007 .... 188–9, 224, 240, 251,
  265–6, 711, 713, 715, 729

(3) Refusal cases

AMF Corp, Decision No DEC 17-REF20-FT (8 December 1982), 1 Iran-US
  CTR 392, 393 (1981–1982) 470, 472, 479
Cascade Overview Development Enterprises Inc, Decision No DEC 4-REF1-FT (4 May
  1982), 1 Iran-US CTR 128 (1981–82) 404
Etka Organization, Decision No DEC78-REF43–1, 19 Iran-US CTR 186
  (1988–II) 408
Glucosan Co, Decision No DEC 80-REF46–1, 19 Iran-US CTR 192
  (1988–II) 408
Helali, Sara, DEC 3-REF11–2 (7 May 1982), 1 Iran-US CTR 134
  (1981–82) 415, 419
Industrial & Mining Bank:
  Decision No DEC 76-REF39–1 19 Iran-US CTR 180 (1988–II) 408
  Decision No DEC 77-REF40–1, (14 July 1988), 19 Iran-US CTR 182, 183
  (1988–II) 407
Iran Brockway Co Ltd, Decision No DEC 67-REF35–2, 17 Iran-US CTR 332
  (1987–IV) 408

Iran Electronics Industries, Decision No DEC 79-REF45-l, 19 Iran-US CTR 189 (1988–II) 408
Iran Helicopter Support and Renewal Co, Decision Nos DEC 88-REF32–3, DEC 89-REF33–3, and DEC 90-REF34–3 23 Iran-US CTR 245, 248 and 251 (1989–III) 408
Iran National Airlines Co, Decision No DEC 69-REF44–2, 17 Iran-US CTR 338 (1987–IV) 408
Iranian Tobacco Co:
(15 December 1982), 7 Iran-US CTR 275 408
Decision No DEC l-A2-FT (26 January 1982), 1 Iran-US CTR 101 408
Decision No DEC 19-REF26-l (9 December 1982), 21 Iran-US CTR 8–9 (1989–I) 407
Decision No DEC 20-REF27–1 (14 December 14, 1982), 7 Iran-US CTR 275–76 (1984–III) 407
Jahanger, Mohammed Sadegk, Decision No DEC 5-REF2-FT (4 May 1982), 1 Iran-US CTR 128 (1981–82) 405
K and S Irrigation Co, Decision No DEC 16-REF29-l (20 October 1982), 1 Iran-US CTR 228–29 (1981–82) 404
Ministry of Mines and Metals and National Iranian Steel Co, Decision No DEC 91-REF36–3, 23 Iran-US CTR 254 (1989–III) 408
Ministry of Roads and Transportation:
Decision No DEC 71-REF48–2, 17 Iran-US CTR 344 (1987–IV) 408
Decision No 92-REF41–3, 23 Iran- US CTR 257 (1989–III) 408
NAHAJA, Ministry of Defence of the Islamic Republic of Iran, Decision No DEC 82-REF51–1, 19 Iran-US CTR 198 (1988–II) 408
National Iranian Copper Industries Co, Decision No DEC 72-REF50–2, 17 Iran-US CTR 347 (1987–IV) 408
National Iranian Oil Co, Decision No DEC 68-REF42–2, 17 Iran-US CTR 335 (1987–IV) 408
Pereira, Victor E, Decision No DEC 2-REF5–2 (10 March 1982), 21 Iran-US CTR 3 (1989–I) 405
Raymond International (UK) Ltd, Decision No DEC18-REF21-FT (8 December 1982), 1 Iran-US CTR 394, 395, 396, 398 (1981–1982) 407, 470, 472, 480, 486
Refusal Cases Nos 1 and 2 401
Refusal Cases 1, 2 and 3, Dissent of Howard M Holtzmann to the Tribunal's Decision Nos DEC 4-REF1-FT (14 May 1982), DEC 5-REF2-FT (14 May 1982), and DEC-REF3-FT (14 February 1983) 404
Satellite Application Project, Decision No DEC 70-REF47–2, 17 Iran-US CTR 341 (1987–IV) 408
Sherkate Tractor Sazi Iran (SahamiKass), Decision No DEC 75-REF38–1, 19 Iran-US CTR 177 (1988–II) 408
Showrai, Atiyeh, Decision No DEC 15-REF28–1 (20 October 1982), 1 Iran-US CTR 226–27 (1981–82) 404
Tehran Regional Electric Company, Decision No DEC 81-REF49–1, 19 Iran-US CTR 195 (1988–II) 408

(4) Other practice

Minutes of the 1st Full Tribunal Meeting of the Iran–United States Claims Tribunal
(1 July 1981) 377, 385
Minutes of the 51st Full Tribunal Meeting of the Iran–US Claims Tribunal
(14 May 1982) 453, 463
Minutes of the 71st Meeting of the Full Tribunal (7 January 1983) 704
Presidential Order No 10 (15 June 1983) 771
Presidential Order No 17 (5 January 1984) 544
Presidential Order No 51 (re Judge Brower) (2 February 1987) 14 Iran-US CTR
353 (1987–I)...282, 292
Presidential Order No 53 (8 April 1987), 14 Iran-US CTR 354 (1987–I).................. 303
Presidential Order No 67 ....253, 267
Presidential Order No 79 (Mr Ahmed Sadek El-Kosheri) 797

B. Practice of Investment and other Tribunals

(1) Awards, decisions, and orders

ADF Group Inc and United States of America, Procedural Order No 2 (1 July 2001)
(ICSID administered)...89–90, 107, 109
Antoine Biloune et al and Ghana Investments Centre et al, Award on Damages and
Costs (30 June 1990) (Ad Hoc Proceeding, 1976 UNCITRAL Rules, special
agreement) 880
Antione Biloune (Syria) and Marine Drive Complex Ltd (Ghana) and Ghana Investment
Centre and Government of Ghana 736
   Award on Liability (27 October 1989), (1994) XIX Ybk Commercial
     Arb 11 ....558, 576, 736
   Award on Damages and Costs (30 June 1990) (Ad Hoc Proceeding), XIX Ybk
     Commercial Arbitration 11, 22–23, 30-1 (1994) 560, 577,
      829, 831, 841, 849
Association of Service Industry Firms and Service Industry Firm:
   Award (27 May 1991) (Ad Hoc Proceeding, 1976 UNCITRAL Rules, Contract),
     (1992) XVII Ybk Commercial Arbitration 11 ....843, 869
   Award (27 May 1991) (Ad Hoc Proceeding, 1976 UNCITRAL Rules, Special
     Agreement), (1992) XVII Ybk Commercial Arb 11 877
Austrian Airlines and Slovak Republic, Final Award (9 October 2009) (PCA administered,
1976UNCITRAL Rules, Austria-Czech/Slovak BIT)... 451
AWG Group Ltd et al and Argentine Republic (ICSID administered, 1976 UNCITRAL
Rules, UK-Argentina BIT)...............................181–2, 197, 201–2, 209, 216, 232, 243
Azinian, Robert, et al and United Mexican States, Award (1 November 1999) (ICSID
administered) 871–4, 885, 887–8, 890
Banque Arabe et Internationale D'Investissement et al and Inter-Arab Investment
Guarantee Corporation, Award (17 November 1994) (Ad Hoc Proceeding,
1976 UNCITRAL Rules, Contract), (1996) XXI Ybk Commercial
Arbitration 13 843
BG Group plc and Republic of Argentina, Award (27 December 2007) (Ad Hoc Proceeding, 1976 UNCITRAL Rules), UK-Argentina BIT 841, 851, 871, 881

Consolidated Canadian Cattle Claims and United States of America (Cases Regarding
   the Border Closure due to BSE Concerns), (20 October 2006)
   (Ad hoc Proceeding) 352, 355, 858, 864
Canfor Corp et al and United States of America (Softwood Lumber Cases) 178
   Procedural Order No 1 (3 November 2003) 855, 858, 863
   Procedural Order No 3 (13 November 2003) 898, 901
   Decision on the Place of Arbitration, Filing of a Statement of Defence and Bifurcation
      of the Proceedings (23 January 2004) 19, 26–7, 90, 100, 109, 424, 433, 462
   Order of the Consolidation Tribunal (7 September 2005) 31, 33, 63, 456–8, 462
   Joint Order on the Costs of Arbitration and for the Termination of Certain Arbitral
      Proceedings (19 July 2007) 842, 866, 870, 875–75, 879, 889
Centurian Health Corp et al and Government of Canada, Order for the Termination of
   the Proceedings and Award on Costs (2 August 2010), (PCA administered) 361
Chemtura Corp and Government of Canada:
   Procedural Order No 1 (12 January 2008) (Ad Hoc Arbitration) 569
   Procedural Order No 1 (21 January 2008) (Ad Hoc Proceeding) 606, 616
   Procedural Order No 1 (21 January 2008) (PCA administered) 864, 897, 902
   Award (2 August 2010) (PCA administered) 86, 841, 851, 857, 866
Chevron Corp et al and Republic of Ecuador:
   Interim Award (1 December 2008) (PCA administered, 1976 UNCITRAL Rules,
      US-Ecuador BIT) 31, 151, 164, 167, 532, 558, 576, 606, 616
   Partial Award on the Merits (20 March 2010) (PCA administered, 1976 UNCITRAL
      Rules, US-Ecuador BIT) 379, 385
   Partial Award (30 March 2010) (PCA administered, 1976 UNCITRAL Rules,
      US-Ecuador BIT) 737
   Procedural Order No 8 (31 March 2010) (PCA administered, 1976 UNCITRAL
      Rules, US-Ecuador BIT) 650
   Order on Interim Measures (14 May 2010) (PCA administered, 1976 UNCITRAL
      Rules, US-Ecuador BIT) 518, 523, 525–6, 531, 539, 607, 638
   Order for Interim Measures (9 February 2011) (PCA administered, 1976 UNCITRAL
      Rules, US-Ecuador BIT) 523–4, 539
   Procedural Order No 8 (18 April 2011) (PCA administered, 1976 UNCITRAL Rules,
      US-Ecuador BIT) 69, 617
   Final Award (31 August 2011) (PCA administered, 1976 UNCITRAL Rules, US-
      Ecuador BIT) 168, 871, 874, 882
   First Interim Award (25 January 2012) (PCA administered, 1976 UNCITRAL Rules,
      US-Ecuador BIT), ...523–5, 541
   Second Interim Award (16 February 2012) (PCA administered, 1976 UNCITRAL
      Rules, US-Ecuador BIT) 516, 519–20, 523, 525, 541
Clayton, William Ralph et al and Government of Canada:
   Procedural Order No 1 (9 April 2009) (PCA administered) 326, 330, 352,
                                                                                                    355, 706, 719
   Procedural Order No 2 (2 May 2009) (PCA administered) 38
   Procedural Order No 3 (3 June 2009) (PCA administered) 569
CME Czech Republic BV and Czech Republic:
   Partial Award (13 September 2001) (Ad Hoc Proceeding, 1976 UNCITRAL Rules,
      Netherlands-Czech Republic BIT), (2002) 14(3) World Trade & Arb Materials 109,
      121, 207–08, 284–5, 287 .... 88, 287, 456, 459, 750, 762, 764, 872, 883

Final Award (14 March 2003) (Ad Hoc Proceeding, 1976 UNCITRAL Rules, Netherlands-Czech Republic BIT), (2003) 15(4) World Trade and Arbitration Materials 83, 91, 99, 109, 100, 114, 180–1 .... 30–1, 73, 119, 129, 164, 166, 370, 605, 614, 625, 629, 736, 739, 762, 872

Eastern Sugar BV and Czech Republic, Partial Award (27 March 2007), para 116 (SCC administered, 1976 UNCITRAL Rules, Netherlands-Czech Republic BIT) 451

Econet Wireless Ltd and First Bank of Nigeria et al, Award (2 June 2005) (Ad Hoc Proceeding, 1976 UNCITRAL Rules, Contract), (2006) XXXI Ybk Commercial Arb 49, 57–58, 63, 64–65 .... 27, 29, 169, 842, 866, 873, 878, 885

EnCana Corp and Government of Ecuador:
   Interim Award (31 January 2004) (LCIA administered, 1976 UNCITRAL Rules, Canada-Ecuador BIT) 520, 523–4, 533
   Award (3 February 2006) (LCIA administered, 1976 UNCITRAL Rules, Canada-Ecuador BIT) 472, 477

Ethyl Corp and Government of Canada:
   Decision Regarding the Place of Arbitration (28 November 1997) (Ad Hoc Proceeding) (1999) 38 ILM 702, 702–06 .... 81, 87–8, 90, 104, 109
   Award on Jurisdiction (24 June 1998), (ICSID administered), (1999) 38 ILM 708, 730 .... 417, 736

Fireman's Fund Insurance Company v Mexico, ICSID Case No ARB(AF)/02/01, Final Award, 17 July 2006 889

Gallo, Vito G and Government of Canada 182, 208, 214, 219–20, 233, 244–7, 272, 289–90, 308, 377
   Procedural Order No 1 (4 June 2008) (PCA 706 administered) 706, 716
   Amended Procedural Order No 1 (10 March 2009) (PCA administered) 248, 385

Glamis Gold Ltd and United States of America 159
   Agreement on Certain Procedural Matters (20 January 2004) (ICSID administered) 19, 26–7, 80, 854, 864
   Procedural Order No 2 (31 May 2005) (ICSID administered) 458, 460
   Decision on Objections to Document Production (20 July 2005) (ICSID administered) 568–9, 578
   Decision on Parties' Requests for Production of Documents withheld on Grounds of Privilege (17 November 2005) (ICSID administered) 566, 570
   Procedural Order No 8 (31 January 2006) (ICSID administered) 33, 40, 63
   Procedural Order No 11 (9 July 2007) (ICSID administered) 33, 40, 63, 604–8, 614
   Procedural Order No 12 (28 August 2007) (ICSID administered) 604, 615
   Award (8 June 2009) (ICSID administered) 82, 871, 873

Grand River Enterprises et al and United States of America:
   Decision on Objections to Jurisdiction (20 July 2006) (ICSID administered Arbitration) 180, 218, 472, 478
   Procedural Order (14 May 2007) (ICSID administered) 569

Guaracachi America Inc et al and Plurinational State of Bolivia (PCA administered, 2010 UNCITRAL Rules, US-Bolivia BIT/UK-Bolivia BIT) 50, 168
   Terms of Appointment and Procedural Order No 1 (9 December 2011) (PCA administered, 2010 UNCITRAL Rules, US-Bolivia BIT/ UK-Bolivia BIT) 168, 326, 330, 605–8, 616, 854, 857–8, 864, 897–8, 902

HICEE BV and Slovak Republic:
  Partial Award (23 May 2011) (PCA administered, 1976 UNCITRAL Rules,
    Netherlands-Slovak Republic BIT) 886
  Supplementary and Final Award (17 October 2011) (PCA administered, 1976
    UNCITRAL Rules, Netherlands-Slovak Republic BIT) 865, 873
Himpurna California Energy Ltd and PT (Persero) Perusahaan Listruik Negara, (2000)
  XXV Ybk Commercial Arb 13 95
  Final Award (4 May 1999) (Ad Hoc Proceeding, 1976 UNCITRAL Rules, Concession
    Agreement), (1999) 14(12) Mealey's International Arb Rep B-12, B41), (2000)
    XXV Ybk Commercial Arb 13, 26, 28–29 .... 20, 22, 29, 469, 473, 475,
                                                                                              765, 869, 873, 882
  Final Award (4 May 1999) (Ad Hoc Proceeding, 1976 UNCITRAL Rules, Special
    Agreement), (2000) XXV Ybk Commercial Arb 13, 107 ....899, 901
Himpurna California Energy Ltd and Republic of Indonesia .. 674–5, 679, 695, 717, 737
  Procedural Order of 7 September 1999 ....98, 766
  Interim Award (26 September 1999) (Ad Hoc Proceeding, 1976 UNCITRAL Rules,
    Concession Agreement), (2000) XXV Ybk Commercial Arb 109, 112, 124–26,
    132–35, 145–48, 167–69, 171–6, 185 .... 95, 97, 674, 679–80, 695
  Interim Award (26 September 1999) (Ad Hoc Proceeding, 1976 UNCITRAL Rules,
    Special Agreement), (2000) XXV Ybk Commercial Arb 109, 146–47,
    152 .... 711, 717, 736–7, 761, 766
  Final Award (4 May 1999) (Ad Hoc Proceeding, 1976, UNCITRAL Rules, Concession
    Agreement), (2000) XXV Ybk Commercial Arbitration 13 674
  Final Award (16 October 1999) (Ad Hoc Proceeding, 1976 UNCITRAL Rules,
    Concession Agreement), (2000) XXV Ybk Commercial Arbitration 186,
    190–1 ....95, 100, 194, 198, 283, 289, 315, 317
Melvin J Howard et al and Government of Canada, Correction of Order for the
  Termination of the Proceedings and Award on Costs (9 August 2010)
  (PCA administered) 813, 815
ICS Inspection and Control Services Ltd and Argentina Republic:
  Decision on Challenge to Arbitrator (17 December 2009) (Ad Hoc Proceeding, 1976
    UNCITRAL Rules UK-Argentina BIT) 182, 218, 234
  Procedural Order No 1 (18 May 2010) 850, 902
  Award on Jurisdiction (10 February 2012) (PCA administered, 1976 UNCITRAL
    Rules, UK-Argentina BIT) 31, 35, 64, 326, 330, 841, 851, 858, 865, 871,
                                                                                874, 890, 898, 900, 902–3
International Thunderbird Gaming Corp and United Mexican States:
  Procedural Order No 5 (12 March 2004) (ICSID administered) 5, 567, 577
  Separate Opinion to Award (December 2005) (ICSID administered) 868, 871,
                                                                                                 873–5, 887, 889
  Award (26 January 2006) (ICSID administered) 558, 706, 718, 871, 874,
                                                                                                      881, 888–9
Karaha Bodas Co LLC and Perusahaan Pertambangan Minyak Dan Gas Bumi Negara:
  Preliminary Award (30 September 1999) (Ad Hoc Proceeding, 1976 UNCITRAL
    Rules Concession Agreement) 492, 494, 496, 841, 850
  Final Award (18 December 2000) (Ad Hoc Proceeding, 1976 UNCITRAL Rules,
    Concession Agreement) 602, 605, 610, 613, 746, 763, 850, 871, 879

Larsen, Lance Paul and Hawaiian Kingdom:
  Procedural Order No 3 (17 July 2000) (PCA administered, 1976 UNCITRAL Rules),
    Special Agreement, (2001) 119 ILR 566, 577–80...................................31, 59, 450
  Award (5 February 2001) (PCA administered, 1976 UNCITRAL Rules, Special
    Agreement), (2001) 119 ILR 566, 579–80, 585–6..................... 25–6, 60, 734, 761
Lauder, Ronald S and Czech Republic:
  Final Award (3 September 2001) (Ad Hoc Proceeding, 1976 UNCITRAL Rules,
    US-Czech Republic BIT), (2002) 14(3) World Trade & Arb Materials 35,
    106–07.. 883
  Final Award (3 September 2001) (Ad Hoc Proceeding, 1976 UNCITRAL Rules,
    US-Czech Republic BIT), (2002) 14(3) World Trade & Arb Materials 35,
    106–07.. 872–3
Link-Trading Joint Stock Co and Dept for Customs Control of the Republic of
  Moldova (18 April 2002) (Ad Hoc Proceeding, 1976 UNCITRAL Rules,
  US-Moldova BIT) 872, 877, 884, 899
  Award on Jurisdiction (16 February 2001) (Ad Hoc Proceeding, 1976 UNCITRAL
    Rules, US-Moldova BIT) 363
Merrill & Ring Forestry LP and Government of Canada:
  Decision on the Place of Arbitration (12 December 2007)
    (ICSID administered)...90, 109
  Decision on Motion to Add a New Party (31 January 2008) (ICSID administered
    Arbitration) 469–71, 473, 478, 873
  Order Concerning Requests for Documents and Certain Evidentiary Matters
    (18 July 2008) (ICSID administered).. 569–70
  Decision of the Tribunal on Production of Documents (18 July 2008)
    (ICSID administered)...32, 64, 579
  Award (31 March 2010) (ICSID administered).. 885
Metalclad Corporation v Mexico 107–8
Methanex Corp and United States of America:
  Minutes of Order of First Procedural Meeting (29 June 2000)
    (ICSID administered)..377, 384, 492, 496
  Minutes of Order of Second Procedural Meeting (7 September 2000)
    (ICSID administered)..493, 497
  Order on the Place of Arbitration (7 September 2000)
    (ICSID administered)..78, 105
  Decision on the Place of Arbitration (7 September 2000) 89–90, 101, 108–9
  Decision on Petitions from Third Persons to Intervene as Amici Curiae
    (15 January 2001) (ICSID administered), (2001) 13(3) World Trade & Arb
    Materials 97, 109–11, 114–15, 118–20 .... 31, 40, 65, 68, 607, 617
  Award on Jurisdiction (7 August 2002), (ICSID administered), (2002) 14(6)
    World Trade & Arb Materials 109, 143, 146, 186–7 ....415, 417–18,
                                                                                              457–9, 473, 477, 736, 762
  Communication to the Parties Regarding Claimant's Request for Interpretation
    (25 September 2002), (ICSID administered) 415
  Letter from the Tribunal to the Parties (25 September 2002) (Ad Hoc Proceeding) 807
  Letter from the Tribunal to the Parties (25 September 2002)
    (ICSID administered)...31, 61
  Award (3 August 2005) (Ad Hoc Proceeding)................................828, 831, 866, 880

Award (3 August 2005) (ICSID administered) 8, 11, 31, 57, 63, 129, 178, 354,
    268, 272, 458, 461, 469, 477, 572, 579, 629, 734, 740, 762, 868
Mytilineos Holdings SA and State Union of Serbia and Montenegro and Republic of
    Serbia, Partial Award on Jurisdiction (8 September 2006) (Ad Hoc Proceeding, 1976
    UNCITRAL Rules, Greece-Yugoslavia BIT) 151, 165, 167, 765
National Grid PLC and Republic of Argentina 271–2
    Decision on the Challenge to Mr Judd L Kessler (3 December 2007)
       (LCIA administered, 1976 UNCITRAL Rules, UK-Argentina BIT) 180, 208,
                                                                                       213, 222, 232
    Procedural Order No 20 (20 December 2007) 649–50
    Award (3 November 2008) (Ad Hoc Proceeding, 1976 UNCITRAL Rules,
       UK-Argentina BIT) 638, 649
Oostergetel and Laurentius and Slovak Republic, Final Award (23 April 2012)
    (Ad Hoc Proceeding, 1976 UNCITRAL Rules, Netherlands-Czech
    Republic BIT) 130, 165, 168, 607, 617, 873, 886
Paushok, Sergei et al and Government of Mongolia:
    Temporary Restraining Order (23 March, 2008) (Ad Hoc Proceeding, 1976
       UNCITRAL Rules, Russia-Mongolia BIT) 535
    Order on Interim Measures (2 September, 2008) (Ad Hoc Proceeding, 1976 UNCI-
       TRAL Rules, Russia-Mongolia BIT) (November 2008) 23 Mealey's International
       Arb Rep, B-1 .... 516, 519–23, 525–6, 531–2, 535
Petrobart and Kyrgyz Republic, Award (13 February 2003) (Ad Hoc Proceeding, 1976
    UNCITRAL Rules, Concession Agreement)..866, 878
Pope & Talbot Inc and Government of Canada:
    Procedural Order No 10 Concerning Crown Privileges (16 November 1999)
       (ICSID administered)...568, 577
    Partial Award (13 February 2000) (Ad Hoc Proceeding), (2001) 40 ILM 1408,
       1409..362, 369
    Interim Award (26 June 2000), (Ad Hoc Proceeding) (2000) 13(4) World Trade & Arb
       Materials 19 737
    Decision on Privileges (6 September 2000) (Ad Hoc Proceeding) 32, 35, 60, 570
    Decision (Ad Hoc Proceeding) (27 September 2000) 38
    Partial Award (13 November 2000) (Ad Hoc Proceeding), (2003) 15(1) World Trade &
       Arb Materials 184, 266 ....746, 763
    Award on the Merits of Phase 2 (10 April 2001) (Ad Hoc Proceeding) (No 4, 2001) 13
       World Trade & Arb Materials 61, 153 61
    Second Partial Award, (21 October 2002) (Ad Hoc Proceeding), (2001) 40 ILM 1408,
       1411, 1443, (2003) 15(1) World Trade & Arb Materials 103...... 637, 639, 649, 736
    Award on Costs (26 November 2002) (Ad Hoc Proceeding) 579, 736,
                                                                          841–2, 851, 871–2, 879, 884
Republika Srpska and Federation of Bosnia and Herzegovina (Control Over the Brcko
    Corridor), Award (14 February 1997) (Ad Hoc Proceeding, 1976 UNCITRAL Rules,
    Special Agreement), (1997) 26 ILM 396, 401, 406, 437..................................750, 764
Romak SA and Republic of Uzbekistan, Award, (26 November 2009) (PCA administered
    1976 UNCITRAL Rules), Switzerland-Uzbekistan BIT................. 692, 696, 871, 889
Saluka Investments B V and Czech Republic, Decision on Jurisdiction over the Czech
    Republic's Counterclaim (7 May 2004) (PCA administered, 1976 UNCITRAL Rules,
    Netherlands-Czech Republic BIT) 425, 428, 434

SD Myers Inc and Government of Canada:
  Final Award on Costs (30 December 2002) (Ad Hoc Proceeding) 736, 842,
    867–8, 870–2, 876–7, 880, 885, 897, 901
Softwood Lumber Cases see Canfor Corp et al and United States of America
TCW Group Inc et al and Dominican Republic:
  Procedural Order No 2 (15 August 2008) (PCA administered, 1976 UNCITRAL
    Rules, CAFTA-DR Chapter Ten) 377, 379, 385
  Consent Award (16 July 2009) (PCA administered, 1976 UNCITRAL Rules,
    CAFTA-DR Chapter 10) 784, 792
Ulysseas Inc and Republic of Ecuador, Final Award (12 June 2012) (PCA administered
  1976 UNCITRAL Rules, US-Ecuador BIT) 871, 882, 900, 903
United Parcel Service of America Inc and Government of Canada:
  Decision on the Place of Arbitration (17 October 2001) (ICSID administered), (2002)
    14(1) World Trade & Arb Materials 33, 34–40 .... 89–90, 107, 109
  Decision on Filing of Statement of Defence (17 October 2001)
    (ICSID administered) 424, 432–3
  Decision on Petitions for Intervention and Participation as Amici Curiae (17 October
    2001) (ICSID administered), (2002) 14(1) World Trade & Arb Materials
    41, 64–68 .... 31, 39–41, 67
  Award on Jurisdiction (22 November 2002), (ICSID administered) 413, 418,
    468, 476, 492, 497
  Decision of the Tribunal Relating to Canada's Claim of Cabinet Privilege, (8 October
    2004) 570
Veteran Petroleum Ltd and Russian Federation:
  Interim Award (30 November 2009) (Ad Hoc Proceeding, 1976 UNCITRAL Rules,
  Interim Award (30 November 2009) (PCA administered, 1976 UNCITRAL Rules,
    Energy Charter Treaty) 165, 167
Walter Bau AG and Kingdom of Thailand, Award (1 July 2009) (Ad Hoc Proceeding,
  1976 UNCITRAL Rules, Germany-Thailand BIT) 178, 230
White Industries Australia Ltd and Republic of India, Final Award (30 November 2011)
  (Ad Hoc Proceeding, 1976 UNCITRAL Rules, Australia-India BIT) 625, 629, 849
Wintershall AG et al and Government of Qatar:
  Partial Award on Liability (29 January 1988), Separate Opinion of Professor Ian
    Brownlie (29 January 1988) (Ad Hoc Proceeding 1976 UNCITRAL Rules,
    Concession Agreement), (1989) 28 ILM 827 .... 702, 717
  Partial Award on Liability (5 February 1988) (Ad Hoc Proceeding, 1976 UNCITRAL
    Rules, Concession Agreement), (1989) 28 ILM 795, 798, 801 .... 20, 22, 28, 81,
    96, 637, 648
  Final Award (31 May 1988) (Ad Hoc Proceeding, 1976 UNCITRAL Rules,
    Concession Agreement), (1989) 28 ILM 834, 837 .... 803–6, 807
Wintershall AG et al and International Ocean Resources Inc, Partial Award on Liability
  (5 February 1988), (Ad Hoc Proceeding 1976 UNCITRAL Rules,
  Germany-Argentina BIT), (1989) 28 ILM 798 736
Zeevi Holdings and Bulgaria and Privatization Agency of Bulgaria:
  Final Award (25 October 2006) (Ad Hoc Proceeding, 1976 UNCITRAL Rules,
    Contract) 855, 864
  Final Award (25 October 2006) (Ad Hoc Proceeding, 1976 UNCITRAL Rules,
    Privatization Agreement) 122, 130

(2) Challenge cases

Challenge decision of 15 April 1993, (1997) XXII Ybk Commercial Arbitration
  222, 224, paras 2, 5, 7.1 .... 178–9, 209, 231, 254, 256
Challenge decision of 11 January 1995, (1997) XXII Ybk Commercial Arbitration
  227, 238, paras 37–38 .... 179, 208–9, 218–19, 225, 231, 234
Challenge decision by a Division of the LCIA—October–December 2005 179
Mr Stanimir Alexandrov, Argentine Government's challenge in the ICS arbitration
  2009 .... 182, 218, 234
Mr Judd L Kessler, 2007, LCIA Case No UN 7949, National Grid PLC and Republic of
  Argentina 180–1, 208, 213, 222–3, 232, 271–2
Mr J Christopher Thomas, QC, Challenge in the case of Vito G Gallo and Government
  of Canada, (October 14, 2009) 182, 208–9, 214, 220, 233–4, 244, 246–7, 271–2
Professor James Anaya, Challenge by United States, 2007 .... 180, 218
Professor Gabrielle Kaufmann-Kohler:
  First Challenge by Argentina in the AWG litigation, 2007 181–2
  Second Challenge by Argentina in the AWG litigation,
    2008 .... 181, 197, 201, 209, 216, 232–3

PRACTICE OF OTHER COURTS AND TRIBUNALS

A. International Courts and Tribunals

Aguilar-Amory and Royal Bank of Canada Claims (Tinoco Arbitration) (Great Britain
  and Costa Rica) (18 October 1923) 897–8
Asian Agricultural Products v. Republic of Sri Lanka, ICSID Case 87/3, Award of 27
  June 1990, 6 ICSID Review–Foreign Investment Law Journal 526 (1991) 681
Bengtson and Federal Republic of Germany, Case No 60, II Decision of the Arbitral
  Commission 216 (Wickstrom, Sauser-Hall, Lagergren, Euler Arndt (CO) Marion,
  Phenix (CO) comms, 1959), (1963) 28 ILR 549 229
Benvenuti et Bonfant and People's Republic of Congo, Award of 8 August 1980 (Trolle,
  Bystricky, Razfindralambo, arbitrators), ICSID case, (1982) 21 International Legal
  Materials 740 120
Berchader Russia 890
Braspetro Oil Services Co v Great Man-Made River Project (1999)
  XXIVa ICCA YBCA 296 763
Buraimi Oasis case 253
City Oriente case 536
Compañia de Aguas del Aconquijo S.A. and Vivendi Universal SA v Argentine Republic,
  ICSID Case No ARB/97/3 .... 181–2, 234–5
Corfu Channel Case (UK v Alb), 1949 ICJ 4, 20 .... 587, 637
Deutsche Schachtbau- und Tiefbohrgesellschaft mbH (DST) v Ras Al Khaimah National
  Oil Co (Rakoil), ICC award 115
Esso/BHP v Plowman, (1995) 11(3) Arb International 273 755
  Partial Award on Jurisdiction (27 February 2004) (LCIA administered, 1976 UNCI-
    TRAL Rules, Canada-Ecuador BIT) 32, 62, 450
Franco Tunisian Arbitration [1957] ILR 767, 769, ... 291
Generation Ukraine Inc v Ukraine, ICSID Case No ARB/00/9, Award, 16 September
  2003 889

Guinea-Bissau v Senegal, Case Concerning the Arbitral Award of 31 July 1989 ICJ Rep 1991, 40 702
Haya de la Torre Case (Colom v Peru) 1951 ICJ 79 (June 13) 803
Hoge Raad case, 21 January 1966 NJ 1966, No 214 750
Hot Rolled Lead and Carbon Steel, Order of the Appellate Body of the WTO 68
Hrvatska Elektroprivreda and Republic of Slovenia, ICSID Case No ARB/05/24 350
Iran and Cubic Corporation, ICC arbitration 190, 204–5, 266, 470
Klöckner and Cameroon, Decision of the Ad Hoc Committee, 3 May 1985 (1986) ICSID Rev–Foreign Investment L J 90 33
Kuwait and The American Independent Oil Co (AMINOIL):
  Award of 12 April 1977, (1982) 21 ILM 976, 980 378
  Award of 24 March 1982, 21 ILM 976 (1982) 138, 141, 495
Lena Goldfields Ltd v Union of Soviet Socialist Republics, 36 Cornell LQ 42 (1930) 775
Libyan American Oil Company (LIAMCO) and Government of the Libyan Arab Republic (Award of 12 April 1977) 62 ILR 139 (1982) 138
Military and Paramilitary Activities in and against Nicaragua (Nicaragua v. United States of America), Provisional Measures, ICJ Reports 1984, 169, 179 .... 536, 545
Norsolor, ICC award ((1984) 9 Ybk of Commercial Arb 109) 115
Nuclear Test Case (Australia v France) 1973 ICJ 99; 1974 ICJ 253, 273 (declaration of Lachs, J) and 293–296 (separate opinion of Gros, J.) 723
Parker Case, 4 R Int'l Arb Awards 39 (1926) 581
Pinson Case, 5 R Int'l Arb Awards 327 (1928) 581
Sabotage claims see United States on behalf of Lehigh Valley Ry v Germany
Saipem case 890
Sapphire International Petroleums and National Iranian Oil Co (15 March 1963), (1968) 35 ILR 136, 167 154
Saudi Arabia and Aramco (23 August 1958) 320
Serbian Loans case, 1929 PCIJ series A No 20 (12 July 1929) 116
Southern Pacific (Middle East) Ltd and Arab Republic of Egypt, Case No ARB 84/3, ICSID, Award of 20 May 1992, (1993) 32 ILM 933 470
Telenor Mobile Communications AS v Hungary, ICSID Case No ARB/04/15, Award, 13 September 2006 889
Texaco Overseas Petroleum Company v. Government of the Libyan Arab Republic ('TOPCO'), (Award of 19 January 1977), 53 ILR 389 (1979) 138
Tinoco Arbitration see Aguilar-Amory and Royal Bank of Canada Claims (Great Britain and Costa Rica)
Tokios Tokelés and Ukraine, ICSID Case No ARB/02/18, Decision on Jurisdiction (29 April 2004) 701
Tradex v Albania 890
United States on behalf of Lehigh Valley Ry v Germany (Sabotage Claims), Mixed Claims Commission, United States and Germany:
  Opinions and Decisions (1 October 1926 to 31 December 1932) (1933) 831
  Opinions and Decisions (15 June 1939 and 30 October 1939) 831
  Decisions French Mexican Claims Commission, 5 R International Arb 510–14 (1936) 775
  Decision of Roberts, Umpire and Opinion of Garnett (1939) 775

B. National and European Courts and Tribunals

1. Australia

Esso Australia Resources Lt and ors v The Honourable Sidney James Plowman and ors (1995) 128 Australian L Rep 391; (1995) 183 Commonwealth Reports 10 37

2. Austria

Norsolor 115–16

3. Ecuador

Lago Agrio Case 539–42

4. Europe

Eco Suris China Time Limited v Benetton International NV (Case C–126/97, 1 June 1999, ECR I-3055) 117
Holm v Sweden, ECHR (1993), Series A, Vol 279-A, para 33 213
Nordström-Janzon v Netherlands (528101/95), Decision of the European Commission of Human Rights (27 November 1996) DR 87-A, 112 213

5. France

BKMI and Siemens v Société Dutco, Court of Cassation (7 January 1992), (1993) 18 Ybk of Commercial Arb 140 .... 56, 170–1, 1072
Braspetro Oil Services Co. v. Great Man-Made River Project (1999) XXIVa ICCA YBCA 763
Creighton v Qatar, Court of Cassation, Appeal No A98019.068, (October 2000) 15(10) Mealey's International Arb Rep(s) A-1 744–5
Ets Raumond Gosset v Carapelli, (7 May 1963) JCP G 1963, II, 13 para 405 454
SPP (Middle East) Ltd and Southern Pacific Properties Ltd and Arab Republic of Egypt and the Egyptian General Co for Tourism and Hotels ('Pyramids' case):
(1983) (1984) 23 ILM 1048 (Paris Court of Appeal) 470, 563
(1987) 26 ILM 1004 (Paris Court of Appeal) 470

6. Germany

Judgment of 27 February 1970, 6 Arbitration International 79 (1990) (Bundesgerichtshof) 454

7. Netherlands

Republic of Indonesia v Himpurna California Energy Ltd et al (Dutch Court of First Instance (Arrondissementsrechtbank)), (21 September 1999), translated and (2000) XXV Ybk Commercial Arbitration 469, 471–73 .... 95, 99

8. Nigeria

Total Nigeria Plc v. Morkah (2002) 9 NWLR 492 28

9. Sweden

AI Trade Finance Inc v Bulgarian Foreign Trade Bank Ltd, [1998] Stockholm City Court, Case No T-111–98 37

10. United Kingdom

Ali Shipping Corporation v Shipyard Trogir [1999] 1 Weekly L Rep 314 37
American Cynamid v Ethicon 520
Associated Electric and Gas Insurance Ltd v The European Reinsurance Company of
  Zurich [2003] UKPC 11 37
Dallal, Mark v Bank Mellat, Queens Bench Division (Commercial Court) [1986] 1 All
  ER 239, 254 .... 44, 368
Department of Economic Policy and Development, City of Moscow v Bankers Trust Co.
  and Anr (2004) EWCA 314 39
Deutsche Schachtbau- und Tiefbohrgesellschaft mbH (DST) v Ras Al Khaimah National
  Oil Co (Rakoil) (1987) 3 WLR 1023 (CA) 115
Harbour Assurance Co (UK) Ltd v Kansas General International Insurance Co Ltd
  [1992] 1 Lloyd's Rep. 81, 92–3 (QB) 454
Holland v Cassidy (1888) 13 App Cas. 170 (PC) 258
Modern Engineering v Miskin [1981] Lloyd's L Rep 135, 138 235
Salomon v Salomon 683

11. United States of America

Baar v Tigerman, 140 Cal App 3d 979, 985; 189 Cal Rptr 834, 839 (1983) 288
Buckeye Check Cashing Inc v Cardegna, 546 US 440 (2006) 454
Colombia v Cauca Co, 290 US 524, 527–28 (1903) 316
Columbia v Cauca Co, 190 US 524; 47 L Ed 1159 (1902) 775
Commonwealth Coatings v Continental Casualty, 393 US 145 (1968) 195
Edmonds v Stratton, MO. APP, 457 SW 2d 228, 232, Black's Law Dictionary 445
Federal Reserve Bank of New York v Gordon Williams, 708 F Supp. 4–8
  (SDNY 1989) 354
International Thunderbird Corporation v. Mexico, U.S. District Court for the District of
  Columbia, Civil Action 06-00748, 14 February 2007 889
Iran Aircraft Industries and Iran Helicopter Support and Renewal Company v Avco
  Corporation, 980 F 2d 141, 146 (2nd Cir, 1992), (1992) 7(12) Mealey's International
  Arb Rep A-1 .... 44, 754
Mack v Hugger Bros Constr S 153 Tenn 260, 283 SW 448, 46 ALR 389 Ballentine's
  Law Dictionary 445
Mitsubishi v Soler, 473 US 614 (1985) 82
Prima Paint Corporation v Flood and Conklin Manufacturing Co, 388
  US 395 (1967) 454
Publicis Communications v True North Communications Inc, 203 F.3d 725 (7th Cir
  2000); (2000) XXV ICCA YBCA 1152 .... 735, 763
United States v Panhandle Eastern Corp (1988) 118 Federal Rules Decisions 346
  (D Del) 37–8
United States v Sperry Corp, 387 US 52 (1989) 848

Table of Instruments

UNCITRAL INSTRUMENTS

UNCITRAL Arbitration Rules 7, 11, 23, 34–5, 37–8, 40–1,
56, 58, 81, 83, 85, 90, 109, 127, 216, 286, 751, 755
UNCITRAL Arbitration Rules 1976 .... 2–4, 6, 8–10, 16–18, 24–8, 31–2,
35, 38–40, 42, 49–52, 59–61, 64–5, 68, 79, 84, 90,
92–3, 95, 97, 99–100, 109, 112–14, 117, 120–2,
124–6, 129–30, 150–1, 155, 158–9, 168–9, 172–3, 178–9,
181, 184, 191–4, 196–7, 209, 214, 231, 240, 242, 248,
251–2, 255, 258, 263, 269, 273, 275, 281–2, 288–91,
295, 297, 299, 314–15, 319–20, 325, 330, 337, 348–56,
361–2, 366, 368–71, 373, 395, 397, 399–400, 402, 413,
417–18, 428, 431–4, 440–1, 452, 454, 456–7, 459, 463,
471, 513, 516–17, 521, 524–6, 531–3, 535–6, 558, 561,
563–4, 572, 577, 604–5, 612, 628, 638, 647–8, 678–80,
692–3, 695, 700–1, 704, 706–7, 716–20, 722, 733–4,
745, 750, 753, 756, 758–62, 768, 786, 791, 804, 806,
812, 823–5, 830, 842, 844, 846, 848–9, 854, 862–3,
867–70, 877, 882, 889, 891, 901

    Section III 63
    Section IV 63
    Art 1 .... 16, 24–5, 367, 806
    Art 1(1) 18–19, 24–5, 27–8, 864
    Art 1(2) 26, 28–9, 41, 64
    Art 1(3) 79
    Art 2 .... 242, 401, 403, 806
    Art 2(1) 394–5, 399–401, 403
    Art 2(2) 394, 402, 404
    Art 2(3) 401
    Art 3 ....366, 368–70
    Art 3(1) 156, 360
    Art 3(2) 360, 362, 368
    Art 3(3) 360, 362
    Art 3(3)(b)–(e) 368
    Art 3(4) 360, 364
    Art 4 ....347–50, 352, 354–5
    Art 4(3) 361
    Art 5 ....157, 172
    Art 6 ....148–9, 156, 163–4, 172–3, 219, 253, 273
    Art 6(1) 162–3
    Art 6(1)(b) 172
    Art 6(2) 162, 172, 268–9
    Art 6(3) 162, 167

Art 6(3)(d)	167
Art 6(4)	162, 172
Art 6(7)	163
Art 7	28, 148–9, 164, 172–3
Art 7(1)	28, 62, 164, 167, 178
Art 7(2)	28, 164
Art 7(2)(b)	167, 172–3
Art 7(3)	28, 165, 167
Art 8	148–9, 172
Art 8(1)	154
Art 8(2)	172
Art 9	105, 177, 194–5, 197, 201, 223, 227, 231
Arts 9–12, Note 5	299
Art 10	105, 156, 177, 193, 207, 211, 214, 221, 223, 227, 314
Art 10(1)	209, 212, 228–9, 250, 274
Art 10(2)	274, 760
Art 11	2–4, 6, 8–10, 16–18, 24–8, 31–2, 35, 38–40, 42, 49–52, 59–61, 64–5, 68, 79, 84, 90, 92–3, 95, 97, 99–100, 105, 109, 112–14, 117, 120–2, 124–6, 129–30, 150–1, 155–6, 158–9, 168–9, 172–3, 177–9, 181, 184, 191–7, 199–200, 223, 226, 242, 245–6, 249–50, 269, 271, 314
Art 11(1)	241–4, 253, 275
Art 11(2)	241, 248, 275
Art 11(3)	241, 253–4, 256, 275
Art 12	156, 177, 192–3, 196–7, 223, 226, 314
Art 12(1)	196, 228, 268, 272, 275
Art 12(1)(a)–(b)	268–9, 273
Art 12(1)(c)	156, 219, 268, 270, 273
Art 12(2)	195, 268, 275
Art 13	177, 223, 228, 290, 296, 302, 311, 314
Art 13(1)	290, 305–7, 314, 316
Art 13(2)	49, 223, 228–30, 274, 278–80, 282, 289–92, 296–302, 305, 314–17
Art 13(3)	49
Art 13(5)	290, 303
Art 14	48, 177, 318–22
Art 15	29, 58, 60–1, 64–5, 69, 355, 419, 476, 579
Art 15(1)	31, 33, 40, 47, 58–60, 62–9, 315–16, 355, 456, 535, 569, 578–9, 831–2
Art 15(2)	49–51, 59, 63, 832
Art 15(3)	54, 62
Art 16	77, 79, 95–7, 99
Art 16(1)	27, 77–9, 95–7, 99, 105, 107–8
Art 16(2)	77, 93, 98, 100, 102, 106
Art 16(3)	77, 96
Art 16(4)	77–8, 92, 95–6, 745, 760
Art 17	376–7, 384
Art 17(1)	48, 379–80, 828, 853

Art 17(2)	48–9, 384
Art 18	65, 362, 414–21
Art 18(1)	410, 413, 416, 419
Art 18(1)(b)–(c)	417
Art 18(2)	410, 412, 416–19, 421
Art 18(2)(b)	417
Art 19	419, 422, 429–31, 496
Art 19(1)	432–3
Art 19(2)	65, 431
Art 19(3)	426, 429–31, 434, 440–1, 446
Art 19(4)	434, 447
Art 20	414–15, 417–19, 456, 467–9, 473, 475, 477–80, 496, 674
Art 20(2)(c)	369
Art 21	432, 458, 461, 463, 674
Art 21(1)	450–2
Art 21(2)	450, 452–4, 458
Art 21(3)	433–4, 450, 455, 458–9
Art 21(4)	433, 450, 457, 459–62
Art 22	415, 418–19, 491, 496–7, 505, 508
Art 23	418, 433, 505
Art 24	419, 557, 574, 578
Art 24(1)	574
Art 24(2)	574–5
Art 24(3)	31, 570, 574, 578
Art 25	574, 602, 674
Art 25(1)	612
Art 25(2)	575, 605, 612
Art 25(3)	610, 612
Art 25(4)	66–9, 609, 612, 617
Art 25(5)	557, 564–5, 574, 611
Art 25(6)	66, 557, 571, 574, 579, 581, 611
Art 26	514–15, 518, 530, 533–4, 537, 540–1, 543, 740
Art 26(1)	535, 539
Art 26(2)	518, 524, 533, 535
Art 26(3)	529
Art 26(6)	741
Art 27	648–50
Art 27(1)	576, 648–9
Art 27(2)	576–7
Art 27(3)	577, 674, 677
Art 27(4)	571–2, 574, 579
Art 28	419, 672–5, 678, 680–3, 718, 761
Art 28(1)	671, 674, 678–9, 790
Art 28(2)	672
Art 28(3)	672, 675, 679, 683
Art 29	624, 628–9
Art 29(1)–(2)	629

Art 30	691–2, 695–6, 718, 825
Art 30(1)(a)	901
Art 31	701, 704, 716–18
Art 31(1)–(2)	700
Art 31(2)	303, 710, 718
Art 32	61, 63, 540–1, 718, 759, 761–2, 832
Art 32(1)	60, 540–1, 732, 734–5, 759, 761–3
Art 32(2)	321, 540–1, 732, 738, 745, 760, 762–3, 831
Art 32(3)	732, 747, 751, 760
Art 32(4)	717–18, 732, 745–6, 748, 760, 763–5, 792
Art 32(5)	732, 756, 760
Art 32(6)	732, 757, 760
Art 32(7)	732, 759–60, 765, 792
Art 33	123, 128, 130
Art 33(1)	112, 114, 118, 123–6, 129
Art 33(2)	112, 120, 127, 129
Art 33(3)	112, 123, 127, 130
Art 34	781, 790
Art 34(1)	790, 792
Art 34(2)	782, 790–1, 842
Art 34(3)	790
Art 34(4)–(5)	782, 790
Art 35	741, 762, 802–4, 806–8, 831
Art 35(1)	762
Art 36	741, 803, 811–13, 831, 842, 901
Art 36(1)	812
Art 37	48, 803, 807, 822–4, 831
Art 37(2)	759, 824
Art 38	48, 841, 843, 848–51, 861, 888
Art 38(3)	853
Art 38(4)	853
Art 38(a)	852–3, 878
Art 38(b)	852, 878
Art 38(c)–(d)	848, 852
Art 38(e)	848–9, 881, 890
Art 39	27, 48, 805, 852, 858, 862, 864
Art 39(1)	862
Art 39(2)	855, 862–4
Art 39(3)–(4)	855, 862–3
Art 40	865, 877–8, 881, 886, 888
Art 40(1)	865, 868, 877, 879–80, 882, 886, 889–90
Art 40(2)	865, 868, 877, 879, 881, 886, 889–90
Art 40(3)	865, 877
Art 40(4)	807, 865, 877
Art 41	851, 896–7, 900–1
Art 41(1)	896
Art 41(2)	896, 902–3

Art 41(3)	896, 899
Art 41(4)	896, 900
Art 41(5)	896, 901, 903
Art I	761
UNCITRAL Arbitration Rules 2010	2–3, 8, 10, 16, 18, 21–2, 24–6, 47, 49–50, 54, 59, 83, 92, 94, 115, 117, 119, 121–2, 145–6, 148, 150–1, 170, 172–3, 178, 198, 216, 256, 269–70, 326, 337, 339–41, 343, 352, 365, 370, 393, 396–7, 399, 411, 452, 459, 527, 530, 532, 561–2, 566, 575, 604–5, 607, 612, 640, 669, 676, 691–3, 695, 697, 699, 732, 742, 745, 750, 752, 759–60, 790, 806, 844, 849, 855, 862–3, 868
Art 1	13, 24, 26, 30, 751
Art 1(1)	16, 18–19, 24, 34, 36, 38, 78, 86, 96, 492, 505–6, 555, 714
Art 1(2)	16–17, 21–2, 26, 34, 36, 452, 561–2, 732
Art 1(3)	16–17, 22, 26, 41, 45, 49, 86, 328, 760, 866
Art 2	53, 83, 345, 352, 355, 368, 394–5, 397–8, 403
Art 2(1)	393–5, 397, 400
Art 2(2)	362, 394, 397, 399–400, 402–3
Art 2(3)	394, 397, 400, 402–3
Art 2(4)	394, 397, 400, 402–3
Art 2(5)–(6)	394, 402, 404
Art 3	123, 345, 359, 362, 368, 410, 412–13, 416, 423
Art 3(1)	359–61, 368
Art 3(2)	359–60, 362, 368
Art 3(2)(g)	362
Art 3(3)	359–60, 362, 366
Art 3(3)(b)–(e)	368
Art 3(4)	359–60, 362, 364, 369
Art 3(4)(a)	149
Art 3(4)(a)–(c)	364
Art 3(4)(b)	163
Art 3(5)	359–60, 364–5, 369
Art 3(b)	373
Art 3(c)–(e)	372–3
Art 3(f)–(g)	372
Art 4	370, 373
Art 4(1)	359, 370–3
Art 4(1)(a)–(b)	372
Art 4(2)	359, 370, 372–3
Art 4(2)(a)	149
Art 4(2)(c)	163
Art 4(3)	359, 370, 372–3, 398
Art 4(4)	370
Art 5	347–8, 350–5, 1020
Art 6	149, 172
Art 6(1)	148–51, 172, 339, 364
Art 6(2)	148, 151, 172

Art 6(3)	148, 153, 171
Art 6(4)	148, 151, 153, 172
Art 6(5)	148, 153–5, 172
Art 6(6)	148, 153–4, 172
Art 6(7)	149, 153, 155, 164
Art 7	157, 161
Art 7(1)	157, 172–3, 338–9
Art 7(2)	157, 160–1, 173, 339
Art 8	154, 162, 164, 173, 289, 307, 700, 846
Art 8(1)	162–3, 338, 364
Art 8(2)	162, 339
Art 9	154, 164, 166, 173, 289, 307, 311, 364, 846
Art 9(1)	164, 169, 338
Art 9(2)	164, 338–9
Art 9(3)	164–5, 339
Art 10	154, 169, 173, 289, 308, 364
Art 10(1)	169
Art 10(2)	161, 169–70
Art 10(3)	169–71
Art 11	212, 274, 289
Art 12	154, 214, 274, 329
Art 12(1)	207–9, 212, 228–9, 274, 278
Art 12(2)	207–8
Art 12(3)	207–8, 228–9, 278–80, 289
Art 13	154, 241, 268–9, 274, 329
Art 13(1)	241, 243, 245, 268, 275, 338, 642
Art 13(2)	241, 248, 275
Art 13(3)	241, 253–5, 275
Art 13(4)	153, 241, 256, 268, 275
Art 14	154, 278, 305, 307, 314, 323, 329
Art 14(1)	289, 305, 307–8
Art 14(2)	283, 288, 305, 308, 311–14
Art 15	278, 318–20
Art 15(2)	311
Art 16	325–30
Art 17	13, 16, 29–30, 32, 34, 58, 85–6, 365, 505, 575, 625
Art 17(1)	16, 22, 29–33, 35–6, 38, 40, 45–7, 52–3, 57–9, 77, 92, 94, 96, 272, 329, 348, 415, 424, 429, 456, 557, 571, 604, 609–10, 626, 645, 859, 861–2
Art 17(2)	16, 29, 35, 46–7, 59, 492
Art 17(3)	16, 30, 49–53, 59, 457, 561, 601, 628, 636, 638, 647
Art 17(4)	30, 53, 59
Art 17(5)	30, 54–9, 469
Art 18	13, 16, 45, 77–8, 93, 95, 123, 709
Art 18(1)	36, 77–8, 80, 89, 92–6, 113
Art 18(2)	77–8, 91, 93–4, 96
Art 18(4)	745
Art 19	32, 345, 375–6, 380–1, 384, 610

Art 19(1)	375–6, 381–2
Art 19(2)	375–6, 379, 382–3
Art 19(3)	58
Art 20	345, 364, 410, 414, 416, 422–3, 493, 576
Art 20(1)	362, 410–11, 416
Art 20(2)	410–12, 414–16, 423, 429
Art 20(2)(a)	369
Art 20(2)(d)	369
Art 20(3)	411–13, 416, 423
Art 20(4)	411–12, 416–17, 424, 429, 575
Art 21	345, 410, 421, 423, 429, 431, 576
Art 21(1)	362, 422, 431
Art 21(2)	422–4, 431, 575
Art 21(3)	422, 425–9
Art 21(4)	422, 429
Art 22	345, 410, 413, 456, 467–71, 473–5, 480
Art 23	83, 345, 410, 421, 449, 458
Art 23(1)	449–54, 458
Art 23(2)	372–3, 424, 449–50, 455–6, 458–9
Art 23(3)	449–50, 457–9
Art 24	491–2, 494–6, 566, 570, 625, 646
Art 24(1)	576
Art 24(3)	565, 567
Art 25	46, 48, 345, 411, 415, 423, 491, 495, 505–8, 570, 625, 646
Note 5	608
Note 6(a)	644
Notes	611
Art 25(2)	576, 618–19
Art 25(4)	608
Art 26	345, 493, 513, 516–17, 520, 524–5, 530–2, 571
Art 26(1)	513–14, 516–17, 532
Art 26(2)	513–14, 517, 527, 533
Art 26(3)	513–14, 517, 520–1, 524, 533
Art 26(4)	514, 520, 524, 533
Art 26(5)	514–15, 523, 525–6, 533
Art 26(6)	514–15, 523, 526, 528, 533
Art 26(7)	514–15, 533
Art 26(8)	514–15, 523, 528, 533
Art 26(9)	85, 514–15, 529–30, 533, 571
Art 27	553, 555, 557, 571, 574, 602, 611, 636
Note 2	643–4
Art 27(1)	243, 245, 557–9, 561
Art 27(2)	83, 557, 561–5, 574, 576, 647
Art 27(3)	31, 557, 559, 565–7, 569–70, 574
Art 27(4)	557–9, 565, 571–4, 610, 625
Art 28	507, 553, 555, 557, 601–2, 604, 610–11, 636–7, 646
Art 28(1)	602, 612

Art 28(2) 561, 602, 604–7, 609–10, 647
Art 28(3) 36–7, 40, 602, 604, 607–9, 612, 647, 749
Art 28(4) 602, 604, 609, 647
Art 29 .... 329, 553, 561, 566, 635–6, 638, 648, 825
Art 29(1) 636, 638, 640–1, 643, 648
Art 29(2) 638, 640, 642–3, 648, 665
Art 29(3) 636, 644–5
Art 29(4) 636, 645–6
Art 29(5) 413, 636–7, 645–7
Art 30 .... 246, 415, 625, 669, 671–4, 676–9
Art 30(1) 414, 507, 671–2, 675–6, 678–9
Art 30(1)(a) 675, 789–90, 900–1
Art 30(1)(b) 423, 676–7, 679
Art 30(2) 672, 677
Art 30(3) 570, 672, 677–9
Art 31 .... 624–5, 628
Art 31(1) 624–6
Art 31(2) 626–8
Art 32 .... 34, 669, 691–5
Art 33 .... 91, 697, 699–702, 706–7, 716, 804, 812
Art 33(1) 91, 699–702, 704, 710
Art 33(2) 384, 474, 699–701, 706–7, 709, 739
Art 34 .... 697, 732, 735, 742, 759
Art 34(1) 732–6, 759, 812
Art 34(2) 87, 733, 735, 738–9, 742, 745, 757, 760, 789, 804, 812, 828
Art 34(3) 733, 739, 750, 760, 812
Art 34(4) 714, 732–3, 739, 745–6, 749, 760, 792, 806, 812
Art 34(5) 37, 733, 749, 755–6, 760, 806, 812
Art 34(6) 733, 739, 757, 760, 792, 804, 806, 812
Art 35 .... 13, 111, 115, 117–18, 128
Art 35(1) 83, 111–14, 116–19, 121, 124
Art 35(2) 83, 111–12, 114–15, 119, 127
Art 35(3) 111–12, 117, 121–3
Art 36 .... 697, 781, 788, 790, 901
Art 36(1) 782, 784, 788, 791
Art 36(2) 783, 788–91, 900
Art 36(3) 790, 792
Art 37 .... 697, 757, 802–5, 828
Art 37(1) 802
Art 37(2) 802, 806
Art 38 .... 697, 757, 802, 812, 828
Art 38(1)–(2) 811
Art 38(3) 811
Art 39 .... 697, 757, 802–3, 822–4, 828, 877
Art 39(2) 823–5
Art 40 .... 697, 840, 843–4, 846, 848–9
Art 40(1) 841, 848, 867, 870

Art 40(2) 841, 843, 867
Art 40(2)(a) 842, 852, 860, 867, 897
Art 40(2)(b) 842, 849, 852, 860, 867, 897
Art 40(2)(c) 842, 849, 867, 897
Art 40(2)(d) 849, 867
Art 40(2)(e) 849, 876
Art 40(2)(f) 867, 1021
Art 40(3) 841, 848–9, 877
Art 40(4) 849
Art 41 .... 337, 697, 840, 842, 852, 856, 876, 901
Art 41(1) 853–4, 858, 861–2
Art 41(2) 853, 862
Art 41(3) 847, 855–60, 862
Art 41(4) 153, 172, 847, 855, 858–62
Art 41(4)(a) 860
Art 41(4)(b) 847
Art 41(4)(c) 860–1
Art 41(4)(d) 861
Art 41(5) 855–6, 859–62, 903
Art 41(6) 855, 860–2
Art 42 .... 672, 697, 840, 843, 849, 865, 867, 869, 877
Art 42(1) 855, 865–7, 869–70, 874
Art 42(2) 842, 865, 869–70
Art 42(3) 849
Art 43 .... 638–9, 697, 840, 843, 896–7, 901
Art 43(1) 896–7
Art 43(2) 625, 896–8
Art 43(3) 896, 899
Art 43(4) 789, 899–900
Art 43(5) 900–1
Annex 149, 198, 200, 733, 744
   Model Arbitration Clause for Contracts 17, 376
   Note 149
UNCITRAL Conciliation Rules 1980 3
  Art 14 787
  Art 19 787
  Art 20 787–8
UNCITRAL Model Law on Electronic Commerce 1996 397
  Art 15(2)–(4) 402
UNCITRAL Model Law on International Commercial Arbitration 1985 .... 2–3, 6,
37, 49, 84–5, 87, 91, 94, 104, 114–16, 118, 120, 123–5,
127, 161, 194, 295, 297, 329, 367, 393, 413, 429, 458,
469, 496, 515–16, 518–19, 521–2, 524–7, 531, 537, 558,
564, 571, 602, 626, 644, 694–5, 706–7, 709, 735, 744,
785, 807, 825
  Art 2 429
  Art 3 397

Art 4	695
Art 7	19
Art 7(1)	18
Art 12	196
Art 12(1)	196
Art 13	259
Art 14	297
Art 16	457
Art 16(1)	451, 454, 456
Art 16(2)	456, 459
Art 16(3)	457–8
Art 17	515–17, 520–1, 524, 530–2
Art 17(2)	525
Art 17(2)(a)–(c)	520
Art 17A	517, 520, 531, 537
Art 17A(1)(a)	531
Art 17B	530
Art 17B(1)	530
Art 17G	525, 528
Art 18	30, 33, 527
Art 19	30
Art 19(2)	520, 572
Art 20	79–80
Art 20(2)	94, 932
Art 22	377, 381
Art 23(1)	411, 423
Art 23(2)	468–9, 471, 474
Art 24(1)	49–52, 602
Art 24(3)	54, 527
Art 25	678
Art 25(b)	676
Art 26	639
Art 27	571
Art 28	114, 125
Art 28(1)	112, 124
Art 28(2)	118, 120, 125
Art 28(4)	121
Art 29	701, 703, 706–7
Art 30(2)	783
Art 31	759
Art 31(3)	92
Art 32	739
Art 32(1)	822
Art 32(2)(a)	424, 788
Art 33	807
Art 33(1)(b)	804, 807, 847
Art 33(3)	823

Art 33(4) 823–4
Art 34 .... 84, 87, 306, 740, 743–4
Art 34(2) 84
Art 34(2)(ii) 692
Art 34(4) 740
Art 35 .... 87, 807
Art 36 .... 87, 744
Art 36(1)(a)(ii) 393
Art 36(1)(a)(iv) 56
UNCITRAL Model Law on International Commercial Conciliation 2002 .... 3, 788
UNCITRAL Notes on Organizing Arbitral Proceedings 1996 .... 3, 100–1, 103, 106, 384, 602
 complete text 925–43
 para 2 101
 para 20 384
 para 21 92
 para 22 .... 100, 107
 para 22(c)–(e) 89
 para 23 91

IRAN–US CLAIMS TRIBUNAL

Rules of Procedure 1983 .... 25, 30–2, 41–2, 46, 50–1, 53, 70, 73, 75, 128, 260–1, 282, 290, 351, 353, 414–15, 430, 439, 500, 503, 596, 608, 694, 704, 713, 726, 728, 768, 778, 810, 832, 848, 900
 Art 1(1) 25, 835
 Art 1(3) 367
 Art 2, Note 1 402–3
 Art 2(1) 404–5
 Art 2(2) 405
 Art 2(3) 403, 405–7
 Art 2(4)–(5) 407
 Art 3 239
 Art 4 .... 239, 354
 Art 5 239
 Art 6 .... 270–1, 294
 Art 6(2) 270
 Art 7 .... 280, 287, 294
 Art 8 294
 Art 9 .... 201, 203–4, 216, 239, 243, 260, 294, 651, 686
 Arts 9–12
  Note 1 .... 264, 274
  Note 4 .... 253, 267
 Art 10 .... 185, 201, 235, 237, 239, 243, 260, 294, 648, 651, 686
 Art 10(1) 235, 237–8

Art 10(2)	240, 258
Art 11	201, 239, 243, 252, 257, 259–60, 262, 264–5, 274, 294, 648
Art 11(1)	185, 204, 238, 257–61, 263–4, 651
Art 11(2)	248, 263–5
Art 11(3)	264–5, 267, 295, 322
Art 12	201, 239, 243, 264, 270–1, 294
Art 12(b)	274, 294
Art 12(1)	270
Art 12(1)(6)	249
Art 12(2)	274
Art 13	230, 238–9, 283, 288, 302, 403
Art 13(1)	286–7, 708
Art 13(2)	230, 281, 283, 286, 292–6, 301, 708
Art 13(3)	282–3, 302
Art 13(4)	283, 302, 317
Art 13(5)	283, 288–9, 293, 302–4, 707–8, 722, 772
Art 14	302, 304
Art 14(5)	722
Art 15	70, 73, 354, 500, 503–4, 629–30
Note 3	53
Note 4	52
Note 5	40, 46, 70
Art 15(1)	30, 69, 72–3, 503, 628, 631
Art 15(2)	74, 76–7, 632–3, 688
Art 15(5)	722
Art 17	386, 388, 390, 402
Note 2	377, 387
Note 3	382, 387–8, 391, 620
Note 3(a)–(d)	389
Note 4	382, 388
Art 17(1)	385, 678
Art 17(2)	382, 387
Art 18	366, 414, 484, 505
Note 1	416
Art 18(1)(h)	354
Art 19	435–6, 442, 484
Note 1	423, 435
Note 2	429
Notes	493
Art 19(1)	422–3
Art 19(2)	354, 424, 429, 436
Art 19(3)	427, 436–7, 440, 442–3, 446, 657
Art 20	442, 480–1, 483–4, 486–9
Art 21, Note 2	224
Art 21(2)	463
Art 21(3)	464
Art 21(4)	464–6

Art 22	72–3, 500–4, 629
Art 22(2)	470
Art 23	73, 500, 504–5, 629
Art 24(1)	580, 584–7, 596
Art 24(3)	588–9
Art 25	498, 596, 620
Note 2	612–13, 619–20, 622
Note 3	611
Note 4	623
Note 5	624
Note 6(a)	597, 600, 607, 620
Note 6(b)	606
Note 7	611, 623
Art 25(1)	617
Art 25(2)	563–4, 619–20, 622
Art 25(3)	623
Art 25(4)	624
Art 25(5)	593
Art 25(6)	72, 503, 564, 594, 596–7, 620, 628
Art 26	589, 737
Art 26(1)	543, 548
Art 26(2)	550–1
Art 26(3)	550
Art 27	650, 653, 664
Art 27(1)	650
Art 27(2)	662
Art 27(3)	663
Art 27(4)	667
Art 28	73, 484, 504, 629, 683–5
Art 28(1)	684
Art 28(2)	677, 685–7
Art 28(3)	384, 390, 501–2, 678, 687–9
Art 29	261
Art 29(1)	630
Art 29(2)	72, 503, 627, 630, 632–3
Art 29(4)	646
Art 30(1)(a)	900
Art 31	185, 228, 754
Note 1	700
Note 2	189, 704, 706, 711–12, 715–16, 723–6, 728–30
Art 31(1)	719–20
Art 31(2)	707–8, 722
Art 32	778
Art 32(1)	736, 766–7
Art 32(2)	185, 739, 767, 776, 829, 837
Art 32(3)	728, 753, 767–8, 776
Art 32(4)	714, 767, 769–70, 772–3, 775

Art 32(5) 776–9
Art 33 822
Art 33(1) 128, 131
Art 33(2) 129, 140
Art 33(3) 140
Art 34 .... 380, 793, 798–800
Art 34(1) 380, 782–3, 793, 797
Art 34(2) 798–800
Art 35 .... 405, 739, 808–11, 821, 829–30, 836
Art 35(1) 809
Art 36 .... 389, 406, 739, 808, 810–13, 818–19, 821, 829–30, 833–4, 836
Art 36(1) 818–20
Art 36(2) 900
Art 37 .... 386, 406–7, 739, 810–11, 821, 825, 827, 829–30, 833–4, 836
Art 37(1) 386
Art 38 .... 891, 894
Art 38(1)(a) 894, 897
Art 38(1)(b) 894
Art 38(1)(c) 891
Art 38(2) 848
Art 39 379
Art 40 894–5
Art 40(1)–(2) 891–2
Art 41 899
Art 41(2) 551, 659, 897, 904
Art 41(3) 899–900
Art 43(4)–(5) 900
Art 83 891
Art 83(1)(c) 891
Art 85 818
Art 86 818
   Note 2(4) 416
   Note 5 383

OTHER INSTITUTIONS' RULES

AAA Commercial Rules of Arbitration
   R-12, 17 209
   Section 7 361
AAA Rules 2010 .... 215, 704
   Art 16(2) 34
   Arts 10–11 313
   Art 14 377
   Art 27(1) 759
   Art 28(3) 120
   Art 34 .... 37, 755
   Art 35 327

Australian Centre for International Commercial Arbitration Rules 2005, Art 4.5....... 365
CPR International Rules, r 7.1 209
ECAFE Rules for International Commercial Arbitration 1966
    Art II(3) 361
    Art VI(8) 349
Economic Commission for Europe (ECE) Arbitration Rules
    Art 3 361
    Art 38 125
Hague Rules, Art 3(6) 133
Hamburg Rules 88
IBA Rules of Ethics for International Arbitrators 1987 .... 198, 215
    Rule 8 787
    Rule 9 711
IBA Rules on Taking of Evidence in International Commercial
    Arbitration 1999 .... 31, 520, 555–6, 569, 577–8, 602, 642–3
    Art 3(a)(ii) 578
    Art 3(b) 578
    Art 3(3) 569
    Art 3(3)(c) 569
    Art 4 563
    Art 5(3) 647
    Art 6 642–3
    Art 6(2) 642
    Art 9 569
IBA Rules 2010 569
    Art 8.1 609
    Art 9(5) 571
IBA Supplementary Rules on the Taking of Evidence in International Commercial
    Arbitration 46
ICC Internal Rules of the Court of Arbitration, r 2(2) 723
ICC Rules of Arbitration 58, 122, 125, 319, 701, 703, 744
    Art 2(8) 259
    Art 14(1) 80
    Art 17(3) 120, 129
    Art 30(5) 864
ICC Rules of Arbitration 1975, Art 24 745
ICC Rules of Arbitration 1998 .... 171, 329, 352, 692
    Art 3(3) 399
    Art 4(6) 57
    Art 7(3) 199
    Art 10 171
    Art 17 119
    Art 21(4) 352
    Art 31(3) 866
    Art 34 329

ICC Rules of Arbitration 2012 715
    Art 3(2) 397
    Art 4(4) 365
    Art 5 371
    Art 6(3) 449
    Art 11 196–7
    Art 18(2) 94
    Art 21(1) 112
    Art 22(2) 122
    Art 30(1) 758
    Art 33 .... 694, 715
    Art 34(6) 743
    Art 39 692
    Art 40 329
    r 41 742
ICDR Rules 2009, Art 15 449
ICDR International Arbitration Rules 2010
    Art 7 .... 194, 196
    Art 18(1) 397
ICSID Arbitration Rules 269, 871
    Art 48(4) 755
    r 9(4) 181, 192
    r 35(2) 607, 615
    r 35(3) 615, 643
    r 37(2) 41
    r 46 758
ICSID Additional Facility Rules 2006
    Art 45(1) 449
    Art 46(2) 517
Incoterms 118
Inter-American Commercial Arbitration Commission Rules of Procedure
    2002, Art 6 194
International Court of Justice, Statute of the 834
    Arts 34–35 68
    Art 54(3) 711, 723
    Art 61 .... 68, 828, 831
    Arts 62–64 68
JAMS International Rules, Art 8.1 209
Japan Commercial Arbitration Association (JCAA) Administrative and Procedural Rules
    for Arbitration under the UNCITRAL Arbitration Rules 2009 1021
London Court of International Arbitration (LCIA) Rules 1998 .... 55, 703
    Art 3 371
    Art 4.1 397
    Art 5.3 196
    Art 5.4 365
    Art 11.1 313
    Art 14.1(ii) 34

Art 15.6	414
Art 16	79
Art 16.2	94
Art 17.3	377
Art 20.7	563
Art 22.1(h)	55–6
Art 22.4	120
Art 23.1	449
Art 26.5	758
Art 26.7	733, 735
Art 26.9	743
Art 28	758
Art 30	755
Art 30.1	37, 756
Art 31.1	327, 329
Netherlands Arbitration Institute Rules, Art 48(2)	703
Permanent Court of Arbitration Optional Rules for Arbitrating Disputes between Two States 1992	7
r 575	7
Rules and Procedures of the Inter-American Commercial Arbitration Commission, Section 7	361
Stockholm Chamber of Commerce (SCC) Rules 2010	
Art 5	371
Art 19(2)	34
Swiss Rules of International Arbitration	6, 55, 319
Art 4(2)	57
Art 14	319
Art 44(1)	328
Swiss Rules of International Arbitration 2004	160
Swiss Rules of International Arbitration 2012	
Art 6	160
Art 6(1)–(4)	160
Art 13(2)	313
Art 21	449
Art 25(2)	563
Unidroit Principles of International Commercial Contracts	118
Art 1(8)	122
Uniform Customs and Practices for Documentary Credit	118
WIPO Arbitration Rules 2001	
Art 38(c)	34
Art 40	377
Art 52	37
Art 63	758
WIPO Arbitration Rules 2002, Art 41(c)	414

INTERNATIONAL CONVENTIONS, TREATIES, AGREEMENTS etc

Agreement among the Government of Brunei Darussalam, the Republic of Indonesia, Malaysia, the Republic of the Philippines, the Republic of Singapore and the Kingdom of Thailand for the Promotion and Protection of Investments, Manila *see* Association of Southeast Asian Nations Regional Investment Agreement

Agreement between Finland and Estonia for the Promotion and Protection of Investments, Art 8 7

Algiers Accords 5, 137, 186, 342, 366–7, 444, 530, 552, 737, 873

Algiers Declarations 1981 .... 25, 142, 205–6, 223, 259, 367, 401–2, 407–8, 453, 543–5, 548–9, 767, 777–8, 786, 810, 833–5, 874

    Article IV(1) 837

    Article IV(3) 837

Association of Southeast Asian Nations Regional Investment Agreement 8

    Art X(2) 8

Canada-Ecuador Agreement for the Promotion and Reciprocal Protection of Investments (BIT)

    Art II 534–535

    Art XII(l) 534–5

    Art XIII(8) 524, 533–4

Claims Settlement Declaration (Iran and United States of America) 5, 87, 156, 192–3, 315, 354, 367, 407, 439, 446, 487, 724, 775, 830, 834–5

    Art I 416, 835

    Art II 835

    Art II(1) 41, 430, 437–40, 442, 444, 446, 453

    Art II(2) 5, 290, 299, 446

    Art III 5, 249, 267

    Art III(1) 5, 379

    Art III(1)–(2) 775

    Art III(2) 25, 193, 296, 315, 404

    Art III(3) 5, 808, 818, 848

    Art III(4) 404, 416, 480, 487, 505

    Art IV(1) 767, 834–5

    Art V 128–9, 131, 133, 137, 139–40, 142–3

    Art VI(1) 87, 109

    Art VI(2) 406, 686

    Art VI(3) 848, 873

    Art VI(4) 5

    Art VI(I) 342

    Art VII 469

    Art VII(1) 511

    Art VII(2) 481

Convention on the Limitation Period in the International Sale of Goods 1974 402

    Art 14 362

Czech-Netherlands BIT, Art 8 434

Dominican Republic–Central America–United States Free Trade Agreement
    (CAFTA-DR) 166, 365
    Art 10.16.2 365
    Art 10.16.5 22
    Art 10.16.6 365
    Art 10.19.1 166
    Art 10.19.3 166
    Art 10.21 757
    Art 10.25 58
EC Convention on the law applicable to contractual relations (Convention 80/934 EEC
    of 19 June 1980) 115
Energy Charter Treaty, Art 26(4)(b) 8
Escrow Agreement 778
European Convention on International Commercial Arbitration 1961 .... 123, 125
Art VII(1) 125
Art VII(2) 115
European Convention on the Protection of Human Rights and Fundamental Freedoms 171
    Art 6 213
Final Act of the Conference on Security and Cooperation in Europe (Helsinki, 1975) 88
GATT litigation 887
Geneva Convention 1927 .... 86, 740–1
    Art 1(2)(d) 740–1
Geneva Convention 1958, Art 4(2) 741
Hague Convention on the Law Applicable to International Sale of Goods 1985 115
    Art 15 115
Hague Convention on the Law Applicable to Matrimonial Property
    Regimes 1976, Art 4 139
Hague Convention for the Pacific Settlement of International Disputes 1899 834
ICSID Convention 834, 872
    Art 48(5) 755
    Art 51 .... 828, 831
ICSID Convention 1965 .... 89, 805
    Art 41(1) 451
    Art 56(1) 350
Inter-American Convention on Extraterritorial Validity of Foreign Judgments and
    Arbitral Awards, Art 2(g) 741
Inter-American Panama Convention 1975 86
NAFTA 8, 37, 39, 60, 65–6, 68, 89, 101, 105–6, 108,
                                                         129, 183, 220, 234, 432–3, 493, 498, 740, 757
    Chapter 11 .... 67–8, 80–1, 89, 92, 101, 103, 106–8,
                                                         112, 178, 182, 233, 418, 432, 457, 757
        Section B 20, 66, 129, 166, 477
    Chapter 19 433
    Art 115 61
    Art 1101 .... 417, 477
    Art 1101(1) 415, 417, 460, 477, 762
    Art 1102 .... 105, 879

Art 1105 .... 879, 884
Art 1106 .... 105, 879
Art 1110 .... 105, 879–80
Art 1120 462–3
Art 1120(1) 129–30
Art 1120(1)(c) 8
Art 1120(2) 20, 129–30
Art 1123 166
Art 1126 .... 63, 462–3
Art 1126(2) 462
Art 1126(8) 462
Art 1128 .... 183, 220, 233–4, 493, 497
Art 1130 101
Art 1130(b) 89, 105
Art 1131 129
Art 1135 888
Art 1137(4) 37
Netherlands-Czech Republic BIT 762
   Art 8(7) 762
New York Convention on the Recognition and Enforcement of Foreign Arbitral
   Awards 1958 .... 1, 3, 18, 25–6, 32, 42–4, 86–7, 89, 102, 105, 107, 115, 366,
                                  428, 454, 515, 524, 540, 626, 674, 710, 740–2, 762
   Art II 18, 366–7
   Art II(1) 19, 44
   Art II(2) 19
   Art III 741
   Art IV 366
   Art IV(1)(a) 381, 745, 757
   Art IV(2) 376
   Art V 84, 87, 117, 744
   Art V(1) 86
   Art V(1)(b) 44, 393, 674
   Art V(1)(d) 32, 43, 54, 56, 692
   Art V(1)(e) 87
   Art V(2)(b) 117, 125, 828
   Art VI(1)(e) 741
Russia-Mongolia BIT
   Art 2 535
   Art 3 535
   Art 3(1) 535
   Art 4 535
Treaty of Amity, Economic Relations, and Consular Rights between the United States of
   America and Iran 1955 .... 133, 143
   Art IV(2) 136
Treaty of the Windfall Profit Tax 535
   Art 2 535

    Art 3 535
    Art 3(1) 535
    Art 4 535
UK–Argentina BIT
    Art 3 890
    Art 9(5) 890
UN Convention on Contracts for the International Sale of Goods 118
    Art 9 122
UN Convention on the Law of the Sea 1994 7
    Art 188(c) 7
UN Convention on the Use of Electronic Communications in International
    Contracts 2005 397
    Art 10 402
United Nations Convention on Independent Guarantees and Stand-by
    Letters of Credit 396
US–Ecuador BIT 62, 540, 542, 737
    Art VI.3(6) 540–1
    Art VI.3(a)(iii) 540–1
US–Uruguay BIT, Art 37(3) 873
Vienna Convention on the Law of Treaties 1969 381
    Arts 31–32 21
Washington Convention on the Settlement of Investment Disputes between States and
    Nationals of Other States 1965 .... 7, 101, 114
    art 41(1) 450

NATIONAL LEGISLATION

Austria
Code of Civil Procedure, § 2 750
ZPO 2006, § 594 328

Belgium
Code of Civil Procedure, Art 1717 84
Judicial Code, Art 1694(4) 350
Law of 27 March 1985 84

Canada
Access to Information Act 39
Canada Evidence Act 1985 .... 61, 577
    § 39 577
Commercial Arbitration Act 1985 104
MMT Act 476

China
Arbitration Law
    Art 34(4) 328
    Art 38 328

Art 58(6) 328

Finland
Arbitration Act 1992, § 31(3) 120

France
Civil Code, Art 1290 445
Code of Civil Procedure, Arbitration
    Art 1482 744
    Art 1484 744
New Code of Civil Procedure, Art 1442 454

Germany
Civil Code, § 839 328
Code of Civil Procedure, Art 1027 694

Indonesia
Code of Civil Procedure 765
    Art 634 765–6
    Art 635 766
    Art 1245 680

Iran
Act concerning Development of Petrochemical Industries of 15 July 1965 135
    Art 1 135
    Art 3 135
Civil Code
    Art 193 132
    Arts 224–225 138
    Art 294 445
    Arts 301–306 133
    Art 336 133
    Art 963 139
    Art 966 139
    Art 968 136
    Art 1306 132
    Art 1310 132
Civil Procedure Code 548
    Art 3 138
Commercial Code, Art 141 445
Single Article Act concerning the Nationalization of the Oil Industry of Iran 1980 137

Italy
Code of Civil Procedure Art 813(2) 288

Lebanon
New Code of Civil Procedure, Art 769(3) 288

Netherlands
Code of Civil Procedure 42, 288, 366
    Art 623(1) 366

Art 628	288
Netherlands Arbitration Act 1986	804, 806–7
Art 48, § 2	750
Art 1036	806
Art 1041(1)	643
Art 1042(6)	643
Art 1057, § 3	750
Art 1059	807
Art 1061	804, 807
Art 1061(3)	805, 807
Netherlands Arbitration Law	97
New Dutch Arbitration Act, Art 1029	288

New Zealand

Arbitration law, Art 14(1)–(2)	38

Portugal

Law on Voluntary Arbitration, Art 9(3)	288

Spain

Arbitration Act, Art 21(1)	328

Sweden

Arbitration Act	866

Switzerland

Code of Obligations, Art 104(2)	143
Law on Private International Law, Art 178(2)–(3)	454

Turkey

Act on International Arbitration	413

United Kingdom

Arbitration Act 1996	78
Arbitration Act, §§ 67–69	744

United States of America

18 USC § 1782 28	62
Arbitration Act, 9 USC, §10	828, 831
Claims Settlement Act, USC § 1701 (1985)	848
Federal Arbitration Act	102, 828
§ 203	43–4
Freedom of Information Act	39
Intelligence Authorization Act for Fiscal Year 1996	591
§ 102	591
Iowa Code 1965, §§ 554.1101–09	132
Model BIT 2012, Art 24(3)(b)	8
Uniform Commercial Code	132, 142

List of Abbreviations

AAA	American Arbitration Association
AJIL	American Journal of International Law
ASEAN	Association of Southeast Asian Nations
BITs	Bilateral Investment Treaties
CERD	Committee on the Elimination of Racial Discrimination
FTAs	free trade agreements
IBA	International Bar Association
ICC	International Chamber of Commerce
ICDR	International Centre for Dispute Resolution
ICJ	International Court of Justice
ICLQ	International Comparative Law Quarterly
ICSID	International Centre for the Settlement of Investment Disputes
IIAs	international investment agreements
ILM	International Legal Materials
ILR	International Legal Reports
LCIA	London Court of International Arbitration
NAFTA	North American Free Trade Agreement
PCA	Permanent Court of Arbitration
UNCITRAL	United Nations Commission on International Trade Law

Chapter 1

Introduction

1. Introduction	1
2. The International Arbitral Process and the Work of UNCITRAL	2
3. The Development of the UNCITRAL Rules of Procedure	3
A. The Drafting of the 1976 Rules	3
B. The UNCITRAL Rules and the Iran–US Claims Tribunal	4
(1) The Origins and Structure of the Iran–US Claims Tribunal	4
(2) The Tribunal's Use of the UNCITRAL Arbitration Rules	5
C. The UNCITRAL Rules and the 1985 UNCITRAL Model Law	6
D. Adoption of the UNCITRAL Rules in other Public and Private Institutions	6
E. Investor–State Arbitration and the UNCITRAL Rules	7
F. The 2010 UNCITRAL Rules	8
G. The Work of UNCITRAL on Rules for Transparency in Investor–State Arbitration	9
4. How to Use this Commentary	10
A. Navigating the Text	10
B. The Interplay between the 1976 Rules and 2010 Rules in Application and Interpretation	10
C. The Extracts	10
D. Further Research	11
5. Conclusion	11

1. Introduction

The evolution of an effective and trustworthy private international arbitration system over the last half a century has had three major strands and the United Nations Commission on International Trade Law (UNCITRAL) is an international organization centrally involved with the evolution of all three. The first strand is embodied in the 1958 Convention on the Recognition and Enforcement of Foreign Arbitral Awards (The "New York Convention")[1] that obliges the courts of state parties (1) to respect the agreement of parties to arbitrate and (2) to recognize and enforce—within certain limits—the awards that result from such an arbitration. In essence, the Convention allows private parties to use the coercive power of national courts to implement private dispute settlement arrangements. The second strand seeks the harmonization of national arbitration statutes, that is, the national law within which the private arbitral arrangement operates and, in a sense, is regulated. This task was

---

[1] New York, June 10, 1958; 330 UN Treaty Series 3 (1959). For more discussion of the Convention, see Chapter 2, discussing Article 1.

substantially advanced by UNCITRAL's adoption of a Model Law on International Commercial Arbitration in 1985.[2] If the second strand aimed at harmonizing the national overlay of the arbitral process, the third strand sought to provide a model for the process of arbitration itself. Many sets of procedural rules defining that process exist, including, for example, the rules of the International Chamber of Commerce (ICC) or the American Arbitration Association (AAA). Despite the presence of such rules, however, there was a need for rules that the international community as a whole would recognize as meeting its needs. This third strand is addressed by the UNCITRAL Arbitration Rules, first recommended for use in 1976, and most recently revised in 2010. The new edition of our commentary addresses the revised UNCITRAL Arbitration Rules.

The construction of the international arbitration framework is one of the great legal accomplishments of the twentieth century. This effort necessarily involved both the public and private sectors. As mentioned, one key dimension to this system is the procedural rules that construct and order arbitrations around the world. Although less than four decades old, the UNCITRAL Rules have emerged globally as the dominant and most influential set of arbitration rules.

This book is concerned with advancing our understanding of the set of rules that were the product of this third strand of effort. This book seeks to enhance the utility of these Rules by analyzing both the drafting history of the Rules, and the main sources of practice interpreting and applying the Rules. This practice includes the Iran–US Claims Tribunal, investor–state tribunals and *ad hoc* tribunals constituted in accordance with the UNCITRAL Rules. Because the practice of the Iran–US Claims Tribunal is so extensive and, for the time being, continues to be paramount among these sources, two of the following sections briefly introduce the origins and structure of the Iran–US Claims Tribunal and the significance of its practice for the UNCITRAL Arbitration Rules. Since the Iran–US Claims Tribunal is near the end of its docket, if not its work, while the investor–state arbitrations and other *ad hoc* tribunals will continue indefinitely, the latter sources clearly will grow in influence with time.

This book explains the UNCITRAL Rules, both in their origins and as they have been used in practice. An effective system of international dispute resolution is indispensable to the growth of more complex transnational arrangements, and—for the foreseeable future—that system of resolution is primarily international arbitration. This book seeks to make that system more accessible, more reliable and ultimately, more effective.

2. The International Arbitral Process and the Work of UNCITRAL

UNCITRAL was created in 1966 by the UN General Assembly, in part as a component of the effort at that time to change the direction of the international economic order, to open it up to more actors. Its mandate includes "(c) Preparing or promoting the adoption of new international conventions, model laws and uniform laws."[3] In design, the membership of UNCITRAL does not mirror the general membership of the UN. Its

---

[2] See generally H Holtzmann and J Neuhaus, *A Guide to the UNCITRAL Model Law on International Commercial Arbitration: Legislative History and Commentary* (1989). The Model Law was revised in 2006.

[3] UNCITRAL was created by the General Assembly on December 17, 1966 in Resolution 2205 (XXI). Arbitration was only one portion of the substantive area it was thought UNCITRAL would address.

authorized membership level has grown since its creation. Membership currently is 60 States (it was only 36 States at the time of the drafting of the 1976 UNCITRAL Arbitration Rules).

At the outset, UNCITRAL worked as a whole, today it conducts its work through "working groups," of which there are six. Their earlier work on arbitration was as a whole, but since 2000, Working Group II has been the specific working group dedicated to arbitration. This Working Group has worked in two sessions per year. The UNCITRAL documents referred to in this commentary reflect documents prepared in anticipation of such sessions, records of the sessions as well as reports on each session.

Since its inception, UNCITRAL has worked on seven major international arbitration initiatives:

1976 UNCITRAL Arbitration Rules
1980 UNCITRAL Conciliation Rules
1985 UNCITRAL Model Law on International Commercial Arbitration
1996 UNCITRAL Notes on Organizing Arbitral Proceedings
2002 UNCITRAL Model Law on International Commercial Conciliation
2006 Amendments to 1985 Model Law on International Commercial Arbitration
2010 UNCITRAL Arbitration Rules (Revision of the 1976 UNCITRAL Arbitration Rules)

In addition, the 1958 New York Convention (which was concluded under the auspices of the United Nations but predated the creation of UNCITRAL) is seen as falling within the ambit of UNCITRAL and it can be expected that any revisiting of the Convention will occur in the UNCITRAL framework.

This responsibility for and work in all aspects of the international arbitration framework yields an insight that greatly influences all UNCITRAL efforts, including the 2010 revision of the UNCITRAL Arbitration Rules. In particular, as UNCITRAL works on any project, it necessarily has a constant concern for the impact changes in one document may have for all of the other UNCITRAL instruments. A private institution that promulgates only procedural rules does not, when revising those rules, have the same level of concern for the interpretive effect their revision may have on national statutes or treaties that use the same terms. The delegates who worked on the 2010 revision of the UNCITRAL Arbitration Rules are informed by, educated by, and indeed limited by, the work done earlier on the Model Law. As will be seen throughout this volume, both the New York Convention and the Model Law greatly influence the structure and wording of changes in the Rules. A particular focus is thus on the drafting of revisions that are consistent with the Model Law and the New York Convention, and that certainly do not imply, for example, that the common understandings of the Model Law are incorrect.

3. The Development of the UNCITRAL Rules of Procedure

A. The Drafting of the 1976 Rules

After several years' work, on 28 April 1976, UNCITRAL adopted a set of procedural rules, primarily for international commercial arbitration—the UNCITRAL Arbitration Rules.[4]

---

[4] Reprinted in (1977) II Ybk Commercial Arb ii 161; (1976) 15 ILM 702.

On December 15 of that same year, the UN General Assembly adopted a resolution,[5] stating, *inter alia*, "that the establishment of rules for *ad hoc* arbitration that are acceptable in countries with different legal, social and economic systems would significantly contribute to the development of harmonious international economic relations." In the operative part of the Resolution, the General Assembly:

1. *Recommends* the use of the Arbitration Rules of the United Nations Commission on International Trade Law in the settlement of disputes arising in the context of international commercial relations, particularly by reference to the UNCITRAL Arbitration Rules in commercial contracts;
2. *Requests* the Secretary General to arrange for the widest possible distribution of the Arbitration Rules.[6]

The UNCITRAL Rules were recommended for use in a world where a number of private arbitration institutions, such as the ICC, offered their own rules and administered arbitration proceedings in specific cities around the world. The drafting of the UNCITRAL Rules was undertaken in part as an alternative to private institutions that were seen by some as providing their service at too great a cost or which were possibly biased in subtle ways toward the western developed world. It is partly for this reason that the UNCITRAL Rules are designed to operate without the service (or cost) of a supervising institution (ie, "non administered" arbitration). It must be said that in 1976, some individuals involved in the original negotiation indicated to the authors that they wondered whether the Rules would be used to any significant extent.

B. The UNCITRAL Rules and the Iran–US Claims Tribunal

(1) *The Origins and Structure of the Iran–US Claims Tribunal*

The 1979 Islamic Revolution in Iran led to a disruption of extensive economic relations, as well as to a political crisis, between Iran and the United States of America. On January 19, 1981, the conclusion of several agreements led to the release of Americans held hostage since November 1979 and the release of frozen Iranian assets. To address many outstanding claims, it was also agreed that US $1 billion of the released Iranian assets would be held in a Security Account for possible satisfaction of the claims of Americans. The validity of those claims in turn was to be adjudicated by an international arbitral tribunal: the Iran–US Claims Tribunal (the Tribunal).[7]

---

[5] Reprinted in (1977) II Ybk Commercial Arb xi (Introduction by P Sanders).

[6] Regarding UNCITRAL and its workings, see the references included in the Select Bibliography at the end of this commentary.

[7] The Iran–US Claims Tribunal and its practice have triggered an abundance of legal writing. References to various books and articles are made throughout the present work and are incorporated in the Select Bibliography. A few important contributions of a general nature may be mentioned here: D Caron and J Crook (eds), *The Iran–United States Claims Tribunal and the Process of International Claims Resolution* (2000); M Mohebi, *The International Law Character of the Iran–United States Claims Tribunal* (1999); C Brower and J Brueschke, *The Iran–United States Claims Tribunal* (1998); R Lillich and D Magraw (eds), *The Iran–United States Claims Tribunal: Its Contribution to the Law of State Responsibility* (1998); G Aldrich, *The Jurisprudence of the Iran–United States Claims Tribunal* (1996); C Brower, "The Iran–United States Claims Tribunal," 224 *Recueil des Cours* (1990–V) 123; D Caron, "The Nature of the Iran–United States Claims Tribunal and the Evolving Structure of International Dispute Resolution," (1990) 84 AJIL 104; R Khan, *The Iran–United States Claims Tribunal: Controversies, Cases and Contribution* (1990); A Mouri, *The International Law of Expropriation as Reflected in the Work of the Iran–U.S. Claims Tribunal* (1994); J Westberg, *International Transactions and Claims involving Government Parties: Case Law of the Iran–United States Claims Tribunal* (1991).

The settlement agreements consist of seven interrelated documents. One of them, the Claims Settlement Declaration (the Declaration),[8] created the Tribunal and set forth the procedural and substantive law framework for the settlement of the claims through arbitration. The Declaration contains eight articles. According to Article III(1), "the Tribunal shall consist of nine members or such larger multiple of three as Iran and the United States may agree are necessary to conduct its business expeditiously." Given the fact that no agreement on a larger multiple of three was reached, three of the nine members have been appointed by Iran, three by the United States, and three others have been appointed by the six party-appointed arbitrators (or, failing their agreement, by a designated third party called the Appointing Authority).[9] Most of the work of the Tribunal has been conducted in three Chambers consisting of an Iranian, an American and a third country presiding arbitrator. One of the third country arbitrators also serves as President of the Full Tribunal.

The bulk of the Tribunal's caseload consists of the claims by US nationals against Iran, broadly defined elsewhere in the Declaration. Between October 20, 1981 and January 19, 1982, 965 claims by nationals seeking over US $250,000 were filed and 2,795 claims by nationals seeking less than US $250,000 were filed. As of 2002, all claims by nationals had been resolved. In addition to claims by nationals, the Tribunal has jurisdiction over "official claims of the United States and Iran against each other arising out of contractual arrangements between them for the purchase and sale of goods and services,"[10] as well as over certain interpretative disputes concerning the Algiers Accords (the Accords).[11] As of mid-2012, a small number of official claims and interpretative disputes of considerable significance remain.

(2) *The Tribunal's Use of the UNCITRAL Arbitration Rules*

In seeking to design an international arbitral tribunal quickly, the negotiators of the Accords found that they, fortunately, had a set of procedural rules prepared by distinguished experts representing various legal systems of the world, namely the UNCITRAL Arbitration Rules. Instead of lengthy negotiations on the subject, the drafters of the Declaration simply make reference to the UNCITRAL Arbitration Rules. Article III of that Declaration reads:

> Members of the Tribunal shall be appointed and the Tribunal shall conduct its business in accordance with the arbitration rules of the United Nations Commission on International Trade Law (UNCITRAL) except to the extent modified by the Parties or by the Tribunal to ensure that this Agreement can be carried out. The UNCITRAL rules for appointing members of three-member tribunals shall apply *mutatis mutandis* to the appointment of the Tribunal.

The Tribunal Rules, adopted provisionally on March 10, 1982 and finally on May 3, 1983, as the procedural rules of the Iran–US Claims Tribunal were based on the UNCITRAL Rules, in accordance with the above-quoted provision of the Declaration. If there had been concern in 1976 that the UNCITRAL Rules might not be used to any significant extent, that situation changed dramatically as the Tribunal began its work. The

---

[8] Declaration of the Government of the Democratic and Popular Republic of Algeria, Concerning the Settlement of Claims by the Government of the United States of America and the Government of the Islamic Republic of Iran, reprinted in (1981–82) 1 Iran–US CTR 9; (1981) 20 ILM 230.

[9] The appointment of the arbitrators is discussed in Chapter 4.

[10] Article II(2) of the Declaration.

[11] See Articles III(3) and VI(4) of the Declaration, n 8. R Bettauer, "The Task Remaining: The Government Cases," in D Caron and J Crook (eds), *The Iran–United States Claims Tribunal and The Process of International Claims Resolution* (2000) 355.

Tribunal's practice in applying its rules currently represents the most extensive body of practice concerning the UNCITRAL Rules because the Tribunal's docket was large and, most importantly, because the practice of the Tribunal is public.

Even though the UNCITRAL Rules have come to be used widely in many other institutions and settings, the experience of the Tribunal with its wide range of cases remains central to understanding the UNCITRAL Rules.[12] The Tribunal has, more than any other body, grappled with the application of these Rules. Quickly gaining in significance is, however, the practice of investment arbitration under both Chapter Eleven of the NAFTA and under various Bilateral Investment Treaties (BITs).

C. The UNCITRAL Rules and the 1985 UNCITRAL Model Law

Even as the Tribunal began its work in earnest, UNCITRAL undertook the drafting of a model national statute to govern international commercial arbitration: the 1985 UNCITRAL Model Law. A national arbitration statute is primarily concerned with the relationship of the courts to international arbitrations taking place in that state, to the possibility of an award being annulled by those same courts, and to detailing a set of default rules of arbitral procedure to be employed assuming that the parties do not agree otherwise. These default rules in the Model law followed the 1976 Rules closely.

Two observations are important at this point. First, the Iran–US Claims Tribunal was already providing significant lessons concerning the 1976 Rules and some of these lessons were addressed in the Model Law through changes to those rules. Second, as the 1985 UNCITRAL Model law was used as at least the basic framework for arbitration statutes around the world (over 60 states by the middle of 2012), the use of the 1976 Rules was becoming more widespread and gaining influence.

D. Adoption of the UNCITRAL Rules in other Public and Private Institutions

Although the UNCITRAL Rules were originally intended to provide a procedural framework for non-administered commercial arbitration, they may be adapted quite easily to serve as the rules for arbitrations conducted under the auspices of arbitral centers. For example, the Rules of the Inter-American Commercial Arbitration Commission, the Cairo International Commercial Arbitration Centre, the Kuala Lumpur Regional Centre for Arbitration, and the Hong Kong International Arbitration Centre are all based on the UNCITRAL Rules. Indeed, the Swiss Rules of International Arbitration, in an earlier version, explicitly stated that these "Rules are based on the UNCITRAL Arbitration Rules" with "[c]hanges and additions reflecting modern practice."[13] This is also the case with at least one global arbitration institution. The International Centre for Dispute Resolution (ICDR), a major global supervising institution, based its rules of procedure on the UNCITRAL Rules.[14] In addition, several well known arbitral institutions with their own

---

[12] For other commentary on the UNCITRAL Rules as practiced by the Iran–US Claims Tribunal, reference can be made to: S Baker and M Davis, *The UNCITRAL Arbitration Rules in Practice: The Experience of the Iran–United States Claims Tribunal* (1992); J van Hof, *Commentary on the UNCITRAL Arbitration Rules: The Application by the Iran–U.S. Claims Tribunal* (1991).

[13] Swiss Rules of International Arbitration (2004) at 7.

[14] The leading commentary on the ICDR Rules states that "[t]he 1996 Revised ICDR Rules continued to reflect the model of the UNCITRAL Rules..." M Gusy, J Hosking, and F Schwarz, *A Guide to the ICDR International Arbitration Rules* (2011) 16.

procedural rules nonetheless will provide services as appointing authority as well as administrative services for arbitrations conducted under the UNCITRAL Rules.[15]

The UNCITRAL Rules likewise have been adopted as the procedural rules in inter-state cases with public law elements. For example, the UNCITRAL Rules play a role in the dispute settlement under the 1994 UN Convention on the Law of the Sea.[16] And in 1992 the Permanent Court of Arbitration adopted Optional Rules for Arbitrating Disputes Between two States, which are based on the UNCITRAL Rules.[17] The Introduction to those Rules states:

Experience since 1981 suggests that the UNCITRAL Arbitration Rules provide fair and effective procedures for peaceful resolution of disputes between States concerning the interpretation, application and performance of treaties and other agreements, although they were originally designed for commercial arbitration.[18]

Undoubtedly, it was the experience of the Iran–US Claims Tribunal with respect to all its categories of claims that was in the minds of the drafters of this passage.

E. Investor–State Arbitration and the UNCITRAL Rules

The UNCITRAL Rules have also been used extensively in the investment arbitration context, as evidenced by many references to the UNCITRAL Rules in BITs and investment chapters in free trade agreements (FTAs). In such treaties, arbitration under the UNCITRAL Rules is envisaged as the dispute settlement mechanism between a host state and the investor more often than any other procedure except for arbitration under the auspices of the International Centre for the Settlement of Investment Disputes (ICSID).[19]

Disputes resolved under international investment treaties are another important and growing source of awards and decisions rendered under the UNCITRAL Rules. Since the 1990s there has been a proliferation of international investment agreements (IIAs) at the bilateral, regional, and multilateral level.[20] UNCTAD reports that, by the end of 2011 the

---

[15] Examples include the American Arbitration Association (AAA), the London Court of International Arbitration (LCIA), and the Stockholm Chamber of Commerce (SCC). See Rules of ICC as Appointing Authority in UNCITRAL or Other *Ad Hoc* Arbitration Proceedings, in force as from January 1, 2004, reprinted at (Fall 2003) 14 ICC Intl Court of Arbitration Bulletin 8.

[16] See, eg, Article 188(c) of the 1994 UN Convention on the Law of the Sea.

[17] Permanent Court of Arbitration: Optional Rules for Arbitrating Disputes between Two States, effective October 20, 1992, reprinted in (1993) 32 ILM 572.

[18] Permanent Court of Arbitration, Optional Rules 575.

[19] See P Peters, "Dispute Settlement Arrangements in Investment Treaties," (1991) 22 Netherlands Ybk Intl L 90, 125: "Of the BITs that indicate which arbitration system is to be used, a large majority express a preference for the ICSID Rules and some others give ICSID as an option. UNCITRAL comes second and ICC arbitration as a poor third." For example, Article 8 of the Agreement between Finland and Estonia for the Promotion and Protection of Investments (Finnish Treaty Series 104 (1992)) provides for the submission of such disputes either to:

(a) the International Centre for Settlement of Investment Disputes . . . having regard to the applicable provisions of the Convention on the Settlement of Investment Disputes between States and Nationals of other States . . . in the event both Contracting Parties shall have become a party to the Convention; or
(b) an international ad hoc arbitral tribunal established under the Arbitration Rules of the United Nations Commission on International Trade Law as then in force. The Parties to the dispute may agree in writing to modify these Rules.

[20] See generally J Salacuse and N Sullivan, "Do BITs Really Work?: An Evaluation of Bilateral Investment Treaties and Their Grand Bargain," (2005) 46 Harvard Intl L J 1.

overall IIA universe consisted of 3,164 agreements, which include 2,833 BITs and 331 "other IIAs," including, principally, FTAs with investment provisions, economic partnership agreements and regional agreements (not including double taxation treaties).[21] Almost all of these agreements contain dispute settlement provisions granting foreign investors recourse to various mechanisms of international arbitration, often including arbitration under the UNCITRAL Arbitration Rules. The NAFTA, the Energy Charter and the Association of Southeast Asian Nations (ASEAN) Regional Investment Agreement are examples of regional and multilateral investment agreements that contain such provisions.[22] Similar provisions are also contained in many BITs, including those influenced by the United States Model BIT program.[23]

The awards and decisions of international tribunals in this area have already enhanced our understanding of the interpretation and application of the UNCITRAL Arbitration Rules, and will likely grow in influence with time.

F. The 2010 UNCITRAL Rules

The prompt toward revision of the 1976 UNCITRAL Rules began with an article published in 2004 by the primary drafter of the 1976 Rules, Pieter Sanders.[24] That impetus was followed by a study by Jan Paulsson and Georgios Petrochilos and submitted to UNCITRAL for consideration.[25] Working Group II of UNCITRAL began its work on the Revision at its 45th Session in the Fall of 2006. This commentary is, in significant part, a summary and analysis of the drafting effort that followed.

The important point at the outset is to stress the guiding principles adopted by consensus by the drafters at the start of their work. In particular, Working Group II in undertaking the drafting of the 2010 Rules:

> viewed the UNCITRAL Arbitration Rules as one of the most successful instruments of UNCITRAL and therefore cautioned against any unnecessary amendments or statements being included in the *travaux préparatoires* that would call into question the legitimacy of prior applications of the Rules in specific cases. It was considered that the focus of the revision should be on updating the Rules to meet changes that had taken place over the last thirty years in arbitral practice, not on simply making them more complex.[26]

This statement of principles is important because, as will be seen, these principles would come to be decisive regarding a number of controversial points in the negotiations.

---

[21] United Nations Conference on Trade and Development (UNCTAD), World Investment Report, 2012.

[22] Article 1120(1)(c), NAFTA; Article 26(4)(b), The Energy Charter Treaty; Article X(2), Agreement among the Government of Brunei Darussalam, the Republic of Indonesia, Malaysia, the Republic of the Philippines, the Republic of Singapore and the Kingdom of Thailand for the Promotion and Protection of Investments, Manila (ASEAN Investment Agreement).

[23] See Article 24(3)(b), 2012 Model BIT, available at <http://www.ustr.gov/sites/default/files/BIT%20text%20for%20ACIEP%20Meeting.pdf.> On the dispute resolution provisions of earlier Model BITs, see K Vandevelde, *United States Investment Treaties: Policy and Practice* (1992) 163. On the dispute resolution provision in bilateral investment treaties generally, see R Dolzer and M Stevens, *Bilateral Investment Treaties* (1995) 147.

[24] P Sanders, "Has the Moment Come to Revise the UNCITRAL Rules of Arbitration?" (2004) 20 Arb Intl 243.

[25] J Paulsson and G Petrochilos, *Revision of the UNCITRAL Arbitration Rules, A Report* (2006).

[26] *Report of the Working Group on Arbitration and Conciliation on the Work of its Forty-Fifth Session* (Vienna, September 11–15, 2006), UNCITRAL, 40th Session, UN Doc A/CN.9/614, at 5, para 16 (2006).

G. The Work of UNCITRAL on Rules for Transparency in Investor–State Arbitration

During discussions to revise the UNCITRAL Arbitration Rules, it was generally agreed that, because the Rules were frequently used in investor–state arbitration, it would be desirable to address the subject of transparency in that context. Many delegations recognized that investor–state arbitration would benefit from transparency, given it often involved considerations of public policy and the potential for large monetary awards rendered against public treasuries. Many also believed that transparency in investor–state arbitration would enhance public understanding of the process and thus boost its overall legitimacy. The Working Group, and later the Commission, therefore concluded that, in line with ICSID's revisions to its arbitration rules in 2006, UNCITRAL should take up the work of developing rules of transparency for investor–state arbitration.[27]

Despite support for transparency rules, the Working Group waited to begin work in this area until completion of its revision of the UNCITRAL Rules. The aim was to avoid delaying the important work on the revised Rules that was already well advanced and which had already consumed a significant amount of time. At the time of this writing, the Working Group was nearing completion of its work on developing transparency rules for investor–state arbitration, with the aim of having new rules adopted in 2013.

Those who practice in the field of investor–state arbitration therefore may wish to monitor the Working Group's efforts in this area closely. In their present form, the draft transparency rules contain provisions on scope of application, publication of information at the commencement of the arbitral proceedings, publication of documents, submission by a third person, submission by a non-disputing state party to the investment treaty, hearings, exceptions to transparency, and the repository of published information.[28] Though consensus has been forming around the text of many of these draft provisions, one threshold issue, the scope of application of the transparency rules, continues to divide the Working Group. As explained in Chapter 2, some delegations want the transparency rules to be capable of the broadest application, in accordance with international law rules of treaty interpretation, to existing and future investment treaties that refer to the UNCITRAL Arbitration Rules. Other delegations prefer a more limited application of the transparency rules under such treaties, including a rule of application with respect to future treaties, but a requirement of express consent to application with respect to existing treaties.[29] The manner in which the Working Group resolves the debate over scope of application, as well as the final form of the substantive rules on transparency, will have an important impact on whether and how the transparency rules will apply in future investor–state arbitrations under the UNCITRAL Arbitration Rules.

---

[27] For discussion, see *Report of the Working Group on Arbitration and Conciliation on the Work of its Forty-Eighth Session* (New York, February 4–8, 2008), UNCITRAL, 41st Session, UN Doc A/CN.9/646, at 13–16, paras 54–69 (2008); *Report of the United Nations Commission on International Trade Law* (New York, June 16-July 3, 2008), 41st Session, UN Doc A/63/17, at 60, para 314.

[28] See *Settlement of Commercial Disputes: Preparation of a Legal Standard on Transparency in Treaty-Based Investor-State Arbitration, Note by the Secretariat*, UNCITRAL, UN Doc A/CN.9/WG.II/WP.169 (2011).

[29] *Report of the Working Group on Arbitration and Conciliation on the Work of its Fifty-Sixth Session* (New York, February 6–10, 2012), UNCITRAL, 45th Session, UN Doc A/CN.9/741, at 4–13, paras 13–58 (2012).

4. How to Use this Commentary

A. Navigating the Text

In preparing this commentary, we are well aware that in all likelihood it will be consulted in the context of a particular situation or rule. That awareness led us to several choices in the structuring of the commentary. First, an attempt is made to make each chapter complete unto itself. For example, references to the literature are introduced anew in each chapter. Second, the commentary is organized basically by the situation presented. Although that organization tracks for the most part the numerical order of the rules, that ordering is not exactly the same. We chose this ordering because someone who wishes to better understand a particular rule, is likely to have been led to that question because of the particular situation they find themselves in and that situation in fact may be addressed by several rules. Having said this, we have also attempted to indicate particular rules in chapter headings as well.

The chapters all have a similar structure, each including three major parts: (1) the text of the relevant 2010 rule is stated, (2) a commentary on that rule drawing on UNCITRAL's negotiating history and international arbitral practice is provided along with a comparison with the corresponding predecessor 1976 rule, and (3) relevant extracts from the practice of arbitral tribunals, including awards and orders are reprinted. In those instances where a chapter addresses more than one rule, this basic structure is repeated for each rule.

B. The Interplay between the 1976 Rules and 2010 Rules in Application and Interpretation

This commentary addresses both the 2010 Rules and the 1976 Rules for three reasons. First, in drafting the 2010 Rules the Working Group primarily discussed the rationales for proposed changes, but did not always reiterate or discuss the rationales for the original language. In this sense, the bulk of relevant negotiating history is still to be found in the discussions leading up to adoption of the 1976 Rules. Second, although the 2010 Rules are quickly being applied in practice, there is still little publicly available practice under them. Thus, the extracts in this commentary are necessarily drawn from arbitrations that utilized the 1976 Rules, much of which, as mentioned, remains relevant in relation to many aspects of the 2010 Rules. However, while these extracts very often are relevant to understanding the meaning of both the 1976 Rules and the 2010 Rules, obviously due care must be used in doing so. Third, as discussed in Chapter 2, it is entirely possible that the 1976 Rules—particularly in the context of investor–state arbitration—will continue to apply. For this reason, although the commentary deals primarily with the text of the 2010 Rules, incorporating relevant aspects of the 1976 Rules, the last subsection of the commentary in each chapter compares each 2010 rule to its 1976 predecessor.

C. The Extracts

Although extensive commentaries are provided, we nonetheless felt it important to provide the extracts upon which those commentaries are based, for two reasons. First, in our experience in practice, the authors of commentaries rarely address specific situations, leaving the practitioner or arbitral tribunal to triangulate the meaning to be given to a rule from the existing commentary and the most relevant arbitral decisions from practice. Second, although awards are increasingly becoming available in online resources, some awards and most procedural orders remain difficult to obtain.

In ordering the extracts, we first provide those from investor–state arbitration or *ad hoc* arbitration, followed by those from the Iran–US Claims Tribunal. In both cases, they are ordered chronologically (from oldest to newest) rather than by case name. The citation to these extracts attempts to convey both the essential identifying information of the original award, decision or order (including the arbitral venue, the applicable version of the UNCITRAL Rules, and the instrument under which the dispute arose) and, in some cases, where it may be found in a printed source. Online sources are not typically provided inasmuch as there are usually multiple online locations, and that the URLs for such locations often change.

D. Further Research

For further research, a Select Bibliography is provided at the end of this commentary.

5. Conclusion

Since the 1980s, the UNCITRAL Rules have come to be very widely used and, more importantly, the most influential global procedural framework for international dispute settlement. The various references to UNCITRAL Rules underline their increased importance—an importance that is unique in that such references are not limited to commercial arbitration, but also extend to inter-state arbitration and arbitration between states and private investors.

PART I

FUNDAMENTAL PRINCIPLES AND THE LEGAL FRAMEWORK WITHIN WHICH THE ARBITRAL TRIBUNAL OPERATES

Introduction

It has been rightly said that "the practice of resolving disputes by international arbitration only works effectively because it is held in place by a complex system of national laws and international treaties."[1] While the importance of arbitral autonomy is recognized, so is the principle that certain fundamental guarantees of fairness must apply to the exercise of that autonomy. For the enforcement and supervision of these guarantees, some outside control is needed. Normally this can only be provided by domestic courts. As the basic legal framework for these courts is national law, the relationship between arbitral procedure and domestic law—especially the law regarding arbitration—in the country where the arbitration takes place is of utmost importance. In addition to the limitations imposed by domestic arbitration law, the arbitrators may be bound to apply a certain law to the substance of the dispute. Often they also have to take into account legal considerations likely to govern the enforcement of the award. This may bring into play the law of the likely place of enforcement, since an award rendered in defiance of mandatory norms of that place may stand in the way of successful recognition and enforcement.

Thus, arbitration is in many ways circumscribed by laws pertaining to the proceedings. Articles 1 and 17 of the 2010 UNCITRAL Rules contain certain fundamental principles relevant in this regard. Their application is largely dependent on the jurisdiction chosen as the place of arbitration in accordance with Article 18. Hence Articles 1, 17 and 18 have been grouped together in the following Chapter 2. Article 35 (on applicable substantive law) is dealt with in Chapter 3.

---

[1] N Blackaby and C Partasides with A Redfern and M Hunter, *Redfern and Hunter on International Commercial Arbitration* (5th edn 2009) 3.

Chapter 2

Scope of Application, General Provisions, and Place of Arbitration

1. Introduction	16
2. Scope of Application—Article 1	16
A. Text of the 2010 UNCITRAL Rule	16
B. Commentary	17
(1) General comments	17
(2) Scope of application—Article 1(1)	18
(3) No writing requirement for agreement to arbitration—Article 1(1)	18
(4) Party autonomy and modification of the Rules—Article 1(1)	19
(5) Presumptive scope of application—Article 1(2) and (3)	20
(6) Future transparency rules for investor–state arbitration	23
(7) Model arbitration clause	24
(8) Comparison to the 1976 UNCITRAL Rules	24
C. Extracts from the Practice of Investment and other Tribunals	26
(1) Article 1(1) (1976 Rules)—scope and modification	26
(2) Article 1(2) (1976 Rules)—non-derogation from mandatory law	28
3. General Provisions—Article 17	29
A. Text of the 2010 UNCITRAL Rule	29
B. Commentary	30
(1) Basic principles—Article 17(1)	30
(a) Arbitral autonomy and its limits	30
(b) Confidentiality in UNCITRAL arbitration	36
(c) Non-disputing party (*amicus*) participation in UNCITRAL arbitration	39
(d) The nature of the proceedings before the Iran–US Claims Tribunal	41
(e) Concluding comments	45
(2) Provisional timetable and modification of time periods—Article 17(2)	46
(a) Provisional timetable	46
(b) Modifications of time periods	47
(c) Issues of general application	49
(3) Right to a hearing—Article 17(3)	49
(a) Scope of hearings	49
(b) Timing of hearing requests	51
(c) Preliminary meetings	52
(4) Communication of documents—Article 17(4)	53
(5) Joinder of third persons—Article 17(5)	54
(6) Consolidation of claims	57
(7) Comparison to the 1976 UNCITRAL Rules	58
C. Extracts from the Practice of Investment and other Tribunals	59
(1) Article 15(1) (1976 Rules)—general	59
(2) Article 15(1) (1976 Rules)—*amicus* submissions	65
D. Extracts from the Practice of the Iran–US Claims Tribunal	69

		(1) General and Tribunal Rules (1983), Article 15(1)	69
		(2) Tribunal Rules (1983), Article 15(2)	74
4.	Place of Arbitration—Article 18		77
	A.	Text of the 2010 UNCITRAL Rule	77
	B.	Commentary	78
		(1) Meaning of "place of arbitration"	78
		(2) Selection of the place of arbitration—Article 18(1)	80
		(a) Considerations to be taken into account	80
		(1) Nature and suitability of the local law	81
		(2) Enforceability of the award	85
		(3) Neutrality	87
		(4) Practical considerations	89
		(b) Decision on place of arbitration not procedural; consultation with the parties	91
		(3) Where the award is "deemed to have been made" —Article 18(1)	92
		(4) The location of tribunal deliberations and meetings "for any other purpose, including hearings"—Article 18(2)	93
		(5) Comparison to the 1976 UNCITRAL Rules	95
	C.	Extracts from the Practice of Investment Tribunals	96
	D.	Extracts from the Practice of the Iran–US Claims Tribunal	109

1. Introduction

This chapter addresses those rules that generally frame arbitration under the UNCITRAL Rules. The 2010 UNCITRAL Rules address in Article 1(1) the general scope of application of the Rules, in Article 1(2) the applicable version of the Rules (2010 or 1976), and in Article 1(3) the relationship between the proceedings and the mandatory norms of law of the place of arbitration. The focus of Article 1(3) is closely related to the principle, expressed in Article 17(1), that "the arbitral tribunal may conduct the arbitration in such manner as it considers appropriate,..." In addition, Articles 17(2) and 17(3) concern the right to a hearing and the communication of documents, respectively. The actual role in concrete arbitrations of some of the basic principles expressed in Articles 1 and 17 is largely dependent on the place of arbitration, the subject matter of Article 18.

2. Scope of Application—Article 1

A. Text of the 2010 UNCITRAL Rule[1]

Article 1 of the 2010 UNCITRAL Rules provides:

1. Where parties have agreed that disputes between them in respect of a defined legal relationship, whether contractual or not, shall be referred to arbitration under the UNCITRAL Arbitration Rules, then such disputes shall be settled in accordance with these Rules subject to such modification as the parties may agree.

---

[1] Corresponding Article 1 of the 1976 UNCITRAL Rules provides:

1. Where the parties to a contract have agreed in writing* that disputes in relation to that contract shall be referred to arbitration under the UNCITRAL Arbitration Rules, then such disputes shall be settled in accordance with these Rules subject to such modification as the parties may agree in writing.
2. These Rules shall govern the arbitration except that where any of these Rules is in conflict with a provision of the law applicable to the arbitration from which the parties cannot derogate, that provision shall prevail.

2. The parties to an arbitration agreement concluded after August 15, 2010 shall be presumed to have referred to the Rules in effect on the date of commencement of the arbitration, unless the parties have agreed to apply a particular version of the Rules. That presumption does not apply where the arbitration agreement has been concluded by accepting after August 15, 2010 an offer made before that date.
3. These Rules shall govern the arbitration except that where any of these Rules is in conflict with a provision of the law applicable to the arbitration from which the parties cannot derogate, that provision shall prevail.

MODEL ARBITRATION CLAUSE FOR CONTRACTS (Located in the Annex to the Rules)
Any dispute, controversy or claim arising out of or relating to this contract, or the breach, termination or invalidity thereof, shall be settled by arbitration in accordance with the UNCITRAL Arbitration Rules.

Note—Parties should consider adding:

(a) The appointing authority shall be … (name of institution or person);
(b) The number of arbitrators shall be … (one or three);
(c) The place of arbitration shall be … (town and country);
(d) The language(s) to be used in the arbitral proceedings shall be …

B. Commentary

(1) General comments

Arbitration is a form of dispute settlement based on agreement between parties who may wish for various reasons to avoid proceedings before domestic courts.[2] The parties may select an arbitral institution to oversee the resolution of their dispute, in which case the procedural rules of that institution are applied. They may, however, also wish to arrange their arbitration on an *ad hoc* basis outside any institution. In doing so, they are, in principle, free to create their own rules of procedure. As agreeing on such rules for a particular case may pose many difficulties, it is useful to have a ready-made set of procedural rules to which the parties may resort if they so agree. The UNCITRAL Rules are such a set of procedural rules.[3] The 1976 UNCITRAL Rules have proven to be so useful that many arbitration institutions have based their own rules of procedure on them,[4] and the same is almost certainly to be the case for the 2010 version of the Rules as they gain widespread acceptance.

Note (*) to Article 1(1) contains the following Model Arbitration Clause:
  Any dispute, controversy or claim arising out of or relating to this contract, or the breach, termination or invalidity thereof, shall be settled by arbitration in accordance with the UNCITRAL Arbitration Rules as at present in force.
Note—Parties may wish to consider adding:
(a) The appointing authority shall be (name of institution or person)
(b) The number of arbitrators shall be (one or three)
(c) The place of arbitration shall be (town or country)
(d) The language(s) to be used in the arbitral proceedings shall be …

[2] For a discussion of the advantages and disadvantages of arbitration as compared to other forms of dispute settlement, see N Blackaby and C Partasides with A Redfern and M Hunter, *Redfern and Hunter on International Arbitration* (5th edn 2009) 31 et seq.

[3] On the use of the UNCITRAL Rules, see Chapter 1.

[4] "[T]he Rules are used in international commercial arbitrations administered by regional and international arbitral institutions whose rules are modelled on the Rules (such as the Australian Centre for International

(2) Scope of application—Article 1(1)

According to Article 1(1), the 2010 UNCITRAL Rules apply to disputes between the parties "in respect of a defined legal relationship, whether contractual or not." This broad language contrasts with the narrower scope of the 1976 UNCITRAL Rules, which cover only disputes "in relation to [a] contract."[5] Indeed, the phrase "defined legal relationship" in the 2010 Rules is meant to encompass a wide range of both contractual and non-contractual disputes.[6] For example, the Rules may be utilized to resolve not only claims of contract breach, but also claims of third-party interference with contractual relations, trademark infringement, or other unfair competition.[7] The Rules may also be used in resolving disputes arising under investment treaties in which non-contractual questions of state responsibility under international law are at issue.[8] Further, nothing in Article 1(1) prevents the Rules from being utilized in purely domestic arbitration, even though they were developed specifically with international commercial arbitration in mind.[9]

The broader formulation in Article 1(1) also promotes consistency with Article II(2) of the New York Convention on the Recognition and Enforcement of Foreign Arbitral Awards,[10] and Article 7(1) of the UNCITRAL Arbitration Model Law, both of which contain identical language.[11]

(3) No writing requirement for agreement to arbitration—Article 1(1)

Article 1(1) does not require that the arbitration agreement be in writing in contrast to the 1976 UNCITRAL Rules, which contained such a requirement to "avoid uncertainty as to

---

Commercial Arbitration ('ACICA'), Kuala Lumpur Regional Centre for Arbitration, Cairo Regional Centre for International Arbitration, the Swiss Chambers' Court of Arbitration and Mediation, and the Permanent Court of Arbitration ('PCA'))." J Levine, "Current Trends in International Arbitral Practice as Reflected in the Revision of the UNCITRAL Arbitration Rules" (2008) 31(1) *U New South Wales L J* 266, 267.

[5] The text of Article 1(1) of the 1976 UNCITRAL Rules appears in note 1. The new language of Article 1(1) met with only minimal criticism in the Working Group. Some delegates objected to the new language "as simply replac[ing] one restriction with another, which unnecessarily limited the scope of the Rules and could raise interpretive questions that would undermine the certainty of the text." *Report of the Working Group on Arbitration and Conciliation on the Work of its Forty-Fifth Session* (Vienna, 11–15 September 2006), UNCITRAL, 40th Session, UN Doc A/CN.9/614, at 8, para 33 (2007). Their preferred approach was to include no limitation at all. Others believed that a reference to "defined legal relationship" might not be accommodated in certain legal systems. *Report of the Working Group on Arbitration and Conciliation on the Work of its Forty-Sixth Session* (New York, 5–9 February 2007), UNCITRAL, 40th Session, UN Doc A/CN.9/619, at 6, para 22 (2007). These arguments ultimately did not persuade the Working Group.

[6] Many delegates of the Revision Working Group believed that the application of the Rules should not be limited to disputes of only a contractual nature. See UNCITRAL, 40th Session, UN Doc A/CN.9/619, n 5, at 6, para 21. As to the applicability of the New York Convention to non-commercial disputes, see I Eliasoph, "A Missing Link: International Arbitration and the Ability of Private Actors to Enforce Human Rights Norms," (2004) 10 New England J Intl and Comparative L 83.

[7] For a discussion of the meaning of the phrase "defined legal relationship, whether contractual or not" as used in the Model Law, see *Seventh Secretariat Note: Analytical Commentary on Draft Text*, UN Doc A/CN.9/264, para 4 (March 25, 1985), an excerpt of which is included in H Holtzmann and J Neuhaus, *A Guide to the UNCITRAL Model Law on International Commercial Arbitration: Legislative History and Commentary* (1989) 290.

[8] UNCITRAL, 40th Session, UN Doc A/CN.9/614, n 5, at 8, para 33. See also J Castello, "Unveiling the 2010 UNCITRAL Arbitration Rules" (2010) 65 (2/3) Dispute Resolution J 21, 147.

[9] See S Baker and M Davis, *The UNCITRAL Arbitration Rules in Practice: The Experience of the Iran-United States Claims Tribunal* (1992) 7; J van Hof, *Commentary on the UNCITRAL Arbitration Rules: The Application by the Iran-U.S. Claims Tribunal* (1991) 13–14. The adaptability of the UNCITRAL Rules is of course a separate question from limitations in law of the place of arbitration or in the New York Convention.

[10] Hereinafter the New York Convention (New York, June 10, 1958; 330 TS 3 (1959)). Article II requires an "agreement in writing."

[11] New York Convention, art II.

whether the Rules have been made applicable" and to ensure conformity with Article II(1)–(2) of the New York Convention.[12] This omission in the 2010 Rules thus represents a significant departure in approach. During Working Group discussions, some delegates cautioned against the change, citing some of the same reasons as the original drafters of the Rules, clarity and conformity.[13] Others proposed new justifications for a writing requirement, including that, in the absence of uniform practice under national arbitration laws,[14] a writing requirement would remind the parties that the arbitration agreement might be valid only if in writing.[15]

Elimination of the writing requirement ultimately attracted a consensus, however. Many delegates believed the form of the arbitration agreement was a question that was better addressed by the applicable arbitration law, particularly since approaches varied across jurisdictions.[16] In addition, it was noted that if the Rules contained a writing requirement, it would conflict with the laws in jurisdictions that no longer imposed such a requirement; thus, the absence of the requirement would better harmonize international arbitration law.[17] Option II for Article 7 of the Model Law, as amended, does not contain a writing requirement, for example.[18] Still others pointed out that the question of whether the writing requirement had been met had given rise to substantial amounts of litigation.[19]

(4) Party autonomy and modification of the Rules—Article 1(1)

In conformity with the contractual nature of arbitration and the principle of party autonomy, the UNCITRAL Rules do not require that they be adopted as a "package." Under Article 1(1), the parties may agree to modify the Rules to the extent they are not inconsistent with the law of the place of arbitration.[20] In a typical *ad hoc* arbitration, modifications to the UNCITRAL Rules can be made in the arbitration agreement or in a separate agreement which can be concluded between the parties even after the commencement of the arbitral proceedings. Unlike the 1976 UNCITRAL Rules, Article 1(1) of the 2010 UNCITRAL Rules does not require that modification of the Rules be in writing. While some Working Group delegates supported the requirement as necessary to confirm the existence and scope of a modification agreement,[21] others pointed out that arbitration practice had

---

[12] *Report of the Secretary General on the Revised Draft Set of Arbitration Rules*, UNCITRAL, 9th Session, Introduction, para 7, UN Doc A/CN.9/112 (1975), reprinted in (1976) VII UNCITRAL Ybk 157, 167.

[13] UNCITRAL, 40th Session, UN Doc A/CN.9/614, n 5, at 7, para 28.

[14] UNCITRAL, 40th Session, UN Doc A/CN.9/614, n 5, at 8, para 30.

[15] Other proposed reasons for a writing requirement included providing a basis upon which an appointing authority could appoint arbitrators or an opportunity for parties to clarify which version of the rules would apply, UNCITRAL, 40th Session, UN Doc A/CN.9/619, n 5, at 7–8, para 30.

[16] UNCITRAL, 40th Session, UN Doc A/CN.9/614, n 5, at 7–8, para 29.

[17] UNCITRAL, 40th Session, UN Doc A/CN.9/619, n 5, at 7, para 28; UNCITRAL, 40th Session, UN Doc A/CN.9/614, n 5, at 7–8, para 29. Others said if the requirement remained it would have to be defined and that would go beyond the usual scope of arbitration rules. UNCITRAL, 40th Session, UN Doc A/CN.9/619, at 7, para 28.

[18] For examples of approaches to the writing requirement in various jurisdictions see T Webster, *Handbook of UNCITRAL Arbitration: Commentary, Precedents and Materials for UNCITRAL Based Arbitration Rules* (2010) 20–32.

[19] UNCITRAL, 40th Session, UN Doc A/CN.9/619, n 5, at 7, para 29. It was also noted that there was uncertainty as to whether the writing requirement applied to the agreement to arbitrate or to the parties' agreement on application of the UNCITRAL Rules. Id. 29.

[20] Such modification has occurred in the context of NAFTA Chapter Eleven arbitrations. See *Canfor Corp* (1976 Rules); and *Glamis Gold Ltd* (1976 Rules); both reprinted in section 2(C).

[21] *Settlement of Commercial Disputes: Revision of the UNCITRAL Arbitration Rules, Note by the Secretariat*, UNCITRAL, UN Doc A/CN.9/WG.II/WP.143 at 5, para 20 (2006). "A concern was expressed that the deletion of the requirement that the arbitration agreement be in writing might create difficulties in practice, and therefore

developed toward a more flexible approach.[22] For example, Article 19(1) of the Model Law, as amended, and many institutional procedural rules do not include a writing requirement.[23] In addition, Paulsson and Petrochilos, in their advisory report to UNCITRAL, noted that "the parties are better placed to evaluate whether the modifications they desire are of such importance or detail as to call for a written agreement or document."[24] Like the writing requirement for an arbitration agreement, the writing requirement for modification of the Rules was deemed to be outmoded and thus was dropped from the Rules.

While the freedom of the parties to modify the Rules and the discretion of the arbitral tribunal in their application[25] is considerable, Article 1(3) contains an important limitation to be taken into account in both respects. According to that provision, the UNCITRAL Rules "shall govern the arbitration except that where any of these Rules is in conflict with a provision of the law applicable to the arbitration from which the parties cannot derogate, that provision shall prevail." Article 1(3), which requires the respect of mandatory norms of the applicable procedural law, reflects the fact that arbitration is in many ways circumscribed by laws pertaining to it,[26] whether of domestic or international origin.[27] The scope and meaning of the requirement, and its relation to certain other fundamental principles concerning arbitration, will be further discussed in the next section.[28]

(5) *Presumptive scope of application—Article 1(2) and (3)*

The existence of two versions of the UNCITRAL Rules, the original 1976 version and the revised 2010 version, may raise important questions as to which version of the Rules applies in a dispute.[29] If the parties have agreed to apply "a particular version of the Rules,"

---

there should be convincing evidence indicating the existence of such agreement." *Report of Working Group II (Arbitration and Conciliation) on the Work of its Forty-Ninth Session* (Vienna, 15–19 September 2008), UNCITRAL, 42nd Session, UN Doc A/CN.9/665, at 6, para 18 (2008).

[22] UNCITRAL, 42nd Session, UN Doc A/CN.9/665, n 21, at 5, paras 21–22 (citing examples). See also 6, para 18.

[23] UNCITRAL, 40th Session, UN Doc A/CN.9/619, n 5, at 7, para 28. The provision of the Model Law, as amended, provides: "Subject to the provisions of this Law, the parties are free to agree on the procedure to be followed by the arbitral tribunal in conducting the proceedings."

[24] J Paulsson and G Petrochilos, "Revision of the UNCITRAL Rules," (A Report Commissioned by the UNCITRAL Secretariat), March 31, 2006, at 12, para 21.

[25] According to Article 17(1), discussed in section 3, "[s]ubject to these Rules, the arbitral tribunal may conduct the arbitration in such manner as it considers appropriate..."

[26] This fundamental tenet of international arbitration is widely recognized by international tribunals. See, eg *Wintershall AG* (1976 Rules); and *Himpurna California Energy Ltd* (1976 Rules); both reprinted in section 2(C)(2).

[27] In the case of arbitration arising under international investment agreements, the procedural law may be circumscribed by the specific terms of the treaty. See, eg, NAFTA, Chapter Eleven, Subchapter B, art 1120(2) ("The applicable arbitration rules shall govern the arbitration except to the extent modified by this subchapter."). The Working Group tasked with revising the Rules found the phrase "the law applicable to the arbitration from which the parties cannot derogate" to sufficiently cover cases in which international law, by way of an international investment agreement, imposed mandatory rules on the arbitration. See *Report of the Working Group on Arbitration and Conciliation on the Work of its Forty-Fifth Session* (Vienna, 11–15 September 2006), UNCITRAL, 40th Session, UN Doc A/CN.9/614, at 9, para 35 (2007).

[28] For a general discussion, see K H Böckstiegel, "The Relevance of National Arbitration Law for Arbitrations Under the UNCITRAL Rules," (1984) 1 J Intl Arb 223–236.

[29] This question arises in the context not only of commercial arbitration, but also investment arbitration as many investment treaties contain provisions on dispute settlement that makes only general reference to the UNCITRAL Arbitration Rules.

then the inquiry is straightforward: Article 1(2) indicates that their choice shall be determinative.[30] In other cases where the agreement of the parties is not express or otherwise clear—namely where the arbitration agreement contains only a general reference to the "UNCITRAL Arbitration Rules"—it falls to the arbitral tribunal to decide which version of the Rules is operative.[31] With the aim of assisting the tribunal's analysis, Article 1(2) offers two presumptions of applicability for disputes arising either out of a contract or under an investment treaty.

These presumptions are clearly not binding on the arbitral tribunal or the parties. Indeed, at the stage of the proceedings when it would be useful to refer to them, the tribunal's determination as to whether the 2010 Rules apply has yet to be made. Thus, the presumptions contained in Article 1(2) do not replace traditional techniques of contract or treaty interpretation used to determine which version of the Rules the parties intended to have apply. For example, in the context of interpreting a general reference to the "UNCITRAL Arbitration Rules" in an investment treaty, the arbitral tribunal may be required, where the text itself is ambiguous, to examine whether the negotiating history or subsequent practice of the state parties to the treaty inform the meaning of the reference.[32] In many cases, however, the disputing parties' intent will be difficult, if not impossible, to ascertain, leaving the presumptions in Article 1(2) as useful guides.

The first sentence of Article 1(2) establishes a presumption that the parties have agreed to adopt the 2010 Rules if their arbitration agreement was concluded *after* August 15, 2010, the date on which UNCITRAL adopted the 2010 Rules.[33] As Castello notes, this presumption reflects the Working Group's belief that, unless otherwise specified, the disputing parties "want the most recent version of the Rules to apply to any arbitration that arises under [the arbitration] agreement...."[34] Thus, a general reference to the "UNCITRAL Arbitration Rules" after adoption of the revised Rules is understood to mean the 2010 UNCITRAL Rules. The benefit of this approach is that it respects the consent-based nature of arbitration by assuming that the disputing parties could only agree to apply a version of the Rules that was in effect at the time the arbitration agreement was concluded.[35] Some Working Group delegates supported retroactive application of the Rules, whereby in the absence of party agreement the applicable version of the Rules would be the latest version of the Rules in effect when the arbitration commenced, ie, the 2010 UNCITRAL Rules, even if the arbitration agreement was concluded before adoption of that

---

[30] The Working Group replaced the phrase "another version of the Rules" in the first line of Article 1(2) with the phrase "a particular version of the Rules" in order to "clarify that the will of the parties would in all circumstances prevail." UNCITRAL, 42nd Session, UN Doc A/CN.9/665, n 21, at 6, para 19.

[31] "It was widely felt [among Revision Working Group delegates] that, in the case of disagreement or doubt regarding the chosen version of the Rules, it would be for the arbitral tribunal to interpret the will of the parties." UNCITRAL, 40th Session, UN Doc A/CN.9/619, n 5, at 8–9, para 37.

[32] Vienna Convention on the Law of Treaties (1969), arts 31 and 32.

[33] The straightforward approach of this rule was intended to ensure "the maximum degree of clarity to avoid disputes concerning which version of the Rules to apply in a given proceeding [particularly in *ad hoc* arbitration where an administering institution is not available to provide guidance]." *Report of the Working Group on Arbitration and Conciliation on the Work of its Forty-Eighth Session* (New York, 4–8 February 2008), UNCITRAL, 41st Session, UN Doc A/CN.9/646, at 17, para 74 (2008).

[34] J Castello, "UNCITRAL Rules," in F Weigand (ed) *Practitioner's Handbook on International Commercial Arbitration* (2009) 1417–18.

[35] UNCITRAL, 41st Session, UN Doc A/CN.9/646, n 33, at 16–17, para 72. See also UNCITRAL, 40th Session, UN Doc A/CN.9/614, n 5, at 7, para 25 (reporting that it was observed that "[n]o version of the Rules could be considered to be 'in force' in and of itself outside the context of an agreement between the parties to the dispute").

version of the Rules.[36] However, in the end, retroactive application was disfavored as it was inconsistent with the contractual nature of arbitration.[37]

The second sentence of Article 1(2) governs the special case where offer and acceptance of an agreement to arbitration are not simultaneous, namely in the context of investor–state arbitration. A state party to an investment treaty, for example, often provides foreign investors a standing offer to arbitrate disputes, though it is not sometimes until many years later that an investor accepts the offer by filing its arbitration claim against the state party. In this situation, the 2010 UNCITRAL Rules are presumed to apply only if both offer and acceptance occur after adoption of the 2010 Rules. Thus, for example, the 2010 Rules would not apply if an offer to arbitrate was made in an investment treaty concluded before August 15, 2010, even if an investor filed a claim—and accepted the arbitration agreement—after that date. Like the first sentence of Article 1(2), the second sentence proceeds on a theory of consent and avoids retroactive application of the 2010 Rules where both parties could not have reasonably assented to their application.[38] That said, the terms of some investment treaties expressly allow for retroactive application of the 2010 Rules (thus superseding any contrary presumption), such as where the standing offer to arbitrate is with respect to the version of the UNCITRAL Rules "in effect on the date the claim or claims were submitted to arbitration."[39] While the freedom of the parties to modify the Rules and the discretion of the arbitral tribunal in their application[40] is considerable, Article 1(3) contains an important limitation to be taken into account in both respects. According to that provision, the UNCITRAL Rules "shall govern the arbitration except that where any of these Rules is in conflict with a provision of the law applicable to the arbitration from which the parties cannot derogate, that provision shall prevail." Article 1(3), which requires the respect of mandatory norms of the applicable procedural law, reflects the fact, touched upon in the introduction to the present chapter, that arbitration is in many ways circumscribed by laws pertaining to it,[41] whether of domestic or international origin.[42] The scope and meaning of the requirement, and its relation to certain other fundamental principles concerning arbitration, will be further discussed in the next section.[43]

---

[36] Proponents of this approach argued that many parties expected that the latest version of a particular set of procedural rules would apply, that many arbitral institutions adopted this approach when revising their procedural rules, and that this approach would promote application of the latest version of the UNCITRAL Rules in the greatest number of situations. UNCITRAL, 41st Session, UN Doc A/CN.9/646, n 33, at 16–17, paras. 72–73. See also UNCITRAL, 40th Session, UN Doc A/CN.9/614, n 5, at 6–7, para 23.

[37] UNCITRAL, 40th Session, UN Doc A/CN.9/614, n 5, at 7, para 25.

[38] UNCITRAL, 41st Session, UN Doc A/CN.9/646, n 33, at 17, para 76.

[39] See, eg, CAFTA-DR, art 10.16.5.

[40] According to Article 17(1), discussed in section 3, "[s]ubject to these Rules, the arbitral tribunal may conduct the arbitration in such manner as it considers appropriate..."

[41] This fundamental tenet of international arbitration is widely recognized by international tribunals. See, eg *Wintershall AG* (1976 Rules); *Himpurna California Energy Ltd* (1976 Rules); both reprinted in section 2(C)(2).

[42] In the case of arbitration arising under international investment agreements, the procedural law may be circumscribed by the specific terms of the treaty. See, eg, NAFTA, Chapter Eleven, Subchapter B, Art 1120(2) ("The applicable arbitration rules shall govern the arbitration except to the extent modified by this subchapter.") The Working Group found the phrase "the law applicable to the arbitration from which the parties cannot derogate" to sufficiently cover cases in which international law, by way of an international investment agreement, imposed mandatory rules on the arbitration. See UNCITRAL, 40th Session, UN Doc A/CN.9/614, n 5, at 9, para 35.

[43] For a general discussion, see K H Böckstiegel, "The Relevance of National Arbitration Law", n 28, 223–36.

(6) Future transparency rules for investor–state arbitration

Users of the UNCITRAL Rules in the context of investor–state arbitration should be aware of UNCITRAL's work to develop rules of transparency for investor–state arbitration, a project nearing completion at the time of this writing. The precise scope of application of the transparency rules is still under debate. Throughout Working Group discussions, two distinct camps emerged. The majority of delegations supported the "opt in" approach. They favored application of the transparency rules only by express agreement of the parties in a future treaty or through some other instrument of consent. Thus, the transparency rules would take the form of a stand-alone set of procedural rules, either specific to UNCITRAL arbitration or more generally applicable, into which the parties to an investment treaty could opt if they so desired. According to those favoring the "opt in" direction, this approach would ensure that parties to an investment treaty could not be surprised by a tribunal as to application of the transparency rules to a particular investor–state arbitration.[44]

A minority of delegations expressed strong support for the "opt-out" position. The "opt out" proponents supported inclusion of the transparency rules as part of the UNCITRAL Rules, either as an annex to those Rules or as an addition to the main body of the Rules. They also advocated for a presumption in the transparency rules, according to which a general reference to the "UNCITRAL Arbitration Rules" in a future investment treaty would mean, subject to rules of treaty interpretation, that the transparency rules would apply (since they are part of the UNCITRAL Rules), unless the parties to an investment treaty expressly opted out of their application. The "opt out" camp believed that such a presumption of application under future treaties, along with no express limitation of application under existing treaties, furthered the aims of transparency better, particularly because it did not limit the possibility that thousands of existing investment treaties might therefore involve the application of the transparency rules.[45]

The question of the scope of application of the transparency rules was heavily debated at the Working Group's fifty-sixth session, with the outlines of a compromise slowly emerging. The compromise proposal provided generally that the transparency rules would apply only when the parties to an investment treaty or the disputing parties in an investor–state arbitration had expressly agreed to their application.[46] It further provided that a generic reference to the UNCITRAL Arbitration Rules in a treaty concluded after the date of adoption of the transparency rules would be presumed to include the transparency rules.[47] Thus, the basis of the compromise was the "opt out" approach, but only with respect to future investment treaties concluded after the transparency rules come into effect. If such a compromise is ultimately adopted by UNCITRAL, it may very well require a revision to

---

[44] For the development of this position throughout the discussions, see *Report of the Working Group on Arbitration and Conciliation on the Work of its Fifty-Fourth Session* (New York, 7–11 February 2011), UNCITRAL, 44th Session, UN Doc A/CN.9/717, at 7, para 19–20 (2011); *Report of the Working Group on Arbitration and Conciliation on the Work of its Fifty-Fifth Session* (Vienna, 3–7 October 2011), UNCITRAL, 45th Session, UN Doc A/CN.9/736, at 5–7, paras 20–24 (2011); and *Report of the Working Group on Arbitration and Conciliation on the Work of its Fifty-Sixth Session* (New York, 6–10 February 2012), UNCITRAL, 45th Session, UN Doc A/CN.9/741, at 5–6, paras 17–23 (2012).

[45] The progression of this position throughout the discussions can be found in UNCITRAL, 44th Session, UN Doc A/CN.9/717, n 44, at 7, 8, para 19, 21; UNCITRAL, 45th Session, UN Doc A/CN.9/736, n 44, at 7–8, paras 25–30; and UNCITRAL, 45th Session, UN Doc A/CN.9/741, n 44, at 6–7, paras 24–27.

[46] UNCITRAL, 45th Session, UN Doc A/CN.9/741, n 44, at 8, para 33.

[47] UNCITRAL, 45th Session, UN Doc A/CN.9/741, n 44, at 8, para 33.

Article 1(1) of the 2010 UNCITRAL Rules to clarify the relationship between those Rules and the transparency rules. Or it may even result in a re-issuing of the UNCITRAL Arbitration Rules to include the general procedural rules, adopted in 2010, and the transparency rules in one instrument.

(7) Model arbitration clause

The Rules also include a model arbitration clause to assist the parties in drafting a complete and enforceable agreement to arbitrate. Despite the wide scope of application of the Rules themselves ("in respect of a defined legal relationship, whether contractual or not"), the model arbitration clause applies only with respect to "any dispute, controversy, or claim arising out of or relating to this contract, or the breach, termination or invalidity thereof....". The Working Group tasked with revising the Rules considered whether to delete the reference to contract, but ultimately concluded that the purpose of the clause was "precisely to provide a recommendation for the parties wishing to include a clause in their contract."[48] A note to the model arbitration clause identifies key information that the parties should consider including in their arbitration clause. This information includes: (a) the name of the institution or person that is to act as appointing authority,[49] (b) the number of arbitrators (one or three), (c) the town and country that is to serve as the "place," or legal seat, of arbitration,[50] and (d) the language(s) to be used in the proceedings.[51]

(8) Comparison to the 1976 UNCITRAL Rules

Article 1 of the 2010 UNCITRAL Rules bears similarities to corresponding Article 1 of the 1976 UNCITRAL Rules, but with certain notable differences.

Article 1(1) of the 2010 Rules applies to disputes "in respect of a defined legal relationship, whether contractual or not,"[52] whereas Article 1(1) of the 1976 Rules only covers disputes in relation to a "contract."[53] Thus, the scope of application of the 1976 Rules is decidedly narrower than the 2010 Rules. Despite their more limited scope of application, the 1976 Rules have proven to be highly adaptable to a wide range of both contractual and

---

[48] UNCITRAL, 40th Session, UN Doc A/CN.9/614, n 5, at 9, para 36.

[49] Note that the Working Group rejected a proposal to delete the word "person" because removal of the possibility to appoint a person [as appointing authority] would run counter to existing practice..." UNCITRAL, 40th Session, UN Doc A/CN.9/619, n 5, at 9, para 40.

[50] The model arbitration clause contained in the 2010 Rules uses the phrase "town and country," in contrast to the phrase "town or country" used in the model clause contained in the 1976 Rules. The change was made because it was believed that the words "town or country" failed to capture "all factual possibilities" for designating the place of arbitration and thus did not adequately convey the important legal consequences that flow from the designation of the place of arbitration. UNCITRAL, 40th Session, UN Doc A/CN.9/619, n 5, at 9, para 41. For example, designation of a "country" alone may be insufficient where that country has more than one legal system for governing arbitral procedure, eg, in the United States arbitration law may vary at the sub-federal level from state to state.

[51] The Working Group considered, but did not adopt, proposals to add a subparagraph (e) to the model arbitration clause with references to the law governing the arbitration agreement or the law applicable to the substance of the dispute, or with a clarification about the relationship between the place of arbitration on the law applicable to the arbitral proceedings. UNCITRAL, 40th Session, UN Doc A/CN.9/619, n 5, at 9, para 41. The Working Group also did not adopt a proposal to include a reference to conciliation, possibly in the form of an optional conciliation clause, "to avoid unnecessarily complicating" the model arbitration clause. UNCITRAL, 40th Session, UN Doc A/CN.9/619 at 10, para 43. Nor did it adopt a proposal to include a footnote to the model arbitration clause bringing to the parties' attention the possibility of including a provision on confidentiality given the absence of one in the Rules. UNCITRAL, 40th Session, UN Doc A/CN.9/619 at 25, para 132.

[52] See section 2(A).

[53] See text of Article 1(1) in n 1.

non-contractual disputes for two primary reasons. First, Article 1(1) does not limit application of the 1976 Rules to commercial transactions of only an international nature.[54] Although the Rules were developed with international commercial arbitration in mind, nothing prevents them from being utilized in purely domestic arbitration. Second, because Article 1(1) affords the parties substantial flexibility to modify the Rules, they may in many cases agree to expand the scope of application to cover disputes involving non-contractual issues, such as issues of tort or public international law.[55] The Iran–US Claims Tribunal, for example, expanded the scope of Article 1 of the 1976 Rules to include claims permitted within the framework of the Algiers Declarations, ie, "debts, contracts..., expropriation or other measures affecting property rights."[56] One *ad hoc* arbitral tribunal applying the Rules found that the parties were free to adapt the UNCITRAL Rules to apply to their dispute over the annexation of the Hawaiian Kingdom by the United States.[57]

Another significant difference is that the 2010 Rules no longer require, as the 1976 Rules did, that an agreement to arbitrate under the Rules be made in writing. While the desirability of this requirement under the 1976 Rules drew differing views during UNCITRAL's preparatory discussions, it was ultimately concluded that "[w]riting is required in order to avoid uncertainty as to whether the Rules have been made applicable."[58] Delegates believed that by guaranteeing both certainty and compliance with most national

---

[54] See S Baker and M Davis, *The UNCITRAL Arbitration Rules in Practice*, n 9, 7; J van Hof, *Commentary on the UNCITRAL Arbitration Rules*, n 9, 13–14. The adaptability of the UNCITRAL Rules is of course a separate question from limitations in law of the place of arbitration or in the New York Convention. As to the applicability of the New York Convention to non-contractual disputes, see I Eliasoph "A Missing Link", n 6, 83.

[55] However, they may only do so subject to "a provision of the law applicable to the arbitration from which the parties cannot derogate...." Article 1(2).

[56] 1983 Rules of Procedure of the Iran–US Claims Tribunal, reprinted in Appendix 5. The 1983 Tribunal Rules constitute a modified version of the 1976 Rules. The Tribunal Rules were adopted by the Tribunal provisionally on March 10, 1982 and finally on May 3, 1983. Due to the special nature of this Tribunal, the power to make such modifications has been conferred on the two Governments and the Tribunal itself, the private parties being excluded. According to Article III(2) of the Claims Settlement Declaration, "the Tribunal shall conduct its business in accordance with the [UNCITRAL Rules] except to the extent modified by the Parties or by the Tribunal to ensure that this Agreement can be carried out." See also Article 1(1) of Tribunal Rules, reprinted in Appendix 5. See also para 3 of the last-mentioned Article, according to which the "[t]he Claims Settlement Declaration constitutes an agreement in writing by Iran and the United States...on behalf of their nationals..." See Chapter 10 section 2(B)(7). In these modified UNCITRAL Rules, some of the original articles have been left intact, while others have been rewritten, mainly to serve the specific needs arising from the institutional structure of the Tribunal. Several Rules have been supplemented by "Notes" indicating how the Tribunal intends to interpret and apply the Rule in question. On the drafting of the Tribunal Rules, see H Holtzmann, "Drafting the Rules of the Tribunal," in D Caron and J Crook (eds), *The Iran-United States Claims Tribunal and The Process of International Claims Resolution* (2000) 75.

[57] In the *Larsen* arbitration, the selection of the UNCITRAL Rules raised an important preliminary question for the tribunal, namely the applicability of the UNCITRAL Rules to a non-contractual dispute. The tribunal found "no reason why the UNCITRAL Rules cannot be adapted to apply to a non-contractual dispute." See *Lance Paul Larsen* (1976 Rules), para 10.7, reprinted in section 2(C)(1). Noting the "non-prescriptive" and "non-coercive" nature of the Rules, the tribunal concluded that parties who agree to arbitrate under the Rules are able to adapt the terms of the Rules, either expressly or by implication, to suit their dispute, including a dispute where one of the parties is alleged to be a state. *Lance Paul Larsen*, paras 10.5–10.7. Specifically, the tribunal found that "[t]he parties to this arbitration effectively have agreed to apply the UNCITRAL Rules with such necessary adaptations as arise from the terms of the Arbitration Agreement and the nature of the issues referred to arbitration." *Lance Paul Larsen*, para 10.10.

[58] *Report of the Secretary-General on the Revised Draft Set of Arbitration Rules*, UNCITRAL, 9th Session, Addendum 1 (Commentary), UN Doc. A/CN.9/112/Add.1 (1975), reprinted in (1976) VII UNCITRAL Ybk 166, 167. See also S Baker and M Davis *The UNCITRAL Arbitration Rules in Practice*, n 9, 8; J van Hof, *Commentary on the UNCITRAL Arbitration Rules*, n 9, 15.

laws of the day, as well as with the New York Convention, a written arbitration agreement would enhance acceptance and enforceability of any award resulting from the proceedings.[59] Similarly, there is a requirement that any "modification [of the 1976 Rules] must be in writing in order to ensure certainty as to its existence and precise ambit."[60] For reasons explained in the preceding section, Article 1 of the 2010 Rules no longer includes any writing requirements.

Article 1(2) of the 2010 Rules provides presumptions for determining which version of the Rules is applicable to a particular dispute where there is no agreement rather between the disputing parties. No such provisions appear in the 1976 Rules, although the 1976 model arbitration clause anticipates new versions of the Rules, providing that resolution of a contractual dispute will be in accordance with the UNCITRAL Rules "as at present in force."[61] Thus, parties that have incorporated the model clause into their contracts, even prior to adoption of the 2010 Rules on August 15, 2010, have agreed to apply the revised Rules to any dispute arising thereafter.

Article 1(3) of the 2010 Rules is identical to Article 1(2) of the 1976 Rules.

The 2010 and 1976 model arbitration clauses are substantially similar, with minor differences. The 1976 model clause, as noted, contains the phrase "shall be settled by arbitration in accordance with the UNCITRAL Arbitration Rules as at present in force,"[62] whereas the 2010 model clause drops "as at present in force." Instead, the 2010 Rules contain separate provisions on applicability of a particular version of the Rules.[63] A second change is the strengthening of the suggestion to include additional provisions. The note to the 1976 model clause provides that the parties "may wish to consider" including certain key information in their arbitration clause, whereas the 2010 Rules changes this to "should consider." The 1976 model clause also encourages the parties to identify the "town *or* country" when designating the place of arbitration. In contrast, the 2010 Rules include the words "town *and* country" to encourage greater specificity in the parties' designation.[64] Finally, the reference to "language(s)" of the arbitration in the 1976 Rules is replaced by "language" in the 2010 Rules in order not to unnecessarily encourage dual-language arbitration.

C. Extracts from the Practice of Investment and other Tribunals

(1) Article 1(1) (1976 Rules)—scope and modification

Lance Paul Larsen and *Hawaiian Kingdom*, Award (February 5, 2001) (PCA administered, 1976 UNCITRAL Rules, Special Agreement), reprinted in (2001) 119 Intl L Rep 566, 585–86:

---

[59] For a discussion of the acceptance of an arbitration agreement in the course of electronic commerce or by tacit or oral conduct, see *Possible Future Work in the Area of International Commercial Arbitration*, UNCITRAL, 32nd Session, UN Doc A/CN.9/460 (1999), paras 20–31, reprinted in (1999) XXX UNCITRAL Ybk 395, 398–9 [hereinafter "*Possible Future Work*"].

[60] P Sanders, "Commentary on UNCITRAL Arbitration Rules," (1977) II Ybk Commercial Arb 177, 179. Such modification has occurred in the context of NAFTA Chapter Eleven arbitrations. See *Canfor Corp* (1976 Rules); and *Glamis Gold Ltd* (1976 Rules); both reprinted in section 2(C).

[61] During the revision of the Rules, some proposed that the phrase "as at present in force" should be replaced with the phrase "as at present in effect" to "better reflect that the Rules have a contractual rather than legislative nature *Settlement of Commercial Disputes: Revision of the UNCITRAL Arbitration Rules, Note by the Secretariat*, UNCITRAL, UN Doc A/CN.9/WG.II/WP.145 at 6, para 21 (2006). Because the 2010 Rules contain a separate provision to address the applicability of a particular version of the Rules, the phrase "as at present in force" was dropped from the 2010 model arbitration clause.

[62] The complete text of the 1976 model arbitration clause appears in n 1.

[63] Article 1(2) states which version of the Rules will be presumed to apply unless the parties agree otherwise.

[64] See J Castello "UNCITRAL Rules," n 34, 1418.

10.7 ... When regard is had to the non-prescriptive and non-coercive nature of the [1976] UNCITRAL Rules as a standard regime available for parties to apply to resolve disputes between them, however, there appears no reason why the [1976] UNCITRAL Rules cannot be adapted to apply to a non-contractual dispute. For example, the parties could agree that a dispute as to tort, or occupier's or environmental liability might be determined in an arbitration applying the [1976] UNCITRAL Rules. Moreover they could so agree in relation to a dispute which had already arisen independently of any contractual relationship between them. In this manner the parties to an arbitration may specifically or by implication adopt or apply the [1976] UNCITRAL Rules to any dispute.

10.8 Further, although the [1976] UNCITRAL Rules were primarily drawn for the purposes of the arbitration of contractual disputes between parties or corporations, a State entity, or a State itself, may become a principal party to an agreement to arbitrate subject to [1976] UNCITRAL Rules. A State may agree to arbitrate under the [1976] UNCITRAL Rules before or after a dispute arises. Indeed, State parties commonly agree to apply the [1976] UNCITRAL Rules, modified as may be appropriate, to disputes that they have agreed to arbitrate with a non-state party. In the context of international arbitration this often enough occurs in disputes over procurement or "build, operate and transfer" contracts and other transactions involving a State and a non-State foreign party.

...

10.10 For these reasons the Tribunal approaches the issue of the applicable rules on the basis that the [1976] UNCITRAL Rules may be applied to an agreement to arbitrate a non-contractual dispute, including a dispute where one of the parties is or is said to be a State. The Tribunal finds that the parties to this arbitration effectively have agreed to apply the [1976] UNCITRAL Rules with such necessary adaptations as arise from the terms of the Arbitration Agreement and the nature of the issues referred to arbitration.

Glamis Gold Ltd and *United States of America*, Agreement on Certain Procedural Matters (January 20, 2004) (ICSID administered, 1976 UNCITRAL Rules, NAFTA Chapter Eleven), at 1:

3. As contemplated by Article 1.1 of [1976] UNCITRAL Arbitration Rules, the disputing parties hereby agree to modify Article 39 of the [1976] UNCITRAL Arbitration Rules to provide as follows: "Compensation for the arbitration tribunal shall be at the rates specified in the International Centre for Settlement of Investment Disputes (ICSID) Schedule of Fees, and administered as provided in ICSID's Administrative and Financial Regulation 14."

Canfor Corp and *United States of America*, Decision on the Place of Arbitration, Filing of a Statement of Defence and Bifurcation of the Proceedings (January 23, 2004) (ICSID administered, 1976 UNCITRAL Rules, NAFTA Chapter Eleven), at 2:

8. By letter of November 18, 2003, the parties advised the Tribunal that they had agreed, pursuant to Article 1(1) of the [1976] UNCITRAL Arbitration Rules, to modify Article 16(1) of those Rules to provide that, "[u]*nless the parties have agreed upon the place where the arbitration is to be held, the Tribunal shall fix the place of arbitration at a city in Canada or the United States of America, having regard to the circumstances of the arbitration.*"

Econet Wireless Ltd and *First Bank of Nigeria,* et al, Award (June 2, 2005) (*Ad Hoc* Proceeding, 1976 UNCITRAL Rules, Contract), reprinted in (2006) XXXI Ybk Commercial Arb 49, 57–58, 63:

[18] The Claimant argues that by adopting an alternative appointment procedure to replace Art. 7(1) of the UNCITRAL Rules, the Parties *implicitly* agreed to modify Art. 7(2) and 7(3) as necessary to make these provisions consistent with the procedure they chose. According to the Claimant, the Parties made this 'implicit' modification to ensure the same outcome as would arise where one of the parties fails to appoint under the standard UNCITRAL Rules: the vacancies on the Tribunal are filled by an appointing authority selected by the PCA.

[19] Through their arbitration agreement, the parties have the power to alter the UNCITRAL Rules as they see fit. As already noted, this is expressly authorised in Art. 1(1) of the Rules. While the UNCITRAL Rules require that modification be 'in writing', this requirement is interpreted broadly in modern arbitration practice. The Parties indeed modified the UNCITRAL Rules 'in writing', through Art. 25.1 of the Shareholders' Agreement; the question remains as to the contours of the arbitration procedure so modified.

[20] The Tribunal's task is to enforce the Parties' bargain, reconstructing as closely as possible the dispute resolution structures that the Parties contemplated when they signed their agreement. *Total Nigeria Plc v. Morkah,* (2002) 9 NWLR 492 at 519. This is no simple matter now that a dispute has arisen between them, perhaps changing each side's view of what the optimal arbitration procedure should have been. The difficulty in deciding a case such as this one is not that one must choose between a logical and an illogical interpretation, but rather between two logical but inconsistent interpretations.

[21] The implicit modification of UNCITRAL Rules Art. 7 suggested by the Claimant would require substantial wordsmithing to be effective...

. . .

[40] We find there to be insufficient evidence as to the ex ante expectation of the Parties with regard to whether NACA Sect. 7(3) would serve as a reliable backstop provision to complement their agreed system for composing the arbitral tribunal. More importantly, there is insufficient evidence to support the notion that, regardless of their view of the NACA's sufficiency in this regard, the Parties agreed to the PCA as the appropriate alternative recourse. As explained above, to accept this assumption the Tribunal must substantially alter the Parties' express contractual agreement, as expressed in the UNCITRAL Rules. This the Tribunal cannot do, in the absence of persuasive evidence that this change was indeed the Parties' intent. While the Parties may have signed an imperfect arbitration agreement, and one which leads to an undesired result for the Claimants in the present specific circumstances, it is not for us to repair it for them after the fact.

(2) Article 1(2) (1976 Rules)—non-derogation from mandatory law

Wintershall AG, et al and *Government of Qatar,* Partial Award on Liability (February 5, 1988) (*Ad Hoc* Proceeding, 1976 UNCITRAL Rules, Concession Agreement), reprinted in (1989) 28 ILM 798, 801:

By the second sentence of paragraph 1 of its Order of March 18, 1987, the Tribunal provided that the procedure of the arbitration shall be governed by the [1976] UNCITRAL Arbitration Rules, as agreed by the Parties in the Agreement of October 22, 1986, subject to any mandatory provisions of the Netherlands Arbitration Law, which, in the event of conflict with any of the [1976] UNCITRAL Rules shall prevail. The Tribunal has concluded that its Partial Award on Liability, determining the substance of the claims on both jurisdiction and the merits, and proposed Final Award (See XX hereof) are consistent with the [1976] UNCITRAL Arbitration Rules and in no respect in conflict with any of the mandatory provisions of the Netherlands Arbitration Law.

Himpurna California Energy Ltd and *PT (Persaro) Perusahaan Listruik Negara*, Final Award (May 4, 1999) (*Ad Hoc* Proceeding, 1976 UNCITRAL Rules, Concession Agreement), reprinted in (2000) XXV Ybk Commercial Arb 13, 26:

> [44] With respect to matters of procedure, the Arbitral Tribunal is bound to follow the agreement of the Parties, which in this case means the [1976] UNCITRAL Arbitration Rules to which their contract refers. The Arbitral Tribunal is not required to apply any national rules of procedure unless a Party has shown that the application of such a rule is mandatory. This is the consequence of Art. 1(2) of the [1976] UNCITRAL Rules which provides:
>
>> These Rules shall govern the arbitration except that where any of these Rules is in conflict with a provision of the law applicable to the arbitration from which the parties cannot derogate, the provision shall prevail.

Econet Wireless Ltd and *First Bank of Nigeria,* et al, Award (June 2, 2005) (*Ad Hoc* Proceeding, 1976 UNCITRAL Rules, Contract), reprinted in (2006) XXXI Ybk Commercial Arb 49, 57–58, 63:

> [25] But this is not the end of the analysis. The Parties' reference to Nigerian law as the procedural system applicable to their dispute only serves to reinforce the gap-filling function served by the lex arbitri where the parties have not chosen another procedural regime. The NACA, along with any relevant jurisprudence interpreting the statute, is therefore the Tribunal's next port of call, since neither the Shareholders' Agreement nor the UNCITRAL Rules provide a satisfactory answer to the question at hand.

3. General Provisions—Article 17

A. Text of the 2010 UNCITRAL Rule[65]

Article 17 of the 2010 UNCITRAL Rules provides:
General provisions

1. Subject to these Rules, the arbitral tribunal may conduct the arbitration in such manner as it considers appropriate, provided that the parties are treated with equality and that at an appropriate stage of the proceedings each party is given a reasonable opportunity of presenting its case. The arbitral tribunal, in exercising its discretion, shall conduct the proceedings so as to avoid unnecessary delay and expense and to provide a fair and efficient process for resolving the parties' dispute.
2. As soon as practicable after its constitution and after inviting the parties to express their views, the arbitral tribunal shall establish the provisional timetable of the arbitration. The arbitral tribunal may, at any time, after inviting the parties to express their views, extend or abridge any period of time prescribed under these Rules or agreed by the parties.

---

[65] Corresponding Article 15 of the 1976 UNCITRAL Rules provides:
1. Subject to these Rules, the arbitral tribunal may conduct the arbitration in such manner as it considers appropriate, provided that the parties are treated with equality and that at any stage of the proceedings each party is given a full opportunity of presenting his case.
2. If either party so requests at any stage of the proceedings, the arbitral tribunal shall hold hearings for the presentation of evidence by witnesses, including expert witnesses, or for oral argument. In the absence of such a request, the arbitral tribunal shall decide whether to hold such hearings or whether the proceedings shall be conducted on the basis of documents and other materials.
3. All documents or information supplied to the arbitral tribunal by one party shall at the same time be communicated by that party to the other party.

3. If at an appropriate stage of the proceedings any party so requests, the arbitral tribunal shall hold hearings for the presentation of evidence by witnesses, including expert witnesses, or for oral argument. In the absence of such a request, the arbitral tribunal shall decide whether to hold such hearings or whether the proceedings shall be conducted on the basis of documents and other materials.
4. All communications to the arbitral tribunal by one party shall be communicated by that party to all other parties. Such communications shall be made at the same time, except as otherwise permitted by the arbitral tribunal if it may do so under applicable law.
5. The arbitral tribunal may, at the request of any party, allow one or more third persons to be joined in the arbitration as a party provided such person is a party to the arbitration agreement, unless the arbitral tribunal finds, after giving all parties, including the person or persons to be joined, the opportunity to be heard, that joinder should not be permitted because of prejudice to any of those parties. The arbitral tribunal may make a single award or several awards in respect of all parties so involved in the arbitration.

B. Commentary

Article 17 contains "General Provisions" and is one of the most important articles of the UNCITRAL Rules. It spells out certain fundamental principles which must be taken into account in the application of the more specific rules "during the arbitral proceedings," that is, until the issuance of the award or other termination of the proceedings.[66] Although at first reading Article 17 may not appear to provide answers to so many concrete questions, it does in fact provide the key to a variety of problems not regulated elsewhere in the Rules. Therefore, Article 17 should be carefully studied prior to commencement of the arbitral proceedings.

(1) Basic principles—Article 17(1)

(a) Arbitral autonomy and its limits

Article 17(1) has rightly been referred to as the "heart" of the UNCITRAL Rules.[67] By providing that "the arbitral tribunal may conduct the arbitration in such manner as it considers appropriate" the provision reflects the procedural flexibility which is generally regarded as one of the main advantages of arbitration.[68] Tribunal practice evidences the wide application of this authority.[69] In international cases there is also a special need for freedom from

---

[66] See *Dames & Moore* (1983 Tribunal Rules), reprinted in section 3(D)(1).

[67] H Bagner, "Enforcement of International Commercial Contracts by Arbitration: Recent Developments," (1982) 14 Case Western Reserve J Intl L 573, 577. In the Model Law, as amended, the main elements of the present provision are contained in two separate articles, Articles 18 and 19. Together they have been called the "Magna Charta of Arbitral Procedure." See H Holtzmann and J Neuhaus, *A Guide to the UNCITRAL Model Law*, n 7, 550, 564.

[68] See N Blackaby and C Partasides, *Redfern and Hunter on International Arbitration*, n 2, 33. See also S Baker and M Davis, *The UNCITRAL Arbitration Rules in Practice*, n 9, 75–6 (discussion on the "principle of flexibility" as applied by the Iran–US Claims Tribunal); *UNCITRAL Notes on Organizing Arbitral Proceedings*, UNCITRAL, UN GAOR, 51st Session, para 4, UN Doc A/51/17 (1996), reprinted in (1996) XXVII UNCITRAL Ybk 45, 46 [hereinafter "UNCITRAL Notes"] ("This [procedural flexibility] is useful in that it enables the arbitral tribunal to take decisions on the organization of proceedings that take into account the circumstances of the case, the expectations of the parties and of the members of the arbitral tribunal, and the need for a just and cost-efficient resolution of the dispute.").

[69] Examples of the application of powers by the Iran–US Claims Tribunal under corresponding Article 15(1) of the 1983 Tribunal Rules are reprinted in section 3(D): *Watkins-Johnson Co* (1983 Tribunal Rules) (rejecting submission after closure of written record); *General Electric Co* (1983 Tribunal Rules) (same); *Gloria Jean Cherafat* (1983 Tribunal Rules) (refusing to reinstate terminated case), *The Austin Co* (holding settlement conference) (1983 Tribunal Rules); *White Consolidated Industries Inc* (1983 Tribunal Rules) (refusing to hold

unfamiliar local standards and requirements.[70] The desire for flexibility, however, must be balanced against other interests, such as the need for some ultimate control of procedural fairness and legal certainty concerning the international acceptance of the award.[71] Thus, the ostensibly wide discretion of the arbitrators is subject to certain limitations; some follow directly from Article 17(1), while others flow from other provisions in the Rules.[72]

The first limitation is that the freedom of the arbitral tribunal is "[s]ubject to these Rules," ie, limited by the more specific provisions of the UNCITRAL Rules regarding the conduct of the arbitration.[73] The UNCITRAL Rules in many cases provide a limiting framework for the exercise of arbitral discretion.[74] For example, Article 27(3) provides that "[a]t any time during the arbitral proceedings the arbitral tribunal may require the parties to produce documents, exhibits or other evidence within such a period of time as the tribunal shall determine."[75] In other cases, however, the Rules provide almost no structure at all and it is the arbitrators who must develop the particulars in accordance with the general principle enunciated in Article 17(1). For example, the question of whether a tribunal applying the Rules has the power to accept *amicus* submissions from third parties arose in various investor–state arbitrations.[76] In these cases, it was found that allowing third parties to make *amicus* submissions fell within the tribunal's powers to conduct the arbitration in an appropriate manner.[77] Whenever the Rules impose more definite limitations on arbitral

---

preliminary hearing); *Parvin Mariam Samrad* (1983 Tribunal Rules) (granting request to extend filing deadline); *World Farmers Trading Inc* (1983 Tribunal Rules) (refusing to hold oral hearing unless requested by parties); *New York Blower Co* (1983 Tribunal Rules) (same); *Tai Inc* (1983 Tribunal Rules) (rejecting request to make interlocutory award); Case Nos A3, A8, A9, A14 and B16 (1983 Tribunal Rules) (holding pre-hearing conference); *Dadras Intl* (1983 Tribunal Rules) (refusing to admit unauthorized, late-filed documents into evidence); *Vivian Mai Tavakoli* (1983 Tribunal Rules) (same); and *Vera-Jo Miller Aryeh* (1983 Tribunal Rules) (same). Examples from investment tribunals are reprinted in section 3(C): *Methanex Corp* (1976 Rules), Tribunal Letter (admission of *amicus* submissions and establishing deadlines); *United Parcel Services of America Inc* (1976 Rules) (admission of *amicus* submissions); and *CME Czech Republic BV* (1976 Rules) (adopting, as appropriate, the IBA Rules on Taking Evidence). Another example from an *ad hoc* tribunal is found in *Lance Paul Larsen* (1976 Rules) (determining preliminary issues but refusing to issue preliminary award), reprinted in section 3(C)(1).

[70] H Holtzmann and J Neuhaus, *A Guide to the UNCITRAL Model Law*, n 7, 564.
[71] See J Castello, "UNCITRAL Rules," n 34, 1465.
[72] Cf *ICS Inspection and Control Services Ltd* (1976 Rules), Award on Jurisdiction, reprinted in section 3(C)(1) (recognizing some, but not all, limitations on a tribunal's general authority).
[73] Article 17(1) grants the arbitral tribunal's discretion only with respect to the "conduct [of] the arbitration." Thus, a NAFTA Chapter Eleven tribunal found that corresponding Article 15(1) of the 1976 UNCITRAL Rules did not authorize it to reconsider a final and binding award. See *Methanex Corp* (1976 Rules), Final Award, reprinted in Section 3(C)(1).
[74] For a discussion on the various limitations imposed by the Rules see K P Berger, "Art. 15 UNCITRAL Arbitration Rules: The Eternal Conflict Between Arbitral Discretion and the Parties Due Process Rights" (2006) 21(4) Mealey's Intl Arb Rep 29.
[75] According to the drafters of the 1976 UNCITRAL Rules, Article 24(3) of the original Rules (which is identical to Article 27(3) of the 2010 UNCITRAL Rules) is "a specific example of the general rule in article [15(1) of the 1976 UNCITRAL Rules, revised as Article 17(1) of the 2010 UNCITRAL Rules] to the effect that 'the arbitrators may conduct the arbitration in such a manner as they consider appropriate.'" *Report of the Secretary General on the Revised Draft Set of Arbitration Rules*, UNCITRAL, 9th Session, Introduction, para 17, UN Doc A/CN.9/112 (1975), reprinted in (1976) VII UNCITRAL Ybk 157, 160.
[76] See *Methanex Corp* (1976 Rules); *United Parcel Service of America, Inc* (1976 Rules); and *Chevron Corp* (1976 Rules); all reprinted in section 3(C)(2).
[77] Notably, both tribunals found that the scope of Article 15(1) of the 1976 UNCITRAL Rules was limited to procedural matters internal to the arbitration and thus granted no authority to treat third parties as parties to the arbitration. See *Methanex Corp* (1976 Rules), para 29; and *United Parcel Services of America Inc* (1976 Rules), para 39 both reprinted in section 3(C)(2).

discretion, these should be taken into account. A major departure from them could provide a ground for setting aside the award[78] or endanger an award's enforceability under the New York Convention.[79]

A second fundamental limitation on the discretionary powers granted by Article 17 is found in the principle of equality,[80] a concept closely connected with the principle of *audiatur et altera pars*.[81] The Preliminary Draft of the 1976 UNCITRAL Rules required that the parties be treated "with absolute equality."[82] The abolition of the word "absolute" from the rule as finally adopted indicates that the provision aims to guarantee not so much formal equality as equality in the sense of justice and fairness.[83] The arbitral tribunal may, for example, deviate from a "mechanical" application of equality[84] as between the respective national languages of the parties (assuming both are used in arbitration), provided it does not prejudice any party's right to present its case and receive justice on the basis of material equality.[85] On the other hand, a party's rights would unavoidably be prejudiced should its opponent be consulted ex parte by the arbitrators,[86] or be "permitted to present an extensive Memorial and additional exhibits, without providing an opportunity for the other party to file a memorial in response."[87] This understanding of equality is reflected in the wording of Article 17(1), which does not include the word "absolute." Arbitral tribunals have drawn on the principle of equal treatment to address a number of procedural matters.[88]

The principle of equality has been closely tied with the requirement "that at an appropriate stage of the proceedings each party is given a reasonable opportunity of presenting

---

[78] See M Aden, *Internationale Handelsschiedsgerichtbarkeit* (1988) 24–5 (a violation of the procedure agreed upon by the parties may lead to the setting aside (*Aufhebung*) of the award under German Law).

[79] According to Article V(1)(d) of the Convention recognition and enforcement may be refused, *inter alia*, where the "arbitral procedure was not in accordance with the agreement of the parties..." See also W Craig, "Uses and Abuses of Appeal from Awards," (1988) 4 Arb Intl 174, 189.

[80] See generally N Blackaby and C Partasides, *Redfern and Hunter on International Arbitration*, n 2, 366.

[81] For a discussion of the principle of *audiatur et altera pars*, see B Cheng, *General Principles of Law as Applied by International Courts and Tribunals* (1987) 290–8.

[82] *Report of the Secretary-General on the Preliminary Draft Set of Arbitration Rules*, UNCITRAL, 8th Session, UN Doc A/CN.9/97 (1974), reprinted in (1975) VI UNCITRAL Ybk 163, 172–3.

[83] See *Report of the UNCITRAL*, 8th Session, Summary of Discussion of the Preliminary Draft, UN Doc A/10017, para 99 (1975), reprinted in (1975) VI UNCITRAL Ybk 24, 35 ("In this context, the comment was made that what was important was not the imposition of an obligation to observe the principle of equal treatment, since in certain circumstances (such as where the parties made conflicting requests to an arbitral tribunal) such treatment was impossible; the real need was to stress that both parties should receive fair treatment. It was suggested, however, that the best course might be to modify the paragraph so as to impose an obligation on the arbitrators to treat the parties both with equality and fairness."). For further discussion concerning the amendment in question and its legislative history, see S Baker and M Davis, *The UNCITRAL Arbitration Rules in Practice*, n 9, 76–7; J van Hof, *Commentary on the UNCITRAL Arbitration Rules*, n 9, 102. For an application of the principle of equality by a NAFTA Chapter Eleven tribunal, see *Pope & Talbot Inc* (1976 Rules), reprinted in section 3(C)(1).

[84] Van Hof comments that equality "in this provision is not necessarily aimed at guaranteeing a mechanical application of equality in all circumstances, but rather is aimed at guaranteeing equality in the material sense of justice and fairness." J van Hof, "UNCITRAL Arbitration Rules, Section III, Article 15 [General provisions]" in L Mistelis (ed) *Concise International Arbitration* (2010) 191.

[85] The language of arbitration is discussed in connection with Article 19 in Chapter 11.

[86] Although special circumstances may exist in the case of a preliminary request for interim measures, see Chapter 17.

[87] See *Foremost Tehran Inc* (1983 Tribunal Rules), reprinted in section 3(D)(1).

[88] Examples are reprinted in section 3(C)(1): *EnCana Corp* (1976 Rules) (in addressing confidentiality where the same arbitrator was appointed in two related arbitrations); *Softwood Lumber Consolidated Proceeding* (1976 Rules) (in consolidating multiple arbitrations); and *Merrill & Ring Forestry* (1976 Rules) (in considering the application of an asserted privilege).

his case." This requirement not only prohibits relative differences in treatment of the parties with respect to the presentation of their cases, but also establishes an absolute prohibition against depriving a party of the right to present its case, even if the tribunal's treatment affects both parties "equally." Even "equal treatment" in some cases can amount to arbitrariness when it benefits one party to the detriment of another, ie, by negating equality in the material sense discussed earlier.[89] At the same time, a party's right to present its case is not without limits. According to Article 17(1), a party is entitled to a reasonable opportunity to present its case "at an appropriate stage of the proceedings," as opposed to *any* stage of the proceedings.[90] The arbitral tribunal thus retains significant discretion in determining *when* the parties should have an opportunity to present their cases.[91]

In the practice of international tribunals, the issue of equality has mainly arisen as a question concerning the right to present one's case, most particularly in connection with orders and other decisions on written submissions.[92] The delicate and difficult questions that the requirement of equality may raise are reflected in some of the dissenting opinions of party-appointed arbitrators.[93]

A party who feels that its right to equal treatment has been violated is advised to object promptly. Failure of timely protest may not only deprive the arbitral tribunal of the opportunity to reconsider the matter immediately, but also, in subsequent court proceedings, it may be regarded as indirect proof that the requirement of fair treatment of the parties was in fact fulfilled.[94] Denial of a party's reasonable opportunity to present its case may lead to

---

[89] It may be noted that the Revised Draft which followed the Preliminary Draft (but preceded the final text) required treatment "with equality and with fairness." The text of the Revised Draft is reproduced in (1976) VII UNCITRAL Ybk 160. The Preliminary Draft had contained only the provision on "absolute equality."

[90] In this aspect, the differences between Article 17(1) and corresponding Article 15(1) of the 1976 UNCITRAL Rules, which includes the phrase "any stage of the proceedings," are discussed in Section 3(B)(7) entitled "Comparison to the 1976 UNCITRAL Rules." Note that Article 18 of the amended Model Law ("the parties shall be treated with equality and each party shall be given a full opportunity of presenting his case") does not contain the words "at any stage." This phrase was omitted because "it was feared that it might be relied upon to prolong the proceedings unnecessarily." H Holtzmann and J Neuhaus, *A Guide to the UNCITRAL Model Law*, n 7, 552.

[91] In the context of a party's right to present its case, Article 15(1) of the 1976 UNCITRAL Rules guarantees "a full opportunity," whereas Article 17(1) of the 2010 UNCITRAL Rules ensures "an opportunity." According to the *travaux préparatoires*, the word "full" was omitted out of concerns that the term could be "contentious," apparently meaning that a party, based on its own subjective assessment, might argue that it was entitled to a fuller opportunity to present its case than it received. However, it was recognized that there was no information before the Working Group to suggest that the current text has given rise to any difficulties in practice. UNCITRAL, 40th Session, UN Doc A/CN.9/614, n 5, at 17, para 77.

[92] For examples from the practice of the Iran–US Claims Tribunal, see *Foremost Tehran* (1983 Tribunal Rules); *Watkins-Johnson Co* (1983 Tribunal Rules); and *General Electric Co* (1983 Tribunal Rules); all reprinted in section 3(D)(1). See generally J van Hof, *Commentary on the UNCITRAL Arbitration Rules*, n 9, 103–5. For examples from the practice of a NAFTA Chapter Eleven tribunals, see *Methanex Corp* (1976 Rules); and *Glamis Gold Ltd* (1976 Rules); both reprinted in section 3(C)(1).

[93] See, eg, Case Nos 33, 87 and 174, Dissent of Howard M Holtzmann from Orders Permitting Post-Hearing Statements, June 20, 1983, reprinted in 3 Iran-US CTR 87–88 (1983–11); *Ford Aerospace & Communications Corp* and *Islamic Republic of Iran*, Case No 93, Dissenting Opinion of Mohsen Mostafavi to the Order of February 28, 1986, March 4, 1986, reprinted in 10 Iran-US CTR 108, 109 (1986–1).

[94] See *Klöckner* and *Cameroon*, Decision of the *Ad Hoc* Committee, May 3, 1985, reprinted in (1986) ICSID Rev—Foreign Investment L J 90, para 88 ("it suffices to note that the Claimant has not established that it made a timely protest against the serious procedural irregularities it now complains of."). See also J Thieffry, "The Finality of Awards in International Arbitration," (1985) 1(3) J Intl Arb 27, 45 ("In practice, it appears that the courts will take into consideration a violation of the adversarial principle to deny enforcement of an international arbitral award only where such violation is serious in nature.").

the non-enforcement of the award,[95] as was the case with the award in *Avco*, discussed later in section 3(B)(1)(d).

A third limitation is rooted in the arbitral tribunal's duty to conduct the proceedings "so as to avoid unnecessary delay and expense and to provide a fair and efficient process for resolving the parties' dispute."[96] The negotiating history reports that some delegations found express reference to the duty to be unnecessary, presumably because they believed it was implied.[97] Nevertheless, such a duty may serve as a useful reminder that the parties have a right—in addition to the right to equal treatment and an opportunity to present their cases—to an arbitral process that is conducted expeditiously, cost-effectively, fairly and efficiently.[98] Failure to comply with this duty may expose the tribunal to criticism by the parties or in some cases even litigation by the parties.[99]

A fourth limitation on the discretion of the arbitrators stems from Article 1(1), according to which the UNCITRAL Rules govern arbitration "subject to such modifications as the parties may agree." Thus, the parties have freedom to modify the rules, and the arbitral tribunal should afford due respect to such modifications.[100] The proceedings before the Iran–US Claims Tribunal exemplify the application of the UNCITRAL Rules in a modified fashion. Such modifications have been created through article-by-article specifications in the "Tribunal Rules." Furthermore, the provisions of the Algiers Accords (insofar as they relate to the Tribunal proceedings) amount to written modifications of the UNCITRAL Rules which the Tribunal must respect.[101]

A fifth basic limitation to be taken into account in the application of Article 17(1) follows from Article 1(2). It provides that the UNCITRAL Rules (whether intended to apply as such or in a version modified by the parties) prevail only to the extent that they are not "in conflict with a provision of the law applicable to the arbitration from which the parties cannot derogate."[102] This means, on the one hand, that the parties cannot

---

On the other hand, it is doubtful whether in domestic judicial proceedings, a mere lack of objection can automatically cure clearly discriminatory treatment by virtue of Article 32 of the Rules, according to which "[a] failure by any party to object promptly to any non-compliance with these Rules or with any requirement of the arbitration agreement shall be deemed to be a waiver of the right of such party to make such an objection, unless such party can show that, under the circumstances, its failure was justified." As the principles of non-discrimination and *audi alterem partem* are likely to be mandatory norms in most domestic systems, courts might be reluctant to accept that their violation can be made good on the basis of the quoted provision. The same is the case with excess of jurisdiction. The question of mandatory norms is discussed later in this section.

[95] See P Sanders, *The Work of UNCITRAL on Arbitration and Conciliation* (2001) 6 ("Non-observance of equal treatment or not giving parties a full opportunity to present their case will make the award subject to an action for setting aside.").

[96] This duty of the arbitral tribunal was added to the 2010 UNCITRAL Rules, thus bringing the Rules in line with other leading arbitration rules. See, eg, 1998 LCIA Rules, art 14.1(ii); 2010 SCC Rules, art 19(2); 2010 AAA Rules, art 16(2); 2001 WIPO Rules, art 38(c).

[97] UNCITRAL, 40th Session, UN Doc A/CN.9/614, n 5, at 17, para 76.

[98] In Working Group discussions, an express statement of the duty was also said to be "useful to provide leverage for arbitral tribunals to take certain steps both vis-à-vis the other arbitrators and the parties." UNCITRAL, 40th Session, UN Doc A/CN.9/614, n 5, at 17, para 76.

[99] UNCITRAL, 40th Session, UN Doc A/CN.9/614, n 5, at 17, para 76.

[100] But see M Pryles, "Limits to Party Autonomy in Arbitral Procedure," (2007) 24 J Intl Arb 335 (noting "it would appear that the arbitral tribunal is not bound to accept an agreement of the parties as to a period of time"). On the 1976 version of the rule, see P Sanders, n 60, 179. See also section 2(B).

[101] See Article 1(1) of the 2010 UNCITRAL Rules, section 2. See also J Selby and D Stewart, "Practical Aspects of Arbitrating Claims Before the Iran-United States Claims Tribunal," (1984) 18 Intl Lawyer 211, 219, n 23 ("It is not possible... to waive mandatory requirements set forth in the Algiers Accords.").

[102] See Article 1(2) in section 2(B)(5).

agree to modifications which are in conflict with mandatory provisions of the law applicable to the arbitration, nor is it possible for the arbitrators to derogate from such provisions. On the other hand, the combined effect of Articles 17(1) and 1(2) is that "a choice of the UNCITRAL Rules is to be understood as an exclusion of all national arbitration law, except for its mandatory provisions."[103] In other words, unless the parties have agreed to abide by a given law, or the arbitral tribunal has decided, in accordance with Article 17(1), to apply procedural norms of a designated national law, the arbitrators are not obliged to follow any domestic law in solving procedural problems not covered by the UNCITRAL Rules.[104] They must, however, ensure that the mandatory norms of "the law applicable to the arbitration" are not circumvented.

If no national procedural law has been specifically designated, "the law applicable to the arbitration" presumptively is the law of the place of arbitration (*lex loci arbitri*).[105] Even when another law has been chosen as the procedural law of the arbitration, any mandatory norms of the law of the place prevail by virtue of the sovereignty of the territorial state,[106] or—to put it differently—"an international arbitral tribunal is only free of the constraints of local law if the local law itself allows it to be so."[107] In order to avoid confusion, and also practical difficulties caused by applying different domestic norms, an arbitral tribunal should avoid designating a law other than the *lex loci arbitri* as the applicable procedural law.[108]

The normal sanction for non-observance of the mandatory norms of the local law is that the award may be set aside by the courts of the seat of arbitration. This, in turn, may prevent the award from being recognized and enforced in other countries.[109] The contents of typical mandatory norms are discussed later in this chapter in connection with Article 18(1) in section 4.

While, at least as a general principle, the mandatory provisions of the law of the place of arbitration must be respected, the question remains whether exceptions to this rule are ever

---

[103] K H Böckstiegel, "The Relevance of National Arbitration Law," n 28, 227.

[104] For a NAFTA Chapter Eleven tribunal's treatment of Canada's refusal to comply with a document production request based on Crown privilege under Canadian law, see *Pope & Talbot Inc* (1976 Rules), reprinted in section 3C(1). See *ICS Inspection and Control Services Ltd* (1976 Rules), Procedural Order, reprinted in section 3(C)(1). Despite the *ICS* Tribunal's recognition of the limitations on its assertion of authority, the authors regard the view expressed in this opinion as overly broad.

[105] This is a generally accepted principle in international arbitration law and theory. See N Blackaby and C Partasides, *Redfern and Hunter on International Arbitration*, n 2, 180–1; K H Böckstiegel, "The Relevance of National Arbitration Law," n 28, 230–1; P Sanders, n 60, 195; G Sacerdoti, "The New Arbitration Rules of ICC and UNCITRAL," (1977) 11 J World Trade L 2 (on the standard adopted in the New York Convention of 1958); W Park, "The *Lex loci Arbitri* and International Commercial Arbitration," (1983) 32 ICLQ 21, 23; F Mann, "*Lex Facit Arbitrum*," in P Sanders (ed), *International Arbitration*—Liber Amicorum *for Martin Domke* (1967) 157, 160–1.

[106] See K Böckstiegel, "The Relevance of National Arbitration Law," n 28, 231; F Mann, "*Lex Facit Arbitrum*," n 105, 161. See also M Ferrante, "About the nature (national or a-national, contractual or jurisdictional) of ICC awards under the *New York Convention*," in J Schultsz and A van den Berg (eds), *The Art of Arbitration* (1982) 129, 134–5; and Y Derains, "France as a Place for International Arbitration," in *The Art of Arbitration*, 111, 112. See also M Aden, *Internationale Handelsschiedsgerichtbarkeit*, n 778, 24.

[107] A Redfern and M Hunter, *Law and Practice of International Commercial Arbitration* (2nd edn 1991) 88. See also W Craig "Uses and Abuses of Appeal from Awards," n 79, 180 ("The State where the arbitration takes place has the power to regulate how an arbitration procedure shall be held on its territory or, for that matter, whether it shall be held at all.").

[108] In practice this has not been frequently done either. See A J van den Berg, *The New York Arbitration Convention of 1958: Towards a Uniform Judicial Interpretation* (1981) 292.

[109] See, eg, W Craig, "Uses and Abuses of Appeal from Awards," n 79, 183.

possible. In other words, do the UNCITRAL Rules envisage the possibility of "a-national" arbitration, detached from any control exercised by the local law?[110]

The relevant wording allows the interpretation "that Article 1(2) only provides for national law 'if applicable,' and, thereby does not exclude the possibility that none is applicable."[111] Although the sovereignty aspect usually does exclude such a possibility, this is not the case where the territorial state has accepted the non-applicability of its own mandatory norms, or where it has no mandatory norms. In the latter, perhaps somewhat theoretical[112] case, it is clear that Article 1(2) has no practical relevance. If, on the other hand, the territorial state does have mandatory norms from which derogations are permitted (eg in international arbitrations), the detachment of the proceedings from the national law is conceivable, provided the parties, in accordance with Article 1(1), or the arbitral tribunal, by virtue of Article 17(1), are in agreement. However, in the absence of a clear agreement between the parties, the tribunal should not detach the proceeding from national law. The very existence of Article 1(2) in the applicable procedural rules might be understood by courts to signify the parties' intention to keep the arbitration under the control of the local law. Further, as indicated earlier, non-observance of the party agreement may, in turn, have harmful consequences.[113]

(b) Confidentiality in UNCITRAL arbitration

Privacy is a long-established hallmark of international commercial arbitration. One of the principal attractions of arbitration is the ability to resolve commercial disputes discreetly, without exposure to the public scrutiny often associated with national court proceedings.[114] In most arbitrations, the discretion of the parties is enough to prevent sensitive information from being disclosed to the public. However, privacy, even if deeply established in custom, does not equate to confidentiality, which implicates a legal obligation to avoid public disclosure of sensitive information. Thus, it is not imprudent to expect that international arbitration will take place in a completely closed environment in which all sensitive information and documents remain private *and* confidential. As we will explain, the degree of disclosure may depend on other important factors, such as the existence and scope of a confidentiality agreement and/or confidentiality order, and the mandatory provisions of any governing law on confidentiality. Further, the participation of non-disputing parties in the arbitral process, namely as *amicus curiae*, may be determined by the public character of the arbitration.

The UNCITRAL Rules address only a handful of issues relating to the exclusivity of the arbitral process. Article 28(3) requires that the *hearings* "be held *in camera*." According to

---

[110] On the concept of "a-national" (also called "floating" or "delocalised") arbitration, as well as on *pros* and *cons* regarding that concept, see generally G Petrochilos, *Procedural Law in International Arbitration* (2004), Chapter 8; A Avanessian, *Iran-US Claims Tribunal in Action* (1993) 283–90; W Park, "Judicial Controls in the Arbitral Process," (1991) 3 Arb Intl 230, 242–54; J Paulsson, "Delocalisation of International Commercial Arbitration; When and Why it Matters," (1983) 32 ICLQ 53; N Blackaby and C Partasides, *Redfern and Hunter on International Arbitration*, n 2, 180–1; S Toope, *Mixed International Arbitration* (1990) 17 et seq.

[111] K H Böckstiegel, "The Relevance of National Arbitration Law," n 28, 230. This, however, is not the interpretation preferred by Böckstiegel himself.

[112] But see the Belgian law on international arbitration as discussed in connection with Article 18(1). See N Blackaby and C Partasides, *Redfern and Hunter on International Arbitration*, n 2, 191.

[113] See n 78 and n 79.

[114] See P Sanders, *The Work of UNCITRAL on Arbitration and Conciliation* (2nd rev edn 2004) 173–4; N Blackaby and C Partasides, *Redfern and Hunter on International Arbitration*, n 2, 33–4; W Craig, W Park, J Paulsson, *International Chamber of Commerce Arbitration* (3rd edn 2000) 311.

Article 34(5), the *award* may be published "only with consent of both parties." However, other important issues regarding confidentiality are not addressed, such as the extent to which written submissions or supporting materials, such as witness statements, expert reports, or documentary evidence, may be made public. The arbitration rules of various arbitral institutions have addressed these issues with notably greater specificity and depth than the UNCITRAL Rules.[115] The limited approach of the Rules toward confidentiality matters raises two important issues: (1) whether a general duty of confidentiality can be inferred from the existing provisions of the Rules or from the arbitral process in general; and (2) whether, in the absence of such a general duty, confidentiality can be preserved through a confidentiality agreement by the parties or a procedural order by the arbitral tribunal.

Since Articles 28(3) and 34(5) of the Rules affirmatively address discrete aspects of the arbitral process (the hearing, the deliberations, and the award), we conclude that they alone cannot give rise to a general duty of confidentiality. Whether a duty of confidentiality can be inferred from the arbitration agreement (perhaps along with the UNCITRAL Rules as incorporated into that agreement) is a more relevant question that has divided many national courts.[116] The common view in English law is that the parties' arbitration agreement gives rise to an implied duty of confidentiality.[117] In contrast, Australia, the United States, and Sweden have taken the view that a party to the arbitral proceedings is not bound by an inherent duty of confidentiality.[118] For example, in *Panhandle Eastern Corporation*, a US district court ruled that absent express provisions on confidentiality in the arbitral rules of procedure "parties to arbitration proceedings or the independent arbitration tribunal which conducts those proceedings" are not bound to keep documents confidential.[119] Some arbitral institutions have followed this approach.[120]

Given the divergence of national law approaches toward confidentiality, the parties to arbitration are well advised to research carefully the *lex arbitri*. The Model Law does not contain any provisions on confidentiality. At least one jurisdiction has adopted a modified version of the Model Law that includes provisions providing for significant protections

---

[115] See, eg, 2001 WIPO Arbitration Rules, art 52; 1998 LCIA Rules, art 30.1; 2010 AAA Rules, Rule 34. For Professor Sanders's views on supplementing the Rules with provisions on confidentiality, see P Sanders, "Has the Moment Come to Revise the Arbitration Rules of UNCITRAL?" (2004) 20(3) Arb Intl 243, 266–7.

[116] The UNCITRAL Notes observe: "there is no uniform answer in national laws as to the extent to which the participants in an arbitration are under the duty to observe the confidentiality of information relating to the case." UNCITRAL Notes, n 68, para 31.

[117] See *Ali Shipping Corporation v Shipyard Trogir* [1999] 1 Weekly L Rep 314. Limitations on the general duty of confidentiality with respect to the award are set forth in *Associated Electric and Gas Insurance Ltd v The European Reinsurance Company of Zurich* [2003] UKPC 11.

[118] *Esso Australia Resources Lt and ors v The Honourable Sidney James Plowman and ors* (1995) 128 Australian L Rep 391, (1995) 183 Commonwealth Reports 10; *United States v Panhandle Eastern Corp*, (1988) 118 Federal Rules Decisions 346 (D Del); *AI Trade Finance Inc v Bulgarian Foreign Trade Bank Ltd*, [1998] Stockholm City Court, Case No T-111-98.

[119] *Panhandle*, 118 Federal Rules Decisions at 349–50.

[120] According to the NAFTA Notes of Interpretation of Certain Chapter 11 Provisions:

Nothing in the NAFTA imposes a general duty of confidentiality on the disputing parties to a Chapter Eleven arbitration, and, subject to the application of Article 1137(4), nothing in the NAFTA precludes the Parties from providing public access to documents submitted to, or issued by a Chapter Eleven tribunal. In ICSID arbitration, the ICSID system does not expressly require the parties to keep awards confidential.

Notes of Interpretation, section A(1), adopted by NAFTA Free Trade Commission on July 31, 2001, reprinted in (2001) 13(6) World Trade & Arb Materials 139. See also M Stevens, "Revisiting Confidentiality," News from ICSID, Spring 2000 (vol 17(1)).

against public disclosure.[121] In addition to the *lex arbitri*, the laws on confidentiality of other relevant jurisdictions should be considered, such as the law of a jurisdiction in which the award might be enforced, since enforcing courts are likely to address claims of confidentiality in accordance with local rules on disclosure.[122]

The best protection against disclosure of sensitive information relating to the arbitral process is a precise and comprehensive agreement by the parties on all confidentiality matters. A confidentiality agreement may assume many forms with equal effectiveness. It may be fashioned as part of the arbitration agreement,[123] as a modification of the Rules, in accordance with Article 1(1), or as a separate agreement reached by the parties during the early phase of arbitration. Regardless of the agreement's form, the arbitral tribunal may wish to issue a procedural order, pursuant to Article 17(1), which endorses any agreed-upon terms of confidentiality or, if agreement has not been reached with respect to one or more terms, establishes such terms to the extent necessary. Once embodied in a procedural order, the terms of confidentiality are binding on the parties and enforceable by the tribunal, if necessary, in accordance with the relevant provisions of the UNCITRAL Rules.[124]

As to the substance of a confidentiality agreement, the UNCITRAL Notes recommend inclusion of one or more of the following matters:

[1] the material or information that is to be kept confidential (e.g. pieces of evidence, written and oral arguments, the fact that the arbitration is taking place, identity of the arbitrators, content of the award); [2] measures for maintaining confidentiality of such information and hearings; [3] whether any special procedures should be employed for maintaining the confidentiality of information transmitted by electronic means (e.g. because communication equipment is shared by several users, or because electronic mail over public networks is considered not sufficiently protected against unauthorized access); [4] circumstances in which confidential information may be disclosed in part or in whole (e.g. in the context of disclosures of information in the public domain, or if required by law or a regulatory body).[125]

---

[121] New Zealand's Arbitration law provides:

14. *Disclosure of information relating to arbitral proceedings and award prohibited*

(1) Subject to subsection (2), an arbitration agreement, unless otherwise agreed by the parties, is deemed to provide that the parties shall not publish, disclose, or communicate any information relating to arbitral proceedings under the agreement or to an award made in these proceedings.
(2) Nothing in subsection (1) prevents the publication, disclosure, or communication of information referred to in that subsection
   (a) If the publication, disclosure, or communication is contemplated by this Act; or
   (b) To a professional or other adviser of any of the parties.

[122] See, eg, *Panhandle*, 118 Federal Rules Decisions at 349–50.

[123] Such a form may also include penalties for disclosure. See L Trakman, "Confidentiality in International Commercial Arbitration," (2002) 18(1) Arb Intl 1, 9.

[124] For example, in accordance with Articles 40 and 43 of the Rules, the arbitral tribunal may apportion the costs of additional proceedings caused by a breach of confidentiality to the breaching party. See *Pope & Talbot Inc* and *Government of Canada*, Decision (*Ad Hoc* Proceeding, 1976 UNCITRAL Rules, NAFTA Chapter Eleven (September 27, 2000) (investor to pay costs of pleadings caused by breach of confidentiality by investor's counsel with understanding that investor's counsel was personally to assume all costs). Where confidentiality measures are in place and a party still refuses to produce information to the tribunal on grounds that it is sensitive, the arbitral tribunal may consider drawing an adverse inference against the defaulting party pursuant to Article 30(3).

[125] UNCITRAL Notes, n 68, para 32 (numbers added). For an example of a comprehensive confidentiality order which defines the scope of protected information covered by the order, establishes procedures for designating material as protected and for resolving disputes concerning proposed designations, establishes procedures for withholding protected information from another party, addresses disclosures required by law, provides rules regarding the confidentiality of hearings, among other things, see *William Ralph Clayton*, et al and *Government of Canada*, Procedural Order No 2 (May 2, 2009) (PCA administered, 1976 UNCITRAL Rules, NAFTA Chapter Eleven).

A party often will find it necessary to disclose confidential information to a third party who is involved in the arbitration, such as counsel, officials or employees of a party, experts or witnesses. Accordingly, to elaborate on matter [2] above, it is good practice to require each such individual to execute a separate confidentiality agreement which establishes the terms of confidentiality and the obligation to return all original documents and copies to the relevant parties when the arbitration concludes.[126]

Even where the duty of confidentiality is firmly established by a confidentiality agreement, a confidentiality order, or by national law, that duty is typically not absolute. Information or materials designated as confidential in arbitration may be subject to disclosure for various reasons. For example, disputing parties may be subject to competing or superseding contractual obligations to disclose information relating to a dispute to shareholders, creditors, insurance companies or auditors. In addition, where one of the disputing parties is a sovereign nation, that party's national laws on public access to government documents may compel disclosure of confidential information.[127]

During revision of the Rules, the issue arose whether to include a general provision on the confidentiality of the proceedings. Proponents highlighted the risks of not containing such a provision, as demonstrated by the opinion of the English Court of Appeal in *City of Moscow v Bankers Trust*, which held that an award challenged in English courts could be made public despite one party's expectation of privacy.[128] Opponents cautioned that a general confidentiality provision in the Rules would limit the flexibility of the tribunal and the parties to respond to a complex and evolving area of the law and practice.[129] They also saw drafting a general provision as "extremely problematic," noting the difficulties in addressing issues such as "when the duty of confidentiality arose and ended, whether that duty extended to persons other than the parties, such as witnesses and experts, and what exceptions should be made to that duty."[130] Some also believed a general provision would contravene the current trend toward greater transparency in international proceedings. Thus, according to the prevailing view in the Working Group, the issue of confidentiality was left to be addressed on a case-by-case basis by the tribunal and the parties.[131]

(c) **Non-disputing party (*amicus*) submissions in UNCITRAL arbitration**

Another issue regarding the openness of the arbitral process is the level of participation in proceedings by non-parties (other than counsel, experts, and witnesses). Non-parties have no standing to bring claims before the arbitral tribunal as interveners if they are not

---

[126] Even then, as leading commentators observe, "the difficulty with confidentiality agreements becomes apparent if a document does become public knowledge. It will never be easy to establish which party is responsible for the document's release, and it may be difficult for the disclosing party to prove that it suffered loss as a result of any breach by its adversary." E Gaillard and J Savage (eds) *Fouchard, Gaillard, Goldman on International Arbitration* (1999) 693. The confidentiality order and the third-party confidentiality agreement used in *United Parcel Services* (1976 Rules) are reprinted in section 3(C).

[127] In the NAFTA context, for example, disclosure may be necessary pursuant to the US Freedom of Information Act or the Canadian Access to Information Act.

[128] *Department of Economic Policy and Development, City of Moscow v Bankers Trust Co. And Anr.* (2004) EWCA 314 (Court of Appeal of England and Wales).

[129] UNCITRAL, 40th Session, UN Doc A/CN.9/614, n 5, at 19, para 85; UNCITRAL, 40th Session, UN Doc A/CN.9/619, n 5, at 25, para 130.

[130] UNCITRAL, 40th Session, UN Doc A/CN.9/619, n 5, at 25, para 129.

[131] UNCITRAL, 40th Session, UN Doc A/CN.9/614, n 5, at 19, para 86. One example in support of retaining maximum flexibility under the Rules with respect to confidentiality was that "contracts relating to intellectual property demanded a high degree of confidentiality." UNCITRAL, 40th Session, UN Doc A/CN.9/619, n 5, at 25, para 131.

contractually bound by the arbitral agreement. The participation of non-disputing parties as *amicus curiae* in special circumstances is another matter, however. The UNCITRAL Rules contain no express provision on *amicus curiae* participation. Investor–state arbitral tribunals, however, have concluded that they may accept submissions by non-disputing parties as *amicus curiae* under their general authority to conduct the proceedings in the manner deemed appropriate.[132] This conclusion is consistent with the practice of the Iran–United States Claims Tribunal, according to which outside involvement by non-disputing parties has been deemed acceptable.[133]

The arbitral tribunal's authority to accept *amicus* submissions is circumscribed by other important provisions of the Rules. The arbitral tribunal's procedural powers under Article 17(1) are tempered by that same provision's requirement to treat the parties with equality. Accordingly, *amicus* submissions may not be used in a way which is unduly burdensome for the parties in terms of time and cost or which complicates or substantially lengthens the arbitral process. An arbitral tribunal thus may wish to place restrictions on the scope and length of any submissions made by non-disputing parties.[134] Moreover, the acceptability of *amicus* submissions does not imply any higher level of participation by non-disputing parties. Article 28(3) expressly bars all non-parties from attending the hearings, unless the parties agree otherwise.[135] Further, with respect to access to confidential information, *amicus curiae* would obtain no greater access to confidential materials than any other member of the public would in accordance with an applicable confidentiality agreement, procedural order, or national law provision.

While generally permissible under the UNCITRAL Rules, *amicus* submissions are unlikely to be utilized in most arbitrations. Traditional resistance by the parties in a commercial arbitration to disclosing any information about their dispute to the public may likely stymie any outside participation.[136] In a more public forum, such as investor–state arbitration, the presence of a sovereign party and "the important public character of the

---

[132] See *Methanex Corp* (1976 Rules); *United Parcel Services of America* (1976 Rules); both reprinted in section 3(C)(2). In another case, the tribunal exercised its discretion by not accepting *amicus* submissions. See *Chevron* (1976 Rules), reprinted in section 3(C)(2). The disputing parties also can agree to allow *amicus* submissions. See *Glamis Gold Ltd* (1976 Rules), reprinted in section 3(C)(2). For further discussion, see generally L Mistelis, "Confidentiality and Third Party Participation: *UPS v. Canada* and *Methanex Corp v. United States*" in T Weiler (ed) *International Investment Law and Arbitration: Leading Cases from the ICSID, NAFTA, Bilateral Treaties and Customary International Law* (2005) 183 et seq.

[133] See 1983 Rules of Procedural of the Iran–US Claims Tribunal, note 5 to art 15, reprinted in Appendix 5. In Case No A/17 between the United States and Iran, the Tribunal applied Note 5 to permit a third-party financial institution to attend Tribunal hearings. *United States of America* and *Islamic Republic of Iran*, Decision No DEC 37-A17-FT (May 13, 1985), reprinted in 8 Iran-US CTR 189, 191 n 5 (1985-I). See also *United Parcel Services of America* (1976 Rules), para 64, reprinted in section 3(C) (citing the practice of the WTO and distinguishing that of the ICJ). UNCITRAL has also recognized that Article 15(1) of the 1976 UNCITRAL Rules, now Article 17(1) of the 2010 UNCITRAL Rules, "could be interpreted as encompassing power of the arbitral tribunal to accept [third-party] interventions, for example in the form of *amicus curiae* briefs." *Settlement of Commercial Disputes: Revision of the UNCITRAL Arbitration Rules, Note by the Secretariat*, UNCITRAL, UN Doc A/CN.9/WG.II/WP.143 at 15, para 69 (2006).

[134] For example, in *United Parcel Services of America*, the tribunal deemed *amicus* submissions on the questions of jurisdiction and the place of arbitration inappropriate. *United Parcel Services of America* (1976 Rules), para 71, reprinted in section 3(C)(2).

[135] According to UNCITRAL, "[w]hile ensuring the privacy of proceedings does not necessarily also ensure confidentiality, privacy assists by limiting the number of people who have access to the arbitration hearing." *Possible Future Work*, n 59, para 63.

[136] Most arbitral institutions facilitate the exclusivity of commercial arbitration by employing strict internal rules and measures on privacy.

matters in issue" are clearly more conducive to the acceptance of *amicus* submissions.[137] This is not to say, however, that non-disputing party participation could not occur in international commercial arbitration where the arbitration arises under a national statute with a public purpose or the issues bear heavily upon the public interest.

Users of the UNCITRAL Rules should also bear in mind the work of the Working Group on rules of transparency in investor–state arbitration.[138] At the time of this writing, the Working Group was close to reaching consensus on a rule on *amicus* submissions. The current draft of the rule incorporates elements of Rule 37(2) of the ICSID Arbitration Rules on non-disputing parties and the NAFTA's Statement of the Free Trade Commission on Non-disputing Party Participation dated October 7, 2004.[139] When requesting leave to file an *amicus* submission, a third person must provide information regarding its identity, its affiliation with any disputing party, its interest in the arbitration, and the issues of fact or law it wishes to address. In determining whether to accept such a submission, the tribunal should consider whether the third person has a significant interest in the arbitration and whether the submission would assist the tribunal in determining issues of fact or law by bringing knowledge, insights, or perspectives that are different from that of the disputing parties.[140]

(d) The nature of the proceedings before the Iran–US Claims Tribunal

The status of the arbitral proceedings before the Iran–US Claims Tribunal, and their relation to the local (ie Dutch) law, is not easily characterized. The ambiguity primarily concerns the "private" element of the Tribunal proceedings, that is, the commercial cases involving private parties on one side. As to the public international arbitration between Iran and the United States, it appears that the proceedings are governed solely by the Algiers Accords and the Tribunal Rules.[141]

The Tribunal's work which resembles private arbitration is filled with ambiguity. On the one hand, factors such as the specification of The Hague as the place of arbitration, the practice according to which the Tribunal deposits its awards with the District Court of The Hague and the adoption of Article 1(2) of the 1976 UNCITRAL Rules in the 1983 Tribunal Rules may be taken to suggest that the proceedings are subject to mandatory Dutch law.[142] On the other hand, all of these factors can be explained otherwise: the specification of The Hague as the place of arbitration was made only in order to provide a neutral seat; the practice concerning deposit can be explained by practical considerations; and Article 1(3) of the 2010 UNCITRAL Rules (formerly Article 1(2) of the 1976 Rules) in itself does not exclude the possibility of no national law being "applicable."[143]

---

[137] *United Parcel Services of America* (1976 Rules), para 70, reprinted in section 3(C)(2).
[138] For a general discussion of the work of UNCITRAL in this area, see Chapter 1, section 3(G).
[139] *Report of the Working Group on Arbitration and Conciliation on the Work of its Fifty-Fifth Session* (Vienna, 3–7 October 2011), UNCITRAL, 45th Session, UN Doc A/CN.9/736, at 15, para 70 (2011).
[140] *Settlement of Commercial Disputes: Preparation of a Legal Standard on Transparency in Treaty-Based Investor-State Arbitration, Note by the Secretariat*, UNCITRAL, UN Doc A/CN.9/WG.II/WP.169 at 12, para 37 (2011).
[141] Thus the Bill on the applicability of Dutch law to the Tribunal proceedings would have governed only the cases mentioned in Article II(1) of the Claims Settlement Declaration ("...Claims of nationals of the United States against Iran and claims of nationals of Iran against the United States, and any counterclaim which arises out of the same contract, transaction or occurrence...").
[142] See W Lake and J Tucker Dana, "Judicial Review of Awards of the Iran-United States Claims Tribunal: Are the Tribunal's Awards Dutch?" (1984) 16 Law and Policy in Intl Business 755, 771–3.
[143] See W Lake and J Tucker Dana, "Judicial Review of Awards," n 142, 733–80; See also n 111.

Given these circumstances, guidance should be sought from the Tribunal's practice. The fact that the Tribunal has never referred to the mandatory norms of Dutch law is hardly alone decisive.[144] It is conceivable that, when applying the 1976 UNCITRAL Rules, as modified, the Tribunal takes for granted that any mandatory requirements of the arbitration law of the Netherlands are automatically complied with. A somewhat more forceful argument supporting the "a-national" characterization of the Tribunal proceedings is found in the Chambers' orders emphasizing that the proceedings are governed "by the Tribunal Rules and by no national procedural system,"[145] or "by the Declaration of the Government of the Democratic and Popular Republic of Algeria and by the Tribunal Rules of Procedure."[146] These statements clearly reflect an understanding that the arbitration before the Tribunal is in no way controlled by Dutch law.

Whether or not this view of the nature of the Tribunal proceedings can be taken as the Tribunal's final word on the issue, it certainly could not overrule any contrary conclusion drawn by the territorial state, the Netherlands, or by courts in the Netherlands. Neither the Dutch courts nor the Dutch government have taken a definite stand. In 1983 the Dutch government proposed a "Bill regarding the Applicability of Dutch Law to the Awards of the Tribunal Sitting in The Hague to Hear Claims between Iran and the United States,"[147] which would have declared the Tribunal's awards rendered in cases involving private parties to be Dutch, and made it possible to challenge them before Dutch courts (though only on very limited grounds). The legislative process, however, was frozen, largely due to criticism leveled against the Bill by Iran.[148] Iran, in turn, agreed to withdraw ten lawsuits filed in 1983 at the District Court of the Hague against the Tribunal's awards allegedly rendered in breach of the Dutch arbitration law.[149]

Thus, the relationship between the Tribunal proceedings and Dutch law remains untested by the courts and authorities of the Netherlands. Opposite views have been put forward in Dutch legal writing,[150] and the following passage from the preamble to the Dutch Bill also shows the ambiguity surrounding the question: "It is by no means clear that the decisions and awards of the Tribunal concerning private claims would be characterized, by Dutch courts, as arbitral decisions or awards under the relevant provisions of the Dutch Code of Civil Procedure."[151]

Faced with this problem, a court of another country should take into account the possibility of the Tribunal awards being "a-national," that is, not under the control of the procedural law of the Netherlands. It is in connection with efforts to enforce Tribunal

---

[144] For an example of a case (not decided by the Iran–US Claims Tribunal) in which the tribunal has explicitly addressed the question of compatibility of its proceedings with mandatory local law, see *Wintershall AG* (1976 Rules), reprinted in section 4(C) (under Article 18).

[145] *Amman & Whitney* (1983 Tribunal Rules), reprinted in section 3(D)(1).

[146] *Fedders Corp* (1983 Tribunal Rules), reprinted in section 3(D)(1).

[147] An English translation can be found in (July 15, 1983) Iranian Assets Litigation Rep 6,899. On the contents of the Bill, see also W Lake and J Tucker Dana, "Judicial Review of Awards," n 142, 783–6.

[148] The Bill was criticized basically on two grounds: first, for facilitating the enforceability of the awards, as Dutch arbitral awards, under the New York Convention and, second, for limiting the grounds of challenge against the awards so as to make the setting aside of them a very unlikely possibility. Letter of Mohammed K Eshragh, the Agent of the Islamic Republic of Iran before the Iran–US Claims Tribunal to the Dutch Ministry of Foreign Affairs of February 24, 1984, reprinted in Mealey's Litigation Reporter 394 (April 6, 1984). See also W Lake and J Tucker Dana, "Judicial Review of Awards," n 142, 778, 786–7.

[149] W Lake and J Tucker Dana, "Judicial Review of Awards," n 142, 759 et seq.

[150] See L Hardenberg, "The Awards of the Iran-United States Claims Tribunal Seen in Connection with the Law of the Netherlands," (September 1984) Intl Business Lawyer 337. See A J van den Berg, "Proposed Dutch Law on the Iran-U.S. Claims Settlement Declaration—A Reaction to Mr. Hardenberg's Article," (September 1984) Intl Business Lawyer 341.

[151] W Lake and J Tucker Dana, "Judicial Review of Awards," n 142, 778.

awards outside the Netherlands that the issue may arise—indeed, has arisen. According to some experts, "the primary international Convention in the field, the New York Arbitration Convention of 1958, does not apply to awards which are not governed by a national arbitration law."[152] However, an equally eminent author has noted that "[t]his is not the black letter of the Convention—in fact, to many it is an impermissible reading."[153]

Such differences of opinion indicate that the enforceability of "a-national" awards under the New York Convention is at least uncertain. Indeed, one of the side effects expected from the Dutch Bill was to guarantee the enforceability of the awards under the Convention.[154]

The question whether the awards of the Iran–US Claims Tribunal fall under the New York Convention arose in connection with the *Gould* case, in which the Tribunal awarded US$3.6 million to the Iranian Respondent on the basis of its counterclaim.[155] It will be recalled that the payment mechanism with a special Security Account works only in favor of US claimants.[156] As Gould refused to comply with its payment obligation, the Iranian party had to seek the enforcement of the award through other avenues. After the Full Tribunal confirmed in Case A/21 that the United States government was not directly responsible for the implementation of the awards rendered against its nationals,[157] the Iranian party commenced enforcement action in the United States. The case first came before the District Court of the Central District of California[158] and then before the Ninth Circuit Court of Appeals.[159] Both courts substantially agreed on the applicability of the New York Convention.[160]

---

[152] A J van den Berg, "Proposed Dutch Law,", n 150, 343. See also A J van den Berg, *The New York Convention*, n 108, 34–40. Support for this argument is believed to be found, *inter alia*, in Article V(1)(d) of the Convention, according to which the recognition and enforcement of an award may be refused if the "composition of the arbitral authority or the arbitral procedure was not in accordance with the agreement of the parties, or, failing such agreement, was not in accordance with *the law of the country where the arbitration took place.*" See A J van den Berg, *The New York Convention*, n 108, 34–9 (emphasis added).

[153] W Craig, "Uses and Abuses of Appeal from Awards," n 79, 201. Indeed, Article V(1) (d) of the New York Convention relied on by the authors referred to in the previous note can also be construed as envisaging control by national law and party agreement as alternatives. Moreover, an award not subject to judicial control at the seat of arbitration as such is not excluded by the basic definition contained in Article 1(1) of the Convention: "This Convention shall apply to the recognition and enforcement of arbitral awards made in the territory of a State other than the State where the recognition and enforcement of such awards are sought...." For views favoring the enforceability under the New York Convention of awards not subject to the law of the place of arbitration, see W Lake and J Tucker Dana, "Judicial Review of Awards," n 142, 789 et seq.; V Saario, "Asianosaisautonomia kansainväliseen kauppaan liittyvässä välimiesmenettelyssä" (Party Autonomy in International Commercial Arbitration), in Finnish, in *Juhlajulkaisu* (Essays in Honor of) *Matti Ylöstalo* (1987) 341, 345.

[154] W Lake and J Tucker Dana, "Judicial Review of Awards," n 142, 778.

[155] *Gould Marketing Inc* and *Ministry of Defence of the Islamic Republic of Iran*, Award No 136–49/50 (June 29, 1984), reprinted in 6 Iran-US CTR 272 (1984-II).

[156] See Chapter 1 section 2(B)(1).

[157] *Islamic Republic of Iran* and *United States of America*, Decision No DEC 62-A21-FT (May 4, 1987), reprinted in 14 Iran-US CTR 324 (1987–1). The Tribunal, however, held that it is "incumbent on each State Party to provide some procedure or mechanism whereby enforcement may be obtained within its national jurisdiction, and to ensure that the successful party has access thereto." Para 15, 14 Iran-US CTR 331 (1987–1).

[158] *Ministry of Defence of the Islamic Republic of Iran v Gould, Inc*, CV 87–03673 RG, Order of January 14, 1988, reprinted in (1988) Mealey's Intl Arb Rep 3.

[159] *Ministry of Defence of the Islamic Republic of Iran v Gould Inc*, Decision filed October 23, 1989, [1989] CDOS 7832.

[160] The District Court concluded that the award could not be recognized and enforced on the basis of "federal question jurisdiction." On this question, which essentially turned on whether the Algiers Accords are "self-executing," see the 14 January Order, n 158, 4–5, and R Lewis, "What Goes Around Comes Around: Can Iran Enforce Awards of the Iran–US Claims Tribunal in the United States," (1987) 26 Columbia J Transnatl L 515, 528–49. The Court of Appeal did not reach the question, because it held that jurisdiction existed under section 203 of the Federal Arbitration Act concerning the New York Convention. *Ministry of Defence of the Islamic Republic of Iran v Gould Inc*, [1989] CDOS at 7836.

Thus it was held that the requirement concerning a written arbitral agreement[161] had been met, despite the fact that the agreement had been concluded by the governments of the respective parties, and not by the parties themselves.[162]

Gould's remaining objection to the jurisdiction was that the New York Convention allegedly contained "an implicit requirement that the Convention applies only to arbitral awards made in accordance with the national arbitration law of a Party State."[163] To this the Ninth Circuit Court of Appeals responded as follows:

> Section 203 does not contain a separate jurisdictional requirement that the award be rendered subject to a "national law." Language pertaining to the "choice of law" issue is not mentioned, or even alluded to, in Article 1, which lays out the Convention's scope of applicability. In addition, although it is a close question, the fairest reading of the Convention itself appears to be that it applies to the enforcement of non-national awards.[164]

The Court then concluded "that an award need not be made 'under a national law' for a court to entertain jurisdiction over its enforcement pursuant to the Convention."[165]

In 1992, the applicability of the New York Convention to Tribunal awards was confirmed by the United States Court of Appeals for the Second Circuit in *Avco*.[166] In the circumstances of that case, however, the enforcement of an award made in favor of Iran was refused on the ground that, before the Tribunal, Avco had been "unable to present [its] case" within the meaning of Article V(I)(b) of the New York Convention.[167] The Court held that, while enforceable under the Convention, the Tribunal awards are also "subject to the defences to enforcement provided for in the Convention."[168] According to the Court, Avco had been denied due process before the Tribunal in such a way as to justify the non-enforcement of the award rendered against the company.[169]

The *Gould* and *Avco* cases set important precedents regarding both the scope of the New York Convention in general and the enforcement of Tribunal awards in particular. *Avco*, in particular, shows that the New York Convention provides the competent court with power to exercise certain ultimate control over the fairness of the Tribunal

---

[161] New York Convention, art II(1).

[162] See *Ministry of Defence of the Islamic Republic of Iran v Gould, Inc*, [1989] CDOS at 7835. The Court of Appeal distinguished the English case *Dallal v Bank Mellat*, Queens Bench Division (Commercial Court), [1986] 1 All ER 239, in which what appears to be a contrary conclusion concerning the arbitration agreement was reached. In *Dallal*, the Tribunal award was, however, recognized on the basis of "international comity," as a consequence of which the claim before the English Court was struck out. For the award by the Tribunal, see *Dallal* and *Islamic Republic of Iran*, Award No 53–149–1 (June 10, 1983), reprinted in 3 Iran-US CTR 10 (1983-III).

[163] *Gould, Inc*, at 7835.

[164] *Gould, Inc*, at 7835.

[165] *Gould, Inc*, at 7836.

[166] *Iran Aircraft Industries and Iran Helicopter Support and Renewal Company v Avco Corporation*, 980 F 2d 141 (US Ct of Apps 2nd Cir, 1992), reprinted in (1992) 7(12) Mealey's Intl Arb Rep A-1.

[167] *Avco*, at A-6.

[168] *Avco*, at A-5.

[169] Certain of Avco's claims were based on a large number of invoices which were not presented to the Tribunal. At the pre-hearing conference held in May 1985 Avco was notified by the then Chairman of the Chamber, Judge Mangård, that the Tribunal was not "very much enthusiastic" (at A-3) about getting all the invoices, but that Avco should have an independent audit of the invoices. In its Award of 18 July 1988, the Tribunal, in a different composition, held—as stated with regard to one of the claims in question—that it "cannot grant Avco's claim solely on the basis of an affidavit and a list of invoices, even if the existence of the invoices was certified by an independent audit." *Avco Corp* and *Iran Aircraft Industries*, Award No 377–261–3 (July 18, 1988), reprinted in 19 Iran-US CTR 200, 214 (1988-II). Respondents (and Counterclaimants) Iran Aircraft Industries and Iran Helicopter Support and Renewal Co were awarded $ 3.5 million (against the dissent of Judge Brower, at 231).

proceedings.[170] However, in the absence of Dutch judicial pronouncements, the cases discussed do not definitively settle the question concerning the relationship of the Tribunal proceedings to Dutch law.[171]

Another remaining question is whether the Tribunal has inherent power to reopen its proceedings in exceptional circumstances.[172] In one decision the Tribunal, while leaving the question open, cautiously suggested in an *obiter*-like manner that "it might possibly be concluded that a tribunal, like the present one, which is to adjudicate a large group of cases and for a protracted period of time would by implication, until the adjournment and dissolution of the tribunal, have the authority to revise decisions induced by fraud."[173]

(e) Concluding comments

Whatever the nature of the Tribunal proceedings or Tribunal awards, a completely a-national arbitration under the UNCITRAL Rules does not seem practically possible or desirable in normal *ad hoc* arbitration. In such proceedings the effect of Articles 1(3) and 17(1) is to subject the arbitration to at least the mandatory procedural norms of the *lex loci arbitri*. Normally this is not likely to hamper the proceedings in any substantial way, as the concurrent observance of the UNCITRAL Rules guarantees that no non-derogable national norms are circumvented. On the other hand, considering the uncertainties and differing attitudes among various jurisdictions concerning the applicability of the New York Convention to "a-national" awards, this kind of connection with a national legal system is likely to facilitate the enforcement of the award in other jurisdictions. These questions are explored further when the place of arbitration is discussed under Article 18. In this connection a few final comments on the scope of Article 17(1) are due.

Subject to the limitations discussed above, "the arbitral tribunal may conduct the arbitration in such manner as it considers appropriate." Except for the mandatory norms of the *lex loci arbitri*, it does not have to follow any national rules; on the other hand, if they deem it useful, the arbitrators can choose a specific national law of procedure.[174] As already noted, if they do choose a specific national law, the arbitrators should give preference to the law of the place of arbitration. General reliance on any national law, however, can

---

[170] As long as awards against Iran are satisfied from the Security Account, this control, of course, may only work in favor of unsuccessful American parties before the Tribunal. This lack of balance is compensated only to a very limited extent by the control exercised in connection with payments made by the Federal Reserve to American claimants. In *Gordon Williams*, Award No 342–187–3 (December 18, 1987), reprinted in 17 Iran-US CTR 269 (1987-III), in which the named claimant turned out to be a fictitious entity created by an Iranian national, no payment was made. The funds were returned to The Hague after a US court had concluded that the award had been obtained by fraud. See D Bederman, "Nationality of Individual Claimants before the Iran-United States Claims Tribunal," (1993) 42 ICLQ 119, 121.

[171] Although the question is open in light of the case law, much can be said in favor of the view that the Tribunal proceedings are governed by the Dutch legal system. For an extensive analysis to this effect, see D Caron, "The Nature of the Iran-United States Claims Tribunal and the Evolving Structure of International Dispute Resolution," (1990) 84 AJIL 104. See also Chapter 10. For further discussion on this question, see S Toope, *Mixed International Arbitration*, n 110, 263 et seq.; A Avanessian, *Iran-US Claims Tribunal in Action*, n 110, 272 et seq.; and D Jones, "The Iran-United States Claims Tribunal: Private Rights and State Responsibility," (1984) 24 Virginia J Intl L 259.

[172] The question is addressed in detail in section 5 of Chapter 26 on inherent power to reconsider.

[173] *Ram Intl Industries* and *Air Force of the Islamic Republic of Iran*, Decision No DEC 118–148–1 (December 28, 1993), para 20 (footnote omitted). See also *Cherafat* (1983 Tribunal Rules), reprinted in section 3(D)(1). The *Gordon Williams* Award, n 170, has not been vacated by the Tribunal. See also A Mouri, "Striking a Balance between the Finality of Award and the Right to a Fair Judgment: What is the Contribution of the Iran-United States Claims Tribunal?" (1993) IV Finnish Ybk Intl L 1.

[174] K H Böckstiegel, "The Relevance of National Arbitration Law," n 28, 232.

be dispensed with, as the UNCITRAL Rules themselves contain a rather comprehensive procedural order.[175] Any lacunae that the rules may leave can be filled by creative application of discretion, whereby procedural models may be borrowed from various legal systems. For example, without selecting any procedural system as a whole, the arbitral tribunal may follow common law or civil law principles, or a mixture of both, concerning witnesses and evidence, depending on which kind of legal system with which the parties are most familiar.[176] They may also establish specific procedural devices, such as the possibility, provided for in note 5 to the Tribunal Rules of the Iran–US Claims Tribunal, of utilizing non-parties as a kind of *amicus curiae*.[177] As the Rules contain no provision on power of attorney, it is (unless the mandatory provisions of the *lex loci arbitri* provide otherwise) up to the arbitral tribunal to decide whether this is required of counsel of the parties. By virtue of its wide discretion under Article 17(1), the tribunal is also free to use the administrative and technical services of an arbitral institution.[178]

(2) *Provisional timetable and modifications of time periods—Article 17(2)*

(a) Provisional timetable

Once constituted, the arbitral tribunal has principal responsibility for directing the progress of the arbitration, including the timing of the proceedings. Beyond the exchange of the notice of arbitration and the response to the notice (which is likely to occur before constitution of the tribunal), the Rules recommend only that the time period for submitting written pleadings should not exceed 45 days.[179] While such matters would in any event fall within the tribunal's discretion under the Rules to conduct the proceedings, the first sentence of Article 17(2), which is new to the 2010 Rules, expressly requires the arbitral tribunal to establish a "provisional timetable of the arbitration."[180]

The addition of Article 17(2) principally aims to enhance the efficiency of the proceedings,[181] a goal confirmed by the requirement that the tribunal create the provisional timetable "as soon as practicable after its constitution." Without a provisional timetable, the parties would unquestionably be at a loss as to how to organize themselves and when to apply their resources in order to meet the demands of the arbitration.[182] Article 17(2) thus serves the goal of efficiency by requiring ("shall") the arbitral tribunal to establish a

---

[175] See P Sanders, "Commentary on UNCITRAL Arbitration Rules," n 60, 195; M Aden, *Internationale Handelsschiedsgerichtbarkeit*, n 778, 50–1.

[176] In this particular respect resort may be had to the supplementary IBA Rules on the Taking of Evidence in International Commercial Arbitration. See Introduction to Chapter 18 on Article 27.

[177] For the text of note 5 of the 1983 Rules of Procedure of the Iran—US Claims Tribunal, see Appendix 5. For the application, see *Drucker* (1983 Tribunal Rules); and *E-Systems* (1983 Tribunal Rules); both reprinted in section 3(D)(1). For a general discussion of the involvement of non-disputing parties, such as *amicus curiae*, see section 3(B)(1)(c).

[178] In 1982 UNCITRAL adopted certain guidelines for both arbitral and related institutions willing to conduct administered arbitration under the UNCITRAL Rules and those ready to take a more limited role as appointing authority and a provider of administrative services. See *Recommendations to Assist Arbitral Institutions and Other Interested Bodies with regard to Arbitrations under the UNCITRAL Arbitration Rules*, reprinted in (1982) XIII UNCITRAL Ybk 420, and in I Dore, *Arbitration and Conciliation under the UNCITRAL Rules: A textual Analysis*, Appendix 3 (1986). See also Chapter 1.

[179] 2010 UNCITRAL Arbitration Rules, art 25.

[180] For the origins of the rule, see J Paulsson and G Petrochilos, "Revision of the UNCITRAL Rules," (A Report Commissioned by the UNCITRAL Secretariat), March 31, 2006, at 63–4.

[181] Report of Working Group II (Arbitration and Conciliation) on the Work of its Fifty-Second Session (New York, 1–5 February 2010), UNCITRAL, 43rd Session, UN Doc A/CN.9/688, at 19, para 85 (2010).

[182] G Born, *International Commercial Arbitration* (2009) 1813–15.

provisional timetable, leaving no discretion under the Rules to do otherwise, and by ensuring that it take this step as one of its first orders of business.[183]

At the same time, the provisional timetable cannot be established without first "inviting the parties to express their views." Thus, the Rules seek to strike a careful balance between efficiency of the proceedings and fairness to the parties. Consultation with the parties on the provisional timetable is certain to yield practical information, such as the existing of scheduling conflicts or the occurrence of holidays. Moreover, it may serve to provide the arbitral tribunal with an understanding of the parties' capabilities (or limitations) with respect to their participation in the arbitral proceedings, thus allowing for consideration of how best to schedule the proceedings in a manner consistent with the principles of equal treatment and reasonable opportunity to present a case established in Article 17(1).[184]

Article 17(2) does not specify the mode or venue for establishing the provisional timetable. These matters are left to the arbitral tribunal's discretion under Article 17(1). In practice, issues of scheduling are commonly addressed, along with other preliminary matters, at an initial procedural conference of the parties.[185]

Finally, the provisional timetable is, by its own terms, only "provisional." As explained below, the second sentence of Article 17(2) affords the arbitral tribunal discretion to modify not only the agreed schedule established in the provisional timetable, but also any other time period applicable to the arbitration.

(b) Modifications of time periods

The second sentence of Article 17(2) is also new to the UNCITRAL Rules and authorizes the tribunal at any time to "extend or abridge" any time periods applicable to the arbitration.[186] Inclusion of the provision in the 2010 Rules aimed to ensure that the arbitral tribunal, where necessary, could modify any time period in the interest of a "fair and efficient process of resolving the parties' dispute."[187] The prevailing view of the Working Group was that a new provision was necessary to achieve this goal because the arbitral tribunal's general authority to conduct the proceedings under Article 15(1) of the 1976 Rules (now Article 17(1)) was cabined by the phrase "subject to these Rules";[188] thus, it was believed that express time periods could not be changed, except by mutual agreement of the parties.

---

[183] D Kozlowska notes that a provisional timetable is important to the organization, *inter alia*, of issues regarding electronic evidence. D Kozlowska, "The Revised UNCITRAL Arbitration Rules Seen through the Prism of Electronic Disclosure," (2011) 28(1) J Intl Arb 58–61.

[184] However, there is an important balance: "[t]he arbitral tribunal may put pressure on the parties to tailor their presentations to fit within an agreed timetable; but each party must be allowed a reasonable period of time in which to present its case" N Blackaby and C Partasides, *Redfern and Hunter on International Arbitration*, n 2, 299.

[185] The UNCITRAL Rules leave broad discretion to the arbitral tribunal to schedule procedural conferences. Indeed, a proposal to revise the Rules by expressly allowing the arbitral tribunal to "hold one or more procedural conferences with the parties at any appropriate stage in the arbitral proceedings, was rejected as it was said to "overregulate the matter." *Report of Working Group II (Arbitration and Conciliation) on the Work of its Fifty-Second Session* (New York, 1–5 February 2010), UNCITRAL, 43rd Session, UN Doc A/CN.9/688, at 19, para 90 (2010).

[186] Note that Article 25 of the Rules, discussed in Chapter 16 section 3, is more limited in scope, allowing the arbitral tribunal to extend, but not abridge, the time limits for the communication of written statements beyond 45 days.

[187] UNCITRAL, 40th Session, UN Doc A/CN.9/614, n 5, at 10, para 41.

[188] UNCITRAL, 40th Session, UN Doc A/CN.9/614, n 5, at 10, para 44. See J Castello, "UNCITRAL Rules," n 34, 1469. It should be noted that some Working Group delegates believed such a provision was unnecessary because the modification of time periods under the Rules was an inherent power of the tribunal. UNCITRAL, 40th Session, UN Doc A/CN.9/614, at 10, para 43.

The power to extend or abridge time periods extends to two situations. First, the tribunal may modify any time period prescribed under the Rules, such as the express 30-day time periods for replacing an arbitrator in Article 14 or for requesting an interpretation or correction of an award or an additional award in Articles 37, 38, and 39 of the Rules. Second, it may modify any time periods "agreed by the parties," such as in the arbitration agreement or in an order or agreement memorializing the time periods established by the provisional timetable discussed. The latter power to modify, of course, does not extend beyond questions of time periods.[189]

Ultimate authority to extend or abridge a time period under the Rules resides with the arbitral tribunal.[190] However, Article 17(2) prevents a tribunal from acting before "inviting the parties to express their views." This precondition thus presupposes the existence of a proposal for modification on which the parties can comment. Though Article 17(2) does not expressly address who may make a proposal for modification, the absence of any restrictive language in Article 17(2) (eg "at the request of a party") clearly leaves it to either the parties or the arbitral tribunal. Indeed, in most cases, it will be a party who needs more time that will request an extension of a deadline. At the same time, the arbitral tribunal may propose *sua sponte* to change a time period, eg, where the arbitral tribunal legitimately requires more time than the 45 days allotted under the Rules to render an interpretation of the award.

The notion that the arbitral tribunal would have authority under Article 17(2) both to propose and decide a change to the time periods under the Rules gave many in the Working Group pause. One specific concern was that the arbitral tribunal might modify the parties' agreement on time periods, such as to complete the arbitration within a specified period of time.[191] The concern about unilateral action by the tribunal prompted numerous proposals to include language in Article 17(2) that guaranteed that the tribunal's powers would apply only "if necessary," "in exceptional circumstances," or, similar to the approach in Article 25 of the Rules, "on justified grounds."[192] No such language ultimately appears in the final version of the rule, as it appears that the requirement of "inviting the parties to express their views" was seen as an adequate check on abuse by a tribunal.[193] Further, the arbitral tribunal's powers of modification are also prescribed by the arbitral tribunal's Article 17(1) duties to treat the parties with equality, to provide them a reasonable opportunity to present their cases, to avoid unnecessary delay and expense, and to provide a fair and efficient arbitral process.

---

[189] As Webster notes, Article 17(2) does not apply to the parties' agreement on non-timing issues, such as an agreement to bifurcate issues of liability and quantum. T Webster, *Handbook of UNCITRAL Arbitration: Commentary, Precedents and Materials for UNCITRAL Based Arbitration Rules* (2010) 277 n 28.

[190] Naturally, these powers do not apply before constitution of the tribunal, as only the "arbitral tribunal" may modify time periods. One proposal before the Working Group was to grant the appointing authority the power to modify time periods pending constitution of the arbitral tribunal, but concerns were expressed that this power might create the risk of delaying the tribunal's constitution. UNCITRAL, 40th Session, UN Doc A/CN.9/619, n 5, at 26, para 135. However, time periods relevant to the replacement of an arbitrator would be covered.

[191] UNCITRAL, 40th Session, UN Doc A/CN.9/619, n 5, at 26, para 135; UNCITRAL, 42nd Session, UN Doc A/CN.9/665, n 21, at 23–4, para 124.

[192] UNCITRAL, 42nd Session, UN Doc A/CN.9/665, n 21, at 23–4, paras. 124–25. See also UNCITRAL, 40th Session, UN Doc A/CN.9/619, n 5, at 26, para 135 (noting a suggestion that the arbitral tribunal "should be required to provide reasons justifying any change to the procedural time periods").

[193] "The Working Group agreed that the Rules should establish the authority of the arbitral tribunal to modify the periods of time prescribed in the Rules but not to alter the general time frames that might be set by the parties in their agreements without prior consultation with the parties." UNCITRAL, 40th Session, UN Doc A/CN.9/619, at 26, para 136.

(c) Issues of general application

Article 17(2) contains new express consultation requirements ("inviting the parties to express their views") that do not appear elsewhere in the Rules. Some Working Group delegations raised concerns that their inclusion in Article 17(2) might create a negative inference with respect to other provisions of the Rules that lacked the requirement.[194] The *travaux préparatoires* thus make clear that express reference to consultation in Article 17(2) is for purposes of emphasis only; it is merely meant to "signal to the arbitral tribunals the significance of not amending periods of time without the parties being involved in that decision-making process."[195] Consultation is consequently no less appropriate in other contexts under the Rules where the rights of the disputing parties may be directly affected, and where hearing from the parties may assist the tribunal in reaching a decision that is less susceptible to criticism that a party was mistreated.

Like all provisions of the Rules, the arbitral tribunal's powers to establish a provisional timetable and extend or abridge time periods is subject to any non-derogable provisions of the applicable arbitration law, in accordance with Article 1(3).[196] Thus, any mandatory time periods established under a national arbitration law or an international investment agreement cannot be modified.

(3) Right to a hearing—Article 17(3)

Article 17(3) elaborates upon the "reasonable opportunity" of each party to present its case. According to paragraph 3, the tribunal shall hold hearings at the request of either party "at an appropriate stage of the proceedings." Hearings may be held for "the presentation of evidence by witnesses, including expert witnesses" or "oral argument."

(a) Scope of hearings

In the Preliminary Draft of the 1976 Rules, the hearing requirement was intended to apply only to hearings for the production of evidence by witnesses, whereas hearings for the presentation of oral argument were to be discretionary, unless requested by *both* parties.[197] The New Delhi Arbitration Congress, at which the Draft was discussed, "disclosed a preponderant opinion that the presentation of oral argument was a right generally available in [domestic] legal proceedings which should also be available in arbitral proceedings at the request of either party."[198] Hence, under Article 15(2) of the 1976 UNCITRAL Rules, like Article 17(3), any party has the right to have hearings not only for the presentation of witness evidence, but also for oral argument.

The scope of hearings under the UNCITRAL Model Law is broader on its face. Instead of referring to the presentation of evidence by "witnesses," Article 24(1) of the Model Law

---

[194] In Working Group discussions, it was said that the right to express views "applied in many different instances under the Rules, and it might be awkward to expressly refer to that right in [Article 17(2)] only." UNCITRAL, 42nd Session, UN Doc A/CN.9/665, n 21, at 23, paras 122.

[195] UNCITRAL, 42nd Session, UN Doc A/CN.9/665, n 21, at 23, para 122.

[196] For the Working Group's discussion on this issue, see UNCITRAL, 42nd Session, UN Doc A/CN.9/665, n 21, at 23, para 121.

[197] See *Report of the Secretary-General on the Preliminary Draft Set of Arbitration Rules*, UNCITRAL, 8th Session, UN Doc A/CN.9/97 (1974), reprinted in (1975) VI UNCITRAL Ybk 163, 173 (Draft Articles 13(2) and (3) of the 1976 Rules).

[198] See *Report of the Secretary-General on the Preliminary Draft Set of Arbitration Rules*, UNCITRAL, 8th Session, Addendum 2 (Suggested Modifications), UN Doc A/CN.9/97/Add 2, para 15 (1975), reprinted in (1975) VI UNCITRAL Ybk 182, 183. See also *Summary Record of the 6th Meeting of the Committee of the Whole (II)*, UNCITRAL, 9th Session, UN Doc A/CN.9/9/C.2/SR.6, at 2–4, paras 9–28 (1976).

provides for hearings "for the presentation of evidence" in general.[199] This wording "was intended to ensure that the provision would not be interpreted to bar types of evidence that might be deemed in some systems not to be "testimony of witnesses," such as cross-examination or the testimony of a party."[200] While the clarification may be welcomed, it is submitted that in the UNCITRAL Rules, intended for worldwide use, the concept of "witness" can and should be interpreted in a broad, non-technical sense. This has been the practice of the Iran–US Claims Tribunal where, on the one hand, a distinction has been made between witnesses in a strict sense and "party witnesses," but where, on the other hand, both categories of witnesses have been allowed to testify at hearings.[201] The practice of investor–state arbitration tribunals is similar.[202]

The limits on the right to a hearing guaranteed by Article 17(3) are not entirely clear, however. At face value, the provision appears to include the right to request hearings not only on the merits, but also on jurisdictional and other preliminary questions and even procedural matters. On the other hand, the participants of the New Delhi Congress, when referring to a right "generally available in legal proceedings," plainly did not contemplate a right to have a separate hearing on any kind of preliminary issue. Further, the inclusion of the phrase "any stage of the proceedings" in the 1976 Rules (which was not included in the Preliminary Draft) does not contradict this conclusion. The quoted phrase was added in response to the suggestion of the representative of the Soviet Union who "proposed an amendment to the effect that a party might request an oral hearing at any stage in the proceedings, not just at the beginning."[203] Thus the altered wording was not intended to have any bearing on the question of whether there is a right to a hearing on procedural and other issues, but only to clarify when a hearing can be requested. (As explained below, the phrase "any stage of the proceedings" was replaced by "an appropriate stage of the proceedings" in the 2010 UNCITRAL Rules.)

The Iran–US Claims Tribunal has interpreted corresponding Article 15(2) of the 1976 Rules so as to make the right to a hearing dependent on whether or not the question regards "procedural matters."[204] If it does, a hearing can be dispensed with, notwithstanding a party's request concerning it. The right to a hearing has been considered excluded, *inter alia*, for requests for interim measures and preliminary jurisdictional questions.[205] However, in *ad hoc* arbitration, an arbitral tribunal is advised not to proceed from such a general distinction between substantive and procedural questions unless authorized to do so by the parties. In investor–state arbitration under the UNCITRAL Rules hearings on jurisdictional matters are commonplace.

---

[199] Article 24(1) of the Model Law, as amended, provides:

Subject to any contrary agreement by the parties, the arbitral tribunal shall decide whether to hold oral hearings for the presentation of evidence or for oral argument, or whether the proceedings shall be conducted on the basis of documents and other materials. However, unless the parties have agreed that no hearings shall be held, the arbitral tribunal shall hold such hearings at an appropriate stage of the proceedings, if so requested by a party.

[200] H Holtzmann and J Neuhaus, *A Guide to the UNCITRAL Model Law*, n 7, 673.
[201] See Chapter 19 on Article 28.
[202] See, eg, *Guaracachi America Inc*, et al and *Plurinational State of Bolivia*, Terms of Appointment and Procedural Order No 1 (PCA administered, 2010 UNCITRAL Rules, US-Bolivia BIT/UK-Bolivia BIT), para 13 (establishing procedures for allowing Party witnesses to testify).
[203] *Summary Record of the 6th Meeting of the Committee of the Whole (II)*, UNCITRAL, 9th Session, UN Doc A/CN.9/9/C.2/SR.6, at 4, para 24 (1976) (Comment by Mr Lebedev, USSR).
[204] See 1983 Rules of Procedure of the Iran–US Claims Tribunal, Note 2 to Article 17, reprinted in Appendix 5.
[205] See *Component Builders* (1983 Tribunal Rules), reprinted in section 3(D)(2). But see *Ninni Ladjevardi* (1983 Tribunal Rules), reprinted in section 3(D)(2).

In light of the questions surrounding Article 17(3), exempting procedural or jurisdictional questions from the scope of the right to a hearing could be regarded as such a departure from the agreement of the parties as to subject the award to a challenge at the place of arbitration or non-recognition in another jurisdiction.[206] In this regard, the legislative history of Article 24(1) of the Model Law is illustrative. In that context a proposal was made to limit the right to a hearing to "the substance of the dispute," to the exclusion of procedural or jurisdictional questions. From the rejection of this proposal it has been concluded that "the party's right to a hearing should not be considered limited to substantive issues."[207] There are no strong reasons why Article 17(3) of the UNCITRAL Rule should be construed differently.

The broad scope of Article 17(3) should not be interpreted as granting the parties unlimited rights to have separate hearings on all kinds of procedural or preliminary questions. To conduct the proceedings efficiently, the arbitral tribunal must have considerable control over such matters as the number of hearing days and the hearing procedure. By virtue of this control, the tribunal normally can, for example, join jurisdictional issues to the merits or decide minor procedural questions without a hearing, even if a party requests one. Whenever a decision on a preliminary question may lead to the final disposition of the rights of the parties, or to the termination of the proceedings, a hearing normally should be granted if requested by a party.

As to decisions on interim measures (those which neither affect the final disposition of the rights of the parties nor terminate the whole proceedings), the decision whether or not to grant a requested hearing should be made in light of the particular circumstances. Sometimes the urgency of the matter may not allow a hearing; in other cases, the very nature of the measure requested may require that oral argument be heard. The principle of party autonomy suggests that a hearing be granted whenever requested by both parties. Even where requested by only one of the parties, the arbitral tribunal should keep in mind that Article 17(3) provides an opportunity for a hearing. Should a party request a hearing abusively, that party may be forced to bear the costs resulting from an unnecessary hearing.[208]

(b) Timing of hearing requests

The hearing can be requested at "an appropriate stage of the proceedings." This formulation has been changed from the 1976 UNCITRAL Rules, which allowed a party to request a hearing "at any stage of the proceedings." As already noted, the original wording was chosen in order to clarify that the right does not necessarily have to be exercised in the beginning of the proceedings. It was not a license for the parties to demand a hearing whenever it pleased, as this would open up the possibility for disruptive requests made, for example, very late in the proceedings. In applying corresponding Article 15(2) of the 1976 Rules, the Iran–US Claims Tribunal has held that the hearing requirement "should be interpreted, in the light of the particular circumstances of each case, to mean that hearings are to be held upon reasonable request of a party at an appropriate stage of the proceedings."[209] Similarly,

---

[206] See n 78 and n 79.
[207] H Holtzmann and J Neuhaus, *A Guide to the UNCITRAL Model Law*, n 7, 674.
[208] See *Report of the Secretary-General on the Preliminary Draft Set of Arbitration Rules*, UNCITRAL, 8th Session, Addendum 2 (Suggested Modifications), UN Doc A/CN.9/97/Add. 2, para 15 (1975), reprinted in (1975) VI UNCITRAL Ybk 182, 183; see generally Chapter 27, section 4 on apportionment of costs.
[209] See *Tchacosh Co* (1983 Tribunal Rules), reprinted in section 3(D)(2), and the other case mentioned therein. See also J van Hof, *Commentary on the UNCITRAL Arbitration Rules*, n 9, 107.

Article 24(1) of the Model Law provides a right to request a hearing "at an appropriate stage of the proceedings."

In revising the UNCITRAL Rules, the Working Group was cognizant of the need to clarify when a disputing party could request a hearing. The issue arose first in discussions regarding the arbitral tribunal's general discretion to conduct the proceedings. In that context, it was suggested that "to avoid a situation where a party would insist on submission at an inappropriate stage of the arbitration," the phrase "at any stage of the proceedings," as used in the 1976 Rules, should be replaced by the words "at an appropriate stage of the proceedings."[210] On the same rationale, the latter phrase was also adopted in Article 17(3).[211] The arbitral tribunal can, whenever it intends to proceed without a hearing, inform the parties and invite them to exercise their right to request a hearing by a certain date.[212]

(c) Preliminary meetings

In addition to hearings for the presentation of evidence and oral argument, the arbitral tribunal, by virtue of its power to "conduct arbitration in such manner as it considers appropriate" under Article 17(1), may summon the parties for more informal meetings according to the needs of the particular arbitration. The practice of holding "preliminary meetings," also known as "preliminary conferences," in international arbitration has been described as follows:

> [E]specially where the parties and their representatives come from different cultural backgrounds, or from different legal systems, it is sensible for the arbitral tribunal to convene a meeting with the parties as early as possible in the proceedings. This ensures that the arbitral tribunal and the parties have a common understanding of how the arbitration is to be conducted and enables a carefully designated framework for the conduct of the arbitration to be established.[213]

The UNCITRAL Notes provide a useful list of matters for possible consideration in organizing arbitral proceedings, many of which can be addressed in the context of preliminary meetings. In investor–state arbitration under the UNCITRAL Rules, preliminary meetings have been a matter of course. In the practice of the Iran–US Claims Tribunal, meetings with basically similar functions have been institutionalized in the form of "pre-hearing conferences" mentioned in note 4 to Article 15 of the 1983 Tribunal Rules.[214] The arranging of such preliminary meetings is within the discretion of the arbitrators.[215] In the early years of the Iran–US Claims Tribunal they were very common in more substantial cases. Generally, these conferences served the purpose of clarifying and narrowing issues, especially jurisdictional questions. They also provided an opportunity to examine the possibilities of a settlement and to discuss the further proceedings, as well as settle questions such as

---

[210] UNCITRAL, 40th Session, UN Doc A/CN.9/614, n 5, at 17, para 77.

[211] J Castello notes that the changes were necessary because the Rules had been written in such a way that "parties could invoke them for an abusive purpose—for example, to delay an award by seeking an unnecessary additional hearing very late in the proceedings," J Castello, "Unveiling the 2010 UNCITRAL Arbitration Rules," (2010) 65(2/3) Dispute Resolution J 21, 152.

[212] See *Tchacosh Co* (1983 Tribunal Rules), reprinted in section 3(D)(2). See *Sylvania Technical Systems* (1983 Tribunal Rules); and *World Farmers Trading* (1983 Tribunal Rules); both reprinted in section 3(D)(2).

[213] N Blackaby and C Partasides, *Redfern and Hunter on International Arbitration*, n 2, 371.

[214] 1983 Rules of Procedure of the Iran–US Claims Tribunal, reprinted in Appendix 5. Although "pre-hearing conferences" or the like find their basis in Article 17(1) rather than 17(3), they can conveniently be discussed in connection with hearings.

[215] See *Phelps Dodge Corp* (1983 Tribunal Rules), reprinted in section 3(D)(2).

production of documents.²¹⁶ There are differing views on the usefulness of the pre-hearing conferences, and their utility at the Tribunal would appear to depend on the particular circumstances of each case. In simple cases, especially where it is clear that a hearing is going to be held, they may be unnecessary. In more complex cases they may be useful both to the parties and the arbitrators, for example, to determine whether some jurisdictional or other preliminary question deserves to be treated separately.²¹⁷ While a preliminary meeting or conference is not a hearing in the sense of Article 17(3), it may help the tribunal in deciding whether and to what extent hearings are needed.²¹⁸

(4) Communication of documents—Article 17(4)

Article 17(1) requires equal treatment of the parties by the arbitral tribunal. Article 17(4) extends the principle of "[e]qual treatment and equal opportunity for both parties"²¹⁹ to the conduct of the parties themselves by requiring them to submit all communications supplied to the arbitral tribunal simultaneously to all other parties.²²⁰ Such elaboration of the principle of *audiatur et altera pars* creates an important safeguard against unenforceability of the arbitral award on the ground that it has been based on documents not communicated to the losing party.²²¹ Article 2 sets forth the details concerning the mode of communication of documents to the other party.²²²

In its overall control of the arbitral proceedings, the tribunal should see to it that the parties act in accordance with Article 17(4). Therefore, if it ascertains that certain documents or other pieces of information supplied to it have not been communicated to the other party, then the Tribunal should, if necessary, convey the information to the other party itself.

Indeed, the parties may consider the possibility of modifying Article 17(4) so as to entrust the arbitral tribunal with the task of acting as a "clearinghouse" to which the

---

²¹⁶ See *The Austin Co* (1983 Tribunal Rules), reprinted in section 3(D)(2). See generally J Selby and D Stewart, "Practical Aspects of Arbitrating Claims," n 101, 222–6 and S Baker and M Davis, *The UNCITRAL Arbitration Rules in Practice*, n 9, 123 ("The purported goals of pre-hearing conferences at the Tribunal were twofold: (1) to allow parties to exchange views; and (2) to narrow and clarify issues.").

²¹⁷ There are differing views on the usefulness of the pre-hearing conferences at the Tribunal, and their utility would appear to depend on the particular circumstances of each case. See, on the one hand, J Selby and D Stewart, "Practical Aspects of Arbitrating Claims," n 101, 222, according to whom the utility of the conferences "is in many cases doubtful," and, on the other, S Belland, "The Iran-United States Claims Tribunal: Some Reflections on Trying a Claim," (1984) 1 J Intl Arb 240–41, who regards the pre-hearing conference as "a good idea" and the guidance afforded by comments made during it as "invaluable." In simple cases, especially where it is clear that a hearing is going to be held, they may be unnecessary. In more complex cases they may be useful both to the parties and the arbitrators, for example, to determine whether some jurisdictional or other preliminary question deserves to be treated separately. See *Tai Inc* (1983 Tribunal Rules); and *Islamic Republic of Iran* and *United States of America* (Case Nos A3, A8, A9, A14 and B16) (1983 Tribunal Rules), Order of December 3, 1992; both reprinted in section 3(D)(2).

²¹⁸ See *Tai Inc* (1983 Tribunal Rules), reprinted in section 3(D)(2). The additional benefits of a pre-hearing conference are described in P Sanders, *The Work of UNCITRAL on Arbitration and Conciliation*, n 95, 7–8.

²¹⁹ See *Report of the Secretary-General on the Preliminary Draft Set of Arbitration Rules*, UNCITRAL, 8th Session, UN Doc A/CN.9/97 (1974), reprinted in (1975) VI UNCITRAL Ybk 163, 173 (Commentary of Draft Article 13(4)).

²²⁰ The word "communications" replaced the words "documents or information" used in corresponding Article 15(3) of the 1976 UNCITRAL Rules, but without any intended change in meaning. *Settlement of Commercial Disputes: Revision of the UNCITRAL Arbitration Rules, Note by the Secretariat*, UNCITRAL, UN Doc A/CN.9/WG.II/WP.151 at 15–16, para 36 (2008).

²²¹ See J Thieffry, "The Finality of Awards," n 94, 44–5.

²²² See Note 3 to Article 15 of the 1983 Rules of Procedure of the Iran–US Claims Tribunal, reprinted in Appendix 5. See also Chapter 12.

documents and other information are first supplied, and which then transmits them to the other party.[223]

The obligation to simultaneously transmit communications to all parties is potentially subject to an important exception in the case of preliminary requests for interim measures.[224]

(5) Joinder of third persons—Article 17(5)

An arbitration may already be in progress when a disputing party realizes it needs to bring an additional person or entity into the proceedings.[225] This situation may arise, for example, in the case of a dispute involving multiple players, not all of which are before the tribunal, and it becomes evident that full resolution of the entire dispute would benefit from the participation of them all.[226] By joining as many parties as possible into a single proceeding, joinder reduces the possibility of concurrent or successive proceedings, thus enhancing the efficiency of the dispute resolution process.[227] Further, joinder can minimize the problem of inconsistent rulings from multiple tribunals on the same matters of law and fact. To further these aims, Article 17(5) contains a provision on joinder, which is new to the 2010 UNCITRAL Rules.[228]

Consent is a cornerstone principle of arbitration and is no less applicable in the case of joinder. As a rule, the parties to a dispute must agree with one another to subject themselves to arbitration; the same can be said about expanding an existing arbitration to include additional actors.[229] Failure to gain the consent of all involved in a joinder may expose the award to challenges at the seat or complicate enforcement efforts.[230] Article 17(5) deals with the issue of consent by allowing joinder of a third person "provided such person is a party to the arbitration agreement." This condition limits joinder to situations in which the third person to be added is a party to the arbitration agreement pursuant to which the arbitration is

---

[223] Article 24(3) of the Model Law, as amended, reads as follows: "[a]ll statements, documents or other information supplied to the arbitral tribunal by one party shall be communicated to the other party. Also any expert report or evidentiary document on which the arbitral tribunal may rely in making its decision shall be communicated to the parties." The wording of the first sentence differs from that of Article 15(3) of the 1976 UNCITRAL Rules "in order to accommodate the practices of some arbitral institutions, under which documents are sent first to the institution or the tribunal which then transmits them to the arbitrators and the other party." H Holtzmann and J Neuhaus, *A Guide to the UNCITRAL Model Law*, n 7, 674.

[224] UNCITRAL, 42nd Session, UN Doc A/CN.9/665, n 21, at 24, para 127. See also Chapter 17.

[225] For a general discussion on joinder, see G Born, *International Commercial Arbitration*, n 182, 2073 et seq.

[226] See N Blackaby and C Partasides, *Redfern and Hunter on International Arbitration*, n 2, 39.

[227] Commentators have noted that "[i]n practice, an application for joinder will therefore require both a hearing and an interim award" M Skinner et al, "The UNCITRAL Arbitration Rules 2010" (2011) 7(1) Asian Intl Arb J 76.

[228] In deciding to add a rule on joinder, the Working Group closely considered the practice of the International Court of Arbitration of the International Chamber of Commerce, the London Court of International Arbitration, and the Swiss Arbitration Association. There has been very little publicly available practice on joinder under the 1976 UNCITRAL Rules. For a description of an unpublished *ad hoc* UNCITRAL award in which the tribunal ordered joinder over the respondents' objections, see M de Boisséson, "Joinder of Parties to Arbitral Proceedings: Two Contrasting Decisions," in (2003) ICC Bulletin: Complex Arbitration (Special Supplement) 23.

[229] See N Blackaby and C Partasides, *Redfern and Hunter on International Arbitration*, n 2, at 105 ("The tribunal's jurisdiction derives from the will of the parties to the arbitration agreement and therefore joinder or intervention is generally only possible with the consent of all parties concerned.").

[230] See G Born, *International Commercial Arbitration*, n 182, 2074–5 ("In the context of recognizing arbitral awards, Article V(1)(d) of the [New York] Convention provides for the non-recognition of awards that are rendered following arbitral proceedings where consolidation, joinder, or intervention was ordered, notwithstanding an arbitration agreement that did not permit such actions.").

proceeding.²³¹ According to the *travaux préparatoires*, this condition is based on a theory of implied consent: by agreeing in the arbitration agreement to arbitrate under the Rules, in particular Article 17(5) on joinder, all parties to that agreement consent to any future application of the joinder provision, whether or not they are the original parties to the existing arbitration.²³²

Article 17(5) is thus more restrictive in scope than, for example, Article 22.1(h) of the London Court of International Arbitration (LCIA) Rules, on which an earlier proposed version of Article 17(5) was closely modelled.²³³ Article 22.1(h) permits joinder where any third person and the party to the arbitration that is requesting joinder "have consented thereto in writing." That provision notably does not limit the scope of joinder only to third persons who are parties to the arbitration agreement. Thus, joinder under Article 22.1(h) may occur solely on the basis that a third person has consented in writing to a request for joinder, ie the third person is not a party to the arbitration agreement but has agreed to accept the specific request to join the existing arbitration.²³⁴ In contrast, Article 17(5) would preclude joinder under these same circumstances, as only third persons who are parties to the arbitration agreement may be joined. At the same time, Article 17(5) contains no requirement to consent in writing, as Article 22.1(h) of the LCIA Rules does. Thus, under the UNCITRAL Rules, a third party (who is also a party to the arbitration agreement) cannot veto a request for joinder by withholding its written consent.

The more conservative approach of Article 17(5), as compared to Article 22.1(h), resolved an important concern of the UNCITRAL drafters. In Working Group discussions, many delegations feared that under a broader approach a third person could be joined to the proceedings without the consent of the non-requesting parties to the arbitration. This situation was believed to "run counter to the fundamental principle of consent of the parties to the arbitration."²³⁵ On the theory of implied consent that underlies Article 17(5), however, this problem is solved because a non-requesting party to the arbitration is deemed to have consented to any request to join a third person who is also a party to the arbitration agreement.²³⁶

The requirement that a joined person be a party to the arbitration agreement places significant limitations on the practical application of Article 17(5). Joinder may be allowed in the case of a multi-party contract, such as one between a consortium of business partners

---

²³¹ J Castello, "UNCITRAL Rules," n 34, 1470.
²³² UNCITRAL, 42nd Session, UN Doc A/CN.9/665, n 21, at 24–25, para 130. Further, a third person to be joined need not provide its specific consent to a request for joinder. This is clear from the *travaux préparatoires*, which report that a proposal in which the words "provided such person is a party to the arbitration agreement" was followed by "and has consented to be joined" was rejected out of concerns that it would empower the third person to veto a request for joinder, even if it were a party to the arbitration agreement, thus hampering operation of Article 17(5).
²³³ *Settlement of Commercial Disputes: Revision of the UNCITRAL Arbitration Rules, Note by the Secretariat*, UNCITRAL, UN Doc A/CN.9/WG.II/WP.147/Add.1 at 3, para 5 (2007) (Draft Article 15(4)).
²³⁴ P Turner and R Mohtashami, *A Guide to the LCIA Arbitration Rules* (2009) 149 (commenting that Article 22.1(h) provides "an express power to join third parties who may not necessarily be parties to the arbitration agreement.").
²³⁵ UNCITRAL, 40th Session, UN Doc A/CN.9/619, n 5, at 24, para 122.
²³⁶ Castello and Digon note also that the Working Group's conservative approach flowed from the apparent paucity of practice on joinder under the LCIA and Swiss Rules. As they explain: "[T]he cold facts about how rarely the LCIA and Swiss Rules provisions had been used gave delegates further pause about the risks of innovating too far on the subject of joinder...." J Castello and R Digon, "Maximizing Possibilities for Joinder in International Arbitration," forthcoming in A Rovine (ed) *Contemporary Issues in International Arbitration and Mediation: The Fordham Papers (2011)* (2012) 116.

which contains an agreement to arbitrate under the Rules. Under these circumstances, all parties to the dispute are parties to the arbitration agreement and, thus, any who are not already before the tribunal may be joined. In contrast, joinder is precluded where there are multiple contracts between multiple parties. For example, in a construction arbitration between an employer and the main contractor, it may be desirable to join a subcontractor of the main contractor. However, if the employer and the main contractor are parties to one contract and the main contractor and the subcontractor to another (which is often the case), the subcontractor cannot be joined under Article 17(5) since it is not a party to the arbitration agreement on which the existing arbitration is based. Apart from Article 17(5), joinder can only be accomplished by amending the arbitration agreement to add a third person.

Inclusion of the term "third persons" in Article 17(5)—a term borrowed from Article 22.1(h) of the 1998 LCIA Rules—is meant to complement the requirement that the third person to be joined be a party to the arbitration agreement. The drafters of the UNCITRAL Rules preferred to use the term "third persons" over "third parties" in order to emphasize that the person to be joined was not a "third party" in the sense of a non-party to the arbitration agreement.[237] In light of its intended purpose in Article 17(5), the term "third persons" should not be construed as limiting the scope of joinder to natural persons; both natural person and juridical entities may be joined so long as the conditions established under the Rules are satisfied.

A more specific problem of consent is that "third persons" that have been joined to an existing arbitration often do not have the opportunity to participate in the process of appointing arbitrators, having joined the proceedings after constitution of the tribunal. Depriving a party of this important right could expose any subsequent award to challenge on the basis of an alleged improper constitution of the tribunal.[238] Article 17(5) addresses this problem in two ways. First, under the theory of implied consent, a third person so joined, having agreed to arbitrate under the Rules, is deemed to have consented to the possibility that the tribunal will be constituted without their consent.[239] Second, Article 17(5) permits joinder "unless the arbitral tribunal finds, after giving all parties, including the person or persons to be joined, the opportunity to be heard, that joinder should not be permitted because of prejudice to any of those parties." Consultation is thus meant to facilitate an exchange of views that may assist the arbitral tribunal in assessing whether any of the parties stands to suffer prejudice as a result of the joinder, particularly a third person who may be deprived of an opportunity to appoint an arbitrator.[240]

---

[237] UNCITRAL, 42nd Session, UN Doc A/CN.9/665, n 21, at 24, para 129.

[238] The *travaux préparatoires* state: "Concerns were expressed that the absence of explicit consent of a party to be joined might entail the consequence that, at the stage of recognition and enforcement of the arbitral award, the party so joined might raise the argument that it did not participate in the constitution of the arbitral tribunal, and therefore the arbitral tribunal was not composed in accordance with the agreement of the parties." UNCITRAL, 42nd Session, UN Doc A/CN.9/665, n 21, at 25, para 131. The source of such a challenge could be Article 36(1)(a)(iv) of the Model Law and/or Article V(1)(d) of the New York Convention. In one case, for example, an award was set aside because, pursuant to an arbitration agreement, multiple respondents had to compromise in choosing an arbitrator or have the arbitrator chosen by an appointing authority, and this arrangement was determined to violate the principle of equal treatment of the parties. See *Sociétés BKMI et Siemens c/ Société Dutco,* Cour de Cassation (January 7, 1992), reprinted in (1993) 18 Ybk of Commercial Arb 140.

[239] UNCITRAL, 42nd Session, UN Doc A/CN.9/665, n 21, at 24–5, para 130.

[240] As to third persons to be joined, Castello and Digon identify multiple reasons why joinder may not cause prejudice: (1) when all parties agree to the joinder; (2) when an appointing authority has appointed the tribunal, thus putting all parties in the same position of non-participation; (3) when the new party's interests are closely

The assessment of prejudice under Article 17(5) is only one aspect to consider before joinder may occur. During Working Group discussions, a proposal was made to replace the phrase "because of prejudice to any of those parties" with the words "taking into consideration fairness to each of the parties" to ensure wider consideration of the interests at stake.[241] It was noted, however, that this change was unnecessary because the general principles of equal treatment, avoidance of unnecessary delay and cost, and fair and efficient proceedings established in Article 17(1) of the Rules in any event overlay the requirements of Article 17(5).[242] Further, the powers of the arbitral tribunal to join a third person under Article 17(1) are ultimately permissive; the tribunal "may" allow joinder. Thus, even if all the conditions established in Article 17(5) are satisfied, a tribunal has discretion to deny a request for joinder that fails to comport with the general principles of Article 17(1).

Article 17(5) provides that joinder of one or more third persons may be considered "at the request of any party." This condition naturally precludes the arbitral tribunal or any third person from validly proposing joinder, as neither of these actors is a "party" to the arbitration. Further, it grants a party to the arbitration the right to request joinder unilaterally, over objections of other original parties, who are in any event deemed to have agreed to the joinder process under a theory of implied consent.

The last sentence of Article 17(5) confirms the authority of the arbitral tribunal to render awards with respect to all parties to the arbitration, including any third persons that have been joined to the proceedings.

(6) Consolidation of claims

The UNCITRAL Rules do not contain a general provision on consolidation of claims. During Working Group discussions to revise the Rules, the issue of consolidation was discussed in some detail. Some delegations expressed support for inclusion of a consolidation provision along the lines of Article 4(6) of 1998 ICC Rules.[243] It was noted that consolidation could be beneficial:

> where several distinct disputes arose between the same parties under separate contracts (e.g., related contracts or a chain of contracts) containing separate arbitration clauses or to avoid a situation where a party initiated a separate arbitration in respect of a distinct claim under the same contract in order to gain a tactical advantage.[244]

In these situations, some delegations believed consolidation could resolve disputes more efficiently and minimize the possibility of inconsistent awards.[245]

---

aligned with those of an original party; and (4) when a respondent seeking to join a jointly and severally liable co-respondent agrees to replace a previously designated party-appointed arbitrator with a jointly-appointed new arbitrator. J Castello and R Digon, "Maximizing Possibilities for Joinder," n 236, 118.

[241] UNCITRAL, 43rd Session, UN Doc A/CN.9/688, n 181, at 19, para 88. An earlier proposal was to add language, such as "all circumstances that the arbitral tribunal deems relevant and applicable," along the lines of Article 4.2 of the Swiss Rules of International Arbitration. UNCITRAL, 42nd Session, UN Doc A/CN.9/665, n 21, at 25, para 134.

[242] UNCITRAL, 43rd Session, UN Doc A/CN.9/688, n 21, at 19, para 88.

[243] For general discussion of the ICC rule, see Y Derains and E Schwartz, *A Guide to the New ICC Rules of Arbitration* (2005) 62–5. For recent practice of the ICC on consolidation, see A M Whitesell and E Silva-Romero, "Multiparty and Multicontract Arbitration: Recent ICC Experience," (2003) ICC Bulletin: Complex Arbitrations (Special Supplement).

[244] UNCITRAL, 40th Session, UN Doc A/CN.9/619, n 5, at 23, para 117.

[245] UNCITRAL, 40th Session, UN Doc A/CN.9/619, n 5, at 23, para 117.

Other delegations raised concerns about including a consolidation provision in the Rules. Unlike the International Chamber of Commerce (ICC) Rules, the UNCITRAL Rules in many cases would be applied in non-administered arbitration, and there were doubts about the feasibility of applying such a provision in this context.[246] Concerns with respect to the reach of a consolidation provision were also voiced. To the extent the provision was to address new claims raised under the same contract, some believed that the provision on amendment of the statement of claim contained in the Rules might already apply. To the extent a consolidation provision would address several distinct disputes arising between the same parties under separate contracts, each with its own distinct arbitration clause, problems of consent were identified.[247] For example, in consolidated proceedings, some worried that a party might be forced to participate in the arbitration on terms which differed from those in its arbitration agreement.[248]

To facilitate the discussion on consolidation under the Rules, UNCITRAL's Secretariat prepared the following draft provision:

The arbitral tribunal may, on the application of any party, ... assume jurisdiction over any claim involving the same parties and arising out of the same legal relationship, provided that such claims are subject to arbitration under these Rules and that the arbitration proceedings in relation to those claims have not yet commenced.[249]

While addressing some of the concerns of the Working Group,[250] the draft provision was never adopted. Instead, the Working Group turned its efforts toward drafting a provision on joinder, which was thought to deal with many of the same issues of multi-party arbitration as consolidation. Article 17(5) on joinder is discussed in section (5) Joinder of third persons—Article 17(5).

Parties involved in investor–state arbitration under the UNCITRAL Rules should be aware that some international investment agreements contain provisions on consolidation.[251]

(7) Comparison to the 1976 UNCITRAL Rules

Article 17 is similar to Article 15 of the 1976 UNCITRAL Rules in many important respects, while adding new substantive provisions to the Rules.

The first sentence of Article 17(1) on the arbitral tribunal's general duties contains clarifying revisions to the 1976 UNCITRAL Rules. The opportunity for a party to present its case is no longer characterized as a "full opportunity," but simply "a reasonable opportunity," and under the revised rule such opportunity must be provided "at an appropriate stage" of the arbitration, as opposed to "at any stage," as permitted under Article 15(1) of the 1976 Rules. Both changes were intended to moderate language that might cause a party

---

[246] UNCITRAL, 40th Session, UN Doc A/CN.9/619, n 5, at 23, para 119.
[247] It was also recognized that a respondent could raise a counterclaim under Article 19(3).
[248] UNCITRAL, 40th Session, UN Doc A/CN.9/619, n 5, at 23, para 119.
[249] *Settlement of Commercial Disputes: Revision of the UNCITRAL Arbitration Rules, Note by the Secretariat*, UNCITRAL, UN Doc A/CN.9/WG.II/WP.145/Add.1 at 2–3, para 5 (2006) (Draft Article 15(4)(a)).
[250] Some delegations maintained that a consolidation provision "should be carefully drafted in order to clarify that consolidation would only be possible if either the claim was already subject to the UNCITRAL Rules, or the parties expressly agreed that the claim should be subject to consolidation." UNCITRAL, 40th Session, UN Doc A/CN.9/619, n 5, at 23, para 118.
[251] See, eg, Dominican Republic–Central America–United States Free Trade Agreement (CAFTA-DR), art 10.25.

to have unreasonable expectations concerning its rights under the Rules.[252] The second sentence of Article 17(1) of the 2010 Rules is entirely new. While some Working Group delegations believed the duty to conduct the proceedings so as to avoid unnecessary delay and expense and to provide a fair and efficient process was implied under the Rules,[253] others believed an express statement of the duty would afford the tribunal a certain "leverage" in relation to the parties, and possibly an arbitrator, to take action under the Rules.[254] At the same time, the express duty may provide new grounds for complaining about the arbitral tribunal's conduct of the proceedings.

Article 17(2) is new to the 2010 Rules. The first sentence requires that the arbitral tribunal establish a provisional timetable for the arbitration, whereas under the 1976 Rules that task was left to the tribunal's discretion. The second sentence of the paragraph changes the Rules substantively by granting the arbitral tribunal new authority to extend or abridge any time periods under the Rules or agreed to by the parties.

Article 17(3) is identical to corresponding Article 15(2) of the 1976 Rules, save for one revision. Under the 2010 Rules a party may request a hearing "at an appropriate stage" of the arbitration, as opposed to "at any stage" of the arbitration, as permitted under the 1976 Rules. This revision was made for the same reasons as those underlying a similar revision to Article 17(1), described above.

Article 17(4) is similar to corresponding Article 15(3) of the 1976 Rules. Under the 2010 rule, the simultaneous communication requirement applies to all "communications," whereas under the 1976 rule, it applies to "documents or information." There is no substantive difference in the respective texts, the revision was made simply for the sake of consistency with the terminology under the Rules.[255] In addition, Article 17(4) contains an exception to simultaneous communication where otherwise permitted by the applicable law.

Article 17(5) finds no analogue in the 1976 Rules. As discussed, the provision permits joinder of third persons to the arbitral proceedings in limited situations. Parties arbitrating under the 1976 Rules may wish to consider modifying those rules by including the provision on joinder, if they foresee the need to include third persons in the arbitration.

C. Extracts from the Practice of Investment and other Tribunals

(1) Article 15(1) (1976 Rules)—general

Lance Paul Larsen and *Hawaiian Kingdom*, Procedural Order No 3 (July 17, 2000) (PCA administered, 1976 UNCITRAL Rules, Special Agreement, reprinted in (2001) 119 ILR 566, 577, 578:

6. The parties subsequently filed Memorials and Counter-Memorials dated respectively 22 May 2000 and 22/23 June. These were supported by a substantial number of annexes. The Tribunal has carefully considered these. However, before proceeding to the substance of the issues the parties have sought to place before it, the Tribunal wishes to raise a number of preliminary issues. In short, there are questions whether the "dispute" identified in Article 1 of the

---

[252] See J Castello, "UNCITRAL Rules," n 34, 1468; D Kozlowska, "The Revised UNCITRAL Arbitration Rules Seen through the Prism of Electronic Disclosure" (2011), 28(1) J Intl Arb 51, 53–6.
[253] UNCITRAL, 40th Session, UN Doc A/CN.9/614, n 5, at 17, para 76.
[254] UNCITRAL, 40th Session, UN Doc A/CN.9/614, n 5, at 17, para 76.
[255] *Settlement of Commercial Disputes: Revision of the UNCITRAL Arbitration Rules, Note by the Secretariat*, UNCITRAL, UN Doc A/CN.9/WG.II/WP.151 at 15–16, para 36 (2008).

Arbitration Agreement is one which is capable of reference to arbitration under the [1976] UNCITRAL Rules, or which the Tribunal has jurisdiction to decide in accordance with international law. It does not matter that the parties have failed to raise these issues. The Tribunal has the power to do so, by virtue of Article 6 of the Agreement and Article 15(1) of the [1976] Rules. Indeed, the jurisprudence of international tribunals suggests that it has the duty to do so.

...

14. In accordance with Article 15(1) of the [1976] Rules, the parties must have a full opportunity to deal with these questions before the Tribunal proceeds to consider them further, or to reach any conclusion on them. The pleadings currently before the Tribunal do not consider these questions.
15. The Tribunal believes that the parties should have an opportunity to decide whether they wish to undertake a separate round of pleadings or should include an oral phase. If the parties do not wish to engage in a separate round of pleadings, the Tribunal is presently of the view that it should then proceed to consider these issues as preliminary issues and to make an award thereon.
16. The Tribunal accordingly gives the parties until 7 August 2000 to present, jointly or separately, their views on the procedure that should now be followed....

Pope & Talbot Inc and *Government of Canada*, Decision on Privileges (September 6, 2000) (*Ad Hoc* Proceeding, 1976 UNCITRAL Rules, NAFTA Chapter Eleven), at 2–3:

1.5 In the specific context of a NAFTA arbitration where the parties have agreed to operate by [1976] UNCITRAL Rules, it is an overriding principle (Article 15) that the parties be treated with equality. The other NAFTA Parties do not, so far as the Tribunal has become aware, have domestic law that would permit or requires them to withhold documents from Chapter 11 Tribunals without any justification beyond a simple certification that they are some kind of state secret. In these circumstances, Canada, if it could simply rely on s. 39 [of the Canada Evidence Act], might be in an unfairly advantaged position under Chapter 11 by comparison with the United States and Mexico.

Lance Paul Larsen and *Hawaiian Kingdom*, Award (February 5, 2001) (PCA administered, 1976 UNCITRAL Rules, Special Agreement), reprinted in (2001) 119 ILR 566, 579–80:

6.4. Following the delivery of the Tribunal's Procedural Order No 3 the parties entered into Special Agreement No 2 of 2 August 2000 and sought to raise a preliminary issue to be determined by the Tribunal in the following terms:

Pursuant to Article 32(1) of the [1976] UNCITRAL Rules, the Parties request the Arbitral Tribunal to issue an Interlocutory Award, on the basis of the 1843 Anglo-Franco Proclamation of 28 November 1843 and the rules and principles of international law, verifying the continued existence of Hawaiian Statehood with the Hawaiian Kingdom as its government.

6.5. The Tribunal responded to the making of Special Agreement No 2 with its Procedural Order No 4 of 5 September 2000, which read as follows:

...

3. The Tribunal set out in its Order No 3 the questions which, in its view, are raised before it can proceed to the merits of the dispute. The issue identified in Article 1 of Special Agreement No 2 is not one of these. Rather it appears to be a reformulation of the first substantive issue identified as being in dispute.
4. It is not open to the parties by way of an amendment to the Special Agreement to seek to redefine the essential issues, so as to convert them into "interim" or "interlocutory" issues.

In accordance with article 32 of the [1976] UNCITRAL Rules, and with the general principles of arbitral procedure, it is for the Tribunal to determine which issues need to be dealt with and in what order. For the reasons already given, the Tribunal cannot at this stage proceed to the merits of the dispute; these merits include the question sought to be raised as a preliminary issue by Article 1. If the arbitration is to proceed it is first necessary that the preliminary issues identified in its Order No 3 should have been dealt with.

5. If the parties are not content with the submission of the dispute to arbitration under the [1976] UNCITRAL Rules and under the auspices of the Permanent Court of Arbitration, they may no doubt, by agreement notified to the Permanent Court, terminate the arbitration. What they cannot do, in the Tribunal's view, is by agreement to change the essential basis on which the Tribunal itself is constituted, or require the Tribunal to act other than in accordance with the applicable law.

Pope & Talbot Inc and *Government of Canada*, Award on the Merits of Phase 2 (April 10, 2001) (*Ad Hoc* Proceeding, 1976 UNCITRAL Rules, NAFTA Chapter Eleven), reprinted in (No 4, 2001) 13 World Trade & Arb Materials 61, 153:

193. As noted, during the course of discovery in this proceeding, Canada objected to producing certain items on the ground that, as Privy Council documents, their disclosure was prohibited by the Canada Evidence Act. The Tribunal rules that that Act by its terms did not apply to a Chapter 11 tribunal, and Canada did not contest that ruling. However, it nonetheless refused to produce or even identify the documents in order to permit the Tribunal to make a reasoned judgment as to their relevance and materiality. In the result, this refusal did not appear prejudicial to the Investor, and the Tribunal proceeded upon the basis of the materials actually before it. However, the Tribunal deplores the decision of Canada in this matter. As the Tribunal noted in its decision on this matter dated September 6, 2000, Canada's position could well be a derogation from the "overriding principle" found in Article 15 of the [1976] UNCITRAL Arbitration Rules, under which these proceedings have been conducted, that all Parties should be treated with equality. Moreover, Article 115 of NAFTA declares that there shall be "equal treatment among investors of the Parties." As Canada's refusal to disclose or identify documents in these circumstances is at variance with the practice of other NAFTA Parties, at least of the United States, that refusal could well result in a denial of equality of treatment of investors and investments of the Parties bringing claims under Chapter 11.

Methanex Corp and *United States of America*, Letter from the Tribunal to the Parties (September 25, 2002) (ICSID administered, 1976 UNCITRAL Rules, NAFTA Chapter Eleven), at 9–10:

20. ... Methanex seeks confirmation that it is not now required to produce all evidence on which the presentation of its case on the merits will rely, thereby foreclosing the development and presentation of additional evidence at a later stage. Methanex also seeks clarification as to whether it is required to produce "essentially final reports from all its experts" within the ninety day time limit imposed by the Tribunal; and it seeks confirmation now that the Tribunal is not planning to proceed directly to a hearing on the merits.

21. It is difficult for the Tribunal to follow Methanex's apparent difficulties. As the Partial Award states in Paragraph 163 (page 69), Methanex must file with its fresh pleading copies of all evidential documents on which it relies. This direction is clear both as to the ambit of the evidence required ("as regards the USA's alleged liability"; but "we exclude evidential materials relating to the alleged quantum") and the extent ("all evidential documents"). Similarly there is no ambiguity with respect to the Tribunal's direction on the submission of expert reports, and there is no suggestion that these should be draft reports or reports that are otherwise incomplete: see Paragraphs 163 and 165 of the Partial Award (pages 69 & 70).

22. Nonetheless, insofar as Methanex may find insuperable difficulty in complying with the ninety day limit imposed by the Partial Award, it remains open to Methanex to seek an

extension of that deadline from the Tribunal. Moreover, if for good cause shown, Methanex is unable timeously to complete its filing of all relevant evidential materials, it remains equally open to Methanex to seek dispensation from the Tribunal in regard to missing materials; e.g. an outstanding application against a third person under 18 U.S.C. § 1782 28 (if applicable), as raised at page 6 of Methanex's letter.

23. It is the Tribunal's intention, both in the Partial Award and now, that Methanex and its legal advisers should have the best opportunity to advance Methanex's best case. It is not the Tribunal's intention to deprive either Disputing Party of its procedural rights under Article 15(1) of the [1976] UNCITRAL Arbitration Rules, or otherwise. However, as regards Methanex's present exercise, given the long history of this arbitration (on which Methanex rightly comments at page 7 of its letter), that can only be a reasonable opportunity. There must therefore be a reasonable deadline. In all the circumstances, from the Tribunal's current perspective, ninety days is a reasonable period of time. It could be extended by the Tribunal if necessary; but an extension should be sought by means of a reasoned application to the Tribunal and not by a request for interpretation of the Partial Award.

24. There is no suggestion in the Partial Award that if, at a later stage Methanex sought to submit further relevant evidence, it would be debarred automatically from doing so—nor could there be. This would be a matter for consideration by the Tribunal in the future, if and when that issue arose and after hearing both Disputing Parties.

CME Czech Republic BV and *Czech Republic*, Final Award (March 14, 2003) (*Ad Hoc* Proceeding, 1976 UNCITRAL Rules, Netherlands-Czech BIT), reprinted in (2003) 15(4) World Trade & Arb Materials 83, 100:

43. In accordance with Article 15.1 of the [1976] UNCITRAL Arbitration Rules, the Tribunal decided to conduct the arbitration in the manner it considers appropriate. For this purpose, the Tribunal decided, to the extent appropriate, to apply the IBA Rules [in Taking Evidence in International Commercial Arbitration].

EnCana Corp and *Republic of Ecuador*, Partial Award on Jurisdiction (February 27, 2004) (LCIA administered, 1976 UNCITRAL Rules, Canada-Ecuador BIT), at 19–20:

44 As to the question of the confidentiality of pleadings in the parallel arbitration under the United States-Ecuador Treaty, the Tribunal notes that the Respondent has chosen the same arbitrator in the two proceedings, as it was entitled to do under Article 7(1) of the [1976] UNCITRAL Rules.... The Respondent is also represented by the same legal firm, again something which is a matter for it to decide. Evidently the Respondent and its legal advisers have a synoptic view of the various disputes related to the oil industry in Ecuador which may be denied to the Claimant and its legal advisers. But that is a natural inequality as between private companies and a host State, one which arises from their respective status and roles and which cannot be reversed *en tant que tel*.

45 A problem of procedural equality could nonetheless arise. In this respect the Tribunal notes the requirements of Article 15(1) and (3) of the [1976] UNCITRAL Rules. Under Article 15(1) the tribunal must treat the parties with equality; under Article 15(3) all documents or information supplied to the arbitral tribunal by one party shall at the same time be communicated to the other party....

46 ...as soon as Dr. Barrera [appointed by Respondent] uses information gained from the other Tribunal in relation to the present arbitration, a problem arises with respect to the equality of the parties. Furthermore Dr. Barrera cannot reasonably be asked to maintain a "Chinese wall" in his own mind: his understanding of the situation may well be affected by information acquired in the other arbitration. The most he can be asked to do is to disclose facts so derived whenever they appear to be relevant to any issue before this Tribunal.

47 The Tribunal does not propose to deal with this question in a categorical way by ordering full advance disclosure to the Claimant of the pleadings in the other arbitration. Even assuming it

has authority to do so, it is not persuaded that such an order is necessary. In particular it notes that the joined issues of jurisdiction and merits in the other arbitration have recently been the subject of an oral hearing, and that the decision of that Tribunal may be expected to become available before the pleadings in the present case are closed. It does however believe that the award of the other Tribunal should be made available to the Claimant as soon as may be after it is issued, and it calls on the Respondent to do what it can to ensure that this happens. If extra time is needed for the Claimant to respond to such award, it may request this.

Methanex Corp and *United States of America*, Final Award of the Tribunal on Jurisdiction and Merits (August 3, 2005) (ICSID administered, 1976 UNCITRAL Rules, NAFTA Chapter Eleven), Part II, Chapter E, at 19:

33. Turning to the issue under Article 15(1) of the [1976] UNCITRAL Rules, there is nothing there to suggest that an arbitration tribunal has a broad jurisdiction to reconsider a final and binding award that it has already made. (The possible exception for fraud by a party is here irrelevant). To the contrary, both the ordinary meaning and the context of Article 15(1) lead to the opposite conclusion. Article 15(1) is located in Section III of the [1976] Rules, "Arbitral Proceedings"; and it is a general provision that regulates the conduct of the arbitral proceedings. By contrast, Article 32 is to be found in Section IV, "The Award"; and it is concerned with the form and effect of an award. Article 15(1) cannot be read as creating such a huge derogation from Article 32; it has a significantly different subject-matter. Moreover, Article 15(1) requires that a party be given a full opportunity of presenting its case "*at any stage of the proceedings*". This accepts that arbitral proceedings may comprise differing stages, as also appears from Article 15(2), and a given stage in the proceedings may of course be brought to an end by a final and binding award. It would both undermine Article 32 and lead to an inequality between the parties if at any time the losing party could seek to re-litigate matters contained in an award simply by invoking Article 15(1) of the [1976] UNCITRAL Rules.

Softwood Lumber Consolidated Proceeding (*Canfor Corporation,* et al and *United States of America*, Order of the Consolidation Tribunal (September 7, 2005) (ICSID administered, 1976 UNCITRAL Rules, NAFTA Chapter Eleven), at 48:

125. In making that determination, an Article 1126 Tribunal is also to consider what is "fair." That requirement indicates that the interests of all parties involved should be balanced in determining what is the procedural economy in the given situation. For example, a balance needs to be struck between a hearing that is longer for one party but at the same time shorter for another. It may also happen that what is procedurally less efficient for one party is procedurally more efficient for another. In that respect, the procedural economy that will redound to the benefit of a disputing State Party is another relevant factor, for the reasons explained earlier. The necessary balancing further includes the consideration that all parties shall continue to receive the fundamental right of due process as it is set forth in Article 15(1) of the [1976] UNCITRAL Arbitration Rules ("... the parties are treated with equality and each party is given a full opportunity of presenting his case").

Glamis Gold Ltd and *United States of America*, Procedural Order No 8 (January 31, 2006) (ICSID administered, 1976 UNCITRAL Rules, NAFTA Chapter Eleven), at 5, 7:

9. The Tribunal recognizes that the production of documents phase of this arbitration has been relatively extensive and that this process has been burdensome for the Parties, especially in light of the tight arbitral schedule....
12. Due to the extensive nature of this document production process and the desire to have evidence available to the Parties prior to their memorial submissions, the Tribunal finds the current arbitral schedule unsustainable. Therefore, despite the desire not to delay the arbitral hearing, the Tribunal determines that the schedule must be extended to accommodate these additional production procedures. In adjusting the schedule, the Tribunal is cognizant of

Respondent's arguments that the Parties must be treated equally with respect to the completion of submissions to the Tribunal. The Tribunal notes that Article 15(1) of the [1976] UNCITRAL Rules provides that "[s]ubject to these Rules...the parties are treated with equality and that at any stage of the proceedings each party is given a full opportunity of presenting its case." As to the requirement that each party be given a full opportunity to present its case, the Tribunal observes that a period of approximately four months to prepare a memorial, whether that be the memorial or counter-memorial, is customarily an adequate amount of time, absent unusual circumstances. A general delay in the proceedings, which as a consequence in theory provides more time to the Claimant for the preparation of its memorial, does not require under Article 15(1), absent unusual circumstances not present in this case, the granting of an equally long extended period of time to the Respondent for the preparation of its counter-memorial. Therefore, the Tribunal amends the arbitral schedule as follows: [Schedule omitted]

Merrill & Ring Forestry LP and *Government of Canada*, Decision of the Tribunal on Production of Documents (July 18, 2008) (ICSID administered, 1976 UNCITRAL Rules, NAFTA Chapter Eleven), at 8:

20. Canada has asserted in its letter of July 10, 2008, that claims on privileges have already been made in its submissions on refusals and there is thus no need to further elaborate on this question. But even if that were the case such claims are not specific in respect of identification and justification. Canada has also explained that at this stage it is only advising the Investor that the case may arise in its search for documents.
21. In the absence of this specific information the Investor is unable to agree or disagree with such refusal just as the Tribunal is unable to decide on a privilege which at present has no connection to specific documents or even less so justified or explained. The principle of equality in the treatment of the parties laid down by Article 15 of the [1976] UNCITRAL Arbitration Rules governing these proceedings also requires that such privileges be clearly explained so as to allow the Investor the opportunity to provide informed comments on the matter.
22. The Tribunal accordingly directs Canada that if it believes that a document will need to be protected under paragraph 6 (f) of the Document Production Order, it shall need to identify such document specifically, its date and description of its general contents. At the same time, Canada is required to provide the appropriate explanations about why it considers that the privilege must be asserted.

ICS Inspection and Control Services Ltd and *Argentine Republic*, Award on Jurisdiction (February 10, 2012) (PCA administered, 1976 UNCITRAL Rules, UK-Argentina BIT), at 13 (reprinting Procedural Order No 1 dated May 18, 2010):

4.2 For issues not dealt with in the [1976] UNCITRAL Rules or in the Treaty, the Tribunal shall apply the rules it deems appropriate, subject to Article 1(2) of the UNCITRAL Rules.

ICS Inspection and Control Services Ltd and *Argentine Republic*, Award on Jurisdiction (February 10, 2012) (PCA administered, 1976 UNCITRAL Rules, UK-Argentina BIT), at 84 (footnote omitted):

253. The Tribunal holds an inherent power over procedure. This power is implicit, but is also set out in Article 15(1) of the [1976] UNCITRAL Arbitration Rules...
254. Within the bounds of equality, due process, and the explicit stipulations of the [1976] UNCITRAL Arbitration Rules, the Tribunal has nearly unlimited discretion in relation to procedural matters. It has even been noted that under the [1976] UNCITRAL Arbitration Rules, as opposed to other procedural frameworks, a tribunal may even enjoy broad power in certain cases to overrule the parties' agreements on procedural matters.

(2) Article 15(1) (1976 Rules)—amicus submissions

Methanex Corp and *United States of America*, Decision on Petitions from Third Persons to Intervene as *Amici Curiae* (January 15, 2001) (ICSID administered, 1976 UNCITRAL Rules, NAFTA Chapter Eleven), reprinted in (2001) 13(3) World Trade & Arb Materials 97, 109–11, 114–15, 118–20:

24. ...In the Tribunal's view, there is nothing in either the [1976] UNCITRAL Arbitration rules or Chapter 11, Section B, that either expressly confers upon the Tribunal the power to accept *amicus* submissions or expressly provides that the Tribunal shall have no such power.

25. It follows that the Tribunal's powers in this respect must be inferred, if at all, from its more general procedural powers. In the Tribunal's view, the Petitioner's requests must be considered against Article 15(1) of the [1976] UNCITRAL Arbitration Rules; and it is not possible or appropriate to look elsewhere for any broader power or jurisdiction.

26. Article 15(1) of the [1976] UNCITRAL Arbitration Rules grants to the Tribunal a broad discretion as to the conduct of this arbitration, subject always to the requirements of procedural equality and fairness towards the Disputing Parties. It provides, broken down into numbered sub-paragraphs for ease of reference below, as follows:

"[1] Subject to these Rules, [2] the arbitral tribunal may conduct the arbitration in such manner as it considers appropriate, [3] provided that the parties are treated with equality and that at any stage in the proceedings each party is given a full opportunity of presenting its case."

This provision constitutes one of the essential "hallmarks" of an international arbitration under the [1976] UNCITRAL Arbitration Rules, according to the *travaux préparatoires*. Article 15 has also been described as the "heart" of the [1976] UNCITRAL Arbitration Rules; and its terms have since been adopted in Article 18 and 19(2) of the [1976] UNCITRAL Model Law on International Commercial Arbitration, where these provisions were considered as the procedural "Magna Carta" of international commercial arbitration. Article 15(1) is plainly a very important provision.

[The Tribunal turned to the issue of "whether the Tribunal's acceptance of *amicus* submissions falls within the general scope of the sub-paragraph numbered [2] of Article 15(1)"]

...

28. In addressing this issue, there are four principal matters to be considered:

   (i) whether the Tribunal's acceptance of *amicus* submissions falls within the general scope of...Article 15(1);
   (ii) if so, whether the acceptance of *amicus* submissions could affect the equal treatment of the Disputing Parties and the opportunity of each to present its case, under...Article 15(1);
   (iii) whether there are any provisions in Chapter 11, Section B, of NAFTA that modify the application of Article 15(1) for present purposes; and
   (iv) whether other provisions of the [1976] UNCITRAL Rules likewise modify the application of Article 15(1) in regard to this particular case, given the introductory words...of Article 15(1).

It is convenient to consider each matter in turn.

(i) The General Scope of Article 15(1) of the [1976] UNCITRAL Arbitration Rules

...

29. The Tribunal is required to decide a substantive dispute between the Claimant and the Respondent. The Tribunal has no mandate to decide any other substantive dispute or any dispute determining the legal rights of third persons. The legal boundaries of the arbitration are set by this essential legal fact. It is thus self-evident that if the Tribunal cannot directly, without consent, add another person as a party to this dispute or treat a third person as a party to the arbitration or NAFTA, it is equally precluded from achieving this result indirectly by

exercising a power over the conduct of the arbitration. Accordingly, in the Tribunal's view, the power under Article 15(1) must be confined to procedural matters. Treating non-parties as Disputing Parties or as NAFTA Parties cannot be matters of mere procedure; and such matters cannot fall within Article 15(1) of the [1976] UNCITRAL Rules.
30. However, in the Tribunal's view, its receipt of written submissions from a person other than the Disputing Parties is not equivalent to adding that person as a party to the arbitration....
31. The Tribunal considers that allowing a third person to make an *amicus* submission could fall within its procedural powers over the conduct of the arbitration, within the general scope of Article 15(1) of the [1976] UNCITRAL Arbitration Rules. The wording of...Article 15(1) suffices, in the Tribunal's view, to support its conclusion; but its approach is supported by the practice of the Iran-US Claims Tribunal and the World Trade Organisation.

[The Tribunal's discussion of the practice of these institutions, as well as that of the International Court of Justice, has been omitted.]

...

(ii) Safeguarding Equal Treatment

...

36. However, at least initially, the burden in meeting the Petitioners' written submissions would be shared by both Disputing Parties; and moreover, that burden cannot be regarded as inevitably excessive for either Disputing Party. As envisaged by the Tribunal, the Petitioners would make their submissions in writing, in a form and subject to limitations decided by the Tribunal. The Petitioners could not adduce the evidence of any factual or expert witness; and it would not therefore be necessary for either Disputing Party to cross-examine a witness proffered by the Petitioners: there could be no such witness. As to the contents of the Petitioners' written submissions; it would always be for the Tribunal to decide what weight (if any) to attribute to those submissions. Even if any part of those submissions were arguably to constitute written "evidence", the Tribunal would still retain a complete discretion under Article 25.6 of the [1976] UNCITRAL Arbitration Rules to determine its admissibility, relevance, materiality and weight. Of course, if either Disputing Party could not then complain at that burden: it was always required to meet its opponent's case; and that case, however supplemented, can form no extra unfair burden or unequal treatment.
37. It would always be the Tribunal's task, assisted by the Disputing Parties, to adopt procedures whereby any burden in meeting written submissions from a Petitioner was mitigated or extinguished. In theory, a difficulty could remain if a point was advanced by a Petitioner to which both Disputing Parties were opposed; but in practice, that risk appears small in this arbitration. In any case, it is not a risk the size or nature of which should swallow the general principle permitting written submissions from third persons. Accordingly, whilst there is a possible risk of unfair treatment as raised by the Claimant, the Tribunal is aware of that risk and considers that it must be addressed as and when it may arise. There is no immediate risk of unfair or unequal treatment for any Disputing Party or Party.

(iii) Relevant Provisions in Chapter 11, Section B, of NAFTA

...

(iv) Other [1976] UNCITRAL Rules

40. The Claimant's reliance on Article 25(4) of the [1976] UNCITRAL Arbitration Rules to the effect that hearings are to be held in camera is not relevant to the Petitioners' request to serve written submissions to the Tribunal. In the Tribunal's view, there are no further provisions under the [1976] UNCITRAL Arbitration Rules that modify the application of its general power under Article 15(1) to allow the Petitioners to make such submissions in this arbitration.
41. However, the Claimant's reliance on Article 25(4) is relevant to the Petitioners' request to attend hearings and to receive copies of all submissions and materials adduced before the Tribunal. [The

Tribunal declined to grant Petitioners these rights because the Parties had not consented in this regard pursuant to Article 25(4).] Article 25(4) provides that: "[Oral] Hearings shall be held in camera unless the parties agree otherwise…". The phrase "in camera" is clearly intended to exclude members of the public, i.e. non-party third persons such as the Petitioners. As the travaux préparatoires disclose, the UNCITRAL drafting committee deleted a different provision in an earlier draft which could have allowed the arbitration tribunal to admit into an oral hearing persons other than the parties. However, as discussed further below, Article 25(4) relates to the privacy of the oral hearings of the arbitration; and it does not in like terms address the confidentiality of the arbitration.

42. As to privacy, the Respondent has accepted that, as a result of Article 25(4), hearings are to be held in camera unless both Disputing Parties consent otherwise. The Respondent has given such consent. The Claimant has given no such consent. The Tribunal must therefore apply Article 25(4); and it has no power (or inclination) to undermine the effect of its terms. It follows that the Tribunal must reject the Petitioners' requests to attend oral hearings of the arbitration.

43. As to confidentiality, the Tribunal notes the conflicting legal materials as to whether Article 25(4) of the [1976] UNCITRAL Arbitration Rules imposes upon the Disputing Parties a further duty of confidentiality (beyond privacy) in regard to materials generated by parties within the arbitration….

…

46. This is however a difficult area; and for the present purposes, the Tribunal does not have to decide the point. Confidentiality is determined by the agreement of the Disputing Parties as recorded in the Consent Order regarding Disclosure and Confidentiality, forming part of the Minutes of Order of the Second Procedural meeting of 7th September 2000. As amici have no rights under Chapter 11 of NAFTA to receive any materials generated within the arbitration (or indeed any rights at all), they are to be treated by the Tribunal as any other members of the public….

(v) The Tribunal's Conclusion

47. *Power.* The Tribunal concludes that by Article 15(1) of the [1976] UNCITRAL Arbitration Rules it has the power to accept amicus submissions (in writing) from each of the Petitioners, to be copied simultaneously to the legal representatives of the Disputing Parties, Canada and Mexico…. The Tribunal also concludes that it has no power to accept the Petitioners' requests to receive materials generated within the arbitration or to attend oral hearings of the arbitration. Such materials may however may be derived from the public domain or disclosed into the public domain within the terms of the Consent Order regarding Disclosure and Confidentiality, or otherwise lawfully; but that is a quite separate matter outwith the scope of this decision.

…

(vi) The Tribunal's Order

53. For the reasons set out above, pursuant to Article 15(1) of the [1976] UNCITRAL Arbitration Rules, the Tribunal declares that it has the power to accept amicus written submissions from the Petitioners.

United Parcel Service of America Inc and *Government of Canada*, Decision on Petitions for Intervention and Participation as *Amici Curiae* (October 17, 2001) (ICSID administered, 1976 UNCITRAL Rules, NAFTA Chapter Eleven), *reprinted in* (2002) 14(1) World Trade & Arb Materials 41, 64–68:

[The Tribunal's discussion of the general nature of Article 15(1) of the 1976 UNCITRAL Rules in paragraphs 37 to 39 is omitted.]

The Tribunal's opinion and conclusion on the participation of amici curiae

59. The submission by Mexico raises a threshold issue: does the Tribunal have any power at all to allow third parties to participate in these proceedings? The Tribunal has already ruled that they cannot participate as parties to the proceedings. But is a less, *amicus curiae* role, permitted?

60. As all those making submissions agree, the answer is to be found in the powers conferred by article 15(1) [of the 1976 UNCITRAL Rules], read of course in its context. Those powers are limited to matters of procedure and they are constrained by other relevant rules and NAFTA provisions and by the principles of equality and fairness. They cannot be used to turn the dispute the subject of the arbitration into a different dispute, for instance by adding a new party to the arbitration. Rather, the powers are to be used to facilitate the Tribunal's process of inquiry into, understanding of, and resolving, that very dispute which has been submitted to it in accordance with the consent of the disputing parties.

61. Is it within the scope of article 15(1) for the Tribunal to receive submissions offered by third parties with the purpose of assisting the Tribunal in that process? The Tribunal considers that it is. It is part of its power to conduct the arbitration in such manner as it considers appropriate. As the *Methanex* Tribunal said, the receiving of such submissions from a third person is not equivalent to making that person a party to the arbitration. That person does not have any rights as a party or as a non-disputing Party. It is not participating to vindicate its rights. Rather, the Tribunal has exercised its power to permit that person to make the submission. It is a matter of its power rather than of third party right. The rights of the disputing Parties are not altered (although in exercise of their procedural rights they will have the rights to respond to any submission) and the legal nature of the arbitration remains unchanged.

...

63. We consider that article 15(1) supports a power to allow submissions by *amici curiae*.

64. In support of that conclusion, we call attention to the practice mentioned by the *Methanex* Tribunal of the Iran-US Claims Tribunal and the WTO Appellate Body which supports a power (but not a duty) to receive third party submission: *Iran v. United States* case A/15 Award No 63-A/15-FT; 2 Iran-US CTR 40, 43; and *Hot Rolled Lead and Carbon Steel*, order of the Appellate Body of the WTO. It is true that in contentious cases in the International Court of Justice only states and in certain circumstances public international organizations may have access to the Court (the latter only to provide information relevant to cases before it.) But that limit appears to result directly from the wording of articles 34, 35 and 61–64 of the Statute of the Court which carefully regulate those matters as well as from the practice under them extending over several decades; see Shabtai Rosenne *The Law and Practice of International Court, 1920–1966* (1997) chs 10 and 26.

...

Relevant provisions of NAFTA and the [1976] UNCITRAL Rules

...

67. The relevant provision of the [1976] UNCITRAL rules to which attention is given in the submissions is article 25(4) under which hearings are *in camera* unless the parties agree otherwise. They have not so agreed. The provision does not however prevent the Tribunal receiving written submissions. But it does prevent third parties or their representatives attending the hearings in the absence of both parties agreeing.

68. Next there is the difficult question of the confidentiality of the pleadings and other documents generated in the course of the proceeding... The privacy of the hearing is perhaps to be distinguished from the confidentiality or availability of documents. Under Chapter 11 and the [1976] UNCITRAL Rules provision is made for the communication of pleadings, documents and evidence to the other disputing party, the other NAFTA Parties, the Tribunal and the Secretariat—and to no one else. The matter is also subject to any agreement between the parties or order in respect of confidentiality....

The requirement of equality and of the full opportunity of parties to present their case

69. The requirement of equality and the parties' right to present their cases do limit the power of the Tribunal to conduct the arbitration in such manner as it considers

appropriate. That power is to be used not only to protect those rights of the parties, but also to investigate and determine the matter subject to arbitration in a just, efficient and expeditious manner. The power of the Tribunal to permit *amicus* submissions is not to be used in a way which is unduly burdensome for the parties or which unnecessarily complicates the Tribunal process. The Tribunal envisages that it will place limits on the submissions to be made in writing in terms for instance of the length. The third parties would not have the opportunity to call witnesses (given the effect of article 25(4)) with the result that the disputing parties would not face the need to cross-examine them or call contradictory evidence. The parties would also be entitled to have the opportunity to respond to any such submissions.

The Tribunal's assessment

70. The Tribunal returns to the emphasis which the petitioners, with considerable cogency, have placed on the important public character of the matters in issue in this arbitration and on their own real interests in these matters. It recalls as well the emphasis placed on the value of greater transparency for proceedings such as these. Such proceedings are not now, if they ever were, to be equated to the standard run of international commercial arbitration between private parties....

71. The Tribunal does not consider that among the matters on which it is appropriate for the Petitioners to make submissions are questions of jurisdiction and the place of arbitration. On both, the parties are fully able to present the competing contentions and in significant degree have already done so. In any event it is for the respondent to take jurisdictional points and the parties themselves have the power to fix the place of arbitration by agreement between them. The Tribunal does not consider that any other procedural matters of which it is award should be the subject of *amicus* submissions.

72. The circumstances and the detail of the making of any *amicus* submissions would be the subject of consultation with the parties.

Chevron Corp, et al and *Republic of Ecuador*, Procedural Order No 8 (April 18, 2011) (PCA administered, 1976 UNCITRAL Rules, US-Ecuador BIT), at 5:

18. As regards the two other orders sought by the Petitioners, the Tribunal notes that the Parties agree that they do not believe that the *amicus* submissions will be helpful to the Tribunal and neither side favours the participation of the petitioners during the jurisdictional phase of the arbitration, in which the issues to be decided are primarily legal and have already been extensively addressed by the Parties' submissions.

19. The Tribunal has yet to decide these issues of jurisdiction and admissibility; and it is not anticipated that the Parties will make further submissions to the Tribunal as regards these issues before the Tribunal's decision.

20. Accordingly, having considered the Amicus Petitions in all the circumstances currently prevailing in these arbitration proceedings, the Tribunal decides to exercise its discretion (*inter alia*) under Article 15(1) of the [1976] UNCITRAL Arbitration Rules not to permit the participation of the Petitioners as *amici curiae* at this stage of the arbitration.

D. Extracts from the Practice of the Iran–US Claims Tribunal

(1) General and Tribunal Rules (1983), Article 15(1)

E-Systems, Inc and *Islamic Republic of Iran*, Award No ITM 13–388-FT (February 4, 1983) at 6, reprinted in 2 Iran-US CTR 51, 54 (1983-II):

Upon invitation of the Tribunal in accordance with Note 5 to Article 15 of the [1983] Provisionally Adopted Tribunal Rules the Government of the United States has submitted oral and written statements with a view to assisting the Tribunal in carrying out its task.

Foremost Tehran Inc and *Islamic Republic of Iran*, Case Nos 37 and 231, Chamber One, Order of September 15, 1983, reprinted in 3 Iran-US CTR 361, 362 (1983-II):

> Article 15 of the [1983] Tribunal Rules requires that the Tribunal treat the parties equally. This is a fundamental principle of justice. In the circumstances of these cases, the delicate balance of equality would be tipped if one party were to be permitted to present an extensive Memorial and additional exhibits, without providing an opportunity for the other party to file a memorial in response. While the filing by Claimants of their Memorial on the Merits prior to the Hearing may be an advantage to the Respondents in that it informs them in detail of Claimants' contentions and arguments and may be of assistance to the Tribunal in analyzing the case, nevertheless it cannot be accepted without providing the Respondents an equal opportunity to make a written submission.

Amman & Whitney and *Ministry of Housing and Urban Development* (Khuzestan Department of Housing and Urban Development), Case No 198, Chamber One, Order of January 30, 1984:

> The conduct of proceedings before this Tribunal is governed by the [1983] Tribunal Rules and by no national procedural system.

Dames & Moore and *Islamic Republic of Iran*, Decision No DEC 36–54–3 (April 23, 1985) at 15, reprinted in 8 Iran-US CTR 107, 115 (1985-I):

> It is clear from the language and context of Article 15 [of the 1983 Tribunal Rules] that its operative terms apply during the arbitral proceedings themselves, prior to the issuance of an award. Its applicability terminates with the rendering of an award. This is especially apparent when Article 15 is compared with Article 29(2),...

George W Drucker Jr and *Foreign Transaction Co*, Case No 121, Chamber Two, Order of May 2, 1986:

> The Tribunal notes a document received by the Tribunal's Registry on 25 April 1986, submitted by M. A. Saheb, who identifies himself as the Chairman and Managing Director of South Gulf Trading and Shipping Limited of Dubai, who is not a party in this Case.
>
> Pursuant to note 5 to Article 15 of the [1983] Tribunal Rules and taking into consideration that the above-mentioned document may assist the Tribunal in deciding the jurisdictional issue regarding the Claimant's ownership and control of SGTC, the Tribunal decides that such document should be filed by the Registry and served on the Parties.

Watkins-Johnson Company and *Islamic Republic of Iran*, Case No 370, Chamber One, Order of December 3, 1987:

> On 27 November 1987 the Claimants filed a request for permission to file a "Supplemental Memorial and Summary of Evidence" in response to "Respondents' Brief and Evidence and Rebuttal Memorial" filed on 15 September 1987 (Doc. No 178). The Claimants did not allege that Respondents' Doc. no. 178 contains improper rebuttal material and identified no new material. Together with this request, the Claimants filed the "Supplemental Memorial and Summary of Evidence" that it requested be admitted.
>
> It has been the established practice of the Tribunal to close the exchange of written pleadings after the submission of Memorials in Rebuttal. In order to secure equal treatment of the Parties and an orderly conduct of the proceedings, the Tribunal admits further written submission close to the Hearing date only in exceptional circumstances. It finds no reason to depart from this practice in the circumstances of this Case, particularly in view of the fact that the Hearing has already been postponed once to afford the Parties another round of written pleadings.

General Electric Co and *Islamic Republic of Iran*, Case No 386, Chamber One, Order of December 10, 1987:

On 30 November 1987 the Claimant filed a Request for an Order authorizing the Parties in this Case to file simultaneous surrebuttals. In the Request it is stated that the Respondents' rebuttal Memorial and Exhibits filed on 3 August 1987 contain new arguments and evidence. It is also stated that a round of surrebuttal pleadings would afford the Respondents a further opportunity to respond fully to Claimant's evidence and arguments.

It has been the established practice of the Tribunal to close the exchange of written pleadings after the submission of Memorials in Rebuttal. In order to secure equal treatment of the Parties and an orderly conduct of the proceedings, the Tribunal admits further written submissions close to the Hearing date only in exceptional circumstances.

The Tribunal finds no reason to allow a further round of submissions in the present Case. If any of the material filed by the Respondents on 3 August 1987 is found not to fall within the definition of rebuttal evidence, it will be ruled inadmissible and disregarded. The Claimant's request is therefore denied.

Fedders Corp and *Loristan Refrigeration Industries*, Case No 250, Chamber Three, Order of January 5, 1988:

On that date the Tribunal also received the documents in French language, dated 6 March, 15 April and 5 October 1987, allegedly related to the criminal proceedings at the Swiss court initiated by the Respondents. The above submissions were made in support of the Respondents' request to "suspend the proceedings in this Case, pending determination of suit" in the Swiss court.

On 30 October 1987 the Claimant objected to the above request and to the submission of the above documents.

The Tribunal's proceedings are governed by the Declaration of the Government of the Democratic and Popular Republic of Algeria and by the Tribunal Rules of Procedure. None of these texts obliges the Tribunal to suspend the proceedings before it for the reason of an alleged initiation of the criminal proceedings in a national court by one of the Parties. Such a suspension could be only a matter of convenience.

Gloria Jean Cherafat and *Islamic Republic of Iran*, Decision No DEC 106–277–2 (June 25, 1992), reprinted in 28 Iran-US CTR 216, 221–23 (1992) (footnotes omitted):

19. As to the existence, or the exercise of any inherent power to reinstate a terminated Case, the Tribunal practice fails to provide conclusive guidance; indeed, the Tribunal has specifically reserved its position as to whether it has inherent power to revise an award under exceptional circumstances. *See,* e.g. *World Farmers Trading Inc.* and *Government Trading Corporation,* et al., Decision No DEC 93–764–1, para 3 (3 Oct. 1990), *reprinted in* 25 Iran-U.S. C.T.R. 186, 187 (1990-II); *Dames & Moore* and *The Islamic Republic of Iran,* Decision No DEC 36–54–3, pp. 18–21 (23 Apr. 1985), *reprinted in* 5 Iran-U.S. C.T.R. 107, 117–18 (1984-I); *Mark Dallal* and *Islamic Republic of Iran,* Decision No DEC 30–149–1 (12 Jan. 1984), *reprinted in* 5 Iran-U.S. C.T.R. 74, 745 (1984-I); *Henry Morris* and *Government of the Islamic Republic of Iran* et al., Decision No DEC 26–200–1, p. 2 (16 Sept. 1983), *reprinted in* 3 Iran-U.S. C.T.R. 364, 365 (1983-II).

20. Of the Decisions cited above, the Decision most on point is *Dames & Moore*. There, the Tribunal rejected the Respondent's request to reopen a case allegedly based on forged documents and perjured affidavits. The Tribunal concluded that even a generous reading of the Respondent's allegations of fraud did "not raise justified concern that the processes of the Tribunal [had] been subverted." The Tribunal thus did not need to decide whether it possessed inherent authority to reopen a case procured by fraud:

> In the absence of an express grant of authority to the Tribunal to reopen and reconsider cases in the merits after issuance of an award, the question has been posed as to whether

an "inherent power" to do so may exist "under exceptional circumstances", at least where an award "was based on forged documents or perjury." [citing *Henry Morris* and *Mark Dallal*, above]. The implied or inherent power of an international claims tribunal in this area is an issue which has been subjected to learned analysis and limited judicial scrutiny, with wholly inconsistent results. [...] The instant request for reopening and reconsideration, however, falls well short of justifying any such effort to ascertain the precise balance struck between finality of Tribunal dispositions, on the one hand, and the integrity of its processes on the other.

21. As in *Dames and Moore*, the Tribunal has first to examine the request to determine whether there exists a *prima facie* case to justify reinstatement and if such a case exists, whether the Tribunal possesses inherent power to do so under the circumstances.

...

24. The evidence submitted by the Applicants falls short of establishing a *prima facie* case...

Dadras Intl, et al and *Islamic Republic of Iran,* et al, Award No 567–213/215–3 (November 7, 1995), reprinted in 31 Iran-US CTR 127, 135–36, 143–44 (1995) (footnotes omitted):

27. The Tribunal Rules grant considerable discretion to the Tribunal to admit or exclude written submissions. This discretion includes the power to accept unauthorized post-Hearing submissions, as derived from Article 15, paragraph 1; Article 22; Article 25, paragraph 6; and Article 29, paragraph 2 of the [1983] Tribunal Rules.
28. Tribunal precedent is, however, strongly against the admission into evidence of unauthorized late-filed documents. The Tribunal has expressed a particular aversion to admitting documents that are submitted not only after filing deadlines, but also after the Hearing itself. The most extensive treatment of this issue is to be found in *Harris International Telecommunications, Inc.* and *The Islamic Republic of Iran,* et al, Award No 323–409–1 (2 November 1987), *reprinted in* 17 Iran-U.S. C.T.R. 31, 45–50.
29. Harris emphasizes that in deciding whether to admit a late submission, it is important that the Tribunal treat the parties equally and fairly, bearing in mind that accepting late-filed documents from one party can result in prejudice to the other. A further consideration is the "orderly conduct of the proceedings." In applying these principles to the facts of a given case, the Tribunal should consider the "character and contents of late-filed documents and the length and cause of the delay." Late-filed submissions containing new facts and evidence "are the most likely to cause prejudice to the other Party and to disrupt the arbitral process if filed late."
30. Thus the considerations that are generally relevant when deciding whether to admit late-filed documents are the possibility of prejudice, the equality of treatment of the Parties, the disruption of the arbitral process caused by the delay and the reason for the delay.

...

59. The Agent of Iran also cited Article 15, paragraph 1 of the [1983] Rules as authority for the Respondents' request to reopen [the hearing].... The Agent of Iran argued that

> [t]here is no doubt that if an affidavit is accepted as evidence in a case while, on the other hand, the adverse party is not given the permission to orally and directly examine the said witness at the hearing session, the latter will be completely deprived of the "full opportunity" he is supposed to be given for presenting his Case. In other words, it is not possible to deprive a party of the right of examining a witness whose written testimony has been accepted and still claim that the latter party has been granted a "full opportunity" of presenting his case.

60. The Tribunal need hardly point out, however, that this Tribunal (like many others) customarily accepts affidavits into evidence and takes account of those affidavits without the opposing party necessarily being given the opportunity to cross-examine the affiant. Several examples (unchallenged by either of the Parties) are to be found in these very Cases.
61. Furthermore, the Tribunal is unpersuaded that any Party can credibly claim that it has been denied a "full opportunity of presenting [its] case" given the procedural history of these Cases.

The key word is "opportunity": the Tribunal is obliged to provide the framework within which the parties may present their cases, but is by no means obliged to acquiesce in a party's desire for a particular sequence of proceedings or to permit repetitious proceedings.

Vivian Mai Tavakoli, et al and *Government of the Islamic Republic of Iran,* Award No 580–832–3 (April 23, 1997), reprinted in 33 Iran-US CTR 206, 211 (1997):

9. Under the [1983] Tribunal Rules the Tribunal has the discretion to accept unauthorized late submissions from the Parties. See Article 15, paragraph 1, and Article 22 of the [1983] Tribunal Rules. However, in the interests of the orderly conduct of the proceedings and in order to maintain "equality of arms," it has in general taken a restrictive approach to the exercise of this discretion. *See,* for example, *Dadras International, et al.* and *Islamic Republic of Iran, et al.*, Award No 567–213/215–3, paras 27–28 (7 Nov. 1995), *reprinted in* 31 Iran-U.S. C.T.R. 127, 135–36; *Edgar Protiva, et al.* and *Government of the Islamic Republic of Iran,* Award No 566–316–2, paras 30–36 (14 July 1995), *reprinted in* 31 Iran-U.S. C.T.R. 89, 102–03 ("Protiva"); *Reza Said Malek and Government of the Islamic Republic of Iran,* Award No 534–193–3, para 12 (11 Aug. 1992), *reprinted in* 28 Iran-U.S. C.T.R. 246, 249–50; *Harris International Telecommunications, Inc.* and *Islamic Republic of Iran, et al.*, Award No 323–409–1 (2 Nov. 1987), *reprinted in* 17 Iran-U.S. C.T.R. 31, 45–50. In the present Case, the Tribunal's Order of 17 April 1996 clearly restricted the scope of the submissions to be made by both Parties. In light of these restrictions and in the absence of any other justifying circumstances, the Tribunal excludes from the record items 3, 4 and 6 of the Respondent's submission of 27 June 1996, the Claimant's entire submission of 22 July 1996 and the Respondent's entire submission of 20 August 1996.

Vera-Jo Miller Aryeh, et al and *Islamic Republic of Iran,* Award No 581–842/843/844–1 (May 22, 1997), reprinted in 33 Iran-US CTR 272, 287–88 (1997):

48. The Tribunal notes that, according to its practice reflected in *Harris International Telecommunications, Inc.* and *The Islamic Republic of Iran, et al.*, Partial Award No 323–409–1, paras 57–75 (2 Nov. 1987), *reprinted* in 17 Iran-U.S. C.T.R. 31, 45–52, Articles 15, 22, 23, and 28 of the [1983] Tribunal Rules are the primary rules regulating the status of late-filed documents....

49. Furthermore, on the basis of Article 15 [of the 1983 Tribunal Rules], both parties to the case have to be treated equally. This means that both parties to the case are entitled to have an equal opportunity to present written submissions and to respond to each other's submissions. This also means that the parties must have an equal opportunity to go through the evidence and the arguments submitted by the other party, and to prepare their own position and arguments in advance of the hearing.

50. Chamber One has taken a strict stance on these matters: no new evidence is permitted prior to the hearing unless the Tribunal finds that it is justified by exceptional circumstances and is filed no later than two months before the hearing in the case. Moreover, as a matter of routine in its orders scheduling a hearing the Chamber advises the parties that any party is free to make whatever arguments it wishes at the hearing; however, parties may not introduce new documents into evidence absent the Tribunal's permission. Such permission normally is not granted except for rebuttal evidence introduced to rebut evidence produced at the hearing.

...

52. Typically, the practice not to allow new evidence in the record encompasses not only the two-month period directly preceding the hearing but also the post-hearing period preceding the filing of an award. The practice of Chamber One has been strict, even though the Chamber has taken into consideration the nature of these documents, the elapsed period of time, and the reasons for the delay, when deciding on the admissibility of late-filed, unauthorized documents. Usually, the Tribunal has rejected the late-filed unauthorized documents in order to prevent any party from using "tactical" filings at the hearing or thereafter.

(2) Tribunal Rules (1983), Article 15(2)

The Austin Co and *Machine Sazi Arak*, Case No 295, Chamber Two, Order of July 30, 1982:

The Parties are hereby notified that a settlement or pre-hearing conference in this case will be held on Thursday 16 December at 9.00 am at Parkweg 13, The Hague. The Parties should be prepared to discuss the matters indicated in the schedule annexed. The Parties are requested in particular to have available all necessary authorizations and approvals in the event that a settlement should result.

ANNEX

(a) Clarification of the issues presented and relief sought;
(b) identification and clarification of any issues to be considered as preliminary questions and particularly the issue of jurisdiction;
(c) status of any settlement discussions;
(d) whether any further documents or written statements, including any reply or rejoinder, are requested by the arbitrating parties or required by the arbitral tribunal;
(e) fixing a schedule for submission by each arbitrating party of a summary of the documents or lists of witness or other evidence it intends to present at the hearing;
(f) fixing a schedule for submission of any documents, exhibits or other evidence which the arbitral tribunal may require;
(g) desirability of appointing an expert by the arbitral tribunal and, if so, the expert's qualifications and terms of reference; whether the arbitrating parties intend to present experts and, if so, the qualification of and the areas of expertise to be covered by any such expert;
(h) determining what documentary evidence will require translation;
(i) fixing a schedule of hearings;
(j) other appropriate matters.

Sylvania Technical Systems, Inc and *Islamic Republic of Iran*, Case No 64, Chamber One, Order of May 10, 1983:

The Tribunal intends to decide on the basis of the documents submitted (i) whether the forum selection clause in the Contract excludes jurisdiction of the Tribunal and (ii) whether the claim is a claim by a national of the United States as defined in Article VII of the Claims Settlement Declaration.

Phelps Dodge Corp and Overseas Private Investment Corp and *Islamic Republic of Iran*, Case No 99, Chamber Two, Order of May 8, 1984:

The Tribunal wishes to point out that, contrary to the provisions relating to Hearings, the Tribunal Rules do not contain any provision by which the Parties are entitled to a Pre-hearing Conference when they make a request to that effect. Moreover, the practice of the Tribunal to date has been to schedule Pre-hearing Conferences only when the Tribunal deems it necessary for the proper scheduling of further proceedings. In quite a number of cases this is not necessary, such as in the present case.

White Consolidated Industries Inc and *Iran Compressor Manufacturing Co*, Case No 126, Chamber Two, Order of December 7, 1984:

In view of the large number of pending cases and the practical limits on the number of hearings and deliberations that can be held during each year, the Tribunal cannot afford, as a general practice, to separate certain issues for preliminary hearing and decision but must normally join such issues to the merits.

Component Builders, Inc and *Islamic Republic of Iran*, Case No 395, Chamber Three, Order of February 19, 1985:

> ...neither the [1983] Tribunal Rules nor Tribunal practice requires that there be a Pre-Hearing Conference or that a Hearing be held on requests for interim measures or preliminary issues such as jurisdiction.

Parvin Mariam Samrad and *Islamic Republic of Iran*, Case No 465, Chamber Two, Order of July 28, 1986:

> The Tribunal does not find that the reasons invoked by the Respondent in this submission constitute strong and compelling reasons. Nevertheless, it is prepared to grant a last extension for the filing of Respondent's submission until 21 October 1986. After that date, the Tribunal will take a decision regarding its jurisdiction on the basis of the briefs and evidence before it.

World Farmers Trading Inc and *Government Trading Corp*, Case No 764, Chamber One, Order of August 4, 1986:

> Unless by 18 February 1987 either Party has filed a request for an oral Hearing, both the jurisdictional issues and the merits of the Case will be decided thereafter by the Tribunal on the basis of the documents submitted.

Tai, Inc and *Islamic Republic of Iran*, Case No 421, Chamber One, Order of August 12, 1986:

> The Tribunal makes the following order pursuant to the pre-hearing conference held on 1 July 1986:
>
> 1 The Tribunal does not consider it appropriate at the present stage of the proceedings to issue an interlocutory Award disposing of jurisdictional or other preliminary issues.
>
> It is the present intention of the Tribunal that the issues raised in paragraphs 2 and 3 above shall thereafter be decided on the basis of the documents submitted.

United States of America on behalf and for the benefit of the New York Blower Co and *Islamic Republic of Iran*, Case No 10418, Chamber Two, Order of September 1, 1986:

> 1. Considering the nature of the dispute and the amount involved in the claim in relation to the costs that will be incurred by the parties in the event of a hearing, the Tribunal is prepared to decide this claim on the basis of the documents submitted.
> 2. The Tribunal will decide the claim without a hearing unless a request for a hearing is filed by either party not later than 22 September 1986. In the event such a request is filed, the hearing will be held on October 20, 1986 at Parkweg 13, The Hague starting at 9.30 am.

Tchacosh Co, Inc and *Islamic Republic of Iran*, Award No 540–192–1 (December 9, 1992), reprinted in 28 Iran-US CTR 371, 379–80 (1992):

> 21. As noted above, ... Iran withdrew its earlier request for a hearing on jurisdictional issues by its submission filed on 5 February 1992. As noted also in para 11, Siporex California requested in its submission filed on 22 June 1992 "a formal hearing and the presentation of evidence since the respondents have criticized and slandered the evidence presented on behalf of the claimant in support of its claim contending it is unreliable and fabricated." This request for hearing must be denied. More than a year before Siporex California requested a hearing, the Tribunal had, by Order filed on 14 March 1991, informed the Parties that it "intends to take a decision regarding its jurisdiction on the basis of the evidence before it..." The Tribunal notes that the Claimant was free at that time to request a hearing, but it chose not to do so. Instead, it and the Respondents filed extensive pleadings within the framework of the Tribunal's Order, without any mention of a request for a hearing. In the circumstances, the request for a hearing was not made at an appropriate time. Although Article 15, paragraph 2, of the

[1983] Tribunal Rules states that a party may request a hearing at "any stage of the proceedings", the Tribunal has previously held that "such provision should be interpreted, in the light of the particular circumstance of each case, to mean that Hearings are to be held upon the reasonable request of a party made at an appropriate stage of the proceedings." *See World Farmers Trading Inc.* and *Government Trading Corporation, et al.*, Award No 428–764–1 (7 July 1989), para 16, *reprinted in* 22 Iran-U.S. C.T.R. 204, at 209 (1989–II). Further, it is clear from its request that the Claimant seeks a hearing in order to present evidence in connection with the authenticity of certain documents that Iran asserts were fabricated. However, no hearing for that purpose is needed because, for reasons stated below,... the Tribunal decides that it has no jurisdiction in this Case regardless of the Parties' dispute on the authenticity of those documents.

Islamic Republic of Iran and *United States of America*, Case Nos A3, A8, A9, A14 and B16, Full Tribunal, Order of December 3, 1992:

3. The Tribunal notes that the Parties appear to disagree about the controlling precedent in these Cases, the Claimant citing Award No 382-B 1-FT (31 Aug. 1988) and the Respondent citing Award No 529-A15 (II:A and II:B)-FT (6 May 1992). The Tribunal also notes that the Parties appear to envisage somewhat different proceedings and filings.
4. In these circumstances, the Tribunal believes that it would be desirable to have a Pre-Hearing Conference with the Parties prior to its decision on the further proceedings in these consolidated Cases.
5. Accordingly, the Parties are requested to attend a Pre-Hearing Conference in these consolidated Cases to be held at Parkweg 13 on 10 February 1993, commencing at 9:30 a.m.
6. The following matters will be considered at the Pre-Hearing Conference:
    (a) identification of any issues that the Parties believe the Tribunal should consider as preliminary questions;
    (b) procedures for avoiding overlap between properties at issue in these consolidated Cases and properties at issue in Case No A15 (II:A);
    (c) further proceedings in these consolidated Cases, including the schedule for further submissions by the Parties:
    (d) any other procedural issues relating to these consolidated Cases that the Parties or the Tribunal may wish to raise at the Pre-Hearing Conference.

Ninni Ladjevardi (formerly Burgel) and *Islamic Republic of Iran*, Case No 118, Chamber One, Order of March 24, 1993:

On March 1993, the Respondent filed "Respondent's Rebuttal Brief on the Issue of Claimant's Dominant and Effective Nationality". Both Parties having now filed their rebuttals, the Tribunal takes note of the Claimant's request for "oral argument on the issue of the dominant and effective nationality" contained in her submission, filed on 31 October 1991, and in accordance with Article 15, paragraph 2 of the [1983] Tribunal Rules, orders as follows:

The Parties are requested to appear before Chamber One of the Tribunal for a Hearing, restricted to the issue of the Claimant's dominant and effective nationality, which is scheduled to take place on 11 June 1993 at Parkweg 13, The Hague, starting at 9:30 a.m.

Dadras Intl, et al and *Islamic Republic of Iran*, et al, Award No 567–213/215–3 (November 7, 1995), reprinted in (1995) 31 Iran-US CTR 127, 143 (footnotes omitted):

56. The Tribunal concludes that Article 15, paragraph 2 [of the 1983 Tribunal Rules] is primarily applicable to the situation where there has not yet been a hearing and one of the parties requests one. The right of the parties to request a hearing under Article 15, paragraph 2 is not, however, an absolute right. For example, in *World Farmers Trading, Inc.* and *Government Trading Corporation, et al.*, Award No 428–764–1 (7 July 1989), *reprinted in* 22 Iran-U.S. C.T.R. 204, 209, the Tribunal held that although Article 15, paragraph 2 of the [1983] Tribunal

Rules states that a party may request a hearing "at any stage of the proceedings," "[t]his provision should be interpreted, in light of the particular circumstances of each case, to mean that Hearings are to be held upon the reasonable request of a party made at an appropriate stage of the proceedings." This interpretation of Article 15, paragraph 2 was followed in *Tchacosh Company, Inc., et al.* and *The Government of the Islamic Republic of Iran, et al.*, Award No 540–192–1, para 21 (9 December 1992), *reprinted in* 28 Iran-U.S. C.T.R. 37, 380, in which the Tribunal refused to grant the claimant's request for a hearing, saying that the request had not been made at an "appropriate time" because it was made more than one year after the Tribunal had informed the Parties of its intention to take a decision on jurisdiction on the basis of the written evidence before it.

57. Thus even where no hearing has been held, Article 15, paragraph 2 does not oblige the Tribunal to accede to any request by a party for a hearing. The applicable criteria in evaluating each request are whether the request is both reasonable and made at an appropriate stage of the proceedings. In a context such as the present, where a Hearing has already been held, the reasonableness of the request and the appropriateness of the timing become even more important because the disruption of the arbitral process is that much greater and because the parties have already had an extensive opportunity to present their cases.

58. For the foregoing reasons, the Tribunal does not consider Article 15, paragraph 2 to be capable of justifying the reopening of the Hearing in the present situation.

4. Place of Arbitration—Article 18

As the preceding discussion concerning Article 17(1) indicated, the choice of the place of arbitration is not only a practical matter, but also may involve significant legal consequences in the form of local mandatory norms. Given that such a choice may decisively affect the validity and enforceability of an award, the issue is much more important than might appear at first blush.

A. Text of the 2010 UNCITRAL Rule[256]

Article 18 of the 2010 UNCITRAL Rules provides:

1. If the parties have not previously agreed on the place of arbitration, the place of arbitration shall be determined by the arbitral tribunal having regard to the circumstances of the case. The award shall be deemed to have been made at the place of arbitration.
2. The arbitral tribunal may meet at any location it considers appropriate for deliberations. Unless otherwise agreed by the parties, the arbitral tribunal may also meet at any location it considers appropriate for any other purpose, including hearings.

---

[256] Corresponding Article 16 of the 1976 UNCITRAL Rule provides:

1. Unless the parties have agreed upon the place where the arbitration is to be held, such place shall be determined by the arbitral tribunal, having regard to the circumstances of the arbitration.
2. The arbitral tribunal may determine the locale of the arbitration within the country agreed upon by the parties. It may hear witnesses and hold meetings for consultation among its members at any place it deems appropriate, having regard to the circumstances of the arbitration.
3. The arbitral tribunal may meet at any place it deems appropriate for the inspection of goods, other property or documents. The parties shall be given sufficient notice to enable them to be present at such inspection.
4. The award shall be made at the place of arbitration.

Article 16 was adopted by the Iran–US Claims Tribunal without modification.

B. Commentary

(1) Meaning of "place of arbitration"

Article 18(1) includes the phrase "place of arbitration," a term of art referring to the legal seat of the arbitration. In international arbitration, the selection of the place of arbitration typically denotes the jurisdiction whose national arbitration law, or *lex arbitri*, governs the arbitration and, in some cases, the concomitant supervisory jurisdiction of the courts of that jurisdiction.[257] Thus, for example, where the parties choose London as the place of arbitration, that choice would translate into the application of the United Kingdom's Arbitration Act 1996 to the arbitration.[258] The law of the place of arbitration may regulate matters, such as the validity of an agreement to arbitrate, the non-arbitrability of certain subject matter, interim measures, the form and validity of the arbitral award, and the parties' respective rights to challenge and enforce the award. The terms of the *lex arbitri* may not always be attractive to one or both of the disputing parties.[259] In addition, in some cases they may supersede the terms of the UNCITRAL Rules.[260] Consequently, the law of the place of arbitration should be studied carefully before the place of arbitration is selected.

The "place of arbitration" has a significance that is sharply distinct from the "location" of certain meetings that comprise significant aspects of the arbitration, such as the hearings and deliberations. As Born notes, "It is critical to appreciate that the concept of the arbitral 'seat' (or 'place') is a legal construct, not a geographic or physical location."[261] The term "location," as used in Article 18(2), thus refers only to the physical or geographical place of arbitral meetings.[262] Consequently, under the Rules, these types of meetings may occur outside the jurisdiction of the law governing the arbitration, typically for purposes of convenience, without any legal effect on the choice of the place of arbitration. Thus, for example, if the place of arbitration is London and the hearings are held outside the UK, eg, in Paris, the arbitration remains subject to the UK Arbitration Act 1996. The bifurcation of Article 18 into two paragraphs—the first to address the place of arbitration, the second

---

[257] See E Gaillard and J Savage, *Fouchard, Gaillard, Goldman*, n 126, 651. For general discussion on the place of arbitration, see M Storme and F De Ly, *The Place of Arbitration* (1992); Y Derains, "The Choice of the Place of Arbitration," (1986) Intl Business L J 109. See also *Report of the Secretary-General on the Revised Draft Set of Arbitration Rules*, UNCITRAL, 9th Session, Addendum 1 (Commentary), UN Doc A/CN.9/112/Add.1 (1975), reprinted in (1976) VII UNCITRAL Ybk 166, 172 (Commentary on Draft Article 15(4)). Article 16(4) of the 1976 UNCITRAL Rules may be read as equating the place "where the award is made" with the "place of arbitration."

For a general discussion on the impact that the seat of arbitration has on the *lex arbitri* see L Mistelis, "Reality Test: Current State of Affairs in Theory and Practice Relating to 'Lex Arbitri'" (2006) 17 American Rev Intl Arb 172–74.

[258] The choice of the law governing the procedure, of course, may be different from the law governing the substance of the dispute.

[259] As one example leading practitioners identify the power of local courts or arbitrators to consolidate arbitral claims. N Blackaby and C Partasides, *Redfern and Hunter on International Arbitration*, n 2, 177–8 (citing Article 1046 of the Netherlands Arbitration Act 1986).

[260] 2010 UNCITRAL Arbitration Rules, art 1(1).

[261] G Born, *International Commercial Arbitration*, n 182, 1248. See also A J van den Berg, "Organizing an International Arbitration: Practice Pointers," in L Newman and R Hill (eds) *The Leading Arbitrators' Guide to International Arbitration* (2004) 182.

[262] See *Methanex Corp* and *United States of America*, Order on the Place of Arbitration (September 7, 2000) (ICSID administered, 1976 UNCITRAL Rules, NAFTA Chapter Eleven), at 3, para 2 (observing that "[corresponding] Article 16(1)[of the 1976 UNCITRAL Rules] refers to the legal place or seat of the arbitration as distinct from the geographical place of the arbitration's hearing or hearings and deliberations by the Tribunal").

concerning the geographical location of meetings—is meant to reinforce this important difference in concept.[263]

Inclusion of the term "place of arbitration" improves the clarity of the Rules. Corresponding Article 16(1) of the 1976 UNCITRAL Rules previously contained the phrase "the place where the arbitration is to be held" to indicate the legal seat of the arbitration.[264] As leading commentators observed, "[t]he existing expression in many cases creates the mistaken impression that the place chosen for occasional meetings is also the formal place of arbitration."[265] During revision of the Rules, some proposed use of the terms "seat," "legal seat," or "juridical seat" of arbitration,[266] rather than "place of arbitration," as clearer terminology for signaling to users of the Rules the legal, rather than geographical, implications of choosing the place whose domestic law is to govern the arbitral procedure.[267] Though any of these proposed terms would serve as synonymous substitutes,[268] some Working Group delegates noted that "new terminology" might complicate existing contractual practice where parties had already included the phrase "place of arbitration" in their agreements to indicate the legal place of arbitration.[269] In the end, the Working Group adopted the phrase "place of arbitration" largely to ensure consistency with the terminology of the UNCITRAL Model Law.[270]

The Rules do not address the legal effect of the selection of the place of arbitration as a matter of domestic law. During Working Group discussions, it was proposed that the Rules should clarify that this choice determined the law applicable to the arbitral procedure, including court jurisdiction. The Working Group did not adopt this proposal, on grounds that "the legal consequences arising from the choice of the seat of arbitration might differ in different legal systems, and that the Rules were not the appropriate instrument to codify the matter."[271] This interpretation is consistent with the aim of Article 1(3) of the Rules, which clearly establishes that the Rules regulate the internal process of the arbitral proceedings, subject to the mandatory terms of the law governing the arbitration, and do not themselves speak to that law.

---

[263] UNCITRAL, 40th Session, UN Doc A/CN.9/619, n 5, at 27, para 142. See also J Castello, "UNCITRAL Rules," n 34, 1473 ("In using the word 'location' to identify alternative meeting sites, the Working Group hopes to reduce confusion by reserving the word 'place' to designate only where the arbitration is legally seated."); J Levine, "Current Trends in International Arbitral Practice as Reflected in the Revision of the UNCITRAL Arbitration Rules" (2007) 14(1) U New South Wales L J 266, 274.

[264] In other provisions of Article 16 of the 1976 UNCITRAL Rules, the "locale" of the arbitration and the "place" for the inspection of goods are referred to, which may cause additional confusion.

[265] Paulsson and Petrochilos observe that "[t]he existing expression in the many cases creates the mistaken impression that the place chosen for occasional meetings is also the formal place of arbitration." J Paulsson and G Petrochilos, "Revision of the UNCITRAL Rules," (A Report Commissioned by the UNCITRAL Secretariat), March 31, 2006, at 12, para 141.

[266] UNCITRAL, 40th Session, UN Doc A/CN.9/614, n 5, at 19, para 88; UNCITRAL, 40th Session, UN Doc A/CN.9/619, n 5, at 27, para 139. Similarly, Article 16 of the 1998 LCIA Arbitration Rules uses the phrase "the seat (or legal place)" of arbitration.

[267] UNCITRAL, 40th Session, UN Doc A/CN.9/614, n 5, at 19, para 88.

[268] See G Born, *International Commercial Arbitration*, n 182, 1250 (noting synonymous terms like "seat," "place," "situs," and "forum," but preferring "seat" because it avoids "the arguably geographical connotation of the 'place' of arbitration, and instead connotes an arbitration's connection to, or rootedness in, a legal regime").

[269] UNCITRAL, 40th Session, UN Doc A/CN.9/619, n 5, at 27, para 141.

[270] According to the UNCITRAL Secretariat, a draft containing the phrase "place of arbitration" aims to "distinguish between the place of arbitration (meaning the legal seat) and the location where meetings could be held, in terms similar to those adopted under article 20 of the UNCITRAL Model Law on International Commercial Arbitration." *Settlement of Commercial Disputes: Revision of the UNCITRAL Arbitration Rules, Note by the Secretariat*, UNCITRAL, UN Doc A/CN.9/WG.II/WP.151 at 17, para 38 (2008).

[271] UNCITRAL, 40th Session, UN Doc A/CN.9/619, n 5, at 27, para 143.

(2) Selection of the place of arbitration—Article 18(1)

(a) Considerations to be taken into account

Article 18(1) grants the arbitral tribunal authority, in the absence of party agreement,[272] to determine the place of arbitration—an authority that helps to avoid delay in the proceedings.[273] The tribunal's authority only arises "[i]f the parties have not previously agreed on the place of arbitration." Article 18(1) thus defers to the parties' choice as to the place of arbitration prior to the constitution of the tribunal, or even thereafter so long as the arbitrators have not yet made the determination.[274] The wording of the provision, however, appears to bar the parties from determining the place of arbitration *after* the tribunal has decided the matter.[275] Nevertheless, there is nothing to prevent the tribunal from revisiting its determination upon a unanimous request by the parties.[276] Further, as the parties are the "masters" of the proceedings, that is, they can simply terminate the arbitration if their request is not complied with, the tribunal should always follow such a unanimous request.[277]

It is generally preferable that the parties expressly determine the place of arbitration in their arbitration clause or agreement.[278] In some cases, however, this may not be advisable, as "the identity of the most suitable place of arbitration may depend on the nature and circumstances of the particular dispute that will be submitted to arbitration,"[279] and the nature of the dispute may not be foreseeable at the time the agreement is concluded. In such circumstances, the parties may wish to leave the place of arbitration to be decided by the tribunal. In other cases, prior designation of the place of arbitration may not be possible, such as in investor–state arbitration where the terms of arbitration are laid out in the investment treaty, which typically does not identify the place of arbitration.

Where the parties have not agreed on the place of arbitration, the arbitral tribunal must carry out the task "having regard to the circumstances of the case." The arbitral tribunal's analysis may be guided by the UNCITRAL Notes, which observes:

---

[272] See generally L Mistelis, "Reality Test," n 257, 155, 158 ("Only to the extent that there is no express or clear reference to the *lex arbitri* in the arbitrational agreement or the contract of the parties, will the tribunal *lastly* attempt to find rules applicable to the arbitration.").

[273] H Holtzmann, "The Importance of Choosing the Right Place to Arbitrate an International Case," in *Private Investors Abroad–Problems and Solutions in International Business* (1977) 183, 189. A similar provision is found, *inter alia*, in Article 14(1) of the ICC Arbitration Rules, which provides: "The place of arbitration shall be fixed by the Court unless agreed upon by the parties," and in Article 20(1) of the UNCITRAL Model Law, as amended, which provides: "The parties are free to agree on the place of arbitration. Failing such agreement, the place of arbitration shall be determined by the arbitral tribunal having regard to the circumstances of the case, including the convenience of the parties."

[274] In a recent NAFTA Chapter Eleven arbitration the parties, Glamis Gold Ltd and the United States of America, agreed on Washington, DC as the place of arbitration, in their Agreement on Certain Procedural Matters, dated January 20, 2004.

[275] See P Sanders, "Commentary on UNCITRAL Arbitration Rules," n 60, 194; K Rauh, *Die Schieds- und Schlichtungs-Ordnungen der UNCITRAL* 89 (1983).

[276] See P Sanders, "Commentary on UNCITRAL Arbitration Rules," n 60, 194.

[277] See M Aden, *Internationale Handelsschiedsgerichtbarkeit*, n 778, 230.

[278] See N Blackaby and C Partasides, *Redfern and Hunter on International Arbitration*, n 2, 114; H Holtzmann, "The Importance of Choosing the Right Place to Arbitrate an International Case," n 273, 188–91; K Lionnet, "Erfahrungen mit der internationalen Schieds-gerichtsbarkeit im Anlagenbau aus der Sicht der Partei," in K H Böckstiegel (ed), *Vertragsgestaltung und Streiterledigung in der Bauindustrie und im Anlagenbau* (1984) 291, 302. See the Model Arbitration Clause in n 1. See also *Report of the Secretary General on the Revised Draft Set of Arbitration Rules*, UNCITRAL, 9th Session, Introduction, para 17, UN Doc A/CN.9/112 (1975), reprinted in (1976) VII UNCITRAL Ybk 157, 160.

[279] UNCITRAL, 9th Session, Introduction, para 17, UN Doc A/CN.9/112. See also R David, *Arbitration in International Trade* (1985) 282.

Various factual and legal factors influence the choice of the place of arbitration, and their relative importance varies from case to case. Among the more prominent factors are: (a) suitability of the law of arbitral procedure of the place of arbitration; (b) whether there is a multilateral or bilateral treaty on enforcement of arbitral awards between the State where the arbitration takes place and the State or States where the award may have to be enforced; (c) convenience of the parties and the arbitrators, including the travel distances; (d) availability and cost of support services needed; and (e) location of the subject-matter in dispute and proximity of evidence.[280]

As the Notes themselves indicate, the enumerated list of factors is non-exhaustive, nor is any one enumerated factor in the list given more weight in relation to another.[281] Other factors, therefore, such as the neutrality of the place of arbitration may also be important in determining the place of arbitration, as has been the case in investor–state arbitration under NAFTA Chapter Eleven.[282] The following factors relating to the place of arbitration are addressed in the following sections: the nature and suitability of the local law; the enforceability of the award; neutrality; and practical considerations.

(1) Nature and suitability of the local law

Where a place of arbitration is chosen, "[i]t is generally accepted ... that a state should insist upon the observance of a minimum standard of objectivity and justice in quasi-judicial proceedings held within its territory, whether they are the proceedings of a jockey club or of an arbitral tribunal."[283]

In addition to its own legitimate interest in controlling the proceedings, the chosen jurisdiction may also be involved in providing the support of its courts for such purposes as gathering evidence and ordering interim measures of protection. The tribunal thus should take into account the contents and nature of the local law.[284]

As to control over the proceedings, an arbitral tribunal's wide discretion under the UNCITRAL Rules to conduct the arbitral proceedings in the manner it considers appropriate is restricted by the tribunal's duty to respect mandatory norms of the law of the place of arbitration.[285] This, of course, is also the case where the country of one of the parties has been chosen as the venue. Therefore the arbitrators, as well as the parties, should carefully examine the requirements of the law of the place or proposed place of arbitration in this respect.[286] This is not always an easy task, if only for the reason that the mandatory or non-mandatory character of a particular norm may be difficult to determine even for a lawyer educated in the country in question.[287]

---

[280] UNCITRAL Notes, n 68, para 22.

[281] One investor–state tribunal applying the 1976 UNCITRAL Rules has observed that "having regard to the circumstances of the arbitration," means having regard to "*all* such circumstances, including those elements offered for consideration in paragraph 22 of the Notes, and without any individual circumstance being accorded paramount weight irrespective of its comparative merits." *Ethyl Corp* and *Government of Canada*, Decision Regarding the Place of Arbitration, (November 28, 1997) (*Ad Hoc* Proceeding, 1976 UNCITRAL Rules, NAFTA Chapter Eleven), at 4 (emphasis in the original)

[282] See section 4(B)(1)–(3).

[283] A Redfern and M Hunter, *Law and Practice of International Commercial Arbitration* (2nd edn 1991) 429.

[284] See G Born, *International Arbitration and Forum Selection Agreements: Drafting and Enforcing* (3rd edn 2010) 67–8 (observing "the arbitral seat must have both national arbitration legislation and national courts that are hospitable to and supportive of international arbitration").

[285] See discussion concerning Article 17(1) in section 3(B)(1).

[286] See *Wintershall AG* (1976 Rules), reprinted in section 4(C).

[287] See K Böckstiegel, "The Relevance of National Arbitration Law," n 28, 223–34.

Such local expertise or at least commentaries or other literature on the arbitration law of the country in question[288] should be consulted in case of doubt. Here it suffices to outline generally the impact which the mandatory norms of the *lex loci arbitri*, as well as the challenge and appeal possibilities provided by it, may have on the arbitration process. In addition to the actual proceedings, mandatory requirements of the local law may also impose conditions as to what may be arbitrated and who can arbitrate.[289] In a worst case scenario, the failure to comply with such requirements may lead to the setting aside of the award. This in turn may make it impossible to have the award enforced.[290]

Many national laws restrict what issues are arbitrable.[291] Such limitations usually concern disputes on matters with public law elements, such as employment, antitrust rules, competition law and intellectual property rights. These limitations should be taken into account when selecting the place of arbitration. Fortunately for international arbitration, the trend in various countries having such restrictions has been to adopt a more flexible attitude regarding international arbitrations.[292]

Thus, in international cases, "most commercial disputes are arbitrable under the laws of most countries."[293] Some caution is nevertheless needed, as indicated by cases in which a party relying on an arbitration clause has been unable to enforce it on the ground of non-arbitrability of the issue according to the law of the country in question.[294]

Local law may also deny to certain parties, such as state entities, the capacity to arbitrate.[295] Although the principle of estoppel may be applied against an entity which, in contravention of such a prohibition,[296] has consented to arbitration, the other party should be aware of any limitations of this kind. If the arbitration takes place in the home country of such an entity (instead of a neutral venue), the free consent to arbitration by the entity may not cure the legal impediment in question.

---

[288] Surveys on various domestic arbitration laws and regimes are conveniently located in the ICC publication *Arbitration Law in Europe* and in the ICCA publication, *Ybk Commercial Arb*, which cover national reports on the subject from 1976 to 1988, and *The International Handbook on Commercial Arbitration*, where the national reports are covered since 1989.

[289] See H Holtzmann, "The Importance of Choosing the Right Place to Arbitrate an International Case," n 273, 183.

[290] See section 4(B)(2)(a)(2).

[291] In general, see N Blackaby and C Partasides, *Redfern and Hunter on International Arbitration*, n 2, 123–35; H Arfazadeh, *Ordre public et arbitrage international à l'épreuve de la mondialisation* (2005) 79–109; H Holtzmann, "The Importance of Choosing the Right Place to Arbitrate an International Case," n 273, 198–204; K Böckstiegel, "The Relevance of National Arbitration Law," n 28, 234.

[292] See N Blackaby and C Partasides, *Redfern and Hunter on International Arbitration*, n 2, 124; W Park, "Judicial Controls in the Arbitral Process," (1991) 3 Arb Intl 230, 253–4. An important US decision confirming, in principle, the arbitrability of international antitrust disputes was rendered by the Supreme Court in 1985 in *Mitsubishi v Soler*, 473 US 614 (1985). For a comment, see S Jarvin, "Arbitrability of Anti-Trust Disputes: The *Mitsubishi v Soler* Case," (1985) 2(3) J Intl Arb 69. See also PD O'Neill, Jr, "Recent Developments in International Commercial Arbitration: an American Perspective," (1987) 4(1) J Intl Arb 7. See also R Brand, "International Trade Law and the Arbitration of Administrative Law Matters: *Farrel Corp v US International Trade Commission*," (1993) 31 Columbia J Transnatl L 181.

[293] N Blackaby and C Partasides, *Redfern and Hunter on International Arbitration*, n 2, 135.

[294] See N Blackaby and C Partasides, *Redfern and Hunter on International Arbitration*, n 2, 135 (references to two cases involving an exclusive distributorship agreement and an international employment contract respectively).

[295] See N Blackaby and C Partasides, *Redfern and Hunter on International Arbitration*, n 2, 109–10.

[296] See n 340.

Mandatory norms of the locale may also exclude certain categories of persons as arbitrators.[297] General exclusion of foreigners by such rules may provide enough impediment not to choose the country in question as the venue of arbitration. However, a trend towards more flexibility in international, as distinct from domestic, arbitration is discernible.[298]

While the choice of the place of arbitration may only exceptionally have impact on the question of substantive law governing the dispute,[299] the way in which the mandatory procedural norms of the *lex loci arbitri* control the arbitration is one of the most important considerations to be taken into account in the selection of the place.[300] The more extensively the local law imposes mandatory requirements, the greater the risk of the award being set aside by a domestic court, and the greater the likelihood that the proceedings will be hampered by judicial interference.[301] The extent of the possibility of such an interference is one consideration to be taken into account in the selection of the place.[302] After making the choice of location, the arbitral tribunal should see to it that those norms of the venue, the non-application of which may subject the proceedings or the award to a successful attack before a court, are followed.

Insofar as non-derogable national rules are limited to such fundamental procedural principles as *audiatur et altera pars*, they do not present any particular problems, as strict application of the UNCITRAL Rules guarantees that universally accepted principles are observed to the extent necessary.[303] The arbitral tribunal, however, should be aware that various domestic laws may contain mandatory norms which are less universal in character, but nevertheless may be in conflict with the UNCITRAL Rules. Such norms may relate to questions such as the acceptability of written affidavits as evidence,[304] notice provisions contained in Article 2, dissenting opinions and the allowability of decisions *ex aequo et bono*.[305] The power of the arbitral tribunal to decide its own jurisdiction in accordance with Article 23 is often circumscribed by the local courts' power to determine whether the tribunal has exceeded its jurisdiction.[306]

As to the control which the local law and local courts exercise over arbitration proceedings, the general trend is clearly towards more autonomy of international arbitration. Thus, while violation of *ordre public* or public policy is frequently a ground for setting aside an

---

[297] See H Holtzmann, "The Importance of Choosing the Right Place to Arbitrate an International Case," n 273, 204–6.

[298] Thus under the general rule of Saudi Arabian law an "arbitrator shall be a Saudi national or Muslim expatriate." According to an authority on that law, what in this respect "is applicable in national arbitration is not necessarily so in international arbitration." A El-Ahdab, "Arbitration in Saudi-Arabia under the New Arbitration Act, 1983 and its Implementation Rules of 1985," Part One, (1986) 3(3) J Intl Arb 27 and Part Two, and at (No 4, 1986) 23. See also N Blackaby and C Partasides, *Redfern and Hunter on International Arbitration*, n 2, 259.

[299] Further, see Chapter 3 on Article 35(1).

[300] If no particular procedural law has been designated for the arbitration, the law of the place presumptively is also the law applicable to the interpretation of the UNCITRAL Rules. See M Aden, *Internationale Handelsschiedsgerichtbarkeit*, n 78, 34–5. This aspect, however, is likely to be of such a limited importance as not to play a role in the choice of the place.

[301] As will be discussed later in this section, non-compliance with the mandatory rules of the law of the place of arbitration may also negatively influence the chances of having the award enforced in other jurisdictions.

[302] For a comparative analysis of the appeal and review possibilities under the arbitration laws of selected countries, see D Kolkey, "Attacking Arbitral Awards. Rights of Appeal and Review In International Arbitrations," (1988) 22 Intl Lawyer 693.

[303] See K Böckstiegel, "The Relevance of National Arbitration Law," n 28, 233. See also M Aden, *Internationale Handelsschiedsgerichtbarkeit*, n 78, 24, 50.

[304] See Chapter 18 on Article 27(2).

[305] See N Blackaby and C Partasides, *Redfern and Hunter on International Arbitration*, n 2, 575 and Chapter 3, section 2(B)(2) on Article 35(2).

[306] N Blackaby and C Partasides, *Redfern and Hunter on International Arbitration*, n 2, 358. See Chapter 14 on Article 23.

award, a distinction is increasingly made between domestic and international public policy in the sense that mandatory norms originally based on domestic public policy considerations are not necessarily applied to international cases.[307] The consequence is that:

> where an arbitration under the [1976] UNCITRAL Rules is of an international character, provisions in the Rules although in conflict with national public policy for domestic arbitration, may nevertheless be upheld, when the more restrictive standard of international public policy is applied.[308]

As a result, the validity and arbitrability of a contract involving international sales may be upheld, even if a similar contract involving domestic sales were void,[309] or a procedural practice not accepted in purely domestic contexts may be tolerated in international arbitration. The trend toward more autonomy of international arbitration is evident in recent legislative changes carried out in various countries with a view to reducing court interference—and to increasing the attractiveness of the country as a venue for international commercial arbitration. Probably the most radical step was taken by Belgium, where, in cases in which none of the parties is a Belgian national or resident, the arbitration was, by law of 1985, placed totally outside the control of national judges.[310] The law, however, has been changed.[311]

The trend towards limitations on appeals against arbitral awards—and at the same time towards harmonization of national laws—is likely to continue in light of the increasingly broad adoption of the UNCITRAL Model Law, under which the "grounds for challenge of an arbitral award are strictly limited."[312] The setting aside procedure regulated in Article 34 of the Model Law is the sole means for recourse to courts, and it is possible only on the following narrow grounds modeled on Article V of the New York Convention.[313]

Legislation influenced by the Model Law has been adopted in a number of countries.[314] To a varying degree, the Model Law has affected the contents of legislative reforms carried out in other countries.[315]

---

[307] The underlying philosophy behind this distinction is well illustrated in the following example by Craig: "Think of the difference between the criminal procedure that the Anglo-American observer is familiar with and criminal proceedings in any other country. If judged by these standards, any Japanese, French ... case, for example, would be found to have numerous 'errors.' However, we can still look at the same case and say it was procedurally just. When we do, we are making a judgment about procedural fairness that is no longer tied to our own national standards." See W Craig, "Uses and Abuses of Appeal from Awards," n 79, 197–8.

[308] P Sanders, "Commentary on UNCITRAL Arbitration Rules," n 60, 179–80. "More restrictive" here denotes the narrower scope of public policy considerations which in international cases, as distinct from domestic cases, may affect the validity of the award.

[309] See W Craig, "Uses and Abuses of Appeal from Awards," n 79, 197, and the French cases referred to therein.

[310] Law of March 27, 1985 amending Article 1717 of the Code of Civil Procedure. For the text in English with an Introductory Note by E Gaillard, see (1986) 25 ILM 725. The Belgian solution has been the subject of criticism. Thus the shifting of all judicial control from the place of arbitration (a neutral site) to the courts of the country of enforcement (usually the home country of one of the parties) may run counter to the very purpose why the neutral place was selected. See W Craig, "Uses and Abuses of Appeal from Awards," n 79, 201–2. As to the argument that this kind of "non-national" award is not enforceable at all under the New York Convention, see section 3(B)(1).

[311] Now the parties to an international arbitration are allowed to opt out of local control. See N Blackaby and C Partasides, *Redfern and Hunter on International Arbitration*, n 2, 191. See B Hanotiau and G Block, "The Law of 19 May 1998 amending Belgian Arbitration Legislation," (1999) 15, 1 Arb Int 97–102.

[312] N Blackaby and C Partasides, *Redfern and Hunter on International Arbitration*, n 2, 595–617.

[313] Model Law, as amended, Article 34(2). See H Holtzmann and J Neuhaus, *A Guide to the UNCITRAL Model Law*, n 7, 911 et seq. See also M Kerr, "Arbitration and the Courts: the UNCITRAL Model Law," (1985) 34 ICLQ.

[314] This is the case, for example, with the Spanish arbitration law adopted in 2003. See F Mantilla-Serrano, *Ley de Arbitraje: Una Perspectiva International* (2005) 31–3.

[315] See generally P Binder, *International Commercial Arbitration and Conciliation in UNCITRAL Model Law Jurisdictions* (3rd edn 2010) 12–19.

As the Model Law continues to proliferate, domestic laws allowing extensive court interferences during arbitral proceedings or appeals on the merits are likely to become rare. They will not disappear, however; while the Model Law has opted in favor of only limited judicial control, at the same time it firmly allows some judicial control to be exercised by domestic courts. This is the compromise the Model Law strikes between arbitral autonomy and the need for some minimum level of official control over procedural fairness, as well as between the conflicting expectations the parties may have in this respect.[316] In light of recent legislative trends, which in some countries has led to more limited judicial control than the Model Law compromise, it appears that on a worldwide level, the Model Law approach will, more and more, represent the maximum of judicial control over arbitral proceedings.

The position adopted in the Model Law can also be understood to recognize that arbitration cannot completely cut off its ties with courts, but may need their support at various stages, such as for the constitution of the tribunal and gathering of evidence.[317] In the application of the UNCITRAL Rules, such support is not needed so much because the Rules themselves contain complete provisions on the appointment of arbitrators and challenges against them.[318] However, in certain respects, the availability of the supportive role of domestic courts should also be taken into account as a pertinent consideration in the choice of the place of arbitration for proceedings under these rules.[319]

The recognition in the UNCITRAL Model Law of the connection between arbitral proceedings and the legal system of the place of arbitration is also important in that it increases the enforceability of the arbitral award in other jurisdictions.[320] This leads to a very important criterion to be considered when selecting the place of arbitration.

(2) Enforceability of the award

It is rare that the losing party has assets in any neutral country which would be suitable as the place of arbitration.[321] If it has, the enforcement of the award does not usually pose any particular problems but takes place in the same way as the enforcement of "purely" domestic awards.[322] Normally a party to an international arbitration, however, must be prepared for the possibility of having to seek the enforcement of the award outside the place of arbitration. The selection of that place in turn influences the international enforceability of the award. This, consequently, is one factor to be taken into account in the choice of the arbitration place. This is the case notwithstanding the fact that, in an overwhelming majority of cases, an international award is complied with voluntarily.

Usually the enforcement (if any is needed) of awards rendered in international commercial arbitration takes place by virtue of international agreements, whether bilateral treaties

---

[316] See N Blackaby and C Partasides, *Redfern and Hunter on International Arbitration*, n 2, 191 n. 103, who point out that while a claimant may be interested in speedy proceedings which are not interrupted by court, the respondent may formulate his priorities quite differently.

[317] N Blackaby and C Partasides, *Redfern and Hunter on International Arbitration*, n 2, 441–2.

[318] See Chapters 4–6.

[319] See discussion on Article 26(9) concerning interim measures ordered by a court in Chapter 17, section 2(B)(10).

[320] As noted in connection with Article 17, there is some uncertainty as to the international enforceability of a-national awards.

[321] See N Blackaby and C Partasides, *Redfern and Hunter on International Arbitration*, n 2, 630.

[322] It is for this reason that arbitration in the respondent's home country, instead of in a neutral place, is recommended in some cases. See *UNCITRAL, Legal Guide on Drawing Up International Contracts for the Construction of Industrial Works* (1988) 317 ("The enforcement of an award against a party in his own country that was rendered in that country would not encounter the problems associated with the enforcement of a foreign award.").

or regional[323] or general conventions. The most important general convention (and most important international agreement on the enforcement of arbitral awards in general) is the 1958 New York Convention on the Recognition and Enforcement of Foreign Arbitral Awards.[324]

As the New York Convention provides the most effective mechanism for the enforcement of international arbitral awards, it is important to select the place of arbitration so as to guarantee that the award falls under the Convention. The place of arbitration is frequently determinative in this respect due to a provision according to which a state, party to the Convention, "may on the basis of reciprocity declare that it will apply the Convention to the recognition and enforcement of awards made only in the territory of another Contracting state."[325] In fact, the majority of the 137 contracting states has accepted the Convention with such a "reciprocity reservation," and thus enforce by virtue of the Convention only awards rendered in the territory of another state party.[326] Accordingly, "[c]hoosing a country that is a signatory to the New York Convention is of fundamental importance in ensuring the enforceability of an award."[327] Should this not seem practical, the existence of a bilateral treaty on the subject between the prospective place of arbitration and the likely place of enforcement should be studied.

The choice of the place of arbitration is important because enforcement may be denied on grounds related to the law of the place of arbitration. Among other reasons set out in Article V of the Convention,[328] recognition and enforcement may be denied if the party

---

[323] See, eg, the Inter-American Panama Convention of 1975, reproduced in (1978) III Ybk Commercial Arb 15.

[324] 330 UNTS 3 (New York, June 10, 1958). On the "predecessor" of this Convention, the Geneva Convention of 1927, see N Blackaby and C Partasides, *Redfern and Hunter on International Arbitration*, n 2, 70–2. A thorough commentary is provided by A J van den Berg *The New York Convention*, n 108. See also H Holtzmann, "The Importance of Choosing the Right Place to Arbitrate an International Case," n 273, 195–7. As to the New York Convention and a-national awards, see, n 152–153, section 3(B)(1) dealing with Article 17.

[325] Article 1(3). According to this provision, a state may also declare that it will apply the Convention only to differences arising out of legal relationships, whether contractual or not, "which are considered commercial under the national law of the state making such declaration." A "commercial reservation" is rarely likely to hamper the enforcement of an award rendered by a tribunal applying the UNCITRAL Rules. See generally N Blackaby and C Partasides *Redfern and Hunter on International Arbitration*, n 2, 636–7.

[326] States which have not made any of the two reservations mentioned apply to the main rule of Article I(1) according to which:

This convention shall apply to the recognition and enforcement of arbitral awards made in the territory of a State other than the state where the recognition and enforcement of such awards are sought, and arising out of differences between persons, whether physical or legal. It shall also apply to arbitral awards not considered as domestic awards in the State where the recognition and enforcement are sought.

[327] A Redfern and M Hunter with N Blackaby and C Partasides, *Law and Practice of International Commercial Arbitration* (4th edn, 2004) 326. See also H Holtzmann, "The Importance of Choosing the Right Place to Arbitrate an International Case," n 273, 196; J van Hof, "UNCITRAL Arbitration Rules, Section III, Article 16 [Place or Arbitration]," in L Mistelis (ed) *Concise International Arbitration* (2010) 193.

[328] Article V reads as follows:

1. Recognition and enforcement of the award may be refused, at the request of the party against whom it is invoked, only if that party furnishes to the competent authority where the recognition and enforcement is sought, proof that:
   (a) the parties to the agreement referred to in article II were, under the law applicable to them, under some incapacity, or the said agreement is not valid under the law to which the parties have subjected it or, failing any indication thereon, under the law of the country where the award was made; or
   (b) the party against whom the award is invoked was not given proper notice of the appointment of the arbitrator or of the arbitration proceedings or was otherwise unable to present his case; or
   (c) the award deals with a difference not contemplated by or not falling within the terms of the submission to arbitration, or it contains decisions on matters beyond the scope of the submission to arbitration, provided

against whom the award is invoked shows that the Convention "has not yet become binding on the parties, or has been set aside or suspended by a competent authority of the country in which, or under the law of which, that award was made."[329] Although not all the grounds for enforcement under the New York Convention are judged under the standards of the law of the place of arbitration, Article V of the Convention emphasizes that, to produce an enforceable award, the arbitrators should assure that the mandatory requirements of the law of the place of arbitration are respected.[330] As the UNCITRAL Model Law gains acceptance, the mandatory requirements justifying the setting aside of the award at the place of arbitration, on the one hand, and those justifying the denial of recognition and enforcement, on the other hand, are likely to be harmonized. The Model Law, which was modeled after Article V of the New York Convention, defines both in substantially similar terms.[331]

The seat of the Iran–US Claims Tribunal was specified in the Claims Settlement Declaration. According to this declaration, the seat "shall be The Hague, The Netherlands, or any other place agreed by Iran and the United States."[332] The parties did not reach any such agreement, so the proceedings have taken place in The Hague.[333]

(3) Neutrality

Even though neutrality is not a factor expressly enumerated in the UNCITRAL Notes,[334] psychological considerations, as well as the principle of equality of the parties, may favor holding the arbitration "in a country that is 'neutral', in the sense that it is not the home country of any of the parties to the dispute."[335] As the *Ethyl* tribunal observed,

---

that, if the decisions on matters submitted to arbitration can be separated from those not so submitted, that part of the award which contains decisions on matters submitted to arbitration may be recognized and enforced; or

(d) The composition of the arbitral authority or the arbitral procedure was not in accordance with the agreement of the parties, or, failing such agreement, was not in accordance with the law of the country where the arbitration took place; or

(e) the award has not yet become binding on the parties, or has been set aside or suspended by a competent authority of the country in which, or under the law of which, that award was made.

[329] Article V(1) (e). As indicated earlier in the application of the UNCITRAL Rules, law other than the *lex loci arbitri* should never be designated as the applicable procedural law (*lex arbitri*). For discussion of the requirement in Article V(1)(e) that an award be binding on the parties, see Chapter 24, section (2)(B)(2) on Article 34(2) of the UNCITRAL Arbitration Rules. See also A J van den Berg, *The New York Convention*, n 108, 333 et seq.

[330] For more detailed discussion concerning Article V of the New York Convention, see A J van den Berg, *The New York Convention*, n 108, 275 et seq.; N Blackaby and C Partasides, *Redfern and Hunter on International Arbitration*, n 2, 638–62.

[331] UNCITRAL Model Law, as amended, arts 34, 35 and 36. See H Holtzmann and J Neuhaus, *A Guide to the UNCITRAL Model Law*, n 7, 1006 et seq.

[332] Article VI(1), reprinted in section 4(D).

[333] Initially there had been some discussion about locating at least one Chamber in London, but these plans never materialized. S Baker and M Davis, *The UNCITRAL Arbitration Rules in Practice*, n 9, 78.

[334] As the *Ethyl* tribunal noted:

The fact that the UNCITRAL Notes omitted the "perception of a place as being neutral" from its list of criteria for selection of a place of arbitration because it was "unclear, potentially confusing" does not mean that such criterion cannot be considered. UNCITRAL, in taking this step, itself indicated "that the arbitral tribunal, before deciding on the place of arbitration, might wish to discuss that with the parties."

Ethyl Corp and *Government of Canada*, Decision Regarding the Place of Arbitration (November 28, 1997) (*Ad Hoc* Proceeding, 1976 UNCITRAL Rules, NAFTA Chapter Eleven), at 10, n 12.

[335] N Blackaby and C Partasides, *Redfern and Hunter on International Arbitration*, n 2, 173. See also, eg, Y Derains, "France as a Place for International Arbitration," n 106, 111–12; K Lionnet, "Erfahrungen," n 278,

"[t]raditionally arbitrating parties, desiring both the reality and the appearance of a neutral forum, incline to agree on a place of arbitration outside their respective national jurisdictions."[336] The neutrality aspect is particularly relevant in arbitrations involving parties from different socio-economic systems[337] or where a sovereign party is involved.[338] Although this consideration has lost much of its relevance in recent years, the tribunal (and the parties, if they make the determination) is normally recommended to follow the prevailing practice[339] of choosing a neutral country as the place of arbitration.[340] For example, arbitration in the country of the respondent is normally not recommended to avoid giving an unfair advantage to one party with greater familiarity with the local law.[341] Although choosing a neutral location may appear reasonable, there arise potential difficulties since the arbitral proceedings may differ from those conducted in the respective home countries of both parties.[342] However, the increased harmonization of national arbitration laws has

---

303. The Final Act of the Conference on Security and Cooperation in Europe, signed in Helsinki in 1975, urges the participating states, *inter alia*, to "[r]ecommend, where appropriate, to organizations, enterprises and firms in their countries, to include arbitration clauses in commercial contracts...and permit arbitration in a third country..." (1975) 14 ILM 1292, 1304.

[336] *Ethyl Corp* and *Government of Canada*, Decision Regarding the Place of Arbitration, November 28, 1997 (*Ad Hoc* Proceeding, 1976 UNCITRAL Rules, NAFTA Chapter Eleven), at 9.

[337] H Holtzmann, "The Importance of Choosing the Right Place to Arbitrate an International Case," n 273, 187.

[338] *Ethyl Corp* and *Government of Canada*, Decision Regarding the Place of Arbitration, November 28, 1997 (*Ad Hoc* Proceeding, 1976 UNCITRAL Rules, NAFTA Chapter Eleven), at 9.

[339] See, eg, N Blackaby and C Partasides, *Redfern and Hunter on International Arbitration*, n 2, 173; Y Derains, "France as a Place for International Arbitration," n 106, 111.

[340] In some cases, however, the parties may have difficulties in agreeing on a neutral venue. Thus certain developing countries may refuse, or at least be very reluctant, to submit disputes involving their governmental entities or agencies for settlement outside their own boundaries. See J McLaughlin, "Arbitration and Developing Countries," (1979) 13 Intl Lawyer 211, 217–19. This attitude used to be shared by some Eastern European countries, but the situation has changed decisively. In certain Latin American countries arbitration concerning investment and related contracts is prohibited unless it takes place in the country which received the investment. H Holtzmann, "The Importance of Choosing the Right Place to Arbitrate an International Case," n 273, 201–2. On investment arbitration and Latin America, see also G Naón, "Arbitration in Latin America: Overcoming Traditional Hostilities," (1989) 5 Arb Intl 131, 141–2. It should be noted, however, that where a state or state entity has, in derogation from its domestic law, consented to arbitration in a neutral venue, it should be regarded as estopped from relying on the national rules in order to get rid of its commitment. See G Delaume, "The Finality of Arbitration Involving States," (1989) 5 Arb Intl 21, 26 and the cases mentioned therein. Note also that in maritime cases the parties' freedom to choose a neutral place may be curtailed by international regulations such as the Hamburg rules. See H Holtzmann and J Neuhaus, *A Guide to the UNCITRAL Model Law*, n 7, 595.

[341] For example, in an arbitration initiated by a Dutch corporation against the Czech Republic the place of arbitration was determined to be Stockholm. See *CME Czech Republic BV* and *Czech Republic*, Partial Award (September 13, 2001) (*Ad Hoc* Proceeding, 1976 UNCITRAL Rules, Netherlands-Czech Republic BIT), reprinted in (No 3, 2002) 14 World Trade & Arb Materials 109, 121.

[342] Thus "[t]he legal rules applicable to arbitral proceedings in the respective countries may differ, and they could be more burdensome or otherwise less satisfactory to a party in one country than in the other. In addition, arbitral proceedings conducted in the respective countries will be controlled by different courts, which may exercise differing degrees of control over the proceedings." *UNCITRAL, Legal Guide*, n 322, 317. See also I Hertzfeld, "Applicable Law and Dispute Settlement in Soviet Joint Ventures," (1988) 3 ICSID Rev-Foreign Investment L J 249, 258, which provides:

[S]uch split jurisdictional clauses, which leave doubt as to the ultimate forum for litigation, may pose certain problems in practice. They may, for example, cause a party to act in such a manner as to oblige the opposing party to commence an action, in order that the action be brought in the first party's home jurisdiction. They may also give rise to multiple actions in different jurisdictions with the rise of contradictory decisions.

The author refers to agreements concluded between the former USSR Chamber of Commerce and certain foreign chambers in which arbitration in the respondent's country is recommended.

minimized this concern. Thus, other considerations may prevail over neutrality with the consequence that the parties and the arbitrators should not always be discouraged from selecting the country of one of the parties as the place of arbitration.

The question of neutrality has played a significant role in resolving disputes regarding the place of arbitration in investor–state arbitrations under NAFTA Chapter Eleven. Article 1130(b) of the NAFTA limits the parties' choice of the place of arbitration to the territory of a NAFTA Party that is a party to the New York Convention: in this case, the United States, Canada, or Mexico.[343] In *ADF*, the United States argued in favor of Washington, DC as the place of arbitration. The arbitral tribunal found, in line with other tribunals, the location of ICSID in Washington, DC to be decisive in its analysis because of the fact that ICSID is "widely perceived to be . . . a 'neutral' forum and institution."[344]

(4) Practical considerations

In addition to neutrality and other important legal considerations discussed above, there are other factors to be taken into account in the selection of the place of arbitration. The place should also be suitable from a functional point of view.[345] Subparagraphs (c), (d), and (e) of Paragraph 22 of the UNCITRAL Notes speak of these considerations with respect to the convenience of the place of arbitration to the parties and the arbitrators, the availability and costs of support services, and the location of the subject matter in dispute and the proximity of evidence.

Convenience of the parties and the arbitrators is often a factor in determining the place of arbitration.[346] It is commonplace in international arbitration for the disputing parties to come from different countries. The makeup of international arbitral tribunals is also frequently international in character, with members originating from diverse parts of the world, especially where the parties wish to appoint arbitrators of their own nationality or where the presiding arbitrator is deliberately chosen because he or she is from a country other than that of the parties. In choosing the place of arbitration, a comparison between the ease and cost of travel to one or another proposed place of arbitration may be in order, as travel may be particularly burdensome in some cases.[347] NAFTA Chapter Eleven

---

[343] That provision provides: "Unless the disputing parties agree otherwise, a Tribunal shall hold an arbitration in the territory of a Party that is a party to the New York Convention, selected in accordance with: (a) the ICSID Additional Facility Rules if the arbitration is under those Rules or the ICSID Convention; or (b) the UNCITRAL Arbitration Rules if the arbitration is under those Rules."

[344] See *ADF Group Inc* (1976 Rules), at 15, reprinted in section 4(C). See also *United Parcel Service of America Inc* and *Government of Canada*, Decision of the Tribunal on the Place of Arbitration (October 17, 2001) (ICSID administered, 1976 UNCITRAL Rules, NAFTA Chapter Eleven), at 8, para 18; *Methanex Corp* and *United States of America*, Written Reasons for the Tribunal's Decision of September 7th, 2000 on the Place of the Arbitration (December 31, 2000) (ICSID administered, 1976 UNCITRAL Rules, NAFTA Chapter Eleven), at 14, para 39.

[345] In general, see H Holtzmann, "The Importance of Choosing the Right Place to Arbitrate an International Case," n 273, 206–10; A Redfern and M Hunter with N Blackaby and C Partasides, *Law and Practice of International Arbitration* (4th edn 2004) 322.

[346] While potentially important, convenience is not the only factor to consider when determining the place of arbitration. The Working Group that revised the Rules recognized this fact when it agreed to delete the last clause of the phrase "having regard to the circumstances of the case, including the convenience of the parties" in an earlier version of Article 18(1). The Working Group concluded that "mentioning one circumstance only was not justified and there were other circumstances which might be more important." UNCITRAL, 49th Session, UN Doc A/CN.9/665, n 21, at 25 para 136.

[347] In the *ADF* case, the arbitral tribunal recognized that in investor–state arbitration a state party could be inconvenienced if multiple governmental agencies were required to travel to a foreign location. See *ADF Group Inc* and *United States of America*, Procedural Order No 2 (July 1, 2001 (ICSID administered, 1976 UNCITRAL Rules, NAFTA Chapter Eleven), at 13, para 18.

tribunals have considered travel as an element of convenience in several cases,[348] with tribunals finding that the convenience of counsel was also a relevant consideration.[349]

The availability and costs of support services, such as suitable hearing rooms and accommodation, are also factors to consider. The accommodation must be convenient and guarantee the necessary privacy for a party, its counsel, and witnesses. The availability of competent interpreters, stenographers, and the existence of a competent local bar able to advise on the requirements of the local law are factors to be taken into account when the place of arbitration is being chosen. An experienced arbitral institution that is willing to offer its facilities for arbitrations under the UNCITRAL Rules normally guarantees these practical requirements. When a particular institution of that kind has been, or is going to be, designated as appointing authority by the parties, it more often than not would be natural to have the place of arbitration coincide with the seat of the institution in question.[350] On the other hand, if no appointing authority has been designated, the parties and the arbitrators should be aware that the designation of the place of arbitration will likely determine the nationality of the appointing authority, if any, designated by the Secretary-General of the Permanent Court of Arbitration.[351] The costs of support services will inevitably vary in relation to the general cost of living of the city in which the support services are provided.[352]

Another factor for consideration is the location of the subject matter in dispute and the proximity of evidence. In construction cases, the location of the subject matter in dispute may likely correspond to the location of the physical facilities or construction project at issue. By contrast, investor–state arbitration often deals with the alleged effects of government measures on an investment. In this situation, arbitral tribunals have found that the location of the subject matter in dispute was the city where the relevant government authorities adopted the measures in question.[353] The relevance of the proximity of evidence may depend on

---

[348] See, eg, *Merrill & Ring Forestry LP* and *Government of Canada*, Decision on the Place of Arbitration (December 12, 2007) (ICSID administered, 1976 UNCITRAL Rules, NAFTA Chapter Eleven), at 4–5; *Canfor Corp* and *United States of America*, Decision on the Place of Arbitration, Filing of a Statement of Defence and Bifurcation of the Proceedings (January 23, 2004) (ICSID administered, 1976 UNCITRAL Rules, NAFTA Chapter Eleven), at 6; *United Parcel Service of America, Inc* and *Government of Canada*, Decision of the Tribunal on the Place of Arbitration (October 17, 2001) (ICSID administered, 1976 UNCITRAL Rules, NAFTA Chapter Eleven), at 6; *Methanex Corp* and *United States of America*, Written Reasons for the Tribunal's Decision of September 7th, 2000 on the Place of the Arbitration (December 31, 2000) (ICSID administered, 1976 UNCITRAL Rules, NAFTA Chapter Eleven), at 11–12; *ADF Group Inc* and *United States of America*, Procedural Order No 2 (July 1, 2001) (ICSID administered, 1976 UNCITRAL Rules, NAFTA Chapter Eleven), at 12–13; all reprinted in relevant part in section 4(C).

[349] See, eg, *Ethyl Corp* and *Government of Canada*, Decision Regarding the Place of Arbitration (November 28, 1997) (*Ad Hoc* Proceeding, 1976 UNCITRAL Rules, NAFTA Chapter Eleven), at 7 (finding "[c]ertainly the convenience of attorneys appointed by the parties, which translates into cost factors, affects their clients").

[350] See P Sanders, "Commentary on UNCITRAL Arbitration Rules," n 60, at 194–5.

[351] In two relevant cases, the Secretary-General has acted in the way just indicated. He appointed the President of the Supreme Court of the Netherlands as Appointing Authority for the Iran–US Claims Tribunal at The Hague, and the principal arbitral institution of the Federal Republic of Germany as Appointing Authority for an arbitration in which the parties had chosen the Federal Republic as the place of arbitration. See A Redfern and M Hunter, *Law and Practice of International Commercial Arbitration* (2nd edn 1991) 482–5; see generally N Blackaby and C Partasides, *Redfern and Hunter on International Arbitration*, n 2, 257–8; and the Commentary of Article 9 in Chapter 4 section 5.

[352] *Ethyl Corp* and *Government of Canada*, Decision Regarding the Place of Arbitration (November 28, 1997) (*Ad Hoc* Proceeding, 1976 UNCITRAL Rules, NAFTA Chapter Eleven), at 7 (noting the cost difference between New York City and Ottawa or Toronto). One exception may be arbitration in Washington, DC at ICSID because of ICSID's comparatively cheaper fee schedule and administrative expenses.

[353] See, eg, *ADF Group Inc* and *United States of America*, Procedural Order No 2 (July 1, 2001) (ICSID administered, 1976 UNCITRAL Rules, NAFTA Chapter Eleven), at 15, para 20.

the necessity for witness testimony or documents or other materials that cannot be readily submitted to the tribunal. Additionally, in some situations, such as construction cases, arbitration in a country near the site may be desirable, as a visit to the site may become necessary.[354]

Finally, communications between the prospective place of arbitration and the outside world is another pertinent consideration. Any potential restrictions (including visa requirements) on the entry of the persons involved, and on the right of the parties to communicate with their home bases, should be carefully considered. The distances between the place of arbitration and the headquarters of the parties are important but purely geographical considerations should not be over-emphasized. Desirable as it is to minimize the costs and inconveniences caused by distances between the place of arbitration and the various participants in the arbitration process, such inconveniences can be mitigated by hearing witnesses and having other special meetings take place outside the place of arbitration.[355]

(b) **Decision on place of arbitration not procedural; consultation with the parties**

There are several suitable places to conduct an international arbitration, and the number is increasing as states adopt the UNCITRAL Model Law and otherwise take steps to improve their attractiveness as a possible venue.[356] Nevertheless, not every jurisdiction has the necessary qualifications, and so the decision should be made only after careful weighing of the various considerations involved, especially those of a legal nature.[357] It is the legal consequences of the choice of the place of arbitration that have prompted leading commentators to argue that such a decision, where it is made by the arbitral tribunal, should not be regarded as a procedural matter which, in the absence of a majority, could be decided by the presiding arbitrator alone.[358] Sanders, for example, observes that a rule on the place of arbitration:

not only refers to practical considerations in connection with the arbitral proceedings, such as the least possible displacement of parties, witnesses and arbitrators, but also... to the legal consequences of the choice, and more especially to the recognition and enforcement of the award.[359]

Accordingly, in the context of revising the Rules, Paulsson and Petrochilos recommended including an express provision that required an arbitral tribunal to select the place of arbitration by a majority decision in accordance with Article 33(1).[360] Despite the merits of the recommendation, the Working Group did not adopt the recommendation.

---

[354] UNCITRAL *Legal Guide*, n 322, 317. See also section 4(B)(3).

[355] See UNCITRAL Notes, n 68, para 23 (geographical flexibility allows the "arbitral proceedings to be carried out in a manner that is most efficient and economical"); K Lionnet, "Erfahrungen," n 278, 302 and the commentary on para 2 of Article 18 in section 4(B)(3).

[356] As to certain concrete indications, see G Born, *International Arbitration and Forum Selection Agreements: Drafting and Enforcing* (3rd edn 2010) 67–9; see also H Holtzmann, "The Importance of Choosing the Right Place to Arbitrate an International Case," n 273, 211–21, who tests (with positive results) the suitability of Sweden and the United States as places of arbitration according to the various relevant criteria.

[357] For example, there are clear limitations on the place of arbitration in UNCITRAL Model Law jurisdictions. See P Binder, *International Commercial Arbitration and Conciliation in UNCITRAL Model Law Jurisdictions* (3rd edn 2010) 288–9.

[358] P Sanders, "Commentary on UNCITRAL Arbitration Rules," n 60, 194. Similarly see K Rauh, *Die Shieds-und Schlichtungs-Ordnungen der UNCITRAL*, n 275, 80, and M Aden, *Internationale Handelsschiedsgerichtbarkeit*, n 78, 230. Aden indicates—correctly, it is believed—that the presiding arbitrator can only decide "purely procedural questions" (reine Verfahrensfragen). Decision-making is dealt with in Article 33 of the UNCITRAL Rules discussed in Chapter 23. See also N Blackaby and C Partasides, *Redfern and Hunter on International Arbitration*, n 2, 570.

[359] P Sanders, "Commentary on UNCITRAL Arbitration Rules," n 60, 194.

[360] J Paulsson and G Petrochilos, "Revision of the UNCITRAL Rules," (A Report Commissioned by the UNCITRAL Secretariat), March 31, 2006, at 12, para 142.

In light of the legal significance of the choice of the place of arbitration, the arbitral tribunal is well advised to consult with the parties before making its determination.[361] Though not expressly required by the Rules, in many cases consultation will yield useful information about the parties' relative interest and is consistent with the tribunal's duties in Article 17(1) to afford equal treatment to the parties and provide them with a reasonable opportunity to present their case. In UNCITRAL cases under NAFTA Chapter Eleven where the disputing parties had not agreed on the place of arbitration, the disputing parties have been afforded the opportunity to brief the issue.

(3) Where the award is "deemed to have been made"—Article 18(1)

In international arbitration, the award is frequently not signed by the arbitrators in the city or locale designated as the place of arbitration. Practical considerations often make it inconvenient and costly for the parties to return to the place of arbitration simply to deliberate and sign the award. Article 18(1) therefore provides that "[t]he award shall be deemed to have been made at the place of arbitration." This construction, particularly the phrase "deemed to have been made" is new to the 2010 UNCITRAL Rules and replaces the phrase "the award shall be made at the place of arbitration."[362] The revision, which tracks the language of Article 31(3) of the Model Law, was clearly intended "to avoid the risk that an award be declared invalid if it was signed in a place other than the seat of arbitration."[363] As leading commentators note, by so doing the arbitral tribunal may avoid the risk of the award being regarded by a court as having been rendered in breach of the agreement by the parties.[364]

Article 18(1) brings needed clarity to the question of where an award is made under the Rules and rectifies the ambiguity in corresponding Article 16(4) of the 1976 UNCITRAL Rules as to whether the arbitrators are required to travel to the place of arbitration merely for a signing ceremony.[365] While on the one hand, it is almost always more convenient to have the award circulated electronically from one arbitrator to another for signing, including to locations outside the place of arbitration,[366] on the other hand, the clear wording of Article 16(4) of the 1976 UNCITRAL Rules ("shall be made at the place"), especially when compared to that of Article 31(3) of the UNCITRAL Model Law, could have been construed to require the signing at the place of arbitration.[367] The *travaux préparatoires* of the 1976 Rules did not provide for a conclusive answer, although

---

[361] See UNCITRAL Notes, n 68, para 21.

[362] Corresponding Article 16(4) of the 1976 UNCITRAL Rules provided that "[t]he award shall be made at the place of arbitration."

[363] UNCITRAL, 40th Session, UN Doc A/CN.9/614, n 5, at 19, para 90. The UNCITRAL Secretariat described the provision as designed "to avoid the uncertainty as to the jurisdiction of courts regarding the award if it was signed in a place other than the seat of arbitration": *Settlement of Commercial Disputes: Revision of the UNCITRAL Arbitration Rules, Note by the Secretariat*, UNCITRAL, UN Doc A/CN.9/WG.II/WP.145/Add.1 at 2–3, para 10 (2006).

[364] A Redfern and M Hunter with N Blackaby and C Partasides, *Law and Practice of International Commercial Arbitration* (4th edn 2004) 328; see generally G Born, *International Arbitration and Forum Selection Agreements*, n 356, 2408–9.

[365] See J Waincymer, "The New UNCITRAL Arbitration Rules: An Introduction and Evaluation," (2010) 14 Vindobona J Intl Commercial L and Arb 223, 238–9.

[366] See A J van den Berg, n 108, 295; N Blackaby and C Partasides, *Redfern and Hunter on International Arbitration*, n 2, 187.

[367] See F Mann, "Where is an Award 'made'?" (1989) 5 Arb Intl 107, 108 (while arguing that, regardless of the actual place of the signing of the award, an award is "made" at the place of arbitration admits that "the view suggested ... attributes a somewhat strained meaning to the word 'made'").

the preponderant view seems to have been that signing at the place of arbitration was not required.[368]

If the law applicable to the arbitration requires the signing at the place where the award is deemed to be made,[369] it is especially important that the arbitrators meet there. The award, of course, can be drafted elsewhere. Even where the applicable procedural law allows signature of the award outside the place of arbitration, the award should always state that it has been made at the place of arbitration.[370] In the practice of the Iran–US Claims Tribunal, awards have occasionally been signed by one or more arbitrators outside The Hague. The signatures of the arbitrators are nevertheless always preceded by the words: "Dated, The Hague" (the date). A similar practice has been followed by other tribunals, including investor–state arbitration tribunals.

(4) *The location of tribunal deliberations and meetings "for any other purpose, including hearings"—Article 18(2)*

As explained above, the structure and terminology of Article 18 reflects the difference in concept between the *legal* and the *physical* place of arbitration. Whereas Article 18(1) uses the term "place of arbitration" to denote the legal seat of the arbitration and thus the jurisdiction whose law governs the arbitral process, Article 18(2) refers to the "location" of meetings related to the arbitration in the physical or geographical sense.[371] These meetings may include conferences, hearings, and deliberations of the arbitral tribunal.[372] Selection of the location of these meetings, even if outside the jurisdiction of the place of arbitration, is not meant to affect the choice of law governing the arbitral proceedings.

Article 18(2) revises the approach of corresponding Article 16(2) of the 1976 UNCITRAL Rules that provided for only "limited flexibility"[373] to hold meetings outside the place of the arbitration. Article 16(2) of the 1976 UNCITRAL Rules provided:

> The arbitral tribunal may determine the locale of the arbitration within the country agreed upon by the parties. It may hear witnesses and hold meetings for consultation among its members at any place it deems appropriate, having regard to the circumstances of the arbitration.[374]

Designation of the locale under the 1976 UNCITRAL Rules likely determined where the main oral proceedings, ie, hearing and pre-hearing conferences, if any, were to be held. In contrast to Article 16(2) of the 1976 UNCITRAL Rules, Article 18(2) eliminates the notion of selecting a "locale" of the arbitration and broadens the tribunal's discretion to

---

[368] See *Summary Record of the 6th Meeting of the Committee of the Whole (II)*, UNCITRAL, 9th Session, UN Doc A/CN.9/9/C.2/SR.6, at 8–10, paras 70–89 (1976). See also P Sanders, *The Work of UNCITRAL on Arbitration and Conciliation*, n 95, 9 ("An award may be circulated to the arbitrators for signing at their convenience.").
[369] See M Aden, *Internationale Handelsschiedsgerichtbarkeit*, n 78, 231–2.
[370] H Holtzmann and J Neuhaus, *A Guide to the UNCITRAL Model Law*, n 7, 596.
[371] UNCITRAL, 40th Session, UN Doc A/CN.9/619, n 5, at 27, para 139. As an alternative, the term "venue" was also proposed but not adopted. See para 137.
[372] An earlier version of Article 18(2) included a broad, but closed list of "consultations, hearings, meetings and deliberations." *Settlement of Commercial Disputes: Revision of the UNCITRAL Arbitration Rules, Note by the Secretariat*, UNCITRAL, UN Doc A/CN.9/WG.II/WP.151 at 17 (draft article 16(2) (2008). The Working Group deleted the word "consultations" as redundant of "meetings and deliberations." UNCITRAL, 42nd Session, UN Doc A/CN.9/665, n 21, at 26, para 138. The final version of the rule maintains maximum flexibility by referring to meetings "for any other purpose, including hearings."
[373] See *Report of the Secretary-General on the Revised Draft Set of Arbitration Rules*, UNCITRAL, 9th Session, Addendum 1 (Commentary), UN Doc A/CN.9/112/Add.1 (1975), reprinted in (1976) VII UNCITRAL Ybk 166, 172 (Commentary on Draft Articles 15(2) and (3)).
[374] 1976 UNCITRAL Arbitration Rules, art 16(2).

choose the location of meetings. Under the 2010 UNCITRAL Rules, the tribunal may deliberate and, unless otherwise agreed by the parties, may hold other meetings, including hearings, "at any location it considers appropriate."[375] While in some cases this added flexibility may enhance the efficiency and convenience of an arbitration, the parties should be aware that overly attenuated ties between the legal place of arbitration and the actual proceedings may, depending on the nature of the domestic laws involved, have negative repercussions.

At first blush, eliminating the phrase "having regard to the circumstances of the arbitration" from the rule on location of meetings may seem to limit the safeguards against an abuse of tribunal discretion. As Professor Sanders has observed, emphasis on such circumstances was intended to reduce the temptation to choose "attractive meeting places such as the Riviera or the Bahamas which have no relationship whatsoever with the arbitration or the domicile of arbitrators."[376] At the same time, the arbitral tribunal's duties contained in Article 17(1) of the Rules, among others, to "conduct the proceedings so as to avoid unnecessary delay and expense" should serve to offset any frivolous or self-interested choice of the location of meetings.

The revisions reflected in Article 18(2) bring the Rules in line with Article 20(2) of the UNCITRAL Model Law,[377] which deliberately increased the tribunal's flexibility in choosing the location of meetings. In the Model Law, the hearing of "experts or the parties" was added to the list of purposes for which the arbitral tribunal may meet "at any place it considers appropriate."[378] The approach under the Rules is also consistent with the procedural rules of some of the leading arbitral institutions.[379]

Article 18(2) affords the arbitral tribunal discretion, subject to the overriding will of the parties, to determine the location of meetings "for any other purpose." This phrase, when read in the context of Article 18(1), plainly means for any purpose other than deliberations of the tribunal members. Article 18(2) expressly provides that "hearings," if necessary, would fall within the scope of the rule. The rule also clearly contemplates other types of meetings, including conferences of the parties and site visits for the inspection of evidence or documents. As to the latter, the flexibility provided for in Article 18(2) is particularly relevant because it may be impossible as well as impractical to transfer items such as goods stored in a warehouse to the tribunal location of the hearings.

Should the home country of one of the parties be chosen as the place of arbitration, then as a general matter the tribunal should avoid holding the arbitral proceedings at the office

---

[375] The formulation of Article 18(2) leaves no doubt that tribunal members have complete discretion to decide where to meet for deliberations as opposed to the location of other meetings, which are at the tribunal's discretion "[u]nless otherwise agreed by the parties." UNCITRAL, 42nd Session, UN Doc A/CN.9/665, n 21, at 25–6, para 137 (noting concerns regarding an earlier draft of Article 18(1) (A/CN.9/WG.II/WP.151 (draft article 16(2)), which was not clear on this matter).

[376] P Sanders, "Commentary on UNCITRAL Arbitration Rules," n 60, 196.

[377] Article 20(2) of the UNCITRAL Model Law, as amended, reads as follows: "Notwithstanding the provisions of paragraph (1) of this article, the arbitral tribunal may, unless otherwise agreed by the parties, meet at any place it considers appropriate for consultation among its members, for hearing witnesses, experts or the parties, or for inspection of goods, other property or documents."

[378] See H Holtzmann and J Neuhaus, *A Guide to the UNCITRAL Model Law*, n 7, 595–6.

[379] Under the 1998 LCIA Rules, Article 16.2 provides: "The Arbitral Tribunal may hold hearings, meetings and deliberations at any convenient geographical place in its discretion…" Similarly, Article 18(2) of the 2012 ICC Rules of Arbitration provides: "The Arbitral Tribunal may, after consultation with the parties, conduct hearings and meetings at any location it considers appropriate, unless otherwise agreed by the parties."

of the party[380] or of a party-appointed arbitrator.[381] The premises of the law firm of the chairman may be a natural meeting, if available and otherwise suitable for the purpose. The premises of an arbitral institution situated within the designated jurisdictional area may also be desirable. Facilities provided by large hotels are often utilized for this purpose.

In exceptional cases, circumstances may compel the arbitral tribunal to move the physical venue of the proceedings from the designated place of arbitration, such as when a party engages in inappropriate conduct at the legal seat of arbitration designed to undermine the work of the tribunal. The *Himpurna* arbitrations provide a good example. In the first arbitration against PT Perusahaan Listruik ("PLN"), an entity controlled by Indonesia, the claimant, Himpurna, obtained a favorable arbitral award,[382] which PLN failed to pay. Himpurna then brought a second arbitration against Indonesia for its failure to ensure PLN's payment of the award.[383] Soon after, Pertamina, another entity controlled by Indonesia, successfully moved in a Jakarta court to enjoin the arbitral proceedings, and the court imposed a fine of US $1 million per day for any breach of the injunction. Recognizing the "exceptional circumstances," the arbitral tribunal decided to move the hearing from Jakarta to The Hague, though without changing the legal seat of the arbitration, which remained Jakarta.[384]

In all cases when an arbitral tribunal, with its seat in one jurisdiction, holds a meeting in another jurisdiction for the purpose of a particular proceeding, it should respect the laws of the latter jurisdiction. If, for example, the purpose of the visit is to take witness evidence, the tribunal should follow the mandatory provisions concerning the taking of such evidence in that jurisdiction.[385] Any inspection of goods, property and documents must also take place in accordance with the mandatory norms of the law of the place where the goods are situated.

(5) Comparison to the 1976 UNCITRAL Rules

Article 18 contains a clearer, more streamlined set of rules than those in corresponding Article 16 of the 1976 Rules. In essence, however, the original and revised articles achieve the same purpose of affording the arbitral tribunal authority to determine, in certain circumstances, the legal seat of the arbitration and the location of the meetings related to the arbitral proceedings.

Article 18(1) consolidates into one provision the rules previously found in Article 16(1) and 16(4) of the 1976 UNCITRAL Rules regarding, respectively, the selection of the place of arbitration and the place where the award is made. In the first sentence of Article 18(1),

---

[380] Failure to do this is about the only conceivable situation in which the determination of the locale (as distinct from the place) of arbitration could entail legal consequences (because of breach of the principle of equality of the parties).

[381] P Sanders, "Commentary on UNCITRAL Arbitration Rules," n 60, 196.

[382] See *Himpurna California Energy Ltd and PT (Persero) Perusahaan Listruik Negara*, reprinted in (2000) XXV Ybk Commericial Arb 13.

[383] See *Himpurna California Energy Ltd and Republic of Indonesia*, (2000) XXV Ybk Commercial Arb 112.

[384] See *Himpurna California Energy* (1976 Rules), Interim Award, reprinted in section 4(C). In an effort to block the tribunal's decision, Indonesia unsuccessfully sought in the Dutch court to enjoin the arbitral tribunal from holding the hearing in The Hague. See *Himpurna California Energy* (1976 Rules), Dutch Decision; *Himpurna California Energy* (1976 Rules), Final Award; both reprinted in section 4(C).

[385] N Blackaby and C Partasides, *Redfern and Hunter on International Arbitration*, n 2, 183. Similar respect for the sovereignty of the territorial state, which always makes it incumbent on the arbitral tribunal to pay due respect to the mandatory norms of the place of arbitration, should also be taken into account where a part of the proceedings are conducted outside the principal place.

the more concise term "place of arbitration" replaced the potentially confusing phrase "place where the arbitration is to be held." This revision notwithstanding, it was observed in Working Group discussions that the word "place," as used in Article 16(1) and 16(4) of the 1976 UNCITRAL Rules, referred to "the seat of arbitration, which determined the law applicable to the arbitral procedure and court jurisdiction."[386] Nevertheless, in the interest of clarity, users of the 1976 UNCITRAL Rules may wish to modify Article 16 accordingly.

As explained, Article 18(1) clarifies the rule in Article 16(4) of the 1976 UNCITRAL Rules by providing: "The award shall *be deemed to have been* made at the place of arbitration." The additional language (in italics) leaves no doubt that the award may be signed outside the place of arbitration, provided the applicable procedural law allows it.[387] Article 16(4) of the 1976 UNCITRAL Rules lacked the same clarity such that there were possible negative consequences for an overly literal reading of the rule.[388] Parties may consider modifying, in accordance with Article 1(1), original Article 16(4) to include the language of Article 18(1) that provides the arbitrators wider discretion. When contemplating this kind of modification, however, the parties should consider that very loose ties between the legal place of arbitration and the actual proceedings may, depending on the nature of the domestic laws involved, have negative repercussions.

In simplifying and reducing the rules previously found in Articles 16(2) and 16(3) of the 1976 UNCITRAL Rules, Article 18(2) clarifies the broad scope of the arbitral tribunal's discretion in determining the location of meetings, hearings, and deliberations. Absent from the revised Rule is the notion that the arbitral tribunal may determine "the locale within the country agreed upon by the parties," which would likely determine the location of the hearings, and the requirement that the tribunal determine the location to hold hearings and deliberations "having regard to the circumstances of the arbitration." Rather, Article 18(2) leaves it largely to the arbitral tribunal, subject to the overriding will of the parties, to determine the location of any meetings, hearings, and deliberations "as it considers appropriate."

Article 18(2) also omits the express rules on deciding to meet at a location to inspect goods, other property or documents and the related notice requirement previously contained in Article 16(3) of the 1976 UNCITRAL Rules. These revisions have little, if any, effect on the operation of the Rules as the arbitral tribunal has discretion under Article 18(2) to order a meeting at any location for any "other purpose," including site visits and must in any event treat the parties equally and fairly under Article 17(1), which would include providing sufficient notice to the parties of a site visit.[389]

C. Extracts from the Practice of Investment Tribunals

Wintershall AG, et al and *Government of Qatar*, Partial Award (February 5, 1988) (*Ad Hoc* Proceeding, 1976 UNCITRAL Rules, Concession Agreement), reprinted in (1989) 28 ILM 795, 801:

---

[386] UNCITRAL, 40th Session, UN Doc A/CN.9/614, n 5, at 19, para 87.

[387] See P Viscasillas, "Place of Arbitration (Article 16) and Language of Proceedings (Article 17) in the UNCITRAL Arbitration Rules: Some Proposals for a Revision," (2006) 13 Croatian Arb Ybk 205, 215.

[388] However, the few countries that contained strict provisions requiring physical presence at the place of arbitration to make the award, in practice, were rarely chosen as the place of arbitration. *Summary Record of the 6th Meeting of the Committee of the Whole (II)*, UNCITRAL, 9th Session, UN Doc A/CN.9/9/C.2/SR.6, at 10, para 81 (Comment by Mr Melia, Austria) (1976).

[389] Note, however, that by accepting Article 16(3) of the 1976 UNCITRAL Rules without modification, the party with control over the goods to be inspected is generally understood to waive any right to deny access to the goods.

B. III. *Place of Arbitration*

By the first sentence of paragraph 1 of its Order of March 18, 1987, the Tribunal decided that "Having regard to the circumstances of these arbitral proceedings, the place of arbitration shall be The Hague, the Netherlands." This determination is in accordance with Article 16(1) of the [1976] UNCITRAL Arbitration Rules.

B. IV. *Arbitral Law*

By the second sentence of paragraph 1 of its Order of March 18, 1987, the Tribunal provided that the procedure of the arbitration shall be governed by the [1976] UNCITRAL Arbitration Rules, as agreed by the Parties in the Agreement of October 22, 1986, subject to any mandatory provisions of the Netherlands Arbitration Law, which, in the event of conflict with any of the UNCITRAL Rules, shall prevail. The Tribunal has concluded that its Partial Award on Liability, determining the substance of the claims on both jurisdiction and the merits, and proposed Final Award (*See* XX hereof) are consistent with the [1976] UNCITRAL Arbitration Rules and in no respect in conflict with any of the mandatory provisions of the Netherlands Arbitration Law.

Himpurna California Energy Ltd and *Republic of Indonesia*, Interim Award (September 26, 1999) (*Ad Hoc* Proceeding, 1976 UNCITRAL Rules, Concession Agreement), reprinted in (2000) XXV Ybk Commercial Arb 112, 124–26, 145–46, 168–69:

[32] The Republic of Indonesia's conduct, according to the claimant, was a "naked use of... powers to deny claimants effective representation". The claimant accordingly asked the Arbitral Tribunal that in the absence of unequivocal assurances that the claimant's employees, witnesses, counsel and the arbitral tribunal itself will be free from harassment or arrest... we will request that the Tribunal convene the hearings at another appropriate location in accord with Art. 16 of the [1976] UNCITRAL Rules.

...

[35] In its letter to the Parties of 12 July 1999, the Arbitral Tribunal replied as follows:
the Arbitral Tribunal wishes first of all to remind counsel that these are extremely serious proceedings involving large financial stakes and, directly or indirectly, bilateral relations between two important countries. Your clients are entitled to a respectful debate. The claimants are part of a publicly traded company whose shareholders are entitled to a resolute defence of their economic interests; the Republic of Indonesia is equally entitled to a resolute protection of its own position. The economic problems at the heart of this case have hurt many people, and each side must understand that the other has weighty responsibilities. This is a most inappropriate forum for counsel to indulge in inflammatory rhetoric which the Arbitral Tribunal finds neither helpful nor humorous. Misplaced similes ("like *wayang* puppets"), ill-considered metaphors ("ever ready to rattle the government's saber"), or chatty language used for sarcastic effect ("whine to this Tribunal", "we are not qualified in psychiatry") have no place before this Arbitral Tribunal, and will not advance the interests of either side. The Arbitral Tribunal is interested in precise and reliable factual information, and in cogent arguments of law. Counsel would make a better impression on the Arbitral Tribunal if they resisted the temptation to speculate on the motives of opposite counsel, and did not proffer lectures on proper forensic behaviour. The Arbitral Tribunal feels it must admonish you that you are crossing the line of acceptable discourse.

This being said, the concerns raised by Messrs Lathams & Watkins are serious, and have not, behind the rhetoric, been assuaged by Messrs Karim Sani's letter of 9 July. As that letter itself recognises, there may be exceptional circumstances when the physical venue of proceeding under the [1976] UNCITRAL Rules is moved. (Of course Karim Sani does not accept that they are extant in this case, but that does not affect the principle.)

If the Republic of Indonesia fails to disprove the claimants' contentions that, as a matter of fact:

— a government-controlled entity has instituted legal proceedings in Indonesian courts designed to obstruct the implementation of the Terms of Appointment signed by the Republic of Indonesia;

— although a party to those proceedings, the Republic of Indonesia has not only failed to oppose this attempted obstruction, but has to the contrary manifested a degree of complicity;
— another government-controlled entity has threatened to bring a criminal complaint against the claimants' counsel on account of comments on the dispute attributed to him—but denied by him—which as a matter of principle could lead to a sentence of imprisonment;
— government officials have harassed the claimants, with the result that witnesses have been intimidated;
— although the Republic of Indonesia says it will formally oppose the motion for injunction, it nevertheless reserves the right to initiate court actions for "fines... and/or imprisonment" if the arbitrators were to proceed in accordance with the Terms of Appointment; and ultimately
— rather than use its judicial and governmental processes to implement the Terms of Reference signed by it, the Republic of Indonesia is attempting to use them to divest this Arbitral Tribunal of its jurisdiction;

the Arbitral Tribunal must seriously reconsider the physical venue for any hearings in this case.

Messrs Karim Sani are therefore invited to furnish any further factual information that would bear on these issues, in particular proof as to the position taken by the Republic of Indonesia in relation to the Indonesian court proceedings, such as previous pleadings; previous correspondence between the Government, on the one hand, and Pertamina and PLN, on the other hand; or any other evidence of the respondent's sincerity in seeking to implement the Terms of Appointment as signed.

...

[73] After extensive deliberations among all its members, the Arbitral Tribunal delivered the following Procedural Order on 7 September 1999 [which provides in relevant part]:

...the Arbitral Tribunal hereby decides and orders that:
The Republic of Indonesia is in default under the Terms of Appointment.

Hearings are hereby convened in the small Hall of Justice in the Peace Palace, The Hague, beginning at 10.30 a.m. on Wednesday 22 September and continuing as far as necessary the two following days. Given the Republic of Indonesia's default, as well as its affirmation that it will not participate in the arbitration, the convenience of its counsel, or such witnesses as it might have presented if it had not been in default, will not be taken into account. The Arbitral Tribunal will test the evidence presented by the claimants, who will be required to prove their case to the satisfaction of the arbitrators irrespective of the default of the Republic of Indonesia; and will consider all arguments raised by the Republic of Indonesia.

The Arbitral Tribunal has chosen the place for this hearing in the exercise of its authority under Art. 16(2) of the [1976] UNCITRAL Rules without changing the legal seat of the arbitration, which, in accordance with paragraph 3(c) of the Terms of Appointment, remains Jakarta.

In the exercise of its procedural discretion the Arbitral Tribunal hereby informs counsel to the Republic of Indonesia that in the event they formally advise the Arbitral Tribunal on or before 17 September 1999 that the injunction has been withdrawn, and that they are authorised to stipulate that the Republic of Indonesia will fully and irrevocably participate in these arbitral proceedings, then the schedule would be modified as an extraordinary accommodation to the Republic of Indonesia. If said stipulation is made to the Arbitral Tribunal, the Republic of Indonesia's submission of documentary evidence, including statements of all witnesses upon whom it intends to rely, as defined in paragraph 5(f) of the Terms of Appointment, should also be made on 17 September 1999, and the hearing would be rescheduled thereafter.

...

[111] The position of the Arbitral Tribunal is thus based on its appreciation of the facts of this case, and founded on the authority granted by the Parties when they agreed to arbitration under the [1976] UNCITRAL Arbitration Rules.

...

[114] Nor did the decision to hear witnesses at a location outside Indonesia crystallise into any imaginary struggle between the Indonesian courts and the Arbitral Tribunal—to the contrary. The Jakarta Court's injunction purported to forbid pursuit of the arbitration. The jurisdiction of that court is perforce limited to Indonesian territory. Whether or not the Arbitral Tribunal is to be deemed to be "international", it avoided offending the Jakarta court by convening the hearing of witnesses outside Indonesia. It did so pursuant to Art. 16 of the [1976] UNCITRAL Rules, with the compelling justification that the cause of this choice of physical meeting place was directly attributable to an event which the Republic of Indonesia could have avoided.

[115] The Republic of Indonesia is in no position to contend that the Arbitral Tribunal was precluded in principle from hearing witnesses outside Indonesia. For not only is such a possibility consistent with Art. 16 of the [1976] UNCITRAL Rules, but the Republic of Indonesia itself acknowledged, in the letter of 9 July 1999 from its counsel quoted in Paragraph [33] as well as in the further letter of 26 August 1999 (see Paragraph [65]) that Art. 16 would allow hearings in another location in the event of "extraordinary circumstances". Moreover, as seen in Paragraph [69], on 31 August 1999 the Republic of Indonesia proposed a hearing in London devoted to the expert testimony of Professors Lalive and Rogers, to be followed by "further deliberations of the Tribunal". Having admitted that "extraordinary circumstances" permit hearings outside Indonesia, one of the Parties is not entitled to impose its evaluation of what constitutes "extraordinary circumstances", or to insist that the Arbitral Tribunal bow to its preference for London over The Hague.

Republic of Indonesia v Himpurna California Energy Ltd, et al (Dutch Court of First Instance (Arrondissementsrechtbank)), (September 21, 1999), translated and reprinted in (2000) XXV Ybk Commercial Arb 469, 471–73:

I. The Parties' Position
...

[3] Indonesia maintains that the arbitral tribunal may not hold a hearing in The Hague rather than in the contractually agreed place of arbitration, Jakarta. Indonesia alleges breach of contract (*wanprestatie*) or unlawful behaviour (*onrechtmatige daad*) under the parties' agreements, including the Terms of Reference. The Terms of Appointment indicate Jakarta as the place of arbitration. Art. 16(1) of the [1976] UNCITRAL Arbitration Rules, which the parties declared applicable, provides that the place of arbitration is (in principle) the place chosen by the parties. It is certainly not in the Minister of Finance's interest to deviate from this general rule, since by choosing a different venue he does not escape the prohibition and the penalty of the Indonesian court's injunction, as is the case with Himpurna and Patuha, whose seat is [not in Indonesia]. On the other hand, his failure to appear at the hearing of 22 September may result in his being ordered to pay US $573 million.

[4] Himpurna, Patuha and Paulsson maintain that the present case is an international arbitration, in which national courts play no or a very limited role. (International) arbitrators examine and ascertain their own jurisdiction according to, inter alia, the [1976] UNCITRAL Rules; proceedings are regulated by the applicable arbitration rules, as provided in the Terms of Reference and/or the Terms of Appointment, and enforcement takes place at the parties' initiative, possibly with the assistance of the national courts. Dutch courts must refrain as much as possible from any intervention in the arbitral process, and promote the smooth flow of the arbitration. Further, Dutch courts have no jurisdiction if there are no sufficient connecting factors.

...

II. The Court's Decision

[7] First, we must examine whether Dutch courts have international jurisdiction. On this issue we reason as follows. The fact that in the present international arbitration a hearing is to be held on Dutch territory is in itself a connecting factor with the Dutch legal system. The hearing shall take place in the Peace Palace in The Hague. The arbitrators apparently obtained the permission therefor from the International [rectius] Permanent Court of Arbitration ["PCA"]. This does not in itself mean that the arbitration takes place "under the auspices" of the PCA, a case which is regulated in the agreement concluded by the Netherlands on 30 March 1999 in replacement of the 1899 agreement. If this were an arbitration "under the auspices" of the PCA, defendants 3 through 5 [Jan Paulsson, Antonino Albert De Fina and Priyatna Abdurrasyid] would be, according to the new agreement as submitted, PCA arbitrators and would enjoy immunity. If this were the case, it would be logical to presume that there is insufficient connection with the Dutch legal system. [However], since the status of the arbitrators is unclear, we must presume in this summary proceedings that the arbitration at issue does have sufficient connection with the Dutch legal system and that, therefore, Dutch courts have jurisdiction.

[8] Subsequently, we must examine whether the arbitrators violated their mandate by deciding that a hearing would take place in The Hague and/or whether Himpurna and Patuha would be in breach of their contract with Indonesia by participating in this hearing. Indonesia maintains that this is the crux of the dispute.

[9] The President leaves aside the question whether the arbitration at issue must be considered a domestic arbitration according to the Indonesian legal view, as alleged by Indonesia. The parties stipulated in their Terms of Appointment that the [1976] UNCITRAL Arbitration Rules apply where the parties have not otherwise agreed. Art. 16(2) of the [1976] Rules explicitly allows the arbitral tribunal to hear witnesses and to hold meetings "at any place it deems appropriate". This power is not limited by the [1976] UNCITRAL Rules or by the Terms of Appointment. Hence, we must conclude that the arbitral tribunal may decide that a hearing shall take place here in The Hague. The question under [[8]] must therefore be answered in the negative.

Himpurna Energy Ltd and *Republic of Indonesia*, Final Award (October 16, 1999) (*Ad Hoc* Proceeding, 1976 UNCITRAL Rules, Concession Agreement), reprinted in (2000) XXV Ybk Commercial Arb 186, 190:

[22] The session before the District Court lasted four and one-half hours. The following morning, at 9 a.m., the Court issued its judgment rejecting the Republic of Indonesia's request for injunction. The written judgment disposed of, *inter alia*, the two following arguments raised by the Republic of Indonesia:

(i) that the Arbitral Tribunal had violated its mandate by determining that a hearing should take place in The Hague; the District Court rejected this argument by noting that Art. 16(2) of the [1976] UNCITRAL Rules explicitly permits arbitrators to hear witnesses and to hold meetings "at any place it deems appropriate."

Canfor Corp and *United States of America*, Decision on the Place of Arbitration, Filing of a Statement of Defence and Bifurcation of the Proceedings (January 23, 2004) (ICSID administered, 1976 UNCITRAL Rules, NAFTA Chapter Eleven), at 3–9 (citations omitted):

13. In order to provide guidelines to the Tribunal in the determination of the place of arbitration, the parties have referred to the UNCITRAL Notes on Organizing Arbitral Proceedings (hereafter "UNCITRAL Notes") and, in particular, Paragraph 22 of the Notes which discusses various factual and legal factors.

...

15. The Tribunal considers that it must determine the place of arbitration in light of any relevant circumstances in this arbitration and that the factors enumerated in the UNCITRAL Notes

provide no more than non-binding guidelines, as Paragraph 2 of the Notes makes clear (*"The arbitral tribunal remains free to use the Notes as it sees fit and is not required to give reasons for disregarding them"*).

16. The Tribunal will therefore examine each of the factors offered for consideration by the parties, without according particular weight to any individual circumstance over another. These factors include neutrality, which is not referred to in the UNCITRAL Notes but which constitutes one of the key features of international arbitration.

(1) The neutrality factor

17. ... [T]he Claimant contends that the factor of neutrality, or perceived neutrality, should direct the Tribunal to determine the place of arbitration in Canada. The Claimant argues that, unlike in those cases where Washington, D.C. was held to be the appropriate place of arbitration, in this case the Tribunal should consider Vancouver as an appropriate place of arbitration given its substantial connection to the proceedings; should Vancouver not be perceived as neutral, Toronto could in the alternative be determined as the place of arbitration where neutrality would be best ensured...

18. ... [T]he Claimant maintains that Washington, D.C., which is not only the seat of the United States Government but also the place where the disputed measures were taken, is the least neutral location for the place of arbitration...

19. The Respondent considers, for its part, that the venues proposed by each party are equally neutral... First, relying on the *Methanex v. USA* case, the Respondent argues that a neutral national venue is not possible in this case... Second, the Respondent submits that neutrality is not an important factor to be taken into consideration, given that it was excluded from the UNCITRAL Notes, that Chapter Eleven limits the place of arbitration to one of the three NAFTA Parties, and the fact that the parties have agreed to exclude Mexico as an alternative place of arbitration. Only if the five factors set forth in the UNCITRAL Notes do not result in the determination of a place of arbitration could neutrality be considered as a tie-breaking factor. Third, the Respondent submits that neutrality could be addressed by holding the hearings in ICSID's headquarters in Washington, D.C. In addition, the Respondent has emphasized that the softwood lumber issue is an important local issue in British Columbia and Ontario and that, should neutrality be weighed at all, it should not be considered a factor favoring a Canadian venue...

20. The Tribunal is not convinced by the parties' arguments.

21. The Tribunal observes that Article 1130 of the NAFTA has limited the choice of the place of arbitration, absent an agreement between the disputing parties, to one of the three NAFTA Parties. In the present arbitration, had the disputing parties intended to ensure neutrality, they were at liberty to agree to a neutral forum outside any of the three NAFTA Parties. In the alternative, the disputing parties were at liberty to leave open the option of Mexico. Rather, the parties have chosen expressly to exclude such options and to limit the scope of the Tribunal's choice to a venue in either Canada or the United States. As a result, because of the choice made by the negotiators of the NAFTA and because of the procedural choices made by the disputing parties in this arbitration, the Tribunal considers that, with regard to the place of arbitration, a neutral venue is not available.

22. Further, the Tribunal is not persuaded, in the circumstances of this arbitration, by the argument of perceived neutrality. In particular, the Tribunal finds little assistance in the Respondent's argument that any concern of neutrality in this arbitration could be addressed by holding the hearings at the ICSID facilities in Washington, D.C. First, the Respondent's implication that the mere physical location of a building may ensure the neutrality of the place of arbitration is at odds with the distinction, on which it has laid emphasis, between the legal seat of an arbitration and the physical location of hearings.... Second, the Tribunal does not find any reason in the facts of this case to give consideration to ICSID as a weighing circumstance with respect to the determination of the place of arbitration. Absent the ratification of the Washington Convention by Canada, the guarantees offered by ICSID, including the true

neutrality provided by a system which is genuinely independent from any national legal order, are not available to the disputing parties in this arbitration.

23. As a result, the Tribunal concludes that the neutrality factor does not favor either the United States or Canada. To the contrary, by the very choice of the disputing parties, any decision on the place of arbitration taken by the Tribunal will result in having one of the parties arbitrate in the other's forum....

(2) The suitability of the law on arbitral procedure

24. The Claimant and the Respondent agree on the suitability of both U.S. and Canadian arbitral laws....
25. The Tribunal agrees with the parties that this factor weighs neutrally, and that the laws applicable in British Columbia and in Ontario as well as the Federal Arbitration Act are equally suitable, including on questions concerning the applicable standards of review for Chapter Eleven arbitral awards....

(3) The existence of a multilateral treaty on enforcement of arbitral awards

[The Tribunal found that this factor was neutral because both the United States and Canada are parties to the New York Convention.]

(4) The convenience of the parties and the arbitrators

27. ...The Claimant argues that [this factor] weighs neutrally and does not point to any one place over another since the parties have agreed, in accordance with Article 16(2) of the [1976] UNCITRAL Arbitration Rules, that the seat of the arbitration and the place of hearings need not coincide and that hearings or meetings may take place at any appropriate place, including Washington, D.C., Vancouver or Toronto....The Respondent does not agree. It contends that holding the arbitration in Washington, D.C. would be less inconvenient than Vancouver or Toronto for the members of the Tribunal as well as for the U.S. officers from the various governmental agencies involved in this arbitration, without such venue being inconvenient for Canfor...
28. The Tribunal agrees with the Claimant and considers that this factor, which should not be accorded a great weight in this arbitration, is neutral. The Tribunal is attentive to the Respondent's argument regarding the convenience of Washington, D.C. The Tribunal is also mindful that, as emphasized by the Respondent, a distinction should accurately be drawn between the legal seat of an arbitration and the geographical location of hearings.... However, in light of Paragraph 13 of the Terms of Agreement signed by the parties at the Hearing of October 28, 2003, the Tribunal considers that the parties' agreement, without prejudice to the legal seat of the arbitration, to hold the hearings and the meetings at any appropriate place—which may include, as need be, Washington, D.C.—adequately satisfies, in the circumstances of this arbitration, the convenience factor.

(5) The availability of cost and support services

29. ...The Claimant argues that the availability and cost of support services is neutral, and that the cost of support services may become relevant at the time of the determination of the place where particular hearings will be held....The Claimant further argues that the facilities of ICSID in Washington, D.C. may be compared, in terms of costs, to equivalent facilities in either Vancouver or Toronto....The Respondent contends that this factor favors Washington, D.C. as a less costly venue. The relevant factors considered by the Respondent are travel costs for the members of the Tribunal, the parties and their attorneys, and the fact that ICSID facilities are available for use at rates that are likely more competitive than equivalent facilities in Vancouver or Toronto...
30. The Tribunal finds that this factor does not favor any venue over the other and considers that the parties' agreement to hold the hearings and the meetings at any appropriate place allows the Tribunal to conduct the arbitration in a cost-effective manner.

(6) The location of the subject matter in dispute and the proximity of evidence

31. The final factor set forth in the UNCITRAL Notes, that of the location of the subject matter in dispute and the proximity of evidence, sharply divides the parties. The Claimant finds it to be neutral.... In particular, the Claimant disputes the Respondent's submission that the subject matter of the dispute is located exclusively in Washington, D.C.: according to the Claimant, the subject matter in dispute relates to decisions made by the United States in relation to the alleged conduct of Canadian softwood lumber companies operating in British Columbia...

32. The Respondent argues to the contrary that the subject matter in dispute is located in Washington, D.C. for the following reasons: the Claimant's allegations are based on anti-dumping and countervailing duty determinations which were made in Washington, D.C. by the U.S. Department of Commerce and the International Trade Commission; the significant events underlying the Claimant's allegations took place in Washington, D.C.; and most or all of the relevant evidence is located in Washington, D.C. In contrast, the Respondent finds no connection between either Vancouver or Toronto and the subject matter in dispute... The Respondent further argues that the subject matter in dispute points to a U.S. venue given that the Claimant's allegations that it has been denied national treatment or most-favored nation treatment may only be made with respect to its U.S. investments...

33. The Tribunal finds that, as regards the proximity of evidence, it is irrelevant in this arbitration given the parties' agreement to hold hearings and meetings at any appropriate place... As regards the subject matter in dispute, the parties have not presented the Tribunal with a uniform definition of what constitutes the "subject matter". The Claimant refers to the determination of the location of a particular hearing and considers that *"[t]he 'subject matter' of the dispute is the treatment of a Canadian investor situate in Canada and the United States, by organs of the United States government situate in Washington, D.C."*.... The Claimant further refers to the *"physical subject-matter of the dispute"* which it situates in British Columbia and to *"legal facts"* it claims have occurred in British Columbia... The Respondent, referring to the decision rendered in *ADF v. United States*, considers *"the 'subject-matter' of the dispute as 'the issue presented for consideration; the thing in which [or in respect of which] a right or duty has been asserted'* [...] "...

35. The Tribunal considers that the subject matter, independently from the proximity of evidence, does not, in this arbitration, relate to the Claimant's conduct in British Columbia. It rather relates to the Respondent's measures determining the Claimant's softwood lumber importations into the United States as subsidized or dumped, which are alleged by the Claimant to have affected its investments in the United States and breached Chapter Eleven of the NAFTA....

...

36. The Tribunal therefore finds that, with respect to the subject matter in dispute in this arbitration, substantial connections point to a venue in the United States: the United States is the territory in which the Claimant's investments are alleged to have been made...; it is the place where the alleged measures were taken; it also happens to be the country of the defendant's domicile in this case.

(7) The Tribunal's decision

37. The Tribunal has carefully balanced each of the factors discussed by the parties and has found most of these factors to weigh equally between a venue in Canada and a venue in the United States. The Tribunal finds however that the location of the subject matter in dispute is a factor pointing to a venue in the United States. As a result, the Tribunal considers that Washington, D.C. (United States) should be designated as the place of arbitration.

Ethyl Corp and *Government of Canada*, Decision Regarding the Place of Arbitration (November 28, 1997) (*Ad Hoc* Proceeding, 1976 UNCITRAL Rules, NAFTA Chapter Eleven), reprinted in (1999) 38 ILM 702, 702–06:

> ... [T]he Tribunal now turns its attention to the four factors relevant under the UNCITRAL Notes, considering each of them in relation to the respective proposed places of arbitration: Ottawa (or, alternatively, Toronto) and New York City.
>
> As to criterion (a) of the Notes—"suitability of the law on arbitral procedure"—the Tribunal concludes that all proposed fora are all equally suitable. It appears undisputed that Canada's Commercial Arbitration Act is based on the UNCITRAL Model Law on International Commercial Arbitration and by its terms would apply to this arbitration under NAFTA Chapter 11. It appears to be equally undisputed that the relevant laws of the United States, and, to the extent relevant, the State of New York, are no less suitable. The fact that the laws applicable to this arbitration, were it situated in New York City, have been in place longer than Canada's Commercial Arbitration Act, and therefore are judicially more elaborated, does not, in the view of the Tribunal, significantly affect their comparative suitability.
>
> Criterion (c) of the Notes—"the convenience of the parties and the arbitrators, including the travel distances"—likewise seems not be significantly better served by one proposed alternative as opposed to any other. As to the Tribunal, the President, who normally is resident in Cologne, Germany, can travel with more or less equal ease to New York City, Ottawa and Toronto. Mr. Lalonde, a resident of Montreal, can travel to Ottawa or Toronto just as well as Judge Brower can from his Washington, DC residence to New York City. By the same token, Judge Brower would be no more and no less inconvenienced by travel to Ottawa or Toronto than would Mr. Lalonde be by the need to appear in New York City.
>
> The situation of the parties is substantially similar. Canada has noted ... that:
>
>> The investment which Ethyl Corporation alleges has been damaged is the wholly owned subsidiary, Ethyl Canada, which has its head office in Mississauga, adjoining the City of Toronto, in the Province of Ontario. Its blending facility, where it processes MMT, is in Coronna, in the Province of Ontario.
>
> In response to this Ethyl simply contends ... that it has "its head office in [the Commonwealth of] Virginia" and that the "location of subsidiary offices is not a relevant factor for this arbitration." For purposes of criterion (c) alone this may well be correct. If it is, there is no significant difference in the convenience factor between Canada having to travel to New York City and Ethyl having to be present in Ottawa or Toronto. If it is not, then a degree of preference would be indicated for a Canadian venue.
>
> Canada has introduced as a consideration the location of counsel to the parties, emphasizing that Ethyl's counsel has an office in Toronto as well as in New York City. Ethyl disputes the relevance of counsel's convenience, while nonetheless pointing out ... that "The Government of Canada also maintains a large consulate in New York City as well as a Permanent Mission to the United Nations which can support the needs of the Government of Canada's legal team ... " Canada terms this latter assertion "incorrect," as "[t]hese are diplomatic offices and are not set up to act as alternative legal offices, such as [Claimant's counsel] apparently [sic] has available to him."
>
> The Tribunal is inclined to the view that the convenience of counsel is a relevant consideration, subsumed under the "convenience of the parties." Certainly the convenience of attorneys appointed by the parties, which translates into cost factors, affects their clients. The Tribunal also believes that the availability for temporary use by government lawyers of facilities at a consular post or diplomatic mission is not comparable to a dedicated office of counsel. Accordingly, the Tribunal concludes that it is relevant to consider that fixing the place of arbitration in either Ottawa or Toronto will serve the convenience of counsel collectively better than New York City.
>
> We now turn to criterion (d), "availability and cost of support services needed." It is clear that all necessary support services for this arbitration are available in all three of the cities that have been proposed. The Tribunal believes it appropriate to take judicial notice of the fact that such services

inevitably will be more costly in New York City than in either Ottawa or Toronto. This includes transportation, hotels, meal service, hearing rooms and counsel rooms, and certified stenographic reporting services. Therefore application of criterion (d) favors Ottawa or Toronto over New York City, but does not discriminate between them.

The Tribunal does not, however, take into consideration in this regard, as Canada has proposed, the presence and availability in Ottawa of NAFTA Secretariat facilities.... [T]o avail itself of such facilities could be viewed as inconsistent with at least the spirit of the requirement of the [1976] UNCITRAL Rules (Articles 9–10) that it act so as to leave no doubt whatsoever as to its complete independence of any party. This is all the more so where, as here, Ethyl has registered its objection... that the use of such facilities "would be inappropriate."

The last criterion of the Notes—"(e) location of the subject-matter in dispute and proximity of evidence"—finally turns the Tribunal definitely to selection of a place of arbitration in Canada. Clearly the subject-matter in dispute is fixed in Canada. Ethyl charges...—that certain legislative and other acts of Canada "remov[ing] MMT [...] from Canadian gasoline" have resulted in breaches by Canada of Article 1102, 1106 and 1110 of NAFTA, thereby "harm[ing] Ethyl Corporation and the value of its Canadian investment, Ethyl Canada." The "location of the subject-matter in dispute" is not subject to serious debate.

The parties have little to say as regards "the proximity of evidence."... Thus the Tribunal is afforded little insight into just how any considerations of the proximity of evidence should affect its decision.

Traditionally arbitrating parties, desiring both the reality and the appearance of a neutral forum, incline to agree on a place of arbitration outside their respective national jurisdictions. This is especially the case where a sovereign party is involved. Where an arbitral institution or a tribunal must make the selection, this tendency is, if anything, even greater, and for the same reasons. Article 16(1) of the [1976] UNCITRAL Rules easily accommodates this consideration as one of the "circumstances of the arbitration."

The Tribunal concludes on the basis of all of the foregoing that, on balance, the place of arbitration should be in Canada.... Most significantly, Canada indisputably is the location of the subject-matter in dispute. In addition, a Canadian venue offers less costly support services and overall would better suit the convenience of counsel for the parties. It is far less certain, but likely, that Canada overall is more convenient for the parties themselves and as regards the proximity of evidence....

Once the Tribunal has determined to select a Canadian venue, none of the specific factors considered weighs strongly in favor of Toronto, Canada's alternative proposal, rather than Ottawa. The Tribunal has some reluctance, however, to choose Ottawa. This is due to the fact that it is the capital of Canada. The Tribunal therefore has determined to designate Toronto as the place of arbitration, for the reason that while it is no more, and no less, appropriate than Ottawa when measured by the other applicable criteria, it is likely to be perceived as a more "neutral" forum.

Methanex Corp and *United States of America*, Order on the Place of Arbitration (September 7, 2000) (ICSID administered, 1976 UNCITRAL Rules, NAFTA Chapter Eleven), at 3, 9–15:

III—The Tribunal's Reasons

23. In the absence of the parties' agreement on the place of arbitration (save to exclude any place outside Canada and the USA), the Tribunal is required to choose for this arbitration a place of arbitration in either Canada or the USA in accordance with Article 1130(b) of NAFTA and Article 16(1) of the [1976] UNCITRAL Rules. Both Canada and the USA have enacted the 1958 New York Convention, satisfying the requirements of Article 1130(b); and the issue turns on the application of Article 16(1) to the particular circumstances of this arbitration.

24. Under Article 16(1) of the [1976] UNCITRAL Rules, the place of the arbitration is the legal place, or "seat", of the arbitration; and the Tribunal here makes no decision as to the

geographical place of any particular hearing. Any such hearing could be held at a geographical place elsewhere than the legal place of arbitration in accordance with Article 16(2) of the [1976] UNCITRAL Rules, depending upon the convenience of witnesses, the parties and their legal representatives, together with other relevant circumstances....

26. The Tribunal begins, as did the parties, with the factors listed in the UNCITRAL Notes. As regards Factors A and B, the Tribunal accepts that there is little to choose between Toronto and Washington DC in regard to suitability of the law on arbitral procedure and enforcement. The Tribunal concludes that, for all practical purposes in regard to this arbitration, the two potential places of arbitration may be considered equally in terms of the law on arbitral procedure and enforcement.

...

28. As to Factor C, the Tribunal considers that the convenience of the three arbitrators is irrelevant in this case when measured against other factors invoked by the Disputing Parties. As regards the convenience of the parties, the Claimant is correct in describing it here more as the balance of "inconvenience" rather than "convenience". The Tribunal also accepts that this balancing exercise must take into account both the parties and their Counsel, because the latter's extra traveling time and expenses will be borne ultimately as costs by the parties. [The Tribunal finds that Washington, DC is not inconvenient for the Claimant, which has a substantial permanent office in that city, while Toronto is unduly inconvenient for the Respondent whose various government departments involved in the dispute are located in Washington, DC.]

32. As to Factor D relating to the availability and costs of support services, the necessary support services would be available in both Toronto and Washington DC....

33. As to Factor E relating to the location of the subject-matter of the dispute, the Tribunal considers that it points to a place in the USA as the place of arbitration. [Noting that Claimant's arbitral claims involve actions of the State of California, the Tribunal concludes that] the subject-matter of the dispute is not located in Canada; and accordingly, whilst this factor bears only slight importance on this arbitration, the Tribunal considers that it favours Washington DC over Toronto.

34. In summary, in the Tribunal's considerations so far, the factors cited from the UNCITRAL Notes favour Washington DC over Toronto. The Tribunal now turns to the separate issue of neutrality, or perceived neutrality, which the claimant invokes to favour Toronto over Washington DC.

35. For the purpose of the present case, the Tribunal does not place any great weight on the fact that neutrality as a factor was removed from the final version of the UNCITRAL Notes. The Tribunal's discretion turns on the broad concept of "circumstances" in Article 16(2) of the [1976] UNCITRAL Rules; and there is no linguistic or logical basis for excluding neutrality as a factor in an appropriate case. Accordingly, the Tribunal has considered neutrality as a possible circumstance in this arbitration.

36. However, in assessing the significance of neutrality or perceived neutrality, the Tribunal bears in mind (i) that it was open to the NAFTA Parties to agree that in the interests of neutrality Chapter Eleven disputes should be arbitrated in the territory of any third Party not directly involved in the dispute, yet they did not do so; and (ii) that in circumstances where (as in this case) the disputing parties have further limited the choice of place of arbitration by their arbitration tribunal to one or the other's state, a neutral national venue is simply not possible....

...

38. For this arbitration, the Tribunal considers that the requirements of neutrality are sufficiently met if the place of arbitration lies outside British Colombia (as the home of the Claimant), California (responsible for the legislative measure in issue) and Texas (as the home of Methanex US). Once these three locations are excluded, the question then arises whether Washington DC should also be excluded on grounds of neutrality because it is the Respondent's capital city, thereby (it might be said in sporting terms) requiring the Claimant to play away from home in its opponent's home stadium.

39. As to actual neutrality, from the information currently available before it, the Tribunal can find no evidence of any difficulties for the Claimant. As to perceived neutrality, the point is

answered by accepting ICSID's offer of the World Bank's facilities... Whilst Washington DC is of course the seat of federal government in the USA, it is also the seat of the World Bank and ICSID. The World Bank is an independent international organisation with juridical personality and broad jurisdictional immunities and freedoms...; and ICSID similarly has international legal personality and benefits from a wide jurisdiction immunity.... The Tribunal considers that the requirements of perceived neutrality in this case will be satisfied by holding such hearings in Washington DC as the seat of the World Bank, as distinct from the seat of the USA's federal government.

40. *Decision*: Balancing all these factors as circumstances relevant to the exercise of its discretion under Article 16(1) of the [1976] UNCITRAL Rules, the Tribunal considers that Washington DC, USA should be designated as the place of the arbitration...

ADF Group Inc and *United States of America*, Procedural Order No 2 (July 1, 2001) (ICSID administered, 1976 UNCITRAL Rules, NAFTA Chapter Eleven), at 5:

10. It appears to us that the "suitability" in international arbitration of the law on arbitral procedure of a suggested place of arbitration, has multiple dimensions. These dimensions include the extent to which that law, e.g., protects the integrity of and gives effect to the parties' arbitration agreement; accords broad discretion to the parties and to the arbitrators they choose to determine and control the conduct of arbitration proceedings; provides for the availability of interim measures of protection and of means of compelling the production of documents and other evidence and the attendance of reluctant witnesses; consistently recognizes and enforces, in accordance with the terms of widely accepted international conventions, international arbitral awards when rendered; insists on principled restraint in establishing grounds for reviewing and setting aside international arbitral awards; and so on.

United Parcel Service of America Inc and *Government of Canada*, Decision on the Place of Arbitration (October 17, 2001) (ICSID administered, 1976 UNCITRAL Rules, NAFTA Chapter Eleven), reprinted in (2002) 14(1) World Trade & Arb Materials 33, 34–40:

7. We consider [the five factors enumerated in Paragraph 22 of the UNCITRAL notes] in turn.

    A. Suitability of the law on arbitral procedure of the place of arbitration

8. UPS contends that the position of the Canadian government in litigation relating to another NAFTA arbitration (the *Metalclad Corporation v Mexico* case) and the position of the Canadian courts provide insufficient deference to the rulings of chapter 11 Tribunal. It calls attention in particular to the fact that in argument in that case Canada submitted that the leading Canadian authorities supporting deference to arbitral tribunals ought to be rejected and that

    awards of chapter 11 Tribunals "are not worthy of judicial deference and are not supposed to be protected by a high standard of review". The submission continued that chapter 11 Tribunals are neither expert nor specialised Tribunals....

11. The Tribunal is troubled by Canada's submission on this issue in the *Metalclad* case.

    [The Tribunal finds the second factor, the existence of an applicable treaty on the enforcement of arbitral awards, to be neutral because Canada and the United States are both parties to the New York Convention.]

    C. *Convenience of the Parties and the arbitrators including travel distances*

13. ... [T]his factor includes not just the Parties but also their counsel because their extra travelling time and expenses will ultimately be borne as costs by the disputing Parties. [Because the Canadian agencies involved in the dispute, Canada's counsel, and its investment UPS Canada are all in Canada], [t]he balance of the convenience therefore strongly favours Canada over the United States....

D. Availability and cost of support services

14. ... [UPS] calls attention to the fact that the Tribunal has ... proposed that the administrative services of ICSID be used and if that decision were made this would be a strong reason in favour of Washington as a convenient location for the arbitration. Canada responds to that point by recalling that, when the Tribunal suggested to the parties that they consider ICSID as the body to provide administrative services, the Tribunal made it clear that that suggestion was without prejudice to the determination of the place of arbitration....

E. Location of the subject matter in dispute and the proximity of the evidence

15. Canada argues that this factor weighs very heavily in favour of Canada and in particular Ottawa.... All the records relating to the impugned measures and the individual decision-makers implicated by the Investor in its claim are in Canada. [As to the argument that the place of arbitration should be Canada because Canada is alleged to have breached NAFTA Chapter 11, UPS states] [t]o give this criterion undue weight would lead to the result that the place of arbitration under chapter 11 arbitrations would nearly always be in the territory of the respondent party. This was clearly not the intention of the NAFTA parties and the text does not provide for that result.... So far as the evidence is concerned, although it is difficult to assess this issue at this early stage in the arbitration, it can be said with some certainty that the arbitration will be largely based on documentation and expert evidence. With modern information technology, the handling of documentation should not be an issue in this arbitration particularly given that the disputing parties have a high degree of expertise and sophistication in the handling of information. So far as witnesses and experts are concerned, there is no clear balance of convenience. Witnesses will be from throughout North America and likely from Europe. There is neither advantage nor disadvantage for either disputing party if the arbitration is located in either the United States or Canada.

The Tribunal's assessment

16. Of the factors mentioned so far two are neutral—B and C (although in the usual course travel from New Zealand to the United States is marginally more convenient than it is to Canada); two weigh slightly in UPS's favour (A, because of the attitude of the Canadian government in the *Metalclad* litigation and D because the Tribunal, although without prejudice, has already suggested to the Parties that they consider ICSID as its registry); and another is in Canada's favour (E, but the importance of that factor in the arbitration is not clear at present).
17. Neutrality had been identified as a factor relevant to the place of arbitration (although it is not in the UNCITRAL list), for instance in the *Methanex* decision paras 35–39. Canada addressed it in its submission. That factor is plainly relevant given the broad reference to "the circumstances of the arbitration" in Article 16(1) of the [1976] UNCITRAL rules (para 2 above).
18. In one sense a neutral place is not available given that the claimant is a United States corporation and Canada is the respondent and the place of the arbitration is to be in one or other country. It is however relevant that it is Canada's measures that are in issue, even if it has been the place of arbitration in all chapter 11 investment disputes in which it has been the respondent. It is also relevant that Washington DC can be seen as having the neutrality of being the seat of the World Bank and ICSID, rather than the seat of federal government in the United States of America. And UPS's headquarters are in Atlanta, GA.
19. While the matter is finely balanced, the Tribunal considers that the balance does favour the United States of America as the place of arbitration and in particular Washington, DC. The Tribunal so decides.

Merrill & Ring Forestry LP and *Government of Canada*, Decision on the Place of Arbitration, (December 12, 2007) (ICSID administered, 1976 UNCITRAL Rules, NAFTA Chapter Eleven), at 7–8:

> 27. Both Ottawa and Washington, D.C. end-up, after all elements having been considered, in an almost identical situation from the point of view of their suitability as the place of arbitration. In order to arrive at a determination the Tribunal thus needs to weigh further some particular arguments made by the parties in support of their respective proposals.
> 28. The first such argument concerns the location of the subject matter in dispute and the proximity of evidence. While these factors are likely to be more readily available in Ottawa as the place where many or most of the challenged measures have been adopted by the Canadian government and its services, a criterion accepted by several NAFTA tribunals (Ethyl (at 705), ADF (para. 20) and Canfor (para. 35), the Tribunal does not believe that this is a crucial factor in the age of electronic communications and availability of records.
> 29. The second argument to be taken into account relates to the travel facilities servicing one or other venue. Although this particular aspect is related more to the place of hearings than to the place of arbitration, the Tribunal will consider it for the sake of completeness, particularly in view that both the UNCITRAL Rules and the parties' submissions refer to it in connection with the place of arbitration.
> 30. In consideration of the fact that one arbitrator has a residence in Washington, D.C. or will be traveling from Chicago, that another arbitrator shall be coming from either Toronto or London, that the Presiding arbitrator will be arriving either from New York or Miami as the most convenient ports of entry to the United States coming from Santiago, that one party will be traveling from Seattle and its counsel from Toronto, the Tribunal is persuaded that flight connections with Washington, D.C. are more readily available than with Ottawa. In this last case travel is many times routed through Toronto. In any event, connections between Ottawa and Washington, D.C. are also adequate enough so as not to inconvenience counsel for the Respondent.
> 31. In addition to the above considerations, the Tribunal also notes that Washington, D.C. is the seat of ICSID, the administering institution of this case, that it has been accepted on various occasions as the place of arbitration and that it has developed the reputation of being an independent venue for many international organizations (See UPS (para. 18), ADF (para. 21); Methanex (para. 39)). While some cases were brought under the ICSID Additional Facility Rules of Arbitration, and hence were held at and administered by ICSID itself, there are also cases brought under the UNCITRAL Rules that have been held in the ICSID facilities, just as the present case.
> 32. Having considered all the arguments made in favour of the different venues indicated, the Tribunal can conclude, like the *UPS* tribunal, that,
>
>> While the matter is finely balanced, the Tribunal considers that the balance does favour the United States of America as the place of arbitration and in particular Washington, DC *(UPS,* para. 19).
>
> 33. The Tribunal appreciates, of course, that the Claimant is a national of, and distinct from, the United States, and that this factor is sufficient guarantee that the impartiality of the courts will not be in any way affected as the United States Federal judiciary is also fully independent. In this connection, Washington, D.C. is favoured, not because of being the capital of the United States but because it is the seat of ICSID and offers some advantages in terms of practical conveniences.

D. Extracts from the Practice of the Iran–US Claims Tribunal

Article VI, paragraph 1 of the Claims Settlement Declaration:

> The seat of the Tribunal shall be the Hague, The Netherlands, or any other place agreed by Iran and the United States.

Chapter 3

Applicable Law, *Amiable Compositeur*

1. Introduction	111
2. Applicable Law—Article 35	112
A. Text of the 2010 UNCITRAL Rule	112
B. Commentary	112
(1) The primary rule—Article 35(1)	112
(a) The principle of party autonomy and its application	112
(b) Choice of applicable law where not designated by the parties	118
(2) *Amiable compositeur or ex aequo et bono*—Article 35(2)	119
(3) The significance of the contract and of trade usages—Article 35(3)	121
(4) Comparison to the 1976 UNCITRAL Rules	123
(5) A note on the Iran–US Claims Tribunal	128
C. Extracts from the Practice of Investment Tribunals	129
D. Extracts from the Practice of the Iran–US Claims Tribunal	131
(1) Tribunal Rules (1983), Article 33(1)	131
(2) Tribunal Rules (1983), Article 33(2)	140
(3) Tribunal Rules (1983), Article 33(3)	140
(4) Other practice of the Iran–US Claims Tribunal	142

1. Introduction

The rules of law applied by the arbitrators to decide the substance of the dispute is the focus of Article 35 of the 2010 UNCITRAL Rules and this chapter. The applicable substantive law is distinct from the legal system regulating the arbitral proceedings, that is, the *lex arbitri*.[1] Article 35(1) expresses the overriding principle of party autonomy in choosing the applicable rules of law, with provision for those instances where the parties fail to designate applicable rules of law. Article 35(2) addresses the authority of the arbitral tribunal to decide as *amiable compositeur* or *ex aequo et bono*. Finally, Article 35(3) emphasizes the importance of the terms of the contract and applicable trade usages. As will be seen, Article 35 contains basic elements found in many other arbitration rules.[2]

---

[1] Chapter 2 addresses the regulatory relationship of the legal system of the place of the arbitration to the arbitral proceedings. Finer distinctions between the different meanings of "applicable law" are possible, distinguishing, for example, between the applicable "governing law," "procedural law" and "substantive law." See V Heiskanen, "Theory and Meaning of the Law Applicable in International Commercial Arbitration," (1993) IV Finnish Ybk of Intl L 98, 111.

[2] See *Report of the Secretary-General on the Preliminary Draft Set of Arbitration Rules*, UNCITRAL, 8th Session, UN Doc A/CN.9/97 (1974), reprinted in (1975) VI UNCITRAL Ybk 163, 178 (Commentary on Draft Article 27).

2. Applicable Law—Article 35

A. Text of the 2010 UNCITRAL Rule[3]

Article 35 of the 2010 UNCITRAL Rules provides:

1. The arbitral tribunal shall apply the rules of law designated by the parties as applicable to the substance of the dispute. Failing such designation by the parties, the arbitral tribunal shall apply the law which it determines to be appropriate.
2. The arbitral tribunal shall decide as *amiable compositeur* or *ex aequo et bono* only if the parties have expressly authorized the arbitral tribunal to do so.
3. In all cases, the arbitral tribunal shall decide in accordance with the terms of the contract, if any, and shall take into account any usage of trade applicable to the transaction.

B. Commentary

(1) The primary rule—Article 35(1)

(a) The principle of party autonomy and its application

Article 35(1), like its predecessor in the 1976 UNCITRAL Rules, "is based on the principle of party autonomy for the choice of the law applicable to the substance of a dispute that is referred to arbitration."[4] This principle, which has found expression in other arbitration rules,[5] is generally accepted in international arbitral theory and practice, as well as in national laws.[6] The Tribunal thus is directed by Article 35(1) to observe the principle of party autonomy and "shall" apply the rules of law designated by the parties.

To exercise their autonomy, the parties must "designate" the applicable substantive rules of law.[7] Although the rules of law need not be "expressly designated" as would have

---

[3] Article 33 of the 1976 UNCITRAL Rules provides:

1. The arbitral tribunal shall apply the law designated by the parties as applicable to the substance of the dispute. Failing such designation by the parties, the arbitral tribunal shall apply the law determined by the conflict of laws rules which it considers applicable.
2. The arbitral tribunal shall decide as *amiable compositeur* or *ex aequo et bono* only if the parties have expressly authorized the arbitral tribunal to do so and if the law applicable to the arbitral procedure permits such arbitration.
3. In all cases, the arbitral tribunal shall decide in accordance with the terms of the contract and shall take into account the usages of the trade applicable to the transaction.

[4] *Report of the Secretary-General on the Revised Draft Set of Arbitration Rules*, UNCITRAL, 9th Session, Addendum 1 (Commentary), UN Doc A/CN.9/112/Add.1 (1975), reprinted in (1976) VII UNCITRAL Ybk 166, 178 (Commentary on Draft Article 28(1)).

[5] For example, according to Article 21(1) of the ICC Rules as revised in 2012, "[t]he parties shall be free to agree upon the rules of arbitration to be applied by the arbitral tribunal to the merits of the dispute."

[6] Article 28(1) of the UNCITRAL Model Law provides: "The arbitral tribunal shall decide the dispute in accordance with such rules of law as are chosen by the parties as applicable to the substance of the dispute. Any designation of the law or legal system of a given State shall be construed, unless otherwise expressed, as directly referring to the substantive law of that State and not to its conflict of laws rules."

On party autonomy see also N Blackaby and C Partasides with A Redfern and M Hunter, *Redfern and Hunter on International Arbitration* (5th edn 2009) 195–9; J Lew, *Applicable Law in International Commercial Arbitration* (1978) 72 et seq; O Lando, "The law applicable to the merits of the dispute," (1986) 2 Arb Intl 104, 107; C Croff, "The Applicable Law in International Commercial Arbitration: Is It Still a Conflict of Laws Problem?" (1982) 16 Intl Lawyer 613, 615, 642; *American Bell Intl, Inc*, Concurring and Dissenting Opinion of Judge Mosk, reprinted in section 2(D)(1).

[7] This designation is clear, for example, when the parties have agreed to arbitration under NAFTA Chapter Eleven. See *Methanex Corp* (1976 Rules), reprinted in section 2(C).

been required in the Preliminary Draft of the 1976 Rules,[8] the use of the word "designate" implies that there must exist a rather unambiguous choice of law. Although the arbitral tribunal could attempt to analyze the presumed intentions of the parties and derive a "tacit" designation of the applicable law; in most cases that law could, and preferably should, be determined by the tribunal under the provision applicable when the parties do not designate applicable rules of law, a topic considered below.[9] Under the UNCITRAL Rules, a "designation" of the applicable substantive law should not be inferred merely from the selection of the place of arbitration. The selection of the place of arbitration can and often does reflect quite different considerations.[10] To avoid confusion, the parties should designate the applicable rules of law in a choice of law clause included in the main contract or in the arbitration agreement.[11] In keeping with the principle of party autonomy, the parties may even designate the applicable law separately, for example, by conveying their agreement to the tribunal in the course of oral or written proceedings.[12]

Unless otherwise specifically indicated by the parties, a choice of law clause referring to a particular law does not include the conflict of laws rules of that law, including provisions on *renvoi*. The Working Group declined a suggestion to clarify that any designation of a law or legal system of a given state by the parties should be construed as referring to the substantive law of that state and not to its conflict of law rules, finding that this addition was not necessary under the Rules.[13] Thus Article 35(1) assumes the parties intend to exclude conflict of laws rules from an otherwise general designation of an applicable law unless they expressly state otherwise. In the past, parties were advised in some situations to expressly exclude the conflict rules in the

---

[8] Article 27(1) of the Preliminary Draft to the 1976 Rules provided: "The arbitrators shall apply the law expressly designated by the parties as applicable to their contract." The delegations of France, Hungary and the United States proposed the replacement of this by a provision to the effect that "[t]he arbitral tribunal shall apply the law designated by the parties... Such designation must be contained in an express clause, or unambiguously result from the contract..." See *Summary Record of the 14th Meeting of the Committee of the Whole (II)*, UNCITRAL, 9th Session, UN Doc A/CN.9/9/C.2/SR.14, at 2, para 1 (1976). On suggestion by the UK representative, Mr Guest, the second sentence quoted above was deleted, "since it would not necessarily be in accordance with all legal systems." See 2, para 2.

[9] For example, the fact that the parties have used a contractual formula known in a particular country which moreover happens to be the place of performance of the contract might be considered tacit designation of the law of that country as the applicable substantive law. See O Lando, "The law applicable to the merits of the dispute," n 6, 107–8. The same result, however, in most cases is probably obtainable with the help of the principle expressed in the second sentence of Article 35(1), discussed below. As the inferring of a tacit designation could in some jurisdictions create the risk of a successful court challenge on the ground of excess jurisdiction by the arbitrators, the alternative based on the second sentence is preferable.

[10] See Chapter 2, section 4 on Article 18(1). Although at one time the choice of the place of arbitration was seen on occasion to constitute a tacit choice of the law of the country. Von Mehren even referred to "a developing tendency to link the situs of the arbitration with the choice of substantive law," R von Mehren, "Arbitration in Central and Eastern Europe," (September 1992) 47 Arb J 38, 40. However, we tend to agree with Lando that even then "an opposite trend [was] discernible" in this regard. O Lando, "The law applicable to the merits of the dispute," n 6, 136. Today, we would think it quite unusual for such a link to be made.

[11] A choice of law clause may read for example as follows: "'This contract shall be governed by and construed in accordance with the law of...'"

[12] See J Lew, *Applicable Law*, n 6, 140–5.

[13] *Report on the Work of the Session*, 51st Session, Second Reading, A/CN.9/684, para 92 (2009). Indeed, this principle underlies Article 33(1) of the 1976 Rules as well, which, according to a statement in the Report of the Committee of the Whole II, "was intended as a reference to the internal law of that country not including its rules on conflict of laws or *renvoi*," *Report of the UN Commission on International Trade Law on the Work of its Ninth Session*, UN GAOR, 31st Session, Supp No 17, UN Doc A/31/17, para 172 (1976), reprinted in (1976) VII UNCITRAL Ybk 66, 78 (Commentary on Draft Article 28(1)).

arbitration clause or agreement.[14] Under Article 35(1), such an express exclusion is not necessary, although it must be also noted that this exclusion is not expressly stated in the text.

Similarly, parties who designate a general applicable law are presumed to have chosen that law as it evolves.[15] However, "stabilization clauses" or other provisions designed to protect a private party against unilateral changes made by the sovereign have been used in investment agreements between private companies and states.[16]

The text of Article 35(1) and the *travaux préparatoires* suggest that the article certainly clarifies, and potentially expands, the scope of party autonomy in choosing the rules of law applicable to the dispute beyond that which was permitted by the text of former Article 33(1). Article 35(1) provides that the arbitral tribunal shall apply the "rules of law" designated by the parties as applicable to the substance of the dispute. The *travaux préparatoires* note that the term "rules of law" was preferred "essentially because of its broad scope, respecting party autonomy to elect, for example, different legal systems to govern different aspects of the relationship."[17] The Working Group noted that the term "rules of law" was consistent with Article 28 of the UNCITRAL Model Law, which provided that the parties might designate the "rules of law" applicable to the substance of the dispute.[18] The term "rules of law," prior to its inclusion in the Model Law, had only been used in the 1965 Washington Conference on the Settlement of Investment Disputes, and the arbitration laws of France and Djibouti.[19] The Working Group understood the term "rules of law" to be wider than the term "law," allowing the parties "to designate as applicable to their case rules of more than one legal system, including rules of law which have been elaborated on the international level."[20]

Whether the substitution of "rules of law" for the word "law" in Article 33(1) of the 1976 UNCITRAL Rules implies that the autonomy available to parties under the 1976 Rules is narrower is open to some debate. That debate, discussed below, centers particularly on whether the 1976 UNCITRAL Rules recognize the power of the parties to designate *lex mercatoria* as the applicable law. The term, "rules of law," arguably implies that a sufficient degree of precision exists and that such rules are ascertainable by the parties and tribunal. This precision is an essential distinction from a tribunal decision made *ex aequo et bono*; a basis of decision which requires, under Article 35(2), the express authorization of the

---

[14] This kind of caution was recommended for those concluding joint venture agreements, for example, with the former Soviet partners. See J Hertzfeld, "Applicable Law and Dispute Settlement in Soviet Joint Ventures," (1988) 31 ICSID Rev—Foreign Investment L J 249, 254 ("When inserting foreign law provisions in their agreements, parties should draft them carefully. If, for example, the parties intend to choose Swedish material law to govern their rights and obligations, they should be careful to exclude Swedish choice of law principles from their clause, since the application of such principles is likely to lead to a *renvoi* to some other legal system to the parties' mutual surprise."). Even after the collapse of the Soviet Union similar caution may be recommendable in relations with parties from former Soviet Republics. See also G Delaume, *Law and Practice of Transnational Contracts* (1988) 5–6.

[15] See G Delaume, *Law and Practice*, n 14, 30; W Peter, *Arbitration and Renegotiation of International Investment Agreements* (1988) 88. On arbitral practice (which is not uniform) in this regard, see J Lew, *Applicable Law*, n 6, 136 et seq.

[16] See *Mobil Oil Iran* (1983 Tribunal Rules), reprinted in section 2(D)(4) at para 59 (showing one version of such a provision).

[17] J Paulsson and G Petrochilos, "Revision of the UNCITRAL Rules," (A Report Commissioned by the UNCITRAL Secretariat), March 31, 2006, 138–9.

[18] *Settlement of Commercial Disputes: Revision of the UNCITRAL Arbitration Rules, Note by the Secretariat*, UNCITRAL, UN Doc A/CN.9/WG.II/WP.143/Add.1 at 9, para 30 (2006).

[19] See UNCITRAL, UN Doc A/CN.9/WG.II/WP.143/Add.1 at 9, para 30; see also Washington Convention on the Settlement of Investment Disputes Between States and Nationals of Other States, Oct 14, 1966, 17 UST 1270, TIAS 6090, 575 UNTS 159, art 42.

[20] See UNCITRAL, UN Doc A/CN.9/WG.II/ /WP.143/Add.1, n 19, at para 42.

parties. It is this question of precision that in part drives debates concerning the designation of either *lex mercatoria* or "general principles." The drafters of the 2010 Rules did not clarify whether the parties may designate the *lex mercatoria* to the substance of the dispute, although their discussion on the choice of applicable law where not designated by the parties clearly indicates that the 2010 Rules recognize the ability of the tribunal on its own authority to choose *lex mercatoria*, a provision that in our opinion supports the power of the parties to do so as well.

If the relevant domestic laws indicate that the parties' agreement to use *lex mercatoria* or "general principles of commercial law" as the applicable substantive law is accepted by national courts,[21] then an arbitral tribunal operating under the UNCITRAL Rules should respect such a choice. This is *a fortiori* supported by Article 35(2), which allows decisions made *ex aequo et bono* or by *amiable compositeur* when authorized by the parties and when the law applicable to the arbitral procedure permits such arbitration. As "the *lex mercatoria* will tie arbitrators to legal rules more than decisions made by an *amiable compositeur*,"[22] there should be no "policy" reasons against the application of *lex mercatoria* on conditions similar to those expressed in Article 35(2). It is possible that the reference by the UNCITRAL Model Law and Article 35 of the 2010 UNCITRAL Rules to "such rules of law as are chosen by the parties" will increase the acceptability of *lex mercatoria* in various domestic arbitration laws.[23] Moreover, as discussed below, the Iran–US Claims Tribunal has applied general principles of law in many cases.[24]

---

[21] A well known "successful" application of *lex mercatoria* by an international tribunal is the *Norsolor* case. In it, an ICC arbitral tribunal, with its seat in Vienna, applied *lex mercatoria* to a dispute between a Turkish and a French party. The award (reprinted in (1984) 9 Ybk of Commercial Arb 109) was annulled by an Austrian Court of Appeal which regarded *lex mercatoria* as of questionable value. This decision was subsequently reversed by the Supreme Court and the award enforced in France. Another important decision was rendered by the English Court of Appeal in *Deutsche Schachtbau- und Tiefbohrgesellschaft mbH (DST) v Ras Al Khaimah National Oil Co (Rakoil)*, (1987) 3 WLR 1023. In the ICC award made in Switzerland, the tribunal applied "internationally accepted principles of law governing contractual relations." The Court of Appeal held that the award was enforceable under the New York Convention. On these cases and other relevant practice, see C Stoecker "The *Lex Mercatoria:* To what Extent does it Exist?" (1990) 7(1) J Intl Arb 101, 123–4; E Paasivirta, *Participation of States in International Contracts and the Arbitral Settlement of Disputes* (1990) 134–6; B Goldman "Lex mercatoria," (November 1983) 3 Forum Internationale, 15–17; D Rivkin, "Enforceability of Arbitral Awards Based on Lex Mercatoria," (1993) 9(1) Arb Intl 67–84. In the cases mentioned above the question was of the arbitrators' choice of non-national law. This would appear to support the proposition that the parties *a fortiori* may make such a choice. See Rivkin, 78. For a comparative review of the situation in a number of countries, see F Dasser, *Internationale Schiedsgerichte und lex mercatoria* (1989) 200 et seq. See also O Lando, "The Lex Mercatoria in International Commercial Arbitration," (1985) 34 ICLQ 747, 755–63 and I Schultsz, "Ein neues Schiedsgerichtsgesetz für die Niederlande," (1987) 7 Praxis des Internationalen Privat und Verfahrensrechts 383, 384 (Dutch arbitration law allows the parties to select *lex mercatoria* as applicable substantive law).

[22] O Lando, "The Lex Mercatoria," n 21, 756 (referring to Article VII (2) of the ECCA).

[23] See R David, *Arbitration in International Trade* (1985) 341–2. The *travaux préparatoires* to the 1976 Rules do not, however, show any explicit intention to have *lex mercatoria* included in the "rules of law." The wording seems to have been chosen with a view to facilitating both the application of various national laws and the acceptability of the selection of "rules embodied in a convention or a similar legal text elaborated on the international level, even if not yet in force or not in force in any State connected with the parties or their transaction." *Report of the UN Commission on International Trade Law on the Work of its Eighteenth Session*, UN GAOR, 40th Session, Supp No 17, UN Doc A/40/17, at 45, para 232 (1985). With respect to the 1985 Hague Convention on the Law Applicable to International Sale of Goods it is questionable whether *lex mercatoria* is an acceptable choice of law. In Article 15 "law" is defined to mean "the law in force in a State other than its choice of law rules." Some would read this to exclude *lex mercatoria*, while others are against such an interpretation. See O Lando, "The 1986 Hague Convention on the Law Applicable to Sales," (1987) 51 *Rabels Zeitschrift* 60, 66–7. The EC Convention on the law applicable to contractual relations (Convention 80/934 EEC of June 19, 1980) has been argued to exclude *lex mercatoria*. See A Kassis, *Le nouveau droit européen des contrats internationaux* (1993) 373 et seq.

[24] See section 2(B)(5) (A Note on the Iran–US Claims Tribunal).

If the arbitrators have any hesitation about the acceptability of *lex mercatoria* by the parties, they should try to accommodate party autonomy by giving due consideration to the relevant domestic laws. Thus, if possible, the award should make it clear that the application of *lex mercatoria* does not lead to results incompatible with any domestic law that might otherwise be applicable, or that the application of a domestic law suggested by appropriate conflict rules does not contradict the *lex mercatoria* referred to in the arbitration clause or agreement.[25]

In our opinion, there should be no hesitation to accept public international law as the applicable law if the parties have so agreed. Public international law fulfils the criteria of "law" within the meaning of Article 35(1), regardless of any disagreement surrounding the concept of *lex mercatoria*. Although public international law in relations between private enterprises is not likely to provide the most appropriate legal framework,[26] in relations between a state or a state entity on the one hand and a private enterprise on the other, a non-domestic law such as public international law may be the suitable applicable substantive law.[27] In practice, certain significant state contracts have included choice of law clauses that combine domestic law, international law and general principles of law.[28]

The "rules of law" need not be in force. Indeed, it was exactly with the purpose of enabling a tribunal to apply, for example, a convention not yet in force that the Model Law employs the words "rules of law chosen by the parties" instead of simply referring to "law."[29] As party autonomy is the overriding principle in the application of the UNCITRAL Rules, the parties' choice of a "law" not in force should be respected to the extent possible.[30] Accordingly, a convention not in force, but which has been designated as applicable law, should be applied along the same principle and with similar reservations as applicable to *lex mercatoria*.[31]

---

[25] In *Norsolor*, the Austrian Supreme Court held that the application of *lex mercatoria* "neither contradicts nor violates any of the imperative rules to be found in the law in vigor in either of the two concerned States…" cited in B Goldman, "Lex mercatoria,", n 21, 17. See also *American Bell Intl*, section 2(D)(1) (finding it unnecessary to discuss the applicable law as the result would be the same under any such law, whether international or national).

[26] The famous statement by the Permanent Court of International Justice in the *Serbian Loans* case that "[a]ny contract which is not a contract between states acting in their capacity as subjects of international law, is based on the municipal law of some country," 1929 PCIJ series A No 20, at 41 (July 12, 1929), cannot be regarded as valid law today. Yet, according to J Lew, *Applicable Law*, n 6, 405, "no award has been found where arbitrators have actually applied positive rule of public international law to the substance of a private commercial dispute." But see O Lando, "The Law Applicable to the Merits of the Dispute," in P Šarčević (ed) *Essays on International Commercial Arbitration* (1989) 129, 145 ("Rules of public international law may also be applied to disputes between private enterprises.").

[27] See Case No B36 (1983 Tribunal Rules), reprinted in section 2(D)(1). The questions concerning the law applicable to state contracts and related issues have generated an abundance of literature. See, eg, G Delaume, *Law and Practice*, n 14; W Peter, *Arbitration and Renegotiation*, n 15; E Paasivirta, *Participation of States in International Contracts*, n 21; J-P Regli, *Contrats d'Etat et arbitrage entre Etats et personnes privées* (1983).

[28] See *Mobil Oil Iran* (1983 Tribunal Rules), reprinted in section 2(D)(4), in which the Iran–US Claims Tribunal held, when interpreting the relevant clause of the Contract (Award, para 59), "that the law applicable to the Agreement is Iranian law for interpretative issues, and the general principles of commercial and international law for all other issues" (para 81).

[29] See n 6, and H Holtzmann and J Neuhaus, *A Guide to the UNCITRAL Model Law on International Commercial Arbitration: Legislative History and Commentary* (1989) 766–8.

[30] For some, the term "law" is taken to limit legal rules and principles to those in force, thus excluding, for example, Roman law or other ancient laws, except insofar as they form part of an existing legal system. See *Ouziel Aryeh* (1983 Tribunal Rules), reprinted in section 2(D)(1) (considering the application of Jewish law as it relates to Iranian law). However, as discussed in the text in regard to *lex mercatoria*, this appears to be a minority view.

[31] Indeed, international conventions not in force for the state in question are sometimes regarded as one source on the basis of which the contents of *lex mercatoria* can be determined. See, eg, F Dasser, *Internationale Schiedsgerichte*, n 21, 102–3.

Beyond limitations on party autonomy within Article 35(1) itself, there are three other sources of possible limitations.

First, and discussed in more detail in section 2(B)(3), Article 35(3) in directing the tribunal to apply the terms of the contract "in all cases" potentially limits the choice of the parties in Article 35(1).

Second, it should be recalled that under Article 1 of the UNCITRAL Rules, a provision of the legal system governing the arbitration (ie the *lex arbitri*) from which no derogation is possible supersedes the Rules, including Article 35. The *travaux préparatoires* of the 1976 Rules observe that at that time "in some jurisdictions parties may only choose as the law applicable to the substance of their dispute the law of a jurisdiction having some real connection with the transaction."[32] Issues of public policy may be present, for example, in competition and antitrust cases, in so far as they are arbitrable at all.[33]

Third, it is prudent for the tribunal to be aware of the public policy of relevant jurisdictions that may bear on the enforceability of the award. It is for this reason that arbitral tribunals are sometimes urged to be cautious in their treatment of punitive damages and other penalties.[34] Although such cautions should be kept in mind, the tribunal should respect the clear choice of the parties. Similarly, such a cautionary note should not discourage the parties from choosing a neutral, well-developed law for fear of its rejection for lack of a sufficient connection to the subject matter of the dispute. Such fears are likely to be unfounded, as indicated by the fact that "[n]o case is known in which an arbitrator has set aside the parties' express choice of law on the ground of lack of connection with the intended legal system."[35]

---

[32] *Report of the Secretary-General on the Revised Draft Set of Arbitration Rules*, UNCITRAL, 9th Session, Addendum 1 (Commentary), UN Doc A/CN.9/112/Add.1 (1975), reprinted in (1976) VII UNCITRAL Ybk 166, 178 (Commentary on Draft Article 28, para 3). On the discussion on the preparatory stage, see S Baker and M Davis, *The UNCITRAL Arbitration Rules in Practice: The Experience of the Iran-United States Claims Tribunal* (1992) 175–7.

[33] See Lando, "The Law Applicable to the Merits of the Dispute,", n 26, 156–9. See also S Jarvin, "Arbitrability of Anti-Trust Disputes: The *Mitsubishi v. Soler* Case," (1985) 2(3) J Intl Arb 69. EC competition law for the member states is largely of a public policy nature. A court of a member state to which an application is made may be bound under EC law to annul the award. See *Eco Suris China Time Limited v Benetton International NV* (Case C-126/97, judgment June 1, 1999, ECR I-3055). See also G Zekos, "Eco Swiss China Ltd v. Benetton International NV–Court's involvement in arbitration," (2000) 17(2) J Intl Arb 91–4; N Blackaby and C Partasides, *Redfern and Hunter on International Arbitration*, n 6, 205–7.

[34] See N Blackaby and C Partasides, *Redfern and Hunter on International Arbitration*, n 6, 530–1. According to Article V(2)(b) recognition and enforcement of an arbitral award may be denied if it would be against the public policy of the country. See C Croff, "The Applicable Law in International Commercial Arbitration," n 6, 619, for an example of a dispute relating to the installation of a nuclear plant, in which the enforcement might be against public policy for reasons of substantive law. If such a dispute has been arbitrated with the application of substantive law other than that of the country where the plant is sited, the award might not be enforceable in that country. But see Croff, 638–9 (arguing that Art V of the New York Convention could not be invoked at all for reasons related to the applicable substantive law).

[35] O Lando, "The law applicable to the merits of the dispute," n 6, 107. But see J Lew, *Applicable Law*, n 6, 132–5 (citing a few cases where the parties' choice has been rejected by the arbitrators). As noted by Lew, "these few awards show no tendency sufficient to give rise to some exception to the general rule." Lew, 132. One author has concluded that "[t]he prevailing trend at present, reinforced by international Conventions, is to allow parties complete freedom of choice as regards the law applicable to the substance of the award." R David, *Arbitration in International Trade*, n 23, 343.

(b) Choice of applicable law where not designated by the parties

When the parties have not designated the rules of law applicable to the substance of the dispute, the arbitral tribunal "shall apply the law which it determines to be appropriate."[36] In contrast with the formulation under former Article 33(1) of the 1976 Rules, the arbitral tribunal is no longer required to "choose" the law in accordance with the "conflict of law rules which it considers applicable." Rather, the text of Article 35(1) appears at first glance to provide the tribunal with greater flexibility to "determine" the applicable law to the substance of the dispute (although the tribunal may only determine "law," whereas the parties may designate "rules of law" applicable to the substance of the dispute).

The *travaux préparatoires* reflect that the Working Group considered several different variants of the rule before arriving at the text of Article 35(1). The Working Group considered whether to use the term "law" or "rules of law."[37] Opinion diverged over whether the arbitral tribunal should be given the same discretion to designate "rules of law" where the parties had failed to designate the applicable law. Comparison was made with Article 28(2) of the UNCITRAL Model Law, which referred to the arbitral tribunal applying the "law determined by the conflict of law rules which it considers applicable."[38] To ensure consistency with the Model Law, it was suggested that the Rules adopt the same approach.[39]

The Working Group also considered a proposal to replace the rule in the original text (that reference be made to conflict of laws rules failing designation by the parties) with a reference to a direct choice of the rules of law most closely connected to the dispute.[40] There was some support for a variant that referred to conflict of law rules, which could only result in the application of a national law.[41] This variant placed the arbitral tribunal in the same situation as a state court having to determine which law should govern a dispute in the absence of designation by the parties, although the tribunal would have the additional obligation to choose the conflict of laws rules to be used for that determination.[42]

There was broader support, however, for the variant that would allow the arbitral tribunal to directly choose the law most closely connected to the dispute.[43] It was noted that this would:

offer the opportunity to modernize the Rules by allowing the arbitral tribunal to decide directly on the applicability of such instruments as e.g., the United Nations Convention on Contracts for the International Sale of Goods, the Unidroit Principles of International Commercial Contracts, texts adopted by the International Chamber of Commerce, such as the Incoterms and the Uniform Customs and Practices for Documentary Credit, or lex mercatoria.[44]

---

[36] Webster argues that "if the parties have not agreed on the applicable law, then one of the issues to be dealt with in the Statement of Claim should be the applicable law or laws that are applicable to the dispute pursuant to Art. 35." T Webster, *Handbook of UNCITRAL Arbitration—Commentary, Precedents and Materials for UNCITRAL Based Arbitration Rules* (2010) 308.

[37] *Report of the Working Group on Arbitration and Conciliation on the Work of its Forty-Seventh Session* (Vienna, 10–14 September 2007), UNCITRAL, 41st Session, UN Doc A/CN.9/641, at 21, para 108 (2007).

[38] See UNCITRAL 47th Session, UN Doc A/CN.9/641, n 37, para 108; see also, UNCITRAL Model Law, as amended, art. 28(2).

[39] UNCITRAL 47th Session, UN Doc A/CN.9/641, n 37, para 108.

[40] *Settlement of Commercial Disputes: Revision of the UNCITRAL Arbitration Rules Note by the Secretariat*, UNICTRAL, UN Doc A/CN.9/WG.II/WP.145/Add.1 at 18, para 38 (2006).

[41] UNCITRAL 47th Session, UN Doc A/CN.9/641 (2007), n 37, para 110.

[42] UNCITRAL 47th Session, UN Doc A/CN.9/641 (2007), n 37, para 110.

[43] UNCITRAL 47th Session, UN Doc A/CN.9/641 (2007), n 37, para 110.

[44] UNCITRAL 47th Session, UN Doc A/CN.9/641 (2007), n 37, para 110.

It was proposed, however, that the Rules should provide the arbitral tribunal with broader discretion in the determination of the applicable law by adopting wording along the lines of Article 17 of the then applicable 1998 ICC Rules.[45] The *travaux préparatoires* note that this option received "broad support."[46] It was also suggested that the discretion of the arbitral tribunal should be limited by language referring to conflict of law rules or by requiring that the arbitral tribunal determine the choice of law "based on objective criteria."[47] The Working Group noted that the broad discretion of the arbitral tribunal to determine the appropriate law was bound already by the obligation of the tribunal to render a reasoned award, and that further safeguards were unnecessary.[48]

In addition, it was suggested that the provision referring to the application of "the law" could be understood as limiting the choice of the tribunal to one law only, which might impact the enforceability of the award.[49] In international arbitration, however, it was not infrequently required that more than one law had to be applied to deal with different issues arising in the dispute.[50] After discussion, the Working Group concluded that the provision was drafted in sufficiently broad terms and it was understood that the tribunal might apply different laws, depending on the issues at stake in the dispute.[51]

As indicated by the text of Article 35(1) and the *travaux préparatoires*, the Working Group ultimately chose language that modernized the Rules by granting broad discretion to the arbitral tribunal to choose the law applicable to the dispute where the parties did not designate the applicable law. Importantly, while the discretion accorded to the arbitral tribunal is less than that accorded to the parties under the principle of party autonomy, the Working Group seems to have intended to expand the discretion of the tribunal to choose and apply international law instruments, as well as *lex mercatoria*.

(2) Amiable compositeur or ex aequo et bono—Article 35(2)

Article 35(1), as discussed above, assumes that the arbitrators decide on the basis of law. This general rule is confirmed by Article 35(2), which makes clear that the arbitral tribunal may assume the role of *amiable compositeur* or decide *ex aequo et bono* only under strictly defined conditions.[52] Although both terms in Article 35(2) denote the same idea of equitable considerations,[53] they were retained in the provision as separate concepts on the ground that they "had different connotations in the various national legal systems."[54]

---

[45] UNCITRAL 47th Session, UN Doc A/CN.9/641 (2007), n 37, para 111. The proposed wording was as follows: "In the absence of any such agreement, the Arbitral Tribunal shall apply the rules of law which it determines to be appropriate."

[46] *Report of Working Group II (Arbitration and Conciliation) on the Work of its Fifty-First Session* (Vienna, 14-18 September 2009), UNCITRAL, 43rd Session, UN Doc A/CN.9/684, at 21, para 94 (2009).

[47] UNCITRAL 43rd Session, UN Doc A/CN.9/684, n 46, para 95.

[48] UNCITRAL 43rd Session, UN Doc A/CN.9/684, n 46, para 95.

[49] UNCITRAL 43rd Session, UN Doc A/CN.9/684, n 46, para 96.

[50] UNCITRAL 43rd Session, UN Doc A/CN.9/684, n 46, para 96.

[51] UNCITRAL 43rd Session, UN Doc A/CN.9/684, n 46, para 96.

[52] See *CME Czech Republic BV* (1976 Rules), reprinted in Section 2(C).

[53] See N Blackaby and C Partasides, *Redfern and Hunter on International Arbitration*, n 6, 228–9.

[54] *Report of the UN Commission on International Trade Law on the Work of its Ninth Session*, UN GAOR, 31st Session, Supp No 17, UN Doc A/31/17, para 172 (1976), reprinted in (1976) VII UNCITRAL Ybk 66, 78 (1976) (Commentary on Draft Article 28(3)). More clarification on the issue is cast by the following quotation from Mr Holtzmann (United States) who said "that different legal systems placed different interpretations on the two terms. Furthermore, there was disagreement among legal scholars as to their exact meaning. Consequently, the sponsors of the proposal had decided to include both terms in the text so that parties would be free to use either, depending on the legal system to be applied." *Summary Record of the 14th Meeting of the Committee of the Whole (II)*, UNCITRAL, 9th Session, UN Doc A/CN.9/9/C.2/SR.14, at para 19 (1976).

It is possible to decide "as *amiable compositeur* or *ex aequo et bono* only if the parties have expressly authorized the arbitral tribunal to do." Thus the very basic condition is that the parties explicitly authorize a departure from the application of law in favor of what is regarded as reasonable or equitable in the circumstances. Such an authorization may be jointly given by the parties in the arbitration agreement, in a separate agreement, or even orally before the arbitrators (at a pre-hearing conference or a hearing).[55]

The authorization by the parties, however, is not the only necessary condition for the arbitrators to award *ex aequo et bono* (or act as *amiable compositeur*). In addition, the arbitrators must make sure that "the law applicable to the arbitral procedure permits such arbitration."[56] This quoted language is an explicit requirement in corresponding Article 33(2) of the 1976 Rules. Its deletion was suggested by the UNCITRAL Secretariat at the outset of the revision of the 1976 Rules, but not adopted by the Working Group until the 52nd Session in 2010. The proposal was made in part so as to align the rule with the approach taken in other major arbitration rules.[57] The requirement is also not necessary since such a mandatory rule of the *lex arbitri* would supersede the rule in any event. In most cases, this means that the law of the place of arbitration must accept decision-making on the basis of equitable or other similar considerations.[58] Many civil law and other countries recognize this kind of extra-legal arbitration, often on the same primary condition as expressed in the UNCITRAL Rules, ie, that the parties have given their express authorization thereto.[59] Jurisdictions adopting the UNCITRAL Model Law recognize the power of the arbitrators to decide *ex aequo et bono* or as *amiable compositeur* subject to the authorization of the parties.[60] Further, the line between the application of law and equity may be very thin, as equitable considerations are increasingly accepted as a part of law in various legal systems.[61]

The words "shall decide" in Article 35(2) indicate that, upon the fulfilment of the condition just discussed, the arbitrators are required to act as *amiable compositeur* or to decide

---

[55] While no *ex aequo et bono* or *amiable compositeur* award rendered under the UNCITRAL Rules is known to the authors, the ICSID case *Benvenuti et Bonfant* and *People's Republic of Congo*, Award of August 8, 1980 (Trolle, Bystricky, Razfindralambo, arbitrators), reprinted in (1982) 21 ILM 740, can be cited as an example of an *ex aequo et bono* decision made with the authorization of the parties. The agreement of the parties to allow the tribunal to decide *ex aequo et bono* was presented to the arbitrators, in the form of minutes of a meeting, during the hearings and subsequently recorded in an order by the arbitral tribunal. See (1982) 21 ILM at 746, para 122.

[56] See *UNCITRAL Legal Guide on Drawing Up International Contracts for the Construction of Industrial Works* 313, para 29 (1988) ("It is advisable for the parties to be cautious about authorizing the arbitral tribunal to decide disputes *ex aequo et bono* or to act as *amiable compositeur*, since arbitrators are not permitted to do so under some legal systems. In addition, such authorization may be interpreted in different ways and lead to legal insecurity.").

[57] *Settlement of Commercial Disputes: Revision of the UNCITRAL Arbitration Rules, Note by the Secretariat*, UNCITRAL, UN Doc A/CN.9/WG.II/WP.143/Add.1, at 9–10, para 31 (2006) ("The Working Group might wish to note that rules of certain arbitration centres (article 17.3 of the ICC Rules, article 22.4 of the LCIA Rules and article 28.3 of the AAA Rules) require authorization by the parties for the arbitral tribunal to decide as amiable compositeur or *ex aequo et bono* and do not include a requirement that the law applicable to the arbitral procedure permit an arbitration to be decided *ex aequo et bono*.").

[58] See generally Chapter 2. See also *Summary Record of the 14th Meeting of the Committee of the Whole (II)*, UNCITRAL, 9th Session, UN Doc A/CN.9/9/C.2/SR.6, at 4–5, paras 22–31 (1976).

[59] For example, according to § 31(3) of the Finnish Arbitration Act of 1992, the award may be based on what the arbitrators find reasonable (*ex aequo et bono*), provided the parties have expressly authorized them to do so.

[60] According to Article 28(3) of the Model Law, as amended, "[t]he arbitral tribunal shall decide *ex aequo et bono* or as *amiable compositeur* only if the parties have expressly authorized them to do so."

[61] See *American Bell Intl, Inc* (1983 Tribunal Rules), reprinted in section 2(D)(3).

ex aequo et bono. However, because the provision requires authorization by the parties, it seems that a better interpretation—and at the same time one in accordance with the general concept of *amiable compositeur*[62]—is to regard the provision as granting an authorization rather than imposing a duty to decide *ex aequo et bono*. Of course, the arbitrators could apply an applicable law that they deem will lead to an equitable solution. Even where the law and equity do not fully coalesce in this way, the arbitral tribunal may have sufficient reason to give precedence to law despite the authorization to act as *amiable compositeur*. This is the case where the arbitrators have strong reasons to believe that, despite the fact that the law governing the arbitral procedure recognizes extra-legal arbitration, difficulties would be likely to ensue in later enforcement proceedings on the ground that the law of the likely place of enforcement rejects the notions of *amiable compositeur* and *ex aequo et bono*.[63] Equitable considerations also cannot be given effect where they result in contravention of clear terms of the contract in question, as discussed in the next sub-section.

(3) *The significance of the contract and of trade usages—Article 35(3)*

The significance of Article 35(3) is subtle and potentially important. First, it need be stressed that the article opens "[i]n all cases," meaning that if the parties have (or have not) designated the rules of law applicable to the substance of the dispute or have (or have not) authorized the tribunal to decide as *amiable compositeur*, the arbitral tribunal also "shall decide in accordance with the terms of the contract and shall take into account the usages of the trade applicable to the transaction."[64] Putting aside momentarily what Article 35(3) precisely requires, the critical point at the outset is that Article 35(3) requires the tribunal to consider rules that may or may not be compatible with, for example, the rules of law designated by the parties. In essence, it could be said that in choosing the UNCITRAL Rules, the parties—in addition to, for example, making an explicit choice as to applicable rules of law—also direct the tribunal to decide in accordance with the terms of the contract. This is sometimes surprising to some: having chosen the applicable rules of law, the tribunal is nonetheless directed by Article 35(3) to decide in accordance with the terms of the contract. This twist is in part a device aimed at fulfilling party expectations by avoiding surprises in the rules of law chosen that otherwise would disturb expectations expressed in the contract.

Thus, the arbitral tribunal should first apply the terms of the contract in cases even where there is an applicable law designated in accordance with Article 35(1) and where the arbitrators have been authorized to act as *amiable compositeur* or *ex aequo et bono*.[65]

The strict primacy of the contract was intentionally emphasized by a change of wording that took place in the course of the drafting of the 1976 Rules. While both the Preliminary and Revised Drafts of the 1976 Rules referred to the need to "take into account the terms

---

[62] See B Poznanski, "The Nature and Extent of an Arbitrator's Powers in International Commercial Arbitration," (1987) 4(3) J Intl Arb 71, 79 ("Amiable composition does not mean that an arbitrator cannot apply rules of substantive law, it simply removes the imperative and obligatory character of such law and allows the arbitrator to choose that which he wishes to apply.").

[63] See B Poznanski, "The Nature and Extent of an Arbitrator's Powers," n 62, 80; S Stein and D Wotman, "International Commercial Arbitration in the 1980s: A Comparison of the Major Arbitral Systems and Rules," (1983) 38 Business Lawyer 1685, 1714.

[64] An almost identical provision is contained in Article 28(4) of the Model Law, as amended.

[65] See *Report of the Secretary-General on the Revised Draft Set of Arbitration Rules*, UNCITRAL, 9th Session, Addendum 1 (Commentary), UN Doc A/CN.9/112/Add.1 (1975), reprinted in (1976) VII UNCITRAL Ybk 166, 179 (Commentary on Draft Article 28).

of the contract and the usages of the trade,"⁶⁶ a more obligatory formulation ("in accordance with") was eventually chosen to make clear the primary role of the contract.⁶⁷

In practice, most arbitration cases are decided on the basis of the terms of the contract.⁶⁸ The applicable law, ie, the law "governing" the contract, only rarely plays a role in the interpretation of such terms.⁶⁹ The applicable law, however, has relevance if the contract is defective or silent with regard to certain situations or issues (eg the rate of interest).⁷⁰ It is in such circumstances that the authorization to act as *amiable compositeur* or *ex aequo et bono* may greatly influence the decision-making, since Article 35(3) states unambiguously that contractual terms are binding on a tribunal deciding *ex aequo et bono*. As a part of the law, equitable considerations may be important in the interpretation of the contract, thus diminishing the distinction between equity and contract.⁷¹ The applicable law also may play a role in deciding whether a contract exists or not: "[i]t is a generally accepted principle of private international law that the formation of and the requirements as to the form of a contract are governed by that law which would be the proper law of the contract, if the contract was validly concluded."⁷²

In addition to being bound by the contract, the arbitrators "shall take into account the usages of trade applicable to the transaction." The drafting histories of the 1976 and 2010 Rules do not provide guidance as to what shall be regarded as a usage of the trade, although some commentators have suggested that it may be understood generally by reference to Article 1(8) of the UNIDROIT Principles of International Contracts.⁷³ As already

---

⁶⁶ Article 27(4) of the Preliminary Draft; Article 28(4) of the Revised Draft.

⁶⁷ The reasons behind the change were explained by Mr Holtzmann (USA) who noted, *inter alia*, that "[t]he ECE arbitration rules had not been used by many American corporations precisely because they contained" the more ambiguous wording "take into account." *Summary Record of the 17th Meeting of the Committee of the Whole (II)*, UNCITRAL, 9th Session, UN Doc A/CN.9/9/C.2/SR.17, at 4, para 23 (1976).

Mr Sanders (Special Consultant of the UNCITRAL Secretariat) commented that "although in practice arbitrators normally applied the terms of the contract very strictly in any case, the words 'in accordance with' underlined the primary importance of the contract and were therefore acceptable." UNCITRAL, 9th Session, UN Doc A/CN.9/9/C.2/SR.17, n 67, at 5, para 24. For further discussion, see also UNCITRAL, paras 25–33. See also *Summary Record of the 18th Meeting of the Committee of the Whole (II)*, UNCITRAL, 9th Session, UN Doc A/CN.9/9/C.2./SR.18, at 2, para 1 (1976).

In contrast, Article 22(2) of the 2012 ICC Rules states: "The arbitral tribunal shall *take account of* the provisions of the contract, if any, between the parties and of any relevant trade usages." (Emphasis added.) Yves Derains and Eric Schwartz looking to this same language in an earlier version of the ICC Rules note that the language merely obliges the Arbitral tribunal "to take account of its provisions, and, unlike some other rules [citing *inter alia* the UNCITRAL Rules], does not explicitly require the tribunal to render its decision 'in accordance' therewith." Y Derains and E Schwartz, *A Guide to the New ICC Rules of Arbitration* (2005) 224.

⁶⁸ See, eg, *Zeevi Holdings* (1976 Rules), at para 106, reprinted in section 2(C).

⁶⁹ See M Mustill, "The New Lex Mercatoria: The First Twenty-Five Years," in I Brownlie and M Bos (eds) *Liber Amicorum for the Rt. Hon. Lord Wilberforce* (1987) 149, 153 ("most disputes turn on the facts and on the words of the contract"); J Crook, "Applicable Law in International Arbitration: The Iran-U.S. Claims Tribunal Experience," (1989) 83 AJIL 278, 280 ("A majority of the claims have been decided entirely or substantially on the basis of the parties' contracts"); O Lando, "The law applicable to the merits of the dispute," n 6, 148 ("Many arbitrations turn upon the interpretation of a contract. Although continental countries have statutory rules on interpretation, arbitrators seldom invoke them. The interpretation of a contract is generally based on reason and logic, and they are communal property.").

⁷⁰ See *Rexnord, Inc* (1983 Tribunal Rules), reprinted in section 2(D)(1).

⁷¹ See *American Bell Intl, Inc* (1983 Tribunal Rules), Final Award, at para 54, reprinted in section 2(D)(3).

⁷² *Economy Forms Corp* (1983 Tribunal Rules), reprinted in section 2(D)(1). See *DIC of Delaware, Inc* (1983 Tribunal Rules), reprinted in section 2(D)(1).

⁷³ Article 1(8) provides that "(1) The parties are bound by any usage to which they have agreed and by any practice which they have established between themselves. (2) The parties are bound by a usage that is widely known and regularly observed in international trade by parties in the particular trade concerned except where the application of such usage would be unreasonable." See also Article 9 of the UN Convention on Contracts for the International Sale of Goods.

indicated, Article 35(3) establishes a clear hierarchy between the contract and trade usages. The latter have only a supplementary role, for "[i]f the contract is clear, trade usages cannot justify a deviation from it."[74]

While Article 35(3) of the 2010 UNCITRAL Rules essentially follows Article 33(3) of the 1976 Rules, particularly in establishing a hierarchy between contract and trade usages, new language has been added to ensure the broader applicability of the Rules in situations where a contract was not necessarily the basis of the dispute, such as in investor–state disputes.[75] The *travaux préparatoires* reflect the efforts of the Working Group to accommodate situations where a contract was not necessarily the basis of the dispute, by referring to the word "any applicable" in relation to "contract" and "any" in relation to "usage of trade."[76] Later in the drafting process, however, this language was replaced by the formulation included in Article 35(3) for purposes of increasing the clarity of the provision.[77]

During the drafting of the 2010 Rule, a question was raised whether the word "contract" was broad enough to encompass all types of agreements that might form the basis of a transaction.[78] In order to broaden the scope of the provision, it was suggested that the word "contract" be replaced by the word "agreement," since the word "agreement" was understood in some jurisdictions as including contracts as well as other agreements on which commercial transactions would usually be based.[79] This proposal was objected to on the basis that in some jurisdictions a contract was legally enforceable, which would not necessarily be the case of an agreement.[80] Moreover, it was noted that the term "contract" was used in the UNCITRAL Model Law and in the European Convention on International Commercial Arbitration of 1961.[81] Accordingly, the proposal was rejected.[82] Another proposal was made to add the words "or any legal instrument" after the word "contract" in order to reflect the language adopted by the Working Group when revising Articles 3 and 18 of the Rules.[83] This proposal was also rejected, on the grounds that the term "legal instruments" would be understood to include investment treaties, the application of which was not intended to be regulated under the Article.[84]

(4) Comparison to the 1976 UNCITRAL Rules

As the topic of applicable law is central to the operation of international arbitration, it should not be surprising that the revision of Article 33 of the 1976 Rules received substantial attention. The differences in Article 33 of the 1976 Rules that are of particular significance are in Article 33(1).

---

[74] See P Sanders, "Commentary on UNCITRAL Arbitration Rules," (1977) II Ybk Commercial Arb 177, 211. The Paulsson and Petrochilos study preceding the 2010 Revision recommended that the tribunal decide in accordance with both terms of the contract and trade usages. J Paulsson and G Petrochilos, "Revision of the UNCITRAL Rules," (A Report Commissioned by the UNCITRAL Secretariat), March 31, 2006, at para 20. That extension was not raised in the initial Secretariat Note and is not mentioned anywhere in the official record of the revision effort.
[75] UNCITRAL, 41st Session, UN Doc A/CN.9/641, n 37, at 22, para 113.
[76] UNCITRAL 41st Session, UN Doc A/CN.9/641, n 37, para 113.
[77] UNCITRAL, 43rd Session, UN Doc A/CN.9/684, n 46, at 22, para 98.
[78] UNCITRAL 43rd Session, UN Doc A/CN.9/684, n 46, para 99.
[79] UNCITRAL 43rd Session, UN Doc A/CN.9/684, n 46, para 99.
[80] UNCITRAL 43rd Session, UN Doc A/CN.9/684, n 46, para 99.
[81] UNCITRAL 43rd Session, UN Doc A/CN.9/684, n 46, para 99.
[82] UNCITRAL 43rd Session, UN Doc A/CN.9/684, n 46, para 99.
[83] UNCITRAL 43rd Session, UN Doc A/CN.9/684, n 46, para 99.
[84] UNCITRAL 43rd Session, UN Doc A/CN.9/684, n 46, para 99.

The changes in wording of Article 35(1) of the 2010 UNCITRAL Rules from Article 33(1) of the 1976 UNCITRAL Rules reflect (1) a desire to clarify, perhaps expand, the broad capacity of the parties to designate, and tribunal to determine, the applicable law; and (2) the belief that the language should be consistent with Article 28(1) of the UNCITRAL Model Law. The choice to substitute "rules of law" for "law" in the first sentence reflected the view that the term "rules of law" is understood to be wider than the term "law," allowing the parties "to designate as applicable to their case rules of more than one legal system, including rules of law which have been elaborated on the international level."[85] The choice to change the first sentence to say "rules of law" and the choice to retain "law" in the second sentence both reflect the priority placed on being consistent with the UNCITRAL Model Law. The key question is whether these changes should be viewed as a departure from, or a clarification of, Article 33(1) of the 1976 UNCITRAL Rules.

Both the text and negotiating history of Article 33(1) of the 1976 UNCITRAL Rules suggest that the law designated as applicable should be a definite set of rules, typically the national law of a particular country. In our opinion, however, this limitation quite clearly was not intended to preclude the parties from designating one law to apply, for example, to the modalities and rate of interest, and another to the rest of the merits of the case (*dépecage*).[86]

The area open to debate is whether the so-called *lex mercatoria* (a set of general rules and principles of commercial law transcending the confines of one particular legal system),[87] can be designated as the "law" applicable to the substance of the dispute under Article 33(1). There is no straightforward answer to this question, but in our opinion the answer is yes.[88] The principle of party autonomy strongly suggests the acceptance of such a choice.

Where the parties have failed to designate the applicable law,[89] "the arbitral tribunal shall apply the law determined by the conflict of laws rules which it considers applicable." Thus,

---

[85] *Note by the Secretariat*, UNCITRAL 49th Session, UN Doc A/CN.9/WG.II/WP.143/Add.1, at para 30 (2006).

[86] The Model Law's reference to "rules of law" (instead of "law") was chosen on the explicit understanding that it would allow the parties "to choose provisions of different laws to govern different parts of their relationship, or to select the law of a given State except for certain provisions..." *Report of the UN Commission on International Trade Law on the Work of its Eighteenth Session*, UN GAOR, 40th Session, Supp No 17, UN Doc A/40/17, at 45, para 232 (1985), reprinted in H Holtzmann and J Neuhaus, *A Guide to the UNCITRAL Model Law*, n 29, 550, 804–5. In the Report referred to it was noted, however, "that the right to select provisions of different laws for different parts of the relationship (the so-called *dépecage*) was recognized by most legal systems even under the more traditional approach" represented, *inter alia*, by Article 33(1) of the UNCITRAL Rules. *Report*, para 233. Thus in the application of Article 33(1) such a selection of various laws should be considered precluded only (in the unlikely case) where it violates the *ordre public* of the law of the place of arbitration or, if known, the probable place of enforcement.

As to the practice generally, see V Heiskanen, "Forbidding *Dépecage*: Law Governing Investment Treaty Arbitration," 32 Suffolk Transnatl L Rev 367 (concluding "*dépecage* may be here to stay").

[87] See M Pryles, "Application of the *Lex Mercatoria* in International Commercial Arbitration," (2004) 78 Australian L J 396; M Brunetti, "The *Lex Mercatoria* in Practice: The Experience of the Iran-United States Claims Tribunal," (2002) 18 Arb Intl 355; T Carbonneau, Lex Mercatoria *and Arbitration* (1990); O Lando, "The Lex Mercatoria," n 21, 747; M Mustill, "The New Lex Mercatoria," n 69; B Goldman, "Lex mercatoria," n 21; F Dasser, *Internationale Schiedsgerichte*, n 21; C Stoecker, "The *Lex Mercatoria:* To what Extent does it Exist?" n 21.

[88] But see M Mustill, "The New Lex Mercatoria," n 69, 160 ("I suggest that the answer must surely be no."). Also David interprets the 1976 UNCITRAL Rule as providing "that a particular national law will always ultimately be applied by the arbitral tribunal..." R David, *Arbitration in International Trade*, n 23, 342.

[89] Reasons for such a failure may be many: negotiators are more concerned with commercial clauses than the applicable law; they may not foresee the possibility of the terms of the contract themselves not being able to regulate any possible situation; if they do foresee such a situation, they may not be able to agree on the applicable law. See C Croff, "The Applicable Law in International Commercial Arbitration," n 6, 623. See also J Lew, *Applicable Law*, n 6, 221–2.

the UNCITRAL Rules proceed from the principle that the applicable substantive law should be determined by the arbitrators on the basis of a conflict-of-laws system, rather than by way of a "direct" determination of the applicable law. The same approach exists in the Model Law.[90]

Although, the formulation of Article 33(1) appears to provide considerable flexibility in determining the conflict-of-laws rules, it should not be interpreted to allow the tribunal to choose the applicable conflict-of-laws system without any restraints.[91] The provision was intended to permit "the arbitrators to exercise their discretion in choosing the applicable conflict of laws rules in the light of the particular circumstances of the dispute."[92] Thus, priority is not given to the conflict rules of the *lex loci arbitri*,[93] and it is not impermissible to apply them.[94] Unlike courts, which generally are bound to apply the conflict rules of the *lex fori*, "most countries will permit the arbitrator to select the choice-of-law rule which he deems applicable if a rule of the arbitration institution, or other rules adopted by the parties, such as the ICC Rules or the UNCITRAL rules of 1976, authorise him to do so."[95]

Sometimes it is preferable to refer to a conflict system, or systems, other than that of the law of the place of arbitration. This is the case where the private international law rules of the home countries of both parties point to the same applicable substantive law, while the application of the conflict of laws system of the place of arbitration would lead to another

---

[90] Article 28(2): "Failing any designation by the parties, the arbitral tribunal shall apply the law determined by the conflict of laws rules which it considers applicable." It was noted, however, that "since the Model Law did not provide for court review of an award on the ground of wrong application of Article 28, it served as little more than a guideline for the arbitral tribunal." *Report of the UN Commission on International Trade Law on the Work of its Eighteenth Session*, UN GAOR, 40th Session, Supp No 17, UN Doc A/40/17, at 47, para 238 (1985). See also H Holtzmann and J Neuhaus, *A Guide to the UNCITRAL Model Law*, n 29, 769–70. Even pending the adoption of the Model Law in various countries, the same is the case with the UNCITRAL Rules in so far as the choice of the applicable conflict norms is very rarely likely to be a ground for successful setting aside or similar proceedings. Yet it is not totally excluded that a flagrantly arbitrary determination of the applicable law might in some jurisdictions be a ground for rejecting the recognition and enforcement of the award for public policy reasons by virtue of Article V(2)(b) of the New York Convention. See O Lando, "The law applicable to the merits of the dispute," n 6, 110; C Croff, "The Applicable Law in International Commercial Arbitration," n 6, 628. Therefore due consideration should be given to the issue.

[91] This is confirmed by the discussion which took place in the course of the drafting process. While there was a suggestion for a wording to the effect that "the arbitral tribunal shall apply the law determined by the conflict of laws rules which it *chooses*" (instead of "deem applicable" as in both the Preliminary and Revised Draft—emphasis added), this was successfully opposed by several delegates, among them Mr Pirrung (Federal Republic of Germany) who "said that the use of the word 'chooses'... suggested that the arbitrators would have complete freedom with regard to the conflict of laws rules to be applied." *Summary Record of the 14th Meeting of the Committee of the Whole (II)*, UNCITRAL, 9th Session, UN Doc A/CN.9/9/C.2/SR.14, at 3, para 6 (1976). See also paras 1–15.

[92] *Report of the Secretary-General on the Revised Draft Set of Arbitration Rules*, UNCITRAL, 9th Session, Addendum 1 (Commentary), UN Doc A/CN.9/112/Add.1 (1975), reprinted in (1976) VII UNCITRAL Ybk 166, 179 (Commentary on Draft Article 28(2)). The same approach is to be found also in Article VII(1) of the ECCA and in Article 38 of the ECE Arbitration Rules, both of which are referred to in the document just quoted. On the European Convention in this regard, see J Gentinetta, *Die Lex Fori Internationaler Handelsschiedsgerichte* (1973) 329–30.

[93] O Lando, "The law applicable to the merits of the dispute," n 6, 110.

[94] On the selection of conflict-of-laws rules by arbitral tribunals, see J Lew, *Applicable Law*, n 6, 221 et seq.; O Lando, "The law applicable to the merits of the dispute," n 6, 110–12; C Croff, "The Applicable Law in International Commercial Arbitration," n 6, 341.

[95] O Lando, "The 1986 Hague Convention," n 23, 95. See also N Blackaby and C Partasides, *Redfern and Hunter on International Arbitration*, n 6, 144–5. However, the rules of arbitration institutions in socialist countries used to provide for the application of the conflict rules of the place of arbitration. See R David, *Arbitration in International Trade*, n 23, 341.

result. Under such circumstances the principle of foreseeability, and presumably the will of the parties, make it desirable to select the conflict-of-laws systems of the parties rather than that of the place of arbitration. The UNCITRAL Rules do not prohibit such a reference to two (or even more) conflict-of-laws systems; it is in fact a common feature in international arbitral practice. Such a practice ensures that the choice of law has been made properly under any conceivable conflict-of-laws systems that could be considered appropriate in court proceedings.[96] It is also possible that, although the various conflict-of-laws systems in question point to different national laws, the material result of the dispute would be the same regardless of which law is deemed applicable.[97] In this kind of situation, a statement by the arbitral tribunal that the selection of any law by any applicable choice of law rules leads to the same outcome would likely meet the requirements of Article 33(1).[98]

The degree of flexibility in the choice of law approach prescribed in Article 33(1) also depends on the laws and judicial attitudes of the country where the arbitration takes place, as well as of the jurisdiction of the likely enforcement of the award, if foreseeable. If these are known to have a flexible attitude towards issues such as *lex mercatoria*, they are also likely to accept the application of "general principles of private international law" as the method for determining the applicable substantive law. As such principles refer to certain widely accepted connecting factors in the search for the "proper law" of the contract, the application of general principles may come very close to a direct determination of the applicable law.[99] If the relevant domestic laws are receptive to the concept of *lex mercatoria*, reference to general principles of private international law may justify the application of *lex mercatoria* by the arbitrators even in the absence of a party agreement to that effect.

Generally, arbitrators are well advised to proceed with caution when contemplating a departure from what may be called a "strict" conflict-of-laws approach. If any risk of a successful challenge to such a departure exists, the tribunal should apply the choice-of-law rules of a particular jurisdiction or jurisdictions. Where the law cannot be determined by way of cumulative application of the several conflict systems connected with the case, the conflict-of-laws rules of the place of arbitration can be the most neutral solution. When the place has been selected by the parties (rather than by the arbitral tribunal), the application of the conflict-of-laws rules of that jurisdiction is likely to be a better solution than using conflict norms of the seller's country which point in another direction than the private international law of the buyer.[100]

Whenever it is difficult to determine the applicable law, the arbitral tribunal may find it appropriate to ask the parties to address the issue specifically, if they have not already

---

[96] See O Lando, "The law applicable to the merits of the dispute," n 6, 110.

[97] This result is often possible due to the pre-eminence of the relevant contract. See section 2(B)(3) on Article 33(3).

[98] See *Carolina Brass, Inc* (1983 Tribunal Rules), in section 2(D)(1). The case is discussed by J van Hof, *Commentary on the UNCITRAL Arbitration Rules: The Application by the Iran-U.S. Claims Tribunal* (1991) 236–8. See also O Lando, "The 1986 Hague Convention," n 23, 140.

[99] See the discussion by H Holtzmann and J Neuhaus concerning the question whether "direct" determination of the applicable law should have been accepted under the UNCITRAL Model Law, in *A Guide to the UNCITRAL Model Law*, n 29, at 770 ("In the end, though it was widely recognized that the practical result would generally be the same regardless of which formulation were chosen, particularly with respect to whether reference to conflict of law rules was required. It was said that the reasons invoked by arbitral tribunals when they select the governing law directly, without separate reference to conflicts rules, are often similar to the connecting factors used in such rules."). See *Economy Forms Corp* (1983 Tribunal Rules), reprinted in section 2(D)(1). On "non-national" conflict-of-laws systems generally, see J Lew, *Applicable Law*, n 6, 285 et seq.

[100] See C Croff, "The Applicable Law in International Commercial Arbitration," n 6, 625.

done so.[101] Similar party views should be taken into account as an important factor in the determination of the applicable law, although not necessarily regarded as a designation of the applicable law by the parties.[102]

The chosen conflict-of-laws system determines the applicable substantive law, which is likely to be other than the procedural law controlling the arbitration (normally the law of the place). Sometimes a problem may arise as to whether a particular rule or problem—eg the quantification of damages[103]—is to be classified as substantive or procedural in nature. As the classification of rules and concepts under most legal systems is considered a part of the conflict of laws, the chosen conflict-of-laws system can be utilized also for the purpose of classification. There is considerable support for the proposition that questions of evidence, including its admissibility, should be considered a procedural question regardless of the classification in the relevant domestic law.[104]

The only change in wording in Article 35(2) of the 2010 UNCITRAL Rules from Article 33(2) of the 1976 UNCITRAL Rules is the deletion of the clause at the end of Article 33(2) which provided that a tribunal could decide as *amiable compositeur* or *ex aequo et bono* only "if the law applicable to the arbitral procedure permits such arbitration." In practice and in the revision discussions, this deletion was not viewed as a significant change because the requirement strictly speaking is not necessary since such a mandatory rule of the *lex arbitri* would supersede the rule in any event. The proposal was made in part so as to align the rule with the approach taken in other major arbitration rules.

Two changes were made to Article 33(3) of the 1976 UNCITRAL Rules to clarify the provision and to ensure its broader application in cases where the contract is not necessarily the basis of the dispute, such as investor–state disputes. First, the phrase "if any" was inserted to reflect the general drafting decision in the 2010 revision to broaden applicability by providing for situations where the arbitration proceeding was based not on a contract, but rather, for example, on a bilateral investment treaty.[105] Second, the substitution of the word "any" for "the" prior to trade usages likewise reflected a desire "to ensure broader applicability of the Rules in situations where a contract was not necessarily the basis of the dispute."[106] Despite this effort to broaden the applicability of the rule, the Working Group was cautious to prevent the language from extending to agreements other than contracts. Additionally, while the revision of the language of former Article 33(3) was intended to broaden the applicability of the rule to investor–state disputes, the rule was not intended to regulate investment treaties.

---

[101] See *Haus Intl, Inc* (1983 Tribunal Rules), reprinted in section 2(D)(1). See also *Anaconda-Iran, Inc* (1983 Tribunal Rules), reprinted in section 2(D)(4), at para 133.

[102] See the ICC Award No 1434 of 1975, reported in (1976) 103 Journal du Droit International, in which the parties' common view was that French law played an important—though not exclusive—role in the determination of that law as applicable.

[103] In England this would be regarded as a procedural issue, while in Sweden (and probably in most other civil law countries) the question would be classified as substantive. See also R Schütze, D Tscherning and W Wais, *Handbuch des Schiedsverfahrens* (1985) (in Germany the question of statute of limitation is a substantive law issue, whereas in England and the United States it would be regarded as a procedural matter) 332–3 (para 605).

[104] See H Holtzmann and J Neuhaus, *A Guide to the UNCITRAL Model Law*, n 29, 367, 768–9 (from the point of view of the Model Law, which in the present respect does not differ from the UNCITRAL Rules). See also *DIC of Delaware, Inc* (1983 Tribunal Rules), reprinted in section 2(D)(1).

[105] *Report of the Working Group on Arbitration and Conciliation on the Work of its Forty-Seventh Session* (Vienna, September 10–14, 2007), UNCITRAL, 47th Session, UN Doc A/CN.9/641, at 22, para 113 (2007).

[106] *Report of the Working Group on Arbitration and Conciliation on the Work of its Forty-Eighth Session* (New York, February 4–8, 2008), UNCITRAL, 48th Session, UN Doc A/CN.9/646, at 15, para 65 (2008); and *Report of Working Group II (Arbitration and Conciliation) on the Work of its Fifty-First Session* (Vienna, September 14–18, 2009), UNCITRAL, 51st Session, UN Doc A/CN.9/684, at 22, para 98 (2009).

(5) A note on the Iran–US Claims Tribunal

In the 1983 Tribunal Rules of the Iran–US Claims Tribunal, Article 33 of the 1976 UNCITRAL Rules has been modified considerably. The modified text corresponds to Article V of the Claims Settlement Declaration[107] and grants the Tribunal wider discretion in the choice of the applicable law than is the case with the original UNCITRAL Rule. According to Article 33(1) of the 1983 Tribunal Rules, the Tribunal "shall decide all cases on the basis of respect for law, applying such choice of law rules and principles of commercial and international law as the tribunal determines to be applicable, taking into account relevant usages of the trade, contract provisions and changed circumstances."

Article 33(1) of the 1983 Tribunal Rules and Article V of the Claims Settlement Declaration do not require the Tribunal to apply any system of conflict-of-law rules.[108] Indeed, they do not even strictly oblige the Tribunal to follow a contractual choice of law clause, although such rules, of course, are taken "seriously into consideration."[109] Nevertheless, "the Tribunal is vested with extensive freedom in determining the applicable law in each case."[110] As explained in one Tribunal award, such freedom is thought to be "consistent with, and perhaps almost essential to, the scope of the tasks confronting the Tribunal, which include not only claims of a commercial nature...but also claims involving alleged expropriations or other public acts, claims between the two Governments, certain claims between banking institutions, and issues of interpretation and implementation of the Algiers Declarations."[111]

The special nature of the Tribunal and the provisions on applicable law applied by it, however, do not mean that the Tribunal's practice is without general relevance for applicable law and the interpretation of Article 35 of the UNCITRAL Rules. First, in many cases the Tribunal in practice has proceeded in the way any commercial arbitral tribunal would, applying the contract provisions[112] and choice-of-law clauses agreed upon by the parties.[113] In doing this, the Tribunal awards have contributed to the general arbitral practice on questions concerning applicable law.

---

[107] Article 33 of the 1976 Rules, as modified in the Tribunal Rules, reprinted in Appendix 5. Article V of the Claims Settlement Declaration reads as follows:

The Tribunal shall decide all cases on the basis of respect for law, applying such choice of law rules and principles of commercial and international law as the Tribunal determines to be applicable, taking into account relevant usages of the trade, contract provisions and changed circumstances.

[108] See J Crook, "Applicable law in International Arbitration," n 69, 282; S Baker and M Davis, *The UNCITRAL Arbitration Rules in Practice*, n 32, 180–1.

[109] *Anaconda-Iran, Inc* (1983 Tribunal Rules), reprinted in section 2(D)(4), at para 131. See also *CMI Intl, Inc* (1983 Tribunal Rules), reprinted in section 2(D)(4), and G Hanessian, "General Principles of Law in the Iran-U.S. Claims Tribunal," 27 Columbia J Transnatl L (1989) 309, 330 (discussing the reasons which led to a departure from the contractually agreed-upon choice of law clause).

[110] *Anaconda-Iran, Inc* (1983 Tribunal Rules), reprinted in section 2(D)(4), at para 130.

[111] *CMI Intl, Inc* (1983 Tribunal Rules), reprinted in section 2(D)(4). In accordance with this flexibility, the Tribunal's "case law should be seen on a sliding scale from cases where national law is applied fully, to cases where national law is not applied at all but 'overruled' by general principles of international law, to cases where international law was applied directly, without any reference to national law." J van Hof, n 98, 232. For examples of the Tribunal's approach in this regard, see, eg, *Harnischfeger Corp* (1983 Tribunal Rules); *Sedco, Inc* (1983 Tribunal Rules); *United Painting Co, Inc* (1983 Tribunal Rules); all reprinted in section 2(D)(1). See also *Benjam R Isaiah* (1983 Tribunal Rules), reprinted in section 2(D)(3), *RJ Reynolds Tobacco Co* (1983 Tribunal Rules), reprinted in section 2(D)(4), and *Jack Rankin* (1983 Tribunal Rules), reprinted in section 2(D)(4).

[112] *Civil International Inc* (1983 Tribunal Rules), reprinted in section 2(D)(4).

[113] See cases reprinted in section 2(D)(1).

More importantly in the long run, however, is the portion of the Tribunal's practice in which the "novel system of determining applicable law"[114] established by Article V of the Claims Settlement Declaration has been utilized with all the flexibility it allows. By its extensive application of general principles of law, including general principles of private international law, the Tribunal has provided much-needed clarification concerning the contents of *lex mercatoria*[115] for other tribunals contemplating resort to it according to the principles discussed earlier.[116] The Tribunal's docket, which comprises issues of a private law nature as well as claims involving state responsibility and other public international law questions, has given this arbitral body an opportunity to discuss questions such as applicable law in "state contracts."[117] A more extensive discussion of these developments is covered elsewhere.[118]

Despite the flexibility of the choice-of-law provision in Article V of the Claims Settlement Declaration, the rule is limited by the need to decide cases "on the basis of respect for law." According to Article 33(2) of the 1983 Tribunal Rules, *ex aequo et bono* and *amiable compositeur* decisions are only possible upon specific authorization by the parties. In no case has such an authorization been given.

C. Extracts from the Practice of Investment Tribunals

CME Czech Republic BV and *Czech Republic*, Final Award (March 14, 2003) (*Ad Hoc* Proceeding, 1976 UNCITRAL Rules, Netherlands-Czech Republic BIT), reprinted in 15 World Trade and Arb Materials 83 (2003).

> 403. The basic mandate of the Treaty obligates the Tribunal to "*decide on the basis of law*", which is a self-explanatory confirmation of the basic principle of law to be applied in international arbitration according to which the arbitral tribunal is not allowed to decide *ex aequo et bono* without authorization by the parties (see Art. 33 (2) [1976] UNCITRAL Arbitration Rules and Art. 17 (3) ICC Arbitration Rules).

Methanex Corp and *United States of America*, Award (August 3, 2005) (ICSID administered, 1976 UNCITRAL Rules, NAFTA Chapter Eleven), Part II, Chapter B, at 4–5:

> 7. Pursuant to Article 1120(1) NAFTA, Methanex submitted its claim to arbitration under the [1976] UNCITRAL Arbitration Rules (the "UNCITRAL Rules")[8]. It follows from Article 1120(2) NAFTA that the [1976] UNCITRAL Rules govern the procedure of the arbitration (except to the extent modified by Section B of Chapter 11)[9].
> 8. By Article 33(1) of the [1976] UNCITRAL Rules, the Tribunal is required to apply the law designated by the parties as applicable to the substance of the dispute, namely NAFTA itself (including Article 1131) and applicable rules of international law.

---

[114] *Anaconda-Iran, Inc* (1983 Tribunal Rules), para 130, reprinted in section 2(D)(4).
[115] See M Brunetti, *The Lex Mercatoria in Practice*, n 87; G Hanessian, "General Principles of Law," n 109.
[116] See section 2(B)(4) on Article 33(1).
[117] See *Amoco International Finance Corporation* and *Mobil Oil Iran Inc* (1983 Tribunal Rules), reprinted in section 2(D)(1).
[118] See J Crook, "Applicable Law in International Arbitration," n 69; G Hanessian, "General Principles of Law," n 109; J Westberg, "Applicable Law, Expropriatory Takings and Compensation in Cases of Expropriation," (1993) 8 ICSID Rev-Foreign Investment L J 5; J Westberg, "The Applicable Law Issue in International Business Transactions with Government Parties—Rulings of the Iran-United States Claims Tribunal," (1987) 2 ICSID Rev-Foreign Investment L J 473.

9. To a limited extent, where the [1976] UNCITRAL Rules make no provision and the Disputing Parties have not agreed otherwise, the procedure of the arbitration may also be governed by the lex loci arbitri and any laws or rules of law thereby designated. This is an issue to which the Tribunal returns in part below in Chapter III of this Award with regard to the USA's Application to Exclude Certain of Methanex's Evidence.

[Footnote]8. . . . Article 1120(1) NAFTA provides: "*Except as provided in Annex 1120.1, and provided that six months have elapsed since the events giving rise to a claim, a disputing investor may submit the claim to arbitration under: . . . (c) the [1976] UNCITRAL Arbitration Rules.*"

[Footnote] 9. Article 1120(2) NAFTA provides: "*The applicable arbitration rules shall govern the arbitration except to the extent modified by this Section.*"

Zeevi Holdings and *Bulgaria and The Privatization Agency of Bulgaria*, Final Award, (October 25, 2006) (*Ad Hoc* Proceeding, 1976 UNCITRAL Rules, Privatization Agreement):

104. Pursuant to para. 15.1 of the PA the Parties have agreed to settle any claim or dispute arising out of or in relation to this contract by arbitration to be conducted under the Rules of Arbitration of the United Nations Commission on International Trade (UNCITRAL Rules). Regarding the substantive law to be applied by the tribunal, Article 33 UNCITRAL Rules provides:

"Article 33
　　1. The arbitral tribunal shall apply the law designated by the parties as applicable to the substance of the dispute."

105. In Section 14.1 of the PA the Parties have agreed that the PA "shall be governed by and construed in accordance with the laws Bulgaria." Therefore, concerning the merits of the case the law of the Republic of Bulgaria will be applied.
106. Since it has not been contested by the Parties that under the law of the Republic of Bulgaria, generally and subject to mandatory provisions of the law, the terms of the parties' contract have the force of law between them, and the parties must comply with what is expressly stated in the contract the PA is the primary legal source for the Tribunal's findings.
107. Additionally, Bulgarian Law may be applied where the PA lacks an agreement on certain issues.
108. Furthermore, pursuant to Article 33 (3) [1976] UNCITRAL Rules "usages of trade applicable to the transaction" might be pertinent, although they are cautiously applied.

Oostergetel and Laurentius and*Slovak Republic,* Final Award (April 23, 2012) (*Ad Hoc* Proceeding, 1976 UNCITRAL Rules, Netherlands-Czech Republic BIT):

141. As regards the method for establishing the content of the governing law, the Tribunal observes that the BIT and the [1976] UNCITRAL Arbitration Rules are silent on this issue. By contrast, under Swiss international arbitration law which governs these proceedings, the principle of *iura novit iuria*—or better *iura novit arbiter*—does apply to an arbitral tribunal.[10] Thus, the arbitral tribunal is under an obligation to apply the law *ex officio* without being bound by the arguments and sources invoked by the Parties. However, the Tribunal should not base its decision on a legal theory which was not part of the debate and which the parties could not expect to be relevant.

　　[10] Swiss Supreme Court decision of 19 December 2001, P. 114/2001, section 3.a, ASA Bulletin 2002 p. 493; see also G. Kaufmann-Kohler, "The Governing Law: Fact or Law?—A Transnational Rule on Establishing its Content," in *Best Practices in International Arbitration.* ASA Special Series No 26, at 79 (M. Wirth, Ed. 2006).

D. Extracts from the practice of the Iran–US Claims Tribunal

(1) Tribunal Rules (1983), Article 33(1)

Rexnord Inc and *Islamic Republic of Iran*, Award No 21–132–3 (January 10, 1983) at 13, reprinted in 2 Iran–US CTR 6, 12 (1983-I):

> c. Interest
> The law applicable to the agreements is that of the United Kingdom. Under English law, where a bill is dishonored by non-payment, interest on the principal debt is awarded at a rate reflecting the rates which would have been incurred had the prevailing party borrowed the amount at the time it fell due. The date from which the interest is to be calculated is the time of the maturity of the bill except in cases where the bill is payable on demand.

Haus Intl, Inc and *Islamic Republic of Iran*, Case No 174, Chamber One, Order of January 17, 1984:

> The Claimant is ordered to file with the Tribunal by 5 April 1984 a Memorial addressing the following questions:
> 1. What law determines the relationship between Haus International, Inc. ("Haus") and Meaplan A.G. ("Meaplan") created by ("the Architect's Agreement,") dated December 5, 1977, signed by Haus and Meaplan, on the one hand, and Tehran Development Corporation on the other, and (ii) the "Joint Venture Agreement," dated December 10, 1977, between Haus and Meaplan, both of those agreements read together? Under that law, did those agreements create a partnership or other form of association?
> 2. If a partnership or other form of association was created under the applicable law, has Haus by itself the right under that law, or under International law, to assert a claim before the Tribunal for damages allegedly sustained by the partnership or association?

American Bell Intl Inc and *Islamic Republic of Iran*, Award No ITL 41–48–3 (June 11, 1984), Concurring and Dissenting Opinion of Richard Mosk on Preliminary Legal Issues, at 6 (June 11, 1984), reprinted in 6 Iran-US CTR 95, 97–98 (1984-II) (footnote omitted):

> That a limitation of amount of liability clause is valid is supported by whatever law is applicable. Article 10 of the contracts provides that the contracts are subject to the Laws of the Imperial Government of Iran and the United States in every respect, but however the governing law of [the contracts] is the law of Iran. It has been said that "the parties' freedom to choose the law which governs their contract seems to be so widely accepted that it must be said to be a "general principle of law recognized by civilized nations." O Lando, *Contracts*, Ch. 24, in III International Encyclopedia of Comparative Law 33 (1976). It might be that by virtue of Article V of the Claims Settlement Declaration, which gives the Tribunal the power to apply "such choice of law rules and principles of commercial and international law as the Tribunal determines to be applicable, taking into account relevant usages of the trade, contract provisions and changed circumstances," the Tribunal can apply law other than that designated by the parties to the contract. The tribunal has not provided much guidance as to the applicable law. As a practical matter, in many cases the choice of whether to utilize public international law, general principles of law, municipal law (past or present) or some other law will not affect the result. As to the applicable law, see *Oil Field of Texas, Inc.* and *Iran*, ITL 10–43-FT (9 Dec 1982), (Concurring Opinion of Richard M Mosk (10 Dec 1982)); *Settlement of Disputes*, in I Encyclopedia of Public International Law 130, 144, 147 (1981); A Feller, *The Mexican Claims Commissions* 223 (1935).

Economy Forms Corp and *Islamic Republic of Iran*, Award No 55–165–1 (June 14, 1983) at 11–12, reprinted in 3 Iran–US CTR 42, 47–48 (1983-II):

> 1. Applicable law
>
> It is a generally accepted principle of private international law that the formation of and the requirements as to the form of a contract are governed by that law which would be the proper law of the contract, if the contract was validly concluded. *See* 2 Dicey & Morris, *The Conflict of Laws Rule* 146 at 775 and Rule 148 at 784 (10th ed. 1980), O. Lando, "Contracts," in III *International Encyclopedia of Comparative Law* Chapter 24 at 102–103.
>
> The goods were to be manufactured in Iowa by Economy Forms and delivery and payment had also to be made in the United States. In view of these circumstances the Tribunal holds that United States law governs the contract, since the centre of gravity of these business dealings was in the United States; that being the test under general principles of conflicts of law. Consequently, the law applicable to the contract, including its formation, is the Uniform Commercial Code, enacted e.g. as Iowa Code §§ 554.1101–09 by the Iowa legislature, 1965, (61 G.A.) c. 413 (effective 4 July 1966; hereinafter "UCC").

Harnischfeger Corp and *Ministry of Roads and Transportation*, Partial Award No 144–180–3 (July 13, 1984) at 15–16, reprinted in 7 Iran–US CTR 90, 99 (1984-III) (footnote omitted):

> The agreement between MSA and Harnco makes no reference to governing law; however, under general choice of law principles, the law of the United States, the jurisdiction with the most significant connection with the transaction and the parties, must be taken to govern in this specific case. Not only was the agreement accepted in the United States by Harnco, a Delaware Corporation, but the component parts were manufactured in the United States, and Harnco completed its performance by delivering the equipment FOB its Iowa plant. *See Economy Forms Corporation* and *The Government of the Islamic Republic of Iran, et al.*, Award No 55–165–1 (14 June 1983).
>
> The United States law applicable to this commercial transaction is the Uniform Commercial Code ("UCC") which, with minor variations, has been adopted by 49 of the 50 states, including each of the United States jurisdictions with contacts with this transaction.

DIC of Delaware, Inc and *Tehran Redevelopment Corp*, Award No 176–255–3 (April 26, 1985) at 22–24, reprinted in 8 Iran–US CTR 144, 160–162 (1985-I):

> The only issue of the existence and enforceability of a contract relates to the alleged Phase III Contract. TRC contends that it did not enter into a contract for Phase III with the Contractors; that the unsigned, draft Phase III contract submitted by the Claimants was of no effect; that the matter never progressed beyond the stage of oral negotiations; and that no work was performed or payments made under any such alleged contract.
>
> ...
>
> If there were an oral agreement, it would be enforceable under Iranian law, which would seem to be the law of the contract because of the connection between the project and Iran and because of the fact that Iranian law was chosen to be the applicable law in the contracts for the other phases. *See Economy Forms Corporation* and *Iran*, Award No 55–165–1 (14 June 1983).
>
> Under Iranian law, a contract not in writing and involving an amount exceeding over 500 rials in value cannot be proved by oral or written testimony alone. *See* The Civil Code of Iran, Arts. 1306 and 1310. In the present case the Claimants rely on contemporaneous documents recording the understandings reached with IRC, and demonstrating part performance of the contract. It appears that acceptance of part performance can be proof of a binding contract under Iranian law. *See, e.g.* The Civil Code of Iran, Art. 193. Moreover, although the governing law of the contract itself must be taken to be that of Iran, each forum applies its own procedural and evidentiary rules to the disputes before it, and it is arguable that the type of evidence admissible to establish a contract is a

procedural or evidentiary matter. Under Article V of the Claims Settlement Declaration the Tribunal must look to "principles of commercial and international law" for guidance. It is widely accepted by municipal systems of law that one can prove the existence of an enforceable oral contract through evidence demonstrating part performance. *See*, e.g. II K. Zweigert & H. Kötz, *An Introduction to Comparative Law: The Institutions of Private Law* 40–41, 48–50 (1977). Such a principle must be taken to constitute a general principle of law. Moreover, it could be argued that, by its conduct, TRC is estopped to assert the non-existence of the contract.

…

Accordingly, if there were an agreement, there is not sufficient evidence of its definiteness of terms to be enforceable. Nevertheless, the Contractors performed work at the request of and with the knowledge of TRC and should be compensated therefore. It is well established under Iranian law and general principles of law that under the doctrine of *quantum meruit* there may be a recovery for work performed. *See* The Civil Code of Iran, Arts. 301–06, 336; 3 M. Whiteman, *Damages in International Law* 1732–61 (1943); 12 *Williston on Contracts* §§ 1452–1459A at 68–108 (3d ed. 1970); *Benjamin R. Isaiah* and *Bank Mellat*, Award No 35–219–2 (30 Mar. 1983).

Carolina Brass, Inc and *Arya Shipping Lines*, Award No 252–10035–2 (September 12, 1986), reprinted in 12 Iran–US CTR 139, 144–145 (1986-III):

20. The Tribunal notes that the Islamic Republic of Iran, the United States, and India, being the Countries connected with the formation and execution of the Bills of Lading, have all adopted the Hague Rules in their domestic legislation, thus embodying the one year limitation of time in their national laws. The Tribunal also notes that the Hague Rules are widely accepted as the standard regime for bills of lading in international maritime trade. The Netherlands also, whose law the Claimant argues is applicable due to the seat of this Tribunal in The Hague, has adopted the Hague Rules and embodied the one year time limitation in its domestic legislation.

21. The Tribunal need not decide whether the law of the Islamic Republic of Iran, the United States, India, or the Netherlands should apply to this particular Case in order to establish that the time limitation contained in Article 3 (6) of the Hague Rules and in Paragraph 21 of the Bills of Lading is applicable in this Case, since the law in each of these countries is similar, and all are in conformity with the widespread practice reflected in the Hague Rules.

Sedco, Inc and *National Iranian Oil Co*, Award No 309–129–3 (July 7, 1987), reprinted in 15 Iran–US CTR 23, 29 (1987-II):

a) The Applicable Law

17. The Tribunal has held in this Case that in the event of an expropriation implicating the rules of public international law the Treaty of Amity, Economic Relations, and Consular Rights between the United States of America and Iran, *signed* 15 August 1955, *entered into force* 16 June 1957, 284 U.N.T.S. 94, T.I.A.S. No 3853, 8 U.S.T. 899 ("Treaty of Amity"), "is applicable to the issue of compensation due Claimant …". March Interlocutory Award, p. 7. Further, the Tribunal has stated that "the Treaty of Amity on the particular issue of what constitutes a taking incorporates the rules of customary international law …". October Interlocutory Award, p. 34. To the extent the taking here alleged is seen as a non-governmental appropriation, general principles of commercial law then become controlling.

Amoco Intl Finance Corp and *Islamic Republic of Iran*, Award No 310 56 3 (July 14, 1987), reprinted in 15 Iran–US CTR 189, 236–41 (1987-II):

b) The Law of the Contract

154. In the present context the issue of the applicable law is quite different from the question of the law applicable to expropriation. It relates to the problem known in conflicts of laws, or private international law, as "the law of the contract," namely the law governing the validity, interpretation and implementation of the Khemco Agreement. Although such a distinction

is rather simple, the discussion of the two issues by the Parties was not always pursued without some confusion.

155. The choice of the parties relating to the law of the Khemco Agreement appears in Article 30, headed "Applicable Laws," which reads as follows:
   1. This Agreement shall be construed and interpreted in accordance with the plain meaning of its terms, but subject thereto, shall be governed and construed in accordance with the laws of Iran.
   2. The provisions of any current laws and regulations which may be wholly or partly inconsistent with the provisions of this Agreement shall, to the extent of any such inconsistency, be of no effect in respect of the provisions of this Agreement.

156. Construed according to the ordinary meaning of the terms, Article 30, paragraph 1 provides that an interpretation of the Khemco Agreement must be based first on the terms thereof. This is, of course, the normal way of interpreting a contract. If problems arise which cannot be solved in this way, the interpreter will have to look at the laws of Iran, which is also the usual way of applying the law of the contract in practice. On the basis of this reading, the Tribunal cannot accept that Iranian law plays only a subordinate role, as contended by the claimant. Nor is the Tribunal convinced that the Khemco Agreement should be characterized as an agreement governed, by nature, by international law. Such a Construction is manifestly contrary to the plain meaning of the terms of Article 30, paragraph 1. It is clear that the parties chose Iranian law as the law of the contract and no reason appears for reading the provisions otherwise.

157. Paragraph 2 of Article 30 does not change this conclusion; it only qualifies it. The purpose of this paragraph was not to submit the Khemco Agreement to law other than Iranian law, but only to solve any question which may arise in case of inconsistency between the "current laws and regulations" of Iran and the terms of the Khemco Agreement itself. In such a case the terms of the Khemco Agreement would nevertheless be considered as valid and binding on the parties. Thus, the contractual regime established by the Khemco Agreement may constitute an exception to the legal regime otherwise existing in Iran.

158. The Khemco Agreement was thus of a specific nature, since its provisions could be contrary to Iranian law without losing their binding force on the parties. In fact, a series of clauses of the Khemco Agreement determine how a number of public laws of Iran would apply to the parties in the implementation of the Khemco Agreement (see, *inter alia*, Articles 9, 10, 14, 15, 16, 17 and 18). For this reason, the provisions of Article 2 required NPC to submit the Khemco Agreement for approval and ratification by the High Council for Petroleum Industries, NIOC, the Council of Ministers and the Joint Economic and Financial Committees of the Majlis.

159. Nothing in Article 30, paragraph 2 or Article 2 militates against the choice of Iranian law as the law of the contract made in Article 30, paragraph 1. Article 2 only provides for the approval by the competent Iranian authorities necessary to authorize those articles of the Khemco Agreement which establish a special regime within the framework of Iranian law. Article 30, paragraph 2, clearly intended that articles which are not inconsistent with Iranian law, as it existed at the time of execution of the Khemco Agreement, are subject to it as provided in Article 30, paragraph 1.

160. The law of the contract applies only to the interpretation and implementation of the Khemco Agreement (and possibly to its validity) as between the parties. Therefore, while it certainly applies to NPC and Amoco, as well as to Khemco, it does not apply to NPC, which was not a party to the Khemco Agreement. The issue then arises as to whether the law of the contract applies to the other Respondent, namely Iran.

161. It cannot easily be found that Iran became a party to the Khemco Agreement through approval and ratification thereof pursuant to Article 2. The Preamble clearly identifies the parties between which the Khemco Agreement is concluded as NPC and Amoco, and makes reference, several times, to them as "both parties." While NPC is controlled by Iran and was established pursuant to a State law, it has a legal personality distinct from that of the State and NPC contracted only for itself.

162. It can be admitted that, in certain circumstances, the separate personality of an entity fully controlled by a State can be discarded and the State considered as bound by the terms of a contract entered into by such an entity. See K.H. Böckstiegel, *Arbitration and State Enterprises* 34–48 (1984); K. H. Böckstiegel, "The Legal Rules Applicable in International Commercial Arbitration involving States or State-Controlled Enterprises," in International Chamber of Commerce, 60 *Years On—A look at the Future* 117, 130–46 (1984). Such a conclusion, however, can legitimately be drawn only if this entity acted as an instrument of the State. The Tribunal is not satisfied that such was the case in the present instance. It is true that the development of petrochemical industries was considered by the Iranian Government as an important goal of the development policy of the country, and was promoted by the enactment in 1965 of an Act authorizing NPC to enter into joint ventures with foreign companies to this effect, and providing for tax exemptions and other privileges beneficial to such joint ventures. Such legislation, however, clearly shows that the State had no intention itself to engage in such industrial and commercial endeavors and left NPC to take the financial and commercial risks associated with them. In approving and ratifying the Khemco Agreement, the Iranian authorities only acted pursuant to Article 1 of the Act concerning Development of Petrochemical Industries of 15 July 1965 ("the Act of 15 July 1965"), in order to permit Khemco to enjoy the statutory exceptions and privileges defined by Article 3 thereof. This approval and ratification were the conditions of application of the Act of 15 July 1965 to the Khemco Agreement but, for the reasons just set forth, cannot be considered binding Iran as a party to the Khemco Agreement.

c) The "Stabilization" Clauses

165. The Claimant alleges that the conduct of Iran in terminating the Khemco Agreement violated two articles thereof which the Claimant characterizes as "stabilization" clauses, namely Article 21, paragraph 2 and Article 30, paragraph 2. These clauses are actually quite different in nature, as revealed by the heading of the respective articles. Article 21 is headed "Guarantee of Performance and Continuity" and Article 30 "Applicable Laws."

166. Article 30, paragraph 2, as discussed above, had the effect of affirming the validity of contractual clauses inconsistent with Iranian laws and regulations. This cannot be considered as a stabilization clause in the usual meaning of the term, however, since that term normally refers to contract language "which freeze the provisions of a national system of law chosen as the law of the contract as of the date of the contract, in order to prevent the application to the contract of any future alterations of this system. Article 30, paragraph 2 applied only to the provisions of any *current* laws and regulations, clearly referring solely to the laws and regulations existing at the time of execution of the Khemco Agreement. Therefore it provided no guarantee for the future and is not a stabilization clause.

167. Article 30, paragraph 2, furthermore, must be read in conjunction with Article 2, which, as already noted, referred to the grant of facilities and privileges conferred by the Government under the two Acts, but with the *proviso* that "any future amendments to such Acts" would also apply. This is the contrary of a stabilization clause.

168. Article 21, paragraph 2 is of a quite different nature. It does not relate to applicable law but to performance of the Khemco Agreement. It reads as follows:
Measures of any nature to annul, amend or modify the provisions of this Agreement shall only be made possible by the mutual consent of NPC and AMOCO.

...

173. In conclusion, the Tribunal does not find that the Khemco Agreement contains any "stabilization" clauses binding on the government. The clauses referred to by the Claimant bind only the parties to the Khemco Agreement, namely NPC and Amoco. According to its own terms, Article 30, paragraph 2 cannot be construed as a stabilization clause and Article 21, paragraph 2 only prohibits unilateral measures by NPC or Amoco to "annul, amend or modify" the provisions of the Khemco Agreement.

Mobil Oil Iran, Inc, et al and *Islamic Republic of Iran* Award No 311–74/76/81/150–3 (July 14, 1987), reprinted in 16 Iran–US CTR 3, 20–28 (1987-III):

1. Applicable Law

a) *The Claimants' Contentions*

59. The first issue raised by the Claimants in relation to applicable law concerns the law of the contract. This question is dealt with in Article 29 of the Agreement, which reads as follows:

   This Agreement shall be interpreted in accordance with the laws of Iran. The rights and obligations of the Parties shall be governed by and according to the provisions of this Agreement. The termination before expiry date or any alteration of this Agreement shall be subject to the mutual agreement of the Parties.

60. According to the Claimants, "Article 29 thus identifies only one source of mandatory rules that will govern the parties' rights and obligations—the Agreement itself. By this provision, the parties plainly intended to exclude any law that would alter or terminate the Agreement by any means other than mutual consent. The Claimants further note that the parties drew a sharp line between the rules that would be used to *interpret* the Agreement and those that would *govern* the parties' rights and obligations." In support of this contention, the Claimants refer to the initial negotiation of the Agreement and conclude that "Article 29 does not say what systems of law may be used to determine the Agreement's validity or to enforce its implementation."

61. In view of the limited scope which they accord to Article 29, the Claimants state that the Tribunal must look elsewhere to determine the law governing the implementation of the Agreement. They therefore suggest that "both the nature of the Agreement and its provisions demonstrate that the Agreement and claims arising thereunder are governed by international law, including general principles of law." In support of this position, the Claimants essentially rely on four factors: (1) the Agreement was a long-term contract; (2) it was concluded between a State or a State agency and a private foreign company; (3) its purpose was to assist in developing an important national resource through complex arrangements; and (4) it contained a clause requiring international arbitration of all disputes arising out of its interpretation and performance. According to the Claimants, these elements define the SPA as an "internationalized contract" which, as is generally recognized by arbitral tribunals and scholars, is governed by international law, including general principles of law.

65. Finally, the Claimants assert that the repudiation of the SPA also was expropriation of the Companies' property interests. This uncompensated expropriation allegedly violated both customary international law and Iran's treaty obligations. More specifically, the Claimants argue that it was contrary to Article IV, paragraph 2, of the 1955 Treaty of Amity, Economic Relations and Consular Rights ("Treaty") between the United States of America and Iran, *signed* 15 August 1955, *entered into force* 16 June 1957, 284 U.N.T.S. 92, T.I.A.S. No 3853, 8 U.S.T. 900.

b) *The Respondents' Contentions*

66. To some extent, the Respondents arrive at similar conclusions as to the law applicable to the issue of liability. They assert that the claims may succeed only if "the facts invoked by the Claimants give rise to the responsibility in international law of the Government of Iran." This is because the Tribunal is a truly international tribunal, which, as such, is concerned with the rights and duties of States in public international law. In the case before it, therefore, "the responsibility engaged is that of the Respondent State for a breach of public international law."

67. In the present Cases, the Respondents contend that a breach of contract can be established only by reference to the proper law of the SPA, which undoubtedly is Iranian law, as clearly stated in Article 29 of the Agreement. According to the Respondents, this conclusion conforms to Article 968 of the Iranian Civil Code, which provides that the law of the contract is the law of the place where the contract was concluded, except if the parties have explicitly or impliedly declared the transaction to be subject to the law of another country (and if those parties are all foreign nationals). The Respondents further note that Iranian law also is specified in the Iranian petroleum legislation of 1957 as the law applicable to contracts concluded by NIOC. Similarly, they point out that a presumption exists in international law that the law applicable to a contract to which a State is a party is the domestic law of that State.

c) *The Tribunal's Findings*
72. Initially, the Tribunal notes that, when dealing with an issue of applicable law, it first must comply with the relevant provisions of the Algiers Accords, found in Article V of the CSD. Article V reads as follows: The Tribunal shall decide all cases on the basis of respect for law, applying such choice of law rules and principles of commercial and international law as the Tribunal determines to be applicable, taking into account relevant usages of the trade, contract provisions and changed circumstances.

    Accordingly, in determining the choice of law in a given case, the Tribunal should examine relevant legal principles and rules as well as the specific factual and legal circumstances of the case, giving special regard to relevant usages of the trade, contract provisions and changed circumstances.
73. In these cases, the Tribunal concludes, and the Parties agree, that the lawfulness of an expropriation must be judged by reference to international law. This holds true even when the expropriation is of contractual rights. A concession, for instance, may be the object of a nationalization regardless of the law the parties chose as the law of the contract. In the instant Cases, the validity under international law of the Single Article Act and of its application to the SPA or any other agreement is not dependent upon the law which the Parties chose to govern the Agreement.
74. In this regard, the Tribunal finds that the Treaty sets forth the governing obligations of the Parties as to the expropriation.

...

75. The claim for alleged breach and repudiation of the Agreement, however, raises quite different issues. At the outset, the Tribunal notes that, when determining the alleged liability of Iran or the United States, the Tribunal must act pursuant to the principles and rules of international law, as it is empowered to do by Article V of the CSD. However, when a claim is based on an alleged breach of contract, the Tribunal first must determine whether the alleged breach actually took place. Obviously, such a determination is made by reference to the terms of the relevant contract, but it also may depend upon legal issues to which the provisions of the contract do not provide a solution. Whether certain conduct of a party constitutes a repudiation of the contract or whether certain dealings of the parties constitute an agreement altering the initial contract are examples of such issues. In questions of this kind, it becomes necessary to rely upon the law applicable to the contract. This is also the case when the Tribunal must decide upon the alleged liability of an entity other than Iran or the United States, when the entity is not a subject of international law.
76. The only provisions of the SPA concerning the applicable law are those contained in Article 29, quoted above in paragraph 59. As the dispute between the Parties over the interpretation of Article 29 demonstrates, these provisions are remarkably—and perhaps intentionally—ambiguous.
77. The sentence providing that "[t]he rights and obligations of the Parties shall be governed by and according to the provisions of this Agreement" states only the obvious. It is nothing more than reaffirmation of the basic rule of contract law that a contract is the law of the parties. It therefore does not impose any specific system of law. Nor can it be construed as meaning that the contract is self-sufficient and is not governed by a system of law. Apart from the fact that some of the issues cannot be resolved by reference to the terms of the Agreement alone, it is sufficient to note that such a radical conclusion cannot be drawn from an article which specifically refers to a domestic system of law, even if it is only for the interpretation of the Agreement. Indeed, the first sentence of Article 29 states that the SPA "shall be interpreted in accordance with the laws of Iran." This is a clear recognition by the parties that the Agreement alone could not provide a solution for all the difficulties which might occur in relation to its performance.
78. It is noteworthy that the usual choice of law clause, which can be found in many international contracts and refers to the interpretation *and* implementation of the contract, was studiously avoided, and that reference is made to Iranian law solely for interpretation of the Agreement. The emphasis put on Iranian law as applicable to interpretation is, at first glance, surprising,

since the rules of interpretation of contracts set forth in Article 224 and 225 of the Iranian Civil Code and the general rules of interpretation set forth in Article 3 of the Civil Procedure Code are rather terse and do not differ from the rules generally applied in most systems of law, including international law. The provision, however, draws some importance from the fact that the Agreement relies on specific Iranian laws, notably tax law and law applicable to the ownership of hydrocarbon reserves.

79. Read in its entirety, Article 29 appears to have had as its main objective to ensure that the Agreement would not be unilaterally amended, but, as expressly stated in the last sentence, be terminated before the expiry date or altered only by "the mutual agreement of the Parties." In light of this objective, the second sentence becomes legally meaningful. Such language is particularly significant in a contract such as the SPA, which relates to the oil industry, where it has often been held that the contracts executed between a State or a State agency and a foreign company may be unilaterally altered by the former. This was especially relevant at the time of negotiation of the Agreement, when important changes in contractual relationship between the Persian Gulf Countries and foreign companies were introduced by unilateral measures decided by the governments of the former. Even in relations between Iran and the Consortium, the negotiation of the SPA was prompted by a decision by Iran not to permit the 1954 Consortium Agreement to be extended beyond 1979, in spite of a clause in that agreement reserving to the Consortium the right to such an extension.

80. In sum, Article 29 is only partially and secondarily concerned with a choice of law. The fact that this choice only applied to the issue of interpretation, in contrast with the usual practice, does not justify an extension of this choice to other issues. *Expressio unius exclusio alterlus est.* The only possible interpretation is that the parties were unable to arrive at an agreement beyond the question of interpretation and that no choice of law was made in the Agreement in relation to the law applicable to any other issue.

81. In the absence of contract provisions, the Tribunal must decide what choice of law is applicable by taking into consideration all circumstances that it deems relevant. In view of the international character of the SPA, concluded between a State, a State agency and a number of major foreign companies, of the magnitude of the interests involved, of the complex set of rights and obligations which it established, and of the link created between this Agreement and the sharing of oil industry benefits throughout the Persian Gulf Countries, the Tribunal does not consider it appropriate that such an Agreement be governed by the law of one Party. This conclusion is in accord with the spirit of Article 29 and with the usages of trade, as expressed in agreements between States and foreign companies, notably in the oil industry, and confirmed in several recent arbitral awards. *See Libyan American Oil Company* (LIAMCO) and *Government of the Libyan Arab Republic* (Mahmassani arb., Award of 12 Apr. 1977), *reprinted in* 62 *I.L.R.* 139 (1982), *Kuwait* and *American Independent Oil Company* (AMINOIL) (Reuter, Sultan & Fizmaurice arbs., Award of 24 Mar. 1982), *reprinted in* 21 *International Legal Materials* 976 (1982); *Texaco Overseas Petroleum Company v. Government of the Libyan Arab Republic* ("TOPCO"), (Dupuy arb., Award of 19 Jan. 1977), *reprinted in* 53 *I.L.R.* 389 (1979). Accordingly, the Tribunal determines that the law applicable to the Agreement is Iranian law for interpretative issues, and the general principles of commercial and international law for all other issues. For reasons previously set forth, the law applicable to the liability of Iran, as well as of NIOC, which acted as an instrumentality of the Iranian Government in these Cases, is international law.

United Painting Co, Inc, a claim of less than US $250,000 presented by the United States of America and *Islamic Republic of Iran*, Award No 458–11286–3 (December 20, 1989), reprinted in 23 Iran-US CTR 351, 356–57 (1989-III):

22. In *Housing and Urban Services International, Inc.* and *The Government of the Islamic Republic of Iran, et al.*, Award No 201–174–1, p. 22 (22 Nov 1985), *reprinted in* 9 Iran-U.S. C.T.R. 313, 329 ("*Haus*"), the Tribunal addressed this question under Iranian law. It concluded that there is substantial authority for the proposition that where there is a civil partnership, a claim

must be pursued in the names of all the partners as its joint owners. The Tribunal therefore held that under the laws of Iran the Claimant might not have standing to sue. At the same time, the Tribunal noted that due to its international position, while municipal law may serve as its "point of departure," the Tribunal must also look to international law. *See id.* at 23–24, *reprinted in* 9 Iran-U.S. C.T.R. 330.

23. Article 20 of the Joint Venture Agreement states that the agreement shall be governed in all respects by the laws of the State of New York. NIOC argues that under the laws of New York a partner is generally not permitted to sue alone on rights belonging to the partnership. Yet even if it were established that the laws of the State of New York prevent a partner from bringing suit without its partner acting as co-claimant as the laws of Iran appear to do the Tribunal would, as confirmed by *Haus*, have to take into account international law. *See id.* This is consistent with Article V of the Claims Settlement Declaration, which forms the basis for the Tribunal's awards.

24. As the Tribunal concluded in *Haus*,

> [w]hile international law seems to accept that as a rule a partner may not sue in his own name alone on a cause of action accruing to the partnership, where special reasons or circumstances required it, "international tribunals have little difficulty in disaggregating the interests of partners and in permitting" partners to recover their *pro rata* share of partnership claims. The most relevant "special circumstance" in this sense exists when a partner's claim is for its own interest, which is independent and readily distinguishable from a claim of the partnership as such.

Id. at 24–25, *reprinted in* 9 Iran-U.S. C.T.R. at 330. The primary reason for allowing a partner to bring a claim individually is that he "would otherwise be prevented from claiming before an international forum because of a foreign partner's disability". *Id.* at 27, *reprinted in* 9 Iran-U.S. C.T.R. at 332. The Tribunal observes that this rationale applies in the present Case.

Catherine Etezadi and *Government of the Islamic Republic of Iran*, Award No 554–319–1 (March 23, 1994), Dissenting Opinion of Richard M Mosk (March 23, 1994), reprinted in 30 Iran–US CTR 45, 45, 49–50 (1994):

I dissent from the award because I believe Claimant Catherine Etezadi, by virtue of her agreement with her husband and under applicable law, has a beneficial, and therefore enforceable, interest in certain assets that were held in her husband's name and that were wrongfully taken by Respondent, the Government of the Islamic Republic of Iran (hereinafter sometimes referred to as "Iran").

…

The issue of choice-of-law with respect to marital rights in property normally arises in the context of death or divorce or, occasionally, in a claim by a creditor of the marital estate or of one of the spouses. This case is unusual in that the wife, with the husband's backing, is asserting certain beneficial rights in properties vis-a-vis a non-creditor third party. If there were a choice-of-law issue, the laws of several jurisdictions could be invoked.

At the time of marriage, the Etezadis were domiciled in New York; therefore, the law of New York could apply to any pre-marital or immediate post-marital agreements. *See Hague Convention on the Law Applicable to Matrimonial Property Regimes* (1976), art. 4, in 25 *Am. J. of Comp. Law* 393, 395 (1977) (applicable law is that of "the State in which both spouses establish their first habitual residence after marriage"), 2 *Dicey and Morris on the Conflict of Laws* 1058–59 (L. Collins 11th ed. 1987) (Rule 154(2)) (husband's domicile upon marriage); see also, E. Scoles, *Choice of Law in Family Transactions*, 209 *Recueil des Cours* 9, 28–30 (1989), and authorities cited therein (discussing "immutability of marital rights").

The situs of the properties in issue are located in Iran, and thus Iran contends that Iranian law applies. *See* Civil Code of Iran, art. 966; *see also id.*, art. 963 ("If husband and wife are not nationals of the same country, their personal and financial relations with one another will be subject to the laws of the country of the husband").

California has been the marital domicile of the Etezadis since 1974. As such, its laws could be applied. See E. Scoles & P. Hay, *Conflict of Laws* § 14.4, at 468 (2d ed. 1992) ("In most instances, the state of dominant interest, as in other matters involving family and marital concerns, is the domicile of the parties").

As I shall discuss, the relevant laws of these jurisdictions that can be applied in this case are consistent. See *DIC of Delaware, et al. v. Tehran Redevelopment Corp., et al.*, Award No 176–255–3, p. 17 (26 Apr. 1985), *reprinted in* 8 Iran-U.S. C.T.R. 144, 156–57. The Tribunal is not restricted to applying the law of any specific place, for under Article V of the Claims Settlement Declaration, the Tribunal "shall decide all cases on the basis of respect for law, applying such choice-of-law rules and principles of commercial and international law as the Tribunal determines to be applicable, taking into account relevant usages of the trade, contract provisions and changed circumstances."

There is not, however, a true conflict of laws, for under the law of the marital domicile at the relevant times—California—Mrs. Etezadi effectively obtained a one-half interest in the entire marital estate, including a beneficial interest in any property solely in the name of Mr. Etezadi. Under Tribunal jurisprudence, such beneficial interests are enforceable. See below.

United States of America and *Islamic Republic of Iran* (Case No B36), Award No 574-B-36–2 (December 3, 1996), reprinted in 32 Iran–US CTR 162, 180 (1996):

> 71. In the Tribunal's view, several factors in the present Case give strong support to the conclusion that the 1948 Contract was of an intergovernmental character, the governing law of which should be international law. The Contract was concluded between two sovereign States. It concerned the sale of military equipment belonging to the United States government. The terms of the Contract took effect on approval by the Majlis (the Iranian parliament), and the U.S. Congress approved a special appropriation to cover PHT costs. When the debts became due, the United States pursued the matter at the highest diplomatic levels and did not take the matter before any municipal forum. The foregoing points, in the absence of a choice of law provision, compel the Tribunal to determine that the applicable law of the 1948 Contract is international law.

Ouziel Aryeh, et al and *Islamic Republic of Iran*, Award No 584–839/840–3 (September 25, 1997), reprinted in 33 Iran–US CTR 460, 477 (1997) (footnotes omitted):

> 67. The Respondent's second objection to the validity of the Will is based on its alleged inconsistency with Jewish law. This contention, however, is supported only by a general statement of its invalidity by a Jewish authority in Tehran. By contrast, the legal opinion obtained by the Claimants is detailed and contains reference to authorities. The Tribunal notes that it generally makes more credible reading. Its facial credibility is further enhanced by the credentials of its author, who had been Chief Rabbi of Tehran for many years, including the relevant period. The Tribunal therefore decides that on its face, the Will appears not to be inconsistent with Jewish law and not for that reason invalid.

(2) *Tribunal Rules (1983), Article 33(2)*

The Iran–United States Claims Tribunal has not been authorized by the parties in any case to decide *ex aequo et bono* or as *amiable compositeur*.

(3) *Tribunal Rules (1983), Article 33(3)*

American Bell Intl Inc and *Islamic Republic of Iran*, Final Award No 255–48–3 (September 19, 1986), reprinted in 12 Iran–US CTR 170, 186–87 (1986-III):

> 54. That does not mean that *force majeure* was of no consequence to the question of termination costs. The Tribunal has decided that a portion of the departure was attributable to *force*

majeure, and that *force majeure* prevented the negotiations relating to the financial consequences of the force reductions from being concluded. Thus *force majeure*. Although not the ultimate cause to which Claimant's termination costs can be attributed, created conditions which made it impossible for Claimant to recover what it was entitled to under the contract. Unlike those situations in which costs are directly attributable to *force majeure*, this does not reflect the allocation of risks as contemplated by Contract 138, but rather is a consequence of a situation unforeseen in the contract. In such circumstances the determination of the rights and liabilities of the parties is subject "to the Tribunal's equitable discretion, using the contract as a framework and reference point." *Queens Office Tower Associates* and *Iran National Airlines Corp.*, Award No 37172–1 at 14 (15 April 1983), *reprinted in* 2 Iran-U.S. C.T.R. 247, 254, *International School Services Inc.* and *National Iranian Copper Industries Co.*, Award No 194–111–1 at 14 (10 Oct. 1985). In exercising its equitable discretion, the Tribunal must determine what the parties, in the light of their intentions as reflected in the contract, would have agreed upon as to the financial consequences of the force reductions, and what consequently is the reasonable compensation for the costs incurred.[1]

...

[Footnote] 1. The Tribunal notes that its task in the present respect is very similar to that faced by the arbitration tribunal in *Kuwait v. The American Independent Oil Company (Aminoil)*, Award of 24 March 1982, (Reuter, Sultan, Fitzmaurice, arbs.), *reprinted in* 21 *Int'l Legal Mat'ls* 976 (1982), where the parties had conducted negotiations on the application of a new price formula without being able to complete these negotiations. The tribunal stated that "it thinks that it is not really a question of modifying or completing the contract... The Tribunal is not expected to devise new provisions that will govern the contractual relations of the Parties for the future, but to liquidate the various consequences of their past conduct, and of the contractual clauses that once bound them but are now at an end." *Id.* at paragraph 75.

Iran National Airlines Co and *United States of America*, Award No 337-B10–2 (November 30, 1987), reprinted in 17 Iran–US CTR 238, 239–40 (1987-III):

1. Time Limitation and Applicable Law
4. The Tribunal notes that the Parties dispute the question of the law applicable to these transactions. The Respondent contends that GBL and GTR transactions are governed by U.S. law. The Claimant denies that U.S. law is applicable to these transactions, contending that Iranian law governs Iran Air passenger tickets and airwaybills. It argues generally that its submission of the relevant U.S. forms for air cargo and air travel together with its invoices should not be construed as an admission by the Claimant to the application of U.S. laws and regulations in the event of disputes.
5. For the reasons set forth in Case No B9 in relation to carriage of goods by air, Award No 335-B9–2, and in Case No B12 in relation to passenger transportation services, Award No 336-B12–2, the Tribunal finds that it is able to resolve all issues by reference to the practice of the Parties and to the terms of the contractual documents themselves, without entering into a discussion of the applicable law.

Benjam R Isaiah and *Bank Mellat (as successor to International Bank of Iran)*, Award No 35–219–2 (March 30, 1983) at 10–11, reprinted in 2 Iran–US CTR 232, 237 (1983-I) (footnote omitted):

While it might be argued that Iranian law must be applied to this claim on the ground that the act giving rise to the unjust enrichment took place at least partly in Iran, and that the enrichment occurred there, it might also be argued that this is unnecessarily restrictive in view of the fact that the dishonored check was drawn on a New York bank and much of the underlying transaction occurred outside Iran.

Article V of the Claims Settlement Declaration leaves the Tribunal with considerable flexibility in this regard. It provides as follows:
Article V
The Tribunal shall decide all cases on the basis of respect for law, applying such choice of law rules and principles of commercial and international law as the Tribunal determines to be applicable, taking into account relevant usages of the trade, contract provisions and changed circumstances.

Under this rule, the Tribunal is free to apply general principles of law in a case such as this, although there is no reason to believe the result would be different if only Iranian law were applied.

(4) Other practice of the Iran–US Claims Tribunal

CMI Intl, Inc and *Ministry of Roads and Transportation of Islamic Republic of Iran*, Award No 99–245–2 (December 27, 1983) at 8–9, reprinted in 4 Iran–US CTR 263, 267–68 (1983-III):

B. Damages

1. Choice of Law

The Claimant argued the damage questions in terms of the statutory law of Idaho, which in this case is essentially the Uniform Commercial Code. As noted above, the purchase orders provided that they were governed by the laws of Idaho. The Tribunal does not believe, however, that it is rigidly tied to the law of the contract, at least insofar as the assessment of damages is concerned. Article V of the Claims Settlement Declaration provides:

The Tribunal shall decide all cases on the basis of respect for law applying such choice of law rules and principles of commercial and international law as the Tribunal determines to be applicable, taking into account relevant usages of the trade, contract provisions and changed circumstances.

It is difficult to conceive of a choice of law provision that would give the Tribunal greater freedom in determining case by case the law relevant to the issues before it. Such freedom is consistent with, and perhaps almost essential to, the scope of the tasks confronting the Tribunal, which include not only claims between the two Governments, certain claims between banking institutions, and issues of interpretation and implementation of the Algiers Declarations. Thus the Tribunal may often find it necessary to interpret and apply treaties, customary international law, general principles of law and national laws, "taking into account relevant usages of the trade, contract provisions and changed circumstances," as Article V directs.

With respect to the assessment of damages, the Tribunal considers its main task to be determining what are the losses suffered by the Claimant and to award compensation therefor. Our search is for justice and equity, even in cases where arguably relevant national laws might be designed to further other and doubtless quite legitimate goals. In the present case, while application of the Uniform Commercial Code may not lead to substantially different conclusions from those adopted by the Tribunal (except with respect to accounting for profits on resales, which will be discussed below), the Tribunal prefers to analyze the damage questions in accordance with general principles of law, rather than by reference to the Code as incorporated in the statutory law of Idaho.

R J Reynolds Tobacco Co and *Islamic Republic of Iran*, Award No 145–35–3 (August 6, 1984) at 18–19, reprinted in 7 Iran–US CTR 181, 191–92 (1984-III):

4. The Tribunal's Findings on the Interest Claim

Claimant contends that it is entitled to interest based on the following terms and conditions appearing on the order acknowledgement form used in connection with the goods that are the subject of the claim:

Buyer [ITC] agrees to pay to Seller interest at three months libor [London International Offering Rate] (as quoted by the Financial Times of London) plus 2 per cent p.a. on all sums and for the duration such sums remain unpaid in excess of the agreed payment terms. Seller's occasional or continued omission to claim interest hereunder shall not be construed as a waiver.

The order acknowledgement form provides for the application of Swiss law to the sale. Under Swiss law, a contractually agreed upon rate of interest is binding on the parties to the contract. Swiss Code of Obligations, Article 104, Paragraph 2.

Claimant asserts that this clause permits the compounding of interest. Also the large profits of ITC from the sale of the unpaid cigarettes have been referred to by Claimant as a particular justification for compound interest.

The Tribunal, however, does not find that there are any special reasons for departing from international precedents which normally do not allow the awarding of compound interest. As noted by one authority, "[t]here are few rules within the scope of the subject of damages in international law that are better settled than the one that compound interest is not allowable." III M. Whiteman, *Damages in International Law* 1997 (1943). Even though the term "all sums" could be construed to include interest and thereby to allow compound interest, the Tribunal, due to the ambiguity of the language, interprets the clause in the light of the international rule just stated, and thus excludes compound interest.

Anaconda-Iran, Inc and *Islamic Republic of Iran*, Award No ITL 65–167–3 (December 10, 1986), reprinted in 13 Iran–US CTR 199, 232–33 (1986-III):

130   … This Article [V of the Claims Settlement Declaration] has a vast scope of application. The Algiers Accords apply to a great number of claims arising out of contracts which may contain very differing provisions regarding applicable law. More importantly, Article V creates a novel system of determining applicable law. Contrary to NICIC's contentions, the Tribunal finds that according to this system the Tribunal is not required to apply any particular national or international legal system. On the contrary, the Tribunal is vested with extensive freedom in determining the applicable law in each case. This freedom is not a discretionary freedom, however, as the Tribunal is given a rather precise indication as to the factors which should guide its decision.

131. Contract provisions constitute one of these factors, but it is noteworthy that they are not listed first, nor foremost, among the factors enumerated. The Tribunal is of course required to take seriously into consideration the pertinent contractual choice of law rules, but it is not obliged to apply these if it considers it has good reasons not to do so.

132. In the present Case the TAA [Technical Assistance Agreement] does not contain any choice of law rules. For the reasons developed above, the Tribunal cannot on that ground conclude, as does the Claimant, that the TAA is self-sufficient under all circumstances and that no law shall govern the TAA. No more can the Tribunal conclude, as does the Respondent, that Iranian law is applicable because the place of conclusion and execution of the TAA was Iran. In most contract cases before the Tribunal the contracts actually were concluded and executed in Iran. If the States Parties to the Algiers Accords had intended that Iranian law would apply to all such cases which do not contain a contractual clause to the contrary, the Algiers Accords undoubtedly would have contained specific provisions to that effect. As we have seen, however, Article V created quite a different system.

133. In conclusion, the Tribunal notes that contractual limitations of remedies similar to the provision in Article 9 of the TAA frequently are included in international commercial contracts. In deciding the remaining issues in this Case, the Tribunal therefore must give particular consideration to the usages of the trade as well as principles of commercial and international law mentioned in Article V of the CSD. One of the legal issues which the Parties should brief in their future pleadings therefore is the relevant usages of the trade in respect of contractual limitations of remedies similar to the provisions contained in Article 9 of the TAA.

Jack Rankin (a claim of less than $250,000 presented by United States of America) and *Islamic Republic of Iran*, Award No 326–10913–2 (November 3, 1987), reprinted in 17 Iran–US CTR 135, 142–43 (1987-III):

1. Applicable Law
21. Pursuant to Article V of the Claimant Settlement Declaration, the Tribunal is directed to decide all cases "on the basis of respect for law" and to apply "such choice of law rules and principles of commercial and international law as the Tribunal determines to be applicable." With respect to these expulsion cases, however, it is clear that, contractual questions aside, only Iranian law and international law can be relevant. In the present Case there has been no allegation that the Claimant's departure involved violations of Iranian law, so the allegation of wrongfulness is to be determined by the standards of international law.
23. For the reasons stated in *Phelps Dodge Corp. et al.*, and *The Islamic Republic of Iran*, Award No 217–99–2 (19 March 1986) and *Amoco International Finance Corporation* and *The Government of the Islamic Republic of Iran, et al.*, Award No 310–56–3 (14 July 1987), the Tribunal need not determine whether the Treaty of Amity today remains in force between the two State Parties, as it was clearly applicable at the time the claim arose and is, pursuant to Article V of the Claims Settlement Declaration, a relevant source of law on which the Tribunal is justified in relying in reaching its decision.

PART II

ARBITRAL PROCEDURES TO CONTROL THE SELECTION AND CONDUCT OF ARBITRATORS

Introduction

Following the initiation of the arbitral process, a crucial task facing the parties is the constitution of the tribunal.[1] Setting up the tribunal can be one of the most difficult processes in an arbitration. The membership of the panel is very important because so much of what occurs later in the arbitration, especially crucial decision-making, depends upon the knowledge, skill and interpersonal dynamics of the arbitrators chosen. The process may be frustrating. Parties may find themselves avidly studying the backgrounds of several possible arbitrators, often to discover that the one desired is not available because of conflicts or scheduling issues. Even more trying is when a reluctant party cleverly opposes constitution of the panel at every turn. A great deal of effort has been exerted in both interstate and private international arbitration to ensure that arbitral panels can always be constituted while simultaneously respecting the rights of the parties in the process.

This Part examines the success of such efforts in terms of the 2010 UNCITRAL Rules. The experience of the Iran–US Claims Tribunal and investor–state arbitration tribunals is particularly significant. The constitution of the tribunal is an area of arbitral procedure where until quite recently practice was difficult to ascertain. This problem has been mitigated in the case of the Tribunal and, in some cases, investor–state arbitration through the publication of challenge decisions which have generated a growing body of case law. The scarcity of commentary is also due to the fact that, although appointments are routinely made, actions such as the challenge of an arbitrator have been rare. While the Iran–U.S. Claims Tribunal remains far and away the leading source of practice in the area under the Rules, having been involved in sixteen challenges, the five publicly available challenge decisions from the field of investor–state arbitration also usefully add to corpus of practice.

The initial constitution of a tribunal involves three distinct stages: (1) the appointment of an arbitrator, (2) the disclosure by that arbitrator, to all parties not involved in his appointment, of any circumstances which might give rise to justified doubts as to his impartiality, and (3) objection to that arbitrator by any parties who believe the circumstances disclosed

---

[1] "[T]he constitution of the tribunal is, on the whole, the *fundamental* problem of arbitration, because without a tribunal there can be no arbitration." D Johnson, "The Constitution of an Arbitral Tribunal," (1953) 30 BYIL 152.

warrant a challenge. At every step, the 2010 UNCITRAL Rules prefer that the parties mutually agree on the composition of the panel. However, the Rules also place limits on how long any party must wait for mutual agreement. Finally, behind all of these time limits is a third party, the "appointing authority" who will, if necessary, make impartial appointments or decide upon challenges.

The following chapters examine all these stages and the central, yet often neglected, role of the appointing authority. Specifically, in light of the experience of the Iran–US Claims Tribunal and other tribunals, including investor–state arbitration tribunals, the approach of the UNCITRAL Rules to formation of the arbitral panel is evaluated.

Chapter 4
The Number and Selection of Arbitrators

1. Introduction	148
2. Designating and Appointing Authorities—Article 6	148
A. Text of the 2010 UNCITRAL Rule	148
B. Commentary	149
(1) Opportunities for agreement on an appointing authority—Article 6(1)	149
(2) The role of the designating authority—Article 6(2) and(4)	151
(3) Suspension of time periods in the absence of an appointing authority—Article 6(3)	153
(4) The role of the appointing authority—Article 6(5)–(7)	153
C. Extracts from the Practice of the Iran–US Claims Tribunal	155
3. The Number of Arbitrators—Article 7	157
A. Text of the 2010 UNCITRAL Rule	157
B. Commentary	157
(1) The default rule on the number of arbitrators—Article 7(1)	157
(2) The exception to the default rule of three arbitrators—Article 7(2)	160
(3) A number of arbitrators other than one or three	161
4. Appointment of the Sole Arbitrator—Article 8	162
A. Text of the 2010 UNCITRAL Rule	162
B. Commentary	163
5. Appointment of a Three-Person Panel—Article 9	164
A. Text of the 2010 UNCITRAL Rule	164
B. Commentary	164
(1) The right of each party to appoint an arbitrator	164
(2) The appointment of the presiding arbitrator	165
C. Extracts from the Practice of Investment Tribunals	166
6. Appointment in Multi-Party Arbitration—Article 10	169
A. Text of the 2010 UNCITRAL Rule	169
B. Commentary	169
(1) The requirements for appointment—Article 10(1) and (2)	169
(2) The power of the appointing authority to appoint and reappoint—Article 10(3)	170
7. Comparison to the 1976 UNCITRAL Rules	172

1. Introduction

Appointment of arbitrators under the UNCITRAL Rules presents two topics for discussion: the proper number of arbitrators—a sole arbitrator or a panel of three—and the process by which the arbitrator or arbitrators are appointed.[1]

2. Designating and Appointing Authorities—Article 6

A. Text of the 2010 UNCITRAL Rule[2]

Article 6 of the 2010 UNCITRAL Rules provides:

1. Unless the parties have already agreed on the choice of an appointing authority, a party may at any time propose the name or names of one or more institutions or persons, including the Secretary-General of the Permanent Court of Arbitration at The Hague (hereinafter called the "PCA"), one of whom would serve as appointing authority.
2. If all parties have not agreed on the choice of an appointing authority within 30 days after a proposal made in accordance with paragraph 1 has been received by all other parties, any party may request the Secretary-General of the PCA to designate the appointing authority.
3. Where these Rules provide for a period of time within which a party must refer a matter to an appointing authority and no appointing authority has been agreed on or designated, the period is suspended from the date on which a party initiates the procedure for agreeing on or designating an appointing authority until the date of such agreement or designation.
4. Except as referred to in article 41, paragraph 4, if the appointing authority refuses to act, or if it fails to appoint an arbitrator within 30 days after it receives a party's request to do so, fails to act within any other period provided by these Rules, or fails to decide on a challenge to an arbitrator within a reasonable time after receiving a party's request to do so, any party may request the Secretary-General of the PCA to designate a substitute appointing authority.
5. In exercising their functions under these Rules, the appointing authority and the Secretary-General of the PCA may require from any party and the arbitrators the information they deem necessary and they shall give the parties and, where appropriate, the arbitrators, an opportunity to present their views in any manner they consider appropriate. All such communications to and from the appointing authority and the Secretary-General of the PCA shall also be provided by the sender to all other parties.
6. When the appointing authority is requested to appoint an arbitrator pursuant to articles 8, 9, 10 or 14, the party making the request shall send to the appointing authority copies of the notice of arbitration and, if it exists, any response to the notice of arbitration.

---

[1] The characteristics to be sought in an arbitrator, other than by contradistinction from the limits set by challenge, are not addressed by the UNCITRAL Rules. These are more properly a question for the parties in light of the nature of the dispute. Whether that absence is satisfactory when the UNCITRAL Rules are utilized in proceedings with a higher degree of public interest in the outcome, such as investment arbitrations, is an open question.

[2] Article 6 draws from and consolidates provisions in corresponding Articles 6, 7, and 8 of the 1976 UNCITRAL Rules, while also adding new provisions.

7. The appointing authority shall have regard to such considerations as are likely to secure the appointment of an independent and impartial arbitrator and shall take into account the advisability of appointing an arbitrator of a nationality other than the nationalities of the parties.

B. Commentary

Where a disputing party fails to make or agree on a required appointment, ie, of a party-appointed arbitrator or a sole arbitrator, or the appointed arbitrators fail to agree on the appointment of a presiding arbitrator, the appointing authority assumes a critical role in the arbitration. Without an appointing authority to make necessary appointments, the process of arbitration would come to a halt. Article 6 underscores "the importance of the role of the appointing authority, particularly in the context of non-administered arbitration."[3] It covers four essential matters: the opportunity for agreement among the parties on an appointing authority, the process for designating an appointing authority when the parties cannot agree, suspension of time periods pending referral of matters to the appointing authority, and the appointing authority's discretion in making appointments.[4] Other matters regarding the appointing authority's role in deciding requests to remove arbitrators are addressed in Chapters 5, 6, and 7.

(1) Opportunities for agreement on an appointing authority—Article 6(1)

Under the basic principle of party autonomy, the parties are entitled to agree on the person or institution to serve as appointing authority in the arbitration. While agreement may be reached at any time, the Rules clearly encourage the parties to do so as early as possible, even before a dispute giving rise to a notice of arbitration, where feasible. To illustrate, the note to the UNCITRAL Model Arbitration Clause for Contracts encourages the parties to consider naming the appointing authority in the underlying contract.[5] If no pre-dispute designation is made, the Rules recommend a process for facilitating agreement on an appointing authority in the earliest phase of the proceedings. Under Article 3(4)(a), the claimant may make a proposal for the appointment of the appointing authority in its notice of arbitration.[6] When submitting its response to the notice of arbitration, pursuant to Article 4(2)(a), a respondent may accept the claimant's proposal or propose a different person or institution for the claimant's consideration.

Article 6(1) also allows the parties to make proposals for the person or institution to serve as appointing authority "at any time" during the arbitration. Article 6(1) thus clarifies that the parties are not required to wait to reach agreement until the Rules indicate an

---

[3] *Report of the Working Group on Arbitration and Conciliation on the Work of its Forty-Sixth Session* (New York, February 5–9, 2007), UNCITRAL, 40th Session, UN Doc A/CN.9/619, at 15, para 69 (2007).

[4] Whereas some of the provisions contained in Article 6 are new to the 2010 UNCITRAL Rules, others draw on pre-existing provisions in corresponding Articles 6, 7, and 8 of the 1976 UNCITRAL Rules.

[5] See Model Arbitration Clause For Contracts (Located in the Annex to the 2010 UNCITRAL Rules), sub-paragraph (a), extracted in Chapter 2 section 2(A). As the *travaux préparatoires* indicate, because "the designation of an appointing authority by the parties prior to the commencement of the arbitral proceedings can expedite both the appointment of arbitrators and the decision on possible challenges, it is recommended that the appointing authority should be designated in the arbitration clause or separate arbitration agreement...." *Report of the Secretary-General on the Revised Draft Set of Arbitration Rules*, UNCITRAL, 9th Session, UN Doc. A/CN.9/112, para 15 (1975), reprinted in VII UNCITRAL Ybk (part 2) 159 (1976).

[6] 2010 UNCITRAL Arbitration Rules, art 3(4)(a).

opportunity to choose the appointing authority, such as the respondent's response to the claimant's proposal in the notice of arbitration, or a particular need for an appointing authority arises, such as a party's failure to exercise its right of appointment or the challenge of an arbitrator.[7] As the *travaux préparatoires* note, the phrase "at any time" was meant to indicate that possibilities for choosing the appointing authority exist continuously throughout the proceedings, "not only in circumstances currently provided for in the Rules."[8]

The Rules place no limitations on who or what institution the parties may agree on to serve as appointing authority. In practice, the choice may include an eminent jurist, such as Judge W.E. Haak, former judge in the Supreme Court of the Netherlands, who serves as appointing authority for the Iran–US Claims Tribunal, or an institution, such as the London Court of International Arbitration.[9] Article 6(1) also expressly indicates that the Secretary-General of the Permanent Court of Arbitration (PCA) may serve as appointing authority. This reference is to clarify that while the PCA Secretary-General functions generally as the default authority under the Rules for designating the appointing authority when the parties cannot reach agreement, he may also be chosen directly to serve as appointing authority.[10]

During discussions to revise the Rules, the Working Group considered a proposal that would give the PCA a more active role in the appointment process than it had under the 1976 UNCITRAL Rules. Rather than functioning only as designating authority (or appointing authority when agreed to by the parties), some delegates envisioned the PCA Secretary-General acting as the default appointing authority, when the parties could not reach agreement. Proponents of the proposal believed that it would provide the parties with a "simple, streamlined, and efficient" process of appointment with greater "predictability," without compromising the parties' rights, since they would always be free to agree on an appointing authority other the PCA Secretary-General.[11] The PCA's status as an intergovernmental organization with broad membership was seen as uniquely qualifying the institution to carry out the task of appointment of arbitrators.

Other delegates strongly opposed the proposal. Concerns were raised that it did not sufficiently take into account "the multi-regional applicability of the UNCITRAL Arbitration Rules" and would "centraliz[e] all cases where the parties had not designated an appointing authority in the hands of one organization."[12] While some regarded the proposal as possibly

---

[7] As Castello observes:

A principal purpose of this restructuring is to encourage parties to put an appointing authority in place as soon as possible. Moreover, by consolidating provisions relating to the appointing authority in a separate Article, the revised Rules would, for example, eliminate the uncertainty as to whether the Rules require a party to propose candidates for appointing authority and candidates for sole arbitrator together.

J Castello, "UNCITRAL Rules" in F Weigand (ed) *Practitioner's Handbook on International Commercial Arbitration* (2nd edn 2009) 1435. See also J Castello, "Unveiling the 2010 UNCITRAL Arbitration Rules," (May/October 2010) 65 Dispute Resolution J 151.

[8] UNCITRAL, 40th Session, UN Doc A/CN.9/619, n 3, at 15, para 69.

[9] In general, arbitral institutions provide advantages over individuals because institutions typically possess greater knowledge of, and have better access to, highly qualified arbitrators. See N Blackaby and C Partasides with A Redfern and M Hunter, *Redfern and Hunter on International Arbitration* (2009) 252; G Born, *International Commercial Arbitration*, (2009) 1409.

[10] The PCA Secretary-General has served as appointing authority. See, eg, *Veteran Petroleum Ltd* and *Russian Federation*, Interim Award (November 30, 2009) (*Ad Hoc* Proceeding, 1976 UNCITRAL Rules, Energy Charter Treaty), paras 8–9.

[11] UNCITRAL, 40th Session, UN Doc A/CN.9/619, n 3, at 16, paras 71, 73.

[12] UNCITRAL, 40th Session, UN Doc A/CN.9/619, n 3, at 16, at para 72.

appropriate for investor–state arbitration, many believed that it would not be as useful in regional or domestic arbitration.[13] It was also noted that the mechanism provided in the 1976 UNCITRAL Rules did not raise problems in practice and thus required no change.[14] In the end, it was viewed as "a major and unnecessary departure from the existing UNCITRAL Arbitration Rules."[15] With a view toward reconciling conflicting views, as discussed, the 2010 UNCITRAL Rules retain the parties' right to request the PCA Secretary-General to designate an appointing authority, while clarifying expressly that the PCA Secretary-General himself may serve as appointing authority.

(2) The role of the designating authority—Article 6(2) and (4)

Paragraphs 2 and 4 of Article 6 establish a special role for the PCA Secretary-General as the entity empowered to designate the appointing authority in certain situations. The PCA Secretary-General may serve as the designator of the appointing authority when the parties to the arbitration cannot agree on the choice of appointing authority within 30 days of any proposal communicated in accordance with Article 6(1),[16] or a previously selected appointing authority refuses to act or fails to appoint an arbitrator within 30 days after it receives a party's request to do so.[17] Thus, the 2010 UNCITRAL Rules, like the 1976 UNCITRAL Rules, utilize a two-step process of indirect appointment to resolve more difficult cases of disagreement between the parties or inaction by the appointing authority.

Before adopting this mechanism for indirect appointment, the drafters of the 1976 UNCITRAL Rules explored the possibility of direct appointment, but without success. Three leading proposals emerged, each of which would allow the claimant, if necessary, to appeal directly to a default appointing authority: either (1) an appointing authority designated, pursuant to a United Nations General Assembly resolution, by the government of the country where the respondent has his principal place of business or habitual residence, (2) an arbitral institution in the country where the respondent has his principal place of business or habitual residence or a chamber of commerce in that country with experience in appointing arbitrators, or (3) an appointing authority established within the United Nations system, either an organ under the direction of the UNCITRAL Secretariat or a separate organ.[18]

---

[13] UNCITRAL, 40th Session, UN Doc A/CN.9/619, n 3, at 16, at para 72.

[14] UNCITRAL, 40th Session, UN Doc A/CN.9/619, n 3, at 16, at para 72.

[15] UNCITRAL, 40th Session, UN Doc A/CN.9/619, n 3, at 16, at para 74. For further discussion of these issues, see also transcript of roundtable discussion between James Castello, Georgios Petrochilos, Michael Schneider, Josefa Sicard-Mirabal, William Slate and Christopher To, reprinted in "Assessment of the UNCITRAL Rules Revision: A Roundtable," *50 Years of the New York Convention: ICCA International Arbitration Conference*, Dublin 615–35 (ICCA Congress Series No 14, 2009).

[16] Consultations between the disputing parties regarding selection of the appointing authority are not a prerequisite for engaging the PCA Secretary-General as the designator of the appointing authority. See Decision of the Appointing Authority (March 5, 1982), reprinted in section 2(C) (finding such an obligation would be in tension with the policy under the Rules of quickly designating an appointing authority to carry out its work). However, in most cases, attempts at reaching agreement are likely to be useful.

[17] The PCA Secretary-General designated the appointing authority in *Chevron Corp* (1976 Rules) and *Mystilineos Holdings* (1976 Rules); both reprinted in section 5(C). Note that the Rules do not require the parties to consult.

[18] Proposals (1) and (2) were contained in the preliminary draft of Article 6. UN Doc. A/CN.9/97 (1974) (draft Article 6) (1974), VI UNCITRAL Ybk (part 2) 168 (1975). Proposal (3) was made thereafter. *Summary Record of the 163rd Meeting of the UNCITRAL*, 8th Session, UN Doc A/CN.9/SR.163, at 142 (1975) (comment by Mr Jenard, Belgium) (proposing that the UNCITRAL Secretariat might act as appointing authority); also at 142 (comment by Mr Sumulong, Philippines) (proposing that the UNCITRAL Secretariat create a panel of arbitrators); at 143 (Comment by Mr Jakubowski, Poland) (supporting the proposal); and at 144 (Comment by

The Committee considered, but ultimately rejected, each of these proposals. The first failed because of the potential difficulty in obtaining the requisite UN resolution and because the designation of the appointing authority by the respondent's government would be inconsistent with the principle of neutrality.[19] The second proposal was inadequate because, not only did it raise concerns of impartiality like the first, but also because the institutions referenced, whether arbitral institutions or chambers of commerce, might not exist in some countries.[20] The third proposal was dropped, in large part, because it was believed that there would not be sufficient demand for the services of a default appointing authority to justify creation of a special UN body especially for this purpose.[21] Thus, the Committee was unable to agree on a procedure that would provide direct appointment of the appointing authority.

The Committee's decision to establish the PCA Secretary-General as the designating authority was widely supported, but not without diverging views. Some delegates questioned whether the PCA was "sufficiently universal" to perform the role, given that not all countries were represented on the Permanent Court of Arbitration.[22] They feared the "over-centralization" of the designation process.[23] Others noted, as a practical matter, that a process of indirect appointment could give rise to delays.[24] Still others thought that the role of designator of the appointing authority was not enough for the PCA, which should serve as the default.[25] However, the PCA's own unwillingness to take on this responsibility put an end to this proposal.[26] Thus, the Committee decided to endorse a process of indirect appointment through the PCA as the designator of the appointing authority.[27]

In the end, the process of indirect appointment is arguably best suited for the UNCITRAL Rules, which are designed primarily for use in *ad hoc* arbitration and which may be applied to disputes arising from all corners of the world. The Rules unquestionably require some procedural mechanism to ensure that the arbitral process will advance, even in the face of party disagreement or an appointing authority's failure to act. Designating a default appointing authority under the Rules, though perhaps most efficient for the parties, may not provide the most equitable result, as it would be difficult for any one institution to possess the resources and expertise to be able to appoint the most appropriate arbitrator in every situation arising under the Rules, from the small contract arbitration in Indonesia to the sizable investor–state arbitration in Germany. Though indirect appointment by the

---

Mr Khoo, Singapore) (supporting the proposal). Yet another proposal provided: "if the parties were agreed on the place of arbitration (and if the place were a country other than a country of the parties), the appointing authority would be designated by an arbitral institution of the country where the arbitration took place, or by a chamber of commerce in that country with experience in appointing arbitrators." *Summary Record of the 163rd Meeting of the UNCITRAL*, 8th Session, UN Doc A/CN.9/SR.163, at 143 (1975) (comment by Mr Réczei, Hungary).

[19] UN Doc A/CN.9/SR.163, n 18, at 145 (comment by the Chairman).
[20] UN Doc A/CN.9/SR.163, n 18, at 145.
[21] *Report of the UNCITRAL on the Work of its Ninth Session*, UN GAOR, 31st Session, Supp No 17, UN Doc A/31/17, para 38 (1976), reprinted in VII UNCITRAL Ybk 66, 69. Others questioned the resources, expertise, or the universality of the UNCITRAL Secretariat in carrying out this task. See UN Doc A/CN.9/SR.163, n 18, at 143 (comment by Mr Gueiros, Brazil); also at 143 (comment by Mr Bennett, Australia); and at 144 (comment by Mr Bennett, Australia).
[22] UN Doc A/CN.9/SR.163, n 18, at 143 (Comment by Mr Jakubowski, Poland).
[23] UN Doc A/CN.9/SR.163, n 18, at 144 (Comment by Mr Jenard, Belgium).
[24] UN Doc A/CN.9/SR.163, n 18, at 145 (Comment by the Chairman).
[25] UN Doc A/CN.9/SR.163, n 18, at 141–2 (Comment by Mr Pirrung, Federal Republic of Germany).
[26] UN Doc A/31/17, n 21, para 39, reprinted in VII UNCITRAL Ybk 66, 69.
[27] UN Doc A/31/17, n 21, para 40.

PCA adds time and expense to the process, it provides a global system that is likely to yield a particularly knowledgeable appointing authority. In practice, the PCA's role as the designator of the appointing authority has functioned well under the Rules.[28]

As referenced in Article 6(4), the PCA Secretary-General has additional powers pursuant to Article 41(4), discussed in Chapter 27, where an appointing authority fails to act within 30 days on a request by a party to make a decision on the appropriateness of arbitrator fees.

(3) Suspension of time periods in the absence of an appointing authority—Article 6(3)

The UNCITRAL Rules contain a number of time periods within which a party must refer a matter to the appointing authority. For example, pursuant to Article 13(4), a party can pursue a decision on a challenge only after 15 days, but before 30 days, have passed since it submitted its notice of challenge to seek a decision from the appointing authority resolving the matter. Where an appointing authority has not already been designated at the time the notice was filed, such time period would almost certainly elapse while the parties sought agreement on an appointing authority or, if no agreement was reached, enlisted the services of the PCA Secretary-General to designate an appointing authority. In the interests of fairness, practicality, and respect for the parties' rights under the Rules, Article 6(3) allows any time periods for referral to the appointing authority to be "suspended" pending agreement on or designation of an appointing authority. A suspension does not come about automatically when a party pursues a matter to be referred to the appointing authority in the absence of an appointing authority. Rather, according to Article 6(3), a suspension will occur "from the date on which a party initiates the procedure for agreeing on or designating an appointing authority until the date of such agreement or designation." Thus, the party that submits a notice of challenge in the absence of an appointing authority, but fails to seek agreement on or designation of the appointing authority, will not benefit from a suspension of the time period for bringing a challenge, and may ultimately waive its right to have the challenge resolved by the appointing authority.

(4) The role of the appointing authority—Article 6(5)–(7)

In the context of appointing arbitrators, the role of the appointing authority under the UNCITRAL Rules is a limited one. Once the appointing authority confirms its authority to act on behalf of the party, determines its responsibility, and makes the requested appointment, its mandate extinguishes. The appointing authority's duty does not extend beyond considerations of form and process, such as to considering the admissibility of the dispute under the arbitration agreement invoked. According to a former President of the International Court of Justice, Sir Muhammad Zafrulla Khan, such limited review is justified because the appointing authority "is not acting on behalf of the two parties, on the basis of the view of the legal situation which they share . . . [rather] [the appointing authority] is acting on behalf of the party which has requested him to act and on the basis of that party's view of the legal situation."[29] In this sense, the task delegated in advance by the parties to

---

[28] For information on the PCA's process for requesting a designation, see <http://www.pca-cpa.org/showpage.asp?pag_id=1062>.

[29] M Khan, "The Appointment of Arbitrators by the President of the International Court of Justice," (1975) 14 Communicazioni e Studi 1021.

the appointing authority, given certain stipulated conditions of form, is to make a selection on behalf of a party or the parties. The *right* to appoint is with the parties; they have merely delegated the *task* of choosing or selecting the particular person to a third party.

The role of the appointing authority in resolving a challenge to an arbitrator pursuant to Articles 12 and 13 is decidedly broader, though by no means unlimited. As described in detail in Chapter 5, the appointing authority, when requested, is responsible for determining whether doubts as to an arbitrator's impartiality or independence are justifiable, as substantive inquiry which is beyond the purview of the arbitral tribunal. However, this function, like that of appointing arbitrators, does not allow the appointing authority to address the merits of the underlying dispute.

When a referral is made to an institution or a person to serve as appointing authority, the first order of business is for the recipient of the request to confirm whether it has the requisite authority to do so.[30] Only after this confirmation can the individual or institution asked to serve as appointing authority turn to the substance of the matter referred by the party.

Article 6(5) contains general rules governing the process by which the appointing authority exercises its functions under the Rules. On the one hand, the provision grants the appointing authority, in fulfilling its tasks, the power to "require from any party and the arbitrators the information [it] deem[s] necessary." This power may be especially useful in the context of making appointments if more information is required than is found in the notice of arbitration and the response to the notice of arbitration, as discussed below, or in deciding a challenge request based on complex or difficult to obtain factual information. On the other hand, the provision requires that the appointing authority give "the parties, and where appropriate, the arbitrators an opportunity to present their views," though it may do so "in any manner [it] consider[s] appropriate."

Article 6(6) establishes requirements for information production in the specific context of the appointment of arbitrators. Where an appointment is requested pursuant to Article 8, 9, 10, or 14, the requesting party must "send to the appointing authority copies of the notice of arbitration and, if it exists, any response to the notice of arbitration." These documents may be essential in confirming that the recipient of the request has been duly selected to serve as appointing authority and clarifying the task at hand, ie, appointing a sole arbitrator, a presiding arbitrator, or a party-appointed arbitrator.[31] The notice of arbitration, for example, must identify the arbitration agreement, which may indicate the parties' choice of appointing authority and the number of arbitrators, or may contain the claimant's proposals

---

[30] The appointing authority "is necessarily also competent to examine first of all whether the [pre]conditions [necessary] for an appointment have been satisfied." *Sapphire Intl Petroleums* and *National Iranian Oil Co* (Cavin sole arb, March 15, 1963), reprinted in (1968) 35 ILR 136, 167.

[31] Corresponding Article 8(1) of the 1976 UNCITRAL Rules was not discussed in depth during its drafting. It was intended to ensure that appointments by the appointing authority are successful, an objective which in the opinion of the original drafters required that the appointing authority had sufficient information to complete his or her tasks. Thus, as the representative of Mexico stated: "The important point was that the appointing authority should know what the dispute involved; accordingly, the claimant should enclose a summary of the dispute in the application and, possibly, a copy of the arbitration agreement." *Summary Record of the 4th Meeting of the Committee of the Whole (II)*, UNCITRAL, 9th Session, UN Doc A/CN.9/9/C.2/SR.4, at 7, para 51 (1976) (Comment by Mr Mantilla-Molina, Mexico). Leading commentators also note:

> The UNCITRAL Rules do not specify the information that must be supplied to the Secretary-General for the purpose of designating an appointing authority, but in practice the Bureau asks for the same documents that are to be provided to an appointing authority under Article 8.1 of the [1976] Rules for the purposes of appointing and arbitrator. These include notice of arbitration, the contract out of or in relation to which the dispute has arisen, and (if it is not contained in that contract) the arbitration agreement. The Secretary-General

on these matters, if no agreement has been reached. The response to the notice of arbitration may indicate the respondent's willingness to agree to any proposals by the claimant.

Article 6(7) states broad criteria for consideration by the appointing authority when making an appointment of an arbitrator. The appointing authority must factor into its decision "considerations as are likely to secure the appointment of an independent and impartial arbitrator." This requirement does not require the appointing authority to appoint an arbitrator that *is* impartial and independent—an unreasonably high standard in practice—but rather one that is *likely* to have these characteristics. Additionally, the appointing authority must consider "the advisability of appointing an arbitrator of a nationality other than the nationalities of the parties." Thus, for example, the appointing authority must determine whether a person who could serve as arbitrator with impartiality and independence would nonetheless be an inappropriate choice because he or she shares the nationality of a party.[32] While this requirement applies generally with respect to all appointments, it is of particular importance with respect to the legitimacy and credibility of the arbitral tribunal in the case of appointment of a sole or presiding arbitrator.

Finally, Article 6(5) contains a general requirement of disclosure of all communications to and from the appointing authority in response to requests for information from the appointing authority or the presentation of views from the parties or, where appropriate, the arbitrators. This rule is useful in keeping all parties apprised of developments in a matter pending before the appointing authority and in ensuring transparency and fairness in the appointing authority's resolution of the matter.

C. Extracts from the Practice of the Iran–US Claims Tribunal

Decision of the Appointing Authority on Iran's Objections to Judge Mangård, March 5, 1982 at 1, 2, 7–9, reprinted in 1 Iran–US CTR 509–19 (1981–1982):

1. *The documents lodged*
    (a) In a letter of January 1, 1982 (with enclosure) addressed to Mr. N. Mangård, a copy of which was sent to the Agent of the United States of America and the Members of the Iran-United States Claims Tribunal, the Agent of the Islamic Republic of Iran stated that Mr. Mangård was disqualified from acting as a "neutral" arbitrator for the Iran-United States Claims Tribunal and chairman of its number 3 chamber.
    (b) In a letter of January 8, 1982 addressed to the Secretary-General of the Permanent Court of Arbitration, the Agent of the United States did not agree to the challenge, and requested the Secretary-General to designate an Appointing Authority.
    ...
    (e) The Secretary-General of the Permanent Court of Arbitration designated Us to be the Appointing Authority in a letter of January 13, 1982.
    (f) In his letter of January 15, 1982 to the Secretary-General of the Permanent Court of Arbitration the Agent of the Islamic Republic of Iran submitted that the contents of his letter referred to above under (a) cannot be described as a "challenge" within the meaning of the [1976] UNCITRAL Rules, and furthermore that the procedure set out

---

will usually also request copies of correspondence indicating that the designation of an appointing authority is necessary because a party has failed to appoint an arbitrator; it has been impossible to reach agreement on a sole or presiding arbitrator or there is a contested challenge of an arbitrator.

N Blackaby and C Partasides, *Redfern and Hunter on International Arbitration*, n 9, 257.

[32] On determining the nationality of a party that is a corporation, see T Webster, *Handbook of UNCITRAL Arbitration: Commentary, Precedents and Materials for UNCITRAL Based Arbitration Rules* (2010) 121.

in Article 6 of the [1976] UNCITRAL Rules was not observed when the Appointing Authority was designated, whereas it should have been.

(g) From the contents of his letter of January 19, 1982 to the Secretary-General of the Permanent Court of Arbitration, it is evident that the Agent of the United States contests the view of the Agent of the Islamic Republic of Iran contained in the letter referred to above under (f).

(h) In a letter of January 21, 1982 to the Agent of the Islamic Republic of Iran, copies of which were sent to the President of the Iran-United States Claims Tribunal, the Agent of the United States and Ourselves, the Secretary-General of the Permanent Court of Arbitration confirmed Our designation as Appointing Authority.

...

3.3 The combined effect of [the Claims Settlement Declaration and Articles 6 and 10–12 of the [1976] UNCITRAL Rules], which to date have not been amended either by the Parties or the Tribunal, is that the person designated as Appointing Authority by the Secretary-General of the Permanent Court of Arbitration at The Hague pursuant to Article 12(1)(c) in conjunction with Article 6 is empowered to interpret both the agreement referred to above under 3.1 and the [1976] UNCITRAL Rules, in so far as they are relevant to the matter instituted before him.

3.4 According to the documents lodged in the case, the Islamic Republic of Iran bases its assertion that We are not competent to hear the case instituted before Us, on the contention that the designation referred to above under 1(e) is not valid in law. This contention cannot be accepted as correct for the following reasons.

...

3.6 The contention that pursuant to the provisions of Article 12(1)(c), in conjunction with Article 6, of the [1976] UNCITRAL Rules, the Secretary-General of the Permanent Court of Arbitration at The Hague is not empowered to designate an Appointing Authority until the Parties have been unable to reach agreement on the designation by them in mutual consultation of an Appointing Authority is based on an incorrect interpretation of the provisions in question. The arrangement provided for in Article 12(1)(a) and (b) relates to cases in which the appointment of the challenged arbitrator was made by an Appointing Authority or, alternatively, in which an Appointing Authority was designated during the procedure leading to the appointment of the challenged arbitrator.

Article 12 provides that in such cases the decision on the challenge shall be made by the Appointing Authority. The clear intention of this rule is to ensure that a speedy decision can be taken on the challenge.

In the light of this, it must be assumed that the rule contained in Article 12(1)(c) is also intended to make it possible in the cases referred to therein to designate an Appointing Authority to decide on the challenge as quickly and as simply as possible.

Therefore, the rule which Article 12(1)(c) contains to the effect that the designation of the Appointing Authority must be "in accordance with the procedure for designating an appointing authority as provided for in Article 6" has to be interpreted as meaning that except in cases in which the Parties have agreed upon an Appointing Authority in the context of the procedure relating to the appointment of an arbitrator, the Secretary-General of the Permanent Court of Arbitration at The Hague is empowered to designate an Appointing Authority to decide on a challenge, if he receives a request to that effect from one of the Parties.

This interpretation is supported by the history of the proceedings leading to the adoption of the [1976] UNCITRAL Rules. At the conference which adopted the rules, a draft of Article 6 prepared by the Secretariat requiring that the Parties endeavour to reach agreement on the choice of an Appointing Authority, was rejected in favour of a Belgian proposal in which there was no requirement to seek agreement (UN Doc. A/CN.9/112; UN Doc. A/CN.9/112/Add. 1; UN Doc. A/CN.9/9/C.2/SR.3).

3. The Number of Arbitrators—Article 7

A. Text of the 2010 UNCITRAL Rule[33]

Article 7 of the 2010 UNCITRAL Rules provides:

1. If the parties have not previously agreed on the number of arbitrators, and if within 30 days after the receipt by the respondent of the notice of arbitration the parties have not agreed that there shall be only one arbitrator, three arbitrators shall be appointed.
2. Notwithstanding paragraph 1, if no other parties have responded to a party's proposal to appoint a sole arbitrator within the time limit provided for in paragraph 1 and the party or parties concerned have failed to appoint a second arbitrator in accordance with article 9 or 10, the appointing authority may, at the request of a party, appoint a sole arbitrator pursuant to the procedure provided for in article 8, paragraph 2, if it determines that, in view of the circumstances of the case, this is more appropriate.

B. Commentary

(1) The default rule on the number of arbitrators—Article 7(1)

Article 7(1) establishes the default rule on the number of arbitrators. If the parties have not agreed on the number of arbitrators, including whether to employ a sole arbitrator, the arbitral tribunal shall be comprised of three arbitrators. This default rule takes effect 30 days from the date of respondent's receipt of the notice of arbitration, the same time period that the respondent has to communicate its response to the notice of arbitration, which must include the respondent's proposal on the number of arbitrators.[34] Thus, if the parties fail to reach agreement on the number of arbitrators after the notice of arbitration and response are exchanged, a three-member tribunal will decide the dispute.

During discussions of corresponding Article 5 of the 1976 UNCITRAL Rules, some delegates favored a default rule that resulted in a sole arbitrator if the parties could not agree on the number of arbitrators. Proponents of this approach argued that: (1) the arbitration would be less expensive if only one arbitrator was used;[35] (2) such expense may be of great significance when the "parties [are] of different economic strength, [and] the weaker party would be at an economic disadvantage if the stronger party insisted on a three-member

---

[33] Corresponding Article 5 of the 1976 UNCITRAL Rules provides: "If the parties have not previously agreed on the number of arbitrators (i.e. one or three), and if within fifteen days after the receipt by the respondent of the notice of arbitration the parties have not agreed that there shall be only one arbitrator, three arbitrators shall be appointed."

[34] For consistency with the time limits in other revised provisions, the Working Group expanded the time limit in Article 7(1) from 15 to 30 days. *Report of Working Group II (Arbitration and Conciliation) on the Work of its Forty-Ninth Session* (Vienna, September 15–19, 2008), UNCITRAL, 42nd Session, UN Doc A/CN.9/665, at 13, para 65 (2008). During the drafting of corresponding Article 5 of the 1976 UNCITRAL Rules, the technical question of how long the parties should be given to agree upon the number of arbitrators after receipt by the respondent of the notice of arbitration was the only other issue discussed at any length. The preliminary draft proposed for this Article allowed only eight days for agreements to be reached. *Report of the Secretary-General on the Preliminary Draft Set of Arbitration Rules*, UNCITRAL, 8th Session, UN Doc A/CN.9/97 (1974), reprinted in (1975) VI UNCITRAL Ybk 163, 168 (1975): "The 8-day period is believed sufficient to allow the parties to communicate and reach an agreement as to the desired number of arbitrators." "There was general agreement that the period of eight days . . . was too short and should be extended." *Report of the UNCITRAL*, 8th Session, Summary of Discussion of the Preliminary Draft, UN Doc A/10017, para 41 (1975), reprinted in (1975) VI UNCITRAL Ybk 24, 29.

[35] UN Doc A/10017, n 34, para 39.

tribunal";[36] (3) "[i]t was not for the arbitrators to act [as is 'traditional and statistical' of the party-appointed arbitrators] as lawyers for the parties [and a] single arbitrator would therefore be preferable";[37] and (4) the arbitral proceeding would be speedier.[38]

The discussions to revise the Rules some 35 years later heard many of the same arguments as originally proposed.[39] Some delegates, for example, maintained that a sole arbitrator would render arbitration "less costly," thus making it "more accessible, particularly to poorer parties in less complex cases."[40] Because many disputes under the UNCITRAL Rules that were brought to the PCA's attention involved small claims, it was believed that a default rule requiring three arbitrators would be "overly burdensome" to the parties in many cases.[41]

These arguments, both then and now, stand in stark contrast to others in favor of a three-arbitrator default rule. The *travaux préparatoires* indicate that many of the original drafters of the 1976 UNCITRAL Rules contended that: (1) customary practice endorsed the appointment of three arbitrators;[42] (2) "the presence of three arbitrators was necessary to ensure that the tribunal possessed a sufficient degree of competence and expertise";[43] and (3) the two party-appointed arbitrators often "brought to the tribunal a special knowledge of the commercial law and practice of the country to which the party who nominated him belonged."[44] In addition to similar arguments with respect to arbitral practice,[45] some delegates of the Working Group charged with revising the Rules noted more recently that a three-member tribunal could "enhance the legitimacy of the arbitral tribunal and better guarantee impartiality and fairness of the proceedings."[46] In complex cases, some also argued that a default rule requiring a sole arbitrator might not be appropriate.[47]

---

[36] *Summary Record of the 3rd Meeting of the Committee of the Whole (II)*, UNCITRAL, 9th Session, UN Doc A/CN.9/9/C.2/SR.3, at 2, para 5 (1976) (Comment by Mr Melis, Australia).

[37] UN Doc A/CN.9/9/C.2/SR.3, n 36, para 3 (Comment by Mr Mantilla-Molina, Mexico).

[38] UN Doc A/31/17, n 21, para 127, reprinted in (1976) VII UNCITRAL Ybk 66, 68 (Commentary on Draft Article 6).

[39] One proposal in support of a sole arbitrator provided: "If the parties have not previously agreed on the number of arbitrators, one arbitrator shall be appointed, unless either the claimant, in its notice of arbitration, or the respondent, within thirty days after receipt of the notice of arbitration, requests that there be three, in which case three arbitrators shall be appointed." *Settlement of Commercial Disputes: Revision of the UNCITRAL Arbitration Rules, Note by the Secretariat*, UNCITRAL, UN Doc A/CN.9/WG.II/WP.147 at 12, para 34 (2007).

[40] *Report of the Working Group on Arbitration and Conciliation on the Work of its Forty-Fifth Session* (Vienna, September 11–15, 2006), UNCITRAL, 40th Session, UN Doc A/CN.9/614, at 13–14, para 60 (2007).

[41] *Report of Working Group II (Arbitration and Conciliation) on the Work of its Forty-Ninth Session* (Vienna, September 15–19, 2008], UNCITRAL, 42nd Session, UN Doc A/CN.9/665, at 12, para 59 (2008); *Report of the Working Group on Arbitration and Conciliation on the Work of its Forty-Sixth Session* (New York, February 5–9, 2007), UNCITRAL, 40th Session, UN Doc A/CN.9/619, at 17–18, para 81 (2007).

[42] UN Doc A/10017, n 34, para 39, reprinted in (1975) VI UNCITRAL Ybk 24, 28. It is certainly true that the customary practice of public international arbitration supports the appointment of three members. See G Raymond, *Conflict Resolution and the Structure of the State System—An Analysis of Arbitrative Settlements* (1980) 21 ("When the raw data were coded according to the type of arbitrator utilized, only thirty percent of the arbitrations since the Congress of Vienna were seen to have employed individual arbitrators. Furthermore, regardless of the diplomatic period analyzed, tribunals were clearly utilized more than individuals . . .").

[43] UN Doc A/10017, n 34, para 39, reprinted in (1975) VI UNCITRAL Ybk 24, 28.

[44] UN Doc A/10017, n 34, para 39.

[45] They said that arbitral practice indicated that parties preferred a "three member panel which allowed them to choose at least one arbitrator." *Report of the Working Group on Arbitration and Conciliation on the Work of its Forty-Fifth Session* (Vienna, September 11–15, 2006), UNCITRAL, 40th Session, UN Doc A/CN.9/614, at 13–14, para 60 (2007).

[46] UNCITRAL, 42nd Session, UN Doc A/CN.9/665, n 34, at 12, para 58.

[47] UN Doc A/CN.9/665, n 34, at 12, para 58.

The age-old debate over a sole arbitrator versus three arbitrators has twice ended in deep division, but with a preference for using a three-arbitrator tribunal as the default structure.[48] More recently, in revising the Rules a failure to reach consensus on the issue resulted in retention of the default rule under the 1976 UNCITRAL Rules, with a minor revision to ensure consistency with other changes to the Rules.[49]

The three-member default rule twice adopted by UNCITRAL represents a choice that has worked well in practice under the Rules, including the experience of party-appointed arbitrators in investor–state arbitrations and both Iranian and American arbitrators with the Iran–US Claims Tribunal. A three-member panel has been preferable for these tribunals for exactly the reasons stated by the members of the original UNCITRAL Drafting Committee: the party-appointed arbitrators, particularly those appointed by the respondent, in many investor–state arbitrations, like the Iranian and American arbitrators on the Iran–US Claims Tribunal, have often found themselves, for example, explaining aspects of the respondent's national laws and regulations.[50]

A further reason in favor of the three-arbitrator rule is more psychological: the presence of a colleague sets up a dialogue that yields deliberations that are necessarily more refined and exacting.[51] It is all too easy for a sole arbitrator to focus upon one particular aspect of a complex case and for his views on that aspect to not benefit from discussion. It is true that national trial courts often are presided over by one judge, but such courts allow appeals unlike arbitral decisions. This psychological factor supports the three-member panel position, but to a large degree does not require that the two be party-appointed. The practice of party-appointed arbitrators is discussed further below. Suffice to say here that there is significant precedent for the UNCITRAL Rules to include party-appointed arbitrators as part of the panel. Moreover, party-appointed arbitrators strive to ensure that the position of the party that appointed them is fully considered, which increases the thoroughness, if not also the intensity, of the dialogue.

Pragmatically, a three-member panel is also desirable because it increases the probability of the tribunal possessing the required degree of competence. Persons who dealt with appointments at the Iran–US Claims Tribunal, for example, universally found it difficult to predict how competent a particular arbitrator would be. The competence of arbitrators may be surprising even when the reputation and personal history of the arbitrator and the personal views of others who have appeared before him are known.[52]

Given that "experience shows that at least one of the parties will insist on a three-member panel," the approach of the UNCITRAL Rules means that a panel of three will virtually always be used.[53]

---

[48] But see UN Doc A/31/17, n 21, para 29, reprinted in (1976) VII UNCITRAL Ybk 66, 68 ("Three representatives expressed their reservation and noted their preference for the constitution of a tribunal composed of one arbitrator in the case of failure of the parties to agree on the arbitrators").

[49] The original 15-day time limit was extended to 30 days in order to correspond with the respondent's time limit for communicating a response to the notice of arbitration, which must contain a proposal on the number of arbitrators. UNCITRAL, 42nd Session, UN Doc A/CN.9/665, n 34, at 13, para 61.

[50] Indeed, the national law of one of the state parties can be so central to the dispute that both parties appoint an arbitrator with knowledge of that particular law. In the NAFTA Chapter Eleven arbitration between *Glamis Gold Ltd* and *United States*, for example, all three members of the arbitral panel were nationals of the United States.

[51] See R D Bishop, "The Quality of Arbitral Decision-Making and Justification," 6 World Arb and Mediation Rev (forthcoming 2013).

[52] See W Craig, W Park and J Paulsson, *International Chamber of Commerce Arbitration* §12.02, (3rd edn 2000) 190–1.

[53] Craig, et al, *International Chamber of Commerce Arbitration*, n 52, 190–1. See also G Raymond, *Conflict Resolution and the Structure of the State System*, n 42.

(2) The exception to the default rule of three arbitrators—Article 7(2)

Article 7(2) establishes a limited exception to the default rule of three arbitrators. During Working Group discussions to revise the Rules, concerns were raised that the default rule could be counter-productive in situations "where, despite the claimant's proposal in its notice of arbitration to appoint a sole arbitrator, a three-member arbitral tribunal had to be constituted due to the respondent's failure to react to that proposal."[54] If the cases did not warrant a three-member tribunal, many believed that the Rules should contain a "corrective mechanism" to allow for the option, if appropriate, of appointing a sole arbitrator.[55] The solution was found in involving the appointing authority in the process. Pursuant to Article 7(2), where a party has failed to respond to a proposal on the number of arbitrators within 30 days after the claimant has submitted its notice of arbitration, the appointing authority, at the request of the claimant, may appoint a sole arbitrator.

Enhancing the role of the appointing authority in this regard was a step that the Working Group took cautiously. The issue of greater involvement by the appointing authority arose initially during discussions over an appropriate default rule on the number of arbitrators. Delegates noted that under the rules of some arbitral institutions, a sole arbitrator was appointed by default, but that the institution retained discretion to appoint three arbitrators, if appropriate, subject to contrary agreement by the parties.[56] Since the UNCITRAL Rules were designed primarily for application in *ad hoc* arbitration, outside the framework of an arbitral institution, it was suggested that the appointing authority could be granted the discretion to intervene and reverse the default rule in favor of three arbitrators.[57]

This proposal was strongly opposed on various grounds: (1) "such discretion fell outside the traditional role for appointing authorities"; (2) it could "introduce a further level of delay in the arbitral proceedings"; (3) "at the time of appointment of arbitrators, there might not be an appointing authority"; and (4) "leaving the question of the number of arbitrators to the appointing authority based on the subjective question of whether or not

---

[54] UNCITRAL, 42nd Session, UN Doc A/CN.9/665, n 34, at 13, para 62.
[55] UNCITRAL, 42nd Session, UN Doc A/CN.9/665, n 34, at 13, para 63.
[56] UNCITRAL, 40th Session, UN Doc A/CN.9/614, n 40, at 13–14, para 60.

The Swiss Rules of International Arbitration for example, which in their 2004 version were stated to be based on the UNCITRAL Rules with "[c]hanges and additions reflecting modern practice," have a default toward a sole arbitrator unless circumstances justify otherwise. Article 6 of the 2012 Swiss Rules (which is substantially similar to the 2004 version) provides:

NUMBER OF ARBITRATORS
Article 6
1. If the parties have not agreed upon the number of arbitrators, the Court shall decide whether the case shall be referred to a sole arbitrator or to a three-member arbitral tribunal, taking into account all relevant circumstances.
2. As a rule, the Court shall refer the case to a sole arbitrator, unless the complexity of the subject matter and/or the amount in dispute justify that the case be referred to a three-member arbitral tribunal.
3. If the arbitration agreement provides for an arbitral tribunal composed of more than one arbitrator, and this appears inappropriate in view of the amount in dispute or of other circumstances, the Court shall invite the parties to agree to refer the case to a sole arbitrator.
4. Where the amount in dispute does not exceed CHF 1,000,000 (one million Swiss francs), Article 42(2) (Expedited Procedure) shall apply.

[57] UNCITRAL, 40th Session, UN Doc A/CN.9/614, n 40, at 13–14, para 60.

a case was complex introduced a level of uncertainty."[58] In the end, the Working Group decided to expand the role of the designating authority only to the extent provided for in Article 7(2).

In contrast to the initial, broad proposal, the role for the appointing authority under Article 7(2) was meant to be limited. The Working Group recognized that the new procedural mechanism would likely not create significantly longer delays—a principal concern of many of the drafters—than already expected in a case where the respondent had failed to appoint an arbitrator and the appointing authority's involvement was required in any event.[59] Still, the provision adds a new dimension to the responsibilities of the appointing authority, who must already make an appointment likely to secure the appointment of an impartial and independent arbitrator, taking into account the nationality of the appointed arbitrator. Article 7(2) further requires that the appointing authority understand the substance and nature of the underlying dispute, at least well enough to determine whether a sole arbitrator would be most appropriate for resolving the dispute.

(3) A number of arbitrators other than one or three

Although the UNCITRAL Rules expressly contemplate arbitration under a one- or three-member tribunal, they do not exclude the possibility of a tribunal comprised of a different number of arbitrators.[60] Some systems of arbitration, such as the one established under the UNCITRAL Model Law, permit other options such as two-member tribunals. The UNCITRAL drafters considered revising the Rules to include a provision clarifying that the parties were free to derogate from Article 7, if they so desired.[61] The draft provision provided: "If the parties decide that the arbitral tribunal is to be composed of a number of arbitrators other than one or three, the arbitrators shall be appointed according to the methods agreed upon by the parties."[62] The stated purpose of the draft provision was "to clarify that... if the parties wish to derogate from that rule [of one or three arbitrators] (e.g., to have a two-member arbitral tribunal, which is allowed by the UNCITRAL Model Law), they should define their own method for the constitution of the arbitral tribunal."[63]

Without any recorded discussion, the provision was dropped from the 2010 Rules, perhaps because the draft provision was redundant of Article 1 of the Rules, under which the parties may modify any rule to the extent permissible under mandatory laws.[64] However, should the parties seek to have a tribunal constituted with a number of arbitrators other than one or three, they should carefully consider whether such an alternative structure will function effectively with other provisions in the UNCITRAL Rules.

---

[58] UNCITRAL, 40th Session, UN Doc A/CN.9/614, n 40, at 13–14, para 60. On the problem of delays, UNCITRAL, 40th Session, UN Doc A/CN.9/619, n 3, at 17, para 80, and UNCITRAL, 42nd Session, UN Doc A/CN.9/665, n 34, at 13, para 60.

[59] UNCITRAL, 42nd Session, UN Doc A/CN.9/665, n 34, at 13, para 63.

[60] To the contrary, Article 10(2), discussed below, expressly recognizes this possibility: "If the parties have agreed that the arbitral tribunal is to be composed of a number of arbitrators other than one or three, the arbitrators shall be appointed according to the method agreed upon by the parties."

[61] *Settlement of Commercial Disputes: Revision of the UNCITRAL Arbitration Rules, Note by the Secretariat*, UNCITRAL, UN Doc A/CN.9/WG.II/WP.145 at 13 (2006) (Draft Article 5(2).

[62] UNCITRAL, UN Doc A/CN.9/WG.II/WP.145, n 61, at 13 (Draft Article 5(2).

[63] UNCITRAL, UN Doc A/CN.9/WG.II/WP.145, n 61, at 13 (Draft Article 5(2), para 44.

[64] Note that some countries prohibit arbitration by an uneven number of arbitrators, such as in France (in domestic arbitrations), the Netherlands, Belgium, Italy, Portugal, Egypt and Tunisia. See G Born, *International Commercial Arbitration*, n 9, 1352.

4. Appointment of the Sole Arbitrator—Article 8

A. Text of the 2010 UNCITRAL Rule[65]

Article 8 of the 2010 UNCITRAL Rules provides:

1. If the parties have agreed that a sole arbitrator is to be appointed and if within 30 days after receipt by all other parties of a proposal for the appointment of a sole arbitrator the parties have not reached agreement thereon, a sole arbitrator shall, at the request of a party, be appointed by the appointing authority.
2. The appointing authority shall appoint the sole arbitrator as promptly as possible. In making the appointment, the appointing authority shall use the following list-procedure, unless the parties agree that the list-procedure should not be used or unless the appointing authority determines in its discretion that the use of the list-procedure is not appropriate for the case:
   (a) The appointing authority shall communicate to each of the parties an identical list containing at least three names;
   (b) Within 15 days after the receipt of this list, each party may return the list to the appointing authority after having deleted the name or names to which it objects and numbered the remaining names on the list in the order of its preference;
   (c) After the expiration of the above period of time the appointing authority shall appoint the sole arbitrator from among the names approved on the lists returned to it and in accordance with the order of preference indicated by the parties;
   (d) If for any reason the appointment cannot be made according to this procedure, the appointing authority may exercise its discretion in appointing the sole arbitrator.

---

[65] Corresponding Article 6 of the 1976 UNCITRAL Rules provides:
1. If a sole arbitrator is to be appointed, either party may propose to the other:
   (a) The names of one or more persons, one of whom would serve as the sole arbitrator; and
   (b) If no appointing authority has been agreed upon by the parties, the name or names of one or more institutions or persons, one of whom would serve as appointing authority.
2. If within thirty days after receipt by a party of a proposal made in accordance with paragraph 1 the parties have not reached agreement on the choice of a sole arbitrator, the sole arbitrator shall be appointed by the appointing authority agreed upon by the parties. If no appointing authority has been agreed upon by the parties, or if the appointing authority agreed upon refuses to act or fails to appoint the arbitrator within sixty days of the receipt of a party's request therefor, either party may request the Secretary-General of the Permanent Court of Arbitration at The Hague to designate an appointing authority.
3. The appointing authority shall, at the request of one of the parties, appoint the sole arbitrator as promptly as possible. In making the appointment the appointing authority shall use the following list-procedure, unless both parties agree that the list-procedure should not be used or unless the appointing authority determines in its discretion that the use of the list-procedure is not appropriate for the case:
   (a) At the request of one of the parties the appointing authority shall communicate to both parties an identical list containing at least three names;
   (b) Within fifteen days after the receipt of this list, each party may return the list to the appointing authority after having deleted the name or names to which he objects and numbered the remaining names on the list in the order of his preference;
   (c) After the expiration of the above period of time the appointing authority shall appoint the sole arbitrator from among the names approved on the lists returned to it and in accordance with the order of preference indicated by the parties;
   (d) If for any reason the appointment cannot be made according to this procedure, the appointing authority may exercise its discretion in appointing the sole arbitrator.
4. In making the appointment, the appointing authority shall have regard to such considerations as are likely to secure the appointment of an independent and impartial arbitrator and shall take into account as well the advisability of appointing an arbitrator of a nationality other than the nationalities of the parties.

B. Commentary

Where the parties have agreed that a sole arbitrator will preside but have not chosen the particular individual to serve in that capacity, Article 8 dictates the appointment procedure. Article 8(1) establishes the appointing authority's power to appoint, which arises 30 days after receipt by all other parties of a party's proposal to name a sole arbitrator. Under the Rules, the claimant typically has the first opportunity to propose the name of a sole arbitrator in its notice of arbitration, pursuant to Article 3(4)(b), though proposals can be made later by either the claimant or the respondent.[66]

The Rules place no restrictions on the nationality of the person who may be selected to serve as sole arbitrator. The issue arose during negotiation of the preliminary draft of corresponding Article 6 of the 1976 UNCITRAL Rules, which provided that the sole arbitrator "shall be of a nationality other than the nationality of the parties."[67] The provision was "designed to ensure the neutrality of the sole arbitrator."[68] This limitation was deleted, however, because it was viewed as an unnecessary limitation on "the autonomy of the parties" that might lead to the disqualification of "the most competent person."[69]

Where no agreement has been reached on the choice of the sole arbitrator within 30 days after a proposal has been properly communicated, the appointing authority, at the request of a party, may make the necessary appointment pursuant to the following requirements.

The appointing authority shall under Article 8(2) appoint a sole arbitrator "as promptly as possible." It must also use a "list-procedure" to perform the appointment, unless the parties unanimously object to use of the list-procedure or the appointing authority concludes that the procedure "is not appropriate for the case."[70] The list-procedure entails the following:

(a) The appointing authority shall communicate to each of the parties an identical list containing at least three names;
(b) Within 15 days after the receipt of this list, each party may return the list to the appointing authority after having deleted the name or names to which it objects and numbered the remaining names on the list in the order of its preference;
(c) After the expiration of the above period of time the appointing authority shall appoint the sole arbitrator from among the names approved on the lists returned to it and in accordance with the order of preference indicated by the parties.

If the list-procedure fails to produce a mutually agreeable choice of sole arbitrator, the appointing authority may exercise its discretion and appoint a sole arbitrator. Given that 30 days must elapse before an appointing authority becomes authorized to make the

---

[66] If the claimant has not made a proposal, then the respondent may wish to do so in its response to the notice of arbitration, pursuant to Article 4(2)(c).

[67] *Report of the Secretary-General on the Preliminary Draft Set of Arbitration Rules*, UNCITRAL 8th Session, UN Doc A/CN.9/97 (1974), reprinted in (1975) VI UNCITRAL Ybk 163, 168 (Draft Article 6(1)). Article 6(1) of the 1976 UNCITRAL Rules provides that "either party may propose to the other . . . [t]he names of one or more persons, one of whom would serve as the sole arbitrator . . ."

[68] UNCITRAL 8th Session, UN Doc A/CN.9/97, n 67, (Commentary on Draft Article 6(1)).

[69] *Report of the UNCITRAL*, 8th Session, Summary of Discussion of the Preliminary Draft, UN Doc A/10017, para 44 (1975), reprinted in (1975) VI UNCITRAL Ybk 24, 30. It was also noted that "a determination as to the nationality of the parties might cause serious difficulties where one or both of the parties was a firm, corporation or enterprise." (Para 48). See Article 6(7) for the emergence of this factor in the considerations of the appointing authority.

[70] One commentator proposes avoiding use of the list-procedure "[i]f it is urgent that proceedings be commenced" or "if [the appointing authority] is concerned it will result in systematic rejection of names on the list by one party." T Webster, *Handbook of UNCITRAL Arbitration*, n 32, 131–2.

appointment and that at least 30 days are required to exhaust the steps of the list-procedure, appointment of a sole arbitrator over the opposition of a party would require at least, and probably more than, 60 days under the Rules and closer to 90 to 120 days in practice. Appointment of a sole arbitrator by the appointing authority, pursuant to Article 8, is subject to the requirements of Article 6, discussed above, which apply to the appointment process more generally. Noteworthy is the general requirement that the appointing authority take into account "the advisability of appointing an arbitrator of a nationality other than the nationalities of the parties."[71] While, as discussed above, the parties themselves enjoy complete freedom to select a sole arbitrator that shares the nationality of a party, the appointing authority must consider the broader implications of such an appointment, such as its effect on the legitimacy of the arbitral process.

5. Appointment of a Three-Person Panel—Article 9

A. Text of the 2010 UNCITRAL Rule[72]

Article 9 of the 2010 UNCITRAL Rules provides:

1. If three arbitrators are to be appointed, each party shall appoint one arbitrator. The two arbitrators thus appointed shall choose the third arbitrator who will act as the presiding arbitrator of the arbitral tribunal.
2. If within 30 days after the receipt of a party's notification of the appointment of an arbitrator the other party has not notified the first party of the arbitrator it has appointed, the first party may request the appointing authority to appoint the second arbitrator.
3. If within 30 days after the appointment of the second arbitrator the two arbitrators have not agreed on the choice of the presiding arbitrator, the presiding arbitrator shall be appointed by the appointing authority in the same way as a sole arbitrator would be appointed under article 8.

B. Commentary

(1) The right of each party to appoint an arbitrator

Article 9 provides that when a three-member tribunal is to be appointed "each party shall appoint one arbitrator." Except for the provision for challenge by the other party, the Rules

---

[71] 2010 UNCITRAL Arbitration Rules, art 6(7).
[72] Corresponding Article 7 of the 1976 UNCITRAL Rules provides:

1. If three arbitrators are to be appointed, each party shall appoint one arbitrator. The two arbitrators thus appointed shall choose the third arbitrator who will act as the presiding arbitrator of the tribunal.
2. If within thirty days after the receipt of a party's notification of the appointment of an arbitrator the other party has not notified the first party of the arbitrator he has appointed:
    (a) The first party may request the appointing authority previously designated by the parties to appoint the second arbitrator; or
    (b) If no such authority has been previously designated by the parties, or if the appointing authority previously designated refuses to act or fails to appoint the arbitrator within thirty days after receipt of a party's request therefor, the first party may request the Secretary-General of the Permanent Court of Arbitration at The Hague to designate the appointing authority. The first party may then request the appointing authority so designated to appoint the second arbitrator. In either case, the appointing authority may exercise its discretion in appointing the arbitrator.

specify no limits on this choice. Indeed, a party could even appoint a national of the opposing party's country.

In the past, parties have failed, or even refused, to exercise their rights to appoint a member of a tribunal.[73] The UNCITRAL Rules therefore anticipate this possibility. Thirty days after a party receives notice of the other party's appointment of an arbitrator, the notified party's right to appoint its arbitrator, if it has not yet done so, continues only with prejudice to the party who has appointed. When after the thirty days no appointment has been made by the other party, then the party who has appointed its arbitrator may request the appointing authority to appoint the opposing party's arbitrator.[74]

(2) The appointment of the presiding arbitrator

The two party arbitrators, whether appointed by a party or by the appointing authority, "shall choose the third arbitrator who will act as presiding arbitrator of the tribunal."[75] Thirty days after the appointment of the second party arbitrator, whether such appointment is made by a party or by the appointing authority, if the two arbitrators have not agreed upon a presiding arbitrator, then the appointing authority shall appoint the presiding arbitrator in the same way it would appoint a sole arbitrator.[76]

The ability of the party arbitrators to agree on a third arbitrator rests primarily on the good faith of the arbitrators. The Iran–US Claims Tribunal's party-appointed arbitrators were successful three times in reaching agreement: first in the initial selection of Judges Lagergren, Bellet and Mangård, second in the selection of Judges Briner and Virally, third in the selection of Judges Broms and Arangio-Ruiz.[77] The first time benefited from the air of goodwill present at the inception of the Tribunal. The second followed Iran's internal renewal of its commitment to the Tribunal process, a renewal evidenced by its replacement of Judges Kashani and Shafeiei with Judges Mostafavi and Bahrami. In between these instances were failures at negotiation which led to the appointing authority's selection of Judges Riphagen and Böckstiegel. The third instance of successful negotiation was the agreement to appoint Judges Broms and Arangio-Ruiz. This success, and the subsequent failures in negotiation resulting in the appointing authority's selection of Judges Ruda, Skubiszewski, and van Houtte point to an additional factor possibly explaining the success or failure of such negotiations. In particular, negotiations are more likely to succeed when the party-appointed arbitrators have two, rather than one, position to fill.

---

3. If within thirty days after the appointment of the second arbitrator the two arbitrators have not agreed on the choice of the presiding arbitrator, the presiding arbitrator shall be appointed by an appointing authority in the same way as a sole arbitrator would be appointed under article 6.

[73] See, eg, "*Interpretation of Peace Treaties*," ICJ Reports (1950) 227.

[74] Such an appointment was required in the *Chevron Corp* (1976 Rules), reprinted in section 5(C).

[75] For an application of this same rule under corresponding Article 7(1) of the 1976 UNCITRAL Rules, see *CME Czech Republic* (1976 Rules), and *Jan Oostergetel* (1976 Rules), both reprinted in section 5(C).

[76] 2010 UNCITRAL Arbitration Rules, art 9(3). Although Article 9(3) is silent on the question, the general approach of these articles makes clear that the appointing authority will not act to appoint the presiding arbitrator unless requested to do so by one of the parties. For examples in which the list-procedure was successfully used to appoint the presiding arbitrator under corresponding Article 7(3) of the 1976 UNCITRAL Rules, see *Mystilineos Holdings* (1976 Rules), and *Guaracachi America, Inc* (2010 Rules), both reprinted in section 5(C). For an example in which the list-procedure failed under the same rule, see *Veteran Petroleum Ltd* (1976 Rules), reprinted in section 5(C).

[77] For a discussion of the selection process by an American arbitrator on the Tribunal, see G Aldrich, "The Selection of Arbitrators," in D Caron and J Crook (eds), *The Iran-United States Claims Tribunal and the Process of International Claims Resolution* (2000).

Negotiations between party-appointed arbitrators at the Iran–US Claims Tribunal usually consisted of meetings where a very limited number of names were proposed by each side. The meeting would then adjourn for study of the proposed names. Several difficulties arose. First, it was simply not possible, and equally not always appropriate, to ascertain beforehand whether the proposed individuals would be able or willing to serve. This is most likely far more of a concern, however, for an institution such as the Tribunal where the time commitment required is great. More importantly, the party-appointed arbitrators, in contact on this issue with Agents of the Governments that appointed them, were reluctant to propose all of the individuals in whom they were most interested out of the concern that one of the Governments would later exclude that individual from consideration by the appointing authority.[78] This tendency was most present when a Party suspected that the other was not seriously negotiating. Thus it is not only the lack of good faith but even the perception of lack of good faith that can cripple such negotiations.

The Tribunal's experience indicates that the 30-day period for agreement by the arbitrators on a presiding arbitrator is sufficient. Negotiations for the initial selection of presiding arbitrators began on May 18, 1981 and were concluded on June 4, 1981. Moreover, when negotiations appear productive, it is quite easy to extend the 30-day period simply by refraining from requesting the appointing authority for assistance. This was the case with the appointments of Judges Briner and Virally and Judges Broms and Arangio-Ruiz.[79]

Parties involved in investor–state arbitration under the UNCITRAL Rules should be aware of possible modifications to the selection procedures established in Article 9. The Dominican Republic–Central America–United States Free Trade Agreement ("CAFTA–DR"), for example, pre-empts the default rule in the UNCITRAL Rules by providing that the presiding arbitrator "shall be...appointed by agreement of the disputing parties."[80] If agreement between the parties cannot be reached, the Secretary-General of ICSID, acting as appointing authority, has discretion to make the appointment.[81]

C. Extracts from the Practice of Investment Tribunals

CME Czech Republic BV and *Czech Republic*, Final Award (March 14, 2003) (*Ad Hoc* Proceeding, 1976 UNCITRAL Rules, Netherlands-Czech Republic BIT), reprinted in (2003) 15(4) World Trade & Arbitration Materials 83, 99:

> 34. After having initiated the arbitration proceedings, the Claimant appointed Judge Stephen M. Schwebel, Washington, and the Respondent JUDr. Jaroslav Hándl, Prague, as party-appointed arbitrators. Both arbitrators appointed Dr. Wolfgang Kühn, Düsseldorf, as Chairman of the

---

[78] For a discussion on consultations between co-arbitrators and the parties about the appointment of a presiding arbitrator see G Born, *International Commercial Arbitration*, n 9, 1404 ("At the outset of an arbitration, the co-arbitrators will know relatively little about the parties' dispute or procedural expectations. They will also have little basis for identifying potential conflicts, including positional or similar conflicts, that could make particular proposals for a presiding arbitrator inappropriate or worse. As a consequence, consultations between the co-arbitrators and the parties provide a vital source of information, necessary to select a suitable presiding arbitrator. At the same time, the parties' continued participation in the selection process helps maximize the likelihood that they will have confidence in the arbitral tribunal.").

[79] See Iranian Assets Litigation Rep 10101 (February 22, 1985).

[80] CAFTA–DR, art 10.19(1).

[81] CAFTA–DR, art 10.19(3). See also NAFTA Subchapter B, art 1123.

Arbitral Tribunal on July 19, 2000, which appointment was accepted by the Chairman on July 21, 2000. On September 19, 2000, Dr. Hándl resigned as arbitrator (after the Tribunal rendered a Partial Award on September 13, 2001 (PA), which Dr. Hándl refused to sign). On October 18, 2001 the Respondent appointed Mr. Ian Brownlie C.B.E., Q.C. as arbitrator.

Mystilineos Holdings SA and *State Union of Serbia and Montenegro and Republic of Serbia*, Partial Award on Jurisdiction (September 8, 2006) (*Ad Hoc* Proceeding, 1976 UNCITRAL Rules, Greece-Yugoslavia BIT), at 4–5:

9. On 8 April 2005, Claimant appointed Professor Dr. Stelios Koussoulis as its arbitrator under Article 7(1) of the [1976] UNCITRAL Rules. Professor Dr. Christoph Schreuer was designated as an appointing authority by the Secretary-General of the Permanent Court of Arbitration (the "PCA") under Article 7(2)(b) of the [1976] UNCITRAL Rules on 30 June 2005.
10. On 1 August 2005, Professor Dr. Schreuer appointed Professor Dr. Dobrosav Mitrović as second arbitrator on behalf of Respondents under Article 7(2)(b) of the [1976] UNCITRAL Rules.
11. In accordance with the list-procedure provided for in Articles 7(3) and 6(3) of the [1976] UNCITRAL Rules, during the process of which both parties expressed their preference for the same candidate, the appointing authority appointed Professor Dr. August Reinisch as presiding arbitrator on 20 September 2005 (together with Professors Koussoulis and Mitrović, the "Tribunal").

Chevron Corp, et al and *Republic of Ecuador*, Interim Award (December 1, 2008) (PCA administered), 1976 UNCITRAL Rules, US-Ecuador BIT), at 20–21:

11. On January 16, 2007, the Claimants appointed The Honorable Charles N. Brower as arbitrator.
12. Pursuant to a letter to the Secretary-General of the Permanent Court of Arbitration (the "SG-PCA") dated February 26, 2007, the Claimants formally requested that the SG-PCA designate an appointing authority due to the Respondent's failure to designate an arbitrator within the thirty day period allotted under Article 7(2) [of the 1976] UNCITRAL Arbitration Rules. By letter dated March 2, 2007, the SG-PCA invited the Respondent to comment on the request for designation of an appointing authority. The SG-PCA designated Dr. Robert Briner as appointing authority on March 20, 2007.
13. By letter dated March 21, 2007, the Claimants requested that Dr. Briner, as appointing authority, appoint the second arbitrator on behalf of the Respondent.
14. By letter dated March 26, 2007, the Respondent appointed Prof. Albert Jan van den Berg as the second arbitrator. Dr. Briner, by letter dated April 13, 2007, informed the Parties that he had not yet been able to make any appointment on behalf of the Respondent in his capacity as appointing authority and considered that the issue had become moot.
15. By letter dated May 8, 2007, the two party-appointed arbitrators confirmed, with the consent of the Parties, their appointment of Prof. Dr. Karl-Heinz Böckstiegel as presiding arbitrator.

Veteran Petroleum Ltd and *Russian Federation*, Interim Award (November 30, 2009) (PCA administered, 1976 UNCITRAL Rules, Energy Charter Treaty), at 2–3:

9. By letter dated 4 July 2005, the PCA communicated to the Parties a list of three prospective presiding arbitrators in accordance with the list procedure foreseen in Articles 6(3) and 7(3) of the [1976] UNCITRAL Rules. On 19 July 2005, the Parties communicated their choices to the PCA, but no arbitrator set forth on the list was considered acceptable to both sides. On 20 July 2005, the PCA notified the Parties that the list procedure had failed and on 21 July 2005 the PCA Secretary-General exercised his discretion, pursuant to Article 6(3)(d) of the [1976] UNCITRAL Rules, and directly appointed Maître L. Yves Fortier, CC, QC (the "**Chairman**") as presiding arbitrator.

Guaracachi America, Inc, et al and *Plurinational State of Bolivia*, Letter from the Appointing Authority, Gilbert Guillaume (August 8, 2011) (PCA administered, 2010 UNCITRAL Rules, US-Bolivia BIT/UK-Bolivia BIT), at 1–2:

> On June 20, 2011, the Claimants, following the failure of the co-arbitrators to reach an agreement on the appointment of the presiding arbitrator, requested that I proceed with the appointment of the presiding arbitrator and provided their comments on their desired profile of presiding arbitrator.
>
> On July 1, 2011, the Respondent provided its comments with respect to the Claimants letter and its desired profile of presiding arbitrator.
>
> On July 20, 2011, the PCA, on my behalf sent the Parties a list of five prospective presiding arbitrators, together with the candidates' *curricula vitae* and the disclosure of one candidate, inviting the Parties to return the list of prospective presiding arbitrators by August 4, 2011.
>
> On August 4, 2011, the Parties returned the list of prospective presiding arbitrators, each indicating their preferences.
>
> On the basis of the above, I, Gilbert Guillaume, acting as appointing authority in the above-referenced matter, in accordance with the UNCITRAL Rules, and
>
> (1) having established to my satisfaction my competence to appoint the presiding arbitrator in this matter;
> (2) having confirmed that the person named below is available and willing to act in this matter; and
> (3) that the person named below has declared that he is impartial and independent with respect to each of the Parties and intends to remain so; hereby appoint as presiding arbitrator in the above-referenced matter: Dr. José Miguel Júdice

Chevron Corp, et al and *Republic of Ecuador*, Final Award (August 31, 2011) (PCA administered, 1976 UNCITRAL Rules, US-Ecuador BIT), at 42:

> 94. Pursuant to a letter to the SG-PCA dated February 26, 2007, the Claimants formally requested that the SG-PCA designate an appointing authority due to the Respondent's failure to designate an arbitrator within the thirty-day period allotted under Article 7(2) of the [1976] UNCITRAL Arbitration Rules. By letter dated March 2, 2007, the SG-PCA invited the Respondent to comment on the request for designation of an appointing authority by March 16, 2007. No comments were submitted by the Respondent. The SG-PCA designated Dr. Robert Briner as appointing authority on March 20, 2007.

Guaracachi America, Inc, et al *and Plurinational State of Bolivia,* Terms of Appointment and Procedural Order No 1 (December 9, 2011) (PCA administered, 2010 UNCITRAL Rules, US-Bolivia BIT/UK-Bolivia BIT), at 1–2:

> 4.4 The Parties confirm that the members of the Tribunal have been validly appointed in accordance with the Treaty and the UNCITRAL Rules (as defined in section 5 below).

Jan Oostergetel, et al and *Slovak Republic,* Final Award (April 23, 2012) (*Ad Hoc* Proceeding, 1976 UNCITRAL Rules, Netherlands-Slovak Republic BIT), at 13:

> 51. Following the resignation of Dr. Briner on 28 July 2009, the Party-appointed arbitrators appointed Prof. Kaufmann-Kohler to act as the President of the Tribunal. On 7 September 2009, Prof. Kaufman-Kohler advised the Parties that she had accepted her appointment as President of the Tribunal.

6. Appointment in Multi-Party Arbitration—Article 10

A. Text of the 2010 UNCITRAL Rule[82]

Article 10 of the 2010 UNCITRAL Rules provides:

1. For the purposes of article 9, paragraph 1, where three arbitrators are to be appointed and there are multiple parties as claimant or as respondent, unless the parties have agreed to another method of appointment of arbitrators, the multiple parties jointly, whether as claimant or as respondent, shall appoint an arbitrator.
2. If the parties have agreed that the arbitral tribunal is to be composed of a number of arbitrators other than one or three, the arbitrators shall be appointed according to the method agreed upon by the parties.
3. In the event of any failure to constitute the arbitral tribunal under these Rules, the appointing authority shall, at the request of any party, constitute the arbitral tribunal and, in doing so, may revoke any appointment already made and appoint or reappoint each of the arbitrators and designate one of them as the presiding arbitrator.

B. Commentary

The involvement of multiple parties in an arbitration poses unique challenges for the appointment of arbitrators. Competing interests among a group of claimants or respondents may impede the consensus typically required to make arbitrator appointments. The problem may arise, for example, in arbitration involving a large group of shareholders that "d[o] not form a single group with common rights and obligations."[83] Article 10 addresses the problem by requiring claimants or respondents to appoint their respective arbitrators jointly, while empowering the appointing authority to make any necessary appointments in the event agreement on a joint appointment cannot be reached.

(1) *The requirements for appointment—Article 10(1) and (2)*

Article 10(1) modifies the basic rules of appointment established in Article 9(1), which allows "each party" to appoint "one arbitrator." Under Article 10(1), a group of claimants or respondents must make their appointment "jointly." An express exception to this requirement applies where the parties have "agreed to another method of appointment of arbitrators."[84]

Article 10(2) contains a rule for special cases in which the parties have agreed that the arbitral tribunal will be composed of a number of arbitrators other than one or three. In that situation, the arbitrators are to be appointed pursuant to the agreed upon method.

---

[82] No corresponding provision exists in the 1976 UNCITRAL Rules.

[83] *Report of the Working Group on Arbitration and Conciliation on the Work of its Forty-Fifth Session* (Vienna, September 11–15, 2006), UNCITRAL, 40th Session, UN Doc A/CN.9/614, at 14, para 63 (2007).

[84] In one case, 21 parties to a telecommunications shareholder's agreement derogated from the appointment procedures of the 1976 UNCITRAL Rules and devised their own appointment process that delegated responsibility for all appointments to a three-arbitrator tribunal to the Chief Judge of the Federal High Court of Nigeria. See *Econet Wireless Ltd* and *First Bank of Nigeria,* et al, Award (June 2, 2005) (*Ad Hoc* Proceeding, 1976 UNCITRAL Rules, Contract).

(2) The power of the appointing authority to appoint and reappoint—Article 10(3)

Where a group of claimants or respondents fails to jointly appoint an arbitrator pursuant to Article 10(1), the appointing authority is empowered, at the request of any party, to "constitute the arbitral tribunal."[85]

The appointing authority's power in this regard is significant.[86] It includes not only the authority to appoint an arbitrator on behalf of a group of claimants or respondents, but also to "revoke" any previously made appointment and to "reappoint" any arbitrators, including by designating one of them the presiding arbitrator. Thus, Article 10(3) may be applied to "deprive[] all parties of their right to appoint an arbitrator if the parties on either side were unable to make such an appointment."[87] For example, if a single respondent has appointed an arbitrator, but a group of claimants has failed to make an appointment within the required time period, the appointing authority may not only appoint an arbitrator on behalf of the claimants, but also may revoke the respondent's appointment and re-appoint an arbitrator on behalf of the respondent. The drafters' rationale for inclusion of Article 10(3) is rooted in the principle of party equality and is best understood by reference to the French Court of Cassation's decision in *Dutco v BKMI and Siemens*.

In the *Dutco* case, BKMI Industrian Lagen GmBH ("BKMI"), a German company, entered into a contract for the construction of a cement plant in Oman. BKMI further entered into a consortium agreement with Siemens AG ("Siemens") and Dutco Construction Co. ("Dutco") in order to satisfy the terms of the underlying contract. The consortium agreement called for arbitration in Paris under the ICC Rules before a three-member arbitral tribunal. When disputes arose, Dutco initiated a single arbitration at the ICC, alleging separate claims for breach of the consortium agreement against Siemens and BKMI. Dutco appointed an arbitrator and requested that Siemens and BKMI jointly appoint an arbitrator, which they ultimately did under protest and with reservations. In a partial award, the Tribunal ruled that it had been validly constituted and that the proceedings could continue as a multi-party arbitration. BKMI and Siemens sought to annul the award before the Paris Court of Appeal on the grounds that the arbitral tribunal was irregularly constituted and that the enforcement of its partial award would be contrary to international public policy. The Court of Appeal rejected the request for annulment, holding that there had been no violation of public policy and the tribunal had been properly constituted. It found further that the arbitral clause in question "unambiguously expressed the common will of the parties," whose differences in the arbitral appointment process were a "foreseeable possibility"

---

[85] Without such authority granted through the choice of the UNCITRAL Rules by the parties, the award may be susceptible to challenge. On the risks, see N Blackaby and C Partasides, *Redfern and Hunter on International Arbitration*, n 9, 151.

[86] It also places the 2010 UNCITRAL Rules on the leading edge of arbitral practice. See R Ugarte and T Bevilacqua, "Ensuring Party Equality in the Process of Designating Arbitrators in Multiparty Arbitration: An Update on the Governing Provisions," (2010) 27 J Intl Arb 1, 18 (noting that the 2010 UNCITRAL Rules represent "the most explicit of any major set of arbitration rules regarding the possibility for the appointing authority to confirm an arbitrator that had already been designated by a party or multiple parties when the designation process ran aground"). See also M Kramer, *et al*, "The Arbitrator and the Arbitration Procedure—Equal Treatment in Multi-Party Arbitration and the Specific Issue of the Appointment of Arbitrators," in C Klausegger, *et al* (eds), *Austrian Arbitration Ybk 2009* (2009) 149, 158–9.

[87] *Report of the Working Group on Arbitration and Conciliation on the Work of its Forty-Fifth Session* (Vienna, September 11–15, 2006), UNCITRAL, 40th Session, UN Doc A/CN.9/614, at 14, para 63 (2007).

that was accepted at the time of agreement.[88] The French Court of Cassation, however, overturned the decision of the Court of Appeal and annulled the Tribunal's partial award, holding "that the principle of the equality of the parties in the appointment of arbitrators is a matter of public policy (*ordre public*) which can be waived only after a dispute has arisen."[89]

The *Dutco* case caused the ICC Court of Arbitration and other arbitral institutions to revise their institutional rules of arbitral procedure. According to the then Secretary-General of the ICC's International Court of Arbitration, Dr. Horacio A Grigera Naón, "[a] way of avoiding any unequal treatment of the parties [as was deemed to be the case in *Dutco*] would be to vest the appointing authority with the power to appoint all three panel members."[90] Thus, under Article 10 of the 1998 ICC Rules, where multiple parties are unable to agree on an appointment, the ICC Court thus "may appoint each member of the Arbitral Tribunal and shall designate one of them to act as chairman." When drafting Article 10(3) of the 2010 UNCITRAL Rules, the Working Group was keenly aware of the *Dutco* problem and the ICC's approach in addressing it. Thus, it is not surprising that Article 10(3) draws heavily on the 1998 ICC rule, and is meant primarily to address the demands of arbitration "in all countries bound by article 6 of the European Convention on the Protection of Human Rights and Fundamental Freedoms...."[91] However, even in jurisdictions that do not impose a requirement of equal treatment, Article 10(3) is sufficiently flexible "to accommodate the wide variety of situations arising in practice."[92]

With the appointing authority's significant discretion to appoint and, if necessary, revoke and reappoint arbitrators comes the responsibility of ensuring that all parties concerned are heard. The Working Group that revised the Rules considered whether to include in Article 10 an express provision on the right to be heard.[93] While the draft provision was never adopted, presumably because such a right already exists under Article 6(3), the proposal reflects legitimate concerns about the need to provide the parties ample notice and opportunity to comment on a decision by the appointing authority under Article 10(3). This is particularly the case if that decision compels one or more parties to accept an appointment on their behalf of an arbitrator who was not their first choice.

Appointments made pursuant to Article 10(3) are not subject to any time limits. The Working Group considered the need for time limits in multi-party litigation but ultimately concluded they were not necessary; the international arbitration rules of other arbitral institutions, which were similar to Article 10(3), "did not create any difficulty in practice."[94] The parties are naturally free to include any time limits that they can agree upon.

---

[88] January 7, 1992—Cour de Cassation [Supreme Court] in A J van den Berg (ed), Ybk Commercial Arb Volume XVIII—1993, Volume XVIII (1993) 140–2.

[89] A J van den Berg (ed), Ybk Commercial Arb Volume XVIII—1993, Volume XVIII (1993) 140–2.

[90] Dr H Grigera Naón, "The Administration of Arbitral Cases under the 1988 Rules of Arbitration of the International Chamber of Commerce," Section 3(b) (October 24, 1997).

[91] UNCITRAL, 40th Session, UN Doc A/CN.9/619, n 3, at 19, para 90.

[92] UNCITRAL, 40th Session, UN Doc A/CN.9/619, n 3, at 19, para 90.

[93] *Settlement of Commercial Disputes: Revision of the UNCITRAL Arbitration Rules, Note by the Secretariat*, UNCITRAL, UN Doc A/CN.9/WG.II/WP.147 at 15, para 44 (2007).

[94] *Report of Working Group II (Arbitration and Conciliation) on the Work of its Forty-Ninth Session* (Vienna, September 15–19, 2008), UNCITRAL, 42nd Session, UN Doc A/CN.9/665, at 14, para 70 (2008).

7. Comparison to the 1976 UNCITRAL Rules

With some significant differences, the 2010 UNCITRAL Rules generally track the approach of the 1976 UNCITRAL Rules with respect to the number of arbitrators and the processes both for designating an appointing authority and appointing arbitrators. Article 6, which addresses the role of the designating and appointing authorities generally, consolidates various provisions originally appearing throughout corresponding Articles 6, 7, and 8 of the 1976 UNCITRAL Rules. Notwithstanding this restructuring, revised Article 6 remains true to the original rules in many respects, but with some useful revisions. For example, revised Article 6(1) restates the basic rule, originally contained in original Article 6(1)(b), that unless the parties have already agreed upon an appointing authority, any party may propose the name or names of one of more institutions or persons to serve as appointing authority.[95] Revised Article 6(1) now also provides that the PCA Secretary-General, though functioning as designating authority under the Rules, may also be chosen to serve as appointing authority, a possibility that is already implicit under the 1976 UNCITRAL Rules.

Revised Articles 6(2) and 6(4) adopt the rule contained in corresponding Articles 6(2) and 7(2)(b) of the 1976 UNCITRAL Rules, which empower the PCA Secretary-General to designate the appointing authority where the parties are unable to reach agreement on who shall serve, or where the existing appointing authority fails to perform its functions. One notable difference in revised Article 6(4) is the reference to Article 41(4) of the 2010 UNCITRAL Rules, a new provision which authorizes the PCA Secretary-General to resolve disputes over arbitrator fees where the appointing authority fails to do so.

Articles 6(5) through 6(6) incorporate the same rules concerning the discretion and power of the appointing authority that originally appeared in corresponding Article 6(4) and Article 8 of the 1976 UNCITRAL Rules, while at the same time adding new rules. For example, whereas under both the original and revised Rules the appointing authority may compel a party to produce relevant information, only under the revised Rules is the appointing authority required to "give the parties an opportunity to present their views." In addition, under the revised Rules, the party requesting an appointment must send the appointing authority not only a copy of the notice of arbitration (as in the original rule), but also the response to the notice of arbitration, thus accounting for this additional procedural step contained only in the revised Rules. The requirement in revised Article 6 for the provision of communications to all parties is new to the 2010 UNCITRAL Rules, but merely makes explicit what was already sound practice.

With respect to the number of arbitrators, Article 7(1) of the 2010 UNCITRAL Rules and corresponding Article 5 of the 1976 UNCITRAL Rules are virtually identical, save for the lengthening of the time period (from 15 to 30 days) before the default rule of three

---

[95] This provision did not appear in Article 7 of the 1976 UNCITRAL Rules on the constitution of a three-member tribunal. Another provision that did not carry over from the 1976 UNCITRAL Rules is original Article 8(2): "Where the names of one or more persons are proposed for appointment as arbitrators, their full names, addresses and nationalities shall be indicated, together with a description of their qualifications." Given the extensive discussion of the drafters over whether arbitrators appointed by the appointing authority need be of a nationality other than the nationalities of the parties, original Article 8(2) was once thought to be useful in that it facilitated the appointment of well-qualified arbitrators. See, eg, *Report of UNCITRAL on the work of its Ninth Session*, UN GAOR, 31st Session, Supp No 17, UN Doc A/31/17, para 43 (1976), reprinted in (1976) VII UNCITRAL Ybk 66, 69. Its omission from the 2010 UNCITRAL Rules is inconsequential, however, since such information is likely to be conveyed in any event.

arbitrators becomes effective.[96] The second paragraph of revised Article 7 is new to the Rules, however. It provides an exception to the default rule where one party proposes the appointment of a sole arbitrator and the other party fails to respond within the prescribed time limit. In that event, the appointing authority, at the request of a party, has discretion to appoint a sole arbitrator. By accounting for such a situation, revised Article 7(1) can enhance the efficiency of arbitration in a way that the 1976 UNCITRAL Rules cannot.

The basic rules for appointing a sole arbitrator are also substantially similar under both the 1976 and 2010 UNCITRAL Rules. Under both revised Article 8 and original Article 6, if the parties agree that a sole arbitrator will decide the case, but cannot agree on who should serve in this capacity, the appointing authority may make the appointment using the list-procedure, unless the parties prefer another method or the appointing authority determines the list-procedure is inappropriate.

The method of appointing a three-member tribunal is also the same in both Article 9 of the 2010 UNCITRAL Rules and corresponding Article 7 of the 1976 UNCITRAL Rules. Each party may appoint one arbitrator and the two appointed arbitrators are responsible for appointing the presiding arbitrator. The appointing authority may be called upon to make appointments if one of the parties fails to appoint an arbitrator after the other has made its appointment. The omission of the last sentence in original Article 7(2)(b), providing that the appointing authority may "exercise its discretion" in appointing the second party-appointed arbitrator, is inconsequential, since that provision was merely redundant of the appointing authority's inherent authority to appoint. Finally, both the revised and old rules delegate the appointment power to the appointing authority when the two previously appointed arbitrators are unable to agree on a presiding arbitrator.

Article 10 of the 2010 UNCITRAL Rules has no counterpart in the 1976 UNCITRAL Rules. As discussed above, that provision usefully regulates the appointment process in the context of multi-party arbitration when joint agreement on the appointment of an arbitrator becomes impossible. Parties litigating under the 1976 UNCITRAL Rules in a multi-party setting may wish to consider whether to incorporate the substance of Article 10 into their procedural terms of reference.

---

[96] Another minor change is that the phrase "(i.e. one or three)" referring to the possible number of arbitrators has been deleted to better reflect the fact that tribunals comprised of different numbers of arbitrators, including an even number of arbitrators, are permissible under the Rules.

5
The Challenge of Arbitrators

1. **Introduction**   177
   - A. An Overview of Challenges before Investment and other Tribunals   178
     - (1) Challenge decision of April 15, 1993   178
     - (2) Challenge decision of January 11, 1995   179
     - (3) Challenge decision by a Division of the LCIA—October–December 2005   179
     - (4) The US Government challenge of Professor James Anaya in the Grand River arbitration—2007   180
     - (5) The Argentine Government's challenge of Mr Judd L Kessler in the National Grid arbitration—2007   180
     - (6) The Argentine Government's challenges of Professor Gabrielle Kaufmann-Kohler in the AWG Group arbitration—2007–2008   181
       - (a) The Argentine Government's first challenge—2007   181
       - (b) The Argentine Government's second challenge—2008   181
     - (7) The Argentine Government's challenge of Mr Stanimir Alexandrov in the ICS arbitration 2009   182
     - (8) The claimant's challenge to Mr J Christopher Thomas in the Gallo arbitration—2009   182
   - B. An Overview of the Challenges before the Iran–US Claims Tribunal   183
     - (1) The Iranian Government challenge of Nils Mangård—1982   183
     - (2) The US Government challenge of Judges Kashani and Shafeiei—1984   184
     - (3) The first Iranian Government challenge of Judge Briner in Case No 55, *Amoco Iran* and *Islamic Republic of Iran*—1988   184
     - (4) The second Iranian Government challenge of Judge Briner—1989   184
     - (5) The third Iranian Government challenge of Judge Briner—1989   185
     - (6) The US claimant's challenge of Judge Noori in Case No 248, *Carlson* and *Melli Industrial Group*—1990   186
     - (7) The Iranian Government challenge of Judge Arangio-Ruiz—1991   186
     - (8) The Iranian Government challenges of Judge Krzysztof Skubiszewski—1999   186
     - (9) The US Government challenge of Judge Bengt Broms—2001   187
     - (10) The US claimant's challenge of Judge Bengt Broms in connection with Case No 485, *Frederica Lincoln Riahi*—2004   187
     - (11) The US Government challenge of Judges Assadollah Noori, Koorosh Ameli, and Mohsen Aghahosseini—2005–2006   188
     - (12) The Iranian Government Challenge of Judge Krzysztof Skubiszewski and the US Government Challenge of Judge Hamid Reza Oloumi Yazdi—2007   188
     - (13) The Iranian Government challenge of Judge Krzysztof Skubiszewski and Judge Gaetano Arangio-Ruiz—2009   189
     - (14) The US Government challenge of Judge Seyed Jamal Seifi—2010   190
     - (15) The Iranian Government challenge of Judge Charles Brower—2010   190
   - C. The Exclusivity of the UNCITRAL Challenge Procedure   191

2. The Duty to Disclose—Article 11 — 194
A. Text of the 2010 UNCITRAL Rule — 194
B. Commentary — 195
(1) The duty to disclose — 195
(2) Model statements of independence — 198
(3) Disclosure guidelines of the Iran–US Claims Tribunal — 200
C. Extracts from the Practice of Investment Tribunals — 201
D. Extracts from the Practice of the Iran–US Claims Tribunal — 202
(1) General — 202
(2) Disclosure by the US Arbitrators — 205

3. The Grounds for Challenge—Article 12 — 207
A. Text of the 2010 UNCITRAL Rule — 207
B. Commentary — 208
(1) Challenge on the ground of justifiable doubts as to impartiality or independence—general remarks on Article 12(1) — 208
  (a) The standard for impartiality and independence is objective — 208
  (b) The same standard applies to party-appointed and non-party appointed arbitrators — 209
  (c) Criteria regarding and examples of justifiable doubts — 211
(2) Challenge on the ground of justifiable doubts as to impartiality or independence — 212
  (a) The meaning of "impartiality" and "independence" — 213
  (b) When are doubts as to impartiality or independence justified? — 213
    (1) An arbitrator's relationship with a witness — 215
    (2) An arbitrator's financial relationship with a party (shareholding) — 216
    (3) An arbitrator's financial relationship with a party (salary) — 217
    (4) An arbitrator's previous employment by a parent corporation of a party — 217
    (5) An arbitrator's representation in another forum that is adverse to a party — 218
    (6) An arbitrator's previous advocacy on behalf of a country formerly adverse to a sovereign party — 218
    (7) An arbitrator's representation of a third party with a right to intervene in the proceedings — 219
    (8) An arbitrator's handling of the proceedings — 220
    (9) An arbitrator's statement regarding a party or the dispute — 222
    (10) An arbitrator's decision-making — 222
    (11) An arbitrator's breach of the confidentiality of deliberations — 223
    (12) An arbitrator's physical assault of a fellow arbitrator — 225
  (c) The standard of independence and impartiality does not vary according to the stage of the proceedings — 225
  (d) A failure to disclose under article 11 may give rise to, but does not per se establish, justifiable doubts as to impartiality or independence — 226
  (e) Are there any limitations on the circumstances which may be used as the basis for justifiable doubts? — 228
(3) Article 12(1) as providing the exclusive grounds for challenge — 228
(4) When may a party challenge the arbitrator it has appointed—Article 12(2) — 230
C. Extracts from the Practice of Investment and other Tribunals — 231
D. Extracts from the Practice of the Iran–US Claims Tribunal — 235
(1) Tribunal Rules (1983), Article 10(1) — 235
(2) Tribunal Rules (1983), Article 10(2) — 240

4. The Initiation of the Challenge and the Potential for Agreement to the Challenge—Article 13 — 241
A. Text of the 2010 UNCITRAL Rule — 241
B. Commentary — 241
(1) When notice of challenge must be made—Article 13(1) — 241

	(a) General comments on the travaux préparatoires	241
	(b) When circumstances "became known" to the challenging party	243
	(1) Burden of proof	243
	(2) Actual prior knowledge	245
	(2) To whom should notice be sent; what form should notice take; sufficiency of the notice; who may send notice—Article 13(2)	248
	(3) Procedure if challenge is accepted by all parties or challenged arbitrator withdraws—Article 13(3)	253
	(4) Timeline for seeking a decision on a challenge—Article 13(4)	256
C.	Extracts from the Practice of Investment Tribunals	256
D.	Extracts from the Practice of the Iran–US Claims Tribunal	257
	(1) Tribunal Rules (1983), Article 11(1)	257
	(2) Tribunal Rules (1983), Article 11(2)	263
	(3) Tribunal Rules (1983), Article 11(3)	267
5. The Resolution of the Challenge		268
A.	Text of the 2010 UNCITRAL Rule	268
B.	Commentary	268
	(1) Which authority shall make the decision on the challenge if the other party does not agree to the challenge or the challenged arbitrator does not withdraw?	268
	(2) When may a party seek the assistance of the PCA Secretary-General in designating an appointing authority?	270
	(3) What procedures the appointing authority may follow in deciding the challenge	271
	(4) Limitations on the powers of the appointing authority	272
C.	Extracts from the Practice of Investment Tribunals	272
D.	Extracts from the Practice of the Iran–US Claims Tribunal	273
	(1) Tribunal Rules (1983), Article 12(1)	273
	(2) Tribunal Rules (1983), Article 12(2)	274
6. Comparison to the 1976 UNCITRAL Rules		274

1. Introduction

The challenge is a device to maintain minimal standards of independence and impartiality in arbitrators. Challenge is an exceptional and serious mechanism. It is a process that is infrequently initiated; it may be used more today than in the past, but that conclusion is difficult to assert with confidence given the rareness of published decisions. A challenge may be lodged in response to the appointment of an arbitrator at the commencement of an arbitration or at any time throughout the arbitration when, for example, new circumstances give rise to justifiable doubts as to an arbitrator's impartiality or independence or because of an arbitrator's failure to perform. The UNCITRAL Rules address the challenge process in Articles 11 through 13, the subject of this chapter.[1] Article 14, the subject of Chapter 6, among other things, addresses the process for replacing an arbitrator who has been successfully challenged or is found to have failed to perform.

---

[1] Articles 9 through 12 of the 1976 UNCITRAL Arbitration Rules and the Iran–US Claims Tribunal's experience with the subjects discussed in those articles has been discussed elsewhere. The main works to be consulted are S Baker and M Davis, *The UNCITRAL Rules in Practice: The Experience of the Iran-United States Claims Tribunal* (1992) 37–74; and C Brower, "The Iran-United States Claims Tribunal," (1990–V) 224 Recueil des Cours 200–11. Other works include I Dore, *The UNCITRAL Framework for Arbitration in Contemporary Perspective* (1993) 59–65; J van Hof, *Commentary on the UNCITRAL Arbitration Rules: The Application by the Iran-U.S.*

A. An Overview of Challenges before Investment and other Tribunals

The fields of commercial and investor–state arbitration have increasingly yielded publicly available challenge decisions arising in connection with UNCITRAL proceedings.[2] Throughout this chapter, these challenge incidents are used to gain insights into the process of challenge in general and the UNCITRAL challenge process in particular. All of these incidents arose under the 1976 UNCITRAL Rules, though they remain relevant to the application of the 2010 UNCITRAL Rules, which contain identical standards of conduct. These challenge incidents are summarized briefly below.

(1) Challenge decision of April 15, 1993

The dispute giving rise to this challenge involved a contract between the claimant, an Italian contractor, and the respondent, a state agency, for the construction of an embassy building for the respondent in a third country. A disagreement over payment terms was ultimately put to arbitration in Paris, under the 1976 UNCITRAL Rules. According to Article 7(1) of the Rules, each party appointed an arbitrator and the two party-appointed arbitrators appointed the presiding arbitrator.

The respondent's challenge to the claimant-appointed arbitrator eventually prompted both party-appointed arbitrators to resign, and the parties appointed new replacement arbitrators. Thereafter, the respondent challenged the presiding arbitrator, arguing that he lacked legitimacy "because he was elected with the help of a Party Arbitrator too closely connected with the claimant; and [was] inescapably influenced by too close cooperation with the same in the Tribunal's work and decisions."[3] The presiding arbitrator refused to resign.

The Secretary-General of the Permanent Court of Arbitration designated Pierre Pescatore as appointing authority to adjudicate the challenge. Pescatore dismissed the challenge, ruling that "the respondent cannot avail itself of the reasons adduced against the claimant's first Party Arbitrator to put into question indirectly the status of the Presiding Arbitrator."[4] Indeed, the simultaneous withdrawal of the two party-appointed arbitrators "left untouched the existence and identity of the arbitral tribunal and the office of the Presiding Arbitrator."[5]

Claims Tribunal (1991) 58–89; R Mosk, "The Role of Party-Appointed Arbitrators in International Arbitration," (1988) 1 Transnatl Lawyer 253; R Teitelbaum, "Challenges of Arbitrators at the Iran-United States Claims Tribunal: Defining the Role of the Appointing Authority" (2006) 23(6) J Intl Arb 547.

This chapter originally drew upon D Caron, *The Iran-United States Claims Tribunal and The Intl Arbitral Process*, 119–206 (unpublished dissertation, Dr. jur, Leiden University, 1990).

[2] Other challenges pursuant to the UNCITRAL Rules have not resulted in decisions because the challenged arbitrator resigned. See, eg, *Walter Bau AG* and *Kingdom of Thailand*, Award (July 1, 2009) (*Ad Hoc* Proceeding, 1976 UNCITRAL Rules, Germany-Thailand BIT), at paras 1.36–1.42 (Dr Suvarn Valaisathien resigned after challenged based on his alleged nominal shareholdings of a company that was a member of a consortium of companies in which the investment company was also a member); *Methanex Corp* and *United States of America*, Award (August 3, 2005) (ICSID administered, 1976 UNCITRAL Rules, NAFTA Chapter Eleven), Part II, Chapter E, at 19 (Mr Warren Christopher resigned after challenged based on his law firm's representation of the State of California in other matters). For another example arising in *Canfor Corp* and *United States*, an UNCITRAL arbitration under NAFTA Chapter Eleven, see B Legum, "Investor-State Arbitrator Disqualified for Pre-appointment Statements on Challenged Measures," (November 2, 2005) 21 Arb Intl 241.

[3] Challenge Decision of April 15, 1993, reprinted in part in (1997) XXII Ybk Commercial Arbitration 222, 224, para 2 (argument summarized by the appointing authority). Extracts reprinted in sections 3(C) and 4(C).

[4] Challenge Decision of April 15, 1993, n 3, para 5.

[5] Challenge Decision of April 15, 1993, n 3, para 7.I.

Following the appointing authority's decision, the tribunal, composed of the original presiding arbitrator and the two replacement party arbitrators, rendered a final award on the merits. The respondent's subsequent challenge of the award in the French court on this same basis was denied.[6]

(2) Challenge decision of January 11, 1995

This challenge arose out of a dispute over a five-year sales contract between the claimant, Country X, and the respondent, Company Q, for the purchase of agricultural products. The claimant challenged the respondent-appointed arbitrator on grounds that justifiable doubts existed as to his impartiality, because he had served as a legal advisor to Country A during a period of hostility with Country X, the claimant, and had served as legal counsel to a government official of Country A in connection with an investigation of Country A's military activities in Country X.

Although the appointing authority, whose identity is unknown, recognized the important "political overtones" of the dispute, he dismissed the challenge. He concluded, in particular, that the evidence, a legal opinion and brief drafted by the respondent-appointed arbitrator in his governmental capacities, did not demonstrate a direct link between the political background and the alleged partiality on the part of the challenged arbitrator.[7]

(3) Challenge decision by a Division of the LCIA—October–December 2005

This challenge arose in connection with a dispute arising out of a shareholders' agreement providing for arbitration in London under the 1976 UNCITRAL Rules before a sole arbitrator appointed by the LCIA. The challenge was decided by a Division of the LCIA comprised of Dr Laurent Lévy, Professor Bernard Hanotiau, and J William Rowley QC.[8]

The Division upheld the challenge, deciding on three grounds that the conduct of the sole arbitrator gave rise to an appearance of bias, if not the real possibility of actual bias. First, the arbitrator inappropriately met with claimant's counsel in private on two occasions. Not only did the arbitrator provide inconsistent explanations of the substance of the first meeting, but the substance of the second meeting, whether the respondent had committed a breach of confidentiality, related to issues material to the arbitration.[9] Second, the arbitrator inappropriately ordered the deletion of a portion of the transcript reflecting an exchange between opposing counsel about costs, in disregard of the arbitrator's duty under the UNCITRAL Rules to maintain a record of the proceedings.[10] Third, the arbitrator made accusations of lying and trespassing against one of the respondent's counsel, which regardless of their veracity, were incompatible with the conduct expected of the arbitrator.[11]

---

[6] Challenge Decision of April 15, 1993, n 3, at 222 (summary of facts).
[7] Challenge Decision of January 11, 1995, (1997) XXII Ybk Commercial Arb 227, 238, paras 37–38. Extract reprinted section 3(C).
[8] An abstract of the challenge decision appears in "LCIA Court Decisions on Challenges to Arbitrators" Reference No UN3490, October 21, 2005 and December 27, 2005, summarized in 27(3) Arb Intl 377.
[9] "LCIA Court Decisions," n 8, at 388.
[10] "LCIA Court Decisions," n 8, at 389.
[11] "LCIA Court Decisions," n 8, at 389.

(4) *The US Government's challenge of Professor James Anaya in the* Grand River *arbitration—2007*

The US Government challenged Professor James Anaya, who was appointed by the claimants, certain Native American persons, in the *Grand River* arbitration brought against the United States under NAFTA Chapter Eleven. The circumstances underlying the US government challenge was that Professor Anaya was simultaneously serving as claimant-appointed arbitrator in the *Grand River* arbitration on behalf of certain Native American persons and representing or assisting the same or other Native American persons before the Inter-American Commission on Human Rights and before the United Nations Committee on the Elimination of Racial Discrimination ("CERD"). Given the "basic similarity" of the two proceedings—in which the United States' compliance with its international commitments was at issue—the appointing authority, The ICSID Secretary-General, found that Professor Anaya's continued representation or assistance was "incompatible with simultaneous service as arbitrator in the NAFTA proceeding."[12] Consequently, Professor Anaya was given the choice either to continue to represent or assist parties in the non-NAFTA procedures or resign as arbitrator.[13]

Professor Anaya agreed to cease his involvement in the non-NAFTA proceedings and at the same time notified the appointing authority that he was also currently instructing law students in a clinical course in connection with their work concerning certain Native-American persons and the CERD. The appointing authority found that such instruction did not give rise to doubts as to Professor Anaya's impartiality and independence.[14]

(5) *The Argentine Government's challenge of Mr Judd L Kessler in the* National Grid *arbitration—2007*

In the *National Grid* arbitration, Argentina challenged Mr Kessler, the claimant-appointed arbitrator, as a result of an intervention that he made in Spanish during cross-examination of the claimant's expert witness. The portion of the intervention on which Argentina based its challenge was Mr Kessler's statement: "We know the facts generally speaking that there was major harm or major change in the expectations of the investment." According to Argentina, this statement evidenced Mr Kessler's prejudgment of the key issue of Argentina's alleged liability and thus the final outcome of the arbitration. The claimant disagreed, arguing that the intervention by Mr Kessler, whose native language is English, was misinterpreted by Argentina and was meant only to facilitate cross-examination by suggesting that the witness be asked hypothetical questions.[15]

The appointing authority, a Division of the LCIA, dismissed the challenge. The Division found it was inappropriate to view Mr Kessler's statement in isolation, because immediately after his statement Mr Kessler explained his intent and proposed examples of hypothetical questions that could be posed to the expert witness. This context, along with the

---

[12] *Grand River Enterprises, Six Nations Ltd*, et al, and *United States of America*, Letter from Ms. Ana Palacio, ICSID Secretary-General, to Professor James Anaya (November 28, 2007) (ICSID administered, 1976 UNCITRAL Rules, NAFTA Chapter Eleven), at 1.
[13] *Grand River Enterprises* (1976 Rules), Letter, at 1.
[14] *Grand River Enterprises* (1976 Rules), Letter, at 2.
[15] *National Grid PLC* and *Republic of Argentina*, Decision on the Challenge to Mr Judd L Kessler (December 3, 2007) (LCIA administered UN 7949, 1976 UNCITRAL Rules, UK-Argentina BIT), at 7–13. Extract reprinted in section 3(C).

fact that Mr Kessler was not a native Spanish speaker, eliminated any concerns raised by Mr Kessler's statement in question.[16]

(6) The Argentine Government's challenges of Professor Gabrielle Kaufmann-Kohler in the AWG Group arbitration—2007–2008

Argentina challenged Professor Gabrielle Kaufmann-Kohler, claimant-appointed arbitrator, on two occasions during a consolidated arbitration between Argentina and claimants Suez, Sociedad General de Aguas de Barcelona S.A. and Vivendi Universal S.A., ("Vivendi"), Suez, Sociedad General de Aguas de Barcelona S.A. and InterAguas Servicios Integrales del Agua ("InterAguas"), and AWG Group Ltd ("AWG"), all of which did business in Argentina's water sector. By agreement of the parties, the claims of Vivendi and InterAguas were to be arbitrated pursuant to the ICSID Convention and the ICSID Arbitration Rules, whereas the claims of AWG were to be arbitrated pursuant to the 1976 UNCITRAL Arbitration Rules. The consolidated proceedings were administered by the ICSID Secretariat. Argentina's two challenges in relation to the *AWG* proceedings are described below.

(a) The Argentine Government's first challenge—2007

Argentina first challenged Professor Kaufmann-Kohler because she had participated as a member of the ICSID tribunal in the case of *Compañia de Aguas del Aconquijo S.A. and Vivendi Universal S.A. v Argentine Republic*, which rendered an award against Argentina on August 20, 2007.[17] According to Argentina, the award in that case was so flawed that Professor Kaufmann-Kohler's very participation in the decision-making process "reveals a prima facie lack of impartiality."[18]

Pursuant to the agreement of the parties, the two members of the arbitral tribunal other than Professor Kaufmann-Kohler decided the challenge and, in relation to the *AWG* arbitration, applied the UNCITRAL Rules.[19] The two members dismissed the challenge as untimely as Argentina failed to lodge its proposal for disqualification until well after the 15-day time limit for initiating a challenge.[20]

(b) The Argentine Government's second challenge—2008

Argentina challenged Professor Kaufmann-Kohler a second time based on her election to the board of directors of the UBS Group ("UBS"), a large financial services firm, two years after the arbitral tribunal was constituted. According to Argentina, Professor Kaufman-Kohler had an inappropriate financial relationship with certain claimants; as a UBS director, she was a shareholder in the firm which, in turn, held shares in two of the claimants, Suez, Sociedad General de Aguas de Barcelona S.A. ("Suez") and Vivendi Universal S.A., ("Vivendi"). Argentina alleged that Professor Kaufmann-Kohler breached her duty to disclose these relationships.[21]

---

[16] *National Grid PLC* (1976 Rules), at 22–4.
[17] ICSID Case No ARB/97/3.
[18] *AWG Group Ltd* and *Argentine Republic*, Decision on the Proposal for the Disqualification of a Member of the Arbitral Tribunal (October 22, 2007) (ICSID administered, 1976 UNCITRAL Rules, UK-Argentina BIT), at 7.
[19] ICSID Arbitration Rule 9(4) was applied.
[20] *AWG Group Ltd* and *Argentine Republic*, Decision on the Proposal for the Disqualification of a Member of the Arbitral Tribunal (October 22, 2007) (ICSID administered, 1976 UNCITRAL Rules, UK-Argentina BIT), at 9–10.
[21] *AWG Group Ltd* and *Argentine Republic*, Decision on a Second Proposal for the Disqualification of a Member of the Arbitral Tribunal (May 12, 2008) (ICSID administered, 1976 UNCITRAL Rules, UK-Argentina BIT), at 5–10. Extracts reprinted in sections 2(C) and 3(C).

The truncated tribunal that decided the challenge recognized that UBS was not a shareholder in AWG. Therefore, it observed that the only "circumstance" that could give rise to justifiable doubts as to Professor Kaufmann-Kohler's impartiality and independence was that fact that she was a UBS director and that UBS conducted research and developed financial products related to the water sector. However, the truncated tribunal found Professor Kaufmann-Kohler's alleged connection with AWG to be "too remote and tenuous as to hardly be called a connection or relationship at all."[22] On the question of the failure to disclose her position as UBS director, the truncated tribunal found that because Professor Kaufmann-Kohler's election as UBS director did not give rise to justifiable doubts as to her impartiality or independence, she was not required to disclose such circumstance. On these grounds, the truncated tribunal dismissed Argentina's challenge.[23]

(7) The Argentine Government's challenge of Mr Stanimir Alexandrov in the ICS arbitration—2009

In the case of *ICS Inspection and Control Services Ltd* ("*ICS* arbitration"), Argentina challenged Mr Stanimir Alexandrov, claimant-appointed arbitrator. Upon his appointment, Mr Alexandrov had disclosed, among other information, that he and his law firm were representing other private claimants in another arbitration against Argentina (*Compañia de Aguas del Aconquija S.A. and Vivendi S.A. v Argentine Republic* ("*Vivendi* arbitration")),[24] but stated that he did not believe these circumstances affected his impartiality and independence as arbitrator in the *ICS* arbitration.[25]

Thereafter Argentina challenged the appointment of Mr Alexandrov on the basis of his participation in the *Vivendi* arbitration. The appointing authority, Mr Jernej Sekolec, upheld the challenge. While the claimant argued that the *Vivendi* arbitration may soon come to a close and was unrelated to the *ICS* arbitration, the appointing authority emphasized that Mr Alexandrov's participation in the *Vivendi* arbitration was "not merely a case in which the arbitrator's firm is acting adversely to one of the parties in the dispute, but rather a case where the arbitrator has personally and recently acted adversely to one of the parties to the dispute."[26]

(8) The claimant's challenge to Mr J Christopher Thomas in the Gallo arbitration—2009

In a case pursued under Chapter Eleven of the NAFTA, the claimant challenged Mr J Christopher Thomas, who was appointed by the respondent, the Canadian Government. Upon the appointment of Mr Thomas, the respondent provided the claimant with a copy of his curriculum vitae, which indicated that he was currently a managing partner of his firm but was due to retire from counsel work and withdraw from his firm by a certain date in the near future. Several months later, Mr Thomas became engaged again in counsel work as independent counsel to a new law firm, which the partners of his old firm had joined. Mr Thomas sought to inform the parties about his change in status in an email letter, including in particular that Mexico had retained his new law firm and wished for him to provide

---

[22] *AWG Group Ltd* (1976 Rules), Decision on a Second Proposal at 13.
[23] *AWG Group Ltd* (1976 Rules), Decision on a Second Proposal at 13–14.
[24] ICSID Case No ARB/97/3.
[25] *ICS Inspection and Control Services Ltd* and *Republic of Argentina*, Decision on Challenge to Arbitrator, Jernej Sekolec, Appointing Authority (December 17, 2009) (PCA administered, 1976 UNCITRAL Rules, UK-Argentina BIT), at 4–5. Extract reprinted in section 3(C).
[26] *ICS Inspection and Control Services Ltd* (1976 Rules), at 4–5.

advice on certain legal matters. Due to a technical error, however, Mr Thomas's letter was not received by the parties until several months after it was sent.[27]

In response, the claimant asked Mr Thomas to clarify whether any work that he had performed for Mexico involved the "provision of legal research, advice or representation with respect to the interpretation or application of the provisions of NAFTA Chapter 11, or similar provisions in Mexico's Bilateral Investment Treaties." Mr Thomas responded that while he had not performed work of this specific nature, he had done a small amount of work for his new law firm "consisting principally of reviewing its advice in respect of matters that fall within the rubric of international trade and investment law." This response prompted the claimant to challenge Mr Thomas.[28]

The appointing authority, the Deputy Secretary-General of ICSID, dismissed the claimant's challenge conditionally. Of greatest concern was the fact that Mr Thomas was currently advising Mexico, a NAFTA Party, which had a legal right under the NAFTA to intervene in the current arbitration to provide views on the proper interpretation of the NAFTA's provisions.[29] This situation led the appointing authority to conclude that Mr Thomas could not avoid "the appearance of an inability to distance himself from the interests of Mexico." The appointing authority rejected the claimant's challenge, however, providing Mr Thomas the opportunity to choose either to advise Mexico or continue to serve as an arbitrator in the current arbitration.[30]

B. An Overview of the Challenges before the Iran–US Claims Tribunal

Although the number of challenges in the context of commercial and investor–state arbitration continues to grow, the Iran–US Tribunal remains the most significant source of challenge practice. Throughout this chapter, the numerous challenge incidents before the Tribunal are used to gain insights into the process of challenge in general and the UNCITRAL challenge process in particular. In this section, we provide a very brief overview of these incidents so that they may be discussed in perspective later.

(1) The Iranian Government challenge of Nils Mangård—1982

During a meeting of the arbitrators in Chamber Three near the end of 1981, Nils Mangård made an informal remark whose content is disputed but which resulted in a request by Iran for his resignation.[31] The Iranian arbitrator, Seyyed Hossein Enayad believed the remark to be critical of the Iranian judicial system[32] and the executions that were then taking place in Iran.[33] Judge Mangård later stated that the remark was misunderstood.[34]

---

[27] *Vito G Gallo* and *Government of Canada,* Decision on the Challenge to Mr J Christopher Thomas, QC, (Nassib G Ziadé, ICSID Deputy Secretary-General, Appointing Authority) (October 14, 2009) (ICSID administered, 1976 UNCITRAL Rules, NAFTA Chapter Eleven), at 2–3. Extract reprinted in section 3(C).
[28] *Vito G Gallo* (1976 Rules), at 3–4.
[29] Article 1128 of the NAFTA entitles the Parties to "make submissions to a Tribunal on a question of interpretation of this Agreement."
[30] In his letter of October 21, 2009 to Mr Nassib G Ziadé, Deputy Secretary-General of ICSID, Mr Thomas resigned from the arbitral tribunal.
[31] The events described in this section are primarily based upon the Decision of the Appointing Authority, Ch M J A Moons, on the Objections by Iran to Judge Mangård, March 5, 1982, reprinted in 1 Iran-US CTR 509 (1981–82) and Intl Arb L Rev 4399 (March 19, 1982).
[32] See Intl Arb L Rev 4235 (February 19, 1982).
[33] See Letter of the Iranian Government to Nils Mangård, delivered by M K Eshragh in Stockholm on December 28, 1981, attached to the letter of the Agent of the Government of Iran's letter to Nils Mangård of January 1, 1982, reprinted in Decision of the Appointing Authority, n 31, at para 4.1.
[34] Intl Arb L Rev 4235 (February 19, 1982).

Within a month's time, the Iranian Government sent a letter to Judge Mangård informing him that "the Islamic Republic of Iran hereby disqualifies Your Honour as a 'neutral' arbitrator…"[35] Ultimately, the Iranian action resulted in the designation of Charles M J A Moons, then Chief Justice of the Hoge Raad, the Supreme Court of the Netherlands, as the Appointing Authority for the Iran–US Claims Tribunal. Justice Moons ultimately disagreed with Iran, albeit for different and more cogent reasons, that its letter did not constitute a challenge under the 1976 UNCITRAL Rules and that no further action was therefore required.

(2) The US Government challenge of Judges Kashani and Shafeiei—1984

On September 3, 1984, Mahmoud Kashani and Shafie Shafeiei, Iranian arbitrators, physically assaulted a fellow member of the Iran–US Claims Tribunal, Nils Mangård. This act was followed by continued threats of violence by Judges Kashani and Shafeiei. A challenge against Judges Kashani and Shafeiei was filed by the US Government on September 17, 1984.[36]

The work of the Tribunal came to a halt. At the urging of Iran, the US Government did not press for an immediate resolution of the challenge by the Appointing Authority. Toward the end of 1984, the Iranian government withdrew and, not long after, replaced Judges Kashani and Shafeiei.

(3) The first Iranian Government challenge of Judge Briner in Case No 55, Amoco Iran and Islamic Republic of Iran—1988

On September 13, 1988, the Government of Iran initiated a challenge against Judge Briner in regard to his participating in the arbitration of Case No 55, *Amoco* and *Islamic Republic of Iran*. Iran alleged that Briner had a past relationship with the Swiss subsidiary of Morgan Stanley, an important expert witness for the Claimant in the case, and that he had failed to disclose that relationship. The Iranians were concerned because Morgan Stanley's testimony was heavily relied upon by the Claimant in quantifying the relief it sought and because an "arbitrator related to an expert witness cannot be assumed to be impartial in the treatment of such a witness vis-à-vis other witnesses."[37] On December 6, 1988, Judge Briner withdrew from Case No 55 under protest, approximately three months after the challenge was formally made by the Iranians.[38]

(4) The second Iranian Government challenge of Judge Briner—1989

On July 28, 1989, the Iranians again raised a challenge to Judge Briner. This time the challenge, although arising in part out of a specific case, was directed generally at Judge Briner's continued service in the Tribunal. The basis for the challenge was Judge Briner's handling of Case No 39, primarily the manner in which the amount of the Award was determined:

---

[35] Reprinted in Decision of the Appointing Authority on the Objections by Iran to Judge Mangård, n 31, at para 4.1; also reprinted in section 1(C).

[36] Letter and Memorandum of the Agent of the United States to the Appointing Authority initiating the Challenge of Judges Kashani and Shafeiei, September 17, 1984, reprinted in Intl Arb L Rev 9344, reprinted in section 3(D)(1). Also see discussion in section 3(B)(2)(b)(12).

[37] Letter of the Agent of the Government of Iran to the Appointing Authority initiating the First Challenge by Iran of Judge Briner, September 13, 1988, reprinted in 20 Iran-US CTR 181, 182 (1988–III). See also extract reprinted in sections 3(D)(1) and 4(D)(2).

[38] Letter of Judge Robert Briner to the Appointing Authority, December 6, 1988, reprinted in 20 Iran-US CTR 329–30 (1988–III).

"The circumstances warranting a challenge under the 1983 Tribunal Rules, Article 10, are Mr. Briner's totally improper course of conduct in the proceedings of Case No 39, *Phillips Petroleum Company Iran* and *The Islamic Republic of Iran and the National Iranian Oil Company*."[39]

The Government of Iran claimed that Judge Briner had used a secret memorandum given to him by the American arbitrator, Judge Aldrich, to determine the amount of the Award and then withheld that same memorandum from the Iranian arbitrator in the case. Other charges leveled against Judge Briner were that he used the disputed testimony of Morgan Stanley from Case No 55; that the Award was tainted with efforts to conceal and slant evidence in the Claimant's favor; that there were significant inaccuracies in the Award which served to increase the amount awarded to the Claimant; and finally, that Judge Briner had ignored Tribunal practice and made inconsistent decisions during the course of the proceedings without any explanation and which served mainly to benefit the Claimant.[40]

The challenge was brought by the Iranians after the majority had signed the English Award. The timing of the challenge suggested that the Iranians were trying to circumvent Article 32(2), which made all Tribunal Awards final and binding, and were attempting to use the challenge mechanism as a means in essence to appeal the Award.

On September 19, 1989, the Appointing Authority, Justice Moons, delivered a decision dismissing the challenge largely on technical grounds. First, because the Iranians did not meet the 15-day deadline established under Article 11(1). Second, because much of the material Iran wanted to use to support its challenge came from *in camera* deliberations which are considered confidential under Article 31 and which, therefore, generally should not be examined by the appointing authority in making a decision on the merits of a challenge.[41]

(5) The third Iranian Government challenge of Judge Briner—1989

The third challenge of Judge Briner was in many ways an extension of the second. On September 11, 1989, just days prior to the Appointing Authority's decision on the second challenge, the Iranian government initiated a further challenge on the ground that Iran had just learned of possible violations of India's foreign exchange laws by Judge Briner.[42] Iran also argued that these alleged violations should bear on the Appointing Authority's decision in the then still-pending second challenge. The Appointing Authority decided this challenge in his decision of September 25, 1989, finding that Judge Briner, regardless of whether there "theoretically" was a violation, had acted in good faith and that the act did not thus raise "justifiable doubts as to Mr. Briner's impartiality or independence."[43]

---

[39] Letter of the Agent of Iran to the Appointing Authority initiating the Second Challenge by Iran of Judge Briner, July 28, 1989, reprinted in 21 Iran-US CTR 318 (1989–I). For additional context, see also Letter (of Agent of Iran), dated August 29, 1989; extracts from both reprinted in sections 3(D)(1) and 4(D)(2).
[40] Letters dated July 28 and August 29, 1989, n 39.
[41] Decision of the Appointing Authority on the Second Challenge by Iran of Judge Briner, September 19, 1989, reprinted in 21 Iran-US CTR 384 (1989–I). See also extract reprinted in section 3(D)(1).
[42] Letter of the Agent of the Government of Iran to the Appointing Authority initiating the Third Challenge by Iran of Judge Briner, September 11, 1989, reprinted in 21 Iran-US CTR 380 (1989–I). See also extract reprinted below, section 3(D)(1).
[43] Decision of the Appointing Authority on the Third Challenge by Iran to Judge Briner, September 25, 1989, reprinted in 21 Iran-US CTR 396, 398 (1989–I) and (October 13, 1989) 4(17) Mealey's Intl Arb Rep A–3. See

(6) *The US claimant's challenge of Judge Noori in Case No 248,* Carlson *and* Melli Industrial Group—*1990*

The US claimant in Case No 248 challenged the participation of Judge Noori, the Iranian-appointed member of the Chamber, who had earlier served as general counsel of the parent corporation of the respondent.[44] The Appointing Authority denied the challenge, concluding that even if "his service as Head of the NIOI legal office [the parent corporation of the Respondent] and his failure to disclose this to the President of the Tribunal were true, I do not feel this doubt can be termed justifiable doubt."[45]

(7) *The Iranian Government challenge of Judge Arangio-Ruiz—1991*

On August 8, 1991, the Iranian Government challenged Judge Arangio-Ruiz, alleging a failure to act on his part. Iran did not allege that Judge Arangio-Ruiz was totally inactive, but that his neglect of his duties constituted a failure to act. The Appointing Authority upon review of the evidence concluded on September 24, 1991 that "Mr. Arangio-Ruiz has not consciously neglected his arbitral duties in such a way that his overall conduct as an arbitrator and chairman of one of the Tribunal's Chambers falls clearly below the standard of what may be reasonably expected of an arbitrator in a Tribunal such as the Iran-United States Claims Tribunal."[46]

(8) *The Iranian Government challenges of Judge Krzysztof Skubiszewski—1999*

Iran based two related challenges against Judge Skubiszewski on events surrounding an inquiry by the Tribunal's Deputy Secretary-General into the balance of the Security Account, which Iran is required by the Algiers Accords to maintain at a minimum level.

On May 20, 1999, Iran raised its first challenge. It alleged partiality and prejudgment of the issues by Judge Skubiszewski for collecting evidence on a "central issue" in Case No A/28, which dealt with Iran's obligation to maintain the Security Account at US $500 million. Iran's second challenge raised on June 3, 1999 alleged that Judge Skubiszewski lied when denying that he instructed the Tribunal's Deputy Secretary-General to inquire into the account balance.

On August 30, 1999, the Appointing Authority, Sir Robert Jennings, dismissed both challenges. He found not only that the inquiry into the account balance was proper to update information relating to a pending case, regardless of who directed it, but also that Iran presented no credible evidence that Judge Skubiszewski had directed or was complicit in making the inquiry, or that he lied about any involvement.[47]

---

also extract reprinted in sections 3(D)(1) and 4(D)(1). S Baker and M Davis, *The UNCITRAL Rules in Practice*, n 1, 45, incorrectly suggest that the Appointing Authority decided the third challenge in his decision regarding the second challenge. For additional context, see also letters from Agent of United States, dated September 15, 1989 and September 19, 1989; extracts reprinted in section 3(D)(1).

[44] Letter of Claimant in Case No 248 to the Appointing Authority, Ch M J A Moons, initiating the challenge of Judge Noori in Case No 248, February 20, 1990, reprinted in 24 Iran-US CTR 309 (1990–I).

[45] Decision of the Appointing Authority on the Challenge of Judge Noori, August 31, 1990, reprinted in 24 Iran-US CTR 314, 324 (1990–I). See also extract reprinted in section 3(D)(1).

[46] Decision of the Appointing Authority on the Challenge by Iran of Judge Arangio-Ruiz, September 24, 1991, reprinted in 27 Iran-US CTR 328, 336 (1991–II).

[47] Decision of the Appointing Authority on the Challenge of Judge Skubiszewski, August 30, 1999, reprinted in 14 Mealey's Intl Arb Rep A/1 (No 9, September 1999).

(9) The US Government challenge of Judge Bengt Broms—2001

On January 4, 2001, the US Government challenged Judge Broms based on his concurring and dissenting opinion in Case No A/28, which contained revelations about the secret deliberations of the Tribunal.[48] The US Government argued that Judge Broms's opinion "intentionally and repeatedly undercut the legitimacy of those portions of the Tribunal's ruling favorable to the United States, demonstrate[d] his favorable disposition towards Iran, and strip[ped] those arbitrators who had voted in favor of the United States from the protections and respect accorded by the requirement of confidentiality of deliberations."[49]

On March 10, 2001, the US Government renewed its request for challenge based on responsive submissions by Judge Broms that, according to the US Government, "exacerbate[d] his wrongful conduct both by compounding his original disclosures of confidential deliberations and by gratuitously exhibiting anti-American bias in a surprisingly raw manner."[50]

On May 7, 2001, the Appointing Authority, Sir Robert Jennings, dismissed the US Government's applications for challenge.[51]

(10) The US claimant's challenge of Judge Bengt Broms in connection with Case No 485, Frederica Lincoln Riahi—2004

On March 28, 2003, the US claimant requested that the Tribunal reopen Case No 485, presided over by Judge Bengt Broms, on grounds that the award rendered in that case was fundamentally biased and unfair. On July 2, 2003, the claimant reaffirmed her request and asked that Judge Broms recuse himself from any further involvement in the matter because his conduct of the proceedings and exercise of judgment in rendering the award were central issues raised by her application. On January 26, 2004, the US claimant challenged Judge Broms, for his continued participation in the claimant's post-award application.

The Appointing Authority, Sir Robert Jennings, rejected the challenge as untimely since the circumstances giving rise to the challenge were set forth in the claimant's July 2003 application, but the challenge was not formally raised until January 2004, well after the 15-day time limit had expired.[52]

---

[48] See Memorandum in Support of the Challenge by the US of Mr Bengt Broms, Member and Chairman of Chamber One of the Iran-US Claims Tribunal, January 4, 2001. Also see discussion in section 3(B)(2)(b)(11).

[49] Letter from the US Agent to the Appointing Authority, Sir Robert Jennings, January 4, 2001, at 1. The US Government also argued that the opinion demonstrated that Judge Broms had violated Article 33 of the Tribunal Rules and Article V of the Settlement Declaration, because he failed to decide Case No A/28 on the applicable law.

[50] Reply of United States to the Submission of Iran and Mr Bengt Broms Concerning the Challenge by the United States of Mr Broms, March 10, 2001, at 1.

[51] See Decision of the Appointing Authority on the Challenge of Judge Bengt Broms, May 7, 2001, reprinted in 38 Iran-US CTR 386. See also extract reprinted below, section 3(D)(1).

[52] Decision of the Appointing Authority on the Challenge of Judge Bengt Broms, September 30, 2004, reprinted in (No October 10, 2004) 19 Mealey's Intl Arb Rep B-1; 38 Iran-US CTR 398, also reprinted in section 2(D)(1). See also "Challenge of Iran-U.S. Claims Tribunal Judge Bengt Broms" in "Contemporary Practice of the United States," (2001) 95 AJIL 895.

(11) The US Government challenge of Judges Assadollah Noori, Koorosh Ameli, and Mohsen Aghahosseini—2005–2006

On December 21, 2005, the US Government challenged all three Iranian arbitrators, Judges Assadollah Noori, Koorosh Ameli, and Mohsen Aghahosseini.[53] The challenge was submitted on the basis of a statement made by Judge Noori on December 6, 2005, in a Full Tribunal meeting on the subject of a new Tribunal budget. In that meeting Judge Noori stated that any increase in arbitrator salaries would not affect the personal situation of the Iranian arbitrators substantially because they remit a portion of their remuneration to the Iranian Government. The United States argued that this statement proved that the Iranian arbitrators were financially dependent on Iran, as Iran had the power to reward or sanction the conduct of Iranian arbitrators by adjusting the level of income that they were allowed to keep.[54]

The Iranian arbitrators and Iran argued that the US challenge was untimely because the practice of remitting arbitrator payments was made known to the United States in the early days of the Tribunal.[55] The Iranian arbitrators and Iran also argued that the payments in question were not illicit, but rather made pursuant to Iranian tax law.

On April 19, 2006, after holding individual fact-finding meetings with the three Iranian arbitrators and the Secretary-General of the Tribunal, the Appointing Authority, Judge W E Haak, dismissed the US challenge as untimely. His decision was based on two pieces of evidence which he believed demonstrated that the United States had prior knowledge of the Iranian practice: handwritten notes of the Secretary-General from a 1984 budget meeting, according to which a former Iranian arbitrator explained the Iranian practice in the presence of the US Agent; and a 2006 letter from a former Iranian arbitrator stating that a US arbitrator suggested in a 1981 Tribunal meeting, in which the US Agent was present, that the Iranian arbitrators may wish to return the portion of their salaries that Iran found to be objectionable.[56] Judge Haak also found that even were the challenge timely, he would have rejected it on the merits because the United States failed to prove that the payments to Iran were anything other than legal contributions, pursuant to Iranian tax law.[57]

(12) The Iranian Government Challenge of Judge Krzysztof Skubiszewski and the US Government Challenge of Judge Hamid Reza Oloumi Yazdi—2007

The challenges of Judges Skubiszewski and Oloumi arose out of the same general factual background. In November 2006, Judge Noori, an Iranian arbitrator, submitted his resignation, effective on the day after the hearings in Case No B61 were concluded and refused to participate in the deliberations of that case.[58] Judge Oloumi ultimately replaced Judge

---

[53] Letter from the US Agent, Mr Clifton Johnson, to the Appointing Authority, Judge W E Haak, regarding notice of challenge of Arbitrators Assadollah Noori, Koorosh H Ameli, Mohsen Aghahosseini, December 21, 2005.

[54] Letter from the US Agent, n 53, at 1. See also Letter from the US Agent, Mr Clifton Johnson, to the Appointing Authority, Judge W E Haak, regarding the challenge of Mr Assadollah Noori, Mr Koorosh H Ameli, and Mr Mohsen Aghahoseeini, February 3, 2006, at 7.

[55] For a more detailed discussion on this aspect, see section 4(B)(1)(b).

[56] Decision by the Appointing Authority, Judge W E Haak, on the Challenge against Judges Assadollah Noori, Koorosh H Ameli, and Mohsen Aghahosseini, April 19, 2006, at 4–5, paras 26–28. See also extracts reprinted in sections 2(D)(1) and 3(D)(1).

[57] Decision by the Appointing Authority, n 56, at 5, para 29.

[58] As discussed in Chapter 6, section 2, Judge Noori's conduct was inconsistent with Article 13(5) of the 1983 Tribunal Rules, also known as the "Mosk Rule."

Noori and by a decision dated May 1, 2007, the Full Tribunal decided that "Mr. Oloumi Yazdi will be afforded the time he requires fully and adequately to prepare for deliberations in Case No B61." Citing the May 1, 2007 decision, Judge Oloumi submitted a memorandum to the President of the Tribunal on November 23, 2007, formally requesting a rehearing of certain issues in the case and a postponement of all deliberations in the case until April 2008 to allow him adequate time to prepare for further deliberations.

On November 30, 2007, Iran challenged Judge Skubiszewski, alleging that the President "virtually eliminated Judge Oloumi from deliberations of Case B61" by turning down his request for a postponement of deliberations through "most irregular action committed clandestinely with obvious prejudice" to Iran.[59] Iran further argued that the Full Tribunal's decision of May 1, 2007, as formulated, denied the President any discretion to reverse that decision. In response, the United States challenged Judge Oloumi on December 10, 2007, alleging that he disclosed to Iran and the United States the substance of confidential discussions on the possible postponement of Case B61 in breach of Article 31, Note 2 of the 1983 Tribunal Rules. The breach, the United States argued, "appear[ed] to be calculated to enable the party that appointed him, Iran, to seek to influence the Tribunal's ongoing deliberations in Case B61 and alter the composition of the Tribunal in the midst of deliberations."[60] On April 2, 2008, the Appointing Authority, Judge W E Haak, dismissed both challenges in a joint decision, finding that Judge Skubiszewski appeared to have appropriately submitted Judge Oloumi's request to the Full Tribunal for decision and that while Judge Oloumi did breach the Tribunal's confidentiality rules, he did not do so in bad faith.

(13) The Iranian Government challenge of Judge Krzysztof Skubiszewski and Judge Gaetano Arangio-Ruiz—2009

On August 5, 2009, shortly after the Tribunal had rendered its partial award in Case No B61, Iran submitted a request to revise the partial award and a challenge against Judge Skubiszewski, President of the Tribunal, and Judge Gaetano Arangio-Ruiz, third-country arbitrator. The challenge alleged that the two arbitrators had been involved in "a calculated scheme to covertly and illegally revise the Tribunal's partial award" in Case No A15(II:A & II:B) on which Iran argued it had based many of its representations in Case No B61. Thus, according to the Iranian Government, it therefore had not been given the opportunity to present its case on the issues on which the B61 partial award was decided.[61] Iran further argued that the refusal of Judges Skubiszewski and Arangio-Ruiz to recuse themselves from deciding the request for revision created additional doubts as to their impartiality and independence.[62] The Appointing Authority, Judge W E Haak, disagreed, dismissing the challenge based on a combination of grounds.[63]

---

[59] Joint Decision of the Appointing Authority, Judge W E Haak, on the Challenges of Judges Krzysztof Skubiszewski and Hamid Reza Oloumi Yazdi, dated April 2, 2008, at 9 (citing Iran's Notice of Challenge dated November 30, 2007). See also extracts reprinted in sections 3(D)(1) and 4(D)(1), and discussion in section 3(B)(2)(b)(11).

[60] Joint Decision of the Appointing Authority, n 59, at 24–5.

[61] Decision of the Appointing Authority, Judge W E Haak, on the Challenges against Judges Krzysztof Skubiszewski and Gaetano Arangio-Ruiz, March 5, 2010, at 1, para 2.1 (citing Iran's challenge letter). See also discussion at section 3(B)(2)(b)(10).

[62] Decision of the Appointing Authority, n 61, at 1, para 2.1.

[63] In the course of the challenge, Judge Skubiszewski sadly passed away, though the Appointing Authority continued to decide the challenge against the former President in the absence of agreement between the United States and Iran that the matter was moot. Decision of the Appointing Authority, n 61, at 7, paras 28–31.

These grounds included: that while Iran had timely lodged its challenge within 15 days of the issuance of the B61 partial award, any "other circumstances" leading up to that decision which gave rise to Iran's doubts in Case No B61 would have occurred beyond that time period;[64] that Iran's "calculated scheme" allegation had not been sufficiently substantiated, leaving as Iran's principal claim that the challenged arbitrators illegally revised the prior partial award in Case No A15(II:A & II:B) in violation of the principle of *res judicata*;[65] that neither the challenged arbitrators' defense of themselves in the challenges, nor their refusal to recuse themselves from deciding Iran's request for revision or to step down entirely, in any way provide additional grounds for challenge;[66] that by choosing to challenge only two arbitrators, as opposed to all arbitrators who formed the majority behind the B61 partial award, Iran "fatally weakened" its challenge because it would require the appointing authority to agree to hold the party-appointed arbitrator to a lower standard of impartiality and independence;[67] that since the appointing authority does not serve as an appellate body, he must approach an alleged *res judicata* violation with special caution, having authority only to sustain a challenge where (as was not the case here) "the two awards are so clearly divergent on their face" as to demonstrate a lack of impartiality and independence.[68]

(14) *The US Government challenge of Judge Seyed Jamal Seifi—2010*

On April 22, 2010, the US Government challenged Judge Seifi on the basis of his prior involvement as an arbitrator in an ICC arbitration between Iran and Cubic Corporation, a US corporation. The ICC tribunal rendered its award in 1997. The US Government alleged that both Iran's claims in the ICC arbitration and one of its claims in Case No B61 related to the same sale and installation of military equipment under contracts between Iran and Cubic. The US Government therefore claimed that Judge Seifi impermissibly failed to disclose his prior participation in the ICC arbitration, which was likely to influence his participation in any future proceedings in Case No B61. The Appointing Authority, Judge W E Haak, dismissed the challenge, finding that Judge Seifi did not have a duty to disclose his prior involvement in the ICC arbitration given the differences in the legal bases of the two proceedings and that the US Government was time-barred from bringing the challenge since it had relied upon Judge Seifi's dissent in the ICC arbitration in its 2009 pleadings in Case No B61.[69]

(15) *The Iranian Government Challenge of Judge Charles Brower—2010*

On May 10, 2010, Iran challenged Judge Charles Brower, a US-appointed arbitrator, for his allegedly unauthorized interference with the functions of the appointing authority in appointing a new third-country arbitrator. At issue was Judge Brower's phone call to Professor Pierre-Marie Dupuy to explain the various aspects of the position placed after the appointing authority had selected Professor Dupuy as third-country arbitrator with the support of both the United States and Iran. Iran alleged that Judge Brower's phone call was

---

[64] Decision of the Appointing Authority, n 61, at 11, para 47.
[65] Decision of the Appointing Authority, n 61, at 12, para 54.
[66] Decision of the Appointing Authority, n 61, at 14–15, paras 58–62.
[67] Decision of the Appointing Authority, n 61, at 16, para 68.
[68] Decision of the Appointing Authority, n 61, at 21–2, paras 86–87.
[69] Decision by the Appointing Authority, Judge W E Haak, on the Challenge against Judge Seyed Jamal Seifi, September 3, 2010, reprinted in section 2(D)(1).

inconsistent with the Tribunal Rules, contravened the orders of the Appointing Authority and was pursued on behalf of the United States. The Appointing Authority dismissed the challenge on September 3, 2010 rather summarily, finding no breach of the appointment procedures and no violation of the standard of impartiality and independence.[70]

C. The Exclusivity of the UNCITRAL Challenge Procedure

Before discussing the challenge mechanism provided for in the UNCITRAL Rules, one must consider whether the bases and means for removal of an arbitrator are exclusively provided by the UNCITRAL Rules or whether other grounds or indeed other mechanisms exist independently of the Rules.[71] Iran asserted a basis for removal of an arbitrator outside the Rules in its "challenge" of Nils Mangård in January, 1982.

On December 28, 1981, Mohammed K Eshragh, the Agent of the Islamic Republic of Iran delivered a letter to Judge Mangård in Stockholm stating:

Neutrality and impartiality of the jurists composing the Iran-United States Claims Tribunal has been the most significant condition upon which the Islamic Republic of Iran has submitted its disputes to adjudication by this Tribunal. The Islamic Republic of Iran requires the complete neutrality and independence and lack of the slightest political prejudice from the arbitrators of this Tribunal, particularly from those commonly appointed as "neutral."

It has come to our attention that despite the responsibility of neutral arbitrators to disassociate themselves from unsound political propaganda, you have unfortunately taken a position accusing the Islamic Republic of Iran of condemning executions. [sic] The obvious implication of such statement is nothing but a groundless prejudgment against a political system whose acts will be brought before you for evaluation and neutral decision.

Such political approach on your part morally and legally disqualifies you from rendering any fair judgment in connection with acts attributed to the Islamic Republic before this Tribunal…

For these reasons and for avoiding recourse to challenge procedure by the Islamic Republic of Iran, it is respectfully suggested that you opt to resign from the membership of the Tribunal, so that the Islamic Republic and the United States be able to select another arbitrator and hopefully to resolve their disputes smoothly and in the best interests of their nations. To respect you as an international arbitrator, the content of this letter will be considered confidential should you, by your resignation, relieve the Islamic Republic of Iran from the unpleasant task of disqualification procedure, which as you are aware is quite substantial in this case.[72]

---

[70] Decision of the Appointing Authority, Judge W E Haak, on the Challenge of Judge Charles Brower, September 3, 2010.

[71] Of course the mechanisms provided for in the UNCITRAL Rules are always subject to the municipal law at the place of arbitration. The Summary of Discussion on the Preliminary Draft, 8th Session, paragraph 77, noted that the question of challenge of arbitrators ultimately is regulated by the provisions of the applicable municipal law. UN Doc A/10017 (1975), reprinted in (1975) VI UNCITRAL Ybk 24, 33. As stated in the Commentary on the Revised Draft, 9th Session, paragraph 1, "provisions contained in this article are subject to the mandatory rules relating to these issues contained in the applicable national law." UN Doc A/CN.9/112/Add.1 (1975), reprinted in (1976) VII UNCITRAL Ybk 166, 170 (Commentary on Draft Article 9). In practice, municipal law, however, places few restrictions on the challenge mechanism in the UNCITRAL Rules. Yet, as Richard Mosk notes: "The ICC has the authority to disapprove a party-appointed arbitrator on the basis of lack of independence, but the parties may agree to waive the requirement of independence of party-appointed arbitrators. Such express agreements are 'rare in ICC practice,' which could reflect the fact that impartiality of party appointed arbitrators may be required by local law." R Mosk, "The Role of Party-Appointed Arbitrators," n 1, 261.

[72] Reprinted in Decision of the Appointing Authority on the Objections by Iran to Judge Mangård, n 31, para 4.1.

The Iranian Agent, in a further letter to Mangård dated January 1, 1982, emboldened the position of Iran. No longer was Mangård "suggested" to resign and thereby relieve all "from the unpleasant task of disqualification procedure." Now quite simply the Agent wrote: "[w]ith utmost regret I have been instructed to notify you that the Islamic Republic of Iran hereby disqualifies Your Honour as a 'neutral' arbitrator...."[73] A copy of the letter was sent to the other members of the Tribunal and the Agent of the United States.

The UNCITRAL Rules, in addressing the question of challenge of an arbitrator, provide that ultimately a challenge will be decided by a third party called an "appointing authority." The Government of Iran, however, asserted that it possessed the power to unilaterally disqualify a third-country arbitrator.

Although ostensibly a challenge is not a matter for a tribunal to consider under the UNCITRAL Rules,[74] the Iran–US Claims Tribunal was forced to address the "disqualification" in part because the Agent of Iran requested that no meeting be held until Judge Mangård had been replaced.[75]

The Agents of the two governments submitted their views in writing[76] and by oral argument[77] to the Tribunal. Iran argued that it had exercised its sovereign right to disqualify Judge Mangård; that "the disqualification by Iran is *above and outside* the procedure laid down in the [1976] UNCITRAL Rules; and the challenge procedure provided for in Articles 11 and 12 of the [1976] UNCITRAL Rules is not applicable."[78] The United States, on the other hand, argued that neither state party had the legal capacity to unilaterally disqualify a member of the Tribunal and that the only procedure provided for removal of a member was that set forth in the UNCITRAL Rules.

Considering Iran's sovereign rights argument, the Tribunal stated:

Iran has not submitted any reference to international law, precedents, the Agreements between Iran and the United States or any other source of law in support of its position. Indeed, there is no such support. On the contrary, it is an element of absolutely fundamental importance in international law that sovereign States must respect the international agreements to which they have become Parties.[79]

The Tribunal went on to conclude:

Neither the Claims Settlement Declaration nor any of the other instruments relating to the settlement of disputes between Iran and the United States contains anything that can be interpreted as indicating that alternative means for removing an arbitrator exist. Thus, Article III, paragraph 2 of the Claims Settlement Declaration makes it abundantly clear that the only method by which an arbitrator may be removed from office is through challenge by a party and decision by the Appointing Authority pursuant to Article 11 and 12 of the [1976] UNCITRAL Rules.[80]

---

[73] Decision of the Appointing Authority, n 31, para 4.1.

[74] Exceptions are possible where the parties mutually agreed to such an arrangement, as was the case in the *AWG Group* arbitration in which the parties agreed the challenge would be decided by the two remaining unchallenged arbitrators, pursuant to ICSID Arbitration Rule 9(4). See also above discussion in section 1(A)(6).

[75] See Section IV of the Majority Decision of the Full Tribunal, January 15, 1982 (hereinafter cited as "Tribunal Decision"), referring to the January 11, 1982 Letter of the Agent of the Government of Iran to the Tribunal.

[76] Letter of the Agent of the Government of the United States, January 7, 1982; Letter of the Agent of the Government of Iran, January 11, 1982.

[77] The Full Tribunal heard oral argument on January 11, 1982.

[78] Tribunal Decision, n 31, Section II (emphasis added).

[79] Tribunal Decision, n 31, Section V.

[80] Tribunal Decision, n 31, Section V.

The Tribunal's Decision is an obviously correct one. As noted by the Tribunal, to have decided otherwise and granted a unilateral disqualification right "would seriously impair the integrity of the arbitration process and would be contrary to all general principles of justice."[81]

Charles M J A Moons, the Appointing Authority, ultimately agreed with the Tribunal in his March 5, 1982 "Decision on the objections to Mr. N. Mangård as a Member of the Iran-United States Claims Tribunal, lodged by the Islamic Republic of Iran":

> 4.2 If the High Contracting Parties wish to remove a duly Appointed arbitrator from office, the only option open to them under the agreement [Claims Settlement Declaration] is to use the challenge procedure provided for in articles 10 to 12 of the [1976] UNCITRAL rules.
>
>> It has been contended on behalf of the Islamic Republic of Iran that in addition to the power to challenge an arbitrator on the ground of circumstances that "give rise to justifiable doubts as to the arbitrator's impartiality of independence", Iran also has the right as a sovereign state to disqualify a duly appointed arbitrator if he has lost the confidence of Iran. This proposition cannot be accepted as correct.
>>
>> It is inconsistent with the provision of Article III, paragraph 2, of the Claims Settlement Agreement set out above under 3.1, which cannot reasonably be interpreted in any other way than as meaning that the High Contracting Parties thereby agreed that a duly appointed arbitrator could be removed from office only in accordance with the challenge procedure provided for in Articles 10 to 12 of the [1976] UNCITRAL Rules. Furthermore, neither the Claims Settlement Declaration nor any of the other instruments relating to the settlement of disputes between Iran and the United States contains anything which could justify the conclusion that, contrary to the foregoing, the Islamic Republic of Iran reserved itself the right referred to in the above-mentioned proposition.
>>
>> The independence of the arbitrators, which is aimed at by the Claims Settlement Agreement, is also scarcely reconcilable with the notion that the arbitrators can be disqualified by a unilateral statement by one of the High Contracting Parties that it no longer has confidence in them.
>
> 4.3 It is an established fact that the three members of the Iran-United States Claims Tribunal appointed by Iran and the three members appointed by the United States, acting within the framework of the Declaration referred to under 3.1, mutually agreed on 4 June 1981 to appoint Gunnar Lagergren, Pierre Bellet and Nils Mangård as the remaining three members of the Tribunal.

Since the [1976] UNCITRAL Rules, which are applicable in the present matter by virtue of Article III, paragraph 2, of the Claims Settlement Agreement, do not provide that the power of the six party-appointed arbitrators to designate the remaining three arbitrators by mutual agreement is subject in any way to the consent of one or more of the High Contracting Parties and allocate no role to such Parties in regard to the exercise of such power, the appointment of Mr. Mangård, which took place as described above, cannot be nullified by a later withdrawal of such consent.[82]

Although obvious from the above decision, it is worth emphasizing that a party does not even have the right to recall the arbitrator it appointed. Indeed, even *both* parties cannot force the resignation of an arbitrator, although such a result could be achieved by termination of the entire proceedings or by challenge by one party and the agreement of the other party to the challenge.[83]

---

[81] Tribunal Decision, n 31, Section V.
[82] Decision of the Appointing Authority on the Objections by Iran to Judge Mangård, n 31, para 4.2.
[83] An unanswered question raised by the physical attack of Judges Shafeiei and Kashani on Judge Mangård was whether the Tribunal had the express, implied or inherent power to either expel the Iranian arbitrators, declaring their seats to be vacant, or expel the Iranian arbitrators from the premises of the Tribunal unless assurances as to their future conduct were given. See Memorandum to President Lagergren from D Caron and R Lahne, American Legal Assistants, "The Power of the Tribunal and Its President to Take Such Steps as May Be Necessary to Restore the Tribunal to Proper Functioning," dated September 11, 1984, reprinted in Intl Arb L Rev (September 28, 1984) 9374.

2. The Duty to Disclose—Article 11

Article 11 addresses the duty of a prospective arbitrator or an appointed or chosen arbitrator to disclose circumstances "likely to give rise to justifiable doubts as to his impartiality or independence."[84] As Professor Sanders stated in his commentary to the almost identical provision in the preliminary draft of the 1976 UNCITRAL Rules, "[n]o one knows better than the arbitrator himself whether such circumstances exist."[85]

A. Text of the 2010 UNCITRAL Rule[86]

Article 11 of the 2010 UNCITRAL Rules provides:

When a person is approached in connection with his or her possible appointment as an arbitrator, he or she shall disclose any circumstances likely to give rise to justifiable doubts as to his or her impartiality or independence. An arbitrator, from the time of his or her appointment and throughout the arbitral proceedings, shall without delay disclose any such circumstances to the parties and the other arbitrators unless they have already been informed by him or her of these circumstances.

Model statements of independence pursuant to article 11 of the Rules[87]

No circumstances to disclose

I am impartial and independent of each of the parties and intend to remain so. To the best of my knowledge, there are no circumstances, past or present, likely to give rise to justifiable doubts as to my impartiality or independence. I shall promptly notify the parties and the other arbitrators of any such circumstances that may subsequently come to my attention during this arbitration.

Circumstances to disclose

I am impartial and independent of each of the parties and intend to remain so. Attached is a statement made pursuant to article 11 of the UNCITRAL Arbitration Rules of (a) my past and present professional, business and other relationships with the parties and (b) any other relevant circumstances. [Include statement.] I confirm that those circumstances do not affect my independence and impartiality. I shall promptly notify the parties and the other arbitrators of any such further relationships or circumstances that may subsequently come to my attention during this arbitration.

Note. Any party may consider requesting from the arbitrator the following addition to the statement of independence:

I confirm, on the basis of the information presently available to me, that I can devote the time necessary to conduct this arbitration diligently, efficiently and in accordance with the time limits in the Rules.

---

[84] Similar provision may be found in other arbitral rules. See, eg, 2002 Inter-American Commercial Arbitration Commission Rules of Procedure, art 6; 2010 ICDR International Arbitration Rules, art 7; 2012 ICC Arbitration Rules, art 11.

[85] *Report of the Secretary-General on the Preliminary Draft Set of Arbitration Rules*, UNCITRAL, 8th Session, UN Doc A/CN.9/97 (1974), reprinted in (1975) VI UNCITRAL Ybk. 163, 171 (Commentary on Draft Article 8(3)).

[86] Corresponding Article 9 of the 1976 UNCITRAL Rules provides:

A prospective arbitrator shall disclose to those who approach him in connexion with his possible appointment any circumstances likely to give rise to justifiable doubts as to his impartiality or independence. An arbitrator, once appointed or chosen, shall disclose such circumstances to the parties unless they have already been informed by him of these circumstances.

[87] The Model statements of independence pursuant to article 11 are found in the annex to the Rules.

B. Commentary

(1) The duty to disclose

The duty to disclose arises in two stages. First, a prospective arbitrator has a duty of disclosure to those who approach him or her in regard to possible appointment.[88] Second, the arbitrator, once appointed, bears the same duty of disclosure to the parties he or she has not already informed. Thus in the case of one party having approached a prospective arbitrator, all other parties must be disclosed to following the appointment of that arbitrator. When an appointing authority has approached the prospective arbitrator, then all parties should later be provided the disclosure. In this sense, the duty to disclose in the first stage is to whomsoever may approach the prospective arbitrator and thus may include even a non-party such as the appointing authority.

During the second stage, however, the duty to disclose is limited to the parties to the arbitration and the other members of the tribunal.[89] There is, of course, "no corollary obligation upon the non-appointing party [or parties] to conduct independent research into the background and experience of the nominated arbitrator."[90]

Disclosure at both the pre- and post-appointment stages helps avoid selection of an arbitrator who may be successfully challenged later and thereby avoids interruption of arbitral proceedings.[91] Disclosure to all parties is also important for reasons of estoppel. Acceptance of arbitrators in the face of circumstances likely to give rise to justifiable doubts as to impartiality or independence lays the basis for possible estoppel of the accepting party later seeking to challenge the arbitrator on the basis of the same circumstances (see Article 12(2)) or to challenge the award in the appropriate municipal court.[92]

Article 11 places on the arbitrator a duty to disclose circumstances "from the time of his or her appointment and throughout the arbitral proceedings," thus expressly establishing a continuing duty to disclose. Corresponding Article 9 of the 1976 UNCITRAL Rules referred only to the duty of disclosure "once [the arbitrator was] appointed or chosen."

---

[88] P Sanders, "Procedures and Practices under the UNCITRAL Rules," (1979) 27 American J Comparative L 453, 458.

[89] The UNCITRAL Working Group that revised the Rules added the words "and the other members of the arbitral tribunal" after the word "parties" in the second sentence of corresponding Article 9 of the 1976 UNCITRAL Rules to clarify that an arbitrator should disclose not only to the parties, but also to the other members of the arbitral tribunal. *Report of Working Group II (Arbitration and Conciliation) on the Work of its Forty-Ninth Session* (Vienna, September 15–19, 2008), UNCITRAL, 42nd Session, UN Doc A/CN.9/665, at 15, para 74 (2008). The Preliminary Draft of the 1976 UNCITRAL Rules included a duty to disclose upon appointment to "the arbitral institution," assuming that the institution had not already been informed. *Report of the Secretary-General on the Preliminary Draft Set of Arbitration Rules*, UNCITRAL, 8th Session, UN Doc A/CN.9/97 (1974), reprinted in (1975) VI UNCITRAL Ybk 163, 171 (Draft Article 8(3)). The term, however, was deleted from the Revised Draft of the 1976 UNCITRAL Rules, which generally dropped references to arbitration administered by an arbitral institution.

[90] Decision by the Appointing Authority, Judge W E Haak, on the Challenge against Judge Seyed Jamal Seifi, September 3, 2010, at 6, para 23.

[91] Disclosure and challenge are mutually exclusive mechanisms for an arbitrator and a party, respectively. A violation of corresponding Article 9 of the 1976 Rules was found to be not in and of itself a basis for disqualifying an arbitrator. See Decision of the Appointing Authority in the Challenge of Judge Bengt Broms, para 29 (September 30, 2004), reprinted in section 2(D)(1).

[92] The US Supreme Court in setting aside an award because of the appearance of bias stated: "We can perceive no way in which the effectiveness of the arbitration process will be hampered by the simple requirement that arbitrators disclose to the parties any dealings that might create an impression of possible bias." *Commonwealth Coatings v Continental Casualty*, 393 US 145, 148–9 (1968).

Although not expressly stated in that provision, such a continuing duty is indicated in the *travaux préparatoires* of the 1976 UNCITRAL Rules,[93] is consistent with disclosure requirements in other rules of arbitral procedure,[94] and is consistent with policies underlying the rule.[95] The Working Group that revised the Rules added the new language to Article 11 "in order to put that matter [of the continuing duty to disclosure] beyond doubt and in the interests of achieving consistency with [Article 12(1) of] the Model Law."[96]

Likewise, although not express, the Article 11 pre-appointment duty to disclose exists not only at the moment the prospective arbitrator is first approached, but rather up to the point that the arbitrator is or is not appointed. Thus a prospective arbitrator has a duty to disclose, to those who approach him, circumstances likely to give rise to justifiable doubts, even when those circumstances arise after he is initially approached but before he is appointed or chosen.

The circumstances which should be disclosed are those which are "likely" to give rise to "justifiable doubts as to his impartiality or independence," and thus constitute a basis for challenge under Article 12(1) of the Rules.[97] Article 11 thus implicitly recognizes that although there can be many relationships between the arbitrator and the parties, the duty to disclose does not require disclosure of *all* circumstances which might support a challenge under Article 12. Rather the duty extends only to those circumstances which more likely than not would support a challenge.[98] When in doubt, it is often good practice for an arbitrator to disclose particular facts about his or her background to the fullest extent possible in order to "build confidence between an arbitrator and the Parties."[99]

Importantly, the standards for disclosure under Article 11 and for sustaining a challenge under Article 12 are not identical. On the contrary, while Article 11 requires an arbitrator to disclose any circumstances "likely" to give rise to justifiable doubts, an arbitrator can be disqualified under Article 12 if such circumstances, in fact, "exist." Thus, an arbitrator may

---

[93] See *Report of the Secretary-General on the Preliminary Draft Set of Arbitration Rules*, UNCITRAL, 8th Session, UN Doc. A/CN.9/97 (1974), reprinted in (1975) VI UNCITRAL Ybk 163, 171.

[94] Such a continuing obligation is clearly provided for in, for example, Article 7 of the 2010 ICDR International Arbitration Rules, Article 11 of the 2012 ICC Arbitration Rules and Article 5.3 of the 1998 LCIA Arbitration Rules, as well as Article 12 of the UNCITRAL Model Law, as amended. On the latter, see H Holtzmann and J Neuhaus, *A Guide to the UNCITRAL Model Law on International Commercial Arbitration: Legislative History and Commentary* (1989) 390.

[95] Other commentators agree that the obligation is continuing. S Baker and M Davis, *The UNCITRAL Rules in Practice*, n 1, 46; I Dore, *The UNCITRAL Framework for Arbitration*, n 1, 11–12. Stressing the wording of the article, Blessing asserts there is not a continuing obligation. M Blessing, "The Major Western and Soviet Arbitration Rules: A Comparison of the Rules of UNCITRAL, UNCITRAL Model Law, LCIA, ICC, AAA, and the Rules of the USSR Chamber of Commerce and Industry," (1989) 6(3) J Intl Arb 7, 38. In addition, J van Hof, without a clear conclusion, questions the adequacy of the support of the drafting history as to whether there is a continuing obligation. J van Hof, *Commentary on the UNCITRAL Arbitration Rules*, n 1, 58 n 97.

[96] *Report of the Working Group on Arbitration and Conciliation on the Work of its Forty-Fifth Session* (Vienna, September 11–15, 2006), UNCITRAL, 40th Session, UN Doc A/CN.9/614, at 14–15, para 64 (2007).

[97] This conclusion is supported by the parallel wording of Articles 11 and 12(1) and the fact that these two provisions were originally proposed respectively as paragraphs 1 and 3 of Article 8 of the Preliminary Draft of the 1976 UNCITRAL Rules.

[98] Sanders provides such an example: "[I]f a lawyer has been appointed as arbitrator and his law firm merges with another law firm of which one of the partners acts as lawyer of one of the parties, this circumstance should immediately be disclosed." P Sanders, *The Work of UNCITRAL on Arbitration and Conciliation* (2001) 5. On the other hand, the passage of extended time may weigh against the need to disclose. See Decision by the Appointing Authority, Judge W E Haak, on the Challenge against Judge Seyed Jamal Seifi (September 3, 2010), at 10, para 32, (noting that the passage of 13 years between an arbitrator's involvement in a prior arbitration "should, by any reasonable measure, reduce the expectation of disclosure").

[99] Decision by the Appointing Authority, n 98, para 24, reprinted in section 2(D)(1).

have a duty under Article 11 to disclose circumstances which he or she believes more likely than not would support a challenge but that, in fact, do not cause a party to bring a challenge or, if a challenge is brought, are not found by the appointing authority to give rise to justifiable doubts under Article 12. If the standards in Articles 11 and 12 were coterminous, every disclosure under Article 11 would necessarily result in the disqualification of the disclosing arbitrator, unless all parties were to agree nevertheless to allow an arbitrator to serve on the arbitral tribunal. As discussed in the following section, the model statement of independence to be used in cases of disclosure contemplates the possibility that a person chosen to be an arbitrator may disclose circumstances "likely" to give rise to justifiable doubts, but simultaneously believe that he or she can still serve as an impartial and independent arbitrator.

The decision on the challenge to Professor Gabrielle Kaufmann-Kohler in the *AWG* arbitration underscores the complexity in applying the two similar, but distinct standards.[100] In that situation, Professor Kaufmann-Kohler, the claimant-appointed arbitrator, had been recently elected to the board of the UBS Group ("UBS"), which held nominal shareholdings in two of the three claimants in the consolidated arbitration, Suez and Vivendi, but not in the third, AWG Group. Unlike the others, AWG Group's arbitration was proceeding pursuant to the 1976 UNCITRAL Rules.[101] Professor Kaufmann-Kohler did not inform the parties or her co-arbitrators of her new position. Upon learning of her appointment, the Argentine Government challenged Professor Kaufmann-Kohler on the basis of not only an alleged conflict of interest, but also her failure to disclose her new position as board member.

On the question of whether Professor Kaufmann-Kohler had a duty to disclose her position as UBS director, the truncated tribunal interpreted corresponding Article 9 of the 1976 UNCITRAL Rules as requiring disclosure of facts that "if disclosed might give rise to justifiable doubts as to the impartiality."[102] At the same time, it found that because Professor Kaufmann-Kohler's appointment, in fact, did not give rise to justifiable doubts, she therefore had no obligation to disclose this fact to the parties.[103]

In our view, this decision does not adequately recognize the distinction between the disclosure requirements and justifiable grounds for challenge under the Rules. In fact, a person chosen to be an arbitrator may in some situations have a duty to disclose a particular circumstance, even though that circumstance is later determined by the appointing authority not to give rise to justifiable doubts.

The challenge to Professor Kaufmann-Kohler is useful, nevertheless, in demonstrating the appropriate due diligence to be performed by an arbitrator when assessing whether circumstances exist that are likely to give rise to justifiable doubts. For example, when nominated for the position of UBS director, Professor Kaufmann-Kohler submitted to UBS a list of the arbitrations in which she was involved and was informed by the company that no conflicts of interest existed.[104] In addition, she understood that, according to Swiss banking law, the position for which she was nominated was independent from the

---

[100] For an extract from the decision, see infra section 2(C). See also discussion in section 1(A)(6) and section 2(B)(2)(b)(2).
[101] For a more detailed explanation of the proceedings, see section 1(B)(6).
[102] Decision by the Appointing Authority, n 98, at 13.
[103] Decision by the Appointing Authority, n 98, at 13–14.
[104] Decision by the Appointing Authority, n 98, at 7, 9.

management of UBS, including its investment decisions, and thus her responsibilities would be limited to supervision and control only.[105] These steps enabled Professor Kaufmann-Kohler to reach in good faith the conclusion that her appointment would not affect her impartiality and independence as an arbitrator and helped reduce her exposure to disqualification.[106]

Unaddressed by the Rules is the issue of what consequences flow from a failure to disclose. In particular, should a failure to disclose be taken to support the existence of "justifiable doubts as to . . . impartiality or independence" and thus summarily support a challenge? This question is considered below in our discussion of Article 12.

(2) Model statements of independence

The Annex to the 2010 UNCITRAL Rules includes two "model statements of independence pursuant to Article 11 of the Rules." According to the *travaux préparatoires*, these statements offer "guidance" as to "the required content of disclosure."[107] The model statements of independence are a new addition to the UNCITRAL Rules, though the use of disclosure statements has been common practice in international arbitration for many years.[108]

The model statements of independence contemplate two distinct situations that a prospective arbitrator might face. Use of the first statement conveys the prospective arbitrator's decision against disclosure because of the belief that "there are no circumstances, past or present, likely to give rise to justifiable doubts" as to his or her impartiality or independence. Use of the second statement indicates the prospective arbitrator's wish to disclose certain "past and present professional, business and other relationships with the parties" or "any other relevant circumstances," while maintaining the view that "those circumstances do not affect [his or her] independence and impartiality." Thus, the use of both model statements is predicated on a prospective arbitrator's express conviction: "I am impartial and independent of the parties and intend to remain so." Were a prospective arbitrator to feel otherwise, he or she should decline the request for appointment altogether.

Whether to disclose under the second model statement, however, depends not on a prospective arbitrator's subjective opinion as to his or her ability to serve ethically, but on the disclosure requirements of Article 11. That provision requires disclosure of any circumstances "likely," but not necessarily, to give rise to justifiable doubts as to an arbitrator's impartiality and independence, which requires an objective assessment of the relevant circumstances. Thus, where the second statement is used, the prospective arbitrator has decided to disclose "past and present professional, business and other relationships with the parties and . . . any other relevant circumstances" not because that person believes that he or she cannot satisfy the standard for impartiality and independence under the Rules, but because one of the parties to the arbitration might reasonably disagree with that conclusion.

---

[105] Decision by the Appointing Authority, n 98, at 7, 9–10.
[106] Decision by the Appointing Authority, n 98, at 7, 10.
[107] *Report of the Working Group on Arbitration and Conciliation on the Work of its Forty-Sixth Session* (New York, February 5–9, 2007), UNCITRAL, 40th Session, UN Doc A/CN.9/619, at 20, para 96 (2007).
[108] See 1987 IBA Rules of Ethics for International Arbitrators; 2004 IBA Guidelines on Conflicts of Interest in International Arbitration. The PCA has incorporated the model statements of independence into its procedures for administering UNCITRAL arbitration. See *Arbitrator's Declaration of Acceptance and Statement of Impartiality and Independence*, reprinted in section 2(C).

The *travaux préparatoires* confirm the strict symmetry between the second model statement and the disclosure requirements of Article 11. Early drafts of the second statement that failed to achieve this aim were rejected. For example, one draft required disclosure of any circumstance that "might cause a party to question [the arbitrator's] impartiality or independence."[109] When criticized as inconsistent with Article 11, which uses the different formulation "likely to give rise to," it was proposed to add a sentence to the provision following a description of the circumstances disclosed by the arbitrator: "Nevertheless, I do not regard such circumstances as likely to give rise to justifiable doubts as to my impartiality or independence."[110] The addition of that sentence, however, only further confused the issue by suggesting that a prospective arbitrator was disclosing circumstances even though he or she believed disclosure was not required under Article 11. Consequently, the final version of the second statement omits this sentence, along with the "might cause" phrase, in the interest of maintaining parity between the second model statement and the disclosure requirements of Article 11.[111]

The last sentence of both model statements references the continuous duty of disclosure contained in Article 11. Under both statements, the prospective arbitrator undertakes, respectively, to notify the parties and the other members of the tribunal promptly of "any ... circumstances," if the arbitrator did not initially make a disclosure, or "any ... further relationship or circumstances," if the arbitrator has already disclosed, that are likely to give rise to justifiable doubts as to the arbitrator's impartiality or independence and that "subsequently come to [the arbitrator's] attention during this arbitration."

Neither the model statements nor Article 11 itself indicates when a statement of independence should be made. The Working Group appears to have preferred to leave the issue open in order to avoid placing undue restrictions on the use of the statements.[112] Statements are most efficiently used when they are made at the time a person accepts an appointment as arbitrator, or shortly thereafter, to allow any party that wishes to challenge the appointment an opportunity to do so early in the arbitral proceedings before substantive consideration of the issue has begun. A statement may also be used later in an arbitration if new circumstances arise that are likely to raise doubts as to an arbitrator's impartiality and independence.[113]

---

[109] *Settlement of Commercial Disputes: Revision of the UNCITRAL Arbitration Rules, Note by the Secretariat*, UNCITRAL, UN Doc A/CN.9/WG.II/WP.151 at 11–12, para 23 (2008) (Draft model statement of independence). An even earlier formulation contained the phrase: "that might cause [the arbitrator's] reliability for independent and impartial judgment to be questioned by a party." *Settlement of Commercial Disputes: Revision of the UNCITRAL Arbitration Rules, Note by the Secretariat*, UNCITRAL, UN Doc A/CN.9/WG.II/WP.145 at 16–17, para 50 (2006) (Draft model statement of independence).

[110] UNCITRAL, 42nd Session, UN Doc A/CN.9/665, n 89, at 15–16, paras 78–79.

[111] According to the UNCITRAL Secretariat's note: "The purpose of the second statement of independence is to allow parties to decide whether there are actually circumstances that give rise to justifiable doubts as to the arbitrator's impartiality or independence. The modifications made to the second statement of independence aim at ensuring consistency of the statement with article 11." *Settlement of Commercial Disputes: Revision of the UNCITRAL Arbitration Rules, Note by the Secretariat*, UNCITRAL, UN Doc A/CN.9/WG.II/WP.154 at 12, para 29 (2008).

[112] A suggestion was made that the point in time when the arbitrator should provide a statement should be clarified. That suggestion did not receive support. UNCITRAL, 40th Session, UN Doc A/CN.9/619, n 107, at 20, para 98.

[113] N Blackaby and C Partasides with A Redfern and M Hunter, *Redfern and Hunter on International Arbitration* (5th edn 2009) 268–9. See also in context of a similar continuing duty to disclose under Article 11(3) of the 2012 ICC Rules. See M Buhler and S Jarvin, "The Arbitration Rules of the International Chamber of Commerce (ICC)," in F Weigand (ed) *Practitioner's Handbook on International Commercial Arbitration* (2nd edn 2009) 1209–10 (discussing comparable Article 7(3) of the 1998 ICC Rules).

Finally, the Annex to the UNCITRAL Rules includes text that "[a]ny party may consider requesting from the arbitrator" in addition to a statement of independence: "I confirm, on the basis of the information presently available to me, that I can devote the time necessary to conduct this arbitration diligently, efficiently and in accordance with the time limits in the Rules." This addition reflects a growing concern in the arbitration community with the possibility that a prospective arbitrator will accept an appointment even though he or she cannot perform in a timely fashion because of other commitments. This possibility certainly bears on the wisdom of any particular appointment, but delays due to conflicts do not themselves necessarily provide grounds for a challenge under Article 12. Rather, this additional confirmation reflects a broader functional scope for the prospective arbitrator's statement, which concerns not only disclosure, but also pledges as to performance that were previously thought to be implicit in acceptance of the appointment.

(3) *Disclosure guidelines of the Iran–US Claims Tribunal*

For at least the initial appointments made to the Iran–US Claims Tribunal in 1981, pursuant to a rule very similar to Article 11, "disclosure guidelines" were used by the prospective arbitrators.[114] For the three Iranian arbitrators, this statement of guidelines was used directly as a "form" for disclosure. The guidelines were also the point of departure for the drafting of a disclosure letter for the initial three American arbitrators.

In the case of the US party-appointed arbitrators, a general disclosure was made on behalf of these arbitrators following appointment by the Agent for the United States in fairly detailed letters to the Agent for Iran and to the President of the Tribunal.[115] In the case of the appointment of Charles Brower by the United States, the Agent for Iran requested additional information.[116] Such additional information was provided "as a matter of courtesy" given that "the initial 15 day challenge period with respect to Mr. Brower's appointment ha[d] run" and the "earlier disclosure...was thorough, candid and more than sufficient to satisfy...the rules."[117]

As with Iran's initial appointments, the guidelines were used as a "form" by Judge Mostafa Jahangir Sani in 1982. The disclosure statements for Iranian arbitrators

---

[114] Reprinted in section 2(D).

[115] See, eg, Letter of the Agent for the Government of the United States, Arthur W Rovine, to the Agent for the Government of Iran, M K Eshragh, May 24, 1981 (information concerning Howard M Holtzmann, Richard M Mosk, and George H Aldrich, arbitrators); Letter of Agent for the Government of the United States, Arthur W Rovine, to the President of the Tribunal, Gunnar Lagergren, April 20, 1983 (information concerning Charles N Brower, arbitrator), reprinted in section 2(D)(2); Letters of the Agent for the Government of the United States, John R Crook, to the Agent for the Government of Iran, Mohammad K Eshragh, and to the President of the Tribunal, Gunnar Lagergren, both dated October 31, 1984 (information concerning Richard M Mosk, substitute arbitrator); Letters of the Agent for the Government of the United States, John R Crook, to the Agent for the Government of Iran, Mohammad K Eshragh, and to the President of the Tribunal, Gunnar Lagergren, both dated February 17, 1984 (information concerning Carl F Salans, substitute arbitrator); and Letters of the Agent for the Government of the United States John R Crook, to the Agent for the Government of Iran, Mohammad K Eshragh, and to the President of the Tribunal, Gunnar Lagergren, both dated March 14, 1984 (information concerning William H Levit, Jr, substitute arbitrator). See also R Mosk, "The Role of Party-Appointed Arbitrators," n 1, at 267 (describing US government's questioning of prospective arbitrators as to "any connection with prospective American claimants or claims" and the internal disqualification of one candidate for the existence of such connections).

[116] See Letter of the Agent of Iran to the Agent of the United States, December 13, 1983, cited in Letter of the Agent of the United States to the Agent of Iran, January 5, 1984, both reprinted in section 2(D)(2).

[117] Letter of the Agent of the Government of the United States to the Agent of the Government of Iran, January 5, 1984, reprinted in section 2(D)(2).

appointed following Judge Sani were provided by the Agent of Iran. As mentioned above, these statements were relatively brief and occasionally were objected to on that basis by the Agent for the United States.[118]

The Tribunal's addition to Article 9 of the 1976 UNCITRAL Rules reflects the multi-claim nature of the Tribunal and a related decision of the Tribunal. Specifically, a challenge seeking to remove an arbitrator entirely from the Tribunal might be initiated only by one of the state parties, while a challenge of an arbitrator's hearing of a particular case might be raised by both the particular parties to the case in question and the state parties.[119] The addition to Article 9 placed the President of the Tribunal in the position of gatekeeper as to whether the disclosure made by an arbitrator to the two governments should also be made to the particular parties involved.[120]

C. Extracts from the Practice of Investment Tribunals

AWG Group Ltd and *Argentine Republic,* Decision on a Second Proposal for the Disqualification of a Member of the Arbitral Tribunal (May 12, 2008) (ICSID administered, 1976 UNCITRAL Rules, UK-Argentina BIT) (footnotes omitted), at 13–14:

25. The Respondent also alleges that Professor Kaufmann-Kohler had a duty to disclose to the parties in the *AWG Case* that she was a director of UBS and that UBS carried out certain activities relating to the international water sector. Does her failure to disclose these facts also create a "circumstance" that raises a justifiable doubt as to her impartiality or independence? Article 9 of the [1976] UNCITRAL Arbitration Rules states an arbitrator's obligations of disclosure to the parties. It provides: "A prospective arbitrator shall disclose to those who approach him in connexion with his possible appointment any circumstances likely to give rise to justifiable doubts as to his impartiality or independence. An arbitrator, once appointed or chosen, shall disclose such circumstances to the parties unless they have already been informed by him of these circumstances." Thus, Article 9 makes clear that Professor Kaufmann-Kohler, once appointed in the *AGW Case*, had a continuing obligation to disclose to the parties any circumstances that may subsequently arise, which would be likely to give rise to justifiable doubts as to her impartiality.

26. We interpret Article 9 to require disclosure of such facts that if disclosed might give rise to justifiable doubts as to impartiality and that an arbitrator has no obligation to disclose facts which do not meet this test. Having decided that Professor Kaufmann-Kohler's appointment as a director of UBS did not create a circumstance giving rise to justifiable doubts as to her impartiality or independence in the *AWG Case*, because of the lack of any business relationship between UBS or Professor Kaufmann-Kohler on the one hand and AWG Group Limited on the other, we also conclude that she had no obligation under Article 9 of the [1976] UNCITRAL Arbitration Rules to disclose the fact of her directorship in UBS to the parties in the *AWG Case*. In view of the foregoing, the remaining members of the Tribunal have

---

[118] See Letters of the Agent of the United States to the Agent of Iran, September 16, 1983 and December 5, 1983. A special issue beyond the scope of this Chapter is the disclosure requirements of legal secretaries to a tribunal or, in the case of the Tribunal, legal assistants to the arbitrators. In this regard the authors will only note that (1) it was generally believed at the Tribunal that legal assistants should provide disclosure to the arbitrator they served and recuse themselves from cases with which they had a possible conflict of interest and that (2) because the legal assistant is not the arbitrator, disclosure of possible conflicts to a small degree can cure such conflicts because the arbitrators can incorporate such circumstances in their evaluation of the work of the assistant.

[119] See Note 1 of Articles 9 to 12 of the 1983 Rules of Procedure of the Iran–US Claims Tribunal, reprinted in Appendix 5.

[120] For a discussion of this role, see I Dore, *The UNCITRAL Framework for Arbitration*, n 1, at 59–61.

concluded that the Respondent has not established the existence of circumstances in the *AWG Case* that give rise to justifiable doubts as to Professor Kaufmann-Kohler's impartiality and independence and that Respondent's proposal to disqualify her as an arbitrator in that case must be dismissed.

Permanent Court of Arbitration, *Arbitrator's Declaration of Acceptance and Statement of Impartiality and Independence for Cases Under the UNCITRAL Arbitration Rules*:

PCA CASE N° _____
**ARBITRATOR'S DECLARATION OF ACCEPTANCE
AND STATEMENT OF IMPARTIALITY AND INDEPENDENCE
FOR CASES UNDER THE UNCITRAL ARBITRATION RULES**
(Please check the relevant box or boxes)

I, the undersigned,
Last Name: _____ First Name: _____

NON-ACCEPTANCE

❏ hereby declare that **I decline** to serve as arbitrator in the subject case. (If you wish to state the reasons for checking this box, please do so.)

ACCEPTANCE

❏ hereby declare that **I accept** to serve as arbitrator under the UNCITRAL Arbitration Rules ("UNCITRAL Rules") in the instant case. In so declaring, I confirm that I have familiarized myself with the requirements of the UNCITRAL Rules and am able and available to serve as an arbitrator in accordance with all of the requirements of those Rules.

IMPARTIALITY AND INDEPENDENCE

(If you accept to serve as arbitrator, please <u>also</u> check one of the two following boxes. The choice of which box to check will be determined after you have taken into account, <u>inter alia</u>, whether there exists any past or present relationship, direct or indirect, with any of the parties or their counsel, whether financial, professional or of another kind and whether the nature of any such relationship is such that disclosure is called for pursuant to the criteria set out below. <u>Any doubt should be resolved in favor of disclosure.</u>)

❏ **I am impartial and independent** with respect to each of the parties and intend to remain so; to the best of my knowledge, there are no facts or circumstances, past or present, that need be disclosed because they are likely to give rise to justifiable doubts as to my impartiality or independence.

OR

❏ **I am impartial and independent** with respect to each of the parties and intend to remain so; **however**, in consideration of the UNCITRAL Rules, I wish to call your attention to the following facts or circumstances which I hereafter disclose because they might be of such a nature as to give rise to justifiable doubts as to my impartiality or independence. (Use separate sheet.)

Date: _____ Signature: _____

D. Extracts from the Practice of the Iran–US Claims Tribunal

(1) General

During at least the initial establishment period of the Tribunal in 1981, the following disclosure guidelines were used:

GUIDELINES FOR WRITTEN STATEMENT TO BE FURNISHED BY EACH MEMBER OF THE TRIBUNAL

1. Name
2. Place and Date of Birth
3. Citizenship
4. Place of Residence
5. List of all Academic Degrees, stating
    —degree
    —institution
    —year degree granted
6. Description of present employment, stating
    —name of present employer
    —date present employment began
    —title or function with present employer
    —whether the Member, or any law firm with which he is associated has acted or is acting as lawyer, adviser or representative on any claim, counterclaim or dispute intended to be presented to the Iran–U.S. Claims Tribunal
7. Description of other major professional, business or governmental organization
    —name of the professional, business or governmental organization
    —title or function
8. Description of past employment, stating
    —name of each past employer
    —years of each past employment
    —title or function with each past employer
9. Knowledge of any claim, counterclaim or dispute intended to be presented to the Iran–U.S. Claims Tribunal by any business entity in which the Member has an investment or financial interest.

This statement of guidelines was used directly as a form for disclosure by the initial three Iranian arbitrators, in part used directly as a form by the initial three third-country arbitrators, and used directly as a form in 1982 by the Iranian arbitrator, Judge Mostafa Jahangir Sani. This statement was used as a guideline for the drafting of a disclosure letter for the initial three American arbitrators and in part used in the same manner by the initial third-country arbitrators. The form does not appear to have been directly used or referred to following these disclosures early in the life of the Tribunal.

Decision of the Appointing Authority, W E Haak, in the Challenge of Judge Bengt Broms (September 30, 2004), reprinted in (October 2004) 19(10) Mealey's Intl Arb Rep B-1, B-2 (emphasizing the general and foundational observation that the duties contained in Article 9 of the Tribunal Rules are directed at the arbitrator):

> 29. In the present case...Ms. Riahi and her counsel elected to invoke Article 9 of the Tribunal Rules, requesting that Judge Broms disqualify himself, and asking for a preliminary decision of this recusal. That article, however, deals with the situation in which an *arbitrator*, rather than a party, obtains knowledge of circumstances likely to give rise to justifiable doubts as to his impartiality or independence in a particular case. It focuses primarily on the disclosure of these circumstances, initially to the Tribunal's President. While the arbitrator is directed, if appropriate, to disqualify himself as to that case, this appears to be discretionary. There is no time limit provided for such recusal, and no procedure prescribed whereby a party to the arbitration may seek recusal or object to an arbitrator's failure to resign. As set forth in the Tribunal Rules, challenge [is] the proper procedure for dealing with a *party's* justifiable doubts concerning an arbitrator.

Decision of the Appointing Authority, Judge W E Haak, in the Challenge of Judges Assadollah Noori, Koorosh Ameli, Mohsen Aghahosseini, April 19, 2006:

24. Iran and the Iranian arbitrators claim that the payments have occurred since the creation of the Tribunal and that the United States has been aware of such payments since 1981. The United States argues that it only became aware of the payments from Judge Noori's statement of 6 December 2005. The United States further argues that actual prior knowledge of the facts (as opposed to constructive knowledge) is required to be shown. The United States asserts that in the present case, only "vague statements or rumors" existed prior to Judge Noori's statement of 6 December 2005 (Letter of the United States dated 10 March 2006).

25. The United States is correct in stating that evidence of actual prior knowledge on the part of the challenging party of circumstances giving rise to a challenge must be shown. Whether such actual knowledge existed or not is a matter for me as appointing authority to determine on the basis of evidence submitted. In the past history of the Tribunal such evidence has included, for example, a prior statement made by the challenging party (Decision of the appointing authority in the challenge of Judge Briner, 19 September 1989).

26. In the present case, the evidence submitted to me includes a Statement by Secretary-General Pinto that he and the Tribunal had been aware for more than twenty years that the Iranian arbitrators made payments to Iran. Mr. Pinto supported his declaration with handwritten notes from a meeting of the Committee on Administrative and Financial Questions on 26 April 1984, where a then Iranian appointed arbitrator, Mr. Kashani, stated in the presence of the Agent of the United States that the Iranian arbitrators returned part of their salaries to Iran.

27. In addition to Mr. Pinto's statement, the appointing authority was also provided with a letter dated 1 February 2006 from Dr. Seyyed Hossein Enayat, a former Iranian arbitrator, indicating that during a meeting of the Tribunal in 1981, an arbitrator appointed by the United States suggested that Iranian arbitrators may wish to return part of their salaries to Iran, should Iran deem the salaries to be too high. Dr. Enayat states that the United States Agent, who was present at the meeting, did not object to this proposal.

28. This evidence is sufficient to convince me that the United States had actual knowledge of payment by the Iranian arbitrators of a part of their salaries to Iran since at least 1984. Consequently, the Challenge brought by the United States on 21 December 2005 was made well after the time limit set out in Article 11(1) of the [1983] Tribunal Rules, and the Challenge, having failed to comply with this time limit, shall be declared inadmissible.

Decision by the Appointing Authority, Judge W E Haak, on the Challenge against Judge Seyed Jamal Seifi, September 3, 2010, at 6–7, 9–10, para 24, 26–27, 31:

24. Given this purpose, arbitrators should, as a general principle, resolve all doubts about whether or not to disclose particular facts in favor of disclosure. The fullest possible disclosure is far more likely to build confidence between an arbitrator and the Parties than a selective or incomplete disclosure of the arbitrator's personal details and experience. Indeed, full disclosure of an arbitrator's past cases in which he or she acted as either counsel or arbitrator (to the extent allowed by confidentiality obligations) has evolved into a "best practices" standard in modern arbitral proceedings, precisely in order to help forestall doubts on the part of parties and, equally important, to resolve potential conflicts of interest decisively at the soonest possible time to ensure a minimal disruption of proceedings.

26. As discussed above, arbitrators should as a general rule err on the side of caution and disclose any and all prior professional activities and other circumstances that might lead any of the parties to harbor justifiable doubts as to their impartiality or independence. Indeed, the present Challenge might have been avoided or at least been dealt with earlier had disclosure of the Cubic Arbitration been made at the time Judge Seifi first took office in August 2009. Following the practice of full disclosure would thus have precluded or greatly simplified these proceedings.

27. That said, Article 9 of the Tribunal Rules does not impose such a thorough level of disclosure as a legal requirement, stating only that an arbitrator shall disclose "any circumstances likely

to give rise to justifiable doubts as to his impartiality or independence." Even interpreting Article 9 in the manner most conducive to full disclosure, one cannot reasonably argue that it provides for a legal obligation on the part of arbitrators to disclose every previous professional engagement. If an arbitrator does not think that something he or she has done in the past meets the justifiable doubts standard, to what extent should a decision not to disclose that activity be considered consistent with the Tribunal Rules' disclosure obligation? This is not a question that easily lends itself to general formulae; every instance must be decided based on the specific circumstances alleged by the challenging party. In this case, an analysis of the extent to which an actual issue conflict exists due to Judge Seifi's membership in both the Tribunal (which will decide the remaining issues in Case B/61) and the ICC Tribunal (which decided the Cubic Arbitration) is unavoidable.

...

31. ...I am not convinced that Judge Seifi had an obligation to disclose his participation in the Cubic Arbitration, as those proceedings have not created a conflict in a manner that would lead to justifiable doubts as to Judge Seifi's capacity to decide Case B/61 in an independent and impartial manner. It is clear from a cursory reading of the Cubic Arbitration award and Case B/61's partial award that the legal bases of the cases are different – unlike the Cubic Arbitration which was a contractual claim focused on the performance of contracts related to the sale of goods and services, Case B/61 concerns the United States' obligation under the Algiers Declarations to arrange for the return of certain Iranian properties and focuses on the alleged losses suffered by Iran as the result of the United States' non-export of Iranian properties. While Judge Seifi is undoubtedly familiar with the facts and arguments leading up to the Cubic Arbitration award in 1997, the United States has not provided sufficient evidence to demonstrate that Judge Seifi would be influenced by his experience in that arbitration when hearing the remaining issues contained in Case B/61. That common facts may exist in the two cases cannot, of itself, justify the Challenge. Given the significant differences between the two proceedings, Judge Seifi's membership in the ICC Tribunal is insufficient to disqualify him from Case B/61.

(2) *Disclosure by the US Arbitrators*

Following appointment, a general disclosure was made on behalf of the US party-appointed arbitrators and substitute arbitrators by the Agent for the United States in letters to the Agent for Iran and to the President of the Tribunal.[121]

We are aware of Iranian comments upon these disclosures only in respect of Charles N. Brower; the relevant correspondence follows. Mr. Brower's original appointment as a substitute arbitrator was briefly announced March 7, 1983. A further detailed letter was sent on April 20, 1983; this letter is in a format typical of the American disclosure statement:

> With reference to Article 9 of the Provisionally Adopted Tribunal Rules, I am pleased to provide the following information concerning Charles N. Brower, recently appointed by the United States as a substitute Arbitrator on the Iran-United States Claims Tribunal.
>
> Mr. Brower was born in Plainfield, New Jersey, in 1935. He is a citizen of the United States and resides in Bethesda, Maryland.
>
> His academic degrees are: Bachelor of Arts, Harvard College, 1957; Doctor of Jurisprudence, Harvard Law School, 1961...
>
> Mr. Brower is a lawyer. Since 1961, he has been with the law firm of White & Case, with the exception of his government service during 1969–73.
>
> Mr. Brower is past Chairman of the Section of International Law and Practice of the American Bar Association, a member of the Executive Committee, American Branch of the International Law Association, and a member of the Executive Council of the American Society of International Law.

---

[121] See n 115.

He is also a member of the Panel of Arbitrators of the American Arbitration Association, the Committee on Arbitration for the United States Council for International Business, the American Law Institute, and various other professional organizations.

During 1969 to 1973, Mr. Brower held a number of senior positions in the Office of the Legal Adviser of the Department of State, including service as Acting Legal Adviser. In that capacity, he participated in numerous international negotiations and conferences... He has served as... Chairman of the Interagency Task Force on the Law of the Sea.

Over the course of 17 years of private practice Mr. Brower has represented a wide variety of diverse interests. The law firm in which Mr. Brower practices works with and against various individuals, entities and other law firms...

Mr. Brower has had no responsibility in either his private practice or government service for the negotiations or implementation of the Declaration of Algiers of January 19, 1981 or the preparation or presentation of any claim by or against the United States thereunder. Mr. Brower has not appeared for any U.S. national before the Tribunal. Other members of Mr. Brower's law firm represent four U.S. nationals in claims before the Tribunal, and the firm has advised three clients with respect to such claims but has not acted for them at the Tribunal. Mr. Brower has from time to time in the past been consulted with respect to certain of those claims. (A list of these clients is attached.) Other clients of the firm have or may have presented claims to the Tribunal as to which Mr. Brower's firm has not been consulted, but Mr. Brower has no knowledge as to the details of such claims. Mr. Brower will not act as substitute Arbitrator with regard to any matter involving a client of his law firm.

Mr. Brower is not aware that he or any member of his immediate family has any investment in any entity which is a party before the Tribunal.

Mr. Brower's appointment as the Arbitrator to succeed Richard Mosk was made on October 31, 1983, in a letter which incorporated by reference the previous disclosure statement.

The Agent for Iran in a letter to the Agent for the United States dated December 13, 1983, among other things, posed the following questions:

I would like to have the following information and disclosures about Mr. Charles Nelson Brower for review and consideration by my Government.

1. Although not indicated in your or Mr. Rovine's letters, it appears that the Inter-Agency Task Force on the Law of the Sea, of which Mr. Brower has been chairman, has been part of the National Security Council of the Government of the United States. You are requested to furnish us with detailed information in that respect including the exact date, extent of period and the nature of his engagement with the United States National Security Council.
2. Likewise, although you or Mr. Rovine's letters do not indicate, it appears that Mr. Brower has been a member of the Council on Foreign Relations. You are also requested to give full information about the functions of that Council and the period of Mr. Brower's membership as well as the extent, the role and the nature of Mr. Brower's engagement there.
3. You are requested to provide details of the cases that Mr. Brower or his firm advocated before the United States courts against Iran or Iranian entities, including copies of the pleadings, briefs and documents that Mr. Brower or his firm had or has filed in such cases.
4. You are requested to give the names of other American or non-American firms and persons in partnership or association with Mr. Brower or his firm... and the extent and nature of their works (if any—in connection with Iranian persons or entities in this Tribunal or elsewhere).
5. All articles and papers circulated and lectures given by Mr. Brower on the Algiers Accords, the functioning of the Tribunal, the subjects to be dealt with by the Tribunal, or how United States parties may act vis-à-vis the Government of Iran are also requested to be provided.

Additional information may be requested to enable the Government of the Islamic Republic of Iran to determine whether Mr. Brower is legally qualified to replace Mr. Mosk.

The Agent for the United States replied to this request in a letter dated January 5, 1984 which reads:

> Mr. Brower's earlier disclosure of the circumstances bearing upon his service as an arbitrator was thorough, candid, and more than sufficient to satisfy Part II of the Rules. Mr. Brower has asked, however, that as a matter of courtesy, I provide the following further information.
>
> (1) As indicated in Mr. Rovine's letter of April 20 (which was attached to my October 31 notification to you), Mr. Brower served as Acting Legal Adviser of the Department of State for eight months, from January 2 through August 31, 1973. During that period, he also served as Chairman of the United States Interagency Task Force on the Law of the Sea... The group was not itself part of the National Security Council, which is a statutory body of limited membership.
> (2) Mr. Brower is a member of the Council on Foreign Relations. The Council is a private, not-for-profit body concerned about foreign policy questions. It has no official responsibility or functions. Mr. Brower is also a member of several other clubs and associations but does not believe that such memberships are material to service as an arbitrator.
> (3) Mr. Brower or his firm have appeared as counsel in the following cases in United States Courts against Iran or Iranian entities:... Copies of the pleadings, briefs and other documents filed in such cases are available to the public for inspection at the courts and under the docket numbers indicated.
> (4) There are no other American or non-American persons in partnership or employment relations with Mr. Brower or his firm having any "works... in connection with Iranian persons or entities in this Tribunal or elsewhere" except as already disclosed by Mr. Brower through Mr. Rovine's letter of April 20 and my letter of October 31.
>
> Finally, Mr. Brower asked that I give to you the enclosed bibliography of his writings.

3. The Grounds for Challenge—Article 12

To protect the integrity of the arbitral proceedings, parties to those proceedings must have confidence that the presiding arbitrator or arbitrators will make every effort to reach a fair and timely result. Therefore, the requirements that the arbitrators be impartial and independent and that they not fail to act are essential if the institution of arbitration is to maintain the respect needed to be an effective means of settling international commercial disputes.

Article 12(1)–(2) defines which arbitrators may be challenged and the grounds for challenge based on lack of impartiality or independence under the UNCITRAL Rules. Article 12(3) also provides that arbitrators may also be removed under the challenge procedure for failure to act or in the event of *de jure* or *de facto* impossibility to perform, a topic addressed in Chapter 6.

A. Text of the 2010 UNCITRAL Rule[122]

Article 12(1)–(2) of the 2010 UNCITRAL Rules provides:

---

[122] Corresponding Article 10 of the 1976 UNCITRAL Rules provides:
1. Any arbitrator may be challenged if circumstances exist that give rise to justifiable doubts as to the arbitrator's impartiality or independence.

1. Any arbitrator may be challenged if circumstances exist that give rise to justifiable doubts as to the arbitrator's impartiality or independence.
2. A party may challenge the arbitrator appointed by it only for reasons of which it becomes aware after the appointment has been made.
3. ... [This provision is addressed in Chapter 6]

B. Commentary

(1) Challenge on the ground of justifiable doubts as to impartiality or independence—general remarks on Article 12(1)

Article 12(1) provides that: "Any arbitrator may be challenged if circumstances exist that give rise to justifiable doubts as to the arbitrator's impartiality or independence." Several issues emerging out of the drafting of the rule and its application by international tribunals are noteworthy.

(a) The standard for impartiality and independence is objective

The inclusion of the word "justifiable" in Article 12(1), to define the kind of doubt required to sustain a challenge, reflects UNCITRAL's clear intention of establishing an objective standard for impartiality and independence. While a party's subjective concerns about an arbitrator's bias may prompt a challenge, it is the objective reasonableness of these concerns that is ultimately determinative. The appointing authority in the Challenge Decision of January 11, 1995 aptly explained the standard:

> If the doubt had merely to arise in the mind of a party contesting the impartiality of an arbitrator, "justifiable" would have been almost redundant. The word must import some other standard—a doubt that is justifiable in an objective sense. In other words, the claimant here has to furnish adequate and solid grounds for its doubts. Those grounds must respond to reasonable criteria. In sum, would a reasonably well informed person believe that the perceived apprehension—the doubt—is justifiable? Is it ascertainable by that person and so serious as to warrant the removal of the arbitrators?[123]

In short, "the test to be applied is that the doubts existing on the part of the [party raising the challenge] must be 'justifiable' on some objective basis."[124] More recent decisions resolving challenges raised in the context of investment arbitration confirm this interpretation of Article 12(1).[125]

---

2. A party may challenge the arbitrator appointed by him only for reasons of which he becomes aware after the appointment has been made.

[123] Challenge Decision of January 11, 1995, para 23, reprinted in (1997) XXII Ybk Commercial Arb 227, 234. Additional text from the decision is reprinted in section 3(C).

[124] Challenge Decision of January 11, 1995, n 123, para 30. The appointing authority's conception of the "objective observer" was a "well informed but disinterested commercial person assessing the matter without specific expertise but aware of the political background against which the matter arises and of the nature of a lawyer's professional services." Para 31.

[125] See *National Grid PLC* and *Republic of Argentina*, Decision on the Challenge to Mr Judd L Kessler (December 3, 2007) (LCIA Case No UN 7949, 1976 UNCITRAL Rules, UK-Argentina BIT), at 18–19, paras 75–87 (applying an objective test, "pursuant to which it has to be determined whether a reasonable, fair-minded and informed person has justifiable doubts as to the arbitrator's impartiality"); *Vito G Gallo* and *Government of Canada*, Decision on the Challenge to Mr J Christopher Thomas, QC (October 14, 2009) (ICSID administered, 1976 UNCITRAL Rules, NAFTA Chapter Eleven Proceeding), at 6, para 19 (finding the standard is objective as it "requires not only doubt, but doubt that is justifiable"); *AWG Group Ltd* and *Argentine Republic,* Decision

(b) The same standard applies to party-appointed and non-party-appointed arbitrators

Discussions on the preliminary draft of Article 10(1) of the 1976 UNCITRAL Rules (corresponding and identical to Article 12(1) of the 2010 UNCITRAL Rules) concerned whether the rule on impartiality and independence of arbitrators should apply to both party-appointed arbitrators and non-party-appointed arbitrators (eg sole or presiding arbitrators).[126]

The issue arose in part because of differences in state practice in this regard. In the United States, for example, the prevailing practice had been that the parties could agree that party-appointed arbitrators will be subject to the same standard as the non-party-appointed arbitrators or be subject to a lesser standard, implicitly recognizing the different position of the party-appointed arbitrator.[127]

In contrast, most other countries, including most European countries, employ a single standard of conduct for both party-appointed and non-party-appointed arbitrators.[128]

During the drafting of the 1976 UNCITRAL Rules, some argued that requiring impartiality of all arbitrators (1) would lead the institution of arbitration to gain greater respect, (2) was in accord with the arbitration laws of many countries, and (3) would therefore be widely acceptable and would not conflict with applicable laws governing the arbitration.[129] The main argument raised against requiring a party-appointed arbitrator to be neutral was that it was impractical and unrealistic to impose such an obligation, if for no other reason than that such arbitrators were dependent on the party who appointed him for fees.[130]

In the end, the UNCITRAL drafters concluded that the rule embodied in Article 10(1) of the 1976 UNCITRAL Rules as to arbitrator impartiality and independence should apply to every arbitrator.[131] The same rule holds for identical Article 12(1) of the 2010

---

on the Second Proposal for the Disqualification of a Member of the Arbitral Tribunal (May 12, 2008) (ICSID administered, 1976 UNCITRAL Rules, UK-Argentina BIT), at 11, para 22 (finding the operative question to be: "Would a reasonable, informed person viewing the facts be led to conclude that there is a justifiable doubt as to the challenged arbitrator's independence and impartiality?"); all reprinted in section 3(C). See also "LCIA Court Decisions on Challenges to Arbitrators Reference No UN 3490, October 21, 2005 and December 27, 2005," summarized in 27(3) Arb Intl 377, 384–6 (recognizing a reasonable man test).

[126] UN Doc A/10017, n 71, paras 65–69, reprinted in (1975) VI UNCITRAL Ybk 24, 32.

[127] The situation has since reversed. See P Rutledge, R Kent and C Henel, "United States", in F Weigand (ed) *Practitioner's Handbook on International Commercial Arbitration* (2nd edn 2009) 897. See also AAA/ABA Code of Ethics, Note on Neutrality (effective March 1, 2004), AAA Commercial Rules, R-12,17; CPR International Rules, r 7.1; JAMS International Rules, Article 8.1. See also J Poudret and S Besson, *Comparative Law of International Arbitration* (2nd edn 2007) 346.

[128] See R Mosk, "The Role of Party-Appointed Arbitrators," n 1, 260 ("Most rules for institutional international arbitrations and European arbitration laws make no distinction between party-appointed and non-party-appointed arbitrators for purposes of their independence and impartiality"). See also J Poudret and S Besson, *Comparative Law*, n 127.

[129] UN Doc A/10017, n 71, para 68, reprinted in (1975) VI UNCITRAL Ybk 24, 32.

[130] UN Doc A/10017, n 71, para 69.

[131] See *Report of the Secretary-General on the Revised Draft Set of Arbitration Rules*, UNCITRAL, 9th Session, Addendum 1 (Commentary), UN Doc A/CN.9/112/Add.1 (1975), reprinted in (1976) VII UNCITRAL Ybk 166, 170 (Commentary on Draft Article 9(1)). See also Decision of the Appointing Authority on the Challenge of Judge Broms, May 7, 2001, at 11, reprinted in section 3(D)(1); Challenge of April 15, 1993 para 1, and Challenge of January 11, 1995, para 8, both reprinted in section 3(C).

UNCITRAL Rules. Since this basis for challenge has general application, a party-appointed arbitrator on a three-member arbitral tribunal can be challenged on the ground that circumstances exist that give rise to justifiable doubts as to such arbitrator's impartiality or independence, even if such doubts are due to his relationship to the party who appointed him.

Of course, the decision to adopt a single standard does not alter the fact that the party-appointed arbitrator is appointed by a party who has made their selection strategically and often after much research into the prospective arbitrator's background. Moreover, it has been argued that the party-appointed arbitrator has the additional ethical duty of ensuring that the case of the party that appointed him or her has been fully considered by the tribunal. In our opinion, however, each arbitrator has the duty to ensure that the case of each party has been fully considered.

The fact that there is tolerance of some party-appointed arbitrators who exhibit a degree of partiality toward, or dependence on, the party that appointed him or her does not alter the fact that there is only one standard applicable. Instead, such tolerance should be viewed as either evidence of a strategic decision of a party to not challenge or as a characteristic of an institution such as the Iran–US Claims Tribunal.

At the Iran–US Claims Tribunal, most, but not all, challenges involved the third-country arbitrators. Given that the US government and the US claimant community viewed the Iranian arbitrators for the most part as not independent or impartial, this practice arguably reflects a tolerance of some partiality or dependence on the part of those party-appointed arbitrators. The practice possibly also reflected the strategic judgment of the US agent and US claimant community that (1) a challenge against an Iranian party-appointed arbitrator would be pointless because it would be time-consuming and, even if successful, would result only in Iran's appointment of another equally objectionable person, and (2) the belief that arbitrators obviously lacking independence and impartiality tend not to be particularly effective in deliberations. Of course, such a strategic judgment necessarily also involves a failure to raise a challenge in a timely manner and therefore a loss of the right to do so on the particular basis involved.

Over time, as indicated above, the disclosure statements from Iranians were relevant primarily for identifying the cases they had directly worked on as counsel. Often these cases were limited to those where their involvement would have been reported by others in any event. This became evident in the context of a challenge to Judge Noori for serving (but not disclosing his role) as General Counsel of the parent corporation of the respondent. In 1999, Judge Briner, then President of the Tribunal, stated to the appointing authority that Tribunal practice was for arbitrators to disclose "one's previous participation as counsel or advocate for one of the parties in a particular case pending before the Tribunal."[132] The appointing authority, citing this narrow disclosure requirement, found both that Judge Noori's earlier position did not give rise to justifiable doubts and that Judge Noori "has been wrongly accused of having infringed Article 9."[133]

---

[132] Decision of the Appointing Authority on the Challenge of Judge Noori, August 31, 1990, n 45, at 317. Note the President did not say that this was all that was thought required in disclosure by arbitrators, but rather implicitly that it was all that had come to be expected of the Iranian arbitrators.

[133] Decision of the Appointing Authority, n 45, at 324.

In our view, the appointing authority's reasoning should not be taken as an accurate interpretation of corresponding Article 10 of the 1976 UNCITRAL Rules, but rather as a decision confined to the facts of a particular case and institution. As Baker and Davis note: "Is there any doubt that if Judge Briner had concealed a past position as, for example, general counsel of Amoco Iran's parent company he would not have been permitted to decide the case?"[134]

More recently, the Appointing Authority, Judge W E Haak, has taken an admirably principled view on the matter. In the challenges of Judges Skubizsewski and Arangio-Ruiz, Judge Haak strongly criticized Iran's decision to challenge only the two third-country arbitrators, but not the party-appointed arbitrators, who joined in the majority in the partial award in Case No B61. Iran had argued that "a challenge against party-appointed arbitrators even if sustained may not ultimately bring any real changes to the Tribunal or its decisions."[135] Judge Haak rejected this assertion on principle, finding that it would be "tantamount to the Appointing Authority agreeing to hold party-appointed arbitrators to a lower standard of impartiality than third-country arbitrators," a situation not contemplated under the UNCITRAL Rules.[136]

(c) Criteria regarding and examples of justifiable doubts

Concerned that the language of [corresponding] Article 10(1) of the 1976 UNCITRAL Rules alone would not provide sufficient guidance, the original drafters of the Rules considered adding an additional paragraph to make the grounds for challenge of arbitrators more explicit. They attempted to create a list of examples of possible partiality or dependence which would give rise to "justifiable doubt." Their discussion focused on two specific examples which seemed clearly to raise justifiable doubts: a financial or personal interest in the outcome of the arbitration, or family or commercial ties with either party or with a party's counsel or agent.[137] The drafters concluded, however, that the creation of such a list was fraught with difficulties. The list would need to be exhaustive, an impossible task.[138] There was always a chance that cases might fall outside the list, yet nonetheless raise justifiable grounds for challenge.[139] The other main concern with such a list was how to define exactly what types of commercial ties would prove disqualifying. Arbitrators often have some relationship with one or both of the parties and many of these relationships, even when commercial, could be trivial and not raise justifiable doubts as to impartiality or independence.[140]

As an alternative to creating a list, some members of the original Drafting Committee recommended the creation of categories of circumstances giving rise to justifiable doubts. "Absolute" grounds would only include a direct financial or personal interest in the

---

[134] S Baker and M Davis, *The UNCITRAL Rules in Practice*, n 1, at 56.
[135] Decision of the Appointing Authority, Judge W E Haak, on the Challenges against Judges Krzysztof Skubiszewski and Gaetano Arangio-Ruiz, March 5, 2010, at 16, para 67 (citing Iran's Second Submission dated October 22, 2009, at 6 n 4). See also generally n 61.
[136] Decision of the Appointing Authority, n 135, at 16, para 67.
[137] *Report of the Secretary General on the Preliminary Draft Set of Arbitration Rules*, UNCITRAL, 8th Session, UN Doc A/CN.9/97 (1974), reprinted in (1975) VI UNCITRAL Ybk 163, 171 (Commentary on Draft Article 8(2)); UN Doc A/10017, n 71, paras 70–72, reprinted in (1975) VI UNCITRAL Ybk 24, 32 (Commentary on Draft Article 8(2)).
[138] See UNCITRAL, 8th Session, UN Doc A/CN.9/97, n 137, para 73.
[139] UNCITRAL, 8th Session, UN Doc A/CN.9/97, n 137, para 73.
[140] UNCITRAL, 8th Session, UN Doc A/CN.9/97, n 137, para 73.

outcome of the dispute and certain specified close ties, such as close family ties, between the arbitrator and a party. Proof of these grounds would result automatically in a successful challenge.[141] "Relative" grounds would include all other grounds for challenge. For a challenge on "relative" grounds to succeed, it would be necessary to prove not just that the grounds existed, but that they gave rise to justifiable doubts as to the impartiality or independence of any arbitrator.[142] A problem with this type of categorization was that it did not really help in defining the type of circumstances that would be required to sustain a challenge, since the challenging party often would still need to prove into which category the circumstances fit.

In the end, but not without dissent,[143] the Drafting Committee agreed to delete the proposed paragraph 2 of the Preliminary Draft, which included specific grounds for challenge, and to retain the general statement in paragraph 1 as the standard for determining the validity of a challenge.[144] The difficulties in defining, in the time available, what relationships to the dispute or parties would be disqualifying, without also complicating the identification of competent arbitrators overwhelmed the attempt to define more specific criteria. The result is that the content of Article 10(1) of the 1976 UNCITRAL Rules, and corresponding Article 12(1) of the 2010 UNCITRAL Rules, is to be determined in practice by the parties, arbitrators, and, ultimately, the appointing authority. The practice of the Iran–US Claims Tribunal shows that the decision to leave the language of Article 10(1) of the 1976 UNCITRAL Rules sufficiently broad to encompass a wide variety of situations was wise. A variety of circumstances not envisioned or considered by the original drafters have been addressed during challenge procedures at the Tribunal and in investment arbitration.

(2) Challenge on the ground of justifiable doubts as to impartiality or independence

Although the grounds for challenge in Article 12(1), like in corresponding Article 10(1) of the 1976 UNCITRAL Rules, appear quite encompassing, they leave a great deal to interpretation.

Given the general objective of ensuring that arbitrators are impartial and independent, how is a lack of impartiality or independence to be established? Article 12(1) provides that any arbitrator can be challenged on the basis of "circumstances which give rise to justifiable doubts" as to impartiality or independence. A party therefore needs to (1) establish the existence of certain "circumstances" and (2) establish that these circumstances "give rise to *justifiable* doubts" as to impartiality or independence. The challenging party need not establish a lack of impartiality or independence, but only justifiable doubts regarding those qualities. The following sections address five issues: (a) what is meant by "impartiality" and "independence"; (b) when are doubts as to impartiality or independence "justified"; (c) does the stage of the proceeding at which the challenge is raised bear on the standard to be employed in evaluating whether doubts as to impartiality or independence are justified; (d) does a failure to disclose under Article 11 per se establish justifiable doubts as to

---

[141] UNCITRAL, 8th Session, UN Doc A/CN.9/97, n 137, para 73.
[142] UNCITRAL, 8th Session, UN Doc A/CN.9/97, n 137, para 73.
[143] See *Summary Record of the 3rd Meeting of the Committee of the Whole (II)*, UNCITRAL, 9th Session, UN Doc A/CN.9/9/C.2/SR.3, at 3, para 17 (1976) (Comment by Mr Holtzmann, United States).
[144] *Summary Record*, n 143, at 4.

impartiality or independence; and (e) are there any limitations on the "circumstances" which may be used as the basis for justifiable doubts?

(a) The meaning of "impartiality" and "independence"

What does it mean for an arbitrator to be impartial and independent? In general, impartiality means that an arbitrator will not favor one party more than another, while independence requires that the arbitrator remain free from the control of either party. Impartiality thus refers to the arbitrator's internal disposition, while independence refers to external control over the arbitrator. Impartiality is a state of mind and thus somewhat elusive, while independence involves some relationship and is thus much more a question of fact. There is, however, no strict division between the two concepts, as external factors or conditions—although not necessarily sufficient to put in question the arbitrator's independence—might strengthen the objective justifiability of the doubts expressed by a party about an arbitrator's impartiality.[145] The distinction in concepts has been recognized in the practice of arbitral tribunals.[146]

(b) When are doubts as to impartiality or independence justified?

How, and on what basis, is the appointing authority to decide that doubts as to impartiality and independence are justified (ie, would a reasonable person find the doubts to be justified)? Application of a "reasonable person" standard in a multi-cultural setting would be difficult. Yet, although the parties may represent a multi-cultural context, it is also true that the community of international commercial arbitrators have many shared values. For example, the circumstances thought to provide "absolute" grounds for challenge are sufficiently shared to be a basis for impartiality or independence. In addition, the shared values of the international arbitration community are reflected in codes of ethics such as those issued by the International Bar Association.[147] Although these codes of ethics are not mandatory for most tribunals, their invocation by disputing parties and their citation by appointing authorities and tribunals in practice suggests that such ethical rules may provide particularly important guideposts as to whether certain circumstances should be viewed as giving rise to justifiable doubts.[148] Yet other circumstances will be more difficult

---

[145] See generally section 3(B)(1)(a). In its case law regarding the independence and impartiality of a tribunal (under Article 6 of the European Convention on Human Rights), the European Court of Human Rights (ECHR) has on many occasions recognized the difficulty in separating the two concepts. For example, this was the case in *Holm v Sweden* involving a freedom of speech trial with a jury largely consisting of members of one political party. The Court examined the issues of independence and impartiality together and concluded that "the independence and impartiality of the District Court were open to doubt and that the applicant's fears in this respect were objectively justified." *Holm*, ECHR (1993), Series A, Vol 279-A, para 33. For the sake of clarity, it should be noted that the requirements of Article 6 do not apply fully to arbitration. Within certain limits it is possible to waive Convention rights, and the conclusion of an arbitration agreement can be regarded as such a waiver. See, eg, *Nordström-Janzon v Netherlands* 528101/95), Decision of the European Commission of Human Rights (November 27, 1996) DR 87-A, 112. See also N Blackaby and C Partasides, *Redfern and Hunter on International Arbitration*, n 113, 266–8, 274–7.

[146] See, eg, *National Grid PLC* and *Republic of Argentina,* Decision on the Challenge to Mr Judd L Kessler (December 3, 2007) (LCIA administered UN 7949, 1976 UNCITRAL Rules, UK-Argentina BIT), at 18, paras 76–77.

[147] See 2004 IBA Guidelines on Conflicts of Interest in International Arbitration.

[148] See Decision of the Appointing Authority, Judge W E Haak, on the Challenges against Judges Krzysztof Skubiszewski and Gaetano Arangio-Ruiz, March 5, 2010, at 10, para 43 (finding that "[t]ogether with the case precedents of the Tribunal established through past challenges, the IBA Guidelines will inform my analysis in this Challenge").

to evaluate and, ultimately, it will be up to the appointing authority to decide whether doubts based on such other circumstances are justified.

Another issue to be addressed is: against what degree of knowledge of the circumstances is the justifiability of the doubts to be assessed? In the second challenge by Iran of Judge Briner, the parties argued two different notions of how a reasonable person standard should be applied in challenge proceedings. For Amoco, the test was whether a reasonable person, *after reviewing the evidence* adduced in support of the challenge, would conclude that justifiable doubts existed. For the Iranians, "the controlling term 'doubt' is formed *on the basis of appearances*, not as a result of the careful analysis of the evidence."[149] Clearly, the more objective view proposed by Amoco must be accepted given that the Iranian view can result in easy manipulation by the challenging party. Thus in his decision on the second Briner challenge, the appointing authority drew a distinction between challenges based on serious doubts and justifiable doubts, ie, the fact that one side has its own doubts does not mean those doubts are justifiable. In drafting corresponding Article 10 of the 1976 UNCITRAL Rules, the Committee also discussed the distinction between serious and justifiable doubts.[150] The Mexican representative did not find it appropriate to speak of serious doubts since a party would always consider its doubts serious.[151] The United States representative agreed and emphasized the importance of the term "justifiable" as a limitation on areas of challenge: "omission of the word 'justifiable' could open up too many areas for challenge."[152]

Finally, sustaining a challenge of an arbitrator under Article 12 does not necessarily require proof of an arbitrator's *actual* lack of impartiality or independence. The *appearance* of these deficiencies may alone suffice in certain circumstances to disqualify an arbitrator. Article 12 notably requires only that "doubts" as to an arbitrator's impartiality or independence be proven to be justifiable, not that an arbitrator is, in fact, biased or dependent on a party. Article 12 thus establishes a standard with sufficient flexibility to address situations which, even in the absence of actual bias or dependence, nevertheless create a sufficiently negative perception about an arbitrator's impartiality and independence to justify his or her removal.[153]

Appointing authorities, arbitral tribunals, and parties have considered several circumstances that could potentially justify doubts as to an arbitrator's impartiality and independence, such as an arbitrator's (1) relationship with a witness; (2) financial relationship with a party through shareholdings; (3) financial relationship with a party through potential control over arbitrator salaries; (4) previous employment by the parent corporation of a party; (5) representation in another forum that is adverse to a party; (6) previous advocacy on behalf of a country formerly adverse to a sovereign party; (7) representation of a third party with a right to intervene in the proceedings; (8) handling of the proceedings; (9)

---

[149] Reply Memorandum of Iran regarding the Challenge of Judge Briner in Case No 55, November 28, 1988, reprinted in 20 Iran-US CTR 260, 273 (1988–III). See also, extract reprinted in section 3(D)(2).

[150] See Decision of the Appointing Authority on the Second Challenge by Iran of Judge Briner, September 19, 1989 at 4–6, 8–9, reprinted in 21 Iran-US CTR 384, 387–91 (1989–I). See also discussion at section 1(B)(4) and extract reprinted in section 3(D)(1)

[151] See *Summary Record of the 15th Meeting of the Committee of the Whole (II)*, UNCITRAL, 9th Session, UN Doc A/CN.9/9/C.2/SR.15, at 7, para 65 (1976) (Comment by Mr Mantilla-Molina).

[152] *Summary Record*, n 151, para 63 (Comment by Mr Holtzmann, United States).

[153] See section 1(A)(8), for a discussion of the appointing authority's decision in the challenge to Mr Christopher Thomas in the *Gallo* arbitration.

statement regarding a party or the dispute; (10) decision-making; (11) breach of the confidentiality of deliberations; (12) physical assault of a fellow arbitrator.

(1) An arbitrator's relationship with a witness

The first Iranian challenge of Judge Briner over his participation in Case No 55 raised the question of whether a past professional relationship with an expert witness gave rise to justifiable doubts.[154] The preparatory work for the 1976 UNCITRAL Rules did not discuss this as a category of circumstances, in part because the original drafters focused exclusively on relationships that arbitrators might have with the parties. There was never any mention by the drafters of an arbitrator's relationship with a witness as a circumstance giving rise to justifiable doubts. However, as two commentators have pointed out, "there can be no doubt that in some cases close family or financial ties to an important witness could be legitimate concern—especially if the nature of the relationship renders the arbitrator incapable of assessing the witness's credibility with objectivity."[155] Indeed, both the Iranian and Amoco memoranda agreed that in some cases an arbitrator's relationship with a witness could give rise to justifiable doubts as to impartiality and independence, even though neither party could find a case of an arbitrator being disqualified for a relationship with an expert witness.

The two parties disagreed vehemently, however, as to whether Judge Briner's relationship with Morgan Stanley was the type that would give rise to justifiable doubts. Amoco argued that relationships between arbitrators and witnesses should rarely if ever be considered disqualifying. Amoco looked to national statutes and rules of arbitration associations and concluded that:

> the fact that relations of arbitrators with parties are always specifically mentioned, while relations with witnesses almost never are, has at least three implications: (1) a relation with a witness is much less likely to be considered disqualifying than a relation with a party; (2) in fulfilling a disclosure obligation, an arbitrator will quite naturally and reasonably focus on his relations with parties rather than with witnesses; (3) in assessing whether a relationship is significant enough to require disclosure or disqualification, a reasonable man will conclude that a relation with a witness need not lead to these results unless it is considerably more extensive and significant than a relation with a party that may produce one or both of these results.[156]

Iran, on the other hand, relied heavily on the ethical standards on disclosure set forth in the IBA and the AAA Rules to show that an arbitrator's relations with a witness could give rise to justifiable doubts as to impartiality and independence. Paragraph 3.3 of the Draft Guidelines of the IBA on Ethics for Arbitrators, for example, provided: "Any current direct or indirect business relationship between an arbitrator and a party, or with a person who is known to be a potentially important witness, will normally give rise to justifiable doubts as to a prospective arbitrator's impartiality or independence."[157]

---

[154] See also discussion at section 1(B)(3).
[155] See S Baker and M Davis, *The UNCITRAL Rules in Practice*, n 1, 49.
[156] Memorandum of Amoco Iran Oil regarding the Challenge of Judge Briner in Case No 55 by Iran, November 2, 1988, reprinted in 20 Iran-US CTR 233, 250 (1988–III). See also extracts reprinted in section 3(D)(1).
[157] Cited in Memorandum of Iran regarding its Challenge of Judge Briner in Case No 55, September 28, 1988, reprinted in 20 Iran-US CTR 190, 212 (1988–III). The IBA Rules of Ethics for International Arbitrators, adopted in 1987, were reprinted in (1987) 15 Intl Business Lawyer 332. For a later related effort, see the 2004 IBA Guidelines on Conflicts of Interest in International Arbitration.

By what measure should an appointing authority decide whether an arbitrator's past relationship with a multinational corporation currently acting as an expert witness is trivial or substantial? Judge Briner noted that, although he was a director of Morgan Stanley's inactive Swiss affiliate, he had very little contact with Morgan Stanley personnel and none with the individuals responsible for the valuation of the claim in Case No 55. He therefore considered his relationship not significant and not even subject to the disclosure requirement under Article 9 of the Tribunal Rules. Such an attenuated relationship was, in his view, not even likely to give rise to, never mind support, justifiable doubts about his impartiality or independence. Needless to say, Iran did not accept this view and argued instead that as a former director and employee of a part of the corporation now serving as a key expert witness, Judge Briner's relationship did give rise to justifiable doubts. There does not appear to be any clear answer to whether an arbitrator's relationship with a subsidiary or affiliate of a large multinational corporation acting as an expert witness or even as a party would be disqualifying. The spirit of the UNCITRAL Rules suggests that such a relationship would not be automatically disqualifying, given the interest in finding experienced arbitrators and the varied business contacts of many arbitrators. On the other hand, the relationship of an arbitrator with one part of a company could affect his ability to judge objectively the credibility of another.

Upon withdrawing from the case, Judge Briner mentioned his concern for avoidance of further delay to the claimant. Implicitly, his withdrawal also suggests that he was at least somewhat concerned that the basis for the challenge might be sustained. This concern, however, either could reflect an assessment of the merits or Judge Briner's conclusion that, as in other areas of Tribunal procedure, concerns for upholding the legitimacy of the Tribunal's authority in the face of Iranian protests would lead to an overly strict application of the standard of impartiality and independence in his case.

(2) An arbitrator's financial relationship with a party (shareholding)

In the *AWG* arbitration against Argentina, Professor Kaufmann-Kohler was challenged because of her appointment as a director of the UBS Group ("UBS").[158] After constitution of the arbitral tribunal, it became known that Professor Kaufmann-Kohler was serving as director and that UBS held nominal shareholdings in two of the claimants involved in the consolidated proceedings, though not in the third, AWG Group Ltd. Thus, the two arbitrators deciding the challenge as a truncated tribunal observed that "the only connection, if one may call it that, between Professor Kaufmann-Kohler and the Claimant AWG Group Ltd is the fact that she is a director of UBS and that UBS, among its many other activities and interests through the world, conducts research and develops financial products related to the water sector."[159] On the question of whether that situation justified sustaining the challenge, the truncated tribunal found:

The existence of such purported connection is not enough to establish a "circumstance" giving rise to justifiable doubts as to an arbitrator's independence and impartiality. Such a connection must be significant and direct, such as an economic relationship causing an arbitrator to be dependent in

---

[158] For a discussion, see section 1(A)(6).
[159] Decision on a Second Proposal for the Disqualification of a Member of the Arbitral Tribunal, May 12, 2008, at 12–13, *Suez, Sociedad General de Aguas de Barcelona SA and Vivendi Universal SA* and *Argentine Republic, Suez, Sociedad General de Aguas de Barcelona SA and InterAguas Servicios Integrales del Agua* and *Argentine Republic, and AWG Group Ltd* and *Argentine Republic*. For additional text from the decision, see section 3(C).

some way on a party. Such Connection between Professor Kaufmann Kohler and AWG Group Limited, as suggested though not specifically alleged by the Respondent, is too remote and tenuous as to hardly be called a connection or relationship at all.[160]

(3) An arbitrator's financial relationship with a party (salary)

After one Iranian arbitrator, Judge Noori, mentioned at a budget meeting of the Full Tribunal that the Iranian arbitrators remit a portion of their salaries back to Iran, the United States challenged all three of them.[161] The United States argued that the Iranian arbitrators were impermissibly "financially dependent" on Iran because Iran "effectively determines the income received by each of its appointed arbitrators."[162] In a subsequent submission, the United States elaborated on its concern:

> In such circumstances, a party-appointed arbitrator, especially one for whom his service as a Tribunal member is his sole or main support, is completely at the mercy of the Party that appointed him for the quality of his life and the well-being of his family. That Party can lower the authorized base amount to punish, or raise it to reward, the behaviour of the arbitrator.[163]

If it were proven that the Iranian payments functioned as illicit "kickbacks," as the United States argued, such an arrangement of significant financial dependency would most likely give rise to justifiable doubts as to an arbitrator's impartiality and independence under prevailing practice. However, the appointing authority dismissed the US challenge in light of explanations provided by Iran and the Iranian arbitrators that the payments in question were made legitimately pursuant to Iranian tax law, a process which they argued deprived Iran of any undue power over the arbitrators who it appointed to the tribunal.[164]

(4) An arbitrator's previous employment by the parent corporation of a party

In Case No 248 before the Iran–US Claims Tribunal, Judge Noori was challenged for his failure to disclose that he had earlier served as general counsel of the parent corporation of the respondent. In this challenge, the appointing authority applied a quite different standard. The appointing authority concluded that even if "his service as Head of the NIOI legal office [the parent corporation of the Respondent] and his failure to disclose this to the President of the Tribunal were true, I do not feel this doubt can be termed justifiable doubt."[165] Justice Moons dismissed this circumstance much too readily and, in this sense, we view his decision primarily as reflecting the low expectations of impartiality that came to be placed on the Iranian-appointed arbitrators.

---

[160] Decision on a Second Proposal for the Disqualification of a Member of the Arbitral Tribunal, n 159, at 13.
[161] For a discussion, see also section 1(B)(11).
[162] Letter from the US Agent, Mr Clifton Johnson, to the Appointing Authority, Judge W E. Haak, regarding Notice of Challenge of Mr Assadollah Noori, Mr Koorosh H Ameli, and Mr Mohsen Aghahoseeini, December 21, 2005, at 1.
[163] Letter from the US Agent, Mr Clifton Johnson, to the Appointing Authority, Judge W E Haak, regarding the Challenge of Mr Assadollah Noori, Mr Koorosh H Ameli, and Mr Mohsen Aghahoseeini, February 3, 2006, at 7. For additional text of the decision, see section 3(D)(1).
[164] Decision by the Appointing Authority, Judge W E Haak, on the Challenge against Judges Assadollah Noori, Koorosh H Ameli, and Mohsen Aghahosseini, at 5–6, paras 31–33. For the text of the decision, see section 3(D)(1).
[165] Decision of the Appointing Authority on the Challenge of Judge Noori, n 56, at 324.

(5) An arbitrator's representation in another forum that is adverse to a party

Upon appointment by the claimant as arbitrator in the *ICS* arbitration against Argentina, Mr Stanimir Alexandrov disclosed that his law firm and he personally represented two different claimants in another arbitration against Argentina. The Appointing Authority found that:

> this puts Mr. Alexandrov in a situation of adversity towards Argentina, a situation that is often a source of justified concerns and that I believe in principle should be avoided, except where circumstances exist that eliminate justifiable doubts as to the arbitrator's impartiality or independence.[166]

In sustaining Argentina's challenge request, the Appointing Authority found support in two sections of the "Orange List" of the IBA Guidelines on Conflicts of Interest in International Arbitration: Section 3.1.2 addressing circumstances in which "[t]he arbitrator has within the past three years served as counsel against one of the parties or an affiliate of one of the parties in an unrelated matter and Section 3.4.1 covering circumstances in which "[t]he arbitrator's law firm is currently acting adverse to one of the parties or an affiliate of one of the parties."[167] The Appointing Authority emphasized that "this is not merely a case in which the arbitrator's law firm is acting adversely to one of the parties in the dispute, but rather a case where the arbitrator has personally and recently acted adversely to one of the parties to the dispute."[168]

A similar situation arose in the *Grand River* arbitration, in which the US Government challenged Professor James Anaya, who was appointed as arbitrator by Native American persons in the NAFTA Chapter Eleven proceeding against the United States, while simultaneously representing or assisting other Native American persons in procedures before the Inter-American Commission on Human Rights and the UN CERD. The Appointing Authority found these circumstances would justify the US Government's challenge, unless Professor Anaya ceased his non-NAFTA work, which he agreed to do. At the same time, the Appointing Authority found that Professor Anaya's continued instruction of his law students in a clinical course involving work concerning Native American peoples and the CERD. As justification, the Appointing Authority reasoned:

> A reasonable distinction can be made between: (i) representing parties in international fora where the underlying aim is similar to the aim of the current arbitration (i.e., assessing whether the United States is in compliance with its international legal obligations); and (ii) supervising students as part of a clinical course. The former requires advocacy of a position; the latter involves instruction and mentoring.[169]

(6) An arbitrator's previous advocacy on behalf of a country formerly adverse to a sovereign party

In the challenge decision of January 11, 1995, published anonymously,[170] the claimant, Country X, challenged the arbitrator appointed by the respondent, Company Q, on

---

[166] *ICS Inspection and Control Services Ltd* and *Republic of Argentina*, Decision on Challenge to Arbitrator (Jernej Sekolec, Appointing Authority) (December 17, 2009), at 4 (PCA administered, 1976 UNCITRAL Rules, UK-Argentina BIT). For additional text of the decision, see section 3C.

[167] *ICS Inspection and Control Services Ltd* (1976 Rules), at 4.

[168] *ICS Inspection and Control Services Ltd* (1976 Rules), at 5. For a discussion, see also section 1(A)(7).

[169] Letter from Ms Ana Palacio, ICSID Secretary-General, to Professor James Anaya (November 28, 2007), n 12, at 2. For a discussion, see also section 1(A)(4).

[170] For a discussion, see also section 1(A)(2). See Challenge Decision of January 11, 1995, reprinted in part, in (1997) XXII Ybk Commercial Arb 227.

grounds that justifiable doubts existed as to his impartiality. The claimant alleged that the respondent's arbitrator had served as a high-ranking legal advisor to Country A during a period of demonstrably hostile relations with Country X. The claimant also alleged that the respondent's arbitrator had served as legal counsel to an official of Country A in connection with Country A's military activities in Country X.[171] The upshot of the challenge was thus the concern that the respondent's arbitrator would be partial since his previous advocacy on behalf of Country A had aligned him so closely with the policies of Country A, which historically were adverse to Country X. Of significant concern was the fact that "some of the underlying questions in the arbitration, ha[d] to do with the actions of the claimant government [Country X] and its Ministers whose credibility... will be in issue."[172]

The challenge was adjudicated by an Appointing Authority designated by the Secretary-General of the Permanent Court of Arbitration pursuant to Articles 6 and 12(1)(c) of the 1976 UNCITRAL Rules. In support of its challenge, the claimant, Country X, submitted a legal opinion and a brief written by the respondent's arbitrator in his respective capacities as legal advisor and legal counsel.

The Appointing Authority recognized that the unique political backdrop between Country X and Country A distinguished the dispute from the typical commercial arbitration. The Appointing Authority thus concluded that the standard for resolving the challenge "cannot... be a uniquely commercial one in a case such as this" and that the "general political factors" require "a most careful weighing of all elements."[173] Though highly relevant, the politics surrounding the case were not dispositive. The Appointing Authority rightly concluded that the real test was whether there was "some direct relationship, something of real substance, that establishes a link on the record in the case, with that [political] background and that points to possible eventual partiality on the arbitrator's part."[174]

A review of the evidence demonstrated no signs of partiality on the part of the respondent's arbitrator. The Appointing Authority found the legal brief drafted on behalf of an official of Country A to be nothing more than "a robust defence of his client's position," which properly cast "his [client's] position in as persuasive and as forceful terms as possible."[175] According to the Appointing Authority, the legal opinion was also innocuous because: it addressed "a peripheral but not directly related issue"; it contained "no evidence whatsoever of the arbitrator's personal views on the matter... [nor] evidence of his involvement in policy making for Country X"; it was given in "the discharge of his duties as legal counsel" in which he was required to consider "the important legal, as distinct from the policy, questions"; and the "legal issues [were] unconnected with the arbitration at hand." Accordingly, the Appointing Authority dismissed the challenge.

(7) An arbitrator's representation of a third party with a right to intervene in the proceedings

In the NAFTA Chapter Eleven case between Mr Vito Gallo and Canada, Mr J Christopher Thomas, appointed by Canada, disclosed to the parties upon his appointment a significant

---

[171] The claimant also alleged that the arbitrator "had a recent connection with a matter relevant to the underpinnings of the dispute in his capacity as one of the attorneys for a former government official." Challenge Decision, n 170, para 3.
[172] Challenge Decision, n 170, para 35.
[173] Challenge Decision, n 170, paras 37–38.
[174] Challenge Decision, n 170, paras 37–38.
[175] Challenge Decision, n 170, para 44.

amount of prior and current work for Mexico. At the same time, Mr Thomas informed the parties of plans to retire from counsel work and withdraw from his law firm by a certain date in the near term. Later, it became known that Mr Thomas's plans had changed and that he had joined a new law firm as independent counsel where he had and might continue to provide Mexico legal advice on matters affecting "international trade and investment law."[176] Subsequently, the claimant challenged Mr Thomas.

The Appointing Authority found that the circumstances, while not entirely ripe for decision, could give rise to justifiable doubts as to Mr Thomas's impartiality and independence. The fact that Mr Thomas changed his mind about performing counsel work was not per se problematic as acting as arbitrator in one case and counsel in another was insufficient to disqualify an arbitrator, absent other evidence of an ethical conflict.[177] However, Mr Thomas's representation of Mexico raised significant concerns since Mexico, as a NAFTA Party, had a legal right to participate in the current proceedings on any matter of interpretation of the NAFTA.[178] The Appointing Authority found:

> In an arrangement like the one presently at issue, the arbitrator could be perceived as attentive to the interests of the advised State Party [Mexico]. His judgment may appear to be impaired by the potential interest of the advised State Party [Mexico] in the proceedings. Moreover, if the advised State Party [Mexico] were formally to intervene under Article 1128, this would necessarily lead to the reconstitution of the tribunal.[179]

Because of "the appearance of an inability to distance himself from the interests of Mexico," the appointing authority required Mr Thomas either to resign as arbitrator or discontinue his work with Mexico.[180]

(8) An arbitrator's handling of the proceedings

Iran's second challenge of Judge Briner pointed to his handling of the proceedings in Case No 39 as the "circumstances" giving rise to justifiable doubts. Even though the Appointing Authority dismissed the case on largely technical grounds, Justice Moons' decision also addressed Iran's specific allegations against Briner. His comments are helpful in demonstrating how challenges based solely on an arbitrator's conduct of arbitral proceedings are likely to fail, unless the conduct is obviously inappropriate.

Justice Moons' decision indicates that challenges based on an arbitrator's choices in admitting and evaluating evidence will almost necessarily fail:

> The appointing authority is not competent to assess the correctness of the arbitrator's judgment whether evidence is or is not convincing nor of their decision to accept some evidence as a basis for their award and put other evidence aside... Given the freedom granted arbitrators... to make their awards to the best of their knowledge and conviction, it cannot be concluded from an arbitrator's choices in this area that he is not impartial or independent.[181]

However, Justice Moons also recognized that there may be some grounds for challenge if the admission of the evidence produces a blatantly biased result. In addressing the Iranians'

---

[176] *Vito G Gallo* and *Government of Canada,* Decision on the Challenge to Mr J Christopher Thomas, QC (Nassib G Ziadé, ICSID Deputy Secretary-General, Appointing Authority) (October 14, 2009) (ICSID administered, 1976 UNCITRAL Rules, NAFTA Chapter Eleven). For a partial text of the decision, see section 3(C).

[177] Decision on the Challenge to Mr J Christopher Thomas, n 176, at 9. For additional discussion, see also section 1(A)(8).

[178] NAFTA, art 1128.

[179] Decision on the Challenge to Mr J Christopher Thomas, n 176, at 10.

[180] Decision on the Challenge to Mr J Christopher Thomas, n 176, at 11.

[181] Decision of the Appointing Authority on the Second Challenge by Iran of Judge Briner, n 41, at 387.

allegation that Judge Briner used testimony provided by Morgan Stanley in Case No 55 about the Chase Econometrics Forecast for the Award in Case No 39, Moons states:

This allegation can serve as support for the contention that justifiable doubts within the meaning of Article 10... have arisen, only if it is established beyond doubt that consideration in Case No 39 of testimony provided in Case No 55 intended to be or had for result either an impediment of the Respondent's position or possibilities in legal proceedings or an unjustified favoring of the Claimant.[182]

Challenges based on infringement or misapplication of the rules can succeed only if "the infringement or misapplication admits of no other explanation than that it has its cause in lack of impartiality or independence on the part of the challenged arbitrator and that any other cause, such as an error or misunderstanding... can be ruled out."[183] Thus one can conclude from Moons' analysis that an attempt to appeal an arbitral award that is considered final and binding under the Rules by resorting to the challenge mechanism generally should not be considered unless evidence of bias is substantial.

The line between appropriate and inappropriate conduct of an arbitrator was carefully drawn by a Division of the LCIA upholding a challenge against a sole arbitrator brought under the UNCITRAL Rules. In that instance, the arbitrator had twice met privately with claimant's counsel and had discussed matters relevant to the arbitration on at least one of these occasions. While recognizing that "courtesy may move an arbitrator to greet an uninvited Counsel entering his private retiring room," the Division concluded that ex parte communications are generally not recommended as they may cause suspicions about the arbitrator's lack of impartiality.[184] On the facts before it, the Division found that "accepting a meeting behind closed doors and addressing live issues in the arbitration was a step too far and would, indeed, raise suspicions of unequal treatment between the parties."[185]

The arbitrator's order to strike an oral exchange between opposing counsel regarding costs from the record of the hearing was also problematic. The Division found such conduct to be inconsistent with the arbitrators' duty to maintain a record of the proceedings under the UNCITRAL Rules.[186] Moreover, consistent with Moons' approach in the second challenge of Judge Briner, discussed above, the Division was unable to discern any basis for the arbitrator's conduct other than a lack of impartiality and independence. Thus, because the arbitrator's discretion "did not extend to allowing him to decide unilaterally that certain parts of the hearing simply never existed," the Division concluded his behavior gave rise to an appearance of bias, if not the real possibility that he was biased.[187]

Finally, accusations aimed at counsel by an arbitrator crossed the line. Part of the exchange was made in jest, that respondent's counsel entered his retiring room uninvited to steal his grapes. But "[a]lthough acknowledging that humour was not reprehensible and that the theft of the grapes may have been tantamount to a joke having turned sour," the Division found "what could not be taken lightly was the arbitrator's heated controversy with Counsel, accusing her of lying and trespassing, and maintaining these accusations

---

[182] Decision of the Appointing Authority, n 41, at 390.
[183] Decision of the Appointing Authority, n 41, at 388.
[184] Abstract of decision found in "LCIA Court Decisions on Challenges to Arbitrators Reference No UN3490, October 21, 2005 and December 27, 2005," summarized in 27(3) Arb Intl 377, 388, para 6.6.
[185] LCIA Court Decisions on Challenges, n 184, at para 6.7.
[186] LCIA Court Decisions on Challenges, n 184, at para 6.11.
[187] LCIA Court Decisions on Challenges, n 184, at para 6.10.

notwithstanding the fact that their veracity had been vehemently disputed."[188] Thus, the Division concluded that such conduct was "incompatible with the expected behaviour of an arbitrator."[189]

(9) An arbitrator's statement regarding a party or the dispute

In its decision on the challenge of Mr Kessler in *National Grid PLC* and *Republic of Argentina*, the LCIA observed that given a statement by Mr Kessler during the examination of a witness "a reasonable third person might indeed gain the impression that Mr Kessler had already taken a firm view on issues which are key to the final result of the arbitration."[190] The LCIA took the position, correct in our view, that "it would be inappropriate under a reasonable third person test to determine Mr Kessler's impartiality by looking at the challenged statement in isolation without considering Mr Kessler's intervention as a whole and the context of the intervention."[191] In particular, the LCIA examined the statements that immediately followed and concluded that "any appearance of bias which may have been created by the challenged sentence was eliminated."[192]

A statement certainly may be evidence of a lack of partiality, but it must be evaluated in context.

(10) An arbitrator's decision-making

The Iranian Government's challenge of Judges Skubiszewski and Arangio-Ruiz raised the question of whether an arbitrator's decision to join a voting majority in rendering an award that, according to Iran, had "illegally revised" a prior Tribunal decision in violation of the principle of *res judicata* could raise justifiable doubts as to those arbitrators' impartiality and independence.[193]

As an initial matter, the Appointing Authority, Judge W E Haak, was careful to acknowledge the limitations on his authority in this area:

[T]he Appointing Authority's role in challenge proceedings is not to assess the correctness of the arbitrators' decision, nor to assume the functions of an appellate magistrate in review of the procedural and substantive matters surround the issuance of [an award]. The Parties' consent, as expressed through the Tribunal Rules, simply does not vest this function to the Appointing Authority.[194]

Judge Haak therefore concluded that he "will not consider any grounds alleged by the Parties in favor or against the Challenge that would effectively substitute an arbitrator's judgment with my own."[195]

As to the Iranian Government's challenge, Judge Haak noted that Iran had only challenged two members of the Tribunal's majority—the two it argued "ha[d] a decisive role in forming [the] narrow majority [in the award]." To Judge Haak, this fact "fatally weakened" Iran's case by placing him in the untenable position of having to "agree[] to hold party-appointed arbitrators to a lower standard of impartiality than third-country arbitrators."[196]

---

[188] LCIA Court Decisions on Challenges, n 184, at para 6.13.
[189] LCIA Court Decisions on Challenges, n 184, at para 6.13.
[190] *National Grid PLC* and *Republic of Argentina*, Decision on the Challenge to Mr Judd L Kessler (December 3, 2007) (LCIA administered, 1976 UNCITRAL Rules, UK-Argentina BIT), at 22–3, para 92.
[191] Decision on the Challenge to Mr Judd L Kessler, para 93.
[192] Decision on the Challenge to Mr Judd L Kessler, para 96.
[193] For a more detailed description of the challenge, see section 1(B)(13).
[194] Decision of the Appointing Authority, Judge W E Haak, on the Challenges against Judges Krzysztof Skubiszewski and Gaetano Arangio-Ruiz, March 5, 2010, at 8, para 33.
[195] Decision of the Appointing Authority, n 194, at 8, para 33.
[196] Decision of the Appointing Authority, n 194, at 16, para 67.

But even assuming *arguendo* that the challenge could proceed, Judge Haak found on the facts before him it nonetheless would have been without merit because, as a general matter, "[t]he appointing authority is not competent to judge whether and to what extent arbitrators have rightly departed from previous Tribunal awards."[197]

At the same time, Judge Haak observed that in exceptional circumstances he would be empowered to sustain a challenge based on an alleged *res judicata* violation:

Only if the two awards are so clearly divergent on their face as to demonstrate that the only way [the award] could have been decided in that manner is that the Challenged Arbitrators lack independence and impartiality.[198]

(11) An arbitrator's breach of the confidentiality of deliberations

The US Government's challenge of Judge Broms was based primarily on his concurring and dissenting opinion in Case No A/28.[199] In that case, the majority ruled that Iran was expected to replenish the Security Account (from which awards against Iran are paid) to the amount of US $500 million, consistent with its obligations under the Algiers Declarations.[200] Despite voting with the majority, Judge Broms filed a separate opinion in which in the course of criticizing the majority's decision he disclosed information on the method and substance of Tribunal deliberations. In particular, the opinion revealed that Judge Broms (and other members of the minority) had argued strenuously for deferring treatment of the replenishment question until the related issue of the Tribunal's jurisdiction over the US counterclaim in Case No B1 could be resolved.[201]

The US Government argued that Judge Broms's opinion not only breached the rule of confidentiality of deliberations, but also raised serious doubts about Judge Broms's independence and impartiality.[202] According to the US Government, the opinion affirmatively

---

[197] Decision of the Appointing Authority, n 194, at 21, para 85 (citing Decision of the Appointing Authority, Justice Ch M J A Moons, on the Challenge against Judge Briner, September 19, 1989, at 5, reprinted in 21 Iran-US CTR 384, 388).

[198] Decision of the Appointing Authority, n 194, at 22, para 87. Similarly, Justice Moon as Appointing Authority found:

Complaints alleging infringement or misapplication of the rules of procedure can succeed only if the alleged infringement or misapplication justifies doubts about the impartiality or independence of the arbitrator concerned. This can only be so if the infringement or misapplication admits of no other explanation than that it has its cause in lack of impartiality and independence on the part of the challenged arbitrator and that any other cause, such as an error or misunderstanding which, as experience has taught, may happen to the most conscientious judges, can be ruled out.

Decision of the Appointing Authority, Justice Ch M J A Moons, on the Challenge against Judge Briner, September 19, 1989, at 5–6, reprinted in 21 Iran US CTR 384, 388.

[199] See Memorandum in Support of the Challenge by the United States of Mr Bengt Broms, Member and Chairman of Chamber One of the Iran-United States Claims Tribunal dated January 4, 2001. See also discussion at section 1(B)(9).

[200] See *The United States,* et al and *the Islamic Republic of Iran,* et al (Case No A/28), Decision No DEC 130-A28-FT (December 19, 2000), para 95.

[201] Dissenting Opinion by Judge Broms, para 1. The minority view in deliberations, according to which an order for replenishment might be unnecessary, given the small size of private claims pending against Iran, if it was proven that the Tribunal did not have jurisdiction over the US Government's largest remaining claim against Iran, the counterclaim in Case No B1 for over US $1 billion. Judge Broms' opinion also alleged improprieties in the manner in which negotiation of the decision's operative replenishment language took place.

[202] The US Government simultaneously argued that Judge Broms' alleged misconduct served as a basis for challenge under Article 13(2) of the Tribunal Rules for failure to act. Sir Robert rejected these grounds. Decision of the Appointing Authority, Sir Robert Jennings, on the challenge of Judge Bengt Broms (May 7, 2001), at 4 ("Article 13 was not intended to be used to supplement or qualify the meanings of 'independence' and 'impartiality' in Articles 9 to 12…").

encouraged non-compliance with the remedy of replenishment afforded the US. It also allegedly contained statements that prejudged the issue of the Tribunal's jurisdiction over the counterclaim in Case No B1, raising questions about Judge Broms's impartiality in future matters before the Tribunal.

While recognizing the serious nature of Judge Broms's breaches of confidentiality, Sir Robert Jennings assigned only limited weight to them; they were "a factor" to be considered in the challenge decision.[203] The key inquiry, according to Sir Robert, was whether those breaches were "consciously and intentionally deployed so as to assist the calling in question of the fairness of the Tribunal's decision." Sir Robert found that the evidence before him could not support an affirmative answer. Rather, he concluded that Judge Broms's breaches of confidentiality most likely were motivated by the arbitrator's inability in the face of successful opposition "to resist the temptation to continue arguing with his colleagues."[204]

Sir Robert also was unable to conclude that the US Government's doubts about Judge Broms's independence and impartiality were justified. The evidence did not indicate that Judge Broms was "so beholden in some way to the Iranian Government such that he has lost his independence of thought and action."[205] Nor did it suggest that Judge Broms's convictions in favor of Iran had exceeded the level of partiality to be expected of an arbitrator with views in opposition to the majority's. According to Sir Robert, it was within Judge Broms's rights as an arbitrator to favor one side in the dispute ultimately and to criticize— even dissent from—the majority's decision if he disagreed with its reasoning.

The significance of an arbitrator's breach of confidentiality arose again in the context of the US Government's challenge of Judge Oloumi. The US Government argued that Oloumi's disclosure of the circumstances relating to his request for the postponement of deliberations, and the denial of that request, in Case No B61 not only breached the rule of confidentiality, but also was "intended to give the party that appointed him—Iran—the opportunity to seek to alter the course of deliberations, change the composition of the Tribunal or, by seeking to force a rehearing of select position portions of Case B61, possibly even change the outcome of the case."[206] Judge Oloumi's disclosures caused Iran to challenge Judge Skubizsewski, the President of the Tribunal, on the alleged basis that the President had inappropriately denied Judge Oloumi's request for a postponement. The Appointing Authority, Judge Haak, agreed with the United States that Judge Oloumi's disclosures breached the rule of confidentiality in Article 21, Note 2 of the 1983 Tribunal Rules. However, he found that this breach did not give rise to justifiable doubts as to Judge Oloumi's impartiality and independence in the absence of compelling evidence that his disclosure was intended to create the opportunity to challenge Judge Skubizsewski. Rather, the appointing authority found that the evidence indicated at most that Judge Oloumi's conduct was based on a mistake or misunderstanding about his right to a postponement of deliberations in Case B61 and the scope of Tribunal deliberations in general.[207]

---

[203] Decision of the Appointing Authority, Sir Robert Jennings, n 202, at 11. Given the Tribunal's unique institutional setting, Sir Robert noted, however, that "any sign of a repetition [by Judge Broms] might change the balance of a decision in respect of any further challenge."
[204] Decision of the Appointing Authority, Sir Robert Jennings, n 202, at 6.
[205] Decision of the Appointing Authority, Sir Robert Jennings, n 202, at 8.
[206] Joint Decision by the Appointing Authority, Judge W E Haak, on the Challenges against Judge Krzysztof Skubiszewski and Judge Hamid Reza Oloumi Yazdi, April 2, 2008, at 25.
[207] Joint Decision by the Appointing Authority, Judge W E Haak, n 206, at 25. See also discussion at section 1(B)(12).

(12) An arbitrator's physical assault of a fellow arbitrator

In the US challenge of Judges Kashani and Shafeiei for their assault on Judge Mangård, the US Agent argued that:

> A violent physical attack by two arbitrators upon a third who, in their view, is opposed to the interests of the party that appointed them, demonstrates a total lack of the necessary impartiality and independence envisioned by Article 10 [of the Tribunal Rules]....
>
> Mr. Kashani and Mr. Shafeiei assert in their September 6 communication to President Lagergren that Mr. Mangård "has totally hostile feelings specifically directed against the Islamic Republic of Iran." This conduct shows that Mr. Kashani and Mr. Shafeiei identify themselves so completely with what they consider to be the interests of the Islamic Republic of Iran that they will resort to unprecedented physical violence to protect those interests...Arbitrators who resort to physical violence in order to protect the interests of the party that appointed them demonstrate such a deep-seated bias that they must be presumed to display similar partisanship in all matters in the future.[208]

Although Iran withdrew Judges Kashani and Shafeiei before a decision on the challenge, the argument of the US Agent appears correct, particularly when, as in the case of the assault on Judge Mangård, statements indicate that the assault is motivated by an apparent identity of interests between the arbitrator and the party who appointed the arbitrator.

(c) The standard of independence and impartiality does not vary according to the stage of the proceedings

In response to the first Iranian challenge of Judge Briner, Amoco argued that challenges brought at a late stage of the proceeding should be subject to a higher standard for success than challenges brought at the outset. The rationale for the higher standard is that late challenges are more likely to "create delay, disruption and therefore injustice." Amoco quoted AAA practice to support its argument:

> Given the serious consequences resulting from the disqualification of an arbitrator after hearings have commenced, the approach employed by the AAA at this stage of the process is less liberal—an arbitrator will only be disqualified if the disclosed information reflects, or a party demonstrates, such an interest on the part of the arbitrator as would justify judicial vacatur of the arbitral award. In this regard, the courts have generally held that an arbitration award will not be set aside for allegations of arbitrator bias unless such bias is adequately proven.[209]

Conversely, in Challenge Decision of January 11, 1995, the claimant suggested that the standard for impartiality was lower at the inception of the proceedings.[210] The Appointing Authority recognized the "natural tendency to protect the [arbitral] process at the outset rather than having to support it at its conclusion."[211] He noted that "[p]articular prudence" was required when making threshold decisions on partiality, and that "if matters are evenly balanced, there may be reasons...for great caution and possible admission of the challenge."[212]

---

[208] Letter and Memorandum of the Agent of the United States to the Appointing Authority initiating its Challenge of Judges Kashani and Shafeiei, n 36. See also discussion at section 1(B)(2).

[209] Memorandum of Amoco Iran Oil regarding the Challenge of Judge Briner in Case No 55 by Iran, November 2, 1988 (quoting from a speech by M Hoellering), n 156, at 248. See also extracts reprinted in sections 3(D)(1) and 4(D); and discussion at section 1(B)(3).

[210] Challenge Decision of January 11, 1995, para 11, reprinted in section 3(C). See also discussion at section 1(A)(2).

[211] Challenge Decision of January 11, 1995, para 10. See also S Baker and M Davis, *The UNCITRAL Rules in Practice*, n 1, 51 ("A prudent appointing authority may be tempted to sustain an early challenge simply to be on the safe side and avoid the potential for delay and disruption later.").

[212] Challenge Decision of January 11, 1995, paras 10–11, reprinted in section 3(C).

Still the language of Article 12 does not allow for a differentiation in the standard of independence or impartiality based on the stage of the proceeding. Indeed, as the appointing authority in the Challenge Decision of January 11, 1995 concluded, "The standard to be applied...and the proof required...should, in theory, be no different according to whether the issue is raised at the threshold or at the conclusion of the proceedings."[213] To conclude otherwise would only serve to "muddle the standard for arbitrator impartiality."[214]

(d) A failure to disclose under article 11 may give rise to, but does not per se establish, justifiable doubts as to impartiality or independence

It is not always an easy task to establish the grounds for challenge. Much of the information that would be most helpful in the most egregious cases will be in the control of the arbitrator and not the parties. That the arbitrator may know better than any other of likely grounds for challenge, returns us to the importance and desirability of the early disclosure required by Article 11. Although arbitrators cannot be forced to provide the required disclosure, sanctions for failure to do so could encourage them to disclose. A claimant with an interest in speedy and unassailable proceedings may encourage the arbitrator appointed by it to provide a full disclosure, as well as seek an arbitrator not subject to potential challenge. The interest of the presiding arbitrator in maintaining a reputation for professionalism likewise motivates disclosure. A problem arises, however, with the arbitrator appointed by the respondent. A difficult respondent, for one reason or another, may appoint an objectionable arbitrator. The possibility of a lengthy challenge of the arbitrator will not deter such conduct; indeed the delays involved in a challenge might do just the opposite. In such instances, the claimant faces the dilemma of proceeding with the arbitration despite the presence of a possibly objectionable arbitrator or initiating a potentially lengthy challenge which may ultimately just result in the appointment of a new, but equally objectionable arbitrator.[215] The reluctance to challenge stems from a desire to avoid lengthy ancillary proceedings, the fear that ultimately nothing will be gained, and the simple fact that without disclosure it may be very difficult to articulate the basis for challenge.

All of these objections are avoided, however, if the failure to provide a disclosure statement or to respond to reasonable inquiries from the other party is treated as a circumstance not only *potentially* giving rise to justifiable doubts as to the arbitrator's impartiality or independence, but rather as *establishing* such lack of impartiality or independence. The failure to disclose would thus itself be the basis for the challenge, would result in a rather summary challenge procedure, and perhaps ultimately would encourage disclosure by arbitrators.

The Iran–US Claims Tribunal twice confronted a failure to disclose, although the appointing authority did not ultimately decide the issue in either instance. In a more recent investment arbitration, the issue was addressed more directly, but without fully resolving when a failure to disclose is problematic. In our view, a failure to disclose may give rise to justifiable doubts, depending on the circumstances, but does not, per se, establish such justifiable doubts.

---

[213] Challenge Decision of January 11, 1995, para 9, n 210.
[214] S Baker and M Davis, *UNCITRAL Rules in Practice*, n 1, 51.
[215] As mentioned above, this choice was presented to the Agent of the United States on several occasions, by Iran's appointment of attorneys as arbitrators with Iran's Bureau of International Legal Services, the organization

In the first Briner challenge, the Iranians claimed that Judge Briner's failure to disclose his relationship with Morgan Stanley should disqualify him even if the relationship itself did not warrant disqualification. While there may be instances where nondisclosure would give rise to justifiable doubts, such a per se rule is not supported by the text of the rules. The duty to disclose circumstances "likely" to give rise to justifiable doubts involves an element of judgment on the part of the arbitrator.[216] A failure to disclose is not in itself a ground for challenge in addition to those set forth expressly in the UNCITRAL Rules. As stated in the Amoco memorandum, the "UNCITRAL/Tribunal Rules contain no such provision; they provide only that an arbitrator may be disqualified on grounds of lack of impartiality or independence, not failure to disclose."[217] As noted by Baker and Davis:

Failure to disclose may nonetheless give rise to doubts as to an arbitrator's impartiality under Article 10 [of the 1976 UNCITRAL Rules]. Whether nondisclosure raises such doubts depends on whether the failure to disclose was inadvertent or intentional, whether it was the result of an honest exercise of discretion, whether the facts that were not disclosed raised obvious questions about impartiality and independence, and whether the nondisclosure is an aberration on the part of a conscientious arbitrator or part of a pattern of circumstances raising doubts as to impartiality.[218]

The conclusion is strengthened when one considers whether the Iranians would have challenged Judge Briner at the time of his appointment had he disclosed his relationship with Morgan Stanley. In making a determination as to what was likely to give rise to justifiable doubts, it was, at a minimum, reasonable for Judge Briner to assume that the Iranians would not object to his relationship with a witness. Unfortunately, the issue was never addressed by the Appointing Authority because of Judge Briner's withdrawal.

A failure to disclose also arose in the context of the claimant's challenge of Judge Noori in Case No 248. In this instance, Judge Noori had failed to disclose that he had earlier served as general counsel of the parent corporation of the respondent. Although the challenging party repeatedly stated that Judge Noori violated Article 9 of the 1976 UNCITRAL Rules, the challenging party did not expressly assert that the failure to disclose was an independent ground for challenge. Rather, the challenging party argued that Judge Noori's "position as head of the NIOI's legal department gives rise to justifiable doubts as to his impartiality or independence."[219] The appointing authority concluded that even if "his service as Head of the NIOI legal office and his failure to disclose this to the President of the Tribunal were true, I do not feel this doubt can be termed justifiable doubt."[220] This conclusion supports the view of Amoco that although a failure to disclose may give rise to doubts, it does not, per se, establish a basis for justified doubts.[221]

---

representing Iran before the Tribunal. In each case, very summary disclosure statements or no statements were provided. The response of the United States was to object to the lack of full disclosure, but not to challenge such arbitrators.

[216] See S Baker and M Davis, *UNCITRAL Rules in Practice*, n 1, 50 ("The decision whether to disclose is left to the arbitrator's good faith discretion, after all, and there is room for necessarily an honest difference of opinion about whether a particular relationship should have been disclosed").

[217] Memorandum of Amoco Iran Oil regarding the Challenge by Iran of Judge Briner in Case No 55, November 2, 1988, n 209, at 255.

[218] S Baker and M Davis, *UNCITRAL Rules in Practice*, n 1, 50.

[219] Letter of Claimant in Case No 248 to the Appointing Authority initiating the Challenge of Judge Noori in Case No 248, February 20, n 44. See also discussion at section 1(B)(6).

[220] Decision of the Appointing Authority on the Challenge of Judge Noori, n 45, at 324.

[221] The inexplicable aspect of the decision is the Appointing Authority's wording of his holding—"Mr. Noori has wrongly been accused of having infringed article 9 . . . the challenge ought to be dismissed"—which implies that the issue was the alleged failure to disclose rather than whether, first and foremost, the earlier position of Judge Noori *and*, secondarily, his failure to disclose that position, gave rise to justifiable doubts.

(e) Are there any limitations on the circumstances which may be used as the basis for justifiable doubts?

Finally, Justice Moons' decision on Iran's second challenge of Judge Briner suggests that certain circumstances, at least as a general matter, may not give rise to justifiable doubts. In particular, Justice Moons' reluctance to refer to the circumstances of deliberations constitutes one such category:

> b. Article 31 of the Tribunal Rules... prescribes that deliberations in camera are confidential and must remain so.
> In the interest of a proper functioning of the Tribunal this rule should be strictly observed, so that every Arbitrator may put forward his opinions and arguments in camera in full freedom, without fear of being called upon by the parties to account for them.
> To my mind it would not be consonant with this interest if an appointing authority, as provided for in the Tribunal Rules, were to consider in deciding a challenge, also information which should have remained confidential pursuant to the said Article 31.[222]

We agree with Justice Moons' analysis, although we note that his juxtaposition of interests also suggests that there might be some extreme circumstance in deliberations so egregious that it should be allowed to form the basis for a challenge.

(3) Article 12(1) as providing the exclusive grounds for challenge

An issue more subtle than whether the UNCITRAL Rules provide the exclusive *mechanism* for challenge of a member[223] is whether they delimitate the exclusive *grounds* for challenge. The question of whether a challenge could be based on a general duty "to adhere to proper judicial decorum and demeanor" and on Article 13 of the 1976 UNCITRAL Rules has arisen in two situations before the Iran–US Claims Tribunal.

The first situation involved the US challenge of Judges Kashani and Shafeiei in September 1984. On September 3, 1984, Mahmoud Kashani and Shafie Shafeiei, members of the Iran–US Claims Tribunal, physically assaulted a fellow member of the Tribunal, Nils Mangård. This act was followed by continued threats of violence by Judges Kashani and Shafeiei. At this point there was intense consideration as to the scope of the grounds for challenge under Articles 10(1) and 13(2) of the Tribunal Rules.[224] Does physical assault give rise to justifiable doubts as to impartiality or independence? Judges Kashani and Shafeiei were still reporting daily for work at the Tribunal: was there failure to act or impossibility of doing so? What would be the effect on any existing basis for challenge, if Judges Kashani and Shafeiei rendered a formal, perhaps even ambiguous apology? A challenge against Judges Kashani and Shafeiei was filed by the US Government on September 17, 1984.

The US Memorandum setting forth the legal basis for challenge and summarizing the position of the US notably contended that Judges Kashani and Shafeiei violated Article 10(1), Article 13(2) of the Tribunal Rules *and* the duty "to adhere to proper judicial decorum and demeanor," a part of "civilized behavior and a basic respect for law."[225] The

---

[222] Decision of the Appointing Authority on the Second Challenge by Iran of Judge Briner, n 39, at 387. See also discussion at section 1(B)(4).
[223] See section 1(C).
[224] These provisions correspond to Articles 12(1) and 12(3) of the 2010 UNCITRAL Rules.
[225] "Memorandum Re: Challenge to Arbitrators Kashani and Shafeiei by the Government of the United States of America" at 8, attached to Letter of the Agent of the United States to the Appointing Authority, n 36, at 9347–8.

memorandum separately addressed each of these sources of challenge, the last source being treated in a section entitled "The Attack and Continuing Threats Violate Fundamental Legal Principles Governing International Arbitration." In citing "broader and more fundamental principles ['due process, fairness and justice'], which *also* entail the attributes of arbitrator impartiality and independence," the US Government in essence argued that this source of challenge based on "fundamental legal principles" is broader than and encompasses within it Article 10(1).[226]

As precedent for its position, the US Government cited the arbitration between *Bengtson* and *Federal Republic of Germany*.[227] In *Bengtson*, the Arbitral Commission on Property, Rights and Interests in Germany in Plenary Session was presented with an appeal of the decision of the Second Chamber to reject an application for disqualification of a commissioner for fear of partiality, given the past employment of that commissioner with the defendant in the case. The Commission dismissed the appeal, holding that disqualification could not be based on "the Commission's Charter *or* on the general principles of international law."[228] The US Government cited this holding as support for general principles of international law as a residual independent source of grounds for challenge.[229] The reasoning in *Bengtson* in support of this holding, however, reveals that recourse was made to general principles of international law not because that is always an independent source for challenge or disqualification but rather because Article 8(1) of the Charter directed the Commission to do so. This Article provides:

In arriving at its decisions, the Commission shall apply the provisions of the Convention … Where necessary to supplement or interpret such provisions, or in the absence of any relevant provisions, it shall apply the general principles of international law and of justice and equity.[230]

As a matter of policy, denying a source for challenge outside Articles 12(1) and 12(3) is appropriate. The challenge process is time-consuming and confusing enough without expanding the bases for asserting a challenge to general sources of law. Even if challenges might be sustained under a broader residual source, the parties could very well desire instead to operate under a narrow, more limited enumeration of the basis for challenges.[231] Having said this, one must note that Articles 12(1) and 12(3) are on their face very broad in scope[232]

---

[226] Memorandum Re: Challenge to Arbitrators Kashani and Shafeiei," n 225, at 9 (emphasis added).

[227] Case No 60, II Decision of the Arbitral Commission 216 (Wickstrom, Sauser-Hall, Lagergren, Euler, Arndt (CO) Marion, Phenix (CO) comms, 1959), reprinted in (1963) 28 ILR 549.

[228] Intl L Rep, n 227, 552 (emphasis added).

[229] Memorandum, n 225, at 8.

[230] But see Separate Opinion of Mr Phenix concurring in the result but contending that Article 4(2) is exhaustive and that Article 8(1) may not be used to expand Article 4(2).

[231] See *Bengtson*, n 227, at 554:

… [T]he question might be put whether a strict interpretation of the Charter does not show that the Signatories to the Settlement Convention had intended to recognize only the narrowly defined reasons laid down in Article 4, paragraph 2, of the Charter, because, taking into consideration the special composition of the Commission, neither of the parties should be given the power of obstructing the work of the Commission by applying for disqualification. In fact, in national jurisdictions, a challenged judge may be replaced immediately, whereas the replacement of a non-German member of the Commission would necessitate the appointment of a new member by the Power which had appointed him or, in the case of a neutral member, an agreement between the four Signatories to the Settlement Convention a replacement procedure which would, in each case take up a great deal of time.

[232] Indeed, Article 13(2) of the 1976 UNCITRAL Rules was intended to cover all circumstances that make it impossible for an arbitrator to perform his functions. *Report of the UNCITRAL on the Work of its Ninth Session*, UN GAOR, 31st Session, Supp No 17, UN Doc A/31/17, para 70 (1976), reprinted in (1976) VII UNCITRAL Ybk 66, 71.

and that they alone would have likely supplied a basis for the US challenge of Judges Kashani and Shafeiei. In this sense, the position of the US Government as to this general source for challenge is better viewed as the product of a thorough litigator rather than a correct statement of law. "The Tribunal's Rules governing challenges exist to safeguard against unfairness and injustice, and to ensure that the arbitration process is not frustrated or tainted by arbitrators who are unwilling to perform, or incapable of performing, their functions."[233] Given this accurately described scope, there is, if nothing else, little need for a general source of grounds for challenge outside the UNCITRAL Rules.

The second situation involved the US challenge of Judge Broms in 2001 in connection with his dissenting opinion in Case No A/28. The US Government maintained that the opinion contained revelations about the confidential deliberations of the Full Tribunal, which, among other things, undermined the remedy afforded the US by the majority of the Tribunal.[234] One of the arguments in the US challenge was that Judge Broms's disclosures, in addition to showing his partiality, demonstrated his failure to perform his function as an arbitrator and his desire to hinder the work of the Tribunal in subsequent related cases. According to the US Government, Judge Broms's conduct, particularly in light of the Tribunal's institutional setting, made him subject to challenge pursuant to Article 13(2) of the Tribunal Rules.

The Appointing Authority, Sir Robert Jennings, found that argument unpersuasive. In his decision dated May 7, 2001, he concluded that Article 13(2) of the Tribunal Rules was meant to address the "actual," rather than the "metaphorical" failure or impossibility to act, such as when an arbitrator is temporarily ill or absent from the proceedings.[235] Accordingly, he rejected the US interpretation of Article 13 because that provision "was not intended to be used to supplement or qualify the meanings of 'independence' and 'impartiality' in Articles 9 to 12."[236] The same analysis should apply with respect to corresponding Articles 11 through 13 of the 2010 UNCITRAL Rules.

(4) When may a party challenge the arbitrator it has appointed—Article 12(2)

Should a party be able to challenge the arbitrator it has nominated or only the arbitrator nominated by the other party? According to the UNCITRAL drafters: "The prevailing view...was that a party should be permitted to challenge even the arbitrator nominated by him. For circumstances unknown at the time of the nomination may emerge thereafter revealing that the arbitrator had a bias against the party nominating him, or in favor of the other party."[237]

Tribunal practice indicates that in at least one case, a party exercised this right. In the *Walter Bau* arbitration, the respondent challenged the arbitrator it had appointed on grounds that he had previously provided advice to and had nominal equity holdings in a company connected with the investment project at issue in the case.[238]

---

[233] Memorandum, n 225, at 9.
[234] See generally US Notice of Challenge of Arbitrator Bengt Broms from the Agent of the United States to the Appointing Authority (January 4, 2001).
[235] Decision of the Appointing Authority, Sir Robert Jennings, on the challenge of Judge Bengt Broms, May 7, 2001, at 4.
[236] Decision of the Appointing Authority, Sir Robert Jennings, n 235, at 4. For the text of the decision relating to Article 13, see section 3(D)(1).
[237] UN Doc A/10017, n 71, para 67, reprinted in (1975) VI UNCITRAL Ybk 24, 32.
[238] *Walter Bau AG* and *Kingdom of Thailand*, Award (July 1, 2009) (*Ad Hoc* Proceeding, 1976 UNCITRAL Rules, Germany-Thailand BIT), at paras 1.36–1.42. The arbitrator ultimately resigned. Para 1.42.

C. Extracts from the Practice of Investment and other Tribunals

Challenge Decision of April 15, 1993, reprinted in part in (1997) XXII Ybk Commercial Arb 222, 224:

[1] My decision calls for a preliminary clarification of a point of terminology which was raised by the claimant and which covers an important matter of substance. I have to refer throughout this decision to "Party Arbitrators" according to the general use in arbitral matters, adopted also by the parties. It must however be made clear that this expression refers exclusively to the mode of appointment of the said arbitrators and that it may not be understood as conveying any idea of dependency, allegiance or accountability of an arbitrator in relation to the appointing party. Party Arbitrators appointed in conformity with the requirement of Art. 9 of the [1976] UNCITRAL Rules must therefore be considered to have the same status of independence as a single arbitrator or the presiding arbitrator, as the case may be. This status must be recognized and respected by all concerned as long as a possible lack of impartiality or independence has not been established by a competent authority.

Challenge Decision of January 11, 1995, reprinted in part in (1997) XXII Ybk Commercial Arb 227, 230–31:

B. Standards for Party Appointed Arbitrators

[8] The first bench mark or guidepost has to do with whether different standards with respect to impartiality apply to party appointed arbitrators. The matter, as far as I am concerned, is clear. The criteria mandated by the [1976] UNCITRAL Arbitration Rules apply equally to all arbitrators. There is no lesser standard for party nominated arbitrators than for a neutral arbitrator. I detect no dispute whatsoever between the parties on this point. In this regard, authorities which are predicated on different standards and régimes are largely irrelevant to this enquiry....

C. Effect of the Timing of the Challenge or Its Disposition

[9] The next guidepost involves the timing of the challenge to an arbitrator. Does the standard of impartiality take on a shifting or ambulatory character depending on the stage of the proceeding? The standard to be applied for impartiality and the proof required to establish a lack thereof should, in theory, be no different according to whether the issue is raised at the threshold or at the conclusion of the proceedings....

[10] It must nevertheless, be conceded that there may be a natural tendency to protect the process at the outset rather than having to support it at its conclusion.... As a practical matter, if a reviewing judicial authority at the conclusion of proceedings were to disagree with a threshold conclusion that an arbitrator is not partial, the entire arbitration is at risk. Particular prudence is, therefore, called for in making a threshold decision on partiality as well as a scrupulously fair appreciation of all of the circumstances that may bear on the assessment.

[11] While the claimant applied inferentially to advance in its Challenge the view that somehow the standard is more relaxed at the inception of proceedings, I believe that the most one can say is that, if matters are evenly balanced, there may be reasons... for great caution and possible admission of the challenge....

[12] In a parallel submission, the claimant also argued with considerable persuasiveness that the arbitration process could, and should here, be safeguarded at the threshold. The way to do this was to reject the respondents' arbitrator. There are, they suggested, many other experienced, and no doubt willing, candidates available. While many of the reasons advanced in support of this position may in themselves be unobjectionable, the test which I must apply is not a pragmatic or discretionary one, but rather one based on whether there are justifiable doubts as to the arbitrator's impartiality. I cannot supplant the standard in the [1976] UNCITRAL Arbitration Rules with a largely subjective view based on essentially peripheral considerations which, although possibly otherwise cogent, may be shifting in character and unrelated to that objective criterion. I should also add here that a challenge should not be upheld simply to avoid controversy. Otherwise challenges would be resorted to for their *in terrorem* effect.

National Grid PLC and *Republic of Argentina,* Decision on the Challenge to Mr Judd L Kessler (December 3, 2007) (LCIA administered, 1976 UNCITRAL Rules, UK-Argentina BIT), at 22–23:

92. Taking the statement quoted by Argentina in its Challenge in isolation, i.e., in particular that "*[…] and it is not hypothetical because everyone present here knows the facts in general, that there has been an important damage or a very important change in the expectations of the investment*", the Division admits that a reasonable third person might indeed gain the impression that Mr Kessler had already taken a firm view on issues which are key to the final result of the arbitration.

93. However, the Division is of the opinion that it would be inappropriate under a reasonable third person test to determine Mr Kessler's impartiality by looking at the challenged statement in isolation without considering Mr Kessler's intervention as a whole and the context of the intervention.

94. The transcript shows that Mr Kessler started his intervention by suggesting, in Spanish, to Mr Guglielmino that he pose to the expert witness hypothetical questions. The preceding pages of the transcript show that this suggestion was triggered by a discussion between counsel and the Tribunal as to whether certain questions were factual and thus improper to be put to a legal expert.

95. It is true that this suggestion by Mr Kessler was followed by the challenged statement that "*[…] and it is not hypothetical because everyone present here knows the facts in general, that there has been an important damage or a very important change in the expectations of the investment*". However, immediately after this statement, and before being asked by Mr. Guglielmino for clarification, Mr Kessler went on to explain his suggestion by formulating examples for hypothetical questions to be posed to the expert.

   "*If you want to ask him questions. If there were major harm, what would the result be under Argentine law? Is there protection? Is there not protection?*

   Does the law apply? Does it not apply? I state this merely as a suggestion".

96. From a reasonable point of view, by formulating such questions, any appearance of bias which may have been created by the challenged sentence was eliminated. Even if one were to admit remaining doubts, they were then clearly eliminated by Mr Kessler's clarification in response to Mr. Guglielmino's question.

97. Following Mr Kessler's intervention, Argentina's counsel Mr Guglielmino sought immediate clarification and asked:

   "*You state that at this stage we already know that there was harm?*" 36

98. Mr Kessler responded:

   "*I merely say that we are here because there is an allegation of harm of a change in the contract that caused problems to the investor. As we were saying before, we are not speaking in abstract. I don't know. I'm trying to help, but perhaps what I have had to say isn't all that helpful*".

99. Thus, by stating that the subject of the arbitration was "*an allegation of harm of a change in the contract that caused problems to the investor*", Mr Kessler made clear beyond any reasonable doubt that he was not prejudiced.

AWG Group Ltd and *Argentine Republic,* Decision on a Second Proposal for the Disqualification of a Member of the Arbitral Tribunal (May 12, 2008) (footnotes omitted), (ICSID administered, 1976 UNCITRAL Rules, UK-Argentina BIT), at 12–13:

23. What then is the "circumstance" in the case of *AWG Group Limited v. The Argentine Republic* that the Respondent alleges gives rise to a justifiable doubt as to the impartiality or independence of Professor Kaufmann-Kohler? The Respondent's submissions, which it must be

acknowledged tend to focus more heavily on the circumstances in the other two cases, point to the fact that Professor-Kauffman-Kohler is a director of UBS and that UBS has engaged in certain research activities in the water sector and has developed financial products to allow its clients to invest in the water sector. At paragraph 29 of its Second Proposal, the Respondent refers to one such product, the UBS Global Water Utilities Index TR-Index-Zertificat (UBOWAS), which includes "...12 companies, mostly British..."; however, the Respondent does not allege that AWG Group Limited is among the twelve or even that companies in which UBS conducts research or the financial products developed by UBS include investments in AWG Group Limited. Indeed, the Respondent does not specifically allege the existence any sort of a business relationship, direct or indirect, between UBS and AWG Group Limited. In particular, the Respondent does not assert that UBS owns shares in or has any other type of financial connection to AWG Group Limited. Moreover, as will be discussed more extensively below, Professor Kaufmann-Kohler states that as a director of UBS she is not involved in the management of UBS business, does not participate in the development and management of the company's financial products or its research activities, and indeed was unaware of its activities with respect to the water sector. The Respondent offers no evidence to the contrary.

24. Thus the only connection, if one may call it that, between Professor Kaufmann-Kohler and the Claimant AWG Group Limited is the fact that she is a director of UBS and that UBS, among its many other activities and interests throughout the world, conducts research and develops financial products related to the water sector. The existence of such purported connection is not enough to establish a "circumstance" giving rise to justifiable doubts as to an arbitrator's independence and impartiality. Such a connection must be significant and direct, such as an economic relationship causing an arbitrator to be dependent in some way on a party. Such connection between Professor Kaufmann-Kohler and AWG Group Limited, as suggested though not specifically alleged by the Respondent, is too remote and tenuous as to hardly be called a connection or relationship at all. An objective analysis of the facts as alleged by the Respondent does not establish a circumstance that would lead a reasonable, informed person to conclude that a justifiable doubt exists as to Professor Kaufmann-Kohler's impartiality or independence in the case of *AWG Group Limited v. The Argentine Republic*.

Vito G Gallo and *Government of Canada,* Decision on the Challenge to Mr J Christopher Thomas, QC (October 14, 2009) (ICSID administered, 1976 UNCITRAL Rules, NAFTA Chapter Eleven), at 9–11:

29. It would have been preferable for Mr. Thomas not to have stated in a CV provided to the parties that he intended to retire as counsel if his intentions were not entirely certain. As things stand today, and irrespective of the advisability of such a situation, one may as a general matter be simultaneously an arbitrator in one case and a counsel in another. There is no need to disavow the possibility of assuming either role. The fact that one makes such a statement and then changes one's mind is therefore hardly sufficient to sustain a challenge absent other evidence of a conflict. Thus, the Claimant's assertion that it relied on Mr. Thomas' statement in his CV in evaluating his acceptability as an arbitrator does not by itself sustain the challenge raised against Mr. Thomas.

30. The real issue is that Mr. Thomas is presently advising Mexico, a State Party to the NAFTA and a potential participant in this case pursuant to NAFTA Article 1128. In his letter of June 22, 2009, Mr. Thomas stated that he had not since March 2009 represented Mexico "in respect of the interpretation or application of the provisions of NAFTA Chapter 11 or similar provisions in Mexico's Bilateral Investment Treaties," but has done "a small amount of work for BLG on Mexico-related matters, consisting principally of reviewing its advice in respect of matters that fall within the rubric of international trade and investment law."

31. In the particular context of NAFTA Article 1128, this is too fine a distinction to dispel doubt. By serving on a tribunal in a NAFTA arbitration involving a NAFTA State Party, while simultaneously acting as an advisor to another NAFTA State Party which has a legal right to participate in the proceedings, an arbitrator inevitably risks creating justifiable doubts as to his impartiality and independence.

32. The Respondent opines that there can be no conflict of interest since the amount of legal advice provided by Mr. Thomas to Mexico is *de minimis*. The Respondent misses the point, however. Where arbitral functions are concerned, any paid or *gratis* service provided to a third party with a right to intervene can create a perception of a lack of impartiality. The amount of work done makes no difference. What matters is the mere fact that work is being performed.

33. Mr. Thomas' personal integrity is unquestioned, and he is to be commended for disclosing his advisory services to Mexico in a forthright manner. Nevertheless, in an arrangement like the one presently at issue, the arbitrator could be perceived as attentive to the interests of the advised State Party. His judgment may appear to be impaired by the potential interest of the advised State Party in the proceedings. Moreover, if the advised State Party were formally to intervene under Article 1128, this would necessarily lead to the reconstitution of the tribunal. In any event, the arbitrator's involvement is problematic.

34. The Claimant demands Mr. Thomas' disqualification on the basis that "there is no way to 'un-ring' the bell." But the bell has not yet actually been rung. Mexico has not stated an interest in this case by participating under Article 1128, or otherwise. Had Mexico intervened, this would have required Mr. Thomas' immediate disqualification. The fact is, however, that Mexico has not yet done so. The claimant's request must therefore be rejected.

35. Nevertheless, because Mexico has the immanent right under Article 1128 formally to state its interest by participating in the case, an apparent conflict of interest is perceptible. Even if Mexico were not in the end to intervene, the arbitration would have had to proceed under the shadow of this possibility. The parties would inevitably be in a distracting and unsettled situation. It would be next to impossible for Mr. Thomas to avoid altogether, in his work as an arbitrator, the appearance of an inability to distance himself fully from the interests of Mexico, the advised NAFTA State Party and a potential participant in the present case.

36. In the instant case, from the point of view of a "reasonable and informed third party" (General Standard 2(c) of the IBA Guidelines on Conflicts of Interest in International Arbitration), i.e., a "fair minded, rational, objective observer" (Challenge Decision of 11 January 1995, *op. cit.* at 236), there would be justifiable doubts about Mr. Thomas' impartiality and independence as an arbitrator if he were not to discontinue his advisory services to Mexico for the remainder of this arbitration. Mr. Thomas must therefore now choose whether he will continue to advise Mexico, or continue to serve as an arbitrator in this case. Mr. Thomas shall inform me of his choice (with copies being sent to the parties, the two other arbitrators and the PCA) within seven (7) days of his receipt of the present decision.

ICS Inspection and Control Services Ltd and *Republic of Argentina,* Decision on Challenge to Arbitrator (December 17, 2009) (*Ad Hoc* Proceeding, 1976 UNCITRAL Rules, UK-Argentina BIT), at 4–5:

1. In his disclosure, Mr. Alexandrov indicates that he and his law firm currently represent the claimants in the long-running investment treaty proceedings, *Compania de Aguas del Aconquija S.A. and Vivendi S.A. v. Argentine Republic* (the "*Vivendi*" case). This puts Mr. Alexandrov in a situation of adversity towards Argentina, a situation that is often a source of justified concerns and that I believe should in principle be avoided, except where circumstances exist that eliminate any justifiable doubts as to the arbitrator's impartiality or independence.

2. It is noted that, in their submissions on the challenge, both Parties have referred to the IBA Guidelines on Conflicts of Interest in International Arbitration (the "IBA Guidelines"). Although the IBA Guidelines have no binding status in the present proceedings, they reflect international best practices and offer examples of situations that may give rise to objectively

justifiable doubts as to an arbitrator's impartiality or independence. Specifically, in support of its challenge, the Respondent relied on the scenario set forth at section 3.4.1 of the "Orange List" of the IBA Guidelines which provides that circumstances in which "[t]he arbitrator's law firm is currently acting adverse to one of the parties or an affiliate of one of the parties" may give rise to justifiable doubts as to the arbitrator's impartiality or independence. I also note that the scenario posited at section 3.1.2 of the "Orange List" provides that circumstances in which "[t]he arbitrator has within the past three years served as counsel against one of the parties or an affiliate of one of the parties in an unrelated matter" may give rise to justifiable doubts as to the arbitrator's impartiality or independence. Given that the facts underlying Mr. Alexandrov's disclosure are reflected in both of theses scenarios, I am of the opinion that the conflict in question is sufficiently serious to give rise to objectively justifiable doubts as to Mr. Alexandrov's impartiality and independence.

3. It has been argued in opposition to the challenge, *inter alia*, that the *Vivendi* case may soon come to a close and is unrelated to the present case. However, I do not consider that these circumstances resolve all justifiable doubts. While no more action appears to be required from Mr. Alexandrov in the current annulment proceedings in the above case, I do not consider that this possibility entirely negates Mr. Alexandrov's conflict as envisaged in section 3.4.1 of the IBA Guidelines inasmuch as the possibility exists that the case may continue in some form and engage Mr. Alexandrov's firm's continued representation.

4. As to the relation between the cases, I note again that this is not merely a case in which the arbitrator's law firm is acting adversely to one of the parties in the dispute, but rather a case where the arbitrator has personally and recently acted adversely to one of the parties to the dispute. The scenario set forth in section 3.1.2 of the IBA Guidelines provides that past, personal representation against one of the parties "in an unrelated matter" can be sufficient to give rise to justifiable doubts. Moreover, while the Claimant has argued that the cases are unrelated and there are technical differences between the issues raised in the two cases, they are not entirely dissimilar. Both matters are investment protection actions of considerable magnitude which raise broadly similar concerns against the same State party in a manner that reinforces any justifiable doubts as to the arbitrator's impartiality or independence.

D. Extracts from the Practice of the Iran–US Claims Tribunal

(1) *Tribunal Rules (1983), Article 10(1)*

Letter of the Agent of the United States to the Appointing Authority initiating the Challenge of Judges Kashani and Shafeiei, September 17, 1984 (footnote omitted), reprinted in Intl Arb L Rev 9344:

> A violent physical attack by two arbitrators upon a third who, in their view, is opposed to the interests of the party that appointed them, demonstrates a total lack of the necessary impartiality and independence envisioned by Article 10 [of the 1983 Tribunal Rules]. Further, such conduct compels strong doubts as to whether the two attackers can in the future act with impartiality or independence.
>
> Mr. Kashani and Mr. Shafeiei assert in their September 6 communication to President Lagergren that Mr. Mangård "has totally hostile feelings specifically directed against the Islamic Republic of Iran." Their memorandum goes on to criticize Mr. Mangård for deciding cases against Iranian respondents. The response of Messrs. Kashani and Shafeiei to this asserted hostility on the part of Mr. Mangård was to attack him physically.
>
> This conduct shows that Mr. Kashani and Mr. Shafeiei identify themselves so completely with what they consider to be the interests of Islamic Republic of Iran that they will resort to unprecedented physical violence to protect those interests. As Lord Denning ruled, in deciding on the disqualification of an arbitrator, the key consideration is confidence in "his ability to come to a fair and just conclusion." *Modern Engineering v. Miskin*, [1981] Lloyd's L. Rep. 135, 138 (per Lord Denning, M.R.). Arbitrators who resort to physical violence in order to protect the interests of the

party that appointed them demonstrate such a deep-seated bias that they must be presumed to display similar partisanship in all matters in the future.

Impartiality requires that an arbitrator listen carefully to contending arguments and weigh them thoughtfully with due regard for applicable principles of law and proper procedure.

The conduct involved here is the antithesis of such impartiality. Instead of demonstrating even-handedness and reasoned deliberation, Mr. Kashani and Mr. Shafeiei have resorted to threats and violence against those whom they consider the enemies of the party that appointed them. They have thereby compelled doubts as to their future impartiality and independence. These doubts would persist even if Messrs. Kashani and Shafeiei, in the face of this challenge, were now to apologize and agree to refrain from violence in the future.

Letter of the Agent of the Government of Iran to the Appointing Authority initiating the First Challenge by Iran of Judge Briner, September 13, 1988, at 3, reprinted in 20 Iran-US CTR 182, 183 (1988–III):

> Mr. Briner's relationship with Morgan Stanley, given the circumstances, obviously raises justifiable doubts as to his impartiality and independence, and is, thus, a ground for challenge according to the Tribunal's Rules and fundamental legal principles governing international arbitration. Mr. Briner's failure to fulfill his disclosure obligation is also an additional basis for challenge. For these reasons, the Government of the Islamic Republic of Iran, for itself and on behalf of other Respondents in Case No 55, hereby challenges Mr. Briner . . . according to Article 10 of the [1983] Tribunal Rules.

Memorandum of Amoco Iran Oil regarding the Challenge by Iran of Judge Briner in Case No 55, November 2, 1988, reprinted in 20 Iran-US CTR 233, 241 (1988–III):

> Under the [1983] Tribunal Rules, the test for disqualification is whether circumstances exist that give rise to justifiable doubts as to the arbitrator's impartiality or independence (Article 10(1)). The challenging party, in this case Iran, bears the burden of proof on this issue. The standard is an objective one: whether a reasonable man would conclude, after reviewing the evidence, that justifiable doubts exist. The standard is not whether the challenging party itself doubts the arbitrator's impartiality or independence, but whether a reasonable man would do so.

Letter of the Agent of Iran to the Appointing Authority initiating the Second Challenge by Iran of Judge Briner, July 28, 1989 at 1–2, reprinted in 21 Iran-US CTR 318 (1989–I):

> This challenge is made of respect to all functions he presently performs either as an arbitrator or as the President of the Iran-US Claims Tribunal in regard to any and all cases, inasmuch as the circumstances prompting the challenge raised such serious doubts about his impartiality and independence that he is no more worthy of trust by any standards, and therefore no longer fit to serve as the President of the Tribunal or as a member of it.
>
> The circumstances warranting a challenge under the [1983] Tribunal Rules, Article 10, are Mr. Briner's totally improper course of conduct in the proceedings of Case No 39, *Phillips Petroleum Co. Iran v. The Islamic Republic of Iran and National Iranian Oil Co.*

Letter of the Agent of Iran to the Appointing Authority initiating the Second Challenge by Iran of Judge Briner, August 29, 1989 at 2, reprinted in 21 Iran-US CTR 355 (1989–I):

> As to the merit of the Challenge, it should be borne in mind that all challenging party has to prove is that "circumstances exist that give rise to justifiable doubts as to the arbitrator's impartiality or independence". Such is the criterion to uphold a challenge under the [1983] Tribunal Rules, Article 10(1). According to that standard, no actual bias, but simple uncertainty or doubts

engendered in the mind of a reasonable man because of no matter what circumstances would suffice for the success of the challenge.

Decision of the Appointing Authority on the Second Challenge by Iran of Judge Briner, September 19, 1989 at 4–6, 8–9, reprinted in 21 Iran-US CTR 384, 387–91 (1989–I):

C. General Considerations

a. Under the Tribunal Rules, an Arbitrator can be challenged not on the ground of circumstances which have given rise to serious doubts about that Arbitrator's impartiality and independence, but solely on the ground of circumstances which give rise to justifiable doubts on that score.

...

c. The appointing authority is not competent to assess the correctness of the arbitrators' judgment whether evidence is or is not convincing nor of their decision to accept some evidence as a basis for their award and put other evidence aside... Given the freedom granted the arbitrators... to make their awards to the best of their knowledge and conviction, it cannot be concluded from an arbitrator's choices in this area that he is not impartial or independent.

d. ...Complaints alleging infringement or misapplication of the rules of procedure can succeed only if the alleged infringement or misapplication justifies doubts about the impartiality or independence of the arbitrator concerned. This can only be so if the infringement or misapplication admits of no other explanation than that it has its cause in lack of impartiality or independence on the part of the challenged arbitrator and that any other cause, such as an error or misunderstanding—which, as experience has taught, may happen to the most conscientious judge—can be ruled out.

...

As to the allegation mentioned above under B.2 [that Mr. Briner used the testimony provided in Case No 55 by Morgan Stanley about the Chase Econometrics Forecast for the award in Case No 39].

This allegation can serve as support for the contention that justifiable doubts within the meaning of Article 10 of the Tribunal Rules have arisen, only if it is established beyond doubt that consideration in Case No 39 of testimony provided in Case No 55 by Morgan Stanley about the Chase Econometric Forecast—...—intended to be or had for result either an impediment of the Respondent's position or possibilities in legal proceedings or an unjustified favoring of the Claimant.

To my mind this condition is not fulfilled.

...

As to the allegation mentioned above under B.4...

...

The mistakes and inaccuracies in the Award... have been found not to be of such a nature as to warrant the conclusion that they provide grounds for justifiable doubts about Mr. Briner's impartiality and independence.

Letter of the Agent of the United States to the Appointing Authority concerning the Third Challenge by Iran of Judge Briner, September 15, 1989, at 1, reprinted in 21 Iran-US CTR 383 (1989–I):

The newspaper articles, in which President Briner is mentioned only peripherally, contain assertions that he made a loan for the purchase of certain equipment. Even if one were to accept the statements made in these newspaper articles as true, there is nothing in them to suggest impropriety on the part of President Briner as alleged... Most important for present purposes, these materials could not possibly form the basis of a challenge, since they contain nothing to suggest the existence of circumstances "that give rise to justifiable doubts as to [President Briner's] impartiality or independence". ([1983] Tribunal Rules of Procedure, Article 10, paragraph 1).

Letter of the Agent of the United States to the Appointing Authority concerning the Third Challenge by Iran of Judge Briner, September 19, 1989 at 1, reprinted in 21 Iran-US CTR 395 (1989–1):

> While consideration of this "whole context" could not in any case lend substance to this meritless challenge, Mr. Nobari's suggestion should be seen for what it is—an effort to circumvent the Tribunal Rules of Procedure. Article 10, paragraph 1 of the [1983] Tribunal Rules provides that an arbitrator may be challenged "if circumstances exist that give rise to justifiable doubts as to the arbitrator's impartiality or independence". Article 11, paragraph 1 requires that a party who intends to challenge an arbitrator send notice of the challenge "within 15 days after the circumstances mentioned in articles 9 and 10 become known to that party". These provisions simply afford no basis for consideration of various alleged circumstances of which Iran has been aware for more than 15 days.

Decision of the Appointing Authority on the Third Challenge by Iran to Judge Briner, September 25, 1989 at 2, 3, reprinted in 21 Iran-US CTR 396, 397–98 (1989–I):

> a. Only questions of fact, not mere qualifications or presumptions can properly form the basis of a challenge.
>
> ...
>
> In view of these circumstances, and satisfied as I am that Mr. Briner acted in good faith, the advance payment, even if theoretically it could be shown to have breached the Indian Foreign Exchange Regulations Act, cannot give rise to justifiable doubts as to Mr. Briner's impartiality or independence as an Arbitrator or as President of the Tribunal.

Decision of the Appointing Authority on the Challenge to Judge Noori, August 31, 1990 at 13–14, reprinted in 24 Iran-US CTR 314, 324 (1990–I):

> ...even if for the sake of argument it were assumed that this claim and the other grounds put forward in the challenge for doubting Mr. Noori's impartiality and independence—to wit his service as Head of the NIOI Legal Office and his failure to disclose this to the President of the Tribunal—were true, I do not feel that, in connection with the circumstances to be mentioned hereafter, this doubt can be termed justifiable doubt within the meaning of Article 10 of the [1983] Tribunal Rule:
>
> 1. The circumstances that Mr. Noori served with NIOI as Head of the Legal Office a long time ago—from mid–1980 to mid–1982—and was in that capacity a member of the NIOI Council for a few months only during that period;
> 2. The circumstances that...MIG was falling under the purview of NIOI as only one of very many companies;
> 3. The circumstances that Mr. Noori's duties as a member of the NIOI Council were limited to providing legal advice to the NIOI authorities only on internal legal matters and, as Head of the NIOI Legal Office, to provide services in connection with internal legal works;
> 4. The circumstances that Mr. Noori, prior to his appointment as an Arbitrator in the Tribunal, had in no way been involved in Case No 248, especially not as Head of the NIOI Legal Office or as counsellor or advisor to any of the respondents in this Case;
> 5. The circumstances that NIOI is not a party to Case No 248 nor has ever been one.

Decision of the Appointing Authority Sir Robert Jennings on the Challenge by the United States to Judge Broms, May 7, 2001 at 3–4, 11:

> ...The United States describes Judge Broms having by his conduct made it *de jure* and *de facto* impossible for him to act as an arbitrator, thus, in the view of the United States bringing into operation the Article 13 [of the 1983 Tribunal Rules] provisions for "replacement of a member".

This suggested device and its effect appears in several places in the Memorandum attached to the challenge, and is conveniently summarized in the Agent for the United States' Notice of Challenge, dated 4 January, when he says that, besides the lack of independence and impartiality, Judge Broms '*in addition* [emphasis supplied] demonstrates his unfitness to continue as a member of the Tribunal because of his failure to act and the *de facto* impossibility of his performing his functions'.

This argument is unpersuasive. In the circumstances described in Article 13, of an impossibility of an arbitrator performing, the resulting problem of the need for a substitute arbitrator is dealt with by a simple cross-reference to the procedures of substitution set out in Articles 9 to 12. But it does not follow that lack of independence or impartiality can also be used to activate the triggering provisions of Article 13. Justifiable doubts about impartiality and about lack of independence are adequately dealt with under Articles 9–12.

Moreover, paragraphs 3, 4, and 5, of Article 13 of the [1983] Tribunal's Rules—that is to say the ones that are additional to the original [1976] UNCITRAL Article 13—are clearly intended to deal with what should be done in the event of actual failure to act, or "the impossibility of his performing his functions", rather than a metaphorical failure or impossibility inferred from his views expressed when acting. Thus they provide *inter alia* for a "temporary illness" and for a "temporary absence", which suggests that Article 13 was not intended to be used to supplement or qualify the meanings of "independence" and "impartiality" in Articles 9 to 12 but to provide for a quite different situation that clearly needs to be provided for.

Accordingly I am not persuaded to regard Judge Broms as having behaved in such a way as to amount to failure to act or to a *de jure* or *de facto* impossibility of performing his functions within the meaning of Article 13.

...

One ought to resist an assumption that the independence and the impartiality of the Members of the Tribunal who are nominated by a party are different in their juridical nature from the requirements for one of the "neutral" judges. No such distinction in made in the [1983] Rules governing challenges.

Decision of the Appointing Authority, W E Haak, in the Challenge of Judges Assadollah Noori, Koorosh H Ameli, Mohsen Aghahosseini, April 19, 2006:

29. ... [T]he United States fails to demonstrate that the payments made to Iran by the Challenged Arbitrators constitute a circumstance giving rise to justifiable doubts about these arbitrators' Independence or impartiality. The United States has not convinced me that these payments, said to currently amount to approximately forty percent of the remuneration of the Challenged Arbitrators, are anything other than legally made contributions, required by Iranian tax law. At any rate, I cannot find any evidence supporting the United States' theory that these payments should be labeled as illicit "kickbacks".

30. The United States bases its Challenge on the statement made by Judge Noori on 6 December 2005. The United States asserts in its Notice of Challenge that this statement demonstrates that the Iranian arbitrators are financially dependent on the Government of Iran, which "effectively determines the income received by each of its appointed arbitrators". The United States claims that this gives rise to "justifiable doubts" as to the impartiality and independence required of arbitrators under Article 10 of the [1983] Tribunal Rules. In later submissions, the United States refers to the payments as "Party-mandated arbitrator kickbacks".

31. Iran and the Challenged Arbitrators concede that payments were made to Iran. They explained that these payments constitute income tax payments made pursuant to Iranian law. During the individual fact-finding meetings held on 6 February 2006, the Iranian arbitrators provided practical explanation. on how the payments are made, through a representative of the Ministry of Finance at the Iranian Centre for International Legal Affairs in The Hague. Some relevant provisions of Iranian tax law were provided by the Agent of Iran to the appointing authority on 17 February 2006.

32. It therefore falls to the United States to demonstrate that the payments are not legal contributions, but rather "illicit kickbacks" as it alleges.

39. ... [T]he United States does not show that the payments made by the Iranian arbitrators to Iran are anything other than what Iran and the Challenged Arbitrators assert they are: regular periodical payments under Iranian income tax law. The United States does not assert that normal payments under ordinary income tax law would result in a breach of the arbitrators' obligation of impartiality and independence.

40. Neither do I believe that ordinary tax payments should be considered to give rise to justifiable doubts as to an arbitrator's independence, because payment of taxes to the state conforms to legally established rules equally applicable to all taxpayers in an identical situation; nor does it give rise to justifiable doubts as to an arbitrator's impartiality, as payment of taxes is neither likely to prejudice an arbitrator in favor of the state to which it pays taxes; nor against it, since taxation will occur in any event. From the foregoing it should be clear that I am of the opinion that there is no ground for any appearance of bias whatsoever.

Joint Decision by the Appointing Authority, Judge W E Haak, on the Challenges against Judge Krzysztop Skubiszewski and Judge Hamid Reza Oloumi Yazdi, April 2, 2008, at 25:

The United States did argue that "the only explanation for Judge Oloumi's disclosure is that he intended to give the party that appointed him – Iran – the opportunity to seek to alter the course of deliberations, change the composition of the Tribunal or, by seeking to force a rehearing of select portions of Case B61, possibly even change the outcome of a case" (United States' submission of February 1, 2008, p. 8). According to the United States, such a serious breach of the Rules would warrant Judge Oloumi's withdrawal from the Tribunal.

It may well be that if there were compelling evidence that an arbitrator intentionally disclosed confidential information in order to provide ammunition for a party to challenge another arbitrator, such disclosures would amount to circumstances giving rise to justifiable doubts within the meaning of article 10 of the Rules. However, having reviewed the file carefully, I have not found any proof that Judge Oloumi ever intended to create an opportunity for Iran to challenge President Skubiszewski. Judge Oloumi has constantly stated that he honestly believed that the issues discussed in his memorandum were not confidential Judge Oloumi's disclosures should rather be seen as the fruit of an error or a misunderstanding as to the interpretation of the May 1, 2007 Full Tribunal Decision and the scope of the deliberations.

The breach is thus not as serious as the United States claims, due to the lack of intention to disclose confidential information and to the vagueness of Judge Oloumi's statements. Nevertheless, it has had highly regrettable consequences for the integrity and the prosperity of the Tribunal's proceedings. While Judge Oloumi's unfortunate initiative cannot be analyzed as a circumstance giving rise to justifiable doubts as to Judge Oloumi's impartiality or independence, much greater care should be taken in the future in order to comply with this fundamental rule of procedure and avoid the harmful effects of forbidden disclosures.

(2) *Tribunal Rules (1983), Article 10(2)*

Reply Memorandum of the Islamic Republic of Iran regarding the Challenge of Judge Briner in Case No 55, November 28, 1988, reprinted in 20 Iran-US CTR 260, 315 (1988–III):

...Article 10(2) states that "(A) party may challenge the arbitrator appointed by him only for reasons of which he becomes aware after the appointment has been made". Thus, for party-appointed arbitrators, there may be an implied burden of proof of the kind proposed by Amoco to show that *prior to the appointment* such reasons were unknown. Indeed, Amoco's reference to the *oeuvres préparatoires* of the [1976] UNCITRAL Rules confirms this implication. However, Mr. Briner is not a party-appointed arbitrator but a neutral arbitrator appointed by the 2 party-appointed arbitrators. There is no suggestion whatsoever that such a rule applies in the cases of a neutral arbitrator so appointed. Indeed, the inclusion of such a specific provision in the [1976]

UNCITRAL Rules relating only to party-appointed arbitrators implies that the opposite is true in the case of neutral arbitrators.

4. The Initiation of the Challenge and the Potential for Agreement to the Challenge—Article 13

Challenges are a serious matter which may greatly delay arbitral proceedings. For this reason, Article 13 of the UNCITRAL Rules sets forth several formal requirements intended to prevent untimely or unsubstantiated challenges. Similarly, it specifies how the agreement of a party or the arbitrator challenged may resolve the challenge.

A. Text of the 2010 UNCITRAL Rule[239]

Article 13 of the 2010 UNCITRAL Rules provides:

1. A party that intends to challenge an arbitrator shall send notice of its challenge within 15 days after it has been notified of the appointment of the challenged arbitrator, or within 15 days after the circumstances mentioned in articles 11 and 12 became known to that party.
2. The notice of challenge shall be communicated to all other parties, to the arbitrator who is challenged and to the other arbitrators. The notice of challenge shall state the reasons for the challenge.
3. When an arbitrator has been challenged by a party, all parties may agree to the challenge. The arbitrator may also, after the challenge, withdraw from his or her office. In neither case does this imply acceptance of the validity of the grounds for the challenge.
4. If, within 15 days from the date of the notice of challenge, all parties do not agree to the challenge or the challenged arbitrator does not withdraw, the party making the challenge may elect to pursue it. In that case, within 30 days from the date of the notice of challenge, it shall seek a decision on the challenge by the appointing authority.

B. Commentary

(1) When notice of challenge must be made—Article 13(1)

(a) **General comments on the** *travaux préparatoires*

Article 13(1) establishes the period within which a challenge must be made. Under this provision, a notice of challenge must be sent within fifteen days after the appointment of the challenged arbitrator has been notified to the challenging party, or fifteen days after the

---

[239] Corresponding Article 11 of the 1976 UNCITRAL Rules provides:

1. A party who intends to challenge an arbitrator shall send notice of his challenge within fifteen days after the appointment of the challenged arbitrator has been notified to the challenging party or within fifteen days after the circumstances mentioned in articles 9 and 10 became known to that party.
2. The challenge shall be notified to the other party, to the arbitrator who is challenged and to the other members of the arbitral tribunal. The notification shall be in writing and shall state the reasons for the challenge.
3. When an arbitrator has been challenged by one party, the other party may agree to the challenge. The arbitrator may also, after the challenge, withdraw from his office. In neither case does this imply acceptance of the validity of the grounds for the challenge. In both cases the procedure provided for in article 6 or 7 shall be used in full for the appointment of the substitute arbitrator, even if during the process of appointing the challenged arbitrator a party had failed to exercise his right to appoint or to participate in the appointment.

circumstances constituting the basis for the challenge first become known to the challenging party. If, for example, facts believed to constitute a ground for challenge become known for the first time *via* disclosure in accordance with Article 11 and disclosure occurs after appointment, then the 15-day period runs from the date of disclosure to the challenging party and not the date of appointment. The 15-day period can never commence before the appointment of the challenged arbitrator, given that only an "arbitrator" may be challenged.

The drafters of the 1976 UNCITRAL Rules wanted to ensure that challenges were made at the earliest possible stage of the arbitral proceedings due to the high costs of challenges made once proceedings are well under way. Challenges result in the interruption of the course of proceedings, and a successful challenge creates serious delays because a substitute must be appointed and there may be a need to repeat hearings.[240] This is particularly so where a sole arbitrator is challenged.

The preliminary draft of Article 11(1) of the 1976 UNCITRAL Rules set a time limit of 15 days for making notice of a challenge. There was some discussion of whether to extend the limit to 30 days or reduce it to immediate notification. A limit of 15 days was finally agreed upon as fair, since it gave the challenging party some time to consider what actions to take without allowing the proceedings to progress too far. In other words, it served "to avoid the possibility of a party awaiting the completion of the arbitration procedure before making his challenge."[241]

Discussion of the preliminary draft of Article 11 of the 1976 UNCITRAL Rules apparently provoked a question of whether a time limit was needed at all, since "the time within which a challenge should be made would be determined under applicable municipal law and under the arbitration laws of many countries, a challenge was permissible at any stage of the hearing."[242]

However, the decision was made to keep the time limit for two reasons. First, it was argued that municipal law would not adequately govern challenges in all cases. Second, the drafters agreed that parties should be permitted to contractually agree to time limits for the challenge of arbitrators.[243]

The drafters made it clear that after 15 days the right to challenge was waived.[244] Again, the purpose was to prevent parties from abusing the challenge mechanism by bringing up areas of concern of which they had been aware for some time, just to delay proceedings that appeared to be going against them.

The final issue addressed by the drafting Committee was whether the 15-day limit should be based on the sending or receipt of the notice of challenge. The preliminary draft of Article 11(1) of the 1976 UNCITRAL Rules said the challenge "should be made" within 15 days. The German representative stated that this implied that the notice of challenge should be received within 15 days, especially since Article 2 of the 1976 UNCITRAL Rules

---

[240] Accord *Report of the Secretary-General on the Revised Draft Set of Arbitration Rules*, UNCITRAL, 9th Session, Addendum 1 (Commentary), UN Doc A/CN.9/112/Add.1 (1975), reprinted in (1976) VII UNCITRAL Ybk 166, 170.

[241] *Summary Record of the 3rd Meeting of the Committee of the Whole (II)*, UNCITRAL, 9th Session, UN Doc A/CN.9/9/C.2/SR.3, at 4–5, para 25 (1976) (Comment by Mr Pirrung, Federal Republic of Germany).

[242] UN Doc A/10017, n 71, para 78, reprinted in (1975) VI UNCITRAL Ybk 24, 33.

[243] *Report of the UNCITRAL*, 8th Session, n 242, para 79.

[244] *Report of the Secretary-General on the Revised Draft Set of Arbitration Rules*, UNCITRAL, 9th Session, Addendum 1 (Commentary), UN Doc A/CN.9/112/Add.1 (1975), reprinted in (1976) VII UNCITRAL Ybk 166, 170 (Commentary on Draft Article 10(1)).

established the general rule that all notifications were effective on receipt. Although it was argued that clarification was needed, the Committee in the end decided to require only that the challenging party "send" notice within 15 days, on the theory that the time limit "was important not so much for the party receiving notification of challenge, but for the challenging party."[245] In other words, the purpose of the 15-day rule was to ensure that the challenging party acts expeditiously, a purpose fulfilled by proof of sending. Corresponding Article 13(1) of the 2010 UNCITRAL Rules, which is identical to Article 11(1) of the 1976 UNCITRAL Rules in substance, is subject to the same policy.

(b) When circumstances "became known" to the challenging party

Determining when the circumstances underlying a challenge "became known" to the challenging party is often a simple task when the information about those circumstances is based on some widely known event or circumstance. Such was the case with the first challenge in the *AWG* arbitration in which the Argentine Government challenged an arbitrator for serving on another tribunal that had rendered an award against Argentina. The challenge was dismissed as untimely because the date on which Argentina received the adverse award was undisputed, and Argentina filed its notice of challenge several days after the 15-day limit had expired.[246] Other situations may not be as straightforward, however, such as where an arbitrator's general or recurring conduct is questioned.

The practice of the Iran–US Claims Tribunal and investment tribunals is illuminating with respect to two important questions related to the 15-day limit on challenges: (1) who bears the burden of proving when circumstances "became known" to a challenging party; and (2) what constitutes actual prior knowledge of the circumstances giving rise to the challenge.[247]

(1) Burden of proof

In Iran's challenge of Judge Briner in Case No 55, one of the key areas of disagreement between Iran and Amoco was whether or not Iran knew of Briner's relationship with Morgan Stanley's Swiss subsidiary long before it decided to bring a challenge.[248]

The memoranda of the two parties addressed the question of who should bear the burden of proving when a challenging party becomes aware of the circumstances on which the challenge is based. Amoco argued that Iran "has the burden of proof in establishing that it has standing to bring the challenge—that is, that it learned of the circumstances that gave rise to the challenge no more than 15 days before acting on that information."[249] The

---

[245] *Summary Record of the 15th Meeting of the Committee of the Whole (II)*, UNCITRAL, 9th Session, UN Doc A/CN.9/9/C.2/SR.15, at 8, para 70 (1976) (Comment by the Chairman).

[246] Decision on the Proposal for the Disqualification of a Member of the Arbitral Tribunal *Suez, Sociedad General de Aguas de Barcelona SA and Vivendi Universal SA* and *Argentina Republic, Suez, Sociedad General de Aguas de Barcelona SA and InterAguas Servicios Integrales del Agua* and *Argentine Republic, and AWG Group Ltd* and *Argentine Republic* (October 22, 2007), at 9–10.

[247] As to challenges raised in proceedings before the Iran–US Claims Tribunal, Note 2 to Articles 9 through 12 of the 1983 Tribunal Rules explains how Article 11(1) of the 1976 UNCITRAL Arbitration Rules is applied in this specific setting. For the Tribunal, the period for making a challenge to a member of the Chamber to which the case has been assigned is 15 days after the challenging party is given notice of the Chamber to which the case has been assigned, or 15 days after circumstances giving rise to the challenge become known.

[248] Recall that the challenge involved whether Judge Briner's failure to disclose his relationship, given the Claimant's use of Morgan Stanley as an expert witness in the case, gave rise to justifiable doubts as to his impartiality or independence.

[249] Memorandum of Amoco Iran Oil regarding the Challenge of Judge Briner in Case No 55 by Iran, n 156, at 234; reprinted in section 4(D)(1).

Iranians replied that Article 11(1) of the Tribunal Rules "says nothing about having to fulfill any alleged burden of proof."[250] Inasmuch as Judge Briner withdrew from Case No 55, the appointing authority did not have the opportunity to address the issue.

While the rules do not explicitly address the question of burden of proof in the context of a challenge,[251] Article 27(1) provides that "each party shall have the burden of proving the facts relied on to support his claim or defence."[252] Given the serious consequences of a challenge and the concern of the UNCITRAL drafters that the procedure not be abused, it seems appropriate that the party bringing a challenge should be required, analogously to Article 27(1), to make some showing that its awareness of the circumstances forming the basis of the challenge arose within the 15-day limit.[253] As the attorney for Amoco pointed out in a letter to the appointing authority: "when the facts are wholly within the possession of one party and inaccessible to the other party, it is the first party that should bear the burden of proof."[254]

The party resisting a challenge as untimely bears the burden of proving that the notice of challenge was submitted beyond the 15-day time limit. This issue arose during the challenge to Mr Christopher Thomas in a NAFTA Chapter Eleven arbitration between a US claimant and Canada. Upon his appointment, Mr Thomas disclosed his plans to discontinue his counsel work by a certain specified date. Sometime later, he informed the parties that he had returned to counsel work and, in particular, had performed legal work for the Mexican Government. In a later disclosure, Mr Thomas stated that he had advised the Mexican Government on "matters that fall within the rubric of international trade and investment law," though not "in respect of the interpretation or application of the NAFTA Chapter 11 or similar provisions in Mexico's Bilateral Investment Treaties."[255] Within 15 days of the second disclosure, the claimant filed its notice of challenge against Mr Thomas.

Canada argued that the challenge was untimely because Mr Thomas had returned to counsel work well before his disclosures were received by the parties, a fact which the claimant knew or should have known. In assessing Canada's claim, the Appointing Authority found: "While the Claimant as the party raising the challenge must show that justifiable doubts exist as to the arbitrator's impartiality or independence, the burden of proving the Claimant knew of relevant circumstances more than fifteen days prior to bringing the challenge falls upon the Respondent."[256]

---

[250] Reply Memorandum of Iran regarding the Challenge of Judge Briner in Case No 55, n 149, at 319; reprinted in section 4(D)(1).

[251] See *Summary Record of the 3rd Meeting of the Committee of the Whole (II)*, UNCITRAL, 9th Session, UN Doc A/CN.9/9/C.2/SR.3, at 4–6 (1976).

[252] See Chapter 18.

[253] The 15-day limit has typically been followed strictly. See also Decision of the Appointing Authority on the Challenge of Judge Bengt Broms, n 51, Letter of the Agent of the Government of the United States to the Appointing Authority, n 43; both reprinted in section 4(D)(1).

[254] Letter of Attorney for Amoco Iran Oil, Mr Brice M Clagett, to the Appointing authority regarding the Challenge by Iran of Judge Briner in Case No 55, December 1, 1988, at 1–2, reprinted in 20 Iran-US CTR 325 (1988–III); reprinted in section 4(D)(1).

[255] *Vito G Gallo* and *Government of Canada,* Decision on the Challenge to Mr J Christopher Thomas, QC, (Nassib G Ziadé, ICSID Deputy Secretary-General, Appointing Authority) (14 Oct 2009) (ICSID administered, 1976 UNCITRAL Rules, NAFTA Chapter Eleven), at 4, para 11 (citing Mr Thomas's reply of 22 June 2009).

[256] Decision on the Challenge to Mr J Christopher Thomas, at 7.

We agree with the Appointing Authority that the party resisting a challenge bears the burden of proving that the challenge was untimely. At the same time, in many circumstances it may also be necessary for the challenging part to establish the timeliness of its notice of arbitration. Such proof was not necessary in the challenge to Mr Thomas because it was undisputed that the claimant filed its challenge within 15 days of Mr Thomas's second disclosure. Nevertheless, consistent with Article 27(1), the challenging party not only must demonstrate its justifiable doubts, but must also prove that its challenge request was filed within 15 days of becoming aware of the circumstances underlying the challenge. A failure to do so would result in dismissal of the challenge, regardless of whether the resisting party has proven that the challenge was untimely.

One example of a challenging party failing to satisfy its burden of proof is the third challenge to Briner in which Iran alleged that Briner violated India's foreign exchange laws.[257] The Appointing Authority dismissed the challenge because, among other reasons, Iran based the challenge on information in articles which appeared in *India Today* in 1987, two years before the challenge:

b. It is not consistent with the system of the Tribunal Rules that the Appointing Authority, deciding on a challenge, should take into account circumstances that came to the knowledge of the challenging party earlier than the beginning of the period of 15 days mentioned in article 11 of those rules.[258]

The prior publication of the newspaper articles therefore appears to have raised sufficient doubts as to whether Iran had demonstrated that it gained knowledge of the situation more recently and, thus, within 15 days of submitting its challenge request.[259]

(2) Actual prior knowledge

Article 13(1) requires that a party send notice of challenge within 15 days after the circumstances underlying the challenge "became known" to that party. The provision could have, but notably does not include, the phrase "should have known" or "ought to have known."[260]

---

[257] See section 1(B)(5).

[258] Decision of the Appointing Authority on the Challenge by Iran of Judge Briner, September 25, 1989, reprinted in 21 Iran-US CTR 398 (1989–I); reprinted in section 4(D)(1).

[259] In spite of the strict application of the 15-day limit in the two Briner decisions, Tribunal practice implicity suggests that extensions of the time limit may be granted in some instances. Baker and Davis point, for example, to the instance involving Judge Virally:

...President Böckstiegel refused a request by Iran for a two month extension of time within which to bring a possible challenge to Virally as to a particular case, stating that in view of the 15-day time limit there was "no room for extensions." This would appear to support a view of the time limit as absolute and nonextendable, except that President Böckstiegel had already permitted the parties much more than 15 days. Judge Virally's disclosure statement containing the professional relationships in question was made available to the Iranian agent no later than May 22, 1985, but President Böckstiegel stated that he would accept comments or objections until June 28, 1985. Because no challenge was ultimately made, the issue whether the 15-day limit is jurisdictional and nonextendable was never specifically addressed, but President Böckstiegel's action suggests that he at least believed the 15-day limit could be extended in proper circumstances.

S Baker and M Davis, *The UNCITRAL Rules in Practice*, n 1, 63–4. Of course, the other party can waive the time limit, since by agreement of the parties any provision of the rules can be modified.

[260] In discussions to revise the Rules, members of the Working Group considered the addition of a provision that granted the appointing authority discretion to dismiss a challenge if the challenging party "ought reasonably to have known the grounds for challenge at an earlier stage of the procedure." *Settlement of Commercial Disputes: Revision of the UNCITRAL Arbitration Rules, Note by the Secretariat*, UNCITRAL, UN Doc A/CN.9/WG.II/WP.151 at 13, para 28 (2008) (Draft Article 12(2)). The proposed language was rejected, among other reasons as it would create a standard of "imputed knowledge that would constitute a novelty in the Rules." UNCITRAL, 42nd Session, UN Doc A/CN.9/665, n 89, at 19, para 101.

In the challenge by the United States of the three Iranian arbitrators on the Iran–US Claims Tribunal, the Appointing Authority interpreted corresponding Article 11 of the Tribunal Rules as requiring "evidence of actual prior knowledge."[261] The Appointing Authority, Judge Haak, thus accepted the US position that Article 11 of the Tribunal Rules did not contain a standard of constructive knowledge, which could result in a party waiving its right to challenge too easily. The United States noted that Article 30 of the Tribunal Rules on waiver contained the same standard of actual knowledge ("knows"), and that the drafters of the Rules carefully considered and rejected additional language on constructive knowledge ("should have known") in that provision.[262] Further, the United States persuasively argued:

> The UNCITRAL drafters were appropriately cautious about depriving a party of its right to object under Article [30 of the 1976 UNCITRAL Rules], which was intended to address "minor violations of the procedure." Article 11(1), in contrast, deals with a party's fundamental right to an impartial and independent tribunal. Accordingly, where deprivation of a party's fundamental – as opposed to minor—rights are at risk, a constructive waiver test is, *a fortiori*, unwarranted and inappropriate.[263]

The Appointing Authority who decided the challenge to Mr Thomas in the *Gallo* arbitration also applied an actual knowledge test. In that challenge, the respondent, the Canadian Government, argued that the claimant should have known that Mr Thomas had resumed his counsel work because news of Mr Thomas's association with a new law firm had been reported in the Canadian press.[264] The appointing authority rejected the Canadian Government's assertion that claimant's counsel was "almost certainly aware" of Mr Thomas's new status because "[s]uch speculative statements cannot replace proof of actual knowledge."[265]

What type of evidence then is sufficient to establish actual knowledge beyond the 15-day time limit? In its challenge to the three Iranian arbitrators, the United States argued that the only sufficient evidence was "conclusive evidence (usually in the form of written documents) that the challenging party had full and accurate knowledge of the circumstances giving rise to a challenge."[266] The practice of appointing authorities generally confirms that the standard for establishing actual knowledge is generally high. In two leading cases, the appointing authorities respectively found a challenge request to be untimely only when the challenging party had directly received the information that formed the basis for the challenge more than 15 days before the notice of challenge was submitted.

In the US challenge to the three Iranian arbitrators, Iran and the Iranian arbitrators argued generally that the United States knew of the Iranian arbitrators' practice of

---

[261] Decision by the Appointing Authority, Mr W E Haak, on the US Challenge to the three Iranian Arbitrators, April 19, 2006, para 25 at 4. Extracts of the decision are found in section 4(D)(1).

[262] Letter from the US Agent, Mr Clifton Johnson, to the Appointing Authority, Mr W E Haak, March 10, 2006, at 14–15. For excerpts of the letter, see section 4(D)(1).

[263] Letter from the US Agent, Mr Clifton Johnson, n 262, at 15.

[264] *Vito G Gallo* and *Government of Canada*, Decision on the Challenge to Mr J Christopher Thomas, QC (Nassib G. Ziadé, ICSID Deputy Secretary-General, Appointing Authority) (October 14, 2009) (ICSID administered, 1976 UNCITRAL Rules, NAFTA Chapter Eleven), at 7, para 23.

[265] Decision on the challenge to Mr J Christopher Thomas at 8, para 24. The appointing authority also found that "[a]llowing the Respondent to invoke evidence of constructive knowledge (even if reasonably proved) would relieve the arbitrator of the continuing duty to disclose. This would unfairly place the burden on the Claimant to seek elsewhere the notice it should have received from the arbitrator."

[266] Letter from the US Agent, Mr Clifton Johnson, to the Appointing Authority, Mr W E Haak (March 10, 2006), at 15–16. An excerpt of the letter canvassing Tribunal practice is included at section 4(D)(1).

remitting a portion of their salary to the Iranian government long before it submitted its notice of challenge.[267] In response to this allegation, the United States noted that it had "long harbored doubts" about the impartiality and independence of the Iranian arbitrators and had been "aware of rumors" about the Iranian practice.[268] However, it argued that nevertheless "doubts, beliefs and rumors alone are not sufficient to sustain a challenge, which requires that doubts be justifiable."[269] The Iranian arbitrators and Iran immediately cited the US response as proof of prior knowledge of the Iranian practice.

The Appointing Authority rejected the Iranian position. In defining what evidence of actual knowledge entails, the Appointing Authority observed that, according to Tribunal practice, such evidence has included more conclusive evidence, such as "a prior statement by the challenging party."[270] The Appointing Authority's decision in the specific challenge before him rested on two pieces of evidence to which he assigned significant probative value: (1) a recent statement by the Tribunal's Secretary-General and his handwritten notes from a 1984 meeting indicating that a former Iranian arbitrator had stated in the presence of the US Agent that the Iranian arbitrators returned part of their salaries to Iran; and (2) a recent letter from a former Iranian arbitrator stating that a US arbitrator suggested at a 1981 Tribunal meeting that Iranian arbitrators may wish to return part of their salaries to Iran, if Iran deemed the salaries to be too high, and that the US Agent present at the meeting did not object to this proposal.[271] Thus, in dismissing the US challenge as untimely, the Appointing Authority emphasized the evidence that he concluded demonstrated that the United States had been directly informed of the circumstances underlying the challenge.

In the challenge to Mr Thomas in the *Gallo* arbitration, the Canadian Government, the party resisting the challenge, argued that the claimant knew or should have known about the resumption of Mr Thomas's counsel work. In that case, Mr Thomas informed the parties that he was retiring from counsel work and withdrawing from his current law firm, Thomas & Partners, but later joined a new firm where he continued his work as counsel. Canada noted that, after Mr Thomas's disclosure of his planned retirement, the claimant continued to send submissions to him at the address of his prior law firm, that a procedural order of the tribunal listed the same address as his contact information, and that when Mr Thomas later notified the parties of his change of address, he referred to his "former office premises."[272] Thus, the Canadian Government argued that the claimant was on notice of

---

[267] Decision by the Appointing Authority, Judge W E Haak, on the Challenge against Judges Assadollah Noori, Koorosh H Ameli, and Mohsen Aghahosseini, April 19, 2006, at 4–5, paras 26–28, n 56.

[268] Letter from the US Agent, Clifton Johnson, to the Appointing Authority, Judge W E Haak, regarding the Challenge of Arbitrators Assadollah Noori, Koorosh H Ameli and Mohsen Aghahosseini (February 3, 2006), at 9.

[269] Letter from the US Agent, Clifton Johnson, n 268, at 9.

[270] Decision by the Appointing Authority, Mr W E Haak, on the Challenge against Judges Assadollah Noori, Koorosh H Ameli, and Mohsen Aghahosseini (April 19, 2006), at 4, para 25.

[271] Decision by the Appointing Authority, Mr W E Haak, n 270, at 5, paras 26–27. The decision cites the appointing authority's decision of September 19, 1989, on the second challenge to Judge Briner. In that, the Appointing Authority, Judge Moons, rejected the challenge based on Briner's handling of Case No 39 as untimely. Moons calculated the relevant time period based on the fact that "all the allegations on which the challenge is based are mentioned in Mr. Khalilian's statement of June 30, 1989," which exceeded the 15-day time limit." Decision of the Appointing Authority on the Second Challenge by Iran of Judge Briner, September 19, 1989, n 41, at 394.

[272] *Vito G Gallo* and *Government of Canada*, Decision on the Challenge to Mr J Christopher Thomas, QC, (Nassib G. Ziadé, ICSID Deputy Secretary-General, Appointing Authority) (14 Oct 2009) (ICSID administered, 1976 UNCITRAL Rules, NAFTA Chapter Eleven), at 7 para 21.

Mr Thomas's continued counsel work well before it submitted its notice of challenge.[273] The Appointing Authority did not find this evidence to be conclusive: "Merely maintaining an address at a law firm for some months after a declared date of departure does not by itself indicate continuing work as to counsel."[274]

The Canadian Government also argued that the claimant should have known about Mr Thomas's continued counsel work because of press coverage of what Canada described as the "merger" between Mr Thomas's old law firm and a new law firm with which he became associated. The Canadian Government further argued that because of the modest size of the Canadian trade and investment bar, the claimant should have known of Mr. Thomas's status. As noted above, the Appointing Authority rejected the notion that the Rules contained a test of constructive knowledge of the circumstances underlying the challenge.[275]

(2) To whom should notice be sent; what form should notice take; sufficiency of the notice; who may send notice—Article 13(2)

Article 13(2) establishes who should be notified in the event of a challenge, as well as the form and contents of the notification. It requires that notice be sent to all other parties, to the arbitrator being challenged, and to the other members of the arbitral tribunal.

Article 13(2) also specifies that the notice of challenge must state the reasons for the challenge. The form in which notice of challenge should be communicated is not expressly addressed in the rule, but like all communications, this issue is governed by Article 2 of the Rules.[276] Thus, a notice may be communicated "by any means of communication that provide a record of its transmission." Oral challenges, even if capable of meeting this standard, are too easily made and thus not advisable; the act is serious and deserves the time for reflection provided by reduction to writing. Nor may a challenge be vague. The notice must state the reasons, although not necessarily providing the evidence justifying the challenge, or the challenge will be declared inadmissible.[277]

As far as the drafters of the 1976 UNCITRAL Rules were concerned, the purpose of the notice is to enable the other party to decide whether it will agree to the challenge and the challenged arbitrator to decide whether he will withdraw from office.[278]

The Iran–US Claims Tribunal and its appointing authority offer extensive practice in evaluating whether different notices of challenge presented to the Tribunal meet the formalities required under Article 11(2) of the Tribunal Rules, which is substantively identical to Article 13(2) of the 2010 UNCITRAL Rules.[279]

---

[273] Decision on the challenge to Mr J Christopher Thomas, at 7, para 21.
[274] Decision on the challenge to Mr J Christopher Thomas, at 7, para 22.
[275] Decision on the challenge to Mr J Christopher Thomas, at 7–8, paras 22–23.
[276] Article 13(2) omits the writing requirement found in corresponding Article 11(2) of the 1976 UNCITRAL Rules because "the manner in which the information should be exchanged is already dealt with under article 2." *Settlement of Commercial Disputes: Revision of the UNCITRAL Arbitration Rules, Note by the Secretariat*, UNCITRAL, UN Doc A/CN.9/WG.II/WP.151 at 13, para 26 (2008).
[277] See, eg, Letter of the Agent of the Government of Iran to the Appointing Authority, Ch M J A Moons, September 27, 1988, at 2, reprinted in 20 Iran-US CTR 188–9 (1988–III); reprinted in section 4(D)(2).
[278] *Report of the Secretary-General on the Revised Draft Set of Arbitration Rules*, UNCITRAL, 9th Session, Addendum 1 (Commentary), UN Doc A/CN.9/112/Add.1 (1975), reprinted in (1976) VII UNCITRAL Ybk 166, 170 (Commentary on Draft Article 10(2)).
[279] See, eg, Letter of the Agent of Iran to the Appointing Authority initiating the Second Challenge, n 39, reprinted in section 4(D)(2).

The challenge of Judges Kashani and Shafeiei, for example, appeared to meet all of these formal requirements. The Agent for the US wrote to the Appointing Authority on September 17, 1984, stating "[w]e have waited the full fifteen day period provided in the Rules...."[280] The challenge was "notified" to the other party, the challenged arbitrators, and the other members of the Tribunal by the delivery of copies. That the letter was addressed to the Appointing Authority is not contrary to the Rules and was appropriate, given that Article 12(1)(6) of the Tribunal Rules provided for the Appointing Authority to decide upon the challenge. The operative paragraph of the cover letter stated:

[T]he Government of the United States, in accordance with Article III of the Claims Settlement Declaration and Articles 9–13 of the Tribunal Rules, is compelled to, and hereby does, challenge Arbitrators Kashani and Shafeiei. In the event that the Government of Iran does not expeditiously agree to the challenge, or that the challenged arbitrators do not quickly withdraw voluntarily, the United States requests, pursuant to Article 12(1)(6) of the Tribunal Rules, that you decide and sustain the challenge.[281]

Attached to this cover letter was a 17-page memorandum setting forth the factual and legal basis for the challenge. The three challenges by Iran of Judge Briner, the challenge by Iran of Judge Arangio-Ruiz, and the claimant's challenge of Judge Noori in Case No 248 likewise all met the formal requirements of a challenge in Article 11.

In stark contrast to these challenges is the January 1, 1982 letter from the Government of Iran to Nils Mangård objecting to his continued service as an arbitrator. The status of this letter was considered both by the Tribunal and the appointing authority.

The Tribunal having, as described above, resolved the problem of the merits of the Iranian objection to the Tribunal proceeding with its work as long as Judge Mangård remained a member, the Tribunal with little explanation set itself a new task: deciding whether the Iranian letter of January 1, 1982 to Judge Mangård constituted a challenge under Article 11 of the 1976 UNCITRAL Rules. The lack of any *need* for the Tribunal to take up this question, given its holding rendered on the first question, is clear. Moreover, the question of whether the January 1, 1982 letter constituted a challenge under the UNCITRAL Rules was clearly for the appointing authority to decide. Nonetheless, the Tribunal addressed the question briefly and concluded "that the letter of January 1, 1982, and its attachment constitute a challenge pursuant to Article 11 of the UNCITRAL Rules."[282] In contrast, Justice

---

[280] Letter from the US Agent to the Appointing Authority dated September 17, 1984, at 3; reprinted in section 4(D)(2). Applying Article 2(2) of the UNCITRAL Rules, the 15 days "shall begin to run on the day following the day" that the circumstances become known to the challenging party. Therefore, because the attack occurred on September 3, the 15-day period commenced on September 4 and would have run to the end of business on September 18.

[281] Letter from the US Agent, n 280, at 2.

[282] Letter from the US Agent, n 280, at 2. Inasmuch as the Secretary-General of the Tribunal forwarded a copy of the Decision to the appointing authority on January 15, it might be thought that the Tribunal was merely attempting to decide internally whether the letter of January 1 was one they should refer to the appointing authority. If this was the case, however, then it is strange that the Tribunal did not consider that 1976 UNCITRAL Rule 11 speaks only of a party raising a challenge and does not address the power of the Tribunal to do so. In short, we must agree with the dissent of Judges Kashani and Shafeiei when they wrote "no mandate has been envisaged for this Tribunal either under the Declarations or even the UNCITRAL Rules in connection with the question of challenge or disqualification of the arbitrators." Letter of Mahmoud M Kashani and Shafie Shafeiei, January 18, 1982. The Tribunal certainly was within its rights to inform the appointing authority of the first portion of its decision, but it need not have decided the status of the January 1 letter in order to do so.

If anything, it appears that the Tribunal may have decided that the January 1 letter constituted a challenge in order to indirectly help preserve the rights of Iran, the Agent of Iran having argued before the Tribunal that

Moons later concluded that the notification was not intended as a challenge and cannot "be said to state the reason for the challenge within the meaning of Article 11 of the [1976] UNCITRAL Rules."[283]

Justice Moons established a two-step test when considering whether a challenge is made:

objections lodged by a High Contracting Party to a duly appointed arbitrator will be admissible only if they satisfy *inter alia* the following conditions:

(a) the High Contracting Party must intend to use the legal remedy of a challenge as provided for in the UNCITRAL Rules;
(b) the regulations contained in Article 11 of the [1976] Rules must have been observed.[284]

Thus to be *admissible* the objections must be intended to be a challenge under the UNCITRAL Rules and must meet the *formalities* of a challenge required by the UNCITRAL Rules.

As to the first requirement, Justice Moons noted a letter of the Agent of Iran dated February 3, 1982:

My letter of January 1, 1982 and the enclosure in clear terms stated the position of my Government that due to Mr. Mangård's lack of neutrality, the Islamic Republic of Iran disqualified him and requested his resignation. In taking that position the Islamic Republic of Iran would see no relevance to Article 11 of the [1976] UNCITRAL Rules.[285]

Justice Moons concluded that the Government of Iran had not intended by its January 1, 1982 letter to initiate the UNCITRAL challenge procedure.[286]

The Appointing Authority also concluded that the formalities required to initiate a challenge had not been fulfilled. In his view these formalities, including the statement of reasons for the challenge, are intended to provide an opportunity:

(i) to the other party: to determine whether there is any reason for it to agree to the challenge;
(ii) to the challenged arbitrator: to determine whether there is any reason for him to withdraw from his office;
(iii) to the Appointing Authority: to determine whether the notification of the challenge was made in good time and whether what is set out in the notification can be construed as an allegation that the circumstances referred to in Article 10(1) [of the 1976 UNCITRAL Rules] have been satisfied.[287]

"although the [1976] UNCITRAL Rules are not needed, no rights should be taken away from it." Tribunal Decision, Section II. Thus the Tribunal states at the end of its Decision: "In view of the decision by the Tribunal that the [1976] UNCITRAL Rules provide the only means by which a member of the Tribunal may be challenged [and given the 15-day limit] to hold [other than that the letter of January 1 constitutes a challenge] would deprive Iran of the only means of challenge available to it." Tribunal Decision, Section V.

The later decision of the appointing authority does not state that this holding of the Tribunal was unauthorized but does state that it was unnecessary. Justice Moons writes that "it is not relevant whether the said Tribunal was competent to give the decision referred to above…". Decision of the Appointing Authority on the Objections by Iran to Judge Mangård, n 31, para 3.5.

[283] Decision of the Appointing Authority, n 31, para 4.8.
[284] Decision of the Appointing Authority, n 31, para 4.4; reprinted in section 4(D)(2).
[285] Decision of the Appointing Authority, n 31, para 4.5 (italics removed).
[286] Decision of the Appointing Authority, n 31, para 4.5.
[287] Decision of the Appointing Authority, n 31, para 4.7.

Finding that the January 1, 1982 letter and its enclosure "contain neither a sufficiently clear description of the circumstances giving rise to the accusation against Mr. Mangård..., nor any indication of the dates on which the actual event on which the disqualification is based... and on which this event came to the knowledge of the party alleging disqualification," the Appointing Authority concluded that the letter was not admissible as a challenge under the 1976 UNCITRAL Rules.[288]

The Appointing Authority, Judge Haak, would closely examine whether Iran had provided adequate reasons in its notice of challenge in the challenge of Judge Krzysztof Skubiszewski, President of the Tribunal. In that context, the Appointing Authority faced a notice strongly insinuating that the President had unilaterally and secretly acted to deny a request from Judge Oloumi to postpone deliberations in Case No B61, with prejudice to Iran. In view of the seriousness of the accusations, the Appointing Authority emphasized that:

Filing a notice of challenge is not an initiative that should be taken lightly. Challenge proceedings disrupt the normal activities of the Tribunal. The reasons why it is made must therefore readily and clearly appear to the recipients of the notice of challenge.[289]

Further, in reviewing Iran's notice of challenge, the Appointing Authority found that certain basic information was lacking, such as when Judge Oloumi's request for postponement was made and the precise date on which it was rejected, as well as how the decision to reject his request was made and who took the decision.[290] On that basis, the Appointing Authority dismissed Iran's notice of challenge as "too vague."[291]

In subsequent challenge proceedings, Judge Haak, as Appointing Authority, would articulate the sufficiency standard as follows:

A Notice of Challenge must contain "a sufficiently clear description of the circumstances that allegedly gave rise to justifiable doubts as to impartiality and independence of the challenge arbitrators" and the grounds for a challenge are admissible where the respondent party could not reasonably say that they were not sufficiently appraised of the allegations underlying the challenge. Allegations in the Notice of Challenge must therefore contain a sufficiently clear description of the circumstances complained of and of the dates on which those circumstances came to the knowledge of the challenging party.[292]

Thus, the US Government's notice of challenge of Judge Seifi was sufficient because in asserting that the Iranian judge's prior participation in a commercial arbitration would substantially influence his participation in any future proceedings in Case No B61, the notice clearly identified the "purported issue conflict that forms the essence of" the US challenge.[293] Similarly, the subsequent notice of challenge of Judge Brower was adequate because Iran had clearly identified the undisputed fact which purportedly gave rise to

---

[288] Decision of the Appointing Authority, n 31, para 4.8.
[289] Joint Decision by the Appointing Authority, Judge W E Haak, on the Challenges against Judge Krzysztof Skubiszewski and Judge Hamid Reza Oloumi Yazdi, April 2, 2008, at 9.
[290] Joint Decision by the Appointing Authority, n 289, at 10–11, reprinted below, section (4)D(2).
[291] Joint Decision by the Appointing Authority, n 289, at 10–11.
[292] Decision by the Appointing Authority, Judge W E Haak, on the Challenge against Judge Seyed Jamal Seifi, September 3, 2010, at 5–6, para 19 (citing Joint Decision by the Appointing Authority, Judge W E Haak, on the Challenges to Judge Skubiszewski and Judge Oloumi, April 2, 2008, at 8).
[293] Decision by the Appointing Authority, n 292, at 6, para 20, reprinted in section 4(D)(2).

justifiable doubts, a phone conversation between Judge Brower and a candidate for the position of third country arbitrator on the Tribunal.[294]

The central question raised and eventually sidestepped by the drafters of the 1976 UNCITRAL Rules was whether or not some evidentiary material should be provided with the notice to substantiate the statement of reasons for the challenge. In fact, the Ninth Drafting Committee Session seemed to be in general agreement that "[t]he provision that the notification of challenge should simply state the reasons for challenge did not seem adequate."[295] The only dissent came from the German representative who was concerned that requiring documentary evidence might unfairly limit the acceptable reasons for challenge.[296] Ultimately, the drafters did not require the submission of documentary evidence, a decision which appears to have been a consequence of their adoption of the strict 15-day rule on the raising of the challenge. Namely, it would be counterproductive to strictly require not only the notice of challenge, but also the assembly of supporting evidence within fifteen days.

In the challenge to Judge Briner in Case No 55, the Appointing Authority dealt with the question of whether supporting evidence or other supplementary materials would be allowed under Article 11 of the 1983 Tribunal Rules. In the notice of challenge sent to the Appointing Authority and to all the necessary parties, the Iranians requested that they be allowed to supplement their notice of challenge with a "memorandum together with evidence in support of the relevant factual and legal issues."[297] Judge Briner's response to the notice of challenge addressed the Iranian request by suggesting that the Tribunal Rules did not allow the submission of any further memoranda or evidence and that the notice of challenge itself should include all the material necessary to allow the other party and the challenged arbitrator to make a determination on the challenge.[298]

The Appointing Authority disagreed with Judge Briner's reasoning and granted the Iranians' request:

in my opinion Article 11, paragraph 2, of the Tribunal Rules does not oppose your sending me a Memorandum to complement the Notice of Challenge of Mr. Briner with respect to Case No 55 dated 13 September 1988, in which the reasons for this challenge set out in the above Notice will be further developed and in which evidence will be put forward to support these reasons.[299]

Justice Moons' decision makes perfect sense in our view. The 15-day limit and the decision not to require evidence, along with the notice of challenge, indicate the UNCITRAL drafters' awareness that the notice might not include all the information necessary to determine the validity of a challenge.

Lastly, there is the question of who may initiate a challenge. Although not expressly excluding other initiators, the UNCITRAL Rules only provide that a challenge may be

---

[294] See Decision of the Appointing Authority, Judge W E Haak, on the challenge to Judge Charles Brower, September 3, 2010, at 6, para 15, reprinted in section 4(D)(2).

[295] *Summary Record of the 3rd Meeting of the Committee of the Whole (II)*, UNCITRAL, 9th Session, UN Doc A/CN.9/9/C.2/SR.3, at 5, para 33 (1976) (Comment by the Chairman).

[296] *Summary Record*, n 295, para 39 (Comment by Mr Pirrung, Federal Republic of Germany).

[297] Letter of the Agent of the Government of Iran to the Appointing Authority initiating the First Challenge by Iran of Judge Briner, n 37, at 183; reprinted in section 4(D)(2).

[298] Letter of Judge Briner to the Appointing Authority, Ch M J A Moons, September 14, 1988, reprinted in 20 Iran-US CTR 184 (1988–III); reprinted in sections 4(D)(1) and 4(D)(2).

[299] Letter of the Appointing Authority, Ch M J A Moons, to the Agent of the Government of Iran, September 21, 1988, reprinted in 20 Iran-US CTR 187 (1988–III); reprinted in section 4(D)(2).

made by a party to the arbitration.³⁰⁰ This view was supported by the Tribunal in its decision on Iran's challenge of Judge Mangård in 1982: "the only method by which an arbitrator may be removed from office is through challenge by a High Contracting party..."³⁰¹ If one or two members of a panel find their colleague objectionable, yet such colleague is not challenged by a party, the one or two members of the panel have no recourse but to continue with the *status quo* or resign.³⁰²

(3) Procedure if challenge is accepted by all other parties or challenged arbitrator withdraws—Article 13(3)

Article 13(3) sets forth the process for appointing a substitute arbitrator if either all parties agree to the challenge or the challenged arbitrator voluntarily withdraws. There were essentially two issues that arose in the drafting of Article 11(3) of the 1976 UNCITRAL Rules, which is substantially similar to Article 13(3) in many respects. The first entailed defining exactly what procedures would be used to appoint the substitute arbitrator. The preliminary draft of the rule stated simply that "a substitute arbitrator shall be appointed pursuant to the procedure applicable to the initial appointment."³⁰³ There was some confusion among the delegates as to whether this meant that the parties could only use the procedure already used to appoint the challenged arbitrator, eg if the appointing authority had designated the arbitrator then only the appointing authority could appoint the new arbitrator, or whether they could use any procedure available under the relevant rules.³⁰⁴

According to the principal drafter of the original language of the rule, Professor Sanders, the appointing authority should choose the new arbitrator for a simple reason. The fact that the appointing authority had been called upon to make the original appointment meant that the party associated with the challenged arbitrator had not cooperated in the first place by making a nomination of his own.³⁰⁵ The Committee rejected this thinking on the grounds that the parties should not be penalized for failing to make the appointment in the first place, especially in light of the fact that it was the appointing authority who had chosen the challenged arbitrator.³⁰⁶ The adopted language makes it clear that if the other party agrees to the challenge or the challenged arbitrator withdraws, the original procedures on appointment of arbitrators—under Article 8 in the event of a sole arbitrator or Article 9 in

---

³⁰⁰ Article 11(1) ("A *party* who intends to challenge...") (emphasis added).
Under the Tribunal Rules and reflecting the Tribunal's multi-claim nature, a distinction is drawn between the role of the two governments in the institution and the arbitrating parties in a particular case. Only one of the two governments or High Contracting Parties may bring a challenge against an arbitrator on general grounds seeking to remove the arbitrator from the Tribunal entirely. However, the private parties arbitrating particular cases could challenge an arbitrator on the basis of circumstances giving rise to justifiable doubts about his impartiality or independence with regard to their particular case.

³⁰¹ Tribunal Decision, n 31, Section VI.

³⁰² Thus in the *Buraimi Oasis* case where no provision at all for challenge existed, the British-appointed judge, Sir Reader Bullard, finding the Saudi-appointed judge objectionable, concluded that "the only step I can take which is consistent with my own independence and honour is to tender my resignation." See J Wetter, *The International Arbitral Process: Public and Private* (1979) vol III, 372.

³⁰³ See, eg, *Report of the Secretary-General on the Preliminary Draft Set of Arbitration Rules*, UNCITRAL, 8th Session, UN Doc A/CN.9/97 (1974), reprinted in (1975) VI UNCITRAL Ybk 163, 171 (Draft Article 9(3)).

³⁰⁴ See *Summary Record of the 3rd Meeting of the Committee of the Whole (II)*, UNCITRAL, 9th Session, UN Doc A/CN.9/9/C.2/SR.3, at 4, 5, paras 26–30, 32 (1976).

³⁰⁵ UN Doc A/CN.9/9/C.2/SR.3, n 304.

³⁰⁶ UN Doc A/CN.9/9/C.2/SR.3, n 304, at 5.

the case of a three member panel—should be followed, including the right of each party to appoint an arbitrator.[307]

The second issue addressed by the Drafting Committee involved safeguarding a challenged arbitrator's reputation in the event that the challenge was accepted under Article 11(3) of the 1976 UNCITRAL Rules (now Article 13(3) of the 2010 UNCITRAL Rules). For example, the Mexican representative expressed concern that if one party challenged the other party's arbitrator and the other party accepted a reason for the challenge which the arbitrator contested, "the arbitrator's honor would be compromised."[308] The text of Article 11(3) of the 1976 UNCITRAL Rules was therefore modified "in order to remove any implication of dishonor from the voluntary withdrawal of an arbitrator or the removal of an arbitrator by the mutual agreement of the parties." In other words, upon the resignation or withdrawal of a challenged arbitrator there would be no implication of acceptance or acknowledgment that the reasons for the challenge were valid.[309]

Article 13(3) differs from original Article 11(3) of the 1976 UNCITRAL Rules in one important respect. Pursuant to Article 13(3), a challenge is effective if agreed to by "all parties," whereas corresponding Article 11(3) of the 1976 UNCITRAL Rules requires agreement only by "the other party." While the revised language was proposed, in part, to account for the possibility of multi-party arbitration,[310] the Working Group quickly realized that the revision raised the broader question of whether "all parties should be given a right to oppose the challenge, or whether that right should be limited to the party that appointed the challenged arbitrator."[311] Delegates were divided on the answer.

---

[307] See S Baker and M Davis, *The UNCITRAL Rules in Practice*, n 1, 127 (discussing ambiguities in Article 6 of the 1976 Rules).

[308] *Summary Record of the 3rd Meeting of the Committee of the Whole (II)*, UNCITRAL, 9th Session, UN Doc A/CN.9/9/C.2/SR.3, at 6, para 43 (1976) (Comment by Mr Mantilla-Molina, Mexico).

[309] *Report of the UNCITRAL on the Work of its Ninth Session*, UN GAOR, 31st Session, Supp No 17, UN Doc A/31/17, para 65 (1976), reprinted in (1976) VII UNCITRAL Ybk 66, 71. See also *Methanex Corp* (1976 Rules), reprinted in section 4(C), and Challenge of April 15, 1993 (1976 Rules), reprinted in section 4(C). See also, Letter of Judge Robert Briner to the Appointing Authority, Ch M J A Moons, December 6, 1988, regarding the Challenge by Iran to his participation in Case No 55, reprinted in 20 Iran-US CTR 329 (1988–III), March 7, 1989, reprinted in section 4(D)(3).

Judge Briner has been the only arbitrator at the Iran-US Claims Tribunal to withdraw from a case in the face of a challenge. Because of its multi-claim nature, the Tribunal developed formal mechanisms to deal with withdrawal from cases by arbitrators. The Tribunal adopted one such mechanism, transfer of the case to another Chamber, early in its life as Note 4 to Articles 9–12 of the Tribunal Rules demonstrates. Note 4 states that "in the event that a member of a Chamber is challenged with respect to a particular case and withdraws or if the challenge is sustained, the President will order the transfer of the case to another Chamber." In practice, however, the Tribunal came instead, for efficiency reasons, to leave the case in the Chamber and employ a substitute arbitrator. The possible conflict between a formal and informal mechanism became apparent in the withdrawal by Judge Briner.

Shortly after withdrawing from Case No 55, Judge Briner was appointed President of the Tribunal by Justice Moons—under vigorous protest by the Iranians. In his first Presidential Order, Briner appointed Judge Broms as his replacement in Chamber Two for Case No 55. (See Presidential Order No 67.) The Iranians strongly protested this move, arguing that Briner had disregarded the Tribunal Rules by not transferring the Case to another Chamber as Note 4 requires. Judge Briner responded by referring to the evolution of the practice of the Tribunal. (See Letter of President Briner to the Agent of Iran, March 7, 1989, reprinted in section 4(D)(3)). It is interesting to note that Iran in its Reply Memorandum in the Challenge to Judge Briner in Case No 55 stated that "the proceeding in a case when a challenge is brought, may only be delayed if the challenge is sustained. It is only then that the case is transferred to another chamber."

[310] UNCITRAL, 42nd Session, UN Doc A/CN.9/665, n 89, at 16, para 85.

[311] *Settlement of Commercial Disputes: Revision of the UNCITRAL Arbitration Rules, Note by the Secretariat*, UNCITRAL, UN Doc A/CN.9/WG.II/WP.151 at 13, para 27 (2008). See also UNCITRAL, 42nd Session, UN Doc A/CN.9/665, n 89, at 16, para 85.

Those opposing the requirement of unanimous agreement raised concerns that a party's right to object to the challenge could be abused, particularly where "a respondent would have tactical reasons to delay the arbitral proceedings by forcing a lengthier challenge process."[312] According to the *travaux préparatoires*:

[I]t was said that in a case with two respondents, if one of them challenged the arbitrator appointed by a single claimant, the effect of requiring all parties to agree would be to give the second respondent a provisional veto over the challenge. This would force the challenging party to bring its challenge before an appointing authority, despite the willingness of the claimant that had appointed the challenged arbitrator to accept the challenge.[313]

Other members of the Working Group strongly favored the requirement of unanimous agreement. They believed that once a party appointed an arbitrator, that party "should not retain a greater stake [than any other party] in the future service of that arbitrator in the proceedings."[314] Thus, they maintained that "differentiating among the arbitrators based on who appointed them would run contrary to the fundamental principle whereby all arbitrators were equally appointed for the overall purpose of the arbitration."[315] Proponents also noted that this approach was consistent with the 1976 UNCITRAL Rules, where "the other party" was required to agree.[316]

Article 13(3), as adopted, thus gives any party the right to oppose a challenge of an arbitrator, though in practice it is the agreement of the party with the right to appoint the arbitrator that in most cases will cast the deciding vote.

Article 13(3) does not expressly address the legal effect of all the parties' agreement to support the challenge of an arbitrator. During Working Group discussions, a proposal was made to state in the rule that unanimous agreement of the parties would terminate the mandate of the challenged arbitrator whether or not the challenged arbitrator agreed to withdraw.[317] That proposal was seen as providing an opportunity to better clarify the date when the arbitrator's removal would take effect. It was observed that that question was important in practice, namely when the challenge occurred during the arbitral proceedings, when, for instance, provisional measures were to be taken by the arbitral tribunal.[318]

Objections to the proposal were raised on the ground that "in certain jurisdictions, the applicable law included statutory provisions on the mandate of the arbitrators, which could not be merely terminated by agreement of the parties."[319] Considering this objection, and recognizing that the absence of such an express provision in the 1976 UNCITRAL Rules had not created difficulties in practice, the Working Group rejected the proposal for the additional language.[320] Thus, on the important question of termination of the arbitrator's mandate, Article 13(3) defers to the governing arbitration law.

---

[312] UNCITRAL, 42nd Session, UN Doc A/CN.9/665, n 89, at 16–17, para 86. In addition, "It was said that there might be a need to provide for additional language to deal with the case where the challenged arbitrator was either the sole or presiding arbitrator." Para 86.
[313] UNCITRAL, 42nd Session, UN Doc A/CN.9/665, n 89, at 16–17, para 86.
[314] UNCITRAL, 42nd Session, UN Doc A/CN.9/665, n 89, at 17, para 87.
[315] UNCITRAL, 42nd Session, UN Doc A/CN.9/665, n 89, at 17, para 87.
[316] UNCITRAL, 42nd Session, UN Doc A/CN.9/665, n 89, at 16, para 85.
[317] UNCITRAL, 42nd Session, UN Doc A/CN.9/665, n 89, at 17, para 89.
[318] UNCITRAL, 42nd Session, UN Doc A/CN.9/665, n 89, at 17, para 89.
[319] UNCITRAL, 42nd Session, UN Doc A/CN.9/665, n 89, para 90.
[320] UNCITRAL, 42nd Session, UN Doc A/CN.9/665, n 89, para 90.

(4) Timeline for seeking a decision on a challenge—Article 13(4)

Article 13(4) establishes a two-tiered timeline for seeking a decision on the challenge by the appointing authority. Within fifteen days of the date of the notice of challenge, all the parties may agree to the challenge or the challenged arbitrator may withdraw. In either situation, the challenge is resolved and the appointing authority need not be approached for a decision. However, in the absence of agreement or withdrawal, the challenging party may seek a decision on the challenge within 30 days from the date of the notice of challenge. The 30-day time period is, of course, only the outer limit on when a party may seek a decision from the appointing authority. If before expiration of the initial 15-day time period, one of the parties indicates that it does not agree to the challenge or the challenged arbitrator communicates that he or she will not withdraw, the challenging party may immediately enlist the services of the appointing authority to resolve the challenge. After expiration of the 30-day time period, a challenging party's right to seek a decision on the challenge, unless otherwise agreed, is waived.

The timetable on seeking a decision on a challenge is new to the 2010 UNCITRAL Rules, but raised no significant concerns among Working Group delegations.[321]

C. Extracts from the Practice of Investment Tribunals

Methanex Corp and *United States of America*, Award, (August 3, 2005) (ICSID administered, 1976 UNCITRAL Rules, NAFTA Chapter Eleven), Part II, Chapter E, at 19:

> 32 .... Mr. Christopher's resignation was voluntary; and his resignation cannot be treated as an admission of Methanex's factual allegations. To the contrary, Article 11(3) of the [1976] UNCITRAL Rules expressly provides that resignation "does not imply acceptance of the validity of the grounds for the challenge".

Challenge Decision of April 15, 1993, reprinted in part in (1997) XXII Ybk Commercial Arb 222, 224–25:

> [3] It is to be recalled that the claimant's first Party Arbitrator was appointed by the claimant and that his independence had been duly recognized by the respondent's first Party Arbitrator as also by the respondent itself, with a full knowledge of the background of the claimant's first Party Arbitrator's position. The challenge raised later on against the claimant's Party Arbitrator by the respondent, for alleged facts preceding his appointment, could therefore not affect in any way his status as long as no competent authority had removed him from office. The respondent had the possibility of seeking his removal under Arts. 10, 11 and 12 of the [1976] UNCITRAL Rules, but it refrained from doing so.
>
> [4] It follows that claimant's first Party Arbitrator held his office properly throughout, from the moment of his appointment to the moment of his resignation. The resignation in itself cannot be considered to be a recognition of the challenge brought earlier by the respondent against the claimant's first Party Arbitrator. This results explicitly from Art. 11(3) of the [1976] UNCITRAL Rules which provides in this respect that an arbitrator subject to a challenge may "after the challenge, withdraw from his office," but that, in no case, "does this imply acceptance of the validity of the grounds for the challenge."

---

[321] The only significant question was how long the new time periods should be. An early proposal recommended 15 or 30 days and 60 days for the respective time periods, *Settlement of Commercial Disputes: Revision of the UNCITRAL Arbitration Rules, Note by the Secretariat*, UNCITRAL, UN Doc A/CN.9/WG.II/WP.145 at 18, para 53 (2006) (Draft Article 12(1)), but was ultimately rejected in favor of shorter time periods. UNCITRAL, 40th Session, UN Doc A/CN.9/619, n 107, at 21, para 102.

D. Extracts from the Practice of the Iran–US Claims Tribunal

(1) Tribunal Rules (1983), Article 11(1)

Letter of the Agent of the United States to the Appointing Authority initiating the Challenge of Judges Kashani and Shafeiei, September 17, 1984, reprinted in Intl Arb L Rev 9344:

> We have waited the full fifteen day period provided in the Rules before bringing this challenge in order to give the Government of Iran and the President of the Tribunal the fullest opportunity to take appropriate action in response to the (3 September 1984) violent conduct by Messrs. Kashani and Shafeiei.

Memorandum of Amoco Iran Oil regarding the Challenge by Iran of Judge Briner in Case No 55, November 2, 1988, reprinted in 20 Iran-US CTR 233, 234, 237 (1988–III) (footnotes omitted):

> Article 11 of the [1983] Tribunal Rules provides that a challenge to an arbitrator must be presented "within 15 days after the circumstances mentioned in articles 9 and 10 become known to that party". This time limit is jurisdictional; if it has not been observed, the challenge may not be considered. And, just as Iran has—the burden of proof in establishing that its challenge is justified, so also it has the burden of proof in establishing that it has standing to bring the challenge—that is, that it learned of the circumstances that gave rise to the challenge no more than 15 days before acting on that information.
>
> ...
>
> 5. The reasons for the 15-day requirement of Rule 11, and its mandatory nature are apparent. First, a party processing information that could lead to a challenge may be tempted to wait until the proceeding is far enough advanced that he has some feeling for (or information about) its likely result; allowing him to make the challenge at that point is obviously unfair and a perversion of the arbitral process. Second, a party whose purpose is delay may find it in his interest to make a challenge at a time when it will cause the maximum disruption and delay in the arbitral proceedings and, consequently, maximum prejudice to the other party.

Letter of the Appointing Authority, Ch M J A Moons, to the Agent of the Government of Iran, Mohammad K Eshragh, November 10, 1988, at 1:

> I have the honour to confirm herewith the verbal agreement we made on 9 November last to the effect that:
>
> (a) On or before November 28, 1988 you will produce evidence that with respect to the challenge of Mr. Briner the time limit provided in Article 11 of the [1983] Tribunal Rules has been observed; ...

Reply Memorandum of Iran regarding the Challenge of Judge Briner in Case No 55, November 28, 1988 at 6–9 and Exhibit No 4, reprinted in 20 Iran-US CTR 260, 266–67, 314–16, 319 (1988–III) (footnotes omitted):

> *A. Amoco, not Iran, Has to Carry the Burden of Showing that Iran Had Acquired Knowledge of the Relationship Over 15 Days Before Challenge*
>
> 15. Amoco, for the first time in its Memorandum of 2 November 1988, has come up with the idea that Iran, as a requirement of establishing its "standing to bring the challenge," has to show that it *did not* know about the connection between Mr. Briner and Morgan Stanley earlier than 15 days before it brought the challenge. Legal Memorandum at 2. This issue, in Iran's view, has nothing to do with the standing, or *locus standi, in stricto sensu*, to bring the challenge. All there is to prove as a matter of *locus standi* is that the right party, or parties, have

brought the challenge. As stated in the Notice of Challenge, and further explained in the Memorandum, the challenge has been made by the Government of the Islamic Republic of Iran and other Respondents to Case No 55 pursuant to the [1983] Tribunal Rules, Articles 9–12, and Note 1 thereto. This is all there is to show in regard to the standing to bring the challenge and Amoco does not, and cannot possibly, contest the issue of *locus standi*.

16. What Amoco, in fact, means—but does not clearly say it to avoid the burden of proof—is that the issue is not justifiable because the right to challenge has been time-barred, or waived. Amoco alleges, but fails to prove, that Iran acquired knowledge of Mr. Briner-Morgan Stanley's relationship more than 15 days before it brought the challenge, and thus the right to challenge is time barred, or waived in view of 15-day time limit provided in Article 11(1) of the [1983] Tribunal Rules.

17. Once the issue raised by Amoco is rightly named, and put in proper context, it becomes clear that what Amoco is trying to do, though in a contorted manner, is to place the burden of proof for its affirmative assertion on the shoulder of the other party denying the allegation. The general rule governing the burden of proof is that it lies on him who affirms a fact—as Amoco does—not on him who denies it, which is Iran's position. This rule is based on a latin maxim, fundamental to every system of law and justice: *ei qui affirmat, non ei qui negat, incumbit probatio*.

18. This principle, a dictate of common sense, is universally observed at national and international levels. According to Sandifer:

    The broad basic rule of burden of proof adopted, in general, by international tribunals resembles the civil law rule and may be simply stated: that the burden of proof rests upon him who asserts the affirmative of a proposition that if not substantiated will result in a decision adverse to his contention. (Footnote omitted.) D. Sandifer, Evidence Before International Tribunals, Revised Ed. 1975, p. 127.

19. The rule of law specifically dealing with the question at hand is fully in accord with that general principle. The burden of proving a case of waiver and acquiescence is on the person who suggests it. Lord Selbors speaking for the Privy Council in *Holland v. Cassidy* (1888) 13 App. Cas. 170 at 178. The authorities provided by Amoco in support of its assertion that Iran carries the burden of proving that it *did not* know of the relationship earlier than 15 days before the challenge was brought, are too scanty to establish that the general rule of burden of proof is reversed when it comes to the challenge procedure. It follows, therefore, that the Appointing Authority should take a decision adverse to Amoco's contention, and dismiss its claim that Iran's right to challenge has been time barred or waived.

…

Amoco's argument on the issue of burden of proof is irrelevant for a number of legal reasons, as will be shown below. Amoco contends that Iran has a burden of proof under Rule 11(1) of the [1983] Tribunal Rules to show that it learned of the circumstances that gave rise to the challenge no more than 15 days before acting on that information. Amoco contends that this is a jurisdictional requirement which, if not fulfilled, precludes Iran from having the standing to bring the challenge. This argument is wrong and irrelevant.

It is wrong, first, because it misreads the [1983] Tribunal's Rules, Article 10(2) states that "(A) party may challenge the arbitrator appointed *by him* only for reasons of which he becomes aware after the appointment has been made" (emphasis added). Thus, for party-appointed arbitrators, there may be an implied burden of proof of the kind proposed by Amoco to show that *prior to the appointment* such reasons were unknown. Indeed, Amoco's reference to the *oeuvres préparatoires* of the [1976] UNCITRAL Rules (see p. 5 fn. 4 of Amoco's Response) confirms this implication. However, Mr. Briner is not a party-appointed arbitrator but a neutral arbitrator appointed by the two party-appointed arbitrators. There is no suggestion whatsoever that such a rule applies in the case of a neutral arbitrator so appointed. Indeed, the inclusion of such a specific provision in the [1976] UNCITRAL Rules relating only to party-appointed arbitrators implies that the opposite is true in the case of neutral arbitrators.

The assumption made by Amoco that the Government of Iran was involved with the appointment of Mr. Briner because he was appointed "by agreement between the United States and Iranian arbitrators" and that "(I)t stands to reason that Iran would have investigated his (Mr. Briner's) activities thoroughly before agreeing to his appointment" (see Amoco's Response pp. 7–8) is simply wrong. It is a clear rule of law that a party-appointed arbitrator does not act as the agent of the party who appointed him in relation to such questions, especially where the neutrality of party-appointed arbitrators is considered as an important rule of international arbitration, a point which Amoco itself has stressed.

Finally, it would be quite extraordinary if the 15-day limit were a jurisdictional bar of the kind suggested by Amoco, especially where, as here, the Respondents have no specific right to challenge the award under the Algiers Declarations. To see this time-limit as jurisdictional and to make no provision warning a party that failure to meet such a time-limit would deprive that party of all its rights would be an extraordinary conclusion to reach. As comparison, if one looks at time-limits for filing appeals against judgments, they all put a party on notice of the loss of right entailed if the time-limit is not met.

Institutional arbitration bodies want to see the values of arbitration upheld. To effect this they have an administrative discretion quite unlike that in the judicial system. It is for this reason that the General Counsel of the ICC commented on Article 2(8) of the ICC Rules as follows:

Naturellement, la cour dispose d'un pouvoir d'appréciation des difficultés qui pourrait résulter de l'application du délai pour la recusation d'un arbitre fondée sur des motifs survenus en cours de procedure.

An officer of the ICC would not have expressed such a view if the time-limit for the challenge were to be considered as being jurisdictional in nature. Two German authors commenting on Article 11 of the [1976] UNCITRAL Rules, and Article 13 of the UNCITRAL Model Law have come to the same conclusion.
...

All the [1983] Tribunal Rules say in regard to the challenge of a neutral arbitrator is that within 15 days of the circumstances giving rise to justifiable doubts becoming known to a party he shall make a challenge stating the reasons for the challenge. The relevant circumstances became known on and after 1 September with Mr. Briner's disclosures. Indeed the 15 day limit is precisely to prevent parties being dilatory in objecting to such disclosures, the disclosure itself being what triggers the time limit. This being said it will be noted that all the challenger has to do is state the "reasons for challenge", it says nothing about having to fulfill any alleged burden of proof.

Letter of Attorney for Amoco Iran Oil, Mr Brice M Clagett, to the Appointing Authority regarding the Challenge by Iran of Judge Briner in Case No 55, December 1, 1988, at 1–2, reprinted in 20 Iran-US CTR 325 (1988–III):

1. Iran argues elaborately, but wholly unpersuasively, that the burden of proof is on Amoco to show that Iran had prior knowledge of the basis for its challenge. Iran ignores the elementary principle, that, when the facts of a matter are wholly within the possession of one party and inaccessible to the other party, it is the first party that bears the burden of proof... That principle is based on considerations of fairness and practicality that are too obvious to need explanation.

Letter of Judge Robert Briner to the Appointing Authority, Ch M J A Moons, August 3, 1989, at 2, reprinted in 21 Iran-US CTR 348 (1989–I):

I should furthermore like to mention that the fifteen days time limit of Article 11, paragraph 1 of the [1983] Tribunal Rules do not seem to have been respected as all allegations made in the challenge of 28 July 1989 are based either on the award in Case No 39 (document 389) filed on 29 Jun 1989, or on the "Statement by Judge Khalilian as to why it would have been prevented to sign the Award and its annexes (Document 391) filed on 30 June 1989."

Decision of Appointing Authority on the Second Challenge by Iran of Judge Briner, September 19, 1989, at 9–12, reprinted in 21 Iran-US CTR 384, 391–94 (1989–I):

> Under Article 11[1] of the [1983] Tribunal Rules... a party can file a notice of challenge to good effect only within fifteen days after the circumstances mentioned in Articles 9 and 10 of the Tribunal Rules "become known to the party".
>
> The question that arises is at what time should this be deemed to have been so.
>
> ...
>
> With the exception of the allegation that Mr. Briner, after the discovery of computational error in the DCF calculation... arbitrarily reduced the amount of money to be awarded to the claimant by only $10 million and then threatened to increase the amount of gain, all the allegations on which the challenge is based are mentioned in Mr. Khalilian's statement of 30 June 1989, which was received by the Agent of the Islamic Republic on 5 July 1989, and/or the English version of the Award, dated 29 June 1989, which was received by the Agent of the Islamic Republic on 30 June 1989.
>
> The notice of challenge is dated 28 July 1989 and was received in my office on that date.
>
> Hence the notice of challenge—to the extent that the challenge set forth in it is based on the last-mentioned allegations—was not presented within in the period set for that purpose by Article 11 of the [1983] Tribunal rules, so that it cannot to that extent be entertained.

Letter of the Agent of the Government of the United States to the Appointing Authority, September 19, 1989, reprinted in 21 Iran-US CTR 395 (1989–I):

> While consideration of this "whole context" could not in any case lend substance to this meritless challenge, Mr. Nobari's suggestion should be seen for what it is—an effort to circumvent the Tribunal Rules of Procedure. Article 10, paragraph 1 of the [1983] Tribunal Rules provides that an arbitrator may be challenged "if circumstances exist that give rise to justifiable doubts as to the arbitrator's impartiality or independence." Article 11, paragraph 1 requires that a party who intends to challenge an arbitrator send notice of the challenge "within 15 days after the circumstances mentioned in articles 9 and 10 become known to that party." These provisions simply afford no basis for consideration of various alleged circumstances of which Iran has been aware for more than 15 days.

Decision of Appointing Authority on the Third Challenge by Iran of Judge Briner, September 25, 1989, at 3, reprinted in 21 Iran-US CTR 396, 398 (1989–I):

> b. It is not consistent with the system of the [1983] Tribunal Rules that the Appointing Authority, deciding on a challenge, should take into account circumstances that came to the knowledge of the challenging party earlier than the beginning of the period of 15 days mentioned in article 11 of those rules. This prevents me from complying with the request mentioned above under A.d. [that "since the challenge has been made on general grounds, Mr. Briner's participation in the 'money laundering offence' in India should not be considered an isolated incident, but must be related in the whole context of Mr. Briner's past behaviour"].

Decision of the Appointing Authority on the Challenge of Judge Bengt Broms, September 30, 2004, reprinted in (October 2004) 19(10) Mealey's Intl Arb Rep B-1:

> 30. Nor is there anything in the [1983] Tribunal Rules or in the facts and arguments presented by Ms. Riahi and her counsel to suggest that the request for Judge Broms' recusal somehow stopped the running of the fifteen-day time limit for giving notice of challenge. The [1983] Rules do not give a party the option of either seeking recusal or initiating a challenge. It is clear from the record that Ms. Riahi and her counsel were aware, as early as July 2, 2003, of circumstances likely to give rise to the justifiable doubts as to Judge Broms' impartiality or independence with respect to the consideration of the application. Judge Broms' failure to disqualify himself from participating in the review of the application, and his refusal even to respond to the recusal request do not constitute new or independent circumstances giving rise to justifiable doubts as to his impartiality and independence. The [1983] Tribunal Rules place him

under no obligation to disqualify himself or to respond to the request. Ms. Riahi and her counsel cannot therefore argue that prior to January 13, 2004, there were no grounds for challenging Judge Broms, because he might have decided to withdraw voluntarily. The grounds for challenging Judge Broms were those set out in the request of July 2, 2003, in support of his recusal. More than six months elapsed before the notice of challenge was issued on January 26, 2004. This far exceeds the fifteen-day time limit set forth in Article 11(1) of the [1983] Tribunal Rules, and the challenge must be therefore... declared inadmissible for failure to comply with this time limit.

Letter from the US Agent, Mr Clifton Johnson, to the Appointing Authority, Mr W E Haak, March 10, 2006, at 15–17 (footnotes omitted):

The Tribunal Rules require actual prior knowledge, as opposed to constructive prior knowledge, of the circumstances giving rise to a challenge as a prerequisite for waiver.

A plain reading of the [1983] Tribunal Rules demonstrates the very high standard for proving prior knowledge of circumstances that would waive a party's right to bring a challenge. Article 11(1) requires a party to bring a challenge within 15 days *after* the circumstances giving rise to its justifiable doubts "became known" to that party. The inclusion of the phrase "became known," as opposed to "should have known" or "could have known" is of key significance. It establishes that the 15-day time period within which to bring a challenge begins to run only after a party has obtained actual knowledge of the relevant circumstances giving rise to the challenge.

An analysis of Article 29 of the [1983] Tribunal's Rules, which addresses the same concepts of knowledge and waiver, confirms this conclusion. Article 29 provides that a party who "knows" of an incident of noncompliance with the Rules, yet proceeds with the arbitration without objecting, waives the right to object. According to the *travaux préparatoires* of the UNCITRAL Arbitration Rules, upon which the Tribunal Rules are based, early drafts of Article 29 contained the phrase "knows or should have known." However, after careful deliberation, UNCITRAL removed the phrase "should have known," resolving affirmatively "not to add a provision dealing with constructive waiver."

Nor should a constructive waiver test be read into Article 11(1) of the [1983] Tribunal Rules. The UNCITRAL drafters were appropriately cautious about depriving a party of its right to object under Article 29, which was intended to address "minor violations of the procedure." Article 11(1), in contrast, deals with a party's fundamental right to an impartial and independent tribunal Accordingly, where deprivations of a party's fundamental—as opposed to minor—rights are at risk, a constructive waiver test is, *a fortiori,* unwarranted and inappropriate.

The practice of the Appointing Authority regarding waiver is to require conclusive evidence of a party's actual knowledge of the circumstances giving rise to a challenge prior to the 15-day period.

Throughout the life of the Tribunal, the Appointing Authority, whenever called upon to decide a challenge, has carefully confronted claims that a party has waived its right to raise a challenge. The practice in this regard demonstrates the clear rule that, before a party may be deprived of its right to bring a challenge, there must be conclusive evidence (usually in the form of written documents) that the challenging party had full and accurate knowledge of the circumstances giving rise to a challenge more than 15 days before the challenge was brought.

Iran's challenge of former Tribunal President Briner, for example, was dismissed as untimely because Iran was undeniably found to have had prior knowledge through the filing of documents with the Tribunal's Registry that pre-dated the 15-day time limit. Iran's challenge, which was filed on July 28, 1989, claimed that Mr. Briner was responsible for numerous procedural irregularities with respect to the rendering of the award in Case No 39. Nearly a month earlier, however, on June 30, 1989, Iranian Arbitrator Khalilian had filed a statement with the Registry entitled "Why It Would Have Been Premature to Sign the Award," which outlined in detail his concerns with Chamber Two's resolution of Case No 39.

In dismissing most allegations comprising the challenge as untimely, the Appointing Authority found that, with the exception of one allegation:

all the allegations on which the challenge is based are mentioned Mr. Khalilian's statement of 30 June 1989, which was received by the Agent of the Islamic Republic of Iran on 5 July 1989 and/or the English version of the Award, dated 29 June 1989, which was received by the Agent of the Islamic Republic on 30 June 1989.

Iran was deemed to have waived its right to bring the challenge only on conclusive evidence—the filing and subsequent transmittal to the Agent for Iran of Mr. Khalilian's statement—that Iran had prior actual knowledge of the circumstances giving rise to the challenge.

This rule was again applied in the February 20, 1999, challenge of Mr. Noori on the basis that he had a conflict of interest arising from his prior employment as head of the National Industries Organization of Iran ("NIOI"), which allegedly controlled the respondent in Case No 248. The claimant said he had first obtained knowledge of Mr. Noori's alleged conflict of interest on February 18, 1999. Mr. Noori, the Agent for Iran, and the respondent disputed the timeliness of the challenge based on the short time between the dates on which the challenging party claimed to have obtained knowledge and on which the challenge was filed. They argued that it was unlikely that the claimant had not been aware of Mr. Noori's position with NIOI sooner because his others were aware of Mr. Noori's position.

The Appointing Authority rejected Iran's timeliness claim observing:

Failing adequate refutation of the *prima facie* evidence of [the claimant's] ignorance of Mr. Noori's aforesaid position with NIOI up to 18 February 1990, I cannot but assume that the challenge was filed within the time limit of article 11 of the [1983] Tribunal Rules.

Notably, the appointing authority rejected Iran's theory of constructive knowledge, again adhering to the rule that absent conclusive proof that the challenging party had prior knowledge of a full and accurate nature, he cannot be deemed to have waived his right to bring the challenge.

The challenge of Mr. Skubiszewski on May 20, 1999, also confirms this rule. Iran accused Mr. Skubiszewski of inappropriate conduct in connection with his legal assistant's efforts to obtain information relevant to Case No A/28 from a Dutch Bank. The United States argued that Iran was most likely aware of the facts underlying the challenge prior to a letter dated May 6 from the Bank which included a copy of the letter in response to inquiries made by Mr. Skubiszewski's legal assistant.

The Appointing Authority found:

It seems that on both sides of the argument there are matters of speculation and that it would be a doubtful task to try to establish the degree of necessary knowledge in the mind of the Iranian Agent or his colleagues on a particular day of the fifteen available. I therefore take the view that it would be wrong in this case to reject the First Challenge on the basis of speculations about its timeliness?

Thus, "speculations," like general concerns, doubts, or rumors, do not suffice to establish a challenging party's prior actual knowledge.

A final example of application of this rule was the challenge of Judge Broms on January 13, 2004. The appointing authority dismissed the challenge as untimely, finding that claimant's application filed with the Tribunal on July 2, 2003—several months before the challenge—contained clear and unequivocal statements demonstrating her prior knowledge of the circumstances giving rise to her challenge. Referencing the assertions in the application that tracked the assertions in the challenge, the appointing authority ruled that these assertions "leave[] little doubt that at least as early as July 2, 2003, [the claimant] and her counsel were aware of circumstances likely to give rise to justifiable doubts...."

Thus, over the life of the Tribunal, when called upon to resolve a party's challenge, the appointing authority, recognizing the seriousness of depriving a party of its right to challenge an arbitrator, has only dismissed a challenge for lack of timeliness when presented with conclusive evidence establishing that the challenging party had obtained actual knowledge of all relevant circumstances giving rise to the challenge more than 15 days before the challenge was filed. As demonstrated in the following section, the evidence Iran relies on to show that the United States has waived its right to bring the present challenge falls far short of this standard.

Decision of the Appointing Authority, W E Haak, in the Challenge of Judges Assadollah Noori, Koorosh H Ameli, Mohsen Aghahosseini, April 19, 2006:

24. Iran and the Iranian arbitrators claim that the payments have occurred since the creation of the Tribunal and that the United States has been aware of such payments since 1981. The United States argues that it only became aware of the payments from Judge Noori's statement of 6 December 2005. The United States further argues that actual prior knowledge of the facts (as opposed to constructive knowledge) is required to be shown. The United States asserts that in the present case, only "vague statements or rumors" existed prior to Judge Noori's statement of 6 December 2005 (Letter of the United States dated 10 March 2006).

25. The United States is correct in stating that evidence of actual prior knowledge on the part of the challenging party of circumstances giving rise to a challenge must be shown. Whether such actual knowledge existed or not is a matter for me as appointing authority to determine on the basis of evidence submitted. In the past history of the Tribunal such evidence has included, for example, a prior statement made by the challenging party (Decision of the appointing authority in the challenge of Judge Briner, 19 September 1989).

26. In the present case, the evidence submitted to me includes a Statement by Secretary-General Pinto that he and the Tribunal had been aware for more than twenty years that the Iranian arbitrators made payments to Iran. Mr. Pinto supported his declaration with handwritten notes from a meeting of the Committee on Administrative and Financial Questions on 26 April 1984, where a then Iranian appointed arbitrator, Mr. Kashani, stated in the presence of the Agent of the United States that the Iranian arbitrators returned part of their salaries to Iran.

27. In addition to Mr. Pinto's statement, the appointing authority was also provided with a letter dated 1 February 2006 from Dr. Seyyed Hossein Enayat, a former Iranian arbitrator, indicating that during a meeting of the Tribunal in 1981, an arbitrator appointed by the United States suggested that Iranian arbitrators may wish to return part of their salaries to Iran, should Iran deem the salaries to be too high. Dr. Enayat states that the United States Agent, who was present at the meeting, did not object to this proposal.

28. This evidence is sufficient to convince me that the United States had actual knowledge of payment by the Iranian arbitrators of a part of their salaries to Iran since at least 1984. Consequently, the Challenge brought by the United States on 21 December 2005 was made well after the time limit set out in Article 11(1) of the [1983] Tribunal Rules, and the Challenge, having failed to comply with this time limit, shall be declared inadmissible.

(2) *Tribunal Rules (1983), Article 11(2)*

Decision of the Appointing Authority, Ch M J A Moons, on the Objections by Iran to Judge Mangård, March 5, 1982, at 12–14, reprinted in 1 Iran-US CTR 509, 517–18 (1981–82):

4.4 The consequence of the above consideration is that the objections lodged by a High Contracting Party to a duly appointed arbitrator will be admissible only if they satisfy *inter alia* the following conditions:
  (a) the High Contracting Party must intend to use the legal remedy of a challenge as provided for in the [1976] UNCITRAL Rules;
  (b) the regulations contained in Article 11 of the Rules must have been observed.

4.5 In view of the documents lodged with Us, particularly the letter of the Agent of the Islamic Republic of Iran dated 3 February 1982 which contains the following passage: My letter of January 1, 1982 and the enclosure in clear terms stated the position of my Government that due to Mr. Mangård's lack of neutrality, the Islamic Republic of Iran disqualified him and requested his resignation. *In taking that position the Islamic Republic of Iran would see no relevance to Article 11 of the [1976] UNCITRAL Rules*," We consider that the requirement referred to at (a) above cannot be said to have been satisfied.

4.6 Nor has the requirement referred to at (b) above been satisfied. This view is based on the following grounds. The relevant provisions of Article 11 read as follows:
1. A party who intends to challenge an arbitrator shall send notice of his challenge... within fifteen days after the circumstances mentioned in Article... 10 became known to that party.
2. The challenge shall be notified to the other party, to the arbitrator who is challenged and to the other members of the arbitral tribunal. The notification shall be in writing and shall state the reasons for the challenge.
3. When an arbitrator has been challenged by one party, the other party may agree to the challenge. The arbitrator may also, after the challenge, withdraw from his office....

Article 12 also provides that a decision on the challenge will be made "if the other party does not agree to the challenge and the challenged arbitrator does not withdraw."

4.7 In view of this body of rules and the provisions of Article 10(1), it must be assumed that the regulation that the notification must state the reasons for the challenge is intended to provide an opportunity:
   (i) to the other party: to determine whether there is any reason for it to agree to the challenge;
   (ii) to the challenged arbitrator: to determine whether there is any reason for him to withdraw from his office;
   (iii) to the Appointing Authority: to determine whether the notification of the challenge was made in good time and whether what is set out in the notification can be construed as an allegation that the circumstances referred to in Article 10(1) have been satisfied.
4.8 The contents of the letter of the Agent of the Islamic Republic of Iran of 1 January 1982 (with enclosure) offer insufficient opportunity to determine any of the above matters.

These documents contain neither a sufficiently clear description of the circumstances giving rise to the accusation levelled against Mr. Mangård of a "lack of neutrality," nor any indication of the dates on which the actual event on which the disqualification is based took place and on which this event came to the knowledge of the party alleging disqualification.

This notification cannot therefore be said to state "the reason for the challenge" within the meaning of Article 11 of the [1976] UNCITRAL Rules.

Letter of the Agent of the United States to the Appointing Authority initiating the Challenge of Judges Kashani and Shafeiei, September 17, 1984, reprinted in Intl Arb L Rev 9344:

In accordance with Article 11 of the [1983] Tribunal Rules, I have today sent notice of this challenge to the Government of Iran, to the Challenged arbitrators, and to the other members of the Tribunal.

Letter of the Agent of the Government of Iran to the Appointing Authority initiating the First Challenge by Iran of Judge Briner, September 13, 1988 at 3, reprinted in 20 Iran-US CTR 181, 183 (1988–III):

The Notice of Challenge was sent today to the other party, to the challenged arbitrator and to the other members of the Tribunal pursuant to the [1983] Tribunal Rules, Article 11 and Note 1 to Articles 9–12.

Letter of Judge Robert Briner to the Appointing Authority, Ch M J A Moons, September 14, 1988 at 1–2, reprinted in 20 Iran-US CTR 184 (1988–III):

In my opinion, the [1983] Tribunal Rules, with which I know you are familiar, do not provide for any further memorandum and evidence. Under Article 11, paragraph 2, the challenge shall be in writing and shall state the reasons for the challenge. This is obviously necessary in order to allow, under Article 11, paragraph 3 of the [1983] Tribunal Rules, the other party and arbitrator to determine themselves on the challenge. All material necessary for such a determination therefore has to be first notified to the challenged arbitrator and the other party to the arbitration.

Letter of the Appointing Authority, Ch M J A Moons, to the Agent of the Government of Iran, September 21, 1988, at 1, reprinted in 20 Iran-US CTR 187 (1988–III):

> … in my opinion Article 11, paragraph 2, of the [1983] Tribunal Rules does not oppose your sending me a Memorandum to complement the Notice of Challenge of Mr. Briner with respect to Case No 55 dated 13 September 1988, in which the reasons for this challenge set out in the above Notice will be further developed and in which evidence will be put forward to support these reasons.

Letter of the Agent of the Government of Iran to the Appointing Authority, Ch MJA Moons, September 27, 1988, at 2, reprinted in 20 Iran-US CTR 188–89 (1988–III):

> As expressly stated in the [1976] Rule in question [Article 11(2)], the notification is only required to "state the reasons for challenge". Not to *adduce*, but to *state*, reasons; and not a word about documents or evidence in support of stated reasons. If this clear language should still leave any doubt, a short reference to the preparatory work of the Article in question would dispel it. There it will be noticed that a suggestion to include a new provision to Article 11 requiring the notification to contain evidence and supporting documents did not find favour with the members of the UNCITRAL drafting committee.

Letter of the Appointing Authority, Ch M J A Moons, to the Agent of the Government of Iran, Mohammad K Eshragh, November 10, 1988, at 1:

> I have the honour to confirm herewith the verbal agreement we made on 9 November last to the effect that:
>
> (a) …;
> (b) Up to November 28, 1988 you will have the opportunity to carry out your intention to submit further explanatory comment on the challenge.

Letter of the Agent of Iran to the Appointing Authority initiating the Second Challenge by Iran of Judge Briner, July 28, 1989, at 1, reprinted in 21 Iran-US CTR 318 (1989–I):

> On the instructions of the Government of the Islamic Republic of Iran (hereafter "The Islamic Republic") and on behalf of the National Iranian Oil Company ("NIOC"), I am writing to you in your capacity as the AA to the Iran-United States Claims Tribunal to challenge Mr. Robert Briner, the third country arbitrator and the President of the Iran-United States Claims Tribunal. Copies of this letter, as a notice of challenge, are being simultaneously notified to Mr. Briner and other concerned parties pursuant to the [1983] Tribunal Rules, Article 11 and Note 1 to Articles 9–12.

Joint Decision of the Appointing Authority, Judge W E Haak, on the Challenges to Judge Krzysztof Skubiszewski and Judge Hamid Reza Oloumi Yazdi, April 2, 2008, at 10, 11–12:

> In the present case, it is impossible to determine precisely, on the basis of Iran's Notice of Challenge and the exhibits attached to it, when Judge Oloumi's request was made and when its alleged rejection took place. The Notice and its exhibits contain no clear indication either as to how the decision to allegedly reject his request was made. In addition, and most importantly, it is equally impossible to determine with any certainty, on the basis of those documents, who took that decision and what was the exact content of that decision (see Judge Skubiszewski's submission of January 8, 2008, paragraph 10).

The review of the Notice of Challenge and its exhibits reveal that basic information with respect to the timing of the request and its alleged rejection is lacking. In his memorandum, Judge Oloumi does not mention the date of his request, nor the date of the alleged rejection of his request. These dates are not provided either in the Notice of Challenge. The only thing that is clear is that the request was made and allegedly rejected during the Full Tribunal's deliberative sessions.

It is also impossible to determine, on the basis of Judge Oloumi's statement, how the decision to allegedly reject his request was made and who took the decision. While Judge Oloumi addresses his memorandum to the President of the Arbitral Tribunal, he does not state whether the President *took* a decision on his own; he states in rather nebulous terms that the President "*dealt* with [his request] in a way that it met with a negative outcome" (emphasis added). The meaning of this sentence is unclear and in any event it is quite different from stating that the President decided on his own to reject Judge Oloumi's request.

... The Notice does not state either whether the Tribunal authorized the president to render a decision on his own. It does not state whether the Tribunal sought to exercise its power to revise the decision or whether there was any request for revision, by any Member of the Tribunal, including in particular Judge Oloumi. In other words, the Notice of Challenge and Judge Oloumi's memorandum are not sufficiently specific to allow me to verify how the provisions of article 31(2) of the Rules were applied and which of the different decision-making procedures contemplated in this article was followed.

This further confirms that the notice of challenge fails to state sufficiently specific reasons that would enable one to determine how the decision to allegedly reject Judge Oloumi's request was made and who took that decision.

The precise content of the decision that allegedly denied Judge Oloumi's request remains unknown. Judge Olowni merely states that his request was "unexpectedly rejected" and that the President "questioned the merit" of his request. As pointed out by Judge Skubiszewski, neither the Notice nor the memorandum state whether the alleged rejection was complete and definite or only partial (see Judge Skubiszewski's final submission of March 12, 2008, paragraph 8). They do not state what the alleged criticism of that request was thereby preventing any proper assessment of the justifications of the decision.

On the basis of the above, it must be held that the notice of challenge is too vague and that it fails to state reasons for the challenge.

Decision of the Appointing Authority, Judge W E Haak, on the Challenge to Judge Seyed Jamal Seifi, September 3, 2010, at 6 (citations omitted):

20. In my view, the United States met the specificity requirement by alleging at the inception of the Challenge that Judge Seifi's experience as a member of the ICC Tribunal could influence his participation in any future proceedings in Case B/61 despite his obligations to consider the merits of Case B/61 only as presented by the Parties to the Tribunal. The United States alleged in its second submission that any Iranian claim for loss in Case B/61 would necessarily require examination of the same facts and arguments at issue with the Cubic Arbitration, which, in its view, gives rise to justifiable doubts about Judge Seifi's impartiality due to his prior consideration and decision of those issues in the Cubic Arbitration. These statements point toward a purported issue conflict that forms the essence of the United States' challenge against Judge Seifi. In addition, the date in which the United States claimed to first have had actual knowledge of the purported issue conflict—the conversation between Justice Richard Mosk and Ms. Lisa Grosh on April 7, 2010—was clearly indicated in the Notice of Challenge. It cannot reasonably be said that either Iran or Judge Seifi were not sufficiently appraised of the allegations and evidence supporting the Challenge.

Decision of the Appointing Authority, Judge W E Haak, on the Challenge to Judge Charles Brower, September 3, 2010, at 6 (citation omitted):

15. In my view, Iran's reasons for challenging Judge Brower, as contained in the Notice of Challenge, were sufficiently clear to enable the United States to arrive at a position on whether

there is any reason to agree to the Challenge, and for Judge Brower to determine whether there is any reason for him to withdraw from office. Iran has in large measure challenged Judge Brower because of the *fact* that he conversed with Professor Dupuy regarding the potential appointment (regardless of the content of their discussion), which is not disputed. This fact is relied upon as basis for Iran's allegations, and evidence of that fact was presented in the Notice of Challenge through a reprint of Professor Dupuy's e-mail communication of May 3, 2010 (and has not been contested by the United States or Judge Brower). The link between this fact and Iran's allegations of lack of impartiality or independence was stated in sufficient detail, to my mind.

16. That said, I note that Iran did not confine itself to this ground for challenge alone and made further allegations that are far more speculative and unproven, such as Judge Brower's possible motives for contacting Professor Dupuy, and the allegation that Judge Brower acted as an agent of the United States. I shall deal with all these grounds for challenge in turn.

(3) Tribunal Rules (1983), Article 11(3)

Letter of Judge Robert Briner to the Appointing Authority, Ch M J A Moons, December 6, 1988, regarding the Challenge by Iran to his participation in Case No 55, reprinted in 20 Iran-US CTR 329 (1988–III):

> This is to inform you that I have decided to withdraw from Case No 55 and I have so informed the President of the Iran-United States Claim Tribunal in order that he can take the necessary dispositions.
>
> I should like to stress that this action does in no way imply an acceptance of the validity of the grounds put forward for my challenge…

Letter of Judge Robert Briner, President of the Tribunal, to the Agent of the Government of Iran, Mohammad K Eshragh, March 7, 1989 at 1–2:

> I agree with your view that Note 4 to Articles 9–12 of the [1983] Tribunal Rules is relevant in determining which chamber should deal with Case No 55 following my withdrawal from that Case. However, I thought it my duty to ensure that action taken in conformity with that provision should follow any relevant practice of the Tribunal and seek to cause as little disruption as possible in the work of the Tribunal as a whole.
>
> While there has been no previous instance of withdrawal by a Member following a challenge, a practice has been established in cases where a Member disqualified himself pursuant to Article 9 of the Tribunal Report—a situation which you yourself had reasoned in your letter No 21402 of 25 March 1988 was analogous to that where a Member has withdrawn following a challenge. You would recall that in regard to Cases Nos 20 and 21, the Tribunal, following an extensive discussion of the issues involved, implicitly recognized the previous practice of replacing a Party-appointed Member who had disqualified himself, by a Member appointed by the same Party from another Chamber rather than transferring those cases to another chamber which had its own full schedule, and thus increasing the risk of disrupting the orderly functioning of the Tribunal.
>
> The result of such action is, in effect the constitution of a new *ad hoc* chamber composed of two regular Members of the Chamber and one from outside it, and the transfer to it of the case concerned. On the other hand, this procedure would only produce minor consequences elsewhere in the tribunal, and was therefore to be preferred to transfer of the case to another regular Chamber with the attendant disruption of the latter's schedule.
>
> Accordingly, the designation of Mr. Broms to act as Chairman of Chamber Two for Case No 55 was entirely in conformity with the letter and intent of Note 4 to Articles 9–12 of the [1983] Tribunal Rules, as interpreted through Tribunal practice, and within the scope of the powers conferred on me as President of the Tribunal pursuant to Article III of the Claims Settlement Declaration. While the Chamber which, pursuant to Presidential Order No 67, will now deal with Case No 55 would be referred to as "Chamber Two", it differs from Chamber Two as regularly composed, and is, in fact, another Chamber.

5. The Resolution of the Challenge

In the case where a party's challenge to an arbitrator is not accepted by all the parties or the challenged arbitrator does not withdraw within 15 days of the date of the notice of arbitration, as discussed above, the challenging party may seek within 30 days of the date of the notice of challenge a decision on the challenge by the appointing authority. If the challenge is sustained, Article 14 (discussed in chapter 6) provides the procedure for appointment of a substitute arbitrator.

Once the decision on the challenge has been turned over to the appointing authority, the UNCITRAL Rules are silent as to the process for deciding the challenge.[322]

A. Text of the 2010 UNCITRAL Rule

For the text of Article 13 of the 2010 UNCITRAL Rules, see Section 4(A) above.

B. Commentary

(1) Which authority shall make the decision on the challenge if the other party does not agree to the challenge or the challenged arbitrator does not withdraw?

Article 13(4) establishes the rule that an appointing authority will decide a challenge in those cases where the parties do not agree to the challenge or the challenged arbitrator chooses not to withdraw.[323] In this respect, Article 13(4) parallels Article 12(1) of the 1976 UNCITRAL Rules, despite the omission of specific provisions outlining three scenarios for determining how to designate the appointing authority with responsibility for deciding the challenge.[324] Article 12(1) of the 1976 UNCITRAL Rules contained three provisions which the 2010 Rules do not. Under Article 12(1), subsection (a), if an appointing authority made the original appointment of the challenged arbitrator, the challenge will be decided by that authority. Under subsection (b), if an appointing authority did not appoint the challenged arbitrator, but an appointing authority has already been designated by the parties, that authority will make the decision.[325] Finally, subsection (c) covers the remaining cases in

---

[322] Article 12 of the 1976 UNCITRAL Rules provides:
1. If the other party does not agree to the challenge and the challenged arbitrator does not withdraw, the decision on the challenge will be made:
    (a) When the initial appointment was made by an appointing authority, by that authority;
    (b) When the initial appointment was not made by an appointing authority, but an appointing authority has been previously designated, by that authority;
    (c) In all other cases, by the appointing authority to be designated in accordance with the procedure for designating an appointing authority as provided for in article 6.
2. If the appointing authority sustains the challenge, a substitute arbitrator shall be appointed or chosen pursuant to the procedure applicable to the appointment or choice of an arbitrator as provided in articles 6 to 9 except that, when this procedure would call for the designation of an appointing authority, the appointment of the arbitrator shall be made by the appointing authority which decided on the challenge.

[323] For application of a similar rule under the 1976 UNCITRAL Rules (art 12(1)), see *Methanex Corp* (1976 Rules), reprinted in section 5(C) (finding that the tribunal has no jurisdiction to decide upon any aspects of a party's challenge).

[324] Under Article 12(a) of the 1976 UNCITRAL Rules, if an appointing authority made the original appointment of the challenged arbitrator, the challenge will be decided by that authority. Under Article 12(b), if an appointing authority did not appoint the challenged arbitrator, but an appointing authority has already been designated by the parties, that authority will make the decision. Finally, Article 12(c) covers the remaining cases in which an appointing authority will be designated according to the procedures of Article 6(2).

[325] For practice under the original rule, see, eg, Letter of the Agent of the United States to the Appointing Authority initiating the Challenge of Judges Kashani and Shafeiei, September 17, 1984, reprinted in Intl Arb L

which an appointing authority will be designated according to the procedures of Article 6(2) of the 1976 UNCITRAL Rules. The *travaux préparatoires* of the 1976 UNCITRAL Rules nevertheless remain instructive as to the interpretation of the 2010 UNCITRAL Rules.

The primary concern of the UNCITRAL drafters in drafting Article 12(1) of the 1976 UNCITRAL Rules was to ensure that the authority called upon to decide the challenge be an impartial and independent party. In this context, representatives to UNCITRAL expressed some of the same concerns that arose in the discussion of Article 11 of the 1976 UNCITRAL Rules (now Article 13 of the 2010 UNCITRAL Rules) regarding whether the appointing authority who made the original appointment could be trusted to make an impartial decision.[326] As a result, they considered several other possibilities for an authority to decide the challenge. The first was to have the other two members of the arbitral tribunal decide the challenge.[327] The second and more seriously considered possibility was to allow the court of first instance at the place of arbitration to decide the challenge. This possibility was based on the assumption that this court would most likely possess the necessary jurisdiction and competence[328] and in some countries would be required by law to make the final decision on the challenge, or at a minimum have a right to review the challenge decision.[329] If this court did not have the requisite jurisdiction, the president of the chamber of commerce at the place of arbitration could make the decision.[330]

Strong arguments were raised in favor of allowing national courts to decide challenges. Discussion of the Committee considering the Revised Draft of Article 12 of the 1976 UNCITRAL Rules made it clear that the national laws in some key countries ran contrary to the text of the rule as proposed. For example, it was argued that under then Austrian law no person other than a judge was permitted to decide a challenge.[331] Likewise, it was said that under German law the final decision on a challenge must be made by a municipal court judge.[332] While the representatives from these countries did not object to the rule's grant of decision-making authority to an independent appointing authority, they thought that parties subject to arbitration should examine local laws to determine which authority will make the final decision.

Ultimately, the representatives were satisfied that even if the appointing authority who made the original appointment would decide the challenge under Article 12(1)(a) of the 1976 UNCITRAL Rules, the assumption of neutrality and impartiality could be maintained: "[E]xperience had shown that arbitral institutions and appointing authorities acted with complete impartiality even when one of their appointees was challenged. Such institutions and appointing authorities were deeply concerned with preserving their reputation for integrity...."[333] Safeguards for neutrality were also provided under Article 12(1)(b)

Rev 9344; and Letter of the Agent of the Government of Iran to the Appointing Authority initiating the First Challenge, n 37; both reprinted in section 5(D)(1).

[326] UN Doc A/10017, n 71, para 83, reprinted in (1975) VI UNCITRAL Ybk 24, 33.

[327] *Report of the UNCITRAL*, 8th Session, n 326, para 85. This is the practice followed, for example, under the ICSID arbitration rules.

[328] *Report of the UNCITRAL*, 8th Session, n 326, para 85.

[329] See *Summary Record of the 5th Meeting of the Committee of the Whole (II)*, UNCITRAL, 9th Session, UN Doc A/CN.9/9/C.2/SR.5, at 4, paras 22–23 (1976) (Comments by the Chairman and Mr Pirrung, Federal Republic of Germany).

[330] UN Doc A/10017, n 71, para 85, reprinted in (1975) VI UNCITRAL Ybk 24, 34.

[331] *Summary Record of the 5th Meeting of the Committee of the Whole (II)*, UNCITRAL, 9th Session, UN Doc A/CN.9/9/C.2/SR.5, at 4, para 22 (1976) (Comment by the Chairman).

[332] *Summary Record of the 5th Meeting*, n 331, para 23 (Comment by Mr Pirrung, Federal Republic of Germany).

[333] UN Doc A/10017, n 71, para 84, reprinted in (1975) VI UNCITRAL Ybk 24, 33.

since the parties themselves would presumably only appoint an appointing authority they considered neutral,[334] and if the parties failed to agree on a choice of appointing authority, Article 12(1)(c) provides for the Secretary-General of the Permanent Court of Arbitration in The Hague to make the appropriate appointment.

Nothing in the 2010 UNCITRAL Rules suggests that the appointing authority should have any different duties and responsibilities. Under the revised Rules, the appointing authority that made the initial appointment of a challenged arbitrator may decide the challenge and in all cases the appointing authority should act with impartiality and independence. However, it is also clear that the tasks of appointment and challenge are fundamentally different. Appointment is not a particularly legal task, but rather involves knowledge of potential arbitrators and appreciation for the importance of the place of arbitration. Deciding upon a challenge, in contrast, is distinctly legal and judicial requiring both application of the law, assessment of evidence and fair, yet firm, administration of procedure. It may be the case that the institution or person that served as the appointing authority making the original appointment also possesses the skills necessary to decide upon a challenge, but that is not necessarily always the case.

(2) When may a party seek the assistance of the PCA Secretary-General in designating an appointing authority?

In the challenge to Judge Mangård, Iran claimed that the procedures established under Articles 6[335] and 12 of the 1983 Tribunal Rules for the designation of an appointing authority to decide the challenge were not observed. Specifically, Iran charged that the United States had requested that the Secretary-General designate an appointing authority before attempting to reach an agreement on an appointing authority with the Iranians.[336]

On its face, Article 6(2) of the Tribunal Rules does seem to indicate that parties should try to reach an agreement before making a request for the Secretary-General to designate an appointing authority. However, in practical terms, a strict reading of Article 6(2) appears inappropriate in the context of a challenge. If the parties failed to reach an agreement on an appointing authority at the start of the arbitral proceedings, they are unlikely to reach agreement in the tense atmosphere of a challenge.[337]

Justice Moons, the Appointing Authority chosen by the Secretary-General to decide the challenge to Judge Mangård, adopted this more pragmatic reading of Article 6 of the Tribunal Rules. He rejected the Iranian interpretation of Articles 12(1) and 6:

The clear intention of this rule [Article 12 of the Tribunal Rules] is to ensure that a speedy decision can be taken on the challenge.

In the light of this, it must be assumed that the rule contained in Article 12(1)(c) is also intended to make it possible in the cases referred to therein to designate an Appointing Authority to decide on the challenge as quickly and as simply as possible.

Therefore, the rule which Article 12(1)(c) contains to the effect that the designation of the Appointing Authority must be "in accordance with the procedure for designating an appointing

---

[334] *Report of the Secretary-General on the Revised Draft Set of Arbitration Rules*, UNCITRAL, 9th Session, Addendum 1 (Commentary), UN Doc A/CN.9/112/Add.1 (1975), reprinted in (1976) VII UNCITRAL Ybk 166, 171 (Commentary on Draft Article 11(1)(b)).
[335] See discussion of Article 6(2) in Chapter 4.
[336] Decision of the Appointing Authority on the Objections by Iran to Judge Mangård, n 31, at 513–14.
[337] See S Baker and M Davis, *The UNCITRAL Rules in Practice*, n 1, 66.

authority as provided for in Article 6" has to be interpreted as meaning that except in cases in which the Parties have agreed upon an Appointing Authority in the context of the procedure relating to the appointment of an arbitrator, the Secretary-General of the Permanent Court of Arbitration at the Hague is empowered to designate an Appointing Authority to decide on a challenge, if he receives a request to that effect from one of the Parties.[338]

(3) What procedures the appointing authority may follow in deciding the challenge

The UNCITRAL Rules do not define the appointing authority's decision-making process. For example, there is nothing in the Rules to suggest whether parties and the challenged arbitrator have the right to file briefs or to demand a hearing. The drafters of the UNCITRAL Rules apparently chose to leave these issues up to the discretion of the appointing authority, presumably to ensure sufficient flexibility so the process could be tailored to the circumstances of each arbitration and could avoid taking on a life of its own.[339] In practice, appointing authorities have enjoyed wide latitude in developing the terms of procedure for resolving a challenge, including by establishing a schedule for receiving submissions and responses from the parties pursuing and resisting the challenge, as well as from the challenged arbitrator,[340] by conducting individual fact-finding meetings with the challenged arbitrator and other relevant individuals,[341] and by holding hearings, if necessary, to resolve more complicated factual and legal matters related to the challenge.[342] In practice, but less so in recent years, appointing authorities have also decided upon challenges in a manner less formal than the arbitration to which it is related.

In the challenge of Judge Mangård, for example, the first challenge under the 1976 UNCITRAL Rules as modified by the Iran–US Claims Tribunal, the decision process was somewhat informal and expedited. In particular, the Appointing Authority, Justice Moons, on January 25, 1982 requested the views of the Agents of the two state parties and Judge Mangård on specified issues. All three submitted their views in succinct letters in the first part of February. The Agents met with Justice Moons and explained their view orally on February 17, 1982. These statements were summarized and supplemented in further letters sent by the Agents in late February. Justice Moons rendered his decision very shortly thereafter on March 5, 1982. Although the proximity of the appointing authority to the parties may have been a factor, his rapid decision generally reflects the fact that the challenge was denied on a very preliminary issue—that of admissibility.

Several guiding principles should be followed in handling challenges. First, the potential for abuse of the challenge proceedings is great and thus manifestly deficient challenges

---

[338] Decision of the Appointing Authority on the Objections by Iran to Judge Mangård, n 31, at 514, reprinted in section 5(D)(1).

[339] See *Summary Record of the 5th Meeting of the Committee of the Whole (II)*, UNCITRAL, 9th Session, UN Doc A/CN.9/9/C.2/SR.5, at 4–5 (1976). In the Committee discussions on Article 12 of the 1976 UNCITRAL Rules, the Soviet representative once again, as he had in the discussions on Article 11 of the 1976 UNCITRAL Rules, raised the issue of the types of evidence which should be permitted when an arbitrator was challenged. Nevertheless, the issue remained unaddressed.

[340] See, eg, *Vito G Gallo* and *Government of Canada*, Decision on the Challenge to Mr J Christopher Thomas, QC (October 14, 2009) (ICSID administered, 1976 UNCITRAL Rules, NAFTA Chapter Eleven), at 5, para 16.

[341] Decision by the Appointing Authority, Judge W E Haak, on the Challenge against Mr Assadollah Noori, Koorosh H Ameli, Mohsen Aghahosseini (April 19, 2006), n 56, at 2, para 8; reprinted in section 4(D)(1).

[342] *National Grid PLC* and *Republic of Argentina*, Decision on the Challenge to Mr Judd L Kessler (December 3, 2007) (LCIA administered, 1976 UNCITRAL Rules, UK-Argentina BIT), at 7, para 26.

should simply and quickly be declared inadmissible. Second, the challenge exists to further the arbitration. As a result, the decision process must not become so formal and structured that the task of deciding the challenge takes on a life of its own at the cost of the arbitration. We therefore endorse informal investigations that lead to the expeditious resolution of a challenge, as were sometimes pursued in challenges before the Iran–US Claims Tribunal. In the case of a panel of three arbitrators, expedited challenge proceedings theoretically do not substantially prejudice the interests of the party who appointed the challenged arbitrator, for even if the challenge is sustained, that party may appoint a replacement. Moreover, although the challenged arbitrator has a direct and significant interest in his or her reputation, the UNCITRAL Rules protect this interest by providing for withdrawal without prejudice. In fact, given the provisions for agreement and withdrawal, it seems unlikely that a meritorious challenge would ever reach the point of decision.

(4) Limitations on the powers of the appointing authority

Though largely unregulated by the UNCITRAL Rules, the powers of the appointing authority are not limitless. The appointing authority's discretion necessarily ends where the arbitral tribunal's begins. Thus, whereas the appointing authority has sole authority to determine the existence of justifiable doubts as to the impartiality or independence of an arbitrator, unless otherwise agreed by the parties, the appointing authority may not decide the merits of the underlying dispute or any other matters solely within the discretion of the arbitral tribunal. For example, appointing authorities have appropriately declined to rule on requests to apportion the costs of challenge proceedings because, as one appointing authority observed, under the UNCITRAL Rules "the power to fix and apportion costs, including the fees and expenses of the appointing authority and other costs associated with the challenge, is reserved to the arbitral tribunal."[343] In addition, the appointing authority is well advised to adhere to (although technically not bound by) the guiding principles of UNCITRAL Rules on the conduct of the arbitral proceedings, such as equal treatment of the parties, avoidance of unnecessary delay and expense, and fair and efficient process.[344]

C. Extracts from the Practice of Investment Tribunals

Methanex Corp and *United States of America*, Award (August 3, 2005) (ICSID administered, 1976 UNCITRAL Rules, NAFTA Chapter Eleven), Part II, Chapter E, at 19:

 34. Turning next to the impact of Mr. Christopher's resignation, the Tribunal notes that under the [1976] UNCITRAL Rules it has no role (unlike an ICSID tribunal) to decide upon any challenge by a party to any of the arbitrators. All decisions on challenges to members of this Tribunal are reserved to the appointing authority pursuant to Article 12(1) of the [1976] UNCITRAL Rules, in this case the Secretary-General of ICSID or his designated alternate. The Tribunal has therefore no jurisdiction to decide that an undisclosed relationship did or not exist between an arbitrator and a party, as Methanex has alleged. In the Tribunal's view, it likewise lacks any jurisdiction to decide Methanex's further contentions that US law requires reconsideration in such cases and that there is or is not a three month's time-limit under US law....

---

[343] Decision on Challenge to Arbitrator, December 17, 2009, at 5, para 7. See also *National Grid PLC* and *Republic of Argentina,* Decision on the Challenge to Mr Judd L Kessler (December 3, 2007) (LCIA administered, 1976 UNCITRAL Rules, UK-Argentina BIT), at 24, para 104. *But see Vito G Gallo* and *Canada,* Decision on the Challenge to Mr J Christopher Thomas, QC (October 14, 2009) (ICSID administered, 1976 UNCITRAL Rules, NAFTA Chapter Eleven), at 11, para 37.

[344] See 2010 UNCITRAL Rules, art 17(1).

D. Extracts from the Practice of the Iran–US Claims Tribunal

(1) Tribunal Rules (1983), Article 12(1)

Decision of the Appointing Authority, Ch M J A Moons, on the Objections by Iran to Judge Mangård, March 5, 1982 at 7–9, reprinted in 1 Iran-US CTR 509, 513–14 (1981–82):

> The contention that pursuant to the provisions of Article 12(1)(c), in conjunction with Article 6, of the [1976] UNCITRAL Rules, the Secretary-General of the Permanent Court of Arbitration at the Hague is not empowered to designate an Appointing Authority until the Parties have been unable to reach agreement on the designation by them in mutual consultation of an Appointing Authority is based on an incorrect interpretation of the provisions in question. The arrangement provided for in Article 12(1)(a) and (b) relates to cases in which the appointment of the challenged arbitrator was made by an Appointing Authority or, alternatively, in which an Appointing Authority was designated during the procedure leading to the appointment of the challenged arbitrator.
>
> Article 12 provides that in such cases the decision on the challenge shall be made by the Appointing Authority. The clear intention of this rule is to ensure that a speedy decision can be taken on the challenge.
>
> In light of this, it must be assumed that the rule contained in article 12(1)(c) is also intended to make it possible in the cases referred to therein to designate an Appointing Authority to decide on the challenge as quickly and as simply as possible.
>
> Therefore, the rule which Article 12(1)(c) contains to the effect that the designation of the Appointing Authority must be "in accordance with the procedure for designating an appointing authority as provided for in Article 6" has to be interpreted as meaning that except in cases in which the Parties have agreed upon an Appointing Authority in the context of the procedure relating to the appointment of an arbitrator, the Secretary-General of the Permanent Court of Arbitration at the Hague is empowered to designate an Appointing Authority to decide on a challenge, if he receives a request to that effect from one of the Parties.
>
> This interpretation is supported by the history of the proceedings leading to the adoption of the [1976] UNCITRAL Rules. At the conference which adopted the rules, a draft of Article 6 prepared by the Secretariat requiring that the Parties endeavor to reach agreement on the choice of an Appointing Authority, was rejected in favour of a Belgian proposal in which there was no requirement to seek agreement...

Letter of the Agent of the United States to the Appointing Authority initiating the Challenge of Judges Kashani and Shafeiei, September 17, 1984, reprinted in Intl Arb L Rev 9344:

> In the event that the Government of Iran does not expeditiously agree to the challenge, or that the challenged arbitrators do not quickly withdraw voluntarily, the United States requests, pursuant to Article 12(1)(b) of the Tribunal Rules, that you decide and sustain the challenge.

Letter of the Agent of the Government of Iran to the Appointing Authority initiating the First Challenge by Iran of Judge Briner, September 13, 1988 at 1, 3, reprinted in 20 Iran-US CTR 181, 183 (1988–III):

> On the instructions of my Government and the other Respondents to Case No 55 pending before the Iran-United States Claims Tribunal, I am writing to you in your capacity as the Appointing Authority to the Iran-United States Claims Tribunal. The purpose of this letter is to challenge Mr. Robert Briner, the third country arbitrator of Chamber Two, Iran-United States Claim Tribunal with respect to the above-mentioned case and to request you to decide the challenge pursuant to Article 12(1)(b) of the [1983] Tribunal Rules.
>
> ...

The Notice of Challenge was sent today to the other party, to the challenged arbitrator and to the other members of the Tribunal, pursuant to the [1983] Tribunal Rules, Article 11 and Note 1 to Articles 9–12. You are, therefore, requested to decide the challenge if the other party does not agree to the challenge, or Mr. Briner does not withdraw, as is the rule of Article 12 of the [1983] Tribunal Rules.

Letter from the Agent of the Government of Iran to the Appointing Authority for the Iran–US Claims Tribunal, Ch M J A Moons, entitled "Application to Excuse Mr. Gaetano Arangio-Ruiz From His Office for Failure to Perform his Arbitral Functions," August 8, 1991 at 4, reprinted in 27 Iran-US CTR 293, 297 (1991–II):

In case the other party does not agree to this application and Mr. Arangio-Ruiz does not withdraw, you, as the Appointing Authority of the Iran-United States Claims Tribunal are requested to decide upon it pursuant to Article 12(b) of the [1983] Tribunal Rules.

(2) Tribunal Rules (1983), Article 12(2)

No practice is being extracted in this area.

6. Comparison to the 1976 UNCITRAL Rules

Articles 11 through 13 establishes a process for resolving challenges to arbitrators that contains the same standard of arbitrator conduct as found in corresponding Articles 9 through 12 of the 1976 UNCITRAL Rules. The 2010 UNCITRAL Rules are more streamlined, however, and eliminate the redundancies and superfluity of the original articles, while adding new features, such as a model disclosure statement and new deadlines to regulate the time between the submission of a notice of challenge and the request for a decision by the appointing authority.

The first sentence of Article 11 retains the same standard for disclosure as in corresponding Article 9 of the 1976 UNCITRAL Rules: "disclose any circumstances likely to give rise to justifiable doubts as to his [or her] impartiality or independence." Replacement of the term "prospective arbitrator" in the old rule with "a person [who] is approached in connection with his or her possible appointment as an arbitrator" in the revised rule is immaterial to the application of the provision. The second sentence of Article 11 states the rule of the arbitrator's continuing obligation to disclose. Article 11 clarifies that the duty of disclosure continues beyond the time of appointment and applies "throughout the arbitral proceedings." It thus remedies certain drafting deficiencies in Article 9 of the 1976 UNCITRAL Rules, which only requires disclosure by an arbitrator "once appointed or chosen." (However, as mentioned above, we believe the drafting history and policies underlying the original rule favor reading in a continuing duty of disclosure). Article 11 contains the new condition that any disclosure be made "without delay," which complements the goal of arbitral efficiency.

Article 12(1) retains the core standard of arbitrator conduct originally established in the corresponding Article 10(1) of the 1976 UNCITRAL Rules: "if circumstances exist that give rise to justifiable doubts as to the arbitrator's impartiality or independence." Article 12(2) states the identical rule as in original Article 10(2) on a party challenging its own arbitrator. As a result of a re-organization of the Rules, Article 12(3) now contains the identical rule on the procedure for an arbitrator's failure to act that was originally contained in Article 13(2) of the 1976 UNCITRAL Rules.

Without minor revision, Article 13(1) through (3) contains the same rules on providing notice of challenge as originally included in Article 11(1) through (3) of the 1976 UNCITRAL Rules. While the term "notification" in the original rule has been replaced by "notice of challenge" and minor grammatical revisions have been made, these do not change the manner in which the article functions. However, Article 13 does not incorporate the last sentence of original Article 11(3), which largely restates what is already known: that after the parties agree to accept the challenge or the arbitrator withdraws the procedures for appointment of arbitrators under the Rules apply. Notably, Article 13(4) adds two new time periods following the date of the notice of challenge: 15 days for the parties to agree on a challenge or for the challenged arbitrator to withdraw; and 30 days for the challenging party to seek a decision by the appointing authority. In the absence of such time limits in the 1976 UNCITRAL Rules, the Secretary-General of the PCA or the appointing authority, if one has been appointed, has discretion to determine how long the parties should have to reach agreement on the challenge and the arbitrator has to withdraw.[345]

That provision also departs slightly from the formulation of the general prerequisites for seeking a decision on the challenge by the arbitrator. Whereas Article 12(1) of the 1976 UNCITRAL Rules provided "If the other party does not agree *and* the challenged arbitrator does not withdraw," Article 13(4) now provides "If...all parties do not agree to the challenge *or* the challenged arbitrator does not withdraw."[346] According to the *travaux préparatoires*, without the revision the provision "might create a risk that, in the exceptional situation where an arbitrator would refuse to withdrawal despite the parties having agreed on the challenge, such refusal would prevent the parties from pursuing the challenge."[347]

The specific directions on designating an appointing authority that were originally contained in Article 12(1) and (2) of the 1976 UNCITRAL Rules have been omitted, presumably because the Working Group viewed them as largely redundant of other provisions under the Rules.

---

[345] For example, in the case of the Iranian Government challenge of Judge Mangård initiated on January 1, 1982, the Agent for the United States wrote to the Secretary-General of the Permanent Court of Arbitration, Jacob Varekamp, on January 8, 1982, stating that the US Government did not agree to the challenge and requesting that an appointing authority be designated. This designation was made five days later on January 13, 1982. Such speed no doubt reflects in large part the fact that the Tribunal and the Permanent Court of Arbitration are both located in The Hague and thus the Secretary-General of the Permanent Court was intimately familiar with individuals and institutions who could ably serve as appointing authority. In the case of a request for designation of an appointing authority for an *ad hoc* arbitration, such designation may take considerably longer. There is no reason to suppose, however, that the Permanent Court of Arbitration will not handle the matter expeditiously under these circumstances.

[346] Emphases added.

[347] UNCITRAL, 42nd Session, UN Doc A/CN.9/665, n 89, at 18, para 94.

Chapter 6

Failure to Act, other Disruptions, and the Replacement of an Arbitrator

1. Introduction	278
2. Failure to Act and other Disruptions—Article 12(3)	278
A. Text of the 2010 UNCITRAL Rule	278
B. Commentary	278
(1) Drafting history of the rule and general comments	278
(2) Iran–US Claims Tribunal practice with respect to an arbitrator's failure to act	280
(3) Iran–US Claims Tribunal practice with respect to other disruptions	282
(a) A note on substitute arbitrators	282
(b) A note on truncated proceedings	283
(1) The absence of Mr Sani, Fall 1983	284
(2) The absence of Judge Mostafavi, Spring 1988	284
(3) The practice of the Tribunal regarding absence from the hearing	285
(4) The practice of the Tribunal regarding the rendering of awards despite a refusal to sign	286
(5) The practice of the Tribunal regarding the rendering of awards on agreed terms despite no participation by an arbitrator	286
(6) The practice of the Tribunal regarding the holding of pre-hearing conference despite the absence of an arbitrator	286
(c) A note on resignation of an arbitrator	286
(4) Comparison to the 1976 UNCITRAL Rules	289
C. Extracts from the Practice of Investment Tribunals	289
D. Extracts from the Practice of the Iran–US Claims Tribunal	290
(1) Tribunal Rules (1983), Article 13(1)—Resignation	290
(2) Tribunal Rules (1983), Article 13(2)—Failure to act	291
(3) Tribunal Rules (1983), Article 13(3)	302
(4) Tribunal Rules (1983), Article 13(4)	302
(5) Tribunal Rules (1983), Article 13(5)	302
3. Replacement of an Arbitrator—Article 14	305
A. Text of the 2010 UNCITRAL Rule	305
B. Commentary	305
(1) Rationale for the revised approach: the problem of spurious resignations	305
(2) Procedures when an arbitrator "has to be replaced"—Article 14(1)	307
(3) Replacement of an arbitrator in "exceptional circumstances"—Article 14(2)	308
(a) Depriving a party of its right to appoint	308
(b) Procedural requirements	311
(c) Exclusivity of the discretion of the appointing authority	312
(d) Agreement between the parties	313
(4) Comparison to the 1976 UNCITRAL Rules	314
(a) The express power to proceed	315
(b) The inherent power to proceed	317

4. Repetition of Hearings in the Event of Replacement of an Arbitrator—Article 15	318
A. Text of the 2010 UNCITRAL Rule	318
B. Commentary	318
(1) General comments	318
(2) Comparison to the 1976 UNCITRAL Rules	320
C. Extracts from the Practice of the Iran–US Claims Tribunal	322

1. Introduction

Lack of impartiality or independence in an arbitrator is not the only contingency that a set of arbitral rules must anticipate. An arbitrator's failure to perform his or her functions, resignation, absence, or death also have the potential to disrupt the arbitral proceedings.

Article 12(3) addresses an arbitrator's failure to act or the impossibility of performing his or her functions. The problems of resignation, absence, and death have been dealt with extensively in the practice of the Iran–US Claims Tribunal. Article 14 establishes the procedures for replacement of an arbitrator or, in certain circumstances, the continuation of the proceedings without an arbitrator. Finally, Article 15 creates the rule for resumption of a hearing after replacement of an arbitrator. These provisions are the subject of this chapter.

2. Failure to Act and other Disruptions—Article 12(3)

A. Text of the 2010 UNCITRAL Rule[1]

Article 12(3) of the 2010 UNCITRAL Rules provides:

1. ... [This provision is addressed in Chapter 5]
2. ... [This provision is addressed in Chapter 5]
3. In the event that an arbitrator fails to act or in the event of the *de jure* or *de facto* impossibility of his or her performing his or her functions, the procedure in respect of the challenge of an arbitrator as provided in article 13 shall apply.

B. Commentary

(1) Drafting history of the rule and general comments

Article 12(3) provides that if an arbitrator fails to act or if there is the *de jure* or *de facto* impossibility of further performance, the challenge procedures in Article 13 will apply. This provision essentially establishes a second ground for challenge in addition to "circumstances giving rise to justifiable doubts as to arbitrator's impartiality or independence" under Article 12(1).[2]

---

[1] Corresponding Article 13(2) of the 1976 UNCITRAL Rules provides:

In the event that an arbitrator fails to act or in the event of the *de jure* or *de facto* impossibility of his performing his functions, the procedure in respect of the challenge and replacement of an arbitrator as provided in the preceding articles shall apply.

[2] See Chapter 5 on Article 12(1).

Article 12(3) is virtually identical to Article 13(2) of the 1976 UNCITRAL Rules. The Commentary on the revised draft of corresponding Article 13(2) of the 1976 UNCITRAL Rules provides the following summary of proceedings:

> ... the party who alleges that an arbitrator is incapacitated or has failed to act must notify the arbitrator concerned and the other party of this challenge. Upon receipt of this notification, the other party may agree to the removal of the challenged arbitrator or the arbitrator may decide to withdraw from his office; in all other cases, pursuant to the procedures laid down in article 11 [of the 1976 UNCITRAL Rules], the appropriate appointing authority will have to decide on the validity of the challenge made against the arbitrator. When an arbitrator loses his office on the ground of incapacity or of failure to act, regardless of whether such loss of office resulted from the agreement of the other party to the charge, the withdrawal of the arbitrator from his office, or the decision of an appointing authority, a sole arbitrator shall be replaced in accordance with the provisions of article [6] of these [1976 UNCITRAL] Rules, and a party-appointed or presiding arbitrator in accordance with the relevant provisions of Article [7 of the 1976 UNCITRAL Rules].[3]

Article 13(2) of the 1976 UNCITRAL Rules was added to the Rules to highlight the distinction between death and resignation and more ambiguous situations. Like Article 13(2) of the 1976 UNCITRAL Rules, Article 12(3) covers cases in which an arbitrator is incapacitated or has failed to act, such as when an arbitrator has simply failed to perform his duties without officially resigning.

The first issue addressed by the drafters in the debates on Article 13(2) of the 1976 UNCITRAL Rules was whether to fix a time limit to establish a case of failure to act.[4] To give the rule maximum flexibility, the Committee chose not to impose a specific time limit but to leave that issue to the authority who would decide the challenge.[5]

The drafters also spent significant time discussing whether to include the term "incapacitated" in the provision. A summary of this discussion is provided in the Report of Committee II at the Ninth Session:

> It was noted ... that the word "incapacitated" was unduly ambiguous in that it was not clear whether both physical incapacity, such as a serious illness, and legal incapacity, such as minority or insanity on the part of an arbitrator, were covered. The Committee agreed that this word should be replaced by an objective statement establishing that article [13], paragraph 2 [of the 1976 UNCITRAL Rules], extended to all circumstances that made it legally or physically impossible for an arbitrator to perform his functions.[6]

The final language of Article 13(2) of the 1976 UNCITRAL Rules, like Article 12(3) of the 2010 UNCITRAL Rules, uses the terms "*de jure* or *de facto* impossibility of performing functions."

What conduct constitutes a failure to act or a *de jure* or *de facto* impossibility of further performance? The text of Article 12(3) does not expressly address this question. However,

---

[3] *Report of the Secretary-General on the Revised Draft Set of Arbitration Rules*, UNCITRAL, 9th Session, Addendum 1 (Commentary), UN Doc A/CN.9/112/Add. 1 (1975), reprinted in (1976) VII UNCITRAL Ybk 166, 171 (Commentary on Draft Article 12(2)).

[4] *Summary Record of the 5th Meeting of the Committee of the Whole (II)*, UNCITRAL, 9th Session, UN Doc A/CN.9/9/C.2/SR.5, at 5, para 34 (1976) (Comment by Mr Jenard, Belgium).

[5] UNCITRAL, 9th Session, UN Doc A/CN.9/9/C.2/SR.5, n 4, at 5, para 35 (Comment by the Chairman).

[6] *Report of the UNCITRAL on the Work of its Ninth Session*, UN GAOR, 31st Session, Supp No 17, UN Doc A/31/17, para 70 (1976), reprinted in (1976) VII UNCITRAL Ybk 66, 71 (Commentary on Draft Article 12(2)).

when an arbitrator intends only a brief absence, it seems inappropriate to require referral to the lengthy procedure of challenge.[7] The Iran–US Claims Tribunal approached the problem by modifying corresponding Article 13(2) of the 1976 UNCITRAL Rules to provide that in the event of impossibility to perform because of temporary illness or other circumstances of a relatively short duration, the member shall not be replaced but a temporary substitute member shall be appointed.[8] In the context of *ad hoc* arbitration under the Rules, without such a mechanism for temporary substitution, whether the absence of an arbitrator requires action under Article 12(3) will depend on the specific circumstances of the case, as they are understood by the party that is prejudiced by the absence.[9]

The practice of the Iran–US Claims Tribunal, discussed in the following sections, is instructive in terms of defining where the line falls between reasonable inconvenience by an arbitrator and failure to act or impossibility of further performance. Such practice may be drawn upon in interpreting and applying the virtually identical text of Article 12(3) of the 2010 UNCITRAL Rules. The question of remedies other than the challenge procedure reference in Article 12(3) is discussed in section 3 of this chapter on Article 14.

(2) Iran–US Claims Tribunal practice with respect to an arbitrator's failure to act

The Iran–US Claims Tribunal adopted corresponding Article 13(2) of the 1976 UNCITRAL Rules, without modification to the basic rule.[10] The Tribunal confronted two incidents where arbitrators were challenged on the basis of a failure to act under Article 13(2). First, the 1984 challenge by the United States of Judges Kashani and Shafeiei was premised in part on a failure to act. Second, the Iranian government brought a challenge under Article 13(2) of the Tribunal Rules in August 1991 against a third-party arbitrator, Judge Gaetano Arangio-Ruiz.

In the first instance, the Agent for the United States argued that Judges Kashani and Shafeiei had "failed to act" when they attacked Judge Mangård. Specifically they "have repudiated basic principles of conduct governing international arbitration" and "they have refused to work with Mr. Mangård, a duly appointed member of the Tribunal entitled and obligated to perform the duties of an arbitrator."[11] The Agent continued: "By their actions, they have served notice that they will not participate further in the Tribunal

---

[7] See Letter of the Agent of the United States dated August 16, 1983 regarding the absence of Judge Sani:

It is evident that the agreement of the parties cannot be carried out if the only remedy for the willful and unjustified absence of arbitrators is challenge and replacement. This mechanism by itself cannot prevent disruption of Tribunal operations for months at a time. Under Article 7 of the Tribunal Rules, a party has 30 days to appoint a replacement party arbitrator. If the party fails to do so, the appointing authority is allowed in principle another 30 days to make such appointment. If an appointment is named, but does not act, some time must be allowed for the process of challenge. If such challenge is successful, the process of appointment begins anew. Thus, the Tribunal must be empowered to act in the interim, and cannot simply wait for a replacement to be named.

See also discussion of absence of Judge Mostafavi in *Uiterwyk Corp* (1983 Tribunal Rules) in section 2(B)(3)(b).

[8] Note that the service of the substitute member is then governed in part by Article 13(4) of the 1983 Tribunal Rules which states that "[a] substitute member appointed for a temporary period shall continue to serve with respect to any case in which he has participated in the hearing, notwithstanding the member for whom he is a substitute is again available and may work on other Tribunal cases and matters."

[9] For some examples of "failure to act" see T Webster, *Handbook of UNCITRAL Arbitration: Commentary, Precedents and Materials for UNCITRAL Based Arbitration Rules* (2010) 200–1.

[10] Additions made to the rule are discussed in section (2)B(3)(a) on substitute arbitrators.

[11] Memorandum of the Agent of the United States to the Appointing Authority supporting the Initiation of the Challenge of Judges Kashani and Shafeiei, September 17, 1984, at 13–14, reprinted in section 2(D)(1).

as presently, and lawfully, constituted."[12] Concerned that Judges Kashani and Shafeiei might apologize for the attack and argue that they were able to continue to act, the US Agent argued that:

Even if Messrs. Kashani and Shafeiei were to apologize and agree to work... [t]he conduct of Messrs. Kashani and Shafeiei demonstrates their incapacity and unfitness to perform—and hence the *de facto* impossibility of performing—their functions as arbitrators.... Article 13(2) [of the 1983 Tribunal Rules] was drafted to cover all circumstances that make it impossible for an arbitrator to perform his functions.[13]

Judges Kashani and Shafeiei were withdrawn by the Iranian government prior to a decision on the challenge by the Appointing Authority.

The second instance involved an Iranian challenge to Judge Arangio-Ruiz for failure to act and rested on essentially four allegations. First, during the preceding twelve months, Judge Arangio-Ruiz had not spent more than 40 working days at the Tribunal, only 14 of which were spent physically participating in hearings. Second, based on this limited participation, Judge Arangio-Ruiz could not have had sufficient time to read and review carefully the parties' pleadings and relevant evidence. He therefore must have relied exclusively on condensed and selected versions of pleadings and evidence prepared by a legal assistant. Third, Judge Arangio-Ruiz allegedly failed to study proposals concerning the cases brought before his Chamber and several times demonstrated he was insufficiently informed. Lastly, Judge Arangio-Ruiz's attendance at the Tribunal allegedly resulted in a sluggish adjudicating process in Chamber 3, which led to a large backlog of cases.[14]

The Agent for the United States argued in response that, in addition to the inaccuracy of Iran's allegations, the "plain meaning of 'fails to act' is inactivity, not activity of a type that one arbitrating party does not like."[15] The Agent went on to state that "the negotiating history of... the [1976] UNCITRAL Rules... confirms that the 'fails to act' provision was devised to address the case of an arbitrator who, while not formally resigning, had ceased all activity with respect to arbitral proceedings."[16] The Agent for Iran replied "that 'failure to act' is not meant to be absolute and that the level of an arbitrator's performance has to be taken into account in the light of the circumstances of every situation."[17]

The Appointing Authority agreed with Iran that "the phrase 'fails to act' also covers the situation in which an arbitrator, though not completely inactive, consciously neglects his arbitral duties in such a way that his overall conduct falls clearly below the standard of what may be reasonably expected from an arbitrator."[18] However, the appointing authority disagreed with Iran that Judge Arangio-Ruiz's conduct fell below this standard.[19]

---

[12] Memorandum, (1983 Tribunal Rules) n 11, at 16.

[13] Memorandum, (1983 Tribunal Rules) n 11, at 16–17.

[14] Letter of the Agent of Iran to the Appointing Authority initiating the Challenge of Judge Arangio-Ruiz, August 8, 1991, reprinted in 27 Iran-US CTR 293 (1991–II), also reprinted in section 2(D)(2).

[15] Letter of the Agent of the United States to the Appointing Authority regarding the Challenge by Iran of Judge Arangio-Ruiz, September 5, 1991, reprinted in 27 Iran-US CTR 312 (1991–II), also reprinted in section 2(D)(2).

[16] Letter of the Agent of the United States, n 15.

[17] Letter of the Agent of Iran to the Appointing Authority, September 17, 1991, reprinted in 27 Iran-US CTR 324–27 (1991–II), also reprinted in section 2(D)(2).

[18] Decision of the Appointing Authority on the Challenge by Iran to Judge Arangio-Ruiz, September 24, 1991, reprinted in 27 Iran-US CTR 328, 332 (1991–II), also reprinted in section 2(D)(2).

[19] Letter of Judge Arangio-Ruiz to the Appointing Authority, August 14, 1991, at 1–2, reprinted in 27 Iran-US CTR 311 (1991–II), also reprinted below, section 2(D)(2).

(3) Iran—US Claims Tribunal practice with respect to other disruptions

In addition to the mechanism of resolving an alleged failure to act or impossibility of further performance through the challenge process, the Tribunal itself had to consider remedies in the event of an arbitrator's absence from proceedings. The Tribunal essentially came to rely on two mechanisms for dealing with absences: (1) the use of substitute arbitrators to replace members in the event of temporary, justified absences, and (2) the use of truncated tribunals in the face of unjustified absences.

(a) A note on substitute arbitrators

The Iran–US Claims Tribunal anticipated that arbitrators might, for good reasons, be temporarily absent from arbitral proceedings. As a result, it modified Article 13(2) of the 1976 UNCITRAL Rules to provide that if the President of the Tribunal determined that an arbitrator's failure to act or his impossibility to perform his duties was due to a temporary illness or other circumstances of a relatively short duration, the member would not be replaced but rather a temporary substitute member would be appointed.

An example of the Tribunal's application of its modified Article 13(2) of the 1976 UNCITRAL Rules was the appointment of Mr Salans as a substitute for the American arbitrator, Charles N Brower, when he was appointed Deputy Special Counsel to President Ronald Reagan in early 1987.[20] The naming of a substitute in this case was facilitated by the fact that the Americans had taken steps under the Note to Article 13 of the 1983 Tribunal Rules to have pre-qualified substitutes available to step in if a permanent member was temporarily absent. The Iranian government had not appointed pre-qualified substitutes, a practice which guaranteed that the absence of an Iranian arbitrator would lead to disruption of Tribunal proceedings unless the Tribunal could continue to proceed on some other basis.

Article 13(3) of the 1983 Tribunal Rules provides for the replacement of the Tribunal President in the event of his temporary absence. Under this provision, the replacement shall be "the senior other member of the Tribunal not appointed by either of the two Governments." The individual so appointed shall act as President of the Tribunal and Chairman of the Full Tribunal.

In 1989, during the Iranian challenge to Judge Briner in Case No 39 and as President of the Tribunal, the Iranians alleged that Briner was acting improperly by continuing to perform his duties as President in the midst of the challenge proceedings. In a Dissent to Orders dated August 11, 1989, Judge Khalilian tried to equate the Iranian challenge to Briner with a *de jure* or *de facto* impossibility of the President's performance of his functions and called for the President to step aside and allow a replacement to perform his duties under Article 13(3).[21]

In response to the Iranian interpretation of Article 13(3), the Agent for the United States focused on the fact that nothing explicitly stated in either the 1983 Tribunal Rules or the 1976 UNCITRAL Rules requires the President or any arbitrator to relinquish his official duties in the face of a challenge. The Agent further noted that forcing an arbitrator to

---

[20] Presidential Order No 51, February 2, 1987, reprinted in 14 Iran-US CTR 353 (1987–I), partly reprinted in section 2(D)(2).

[21] Dissenting Opinion of Judge Khalilian with Respect to the Orders dated August 11, 1989 in Case Nos B1 (Claim 1), 197 and 476, August 22, 1989, reprinted in 21 Iran-US CTR 279–82 (1989–I), also reprinted in section 2(D)(3).

relinquish those duties prior to the resolution of a contested challenge would disrupt Tribunal proceedings and encourage abuse of the challenge mechanism.[22]

A challenge of the President affected the entire operations of the Tribunal in a way the challenge of an arbitrator in a particular case does not. There was significant evidence that the Iranian challenge to Judge Briner as President was made for the purpose of disrupting proceedings in significant cases. Thus if the Iranian government achieved its goal of having Judge Briner replaced, even temporarily, they would arguably have been rewarded for their attempt to disrupt the proceedings. Nevertheless, in the event of a serious challenge to the President of a multi-claim institution, and certainly the Iranian challenge was regarded by many Iranian representatives as serious, applying the replacement provision of Article 13(3) could be appropriate.

Article 13(4) of the 1983 Tribunal Rules requires that a substitute member appointed for a temporary period under Article 13(2) continue to serve as a member of the Tribunal for those cases in which he participated in a hearing on the merits. It operates like Article 13(5), discussed below, to ensure minimal disruption of the proceedings and avoid the necessity of a re-hearing upon the return of the permanent member.

This rule does not appear to have been applied specifically at the Tribunal, however. Substitute arbitrators have been assigned to cases at the Tribunal, eg, Mr Salans as substitute for Mr Brower from January to April 1987, and presumably, awards could have been rendered under the signature of a substitute who had participated in the hearing.

(b) A note on truncated proceedings

What the Iran–US Claims Tribunal perhaps did not foresee when it adopted the 1983 Tribunal Rules was that arbitrators would use unjustified absences to disrupt Tribunal proceedings, such as where arbitrators were absent for some deliberations and for the signing of awards. In these cases the proceedings had reached an advanced stage and the cases in question had already been heard and, more or less, deliberated. Because the use of the replacement procedures in Article 13 of the 1983 Tribunal Rules would have further frustrated ongoing proceedings, the Tribunal followed a practice of allowing the remaining members to proceed with the arbitration as a truncated tribunal.

Following is a description of that practice that inspired the inclusion in the 2010 UNCITRAL Rules of Article 14(2), a provision empowering the appointing authority in exceptional circumstances to appoint a substitute arbitrator or to authorize the remaining arbitrators to proceed as a truncated tribunal and make an award.[23]

The Absence of Mr Shafeiei, Summer 1983. Judge Bellet submitted his resignation in a letter to President Lagergren dated December 1, 1982. The Tribunal accepted this resignation to be effective August 1, 1983 or upon any earlier date when Judge Bellet's replacement would be available.[24] In view of the August 1, 1983 departure date, "from February to late June the three arbitrators had been in agreement that July would be fully dedicated to final deliberations in...pending cases."[25] On June 23, 1983, Judge Shafeiei in a letter to

---

[22] Letter of the Agent for the Government of the United States to Judge Briner, August 8, 1989, reprinted in 21 Iran-US CTR 351 (1989–I).

[23] For an additional example from the practice of investor–state arbitration, see *Himpurna California Energy Ltd* (1976 Rules), reprinted in section (2)C.

[24] As to this decision, see dissenting letter of Judges Kashani and Shafeiei to President Lagergren, dated January 18, 1983, and the written comments of February 3, 1983 of the American Arbitrators to President Lagergren concerning that dissenting letter.

[25] Statement of Judges Bellet and Aldrich appended to *Gruen Associates* and *Islamic Republic of Iran*, Award No 61–180–2 (July 27, 1983), reprinted in 3 Iran-US CTR 97, 108 (1983–II).

Chairman Bellet informed the Chamber that he would be on vacation until the end of July.[26] Despite the absence of Judge Shafeiei, Chamber Two dealt with the pending cases as planned, rendering Awards on Agreed Terms in Case Nos 449 and 83 and Awards in Case Nos 188 and 220. Tribunal Award No 61 in Case No 188, rendered July 27, 1983, is particularly significant because the Iranian arbitrator apparently did not participate in any deliberations concerning the case.[27] Despite this total absence following the Hearing, the Chamber nonetheless rendered its Award. Judge Aldrich later wrote: "Judge Bellet and I decided that the Chamber was justified, and in fact obligated, by international law and precedent to proceed with the awards on which we could agree... any other conclusion, in a continuing tribunal of this type with many cases on its docket, would permit the Tribunal's work to be sabotaged."[28]

(1) The absence of Mr Sani, Fall 1983

On August 10, 1983, the Agent for Iran informed the Tribunal that Judge Sani had submitted his resignation to the Government of Iran and that such resignation was effective August 10, 1983. President Lagergren declared at the 83rd Meeting of the Full Tribunal "that the Tribunal had, as yet, received no valid reasons for Mr. Sani's absence, and had not authorized that absence [and] that for the time being it would be for Chamber 3 and the Full Tribunal to determine the legal consequences of that absence in the individual cases pending before them." Chairman Mangård informed Judge Sani in a letter dated August 18 that the Chamber still regarded him as a Member, and that six cases would be finalized with Awards signed on September 2, 1983 and an additional seven cases would be finalized with Awards signed the following week. On September 2, 1983, awards were rendered by Chamber Three despite the absence of Judge Sani in Case Nos 185, 346, 124, 67 and 62. In statements attached to each award, Judges Mangård and Mosk indicated that some deliberations in each case had been held in the presence of Judge Sani "after the Hearing... and before the Tribunal's summer recess."[29]

(2) The absence of Judge Mostafavi, Spring 1988

The hearing in *Uiterwyk Corp* and *The Islamic Republic of Iran* was held on November 12 and 13, 1986 before Chamber One, with all three arbitrators of that Chamber present. These arbitrators then held three sessions of oral deliberations on various procedural issues. During the last of these sessions, however, Judge Mostafavi announced that "in view of his dissent from decisions reached by a majority of the Chamber on procedural issues, he did not wish to take part in further deliberations."[30] Judges Böckstiegel and Holtzmann informed Judge Mostafavi that the "Chamber could and would nevertheless continue the

---

[26] Statement of Judges Bellet and Aldrich, n 25. See also "Reason for Absence of Signature of Mr. Shafeiei" filed by Judge Shafeiei in Case No 449 on August 9, 1983.

[27] See Letter of Judge Shafeiei to President Lagergren, dated August 8, 1983, at 26 ("The final hearing in this case was held on May 26, 1983. This was precisely one day prior to Mr. Aldrich's departure on leave. From 27 May until the end of June Mr. George Aldrich was absent... Throughout July, I too was absent.... Naturally, then I neither attended nor played any kind of part or role in the deliberative session..."). See also the statement attached by Judges Bellet and Aldrich to the Award in Case No 188 with the statement attached to the Award in Case No 220.

[28] See "Comment of George H Aldrich" filed October 13, 1983 in Case Nos 449, 220, 83 and 188.

[29] Disputing the extent of deliberations, see the Letter of the Agent of Iran to President Lagergren, dated September 2, 1983, and alleged "testimony" of A H Hosseini cited therein.

[30] *Uiterwyk Corp* and *Islamic Republic of Iran*, Award No 375–381–1 (July 6, 1988), para 30, reprinted in 19 Iran-US CTR 107, 116 (1988–II), reprinted in section 2(D)(2).

deliberations and prepare an award notwithstanding his absence."[31] The truncated Chamber rendered a partial award in the case on July 6, 1988. The majority noted:

> The practice of the Tribunal in this respect is necessary to prevent disruption and frustration by one Member of the Tribunal's performance of its functions and is fully in accordance with recognized principles of international law. As Judge Stephen Schwebel has observed, "the weight of international authority, to which the International Court of Justice has given its support, clearly favors the authority of an international tribunal from which an arbitrator has withdrawn to render a valid award."[32]

Judge Mostafavi refused to sign. In a letter appended to the Partial Award, he explained his refusal to sign and criticized the Chamber's decision to proceed in truncated fashion. On the latter point, Judge Mostafavi wrote:

> [I]t is also clear that even if [my] refusal were found to be unjustified, the provisions of Article 13, para 2 of the [1983] Tribunal Rules will still apply to this issue. That paragraph deals with the matter directly, and provides that:
>
> In the event that an arbitrator fails to act or in the event of the *de jure* or *de facto* impossibility of his performing his functions, the procedure in respect of the challenge and replacement of an arbitrator as provided in the preceding articles shall apply.
>
> ...It will be noted that the above paragraph covers both justified and unjustified cases of refusal to perform an arbitrator's functions....[33]

In a Supplemental Opinion,[34] Judges Böckstiegel and Holtzmann responded:

> Finally, it is appropriate to comment briefly on Mr. Mostafavi's view that when he failed to act he should have been replaced pursuant to Article 13, paragraph 2 of the [1983] Tribunal Rules. That provision permits the challenge and replacement of an arbitrator "who fails to act or in the event of the *de jure* or *de facto* impossibility of his performing his functions." Article 13, paragraph 2 is not, however, the exclusive procedure for dealing with failure of an arbitrator to act. As explained in paragraph 30 of the Partial Award, the established practice of the Tribunal which is in accord with recognized international procedures, is for the majority of the arbitrators to continue their work and issue an award despite the voluntary choice of an arbitrator not to participate. In such circumstances, Article 13, paragraph 2 cannot be invoked to disrupt the orderly process of the Tribunal or to obstruct its functions. Moreover, the Tribunal is aware of no reason why it has been *de jure* or *de facto* impossible for Mr. Mostafavi to perform his functions in this Case either during the months he was still present at the Tribunal in The Hague or after his return to Iran. As noted in paragraph 30 of the Partial Award and confirmed in his letter, he acted in two other cases after his return to Iran.

Thus, the practice of all three Chambers of the Tribunal (and the President who has signed the notifications to the Escrow Agent)[35] constitutes precedent to the effect that at least after the hearing, the majority of a Chamber can continue working without the participation of a member who abstains without what the majority is ready to regard as a valid reason.

(3) *The practice of the Tribunal regarding absence from the hearing*

The Tribunal has not clearly decided whether proceedings at the stage of the hearing may continue despite the absence of an arbitrator. Generally, hearings have been postponed

---

[31] *Uiterwyk Corp* (1983 Tribunal Rules), n 30.
[32] *Uiterwyk Corp* (1983 Tribunal Rules), n 30, at 116–17.
[33] Letter of Judge Mostafavi to President Böckstiegel, dated June 3, 1988, Sections 3.1 and 3.2, reprinted in this volume, section 2(D)(2).
[34] Supplemental Opinion of Judges Böckstiegel and Holtzmann to Award No 375–381–1 (July 6, 1988), reprinted in section 2(D)(2).
[35] See Letter of Judge Shafeiei to President Lagergren, dated August 5, 1983, objecting to notification. In this regard, see also the Letter of President Lagergren to the Iranian Arbitrators, dated September 25, 1984.

when "truncation" was the only option for the Tribunal or one of its Chambers,[36] but no ruling that such a postponement is legally required has been given. Chamber Three conducted two oral proceedings in May 1985 without one party-appointed arbitrator. This cannot serve as a precedent for hearings in general, since one was limited to the taking of witness testimony and the other concerned a pre-hearing conference.

(4) The practice of the Tribunal regarding the rendering of awards despite a refusal to sign

Although a lesser included category of truncated proceedings given the precedent of the Tribunal rendering awards despite both a refusal to sign *and* absence from deliberations, it should be noted that numerous awards were rendered where an arbitrator refused to sign.[37]

(5) The practice of the Tribunal regarding the rendering of awards on agreed terms despite no participation by an arbitrator

Despite the absence and total non-participation of Judge Shafeiei in the summer of 1983, Chamber Two rendered two awards on agreed terms in Case Nos 449 and 83. Apparently, no hearing had been held in either case and neither Joint Request for an Award on Agreed Terms was filed with the Tribunal until after Judge Shafeiei had absented himself from the Tribunal. The second Award on Agreed Terms was rendered despite a strong protest by the Agent of Iran to the first.[38]

(6) The practice of the Tribunal regarding the holding of pre-hearing conference despite the absence of an arbitrator

During an absence of Judge Ansari, Chamber Three nonetheless proceeded to hold a pre-hearing conference in Case No 261 on May 17, 1985.[39] Furthermore, it appears that Chamber One had held at least one pre-hearing conference in the past where an arbitrator, without objection from the panel, absented himself.

Finally, the unjustified absence of an arbitrator in a public international arbitration between nations does not prevent the tribunal from conducting at least certain of its proceedings with a truncated panel. However, in a private international arbitration, the law of the forum may be particularly significant in determining whether the remedy of suing the resigning or absent arbitrator is exclusive or whether additional remedies such as truncated proceedings are available.

(c) **A note on resignation of an arbitrator**

The UNCITRAL Rules are silent as to the duties of the resigning arbitrator vis-à-vis the arbitral tribunal. The hidden issues surfaced, however, with the Iran–US Claims Tribunal. The several occasions the Tribunal has had to interpret Article 13(1) of the 1983 Tribunal Rules provide guidance as to the mechanics of resignation and the duties of resigning arbitrators vis-à-vis the tribunal.

The issue of abrupt resignations arose very early in the life of the Tribunal. On February 1, 1982, Judge Seyyed Hossein Enayat submitted his resignation from the Tribunal to his government, the Islamic Republic of Iran, without providing any notice to the Tribunal.

---

[36] See Dissent of Judge Mosk to Orders in Case Nos 42, 48, 60, 167, 439, filed August 26, 1983 (postponements following the absence of Judge Sani).

[37] For a more detailed discussion of an arbitrator's failure to sign the award, see Chapter 24, section 2(B)(4) on Article 34(4).

[38] See Letter of the Agent of Iran to President Lagergren, dated July 17, 1983, and received July 27, 1983.

[39] See the Chamber's Order, dated June 6, 1985, in Case No 261.

This resignation was ostensibly in protest of certain remarks allegedly made by Nils Mangård, a third-party arbitrator, the previous December.[40] According to the Iranians, the resignation was to be effective immediately. At the time of Enayat's resignation, a hearing was scheduled for March 8, 1982 by the Tribunal in Case A/1, which encompassed four issues relating to the operation of the Security Account.

Article 13(1) of the 1983 Tribunal Rules provides that in the event of resignation, a substitute arbitrator shall be appointed pursuant to the procedure applicable to the original appointment of the resigning arbitrator. In this case, Enayat was a party-appointed arbitrator. Thus, under Article 7 of the 1983 Tribunal Rules, Iran had thirty days to appoint a substitute. Only after this initial thirty days had passed could the United States request the appointing authority to appoint a substitute. Given the opportunities for delay, Enayat's resignation jeopardized the Tribunal's scheduled adjudication of a very important matter. Ultimately, but not until much discussion had ensued, the issue became moot due to the appointment by Iran of Mostafa Jahangir Sani and his timely arrival for the hearing in Case A/1. Once it became clear that a successor would arrive in timely fashion, the Tribunal accepted Enayat's resignation effective February 1, 1982, even though the resignation had not per se been submitted to the Tribunal.

It was thus not until the resignation of Judge Sani in August 1983, that the Tribunal ultimately developed a position with regard to resignations. On August 10, 1983, the Government of Iran informed the Tribunal that Judge Sani had submitted his resignation, effective immediately. Chamber Three, of which Judge Sani was a member at that time, however, had a number of completed cases awaiting only the signature of the arbitrator and a full schedule of hearings set for September. When the Iranians failed to appoint a substitute to undertake Sani's responsibilities, the Tribunal recognized that the issue of sudden and potentially disruptive resignations had to be addressed in a systematic way. Therefore, in the interests of minimizing disruption to Tribunal proceedings and yet maintaining respect for an arbitrator's right to resign, the Tribunal established the following procedures for resignations. First, the resignation must be submitted to the Tribunal, not to the party that initially appointed the arbitrator. Second, the resignation would not be effective until accepted by the Tribunal. Third, the effective date of the resignation would not necessarily be the date suggested by the resigning arbitrator, but rather one determined by the Tribunal taking into account, among other things, the date suggested by the resigning arbitrator.

In addition, the Tribunal has usually made an arbitrator's resignation effective only when a successor has been appointed and is available to take up his or her duties. In short, it is the right of an arbitrator to resign. The freedom to resign, however, is not license to do so. As with all rights, the freedom to resign finds its limits in the rights of others. Accordingly, John Crook, the Agent of the United States, wrote to President Lagergren following Sani's resignation: "we trust that proper consideration will be given to the disruption, cost and potential prejudice to Claimant's rights that will inevitably follow from a precipitous departure from the Tribunal."[41]

In essence, the Tribunal accepted Judge Sani's resignation but at a date significantly later than that given in the original resignation notice. The significance of this action was that for the period between Judge Sani's unilateral attempt to resign and the Tribunal's acceptance of that resignation, his absence from Tribunal proceedings was unjustified in the view of the

---

[40] See Iranian Assets Litigation Reports 4234 (February 19, 1982).
[41] Letter of John Crook to Gunnar Lagergren, dated August 10, 1983.

Tribunal. As discussed below, Article 14(2) of the 2010 UNCITRAL Rules empowers the appointing authority to appoint a substitute arbitrator or allow a truncated tribunal to proceed with the arbitration to conclusion. Thus, the conclusion that an arbitrator is unjustifiably absent potentially allows for one of these extraordinary remedies to be imposed.

Moreover, the law of the forum may be particularly significant as to whether the often available remedy of suing the resigning arbitrator for costs is exclusive. Municipal legal systems widely recognize limits on the right of resignation and indeed may make the arbitrator personally liable for exceeding such limits.[42] Responding more generally to the disruption involved in resignations such as Judge Sani's, the Tribunal also amended Article 13 of the 1983 Tribunal Rules by adding paragraph 5, which made resignations applicable only to future cases and not current ones.[43] The "Mosk Rule," named after Judge Mosk, the first arbitrator to which the rule applied, "was adopted to facilitate efficient proceedings by permitting an arbitrator to continue to participate in deliberations in a case he or she had heard even if he or she resigned prior to the conclusion of deliberations and to prevent arbitrators from frustrating the issuance of an award by resigning during or after deliberations."[44] As a result, arbitrators at the Tribunal are expected to

---

[42] A previous version of The Netherlands Code of Civil Procedure, for example, provided:

Arbitrators who have accepted their mandate cannot withdraw except for reasons to be approved by the Court. They are liable to compensate the damages of the parties, should they, without any justifiable reason, fail to make their award within the period of time fixed for it

Netherlands Code of Civil Procedure, Article 628 (Unofficial translation by the TMC Asser Institute—1980). Article 1029 of the New Dutch Arbitration Act provides: "An arbitrator who has accepted his mandate can at his own request, be relieved of his office by the President of the District Court for compelling reasons only." For other examples see G Born, *International Commercial Arbitration*, (2009) 1635 n 233 (Italian Code of Civil Procedure, Art. 813(2) (implying that arbitrator may resign without liability for "just cause"); Lebanese New Code of Civil Procedure, Art. 769(3) ("Once he has accepted his functions, the arbitrator cannot resign without serious grounds for doing so…"); […] Portuguese Law on Voluntary Arbitration, Art. 9(3) ("An arbitrator who, having accepted his or her functions, refuses, without justification to exercise them, shall be liable for any damages which he or she may cause.").

In a comparative study, Martin Domke wrote: the premature withdrawal of an arbitrator, more often a party-appointed one, may sometimes cause new arbitration proceedings with new expenses to the parties for which no immunity from liability exists. M Domke, "The Arbitrator's Immunity from Liability: A Comparative Survey," (1971) 3 U Toledo L Rev 99, 102. Indeed a California State appeals court permitted a cause of action in breach of contract against an arbitrator who failed to render his award in timely fashion, *Baar v Tigerman*, 140 Cal App 3d 979, 985, 189 Cal Rptr 834, 839 (1983). See also Olesen, "*Baar v. Tigerman*: An Attack on Absolute Immunity for Arbitrators!" (1985) 21 California Western L Rev 564 (1985).

In his Commentary on the 1976 UNCITRAL Arbitration Rules, Professor Sanders wrote:

The Rules do not give any indication as to the circumstances in which a resignation may be justified, and, indeed, they could hardly be expected to do so. Once the arbitrator has agreed to function, he should fulfil his task. Exceptionally there may be good reasons for not continuing, such as a heart attack. If not, an arbitrator who resigns may possibly be sued for damages (costs) consequent upon his resignation.

P Sanders, "Commentary on UNCITRAL Arbitration Rules," (1977) II Ybk Commercial Arb 172, 191. See also P Sanders, "Has the Moment Come to Revise the Arbitration Rules of UNCITRAL?" (2004) 20(3) Arb Intl 243, 262 (proposing a new provision in the UNCITRAL Rules that would empower two arbitrators to render the award when the third withdraws inappropriately).

[43] See section 2(D)(5).

[44] Decision by the Tribunal *Islamic Republic of Iran* and *United States of America*, Case Nos A3, A8, A9, A14 and B61, May 7, 2007, available at Iran Dec A3, 2007 WL 727080. See also S Baker and M Davis, *The UNCITRAL Arbitration Rules in Practice: The Experience of the Iran-United States Claims Tribunal* (1992) 69 (observing that the "Mosk Rule" provides "a common-sense rule of thumb for a resigning arbitrator in a multi-case arbitration." Baker and David also note:

Of course, the Tribunal could not realistically force an arbitrator who wishes to resign to continue deliberations in cases that may take many months or years to resolve. Nevertheless the obligation to continue may have discouraged tactical resignations by a party-appointed arbitrator. Importantly, the rule provided the Tribunal with an

continue to serve as members of the Tribunal for all cases on which they have participated in a hearing in the merits.[45]

The Article 13(5) practice of the Tribunal concerning resignations has been consistently followed by the American and third-country arbitrators, if not always by their Iranian counterparts.[46] The resignations of the American and third-country arbitrators were all submitted to the Tribunal and all recognized that a resigning arbitrator has a duty where possible to ensure an orderly transition of the work.

The history of the Tribunal has seen the death of two great scholars and arbitrators, Professor Michel Virally and Krzysztof Skubiszewski. Given that arbitrators in major international arbitrations are often senior in age due to their pre-eminence in the field, death is a possibility which the Rules must take into account. In the event of the death of an arbitrator, Article 14(1) of the UNCITRAL Rules stipulates that "a substitute arbitrator shall be appointed or chosen pursuant to the procedure provided for in articles 8 to 11 that was applicable to the appointment or choice of the arbitrator being replaced."[47]

(4) Comparison to the 1976 UNCITRAL Rules

Article 12(3) is nearly identical to Article 13(2) of the 1976 UNCITRAL Rules, save for the inclusion of feminine adjectives to reflect modern times and the omission of a reference to the general replacement procedures that in any event apply under the Rules if a claim of failure to act or impossibility of further performance is upheld. The repositioning of the rule from under the heading "Replacement of an Arbitrator" to under the heading "Disclosures by and Challenge of Arbitrators" reflects the close procedural relationship between challenges and determinations of an arbitrator's failure to act of impossibility of further performance.

C. Extracts from the Practice of Investment Tribunals

Himpurna California Energy Ltd and *Republic of Indonesia*, Final Award (October 16, 1999) (*Ad Hoc* Proceeding, 1976 UNCITRAL Rules, Concession Agreement), reprinted in (2000) XXV Ybk Commercial Arb 186, 194, 198:

> [43] Although the Republic of Indonesia's readiness to sabotage these proceedings gave rise to an extraordinary event, the Arbitral Tribunal has not found it necessary to innovate in order to

---

explicit basis on which to complete its deliberations on cases despite the absence of an arbitrator. In a normal, single-case arbitration, however, the "Mosk rule" would rarely be appropriate, since it would in effect prohibit resignation after a hearing, a situation the Rules explicitly contemplate.

S Baker and M Davis, *The UNCITRAL Arbitration Rules in Practice*, n 44, at 69–70.

[45] See in this context, *Whittaker Corp* (1983 Tribunal Rules), Dissenting Opinion of Judge Holtzmann (April 27, 1987), reprinted in 14 Iran-US CTR 271 n 2 (1987–I), also reprinted in section 2(D)(1).

[46] For a comprehensive description of the Tribunal's practice in applying the "Mosk Rule," see Attachment A (Relevant Tribunal Practice) to Decision by the Tribunal, *Islamic Republic of Iran* and *United States of America*, Cases Nos A3, A8, A9, A14 and B61, May 7, 2007, available on Westlaw at Iran Dec A3, 2007 WL 727080. For an example in which an Iranian arbitrator refused to observe the "Mosk Rule" and the Tribunal allowed his successor to participate in deliberations in place of him see *Islamic Republic of Iran* and *United States of America* (1983 Tribunal Rules), reprinted in section 2(D)(5). For other instances of application of "Mosk Rule"/Article 13(5), by the Tribunal, see other cases reprinted in section 2(D)(5), namely, *Morrison-Knudsen Pacific Ltd, Harnischfeger Corp, Sedco Inc, American Bell International Inc, Jimmie B Leach* (all 1983 Tribunal Rules).

[47] In one case, the parties agreed to allow the tribunal to proceed in truncated fashion in the event of the death of an arbitrator. See *Vito G Gallo* (1976 Rules), reprinted in section 2(C).

ensure the fulfilment of its mandate under the Terms of Appointment. The weight of well-established international authority makes clear that an arbitral tribunal has not only the right, but the obligation, to proceed when, without valid excuse, one of its members fails to act, withdraws or—although not the case here—even purports to resign.

...

[58] [The Tribunal noted the Supplemental Opinion by Judges Böckstiegel and Holtzmann in *Uiterwyk Corp. v. The Islamic Republic of Iran*, 26 Iran-U.S. C.T.R. 5 (1991–I), which concluded that Article 13(2) of the [1976] UNCITRAL Rules "is not the exclusive procedure for dealing with failure to act," and "cannot be invoked to disrupt the orderly process of the Tribunal or to obstruct its functions."]

[59] The Arbitral Tribunal concurs with that conclusion. A possible course may be to remove and replace an arbitrator who has withdrawn, if the withdrawal takes place at a sufficiently early stage that his replacement would cause only limited disruption. Such a solution is, however, manifestly inappropriate when an arbitrator withdraws at an advanced stage in the proceedings and that withdrawal is found by the Arbitral Tribunal to be without valid excuse....

...

[63] ... [Where the withdrawal of the arbitrator appointed by Indonesia] is the result of improper behaviour of agents of the Republic of Indonesia... the Republic of Indonesia should not benefit from its own wrong....

Vito G Gallo and *Government of Canada*, Procedural Order No 1 (June 4, 2008) (ICSID administered, 1976 UNCITRAL Rules, NAFTA Chapter Eleven), at 4:18:

...In the event of the death or incapacity of a member of the Arbitral Tribunal, the truncated tribunal may proceed to decide procedural matters.

D. Extracts from the Practice of the Iran–US Claims Tribunal

(1) Tribunal Rules (1983), Article 13(1)—Resignation

Whittaker Corp and *Islamic Republic of Iran*, Award No 301–286–1 (April 22, 1987), Dissenting Opinion of Judge Holtzmann (April 27, 1987), reprinted in 14 Iran-US CTR 271 n 2 (1987–I):

The majority in this case [was] the Chairman and Judge Mostafavi. [Judge] Mostafavi was the proper arbitrator to sign the Award notwithstanding the letter of resignation that he wrote to the President of the Tribunal...

Article 13 of the [1983] Tribunal Rules contemplates the possibility of the resignation of an arbitrator and establishes the procedures for appointing a successor. With respect to the resignation of J. Mostafavi, the Full Tribunal, following its previous practice, determined that (i) the resignation must be submitted to and considered by the Tribunal, (ii) the resignation is not effective until it is accepted by the Tribunal, (iii) the effective date of the resignation is not the date suggested by the resigning arbitrator, but rather a date determined by the Tribunal, and (iv) Judge Mostafavi's resignation would be effective when his successor had been appointed and was available to take up his duties. No successor had been appointed by the date on which the Award was to be signed, and, therefore, J. Mostafavi's resignation had not become effective on that date.

Finally, it is to be noted that even if J. Mostafavi's resignation had become effective by the date of the signature of the Award, he would still be the proper arbitrator to sign the award in this Case in view of Article 13, paragraph 5, of the Tribunal Rules which states that "[a]fter the effective date of a member's resignation he shall continue to serve as a member of the Tribunal with respect to all cases in which he had participated in a hearing on the merits..." This provision is not contained in the [1976] UNCITRAL Arbitration Rules on which the Tribunal Rules are based, but was added by the Tribunal in the exercise of its powers under Article II, paragraph 2 of the Claims Settlement Declaration.

(2) Tribunal Rules (1983), Article 13(2)—Failure to act

Memorandum of the Agent of the United States to the Appointing Authority supporting the Initiation of the Challenge of Judges Kashani and Shafeiei, September 17, 1984, at 13–17 (footnote numbers added):

D. Mr. Kashani's and Mr. Shafeiei's Resort to Violence and Threats Constitutes a Failure to Act Pursuant to the Tribunal Rules and Renders it *De Facto* Impossible for Them to Perform Their Functions as Arbitrators under those Rules.

Article 13(2) of the [1983] Tribunal Rules provides that an arbitrator may be challenged and replaced first if he "fails to act" or, second, "in the event of *de facto* or *de jure* impossibility of his performing his functions." The arbitrators' conduct at issue here justifies a challenge on both grounds.

Messrs. Kashani and Shafeiei have "fail[ed] to act" in two significant respects. First, by their attack and continued threats, Messrs. Kashani and Shafeiei have repudiated basic principles of conduct governing international arbitration. "To act" as an arbitrator entails action in accordance with applicable rules and basic principles of decent conduct. Messrs. Kashani and Shafeiei have renounced those principles and violated those rules. They have thus failed to act as the Rules require.

Second, they have refused to work with Mr. Mangård, a duly appointed member of the Tribunal entitled and obligated to perform the duties of an arbitrator. Each member of the Tribunal has a duty to join with every other member as necessary in deliberations, hearings and other business of the Tribunal. Nevertheless, Messrs. Kashani and Shafeiei have refused to meet with Mr. Mangård in the performance of these required duties. Instead, they have sought to drive Mr. Mangård from the Tribunal by force. Their attack and continued threats violate and abandon their responsibilities as arbitrators. They have thus both failed to act under the first portion of Article 13(2).

...

Where an arbitrator's refusal to sit paralyzes a tribunal, international law requires the removal of that arbitrator. In the Franco-Tunisian Arbitration, the Tunisian Arbitrators refused to participate in Tribunal proceedings because they believed that the convention establishing the tribunal was invalid. Because the convention required the presence of at least two Tunisians on the tribunal, the refusal of the Tunisian arbitrators to sit threatened to paralyze the tribunal. Accordingly, the tribunal removed the two Tunisians, holding that the refusal of a member of a permanent arbitral tribunal to comply with a request to sit cannot, whatever the reasons given and even if his refusal to sit paralyzes the tribunal, result in dissolving the tribunal or putting an end to its mission.[1]

The principle established by these authorities, that an arbitrator who paralyzes the tribunal by refusal to perform arbitral functions shall be removed, is embodied in [1983] Tribunal Rule 13(2). As is now indisputably clear, Messrs. Kashani and Shafeiei adamantly refuse to perform their functions as arbitrators. By their actions, they have served notice that they will not participate further in the Tribunal as presently, and lawfully, constituted. So long as they remain members, the Tribunal will remain paralyzed and its arbitral mission frustrated. Under these circumstances, international law requires, and Article 13(2) permits, their removal and replacement.

Even if Messrs. Kashani and Shafeiei were to apologize and agree to work with Mr. Mangård in some fashion, a second, independent ground for challenge under Article 13(2) is applicable. The conduct of Messrs. Kashani and Shafeiei demonstrates their incapacity and unfitness to perform—and hence *de facto* impossibility of performing—their functions as arbitrators. Arbitrators who physically attack their colleagues and make violent threats against them show a fundamental, irremediable incapacity and unfitness to function as arbitrators.[2] As the Committee Report on the [1976] UNCITRAL Arbitration Rules makes clear, Article 13(2) was drafted to cover all circumstances that make it impossible for an arbitrator to perform his functions. *See* Report of Committee II, 9th Sess. para 70 (A/CN.9/IX/CRP.1). The conduct displayed here shows such a fundamental defect in temperament and character, that it is impossible, *de facto*, for them to perform their functions as arbitrators.

[Footnote] 1. *Case re Franco Tunisian Arbitration*, [1957] Intl L. Rep. 767, 769, quoted in 12 M. Whiteman, *Digest of International Law* 1072 (1971). In this case, there was no challenge procedure available and thus the removal was by action of the tribunal. In the present case, Article 13(2) provides that a challenge is the appropriate means of removal.

[Footnote] 2. Similarly, Witenberg has observed that "l'indignité"—unworthiness or unfitness—is a basis for declaring an arbitrator's seat vacant. J. C. Witenberg, *L'Organisation Judiciaire* 45–46, paras 64–66 (1937).

Blount Bros and *Islamic Republic of Iran*, Award No 216–53–1 (March 6, 1986) at 3, reprinted in 10 Iran-US CTR 95, 96 (1986–I):

>Mr. Richard Mosk participated in the hearing and Award in this case pursuant to Article 13(2) (as amended) of the [1983] Tribunal Rules and pursuant to an agreement between the Governments of the Islamic Republic of Iran and the United States of America.

Presidential Order No 51, February 2, 1987, reprinted in 14 Iran-US CTR 353 (1987–I):

taking due account of:

— Mr. Brower's appointment as Deputy Special Counsellor to the President of the United States of which I have been notified by a letter of Mr. Brower dated January 8, 1987;

— my determination that these are circumstances "of relatively short duration" in the sense of Article 13, paragraph 2 of the [1983] Tribunal Rules;

— the letters of the Agent of the Government of the United States of America dated January 9, 1987 and January 21, 1987, which acting under the Note to Article 13 of the [1983] Tribunal Rules, had appointed Mr. Carl F. Salans as well as Richard M. Mosk as substitute for Mr. Brower in Cases 155, A21, A15 I:C, 830, A19 and 423 and that Mr. Mosk would act as substitute for Mr. Brower in Case 173;

I hereby designate Mr. Salans as member of the Tribunal to act in the Full Tribunal in Cases [see above], and Mr. Mosk to act as a member of Chamber 3 in Case 173.

Uiterwyk and *Islamic Republic of Iran*, Award No 375–381–1 (July 6, 1988), reprinted in 19 Iran-US CTR 107, 116–17 (1988–II) (footnotes omitted):

>30. Mr. Mostafavi took part in the Hearing and in three sessions of oral deliberations on various procedural issues in the Case. However, at the third session, he announced that, in view of his dissent from decisions reached by a majority of the Chamber on procedural issues, he did not wish to take part in further deliberations. The Chairman then informed Mr. Mostafavi that, in accordance with the [1983] Tribunal Rules and Tribunal practice, the Chamber could and would nevertheless continue the deliberations and prepare an Award notwithstanding his absence. Mr. Mostafavi then withdrew from further participation in the arbitration of this Case. The other two Members of the Chamber continued the deliberations and prepared the Award. This is in accordance with the established practice of the tribunal to continue its work and make awards despite the failure of one arbitrator to participate. The practice of the Tribunal in this respect is necessary to prevent disruption and frustration by one Member of the Tribunal's performance of its functions and is fully in accordance with recognized principles of international law. As Judge Stephen Schwebel has observed, "the weight of international authority, to which the International Court of Justice has given its support, clearly favors the authority of an international tribunal from which an arbitrator has withdrawn to render a valid award". During the period while the deliberations were being conducted Mr. Mostafavi submitted his resignation which in accordance with the Tribunal's usual practice was accepted by the Tribunal effective 17 July 1987, the date on which his successor was appointed and available to take up his duties. It is noteworthy that Mr. Mostafavi had voluntarily withdrawn from deliberations more than six months before his resignation as a Member of the Tribunal became effective. Notwithstanding his resignation and the appointment of his successor,

Mr. Mostafavi is a Member of the Tribunal for all purposes of this and certain other Cases pursuant to the provisions of Article 13, paragraph 5 of the [1983] Tribunal Rules.... Pursuant to this provision, after his resignation and return to Iran, Mr. Mostafavi participated in other Cases and signed Awards in those Cases. In accordance with the same provision he has been invited to sign this Award.

Uiterwyk and *Islamic Republic of Iran*, Award No 375–381–1 (July 6, 1988), Supplemental Opinion of Judges Böckstiegel and Holtzmann (July 6, 1988), reprinted in 19 Iran-US CTR 169, 170–71 (1988–II):

Finally, it is appropriate to comment briefly on Mr. Mostafavi's view that when he failed to act he should have been replaced pursuant to Article 13, paragraph 2 of the [1983] Tribunal Rules. That provision permits the challenge and replacement of an arbitrator "who fails to act or in the event of the de jure or de facto impossibility of his performing his functions." Article 13, paragraph 2 is not, however, the exclusive procedure for dealing with the failure of an arbitrator to act. As explained in paragraph 30 of the Partial Award, the established practice of the Tribunal, which is in accord with recognized international procedures is for the majority of the arbitrators to continue their work and issue an award despite the voluntary choice of an arbitrator not to participate. In such circumstances, Article 13, paragraph 2 cannot be invoked to disrupt the orderly process of the Tribunal or to obstruct its other functions.

Letter of Judge Mostafavi (June 3, 1988) regarding *Uiterwyk* and *The Islamic Republic of Iran*, Award No 375–381–1 (July 6, 1988) at 8–10, reprinted in 19 Iran-US CTR 161, 167–69 (1988–II):

3.1 As noted above, both the way you treated the facts in the Case and your unwillingness to respect recognized principles of equitable proceedings, necessarily and justifiably compelled me, by virtue of my duty to the arbitrating Parties, to refuse to participate any further in the proceedings in this Case. However, it is also clear that even if this refusal were found to be unjustified, the provisions of Article 13, paragraph 2 of the [1983] Tribunal Rules will still apply to this issue....

3.2 It will be noted that the above paragraph [text of Article 13, paragraph 2] covers both justified and unjustified cases of refusal to perform an arbitrator's functions and applies both to a current arbitrator and to an arbitrator who has resigned but is still "considered a member of the Tribunal" pursuant to Article 13, paragraph 5 of the [1983] Tribunal Rules....

4.1 I wrote in my letter of 10 April 1988, there is no way that Article 13, para 5 of the [1983] Tribunal Rules—which has been repeatedly invoked for the purpose of establishing that I am still a member of the Tribunal for the purpose of this Case—can be construed as requiring and compelling me to serve in that capacity. Furthermore, the Tribunal's records on the process whereby this paragraph was approved clearly demonstrate that the Tribunal's members were not intent on applying a dictatorial rule.... However, the more fundamental and important point which I insist be kept in mind in this connection, is that even supposing that one were to reject my abovementioned assertion—that is, supposing that Article 13, para 5 were held to be binding in this instance—all that the said paragraph will, in the end, indicate is that my resignation on 1 April 1987 did not affect those cases in which I was serving as an arbitrator at the time that I resigned, and in the hearings in which I participated before my resignation. With respect to the instant Case it is clear, first of all, that I announced my refusal to participate on 17 November 1986; and by applying the provisions of Article 13, para 2 with respect to that same date, the issue of whether to apply the rule set forth in para 5 of that same Article has been altogether extinguished. Second, and more important, Article 13, para 2 deals with an arbitrator's refusal to perform his functions; and applying Article 13, para 5 in connection with any particular case will, in the end, lead to only one conclusion—namely that notwithstanding his resignation, a resigned arbitrator is considered *an arbitrator* in respect of that particular case.

Letter of the Agent of Iran to the Appointing Authority initiating a Challenge of Judge Arangio-Ruiz, August 8, 1991, at 1, 4–5, reprinted in 27 Iran-US CTR 293–97 (1991–II):

> I am writing to you on the basis of Article 13, paragraph 2 of the Iran-United States Claims Tribunal Rules to request you to excuse Mr. Gaetano Arangio-Ruiz from his present office as a third country arbitrator to Iran-United States Claims Tribunal, if he does not voluntarily withdraw. Mr. Arangio-Ruiz now has the post of the Chairman of Chamber Three.
>
> The reason for this motion is that, as the facts described below will show, Mr. Arangio-Ruiz has failed to act as his demanding position requires. Under such circumstances, the above-referenced Provision stipulates that:
>
>> "... the procedure in respect of the challenge and replacement of an arbitrator as provided in the proceeding articles shall apply."
>
> This notice has been essentially prompted by the revelations made in Iranian Arbitrator's, Dr. Aghahosseini's Dissent to Order of 26 July 1991 in Cases Nos 44, 46, 47 and 146, *Shahim S. Ebrahimi* et al. *v. The Government of the Islamic Republic of Iran* (hereinafter Dissent to Order). This document imparts the shocking news that Mr. Arangio-Ruiz for the last 12 months has been present at the Tribunal "no more than 40 working days."
>
> ...
>
> For the above reasons, the Government of the Islamic Republic of Iran believes that Article 13(2) of the [1983] Tribunal Rules concerning an arbitrator's failure to act applies to Mr. Arangio-Ruiz's course of conduct, and thus the procedure in respect of the challenge and replacement of arbitrators provided in Articles 6–12 should be followed to remedy the situation.
>
> And wherefore copies of this letter are sent to Mr. Gaetano Arangio-Ruiz, the Chairman of Chamber Three of the Iran-United States Claims Tribunal, to the other Party (the United States of America) and other Members of the Tribunal in accordance with Article 11(2) of the [1983] Tribunal Rules.
>
> In case the other party does not agree to this application and Mr. Arangio-Ruiz does not withdraw; you, as the Appointing Authority of the Iran-United States Claims Tribunal are requested to decide upon it pursuant to Article 12(b) of the [1983] Tribunal Rules.
>
> The Government of the Islamic Republic of Iran stands ready to file briefs and evidence in support of the legal and factual grounds in this Application, and respond to any points the other Parties might take issue with, according to the schedule you will set for the exchange of memorials.

Letter of Judge Arangio-Ruiz to the Appointing Authority, August 14, 1991, at 1–2, reprinted in 27 Iran-US CTR 311 (1991–II):

> I have this honour to advise you that I consider that my conduct does not constitute a failure to act under Article 13, paragraph 2 of the [1983] Tribunal Rules.
>
> I therefore do not intend to withdraw from my office as a third country member of the Iran-United States Claims Tribunal.
>
> I am prepared to refute the allegations in the above-referenced letter of the Agent of the Government of the Islamic Republic of Iran whenever you so instruct me.
>
> I await your further instructions.

Letter and Memorandum of the Agent of the United States to the Appointing Authority regarding the Challenge by Iran of Judge Arangio-Ruiz, September 5, 1991, at 1–2, 3, 4, 6–7 (footnotes omitted), reprinted in 27 Iran-US CTR 312–23 (1991–II):

> By letter dated 8 August 1991, the Agent of the Government of the Islamic Republic of Iran has requested that you excuse Judge Arangio-Ruiz as a third country arbitrator of the Iran-United States Claims Tribunal on the ground that Judge Arangio-Ruiz has "fail[ed] to act" within the meaning of Article 13(2) of the [1983] Tribunal Rules.

Pursuant to Article 11(3) of the [1983] Tribunal Rules, the United States responds by stating unequivocally that it does not agree to Iran's application. This is not to say that the United States has changed in any way its consistent position that the Tribunal's chambers should expedite their work and that arbitrators should devote full time to their Tribunal responsibilities. This is, however, a matter which must be addressed by the Tribunal itself, and cannot be resolved by filings with the Appointing Authority.

Iran's letter does not set forth grounds for the removal of an arbitrator for failure to act within the meaning of Article 13(2). Analysis of Iran's allegations against Judge Arangio-Ruiz reveals that Iran is proceeding on the basis of a fundamentally flawed notion of the meaning of the phrase "fails to act" as used in Article 13(2). Furthermore, even if Judge Arangio-Ruiz had failed to act, which he has not, Iran has failed to acknowledge the procedures mandated by the last sentence of Article 13(2), which was added to establish a significant role for the President in such a situation.

The plain meaning of "fails to act" is inactivity, not activity of a type that one arbitrating party does not like. And, as set forth in the enclosed Memorandum of Law, the negotiating history of both the [1976] UNCITRAL Rules and the related provision of the UNCITRAL Model Law confirm that the "fails to act" provision was devised to address the case of an arbitrator who, while not formally resigning, had ceased all activity with respect to arbitral proceedings.

When an application is made to remove an arbitrator under Article 13(2), the sole relevant question is whether the arbitrator has in fact been completely inactive with respect to the arbitral tribunal for a sufficiently long period that it is appropriate to replace him. The answer would be affirmative, for example, in a situation in which an arbitrator failed entirely to attend hearings or deliberations.

There is no basis in the plain meaning or the negotiating history of Article 13(2) for an interpretation that would require or permit inquiry into the manner in which an arbitrator has performed his functions. The article does not allow considerations of whether others disagree with an arbitrator's decisions, whether others think that his working methods have been diligent, or whether he has behaved in a way that others do not approve. To the contrary, as shown in the enclosed Memorandum of Law, the negotiating history expressly rejects such an interpretation. This is not surprising because such an interpretation would violate the most basic precepts of modern arbitration practice. An arbitrator cannot be subject to review on issues such as why he has decided in a particular way or what working methods he used in reaching the decision, without ultimately undermining the principle of the independence of the arbitrator and the finality of his decisions.

Particularly in light of the plain meaning of the phrase "fails to act" in Article 13(2), Iran's letter is striking in its silence concerning the extensive activities of Chamber Three while Judge Arangio-Ruiz has been its Chairman. The activity statistics are illuminating. Since 1 January 1989, the date on which Judge Arangio-Ruiz became Chairman of Chamber Three, Chamber Three has issued a total of 36 substantive rulings in contested cases (21 awards and 15 interlocutory awards, interim awards or decisions). During the same period, Chamber Two has issued 22 (20 awards, and 2 interlocutory awards, interim awards or decisions) and Chamber One has issued 33 (27 awards and 6 interlocutory awards, interim awards or decisions).

Similar results are seen with respect to shorter periods within the overall period of Judge Arangio-Ruiz tenure.

...

Thus, for whatever period one considers, the activity statistics for Chamber Three simply do not support the allegations that the Chairman has "failed to act" within the meaning of Article 13(2).

...

Iran's allegations concerning Judge Arangio-Ruiz do not relate to whether he has "failed to act" within the meaning of Article 13(2) but rather, are criticisms of how he has acted.

...

To summarize, Iran's application to remove Judge Arangio-Ruiz is premised on a flawed interpretation of the "fails to act" phrase in Article 13(2). Analysis of objective factors easily reveals that there has been no "failure to act" within the meaning of Article 13(2). Instead, one party—Iran—disapproves of Judge Arangio-Ruiz's manner of acting and disagrees with some of the majority decisions of his Chamber. Both the plain meaning of the "fails to act" phrase and the negotiating history show that such disapproval and disagreement do not Justify an inquiry under Article 13(2), and much less the removal of Judge Arangio-Ruiz.

Accordingly, the United States requests that you summarily reject Iran's application, and allow Chamber Three to proceed apace with the important business before it.

[The accompanying memorandum follows.]

MEMORANDUM OF LAW OF THE UNITED STATES CONCERNING ARTICLE 13(2) OF THE RULES OF THE IRAN-UNITED STATES CLAIMS TRIBUNAL

Article 13(2) of the [1983] Tribunal Rules contains the entire text of Article 13(2) of the [1976] UNCITRAL Arbitration Rules plus an additional last sentence added by the Full Tribunal pursuant to its powers under Article III, paragraph 2, of the Claims Settlement Declaration.

. . .

Proper application of Article 13(2) must take into account both the first sentence, unchanged from the [1976] UNCITRAL Rules, and the last sentence, added for the purposes of the Tribunal.

The negotiating history of Article 13 of the [1976] UNCITRAL Rules reveals clearly the context in which the "failure to act" aspect of the Rule was devised. The preliminary draft of the article that, in relevant part, became Article 13 dealt only with death, incapacity or resignation of an arbitrator. The Summary of Discussion of the preliminary draft at the Eighth Session of UNCITRAL, the first session to take up the drafting of the Rules, notes the following:

> The reference in this paragraph to the "resignation" of an arbitrator was examined. It was pointed out that this term might not be sufficiently wide to cover certain situations which might arise in relation to the conduct of the arbitrator. One such situation arose *where an arbitrator did not formally resign, but simply ceased to attend the arbitral hearings, or otherwise ceased to participate in the arbitral proceedings*. It was suggested that an appropriate provision should be added for a *presumption of resignation* in such cases. Alternatively *it was suggested that the phrase "failure to act" might be added to cover this situation*. . . . It was also suggested that a provision be inserted to the effect that, where an arbitrator resigns or *ceases to act,* he must give his reasons for such action.

United Nations Commission on International Trade Law, Summary of Discussion on Preliminary Draft—Eighth Session, U.N. Doc. A/10017, para 89 (emphasis added). This reflected the views of the representative of Greece that the rule should make some provision for "informal resignation"—the situation in which an arbitrator "stopped attending the proceedings if he realized that they were proceeding unfavorably from the point of view of the party who had appointed him" and of the representative of the United Kingdom who said that "the problem most commonly encountered was . . . [the arbitrator's] failure to take any action." U.N. Doc. A/CN.9/SR.16 (1975), at 157–58. Thus, it is clear what was meant by the phrase "failure to act" at the time it was suggested for inclusion in the Article: intentional and complete non-attendance at and non-participation in arbitral proceedings.

Following the Eighth Session, the draft was revised to include a "failure to act" provision. In the Commentary on the Revised Draft, reference was made to the inclusion of a provision on replacement for "unwillingness to perform the functions of an arbitrator." United Nations Commission on International Trade Law, Commentary on Revised Draft—Considered at Ninth Session, U.N. Doc. A/CN.9/112/Add.1, para 1. In the same document, the "failure to perform the functions of an arbitrator." *Id.*, para 3.

In the discussion at the Ninth Session, the representative of Belgium stated that a time-limit for non-performance should be fixed because "otherwise it would be difficult to know at what stage an arbitrator could be judged to have 'failed to act'." The representative of the Philippines supported this view, stating that "'failure to act' would be difficult to establish if no time-limit was stipulated." The Chairman, however, was of the view that the appropriate authority would decide whether and when an arbitrator had failed to act and that "[e]stablishing a time-limit would lead to a lack of flexibility." No alteration was made in the draft. United Nations Commission on

International Trade Law, Summary of Discussion—Ninth Session. Committee II, U.N. Doc. A/CN.9/9/C.2/SR.5, at 5–6.

Accordingly, all the discussion of the drafters concerning the "failure to act" provision related solely to the question of the length of time that should elapse before complete non-participation in arbitral proceedings could be regarded as constituting a failure to act. There was absolutely no consideration of, much less adoption of, any proposal that would have endorsed the use of the provision as a test of how versus whether, an arbitrator performed his functions.

UNCITRAL revisited the subject of "failure to act" when it considered what became Article 14 of the Model Law. In the Model Law as finally adopted, the phrase was modified by the addition of the clause "without undue delay," so that the procedures set forth in that Article would be invoked.

> [i]f an arbitrator becomes *de jure* or *de facto* unable to perform his functions or for other reasons fails to act *without undue delay*…

(Emphasis added.) Because the negotiating history of the Model Law indicates that "the addition served merely to clarify the text and should not be construed as attaching to the words 'fails to act' a meaning different from the one given to the wording in the [1976] UNCITRAL Arbitration Rules" (Report of the United Nations Commission on International Trade Law on the work of its Eighteenth Session, Official Records of the General Assembly, Fortieth Session, Supplement No 17, 3–21 June 1985 (adopted 21 June 1985) ("Commission Report"), U.N. Doc. A/40/17 (21 Aug. 1985), para 139), this history is instructive in considering the meaning of Article 13(2) of the Rules.

The legislative history of the "failure to act" provision demonstrates the elements that UNCITRAL considered as the term evolved. By the Fifth Draft the wording was identical to Article 13(2) of the Arbitration Rules. Draft Text of a Model Law on International Commercial Arbitration as Adopted by the Working Group, U.N. Doc. A/CN.9/246 (Annex) (6 Mar. 1984). In connection with that Draft, the Secretariat prepared a Commentary for discussion at the next session of the Commission. In that discussion, the Commission reached somewhat different views, as reflected in its Report—and the Report is, of course, the controlling document. Recalling that, as noted above, UNCITRAL expressly stated that it intended the meaning of the Model Law on this point to be the same as in the Arbitration Rules, it is useful in understanding that meaning to analyze both the Secretariat's Commentary and the Commission's later decision, as reflected in its Report.

The Secretariat Commentary states:

> It is submitted that in judging whether an arbitrator failed to act the following considerations may be relevant: Which action was expected or required of him in the light of the arbitration agreement and the specific procedural situation? If he has not done anything in this regard, has the delay been so inordinate as to be unacceptable in the light of the circumstances, including technical difficulties and the complexity of the case? If he has done something and acted in a certain way, did his conduct fall clearly below the standard of what may reasonably be expected from an arbitrator? Amongst the factors influencing the level of expectations are the ability to function efficiently and expeditiously and any special competence or other qualifications required of the arbitrator by agreement of the parties.

Analytical Commentary on Draft Text of a Model Law on International Commercial Arbitration, Report of the Secretary-General, UN Doc A/CN.9/264 (25 Mar 1985), para 4.

Two observations are appropriate concerning the Secretariat Commentary. First, it confirms that the "fails to act" phrase is applicable in the situation where the arbitrator "has not done anything" at which point the relevant question becomes whether the resulting delay has been "unacceptable." In this regard, the Commentary does not go beyond the previous interpretation of the phrase in the [1976] UNCITRAL Rules. Second, the Commentary appears to support an interpretation of the phrase that could include a review of the performance of the arbitrator in certain circumstances—an analysis of whether he functioned "efficiently and expeditiously," whether his conduct reflected his "special competence or other qualifications." This aspect of the Commentary appears to expand upon the interpretation of the phrase as discussed in the context of the Rules, although, even in this expanded form, it is clear that the phrase would apply only where the conduct was "clearly below the standard of what may reasonably be expected from an arbitrator."

It appears that the Secretariat Commentary provoked significant discussion at the next meeting of the Commission in June 1985. A number of representatives suggested changes adding specific language relating to performance of the arbitrator. Thus, for example, the representative of Italy suggested adding specific addition of the phrase "with appropriate speed and efficiency," and the representative of India suggested "with due diligence" or "with due despatch." United Nations Commission on International Trade Law, Eighteenth Session Summary Records of the 305th to 333rd Meetings, 3–21 June 1985, U.N. Doc. A/CN.9/SR.314 (7 June 1985). The Commission's disposition of the issue is summarized in its Report:

> Another suggestion was to describe more precisely what was meant by the words "fails to act," for instance, by adding such words as "with due dispatch and with efficiency" or "with reasonable speed." It was stated in reply that the criteria of speed and efficiency, while important guidelines for the conduct of an arbitration, should not be given the appearance of constituting absolute and primary criteria for assessing the value of an arbitration. *It was pointed out that the criterion of efficiency was particularly inappropriate in the context of Article 14 since it could open the door to court (i.e. appointing authority under the Tribunal Rule) review and assessment of the substantive work of the arbitral tribunal.* There were less reservations to expressing the idea of reasonable speed, which was regarded as a concretization of the time element inherent in the term "failure to act."
>
> While considerable support was expressed for leaving the wording of Article 14 unchanged, which corresponded with the wording of Article 13(2) of the [1976] UNCITRAL Arbitration Rules, the Commission, after deliberation, was agreed that the expression "fails to act" should be qualified by such words as "with reasonable speed."

Commission Report at paras 138–9 (emphasis added).

Two points are significant concerning the Commission's actions as summarized in the Report. First, the addition of the phrase "without undue delay" to Article 14 of the Model Law, as explained by the commission Report, confirms that the phrase "failure to act" in Article 13(2) of the Rules is concerned only with the length of time that an arbitrator must fail to participate in arbitral proceedings before he may be replaced. Second, the Commission expressly rejected the efforts to expand the scope of the provision to include a requirement that the arbitrator perform his functions "efficiently" or "with due diligence." Despite some sentiment for adding such a provision, and despite the Secretariat Commentary which appeared to view some such standard as implicit in the "fails to act" phrase, the Commission refused to expand the "fails to act" provision to include considerations of the manner in which an arbitrator performs his functions. It chose, instead, to maintain the phrase solely as a limitation on complete inactivity by an arbitrator, and the resultant delay.

Even in the context of delay of the proceedings, the drafters of the Model Law showed some flexibility. As the definitive commentary on the Model Law has observed:

> The text finally adopted recognizes that some "delay" is to be expected in arbitration. That is, it does not mean that a court (i.e., appointing authority under the Tribunal Rules) is to ensure that the arbitration is proceeding in a manner that the court (i.e., appointing authority) deems to be "efficient." In fact, a proposal to add the phrase "with appropriate speed and efficiency" was specifically rejected because it might involve the courts in reviewing whether a particular procedural step—such as an extra hearing day or a request for further briefing—was necessary. *Article 14 invites review only of the question whether the arbitration is moving along, not whether the conduct of the proceedings is wise and efficacious. It is intended to catch the egregious cases and not to place a judge with a stopwatch over the shoulder of every arbitrator.*

H. Holtzmann and J. Neuhaus, *A Guide to the UNCITRAL Model Law on International Commercial Arbitration: Legislative History and Commentary* 440 (1989)(emphasis added). The same points obviously also apply in the context of Article 13(2) of the [1976] UNCITRAL Rules.

Strong policy reasons underlie UNCITRAL's refusal to make criticism of an arbitrator's efficiency or manner of working a ground for replacement under either the Rules and the Model Law. Modern arbitration practice is premised on the principle that an arbitrator cannot be challenged, and the validity of a decision cannot be questioned, based on the correctness of the arbitrator's decision on questions of facts or law. It is equally fundamental that a party cannot question the arbitrator's manner of reaching his decision. Just as the grounds for replacement must be strictly limited. To broaden the grounds for replacement to include consideration of the arbitrator's modus operandi—his working habits, his manner of conducting proceedings—in anything but an egregious case where an arbitrator fails to work at all, would be to undermine one of the foundations of contemporary arbitration.

Finally, consideration of the proper scope of Article 13(2) of the Tribunal Rules must take into account the sentence added at the end of the [1976] UNCITRAL Rule provision pursuant to Article II, paragraph 2, of the Claims Settlement Declaration. The addition bears repeating:

> In applying the principles of this paragraph, if the President, after consultation with the other members of the full Tribunal, determines that the failure of a member to act or his impossibility to perform his functions is due to a temporary illness or other circumstance expected to be of relatively short duration, the member shall not be replaced but a substitute member shall be appointed for the temporary period in accordance with the same procedures as are described in Note 5 to Articles 9–12.

This sentence modifies the [1976] UNCITRAL Rule provision as it applies to the Tribunal by specifying an important role for the President of the Tribunal when an allegation of "failure to act" is made. As modified, the Article requires the President to determine, after consultations with the other members of the Tribunal, whether a measure short of replacement of the arbitrator will solve the problem. In a case in which the President determines that the failure to act is the result of temporary illness or other circumstances that are likely to be of short duration, the Article expressly provides for a substitute arbitrator rather than a replacement. In such a case, disruption to the Tribunal is minimized. It follows that if the President were to determine, after consultation with the other members of the Full Tribunal, that the circumstances that allegedly constituted a failure to act no longer existed, the arbitrator would not be replaced.

Letter of the Agent of Iran to the Appointing Authority regarding its Challenge of Judge Arangio-Ruiz, September 17, 1991, at 1, 2–3, reprinted in 27 Iran-US CTR 324–27 (1991–II):

> The main point with which Iran has taken issue is as simple as this: whether an arbitrator who has made a full time commitment—as the United States also appears to concede—to work as an arbitrator at an arbitral tribunal seated in the Hague can be absent from the seat of the Tribunal for a year except for appearances of a few hours duration on 40 days? The irregularities which Iran has discussed with respect to Chamber Three's decisions are merely intended to show some tangible unfortunate results of Mr. Arangio-Ruiz's long absence from the Tribunal and neglect of his arbitral responsibilities. We do not argue—however the US wishes to make believe that we did—the manner in which Mr. Arangio-Ruiz has performed his functions: but rather, our point is that, he has not acted as his demanding position as the Chamber Chairman of the Iran-US Claims Tribunal requires.
>
> ...
>
> The negotiating history of Article 13(2) [of the 1976 UNCITRAL Rules] as presented by the United States is not supportive of its view that "failure to act" means complete inaction. The study of the discussions leading to the formulation of that article cannot but lead one to conclude that "failure to act" is not meant to be absolute and that the level of an arbitrator's performance has to be taken into account in the light of the circumstances of every situation. The United States itself quotes the Secretariat Commentary in a controlling document, in part, as follows:

"It is submitted that in judging whether an arbitrator failed to act the following considerations may be relevant: Which action was expected or required of him in the light of the arbitration agreement and the specific procedural situation? If he has not done anything in this regard, has the delay been so inordinate as to be unacceptable in the light of the circumstances, including technical difficulties and the complexity of the case? If he has done something and acted in a certain way, did his conduct fall clearly below the standard of what may reasonably be expected from an arbitrator? Amongst the factors influencing the level of expectations are the ability to function efficiently and expeditiously and any special competence or other qualifications required of the arbitrator by agreement of the parties." U.S. Memorandum of Law, p. 4.

And for the reasons stated in our application, Mr. Arangio-Ruiz, because of his uncontested absence of almost eleven months of a year from the seat of the Tribunal, has manifestly failed to act as expected or required of him as a Chamber Chairman.

...

[The United States] would have the absurd result that all arbitrators, party appointed and third country arbitrators alike can return to their sweet homes and ask their legal assistants to do their job. If the work of a legal assistant is as good as that of an arbitrator, there should have been no reasons for the parties to bother so much about the appointment of a right arbitrator. If a legal assistant can do everything else, there is no reason for him not to be able to replace an arbitrator at a hearing or a deliberation session.

The fact of the matter is that a legal assistant, by definition, may not be expected to do more than assist an arbitrator. He cannot practically substitute the arbitrator. The Tribunal arbitrators' power of adjudication has been delegated to them by the States parties to the Algiers Declarations and, as such, according to a settled principle of law, they cannot grant that delegated power to someone else, in the absence of a provision to the contrary. *Delegata potestas non potest delegari.*

...

The activity statistics provided by the United States to prove that not only has Mr. Arangio-Ruiz not been less active, but he has been far more productive than the Chairmen of the two other Chambers are irrelevant, misleading and erroneous.

They are irrelevant because the central point at issue is that Mr. Arangio-Ruiz has been absent from the Tribunal's seat for almost a year and thus has not sufficiently attended to his responsibilities as a Chamber's presiding arbitrator; and that, as a result, his arbitral work has been done by his legal assistants to an unacceptable measure.

Decision of the Appointing Authority on the Challenge of Judge Arangio-Ruiz, September 24, 1991 at 3–5, 7–8, reprinted in 27 Iran-US CTR 328–36 (1991–II):

B. GROUNDS OF THE REQUEST

The letter mentioned above under A sub a of the Agent of the Islamic Republic of Iran cites a number of grounds as warranting the complaint that Mr. Arangio-Ruiz failed to act within the meaning of Article 13(2) of the [1983] Tribunal Rules. These grounds may be summarized as follows:

1. during the last 12 months Mr. Arangio-Ruiz did not spend more than 40 working days at the Tribunal, 14 days of which were spent physically participating in hearings;
2. the limited time Mr. Arangio-Ruiz did spend at the Tribunal cannot have been sufficient to read carefully the parties' pleadings and to examine their evidence; therefore it must be assumed that he has been wholly depending on condensed and selective versions of those pleadings and evidence that his legal assistant chose to communicate to him;
3. Mr. Arangio-Ruiz failed to study properly the cases brought before his Chamber and several times demonstrated that he was insufficiently informed; the joinder question discussed in the dissenting opinion of Mr. Aghahosseini, mentioned above under A sub a, shows a "discernible vice" of an arbitrator's insufficient knowledge of the issues to be decided;

4. Mr. Arangio-Ruiz's rare attendance at the Tribunal accounts for the sluggish adjudicating process of Chamber Three, in which Chamber there is a comparatively large backlog of unresolved cases.

C. CONSIDERATIONS ABOUT ARTICLE 13(2) OF THE TRIBUNAL RULES

a. Text of paragraph 2 of the Article 13 of the [1976] UNCITRAL Rules:

...

In the [1983] TRIBUNAL RULES the following is added as the last sentence of paragraph 2 of Article 13 of the [1976] UNCITRAL RULES:

...

This addition does not prevent a party from making a request such as the present to the Appointing Authority, nor does it bar the reviewing of such a request by the latter. However, I share the view expressed in the letter of the Agent of the United States, dated 5 September 1991, mentioned above under A sub c, that, as a consequence of this addition, in the event that the Appointing Authority considers that an arbitrator has failed to act within the meaning of Article 13(2), the removal and replacement of that arbitrator will not be possible if the President of the Tribunal, after consultation with the other members of the Full Tribunal, determines that the failure is due to a temporary illness or other circumstance expected to be of relatively short duration.

b. The meaning of "failed to act" in Article 13(2) of the Tribunal Rules

It is clear that an arbitrator who, while not having formally resigned, has totally ceased to participate in the arbitral proceedings "fails to act" within the meaning of Article 13(2) of the [1983] Tribunal Rules.

It is also clear, in the light of the negotiating history, that the drafters of Article 13(2) of the [1976] UNCITRAL Rules were reluctant to jeopardize the independence of an arbitrator by allowing the efficiency of his working methods to be an object for review.

However, taking into account the purpose of the provision—to safeguard the regular progress of the adjudicatory process—it is reasonable to assume that the phrase "fails to act" also covers the situation in which an arbitrator, though not completely inactive, consciously neglects his arbitral duties in such a way that his overall conduct falls clearly below the standard of what may be reasonably expected from an arbitrator.

...

E. CONCLUSIONS

a. No conclusive evidence has been supplied that the complaints made against Mr. Arangio-Ruiz, mentioned above under B sub 2 to 4, are justified.

The only issue that remains to be decided by me is whether, taking into account all relevant circumstances, the limited number of days Mr. Arangio-Ruiz spent at the Tribunal, as mentioned above under B sub 1, in itself warrants the conclusion that he failed to act within the meaning of Article 13(2) of the [1983] Tribunal Rules.

It is not up to the Appointing Authority or to the President of the Tribunal to answer the question whether a more frequent presence of Mr. Arangio-Ruiz at its seat would have been desirable—and still is to be desired—in the interest of an efficient functioning of the Tribunal.

b. It should be noted: 1. that it appears to me that Mr. Arangio-Ruiz's absences from the Tribunal were not due to any unwillingness to perform his Tribunal duties properly, but in all probability can be attributed to his preference to prepare his cases not at his Tribunal office but at other places where he would not be disturbed, and that his dedication to important work outside the Tribunal demanded of him, while not prejudicing the discharge of his duties as arbitrator of the Tribunal, also required his frequent presence elsewhere than in the Hague; 2. that the absence of arbitrators and of chairmen of a Chamber of the Tribunal for substantial periods of time has not been exceptional and may have appeared to be a regular feature of the Tribunal; 3. that while it is one of the primary responsibilities of a Tribunal President to safeguard the proper functioning of the Tribunal, apparently no President of the Tribunal found sufficient reason to require a more frequent presence of Mr. Arangio-Ruiz at the Tribunal.

For these reasons I must come to the conclusion that Mr. Arangio-Ruiz has not consciously neglected his arbitral duties in such a way that his overall conduct as an arbitrator and chairman of one of the Tribunal's Chambers falls clearly below the standard of what may be reasonably expected of an arbitrator and chairman in a Tribunal such as the Iran-United States Claims Tribunal, and that therefore he cannot be said to have failed to act within the meaning of Article 13(2) of the [1983] Tribunal Rules.

(3) *Tribunal Rules (1983), Article 13(3)*

Dissenting Opinion of Judge Khalilian with Respect to the Orders, dated August 11, 1989, in Case Nos B1 (Claim 1), 197 and 476, August 22, 1989, reprinted in 21 Iran-US CTR 279 (1989–I):

I dissent to the above-mentioned orders canceling the hearings in the three captioned Cases, because of the improper procedure through which they have been issued... Having been recently challenged by the Government of the Islamic Republic of Iran, he [Briner] has obviously forfeited all competence to handle any of the Tribunal's judicial or administrative affairs including issuance of the aforementioned orders...

...

8. Nor should the fact that Mr. Briner is the Tribunal President be construed as conferring upon him the privilege of an interpretation of the Rules which is contrary to the challenge mechanism. A *de jure* or *de facto* impossibility (which may be permanent) of the presiding Member's performance of his functions, is at least a case which is obviously analogous to the president's temporary absence. For this latter case, the Rules have provided as follows:

> "In the event of the temporary absence of the President, the senior other member of the Tribunal not appointed by either of the two Governments shall act as President of the Tribunal and as Chairman at the meetings of the Full Tribunal. Article 13(3)."

This situation could have been applied in the instant case without disrupting the Tribunal's current proceedings.

(4) *Tribunal Rules (1983), Article 13(4)*

No practice is being extracted in this area.

(5) *Tribunal Rules (1983), Article 13(5)*

Amendment to Tribunal Rules, Article 13, reprinted in 7 Iran-US CTR 317 (1984–III):

Provisionally applied by decision of the Tribunal on 7 October 1983 at its 86th meeting (FTM 86, paragraph 9) and definitively adopted as an amendment to the Tribunal Rules by decision of the Tribunal on 7 March 1984 at its 90th meeting (FTM 90, paragraph 14). The following is the text as issued by the Tribunal:

Article 13 of the [1983] Tribunal Rules is amended by the addition of a new paragraph as follows: [See above section 2, paragraph 5 of Article 13 of the Tribunal Rules].

Morrison-Knudsen Pacific Ltd and *Ministry of Roads and Transportation*, Award No 143–127–3 (July 13, 1984) at 4, reprinted in 7 Iran-US CTR 54, 56 (1984–III):

Following the Hearing, the member of the Tribunal appointed by the Islamic Republic of Iran resigned. A new member was appointed. The Tribunal has hereby determined not to repeat the prior hearing (*see* Article 14 of the [1983] Tribunal Rules). As from 15 January 1984, the member appointed by the United States also resigned. Pursuant to an amendment to Article 13 of the Tribunal Rules, provisionally adopted on 7 October 1983 and definitively adopted on 7 March 1984 [Article 13, paragraph 5], the resigned member participated in the Award.

Harnischfeger Corp and *Ministry of Roads and Transport*, Award No 144–180–3 (July 13, 1984) at 4, reprinted in 7 Iran-US CTR 90, 92 (1984–III):

> Pursuant to Article 13, paragraph 5, of the [1983] Tribunal Rules, a member who had resigned after the Hearing on the merits of this claim participated in this Award.

Sedco Inc and *Islamic Republic of Iran*, Decision No DEC 64–129–3 (September 18, 1987) at 3, n 1, reprinted in 16 Iran-US CTR 282, 284 n 8 (1987–III):

> One of NIOC's allegations of procedural error contains a factual error which warrants comment, however. NIOC states that Judge Mangård was "not competent" to participate in the issuance of the Award under Article 13, paragraph 5 of the [1983] Tribunal Rules, since before his resignation from the Tribunal he had not participated in a Hearing on the merits of the Case but only in a Pre-Hearing Conference. In fact, the final Hearing in this Case was held on 21–23 June 1985, before Judge Mangård's resignation took effect on 1 July 1985.

Presidential Order No 53 (April 8, 1987), reprinted in 14 Iran-US CTR 354 (1987–I):

> Having now determined that the aforesaid circumstances expected to be of relatively short duration terminated with effect from 6 April 1987;
>
> I hereby order that, without prejudice to the application, as appropriate, of Article 13, paragraph 5 of the [1983] Tribunal Rules, Presidential Order No 51 shall cease to have effect today.

Letter of the President regarding *American Bell Intl Inc* and *Islamic Republic of Iran* (September 12, 1985), reprinted in 9 Iran-US CTR 409 (1985–II):

> Noting that Article 13, paragraph 5, constitutes a derogation from the normal composition of Chambers (Article III, paragraph 1, Claims Settlement Declaration, Article 5 and Article 13, paragraph 1 of the [1983] Tribunal Rules), and noting further that in the Full Tribunal no majority could be found either for or against the applicability of Article 13, paragraph 5, to Mr. Mangård in Case No 48, it appears to me that Article 13, paragraph 1, should be considered to prevail and that Chamber 3 in its present composition with Mr. Virally as Chairman should further deal with this case.

Dissent by Charles N Brower to the Letter of the President regarding *American Bell Intl Inc* and *Islamic Republic of Iran*, reprinted in 9 Iran-US CTR 410 (1985–II):

> Accepting arguendo the President's premise that Article 13(5) "constitutes a derogation" from the "normal composition" of Chambers..., whatever validity there might have been to the conclusion that such "derogation" not prevail was lost when Chamber Three decided in 1984 thenceforward to apply such "derogation" itself as "the normal composition" in this Case.
>
> ...Thus it is the exclusion of Judge Mangård from further proceedings in this Case (and not his inclusion) that constitutes a "derogation" from the presently established norm. Accordingly, the conclusion that an even division of opinion in the Full Tribunal leaves the status quo intact should lead to confirmation of Judge Mangård's further participation rather than its curtailment.
>
> ...The exclusion of Judge Mangård from completing this Case can mean only one of two things: Either it constitutes an interpretation of Article 13(5) at variance with that previously made by Chamber Three, in which case the previous Award would be called into question; or it means that Article 13(5) thereby is changed, presumably to make its application discretionary (which was not the Tribunal's intention in adopting it). The latter possibility would have the additional problem that a change of Article 13(5) was never discussed in the Full Tribunal, a fact which in turn would cast doubt on the character of the Tribunal deliberations if not on the validity of the amendment itself. Either result would leave the Tribunal undeservedly blemished.
>
> The only course open to the President that would not have impaired our institutional integrity would have been (1) either to note officially that the Tribunal had failed to disaffirm the application of Article 13(5) to Case No 48 by Chamber Three or (2) in the exercise of his powers under Article 31(2) to confirm such application.

Jimmie B Leach and *Islamic Republic of Iran*, Award No 440–12183–1 (October 6, 1989) at 2, para 3, reprinted in 23 Iran-US CTR 233, 234 (1989–III):

> Mr. Karl-Heinz Böckstiegel, whose resignation took effect on 15 December 1988, continued to participate in the Award in this case in accordance with Article 13, paragraph 5 of the [1983] Tribunal Rule.

Decision by the Tribunal, *Islamic Republic of Iran* and *United States of America*, Case Nos A3, A8, A9, A14 and B61, May 7, 2007:

10. The Tribunal finds that it has applied the Mosk Rule to Mr. Noori's participation in Case No B61 by its decisions of 6 November 2006 and 7 March 2007. In light of Mr. Noori's communications to the President of 13, 18, and 22 April 2007, however, the Tribunal decides that he has clearly failed to accept the financial terms fixed by the Tribunal for his participation under the Mosk Rule. The Tribunal notes that Mr. Noori has repeatedly refused to indicate his willingness to serve under the Mosk Rule on the financial terms set by the Tribunal, and, in particular, that he failed to sign and return the document sent to him by the President following the 7 March 2007 meeting of the Tribunal by mid-April 2007 as required, or, indeed, at all. Mr. Noori's refusal to comply already has forced the postponement of deliberations in Case No B61. It would be contrary to an important interest underlying the Mosk Rule – the facilitation of efficient proceedings – to continue to apply the Mosk Rule to Mr. Noori. Article 13, paragraph 5, of the Tribunal Rules of Procedure does not compel the Tribunal or the Member who has resigned to continue his or her services so long as the Tribunal is satisfied, as it is here, that such continuation does not advance the conduct of the proceedings and that the replacement of such Member does not result in undue delay in the proceedings. Accordingly, the Tribunal decides that, under the present circumstances, Mr. Noori has removed himself from application of the Mosk Rule as regards Case No B61.

11. The Tribunal wishes to add that, when it took its 6 November 2007 decision, both it and the States Parties had every reason to believe that Mr. Noori would serve fully under the Mosk Rule until the final disposition of Case No B61. Subsequently, however, as a consequence of Mr. Noori's conduct, both the Tribunal and the States Parties were confronted by a situation they thought had been excluded. The Tribunal would note in that regard that it has no power to compel compliance with the Mosk Rule, that it fixed reasonable financial terms for Mr. Noori's Mosk-Rule service in Case No B61, and that the subsequent actions of Mr. Noori himself have made unavoidable the non-application of that Rule to him in that Case. The Tribunal has acted throughout this matter entirely consistently with the Tribunal Rules of Procedure, its precedents, and practices.

II. THE COMPOSITION OF THE TRIBUNAL

12. In view of its decision with respect to the Mosk Rule as regards Case No B61, the Tribunal must decide the effect of that decision on the composition of the Tribunal for the remaining proceedings in that Case. While the United States asserts that the appropriate composition should be a truncated Tribunal of eight Members, so that all will be persons who participated in the many hearing sessions, the Tribunal decides that such a result would be both unnecessary and inconsistent with its past practice and inconsistent with the structure of the Tribunal as provided in the Algiers Declarations. In that connection, the Tribunal notes that the substantial pleadings and evidence are all available to its new Member and that all hearings, which took place over a period of some fifteen months, were transcribed and are also available to him. Those resources are and will be important for all Members. Furthermore, Mr. Oloumi Yazdi will be afforded the time he requires fully and adequately to prepare for deliberations in Case No B61. The Tribunal notes, further, that it would be open for Mr. Oloumi Yazdi at any time, should he so desire, to avail himself of Article 14 of the Tribunal Rules of Procedure. Consequently, the Tribunal decides that Mr. Oloumi Yazdi will succeed Mr. Noori for all further proceedings in Case No B61.

3. Replacement of an Arbitrator—Article 14

A. Text of the 2010 UNCITRAL Rule[48]

Article 14 of the 2010 UNCITRAL Rules provides:

1. Subject to paragraph 2, in any event where an arbitrator has to be replaced during the course of the arbitral proceedings, a substitute arbitrator shall be appointed or chosen pursuant to the procedure provided for in articles 8 to 11 that was applicable to the appointment or choice of the arbitrator being replaced. This procedure shall apply even if during the process of appointing the arbitrator to be replaced, a party had failed to exercise its right to appoint or to participate in the appointment.
2. If, at the request of a party, the appointing authority determines that, in view of the exceptional circumstances of the case, it would be justified for a party to be deprived of its right to appoint a substitute arbitrator, the appointing authority may, after giving an opportunity to the parties and the remaining arbitrators to express their views: (a) appoint the substitute arbitrator; or (b) after the closure of the hearings, authorize the other arbitrators to proceed with the arbitration and make any decision or award.

B. Commentary

Article 14 determines the consequences of an arbitrator's permanent absence from the arbitral proceedings, whether due to a failure to act or impossibility to perform, or some other disruption, such as the resignation, absence, or death of an arbitrator. Article 14(1) establishes the general rule: where an arbitrator "has to be replaced" a substitute arbitrator is appointed pursuant to the same procedures under which the arbitrator being replaced was originally appointed.[49] Article 14(2) creates an exception to the general rule which may be applied in "exceptional circumstances." Under these circumstances, the appointing authority has discretion to appoint a substitute arbitrator or approve the continuation of the proceedings to conclusion by a truncated tribunal. Article 14 reflects a significant change in approach under the UNCITRAL Rules, designed in large part to avoid a rigid categorization of arbitrator conduct that could limit the effectiveness of the Rules in addressing for example, resignations intended to disrupt the arbitral proceedings.

(1) Rationale for the revised approach: the problem of spurious resignations

Article 13(1) of the 1976 UNCITRAL Rules provided that "[i]n the event of the death or resignation of an arbitrator during the course of the proceedings" an arbitrator "shall" be replaced pursuant to the procedures originally used to make his or her appointment. The Working Group responsible for revising the Rules recognized that this original formulation

---

[48] Corresponding Article 13 of the 1976 UNCITRAL Rules provides:

1. In the event of the death or resignation of an arbitrator during the course of the arbitral proceedings, a substitute arbitrator shall be appointed or chosen pursuant to the procedure provided for in articles 6 to 9 that was applicable to the appointment or choice of the arbitrator being replaced.
2. In the event that an arbitrator fails to act or in the event of the *de jure* or *de facto* impossibility of his performing his functions, the procedure in respect of the challenge and replacement of an arbitrator as provided in the preceding articles shall apply.

[49] *Report of Working Group II (Arbitration and Conciliation) on the Work of its Forty-Ninth Session* (Vienna, September 15–19, 2008), UNCITRAL, 42nd Session, UN Doc A/CN.9/665, at 19, para 103 (2008) (describing Article 14(1) as the "general rule on replacement procedure").

might not function as effectively as possible in dealing with cases of "*mala fide* or tactical resignations of arbitrators."[50] As discussed above, prime examples of such spurious resignations were when an Iranian arbitrator resigned in order to disrupt the arbitral proceedings before the Iran–US Claims Tribunal. In that situation, the re-appointment procedures required under Article 13(1) of the 1976 UNCITRAL Rules may not be effective in preventing a party from appointing another arbitrator who would resign in bad faith at another opportune time for disrupting the proceedings again.

In the course of revising the Rules to address this problem, the Working Group considered the question of "whether the conditions for resignation of an arbitrator should be defined, in order to dissuade spurious resignations, or at least minimize their impact on the overall process."[51] There were significant doubts as to whether to answer this question in the affirmative. Under the prevailing view, any criteria for determining whether a resignation was made in bad faith would likely be "too rigid," and the better approach would be "to permit either the remaining members of the arbitral tribunal or the appointing authority to determine, by reference to the relevant facts and circumstances whether the resignation was acceptable or not."[52]

Another question considered by the Working Group was whether Article 13(1) of the 1976 UNCITRAL Rules was formulated in a way that could preclude the application of certain remedies in the face of a spurious resignation, such as the arbitral tribunal proceeding in truncated fashion. Because Article 13(1) of the 1976 UNCITRAL Rules lacked an express reference to truncated tribunals, some delegates believed that an award rendered pursuant to this unique procedure "might not be recognized under some national laws."[53] Other delegates noted that the original provision risked being interpreted as expressly precluding the use of truncated tribunals because, by its plain terms, in the event of a resignation a substitute arbitrator "shall" be chosen or appointed pursuant to the procedures originally used to choose or appoint the resigning arbitrator.[54]

These drafting issues presented difficulties for the Working Group, particularly as it recognized that two extraordinary remedies may be necessary in effectively addressing the problem of spurious resignations. First, it may be useful in some cases for the appointing authority to appoint a substitute arbitrator, thus depriving the party that initially appointed the resigning arbitrator of its right to appoint a replacement.[55] Second, in certain situations, the best solution may be for the remaining arbitrators to proceed with the arbitration

---

[50] *Report of the Working Group on Arbitration and Conciliation on the Work of its Forty-Fifth Session* (Vienna, September 11–15, 2006), UNCITRAL, 40th Session, UN Doc A/CN.9/614, at 15, para 67 (2007).

[51] UNCITRAL, 40th Session, UN Doc A/CN.9/614, n 50, at 15, para 67.

[52] UNCITRAL, 40th Session, UN Doc A/CN.9/614, n 50, at 15–16, para 69. For examples of "justifiable" reasons for resignation, see G Born, *International Commercial Arbitration*, (2009) 1636.

[53] UNCITRAL, 40th Session, UN Doc A/CN.9/614, n 50, at 16, para 73. The principle concern seemed to be that some jurisdictions imposed strict requirements on the number of arbitrators. See UNCITRAL, 40th Session, UN Doc A/CN.9/614, n 50, para 70 (noting that some national laws "prohibited even-numbered arbitral tribunals"). Some delegates favored addressing the issue concerning the validity of an award at the enforcement stage under the local arbitration law, including under Article 34 of the Model Law, if applicable, or Article V of the New York Convention. The view that gained consensus support in the Working Group, however, was that "it was desirable to provide a solution during the proceedings rather than leave the issue to be dealt with at the enforcement stage." UNCITRAL, 40th Session, UN Doc A/CN.9/614, n 50, para 73.

[54] UNCITRAL, 40th Session, UN Doc A/CN.9/614, n 50, para 73; *Settlement of Commercial Disputes: Revision of the UNCITRAL Arbitration Rules, Note by the Secretariat*, UNCITRAL, UN Doc A/CN.9/WG.II/WP.143 at 12, para 55 (2006).

[55] UNCITRAL, 40th Session, UN Doc A/CN.9/614, n 50, at 16, para 70.

in truncated fashion, "which would preserve the existence of a three-person arbitral tribunal and thus satisfy the provision found in some national laws that prohibited even-numbered arbitral tribunals...."[56]

The considerations described above resulted in substantial revisions to Article 13(1) of the 1976 UNCITRAL Rules. Article 14(1) of the 2010 UNCITRAL Rules omits the original phrase "[i]n the event of the death or resignation of an arbitrator during the course of the proceedings." Instead, the procedures originally used for an arbitrator's initial appointment apply more generally whenever an arbitrator "has to be replaced." This general rule is subject to an exception that permits, "in view of the exceptional circumstances of the case," either the appointment of a substitute arbitrator by the appointing authority or the use of a truncated tribunal in limited situations. The new Rules thus ensure greater flexibility in addressing arbitrator absences. Whereas Article 14 starts from the presumption that any replacement of an arbitrator will be addressed under the normal appointment procedures of the Rules, it also affords the appointing authority discretion to address extreme cases of arbitrator misconduct, such as spurious resignations that may significantly disrupt the arbitral proceedings.

(2) Procedures when an arbitrator "has to be replaced"—Article 14(1)

Article 14(1) establishes the "general rule on the replacement procedure" under the UNCITRAL Rules.[57] The scope of Article 14(1) is broad; it applies "in any event where an arbitrator has to be replaced during the course of the arbitral proceedings." Circumstances falling under Article 14(1) thus include a determination by the appointing authority that an arbitrator must be removed on grounds of a lack of impartiality or independence or a failure to act, and the resignation, death or permanent incapacity of an arbitrator. Whether an arbitrator has to be replaced should be an objective inquiry but, in practice, will depend on whether the party or parties with the right to appoint a replacement arbitrator agree that replacement is necessary. For example, if an arbitrator appointed by the respondent becomes absent from the proceedings for some reason, the respondent will only follow the rule of Article 14(1) if it believes the rule applies, in other words, that the arbitrator who it appointed "has to be replaced." In this sense, the Rules respect a party's right of appointment. At the same time, however, the Rules allow a party to challenge another party's assessment by bringing a complaint before the appointing authority on the basis, for example, that the respondent-appointed arbitrator has failed to act.

The replacement procedures contemplated under Article 14(1) are straightforward: where an arbitrator has to be replaced, a substitute arbitrator shall be chosen or appointed pursuant to the procedure that was applicable to the original appointment or choice of arbitrator. According to the *travaux préparatoires*: "The underlying idea for the [replacement] procedure to be followed in these cases is that the substitute arbitrator will be appointed in the same way as his predecessor."[58] Thus, if a sole arbitrator has to be replaced, the procedures in Article 8 govern, and if a party-appointed arbitrator or the presiding arbitrator has to be replaced, Article 9 procedures should be followed.[59] In the case of

---

[56] UNCITRAL, 40th Session, UN Doc A/CN.9/614, n 50, at 16, para 70.

[57] UNCITRAL, 42nd Session, UN Doc A/CN.9/665, n 49, at 19, para 103.

[58] *Report of the Secretary-General on the Preliminary Draft Set of Arbitration Rules*, UNCITRAL, 8th Session, UN Doc A/CN.9/97 (1974), reprinted in (1975) VI UNCITRAL Ybk 163, 172 (Commentary on Draft Article 11).

[59] These procedures apply even if the two party-appointed arbitrators resign, leaving only the presiding arbitrator in place. As explained in one challenge decision, this situation leaves "untouched the existence and the identity of the Arbitral Tribunal and the office of the Presiding Arbitrator." Challenge of April 15, 1993, reprinted in part in (1997) XXII Ybk Commercial Arb 222, 225.

multi-party arbitration, Article 10 applies. Finally, in all cases of replacement, the substitute arbitrator must follow the disclosure requirements of Article 11.

The last sentence of Article 14(1) provides that the procedures in Articles 8 through 11 apply, as the case may be, "even if during the process of appointing the arbitrator to be replaced, a party had failed to exercise its right to appoint or to participate in the appointment." Thus, a party's right of appointment is revived in full upon re-appointment regardless of whether it waived such rights in the course of the initial appointment.

Finally, the parties should be aware that Article 14(1) is subject to the exception established in Article 14(2). As explained in the following section, the appointing authority has discretion to derogate from the normal appointment procedures under the Rules in exceptional circumstances

(3) Replacement of an arbitrator in "exceptional circumstances"—Article 14(2)

Whereas Article 14(1) establishes the general rule on the appointment of a substitute arbitrator, Article 14(2) establishes an exception whereby the appointing authority has discretion to impose two remedies in exceptional circumstances, such as "spurious resignations" and other "obstructionist behaviour by an arbitrator."[60] First, the appointing authority may decide to appoint a substitute arbitrator itself, as opposed to the party otherwise entitled to do so under the general appointment rules. Second, the appointing authority, after the closure of the hearing, may authorize the remaining arbitrators to proceed with the arbitration as a truncated tribunal, without the appointment of a substitute arbitrator, eg, a three-member tribunal may proceed with the two remaining members.[61] These remedies are extraordinary in nature and can have serious consequences for the parties. As Article 14(2) expressly states, they operate to "deprive [a party] of its right to appoint a substitute arbitrator."

(a) Depriving a party of its right to appoint

Because of the serious consequences of applying Article 14(2),[62] the Working Group discussed at length how best to delimit the appointing authority's powers under Article 14(2).[63] Views among Working Group delegates diverged significantly even as to the basic

---

[60] The problem to be addressed by Article 14(2) was described in Working Group discussions varyingly from "spurious resignations" by arbitrators, UNCITRAL, 40th Session, UN Doc A/CN.9/614, n 50, at 15, para 67, to "mala fide or tactical resignations by arbitrators," para 67, to "obstructionist behaviour by an arbitrator," para 74.

[61] This rule is new to the 2010 Rules, though some tribunals applying the 1976 Rules have adopted express rules on proceeding in truncated fashion. See *Vito G Gallo* (1976 Rules), reprinted in section 2(C) (adopting a rule with respect to procedural matters).

[62] In Working Group discussions, the right to appoint an arbitrator was described as a "fundamental right." UNCITRAL, 42nd Session, UN Doc A/CN.9/665, n 49, at 20, para 105. The act of depriving a party of its right to appoint a substitute arbitrator was thus "a serious act." UNCITRAL, 40th Session, UN Doc A/CN.9/614, n 50, at 16, para 71.

[63] Even before the Working Group discussed the approach of imposing extraordinary measures that deprive a party of its right to appoint a substitute arbitrator, it considered other ways "to avoid spurious resignations, or at least minimize their impact on the overall arbitral process." UNCITRAL, 40th Session, UN Doc A/CN.9/614, n 50, at 15, para 67. Two options were proposed, but ultimately rejected. First, an arbitrator's resignation could be approved by the other arbitrators, which would "require an arbitrator to provide reasons for resigning and to submit to the other arbitrators' scrutiny and judgement...." Para 68. Second, the appointing authority could approve the resignation; "However it was said that the other arbitrators would be in a better position to approve or refuse such resignation as they would be aware of the circumstances and facts of the arbitral proceedings." Para 68. Yet another suggestion was to have resignation "take effect on a date decided upon by the arbitral tribunal [which] would permit arbitral tribunals to continue with the proceedings in an orderly way." *Settlement of Commercial Disputes: Revision of the UNCITRAL Arbitration Rules, Note by the Secretariat*, UNCITRAL, UN Doc A/

purpose of such an extraordinary remedy. Some delegates argued that deprivation of a party's appointment right should occur only as a "sanction in case a party or an arbitrator misbehaved."[64] The precise circumstances under which such a "sanction" should apply were heavily debated, however. Because of its severity, some believed a party's appointment right should only be curtailed to address "the faulty behaviour of a party to the arbitration."[65] Others focused more on the arbitrator's conduct, believing that "the loss of [the appointment] right should not be connected with the need to prove [a party's] collusion with the resigning arbitrator."[66] Yet another view was that deprivation of a party's appointment right should be applied not as a sanction, but simply "in a most efficient manner," even where a party's misconduct was not implicated.[67]

Views among Working Group delegates also differed on how a rule depriving a party of the right to appoint a substitute arbitrator should be drafted. Some argued for an enumerative approach according to which a party could be subject to an extraordinary remedy only after satisfying expressly enumerated conditions.[68] Proponents favored this approach because they believed it would limit the discretion of the appointing authority and thus "provide more safeguards to the parties."[69]

Achieving consensus on the enumerative approach proved to be difficult, however. An early draft of Article 14(2), for example, contained references to situations in which an arbitrator "has resigned for invalid reasons" or "refuses or fails to act."[70] While the latter description of arbitrator conduct was not problematic,[71] the former raised concerns. Opposition was expressed on the basis that the word "invalid" (before "reasons") was too vague and susceptible to divergent interpretations.[72] Other variations on this proposal also failed to gain the support of the Working Group for similar reasons.[73]

Another proposal before the Working Group sought to justify application of Article 14(2) in the more general case of an arbitrator's "improper conduct."[74] This proposal was said to cover more clearly situations of "abuse and manipulation," which the term "invalid reasons," in the context of a resignation, might not adequately capture.[75] This proposal was also unpopular because many delegates believed that use of the term "improper conduct"

CN.9/WG.II/WP.143 at 11–12, para 53 (2006) (citing the so-called "Mosk Rule" followed at the Iran–US Claims Tribunal).
[64] UNCITRAL, 42nd Session, UN Doc A/CN.9/665, n 49, at 21, para 112.
[65] UNCITRAL, 40th Session, UN Doc A/CN.9/614, n 50, at 16, para 71.
[66] UNCITRAL, 40th Session, UN Doc A/CN.9/614, n 50, at 16, para 71.
[67] UNCITRAL, 42nd Session, UN Doc A/CN.9/665, n 49, at 21, para 112.
[68] Some delegates believed that application of Article 15(2) should be "automatic or subject to conditions." UNCITRAL, 40th Session, UN Doc A/CN.9/614, n 50, at 16, para 71.
[69] UNCITRAL, 42nd Session, UN Doc A/CN.9/665, n 49, at 21, para 112.
[70] *Settlement of Commercial Disputes: Revision of the UNCITRAL Arbitration Rules, Note by the Secretariat*, UNCITRAL, UN Doc A/CN.9/WG.II/WP.145 at 19, para 55 (2006) (Draft Article 13(2)).
[71] *Report of the Working Group on Arbitration and Conciliation on the Work of its Forty-Sixth Session* (New York, February 5–9, 2007), UNCITRAL, 40th Session, UN Doc A/CN.9/619, at 22, para 108 (2007) (noting a preference for the phrase "refuses or fails to act" over the prior formulation "failing to perform his or her functions").
[72] UNCITRAL, 42nd Session, UN Doc A/CN.9/665, n 49, at 20, para 109.
[73] UNCITRAL, 42nd Session, UN Doc A/CN.9/665, n 49, at 20, para 109. Other proposals included different qualifying words in place of "invalid," such as "insufficient," "untenable," "unwarranted," "unjustified," or "objectively frivolous." Another suggestion was to include the phrase "without valid reasons," instead of "invalid reasons" in order to emphasize that "the withdrawing arbitrator should provide reasons for his or her withdrawal." Para 109. Still others proposed establishing a higher standard by including the words "manifestly" before "without valid reasons" and "in exceptional circumstances."
[74] UNCITRAL, 42nd Session, UN Doc A/CN.9/665, n 49, at 21, para 110.
[75] UNCITRAL, 42nd Session, UN Doc A/CN.9/665, n 49, at 21, para 111.

would require the appointing authority to make a "subjective assessment of the conduct of the arbitrator."[76] Thus, some feared that the proposal would "run counter to the goal of predictability and consistency in the application of the Rules, particularly where less experienced appointing authorities were involved."[77]

As support for the enumerative approach waned in the Working Group, another approach began receiving more serious consideration—one which favored a "generic description" of the situations in which a party should be deprived of its right to appoint a substitute arbitrator.[78] It was noted that the proposals under the enumerative approach (including those with references to an arbitrator who "resigns for invalid reasons" or "refuses or fails to act") failed to distinguish adequately between "situations that differed in nature."[79] Some of these situations "implied misconduct from either the parties or members of the arbitral tribunal, while others involved the arbitrator being prevented from performing his or her functions for legitimate reasons."[80] One example that seemed to defy classification was where a local court or other public authority enjoined an arbitrator from participating in the arbitral proceedings.[81] Working Group delegates thus believed a more effective approach was to afford the appointing authority greater discretion to "better delineate the cases that triggered the application of the exceptional procedure [of Article 14(2)]."[82]

Article 14(2), in its final form, clearly reflects the shift toward granting the appointing authority wider, albeit not unbounded, discretion to address the problem of an arbitrator's unjustifiable absence. In the absence of precisely defined criteria for exercising authority, the appointing authority must engage in a fact-specific inquiry to determine whether it is appropriate to intervene.[83] At the same time, the appointing authority may exercise such discretion "only in exceptional circumstances."[84] The Rules do not define the phrase "exceptional circumstances," as included in Article 14(2), leaving that interpretation to the appointing authority in evaluating the specific circumstances of a particular case.[85] The *travaux préparatoires* provide some guidance, however. Even before the Working Group had settled on a final formulation for Article 14(2),

---

[76] UNCITRAL, 42nd Session, UN Doc A/CN.9/665, n 49, at 21, para 111.

[77] UNCITRAL, 42nd Session, UN Doc A/CN.9/665, n 49, at 21, para 111. In a later proposal, the use of the term "improper conduct" was objected to on the ground that it "might be too vague a concept." UNCITRAL, 42nd Session, UN Doc A/CN.9/665, at 22, para 116. See also T Webster, *Handbook of UNCITRAL Arbitration: Commentary, Precedents and Materials for UNCITRAL Based Arbitration Rules* (2010) 233 ("to the extent possible, the Appointing Authority should consider the decision that it has rendered and that have been rendered by other Appointing Authorities as to replacement of arbitrators. There should be some attempt at consistency in deciding whether or not to replace arbitrators.").

[78] UNCITRAL, 42nd Session, UN Doc A/CN.9/665, n 49, at 21, para 111.

[79] UNCITRAL, 42nd Session, UN Doc A/CN.9/665, n 49, at 20, para 106.

[80] UNCITRAL, 42nd Session, UN Doc A/CN.9/665, n 49, at 20, para 106.

[81] UNCITRAL, 42nd Session, UN Doc A/CN.9/665, n 49, para 107.

[82] UNCITRAL, 42nd Session, UN Doc A/CN.9/665, n 49, at 20, para 106.

[83] This understanding of the appointing authority's discretion was expressed throughout Working Group discussions. UNCITRAL, 40th Session, UN Doc A/CN.9/614, n 50, at 15–16, para 69 (noting the appointing authority's discretion should be made "by reference to the relevant facts and circumstances, whether the resignation or non-performance was acceptable or not" in a particular case); para 71 (noting that "the loss of that right [of appointment of a substitute arbitrator] should be based on a fact-specific inquiry, and should not be subject to defined criteria").

[84] UNCITRAL, 42nd Session, UN Doc A/CN.9/665, n 49, at 21, para 111.

[85] The *travaux préparatoires* merely state that "a reference to 'exceptional circumstances' should be added to better qualify the conditions under which the provisions of [Article 14(2)] would apply." UNCITRAL, 42nd Session, UN Doc A/CN.9/665, n 49, at 22, para 116.

the written record describes what was the "prevailing view" among the Working Group—that Article 14(2) should apply only in "cases of improper conduct" of an arbitrator or a party.[86] Another view, however, recognized that application of Article 14(2) might still be necessary "in a variety of situations, not limited to misconduct of a party or an arbitrator."[87]

The broad language of Article 14(2) suggests that both views may be relevant to understanding the scope of the appointing authority's authority under that provision. On the one hand, "exceptional circumstances," within the meaning of Article 14(2), would likely exist in the case of demonstrable collusion between a party and an arbitrator with the aim of disrupting the arbitral proceedings. On the other hand, Article 14(2) may also apply where a local court enjoins an arbitrator or a party, or both, from participating in the arbitral proceedings.[88] Though not necessarily a situation involving improper conduct on the part of an arbitrator or a party, application of Article 14(2) may be necessary to ensure the integrity of the arbitral process.

Finally, by its own terms, Article 14(2) can only apply where a party has a "right" to appoint a substitute arbitrator in the first place. The term "right" was chosen by the Working Group over a competing proposal to include the word "opportunity."[89] In practice, Article 14(2) would apply with respect to the appointment of an absent party-appointed arbitrator or sole arbitrator, where the parties have a direct right of appointment, but not in the case of appointment of a substitute presiding arbitrator, where that right has been delegated, pursuant to Article 9, to the two party-appointed arbitrators and those arbitrators have been appointed.

(b) Procedural requirements

Important procedural constraints established in Article 14(2) ensure that the provision is applied only in exceptional circumstances.[90] First, the appointing authority may act only "at the request of a party"; it cannot act *sua sponte*. Second, the appointing authority's decision to apply Article 14(2) must be "justified," meaning that it must take into consideration not only the "exceptional circumstances of the case," but also the serious consequences of depriving a party of its right to appoint a substitute arbitrator. Third, the appointing authority must provide the parties and the remaining arbitrators, along with the absent arbitrator, the opportunity to "express their views." No practice in this regard is currently known to the authors. Nonetheless, the plain terms of Article 14(2) contemplate a

---

[86] UNCITRAL, 42nd Session, UN Doc A/CN.9/665, n 49, at 21, para 112. See also G Born, *International Commercial Arbitration*, (2009) 1589 ("Just as institutional rules validly provide that a party may waive its right to nominate a co-arbitrator, through failure to exercise or otherwise, so a party should be subject to losing its right to nominate a co-arbitrator through the nomination of someone who is obstructive or uncooperative. The counter-argument is that a truncated tribunal is a disproportionate and fundamentally unfair means of addressing a co-arbitrator's obstruction.").

[87] UNCITRAL, 42nd Session, UN Doc A/CN.9/665, n 49, at 21, para 111.

[88] For example: "The Working Group first considered the situation where an arbitrator would refuse to fail to act, and therefore would not exercise its functions, for any reason, not necessarily tainted by misconduct. The attention of the Working Group was drawn to the objective situations where the appointing authority would need to make the appointment, for example, where a court decision or another public authority enjoined an arbitrator from participating in the proceedings." UNCITRAL, 42nd Session, UN Doc A/CN.9/665, n 49, at 20, para 107.

[89] UNCITRAL, 42nd Session, UN Doc A/CN.9/665, n 49, at 22, para 116.

[90] In Working Group discussions, it was observed that "[s]afeguards should be provided ... to ensure that they would apply only in exceptional circumstances." UNCITRAL, 42nd Session, UN Doc A/CN.9/665, n 49, at 20, para 105.

decision-making process that is both considered and objective, with an emphasis on the solicitation and careful consideration of information and arguments provided by the affected parties as to whether the extraordinary procedure of the provision should be applied.

(c) Exclusivity of the discretion of the appointing authority

The discretion to apply the extraordinary remedies of Article 14(2) resides exclusively with the appointing authority. The Working Group considered whether, where an arbitrator is unjustifiably absent, the remaining arbitrators on the tribunal should possess such authority, particularly in cases in which it may be appropriate for the remaining arbitrators to proceed as a truncated tribunal.[91] Some delegates argued that such a provision would be most useful in situations in which other arbitrators on a tribunal knew an arbitrator was failing to act, but "none of the parties were aware of that fact."[92] Others pointed out, however, that to afford the remaining arbitrators exclusive authority to proceed without the replacement of their absent colleague, for example, would not provide "sufficient safeguards" for the parties "in particular in case of collusion between arbitrators."[93] Another proposal was to afford the remaining arbitrators not the power to impose a particular remedy itself, but the same right the parties would have to request action by the appointing authority.[94] None of these suggestions are reflected in the final version of Article 14(2).

An arguable consequence of the inclusion of Article 14(2) is that the tribunal is deprived of its inherent power to proceed in truncated fashion. Given that implied powers are partly justified by the necessity of their implication, the intentional lodging with the appointing authority of the decision of whether the tribunal can and should proceed in truncated tribunal thereby makes it unnecessary for the tribunal to possess such a power. We hesitate to conclude, however, that such inherent power is therefore denied because it remains possible that some set of circumstances we cannot foresee would necessitate such a power with the tribunal.

Article 14(2) does not, however, overlook the potentially important role that the remaining arbitrators may serve in the appointing authority's determination of whether to apply the extraordinary procedure of Article 14(2). As discussed, Article 14(2) requires that before deciding to take action under the provision, the appointing authority must provide "the arbitrators," meaning in this context the remaining arbitrators, an opportunity to express their views. Such an opportunity allows the remaining arbitrators to share information that may be useful to the appointing authority's decision-making process, particularly information known to the remaining arbitrators but not by the parties.

---

[91] For views in favor of involving the remaining arbitrators in the determination to apply Article 14(2), see UNCITRAL, 40th Session, UN Doc A/CN.9/619, n 71, at 22, paras 109–110.

[92] UNCITRAL, 40th Session, UN Doc A/CN.9/619, n 71, at 22, para 109.

[93] UNCITRAL, 40th Session, UN Doc A/CN.9/619, n 71, at 22, para 109.

[94] *Settlement of Commercial Disputes: Revision of the UNCITRAL Arbitration Rules, Note by the Secretariat*, UNCITRAL, UN Doc A/CN.9/WG.II/WP.147 at 19, paras 56–57 (2007) (Draft Article 13(2)). For example, a preliminary draft of Article 15(2) granted to both a party and "the arbitral tribunal" the right to apply to the appointing authority for extraordinary relief following an arbitrator absence. Some opposed this approach because they believed it could pose problems in cases in which the parties had not chosen an appointing authority. Others disagreed, arguing that such an obstacle could be readily overcome by requiring the remaining arbitrators in such cases to refer the matter to the parties, who could then designate an appointing authority. UNCITRAL, 40th Session, UN Doc A/CN.9/619, n 71, at 22, para 109.

(d) Agreement between the parties

In addition to establishing extraordinary remedies to address extreme cases of an arbitrator absence, Article 14(2) functions as an agreement between the disputing parties as to the use of that procedure. This dimension of the provision's operation was important to the Working Group, which early in its discussions considered the question of how best to ensure the validity of an award rendered pursuant to the extraordinary remedies of Article 14(2), particularly with respect to the use of a truncated tribunal.[95] In reviewing corresponding Article 13 of the 1976 UNCITRAL Rules, some delegates of the Working Group believed that because the original provision lacked an express reference to truncated tribunals, an award rendered pursuant to such a unique procedure "might not be recognized under some national laws."[96] Other delegates noted that original Article 13 risked being interpreted as expressly precluding the use of truncated tribunals because, by its plain terms, the procedures for appointment of a substitute arbitrator under the Rules "shall" apply to the appointment of a substitute arbitrator in all situations.[97]

Article 14(2) squarely addresses the principal concerns of the Working Group regarding original Article 13. Both possible extraordinary measures—direct appointment by the appointing authority and the use of a truncated tribunal—are expressly referenced in the revised rule. Application of these measures is regulated by the various conditions on the appointing authority's authority described above, thus creating defined procedural parameters to which the disputing parties have agreed in adopting the Rules. With respect to the use of truncated tribunals, in particular, an additional temporal requirement applies: the appointing authority is further constrained by only having authority to authorize the use of a truncated tribunal "after closure of the hearings."[98] Article 14(2) represents the consent of the parties to applying such remedies in certain situations, which may serve to limit the potential grounds for challenging the validity of an award before local courts on the basis of procedural irregularity.[99]

The Working Group's revisions bring the UNCITRAL Rules in line with the procedural rules of the leading arbitral institutions.[100]

---

[95] *Settlement of Commercial Disputes: Revision of the UNCITRAL Arbitration Rules, Note by the Secretariat*, UNCITRAL, UN Doc A/CN.9/WG.II/WP.143 at 12, para 56 (2006).

[96] UNCITRAL, 40th Session, UN Doc A/CN.9/614, n 50, at 16, para 73.

[97] UNCITRAL, 40th Session, UN Doc A/CN.9/614, n 50, at 16, para 73; *Settlement of Commercial Disputes: Revision of the UNCITRAL Arbitration Rules, Note by the Secretariat*, UNCITRAL, UN Doc A/CN.9/WG.II/WP.143 at 12, para 55 (2006). See also n 48, for the text of the 1976 Rule.

[98] The inclusion of this requirement was a response to Working Group delegates who believed that the unique mechanism of a truncated tribunal should apply "within strict time limits." UNCITRAL, 42nd Session, UN Doc A/CN.9/665, n 49, at 22, para 114. See T Webster, *Handbook of UNCITRAL Arbitration: Commentary, Precedents and Materials for UNCITRAL Based Arbitration Rules* (2010) 234 ("an Appointing Authority may therefore only act if the Tribunal has either expressly or by implication declared that the hearings are closed.... If the deliberations have not yet occurred, then the party whose nominee is not replaced will be at a disadvantage and the Tribunal may not have the benefit of a balanced discussion of the issues.").

[99] See N Blackaby and C Partasides with A Redfern and M Hunter, *Redfern and Hunter on International Arbitration*, (5th edn 2009) 290 ("So far as the UNCITRAL Rules are concerned, there is thus respectable authority supporting the legitimacy of a truncated tribunal's decision to proceed and render an award where appropriate.... It seems clear that the option of proceeding as a truncated tribunal, rather than as a reconstituted full tribunal, will remain as an exceptional measure to be adopted only where the arbitration is nearing its end and where there is clear evidence that the arbitrator concerned, voluntarily or involuntarily, has been associated with an abuse of the process.").

[100] Regarding discretion for whether to follow the original nominating process, compare to the 1998 LCIA Rules, art 11.1; and the 2010 AAA Rules, art 10. Regarding truncated tribunals, compare to the 2010 AAA Rules, art 11; and the 2012 Swiss Rules, art 13(2).

(4) Comparison to the 1976 UNCITRAL Rules

While retaining the basic procedure for replacement of an arbitrator, Article 14 represents a significant departure from the approach of its predecessor Article 13 of the 1976 UNCITRAL Rules, particularly in the treatment of arbitrator conduct that leads to his or her unjustified absence.

The preliminary draft of Article 13(1) of the 1976 UNCITRAL Rules covered replacement procedures for the incapacity of an arbitrator as well as death and resignation. There were two main points of discussion on the Preliminary Draft of the 1976 UNCITRAL Rules. The first was whether the term "resignation" was sufficiently broad to cover situations which were more accurately described as "failures to act." This included, for example, when an arbitrator did not resign, but simply ceased to attend the arbitral hearings, or otherwise ceased to participate in the proceedings.[101] The second addressed how the term "incapacity" was to be defined and what authority would decide when an arbitrator was incapacitated.[102]

To clearly distinguish situations that were perceived to be relatively unambiguous, like death and resignation, from those situations requiring some additional, objective evaluation of the circumstances, the drafters created a separate paragraph (Article 13(2) of the 1976 UNCITRAL Rules) for failure to act and incapacity.[103] In order to replace a member under Article 13(2) of the 1976 UNCITRAL Rules, there first would have to be a challenge proceeding as described in Articles 10–12 of the 1976 UNCITRAL Rules. Once it was established that Article 13(1) of the 1976 UNCITRAL Rules would address only the issue of replacing an arbitrator in the event of death or resignation, discussion at the Ninth Session focused on whether the Rules should require an arbitrator to either provide good reasons for his resignation or to risk the possibility of liability for damages.[104] The Committee decided not to require a statement of reasons: "Even if the reasons for resigning were unsatisfactory, it would be difficult to oblige an arbitrator to fulfill his functions, since the arbitration rules constituted nothing more than a private agreement between two parties."[105]

Article 14, in contrast, eliminates the references to "death or resignation" in Article 13(1) of the 1976 UNCITRAL Rules. As described above, concerns that the general replacement procedures of the Rules may be suited in all cases of resignation, such as spurious resignations designed to disrupt the arbitral proceedings, prompted the change in approach. Under the revised rule, the general replacement procedures under the Rules apply whenever an arbitrator "has to be replaced," but the extraordinary remedies of Article 14(2) may apply to arbitrator absences that give rise to "exceptional circumstances." Article 14(2) thus fills an important procedural gap under the Rules. Under the 1976 UNCITRAL Rules, no procedure exists to address an unjustified arbitrator absence most effectively, giving rise to two threshold questions: does the Tribunal have the *power* to continue its proceedings despite the absence of the arbitrator and, if so empowered, is it

---

[101] *Report of the UNCITRAL*, 8th Session, Summary of Discussion of the Preliminary Draft, UN Doc A/10017, para 89 (1975), reprinted in (1975) VI UNCITRAL Ybk 24, 34.
[102] *Report of the UNCITRAL*, 8th Session, n 101, paras 90–91.
[103] *Report of the UNCITRAL*, 8th Session, n 101, paras 90–91.
[104] *Summary Record of the 5th Meeting of the Committee of the Whole (II)*, UNCITRAL, 9th Session, UN Doc A/CN.9/9/C.2/SR.5, at 5, para 31 (1976) (Comment by Mr Mantilla-Molina, Mexico).
[105] UNCITRAL, 9th Session, UN Doc A/CN.9/9/C.2/SR.5, n 104, para 32 (Comment by the Chairman).

appropriate to so proceed?[106] The question of appropriateness will often, but not always, include a determination of whether the absence is justified.

Whether a tribunal applying the 1976 UNCITRAL Rules should continue with its proceedings despite an absence depends in part on when the absence occurs. On the one hand, it may be appropriate to continue in truncated fashion when the absence occurs during deliberations.[107] On the other hand, it may be inappropriate to do so when a lengthy absence occurs early in arbitration.[108] In such a case application of Article 13(2) of the 1976 UNCITRAL Rules on the basis of failure to act would be more appropriate. But even in such early stages, it may be appropriate to continue through a brief absence. Because absence can take many forms, only the two most difficult cases are addressed here: absence from deliberations and absence from the hearing.[109]

(a) The express power to proceed

One *ad hoc* tribunal applying the 1976 UNCITRAL Rules has held that "an arbitral tribunal has not only the right, but the obligation, to proceed when, without valid excuse, one of its members fails to act, withdraws or . . . even purports to resign."[110] What is the source of such a power to proceed? An examination of a tribunal's power to do any act must begin with an examination of the agreement of the parties expressed in the compromissory clause.

The 1976 UNCITRAL Rules do not specifically address the problem of absence of an arbitrator.[111] Article 15(1), however, provides some basis for the Tribunal to proceed:

Subject to these Rules, the arbitral tribunal may conduct the arbitration in such manner as it considers appropriate, provided that the Parties are treated with equality and that at any stage of the proceedings each Party is given a full opportunity of presenting his case.

The issue is whether it may be "appropriate" for a tribunal to proceed in truncated fashion when an unjustified absence occurs. Such a possibility of truncated proceedings obviously would have to be applied "with equality" to both parties.

The agreement of the parties must be examined for both an express grant of a power and a clear denial of such a power. In the case of the Iran–US Claims Tribunal, the Agent for Iran, for example, repeatedly argued that the provision of Article III(1) of the Claims

---

[106] In addition to the discussion in the text, see S Schwebel, *International Arbitration: Three Salient Problems* (1987) 144–296.
[107] See *Himpurna California Energy Ltd* (1976 Rules), para 59, reprinted in section 2(C).
[108] *Himpurna California Energy Ltd* (1976 Rules), para 5, reprinted in section 2(C).
[109] See Chapter 24, section 2(B)(4) on Article 34(4) for discussion of an arbitrator's failure to sign the award.
[110] *Himpurna California Energy Ltd* (1976 Rules), para 43, reprinted in section 2(C).
[111] Nor were the UNCITRAL Rules modified by the Tribunal in anticipation of such absence. Article III(2) of the Claims Settlement Declaration provides that "the Tribunal shall conduct its business in accordance with the arbitration rules of [UNCITRAL] except to the extent modified by the Parties or by the Tribunal to ensure that this Agreement can be carried out."

The circumstances presented by absence arguably threaten the Tribunal's ability to carry out the provisions of the Claims Settlement Declaration. The Tribunal's express power "to ensure that this agreement can be carried out" is limited only by the requirements of good faith and reasonableness in the determination of what measures are appropriate to ensure the carrying out of the Declaration. It would seem well within the reasonable exercise of this express power for the Tribunal to modify its Rules to provide that the Full Tribunal or the Chambers may proceed with a hearing despite the absence of one of the Members when such absence is unjustified. Such a modification was perhaps not originally made because such absences were not foreseen as likely to occur or because the Tribunal did not desire to commit a great deal of its energy and time to passing a rule which might never be needed.

Settlement Declaration, which states that "[c]laims may be decided by the Full Tribunal or by a panel of three members," established a quorum requirement that renders any proceedings in the absence of an arbitrator legally invalid.[112] The Tribunal interpreted this provision, however, as merely definitional and not as establishing a quorum rule. It was thus not viewed by the Tribunal as a limitation on the power of the Tribunal to proceed in truncated fashion.

Although the language of Article 15(1) of the 1976 UNCITRAL Rules arguably grants a tribunal broad discretion to carry out the arbitration agreement, it can also be argued that the option open to the parties under Article 13(2) of the 1976 UNCITRAL Rules is to raise a challenge to the arbitrator failing to act, not the demand that the tribunal proceed in truncated form. However, it may be a mistake to assume that by expressly providing a mechanism that does not permit a tribunal to resolve the problem presented, the Rules necessarily preclude a tribunal from resorting to its general powers to devise a mechanism that could do so. An arbitration agreement or a set of procedural rules cannot take up in express terms every conceivable problem that may be confronted. Many eventualities are simply too remote to provide for in an arbitration agreement.

For example, in the *Cauca Company* case, differences between a private company and the Government of Colombia were submitted to arbitration pursuant to an agreement which allowed the Arbitral Commission a maximum of 210 days in which to render its award. After the Commission had heard the case and deliberated almost to the point of signing an award, 203 days into the Commission's existence, the Colombian commissioner announced his resignation. The *compromis* provided a procedure through which the resigned arbitrator could have been replaced. However, this express procedure, while applicable, was problematic in view of the short time remaining before the termination of the Commission's mandate. The two remaining commissioners determined that the action of the Colombian commissioner was a bad-faith maneuver to paralyze the commission; they therefore decided to render an award despite the absence of their colleague and without awaiting a replacement. The Government of Colombia attacked this award in the federal courts of the United States. The US Supreme Court, upholding the Commission's decision to proceed in truncated form, observed that the short time remaining to the Commission rendered the expressly provided replacement procedure all but useless: "Manifestly it was possible, if not certain, that [the Commission's] only way of saving the proceedings from coming to naught was to ignore the communication and to proceed to the award. This it did."[113] The Court therefore endorsed the Commission's action, taken in spite of an express provision that, while applicable, was ineffectual in the face of a fraudulent attempt to undercut the arbitral process.

In the case of the 1976 UNCITRAL Rules, Article 13(1) deals with replacement of an arbitrator in "the event of the death or resignation of an arbitrator during the course of the arbitral proceedings." In the case under consideration, however, an arbitrator does not tender a resignation but merely absents himself.

Article 13(2) of the 1976 UNCITRAL Rules provides that if an arbitrator fails to act or if there is the *de jure* or *de facto* impossibility of further performance, the challenge and

---

[112] See Letter of the Agent of Iran in Case No 129, filed May 31, 1985, Letter of the Agent of Iran to the President of the Tribunal, dated July 17, 1983, and received July 27, 1983, regarding an Award on Agreed Terms in Case No 449; Letter of the Agent of Iran to the President of the Tribunal, dated September 1, 1983.

[113] *Colombia v Cauca Co*, 290 US 524, 527–28 (1903) (Holmes, J).

replacement procedures outlined earlier will apply. But when an arbitrator intends only a brief absence, it seems inappropriate to require referral to the lengthy procedure of challenge.[114] Indeed, the Iran–US Claims Tribunal modified Article 13(2) to provide also that in the event of impossibility to perform because of temporary illness or other circumstances of a relatively short duration, the member shall not be replaced but a temporary substitute member shall be appointed.[115]

If an absence from a hearing occurs without notice, the Iran–US Claims Tribunal, as a practical matter, could not invoke the substitute provision provided for in Article 13(2) and still continue with the hearing as scheduled. If several days' flexibility exists in the holding of the hearing, then the Tribunal could have provided the Government of Iran an opportunity to designate a substitute arbitrator. But since Iran, as noted above, did not appoint substitute arbitrators to stand by, the substitution process could not work because there was not a means to arrange for timely disclosure of possible conflicts.

Moreover, in cases where a party is a state, the arbitrator involved may not wish to absent himself but may be required to do so at the order of his government. In the *Himpurna* arbitration, for example, the arbitrator appointed by the Republic of Indonesia went missing during an advanced stage of the proceedings. After rather extraordinary first-hand attempts to locate the arbitrator,[116] the remaining members of the tribunal concluded that the missing arbitrator's absence was the result of an "involuntary departure."[117]

It would be extremely unfortunate if, in such circumstances, a challenge of the state's arbitrator were the only means of addressing the situation. Such a remedy punishes the arbitrator and not the government that ordered the absence. As the *Himpurna* Tribunal rightly concluded, the state party causing the withdrawal "should not benefit from its own wrong."[118] Accordingly, to proceed in truncated fashion offers the only real deterrence to the offending government. Assuming the government has no concern for its arbitrators, the remedy of challenge would only encourage the offending government inasmuch as it further obstructs the proceedings of a tribunal.

(b) The inherent power to proceed

Inherent powers have been characterized as powers necessary to fulfill the objective intentions of the parties. The principles of effectiveness and good faith appear to be applicable whenever the question arises as to whether an agreement to arbitrate should be interpreted as impliedly granting some power necessary for the tribunal to carry out its task in the face of behavior which is, in essence, a threat to the original agreement to submit to arbitration.

The arbitral literature refers to the inherent power of a tribunal to deliberate and to render a judgment despite the absence of one or more arbitrators, when such absence is

---

[114] See Letter of the Agent of the United States dated August 16, 1983, n 7, regarding the absence of Judge Sani.

[115] Note that the service of the substitute member is then governed in part by Article 13(4) of the 1983 Tribunal Rules which states that "[a] substitute member appointed for a temporary period shall continue to serve with respect to any case in which he has participated in the hearing, notwithstanding the member for whom he is a substitute is again available and may work on other Tribunal cases and matters."

[116] The events surrounding the departure are contained in the arbitral tribunal's interim award of September 26, 1999, reprinted in (2000) XXV Ybk Commercial Arb 109, 154–65.

[117] *Himpurna California Energy Ltd* and *Republic of Indonesia*, Final Award (October 16, 1999), at para 26 (*Ad Hoc* Proceeding, 1976 UNCITRAL Rules, Concession Agreement), reprinted in (2000) XXV Ybk Commercial Arb 186, 191.

[118] *Himpurna California Energy Ltd* (1976 Rules), para 63, reprinted in section 2(C).

attributable to a bad-faith attempt to paralyze the tribunal.[119] Lalive observes that this power must be implied from the *compromis*. Specifically, the principles of effectiveness and good faith require the *compromis* to be interpreted as impliedly granting the powers necessary for the tribunal to carry out its task in the face of one party's attempt to frustrate it:

> C'est bien ce principe de l'effectivité qui, en définitive, avec celui de la *bonne foi*, commande d'interpréter l'accord de l'arbitrage en ce sens que le retrait de l'Arbitre, sur la pression ou les ordres d'une Partie, n'empêche pas le tribunal de poursuivre sa tâche et de rendre une sentence obligatoire.[120]

4. Repetition of Hearings in the Event of Replacement of an Arbitrator—Article 15

A. Text of the 2010 UNCITRAL Rule[121]

Article 15 of the 2010 UNCITRAL Rules provides:

> If an arbitrator is replaced, the proceedings shall resume at the stage where the arbitrator who was replaced ceased to perform his or her functions, unless the arbitral tribunal decides otherwise.

B. Commentary

(1) General comments

Article 15 sets forth the procedural rule for continuation of the arbitral proceedings once an arbitrator has been replaced. When revising the UNCITRAL Rules, the Working Group considered two related proposals to modify corresponding Article 14 of the 1976 UNCITRAL Rules. The first proposal was to grant the arbitral tribunal "the power to decide whether or not to repeat a hearing when the sole or presiding arbitrator [i]s replaced,"[122] thereby reversing the rule contained in original Article 14. Under that article, the tribunal had discretion to repeat prior hearings where a party-appointed arbitrator was replaced, but was required to repeat a hearing upon replacement of the sole or presiding arbitrator.

The second proposal considered by the Working Group was to include a general rule that "the proceedings should resume at the stage where the arbitrator who was replaced had ceased his or her functions, unless the tribunal decided otherwise."[123] Thus, a new rule would presume that no aspect of the proceedings would be repeated, unless the tribunal decides that repetition was appropriate under the circumstances. This proposal was based, in part, on the practice of the Iran–US Claims Tribunal, which modified Article 14 of the

---

[119] G Scelle, *Report of Arbitration Procedure*, UN Doc A/CN.4/18, at 33–4 (1950); A Mérignhac, *Traité théorique et pratique de l'arbitrage international* (1895) 277.

[120] P Lalive, "Les règles de conflit de lois appliquées au fond du litige par l'arbitre international siégeant en Suisse" (April 1976) 84, in No 53, Mémoires publiés par la Faculté de Droit de Genève, L'arbitrage international privé et la Suisse (1977) (emphasis in original). Translation: "It is certainly this principle of effectiveness which, definitively, with that of *good faith*, mandates the interpretation of the agreement to arbitrate in such a way that the improper withdrawal of an Arbitrator, under the pressure or the orders of a Party, will not prevent the tribunal from pursuing its task and rendering a binding award."

[121] The corresponding Article of the 1976 UNCITRAL Rules provides:

If under articles 11 to 13 the sole or presiding arbitrator is replaced, any hearings held previously shall be repeated; if any other arbitrator is replaced, such prior hearings may be repeated at the discretion of the arbitral tribunal.

[122] UNCITRAL, 40th Session, UN Doc A/CN.9/614, n 50, at 17, para 75.

[123] UNCITRAL, 40th Session, UN Doc A/CN.9/614, n 50, at 17, para 75.

1976 UNCITRAL Rules in order to afford the Tribunal discretion to decide whether to repeat a hearing regardless of which arbitrator was replaced.[124] The proposal also recognized the similarly broad discretion in the practice of commercial arbitration tribunals applying the ICC Arbitration Rules and the Swiss Arbitration Rules.[125] Notably, Article 15 tracks the language of Article 14 of the Swiss Rules nearly verbatim.[126]

The Working Group adopted both proposals discussed above, thus modifying the approach of the UNCITRAL Rules in certain respects. Under Article 15, whether a hearing is repeated no longer depends on the *type* of arbitrator that is replaced. Namely, the replacement of the sole or presiding arbitrator does not compel repetition of a hearing. While the general rule of Article 15 presumes no break in the proceedings will occur, it reserves to the arbitral tribunal the discretion to "decide otherwise" as to how to proceed. Further, such discretion extends beyond repetition of a hearing repetition of *any* stage of the arbitral proceedings.

This change in approach represents a shift in emphasis under the Rules. As discussed in the following section, the drafters of the 1976 UNCITRAL Rules sought to strike an important balance. On the one side, a party should be able to demand that the hearing be repeated, if such repetition ensures that the substitute arbitrator will sufficiently understand the case that has been recently placed before him or her. On the other side, the need for efficiency in the arbitral process argues against repetition, particularly if a party seeks, for example, to repeat a hearing as a dilatory tactic. As compared to Article 14 of the 1976 UNCITRAL Rules, revised Article 15 shifts this balance of interests more towards the goal of efficiency, leaving all matters concerning the repetition of proceedings to the tribunal to determine on a case-by-case basis.

Finally, it is clear that Article 15 applies in all cases of replacement of an arbitrator under the UNCITRAL Rules. The *travaux préparatoires* of both Article 14 of the 1976 UNCITRAL Rules and Article 15 confirm this rule. Original Article 14 was initially proposed as a second paragraph to the article concerning replacement of arbitrators in the event of "death, incapacity or resignation." The Committee decided later, however, that the paragraph should also apply to replacements resulting from a successful challenge of an arbitrator. The relevant paragraph was thus redrafted as a separate article, which became original Article 14.[127] For greater clarity, Article 14 of the 1976 UNCITRAL Rules included express references to

---

[124] Article 14, as modified and adopted by the Iran–US Claims Tribunal, leaves the question of repetition of any hearings, even in the case of replacement of the presiding arbitrator, to the discretion of the new arbitral tribunal. This modification reflects in part the fact that the Tribunal rendered its awards primarily on the basis of the written record with only one or two day hearings being held. Indeed, this modification was made despite the fact that transcripts of hearings were generally not made. The modification also exemplifies the general tendency of the Tribunal when modifying the 1976 UNCITRAL Rules to increase its discretion. This tendency can be understood in part by noting that the State representatives at UNCITRAL (unlike the arbitrators of the Iran–US Claims Tribunal) generally viewed the Rules from the perspective of an arbitrating party and thus preferred not to leave issues of concern to the discretion of future tribunals of unknown composition.

[125] *Settlement of Commercial Disputes: Revision of the UNCITRAL Arbitration Rules, Note by the Secretariat*, UNCITRAL, UN Doc A/CN.9/WG.II/WP.143 at 13, para 60 (2006).

[126] UNCITRAL, 40th Session, UN Doc A/CN.9/614, n 50, at 17, para 75. Article 14 of the 2006 Swiss Arbitration Rules provides: "If an arbitrator is replaced, the proceedings shall as a rule resume at the stage where the arbitrator who was replaced ceased to perform his functions, unless the arbitral tribunal decides otherwise."

[127] *Summary Record of the 5th Meeting of the Committee of the Whole (II)*, UNCITRAL, 9th Session, UN Doc A/CN.9/9/C.2/SR.5, at 7, paras 46 (Comment by the Chairman), 48 (Comment by Mr Szasz, Hungary), 57 (Comment by Mr Lebedev, USSR) (1976). Given the apparent consensus on that point, the Chairman requested that the representative of the Union of Soviet Socialist Republics redraft the relevant paragraph as a separate Article.

other articles of the UNCITRAL rules under which an arbitrator could be replaced.[128] Though revised Article 15 begins more generally with the words "If an arbitrator is replaced," it is clear from that article's similar relationship to other rules on replacement that this change reflects merely a technical drafting preference.[129]

(2) Comparison to the 1976 UNCITRAL Rules

Whereas Article 15 grants the arbitral tribunal full discretion after replacement of an arbitrator to repeat any phase of the arbitration, including hearings, Article 14 of the 1976 UNCITRAL allowed such discretion only after replacement of a party-appointed arbitrator; after replacement of the sole or presiding arbitrator, repetition was required. The more restrictive rule in original Article 14 was extensively discussed by the UNCITRAL drafters.

The discussion focused on the question of whether all hearings should be repeated regardless of what type of arbitrator was replaced. Some drafters called for the decision on repetition of hearings to be left to the discretion of the new sole arbitrator[130] or the newly re-constituted arbitral tribunal as a whole. Such discretion, it was argued, would avoid needless repetition of hearings when, for example, a verbatim record of the hearings had been kept.[131] Other drafters, on the other hand, argued that because arbitrators (especially sole or presiding arbitrators) play such a crucial part in arbitration, oral arguments and the presentation of evidence should be repeated.[132] There was widespread agreement that the sole or presiding arbitrator plays a "special role" in the arbitration and that therefore the replacement of such arbitrators requires that all hearings previously held be repeated.[133]

Such a special role was not recognized for party-appointed arbitrators. Thus, after the replacement of such arbitrators, the repetition of hearings was at the discretion of the new arbitral tribunal.[134] This rule was adopted despite strong argument that such hearings should be repeated unless the party making the replacement and the tribunal decided to

---

[128] Original Article 14 began: "If under articles 11 to 13...."

[129] The drafting change was made by the UNCITRAL Secretariat, and approved by the Working Group, with little substantive comment. *Settlement of Commercial Disputes: Revision of the UNCITRAL Arbitration Rules, Note by the Secretariat*, UNCITRAL, UN Doc A/CN.9/WG.II/WP.151 at 15, para 33 (2008) (providing that "[t]he reference to articles 11 to 13 which was contained in the 1976 version of that article has been deleted, as it might not be necessary to limit the application of that provision").

[130] See, eg, *Report of the UNCITRAL*, 8th Session, Summary of Discussion of the Preliminary Draft, UN Doc A/10017, para 92 (1975), reprinted in (1975) VI UNCITRAL Ybk 24, 34.

[131] *Report of the UNCITRAL*, 8th Session, n 130. See also *Report of the Secretary-General on the Revised Draft Set of Arbitration Rules*, UNCITRAL, 9th Session, Alternative Provisions to Revised Draft, UN Doc A/CN.9/113 (1975), reprinted in (1976) VII UNCITRAL Ybk 181, 185. It was noted by the representative of Mexico that the many municipal legal systems emphasized use of a written record and not oral proceedings. *Summary Record of the 5th Meeting of the Committee of the Whole (II)*, UNCITRAL, 9th Session, UN Doc A/CN.9/9/C.2/SR.5, at 7, para 53 (1976) (Comment by Mr Mantilla-Molina, Mexico).

In *Saudi Arabia* and *Aramco* (Sauser Hall, Badawi/Hassan and Habacy arbs, August 23, 1958) the arbitrator appointed by Saudi Arabia, Dr Badawi, died following oral argument but prior to the rendering the award. He was replaced by Mahmoud Hassan. Hassan was given time to "study the Memorials exchanged by the parties and hear the tape-recording of the oral arguments and hearings... The proceedings were therefore resumed in the state in which they were at the time of Dr. Badawi's death." (1963) 27 Intl L Rev 117, 137.

[132] *Report of the UNCITRAL*, 8th Session, n 130, para 93 (1975), reprinted in (1975) VI UNCITRAL Ybk 24, 34.

[133] The representative of Belgium did attempt to draw a distinction between sole arbitrators and presiding arbitrators, arguing that in the latter case there was no need to repeat hearings especially when accurate records of proceedings were available. *Summary Record of the 5th Meeting of the Committee of the Whole (II)*, UNCITRAL, 9th Session, UN Doc A/CN.9/9/C.2/SR.5, at 7, para 51 (1976) (Comment by Mr Jenard, Belgium).

[134] The decision must be taken by the *new* arbitral panel inasmuch as the replaced arbitrator is no longer a member.

dispense with such repetition.[135] In this vein, the representative for the United Kingdom stated that "[i]f any arbitrator was replaced, any hearing should be repeated, unless otherwise agreed by the Parties. It should not be possible for the arbitral tribunal to decide, against the will of one or both parties, that hearings should not be repeated."[136]

Other representatives argued that the new arbitrator alone should have the right to insist that hearings be repeated.[137] However, in the end, arguments concerning the considerable expense entailed with rehearings[138] and the possibility that the losing party could insist on all hearings being reheard in order to frustrate the procedure[139] prevailed. As a result, the question of whether to repeat a hearing in the case of a party-appointed arbitrator being replaced was left to the discretion of the new arbitral tribunal.

Article 14 of the 1976 UNCITRAL Rules should be understood to require only *repetition* of the hearing previously held, not the granting of a new hearing that would allow submission of new evidence. A tribunal might separately decide that a round of post-hearing pleadings or a new hearing is needed, but such expanded proceedings are not contemplated under original Article 14. Consistent with this approach, the Iran–US Claims Tribunal did not allow new evidence in the only case thus far in which that Tribunal repeated a hearing for the benefit of a replacement arbitrator. Typically, the Tribunal did not decide to repeat hearings.[140]

Further, it should be noted that "hearing" as used within the 1976 UNCITRAL Rules and as understood by the original UNCITRAL drafters means the oral submission of evidence or the oral presentation of argument. The specification that "any" hearings should be repeated indicates that Article 14 of the 1976 UNCITRAL Rules applies not only to final hearings, but also to hearings held, for example, on interim measures or preliminary jurisdictional questions. The tribunal should take into account that a party has no right to a hearing on preliminary or ancillary questions when considering repetition of hearings after a party-appointed arbitrator has been replaced. This factor is not relevant when the sole or presiding arbitrator is replaced because original Article 14 requires repetition in those cases.

Finally, Article 14 of the 1976 UNCITRAL Rules does not apply to hearings predating a phase of the arbitration that has already been resolved by an award or decision of the tribunal. Thus repetition of "any hearings held previously" does not mean that the replacement of an arbitrator after the final hearing but prior to the award makes original Article 14 applicable to, for example, an earlier hearing as to jurisdiction for which an award has been rendered. In accordance with Article 32(2) of the 1976 UNCITRAL Rules, any previous awards are "final and binding on the parties" and there is thus no basis for considering repetition of such earlier hearings.[141]

Before the Iran–US Claims Tribunal, there were numerous instances of replacement that

---

[135] *Report of the Secretary-General on the Preliminary Draft Set of Arbitration Rules*, UNCITRAL, 8th Session, Addendum 3 (Observations by Norway), UN Doc A/CN.9/97/Add.3, Annex I (1975); and *Report of the UNCITRAL*, 8th Session, n 130, para 94 (1975), reprinted in (1975) VI UNCITRAL Ybk 24, 34.

[136] *Summary Record of the 5th Meeting of the Committee of the Whole (II)*, UNCITRAL, 9th Session, UN Doc A/CN.9/9/C.2/SR.5, at 6–7, para 47 (1976) (Comment by Mr Guest, United Kingdom).

[137] UNCITRAL, 9th Session, UN Doc A/CN.9/9/C.2/SR.5, n 136, at 6–7, para 48 (Comment by Mr Szasz, Hungary).

[138] See, eg, UNCITRAL, 9th Session, UN Doc A/CN.9/9/C.2/SR.5, n 136, at 7, para 52 (1976) (Comment by Mr Melis, Austria).

[139] UNCITRAL, 9th Session, UN Doc A/CN.9/9/C.2/SR.5, n 136, at 7, para 49 (Comment by Mr Straus, Observer).

[140] For the Tribunal practice on this issue, see extracts reprinted in section 4(C).

[141] See Chapter 24, section 2(B)(2) on the final and binding nature of awards.

implicated Article 14 of the 1976 UNCITRAL Rules.[142] One instance was emblematic of the Tribunal's general reluctance to repeat proceedings. In particular, Judge Mostafa Johangir Sani submitted his resignation from the Tribunal to the Government of Iran on August 10, 1983, to take effect on that same date. However, the Tribunal later accepted this resignation as being effective September 13, 1983. Judge Sani's departure on August 10, 1983 thus left thirteen cases under submission undecided. Six of the cases[143] were signed by Chairman Mangård and Judge Mosk prior to the Tribunal's designated effective date for Judge Sani's resignation. This left seven cases[144] under submission with Judge Sani's replacement Judge Parviz Ansari Moin. Judge Ansari requested rehearings in the seven cases under Article 14. However, a rehearing was held in only one of the seven cases,[145] with that rehearing being strictly limited to a repetition of the prior hearing without the introduction of any new evidence.

C. Extracts from the Practice of the Iran–US Claims Tribunal

American Intl Group, Inc and *Islamic Republic of Iran*, Award No 93–2–3 (December 19, 1983) at 3, reprinted in 4 Iran-US CTR 96, 97–98:

> Following the Hearing, the member of the Tribunal appointed by the Islamic Republic of Iran resigned. A new member was appointed. The Tribunal has hereby determined not to repeat the prior hearings (*see* Article 14 of the Tribunal Rules).

(Virtually identical statements are contained in *Dames & Moore* and *Islamic Republic of Iran*, Award No 97–54–3 (December 20, 1983), *Pereira Associates* and *Islamic Republic of Iran*, Award No 116–1–3 (March 19, 1984), *Schering Corp* and *Islamic Republic of Iran*, Award No 122–38–3 (April 16, 1984), and *Morrison-Knudsen Pacific Ltd* and *Islamic Republic of Iran*, Award No 143–127–3 (July 13, 1984).)

R J Reynolds Tobacco Co and *Islamic Republic of Iran*, Case No 35, Chamber Three, Order of December 21, 1983:

> A Hearing was held in this case on 9 and 10 May 1983. Subsequently, the arbitrator appointed by the Islamic Republic of Iran resigned. A new arbitrator was appointed.
>
> The Tribunal has determined, by virtue of Article 14 of the Tribunal Rules, that a Hearing for continued oral argument will be held on 1 March 1984, at 9:30 a.m., at Parkweg 13, The Hague, The Netherlands. No further written submissions will be allowed except for the brief mentioned in the Tribunal Order of 29 November 1983.

R J Reynolds Tobacco Co and *Islamic Republic of Iran*, Case No 35, Chamber Three, Dissent of December 21, 1983 by Richard M Mosk to Order of December 21, 1983:

> The Hearing was held in this case in early May of 1983. There was no reason why an award could not have been issued prior to the resignation of the Iranian arbitrator. Nevertheless, the Tribunal

---

[142] Two other instances, for example, involve Judges Hamid Bahrami-Ahmadi and Judge Seyed Mostafavi-Tafreshi, who were appointed as replacements for Judges Shafeiei and Kashani respectively, the latter Judges having been withdrawn by their Government pursuant to Article 11(3) of the 1983 Tribunal Rules. Judge Bahrami inherited two cases under submission (Case Nos 285 and 179), Judge Mostafavi, eleven (Case Nos 134, 161, 299 (settled), 111, 174, 61, 37 and 231 (consolidated), 18, 24, 480, and 36). Both Judges requested under Article 14 that re-hearings be held; to our knowledge no hearings were repeated.

[143] Case Nos 62, 67, 84, 124, 185, and 346.

[144] Case Nos 1, 2, 35, 38, 54, 100, and 283.

[145] Case No 35.

for months and months after the Hearing continued to allow Respondents additional time to file a memorial on one legal issue. Seven months after the Hearing, that memorial has still not been filed.

In September 1983, the new Iranian arbitrator was appointed. From September 1983 until December 20, 1983 the Tribunal gave no indication that any new hearing was necessary in this case. The case has been fully set forth in writing. Absolutely no reason has been given or exists for a new hearing in this case. Indeed, in other cases in which the new Iranian arbitrator participated and in which decisions were against United States Claimants (*Ultrasystems Incorporated* (Award No 89–84–3) and *Dames & Moore* (Award No 97–54–3)), no new hearings were deemed necessary.

R J Reynolds Tobacco Co and *Islamic Republic of Iran*, Partial Award No 145–35–3 (August 6, 1984) at 3, reprinted in 9 Iran-US CTR 181, 183 (1985–II):

Inasmuch as the arbitrator appointed by the Islamic Republic of Iran who had participated in the above mentioned Hearing had meanwhile resigned, the Tribunal, by Order of 21 December 1983, determined by virtue of Article 14 of the Tribunal Rules that a Hearing for continued oral argument be held on 1 March 1984. After this continued Hearing the matter was taken under consideration.

Chapter 7

Exclusion of Liability for Arbitrators and other Participants

1. Introduction	325
2. Exclusion of Liability for Arbitrators and other Key Actors—Article 16	325
A. Text of the 2010 UNCITRAL Rule	325
B. Commentary	326
(1) General	326
(2) Practice of the Iran–US Claims Tribunal	330
(3) Comparison to the 1976 UNCITRAL Rules	330
C. Extracts from the Practice of Investment Tribunals	330
D. Extracts from the Practice of the Iran–US Claims Tribunal	331

1. Introduction

A losing party in an arbitration, perhaps one which has failed to set aside an award, may be tempted to direct its frustrations toward the arbitral tribunal by suing one or more of the arbitrators in their personal capacities, alleging that they had mishandled the proceedings in some manner. The prospect of lawsuits of this nature can have a serious chilling effect on the process of arbitration, with concerns about exposure to liability possibly translating into a general reluctance by arbitrators to offer their services. In an increasingly litigious environment, Article 16 affords arbitrators, the appointing authority, and persons appointed by the tribunal general immunity from suit, subject to an exception for "intentional wrongdoing" and a qualification designed to ensure conformity with the underlying applicable law.

2. Exclusion of Liability for Arbitrators and other Key Actors—Article 16

A. Text of the 2010 UNCITRAL Rule[1]

Article 16 of the 2010 UNCITRAL Rules provides:

Save for intentional wrongdoing, the parties waive, to the fullest extent permitted under the applicable law, any claim against the arbitrators, the appointing authority and any person appointed by the arbitral tribunal based on any act or omission in connection with the arbitration.

---

[1] Article 16 is new to the 2010 UNCITRAL Rules and thus no corresponding provision appears in the 1976 UNCITRAL Rules.

B. Commentary

(1) General

Article 16 is new to the 2010 UNCITRAL Rules. The prevailing view in Working Group discussions was that the Rules should include a provision establishing a general rule of immunity for arbitrators in connection with their conduct in the arbitration.[2] The concern was that without immunity protection, arbitrators would be "exposed to the threat of potentially large claims by parties dissatisfied with arbitral tribunals' rulings or awards who might claim that such rulings or awards arose from the negligence or fault of an arbitrator."[3] An immunity rule was believed to limit exposure to frivolous lawsuits and thus reinforced the independence of arbitrators, allowing them "to concentrate with a free spirit on the merits and procedures of the case."[4] It was also meant to avoid "an unhealthy situation" in which arbitrators would have to negotiate directly with the disputing parties concerning the degree to which they would be immune from suit.[5]

While the Working Group reached a general consensus that the Rules should include immunity protections, the precise degree of protection was a question requiring further deliberation.[6] Some delegates, for example, asserted that because "protecting the interests of parties to arbitration was a goal of the Rules," a rule of immunity should not be "overly protective" of arbitrators.[7] Article 16 seeks to resolve these competing policy goals by creating a general rule of immunity, subject to an exception for "intentional wrongdoing."[8]

---

[2] In their report to the UNCITRAL Secretariat, Paulsson and Petrochilos proposed inclusion of a similar rule. See J Paulsson and G Petrochilos, *Revision of the UNCITRAL Arbitration Rules*, Report to UNCITRAL Secretariat, at 50, para 88 (2006), available at <http://www.uncitral.org/pdf/english/news/arbrules_report.pdf.>

[3] *Report of Working Group II (Arbitration and Conciliation) on the Work of its Fifty-Second Session* (New York, February 1–5, 2010), UNCITRAL, 43rd Session, UN Doc A/CN.9/688, at 12, para 46 (2010); *Report of the Working Group on Arbitration and Conciliation on the Work of its Forty-Eighth Session* (New York, February 4–8, 2008), UNCITRAL, 41st Session, UN Doc A/CN.9/646, at 9–10, para 39 (2008). Further supporting this view was an assured trend in bringing lawsuits against arbitrators where recourse against the award was unavailable. Para 39.

[4] UNCITRAL, 41st Session, UN Doc A/CN.9/646, n 3, at 9–10, para 39. A broad immunity rule is not without its downsides, however. Commentators have observed that while an immunity rule may foster independence and finality of arbitral awards, there are countervailing policy arguments: "immunity may encourage carelessness; the finality of the decision is given priority over individual justice; disciplinary remedies are generally unavailable against arbitrators; and alternative remedies such as *vacatur* of the award and withholding of fees are inadequate." N Blackaby and C Partasides with A Redfern and M Hunter, *Redfern and Hunter on International Arbitration* (5th edn 2009) 331–2. At least one leading commentator has criticized the trend toward broad immunity protection. P Karrer, "Responsibility of Arbitrators and Arbitral Institutions" in L Newman and R Hill (eds) *The Leading Arbitrators' Guide to International Arbitration* (2008) 607–8.

[5] UNCITRAL, 41st Session, UN Doc A/CN.9/646, n 3, at 9–10, para 39. Commentators have also noted practical difficulties:

> It is in fact difficult for arbitrators, in their relations with the parties, to require a clause limiting or excluding their liability. As we have seen, the acceptance of their functions is rarely embodied in a formal contract, and it is hard to imagine how prospective arbitrators could make that acceptance conditional on the inclusion of a clause restricting or excluding liability.

E Gaillard and J Savage (eds) *Fouchard, Gaillard, Goldman on International Commercial Arbitration* (1999) 621. Even if this effect is accurate, it is possible to negotiate such questions with the parties See *William R Clayton* (1976) (memorializing the parties' agreement on arbitrator liability in a procedural order); *ICS Inspection and Control Services Ltd* (1976 Rules) (same); and *Guaracachi America, Inc,* et al (2010 Rules) (same); all reprinted in section 2(C).

[6] UNCITRAL, 41st Session, UN Doc A/CN.9/646, n 3, at 11, para 45.

[7] UNCITRAL, 41st Session, UN Doc A/CN.9/646, n 3, at 9–10, para 39. Others noted the growing trend in some legal systems of imposing "stricter standards" regarding the liability of judges and believed a similar approach might be appropriate with respect to the treatment of arbitrators. Para 39.

[8] 2010 UNCITRAL Arbitration Rules, art 16.

An initial draft of Article 16 denied immunity in cases of "conscious and deliberate wrongdoing," wording that paralleled the approach of other leading arbitration rules.[9] This proposal prompted a debate over terminology. Some Working Group delegates believed the exception should be framed in terms of "gross" or "extremely serious" negligence, an approach lending itself to a more objective analysis.[10] That view was rejected, however, because of concerns that a reference in the provision to the concept of negligence "could lend itself to divergent interpretations in different countries."[11]

The final version of Article 16 exempts from the scope of immunity protection "intentional wrongdoing," without defining that term. The plain meaning of the language suggests a standard similar, if not identical, to "conscious and deliberate wrongdoing"; the unprotected act or omission is the result of wilful and bad faith conduct. The *travaux préparatoires*, though scant on this point, appear to support this interpretation. Some delegates were reported to believe that the concept of "conscious and deliberate wrongdoing"—similar in content to "intentional wrongdoing"—subsumed and thus exceeded the concept of gross negligence,[12] which is commonly defined as the intentional failure to perform a duty in reckless disregard of the consequences as affecting the interests of another.[13] The ambiguity of this phrase is unfortunate as its meaning in any particular instance will necessarily be adjudicated in various national courts in accordance with different legal traditions. In part, in our opinion, the task of interpretation should be guided by not only the ordinary meaning of the words, but also the alternate wordings that were not adopted. In part, the interpreting court needs to also bear in mind that it is clear that the drafters of the Rules intended that immunity should be denied only in cases of egregious and deliberate misconduct.[14]

---

[9] See LCIA Arbitration Rules, art 31.1; AAA Rules, art 35. Paulsson and Petrochilos had proposed the phrase "except if that act or omission was manifestly in bad faith." See J Paulsson and G Petrochilos, *Revision of the UNCITRAL Arbitration Rules*, Report to UNCITRAL Secretariat, at 50, para 88 (2006), available at <http://www.uncitral.org/pdf/english/news/arbrules_report.pdf.>

[10] UNCITRAL, 41st Session, UN Doc A/CN.9/646, n 3, at 11, para 43. The record indicates no support for denying immunity for less severe forms of negligence, an area of arbitrator conduct commonly protected under domestic liability laws.

[11] It was also reported that in some jurisdictions that do not incorporate the concept of "gross negligence," the same principle was expressed in terms of negligent conduct coupled with "dishonesty" or "conscious and deliberate wrongdoing." UNCITRAL, 41st Session, UN Doc A/CN.9/646, n 3, at 11, para 43.

Other proposals also did not attract a consensus:

"With a view to simplifying the provision, another proposal was made to avoid referring to any specific criterion such a 'conscious and deliberate wrongdoing' and simply indicate that 'The arbitrators or [other participants in the arbitral process] shall be exempt from liability to the fullest extent possible under any applicable law for any act or omission in connection with the arbitration'."

UNCITRAL, 41st Session, UN Doc A/CN.9/646, n 3, para 44;

"An alternative proposal was made along the lines of: 'The arbitrators, the appointing authority and the Permanent Court of Arbitration shall not be liable for any act or omission in connection with the arbitration, except for the consequences of conscious or deliberate wrongdoing.' It was explained that replacing 'conscious and deliberate wrongdoing' by 'conscious or deliberate wrongdoing' might practically produce the same effect as including a reference to 'gross negligence'." Para 45.

[12] UNCITRAL, 41st Session, UN Doc A/CN.9/646, n 3, para 43.

[13] *Black's Law Dictionary* (9th edn 2009) 1133–4.

[14] Born notes that "[a]rbitrators should be immune from claims based upon gross negligence, recklessness, or similar theories, not rising to the level of intentional fraud or similar deliberate wrongdoing. The threat to the independence and impartiality of arbitrators would arise with almost equal force from permitting actions based upon gross negligence, as from claims based upon simple negligence. Only deliberate wrongdoing on the part of an arbitrator should permit civil claims against him or her." G Born, *International Commercial Arbitration* (2009) 1662.

The Working Group also recognized that the Rules were "contractual in nature" and thus subject to the mandatory provisions of the applicable law.[15] Thus, an immunity rule that exceeded the scope of immunity protection permitted under the applicable law might not only be legally "ineffective," it might also lead to varying results across different jurisdictions.[16] In light of these potential problems, Article 16 was also drafted with the aim of avoiding conflicts with the applicable law. Accordingly, the disputing parties' ability to waive claims against the arbitrators, the appointing authority, and tribunal-appointed persons is limited to "the fullest extent permitted under the applicable law." In this regard, Article 16 bears similarities in purpose to Article 1(3) on scope of application, though with one noteworthy difference. Whereas Article 1(3) prevents conflicts between the Rules and "the law applicable to the arbitration," Article 16 avoids conflicts between the Rules and "the applicable law," a broader term which may encompass not only the applicable arbitration law, but also other substantive areas of law, such as tort, contract, and criminal law.

In understanding the extent to which Article 16 may be pre-empted, one should carefully study the applicable law, particularly of the place of arbitration, as standards of liability may vary considerably from jurisdiction to jurisdiction.[17] US courts historically have afforded arbitrators exceptionally broad immunity protection, though more recent US case law contains instances of a more moderate approach.[18] Other common-law courts have adopted similar positions of extending broad immunity to arbitrators in respect of their "judicial" functions, typically with an exception for fraudulent or intentional, bad-faith conduct.[19] Qualified immunity (immunity for all but gross negligence and intentional wrongdoing) is the general rule in Continental Europe and China.[20] In some Middle Eastern countries, it appears that arbitrators enjoy very limited, if any, immunity protection.[21] In yet other Middle Eastern countries, it appears that arbitrators have no immunity and are personally liable

---

[15] UNCITRAL, 41st Session, UN Doc A/CN.9/646, n 3, at 9–10, para 39 (2008) ("It was recognized that any such provision would not interfere with the operation of applicable laws."). Commentators explain that "[t]here are two schools of thought. The first school considers that the relationship between the arbitrator and the parties is established by contract. The second school may be defined as the 'status' school which considers that the judicial nature of an arbitrator's function should result in a treatment assimilated to that of a judge. In some jurisdictions, such assimilations may give rise to immunity; in others it simply results in the application of rules on judicial liability." N Blackaby and C Partasides, *Redfern and Hunter on International Arbitration*, n 4, 329.

[16] UNCITRAL, 41st Session, UN Doc A/CN.9/646, n 3, at 10–11, para 42.

[17] See generally, J Lew (ed) *The Immunity of Arbitrators* (1990).

[18] "U.S. Courts historically held that arbitrators were entitled to extremely broad immunities, extending to negligence, bad faith or intentional misconduct, non-disclosure of conflict and similar malfeasance. More recent U.S. judicial decisions suggest that the contemporary scope of arbitrator immunity may be somewhat more limited, with some U.S. courts denying arbitrators immunity for failing to issue an award in a timely manner...." G Born, *International Commercial Arbitration*, n 14, 1655–6.

[19] G Born, *International Commercial Arbitration*, n 14, 1656–7 (citing case law in England, Canada, New Zealand, Australia, Singapore, Hong Kong and Bermuda).

[20] Swiss, Belgian, Dutch, Finnish, Spanish and Chinese courts and/or legislation generally recognize relatively broader arbitrator immunity, subject to exceptions for fraud or similar intentional misconduct (See eg Swiss International Arbitration Rules, Art 44(1); Spanish Arbitration Act, Art 21(1)). German courts limit liability to cases of gross negligence and intentional wrongdoing (German Civil Code § 839). Austrian law is somewhat less protective, providing immunity except in cases of "fault," and only for acts relating to making of the award and not the "decisional process." Even under the 2006 Austrian ZPO §594, arbitrators are liable for wrongful delay in fulfilling their obligations. While older French decisions suggest that arbitrators had little or no immunity, more recent decisions recognize the need for arbitrator independence and allow claims only for gross fault or fraud. See also Chinese Arbitration Law, Arts. 34(4), 58(6), and 38. G Born, *International Commercial Arbitration*, n 14, 1657–8. Also, see generally, J Lew, *The Immunity of Arbitrators*, n 17.

[21] G Born, *International Commercial Arbitration*, n 14, 1659 (citing the laws of Bahrain, Tunisia, Lebanon, Libya, and Qatar).

for all wrongful actions, though the application of such provisions is unclear.[22] Notably the UNCITRAL Model Law is completely silent on arbitrator liability;[23] adopting states have included provisions on arbitrator liability that differ in approach.[24]

Though Article 16 may limit the parties' rights to bring legal action against arbitrators in judicial proceedings, it in no way absolves arbitrators of their arbitral duties under the UNCITRAL Rules. Chief among these duties are those established in Article 17(1): to treat the parties with equality, to give each a reasonable opportunity to present its case, and to conduct the proceedings so as to avoid unnecessary delay and expense and to provide a fair and efficient process for resolving the dispute. Remedies traditionally available under the system of arbitration remain unaffected by Article 16. To the extent that an alleged breach of duty is thought to affect the impartiality or independence of an arbitrator or constitute a failure to act on his or her part, a party has recourse to the challenge procedures set forth in Articles 12 through 14 of the Rules. Article 16 notwithstanding, a party may also still seek to set aside or challenge enforcement of an award based on an alleged breach of duty.[25]

Immunity protection under Article 16 applies with respect to "acts or omissions in connection with the arbitration." Thus, both active and passive conduct is protected, so long as it does not constitute intentional wrongdoing. The term "in connection with the arbitration," also used in the procedural rules of other arbitral institutions,[26] denotes coverage of a broad range of conduct extending beyond an arbitrator's decision-making duties to his or her general conduct of the arbitral proceedings.

Finally, in addition to arbitrators, Article 16 protects the conduct of the appointing authority and any person appointed by the tribunal, who are equally susceptible to baseless lawsuits by a party.[27] The approach of Article 16 is thus consistent with that of other leading procedural rules, though terms have been tailored to account for use of the Rules in *ad hoc* arbitration. Thus, whereas Article 40 of the 2012 ICC Rules protects the ICC and its employees, Article 16 of the 2010 UNCITRAL Rules safeguards the appointing authority, which may be a natural person or institution, and persons appointed by the tribunal, including administrative staff. Article 16 also covers experts appointed by the tribunal pursuant to Article 29 of the Rules.[28]

---

[22] G Born, *International Commercial Arbitration*, n 14, 1659 (citing the laws of Syria and Kuwait).

[23] See *Report of the Secretary-General on Possible Features of a Model Law on International Commercial Arbitration*, UN Doc. A/CN.9/207, para 70, *reprinted in* XII Ybk UNCITRAL 75 (1981). The report recognized that liability is a much debated issue and being highly controversial, a model law may be inadequate to offer a solution. However, the report urged the Commission to consider preparing a code of conduct and ethics to guide arbitrators, especially because national laws tend to apply the same standard as that for judges. See also S Nappert, *Commentary on the UNCITRAL Arbitration Rules 2010: A Practitioner's Guide* (2012) 63, 64. The protection while exercising a quasi-judicial function should come with a corresponding obligation to perform their functions to a judicial standard. See also *Report of the Working Group on International Contract Practices on the Work of its Third Session*, UN Doc A/CN.9/216, paras 51–52, *reprinted in* XIII Ybk UNCITRAL 287 (1982). The Working Group was in general agreement that the question of liability of an arbitrator could not appropriately be dealt with in a model law and it was agreed to not attempt preparation of a code of ethics. The prevailing view was to envisage replacement of an arbitrator if he failed to act.

[24] For examples, see P Sanders, *The Work of UNCITRAL on Arbitration and Conciliation* (2004) 161.

[25] One commentator has argued that a successful challenge against an award should be a prerequisite for suing an arbitrator for wrongful decision-making. See K Berger, *International Economic Arbitration* (1993) 237.

[26] See 1988 LCIA Rules, Article 31.1; 1998 ICC Rules, Article 34; 2012 ICC Rules, Article 40. Note that Derains and Schwartz conclude that the meaning of similar language in the ICC Rules is ultimately left to the courts to determine. Y Derains and E Schwartz, *A Guide to the ICC Rules of Arbitration* (2nd edn 2005) 382–3.

[27] P Karrer, "Responsibility of Arbitrators and Arbitral Institutions," n 4, 619.

[28] For a similar, though more express approach, see Article 31.1 of the 1998 LCIA Rules.

(2) Practice of the Iran–US Claims Tribunal

The Iran–US Claims Tribunal presents a special case on matters such as immunity and liability because the Tribunal was classified as a bilateral international organization between Iran and the United States, operating with the Netherlands, the host country. Although this situation is unusual, it quite clearly may arise again.

The immunities and privileges of international organizations, their staff and their work are addressed by customary international law, although aspects of that custom are contested. In any event, these questions are normally handled by treaty, a host agreement between the institution and the host country. As a general matter, both custom and such host agreements grant absolute immunity to the institution and arbitrators for official acts. Many of the various aspects of immunities concerning the Iran–US Claims Tribunal, its members, and its staff are addressed in an exchange of letters between the President of the Tribunal and the minister of Foreign Affairs for the Netherlands on September 24, 1990.[29]

(3) Comparison to the 1976 UNCITRAL Rules

Article 16 is new to the 2010 UNCITRAL Rules. There is no corresponding provision in the 1976 UNCITRAL Rules. In arbitration under the 1976 Rules, the disputing parties in some cases have dealt with this lacuna by reaching agreement as to the scope of arbitrator liability, an agreement which was memorialized in a procedural order of the arbitral tribunal.[30]

C. Extracts from the Practice of Investment Tribunals

William R Clayton, et al and *Government of Canada,* Procedural Order No 1 (April 9, 2009) (PCA administered, 1976 UNCITRAL Rules, NAFTA Chapter Eleven), at 6:

> D. Exclusion of Liability
>
> 15. No member of the Arbitral Tribunal nor any expert to the Arbitral Tribunal shall be liable to any party whatsoever for any act or omission in connection with the arbitration, save where the act or omission is shown by that party to constitute conscious and deliberate wrongdoing and committed by the body or person alleged to be liable to that party.

ICS Inspection and Control Services Ltd and *Argentine Republic,* Award on Jurisdiction (February 10, 2012) (PCA administered, 1976 UNCITRAL Rules, UK-Argentina BIT), at 19 (reprinting Procedural Order No 1 dated May 18, 2010):

> 16.1 The Parties shall not seek to make the Tribunal or any of its members liable in respect of any act or omission in connection with any matter related to the arbitration.
>
> 16.2 The Parties shall not require any member of the Tribunal to be a party or witness in any judicial or other proceedings arising out of or in connection with this arbitration.

Guaracachi America, Inc, et al and *Plurinational State of Bolivia,* Terms of Appointment and Procedural Order No 1 (December 9, 2011) (PCA administered, 2010 UNCITRAL Rules, US-Bolivia BIT/UK-Bolivia BIT), at 1–2:

> 17.1 The Parties shall not seek to make the Tribunal or any of its members liable in respect of any act or omission in connection with any matter related to the arbitration.

---

[29] See Exchange of Letters between Robert Briner, President, Iran–United States Claims Tribunal and H. van den Broek, Minister for Foreign Affairs, The Netherlands, dated September 24, 1990, reprinted in section 2(D). For a discussion of the relationship of the host country to international courts and tribunals, and the example of the Iran–US Claims Tribunal in particular, see D Caron "International Tribunals and the Role of the Host Country," in D Caron and J Crook, eds, *The Iran–United States Claims Tribunal: Its Contribution to the Process of International Claims Resolution* 27–36 (2000).

[30] For examples, see extracts from the practice of Investment Tribunals in section 2(C).

D. Extracts from the Practice of the Iran–US Claims Tribunal

Exchange of Letters Between Robert Briner, President, Iran-United States Claims Tribunal and H van den Broek, Minister for Foreign Affairs, The Netherlands, dated September 24, 1990:[31]

IRAN-UNITED STATES CLAIMS TRIBUNAL

...

24 September 1990

His Excellency Mr. H. van den Broek
Minister for Foreign Affairs of the Kingdom of the Netherlands
The Hague

Dear Mr. Minister,

I have the honour to refer to Your Excellency's letter dated 6 September 1990 which reads as follows:

"Dear Mr. President,

Referring to the conversations between the Netherlands authorities and the Secretary-General of the Iran-United States Claims Tribunal concerning the privileges and immunities with respect to the functioning of the Tribunal and to the wish expressed during these conversations on behalf of the Tribunal to specify these privileges and immunities, I have the honour hereby to propose to your Excellency the following:

Article 1

1. The premises of the Tribunal shall be inviolable. The Netherlands authorities may not enter them, except with the consent of the President of the Tribunal or of his designee. Such consent may, however, be assumed in case of fire or other disaster requiring prompt protective action, and only in the event that it has not been possible to obtain the express consent of the President or of his designee.
2. The Netherlands Government is under a special duty to take all appropriate steps to protect the premises of the Tribunal against any intrusion or damage and to prevent any disturbance of the peace of the Tribunal or impairment of its dignity.
3. The premises of the Tribunal, their furnishings and other property thereon shall be immune from search, requisition, attachment or execution.
4. Service of process at the premises of the Tribunal and service of any other procedural instruments relating to a cause of action against the Tribunal shall not constitute breach of inviolability.

Article 2

The archives of the Tribunal and any documents belonging to or held by it shall be inviolable. They should, when necessary, bear visible external marks of identification.

Article 3

1. Subject to the provisions of Article 4, the Tribunal, within the scope of the performance of its tasks, shall enjoy in the Netherlands immunity from jurisdiction and execution, except:
    a. to the extent that the Tribunal shall have expressly waived such immunity in a particular case;

---

[31] Given the inability of the state parties to enter into an agreement with the Netherlands, the host state, on the privileges and immunities of the Tribunal, such privileges and immunities were granted initially by the Netherlands in a series of letters and eventually formalized in the exchange of letters between the President of the Tribunal and the Minister for Foreign Affairs of the Netherlands reprinted in the text.

b. in the case of a civil action brought by a third party for damage resulting from an accident caused by a motor vehicle belonging to, or operated on behalf of, the Tribunal, or in respect of a motor traffic offence involving such a vehicle.

The property and assets of the Tribunal, wherever situated, shall be immune from requisition or attachment. The property and assets of the Tribunal shall also be immune from administrative or provisional judicial constraint, except in so far as may be temporarily necessary in connection with the prevention of, and investigation into, accidents involving motor vehicles belonging to or operated on behalf of the Tribunal.

Article 4

1. If the Tribunal institutes or intervenes in proceedings before a court in the Netherlands, it submits, for the purpose of those proceedings, to the jurisdiction of the Netherlands courts.
2. In such cases the Tribunal cannot claim immunity from the jurisdiction of the courts in respect of a counterclaim if the counterclaim arises from the legal relationship or the facts on which the principal claim is based.

Article 5

If the Tribunal appears before the courts in order to assert immunity, it shall not thereby be deemed to have waived immunity.

Article 6

1. The Netherlands Government shall permit and protect free communication on the part of the Tribunal for all official purposes, and notably with the Parties to the Claims Settlement Declaration.
2. The official correspondence of the Tribunal shall be inviolable. Official correspondence means all correspondence relating to the Tribunal and its functions.

Article 7

The members of the Tribunal shall be inviolable. They shall not be liable to any form of arrest or detention. The Netherlands authorities shall treat them with due respect and shall take all appropriate steps to prevent any attack on their person, freedom or dignity.

Article 8

1. The private residence of a member of the Tribunal shall enjoy the same inviolability and protection as the premises of the Tribunal. The exception provided for by paragraph 4 of Article I shall be applicable *mutatis mutandis*.
2. The papers, correspondence and, except as provided for in paragraph 4 of Article 9, the property of a member of the Tribunal shall likewise enjoy inviolability.

Article 9

1. A member of the Tribunal shall enjoy immunity from the criminal jurisdiction of the Kingdom of the Netherlands.
2. He shall also enjoy immunity from the civil and administrative jurisdiction of the Kingdom of the Netherlands, except in the case of:
    a. a real action relating to private immovable property situated in the Netherlands;
    b. an action relating to succession in which a member of the Tribunal is involved as executor, administrator, heir or legatee;
    c. an action relating to any professional or commercial activity exercised by a member of the Tribunal in the Netherlands outside his official function;
    d. an action for damages arising out of an accident caused by a vehicle used or owned by a member of the Tribunal, where those damages are not recoverable from insurance.

1. A member of the Tribunal is not obliged to give evidence as a witness.
2. No measures of execution may be taken in respect of a member of the Tribunal except in the cases coming under sub-paragraphs (a), (b), (c) and (d) of paragraph 2 of this Article, and provided that the measures concerned can be taken without infringing the inviolability of his person or of his residence.

Article 10

The members of the Tribunal shall be exempt in the Kingdom of the Netherlands from all personal services, from all public services of any kind whatsoever, and from military obligations such as those connected with requisitioning, military contributions and billeting.

Article 11

1. The Secretary-General of the Tribunal shall enjoy the privileges and immunities specified in Articles 7 to 10.
2. The other staff-members of the Tribunal shall enjoy the privileges and immunities specified in Articles 7 and 9 to 10, except that the immunity from criminal, civil and administrative jurisdiction specified in Article 9 shall not extend to acts performed outside the course of their duties.

Article 12

1. Except insofar as additional privileges and immunities may be granted by the Netherlands Government, a member of the Tribunal or a staff-member of the Tribunal who is a Netherlands national or permanently resident in the Netherlands shall enjoy only immunity from jurisdiction, and inviolability, in respect of official acts performed in the exercise of his function.
2. In other respects the Kingdom of the Netherlands shall exercise its jurisdiction over those persons in such a manner as not to interfere unduly with the performance of the functions of the Tribunal.

Article 13

Members of the family of a member of the Tribunal and of the Secretary-General forming part of his household shall, if they are not Netherlands nationals, enjoy the privileges and immunities specified in Articles 7 to 10.

Article 14

1. The purpose of the privileges and immunities provided for in the present Articles is not to benefit individuals but to ensure the unimpeded functioning of the Tribunal.
2. The Tribunal may waive the immunity from jurisdiction of a member of the Tribunal and of the Secretary-General or of any person enjoying immunity under Articles 11 to 13. Immunity shall be waived in any case where, in the opinion of the Tribunal, the immunity would impede the course of justice and waiver would not prejudice the purpose for which the immunity is accorded.
3. Waiver must always be express.
4. The initiation of proceedings by any of the persons referred to in paragraph 2 of this Article shall preclude him from invoking immunity from jurisdiction in respect of any counter-claim directly connected with the principal claim.
5. Waiver of immunity from jurisdiction in respect of judicial proceedings shall not be held to imply waiver of immunity in respect of the execution of the judgment, for which a separate waiver shall be necessary.

Article 15

1. Every person entitled to privileges and immunities shall enjoy them from the moment he enters Netherlands territory for the purpose of performing his functions

with the Tribunal or, if he is already in its territory, from the moment when his appointment is notified to the Netherlands Ministry of Foreign Affairs.
2. When the functions of a person enjoying privileges and immunities have come to an end, such privileges and immunities shall normally cease at the moment when he leaves Netherlands territory, or on expiry of a reasonable period in which to do so, but shall subsist until that time, even in case of armed conflict. However in respect of acts performed by such a person in the exercise of his function, immunity shall continue to subsist.
3. In case of the death of a member of the Tribunal or of a staff-member of the Tribunal, the members of his family and his private servants shall continue to enjoy the privileges and immunities to which they are entitled until the expiry of a reasonable period in which to leave the Netherlands.

Article 16

In the event of the death of a member of the Tribunal or of a staff-member of the Tribunal, or of a member of his family forming part of his household, if the deceased was not a Netherlands national nor permanently resident in the Netherlands, the Kingdom of the Netherlands shall permit the withdrawal of the movable property of the deceased, with the exception of any property acquired in the country the export of which was prohibited at the time of his death.

Article 17

1. A member of the Tribunal, and the Secretary-General shall not practise for personal profit any professional or commercial activity in the Netherlands outside the exercise of his function in the Tribunal.
2. The staff members of the Tribunal referred to in paragraph 2 of Article 11, not being Netherlands nationals or permanently resident in the Netherlands, and the members of the families referred to in Article 13 shall not, when they practise a professional or commercial activity for personal profit, enjoy immunity from criminal jurisdiction in respect of acts performed in the course of or in connection with the practice of such activity. However, the immunity with regard to the execution of the judgement will stand unless waived in accordance with Article 14.

Article 18

The Kingdom of the Netherlands shall, even in case of armed conflict, grant facilities to enable members of the Tribunal and staff-members of the Tribunal, other than Netherlands nationals, and members of the families of such persons irrespective of their nationality, to leave at the earliest possible moment. In particular it must, in case of need, place at their disposal the necessary means of transport for themselves and their property.

Article 19

1. The claimants and respondents or their representatives, counsel and advocates, as well as witnesses and experts and other persons who take part in the proceedings of the Tribunal, shall enjoy immunity from legal process in respect of oral or written statements made, or documents or other evidence submitted by them before or to the Tribunal.
2. In other respects, the Kingdom of the Netherlands shall exercise its jurisdiction over those persons in such a manner as not to interfere unduly with the performance of their functions with the Tribunal.

Article 20

1. The Members of the Tribunal and the Secretary-General shall be exempt from social security provisions in force in the Netherlands.

2. In the event that the Tribunal shall have established its own social security system offering coverage comparable to the coverage under Netherlands legislation, the Tribunal and its employees shall be exempt from social security pro visions in force in the Netherlands, with retroactive effect to May 18, 1981.
3. The provisions of par. 1 and 2 shall apply <u>mutatis mutandis</u> to members of the family forming part of the households of the persons mentioned in those paragraphs, unless they are employed or self-employed in the Netherlands or receive Netherlands social security benefits.

If the foregoing meets with the approval of Your Excellency I have the honour further to propose that this document and your letter in reply shall constitute an agreement between the Kingdom of the Netherlands and the Iran–United States Claims Tribunal which will enter into force on the date of receipt by the Ministry of Foreign Affairs of your Excellency's letter accepting the above.

Sincerely Yours,
(signed) H. van den Broek"

On behalf of the Tribunal, I hereby confirm approval of the terms of Your Excellency's letter set forth above, and accordingly agree that that letter and this reply shall constitute an agreement between the Iran-United States Claims Tribunal and the Kingdom of the Netherlands which will enter into force on the date of receipt of this reply by the Ministry of Foreign Affairs.

Yours sincerely,
(sd.)
Robert Briner,
President

Chapter 8
The Institution of the Appointing Authority

1. Evolution of the UNCITRAL Approach?	337
2. The Appointing Authority and Composition Generally	338
3. Lessons from the Iran–US Claims Tribunal for the Office of the Appointing Authority	340

1. Evolution of the UNCITRAL Approach?

A fundamental dimension of the UNCITRAL approach to its 1976 Rules is that those rules allow for unadministered arbitration, that is, that there need not be a supervising institution such as the International Chamber of Commerce (ICC) or the London Court of International Arbitration (LCIA). However, that choice created the need for some third party to take the place of a supervising institution for a minimum set of situations where the parties themselves are unable to resolve a question. Examples include selection of an arbitrator where one side fails to so appoint or decision on a challenge to an arbitrator. This third party under the 1976 UNCITRAL Rules is the appointing authority. In the case of the Iran–US Claims Tribunal, the model of the appointing authority was the naming of individuals, one after another, to fulfill the functions specified in the 1976 Rules. This chapter comments briefly on the office of the appointing authority, its evolution in practice and in the 2010 Rules.

Two major observations are in order. First, the 2010 Rules increase the number of possible questions that may be referred to the appointing authority, review of the reasonableness of fees requested by the arbitration tribunal being a major example.[1] Many of these questions newly referred to the appointing authority reflect not a concern with the failure of the parties to agree or act as obliged, but rather a concern with the capacity of the arbitrators to self-regulate. Several delegates involved in the drafting of the 2010 UNCITRAL Rules indicated to the authors that one subtle theme—not supported through empirical evidence but rather stoked through anecdotes—was a distrust of some arbitrators to do the right thing. The important point to recognize is that the more questions and functions given to the appointing authority, the more the office of the appointing authority resembles that of a supervising institution. Second, it is important to recognize that in practice, many UNCITRAL investor–state arbitrations are in fact lodged within institutions rather than being non-administered. These two observations suggest a trend to fundamentally move away both in structure and in practice from non-administered arbitration and also suggest that the Iran–US Claims Tribunal model of an individual designated as the appointing authority is giving way to institutions taking on the role of appointing authority.

---

[1] See Chapter 27 discussing, among other Rules, Article 41.

2. The Appointing Authority and Composition Generally

The rules concerning appointment, disclosure and challenge of any tribunal must be evaluated as a system. This evaluation has three dimensions: respect for the rights of parties, furtherance of the particular arbitration, and promotion of the arbitral process generally.

Respect for the rights of the parties and furtherance of the particular arbitration are, to a large degree, competing objectives. The UNCITRAL Rules clearly indicate that the parties, by agreeing to arbitration, have waived any right they had to be free of such a consensual process. In this sense, the UNCITRAL Rules undoubtedly lead to the formation of the arbitral panel, and respect for the rights of the parties is limited to the interests of those parties in the constituted panel.

The UNCITRAL Rules recognize several interests of the parties in the arbitral panel. Particularly pervasive is recognition of the interests of the parties in having a say in the formation of the tribunal, their choice as to a sole arbitrator or panel of three, and their choice of a particular appointing authority. Likewise, there is a general acknowledgment of the right of each party to have their case decided by an impartial and independent panel. Thus all arbitrators are required to disclose circumstances that are likely to give rise to justifiable doubts as to impartiality or independence. Arbitrators may be removed if the circumstances do in fact give rise to such doubts. Finally, there is the recognized interest of each party in having a competent and dedicated panel, a particularly important interest, given that the award is final. This interest manifests itself in the right of each party to an arbitrator appointed by it in any panel of three. This right to a party-appointed arbitrator is obviously somewhat paradoxical. On the one hand, it runs quite contrary to the interest in an impartial panel, while, on the other hand, to a degree it ensures a more thorough and exacting deliberative process.

The Rules also recognize that if such interests are regarded as absolute, then an avenue for sabotage of the formation of the panel exists. Thus, a party might refuse to agree to either the use of a sole arbitrator or panel of three, might delay the raising of a challenge until a later crucial moment in the proceedings, or fail to name its arbitrator in a panel of three.

To avoid such delays, a reasonable limit is placed on the time a party has to exercise its rights. A party must choose to use a sole arbitrator or panel of three within thirty days of receipt of the notice of arbitration.[2] A challenge must be raised within fifteen days of the party learning of the circumstances on which a challenge is based.[3] Parties must reach agreement on appointment of a solo arbitrator within thirty days after receipt by all parties of a proposal for such appointment, where parties have agreed for a sole arbitrator to be appointed.[4] Alternatively, a party must appoint its arbitrator to a panel of three within thirty days after the other party's appointment.[5] And finally, where the parties have agreed upon a panel of three, the two appointed arbitrators must agree on a choice of presiding arbitrator within thirty days after the appointment of the second arbitrator.[6]

These temporal limits are mitigated in two ways. First, the right in a practical sense is generally not immediately or permanently lost when the time limit is passed, but rather

---

[2] 2010 UNCITRAL Rules, art 7 (1).
[3] 2010 UNCITRAL Rules, art 13(1).
[4] 2010 UNCITRAL Rules, art 8(1).
[5] 2010 UNCITRAL Rules, art 9(1).
[6] 2010 UNCITRAL Rules, art 9(2).

continues at the discretion of the other party who must give the limit substance by requesting a third party, namely the appointing authority, to act in place of the reluctant party. Second, although once past the time limit the reluctant party may lose its choice in the matter, generally the Rules provide for the choice to be made for that party in a manner that protects its interest in having an impartial, independent and competent panel. Thus, if a party refuses to choose whether a sole arbitrator or panel of three should be used, the Rules themselves dictate that a panel of three shall be used, thus ensuring greater competence.[7] If a party fails to appoint its arbitrator on a panel, then an appointing authority makes that choice for the party.[8] Indeed, where agreement on a sole or presiding arbitrator is not possible, the appointing authority through the stipulated list procedure[9] also gives limited effect to the interests of the parties in personally choosing the arbitrators of their dispute. The one exception to such mitigating factors is the challenge; it must be raised within fifteen days or it is lost.

There is an apparent weakness both in the Rules' respect for the rights of the parties and in its furtherance of the arbitration. The disclosure provision relies only on the good faith of the arbitrator and the party that appointed the arbitrator. This problem is avoided, however, if the failure to disclose or respond to reasonable inquiries is treated as some evidence of a lack of impartiality and independence thereby abbreviating any challenge procedure.

Although the Rules clearly further the arbitration by ultimately allowing formation of a panel, one must ask whether the envisioned process is so costly and lengthy that in fact the attempt to arbitrate is defeated. As to appointment, the Rules present neither a costly nor a lengthy process. For example, in the case of a party opposing at every step the formation of a three-person panel, the other party would have to make only three requests: (1) that the Secretary-General of the Permanent Court of Arbitration (PCA) designate an appointing authority;[10] (2) that the appointing authority choose the other party's arbitrator;[11] and (3) that the appointing authority choose the presiding arbitrator.[12] The periods of time involved do not seem burdensome compared to, for example, the time a party might have to wait on the docket of many municipal courts.

The challenge process, however, is another matter. Although the challenge must be initiated in fifteen days, the Rules are otherwise silent as to the details or speed of the process by which the challenge is decided. Notably, the scheme of the Rules properly regards the objective of resuming the arbitration as quickly and cheaply as possible as more important than ascertaining with certainty through a formal and lengthy process the truth of a challenge. This choice is most graphically evidenced by the provisions allowing for either party to agree to the challenge *without prejudice*. Thus the challenge is not a device policing the arbitration world, but is rather a mechanism for getting the particular arbitration back on track. Therefore, the appointing authority should act quickly to declare inadmissible a late-filed challenge or an unsubstantiated challenge; should quickly deny patently frivolous or vexatious challenges, and otherwise should conduct the investigation of the challenge in an expeditious manner, treating the parties with equality but not inflating the process, for example, by granting the parties or the arbitrator the right to a formal hearing.

---

[7] 2010 UNCITRAL Rules, art 7(1).
[8] 2010 UNCITRAL Rules, art 7(2).
[9] 2010 UNCITRAL Rules, art 8(2).
[10] 2010 UNCITRAL Rules, art 6(1).
[11] 2010 UNCITRAL Rules, art 9(2).
[12] 2010 UNCITRAL Rules, art 9(3).

The ability of an arbitration under the UNCITRAL Rules to proceed despite a resisting party does much to promote international arbitration. That the provisions choose to continue the practice of party-appointed arbitrators is more problematic. The practice has a long tradition and an equally long list of critics. On the positive side, the presence of party-appointed arbitrators makes the deliberative process more thorough and exacting by ensuring that views of the party that appointed them arefully considered. It also reduces the likelihood of an aberrant decision. Such arbitrators also bring to the panel a knowledge of the local law of both parties. On the negative side, party arbitrators can exceed the appropriate bounds and become aggressive advocates for the party that appointed them. Thus holding party-appointed arbitrators under the Rules to the same standards of impartiality and independence applicable to a presiding arbitrator is problematic, but also welcome.

3. Lessons from the Iran–US Claims Tribunal for the Office of the Appointing Authority

Ultimately, the appointing authority ensures that a party cannot block or frustrate the composition of an impartial and independent arbitral panel.[13] Yet it is an office on which little has been written.[14]

This area of arbitral procedure has a language of its own and deserves some preliminary remarks. The title "appointing authority" as used in the UNCITRAL Rules is somewhat of a misnomer. There are appointing authorities who do only what their name implies: appoint. However, an appointing authority under the UNCITRAL Rules is also called upon to decide challenges to arbitrators. The broader functions of the UNCITRAL appointing authority has important consequences, particularly as to his or her qualifications. The Secretary-General of the PCA referenced in the UNCITRAL Rules is not the appointing authority (although the parties could agree that he should be). Rather the Rules provide that that high office *designates* the appointing authority. The Secretary-General of the PCA *designates* an appointing authority while the parties *agree to (and one could say thereby designate)* an appointing authority. Thus the *right* to agree on an appointing authority resides with the parties; as part of this right, the parties under the Rules and under certain circumstances delegate the *task* of designating the appointing authority to the PCA Secretary-General. Although the Rules do not consistently adhere to this distinction in terminology, we find the distinction useful and employ it in the following text.

The UNCITRAL Rules provide that the parties may agree upon the person or the institution to serve as appointing authority. If there is no such agreed authority or if the previously designated authority refuses to make an appointment, then either party may request

---

[13] It may be argued that the parties in undertaking to arbitrate have a legal duty to cooperate in the constitution of the arbitral panel. As a practical matter, however, it is the appointing authority that ensures such constitution. For one view on the theoretical question, see D Johnson, "The Constitution of an Arbitral Panel," (1953) 30 BYIL 152, 164 ("It is submitted that this question could be answered in the affirmative [for States] only if it could be proved that there is a rule of customary law, or an established rule of interpretation, that a pure undertaking to arbitrate necessarily implies an obligation to take some specific step [other than negotiating in good faith] in the matter of constituting a tribunal. It is believed that the existence of no such rule can be proved.") See also J Simpson and H Fox, *International Arbitration* (1959) 82–3.

[14] For the most extensive article known to the authors, see, M Khan, "The Appointment of Arbitrators by the President of the International Court of Justice," (1975) 14 Comunicazioni e Studi 1021.

the PCA Secretary-General to designate an appointing authority. Unusually, the Rules do not contain a provision stating that "if after fifteen days the parties are unable to agree upon an appointing authority then either party may request...." Instead either party may immediately request the designation of an appointing authority. Thus, for example, in the case of the January 1, 1982 Iranian challenge of Judge Mangård,[15] the Agent of the United States requested the Secretary-General of the PCA on January 8, 1982 to designate an appointing authority. The Secretary-General did so on January 13, 1982. In this sense, the parties may only have time to agree to an appointing authority before the need for such an authority arises.

The functions of an appointing authority under the UNCITRAL Rules involve either the appointment of an arbitrator or decision on the challenge of an arbitrator. A former President of the International Court of Justice (ICJ) in discussing that office's responsibility for the *appointment* of arbitrators asserts that "the function is non-judicial [because] it is a function of *selection* and not of *decision*."[16] This observation on the administrative, rather than judicial nature, of the appointment function has clear implications for the qualifications required of an appointing authority under UNCITRAL Rules where there is also the challenge decision function.[17]

In addition to judicial training or experience, other selection criteria can be seen in the choice of Judge Moons, Chief Justice of the Hoge Raad, as the Appointing Authority for the Tribunal. In particular Judge Moons was *immediately available to take up his duties*, was *ordinarily located at the site of the Tribunal* and therefore was *accessible to the parties* and was knowledgeable as to the *law of the forum* to the extent that such law might bear on his duties.

Several Iranian arbitrators objected strenuously, however, to the Dutch nationality of Judge Moons. In this vein, Mr Kashani in a letter to Judge Moons wrote:

"The Netherlands, which has agreed to become the Host Country to this international arbitral Tribunal, must maintain a strict neutrality towards the States party to the disputes. Such a neutrality, requires, as a minimum, that the Netherlands authorities avoid intervening in the work of this Tribunal in any way which works to the manifest interest of one of the two States and to the injury of the other.

... [I]f you wish to know just how illogical and inequitable it is for you to act in the sensitive capacity of Appointing Authority,... you should reflect a bit on the long-standing ties between the Royal Dutch Government and the United States...

... [T]he special, friendly and highly sentimental political-economic-military-security ties between the Netherlands and the United States, and these two countries' mutual interests, definitely and categorically make it impossible for authorities of the Netherlands to play an impartial and independent role with respect to the relations between the Iranian and American Governments... Furthermore, Mr. Moons, as a high-ranking figure in the Dutch Government, you will never be able to ignore your nation's interests or the identity of interests between Holland and the United States. In fact,... you have a conflict of interests vis-à-vis the Government of the Islamic Republic of Iran and should never be able to intervene in the slightest in Iran's relations with the United States. Even if the Iranian Government

---

[15] See Chapter 5, section B(1) for a more detailed commentary.
[16] M Khan, "The Appointment of Arbitrators," n 14, 1027.
[17] "The fact that the President [of the ICJ] is a judicial officer is irrelevant: no more is expected of him than is expected of, for example, the United Nations Secretary-General, when he is requested to appoint arbitrators under analogous treaty-provision." M Khan, "The Appointment of Arbitrators," at 1027–8. As to the power of the Secretary-General of the United Nations to act as an appointing authority, see "Interpretation of Peace Treaties with Bulgaria, Hungary and Romania," (1950) ICJ Rep 65, 221.

had not expressed its lack of consent, you...ought personally to have announced your incompetence to take any manner of action in this regard, in order to comply with the standards of independence and impartiality and to avoid any possible misgivings as to your having interests in common with one of the Parties, criteria which are prerequisite to service as the Appointing Authority."[18]

Independence and impartiality are important criteria in the selection of an appointing authority and the nationality of the appointing authority could be regarded as a circumstance potentially giving rise to justifiable doubts as to the impartiality of that authority. One method that would give adequate consideration to the nationality issue would be to designate an appointing authority in accordance with the apparent will of the parties. The experience of the Tribunal is again noteworthy.

Iran and the United States showed trust in the Netherlands through their designation of that country as the site of the litigation in the Algiers Accords[19] and in their subsequent confirmation of that choice without objection. The state parties also chose the Netherlands as the site for the depositary bank. In doing so Iran and the United States presumably felt that Netherlands was a nation which through its nationals could serve independently and impartially. The will of the state parties, to the extent ascertainable, thus evidences indeed a preference for the Netherlands. Given that the state parties no doubt also intended to have as an appointing authority someone readily available and accessible, the appointment of Judge Moons, a Dutch national, was both wise and proper.

Mr Kashani argued in his letter that the President of the ICJ should serve as the appointing authority. Douglas Johnson has observed that "[i]n theory there could be no more appropriate choice for this task—which may sometimes be a delicate one—than the President of the Court, who may be relied upon to be an international official of the highest integrity and impartiality."[20] However, it is the sensitivity of the President of the Court to delicacies that in the past has been most criticized.[21] More importantly, the President of the Court has no express authority to serve as an appointing authority. While past practice condones such service, the President's function should not be so extensive as to interfere with his duties to the Court. In this regard, it should be noted that designation as appointing authority for a single *ad hoc* arbitration is significantly less of a commitment than service in such a capacity for a claims commission with thousands of claims, or the ICJ during a busy period. As Simpson and Fox wrote in their 1959 study:

There is...sufficient doubt whether, when the need arises, [the President of the ICJ] will in fact be able and willing to act, to make it advisable to explore whether the parties to an arbitral engagement cannot agree to entrust the delicate task of appointing "neutral" arbitrators to some other impartial authority.[22]

There is a possibility that an appointing authority operating under the UNCITRAL Rules may be called upon later to decide a challenge to one of his appointments or, if the

---

[18] Letter of Mahmoud Kashani to the Appointing Authority, Ch M J A Moons, July 17, 1984, reprinted in (Sep 28, 1984) Iranian Assets Litigation Reporter 9362.
[19] Article VI(I) of the Claims Settlement Declaration provides: "The seat of the Tribunal shall be the Hague, The Netherlands, or any other place agreed by Iran and the United States." See also n 332 in Chapter 2 of this volume (a German arbitral institution designated as appointing authority for an arbitration in Germany).
[20] D Johnson, "The Constitution of an Arbitral Panel," n 13, 155.
[21] D Johnson, "The Constitution of an Arbitral Panel," n 13, 153–8 (discussion of the refusal of the President and Vice-President of the Court to appoint a party arbitrator for Iran as requested by the Anglo-American Oil Company in 1951 on the basis of Article 22 of a Concession Agreement between that Company and Iran).
[22] J Simpson and H Fox, *International Arbitration*, n 13, 85.

challenge is sustained, to appoint a substitute arbitrator. This possibility strengthens the natural tendency for one appointing authority to take care of all the respective tasks for such authority for a given tribunal.

Finally, because a party may hope for a negotiated settlement with a friendly continuation of business relations, he may be reluctant to take the "unfriendly" step of reference to the appointing authority. Settlements are always to be encouraged.[23] But the experience of the Tribunal teaches that nothing encourages settlement more than progress in the arbitration and that the reluctant party is not dismayed but rather only surprised at his success and thus encouraged to seek further delays when the claiming party agrees to actions such as extension of the reasonable period provided by the UNCITRAL Rules for appointment.

---

[23] See Chapter 25 on settlements.

PART III

THE INITIATION OF THE ARBITRATION AND THE IDENTIFICATION AND CLARIFICATION OF THE ISSUES PRESENTED

Introduction

According to Article 3 of the 2010 UNCITRAL Rules, a party wishing to have recourse to arbitration (the "claimant") shall give "a notice of arbitration" to the other party (the "respondent"). Receipt of the notice establishes the date for the commencement of the arbitral proceedings. From that point to the main hearing at which the evidence and arguments are fully put to the arbitral tribunal, the facts and law at issue need to be defined and clarified. This happens above all through written submissions, especially the "statement of claim" and "statement of defence" addressed by Articles 20 and 21 of the 2010 UNCITRAL Rules, respectively. Closely connected with these articles are rules concerning the extent to which amendments to the claim or defence are allowed (Article 22) and further written statements are needed (Article 24). Important for all these aspects of procedure are the rules regulating the calculation of various time limits found in Articles 2 and 25 of the 2010 UNCITRAL Rules.

In addition to ordering the parties to submit written statements, the arbitral tribunal may need to render, as a preliminary matter, decisions narrowing and clarifying the issues or otherwise shaping the proceedings. For example, the tribunal may have to establish the language of the proceedings (Article 19) or decide on pleas concerning the jurisdiction of the tribunal (Article 23). Decisions on incidental questions, such as interim measures of protection (Article 26), also belong to this class of early decisions of the arbitral tribunal.

In this part, we address the initiation of the arbitration and the definition of the issues presented, as well as the related preliminary and incidental decisions referred to above. This part consists of nine chapters dealing with the following matters: representation and assistance (Chapter 9), notice of arbitration and response to the notice of arbitration (Chapter 10), language (Chapter 11), notice and calculation of periods of time (Chapter 12), statements of claim and defence (Chapter 13), pleas as to the jurisdiction of the tribunal (Chapter 14), amendments to the claim or defence (Chapter 15), further written statements and the time allowed for submission (Chapter 16) and interim measures of protection (Chapter 17).

Chapter 9
Representation and Assistance

1. Introduction	347
2. Representation and Assistance—Article 5	347
A. Text of the 2010 UNCITRAL Rule	347
B. Commentary	348
(1) The right to representation and assistance by persons chosen	348
(2) Communicating the identity and role of representatives and advisers	351
(3) Proof of a representative's authority	352
(4) Practice of the Iran–US Claims Tribunal	353
(5) Comparison to the 1976 UNCITRAL Rules	354
C. Extracts from the Practice of Investment Tribunals	355
D. Extracts from the Practice of the Iran–US Claims Tribunal	356

1. Introduction

International arbitration can be a complex and arduous undertaking, one that the disputing parties often do not wish to take on by themselves. In many cases, they may therefore decide to enlist the help of outside persons with qualifications or expertise that can assist in resolving their dispute. Article 5 of the 2010 UNCITRAL Rules confirms a party's right to representation or assistance during the arbitration, whether by legal counsel or other non-legal representative. Article 5 establishes a party's requirement to communicate to the other parties and the arbitral tribunal the identity and role of a chosen representative or adviser. Article 5 expressly grants the arbitral tribunal authority to demand proof of a representative's authority, when necessary.

2. Representation and Assistance—Article 5

A. Text of the 2010 UNCITRAL Rule[1]

Article 5 of the 2010 UNCITRAL Rules provides:

Each party may be represented or assisted by persons chosen by it. The names and addresses of such persons must be communicated to all parties and to the members of the arbitral tribunal. Such communication must specify whether the appointment is being made for purposes of representation or assistance. Where a person is to act as a representative of a party, the arbitral tribunal, on its own initiative or at the request of any party, may at any

---

[1] Corresponding Article 4 of the 1976 UNCITRAL Rules provides:

The parties may be represented or assisted by persons of their choice. The names and addresses of such persons must be communicated in writing to the other party; such communication must specify whether the appointment is being made for purposes of representation or assistance.

time require proof of authority granted to the representative in such a form as the arbitral tribunal may determine.

B. Commentary

(1) *The right to representation and assistance by persons chosen*

The first sentence of Article 5 restates a fundamental rule of international arbitration: that a disputing party may choose whomever it likes to represent or assist it in presenting its case.[2] As Mani observes, the right to representation and assistance is "one of the manifestations of the more cardinal right to be heard."[3] Article 17(1) thus complements Article 5 by requiring the arbitral tribunal to afford each party a reasonable opportunity to present its case. Because the right to representation and assistance continues throughout the arbitration, a party's good faith appointment of persons for these purposes should be respected at any stage of the proceedings.[4] A failure to do so may create grounds for challenging the award on the basis that a disputing party was denied its right to be heard.[5]

The scope of the right to representation and assistance is intentionally broad. A preliminary draft of corresponding Article 4 of the 1976 UNCITRAL Rules was deemed unacceptable because it contemplated that a party could only be "represented by a counsel or agent."[6] Some delegations questioned whether the word "represented" would be interpreted too narrowly as excluding the possibility that a party might be "assisted" by a non-lawyer.[7] Indeed, in some cases a party may wish to be represented by non-lawyers, such as engineers, "commercial men," or other types of technical experts.[8] Proposed use of the words "counsel" and "agent" also raised concerns, as the meaning of those terms might vary

---

[2] The right of representation was so obvious that one Committee delegate believed that it was not necessary to include a provision addressing this matter in the UNCITRAL Rules. See *Summary Record of the 2nd Meeting of the Committee of the Whole (II)* (New York, April 13, 1976), UNCITRAL, 9th Session, UN Doc A/CN.9/9/C.2/SR.2, at 9, para 54 (1976) (comment by Mr Guest, United Kingdom).

[3] V S Mani, *International Adjudication: Procedural Aspects* (1980) 58. Professor Mani argues further at 59 that "[r]epresentation of parties before the tribunal is, indeed, part of the general principles of law and finds clear expression in diverse municipal legal systems."

[4] The *travaux préparatoires* of the 1976 UNCITRAL Rules indicate that "representation may take place at any stage of the arbitral proceedings, including any hearing called by the arbitrators ... or any meeting convened by the arbitrators for the inspection of goods...." *Report of the Secretary-General on the Revised Draft Set of Arbitration Rules* (New York, April 12–May 2, 1976), UNCITRAL, 9th Session, Addendum 1 (Commentary), UN Doc A/CN.9/112/Add.1, para 2 (1975), reprinted in (1976) VII UNCITRAL Ybk 166, 168 (Commentary on Draft Article 5).

[5] Leading commentators note "it would be risky for an arbitral tribunal to proceed [without respecting a party's choice of representation] since, on an application for enforcement, such a course might lead to an argument that the losing party had not had a proper opportunity to present its case, even if the parties were treated with equality and respect." N Blackaby and C Partasides with A Redfern and M Hunter, *Redfern and Hunter on International Arbitration* (2009) 415.

[6] *Report of the Secretary-General on the Preliminary Draft Set of Arbitration Rules* (Geneva, April 1–7, 1975), UNCITRAL, 8th Session, UN Doc A/CN.9/97, para 1 (1974), reprinted in (1975) VI UNCITRAL Ybk 163, 168.

[7] *Report of the United Nations Commission on International Trade Law on the Work of its Ninth Session* (New York, April 12–May 7, 1976), UN GAOR, 31st Session, Supp No 17, UN Doc A/31/17, para 25 (1976), reprinted in (1976) VII UNCITRAL Ybk 66, 68 (Commentary on Draft Article 5).

[8] N Blackaby and C Partasides, *Redfern and Hunter on International Arbitration*, n 5, 415. See also K Berger, *International Economic Arbitration* (1993) 392 (noting that "[i]f it can be foreseen that technical issues will play a dominant role in the arbitration, a party may choose to be represented by an expert in that particular field of technology or to include him in his team of attorneys in order to save the time needed to procure experts or expert witnesses").

significantly across legal cultures.[9] In order to leave no doubt that a party could choose from among a wide range of actors (both legal and non-legal) to serve as its advisers in arbitration, the Committee decided to adopt the more generic and expansive phrase "represented or assisted."[10]

A party's right to representation and assistance is subject to applicable national law and practice. A very few jurisdictions, for example, require that a party in arbitration be represented by a member of the local bar. Though most jurisdictions place few, if any, restrictions in this area, nevertheless, it is prudent to study the law in advance of the arbitration, particularly if the use of foreign counsel is contemplated.[11] Nothing in Article 5 requires a disputing party to be represented by legal counsel, but it is typically advisable to have legal representation, particularly in complex cases.

Separate from a party's right to representation and assistance is the important question of whether a person appointed by a party has authority to act on behalf of the appointing party. The Rules do not regulate this area, but rather defer to the governing law as evident from the *travaux préparatoires* of the Revised Draft of what became the 1976 UNCITRAL Rules. The draft provision on representation provided that a party's communication of the name and address of its representative "is deemed to have been given where an arbitration is initiated by a counsel or agent or where a counsel or agent submits a statement of defence and counter-claim for the other party."[12]

According to the Commentary on the Revised Draft, the draft provision reflected "the fact that, in arbitration practice, the requisite authority always exists and need not be expressly communicated when a counsel or agent acts in the manner described therein."[13] The presumption of representative power under the Rules was ultimately rejected, however, as many delegates believed such important questions could only be resolved under the applicable domestic law.[14]

---

[9] UN GAOR, 31st Session, Supp No 17, UN Doc A/31/17, n 7, at para 25. For the discussion of this problem by Committee delegates, see *Summary Record of the 2nd Meeting of the Committee of the Whole (II)* (New York, April 13, 1976), UNCITRAL, 9th Session, UN Doc A/CN.9/9/C.2/SR.2, at 9, paras. 51–57 (1976).

[10] According to the *travaux préparatoires*: "The Committee decided that, in substance, the first sentence of article 5 should be based on article VI(8) of the 1966 ECAFE Rules for International Commercial Arbitration, which read as follows: 'The parties shall have the right to be represented or assisted at the hearing by persons of their choice.'" UN GAOR, 31st Session, Supp No 17, UN Doc A/31/17, n 7, at para 25.

[11] See E Gaillard and J Savage (eds) *Fouchard, Gaillard, Goldman on International Commercial Arbitration* (1999) 677 (citing David W Rivken, "Keeping Lawyers Out of International Arbitrations," (1990) 9 Intl Financial L Rev 11).

[12] *Report of the Secretary-General on the Revised Draft Set of Arbitration Rules* (New York, April 12–May 7, 1976), UNCITRAL, 9th Session, UN Doc A/CN.9/112 (1975), reprinted in (1976) VII UNCITRAL Ybk 160, 161 (Draft Article 5).

[13] *Report of the Secretary-General on the Revised Draft Set of Arbitration Rules* (New York, April 12–May 7, 1976), UNCITRAL, 9th Session, Addendum 1 (Commentary), UN Doc A/CN.9/112/Add.1, para 3 (1975), reprinted in (1976) VII UNCITRAL Ybk 166, 168 (Commentary on Draft Article 5).

[14] See *Report of the United Nations Commission on International Trade Law on the Work of its Eighth Session* (Geneva, April 1–7, 1975), 8th Session, Summary of Discussion of the Preliminary Draft, UN Doc A/10017, para 30 (1975), reprinted in (1975) VI UNCITRAL Ybk 24, 28 ("It was observed that the second sentence of paragraph 1 appeared to assume that the initiation of an arbitration, or the submission of a statement of defence or counter-claim, by a counsel or agent was sufficient evidence that such counsel or agent possessed the requisite authority to act for the party on whose behalf he purported to act. It was suggested that such an assumption might be unjustified and that therefore the present formulation of this sentence should be reconsidered. It was also suggested that the word 'considered' might be substituted in the second sentence of this paragraph for the word 'deemed' as being more appropriate."). *See also Summary Record of the 2nd Meeting of the Committee of the Whole (II)* (New York, April 13, 1976), UNCITRAL, 9th Session, UN Doc A/CN.9/9/C.2/SR.2, at 9, para 48 (1976) (Comment by Mr Domke) (criticizing the draft provision because "it included a presumption of representation and since the powers conferred on an agent depended on national and local law rather than on UNCITRAL rules").

The practice varies with respect to duly authorized representatives. In some, but not all, jurisdictions, for example, it may be necessary for a party to issue a power of attorney in order for its appointed person to be duly authorized to act before the tribunal on a party's behalf.[15]

Article 5 allows a party to be represented or assisted "by persons chosen by it." In contrast, corresponding Article 4 of the 1976 UNCITRAL Rules used the slightly different phrase "by persons of their choice." Though the distinction in formulation is subtle, it was carefully considered. The Working Group concluded that the formulation "by persons chosen by it" was more appropriate "to avoid the implication that the party had an unrestricted discretion, at any time during the proceedings, to impose the presence of any counsel (for example, a busy practitioner that would be unable to meet reasonable times schedules set by the arbitral tribunal)."[16] Thus, in large part, the revision was meant to clarify that Article 5 does not tolerate a party's abuse of the right of representation or assistance aimed at unduly disrupting the arbitral proceedings.[17]

Depriving a party of its right to representation and assistance should be approached with significant caution since, as mentioned, it could easily invite challenges to the validity of an award. Berger has admonished that such an extreme remedy should be limited to only "the truly blatant cases of disruption."[18] Late appointments or changes in representation in the middle of the proceedings, for example, should be honored so long as they have been pursued in good faith.[19] Further, because the right to representation and assistance exists independently of the procedural requirements found in Article 5,[20] a party should not be deprived of its rights, for example, because it has failed to communicate the names of an appointed adviser to all parties or to respond to the tribunal's request for proof of authority of a representative in a timely manner.

---

[15] In Belgium, for example, a power of attorney may be required, "Each party shall have the right to be represented by a lawyer or by a representative, in possession of a special power of attorney in writing, approved by the arbitral tribunal." Belgian Judicial Code, Art. 1694(4) as quoted in G Born, *International Commercial Arbitration* (2009) 2292.

[16] *Report of the Working Group on Arbitration and Conciliation on the Work of its Forty-Sixth Session* (New York, February 5–9, 2007), UNCITRAL, 40th Session, UN Doc A/CN.9/619, at 14, para 63 (2007).

[17] See J Castello, "UNCITRAL Rules" in F Weigand (ed) *Practitioner's Handbook on International Commercial Arbitration* (2nd edn 2009) 1426.

[18] K Berger, *International Economic Arbitration* (1993) 393. In one interesting ICSID arbitration, the claimant objected to the respondent's plans to add new counsel at the hearing because such counsel was a member of the same chambers as the president of the tribunal. The tribunal upheld the objection and ordered the proposed counsel barred from further participation in the case, finding that the cardinal rule of immutability of the tribunal contained in Article 56(1) of the ICSID Convention outweighed the right to representation in these circumstances. See *Hrvatska Elektroprivreda, DD and Republic of Slovenia*, Tribunal's Ruling Regarding the Participation of David Mildon QC in Further Stages of the Proceedings (May 6, 2008) (ICSID administered, 1976 UNCITRAL Rules, Slovania-Croatia BIT).

[19] The *travaux préparatoires* for the 1976 UNCITRAL Rules, for example, reflect the view that "representation may take place at any stage of the arbitral proceedings, including any hearing called by the arbitrators or any meeting convened by the arbitrators for the inspection of goods." *Report of the Secretary-General on the Revised Draft Set of Arbitration Rules* (New York, April 7–May 7, 1976), UNCITRAL, 9th Session, Addendum 1 (Commentary), UN Doc A/CN.9/112/Add.1, para 2 (1975), reprinted in (1976) VII UNCITRAL Ybk 166, 168 (Commentary on Draft Article 5).

[20] The first sentence of Article 5 clearly establishes the right to representation and assistance without conditioning its existence on any of the procedural requirements set forth in subsequent sentences. Notably, a prior draft of the provision in the 1976 UNCITRAL Rules that followed the opposite approach ("A party may be represented by a counsel or agent *upon the communication* of the name and address of such person to the other party") was rejected. *Report of the Secretary-General on the Revised Draft Set of Arbitration Rules* (New York, April 7–May 7, 1976), UNCITRAL, 9th Session, UN Doc A/CN.9/112 (1975), reprinted in (1976) VII UNCITRAL Ybk 160, 161 (Draft Article 5) (emphasis added).

(2) Communicating the identity and role of representatives and advisers

For the arbitral process to function properly, it is essential to know who each disputing party has designated to serve as its principal advisers in the proceedings, ie, the persons to which the arbitral tribunal and other parties may turn for the views of a party. For example, a duly authorized representative may file an amended claim on a party's behalf or bind a party to a settlement agreement. The second and third sentences of Article 5 thus require the parties to convey the names, addresses, and functions of the persons who they have appointed as their authorized advisers.

Despite the broad wording of Article 5, the provision should not be construed as obligating each party to communicate information about anyone other than those persons providing meaningful support to its case, both in terms of oral and written representations to the arbitral tribunal and the other parties. Thus, not every person who lends assistance to a party's case must be identified. As Baker and David note, an overly broad interpretation of the provision "could lead to absurdities, such as requiring disclosure of the names and addresses of translators, economists, paralegals, secretaries, perhaps even travel agents."[21] A more functional reading of Article 5 is therefore appropriate and consistent with its obvious purpose of identifying the parties' authorized representatives.[22]

A person's designation in a communication as either someone who is representing or assisting a party does not necessarily resolve the question of whether that person is a duly authorized representative of the party. As discussed above, a person's status in this regard is typically determined under the applicable national law, though Article 5 provides a mechanism for conveying who a party wishes to serve as its duly authorized adviser. It is noteworthy that the Iran–US Claims Tribunal modified the 1976 UNCITRAL Rules to assign clear consequences to a party's designation of a person as someone who either "represents" or "assists." Note 2 of the 1983 Tribunal Rules provides that when a party appoints a "representative," that person is "deemed to be authorized to act before the arbitral tribunal on behalf of the appointing party for all purposes of the case and the acts of the representative shall be binding upon the appointing party."[23] A "representative," however, need not be "licensed to practice law."[24] Note 3 provides that a person "chosen to assist" (and not to represent) is "not deemed to be authorized to act before the arbitral tribunal on behalf of the appointing party, to bind the appointing party or to receive notices, communications or documents on behalf of the appointing party."[25] The

---

[21] S Baker and M Davis, *The UNCITRAL Arbitration Rules in Practice: The Experience of the Iran-United States Claims Tribunal* (1992) 13. As the *travaux préparatoires* for the 1976 UNCITRAL Rules indicate, the US delegate raised concerns that a literal reading of the text "would mean that the names and addresses of all persons assisting the parties, and not just those of the legal representatives or agents, would have to be communicated...." *Summary Record of the 15th Meeting of the Committee of the Whole (II)* (New York, April 21, 1976), UNCITRAL, 15th Session, UN Doc A/CN.9/9/C.2/SR.15, at 3, para 23 (Comment by Mr Holtzmann, United States). Although his proposal to use the clarifying phrase "legally represented or assisted" appeared to gain a consensus, no changes to the text were ultimately made. UNCITRAL, 15th Session, UN Doc A/CN.9/9/C.2/SR.15, at 3–4.

[22] Castello agrees, noting that a possible misreading of the provision "results from the drafters' attempt to broaden the Article to include non-lawyers by referring to persons who 'assist' a party." J Castello, "UNCITRAL Rules," n 17, 1425.

[23] See 1983 Procedural Rules of the Iran–US Claims Tribunal, reprinted in Appendix 5.

[24] 1983 Procedural Rules of the Iran–US Claims Tribunal.

[25] 1983 Procedural Rules of the Iran–US Claims Tribunal.

UNCITRAL Rules might have also benefited from greater clarity along this line had varying domestic practices not prevented a clearer rule on authority.[26]

Any communication made pursuant to Article 5 constitutes a "notice," as defined in Article 2 of the Rules and "may be transmitted by any means of communication that provides or allows for a record of its transmission."[27] Consistent with Article 2, Article 5 communications need not be conveyed in writing.[28] However, Counsel's signature on an arbitral submission alone is arguably insufficient to satisfy the communication requirements of Article 5, particularly in light of the fact that it is a party that must specify whether an appointment is being made "for purposes of representation or assistance."[29] That said, a party can easily satisfy the requirements by conveying the appropriate information in one of its initial submissions before the arbitral tribunal or at a preliminary conference of the parties. It has been the practice of some tribunals to memorialize the disputing parties' appointments in the initial procedural order.[30]

(3) Proof of a representative's authority

The fourth sentence of Article 5 empowers the arbitral tribunal to demand proof of a representative's authority to act on behalf of a disputing party. The 1976 UNCITRAL Rules contained no such provision, though the Committee engaged in some discussion regarding proof of representation. The delegate from Hungary, for example, wanted to include a provision to address the matter, believing that in arbitration "it was necessary for the representative to provide evidence of power of attorney."[31] The Chairman, however, cautioned that evidence of a person's representative authority was not a universal requirement, noting, for example, that "proof of power of attorney was not a requirement in the civil law of most Western countries."[32] In addition, as discussed above in section 2(B)(1),

---

[26] In contrast, Article 21(4) of the 1998 ICC Rules, which is closely harmonized with French law, allows a party to "appear" either "in person or through duly authorized representatives," though it also allows a party to be "assisted by advisers." ICC Rules of Arbitration, 1998. For commentary see Y Derains and E Schwartz, *A Guide to the ICC Rules of Arbitration* (2nd edn 2005) 291.

[27] See discussion of Article 2 in Chapter 12.

[28] In contrast, corresponding Article 4 of the 1976 UNCITRAL Rules included a writing requirement. The decision to drop the writing requirement was made to ensure consistency with the manner in which communications were exchanged among the parties in accordance with Article 2 of the 2010 UNCITRAL Rules. *Report of the Working Group on Arbitration and Conciliation on the Work of its Forty-Sixth Session* (New York, February 5–9, 2007), UNCITRAL, 40th Session, UN Doc A/CN.9/619, at 15, para 68 (2007). For discussion of Article 2 see Chapter 12.

[29] The *travaux préparatoires* on this point are scant, though arguably support this conclusion. In developing the 1976 UNCITRAL Rules, it was proposed that the article on representation provide that a communication is "deemed to have been given where the notice of arbitration, the statement of claim, the statement of defence, or a counter-claim is submitted on behalf of a party by a counsel or agent." *Report of the Secretary-General on the Revised Draft Set of Arbitration Rules* (New York, April 12–May 7, 1976), UNCITRAL, 9th Session, UN Doc A/CN.9/112 (1975), reprinted in (1976) VII UNCITRAL Ybk 160, 161 (Draft Article 5). That formulation, which appeared to favor constructive notice, was ultimately rejected, though without explanation.

[30] See, eg, *William Ralph Clayton* et al, and *Government of Canada*, Procedural Order No 1 (April 9, 2009) (PCA administered, 1976 UNCITRAL Rules, NAFTA Chapter Eleven), at 3 para 7; *Consolidated Canadian Cattle Claims* and *United States of America* (October 20, 2006) (Ad Hoc Proceeding, 1976 UNCITRAL Rules, NAFTA Chapter Eleven Arbitration), at 1, para 1.2; both reprinted in section 2(C).

[31] *Summary Record of the 2nd Meeting of the Committee of the Whole (II)* (New York April 13, 1976), UNCITRAL, 9th Session, UN Doc A/CN.9/9/C.2/SR.2, at 8, para 46 (1976) (Comment by Mr Szász, Hungary). He was supported by the delegate from Austria. UNCITRAL, 9th Session, UN Doc A/CN.9/9/C.2/SR.2 at 9, para 50 (Comment by Mr Melis, Austria).

[32] UNCITRAL, 9th Session, UN Doc A/CN.9/9/C.2/SR.2, n 31, at 8, para 47 (Comment by the Chairman).

in drafting the 1976 UNCITRAL Rules, a proposed draft provision that contained a presumption of representative authority when a person filed certain submissions on behalf of a party was rejected in favor of leaving the question of authority to be determined by the applicable law.

In the course of revising the UNCITRAL Rules, the Working Group revisited the issue of addressing proof of authority in the Rules. Some delegates were opposed because "requiring disclosure of the scope of authority might prove difficult in certain circumstances, as it could have the consequence of forcing disclosure of certain communications between the party and its representatives that should be kept confidential, such as for example, a power to settle a claim at a certain amount."[33] Others supported a provision on proof of authority so long as it was drafted with enough flexibility to allow the arbitral tribunal to determine *sua sponte* the extent to which information regarding a person's scope of authority was necessary.[34] According to proponents, "the intention of [such a] provision was not to deprive a party of its right to choose a representative but rather to confirm to the other party that a person was actually the representative of a party to the arbitration."[35]

The fourth sentence of Article 5 thus should not be read as necessitating confirmation of a person's representative authority in every case.[36] Rather, the arbitral tribunal has discretion to clarify questions regarding a person's scope of authority, as appropriate, by demanding proof of authority in the appropriate form in light of the varying approaches of different legal systems.[37] Nevertheless, it is good practice for an arbitral tribunal to take whatever steps necessary at the outset of the proceedings to ensure it is dealing with persons who are in fact duly authorized to speak and act on behalf of a party to the proceedings.[38]

(4) Practice of the Iran–US Claims Tribunal

As explained above, the Tribunal modified Article 4 of the 1976 UNCITRAL Rules so that a party's "appointed representative" is "deemed to be authorized to act before the arbitral tribunal on behalf of the appointing party."[39] The Tribunal Rules also establish a procedure for filing notices of appointment of representatives with the Registrar. In the face of a sizable and fast-moving docket, this framework allowed the Tribunal to assume with reasonable confidence that the appointed representatives before it are duly authorized to act on behalf of and bind their respective parties. Though the modified Tribunal Rules do not

---

[33] *Report of the Working Group on Arbitration and Conciliation on the Work of its Forty-Sixth Session* (New York, February 5–9, 2007), UNCITRAL, 40th Session, UN Doc A/CN.9/619, at 15, para 65 (2007).

[34] UNCITRAL, 40th Session, UN Doc A/CN.9/619, n 33, at 15, para 66.

[35] UNCITRAL, 40th Session, UN Doc A/CN.9/619, n 33, at 15, para 66.

[36] Indeed, according to the Iran–US Claims Tribunal, the similar provisions of the Tribunal Rules "do not contain any requirement for a power of attorney to be submitted, neither prior to the filing date for claims nor later." *Starrett Housing Corp* and *Islamic Republic of Iran*, Order of December 17, 1982, *reprinted in* 1 Iran US CTR 385, 388 (1982). *See also H A Spalding, Inc.* and *Ministry of Roads and Transport of the Islamic Republic of Iran*, et al, Final Award of February 24, 1986, *reprinted in* 10 Iran-US CTR 22, 25 n 7 (1986); *International Technical Products Corp* and *Iran*, *reprinted in* 9 Iran-US CTR 10, 15 (1985 II).

[37] *Report of Working Group II (Arbitration and Conciliation) on the Work of its Forty-Ninth Session* (Vienna, September 15–19, 2008), UNCITRAL, 42nd Session, UN Doc A/CN.9/665, at 10, para 43 (2008).

[38] Born recommends that regardless of national requirements, the arbitral tribunal should "require the parties to supply formal written evidence confirming the authority of their legal representative at the outset of arbitral proceedings" and notes that "[a]lthough tribunals frequently rely on the professional ethics and reputation of counsel, doing so involves some risk of subsequent claims that counsel took procedural steps or made concessions or arguments that were not authorized by the party or that the party was not provided with notice of significant events in the arbitration." G Born, *International Commercial Arbitration* (2009) 2304.

[39] See 1983 Procedural Rules of the Iran–US Claims Tribunal, reprinted in Appendix 5.

require appointed representatives "to be licensed to practice law," in many cases they are. While the general practice of the Tribunal is not to require proof of power of attorney,[40] these are often supplied voluntarily.[41]

Perhaps ironically, the cases before the Tribunal giving rise to the most controversy have been those where additional proof of authority was requested. In the *Flexi-Van Leasing* case, for example, Judge Holtzman dissented from Chamber One's order requesting the claimant to provide an original power of attorney, arguing that not only did the Tribunal Rules not require such proof, but the request was also inequitable because it was directed only at the claimant.[42] Judge Holtzmann would dissent again from orders in six cases requiring the Iranian Deputy Agent to submit further proof of his authority to request the dismissal of claims or, if unavailable, a petition for dismissal signed by a duly authorized representative of the Iranian claimants.[43] Judge Holtzmann saw no reason why requests for dismissal by the Iranian Deputy Agent should be subject to a higher standard of scrutiny than any other actions in proceedings before the Tribunal, as the power of the Iranian Agent and Deputy Agent to act on behalf of Iran was clearly established in the Claims Settlement Declaration. Further, Judge Holtzmann raised concerns that imposing a "rigid standard" of evidence would impose a "new and time-consuming burden on the Tribunal which complicates our procedures and delays action on Cases before us."[44]

The pressures of adjudicating thousands of claims in a timely manner undoubtedly influenced the Tribunal's modifications of the 1976 UNCITRAL Rules and its fairly lenient practice (almost resistance at times) toward requiring further proof of authority from a party's representatives.[45] This is not necessarily the right approach in the context of one-off commercial or investor–state arbitrations which may lack the same institutionalized procedures and practices. The last sentence of Article 5 of the 2010 UNCITRAL Rules confirms that the tribunal has the power to request proof of authority, and it should not hesitate to use it in appropriate cases.

(5) Comparison to the 1976 UNCITRAL Rules

Article 5 of the 2010 UNCITRAL Rules and corresponding Article 4 of the 1976 UNCITRAL Rules, while substantially similar in many respects, also differ in certain ways.

The first sentence of Article 5 includes the phrase "person chosen by it" instead of "persons of their choice," as used in Article 4 of the 1976 UNCITRAL Rules. As

---

[40] *Starrett Housing Corp* and *Islamic Republic of Iran*, Order of December 17, 1982, *reprinted in* 1 Iran US CTR 385, 388 (1982). *See also H A Spalding, Inc* and *Ministry of Roads and Transport of the Islamic Republic of Iran*, et al, Award No 212-437-3 (February 24, 1986), reprinted in 10 Iran-US CTR 22, 25 n 7 (1986); *International Technical Products Corp* and *Iran*, reprinted in 9 Iran-US CTR 10, 15 (1985-II).

[41] C Borris "Die UNCITRAL Schiedsregeln in der Praxis des Iran-United States Claims Tribunal" (1988) 2 Jahrbuch für die Praxis der Schiedsgerichtsbarkeit 3, 8.

[42] *Flexi-Van Leasing, Inc* and *Islamic Republic of Iran*, Judge Holtzmann's Dissent from Order of June 15, 1982 1 Iran-US CTR 166, 167 (June 15, 1982), reprinted in section 2(D).

[43] Judge Holtzmann's Dissent in Case Nos 778, 783, 836, 847, 890, and 945, reprinted in section 2(D). For a discussion of the Iranian Agent's authority over proposed settlement agreements, see J Selby and D Stewart, "Practical Aspects of Arbitrating Claims Before the Iran-United States Claims Tribunal," (1984) 18 Intl Lawyer 211, 241–2.

[44] Judge Holtzmann's Dissent in Case Nos 778, 783, 836, 847, 890, and 945, at 36, reprinted in section 2(D).

[45] In hindsight, this approach does not appear to have been problematic. The authors are aware of only one case in which a request for power of attorney may have exposed a fraudulent claimant. See *Gordon Williams* and *Islamic Republic of Iran*, Award No 342-187-3, reprinted in 17 Iran-US CTR 269, 293 (December 18, 1987); *Federal Reserve Bank of New York v Gordon Williams*, 708 F Supp 4–8 (SDNY 1989).

discussed above, the revision was meant to avoid creating the misimpression that a party could compel the participation of a busy practitioner in the arbitration, particularly as a tactic for delaying the proceedings. However, it is difficult to imagine that a tribunal or reviewing court would construe the 1976 language as a justifiable basis for such misconduct.

The second sentence of Article 5 adds the requirement that the names and addresses of appointed persons must be communicated to "the members of the tribunal" in addition to the parties, as the second sentence of corresponding Article 4 of the 1976 UNCITRAL Rules required. This revision is largely technical, but better reflects the realities of such communications which undoubtedly would be shared with the arbitral tribunal, even under the 1976 UNCITRAL Rules.

The third sentence of Article 5 omits the writing requirement for a communication that previously existed in the second sentence of Article 4 of the 1976 UNCITRAL Rules. This change tracks the general approach of the Rules, as reflected in Article 2, to eliminate writing requirements generally.

The fourth sentence of Article 5 is new to the UNCITRAL Rules, expressly granting the arbitral tribunal authority to require proof of a person's authority to represent a party. The lack of such a provision in the 1976 UNCITRAL Rules is not critical, however, since a tribunal in any event has adequate authority under Article 15(1) to conduct the proceedings in such manner as it considers appropriate, including by requiring proof of a representative's authority.[46] The Iran–US Claims Tribunal exercised such powers, for example, in *Flexi-Van Leasing Inc.*[47]

Finally, Article 5 contain technical revisions (eg, "The parties" is replaced with "Each party") in order to clarify that the Rules may be applicable in the context of multi-party arbitration.

C. Extracts from the Practice of Investment Tribunals

Consolidated Canadian Cattle Claims and *United States of America* (October 20, 2006) (*Ad Hoc* Proceeding, 1976 UNCITRAL Rules, NAFTA Chapter Eleven), at 1:

> 1.2. The representation of the Parties in this procedure is as follows
> (UNCITRAL Rule 4):
> Counsel for Claimants:
> [Counsel's name, firm, address, telephone and fax numbers, and e-mail address]
> Counsel for Respondent:
> [Counsel's name, government agency, address, telephone and fax numbers, and e-mail address]

William Ralph Clayton, et al and *Government of Canada*, Procedural Order No 1 (April 9, 2009) (PCA administered, 1976 UNCITRAL Rules, NAFTA Chapter Eleven), at 3:

> C. Representation of the Disputing Parties (Article 4 of the UNCITRAL Arbitration Rules)

---

[46] See 1976 UNCITRAL Arbitration Rules, art 15(1). For discussion of corresponding revised Article 17(1), see Chapter 2.

[47] *Flexi-Van Leasing Inc* and *Islamic Republic of Iran*, Order dated June 17, 1982, reprinted in 1 Iran-US CTR 166, 167 (1982). In that case, the American arbitrator, Judge Holtzmann, implicitly acknowledged the Tribunal's Article 15 powers in this area, though he dissented from Chamber One's order on the basis that its power had been exercised inequitably against the American claimant. Judge Holtzmann's dissent is reproduced below in section 2(D).

7. The Claimants are represented by:
   [Counsel's name, firm, address, telephone and fax numbers, and e-mail address]
8. The Respondent is represented by:
   [Counsel's name, government agency, address, telephone and fax numbers, and e-mail address]

D. Extracts from the Practice of the Iran–US Claims Tribunal

Judge Holtzmann's Dissent Concerning Order, Flexi-Van Leasing Inc and *Islamic Republic of Iran*, Case No 36, Chamber 1, Order of June 15, 1982, reprinted in 1 Iran-US CTR 166, 167 (1982):

> I respectfully dissent from the inclusion in the Order, dated June 15, 1983, of a requirement that Claimant's counsel submit to the Tribunal a written power of attorney. My reasons are:
> 1. No requirement for such a power of attorney is contained in the "Provisionally Adopted Tribunal Rules" (the "Tribunal Rules") nor in the [1976] UNCITRAL Arbitration Rules on which they are based.
> 2. There is no reasonable basis for questioning the authority of Claimant's counsel in this case, and Respondent asserts none.
> 3. It is inequitable to order Claimant's counsel to submit a written power of attorney without at the same time equally requiring a power of attorney from the counsel representing the Respondent. Article 15 of the [1983] Tribunal Rules permits the arbitral tribunal "to conduct the arbitration in such manner as it considers appropriate, *provided the parties are treated with equality*" (emphasis added). The unequal treatment in this case is particularly glaring when one notes that Claimant has included in its Statement of Claim the name of its counsel in compliance with Article 18, Paragraph 1(h) of the [1983] Tribunal Rules, and has thereby also complied with the requirement of Article 4 of the Tribunal Rules, while the Respondent has been permitted to ignore its similar obligations under both Article 19, Paragraph 2 and Article 4 of the [1983] Tribunal Rules.
> 4. Counsel for Claimant clearly stated at the prehearing conference that he would voluntarily submit a power of attorney in order not to waste everyone's time in discussion on the matter. In these circumstances, there was no need for a written order and the issuance of a one-sided order is highly inappropriate.

Dissenting Opinion of Howard M Holtzmann from Orders Requiring Iranian Officials to Submit Further Proof that they are Authorized Representatives of the Entities for Which They Acted, Case Nos 778, 783, 836, 847, 890, and 945, January 26, 1983, *reprinted in* 2 Iran-US CTR 35, 36 (1983):

> Hundreds, perhaps thousands, of documents have been filed with the Tribunal on behalf of Iranian parties. There has been little consistency with respect to the form of the Iranian signatures on such documents. Often the documents are signed by the Agent or Deputy Agent; indeed requests by Iranian entities for extensions of time and various motions are typically so signed, and have been acted upon even though the Statement of Claim or the Statement of Defense may have been signed by a different Iranian official and may have designated another representative. In a number of Cases, Iranian parties have ignored the requirements of Article 4 and Article 19, paragraph 2 of the [1983] Tribunal Rules which require a party to give written notice of the name of its representative, a matter which I noted in one of my earlier dissents; nevertheless, subsequent documents signed by various officials have been received and acted upon. The title or authority of Iranian signatories is not always clear. However, despite these inconsistencies, the Tribunal has not previously, on its own motion, ordered further proof that a document was signed by an authorized Iranian representative.

While a rigid requirement concerning proof of authority for signing all documents might have been adopted at the outset of the proceeding of the Tribunal, instead a practical approach has been followed in which signatures have been accepted, *prima facie*, as being authorized and authentic. Adopting a rigid standard in these six Cases imposes a new and time-consuming burden on the Tribunal which further complicates our procedures and delays action on Cases before us. Nor do I believe that it is appropriate to apply a higher standard of proof of authenticity to documents requesting withdrawal, as in these Cases, and a more lenient standard to other documents. That is because, in addition to requests for withdrawal, many other documents submitted by Iranian parties also significantly affect the rights of parties or the proceedings of the Tribunal.

. . .

Moreover, the practice of Iran in filing documents with the Tribunal precludes doubts as to their authenticity. It is the Iranian practice for documents to be delivered to the Tribunal Registry, either by the Agent or Deputy Agent or by a representative of the official Iranian Bureau which coordinates or conducts all litigation before the Tribunal.

Chapter 10

The Notice Initiating Arbitration and the Response

1. Introduction	359
2. The Notice Initiating Arbitration—Article 3	360
A. Text of the 2010 UNCITRAL Rule	360
B. Commentary	361
(1) The requirement to communicate a notice of arbitration—Article 3(1)	361
(2) The date of commencement of arbitration proceedings—Article 3(2)	362
(3) Mandatory information provided in the notice of arbitration—Article 3(3)	363
(4) Additional information provided in the notice of arbitration—Article 3(4)	364
(5) Insufficiency of the notice of arbitration—Article 3(5)	364
(6) International investment agreements and the notice of arbitration	365
(7) The notice of arbitration at the Iran–US Claims Tribunal	366
(8) Comparison to the 1976 UNCITRAL Rules	368
C. Extracts from the Practice of Investment Tribunals	369
3. The Response to the Notice of Arbitration—Article 4	370
A. Text of the 2010 UNCITRAL Rule	370
B. Commentary	370
(1) The requirement to respond to the notice of arbitration—Article 4(1)	370
(2) Mandatory contents of the response to the notice of arbitration—Article 4(1)	372
(3) Optional contents of the response to the notice of arbitration—Article 4(2)	373
(4) Absence, lateness, or insufficiency of the response to the notice of arbitration—Article 4(3)	373
(5) Comparison to the 1976 UNCITRAL Rules	373

1. Introduction

Parties bound by an arbitration clause or agreement which provides for disputes to be arbitrated under the UNCITRAL Rules are required by Article 3 to provide a formal notice of arbitration to initiate the proceedings. Article 3(1) explicitly states this notice requirement, while Article 3(2) establishes the date of receipt of notice as the operative date for commencement of the proceedings. Article 3(3) details the information which must be included in the notice of arbitration; Article 3(4) gives claimants the option of accelerating the proceedings by providing additional information. Article 3(5) ensures that any inadequacies in the notice do not prevent the arbitral proceedings from moving forward.

Article 4 governs the procedure for responding to the notice of arbitration. Article 4(1) establishes the general response requirement, the 30-day time limit for a response, and the items of information to be included in the response. Article 4(2) provides the respondent the option of accelerating the proceedings by including additional information in the response. Article 4(3) ensures that the absence, lateness, or insufficiency of the response does not hinder advancement of the arbitral process.

2. The Notice Initiating Arbitration—Article 3

A. Text of the 2010 UNCITRAL Rule[1]

Article 3 of the 2010 UNCITRAL Rules provides:

1. The party or parties initiating recourse to arbitration (hereinafter called the "claimant") shall communicate to the other party or parties (hereinafter called the "respondent") a notice of arbitration.
2. Arbitral proceedings shall be deemed to commence on the date on which the notice of arbitration is received by the respondent.
3. The notice of arbitration shall include the following:
   (a) A demand that the dispute be referred to arbitration;
   (b) The names and contact details of the parties;
   (c) Identification of the arbitration agreement that is invoked;
   (d) Identification of any contract or other legal instrument out of or in relation to which the dispute arises or, in the absence of such contract or instrument, a brief description of the relevant relationship;
   (e) A brief description of the claim and an indication of the amount involved, if any;
   (f) The relief or remedy sought;
   (g) A proposal as to the number of arbitrators, language and place of arbitration, if the parties have not previously agreed thereon.
4. The notice of arbitration may also include:
   (a) A proposal for the designation of an appointing authority referred to in article 6, paragraph 1;
   (b) A proposal for the appointment of a sole arbitrator referred to in article 8, paragraph 1;
   (c) Notification of the appointment of an arbitrator referred to in article 9 or article 10.
5. The constitution of the arbitral tribunal shall not be hindered by any controversy with respect to the sufficiency of the notice of arbitration, which shall be finally resolved by the arbitral tribunal.

---

[1] Corresponding Article 3 of the 1976 UNCITRAL Rules provides:

1. The party initiating recourse to arbitration (hereinafter called the "claimant") shall give to the other party (hereinafter called the "respondent") a notice of arbitration.
2. Arbitral proceedings shall be deemed to commence on the date on which the notice of arbitration is received by the respondent.
3. The notice of arbitration shall include the following:
   (a) A demand that the dispute be referred to arbitration;
   (b) The names and addresses of the parties;
   (c) A reference to the arbitration clause or the separate arbitration agreement that is invoked;
   (d) A reference to the contract out of or in relation to which the dispute arises;
   (e) The general nature of the claim and an indication of the amount involved, if any;
   (f) The relief or remedy sought;
   (g) A proposal as to the number of arbitrators (i.e. one or three), if the parties have not previously agreed thereon.
4. The notice of arbitration may also include:
   (a) The proposals for the appointments of a sole arbitrator and an appointment authority referred to in article 6, paragraph 1;
   (b) The notification of the appointment of an arbitrator referred to in article 7;
   (c) The statement of claim referred to in article 18.

B. Commentary

(1) The requirement to communicate a notice of arbitration—Article 3(1)

Article 3(1) provides that a claimant must send a notice of arbitration to a respondent in order to initiate arbitral proceedings. The purpose of the rule is "to inform the respondent...that arbitral proceedings have been started and that a particular claim will be submitted for arbitration."[2] Since the notice requirement is a standard provision of most procedural rules of arbitration, Article 3(1) was originally adopted as part of the 1976 UNCITRAL Rules after minor revision, without much discussion.[3] The Working Group tasked with revising the Rules made only minor technical changes to the rule.[4]

The notice requirement in Article 3(1) is part of a larger "two-tiered approach" to pleading under the Rules.[5] As originally conceived, the two-tiered approach would allow the claimant either to send the statement of claim together with the notice of arbitration or separately at a later stage of the proceedings.[6] Some representatives favored consolidating the requirements of the notice of arbitration and the statement of claim in the interests of accelerating the proceedings and reducing the cost of arbitration to the parties. The Belgian representative also expressed concern that a two-step process could "give rise to delaying tactics on the part of the respondent."[7]

Others favored maintaining the distinction between the notice of arbitration and the statement of claim. They emphasized the burdens on the claimant of requiring a detailed statement of claim in the early stages of an arbitral proceeding and the value of the two-step process in encouraging parties to resolve their disputes early on, before too much time and money had been expended. For example, one representative stated that it was premature to impose an obligation to communicate details required under original Article 18 at such an early stage in the proceedings, since parties might still be discussing terms of a possible settlement.[8] Another noted that a simple notice of arbitration might lead to early resolution of the dispute with minimum cost to claimants.[9]

---

[2] *Report of the Secretary-General on the Preliminary Draft Set of Arbitration Rules*, UNCITRAL, 8th Session, UN Doc A/CN.9/97 (1974), reprinted in (1975) VI UNCITRAL Ybk 163, 167 (Commentary on Draft Article 3).

[3] As adopted by the Commission, Article 3(1) was modeled after similar provisions in Article 3 of the ECE Arbitration Rules; Article II, paragraph 3 of the ECAFE Arbitration Rules, section 7 of the Commercial Arbitration Rules of the AAA, and section 7 of the Rules and Procedures of the Inter-American Commercial Arbitration Commission. *Report of the Secretary-General on the Revised Draft Set of Arbitration Rules*, UNCITRAL, 9th Session, Addendum (Commentary), UN Doc A/CN.9/112/Add.1 (1975), reprinted in (1976) VII UNCITRAL Ybk 166, 168 (Commentary on Draft Article 4).

[4] See discussion at section 2(B)(8).

[5] *Report of the Working Group on Arbitration and Conciliation on the Work of its Forty-Fifth Session* (Vienna, September 11–15, 2006), UNCITRAL, 40th Session, UN Doc A/CN.9/614, at 11, para 48 (2007); *Summary Record of the 2nd Meeting of the Committee of the Whole (II)*, UNCITRAL, 9th Session, UN Doc A/CN.9/9/C.2/SR.2, at 7, para 35 (1976) (Comment by Mr Guest, United Kingdom).

[6] For an example of this practice, see *Centurian Health Corp*, et al, and *Government of Canada*, Order for the Termination of the Proceedings and Award on Costs (August 2, 2010), at 4, para 9 (PCA administered, 1976 UNCITRAL Rules, NAFTA Chapter Eleven) ("In accordance with Article 3, paragraph 4(3), of the [1976] UNCITRAL Arbitration Rules, the Claimants included their Statement of Claim with the Notice of Arbitration.").

[7] UNCITRAL, 9th Session, UN Doc A/CN.9/9/C.2/SR.2, n 5, at 7–8.

[8] UNCITRAL, 9th Session, UN Doc A/CN.9/9/C.2/SR.2, n 5, at 7–8.

[9] UNCITRAL, 9th Session, UN Doc A/CN.9/9/C.2/SR.2, n 5, at 8.

As a compromise, the Committee decided to maintain a two-tiered system of providing a notice of arbitration and a statement of claim,[10] but to give claimants the option under Article 3(4) of attaching a statement of claim to the notice of arbitration which would satisfy their obligations under original Article 18.

In discussions to revise the UNCITRAL Rules, the Working Group reaffirmed the utility of a two-tiered approach, particularly in cases where there was "an urgent need to start the arbitral proceedings either due to a limitation period, to the need to seek interim relief, or to precipitate negotiation of a settlement."[11] However, as explained below in section 3, it also recognized the importance of allowing the respondent an opportunity to state its views before constitution of the arbitral tribunal. This goal was achieved by requiring the respondent to submit a response to the notice of arbitration within 30 days of receiving the notice of arbitration. With the introduction of this new procedural step under the Rules, the Working Group found it useful to eliminate the option of sending the statement of claim together with the notice of arbitration, in order that the claimant should know the respondent's position before filing its statement of claim.[12] However, as discussed in Chapter 13, the claimant retains the option of indicating at a later stage of the arbitration that its notice of arbitration should serve as its statement of claim.

(2) *The date of commencement of arbitration proceedings—Article 3(2)*

Under Article 3(2), the date of receipt of a notice of arbitration establishes the date for commencement of the arbitral proceedings.[13] Paragraph 2 was added to the Preliminary Draft of Article 3 of the 1976 UNCITRAL Rules after the issue of determining the date of commencement of proceedings was raised by the Hungarians[14] and generally accepted by the representatives as an important issue to be resolved under the rule. As noted in the Commentary on the Revised Draft, "the time of commencement of the arbitral proceedings may have relevance to the question of whether provisions on prescriptions of rights or limitations of actions under national law are operative in relation to the dispute."[15] The original UNCITRAL drafters were concerned that parties have a clear understanding of when the time periods, for example, in statutes of limitations begin to run.

During negotiation of the 1976 UNCITRAL Rules, there was brief discussion of whether such a provision was needed since municipal law likely would have rules governing the commencement of proceedings in relation to prescriptions and limitations.[16] However, in the interests of making the rule explicit for the parties involved and of maintaining uniformity for all UNCITRAL conventions, Article 3(2) was modeled on a similar provision

---

[10] The distinction between Articles 3 and 18 was recognized in *Ethyl Corp* (1976 Rules), reprinted in section 2(C).

[11] UNCITRAL, 40th Session, UN Doc A/CN.9/614, n 5, at 11, para 49.

[12] Under Article 20(1) of the Rules, the claimant may elect to treat the notice of arbitration as its statement of claim *after* constitution of the tribunal when the response to the notice will have already been submitted. Under Article 21(1), the respondent may similarly elect to treat the response to the notice of arbitration as its statement of defence.

[13] See *SD Myers* (1976 Rules), reprinted in section 2(C).

[14] *Report of the Secretary-General on the Preliminary Draft Set of Arbitration Rules*, UNCITRAL, 8th Session, Addendum 3 (Observations), UN Doc A/CN.9/97 (1974), Annex II.

[15] *Report of the Secretary-General on the Revised Draft Set of Arbitration Rules*, UNCITRAL, 9th Session, Addendum 1 (Commentary), UN Doc A/CN.9/112/Add.1 (1975), reprinted in (1976) VII UNCITRAL Ybk 166, 168 (Commentary on Draft Article 4(2)).

[16] *Report of the UNCITRAL*, 8th Session, Summary of Discussion of the Preliminary Draft, UN Doc A/10017, para 24 (1975), reprinted in (1975) VI UNCITRAL Ybk 24, 27.

in Article 14 of the 1974 Convention on the Limitation Period in the International Sale of Goods,[17] and adopted.

The Committee chose not to include any specific language to define receipt, leaving that issue to be resolved under Article 2(1) of the 1976 Rules, now Article 2(2) of the 2010 Rules.

Article 3(2) of the 2010 Rules is identical to the original rule and was adopted by the Working Group without revision.

(3) Mandatory information provided in the notice of arbitration—Article 3(3)

Article 3(3) lists the information which must be included in a valid notice of arbitration. By expressly providing for the contents of the notice, the drafters were trying to ensure that the respondent received information "sufficient to apprise the respondent of the general context of the claim asserted against him"[18] and "to enable him to decide on his future course of action."[19]

Subparagraph (a) explicitly requires the claimant to include in the notice of arbitration a demand that the dispute be referred to arbitration. Subparagraphs (b) through (e) require the claimant to identify the names and contact details of the parties, the arbitration agreement invoked, the contract[20] or any other legal instrument out of which the dispute arises,[21] to provide a brief description of the claim and amount involved. Subparagraph (f) obligates the claimant to include the remedy or relief sought.[22]

Subparagraph (g) requires the claimant to make a proposal regarding the number of arbitrators, the language of the arbitration, and the place of arbitration, if the parties have not previously agreed on these terms. With respect to the number of arbitrators, there was general agreement on this provision during negotiations of the 1976 UNCITRAL Rules.[23] The drafters emphasized, however, that parties should be encouraged to reach agreement on the number of arbitrators when they are in the process of drafting an arbitration clause or agreement as recommended in the model UNCITRAL arbitration clause.[24] The same guidance would apply with respect to choosing the language and place of arbitration, items which were added to Article 3(2)(g) for the first time in the 2010 UNCITRAL Rules.[25]

---

[17] *Report of the Secretary-General on the Revised Draft Set of Arbitration Rules*, UNCITRAL, 9th Session, Addendum 1 (Commentary), UN Doc A/CN.9/112/Add.1 (1975), reprinted in (1976) VII UNCITRAL Ybk 166, 167 (Commentary on Draft Article 3(1)).

[18] *Report of the Secretary-General on the Preliminary Draft Set of Arbitration Rules*, UNCITRAL, 8th Session, UN Doc A/CN.9/97 (1974), reprinted in (1975) VI UNCITRAL Ybk 163, 167 (Commentary on Draft Article 3(2)).

[19] *Report of the Secretary-General on the Revised Draft Set of Arbitration Rules*, UNCITRAL, 9th Session, Addendum 1 (Commentary), UN Doc A/CN.9/112/Add.1 (1975), reprinted in (1976) VII UNCITRAL Ybk 166, 168 (Commentary on Draft Article 4).

[20] The claimant must identify the contract but need not include a copy of it in the notice of arbitration. During discussions to revise the rules, a proposal was made to require inclusion of the contract itself, but it determined that "such a requirement would be unnecessarily burdensome...." UNCITRAL, 40th Session, UN Doc A/CN.9/614, n 5, at 12, para 52.

[21] In investment arbitration, the international investment agreement often serves as the instrument out of or in relation to which the dispute arises. See *Link-Trading* and *Dept for Customs Control of Republic of Moldova*, Award on Jurisdiction (February 16, 2001) (*Ad Hoc* Proceeding, 1976 UNCITRAL Rules, US-Moldova BIT), at 6, para 7.

[22] For a discussion of the technical changes made to corresponding Article 3(3) of the 1976 UNCITRAL Rules, see section 2(B)(8).

[23] See Chapter 2, section 2.

[24] See Chapter 2, section 2.

[25] UNCITRAL, 40th Session, UN Doc A/CN.9/614, n 5, at 12, para 53. These additional contents of the notice of arbitration were included "in the interest of improving efficiency of the arbitral proceedings." *Settlement of Commercial Disputes: Revision of the UNCITRAL Arbitration Rules, Note by the Secretariat*, UNCITRAL, UN Doc A/CN.9/WG.II/WP.145 at 10, para 31 (2006).

(4) Additional information provided in the notice of arbitration—Article 3(4)

The drafters of the 1976 UNCITRAL Rules wanted claimants to be aware that while they were required under Article 3(3) to provide certain information in the notice of arbitration, they were not restricted to providing only the listed information. Article 3(4) is intended to give claimants the option to accelerate certain aspects of the proceedings by providing additional information with the notice of arbitration. The same rationale applies with respect to Article 3(4) of the 2010 UNCITRAL Rules.

Under subparagraph (a), the claimant may include its proposal for the appointment of an appointing authority pursuant to Article 6(1). When arbitration is to be conducted by a single arbitrator, subparagraph (b) allows a claimant to propose the name of a sole arbitrator pursuant to Article 8(1). Under subparagraph (c), the claimant may notify the respondent of his appointment of an arbitrator pursuant to Article 9 or Article 10.

Article 3(4), as revised, no longer permits a claimant to include its statement of claim with its notice of arbitration.[26] This change flows directly from the Working Group's decision, as discussed in section 3 of this chapter, to require the respondent to provide a response to the notice of arbitration. It was believed that allowing the claimant to include the statement of claim with the notice of arbitration was no longer prudent because until the respondent submitted its response the claimant "would not know whether it should further develop its position."[27] Thus, the claimant's decision to treat its notice of arbitration as its statement of claim "should be postponed until the stage of proceedings reflected in article [20 on the statement of claim]."[28]

As explained in Chapter 13 on the statement of claim and statement of defence, the claimant and the respondent may decide at a later stage of the proceedings whether, respectively, to have the notice of arbitration serve as the statement of claim or to have the response to the notice of arbitration serve as the statement of defence.

(5) Insufficiency of the notice of arbitration—Article 3(5)

Given that a claimant is obligated under the UNCITRAL Rules to include certain information in the notice of arbitration, an important question arises concerning how to deal with a notice of arbitration that is incomplete or otherwise insufficient. An insufficient notice has the potential to disrupt the arbitral process just as it is getting under way by raising doubts as to whether the arbitral proceedings have formally commenced. The problem may be even more acute in the context of *ad hoc* arbitration where there is no arbitral institution to provide administrative guidance on how to proceed.[29] The Working Group therefore added Article 3(5) to the Rules to address the problem of an incomplete or otherwise insufficient notice of arbitration.

The Working Group initially considered whether the problem of an insufficient notice of arbitration should be addressed in the text of the revised Rules or left to the discretion of

---

[26] The phrase "statement of claim in accordance with" was deleted. *Report of Working Group II (Arbitration and Conciliation) on the Work of its Forty-Ninth Session* (Vienna, September 15–19, 2008), UNCITRAL, 42nd Session, UN Doc A/CN.9/665, at 9, para 36 (2008). For the same reasons, the Working Group also rejected a proposal to include the following provision: "The claimant may elect to treat its notice of arbitration in article 3, paragraph (3) as a statement of claim." 9, para 36.

[27] UNCITRAL, 42nd Session, UN Doc A/CN.9/665, n 26, at 9, para 36.

[28] *Settlement of Commercial Disputes: Revision of the UNCITRAL Arbitration Rules, Note by the Secretariat*, UNCITRAL, UN Doc A/CN.9/WG.II/WP.154 at 6, para 15 (2008).

[29] *Report of the Working Group on Arbitration and Conciliation on the Work of its Forty-Sixth Session* (New York, February 5–9, 2007), UNCITRAL, 40th Session, UN Doc A/CN.9/619, at 12, para 55 (2007).

the arbitral tribunal.³⁰ Article 3(5) ultimately incorporates both approaches. By providing that constitution of the arbitral tribunal "shall not be hindered by any controversy with respect to the sufficiency of the notice of arbitration," Article 3(5) ensures against procedural paralysis at a time when the key decision-making body, the tribunal, is not yet in place.³¹ Article 3(5) also recognizes that the arbitral tribunal, once constituted, has authority to "finally resolve" any controversy with respect to the sufficiency of the notice of arbitration.

Some delegates of the Working Group proposed that Article 3(5) grant the arbitral tribunal express power to request rectification of a notice of arbitration and to determine the consequences of an insufficient notice, such as whether the date of commencement of the arbitral proceedings should be delayed.³² While the Rules do not contain this level of specificity, they do allow the arbitral tribunal, in the event of a controversy over the sufficiency of a notice of arbitration, to "proceed as it considers appropriate." Under this provision, which merely complements the tribunal's general authority under Article 17 to conduct proceedings as it deems appropriate,³³ the tribunal has ample discretion to resolve any questions of delay caused by the filing of an insufficient notice of arbitration.

With the addition of Article 3(5), the Rules are aligned with the arbitral practice of several of the leading arbitral institutions, including the International Chamber of Commerce and the London Court of International Arbitration, among others.³⁴

(6) International investment agreements and the notice of arbitration

Users of the UNCITRAL Rules should be aware that the terms of the international investment agreement, pursuant to which an UNCITRAL arbitration is proceeding, may add notice requirements not contained in the Rules or may supersede those contained in Article 3. The Dominican Republic-Central American Free Trade Agreement (CAFTA-DR), for example, requires the claimant to submit in advance of the notice of arbitration a notice of intent to submit a claim to arbitration including certain basic information about the claim.³⁵ The CAFTA-DR also requires that the notice of arbitration provide either the name of the arbitrator appointed by the claimant or, if no appointment is made, the claimant's written consent for the ICSID Secretary-General to make the appointment.³⁶

Users of the Rules should also note the current work of UNCITRAL in developing rules for transparency in investor–state arbitration, including with respect to publication of information at the commencement of the arbitration.³⁷ At the time of this writing, the Working Group generally supported a provision requiring, upon receipt of the notice of arbitration by the respondent, publication of the name of the disputing parties, the

---

³⁰ UNCITRAL, 40th Session, UN Doc A/CN.9/614, n 5, Chapter 5, at 12, para 54.
³¹ UNCITRAL, 40th Session, UN Doc A/CN.9/619, n 29, at 12–13, para 56.
³² The language of the proposal provided: "In respect of an incomplete notice of arbitration, the arbitral tribunal may request the claimant to remedy the defect within an appropriate period of time, and may delay the date of commencement of the arbitral proceedings until such defect is remedied." UNCITRAL, 40th Session, UN Doc A/CN.9/619, n 29, at 12–13, para 56.
³³ See Chapter 2, section 3 for a discussion of Article 17.
³⁴ See, eg, 1998 LCIA Rules (art 5.4), 2012 ICC Rules (art 4.4), and 2005 Australian Centre for International Commercial Arbitration Rules (art 4.5).
³⁵ CAFTA-DR, art 10.16.2.
³⁶ CAFTA-DR, art 10.16.6.
³⁷ For a general description of UNCITRAL's work in this area, see Chapter 1, section 3(G).

economic sector involved, and the treaty under which the claim is being made.[38] The draft transparency rules also contemplate publication of the notice of arbitration and the response to the notice of arbitration after constitution of the arbitral tribunal.[39]

(7) The notice of arbitration at the Iran–US Claims Tribunal

Since the UNCITRAL Rules were designed to apply to single claim "*ad hoc* arbitration relating to international trade,"[40] it should not be surprising that certain provisions of the Rules were not appropriate in the context of the Iran–US Claims Tribunal.

In its modification of the 1976 UNCITRAL Rules, the Iran–US Claims Tribunal eliminated the need for claimants to provide a notice of arbitration as required under Article 3. While a notice of arbitration is required in *ad hoc* arbitration both to notify the respondent of the claimant's intent to arbitrate a claim and to commence the arbitral process, the Tribunal determined that the Algiers Accords under which it was established did away with this requirement because procedures were already in place under the Accords.[41] Also, much of the information required by Article 3 for the notice of arbitration was covered by Article 18 of the 1983 Tribunal Rules on the requirements for Statements of Claim to be submitted to the Tribunal.

It was particularly significant for the Tribunal that the Statement of Claim under Article 18 of the 1983 Tribunal Rules included a "demand that the dispute be referred to arbitration by the Tribunal," a required part of the notice called for in Article 3(3). The "demand" is important because the claimant's demand for arbitration coupled with a respondent's unconditional appearance can together constitute an agreement to arbitrate. This raised the question of whether the Tribunal's proceedings were subject to the supervisory jurisdiction of the Dutch legal system inasmuch as Dutch law at that time required that the agreement to arbitrate be in writing and signed by the parties.[42]

Undoubtedly, Iran and the United States, the two state parties to the Algiers Accords, knew they were agreeing to arbitration. Moreover, given Iran's challenges in the Dutch

---

[38] *Report of the Working Group on Arbitration and Conciliation on the Work of its Fifty-Sixth Session* (New York, February 6–10, 2012), UNCITRAL, 45th Session, UN Doc A/CN.9/741, at 20–1, para 109 (2012). For the text of the provision, see A/CN.9/WG.II/WP.169, at 8–9, para 25 (Draft Article 2, Option 1).

[39] For the text of the provision, see *Settlement of Commercial Disputes: Preparation of a Legal Standard on Transparency in Treaty-Based Investor-State Arbitration, Note by the Secretariat*, UNCITRAL, UN Doc A/CN.9/WG.II/WP.169 at 9, para 27 (2011) (Draft Article 3).

[40] *Report of the UNCITRAL on the Work of its Sixth Session*, UN GAOR, 28th Session, Supp No 17, UN Doc A/9017, para 85 (1973).

[41] G Aksen, "The Iran-United States Claims Tribunal and the UNCITRAL Arbitrations Rules, an early comment," in J Schultsz and A J van den Berg (eds), *The Art of Arbitration* (1982) 1. See also Chapter 13, section 2 on revised article 20.

[42] The specific provision of the Dutch Code of Civil Procedure referred to provides that the "arbitration agreement...must be made in writing and signed by the parties...." Dutch Code of Civil Procedure, Art 623(1) (Unofficial translation prepared by the Asser Institute, 1980). The arbitration agreement is also significant because such a writing is essential to the enforceability of the award, given that the "in writing" requirement is also set forth in the New York Convention. In particular, Article IV of the New York Convention requires that to obtain recognition and enforcement, the party applying shall present the award and the arbitration agreement, such agreement, by Article II of the Convention, being in writing by the parties.

Van den Berg states, in the context of the New York Convention, that the purpose of the requirement of a written agreement "is to ensure that a party is aware that he is agreeing to arbitration." A J van den Berg, *The New York Convention of 1958: Toward a Uniform Judicial Interpretation* (1981) 171. In this sense, the agreement in writing is the objective manifestation of the consent of the parties, the voluntary act that underlies the notion and legitimacy of arbitration.

court, it is apparent that Iran, like the United States, was aware that it had agreed to arbitration supervised by the Dutch legal system. Thus, Iran could be regarded as being estopped from raising the issue of its written agreement.[43] Hardenberg argues that in the case of claims of nationals before the Tribunal, however, there clearly is not an arbitration agreement between the litigants.[44] In support he cites the Explanatory Note of the Dutch Foreign Ministry accompanying the Dutch Bill:

Given the absence of voluntary prior contractual agreement between the parties concerned in each individual case and the international nature of the agreement between States underlying the arbitration, doubts may arise as to whether this is indeed arbitration within the meaning of Dutch law.[45]

The issue, therefore, was whether not only the state parties, but also the nationals of each state party can be said to have agreed to arbitration.

Although one could argue that the state as agent can bind its nationals,[46] the consent of nationals to arbitrate before the Tribunal may be based on a theory of direct agreement. In particular, the Accords manifest a written agreement between Iran and the United States to participate in binding arbitration of claims brought not only by the state parties, but also by their nationals, even though such nationals were not parties to the Accords. In this sense, the Accords embody a written offer by the two state parties to the nationals of the other state party to arbitrate certain claims.[47] This offer could be accepted in writing by

---

[43] To van den Berg, estoppel, in the context of the New York Convention, would reflect "a fundamental principle of good faith, which principle overrides the formalities required by Article II(2) of the New York Convention." *The New York Convention of 1958*, n 42, 185.

[44] L Hardenberg, "The Awards of the Iran-United States Claims Tribunal Seen in Connection with the Law of the Netherlands," (September 1984) Intl Business Lawyer 337, 338, originally published in Dutch as "De Uitspraken van het Iran-United States Claims Tribunal naar Nederlands recht bezian," (February 11, 1984) Nederlands Juristenblad 167.

[45] Indeed, this problem may explain a less specific statement of a US Department of State official some months after the signing of the Accords: "Upon examination of Dutch law, it became apparent that awards rendered pursuant to the Claims Settlement Declaration would not meet certain procedural requirements for valid arbitral awards under Dutch civil code." M Feldman, "Implementation of the Iranian Claims Settlement Agreement—Status, Issues and Lessons: A View from the Government's Perspective," in M Landwehr (ed), *Private Investors Abroad—Problems and Solutions in Intl Business* (1981) 75, 98.

[46] In particular, it could be argued that each state party possesses the authority to agree to arbitration on behalf of its nationals. As van den Berg wrote in response to Hardenberg, "[i]t is arguable that an arbitration agreement can be considered to be present if one regards Iran and the United States as also representing the interests of their subjects when bringing about the *Claims Settlement Declaration*." A van den Berg, "Proposed Dutch Law on the Iran-United States Claims Settlement Declaration, A Reaction to Mr. Hardenberg's Article," (September 1984) Intl Business Lawyer 341, 343, originally published in Dutch as "Wetsontwerp Iran-United States Claims Tribunal, Een reactie," (February 11, 1984) Nederlands Juristenblad 170 (emphasis in original). Indeed, this position is supported by Article 1(3) of the 1983 Tribunal Rules, which provides: "The Claims Settlement Declaration constitutes an Agreement in writing by Iran and the United States, on their own behalves and *on behalf of their nationals* submitting to arbitration within the framework of the Algiers Declarations and in accordance with the Tribunal Rules." This provision was added to Article 1 of the 1976 UNCITRAL Rules as a part of the Tribunal's modification of those Rules.

[47] Georges Delaume has argued that such a form of agreement would be sufficient for ICSID arbitration: "Consent may also result from the investor's acceptance of a unilateral offer from the contracting State involved when that State has already consented to ICSID arbitration in relevant provisions...of a bilateral treaty with the Contracting State of which the investor is a national." G Delaume, "ICSID Arbitration: Practical Distinctions," (1984) 1(2) J Intl Arb 101, 104. Indeed, the increase in ICSID arbitration in recent years is largely due to the many cases in which the jurisdiction of the Centre is based on a bilateral investment treaty. See S Manciaux, *Investissements étrangers et arbitrages entre États et ressortissants d'autres États: Trente années d'activité du CIRDI* (2004) 191–2. Similarly, although the UNCITRAL Model Law, as amended, requires a written agreement to arbitrate, a writing exists if there is "an exchange of statements of claim and defence in which the existence of an agreement is alleged by one party and not denied by another." Model Law, as amended, art 7(5). See also

individual claimants by the filing of Statements of Claim prior to January 19, 1982. Indeed, each Statement of Claim included an element not normally required by the UNCITRAL Rules, "[a] demand that the dispute be referred to arbitration by the Tribunal...."[48] Although it is true that the Accords compelled US claimants to abandon their proceedings in US courts, the Accords did not compel them to file or defend claims before the Tribunal. As Mr Justice Hobhouse observed in *Dallal v Bank Mellat:* "It was Mr. Dallal's voluntary act to commence the proceedings before the Hague tribunal. It is true that he may have had no other alternative under the law of the United States if he wished to pursue his rights as he saw them. But that does not make it any the less a voluntary act."[49]

A quick response might be that although Dallal's act appeared voluntary in that he was not coerced, is an act truly voluntary when there is no other choice? However, as Mr Justice Hobhouse notes, what choice does any plaintiff have? "Most plaintiffs who commence proceedings are in a similar position. They have to commence proceedings before the appropriate municipal court or else be without legal remedy."[50]

In this sense, it is important that the Tribunal possesses jurisdiction over the claims of nationals of one state party against the other state party, but not vice versa.[51] Unlike in judicial proceedings the nationals of each state party can choose to be a plaintiff, but cannot be forced to be a defendant. Thus, a written agreement to arbitrate exists in the acceptance by the national of one state party of the written offer of the other state party in the Accords through that national's choice to file a written demand for arbitration.[52]

(8) Comparison to the 1976 UNCITRAL Rules

Article 3 is substantially similar to corresponding Article 3 of the 1976 UNCITRAL Rules, though with certain significant differences.

Article 3(1) contains only minor technical revisions. Whereas the original rule is addressed only to "the party" or "the other party," the revised rule refers to the "party or parties" and the "the other party or parties" to account for the possibility that the Rules may be used in multi-party arbitration.[53] The revised rule also replaces the word "give," appearing in the old rule, with "communicate" to ensure consistency with Article 2 of the 2010 UNCITRAL Rules.[54]

Article 3(2) is identical to corresponding Article 3(2) of the 1976 UNCITRAL Rules.

Article 3(3)(b) through (e) contain relatively minor changes in comparison to the corresponding provisions of the 1976 UNCITRAL Rules. In subparagraph (b), the words

---

D Furnish, "Commercial Arbitration Agreements and the Uniform Commercial Code," (1979) 67 California L Rev 317, 347 ("The arbitration agreement should be made amenable to autonomous creation through the same means recognized for the creation of a sales agreement...").

[48] 1983 Rules of Procedure of the Iran–US Claims Tribunal, art 18(1)(a), reprinted in Appendix 5. See Chapter 13.
[49] *Mark Dallal v Bank Mellat*, [1986] 1 All ER 239, 254.
[50] *Mark Dallal*, n 49.
[51] *Islamic Republic of Iran* and *United States of America* (Jurisdiction Over Claims by a State Party Against Nationals of the Other State Party), Decision 1-A2-FT (January 13, 1982), reprinted in 1 Iran-US CTR 101 (1981–1982).
[52] As to the Tribunal's relationship to the Dutch legal system, see generally D Caron, "The Nature of the Iran-United States Claims Tribunal and the Evolving Structure of International Dispute Resolution," (1990) 84 AJIL 104. See also Chapter 2, section 3 on Article 17.
[53] UNCITRAL, 40th Session, UN Doc A/CN.9/619, n 29, at 12, para 51.
[54] A similar proposal to change the word "give" to "deliver" to be more consistent with Article 2 of the UNCITRAL Rules and to include the appointing authority as a recipient of the notice did not find support, UNCITRAL, 42nd Session, UN Doc A/CN.9/665, n 26, at 9, para 33.

"contact details" replace the word "address" to be consistent with other provisions of the Rules, including Article 20(2)(a).[55] In subparagraph (c), the phrase "arbitration clause" used in the 1976 Rules is deleted because that phrase can be "understood as falling under the more generic definition of arbitration agreement."[56] Under subparagraph (d), the words "or other legal instruments" were added to the revised rule to address the case in which a dispute does not arise out of or in relation to a contract.[57] Under subparagraph (e), the words "brief description" have replaced the words "general nature."[58]

Article 3(4) is slightly reorganized in some respects, though the real difference is the elimination of the option of having the notice of arbitration immediately serve as the statement of claim, as was possible under the 1976 UNCITRAL Rules. As explained above, this option no longer exists as the Rules now require communication of a response to the notice of arbitration, and it was believed that a claimant would not be in the best position to file a statement of claim until after it had reviewed the response to the notice of arbitration.

Article 3(5) on sufficiency of the notice of arbitration is also new to the 2010 UNCITRAL Rules. The provision is useful in avoiding uncertainty as to when the proceedings have formally commenced. As a practical matter, however, it may be difficult for parties arbitrating under the 1976 Rules to benefit from adopting it since its principal benefit accrues before establishment of the arbitral tribunal, when it may be difficult to modify the Rules.

C. Extracts from the Practice of Investment Tribunals

Ethyl Corp and *Government of Canada*, Partial Award on Jurisdiction (June 24, 1998) (*Ad Hoc* Proceeding, 1976 UNCITRAL Rules, NAFTA Chapter Eleven), reprinted in (1999) 38 ILM 708, 730:

> 94. The revised and expanded terminology in the Statement of Claim is not intrinsically of such great significance. This is particularly so, bearing in mind that Article 3 of the [1976] UNCITRAL Arbitration Rules, which in this regard remains unmodified by anything in Part B, and which prescribes the form of a notice of arbitration, requires in (3)(e) simply that such notice include "The general nature of the claim and an indication of the amount involved, if any." By contrast, Article 18 of those Rules, likewise unmodified by Part B, requires at (1) (b) and (c) that a statement of claim set forth a "statement of the facts supporting the claim" and the "points in issue." Thus a greater elaboration of detail in the Statement of Claim is permissible, if not, indeed, required.

SD Myers, Inc and *Government of Canada*, Partial Award (February 13, 2000) (*Ad Hoc* Proceeding, 1976 UNCITRAL Rules, NAFTA Chapter Eleven), reprinted in (2001) 40 ILM 1408, 1409:

> 12. On October 30, 1998, SDMI delivered a Notice of Arbitration pursuant to Article 3 of the [1976] Rules. The arbitration is deemed to have "commenced" on that date pursuant to Article 3.1 of the Rules.

---

[55] UNCITRAL, 40th Session, UN Doc A/CN.9/619, n 29, at 12, 28 paras 52,148.
[56] *Settlement of Commercial Disputes: Revision of the UNCITRAL Arbitration Rules, Note by the Secretariat*, UNCITRAL, UN Doc A/CN.9/WG.II/WP.145 at 10, para 32 (2006).
[57] UNCITRAL, 40th Session, UN Doc A/CN.9/619, n 29, at 12, para 54.
[58] UNCITRAL, 40th Session, UN Doc A/CN.9/614, n 5, at 12, para 53.

CME Czech Republic BV and *Czech Republic*, Final Award (March 14, 2003) (*Ad Hoc* Proceeding, 1976 UNCITRAL Rules, The Netherlands/Czech Republic BIT), reprinted in (2003) 15(4) World Trade & Arbitration Materials 83, 91:

> 2. CME Czech Republic B.V. (CME) initiated these arbitration proceedings on February 22, 2000 by notice of arbitration against the Czech Republic pursuant to Art. 3 of the [1976] Arbitration Rules of the United Nations Commission on International Trade Law (UNCITRAL).

3. The Response to the Notice of Arbitration—Article 4

A. Text of the 2010 UNCITRAL Rule[59]

Article 4 of the 2010 UNCITRAL Rules provides:

1. Within 30 days of the receipt of the notice of arbitration, the respondent shall communicate to the claimant a response to the notice of arbitration, which shall include:
   (a) The name and contact details of each respondent;
   (b) A response to the information set forth in the notice of arbitration, pursuant to article 3, paragraph (3) (c) to (g).
2. The response to the notice of arbitration may also include:
   (a) Any plea that an arbitral tribunal to be constituted under these Rules lacks jurisdiction;
   (b) A proposal for the designation of an appointing authority referred to in article 6, paragraph 1;
   (c) A proposal for the appointment of a sole arbitrator referred to in article 8, paragraph 1;
   (d) Notification of the appointment of an arbitrator referred to in article 9 or article 10;
   (e) A brief description of counterclaims or claims for the purpose of a set-off, if any, including where relevant, an indication of the amounts involved, and the relief or remedy sought.
   (f) A notice of arbitration in accordance with article 3 in case the respondent formulates a claim against a party to the arbitration agreement other than the claimant.
3. The constitution of the arbitral tribunal shall not be hindered by any controversy with respect to the respondent's failure to communicate a response to the notice of arbitration, or an incomplete or late response to the notice of arbitration, which shall be finally resolved by the arbitral tribunal.

B. Commentary

(1) The requirement to respond to the notice of arbitration—Article 4(1)

Article 4(1) requires the respondent to send to the claimant a response to the notice of arbitration within 30 days after receiving the notice of arbitration. This mandatory procedural step is new to the 2010 UNCITRAL Rules and was largely a reaction to the two-tiered

---

[59] Article 4 is new to the 2010 UNCITRAL Rules. There is no corresponding provision in the 1976 UNCITRAL Rules.

approach to initiating proceedings under the Rules, according to which the claimant sends the respondent a notice of arbitration and then a statement of claim later in the proceedings. Thus, under the 1976 UNCITRAL Rules, the claimant had two opportunities to take a position on the merits of the dispute before the respondent had its first chance to respond.

In their advisory report commissioned by UNCITRAL in preparation for revising the Rules, Paulsson and Petrochilos described the two-tiered system as imbalanced and inefficient:

> Not to determine the respondent's position—perhaps for six months—is wasteful. It does not promote reciprocal understanding of the dispute, and therefore impedes efficient preparation for both litigation and amical [sic] settlement. Moreover, it is not good practice to constitute an arbitral tribunal without having any indication of the kind of case that will be mounted in defence, as this may bear on the required attributes of arbitrators, especially if any appointment is to be made by an appointing authority; this goes for *both* of the coarbitrators as well as the presiding arbitrator. Finally, giving the respondent an opportunity to submit a response to the claimant's notice of arbitration permits the inclusion of a requirement that the response should contain any counterclaims that the respondent intends to raise. This would, in turn, permit the claimant to articulate in his statement of claim both his positive case (on its claim) and his defensive case (on the respondent's counterclaim).[60]

In discussions on revising the UNCITRAL Rules, the Working Group accordingly considered whether the respondent, like the claimant, should also have an opportunity to state its position before the arbitral tribunal is constituted.[61] The consensus among the Working Group representatives was that allowing such a response would provide the "appropriate balance [in the Rules] between the applicant and the respondent."[62] It was also believed that giving the respondent the opportunity to respond to the notice of arbitration would have the "advantage of clarifying at an early stage of the procedure the main issues raised by the dispute."[63] The respondent, for its part, could state its position in defense of allegations made in the statement of arbitration. The claimant, with the benefit of knowing the respondent's position, could better prepare its statement of claim by addressing both its positive case (on its claim) and its defensive case (on the respondent's claim).[64]

The requirement to respond to the notice of arbitration contained in Article 4(1) was adopted by the Working Group without significant controversy. Some delegates

---

[60] See J Paulsson and G Petrochilos, *Revision of the UNCITRAL Arbitration Rules*, Report to UNCITRAL Secretariat, at 5, para 12(a) (2006).

[61] UNCITRAL, 40th Session, UN Doc A/CN.9/614, n 5, at 12, para 56. Several arbitral rules follow this approach: For instance, such opportunity is provided for in the 2010 SCC Rules (article 5), the 2012 ICC Rules (article 5), and the 1998 LCIA Rules (article 3).

[62] UNCITRAL, 40th Session, UN Doc A/CN.9/614, n 5, at 13, para 57.

[63] UNCITRAL, 40th Session, UN Doc A/CN.9/614, n 5, at 13, para 57.

[64] *Settlement of Commercial Disputes: Revision of the UNCITRAL Arbitration Rules, Note by the Secretariat*, UNCITRAL, UN Doc A/CN.9/WG.II/WP.143 at 8–9, para 40 (2006). In addition, one UNCITRAL delegate explains:

> The Working Group recognized that the delay in hearing from the respondent could make the constitution of a tribunal more difficult (particularly if an appointing authority becomes involved) since the respondent's view of the disputed issues and even the question of whether it has jurisdictional objections are often unknown. The absence of any statement from the respondent could also complicate the tribunal's prompt adoption of a provisional timetable for the arbitration.

J Castello, "Unveiling the 2010 UNCITRAL Arbitration Rules," (May/October 2010) 65 Dispute Resolution J 151.

questioned whether the response to the notice of arbitration should be only permissive, but in the end the provision remained mandatory.[65] As discussed below, the Working Group included Article 4(3) in the Rules to ensure that any failure on the respondent's part to meet the mandatory requirements of Article 4(1) would not hinder constitution of the tribunal, which could then determine the consequences of the respondent's failure to respond to the notice of arbitration. Other delegates felt that the 30-day time limit for communicating a response might be too short in some cases and might not be well synchronized with other time periods in the Rules that were either shorter or longer.[66]

As discussed above in sections 2(B)(1) and (4) of this chapter, the requirement that the respondent provide a response to the notice of arbitration altered the "two-tiered approach" to pleading by eliminating the claimant's option of providing the statement of claim with the notice of arbitration.

(2) Mandatory contents of the response to the notice of arbitration—Article 4(1)

Article 4(1) enumerates the items of information which the respondent must include in its response to the notice of arbitration. Subparagraph (a) requires that the name and contact details of each respondent be included. Under subparagraph (b), the respondent must provide a response to the following items of information included in the claimant's statement of arbitration: the identification of the arbitration agreement that is invoked (Article 3(c)); the identification of any contract or other legal instrument out of or in relation to which the dispute arises or, in the absence of such contract or instrument, a brief description of the relevant relationship (Article 3(d)); a brief description of the claim and an indication of the amount involved, if any (Article 3(e)); the relief or remedy sought (Article 3(f)); and a proposal as to the number of arbitrators, language and place of arbitration, if the parties have not already reached agreement on these matters (Article 3(g)).

Article 4(1)(a)–(b) was uncontroversial and was adopted by the Working Group with minimal discussion. Apart from minor tweaks to the language and structure,[67] the one issue that the Working Group focused on was how to address any pleas by the respondent that the arbitral tribunal lacked jurisdiction. A preliminary draft of Article 4(1) required the respondent to include such a plea in the response to the notice of arbitration.[68] Some observed, however, the possibility of a conflict between that requirement and the provision that became Article 23(2) of the UNCITRAL Rules, which required that such a plea be raised no later than in the statement of defence.[69] Thus, the Working Group decided to move the reference to any jurisdictional plea by the respondent from Article 4(1) to Article 4(2), which listed optional items that might be included in the response to the notice of arbitration.[70]

---

[65] UNCITRAL, 40th Session, UN Doc A/CN.9/619, n 29, at 13, para 58.
[66] UNCITRAL, 40th Session, UN Doc A/CN.9/619, n 29, at 13, para 59.
[67] A preliminary draft of Article 4 required or permitted the respondent to make "any comment" regarding certain information provided in the notice of arbitration, but this proposal was rejected, and more precise language was used, out of concern that the words "any comment" might "not be appropriate if understood to preclude subsequent comment." UNCITRAL, 40th Session, UN Doc A/CN.9/619, n 29, at 13–14, para 60.
[68] *Settlement of Commercial Disputes: Revision of the UNCITRAL Arbitration Rules, Note by the Secretariat*, UNCITRAL, UN Doc A/CN.9/WG.II/WP.147 at 6–8, para 19 (2007) (Draft Article 3(5)).
[69] UNCITRAL, 42nd Session, UN Doc A/CN.9/665, n 26, at 9–10, para 39.
[70] UNCITRAL, 42nd Session, UN Doc A/CN.9/665, n 26, at 9–10, para 39.

(3) Optional contents of the response to the notice of arbitration—Article 4(2)

Article 4(2) provides a respondent the option of submitting additional information in its response to the notice of arbitration beyond what is required to be included under Article 4(1). Under subparagraph (a), a respondent may include any plea that the arbitral tribunal lacks jurisdiction. As discussed above in section 3(B)(2), the Working Group decided to make inclusion of this item non-mandatory to avoid any potential conflict between Article 4 and Article 23(2), which requires that such a plea be raised no later than in the statement of defence.[71] Subparagraph (b) through (e) permit the respondent to provide the following additional information: a proposal for the appointment of an appointing authority; a proposal for the appointment of a sole arbitrator; notification of the appointment of an arbitrator; and a brief description of counterclaims or claims for the purpose of a set-off, including where relevant, an indication of the amounts involved, and the relief or remedy sought.

(4) Absence, lateness, or insufficiency of the response to the notice of arbitration—Article 4(3)

By adding a new requirement under the UNCITRAL Rules for a respondent to file a response to the notice of arbitration, the Working Group had to address the potential problem of a respondent's failure to satisfy that requirement.[72] The Working Group's approach was similar to how it addressed the problem of an insufficient notice of arbitration under Article 3(5).[73] The first sentence of Article 4(3) establishes the general rule to avoid disruption of the arbitral proceedings. If the respondent fails to communicate a response, or if it submits a late or incomplete response, the constitution of the tribunal "shall not be hindered." Once the tribunal is constituted, it has authority to determine the consequences of an inadequate response. The second sentence of Article 4(3) expressly grants the arbitral tribunal authority in these situations to "proceed as it considers appropriate."

(5) Comparison to the 1976 UNCITRAL Rules

Article 4 is new to the 2010 UNCITRAL Rules with no corresponding provision in the 1976 UNCITRAL Rules.

---

[71] UNCITRAL, 42nd Session, UN Doc A/CN.9/665, n 26, at 9–10, para 39.
[72] For a general summary of the discussion, see UNCITRAL, 40th Session, UN Doc A/CN.9/619, n 29, at 12–13, para 56.
[73] See discussion in section 2(B)(5).

Chapter 11

The Choice of Language

1. Introduction	375
2. The Choice of Language—Article 19	376
A. Text of the 2010 UNCITRAL Rule	376
B. Commentary	376
(1) Determination of the language of arbitration—Article 19(1)	376
(2) Translation of documents and exhibits—Article 19(2)	382
(3) Comparison to the 1976 UNCITRAL Rules	384
C. Extracts from the Practice of Investment Tribunals	384
D. Extracts from the Practice of the Iran–US Claims Tribunal	385
(1) Tribunal Rules (1983), Article 17(1)	385
(2) Tribunal Rules (1983), Article 17(2)	387

1. Introduction

In international arbitration, the parties and other persons involved, such as arbitrators, witnesses and experts, may come from different linguistic backgrounds.[1] Priority given to one language may present issues of fairness, while the right of all involved to operate in their own language can lead to inefficiency and delay. The choice of language of the proceedings presents issues addressed by the UNCITRAL Rules—in particular by Article 19(1). This article contains the general provisions for determining the language of oral proceedings and written statements. Article 19(2) supplements these requirements with provisions on determining the translation of annexes and comparable supporting documents. While the choice of language is often uniform, it is important to recognize that there are different aspects of an arbitral proceeding presenting correspondingly different possible choices of language: the written pleadings, the documents supporting those pleadings, the oral proceedings, as well as the language of the award.

---

[1] For a discussion on the choice of language at the Iran–US Claims Tribunal, see D Reichert, "Issues of Language and Translation," in D Caron and J Crook (eds), *The Iran-United States Claims Tribunal and The Process of International Claims Resolution* (2000) 313. As stated by Howard Holtzmann, "[e]vidence is of little use if the parties and the arbitrators cannot understand the language in which it is presented." H Holtzmann, "Fact-Finding by the Iran-United States Claims Tribunal," in R Lillich (ed) *Fact-Finding by International Tribunals* (1991) 101, 128.

2. The Choice of Language—Article 19

A. Text of the 2010 UNCITRAL Rule[2]

1. Subject to an agreement by the parties, the arbitral tribunal shall, promptly after its appointment, determine the language or languages to be used in the proceedings. This determination shall apply to the statement of claim, the statement of defence, and any further written statements and, if oral hearings take place, to the language or languages to be used in such hearings.
2. The arbitral tribunal may order that any documents annexed to the statement of claim or statement of defence, and any supplementary documents or exhibits submitted in the course of the proceedings, delivered in their original language, shall be accompanied by a translation into the language or languages agreed upon by the parties or determined by the arbitral tribunal.

B. Commentary

(1) Determination of the language of arbitration—Article 19(1)

Selection of the place of arbitration does not determine the language to be used in arbitration proceedings, unless the mandatory law of the place prescribes that country's national language as obligatory. However, this is the case in very few, if any, countries.[3] Rather, the determination of the language is usually subject to party autonomy in the first place. This is clearly the point of departure for the UNCITRAL Rules.

According to Article 19(1), the parties, first and foremost, are entitled to determine the language of the proceedings by mutual agreement. Indeed, it is desirable that the parties determine the language in advance by including a relevant provision in their arbitration clause or agreement.[4] In this way, the parties may eliminate a possible source of contention at the very beginning of the arbitral proceedings and thus ensure that efforts at that crucial stage are focused instead on case preparation.[5]

---

[2] Article 19 in the 2010 Rules was adopted without any revision to the text of corresponding Article 17 of the 1976 UNCITRAL Rules.

[3] See T Várady, *Language and Translation in International Commercial Arbitration: From the Constitution of the Arbitral Tribunal Through Recognition and Enforcement Proceedings* (2006) 14–15 (describing restrictions on the use of foreign languages in arbitration in Saudi Arabia, Turkey, Egypt, Jordan, and Oman).

A different issue is the possibility that, with a view to possible court review of enforcement proceedings, the award may eventually have to be translated into (one of) the official language(s) of the country in question. For example, Article IV(2) of the New York Convention states that "if the said award or agreement is not made in an official language of the country in which the award is relied upon, the party applying for recognition and enforcement of the award shall produce a translation of these documents into such language. The translation shall be certified by an official or sworn translator or by a diplomatic or consular agent."

Although hardly any jurisdiction requires that proceedings be conducted in the local language, in some countries the award has to be rendered (and not just translated) in the local language because of possible court review of enforcement proceedings. This is said to be the case in some Arab countries. H van Houtte, "Conduct of Arbitral Proceedings," in P Šarčević (ed) *Essays on International Commercial Arbitration* (1989) 113, 117.

[4] Of course, it is also possible to conclude a separate agreement on this matter. In ICC arbitration, such an agreement might be reached, for example, during the negotiation of the terms of reference.

[5] See P Sanders, "Commentary on UNCITRAL Arbitration Rules," (1977) II Ybk Commercial Arb 180, 193; H de Vries, "International Commercial Arbitration: A Contractual Substitute for National Courts," (1982) 57 Tulane L Rev 42, 70–1; I Dore, *Arbitration and Conciliation under the UNCITRAL Rules: A Textual Analysis* (1986) 56. See also the Model Arbitration Clause (footnote to Article 1), reprinted in Chapter 2, section 2(A).

Where the parties have not agreed on the language to be used, "the arbitral tribunal shall, promptly after its appointment," determine the working language(s). The requirement of "promptness" emphasizes that the decision as to language is a precondition for the commencement of any exchange of pleadings and thus should normally be among the very first acts of an arbitral tribunal.[6] In investor–state arbitration, for example, language issues are often addressed in one of the first procedural orders issued by the arbitral tribunal.[7]

Strictly construed, Article 19 empowers the arbitrators, in the absence of a prior agreement of the parties, to decide unilaterally the issue of language after their appointment. However, consistent with the spirit of arbitration and the principle of party autonomy, the tribunal should consult with and encourage the parties to reach agreement on the issue.[8] This has been the general practice of investment tribunals. The Iran–US Claims Tribunal also followed this path and was ultimately able to rely on agreements between the Agents of Iran and the United States reached after the arbitrators had been appointed.[9]

---

[6] Promptness is not specifically emphasized in Article 22 of UNCITRAL Model Law, a provision modeled on the UNCITRAL rule of arbitral procedure under consideration and not intended to depart from the general principles in that rule. See H Holtzmann and J Neuhaus, *A Guide to the UNCITRAL Model Law on International Commercial Arbitration: Legislative History and Commentary* (1989) 628–9. Article 22 of the Model Law reads as follows:

(1) The parties are free to agree on the language or languages to be used in the arbitral proceedings. Failing such agreement, the arbitral tribunal shall determine the language or languages to be used in the proceedings. This agreement or determination, unless otherwise specified therein, shall apply to any written statement by a party, any hearing and any award, decision or other communication by the arbitral tribunal.

(2) The arbitral tribunal may order that any documentary evidence shall be accompanied by a translation into the language or languages agreed upon by the parties or determined by the arbitral tribunal.

[7] See, eg, *Methanex Corp* (1976 Rules); *TCW Group, Inc* (1976 Rules); and *Vito Gallo* (1976 Rules); all reprinted in section 2(C).

[8] A suggestion to the effect that a provision on consultation with the parties be added to the text of corresponding Article 17 of the 1976 UNCITRAL Rules was not adopted. This, however, was not due to any rejection of the idea, but rather seems to reflect an understanding "that the suggested additional wording was unnecessary, since any competent arbitrator would invariably [sic] consult with the Parties before determining the language to be used." *Summary Record of the 6th Meeting of the Committee of the Whole (II)*, UNCITRAL, 9th Session, UN Doc A/CN.9/9/C.2/SR.6, para 91 (1976) (Comment by Mr Guest, United Kingdom). But see J van Hof, *Commentary on the UNCITRAL Arbitration Rules: The Application by the Iran-U.S. Claims Tribunal* (1991) 113 (asserting that lack of prior agreement constitutes waiver and that the tribunal must decide the issue). Even if one took the view that the lack of prior agreement constituted a waiver by the parties of their ability by mutual agreement to choose the language of the proceedings, it is clear that a tribunal should base its decision on the expressed preference of the parties. In its efforts to revise the UNCITRAL Rules, the Working Group revisited the issue of including a requirement to consult, an addition that could bring the Rules in line with other leading arbitration rules, such as the 2010 AAA Rules (Article 14), the 1998 LCIA Rules (Article 17.3), and the 2001 WIPO Rules (Article 40). See *Settlement of Commercial Disputes: Revision of the UNCITRAL Arbitration Rules, Note by the Secretariat*, UNCITRAL, UN Doc A/CN.9/WG.II/WP.143/Add.1 at 2, para 3 (2006). The Working Group again decided not to include such a requirement. It reasoned that "[e]ven though...as drafted, the requirement that the arbitral tribunal 'promptly after its appointment, determine the language or languages' could be interpreted as not requiring consultation,...the Rules did not affect the advisability of consulting the parties before the arbitral tribunal took such or any other procedural decision." *Report of the Working Group on Arbitration and Conciliation on the Work of its Forty-Fifth Session* (Vienna, September 11–15, 2006), UNCITRAL, 40th Session, UN Doc A/CN.9/614, at 19–20, para 91 (2007).

[9] See Minutes of the First Full Tribunal Meeting, reprinted below, section 2(D)(1), and Note 2 to Article 17 of the 1983 Tribunal Rules, reprinted in Appendix 5. The text of Note 2 refers to "Farsi" as one of the languages of arbitration, but Iran later indicated its preference for the word "Persian." This wish has been respected by the Tribunal, which explains the difference between the Tribunal's early practice and its decisions of a more recent origin. See H Holtzmann, "Fact-Finding by the Iran-United States Claims Tribunal," n 1, 128 n 91, and, eg, *Richard D Harza* (1983 Tribunal Rules); and *Juliette Allen* (1983 Tribunal Rules); both reprinted in section 2(D)(2).

When guidance from the parties is not available, the arbitrators, in determining the language of the proceedings, must consider various factors, which not surprisingly, are similar to the factors that the parties themselves might consider when deciding upon the choice of language.

One particularly important factor is the language previously used in the commercial dealings between the parties. According to the Preliminary Draft of the 1976 UNCITRAL Rules, it was even suggested that, in the absence of a specific agreement, "either the language of the contract or the language used in correspondence between the parties" should always be the language of the arbitration.[10] Although this rigid rule was rejected as being incompatible with the flexibility needed in international arbitration,[11] such a language should normally be regarded as the most suitable one.[12] The language abilities of the arbitrators, the parties and their attorneys are also important considerations,[13] although care must be taken so as to avoid "gaming" by the parties, for example as to the language capacities of the arbitrators they nominate. If these various factors all point to a single language (frequently English in practice), the choice is simple. Where this is not the case, notably where not only the parties have different languages, but also the contract has been drafted in two equally authentic languages, the adoption of two languages should be considered. But even in such cases the adoption of one language only is generally preferable, as the conduct of the proceedings in multiple languages is likely to increase both the time and cost of arbitration.[14] In cases where the equality of the respective national languages has a symbolic value that exceeds the practical considerations involved, such as at the Iran–US Claims Tribunal, bilingualism may be the only alternative.[15] Another possible compromise under the UNCITRAL Rules is that both parties be allowed to use their own language, while only one language is reserved for the awards and other decisions of the arbitral tribunal.[16] Once the arbitral tribunal

---

[10] *Report of the UNCITRAL*, 8th Session, Summary of Discussion of the Preliminary Draft, UN Doc A/10017, para 111 (1975), reprinted in (1975) VI UNCITRAL Ybk 24, 36.

[11] See *Report of the UNCITRAL*, 8th Session, n 10, at para 112.

[12] According to Viscasillas, "it is general arbitral practice that the language of the arbitration is that of the contract [or] that of the business communications, which in the normal situation is also the language of the arbitration clause ... [or] the language of the sole arbitrator of the common language between the three of them." P Viscasillas, "Place of Arbitration (Article 16) and Language of proceedings (Article 17) in the UNCITRAL Arbitration Rules: Some Proposals for a Revision" (2006) 13 Croatian Arb Ybk 205, 218.

[13] Other factors may include language of the place of the performance of the agreement and language of the place of the arbitration. See T Webster, *Handbook of UNCITRAL Arbitration*, (2010) 296. If the language has been agreed between the parties before the appointment of the arbitrators, such an agreement affects the choice of the arbitrators and counsel rather than vice versa. See S Baker and M Davis, *The UNCITRAL Arbitration Rules in Practice: The Experience of the Iran-United States Claims Tribunal* (1992) 80, n 322.

[14] See P Sanders, "Commentary on UNCITRAL Arbitration Rules," n 5, 193–4; A Redfern and M Hunter with N Blackaby and C Partasides, *Law and Practice of International Commercial Arbitration* (4th edn 2004) 232–3 and, regarding the Iran–US Claims Tribunal, S Baker and M Davis, *The UNCITRAL Arbitration Rules in Practice*, n 13, 81; S Toope, *Mixed International Arbitration: Studies in Arbitration between States and Private Persons* (1990) 341–2. For a general discussion of the problems involved in using multiple languages in arbitration, see T Várady, *Language and Translation in International Commercial Arbitration*, n 3, 24–8.

[15] See J Castello, "UNCITRAL Rules," in F Weigand (ed) *Practitioner's Handbook on International Commercial Arbitration* (2nd edn 2009) 1474.

[16] P Sanders, "Commentary on UNCITRAL Arbitration Rules," n 5, 193; K Rauh, *Die Schieds- und Schlichtungs-Ordnungen der UNCITRAL* (1983) 80. Another possibility would be the solution adopted in the *Aminoil* Case (not arbitrated under the UNCITRAL Rules). According to the Arbitration Agreement: "The language of the proceedings shall be English. However, the parties may put forward references to authorities, decisions, awards, opinions and texts (or quotations therefrom) in French without translation." *The Government and State of Kuwait* and *The American Independent Oil Co*, Award of April 12, 1977, reprinted in (1982) 21 ILM 976, 980.

determines the language, it should not be changed except at the unanimous request of the parties.[17]

The decision concerning the language of the proceedings normally applies to all written statements by the parties,[18] as well as to oral proceedings.[19] Thus, if there are two working languages in the proceedings, all statements must be submitted in both languages; correspondingly, both languages can be employed in hearings, possibly necessitating interpretation. The parties, of course, are always entitled to waive the requirements concerning the use of the two languages, for example, with respect to a particular document.[20] In the absence of any such waiver, the two languages also must be applied to the production of all awards, orders and other decisions rendered by the arbitral tribunal.

A decision on bilingualism, in addition, implies equality between the languages chosen. Thus, as a general matter, documents should be submitted and decisions should be issued in both languages simultaneously.[21] Simultaneity, however, may be difficult to reconcile with competing interests, such as the principle in Article 17(1) that the arbitral tribunal should "conduct the proceedings so as to avoid unnecessary delay and expense."

The practice of the Iran–US Claims Tribunal proved to be flexible in order to cope with a similar requirement in the Claims Settlement Declaration to "conduct its business expeditiously."[22] Namely, the Tribunal permitted the practice of distributing a document received in one language only to the members of the Tribunal pending the receipt of the necessary translation and consequential filing of the document. Instead of summarily rejecting a late filing by a party of the second language version of a document, the Tribunal gave the latter party additional time to prepare its reply in order to avoid any prejudice to the other party.[23] The submission of a document in only one language was also accepted as sufficient for the purpose of calculating time limits such as that prescribed for making a request for an additional award pursuant to Article 39 of the Tribunal Rules.[24] Moreover, occasionally and upon instructions from the respective Chairman, decisions by the Tribunal itself, including awards, were filed in English only pending the preparation and later filing of the Persian version. This practice met with some protests from the Iranian side, which demonstrated the sensitivities involved.

Similar flexibility is evident in the *Chevron* arbitration against Ecuador, in which English and Spanish were the official languages of the arbitration, with English being the authoritative language as between them. Spanish translations of submissions were allowed to proceed on a more flexible timetable than English submissions. In particular, an additional six weeks were given to provide Spanish translations of the award and certain key pleadings.[25]

---

[17] See M Aden, *Internationale Handelsschiedsgerichtsbarkeit* (1988) 232.
[18] The extent to which annexes and exhibits to such statements are covered is discussed in connection with Article 19(2) in section 2(B)(2).
[19] The disputing parties, of course, may agree to modify to this rule, as was the case in *TCW Group, Inc* (1976 Rules) (requiring simultaneous translation into two languages at the hearing), reprinted in section 2(C).
[20] See *Pan American World Airways, Inc* (1983 Tribunal Rules), reprinted in section 2(D)(1).
[21] See *Computer Sciences Corp* (1983 Tribunal Rules), reprinted in section 2(D)(1) (Post-Hearing Memorial authorized to respondents "in the exceptional circumstances" of the case was rejected for untimeliness given that respondent had submitted in timely fashion only the Persian version of the document).
[22] See, eg, Article III(1) of the Iran–US Claims Settlement Declaration.
[23] See *The United States of America on behalf and for the benefit of Thomas A Todd* (1983 Tribunal Rules), reprinted in section 2(D)(1).
[24] See *Hood Corp* (1983 Tribunal Rules), reprinted in section 2(D)(1).
[25] See *Chevron Corp* (1976 Rules), reprinted in section 2(C).

Neither Article 19 nor the general principles of equality and efficiency expressed in Article 17(1) should preclude the kind of flexible practice with respect to bilingualism described above.[26]

The acceptance as timely of a party's submission in one language only, provided the other version is "received within a reasonable period,"[27] is not contrary to the requirement of equality, as long as the rule is applied similarly to both parties and both languages. The reasonableness depends on the degree of prejudice to the other party.[28] Even the practice of filing orders and awards of the Iran–US Claims Tribunal tentatively in English only on an *ad hoc* basis is not necessarily contrary to the UNCITRAL Rules, even though it may mean that an Iranian party becomes fully acquainted with the document later than his American counterpart. As discussed earlier, the principle of equality is not automatically violated by any deviation from formally identical treatment;[29] rather, the crux of the matter is whether a party has been deprived of an equal opportunity to present his case.[30] No prejudice in this respect is caused if, as in the *Hood* case,[31] any relevant periods of time are calculated for each party from the date the document is served on that party in his own language, even if the document was served on the party earlier in the other language. Nevertheless, it should be the rule that an arbitral tribunal with two working languages should depart only exceptionally from the practice of issuing orders or decisions simultaneously in both languages.[32] In

---

[26] For opposing views on a case of arguably extreme flexibility at the Iran–US Claims Tribunal, see the award and dissenting opinion in *George E Davidson* (1983 Tribunal Rules), reprinted in section 2(D)(2).

[27] This condition was set in the case of *Hood Corp* (1983 Tribunal Rules), reprinted in section 2(D)(1).

[28] See *Thomas A Todd* (1983 Tribunal Rules), reprinted in section 2(D)(1).

[29] See commentary regarding Article 17(1) in Chapter 2.

[30] Another commentator agrees. J van Hof, "UNCITRAL Arbitration Rules," in L Mistelis (ed) *Concise International Arbitration* (2010) 171, 194.

[31] *Hood Corp* (1983 Tribunal Rules), reprinted in section 2(D)(1).

[32] A rather unique situation arose in connection with *Phillips Petroleum Co Iran* and *Islamic Republic of Iran*, Award No 425–39–2, reprinted in 21 Iran-US CTR 79 (1989-I), which was filed on June 19, 1989 in English only.

On August 30, 1989, the Respondents (the Iranian Government and the NIOC) filed an "Application to the Full Tribunal for the Revocation, Setting Aside and Annulment of the Award in Case No 39 and for Interim Measures." In response, the President of the Tribunal decided to refrain from notifying the Escrow Agent concerning payment on the award to the American Claimant from the Security Account and (as the Chairman of Chamber 2) from having the Farsi version of the award filed. Before Respondents' Application was heard before the Full Tribunal on January 17, 1990, as Case No A/25, the parties concluded a Settlement Agreement, according to which, *inter alia*, "[t]he English Version of Award No 425–39–2 shall be deemed by the Parties as null and void and of no effect whatsoever." Award on Agreed Terms No 461–39–2 (January 10, 1990), 285, 290. The Agreement providing for the payment of $92 million to the claimant was recorded in an Award on Agreed Terms in accordance with Article 34 of the 1983 Tribunal Rules.

Although the Award on Agreed Terms settled, as between the parties, the claims and counter-claims raised in the case, the question of the precedential value of the Tribunal's Award of June 29, 1989 remains. The Award involved very important issues concerning nationalization. On the one hand, it may be argued that the June 29, 1989 Award is of no relevance. Although the parties had no power over the Tribunal to declare the Award "null and void," the acceptance of the Settlement Agreement as the basis for an award on agreed terms implies that there was no Award until January 10, 1990. This is because a basic condition for the issuance of an award on agreed terms is that the settlement agreement be concluded "before the award is made." See Article 34(1) of the 1983 Tribunal Rules and *Separate Opinion of Seyed Khalil Khalilian* (the then-appointed member of the Chamber in question) to Award on Agreed Terms No 461–39–2 (February 6, 1990), 294. On the other hand, the Award may be said to remain valid. It was neither explicitly rejected by the Chamber issuing the Award on Agreed Terms or by the Full Tribunal, nor was it annulled by any competent court, on the various issues of law and facts present in the case in question. See *Separate Statement of George H Aldrich* (the US appointed member of the deciding Chamber) to Award No 461–39–2 (January 19, 1990), 293. It seems that nothing prevents the Iran–US Claims Tribunal or other Tribunals from regarding the June 29, 1990 Award as a precedent. This is supported by the decision rendered in *Petrolane*, in which the *Phillips* Award had been cited by the Tribunal. The request for

such circumstances, an award rendered in only one language may prove unenforceable, or remain unenforceable as long as the other language version does not exist.[33]

The adoption of two working languages in the arbitration arguably means that the texts submitted in both languages are equally authoritative.[34] This conclusion goes to the very purpose of adopting two languages, namely to enable the parties to work in and rely on a language that they better understand. Therefore, in a bilingual arbitration the requirements of Article 19 are clearly not met by providing only a summary, rather than a full translation, of a submission in the "second" language.[35] However, this principle of equal authenticity in bilingual arbitration, particularly with respect to party submission, is not the same as that provided in the Vienna Convention on the Law of Treaties regarding the interpretation of treaties authenticated in two or more languages. Unlike treaties originally intended to be authentic in several languages, submissions by parties in bilingual commercial arbitration are normally first drafted by legal professionals in one language only and then translated into the other. Moreover, Article 19(1) contains no general requirement that the translation be duly certified.[36] Since the "first" version is more likely to reflect the true intentions of the party in question, it should be given preference in possible cases of discrepancy, especially where the party has explicitly stated that its own language should prevail.[37] A conceivable exception to this rule would arise in those rare cases where the discrepancy is such that it puts into question the good faith of the party that submits the document.

Where inconsistencies between the various languages exist in the awards issued by the arbitral tribunal (a situation where the analogy to treaty law is more appropriate but again not necessarily applicable), those inconsistencies should be corrected under the mechanisms provided for in Article 37 of the UNCITRAL Rules concerning the interpretation of the award.[38] Similarly, deficiencies in orders or other procedural decisions can be corrected by issuing a new order or decision.

Finally, unless otherwise agreed by the parties or determined by the tribunal, the UNCITRAL Rules themselves should be used in the version of the language(s) of the arbitration

---

correction in this regard made by Iran was rejected. See *Petrolane Inc* (1983 Tribunal Rules), reprinted in section 2(D)(1). Nevertheless, the uncertainties of the status of the June 29, 1989 Award also make it legitimate not to regard the Award as having the same precedential value as other awards may have, whatever their general value is in this regard.

[33] Thus, when seeking recognition and enforcement under the New York Convention, the party may be required to provide the award in both languages in order to fulfil the condition of Article IV(1)(a), according to which "[t]he duly authenticated original award or a duly certified copy thereof" shall be submitted. Also, the absence of an award in the other language of the arbitration might constitute a ground for refusal to recognize and enforce the award under Article V of the Convention. Cf para 1(d) ("...the arbitral procedure was not in accordance with the agreement of the parties...") and 1(e) ("The award has not yet become binding on the parties...").

[34] See T Várady, *Language and Translation in International Commercial Arbitration*, n 3, 26–7.

[35] See *Kahen Hooshang* (1983 Tribunal Rules), reprinted in section 2(D)(2).

[36] The same is the case with regard to Article 22 of the Model Law, which, however, is not interpreted as preventing the tribunal from requiring certified translations when deemed appropriate. H Holtzmann and J Neuhaus, *A Guide to the UNCITRAL Model Law on International Commercial Arbitration*, n 6, 630; H van Houtte, "Conduct of Arbitral Proceedings," n 3, 117. Article 19 of the UNCITRAL Rules can be interpreted similarly. Generally, if a party objects to a translation, the arbitrator may order a sworn translation. See T Webster, *Handbook of UNCITRAL Arbitration* (2010) 299.

[37] Before the Iran–US Claims Tribunal, the parties frequently made this kind of reservation which appears to have been tacitly approved by the Tribunal.

[38] See Chapter 24, section 2 on interpretation of awards.

(if available in that language). If there are two such languages, it may be wise to agree or determine that, in case of discrepancy, the original English text (even when English is not among the languages of the arbitration) shall prevail as the one best reflecting the intentions of the drafters.

(2) Translation of documents and exhibits—Article 19(2)

Article 19(2) provides that the arbitral tribunal "may" order that any annexes, supplementary documents or exhibits, which have been submitted in their original language, be accompanied by a translation into the language(s) of the proceedings, as agreed upon by the parties or determined by the tribunal in accordance with Article 19(1). Whereas Article 19(1) only requires the language(s) of the arbitration to be used in the written statements of the parties, any annexes, exhibits and the like mentioned in Article 19(2), ie, documentary evidence, may be submitted in their original language only, unless otherwise ordered by the arbitral tribunal.[39]

While the parties are free to agree, in accordance with Article 19(1), on the language of the arbitration with respect to written statements, hearings and decisions of the arbitral tribunal, that freedom does not extend to the documentary evidence dealt with in Article 19(2).[40] However, nothing prevents the parties from also agreeing on whether and to what extent such documents shall be translated.[41] Any such agreement should be reflected as a modification of Article 19(2) for the particular arbitration, pursuant to Article 1(1). Such a modification or general agreement on the translation of documentary evidence is unlikely in practice. Of course, the tribunal in its discretion under Article 19(2) should attach due importance to any unanimous wishes expressed by the parties.

Where guidance from the parties is unavailable, the decision whether the tribunal should order a particular document to be translated depends, above all, on the nature of the document in question. Documents specifically prepared for the purpose of the arbitration, such as affidavits, are likely to require translation, as they typically relate very closely to the written statements, which automatically must be submitted in the language(s) of the arbitration. Conversely, translation is less crucial with respect to documents that are not prepared specifically for purposes of the arbitration. This is especially so with respect to documents that emanate from previous, routine, business correspondence between the parties and at the relevant time did not require translation. For example, invoices, bills of lading and other documents need not be translated as a rule, especially if they are voluminous.

These kinds of translation criteria were developed in the practice of the Iran–US Claims Tribunal.[42] On the basis of numerous tailor-made orders issued in various

---

[39] Although the wording of the provision might be understood to indicate otherwise, it appears (also in light of the practice of the Iran–US Claims Tribunal) beyond doubt that Article 19(2) not only covers situations where the documents are originally submitted in a language which is not the language of the arbitration, but also those cases in which they are submitted in only one of the two official languages of the arbitration. In a bilingual arbitration, the latter situation, indeed, is likely to be much more frequent than the former.

[40] According to the *UNCITRAL Notes on Organizing Arbitral Proceedings*, "[b]earing in mind the needs of the proceedings and economy, it may be considered whether the arbitral tribunal should order that any of those documents or parts thereof should be accompanied by a translation into the language of the proceedings." *UNCITRAL Notes on Organizing Arbitral Proceedings*, UNCITRAL, UN GAOR, 51st Session, Supp No 17, UN Doc A/51/17, para 18 (1996), reprinted in (1996) XXVII UNCITRAL Ybk 45, 49 [hereinafter "*UNCITRAL Notes*"].

[41] See H Holtzmann and J Neuhaus, *A Guide to the UNCITRAL Model Law on International Commercial Arbitration*, n 6, 628–9.

[42] The contents of Article 17(2) of the 1983 Tribunal Rules were elaborated upon in Notes 3 and 4 to Article 17 of the Tribunal Rules. According to Note 3, any "annexes" to written statements as a main rule have to be

cases,[43] the Tribunal, starting in 1985, adopted "guidelines for the translation of documentary evidence," which are reproduced below in section 2(D)(2). These guidelines, which are included or annexed to the relevant orders, best illustrate the Tribunal's position on translation.

According to the Tribunal guidelines, affidavits and similar written evidence prepared or submitted for the purpose of the arbitration should be filed in both languages. In addition, certain other documents as a rule must be translated. In part, this portion of the guidelines concerns documents, though they are not specifically prepared for the case in question, nevertheless they are new to the other party, eg internal memoranda of a party, and correspondence between a party and a third person or entity. In part, the need for translation is due to the central role that these documents are likely to play among the evidence. This latter point is certainly the case with respect to the contract or other such document relied on, portions of laws, decrees allegedly evidencing taking of property, and such correspondence and communications between the parties which allegedly provide evidence of a taking of property or modify the contractual rights or obligations of the parties.[44]

Material which as a rule does not require translation according to the Tribunal guidelines, comprises two categories of documents. These include, firstly, correspondence and communications between the parties (with the exception mentioned at the end of the previous paragraph) and, secondly, such documents as technical reports, invoices, shipping documents, among others.[45]

The practice of the Iran–US Claims Tribunal provides useful guidelines for other tribunals concerning the interpretation of Article 19(2) of the UNCITRAL Rules. In applying such guidelines, however, a tribunal should keep in mind that its discretion under Article 19(2) should be exercised on a case-by-case basis and that flexibility should be retained. Where the duty of translation is dispensed with, it may be wise for the tribunal to reserve its right to order the translation should it prove appropriate to do so at a later stage of the proceedings. In this spirit, the Tribunal characterizes its own guidelines as follows: "They must be taken as a minimum requirement; the Tribunal may at any stage require the translation of further items of evidence on its own motion. The opposing party may submit for the Tribunal's consideration request, giving reasons, for the translation of specific additional items."[46]

Note 5 to the 1983 Tribunal Rules provides that "[a]ny disputes or difficulties regarding translations shall be resolved by the arbitral tribunal." This, of course, is also the case with

---

submitted in both English and Farsi (Persian). Since most supplementary documents relate to written statements, Note 3, interpreted in isolation, might be understood to mean that, subject to any agreement between the parties, practically all documents relied on may have to be submitted in both languages. Such an interpretation, however, would both render Note 4 virtually redundant and provide a somewhat arbitrary criterion (whether or not a document has been "annexed" to a written statement) for solving the translation problem. No surprise, then, that the Tribunal has not applied such a formal criterion but has rather made its decision dependent on the nature of the document in question. See *Rouholah Karubian* (1983 Tribunal Rules); and *Vera-Jo Miller Aryeh* (1983 Tribunal Rules); both reprinted in section 2(D)(2). In this respect the Notes to the Tribunal Rules cannot be recommended as a model for a possible modification of Article 19(2) of the 2010 UNCITRAL Rules. See also J Baker and M Davis, *The UNCITRAL Arbitration Rules in Practice*, n 13, 80. On the Tribunal's practice, see also J van Hof, *Commentary on the UNCITRAL Arbitration Rules*, n 8, 114–18.

[43] See, eg, *Richard D Harza* (1983 Tribunal Rules), reprinted in section 2(D)(2).

[44] See paragraph 1 of the guidelines annexed to the order rendered in *Fluor Corp* (1983 Tribunal Rules), reprinted in section 2(D)(2).

[45] See *Fluor Corp* (1983 Tribunal Rules), para 2.

[46] *Fluor Corp* (1983 Tribunal Rules); see also *Vera-Jo Miller Aryeh* (1983 Tribunal Rules); both reprinted in section 2(D)(2).

other arbitral tribunals acting under the UNCITRAL Rules. Such disputes may concern not only whether translation is required, but also the consequences of a failure to translate[47] or to translate accurately.[48] Submission in only one language of an annex to a written statement which should have been translated or submission of a deficient translation should not automatically lead to the refusal to accept the statement. Rather, the party should first be provided an opportunity to correct the defect, if correction is possible without undue prejudice to the other party or to the proceedings as a whole.[49] If not, or if the party fails to correct the defect, the document as evidence most likely should be rejected in accordance with the relevant principles.[50] In *Juliette Allen*, the Tribunal proceeded with its deliberations, pursuant to Article 28(3) of the 1983 Tribunal Rules, taking into account only the evidence properly filed in both Farsi and English, and ultimately rejected the claim.[51]

Finally, it should be remembered that decision-making regarding the language of arbitration, including translations, is a procedural matter to which Article 33(2) of the UNCITRAL Rules applies.[52] In addition, as highlighted in the UNCITRAL Notes on Organizing Arbitral Proceedings, "it is advisable to decide whether any or all of the costs [of translation and interpretation] are to be paid directly by a party or whether they will be paid out of the deposits and apportioned between the parties along with other arbitration costs."[53]

(3) Comparison to the 1976 UNCITRAL Rules

Article 19 is identical to corresponding Article 17 of the 1976 UNCITRAL Rules.

C. Extracts from the Practice of Investment Tribunals

Methanex Corp and *United States of America*, Minutes of Order of First Procedural Meeting (June 29, 2000) (ICSID administered, 1976 UNCITRAL Rules, NAFTA Chapter Eleven), at 3:

> Item 8: Language
>
> The disputing parties confirmed that the English language is the agreed language to be used in these proceedings, pursuant to Article 17 of the UNCITRAL Arbitration Rules.

---

[47] Castello notes that the Tribunal has "render[ed] its decision without the translations if [translations are] not filed within the extended deadline." J Castello, "UNCITRAL Rules," n 15, 1475.

[48] On the consequences of inadequate translations in arbitration generally, see T Várady *Language and Translation in International Commercial Arbitration*, n 3, 111–28.

[49] See, eg, *Kahen Hooshang* (1983 Tribunal Rules); *Juliette Allen* (1983 Tribunal Rules); *George E Davidson* (1983 Tribunal Rules), Order; and *Vera-Jo Miller Aryeh* (1983 Tribunal Rules); all reprinted in section 2(D)(2). See also J van Hof, "UNCITRAL Arbitration Rules," in L Mistelis, (ed), *Concise International Arbitration* (2010) 195.

[50] See *Shannon and Wilson, Inc* (1983 Tribunal Rules), reprinted in section 2(D)(2). See also Chapter 14 on Article 23.

[51] "If one of the parties, duly invited to produce documentary evidence, fails to do so within the established period of time, without showing sufficient cause for such failure, the arbitral tribunal may make the award on the evidence before it." *Juliette Allen* (1983 Tribunal Rules), reprinted in section 2(D)(2). To resolve questions of translation the Tribunal has occasionally consulted its own Language Services Division, instead of placing all the burden on the parties. See *Zaman Azar Nourafchan* and *The Islamic Republic of Iran*, Award No 550–412/415–3 (October 19, 1993), paras 17 n 7 and 45. See also *Kahen Hooshang* (1983 Tribunal Rules), section 17(2), reprinted in section 2(D)(2).

[52] K Rauh, *Die Schieds- und Schlichtungs-Ordnungen der UNCITRAL*, n 16, 80. But see M Aden, *Internationale Handelsschiedsgerichtsbarkeit*, n 17, 232. See discussion of Article 33 in Chapter 23 on decisions. On the costs of translations, see Chapter 27.

[53] *UNCITRAL Notes*, n 40, para 20.

TCW Group, Inc, et al and *Dominican Republic*, Procedural Order No 2 (August 15, 2008) (PCA administered, 1976 UNCITRAL Rules, CAFTA-DR Chapter Ten), at 4:

8.1 English shall be the official language of the arbitration.
8.2 Communications by the Tribunal (including orders, decisions and awards) and all submissions and communications by the Parties shall be in English, including translations in full of any witness statements prepared in Spanish and translations in relevant part of documentary evidence and legal authorities in a language other than English.
8.3 Spanish translations of all writings referred to in paragraph 8.2 that are not already in Spanish shall be submitted or communicated with the writings or as soon as possible thereafter, but in no event later than two weeks after their submission or communication, except that the Spanish translation of any award may be submitted up to six weeks after such award is made.
8.4 All oral proceedings shall be simultaneously interpreted into English and Spanish. The PCA as Registry will make the necessary arrangements in this regard.

Vito G Gallo and *Government of Canada*, Amended Procedural Order No 1 (March 10, 2009) (PCA administered, 1976 UNCITRAL Rules, NAFTA Chapter Eleven) at 4:

15. The arbitration shall be conducted in English.
16. All documentary evidence in a language other than English shall be translated to English by the party submitting that evidence at its own cost. Witness testimony in a language other than English shall be translated consecutively to English, the cost of which shall be borne by the party calling the witness.

Chevron Corp, et al and *Republic of Ecuador*, Partial Award on the Merits (March 20, 2010) (PCA administered, 1976 UNCITRAL Rules, US-Ecuador BIT), at 32:

8.1 English and Spanish shall be the official languages of the arbitration and, as between them, English will be the authoritative language.
8.2 Communications by the Tribunal (including orders, decisions and awards) and all submissions and communications by the Parties shall be in English, including translations in full of any witness statements prepared in Spanish and translations in relevant part of documentary evidence and legal authorities in a language other than English.
8.3 Spanish translations of all writings referred to in paragraph 8.2 that are not already in Spanish shall be submitted or communicated with the writings or as soon as possible thereafter, but in no event later than two weeks after their submission or communication, except that the Spanish translation of any award or Claimant's Memorial on the Merits and Respondent's Counter-Memorial on the Merits may be submitted up to six weeks after such award or submission is made.
8.4 All oral proceedings shall be simultaneously interpreted and transcribed into English and Spanish.

D. Extracts from the Practice of the Iran–US Claims Tribunal

(1) Tribunal Rules (1983), Article 17(1)

Minutes of the 1st Full Tribunal Meeting of the Iran–US Claims Tribunal (July 1, 1981) at para 4:

> The Tribunal noted and accepted the report made to them by the Agents, that they had agreed that English and Farsi shall be the official languages to be used for oral hearings, decisions and awards.

Pan American World Airways, Inc and *Islamic Republic of Iran*, Award on Agreed Terms No 96–488–1 (December 19, 1983) at 2, reprinted in 4 Iran-US CTR 205, 205–06 (1983-III):

On 6 December 1983 a Joint Motion for an Arbitral Award on agreed terms was filed with the Tribunal, signed by representatives of Pan American World Airways, Inc.... The Ministry of Defense of the Islamic Republic of Iran ("MOD"), and the Agent of the Government of the Islamic Republic of Iran

...

The Joint Motion having been submitted in English only, the Tribunal deems the Parties to have waived the requirements of Article 17 Note 3(e) of the [1983] Tribunal Rules.

Hood Corp and *Islamic Republic of Iran*, Decision No DEC 34–100–3 (March 1, 1985) at 1–2 (footnote omitted), reprinted in 8 Iran-US CTR 53, 53–4 (1985-I):

Article 37(1) of the [1983] Tribunal Rules states:

Within thirty days after the receipt of the award either party, with notice to the other party, may request the Arbitral Tribunal to make an additional award as to claims presented in the arbitral proceedings but omitted from the award.

Interpreting Article 37 to give full effect to its purpose, the Tribunal decides that the date of "receipt of the award" is the date that the Award in that party's language is served upon the Agent of the relevant State-Party. Likewise the Tribunal decides that for the purpose of meeting the 30-day limitation, the date a "request" is made is the date that the requesting submission, even if in only one language, is received. Such request may not be filed or acted upon, however, until the other language version is received and such other version must be received within a reasonable period. See Article 17, [1983] Tribunal Rules.

In the present case the English version of the Request for additional award was received on 13 August 1984, less than 30 days after receipt of the Award by the Agent for the United States. Moreover, the Farsi version of the request was received in a timely fashion thereafter. Therefore, the request for additional award in the instant case was made in a timely manner.

The tribunal has concluded, however, that it considered all of the claims and the grounds on which they were based, and that the award and the reasons therefore are adequate in form and do not warrant any additional consideration or modifications.

United States of America on behalf and for the benefit of Thomas A Todd and *Islamic Republic of Iran*, Case No 10856, Chamber One, Order of January 9, 1986:

The Tribunal refers to the two letters filed by the Agent of the Government of the Islamic Republic of Iran on 19 December 1985 and 2 January 1986, concerning the late filing by ten days of the Farsi version of the Claimant's documentary evidence and legal brief.

The Tribunal advises the Parties that no final decision as to the admissibility of these late-filed documents will be made until after the Hearing on 15 April 1986.

In the meantime, in order to take account of any prejudice which might have been occasioned to the Respondent by this late filing, the Tribunal allows the Respondent an additional ten days in which to file its documentary evidence and legal brief, i.e. until 10 March 1986.

Computer Sciences Corp and *Islamic Republic of Iran*, Award No 221–65–1 (April 16, 1986) at 4–6, reprinted in 10 Iran-US CTR 269, 272–73 (1986-I):

By Order filed on 2 July 1985 the Tribunal allowed the Respondents "in the exceptional circumstances of this case" to file by 5 August 1985 a Post-Hearing Submission, "having regard to the particular procedural history of this case, including the rendering of Interlocutory Award No ITL 49–65–1, and in view of the submission received after the rendering of that Award". The Post-Hearing Submission was to be restricted to rebuttal of evidence and argument that were offered in support of the Claimant's claims and that were presented for the first time in the Claimant's Pre-Hearing Submission of 1 May 1985. The Tribunal stated in the Order that it would not grant any extensions for the Respondents' Post-Hearing Submission.

On 5 August 1985, the Farsi text of a Post-Hearing Memorial was submitted by ISIRAN. Having been submitted in only one language, this written statement was not formally filed by the

Registry of the Tribunal nor sent to the Claimant. See Article 17, note 2 of the Tribunal Rules. At the same time the Agent of the Government of the Islamic Republic of Iran requested an extension of 15 days to file the English text of this and the other Respondents' Post-Hearing Submissions. The Claimant objected to the Respondents' extension request and reserved its right to request an opportunity to respond to any Post-Hearing Submissions the Respondents might be allowed to file. On 8 August 1985, ISIRAN submitted Annexes to its Post-Hearing Memorial in Farsi. On 14 August 1985, Bank Mellat filed a Post-Hearing Submission. On 20 August 1985, ISIRAN's Post-Hearing Memorial together with the Annexes was filed in English and Farsi. The Claimant requested that the Respondents' Post-Hearing Submissions be disallowed or, in the alternative, that the Claimant be granted leave to submit a response.

By Order filed on 4 September 1985, the Tribunal disallowed the Post-Hearing Submissions of ISIRAN, IACI and Bank Mellat. Pointing to its express statement in its Order filed on 2 July 1985 that it would not grant any extensions for the Post-Hearing Submissions, the Tribunal "not[ed] that no reasons were given by the Respondents for the lateness of their submissions, nor was the Tribunal's attention drawn to any unforeseen circumstances which might have affected the filing" of the Post-Hearing Submissions.

On 24 September 1985, the Agent of the Government of the Islamic Republic of Iran requested that the Tribunal revise its Order filed on 4 September 1985 and admit all of the Respondents' Post-Hearing Submissions.

...

The Tribunal notes that the Iranian Agent's request filed on 24 September 1985 does not point to any unforeseen circumstances which might have affected the filing of the Post-Hearing Submissions, nor does it give any new reasons for their lateness. The Tribunal is aware of the communication problems that Iranian Respondents face, and it has taken them into account in this case. In view of this, the procedural history of this case and the exceptional character of Post-Hearing Submissions, the Tribunal sees no need to reverse its decision not to allow the Respondents' Post-Hearing Submissions.

(2) *Tribunal Rules (1983), Article 17(2)*

Richard D Harza and *Islamic Republic of Iran*, Case No 97, Chamber Two, Order of November 9, 1982, reprinted in 1 Iran-US CTR 234 (1981–82):

> The attention of the Parties is drawn to Note 3 to Article 17 of the [1983] Provisionally Adopted Tribunal Rules which empowers the Tribunal to determine in each case which items of documentary evidence shall be submitted in both English and Farsi.
>
> The Tribunal makes the following Order with regard to the translation of documentary evidence for present purposes only. Translations of other documents may be ordered subsequently if the Tribunal so determines. The Tribunal wishes as a matter of priority to ensure the availability in both languages of important documents such as laws, proclamations, contracts, and *procès-verbaux* as well as communications between a party and third parties and communications internal to a party.
>
> The Tribunal accordingly Orders that the Claimants file with the Tribunal as soon as possible and at the latest by 30 January 1983 Farsi translations of any of the documents listed in the Schedule hereto that they wish to be considered in evidence. The Tribunal does not at present require translations of brochures, invoices, accounts, charts, cheques, technical reports, communications between the Parties or books and newspaper articles.

Shannon and Wilson, Inc and *Atomic Energy Organization of Iran*, Case No 217, Chamber Two, Order of September 14, 1983:

> Pursuant to the Tribunal's Order of 28 July 1983, the Claimant has filed as evidence the so-called "ENEXTEC" contract, in English only: The Tribunal, in view of the contents of the contract, hereby decides that the Claimant should file as soon as possible Farsi translations of those portions of this contract on which it will seek to rely as evidence. It should be noted that any contract provisions which are not translated into Farsi cannot be invoked as evidence.

Should circumstances arise that make further translations necessary in the future, the Tribunal will order the Claimant to provide them.

Development and Resources Corp and *Islamic Republic of Iran*, Case No 60, Chamber Three, Order of January 31, 1985:

2. The Tribunal notes that, by Order of 2 November 1984, Claimant was allowed to submit the documents mentioned in the 26 December 1984 request of Khuzestan Water and Power Authority for the time being in English only. In view of the fact that the documents in question are contract forms, reports and plans which were not originally required to be produced in more than one language, the Tribunal, having inspected the documents, still holds that the documents do not need to be translated for the purposes of this arbitration.

3. However, in order to facilitate Respondents' task in reviewing the documents under submission, the Tribunal grants an extension of time until 31 March 1985 to file any written evidence and reply memorial which Respondents intend to rely on in rebuttal to Claimant's memorial of 17 August 1984, and the related documentary evidence submitted thereafter.

Kahen Hooshang and *Islamic Republic of Iran*, Case No 315, Chamber Two, Order of January 22, 1986:

The Tribunal notes Respondent's letter filed on 14 January 1986 stating that the evidence submitted by the Claimant on 7 October 1985 was not accompanied by a complete Farsi translation and requesting the Tribunal to direct the Claimant to submit such translation.

The Language Services Department of the Tribunal has examined the document under reference, and has found that with only two exceptions (the Claimant's Affidavit and the Naturalization Certification), the Claimant has merely provided a brief Farsi-language description of each English-language document rather than a translation thereof. Therefore, the Claimant is hereby instructed to file by 30 March 1986, a complete and correct Farsi translation of its documentary evidence filed on 7 October 1985.

Rouhollah Karubian and *Islamic Republic of Iran*, Case No 419, Chamber Two, Order of March 17, 1986:

The Tribunal notes Respondent's letter filed on 6 March 1986, reiterating its request to the Tribunal to direct the Claimant to submit a Farsi translation of certain documents.

The Tribunal considers that, while the Claimant's documents in question were appended to its submission of 15 January 1986, they are in essence "… documentary exhibits and written evidence …" within the meaning of Note 4 to Article 17 [of the 1983 Tribunal Rules]. In view thereof and due to the fact that the Tribunal has discretionary power to decide in each particular case which exhibits or written evidence shall be submitted in both languages, English and Farsi, the Tribunal's Order of 13 February 1986 remains in effect.

Fluor Corp and *Islamic Republic of Iran*, Case No 810, Chamber One, Order of February 16, 1987:

Guidelines for the Translation of Documentary Evidence
The Attention of the Parties is drawn to Article 17 of the [1983] Tribunal Rules, and the Notes thereto. In addition to the documents enumerated in Note 3, which are to be submitted in both English and Farsi unless otherwise agreed by the arbitrating parties, Note 4 provides that,

"[t]he arbitral Tribunal shall determine in each particular case what other documentary exhibits and written evidence, or what part thereof, shall be submitted in both English and Farsi."

The following guidelines are issued pursuant to Note 4 in order to facilitate the initial submission of evidence by the Parties. They must be taken as a minimum requirement; the Tribunal may at any stage require the translation of further items of evidence on its own motion. The opposing

Party may submit for the Tribunal's consideration request, giving reasons, for the translation of specific additional items.

1. The following categories of documents should be filed in both English and Farsi:
   (a) Affidavits, depositions and other forms of written evidence prepared or submitted for the purpose of this Case;
   (b) In addition to those documents falling within the provisions of Note 3(a)–(d) to Article 17, any portion of the contract or other document relied upon with respect to matters at issue in the Case should be filed in its original language together with a complete translation. If such a contract or document was signed in both English and Farsi, both versions should be submitted as signed;
   (c) Portions of laws, decrees, proclamations and *proces-verbaux* relied upon, e.g. as evidence of a taking;
   (d) Letters and other written communications, telexes and records of verbal communications between one Party and someone other than the other Party to this Case; provided they do not fall within paragraph 2(b) below;
   (e) Internal reports, memoranda, minutes, etc., prepared by a Party for its internal use; provided they do not fall within paragraph 2(b) below;
   (f) Correspondence and communications that passed between the Parties in one language only and were not required to be translated at that time, where they create or alter the contractual rights or obligations of the parties or are relied upon as primary evidence of a taking.

2. The following categories of documents may, in the first instance, be submitted in their original language only:
   (a) Correspondence and communications that passed between the parties in one language only and were not required to be translated at that time, provided they do not fall within paragraph 1(f) above;
   (b) Contemporaneous material which was not required to be translated at the time it came into existence, such as draft contracts and technical reports (except any extracts which are relied upon as a primary source of evidence), studies; brochures; invoices; financial and other accounting statements shipping documents; charts and plans; blueprints and diagrams; tender documents; checks; newspaper articles and extracts from publications; computer printouts; technical data; and schedules or tables of figures.

Petrolane, Inc and *Islamic Republic of Iran*, Chamber Two, Decision No DEC 101–131–2 (November 25, 1991), reprinted in 27 Iran-US CTR 264–65 (1991-II):

3. In his letter, the Agent asserts that a citation in paragraph 50 of the Award to *Phillips Petroleum Company Iran* and *The Islamic Republic of Iran et al.*, Award No 425–39–2 (19 June 1989), is an incorrect citation because the parties in the *Phillips* Case had agreed in their subsequent Settlement Agreement that the English version of the Award (which was the only version filed) shall "be deemed by the Parties as null and void and of no effect whatsoever". The Agent submits that this request should be dealt with as a request to correct a clerical error pursuant to Article 36 of the Tribunal Rules of Procedure.

...

4. The objection to a citation of an Award on the grounds raised by the Agent's letter does not, in the view of the Tribunal, constitute a request for correction of an error within the meaning of Article 36 of the [1983] Tribunal Rules. The citation was correct and was to an Award rendered by the Tribunal, albeit one rendered in English only. While the parties in their subsequent settlement agreed that they would deem that Award null and void upon the issuance of an Award on Agreed Terms giving effect to their Settlement Agreement, that cannot alter the fact that Award 425 was rendered in English and stated the conclusions and reasoning of the Tribunal. As such, the subsequent citation of that Award cannot be considered erroneous.

Vera-Jo Miller Aryeh, on her behalf, on behalf of Laura Aryeh, on behalf of J M Aryeh and *Islamic Republic of Iran*, Case Nos 842, 843 and 844, Chamber One, Order of January 15, 1992:

On December 1991, the Agent of the Government of the Islamic Republic of Iran, filed a letter, in which he requested the Tribunal to order the Claimant to file with the Tribunal the Persian translation of Volume IV of the Claimant's Exhibits Book (Document No 47). In a letter filed on 9 January 1992, the Claimant objected to the request. Having regard to the above submission, the Tribunal decides as follows:

The Tribunal first notes that the nature of Document No 47 is such that according to Article 17 of the [1983] Tribunal Rules, to the provisions of the Guidelines for the translation of documentary evidence, and to the Tribunal's established practice, it should be filed in both English and Persian. Therefore, the Tribunal requests the Claimant to provide a translation of Document No 47 in Persian by 2 March 1992. For information to the Parties, a copy of the Guidelines for the translation of documentary evidence is attached to this Order.

Juliette Allen and *Islamic Republic of Iran*, Award No 541–930–3 (December 11, 1992), reprinted in 28 Iran-US CTR 382, 382–83 (1992):

5. By Order of 2 October 1990 the Tribunal instructed the Claimant, pursuant to Article 17 of the [1983] Tribunal Rules and in accordance with the Tribunal Guidelines for the translation of documentary evidence, to file by 12 November 1990 a translation of her submission of 6 August 1990. The Respondent having protested, through submissions filed on 3 and 9 October 1990, the incomplete character of the translations the Claimant had provided on 28 September 1990, the Tribunal on 30 November 1990 ordered the Claimant to submit by 28 December 1990 "full English and Persian translations of her submissions filed 6 August and 11 September 1990." The Tribunal further emphasized that, considering the procedural status of the Case, no extension of the time limit was envisaged.

6. Observing that none of the required translations had been filed, the Tribunal on 5 March 1991 issued a further Order in which it informed the Parties that it would consider application of Article 28(3) of the [1983] Tribunal Rules if the Claimant, without showing sufficient cause, failed to submit by 28 March 1991 the said translations. The Tribunal again added that it did not envisage any extension of the time limit set by the Order.

7. By Order of 14 May 1991, the Tribunal noted that the Claimant had not filed the translations within the extended time limit set by its Order of 5 March 1991, nor, the Tribunal noted, had she provided any explanation for her failure to do so. Accordingly, the Tribunal announced its intention, pursuant to Article 28(3) of the [1983] Tribunal Rules, "to proceed with its deliberations on the issue of jurisdiction in this Case on the basis of the evidence properly filed in both Persian and English as of 28 March 1991."

...

8. The Tribunal notes that the Claimant has not filed the translations required pursuant to Article 17 of the [1983] Tribunal Rules of, *inter alia*, her American passport and certificate of naturalization despite the Tribunal's repeated Orders for her to do so. Thus, there is no properly filed evidence indicating that she possesses United States nationality.

George E Davidson (Homayounjah) and *Government of the Islamic Republic of Iran*, Case No 457, Chamber One, Order of February 14, 1995:

On 31 January 1995, the Claimant filed his Rebuttal Memorial and Evidence (Docs. 90–92). On 6 February 1995, the Agent of the Islamic Republic of Iran filed a letter (Doc. 93) in which he stated, *inter alia*, that the Persian version of the Claimant's Rebuttal Memorial and Evidence is incomprehensible, confusing and unusable. Therefore, he requested the Tribunal to order the Claimant to prepare a corrected Persian translation of his Rebuttal Memorial and its Exhibits and have it typed to make it readable. On 13 February 1995, the Tribunal's Translation Department reviewed the Claimant's submissions and confirmed that the Persian text contains several

inaccuracies and does not conform to the English text. (The statement of the Translation Department is enclosed.)
Having regard to these submissions the Tribunal decides as follows:
1. The Tribunal invites the Claimant to submit by 31 March 1995 a revised Persian translation of his Rebuttal Memorial and Evidence. No further extension will be granted without specific and compelling reasons. The Tribunal notifies the Claimant that according to its practice the Tribunal does not require the submissions to be typed but instead accepts also handwritten legible submissions.

Vera-Jo Miller Aryeh, et al and *Islamic Republic of Iran,* Award No 581–842/843/844–1 (May 22, 1997), reprinted in 33 Iran-US CTR 272, 278 (1997):

6. On 31 December 1991, the Agent of the Islamic Republic of Iran filed a letter in which he requested the Tribunal to order the Claimants to file the Persian translation of Volume IV of the Claimants' Exhibit Book (the Valuation Report of Business Valuation Services), the original English version of which was filed on 15 November 1991 with the Claimants' Hearing Memorial. On 9 January 1992, the Claimants filed a response to the Agent's letter. In that response the Claimants argued that, according to the Tribunal's practice, the expert reports were allowed to be submitted without translation. By Order of 15 January 1992, the Tribunal, referring to Article 17 of the Tribunal Rules, requested the Claimants to provide a Persian translation of Volume IV of the Claimants' Exhibit Book by 2 March 1992 and annexed thereto the Tribunal's guidelines for the translation of documentary evidence. In compliance with this Order, the Claimants filed the Persian translation of Volume IV of their Exhibit Book on 19 February 1992.

George F Davidson (Homayounjah) and *Government of the Islamic Republic of Iran,* Award No 585–457–1 (March 5, 1998), reprinted in 34 Iran-US CTR 4, 5–6 (1998):

3. On 6 January 1982 the Claimant sent for filing a letter including his claim with regard to five properties allegedly expropriated by the Revolutionary Courts of Iran. The Tribunal Registry received this letter on 12 January 1982. On 14 January 1982, the Tribunal informed the Claimant that it could not accept the letter for filing since it was only in English and no Persian text was presented with it.
4. On 25 January 1982, the Claimant filed a submission dated 16 January 1982, which he titled "Statement of Claim".... On 1 February 1982, the Tribunal Registry refused to accept the submission since it was overdue, but noted that the refusal was, upon the Claimant's objection, subject to review by the Tribunal within 30 days. The Claimant's objection was received on 12 February 1982. The Claimant explained, *inter alia*, that the letter of 6 January 1982 had been accompanied with a Persian text, but the latter might have been misplaced. Also, the Claimant stated that if the letter of 6 January 1982 is accepted, the filing of 25 January should be considered as "merely a more detailed specification and substantiation" and supplementary to the previously filed Claim. The letter dated 6 January 1981, together with its Persian, was later accepted as a Statement of Claim and was marked as filed on 18 January 1982.

George F Davidson (Homayounjah) and *Government of the Islamic Republic of Iran,* Award No 585–457–1 (March 5, 1998), Dissenting Opinion of Judge Assadollah Noori (February 2, 2000), at 1–2:

1. 2 Anomalies Surrounding the Filing of the Claim
2. I would like to briefly discuss some problems I have with the acceptance of an incomplete and late submission as the Statement of Claim in this Case. As one may also conclude from the Majority's Award (paragraphs 3–6), filing of the incomplete submission was refused on 14 January 1982. The reason expressly stated for the denial was that it was not accompanied by a Persian text, a basic requirement under Note 3 to Article 17 of the [1983] Tribunal Rules.

3. The explanation given by the Claimant, or on his behalf, at the time was that the Persian text of the submission was sent together with the English text on 6 January 1982 and that it might have been misplaced (paragraph 4 of the Majority's Award). This was an afterthought explanation with little, if any, merit. Were we to consider the explanation plausible, one of the possibilities should have been to have two refusals, one for the English text not being accompanied by the Persian text and another for the latter not being accompanied by the former.

Chapter 12

Notice and the Calculation of Periods of Time

1. Introduction	393
2. Notice and Calculation of Periods of Time—Article 2	394
A. Text of the 2010 UNCITRAL Rule	394
B. Commentary	395
(1) What form notice may take—Article 2(1)	395
(2) When notice becomes effective—Article 2(2)–(4)	397
(a) A notice is "deemed to have been received"	397
(b) Means of delivery, including by electronic communication	399
(1) Electronic communications	400
(c) Application of Article 2(1) of the 1976 UNCITRAL Rules by the Iran–US Claims Tribunal	401
(3) How to calculate periods of time under the Rules—Article 2(5)–(6)	402
(4) Comparison to the 1976 UNCITRAL Rules	403
C. Extracts from the Practice of Investment Tribunals	404
D. Extracts from the Practice of the Iran–United States Claims Tribunal	404
(1) Tribunal Rules (1983), Article 2(1)	404
(2) Tribunal Rules (1983), Article 2(2)	405
(3) Tribunal Rules (1983), Article 2(3)	405
(4) Tribunal Rules (1983), Article 2(4)	407
(5) Tribunal Rules (1983), Article 2(5)	407

1. Introduction

Principles of fairness dictate that every party to an arbitration should know when the proceedings were initiated, what documents are before the arbitral tribunal, and what opportunities exist during the arbitration for the party to present its case. In this sense, the right to be notified is closely linked to a party's fundamental right to be heard,[1] and a failure to provide a party adequate notice thus may result in a breach of due process that threatens the validity and enforceability of the award.[2]

In this spirit, the UNCITRAL Rules require parties to provide notices, including notifications, communications and proposals, to each other at certain stages in the arbitral proceedings and within specified periods of time. Article 2(1) clarifies what form a notice

---

[1] V S Mani, *International Adjudication: Procedural Aspects* (1980) 30 (noting that the right to be heard includes "each party's right to know, with sufficient notice, what is up against it ... [and] not to be taken by surprise.")

[2] For example, in an UNCITRAL Model Law jurisdiction, a court may refuse to recognize or enforce an award if "the party against whom the award is invoked was not given proper notice of the appointment of an arbitrator or of the arbitral proceedings or was otherwise unable to present his case." Article 36(1)(a)(ii), UNCITRAL Model Law, as amended. Article 5(1)(b) of the New York Convention contains identical conditions.

may take. Article 2(2) establishes when such notices are deemed to have been received. Article 2(3) specifies how to calculate the periods of time established under the Rules after receipt of notice.

2. Notice and Calculation of Periods of Time—Article 2

A. Text of the 2010 UNCITRAL Rule[3]

Article 2 of the 2010 UNCITRAL Rules provides:

1. A notice, including a notification, communication or proposal, may be transmitted by any means of communication that provides or allows for a record of its transmission.
2. If an address has been designated by a party specifically for this purpose or authorized by the arbitral tribunal, any notice shall be delivered to that party at that address, and if so delivered shall be deemed to have been received. Delivery by electronic means such as facsimile or e-mail may only be made to an address so designated or authorized.
3. In the absence of such designation or authorization, a notice is:
   (a) Received if it is physically delivered to the addressee; or
   (b) Deemed to have been received if it is delivered at the place of business, habitual residence or mailing address of the addressee.
4. If, after reasonable efforts, delivery cannot be effected in accordance with paragraphs 2 or 3, a notice is deemed to have been received if it is sent to the addressee's last-known place of business, habitual residence or mailing address by registered letter or any other means that provides a record of delivery or of attempted delivery.
5. A notice shall be deemed to have been received on the day it is delivered in accordance with paragraphs 2, 3 or 4, or attempted to be delivered in accordance with paragraph 4. A notice transmitted by electronic means is deemed to have been received on the day it is sent, except that a notice of arbitration so transmitted is only deemed to have been received on the day when it reaches the addressee's electronic address.
6. For the purpose of calculating a period of time under these Rules, such period shall begin to run on the day following the day when a notice is received. If the last day of such period is an official holiday or a non-business day at the residence or place of business of the addressee, the period is extended until the first business day which follows. Official holidays or non-business days occurring during the running of the period of time are included in calculating the period.

---

[3] Corresponding Article 2 of the 1976 UNCITRAL Rules provides:

1. For the purposes of these Rules, any notice, including a notification, communication or proposal, is deemed to have been received if it is physically delivered to the addressee or if it is delivered at his habitual residence, place of business or mailing address, or, if none of these can be found after making reasonable inquiry, then at the addressee's last-known residence or place of business. Notice shall be deemed to have been received on the day it is so delivered.
2. For the purposes of calculating a period of time under these Rules, such period shall begin to run on the day following the day when a notice, notification, communication or proposal is received. If the last day of such period is an official holiday or a non-business day at the residence or place of business of the addressee, the period is extended until the first business day which follows. Official holidays or non-business days occurring during the running of the period of time are included in calculating the period.

B. Commentary

(1) What form notice may take—Article 2(1)

Article 2(1) addresses the various forms a notice may take, including notifications, communications and proposals.[4] The broad scope of the provision, which covers notices delivered "by any means of communication" that provide a record of their transmission, covers both traditional forms of communication, such as registered mail, as well as newer forms, such as electronic communication.[5] Article 2(1) is new to the 2010 UNCITRAL Rules. During discussions to revise the 1976 Rules, the delegates concluded it would be useful to clarify that references in the Rules to "physical delivery" of a notice are not intended to preclude valid delivery of notice by other forms of "dematerialized communications."[6]

Several proposals were considered by the Working Group to clarify the scope of permissible forms of communicating a notice. Some delegates proposed modifications to the existing text of the 1976 UNCITRAL Rules that inserted references to "electronic communications" or "any other communications."[7] However, in the interest of clarity and emphasis, the consensus of the Working Group favored addressing the form of notice in a new paragraph appearing at the beginning of Article 2.[8] One proposal, along these lines, expressly stated that a notice could be deliverable "by electronic communication."[9] This

---

[4] The paragraph establishes "a list of the actual modes of communication acceptable delivering...notice." *Report of Working Group II (Arbitration and Conciliation) on the Work of its Forty-Ninth Session* (Vienna, September 15–19, 2008), UNCITRAL, 42nd Session, UN Doc A/CN.9/665, at 7, para 24 (2008).

[5] Article 2(1) is equally broad in the sense of who may be a recipient of a notice. Notably, the provision uses the term "addressee," as opposed to "party," thus covering a wide range of communications between the parties themselves, between a party and the tribunal, between the tribunal and outside actors, etc.

[6] UNCITRAL, 42nd Session, UN Doc A/CN.9/665, n 4, at 7, para 23. Paulsson and Petrochilos raised the semantic problem in their report. See J Paulsson and G Petrochilos, *Revision of the UNCITRAL Arbitration Rules, Report to UNCITRAL Secretariat*, at 19, para 38(a) (2006).

[7] Paragraph 1 of the 1976 Rules would thus read: "For the purposes of these Rules, any notice, including a notification, communication or proposal, is deemed to have been received if it is physically delivered to the addressee or if it is delivered (including by electronic communication that provides a record of its transmission) at its habitual residence, place of business, or designated address." UNCITRAL, 42nd Session, UN Doc A/CN.9/665, n 4, at 7, para 25. An alternative proposal was to replace the words "electronic communication" with the words "any form of communications," which was believed to encompass a broader range of communications, "including both future means of telecommunication and currently existing techniques, such as telefax, that were rapidly becoming obsolete." Para 25. Yet another proposal was to clarify that communication could be sent to a postal or electronic address by amending paragraph 1 of the 1976 UNCITRAL Rules with the following revision: "or if it is delivered at its habitual residence, place of business, mailing or designated electronic address." Para. 26. That proposal did not receive support because while it drew on terminology used in the 2005 United Nations Convention on the Use of Electronic Communications in International Contracts, it "might require extensive explanations and the use of additional concepts, such as 'data message' which was found unnecessary in the context of the Rules." Para 26.

[8] "In favor of maintaining two separate paragraphs, it was observed that it might not be advisable to combine a rule establishing which means of communication might be used by the parties with a rule indicating the conditions under which a presumption as to receipt might flow from the use of such means of communication." UNCITRAL, 42nd Session, UN Doc A/CN.9/665, n 4, at 8, para 27. The provision was originally the second paragraph of the Article, but the decision was made to lead with it because "it was preferable first to describe the acceptable means of communications...and only thereafter to provide for a presumption regarding receipt of a notice of arbitration delivered through such means of communication." Para 28.

[9] *Report of the Working Group on Arbitration and Conciliation on the Work of its Forty-Sixth Session* (New York, February 5–9, 2007), UNCITRAL, 40th Session, UN Doc A/CN.9/619, at 11, para 50 (2007). The proposal was made by the Secretariat. *Settlement of Commercial Disputes: Revision of the UNCITRAL Arbitration Rules, Note by the Secretariat*, UNCITRAL, UN Doc A/CN.9/WG.II/WP.147 at 7, paras 24–25 (2007).

proposal was considered to be too narrow because it contained no express reference to traditional means of delivering notice.[10] Other proposals supported inclusion of a non-exhaustive list of acceptable forms of communication,[11] but these were also abandoned ultimately in favor of the more general, yet equally broad, approach found in the final text of the 2010 UNCITRAL Rules.

The form a notice may take under the 2010 UNCITRAL Rules is subject to an important limitation: a means of communication is permissible only if it provides "a record of its transmission." The Working Group did not seek to define the meaning of the phrase. Rather, it decided to include the phrase in the 2010 UNCITRAL Rules because comparable wording used in some international arbitration rules and in other UNCITRAL instruments, including the United Nations Convention on Independent Guarantees and Stand-by Letters of Credit, had not given to practical difficulties.[12] Nevertheless, the phrase "record of its transmission" requires further discussion.

The phrase itself does not significantly restrict a disputing party's choice of particular means of communicating notice. The word "record" is general and unqualified, thus permitting any reasonable form of written or unwritten documentation, from a postal or courier invoice, to a fax transmittal confirmation sheet, to evidence of an electronic data interchange.[13] Further, the phrase includes an obligation only to record the "transmission" of a notice. Thus, a sender is only required to document the fact of sending a notice to another party, but not necessarily receipt of the notice by the other party.[14] This distinction is confirmed by a comparison between the word "transmission" as used in Article 2(1) and the text of earlier drafts of the provision that would have required a record of both a notice's

---

[10] UNCITRAL, 40th Session, UN Doc A/CN.9/619, n 9, at 11, para 50.

[11] One proposal was: "delivery pursuant to paragraph 1 may be made by facsimile, telex, e-mail or any other means of communication that provides a durable record of dispatch and receipt." UNCITRAL, 40th Session, UN Doc A/CN.9/619, n 9, at 11, para 50. The Secretariat proposed: "Such delivery may be made by registered post, delivery against receipt, courier service or transmitted by telex, telefax or other means of telecommunication, including electronic communication that provide a record of dispatch and receipt thereof." *Settlement of Commercial Disputes: Revision of the UNCITRAL Arbitration Rules, Note by the Secretariat*, UNCITRAL, UN Doc A/CN.9/WG.II/WP.147 at 5–6, para 16 (2007) (Draft Article 2). A second iteration: "Any notice, including a notification, communication or proposal shall be delivered by registered post, delivery against receipt, courier service or transmitted by telex, telefax or other means of telecommunications, including electronic communication, that provide a record of its transmission." *Settlement of Commercial Disputes: Revision of the UNCITRAL Arbitration Rules, Note by the Secretariat*, UNCITRAL, UN Doc A/CN.9/WG.II/WP.151 at 4–5, para 6 (2008) (Draft Article 2).

[12] UNCITRAL, 42nd Session, UN Doc A/CN.9/665, n 4, at 8, para 27. However, some delegates raised concerns that the phrase could raise "technical and legal difficulties that could not be addressed in the context of the Rules." Para 27.

[13] This interpretation is consistent with UNCITRAL's flexible approach to the form requirement for documentation. For example, according to the Explanatory Note by the UNCITRAL Secretariat on the United Nations Convention on Independent Guarantees and Stand-by Letters of Credit (para 26):

As is customary in legal texts of UNCITRAL, the Convention establishes a flexible and forwardlooking form requirement for issuance. By requiring a form that preserves a complete record of the text of the undertaking, rather than referring to "written" form, the Convention accommodates issuance in a non-paper-based medium (e.g. by means of electronic data interchange). It does so by referring to issuance in any form that preserves a complete record of the text of the undertaking and provides a generally acceptable or specifically agreed means of authentication (article 7(2)).

United Nations Convention on Independent Guarantees and Stand-by Letters of Credit, Explanatory Note by the UNCITRAL Secretariat, para 26 (1995).

[14] Castello agrees. J Castello, "UNCITRAL Rules," in F Weigand (ed) *Practitioner's Handbook on International Commercial Arbitration* (2nd edn 2009) 1420.

"dispatch and receipt."[15] In practice, however, certain forms of communication in any event will produce a record of both the sending and receipt of a notice, such as courier service or delivery against receipt post.

The broad, but not limitless, scope of Article 2(1) allows a notice to be delivered through a wide range of both traditional and novel means of communication. Thus, the following means of communication would likely fall within the scope of Article 2(1): registered post, delivery against receipt, courier service, certain means of telecommunication, such as by facsimile transmission, telex, or telegram, and certain means of documentable electronic communication, such as electronic data interchange. Article 2(1) would likely not cover the use of unregistered mail, ie where only evidence of postage paid can be obtained, and undocumented oral communications.

By clarifying that both traditional and novel forms of communication (such as electronic communication) may be used to transmit a notice, Article 2(1) represents the latest in a series of UNCITRAL instruments that have approached communication with increasing flexibility, including Article 3 of the UNCITRAL Model Arbitration Law, the 1996 UNCITRAL Model Law on Electronic Commerce, and the 2005 UN Convention on the Use of Electronic Communications in International Contracts. It also aligns the UNCITRAL Rules more squarely with contemporary arbitration practice.[16]

When choosing the form in which a notice will be communicated, the sender should always keep in mind the requirements for effective delivery of a notice established in Article 2(2) of the Rules, discussed in detail in the following section. A notice is deemed to have been received only if it has been delivered to an addressee, or to his or her habitual residence, or place of business or address, or, if none of these can be found after reasonable inquiry, at the addressee's last-known residence or place of business. Thus, in most instances, particularly when sending a notice of arbitration, a sender will likely want to utilize a form of communication that exceeds the requirements of Article 2(1) in order to ensure that delivery of a notice is properly evidenced.

(2) When notice becomes effective—Article 2(2)–(4)

(a) A notice is "deemed to have been received"

Articles 2(2) through (4) identify the possible methods for providing notice under the Rules, each of which (with the exception of physical delivery to the addressee) is premised generally on the concept of "deemed receipt." During revision of the Rules, Article 2 was expanded, as explained below, to more clearly identify acceptable modes of delivering notice. However, the Working Group did not alter the article's general approach of "effective delivery." The Commission's original discussions in the context of drafting the 1976 UNCITRAL Rules therefore remain relevant.

---

[15] *Settlement of Commercial Disputes: Revision of the UNCITRAL Arbitration Rules, Note by the Secretariat*, UNCITRAL, UN Doc A/CN.9/WG.II/WP.147 at 5–6, para 16 (2007) (Draft Article 2). Some delegates of the Revision Working Group believed that formulation reflected "the importance of effectiveness of delivery, the necessity to keep a record of the issuance and receipt of notices, and the consent of the parties to the means of communication used." UNCITRAL, 40th Session, UN Doc A/CN.9/619, n 9, at 11, para 50. An alternative version of the proposal included the phrase "durable record of dispatch and receipt," but it received little support because the term "durable record" was not used in other UNCITRAL instruments. Para 50.

[16] See 2010 ICDR International Arbitration Rules, art 18(1); 2012 ICC Arbitration Rules, art 3(2); 1998 LCIA Arbitration Rules, art 4.1.

One of the Commission's main concerns with regard to notice was determining if and when delivery and receipt occurred. The preliminary draft of Article 2 included a presumption of receipt for telegrams, telexes and registered air mail based on the lapse of a certain period of time after each form of communication was sent.[17] There was a split among the representatives at the Commission on the desirability of this approach, however. Those opposed argued that presumptions regarding receipt of notice or communications were matters of law which were regulated by the rules of the applicable municipal law, and should not be regulated by a set of optional rules which might not even be enforced by the relevant jurisdiction.[18] Some also questioned the efficacy of the provision since it did not eliminate the problem of possible disputes as to the actual time of receipt if evidence was available to rebut the presumption created by the rule.[19]

Those in favor of the preliminary draft provision felt that since "a communication was to be effective when *received* by the addressee, it was necessary to have a rule as to when receipt took place... In the absence of such a rule, difficulties may arise when a party chooses to ignore the communications of the other party, or claims not to have received them."[20] But even the representatives who supported the proposed provision were concerned that setting a timetable for presumption of receipt that would allow for differences in relative efficiencies of national postal services might be infeasible in practice.[21]

The proposed provision establishing a presumption of receipt based on elapsed time was rejected, but the issue of determining actual delivery, and thus receipt, arose again in the discussions of the Drafting Committee. The Committee considered and rejected two more attempts to create a presumption of receipt. First, the Committee rejected another proposal to establish a presumption of receipt after the passage of a certain period of time. The reasons were similar to the grounds that the Commission delegates had rejected the creation of a specific presumption of receipt for telegrams, telexes, and registered mail: the issue should be left to the applicable national law.[22] However, the Committee did not go so far as to state explicitly that national law should govern the issue. Second, it rejected a proposal that delivery be deemed effective when accomplished in accordance with national law applicable at the place of delivery since "senders of communications would then have the burden of knowing applicable national law at each locality where a communication may have to be effected during the course of the arbitral proceedings."[23]

The Committee's discussions of these problems reflected an effort to balance the interests of senders and recipients. On the one hand, the drafters tried to ensure that a party did not face arbitral proceedings without having first been made aware of it through receipt of a formal notice of arbitration.[24] On the other hand, the Committee did not want to place an undue burden on the sender by requiring that he or she know the rules of law on notice

---

[17] Draft Article 4(3) provided: "It is presumed that a communication sent by telegram or telex has been received one day after it was sent, and a communication by registered air mail five days after it was sent." *Report of the UNCITRAL*, 8th Session, Summary of Discussion of the Preliminary Draft, UN Doc A/10017, para 29 (1975), reprinted in (1975) VI UNCITRAL Ybk 24, 28.

[18] *Report of the UNCITRAL*, 8th Session, n 17, paras 32–33.

[19] *Report of the UNCITRAL*, 8th Session, n 17, paras 32–33.

[20] *Report of the UNCITRAL*, 8th Session, n 17, para 34.

[21] *Report of the UNCITRAL*, 8th Session, n 17, para 36.

[22] *Report of the UNCITRAL on the Work of its Ninth Session*, UN GAOR, 31st Session, Supp No 17, UN Doc A/31/17, paras 14–18 (1976), reprinted in (1976) VII UNCITRAL Ybk 66, 67.

[23] *Report of the UNCITRAL on the Work of its Ninth Session*, n 22, paras 14–18.

[24] *Summary Record of the 14th Meeting of the Committee of the Whole (II)*, UNCITRAL, 9th Session, UN Doc A/CN.9/9/C.2/SR.14, at 10–11 (1976).

and presumption of receipt of the state in which the notice was to be delivered,[25] or that he do more than make "a reasonable inquiry" into the recipient's last known habitual residence, place of business or mailing address.[26]

The Working Group tasked with revising the Rules revisited the topic of "deemed receipt" but ultimately did not change the conceptual approach established by the 1976 UNCITRAL Rules.[27] Some delegates proposed inserting a new rule on "deemed delivery," which would cover situations in which delivery was not possible because "a party had absconded or systematically blocked delivery of notices"[28] or because "an address provided was no longer in existence."[29] Other delegates, however, believed these situations were already adequately addressed in the Rules, particularly because the Rules provide that a notice is deemed to have been received upon delivery to the last known place of business or residence constitutes deemed receipt.[30]

The wording of Article 2(2) of the 2010 UNCITRAL Rules (and corresponding 2(1) of the 1976 UNCITRAL Rules) thus, in the end, represents an attempt by UNCITRAL to formulate a compromise solution to a potentially complicated problem.

(b) Means of delivery, including by electronic communication

The methods of accomplishing "deemed receipt" of a notice, described above, are subject to a specific hierarchy under the Rules.

Article 2(2) establishes the preferred method of delivery to an address that has been "designated by a party" or "authorized by the tribunal." If such an address exists, its use is mandatory in communicating a notice.[31] The concepts of "designated" or "authorized" addresses are new to the 2010 Rules. While the *travaux préparatoires* in this area are nearly silent, the context is illuminating as to the meaning. A "designated" address is one that must be "specifically for this purpose," meaning for the purpose of communicating a notice in arbitration under the Rules. Thus, for example, a party may have previously designated in a contract, contact information for purposes of dispute settlement or may do so at a preliminary conference after a dispute has arisen.

The word "specifically" in the phrase "specifically for this purpose" suggests that the intent of a party to designate an address for purposes of arbitration under the Rules must be reasonably certain. Thus, for example, the mere existence of a company's address on a cover letter accompanying a contract with an UNCITRAL model arbitration clause would not necessarily satisfy the requirements of Article 2(2), because it would not convey the company's specific intent to have that address serve as the company's "designated" address for purposes of arbitration.

---

[25] *Report of the UNCITRAL on the Work of its Ninth Session*, UN GAOR, 31st Session, Supp No 17, UN Doc A/31/17, paras 16 (1976), reprinted in (1976) VII UNCITRAL Ybk 66, 67.

[26] See, eg, Summary Record of the 2nd Meeting of the Committee of the Whole (II), UNCITRAL, 9th Session, UN Doc A/CN.9/9/C.2/SR.2, at 3, para 8 (1976) (Comment by Mr Holtzmann, United States).

[27] *Settlement of Commercial Disputes: Revision of the UNCITRAL Arbitration Rules, Note by the Secretariat*, UNCITRAL, UN Doc A/CN.9/WG.II/WP.147/Add.1 at 6, para 16 (2007).

[28] *Report of the Working Group on Arbitration and Conciliation on the Work of its Forty-Fifth Session* (Vienna, September 11–15, 2006), UNCITRAL, 40th Session, UN Doc A/CN.9/614, at 10, para 40 (2007). The Working Group considered Article 3.3 of the 1998 ICC Arbitration Rules, which provided that "A notification or communication shall be deemed to have been made on the day it was received by the party itself or by its representative, or would have been received if made in accordance with the preceding paragraph." Para 40.

[29] UNCITRAL, 40th Session, UN Doc A/CN.9/619, n 9, at 10–11, para 46.

[30] UNCITRAL, 40th Session, UN Doc A/CN.9/619, n 9, at 10–11, para 46.

[31] The rule uses the word "shall."

An address "authorized by the arbitral tribunal" would be one that the tribunal recognizes by official action, such as in a procedural order. Authorization of the parties' contact information may be useful—even if it merely ratifies each party's unilateral designation—in ensuring that the parties are all working from the same page with respect to the delivery of notices during the proceedings. Any additional benefit from the power would appear to accrue in rare circumstances, for example, where a party is absent from the proceedings and it is impossible to ascertain its last known address, thus requiring the arbitral tribunal to determine the proper address in accordance with the applicable law.

In the absence of "designated" or "authorized" addresses, Article 2(3) allows for physical delivery to the addressee or delivery to the addressee's principal place of business, habitual residence, or mailing address. The text of this rule largely parallels Article 2(1) of the 1976 UNCITRAL Rules, with one minor change. However, the drafters of the revised Rules found it unnecessary to subject the method of "physical delivery" to the rule of deemed receipt, presumably because with physical delivery of a notice actual receipt of the notice is less uncertain.[32]

Article 2(4) provides a failsafe option if "after reasonable efforts" delivery cannot be made in accordance with Article 2(2) or (3), described above.[33] In these situations, consistent with the approach of the 1976 UNCITRAL Rules, delivery is to be made to the addressee's last-known place of business, habitual residence or mailing address. A new condition requires delivery by registered letter "or any other means that provides a record of delivery or attempted delivery." By its own terms, this condition establishes a higher threshold of proof of delivery or attempted delivery than Article 2(1), which requires merely "a record of [a notice's] transmission." Though the *travaux préparatoires* are silent on the matter, the heightened evidentiary requirement can be understood, consistent with the principle of equal treatment of the parties, as necessitating further proof of attempts to deliver a notice to a hard-to-reach addressee where a party's fundamental rights of participation or representation may be at risk, such as where the arbitration may be forced to proceed without the involvement of a party.

(1) Electronic communications

As explained above in Section 2(B)(1), in revising the Rules the drafters confirmed that the use of electronic communications, such as email or facsimile transmissions, was permissible for communicating notice under the Rules. At the same time, the Rules reflect an understanding that electronic addresses may be changed or abandoned more readily than physical addresses, such as a mailing address. Thus, as Castello notes, the Working Group limited the use of electronic communications to situations where they have been "designated by the parties" or "authorized by the tribunal" in accordance with Article 2(2), in order to "avoid unfair surprise."[34] In the case in which the parties agreed to designate an

---

[32] It should be noted that this change has no effect on the ability to physically deliver a notice to an authorized representative of the addressee, as originally intended under the 1976 UNCITRAL Rules. See *Summary Record of the 2nd Meeting of the Committee of the Whole (II)*, UNCITRAL, 9th Session, UN Doc A/CN.9/9/C.2/SR.2, at 5–6, para 21 (1976) (comments by Mr Rognlien, Germany).

[33] The Rules do not define what efforts by a party amount to "reasonable efforts," though these would necessarily depend on "opportunities available in the relevant state or in the recipient's last known state." A Bělohlávek, "Service in International Arbitration in Light of Articles 2 and 23 of the UNCITRAL Rules and International Practice," (2006) 24(4) ASA Bulletin (La Haye) 678, 679 (commenting on the similar requirement to make "reasonable enquiry" under the 1976 UNCITRAL Rules).

[34] J Castello, "Unveiling the 2010 UNCITRAL Arbitration Rules," (May/October 2010) 65 Dispute Resolution J 147–8.

address for notice purposes, the agreement between the parties "would put the designating party on notice of the need to monitor the e-mail account, or to update adverse parties if that e-mail address is replaced or even abandoned."[35]

(c) Application of Article 2(1) of the 1976 UNCITRAL Rules by the Iran–US Claims Tribunal[36]

The broad language of Article 2(1) satisfied the two main concerns of the drafters of the 1976 UNCITRAL Rules—that the article should not be too detailed, nor refer to national legislation.[37] However, in the context of the Iran–US Claims Tribunal, which handles thousands of cases in a highly charged political environment, a much more detailed set of rules for serving documents and giving notice is needed. In particular, modifications and additions to Article 2(1) by the Tribunal are meant to address the main issue left unresolved under the UNCITRAL Rules: the determination and documentation of actual receipt and notice. As a result, the Tribunal modified Article 2(1) to expedite and systematize the process of giving notice.

Under the key provisions of Article 2 of the Tribunal Rules, all documents are filed[38] with the Tribunal when they are physically received by the Registrar (Article 2(1)). Furthermore, the filing of documents with the Tribunal constitutes service on all of the other arbitrating parties and documents are deemed to be received by the arbitrating parties when received by the Agent of their Government (Article 2(3)).

The Tribunal cited Article 2(1) of the Tribunal Rules in a series of cases involving the refusal of claims filed after the January 19, 1982 deadline established by the Algiers Declaration.[39] In fact, the Tribunal enforced the deadline so strictly that claims which were delayed by a severe winter storm and arrived at the Tribunal on January 20 were refused:

> Whatever personal hardship to the Claimant, the mere fact that the mail service took longer than he expected to deliver a claim to the Registrar by January 19 does not permit the Tribunal to make an exception to the time limit established by the Declaration.[40]

In a dissenting opinion regarding the first two refusal cases, Judge Holtzmann argued that the Tribunal had the power to change the rule for determining the time of filing from delivery to the Registrar to "mailing or delivery to a recognized air courier service."[41] Such a change would have permitted the Tribunal to accept the claims arriving on 20 January, which in Holtzmann's view would have been the equitable result. However, changing the rule on filing from the receipt of documents to the mailing of documents would have been contrary to Article 2 of the UNCITRAL Rules and the UNCITRAL drafters' decision to make all notice effective upon receipt.

---

[35] J Castello, "Unveiling the 2010 UNCITRAL Arbitration Rules," n 34, 147–8.
[36] 1983 Rules of Procedure of the Iran–US Claims Tribunal, reprinted in Appendix 5.
[37] 1983 Rules of Procedure of the Iran–US Claims Tribunal, reprinted in Appendix 5.
[38] See J Selby and D Stewart, "Practical Aspects of Arbitrating Claims Before the Iran-US Claims Tribunal," (1984) 18 Intl Lawyer 211. "The Registry accepts documents either as 'filed' or 'received.' The distinction is important because under the 1983 Tribunal Rules a document may be 'filed' only when it is received by the Registry in the correct languages and number of copies. Once filed, it will be distributed to the Chambers and the Agents. In contrast, the 'received' designation has no operative effect." 236.
[39] Refusal Case Nos 1 and 2 (1983 Tribunal Rules), reprinted in section 2(D)(1).
[40] Refusal Case Nos 1 and 2 (1983 Tribunal Rules), n 39.
[41] Dissenting Opinion of Judge Holtzmann to Refusal Case Nos 1 and 2 (1983 Tribunal Rules), reprinted in section 2(D)(1).

Most questions arising under Article 2(3) of the Tribunal Rules have dealt with establishing when the filing of documents and service have been achieved, in order to determine whether deadlines based on receipt of documents and service under the Rules have been met. At the Tribunal, most documents are required to be filed in both English and Farsi (Persian).[42] The issue in many cases arising under Article 2(3) of the Tribunal Rules was not when the document in its original language was filed and received by the Agent, but when the document in that Agent's language was received. The cases under this provision established the rule that "the date of 'receipt of the award' [or other document] is the date that the Award in that party's language is served upon the Agent of the relevant State-Party."[43]

Article 2(5) of the Tribunal Rules gave the Registrar the power to refuse to accept documents which were not received within the required time period or which did not comply with the Algiers Declaration or the Tribunal Rules. It also gave parties whose claims were refused the right to appeal the decision to the arbitral tribunal.

(3) How to calculate periods of time under the Rules—Article 2(5)–(6)

Article 2(5)–(6) sets forth the rules for calculating periods of time under the UNCITRAL Rules, which begin the day after receipt of a notice. Article 2(5) provides the necessary starting point for calculations by defining when a notice is deemed to have been received. As a general rule receipt occurs on the same day delivery was made or properly attempted in accordance with Article 2(2)–(4). A notice transmitted by electronic means is deemed to have been received on the day it is sent, unless it is the notice of arbitration, in which case receipt is "on the day when it reaches the addressee's electronic address."[44] Calculation of time periods begins to run on the day after receipt of a notice in accordance with Article 2(6), which is identical to corresponding Article 2(2) of the 1976 UNCITRAL Rules. The *travaux préparatoires* of the 1976 Rules thus remain highly relevant.

In devising rules for calculation of time periods, the original Drafting Committee was looking for a method of uniform application across all UNCITRAL instruments.[45] The Committee drew its inspiration directly from a provision in the Convention on the Limitation Period in the International Sale of Goods, for the final language of Article 2(2) of the 1976 UNCITRAL Rules.[46] While there was general agreement on adoption of this provision, one area of discussion centered on whether or not periods of time under the Rules should begin to run on the day notice was received or on the following day. In the end, the Committee chose to maintain conformity with the 1974 Convention and established that periods of time would begin to run on the day after receipt of a notice or other communication.

Article 2(2) of the 1976 UNCITRAL Rules became Article 2, Note 1, of the Tribunal Rules of the Iran–US Claims Tribunal. The provision was modified merely by using the all-inclusive term "document" rather than the phrase "notice, including notifications,

---

[42] See 1983 Tribunal Rules, Article 17. See also Chapter 11.
[43] See *Hood Corp* (1983 Tribunal Rules) and other cases reprinted in section 2(D).
[44] Note that Article 10 of the 2005 UN Convention on the Use of Electronic Communications in International Contracts and Article 15(2)–(4) of the 1996 UNCITRAL Model Law on Electronic Commerce provide guidance on the time and place of (dispatch and) receipt of data messages.
[45] *Summary Record of the 2nd Meeting of the Committee of the Whole (II)*, UNCITRAL, 9th Session, UN Doc A/CN.9/9/C.2/SR.2, at 6–7, para 28 (1976).
[46] *Report of the UNCITRAL*, 8th Session, Summary of Discussion of the Preliminary Draft, UN Doc A/10017, para 31 (1975), reprinted in (1975) VI UNCITRAL Ybk 24, 38.

communications and proposals," and by establishing that the Tribunal's own schedule of official holidays and non-business days would govern in calculating periods of time.

In general, most controversies determining periods of time under the rules have revolved around when the period has begun to run, ie, determinations usually judged under Article 2(3) of the Tribunal Rules. However, in the case of the challenge to Judge Briner, the decision of the Appointing Authority indicated that there might be exceptions to the enforcement of deadlines established under Article 2(3) and Article 2, Note 1 under special circumstances, although none were found to exist in that case:

> An exception on this rule [that the contents of a filed award or other document must be deemed to be known to an arbitrating party on the day following the day when the document was received by the Agent of his Government] can only be allowed in case…neither the Agent…nor any of his assistants, are familiar with the language in which the document is couched, or exceptional circumstances…have prevented the Agent…to become acquainted with the contents.…Such a contingency cannot consist of circumstances such as a heavy workload or lack of staff.[47]

Enforcement by the Tribunal of the time limits established under the Rules may also be affected by the nature of the rule. In the decision in the Briner challenge case, the appointing authority noted that "with a view to the potential for disruption occasioned by a challenge, Article 13 of the Tribunal Rules seeks to promote that challenges be made expeditiously."[48] The 15-day deadline should therefore be strictly enforced in the event of a challenge, even though extensions to deadlines have routinely been granted in other situations.

(4) Comparison to the 1976 UNCITRAL Rules

Article 2 is substantially similar in approach and content to corresponding Article 2 of the 1976 UNCITRAL Rules, though with certain differences.

The text of Article 2(1) is separated out from the general rules in the 1976 UNCITRAL Rules, as explained above, in order to emphasize the possibility of communicating by electronic transmission. This new structure should not be construed as expanding the scope of the 2010 Rules. The Working Group that revised the Rules was very careful to note that the addition of the new Article 2(1) "would merely constitute a clarification for the avoidance of doubt, and should not be taken to mean that the current [1976] version of article 2, paragraph (1) excluded electronic means of communication."[49]

Article 2(2) introduces the concepts of "designated" and "authorized" addresses to the UNCITRAL Rules and states a preference for their use. It also limits use of electronic communication of notices to these two types of addresses, a feature that is arguably more limiting than the 1976 UNCITRAL Rules.

Article 2(2)–(4) breaks out the basic rule in Article 2(1) of the 1976 Rules into three paragraphs and includes certain revisions. First, physically delivery is more clearly exempted from the concept of "deemed receipt," as this method of delivery raises fewer doubts about actual delivery of a notice. Second, the rule on delivery to a last-known address applies after "reasonable efforts" are made to accomplish delivery through more reliable means, as opposed to "after making reasonable inquiry," though this revision has little effect on the

---

[47] Decision of the Appointing Authority on the Second Challenge by Iran of Judge Briner, September 19, 1989, reprinted in 21 Iran-US CTR 392 (1989–I).
[48] Decision of the Appointing Authority, n 47, at 393.
[49] *Report of the UNCITRAL*, 8th Session, Summary of Discussion of the Preliminary Draft, UN Doc A/10017, para 31 (1975), reprinted in (1975) VI UNCITRAL Ybk 24, para 39.

application of the Rules. A new requirement to deliver to a last-known address by registered letter or other comparable means arguably provides new protections for parties that are unaware of the initiation of proceedings.

Article 2(5) is new to the Rules and more clearly identifies the day on which notice is received and, thus, the day before which the calculation of time periods begins.

Article 2(6) is identical to Article 2(2) of the 1976 UNCITRAL Rules in purpose and function and contains only slight stylistic revisions.

C. Extracts from the Practice of Investment Tribunals

No practice is being extracted in this area.

D. Extracts from the Practice of the Iran–United States Claims Tribunal

(1) Tribunal Rules (1983), Article 2(1)

Refusal Cases 1, 2 and 3, Dissent of Howard M Holtzmann to the Tribunal's Decision Nos DEC 4-REF1-FT (May 14, 1982), DEC 5-REF2-FT (May 14, 1982), and DEC-REF3-FT (February 14, 1983) Refusing to Accept as Filed Three Claims Received by the Registrar on January 20, 1982, at 3, reprinted in 1 Iran-US CTR 129, 130 (1981–82):

> With due respect, I dissent. It is true, of course, that Article III, paragraph 4 of the Declaration states that "no claim may be filed with the Tribunal" after January 19, 1982. However, the Tribunal has the power to determine what constitutes "filing" for this purpose. It is also correct that Article 2 of the Tribunal Rules provides that filing of the documents shall be deemed to have been made upon delivery to the Registrar. However, the Tribunal, which had the power under Article III, Paragraph 2 to make that general rule, clearly also has the power to amend or vary it to provide that for the limited purpose of applying the January 19, 1982 deadline, "filing" shall be deemed to have been made upon mailing or delivery to a recognized courier service.

Refusal to Accept the Claim of Atiyeh Showrai, Decision No DEC 15-REF28–1 (October 20, 1982) at 1–2, reprinted in 1 Iran-US CTR 226–27 (1981–82); *Refusal to Accept the Claim of K and S Irrigation Co*, Decision No DEC 16-REF29-l (October 20, 1982) at 1–2, reprinted in 1 Iran-US CTR 228–29 (1981–82):

> Furthermore, Article 2, Paragraph 1, of the [1983] Provisionally Adopted Tribunal Rules states that filing of a document with the Tribunal shall be deemed to have been made when it is physically received by the Registrar.
>
> On 6 May 1982 the Co-Registrars of the Tribunal received a claim of Atiyeh Showrai against the Islamic Republic of Iran. This claim was accompanied by a letter in which the Claimant's attorney alleged that the claim in English and Farsi originally was sent to the Tribunal by unregistered mail from Strasbourg, France, on 16 and 17 January 1982 in two separate letters.
>
> On 3 June 1982 the Co-Registrars sent a letter of Refusal to the Claimant's attorney informing him that since the claim had not been received by the Tribunal on or before 19 January 1982 they had to refuse acceptance of the claim.
>
> ...
>
> The letters allegedly mailed by the Claimant's attorney in Strasbourg on 16 and 17 January 1982 have not reached the Tribunal. A mere allegation without supporting evidence that the postal administration failed to deliver unregistered mail, does not entitle the Tribunal to make an exception to the time limit established by the Declaration.

Refusal to Accept the Claim of Cascade Overview Development Enterprises, Inc, Decision No DEC 4-REF1-FT (May 4, 1982) at 1, reprinted in 1 Iran-US CTR 128 (1981–82);

Refusal to Accept the Claim of Mr Mohammed Sadegk Jahanger, Decision No DEC 5-REF2-FT (May 4, 1982), reprinted in 1 Iran-US CTR 128 (1981–82):

> Furthermore, Article 2, Paragraph 1, of the [1983] provisional Tribunal Rules states that filing of a document with the Tribunal shall be deemed to have been made when it is physically received by the Registrar. . . .
>
> . . .
>
> Whatever personal hardship to the claimant, the mere fact that the mail service took longer time than he expected to deliver a claim to the Registrar by January 19, does not permit the Tribunal to make an exception to the time limit established by the Declaration.

(To similar effect, see *Refusal to Accept the Claim of Mr Victor E Pereira*, Decision No DEC 2-REF5–2 (March 10, 1982), reprinted in 21 Iran-US CTR 3 (1989–I))

(2) Tribunal Rules (1983), Article 2(2)

Affidavit of Ali H Nobari, the Agent of the Government of Iran, submitted in Support of the Second Challenge by Iran of Judge Briner, August 29, 1989 at 1, reprinted in 21 Iran-US CTR 370 (1989–I):

> 2. Pursuant to the [1983] Tribunal Rules, Article 2, Modification 2, I am responsible for transmitting to each Iranian arbitrating party one copy of the documents I receive from the Tribunal in every Case.

(3) Tribunal Rules (1983), Article 2(3)

Hood Corp and *Islamic Republic of Iran*, Decision No DEC 34–100 3 (March 1, 1985) at 1–2, reprinted in 8 Iran-US CTR 53, 53–54 (1985–I):

> Interpreting Article 37 [of the 1983 Tribunal Rules] to give full effect to its purpose, the Tribunal decides that the date of "receipt of the award" is the date that the award in that party's language is served upon the Agent of the relevant State-Party. (Note 1 cites text of Article 2, Para 3)

International Technical Products and *Islamic Republic of Iran*, Decision No DEC 41–302–3 (June 16, 1986) at 1–2, reprinted in 11 Iran-US CTR 182, 183 (1986–II):

> According to Art 2(3) of the [1983] Tribunal Rules, a document "shall be deemed to have been received by the arbitrating parties when it is received by the Agent of their Government".
>
> As noted above, the English text of Partial Award No 186–302–3 was received by the Agent of the Islamic Republic of Iran on 20 August 1985, and the Farsi version on 16 December 1985. Accordingly, the Civil Aviation Organization's request filed on 19 March 1986 clearly was not made within "30 days after receipt of the Award" as required by Articles 35, 36, and 37 [of the Tribunal Rules]. The Tribunal therefore dismisses the request for having been filed too late.

McCullough & Co and *The Ministry of Post, Telegraph and Telephone*, Decision No DEC 44–89–3 (July 7, 1986) at 1, reprinted in 11 Iran-US CTR 287 (1986–II):

> Article 35 [of the 1983 Tribunal Rules] requires that a request for interpretation of an award be made "within 30 days after the receipt of the award". Furthermore, according to Article 2, paragraph 3 of the [1983] Tribunal Rules, a document "shall be deemed to have been received by [the] arbitrating parties when it is received by the Agent of the Government".
>
> The English text of Award No 225–89–3 was served on the Agent of the Government of the Islamic Republic of Iran on 29 April 1986 and the Farsi text on 13 May 1986. Accordingly the request of the Ministry [for interpretation of certain portions of the Award] filed on 13 June 1986 was not made within 30 days after the receipt of the award as required by Art. 35 of the [1983] Tribunal Rules and is consequently inadmissible.

Harnischfeger Corp and *Ministry of Roads and Transportation*, Award No 175–180–3 (April 26, 1985) at 21–22, reprinted in 8 Iran-US CTR 119, 134 (1985–I):

> According to Article 2, paragraph 3 of the [1983] Tribunal Rules, a document "shall be deemed to have been received by the arbitrating parties when it is received by the Agent of their Government."... Considering that the serving of the English version of the Partial Award on the US Agent is decisive in the counting as to when the American Claimant shall be deemed to have received the Award, the Tribunal concludes that the Partial Award... was so received by Claimant on 16 July 1984. The request for correction filed on 17 August 1984 was thus not made "within thirty days after receipt of the award", as required by Article 36 [of the 1983 Tribunal Rules]. Therefore, and as the claimant has not presented sufficient explanation in justification for the delay, the Tribunal dismisses the request for having been filed too late.

Memorandum attached to the Letter of the Agent of Iran to the Appointing Authority in Support of its Second Challenge of Judge Briner, August 29, 1989, at 3 (emphasis in original), reprinted in 21 Iran US CTR 360, 361 (1989–I):

> The United States' fundamental mistake in alleging that the 15 day time limit has lapsed lies in the fact that it considers the date of 30 June 1989 on which Mr. Khalilian's Statement was filed as constituting the Challenging Parties' knowledge of the circumstances described therein.
>
> That date, under the [1983] Tribunal Rules, Article 2(3) is simply evidence of the service of that document which is, by the explicit language of the Rule, not only different from the parties' awareness of the contents of the document, but is not even the same as the *receipt* of it.

Letter of the Attorney for Phillips Petroleum Company Iran to the Appointing Authority regarding the Second Challenge by Iran of Judge Briner, September 9, 1989, at 2, reprinted in 21 Iran-US CTR 375, 376 (1989–I):

> The Tribunal's Rules adopt the principle that receipt of notice to an arbitrating party's official representative at the Hague constitutes notice to the party. As Mr. Nobari points out, [1983] Tribunal Rule 2(3) provides that documents filed with the Tribunal "shall be deemed to have been received by [the] arbitrating parties when [they are] received by the Agent of their Government". Note 1 to that rule makes clear that time periods under the Tribunal's Rules begin to run "on the day following the day when the document is received". Mr. Nobari admits that he received formal service copies of the Award on June 30, 1989 and copies of Mr. Khalilian's Statement on July 5, 1989.... Thus, counting forward fifteen days from July 5, in accordance with Tribunal Rule 2, the time limit for this challenge expired on July 20, 1989. Yet, Iran's notice of challenge is dated July 28, 1989.

Letter of the Agent of the United States to the Appointing Authority regarding the Second Challenge by Iran of Judge Briner, September 11, 1989, at 2–3, reprinted in 21 Iran-US CTR 378, 379 (1989–I):

> 5. ...Contrary to Mr. Nobari' s assertion that the Agents serve merely as conduits for documents served on them, Article VI(2) of the Claims Settlement Declaration requires the Agents not only to accept documents but also to represent their governments, including governmental agencies like NIOC. Consequently, [1983] Tribunal Rule 2(3) provides for constructive receipt of official documents by parties through service on their Agents. Given the size and English-language capabilities of Iran's legal staff in the Hague,... Iran clearly had ample opportunity between July 5th and July 20th to digest Judge Khalilian's June 30 Statement, and recognize the grounds for challenge allegedly contained therein.

Reza & Shahnaz Mohajer-Shojaee and *Islamic Republic of Iran*, Decision No DEC 95–273–1 (December 26, 1990), reprinted in 25 Iran-US CTR 274 (1990–II):

> 3. The requirements for the issuance of an additional award are set forth in Article 37 of the [1983] Tribunal Rules. The Article provides in relevant part, as follows: "1. Within thirty days

after the receipt of the award, either party, with notice to the other party may request the arbitral tribunal to make an additional award as to claims presented in the arbitral proceedings but omitted from the award." The Tribunal notes that the Award was served upon the Agent of the United States on 5 October 1990, and that the claimants filed their Request on 29 October 1990. Consequently, the Request was filed within thirty days after the receipt of the Award, as required by Article 2, paragraph 3 and Article 37 of the [1983] Tribunal Rules.

(4) *Tribunal Rules (1983), Article 2(4)*

No practice is being extracted in this area.

(5) *Tribunal Rules (1983), Article 2(5)*

Dissent of Howard M Holtzmann, in which George H Aldrich and Richard M Mosk Join, to Refusal to Accept the Claim of Raymond International (UK) Ltd, Decision No DEC 18-REF21-FT (December 8, 1982) at 5, reprinted in 1 Iran-US CTR 396, 398 (1981–82):

> When they finally received the Statement of Claim, the Co-Registrars wrote on 26 May 1982 to Claimant's counsel in Houston informing him that the Claim was refused as being outside the Tribunal's jurisdiction "since the Claimant is not a national of the United States in the sense of the Claims Settlement Declaration." Claimant's counsel promptly exercised the right under the [1983] Tribunal Rules to object to the refusal and to appeal for review by the Tribunal, Article 2, paragraph 5.

Refusal to File Claim of Iranian Tobacco Co, Decision No DEC 19-REF26-l, (December 9, 1982) at 2–3, reprinted in 21 Iran-US CTR 8–9 (1989–I); and *Refusal to File Claim of Iranian Tobacco Co*, Decision No DEC 20-REF27–1 (December 14, 1982) at 2–3, reprinted in 7 Iran-US CTR 275–76 (1984–III):

> The Co-Registrars may refuse any document which is not received within the required time period or which does not comply with the Algiers Declaration or with the Tribunal Rules. [1983] Provisionally Adopted Tribunal Rules, Article 2(5). In order, however, to determine whether a document such as the Statement of Claim in this case is in compliance with the Algiers Declarations, the Co-Registrars would first need to know what those Declarations require. As to certain questions no special interpretation is needed, as in the cases of claims filed by persons who have alleged neither United States nor Iranian nationality, or claims filed after 19 January 1981. Here the Co-Registrars' refusal must have been based on decisions: (1) as to what conduct is "described" in Paragraph 11 of the General Declaration; (2) as to what might constitute "actions of the United States in response" thereto; and (3) the time frame within which such responsive "actions" must have occurred. The answer to each of these questions requires a judicial determination. The Co-Registrars, however, are limited by our Rules to making non-judicial determinations of compliance with the Algiers Declarations, except to the extent that they may apply interpretations made by the Tribunal as to the meaning of the Declarations. Since that limit was exceeded in this case, we reverse the Co-Registrars' decision to refuse the Statement of Claim.

Refusal to Accept the Claim of Industrial & Mining Bank (July 14, 1988), Decision No DEC 77-REF 40–1, reprinted in 19 Iran-US CTR 182, 183 (1988–II):

> 6. The Tribunal Rules of Procedure provide that the Registrar "may refuse to accept any document which is not received within the required time period or which does not comply with the Algiers Declaration or with the [1983] Tribunal Rules." Article 2, paragraph 5. The Rule further provides that any such refusal is, upon objection within 30 days, subject to review by the Tribunal. *Id.* This grant of refusal authority to the Co-Registrars reserves to the Tribunal those issues requiring judicial determination and spares parties who manifestly are not subject to the Tribunal's jurisdiction or to a particular claim from the burden of responding.
> 7. The Co-Registrars based their refusal on the fact that the Claim was not directed against the United States, and therefore was not in compliance with the Claims Settlement Declaration.

The Tribunal has previously observed that certain questions of compliance with the Algiers Declarations require no special interpretation, such as cases of claims filed by persons who have alleged neither U.S. nor Iranian nationality or claims filed after 19 January 1982. The Tribunal also held that the Co-Registrars may apply decisions of the Tribunal interpreting the meaning of the Declarations. *(Refusal To File Claim of Iranian Tobacco Co.*, 15, December 1982), *reprinted in* 7 Iran-US CTR 275. Prior to the Co-Registrar's refusal of the Statement of Claim in this Case, the Full Tribunal decided that the Claims Settlement Declaration does not confer jurisdiction over claims against nationals of either country. See DEC l-A2-FT (26 January 1982), *reprinted in* 1 Iran-US CTR 101. Thus, as the Tribunal determined in its Order of 22 February 1988 in this Case, the Co-Registrars had a basis to refuse the claim of the Industrial and Mining Bank.

As to other Refusal Cases with similar reasoning:

For Chamber One, see *Refusal to Accept the Claim of Sherkate Tractor Sazi Iran (Sahami Kass)*, Decision No DEC 75-REF38–1, reprinted in 19 Iran-US CTR 177 (1988–II); *Refusal to Accept the Claim of Industrial & Mining Bank*, Decision No DEC 76-REF39–1, reprinted in 19 Iran-US CTR 180 (1988–II); *Refusal to Accept the Claim of Etka Organization*, Decision No DEC78-REF43–1, reprinted in 19 Iran-US CTR 186 (1988–II); *Refusal to Accept the Claim of Iran Electronics Industries*, Decision No DEC 79-REF45-l, reprinted in 19 Iran-US CTR 189 (1988–II); *Refusal to Accept the Claim of Glucosan Co*, Decision No DEC 80-REF46–1, reprinted in 19 Iran-US CTR 192 (1988–II); *Refusal to Accept the Claim of the Tehran Regional Electric Company*, Decision No DEC 81-REF49–1, reprinted in 19 Iran-US CTR 195 (1988–II); *Refusal to Accept the Claim of NAHAJA, Ministry of Defence of the Islamic Republic of Iran*, Decision No DEC 82-REF51–1, reprinted in 19 Iran-US CTR 198 (1988–II), all rendered July 14, 1988.

For Chamber Two, see *Refusal to Accept the Claim of Iran Brockway Co Ltd*, Decision No DEC 67-REF35–2, reprinted in 17 Iran-US CTR 332 (1987–IV); *Refusal to Accept the Claim of the National Iranian Oil Co*, Decision No DEC 68-REF42–2, reprinted in 17 Iran-US CTR 335 (1987–IV); *Refusal to Accept the Claim of the Iran National Airlines Co*, Decision No DEC 69-REF44–2, reprinted in 17 Iran-US CTR 338 (1987–IV); *Refusal to Accept the Claim of the Satellite Application Project*, Decision No DEC 70-REF47–2, reprinted in 17 Iran-US CTR 341 (1987–IV); *Refusal to Accept the Claim of the Ministry of Roads and Transportation*, Decision No DEC 71-REF48–2, reprinted in 17 Iran-US CTR 344 (1987–IV); *Refusal To Accept the Claim of National Iranian Copper Industries Co*, Decision No DEC 72-REF50–2, reprinted in 17 Iran-US CTR 347 (1987–IV), all rendered December 22, 1987.

For Chamber Three, see *Refusal to Accept the Claims of Iran Helicopter Support and Renewal Co*, Decision Nos DEC 88-REF32–3, DEC 89-REF33–3, and DEC 90-REF34–3, reprinted in 23 Iran-US CTR 245, 248 and 251 (1989–III); *Refusal to Accept the Claim of the Ministry of Mines and Metals and National Iranian Steel Co*, Decision No DEC 91-REF36–3, reprinted in 23 Iran-US CTR 254 (1989–III); *Refusal To Accept the Claim of the Ministry of Roads and Transportation*, Decision No 92-REF41–3, reprinted in 23 Iran-US CTR 257 (1989–III), all rendered October 11, 1989.

13

Statements of Claim and Defence

1. Introduction		409
2. The Statement of Claim—Article 20		410
A. Text of the 2010 UNCITRAL Rule		410
B. Commentary		411
(1) Submission of the statement of claim		411
(2) Contents of the statement of claim		412
(3) Sanctions for an inadequate statement of claim		414
(4) A note on the Iran–US Claims Tribunal		415
(5) Comparison to the 1976 UNCITRAL Rules		416
C. Extracts from the Practice of Investment Tribunals		417
D. Extracts from the Practice of the Iran–US Claims Tribunal		419
(1) Tribunal Rules (1983), Article 18(1)		419
(2) Tribunal Rules (1983), Article 18(2)		419
3. The Statement of Defence—Article 21		421
A. Text of the 2010 UNCITRAL Rule		422
B. Commentary		422
(1) Submission of the statement of defence		422
(2) Contents of the statement of defence		423
(3) Submission of counterclaims and claims for the purpose of set-off		424
(a) General issues		424
(b) The counterclaim or the claim for a set-off must be within the jurisdiction of the arbitral tribunal		426
(4) Supplementary provisions on counterclaims and claims for the purpose of set-off		428
(5) Comparison to the 1976 UNCITRAL Rules		429
C. Extracts from the Practice of Investment Tribunals		432
D. Extracts from the Practice of the Iran–US Claims Tribunal		434
(1) Tribunal Rules (1983), Article 19(1)		434
(2) Tribunal Rules (1983), Article 19(2)		436
(3) Tribunal Rules (1983), Article 19(3)		436
(4) Tribunal Rules (1983), Article 19(4)		447

1. Introduction

In an overwhelming majority of cases, the arbitral procedure begins with an exchange of written submissions. Written pleadings are often given primary emphasis throughout the proceedings, with a short oral hearing or no hearing at all. Even when a more comprehensive hearing is envisaged, efficient arbitral proceedings require that the parties, in writing and prior to the hearing, specifically determine the issues to sufficiently delineate their scope. Thus, written pleadings are an essential part of virtually every arbitration.[1] Written pleadings are regulated in Articles 20, 21, 22, and 23 of the UNCITRAL Rules. The present chapter addresses Articles 20 and 21, while the other articles are dealt with in Chapters 14 and 15.

The UNCITRAL Rules emphasize the distinction between the statement of claim and the notice of arbitration addressed in Article 3.[2] As discussed in Chapter 10, it is no longer possible under the Rules, as it once was, to elect when filing the notice of arbitration to treat the notice as the statement of claim. However, the decision to do so may be made later, after constitution of the arbitral tribunal. In this situation, the distinction between the two types of submissions loses its relevance. Otherwise, the basic distinction remains: the notice of arbitration signals the commencement of the arbitral proceedings, whereas the statement of claim is the first step in the written pleadings after the appointment of arbitrators.[3]

2. The Statement of Claim—Article 20

A. Text of the 2010 UNCITRAL Rule[4]

Article 20 of the 2010 UNCITRAL Rules provides:

1. The claimant shall communicate its statement of claim in writing to the respondent and to each of the arbitrators within a period of time to be determined by the arbitral tribunal. The claimant may elect to treat its notice of arbitration referred to in Article 3 as a statement of claim, provided that the notice of arbitration also complies with the requirements of paragraphs 2 to 4 of this article.
2. The statement of claim shall include the following particulars:
   (a) The names and contact details of the parties;
   (b) A statement of the facts supporting the claim;

---

[1] The so-called "look-sniff" arbitrations arising from trading on international commodity markets are, in practice, an exception. N Blackaby and C Partasides with A Redfern and M Hunter, *Redfern and Hunter on International Arbitration* (5th edn 2009) 378. On the function and role of written submissions in international arbitrations, see generally 378–84.

[2] See *Report of the Secretary-General on the Preliminary Draft Set of Arbitration Rules*, UNCITRAL, 8th Session, UN Doc A/CN.9/97 (1974), reprinted in (1975) VI UNCITRAL Ybk 163, 173 (Commentary on Draft Article 13); *Report of the Secretary-General on the Revised Draft Set of Arbitration Rules*, UNCITRAL, 9th Session, Addendum 1 (Commentary), UN Doc A/CN.9/112/Add.1 (1975), reprinted in (1976) VII UNCITRAL Ybk 166, 173 (Commentary on Draft Article 17). On Article 3, see Chapter 10.

For a general discussion on the UNCITRAL's use of the statement of claim and the notice of arbitration as compared with other arbitral rules, see G Born, *International Commercial Arbitration* (2009) 1795–800.

[3] Note that the relevance of the distinction may be limited in domestic law. See M Aden, *Internationale Handelsschiedsgerichtsbarkeit* (1988) 234.

[4] Corresponding Article 18 of the 1976 UNCITRAL Rules provides:

1. Unless the statement of claim was contained in the notice of arbitration, within a period of time to be determined by the arbitral tribunal, the claimant shall communicate his statement of claim in writing to the respondent and to each of the arbitrators. A copy of the contract, and of the arbitration agreement if not contained in the contract, shall be annexed thereto.
2. The statement of claim shall include the following particulars:
   (a) The names and addresses of the parties;
   (b) A statement of the facts supporting the claim;
   (c) The points at issue;
   (d) The relief or remedy sought.

The claimant may annex to his statement of claim all documents he deems relevant or may add a reference to the documents or other evidence he will submit.

(c) The points at issue;
(d) The relief or remedy sought;
(e) The legal grounds or arguments supporting the claim.
3. A copy of any contract or other legal instrument out of or in relation to which the dispute arises and of the arbitration agreement shall be annexed to the statement of claim.
4. The statement of claim should, as far as possible, be accompanied by all documents and other evidence relied upon by the claimant, or contain references to them.

B. Commentary

(1) Submission of the statement of claim

The statement of claim must be prepared in writing[5] and communicated to the respondent(s) and to all of the arbitrators. The claimant may elect to treat its notice as its statement of claim,[6] so long as the notice satisfies the requirements of a statement of claim.[7] In that case, the notice should be communicated to the arbitrators as soon as they have been appointed. The rules in Article 20(1) apply to the mode of communication of the statement of claim.

If the statement of claim is submitted separately, this must be done "within a period of time...determined by the arbitral tribunal." According to Article 25, such a period should not exceed 45 days. Although Article 25 allows the arbitral tribunal the discretion to extend time limits for various filings, an extension for a statement of claim is likely to be granted only in exceptional circumstances. First, because the claimant decides whether, and at what moment, to commence the proceedings, it is responsible for ensuring that enough time

---

[5] See *Jonathan Ainsworth* (1983 Tribunal Rules), reprinted in section 2(D)(2). If the parties specify that a non-written statement of claim shall suffice, they should modify Article 20 accordingly. Only in special situations (eg, so-called quality arbitrations) can exceptions to the requirement of a written statement of claim be recommended. In the UNCITRAL Model Law, the corresponding provision has been intentionally worded so as not to preclude the potential sufficiency of a non-written "statement of claim." See H Holtzmann and J Neuhaus, *A Guide to the UNCITRAL Model Law on International Commercial Arbitration: Legislative History and Commentary* (1989) 646–8. Article 23(1) of the Model Law, as amended, provides as follows:

Within the period of time agreed by the parties or determined by the arbitral tribunal, the claimant shall state the facts supporting his claim, the points at issue and the relief or remedy sought, and the respondent shall state his defence in respect of these particulars, unless the parties have otherwise agreed as to the required elements of such statements. The parties may submit with their statements all documents they consider to be relevant or may add a reference to the documents or other evidence they will submit.

[6] An express sentence to this effect was added to the 2010 UNCITRAL Rules. As the *travaux préparatoires* explain:

The purpose of that sentence was to allow a claimant to postpone its decision on whether its notice of arbitration constituted a statement of claim until the time the arbitral tribunal required the claimant to submit its statement of claim, instead of having to make that decision at the time of the notice of arbitration. It was said that that provision was useful in practice, as it clarified that a party did not need to produce a statement of claim if it considered that its notice of arbitration already fulfilled that purpose.

Report of Working Group II (Arbitration and Conciliation) on the Work of its Fiftieth Session (New York, February 9–13, 2009), UNCITRAL, 42nd Session, UN Doc A/CN.9/669, at 6, para 19 (2009).

[7] The words "provided that the notice of arbitration also complies with the requirements of paragraphs 2, 3, and 4 of this article" were added to the 2010 UNCITRAL Rules "to clarify that a notice of arbitration treated as a statement of claim should also comply with the requirements of...article 20, paragraphs (2) to (4)." *Settlement of Commercial Disputes: Revision of the UNCITRAL Arbitration Rules, Note by the Secretariat*, UNCITRAL, UN Doc A/CN.9/WG.II/WP.154.Add.1 at 3, para 5 (2009). Whereas some questioned the need for such language since the arbitral tribunal has discretion to address the problem of an incomplete statement of claim, others saw value in expressly stating the condition. UNCITRAL, 42nd Session, UN Doc A/CN.9/669, n 6, at 6–7, para 20–22.

remains to submit the claim.[8] Where the language of the arbitration is as yet undetermined and the notice (including the statement of claim) is submitted in another language, a translation of the statement of claim in the language(s) of the arbitration[9] must be submitted within a period determined by the tribunal.[10]

(2) Contents of the statement of claim

Article 20, sub-paragraphs (2)–(4) identify the information to be included in the statement of claim and the documentation to be annexed to the statement of claim. Sub-paragraphs (2) and (3), respectively, set forth the essential elements which a statement of claim *must* contain and the documentation that *must* be annexed to the statement of claim. Sub-paragraph (4) indicates additional evidence, which to the extent possible, *should* accompany the statement of claim.

The annexation of such materials was made discretionary on the grounds that it may be "impossible for a claimant to determine at such an early stage of arbitral proceedings what would be all the relevant documents; for example, the relevance of certain documents would depend on the position taken by the respondent in his defence."[11] However, since the claimant is normally interested in avoiding delays, it is advisable that the claimant annex as many relevant materials as possible to the statement of claim."[12] In this spirit, the Iran–US Claims Tribunal has amended the provision in question to make it "advisable" to annex documentary evidence to the statement of claim.[13]

The claimant must include in its statement the particulars listed in Article 20(2), ie, the name and contact details of the parties,[14] a statement of the facts supporting the claim, the points at issue, the relief or remedy sought,[15] and the legal grounds or arguments supporting the claim.[16] While mandatory, these elements need not be fully elaborated at the time

---

[8] See N Blackaby and C Partasides, *Redfern and Hunter on International Arbitration*, n 1, 383.

[9] P Sanders, "Commentary on UNCITRAL Arbitration Rules," (1977) II Ybk Commercial Arb 192. See also K Rauh, *Die Schieds- und Schlichtungsordnungen der UNCITRAL* (1981) 83. See also *Arthur Young & Co* (1983 Tribunal Rules), reprinted in section 2(D)(1).

[10] See M Aden, *Internationale Handelsschiedsgerichtsbarkeit*, n 3, 233.

[11] *Report of the UNCITRAL*, 8th Session, Summary of Discussion of the Preliminary Draft, UN Doc A/10017, para 116 (1975), reprinted in (1975) VI UNCITRAL Ybk 24, 36. Draft Article 16(1) of the Preliminary Draft envisaged in a mandatory form that "all relevant documents" shall be annexed to the statement of claim together with the contract.

[12] See H van Houtte, "Conduct of Arbitral Proceedings," in P Šarčević (ed), *Essays on International Commercial Arbitration* (1989) 113, 121 ("A wise claimant presents all relevant facts and documents at the first stage because failure to do so will inevitably give the respondent opportunities to create delays.").

[13] See 1983 Rules of Procedure of the Iran–US Claims Tribunal, art 18(2), reprinted in Appendix 5. See also H Holtzmann, "Fact-Finding by the Iran-United States Claims Tribunal," in R Lillich (ed), *Fact-Finding before International Tribunals* (1991) 101, 103.

[14] In revising the UNCITRAL Rules, the Working Group decided to use the phrase "contact details," instead of the word "addresses," to ensure consistency with Article 3 of the Rules. *Report of the Working Group on Arbitration and Conciliation on the Work of its Forty-Sixth Session* (New York, February 5–9, 2007), UNCITRAL, 40th Session, UN Doc A/CN.9/619, at 28, para 148 (2007).

[15] For discussion on potentially available types of relief, see T Webster, *Handbook of UNCITRAL Arbitration: Commentary, Precedents and Materials for UNCITRAL Based Arbitration Rules* (2010) 306–7.

[16] The requirement to identify the "legal grounds or arguments supporting the claim" is new to the 2010 Rules. Its inclusion was thought to be important in light of the various pleading practices that existed under different legal systems. UNCITRAL, 40th Session, UN Doc A/CN.9/619, n 14, at 28, para 149–150. An early version of Article 20 included the phrase "legal principles," which was considered to be too vague and was thus replaced by the final language "legal grounds or arguments." *Settlement of Commercial Disputes: Revision of the UNCITRAL Arbitration Rules, Note by the Secretariat*, UNCITRAL, UN Doc A/CN.9/WG.II/WP.145/Add.1 at 6, para 12 (2006); UNCITRAL, 40th Session, UN Doc A/CN.9/619, at 28, para 149–150.

the statement of claim is submitted.[17] Thus, in place of the "full statement of facts and a summary of evidence supporting the facts" envisaged in an early draft of the rule,[18] a more general description of the alleged facts is sufficient at this stage.[19] The requirement concerning the "legal grounds or arguments" requires an explication of the legal arguments, but not a final elaboration of the legal theories supporting the claim. Similarly, although it is necessary to specify whether monetary damages are sought as a remedy, the exact amount of damages claimed can be determined at a later point in the proceedings.[20] Nevertheless, it is essential that the statement of claim be specific enough that the respondent can reply adequately in its statement of defence.[21] Further elaboration of the case can be left to subsequent written statements, which are usually ordered in keeping with Article 22.[22]

Article 20(3) requires the claimant to annex "[a] copy of the contract or other legal instrument out of or in relation to which the dispute arises and of the arbitration agreement" to the statement of claim. The purpose of this provision is to "apprise the arbitrators of the scope of their jurisdiction and the frame of reference for the dispute."[23] References to the contract or other legal instrument, as well as the arbitration agreement, are meant to correspond with similar references made in Article 3 of the Rules.[24]

Article 20(4) provides that the claimant "should, as far as possible," attach to the statement of claim (or make reference to) all the "documents" and "other evidence"[25] it will rely on in the arbitration. The provision is thus discretionary, accounting for the fact that "it was impossible for a claimant to determine at such an early stage of arbitral proceedings what would be all the relevant documents; for example, the relevance of certain documents

---

[17] See N Blackaby and C Partasides, *Redfern and Hunter on International Arbitration*, n 1, 345 ("The UNCITRAL Rules clearly envisage that the initial written pleadings submitted by the parties are not to be considered final and definitive statements of the parties' respective positions.").

[18] *Report of the Secretary-General: Preliminary Draft Set of Arbitration Rules for Optional Use in Ad Hoc Arbitration Relating to International Trade*, UN Doc A/CN.9/97 (1974), reprinted in VI UNCITRAL Ybk 163, 173 (1975) (Draft Article 16(2)(b)).

[19] Indeed, the Statement of Claim must at least inform the arbitral tribunal of "the essence of the claim." See *United Parcel Service of America, Inc* (1976 Rules), para 127; and *Ethyl Corp* (1976 Rules); both reprinted in section 2(C). See also *United States* and *Islamic Republic of Iran*, Case No A/28; and *Islamic Republic of Iran* and *United States*, Case No B1 (1983 Tribunal Rules); both reprinted in section 2(D)(2).

[20] Note, however, that the governing arbitration law may impose heightened requirements. For example, the Turkish Act on International Arbitration, based on the UNCITRAL Model Law, requires the amount of the dispute to be included in the statement of claim. M Ozsunay, "Chapter III: The Arbitration Procedure: Principles and Rules of the UNCITRAL Model Law as Essentially Adopted by the Turkish Act on International Arbitration," in C Klausegger et al (eds), Austrian Arb Ybk 2008 (2008) 358.

[21] *United Parcel Service of America, Inc* (1976 Rules), para 127, reprinted in section 2(C).

[22] See Chapter 15. Because of the flexibility needed with regard to the application of the Article 29(5) "points at issue" requirement, the utility of this requirement has been questioned with reference to the practice of the Iran–US Claims Tribunal. See S Baker and M Davis, *The UNCITRAL Arbitration Rules in Practice: The Experience of the Iran-United States Claims Tribunal* (1992) 85 ("other arbitral tribunals applying the UNCITRAL Rules would do well to follow the Tribunal's practice declining to attach any special significance to this part of the statement of claim.").

[23] *Report of the Secretary-General on the Revised Draft Set of Arbitration Rules*, UNCITRAL, 9th Session, Addendum 1 (Commentary), UN Doc A/CN.9/112/Add.1 (1975), reprinted in (1976) VII UNCITRAL Ybk 166, 173 (Commentary on Draft Article 17) (describing nearly identical Article 18(1) of the 1976 UNCITRAL Rules).

[24] UNCITRAL, 40th Session, UN Doc A/CN.9/619, n 14, at 28, para 147.

[25] An earlier version of the rule used the words "evidentiary materials," but the Working Group reverted back to "other evidence," as used in the 1976 UNCITRAL Rules, because that term was believed to "cover[] all evidence that could be submitted at the stage of the statement of claim, whereas the term 'evidentiary materials' might be construed in a more limitative manner, for instance, excluding testimony or written witness statements." UNCITRAL, 42nd Session, UN Doc A/CN.9/669, n 6, at 7, para 24.

would depend on the position taken by the respondent in his defence."[26] An earlier version of the provision used the word "shall,"[27] consistent with the approach of other leading arbitration rules.[28] Concerns were raised, however, that the word "shall" might be interpreted as requiring the claimant to communicate a "comprehensive" statement of claim, thereby precluding the opportunity to communicate additional materials after the statement of claim is submitted.[29] The phrase "should, as far as possible" in Article 20(4) represents a compromise, by strongly encouraging claimants to communicate additional documents and evidence "without imposing rigid consequences for departures from that standard."[30] As a general rule, providing as many documents and as much evidence as possible in the statement of claim can enhance the efficiency of the arbitral process.[31]

(3) Sanctions for an inadequate statement of claim

Although the requirements of Article 20(2) may be somewhat flexible depending on the nature of the case, a statement that fails to meet these requirements is not a "statement of claim" within the meaning of Article 20.[32] If the 45-day time limit (or any other time limit required by the arbitral tribunal) passes, the consequences envisaged in Article 30(1) can, in principle, be applied.[33]

It is accepted, both in theory and in practice,[34] that a claimant who has submitted a defective statement of claim may cure the shortcomings by submitting supplementary

---

[26] *Report of the UNCITRAL*, 8th Session, Summary of Discussion of the Preliminary Draft, UN Doc A/10017, para 116 (1975), reprinted in (1975) VI UNCITRAL Ybk 24, 36 (commenting on a corresponding provision of the 1976 UNCITRAL Rules similarly discretionary).

[27] UNCITRAL, 40th Session, UN Doc A/CN.9/619, n 14, at 29, para 152.

[28] Compare to Article 41(c) of the 2002 WIPO Rules and Article 15.6 of the 1998 LCIA Rules.

[29] UNCITRAL, 40th Session, UN Doc A/CN.9/619, n 14, at 29, para 153.

[30] UNCITRAL, 40th Session, UN Doc A/CN.9/619, n 14, at 29, para 153. Castello notes that "the more forceful language" in Article 20(4) is "partly justified by the Working Group's decision to require a response to the notice of arbitration, so that the claimant will be aware of the defence before it has to submit supporting documents with its statement of claim." J Castello, "UNCITRAL Rules," in F Weigand (ed), *Practitioner's Handbook on International Commercial Arbitration"* (2nd edn 2009) 1478.

[31] Waincymer observes that "[i]t is highly desirable that international arbitration force early submission of arguments and documents on which a party intends to rely to minimise delay and surprise and help the other party prepare and determine its final position, including as to settlement." J Waincymer, "The New Uncitral Arbitration Rules: An Introduction and Evaluation," (2010) 14 Vindobona J Intl Commercial Law and Arb 223, 239. See also J Castello, "Unveiling the 2010 UNCITRAL Arbitration Rules," (May/October 2010) 65 Dispute Resolution J 147, 152.

[32] See *Jonathan Ainsworth* (1983 Tribunal Rules), Order, reprinted in section 2(D)(2). Reference to an "amendment" of the statement of claim in accordance with corresponding Article 18 of the 1976 UNCITRAL Rules seems to imply that the existing submission did not amount to a statement of claim; if it had, any amendment would have been considered under Article 20 of the 1976 UNCITRAL Rules. See also *Questech, Inc* (1983 Tribunal Rules), reprinted in section 2(D)(2) (observing that corresponding Article 18 of the 1983 Tribunal Rules could be viewed as establishing minimum requirements). For a description of a statement of claim that was not inadequate under the 1983 Procedural Rules of the Iran–US Claims Tribunal, see *Amoco Iran Oil Co* (1983 Tribunal Rules), reprinted in section 2(D)(2).

[33] Article 30(1) provides that: "If, within the period of time fixed by these Rules or the arbitral tribunal, without showing sufficient cause:

(a) The claimant has failed to communicated its statement of claim, the arbitral tribunal shall issue an order for the termination of the arbitral proceedings, unless there are remaining matters that may need to be decided and the arbitral tribunal considers it appropriate to do so[.]"

For an example under the 1983 Procedural Rules of the Iran–US Claims Tribunal, see *Cyrus Petroleum Ltd* (1983 Tribunal Rules), reprinted below, section 2(D)(2).

[34] See K Rauh, *Die Schieds- und Schlichtungsordnungen der UNCITRAL*, n 9, 84, and the *Mishik Movsession* (1983 Tribunal Rules); *Kay Lerner* (1983 Tribunal Rules); and *Jonathan Ainsworth* (1983 Tribunal Rules); all reprinted in section 2(D)(2).

information. This practice is dictated by the most elementary principles of justice and is rarely prejudicial to the respondent. Authorization to allow the claimant to cure defects to the statement of claim may be inferred from Article 17(1), which provides that "the arbitral tribunal may conduct the arbitration in such manner as it considers appropriate."[35]

Sanctions imposed under Article 30 for failure to submit a claim in a timely manner presuppose that no "sufficient cause" has been presented for the delays. As noted above, the claimant need not elaborate all of his arguments fully in the statement of claim. Additionally, a claimant may have a *bona fide* expectation that his submission, though sketchy, fulfils the requirements of Article 20(2).[36] Moreover, the exact contents of these requirements, as interpreted by the arbitral tribunal, depend on the nature of the case. Therefore, rather than equating a defective submission with non-submission of the statement of claim, the arbitral tribunal should ask the claimant to clarify his position with respect to specified issues. Even if the submission is manifestly defective and does not amount to a statement of claim under any interpretation,[37] a tribunal should consider granting an extension of time to cure the defect. An extension can more easily be justified under Article 25 where at least some kind of document purporting to be a statement of claim has been submitted. Defects in what purports to be the original statement of claim rarely justify termination of the proceedings under Article 30.[38]

(4) A note on the Iran–US Claims Tribunal

The 1983 Tribunal Rules of the Iran–US Claims Tribunal modify the 1976 UNCITRAL Rules to dispense with a separate notice of arbitration and to require insertion of relevant information from Article 3 (Notice of Arbitration) into the modified version of Article 18 (Statement of Claim). Although essential to *ad hoc* arbitration, a distinct notice of arbitration requirement (ie, demand for arbitration and notice of intention to proceed with arbitration), was deemed superfluous in the Tribunal process established by interstate treaties.[39]

Explanations of other features of Tribunal regulation concerning the statement of claim may be derived from the specific nature of the Tribunal's claims settlement proceedings. For example, the provision reducing the importance of the exact date of filing of the

---

[35] One example from the practice of NAFTA tribunals is the *Methanex* case. There, various portions of the claimant's original and amended statement of claim were found to fail the jurisdictional test under Article 1101(1) of the NAFTA. As an alternative to rejecting the claimant's amended statement of claim, the tribunal ordered the claimant to file a "fresh pleading" consistent with its jurisdictional ruling and Articles 18, 20, and 22 of the 1976 UNCITRAL Rules. See *Methanex Corp* (1976 Rules), Partial Award and Communication regarding Interpretation, reprinted in section 2(C).

[36] See generally, N Blackaby and C Partasides, n 1, at 378–80.

[37] See *Kay Lerner* (1983 Tribunal Rules), reprinted in section 2(D)(2).

[38] In *Cyrus Petroleum*, the Iran–US Claims Tribunal dismissed the claim, *inter alia*, on the ground that "[n]either in the statement of claim nor in subsequent filings does the Claimant detail the substance of its allegations," but (as the quotation implies) the claimant had been given ample time to correct the defects in his statement of claim. *The Cyrus Petroleum Ltd and The Islamic Republic of Iran*, Award No 230–624–1 (May 2, 1986), reprinted in 11 Iran-US CTR 70, 71 (1986-II). In *Re Helali* (1983 Tribunal Rules), reprinted in section 2(D)(1), the Registry of the Iran–US Claims Tribunal refused to file an unclear claim at the outset. See also J van Hof, *Commentary on the UNCITRAL Arbitration Rules: The Application by the Iran-U.S. Claims Tribunal* (1991) 123.

[39] See G Aksen, "The Iran-United States Claims Tribunal and the UNCITRAL Rules—An Early Comment," in J Schultz and A van den Berg (eds), *The Art of Arbitration* (1982) 6.

statement of claim, now contained in paragraph 4 of note 2 of the 1983 Tribunal Rules,[40] can best be understood in light of the fact that the Claims Settlement Declaration (Article III, paragraph 4) requires all claims to be filed within a short period of time.[41] Without this provision, there might have been a chaotic "rush to the court room," with all the claimants wishing to be "heard first and have clear access to the billion dollar fund set aside to pay awards."[42] Apart from such features, however, the modified 1983 Tribunal Rule 18 contains essentially the same elements as the 2010 UNCITRAL Rules dealing with the notice of arbitration (Article 3) and statement of claim (Article 20). Accordingly, we agree that the "UNCITRAL procedures for filing claims are capable of providing a framework for tribunals with a large caseload as well as *ad hoc* individual arbitrations."[43]

(5) Comparison to the 1976 UNCITRAL Rules

Article 20 differs in only minor respects from corresponding Article 18 of the 1976 UNCITRAL Rules. Both versions of the rule recognize that a claimant may choose to have its notice of arbitration function as a statement of claim. Original Article 18(1) does so implicitly by beginning with the phrase "Unless the statement of claim was contained in the notice of arbitration," whereas revised Article 20(1) more directly states that the claimant "may elect" to treat its notice of arbitration as a statement of claim. Revised Article 20(1) also clarifies expressly what is implied in original Article 18(1)—that to function as a statement of claim the claimant's notice of arbitration must satisfy the requirements for constituting a statement of claim contained in the article.

Article 20(2), unlike Article 18(2) of the 1976 Rules, contains a subparagraph (e), requiring that the statement of claim include "[t]he legal grounds or arguments supporting the claim."

This provision undoubtedly adds an item to the list of particulars to be included in the statement of claim. Arguably, however, the requirement concerning "the points at issue," which was already contained in original Article 18, presupposes explication of the legal arguments to some degree.

The addition of the phrase "or other legal instrument out of or in relation to which the dispute arises" to revised Article 20(3) (which does not appear in the last sentence of original Article 18(1)) is a change to the Rules that is necessary to accommodate the practicalities of non-contractual disputes, such as disputes arising under international investment agreements.

Finally, claimants are encouraged more strongly in Article 20(4), than in original Article 18(2), to supply with the statement of claim the evidence (or at least references to the evidence) it intends to rely on. Whereas according to original Article 18(2) the claimant "may"

---

[40] See 1983 Rules of Procedure of the Iran–US Claims Tribunal, reprinted in Appendix 5. Originally, the particulars concerning the statement of claim, many of which are now defunct, were contained in the Administrative Directives, but were later transferred to the Tribunal Rules when they were adopted. The Administrative Directives in question are annexed to G Aksen, "The Iran-United States Claims Tribunal and the UNCITRAL Rules," n 39.

[41] According to Article I of the Claims Settlement Declaration, no claim could be filed until the expiration of a six-month settlement period ending July 19, 1981, which could be "extended once by three months at the request of either party." In Administrative Directive No 1 the period was extended, by agreement between the two governments, by three months. Therefore, no claim could be filed before October 20, 1981 or after January 20, 1982. See note 1 to Article 18 of the 1983 Rules of Procedure of the Iran–US Claims Tribunal, reprinted in Appendix 5.

[42] See G Aksen, "The Iran-United States Claims Tribunal and the UNCITRAL Rules," n 39, 10.

[43] G Aksen, "The Iran-United States Claims Tribunal and the UNCITRAL Rules," n 39, 7.

provide such additional information, revised Article 20(4) now provides that the claimant "should, as far as possible" do so. Notably, neither formulation is mandatory. Moreover, since the claimant is often interested in avoiding delays, it may in any event choose to attach as many relevant materials as possible to the statement of claim.[44]

C. Extracts from the Practice of Investment Tribunals

Ethyl Corp and *Government of Canada*, Award on Jurisdiction (June 24, 1998), (ICSID administered, 1976 UNCITRAL Rules, NAFTA Chapter Eleven), at 46, reprinted in (1999) 38 ILM 708, 730:

> 94. ...Article 18 of [the 1976 UNCITRAL Arbitration] Rules, likewise unmodified by Part B, requires (at (1)(b) and (c)) that a statement of claim set forth a "statement of the facts supporting the claim" and the "points in issue." Thus, greater elaboration of detail in the Statement of Claim is permissible, if not, indeed, required.

Methanex Corp and *United States of America*, Partial Award on Jurisdiction (August 7, 2002), (ICSID administered, 1976 UNCITRAL Rules, NAFTA Chapter Eleven), at 78, reprinted in (2002) 14(6) World Trade & Arbitration Materials 109, 186–87.

> 161. *Fresh Pleading:* First, the effect of the Tribunal's decision on Article 1101(1) NAFTA in this Award will require Methanex to re-plead its case in a fresh Statement of Claim. Its Original Statement of Claim fails the jurisdiction test under Article 1101; and potentially only a part of its Amended Statement of Claim. In our view, a fresh pleading is required both for the Tribunal and as a matter of procedural fairness to the USA, which is entitled to know precisely the case advanced against it.
>
> 162. The fresh pleading must not exceed the limits of Methanex's existing case (pleaded and unpleaded); and we do not intend Methanex to make any new claim in its fresh pleading. It must comply with our decisions in this Award and Articles 18 and 20 of the [1976] UNCITRAL Arbitration Rules. As regards the statement of the facts supporting its claim under Article 18(2)(b), Methanex's fresh pleading must set out its specific factual allegations, including all specific inferences to be drawn from those facts.

Methanex Corp and *United States of America*, Communication to the Parties Regarding Claimant's Request for Interpretation (September 25, 2002), (ICSID administered,1976 UNCITRAL Rules, NAFTA Chapter Eleven) at 6–7:

> 12. As to form, the meaning of the term "fresh pleading" is self-evident. The phrase is indeed absent from the [1976] UNCITRAL Arbitration Rules (as Methanex rightly comments); but that can scarcely be the cause of any practical difficulty in this case. As explained in the Partial Award, it will be a pleading "more limited" than the Amended Statement of Claim because that pleading asserts claims for which (as we decided in the Partial Award) the Tribunal had no jurisdiction; and it will be "different" because, as to the intent underlying the US measures, we anticipate that it will include allegations made by Methanex orally and in written submissions subsequent to (and therefore not included in) the Amended Statement of Claim. Accordingly, it will be a new pleading of part of an existing case, partly pleaded and partly unpleaded; and the term "fresh pleading" is a convenient description for that pleading, consistent with

---

[44] See H van Houtte, "Conduct of Arbitral Proceedings," n 12, 113, 121 ("A wise claimant presents all relevant facts and documents at the first stage because failure to do so will inevitably give the respondent opportunities to create delays."). In this spirit, the Iran–US Claims Tribunal has amended the provision in question to make it "advisable" to annex documentary evidence to the statement of claim. See para 2 of Article 18 of the 1983 Tribunal Rules. See H Holtzmann, "Fact-Finding by the Iran-United States Claims Tribunal," in R Lillich (ed), *Fact-Finding before International Tribunals* (1991) 101, 103.

Articles 18, 20 and 22 of the [1976] UNCITRAL Arbitration Rules. If the position were otherwise, the Tribunal might have had no alternative but to reject Methanex's Amended Statement of Claim *in toto*.

13. As to content, subject to the outward boundaries permitted by the Tribunal in the Partial Award, it cannot be for this Tribunal to instruct Methanex what should and should not be pleaded in its fresh pleading, as explained in Paragraph 166 of the Partial Award (page 76). Nonetheless, the Tribunal is prepared to reiterate the following guidelines, taken from the Partial Award.

14. As appears from Paragraphs 46–70 of the Partial Award (pages 18 to 24), Methanex's factual case on "intent" is only comprehensible from certain parts of the Amended Statement of Claim, Methanex's Rejoinder of 25th May 2001, the transcript of the Jurisdictional Hearing of July 2001 and Methanex's Reply Submission of 27th July 2001. It is therefore essential for Methanex to reduce its case into one coherent, formal document, i.e. a fresh pleading to stand as its statement of claim in these arbitration proceedings.

15. The pleading requirements of that statement of claim are set out in Article 18(2) of the [1976] UNCITRAL Rules. These do not call for extended argument, whether factual or legal. Moreover, as to legal argument, only brief cross-references need be made to Methanex's existing legal materials. It is Methanex's factual case which needs to be pleaded, however succinctly. Inevitably, it will be an important pleading; possibly it may be difficult to draft; but given that it will plead a case Methanex has already advanced in these proceedings, the task should be relatively uncomplicated and achievable within a relatively short time. (It may be noted that the period of ninety days exceeds the maximum period of 45 days usually allowable under Article 23 of the [1976] UNCITRAL Arbitration Rules).

United Parcel Service of America Inc and *Government of Canada*, Award on Jurisdiction (November 22, 2002), (ICSID administered, 1976 UNCITRAL Rules, NAFTA Chapter Eleven) at 38–41:

Minimum requirements of pleading

123. In its Memorial Canada sought
    to strike the Amended Statement of Claim ["ASC"] for failure to comply with the requirements of Chapter 11 and [1976] UNCITRAL Rules for advancing a claim. In particular, UPS has failed to

...

(ii) plead the minimum required facts and damages flowing from the alleged breach with sufficient particularity.

According to the Memorial, this objection and that relating to the US Subsidiaries (which we have already rejected) "are, alone, a sufficient basis on which to strike the Amended Statement of Claim in its entirety".

...

127. A statement of claim must be specific enough to put the respondent properly on notice so that it can reply adequately in its statement of defence. The tribunal also must be informed of the essence of the claim. An exhaustive statement of facts or of the evidence supporting the claim is not required. What is required, according to Article 18(2) of the [1976] UNCITRAL Arbitration Rules, is the following:

The statement of claim shall include the following particulars:
(a) The names and addresses of the parties;
(b) A statement of facts supporting the claim;
(c) The points at issue;
(d) The relief or remedy sought.

The claimant may annex to his statement of claim all documents he deems relevant or may add a reference to the documents or other evidence he will submit.

128. The ASC follows the list of particulars set out in article 18(2). Thus it has parts headed *The Parties*, Relevant Entities, Procedural History of Dispute and Jurisdiction, Overview—Breaches of NAFTA, Canada's NAFTA Obligations (under which it states *facts* as well as legal obligations and alleges breaches by reference to both), *Points in Issue* and *Relief Sought and Damages Claimed*. (The italics indicate the four elements included in the list in article 18(2) of the Rules.) The Investor used essentially the same structure in its initial Statement of Claim which was much longer (75 pages plus 26 pages of appendices). . . . In the formal sense at least, the Investor complies with the [1976] UNCITRAL article.

. . .

132. Looking at the ASC as a whole and in the context of principle and the relevant [1976] UNCITRAL Rules [namely Articles 18(2), 20, 22, and 15], the Tribunal considers that it does adequately give notice to Canada of the essential elements of the claim it must meet. It does enable Canada to formulate a statement of defence. As the process of the production of evidence and of proof proceeds (a process supported by the Tribunal's powers mentioned earlier and also article 24 of the [1976] UNCITRAL Rules), the Investor will have the opportunity to give its claims greater precision. It is of course in its interest to do so if it is to establish its claims as a matter of fact.

D. Extracts from the Practice of the Iran–US Claims Tribunal

(1) Tribunal Rules (1983), Article 18(1)

Re Refusal to File Claim Concerning Sara Helali, DEC 3-REF11–2 (May 7, 1982), reprinted in 1 Iran-US CTR 134 (1981–82):

> The Tribunal decides that the Registrar was correct in refusing the Statement of Claim submitted by Sara Helali. The Statement of Claim fails to meet the requirements of Article 18 of the [1983] Provisional Rules of Procedure. To the extent that the Tribunal can understand the claim, it is directed primarily against various individuals, some of them Iranian, for refusal to account for or return funds obtained from Claimant and invested in property within the United States. No Claim against Iran is stated such that a Statement of Defence could reasonably be requested.

Arthur Young & Co and *Islamic Republic of Iran*, Award No 338–484–1 (December 1, 1987), reprinted in 17 Iran-US CTR 245, 253–54 (1987-IV):

> 37. . . . Article 20, read together with Article 18, 19 and 28 of the [1983] Tribunal Rules, makes it clear that the arbitrating parties are obliged to present their claim or defence, in principle, as early as possible and appropriate under the circumstances in each case. Compliance with this obligation is indispensable, in the Tribunal's view, to ensure an orderly conduct of the arbitral proceedings and equal treatment of the parties.

(2) Tribunal Rules (1983), Article 18(2)

Mishik Movsessian and *Islamic Republic of Iran,* Case No 272, Chamber Three, Order of July 9, 1982:

> Claimant is hereby ordered to file with the Tribunal by 16 August 1982 a Statement clarifying the basis for his claim and, in particular, the grounds upon which he asserts the liability of Iran and the ultimate relief sought.

Kay Lerner and *Islamic Republic of Iran*, Case No 242, Chamber Three, Order of August 6, 1982, reprinted in 1 Iran-US CTR 215 (1981–82):

> If the Claimant does not provide additional factual information, the Tribunal must consider whether the claim has been presented with sufficient particularity to be capable of adjudication.

The Claimant is therefore requested to address this point and to file by 7 September 1982 further written submissions which should also include any proposals the Claimant may have for procedures which will both meet the Claimant's asserted need for safeguards and fully protect the Respondent's right of defence.

Amoco Iran Oil Co and *Islamic Republic of Iran*, Case No 55, Chamber Two, Order of February 22, 1983:

> The Respondents in this case filed with the Tribunal on 14 February 1983 a request that the Claimant be required to provide more detailed explanation not only as to the amount of the claim but also as to the manner in which liability is alleged against both Respondents.
>
> The Tribunal notes that the Statement of Claim contains forty pages of explanation dealing with the demand for arbitration (p. 1); the parties (p. 1 and following); the Tribunal's jurisdiction (p. 6); the basis and general nature of the claim (p. 7 to p. 10); the applicable law (p. 11); a statement of the facts (p. 12 to p. 37); the points at issue (p. 38); and the relief sought (p. 39 to p. 40). These explanations have since been supplemented by written and oral submissions particularly concerning the issue of jurisdiction.
>
> Article 18 of the [1976] UNCITRAL Rules, as modified by the Tribunal, imposes on the Claimant the sole obligation of giving the following particulars...
>
> It appears that in the present case the Claimant has complied with that Rule.

Jonathan Ainsworth and *Islamic Republic of Iran*, Case No 454, Order of November 7, 1983, reprinted in 4 Iran-US CTR 26 (1983-II):

> 1. By an Order of January 18, 1983, the Tribunal ordered the Statement of Claim to be amended in conformity with Article 18 of the Tribunal Rules by March 4, 1983. The time limit for such amendment was later extended to April 29, 1983.
> 2. On May 23, 1983, the Claimant filed a copy of a telex from Claimant together with materials which had previously been filed as an annex to the Statement of Claim. On July 18, 1983, the Tribunal received a telex from Claimant Jonathan Ainsworth, containing, *inter alia*, a request for a 30 days' extension "to file supplemental papers in support of claim."
> 3. On July 18, 1983, the Tribunal also received a number of video tapes from Claimant and on September 5, 1983 a written submission supplementing his previous filings.
> 4. Noting that Tribunal Rules do not provide for filing a Statement of Claim or supplements to such Statement through use of video tapes, the Tribunal finds that Claimant has not as yet amended his Statement of Claim in accordance with Article 18 of the Tribunal Rules. In particular, the Statement of Claim and the Claimant's subsequent filings do not contain a satisfactory reference to the "debt, contract...expropriations or other measures affecting property rights out of or in relation to which the dispute arises" or a statement of the facts supporting the claim. Furthermore, the points at issue have not been stated by Claimant.
> 5. In view of the foregoing, the Claimant is hereby ordered to file by December 1, 1983 a written Statement containing the items mentioned under paragraph 4 above.

The Cyrus Petroleum Ltd and *The Islamic Republic of Iran*, Case No 624, Chamber One, Order of May 30, 1985:

> The Respondent on 17 January 1983 filed a Statement of Defence stating, *inter alia*, that it was unable to respond to the Statement of Claim, which it said was "totally vague, the relief sought is unknown, and the action allegedly taken by Respondent is rather obscure and unclear." By Order filed 15 February 1983 Claimant was ordered to respond to these objections by 14 March 1983. Claimant failed to comply with that Order, or even to seek an extension of the time within which to do so. By further Order filed 31 August 1984, the Claimant was ordered to file a Response by 1 October 1984 and was informed that if a Response was not filed by that date the Tribunal would proceed to decide this case on the basis of the pleadings and documents submitted.

...
The Tribunal informs the Parties that it now intends to decide this case on the basis of the pleadings and documents before it.

Questech, Inc and *Ministry of National Defence*, Award No 191–59–1 (September 25, 1985) at 3, reprinted in 9 Iran-US CTR 107, 109 (1985-II):

[T]he language of Article 18, paragraph 2 [of the 1976 UNCITRAL Rules as modified by the Iran-United States Claims Tribunal], is merely advisory in nature, not mandatory. While it is conceivable that Article 18 might be viewed as setting forth certain minimum requirements of an orderly understandable submission, so that in exceptional cases non-conforming submissions might be refused, the submission of the Claimant in this case is not of such an exceptional nature.

United States of America and *Islamic Republic of Iran*, Case No A/28, Full Tribunal, Order of December 3, 1993:

The Tribunal notes that the Claimant's submission consists of the following elements: a brief introduction outlining the claims; a section on jurisdiction; statement of facts; points at issue; and the relief sought. The Tribunal is satisfied that the Claimant's submission, which is labelled as a "Statement of Claim", substantially meets the requirements in Article 18 [of the 1976 UNCITRAL Rules]...

Islamic Republic of Iran and *United States of America*, Case No B1 (Counter-Claim), Award No ITL 83-B1-FT (September 9, 2004) (footnotes omitted):

67. The United States maintains that the Counter-claim meets the requirements of Article 18 of the [1983] Tribunal Rules.
68. In the United States' view, Tribunal practice demonstrates the general nature of, and the low threshold for, the pleading requirements for statements of claim. In particular, the United States contends, it is not necessary to include a detailed statement of facts. In the rare cases where the Tribunal has dismissed preliminarily a claim for defects in pleadings, the claimant typically failed to provide extremely basic information (for instance, the claimant failed to identify clearly the respondent parties). The United States also submits that the Tribunal has indicated that it will refuse cases on the basis of Article 18 of the Tribunal Rules only in "exceptional circumstances."
69. The United States contends that such circumstances are not present in this Case and that sufficient information has been provided in the Counter-claim for Iran to respond to its particulars. The Counter-claim devotes distinct sections to each of the Article 18 requirements and explains with sufficient detail the facts supporting the Counter-claim, the general nature of the claim, the amount requested, and the points at issue. The United States recalls that the annexation of additional evidentiary material is a discretionary matter under Article 18(2) of the [1983] Tribunal Rules. The United States notes that Iran has been able to respond to the Counter-claim repeatedly and not just on jurisdictional issues.

3. The Statement of Defence—Article 21

The second written pleading required in every case is the statement of defence, which represents the second opportunity (after the response to the notice of arbitration) for the respondent to state its views and its last opportunity to raise a jurisdictional objection pursuant to Article 23. Counterclaims relating to the principal claim or claims for the purpose of a set-off must be brought in connection with the submission of the statement of defence.[45] The UNCITRAL Rules therefore address questions concerning the statement of defence, the counterclaim, and the claim for a set-off together.

A. Text of the 2010 UNCITRAL Rule[46]

Article 21 of the 2010 UNCITRAL Rules provides:

1. The respondent shall communicate its statement of defence in writing to the claimant and to each of the arbitrators within a period of time to be determined by the arbitral tribunal. The respondent may elect to treat its response to the notice of arbitration referred to in article 4 as a statement of defence, provided that the response to the notice of arbitration also complies with the requirements of paragraph 2 of this article.
2. The statement of defence shall reply to the particulars (b) to (e) of the statement of claim (art. 20, para. 2). The statement of defence should, as far as possible, be accompanied by all documents and other evidence relied upon by the respondent, or contain references to them.
3. In its statement of defence, or at a later stage in the arbitral proceedings if the arbitral tribunal decides that the delay was justified under the circumstances, the respondent may make a counterclaim or rely on a claim for the purpose of a set-off provided that the arbitral tribunal has jurisdiction over it.
4. The provisions of article 20, paragraphs 2 to 4, shall apply to a counterclaim, a claim under article 4, paragraph 2(f), and a claim relied on for the purpose of a set-off.

B. Commentary

(1) Submission of the statement of defence

After a statement of claim fulfilling the conditions of Article 20 has been submitted, the arbitral tribunal issues an order requiring the respondent(s) to submit a statement of defence both to each claimant and to each arbitrator by a prescribed date. In determining the time frame for the submission of a statement of defence, the arbitrators must consider Article 25,[47] according to which such a period normally "should not" exceed 45 days. If, however, it is clear at the outset that this period is inadequate under the circumstances, the parties may modify the rules to extend it pursuant to Article 1(1).[48] Pursuant to Article 21(1), a respondent may elect to treat its response to the notice of arbitration as its statement of

---

[45] This Article is silent on the permissibility of cross claims. For a discussion on the treatment of cross claims in UNCITRAL proceedings, see T Webster, *Handbook of UNCITRAL Arbitration*, n 15, 314–15.

[46] Corresponding Article 19 of the 1976 UNCITRAL Rules provides:

1. Within a period of time determined by the arbitral tribunal, the respondent shall communicate his statement of defence in writing to the claimant and to each of the arbitrators.
2. The statement of defence shall reply to the particulars (b), (c) and (d) of the statement of claim (article 18, para. 2). The respondent may annex to his statement the documents on which he relies for his defence or may add a reference to the documents or other evidence he will submit.
3. In his statement of defence, or at a later stage in the arbitral proceedings if the arbitral tribunal decides that the delay was justified under the circumstances, the respondent may make a counter-claim arising out of the same contract or rely on a claim arising out of the same contract for the purpose of a set-off.
4. The provisions of article 18, paragraph 2, shall apply to a counter-claim and a claim relied on for the purpose of a set-off.

[47] See Chapter 16, section 3.

[48] Such modifications have occurred in the arbitration process before the Iran–US Claims Tribunal, which involves many respondents who must reply to several claims. Article 19(1) of the 1983 Tribunal Rules sets the time limit at 135 days.

defence, so long as the response qualifies as a statement of defence. This right, which is new to the Rules, corresponds with the new requirement that respondents communicate a response to the notice of arbitration.[49]

According to Article 25, the time limit for submitting the statement of defence may be extended if the tribunal finds that such an extension is "justified." Such a determination is left to the discretion of the arbitral tribunal and depends on the circumstances of each case. Generally speaking, an extension of the 45-day time limit is more likely to be permitted for the submission of the statement of defence rather than the statement of claim.[50] Note 1 to Article 19 of the 1983 Tribunal Rules of the Iran–US Claims Tribunal contains a useful list of factors to be taken into account when deciding whether or not to extend the period of time for the submission of the statement of defence.[51] In case of non-compliance with the time limit, the arbitral tribunal has the power to order that proceedings continue notwithstanding the lack of the statement of defence.[52]

(2) Contents of the statement of defence

The intent of Article 21 is to ensure that the statement of defence responds to the information and contentions included in the statement of claim.[53] If a document purporting to be the statement of claim does not fulfil the requirements of Article 20, then there is no duty to submit a statement of defence in accordance with Article 21.[54] The correspondence between Articles 20(2)–(3) and 21(2) is heightened by the fact that the latter encourages the respondent to provide any documents on which it relies, or to add references to the documents or other evidence it will submit.[55]

---

[49] See Chapter 10, section 2, for relevant discussion on Article 3.

[50] See N Blackaby and C Partasides, *Redfern and Hunter on International Arbitration*, n 1, 383 ("While a claimant should know how long it will take to prepare its initial written pleading (and indeed will often delay starting the arbitral until it is ready to do so) the respondent may not be able to make a realistic evaluation of how long it will take to prepare its answer until it has seen the written material delivered by the claimant."). In the Iran–US Claims Tribunal, where the provision on extensions has been incorporated in Article 19(1) of the modified 1976 UNCITRAL Rules, reprinted in Appendix 5, extensions even of the 135-day period have been rather frequent, probably due to the somewhat unusual nature of this arbitration process. See also S Baker and M Davis, *The UNCITRAL Arbitration Rules in Practice*, n 22, 86 ("Iranian respondents' deadlines were often extended for periods that added up to several years."). The relevant practice of that Tribunal is critically discussed by J Selby and D Stewart, "Practical Aspects of Arbitrating Claims Before the Iran-United States Claims Tribunal," (1984) 18 Intl Lawyer 211, 221. Some of the US-appointed arbitrators have also demonstrated their criticism by dissenting to orders granting extensions, while Iranian arbitrators have occasionally held that the Tribunal has been too strict in rejecting extension requests. See Orders issued in *Pepsico* (1983 Tribunal Rules); and *Phillips Petroleum* (1983 Tribunal Rules); and Dissenting Opinions attached to the Orders (1983 Tribunal Rules); all reprinted in section 3(D)(1).

[51] According to the 1983 Tribunal Rules, Note 1 to Article 19: "In determining and extending periods of time pursuant to this Article, the arbitral tribunal will take into account (i) the complexity of the case, (ii) any special circumstances, including demonstrated hardship to a claimant or respondent, and (iii) such other circumstances as it considers appropriate." 1983 Rules of Procedure of the Iran–US Claims Tribunal, Notes to Article 19, reprinted in Appendix 5.

[52] According to Article 30(1)(b): "If, within the period of time fixed by these Rules or the arbitral tribunal, without showing sufficient cause... The respondent has failed to communicate its response to the notice of arbitration or its statement of defence, the arbitral tribunal shall order that the proceedings continue, without treating such failure in itself as an admission of the claimant's allegations; the provisions of this subparagraph also apply to a claimant's failure to submit a defence to a counterclaim or to a claim for the purpose of a set-off."

[53] *Report of the Secretary-General on the Revised Draft Set of Arbitration Rules*, UNCITRAL, 9th Session, Addendum 1 (Commentary), UN Doc A/CN.9/112/Add.1 (1975), reprinted in (1976) VII UNCITRAL Ybk 166, 173 (Commentary on Draft Article 18(2)). On Article 23(1) of the UNCITRAL Model Law, where both the claim and defence are dealt with in the same provision, see n 5.

[54] See, eg, *Cyrus Petroleum Ltd* (1983 Tribunal Rules), reprinted in section 3(D)(2).

[55] On the desired contents, see T Webster, *Handbook of UNCITRAL Arbitration*, n 15, 313.

Although from the point of view of effective arbitral proceedings it is advisable that the respondent do so,[56] the permissive wording of the second sentence of Article 21(2) makes it clear that the provision is "without prejudice to his right to present additional or substitute documents at a later stage in the arbitral proceedings."[57] According to Article 23(2), the respondent should make any objections to the arbitral tribunal's jurisdiction at the latest when submitting its statement of defence. Whether the filing of a statement of defence should be postponed pending the resolution of jurisdictional objections depends on the circumstances of the case.[58]

Article 21(2) more strongly encourages respondents to include in the statement of defence the "documents or other evidence" that it will rely on, or at least contain references to these materials. A similar provision appears in Article 20(4) on the statement of claim and, as explained above, is meant to enhance efficiency of the arbitral proceedings by avoiding delay and surprise.[59] The second sentence of Article 21(2) serves the same goals.[60]

(3) Submission of counterclaims and claims for the purpose of set-off

(a) General issues

Article 21(3) establishes the respondent's right to present counterclaims or claims relied on for the purpose of a set-off.[61] Generally speaking, a counterclaim is a separate claim, whereas a set-off "claim" is a defensive pleading that money owed by the main claimant to the defendant is to be counter-balanced against the claim.[62] Sanders indicates the hypothetical difference between the two: unlike a set-off, "the counter-claim must still be decided upon by the arbitrators when the original claim is withdrawn or settled."[63] Another difference is that a demand based on a counterclaim may exceed the amount of the original claim while a set-off demand may not.[64]

---

[56] See Article 19(2) of the 1983 Tribunal Rules of the Iran–US Claims Tribunal, reprinted in Appendix 5.

[57] *Report of the Secretary-General on the Revised Draft Set of Arbitration Rules*, UNCITRAL, 9th Session, Addendum 1 (Commentary), UN Doc A/CN.9/112/Add.1 (1975), reprinted in (1976) VII UNCITRAL Ybk 166, 173 (Commentary on Draft Article 18(2)) (commenting on corresponding Article 19(2) of the 1976 UNCITRAL Rules which was substantially similar in content).

[58] Compare *United Parcel Service of America, Inc* (1976 Rules), at para 20, (postponing filing of statement of defence because respondent's jurisdictional objections were "so extensive") with *Canfor Corp* (1976 Rules), para 49; both reprinted in section 3(C) (requiring filing of statement of defence setting forth all jurisdictional objections because respondent "ha[d] not presented the Tribunal with all of its jurisdictional arguments and has made [a] reservation of rights [to raise jurisdictional objections]").

[59] See discussion in section 2(B)(2).

[60] See J Castello, "UNCITRAL Rules," n 30, 1481.

[61] For a general discussion on counterclaims and set-offs in arbitral proceedings, see N Blackaby and C Partasides, *Redfern and Hunter on International Arbitration*, n 1, 383–4.

[62] See, eg, B Garner (ed), *Black's Law Dictionary* (9th edn 2009) 402, 1496.

[63] P Sanders, "Commentary on UNCITRAL Arbitration Rules," n 9, 205. See also I Dore, *Arbitration and Conciliation under the UNCITRAL Rules: A Textual Analysis* (1986) 73, n 76. This has been confirmed in the practice of the Iran–US Claims Tribunal. See *Behring Intl, Inc* (1983 Tribunal Rules); and *Interfirst Bank Dallas* (1983 Tribunal Rules); both reprinted in section 3(D)(3). According to Article 32(2)(a) of the UNCITRAL Model Law, as amended, "[t]he arbitral tribunal shall issue an order for the termination of the arbitral proceedings when: (a) the claimant withdraws his claim, unless the respondent objects thereto and the arbitral tribunal recognizes a legitimate interest on his part in obtaining a final settlement of the dispute...." Presumably the existence of a counterclaim would normally mean such "a legitimate interest." For the discussion of whether the Tribunal has jurisdiction over counterclaims brought by state parties, see *Islamic Republic of Iran* and *United States*, Case No B1 (Counterclaim) (1983 Tribunal Rules), reprinted in section 3(D)(3).

[64] The Iran–US Claims Tribunal has confirmed that a counterclaim otherwise falling within its jurisdiction is within that jurisdiction even if it exceeds the amount of the claim. See A Avanessian, *Iran-United States Claims Tribunal in Action* (1993) 63–4. The *Gould Marketing* case (1983 Tribunal Rules), which led to an award against the US party on the basis of counterclaims, is discussed in Chapter 2, in connection with Article 17(1) (the tribunal's power to conduct the proceedings as appropriate).

Counterclaims can only be presented by parties against other parties to the arbitration case.[65] Article 21(3) indicates that counterclaims and demands for set-off should be asserted in the statement of defence. This means only that counterclaims should be asserted at the same time as the statement of defence. The respondent is not prevented from submitting his counterclaim in a document ("statement of counterclaim") separate from the statement of defence. Moreover, exceptions to the obligation to raise counterclaims in connection with the statement of defence are possible "if the arbitral tribunal decides that the delay was justified under the circumstances."

Since counterclaims submitted after the statement of defence are rarely admitted, "the Respondent has the burden of justifying the delay."[66] Accordingly, in the practice of the Iran–US Claims Tribunal, late counterclaims have frequently been rejected for failure to show circumstances that would justify the delay.[67] If a counterclaim is raised after the submission of the statement of defence without any effort to explain the delay, it will normally be dismissed.[68] Exceptions are, however, conceivable when the delay is minimal.[69]

Where the party does submit explanations to justify its delay, it is up to the arbitral tribunal to judge their sufficiency in light of Article 21(3). Three kinds of considerations must be taken into account and balanced against each other in making such a determination: (1) the respondent's reasons for the delay, (2) possible prejudice caused to the claimant by the acceptance of the late submission of the counterclaim, and (3) the effect of the delay on the arbitral proceedings as a whole.

As to the first consideration, failure to assert the counterclaim in the statement of defence may be justified if the evidence supporting the counterclaim only becomes accessible to the respondent after the submission of the statement of defence. The complicated nature of the case and the volume of the record surrounding it may also provide the respondent and its counsel with an excuse for failing to detect the basis for a counterclaim until after the submission of the statement of defence.[70]

From the respondent's point of view, reasons that would excuse the late submission of the counterclaim necessarily justify delay under Article 21(3). The question of whether the late submission will prejudice the other party must also be taken into account. Such prejudice is most evident where the untimely presentation of the counterclaim makes it difficult for the other party to properly defend itself against the counterclaim. The concept of prejudice must be understood in this procedural sense. On the other hand, the "prejudice" caused to the claimant by the meritorious strength of the counterclaim as such is not an argument against the admissibility of the counterclaim. On the contrary, the weaker the counterclaim appears to be, the less reason there is to burden the other party with the

---

[65] See *Collins Systems Intl, Inc* (1983 Tribunal Rules); and *Morrison-Knudsen Pacific Ltd* (1983 Tribunal Rules); both reprinted in section 3(D)(3). However, if a state or government is a party, it presumptively does not matter through which legally non-independent state entity a counterclaim is asserted. See also *William L Pereira Associates, Iran* (1983 Tribunal Rules), reprinted in section 3(D)(3). As one investment tribunal observed: "It is a cardinal principle relating to the bringing of counterclaims...that the necessary parties to the counterclaim must be the same as the parties to the primary claim." *Saluka Investments B V* and *Czech Republic*, Decision on Jurisdiction over the Czech Republic's Counterclaim (May 7, 2004) (PCA administered, 1976 UNCITRAL Rules, Netherlands-Czech Republic BIT), at 11, para 49.

[66] *Harris Intl Telecommunication, Inc* (1983 Tribunal Rules), para 91, reprinted in section 3(D)(3).

[67] See, eg, *Intrend Intl* (1983 Tribunal Rules), reprinted in section 3(D)(3).

[68] See, eg, *International Technical Products* (1983 Tribunal Rules), reprinted in section 3(D)(3).

[69] See, eg, *Anaconda-Iran, Inc*, (1983 Tribunal Rules), reprinted in section 3(D)(3).

[70] See *American Bell Intl, Inc* (1983 Tribunal Rules), Award No 255–48–3, para 183, reprinted in section 3(D)(3).

obligation to reply.[71] The award of the Iran–US Claims Tribunal in *American Bell International Inc*[72] illustrates these various considerations. The assertion, slightly more than a month before the hearing, of an apparently *prima facie* meritorious[73] and factually simple counterclaim in a per se authorized "Counter-claim Memorial" was justified in view of the fact that the other party had ample time to respond to the counterclaim in a rebuttal memorial that was due about a week before the hearing.[74]

A counterclaim presenting more complicated factual and legal issues should not, however, routinely be admitted as late as three years after the presentation of the statement of defence and one month prior to the hearing, as happened in *American Bell International Inc*. Counterclaims not raised until the very eve of the hearing, at the hearing, or subsequent to it, should be admitted only in exceptional circumstances. Thus, the Iran–US Claims Tribunal "has been particularly reluctant to accept late counterclaims filed shortly before the Hearing, during the Hearing or after the Hearing."[75] Untimeliness, which makes it difficult or impossible for the other party to reply to the counterclaim fully in a written pleading, and to prepare a proper oral defence for the hearing, would normally be considered prejudicial. Postponement of the proceedings in order to provide the second party with an opportunity to prepare a defence has negative effects on the arbitral proceedings as a whole. Thus, the longer the lapse of time following the submission of the statement of defence, the weightier the reasons required to justify admitting a counterclaim.[76]

(b) The counterclaim or the claim for a set-off must be within the jurisdiction of the arbitral tribunal

Article 21(3) states the self-evident rule that the respondent may present a counterclaim or a claim for a set-off "provided that the arbitral tribunal has jurisdiction over it." The Rules themselves therefore place no restrictions on a disputing party's ability to raise counterclaims or claims for a set-off, save for possible limitations when such claims are filed late, as described above. Rather, the arbitral tribunal's jurisdiction over counterclaims and claims for a set-off is determined by reference to the governing law, the terms of the arbitration agreement between the disputing parties, the mandatory requirements of the domestic law, or the terms of a governing international treaty, such as an investment treaty.

The phrase "provided that the arbitral tribunal has jurisdiction over it" was added to the 2010 UNCITRAL Rules primarily to account for increased use of the Rules in investor-state arbitration under investment treaties. Corresponding Article 19(3) of the 1976 UNCITRAL Rules was conceived of in the context of international commercial

---

[71] See *Richard D Harza* (1983 Tribunal Rules), reprinted in section 3(D)(3).

[72] *American Bell Intl Inc* (1983 Tribunal Rules), reprinted in section 3(D)(3). See also *Harris Intl Telecommunications, Inc* (1983 Tribunal Rules), reprinted in section 3(D)(3).

[73] The counterclaim in question was eventually granted in the amount of US $3,500,000. *American Bell Intl Inc*, Award No 255–48–3, paras 184–85.

[74] Some further light is shed in the Concurring Opinion of Judge Brower who stated that "[t]his counterclaim was raised only a month or so before the Hearing and was documented at that time with admissions of Claimant in its correspondence as well as contemporaneous memoranda of meetings. In a subsequent Rebuttal Memorial and evidence Claimant would appear at least tacitly to have conceded this liability." Award No 255–48–3, Concurring Opinion of Judge Brower, at 3 n 5 (September 19, 1986), reprinted in 12 Iran-US CTR 233, 234 (1986–III).

[75] *Harris Intl Telecommunications, Inc* (1983 Tribunal Rules), para 93, reprinted in section 3(D)(3).

[76] Compare the cases just cited with *Anaconda-Iran Inc* (1983 Tribunal Rules), reprinted in section 3(D)

arbitration and thus limited the disputing parties' ability to raise counterclaims and claims for a set-off to those "arising out of the same contract." The Working Group viewed this phrase as "too narrow" in the context of investor–state arbitration "where it might be necessary to adopt a particularly broad understanding of the range of counterclaims and set-off that could be dealt with in the same proceeding."[77]

Various proposals to broaden the arbitral tribunal's potential scope of jurisdiction over counterclaims and claims for set-off were considered by the Working Group.[78] One draft of Article 21(3) included two options: either a counterclaim or a set-off claim could be heard when "arising out of the same defined legal relationship, whether contractual or not" or "provided that [such claim] falls within the scope of the arbitration agreement."[79] Some support was expressed for the second option, subject to textual revisions clarifying that the term "arbitration agreement" was not limited to the arbitration agreement out of which the main claim arose.[80] Others opposed this approach, however, proposing instead to combine the two options in order to restrict the admissibility of counterclaims or claims of set-off in cases of broadly drafted arbitration agreements.[81]

The Swiss delegation proposed yet another version of the rule that would treat set-off claims and counterclaims on different terms to reflect the distinct approaches to set-off claims and counterclaims under different legal systems. In some countries, for example, a claim for a set-off was considered to be a defence that could be raised, regardless of whether it fell within the scope of the arbitration agreement; if proven, the set-off would operate to extinguish the main claim.[82] To reflect this practice, the Swiss proposal allowed claims for a set-off "even if the claim on which the set-off is based does not fall within the scope of the arbitration agreement, and even if such claim is the object of a different arbitration agreement or of a forum selection clause, provided that the requirements for a set-off under the substantive law applicable to the main claim are fulfilled."[83] By contrast, counterclaims were subject to different substantive rules under the proposal because a counterclaim was a claim in its own right, not merely a defence. To be valid under the Swiss proposal, a

---

(3) (one or two days' delay "would not by itself ordinarily result in the dismissal of counter-claims"). See also *Blount Brothers Corp* (1983 Tribunal Rules), reprinted in section 3(D)(3). In this case a counterclaim submitted some 20 days after the statement of defence (April 28 and April 6, 1982 respectively) did not seem to cause problems, whereas counterclaims raised about a year later—two weeks before and at the Hearing—were "rejected pursuant to Article 19(3) of the 1983 Tribunal Rules, no justification for the delay in presenting them having been shown." On the Tribunal's practice, see J van Hof, *Commentary on the UNCITRAL Arbitration Rules*, n 38, 128–31; see also S Baker and M Davis, *The UNCITRAL Arbitration Rules in Practice*, n 22, 90–1.

[77] *Report of the Working Group on Arbitration and Conciliation on the Work of its Forty-Fifth Session* (Vienna, September 11–15, 2006), UNCITRAL, 40th Session, UN Doc A/CN.9/614, at 20, para 96 (2007); UNCITRAL, 40th Session, UN Doc A/CN.9/619, n 14, at 29, para 158. See J Castello, "UNCITRAL Rules," n 30, 1481.

[78] UNCITRAL, 40th Session, UN Doc A/CN.9/619, n 14, at 29, para 158.

[79] *Settlement of Commercial Disputes: Revision of the UNCITRAL Arbitration Rules, Note by the Secretariat*, UNCITRAL, UN Doc A/CN.9/WG.II/WP.145/Add.1 at 7, para 16 (2006). (Draft Article 19(3)). Another proposed variation was that it "falls within the scope of the arbitration agreement." *Settlement of Commercial Disputes: Revision of the UNCITRAL Arbitration Rules, Note by the Secretariat*, UNCITRAL, UN Doc A/CN.9/WG.II/WP.151/Add.1 at 4, para 3 (2008), (Draft Article 19(3), option 2).

[80] UNCITRAL, 42nd Session, UN Doc A/CN.9/669, n 6, at 8–9, para 30.

[81] UNCITRAL, 42nd Session, UN Doc A/CN.9/669, n 6, at 8–9, para 30.

[82] UNCITRAL, 42nd Session, UN Doc A/CN.9/669, n 6, at 8, para 28.

[83] *Settlement of Commercial Disputes: Revision of the UNCITRAL Arbitration Rules, Proposal by the Government of Switzerland, Note by the Secretariat*, UNCITRAL, UN Doc A/CN.9/WG.II/WP.152 at 2, para 3 (2008).

counterclaim had to fall within the scope of an arbitration agreement between the parties and have a "sufficient link" to the main claim.[84]

A number of concerns about the Swiss proposal were raised. Because set-off claims and counterclaims are regulated by domestic procedural law, and such laws can vary from jurisdiction to jurisdiction, some Working Group delegates argued that the proposed rule might not be readily incorporated into all legal systems.[85] Thus, the feasibility of a universal rule on the matter was doubtful. Further, others believed the Swiss proposal "might invite challenges under the New York Convention with respect to the scope of the arbitration agreement even if the parties would have accepted such extension by agreeing on the application of the Rules."[86] In other words, despite the arguably indirect agreement of the parties over counterclaims, such an extension might be viewed, for example, as an excess of jurisdiction.

The problems with the Swiss proposal, along with other proposals, moved the Working Group toward considering a proposal that placed no substantive restrictions on the arbitral tribunal's competence to address counterclaims and set-off claims; such claims could be heard "provided that the tribunal has jurisdiction."[87] Some concern was expressed that such an open-ended approach would not offer sufficient guidance to the arbitral tribunal on the limits of its competence.[88] The proposal ultimately found wide support, however, because it was considered to be "broad enough to encompass a wide range of circumstances," ie, it did not require substantive definitions of the terms "counterclaim" and "claim for purpose of a set-off" and could address the situation in which the main claim had been extinguished by a set-off.[89]

In practice, investor–state tribunals have interpreted the 1976 UNCITRAL Rule, with its narrower language ("arising out of the same contract"), along with applicable investment treaties, as allowing the filing of at least counterclaims.[90] Nevertheless, the revisions in Article 21(3) bring clarity to an important area of the Rules which will undoubtedly enhance the efficiency and flexibility of UNCITRAL arbitration as intended by the drafters.[91]

(4) Supplementary provisions on counterclaims and claims for the purpose of set-off

Insofar as it fulfils the aforementioned conditions relating to the arbitral tribunal's jurisdiction, the arbitral tribunal should treat a counterclaim or a set-off claim on a commensurate

---

[84] UNCITRAL, UN Doc A/CN.9/WG.II/WP.152, n 83, at 2, para 3. Another similar proposal was to modify the language such that counterclaims were "substantially connected to (or arose out of) the initial claim. UNCITRAL, 40th Session, UN Doc A/CN.9/619, n 14, at 29, para 158. On the other hand, another suggestion was that "the provision should not require that there be a connection between the claim and the counterclaim of set-off, leaving to the arbitral tribunal the discretion to decide that question." Para 158.

[85] UNCITRAL, 42nd Session, UN Doc A/CN.9/669, n 6, at 8, para 29.

[86] UNCITRAL, 42nd Session, UN Doc A/CN.9/669, n 6, at 8, para 29. In another context the term "sufficient link" was thought to give rise to interpretive problems. 8–9, para 30.

[87] UNCITRAL, 42nd Session, UN Doc A/CN.9/669, n 6, at 9, para 31. (Concerned that such substantive rules "could be understood in a variety of manners under different legal systems.")

[88] UNCITRAL, 42nd Session, UN Doc A/CN.9/669, n 6, at 9, para 31.

[89] UNCITRAL, 42nd Session, UN Doc A/CN.9/669, n 6, at 9, para 31.

[90] See, eg, *Saluka Investments* (1976 Rules), reprinted in section 3(C).

[91] *Settlement of Commercial Disputes: Revision of the UNCITRAL Arbitration Rules, Note by the Secretariat*, UNCITRAL, UN Doc A/CN.9/WG.II/WP.143/Add.1 at 4, para 8 (2006). (citing *Possible Future Work in the Area of International Commercial Arbitration*, UNCITRAL, 32nd Session, UN Doc A/CN.9/460 (1999), paras 72–79, reprinted in (1999) XXX UNCITRAL Ybk 395, 405, and citing "procedural efficiency" and the "desirability of eliminating disputes between parties").

basis with the principal claim.[92] In this spirit, Article 21(4) provides that a counterclaim shall follow the structure of the statement of claim as prescribed in Article 20(2) and (4). In Note 2 to Article 19 of the 1983 Tribunal Rules of the Iran–US Claims Tribunal, this main provision has been supplemented by additionally providing that the "counterrespondent" (ie, the claimant) has the right to reply to the counterclaim, whereby Article 19(2) on the statement of defence is correspondingly applicable. The same basic principles apply to claims and counterclaims under the UNCITRAL Model Law.[93]

(5) Comparison to the 1976 UNCITRAL Rules

The principal difference between Article 21 and corresponding Article 19 of the 1976 UNCITRAL Rules is the elimination of any substantive rules that regulate the arbitral tribunal's jurisdiction over counterclaims and set-off claims. Whereas revised Article 21 requires only that the arbitral tribunal "have jurisdiction over" counterclaims or set-off claims, original Article 19 allows such claims to be heard only if they arise "out of the same contract" on which the main claim is based.

The requirement that the counterclaim relate to the cause of action of the main claim is in keeping with the general function of a counterclaim. Thus, with respect to counterclaims, the practical differences between revised Article 21(3) and original Article 19(3) are likely to be minimal.

The treatment of a set-off claim may be more complex and, in some cases, may reveal greater differences in approach between the 2010 and 1976 Rules. In some legal systems, such a direct connection between the main contract and the set-off claim is not necessary. For example, a debt[94] owed by a claimant to the respondent need not be based on the contract at issue in the main claim in order to be relied on for the purpose of set-off.[95] Unlike revised Article 21, original Article 19(3) forecloses jurisdiction over such a set-off claim.[96]

---

[92] See Chapter 2 on Article 17(1). For an example in which a counterclaim was filed, see *Herman Blum* (1983 Tribunal Rules), reprinted in section 3(D)(4).

[93] The Model Law, as amended, does not contain a provision comparable to Article 21(4) of the UNCITRAL Rules. Article 2 provides, however, that "[f]or the purposes of this Law: ... (f) where a provision of this Law, other than in Article 25(a) and 32(2)(a), refers to a claim, it also applies to a counter-claim, and where it refers to a defence, it also applies to a defence to such counter-claim." Article 25(a) deals with the termination of the proceedings on the ground of failure to submit the statement of claim. See also H Holtzmann and J Neuhaus, *A Guide to the UNCITRAL Model Law on International Commercial Arbitration*, n 5, 153.

[94] See L B Curzon, *Dictionary of Law* (6th edn 2002) 401 ("Nothing which is not a money claim may be set off.").

[95] See M Aden, *Internationale Handelsschiedsgerichtsbarkeit*, n 3, 235. See also the quotation of the authorities by Judge Khalilian in his Separate Opinion in the *First National Bank of Boston* (1983 Tribunal Rules), reprinted in section 3(D)(3).

[96] This interpretation of original Article 19(3) is also implicit in later UNCITRAL discussions:

> 76. The UNCITRAL Arbitration Rules...do not state expressly that the set-off claim must be covered by the same arbitration agreement as the main claim. If the parties have modelled the arbitration agreement on the model arbitration clause..., both the principal claim and the claim invoked for the purpose of a set-off would be covered by the same arbitration agreement. If, however, the arbitration agreement covering the principal claim does not cover the set-off claims, the question will arise also under the UNCITRAL Arbitration Rules whether the arbitral tribunal has the competence to consider the set-off claim that is not covered by the arbitration agreement.

Possible Future Work in the Area of International Commercial Arbitration, UNCITRAL, 32nd Session, UN Doc A/CN.9/460 (1999), para 76, reprinted in (1999) XXX UNCITRAL Ybk 395, 405.

This is also true if the parties have adopted the UNCITRAL model arbitration clause, which covers "[a]ny dispute, controversy or claim arising out of or relating to *this contract*." Footnote to Article 1 of the UNCITRAL Rules (emphasis added).

If the parties wish to make it possible to rely on such debts as set-off claims, they should modify original Article 19(3) accordingly. In some cases, this may be a practical way of avoiding several proceedings.[97]

Modifications of this kind have not been made to the 1983 Tribunal Rules of the Iran–US Claims Tribunal, which interprets original Article 19(3) in light of Article II(1) of the Claims Settlement Declaration.[98] Where set-off claims and counterclaims are governed by the same jurisdictional standards, the relevance of the separate concept of set-off is somewhat limited.[99] In this case it is preferable to assert a counterclaim instead, which will survive possible withdrawal or dismissal and may exceed the amount of the main claim.

To arise "out of the same contract," a counterclaim or a set-off claim presented under original Article 19 cannot be based on a contract which is not covered by the arbitration clause or agreement, notwithstanding a close connection with the subject matter of the claim.[100] However, original Article 19(3) need not necessarily be construed to mean that a counterclaim must without exception be based on the same contract as the original claim. One could argue that the extent of the arbitral tribunal's jurisdiction as defined in the arbitration clause or agreement should be decisive. Thus where one arbitration agreement covers two contracts, a counterclaim based on either of them should be admissible regardless of whether the claim relies on both. In order to avoid uncertainty, parties contemplating an arbitration agreement comprising several contracts are advised to consider modifying original Article 19(3), for example, to allow counterclaims "arising out of any contract included in the arbitration agreement."

If the arbitration clause or agreement is formulated to cover non-contractual claims, the parties should modify original Article 19(3) accordingly. This has occurred in the context of the proceedings of the Iran–US Claims Tribunal, which has a wide jurisdiction over "debts, contracts expropriations or other measures affecting property rights."[101] The counterclaim jurisdiction of the Tribunal has correspondingly been extended in Article II(1) of the Claims Settlement Declaration to counterclaims arising out of the "same contract, transaction or occurrence that constitutes the subject matter" of the claimant's claim. In the

---

[97] See M Aden, *Internationale Handelsschiedsgerichtsbarkeit*, n 3, 235. Note that UNCITRAL has identified issues concerning set-off claims as part of its future work in the area of international commercial arbitration. *Possible Future Work in the Area of International Commercial Arbitration*, UNCITRAL, 32nd Session, UN Doc A/CN.9/460 (1999), paras 72–79, reprinted in (1999) XXX UNCITRAL Ybk 395, 405.

[98] See *Computer Sciences Corp* (1983 Tribunal Rules), reprinted in section 3(D)(3).

[99] See S Baker and M Davis, *The UNCITRAL Arbitration Rules in Practice*, n 22, at 89–90; see also J van Hof, *Commentary on the UNCITRAL Arbitration Rules*, n 38, at 133–4. In his Separate Opinion in *The First National Bank of Boston* (1983 Tribunal Rules), reprinted in section 3(D)(3), Judge Khalilian criticized the majority of the Tribunal for failing to make a distinction between the concepts of "counter-claim" and "set-off." If directed against the Rules as such the criticism perhaps would have more merit.

[100] In discussions concerning the Preliminary Draft the suggestion was made that the phrase "same contract" be replaced by the "same transaction" to clarify that there may be jurisdiction over counterclaims not arising out of the same contract on which the principal claim is based. The suggestion was made with a view to cases "where there was a series of separate contracts arising out of the same transaction between the same parties, each of which contained an arbitration clause in identical terms." The UNCITRAL Secretariat intervened stating that the intention behind the provision was not to allow counterclaims based on such other contracts. The wording remained unchanged. It was noted that "normal arbitral practice" would be to keep such a counterclaim as a separate claim but to consolidate the hearings of the two claims. *Report of the United Nations Commission on International Trade Law*, 8th Session, Summary of Discussion of the Preliminary Draft, UN Doc A/10017, paras 136–37 (1975), reprinted in (1975) VI UNCITRAL Ybk 24, 37–8.

[101] Article II(1) of the Claims Settlement Declaration.

practice of the Tribunal, a series of separate contracts has occasionally been treated as one "transaction" for the purpose of counterclaims.[102]

In most cases, the determination of whether a counterclaim arises "out of the same contract" in the sense of Article 19(3) of the 1976 UNCITRAL Rules, or out of the contract or transaction relied on by the claimant in the Iran–US Claims Tribunal, is relatively unproblematic. Where the claimant makes a claim for a payment due under contract A, and the respondent submits a counterclaim for defective performance under the same contract, the fulfilment of the jurisdictional requirement in question is apparent. It may be, however, that a purported counterclaim that is related to the contract cannot be said to "arise out" of it. For example, the Iran–US Claims Tribunal has held that obligations to pay taxes or social security premiums in connection with the performance of a contract do not normally fall within the Tribunal's jurisdiction, as these obligations arise out of the application of law to the contract rather than the contract itself. Exceptions to this rule occur when "the contract includes provisions which create specific obligations, which do not exist in the law, of one party towards the other, in relation to the burden of taxes to be paid, or provisions which set forth conditions for payment of amounts earned under the contract in relation to the payment of taxes."[103] Contractual obligations regarding payment of withholding taxes are examples of such obligations.[104]

The above discussion shows that the treatment of counterclaims under the 1976 Rules may raise difficult jurisdictional issues. Where the counterclaim is clearly without merit, arbitrators may avoid taking a stand on jurisdictional issues by dismissing the counterclaim with a reference to the merits. Occasionally, the Iran–US Claims Tribunal has done so and concluded that it need not decide the jurisdictional issues in question.[105]

In addition to the substantive rules on the admissibility of counterclaims and set-offs, Revised Article 21 differs from original Article 19 in two other ways. First, a new sentence in Article 21(1) recognizes that the respondent may elect to treat its response to the notice of arbitration, a new procedural step under the Rules, as its statement of defence, so long as the response satisfies the criteria for a statement of defence outlined in Article 21(2), which requires responses to particulars in the statement of claim. Second, the Rules more strongly encourage ("should, as far as possible" in Article 21(2) as compared to "may" in original Article 19(2)) that the statement of defence include all documents and evidence (or references to such materials) relied upon by the respondent.

---

[102] It should also be noted that in the practice of the Iran–US Claims Tribunal several contracts have been regarded as a "transaction" only exceptionally. This was the case in *American Bell Intl Inc* (1983 Tribunal Rules), (Award No ITL 41-48-3, reprinted in section 3(D)(3)), where three subsequent contracts on the same subject matter meant the implementation of one ten-year project. But see Concurring and Dissenting Opinion of Judge Mosk, reprinted in 6 Iran-US CTR 95, 100–3 (1984–II). Also in *Westinghouse Electric Corp* and *Islamic Republic of Iran*, Award No ITL 67-389-2 (February 2, 1987), reprinted in 14 Iran-US CTR 104 (1987-I), several contracts were held to constitute a transaction for the purpose of counterclaims. See J van Hof, *Commentary on the UNCITRAL Arbitration Rules*, n 38, 132. In *Morrison-Knudsen Pacific Ltd* three contracts were not considered to form a transaction, although they related to the construction of one motorway. See *Morrison-Knudsen Pacific Ltd* (1983 Tribunal Rules), reprinted in section 3(D)(3).

[103] *Houston Contracting Co* (1983 Tribunal Rules), para 120, reprinted in section 3(D)(3).

[104] See *Houston Contracting Co* (1983 Tribunal Rules), para 120. See also *Questech, Inc* (1983 Tribunal Rules); and *TCSB Inc* (1983 Tribunal Rules); both reprinted in section 3(D)(3).

[105] See *CBS Inc* (1983 Tribunal Rules), reprinted in section 3(D)(3).

C. Extracts from the Practice of Investment Tribunals

United Parcel Service of America Inc and *Government of Canada*, Decision on Filing of Statement of Defence (October 17, 2001) (ICSID administered, 1976 UNCITRAL Rules, NAFTA Chapter Eleven), at 3–7:

3. Canada contends that it should not be required to file its statement of defence until the Tribunal rules on whether the claim submitted by UPS is within the terms of NAFTA....

4. Along with its initial submissions, Canada filed its Notice of Motion objecting to the jurisdiction of the Tribunal to address UPS's statement of claim. It had earlier advised the Tribunal that, given the extensive nature of its jurisdictional objections, to file the statement of defence at that stage in the proceedings would be inconsistent with the [1976] UNCITRAL Rules and established practice in both NAFTA and other international arbitrations. Later, it noted that, because substantial parts of the UPS claim are outside the terms of NAFTA Chapter 11 and the statement of claim as a whole is deficient and impossible to respond to, it was premature for it to submit a statement of defence. The only appropriate response was an objection to the jurisdiction of the Tribunal by a notice of motion. [In sum, Canada submitted that compelling the filing of a statement of defence at this stage "would require a disputing party to defend on the merits in the face of a live question whether it is required to do so." (Para 8).]

5. UPS has requested throughout that Canada be required to file its statement of defence.... It refers to the general time limits fixed by the [1976] UNCITRAL rules for the communication of written statements, including the statement of defence. It is also concerned that, were the Tribunal to adopt Canada's proposed procedure, Canada would be entitled to raise its jurisdictional objections to the Tribunal immediately but would presumably still reserve its ability to make further jurisdictional objections in its statement of defence. That would further frustrate the process, including the ability of the disputing parties to create or commence an effective documentary production process to further the hearing of the claim.

...

11. It will be seen that [Article 21 of the [1976] UNCITRAL Rules] does not say that the plea to jurisdiction may be made only in the statement of defence. Rather the filing of the statement of defence marks the latest time at which such a plea may be made. Further, in general, jurisdictional pleas are to be resolved as a preliminary matter, whether they are raised in a statement of defence or in some other way. The parties indeed accept that the rules are not decisive on the present issue.

...

16. We do not see this issue as a matter of clear rules or of precise right. The frequent practice, as the cases to which UPS has referred us demonstrate, is for jurisdictional issues to be raised in the statement of defence and not by separate proceedings. They are then however frequently, as the [1976] UNCITRAL rules indicate they should be, dealt with as a preliminary matter.... [I]n the context of the present case, Canada has, we take it, pleaded all the possible jurisdictional arguments that it would want to raise. It says in both of its submissions that "all of its jurisdictional objections can be efficiently and effectively resolved on the statement of claim alone."

...

19. UPS submits that Canada would not suffer any prejudice, were it to file its statement of defence, in respect of its ability to make jurisdictional arguments to the Tribunal. Canada responds by saying that, regardless of prejudice, there is no legal principle requiring the filing of a defence to matters beyond the Tribunal's authority. In any event, requiring the submission of a statement of defence in these circumstances is prejudicial since it would be compelled to proceed on the assumption that all allegations in the statement of claim are relevant and within the jurisdiction of the Tribunal. Canada would have to waste significant time and effort responding to lengthy complex allegations that prima facie are not properly before the Tribunal and also, according to UPS, begin the document discovery process....

20. In the end the Tribunal has to have in mind the practical administration and determination of the arbitration, while applying the underlying principles. The objections made by Canada are so extensive that it seems to the Tribunal that it is better for them to be resolved in advance and for any necessary amendments to be made to the statement of claim before Canada pleads it.

Canfor Corp and *United States of America*, Decision on the Place of Arbitration, Filing of a Statement of Defence and Bifurcation of the Proceedings (January 23, 2004) (ICSID administered, 1976 UNCITRAL Rules, NAFTA Chapter Eleven), at 10–12 (citations to submission omitted):

45. The Tribunal is not convinced by the Claimant's reading of the provisions of the [1976] UNCITRAL Arbitration Rules. Article 19(1) of the [1976] Rules provides that "[w]*ithin a period of time to be determined by the arbitral tribunal, the respondent shall communicate his statement of defence in writing to the claimant and to each of the arbitrators.*" This provision simply recognizes an arbitral tribunal's discretion to define a period of time for a respondent to submit its statement of defence, the timely submission of which is therefore subject to the deadline fixed by the tribunal. Article 23 of the [1976] Rules provides that "[t]*he periods of time fixed by the arbitral tribunal for the communication of written statements (including the statement of claim and statement of defence) should not exceed forty-five days. However, the arbitral tribunal may extend the time-limits if it concludes that an extension is justified.*" …

46. Further, the Tribunal does not consider that, in this case, the submission of a statement of defence by the Respondent is a prerequisite to the issue of whether or not it can decide the bifurcation of the proceedings. Article 21(3) of the [1976] Rules makes it possible for a respondent to raise jurisdictional objections "*not later than in the statement of defence*", which indicates that it may raise such objections in a separate document before it files its statement of defence. Article 21(4) further allows an arbitral tribunal to rule on its jurisdiction as a preliminary question. Nothing in these provisions limits the Tribunal's power to determine whether it may decide to hold a preliminary phase without having ordered the prior submission of a statement of defence. As a legal as well as practical matter, a statement of defence that would be a formality and that would simply deny all of the Claimant's allegations would not be of great assistance to either the Tribunal or the Claimant.

47. As a result, the Tribunal considers that bifurcation of the proceedings between a preliminary phase on the Respondent's jurisdictional objections and a merits phase—each phase involving issues of a different nature—may be ordered without the submission of a statement of defence. In particular, the Tribunal considers that the bifurcation of the proceedings with respect to the Respondent's Objection to Jurisdiction on the basis of Chapter Nineteen of the NAFTA may be decided without the submission of a statement of defence….

48. The Tribunal's acceptance that the proceedings may be bifurcated in no way implies that, should the Tribunal decide that it has jurisdiction to hear the merits of the Claimant's allegations, the Respondent may seek to raise new jurisdictional objections at the merits phase. Indeed, the Tribunal shares the Claimant's legitimate concern that "*all jurisdictional issues that the United States intends to raise* [be] *articulated now*" and that the Respondent in this case has "*reserved its ability to advance other arguments that may be characterized as jurisdictional, but without articulating what they might be*"….

49. Unlike the respondent in *UPS v. Canada* (Decision on the Filing of a Statement of Defence, October 17, 2001, paras 16–17 …), the Respondent in this case has not presented the Tribunal with all of its jurisdictional arguments and has made [a] reservation of rights in its Objection to Jurisdiction…

…

51. …The Tribunal has no reason to doubt that the Respondent is in a position, at this stage, to make every jurisdictional argument it may have, including those relating to whether or not the Claimant has made investments in the territory of the United States as contemplated by the provisions of the NAFTA….

52. The Respondent may find a strategic advantage in presenting the Tribunal, at this stage, with one jurisdiction argument, "*the only one for which it seeks preliminary treatment*"... However, the Tribunal should not be constrained, when conducting the arbitration, by any of the parties' procedural and strategic choices....

54. On the basis of the above, the Tribunal decides that:
    (1) The Respondent shall file a Statement of Defence limited to and setting forth all of its jurisdictional objections;...

Saluka Investments B V and *Czech Republic*, Decision on Jurisdiction over the Czech Republic's Counterclaim (May 7, 2004) (PCA administered, 1976 UNCITRAL Rules, Netherlands-Czech Republic BIT), at 9 (citations omitted):

37. The first issue which the Tribunal has to determine is whether, in principle (and irrespective of the particular counterclaim advanced in these proceedings by the Respondent), it has jurisdiction under Article 8 of the Treaty to hear and determine counterclaims. The parties were agreed that, as it was put by the Respondent, "there is not a wealth of precedent concerning the specific question whether a State may bring a counterclaim against an investor pursuant to a BIT." Moreover, such precedent as exists is often either based on treaty language different from that in Article 8 of the Czech-Netherlands Treaty, or does not arise in an arbitration applying the [1976] UNCITRAL Rules, or both. To a considerable extent, therefore, this issue has to be dealt with by the Tribunal on a 'first impressions' basis.

38. Both parties have, however, accepted that counterclaims might fall within the scope of the Tribunal's jurisdiction under Article 8: the Respondent has done so by virtue of having presented such a counterclaim, and the Claimant has done so by acknowledging that circumstances could be envisaged in which a counterclaim could properly be made, as where a primary claim was presented on the basis of an investment contract and a counterclaim was presented on the basis of that same contract.

39. The Tribunal agrees that, in principle, the jurisdiction conferred upon it by Article 8, particularly when read with Article 19.3, 19.4 and 21.3 of the [1976] UNCITRAL Rules, is in principle wide enough to encompass counterclaims. The language of Article 8, in referring to "All disputes," is wide enough to include disputes giving rise to counterclaims, so long, of course, as other relevant requirements are also met. The need for a dispute, if it is to fall within the Tribunal's jurisdiction, to be "between one Contracting Party and an investor of the other Contracting Party" carries with it no implication that Article 8 applies only to disputes in which it is an investor which initiates claims.

D. Extracts from the Practice of the Iran–US Claims Tribunal

(1) Tribunal Rules (1983), Article 19(1)

Pepsico, Inc and *Islamic Republic of Iran*, Case No 18, Chamber One, Order of June 30, 1982, reprinted in 1 Iran-US CTR 173 (1981–82):

The Tribunal extends the time within which the Respondents shall file their Statements of Defence to 18 August 1982.

In view of the fact that the Statement of Claim and the Exhibits attached thereto set forth what is owed by each of the Respondents as well as the grounds for each claim, the Tribunal does not find reasons to grant the Respondents' request that the Claimant be directed to address its claims separately to each Respondent.

Pepsico, Inc and *Islamic Republic of Iran*, Howard M Holtzmann, Dissent from Decision Granting Second Extension of Time for Filing Statement of Defence (July 9, 1982), reprinted in 1 Iran-US CTR 174 (1981–82):

I dissent from the decision of the Chamber granting a second extension of time for filing the Statement of Defence in this case.

This claim is one of the earliest cases before the Tribunal, having been filed November 3, 1981. It involves transaction between Pepsico, Inc. and a number of Iranian bottling companies.

...

Article 19 of the [1983] Provisionally Adopted Tribunal Rules provides that a Chamber may extend time limits for filing Statements of Defence only "if it concludes that such an extension is justified." Note 1 to Article 19 sets forth certain criteria which will be taken into account in this regard. The first criterion is the "complexity of the case." That criterion is not met in this instance because the transactions are relatively simple, the underlying contracts are identical and the Statement of Claim includes quite detailed documentation thereby facilitating response.

The second criterion of Note 1 to Article 19 justifying extension is any "special circumstances, including demonstrated hardship." The fact that operations of some of the Iranian bottling companies covered by the claim may have been in what later became a war zone, as alleged by Respondents for the first time on June 3, does not excuse the Respondents not so located from filing their Statements of Defence on time, and may not even be a basis for delay as to those few Respondents who were in the war zone because, as noted above, all of the contracts are identical and there has been no showing that the same basic defences are not applicable to all.

Note 1 to Article 19 also provides that if a Chamber determines that a requirement to file a large number of cases would impose an unfair burden on a Respondent, "it will in some cases extend the time periods." That clearly means that extension will be granted in some, not all, cases. That criterion was never intended to justify delay in responding to even the earliest claims filed, such as this, but was designed to relieve proven cumulative burden, if any, arising in later cases.

In summary, there is no showing to justify permitting a total of over eight months—more than twice the time originally granted—for filing the Statement of Defence in this case.

Phillips Petroleum Co, Iran, et al and *The Islamic Republic of Iran*, Cases Nos 39 and 55, Chamber Two, Order of April 27, 1983, reprinted in 2 Iran-US CTR 283 (1983–I):

In reply to your request for an extension of four months from 30 April 1983 to file a Defence in this case, I confirm by the present letter what I told you in my office and what I told Mr. Kashan in Mr. Lagergren's office, as well as what I told Mr. Mouri yesterday.

Since there were already three extensions of time, it seems difficult to grant a new one. Moreover, as the last given date was ordered by an award, it is impossible to modify it without the consent of all the Parties.

It should be on the other hand possible for the Respondents to give before the deadline a written statement with your counter-claim, if any, even if it is very short, to be completed in your further statements.

I regret not to be able to grant you the requested extension but legally I cannot do anything else.

Phillips Petroleum Co, Iran, et al and *Islamic Republic of Iran*, Cases Nos 39 and 55, Chamber Two, Order of April 27, 1983, Dissenting Opinion of Shafei Shafeiei (June 1, 1983), reprinted in 2 Iran-US CTR 284 (1983–I):

It is incumbent upon the Tribunal to provide all the parties to any given claim with sufficient time to defend its case properly. The interests of justice dictate that this Tribunal offer its sincere co-operation to the parties.

In your letter of 27 April 1983, issued in response to the request by the Agent of the Islamic Republic of Iran for an extension, you write:

Since there were already three extensions of time, it seems difficult to grant a new one. Moreover as the last given date was ordered by an Award, it is impossible to modify it without the consent of the parties.

I wonder to what extension your phrase, "three extensions of time" refers!

...

Therefore, by virtue of the facts briefly dealt with in this letter, I am obliged to point out that the reasons adduced in the Chamber's letter of 27 April 1983, issued in response to Mr. Eshragh's request for an extension, are entirely unjustified and that the Chamber's refusal of an extension is unconscionable on the grounds of justice and legality.

(2) Tribunal Rules (1983), Article 19(2)

The Cyrus Petroleum Ltd and *Islamic Republic of Iran*, Case No 624, Chamber One, Order of May 30, 1985:

> The Respondent on 17 January 1983 filed a Statement of Defence stating, *inter alia*, that it was unable to respond to the Statement of Claim, which it said was "totally vague, the relief sought is unknown, and the action allegedly taken by Respondent is rather obscure and unclear." By Order filed 15 February 1983 Claimant was ordered to respond to these objections by 14 March 1983. Claimant failed to comply with that Order, or even to seek an extension of the time within which to do so. By further Order filed 31 August 1984, the Claimant was ordered to file a Response by 1 October 1984 and was informed that if a Response was not filed by that date the Tribunal would proceed to decide this case on the basis of the pleadings and documents submitted.
>
> ...
>
> The Tribunal informs the Parties that it now intends to decide this case on the basis of the pleadings and documents before it.

(See also related Award No 230–624–1 above, n 38):

(3) Tribunal Rules (1983), Article 19(3)

Intrend Intl, Inc and *Imperial Iranian Air Force*, Award No 59–220–2 (July 27, 1982) at 12, reprinted in 3 Iran-US CTR 110, 116 (1983–II):

> Finally, in a Rejoinder filed 12 October 1982, the Air Force supplemented its Statement of Defence filed 20 April 1982 and added an additional counter-claim for Social Security insurance premium payments. The Tribunal notes that this counter-claim was filed six months after the Statement of Defence. Pursuant to Article 19 of its [1983] rules of procedure, the Tribunal can accept a late counter-claim if satisfied that the delay was justified under the circumstances, but in the present case the Tribunal finds no such justification and declines to accept the late counter-claim.

William L Pereira Associates, Iran and *Islamic Republic of Iran*, Case No 1, Chamber Three, Order of September 22, 1982:

> In the Statement of Claim the Islamic Republic of Iran and the Ministry of Housing and Urban Development are named as Respondents. The Ministry of Housing and Urban Development as well as some other government ministries and agencies have filed Statements of Defence, two of which contain counter-claims.
>
> On 12 July the Claimant filed a "Motion to exclude extraneous parties and strike improper pleadings," stating that only the Ministry of Housing and Urban Development is proper Respondent in this case.
>
> The Tribunal, however, sees no reason for not allowing the Islamic Republic of Iran to file Statements of Defence and/or Counter-claims through the ministries and agencies in question. The Claimant's Motion is therefore dismissed.

Richard D Harza and *Islamic Republic of Iran*, Award No ITL 14–97–2 (February 23, 1983) at 5, reprinted in 2 Iran-US CTR 68, 71 (1983–I):

> No experts will be appointed to study the counter-claims relating to seismology insofar as those counter-claims were presented too late within the terms of Article 19(3) [of the 1983 Tribunal Rules], and our own Order of June, 1982 scheduling the proceedings. The use of our discretion under 19(3), to admit the late filing would be inappropriate in view of the uncertain and speculative nature of the alleged damages.

Blount Brothers Corp and *Ministry of Housing and Urban Development*, Award No 74–62–3 (September 2, 1983) at 2–3, reprinted in 3 Iran-US CTR 225, 226 (1983–II):

On 31 January 1983, Claimant and MHUD filed their arguments and evidence.

On 1 March 1983, Gostaresh Maskan filed a Statement of Defence and sought to raise a counter-claim. MHUD also filed additional papers.

On 11 and 14 March 1983, Gostaresh Maskan filed additional material. Claimant objected to such late filings and moved to strike them from the proceedings. The hearing was held on 14 and 15 March 1983. During the course of the Hearing Gostaresh Maskan submitted a second counter-claim. The matter was submitted to the Tribunal at the conclusion of the Hearing.

By an Order of 19 April 1983, the Tribunal determined that the late filings of Gostaresh Maskan would be accepted, but that its late filed counter-claims would be rejected pursuant to Article 19(3) of the [1983] Tribunal Rules, no justification for the delay in presenting them having been shown. The Tribunal further decided that Claimant would have an opportunity to submit a reply to the accepted late filings, and it did so.

TCSB, Inc and *Islamic Republic of Iran*, Award No 114–140–2 (March 16, 1984) at 15, 23–24, reprinted in 5 Iran-US CTR 160, 168, 173 (1984–I):

As stated above, the Claimant was entitled to receive 255,205,242 rials for its supervisory services under the contract. It has already received 163,748,479 rials, including the 9,864,867 rials withheld for the 5.5 percent contract tax. From the balance of 91,456,763 rials still owing to the Claimant, 5.5 percent of the total amount due under the contract, representing the Iranian contract tax, must be deducted, because the parties agreed that it was to be withheld from all payments made to the Claimant, and it was in fact withheld from all such payments. 5.5 percent of 255,205,242 rials is 14,036,288 rials, of which 9,864,867 rials have already been withheld. Thus, 4,171,421 rials additional should be deducted. The Claimant is thus entitled to receive 87,285,342 rials from the Housing Organization.

...

The Housing Organization has also presented a counter-claim alleging, *inter alia,* that TCSB did not pay social insurance contributions due to the Social Security Organization in respect of TCSB's employees in Iran and owes a sum of money "as his due tax". The former allegation was elaborated upon in a memorial filed 11 November 1983, it appears from a "Supplement" filed on 29 December 1983 that the latter allegation was meant to refer to "taxation in respect of revenues arising out of its (i.e., TCSB's) operations."

Under Article II, paragraph 1, of the Claims Settlement Declaration the Tribunal has jurisdiction to decide

> ... any counter-claim which arises out of the same contract, transaction or occurrence that constitutes the subject matter of that national's claim, if such claims and counter-claims ... arise out of debts, contracts ... expropriations or other measures affecting property rights. ...

Accordingly, a distinction must be made, in particular, between legal relationships arising out of the application of the law to a situation in which either party individually finds itself and the contractual relationship between the parties to the contract *inter se*. In the present case, the Tribunal holds:

(i) that only the 5.5 percent tax withholdings referred to above may be said to arise out of the contractual relationship between the parties to the contract; and
(ii) that the remaining part of the taxes and social insurance contributions referred to in the counter-claim, in the absence of satisfactory evidence establishing the contrary, must be deemed to arise out of the application of the law to the contractor's particular situation and hence to be outside the jurisdiction of the Tribunal.

Since the 5.5. percent tax has been taken into account in the present Award, the tax and social security counter-claims must be dismissed for lack of jurisdiction.

American Bell Intl, Inc and *Islamic Republic of Iran*, Award No ITL 41–48–3 (June 11, 1984) at 16–18, reprinted in 6 Iran-US CTR 74, 83–84 (1984–II) (footnotes omitted):

> 4. Issue: Does the Tribunal lack jurisdiction over any of the counter-claims on the ground that they do not arise out of the same contracts, transactions or occurrences which constitute the subject matter of the claims?
>
> (i) Counter-claims based on Contract No 112.
>
> Respondents base their counter-claims in part on Contract Nos 112, 118 and 138; however, they do not specify which amounts are sought under each of these contracts.
>
> ABII has not challenged the Tribunal's jurisdiction over the counter-claims insofar as they are based on the latter two contracts. The dispute concerns whether or not any counter-claim can be asserted on the basis of Contract No 112. More specifically, the issue is whether such a counter-claim can be held to arise out of "the same contract, transaction or occurrence that constitutes the subject matter of that national's claim," as required under Article II, paragraph 1, of the Claims Settlement Declaration.
>
> The three contracts now mentioned were entered into successively. The first contract, No 112, was a short term contract intended to cover ABII work under the Seek Switch Program during the negotiations of Contract No 118. The Government of Iran entrusted the carrying out of that program to one company only, originally AT & T and later in actual fact ABII. Thus it was apparently foreseen that all the successive contracts would go to ABII. The subject matters of the three contracts were closely interrelated, within the framework of the Seek Switch Program.
>
> In light of these particular circumstances, the Tribunal finds that the linkage between all three contracts must be considered sufficiently strong so as to make them form one single "transaction" within the meaning of the Claims Settlement Declaration.
>
> Accordingly, the Tribunal *concludes* that it has jurisdiction over the counter-claims in so far as they are based on Contract No 112.

Morrison-Knudsen Pacific Ltd and *Ministry of Roads and Transportation*, Award No 143–127–3 (July 13, 1984) at 51–54, reprinted in 7 Iran-US CTR 54, 82–84 (1984-III):

> Article II, paragraph 1, of the Claims Settlement Declaration gives the Tribunal jurisdiction over certain claims of nationals of the United States or Iran and over counter-claims which "arise out of the same contract, transaction or occurrence that constitutes the subject matter of that national's claim."
>
> It is clear from both this language and from the Tribunal Rules that the Tribunal's jurisdiction extends only to counter-claims which are presented against claimants. Therefore, to the extent that the counter-claims seek recovery from Cofraran, they must be dismissed.
>
> ...
>
> Claimant also contends that Contract 81 constitutes the subject matter of its claim and that the Tribunal's jurisdiction is limited to counter-claims which arise out of the same contract. Consequently, Claimant argues, counter-claims based on Contracts 87 and 88 do not fall within the Tribunal's jurisdiction.
>
> MORT contends that Contracts 81, 87 and 88 are all part of the same "transaction", that the claims arise out of this transaction and, therefore, that the counter-claims arise out of the same transaction which constitutes the subject matter of this claim.
>
> The Tribunal, however, cannot share the view that Contracts 81, 87 and 88 are part of one single transaction. Although an early intention, as reflected in MORT's letter of intent of 14 April 1976, was to treat the whole motorway project as one whole in the sense that all the four contracts contemplated were to be given to the consortium, this intention was later abandoned. Thus, by the time that Contract 81 was signed, the prospects for the remaining contracts was a matter to be negotiated. This is supported by the language of Article 2(3) of Contract 81, which provides as follows:
>
>> After the performance of *this* Contract, the EMPLOYER will have no other obligation towards the CONTRACTOR, except what may derive from EMPLOYER's Letters of Intent

to the CONTRACTOR, No 6155 of 9 February 1975 and No 1045/2 of 14 April 1976 to the CONTRACTOR, *and from any subsequent contracts or agreements the parties hereto may have entered into*. (Emphasis supplied.)

...

The contracts were executed on different dates, and involved different services to be performed at different times. There is no relation between the disputes concerning Contract 81, on the one hand, and those concerning Contracts 87 and 88 on the other hand. Findings with respect to Contract 81 would have no effect on claims and defences made in connection with Contracts 87 and 88. That the Contracts may refer to one another or may even contemplate the execution of another does not necessarily make the linkage between them sufficiently strong so as to make them form one single transaction within the meaning of the Claims Settlement Declaration. *Compare American Bell International Inc.* and *The Government of the Islamic Republic of Iran*, Interlocutory Award No 41–48–3 (11 June 1984).

Therefore the Tribunal concludes that, to the extent that they arise out of Contacts 87 and 88, the counter-claims do not arise out of the same contract, transaction or occurrence which constitutes the subject matter of any of the claims.

Anaconda-Iran, Inc and *Islamic Republic of Iran, et al,* Case No 167, Chamber Three, Order of October 11, 1984:

Without prejudice to the final decision the Tribunal... notes that the specific issue raised by the Agent of the Islamic Republic of Iran, a period of delay of one or two days in filing counter-claims, would not by itself ordinarily result in the dismissal of counter-claims.

Behring Intl, Inc and *Islamic Republic Iranian Air Force,* Award No ITM/ITL 52–382–3 (June 21, 1985) at 38, reprinted in 8 Iran-US CTR 238, 265 (1984-I):

The indisputable fact remains that Claimant invoked the jurisdiction of the Tribunal by filing a Statement of Claim here and, under the Claims Settlement Declaration and Tribunal Rules, Respondents were thus entitled to file certain counter-claims. While Claimant remains free to withdraw any and all of its claims for relief, such withdrawal can have no effect on the Tribunal's jurisdiction over the counter-claims, unless the Tribunal were to determine that it had no jurisdiction over the claims as originally filed. To date, the claims have not been withdrawn and in any event the Tribunal finds no basis for holding that they do not fall within the scope of its jurisdictional grant.

Questech, Inc, and *Ministry of National Defence of the Islamic Republic of Iran*, Award No 191–59–1 (September 25, 1985) at 38–40, reprinted in 9 Iran-US CTR 107, 134–36 (1985-II):

cc) Taxes

...

Pursuant to Article II, paragraph 1, of the Claims Settlement Declaration, the Tribunal's jurisdiction over counter-claims is limited to those counter-claims "which arise[] out of the same contract, transaction or occurrence that constitutes the subject matter of" the main claim. The asserted obligation to pay taxes in this case is imposed not by the contract that is the subject matter of the claim, but by operation of the applicable Iranian tax law. The Respondent itself states that "[t]he claim is based on the taxation laws of the Islamic Republic of Iran." The obligation to pay taxes is a legal relationship that arises out of the application of the law to a factual situation of a person or legal entity rather than a contractual relationship that exists between the parties to a contract by virtue of that contract. For these reasons, the Respondent's counter-claim for taxes is outside the Tribunal's jurisdiction.

dd) Social security premiums

...

Pursuant to Article II, paragraph 1, of the Claims Settlement Declaration, the Tribunal's jurisdiction over counter-claims is limited to those counter-claims "which arise[ ] out of the same contract, transaction or occurrence that constitutes the subject matter of" the main claim. The asserted obligation to pay social security premiums in this case is imposed not by the contract that is the subject matter of the claim, but by operation of the applicable Iranian Social Security law. Any such obligation is, as the Tribunal found in Award No 114–140–2 of 16 March 1984 in *T.C.S.B., Inc.*, and *Iran*, at 24, and confirmed in Award No 180–64–1 of 27 June 1985 in *Sylvania Technical Systems, Inc. and The Government of the Islamic Republic of Iran*, at 41, a "legal relationship arising out of the application of the law to a situation in which either party individually finds itself" rather than a "contractual relationship between the parties to the contract *inter se.*" The Tribunal thus has no jurisdiction over the Respondent's counter-claim for social security premiums.

International Technical Products Corp and *Islamic Republic of Iran*, Award No 196–302–3 (October 28, 1985) at 29–30, reprinted in 9 Iran-US CTR 206, 226–27 (1985-II):

In its Memorial filed 2 January 1985, just 22 days before the Hearing, AFIRI sets forth for the first time several counter-claims for damages allegedly caused by ITP Export's breaches of the Civil Works Contract. These counter-claims were not timely filed, and no explanation for the delay has been provided. Tribunal Rules, Article 19, paragraph 3. The Tribunal orders that they be dismissed.

Computer Sciences Corp and *Islamic Republic of Iran*, Award No 221–65–1 (April 16, 1986) at 51–54, reprinted in 10 Iran US CTR 269, 309–11 (1986-I):

The Claimant contends that public law debts may not be offset against private law claims. Even if a tax counter-claim was justifiable as a claim for set-off, in the Claimant's view it is clear from Article II, paragraph 1, of the Claims Settlement Declaration that such a set-off is governed by the same jurisdictional standards as a counter-claim. According to the Claimant, Article 19, paragraph 3, of the Tribunal Rules subjects counter-claims and claims for the purpose of a set-off to the same jurisdictional restrictions.

The Tribunal determines that as far as its jurisdiction is concerned claims for set-off are generally governed by the same standards as counter-claims. The concept of set-off necessarily presupposes the existence of a claim that can be used for such set-off. When a respondent seeks to offset alleged tax arrears against contract claims, he can use his alleged right to the payment of taxes for set-off only if this right is an admissible claim under the Claims Settlement Declaration. As the Full Tribunal has decided in Case No A2, Decision DEC 1-A2-FT (13 Jan. 1982), the Claims Settlement Declaration does not grant the Tribunal jurisdiction over claims against nationals of either State party unless those claims are brought as counter-claims. Claims for taxes can thus only be used for set-off if they fulfil the requirements for counter-claims as laid down in Article II, paragraph 1, of the Claims Settlement Declaration. This conclusion is confirmed by the provision of Article 19, paragraph 3, of the Tribunal Rules which states that

… the Respondent may make a counter-claim or a claim for the purpose of a set-off, *if such counter-claim or set-off is allowed under the Claims Settlement Declaration* (emphasis added).

This provision incorporates by explicit reference the requirements of the Claims Settlement Declaration for counter-claims. The Claims Settlement Declaration does not mention set-off explicitly. But it is clear from a comparison of Article 19, paragraph 3, of the [1976] UNCITRAL Rules with that provision as modified in the Tribunal Rules that counter-claims and claims for the purpose of set-off must meet the same jurisdictional requirements. Article 19, paragraph 3, of the [1976] UNCITRAL Rules stipulates that

… the Respondent may make a counter-claim arising out of the same contract or rely on a claim arising out of the same contract for the purpose of set-off.

Because the description of the qualification of admissible counter-claims in the Claims Settlement Declaration was different from the one in the [1976] UNCITRAL Rule, this qualification was modified accordingly. By substituting the two identical qualifications in the [1976] UNCITRAL Rules of counter-claims and claims for the purpose of set-off with the single reference to the Claims

Settlement Declaration, Article 19, paragraph 3, of the Tribunal Rules makes clear that, as under the original [1976] UNCITRAL Rule, both counter-claims and claims for the purpose of set-off are governed by the same jurisdictional standards.

...

The Tribunal has held in a number of cases that the obligation to pay taxes other than withholding taxes specifically provided for in the parties contract arises from the tax laws of Iran rather than from the contract, even where the contract otherwise identifies which contractual party is responsible for the payment of taxes. It consequently has dismissed, tax counter-claims other than counter-claims for such withholding taxes for lack of jurisdiction, see *International Technical Products Corporation et al and The Government of the Islamic Republic of Iran*, Final Award No 196–302–3; p. 29 (28 October 1985), and decisions cited therein. The Tribunal confirms these holdings in the present case and finds that the Ministry's tax counter-claim does not arise out of the Contracts, none of which required IACI or ISIRAN to deduct income tax from payments.

American Bell Intl Inc, and *Islamic Republic of Iran*, Award No 255–48–3 (September 19, 1986), reprinted in 12 Iran-US CTR 170, 225 (1986-III):

182. This counter-claim, as admitted by Respondents, was not raised until TCI's counter-claim Memorial submitted on 30 August 1985. Therefore it raises questions under Article 19, paragraph 3 of the Tribunal Rules which requires a counter-claim to be made "[i]n the Statement of Defence, or at a later stage in the arbitral proceedings if the arbitral tribunal decides that the delay was justified under the circumstances." In the assessment of the circumstances, among other things, the possible prejudice caused to Claimant by the late presentation of the counter-claim has to be taken into account as an important factor.
183. The Tribunal notes that the counter-claim was presented about five weeks before the Hearing, and four weeks before ABII was due to submit its rebuttal. As to the factual issues involved, this counter-claim belongs to one of the least complicated parts of the whole case. Thus the preparation of a defence would not have caused to ABII such hardships as would amount to undue prejudice, and such prejudice is not even alleged by Claimant. In view of this, and accepting that Respondents may not, at the time of the presentation of the Statement of Defence, have detected the evidence (mainly letters of ABII) supporting this counter-claim among voluminous documentary materials relating to the Seek Switch Program, the Tribunal decides that the late presentation of the Counter-claim was acceptable under the circumstances.

Collins Systems Intl, Inc, and *Navy of the Islamic Republic of Iran*, Case No 431, Chamber Two, Order of September 23, 1987:

The Tribunal notes two Counter-claims filed on 16 June 1987 by the Government of the Islamic Republic of Iran, The Islamic Republic of Iran Navy and Bank Tejarat naming as Counter-Respondents Collins Systems International ("Collins") and City Bank of New York in one and Collins and Bank of America, International, Houston, Texas ("Bank of America") in the other. The Tribunal also notes the Claimant's comments on these Counter-claims filed on 15 September 1987.

The Tribunal further notes that Bank Tejarat, the Government of the Islamic Republic of Iran, City Bank of New York and Bank of America are not Parties in this Case. Therefore, the Counter-claims against City Bank of New York and Bank of America cannot be admitted and neither Bank Tejarat nor the Government of the Islamic Republic of Iran have standing to assert counter-claims in this Case.

Interfirst Bank Dallas, NA and *Islamic Republic of Iran*, Decision No DEC 66–338–2 (October 9, 1987), reprinted in 16 Iran-US CTR 291 (1987-III):

8. With regard to Bank Markazi's argument concerning counter-claim jurisdiction, the Tribunal has already held that claims can "only be used for set-off if they fulfil the requirements for

counter-claims as laid down in Article II, paragraph 1, of the Claims Settlement Declaration." *Computer Sciences Corporation* and *The Government of the Islamic Republic of Iran, et al.*, Award No 221-65-1 (16 April 1986); *Howard Needles Tammen & Bergendoff* and *The Government of the Islamic Republic of Iran, et al.*, Award No 224-68-2 (8 August 1986). However, in view of the fact that the Claim has been withdrawn the question of a possible set-off has become moot.

Harris Intl Telecommunications Inc, and *Islamic Republic of Iran*, Award No 323-409-1 (November 2, 1987), reprinted in 17 Iran-US CTR 31, 57-61 (1987-IV) (footnotes omitted):

c) Late Counter-claim

88. The Tribunal now turns to an examination of the counter-claim filed by the Ministry of Defence on 3 April 1986 on behalf of itself, the Islamic Republic of Iran, and Bank Melli, naming Harris and Chase Manhattan Bank as Respondents.

89. The Claimant and Chase Manhattan Bank contend that this counter-claim should be dismissed because it is untimely, because no reason has been offered for the delay in its filing, and because Chase Manhattan Bank is not a party to this Case.

90. Again, the principles guiding the Tribunal's determination of this issue are to be found in the Tribunal Rules. Article 19, paragraph 3, of the Rules require that a counter-claim be made [i]n the Statement of Defence, or at a later stage in the arbitral proceedings if the arbitral tribunal decides that the delay was justified under the circumstances.

91. In the normal course of events, then, a counter-claim must be contained in the Statement of Defence. When counter-claims are filed late, the Respondent has the burden of justifying the delay. Again, considerations of equality in treatment, prejudice to the other party, and delay of the proceedings underlie this requirement that delays be justified.

92. Consequently, the Tribunal has uniformly rejected late-filed counter-claims when it concludes that the delay was not justified under the circumstances, although it has occasionally rejected late-filed counter-claims without entering into such an analysis.

93. The Tribunal has been particularly reluctant to accept late-filed counter-claims which are filed shortly before the Hearing, during the Hearing, or after the Hearing. *Amman & Whitney* and *Ministry of Housing and Urban Development*, Award No 248-198-1, pp. 8-9 (25 Aug 1986), is a good example of the Tribunal's practice in this area. In that Case, one day after the Hearing, the Respondent filed a "counter-claim arising out of letter of guarantee" on behalf of itself and Bank Melli against the Claimant and Citibank of New York concerning a failure to make payment under a letter of guarantee securing an advance payment made to the Claimant under the contract in question. Neither Bank Melli nor Citibank was a party to the Case. The Tribunal rejected the Counter-claim, that

> [A]side from any question as to the Tribunal's jurisdiction over a counter-claim thus formulated and the parties named in it, the Tribunal is bound to reject a pleading filed not only considerably later than the Statement of Defence (*see* Article 19 and 20 of the Tribunal Rules), but, indeed, after the Hearing itself the more so since no explanation has been advanced as to why such a delay may be justified.

94. Indeed, cases are rare in which the Tribunal accepted late counter-claims. In *Starrett Housing Corp.* and *Government of the Islamic Republic of Iran*, Interlocutory Award No ITL 32-24-1, p. 35 (19 Dec. 1983), the Tribunal, without further explanation, admitted four counter-claims "[i]n accordance with Article 19, paragraph 3, of the Tribunal Rules...although they were not included in the Statement of Defence" and not filed until approximately six weeks before the Hearing. But see Concurring Opinion of Howard M Holtzmann, *Starrett Housing Corp., supra*, at pp. 45-46 (arguing that the late-filed counter-claims should not have been admitted). *Starrett*, however, is a unique case in many respects. Given the drawn-out nature of the proceedings in that case, the Tribunal may have concluded that prejudice to the Claimant was unlikely. In any event, *Starrett* represents the exception rather than the rule.

The predominant practice of the Tribunal is that when it accepts a late-filed counter-claim it bases such a determination on an examination of the possible prejudice to the other party and the explanation, if any, for the delay.

95. A more representative example of this practice is *American Bell International, Inc. and Islamic Republic of Iran*, Award No 255–48–3, pp. 78–79 (19 Sep. 1986), in which the Tribunal accepted a late-filed counter-claim.

In the Case the Counter-claim was filed five weeks before the Hearing and four weeks before the Claimant's rebuttal was due. The Tribunal examined the possible prejudice to the Claimant that might result from the counter-claim, but concluded that there was little likelihood of prejudice because the counter-claim related to one of the least complicated portions of the case and because the Claimant had not alleged prejudice. Further, the Tribunal noted that the Respondent may not have been able to find the evidence supporting the counter-claim earlier. Consequently, the Tribunal accepted the counter-claim.

96. The Tribunal has been less hesitant to accept counter-claims which clarify or provide detail for previous timely-filed counter-claims, or amend previous timely-filed counter-claims.

97. In applying these principles to the Case at hand, the Tribunal notes that this Counter-claim was filed for the first time more than 39 months after the Statement of Defence. Thus, it is apparent that this Counter-claim does not comply with Article 19, paragraph 3, unless the delay can be justified by Iran.

98. The Tribunal notes, however, that this Counter-claim may be distinguished from other late-filed counter-claims as it was originally filed as several direct claims by Bank Melli against Chase Manhattan Bank in Cases Nos 510, 534, 540, 541, 543, 548, and 556. These direct claims were later determined to be outside of the Tribunal's jurisdiction in Award No 108-A-16/582/591-FT, p. 21 (25 Jan. 1984). The Tribunal, however, expressly left open the possibility that the claims might be filed as counter-claims. It stated that

Whether an Iranian bank claim on a standby letter of credit can be joined as a counter-claim against the relevant United States contractor is a matter that each Chamber will have to deal with in accordance with Tribunal Rules concerning jurisdiction over counter-claims. It is up to the Chambers to take the necessary steps in each case, in accordance with the Tribunal Rules and this decision.

Id. at 21.

99. By Order filed on 2 July 1985, Chamber One terminated Cases Nos 510, 534, 536, 540, 541, 543, 548, and 556, among a series of other bank claims, in accordance with Article 34 of the Tribunal Rules. In those Orders the Tribunal drew the Parties' attention again to a paragraph of its Order filed on 24 April 1985 providing: "[i]f a letter of credit involved in the present claim relates to any other claim pending before the Tribunal, then the consequences of that letter of credit should be decided as part of the decision on that other claim, and any request to submit a counter-claim with respect thereto should be made in the case where that other claim is pending." It further announced that it would consider as soon as possible what guidance could be given for the submission of such requests.

100. The Ministry of Defence alleges that the Tribunal failed to issue any clear guidelines concerning the filing of such counter-claims. This is incorrect, at least as far as the Cases in question are concerned. On 16 August 1985, following the Termination Orders and in response to a request of the Agent of the Islamic Republic of Iran for further guidance, the Tribunal, again drawing the Parties' attention to the above-quoted paragraph, stated that the request to submit a counter-claim must be made by a Party to the Case in which the underlying, related claim is pending, and filed in the Case while such Case is still pending. The Tribunal did not specify the precise form in which the request should be made but left this to the discretion of the Parties. It noted, however, that such requests "must be timely filed, not later than six months from the date of this communication."

101. As far as the Cases at issue are concerned, this period expired on 16 February 1986. The Counter-claim filed on 3 April 1986 was therefore submitted late with no justification for the delay offered by the Respondent. In such a case the Tribunal's practice is clear. To permit

such late counter-claims might prejudice the Claimant and would in any event run directly contrary to the plain meaning of Article 19, paragraph 3, of the Tribunal Rules, Accordingly, the Counter-claim is dismissed as untimely.

Houston Contracting Co and *National Iranian Oil Co*, Award No 378–173–3 (July 22, 1988), reprinted in 20 Iran-US CTR 3, 36–38 (1988-III):

115. The Tribunal has consistently held that it has no jurisdiction over counter-claims relating to allegedly unpaid taxes, when the obligation to pay such taxes does not arise out of the contract, transaction or occurrence that constitutes the subject matter of the claim in the same proceedings. (*See International Technical Products Corp.* and *Islamic Republic of Iran*, Award No 196–302–3 (28 October 1985), *reprinted in* 9 Iran-U.S. C.T.R. 206; *General Dynamics Telephone Systems Center* and *Islamic Republic of Iran*, Award No 192–285–2 (4 October 1985), *reprinted in* 9 Iran-U.S. C.T.R. 153; *Questech, Inc.* and *Ministry of National Defence*, Award No 191–59–1 (25 September 1985); *reprinted in* 9 Iran-U.S. C.T.R. 107; *Sylvania Technical Systems, Inc.* and *Islamic Republic of Iran*, Award No 180–64–1 (27 June 1985), *reprinted in* 8 Iran-U.S. C.T.R. 298; *T.C.S.B., Inc.* and *Iran*, Award No 114–140–2 (16 March 1984), *reprinted in* 5 Iran-U.S. C.T.R. 160.) The three Chambers fully concurred on this finding. The Tribunal does not see any reason to depart from these precedents in the instant case.

116. The two States Parties to the Algiers Accords deliberately refrained from giving jurisdiction to the Tribunal over claims of one of them against nationals of the other (see Case A12, Decision No DEC 1-A2-FT (26 January 1982), *reprinted in* 1 Iran-U.S. C.T.R. 101.) This exclusion obviously extends to claims arising out of unpaid taxes. The only exception to this negative rule relates to counter-claims. In order to be admissible, such counter-claims, however, have to meet the conditions set forth in the Claims Settlement Declaration, namely to arise out "of the same contract, transaction or occurrence that constitutes the subject matter" of the claim of the national who initiated the proceedings (Article II, paragraph 1).

117. The obligation to pay taxes finds its source in the domestic law of the State concerned. In the case of income taxes, it arises out of the earning of revenues by a person subject to the law. The fact that these revenues are earned as the result of the performance of a contract is immaterial: it does not change the legal nature of the obligation, which remains statutory and not contractual, and creates no legal link between such an obligation and the contract which allowed the revenue to be earned. It cannot be said, therefore, that the obligation to pay taxes "arises out of" this contract and, accordingly, the conditions set forth by the Claims Settlement Declaration for the admissibility of a counter-claim for allegedly unpaid taxes are not fulfilled. The same is true if reference is made to the "transaction" to which the contract relates since the obligation to pay taxes exists independently of the dealings between the parties to a transaction. The fact that such parties include the amounts to be paid as taxes among the costs to be taken into consideration for the calculations of the price of the contract does not suffice to change the legal situation: as with all the other costs, such as the cost of the items to be delivered or labor costs, the taxes to be paid do not constitute a legal obligation of one party to the contract vis-a-vis the other.

...

120. On the other hand, the situation is quite different if the contract includes provisions which create specific obligations, which do not exist in the law, of one party towards the other, in relation to the burden of the taxes to be paid, or provisions which set forth conditions for payment of amounts earned under the contract in relation to the payment of taxes. Examples of such provisions are those, very frequently encountered, that a certain percentage (usually 5.5%) of the amounts due will be withheld by the buyer and directly paid by it to the Ministry of Economic Affairs and Finance, or that the buyer will reimburse the seller the amount of the taxes paid by it, either as a general rule, or if there is an increase in the rate of these taxes after the execution of the contract. Like all other contractual obligations,

such provisions must be enforced by the Tribunal and may be the subject matter of counter-claims. The counter-claim in this case is not based upon a provision of this kind and, accordingly, is dismissed.

The First National Bank of Boston and *Islamic Republic of Iran*, Decision No DEC 83–202–2 (September 19, 1988), Separate Opinion of Seyed Khalil Khalilian (September 23, 1988) at 3–4, reprinted in 19 Iran-US CTR 310, 311–12 (1988-II):

Distinction between the concepts of "Set-off" and "Counter-claim"

"*Set-off*. Remedy employed by defendant to discharge or reduce plaintiff's demand by an opposite one arising from transaction *extrinsic to plaintiff's cause of action. Edmonds v. Stratton*, MO. APP., 457 S.W. 2d 228, 232." *Black's Law Dictionary*.

"*Set-off*. A *defence* or an independent demand made by the defendant to counterbalance that of plaintiff, in whole or in part. *Mack v. Hugger Bros. Constr.* S. 153 Tenn. 260, 283 SW 448, 46 ALR 389." *Ballentine's Law Dictionary*.

"A counter demand which a defendant holds against a plaintiff, arising out of a transaction extrinsic to the plaintiff's cause of action, 20 Am J2d Council section 2." *Ibid*.

"When two persons are indebted to one another, their mutual debts are to be set off in the manner provided for in the following Articles." *Civil Code of Iran, Article 294*.

"In this connection, it will be immaterial whether the two debts arise from the same or different causes, because a difference of cause does not lead to a different effect. Therefore, [even] if one of those two debts arises from a sale and the other from a loan or lease, the two debts are set off against one another." Emani, *Hoquq-e Madani*, vol. I, p. 345.

"La compensation s'opère de plein droit par la seule force de la loi, même a l'insu des debiteurs; les deux dettes s'èteignent reciproquement, à l'instant où elles se trouvent exister à la fois, jusqu'à concourence de leurs quotités respectives." Article 1290, *French Civil Code*.

"No counter-claim is required if the defendant wants to set off liquidated debt against the plaintiff's claim. Such a set-off, called compensation legale, is considered a *defence on the merits* (Dalloz, *Repertoire de procedure civile et commerciale*, Demande reconventionnelle, at No 14)." P Herzog, *Civil procedure in France*, Martinus Nijhof, 1967, p. 277.

"*Set-off*. Generally, in set-off, it is not necessary that the defendant's claim arise from the contract or transaction sued on or be connected with the subject matter thereof." *80 C.J.S., Section 35*.

"The distinguishing feature of counter-claim, as *opposed to set-off*, is that it arises out of the same transaction as that described in the complaint...." *Ibid*., Section 36.

The Distinction between the two concepts of "counter-claim" and "set-off" can be clearly understood from the legal texts cited above. That is to say, the counter-claim is an independent claim which is brought vis-à-vis the original claim. In other words, the original claim provides the motive or justification for bringing the counter-claim, and the latter must therefore be related to it. As for the set-off, it is brought as a distinct claim as well, but it indicates the existence of a debt which in itself, by the operation of law, sets off and extinguishes all or part of the claimant's claims in advance. Thus, the legal set-off constitutes a substantive rule and principle and, as we saw in the above cited texts, it is one of the respondent's grounds of defence.

CBS Inc and *Islamic Republic of Iran*, Award No 486–197–2 (June 28, 1990), reprinted in 25 Iran-US CTR 131, 149–50 (1990-II):

56. The Tribunal notes that, apart from alleging that the foreign managers violated Article 141 of the Commercial Code of Iran by not calling an extraordinary general meeting of the shareholders after CBS SSK had lost over 50 percent of its share capital, CBS SSK does not indicate the acts and omissions for which it reproaches the foreign managers, and that allegedly led to the damages it claims to have suffered. At any rate, CBS SSK tendered no evidence to prove its alleged damages. Accordingly, the Tribunal must dismiss CBS SSK's Counter-claims for

lack of proof. In view of this finding, the Tribunal need not decide the jurisdictional issues related to these Counter-Claims.

Islamic Republic of Iran and *United States of America* (Case No B1 (Counter-Claim)), Award No ITL 83-B1-FT (September 9, 2004) (footnotes omitted):

97. Article 19(3) of the [1983] Tribunal Rules provides that "the respondent may make a counter-claim or rely on a claim for the purpose of a set-off if such counter-claim or set-off is allowed under the Claims Settlement Declaration." This could be read merely as

> confirming that the Claims Settlement Declaration governs which counter-claims are permitted; pursuant to this interpretation, Article 19(3) of the [1983] Tribunal Rules does not provide any additional information as to whether counter-claims are permitted under Article II, paragraph 2, of the Claims Settlement Declaration.

98. On the other hand, Article 19(3) of the [1983] Tribunal Rules could be read as indicating that official counter-claims are permitted so long as the substantive claim made therein is of the type that could be heard by the Tribunal under Article II, paragraph 2, of the Claims Settlement Declaration, i.e. a claim of one State against the other "arising out of contractual arrangements between them for the purchase and sale of goods and services." Therefore, according to this second interpretation, Article 19(3) of the [1983] Tribunal Rules would confirm that a counter-claim that could have been filed as an autonomous claim under Article II, paragraph 2, of the Claims Settlement Declaration would fall within the Tribunal's jurisdiction.

99. The Tribunal does not consider it necessary to decide which of these interpretations should be adopted; suffice it to say that consideration of Article 19(3) of the [1983] Tribunal Rules does not provide a clear answer to the question of the Tribunal's jurisdiction over official counter-claims.

100. It may also be noted that Article 19(3) of the [1983] Tribunal Rules is a modified version of Article 19(3) of the [1976] UNCITRAL Rules, which provides that "the respondent may make a counter-claim arising out of the same contract." It appears doubtful that the modification of Article 19(3) of the [1976] UNCITRAL Rules was intended to prevent counter-claims arising out of the same contract as the claim. Rather, it seems that this modified version was adopted only to ensure that Article 19(3) conformed with the special jurisdictional regime of Article II, paragraph 1, of the Claims Settlement Declaration. First, the modification was adopted in response to the suggestion of the Iranian Members that the defence of set-off be allowed even if that set-off did not arise out of the same contract, transaction or occurrence that formed the subject matter of the national's claim. Second, because Article II, paragraph 1, of the Claims Settlement Declaration provides that claims and counter-claims must arise out of "debts, contracts..., expropriations or other measures affecting property rights," whereas Article 19(3) of the [1976] UNCITRAL Rules only refers to "contract[s]," Article 19(3)'s counter-claim authorization would otherwise have been inconsistent with the terms of the Claims Settlement Declaration absent modification. This being noted, even if the history of the modifications to Article 19(3) of the [1976] UNCITRAL Rules shows that the Tribunal's concerns were related to Article II, paragraph 1, of the Claims Settlement Declaration, it still does not tell us how—in the face of a general reference to the Claims Settlement Declaration by Article 19(3) of the Tribunal Rules—Article II, paragraph 2, of the Claims Settlement Declaration is to be interpreted. Therefore, the Tribunal cannot draw any firm conclusion from the history of the modifications to Article 19(3) of the [1976] UNCITRAL Rules.

101. In light of the foregoing, the Tribunal finds that the context of Article II, paragraph 2, of the Claims Settlement Declaration does not provide a clear answer to the question of the Tribunal's jurisdiction over official counter-claims.

(4) Tribunal Rules (1983), Article 19(4)

Herman Blum Consulting Engineers, Inc and *Islamic Republic of Iran*, Case No 138, Chamber One, Order of September 20, 1982:

> The Respondents in this case are hereby ordered to submit to the Tribunal by 15 December 1982 their Rejoinder to the Claimant's Reply filed on 9 August 1982. The Respondents are requested in particular to substantiate the basis for the counter-claim.

Chapter 14

Objections to the Jurisdiction of the Arbitral Tribunal

1. Introduction	449
2. Objections to Jurisdiction—Article 23	450
A. Text of the 2010 UNCITRAL Rule	450
B. Commentary	450
(1) The power of the tribunal to determine its own jurisdiction—Article 23(1)	450
(2) Objections to the existence or validity of the contract of which the arbitration agreement is a part and the doctrine of separability—Article 23(1)	453
(3) When objections should be raised—Article 23(2)	455
(4) When objections should be ruled upon—Article 23(3)	457
(5) Comparison to the 1976 UNCITRAL Rules	458
C. Extracts from the Practice of Investment Tribunals	459
D. Extracts from the Practice of the Iran–US Claims Tribunal	463
(1) Tribunal Rules (1983), Article 21(1)	463
(2) Tribunal Rules (1983), Article 21(2)	463
(3) Tribunal Rules (1983), Article 21(3)	464
(4) Tribunal Rules (1983), Article 21(4)	464

1. Introduction

During an arbitration proceeding, particularly at the outset, several issues, often termed objections, can arise in connection with pleas as to the jurisdiction of the arbitral tribunal. Article 23 of the UNCITRAL Rules addresses these issues rather fully.[1] Article 23(1) addresses the extent of the power of the arbitral tribunal to rule on its own jurisdiction, including the separability of the arbitration clause from the contract in dispute. Article 23(2) addresses when the parties should raise pleas as to jurisdiction and the arbitral tribunal's discretion to consider late pleas, while Article 23(3) addresses the arbitral tribunal's discretion to rule on a plea as a preliminary question or in an award on the merits and to continue the proceedings in the event of a pending challenge to its jurisdiction in a local court.

---

[1] Similar provisions are found in other arbitral rules. 2012 ICC Rules, art 6(3); 2009 ICDR Rules, art 15; 2006 ICSID Additional Facility Rules, Rule 45(1); 1998 LCIA Rules, art 23(1); 2012 Swiss International Arbitration Rules, art 21.

2. Objections to Jurisdiction—Article 23

A. Text of the 2010 UNCITRAL Rule[2]

Article 23 of the 2010 UNCITRAL Rules provides:

1. The arbitral tribunal may rule on its own jurisdiction, including any objections with respect to the existence or validity of the arbitration agreement. For that purpose, an arbitration clause which forms part of a contract shall be treated as an agreement independent of the other terms of the contract. A decision by the arbitral tribunal that the contract is null shall not entail automatically the invalidity of the arbitration clause.
2. A plea that the arbitral tribunal does not have jurisdiction shall be raised no later than in the statement of defence or, with respect to a counterclaim or a claim for the purpose of a set-off, in the reply to the counterclaim or to the claim for the purpose of a set-off. A party is not precluded from raising such a plea by the fact that it has appointed, or participated in the appointment of, an arbitrator. A plea that the arbitral tribunal is exceeding the scope of its authority shall be raised as soon as the matter alleged to be beyond the scope of its authority is raised during the arbitral proceedings. The arbitral tribunal may, in either case, admit a later plea if it considers the delay justified.
3. The arbitral tribunal may rule on a plea referred to in paragraph 2 either as a preliminary question or in an award on the merits. The arbitral tribunal may continue the arbitral proceedings and make an award, notwithstanding any pending challenge to its jurisdiction before a court.

B. Commentary

(1) *The power of the tribunal to determine its own jurisdiction—Article 23(1)*

The first sentence of Article 23(1) states the principle of Kompetenz-Kompetenz: the arbitral tribunal has authority to "rule on its own jurisdiction."[3] Incorporating the principle of

---

[2] Corresponding Article 21 of the 1976 UNCITRAL Rules provides:

1. The arbitral tribunal shall have the power to rule on objections that it has no jurisdiction, including any objections with respect to the existence or validity of the arbitration clause or of the separate arbitration agreement.
2. The arbitral tribunal shall have the power to determine the existence or the validity of the contract of which an arbitration clause forms a part. For the purposes of article 21, an arbitration clause which forms part of a contract and which provides for arbitration under these Rules shall be treated as an agreement independent of the other terms of the contract. A decision by the arbitral tribunal that the contract is null and void shall not entail *ipso jure* the invalidity of the arbitration clause.
3. A plea that the arbitral tribunal does not have jurisdiction shall be raised not later than in the statement of defence, or with respect to a counter-claim, in the reply to the counter-claim.
4. In general, the arbitral tribunal should rule on a plea concerning its jurisdiction as a preliminary question. However, the arbitral tribunal may proceed with the arbitration and rule on such a plea in their final award.

[3] The power of tribunals to determine their own jurisdiction is widely accepted. See, eg, G Born, *International Commercial Arbitration* (2009) 853; N Blackaby and C Partasides with A Redfern and M Hunter with, *Redfern and Hunter on International Arbitration*, (5th edn 2009) 346; 1965 Washington Convention on the Settlement of Investment Disputes between States and Nationals of Other States (hereinafter "Washington Convention"), art 41(1) ("The Tribunal shall be the judge of its own competence."). When such power is not expressly provided for, it is generally thought to exist as an inherent power of the tribunal. See generally I Shihata, *The Power of the International Court to Determine Its Own Jurisdiction* (1965) 47. See also H Arfazadeh, *Ordre public et arbitrage international à l'épreuve de la mondialisation* (2005) 46–8. Numerous UNCITRAL tribunals have acknowledged such power. See *Larsen* and *Hawaiian Kingdom*, Procedural Order No 3 (July 17, 2000), para 7 (quoted at para 6.2. of the Award (2001)), 119 Intl L Rep 566; *Encana Corp* and *Republic of Ecuador*, Partial Award on Jurisdiction (February 27, 2004), (LCIA administered, 1976

Kompetenz-Kompetenz into the UNCITRAL Rules is critical to the efficient conduct of the arbitration. As noted by leading commentators, "The concept is important in practice because without it a party could stall the arbitration at any time merely by raising a jurisdictional objection that could then only be resolved in possibly lengthy court proceedings."[4] The language of Article 23(1) was modeled virtually verbatim after Article 16(1) of the UNCITRAL Model Arbitration Law.[5]

The Working Group that revised the UNCITRAL Rules intended that Article 23(1) state clearly that the arbitral tribunal has authority to decide issues concerning its jurisdiction *sua sponte*—that is, in the absence of an objection by a party. Article 21(1) of the 1976 UNCITRAL Rules contained a narrower formulation of the rule that granted the arbitral tribunal the power to rule on "*objections* that it has jurisdiction."[6] The Working Group chose to revise the rule to track the language of Article 16(1) of the Model Arbitration Law in order to clarify that the arbitral tribunal's powers include the authority both to "raise and decide upon issues regarding the existence and scope of its own jurisdiction."[7]

An arbitral tribunal will likely need to rule on its jurisdiction *sua sponte* only in rare instances. The Working Group identified two such situations: first, where a party that might otherwise have raised an objection has not participated in the proceedings and, second, where a party that might otherwise have raised an objection is unaware of a complex jurisdictional issue, eg, the arbitrability of a competition issue.[8] In these instances, where a disputing party is unable to protect the integrity of the arbitral process and, in turn, the validity of the award against possible future challenges, the arbitral tribunal has the power under Article 23(1), and arguably the duty under the Rules, to do so.[9] More typically, however, the arbitral tribunal will apply its powers under Article 23(1) in response to an objection raised by a party.

While Article 23(1) expressly identifies only one example of an arbitral tribunal's authority to resolve objections raised by a party—the power to rule on "objections with respect to the existence and validity of the arbitration agreement"—clearly its power is more extensive. Article 23(2), for example, refers broadly to the parties' rights to raise any "plea that

---

UNCITRAL Rules, Canada-Ecuador BIT), at 8, para 13; *Eastern Sugar BV* and *Czech Republic*, Partial Award (March 27, 2007), (SCC administered, 1976 UNCITRAL Rules, Netherlands-Czech Republic BIT), at 23, para 116; *Austrian Airlines* and *Slovak Republic*, Final Award (October 9, 2009), (PCA administered, 1976 UNCITRAL Rules, Austria-Czech/Slovak BIT), at 30, para 117.

[4] H Holtzmann and J Neuhaus, *A Guide to the UNCITRAL Model Law on International Commercial Arbitration: Legislative History and Commentary* (1989) 479.

[5] The original inspiration for Article 23(1) and its predecessor, Article 21(1) of the 1976 UNCITRAL Rules, however, was Article 41(1) of the 1965 ICSID Convention. See *Report of the Secretary-General on the Preliminary Draft Set of Arbitration Rules*, UNCITRAL, 8th Session, UN Doc A/CN.9/97 (1974), reprinted in (1975) VI UNCITRAL Ybk 163, 174.

[6] Emphasis added. Paulsson and Petrocholis observed that a literal interpretation of the provision would preclude the arbitral tribunal from acting *sua sponte*, a limitation that did not reflect modern arbitration practice. See J Paulsson and G Petrochilos, *Revision of the UNCITRAL Arbitration Rules*, Report to UNCITRAL Secretariat, at 92, para 169 (2006).

[7] *Report of the Working Group on Arbitration and Conciliation on the Work of its Forty-Fifth Session* (Vienna, September 11–15, 2006), UNCITRAL, 40th Session, UN Doc A/CN.9/614, at 21, para 97 (2007).

Article 16(1) of the Model Law on which Article 23(1) is modeled should be interpreted similarly. See *Report of the United Nations Commission on International Trade Law on the Work of its Eighteenth Session* (August 21, 1985), UN Doc. A/40/17, para 150 ("[T]he arbitral tribunal could decide on its own motion if there were doubts or questions as to its jurisdiction, including the issue of arbitrability.").

[8] UNCITRAL, 40th Session, UN Doc A/CN.9/614, n 7, at 21, para 97.

[9] Note, however, one commentator's concerns, presumably in the context of an absence of express authority, that a *sua sponte* jurisdictional decision by an arbitral tribunal would be "a serious violation of the parties' procedural rights." G Born, *International Commercial Arbitration*, n 3, 998.

the arbitral tribunal does not have jurisdiction" or that "the arbitral tribunal is exceeding the scope of its authority."

The *travaux préparatoires* of corresponding Article 21(2) of the 1976 UNCITRAL Rules further confirm this conclusion. Original Article 21(2) established the arbitral tribunal's power to rule on "objections to its jurisdiction, including objections with respect to the existence and validity of the arbitration clause or the separate arbitration agreement." The commentary accompanying the preliminary draft of original Article 21(1) indicated that although the "second clause [of this paragraph] might be deemed to be covered by the more general first clause... it does not seem advisable to leave any doubt on this point and, consequently, the second clause is added in the interest of clarity."[10] The commentary also makes clear that original Article 21(1) "is designed to cover all objections to the jurisdiction of the arbitrators, irrespective of the grounds for and the extent of, such objections."[11] Article 23(1) should be understood to have the same extensive coverage.

In sum, the scope of substantive application of Article 23(1) is comparable to that of Article 21(1) of the 1976 UNCITRAL Rules. Notably, the Working Group, in deciding that substantial revision of the 1976 rule was not necessary, confirmed its understanding that:

> the general power of the arbitral tribunal, referred to in paragraph (1), to decide upon its jurisdiction should be interpreted as including the power of the arbitral tribunal to decide upon the admissibility of the parties' claims or, more generally to exercise its own jurisdiction [and that the provision] applied also to the objections made by a party that the tribunal should not exercise its jurisdiction to examine a claim on the merits.[12]

While the scope of the tribunal's authority under Article 23(1) to resolve a wide array of jurisdictional questions has not changed, under the 2010 Rules the tribunal now has express authority to address these questions *sua sponte*.

The arbitral tribunal's powers under Article 23(1) are subject to any mandatory requirements of the governing law.[13] Thus, although the arbitral tribunal has the power under Article 23(1) to determine its own jurisdiction, in many jurisdictions a local court may have the final word on the matter. For example, any awards of the arbitral tribunal might be subject to challenge under the applicable law, whether in set-aside or enforcement proceedings, for excess of jurisdiction.[14]

---

[10] *Report of the Secretary-General on the Preliminary Draft Set of Arbitration Rules*, UNCITRAL, 8th Session, UN Doc A/CN.9/97 (1974), reprinted in (1975) VI UNCITRAL Ybk 163, 174.

[11] *Report of the Secretary-General on the Revised Draft Set of Arbitration Rules*, UNCITRAL, 9th Session, Addendum 1 (Commentary), UN Doc A/CN.9/112/Add.1 (1975), reprinted in (1976) VII UNCITRAL Ybk 166, 174.

[12] *Report of Working Group II (Arbitration and Conciliation) on the Work of its Fiftieth Session* (New York, February 9–13, 2009), UNCITRAL, 42nd Session, UN Doc A/CN.9/669, at 10, para 39 (2009).

[13] The original drafters of the 1976 UNCITRAL Rules debated whether to state this fact expressly. Some delegates believed a rule on Kompetence-Kompetence "could mislead parties, because questions as to the competence and jurisdiction of arbitrators were ultimately a matter for the courts to settle in accordance with the *lex fori*." *Report of the United Nations Commission on International Trade Law*, 8th Session, Summary of Discussion of the Preliminary Draft, UN Doc A/10017, para 141 (1975), reprinted in (1975) VI UNCITRAL Ybk 24, 38. They proposed including a provision to indicate that original Article 21(1) was subject to the limitations of the law applicable to the arbitration proceedings. *Summary Record of the 8th Meeting of the Committee of the Whole (II)*, UNCITRAL, 9th Session, UN Doc A/CN.9/9/C.2/SR.8, at 3–4, paras 13–25 (1976). However, this proposal was rejected as all of the rules were subject to national law and the insertion of such a provision in only this article would "give rise to an *argumentum a contrario*" elsewhere. Para 28. Therefore it was instead agreed that a general reference to the applicability of national law to all the Rules should be made. Para 28. See Chapter 2, section 2 on Article 1(2).

[14] See P Sanders, "Procedures and Practices under the UNCITRAL Rules," (1979) 27 American J Comparative L 453, 461–2 ("Although the arbitrators may rule on their own competence, courts have the final word."); N Blackaby and C Partasides, *Redfern and Hunter on International Arbitration*, n 3, 354. See also Chapter 2, this volume.

(2) Objections to the existence or validity of the contract of which the arbitration agreement is a part and the doctrine of separability—Article 23(1)

Article 23(1) adopts the widely accepted view that the arbitration clause is an agreement separate from the contract in which it is contained.[15] In the ordinary course of international commercial arbitration, the "contract" refers to the contract under dispute, whereas "arbitration clause" refers to the arbitration clause which confers jurisdiction. The doctrine of separability resolves the conundrum perceived by some of how a tribunal possesses jurisdiction when the arbitration clause that allegedly confers jurisdiction is part of a contract that is allegedly null.[16] As stated by Sanders, the doctrine of separability "reflects the view that the arbitration clause, although contained in, and forming a part of, the contract, is in reality an agreement distinct from the contract itself, having as its object the submission to arbitration of disputes arising from or relating to the contractual relationship."[17]

The doctrine of separability may be "considered to conform with the underlying intention of the parties" and consequently means that "a decision by the arbitrators that a contract is null and void will not affect the validity of the arbitration clause in that contract and will not undermine the competence of the arbitrators to make that decision."[18] Toward the same end, the UNCITRAL model arbitration clause provides that "[a]ny dispute, controversy or claim arising out of or relating to this contract, or the breach, termination or invalidity thereof, shall be settled by arbitration ..."[19]

---

[15] See G Born, *International Commercial Arbitration*, n 3, 350, 397. See also rules of procedure cited in n 1.

[16] See E Gaillard and J Savage (eds), *Fouchard, Gaillard, Goldman on International Commercial Arbitration* (1999) 213:

If [the arbitrators] find the main contract to be ineffective, with on the principle of competence-competence they would have no option but to decline jurisdiction. However, the principle of autonomy [also known as separability] enables arbitrators to declare the main contract ineffective without necessarily concluding that the arbitration agreement is likewise ineffective and therefore declining jurisdiction. In other words, the decision of an arbitrator to retain jurisdiction and then declare a disputed contract ineffective must be founded on the principle of autonomy, and not solely on the "competence-competence" rule.

But see G Born, *International Commercial Arbitration*, n 3, 402–3:

[T]he separability presumption does not in fact explain the competence-competence doctrine. Although the competence-competence doctrine arises from the same basic objectives as the separability presumption ... it is not logically dependent upon, nor explicable by reference to, the separability presumption Rather, the competence-competence doctrine permits an arbitral tribunal to consider and decide upon its own jurisdiction even where the existence or validity of an arbitration agreement ... is disputed.

Although decisions of the Iran–US Claims Tribunal cited Article 21(2) of the 1976 UNCITRAL Rules with approval, the relevance of the Article to that Tribunal is somewhat curious. The Iran–US Claims Tribunal is a permanent tribunal, whose jurisdiction derives from the Algiers Declarations, and not from a clause of a contract in dispute before the Tribunal. The Algiers Declarations provide, however, that a certain type of forum selection clause in a disputed contract would oust the Tribunal of jurisdiction over "claims arising under" that contract. Article II, paragraph 1, of the Claims Settlement Declaration. In this curiously reversed manner, Article 21(2) became relevant to the Tribunal. This relevance, however, was by analogy, rather than by direct application, since the Algiers Declarations conferred jurisdiction generally leaving no jurisdictional conundrum to resolve. Thus, Judges Holtzmann and Mosk properly cited to Article 21(2) as support for the doctrine of separability generally rather than as a rule directly applicable to the issue presented. *Forum Selection Claims Cases* (1983 Tribunal Rules), reprinted in section 2(D)(2).

[17] *Report of the Secretary-General on the Revised Draft Set of Arbitration Rules*, UNCITRAL, 9th Session, Addendum 1 (Commentary), UN Doc A/CN.9/112/Add.1 (1975), reprinted in (1976) VII UNCITRAL Ybk 166, 174.

[18] *Report of the Secretary-General on the Preliminary Draft Set of Arbitration Rules*, UNCITRAL, 8th Session, UN Doc A/CN.9/97 (1974), reprinted in (1975) VI UNCITRAL Ybk 163, 175. The members of the Iran-US Claims Tribunal endorsed this principle in the early history of the Tribunal. See *Minutes of the 51st Full Tribunal Meeting*, reprinted in section 2(D)(2).

[19] See Chapter 2, section 2(A).

Furthermore, the separation of the arbitration clause from the contract places the question of the validity of the contract outside court control under most national laws inasmuch as the validity of the contract in such a case does not involve a decision as to the competence of the arbitrators.[20]

The doctrine of separability is incorporated into other leading arbitral rules[21] and has been endorsed by many municipal systems of law.[22] The inclusion of this provision in the 1976 UNCITRAL Rules was not a contested matter among the original drafters. In revising the Rules, the Working Group's primary focus was to harmonize the texts of Article 23(1) and Article 16(1) of the Model Law, which are now virtually identical, save for two differences.

The first difference reflects a substantive change. The third sentence of the Model Law (and the third sentence of original Article 21(2)) states that an arbitration clause is not automatically invalid when the arbitral tribunal determines the contract is "null and void." By contrast, the third sentence of Article 23(1) includes only the word "null," thus omitting the words "and void." The change was made because the phrase "null and void" was believed to be too narrow to capture all relevant situations in which the contract might be defective, such as where a contract had expired with the passage of time.[23] A proposal to add the language "non-existent or invalid" was made, but rejected, because those terms would be incompatible with the approach of some legal systems.[24] The term "null" by itself was ultimately believed to be of sufficient breadth to cover all relevant situations, including where the contract was "null, void, non-existent, invalid or non-effective."[25]

The second difference between Article 23(1) and Article 16(1) of the Model Law is stylistic. The phrase "*ipso jure*" in the third sentence of Article 16(1) of the Model Law (and the third sentence of original Article 21(2)) was replaced by its English translation "automatically" in the third sentence of Article 23(1) in the interests of simplifying the Rules.[26]

Two additional proposals considered by the Working Group inform the meaning of Article 23(1). The first proposal was to add the words "or legal instrument" after the word "contract" in the second and third sentences of Article 23(1). With this change, the doctrine of separability would apply in situations where a "legal instrument," other than a contract, was deemed to be defective. Proponents of the proposal believed it was consistent with the aim of expanding the scope of application of the Rules to non-contractual disputes

---

[20] See P Sanders, "Procedures and Practices under the UNCITRAL Rules," n 14, 461, 463. Some national laws might nonetheless subject the issue of the validity of the contract to court control.
[21] See n 1. See generally P Sanders, "La separabilité la clause compromissoire," in *Liber Amicorum for Frédéric Eisemann* (1978).
[22] See, eg, England: *Harbour Assurance Co. (UK) Ltd v Kansas General Intl Insurance Co Ltd* [1992] 1 Lloyd's Rep. 81, 92–3 (QB); France: Judgment of May 7, 1963, Ets Raumond Gosset v Carapelli, JCP G 1963, II, 13, para 405 (French Cour de cassation civ le); French New Code of Civil Procedure, Article 1442; Germany: *Judgment of 27 February 1970*, 6 *Arbitration Intl* 79 (1990) (German Bundesgerichtshof); Switzerland: Swiss Law on Private International Law, Articles 178(2) and (3); United States: *Prima Paint Corporation v Flood and Conklin Manufacturing Co*, 388 US 395 (1967); *Buckeye Check Cashing Inc v Cardegna*, 546 US 440 (2006).
[23] UNCITRAL, 42nd Session, UN Doc A/CN.9/669, n 12, at 10–11, para 40. Some argued that the phrase "null and void" should be replaced with the words "non-existent or invalid," but it was noted that those words would give rise to particular difficulties in some legal systems.
[24] UNCITRAL, 42nd Session, UN Doc A/CN.9/669, n 12, at 10–11, paras 40–41. Some in favor of the phrase "null and void" noted that the inclusion of this phrase in the New York Convention and Article 16(1) of the Model Law had not given rise to problems in practice. Paras 40–41.
[25] UNCITRAL, 42nd Session, UN Doc A/CN.9/669, n 12, at 11, para 42.
[26] UNCITRAL, 42nd Session, UN Doc A/CN.9/669, n 12, at 11, para 44.

and, specifically, to disputes arising under international investment treaties.[27] The consensus of the Working Group was that the proposal could not be adopted because the Rules were not meant to regulate matters of public international law, particularly given that the doctrine of separability was "not necessarily recognized in the context of international treaties."[28]

(3) When objections should be raised—Article 23(2)

Article 23(2) places respective time limitations on a party's ability to raise a plea that "the arbitral tribunal does not have jurisdiction" or that "the arbitral tribunal is exceeding the scope of its authority." The former type of plea must be raised no later than in the statement of defence or, with respect to a counterclaim or a claim for the purpose of a set-off, in the reply to the counterclaim or to the claim for the purpose of a set-off,[29] whereas the latter must be raised "as soon as the matter alleged to be beyond the scope of its authority is raised during the arbitral proceedings." The aim of these time limitations is to ensure that any objections to the arbitral tribunal's jurisdiction are raised without delay.[30] Article 23(2) tracks the language of Article 16(2) of the Model Law verbatim. Similar provisions are contained in other arbitration procedure codes.[31]

The two types of plea are to be raised under different circumstances. A plea that "the arbitral tribunal does not have jurisdiction" must be raised by the time a particular pleading is submitted, ie, the statement of defence or a reply to a counterclaim or a set-off claim, indicating that the plea will likely arise in response to an assertion by one party in its submission that the arbitral tribunal has jurisdiction over a particular claim or matter. The circumstances in which a plea will arise that the "the arbitral tribunal is exceeding the scope of its authority" are less apparent from the text of Article 23(2). The negotiating history of Article 16(2) of the Model Law from which the rule derives suggests that this type of plea may be appropriate where the arbitral tribunal has indicated it may exceed the scope of its jurisdiction, such as by requesting or examining evidence relating to a matter outside its scope of authority.[32]

The strict time limits established by Article 23(2) are tempered by the arbitral tribunal's discretion to "admit a later plea if it considers the delay justified." The Rules do not enumerate the circumstances under which a delay is justified. While corresponding Article 21(3) of the 1976 UNCITRAL Rules ultimately did not contain the same moderating language, a preliminary draft of the article provided: "Where delay in raising a plea of incompetence is justified under the circumstances, the arbitrators may declare the plea admissible."[33] According to the commentary accompanying the revised draft, this sentence meant that "the arbitrators may admit a plea... if the delay was justified under the circumstances."[34]

---

[27] UNCITRAL, 42nd Session, UN Doc A/CN.9/669, n 12, at 9–10, para 36.
[28] UNCITRAL, 42nd Session, UN Doc A/CN.9/669, n 12, at 10, para 37.
[29] See, eg, *Chevron Research Co* (1983 Tribunal Rules), reprinted in section 2(D)(3).
[30] *Report of the Secretary-General: Analytical Commentary on Draft Text of Model Law on International Commercial Arbitration* (March 25, 1985), UN Doc. A/CN.9/264, at 38, para 4.
[31] See n 1.
[32] See *Report if the United Nations Commission on International Trade Law on the Work of its Eighteenth Session* (August 21, 1985), UN Doc A/40/17, para 155
[33] *Report of the Secretary-General on the Preliminary Draft Set of Arbitration Rules*, UNCITRAL, 8th Session, UN Doc A/CN.9/97 (1974), reprinted in (1975) VI UNCITRAL Ybk 163, 174 (Draft Article 18(2)).
[34] *Report of the Secretary-General on the Revised Draft Set of Arbitration Rules*, UNCITRAL, 9th Session, Addendum 1 (Commentary), UN Doc A/CN.9/112/Add.1 (1975), reprinted in (1976) VII UNCITRAL Ybk 166, 174.

For example, "a plea based on facts newly discovered" might be admitted despite being raised late.³⁵

UNCITRAL delegates were split, however, as to the need for the sentence regarding the arbitral tribunal's discretion. One representative stated that objections to jurisdiction "should be raised as early as possible and considered no later than the statement of claim or the statement of defence."³⁶ Another representative felt that the second sentence was unnecessary "since such a question could be left to the discretion of the tribunal."³⁷ A third representative felt that the second sentence was of a "special character and should be retained."³⁸ The Conference later adopted the report of a special drafting group,³⁹ recommending that the second sentence be deleted because it was unnecessary, since original Article 20 (now Article 22) provides for possible amendment of a claim or defence and original Article 15(1) (now Article 17(1)) states "the arbitral tribunal may conduct the arbitration in such manner as it considers appropriate."⁴⁰ The last sentence of Article 23(2) thus expressly states what was previously only implicit under the 1976 UNCITRAL Rules: that the arbitral tribunal has discretion in limited circumstances to admit justifiably late pleas, such as due to the discovery of new evidence.⁴¹

Article 23(2) also provides that a party is not precluded from making a plea that the arbitral tribunal lacks jurisdiction "by the fact that it has appointed, or participated in the appointment of, an arbitrator." The negotiating history of the identical sentence in Article 16(2) of the Model Law explains: "Thus, if, despite [a party's] objections, he prefers not to remain passive but to take part in, and exert influence on, the constitution of the arbitral tribunal, which would eventually rule on his objections, he need not make a reservation, as would be necessary under some national laws for excluding the effect of waiver or submission."⁴²

Finally, if a party fails to raise a plea as to the arbitral tribunal's jurisdiction within the appropriate time limit, and the arbitral tribunal chooses not to consider the late plea, the party is generally precluded from raising the objection during the remainder of the arbitral proceedings.⁴³ The extent to which the party may raise the objection in post-award proceedings, such as set-aside and enforcement proceedings, is determined by the applicable law.⁴⁴

---

³⁵ *Report of the Secretary-General*, n 33.
³⁶ *Summary Record of the 8th Meeting of the Committee of the Whole (II)*, UNCITRAL, 9th Session, UN Doc A/CN.9/9/C.2/SR.8, at 5, para 30 (1976) (Comment by Mr Dey, India).
³⁷ UNCITRAL, 9th Session, UN Doc A/CN.9/9/C.2/SR.8, n 36, at 4, para 27 (Comment by Mr Pirrung, Federal Republic of Germany).
³⁸ UNCITRAL, 9th Session, UN Doc A/CN.9/9/C.2/SR.8, n 36, at 5, para 29 (Comment by Mr Lebedev, USSR).
³⁹ See *Report of the Drafting Group on articles 20 and 21 (United Kingdom and USSR)*, UN Doc A/CN.9/IX/C.2/CRP.16. .
⁴⁰ See *Report of the UN Commission on International Trade Law on the Work of its Ninth Session*, UN GAOR, 31st Session, Supp No 17, UN Doc A/31/17, para 108 (1976), reprinted in (1976) VII UNCITRAL Ybk 66, 74.
⁴¹ Note also that the same provision in Article 16(1) of the Model Law has been interpreted as allowing the arbitral tribunal to consider a late plea based on "public policy, including admissibility." H Holtzmann and J Neuhaus, *A Guide to the UNCITRAL Model Law on International Commercial Arbitration*, n 4, 483.
⁴² *Report of the Secretary-General: Analytical Commentary on Draft Text of Model Law on International Commercial Arbitration* (March 25, 1985), UN Doc A/CN.9/264, at 38, para 6.
⁴³ See, eg, *CME Czech Republic* (1976 Rules), and *Canfor Corp* (1976 Rules), para 103, both reprinted in section 2(C).
⁴⁴ Holtzmann and Neuhaus, for example, argue that a failure to raise a timely objection under Article 16 (1) of the Model Law, typically bars a party from raising the objection in post-award proceedings, except where issues of public policy, including arbitrability are concerned. H Holtzmann and J Neuhaus, *A Guide to the UNCITRAL Model Law on International Commercial Arbitration*, n 4, 483.

(4) When objections should be ruled upon—Article 23(3)

Article 23(3) addresses when the arbitral tribunal should rule upon preliminary questions concerning jurisdiction.[45] On the one hand, early resolution of significant preliminary issues may yield substantial savings to the parties by either deciding the case or narrowing the scope of the dispute.[46] On the other hand, preliminary hearings to decide frivolously raised objections to jurisdiction constitute an abuse of process that is costly to all parties.[47] Article 23(3) balances these competing interests by giving the tribunal discretion to rule on such pleas either "as a preliminary question or in an award on the merits."[48] This provision of Article 23(3) is modeled after the first sentence of Article 16(3) of the Model Law. The negotiating history of the Model Law indicates a preference for preliminary treatment of jurisdictional issues "to avoid possible waste of time and costs," while recognizing that "where the question of jurisdiction is intertwined with the substantive issue, it may be appropriate to combine the ruling on jurisdiction with a party or complete decision on the merits of the case."[49]

The degree of delay involved in ruling on a jurisdictional objection as a preliminary matter turns a great deal upon whether the tribunal interprets Article 17(3) as giving each party a right to a hearing in the case of such a preliminary ruling. During discussions of corresponding Article 21(4) of the 1976 UNCITRAL Rules some delegates stated that a hearing would not be necessary under these circumstances. The delegate from Sierra Leone, for example, stated "It should be quite clear that the question of jurisdiction was a preliminary question which must be decided *prior to* the hearing."[50] Likewise, Sanders in his commentary to the revised draft of original Article 21(4) stated that objections to jurisdiction were "procedural matters," a characterization which, as stated in the commentary herein accompanying Article 17(3),[51] may indicate there is no absolute right to a hearing on such questions.

---

[45] On what constitutes a question concerning jurisdiction for purposes of corresponding Article 21(4) of the 1976 UNCITRAL Rules, see *Methanex Corp* (1976 Rules), Partial Award, para 86, reprinted in section 2(C). For a discussion of the meaning of "jurisdiction" in this context of a request to consolidate NAFTA Chapter Eleven proceedings under the 1976 UNCITRAL Rules, see *Canfor Corp* (1976 Rules), reprinted in section 2(C).

[46] This point was raised in discussions regarding the 1976 UNCITRAL Rules. The representative of Nigeria, for example, argued "that pleas as to the arbitrator's jurisdiction should be decided as a preliminary question, not during the final award; if the arbitrators ultimately decided that they did not have jurisdiction, unnecessary expenses would have been incurred." UNCITRAL, 9th Session, UN Doc A/CN.9/9/C.2/SR.8, n 36, at 5, para 32 (Comment by Mrs Oyekunle, Nigeria).
At the Iran-US Claims Tribunal, the question of a dual national claimant's dominant and effective nationality was a significant preliminary issue that was often resolved before addressing the merits. See *Ghaffari* (1983 Tribunal Rules), Dissenting Opinion of Judge Khalilian, reprinted in section 2(D)(4).

[47] In drafting the 1976 UNCITRAL Rules, Mexico's representative voiced the opposing concern that parties "might insist on an immediate ruling merely in order to delay the proceedings." UNCITRAL, 9th Session, UN Doc A/CN.9/9/C.2/SR.8, n 36, at 5, para 37 (Comment by Mr Mantilla-Molina, Mexico).

[48] As discussed in section 2(B)(4), the text of Article 23(3) eliminates the presumption in favor of preliminary treatment of jurisdictional objections previously found in corresponding Article 21(4) of the 1976 UNCITRAL Rules. As Castello observes, the presumption, in fact, may decrease arbitral efficiency "if jurisdictional objections have no merit" or "even where jurisdictional objections had merit, ... they overlap significantly with the merits of the case." J Castello, "Unveiling the 2010 UNCITRAL Arbitration Rules," (May/Oct 2010) 65 Dispute Resolution J 21,152–3.

[49] *Analytical Commentary on Draft Text of a Model Law on International Commercial Arbitration, Report by the Secretary-General*, UNCITRAL, 18th Session, UN Doc A/CN.9/264, at 40, para 11 (1985). See also H Holtzmann and J Neuhaus, *A Guide to the UNCITRAL Model Law on International Commercial Arbitration*, n 4, 510–11.

[50] UNCITRAL, 9th Session, UN Doc A/CN.9/9/C.2/SR.8, n 36, at 5, para 35 (Comment by Mr Boston, Sierra Leone) (emphasis added.)

[51] See Chapter 2.

The above discussion points to efficiency as the prime factor in determining whether a tribunal should rule on objections concerning jurisdiction as a preliminary matter or in an award on the merits. Any decision, therefore, must consider the substantiality of the objection, the cost in time and money to the parties of such a preliminary ruling (eg whether such a ruling would entail written filings or an oral hearing),[52] and the practicality of bifurcating the proceedings to address jurisdiction preliminarily, especially where jurisdictional issues are intertwined with the merits.[53]

Finally, the second sentence of Article 23(3) recognizes that the arbitral tribunal's power to rule on its own jurisdiction may be subject to varying degrees of judicial control, depending on the governing law. Article 16(3) of the Model Law, for example, provides: "If the arbitral tribunal rules as a preliminary question that it has jurisdiction, any party may request, within thirty days after having received notice of that ruling, the [applicable local] court... decide the matter, which decision shall be subject to no appeal."[54] The last sentence of Article 23(3) grants the arbitral tribunal discretion, subject to the governing law, to decide whether to continue with the arbitral proceedings and make an award, "pending challenge to its jurisdiction before a court." An arbitral tribunal's decision in this regard should weigh considerations of efficiency and fairness.

(5) Comparison to the 1976 UNCITRAL Rules

Article 23 tracks more closely the language of Article 16 of the Model Arbitration Law and thus differs in structure and content, but not in overall purpose, from Article 21 of the 1976 UNCITRAL Rules.

Article 23(1) articulates a broader rule with respect to the arbitral tribunal's powers to "rule on its own jurisdiction," as opposed to ruling only on "objections that it has no jurisdiction." In practice, however, this difference may be immaterial, since an arbitral tribunal's power to determine its own competence is widely accepted as inherent, even if not expressly stated in the Rules. In addition, the provisions of original Article 21(2) on the doctrine of separability have been incorporated into revised Article 23(1) with only one substantive change: the words "null and void" used in original Article 21(2) and Article 16(1) of the Model Law are replaced with the word "null." As discussed above, the reason for the change was that some legal systems did not recognize the concept of a "void" contract. If the parties contemplate arbitration subject to such a legal system, they may wish to modify original Article 21(2) accordingly.

Article 23(2) retains the same time limits as original Article 21(3) for raising pleas that the tribunal lacks jurisdiction. However, it now recognizes that pleas concerning the arbitral tribunal's lack of jurisdiction may be applicable in response to claims for the purpose of

---

[52] See *Bank Markazi Iran*, Dissenting Opinion of Judge Aghahosseini (1983 Tribunal Rules); *Starrett-Housing Corp*, Dissenting opinion of Judge Kashani (1983 Tribunal Rules); both reprinted in section 2(D)(4).

[53] For decisions on bifurcation, see *Iran* and *United States,* Case No B1 (1983 Tribunal Rules), reprinted in section 2(D)(4). See also *Methanex Corp* (1976 Rules), Partial Award and Final Award; *Canfor Corp* (1976 Rules); and *Glamis Gold Ltd* (1976 Rules); all reprinted in section 2(C).

[54] National approaches vary. See G Born, *International Commercial Arbitration*, n 3, 971 (observing that "national approaches range across a spectrum, with French, Hong Kong and Indian courts permitting very limited interlocutory judicial consideration of any jurisdiction objections (typically on a *prima facie* basis); US, English, and Canadian courts, as well as the UNCITRAL Model Law, permitting full interlocutory judicial consideration in some, but not all, cases, depending upon the nature of the jurisdictional objection and considerations of efficiency and fairness; and Swedish and Chinese courts permitting full interlocutory judicial consideration of jurisdictional issues in almost all circumstances"); J Barcelo, "Who Decides the Arbitrators' Jurisdiction? Separability and Competence-Competence in Transnational Perspective," (2003) 36 Vanderbilt J Transnatl L 1115, 1124–36.

a set-off. In that situation, like the situation involving counterclaims, a party must make its plea no later than in the response to the claim for a set-off. Article 23(2) adds the rule, derived from Article 16(2) of the Model Law, that a party is not precluded from raising a plea that the arbitral tribunal lacks jurisdiction, even if it has appointed or is participating in the appointment of an arbitrator. In addition, revised Article 23(2) establishes a new time limit for pleas that the arbitral tribunal is exceeding its jurisdiction. Finally, Article 23(3) now states expressly what was implied in original Article 21(3): that the arbitral tribunal has discretion to consider late objections.

Article 23(3) also replaces the express encouragement in original Article 21(4) that the arbitral tribunal "should" rule on a plea that it lacks jurisdiction as a "preliminary matter" with a more neutral rule: the arbitral tribunal may rule on such a plea "as a preliminary question or in an award on the merits." However, the same policy of ensuring a fair and efficient arbitration that underpins both the 1976 and 2010 UNCITRAL Rules would minimize any textual differences in practice. Finally, Article 23(3) adds the rule that the arbitral tribunal has discretion to continue the arbitral proceedings and make an award, despite a pending challenge to its jurisdiction before a local court.

C. Extracts from the Practice of Investment Tribunals

CME Czech Republic BV and *Czech Republic*, Partial Award (September 13, 2001) (*Ad Hoc* Proceeding, 1976 UNCITRAL Rules, Netherlands-Czech Republic BIT), at 99–100, reprinted in (2002) 14(3) World Trade & Arb Materials 109, 207–08:

378. The Respondent, for the first time at the Stockholm hearing, expressed its view that the investment of the Claimant in the Czech Republic within the meaning of the Treaty was (only) made when it purchased in 1997 the CNTS shares held by CME Media Enterprises B.V. The Respondent, in respect to this investment of the Claimant in the Czech Republic, expressly did not raise the defence of lack of jurisdiction. The Respondent is, however, of the opinion that Claimant's investment in 1997 limits timewise the Claimant's claim in substance which, therefore, will be dealt with hereafter when dealing with the merits of the Claim.
379. Any possible defence in respect to lack of jurisdiction related to the Claimant's acquisition of the CNTS shares in 1997, therefore, must be deemed as waived. That also would be consistent with Rule 21.3 of the [1976] UNCITRAL Rules, according to which objections in respect to jurisdiction must have been made in the Statement of Defence.
380. The Arbitral Tribunal considered whether (by disregarding the Respondent's waiver of a defence of lack of jurisdiction in respect to the 1997 share acquisition), the Tribunal is obligated ex officio to decide on this subject. The majority of the Tribunal is of the opinion that, disregarding possible Czech national law requirements, the clear provision of the [1976] UNCITRAL Rules must supersede national law, if deviating. According to the [1976] UNCITRAL Rules, a defence of jurisdiction is deemed to be waived, if not raised in time. This concept derives from the assumption that defences on jurisdiction can be waived by the Parties, with the consequence that a Tribunal is not able to set aside or disregard a Party's waiver in respect to the defence of lack of jurisdiction.
381. Therefore, the Respondent's argument that the investment of the Claimant in the Czech Republic was not made until May 21, 1997 must be dealt with by the Tribunal in accordance with the Respondent's express pleadings as a substantive defence, not as a defence to jurisdiction.

Methanex Corp and *United States of America*, Partial Award on Jurisdiction (August 7, 2002) (ICSID administered, 1976 UNCITRAL Rules, NAFTA Chapter Eleven), at 37 (footnote omitted), reprinted in (2002) 14(6) World Trade & Arb Materials 109, 146, 186, 188–89:86:

...Third, even if it qualified as a jurisdictional challenge (which in our view, it does not), its legal merits are so intertwined with factual issues arising from Methanex's case that we would have been minded, as a matter of discretion, to join that challenge to the merits under Article 21(4) of the [1976] UNCITRAL Arbitration Rules.

...

160. Article 21(4) of the [1976] UNCITRAL Arbitration Rules requires the arbitration tribunal, in general, to rule on a jurisdictional question; and indeed this is the procedure which has so far been followed in these arbitration proceedings. If the Tribunal has no jurisdiction, a decision to that effect could save the Disputing Parties much time and cost. However, as Article 21(4) also provides, the tribunal "*may proceed with the arbitration and rule on such a plea in their final award*". The discretion whether to choose the general or the exceptional procedure lies with the arbitration tribunal; and the exercise of that discretion is not confined to economic factors: e.g. where jurisdictional issues are intertwined with the merits, it may be impossible or impractical to decide the former without also hearing argument and evidence on the latter. In these proceedings, two factors have influenced us in selecting the exceptional procedure.

161. *Fresh Pleading:* First, the effect of the Tribunal's decision on Article 1101(1) NAFTA in this Award will require Methanex to re-plead its case in a fresh Statement of Claim.

...

167. *Evidence:* The second reason is, in our view conclusive. The necessary analysis relating to the credibility of Methanex's allegations remains incomplete without receiving at least some evidence from the Disputing Parties on the assumed, but disputed, facts and factual inferences. This part of the USA's jurisdictional challenge depends critically on issues which are intimately linked to the factual merits of Methanex's case. In our view, it is not appropriate to decide these issues without hearing evidence from Methanex and the USA. In short, the Tribunal cannot continue what has become an impossible forensic exercise, composing a jigsaw of assumed facts and inferences with too many missing and incomplete pieces. These difficulties could be resolved with relative ease at an evidential hearing.

Glamis Gold Ltd and *United States of America*, Procedural Order 2 (May 31, 2005) (ICSID administered, 1976 UNCITRAL Rules, NAFTA Chapter Eleven), at 2–3:

9. Article 21(4) [of the 1976 UNCITRAL Rules] establishes a presumption in favor of the tribunal preliminarily considering objections to jurisdiction. Simultaneously, however, Article 21(4) does not require that pleas as to jurisdiction must be ruled on as preliminary questions. The choice not to do so is left to the tribunal's discretion. [citation omitted]

...

11. In examining the drafting history of Article 21(4) of the [1976] UNCITRAL Rules, the Tribunal finds that the primary motive for the creation of a presumption in favor of the preliminary consideration of a jurisdictional objection was to ensure efficiency in the proceedings. Importantly, the Tribunal reads the presumption in favor of preliminarily considering an objection to jurisdiction as an instruction to the Tribunal and clearly not as an absolute right of the requesting party.

12. This Tribunal in examining the various sources finds that Article 21(4) [of the 1976 UNCITRAL Rules] contains a three fold test.
    a. First, in considering a request for the preliminary consideration of an objection to jurisdiction, the tribunal should take the claim as it is alleged by Claimant.
    b. Second, the "plea" must be one that goes to the "jurisdiction" of the tribunal over the claim. For example, the presumption in Article 21(4) would not apply to a request to bifurcate the proceedings between a liability phase and a damages phase. Likewise, Article 21(4) would not apply to a request that the Tribunal first consider whether the actions complained of were the cause of the loss, even though such a determination might be efficient overall for the proceedings. The Tribunal does not mean to suggest that such a

request can not be made to the Tribunal under, for example, Article 15(1), but rather seeks to emphasize that the presumption in favor of bifurcation contained in Article 21(4) extends only to pleas as to the jurisdiction of the tribunal.

c. Third, if an objection is raised to the jurisdiction of the tribunal and a request is made by either party that the objection be considered as a preliminary matter, the tribunal should do so. The tribunal may decline to do so when doing so is unlikely to bring about increased efficiency in the proceedings. Considerations relevant to this analysis include, *inter alia*, (1) whether the objection is substantial inasmuch as the preliminary consideration of a frivolous objection to jurisdiction is very unlikely to reduce the costs of, or time required for, the proceeding; (2) whether the objection to jurisdiction if granted results in a material reduction of the proceedings at the next phase (in other words, the tribunal should consider whether the costs and time required of a preliminary proceedings, even if the objecting party is successful, will be justified in terms of the reduction in costs at the subsequent phase of proceedings); and (3) whether bifurcation is impractical in that the jurisdictional issue identified is so intertwined with the merits that it is very unlikely that there will be any savings in time or cost. [citation omitted]

Methanex Corp and *United States of America*, Award (August 3, 2005) (ICSID administered, 1976 UNCITRAL Rules, NAFTA Chapter Eleven), Part II, Chapter C, at 5–7:

15. By order of 2nd June 2003, the Tribunal decided not to rule as a preliminary question on the USA's extant jurisdictional challenges. It decided following Methanex's proposal and pursuant to the exceptional procedure set out in Article 21(4), second sentence, of the [1976] UNCITRAL Rules to join all such jurisdictional challenges to the merits of the dispute and to proceed to a main hearing to address all such issues, excluding issues of quantum (which, if appropriate, were to be addressed at a subsequent hearing).

16. The Tribunal's order by letter of 2nd June 2003 is set out in full below:

The Tribunal has now concluded its deliberations on the future form of these arbitration proceedings under Article 21 of the [1976] UNCITRAL Arbitration Rules; and I set out the Tribunal's decision below:

In Paragraphs 166 to 168 of the Partial Award of August 2002 (page 70), the Tribunal indicated that the resumption of the jurisdictional stage after Methanex's fresh pleading was not an attractive option; the USA's jurisdictional challenges depended on issues intimately linked to the merits of Methanex's case; and there was a forensic need for an evidential hearing, at least in part. Nonetheless, the Tribunal was concerned to identify one or more threshold or other determinative issues on which limited testimony could be adduced at that evidential hearing, without proceeding necessarily to a full hearing of all factual and expert witnesses.

Following Methanex's fresh pleading and materials served in January 2003, the USA requested an evidential hearing limited to the issue of discriminatory "intent", namely whether California intended the relevant measures to address suppliers to MTBE producers, such as Methanex. . . . The USA submitted that such an evidential hearing would be appropriate for two principal reasons. (i) it would be the most efficient way for the Tribunal to proceed, given that it would not require the Tribunal at this stage to consider the bulky scientific evidence adduced by Methanex on the MTBE ban or the relative merits of MTBE and ethanol and (ii), by reference to the "general" approach required by Article 21(4) of the [1976] UNCITRAL Arbitration Rules, the Tribunal should rule on the USA's jurisdictional challenges as a preliminary question before holding any full hearing on the merits. On this approach, the USA proposed a procedure leading to an oral hearing in September 2003, lasting not more than three days. Methanex opposed the USA's application in its written and oral submissions. In summary, Methanex contended that the most efficient way to proceed would be a full hearing on the merits, with the Tribunal ruling on the USA's jurisdictional challenges in its final award. On this approach, Methanex proposed an evidential hearing of indeterminate length (but roughly estimated at eight days), originally suggested for January 2004 but on further reflection at the procedural meeting, two or more months later.

The choice for the Tribunal and the Disputing Parties is stark; the practical difference is significant; and whilst the choice is not complicated, the decision for the Tribunal was particularly difficult in this arbitration. After much consideration, given in particular the new shape of Methanex's pleaded case, we have decided broadly in favour of the procedure suggested by Methanex, subject to certain important explanations. Accordingly, the Tribunal decides not to rule as a preliminary question on the USA's extant jurisdictional challenges but, pursuant to the exceptional procedure set out in Article 21(4), second sentence, of the [1976] UNCITRAL Arbitration Rules, to join all such jurisdictional challenges to the merits of the dispute and to proceed to a main hearing currently intended to address all such issues (excluding issues of quantum), resulting in an award in which the Tribunal may rule on both jurisdictional and merit issues. This procedure requires the following time-table:
[Timetable omitted].

See also *Canfor Corp*, et al and *United States of America*, Decision on the Place of Arbitration, Filing of a Statement of Defence and Bifurcation of the Proceedings (January 23, 2004) (ICSID administered, 1976 UNCITRAL Rules, NAFTA Chapter Eleven), paras 46–48, reprinted in Chapter 13, section 3(C).

Canfor Corp, Tembec, Termination Forest Products Ltd and *United States of America*, Order of the Consolidated Tribunal (September 7, 2005) (footnotes omitted) (ICSID administered, 1976 UNCITRAL Rules, NAFTA Chapter Eleven), at 38–39:

97. Article 1126(2) provides that the Tribunal may issue an order to "assume jurisdiction over" all or part of the claims, or one or more claims, that have been submitted to arbitration under Article 1120. Article 1126(8) provides in turn: "A Tribunal established under Article 1120 shall not have jurisdiction to decide a claim, or a part of a claim, over which a Tribunal established under this Article has assumed jurisdiction." The meaning of the term "jurisdiction" in those provisions is examined below in the context of various arguments made with respect to that term.

98. It is argued that this working in Article 1126 means that an Article 1126 Tribunal cannot decide on objections to jurisdiction and, in the alternative, that, if a party requests consolidation, it waives the right to object to jurisdiction. The Consolidation Tribunal disagrees with those arguments for the following reasons.

100. In the case of an order for consolidation under Article 1126(2), the term "assume jurisdiction" in Article 1126(2) and (8) means nothing else than that the Article 1126 Tribunal takes over the proceedings, in the capacity of an arbitral tribunal, to hear and to determine the disputes from the respective Article 1120 Tribunals. That action is of a procedurally administrative nature, in which two or more arbitral tribunals are replaced by one arbitral tribunal with respect to the same dispute.

101. The assumption of jurisdiction in such a context does not have any relevance for the question of whether the jurisdiction of the Article 1120 Tribunals or of the Article 1126 Tribunal is justified. That question has to be addressed in context of Article 21 of the [1976] UNCITRAL Rules, either by the Article or, if the proceedings of the Article 1120 Tribunal have not reached the stage of a ruling on a plea as to jurisdiction by the Article 1126 Tribunal. A request under Article 1126, therefore, cannot be considered a waiver of the right to object to the jurisdiction of an arbitral tribunal, whether it be the Article 1120 one or the Article 1126 one, to hear and to determine a dispute.

102. For the same reasons, the Consolidation Tribunal rejects the argument that having submitted its statement of defence in *Canfor* and *Tembec* without raising any objection to the Article 1120 Tribunals' jurisdiction based on Article 1126, the United States' plea that the jurisdiction over the Claimants' claim properly lies within the Article 1126 Tribunal is untimely under the [1976] UNCITRAL Arbitration Rules. The invocation by a disputing

party of Article 1126 is not, by the ordinary meaning of its terms, a jurisdictional objection to an Article 1120 Tribunal. The issue of whether to consolidate is, as such, separate and apart from the issue jurisdiction.

103. A different question is whether a party can no longer raise a plea as to the jurisdiction in the Article 1126 proceedings if it has not timely raised such a plea in the Article 1120 arbitration. According to Article 21(3) of the [1976] UNCITRAL Arbitration Rules, the plea should have been raised not later than in the statement of defence. Although Article 1126 of the NAFTA (and the [1976] UNCITRAL Rules for that matter) are silent on this different question, the Consolidation Tribunal is of the opinion that this question must in principle be answered in the affirmative. Thus, if a party has failed to raise the pleas as to jurisdiction in the Article 1120 arbitration at the latest in the statement of defence (assuming that the Article 1120 arbitration has reached that stage), a party is in principle barred from raising the pleas in the consolidation proceedings.

D. Extracts from the Practice of the Iran–US Claims Tribunal

(1) Tribunal Rules (1983), Article 21(1)

Concurring and Dissenting Opinions of Howard M Holtzmann with respect to Interlocutory Awards on Jurisdiction in Nine Cases containing various Forum Selection Clauses, (November 5, 1982) at 20, n 26, reprinted in 1 Iran-US CTR 284, 294 (1981–82):

> Arbitral tribunals typically rule on whether they have jurisdiction. Indeed, this Tribunal's own rules—and the [1976] UNCITRAL Arbitration Rules on which they are based in accordance with the Claims Settlement Declaration—provide that the Tribunal shall have power to rule on the question of its own jurisdiction.

(2) Tribunal Rules (1983), Article 21(2)

Minutes of the 51st Full Tribunal Meeting of the Iran–US Claims Tribunal (May 14, 1982):

> During a discussion of Article 21(2), several members expressed views concerning the observation of the Government of Iran (page 4 of its letter) that it "cannot agree to Article 21(2), providing that an arbitration clause may remain valid despite the nullity of the contract." By 5 votes in favour to 1 against, with 2 abstentions, the Tribunal decided to maintain Article 21(2), and Article 21 of the [1976] UNCITRAL Rules as a whole, unchanged.

Concurring and Dissenting Opinions of Howard M Holtzmann with respect to Interlocutory Awards on Jurisdiction in Nine Cases Containing Various Forum Selection Clauses (November 5, 1982) at 16–17 (citation omitted):

> The enforceability of the forum selection clause is typically determined separately from the contract in which it is contained arbitration clauses—which are one kind of forum selection clause—are recognized in international law to be separate from the contract in which they are included. This international principle is reflected in the [1976] UNCITRAL Arbitration Rules...Article 21, paragraph 2.... So widespread is the doctrine of the independence of forum selection clauses that Sanders refers to it as "this famous question of separability" and notes that it "has given rise to many decisions in several countries" supporting this concept.

Dissenting and Concurring Opinion of Richard M Mosk on the Issues of Jurisdiction (November 5, 1982) at 6–7, reprinted in 1 Iran-US CTR 305, 308 (1981–82):

> Indeed, the Tribunal Rules themselves provide that an arbitration clause, which is a type of forum-selection clause, remains "binding" after the contract obligations have been breached or found invalid, [1983] Tribunal Rule 21, paragraph 2, thus, in effect, rendering such a clause separable from the contract.

(3) Tribunal Rules (1983), Article 21(3)

Chevron Research Co and *National Iranian Oil Co*, Case No 19, Chamber One, Order of November 19, 1982; *Sea-Land Service, Inc* and *Islamic Republic of Iran*, Case No 33, Chamber One, Order of November 19, 1982:

> The Statement of Defense filed by the Respondent does not raise any plea that the Tribunal does not have jurisdiction because Claimant has not produced evidence of its United States nationality. This issue was raised for the first time almost eight months later during the course of the Pre-Hearing conference. The objection was made without any evidence or reason being given which is sufficient to raise a substantial doubt as to Claimant's nationality. In these circumstances, the Tribunal finds that the objections to the Claimant's nationality have not been timely raised in accordance with Article 21, paragraph 3, of the [1983] Provisionally Adopted Tribunal Rules....

(4) Tribunal Rules (1983), Article 21(4)

Concurring and Dissenting Opinions of Howard M Holtzmann with respect to Interlocutory Awards on Jurisdiction in Nine Cases containing Various Forum Selection Clauses (November 5, 1982) at 2, reprinted in 1 Iran-US CTR 284–85 (1981–82):

> The Tribunal determined to consider and decide this threshold issue [effect of forum selection clauses] in accordance with procedure contemplated in the [1983] Provisionally Adopted Tribunal Rules...Article 21, Paragraph 4.

Starrett-Housing Corp and *Islamic Republic of Iran*, Interlocutory Award No ITL 32–24–1 (December 21, 1983), Dissenting Opinion of Mahmoud Kashani (September 13, 1984) at 23, reprinted in 7 Iran-US CTR 119, 135–36 (1984-III):

> In the Interlocutory Award, the majority has been content to deny Shah Goli's standing to bring claim before this Tribunal, but states, in an ambiguous and incomprehensible manner, that Shah Goli—through the Claimants—has *locus standi* in this case. I fail to comprehend just how, if Shah Goli has no legal standing, its lack of standing can be changed, "through the Claimants," to possession of standing, or just how this would result in bringing about the Tribunal's jurisdiction. This is some sort of acrobatics, and the Chamber must consider the issue of its nonjurisdiction as a preliminary issue in accordance with Article 21, paragraph 4 of the [1976] UNCITRAL Rules as soon as possible, so as to take a decision as to its lack of jurisdiction before burdening the Parties with any further trouble and expense.

Ghaffari and *Islamic Republic of Iran*, Case No 968, Chamber Two, Order of February 2, 1988, Dissenting Opinion of Judge Khalilian (February 10, 1988), reprinted in 18 Iran-US CTR 79 (1988-I):

> The above-mentioned Order represents a deviation from the practice adopted by all three Chambers of the Tribunal following the Decision in Case No A-18. In claims brought by dual nationals, it has always been the practice of the Tribunal to begin by taking up as a preliminary matter the issue of the claimant's dominant nationality, and on principle to refrain from entering into merits.
>
> Such a practice carries a special weight and authority, for two reasons. *Firstly*, in adopting this practice, the Tribunal has demonstrated that by following a general rule in international proceedings—namely the necessity of separating preliminary objections from the merits—it saves the parties from making an unnecessary waste of energy, time and expense. *Secondly*, the practice can be regarded as an interpretive policy as regards the Decision in Case No A-18 with respect to the adjudicative process in related cases, so that any deviation therefrom can also be deemed to constitute a breach of the spirit of the Full Tribunal's Decision.

For the foregoing reasons, I dissent to the Order in question. These two points are elaborated on as follows:

(a) The principle of the necessity of two-stage proceedings

The basis for the necessity to separate proceedings on jurisdictional objections as an important preliminary issue in the claims of dual nationals may be found, first of all, in the Rules of this very Tribunal where, as a general and peremptory rule, Article 21.4 [of the 1983 Tribunal Rules] provides as follows:

> In general, the arbitral tribunal *should* rule on a plea concerning its jurisdiction as a preliminary question... (emphasis added)

This Article states that it is incumbent upon the Tribunal to make a preliminary examination of jurisdictional pleas. Although the Tribunal has also been given the option of joining the merits to the justifiable grounds, since it constitutes a deviation from the aforementioned principle. Otherwise, the Tribunal may not, arbitrarily and without justification, depart from the rule set forth in the beginning of Article 21.4 [of the 1983 Tribunal Rules], a rule which reflects an international practice in proceedings and whose rationale is well stated by Mani, as follows:

> It is not difficult to perceive the rationale of the concept. In the first place, it is in the interest of sound administration of justice, that, a tribunal should, before first examining the rights or interests in dispute, satisfy itself that there exist no legal obstacle paralysing the action... Fifth, the party has a right to have its claim recognized by a competent tribunal, *the other party has an equal right to see that it is not unnecessarily dragged into an international litigation before a tribunal before which the claim is either non-receivable or otherwise barred. Moreover, preliminary objection procedure demonstrates that the basis of international jurisdiction is the sovereign consent of States.* (emphasis added) Mani, *International Adjudication*, 1980, at 123–4. *See also:* Sir G Fitzmaurice, *The Law and Procedure of the International Court of Justice*, 1986 vol. II, at 758.

Moreover, the Tribunal's practice in numerous other instances, particularly in cases involving a "forum selection clause," confirms its respect for the said principle.

(b) The policy of the three Chambers towards interpretation of Decision No 32-A18-FT

The practice adopted by the three Chambers in dealing with the issue of the dominant nationality of Iranians who have brought claim against their Government may be regarded as an interpretative policy which reflects the spirit of the Full Tribunal's Decision in Case No A-18. Chamber Three states this fact very clearly and unambiguously in its Orders issued in Cases Nos 12756 (Doc. No 24) and 213 (Doc. No 64), as follows:

> The Tribunal notes that the Full Tribunal in the abovementioned Decision held that "it has jurisdiction over claims against Iran by dual Iran-US nationals when the dominant and effective nationality of the claimant during the relevant period from the date the claim arose until 19 January 1981 was that of the United States.
>
> *In previous cases the Tribunal has interpreted this Decision to imply that the issue of the Claimant's nationality should be determined as a preliminary matter.* (emphasis added)

It can thus be easily understood that establishing the dominant nationality of such Iranian claimants is, in the opinion of the Full Tribunal, at least as important as determining its jurisdiction in cases involving a "forum selection clause." Therefore, in implementation of the procedural principle set forth in Article 21.4, this matter should certainly be taken up as a preliminary issue and separated from the merits.

It is also worth noting that Chamber Two has to date adhered to this same practice. Thus, for instance, in Case No 385, after it was learned that the shareholders in the claimant company were Iranian nationals, the Chamber issued an Order wherein it stated that:

> ... the Tribunal agrees [with Respondents] that this Case raises questions concerning the U.S. nationality of the Claimant in view of the alleged dual nationality of the shareholders, and therefore

decides to determine as a preliminary matter, the issue of Claimant's nationality. (Doc. No 138)

In Case No 298 too, Chamber Two, in expressly relying on and quoting from the Decision Case No A-18, proceeded on the basis of this same separation of jurisdiction from the merits and as already observed, all three Chambers have consistently followed this established policy.

Bank Markazi Iran and *Federal Reserve Bank of New York*, Award No 595–823–3 (November 16, 1999), Dissenting Opinion of Mohsen Aghahosseini (June 13, 2000), at 26:

> Our own Tribunal Rules prescribe a more flexible approach. As indicated in Article 21(4) [of the 1983 Tribunal Rules], there is no strict requirement to suspend the proceedings on the merits before deciding the issue of jurisdiction, though this is recommended:
>
> In general, the arbitral tribunal should rule on a plea concerning its jurisdiction as a preliminary question. However, the arbitral tribunal may proceed with the arbitration and rule on such a plea in their final award.[46]
>
> [Footnote] 46. In fact, the Tribunal has at times suspended the proceedings on the merits, especially when there has been a request to that effect. Thus, this very Chamber has stated, in respect of Article 21(4) of the [1983] Tribunal Rules, that: "The intention of this provision is to relieve both the Tribunal and the Parties from the burden of further pleadings and expenses involved in pursuing the claim, since, if the Tribunal determines that it lacks jurisdiction, it will not be required to rule on the merits of the claim. The Tribunal therefore concludes that it is appropriate to decide the issue as preliminary matter …" Doc. No 23 in Case No 11429, Chamber Three.

Islamic Republic of Iran and *United States of America* (Case No B1), Award No ITL 83-B1-FT (September 9, 2004):

> 140. Iran also contends that the Tribunal is without jurisdiction to entertain the Counter-claim in this Case. In this connection, Iran maintains that the United States has not established that the Counter-claim was outstanding on 19 January 1981 and that the Counter-claim does not arise out of the same contracts as Iran's claims in Case No B1. Iran also argues that the Counter-claim is not cognizable.
>
> 141. In accordance with its powers under Article 21(4) of the [1983] Tribunal Rules, the Tribunal decides to join to the merits the issues of whether it has jurisdiction over the Counter-claim in the present Case, and of whether the Counter-claim is cognizable. In light of the above, the Tribunal need not decide now whether its jurisdiction over the Counter-claim would be limited to a set-off: that issue is also joined to the merits.

15

Amendments to the Claim or Defence

1. Introduction	467
2. Amendments to the Claim or Defence—Article 22	467
A. Text of the 2010 UNCITRAL Rule	467
B. Commentary	468
(1) General	468
(2) The amendment must not fall outside the jurisdiction of the arbitral tribunal	469
(3) Grounds for rejecting an amendment: delay, prejudice or other circumstances	471
(4) Procedural questions	474
(5) Comparison to the 1976 UNCITRAL Rules	475
C. Extracts from the Practice of Investment Tribunals	475
D. Extracts from the Practice of the Iran–US Claims Tribunal	479

1. Introduction

A party may wish to modify its claim or defence in the course of the arbitral proceedings. For practical and economic reasons, the tribunal should maintain a flexible attitude towards accepting such modifications, as the alternative may be the commencement of new arbitral proceedings. Giving a party an unlimited right to make amendments, however, could be prejudicial to the other party and hamper the orderly conduct of the proceedings. Article 22 of the 2010 UNCITRAL Rules seeks to balance these competing interests.

2. Amendments to the Claim or Defence—Article 22

A. Text of the 2010 UNCITRAL Rule[1]

Article 22 of the 2010 UNCITRAL Rules provides:

During the course of the arbitral proceedings, a party may amend or supplement its claim or defence, including a counterclaim or a claim for the purpose of a set-off, unless the arbitral tribunal considers it inappropriate to allow such amendment or supplement having regard to the delay in making it or prejudice to the other parties or any other circumstances. However, a claim or defence, including a counterclaim or a claim for the purpose of a

---

[1] Corresponding Article 20 of the 1976 UNCITRAL Rules provides:

During the course of the arbitral proceedings either party may amend or supplement his claim or defence unless the arbitral tribunal considers it inappropriate to allow such amendment having regard to the delay in making it or prejudice to the other party or any other circumstances. However, a claim may not be amended in such a manner that the amended claim falls outside the scope of the arbitration clause or separate arbitration agreement.

set-off, may not be amended or supplemented in such a manner that the amended or supplemented claim or defence falls outside the jurisdiction of the arbitral tribunal.

B. Commentary

(1) General

Key aspects of Article 22 can be understood by reference to the *travaux préparatoires* of corresponding Article 20 of the 1976 UNCITRAL Rules, which is identical in purpose and scope. The article on statement of claims in the Preliminary Draft of the 1976 UNCITRAL Rules contained a provision that "the claim may, with the permission of the arbitrators, be supplemented or altered provided the respondent is given opportunity to express his opinion concerning the change."[2] In the course of the drafting process, the provision in question was not only converted into a separate article that became Article 20 of the 1976 UNCITRAL Rules,[3] but it was also modified in two basic respects.

First, in accordance with the principle of equality,[4] the right to make amendments was extended in the final version of original Article 20 to include defences. Revised Article 22 reflects the same approach but, unlike original Article 20, also expressly clarifies that in terms of defences a party may amend or supplement a counterclaim or claim for a set-off.[5]

Second, instead of stating that amendments are possible with "the permission of the arbitrators" (the wording of the Preliminary Draft), the final version of the original Article 20 stipulates that "either party may amend or supplement his claim or defence unless the arbitral tribunal considers it inappropriate …" Article 22 of the 2010 UNCITRAL Rules does not substantively change this formulation. The shift in emphasis from the Preliminary Draft to original Article 20, and now revised Article 22, is significant because it makes clear that the acceptance of amendments by the arbitral tribunal is not entirely discretionary.[6] Rather, a party has a right to make amendments, which should be accepted by the tribunal, provided they remain within the limits defined by Article 22.[7] The UNCITRAL Rules have thereby adopted a "liberal approach" towards the question of a party's right to make

---

[2] *Report of the Secretary-General on the Preliminary Draft Set of Arbitration Rules*, UNCITRAL, 8th Session, UN Doc A/CN.9/97 (1974), reprinted in (1975) VI UNCITRAL Ybk 163, 173–4 (Draft Article 16(3)).

[3] In the UNCITRAL Model Law, as amended, on the other hand, the provision on amendments is found in Article 23(2) on "Statements of Claim and Defence." Paragraph 2 reads as follows: "Unless otherwise agreed by the parties, either party may amend or supplement his claim or defence during the course of the arbitral proceedings, unless the arbitral tribunal considers it inappropriate to allow such amendment having regard for the delay in making it."

[4] See Chapter 2, discussing Article 17(1).

[5] As explained in, section 2(B)(5), even without this express language, Article 20 of the 1976 UNCITRAL Rules should nevertheless be interpreted to cover amendments to counterclaims and claims for set-off.

[6] See *United Parcel Service of America, Inc* (1976 Rules), para 131, reprinted in section 2(C) ("While the tribunal may exercise control over amendments, its leave need not be sought in the first instance.").

[7] The *travaux préparatoires* indicate that the change of the wording was intended to effectuate the kind of clarification suggested. See *Report of the UNCITRAL on the Work of its Ninth Session*, UN GAOR, 31st Session, Supp No 17, UN Doc A/31/17, para 96 (1976), reprinted in (1976) VII UNCITRAL Ybk 66, 73. For the relevant discussion in the Committee, see *Summary Record of the 7th Meeting of the Committee of the Whole (II)*, UNCITRAL, 9th Session, UN Doc A/CN.9/9/C.2/SR.7, at 4–7, paras 23–46 (1976). See also S Baker and M Davis, *The UNCITRAL Arbitration Rules in Practice: The Experience of the Iran-United States Claims Tribunal* (1992) 92 (concluding that "the *travaux* clearly show that the tribunal's authority is not meant to discourage legitimate amendments to claims and defences, but rather to prevent frivolous or vexatious amendments").

amendments.[8] This interpretation accords with a widely recognized arbitral principle concerning the subject matter of amendments. In arbitration, unlike judicial proceedings, the arbitration agreement sets limits to the jurisdiction of the tribunal.[9] Within these limits, the scope of the proceedings, and, correspondingly, the scope of any amendments are foreseeable to the parties. A "liberal approach" towards amendments is therefore appropriate.

(2) *The amendment must not fall outside the jurisdiction of the arbitral tribunal*

As the preceding discussion implies, there must be limits to the right to amend a claim or defence. A *prima facie* absolute limitation is set by the arbitral tribunal's jurisdiction as defined in the arbitration clause, agreement, or other applicable legal instrument, such as an international investment agreement.[10] As the second sentence of Article 22 states, "a claim or defence... may not be amended or supplemented in such a manner that the amended or supplemented claim or defence falls outside the jurisdiction of the arbitral tribunal."[11] Such a claim or defence cannot be characterized as an "amendment" or "supplement" of the original; it is rather a new claim over which the arbitral tribunal lacks jurisdiction.[12] This is the case where, for example, the amendment seeks to bring into the proceedings an entity which was not a party to the agreement forming the basis of the arbitration, though it might somehow have been involved in the subject matter of the arbitration (for example, a turnkey project with many parties). It is possible to bring an entirely new party into the proceedings by way of an amendment, provided that the amendment keeps within the limits of the arbitration agreement (ie, the new party is bound by the agreement) and meets the other conditions set forth in Article 22,[13] and Article 17(5) on joinder. Borderline cases are, however, conceivable. For example, depending on the construction of the contract and its arbitration clause, or the arbitration agreement, the specification of a wholly-owned subsidiary of the

---

[8] See *Intl Schools Services, Inc* (1983 Tribunal Rules) and Judge Aldrich's separate opinion in *Westinghouse Electric Corp* (1983 Tribunal Rules), both reprinted in section 2(D). On the Tribunal's practice in general, see also J van Hof, *Commentary on the UNCITRAL Arbitration Rules: The Application by the Iran-U.S. Claims Tribunal* (1991) 136–41; J Castello, "UNCITRAL Rules," in F Weigand (ed), *Practitioner's Handbook on International Commercial Arbitration Second Edition* (2nd edn 2009) 1482.

[9] For general commentary on jurisdictional requirements for counterclaims or set-offs, see N Blackaby and C Partasides with A Redfern and M Hunter, *Redfern and Hunter on International Arbitration* (5th edn 2009) 383–4.

[10] See *Merrill & Ring Forestry L P* and *Government of Canada*, Decision on a Motion to Add a New Party (January 31, 2008) (ICSID administered, 1976 UNCITRAL Rules, NAFTA Chapter Eleven Arbitration), at 6, para 18 (finding that corresponding Article 20 of the 1976 UNCITRAL Rules "contains an overall and absolute prohibition against introducing amendments which go beyond the scope of the arbitration clause").

[11] The "claim" which is subject to amendment is typically set forth in the Statement of Claim or Statement of Defence, not the Notice of Arbitration. See *Himpurna California Energy Ltd* (1976 Rules), reprinted in section 2(C). See also *Ethyl Corp* (1976 Rules); and *Methanex Corp* (1976 Rules), Award of August 3, 2005; both reprinted in section 2(C).

[12] This being the case, one can say that the limitation on the power to make amendments, put forward in the second sentence of Article 22, is "inherent" in that it would exist even without the explicit provision in question. In Article 23(2) of the Model Law, as amended, (see n 3) there is no provision corresponding to the second sentence of Article 22 of the UNCITRAL Rules. Yet it is clear that the Model Law as amended in 2006 also prohibits amendments going beyond the arbitration agreement. See H Holtzmann and J Neuhaus, *A Guide to the UNCITRAL Model Law on International Commercial Arbitration: Legislative History and Commentary* (1989) 649.

[13] See *Fedders Corp* (1983 Tribunal Rules); and *Vivian Mai Tavakoli* (1983 Tribunal Rules), both reprinted in section 2(D). In *ad hoc* arbitration, the arbitration clause or agreement usually cannot be interpreted to cover so many parties as is the case with the jurisdiction of the Iran–US Claims Tribunal as defined in Article VII of the Claims Settlement Declaration. For a general discussion on the issues involved in adding a new party to an arbitral proceeding, see J Levine, "Current Trends in International Arbitral Practice as Reflected in the Revision of the UNCITRAL Arbitration Rules" (2009) 31(1)U New South Wales L J 266.

original claimant/respondent as the proper party (instead of, or in addition to, the parent company) could be viewed as an acceptable clarification of the claim, rather than as a new claim falling outside the tribunal's jurisdiction.[14]

On the other hand, where the arbitral tribunal has doubts about the compatibility of the purported amendment with the arbitration clause or agreement, it should proceed with caution before accepting amendments, despite the generally liberal spirit of Article 22. A court challenge on the ground of lack of jurisdiction is a concrete risk which may affect the validity and enforceability of an international arbitral award.[15] Of course, where possible, the parties may conclude a new arbitration agreement and thereby extend the jurisdiction of the arbitral tribunal. In principle, an amendment proposed by one party, if acceptable to the other, may constitute such an agreement.[16]

---

[14] Although in the 1983 Rules of Procedure of the Iran–US Claims Tribunal the second sentence of Article 22 has been modified (see Appendix 5), the Tribunal's practice is illustrative from a more general point of view. Thus even in *ad hoc* arbitration the substitution of a new claimant (not party to the arbitration agreement or clause) would normally mean a new claim falling outside the arbitral tribunal's jurisdiction. The exception to this rule is where it is clear from the circumstances that the original claim concerned on its face the newly introduced party which is owned and controlled by the party in whose name the original claim was submitted. See Refusal Case Nos 20 and 21 (1983 Tribunal Rules), reprinted in section 2(D). As regards *ad hoc* arbitration, whether in circumstances like those in Refusal Case No 20 this kind of modification would be acceptable depends on whether the arbitration clause or agreement could be interpreted to encompass disputes immediately concerning subsidiary or the like dependent companies of the original claimant. Similar considerations would apply to cases such as *American Intl Group*, et al and *Islamic Republic of Iran*, et al, Award No 93–2–3 (December 19, 1983), reprinted in 4 Iran-US CTR 96 (1983-III), in which part of the shares, the nationalization of which was at issue, were owned by the main claimant's wholly owned subsidiary (ALICO), which was not originally named as claimant. The Tribunal accepted the amendment, as it did "not change the amount sought or the factual or legal basis of the claim and cannot be said to prejudice the Respondent." Similarly, the specification of the proper respondent would not be prohibited where the original claim (although not addressed against that respondent) indicated that respondent as party to the transaction in question, and the arbitration clause or agreement can be interpreted to have been concluded on behalf of that party. See *Kimberly-Clark* (1983 Tribunal Rules), reprinted in section 2(D). See also ICC Case No 1434 of 1975, partly reproduced in (1976) 103 Journal du droit international 978. In that case, a state enterprise of a developing country claimed against a multinational group of companies which had contracted to build and operate a company in the country. The arbitration clauses in various contracts in question were of such a nature as to create confusion concerning the parties. Some of the companies challenged the jurisdiction of the tribunal over them. The arbitral tribunal, however, held it was the true intention of the parties that all companies could be subjected to the same arbitral proceedings. The case (in which the amendments were not at issue) is commented upon in J Paulsson, "Third World Participation in International Investment Arbitration," (1987) 2 ICSID Rev–Foreign Investment L J 19, 25–6.

In one investor–state arbitration case, the tribunal rejected the claimants request to amend its claim by adding the claim of its business affiliate. *Merrill & Ring Forestry LP* and *Government of Canada*, Decision on Motion to Add a New Party (January 31, 2008) (ICSID administered, 1976 UNCITRAL Rules, NAFTA Chapter Eleven). Among other reasons, the affiliate's apparent failure to satisfy certain basic jurisdictional requirements of the NAFTA gave the tribunal cause for rejecting the request. Paras 23, 29–30.

[15] In 1984, the Paris Court of Appeal set aside an ICC award rendered in Paris for lack of jurisdiction, in what is known as the *Pyramids* case. The award was successfully challenged by the Egyptian Government, a respondent in the arbitration, who denied that its written approval of the agreement in question on the signature page meant that the Government was a party to the agreement. For the text of the award, see *SPP (Middle East) Ltd and Southern Pacific Properties Ltd and Arab Republic of Egypt and the Egyptian General Co for Tourism and Hotels*, (1983) 22 ILM 752. The Judgment of the Paris court is reproduced in English in (1984) 23 ILM 1048, the affirmation of that decision by the *Cour de Cassation* in (1987) 26 ILM 1004. See also A Redfern and M Hunter, *Law and Practice of International Commercial Arbitration* (2nd edn 1991) 439–41. After the annulment, the claimant instituted proceedings under the auspices of ICSID. These proceedings led to an award on the merits in 1992. See *Southern Pacific (Middle East) Ltd* and *Arab Republic of Egypt*, Case No ARB 84/3, Award of May 20, 1992, reprinted in (1993) 32 ILM 933. See also P Sanders, "Commentary on UNCITRAL Arbitration Rules," (1977) II Ybk Commercial Arb 206 (observing "the arbitrators should not hesitate to reject an amendment of the claim which falls outside the scope of the arbitration agreement").

[16] See H Holtzmann and J Neuhaus, n 12, 649; M Aden, *Internationale Handelsschhiedsgerichtsbarkeit* (1988) 235.

(3) Grounds for rejecting an amendment: delay, prejudice or other circumstances

Whereas the second sentence of Article 22, discussed above, concerns proposed amendments which fall outside the jurisdiction of the arbitral tribunal, the first sentence of Article 22 regulates situations where the amendment alters the subject matter of the original claim or defence as defined, respectively, in the statement of claim or statement of defence.[17] Thus, the amendment must satisfy the conditions of the second sentence before it may be considered under the criteria enunciated in the first sentence.

An amendment that falls within the jurisdiction of the tribunal should be accepted unless it is inappropriate to do so on grounds of: (1) delay, (2) prejudice to the other parties,[18] or (3) any other circumstances. In the words of one leading arbitral tribunal, "the Tribunal must consider whether the other Party would be prejudiced by the proposed amendment, whether the other party has had an opportunity to respond to the newly-added or amended claim, and whether the proposed amendment would needlessly disrupt or delay the arbitral process."[19] The amendment may be inappropriate on a single ground, although in practice more often than not a combination of various interrelated grounds will lead to its rejection.

Under Article 22, the amendment should be rejected if it causes inordinate delay.[20] Whether the delay can be accepted depends, in part, on the reasons why the amendment was not submitted earlier. Delays may be due to circumstances beyond the control of the party seeking the amendment, or excusable for corresponding reasons—for example, the documentary evidence on which the amendment is based has become accessible to the party during the arbitral proceedings through a "discovery" procedure.[21] Delays in these cases will be more readily accepted than in those cases where the party could at the outset have raised the arguments put forward in the proposed amendment.[22]

The acceptance or rejection of the amendment will seldom be based on delay alone;[23] rather the acceptability of the delay will normally be assessed by weighing it against the criterion of "appropriateness" listed in Article 22, ie, possible prejudice to the other party.[24]

---

[17] See *Summary Record of the 7th Meeting of the Committee of the Whole (II)*, UNCITRAL, 9th Session, UN Doc A/CN.9/9/C.2/SR.7, at 5, para 27 (1976) (Comment by Mr Sanders, Special Consultant).
[18] According to Castello, use of the word "parties," as opposed to "party," as appeared in the 1976 version of the rule, is to ensure that the arbitral tribunal takes into consideration prejudice to any of the parties. J Castello, "UNCITRAL Rules," n 8, 1483.
[19] *Harris Intl Telecommunications* (1983 Tribunal Rules), para 85, reprinted in section 2(D). See also *Shahin Shaine Ebrahimi* (1983 Tribunal Rules), reprinted in section 2(D).
[20] See *Merrill & Ring Forestry* (1976 Rules), para 30, reprinted in section 2(C) (rejecting request for amendment because it would delay proceedings by "a number of months"); see *Mohsen Asgari Nazari* (1983 Tribunal Rules), para 11, reprinted in section 2(D) (rejecting request for amendment because of "significant lapse of time involved").
[21] See *Frederica Lincoln Riahi* (1983 Tribunal Rules), reprinted in section 2(D). See also discussion on Article 24(3) in Chapter 16.
[22] See *Sedco Inc* and *Iranian National Oil Co and Islamic Republic of Iran*, Case No 129, Order of January 6, 1986, reprinted in Mealey's Litigation Rep: Iranian Claims 3705 (February 7, 1986). See also *Westinghouse Electric Corp* (1983 Tribunal Rules), reprinted in section 2(D) (rejecting claimant's request at the final hearing to amend its claim by adding an additional remedy).
[23] But see *Arthur Young & Co* (1983 Tribunal Rules), reprinted in section 2(D) ("the Tribunal is to consider delay as . . . a criterion independent from 'prejudice to the other party' . . .").
[24] See Article 23(2) of the Model Law, as amended, where only "delay" is specifically mentioned as a bar to the acceptability of amendments. However, "[t]he result is probably a shift in emphasis rather than an absolute bar on considerations of any factors that might be considered under the [1976] UNCITRAL Arbitration Rules." H Holtzmann and J Neuhaus, *A Guide to the UNCITRAL Model Law on International Commercial Arbitration*, n 12, 649. The authors continue: ". . . it appears to have been intended that prejudice to the other party should be taken into account as a function considering the delay in making the amendment. . ." 649. See *Jack Buckamier* (1983 Tribunal Rules), para 23, reprinted in section 2(D).

An amendment prejudices the other party where it is raised so late as to deprive that party of the opportunity to defend itself properly.[25] An amendment made after the case has been heard on the merits or after the scheduled exchange of written pleadings will therefore only rarely be accepted.[26] The reaction of the party potentially prejudiced by the amendment is of considerable—if not decisive—importance in assessing that prejudice. The Iran–US Claims Tribunal, in some cases, cited the absence of any objection alleging prejudice as a factor for accepting an amendment.[27]

Where such objections are raised, the tribunal must assess their merit in light of all the circumstances. In addition to timeliness, the nature of the proposed amendment must be considered. The tribunal should not immediately reject amendments that change or modify arguments opposed to those that change or modify the factual circumstances as presented in the statement of claim or the relief sought. The presentation of "unjust enrichment" as an alternative legal theory for what originally has been put forward as a contract or expropriation claim in our view is acceptable, provided the other party has an opportunity to respond to it.[28] Nor should the introduction of new facts be considered an amendment of the claim when they merely support existing claims.[29] An amendment seeking an increase in the amount of relief sought should not automatically be barred either, provided that relief is sought on the basis of the original allegations.[30] Hence, where a claim for warehousing charges is added to an original claim based on alleged costs of repairs of equipment held in the warehouse, the factual basis of the claim is not changed so as to warrant the rejection of an amendment.[31] Amendments concerning increases in interest and costs are least likely to cause undue prejudice.[32] Indeed, there is seldom a reason not to accept the presentation of such ancillary claims at a late stage of the proceedings.

On the other hand, prejudice may more easily be established when the amendment contains a claim that is truly new in the sense of being based on a new contract or on factual

---

[25] See, eg, *Reza Said Malek* (1983 Tribunal Rules), reprinted in section 2(D) (amendment submitted eight months after the statement of claim and one month prior to the statement of defence accepted). See T Webster, *Handbook of UNCITRAL Arbitration: Commentary, Precedents and Materials for UNCITRAL Based Arbitration Rules* (2010) 325 (observing "if a new claim is raised in a responsive pleading rather than in a submission shortly before the evidentiary hearing, then the claim is less disruptive and the delay is much less substantial.")

[26] See *Flexi-Van Leasing, Inc* and *Islamic Republic of Iran*, Award No 259-36-1 (October 13, 1986), reprinted in 12 Iran-US CTR 335, 346 n 9 (1986-III) ("Insofar as the Claimant, in its Post-Hearing Memorial to which no written answer was given, purports to modify the essence of the bases of its claim, such modification is not admissible."). In contrast, a request to amend the claim raised even on the last day of the jurisdictional hearing did not cause prejudice because, in light of the tribunal's ruling that it had jurisdiction, the parties could adjust the briefing schedule to allow the respondent time to address the amended claim, and because rejecting the request for amendment would require the claimant to initiate a second, separate arbitration. See *Grand River Enterprises* (1983 Tribunal Rules), reprinted in section 2(C).

[27] See *McCullough* (1983 Tribunal Rules); *Sylvania* (1983 Tribunal Rules); both reprinted in section 2(D). See also *Bank Markazi Iran* (1983 Tribunal Rules), reprinted in section 2(D).

[28] See *Cal-Maine Food* (1983 Tribunal Rules), second quoted paragraph, and *Aeronutronic Overseas Services* (1983 Tribunal Rules); both reprinted in section 2(D). In *Dallal* (1983 Tribunal Rules), reprinted in section 2(D), an amendment presenting unjust enrichment as an alternative legal theory was rejected. The amendment, however, was sought very late, in a post-hearing brief.

[29] See *EnCana* (1976 Rules), reprinted in section 2(C).

[30] See *Intl Schools Services* (1983 Tribunal Rules); *Thomas Earl Payne* (1983 Tribunal Rules) (amendment increasing the amount of compensation accepted, although it involved a new valuation method); *Fereydoon Ghaffari* (1983 Tribunal Rules) (the amount claimed increased, but the "essence of the claim" remained the same); and *Jack Buckamier* (1983 Tribunal Rules), paras 28–29 (while the lost profits in question had not been sought in the original claim, the "basis" for the amended claim was set forth in the Statement of Claim); all reprinted in section 2(D).

[31] See *Litton Systems* (1983 Tribunal Rules), reprinted in section 2(D).

[32] See *Pepsico Inc* (1983 Tribunal Rules), reprinted in section 2(D).

circumstances different from those relied on in the original claim (though not in the sense of exceeding the arbitration clause or agreement).[33] Such is the case where the claimant "seeks an amendment adding a different kind of relief, which raises new factual and legal issues."[34] Although the liberal main tenet of Article 22 accepts even such fundamental amendments if they are raised soon after submission of the statement of claim, rejection may be quite appropriate if the amendment is not sought until a relatively late stage of the proceedings.

The *Cal-Maine* case decided by the Iran–US Claims Tribunal is illustrative. On the basis of the original Article 20 (now Article 22 with minor revisions), the Tribunal rejected a new claim that was raised in the Memorial submitted one and a half years after the filing of the statement of claim and four months before the Hearing, while it acccpted a simultaneous amendment which sought to modify the legal theory behind the original portion of the Claimant's claim.[35] The amendment rejected in *Cal-Maine* can also be compared with that accepted in *McCollough*[36] against the respondent's objection. Whereas in the former case the new claim concerned a legal relationship between the parties which differed from that of the original claim, in the latter case the new claim was based on the very same factual circumstances and alleged infractions which formed the basis of the statement of claim.

According to Article 22, "other circumstances" in addition to delay and prejudice may render an amendment inappropriate. It is somewhat difficult to conceive of additional circumstances that could independently, ie, apart from delay and prejudice, have this effect.[37] The provision can perhaps be interpreted as giving the arbitral tribunal discretion to reject an amendment, even where there is neither inexcusable delay nor any allegation of prejudice, if accepting the amendment (with the consequent opportunity for the other party to respond) would be per se prejudicial to orderly proceedings.[38] Such discretion, however, should be applied restrictively. A disruption of orderly proceedings so severe as to justify the rejection of an amendment would thus seem to be a rare possibility.

---

[33] See *Methanex Corp* (1976 Rules), Award, reprinted in section 2(C).

[34] *Arthur Young & Co* (1983 Tribunal Rules), reprinted in section 2(D). See also *Westinghouse Electric Corp* (1983 Tribunal Rules), reprinted in section 2(D).

[35] *Cal-Maine Foods* (1983 Tribunal Rules), reprinted in section 2(D). See also *Arthur Young & Co* (1983 Tribunal Rules), reprinted in section 2(D).

[36] *McCollough Co* (1983 Tribunal Rules), reprinted in section 2(D).

[37] In *Merrill & Ring Forestry* (1976 Rules), para 31, reprinted in section 2(C), the tribunal found that the assertion of a new claim by a new claimant constituted "other circumstances" that confirmed its decision to reject an amendment.

Note that an authoritative source interpreting corresponding Article 20 of the 1976 UNCITRAL Rules has suggested that the second sentence of the original Article 20 prohibiting amendments falling outside the scope of the arbitration agreement might "be regarded as one of the 'other circumstances'… under which the arbitral tribunal will consider the amendment as inappropriate." P Sanders, "Commentary on UNCITRAL Arbitration Rules," n 15, 206; see also *Fedders Corp* (1983 Tribunal Rules), reprinted in section 2(D) ("a party may amend its claim, unless delay, prejudice or loss of jurisdiction would result"). This does not on its face appear persuasive, as the second sentence contains in principle an absolute limit to amendments, whereas the grounds of inappropriateness mentioned in the first sentence (including "other circumstances") are relative and subject to the discretion of the arbitral tribunal. See Rauh, Karlheinz, *Die Schieds- und Schlichtungsordnungen der UNCITRAL* (1983) 97–8.

[38] See *Harris Intl Telecommunications* (1983 Tribunal Rules), reprinted in section 2(D) ("the proposed amendment would needlessly disrupt or delay the arbitral process."). In the *Himpurna* case, the Tribunal concluded that the phrase "other circumstances" takes into account not only "the fair and efficient administration of arbitral justice," but also "the good principle that procedural rules should not be conceived and applied in such a fashion as to impel the parties to adopt maximalist and confrontational positions." See *Himpurna California Energy Ltd* (1976 Rules), para 113, reprinted in section 2(C). See also T Webster, *Handbook of UNCITRAL Arbitration*, n 25, 326 (noting "other circumstances" might include where "the party proposing the amendments has systematically sought to delay or complicate the proceedings").

There may be borderline cases where it is hard to determine whether the purported amendment falls outside the jurisdiction of the arbitral tribunal. In such cases, the "other circumstances" ground gives the tribunal the opportunity to reject an amendment in order to protect the award from possible attacks before courts,[39] even where the arbitrators find that the amendment more likely than not falls within the limits of the arbitration clause or agreement. In general, the reference to "other circumstances" implies that the decision on amendment should always be based on an assessment of the situation as a whole, keeping in mind that the UNCITRAL Rules have intentionally adopted a liberal approach towards the acceptability of amendments. In keeping with this spirit, the Iran–US Claims Tribunal has emphasized that circumstances which would preclude the acceptance of an amendment should be concrete.[40] Parties that are not satisfied with the liberal approach of the Rules can, of course, modify Article 22 to preclude any amendments to the claims and defences.[41]

(4) Procedural questions

A tribunal could determine whether to accept an amendment as a preliminary issue or as an issue joined to the merits.[42] Although both approaches are possible, amendments sought at a relatively early stage of the proceedings should be decided quickly, to remove any uncertainty as to which points the parties have to concentrate on in their subsequent pleadings. Since Article 22 acknowledges the party's right to amend his claim or defence, the arbitral tribunal cannot be required in every case to get the other party's comments on the acceptability of concrete amendments. If, however, there are any *prima facie* reasons why the amendment might be prejudicial to the other party, it should not be accepted without providing that party an opportunity to comment on the acceptability of the amendment.[43] If the amendment ultimately proves to be inappropriate or frivolous, the amending party may be required to compensate the other party for any costs incurred in responding to the amendment.[44]

Determining the admissibility of an amendment is arguably a procedural matter for the presiding arbitrator to decide according to the conditions set by Article 33(2) of the UNCITRAL Rules.[45] It is, however, advisable that the tribunal ratify any such decision which may have been made by the chairman of the arbitral tribunal in its final award.[46]

---

[39] *Handbook of UNCITRAL Arbitration*, n 25, 326.

[40] See *Intl Schools Services* (1983 Tribunal Rules); *Harris Intl Telecommunications* (1983 Tribunal Rules); both reprinted in section 2(D). See also S Baker and M Davis, *The UNCITRAL Arbitration Rules in Practice*, n 7, 92. It is worth noting that the "other circumstances" ground was omitted from the Model Law for fear that it would give too much discretion to the arbitrators to reject an amendment. See H Holtzmann and J Neuhaus, *A Guide to the UNCITRAL Model Law on International Commercial Arbitration*, n 12, 648–9.

[41] See Article 23(2) of the Model Law, as amended, see n 3.

[42] In practice some tribunals have provisionally admitted new claims, while reserving a final ruling until a subsequent phase of the arbitration. See, eg, *Chevron Corp*, et al and *Republic of Ecuador*, Interim Award (December 1, 2008) (PCA administered, 1976 UNCITRAL Rules, US-Ecuador BIT), para 27.

[43] See *Tai, Inc* (1983 Tribunal Rules), reprinted in section 2(D).

[44] See *Methanex Corp* (1976 Rules), Partial Award, reprinted in section 2(C).

[45] Article 33(2) provides: "In the case of questions of procedure, when there is no majority or when the arbitral tribunal so authorizes, the presiding arbitrator may decide on his own, subject to revision, if any, by the arbitral tribunal." According to paragraph 1, the majority requirement is the main rule concerning the decision-making. For more in-depth discussion, see Chapter 23 on decision-making by the arbitral tribunal.

[46] See *Harold Birnbaum* (1983 Tribunal Rules), reprinted in section 2(D).

(5) Comparison to the 1976 UNCITRAL Rules

Article 22 is identical to corresponding Article 20 of the 1976 UNCITRAL Rules in its object and purpose. The Working Group made only a few revisions to the article in order to clarify its meaning and to harmonize its interface with other revised provisions of the Rules.

The main revision was to clarify that a party's right to amend or supplement its "defence" extends not only to the statement of defence, but also to a counterclaim or a claim for a set-off. Although these types of defensive pleadings were not specifically identified in original Article 20, there is no doubt that their amendment or supplementation must also be treated according to principles enunciated in the article.[47] Accordingly, the Iran–US Claims Tribunal has, without any apparent hesitation, applied original Article 20, as modified, to both claims and counter-claims.[48] Nevertheless, parties using the 1976 UNCITRAL Rules may wish to modify them so as to clarify the broad coverage of original Article 20.

Article 22 of the 2010 UNCITRAL Rules also replaces the phrase "falls outside the scope of the arbitration clause or separate arbitration agreement" in the second sentence of original Article 20 with the words "falls outside the jurisdiction of the arbitral tribunal." This revision is consistent with the approach of Article 1(1) of the 2010 UNCITRAL Rules, which broadens the scope of the Rules to account for arbitration in other contexts, such as investor–state arbitration. The parties may wish to modify this provision of the 1976 UNCITRAL Rules, as necessary, depending on the particular needs of an arbitration.

Article 22 of the 2010 UNCITRAL Rules, as revised, also includes minor changes aimed at achieving greater consistency between the text of the first and second sentences of the article, as well as facilitating the application of the Rules in the context of multi-party arbitration.[49]

C. Extracts from the Practice of Investment Tribunals

Himpurna California Energy Ltd and *PT (Persero) Perusahaan Listruik Negara*, Final Award (May 4, 1999) (*Ad Hoc* Proceeding, 1976 UNCITRAL Rules, Concession Agreement), at 31–32, reprinted in (2000) XXV Ybk Commercial Arb 28, 28–29:

> 2. Scope of the arbitration
>
> [54] PLN has argued that "the dispute" crystallised, with respect to its "subject matter," as of Claimant's initial notices under Section 8 of the ESC. Since those notices complained only of PLN's non-payment of one invoice, failure to provide one letter of credit, and failure to provide requested assurances of its intention to perform the ESC, PLN argues that no other matters are properly within the scope of this arbitration....
>
> ...
>
> [57] In the first place, Article 20 of the [1976] UNCITRAL Rules provides that:
> "either party may amend or supplement his claim unless the arbitral tribunal considers it inappropriate to allow such amendment having regard to the delay in making it or prejudice to the other party or any other circumstances."

---

[47] Counterclaims can either be regarded as a sub-category of "claims" or as something falling under the concept of "defence" as understood in Article 20 of the 1976 UNCITRAL Rules. See Article 19 entitled "Statement of Defence" in which counterclaims are also dealt with.

[48] See, eg, the *Sylvania* case (1983 Tribunal Rules), Order of May 10, 1983, reprinted in section 2(D).

[49] For example, Article 22 adds the words "defence" and "supplement" (or "supplemented") in places throughout the text to parallel the initial use of these terms in the first sentence.

The only limitation is that any claim so amended must fall within the scope of the arbitration clause (*n.b.* not the notice of arbitration).

[58] Secondly, in evaluating the "circumstances" with regard to such amendments [to the Statement of Claim pursuant to Article 20] the Arbitral tribunal takes account of (i) the fair and efficient administration of arbitral justice, a consideration which militates against any unduly static or formalistic rule that would require parties to recommence proceedings every time the adversarial evolution of argument and evidence suggests the need for a different legal articulation of claims; and, yet more importantly (ii) the good principle that procedural rules should not be conceived and applied in such a fashion as to impel the parties to adopt maximalist and confrontational positions, such as demanding rescission at a time when there may still be a hope to save the contract.

[59] In this case, the Claimant should not be penalised for having omitted to ask for termination, or termination damages, in its initial notices.

United Parcel Service of America Inc and *Government of Canada*, Award on Jurisdiction (November 22, 2002) (ICSID administered, 1976 UNCITRAL Rules, NAFTA Chapter Eleven), at 40:

130. ... [Canada argues that] leave to amend the statement of claim to provide greater precision should not be granted if the other party would be prejudiced or the amendment fell outside the submission to arbitration.

131. The last submission refers to one of the controls which the Tribunal has over the development of the claim to ensure that it understands the essential matters and that the other party has proper notice. Under article 20 of the [1976] UNCITRAL Rules, either party may amend or supplement its claim or defence unless the tribunal considers the amendment inappropriate having regard to delay, prejudice or other circumstances; further, a claim may not be amended to take it outside the scope of the arbitration claim. It will be observed that the article does not have quite the balance that Canada would suggest. While the tribunal may exercise control over amendments, its leave need not be sought in the first instance. Article 22 is also relevant, as both parties remind the Tribunal. It has the power to decide whether further written statements, in addition to the statements of claim and defence, should be required from the parties or may be presented by them. Those powers are to be read with the broad powers of the tribunal under article 15 of the [1976] UNCITRAL Rules to conduct the arbitration in such manner as it considers appropriate provided that the parties are treated with equality and given a full opportunity to present their cases.

Ethyl Corp and *Government of Canada*, Award on Jurisdiction (June 24, 1998) (ICSID administered, 1976 UNCITRAL Rules, NAFTA Chapter Eleven), at 45–47 (footnotes omitted), reprinted in 38 ILM 708, 730 (1999):

(d) Has a "New Claim" Been Asserted?

93. The Tribunal finally deals with Canada's contention that reliance in the Statement of Claim on the MMT Act, which was enacted some six months following delivery of the Notice of Arbitration, which Notice was directed at Bill C-29 (which became the MMT Act), and specific reference in the Statement of Claim for the first time to the produce Greenburn, constitute the assertion of "new claims" which the Tribunal is prohibited from considering.

94. The revised and expanded terminology in the Statement of Claim is not intrinsically of such great significance...

95. The nub of the matter, however, is that the specific inclusion of references to the MMT Act and the product Greenburn in the Statement of Claim is not, as the Tribunal sees it, to be viewed as adding "new claims," but rather, if anything, as amending the claim previously described in the Notice of Arbitration. Article 20 of the [1976] UNCITRAL Arbitration Rules, which Part B does not modify, provides that Claimant "may" so amend "unless the arbitral tribunal considers it inappropriate to allow such amendment having regard to the

delay in making it or prejudice to the other party or any other circumstances." An amendment of Ethyl's claim, if one there has been, made as early as in the Statement of Claim hardly can be regarded as involving any "delay." No prejudice or any other circumstances are cited by Canada which would tend to rebut Article 20's presumption of amendability and the Tribunal apprehends none. Therefore, to the extent, if any, that the Statement of Claim amends the claim of Ethyl, the Tribunal accepts such amendment.

Methanex Corp and *United States of America*, Partial Award on Jurisdiction (August 7, 2002) (ICSID administered, 1976 UNCITRAL Rules, NAFTA Chapter Eleven), at 34 (citation omitted), reprinted in (2002) 14(6) World Trade & Arb Materials 109, 143:

78. At the jurisdictional hearing of July 2001, the Tribunal ordered that: "Subject to all jurisdiction and admissibility issues and subject to any order as to costs, the Tribunal will allow the Claimant to amend its Statement of Claim in the form of the draft Amended Statement of Claim".... In short, apart from the jurisdiction and admissibility issues, the Tribunal decided, in principle, that Methanex should be allowed to amend its Original Statement of Claim in the form of its Amended Statement of Claim, subject to an order that Methanex should ultimately bear, regardless of the result of the arbitration on the eventual merits of its claim, the wasted costs of the arbitration thrown away by its amendment (including the legal costs of the USA assessed in a reasonable sum). In the Tribunal's view, subject to recovering such costs, the USA would suffer no unfair prejudice from such an amendment; and the overall interests of fairness and procedural efficiency would have supported an order allowing Methanex to amend its claim, as requested.

Methanex Corp and *United States of America*, Award (August 3, 2005) (ICSID administered, 1976 UNCITRAL Rules, NAFTA Chapter Eleven), Part II, Chapter F, at 9:

19. The Tribunal decides that, insofar as Methanex is relying on the amended § 2262.6(c) as *evidence* of California's intent to harm methanol producers, Methanex should be allowed to amend its Second Amended Statement of claim to that limited effect. This allegation is not a radical development from the existing case; the point is implicitly made in Methanex's existing pleadings, albeit not expressly; and there is no sufficient prejudice to the USA which could make this argument unfair. The Tribunal also decides that Methanex need not formally amend its Second Amended Statement of Claim to advance this argument.
20. However, for the reasons which follow, insofar as Methanex is relying on the amended § 2262.6(c) as an additional "measure" under Article 1101 NAFTA, the Tribunal decides that Methanex cannot advance the proposed amendment to its case in these arbitration proceedings.
21. Methanex has never previously pleaded the amended § 2262.6(c) as an additional measure under Article 1101 NAFTA. Accordingly, any such plea would clearly require an amendment to its Second Amended Statement of Claim; and such an amendment would also require the permission of the Tribunal. Pursuant to Article 20 of the [1976] UNCITRAL Rules, a claim may not be amended in such a manner that the amended claim falls outside the scope of the arbitration clause, in this case, Section B of Chapter 11. In seeking to introduce a new claim relying on amended § 2262.6(c) as a measure for the purposes of Article 1101(1) NAFTA, in the Tribunal's view, Methanex fails to meet the essential requirements for bringing a claim under Section B of Chapter 11 and Article 20 of the [1976] UNCITRAL Rules.

EnCana Corp and *Republic of Ecuador*, Award (February 3, 2006) (LCIA administered, 1976 UNCITRAL Rules, Canada-Ecuador BIT), at 5, 47:

18. Following the filing of the post-hearing briefs, the Respondent wrote objecting that the Claimant had introduced new claims concerning, *inter alia,* the dismissal of most of the judges of the Constitutional Court and the Supreme Court and referring to statements made

by the President of Ecuador in that regard. The Tribunal noted that the information was capable of being relevant to issues pleaded in the arbitration and gave the Respondent an opportunity to reply to the allegations. This the Respondent did by letter of 11 February 2005 (leading to a further exchange of 17 and 18 February 2005).

...

164. In sum, a balance must be struck between, on the one hand, unreasonably requiring that new proceedings be commenced where the substance of a claim of breach of the BIT may arguably have been made out or very nearly made out, and subsequent events put the question of breach beyond doubt, and on the other, allowing what are in essence new claims or new causes of action, which in reality have no real relation to the events initially relied upon, to be added on to existing proceedings on the basis of events subsequent to the commencement of proceedings.

165. As already indicated, the Tribunal is of the view that the events between December 2004-April 2005 in Ecuador, were relied upon by EnCana not for the purpose of introducing a new claim or cause of action, but in order to inform the Tribunal of matters which might be of relevance in relation to the claims which had already been identified when the arbitration proceedings were commenced.

Grand River Enterprises Six Nations, Ltd, et al and *United States of America*, Decision on Objections to Jurisdiction (July 20, 2006) (ICSID administered, 1976 UNCITRAL Rules, NAFTA Chapter Eleven Arbitration), at 43–44 (footnotes omitted):

99. The further issue cited in UNCITRAL Rule 20 [of the 1976 UNCITRAL Rules] is the possibility of prejudice. Respondent contended that it would be prejudiced by the amendment, not least because the United States had already filed its Statement of Defense based upon the Claimants' Notice of Claim and Particularized Statement of Claim, which, as the Tribunal found above, did not identify this issue adequately. Accordingly, (as the Respondent rightly contends) if the amendment is to be allowed, the briefing schedule for future proceedings must take account of this imbalance and make appropriate provisions to assure equal treatment of the Parties. But this circumstance cannot result in denying the Claimants an opportunity to plead changes in the law occurring after March 12, 2001 (in the form of the amendments to the escrow statutes) and their consequent results.

100. In this connection, the Tribunal must take account of the fact that, should the amendment be refused, the Claimants could seek to file a second, separate arbitration against the Respondent before a separate tribunal based on the allocable share amendments. The Tribunal believes that in the interests of judicial economy, efficiency and coherence, it is better for all of the Claimants' claims regarding the MSA and its associated enforcement measures to be considered in the context of a single proceeding.

Merrill & Ring Forestry LP and *Government of Canada*, Decision on a Motion to Add a New Party (January 31, 2008) (ICSID administered, 1976 UNCITRAL Rules, NAFTA Chapter Eleven Arbitration), at 6–7, 22:

17. While, at first sight, it appears that Article 20 of the [1976] UNCITRAL Arbitration Rules facilitates the motion of a party to amend or supplement a Statement of Claim or Defence (by indicating first that a party may do so unless the arbitral tribunal considers it inappropriate in the light of certain standards, and only in the second sentence referring to the prohibition against introducing an amendment if the amended claim falls outside the scope of the arbitration clause), the proper interpretation of the Article leads in the opposite direction.

18. This is because the Article contains an overall and absolute prohibition against introducing amendments which go beyond the scope of the arbitration clause. This is what the literature has considered a *prima facie* "absolute limitation" (David D. Caron, Matti Pellonpää and Lee M. Caplan, THE UNCITRAL ARBITRATION RULES: A COMMENTARY (Oxford

University Press, 2006), 468). It is only if the Tribunal is satisfied that no such result will ensue that it can then proceed to the second step, that is to determine whether the standards set out in the Article have been complied with and do not bar the approval of the motion. These standards envisage the delay in making the pertinent request, prejudice to the other party or any other circumstances. Only after the Tribunal is satisfied that the standards have been met will it be in a position to allow the requested amendment.

...

30. Thus, even if it were to be concluded that Merrill & Ring's and Georgia Basin's claims are similar, the compliance with the above mentioned safeguards would still need to be satisfied. This would take a number of months. If these proceedings were to be delayed by waiting for such compliance there would indeed be a serious procedural prejudice. At that point consolidation would not serve the efficient resolution of the claims as the present proceedings will be much advanced.
31. There is, lastly, one other consideration that relates to the "any other circumstances" that Article 20 offers as a guideline to grant or deny a Motion for Amendment. This is the fact that, in the circumstances of this case, it does not appear that the claim by Georgia Basin is just an amendment of the original claim by Merrill & Ring. Rather, it entails the assertion of an entirely new claim by an entirely new claimant even if such a claim were considered similar in nature to that already before us. This is an added reason why such a new claim needs to comply with the requirements and safeguards of NAFTA Chapter 11. The notion of an amended statement of claim is narrower than that involved in this Motion which makes the Motion before us dissimilar to the minor technical failures that other NAFTA tribunals have considered.

D. Extracts from the Practice of the Iran–US Claims Tribunal

Sylvania Technical Systems, Inc and *Islamic Republic of Iran*, Case No 64, Chamber One, Order of May 10, 1983:

In the absence of any objection by the Parties concerned the Tribunal decides that the Supplementary Statement of Claim and the Supplementary Statement of Counter-claim have been timely filed under Article 20 of the Tribunal Rules.

Bank Markazi Iran and *Bank of Boston Intl, New York*, Case No 733, Chamber Two, Order of December 8, 1983:

In response to the Tribunal's order of 19 December 1983, the First Boston Corporation, named as new Respondent in the Claimant's Amendment to the Statement of Claim filed 25 July 1983, has filed objections thereto. The Tribunal sustains those objections and cannot permit a new, unrelated respondent to be named at this stage of the Proceedings.

Refusal to File Claim of AMF Corp, Decision No DEC 17-REF20-FT (December 8, 1982), reprinted in 1 Iran-US CTR 392, 393 (1981–1982):

In this case, the Statement of Claim on its face showed that it concerned a claim of a non-United States company, but it also indicated clearly that this company was a wholly owned subsidiary. Later papers allege that the parent company is a United States national.

In view of circumstances of this case, the Tribunal considers the 22 June Petition to be a clarification of who is the proper Claimant, and not an amendment whereby a new Claimant is named; thus the Tribunal need not address the question whether such an amendment could be permitted under Article 20 of the Tribunal Rules. In view of the foregoing, the claim should now be regarded as claim of AMF Incorporated on behalf of AMF Overseas Corporation. The Statement of Claim is therefore eligible for filing.

Refusal to Accept the Claim of Raymond Intl (UK) Ltd, Decision No DEC18-REF21-FT (December 8, 1982) (square brackets in the original), reprinted in 1 Iran-US CTR 394, 395 (1981–1982):

> Article 20 of the Provisionally Adopted Tribunal Rules provides that a party during the course of the arbitral proceedings [including the refusal proceedings] may amend or supplement his claim unless the Tribunal considers it inappropriate.... However, to substitute a new Claimant for the original one is tantamount to the filing of a new claim and cannot be regarded simply as an amendment to the existing claim, timely received by the Registry.

Kimberly-Clark Corp and *Bank Markazi Iran* et al, Award No 46–57–2 (May 25, 1983) at 8–9, reprinted in 2 Iran-US CTR 334, 338 (1983-I):

> With respect to the argument that Novzohour could not be named a respondent after 19 January 1982 because Article III, paragraph 4 of the Claims Settlement Declaration said that no claim may be filed after that date, the Tribunal notes that it decided to accept that amendment on 4 June 1982. In explanation, we point out that the original Statement of Claim identified Novzohour as the other party to the License and asserted that the Government of the Islamic Republic of Iran "has nationalized Novzohour and is responsible for the control and debt obligations of Novzohour." In its Statement of Defence filed on 12 March 1982 the Government, which said it was representing Novzohour, presented a counter-claim on Novzohour's behalf. In these circumstances, the Tribunal concluded that acceptance of the amendment pursuant to Article 20 of our Provisional Rules of Procedure would violate neither that Article nor the Claims Settlement Declaration.

Dallal and *Islamic Republic of Iran*, Award No 53–149–1 (June 10, 1983) at 3–4, reprinted in 3 Iran-US CTR 10, 11 (1983-III):

> Furthermore, in a post-hearing brief Mr. Dallal has argued that if the Respondents' defence were to be sustained, the bank would be unjustly enriched from its own culpable act, i.e. it would be the beneficiary of the US $400,000 worth of Rials which it undertook to pay and which it has not.
>
> Since this additional basis for the claim was first presented in a post-hearing brief, the Tribunal holds, in accordance with Article 20 of the Tribunal Rules, that it would be inappropriate to allow this amendment to the claim. Bank Mellat has declared that the Rials could be recovered directly from the bank by the person entitled to them.

Intl Schools Services, Inc and *Islamic Republic of Iran, National Defence Industrial Organization*, Award No ITL 57–123–1 (January 30, 1986) at 10–11, reprinted in 10 Iran-US CTR 6, 12 (1986-I):

> This provision affords wide latitude to a party who seeks to amend a claim, and the Tribunal's practice is in accord with this liberal approach. As Article 20 directs, the Tribunal will permit an amendment unless delay, prejudice or other concrete circumstances make it inappropriate to do so. No such circumstances appear here.
>
> First, the Claimant did not unduly delay before making the Amendment ... Claimant tried as long as possible to limit the proceedings to the implementation of the MOU [Memorandum of Understanding], and it was NDIO's refusal to join in a Request for an Award on agreed terms that caused any "delay" in the making of the amendment.
>
> Likewise, the Amendment did not cause prejudice to the Respondents. Again it was NDIO's own refusal, on two separate occasions, to implement the terms of the MOU that prompted the Claimant to return to the claim arising out of the 1976 agreement. While the relief sought was increased, the factual circumstances on which the amendment is based had been presented in the original Statement of Claim. The Respondents can point to no "prejudice" which does

not ensue from NDIO's own conduct, and thus the MOU presents no bar to the proffered amendment.

Finally, there are no "other circumstances" which make inappropriate to permit the Claimant to amend its original Statement of Claim. Accordingly, the Amendment submitted on 24 February 1983 is allowed.

Sedco Inc and *National Iranian Oil Co and Islamic Republic of Iran*, Award No ITL 55–129–3 (October 28, 1985) at 13–14, 25, reprinted in 9 Iran-US CTR 248, 257, 265–66 (1985-II):

> Claimant Sedco has also filed indirect claims relating to Sediran under Article VII(2) of the Claims Settlement Declaration. Respondents present additional objections to these indirect claims. Alternatively, Claimant presents a direct claim for its shareholding interest in SEDIRAN.
>
> ...
>
> Respondents object to the Tribunal's jurisdiction over a direct claim by Sedco for its shareholding interest in Sediran on the ground that it involves "the presentation of a new statement of claim." The Tribunal finds that the claims of Sedco, whether considered jurisdictionally as direct or indirect claims, rest essentially on the same facts, allegations and legal theories. It is also noted that the Tribunal accepted a change from an indirect to direct claim in a similar pleading context in *Tippetts, Abbett, McCarthy, Stratton and The Islamic Republic of Iran*, Award No 4 1–7–2 (29 June 1984). Respondents' objection is therefore denied.

Cal-Maine Food Inc and *Islamic Republic of Iran*, Award No 133–340–3 (June 11, 1984) at 11–12, 15–16, reprinted in 6 Iran-US CTR 52, 59–60, 62–63 (1984-II):

> Although Claimant noted in its 18 January 1982 Statement of Claim that its participation in the running of Sea-Cal included "among other activities, sending its employees to Iran to help in the running of Sea-Cal", Cal-Maine made then no specific claim on the basis of such activities. In its initial Statement of Claim, Cal-Maine sought relief only for its investment in Sea-Cal, interest thereon for two years, and costs of arbitration. A claim for accounts receivable was not raised at the 7 February 1983 Pre-Hearing Conference and was not in any of Cal-Maine's pleadings until its Memorial of 14 July 1983. It did not seek a formal amendment of its claim. Even assuming that the claim for accounts receivable could be deemed a request for amendment, in this case, the delay in asserting such a claim and the likely prejudice to Respondents of such a delay would preclude the acceptance of such an amendment under Article 20 of the Tribunal Rules. In view of this fact and the fact that no such amendment was proposed, the Tribunal does not consider Cal-Maine's claim for accounts receivable.
>
> Cal-Maine's claim for its investment interest in Sea-Cal was asserted in the Statement of Claim. Claimant, however, later altered its theory for recovery of its investment interest. Claimant's Memorial in which the new legal theory was presented was filed three months prior to the hearing. Seamourgh did not object in its October 1983 Memorial to the argument put forward by Cal-Maine in July. Seamourgh had four months in which to prepare its defence for the Hearing. Accordingly, the Tribunal does not believe that Respondents have been prejudiced by any change of theory so as to make such a change inappropriate. Moreover, Respondents were given the opportunity and did in fact file post-hearing memorials.
>
> Cal-Maine in its Statement of Claim stated that it sought "damages in the amount of US $600,000.00 (US $500,000.00 plus 20% interest)". In the light of Claimant's subsequent submissions this has to be understood as a claim for 10% annual interest for a period of two years which Cal-Maine was entitled to receive on its investment according to the terms of the Letter on Intent. In its July 1983 Memorial Claimant alternatively sought interest from the date of each of its capital contributions until full payment on the basis of general principles concerning contract breaches. The Tribunal does not consider this amendment of the claim inappropriate in the light of Article 20 of the Tribunal Rules.

Pepsico Inc and *Islamic Republic of Iran,* et al, Award No 260–18–1 (October 11, 1986) at 20, reprinted in 13 Iran-US CTR 3, 17 (1986-IV):

> The Tribunal admits the Claimant's request to increase the rate of interest initially sought by it as well as to update the amount of its claim for costs, since both these requests affect only the amounts of calculations and as such do not prejudice the defence by the Respondents.

Aeronutronic Overseas Services, Inc and *Islamic Republic of Iran,* et al, Case No 158, Chamber One, Order of March 9, 1984:

> 4. Pursuant to Article 20 of the Tribunal Rules, the Tribunal allows the Claimant's request alternatively to base its claim for US $547,055 for re-engineering and re-testing costs on the doctrine of unjust enrichment.
>
> ...
>
> 7. The Parties are invited to file by 5 October 1984 any further memorials in advance of the Hearing in this case.

McCollough Co, Inc and *Ministry of Post, Telegraph and Telephone*, Award No 225–89–3 (April 22, 1986), reprinted in 11 Iran-US CTR 3, 17–18 (1986-II):

> 45. The Claimant further seeks payment of five invoices dated 15 March 1983 for sums totalling US $238,605 in respect of expenses incurred or services rendered subsequent to the termination of the Contract.
> 46. The Tribunal notes that the Claimant asserted this part of the claim before the Tribunal for the first time on 18 July 1984 by the submission of certain exhibits. The Tribunal does not deem this amendment of the Claim to be "inappropriate", however, within the terms of Article 20 of the Tribunal Rules, as, in the absence of any allegation to that effect, the amendment does not appear to have prejudiced the Respondent.
>
> ...
>
> 50. In its reply to the Statement of Defence of the Respondent PTT, filed 6 July 1982, the Claimant introduced a claim for "[d]amages to the financial health of" McCollough.
>
> ...
>
> 52. Although the Tribunal does not find sufficient cause to declare this amendment inadmissible, the Tribunal notes the utter lack of evidence.

Thomas Earl Payne and *Islamic Republic of Iran*, Award No 245–335–2 (August 8, 1986), reprinted in 11 Iran-US CTR 3, 6 (1986-III):

> 9. As already noted, the Claimant amended his Statement of Claim to increase the amount of compensation sought. The Respondent objected to the amendment on the ground that an increase in the amount claimed is not a proper amendment. The Tribunal decides that no prejudice could be considered to have been caused to the Respondent by a change in the Claimant's valuation of the property at issue even if this change is caused by using a different method of valuation. The Respondent had ample opportunity to respond, and did respond, to the revised valuation made by the Claimant. Accordingly, the Tribunal decides the Amendment is admissible in accordance with Article 20 of the Tribunal Rules.

Tai, Inc and *Islamic Republic of Iran*, Case No 421, Chamber One, Order of August 12, 1986:

> The Claimant is requested to file by 31 October 1986 further clarification and supporting documentation concerning the basis of its proposed amendment increasing its claim for invoiced amounts to US $162,472.30. By the same date the Respondent NIOC is requested to file comments on the procedural issue of whether the proposed amendment should be admitted.

Litton Systems, Inc and *Islamic Republic of Iran*, Award No 249–769–1 (August 25, 1986) at 8, reprinted in 12 Iran-US CTR 126, 131 (1986-III):

> Litton has sought leave to amend its claim to include the costs of warehousing of the 91 retained LN-33 items of equipment. In the view of the Tribunal, no prejudice would be occasioned to the Respondents by the admission of this amendment, and it is therefore allowed in accordance with Article 20 of the Tribunal Rules.

Fedders Corp and *Loristan Refrigeration Industries*, Decision No DEC 51–250–3 (October 28, 1986) at 2, reprinted in 13 Iran-US CTR 97, 98 (1986-IV):

> As regards NIO's status, Article 20 of the Tribunal Rules states that a party may amend its claim, unless delay, prejudice or loss of jurisdiction would result. Claimant's amendment adding NIO as a Respondent was requested after the Claimant discovered that NIO was the entity directly involved in the alleged expropriation. Therefore such a request cannot be considered as untimely filed. Since NIO acted allegedly as an agent of Iran, also a Respondent in this Case, the amendment cannot be said to prejudice Iran or any other Respondent. Finally, there is no suggestion that the amendment may deprive the Tribunal of jurisdiction over the claim.
>
> In view of the foregoing, the Tribunal finds no reason to disallow such an amendment, and it is accordingly accepted.

Fereydoon Ghaffari (a claim less than US $250,000 presented by The United States of America) and *The Islamic Republic of Iran*, Case No 10792, Chamber Two, Order of September 15, 1987, reprinted in 18 Iran-US CTR 64 (1988-I):

> 1. The Tribunal notes Claimant's submission of August 11, 1987, seeking an amendment to increase the amount claimed in this Case from US $244,155 to US $3,022,147 and to change the date of the alleged expropriation from May 11, 1980 to July 28, 1979.
> 2. The Tribunal further notes that only the Statement of Claim has been filed in this Case.
> 3. As stated in Case No 967, the Tribunal considers that under Article 20 of its Rules of Procedure a party is afforded wide latitude in amending its claims and pleadings during the course of the arbitral proceedings, subject only to a determination by the Tribunal that an amendment would be inappropriate or to the limitation that amendments not render the amended claim "outside the jurisdiction of the arbitral tribunal." The Rule cites delay or prejudice to the other party as specific circumstances which might persuade the Tribunal that an amendment would be inappropriate.
> 4. The Tribunal notes that the essence of the claim in this Case would not be changed by the proposed amendment. The claim remains a claim for compensation for the alleged expropriation of Mr. Ghaffari's ownership interest in an Iranian company. Whether there was an expropriation, the effective date of such expropriation, and the value of the expropriated interest are matters of proof to be resolved by the Tribunal in the course of the proceedings, and the Parties are free to make such arguments in respect of those issues as they may choose.
> 5. Therefore, the Tribunal accepts the amendment filed on August 11, 1987 and directs the Co-Registrars to reclassify the Claim accordingly.

Harris Intl Telecommunications, Inc and *Islamic Republic of Iran*, Award No 323–409–1 (November 2, 1987) (footnotes omitted), reprinted in 17 Iran-US CTR 31, 55–57 (1987-IV):

> 84. In determining the admissibility of the amendments, the Tribunal again begins its analysis by examining the Tribunal Rules. The Tribunal notes that Article 20 provides in part that
>
>> [d]uring the course of the arbitral proceedings either party may amend or supplement his claim . . . *unless* the arbitral tribunal considers it inappropriate to allow such amendment having regard to the delay in making it or prejudice to the other party or any other circumstances (emphasis added).

85. As noted in *International Schools Services, Inc.* and *Islamic Republic of Iran*, Interlocutory Award No ITL 57–123–1, p. 10 (30 Jan. 1986), "[t]his provision affords wide latitude to a party who seeks to amend a claim, and the Tribunal's practice is in accord with this liberal approach." The Tribunal permits amendments unless delay, prejudice, or other "concrete circumstances", *see International Schools Services, supra, Ford Aerospace & Communications Corp.* and *Government of the Islamic Republic of Iran*, Award No 289–93–1 (29 Jan. 1987), make amendment inappropriate, or unless "loss of jurisdiction would result", see *Fedders Corporation* and *Loristan Refrigeration Industries*, Decision No DEC 51–250–3, p. 2 (28 Oct. 1986). The same considerations of prejudice, equality of treatment, and delay of the arbitral proceedings are applicable here. Thus, the Tribunal must consider whether the other Party would be prejudiced by the proposed amendment, whether the other Party has had an opportunity to respond to the newly-added or amended claim, and whether the proposed amendment would needlessly disrupt or delay the arbitral process. *See Thomas Earl Payne* and *Government of the Islamic Republic of Iran*, Award No 245–335–2, para 9 (8 Aug. 1986), *Questech, Inc.* and *Ministry of National Defence of the Islamic Republic of Iran*, Award No 191–59–1, p. 28 (25 Sept. 1985); *Sylvania Technical Systems, Inc.* and *Government of the Islamic Republic of Iran*, Award No 180–64–1, p. 39 (27 June 1985).

86. In the present Case the Tribunal holds that, except for the amendment withdrawing the set-off for the value of the computer, all of the proposed amendments are admitted. It is the practice of the Tribunal to admit requests to increase the rate of interest initially sought as well as to update the amount of costs claimed, since, as stated in *Pepsico, Inc.* and *Government of the Islamic Republic of Iran*, Award No 260–18–1, p 20 (13 Oct. 1986), such amendments "affect only the amounts of calculations and as such do not prejudice the defence by the Respondents". As to the other amendments the Tribunal finds that their admission causes neither delay to the arbitral process nor prejudice to the Respondent, and there are no other "concrete circumstances" which would make amendment inappropriate. There have also been no allegations by the Respondents to that effect.

87. The withdrawal of the offset of the value of the computer at the Hearing, however, is a different matter. Such a withdrawal significantly alters the relief sought by the Claimant and raises new factual and legal issues to which the Respondents have not had a sufficient opportunity to respond. Allowing this amendment, at this stage of the proceedings, would likely prejudice the Respondents. Moreover, no explanation has been offered for the delay in seeking this alteration of the Claim. Therefore, the Tribunal rejects this proposed amendment to the Claim. Accordingly, $196,417 must be deducted from any amount awarded to the Claimant.

Arthur Young & Co and *Islamic Republic of Iran*, Award No 338–484–1 (December 1, 1987), reprinted in 17 Iran-US CTR 245, 253–54 (1987-IV):

37. The question arises, however, whether Claimant's request for a declaration from the Tribunal that certain letters of credit are null and void, first mentioned in its Hearing Memorial, was an admissible amendment to the Claim. Article 20 of the Tribunal Rules provides that:

> [d]uring the course of the arbitral proceedings either party may amend or supplement his claim . . . unless the arbitral tribunal considers it inappropriate to allow such amendment having regard to the delay in making it or prejudice to the other party or any other circumstances.

> Under this provision, the Tribunal is to consider delay in making the amendment as a criterion independent from "prejudice to the other party" or "any other circumstances". Article 20, read together with Articles 18, 19 and 28 of the Tribunal Rules, makes it clear that the arbitrating parties are obliged to present their claim or defence, in principle, as early as possible and appropriate under the circumstances in each case. Compliance with this obligation is indispensable, in the Tribunal's view, to ensure an orderly conduct of the arbitral proceedings and equal treatment of the parties. It is true

that the Tribunal has generally taken a liberal approach in permitting amendments, provided that they neither significantly alter the relief sought, nor raise new factual or legal issues to which the other party could not adequately respond, and that an explanation for the delay has been offered. *Harris International Telecommunications, Inc.* and *The Islamic Republic of Iran, et al.*, Award No 323–409–1, paras 84–87 (2 Nov 1987). The Claimant in this Case, however, seeks an amendment adding a different kind of relief, which raises new factual and legal issues. The Tribunal notes that the Claimant, in its Statement of Claim, did not make reference to the existence of outstanding letters of credit securing advance payments or payment of social security premiums. Rather, it merely stated that "all performance guarantees were thus released by TCI". It was, indeed, the Respondent TCI, in its Statement of Defence and Counter-claim filed on 26 September 1983, which first mentioned these letters of credit. Nonetheless, however, the Claimant did not take up the issue in its "Reply" filed on 10 January 1985. It did so, as stated above, only in the Hearing Memorial which was filed on 25 August 1986. Considering that the Claimant offered no explanation why it raised this request only at such a late stage of the proceedings, the Tribunal finds it inappropriate to allow the amendment sought.

Reza Said Malek and *Islamic Republic of Iran*, Award No ITL 68–193–3 (June 23, 1988), reprinted in 19 Iran-US CTR 48, 52–53 (1988-II):

18. The Statement of Claim, signed by the Claimant himself, alleges that the expropriation, which is the basis of the claim, "took place on 28 February 1981". As the Respondent points out, left unamended, this allegation would place the claim outside the Tribunal's jurisdiction, whatever the dominant and effective nationality of the Claimant. However, on 30 August 1982, the Claimant submitted an letter to the Tribunal in which he stated that he wished "to elaborate on the statement made . . . [the] Statement of Claim" and that in due course he would prove that "the expropriation in question effectively took place between the dates of November 5, 1980 and January 19, 1981".

19. This letter can be considered as an amendment to the Statement of Claim. Such an amendment may be submitted, under Article 20 of the Tribunal Rules, "unless the arbitral tribunal considers it inappropriate to allow such amendment having regard to the delay in making it or prejudice to the other party or any other circumstances". Given the fact that the letter in question was filed eight months subsequent to the filing of the Statement of Claim and one month before the filing of the Statement of Defence, the Tribunal finds that there was no unreasonable delay in making this amendment and that the Respondent is not prejudiced by it. Furthermore, the Tribunal previously has interpreted this Rule as affording "wide latitude" to a party wishing to amend his claim and has noted that "the Tribunal's practice is in accord with this liberal approach": *International School Services* and *Islamic Republic of Iran*, Award No ITL 57–123–1 (30 January 1986). *A priori*, such an amendment can therefore be considered as admissible.

Jack Buckamier and *Islamic Republic of Iran*, Award No 528–941–3 (March 6, 1992), reprinted in 28 Iran-US CTR 53, 60 (1992):

23. The Amended Claim was filed on 24 December 1986, almost two and one-half years before the final Hearing was held. The Tribunal notes that all the named Respondents as well as MIO and the Customs Agency have filed a substantive response to the Amended Claim. In addition, Isiran and the Bank have presented rebuttal memorials. The Tribunal is satisfied, therefore, that the increase of the amount claimed, which increase constitutes an amendment or supplement within the scope on Article 20 of the Tribunal Rules, has not caused prejudice to the Respondents.

24. With respect to certain parts of the Amended Claim, however, the question arises whether they constitute a new claim rather than an amendment or supplement as foreseen by Article

20 of the Tribunal Rules. To the extent they represent a new claim, the Tribunal must reject these items. *See Refusal to Accept the Claim of Raymond International (U.K.) Ltd*, Decision No DEC 18-ref 21-FT, p.3 (8 Dec. 1982), reprinted in 1 Iran-U.S. C.T.R. 394, 395.

25. The claim items to be reviewed in this context all relate to the alleged breach of the TRC Contract. Based on the Amended Claim they may be summarized as follows. First, the Claimant contends that he assisted a business associate in the formation of an Iranian company named Chutco. In return, Mr. Buckamier allegedly was entitled to a 10% commission on all gross sales of Chutco products resulting from his efforts. The TRC Contract also entailed an order to Chutco, but TRC's alleged breach prevented the Claimant from collecting his commission.

26. It is incorrect to state that "there is not even a hint" of the Chutco claim in the Claimant's original pleadings. In addition to being mentioned in the testimony of Mr. Abdulazim Fakhami, the commission arrangement and Chutco's involvement in TRC Contract are described in Part VI of the Statement of Claim. Thus, the original claim and the Amended Claim share the same factual basis. The Tribunal notes, however, that "Mr. Buckamier is not trying to collect the balance owed to him by Chutco." This statement compels the conclusion that the Amended Claim relating to Chutco is a new claim. In view to its filing date, the Tribunal therefore must reject this part of the Amended Claim.

27. The second claim item at issue is Mr. Buckamier's share of the installation fee of US $23,780.00 for twenty-nine of the garbage compactors which HNB was to install under the TRC Contract. The Tribunal notes that the Statement of Claim describes both the basis and the amount of this claim. The Claimant did not include this item in his summary of " 'known' unpaid debts" of TRC, apparently because "Mr. Buckamier isn't sure whether this total amount of US $23,780.00 has been paid and if any amount has been withheld." In the light of the wording of this statement and of the opportunity afforded to the Parties to collect and to present evidence in the course of the proceedings, it would be unreasonable to interpret this statement as an abandonment by the Claimant of this part of his claim. The Tribunal is satisfied, therefore, that the installation fee claim constitutes an amendment or a supplement permitted under Article 20 of the Tribunal Rules.

28. The third part of the Amended Claim to be addressed concerns Mr. Buckamier's share of profits in the amount of US $60,013.18 that he claims HNB lost as a result of the breach by TRC of the TRC Contract. Specifically, Mr. Buckamier claims a sales commission for the twelve compactors, out of the agreed total of 282, that were not delivered due to *force majeure*. He also claims his share of the profits that would have resulted from modification and repair by HNB of the 241 delivered compactors. Mr. Buckamier further seeks his share of the profits that would have been made on the installation of the 253 compactors not installed.

29. Review of the original pleadings reveals that, while these lost profits are not included in the amount originally claimed, Part I of the Statement of Claim as well as the correspondence, the TRC Contract and the testimony submitted therewith, set forth the basis for the claim eventually raised in the Amended Claim. The Tribunal therefore finds that this part of the Amended Claim supplements the Statement of Claim in conformity with Article 20 of the Tribunal Rules.

Harold Birnbaum and *Islamic Republic of Iran*, Award No 549–967–2 (July 6, 1993), reprinted in 29 Iran-US CTR 260, 265 (1993):

17. The Tribunal's Order of 18 February 1987 accepting the Claimant's First Amendment forecloses the Respondent's present objection to that amendment.

Mohsen Asgari Nazari and *Government of the Islamic Republic of Iran*, Award No 559–221–1 (August 24, 1994), reprinted in 30 Iran-US CTR 123, 126 (1994):

11. On 16 June 1992, the Tribunal rendered a Decision, *Mohsen Asgari Nazari* and *The Government of the Islamic Republic of Iran*, Decision No DEC 105–221–1 (16 June 1992), *reprinted in* 28 Iran-US CTR 192, regarding the Claimant's application to amend his Claim. Referring

to Article 20 of the Tribunal Rules and the significant lapse of time involved, and emphasizing that the Tribunal had already issued Interlocutory Award No ITL 79–22–1 in this Case and that the proposed new respondents had not had an opportunity to submit evidence during the preliminary stage of the proceedings or otherwise to participate therein, and the fact that the Claimant had not offered any justification for his delay in making this application, the Tribunal considered it inappropriate to allow the proposed amendment adding seven new respondents to the Case.

Shahin Shaine Ebrahimi, et al and *Government of the Islamic Republic of Iran*, Award No 560–44/46/47–3 (October 12, 1994), reprinted in 30 Iran-US CTR 170, 204 (1994):

103. In regard to the Respondent's request for the rejection of the Claimants' valuation, the Tribunal refers to its Award in *Rockwell International Systems*, in which the Tribunal held:

    In exercising its discretion under Article 20 to permit amendments to claims, the Tribunal must consider whether the other party would be prejudiced by the proposed amendment, whether the other party has had an opportunity to respond to the newly-added or amended claim, and whether the proposed amendment would needlessly disrupt or delay the arbitral process. Subject to these considerations, an amendment is generally admissible if the underlying facts of a dispute, as presented in the Statement of Claim, essentially remain the basis of the dispute, and if the amendment is so closely interrelated to the initial claim that it would be contrary to judicial economy to separate the issues and litigate them separately, or possibly, in different fora.

Rockwell International Systems, Inc. and *The Government of the Islamic Republic of Iran*, Award No 438–430–1, para. 73 (5 September 1989), *reprinted in* 23 Iran-U.S. C.T.R. 150, 166 ("*Rockwell*"). The Tribunal is satisfied that the Claimants' revised valuation of the Company meets the criteria laid down in *Rockwell*. Accordingly, the Respondent's request for dismissal of the valuation, and indeed of the claim, is rejected.

Westinghouse Electric Corp and *Islamic Republic of Iran Air Force*, Award No 579–389–2 (March 20, 1997) (citations omitted), reprinted in 33 Iran-US CTR 60, 75–76 (1997):

44. For the first time at the final Hearing, Westinghouse requested permission to amend its claims by adding to the relief sought a request for a declaration by the Tribunal that all bank guarantees and good performance bonds established in connection with the IED contracts are null and void. The proposed amendment thus adds a different kind of relief— a declaratory relief—to the original monetary relief sought and raises new factual and legal issues which had neither been raised nor discussed before. In the Tribunal's view, therefore, rather than making an amendment as foreseen by Article 20 of the Tribunal Rules, it appears that Westinghouse is in fact asserting a new claim after the deadline for filing of claims provided for in Article III, paragraph 4, of the Claims Settlement Declaration. In addition, due to the substantial delay with which Westinghouse made the amendment, the Air Force was not given a sufficient opportunity to respond to the factual and legal aspects of the amended claim. In light of these circumstances, the Tribunal rejects the amendment as inadmissible...

Westinghouse Electric Corp and *Islamic Republic of Iran Air Force*, Award No 579–389–2 (March 20, 1997), Separate Opinion of George H Aldrich (March 20, 1997), reprinted in 33 Iran-US CTR 195, 198–200 (1997):

9. An examination of Tribunal precedents shows that the Tribunal has been liberal in allowing amendments unless those amendments are made so late that their acceptance would cause prejudice to the other party. Thus, in *McCollough & Co.* and *Iran*, Award No 225–89–3, (22 April 1986), *reprinted in* 11 Iran-US C.T.R. 3, 17, the Tribunal held that an amendment made in 1984 raising new claims for expenses subsequent to the termination of the contract on

which the original claims were based was not inappropriate within the terms of Article 20 of the Tribunal Rules, as it "does not appear to have prejudiced the Respondent." [Other citations omitted.] In several cases, new respondents were added by amendment. [Citations omitted.] In *International Sch. Servs., Inc.* and *Iran*, Award No ITL 57–123–1 (30 January 1986), *reprinted in* 10 Iran-U.S. C.T.R. 6, the Tribunal permitted a claim for the enforcement of a settlement agreement to be amended by adding a claim on the underlying debt. Referring to Article 20, the Tribunal said:

> This provision affords wide latitude to a party who seeks to amend a claim, and the Tribunal's practice is in accord with this liberal approach. As Article 20 directs, the Tribunal will permit an amendment unless delay, prejudice or other concrete circumstances make it inappropriate to do so.
>
> ...
>
> In the present case, the reasons to permit Westinghouse to amend its claims are even more persuasive, as uniquely in Tribunal practice it has been the Respondent that has expanded the case by bringing the contracts in question into the case. Our acceptance of a responsive amendment by Westinghouse would not have prejudiced the Air Force, but our rejection of it seriously prejudices Westinghouse.

Vivian Mai Tavakoli, et al and *Government of the Islamic Republic of Iran*, Award No 580–832–3 (April 23, 1997), reprinted in 33 Iran-US CTR 206, 210 (1997):

4. ... The Tribunal stated that

> The Request ... seeks to add as a Claimant a person who was not mentioned in the Statement of Claim. While such an amendment may be possible under Article 20 of the Tribunal Rules, the Tribunal finds that the Claimants have not provided sufficient and consistent information concerning the ownership of the claimed shares and that consequently the Request can be read as an attempt to add a claim by a new Claimant for shares different from those alleged to be owned by the existing Claimants, which might not be a permissible amendment under Article 20 of the Tribunal Rules but rather might be an assertion of a new claim after the deadline contemplated in the Claims Settlement Declaration.

The Tribunal concluded that it did not have enough information to make a decision on the matter and ordered the Claimants to clarify the identity of the persons who are alleged to own the shares to which the Claim relates. On 1 June 1987 the Claimants withdrew their request to include Bettie Tavakoli as a Claimant.

Frederica Lincoln Riahi and *Government of the Islamic Republic of Iran*, Award No 600–485–1 (February 27, 2003):

C. Admissibility of Late Claims and Amendment of Claims
1. Alterations in the Amount Claimed
55. In her Rebuttal Memorial, the Claimant, relying on Article 20 of the Tribunal Rules, ..., requested that she be permitted to amend and supplement her Claim to conform to the evidence submitted with her Hearing Memorial and with her Rebuttal Memorial. The Claimant alleged that the new amount claimed reflects information from documents recently obtained from Iran, which information was not available when she filed her Claim or made her initial submission of evidence. According to the Claimant, the revised amount also reflects new expert appraisals, which are based in part on information not previously available.
56. Therefore, the amount of compensation sought in the Rebuttal Memorial has been increased to US $40,930,443, plus interest and costs, compared to the Statement of Claim, where the Claimant sought US $6,528,116.90, and the Hearing Memorial, where the compensation

sought was US $16,263,578.44. Although the amount of each of the Claimant's individual claims are not itemized in the Statement of Claim, the amounts are itemized in the Hearing Memorial and in the Rebuttal Memorial. At the Hearing the Claimant sought US $33,508,923, explaining that there had been an error in her valuation calculations.

57. The Respondent is opposed to the increased amounts and to their having been increased over five-fold from the amount originally sought in the Statement of Claim. The Respondent holds that before the filing of the Statement of Claim, the Claimant enjoyed ample time, and was in the best possible position, to appraise her claimed property and shares. Any changes in the value of the alleged property subsequent to the filing of the Statement of Claim cannot affect the amount of compensation, which must be determined as of the date of expropriation. The Respondent argues that the Claimant has produced no acceptable reason for her revised valuation. Hence, it argues that the Tribunal may not accept such an increase in the relief sought.

58. The Tribunal notes that its practice has been to allow claimants to increase the amounts sought in stated claims, whether as a result of new evidence or the application of a different valuation or appraisal method.

[Discussion of practice omitted.]

61. For these reasons, the Tribunal holds that the Respondent will not be prejudiced by the amended Claim, as the Tribunal has afforded it ample opportunity to respond to the amended Claim, both in subsequent filings and at the Hearing. Accordingly, the Tribunal rejects the Respondent's objection and decides that the amendments are admissible in accordance with Article 20 of the Tribunal Rules.

16

Further Written Statements and Time Limits on Submission

1. Introduction	491
2. Further Written Statements—Article 24	491
A. Text of the 2010 UNCITRAL Rule	491
B. Commentary	492
(1) General comments	492
(2) Comparison to the 1976 UNCITRAL Rules	496
C. Extracts from the Practice of Investment Tribunals	496
D. Extracts from the Practice of the Iran–US Claims Tribunal	498
3. Time Limits on Submission—Article 25	505
A. Text of the 2010 UNCITRAL Rule	505
B. Commentary	505
(1) General comments	505
(2) Comparison to the 1976 UNCITRAL Rules	508
C. Extracts from the Practice of Investment Tribunals	508
D. Extracts from the Practice of the Iran–US Claims Tribunal	508

1. Introduction

By the time of the final hearing, the issues to be determined should be well defined, and the facts and arguments should be elaborated in writing. The statement of claim and the statement of defence do not necessarily suffice for this purpose. Article 24 provides for the possibility of requiring further written statements from the parties. Article 25 deals with the time limits to be fixed for the submission of various written statements, including the statement of claim and the statement of defence.

2. Further Written Statements—Article 24

A. Text of the 2010 UNCITRAL Rule[1]

Article 24 of the 2010 UNCITRAL Rules provides:

   The arbitral tribunal shall decide which further written statements, in addition to the statement of claim and the statement of defence, shall be required from the parties or may be presented by them and shall fix the periods of time for communicating such statements.

---

[1] Article 24 was adopted without any revision to the text of corresponding Article 22 of the 1976 UNCITRAL Rules.

B. Commentary

(1) General comments

Article 24 grants the arbitral tribunal discretion to order or authorize the submission of further written statements.[2] The arbitral tribunal may use its discretion to initiate actions independently, or at the request of any of the parties,[3] taking into account the specific needs of the particular arbitration. A pre-hearing conference or similar preliminary meeting can be arranged to provide the tribunal with an opportunity to evaluate such needs in direct consultation with the parties.[4] Typically, the tribunal's decisions on the need for further written statements should be reflected in the provisional timetable, required in accordance with Article 17(2), though new developments in the arbitration also may require changes in scheduling or additional rounds of pleadings.

In a relatively simple arbitration, there may be no need for written statements other than the statements of claim and defence. This, however, normally presupposes not only that the hearing allows sufficient time for both parties to elaborate their cases, but also that the documentary evidence relied on has been submitted in connection with the submission of the statement of claim and the statement of defence. In most international arbitrations, further written statements are likely to be useful, unless the case is disposed of on jurisdictional or other preliminary grounds.[5] Therefore, arrangements should be made for a second round of written pleadings, consisting of a reply (*réplique*) by the claimant to the statement of defence (and any counterclaim) and a rejoinder (*duplique*) by the respondent to the reply.[6] In view of the fact that under the UNCITRAL Rules both the statement of claim and the statement of defence may be concise in nature,[7] the arbitral tribunal may not merely order the parties to answer the points raised in the adversary's first written statement. Rather, the tribunal may schedule time for a second round of comprehensive "memorial" (claimant) and "counter-memorial" (respondent) statements containing elaborate

---

[2] See *United Parcel Service of America, Inc* (1976 Rules), and *KarahaBodas Co LLC* (1976 Rules), both reprinted in section 2(C).

[3] The wording of Article 24 makes it clear that not even an agreement of the parties obliges the arbitral tribunal to order further written statements if it is not itself convinced of their utility. In contrast, both the Preliminary Draft and the Revised Draft (Article 19(2), and Article 10(1) respectively) deferred to the parties on this matter, providing the following sentence: "However, if such parties agree on a further exchange of written statements, the arbitrators shall receive such statements." However, this sentence was eventually deleted from what became Article 22 of the 1976 UNCITRAL Rules. For the relevant discussion in Committee of the Whole (II), see *Summary Record of the 8th Meeting of the Committee of the Whole (II)*, UNCITRAL, 9th Session, UN Doc A/CN.9/9/C.2/SR.8, paras 44–78 (1976). It is clear, however, that a unanimous party request should normally be followed by the Tribunal. Moreover, pursuant to Article 1(1), the parties may, by written agreement, modify the rules including Article 24. See also J van Hof, "UNCITRAL Arbitration Rules, Section III, Article 22 [Further written statements]," in L Mistelis (ed), *Concise International Arbitration* (2010) 202.

[4] See Chapter 2, discussing Article 17(2).

[5] On the considerations motivating further written statements, see M Moses, *The Principles and Practice of International Commercial Arbitration* (2008) 159.

[6] See *Report of the Secretary-General on the Preliminary Draft Set of Arbitration Rules*, UNCITRAL, 8th Session, UN Doc A/CN.9/97 (1974), reprinted in (1975) VI UNCITRAL Ybk 163, 175. P Sanders, "Commentary on UNCITRAL Arbitration Rules," (1977) II Ybk Commercial Arb 204. As to the terminology, see A Redfern and M Hunter with N Blackaby and C Partasides, *Law and Practice of International Commercial Arbitration* (4th edn 2004) 347–8. For an example from the practice of NAFTA tribunals, see *Methanex Corp* (1976 Rules), Minutes of First Procedural Order, reprinted in section 2(C).

[7] See Chapter 13, discussion on articles 20 and 21.

legal argumentation,[8] combined with the submission of documentary evidence, expert reports, and the like.[9]

A two-round exchange of written pleadings is thus quite often advisable; a third round may be added, depending on the particular circumstances of the case. If a very substantial oral hearing is contemplated, the tribunal may dispense with further scheduling of written statements. If, on the other hand, the time allotted for the hearing is limited or no hearing at all is envisaged,[10] a third round of written statements consisting of rebuttal memorials or briefs may be in order. A three-stage or even four-stage schedule has been applied in many cases by the Iran–US Claims Tribunal, whose case load does not permit long hearing sessions.[11] Proceedings before investor–state tribunals may also require additional rounds of submissions to allow for participation by non-disputing state parties[12] or non-party *amicus curiae*.[13]

Further rounds of written statements of a general nature are likely to be redundant.[14] Thus "[i]t has been the established practice of the Iran-US Claims Tribunal to close the exchange of written pleadings after the submission of Memorials in Rebuttal."[15] Special situations may, however, warrant granting the parties an opportunity to file further written statements or comments on some particular issue(s).

Examples of such situations include amendments made to the claim or defence,[16] requests for interim measures by one of the parties,[17] the appointment of an expert and the determination of his terms of reference, or objections to the production of documents or with respect to the testimony of a witness.[18] There may also be jurisdictional issues or preliminary objections ("dilatory pleas"),[19] the practical handling of which calls for separate

---

[8] On "memorials" in the text of inter-state arbitration, see V S Mani, *International Adjudication, Procedural Aspects* (1980) 116–19. Only in complex cases is it advisable to permit reply/rejoinder and memorial/counter-memorial in separate stages in the proceedings. This may, however, be practicable where there is a counterclaim to which the main claimant has the right to reply. See Notes to Article 19 of the 1983 Tribunal Rules of the Iran–US Claims Tribunal, para 2, reprinted in Appendix 5. See also n 9.

[9] For examples of somewhat differently worded orders asking for the submission of memorials, see *Control Data Corp* (1983 Tribunal Rules); and *Varo Intl Corp* (1983 Tribunal Rules); both reprinted in section 2(D).

[10] See N Blackaby and C Partasides with A Redfern and M Hunter, *Redfern and Hunter on International Arbitration* (5th edn 2009) 413 (noting the rarity of "documents only" arbitration).

[11] According to A Mouri, *The International Law of Expropriation as Reflected in the Work of the Iran-U.S. Claims Tribunal* (1994) 11, n 38, "[t]he Tribunal has generally allowed four rounds of filings: i) Statement of Claim and Statement of Defence; ii) Claimant's Reply and Respondent's Rejoinder; iii) Claimant's and Respondent's Memorial and Evidence; and iv) their Rebuttals to each others' Memorials and Evidence." On the other hand, Full Tribunal cases have often been regarded as ripe for a hearing after two rounds of written pleadings. See J Selby and D Stewart, "Practical Aspects of Arbitrating Claims Before the Iran-United States Claims Tribunal," (1984) 18 *Intl Lawyer* 228. For examples of scheduling orders, see *Control Data Corp* (1983 Tribunal Rules); and *Varo Intl Corp* (1983 Tribunal Rules); both reprinted in section 2(D).

[12] See NAFTA, art 1128, allowing submissions by a NAFTA Party on a question of interpretation of the NAFTA. See also *Methanex Corp* (1976 Rules), Minutes of Second Procedural Order, reprinted in section 2(C).

[13] See Chapter 2, section 3(B) on non-party participation in UNCITRAL arbitration.

[14] For an example of an exceptional case of the Iran–US Claims Tribunal in which two rounds of written pleadings were ordered after the Hearing Memorials, see *Fluor Corp* (1983 Tribunal Rules), reprinted in section 2(D).

[15] *General Electric Co* (1983 Tribunal Rules), reprinted in section 2(D).

[16] See Chapter 13 on Article 20.

[17] See Chapter 17 on Article 26.

[18] See T Webster, *Handbook of UNCITRAL Arbitration: Commentary, Precedents and Materials for UNCITRAL Based Arbitration Rules* (2010) 344.

[19] See V S Mani, *International Adjudication, Procedural Aspects*, n 8, 123.

briefing before the exchange of written statements of a more general nature.[20] The fundamental principle of party equality may occasionally necessitate allowing the parties to submit post-hearing memorials or briefs. This may be the case where new arguments or evidence has been submitted, and admitted, by the tribunal on the very eve of or at the hearing, or where the time allotted for the hearing has proved to be too short for comprehensive treatment of all aspects of the case.[21] As the orderly conduct of the proceedings is, however, another important consideration in arbitration, a predisposition against post-hearing submissions is appropriate.[22] The general rule, as emphasized by the Iran–US Claims Tribunal, is that "no party shall submit any document for the first time at the Hearing, or so shortly before the Hearing that the other party cannot respond to it in an appropriate way."[23]

Article 24 deals with "written statements," ie, pleadings and legal argumentation, as distinct from documentary evidence.[24] Efficient management of the arbitration proceedings may, however, make it desirable to have documentary evidence and written statements submitted together in one complementary package. The memorial and counter-memorial may be scheduled for filing together with documentary evidence,[25] as has been the common practice of the Iran–US Claims Tribunal[26] and other tribunals.[27]

---

[20] In the practice of the Iran–US Claims Tribunal, "[l]arge, involved claims, such as the large oil company claims, often were divided into phases—e.g. jurisdiction, liability, quantification, counter-claims—with separate exchanges and possibly separate hearing memorials and evidence for each." See S Baker and M Davis, *The UNCITRAL Arbitration Rules in Practice: The Experience of the Iran-United States Claims Tribunal* (1992) 96, n 413.

[21] See, eg, *American Bell Intl* (1983 Tribunal Rules); and *United States of America on behalf and for the benefit of Harrington & Associates, Inc* (1983 Tribunal Rules); both reprinted in section 2(D). On the practice of the Iran–US Claims Tribunal in this regard, see also J Selby and D Stewart, "Practical Aspects of Arbitrating Claims," n 11, 231.

[22] See, eg, *Commercial Development Centre* (1983 Tribunal Rules), reprinted in section 2(D).

[23] See *Harris Intl Telecommunications* (1983 Tribunal Rules); *Agrostruct Intl* (1983 Tribunal Rules); *Frederica Lincoln Riahi* (1983 Tribunal Rules); *Vera-Jo Miller Aryeh* (1983 Tribunal Rules); *Vivian Mai Tavakoli* (1983 Tribunal Rules); *Dadras Intl* (1983 Tribunal Rules); and *NinniLadjevardi* (1983 Tribunal Rules); all reprinted in section 2(D).

[24] In earlier drafts of the 1976 UNCITRAL Rules, what is now Article 24 was originally included as part of an article which addressed both further written statements and further documentary evidence. (See Article 19 of the Preliminary Draft and Article 20 of the Revised Draft of the 1976 UNCITRAL Rules). The provision concerning further documentary evidence ultimately was separated and became part of Article 24 of the Final Draft (now Article 27). For the discussion in the Committee of the Whole (II) leading to the separation of the two issues, see *Summary Record of the 8th Meeting of the Committee of the Whole (II)*, UNCITRAL, 9th Session, UN Doc A/CN.9/9/C.2/SR.8, paras 61–78 (1976).

[25] Sometimes the very concept of "Memorial" is used to imply that documentary evidence is included. See N Blackaby and C Partasides, *Redfern and Hunter on International Arbitration*, n 10, 382.

[26] See n 8 and accompanying text. This and other filing arrangements for written submissions are illustrated by the Tribunal's early practice, as described by informed authors in 1984:

Chamber Two has the most standardized approach, typically a three-step schedule: (i) claimant files a summary of all evidence on which it will seek to rely, together with all documentary evidence (including affidavits) and any written briefs; (ii) respondent files the same; and (iii) both parties file any rebuttal evidence and briefs. Chambers One and Three have normally issued more varied, tailor-made orders, frequently with detailed descriptions of specific documents and types of evidence to be submitted and often setting a hearing date. Chamber One, in keeping with its general attention to technical and jurisdictional points, is most likely to decide minor preliminary questions or to indicate its intention to decide a given jurisdictional issue (especially corporate nationality) on documents at some future time.

J Selby and D Stewart, "Practical Aspects of Arbitrating Claims," n 11, 226–7. See also the various orders quoted in section 2(D).

[27] See, eg, *Gami Investments Inc* (1976 Rules); and *KarahaBodas Co LLC* (1976 Rules); both reprinted in section 2(C).

Whatever the approach taken, the arbitral tribunal must always state clearly what kind of submission it expects.[28]

In case voluminous submissions containing documentary evidence are expected, the arbitral tribunal should facilitate the later handling of the documents, for example, by instructing the parties to use tabs or exhibit numbers for the identification of the documents.[29]

Article 24 concludes with the provision that the arbitral tribunal "shall fix the periods of time for communicating such statements." Time limits will be discussed in connection with Article 25. Nevertheless, a relevant question here is whether the tribunal should order written statements to be submitted simultaneously or successively. The preceding discussion has already implied that the latter is preferable, "so that the claimant fires the first shot and the respondent answers."[30] As Mani points out, "where the plaintiff-defendant relationship is discernible simultaneous presentation is illogical in that it requires the defendant to produce a complete defence without knowing fully in advance of the arguments of the claimant."[31] Though this statement was made primarily with a view to pleadings discharged in a single round, it applies in principle to pleadings that take place in more than one exchange. Where, however, there has already been a substantial exchange of successively submitted pleadings, the simultaneous communication of final rebuttals (in a third or fourth round) may be a proper method to avoid delays with due respect for the equality of the parties. In the earlier practice of the Iran–US Claims Tribunal, the sequential exchange of statements of claim and defence, replies and rejoinders, as well as memorials and counter-memorials, was often followed by the simultaneous filing of rebuttals.[32] Later, however, the practice was to allow the respondent to file the final rebuttal submission.[33]

Apart from rebuttals, simultaneous submission of written statements may be proper in those exceptional cases in which a clear claimant–respondent relationship is lacking, or where none of the parties agrees to be treated as a respondent.[34] Simultaneous filings should also be ordered if the parties so wish.[35] When ordering simultaneous pleadings, the arbitral tribunal should ensure that a party who intentionally withholds its own submission until it has been able to study that of its adversary obtains no unfair advantage thereby.[36]

---

[28] As leading commentators note:

> The parties must understand what is intended. Otherwise the arbitration may be delayed by inadequate written submissions or, alternatively, time and money may be wasted in making voluminous and exhaustive written presentations when the arbitral tribunal intends to hold a full oral inquiry into the evidence and arguments at hearings that will take place later in the proceedings.

N Blackaby and C Partasides, *Redfern and Hunter on International Arbitration*, n 10, 379–80.

[29] See *Joan Ward Malekzadeh* (1983 Tribunal Rules) reprinted in section 2(D).

[30] N Blackaby and C Partasides, *Redfern and Hunter on International Arbitration*, n 10, 381.

[31] V S Mani, *International Adjudication*, n 8, 107.

[32] Contrast *Control Data Corp* (1983 Tribunal Rules); *Varo Intl Corp* (1983 Tribunal Rules); and *Cabot Intl Capital Corp* (1983 Tribunal Rules); all reprinted in section 2(D).

[33] See *RanaNikpour* (1983 Tribunal Rules), reprinted in section 2(D). See also A Mouri, *The International Law of Expropriation*, n 11, 11, n 38. Even in recent years, however, the Full Tribunal has ordered hearing memorials to be filed simultaneously.

[34] Sovereigns may be reluctant to assume this role. An example is provided by the *Aminoil* case, Chapter 9, n 16. See N Blackaby and C Partasides, *Redfern and Hunter on International Arbitration*, n 10, 381.

[35] A common wish of this kind may be behind the order issued in *Brown & Root* (1983 Tribunal Rules), reprinted in section 2(D).

[36] See *Sterling Drug* (1983 Tribunal Rules), reprinted in section 2(D).

The UNCITRAL Model Law contains no provision corresponding to the present Article 24. Such a provision is indeed more properly covered by a set of arbitration rules than by a law on arbitration.

(2) Comparison to the 1976 UNCITRAL Rules

Article 24 was adopted without any revision to corresponding Article 22 of the 1976 UNCITRAL Rules.

C. Extracts from the Practice of Investment Tribunals

Karaha Bodas Co LLC and *Perusahaan Pertambangan Minyak Dan Gas Bumi Negara,* et al, Preliminary Award (September 30, 1999) (*Ad Hoc* Proceeding, 1976 UNCITRAL Rules, Concession Agreement), at 10–11:

The Arbitral Tribunal has,

...

4. Fixed the procedural time table applicable until the issuing of the preliminary award as follows:
   - the Defendants will file a brief on the above referred preliminary issues by January 10, 1999 with all documents they are relying upon,
   - the Claimant will provide a reply within 45 days maximum from the receipt of the Defendant's brief, with all documents it is relying upon,
   - a hearing will then be held on March 10, 1999 in Paris.
5. Contemplated a provisional time table for the continuation of the procedure in case the Tribunal would retain its jurisdiction as follows:
   - the Claimant may, within one month from the rendering of the preliminary award, revise its Statement of Claim dated November 11, 1998,
   - the Defendants will then have two months to reply starting either from the receipt of the revised brief or from the notification by the Claimant that no revised brief will be filed,
   - the Claimant will submit a rebuttal to the reply of the Defendants within one month from receipt of that reply,
   - the Defendants will then submit a rejoinder to the Claimant's memorial within one month from receipt of that rebuttal.

With all these written statements, the parties are entitled to provide any further documentary evidence; A hearing will then be held within one month after receipt of the last brief.

Methanex Corp and *United States of America*, Minutes of Order of First Procedural Meeting (June 29, 2000) (ICSID administered, 1976 UNCITRAL Rules, NAFTA Chapter Eleven), at 4:

Item 9: Pleadings

The Claimant shall re-serve on each member of the Tribunal copies of its Notice of Arbitration, its Statement of Claim of 3 December 1999 and accompanying schedule(s) as soon as practicable.

As regards service of further pleadings, as set out in their letter dated 29 June 2000 to the Tribunal, the parties agreed the following time-table:

Statement of Defence: 11 August 2000

Statement of Reply (if required): 28 August

Statement of Rejoinder (if required): 14 September

(The timing of any further written pleadings, under Articles 19, 20 and 22 of the [1976] UNCITRAL Arbitration Rules or otherwise, may be addressed at the Second Procedural Meeting or subsequent meetings).

...

Methanex Corp and *United States of America*, Minutes of Order of Second Procedural Meeting (September 7, 2000) (ICSID administered, 1976 UNCITRAL Rules, NAFTA Chapter Eleven), at 2:

> The procedural time-table envisaged by the Tribunal at the meeting was subsequently modified at the request of the Disputing Parties, by further order of the Tribunal communicated by letter dated 10th October 2000 as follows:
>
> (1) *16 October 2000*: Further written submissions of non-state petitioners for "amicus curiae" status;
>
> (2) *27 October 2000*: Methanex and US written statements re (1);
>
> (3) *10 November 2000*: Mexico and Canada written submissions as Non-Disputing State Parties re Article 1128 of Chapter Eleven of NAFTA ("Participation by a Party"); and
>
> (4) *22 November 2000*: Methanex and US written submissions re (3) submissions from Mexico and Canada.
>
> ...

United Parcel Service of America, Inc and *Government of Canada*, Award on Jurisdiction (November 22, 2002) (ICSID administered, 1976 UNCITRAL Rules, NAFTA Chapter Eleven), at 40:

> 131. ... Article 22 [of the 1976 UNCITRAL Rules] is also relevant, as both parties remind the Tribunal. It has the power to decide whether further written statements, in addition to the statements of claim and defence, should be required from the parties or presented by them.

Gami Investments Inc and *Government of The United Mexican States*, Procedural Order No 1 (January 31, 2003) (*Ad Hoc* Proceeding, 1976 UNCITRAL Rules, NAFTA Chapter Eleven), at 2–3:

> 5. Timetable for the Proceedings
>
> 5.1 The timetable for the proceedings shall be as follows:
>
> (a) 10 February 2003
>
> The Claimant shall file its Statement of Claim, together with witness statements, expert reports and such other documentary evidence that it relies upon.
>
> (b) 10 March 2003
>
> The Respondent shall file: (i) comments on whether the proceeding should be separated into different phases (bifurcation); and (ii) notification of any objections to jurisdiction and admissibility.
>
> (c) 8 April 2003
>
> The Respondent shall file its definitive submissions on its objections (if any) to jurisdiction and admissibility.
>
> (d) 8 May 2003
>
> The Claimant shall file its submission in reply to the Respondent's objections (if any) to jurisdiction and admissibility and shall reply to the Respondent's comments on bifurcation.
>
> (e) 22 May 2003
>
> The Arbitral Tribunal shall decide whether the Respondent's objections to jurisdiction and/or admissibility will be resolved separately as preliminary matters or be joined to the merits. If the former, the deadlines which follow shall be vacated.
>
> (f) 9 June 2003
>
> The Respondent shall file its Statement of Defence together with witness statements, expert reports and such other documentary evidence that it relies upon.

(g) 8 July 2003

The Claimant shall file its Reply to the Respondent's Statement of Defence together with any responsive witness statements, expert reports and documentary evidence.

(h) 8 August 2003

The Respondent shall file its Rejoinder to the Claimant's Reply together with any responsive witness statements, expert reports and documentary evidence.

5.2 At the latest following the conclusion of the written submissions referred to above, the Arbitral Tribunal shall fix dates for a status conference call with respect to the hearing and the possible exchange of post-hearing submissions, as well as possible submissions by other NAFTA Parties.

D. Extracts from the Practice of the Iran–US Claims Tribunal

Control Data Corp and *Islamic Republic of Iran*, Case No 88, Chamber Three, Order of December 20, 1985:

Having held the Pre-Hearing Conference in the Case on 17 December 1985 and taking into account the submissions of the Parties, the Tribunal decides as follows:

...

5. With respect to the further proceedings:
   a. By 30 April 1986, the Claimants shall file their memorial on all issues in this Case, including any and all written evidence they wish to rely on.
   b. By 30 September 1986, the Respondents shall file their memorials on all issues in this Case, including any and all written evidence they wish to rely on.
   c. By 1 December 1986, the Parties shall submit any brief and evidence in rebuttal.
   d. In setting these time-limits, the Tribunal has taken into consideration the multiplicity of the Respondents and the potential difficulties related to coordination of their submissions.

Cabot Intl Capital Corp and Overseas Private Investment Corp and *Islamic Republic of Iran*, Case No 96, Chamber One, Order of March 25, 1983:

A Pre-Hearing Conference was held in this case on February 28, 1983. The Chamber sets forth the following as the schedule for further proceedings:

The Government of the Islamic Republic of Iran is granted until 1 June 1983 to file a Statement of Defence in this case.

11 April 1983: Claimants shall file a memorial on the question of whether OPIC is entitled to submit a claim in this case, including comments with respect to any laws governing insurance contracts which may be applicable. Claimants shall attach complete copies of the Contract of Insurance and the Settlement Agreement with OPIC. Claimants shall further file the documents and other written evidence on which they intend to rely, including affidavits of any experts and other witnesses, together with such summaries of evidence as they choose to submit.

10 June 1983: Respondents shall file the documents and other written evidence on which they intend to rely, including affidavits of any experts and other witnesses, together with such summaries of evidence as they choose to submit.

11 July 1983: Claimants shall file any rebuttal evidence they choose to submit in the light of Respondents' submission.

9 September 1983: Respondents shall file any rebuttal evidence they choose to submit in the light of Claimants' submissions.

7 October 1983: The parties shall file a list of witnesses, if any, through whom they intend to present oral evidence, pursuant to Article 25 of the Provisionally Adopted Tribunal Rules.

21–22 November 1983: The Parties are invited to appear at Parkweg 13, The Hague at 9.30 a.m. for the Hearing in this case.

American Bell Intl Inc and *Islamic Republic of Iran*, Award No 255–48–3 (September 19, 1986), reprinted in 12 Iran-US CTR 170, 172 (1986-III):

> 4. The Final Hearing was held on 9 and 10 October 1985. On 8 November 1985 Respondents submitted a Post-Hearing Memorial. This had been authorized by the Tribunal in view of the submission by Claimant on 30 September 1985 of its Counter-Memorial with extensive supporting documents the Farsi version of which, moreover, was not timely submitted.

Sterling Drug Inc and *Islamic Republic of Iran*, Case No 491, Chamber Three, Order of January 11, 1985:

> The time for the Respondents to file any evidence in rebuttal is further extended to 15 February 1985.
>
> In view of the fact that the simultaneous filing envisaged in the Order of 21 September 1984 has been derogated from, the Claimants are invited to inform the Tribunal within 3 weeks of the filing of Respondents' rebuttals of any prejudice which may have resulted from the non-simultaneous filing.
>
> On the basis of such information, the Tribunal will decide whether Claimants will be given an opportunity to comment on the rebuttals.

Varo Intl Corp and *Islamic Republic of Iran*, Case No 275, Chamber One, Order of March 13, 1986:

> Each Party shall file with the Tribunal by 12 June 1986, copies of all written evidence on which it will seek to rely together with a list of all documentary evidence submitted by it in this Case and the location in the record (by tab or Exhibit number) of each such document. By the same date each Party may file a Hearing Memorial explaining the evidence and summarizing the issues in this case.
>
> Each Party shall file by 12 September 1986 copies of any documentary evidence on which it will seek to rely in rebuttal of previously presented evidence together with a supplemental list of such rebuttal evidence and the location of each such document in the record.
>
> In this context the Parties should bear in mind that the following consideration will apply once the Tribunal has scheduled a Hearing:
>
> 1. No new documents may be introduced in evidence prior to the Hearing unless the Tribunal so permits and unless the request for their introduction is filed at least two months before the Hearing.
> 2. At the Hearing, any Party is free to make any arguments it wishes, but new documents may not be introduced in evidence unless the Tribunal so permits, which permission will not normally be granted except for evidence in rebuttal of evidence introduced in the Hearing.
>
> The guidelines for the translation of documentary evidence are attached to this Order.

United States of America on behalf and for the benefit of Harrington & Associates, Inc and *Islamic Republic of Iran*, Case No 10712, Chamber Three, Order of October 23, 1986:

> 1. Reference is made to the order dated 2 July 1986 extending the time limit for the Respondent to submit any further Statement or Brief until 8 September 1986, the submission filed by the Respondent on 25 September 1986 and the "Opposition To Respondent's Late Submission" filed on 30 September 1986 by the Agent of the United States.
> 2. The Tribunal notes that notwithstanding its Order of 2 July 1986, and the Hearing in this Case scheduled for 7 October 1986, the Respondent filed on 25 September 1986 a voluminous submission styled "Rejoinder of Iran Carton Company."
> 3. At the Hearing on 7 October 1986, the Tribunal informed the Parties that it was prepared to consider the Respondent's late submission but that in order to avoid undue prejudice to the Claimant caused by the filing of such a voluminous submission so shortly before the

Hearing date, it would permit the Claimant to submit its reply to this submission after the Hearing.

4. The Claimant is accordingly invited to submit its reply by 21 November 1986.

Fluor Corp, Fluor Intercontinental Inc and *Islamic Republic of Iran*, Case No 810, Chamber One, Order of February 16, 1987:

4 a. The Claimants shall file by 30 May 1987 a Hearing Memorial together with copies of all written evidence on which they will seek to rely, together with a list of all documentary evidence submitted by them in this Case and its location in the record (by tab or Exhibit number).

   b. The Respondent, the National Iranian Oil Company, shall by 30 May 1987 file a Hearing Memorial with respect to the Counter-claim together with copies of all written evidence on which it will seek to rely together with a list of all documentary evidence submitted by it in this case and the location in the record (by tab or Exhibit number) of each such document.

   c. The Respondents shall file by 30 September 1987 a Response to the Memorial and evidence, referred to under paragraph 4 a., and the Claimants shall file by the same date their Response to the Memorial and the evidence, referred to under paragraph 4 b.

   d. The Tribunal, by further Order, will invite each Party to submit simultaneously a Memorial containing only its Comments on the Memorials of the other party submitted pursuant to Para 4(c), together with any evidence in support of such comments.

Harris Intl Telecommunications, Inc and *Islamic Republic of Iran*, Award No 323–409–1 (November 2, 1987), reprinted in 17 Iran-US CTR 31, 45–46 (1987-IV):

57. As noted in the discussion of the procedural history of this case, both Parties have submitted documents after the expiration of the filing deadlines established by the Tribunal's Order of 6 March 1986. At the Hearing, the Tribunal reserved its decision on the admissibility of these documents. The Tribunal now turns to an examination of this issue.

58. The starting point of the analysis must be the [1983] Tribunal Rules themselves. There are four rules relevant to this determination. First, Articles 22 and 23 of the Rules provide authority for the Tribunal to establish deadlines for the submission of written submissions. In establishing such deadlines, however, the Tribunal must be mindful of Article 15, which requires that both Parties be treated with equality.

59. Article 22 provides:

   The arbitral tribunal shall decide which further written statements, in addition to the statement of claim and the statement of defence, shall be required from the parties or may be presented by them and shall fix the periods of time for communicating such statements.

   Moreover, Article 28, paragraph 3, states:
   If one of the parties, duly invited to produce documentary evidence, fails to do so within the established period of time, without showing sufficient cause for such failure, the arbitral tribunal may make the award on the evidence before it.

60. Taken together, these rules provide authority for the Tribunal to make and to enforce deadlines for the filing of written submissions, provided that the Parties are treated with equality. This limitation is important. Equality, a "fundamental principle of justice" implies that the Parties must have equal opportunity to make written submissions and to respond to each other's submissions. *See Foremost Tehran, Inc.* and *Islamic Republic of Iran*, Case Nos 37, 231 (Chamber One) (Order of 15 Sept 1983). The Tribunal "has repeatedly stated that no party shall submit any document only at the Hearing or so shortly before the Hearing that the other Party cannot respond to it without prejudice and in an appropriate way", *Sylvania Technical Systems, Inc.* and *Government of the Islamic Republic of Iran*, Award No 180–64–1,

p. 3–7 June 1985); *Questech, Inc.* and *Ministry of National Defence of the Islamic Republic of Iran*, Award No 191–59–1, p. 4 (25 Sept. 1985).

Commercial Development Centre and *US State Dept (Ex US Embassy in Iran)*, Case No B65, Chamber Two, Order of September 28, 1987:

The Tribunal will decide whether to authorize posthearing submissions only at the end of the Hearing. In the Interest of the efficient conduct of the arbitration, the Tribunal will be reluctant to authorize such submissions unless they are clearly essential.

Brown & Root, Inc and *Islamic Republic of Iran*, Case No 432, Chamber One, Order of December 4, 1987:

Each Party shall file simultaneously by 1 March 1988 with the Tribunal copies of any remaining written evidence on which it will seek to rely together with a list of all documentary evidence submitted by it in this Case and the location in the record (by tab or Exhibit number) of each such document. By the same date each Party may file a Hearing Memorial explaining the evidence and summarizing the issues in this Case.

Each Party shall file simultaneously by 1 June 1988 copies of any documentary evidence on which it will seek to rely in rebuttal of previously presented evidence together with a supplemental list of such rebuttal evidence and the location of each such document in the record.

General Electric Co, on behalf of its Aircraft Engine Business Group, and *Islamic Republic of Iran*, Case No 386 Chamber One, Order of December 10, 1987:

On 30 November 1987 the Claimant filed a Request for an order authorizing the Parties in this Case to file simultaneous surrebuttals. In the Request it is stated that the Respondents' rebuttal Memorial and Exhibits filed on 3 August 1987 contain new arguments and evidence. It is also stated that a round of surrebuttal pleadings would afford the Respondents a further opportunity to respond fully to Claimant's evidence and arguments.

It has been the established practice of the Tribunal to close the exchange of written pleadings after the submission of Memorials in Rebuttal. In order to secure equal treatment of the Parties and an orderly conduct of the proceedings, the Tribunal admits further written submissions close to the Hearing date only in exceptional circumstances.

The Tribunal finds no reason to allow a further round of submissions in the present Case. If any of the material filed by the Respondents on 3 August 1987 is found not to fall within the definition of rebuttal evidence, it will be ruled inadmissible and disregarded. The Claimant's request is therefore denied.

Agrostruct Intl, Inc and *Iran State Cereals Organization*, Award No 358–195–1 (April 15, 1988), reprinted in 18 Iran-US CTR 180, 187 (1988-I):

26. Articles 22 and 28, paragraph 3, of the [1983] Tribunal Rules, taken together, provide authority for the Tribunal to establish and enforce deadlines for the filing of written submissions, provided that the parties are treated with equality. Fundamental principles of equality and fairness between the parties, possible prejudice to either party, as well as the orderly conduct of the proceedings, require that time limits be established and enforced. The Tribunal has therefore repeatedly stated that no party shall submit any document for the first time at the Hearing, or so shortly before the Hearing that the other party cannot respond to it in an appropriate way. In deciding whether, in a particular case, a late-filed submission is nevertheless admissible, the Tribunal considers the character and contents of the submission, its length, and the cause of delay. *See Harris International Telecommunications, Inc.*, and *The Islamic Republic of Iran,* et al., Award No 323–409–1, paras 57 *et seq.* (2 Nov 1987).

RanaNikpour and *Islamic Republic of Iran*, Case No 336, Chamber One, Interlocutory Award No ITL 81–336–1 (February 18, 1993), reprinted in 29 Iran-US CTR 67, 68 (1993):

> 5. On 15 July 1992, the Claimant filed a letter in which she requested an opportunity to reply to the above-mentioned Iran's submission of 26 May 1992 because that submission, according to her, includes new documents not previously submitted to the Tribunal. The Agent of the Government of the Islamic Republic of Iran filed a letter on 24 July 1992 objecting to the request. By a letter of 13 August 1992, the Claimant renewed the request.
>
> 6. Before proceeding further, the Tribunal decides the Claimant's request. Having regard to Iran's rebuttal filing of 26 May 1992, the Tribunal considers that the evidence submitted in that filing is admissible as rebuttal evidence. Further, the Tribunal notes that it has already twice given both the Claimant and the Respondents a full opportunity of presenting their evidence concerning the Claimant's dominant and effective nationality. See, *supra*, paras 2 and 4. Moreover, the Tribunal points out that its practice in conducting the proceedings is that a respondent is entitled to file a final rebuttal submission. Consequently, the Tribunal does not deem it necessary to grant the Claimant's request or to request any further filings concerning the issue of the Claimant's dominant and effective nationality.

Joan Ward Malekzadeh and *Islamic Republic of Iran*, Case No 356, Chamber One, Order of August 12, 1993:

> Having regard to both Parties' submissions and referring to Articles 15.1, 19 and 22 of the Tribunal's Rules, the Tribunal considers it appropriate to set the following schedule for further submissions in this Case:
>
> 1. The Respondent shall file with the Tribunal its Statement of Defence by October 28, 1993.
>
> 2. The Claimant shall file with the Tribunal by January 27, 1994 copies of any documentary evidence on which it will seek to rely with respect to any issues remaining in the Case, including any jurisdictional issues not decided in the Interlocutory Award and the merits, together with a list of all documentary evidence submitted by it in this Case and the location in the record (by tab or Exhibit number) of each such document. By the same date the Claimant may file a Hearing Memorial explaining the evidence and summarizing the issues in this Case.
>
> 3. The Respondent shall file with the Tribunal by April 28, 1994 copies of any remaining written evidence on which it will seek to rely with respect to any issues remaining in the Case, including any jurisdictional issues not decided in the Interlocutory Award and the merits, together with a list of all documentary evidence submitted by it in the Case and the location on the record (by tab or Exhibit number) of each such document. By the same date the Respondent may file a Hearing Memorial explaining the evidence and summarizing the issues in this Case.
>
> 4. The Claimant shall file with the Tribunal by June 27, 1994 copies of any documentary evidence on which it will seek to rely in the rebuttal of previously presented evidence, together with a supplemental list of such rebuttal evidence and the location of each such document in the record. By the same date the Claimant may file a Memorial explaining the evidence and summarizing the issues in this Case.
>
> 5. The Respondent shall file with the Tribunal by August 26. 1994 copies of any documentary evidence on which it will seek to rely in rebuttal of previously presented evidence, together with a supplemental list of such rebuttal evidence and the location of each such document in the record. By the same date the respondent may file a Memorial explaining the evidence and summarizing the issues in this Case.

NinniLadjevardi (formerly Burgel) and *Government of the Islamic Republic of Iran*, Award No 553–118–1 (December 8, 1993), reprinted in 29 Iran-US CTR 367, 377 (1993):

> 33. Turning now to an examination of this issue, the Tribunal first notes that Articles 22 and 28, paragraph 3, of the [1983] Tribunal Rules, taken together, provide authority for the Tribunal to

establish and enforce deadlines for the filing of written submissions, provided that the parties are treated with equality. Fundamental principles of equality and fairness between the parties, possible prejudice to either party, as well as the orderly conduct of the proceedings, require that time limits be established and enforced. The Tribunal has therefore repeatedly stated that no party shall submit any document for the first time at the Hearing, or so shortly before the Hearing that the other party cannot respond to it in an appropriate way. *See Harris International Telecommunications, Inc. v. Islamic Republic of Iran, et al.*, Award No 323–409–1, paras 57 *et seq.* (2 Nov. 1987), *reprinted in* 17 Iran-U.S. C.T.R. 31, 45.

Dadras Intl, et al and *Islamic Republic of Iran,* et al, Award No 567–213/215–3 (November 7, 1995), reprinted in 31 Iran-US CTR 127, 135–36 (1995) (footnotes omitted):

26. By Order dated 23 February 1994, the Tribunal decided to admit the Golzar affidavit into evidence, *see* para 36, below. The Tribunal did not explain the underlying reasons for its decision at that time, however, and proceeds to do so now.
27. The [1983] Tribunal Rules grant considerable discretion to the Tribunal to admit or exclude written submissions. This discretion includes the power to accept unauthorized post-Hearing submissions, as derived from Article 15, paragraph 1; Article 22; Article 25, paragraph 6; and Article 29, paragraph 2 of the Tribunal Rules.
28. Tribunal precedent is, however, strongly against the admission into evidence of unauthorized late-filed documents. The Tribunal has expressed a particular aversion to admitting documents that are submitted not only after filing deadlines, but also after the Hearing itself. The most extensive treatment of this issue is to be found in *Harris International Telecommunications, Inc. and The Islamic Republic of Iran, et al.*, Award No 323–409–1 (2 November 1987), reprinted in 17 Iran-U.S. C.T.R. 31, 45–50.
29. Harris emphasizes that in deciding whether to admit a late submission, it is important that the Tribunal treat the parties equally and fairly, bearing in mind that accepting late-filed documents from one party can result in prejudice to the other. A further consideration is the "orderly conduct of the proceedings." In applying these principles to the facts of a given case, the Tribunal should consider the "character and contents of late-filed documents and the length and cause of the delay." Late-filed submissions containing new facts and evidence "are the most likely to cause prejudice to the other Party and to disrupt the arbitral process if filed late."
30. Thus the considerations that are generally relevant when deciding whether to admit late-filed documents are the possibility of prejudice, the equality of treatment of the Parties, the disruption of the arbitral process caused by the delay and the reason for the delay.

Vivian Mai Tavakoli, et al and *Government of the Islamic Republic of Iran,* Award No 580–832–3 (April 23, 1997), reprinted in 33 Iran-US CTR 206, 211 (1997):

9. Under the [1983] Tribunal Rules the Tribunal has the discretion to accept unauthorized late submissions from the Parties. *See* Article 15, paragraph 1, and Article 22 of the Tribunal Rules. However, in the interests of the orderly conduct of the proceedings and in order to maintain "equality of arms," it has in general taken a restrictive approach to the exercise of this discretion. *See,* for example, *Dadras International, et al.* and *Islamic Republic of Iran, et al.*, Award No 567–213/215–3, paras 27–28 (7 Nov. 1995), *reprinted in* 31 Iran-U.S. C.T.R. 127, 135–36; *Edgar Protiva, et al.* and *Government of the Islamic Republic of Iran,* Award No 566–316–2, paras 30–36

(14 July 1995), *reprinted in* 31 Iran-U.S. C.T.R. 89, 102–03 ("Protiva"); *Reza Said Malek* and *Government of the Islamic Republic of Iran,* Award No 534–193–3, para 12 (11 Aug. 1992), *reprinted in* 28 Iran-U.S. C.T.R. 246, 249–50; *Harris International Telecommunications, Inc.* and *Islamic Republic of Iran, et al.*, Award No 323–409–1 (2 Nov. 1987), *reprinted in* 17 Iran-U.S. C.T.R. 31, 45–50. In the present Case, the Tribunal's Order of 17 April 1996 clearly restricted the scope of the submissions to be made by both Parties. In light of

these restrictions and in the absence of any other justifying circumstances, the Tribunal excludes from the record items 3, 4 and 6 of the Respondent's submission of 27 June 1996, the Claimant's entire submission of 22 July 1996 and the Respondent's entire submission of 20 August 1996.

Vera-Jo Miller Aryeh, et al and *Islamic Republic of Iran*, Award No 581–842/843/844–1 (May 22, 1997), reprinted in 33 Iran-US CTR 272, 287 (1997):

2.1 Admissibility of Late-Filed Documents: Documents Submitted at the Hearings and Post-Hearing Submissions

48. The Tribunal notes that, according to its practice reflected in *Harris International Telecommunications, Inc. and The Islamic Republic of Iran, et al.*, Partial Award No 323–409–1, paras 57–75 (2 Nov. 1987), *reprinted in* 17 Iran-US CTR 31, 45–52, Articles 15, 22, 23, and 28 of the [1983] Tribunal Rules are the primary rules regulating the status of late-filed documents. Generally, based upon Article 22, the Tribunal considers and decides which further submissions in addition to the statement of claim and the statement of defence are to be required from the parties in each case and sets forth the schedule for communicating such statements. Moreover, Article 28 gives the Tribunal the authority to make an award based on the evidence before it, if a party that has had the opportunity to file documentary evidence fails to file within the established period of time, and fails to show sufficient reason for its nonconformity. This rule equally applies to the situation in which a party has properly filed its documents, but subsequently tries to submit additional, unauthorized material for inclusion in the record of the case.

49. Furthermore, on the basis of Article 15, both parties to the case have to be treated equally. This means that both parties to the case are entitled to have an equal opportunity to present written submissions and to respond to each other's submissions. This also means that the parties must have an equal opportunity to go through the evidence and the arguments submitted by the other party, and to prepare their own position and arguments in advance of the hearing.

50. Chamber One has taken a strict stance on these matters: no new evidence is permitted prior to the hearing unless the Tribunal finds that it is justified by exceptional circumstances and is filed no later than two months before the hearing in the case. Moreover, as a matter of routine in its orders scheduling a hearing the Chamber advises the parties that any party is free to make whatever arguments it wishes at the hearing; however, parties may not introduce new documents into evidence absent the Tribunal's permission. Such permission normally is not granted except for rebuttal evidence introduced to rebut evidence produced at the hearing.

Frederica Lincoln Riahi and *Government of the Islamic Republic of Iran*, Award No 600–485–1 (February 27, 2003) (citations omitted):

44. The Tribunal has considered the issue of late-filed documents in several previous Cases. In *Harris International Telecommunications*, the Tribunal stated that "[t]he starting point of the analysis must be the [1983] Tribunal Rules themselves. There are four rules relevant to this determination." The Tribunal referred to Articles 22 and 23 of the Tribunal Rules, which provide authority for the Tribunal to establish deadlines for written submissions. In addition, the Tribunal referred to Article 15, which requires that the parties be treated with equality. Moreover, Article 28 gives the Tribunal the authority to make an award based on the evidence before it, if a party that has had the opportunity to file documentary evidence fails to file that evidence within the established period of time, and fails to show sufficient reason for its nonconformity. As the Tribunal stated in Harris International Telecommunications, "these rules provide authority for the Tribunal to make and to enforce deadlines for the filing of written submissions, provided that the Parties are treated with equality."

45. Chamber One has taken a clear position when deciding the admissibility of late filings. When scheduling hearings, the Chamber routinely informs the parties that it does not permit new

evidence prior to a hearing, unless it determines that admission of the documents is justified by exceptional circumstances, and unless those documents are filed not later than two months before the hearing.

3. Time Limits on Submission—Article 25

A. Text of the 2010 UNCITRAL Rule[37]

Article 25 of the 2010 UNCITRAL Rule provides:

The periods of time fixed by the arbitral tribunal for the communication of written statements (including the statement of claim and statement of defence) should not exceed 45 days. However, the arbitral tribunal may extend the time limits if it concludes that an extension is justified.

B. Commentary

(1) General comments

The contents of Article 25 reflect a compromise between two partly conflicting considerations: the need for speedy proceedings on the one hand and the practical impossibility of prescribing rigid time limits to enhance quick disposition of the cases on the other. A compromise has been achieved by setting a time limit that is "merely intended to serve as a general guideline."[38] Thus, although the periods in question "should not exceed forty-five days," exceptions to this rule are possible within relatively wide limits.[39]

The 45-day rule can be modified initially by written agreement of the parties pursuant to Article 1(1).[40] The Iran–US Claims Tribunal's modification of Article 23 of the 1976 UNCITRAL Rules serves as an example. Pursuant to Article III(4) of the Claims Settlement Declaration, as implemented in Article 18 of the modified 1976 UNCITRAL Rules,[41] all statements of claim must be filed between October 20, 1981 and January 20, 1982, whereas the modified version of Article 19 sets the limit for the submission of statements of defence at 135 days.[42] As modified in the Tribunal Rules, Article 23 sets the limit for additional written statements at 90 days.

The provisions just reviewed, with their rather extensive time periods, reflect the special nature of the arbitration process conducted before the Iran–US Claims Tribunal.[43] However, in more conventional arbitration it is also possible, and sometimes advisable, for the

---

[37] Article 25 was adopted without any modification to the text of corresponding Article 22 of the 1976 UNCITRAL Rules.

[38] *Report of the Secretary-General on the Revised Draft Set of Arbitration Rules*, UNCITRAL, 9th Session, Addendum 1 (Commentary), UN Doc A/CN.9/112/Add.1 (1975), reprinted in (1976) VII UNCITRAL Ybk 166, 175.

[39] See, eg, *GAMI Investments, Inc* (1976 Rules), reprinted in section 2(C) (permitting respondent four months to file statement of defence).

[40] *Report of the Secretary-General on the Revised Draft Set of Arbitration Rules*, UNCITRAL, 9th Session, Addendum 1 (Commentary), UN Doc A/CN.9/112/Add.1 (1975), reprinted in (1976) VII UNCITRAL Ybk 166, 175.

[41] See Chapter 13, n 41.

[42] See Chapter 13, n 48.

[43] Many Iranian entities faced a multitude of claims directed against them—hence the 135-day period reserved for statements of defence was appropriate. The 90-day period stipulated in Article 23 of the 1983 Tribunal Rules in part also accounts for this heavy case load. As the disposition of the claims in any case is bound to take quite some time, it perhaps does not make much difference whether 45 or 90 days is the general period of time for written statements.

parties to agree on modifications to the first sentence of Article 25. Modification with regard to the statement of claim should probably involve a shortening rather than a lengthening of the time limit.

Although the claimant may not have included his statement of claim in the notice of arbitration,[44] by the time the proceedings commence, the claimant likely will already have been able to make necessary preparations and, consequently, may not need as long as 45 days to submit the statement of claim.[45]

The first sentence of Article 25 can be modified by a decision of the tribunal as well as by mutual agreement of the parties. The use of the word "should" rather than "shall" or "must" in Article 25 indicates the time specified is only a guideline to be adapted as necessary. Submission of the statement of claim is less likely to require an extension beyond the 45-day limit than subsequent written statements.

Whatever the period of time originally ordered or agreed upon, "the arbitral tribunal may extend the time-limits if it concludes that an extension is justified." The power of the arbitral tribunal to grant an extension is not limited by any given number of days, nor is the tribunal prohibited from renewing or increasing an extension once granted.[46] The only limitation, in addition to those imposed by the general provisions of Article 17—especially the principle of equality—is that in each case the extension be "justified."

The burden of proving justification lies with the party requesting the extension. Legitimate reasons for an extension may include illness of counsel, communication problems, or unexpected problems in gathering evidence to be submitted in support of the written statement in question.[47] It is up to the arbitral tribunal to assess their weight. The consent of the other party, or even its failure to object, makes it easier for the arbitral tribunal to accept the alleged justification.[48] Whereas an initial extension may be granted fairly readily, further extensions may require more "compelling" reasons.[49] In case of doubt the arbitral tribunal may ask a party to elaborate on the reasons for its request.[50]

The justification presented by a party in support of its extension request must be balanced against the possible prejudice that the extension may cause. An extension necessitating the postponement of previously scheduled oral proceedings, or threatening to hamper the orderly conduct of such proceedings, should be granted only for very exceptional

---

[44] See Chapter 10.

[45] The Revised Draft envisaged a period of only 15 days for the statement of claim, reserving 45 days for other written statements. See *Report of the Secretary-General on the Revised Draft Set of Arbitration Rules*, UNCITRAL, 9th Session, Addendum 1 (Commentary), UN Doc A/CN.9/112/Add.1 (1975), reprinted in (1976) VII UNCITRAL Ybk 166, 175. In the Committee of the Whole II it was "agreed that this article should not contain any special provision concerning the communication of the statement of claim." *Report of the UNCITRAL on the Work of its Ninth Session*, UN GAOR, 31st Session, Supp No 17, UN Doc A/31/17, para 120 (1976), reprinted in (1976) VII UNCITRAL Ybk 66, 75.

However, the parties of course retain their freedom to modify the time limits in accordance with Article 1(1).

[46] See, eg, *United States* and *Iran*, Case No A/33 (1983 Tribunal Rules), reprinted in section 3(D).

[47] Webster notes other possible justifications may depend on the complexity of an arbitration or the involvement of government entities. T Webster, *Handbook of UNCITRAL Arbitration: Commentary, Precedents and Materials for UNCITRAL Based Arbitration Rules* (2010) 346. Even absent reasonable justifications for an extension of time, a tribunal may find it difficult to reject late-filed documents that are material to the claims presented in the arbitration. See *OuzielAryeh* (1983 Tribunal Rules), reprinted in section 3(D).

[48] Although there is no absolute duty to ask the other party to give its comments, in cases involving requests for more significant extensions that party should be provided an opportunity to lodge any protest it may have against the extension requested.

[49] See *Texaco Iran* (1983 Tribunal Rules), reprinted in section 3(D).

[50] See *Thomas Earl Payne* (1983 Tribunal Rules), reprinted in section 3(D).

reasons.[51] The arbitral tribunal can also, of course, grant a shorter extension than that requested by the party. In some of its cases, the Iran–US Claims Tribunal has balanced its decision of granting an extension with the need of orderly proceedings by granting an extension for the submission of the statement of defence until a certain date and at the same time setting the deadline for the hearing memorial on the same date.[52]

Although, as a rule, granting an extension presupposes a request by the party concerned, the arbitrators may in principle also conclude *proprio motu* that an extension is justified by the circumstances. An example is provided by an order of the Iran–US Claims Tribunal in the *Development and Resources Corporation* case. The Tribunal denied Respondents' motion to have the Claimant translate certain documents into Farsi but allowed an extension for Respondents' next submission "in order to facilitate Respondents' task in reviewing the documents under submission."[53] In general, the Tribunal's practice of granting extensions can be characterized as liberal.[54]

One of the most important questions to be addressed in connection with Article 25 pertains to the consequences of a failure to meet time limits (including extensions) set for the submission of written statements. In the unlikely event that the claimant who initiated the proceedings fails without sufficient cause to submit his claim, the arbitral tribunal, "shall" according to Article 30(1), "issue an order for the termination of the arbitral proceedings."[55] Similarly, should the respondent fail to communicate its statement of defence "without showing sufficient cause," the arbitral tribunal shall, according to the same provision, "order that the proceedings continue." The reference to the "showing of sufficient cause" implies that before making any decision under Article 30(1), the arbitral tribunal should provide the party with an opportunity to explain why the statement in question was not received.[56] Although Article 30(1) addresses only the statement of claim and statement of defence, the sanction it provides for the failure to submit these documents on time, ie, continuation of the proceedings, also applies in cases involving untimely submission of other written statements.

A few words are warranted about the consequences of actually filing a submission with the arbitral tribunal after the prescribed time limit. Although logic may require that such a submission be rejected, in arbitration such a drastic measure should be reserved for more significant delays. A delay of a few days should not normally lead to the rejection of a written statement (or of evidence, for that matter).[57] As stated by the Iran–US Claims Tribunal,

---

[51] See *Texaco Iran* (1983 Tribunal Rules), reprinted in section 3(D).
[52] See *Vera-Jo Miller Aryeh* (1983 Tribunal Rules), reprinted in section 3(D).
[53] See Chapter 11, section 2(D)(2).
[54] Baker and Davis summarize this practice as follows:

The arbitral chambers settled into a pattern of granting any party three extensions of three months without requiring any explanation. The order granting the third extension normally included cautionary language warning that no further extensions would be granted "without specific and compelling reasons." Iranian parties routinely responded to these orders by seeking a further extension, often asserting more specific reasons. The Tribunal normally denied fourth requests made without offering any particulars, but it nevertheless ordered that the filing be submitted "forthwith" or within an additional period of time. In egregious cases of delay, the Tribunal considered the filing waived and moved on to the next stage; as a practical matter, however, it normally accepted any submission filed sufficiently in advance of the hearing to provide the opposing party with an opportunity to respond.

S Baker and M Davis, *The UNCITRAL Arbitration Rules in Practice*, n 20, 99–100 (citations omitted). See also S Toope, *Mixed International Arbitration* (1990) 328 et seq. For illustrations of the practice, see section 3(D).

[55] See discussion of Article 28 in Chapter 19.
[56] See P Sanders, "Commentary on UNCITRAL Arbitration Rules," n 6, 206.
[57] See *Anaconda-Iran, Inc* (1983 Tribunal Rules), reprinted in Chapter 13, section 3(D)(3).

"fundamental requirements of equality between, and fairness to, the Parties, and the possible prejudice to either Party" should be considered when deciding whether a late submission can be accepted.[58] If a written statement (eg a rebuttal) from the other party is due after the delayed submission, any prejudice to that other party may be cured by accepting from it a correspondingly late filing.[59] Where, however, the arbitral tribunal has decided not to grant any extension for the submission in question, whether because of previous delays or for other reasons, the orderliness of the proceedings may require that the submission be rejected even in case of a relatively short delay.[60] Lack of explanation for the delay may also justify the rejection of a late-filed document.[61] The decision on the admissibility of late-filed documents may also be reserved pending consideration of further explanations to be given at a forthcoming hearing.[62] If rejection is considered too harsh, the arbitral tribunal may regard a delay in the submission of a document as a relevant consideration in allocating the costs of arbitration between the parties.[63] In certain situations (notably where a post-hearing submission is allowed), undue delays may be prevented by granting an extension request while making it clear that deliberations ("*note en délibéré*") and the finalization of the case will not be deferred pending the receipt of the submission.[64]

(2) Comparison to the 1976 UNCITRAL Rules

Article 25 was adopted without any revision to the text of corresponding Article 22 of the 1976 UNCITRAL Rules.

C. Extracts from the Practice of Investment Tribunals

No practice is being extracted in this area.

D. Extracts from the Practice of the Iran–US Claims Tribunal

Texaco Iran, Ltd and *National Iranian Oil Company and Islamic Republic of Iran*, Case No 72, Chamber Three, Order of September 9, 1983:

> In a letter dated 5 September 1983, the Agent for the Islamic Republic of Iran requested on behalf of the Respondents that the date for filing Statements of Defence in the above case be extended. The Tribunal notes that the deadline for filing the Statements of Defence has been successively extended on five separate occasions from 15 April 1982 for a total extension of over 17 months.
> The Respondents have shown no reasons which would justify a further extension in this case.
> Therefore, and in view of the fact that a Hearing in this case has been fixed for 1 and 2 December 1983, the Tribunal denies the above mentioned request for extension. The Order of 29 August 1983 remains in effect.

---

[58] See *W Jack Buckamier* (1983 Tribunal Rules), reprinted in section 3(D).
[59] See *Phillips Petroleum Co, Iran* (1983 Tribunal Rules); and *United States on behalf of and for the benefit of Thomas A Todd* (1983 Tribunal Rules); both reprinted in section 3(D).
[60] *Computer Sciences Corp* (1983 Tribunal Rules), reprinted in section 3(D).
[61] *Bendix Corp* (1983 Tribunal Rules), reprinted in section 3(D).
[62] See *Arco Exploration, Inc* (1983 Tribunal Rules); and *Unidyne Corp* (1983 Tribunal Rules), reprinted in section 3(D).
[63] *Aeronutronic Overseas Services, Inc* (1983 Tribunal Rules), reprinted in section 3(D).
[64] See *Hoffman Export Corp* (1983 Tribunal Rules), reprinted in section 3(D). This is not the only order of its kind issued by the Iran–US Claims Tribunal.

Hoffman Export Corp (a division of Gould Inc) and *Ministry of National Defence of Iran*, Case No 50, Chamber Two, Order of December 8, 1983:

> The Tribunal notes that the Claimant has filed a request for an extension of time to reply to the Respondent's submission of 27 October 1985.
>
> The Tribunal wishes to make clear that it does not intend to defer its deliberations on the present case. Should Claimant wish to file a reply it shall do so as soon as possible. The Tribunal will treat any such submission as a *note en délibéré*, meaning that pending its receipt, the deliberations will commence.

United States of America on behalf and for the benefit of Thomas A Todd and *Islamic Republic of Iran*, Case No 10856, Chamber One, Order of January 9, 1986:

> The Tribunal refers to the two letters filed by the Agent of the Government of the Islamic Republic of Iran on 19 December 1985 and 2 January 1986, concerning the late filing by ten days of the Farsi version of the Claimants' documentary evidence and legal brief.
>
> The Tribunal advises the Parties that no final decision as to the admissibility of these late-filed documents will be made until after the Hearing on 15 April 1986.
>
> In the meantime, in order to take account of any prejudice which might have been occasioned to the Respondent by this late filing, the Tribunal allows the Respondent an additional ten days in which to file its documentary evidence and legal brief, i.e. until 10 March 1986.

Phillips Petroleum Co, Iran and *Islamic Republic of Iran*, Case No 39, Chamber Two, Order of November 7, 1986:

> As the Tribunal indicated in its Order of 1 October 1986, the Respondents' request for an extension of three months to file this submission cannot be granted. However, the Tribunal understands that the delay until 9 September 1986 in filing one volume of the Claimants' Rebuttal submitted on 1 September 1986 has effectively deprived the Respondents of a part of the time allotted for preparation of their evidence and brief in Rebuttal. In these circumstances, the Tribunal is prepared to accept the evidence and brief in Rebuttal, relating to the Claim only and limited to the issues in the Claimants' Rebuttal, as well as any further evidence and brief regarding the issue of measure [i.e., quantification] of damages (including the issue of quantification of damages with respect to all Counter-claims), if filed by 30 November 1986.
>
> Accordingly, the Claimant shall file any rebuttal to the evidence and brief on quantification of damages sought by the counter-claims by 31 January 1987.
>
> The Tribunal reiterates that the Hearing will be held as scheduled.

Thomas Earl Payne and *Islamic Republic of Iran*, Case No 335, Chamber Two, Order of February 14, 1986:

> The Tribunal notes Claimant's letter of 12 February 1986 requesting a date to be scheduled for the submission of documentary evidence to which it has recently gained access.
>
> The Claimant is hereby instructed to submit not later than 15 March 1986, the above-mentioned evidence and to explain the circumstances that have prevented it from filing such evidence earlier. The Tribunal will then take a decision regarding its admissibility.

Computer Sciences Corp and *Islamic Republic of Iran*, Award No 221–65–1 (April 16, 1986) at 5–6, reprinted in 10 Iran-US CTR 269, 273 (1986-I):

> The Tribunal notes that the Iranian Agent's request filed on 24 September 1985 does not point to any unforeseen circumstances which might have affected the filing of the Post-Hearing Submissions, nor does it give any new reasons for their lateness. The Tribunal is aware of the communication problems that Iranian Respondents face, and it has taken them into account in this case. In view of this, the procedural history of this case and the exceptional character of Post-Hearing Submissions, the Tribunal sees no need to reverse its decision not to allow the Respondents' Post-Hearing Submissions.

Aeronutronic Overseas Services, Inc, and *Telecommunications Co of Iran*, Case No 410, Chamber Three, Order of August 6, 1986:

> Reference is made to the submission of the Agent of the Government of the Islamic Republic of Iran filed on 25 July 1986, whereby the Respondent TCI requests a five-month extension of time to submit its Memorial and any and all evidence concerning the Claim and Counter-claims. Reference is also made to the Claimants' objections filed on 1 August 1986.
>
> The Tribunal notes that this is Respondent's third request for extension and for modification of this schedule since the Tribunal's Order of 28 June 1985. The Tribunal also notes that, for the first time, the Respondent has submitted a detailed schedule for the authorized inspection of Claimants' records and for the preparation and submission of its Memorial and evidence. According to the Tribunal this schedule appears to be reasonable.
>
> Taking into consideration the pattern of conduct adopted by the Respondent which, without convincing explanations delayed its application for visas to dispatch its representatives to inspect the records of the Claimants in the United States, and which submitted unjustified complaints about the Orders of the Tribunal, and considering the fact that such conduct could hardly be interpreted otherwise than amounting to dilatory tactics; the Tribunal added to its last Orders the proviso that no further extension would be granted. Consequently, under normal circumstances, the Tribunal would have denied the request for further extension submitted by the Respondent.
>
> However, the request of 25 July 1986 raises certain exceptional factors including the fact that, for the preparation of its defence, the Respondent depends on the inspection of documents which are held within the territory of the United States. Although Claimants have declared themselves willing to facilitate the inspection of their records, in the present state of relations between the two countries, this circumstance involves for the Respondent specific difficulties which cannot be ignored.
>
> In view of the foregoing, the Tribunal orders as follows:
>
> 1. The Respondents shall submit their Memorials and any or all evidence concerning the claims and counter-claims not later than December 26, 1986.
> 2. The Parties shall submit their Memorials and evidence in rebuttal not later than February 26, 1987.
> 3. The Hearing in this Case set for October 29 and 30, 1986 is rescheduled to take place on March 12 and 13, 1987.
> 4. No further extension will be granted.
>
> Failure to comply with this schedule may result in the continuation of proceedings pursuant to Article 28, paragraph 3 of the [1983] Tribunal Rules.
>
> The Tribunal will take into account in its Award the financial consequences which might be imposed on the Claimant, with no fault on its part, by the postponement of the Hearing.

Arco Exploration Inc and *National Iranian Oil Co*, Case No 20, Chamber One, Order of December 17, 1986:

> On 16 December 1986 the Claimants filed a Request for permission to introduce documents into evidence prior to the Hearing scheduled to take place on 17, 18 and 19 February 1987. The Documents concerned were filed together with the Request in one submission.
>
> The Respondents are invited to submit their comments on the new submission in written form at the latest on 10 February 1987. The Parties are free to also address this matter orally at the Hearing. The Tribunal will decide on the admissibility of the late-filed documents after the Hearing.

The Bendix Corp and *Islamic Republic of Iran*, Case No 208, Chamber Two, Order of September 28, 1987:

> The Tribunal notes Respondent the Air Force of the Islamic Republic of Iran's submission of a "Prehearing memorial and supplementary evidence" filed on 14 September 1987.

The Tribunal observes that this Respondent has not given any explanation of the circumstances that have prevented the filing of the above mentioned submission earlier, as required by paragraph 2 of the Tribunal's Order of 24 August 1987.

In view thereof, the "Prehearing memorial and supplementary evidence" of Respondent the Air Force of the Islamic Republic of Iran cannot be accepted.

W Jack Buckamier and *Islamic Republic of Iran*, Award No 528–941–3 (March 6, 1992), reprinted in 28 Iran-US CTR 353, 60–62 (1992):

30. The Tribunal must determine the admissibility of the Second Supplemental Affidavit filed by the Claimant on 6 June 1988. It is not disputed that this document, which contains new evidence, was filed after the final date set for the submission of pleadings in this Case. Under Tribunal precedent, in determining whether to accept such a late submission, the Tribunal considers "fundamental requirements of equality between, and fairness to, the Parties, and the possible prejudice to either Party." *Harris International Telecommunications, Inc.* and *The Islamic Republic of Iran, et al.*, Partial Award No 323–409–1, para 61 (2 Nov. 1987), reprinted in 17 Iran-U.S. C.T.R. 31, 46–47, and cases cited therein.
31. The Respondent objected to this filing on the grounds that they lacked the opportunity to prepare a proper response prior to the Hearing on 8 July 1988. However, on 9 February 1989 the Tribunal informed the Parties that a new Hearing would be held on 22 May 1989. This allowed the Respondents sufficient time to respond, if they so desired, to the Second Supplemental Affidavit. Considering this, the Tribunal finds that acceptance of the Claimant's submission causes no prejudice to the Respondents. The Tribunal therefore admits the Claimant's filing of 6 June 1988.

Vera-Jo Miller Aryeh and *Islamic Republic of Iran*, Case Nos 842, 843 and 844, Chamber One, Order of February 15, 1993:

1. The Tribunal deems it appropriate to extend to 19 March 1993 the time limit within which the Respondent shall file with the Tribunal a Statement of Defence and copies of any written evidence on which it will seek to rely ... together with a list of all documentary evidence submitted by it in these Cases and the location in the record (by tab or Exhibit number) of each such document. By the same date the Respondent may file a Hearing Memorial explaining the evidence and summarizing the issues in these Cases. In view of the procedural history of these Cases, the Tribunal does not envisage to grant any further extension.
2. The Claimant shall file by 19 May 1993 a Statement of Defence to Counter-claims, if any, and copies of any documentary evidence on which it will seek to rely in rebuttal of previously presented evidence, together with a supplemental list of such rebuttal evidence and the location of each such document in the record. By the same date the Claimant may file a Memorial explaining the evidence and summarizing the issues in these Cases.

Unidyne Corp and *Islamic Republic of Iran*, Award No 551–368–3 (November 10, 1993), reprinted in 29 Iran-US CTR 310, 313 (1993):

7. The Hearing was held on 7 September 1990. At the Hearing, the Claimant attempted to submit in evidence its Articles of Incorporation and the birth and death certificates of Mr. Raymond Watts in support of its position that Unidyne qualifies as a national of the United States under Article VII, Paragraph 1, of the Claims Settlement Declaration. It is evident that Unidyne could have submitted all of the documents in question to the Tribunal together with its earlier filings. Furthermore, Unidyne has given no adequate explanation for the delay in their submission. The Tribunal therefore determines that these documents are inadmissible due to late submission.

Ouziel Aryeh, et al and *Islamic Republic of Iran*, Case Nos 839 and 840, Chamber One, Order of May 13, 1994:

> On 2 May 1994, the Claimants filed a submission entitled "Claimants' Memorial and Evidence, Volume II." On 6 May 1994, a letter was filed by the Agent of the Government of the Islamic Republic of Iran in which he stated that the unauthorized filing of Volume II was done more than a year after the filing of Volume I by the Claimants and after the filing of the "Respondent's Brief on Jurisdictional Issues and Merits" on 28 April 1994, thereby denying the Respondent the opportunity to comment on the Claimants' Volume II in its Brief. It was further requested that the Tribunal strike the late filing from the record of these Cases.
>
> The Tribunal notes that the Claimant's Volume II, consisting, *inter alia*, of an appraisal on the properties that are the subject of the claims, was not filed until 2 May 1994 without any explanation for the delay, although the Claimants had stated in Volume I, filed on 31 March 1993, that they "expected to submit within 30 days, an expert appraisal on the value of the properties that are the subject of their claims as of the date of their taking by Respondent." The Tribunal further notes that it had ordered the Claimants to file all written evidence by 1 April 1993. The Respondent also pointed out in its Brief, filed on 28 April 1994, that the appraisal had not been presented to the Tribunal.
>
> However, the Tribunal also notes that the evidence now proffered consists of an appraisal and an Affidavit which further clarify the Claimants' claim. At this stage of the proceedings, the Tribunal finds it appropriate to admit the Claimants' late filing.
>
> In order to avoid any prejudice to the Respondent, the Tribunal further decides as follows:
>
> (1) The Respondent is invited to file by September 30, 1994 its response to Volume II of the Claimant's Memorial and Evidence.
> (2) After receipt of the Respondent's response, the Tribunal will schedule further proceedings in these Cases.

United States of America and *Islamic Republic of Iran*, Case No A/33, Full Tribunal, Order of February 28, 2002:

> 1. The Tribunal notes the letter from the Agent of the Government of the Islamic Republic of Iran, filed on February 15, 2002 (Doc. 7), requesting an extension of time for the Respondent to submit its Statement of Defense. The Tribunal further notes the United States "Objection to Iran's Second Request for Extension," filed on February 20, 2001 (Doc. 8).
> 2. Having considered the Parties' submissions, the Tribunal extends the time-limit for the Respondent to submit its Statement of Defense to April 15, 2002.

17
Interim Measures

1. Introduction	513
2. Interim Measures—Article 26	514
A. Text of the 2010 UNCITRAL Rule	514
B. Commentary	515
(1) The precondition of a request by a party—Article 26(1)	516
(2) The types of interim measures that may be granted—Article 26(2)	517
(a) Maintain or restore the *status quo*	518
(b) Prevent prejudice to the arbitral process itself	518
(c) Preserve assets for possible satisfaction of award	519
(d) Preserve evidence	519
(3) Conditions for the ordering of interim measures—Article 26(3)	520
(a) A likely harm not adequately reparable by an award of damages	521
(b) An appropriate balance of likely harms	522
(c) A reasonable possibility of success on the merits	522
(d) Further conditions imposed by the agreement of the parties	524
(4) Conditions relaxed for the preservation of evidence—Article 26(4)	524
(5) The form (award or order) in which interim measures are granted	524
(6) Tribunal's power to modify, suspend or terminate interim measures—Article 26(5)	525
(7) Security for the costs of interim measures—Article 26(6)	526
(8) Disclosure by any party of any material change—Article 26(7)	527
(9) Liability for costs and damages—Article 26(8)	528
(10) Relations between the arbitral tribunal and municipal courts in issuing interim measures—Article 26(9)	529
(11) Issuance of preliminary orders	530
(12) Comparison to the 1976 UNCITRAL Rules	532
C. Extracts from the Practice of Investment Tribunals	533
D. Extracts from the Practice of the Iran–US Claims Tribunal	543
(1) Tribunal Rules (1983), Article 26(1)	543
(2) Tribunal Rules (1983), Article 26(2)	550
(3) Tribunal Rules (1983), Article 26(3)	551

1. Introduction

Judicial and arbitral proceedings take time—occasionally a great deal of time. As a result courts and tribunals may be called upon to preserve the alleged rights of the parties during the pendency of the proceedings by ordering interim measures. Article 26 of the 2010 UNCITRAL Arbitration Rules addresses the subject of interim measures. It does so in substantially greater detail than the 1976 UNCITRAL Arbitration Rules.

Article 26(1) provides that the tribunal, on the request of a party, may grant interim measures while Article 26(2), through a non-exhaustive list, describes the types of measures the tribunal can grant. Article 26(3) sets forth the conditions that the requesting party needs to satisfy for the ordering of interim measures, while Article 26(4) potentially relaxes those conditions in the case of a request for the preservation of evidence. Article 26(5) recognizes the tribunal's power to modify, suspend or terminate interim measures when necessary. Article 26(6) authorizes the tribunal to require that the requesting party provide appropriate security in connection with the interim measures. Article 26(7) recognizes the tribunal's power to require any party to disclose material changes in connection with the interim measure. Article 26(8) addresses the requesting party's potential liability for costs and damages. Article 26(9) provides that a request for interim measures to a municipal court is not an act inconsistent with or a waiver to the agreement to arbitrate.

2. Interim Measures—Article 26

A. Text of the 2010 UNCITRAL Rule[1]

Article 26 of the 2010 UNCITRAL Rules provides:

1. The arbitral tribunal may, at the request of a party, grant interim measures.
2. An interim measure is any temporary measure by which, at any time prior to the issuance of the award by which the dispute is finally decided, the arbitral tribunal orders a party, for example and without limitation, to:
   (a) Maintain or restore the status quo pending determination of the dispute;
   (b) Take action that would prevent, or refrain from taking action that is likely to cause, (i) current or imminent harm or (ii) prejudice to the arbitral process itself;
   (c) Provide a means of preserving assets out of which a subsequent award may be satisfied; or
   (d) Preserve evidence that may be relevant and material to the resolution of the dispute.
3. The party requesting an interim measure under paragraphs 2 (a) to (c) shall satisfy the arbitral tribunal that:
   (a) Harm not adequately reparable by an award of damages is likely to result if the measure is not ordered, and such harm substantially outweighs the harm that is likely to result to the party against whom the measure is directed if the measure is granted; and
   (b) There is a reasonable possibility that the requesting party will succeed on the merits of the claim. The determination on this possibility shall not affect the discretion of the arbitral tribunal in making any subsequent determination.
4. With regard to a request for an interim measure under paragraph 2 (d), the requirements in paragraphs 3 (a) and (b) shall apply only to the extent the arbitral tribunal considers appropriate.

---

[1] Corresponding Article 26 of the 1976 UNCITRAL Rules provides:

1. At the request of either party, the arbitral tribunal may take any interim measures it deems necessary in respect of the subject-matter of the dispute, including measures for the conservation of the goods forming the subject-matter in dispute, such as ordering their deposit with a third person or the sale of perishable goods.
2. Such interim measures may be established in the form of an interim award. The arbitral tribunal shall be entitled to require security for the costs of such measures.
3. A request for interim measures addressed by any party to a judicial authority shall not be deemed incompatible with the agreement to arbitrate, or as a waiver of that agreement.

5. The arbitral tribunal may modify, suspend or terminate an interim measure it has granted, upon application of any party or, in exceptional circumstances and upon prior notice to the parties, on the arbitral tribunal's own initiative.
6. The arbitral tribunal may require the party requesting an interim measure to provide appropriate security in connection with the measure.
7. The arbitral tribunal may require any party promptly to disclose any material change in the circumstances on the basis of which the interim measure was requested or granted.
8. The party requesting an interim measure may be liable for any costs and damages caused by the measure to any party if the arbitral tribunal later determines that, in the circumstances then prevailing, the measure should not have been granted. The arbitral tribunal may award such costs and damages at any point during the proceedings.
9. A request for interim measures addressed by any party to a judicial authority shall not be deemed incompatible with the agreement to arbitrate, or as a waiver of that agreement.

B. Commentary

Article 26 of the 2010 UNCITRAL Rules is significantly more detailed than the corresponding article in the 1976 UNCITRAL Rules. In one respect, the dramatic expansion of the article runs counter to the guiding principles the Working Group adopted, namely "any revision of the UNCITRAL Arbitration Rules should not alter the structure of the text, its spirit and drafting style and that it should respect the flexibility of the text rather than make it more complex."[2] However, an additional guiding principle was that the new Rules should be consistent with both the 1958 New York Convention, the 1985 UNCITRAL Model Law on International Commercial Arbitration and the 2006 Amendments to the Model Law. It is this additional principle that explains the dramatic expansion of Article 26. In particular, Article 26 of the 2010 Rules does not so much track the 1976 Rules as it tracks, with some deviations, Article 17 of the Model Law, as amended.[3]

This explanation of course begs the question as to why the Model Law's provision was expanded. As Castello explains, this detailing was thought necessary so that municipal courts might feel more comfortable enforcing interim measures if the law authorizing such

---

[2] The Working Group viewed the UNCITRAL Arbitration Rules as one of the most successful instruments of UNCITRAL and therefore cautioned in the *travaux préparatoires* against any unnecessary amendments or statements being included that would call into question the legitimacy of prior applications of the Rules in specific cases. It was considered that the focus of the revision should be on updating the Rules to meet changes that had taken place over the last thirty years in arbitral practice, not on simply making them more complex. *Report of the Working Group on Arbitration and Conciliation on the Work of its Forty-Fifth Session* (Vienna, September 11–15, 2006), UNCITRAL, 40th Session, UN Doc A/CN.9/614, at 5, para 16 (2006).

[3] The adoption of the long, detailed Article 17 of the Model Law (rather than Article 26 of the 1976 Rules) as the starting point for drafting occurred at the outset of the revision process. Paulsson and Petrochilos in their advisory report to UNCITRAL foresaw the choice, offering both as alternatives: "The current draft Articles 17 . . . of the Model Law . . . would serve both those purposes well (see "alternative one" below). Another possibility would be to preserve the existing text of article 26, making limited changes that would be consistent with—but not fully reflect the tenor of—the proposed revision of the Model Law (see "alternative two")." J Paulsson and G Petrochilos, *Revision of the UNCITRAL Arbitration Rules, Report to UNCITRAL Secretariat*, (2006) para 206. The general view of the Working Group at the first negotiating session was that the revision should use Article 17 as the point of departure. UNCITRAL, 45th Session, UN Doc A/CN.9/614, n 2, para 105.

measures was absolutely clear about the scope of the arbitrator's power.[4] While space for arbitral discretion is a value within the arbitration, the drafters of the Model Law appear to have had concerns about an outside authority not adding its coercive power unless there was a transparent basis of decision.

While Article 26 of the 2010 Rules has Article 17 of the Model Law as its starting point, it does not track it entirely. The Working Group was quick to recognize that not all of Article 17 should carry over given the difference in function and scope. For example, the provisions relating to enforcement of interim measures was a matter for national legislation, not arbitration rules. As a result, not all concepts were included in the 2010 Rules.[5] One author explains that while making significant changes to the interim measures article, the drafters of the 2010 Rules were careful to recognize the ambit of arbitration rules and deliberately excluded issues such as the recognition and enforcement of interim measures and the authority of courts to order interim measures.[6] Simultaneously, the fact that Article 17 was the starting point also became a constraint in drafting in that it was thought important that an addition did not imply that that possibility was not implicit in Article 17 as well.[7] For the purpose of this Commentary, it is critical to recognize that given the strong relationship between Article 17 of the Model Law and Article 26 of the 2010 Rules, the *travaux préparatoires* of the former are also relevant to the latter. This is especially appropriate inasmuch as many of the same delegates were in involved in both processes.

In many, but not all, respects, Article 26, as expanded, is consistent with the practice that developed under the skeletal version of corresponding Article 26 of the 1976 Rules.[8] Some experienced arbitrators may lament the attempt to articulate and confine the manner with which arbitral discretion is utilized. Newer, less-experienced arbitrators and counsel may welcome the stronger guidance provided.

(1) *The precondition of a request by a party—Article 26(1)*

Article 26(1) first and foremost recognizes the authority to grant interim measures. It also contains a significant precondition, namely that the interim measures be requested by a party. The requirement of a request from a party is present in the 1976 UNCITRAL Rules, where the *travaux préparatoires* indicate clearly that a party request is a prerequisite to the

---

[4] J Castello, "Generalizing About the Virtues of Specificity: The Surprising Evolution of the Longest Article in the UNCITRAL Model Law," (2012) 6 *World Arb and Mediation Rev* 7. See also J Castello, "Unveiling the 2010 UNCITRAL Arbitration Rules," (2010) 65 Dispute Resolution J 21.

[5] However, the Working Group noted that: "The view was expressed that the provisions of Chapter IV A that were of a contentious nature and had previously given rise to diverging views in the Working Group should not be included in the UNCITRAL Arbitration Rules, in order not to endanger their wide acceptability." UNCITRAL, 45th Session, UN Doc A/CN.9/614, n 2, at 22, para 105.

[6] G Petrochilos, "Interim Measures Under the Revised UNCITRAL Arbitration Rules," (2010) 28(4) ASA Bulletin 878.

[7] The following is an example of this dynamic:

A proposal was made that paragraph (2)(c) should be amended expressly to refer to security for costs through an addition of the words "or securing funds" after the word "assets". Opposition was expressed to that proposal as it could connote that the corresponding provision in the UNCITRAL Arbitration Model Law was insufficient to provide for security for costs. The Working Group agreed that security for costs was encompassed by the words "preserving assets out of which a subsequent award may be satisfied."

Report on the Working Group on Arbitration and Conciliation on the Work Forty-Seventh Session, UNCITRAL, 47th Session, UN Doc A/CN.9/641, para 48 (2007).

[8] See, eg, *Paushok* (1976 Rules), Order on Interim Measures (applying standards similar to those in 2010 Rules); *Chevron Corp* (1976 Rules), Second Interim Award, para 2 (same); both reprinted in section 2(C).

ordering of interim measures.[9] Thus, in arbitration under the UNCITRAL Rules, a tribunal is not entitled to order interim measures on its own initiative.[10]

Article 26 is silent as to the form of the request by a party. Although Article 26(1) does not preclude the admission of oral requests (made, for example, during a hearing), requests should, whenever possible, be in writing and should "set forth sufficient reasons to enable comments by the other party and deliberations by the tribunal."[11]

An arbitral tribunal is not a court of general jurisdiction and therefore its authority to grant interim measures is circumscribed by its jurisdiction as determined by the agreement of the parties. In particular, as an arbitral tribunal's jurisdiction encompasses only the parties before it, interim measures may not be directed to non-parties.[12] As a result the tribunal cannot order the attachment of properties, which are in the direct possession of a third party; such measures are likely to require the assistance of courts or other competent domestic authorities.

(2) The types of interim measures that may be granted—Article 26(2)

Article 26(2) defines interim measures and provides a non-exhaustive list of types of interim measures a tribunal can order.[13] Article 26(2) describes the circumstances of interim measures while Article 26(3) discussed in section 2(B)(3) sets forth the conditions under which interim measures may be granted.[14]

There is a subtle shift in the definition of interim measures that is an important clarification on their scope and purpose. The chapeau to the definition of interim measures in Article 26(2) is "any temporary measure by which, at any time prior to the issuance of the award by which the dispute is finally decided, the arbitral tribunal orders a party...." This chapeau is followed by four examples. The subtle shift is that the phrase "in respect of the subject-matter of the dispute" present in the 1976 Rules is not present in either Article 17 of the Model Law or Article 26 of the 2010 Rules. In particular, as the four examples demonstrate, it was thought that a focus on the "subject matter" of the dispute is overly restrictive, and that the purpose of interim measures has a broader focus than just the arbitral

---

[9] *Report of the Secretary-General on the Revised Draft Set of Arbitration Rules*, UNCITRAL, 9th Session, Addendum 1 (Commentary), UN Doc A/CN.9/112/Add.1 (1975), reprinted in (1976) VII UNCITRAL Ybk 166, 176 ("Under paragraph l, the arbitrators have discretion to take such measures, but only if requested by one or both parties."). See also *Report of the United Nations Commission on International Trade Law*, 8th Session, Summary of Discussion of the Preliminary Draft, UN Doc A/10017, para 164 (1975), reprinted in (1975) VI UNCITRAL Ybk 24, 40.

[10] See D Caron, "Interim Measures of Protection: Theory and Practice in Light of the Iran-United States Claims Tribunal," (1986) 46 ZaöRV at 465, 466. An updated version of the article can be found in D Caron, *The Iran-United States Claims Tribunal and The International Arbitral Process* 207–83 (unpublished dissertation, Leiden 1990). Compare Article 46(2) of the 2006 ICSID Additional Facility Rules ("The Tribunal may also recommend provisional measures on its own initiative ...").

[11] See Caron, "Interim Measures of Protection," n 10, 480.

[12] However, "it was noted that, even if not directed at a third party, an interim measure may nevertheless affect third persons holding, for example, money or other assets of the party concerned, since they may be obliged to take some action in respect of that property by virtue of the order directed to the party." *Report of the Working Group on Arbitration and Conciliation on the Work of its Thirty-Second Session* (New York, June 12–July 7, 2000), UNCITRAL, 32nd Session, UN Doc A/CN.9/468, at 13, para 64 (2000).

[13] This provision is more detailed than that provided in the 1976 UNCITRAL Rules. The Secretariat Note on revising the Rules indicates that changes were suggested in Article 26(2) so as to clarify "the circumstances, conditions and procedure for the granting of interim measures, consistent with [Article 17] A of the Model Law... ." *Settlement of Commercial Disputes: Revision of the UNCITRAL Arbitration Rules, Note by the Secretariat*, UNCITRAL, UN Doc A/CN.9/WG.II/WP.145 at 12, para 25 (2007).

[14] J Paulsson and G Petrochilos, *Revision of the UNCITRAL Arbitration Rules*, n 3, 198 para 203.

process.[15] In practice, Article 26 of the 1976 Rules had been interpreted in this fashion,[16] but the clarification is nonetheless welcome.

Following this chapeau, Article 26(2) proceeds to lists four broad categories of interim measures a tribunal may issue. However, it must be stressed that the provision explicitly states that these four categories are intended only as examples, and do not limit the arbitral tribunal's power to order other measures that would be appropriate in light of the particular circumstances.[17]

(a) Maintain or restore the *status quo*

Under subparagraph (a), interim measures may be taken to "maintain or restore the *status quo* pending determination of the dispute."[18] Thus, for example, interim measures sought before the Iran–US Claims Tribunal have included the stay of the sale or transfer of goods in possession of the claimant.[19] The Tribunal has also issued an interim order directing the conservation of goods.[20] An order for the stay of a planned auction of immovable properties is another example of this category of interim measures.[21]

(b) Prevent prejudice to the arbitral process itself

The Working Group carefully drafted subparagraph (b) to highlight the fact that the tribunal has the power to order interim measures not only in case of current or imminent harm to a party, but also in case of prejudice to the arbitral process itself.[22] Drafters of the 2006 Amendments to the Model Law selected the words "likely to cause," rather than "would cause," as it was noted that at the time such interim measures are sought, there are often insufficient facts to determine whether the arbitral process would in fact be prejudiced.[23] The Working Group also adopted that approach in revising the Rules. To this end, the tribunal may, for example, order duplicative proceedings taken in another forum terminated or stayed by a respondent state until further notice. In numerous cases, the Iran–US Claims Tribunal granted measures ordering a party to stay duplicative Iranian court proceedings.[24]

---

[15] UNCITRAL, 40th Session, UN Doc A/CN.9/614, n 2, at 22, paras 104, 105.

[16] See *Islamic Republic of Iran and United States of America*, Decision No DEC 116-A15(IV) & A24-FT (1983 Tribunal Rules) reprinted in section 2(D)(1).

[17] The Working Group agreed to add at the end of the chapeau to paragraph (2) the words "including, without limitation," to emphasize the non-exclusive nature of the list contained in paragraph (2). *Report of Working Group II (Arbitration and Conciliation) on the Work of its Fiftieth Session* (New York, February 9–13, 2009), UNCITRAL, 42nd Session, UN Doc A/CN.9/669, at 21, paras 92–94 (2009). See also *Report of the Working Group on Arbitration and Conciliation on the Work of its Thirty-Ninth Session* (Vienna, November 10–14, 2003), UNCITRAL, 39th Session, UN Doc A/CN.9/545, at 8–9, para 21 (2003).

[18] See, eg, *Chevron Corp* (1976 Rules) Order of May 14, 2010, para 1(i)–(iii), reprinted in section 2(C).

[19] See *Avco Corp and Iran Aircraft Industries* (Case No 261) (1983 Tribunal Rules) reprinted in section 2(D)(1).

[20] *Behring Intl, Inc* (1983 Tribunal Rules), reprinted in section 2(D)(1).

[21] See *Iran* and *United States* (Case Nos A/4 and A/15)(1983 Tribunal Rules) reprinted in section 2(D)(1).

[22] Concerns were expressed that the actions to be prevented or refrained from in paragraph (2) (b) could be understood as referring only to prejudice to the arbitral process. To clarify the meaning intended by the drafters of the UNCITRAL Arbitration Model Law, it was suggested to introduce an editorial change to paragraph (2) (b) by inserting "(i)" before the word "current" and "(ii)" before the word "prejudice" so that the situation of "prejudice to the arbitral process" would appear as distinct from "current or imminent harm." UNCITRAL, 42nd Session, UN Doc A/CN.9/669, n 17, at 21, para 95.

[23] UNCITRAL, 39th Session, UN Doc A/CN.9/545, n 17, at 10, para 26.

[24] See, eg, *Ford Aerospace* (1983 Tribunal Rules), reprinted in section 2(D)(1). See also D Caron, "Interim Measures of Protection," n 10, 208–9 and Tables I and II 279–82. Note the drafters of the 2006 Amendments to the Model Law debated at length whether Article 17(2) could be interpreted as encompassing a power of an arbitral tribunal to order an anti-suit injunction. *Report of the Working Group on Arbitration and Conciliation on the*

The function of protection of the arbitral process itself can also be seen in the *Chevron v Ecuador* arbitration. In the *Chevron* arbitration, initiated under a bilateral investment treaty, the claimant investor alleged that an adverse domestic court judgment was rendered in violation of international law principles of due process guaranteed under the treaty. It sought interim measures to avoid enforcement of the judgment pending the resolution of the arbitration. The tribunal granted that request in a series of decisions. In its Second Interim Award of February 16, 2012, the tribunal, pointing to its "mission (required under the arbitration agreement) efficaciously and fairly to decide the parties dispute" ordered the "Respondent (whether by its judicial, legislative or executive branches) to take all measures necessary to suspend or cause to be suspended the enforcement or recognition" of the judgment.[25]

(c) Preserve assets for possible satisfaction of award

Under subparagraph (c), the tribunal may order interim measures that would preserve "assets out of which a subsequent award may be satisfied." An award would be worthless if a party after spending significant time in arbitral proceedings were to find that the assets against which the award was to be executed have been dissipated or moved out of the jurisdiction.[26] An order in *Paushok* and *Mongolia* directing a party to refrain from seizing or obtaining a lien on the assets of the other party pending decision of the dispute is an example of a tribunal confronted with such a situation.[27] The *travaux préparatoires* of the 2006 Amendments to the UNCITRAL Model Law show an intention to include preservation of assets in a broad sense within the functional scope of interim measures.[28] The Working Group debated whether the words "securing funds" should be added after "assets," but ultimately concluded that it was already encompassed in the language of subparagraph (c) and thus unnecessary.[29]

(d) Preserve evidence

Subparagraph (d) places a special emphasis on the protection and conservation of evidence that may be relevant and material to the resolution of the dispute.[30] This topic brings together two controversial topics: the appropriate scope of interim measures and the production of documents. The *travaux préparatoires* of the 2006 Amendments to the UNCITRAL Model Law indicate that "while the view was expressed that in certain legal systems subparagraph (d) was superfluous, the text was considered important as the preservation of evidence was not necessarily dealt with to a sufficient extent by all domestic rules of civil procedure."[31] There was dissent, however. Some, concerned with the scope of production,

---

Work of its Fortieth Session (New York, February 23–27, 2004), UNCITRAL, 40th Session, UN Doc A/CN.9/547, at 21–3 para 75–83 (2004). But see, *Paul Donin de Rosiere, Panacaviar, SA* (1983 Tribunal Rules), reprinted in section 2(D)(1), where the Tribunal declined to issue such an order as no irreparable damage was shown.

[25] See *Chevron Corp* (1976 Rules) Second Interim Award of February 16, 2012, para 3, reprinted in section 2(C).

[26] See, eg, discussion in *Paushok* (1976 Rules), terms and conditions of Interim order paras 3–10, reprinted in section 2(C).

[27] See *Paushok* (1976 Rules), terms and conditions of interim order paras 1–3, reprinted in section 2(C).

[28] UNCITRAL, 39th Session, UN Doc A/CN.9/545, n 17, at 10, para 26. See also *Sergei Paushok, et al* (Interim order) (1976 Rules), para 37, reprinted in section 2(C).

[29] UNCITRAL, 47th Session, UN Doc A/CN.9/614, n 2, at 10, para 48.

[30] See D Kozlowska, "The Revised UNCITRAL Arbitration Rules Seen Through the Prism of Electronic Disclosure," (2011) 28(1) J Intl Arb 51.

[31] UNCITRAL, 39th Session, UN Doc A/CN.9/545, n 17, at 10, para 27.

believed that the reference to evidence that "may be relevant and material" was too broad.[32] Others concerned with the scope of interim measures argued that inasmuch as Article 19(2) of the Model Law provides that the arbitral tribunal possesses the power to determine the admissibility, relevance, materiality and weight of any evidence, the tribunal "should not be requested to prejudge the relevance and materiality of evidence at the stage of a granting of an interim measure."[33] Importantly, however, these concerns were in the minority and the content of subparagraph (d) was adopted as part of Article 17 of the Model Law and later as part of Article 26 of the 2010 Rules.[34] Notably, the drafters of the Rules also recognized that a request of measures for the preservation of evidence is somewhat different from the other categories of measure, and that this difference therefore necessitated Article 26(4) of the Rules, which permits the tribunal discretion to ease the requirements listed in Article 26(3) for the issuance of such measures.[35]

(3) Conditions for the ordering of interim measures—Article 26(3)

Article 26(3) lists three substantive and cumulative conditions that must be satisfied for the issuance of interim measures.[36] The paragraph replicates the provisions contained in the 2006 Amendments of the Model Law.[37] These conditions are not explicit under the 1976 Rules. However, the conditions likely were similar in practice under the 1976 Rules[38] and the articulation of these conditions in the 2010 Rules will likely influence the manner in which tribunals exercise their discretion under the 1976 Rules in the future. The 2008 *Paushok* order granting interim measures under the 1976 Rules draws significantly upon aspects of Article 17 of the Model Law.[39]

During the drafting of the 2006 Amendments to the Model Law it was debated whether the conditions should be formulated (1) as obligations binding on the requesting party, (2)

---

[32] *Report of the Working Group on Arbitration and Conciliation on the Work of its Forty-Third Session* (Vienna, October 3–7, 2005), UNCITRAL, 43rd Session, UN Doc A/CN.9/589, at 7, para 28 (2005).

[33] UNCITRAL, 43rd Session, UN Doc A/CN.9/589, n 32, at 7, para 28.

[34] However, the Working Group observed that the phrase "relevant and material" was already included in the IBA Rules on the Taking of Evidence in International Commercial Arbitration (adopted by resolution of the IBA Council, June 1999), which had been the product of much debate. It was noted that the phrase had taken on a meaning such that the term "relevant" required that the evidence be connected to the dispute and the term "material" referred to the significance of the evidence. In support of its retention, it was said that the phrase was commonly used and understood in international arbitration. UNCITRAL, 43rd Session, UN Doc A/CN.9/589, n 32, at 7, para 29.

[35] Article 26(4) of the 2010 Rules provides: "With regard to a request for an interim measure under paragraph 2(d), the requirements in paragraphs 3 (a) and (b) shall apply only to the extent the arbitral tribunal considers appropriate."

[36] Article 26(3) draws on Anglo-common law jurisprudence and more precisely on the judgment of Lord Diplock in *American Cynamid v Ethicon*, requiring that the applicant for interim protection satisfy the tribunal that (1) there is a real risk of "harm not adequately reparable by an award of damages"; (2) that this harm will outweigh the harm likely to be suffered by the party against whom the measure is directed; and (3) that there is a reasonable possibility of success on the merits. M Skinner *et al* (eds), "The UNCITRAL Arbitration Rules 2010," (2011) 7(1) Asian Intl Arb J 76.

[37] Article 17A of the Model Law provides: "(1) The party requesting an interim measure under article 17(2) (a), (b) and (c) shall satisfy the arbitral tribunal that: *(a)* Harm not adequately reparable by an award of damages is likely to result if the measure is not ordered, and such harm substantially outweighs the harm that is likely to result to the party against whom the measure is directed if the measure is granted; and *(b)* There is a reasonable possibility that the requesting party will succeed on the merits of the claim. The determination on this possibility shall not affect the discretion of the arbitral tribunal in making any subsequent determination."

[38] See *EnCana Corp* (1976 Rules), especially para 13; and *Chevron Corp* (1976 Rules) Second Interim Award of February 16, 2012, para 2; both reprinted in section 2(C).

[39] See section 2(C).

as criteria to be applied by the tribunal when determining whether or not to grant interim measures or (3) as conditions that need to be satisfied by the requesting party.[40] The last approach was followed. The initial language suggested that the requesting party "should furnish proof that..."[41] However, it was determined that different legal systems have different standards of proof and therefore a neutral[42] formulation was preferred whereby the requesting party should only have to satisfy the tribunal of certain conditions.[43] In *Paushok*, the Tribunal granting interim measures under the 1976 Rules wrote: "it is incumbent upon Claimants to demonstrate that their request is meeting the standards internationally recognized as pre-conditions for such measures."[44]

The following subsections discuss the three conditions set forth in Article 26(3) as well as the possibility that the parties by mutual agreement may agree on further conditions.

(a) A likely harm not adequately reparable by an award of damages

Under subparagraph (a), the requesting party must satisfy the tribunal that "harm not adequately reparable by an award of damages is likely to result if the measure is not ordered..." The *travaux préparatoires* of the 2006 Amendments to the UNCITRAL Model Law illustrate the difficulties that were faced and the care that was ultimately used in selecting the language for subparagraph (a).

The intention behind subparagraph (a) is to identify "a particular type of harm occurring in a situation where, even at a preliminary stage when all the facts of the dispute were not before the tribunal, it could be shown that the requesting party should be protected against harm that could not be remedied by an award of damages."[45] The drafters of Article 17 of the Model Law grappled extensively with how to phrase this intent. Initially the drafters considered defining harm as "irreparable," but it soon appeared that the term "irreparable" potentially set too high a barrier to measures since monetary damages arguably can remediate many alleged forms of harm.[46] Similarly, it was concluded that the words "substantial harm" could be remedied by way of substantial damages and adds an unnecessary element

---

[40] *Report of the Working Group on Arbitration and Conciliation on the Work of its Thirty-Sixth Session* (Vienna, 4–8 March 2002), UNCITRAL, 36th Session, UN Doc A/CN.9/508, at 15, paras 55–56 (2002).

[41] "The party requesting the interim measure should furnish proof that...." UNCITRAL, 36th Session, UN Doc A/CN.9/508, n 40, at 13, para 51.

[42] UNCITRAL, 39th Session, UN Doc A/CN.9/545, n 17, at 10–11, para 28.

[43] UNCITRAL, 36th Session, UN Doc A/CN.9/508, n 40, at 15, paras 55–56. It was also determined that the "urgency" requirement that is sometimes associated with interim measures should not be a general feature of interim measures but rather that it should be made a specific requirement for granting an interim measure ex parte. *Report of the Working Group on Arbitration on the Work of its Thirty-Seventh Session* (New York, May 12–16, 2003), UNCITRAL, 37th Session, UN Doc A/CN.9/523, at 13, para 41 (2003).

[44] *Paushok* (1976 Rules), para 40, reprinted in section 2(C).

[45] In addition to the loss of a priceless or unique work of art already mentioned at the previous session (UNCITRAL, 36th Session, UN Doc A/CN.9/508, n 40, at 15, paras 55–56; A/CN.9/545, n 17, para. 29), it was explained that "irreparable harm" would occur, for example, in situations such as a business becoming insolvent, essential evidence being lost, an essential business opportunity (such as the conclusion of a large contract) being lost, or harm being caused to the reputation of a business as a result of a trademark infringement. *Report of the Working Group on Arbitration on the Work of its Fortieth Session* (New York, February 23–27, 2004), UNCITRAL, 40th Session, UN Doc A/CN.9/547, at 13, para 86 (2004).

[46] In the view of some delegations, the term should be used only to refer to a truly irreparable damage such as the loss of a priceless work of art. Other delegations referred to the notion of "irreparable damage" as a means of describing particularly serious types of damage that would outweigh the damage that the party against whom the interim measure would be granted could be expected to suffer if that measure was effectively granted. UNCITRAL, 39th Session, UN Doc A/CN.9/545, n 17, at 11, para 29. For an opinion demonstrating the barrier of "irreparable," see *Iran* and *United States* (Case Nos A/15 & A/24) (1983 Tribunal Rules) at para 21, reprinted in section 2(D)(1).

of quantity to the condition.[47] Among the several other alternatives considered were: "harm that cannot be adequately compensated or that cannot be compensated by an award of money"; "damage that is difficult to repair"; "harm that cannot be compensated"; "important harm which cannot be compensated by damages"; "inevitable harm"; "unavoidable harm"; or "serious harm."[48] In the end, the words "harm not adequately reparable by an award of damages" were adopted. As discussion of the 2006 Amendments to the Model Law indicates: "that proposal addressed the concerns that irreparable harm might present too high a threshold and would more clearly establish the discretion of the arbitral tribunal in deciding upon the issuance of an interim measure."[49]

The application of this test can be seen in the *Paushok* arbitration. The dispute involved validity of the windfall profit tax and the levying of a fee for the import of foreign workers imposed by the Government of Mongolia. The Tribunal was of the view that the possibility of monetary compensation is not always sufficient to bar a request for interim measures. In that context the Tribunal held that the measures requested must be *necessary*, as shown by likely 'substantial' (but not 'irreparable') prejudice to the requesting party.[50]

(b) An appropriate balance of likely harms

Under subparagraph (a), the requesting party must satisfy a second test that "such harm substantially outweighs the harm that is likely to result to the party against whom the measure is directed if the measure is granted." This test represents a balance of hardships. As discussed above, the first test for a likely "harm not adequately reparable by an award of damages" already requires the tribunal to weigh the likely harm to the party requesting the measure. This second test requires that the tribunal also consider the hardships posed for the other party by the granting of such measure. The central condition of this second test somewhat disfavors the granting of measures by stating that the threat of possible harm from not granting the measures must not only outweigh, but *substantially* outweigh, the harm that the party against whom the measure is being sought will suffer from its issuance.

(c) A reasonable possibility of success on the merits

Subparagraph (b) states that there must be "a reasonable possibility that the requesting party will succeed on the merits of the claim." It also provides: "The determination on this possibility shall not affect the discretion of the arbitral tribunal in making any subsequent determination." Thus, subparagraph (b) requires that the tribunal have both a reasonable possibility of possessing jurisdiction over the claim and a reasonable possibility that the substance of the claim is meritorious.

The implicit requirement that the tribunal have jurisdiction over the parties before ordering interim measures is a question that has generated considerable legal writing and caused practical problems for various international courts and tribunals.[51] On the one hand, a party may have legitimate objections to an arbitral tribunal's ordering interim

---

[47] It was stated that a reference to "substantial harm" would more easily lend itself to balancing the degree of harm suffered by the applicant if the interim measure was not granted against the degree of harm suffered by the party opposing the measure if that measure was granted. UNCITRAL, 40th Session, UN Doc A/CN.9/547, n 45, at 13, para 85–86.
[48] UNCITRAL, 40th Session, UN Doc A/CN.9/547, n 45, at 13, para 87.
[49] UNCITRAL, 40th Session, UN Doc A/CN.9/547, n 45, at 13, para 89.
[50] See *Paushok* (1976 Rules), esp paras 45, 68, 69; reprinted in section 2(C).
[51] See J Sztucki, *Interim Measures in the Hague Court: An Attempt at a Scrutiny*, (1983) 221–59.

measures against it if it is unclear whether the tribunal ultimately has jurisdiction to grant the relief sought. On the other hand, the very purpose of interim measures serving as a means of conservation and protection of parties' rights could be forfeited if such measures were postponed pending a full jurisdictional determination. In recent years, the Iran–US Claims Tribunal, still a principal source of practice for UNCITRAL Rules, adopted what is known as the "*prima facie* test."[52] The *prima facie* test was likewise adopted in *Paushok*.[53] Under this test, although the tribunal may not order interim measures in the absence of jurisdiction over the merits of the case, considerations of urgency dictate that a *prima facie* showing of jurisdiction is sufficient and necessary[54] at the stage that interim measures are requested.

Although at the stage of interim measures an arbitral tribunal should not be overly concerned with the merits of the case, a party whose case is clearly without merit should not be granted a request for interim measures. For the tribunal in *Paushok*, this requirement meant that:

the Tribunal need not go beyond whether a reasonable case has been made which if the facts alleged are proven, might possibly lead the Tribunal to the conclusion that an award could be made in favor of Claimants. Essentially, the Tribunal needs to decide only that the claims made are not, on their face, frivolous or obviously outside the competence of the Tribunal.[55]

Finally, two notes of practice. First, when the challenged action *prima facie* poses little prejudice to the rights of the petitioner, the arbitral tribunal should consider carefully the intent behind the request for interim measures. A request for interim measures may be made in bad faith to delay the proceedings or harass the opposing party. A manifestly abusive request should be rejected quickly.[56] Second, it is important that the tribunal make clear that the issuance of interim measures does not prejudice subsequent determinations. Interim measures are temporary and are meant only to preserve the rights of the parties pending a final award.[57] Therefore, the fact that the tribunal granted the requesting party an interim measure does not mean that the final award will be in favor of the requesting party.[58]

---

[52] See *Bendone-Derossi Intl* (1983 Tribunal Rules); *Component Builders* (1983 Tribunal Rules); *Tadjer-Cohen Associates* (1983 Tribunal Rules); all reprinted in section 2(D)(1). For more examples and further discussion on the Tribunal's practice, see also D Caron, "Interim Measures of Protection," n 10, 488–90.

[53] *Paushok* (1976 Rules), para 47, reprinted in section 2(C).

[54] See *Bendone-Derossi Intl* (1983 Tribunal Rules); *Component Builders* (1983 Tribunal Rules); *Tadjer-Cohen Associates* (1983 Tribunal Rules); all reprinted in section 2(D)(1); see also *Chevron Corp* (1976 Rules) Order of February 9, 2011, paras A, D; reprinted in section 2(C).

[55] *Paushok* (1976 Rules), para 55, reprinted in section 2(C).

[56] The importance of a "*prima facie* good case as a cornerstone of an application for interim measures can be seen in three rules which complement this requirement": (1) the power of the tribunal to "modify, suspend, or terminate an interim measure," in exceptional cases even of its own initiative (Article 26(5)) (2) the possibility that the applicant furnish security as a condition for the granting of the measure sought (Article 26(6)); and (3) the applicant's liability for "costs and damages" to the other party if later in the proceedings it transpires that the measure should not have been granted in the first place (Article 26(8)). G Petrochilos, "Interim Measures Under the Revised UNCITRAL Arbitration Rules," n 6. See also section 2(D)(2).

[57] See discussion of Article 26(2) in section 2(B)(2). See also *Tadjer-Cohen Associates* (1983 Tribunal Rules) reprinted in section 2(D)(1).

[58] UNCITRAL, 37th Session, UN Doc A/CN.9/523, n 43, at 13–14 para 43; UNCITRAL, 39th Session, UN Doc A/CN.9/545, n 17, at 12, para 32. See also *EnCana Corp* (1976 Rules), para 19; *Paushok* (Interim order) (1976 Rules), para 46; *Chevron Corp* (1976 Rules) Order of May 14, 2010, para 3; *Chevron Corp* (1976 Rules) Order of February 9, 2011, para J; *Chevron Corp* (1976 Rules) First Interim Award of January 25, 2012, para 4; *Chevron Corp* (1976 Rules) Second Interim Award of February 16, 2012, para 8; all reprinted in section 2(C).

(d) Further conditions imposed by the agreement of the parties

Article 26(3) imposes three conditions on the awarding of interim measures. A separate question is whether the parties fixing the powers of the tribunal can through their mutual agreement impose further conditions or restriction on the power to award interim measures. This is particularly relevant in investor–state arbitration where some bilateral investment treaties specifically limit the power of tribunals to order interim measures. This issue arose specifically in the *EnCana Corp v Ecuador* arbitration where the tribunal noted that Article XIII(8) of the Canada–Ecuador bilateral investment treaty provided in relevant part: "A tribunal may not order attachment or enjoin the application of the measure alleged to constitute a breach of this Agreement." The tribunal ultimately did not need to address the effect of this limitation.[59]

(4) *Conditions relaxed for the preservation of evidence—Article 26(4)*

Article 26(4) provides that with regard to a request for an interim measure under paragraph 2 (d) for the preservation of evidence, "the requirements in paragraphs 3 (a) and (b) shall apply only to the extent the arbitral tribunal considers appropriate." The Working Group for the 2006 Amendments to the UNCITRAL Model Law noted that it is not always appropriate that the requesting party satisfy the tribunal of conditions listed in paragraph (3).[60] It was emphasized that paragraph 4 only potentially lessens (as "appropriate") the conditions stated in paragraph (3) for the preservation of evidence. As a result, tribunals should always take the conditions set forth in Article 26(3) into account when determining whether an interim measure should be granted.[61] Article 26(4) simply allows some discretion in the application of those requirements when the request aims at the preservation of evidence.

(5) *The form (award or order) in which interim measures are granted*

Article 26 of the 2010 Rules does not carry forward a sentence of the 1976 Rules that reads: "Such interim measures may be established in the form of an interim award."[62] Thus, the form in which interim measures are issued is not discussed in Article 26 of the 2010 Rules. As discussed in relation to Article 34, however, arbitral tribunals under the 2010 Rules continue to possess, as they did under the 1976 Rules, broad authority to issue "separate awards on different issues at different times," a phrase that clearly includes awards of interim measures.[63] Further, interim measures issued as "awards" are generally thought to be more enforceable than "orders," as the New York Convention refers only to "awards."[64] To the

---

[59] *EnCana Corp* (1976 Rules), para 11, reprinted in section 2(C).
[60] UNCITRAL, 43rd Session, UN Doc A/CN.9/589, n 32, at 8, para 32.
[61] It was suggested that explanatory material accompanying article 17 could indicate that the fact that the type of measure contained in subparagraph (d) was not subject to paragraph (3) did not mean that an arbitral tribunal would not examine and weigh the circumstances in determining the appropriateness of ordering the measure. UNCITRAL, 43rd Session, UN Doc A/CN.9/589, n 32, at 8, para 33.
[62] 1976 UNCITRAL Arbitration Rules, art 26(2), first sentence.
[63] See Chapter 24.
[64] *Report of the Working Group on Arbitration and Conciliation on the Work of its Forty-Fifth Session* (Vienna, September 10–14, 2007), UNCITRAL, 47th Session, UN Doc A/CN.9/614, at 11, para 51 (2007). "In order to facilitate the enforcement of interim measures taken by the arbitrators pursuant to paragraph 1 of this article, paragraph 2 authorizes the arbitrators to establish these measures in the form of interim awards." *Report of the Secretary-General on the Revised Draft Set of Arbitration Rules,* UNCITRAL, 9th Session, Addendum 1 (Commentary), UN Doc A/CN.9/112/Add.1 (1975), reprinted in (1976) VII UNCITRAL Ybk 166, 176. See *Chevron Corp* (1976 Rules), Order of February 9, 2011, para C read with *Chevron Corp* (1976 Rules), 1st Interim Award of January 25, 2012, para 1; both reprinted in section 2(C).

same end, some legal systems require that an interim measure be issued in the form of an award before it is recognized and enforced.[65]

Not all UNCITRAL delegates supported the granting of interim measures in the form of an award, however. They argued that an "award" is a decision of the tribunal only on the substance of the dispute,[66] and that granting interim measures in the form of an award that is "final" goes against the idea that interim measures are "temporary" and ordered "prior to the issuance of the award."[67] In our opinion, this view is overly formalistic and, even then, not supported by the discussions within the Working Group. It continues to be generally accepted that the granting of interim measures can be made in the form of an award.

(6) Tribunal's power to modify, suspend or terminate interim measures—Article 26(5)

Under Article 26(5), the tribunal has the power to modify, suspend or terminate any interim measure it has issued. The tribunal can do so at the request of a party or on its own initiative.[68]

Under the corresponding provision of the 1976 Rules, a chief factor in determining when a tribunal may revise interim measures is whether the measure has been granted as an "Award" or an "Order." Unlike an order, an award granting interim measures is "final" and cannot be subject to revision.[69] The award may be superseded in effect on its terms or by a subsequent award, but the initial award is not itself revised. As noted above, the Working Group charged with revising the Rules followed the approach taken in the 2006 Amendments to the Model Law[70] to suppress the distinction between "Award" and "Order" in the making of interim measures. Therefore, Article 26 simply states that all interim measures granted by the tribunal can be modified, suspended or terminated.[71] But given that, as explained above, interim measures may still be granted in the form of an award, the question remains as to how interim measures are to be modified.

When the tribunal should modify, suspend or terminate an interim measure is not addressed by Article 26. One commentator explains, correctly in our view, that the determination necessarily takes place at a later time and that the tribunal analyzes the question of modification in

---

[65] UNCITRAL, 40th Session, UN Doc A/CN.9/547, n 45, at 20, para 71.

[66] UNCITRAL, 40th Session, UN Doc A/CN.9/547, n 45, at 20, para 70.

[67] The Working Group noted that maintaining the distinction was potentially confusing in the light of Article 26(5), which recognizes the tribunal's power to modify, suspend or terminate interim measures when necessary. UNCITRAL, 47th Session, UN Doc A/CN.9/614, n 2, at 11, para 51. See discussion of Article 26(5) in section 2(B)(6).

[68] See *Paushok* (1976 Rules), terms and conditions of interim order para 15; *Chevron Corp* (1976 Rules) Order of May 14, 2010, para 2; *Chevron Corp* (1976 Rules) First Interim Award of January 25, 2012, para 4; *Chevron Corp* (1976 Rules) Second Interim Award of February 16, 2012, para 7; all reprinted in section 2(C).

[69] D Caron, *Interim Measures of Protection*, n 10, 513.

[70] G Petrochilos, n 6. The author notes that Article 26(5) is more carefully drafted than a similar provision contained in article 17G of the Model Law.

[71] "It was observed that the words 'whether in the form of an award or another form' which appeared in article 17(2) of the UNCITRAL Arbitration Model Law had been deleted from the corresponding article in the revised Rules (article 26 (2)). It was explained that, while in the past some practitioners might have used the form of an award for interim measures with a view to enhancing their enforceability, this no longer had much purpose given that the UNCITRAL Arbitration Model Law now contained provisions permitting enforcement of interim measures regardless of the form in which they were issued. As well, it was noted that issuing an interim measure in the form of an award under the Rules could create confusion, particularly in light of article 26 (5) of the Rules, which permitted the arbitral tribunal to modify or suspend an interim measure." UNCITRAL, 47th Session, UN Doc A/CN.9/641, n 7, at 10–11 para 51. This strong opinion appears to assume that the potential enforcing jurisdiction has adopted the UNCITRAL Model Law. Although many states indeed have legislation based on the 1985 Model Law, only 17, as of 2012, have such laws based on the Model Law, as amended in 2006.

the light of new elements and circumstances.[72] Indeed, the drafters of the 2006 Amendments to the Model Law considered adding the phrase "in light of additional information or a change of circumstances" to paragraph 5. This additional language was rejected, however, as it was felt to be "superfluous" and restrictive of the arbitrator's decision to grant interim measures.[73] The Working Group noted that "it was not clear whether the power to modify or terminate an interim measure should only be recognized when the conditions for granting the interim measure were no longer met or whether the tribunal should have full discretion in this regard."[74] Some argued that the tribunal should only have the discretion to modify, suspend or terminate an interim measure in exceptional circumstances.[75] To respect the consensual nature of arbitration[76] it was also strongly felt that if the tribunal could act upon its own initiative it should be required to inform the parties.[77] Those in favor of allowing the tribunal to act argued that it was important especially in cases where an interim measure was granted on erroneous or fraudulent grounds.[78] As a compromise, Article 26(5) reads: "…or in exceptional circumstances and upon prior notice to the parties, on the arbitral tribunal's own initiative."

Article 26(5) specifically lists several actions the tribunal can take: modification, suspension or termination. (Actions such as "amending" an interim measure were deliberately left out and considered inappropriate.[79]) The right for the tribunal to modify, suspend or terminate an interim measure of course only applies to measures granted by the tribunal itself and not to interim measures issued by other tribunals or courts.[80]

(7) Security for the costs of interim measures—Article 26(6)

Article 26(6) authorizes the tribunal to require that the requesting party provide appropriate security for potential costs in connection with an interim measure.[81] The 1976

---

[72] G Petrochilos, "Interim Measures Under the Revised UNCITRAL Arbitration Rules," n 6, page. See also *Chevron Corp* (1976 Rules) Order of May 14, 2010, para 1(iv)–(v) (The Tribunal can direct the parties to keep it apprised, in writing and otherwise, of later and/or specific circumstances). See further *Islamic Republic of Iran and United States of America* (Case Nos A/4 and A/15), reprinted in section 2(D)(1), where the Tribunal ultimately granted an interim order which it had formerly declined to grant, while reserving with the party a right to make a fresh application, upon such an application having been made and on showing change of circumstances that would cause the moving party irreparable injury.

[73] UNCITRAL, 39th Session, UN Doc A/CN.9/545, n 17, at 13, para 36.

[74] UNCITRAL, 37th Session, UN Doc A/CN.9/523, n 43, at 15, para 51.

[75] However, it was suggested that, in order not to leave too much discretion to the arbitral tribunal acting of its own initiative, paragraph (5) should clearly establish that, while under normal circumstances an interim measure could only be terminated or modified at the request of a party, specific circumstances might justify modification or termination of an interim measure by the arbitral tribunal on its own initiative. The Working Group proposed the following language: "The arbitral tribunal may modify or terminate an interim measure of protection at any time upon application of any party or, in exceptional circumstances, on the tribunal's own initiative, upon prior notice to the parties." UNCITRAL, 39th Session, UN Doc A/CN.9/545, n 17, at 14, para 40.

[76] UNCITRAL, 39th Session, UN Doc A/CN.9/545, n 17, at 13–14, para 37.

[77] UNCITRAL, 37th Session, UN Doc A/CN.9/523, n 43, at 15, para 50.

[78] UNCITRAL, 39th Session, UN Doc A/CN.9/545, n 17, at 13–14, para 38.

[79] As a matter of drafting, it was pointed out that, whereas article 17 bis (4) referred to "termination, suspension or amendment of that interim measure," paragraph (6) referred to "modify, suspend or terminate an interim measure." It was agreed that the texts should be aligned. Preference was expressed for the word "modify" instead of "amend." UNCITRAL, 40th Session, UN Doc A/CN.9/547, n 45, at 27, para 101.

[80] UNCITRAL, 39th Session, UN Doc A/CN.9/545, n 17, at 13–14, para 37. It was recalled that the words "it has granted" were inserted to reflect the decision of the Working Group that the arbitral tribunal could only modify or terminate the interim measure issued by that tribunal (A/CN.9/545, para. 41). On that basis, it was agreed that the words "it has granted" should be retained in the provision. UNCITRAL, 40th Session, UN Doc A/CN.9/547, n 45, at 27, paras 102, 104.

[81] Since the taking of interim measures may entail "costs of arbitration," paragraph 2 gives arbitrators the power to require security for such costs. *Report of the Secretary-General on the Revised Draft Set of Arbitration Rules,*

UNCITRAL Rules contain a similar provision in Article 26(2). It is possible that a decision to order interim measures will prove to be wrong in light of further information or the final disposition of the rights and duties of the parties. In that case, the party subject to interim measures may have suffered, through no fault of its own, considerable inconvenience in the form of attendant costs. During the discussions on amending the Model Law, some argued in favor of making the provision of security mandatory to guarantee that the party against whom interim measures are granted will not suffer harm.[82] This position was not followed as it was said to be uncommon in practice.[83] The possibility of requiring that both the requesting party and any other party provide security in connection with the interim measure was also raised.[84] However, this was neither included in the final draft of the 2006 Amendments to the Model Law nor in the 2010 UNCITRAL Rules. Therefore, the ordering of security is at the tribunal's discretion.[85] The drafters of the 2006 Amendments to the Model Law noted that requiring security did not need to take place before the interim measure is issued, but rather can be requested at a later time.[86]

(8) Disclosure by any party of any material change—Article 26(7)

Under Article 26(7), the tribunal may require any party to disclose any material change in the circumstances on which the interim measure was requested or granted. Given that an interim measure is only temporary and does not constitute a final award, the tribunal has the discretionary power to ensure that the interim measure remains justified. The issue whether the communication of any material change should also be communicated to the other party was raised in the *travaux préparatoires* to the 2006 Amendments to the Model Law. However, such a requirement was not included either in the Model Law or in the 2010 UNCITRAL Rules.[87] Although not expressly addressed, the tribunal may wish to

---

UNCITRAL, 9th Session, Addendum 1 (Commentary), UN Doc A/CN.9/112/Add.1 (1975), reprinted in (1976) VII UNCITRAL Ybk 166, 176. It was stressed that the requirement for appropriate security to be given by the party seeking interim measures was crucial for the acceptability of the provision. *Report of the Working Group on Arbitration and Conciliation on the Work of its Thirty-Forth Session* (New York, May 21–June 1, 2001), UNCITRAL, 34th Session, UN Doc A/CN.9/487 at 19–20, para 67, 68 (2001).

[82] UNCITRAL, 36th Session, UN Doc A/CN.9/508, n 40, at 16–17, para 59. A general view emerged that the granting of security should not be a condition precedent to the granting of an interim measure. It was pointed out that article 17 of the Model Law as well as article 26 (2) of the UNCITRAL Arbitration Rules did not include such a requirement. *Report of the Working Group on Arbitration and Conciliation on the Work of its Fortieth Session* (New York, February 23–27, 2004), UNCITRAL, 40th Session, UN Doc A/CN.9/547, n 45, at 25, para 92.

[83] UNCITRAL, 40th Session, UN Doc A/CN.9/547, n 45, at 25, para 92.

[84] UNCITRAL, 40th Session, UN Doc A/CN.9/547, n 45, at 25, para 95–96.

[85] UNCITRAL, 39th Session, UN Doc A/CN.9/545, n 17, at 12, para 33. See *Paushok* (Interim order) (1976 Rules), para 90, reprinted in section 2(C). See also *Questech, Inc* (1983 Tribunal Rules) and *Behring Intl, Inc* (1983 Tribunal Rules), both reprinted in section 2(D)(2).

[86] UNCITRAL, 40th Session, UN Doc A/CN.9/547, n 45, at 25, para 93.

[87] A concern was expressed that paragraph (6) did not require the requesting party to notify the other party of a material change in the circumstances. The Working Group noted that paragraph (3) of Article 24 of the Model Law, as amended, provided that "all statements, documents or other information supplied to the arbitral tribunal by one party shall be communicated to the other party." Additionally, Article 18 of the Model Law provided that the parties "shall be treated with equality and each party shall be given a full opportunity of presenting his case." A concern was expressed that duplication of these principles in draft paragraph (6) could be detrimental and that the issue should instead be addressed in a commentary to the Model Law. After discussion, the Working Group agreed that, notwithstanding the obligations set out in Article 24(3) and Article 18 of the Model Law, it would be useful to require expressly in paragraph (6) that all information supplied to the arbitral tribunal by one party pursuant to that paragraph should also be communicated to the other party. UNCITRAL, 39th Session, UN Doc A/CN.9/545, n 17, at 15, para 45.

explicitly require that notice of any material change be communicated to the other party as well.[88]

(9) Liability for costs and damages—Article 26(8)

Users of the UNCITRAL Rules should be aware that under Article 26(8) the arbitral tribunal has the discretion to hold the "requesting party liable for any costs and damages caused by the measure to any party if the tribunal later determines that, in the circumstances then prevailing, the measure should not have been granted." Article 26(8) concludes that the tribunal "may award such costs and damages at any point during the proceedings."

Article 26(8) should be read along with Article 26(6) whereby the tribunal has the power to require that the requesting party provide appropriate security in connection with interim measures. The difference between Article 26(6) and Article 26(8) is that liability for costs and damages does not arise in connection with the impact of the interim measure, but because of the lack of justification for the measure.

While drafting Article 26(8), the Working Group expressed the concern that the provision could be interpreted as holding the requesting party liable for costs and damages if in the end that party lost the arbitration.[89] However, it was agreed that the final award should not be an essential element in determining whether to hold the requesting party liable for costs and damages.[90] As a result, it was suggested that the requesting party should be held liable for costs and damages when the tribunal determines that the interim measure "should not have been granted" or "was not justified."[91]

Given that different legal systems have different approaches to holding a party liable for costs and damages, the Working Group discussed whether the conditions triggering liability for costs and damages should be dealt with under applicable law.[92] However, it was decided that the tribunal should have the discretionary power to establish liability.

---

[88] A suggestion was made that while there was a duty to inform the arbitral tribunal of any material changes in the circumstances affecting the granting of the interim measure, there was no sanction if this duty was breached. In response it was agreed that this matter could adequately be dealt with under paragraph (7). On that basis, no decision was made to change the text of paragraph (6). UNCITRAL, 37th Session, UN Doc A/CN.9/523, n 43, at 15 para 49.

[89] UNCITRAL, 50th Session, UN Doc A/CN.9/614, n 2, at 116, para 29.

[90] *Settlement of Commercial Disputes: Revision of the UNCITRAL Arbitration Rules, Note by the Secretariat*, UNCITRAL, UN Doc A/CN.9/WG.II/WP.154/Add.1 at 10, para 32 (2009). See also UNCITRAL, 40th Session, UN Doc A/CN.9/547, n 45, at 27, para 106.

[91] "Some support was expressed for the inclusion of the words 'should not have been granted' at the end of the first sentence of paragraph (8), for the sake of consistency with the approach taken in article 17 G of the UNCITRAL Model Law. Other views supported the second option in paragraph (8) that the measure 'was not justified', as it was found to better address the situation where a measure was granted in compliance with all conditions, but was later found to cause damages. After discussion, the Working Group agreed to modify the first sentence of paragraph (8), so that it would read as follows: 'The party requesting an interim measure may be liable for any costs and damages caused by the measure to any party if the arbitral tribunal later determines that, in the circumstances then prevailing, the measure should not have been granted'. [The Working Group] ... also observed that similar provisions were found in some national laws and arbitration rules, and served a useful purpose of indicating to the parties the risks associated with a request for an interim measure." UNCITRAL, 47th Session, UN Doc A/CN.9/614, n 2, at 49, para 10. According to one author, it is presumed that liability will be held only if the requesting party obtained an unjustified measure through "incomplete or misleading information." J Waincymer "The New UNCITRAL Arbitration Rules: An Introduction and Evaluation" (2010) 14 Vindobona J Intl Commercial L and Arb 223.

[92] The Working Group suggested the following paragraph: "the arbitral tribunal may rule at any time on claims for compensation of any damage wrongfully caused by the interim measure or preliminary order." However, the word "wrongfully" was deleted as it could receive a variety of interpretations and created legal uncertainty. UNCITRAL, 50th Session, UN Doc A/CN.9/614, n 2, at 117, para 29.

It is important to note that the tribunal can hold the requesting party liable "at any point during the proceedings." This should be understood as meaning that the determination may take place at any time during the proceedings, and not only during the period immediately following the measure.[93] It arguably also suggests that a party becoming aware of continuing damage could request the tribunal to retain jurisdiction so as to determine liability for continuing costs and damages even after a final award as to the original dispute has been issued.

(10) Relations between the arbitral tribunal and municipal courts in issuing interim measures—Article 26(9)

An arbitral tribunal may be precluded from granting interim measures by mandatory norms of local law that reserve such powers to the courts. Much more common, however, are domestic laws allowing concurrent jurisdiction between the arbitral tribunal and municipal courts.[94] The interim measures powers of municipal courts and arbitral tribunals thus may complement each other.

The possibility of cooperation between municipal courts and the arbitral tribunal in issuing interim measures is envisaged by Article 26(9), which provides that "a request for interim measures addressed by one party to a judicial authority shall not be deemed incompatible with the agreement to arbitrate, or as a waiver of that agreement." This provision is identical to Article 26(3) of the 1976 Rules.[95]

Where mandatory norms of applicable national law preclude the arbitral tribunal from ordering interim measures, Article 26(9) guarantees that a party requesting a court to enact such measures does not thereby violate the arbitration agreement. Thus Article 26(9) makes clear that by resorting to courts for interim measures a party does not lose the right to demand arbitration and does not become subject to suit for breach of its agreement to arbitrate.[96]

Moreover, where the powers of the arbitral tribunal and courts to order interim measures may coexist, Article 26(9) also recognizes that even if the arbitrators are competent to act, a party may legitimately "prefer to approach the court instead of addressing himself to the arbitral tribunal."[97] Such a choice may be preferable because a "judicial authority" may provide the only adequate means to address the alleged prejudice. The interim measures powers of municipal courts thus may supplement those possessed by the arbitral tribunal. Article 26(9) allows the parties to approach courts both at the place of arbitration and elsewhere.

Nothing in Article 26(9) should suggest, however, that tribunals are not preferable to municipal courts. Arbitral tribunals may be as effective, if not more so, in issuing interim

---

[93] UNCITRAL, 50th Session, UN Doc A/CN.9/614, n 2, at 118, para 29.
[94] See D Donovan, "The Allocation of Authority Between Courts and Arbitral Tribunals to Order Interim Measures: A Survey of Jurisdictions, the Work of UNCITRAL and a Model Proposal," in A Berg (ed) *New Horizons in International Commercial Arbitration and Beyond* (2005). Donovan offers a thorough analysis of different countries' approaches to the relationship between courts and arbitral tribunals with respect to interim measures.
[95] UNCITRAL, 47th Session, UN Doc A/CN.9/614, n 2, at 52, para 10. "This provision is based on Article IV of the European Convention on International Commercial Arbitration." *Report of the Secretary-General on the Revised Draft Set of Arbitration Rules,* UNCITRAL, 9th Session, Addendum 1 (Commentary), UN Doc A/CN.9/112/Add.1 (1975), reprinted in (1976) VII UNCITRAL Ybk 166, 176.
[96] D Caron, "Interim Measures of Protection," n 10, 507.
[97] P Sanders, "Commentary on UNCITRAL Arbitration Rules," (1977) II Ybk Commercial Arb 197.

measures in support of arbitration. First, the coercive force of a court is often unnecessary when the tribunal issues interim measures as parties will often comply with them voluntarily, often to avoid antagonizing the arbitral decision makers who have not ruled on the merits yet. Second, unlike courts, arbitrators are familiar with the underlying facts of the dispute, and it is usually easier for the arbitrator to entertain requests for relief in the language and under the applicable law chosen by the parties.[98]

The statement in Article 26(9) that resort to a municipal court for interim measures is not incompatible with the agreement to arbitrate does not mean that the order resulting from such an act may not be considered incompatible with the proceedings.[99] For example, interim measures sought by one party before a municipal court may be viewed by the other party as prejudicial to its interests, and the second party may then seek from the tribunal interim measures to stop the actions of the first party. Article 26(9) does not state that interim measures ordered by a court necessarily prevail over conflicting measures deemed appropriate by the tribunal. Such prevalence can hardly be denied orders issued by a court of the place of arbitration, but where "the court involved is of a state other than the place of arbitration ... then the tribunal quite likely is not subordinated to that court by municipal law and, therefore, is not constrained from considering contrary interim measures."[100] The Iran–US Claims Tribunal shared this conclusion in the *Behring* case, insofar as the Tribunal, in one of its own interim measure awards, acknowledged that a US court may order "interim measures not in conflict with this Award."[101]

(11) Issuance of preliminary orders

It can take time for a tribunal to make a decision regarding interim measures. In some circumstances, the tribunal may be called upon to grant preliminary measures (sometimes termed "protective measures") to address the possibility of harm until a decision on interim measures can made. It is possible that these measures could be taken ex parte, although the extent of present day communications tend to ensure that the other party is somewhat involved.

Neither Article 26 of the 2010 Rules nor corresponding Article 26 of the 1976 Rules mentions the tribunal's power to make preliminary orders. However, Article 17 of the 2006 Amendments to the Model Law explicitly grants an arbitral tribunal the authority to grant preliminary orders.[102] Given that Article 26 of the 2010 Rules used Article 17 as a point of departure, one would expect that preliminary orders would be addressed in the 2010 Rules.

---

[98] J Castello, "Unveiling the 2010 UNCITRAL Arbitration Rules" (2010) 65 Dispute Resolution J 21.
[99] D Caron, "Interim Measures of Protection," n 10, 506.
[100] D Caron, "Interim Measures of Protection," n 10, 506.
[101] Reprinted in section 2(D)(3). For further discussion, see Caron, "Interim Measures of Protection," n 10, 504–8. See also J van Hof, *Commentary on the UNCITRAL Arbitration Rules: The Application by the Iran-U.S. Claims Tribunal* (1992) 189. An alternate explanation for the Behring Award was that the interim measures granted of US or Iranian courts were displaced expressly by measures granted by the Tribunal because of the international law undertakings of both states. In particular, it arguably is implicit in the third interim measures award in the *Behring* arbitration that the Iran–US Claims Tribunal believed that although the claimant had the right to apply for interim measures in a US court, those interim measures by virtue of the Algiers Accords could not contradict those of the Tribunal. D Caron, "Interim Measures of Protection," n 10, 507, 508.
[102] Article 17 B of the 2006 Model Law, as amended, provides:

Article 17 B. Applications for preliminary orders and conditions for granting preliminary orders

(1) Unless otherwise agreed by the parties, a party may, without notice to any other party, make a request for an interim measure together with an application for a preliminary order directing a party not to frustrate the purpose of the interim measure requested.

The absence of a provision addressing preliminary orders reflects the fact that it was highly controversial in the context of Article 17 of the Model Law and only narrowly adopted. Although for almost the entire process of the revision of the Rules it appeared that a provision on preliminary orders would be included, the drafters, reprising the controversy during the Model Law, debated at length whether or not to include a similar provision in Article 26. In the very last session, it was removed. In this section, we review the arguments made, but we stress that the silence of Article 26 on this point is inconsequential in our view. Preliminary orders were granted in the context of the Iran–US Claim Tribunal and have been granted since 2006 under the 1976 Rules in the context of two investment arbitrations extracted in section 2(C).[103]

On the one hand, those in favor of granting the tribunal the power to order preliminary measures argue that many legal systems allow a party to obtain temporary injunctions without informing the other party of such a request where the court is satisfied that informing the other party would undermine the effectiveness of the temporary injunction.[104] A party against whom the order would be directed might dispose of the evidence or remove the assets from the jurisdiction if given advance notice that such a measure was being sought.[105] Furthermore, it was noted that arbitrators issue preliminary orders in practice and that including a paragraph was strongly recommended to provide guidance to arbitrators.[106] Excluding a reference to preliminary orders from the UNCITRAL Rules, it was argued, could lead to a misimpression that Article 26 disallows such orders.[107]

On the other hand, it was argued that preliminary orders are contrary to the essence of arbitration where each party should be heard.[108] It was noted that the inclusion of preliminary orders in Article 17 of the Model was controversial[109] and should not be included in the UNCITRAL Rules directed to parties, rather than legislatures, as this would risk undermining their wide acceptability.[110]

Throughout the discussion, the Working Group was generally in favor of including a provision dealing with preliminary orders[111] and it drafted many different versions of a paragraph taking into account all arguments.[112] There even was offered as a compromise

---

(2) The arbitral tribunal may grant a preliminary order provided it considers that prior disclosure of the request for the interim measure to the party against whom it is directed risks frustrating the purpose of the measure.

(3) The conditions defined under article 17A apply to any preliminary order, provided that the harm to be assessed under article 17A(1)(a), is the harm likely to result from the order being granted or not.

For discussion on ex parte in the 2006 Amendments to the UNCITRAL Model Law, see UNCITRAL, 36th Session, UN Doc A/CN.9/508, n 40, at 13–23, para 51–94 and UNCITRAL, 37th Session, UN Doc A/CN.9/523, n 43, at 19–23, para 77–94.

[103] See *Paushok* (1976 Rules); *Chevron Corp* (1976 Rules), both reprinted in section 2(C).
[104] See J Castello, "Arbitral Ex Parte Interim Relief: The View in Favor" (2003) 58 Dispute Resolution J 60.
[105] J Castello, "Arbitral Ex Parte Interim Relief," n 104.
[106] UNCITRAL, 47th Session, UN Doc A/CN.9/614, n 2, at 12, para 56.
[107] UNCITRAL, 50th Session, UN Doc A/CN.9/614, n 2, at 23, para 103.
[108] UNCITRAL, 50th Session, UN Doc A/CN.9/614, n 2, at 22, para 101.
[109] UNCITRAL, 47th Session, UN Doc A/CN.9/614, n 2, at 11, para 54.
[110] UNCITRAL, 47th Session, UN Doc A/CN.9/614, n 2, at 11, para 55; UNCITRAL, 50th Session, UN Doc A/CN.9/614, n 2, at 22, para 101.
[111] UNCITRAL, 47th Session, UN Doc A/CN.9/614, n 2, at 12, para 59 (2007); UNCITRAL, 50th Session, UN Doc A/CN.9/614, n 2, at 23, para 105.
[112] UNCITRAL, 47th Session, UN Doc A/CN.9/614, n 2, at 11–12, para 53–60. UNCITRAL, 50th Session, UN Doc A/CN.9/614, n 2, at 22–5, para 100–112.

that the paragraph additionally indicate that a tribunal would not be able to grant preliminary orders if it is located in a legal system prohibiting preliminary orders.[113]

However, the final draft of the 2010 UNCITRAL Rules is silent on the subject of preliminary orders.[114] In our opinion, tribunals clearly possess such a power as is apparent in their issuance in the *Paushok* and *Chevron* arbitrations. Moreover, although the 2010 UNCITRAL Rules are silent as to the power of a tribunal to issue preliminary measures, it is presumed that a party may potentially seek preliminary orders in the courts of the seat of arbitration.[115]

(12) Comparison to the 1976 UNCITRAL Rules

The 2010 Rules differ significantly from the 1976 Rules with respect to interim measures both in detail and the level of discretion afforded the tribunal. Article 26 of the 2010 Rules is more detailed because it tracks Article 17 of the Model Law that was amended significantly in 2006 in response to the need to clarify the scope of the tribunal's authority to order interim measures.[116] Whether the practice under the different versions of the Rules will differ significantly is not clear at this point and will depend largely on how arbitrators utilize the discretion afforded them under the 1976 Rules. In all likelihood, the detail of the 2010 Rules will come to influence the way discretion is used under the 1976 Rules.

In adopting Article 17 of the Model Law as the point of departure, Article 26 was dramatically expanded[117] and now regulates interim measures in greater detail than most other sets of arbitration rules.[118] As a result, the language and concepts in both the Model Law, as amended, and in the 2010 Rules are very similar. The Working Group favored the approach in Article 17 of the Model Law (providing specifically worded guidance) rather than the approach of Article 26 of the 1976 Rules (framing the rules in broad and conceptual terms). Some delegates believed that these changes were necessary to provide "guidance and legal certainty to arbitrators and parties" unfamiliar with the use of interim measures in the context of international arbitration.[119] Others argue that these changes are confusing and diminish the flexibility of arbitration.

Article 26 now contains nine paragraphs, whereas Article 26 of the 1976 UNCITRAL Rules contained three paragraphs.

Article 26(1) is identical to corresponding Article 26(1) of the 1976 Rules. The only difference is that this rule is held in one paragraph whereas under the 1976 UNCITRAL Rules it is a part of paragraph 1.

---

[113] UNCITRAL, 50th Session, UN Doc A/CN.9/614, n 2, at 23–4, para 106.

[114] In the end, no comment was made on this and it will be left to the *lex arbitri* or other jurisdictional bases. J Waincymer, "The New UNCITRAL Arbitration Rules," n 91.

[115] "If the seat is a Model Law state, this would be an application under Art 17. Where preliminary orders are sought from courts of countries other than the seat, it will be a question of whether the law in that country allows for preliminary orders in aid of foreign-seated proceedings. Other than states that have adopted the 2006 text of the Model Law, few states have laws that permit such measures." M Skinner, et al, "The UNCITRAL Arbitration Rules 2010," n 36, 76; The view was also expressed that preliminary orders, in certain jurisdictions, were within the competence of municipal courts, and the procedure for granting such orders contained many safeguards that might not be present to the same extent as in the arbitration procedure. UNCITRAL, 50th Session, UN Doc A/CN.9/614, n 2, at 22, para 102.

[116] G Petrochilos, "Interim Measures Under the Revised UNCITRAL Arbitration Rules," (2010) 28(4) ASA Bulletin 878.

[117] L Graham, "Interim Measures: Ongoing Regulation and Practices (A View from the UNCITRAL Arbitration Regime)," in A J Berg (ed), *50 Years of the New York Convention: ICCA International Arbitration Conference* (2009); G Petrochilos, "Interim Measures," n 116.

[118] G Petrochilos, "Interim Measures," n 116.

[119] J Castello, "Unveiling the 2010 UNCITRAL Arbitration Rules," (2010) 65 Dispute Resolution J 21.

Article 26(2) contains elements that are not present in Article 26 of the 1976 Rules. It provides a definition of an interim measure, and the distinction between "Order" and "Award" contained in Article 26(2) of the 1976 Rules is removed. Article 26(2) offers four types of interim measure a tribunal may order, whereas Article 26(1) of the 1976 Rules contained two examples. However, both lists of examples were clearly intended to be non-exhaustive.

Article 26(3) poses the conditions a party must satisfy to obtain interim measures. No similar express provision exists under the 1976 Rules. Under the 1976 Rules, similar conditions were articulated as criteria to guide a tribunal's use of its discretion.

Article 26(4) potentially lessens the conditions contained in Article 26(3) that a requesting party must satisfy to "preserve evidence that may be relevant and material to the resolution of the dispute." No similar express provision exists under the 1976 Rules.

Article 26(5) gives the tribunal the power to modify, suspend or terminate an interim measure. No similar express provision exists under the 1976 Rules, although some view the distinction contained in Article 26(2) of the 1976 Rules between interim measures issued as "Awards" or "Orders" as bearing on how the tribunal is to approach modifying, suspending or terminating an interim measure.

Article 26(6) is slightly different from the second sentence of corresponding Article 26(2) of the 1976 Rules. The words "may require" replace "shall be entitled to require." The words "the requesting party" were added as well as "in connection with the measure."

Article 26(7) grants the tribunal the power to request the disclosure by any party of any material change in the circumstances on the basis of which the interim measure was requested or granted. No similar express provision exists under the 1976 Rules.

Article 26(8) grants the tribunal the discretionary power to hold the requesting party liable for costs and damages caused by an unnecessary interim measure at any point during the proceedings. No similar express provision exists under the 1976 Rules.

Article 26(9) is identical to corresponding Article 26(3) of the 1976 Rules.

C. Extracts from the Practice of Investment Tribunals

EnCana Corp and *Government of Ecuador,* Interim Award (January 31, 2004) (LCIA administered, 1976 UNCITRAL Rules, Canada-Ecuador BIT):

5. The Claimant seeks interim measures of protection pursuant to Article 26 of the [1976] UNCITRAL Rules and Article XIII(8) of the Canada-Ecuador Agreement for the Promotion and Reciprocal Protection of Investments, concluded on 29 April 1996 (the BIT). Specifically, it seeks measures to prevent freezing of assets of EnCana subsidiaries and its legal representative pending resolution of the dispute by the present Tribunal.

...

10. Two different provisions are potentially relevant to an order for interim measures of protection in the present case, Article 26 of the [1976] UNCITRAL Rules and Article XIII(8) of the BIT. As a specific provision applicable to investments by Canadian corporations in Ecuador, Article XIII(8) must prevail over the general power in Article 26 of the [1976] UNCITRAL Rules.

11. Article XIII(8) provides:

"A tribunal may order an interim measure of protection to preserve the rights or a disputing party, or to ensure that the tribunal's jurisdiction is made fully effective, including an order to preserve evidence in the possession of control of a disputing party or to protect the tribunal's jurisdiction. A tribunal may not order attachment or enjoin the application of the measure alleged to constitute a breach of this Agreement. For purposes of this paragraph, an order includes a recommendation."

12. Under Article 26 of the [1976] UNCITRAL Rules, by contrast, there is no exclusion of interim measures enjoining "the application of the measure alleged to constitute a breach of this Agreement". [quote of rule deleted.]
13. In the Tribunal's view, three conditions ought in principle to be met before interim measures are established, whether under Article XIII(8) of the BIT or Article 26 of the UNCITRAL Rules. First, there must be an apparent basis of jurisdiction. Second, the measure sought must be urgent. Third, the basis for establishing provisional measures must be that otherwise irreparable damage could be caused to the requesting party.
14. In the present circumstances the Tribunal is satisfied that the measures taken give rise to a situation of urgency. They involve the freezing of accounts and the attempted attachment of substantial sums which are in dispute. The second condition is accordingly fulfilled.
15. Turning to the third condition, it is necessary to consider separately the measures taken against AEC, the EnCana subsidiary, and those taken against Mr. Bustamante, the Respondent's legal representative in Ecuador.
16. As to the measures taken against AEC, in the light of the information before it the Tribunal must proceed on the basis that the measures of enforcement are taken by the IRS within the framework of Ecuadorian law in order to recover back monies said to have been wrongly paid out by way of VAT refunds. The Tribunal notes that according to the Respondent, it is open to the parties against whom the measures have been taken to challenge them in the Ecuadorian tax courts or within IRS's administrative processes, on grounds which are independent of the resolution of the underlying issues in dispute in the present proceedings.
17. AEC is not a Canadian corporation and is not a party to the present arbitration. On the other hand it is part of the EnCana group, a substantial Canadian concern, and it appears that in bringing the present proceedings EnCana is seeking to protect the interests of its subsidiaries. In the circumstances the measures taken by the IRS are no doubt inconvenient, but they are open to challenge before the tax courts of Ecuador, which have shown themselves to be independent of the IRS in decisions so far reached. Ultimately any inconvenience can be addressed by AEC (or EnCana on behalf of AEC) paying the amounts in dispute. The question whether the amounts are actually due is not prejudged by the measures themselves, and would not be prejudged by the return of the amounts refunded. Eventually, if jurisdiction is upheld, it would be open to this Tribunal to provide redress to the Claimant for any losses suffered by enforcement action taken in breach of the BIT, including by payment of interest on sums refunded. In these circumstances there is no necessity to order the withdrawal of IRS's measures against AEC in order to protect the rights at stake in this arbitration from irreparable harm.
18. The position with the measures taken against Dr. Bustamante is not necessarily the same. Circumstances could be imagined where measures of enforcement taken against the legal representative of a party would amount to a form of harassment or an attempt to limit or deny the exercise of due process rights, thereby raising issues under the BIT. Even if the substantive dispute concerned taxation measures within the meaning of Article XII(l), this would not necessarily exempt such conduct from the scope of the BIT, in particular Article II. But the Tribunal is not persuaded, in the light of the information provided to it, that this is the case here. Action has been taken against Mr Bustamante as the general representative of AEC in Ecuador and not by reason of his acting for EnCana or its subsidiaries in relation to the dispute. The measures were taken within the framework of general provisions of Ecuadorian law, and it is open to Mr. Bustamante to challenge them before the Ecuadorian courts. Since these measures too appear to have been taken by way of enforcement action in relation to the VAT refund in dispute, there is no reason to treat them any differently than the measures taken against AEC.
19. In these circumstances the Tribunal is not persuaded that there is any necessity for the measures requested in terms of protecting the rights claimed by EnCana in the present proceedings. This finding is in no way intended to prejudge any issue that may arise before the Ecuadorian courts as to the measures taken.

20. Accordingly the Tribunal need not decide whether there is an apparent basis for jurisdiction in respect of EnCana's underlying claim, or whether the power to establish interim measures is constrained by Article XII(l) or XIII(8) of the BIT, even if there is apparent jurisdiction over the dispute as such.

Sergei Paushok, et al and *Government of Mongolia,* Temporary Restraining Order (March 23, 2008) (*Ad Hoc* Proceeding, 1976 UNCITRAL Rules, Russia-Mongolia BIT) (reprinted in the Tribunal's Order on Interim Measures, September 2, 2008, para 16):

1. Taking into account the undertaking already given, Respondent shall refrain from seizing or obtaining a lien on the assets of Claimants and shall allow Claimants to maintain their ordinary business operations;
2. Claimants shall immediately sign an undertaking not to move assets out of Mongolia nor to take any action which would alter in any way the ownership and/or financial interests of the Claimants with respect to their assets in Mongolia, without prior notice to and agreement of Respondent;
3. Claimants shall, within seven days, provide Respondent with a complete list of their assets in Mongolia;
4. The issue raised by Respondent of the provision of security by Claimants shall be dealt with at the time of the consideration of the Request for Interim Measures;
5. The briefing schedule for any issue related to Claimants' interim measures application shall be decided in a separate procedural order by the Tribunal, after consultation with the Parties.

Pending its decision on interim measures, the Tribunal urges the Parties to refrain from any action which could lead to further injury and aggravation of the dispute between the Parties."

Sergei Paushok, et al and *Government of Mongolia,* Order on Interim Measures (September 2, 2008) (*Ad Hoc* Proceeding, 1976 UNCITRAL Rules, Russia-Mongolia BIT) reprinted in (November 2008) 23 Mealey's Intl Arb Rep, B-1:

II - GENERAL COMMENTS

1- The applicable rules

34. The Tribunal wishes to point out, first, that this case is taking place under the [1976] UNCITRAL Arbitration Rules. The powers of the Tribunal relating to interim (or provisional) measures are set in Articles 15(1), 26(1) and 26(2) of those Rules . . . :

...

2 - What is the subject-matter of the dispute

37. The subject-matter of the dispute is the validity under the Treaty of the Windfall Profit Tax and of the levying of a *fee* for the import of foreign workers imposed by Respondent. In their Notice of Arbitration of November 30, 2007, Claimants request declaratory relief based on Articles 3(1) and 4 of the Treaty as well as damages, interest and costs. And, in their Statement of Claim filed on June 27, 2008, Claimants request declaratory relief with regard to those two types of measures as contrary to Articles 2, 3 and 4 of the Treaty; in addition, they claim damages, interest and costs to be determined by the Tribunal.
38. The Parties have spent some considerable time arguing the issue of disputed rights in this case. These matters will be dealt with in the section of this Order dealing with imminent danger of prejudice.

3 - Interim measures not to be granted lightly

39. It is not contested that interim measures are extraordinary measures not to be granted lightly, as stated in a number of arbitral awards rendered under various arbitration rules. Even under the discretion granted to the Tribunal under the [1976] UNCITRAL Rules, the Tribunal still has to deem those measures urgent and necessary to avoid "irreparable" harm and not only convenient or appropriate.

4 - Evidentiary Burden

40. In requests for interim measures, it is incumbent upon Claimants to demonstrate that their request is meeting the standards internationally recognized as pre-conditions for such measures.

...

III - THE CRITERIA GUIDING THE TRIBUNAL

45. It is internationally recognized that five standards have to be met before a tribunal will issue an order in support of interim measures. They are (1) prima facie jurisdiction, (2) prima facie establishment of the case, (3) urgency, (4) imminent danger of serious prejudice (necessity) and (5) proportionality.

46. In addressing the first two criteria, the Tribunal wishes to make it clear that it does not in any way prejudge the issues of fact or law which may be raised by the Parties during the course of this case concerning the jurisdiction or competence of the Tribunal or the merits of the case.

1 - Prima facie jurisdiction

47. The International Court of Justice described the interpretation to be given to this standard in the *Case Concerning Military and Paramilitary Activities in and Against Nicaragua*:

> "(O)n a request for provisional measures the Court need not, before deciding whether or not to indicate them, finally satisfy itself that it has jurisdiction on the merits of the case, or, as the case may be, that an objection to jurisdiction is well founded, yet it ought not to indicate such measures unless the provisions invoked by the applicant appear, prima facie, to afford a basis on which the jurisdiction of the court might be founded;"

...

2 - Prima facie establishment of the case

55. At this stage, the Tribunal need not go beyond whether a reasonable case has been made which if the facts alleged are proven, might possibly lead the Tribunal to the conclusion that an award could be made in favor of Claimants. Essentially, the Tribunal needs to decide only that the claims made are not, on their face, frivolous or obviously outside the competence of the Tribunal. To do otherwise would require the Tribunal to proceed to a determination of the facts and, in practice, to a hearing on the merits of the case, a lengthy and complicated process which would defeat the very purpose of interim measures.

...

3 - Urgency

...

59. The Tribunal is not called upon to rule on that overall situation but taking cognizance of it helps the Tribunal in understanding whether the condition of urgency alleged by Claimants can be met in the present case.

...

62. The Tribunal is aware of preceding awards concluding that even the possible aggravation of a debt of a claimant did not ("generally" says the *City Oriente* case cited below) open the door to interim measures when, as in this case, the damages suffered could be the subject of monetary compensation, on the basis that no irreparable harm would have been caused. And, were it not for the specific characteristics of this case, the Tribunal might have reached the same conclusion, although it might have expressed reservations about the concept that the possibility of monetary compensation is always sufficient to bar any request for interim measures under the [1976] UNCITRAL Rules. But those specific features point not only to the urgency of action by the Tribunal but also to the necessity of such action in the face of an imminent danger of serious prejudice.

4 - Imminent danger of serious prejudice (necessity)

68. The Tribunal does not agree with Respondent that Claimants are merely requesting damages, as is clearly demonstrated by the text of their request for relief. Moreover, the possibility of monetary compensation does not necessarily eliminate the possible need for interim measures. The Tribunal relies on the opinion of the Iran-U.S. Claims Tribunal in the *Behring* case

to the effect that, in international law, the concept of "irreparable prejudice" does not necessarily require that the injury complained of be not remediable by an award of damages. To quote K.P. Berger who refers specifically to Article 26 of the UNCITRAL Rules:

"To preserve the legitimate rights of the requesting party, the measures must be "necessary". This requirement is satisfied if the delay in the adjudication of the main claim caused by the arbitral proceedings would lead to a "substantial" (but not necessarily "irreparable" as known in common law doctrine) prejudice for the requesting party."[18]

69. The Tribunal shares that view and considers that the "irreparable harm" in international law has a flexible meaning. It is noteworthy in that respect that the UNCITRAL Model Law in its Article 17A does not require the requesting party to demonstrate irreparable harm but merely that "(h)arm not adequately reparable by an award of damages is likely to result if the measure is not ordered, and such harm substantially outweighs the harm that is likely to result to the party against whom the measure is directed if the measure is granted".

...

76. Claimants have raised another argument in support of their request for interim measures on the basis that, in this case, the Tribunal would have reasons to believe that Claimants would encounter serious difficulties in having enforced an award which would be rendered in their favor. They allege in particular the modest financial means of Respondent as well as some recent political turbulence in Mongolia. The Tribunal does not believe that such allegations are sufficient to justify the ordering of interim measures in this case. The Tribunal should not presume that Respondent will not honor its international obligations, if an award is to be eventually rendered against it and nothing in the allegations made by Claimants is of such substance as to justify a different stand.

...

78. While it is true that Claimants would still have a recourse in damages and that other arbitral tribunals have indicated that debt aggravation was not sufficient to award interim measures, the unique circumstances of this case justify a different conclusion. In particular, while not putting in doubt the value of the undertaking of Respondent not to seize or put a lien on GEM's assets, the Tribunal believes that it is preferable to formalize that commitment into an interim measures order.

5 - Proportionality

79. Under proportionality, the Tribunal is called upon to weigh the balance of inconvenience in the imposition of interim measures upon the parties.

...

90. Article 26 of the [1976] UNCITRAL Rules does not mandate any specific type of security. An escrow account is not the exclusive measure of protection from which Respondent could benefit Different measures with equivalent results can also be considered. The Tribunal is retaining one such measure: the provision of a bank guarantee having the same effect.

...

ON THE BASIS OF THE ABOVE, THE TRIBUNAL THEREFORE ORDERS AS FOLLOWS

Claimant's application for interim measures of protection under Article 26 of the [1976] UNCITRAL rules is granted in accordance with the terms and subject to the conditions below:

1. Payment to the Respondent of the Windfall Profit tax owing by GEM (including interest and penalties) is suspended until the Tribunal has ruled on the merits of the Claimant's request for relief.
2. Taking note of the undertaking previously made by Respondent on March 19, 2008 and confirmed at the Hearing, Respondent shall refrain from seizing or obtaining a lien on the assets of GEM and other assets of Claimants in connection with the WPT owing to Respondent or from directly or indirectly taking any other action leading to the same or similar effect, except in accordance with the Tribunal's Orders, and shall allow GEM and Claimants to maintain their ordinary business operations in Mongolia.

3. Following their previous undertaking in that regard on Marche 26, 2998, Claimants shall not move assets out of Mongolia, nor take any action which would alter in any way the ownership and/or financial interests of Claimants with respect to their assets in Mongolia, without prior notice to and agreement of Respondent. Sale and pledges of gold are authorized provided the funds thus obtained are used for the ordinary business operations of GEM. Under no circumstances should such funds be used for other purposes; in particular, no transfer of funds or assets of any kind should be made outside of Mongolia (except for deposit into the escrow account under the conditions described below) or to any of the Claimants or any person, corporation or business related to them, without Respondent's agreement.
4. Claimants shall provide gradually increasing security as described below. The Tribunal may increase of decrease the security for good cause shown premised on the evolution of GEM'S business. Claimants shall submit for approval by the Tribunal, within twenty days of the present Order, a detailed proposal, which will have been discussed with Respondent, concerning the implementation of one of the following measures of protection which they will have selected:
    a. An escrow account in an internationally recognized financial or other institution outside Mongolia and Russia and acceptable to the Tribunal;
    b. The provision of a bank guarantee to the same effect and under the same conditions from an internationally recognized financial or other institution outside Mongolia and Russia and acceptable to the Tribunal.

If Respondent is not satisfied with the arrangement proposed by Claimants, the Tribunal will issue the appropriate order upon request by one of the Parties.

5. The cost of the escrow account shall be borne equally by Claimants and Respondent but can be made part of the claim for compensation by each Party.
6. Claimants shall deposit in the escrow account (if such is the option retained), on the first working day of each month following the establishment of that account, the sum of US$2 million, until a final award is rendered in the present case or until the sum in the escrow account has reached 50 percent of the total amount of the accrued WPT claimed by Respondent, including interest and penalties, whichever comes first. The monies deposited in the escrow account may be invested in financial instruments of high liquidity. The decision regarding the scope of the security is adopted by majority, Dr. Horacio A. Grigera Naon being of the view that tax penalties should be excluded from the determination or calculation of the security.
7. Claimants may use the income resulting from the sale of gold by GEM for deposit into the escrow account, provided that, in no circumstance, such transfer would result in a reduction of shareholders' equity in GEM below the sum of MNT 31,578,323,602.35 mentioned at line 2.3.20 of the Balance Sheet of the Financial Statements of December 31, 2007 (after inclusion in the liabilities of the company the amount of WPT payable at that time—but not actually paid—of MNT 35,241,117,548.00 mentioned at line 2.1.1.12). Each such transfer shall be preceded by an affidavit signed by Director S.V. Paushok and the Chief Accountant of GEM confirming that fact and sent to Respondent and the Tribunal.
8. If, instead of the escrow account, the bank guarantee option is retained, arrangements to the same effect shall be put into place.
9. Claimants shall, every six months, provide Respondent with a complete list of their assets in Mongolia.
10. The scope of this Order does not extend beyond the subject-matter of this dispute and does not prevent Mongolia, after due consideration in good-faith of the Tribunal's direction under paragraph 11 below, from exercising its rights against GEM or Claimants in matters unrelated to this dispute, including taxes owing in other respect than the Windfall Profit Tax.

...

12. The Parties shall refrain, until a final award is rendered in this case, from any action which could lead to further injury and aggravation of the dispute between the Parties.
13. The Tribunal reserves for later consideration its decision on costs arising from these proceedings.

14. The Temporary Restraining Order is terminated
15. The Tribunal reserves the right to amend or revoke the present Order at any time during the proceedings, upon request by one of the Parties demonstrating the need for such action. In particular, failure by Claimants to timely provide or maintain the required security could lead to the immediate revocation of the present Order.

[Footnote] 18. Berger, KP, *International Economic Arbitration, in Studies in Transnational Economic Law,* vol. 9, Kluwer Law and Taxation Publishers, Deventer, Boston, 1993 at p.336.

Chevron Corp, et al and *Republic of Ecuador,* Order on Interim Measures (May 14, 2010) (PCA administered, 1976 UNCITRAL Rules, US-Ecuador BIT), at 5:

THE TRIBUNAL ORDERS AS FOLLOWS:

1. Until further decision the Tribunal takes, pursuant to Article 26(1) of the [1976] UNCITRAL Rules, the following interim measures up to and including the next procedural meeting beginning on November 22, 2010:
   (i) The Claimants and the Respondent are both ordered to maintain, as far as possible the *status quo* and not to exacerbate the procedural and substantive disputes before this Tribunal, including (in particular but without limiting howsoever the generality of the foregoing) the avoidance of any public statement tending to compromise these arbitration proceedings;
   (ii) The Claimants and the Respondent are both ordered to refrain from any conduct likely to impair or otherwise adversely affect, directly or indirectly the ability of the Tribunal to address fairly any issue raised by the Parties before this Tribunal;
   (iii) The Claimants and the Respondent are both ordered not to exert, directly or indirectly, any unlawful influence or pressure on the Court addressing the pending litigation in Ecuador known as the Lago Agrio Case;
   (iv) The Claimants and the Respondent are ordered to inform the Tribunal (in writing) of the likely date for the issue by the Court of its judgment in the Lago Agrio Case as soon as such date becomes known to any of them;
   (v) The Respondent is ordered to communicate (in writing and also by any other appropriate means) the Tribunal's invitation to the Court in the Lago Agrio Case to make known as a professional courtesy to the Tribunal the likely date for the issue by the Court of its judgment in the Lago Agrio Case; and, to that end, the Respondent is ordered to send to the Court the full text in Spanish and English of the Tribunal's present order; and
   (vi) The Respondent is ordered to facilitate and not to discourage, by every appropriate means, the Claimants' engagement of legal experts, advisers and representatives from the Ecuadorian legal profession for the purpose of these arbitration proceedings (at the Claimants' own expense).
2. This Order is and shall remain subject to modification in the light of any future event, upon the Tribunal's own motion or upon any Party's application, particularly in the light of any new development in the Lago Agrio Case and the issue of the Court's judgement in such Case; and any of the Parties may apply to the Tribunal for such modification upon 24 hours' written notice.
3. This Order is made strictly without prejudice to the merits of the Parties' procedural and substantive disputes, including the Respondent's jurisdictional and admissibility objections and the merits of the Claimants' claims.

Chevron Corp, et al and *Republic of Ecuador,* Order for Interim Measures (February 9, 2011) (PCA administered, 1976 UNCITRAL Rules, US-Ecuador BIT), at 3–4:

THE TRIBUNAL NOW DECIDES:
(A) As to jurisdiction, the Tribunal records that it has not yet determined the Respondent's challenge to its jurisdiction (as recorded in the fourth preamble to its Order of January 28,

2011). Nonetheless, for the limited purpose of the present decision, the Tribunal provisionally assumes that it has jurisdiction to decide upon the Claimants' Second Application for Interim Measures on the ground that the Claimants have established, to the satisfaction of the Tribunal, a sufficient case for the existence of such jurisdiction at this preliminary stage of these arbitration proceedings under the written arbitration agreement invoked by the Claimants against the Respondent under the Treaty between the United States of America and the Republic of Ecuador concerning the Encouragement and Reciprocal Protection of Investment (the "BIT"), incorporating by reference the 1976 UNCITRAL Arbitration Rules (the "UNCITRAL Rules");

(B) The Tribunal notes that: (i) Article 26 of the UNCITRAL Rules permits a tribunal, at the request of a party, to take interim measures (established in the form of an order or award) in respect of the subject-matter of the parties' dispute; (ii) Article 32(1) of the UNCITRAL Rules permits a tribunal to make (inter alia) an award in the form of a final, partial or interim award; (iii) Article 32(2) of the UNCITRAL Rules provides that any award is final and binding on the parties, with the parties undertaking to carry out such award without delay; and (iv) Articles VI.3(6) of the BIT provides (inter alia) that an award rendered pursuant to Article VI.3(a)(iii) of the BIT under the UNCITRAL Rules shall be binding on the parties to the dispute, with the Contracting Parties undertaking to carry out without delay the provisions of any such award and to provide in its territory for its enforcement;

(C) As to form, the Tribunal records that, whilst this decision under Article 26 of the UNCITRAL Rules is made in the form of an order and not an interim award, given the urgency required for such decision, the Tribunal may decide (upon its own initiative or any Party's request) to confirm such order at a later date in the form of an interim award under Articles 26 and 32 of the UNCITRAL Rules, without the Tribunal hereby intending conclusively to determine the status of this decision, one way or the other, as an award under the 1958 New York Convention.

(D) As to the grounds for the Claimants' Second Application, the Tribunal concludes that the Claimants have made out a sufficient case, to the Tribunal's satisfaction, under Article 26 of the UNCITRAL Rules, for the order made below in the discretionary exercise of the Tribunal's jurisdiction to take interim measures in respect of the subject-matter of the Parties' dispute;

(E) Bearing in mind the Respondent's several obligations under the BIT and international law, including the Respondent's obligation to carry out and provide for the enforcement of an award on the merits of the Parties' dispute in these arbitration proceedings (assuming this Tribunal's jurisdiction to make such an award), the Tribunal orders:
  (i) the Respondent to take all measures at its disposal to suspend or cause to be suspended the enforcement or recognition within and without Ecuador of any judgment against the First Claimant in the Lago Agrio Case; and
  (ii) the Respondent's Government to inform this Tribunal, by the Respondent's legal representatives in these arbitration proceedings, of all measures which the Respondent has taken for the implementation of this order for interim measures; pending further order or award in these arbitration proceedings, including the Tribunal's award on jurisdiction or (assuming jurisdiction) on the merits;

(F) …;

(H) The Tribunal decides further that the Claimants shall be legally responsible, jointly and severally, to the Respondent for any costs or losses which the Respondent may suffer in performing its obligations under this order, as may be decided by the Tribunal within these arbitration proceedings (to the exclusion of any other jurisdiction);

(I) This order shall be immediately final and binding upon all Parties, subject only to any subsequent variation made by the Tribunal (upon either its own initiative or any Party's request); and

(J) This order, as with the earlier order of January 26, 2011, is made by the Tribunal strictly without prejudice to any Party's case as regards the Tribunal's jurisdiction, the Claimants' First Application made by letter dated December 12, 2010, the Respondent's opposition to such First Application, and to any claim or defence by any Party as to the merits of the Parties' dispute.

Chevron Corp, et al and *Republic of Ecuador*, First Interim Award (January 25, 2012) (PCA administered, 1976 UNCITRAL Rules, US-Ecuador BIT), at 16–17:

THE TRIBUNAL NOW MAKES THIS FIRST INTERIM AWARD AS FOLLOWS:

1. Pursuant to Paragraph (C) of its Order dated February 9, 2011 and upon the following terms, the Tribunal confirms and re-issues such Order as an Interim Award pursuant to Article 26 and 32 of the [1976] UNCITRAL Arbitration Rules, specifically Paragraph (E) of such Order; namely (as here modified):
2. Bearing in mind the Respondent's several obligations under the BIT and international law, including the Respondent's obligation to carry out and provide for the enforcement of an award on the merits of the Parties' dispute in these arbitration proceedings (assuming this Tribunal's jurisdiction to make such an award), the Tribunal orders:
   (i) the Respondent to take all measures at its disposal to suspend or cause to be suspended the enforcement or recognition within and without Ecuador of any judgment against the First Claimant in the Lago Agrio Case; and
   (ii) the Respondent's Government shall continue to inform this Tribunal, by the Respondent's legal representatives in these arbitration proceedings, of all measures which the Respondent has taken from the implementation of this Interim Award;

   pending the February Hearing's completion and any further order or award in these arbitration proceedings,
3. This Interim Award is and shall remain subject to modification (including its extension or termination) by the Tribunal at or after the February Hearing; and, in the meantime, any of the Parties may also apply to the Tribunal for such modification upon /2 hours' written notice for good cause shown;
4. This Interim Award is made strictly without prejudice to the merits of the Parties' substantive and order procedural disputes, including (but not limited to) the Parties' respective applications to be heard at the February Hearing;
5. This Interim Award shall take effect forthwith as an Interim Award, being immediately final and binding upon all Parties as an award subject only to any subsequent modifications hearing provided, whether upon the Tribunal's own initiative or any Party's application; and
6. This interim Award although separately signed by the Tribunal's members on three signing pages, constitutes an "interim award" signed by the arbitrators under Article 32 of the [1976] UNCITRAL Arbitration Rules.

Chevron Corp, et al and *Republic of Ecuador*, Second Interim Award (February 16, 2012) (PCA administered, 1976 UNCITRAL Rules, US-Ecuador BIT), at 2–4:

THE TRIBUNAL NOW MAKES THIS SECOND INTERIM AWARD AS FOLLOWS:

1. The Tribunal determines that: (i) Article 26 of the [1976] UNCITRAL Rules (forming part of the arbitration agreement invoked by the Claimants under the Treaty) permits this Tribunal, at the request of a Party, to take interim measures (established in the form of an order or award) in respect of the subject-matter of the Parties' dispute; (ii) Article 32(1) of the UNCITRAL Rules permits this Tribunal to make (inter alia) an award in the form of an interim award; (iii) Article 32(2) of the [1976] UNCITRAL Rules provides that any award by this Tribunal is final and binding on the Parties, with the Parties undertaking to carry out such award without delay; and (iv) Articles VI.3(6) of the Treaty provides (inter alia) that an award rendered by this Tribunal pursuant to Article VI.3(a)(iii) of the Treaty under the [1976] UNCITRAL Rules shall be binding on the parties to the dispute (i.e. the Claimants and the Respondent), with the Contracting Parties (i.e. here the Respondent) undertaking to carry out without delay the provisions of any such award and to provide in its territory for its enforcement;

2. The Tribunal determines further that the Claimants have established, for the purpose of their said applications for interim measures, (i) a sufficient case as regards both this Tribunal's jurisdiction to decide the merits of the Parties' dispute and the Claimants' case on the merits against the Respondent; (ii) a sufficient urgency given the risk that substantial harm may befall the Claimants before this Tribunal can decide the Parties' dispute by any final award; and (iii) a sufficient likelihood that such harm to the Claimants may be irreparable in the form of monetary compensation payable by the Respondent in the event that the Claimants' case on jurisdiction, admissibility and the merits should prevail before this Tribunal;
3. Bearing in mind the Respondent's several obligations under the Treaty and international law, including the Respondent's obligation to carry out and provide for the enforcement of an award on the merits of the Parties' dispute in these arbitration proceedings and the Tribunal's mission (required under the arbitration agreement) efficaciously and fairly to decide the Parties' dispute by a final award, the Tribunal hereby orders:
   (i) the Respondent (whether by its judicial, legislative or executive branches) to take all measures necessary to suspend or cause to be suspended the enforcement and recognition within and without Ecuador of the judgments by the Provincial Court of Sucumbíos, Sole Division (*Corte Provincial de Justicia de Sucumbíos, Sala Unica de la Corte Provincial de Justicia de Sucumbíos*) of January 3, 2012 and of January 13, 2012 (and, to the extent confirmed by the said judgments, of the judgment by Judge Nicolás Zambrano Lozada of February 14, 2011) against the First Claimant in the Ecuadorian legal proceedings known as "the Lago Agrio Case";
   (ii) in particular, without prejudice to the generality of the foregoing, such measures to preclude any certification by the Respondent that would cause the said judgments to be enforceable against the First Claimant; and
   (iii) the Respondent's Government to continue to inform this Tribunal, by the Respondent's legal representatives in these arbitration proceedings, of all measures which the Respondent has taken for the implementation of its legal obligations under this Second Interim Award;
   until any further order or award made by the Tribunal in these arbitration proceedings;
4. The Tribunal determines that the Claimants shall be legally responsible, jointly and severally, to the Respondent for any costs or losses which the Respondent may suffer in performing its legal obligations under this Second Interim Award, as may be decided by the Tribunal within these arbitration proceedings (to the exclusion of any other jurisdiction); and further that, as security for such contingent responsibility the Claimants shall deposit within thirty days of the date of this Second Interim Award the amount of US$50,000,000.00 (United States Dollars Fifty Million) with the Permanent Court of Arbitration in a manner to be designated separately, to the order of this Tribunal;
5. The Tribunal dismisses the application made by the Respondent to vacate its order for interim measures of February 9, 2011;
6. The Tribunal's existing orders for interim measures (as recited in the First Interim Award) and the First Interim Award shall continue to have effect subject to the terms of this Second Interim Award;
7. This Second Interim Award is and shall remain subject to modification at any time before the Tribunal's final award in these arbitration proceedings; and, in the meantime, any of the Parties may also apply to the Tribunal for such modification upon seventy-two hours' written notice for good cause shown, including any material change in the legal or factual circumstances prevailing as at the date of the Hearing;
8. This Second Interim Award is made strictly without prejudice to the merits of the Parties' substantive and other procedural disputes, including the Respondent's objections as to jurisdiction, admissibility and merits;
9. This Second Interim Award shall take effect forthwith as an Interim Award, being immediately final and binding upon all Parties as an award subject only to any subsequent modification as herein provided, whether upon the Tribunal's own initiative or any Party's application; and

10. This Interim Award, although separately signed by the Tribunal's members on three signing pages constitutes an "interim award" signed by the three arbitrators under Article 32 of the [1976] UNCITRAL Arbitration Rules.

D. Extracts from the Practice of the Iran–US Claims Tribunal

(1) Tribunal Rules (1983), Article 26(1)

Ford Aerospace and Communications Corp and *Government of Iran,* et al, Award No ITM 16-93-2 (April 27, 1983), reprinted in 2 Iran-US CTR 281, 282 (1983-I):

> It appears from the copy of the summons received by Ford Aerospace, that the claim filed against it by the Government of Iran before the General Court of Tehran, is identical to the counterclaim previously filed with the Tribunal in this case.
>
> However, it is provided in paragraph 2 of Article VII of the Claims Settlement Declaration that "claims referred to the Arbitral Tribunal shall, as of the date of filing of such claims with the Tribunal, be considered excluded from the jurisdiction of the Courts of Iran, or of the United States, or any other court. The subject matter of the Counter claim is thus excluded from the jurisdiction of the Courts of Iran from the date the Counterclaim was filed with this Tribunal unless and until this Tribunal decides that is has no jurisdiction over it.
>
> Accordingly, the request for a stay of proceedings in Iran must be granted as an interim measure, even though this Tribunal has not yet decided whether it has jurisdiction, in this case.
>
> For the foregoing reasons,
>
> The Tribunal Awards as follows:
>
> The Government of the Islamic Republic of Iran is requested to seek a stay of the proceedings before the General Court of Tehran, pending termination of the proceedings before the Iran-United States Claims Tribunal.

Rockwell Intl Systems, Inc and *Islamic Republic of Iran, Ministry of Defence,* Award No ITM 20–430–1 (June 6, 1983) at 4–5, reprinted in 2 Iran-US CTR 369, 371 (1983–I):

> As to the contention that the Tribunal does not have power to grant the interim relief sought by Rockwell, the Tribunal notes that the Full Tribunal concluded in its interim Award No ITM 13–388-FT in the Case *E-Systems, Inc.* and *The Government of the Islamic Republic of Iran,* Case No 388, that the Algiers Declarations leave the Government of Iran free in principle to initiate claims before Iranian Courts even where the claim would have been admissible as a counter-claim before the Tribunal. However, in that Interim Award it is also stated that the tribunal has an inherent power to issue such orders as may be necessary to conserve the respective rights of the parties and to ensure its jurisdiction and authority are made fully effective. It is also stated that any award to be rendered in the case by the Tribunal, which was established by inter-governmental agreement, will prevail over any decision inconsistent with it rendered by Iranian or United States courts.
>
> The consistent practice of the Tribunal indicates that this inherent power is in no way restricted by the language in Article 26 of the Tribunal Rules. Further, the Government of Iran and the Government of the United States have agreed in the Algiers Declarations to confer upon this Tribunal jurisdiction over certain claims. It follows that both governments are under an international obligation to comply with any decisions rendered by the Tribunal pursuant to this agreement.
>
> For the foregoing reasons,
>
> The Tribunal requests the Government of the Islamic Republic of Iran to take all appropriate measures to ensure that the proceedings before the Public Court of Tehran be stayed, pending determination of the proceedings in the present case before the Iran-United States Claims Tribunal.

RCA Global Communications, Inc and *Islamic Republic of Iran,* Award No ITM 30–160–1 (October 31, 1983) at 5, reprinted in 4 Iran-US CTR 9, 11–12 (1983–III):

> It follows from the Interim Award by the Full Tribunal in the Case *E- Systems, Inc.* and *The Government of the Islamic Republic et al.,* Case No 388, Award No ITM 13–388-FT, that the Tribunal has an inherent power to issue such orders as may be necessary to conserve the respective rights of the Parties and to ensure that the Tribunal's jurisdiction and authority are made fully effective. In order to achieve this end the Tribunal has the power in its discretion to order a Party to stay proceedings before a domestic court, if such proceedings may lead to decisions that are inconsistent with decisions made in proceedings before the Tribunal.
>
> However, in the instant case the proceedings before the domestic court concerns a dispute arising out of a separate contract, and it involves a Party which is not a Party in the case before the tribunal. The alleged interrelationship between the two cases is not quite clear. Therefore, quite apart from the questions as to whether the Tribunal has power to request the Government of Iran to vacate the judgment entered in the Tehran Court and whether there would be any point in ordering the Government to stay the proceedings in a case which appears to be closed, in the exercise of its discretion the Tribunal does not find sufficient reasons to grant the present request.

Avco Corp and *Iran Aircraft Industries,* Case No 261, Chamber Three, Order of January 27, 1984:

> On 28 November 1983, Respondent Iran Aircraft Industries requested that the Tribunal issue an interim order prohibiting the sale of "its property with AVCO Corporation".
>
> In its submission of 30 December 1983, the Claimant asserts that no sale of any of the goods in question is planned to take place before 1 January 1985. Relying on this assertion, the Tribunal need not now take a decision with regard to the request for interim measures of protection.
>
> The Tribunal notes that this decision does not prevent the Party which has made the request from making a fresh request in the same case on new facts.

Islamic Republic of Iran and *United States of America* (Case Nos A/4 and A/15), Award No ITL 33-A-4/A-15(III)-2 (February 1, 1984) at 2, 5, reprinted in 5 Iran-US CTR 131, 133 (1984–I):

> Within the framework of Claims Nos A–4 and A–15 (III) filed with the Tribunal by the Government of the Islamic Republic of Iran against the Government of the United States of America, seeking the restitution to the Claimant of immovable and movable properties of the Iranian Embassy and Consulates located in the United States, and damages for an alleged breach by the Respondent of its obligations in this respect under the Declaration of the Government of the Democratic and Popular Republic of Algeria of 19 January 1981, the Claimant submitted on 20 December 1983 a Request for an interim measure to prevent the Government of the United States of America from auctioning the movable properties of the Iranian Embassy and Consulates in the United States and to cancel any transaction entered into pursuant to such auctions.
>
> In an Order filed on 18 January 1984, Chamber Two of the Tribunal, which had been appointed to deal with this request by Presidential Order No 17 of 5 January 1984, held that the circumstances as presented to the Tribunal at the time were not such as to require the exercise of its power to order the requested interim measure of protection, as these circumstances did not appear to create a risk of an irreparable prejudice, not capable of reparation by the payment of damages. In this Order it was further noted that this decision did not prevent the Party which had made the request from making a fresh request based on new facts.
>
> ...
>
> The Tribunal holds that the circumstances, as they are now presented to it, are such as to require the exercise of the Tribunal's power to order an interim measure of protection, pending the decision of the Full Tribunal in cases A-4 and A-15.

The Tribunal urgently requests the Government of the United States of America to take all necessary and appropriate measures to prevent the sale of Iran's diplomatic and consular properties in the United States which possess important historical, cultural, or other unique features, and which, by their nature, are irreplaceable.

Bendone-Derossi Intl and *Islamic Republic of Iran,* Award No ITM 40–375–1 (June 7, 1984) at 3–4, 6, reprinted in 6 Iran-US CTR 130, 131–132, 133 (1984–II):

In an appropriate case, an international tribunal will grant interim measures of protection before determining its jurisdiction over the merits of the claim, provided that it is satisfied that there is, at least, a *prima facie* showing that it has jurisdiction over the substantive claim. This test was most recently applied by the International Court of Justice in its Order of 10 May 1984 in *Military and Paramilitary Activities in and against Nicaragua (Nicaragua v. United States of America), Provisional Measures,* I.C.J. Reports 1984, 169, 179. The Court stated, at paragraph 24 of the Order:

[O]n a request for provisional measures the Court need not, before deciding whether or not to indicate them, finally satisfy itself that it has jurisdiction on the merits of the case, or, as the case may be, that an objection taken to jurisdiction is well-founded, yet it ought not to indicate such measures unless the provisions invoked by the Applicant appear, *prima facie,* to afford a basis on which the jurisdiction of the Court might be founded.

Without prejudice to the final determination of the jurisdictional issue, the Tribunal is not at present satisfied that it appears, *prima facie,* that there exists a basis on which it can exercise jurisdiction over the present claim.

...

The request of the Respondent for an Order granting interim measures of protection is denied.

Atlantic Richfield Co and *Islamic Republic of Iran,* Award No ITM 50–396–1 (May 8, 1985) at 4–6, reprinted in 8 Iran-US CTR 179, 181–182 (1985–I):

NIOC requests the Tribunal to issue an Order requiring the Government of the United States of America and Atlantic Richfield to take all appropriate measures to ensure that the latter accepts the applicability of the Algiers Declarations, and to withdraw the writs of attachment obtained in the United States Courts, or, in the alternative, an order requiring Atlantic Richfield to withdraw Case No 396 from the Tribunal.

In its Comments filed on 15 February 1985, the Government of the United States of America asserted that since it was not a party to Case No 396, no relief could be sought against it.

Atlantic Richfield also filed Comments on 15 February 1985, in which it contended that there was no necessary contradiction in its respective arguments before the New York Court and the Tribunal because the legal basis on which the attachment had been obtained, that of beneficial ownership of the money in the account, did not depend on whether LAPCO was deemed to be an entity controlled by Iran. Nor was there any inconsistency present in the different claim it had made before the Tribunal for breaches of international law. Atlantic Richfield further argued that as long as the New York Court proceedings remained suspended and the account blocked, there was no prejudice to either party and no risk of inconsistent rulings.

The Tribunal holds that, as to the claim for interim relief against the Government of the United States of America, it cannot grant the relief sought because the Government of the United States of America is not a party to Case No 396. The Tribunal notes, however, that the subject-matter of the present request is before the Full Tribunal as part of Case A-15, and the present decision in no way prejudices the eventual outcome of that Case.

As to the relief sought against Atlantic Richfield, the Tribunal does not consider that there exists any threat of grave or irreparable damage to NIOC, or to the Tribunal's jurisdiction, such as to justify the granting of interim measures. On the contrary, the preservation of the status quo appears to be assured by the continued blocking of the LAPCO account and the suspension of the New York Court proceedings pending the Tribunal's determination of the present case.

Atlantic Richfield admits that it is "true that [it] has resisted transfer of the funds in the LAPCO bank account to Iran on the ground that LAPCO was not an entity controlled by Iran for purposes of the transfer order." While this may indicate the existence of a contradiction between the position taken by Atlantic Richfield respectively as Claimant in the present case and as Plaintiff in the New York court proceedings, this is not *per se* relevant to the question of whether the grant of interim relief is appropriate. Nor is it necessary for the Tribunal to make any decision on this point at the present stage of the proceedings. It is rather an issue to be considered by the Tribunal as part of the merits of Case No 396.

For the foregoing reasons,

The request of the Respondent NIOC for interim relief against Atlantic Richfield and the Government of the United States of America is denied.

Component Builders, Inc and *Islamic Republic of Iran,* Award No ITM/ITL 51–395–3 (May 27, 1985) at 6, 12–13, 14–15, reprinted in 8 Iran-US CTR 216, 220, 225–26 (1985–I):

One requirement for the issuance of interim measures is that there be, at least *prima facie,* a basis on which the jurisdiction of the Tribunal might be founded.

The Full Tribunal has ruled that the Tribunal has "an inherent power to issue such orders as may be necessary to conserve the respective rights of the Parties and to ensure that this Tribunal's jurisdiction and authority are made fully effective," *E-Systems Inc.* and *The Islamic Republic of Iran,* Interim Award No 13–388-FT (4 February 1983) at 10, 2 Iran-US CTR 51, 57. It has exercised such power to require a stay to Tehran court proceedings pending completion of Tribunal action where "it is obvious that the claim initiated before the Iran Court had been admissible as a counter-claim before the Tribunal", even though no counter-claim had been asserted. *E-Systems* at 7, 2 Iran-US CTR at 55.

Moreover, the Full Tribunal has ruled "that once a counter-claim has been initiated before the Tribunal, such claim is excluded from the jurisdiction of any court". *E-Systems* at 9, 2 Iran-US CTR at 5, relying on Article VII(2) of the Claims Settlement Declaration.

...

Examination of the suit filed by Bank Maskan and of Claim 1 and 2 filed by Claimants before this Tribunal also makes clear that both actions seek to adjudicate the same issues. Claimants allege that they have satisfactorily performed under the Contract and under Claim 1 seek monies due and payable by the terms of the Contract and by Claim 2 seek monies allegedly owing as a result of Bank Maskan's failure to fulfill its duties under the Contract. Bank Maskan on the other hand alleges that Claimants' performance was unsatisfactory and seeks the refund of advance payments, damages "representing costs for repairing defects in the grading of terrace floors, roof facades, etc.," and damages "representing costs of repainting". Indeed, Bank Maskan's Statement of Defence, in responding to Claims 1 and 2, repeatedly supports its pleas with reference to the lawsuit in Tehran (see Bank Maskan Statement of Defence at 68, 69, 71, 72 and 74).

The Tribunal therefore concludes, as the Full Tribunal did in E-Systems, that in order "to conserve the respective rights of the Parties and to ensure that this Tribunal's jurisdiction and authority are made effective," it is appropriate that interim measures requiring a stay of the proceedings in the Public Court of Tehran be issued in this case. As the Tribunal noted in *Aeronutronics Overseas Services, Inc.* and *The Islamic Republic of Iran et al.,* Interim Award No 47–158–1 (14 March 1985) at 5, Respondent Iran "has . . . assumed an international obligation to take whatever steps may be necessary to comply with" this Interim Award.

Behring Intl, Inc and *Islamic Republic Iranian Air Force,* Award No ITM/ITL 52–382–3 (June 21, 1985) at 49–50, 53–54, reprinted in 8 Iran-US CTR 238, 273, 275–76 (1985–I):

In support of their request for an Interim Award ordering, *inter alia,* Claimant to release their property from its New Jersey warehouse. Respondents contend that they will suffer irreparable injury if such relief is not granted. Respondents allege as follows:

Respondents' properties are stored under conditions wholly unsuited to the maintenance and preservation of the delicate electronic equipment, computers and aircraft spare parts...worth scores of millions of dollars. The properties are deteriorating rapidly, and the damages incurred by Respondents are irreparable, since some of the properties are irreplaceable. In addition, there are now strong indications that some items of properties are missing from Claimant's warehouse. It is manifest now that the only reason Claimant seeks to retain custody of the properties is to use that custody as a leverage to extract from Respondents a total relinquishment of their counter-claims for losses incurred as a result of Claimant's negligence and wilful breach of its duties as a warehouseman.

...

Applying these standards, the Tribunal determines that the conservation of both the goods and the rights of the Parties requires that the Respondents' property be transferred to an alternate location. Accordingly, we grant the request for interim measures, subject to the conditions set forth below.

The Tribunal first finds that Respondents' property must be removed from its present location in the annex portion of Claimant's Edison, New Jersey warehouse facility in order to prevent unnecessary damage and/or deterioration. The conditions under which the goods are presently stored are inadequate to conserve and protect them and irreparable prejudice to Respondent's asserted rights may result if they are not transferred to a more appropriate facility.[42] The Tribunal made this finding in its Interim Award of 22 February 1985 and reaffirms that conclusion.

...

A definition of "irreparable prejudice" is elusive; however, the concept of irreparable prejudice in international law arguably is broader than the Anglo-American law concept of irreparable injury. While the latter formulation requires a showing that the injury complained of is not remediable by an award of damages (i.e., where there is no certain pecuniary standard for the measure of damages, 43 C.J.S. *Injunctions* § 23), the former does not necessarily so require.

[Footnote] 42. Irreparable prejudice has long been recognized as a basis for ordering provisional relief in international law.

United States of America on behalf and for the benefit of Tadjer-Cohen Associates Inc and *Islamic Republic of Iran,* Award No ITM 50–12118–3 (November 11, 1985), reprinted in 9 Iran-US CTR 302, 304–05 (1985–II):

1. On 19 January 1982, the Government of the United States of America filed the present claim on behalf and for the benefit of the Claimant, Tadjer-Cohen Associates, Incorporated ("TCA"). The Claim names as the Respondent the Islamic Republic of Iran ("Iran"), including Bank Rahni Iran ("Bank Rahni") and seek damages of US $200,222 plus interest for the alleged breach of two contracts entered into between TCSB Incorporated ("TCSB") and Bank Rahni. The contracts relate to the provision of engineering consultancy services for a project for the manufacture and erection of five hundred prefabricated housing units.

...

9. It is evident from the documents in this case that the proceedings before the Public Court of Tehran involve the same contract and work that comprise the subject matter of the claim TCSB assigned to TCA and which is currently before the Tribunal. A decision made in the proceedings before the Public Court of Tehran may lead to decisions that are inconsistent with decisions made in the proceedings before the Tribunal. *See RCA Globcom Communications* and *The Islamic Republic of Iran,* Interim Award No ITM 30–160– 1 at 5 (31 October 1983).

10. The Tribunal is satisfied that there is at least *a prima facie* showing that it has jurisdiction over the substantive claim pending before it. Such preliminary determination is, however, without prejudice to the Tribunal's final decision on jurisdiction, including any issues relating to the assignment from TCSB to TCA or the forum selection clauses.

11. The Tribunal ruled in *E-Systems, Inc.* and *The Islamic Republic of Iran,* Interim Award No ITM 13–388-FT at 10 (4 February 1983) that "[t]his Tribunal has an inherent power to issue such

Orders as may be necessary to conserve the respective rights of the Parties and to ensure that this Tribunal's jurisdiction and authority are made fully effective."

12. The Tribunal notes the Respondent's submissions on the requirements of the Civil Procedure Code of Iran. The Government of the Islamic Republic of Iran and the Government of the United States of America, however, having agreed in the Algiers Declarations to confer upon this Tribunal jurisdiction over certain claims, are under an international obligation to comply with any decisions rendered by the Tribunal. *See Aeronutronics Overseas Services, Inc.* and *The Islamic Republic of Iran*, Interim Award No ITM 47–158–1 at 5 (14 March 1985).

13. The Tribunal therefore concludes that the proceedings in the Public Court of Tehran in so far as they relate to TCJSB should be stayed pending termination of the proceedings before the Tribunal.

INTERIM AWARD For the foregoing reasons,
THE TRIBUNAL AWARDS AS FOLLOWS:
The Tribunal requests the Government of the Islamic public of Iran to take all appropriate measures to ensure that the proceedings before the Public Court of Tehran in so far as they relate to T.C.S.B. Incorporated be stayed pending the termination of the proceedings before the Tribunal.

Paul Donin de Rosiere, Panacaviar, SA and *Islamic Republic of Iran*, Award No ITM 64–498–1 (December 4, 1986), reprinted in 13 Iran-US CTR 193, 194, 196–98 (1986–IV):

6. The Tribunal has before it two related requests for interim measures of protection. The first is that the Tribunal order Panacaviar to withdraw the action it commenced in the courts of Basel prior to the commencement of the present proceedings, in connection with the same contract. The second, more specific, request is that the Tribunal order Panacaviar to obtain a stay of a "hearing" scheduled to take place in the same legal action in the Basel Court of Appeal on 5 December 1986.

...

13. Article 26, paragraph 1, of the Tribunal Rules of Procedure empowers the Tribunal, at the request of either Party, to "take any interim measures it deems necessary in respect of the subject-matter of the dispute..." Apart from so protecting the physical subject-matter of a case before it, or the rights of the respective parties where appropriate, the Tribunal has also exercised its inherent power to protect its own jurisdiction in cases where the risk of inconsistent decisions in parallel and duplicative proceedings instituted in other fora have rendered this necessary. *See, eg, E- Systems, Inc* and *The Islamic Republic of Iran*, Award No ITM 13–388-FT (4 February 1983).

14. The Tribunal must determine whether interim measures of the type requested are necessary and appropriate for either of the above reasons in the present Case. It does so on the basis of the Parties' own descriptions of the course and present status of the Basel proceedings, as the only document before the Tribunal in relation to those proceedings is Panacaviar's "Writ" and "Cause of Plaint" filed in 1980 contained in the Respondents' Rejoinder filed on 28 November 1986.

16. In deciding whether there are grounds for granting interim relief, the Tribunal can only rely on Panacaviar's more detailed characterization of the nature of the Swiss proceedings, which neither Respondent has challenged. The Tribunal is thus prepared to accept, for the sole purpose of deciding the application for interim relief, that the damage claim filed by Panacaviar in Basel was a necessary ancillary proceeding to its application for an attachment of the bank guarantee. Though that suit is founded on the same allegations of breach of contract that form part of the claim before this Tribunal, the Tribunal accepts the Claimants' statement that it is not Panacaviar's intention "to obtain a judgment from another court on the merits of the issues before this Tribunal." Thus, the Tribunal does not find sufficient grounds on the basis of the information presently before it to support the conclusion that the existence of such a suit,

commenced before the Statement of Claim was filed in the present Case, and apparently with a view to achieving an entirely different result, constitutes a violation of Article VII, paragraph 2, of the Claims Settlement Declaration so as to justify the grant of interim relief at this time. Should the Respondents later become aware of circumstances which indicate that the Claimants intend to use the Basel proceedings to obtain and enforce a judgment on the merits of the issues before this Tribunal in a manner inconsistent with the limited objective described by them in the present Case, it is open to the Respondents to apply to this Tribunal for interim measures of protection against such actions.

17. As to the attachment of the BNP bank guarantee obtained by Panacaviar in Basel, the Tribunal considers that its effect is to preserve the *status quo* as between the parties to the present Case rather than to jeopardize the position of either *visa a vis* the Tribunal. Such an attachment means, in effect, that Shilat will, for the present, be unable to obtain the proceeds of its demand under the letter of guarantee issued by Bank Etebarate Iran—a demand the legality of which is currently in issue in the proceedings in the Tribunal. That issue can and will be resolved by the Tribunal in due course when it pronounces upon the merits of the respective claim and counter-claim in its final Award.

18. Thus, the Tribunal can see no risk of grave or irreparable harm resulting to either Party, or to the jurisdiction of this tribunal, which would justify the granting of either of the measures currently sought by Shilat or Iran.

Islamic Republic of Iran and *United States of America,* Decision No DEC 116-A15(IV) & A24-FT (May 18, 1993), reprinted in 29 Iran-US CTR 214, 218, 220 (1993):

20. As to the substance of Iran's Request, the Tribunal notes that, under Tribunal precedent, interim relief can be granted only if it is necessary to protect a party from irreparable harm or to avoid prejudice to the jurisdiction of the Tribunal. *See Boeing Co., et al.,* and *Government of the Islamic Republic of Iran,* Award No ITM 34-222-1, at 4 (17 Feb. 1984), *reprinted in* 5 Iran U.S. C.T.R. 152, 154 ("Boeing"). The Tribunal has determined that this standard also applies in government-to-government cases. *See Islamic Republic of Iran* and *United States of America,* Decision No DEC 85-B1-FT (18 May 1989), *reprinted in* 22 Iran-U.S. C.T.R. 105, 108 ("Case No B1").

21. The Tribunal is not satisfied that Iran has discharged its burden of show that it risks irreparable harm if its Request is not granted. Should the Tribunal eventually determine in *Case No A24* that the United States has not complied with its obligations under the Algiers Declarations by allowing the Foremost/OPIC lawsuit to proceed in the United States, the Tribunal can compensate Iran for any damages that the Tribunal finds Iran has sustained by awarding an adequate monetary relief. The Tribunal has previously held that "injury that can be made whole by monetary relief does not constitute irreparable harm." *Case No B1,* para 11, *supra,* 22 Iran- U.S. C.T.R. at 109 (citing *Boeing, supra*). Although Iran refers to "Foremost's vexatious tactics," *supra,* para 9, and alleges that in the proceedings before U.S. courts, it has failed to demonstrate how this would lead to infliction of irreparable harm on Iran.

22. The issue as to whether there exists a threat to the Tribunal's jurisdiction requires a more intricate analysis. According to Iran's Statement of Claim in *Case No A24,* Iran seeks, *inter alia,* a declaratory judgment holding the United States liable for a breach of the Algiers Declaration by allowing the Foremost/OPIC lawsuit to proceed in the United States; an order directing the United States to terminate the Foremost/OPIC lawsuit; and damages to compensate Iran for any losses it may have incurred, as a result of the United States' breach. Therefore, the Tribunal must determine whether the Tribunal's jurisdiction to arbitrate Iran's claim is prejudiced if its Request is not granted.

23. In this connection, there are two possibilities. Either the Foremost/OPIC lawsuit in the United States will be decided before the Tribunal issues its decision in Cases Nos A15(IV) and A24, or Foremost/OPIC lawsuit will not have been decided when the Tribunal issues its

decision in Cases Nos A15 (IV) and A24. The Tribunal finds that in either event, it will be in a position to render an affective decision upon Iran's claim and, consequently, that there exists no threat to the Tribunal's jurisdiction.

...

26. Finally, the Tribunal also notes that an order granting Iran's Request would not operate so as to maintain the *status quo* pending the Tribunal's decision in *Case No A24,* as alleged by Iran. Quite the contrary, the interim measures sought by Iran would not operate so as to maintain the *status quo* the continuing proceedings before the District Court—but would modify that *"status quo"* by suspending those proceedings. Consequently, should the Tribunal grant Iran's Request, it would, in effect, make an interim judgment in favor of Iran on the merits. Absent compelling reasons for doing so, such as the protection of the Tribunal's jurisdiction or a risk of irreparable damage, Iran's Request cannot be granted. *See Behring International, Inc.* and *Islamic Republic of Iran, et al.,* Award No ITM 46–382–3 (22 Feb. 1985), *reprinted in* 8 Iran- U.S. C.T.R. 44 (dismissing the Respondents' request for interim relief because it would have been "tantamount to awarding Respondents the final relief sought in their counter-claim.")

(2) Tribunal Rules (1983), Article 26(2)

RCA Global Communications, Inc and *Islamic Republic of Iran,* Case No 160, Chamber One, Order of June 2, 1983, reprinted in 3 Iran-US CTR 8 (1983–II):

In a Motion filed with the Tribunal on 6 May 1983 the Claimants have requested the Tribunal to direct the Government of Iran to stay further proceedings regarding a claim filed with the Public Court of Tehran by Iran Insurance Company against RCA Global Communications, Inc. and RCA Global Communications Disc., Inc.

RCA Global Communications, Inc. has been requested to appear before the Public Court of Tehran on 8 June 1983.

In its Order of 12 May 1983 the Tribunal has requested the Respondents to file a Reply to the Claimant's Motion by 23 May 1983, addressing in particular the question as to whether the litigation before the Public Court of Tehran involves any issue that can lead to decisions by the Tribunal inconsistent with decisions by the Public Court of Tehran.

Following a request for an extension submitted by the Deputy Agent of the Islamic Republic of Iran on 23 May 1983, the Tribunal has granted an extension to file said Reply by 1 August 1983.

However, in view of the Claimants' statement that RCA Global Communications, Inc., has been ordered to appear before the Public Court of Tehran on 8 June 1983 and the Tribunal's inherent power to issue orders to conserve the respective rights of the Parties and to ensure that its jurisdiction and authority are made fully effective, the Tribunal finds it appropriate immediately to request the Government of Iran to move for a stay of the proceedings before the Public Court of Tehran until such time that the Tribunal can make a decision on the Claimants' request based on the views of both Parties.

For these reasons, the Tribunal requests the Government of the Islamic Republic of Iran to take all appropriate measures to ensure that the proceedings before the Public Court of Tehran be stayed until 15 August 1983.

Questech, Inc and *Ministry of National Defence of the Islamic Republic of Iran,* Case No 59, Chamber One, Order of March 2, 1984:

1. Reconsidering the requests made by Claimant in its "Motion to Require Respondent to comply with Interim Award or in the alternative for Sanctions", the Tribunal holds that such measures as requested under paragraphs A, B, C and D, on page 4 of this Motion are not provided for under the Tribunal Rules.

Behring Intl, Inc and *Islamic Republic Iranian Air Force,* Award No ITM 46–382–3 (February 22, 1985) at 4–6, reprinted in 8 Iran-US CTR 44, 46, 47–48 (1985–I):

4. The Tribunal decides that certain interim measures requested by Respondents nonetheless are appropriate at this time to preserve the rights of the Parties pending the Tribunal's final determination concerning its jurisdiction. In this respect, the Tribunal notes in particular that the parties agree that the facility in which the goods are currently stored is inadequate to preserve and protect the goods and the Tribunal deems their removal to a more modern air-conditioned and humidity-controlled facility to be essential to conserve the goods. Accordingly:

...

(d) The Tribunal orders that, in accordance with Article 26, paragraph 2 and Article 41, paragraph 2, of the Tribunal Rules, Respondents shall provide an additional $70,000 (for a total deposit outstanding of $100,000) toward the expenses of the expert and costs associated with his work, including the leasing of the full Behring warehouse, to be deposited within 30 days from the date of this Decision (and prior to the actual commencement of inventorying and the other tasks assigned specifically to the expert). This amount shall be remitted to account number 24.58.28.583 (Dollar Account) at Pierson, Heldring and Pierson, Korte Vijverberg 2, 2513 AB The Hague, in the name of the Secretary-General of the Iran-United States Claims Tribunal (Account No II). The account shall be administered by the Secretary-General of the Tribunal, who shall consult with the Tribunal.

The Tribunal further retains jurisdiction to request from arbitrating parties such other amounts as may be required from time to time in connection with the expert's work, or to decide any disputes which may arise in connection with that work. The Tribunal shall later determine which party will ultimately bear the cost of the expert's work.

United States of America, on behalf and for the benefit of Tadjer-Cohen Associates, Inc and *Islamic Republic of Iran,* Case No 12118, Chamber Three, Order of August 4, 1986:

Reference is made to the letter of the Agent of the United States submitted on 28 July 1986, and entitled "Notice to Tribunal of receipt of New Summons to Appear before the Tehran Public Court on August 27, 1986."

Attached to this submission is a copy of a transmittal letter directed to T.S.C.B. Inc. from the Embassy of the Democratic and Popular Republic of Algeria, Interests Section of the Islamic Republic of Iran together with a copy of "Summons No 1227/61" directing T.C.S.B. to appear before Tehran's Public Court No 26 on August 27, 1986 for proceedings concerning the "Claim of Bank Maskan."

The Tribunal notes that the Interim Award No ITM 56–12118–3 filed on 11 November 1985 remains in force. Therefore it continues to be incumbent on "the Government of the Islamic Republic of Iran to take all appropriate measures to ensure that the proceedings before the Public Court of Tehran in so far as they relate to T.C.S.B. Incorporated be stayed pending the termination of the proceedings before the Tribunal."

(3) Tribunal Rules (1983), Article 26(3)

Behring Intl Inc and *Islamic Republic Iranian Air Force,* Award No ITM/ITL 52–382–3 (June 21, 1985) at 60 (footnotes omitted), reprinted in 8 Iran-US CTR 238, 280 (1985–I):

Nonetheless, the Tribunal may allow for a court of the United States, if and to the extent it deems it appropriate, to take interim measures not in conflict with this Award to safeguard such security interest and stay its order transferring the goods to afford Claimant an opportunity to petition a court of competent jurisdiction for such provisional relief and to implement any order issued by such court. See Article 26(3) of Tribunal Rules. Such cooperation between this international Tribunal and the municipal courts of one of the States Parties to the Algiers Accords is made necessary by the operation of the peculiar jurisdictional provisions of the Accords upon the even more peculiar facts and circumstances of this case. Simply stated, our jurisdiction does not encompass the entirety of the transaction in which the Parties are involved, yet those aspects within our jurisdiction cannot be adjudicated without potentially prejudicing the rights of the Parties in related disputes outside our jurisdiction.

PART IV

THE PRESENTATION OF THE CASE: EVIDENCE AND HEARINGS

Introduction

After sufficient clarification of the issues, the arbitral case is often presented to the arbitral tribunal at an oral hearing. The effective conduct of the hearing assumes that the factual background and evidence of the case have been presented adequately to the tribunal as much in advance as possible. That said, the hearings may be a forum for further clarification and refinements of arguments and evidence. Accordingly, questions concerning hearings and evidence are typically closely interrelated, a fact reflected in the proximity of Article 27 on evidence and Article 28 on hearings in the 2010 UNCITRAL Rules. These articles are addressed in Chapters 18 and 19, respectively. Chapter 20 deals with Article 29, which concerns the use of experts during the arbitral proceedings.

18
Evidence

1. Introduction	555
2. Evidence—Article 27	557
A. Text of the 2010 UNCITRAL Rule	557
B. Commentary	557
(1) Burden of proof—Article 27(1)	557
(2) Definition of "witnesses"—Article 27(2)	561
(a) General comments	561
(b) Practice of the Iran–US Claims Tribunal	563
(3) Written witness statements—Article 27(2)	564
(4) Production of documents—Article 27(3)	565
(a) General comments	565
(b) Production of documents at the request of a party	567
(c) "Enforcement" of production orders	570
(5) Admissibility, relevance, materiality, and weight of the evidence—Article 27(4)	571
(6) Comparison to the 1976 UNCITRAL Rules	574
C. Extracts from the Practice of Investment Tribunals	576
(1) Article 27(1) (1976 Rules)—Burden of proof	576
(2) Article 27(2) (1976 Rules)—Definition of "witnesses"	577
(3) Article 27(2) (1976 Rules)—Written witness statements	577
(4) Article 27(3) (1976 Rules)—Production of documents	577
(5) Article 27(4) (1976 Rules)—Admissibility, relevance, materiality, and weight of the evidence	579
D. Extracts from the Practice of the Iran–US Claims Tribunal	580
(1) Tribunal Rules (1983), Article 24(1)—Burden of proof	580
(2) Tribunal Rules (1983), Article 24(2)—Summary of evidence	587
(3) Tribunal Rules (1983), Article 24(3)—Document production	588
(4) Tribunal Rules (1983), Article 25(5)—Written witness statements	593
(5) Tribunal Rules (1983), Article 25(6)—Admissibility, relevance, materiality, and weight of the evidence	594

1. Introduction

Questions of evidence are among the most problematic aspects of any regulation of international arbitration. This is especially so in case of arbitration under the UNCITRAL Rules, which are intended for application in proceedings involving parties from around the world and from various legal systems, including common and civil law. The expectations of parties from different legal systems are never so likely to conflict as with questions of evidence. In the "adversarial" system of common law, the parties generate the evidence in accordance with relatively technical rules on admissibility, under the supervision of the adjudicating body. The adjudicating body enforces the observance of these rules and weighs the significance of the evidence presented. In the "inquisitorial" system of civil law, the court or tribunal generally takes more initiative in administering the production of evidence and has more discretion in questions concerning admissibility.[1]

While being careful not to over-generalize or exaggerate the gulf between common law and civil law systems,[2] one should nevertheless note that there are often fundamental differences. Not surprisingly, the UNCITRAL Rules have adopted the evidentiary principles of neither system as such, but rather have aimed at creating a relatively flexible framework within which the arbitrators are "freed from having to observe the strict legal rules of evidence"[3] of any particular domestic regime.[4]

The skeletal nature of Articles 27 and 28 of the UNCITRAL Rules inevitably leaves lacunae to be filled during arbitration. The parties can prepare for this in advance by agreeing, in accordance with Article 1(1),[5] on a particular national law to govern the proceedings with regard to evidence.[6] This solution is advisable only for arbitrations involving parties from legal systems with similar traditions and concepts (eg a company from England and another from Australia). Where the legal systems differ, the parties may consider supplementing the UNCITRAL Rules with the International Bar Association (IBA) Rules on the Taking of Evidence in International Commercial Arbitration, a somewhat more detailed set of rules intended to serve the special needs arising in arbitration under these circumstances.[7] Even if the IBA Rules are

---

[1] On the difference between the two systems and its relevance to international arbitration and adjudication generally, see, eg, P J Martinez-Fraga, "Good Faith, Bad Faith: A Commentary on the 2010 IBA Rules on the Taking of Evidence in International Arbitration," (2012) 43 Georgetown J Intl L 387; D Shenton, "An Introduction to the IBA Rules of Evidence," (1985) 1 Arb Intl 118, 120–3; M Rubino-Sammartano, "Rules of Evidence in International Arbitration, A Need for Discipline and Harmonization," (1986) 3(2) J Intl Arb 87. See also J Robert, "Administration of Evidence in International Commercial Arbitration," (1976) Intl Ybk Commercial Arb 221; N Blackaby and C Partasides with A Redfern and M Hunter, *Redfern and Hunter on International Arbitration* (5th edn 2009) 385–7, 418–19; C Brower, "Evidence Before International Tribunals: The Need for Some Standard Rules," (1994) 28 Intl Lawyer 47; See also R Mosk, "The Role of Facts in International Dispute Resolution," 304 (2003) Recueil des Cours—Collected Courses of the Hague Academy of International Law 58, 62–6.

[2] In common law countries, the rules of evidence, whose rationale can be connected with the particular requirements of trial by jury, are often not applied strictly in arbitration. See R Bernstein *et al*, "Discovery, Inspection of Documents and Interrogatories," in R Bernstein, *et al* (eds), *Handbook of Arbitration Practice* (1998) 138; "Conduct of Hearings" in L Edmonson, *Domke on Commercial Arbitration* (3rd edn 2011) § 29:9 ("It is a well-established principle of arbitration law and practice that the usual common-law rules regarding the admission and rejection of evidence are not strictly observed in arbitration."). See also R Buxton, "The Rules of Evidence as Applied to Arbitrations," (2004) 58(4) J Chartered Institute of Arbitrators 229 ("Contrary to what is generally believed to be the law, the technical rules of evidence have never applied in arbitrations subject to English law."). On the other hand, the procedural law of some civil law countries has been developing towards the adversarial system. See Stockholm Chamber of Commerce, *Arbitration in Sweden* (1984) 117. In contrast, under the inquisitorial system it is properly the parties who determine what evidence is submitted in support of the claim or defence. See A Marriot, "Evidence in International Arbitration," 5 Arb Intl (1989) 280, 289.

[3] *Report of the Secretary-General on the Preliminary Draft Set of Arbitration Rules*, UNCITRAL, 8th Session, UN Doc A/CN.9/97 (1974), reprinted in (1975) VI UNCITRAL Ybk (1975) 163, 176 (Commentary on Draft Article 21(5)).

[4] The Rules, however, have been criticized for being closer to the continental tradition. See W Morgan, "Discovery in Arbitration," (1986) 3(3) J Intl Arb 9, 23 ("the Rules do not constitute anything like an evenly balanced compromise between the different jurisdictions, being heavily slanted towards continental practice . . ."). But see n 2.

[5] See Chapter 2(2).

[6] See K Böckstiegel, "The Relevance of National Arbitration Law for Arbitrations under the UNCITRAL Rules," (1984) 1(3) J Intl Arb 224, 227.

[7] International Bar Association, "IBA Rules on the Taking of Evidence in International Commercial Arbitration," May 29, 2010. See also J Tackaberry, "Evidence at Hearings and in Documents-Only Arbitration," in R Bernstein (ed), *Handbook of Arbitration Practice* (1998). In general see P J Martinez-Fraga, "Good Faith, Bad Faith," n 1; D Shenton, "An Introduction to the IBA Rules of Evidence," n 1. See also C Brower, "The Anatomy

not specifically adopted by the parties, the arbitral tribunal may turn to them for guidance in fleshing out Articles 27 and 28 "in such manner as it considers appropriate."[8] Any mandatory norms of the applicable procedural law, of course, also have to be taken into account.[9]

2. Evidence—Article 27

A. Text of the 2010 UNCITRAL Rule[10]

Article 27 of the 2010 UNCITRAL Rules provides:

1. Each party shall have the burden of proving the facts relied on to support its claim or defence.
2. Witnesses, including expert witnesses, who are presented by the parties to testify to the arbitral tribunal on any issue of fact or expertise may be any individual, notwithstanding that the individual is a party to the arbitration or in any way related to a party. Unless otherwise directed by the arbitral tribunal, statements by witnesses, including expert witnesses, may be presented in writing and signed by them.
3. At any time during the arbitral proceedings the arbitral tribunal may require the parties to produce documents, exhibits or other evidence within such a period of time as the arbitral tribunal shall determine.
4. The arbitral tribunal shall determine the admissibility, relevance, materiality and weight of the evidence offered.

B. Commentary

(1) Burden of proof—Article 27(1)

Legal rules and principles concerning the presentation of evidence aim at establishing relevant facts.[11] According to Article 27(1), "[e]ach party shall have the burden of proving the facts relied on to support its claim or defence."

---

of Fact-Finding Before International Tribunals: An Analysis and a Proposal Concerning the Evaluation of Evidence," in R Lillich (ed), *Fact-Finding Before International Tribunals* (1992) 147, 172–3.

[8] Article 17(1), discussed in Chapter 2(3).

[9] Thus, if the arbitration takes place in a common law jurisdiction, total disregard of the local rules of evidence may threaten the validity of the award. See J Tackaberry, "Evidence at Hearings," n 7, 160 ("An arbitrator who rejects the rules of evidence wholesale might well be guilty of misconduct. An arbitrator who accepts those rules but who modifies them intelligently in the light of the difference between trial by jury and trial by judge alone . . . can in most cases reach a fair result by wholly legitimate means.").

[10] Corresponding Article 24 of the 1976 UNCITRAL Rules provides:

1. Each party shall have the burden of proving the facts relied on to support his claim or defence.
2. The arbitral tribunal may, if it considers it appropriate, require a party to deliver to the tribunal and to the other party, within such a period of time as the arbitral tribunal shall decide, a summary of the documents and other evidence which that party intends to present in support of the facts in issue set out in his statement of claim or statement of defence.
3. At any time during the arbitral proceedings the arbitral tribunal may require the parties to produce documents, exhibits or other evidence within such a period of time as the tribunal shall determine.

Corresponding Article 25(5) of the 1976 UNCITRAL Rules provides: "Evidence of witnesses may also be presented in the form of written statements signed by them."

Corresponding Article 25(6) of the 1976 UNCITRAL Rules provides: "The arbitral tribunal shall determine the admissibility, relevance, materiality and weight of the evidence offered."

[11] It has been said that "most international arbitrations are fact-driven." A Marriot, "Evidence in International Arbitration," n 2, 281. See generally R Mosk, "The Role of Facts," n 1.

This provision originates in the 1976 UNCITRAL Rules, having been added at the very final stage of that drafting process. No thorough discussion of the subject is recorded in the available *travaux préparatoires* beyond the basic statement that parties are "expected to provide evidence to support their allegations."[12] Nevertheless, it is clear that the provision is simply a restatement of "the general principle that each party has the burden of proving the facts on which he relied in his claim or in his defence,"[13] or else risk an adverse decision.[14] Article 27(1) therefore scarcely represents a modification of pre-existing principles.[15] Nor does the provision, though limited to the question of burden of proof as to the asserted facts, alter the standard rule that the claimant has the burden of demonstrating the legal obligation on which its claim is based.[16]

As to the division of burden of proof between the parties, the general principle was expressed in *Reza Said Malek* as follows: "it is the Claimant who carries the initial burden of proving the facts upon which he relies. There is a point, however, at which the claimant may be considered to have made a sufficient showing to shift the burden of proof to the respondent."[17] In addition, a respondent has the burden of proving any allegations, such as abuse of process, estoppel, or waiver, the nature of which negates a claimant's claim.[18]

Article 27(1), however, does not address the standard of proof, that is, the level, or degree, of proof required to satisfy the burden mentioned in *Reza Said Malek*. Moreover, Article 27(4) gives the arbitral tribunal wide discretion to determine freely, *inter alia*, the "weight of the evidence offered" in particular cases.[19] Rules on proof and evidence in the arbitral (or for that matter judicial) process do not envisage a search for absolute, unchallengeable proof as a scientific matter. Very often such proof is unattainable[20] and the decision is left to

---

[12] *Report of Working Group II (Arbitration and Conciliation) on the Work of its Fifty-Second Session* (New York, February 1–5, 2010), UNCITRAL, 43rd Session, UN Doc A/CN.9/688, at 20, para 97 (2009). No negotiating history is available for Article 24(1) and the issue of burden of proof. See M Kazazi, *Burden of Proof and Related Issues* (1996) 103.

[13] *Report of the UNCITRAL on the Work of its Ninth Session*, UN GAOR, 31st Session, Supp No 17, UN Doc A/31/17, para 116 (1976), reprinted in (1976) VII UNCITRAL Ybk 66, 75; See also P Sanders, "Commentary on the UNCITRAL Arbitration Rules," (1977) II Ybk Commercial Arb 203; S Baker and M Davis, *The UNCITRAL Arbitration Rules: The Experience of the Iran-United States Claims Tribunal* (1992) 109.

[14] See D Sandifer, *Evidence before International Tribunals* (1975) 127.

[15] See M Aden, *Internationale Handelsschiedsgerichtsbarkeit* (1988) 53 (Article 24(1) is "eigentlich überflussig"); A Marriot, "Evidence in International Arbitration," n 2, 282; N Blackaby and C Partisides, n 1, at 387–389, 425. In the UNCITRAL Model Law there is no provision comparable to Article 27(1), although the drafters noted that "it was a generally recognized principle that reliance by a party on a fact required that party to prove that fact. . ." H Holtzmann and J Neuhaus, *A Guide to UNCITRAL Model Law on International Commercial Arbitration: Legislative History and Commentary* (1989) 568.

[16] See J Robert, "Administration of Evidence in International Commercial Arbitration," n 1, 221–2. Article 27(1) also does not prevent the arbitrators from treating the contents of applicable substantive law as a "fact" needing proof in the way foreign law needs proof in some private international law systems. See A Marriot, "Evidence in International Arbitration," n 2, 282. See also n 9. See *Antoine Biloune*, (1976 Rules), reprinted in section 2(C)(1).

[17] See *Reza Said Malek* (1983 Tribunal Rules), reprinted in section 2(D)(1). See also *International Thunderbird Gaming Corp* and *United Mexican States*, Arbitral Award (January 26, 2006) (ICSID administered, 1976 UNCITRAL Rules, NAFTA Chapter Eleven), at 32–3.

[18] For a discussion of burden-shifting in this context, see *Chevron Corp* (1976 Rules), reprinted in section 2(C)(1).

[19] Article 27(4) is discussed in more detail in section 2(B)(5). See also *Flexi-Van Leasing* (1983 Tribunal Rules), reprinted in section 2(D)(1) and 2(D)(5).

[20] See D Sandifer, *Evidence before International Tribunals*, n 14, 22 ("[T]he constantly recurring complaint of tribunal after tribunal is that they are compelled to act upon the basis of meager, incomplete, and unsatisfactory evidence.").

the sometimes subjective judgment of the arbitrators.[21] Thus, understandably, individual arbitrators may frequently reach contrary conclusions on the question of proof, as has been the case in the practice of the Iran–US Claims Tribunal.[22] In contrast, where the types of claims alleged were of a serious or criminal nature, ie, forgery of documents, the Tribunal has at times agreed to apply a heightened standard of proof, such as "clear and convincing" or "beyond a reasonable doubt."[23]

The dissenting or concurring American judges seemed, in some cases, to consider that, due to the special nature of the arbitration in question,[24] *prima facie* evidence submitted by the claimant is generally sufficient to shift the burden of proof onto the respondent.[25] The main awards, however, have not adopted a general assumption of this kind. Nevertheless, in some circumstances *prima facie* evidence clearly was regarded as sufficient to satisfy the initial burden of proof.[26]

Thus, the Tribunal practice does not support the proposition that a claimant would have to prove its case beyond all reasonable doubt. No such proposition is expressed by Article 27(1). Rather, the standard of proof varies according to the circumstances. Notoriously known facts do not need any proof at all,[27] and uncontested facts are usually accepted as such.[28]

While in contested cases, it may be said that at least *prima facie* proof is needed,[29] such proof alone may fail to satisfy the burden of proof. This is the case where the claimant has

---

[21] See J Selby, "Fact Finding Before the Iran-United States Claims Tribunal: The View from the Trenches," in R Lillich (ed), *Fact-Finding Before International Tribunals* (1992) 144 ("[T]he concept of a *quantum* of proof is elusive, if not illusory. The fact seems to be that, as stated by a former president of the Tribunal, 'the burden of proof is that you have to convince me.'").

[22] See *Schering Corp* (1983 Tribunal Rules); *Frederica Lincoln Riahi* (1983 Tribunal Rules), Concurring and Dissenting Opinion of Judge Brower, both reprinted in section 2(D)(1). See also *JL Case Co* and *Islamic Republic of Iran*, Award No 57–224–1 (June 15, 1983), Dissenting Opinion of Judge Holtzmann (July 27, 1983), reprinted in 3 Iran-US CTR 62, 66 et seq (1983-II) (discussing evidence and burden of proof and criticizing the majority award); *Internationall Ore & Fertilizer Corp* and *Razi Chemical Co Ltd*, Award No 351–468–3 (February 19, 1988), Dissenting Opinion of Judge Brower (February 29, 1988), reprinted in 18 Iran-US CTR 98, 102 et seq (1988-I) (similarly discussing, *inter alia*, the treatment of the burden of proof by the majority award). See *Pepsico, Inc* and *Islamic Republic of Iran*, Award No 260–18–1 (October 13, 1986), Dissenting Opinion of Judge Ameli (October 27, 1986), reprinted in 13 Iran-US CTR 45, 54–5 (1986-IV). On the Tribunal's practice regarding the burden of proof, see also S Baker and M Davis, *The UNCITRAL Arbitration Rules*, n 13, 109–11; J van Hof, *Commentary on the UNCITRAL Arbitration Rules: The Application by the Iran-US Claims Tribunal* (1991) 160–3.

[23] See *Dadras Intl* (1983 Tribunal Rules); *Vera-Jo Miller Aryeh* (1983 Tribunal Rules), both reprinted in section 2(D)(1). See also *Oil Field of Texas, Inc* and *Government of Islamic Republic of Iran*, et al, Award No 258–43–1, para 25 (October 8, 1986), reprinted in 12 Iran-US CTR 308, 315 (1986-III).

[24] See *Cal-Maine Foods, Inc* and *Islamic Republic of Iran and Sherkat Seamourgh Co, Inc*, Award No 133–240–3 (June 11, 1984), reprinted in 6 Iran-US CTR 52 (1984-II). See also Concurring Opinion of Judge Mosk, 6 Iran-US CTR at 65: "It appears that Claimant had difficulties obtaining information and material concerning its claim. Much of the information existed in Iran and was available to Respondents. This is another example of the problems parties have in obtaining and submitting evidence to the Tribunal." See also discussion on Articles 27(3) and 27(4), in sections 2(B)(4) and 2(B)(5) respectively, herein.

[25] See Dissenting Opinion of Richard M Mosk, reprinted in section 2(D)(1). See also Dissent of Howard M Holtzmann in *JL Case Co* (1983 Tribunal Rules), n 22, reprinted in 3 Iran-US CTR 62, 72 (1983-II) ("The evidence is sufficient to constitute *prima facie* proof of the facts alleged . . .").

[26] See *Abraham Rahman Golshani* (1983 Tribunal Rules), reprinted in section 2(D)(1). For a thorough discussion of *prima facie* evidence, see M Kazazi, *Burden of Proof and Related Issues*, n 12, 326–43.

[27] See, eg, R Schütze, D Tscherning and W Wais, *Handbuch des Schiedsverfahrens* (1985) 212 (§ 421).

[28] See *Harris Intl Telecommunications Inc* and *Islamic Republic of Iran*, Award No 323–409–1 (November 2, 1987), reprinted in 17 Iran-US CTR 31, 47 (1987-IV) (the burden of proof is "heavier" if the allegations are contested). The proceedings can be facilitated if the parties can agree to submit a joint declaration of uncontested facts. See H Houtte, "Conduct of Arbitral Proceedings," in P Šarčević (ed), *Essays on International Commercial Arbitration* (1989) 117, 119.

[29] See *RN Pomeroy* (1983 Tribunal Rules), reprinted in section 2(D)(1).

access to confirming evidence but fails to provide it.[30] Conversely, a *prima facie* case made by the claimant will often suffice provided that the respondent has access to any rebutting evidence which is not produced.[31] The obvious difficulty which the applicant may have in trying to obtain corroborative evidence should be considered in assessing whether *prima facie* evidence is sufficient.[32] *Prima facie* proof may also suffice where the experience of the tribunal leads it to conclude that the evidence indicates the probable existence of a certain state of affairs. International tribunals have in fact relied strongly on such presumptions.[33] A good example is provided by the evidentiary issue of the nationality of publicly held US corporations appearing as claimants before the Iran–US Claims Tribunal. In the practice of the Tribunal, a publicly held US corporation has only to provide *prima facie* evidence of the kind defined in the oft-cited *Flexi-Van* order. Such evidence, if not successfully rebutted by the respondent, is taken as sufficient proof of the corporation's US nationality in the meaning of Article VII(l) of the Claims Settlement Declaration.[34]

In addition to the statistical probabilities involved in the *Flexi-Van* case, the testimony offered by customary trade practices may lend qualifying support to evidence which otherwise fails to meet the "reasonable doubt" standard. Hence the contemporary approval of invoices has been held to constitute a *prima facie* claim for the amount at issue, shifting the burden onto the respondent to show "that such approval was erroneous."[35] Similarly, "contemporaneous books and records of a company regularly kept in the normal course of business should be accorded substantial evidentiary weight."[36] In some cases, presumptions of this kind are based neither on statistical nor on other experience, and therefore more than *prima facie* evidence in the above sense may be needed. In this light, we may understand the reference to the burden of proof difficulties facing the claimant who alleged lost profits as a "lost volume seller" in the *CMI* case.[37]

---

[30] See *Dallal* (1983 Tribunal Rules), reprinted in section 2(D)(1).

[31] See *Benjamin R Isaiah* (1983 Tribunal Rules), reprinted in section 2(D)(1): "These documents, buttressed by credible testimony at the Hearing, constitute a *prima facie* case that the money, represented by the check was Isaiah's money and that he had held the claim for that money from the time the check was dishonored. In the absence of evidence to the contrary, that evidence is decisive."

[32] See *Leonard and Mavis Daley* (1983 Tribunal Rules), reprinted in section 2(D)(1). See also *W Jack Buckamier* (1983 Tribunal Rules), reprinted in section 2(D)(5).

[33] See V S Mani, *International Adjudication: Procedural Aspects* (1980) 207–8; D Sandifer, *Evidence before International Tribunals*, n 14, 141–6; *Flexi-Van Leasing Inc.* (1983 Tribunal Rules), reprinted in section 2(D)(1); *Islamic Republic of Iran* and *United States of America (Case No A/20)*, Decision No DEC 45-A20-FT (June 26, 1986), reprinted in 11 Iran-US CTR 271, 276 (1986-II) ("The States Parties . . . agree that the use of presumptions can constitute a perfectly legitimate method of evaluating the evidence in cases before the Tribunal.").

[34] On the detailed contents of the documentary evidence required, see *Flexi-Van* (1983 Tribunal Rules), Order of December 15, 1982, reprinted in section 2(D)(1). The "Flexi-Van" standard was supplemented by a further requirement imposed in subsequent cases. See *General Motors Corp* and *Islamic Republic Iran*, Case No 94, Chamber One, Order of January 18, 1983, reprinted in Iranian Assets Litigation Reporter 6247 (March 18, 1983). See also D Stewart, "The Iran-United States Claims Tribunal: A Review of Developments 1983–1984," (1984) 16 Law and Policy in Intl Business 677, 694–6. The Iranian member of Chamber One, Judge Kashani, filed a strong dissent to the *Flexi-Van* order, apparently contending that what virtually amounts to absolute proof is needed to demonstrate the nationality of publicly held corporations. See Dissenting Opinion of Mahmoud K Kashani Regarding Order of December 15, 1982, reprinted in 1 Iran-US CTR 463 (1981–82). See also H Holtzmann, "Fact finding by the Iran-United States Claims Tribunal," in R Lillich (ed), *Fact-Finding Before International Tribunals* (1991) 105–14.

[35] *Time, Inc* (1983 Tribunal Rules), reprinted in section 2(D)(1). See also *Howard Needles* (1983 Tribunal Rules); *Arthur Young and Co* (1983 Tribunal Rules); *RJ Reynolds Tobacco Co* (1983 Tribunal Rules); all reprinted in section 2(D)(1).

[36] See *Antoine Biloune*, Award on Damages and Costs, para 36 (1976 Rules), reprinted in section 2(C)(2).

[37] *CMI Intl* (1983 Tribunal Rules), reprinted in section 2(D)(1).

A different, though related, matter is that sometimes the applicable substantive law may create legal presumptions concerning, for example, fault or liability; Article 27(1) of the UNCITRAL Rules clearly leaves intact presumptions of this kind, which do not affect the general principle of burden of proof stated therein. This is clear not only from the rule of pre-emption stated in Article 1(2) of the Rules, but also from the *travaux préparatoires* that indicate the understanding that Article 27(1) does "not prevent application of regulations on the burden of proof in the applicable law."[38]

That "there has been relatively little discussion of precisely what the proper burden of proof should be and on whom it should rest"[39] is thus at least in part explained by the fact that very precise general rules regarding this problem are difficult to formulate. There may be certain categories of case or circumstance in which *prima facie* evidence is sufficient to shift the onus to the respondent. There are others, however, in which the claimant may be required to make more than just a *prima facie* showing. In general, a "balance of probability" standard may be said to reflect the arbitral practice and also to accord with Article 27(1).[40] In borderline cases the arbitral tribunal may, instead of dismissing the claim straight away, provide the party having the burden of proof with an opportunity to submit further evidence.[41] Matters closely related to the question of the burden of proof are discussed further in section 2(B)(4).

(2) Definition of "witnesses"—Article 27(2)

(a) General comments

Under the UNCITRAL Rules, a party has a right to present "witnesses."[42] A new provision in the 2010 Rules contained in the first sentence in Article 27(2) gives meaning to that term, describing "witnesses" as persons who a party may present to testify "on any issue of fact or expertise."[43] Thus, the Rules allow for the use of both fact witnesses and expert witnesses. The former may assist the tribunal in determining facts that are disputed by the parties, whereas the latter may help resolve disputed matters of opinion where the arbitral tribunal itself lacks the necessary expertise to do so.[44] By its own terms, Article 27(2) applies only to party-chosen witnesses ("who are presented by the parties"). Accordingly, the use of expert witnesses appointed by the arbitral tribunal is regulated principally under Article 29 of the Rules on tribunal-appointed experts and Article 17(1), which recognizes the arbitral tribunal's general authority to conduct the proceedings in such manner as it deems appropriate. The appointment of experts by the arbitral tribunal, however, does not in any way infringe upon a party's right to present its own expert witnesses in support of its case.[45]

---

[38] *Report of Working Group II (Arbitration and Conciliation) on the Work of its Fifty-Second Session* (New York, February 1–5, 2010), UNCITRAL, 43rd Session, UN Doc A/CN.9/688, at 21, para 99 (2009).

[39] D Stewart, "The Iran-United States Claims Tribunal," n 34, 740. See N Blackaby and C Partisides, *Redfern and Hunter on International Arbitration*, n 1, 388 ("The degree, or level, of proof that must be achieved in practice before an international arbitral tribunal is not capable, of precise definition . . .").

[40] A Marriot, "Evidence in International Arbitration," n 2, 282–3.

[41] See *George W Drucker* (1983 Tribunal Rules), reprinted in section 2(D)(1). D Sandifer, *Evidence before International Tribunals*, n 14, 131.

[42] See 2010 UNCITRAL Rules, arts 17(3) and 28(2).

[43] The 1976 UNCITRAL Rules did not provide a definition of "witnesses."

[44] N Blackaby and C Partisides, *Redfern and Hunter on International Arbitration*, n 1, 401, 406.

[45] As the *travaux préparatoires* indicate, the Rules "should not cause doubt on the right of a party to present expert evidence on its own initiative irrespective of whether the arbitral tribunal appointed an expert." *Report of*

The definition of "witnesses" also includes party witnesses. Article 27(2) expressly provides that a party may act as a witness in support of its own case. Inclusion of this rule for the first time in the 2010 UNCITRAL Rules was strongly supported by the Working Group, though with some opposition. Some delegates opposed inclusion of an express rule, believing it might raise problems in the enforcement of an award because in certain jurisdictions a disputing party is prohibited from serving as a witness.[46] Indeed, common law and civil law legal systems sometimes differ in their approach. While in the common law system it is not unusual for a party to be called as a witness, the civil law tradition generally is reluctant to accept testimony from a party or a person who, because of his affiliation to a party, is likely to have a financial interest in the matter.[47]

These differences only solidified the prevailing view that the Rules required "an international standard to overcome these national differences."[48] Most delegates saw no practical downside to this approach, particularly since in the case of a conflict with a mandatory rule of evidence in the applicable domestic law, the latter would prevail over Article 27(2) in any event, pursuant to Article 1(2) of the Rules.[49] Further, it was believed that an express rule could be beneficial in the context of investor–state arbitration to fill the gap where domestic law did not apply[50] and would clarify that the Rules themselves do not bar a government official from giving evidence in support of the respondent state.[51]

The rule on party witnesses, as adopted by the Working Group, is broad in scope, covering not only persons who are parties to the dispute, but also those who are "in any way related to a party."[52] Earlier drafts of the rule enumerated specific categories of individuals who could serve as witnesses, including "officers, employees or shareholders" of a party.[53] This approach was ultimately rejected, however, out of concerns that it might exclude other possible categories of witnesses such as "associates, partners or legal counsel of the parties."[54]

By including in the final text of Article 27(2) what it described as an "encompassing term," instead of enumerated categories of possible witnesses, the Working Group also sought to avoid conflicts with the potentially varying terminology and approaches of

---

the Working Group on Arbitration and Conciliation on the Work of its Forty-Seventh Session (Vienna, September 10–14, 2007), UNCITRAL, 41st Session, UN Doc A/CN.9/641, at 12–13, para 61 (2007).

[46] *Report of Working Group II (Arbitration and Conciliation) on the Work of its Fiftieth Session* (New York, February 9–13, 2009), UNCITRAL, 42nd Session, UN Doc A/CN.9/669, at 13, 17, para 60, 77 (2009); UNCITRAL, 41st Session, UN Doc A/CN.9/641, n 45, at 8, para 35.

[47] See generally E Gaillard and J Savage (eds), *Fouchard, Gaillard, Goldman on International Commercial Arbitration* (1999) 699–701. Objections to "party witnesses" have also come from common law parties and their counsel, see D Sandifer, *Evidence Before International Tribunals*, n 14, 349–50. On the other hand, some civil law countries recognize procedures by which parties may give oral testimony in a manner very similar to that of witnesses.

[48] UNCITRAL, 41st Session, UN Doc A/CN.9/641, n 45, at 7, para 30.

[49] UNCITRAL, 41st Session, UN Doc A/CN.9/641, n 45, at 8, para 35.

[50] UNCITRAL, 42nd Session, UN Doc A/CN.9/669, n 46, at 13, para 60.

[51] UNCITRAL, 41st Session, UN Doc A/CN.9/641, n 45, at 7–8, para 30.

[52] "Broad support was expressed for the principle that any person could be heard on an issue of fact or expertise." UNCITRAL, 41st Session, UN Doc A/CN.9/641, n 45, at 8–9, para 36.

[53] *Settlement of Commercial Disputes: Revision of the UNCITRAL Arbitration Rules, Note by the Secretariat*, UNCITRAL, UN Doc A/CN.9/WG.II/WP.145/Add.1 at 10, para 23 (2006) (Draft Article 25(2bis)); UNCITRAL, 41st Session, UN Doc A/CN.9/641, n 45, at 7, para 29.

[54] UNCITRAL, 41st Session, UN Doc A/CN.9/641, n 45, at 8, para 32. Non-exhaustive or no list considered better. One version had no list. It was observed that "any way relating to any party" was broad allowing legal counsel of parties to testify as witness. UNCITRAL, 42nd Session, UN Doc A/CN.9/669, n 46, at 17, para 77.

national legal systems concerning the status and treatment of persons acting on behalf of a legal person.[55]

By broadly defining the term "witnesses" as including both fact and expert witnesses and as not precluding party witnesses, Article 27(2) clarifies an important lacuna in the 1976 Rules. With respect to the use of party witnesses, in particular, the Rules favor an "international standard." At the same time, the Working Group deliberately chose to make the rule permissive ("may") in order to ensure greater harmonization with the applicable law.[56] In so doing, the UNCITRAL Rules have become more consistent with prevailing practice in international arbitration.[57]

(b) Practice of the Iran–US Claims Tribunal

The hearing of the parties themselves or their officers and employees as witnesses was an issue addressed by the Iran–US Claims Tribunal under its Tribunal Rules based on the 1976 UNCITRAL Rules.[58] Article 25(2) of the 1983 Tribunal Rules on witnesses does not specify whether parties may serve as witnesses. The Iran–US Claims Tribunal has struck a rather peculiar "compromise" between the common law and civil law approaches to party-witnesses.[59] On the one hand, the Tribunal has rejected the Iranian stand that evidence presented by, for instance, responsible company officials should be rejected, since "[r]efusing categorically to accept evidence from those most closely associated with the subject matter of a claim would not likely further the cause of establishing truth."[60] On the other hand, the Chambers of the Tribunal have generally refused to hear parties or their officials, especially senior level officials, as "witnesses,"[61] with the consequence that the notice requirement of Article 25(2) of the 1983 Tribunal Rules does not apply to them. Instead of being treated as witnesses, such interested persons may be allowed to give "information" or "statements" as "party representatives"[62] or "party witnesses."[63] The probative value of the

---

[55] UNCITRAL, 42nd Session, UN Doc A/CN.9/669, n 46, at 18, para 78.

[56] Emphasis added. Opposition was raised to a preliminary draft of the rule that included the word "shall" instead of "may." UNCITRAL, 42nd Session, UN Doc A/CN.9/669, n 46, at 17, para 77.

[57] See 1999 IBA Rules on Taking of Evidence in Commercial Arbitration, art 4; 2012 Swiss Rules, art 25(2); and 1998 LCIA Rules, art 20.7.

[58] See M Straus, "The Practice of the Iran-United States Claims Tribunal in Receiving Evidence from Parties and from Experts," (1986) 3(3) J Intl Arb 57, 58–63.

[59] See generally M Kazazi, *Burden of Proof and Related Issues* (1996) 105–6.

[60] *Sedco, Inc* (1983 Tribunal Rules), para 75, reprinted in, section 2(D)(5). This kind of attitude, it is submitted, is sounder than that adopted by the French Court of Appeal setting aside the ICC award in the so-called *Pyramids* case. The court held that the position of the vice president of the involved companies prevented "lending any credibility to his statements, even though accepted by the arbitral tribunal, which would be sufficient to convince this court." *Arab Republic of Egypt v Southern Pacific Properties Ltd*, Judgment of July 12, 1984, Cour d'appel, Paris, reprinted in (1984) 23 ILM 1048, 1056. See also W Craig, "Uses and Abuses of Appeal from Awards," (1988) 4 Arb Intl 174, 193–4; M Straus, "The Practice of the Iran-United States Claims Tribunal," n 58, 58. See also *Otis Elevator Co* (1983 Tribunal Rules), reprinted in section 2(D)(5).

[61] See *Harris Intl Telecommunications* (1983 Tribunal Rules), para 107 (citing *Economy Forms* (1983 Tribunal Rules); *Kaysons Intl Corp* (1983 Tribunal Rules); both reprinted in section 2(D)(5).

[62] See *Harris Intl Telecommunications* (1983 Tribunal Rules), para 107, reprinted in section 2(D)(5) ("… any Party is free to choose the persons it wishes to present its case, including those not accepted by the Tribunal as witnesses …").

[63] See also *Kaysons Intl Corp* (1983 Tribunal Rules), reprinted in section 2(D)(5). The practice and denominations employed have differed between various chambers and various cases. See M Straus, "The Practice of the Iran-United States Claims Tribunal," n 58, 58–63; J Selby and D Stewart, "Practical Aspects of Arbitrating Claims Before the Iran-United States Claims Tribunal," (1984) 18 Intl Lawyer 211, 231.On the practice of other claims tribunals and similar bodies concerning this issue, see D Sandifer, *Evidence Before International Tribunals*, n 14, 349 et seq.

information thus provided is then freely weighed in accordance with Article 25(6) of the 1983 Tribunal Rules, with the consequence that the Tribunal "may attach a different 'weight' to information provided by such persons as compared to the testimony of witnesses."[64] It has been concluded, however, that the Tribunal has not generally discredited the statements of such "non-witnesses."[65] An interesting discussion by the late Professor Virally, former Chairman of Chamber Three of the Tribunal, concerning the evidentiary value of affidavits or other statements by persons affiliated with the party is contained in the award rendered in the *W Jack Buckamier* case.[66]

The solution adopted by the Iran–US Claims Tribunal is not recommended for use elsewhere as a general matter. Depending on the circumstances, particularly the respective backgrounds of the parties, an arbitral tribunal may or may not admit oral evidence presented by persons closely affiliated with the party. If it does admit such evidence and is prepared to give it weight, however, both the rationale behind Article 25(2) of the 1983 Tribunal Rules and the general requirement of fairness as expressed notably in Article 15(1) of those Rules require that the adversary should have an opportunity to decide whether any rebuttal evidence is necessary.[67] Should the tribunal be reluctant to call the persons in question "witnesses," and therefore regard them as excluded from original Article 25(2) of the 1983 Tribunal Rules, it could nevertheless make the admissibility of their statements dependent on the communication of advance information similar to that required of witnesses under that provision. Support for this approach may be found in Article 25(6) of the 1983 Tribunal Rules, which grants the arbitral tribunal wide discretion in determining, *inter alia*, the admissibility and weight of any evidence offered.

(3) Written witness statements—Article 27(2)

The second sentence in Article 27(2) contains the rule that "statements by witnesses, including expert witnesses, may be presented in writing and signed by them." The rule is very similar to that contained in Article 25(5) of the 1976 UNCITRAL Rules. That provision was the subject of some controversy among the original drafters. It was not included in the Preliminary Draft of the 1976 UNCITRAL Rules, and the Committee of the Whole (II) had serious reservations about its inclusion generally. The representative of Austria reflected the Committee's attitude when he noted that "because under Austrian law evidence of witnesses in written form was not acceptable [it] would be regarded as contrary to public order."[68] Despite such concerns, the provision on the permissibility of witness statements was retained in the 1976 UNCITRAL Rules.[69] The second sentence in Article 27(2) of the 2010 UNCITRAL Rules contains a very similar rule.

---

[64] *Harris Intl Telecommunications* (1983 Tribunal Rules), para 107, reprinted in section 2(D)(5).
[65] See M Straus, "The Practice of the Iran-United States Claims Tribunal," n 58, 60–1.
[66] See section 2(D)(5).
[67] See M Straus, "The Practice of the Iran-United States Claims Tribunal," n 58, 62.
[68] *Summary Record of the 9th Meeting of the Committee of the Whole (II)*, UNCITRAL, 9th Session, UN Doc A/CN.9/9/C.2/SR.9, at 5, para 38 (1976). See also, M Aden, *Internationale Handelsschiedsgerichtsbarkeit*, n 15, 242 ("Nicht unproblematisch …").
[69] For the discussion by the Committee of the Whole (II), see UNCITRAL, 9th Session, UN Doc A/CN.9/9/C.2/SR.9, n 68, at 5–6, paras 38–50. In the UNCITRAL Model Law there is no provision corresponding to Article 27(2) of the present Rules. H Holtzmann and J Neuhaus, *A Guide to the UNCITRAL Model Law on International Commercial Arbitration*, n 15, 567–8 ("The Commission did not consider it necessary to include such a provision in the Model Law, preferring to leave this point of detail to the agreement of the Parties or the discretion of the arbitrators.").

Without doubt, the use of written statements in international arbitration has obvious advantages where it may be difficult in practice to have witnesses appear in person.[70] Accordingly, many domestic laws that prohibit written witness statements in litigation are typically more receptive to this form of evidence in the context of arbitration. The use of written statements signed by the witness is common practice among international arbitral tribunals.[71] Nevertheless, before relying on written statements in accordance with Article 27(2), the arbitral tribunal should ensure that it is not acting contrary to any mandatory rule of the applicable domestic law.[72] On the other hand, where non-mandatory provisions of the applicable procedural law prohibit affidavit testimony, it is of special importance to have the provisions of Article 27(2) included in the arbitration rules or agreement. Without such explicit provision the use of written statements might be considered a violation of the party agreement.[73] The tribunal also has the option of ordering the party that has submitted the written statements to produce its witness in person.[74] That the rule in Article 27(2) begins with the phrase "Unless otherwise directed by the arbitral tribunal" expressly grants the arbitral tribunal authority to manage the use of written witness statements as it deems appropriate.

Apart from possible mandatory requirements of domestic law, Article 27(2) does not impose any specific conditions on the form that written statements must take. Thus, as the *travaux préparatoires* of the corresponding 1976 rule indicate, "it is not required under this paragraph that the witnesses signing such statements also swear to their veracity."[75] However, the party may have the affidavit sworn in before a competent authority.[76] Whether to give this kind of affidavit more weight than an unsworn statement is a matter which the arbitral tribunal must determine in accordance with Article 27(4), discussed below.

Because affidavits submitted under Article 27(2) are documentary evidence, they are subject to the time limits applied to documentary evidence.[77]

(4) Production of documents—Article 27(3)

(a) General comments

As a leading tribunal has observed, the general rule is "that the Party who carries the burden of proof determines at its discretion what evidence it wishes to submit in support of its claim."[78] In order to conduct the proceeding effectively, however, the arbitral tribunal may need to order a party to produce documents that it has not submitted on its own initiative.

---

[70] See *Chas T Main Intl* (1983 Tribunal Rules), reprinted in section 2(D)(4). See also P Sanders, "Commentary on the UNCITRAL Arbitration Rules," n 13, 202.

[71] See *Thomas Earl Payne* (1983 Tribunal Rules) and other cases reprinted in section 2(D)(4).

[72] See J Wetter, *The International Arbitral Process: Public and Private* II (1979) 505 ("An illustrative example of provisions that may have to yield to rules of [domestic] law is Article 25, paragraph 5, of the [1976] UNCITRAL Rules which permits testimony in the form of written affidavits. It is questionable whether an award based on such evidence, if contested, would be upheld, eg by Zurich courts.").

[73] See *Harris Intl Telecommunications* (1983 Tribunal Rules), reprinted in section 2(D)(4), para 75 *in finem* ("Article 25, para 5 [of the 1976 UNCITRAL Rules] merely clarifies the admissibility of affidavits of witnesses, since not all national legal systems admit such written evidence.").

[74] See discussion on Article 24(3) in section 2(B), Chapter 16.

[75] *Report of the Secretary-General on the Revised Draft Set of Arbitration Rules*, UNCITRAL, 9th Sess., Addendum 1 (Commentary), UN Doc. A/CN.9/112/Add.1 (1975), reprinted in (1976) VII UNCITRAL Ybk 166, 176.

[76] See *Chas T Main Intl* (1983 Tribunal Rules), reprinted in section 2(D)(4).

[77] See *Harris Intl Telecommunications* (1983 Tribunal Rules), reprinted in section 2(D)(4).

[78] *The Offshore Co* (1983 Tribunal Rules), reprinted in section 2(D)(3).

Article 27(3) of the UNCITRAL Rules provides the arbitral tribunal with the power to make such directions.[79]

While the subject matter of the provision (production of documents and other evidentiary material) is reminiscent of the "discovery" procedure typical of common law,[80] the emphasis on the discretion of the arbitral tribunal is closer to the practice of civil law. The parties possess no right to have evidence produced by their opponents; it is the arbitrators who "[a]t any time during the arbitral proceedings may require the parties to produce" it.[81]

The materials subject to production orders are defined in Article 27(3) as "documents, exhibits or other evidence."[82] The provision is also taken to encompass evidence by witnesses, including affidavits.[83] However, some dispute this view on the basis of the wording of the rule and its *travaux préparatoires*.[84] Due to the fact that documentary evidence

---

[79] In drafting the 2010 UNCITRAL Rules, the Working Group considered whether to revise the rule to provide that this power may be exercised either on the arbitral tribunal's own motion or on the application of any party, but it decided not to do so. *Report of the Working Group on Arbitration and Conciliation on the Work of its Forty-Fifth Session* (Vienna, September 11–15, 2006), UNCITRAL, 40th Session, UN Doc A/CN.9/614, at 22, para 103 (2007).

[80] In the adversarial system of common law it is thought "fundamental that each party disclose to the other side all the relevant written material, whether such material is supportive of that party's case or not." D Shenton, "An Introduction to the IBA Rules of Evidence," n 1, 120. The procedure whereby a party can force the other to such a disclosure is called "discovery." Its actual scope and contents vary, for example, as between the United States and England. See, eg, W Morgan, "Discovery in Arbitration," n 4, 9 et seq. On discovery (or proceedings similar to discovery) as applied in interstate arbitration, see V Mani, *International Adjudication: Procedural Aspects*, n 33, 216–19; D Sandifer, *Evidence Before International Tribunals*, n 14, 97–100.

[81] See P Sanders, "Commentary on the UNCITRAL Arbitration Rules," n 13, 203. Although the concept of discovery is alien to civil law, judges in continental countries commonly order the production of documents regarded as relevant to the dispute. See R Schütze, D Tscherning and W Wais, *Handbuch des Schiedsverfahrens*, n 27, 212 (§417); W Morgan, "Discovery in Arbitration," n 4, 21–2; D Shenton, "An Introduction to the IBA Rules of Evidence," n 1, 122. Moreover, even in common law, discovery in arbitration, as distinct from court litigation, leaves much to the discretion of the arbitrators. There may be "rather less difference between the Common Law and Civil Law procedures than their quite alien basic approaches would suggest." W Morgan, "Discovery in Arbitration," n 4, 22. For discovery in English and US arbitrations, see Morgan 12–20. On the US, see also M McCabe, "Arbitral Discovery and the Iran-United States Claims Tribunal Experience," (1986) 20 Intl Lawyer 499, 502–11. On English law, see J Tackaberry, "Evidence at Hearings," n 7, 160 et seq. For the Tribunal's practice regarding "discovery," see also S Baker and M Davis, *The UNCITRAL Arbitration Rules*, n 13, 111–14; J van Hof, *Commentary on the UNCITRAL Arbitration Rules*, n 22, 163–5. The parties' obligation to produce documents to an expert appointed by virtue of Article 29 is regulated in paragraph 3 of that article.

[82] A party may not resort to Article 27(3) to cause another party to create a new document. See *Ouziel Aryeh* (1983 Tribunal Rules), reprinted in section 2(D)(3) (rejecting claimants' request that respondent provide a written report on the status of properties that form the basis of the claims). Note also that a tribunal may need to consider the effect of certain privileges, such as attorney-client and deliberative process privilege, when addressing document production. See generally *Glamis Gold Ltd* and *United States of America*, Decision on Parties' Requests for Production of Documents withheld on Grounds of Privilege (November 17, 2005) (ICSID administered, 1976 UNCITRAL Rules, NAFTA Chapter Eleven).

[83] The original version of Article 27(3) was first contained in what is now Article 24 ("Further Written Statements"). This early version of the provision in question mentioned only "supplementary documents or exhibits." *Report of the Secretary-General on the Preliminary Draft Set of Arbitration Rules*, UNCITRAL, 8th Session, UN Doc A/CN.9/97 (1974), reprinted in (1975) VI UNCITRAL Ybk 163, 1 (Draft Article 19(3)). The words "other evidence" were added when the paragraph in question was designated to be treated with evidence rather than written statements. On the discussions in the Committee of the Whole II, see *Summary Record of the 8th Meeting of the Committee of the Whole (II)*, UNCITRAL, 9th Session, UN Doc A/CN.9/9/C.2/SR.8, paras 61–78 (1976). See also S Stein and D Wotman, "International Commercial Arbitration in the 1980s: A Comparison of the Major Arbitral Systems and Rules," (1983) 38 Business Lawyer 1685, 1707; P Sanders, "Commentary on the UNCITRAL Arbitration Rules," n 13, 203.

[84] See M McCabe, "Arbitral Discovery," n 81, 522 n 131.

normally plays a paramount role in international proceedings for reasons such as geographic distance,[85] Article 27(3) has been applied for the most part to "documents and exhibits," excluding affidavits, rather than to "other evidence."[86] This has been the case, for example, at the Iran–US Claims Tribunal.

As McCabe notes, the Tribunal has in several cases, without any specific request, ordered the production of materials such as "documentary proof of patents, corporate ledgers, balance sheets, bank statements, asset and account documents, copies of decisions in the Iranian courts and invoices."[87] Where one party possesses documents of this kind which are necessary to the resolution of the dispute, the arbitral tribunal may legitimately order them to be produced. The principle of equality should always be followed so that where the adversary has primary access to some similarly important materials, the tribunal should order them to be produced as well.[88]

(b) **Production of documents at the request of a party**

While Article 27(3) has no exact analogy in any domestic discovery proceedings,[89] the provision can be applied to serve the purpose of such proceedings. In other words, the tribunal may grant a party's request for the production of documents (or other evidence) by the other party. While the arbitral tribunal has discretion to refuse to order discovery notwithstanding a party's request,[90] a specific request is nevertheless likely to further the cause of the party wishing access to some particular documents.[91] The request may be made as a separate motion, included in some other submission, or during a pre-hearing conference or similar preliminary meeting, if any is arranged.[92]

Although Article 27(3) grants the arbitral tribunal wide discretion, the tribunal should not accept non-specific requests or permit so-called "fishing expeditions" by granting requests, for example, for "all possibly relevant material." Requests of this kind are rarely tolerated even in court litigation in countries whose legal systems include liberal forms of document production.[93] Rather than a standard of possibly relevant, the party requesting the production must establish the materiality of the documents to a claim or defence. It should come as no surprise, then, that the Iran–US Claims Tribunal has not granted requests which fail to specify the documents in question.[94] In addition to requiring the

---

[85] See J Robert, "Administration of Evidence in International Commercial Arbitration," n 1, 223.

[86] See R Schütze, D Tscherning and W Wais, *Handbuch des Schiedsverfahrens*, n 27, 212 (§419).

[87] M McCabe, "Arbitral Discovery," n 81, 514 n 115. See also *Dresser Industries* (1983 Tribunal Rules), reprinted in section 2(D)(3).

[88] Judge Mosk filed a dissent to the Order, partly reprinted in section 2(D)(3), in Case No B1, indicating to the effect that the rejection of the request, made by the United States party, involved derogation from the equality principle. See Richard M Mosk, Dissent to Order, reprinted in 4 Iran-US CTR 58 (1983-III).

[89] In principle, though, there is nothing that prevents a tribunal from following, for example, English or American discovery rules when applying Article 24(3). Such conduct, however, is only advisable where the rules in question are familiar to both parties. See A Marriot, "Evidence in International Arbitration," n 2, 284.

[90] See, eg, Case B1 (1983 Tribunal Rules), reprinted in section 2(D)(3). See also *International Thunderbird Gaming Corp* (1976 UNCITRAL Rules), reprinted in section 2(C)(4).

[91] See *Weatherford Intl* (1983 Tribunal Rules), reprinted in section 2(D)(3).

[92] See M McCabe, "Arbitral Discovery," n 81, 515; J Selby and D Stewart, "Practical Aspects of Arbitrating Claims," n 63.

[93] See S Stein and D Wotman, "International Commercial Arbitration in the 1980s," n 83, 1707 ("However, as in English litigation generally, fishing expeditions will not be tolerated."). Other international tribunals have had similarly negative attitudes to unspecified discovery requests. See I Seidl-Hohenveldern, *Corporations In and Under International Law* (1987) 15–16 (referring to a case before an Austro-German Arbitral Tribunal).

[94] See *MCA Inc* (1983 Tribunal Rules), reprinted in section 2(D)(3). See also M McCabe, "Arbitral Discovery," n 81, 516.

specification of documents, the Tribunal may require explanation "as to which steps were taken by the Claimant . . . to acquire the necessary materials."[95] If no specific efforts are demonstrated, the Tribunal may regard the production request as inadmissible.[96] This must be understood in light of the principle that it is primarily the responsibility of each party to submit the evidence upon which it wishes to rely. Additionally, particularly when sovereigns are a party to the arbitration, the Tribunal must consider the effect of claims of privilege on a request for document production.[97]

Before issuing the discovery order, the Tribunal normally asks the opposing party to comment on the request.[98] The Tribunal may also postpone the production order pending a preliminary jurisdictional decision.[99] When the Iran–US Claims Tribunal is satisfied that the production of the specified documents is 1) "necessary,"[100] "justifiable,"[101] "warranted" or "appropriate,"[102] "material" to a claim or defence[103] and that 2) "all reasonable steps"[104] to obtain the document(s) have been taken by the requesting party itself, it usually grants the request.[105] The discovery order may ask the party in possession of the document(s) either to submit copies of the document(s) and/or to make the original(s) available for investigation and, if appropriate, reproduction by the other party.[106] Instead of issuing an order firmly requesting the production of the documents, the Tribunal may advise the requesting party to deal directly with the adversary in order to obtain the material.[107]

The Iran–US Claims Tribunal's standard as to document production has been characterized as "much narrower than the all relevant information standard employed in U.S. courts or standards used in other kinds of arbitration."[108] Apart from the fact that it is doubtful whether the Tribunal standard really differs so much from that of general international arbitration practice,[109] the standard appears quite reasonable. Failure to fulfill the basic conditions (specification of the documents, explanation concerning alternative efforts to obtain them) neither necessarily leads to a definitive rejection of the request for production,[110] nor prejudices the evidentiary significance which may attach to a request

---

[95] *MCA Inc* (1983 Tribunal Rules), reprinted in section 2(D)(3).
[96] See *Vera-Jo Miller Aryeh* (1983 Tribunal Rules), reprinted in section 2(D)(3).
[97] See, eg, Case No A/30 (1983 Tribunal Rules), reprinted in section 2(D)(3), and *SD Myers* (1976 Rules), reprinted in section 2(C)(4).
[98] See *Frederica Lincoln Riahi* (1983 Tribunal Rules), reprinted in section 2(D)(3).
[99] See M McCabe, "Arbitral Discovery," n 81, 516–17.
[100] See *Weatherford Intl* (1983 Tribunal Rules), reprinted in section 2(D)(3).
[101] See M McCabe, "Arbitral Discovery," n 81, 517.
[102] See *Brown & Root, Inc* (1983 Tribunal Rules), Order of January 4, 1993, reprinted in section 2(D)(3).
[103] See *Glamis Gold Ltd* (1976 Rules), reprinted in section 2(C)(4).
[104] See M McCabe, "Arbitral Discovery," n 81, 517. See also *MCA Inc* (1983 Tribunal Rules), reprinted in section 2(D)(3). For an example of a case in which a discovery order has, in part, been found unnecessary because documents were obtainable by the requesting party without such an order, see *RPM Carlson* (1983 Tribunal Rules), reprinted in section 2(D)(3).
[105] See M McCabe, "Arbitral Discovery," n 81, 516.
[106] See *Dresser Industries* (1983 Tribunal Rules), reprinted in section 2(D)(3).
[107] See M McCabe, "Arbitral Discovery," n 81, 516. If such voluntary cooperation does not work, however, the arbitral tribunal should resort to its power to order the discovery.
[108] M McCabe, "Arbitral Discovery," n 81, 517.
[109] See S Stein and D Wotman, "International Commercial Arbitration in the 1980s," n 83, 1705–7; A Marriot, "Evidence in International Arbitration," n 2, 282–3; I Seidl-Hohenveldern, *Corporations In and Under International Law*, n 93, 15–16.
[110] See *MCA Inc* (1983 Tribunal Rules); *RPM Carlson* (1983 Tribunal Rules); both reprinted in section 2(D)(3).

for production and the negative reaction to it given by the other party.[111] The Tribunal's practice in granting and rejecting requests for production of documents can therefore be regarded as a conservative example of practice under the relatively wide discretion granted by Article 27(3). The parties may naturally agree in advance on the extent of any production request.[112]

Investor–state arbitral tribunals applying the UNCITRAL Rules have followed an equally measured approach to document production. Increasingly, these tribunals have drawn on the IBA's Rules on the Taking of Evidence in International Commercial Arbitration to flesh out what one tribunal described as the "skeletal guidance" provided by the UNCITRAL Rules.[113] While the IBA Rules are not binding on a tribunal, except to the extent that the parties agree they will apply, they may usefully give shape to the largely undefined authority over document production provided for in Article 27(3). Article 3(3) of the 1999 IBA Rules, which has guided tribunals, requires the requesting party to provide: (a) a description of the requested document sufficient to identify it, or a description in sufficient detail of a "narrow and specific" category of documents "that are reasonably believed to exist"; (b) a statement as to how documents requested are "relevant to the case and material to its outcome"; and (c) a statement that the documents requested are "not in the possession, custody or control" of the requesting party, and of the reason why the party "assumes the documents requested are in the possession, custody or control of the other party."[114] The 2010 IBA Rules are likely to provide similarly useful direction, adding to Article 3(3)(c) the requirement of a statement as to "why it would be unreasonably burdensome for the requesting Party to produce" the requested documents itself.[115]

As investor–state arbitration claims typically center on the effects of an allegedly offensive government measure, the investor's production request under the UNCITRAL Rules may target the documents relating to the government's internal deliberations concerning that measure. This type of request has often prompted objections from the respondent state that the requested documents were protected from production pursuant to governmental privilege, sometimes known as executive, deliberative process, or cabinet privilege. In these circumstances, some investor–state tribunals applying the UNCITRAL Rules have found guidance, in the absence of an agreed governing law on privileges,[116] in Article 9 of the IBA

---

[111] See *Brown and Root, Inc* (1983 Tribunal Rules), Order of January 4, 1993, para 3; *Intl Systems and Controls* (1983 Tribunal Rues); both reprinted in section 2(D)(3).

[112] See discussion on Article 1(1) in Chapter 2, section 2(B).

[113] See *Glamis Gold Ltd* (1976 Rules), reprinted in section 2(C)(4).

[114] *Glamis Gold Ltd* (1976 Rules) (finding that "[a]s part of the exercise of its authority under Article 15(1) [of the 1976 UNCITRAL Rules on the conduct of the proceedings]... the Tribunal may look to the IBA Rules on Evidence for guidance"). See also *William Clayton*, et al and *Government of Canada*, Procedural Order No 3 (June 3, 2009) (PCA administered, 1976 UNCITRAL Rules, NAFTA Chapter Eleven); *Merrill & Ring Forestry LP* and *Government of Canada*, Order Concerning Requests for Documents and Certain Evidentiary Matters (July 18, 2008) (ICSID administered, 1976 UNCITRAL Rules, NAFTA Chapter Eleven), reprinted below, section 2(C)(4); *Chemtura Corp* and *Government of Canada*, Procedural Order No 1 (January 12, 2008) (*Ad Hoc* Arbitration, 1976 UNCITRAL Rules, NAFTA Chapter Eleven); *Grand River Enterprises*, et al and *United States of America*, Procedural Order (May 14, 2007) (ICSID administered, 1976 UNCITRAL Rules, NAFTA Chapter Eleven). For a discussion of similar criteria, as applied by UNCITRAL tribunals, see C Brower and J Sharpe, "Determining the Extent of Discovery and Dealing with Requests for Discovery: Perspectives from the Common Law," in (L Newman and R Hill, eds) *The Leading Arbitrators' Guide to International Arbitration* (2008) 311-23.

[115] International Bar Association, "IBA Rules on the Taking of Evidence in International Commercial Arbitration," May 29, 2010.

[116] *Glamis Gold Ltd* (1976 Rules), reprinted in section 2(C)(4).

Rules. That provision exempts requested materials from production on "grounds of special political or institutional sensitivity (including evidence that has been classified as secret by a government or a public international institution) that the Arbitral Tribunal determines to be compelling."[117] A general assertion of the objection, however, has generally been considered insufficient to sustain the objection, with tribunals requiring the respondent state in the interest of equal treatment to identify the documents to which the exemption applies with sufficient specificity.[118] Investor–state tribunals have also addressed objections to document production requests based on attorney-client privilege.[119]

(c) "Enforcement" of production orders

Whatever the standard justifying the issuance of production orders, compliance with such orders is quite another matter.[120] An international tribunal like the Iran–US Claims Tribunal has no direct means of enforcing its orders;[121] nor do the UNCITRAL Rules provide for any sanctions in case of non-compliance.[122] This, however, does not mean that the arbitral tribunal is entirely without means to elicit respect for its orders. Instead of waiting silently[123] it may ask a party to submit specific explanations as to why it has not followed a production order.[124] If the documents are not produced and no satisfactory explanations are provided, the arbitral tribunal may in some cases entertain the possibility of drawing a negative inference from the party's failure to respond.[125] This sanction, however, presupposes that the arbitrators are convinced that the party in question has access to the

---

[117] International Bar Association, "IBA Rules on the Taking of Evidence in International Commercial Arbitration," May 29, 2010.

[118] *Merrill & Ring Forestry LP* (1976 Rules), at 8, paras 21–22, reprinted in section 2(C)(4). See also *Pope & Talbot Inc* and *Government of Canada*, Decision by Tribunal (September 6, 2000) (ICSID administered, 1976 UNCITRAL Rules, NAFTA Chapter Eleven), at 2, para 1.4–1.5 (requiring that respondent state to identify with sufficient specificity the documents which it believes should be exempt under the state secrets privilege).
See generally *Glamis Gold Ltd* and *United States of America*, Decision on Parties' Requests for Production of Documents withheld on Grounds of Privilege (November 17, 2005) (ICSID administered, 1976 UNCITRAL Rules, NAFTA Chapter Eleven).

[119] For an in-depth discussion of privilege, see M Büehler and T Webster, *Handbook of ICC Arbitration* (2008) 303–4; R Mosk and T Ginsburg, "Evidentiary Privileges in International Arbitration," (2001) ICLQ 345 et seq; F Schlabrendorff and A Sheppard, "Conflict of Legal Privileges in International Arbitration: An Attempt to Find a Holistic Solution," in: G Aksen *et al* (eds) *Global Reflections on International Law, Commerce and Dispute Resolution: Liber Amicorum in honour of Robert Briner, Paris* (2005). See also R Bernstein *et al*, "Discovery, Inspection of Documents and Interrogatories," in R Bernstein *et al*, *Handbook of Arbitration Practice* (1998) 139–41, 148–9.

[120] McCabe has calculated that only about half of the production orders issued by the Iran–US Claims Tribunal have in fact been fully complied with. See M McCabe, "Arbitral Discovery," n 81, 518–19.

[121] See *Pope & Talbot Inc* (1976 Rules), n 118, at 2, para 1.3 (finding "[w]hile [corresponding] Article 24(3) of [the 1976 UNCITRAL Rules] empowers to 'require the parties to produce documents, exhibits or other evidence,' there is no power to compel production").

[122] Article 30(3) provides that "the arbitral tribunal may make the award on the evidence before it" in case a party invited to produce documentary evidence fails to do so. This, however, hardly provides for a sanction in non-compliance with a discovery order. The making of an award based on documentary evidence other than that required to be produced is on the contrary likely to be beneficial to the party which has failed to comply with the order.

[123] According to Article 27(3) the documents or other evidence should be produced "within such a period of time as the tribunal shall determine." The time limits and possible extension should be fixed in accordance with Articles 24 and 25. See Chapter 16.

[124] See M McCabe, "Arbitral Discovery," n 81, 520–1.

[125] This was the case in *INA Corp* (1983 Tribunal Rules), reprinted in section 2(D)(3). See also *Brown & Root, Inc* (1983 Tribunal Rules), Order of January 4, 1993, para 3; *Frederica Lincoln Riahi* (1983 Tribunal Rules), Concurring and Dissenting Opinion of Judge Brower, para 20; both reprinted in section 2(D)(3); *United Parcel Service of America, Inc* and *Government of Canada*, Decision of the Tribunal Relating to Canada's Claim of

documents and that these documents are essential to the disposition of the case. Otherwise, the possibility of a successful court challenge against the award, or difficulties in its enforcement, may arise.[126]

Although a party seeking production may not rely on the arbitral tribunal to enforce a production order, the question remains whether that party, or the arbitral tribunal, can turn to local courts in an effort to compel production. Unlike Article 26 on interim measures,[127] Article 27 does not contain any specific provision on a party's right to address judicial authorities. This is true in spite of the fact that some commentators conclude that under the UNCITRAL Rules "the parties are not precluded from applying to the local courts for assistance concerning both documentary evidence and witness evidence in the form of subpoenas assistance."[128] Since the interim measures regulated by Article 26 normally involve greater interference with the adversary's conduct, that Article's explicit provision allowing court assistance can be taken to support *a fortiori* the conclusion that discovery matters may also be addressed to local courts.

It seems clear that, by virtue of its power to "conduct the arbitration in such manner as it considers appropriate,"[129] the arbitral tribunal itself may seek the assistance of courts or authorize a party to do so. It is less clear whether the parties should be allowed to address courts unilaterally. Orderly proceedings require in any case that the parties first ask the arbitral tribunal to order the production of documents and turn to the courts only as a last resort. The court's ability to provide assistance is dependent on local law. Local law often requires that the parties address the court only with the approval of the arbitral tribunal.[130] This is the requirement in the UNCITRAL Model Law.[131]

(5) Admissibility, relevance, materiality, and weight of the evidence—Article 27(4)

Article 27(4) is a cornerstone evidentiary rule, which appears in identical form in both the 1976 and 2010 UNCITRAL Rules.[132] This provision makes clear that rigid rules of

---

Cabinet Privilege, October 8, 2004, at 5, para 15 ("A failure to disclose, found by the Tribunal to be unjustifiable, may lead to the Tribunal drawing adverse inferences on the issue in question."). Article 9(5) of the 2010 IBA Rules grants the same authority. See also E Gaillard and J Savage (eds), *Fouchard, Gaillard, Goldman on International Commercial Arbitration* (1999) 699–701 ("Arbitrators faced with a party refusing, for no valid reason, to comply with their order to disclose certain documents can also 'draw all necessary inferences' from that refusal and thus effectively penalize that party in their award on the merits."); A Marriot, "Evidence in International Arbitration," n 2, 283 ("Arbitrators are free to draw an adverse inference from a party's failure to produce documents which might be harmful to his case.").

[126] See M McCabe, "Arbitral Discovery," n 81, 530–1; See also H Holtzmann, "Fact finding by the Iran-United States Claims Tribunal," n 34, 127.

[127] See discussion on Article 26(9) in Chapter 17, section 2(B)(10).

[128] See S Stein and D Wotman, "International Commercial Arbitration in the 1980s," n 83, 1707.

[129] Article 17(1) is discussed in Chapter 2, section 3.

[130] For further domestic systems in this regard, see L Newman and R Castilla, "Production of Evidence through US Courts for Use in International Arbitration," (1992) 9(2) J Intl Arb 61; M McCabe, "Arbitral Discovery," n 81, 532–3; S Stein and D Wotman, "International Commercial Arbitration in the 1980s," n 83, 1705–7; A Marriot, "Evidence in International Arbitration," n 2, 286–8.

[131] Article 27 of the Model Law, as amended, ("Court Assistance in Taking Evidence") reads as follows: "The arbitral tribunal or a party with the approval of the arbitral tribunal may request from a competent court of this State assistance in taking evidence. The court may execute the request within its competence and according to its rules on taking evidence."

As noted by leading commentators, "Article 27 applies to court assistance in obtaining evidence for arbitrators within the same States as the court receiving the request but does not reach abroad." H Holtzmann and J Neuhaus, *A Guide to the UNCITRAL Model Law on International Commercial Arbitration*, n 15, 738.

[132] Article 27(4) of the 2010 UNCITRAL Rules originally appeared in Article 25(6) of the 1976 UNCITRAL Rules. See n 10. The restructuring was done in accordance with the Working Group's decision to group all

evidence are unsuitable for international arbitral proceedings.[133] Instead, as emphasized in the *travaux préparatoires* of the 1976 UNCITRAL Rules, "[i]n making rulings on the evidence, arbitrators should enjoy the greatest possible freedom and they are therefore freed from having to observe the strict legal rules of evidence."[134]

Such freedom is expressed in the wording of Article 27(4), according to which it is up to the arbitral tribunal to "determine the admissibility, relevance, materiality and weight of the evidence offered." Its wording and the interpretive history supplied by the negotiating history and the practice of international tribunals clearly show that it confers discretion on the tribunal with respect to *all* forms of evidence.[135]

Among the aspects covered by Article 27(4) (admissibility, relevance, materiality, and weight of the evidence) admissibility merits separate discussion. The UNCITRAL Rules do not contain strict rules regarding admissibility, thereby allowing the arbitral tribunal to exercise a liberal policy in this area, as is customary in international arbitration.[136] On the other hand, nothing in Article 27(4) prevents the arbitral tribunal from following the formal rules of evidence of a national system familiar to both parties. Should the tribunal choose to adopt its own policy consistent with the liberal tone of Article 27(4), it should not construe the rule as permitting the unrestricted admission of evidence. Where, for instance, a strict deadline for the submission of documentary evidence has been set, any significant delay in filing the evidence normally should lead to its rejection.[137] Certain kinds of evidence, such as information concerning confidential negotiations between the parties prior to the arbitral proceedings, are generally considered inadmissible as evidence, and should therefore be rejected.[138] The arbitral tribunal also

---

provisions relating to evidence under one article. *Settlement of Commercial Disputes: Revision of the UNCITRAL Arbitration Rules, Note by the Secretariat*, UNCITRAL, UN Doc A/CN.9/WG.II/WP.154.Add.1 at 11, para 38 (2009).

[133] See V S Mani, *International Adjudication: Procedural Aspects*, n 33, 192, who, speaking of interstate adjudication, notes that "[f]lexibility is, indeed, a virtue of the whole international procedure." See also D Sandifer, *Evidence before International Tribunals*, n 14, 16, 176; M Kazazi, *Burden of Proof and Related Issues*, n 59, 323 (international tribunals "are not usually bound by strict rules of evidence but enjoy considerable freedom"); H Holtzmann and J Neuhaus, *A Guide to the UNCITRAL Model Law on International Commercial Arbitration*, n 15, 567 ("As a matter of policy, it is desirable for arbitration to avoid the application of technical rules of evidence where possible"). Holtzmann and Neuhaus discuss Article 19(2) of the Model Law which provides that "[t]he power conferred upon the arbitral tribunal [to conduct the arbitration in such manner as it considers appropriate] includes the power to determine the admissibility, relevance, materiality and weight of any evidence."

[134] *Report of the Secretary-General on the Preliminary Draft Set of Arbitration Rules*, UNCITRAL, 8th Session, UN Doc A/CN.9/97 (1974), reprinted in (1975) VI UNCITRAL Ybk 163, 176 (Commentary on Draft Article 21(5)).

[135] See *Report of the Secretary-General on the Revised Draft Set of Arbitration Rules*, UNCITRAL, 9th Session, Addendum 1 (Commentary), UN Doc A/CN.9/112/Add.1 (1975), reprinted in (1976) VII UNCITRAL Ybk 166, 175–6 (Commentary on Draft Article 22).

[136] See J Selby and D Stewart, "Practical Aspects of Arbitrating Claims," n 63, 238; D Sandifer, *Evidence before International Tribunals*, n 14, 176. See also Case No A/20 (1983 Tribunal Rules), reprinted in section 2(D)(5) ("... the Rules reflect generally accepted principles of international arbitration ...").

[137] See Case No A/16 (1983 Tribunal Rules); *Chas T Main* (1983 Tribunal Rules); *Uiterwyk Corp* (1983 Tribunal Rules); all reprinted in section 2(D)(5). But see *Ultrasystems, Inc* (1983 Tribunal Rules), reprinted in section 2(D)(5) (unauthorized post-Hearing evidence admitted "as supporting evidence."). See also D Sandifer, *Evidence before International Tribunals*, n 14, 179.

[138] See Case No A/1 (1983 Tribunal Rules), reprinted in section 2(D)(5), and S Baker and M Davis, *The UNCITRAL Arbitration Rules*, n 13, 115 ("The Tribunal did adopt one clear rule of exclusion. It refused to consider a party's settlement proposals as evidence against that party."). See also J Tackaberry, "Evidence at Hearings," n 7, 158, 163. In *Methanex Corp* (1976 Rules), Award of August 3, 2005, para 59, reprinted in section 2(C)(5), a NAFTA Chapter Eleven tribunal excluded evidence obtained illegally by the claimant because it "offended basic principles of justice and fairness required in every international arbitration."

has the power to refuse to hear a witness, if it is clear at the outset that the testimony is unnecessary.[139]

But aside from these circumstances (and the exceptional case in which some strict domestic evidentiary system is applied), evidence should not be rejected on any formal or technical grounds. Thus, there is, in principle, no prohibition of what is known in common law as "hearsay evidence,"[140] although characterizing the evidence in this way may affect its probative value.[141] Even the principle that information concerning confidential negotiations between the parties lacks evidentiary value could be based on the irrelevance of such information rather than on its inadmissibility per se.[142] In any case, a liberal attitude towards admissibility, with objections restricted to the "relevance, materiality and weight of the evidence offered," accords best with both the spirit of Article 27(4) and arbitral practice in general.[143] This is also the general approach adopted by international tribunals.[144]

Therefore, rather than summarily rejecting evidence, the arbitral tribunal should normally make an effort to determine its relevance and materiality.[145] As this is not likely to cause difficulties warranting lengthy discussion, we come finally to the issue concerning the "weight" of the evidence. This term was added to the text at the final stage of the drafting process so as to emphasize the wide discretion which the arbitrators were to have.[146]

Because this discretion is applied in light of concrete circumstances, general rules on the weighing of evidence cannot be predetermined. Nevertheless, illustrations provided by the case history of the Iran–US Claims Tribunal may be helpful. For example, although there is no formal prohibition against hearsay evidence, the Tribunal could accord less weight to the testimony of a witness who lacks direct personal knowledge of the subject matter at issue than to the testimony of a witness who does have such personal knowledge.[147] Similarly, although "company witnesses"[148] can be heard, circumstances may demand a cautious assessment of their testimony.[149] Consequently, certain kinds of evidence may be

---

[139] An example from the practice of the ICJ is mentioned by D Sandifer, *Evidence before International Tribunals*, n 14, 290–1. In this kind of case the admissibility of the evidence is closely intertwined with its relevance.

[140] This is the case in international proceedings in general. See D Sandifer, *Evidence before International Tribunals*, n 14, 366 et seq.

[141] See *Sedco Inc* (1983 Tribunal Rules), reprinted in section 2(D)(5) (lack of personal knowledge concerning the subject of testimony considered relevant).

[142] See H Thirlway, "Dilemma or Chimera?—Admissibility of Illegally Obtained Evidence in International Adjudication," (1984) 78 AJIL (1984) 622, 625. Thirlway discusses certain cases of the Permanent Court of International Justice that have evoked differing views on whether certain rulings on arguments based on negotiations between the litigating parties pertain to the question of admissibility of evidence or to relevance.

[143] See J Selby and D Stewart, "Practical Aspects of Arbitrating Claims," n 63, 238.

[144] J Selby and D Stewart, "Practical Aspects of Arbitrating Claims," n 63, 238. See also *INA Corp* (1983 Tribunal Rules); *Sylvania Technical Systems* (1983 Tribunal Rules); both reprinted in section 2(D)(5). But see *Chas T Main Intl* (1983 Tribunal Rules), reprinted in section 2(D)(5).

[145] In concrete cases admissibility and the other issues discussed may be closely intertwined, so that—to use the example already mentioned—the hearing of an irrelevant witness may be rejected, ie, evidence not admitted because of the lack of relevance.

[146] *Report of the UNCITRAL on the Work of its Ninth Session*, UN GAOR, 31st Session, Supp No 17, UN Doc A/31/17, para 130 (1976), reprinted in (1976) VII UNCITRAL Ybk 66, 75 (Commentary on Draft Article 28(1)).

[147] See Chapter 19, section 2, for a discussion on Article 28(2).

[148] Chapter 19, section 2.

[149] See *Sedco Inc* (1983 Tribunal Rules), reprinted in section 2(D)(5). See also *JL Case Co* and *Islamic Republic of Iran*, reprinted in 3 Iran-US CTR 62 (1983–II), n 22, where the Tribunal's inability to "find the available evidence sufficient, even in the absence of any evidence to the contrary" may have been due to the fact that the Claimant's evidence was in the form of testimonies by two sales managers of the Claimant company. See 64–5. See Dissent of Howard M Holtzmann, at 66–7. It should be stressed that there has been no general policy of

regarded as sufficient to create only tentative, or *prima facie*, proof which requires the corroboration of further evidence. On the other hand, evidence which does not suffer from the kinds of deficiencies just discussed may have to be disregarded if contradicted by other evidence emanating from the same party; it has been called a "general rule of evidence that contradictory statements of an interested party should be construed against that party."[150]

In conclusion, under Article 27(4), the discretion "of arbitrators to evaluate the evidence offered by the parties is phrased in the broadest terms possible."[151] Certain principles based on common sense are a good guide in the exercise of that discretion.[152]

During discussions to revise the Rules, the Working Group considered a proposal to include additional language in Article 27(4) to clarify that the arbitral tribunal had authority to refuse to accept late-filed evidence.[153] It was concluded that such a change to the article was not necessary because the matter was already regulated under Article 27(3) on production of evidence.[154]

(6) Comparison to the 1976 UNCITRAL Rules

Article 27 of the 2010 UNCITRAL Rules represents a restructuring of provisions originally appearing in Articles 24 and 25 of the 1976 UNCITRAL Rules, respectively on evidence and hearings. The reorganization was motivated by proper alignment of the rules regulating the use of evidence before the hearing and at the hearing.[155] Articles 27(1) on burden of proof, 27(3) on document production, and 27(4) on admissibility are identical to original Articles 24(1), 24(3), and 25(6).

The second sentence of Article 27(2) on written affidavits is substantially similar to corresponding Article 25(5) of the 1976 UNCITRAL Rules. However, stylistic revisions to the rule clarify its application to witness affidavits, including those by expert witnesses. Inclusion of the phrase "Unless otherwise directed by the arbitral tribunal" provides the tribunal clearer discretion to manage witness evidence but should not be exercised in a manner that deprives a party of a reasonable opportunity to present its case.

At the same time, Article 27 differs from original Article 24 in two ways. First, Article 27 no longer contains the provisions of original Article 24(2) that expressly granted the arbitral tribunal authority to require a party to provide a "summary of the documents and other evidence" that that party intends to rely on in the arbitration.[156] The Working Group agreed that these provisions did not reflect common arbitration practice.[157] Moreover, concerns

---

specifically discrediting evidence from persons affiliated with a party. See M Straus, "The Practice of the Iran-United States Claims Tribunal," n 58, 63. See also the discussion by the late Judge Virally in the *Buckamier* case (1983 Tribunal Rules), reprinted in section 2(D)(5).

[150] *Woodward-Clyde Consultants* (1983 Tribunal Rules), reprinted in section 2(D)(5).
[151] P Sanders, "Commentary on the UNCITRAL Arbitration Rules," n 13, 203.
[152] See C Brower, "Evidence Before International Tribunals," n 1, 54, enumerates certain such principles applied by the Iran–US Claims Tribunal including: primacy of contemporaneous written evidence; importance of the actual conduct of the parties for the interpretation of their contract; failure of timely objection of an invoice is a strong evidence of its acceptance; contradictory positions taken by a party weakens his case; failure of a party having access to certain evidence to produce such evidence justifies inferences against that party.
[153] The proposal would add at the end of Article 24(4) of the 1976 UNCITRAL Rules a sentence along the following lines: "The arbitral tribunal may disregard evidence that is submitted late." UNCITRAL, 42nd Session, UN Doc A/CN.9/669, n 46, at 17, para 74.
[154] UNCITRAL, 42nd Session, UN Doc A/CN.9/669, n 46, at 17, para 74–75.
[155] UNCITRAL, 42nd Session, UN Doc A/CN.9/669, n 46, at 15–16, paras 70–71.
[156] See 1976 UNCITRAL Rules, art 24(2) at n 10.
[157] UNCITRAL, 41st Session, UN Doc A/CN.9/641, n 45, at 6–7, para 22–23. The Working Group stated that summaries of evidence were "rarely, if at all, used in practice." Para 23.

were raised that original Article 24(2) might create uncertainty regarding "the optimal form" in which evidence should be submitted by the parties under the Rules, particularly since Articles 20(4) and 21(2) of the 2010 Rules encourage the parties to provide documents or other evidence with their initial filings.[158] While some Working Group delegates believed the use of summaries could benefit the arbitral process,[159] the prevailing view was that original Article 24(2) should not be adopted as part of the 2010 UNCITRAL Rules. This decision was subject to the understanding that such an omission would not diminish the arbitral tribunal's broad discretion under Article 17 to conduct the arbitral proceedings in an appropriate manner, including by requiring summaries of the evidence, if useful.[160]

The negotiating history and practice concerning original Article 24(2) remains relevant for parties involved in arbitration under the 1976 UNCITRAL Rules, as well as for tribunals applying the 2010 UNCITRAL Rules that wish to request a summary of the evidence from the parties under their general authority. Article 24(2) was added to the 1976 UNCITRAL Rules by the Committee of the Whole II at the very final stage of the drafting process. The Committee agreed that "in order to prevent surprise at hearings the arbitral tribunal may require delivery in advance to the other party and to the arbitral tribunal of a summary of the documents and other evidence which a party intends to present."[161] Original Article 24(2) emphasizes the active role which the arbitral tribunal may take.[162]

Under the 1976 UNCITRAL Rules, the submission of notice in the form of "a summary of documents and other evidence" is not obligatory unless the arbitral tribunal so rules.[163] Very often, however, the tribunal will require such a summary, deeming it appropriate to ensure fair treatment of the parties and conducive to orderly proceedings. As regards documentary evidence, the tribunal is well advised to order the submission of the documents themselves, in addition to a summary, well ahead of the hearing.[164]

The submission of documentary evidence should preferably be combined with the submission of written statements. If the tribunal orders a second (or third) round of written statements (eg, in the form of a hearing memorial), it may order the simultaneous submission of documentary evidence together with the summary of all the evidence, or the remainder of the evidence to be relied upon.[165]

The arbitral tribunal may in some circumstances consider it appropriate to order the parties to submit the summary of the evidence to be produced at the hearing *after* the

---

[158] UNCITRAL, 41st Session, UN Doc A/CN.9/641, n 45. UNCITRAL, 42nd Session, UN Doc A/CN.9/669, n 46, at 12, para 50.

[159] Proponents of retaining original Article 24(2) in the Rules noted that the provision could "provide the arbitral tribunal with the opportunity to obtain from the parties an overview of the dispute, particularly in complex matters," and could "assist in imposing a discipline on the parties to rationalize the evidence upon which they wished to rely." UNCITRAL, 41st Session, UN Doc A/CN.9/641, n 45, at 7, para 24. In response, it was argued that Article 24(2) was unnecessary since the arbitral tribunal already had the authority to request a summary of the evidence under Article 17, and that practice of requesting summaries might "risk increasing the tribunal's work rather than simplifying it." Para 24.

[160] UNCITRAL, 41st Session, UN Doc A/CN.9/641, n 45, at 7, para 25.

[161] *Report of the UNCITRAL on the Work of its Ninth Session*, UN GAOR, 31st Session, Supp No 17, UN Doc A/31/17, para 118 (1976), reprinted in (1976) VII UNCITRAL Ybk 66, 75.

[162] P Sanders, "Commentary on the UNCITRAL Arbitration Rules," n 13, 203.

[163] However, as regards witness evidence, certain information must be provided prior to the oral proceedings by virtue of Article 25(2) of the 1976 UNCITRAL Rules. See Chapter 19.

[164] This has been the practice of the Iran–US Claims Tribunal. See *Brown & Root, Inc* (1983 Tribunal Rules), reprinted in section 2(D)(2), as well as the various orders quoted in connection with Article 24 in Chapter 16.

[165] If the documentary evidence is produced as such, the separate summary of the same may be redundant.

exchange of written statements. In such cases, the submission of the summary can be combined with the submission of the witness information, referred to in Article 25(2).[166]

Particularly where the record of the case is likely to be voluminous, the arbitral tribunal can make the location of each document easier by ordering the parties to number them consecutively.[167] The parties themselves can contribute to efficient proceedings by using tabs, documents with colored covers, and similar means by which the identification of a document is facilitated.[168]

As discussed previously, Articles 20 and 21 of the 2010 UNCITRAL Rules encourage the claimant or respondent to include "all documents and other evidence relied upon" or "references to them" at as early a stage as the presentation of the statement of claim or statement of defence.[169]

A second major difference between the revised and original UNCITRAL Rules is the addition in the first sentence of Article 27(2) of a definition of "witnesses" which, as discussed above, clarifies the broad range of possible witnesses, including party witnesses. Parties arbitrating under the 1976 UNCITRAL Rules may wish to consider a modification to incorporate the first sentence of Article 27(2), particularly if the use of party witnesses is contemplated.

C. Extracts from the Practice of Investment Tribunals

(1) Article 27(1) (1976 Rules)—Burden of proof

Antoine Biloune, et al and *Ghana Investments Centre,* et al, Award on Jurisdiction and Liability (October 27, 1989), (*Ad Hoc* Proceeding, 1976 UNCITRAL Rules, Contract), reprinted in (1994) XIX Ybk Commercial Arb 11, 20:

> 25. The fundamental outlines of the relevant events are clear. Where differences between the parties on the facts remain, the Tribunal has had recourse to the principle recorded in the [1976] UNCITRAL Rules that each party has the burden of proving the facts upon which it relies for its claim or defence. [1976] UNCITRAL Rules, Art. 24.

Chevron Corp, et al and *Republic of Ecuador,* Interim Award (December 1, 2008) (PCA administered, 1976 UNCITRAL Rules, US-Ecuador BIT), at 78–80:

> 138. As a general rule, the holder of a right raising a claim on the basis of that right in legal proceedings bears the burden of proof for all elements required for the UNCITRAL Chevron-Texaco v. Ecuador Interim Award claim. However, an exception to this rule occurs when a respondent raises a defense to the effect that the claim is precluded despite the normal conditions being met. In that case, the respondent must assume the burden of proof for the elements necessary for the exception to be allowed.
>
> 139. The nature of these defenses as exceptions to a general rule that lead to the reversal of the burden of proof stem from, among other factors, the presumption of good faith. A claimant is not required to prove that its claim is asserted in a non-abusive manner; it is for the respondent to raise and prove an abuse as a defense. A respondent whose defense overcomes the presumption of good faith reveals the hierarchy between these norms, as even a well-founded claim will be rejected by the tribunal if it is found to be abusive. Burden-shifting in the present context is consistent with Article 24(1) of the UNCITRAL Arbitration Rules,

---

[166] As to the witnesses, see commentary on Article 25(2) of the 1976 UNCITRAL Rules in Chapter 19.
[167] See *Brown & Root, Inc* (1983 Tribunal Rules), reprinted in, section 2(D)(2).
[168] See N Blackaby and C Partisides,, *Redfern and Hunter on International Arbitration*, n 1, 400.
[169] See Chapter 13 on Articles 20 and 21.

which provides that "[e]ach party shall have the burden of proving the facts relied on to support his claim or defence." Thus, in accordance with that provision, the Iran-U.S. Claims Tribunal in *Sabet v. Iran* stated: "[a]s it was the Respondents who brought the assignment argument as an affirmative defense, they bear the burden of proof on the issue...."

(2) Article 27(2) (1976 Rules)—Definition of "witnesses"

Antoine Biloune, et al and *Ghana Investments Centre,* et al, Award on Damages and Costs (June 30, 1990) (*Ad Hoc* Proceeding, 1976 UNCITRAL Rules, Contract), reprinted in (1994) XIX Ybk Commercial Arb 22, 24:

36. Under the [1976] UNCITRAL Rules, "Each party shall have the burden of proving the facts relied on to support his claim or defence". The Tribunal, governed by the [1976] UNCITRAL Rules, has proceeded in accordance with this principle. The Tribunal has reviewed the accounting records submitted to it, as well as the reports analyzing those records by both the claimants' and the respondents' accountants. The Tribunal holds that, in general, the contemporaneous books and records of a company regularly kept in the normal course of business should be accorded substantial evidentiary weight. In the present case, it appears that a firm of Ghanaian chartered accountants, licensed to pursue their profession by the Government of Ghana, designed MDCL's accounting system and controls and periodically performed audits. This same firm has provided its opinion to this Tribunal that the company's books in fact accurately reflect MDCL's financial status. MDCL's records are thus accepted by the Tribunal as presumptively accurate, subject to proof to the contrary by the respondents.

(3) Article 27(2) (1976 Rules)—Written witness statements

No practice is being extracted in this area.

(4) Article 27(3) (1976 Rules)—Production of documents

SD Myers, Inc and *Government of Canada,* Procedural Order No 10 Concerning Crown Privileges (November 16, 1999) (ICSID administered, 1976 UNCITRAL Rules, NAFTA Chapter Eleven), at 1–2: Crown Privilege

1. CANADA shall not at this stage be required to produce any documents in respect of which a "certificate" of the appropriate authority has been provided pursuant to section 39 of the Canada Evidence Act 1985.
2. It shall be a matter for each party to determine the manner in which it will proceed in the light of the Tribunal's decision to make any order concerning documents in respect of which a Canada Evidence Act "certificate" has been produced, bearing in mind that the closing date for the production of documents is November 30, 1999.
3. If MYERS elects to renew its application for an order for production of documents in respect of which a "certificate" of the appropriate authority has been provided the Tribunal will give directions for the parties to submit memoranda dealing with the issues mentioned in the Tribunal's "Explanatory Note" that accompanies this Procedural Order.
4. Any questions relating to the drawing of "adverse inferences" and/or the discharge of any burden of proof by either party will be determined by the tribunal after consideration of written or oral statements when the evidentiary record is closed.

International Thunderbird Gaming Corp and *United Mexican States,* Procedural Order No 5 (March 12, 2004) (ICSID administered, 1976 UNCITRAL Rules, NAFTA Chapter Eleven), at 1–2: *Considering:*

(A) The previous Procedural Orders
(B) Respondent's letter of February 24, 2004, submitting a Request for the Production of Documents (of which a courtesy English translation was filed on February 27, 2004);

(C) Claimant's letter of March 3, 2004 in response to Respondent's request, as directed by the Tribunal by letter of February 27, 2004;

(D) Respondent's letter of March 4, 2004 in response to Claimant's letter of March 3, 2004;

(E) The written submissions of the Parties subsequent to the Tribunal's ruling on Respondent's request for the production of documents in its Procedural Order No 3;

(F) Article 24(3) of the [1976] UNCITRAL Arbitration Rules, according to which at any time during the arbitral proceedings the Arbitral Tribunal may require the parties to produce documents, exhibits or other evidence within such period of time as the Tribunal shall determine;

The Arbitral Tribunal Hereby Decides As Follows:

[1] Respondent's Request I (Game Specifications) set forth in its letter of February 24, 2004 is denied.

[2] Claimant is ordered to produce the documents identified in Requests II.A (Messrs. Oien and Ong), last paragraph, and II.B (Messrs. Aspe and Arroyo), last paragraph, of Respondent's letter of February 24, 2004, by submitting copies to the Respondent and the Arbitral Tribunal on or before Friday March 19, 2004.

[3] The time limit for filing the Statement of Rejoinder by Respondent, mentioned in paragraph 7.2(d) of Order No 1 (as subsequently amended), is extended until Thursday April 1, 2004 so that Respondent will be able to comment on the documents produced by Claimant under the present Order in the Statement of Rejoinder.

[4] The date of notification of the witnesses, mentioned in paragraph 7.2(e) of Order No 1 (as subsequently amended), is extended until Tuesday April 6, 2004.

[5] The schedule of the proceedings is maintained in all other respects.

Glamis Gold Ltd and *United States of America*, Decision on Objections to Document Production (July 20, 2005) (ICSID administered, 1976 UNCITRAL Rules, NAFTA Chapter Eleven), at 3:

8. …Article 24 [of the 1976 UNCITRAL Rules] is general in its terms, making clear the authority of the Tribunal to order the production of "documents, exhibits or other evidence" but providing only skeletal guidance as to the exercise of that authority. Under Article 15(1) of the [1976] Rules, "the arbitral tribunal may conduct the arbitration in such manner as it considers appropriate, provided that the parties are treated with equality and that at any stage of the proceedings each party is given a full opportunity of presenting his case."

9. The International Bar Associations Rules on the Taking of Evidence in International Commercial Arbitration ("IBA Rules on Evidence") are not directly applicable to this proceeding.1 As a part of the exercise of its authority under Article 15(1) [of the 1976 UNCITRAL Rules], however, the Tribunal may look to the IBA Rules on Evidence for guidance.

10. The Tribunal notes in particular the standards for production referenced in the IBA Rules on Evidence. Article 3(a)(ii) emphasizes that requests for documents should be of a "narrow and specific" nature and of documents that "are reasonably believed to exist." Article 3(b) underscores the need for documents to be "relevant and material to the outcome of the case." On the basis of this general guidance, the Tribunal has endeavored to ensure that any documents which it compels a Party to produce should be of a "narrow and specific" nature, "reasonably believed to exist", and likely "material to the outcome of the case."

…

15. In the interest of avoiding the burdens of litigation and protecting the expectations of the parties in the arbitration process, the Tribunal has endeavored to make its decisions regarding the Parties' Objections in such a manner as to focus on the articulated materiality of a given document or category of documents. The Tribunal believes that as the document production efforts proceed the Parties will have evaluated the publicly available records and will be in a better position to articulate which additional documents will be necessary for the Parties to prepare their arguments.

Merrill & Ring Forestry LP and *Government of Canada*, Decision of the Tribunal on Production of Documents, (July 18, 2008) (ICSID administered, 1976 UNCITRAL Rules, NAFTA Chapter Eleven), at 7–8:

19. The Tribunal is also persuaded, however, that the privilege, as held in *Pope & Talbot* and the *Canada-Aircraft* decisions invoked by the Investor, can only be asserted in respect of sufficiently identified documents together with a clear explanation about the reasons for claiming such privilege. The parties would need such information in order to assess whether they agree or disagree about a refusal on these grounds, just as the Tribunal needs it to decide in case of disagreement between the parties.
21. In the absence of this specific information the Investor is unable to agree or disagree with such refusal just as the Tribunal is unable to decide on a privilege which at present has no connection to specific documents or even less so justified or explained. The principle of equality in the treatment of the parties laid down by Article 15 of the [1976] UNCITRAL Arbitration Rules governing these proceedings also requires that such privileges be clearly explained so as to allow the Investor the opportunity to provide informed comments on the matter.
22. The Tribunal accordingly directs Canada that if it believes that a document will need to be protected under paragraph 6 (f) of the Document Production Order, it shall need to identify such document specifically, its date and description of its general contents. At the same time, Canada is required to provide the appropriate explanations about why it considers that the privilege must be asserted.

(5) Article 27(4) (1976 Rules)—Admissibility, relevance, materiality, and weight of the evidence

Methanex Corp and *United States of America*, Award (August 3, 2005) (ICSID administered, 1976 UNCITRAL Rules, NAFTA Chapter Eleven), Part II, Chapter I, at 1–2, 26–29 (footnotes omitted):

1. … By Motion dated 18th May 2004, the USA then applied for the exclusion of certain categories of evidence submitted by Methanex, by reference to Article 25(6) of the [1976] UNCITRAL Rules, which provides that: "The arbitral tribunal shall determine the admissibility, relevance, materiality and weight of the evidence offered".
2. There were four categories to which the USA objected as evidence in these proceedings. First, the USA submitted that several documents submitted into evidence by Methanex were illegally copied from the private files of Mr. Vind and his company, Regent International: Exhibits 52–61, 64, 66, 151–153, 155–156, 159–160, 162, 165, 202, 216–219, 222–223, 226 and 258–259 to the Second Amended Statement of Claim (referred to as the "Vind Documents"). The USA submitted that the admission of illegally obtained evidence by Methanex was inconsistent with the principle of good faith inherent in any arbitration agreement….

…

53. On 15th June 2004, having read the Vind Documents de bene esse, heard the relevant witnesses and considered the submissions of the Disputing Parties, the Tribunal decided to uphold the USA's challenge to the admissibility of the Vind Documents and ordered that they would form no part of the evidential record in the arbitration proceedings. The reasons for the Tribunal's order are set out below.
54. In the Tribunal's view, the Disputing Parties each owed in this arbitration a general legal duty to the other and to the Tribunal to conduct themselves in good faith during these arbitration proceedings and to respect the equality of arms between them, the principles of "equal treatment" and procedural fairness being also required by Article 15(1) of the [1976] UNCITRAL Rules. As a general principle, therefore, just as it would be wrong for the USA ex hypothesi to misuse its intelligence assets to spy on Methanex (and its witnesses) and to introduce into evidence the resulting materials into this arbitration, so too would it be wrong for Methanex to introduce evidential materials obtained by Methanex unlawfully.

55. The first issue here is whether Methanex obtained the Vind Documents unlawfully by deliberately trespassing onto private property and rummaging through dumpsters inside the office-building for other persons' documentation. Whilst certain of Methanex's agents may have held an honest belief that no criminal violation was committed under the City of Brea's Ordinance, given the legal advice allegedly proffered by the un-named DC law firm, the evidence demonstrates at least a reckless indifference by Methanex as to whether civil trespass was committed by its collection-agents in procuring the Vind Documents from Mr. Vind's office-building in Brea. Once the USA demonstrated prima facie that the evidence which Methanex was proffering had been secured unlawfully, if not criminally, the burden of proof with respect to its admissibility shifted to Methanex, yet Methanex elected not to call the relevant partners of the unnamed law firm, whose testimony might have clarified the issue. The Tribunal is unable to see why these partners could not have testified before it. On the materials before the Tribunal, the evidence shows beyond any reasonable doubt that Methanex unlawfully committed multiple acts of trespass over many months in surreptitiously procuring the Vind Documents. Such unlawful conduct is not mitigated by the fact that the doors to the trash-area were not always closed but sometimes ajar: the entry into this area behind the doors remained unlawful; and Methanex made no attempt to distinguish between documents obtained when the doors were ajar and when they were closed.

...

59. ...There is no doubt on the evidence adduced by Methanex that this documentation was obtained by successive and multiple acts of trespass committed by Methanex over five and a half months in order to obtain an unfair advantage over the USA as a Disputing Party to these pending arbitration proceedings. The dates are illuminating: in August 2000, when this unlawful collection began, Methanex had made no application to the Tribunal for additional evidence from third persons; but when Methanex made its application, particularly at the procedural meeting on 31st March 2003, Methanex was already in possession of certain of the original documents which it purportedly sought from others. In these circumstances, the Tribunal likewise decided that it would be wrong to allow Methanex to introduce this documentation into these proceedings in violation of its general duty of good faith and, moreover, that Methanex's conduct, committed during these arbitration proceedings, offended basic principles of justice and fairness required of all parties in every international arbitration.

D. Extracts from the Practice of the Iran–US Claims Tribunal

(1) Tribunal Rules (1983), Article 24(1)—Burden of Proof

Flexi-Van Leasing Inc and *Islamic Republic of Iran*, Case No 36, Chamber One, Order of December 15, 1982, reprinted in 1 Iran-US CTR, 455 (1981–82):

The Respondent in its Statement of Defence challenges the jurisdiction of the Tribunal on the ground, *inter alia*, that the Claimant has not presented evidence to prove that it is a national of the United States which has owned the claim continuously from the time it arose until January 19, 1981, as required by Article VII, Paragraph 1 and 2 of the Claims Settlement Declaration.

Questions thus arise in this case—and in many other cases before this Chamber—concerning what evidence is to be presented by a Claimant

(a) That a parent corporation is a national of the United States;
(b) That a subsidiary corporation is a national of the United States; and
(c) That a claim has been owned by a national of the United States continuously from the time it arose until January 19, 1981.

...

In these circumstances, it must be recognized that it is neither possible nor necessary to require submission, as the Respondent proposes, of detailed evidence such as either passports, birth certificates or certified copies of naturalization documents for each of the thousands of individuals who collectively own, directly or indirectly, more than 50% of the capital stock of Flexi-Van Corporation. Also, it is not practical to adopt the suggestion of the Respondent to require submission of voluminous lists of the names and addresses of all shareholders, particularly because the identity of shareholders of United States publicly-traded corporations is safeguarded to protect confidentiality.

Any such requirements as Respondent proposes, would impose excessive burdens on the Parties and the Tribunal. The burden on the Claimant would be to attempt to gather such evidence, much of which is not in its possession; the burden on the Respondent would be to review it; and the burden on the Tribunal would be to receive and evaluate it. It is not possible for the Tribunal to estimate the amount of time which would be needed by the Parties and itself to accomplish such tasks, but it is likely that any such requirement would significantly delay the arbitral proceedings in this and many other cases.

Other Tribunals which have adjudicated international claims in the past have also faced similar problems. They have required what they considered to be sufficient evidence and from that have drawn reasonable inferences. *See,* e.g. Mexican-United States General Claims Commission, Foreign Claims Settlement Commission of the United States. A Respondent is, of course, always free to produce evidence in rebuttal. However, as the Mexican United States General Claims Commission held:

> [W]hen the claimant has established a *prima facie* case and Respondent has offered no evidence in rebuttal, the latter may not insist that the former pile up evidence to establish its allegations beyond a reasonable doubt without pointing out some reason for doubting.

Parker Case, 4 R. Int'l Arb. Awards 39 (1926). The same principle was followed by the French-Mexican Claims Commission which determined that an international arbitral tribunal in determining nationality may apply less strict requirements where it does not appear to be reasonably necessary to set in motion the entire process of formal proofs. *Pinson Case,* 5 R. Int'l Arb. Awards 327 (1928).

...

The type of evidence to be submitted by a Claimant depends on the circumstances of each particular case, as viewed by the Chamber. In this case, the evidence described below will, *prima facie,* be considered sufficient as to corporate nationality. Such evidence is in the form of documents officially filed with governmental agencies or is from an independent certified public accountant. Respondent will be free to offer rebuttal evidence. From the totality of such evidence the Chamber will draw reasonable inferences and reach conclusions as to whether the Claimant was, or was not, a national of the United States, as defined in the Declaration, during the necessary period. It is within the power of the Chamber to do this based on accepted principles of international law and also upon the Provisionally Adopted Tribunal Rules which state that:

> The arbitral tribunal shall determine the admissibility, relevance, materiality and weight of the evidence offered.

Article 25, Paragraph 6. Moreover, in view of the impracticality of any other course, this procedure is necessary to ensure that the Declaration can be carried out effectively. See Declaration, Article III, Paragraph 2.

Benjamin R Isaiah and *Bank Mellat,* Award No 35–219–2 (March 30, 1983) at 13, reprinted in 2 Iran-US CTR 232, 238–39 (1983-I):

> The Tribunal has copies of (a) the agreement of 10 January 1978 between Karayesh Co. and Isaiah for the purchase of beer abroad and its sale in Iran which allocates to Isaiah 25 per cent of the profits; (b) the agreement of 22 January 1978 appointing Farkash as Isaiah's representative to develop and manage the beer business in Iran, (c) Alikhani's letter of 3 November 1978 informing Isaiah that his share of profit to the end of October was $380,000; (d) Isaiah's letter to Alikhani of 18 December 1978 asking that the money be sent to Haim Farkash's account in Israel as soon as possible after the first of the year; (e) Alikhani's letter to Isaiah of 4 January 1979 saying that the check representing Isaiah's share of the profits had been purchased from the International Bank of Iran and had been given, as instructed, to Haim Farkash; and (f) Farkash's letter of 4 January 1979 informing Isaiah that he had received the money and would hold it in his account pending directions from Isaiah. These documents, buttressed by credible testimony at the Hearing, constitute a

prima facie case that the money represented by the check was Isaiah's money and that he has held the claim for that money from the time the check was dishonored. In the absence of evidence to the contrary, that evidence is decisive.

RN Pomeroy and *Islamic Republic of Iran*, Award No 50–40–3 (June 8, 1983) at 20, reprinted in 2 Iran-US CTR 372, 382 (1983-I):

Finally, the Navy has not produced any evidence in support of its contention that Pomeroy Corporation breached its duties under the Contract by failing to supply qualified personnel or failing to point out defects in the work of other contractors. By failing to establish even a *prima facie* case or contract breach, the Navy has not met its burden of proof on this defence, and it must be rejected.

Dallal and *Islamic Republic of Iran, Bank Mellat*, Award No 53–149–1 (June 10, 1983) at 12, reprinted in 3 Iran-US CTR 10, 17 (1983-II):

In this case Mr. Dallal has chosen not to provide any further information regarding the transaction. His reticence to provide information about the character of the transaction cannot be sufficiently justified by his alleged concern for the safety of relatives and business connections in Iran, since it had been quite possible for him to give further details—e.g. regarding time and money spent by him for the project—without revealing the identity of his relatives and business connections.[1] The Tribunal therefore reaches the conclusion that the two cheques must be assumed to have been issued as part of a capital transfer, intended merely to exchange Rials for Dollars and to transfer the dollar amount to the United States. The Tribunal therefore concludes that it is unable to issue an award in favour of the Claimant.

[Footnote] 1. The Tribunal reminds [us] of the truism that a man may have a good case, but if he cannot prove it, he cannot prevail.

CMI Intl, Inc and *Ministry of Roads and Transportation and Islamic Republic of Iran*, Award No 99–245–2 (December 27, 1983) at 9–10, reprinted in 4 Iran-US CTR 263, 268 (1983-III):

The Claimant asserts that it is entitled to its lost profits in the amount of U.S. $1,427,608 on the two sales at issue in this case under the theory that it is a "lost volume" seller, that is, a seller whose capacity to sell exceeded the available market and who would have sold other, identical machines to the buyers who eventually bought the machines produced under the purchase orders breached by MORT. The argument is that such a seller would not be made whole merely by being compensated for any losses on resale and for incidental expenses or other damages, because its profits for the year would have been diminished by the profits on the one sale it had lost. While the Tribunal understands that argument, its application to the Claimant's case raises some difficult problems, including those of proof, and the burden of proving entitlement to lost profits as a lost-volume seller is on the Claimant. *See*, Article 24, paragraph 1 of the Tribunal Rules; J White & R Summers, *Uniform Commercial Code* section 7–13 (2d ed. 1980); Harris, "A Radical Restatement of the Law of Seller's Damages," 18 *Stanford Law Review* 66, 81 (1965).

Schering Corp and *Islamic Republic of Iran*, Award No 122– 38–3 (April 16, 1984) at 12–13, reprinted in 5 Iran-US CTR 361, 367–68 (1984-I):

In addition to the two drafts now dealt with, Claimant asserts that Bank Markazi rejected several additional drafts from Schering's Plough Division for at least U.S. $1,195,657,70, all of these drafts allegedly relating to purchase of raw materials from Essex and Schering's Plough Division. Respondent denies that Bank Markazi ever received requests for permission to have these additional drafts paid. In support of its allegations with regard to these drafts, Claimant relies on an affidavit by the Controller of Schering-Iran at the relevant time, Mr. Browning; two internal company memos of 10 and 14 December 1979 signed by Mr. Browning; and a chart of intercompany payables also drawn up by Mr. Browning. However, neither the request for permission, nor any bank correspondence or other similar documents reflecting the decisions allegedly taken by Bank Markazi with regard to the additional drafts have been submitted. In view of this, the Tribunal does not consider it clear from the evidence that requests for permission to transfer payments were submitted to Bank Markazi but were not dealt with or were rejected, by that bank—let alone which were the grounds for such rejections. The conclusion must therefore be that there is insufficient ground for holding the Government of Iran liable for any action or omission by Bank Markazi with regard to the intercompany debts now discussed.

Schering Corp and *Islamic Republic of Iran*, Award No 122–38–3 (April 16, 1984), Dissenting Opinion of Richard M Mosk (April 18, 1984) at 5, reprinted in 5 Iran-US CTR 374, 376 (1984-I):

The material submitted by Claimant at least constitutes *prima facie* evidence that the drafts were submitted. Claimant explained that the Workers' Council prevented Claimant from obtaining more evidence in Iran. A mere assertion that the drafts were not received cannot be deemed to be an adequate rebuttal. Indeed, the relevant Iranian banks should have records listing the submissions of drafts for foreign exchange transfers during the period in question; yet, they failed to produce them. Such records would likely indicate if the drafts in question were submitted or not.

George W Drucker Jr and *Foreign Transaction Co*, Case No 121, Chamber Two, Order of May 8, 1984:

The Tribunal notes the absence of evidence supporting Claimant's ownership and control of South Gulf Trading and Shipping Company Ltd. The Tribunal further notes Claimant's explanation as to its inability to adduce such evidence. In view of the place of incorporation of the Company, the Tribunal believes that the Claimant should provide further explanation as to why evidence of ownership of the Company cannot be provided.

The Claimant is hereby ordered to provide such explanations no later than 1 June 1984.

RJ Reynolds Tobacco Co and *Islamic Republic of Iran, Iranian Tobacco Company*, Award No 145–35–3 (August 6, 1984) at 17, reprinted in 7 Iran-US CTR 181, 190 (1984-III):

It has not been alleged that ITC objected within a reasonable time period to Reynolds' statement of account of 31 October 1979 or to the subsequent invoice of 9 November 1979. In fact, there is no evidence that these specific amounts were disputed until Claimant indicated that it intended to bring this claim before the Tribunal. In view of this, the burden is now on ITC to demonstrate any facts supporting its contention that U.S. $1,886,461.43 should be deducted from Claimant's claim. ITC, however, has not offered sufficient evidence on this point. See *Time Inc* and *Islamic Republic of Iran et al*, Award No 139–166–2 (29 June 1984).

Time, Inc and *Islamic Republic of Iran*, Award No 139–166–2 (June 22, 1984) at 4–5, reprinted in 7 Iran-US CTR 8, 10–11 (1984-III):

The evidence in this case indicated that the invoices covering the months of July through November 1978 were approved by Danesheh Now with certain minor adjustments. The approved total of those five invoices was U.S. $235,047. This total was not, however, paid, apparently initially because of disruption of banking services caused by the Iranian revolution and then by a suspension of payment instructions on 10 March 1979 by the new management of Danesheh Now installed following the revolution. The approval of these invoices in the total amount noted above by the appropriate officials of Danesheh Now establishes a *prima facie* claim for that amount. In the absence of persuasive evidence that such approval was erroneous, the Tribunal holds that the claim for these invoices is valid and that the Respondent, Danesheh Now, therefore owes the Claimant U.S. $235,047.

Howard Needles Tammen & Bergendoff and *Islamic Republic of Iran*, Award No 244–68–2 (August 8, 1986), reprinted in 11 Iran-US CTR 302, 327 (1986-II):

> 92. MORT objects to a sum of 238,080 Rials included in this invoice dated 23 May 1979, allegedly representing the salary and multiplier charges relating to one Gilian Ajanasian. MORT contends he was no longer employed during the period represented by the invoice.
> 93. The Claimant asserts that it no longer possesses a copy of the backup documentation submitted to MORT with Invoice No 53. The Claimant contends that, as MORT has failed to submit copies of this documentation or other evidence in support of its position, its defence must fail.
> 94. The evidence indicates that after receiving the invoice MORT simply disapproved an amount for salaries without offering any explanation. MORT apparently did not notify the Claimant of the reason for its action until filing its Rejoinder with the Tribunal on 30 December 1982. Having delayed over three years in detailing its objection to a particular invoice item, MORT bears the burden of proving its justification. Having submitted neither the invoice backup documentation nor other evidence in support of its contention, MORT's defence must fail. Article 24, paragraph 1, of the [1983] Tribunal Rules. *See* also D Sandifer, *Evidence Before International Tribunals* 127 (rev. ed 1975). Therefore, the Tribunal finds that the amount objected to in Invoice No 53, totalling 238,080 Rials, is payable.

Arthur Young & Co and *Islamic Republic of Iran*, Award No 338–484–1 (November 30, 1987), reprinted in 17 Iran-US CTR 245, 262–63 (1987-IV):

> 73. It is not disputed that TCI, initially, reimbursed the Claimant for social security premiums paid for employees working on the TCI contract. TCI argues that former TCI officials made these reimbursements erroneously. It now raises a Counterclaim for repayment of those reimbursements made in the amount of 3,551,700 Rials.
> 74. As stated in Article 24, paragraph l of the [1983] Tribunal Rules, TCI has the burden of proving the facts relied on that the Claimant was, in fact, not entitled to the reimbursements.
> 75. TCI, in principle, is bound by acts of its former officials, and the very fact that they made payments strongly suggests that the payments were made pursuant to an agreement between the Parties. The Respondent TCI, in any event, did not offer any evidence to support the allegation that its former officials acted erroneously. Consequently, the Counterclaim is dismissed for lack of evidence.

Leonard and Mavis Daley, a claim less than US $250,000 presented by United States of America and *Islamic Republic of Iran*, Award No 360–10514–1 (April 20, 1988), reprinted in 18 Iran-US CTR 232, 242 (1988-I):

> 33. As to the events which are alleged to have preceded Mr. and Mrs. Daley's departure from Mehrabad Airport on 25 June 1979, Mr. Daley's evidence is detailed and convincing, though uncorroborated. The Tribunal is mindful, however, of the obvious difficulty in obtaining corroborative evidence from those who might have witnessed the events described.

Reza Said Malek and *Islamic Republic of Iran*, Award No 534–193–3 (August 11, 1992), reprinted in 28 Iran-US CTR 246, 287–88, 291–92 (1992):

> 111. That being the case, the Tribunal believes the Claim for the Shemiran Properties is best decided by reference to Article 24, paragraph I of the [1983] Tribunal Rules according to which "[e]ach party shall have the burden of proving the facts relied on to support his claim of defence." It goes without saying that it is the Claimant who carries the initial burden of proving the facts upon which he relies. There is a point, however, at which the Claimant may be considered to have made a sufficient showing to shift the burden of proof to the Respondent.

112. In considering whether the Parties have met their respective burdens of proof, the Tribunal is guided by the reflections of the late Professor Virally, former Member of the Tribunal and Chairman of Chamber Three as reflected in *W. Jack Buckamier* and *Islamic Republic of Iran, et al.*, Award No 528–941–3 para 67 (6 Mar 1992), reprinted in 28 Iran-U.S. C.T.R.

...

123. On balance, the Tribunal believes that the deficiencies in the Claimant's presentation concerning the date on which the Claim arose—an issue, which, in light of the jurisdictional parameters laid down in the Partial Award, is central to this Case—are too important to accept that the burden of proof with regard to the issue of whether the Parental Home was unreasonably interfered with between 5 November 1980 and 19 January 1981 has shifted to the Respondent. The Tribunal, therefore, believes that the Claim for the interest in the Parental Home also should be denied for lack of jurisdiction.

Abrahim Rahman Golshani and *Islamic Republic of Iran*, Award No 546–812–3 (March 2, 1993), reprinted in 29 Iran-US CTR 78, 93, 116 (1993):

49. The Tribunal believes that the analysis of the distribution of the burden of proof in this Case should be centered around Article 24, paragraph 1 of The [1983] Tribunal Rules which states that "[e]ach party shall have the burden of proving the facts relied on to support his claim or defence." It was the Respondent who, at one point during the proceedings in the Case, raised the defence that the Deed is a forgery. Specifically, the Respondent has contended that the Deed, dated 15 August 1978, was in fact fabricated in 1982. Having made that factual allegation, the Respondent has the Burden of proving it. However, the Tribunal need only concern itself with the question whether the Respondent has met that burden if the Claimant has submitted a document inspiring a minimally sufficient degree of confidence in its authenticity. It is therefore up to the Claimant first to demonstrate *prima facie* that the Deed is authentic.

...

122. Taking into account all the considerations expressed in the foregoing, including TRC's statements made during the Paris Litigation, the Tribunal believes that the Deed and the affidavits of its signatories do not inspire the minimal degree of confidence in the Deed's authenticity required to shift the burden of proof to the Respondent. The Tribunal thus decided that the Claimant's presentation does not make out a *prima facie* case of authenticity and that, consequently, it need not address the question whether the Respondent has met is burden of proving that the Deed is a forgery. In view of this determination, the Claim is dismissed for lack of proof of ownership.

Dadras Intl, et al and *Islamic Republic of Iran,* et al, Award No 567–213/215–3 (November 7, 1995), reprinted in 31 Iran-US CTR 127, 162 (1995) (footnotes omitted):

B The Standard of Proof

123. In these Cases, the Tribunal is confronted with allegations of forgery that, because of their implications of fraudulent conduct and intent to deceive, are particularly grave. The Tribunal has considered whether the nature of the allegation of forgery is such that it requires the application of a standard of proof greater than the customary civil standard of "preponderance of the evidence." Support for the view that a higher standard is required may be found in American law and English law, both of which apply heightened proof requirements to allegations of fraudulent behavior. In American law the burden imposed is described as "clear and convincing" evidence, and English law speaks of a flexible civil standard that raises the burden of proof where the commission of a fraud or a crime is alleged in civil proceedings.

124. The allegations of forgery in these Cases seem to the Tribunal to be of a character that requires an enhanced standard of proof. Consistent with its past practice, the

Tribunal therefore holds that the allegation of forgery must be proved with a higher degree of probability than other allegations in these Cases. *See Oil Field of Texas, Inc* and *Government of Islamic Republic of Iran, et al.*, Award No 258–43–1 (8 October 1986), reprinted in 12 Iran-U.S. C.T.R. 308, 315 (holding that alleged bribery would not be established if, on the evidence presented, "reasonable doubts remain"). The minimum quantum of evidence that will be required to satisfy the Tribunal may be described as "clear and convincing evidence," although the Tribunal deems that precise terminology less important than the enhanced proof requirement that it expresses.

Vera-Jo Miller Aryeh, et al and *Islamic Republic of Iran*, Award No 581–842/843/844–1 (May 22, 1997), reprinted in 33 Iran-US CTR 272, 316–17 (1997) (footnote omitted):

157. The Tribunal notes that the basic rule on the allocation of the burden of proof is expressed in Article 24, paragraph 1, of the [1983] Tribunal Rules which states that "[e]ach party shall have the burden of proving the facts relied on to support his claim or defence." Further, as described by Sandifer in his work on the practice of international tribunals:

> [t]he broad basic rule of burden of proof adopted, in general, by international tribunals resembles the civil law rule and may be simply stated: that the burden of proof rests upon him who asserts the affirmative of a proposition that if not substantiated will result in a decision adverse to his contention. This burden may rest on the defendant, if there be a defendant, equally with the plaintiff, as the former may incur the burden of substantiating any proposition he asserts in answer to the allegations of the plaintiff.

158. In the present Cases, it was the Respondent who raised the defence that some of the Claimants' documents have been forged. Therefore, the burden of proving that a forgery was committed falls on the Respondent.

159. As was the case in *Dadras International, et al* and *Islamic Republic of Iran, et al*, Award No 567–213/215–3 (7 Nov. 1995), reprinted in 31 Iran-US CTR 127 ("*Dadras*"), the Tribunal, in the present Cases, is confronted with allegations of forgery that are particularly grave, because of their implications of fraudulent conduct and intent to deceive. The Tribunal considers that the allegations of forgery in these Cases are of a character that requires an enhanced standard of proof. Therefore, consistent with its past practice, the Tribunal holds that the allegation of forgery must be proven with a higher degree of probability than other allegations in these Cases. *See,* e.g. Dadras, supra, para 124. The proper standard of proof, as articulated in *Dadras*, was that of "clear and convincing evidence." *Id.* This heightened standard of proof was first propounded in *Oil Field of Texas, Inc* and *Government of Islamic Republic of Iran, et al*, Award No 258–43–1, para 25 (8 Oct 1986), *reprinted in* 12 Iran-U.S. C.T.R. 308, 315.

Frederica Lincoln Riahi and *Islamic Republic of Iran*, Award No 600–485–1 (February 27, 2003), Concurring and Dissenting Opinion of Judge Charles N Brower (February 27, 2003) (footnotes omitted):

3. Second, the Award requires the Claimant to "prov[e] the facts relied on to support [her] claim," as required by Article 24(1) of the [1983] Tribunal Rules, not just by a "convincing" preponderance of the evidence ("it is more likely than not"), which is the accepted norm, but effectively "beyond a reasonable doubt," i.e. the very high standard for securing criminal convictions in common law jurisdictions. This is glaringly evident from the fact that with the exception of one expropriated foal ($2,800 awarded) and one expropriated used Toyota automobile ($7,351 awarded) the Claimant has recovered here only to the extent of properties that the Respondent ultimately conceded in the face of overwhelming evidence that she indeed owned, or, in one case (Khoshkeh), as to which the Respondent's own evidence included, as it turned out, conclusive documentary proof of her ownership (e.g. authentic public records). *See* Award, paras 78, 82, 89, 118 and 179.

As Bin Cheng notes, however:

[W]hen the claimant has established a prima facie case and the respondent has afforded no evidence in rebuttal the latter may not insist that the former pile up evidence to establish its allegations beyond a reasonable doubt without pointing out some reason for doubting.

Or, as Judge Azevedo stated in his Dissenting Opinion in the Corfu Channel Case:

It would be going too far for an international court to insist on direct and visual evidence and to refuse to admit, after reflection, a reasonable amount of human presumptions with a view to reaching that state of moral, human certainty with which, despite the risk of occasional errors, a court of justice must be content.

In my opinion the Tribunal in the instant Case has gone far beyond "too far."

...

2. Burden of Proof
   18. It is axiomatic that the burden of proving a claim lies with the party presenting it. This principle is enshrined in Article 24(1) of the [1983] Tribunal Rules, providing that each party shall have the burden of proving the facts relied upon to establish its claim or defence. Nevertheless, the Tribunal must take into consideration the difficulties faced by claimants presenting expropriation claims. This is particularly so for an individual claimant, such as the one presenting this Case, who was forced to leave Iran with only a few suitcases and, unlike multinational corporate claimants, was not in the practice of sending copies of relevant documents to an office outside of Iran. As stated in the Tribunal's award in *Sola Tiles*, "the Tribunal must be prepared to take some account of the disadvantages suffered by the Claimant, namely its lack of access to detailed documentation, as an inevitable consequence of the circumstances in which the expropriation took place."
   19. Professor Virally addressed the predicament faced by claimants before the Tribunal in a memorandum excerpted in the *Buckamier* award: [Extracts of Professor Virally's memorandum are omitted here, but are reprinted below, section 2(D)(5) on the admissibility, relevance, and materiality of evidence.]
   20. The Claimant in this Case has made a valiant effort to produce documents, and, applying the standard just recited, has been to a large extent successful in that effort. The Tribunal failed to bear this in mind properly when it considered the sufficiency of the Claimant's evidence. Moreover, as noted just below, her Case is definitively established by inferences that the Tribunal not only was permitted to make, but was required to make, given the Respondent's repeated refusal to produce key documents in the face of successive Tribunal Orders to do so, whose existence in the Respondent's possession, custody and control could not be, and was not, denied and indeed was confirmed.

(2) Tribunal Rules (1983), Article 24(2)—Summary of evidence

Brown & Root, Inc and *Islamic Republic of Iran*, Case No 432, Chamber One, Order of December 4, 1987:

Each Party shall file simultaneously by 1 March 1988 with the Tribunal copies of any remaining written evidence on which it will seek to rely together with a list of all documentary evidence submitted by it in this Case and the location in the record (by tab or exhibit number) of each such document. By the same date each Party may file a Hearing Memorial explaining the evidence and summarizing the issues in the Case.

Each Party shall file simultaneously by 1 June 1988 copies of any documentary evidence on which it will seek to rely in rebuttal of previously presented evidence together with a supplemental list of such rebuttal evidence and the location of each such document in the record.

In this context the Parties should bear in mind that the following considerations will apply once the Tribunal has scheduled a Hearing.
1. The Tribunal will not permit the introduction of new documents in evidence prior to the Hearing unless it finds that this is justified by exceptional circumstances and unless such documents are filed not later than two months before the Hearing.

> 2. At the Hearing, any Party is free to make any arguments it wishes, but new documents may not be introduced in evidence unless the Tribunal so permits, which permission will not normally be granted except for evidence in rebuttal of evidence introduced in the Hearing.
>
> The guidelines for the translation of documentary evidence are attached to this Order.

(3) Tribunal Rules (1983), Article 24(3)—Document production

Dresser Industries, Inc and *Islamic Republic of Iran and SSK Magcobar Iran*, Case Nos 107, 109 and 110, Chamber Three, Order of January 27, 1983:

> A Pre-hearing Conference having been held in the above cases on 12 January 1983, the Tribunal orders as follows:
>
> 1. On or before August 27, 1983 each of the Parties shall file with the Tribunal legible copies of all documents upon which it intends to rely in support of its case.
> 2. In addition to the above requirement, the Respondents shall produce the following documents:
>   (a) all general ledgers and subledger books of S.S.K. Magcobar Iran for fiscal years 1977 through 1980, inclusive;
>   (b) all balance sheets and audit reports of or concerning S.S.K. Magcobar Iran for the 1979 and 1980 fiscal years;
>   (c) all bank statements and deposit reports for S.S.K. Magcobar Iran for the fiscal years 1977 through 1980, inclusive;
>   (d) any and all asset account prepared for fiscal years 1977 through 1980, inclusive.
>
> If any of the above materials are in the possession of Respondent S.S.K. Magcobar, said Respondent shall either make the originals of the materials available at the Tribunal for the purpose of inspection and copying by the parties from 27 August 1983 until 27 October 1983 or shall file two copies of each item with the Tribunal by 27 June 1983.
>
> If any of the above materials are in the possession of the Respondent Government of the Islamic Republic of Iran or in the possession of any other person or entity as the result of judicial process of any court of Iran, the Government of the Islamic Republic of Iran shall either make the originals of the materials available at the Tribunal for the purpose of inspection and copying by the Parties from 27 August 1983 to 27 October 1983 or shall file two copies of each item with the Tribunal by 27 June 1983.

MCA Inc and *Islamic Republic of Iran*, Case No 768, Chamber Two, Order of October 6, 1983:

> The Tribunal notes that the Claimant has filed on 15 September 1983 a document requesting, inter alia, the production of certain documents by the Respondents, and more time to continue its search for materials, as well as to amplify and clarify its claim, as directed by the order of 19 July 1983.
>
> Failing any indication by the Claimant as to which documents precisely it wishes to be produced, and failing any information to the Tribunal as to which steps were taken by the Claimant itself to acquire the necessary materials, the Tribunal cannot, at present, make any Order as requested by the Claimant.

Ministry of National Defence of the Islamic Republic of Iran and *Department of Defense of the United States of America*, Case No B1, Full Tribunal, Order of November 18, 1983, reprinted in 4 Iran-US CTR 57, 58 (1983-III):

> (4) With respect to the Counterclaim, the Respondent has requested, pursuant to Article 24, paragraph 3, and Article 26 of the [1983] Tribunal Rules that the Tribunal order the Claimant to render a full and immediate accounting with respect to all classified military equipment and related classified information acquired by Iran under the FMS program. The Tribunal is not

convinced that the requested measures are warranted at the present stage of the proceedings, either under Article 24 paragraph 3, or Article 26 of the [1983] Tribunal Rules.
The Representative of the United States may return to this matter at any time.

Weatherford Intl Inc and *Islamic Republic of Iran*, Case No 305, Chamber Two, Order of February 15, 1985:

Noting Respondent National Iranian Oil Company's comments concerning its difficulties in gaining access to certain documents, the Tribunal wishes to point out that it could require either Party to produce documents, if it deems this necessary, in accordance with Article 24 paragraph 3 of the [1983] Tribunal Rules.

If the National Iranian Oil Company has any specific request in this regard, it should file such request not later than 31 March 1985.

INA Corp and *Islamic Republic of Iran*, Award No 184–161–1 (August 12, 1985) at 14, reprinted in 8 Iran-US CTR 373, 382 (1985-I) (footnote omitted):

The report's numerous references to special rules and directives of CLI also make it impossible for the Tribunal to judge the validity of the valuation techniques used. The Respondent has furnished neither the texts of such rules and directives nor the underlying documents, although it was ordered to do so. The Respondent's attempt to excuse its noncompliance with the Tribunal's Order by merely stating that the documents were "voluminous" is not convincing. The Respondent did not raise this asserted excuse until the hearing, long after the date for submission of these materials had passed; even then, the Respondent gave no indication of the actual amounts of material involved or any description of the alleged problems involved which prevented submission of the materials by the Respondent or their Inspection by INA. In assessing the evidentiary weight of the Amin report, the Tribunal must draw negative inferences from the Respondents failure to submit the documents which it was ordered to produce. In sum, the Amin report is so qualified and limited, and so influenced by unexplained, specially adopted (and not generally accepted) accounting techniques, that it cannot be considered the value of Shargh at the time of nationalisation.

Offshore Co and *National Iranian Oil Co*, Case No 133, Chamber Two, Order of June 26, 1986:

The Tribunal notes Respondent National Iranian Oil Company's submission of 10 June 1986, requesting the Tribunal to direct the Claimant to produce certain documents.

The Tribunal further notes Claimant's letter of 20 June 1986 objecting to such request and stating that "it is willing to make available to NIOC for inspection . . . the original inventory and equipment records . . . at Offshore's premises in Houston."

The Tribunal wishes to point out that the Party who carries the burden of proof determines at its discretion what evidence it wishes to submit in support of its Claim.

It is normally not up to the Tribunal to give directions to any of the Parties regarding the evidence to be submitted by them.

1. In view thereof, the Tribunal denies Respondent National Iranian Oil Company's request for the production of certain documents by the Claimant. However, if Respondent NIOC wishes to take advantage of the Claimant's offer, any report in connection with its inspection of the above mentioned original inventory and equipment records shall be filed not later than August 26, 1986.
2. In view of the filing date of this Order, the time for Respondent NIOC to file its Rebuttal evidence and brief, due on June 29, 1986, is hereby extended to July 15, 1986. As stated in the Tribunal's Order of April 7, 1986, no further extension shall be granted. Therefore, if the new filing authorized by the present Order is made, it shall be limited to the expert's report.
3. The Tribunal intends to schedule a Hearing in this Case during the first half of 1987.

RPM Carlson and *Islamic Republic of Iran*, Case No 248, Chamber One, Order of August 12, 1986:

> Reference is made to the Tribunal's Order of 7 June 1984 and to the documents subsequently filed by the Parties. In view of the fact that the Claimant has requested a hearing on the issues of *locus standi* and jurisdiction described in paragraph 3 of the Order referred to, the Tribunal decides that all such issues shall be joined to the merits of the Case.
>
> It remains open to the Claimant to establish jurisdiction either directly or indirectly over any part of the claim.
>
> The Respondents are requested to file a Rejoinder on the merits by 31 October 1986 including, in particular, a detailed clarification of the counterclaims raised by Melli Industrial Group.
>
> As to the Claimant's Motion for Production of Documents, filed on 30 May 1983 and supplemented by a further filing on 12 June 1984, the Tribunal notes from statements made by the respective Parties at the prehearing conference that the Respondents are prepared to make available for inspection by the claimant at the Tribunal's Registry, the share registers described in paragraph I of the Motion, and also such of the documents itemised in paragraphs 2 and 3 as pertain to the registration, transfer or ownership of shares in the companies enumerated in that Motion.
>
> With regard to the documents described in paragraphs 4, 5, 6, 7 and 8 to 15 inclusive, the Respondents are requested to include in the Rejoinder their comments as to the availability and relevance of such documents.
>
> The Claimant is requested to inform the Tribunal by 30 January 1987 whether, in the light of the Rejoinder, he wishes to maintain his request for production in respect of the documents described in paragraphs 4, 5, 6, 7 and 8 to 15 inclusive of the Motion.

Intl Systems & Controls and *National Iranian Gas Co*, Case No 494, Chamber Three, Order of December 24, 1986:

> Reference is made to the submission filed on 2 December 1986 in which the Agent of the Government of the Islamic Republic of Iran requested the Tribunal to order the Claimant to produce a copy of the contract, dated 15 April 1985 and referred to in Document No 50, filed on 30 June 1986 by which the Claimant assigned its Claim to Geogas Inc
>
> The Tribunal notes that the above-mentioned assignment occurred after 19 January 1981 and therefore has no bearing on the Claimant's locus standi, according to Article VII, paragraph 2, of the Claims Settlement Declaration. Consequently, the request is denied.

Vera-Jo Miller on her own behalf, on behalf of Laura Aryeh, on behalf of JM Aryeh and *Islamic Republic of Iran*, Case No 842, 843 and 844, Chamber One, Order of March 6, 1992:

> On 15 November 1991, the Claimant filed a submission entitled "Request for Production of Documents." On 21 February 1992, the Respondent filed its comments on that request. Having regard to the Respondent's submission and in view of the fact that the record does not demonstrate what specific efforts, if any, the Claimant has made to obtain the documents through other sources, the Tribunal finds the Claimant's request inadmissible.

Brown & Root, Inc and *Islamic Republic of Iran*, Case No 432, Chamber One, Order of January 4, 1993:

> This order is a response to the Respondents' request of 28 April 1992 and the Parties' subsequent comments, to the Respondents' request of 7 August 1992 and the Claimants' subsequent comments, and to the Respondents' requests of 16 October 1992 and of 16 December 1992.
>
> 1. On April 28, 1992, the Respondents filed a letter in which they requested the production of various documents. The Respondents state that their auditors have informed them that they

need the documents requested in their submission "in order to carry out a general and precise audit of the Chahbaha and Bandar projects." The Respondents also contend that the Claimants have conceded the necessity of such an audit.

2. On June 9, 1992, the Claimants filed submission entitled "Claimants' Comments in Response to Respondents' Request for Production of Documents for Auditing" in which they advance several arguments for denying the Respondents' request. The Claimants state that to the extent that the documentation requested by the Respondents is in the possession of the Claimants, it is contained in hundreds of boxes located in Houston, Texas and can only be procured with the expenditure of an enormous amount of time and at great cost to the Claimants. Further the Claimants contend that the Respondents' request for documents at this stage of the proceedings is "unreasonable, unnecessary and too late."

3. Having noted the positions taken up by the Parties, the Tribunal now decides the Respondents' request of April 28, 1992. Considering the circumstances as a whole, the Tribunal does not deem it appropriate to require the Claimants to produce the documents requested by the Respondents. However, the Tribunal points out that this decision is without prejudice to the Tribunal, if and when it eventually considers the merits of the Case, weighing the evidentiary significance if any, that flows from the above-mentioned Respondents' request for production of documents and the Claimants position taken in their respective submissions.

Frederica Lincoln Riahi and *Islamic Republic of Iran*, Case No 485, Chamber One, Order of February 23, 1993:

On 12 February, 1993 the Claimant filed her "Claimant's Memorial and Request for Production of Documents" (Doc. 53) in which the Claimant on pages 54 and 55 requested the Tribunal to order the Respondent to submit the documents a) contained in the Claimant's safe deposit box at Bank Tehran, Main Office, Vali Assr Avenue Tehran, Iran, including among other things her share certificates in Rahmatabad in the summer of 1979 which were kept at Rahmatabad office in Rahmatabad farm.

The Respondent is invited to submit its comments as to whether it is possible to submit the documents, as well as copies at the minutes requested, and if so, to submit these documents by 26 April 1993.

Ouziel Aryeh, et al and *Islamic Republic of Iran*, Case Nos 839 and 840, Chamber Three, Order of January 18, 1996:

6. With respect to the Claimants' request that the Tribunal direct the Respondent to provide a written report on the current status of each of the properties that are the subject of the Claims, the Tribunal notes that this is also a late request. Furthermore, it is a request, not for a document in the possession of the Respondent, but for the preparation of a report by the Respondent. Consequently, the Tribunal finds that granting this request would impose an improper and late burden on the Respondent and be likely to disrupt the orderly conduct of the Tribunal's proceedings. The Tribunal therefore declines to grant the Claimant's request that it direct the Respondent to provide such a report.

Islamic Republic of Iran and *United States of America*, Case No A/30, Full Tribunal, Order of November 4, 1999:

1. On 26 January 1998, in Document 22, Iran requested the Tribunal to issue an Order to the United States to produce the "classified Schedule of Authorization" incorporated into the Intelligence Authorization Act for Fiscal Year 1996 by Section 102 of that Act. Iran argued that the document was relevant to and necessary for its claim and that the document was available to the United States and to the United States alone.

2. On 27 April 1998, in Document 28, the United States asserted that the request was without merit and asked that it be denied. The United States asserted . . . that the document was a

privileged, national security document. . . . The United States stated that, in fact, it would not be able to produce the document requested by Iran and that its refusal should not lead to the drawing of any adverse inference by the Tribunal.

...

5. In response to these pleadings, the Tribunal decides as follows:
   a. Iran's request that the Tribunal issue an order requesting production of that part of the Schedule of Authorizations that relates to Iran is a request within the jurisdiction of the Tribunal.
   b. Nevertheless, the statement by the United States that it could not produce the Schedule or any part of the Schedule relating to Iran, even if the Tribunal should so request, makes it unnecessary for the Tribunal to issue any order pursuant to Iran's request and raises the consequent question whether it would be appropriate for the Tribunal to draw any adverse inference and, if so, the nature of any such inference.
   c. The Parties are requested to address those questions of adverse inference in their further pleadings.

Frederica Lincoln Riahi and *Government of the Islamic Republic of Iran*, Award No 600–485–1 (February 27, 2003), Concurring and Dissenting Opinion of Judge Charles N Brower (February 27, 2003) (footnotes omitted):

3. Drawing Adverse Inferences
   a) The Respondent's repeated and express refusal to comply with document production orders

21. Pursuant to the Claimant's multiple requests, the Tribunal repeatedly has ordered the Respondent to produce various documents relevant to the Claimant's ownership interests in the companies at issue in this Case, or to explain its failure to do so. These documents include, *inter alia*, minutes of shareholders' and Board of Directors' meetings, share registers, registration files and financial documents. The Respondent has clearly and egregiously failed to produce the vast majority of these documents—which the Claimant believes would substantiate her Claim—despite its obligation to do so. The Tribunal itself acknowledged the Respondent's failure in this regard. In its final Order requiring production, dated 18 May 1995, the Tribunal determined that it was not satisfied that the Respondent had complied with its previous document production Orders. Upon receiving the Respondent's cursory response, the Tribunal concluded that the determination of whether the Respondent had complied with its document production Orders would be made at a later date. In its present Award, the Tribunal should have made that determination and generally confirmed as a fact its earlier intimation that the Respondent has failed to comply with its Orders. As a result of this failure, the Tribunal should have drawn inferences adverse to the Respondent and assumed that the requested documents, if submitted, would have substantiated the Claimant's assertions. Specifically, the Claimant should not have been faulted when the evidence offered in support of certain aspects of her Claim was sparse, and instead the Tribunal should have inferred that the documents withheld by the Respondent would have established further the Claimant's position.

...

   b) The Tribunal's authority to draw adverse inferences

30. The Tribunal is empowered to draw adverse inferences due to the non-production of documents, and repeatedly has done so. Under the Tribunal's jurisprudence, several requirements must be met in order to draw an adverse inference. First, the requested documents must be relevant and material to the proceedings. This has also been phrased as requiring them to be "essential" to the resolution of the case. The documents requested in this Case clearly are relevant to the Claim, as the Tribunal's Orders of 18 November 1994 and 18 May 1995 necessarily found. Second, the Tribunal must be convinced that the requested documents are at the disposal of the requested party. In this Case, the Respondent has never

denied its possession, custody or control of the bulk of the requested documents. To the contrary, in asserting that they are publicly available documents accessible to the Claimant (which she has denied in detail), the Respondent necessarily admits their availability to it. The highly selective submission by the Respondent of some of the documents ordered to be produced, e.g. the share register of Tarvandan, and its express reliance in its Hearing Memorial and Evidence on extensive financial documentation of various companies graphically confirm that it does have access to the types of documents ordered produced. Third, the claim must otherwise appear to be substantial, meaning that the claimant should have made out a prima facie case. The Claimant clearly has established a prima facie case that she owned the property that is the subject of her Claim and that the property was expropriated by the Respondent. Fourth, the party failing to produce must have offered no satisfactory explanation for such failure. This is an essential requirement, as the justification for drawing an adverse inference is that a party possessing evidence that supports its position, or which disproves that of its opponent, will either submit that evidence upon being so ordered or provide a reasonable explanation for its failure to do so. As discussed, the Respondent has not justified its failure to produce the requested documents. Therefore, all of the requirements for drawing adverse inferences have been met in this Case and the Tribunal should have drawn appropriate inferences. Such adverse inferences must be taken into account when examining the amount and sort of evidence submitted by the Claimant and the value given to individual pieces of evidence, such as Mr. Riahi's diary and ledger and Mr. and Mrs. Riahi's affidavits.

(4) Tribunal Rules (1983), Article 25(5)—Written witness statements

Thomas Earl Payne and *Islamic Republic of Iran*, Case No 335, Chamber Two, Order of December 12, 1983:

> The Tribunal notes that the Claimant has filed, on 21 November 1983, a request for instructions concerning the form of its evidence.
>
> Article 25(5) of the [1983] Tribunal Rules requires that "(e)vidence of witnesses may also be presented in the form of written statements *signed by* them" (emphasis added).
>
> For present purposes, it will be sufficient for the Claimant to file unsigned copies of the deposition transcripts it wishes to submit. However, signed copies must be filed before the file in this case is complete.

Chas T Main Intl Inc and *Khuzestan Water & Power Authority*, Case No 120, Chamber Two, Order of February 14, 1986:

> The Tribunal notes Claimant's letter of 5 February 1986 requesting certain clarifications and permission to submit additional documents. In view thereof, the Tribunal hereby orders as follows.
>
> ...
>
> 2. Claimant may submit a sworn statement by Mr. Benziger, no later than 7 March 1986, in view of Mr. Benziger's inability to attend the Hearing. This statement must be submitted in both English and Farsi.

Harris Intl Telecommunications, Inc and *Islamic Republic of Iran*, Award No 323-409-1 (November 2, 1987), reprinted in 17 Iran-US CTR 31, 52 (1987–IV):

> 75. With respect to these Affidavits, the Tribunal cannot accept as an excuse that the Claimant may have been misled by Article 25, paragraph 5, of the [1983] Tribunal Rules stating that "[e]vidence of witnesses may also be presented in the form of written statements signed by them". Affidavits constitute documentary evidence which must be submitted in accordance with the time-limits set in the Tribunal's orders so that the other Party is able to respond. Article 25, paragraph 5, merely clarifies the admissibility of affidavits of witnesses, since not all national legal systems admit such written evidence.

(5) Tribunal Rules (1983), Article 25(6)—Admissibility, relevance, materiality, and weight of the evidence

Flexi-Van Leasing, Inc and *Islamic Republic of Iran*, Case No 36, Chamber One, Order of December 20, 1982, reprinted in 1 Iran-US CTR 455 (1981–82):

> The type of evidence to be submitted by a Claimant depends on the circumstances of each particular case, as viewed by the Chamber. In this case, the evidence described below will, *prima facie*, be considered sufficient as to corporate nationality. Such evidence is in the form of documents officially filed with governmental agencies or is from an independent certified public accountant. Respondent will be free to offer rebuttal evidence. From the totality of such evidence the Chamber will draw reasonable inferences and reach conclusions as to whether the Claimant was, or was not, a national of the United States, as defined in the Declaration, during the necessary period. It is within the power of the Chamber to do this based on accepted principles of international law and also upon the Provisionally adopted [1983] Tribunal Rules which state that:
>
> The arbitral tribunal shall determine the admissibility, relevance, materiality and weight of the evidence offered.
>
> Article 25, Paragraph 6. Moreover, in view of the impracticality of any other course, this procedure is necessary to ensure that the Declaration can be carried out effectively. *See* Declaration, Article III, Paragraph 2.

Islamic Republic of Iran and *United States of America*, Case A/1 (Issues, I, III and IV), Decision of July 30, 1982 at 3, reprinted in 1 Iran-US CTR 187, 490–191 (1981–82):

> With respect to point (a), and Iran's reference to settlement negotiations held in August, 1981, a court cannot take account of that which one party proposes to another in a confidential manner in an effort to achieve a resolution of their disputes...

Woodward-Clyde Consultants and *Islamic Republic of Iran*, Award No 73–67–3 (September 2, 1983) at 15–16, reprinted in 3 Iran-US CTR 239, 248–49 (1983–II):

> To support its claim for amounts retained as security for the payment of social insurance obligations, Claimant originally referred to a telex from its Iranian accountant stating that a clearance certificate had previously been issued by the Iranian Social Insurance Organization on 17 October 1979. Subsequent to the Hearing, Claimant obtained and submitted a copy of that clearance. In support of its allegation that the Claimant continues to have outstanding social insurance payment obligations, AEOI has submitted letters from the Social Insurance Organization announcing that Claimant and Woodward Noorany owe substantial amounts as specified in the letters. No mention is made of the clearance having been granted, no reference is made to any payments having been made in the years in question and the method used to calculate the amount alleged to be due is not explained.
>
> While there is no doubt about the authenticity of either the clearance certificate presented by Claimant or the letters submitted by AEOI, they represent totally contradictory conclusions by the Social Insurance Organization which are impossible to reconcile. Given the fact that one conclusion was stated close in time to the events in issue and that the other was stated in the course of this litigation, and considering the general rule of evidence that contradictory statements of an interested party should be construed against that party, the Tribunal finds that the Claimant has obtained the clearance required by the Agreement and is entitled to payment of the amount retained under the social insurance guarantee.

United States of America and *Islamic Republic of Iran*, Case No A/16, *Bank Mellat* and *United States of America*, et al, Case Nos 582 and 591, Full Tribunal, Order of October 10, 1983:

> At the Hearing in these cases on 6–7 October 1983 Mr. Daniel Levitt, the attorney of the Government of the Islamic Republic of Iran, on behalf also of Rank Markazi Iran and Bank Mellat

informed the Tribunal that he wished to submit as evidence some documents relating to the subsequent practice in the application of paragraph 2(B) of the Undertakings. He further informed the Tribunal that these documents were not immediately available to him but that they could be submitted to the Tribunal within one week.

The Tribunal finds it important that a Party submits written evidence well in advance of a Hearing so as to allow other Parties and the Members of the Tribunal to study such evidence before the Hearing and to discuss it in the course of the Hearing. However, in view of the importance of the instant cases for a large number of other cases before the Tribunal, the Tribunal finds it appropriate to accept said evidence despite the intended late filing of it.

The Government of the Islamic Republic of Iran is permitted to submit to the Tribunal on or before 17 October 1983 the further evidence referred to at the Hearing.

The Government of the United States of America, Manufacturers Hanover Trust Co., GTE International Inc, Crocker National Bank and Harris International Telecommunications, Inc are invited to file with the Tribunal on or before 7 November 1983 any comments and rebuttal evidence that they would like to submit in respect of new evidence provided by the Government of the Islamic Republic of Iran.

Ultrasystems Inc and *Islamic Republic of Iran*, Award No 89–84–3 (December 7, 1983) at 2–3, reprinted in 4 Iran-US CTR 77, 78 (1983–III):

Iran submitted on 25 April 1983, *inter alia*, a Statement by Bank Tejarat dated 11 April 1983 concerning the movements on Ultrasystems' account with that bank from 1 August 1978 to 31 March 1979 and a bank statement with regard to Isiran's bank account. Isiran further submitted photocopies of a great number of cheques drawn on Ultrasystem's account between the middle of October and the end of November 1978 and bearing the signature of Mr. Fred C. Feupel, Ultrasystems' principal representative in Iran. Although it must be noted that, pursuant to the Tribunal's pre-hearing order, all evidence that the parties wished to rely on should have been submitted prior to the Hearing, the Tribunal decides in this case to admit this material as supporting evidence.

INA Corp and *Islamic Republic of Iran*, Award No 184–61–1 (August 13, 1985) at 6, reprinted in 8 Iran-US CTR 373, 377 (1985–I):

INA argues that the Tribunal has been furnished with insufficient information as to the basis of the Amin valuation, the principles on which it was undertaken and the documents and data on which it was based, for it to be accorded any evidential value. The Tribunal's Order of 21 January 1983 required production, *inter alia*, of the material which had been made available to Amin & Co., but no such material was filed and the Respondent contended at the hearing that it was too voluminous to be conveniently assembled. The Tribunal decided to admit the Amin Report as evidence but to take account of the lack of supporting documentation in assessing the evidential weight to be accorded to it.

Sylvania Technical Systems Inc and *Islamic Republic of Iran*, Award No 180–64–1 (June 27, 1985) at 3, reprinted in 8 Iran-US CTR 298, 300 (1985–I):

Third, the Respondent has objected on grounds of irrelevance and prejudice to the filing by the Claimant of copies of a number of newspaper and magazine articles submitted as Exhibit 1 in the Claimant's Documentary Evidence filed on 3 January 1984. The Tribunal finds no need to exclude this evidence. As with any evidence, the Tribunal is able to assess its bearing on the case as well as its evidentiary value.

Chas T Main Intl, Inc and *Khuzestan Water & Power Utility*, Case No 120, Order of February 14, 1986:

Claimant's request to submit minutes of witness testimony heard by the Experts in Boston and/or statements of these witnesses is denied. The Tribunal decides that notes taken by assistant clerks of testimony given by witnesses before the Experts cannot be considered appropriate evidence. As to the submission of statements by the witnesses themselves, Claimant has offered no justification or excuse for its delay in submitting such statements. In view of the potential prejudice to respondents, the Tribunal cannot accept them at this late stage in the proceedings without such justification.

Islamic Republic of Iran and *United States of America*, Case No A/20, Decision No DEC 45-A20-FT (July 10, 1986), reprinted in 11 Iran-US CTR 271, 274 (1986–II):

10. Insofar as Iran's case might be interpreted as a request that the Full Tribunal lay down a uniform rule of evidence applicable to the establishment of corporate nationality, the Tribunal holds that the request does not pose a question concerning the interpretation or application of the Declaration. The questions raised by Iran relate to burden of proof, to the evidence required to establish to the satisfaction of the Tribunal the existence of the facts on which its jurisdiction is based, and to the weighing of such evidence by the Tribunal. These issues are obviously not questions concerning the interpretation or application of the Declaration, but, rather, relate to the application of the [1983] Tribunal Rules governing burden of proof and evidence. Article 24, paragraph 1, of the [1983] Tribunal Rules provides that "[e]ach party shall have the burden of proving the facts relied on to support his claim or defence". Article 25, paragraph 6, states that "[t]he arbitral tribunal shall determine the admissibility, relevance, materiality and weight of the evidence offered". These provisions are taken without change from the [1976] UNCITRAL Arbitration Rules, which Article III, paragraph 2, of the Declaration requires the Tribunal to follow in conducting its business, except to the extent modified by the States Parties or the Tribunal to ensure that the Declaration can be carried out effectively. Neither the Tribunal nor the States Parties have considered in necessary to modify any of these provisions. To the contrary, the Rules reflect generally accepted principles of international arbitration practice and contribute to the effective resolution of cases before the Tribunal.

Flexi-Van Leasing Inc and *Islamic Republic of Iran*, Award No 259–36–1 (October 13, 1986) at 14, 15, reprinted in 12 Iran-US CTR 335, 344–45 (1986–III):

Flexi-Van has requested that the Tribunal refuse to consider the evidence appended to the Respondent's Post Hearing Memorial. Submission of such evidence, Flexi-Van contends, was not authorized by the Tribunal, and considering it would be unfair and unwarranted in light of Tribunal practice and the Tribunal Rules of Procedure. The Government has not commented on this request.

...

The Tribunal admits all evidence submitted during the course of the proceedings since none was such as to cause any prejudice.

Sedco Inc and *National Iranian Oil Company and Islamic Republic of Iran*, Award No 309–129–3 (July 7, 1987), reprinted in 15 Iran-US CTR 23, 49 (1987–II) (footnote omitted):

75. Although for these reasons the Tribunal is persuaded that Claimant's valuation forms a more credible basis for a determination of the fair market value of the six SISA rigs than the valuation offered by NIOC, nevertheless Claimant's appraisal must be approached with some caution. The task of the Tribunal is to appraise the value of these specific rigs on the evidence before it. In that process certain inferences may of course be drawn from rig values in the drilling industry in general. One of the most important elements on which to base the value of a particular rig, however, appears to be the operating condition of that rig at the valuation date. The only one of Claimant's expert witnesses who had personal knowledge of the SISA rigs during the five years preceding the appropriation is Mr. Thorne, who stated that the rigs were maintained in "first class operating condition," consistent with SEDCO's operating philosophy and that the equipment was "top quality." Other experts who have confirmed Mr. Thorne's appraisal have based their opinion on Mr. Thorne's assessment of the operating condition of

the rigs. Their opinions on this point must be approached with the same caution as that of Mr. Thorne. Mr. Thorne is a leading officer of the Claimant company and the President of SISA. In that last capacity he was ultimately responsible for the maintenance of the rigs. Although the Tribunal in principle does not accept NIOC's objection to Claimant's experts as unreliable because of their alleged master-servant relationship with Claimant,[25] Mr. Thorne's close affiliation to Claimant and SISA could quite naturally have caused a certain subjectivity (which must be distinguished from bad faith) to taint his assessment.

...

[Footnote] 25: Refusing categorically to accept evidence from those most closely associated with the subject matter of a claim would not likely further the cause of establishing truth. The Tribunal notes that many of NIOC's evidentiary submissions were prepared by its employees as well.

Otis Elevator Co and *Islamic Republic of Iran*, Award No 304–284–2 (April 29, 1987), reprinted in 14 Iran-US CTR 283, 284, 291 (1988–I):

21. On 20 August 1986 the Claimant filed a notification of three witnesses: Mr. Jaulin, Mr. Fayek, and Mr. McGraw. Pursuant to Article 25 of the [1983] Tribunal Rules, the Claimant was required to file this notification at least thirty days before the Hearing. The Tribunal ruled that Mr. Jaulin and Mr. Fayek, both officers of Otis at the relevant times, would be permitted to give evidence but that Mr. McGraw, from Standard Research Consultants who had prepared a valuation report, could not be presented as a witness except to the extent, if any, justified in rebuttal to the presentations made by the Respondents at the Hearing. The Claimant presented only Mr. Jaulin as a witness and Mr. McGraw was called on briefly in rebuttal.

Harris Intl Telecommunications, Inc and *Islamic Republic of Iran*, Award No 323–409–1 (November 2, 1987), reprinted in 17 Iran-US CTR 31, 62–63 (1987–II) (other footnotes omitted):

f) Witnesses

107. Although refusing to admit the persons named by the Claimant in its late filing as witnesses, the Tribunal noted at the Hearing that any Party is free to choose the persons it wishes to present its case, including those not accepted by the Tribunal as witnesses and may receive information from them. See *Economy Forms Corp* and *Government of the Islamic Republic of Iran*, Award No 55–165–1 (14 June 1983). Such persons do not make the declaration that witnesses are required to make in accordance with Note 6(a) to Article 25 of the [1983] Tribunal Rules. The Tribunal, of course, may attach a different "weight" (Article 25, paragraph 6) to information provided by such persons as compared to the testimony of witnesses.

108. For the foregoing reasons, in assessing the evidence before it, the Tribunal does not consider the statements made at the Hearing on behalf of the Claimant by Mr. Stitt and Mr. Scott, who were both on the witness list, as those of witnesses, but does consider them as part of the presentation of the Case by the Claimant in the Hearing.

[Footnote] 19. However, it should be noted that in *Otis Elevator Company* and *The Islamic Republic of Iran et al.* Award No 304–284–2, para 21 (29 Apr. 1987), 14 Iran-US CTR 283 at 291 (1987–I), the Tribunal permitted two witnesses, both officers of the Claimant at the relevant times, to give evidence although the notification was filed only eighteen days before the Hearing. It did not accept the presentation of a third witness who had prepared a valuation report "except to the extent, if any, justified in rebuttal to the presentations made by the Respondents at the Hearing."

Uiterwyk Corp and *Islamic Republic of Iran*, Award No 375–381–1 (July 6, 1988), reprinted in 19 Iran-US CTR 107, 113–116 (1988–II):

28. Absent any convincing explanation by the Respondents, the Tribunal cannot accept a tactic that unveils previously-existing evidence at literally the last moments of the hearing, without

prior notice having been given that the witness would testify, without showing that the evidence is presented in rebuttal, and when the documents the witness proffered had not been included with—or even referred to in—the Respondents' various prior submissions. For procedural reasons the documents cannot therefore be accepted. It might be added, however, that, given the nature of the issue and the conflicting evidence of the Parties with respect to it, it is far from certain that the matter would be clarified by further briefing or an additional hearing. Moreover, even if the evidence sought to be offered by Mr. Paksima were admitted and believed, its principal consequence would be to reflect adversely upon the credibility of various members of the Uiterwyk family. The tribunal need not resolve this thorny issue because, as shown below, it has adequate evidence upon which to determine the issue in this Case without relying upon the affidavits or testimony of the members of the Uiterwyk family. Accordingly, the Tribunal does not consider it procedurally sound or substantively necessary to admit the late proffered evidence by both sides, or to prolong the proceedings by further briefing or an additional hearing.

29. The Tribunal therefore declines to accept the documents offered by Mr. Ali Paksima at the end of the hearing, as well as the document offered by the Claimants in response. No further briefings or oral hearings are found to be necessary.

W Jack Buckamier and *Islamic Republic of Iran*, Award No 528–94 1–3 (March 6, 1992), reprinted in 28 Iran-US CTR 53, 74–76 (1992):

67. The virtual absence of documentary support for Mr. Buckamier's claim raises the issue what the probative value is of the Claimant's affidavit. The importance of this question makes it appropriate to elaborate on the considerations the Tribunal must take into account in weighing this kind of evidence. In a memorandum dated 17 February 1988 the Tribunal's distinguished former member and Chairman of this Chamber, the late Professor Virally, expressed these considerations as follows.

The Tribunal has often been presented with notarized affidavits or oral testimony of claimants or their employees. [Rare] are the cases where such an issue does not arise. The probative value of such written or oral declarations is usually hotly debated between the parties, each of them relying on the peculiarities of its own judicial system. The U.S. parties insist that such evidence must be recognized with full probative value, as would be the case before the U.S. courts. The Iranian parties contend that such declarations are not admissible as evidence under Iranian law, because they emanate from persons whose interests are at stake in the proceedings, or who are, or were, dependent upon the claimants.

The Tribunal has, in the past, adopted a pragmatic and moderate approach towards this problem by deciding, on a case by case basis, whether the burden of proof has been properly sustained by each contending party, taking into consideration those declarations together with all other evidence submitted in the case, the particulars of the case and the attitude of both parties in the proceedings. This pragmatic approach does not always seem to have been well understood, since the same debate continues to arise, often in the same terms, in case after case

As an international Tribunal established by agreement between two sovereign States, the Tribunal cannot, in the field of evidence as in any other field, make the domestic rules or judicial practices of one party prevail over the rules and practices of the other, in so far as such rules and practices do not coincide with those generally accepted by international Tribunals. In this context, it can be observed that the declarations by the parties, or employees of the parties, in the form of notarized affidavits or oral testimony, are often submitted as evidence before such Tribunals. They are usually accepted, but, cautiously, in a manner generally comparable to the attitude of this Tribunal as just described.

It is clear that the value attributed to this kind of evidence is directly related not only to the legal and moral traditions of each country, but also to a system of sanctions in case of perjury, which can easily and promptly be put into action and is rigorous enough to deter witnesses from making false statements. Such a system does not exist within international Tribunals and recourse to the domestic courts of the witness or affiant by the other party would be difficult, lengthy, costly and uncertain. In the absence of any practical sanction (other than the rejection by the international Tribunal of the discredited evidence), oral or written evidence of this kind cannot be accorded the value given to them in some domestic systems. Also it cannot be discounted that the ethical barriers which prevent the making of statements not in conformity with the truth before national courts will not have the same strength in international proceedings, notably when the other party is a foreign government, the conduct of which was severely condemned by public opinion in the country of the other party.

On the other hand, it must be recognized that in many claims filed with the Tribunal, claimants face specific difficulties in the matter of evidence, for which they are not responsible. Such is particularly the case when U.S. claimants were forced by revolutionary events and the chaotic situation prevailing in Iran at the time, to rush out of Iran without having the opportunity or the time to take with them their files, including documents which normally should be submitted as evidence in support of their claims. In many instances, the situation in Iran between the establishment of the Revolutionary Islamic government on 11 February 1979 and the taking of the American Embassy on 4 November 1979 was not sufficiently settled to permit a return in Iran or, in case of return, . . . to recover the files left behind. After 4 November 1979, and up to the critical dates of 19 January 1981 and 19 January 1982, collection of documents in Iran by U.S. nationals was almost impossible. Obviously, these facts made it very difficult for the claimants who did not keep copies of their files outside Iran to sustain the burden of proof in the ways which would be expected in normal circumstances. In view of these facts, the Tribunal could not apply a rigorous standard of evidence to the claimants without injustice. In adopting a flexible approach to this issue, however, it must not lose sight of its duty to protect the respondents against claims not properly evidenced. At any rate, it must be satisfied that the facts on which its awards rely are well established and fully comply with the provisions of . . . its Rules of procedure.

In order to keep an equitable and reasonable balance between those contradictory requisites, the Tribunal must take into consideration the specific circumstance of each case, as well as the elements which can confirm or contradict the declarations submitted by the Claimants. The list of such elements is practically unlimited and varies from case to case. The absence or existence of internal contradictions within these declarations, or between them and events or facts which are known by other means, is obviously one of them. Explicit or implied admission by the other party is another, as well as the lack of contest or the failure to adduce contrary evidence, when such evidence is apparently available or easily accessible. In relation to this last element, however the Tribunal must not disregard the fact that destruction due to revolutionary events or to the war, the departure from Iran of persons responsible for the conduct of the business at the time of the facts referred to in the claim, changes in the direction or the management of the undertakings concerned, can also impair the Respondents' ability to produce evidence. It is often a delicate task to determine if and to what extent respondents would be responsible for such a difficulty.

Kaysons Intl Corp and *Islamic Republic of Iran,* et al, Case No 367, Chamber Two, Order of October 8, 1992:

> The Tribunal refers to the Claimant's notification of witnesses filed on 18 September 1992 (Doc. 104) and to the submission from the Agent of the Government of Iran filed on 28 September 1992 (Doc. 106), objecting to the Claimant's notification and requesting the Tribunal to disallow the testimony of the designated witnesses. The Tribunal also notes the Claimant's submission of 1 October 1992, commenting on the Respondent's objections.
>
> The Tribunal rules on the Parties' submissions as follows:
>
> 1. The Tribunal notes that Mr. Nasrollah Khosrowshahi and Mrs. Faith Lita Khosrowshahi allege to be shareholders in the Claimant company. Consequently, because Mr. and Mrs. Khosrowshahi have an interest in the outcome of the instant Case, they may be presented by

the Claimant at the Hearing as part of the presentation of the Claimant's Case, but they will not be requested to make the declaration provided for in Note 6(a) to Article 25 of the [1983] Tribunal Rules.
2. The Tribunal notes that Mrs. Phyllis Ball is the corporate secretary of the Claimant company and Mr. Richard T. Blancato is the corporate attorney of the Claimant company. Accordingly, Mrs. Ball and Mr. Blancato may be presented by the Claimant as part of the presentation of the Claimant's Case, but they will not be requested to make the declaration provided for in Note 6(a) to Article 25 of the [1983] Tribunal Rules.
3. Mr. Walter L. Dougherty may testify at the Hearing as a witness, provided that he informs the Tribunal prior to or at the Hearing that he has no personal interest in the outcome of the instant Case.

19

The Hearings

1. Introduction	601
2. The Hearings—Article 28	602
A. Text of the 2010 UNCITRAL Rule	602
B. Commentary	602
(1) Notice of hearing—Article 28(1)	602
(2) The conduct of the hearing—Article 28(2)–(4)	604
(a) The conditions for and manner of witness examination	604
(1) Notice of hearing and witness testimony	605
(2) Cross-examination	605
(3) Declarations	606
(b) Hearings normally held *in camera*	607
(c) Retirement of witnesses	608
(d) Examination without physical presence of witness	609
(e) Translation of oral statements, record of the hearing	610
(3) Comparison to the 1976 UNCITRAL Rules	611
C. Extracts from the Practice of Investment Tribunals	613
(1) The conditions for and manner of witness examination	613
(2) Hearings held in camera	617
D. Extracts from the Practice of the Iran–US Claims Tribunal	617
(1) Tribunal Rules (1983), Article 25(1)	617
(2) Tribunal Rules (1983), Article 25(2)	619
(3) Tribunal Rules (1983), Article 25(3)	623
(4) Tribunal Rules (1983), Article 25(4)	624
3. Closure of the Hearing—Article 31	624
A. Text of the 2010 UNCITRAL Rule	624
B. Commentary	625
(1) Closure of the hearing—Article 31(1)	625
(2) Reopening of the hearing—Article 31(2)	626
(3) Comparison to the 1976 UNCITRAL Rules	628
C. Extracts from the Practice of Investment Tribunals	629
D. Extracts from the Practice of the Iran–US Claims Tribunal	629
(1) Tribunal Rules (1983), Article 29(1)	629
(2) Tribunal Rules (1983), Article 29(2)	630

1. Introduction

The right to a hearing is often regarded as essential to the notion of a "fair trial." Article 17(3), which addresses certain fundamental principles applicable to the conduct of arbitration proceedings, expresses that basic right.[1] Article 28 deals with the more technical aspects of the arrangement and conduct of a hearing and it is closely connected with Article

---

[1] See discussion on Article 17(3) in Chapter 2.

27 on evidence, discussed in Chapter 18. The parties are free to supplement these somewhat skeletal rules on hearings and evidence with, for example, the International Bar Association Rules on the Taking of Evidence in International Commercial Arbitration.[2]

2. The Hearings—Article 28

A. Text of the 2010 UNCITRAL Rule[3]

Article 28 of the 2010 UNCITRAL Rules provides:

1. In the event of an oral hearing, the arbitral tribunal shall give the parties adequate advance notice of the date, time and place thereof.
2. Witnesses, including expert witnesses, may be heard under the conditions and examined in the manner set by the arbitral tribunal.
3. Hearings shall be held in camera unless the parties agree otherwise. The arbitral tribunal may require the retirement of any witness or witnesses, including expert witnesses, during the testimony of such other witnesses, except that a witness, including an expert witness, who is a party to the arbitration shall not, in principle, be asked to retire.
4. The arbitral tribunal may direct that witnesses, including expert witnesses, be examined through means of telecommunication that do not require their physical presence at the hearing (such as videoconference).

B. Commentary

(1) Notice of hearing—Article 28(1)

Article 28(1) stipulates that "the arbitral tribunal shall give the parties adequate advance notice of the date, time and place" of any oral hearing.[4] The applicable law may impose its own requirements.[5] As the UNCITRAL Notes on Organizing Arbitral Proceedings explain, "[l]aws on arbitral procedure and arbitration rules often have provisions as to the cases in

---

[2] As revised in 2010.
[3] Corresponding Article 25 of the 1976 UNCITRAL Rules provides:
1. In the event of an oral hearing, the arbitral tribunal shall give the parties adequate notice of the date, time and place thereof.
2. If witnesses are to be heard, at least fifteen days before the hearing each party shall communicate to the arbitral tribunal and to the other party the names and addresses of the witnesses he intends to present, the subject upon and the languages in which such witnesses will give their testimony.
3. The arbitral tribunal shall make arrangements for the translation of oral statements made at the hearing and for a record of the hearing if either is deemed necessary by the tribunal under the circumstances of the case, or if the parties have agreed thereto and have communicated such agreement to the tribunal at least fifteen days before the hearing.
4. Hearings shall be held *in camera* unless the parties agree otherwise. The arbitral tribunal may require the retirement of any witness or witnesses during the testimony of other witnesses. The arbitral tribunal is free to determine the manner in which witnesses are examined.
5. Evidence of witnesses may also be presented in the form of written statements signed by them.
6. The arbitral tribunal shall determine the admissibility, relevance, materiality and weight of the evidence offered.

[4] For an example of such notice, see *Karaha Bodas Co LLC* (1976 Rules), paras 1–2, reprinted in section 2(C).
[5] The UNCITRAL Model Law, however, does not. Article 24(1) merely requires that "[t]he parties shall be given sufficient advance notice of any hearing...."

which oral hearings must be held and as to when the arbitral tribunal has discretion to decide whether to hold hearings."[6]

The adequacy of prior notice depends on the nature of the case and the circumstances, such as how busy the lawyers, arbitrators, and witnesses are and how far they must travel to attend the hearing. In any event, hearings should be planned "long in advance."[7] In a claims settlement process like the one before the Iran–US Claims Tribunal, the case load and the consequent necessity of coordinating numerous schedules tended to guarantee the provision of sufficient notice. Parties to proceedings before that Tribunal typically received notice about six months prior to the hearing. In *ad hoc* arbitration, shorter periods of even as little as one or two months may be sufficient. In investor–state arbitration, the notice period—reflecting the scheduling difficulties for such large and often significant disputes—is often a year or more.

The notice concerning the hearing must indicate "the date, time and place thereof." The hearing is normally held in the jurisdiction designated as the place of arbitration. The exact locale is specified in the notice.[8] When selecting the locale, an *ad hoc* arbitral tribunal may wish to research the availability of an arbitral institution to render its administrative services in accordance with the *Recommendations to Assist Arbitral Institutions and Other Interested Bodies with regard to Arbitrations under the UNCITRAL Arbitration Rules as Revised in 2010.*[9]

As to the requirement to indicate "time," the hearing notice should provide information about the projected length of the hearing as well as the exact time it will commence.[10] The length of the hearing is an issue about which no general rule can be formulated: the time needed may range from one day for a relatively simple case, to 14 weeks over an 18-month period, as was required in the extremely complicated Case B61 before the Iran–US Claims Tribunal.

In many cases, a few days are likely to suffice,[11] given the predominant role which documentary evidence normally plays in international proceedings.[12] The arbitral tribunal may reduce the need for lengthy (and costly) hearings by specifying in appropriate cases—preferably after consultation with the parties—the issues on which oral evidence and argument should concentrate.[13] This may in turn make it desirable to postpone the scheduling of the hearing until a relatively advanced stage of the written proceedings, so as to facilitate the arbitral tribunal's task of determining how many hearing days are needed.[14]

---

[6] *UNCITRAL Notes on Organizing Arbitral Proceedings*, UNCITRAL, UN GAOR, 51st Session, Supp No 17, UN Doc A/51/17, para 75 (1996), reprinted in (1996) XXVII UNCITRAL Ybk 45, 54.

[7] B Hanotiau, "The Conduct of the Hearings," in L Newman and R Hill (eds), *The Leading Arbitrators' Guide to International Arbitration* (2008) 367.

[8] See *Rockwell Intl Systems* (1983 Tribunal Rules); and *Frederica Lincoln Riahi* (1983 Tribunal Rules); both reprinted below, in section 2(D)(1). On the place of arbitration, see Chapter 2.

[9] The revised Recommendations, pre-released by UNCITRAL on August 23, 2012, and reprinted in Appendix 6. The original version of the Recommendations, prepared by UNCITRAL in 1982, are reprinted in (1982) XIII UNCITRAL Ybk 420 and in I Dore, *Arbitration and Conciliation under the UNCITRAL Rules* (1986) 213 (Appendix).

[10] As a rule, the arbitral tribunal should seek to establish firm dates for the hearing, although in exceptional cases only "target dates" may be possible. *UNCITRAL Notes*, n 6, para 77.

[11] When more than a few days are needed to complete the hearing, the arbitral tribunal may wish to consider whether the hearing should be comprised of one period or separate periods. *UNCITRAL Notes*, n 6, para 76.

[12] See discussion on Article 27(3) in Chapter 18.

[13] See A Redfern, "The Arbitration between the Government of Kuwait and Aminoil," (1984) 55 BYIL 75. It is of course necessary to specify when the hearing is to be limited, for example, to jurisdictional questions.

[14] In the practice of the Iran–US Claims Tribunal most hearing sessions were scheduled for only one or two days, although this brevity was probably a result of the heavy case load of the Tribunal rather than an assessment of what would be the optimal length of hearing for each case. See J Selby and D Stewart, "Practical Aspects of

In order to help the parties prepare for the hearing, the arbitral tribunal may provide, in addition to notice of time and place, more detailed information about the organization of the hearing, such as the number of hours allotted to each party for presentation of arguments, witnesses, or experts, and to the tribunal for questions to the parties, witnesses, or experts.[15] In scheduling the dates of the hearing and apportioning presentation time between the parties during the hearing, the arbitral tribunal's decision-making is guided by the principles of equal treatment, fairness, and efficiency, as set forth in Article 17(1).[16]

The notice of hearing normally takes the form of an order issued by the arbitral tribunal. In *ad hoc* arbitration, however, nothing prevents the tribunal from using an arbitral institution whose services may include "[a]ssisting the arbitral tribunal in establishing the date, time and place of hearings," as well as giving advance notice to the parties.[17]

If a party, duly notified of the hearing, fails to appear without showing sufficient cause, the tribunal may proceed with the arbitration, under Article 30(2), in the absence of that party.[18]

(2) The conduct of the hearing—Article 28(2)–(4)

Paragraphs (2) through (4) of Article 28 contain framework rules for the conduct of the hearing. Under these provisions, the arbitral tribunal has broad discretion to conduct the hearing in a manner it deems appropriate. As the *travaux préparatoires* indicate, Article 28 (2)–(4) reflects a compromise between the Working Group's delegates, some of whom eschewed any limitations on the arbitral tribunal's discretion to manage the hearing and others who viewed the hearing process as benefiting from more specific regulation. The final version of Article 28, as revised in 2010, reflects the aim of establishing "a general framework on the conduct of hearings"[19] while recognizing the need to enumerate certain specific rules for the sake of clarity, consistency, or emphasis. The rules of Article 28 are discussed separately in the following sub-sections. The differences in approach between the 2010 UNCITRAL Rules and the 1976 UNCITRAL Rules are addressed below in section 2(B)(3).[20]

(a) The conditions for and manner of witness examination

Article 28(2) provides the general rule that "[w]itnesses, including expert witnesses, may be heard under the conditions and examined in the manner set by the arbitral tribunal." The

---

Arbitrating Claims before the Iran-United States Claims Tribunal," (1984) 18 Intl Lawyer 211, 228. See also J van Hof, *Commentary on the UNCITRAL Arbitration Rules: The Application by the Iran-U.S. Claims Tribunal* (1991) 172 ("In cases where hearings were held, they were short, usually lasting one or two days, sometimes three to five days and only once ten days."). The impossibility of long hearings also in part explains the relatively general practice of this Tribunal to schedule the hearing simultaneously with the submission of further written statements. See discussion on Article 25 in Chapter 16.

[15] See *Glamis Gold Ltd* (1976 Rules), Procedural Order No 11, para 18, reprinted in section 2(C)(1); *Chas T Main Intl* (1983 Tribunal Rules), reprinted in section 2(D)(1).

[16] See *Glamis Gold Ltd* (1976 Rules), Procedural Order No 12, reprinted in section 2(C)(1).

[17] *Recommendations to Assist Arbitral Institutions*, n 9, para 23(c)(i).

[18] See *Plicoflex Inc* (1983 Tribunal Rules), reprinted in section 2(D)(1). During Working Group discussions to revise the UNCITRAL Rules a proposal to state expressly the consequences of a party's failure to appear at a hearing without sufficient cause was made, but not accepted. *Settlement of Commercial Disputes: Revision of the UNCITRAL Arbitration Rules, Note by the Secretariat*, UNCITRAL, UN Doc A/CN.9/WG.II/WP.154.Add.1 at 13, para 47 (2009).

[19] *Report of Working Group II (Arbitration and Conciliation) on the Work of its Fiftieth Session* (New York, February 9–13, 2009), UNCITRAL, 42nd Session, UN Doc A/CN.9/669, at 15–16, para 70 (2009).

[20] UNCITRAL, 42nd Session, UN Doc A/CN.9/669, n 19, at 13, para 55. In revising the UNCITRAL Rules, the Working Group indicated its preferred approach of keeping the rules on conducting the hearing as generic as possible to avoid "overregulating" the hearing process. See 15, para 69. Consistent with this approach, certain provisions of the 1976 UNCITRAL Rules were not incorporated into the 2010 UNCITRAL Rules.

arbitral tribunal's discretion in this regard extends to any number of issues relating to the examination of witnesses, including advance notice of witness testimony, the administration of declarations of truthfulness, and cross-examination.[21]

(1) Notice of hearing and witness testimony

Article 28(2) does not expressly require a party to provide advance notice regarding the witness(es) it intends to present at the hearing. This represents a departure from Article 25(2) of the 1976 UNCITRAL Rules, which required at least 15 days' notice of the names and addresses of a party's witnesses and the subject matter on which he or she will give testimony. The change to the 2010 Rules was made to avoid "overregulating" the hearing process[22] and because it was believed that the arbitral tribunal's general duty to provide advance notice of the hearings would in any event encompass "the identification of persons who were to be examined at the hearing."[23]

The change therefore should not be understood as discouraging an exchange of basic information between the parties about their respective witnesses prior to the hearing and, in fact, it remains good practice to do so.[24] For example, information concerning language may be necessary to determine whether translation must be arranged. Even a description of the subject matter to be addressed by a witness—for example, "liability for the breach of sales contract," "delays and deficiencies in the construction" or "the elements of damages"—may be enough to ensure the other party has a reasonable opportunity to prepare for the hearing. However, a party is not precluded from submitting additional information—for instance, whether the witness to be produced is a fact or an expert witness.[25] In some cases, such as where the subject matter of the dispute is rather complex, it may be appropriate for the arbitral tribunal to request additional information from the parties.[26]

(2) Cross-examination

The regulation of cross-examination is another area squarely within the arbitral tribunal's Article 28(2) general authority. This is clear from the discussions of the Working Group tasked with revising the Rules, in which a proposal to include an express rule on cross-examination was rejected as unnecessary because the Rules already clearly permit such regulation.[27] The drafters of the 1976 UNCITRAL Rules had reached the same conclusion. The Report of the Secretary-General on the Revised Draft of the 1976 UNCITRAL

---

[21] See *Karaha Bodas Co LLC* (1976 Rules), paras 3–5, 8; *Glamis Gold Ltd* (1976 Rules), Procedural Order 11, paras 18–20, 22–23; reprinted below, section 2(C)(1).
[22] UNCITRAL, 42nd Session, UN Doc A/CN.9/669, n 19, at 15, para 69.
[23] UNCITRAL, 42nd Session, UN Doc A/CN.9/669, n 19, at 18, para 80.
[24] For an example of good practice under the 2010 UNCITRAL Rules, see *Guaracachi America, Inc* (2010 Rules), para 13.2, reprinted in section 2(C)(1).
[25] This guideline is corroborated by the *travaux préparatoires*. Neither the Preliminary Draft nor the Revised Draft of the 1976 UNCITRAL Rules includes the requirement concerning the subject matter of the testimony, which was added by the Committee of the Whole (II) upon the initiative of Mrs Beleva (Bulgaria) on the ground that "a party intending to produce witnesses should give not only the name and addresses of those witnesses but also the facts to be established by their testimony...." This proposition was supported, *inter alia*, by Mr Holtzmann (United States) who, however, "suggested that a party should be required to provide information not on the facts to be established but on the subject-matter to be covered by the testimony, since to list each fact would prove too complex." This modification of the Bulgarian suggestion found its way into the final text of the 1976 UNCITRAL Rules. *Summary Record of the 9th Meeting of the Committee of the Whole (II)*, UNCITRAL, 9th Session, UN Doc A/CN.9/9/C.2/SR.9, paras 3–11 (1976).
[26] See, eg, *CME Czech Republic BV* (1976 Rules), reprinted in section 2(C)(1).
[27] UNCITRAL, 42nd Session, UN Doc A/CN.9/669, n 19, at 14, para 61.

Rules states that "the arbitrators may decide whether cross-examination of the witnesses is or is not to be permitted."[28] Examples of the practice of arbitral tribunals with respect to examination, including cross-examination procedures, are found below in sections 2(C) and (D).[29]

Further, Article 28(2) empowers an arbitral tribunal to moderate the practice of cross-examination where the parties may come from legal systems with quite different approaches. For example, common law jurisdictions traditionally subject a witness to cross-examination by the opposing party after he is questioned by the party that produced him. Parties from other types of jurisdictions may be unfamiliar with such procedures.[30] An arbitral tribunal's approach, therefore, should take into consideration the fact that parties to international arbitration often come from different legal backgrounds.[31] At the Iran–US Claims Tribunal, for example, Note 6(b) to Article 25 of the Tribunal Rules on the examination of witnesses proceeds from the assumption that witnesses are questioned initially by the arbitrators, who may then allow the parties to submit questions, "subject to the control of the presiding member."

(3) Declarations

The UNCITRAL Rules do not contain model declarations concerning the truthfulness of a witness's testimony, though the administration of oaths is within the arbitral tribunal's discretion under Article 28(2).[32] In most cases, an arbitral tribunal lacks the power to swear in witnesses,[33] as the hearing of oaths by arbitrators can be prohibited by domestic rules, some of which are mandatory.[34] However, local law does not usually address the kind of declaration required of a witness[35] appearing before ICSID tribunals and the Iran–US Claims Tribunal: "I solemnly declare upon my honour and conscience that I will speak the

---

[28] *Report of the Secretary-General on the Revised Draft Set of Arbitration Rules*, UNCITRAL, 9th Session, Addendum 1 (Commentary), UN Doc A/CN.9/112/Add.1 (1975), reprinted in (1976) VII UNCITRAL Ybk 166, 175–6. The Report continues: "Cross-examination is a technique that is customarily employed in many areas of the world and cannot...be prescribed for international arbitration. Consequently, in cases where both parties or their counsel are accustomed to the technique of cross-examination, the arbitrators may in their discretion permit it, while in cases where one or both parties are unacquainted with this technique the arbitrators may find it inappropriate to permit." See also P Sanders, "Commentary on UNCITRAL Arbitration Rules," (1977) II Ybk Commercial Arb 202.

[29] In the field of investment arbitration, see, in particular, Guaracachi America, Inc (2010 Rules), para 13.5; *Glamis Gold Ltd* (1976 Rules), Procedural Order No 11, para 19; *Chemtura Corp* (1976 Rules), para 54; and *Chevron Corp* (1976 Rules), para 3; all reprinted in section 2(C)(1).

[30] See J Robert, "Administration of Evidence in International Commercial Arbitration," (1976) I Ybk Commercial Arb 224.

[31] Such was the case at the Iran–US Claims Tribunal. Note 6(b) to Article 25 of the 1983 Tribunal Rules of the Iran–US Claims Tribunal on the examination of witnesses proceeds from the assumption that witnesses are questioned initially by the arbitrators, who may then allow the parties to submit questions, "subject to the control of the presiding member."

[32] For practice in this regard, see *Guaracachi America, Inc* (2010 Rules), para 13.4; *Glamis Gold Ltd* (1976 Rules), Procedural Order No 11, para 11; and *Chevron Corp* (1976 Rules), para 3(a); all reprinted in section 2(C)(1).

[33] See J Robert, "Administration of Evidence," n 30, 225; T Esko, "The arbitral proceedings," in M Savola (ed), *Law and Practice of Arbitration in Finland* (2004) 44 ("a party may insist on having a witness to be heard under oath, or having a document produced. If the party succeeds in convincing the arbitrators of the necessity of these measures, the party can file an application to a state court for such action").

[34] See, eg K Rauh, *Die Schieds- und Schlichtungsordnungen der UNCITRAL* (1983) 94 (discussing German law). But see, M Aden, *Internationale Handelsschiedsgerichtsbarkeit* (1988) 242, who questions whether the taking of an oath by the arbitral tribunal in breach of German procedural law could constitute a procedural error rendering the award assailable.

[35] But not party "witnesses" or representatives. See also section (2) on Article 28(2)–(4).

truth, the whole truth and nothing but the truth."[36] An arbitral tribunal has, of course, no power to back the declaration with sanctions comparable to those applicable in domestic law to persons guilty of perjury, but the very formality of the procedure may be conducive to the discovery of the truth. Of course, an oath may be heard by a court which assists an arbitral tribunal by hearing a witness.

As indicated by the phrase "set by the arbitral tribunal" in Article 28(2), final authority to establish the conditions and procedures for witness examination ultimately resides with the arbitral tribunal. Nevertheless, an arbitral tribunal should solicit and carefully consider the views of the parties with respect to witness examination procedures, particularly when those views are jointly presented by the parties.

(b) Hearings normally held *in camera*

The first sentence of Article 28(3) requires that, unless otherwise agreed by the parties, the hearings be held *in camera*. "The phrase '*in camera*' is clearly intended to exclude members of the public, i.e. non-party third persons, from the hearing."[37] This provision reflects the privacy that is characteristic of the hearing phase of a commercial arbitration.[38] The disputing parties, however, may agree to the presence at the hearing of persons other than the parties and their representatives and assistants. If the arbitral tribunal wishes to allow the attendance of an outsider, eg an academic arbitration expert,[39] it must obtain permission from the parties.[40] While Article 28(3) establishes the rule of privacy for the hearing, it does not set forth a general rule of privacy or confidentiality with respect to the entire arbitral process.[41]

The Practice of Investment Tribunals. A growing number of international investment treaties, in particular those concluded by the United States and Canada, impose a requirement of open hearings from which the disputing parties cannot derogate, thus preempting the rule of confidential hearings under the UNCITRAL Rules.[42] In one arbitration under the 2010 UNCITRAL Rules and a BIT without the transparency requirement, the parties agreed to a general rule of open hearings.[43] We also note the work of UNCITRAL to develop rules of transparency for investor–state arbitration, including with regard to open hearings. At the time of this writing, the Working Group had arrived at a general consensus that the hearing should, in principle, be open to the

---

[36] ICSID Arbitration Rule 35(2); Note 6(a) to Article 25 of the 1983 Tribunal Rules of the Iran–US Claims Tribunal. The ICSID declaration has been administered in investor–state arbitration under the 1976 UNCITRAL Rules. See *Glamis Gold Ltd* (1976 Rules), para 23, reprinted in section 2(C)(1).

[37] *Methanex Corp* (1976 Rules); *Chevron Corp* (1976 Rules); and *Jan Oostergetel* (1976 Rules); all reprinted in section 2(C)(2). This is the rule even if the arbitral tribunal has accepted *amicus* submissions by interested non-parties. For more discussion, see Chapter 2, section 3(B)(1)(b) The exclusivity of the hearing is confirmed by the *travaux préparatoires*. The drafters ultimately rejected an earlier draft of the UNCITRAL Rules allowing the arbitral tribunal to admit non-parties to the hearing. See *Report of the Secretary-General on the Preliminary Draft Set of Arbitration Rules*, UNCITRAL, 8th Session, UN Doc A/CN.9/97 (1974), reprinted in (1975) VI UNCITRAL Ybk 163, 176 (Draft Article 21(3) provided: "The arbitrators may decide whether persons other than the parties and their counsel or agent may be present at the hearing.").

[38] *Report of the Secretary-General on the Revised Draft Set of Arbitration Rules*, UNCITRAL, 9th Session, Addendum 1 (Commentary), UN Doc A/CN.9/112/Add.1 (1975), reprinted in (1976) VII UNCITRAL Ybk 166, 175 (Commentary on Draft Article 22).

[39] P Sanders, "Commentary on UNCITRAL Arbitration Rules," n 28, 177.

[40] See *Dadras Intl* (1983 Tribunal Rules), reprinted in section 2(D)(4).

[41] For more discussion, see Chapter 2, section 3(B)(1)(b) on confidentiality and participation by non-parties in UNCITRAL Arbitration.

[42] See, eg, Dominican Republic-Central America-United States Free Trade Agreement, Article 10.21.2.

[43] See *Guaracachi America, Inc* (2010 Rules), reprinted section 2(C)(1).

public, subject to exceptions for the protection of confidential information and the integrity of the arbitral process.[44] However, it remained to be resolved whether the arbitral tribunal should have any broader discretion, after consultation with the disputing parties, to close the hearings.

The Practice of the Iran–US Claims Tribunal. Article 25, Note 5, of the 1983 Tribunal Rules of the Iran–US Claims Tribunal qualifies the rule on privacy of the hearing by taking into account the particular nature of the arbitrations before it.[45] The provision provides that, subject to agreement by the parties, the Tribunal may permit "representatives of arbitrating parties in other cases which present similar issues of law" to attend the hearing. Even where the parties would not object to such attendance, the Tribunal retains discretion to grant or reject requests for "observer" status.[46] The Agents of the two Governments, are, however, always (ie, even when they do not represent the Parties) permitted to be present at hearings and pre-hearing conferences.[47] Note 5 does not mean that the Tribunal is precluded from allowing other persons to attend hearings subject to the conditions of Article 25(4) of the 1983 Tribunal Rules. In fact, persons falling under either of the categories described in Note 5 have occasionally been permitted to observe hearings. Legal assistants of arbitrators could always be present at hearings.

(c) Retirement of witnesses

The second sentence of Article 28(3) provides that the "tribunal may require the retirement of any witness or witnesses, including expert witnesses, during the testimony of such other witnesses, except that a witness, including an expert witness, who is a party to the arbitration shall not, in principle, be asked to retire." According to general arbitral practice, witnesses are not allowed in the hearing room until they testify, but may remain in the hearing room after their testimony.[48] However, pursuant to Article 28(3), the arbitral tribunal ultimately decides, depending on the circumstances of the case, whether and to what extent witnesses may be present in the hearing room when they are not giving testimony.[49] The exception for party witnesses is meant to soften the general rule which if applied too rigidly

---

[44] For the latest version of the proposed provision on hearings as of summer 2012, see *Settlement of Commercial Disputes: Preparation of a Legal Standard on Transparency in Treaty-Based Investor-State Arbitration, Note by the Secretariat*, UNCITRAL, UN Doc A/CN.9/WG.II/WP.169 at 13, para 41 (2011).

[45] The 1983 Procedural Rules of the Iran–US Claims Tribunal are reprinted in Appendix 5.

[46] See Case No A/16 (1983 Tribunal Rules), reprinted in section 2(D)(4).

[47] As to the Agents, see Chapter 12 on Article 2.

[48] See N Blackaby and C Partasides with A Redfern and M Hunter, *Redfern and Hunter on International Arbitration* (5th edn 2009) 421 (noting that the practice often "depends on whether or not a party is likely to gain an unfair advantage by having a particular witness present while the corresponding witness presented by the opposing party gives evidence).

[49] For example, in *Guaracachi*, proceeding under the 2010 UNCITRAL Rules, the tribunal followed the prevailing rule and barred witnesses from the hearing until they presented their testimony. See *Guaracachi America, Inc* (2010 Rules), para 13.7, reprinted in section 2(C)(1). To accommodate witnesses who also served as party representatives, these witnesses were to be presented before all other witnesses. Para 13.7. However, in *Glamis*, decided under the 1976 UNCITRAL Rules, the arbitral tribunal decided not to retire any witnesses because to do so would have allowed the claimant's witnesses greater access to the proceedings than respondent's witnesses. See *Glamis Gold Ltd* (1976 Rules), Procedural Order No 11, paras 12 & 24, reprinted in section 2(C)(1).

An ancillary issue is determining who qualifies as a witness. The Working Group contemplated a revision to give the tribunal guidance on who may qualify as a witness, "any person 'admitted to testify...on any issue of fact or expertise shall be treated as a witness under these Rules.'" Ultimately, however, this provision was not adopted. See J Castello, "UNCITRAL Rules" in F Weigand (ed) *Practitioner's Handbook on International Commercial Arbitration* (2nd edn 2009) 1495.

in the case of a party acting as a witness might adversely affect that party's "ability to present its case."[50]

The necessity of an express rule on retirement of witnesses was debated by the Working Group when revising the Rules. Article 25(4) of the 1976 UNCITRAL Rules contained the basic rule on retirement.[51] Some proponents for retaining that rule, as revised to account for party witnesses, argued that express language was required, as ordering a witness to retire "might be seen as interfering with the right of a party."[52] Yet other proponents believed that omitting the express rule might create the misimpression that witness retirement was no longer a preferred method under the Rules.[53] Though Article 28(3) retains the rule on retirement, as revised, its presence in the 2010 Rules is clearly not essential, given the arbitral tribunal's general authorities under Article 28(2) with respect to witness examination and Article 17(1) with respect to management of the proceedings.

An important consideration in applying the rule on witness retirement is how the matter is regulated in the respective national legal systems of the parties.[54] If the parties share common expectations, decision-making is facilitated. If they do not, principles of the local law may be given preference in the absence of other criteria, or the arbitral tribunal may choose, regardless of local law (unless mandatory), to let the witness stay after his testimony so that he may be readily available for further questioning should the need arise.[55]

(d) Examination without physical presence of witnesses

Article 28(4) includes a new rule that allows the arbitral tribunal to direct that witnesses "be examined through means of telecommunication that do not require their physical presence at the hearing (such as videoconference)."[56] The term "telecommunication" is deliberately broad to ensure that the rule applies when new forms of communication are developed and utilized in arbitration;[57] "videoconference" is referenced only as an example of one means of telecommunication. The rule in Article 28(4) serves merely as a clarification that

---

[50] *Report of the Working Group on Arbitration and Conciliation on the Work of its Forty-Seventh Session* (Vienna, September 10–14, 2007), UNCITRAL, 41st Session, UN Doc A/CN.9/641, at 9, para 41 (2007).

[51] Provision reprinted in n 3.

[52] UNCITRAL, 42nd Session, UN Doc A/CN.9/669, n 19, at 18–19, para 82.

[53] UNCITRAL, 42nd Session, UN Doc A/CN.9/669, n 19, at 18–19, para 82. Opponents had concerns that express inclusion of a rule on witness retirement would suggest that this was the preferred method of witness management under the Rules. They also argued that sufficient jurisprudence existed to guide an arbitral tribunal in this area without an express rule. Para 82. Another concern related to the limiting effect of a particular formulation of an earlier draft of the provision: "The arbitral tribunal may require the retirement of any witness or witnesses during the testimony of other witnesses, *save when the witness is a party to the arbitration*." *Settlement of Commercial Disputes: Revision of the UNCITRAL Arbitration Rules, Note by the Secretariat*, UNCITRAL, UN Doc A/CN.9/WG.II/WP.151/Add.1 at 6–7, para 8 (2008) (Draft Article 25(4), second sentence). Some Working Group delegates had concerns that this formulation would prevent an arbitral tribunal from requiring, if necessary, a representative of a party to retire during the testimony of another representative of the same party. UNCITRAL, 42nd Session, UN Doc A/CN.9/669, n 19, at 18–19, para 82. The final version of the rule, which includes the phrase "shall not, in principle, be asked to retire" arguably affords the arbitral tribunal greater discretion in this regard.

[54] See *Report of the UNCITRAL on the Work of its Ninth Session*, UN GAOR, 31st Session, Supp No 17, UN Doc A/31/17, para 127 (1976), reprinted in (1976) VII UNCITRAL Ybk 66, 75 ("It was noted that in some legal systems witnesses were permitted to be present only when testifying, while in other legal systems, witnesses, particularly expert witnesses, were not formally excluded.").

[55] See N Blackaby and C Partasides, *Redfern and Hunter on International Arbitration*, n 48, 403. On the ICJ, see V S Mani, *International Adjudication: Procedural Aspects* (1980) 231.

[56] Article 28(4) is in line with the general practice in international arbitration. See, eg, Article 8.1, 2010 IBA Rules of the Taking of Evidence in International Commercial Arbitration.

[57] UNCITRAL, 41st Session, UN Doc A/CN.9/641, n 50, at 9–10, para 43.

witnesses may be heard by telecommunication under appropriate circumstances, a method of examination which an arbitral tribunal could already require pursuant to Article 28(2).[58] The arbitral tribunal has authority to determine the admissibility, relevance, materiality and weight of any evidence provided remotely by telecommunication under Article 27(4).

(e) Translation of oral statements, record of the hearing

Article 28 contains no specific rules on translation of oral testimony or the creation of a record of the hearing, leaving these matters for the arbitral tribunal to decide under its general discretion to manage the proceedings pursuant to Article 17(1). In contrast, Article 25(3) of the 1976 UNCITRAL Rules required that the arbitral tribunal make such arrangements "to ensure that the hearings run smoothly."[59] Though considered "too detailed to be included in modern arbitration rules,"[60] arrangements for the translation of oral statements made at the hearing and for a record of the hearing should nevertheless be made in consideration of the parties' agreement or as deemed necessary by the arbitral tribunal.

In the absence of party agreement, the translation arrangements depend primarily on the general determination of the language of the arbitration made pursuant to Article 19. If, for example, the arbitration is conducted in two languages and both are to be utilized at the hearing, translation facilities will be required.[61] Where, however, it is clear that the parties (and their witnesses) have a common language, or can understand each other's language, translation from one official language into the other, with the consent of the parties, can be avoided. Translation may be needed in monolingual arbitration if the parties bring witnesses who testify in a language other than the language of the arbitration.

It is advisable for the arbitral tribunal to keep some kind of authoritative record of the hearing, should statements made at the hearing become an issue later.[62] The nature of the record depends on the particular features of the arbitration. The more central a role the hearing is likely to play in the proceedings, the more detailed the record should be. Conversely, in cases which center on written proceedings, the record can be limited to minutes in which only the main contentions, especially changes made in written pleadings, are

---

[58] In Working Group discussions to revise the Rules, some argued that the 1976 UNCITRAL Rules, particularly Article 25(4) on in camera hearings and Article 25(5) on written witness statements, could be construed as limiting the arbitral tribunal's discretion to hear witnesses remotely, whereas other delegates believed a rule on videoconferencing would "overburden the Rules and reduce their flexibility." UNCITRAL, 41st Session, UN Doc A/CN.9/641, n 50, at 9–10, para 43.

[59] That provision was meant to deal with "certain preparatory measures for hearings that the arbitrators must take in order to ensure that the hearings run smoothly." *Report of the Secretary-General on the Revised Draft Set of Arbitration Rules*, UNCITRAL, 9th Session, Addendum 1 (Commentary), UN Doc A/CN.9/112/Add.1 (1975), reprinted in (1976) VII UNCITRAL Ybk 166, 175.

[60] UNCITRAL, 42nd Session, UN Doc A/CN.9/669, n 19, at 18, para 81. Like original Article 25(2), original Article 25(3) was also seen as "overregulating" the hearing process. Para 69.

[61] See Chapter 11 on Article 19. According to the *UNCITRAL Notes*, "it is advisable to consider whether the interpretation [during oral hearings] will be simultaneous or consecutive and whether the arrangements should be the responsibility of a party or the arbitral tribunal." *UNCITRAL Notes*, n 6, para 19. In an administered arbitration, interpretation and translation typically are handled by the arbitral institution. Para 19.

[62] Problems have arisen in arbitration proceeding under the 1976 UNCITRAL Arbitration Rules. See *Flexi-Van Leasing* (1983 Tribunal Rules), reprinted below, section 2(D)(3); *Karaha Bodas Co LLC* (1976 Rules), para 7, reprinted in section 2(C)(1). The *UNCITRAL Notes* identify several methods: (1) the members of the arbitral tribunal take personal notes; (2) the presiding arbitrator dictates to a typist a summary of oral statements and testimony during the hearing; and (3) a secretary of the tribunal, where one has been appointed, prepares a summary record; (4) professional stenographers prepare verbatim transcripts; and (5) a tape-recording of the proceedings is made. *UNCITRAL Notes*, n 6, para 82.

recorded.[63] The request of a party for a detailed or verbatim record is, of course, a relevant consideration.[64] Such a record can be prepared with the help of audio recording facilities or a stenographer.[65] Both parties, of course, must be guaranteed access to any transcript made of such a record.[66] Arrangements for translating oral statements and providing a record of the hearing usually require the assistance of an arbitral institution. As regards *ad hoc* arbitration, arranging for "stenographic transcripts of hearings," *inter alia*, is something an arbitral institution willing to render administrative services should be able to provide.[67]

In administered arbitration, the administering body normally has the necessary facilities, or at least the capacity and experience to provide for them. Thus, the Language Services of the Iran–US Claims Tribunal provide for interpretation needed at each hearing held at the Tribunal, and the Notes to Article 25 give the Secretary-General instructions in case the Tribunal decides to record a hearing.[68] In actual practice, it should be noted that the Tribunal has arranged to have a hearing taped on very rare occasions. One such occasion was the *Sedco* case in which oral proceedings were held "for the limited purpose of hearing Claimant's expert witness" in spite of the absences of the Respondents and one arbitrator.[69] In normal cases, the Tribunal staff has prepared relatively concise minutes of the hearing. The parties themselves, of course, are free to make stenographic records at their own expense, provided they make the transcript freely available to the Tribunal. Some tribunals prohibit parties from audio recording oral proceedings, apparently because such efforts are not considered conducive to building a constructive and friendly atmosphere.[70] The Tribunal practice, as reflected in the notes to Article 25, can provide guidance for other arbitral tribunals.[71]

(3) Comparison to the 1976 UNCITRAL Rules

Article 28 has been streamlined and reorganized to address only those provisions relating to the hearing process. Thus, Article 25(5) and Article 25(6) of the 1976 UNCITRAL Rules, respectively on written witness statements and admissibility, relevance, materiality, and weight of evidence, have been relocated to Article 27. In substance, Article 28 follows the same basic approach of original Article 25 with respect to hearings, though with some differences.

---

[63] See *Report of the UNCITRAL on the Work of its Ninth Session*, UN GAOR, 31st Session, Supp No 17, UN Doc A/31/17, para 125 (1976), reprinted in (1976) VII UNCITRAL Ybk 66, 75 ("Although the Committee changed the words 'verbatim record' to 'record,' it was agreed that verbatim records were not thereby precluded.").

[64] If parties have unilateral requests concerning translation or records, they should be made in good time prior to the hearing so as to provide the tribunal with an opportunity to make any advance arrangements it may find necessary.

[65] See Note 3 to Article 25 of the 1983 Procedural Rules of the Iran–US Claims Tribunal, reprinted in Appendix 5.

[66] See Notes 3 and 7 to Article 25, reprinted in Appendix 5.

[67] See *Recommendations to Assist Arbitral Institutions*, n 9, para 23(c)(iv).

[68] Reprinted in Appendix 5.

[69] *Sedco, Inc* (1983 Tribunal Rules), see section 2(D)(3).

[70] *Aram Sabet* (1983 Tribunal Rules), reprinted in section 2(D)(3).

[71] On the Tribunal's practice, see S Baker and M Davis, *The UNCITRAL Arbitration Rules in Practice: The Experience of the Iran-United States Claims Tribunal* (1992) 121–2. See also C Brower, "Evidence Before International Tribunals: The Need for Some Standard Rules," (1994) 28 Intl Lawyer 47, 51 n 18 ("in practice few stenographic records have been prepared" by the Tribunal).

The rule on notice of hearing in Article 28(1) is virtually identical to corresponding Rule Article 25(1) of the 1976 UNCITRAL Rules; only the word "advance" has been added before "notice" with no practical effect on the operation of the provision. The same rule on *in camera* hearings appears in both versions of the Rules. Article 28(2) imports and modifies slightly the last sentence of Article 25(4) of the 1976 UNCITRAL Rules to expressly cover "expert witnesses."

Article 28(3) contains the basic rule on witness retirement found in corresponding Article 25(4) of the 1976 UNCITRAL Rules, but the revised provision adds an exception for party witnesses who, in principle, shall not be asked to retire.[72] The arbitral tribunal, of course, has discretion, pursuant to Article 17(1), to reverse this presumption if doing so furthers the aims of equal treatment of the parties, fairness, or efficiency.

Article 25(2)–(3) of the 1976 UNCITRAL Rules, which addressed party notice requirements and logistical arrangements for translation and transcripts, were seen as "overregulating" the hearing process and thus not incorporated into the 2010 UNCITRAL Rules. Though application of original Article 25(2)–(3), in our experience, has not been unduly burdensome in practice, ultimately it is for the parties using the 1976 UNCITRAL Rules to determine whether these provisions serve the needs of their particular arbitration.

Where Article 25(2) of the 1976 UNCITRAL Rules applies, it is useful to understand that it only addresses what may be called a party's "principal" witnesses, as distinct from rebuttal witnesses who may be produced by the other party in response to the witness notice made by the first party.[73] Although this distinction is implicit in the 1976 UNCITRAL Rules, the Iran–US Claims Tribunal has made it explicit in Note 2 to Article 25 of the 1983 Tribunal Rules.[74] Apart from the time factor, which may make it difficult to provide a 15-day advance notice of such rebuttal witnesses, the very definition of a rebuttal witness requires that the subject matter of the testimony is not a surprise.[75] On the other hand, the exception with regard to rebuttal witnesses should be narrowly construed. In this spirit, the Iran–US Claims Tribunal has emphasized that "the exception for rebuttal witnesses created by the first sentence of Note 2 applies only to witnesses who are called to rebut evidence presented at the hearing or so soon before it as to render the normal period of notice impossible."[76] The testimony of the rebuttal witness must be limited to rebuttal of the testimony of the "principal" witness.

Although an arbitral tribunal applying the 1976 UNCITRAL Rules may dispense with strict requirements concerning advance notice of rebuttal witnesses, it may nevertheless

---

[72] The Iran–US Claims Tribunal, which adopted Article 25(4) of the 1976 UNCITRAL Rules on witness retirement, with modifications, in practice followed this exception. Witnesses in the strict sense were not allowed to be present except during their testimony, whereas party representatives who may give evidence de facto as witnesses were allowed to stay.

[73] Accord J van Hof, "UNCITRAL Arbitration Rules, Section III, Article 25 [Hearings]," in L Mistelis (ed) *Concise International Arbitration* (2010) 206.

[74] To eliminate doubt, the parties may modify Article 25(2) to exclude rebuttal witnesses explicitly from the notice requirement.

[75] See *Dadras Intl* (1983 Tribunal Rules), reprinted in section 2(D)(2). Should a party's "rebuttal witness," of whom no notice has been made in accordance with Article 25(2) of the 1976 UNCITRAL Rules, in fact present evidence not related to evidence presented by the other party, the Tribunal should either reject it (see *Uiterwyk Corp* (1983 Tribunal Rules), paras 26–30, reprinted in section 2(D)(2)), not treat it as witness evidence (see *Harris Intl Telecommunications* (1983 Tribunal Rules), paras 106–07, reprinted section 2(D)(2)), or provide the other party with an opportunity (eg post-hearing brief) to respond to it. See also J van Hof, *Commentary on the UNCITRAL Arbitration Rules*, n 14, 170–1.

[76] *Levitt* (1983 Tribunal Rules), para 23, reprinted in section 2(D)(2). See also *Harris Intl Telecommunications* (1983 Tribunal Rules), para 105, reprinted in section 2(D)(2).

require, following the practice of the Iran–US Claims Tribunal, that "information concerning any rebuttal witness shall be communicated to the arbitral tribunal and the other arbitrating parties as far in advance of hearing the witness as is reasonably possible."[77]

C. Extracts from the Practice of Investment Tribunals

(1) *The conditions for and manner of witness examination*

Karaha Bodas Co LLC and *Perusahaan Pertambangan Minyak Dan Gas Bumi Negara,* et al, Final Award (December 18, 2000) (*Ad Hoc* Proceeding, 1976 UNCITRAL Rules, Concession Agreement), at 10–11:

> THE ARBITRAL TRIBUNAL GIVES THE FOLLOWING DIRECTIONS,
>
> 1 —The hearing dedicated to the witnesses and experts (including legal experts) evidence to be held from June 19, 2000 until June 30th, 2000 in the Mercure Hotel in Paris:
> The Arbitral Tribunal intends to convene each day at 9.30 am and break for lunch at 1.00 pm. The afternoon sessions are scheduled from 2.00 to 6.00 pm.
> A break of thirty minutes will be provided in the morning and in the afternoon.
>
> 2 —The hearing will consist of 10 days of 6.30 working hours each. This amounts to 65 hours, allocated as follows:
> 27 hours to each side, for opening statement, cross examination and redirect examination of the witnesses and experts. Each side will be free to use this time in the manner it deems appropriate.
> 11 hours to the Arbitral Tribunal (questions to the witnesses, internal meetings or time to be allocated by the Arbitral Tribunal to meet whatever circumstances may arise).
>
> 3 —Direct testimony has been submitted in writing pursuant to the Tribunal's instructions. Consequently, no direct examination of the witnesses will be admitted, unless expressly authorized by the Arbitral Tribunal for good cause shown. Oral testimony shall consist mainly of cross-examination and re-direct examination shall be limited to the subject matters of cross-examination.
>
> 4 —Witnesses and experts presented by the Claimant will be heard first and then witnesses and experts from the Respondents.
>
> 5 —The Arbitral Tribunal reserves the right to put questions to witnesses and/or experts and organize confrontations between witnesses and/or experts.
>
> 6 —As English is the language of the proceedings, if a witness and/or an expert is not able to give evidence in this language, the party which is relying on the evidence of that person has to provide simultaneous interpretation into English.
>
> 7 —The Arbitral Tribunal has retained the services of a Court reporter to record the hearing.
>
> 8 —The list of the witnesses and experts each party wants to present or to cross examine, will be submitted by June 9, 2000 before 6.00 pm Paris time. If the Respondents provide additional witnesses and/or expert's statements with their Rejoinder due on June 9, 2000, the Claimant shall have until June 12, 2000, before 6.00 pm Paris time to submit a revised list including new witnesses and/or experts. The parties would schedule the order of witnesses after the exchange of witness lists.
>
> Each side must submit an outline of its opening statement to the Arbitral Tribunal and to the other side by June 14, 2000 before 6.00 pm Paris time.
>
> The persons that will be heard during the hearing have to be those who have already submitted a witness statement or an expert report for the Claimant or for the Respondents.
>
> In case a witness whose presence at the hearing was requested does not show up, his or her written statement shall be disregarded. This rule will not apply to expert's reports.

---

[77] Note 2 to Article 25 of the 1983 Procedural Rules of the Iran–US Claims Tribunal, reprinted in Appendix 5.

9 —The fact that an opinion or assertion of fact in a witness statement has not been cross-examined will not be taken as an admission of agreement with that portion of the witness statement.
10 —The Tribunal shall treat the materials submitted by each side pursuant to the Tribunal's Procedural Orders, and the oral testimony at the hearing and any opening statements, as the materials which accurately record the submissions which each side wishes to make.
11 —No oral closing statement is expected. Instead the parties will be authorized to file a post-hearing memorial.

CME Czech Republic BV and *Czech Republic*, Final Award (March 14, 2003) (*Ad Hoc* Proceeding, 1976 UNCITRAL Rules, Netherlands-Czech Republic BIT), reprinted in (2003) 15(4) World Trade & Arbitration Materials 83, 108 (2003):

72. The Tribunal … issued Order No Q 11 (excerpt):

…

The Respondent shall at the latest by August 16, 2002 identify with greater specificity the subjects relevant to quantum on which they propose to examine these witnesses, preferably by listing the key questions relevant to quantum for the witnesses (Art. 25.2 [1976] UNCITRAL Rules).

Glamis Gold, Ltd and *United States of America*, Procedural Order No 11 (July 9, 2007) (ICSID administered, 1976 UNCITRAL Rules, NAFTA Chapter Eleven), at 3–7:

12. The Tribunal additionally requested the Parties' comments regarding whether witnesses and experts should be permitted to attend the hearing prior to their testimony and/or stay afterwards. The Tribunal stated its understanding that, generally, such witnesses were not allowed to attend the hearing prior to their testimony, but could remain after. During the hearing, Respondent expressed concern over a possible imbalance if witnesses were allowed to remain after the testimony but not attend the hearing prior, as Claimant would be presenting its witnesses substantially prior to when Respondent would present its witnesses. Respondent responded by email subsequent to the hearing, however, that it did not consider necessary such a post testimony restriction for witnesses. Claimant did not express an opinion on the subject.

…

16. With respect to the schedule of the hearing, the Tribunal greatly appreciates the efforts of the Parties to think creatively and work together to keep the hearing length to a minimum. After discussion with the Parties, the Tribunal adopted an eight-day hearing schedule. There will be six days starting on Sunday, August 12, 2007 and continuing through Friday, August 17, 2007. In addition, the first two days of the scheduled September hearing dates—Monday, September 17, 2007, and Tuesday, September 18, 2007—were maintained for closing remarks, as well as any rebuttal arguments, and final questions from the Tribunal.
17. Each hearing day will begin at 9:00 a.m. EDT and continue until 6:00 p.m., with a morning break from 10:30 a.m. to 11:00 a.m., lunch from 1:00 p.m. to 2:15 p.m., and a healthy break from 3:30 p.m. to 4:00 p.m. The days of closing arguments—September 17 and 18, 2007—may only require the morning hours of each of the days, however, depending on the number and scope of the Tribunal's questions.
18. Within these scheduled days, it is expected that the Parties will present opening arguments on Sunday, August 12, 2007 and, time allowing, one or two witnesses will be called by the Claimant. Including this time used for opening remarks, the Parties will each have seventeen (17) hours to present their arguments in the first week of the hearing, as they wish. This total includes any time used for the cross examination of witnesses, as well as questions from the Tribunal to counsel. The Tribunal reserved five (5) hours, including all of the afternoon of Friday, August 17, 2007, for its questions to witnesses and procedural issues. During this first week, Claimant will present first, followed by Respondent. In the first two days of the second week of hearings, each Party will have an additional four hours to present its closing remarks, with Claimant again preceding Respondent in presentation, though each party may reserve

up to one hour of its time for rebuttal statements following the other party's summation comments, should it so choose.

19. In an effort to limit the extent of direct witness testimony at the hearing, the Tribunal requests that all witness testimony presented by either party that is "new," in that it responds to new items in Respondent's Rejoinder or addresses events that have occurred subsequently to the filing of the Rejoinder, be provided to the Tribunal and other Party in writing, no later than Monday, July 16, 2007, and be provided only by witnesses already identified in the Parties' respective witness lists. In addition, any rebuttal testimony that the Parties intend to present at the hearing in reply to the written statements submitted on July 16, 2007, is also to be submitted to the Tribunal and the other Party in writing. These rebuttal statements are requested no later than August 7, 2007.
20. In addition to the witnesses' written statements, the Tribunal also requests no later than July 23, 2007, an estimate of the time each Party plans to use for the cross examination of each witness and the sequence of witnesses that it intends to call. The Tribunal intends to use this information to prepare a tentative schedule for witness testimony, thus hopefully reducing the time each witness needs to spend waiting to testify. The Tribunal confirms its desire that all witnesses speak to factual issues, but will permit limited legal testimony as the Parties wish.
22. As regarding the attendance of witnesses at the hearing, the Tribunal decides that witnesses and experts will be permitted in the hearing room throughout the arbitration, except during discussions of confidential information to which the witnesses or experts have not been made privy. The Tribunal requests, however, that the Parties restrict communication with experts and witnesses to breaks and try to limit the overall number of people in the hearing room.
23. All witnesses will be sworn in per Rules 35(2) and 35(3) of the ICSID Arbitration Rules.
24. With respect to the provision of documents for reference in the hearing, the Tribunal accepts the differing approaches as suggested by the Parties, but requests that all documents used—whether physical or electronic—be provided to the Tribunal in a physical form that is clearly marked: (1) as to what the document is and (2) as to where it is to be found in the pleadings.
27. The Tribunal, therefore, confirms the following arbitral schedule:

...

July 16, 2007	Submission of direct witness statements provided to rebut new information in Respondent's rejoinder or provide new facts that have developed since the filing of the Rejoinder
July 23, 2007	Submission of estimates of time necessary for witness cross examinations and the expected sequence of witnesses August 7, 2007 Submission of written statements of any rebuttal witnesses Advisement to the Tribunal of the estimated time required for opening arguments
August 12–17, 2007 and September 17–18, 2007	Arbitral Hearing

---

Glamis Gold, Ltd and *United States of America*, Procedural Order No 12 (August 28, 2007) (ICSID administered, 1976 UNCITRAL Rules, NAFTA Chapter Eleven), at 3:

10. The Tribunal explained that, in approaching the scheduling of the hearing both at the Pre-Hearing Procedural Meeting and at that point, it was guided by four considerations:
    (1) that the parties be treated equally and that one way that this equality is achieved is through an equal allocation of time to each side during the hearing;
    (2) that the basic structure of the hearing should be that Claimant present its case, that Respondent present its defense, that Claimant present its rebuttal and Respondent present its rebuttal;
    (3) that the manner in which each party is to present its case or defense is left to that party; and
    (4) the division of the Hearing over two separate weeks should not work to the disadvantage of either party.

Chemtura Corp and *Government of Canada*, Procedural Order No 1 (January 21, 2008) (*Ad Hoc* Proceeding, 1976 UNCITRAL Rules, NAFTA Chapter Eleven), at 10–11:

> 54. At the hearing, the examination of each witness shall proceed as follows:
>   a) the disputing party summoning the witness may briefly examine the witness, if it is considered necessary to complete the witness statement;
>   b) the adverse disputing party may then cross-examine the witness;
>   c) the disputing party summoning the witness may then re-examine the witness with respect to any matters or issues arising out of the cross-examination, with re-cross examination in the discretion of the Arbitral Tribunal; and
>   d) the Arbitral Tribunal may examine the witness at any time, either before, during or after examination by one of the disputing parties.

Chevron Corp, et al and *Republic of Ecuador*, Interim Award (December 1, 2008) (PCA administered, 1976 UNCITRAL Rules, US-Ecuador BIT) (reprinting Procedural Order No 3 dated April 21, 2008), at 32:

> 3. Unless otherwise agreed by the Parties: Examination of witnesses and experts presented by Respondent. For each:
>   a) Affirmation of witness or expert to tell the truth.
>   b) Short introduction by Respondent (This may include a short direct examination on new developments after the last written statement of the witness or expert).
>   c) Cross examination by Claimants.
>   d) Re-direct examination by Respondent, but only on issues raised in cross-examination
>   e) Re-Cross examination by Claimants.
>   f) Remaining questions by members of the Tribunal, but they may raise questions at any time.

Guaracachi America, Inc, et al and *Plurinational State of Bolivia*, Terms of Appointment and Procedural Order No 1 (December 9, 2011) (PCA administered, 2010 UNCITRAL Rules, US-Bolivia BIT/UK-Bolivia BIT), at 9:

> 13.1 Any person may present evidence as a witness, including a Party or its officials, officers, employees or other representatives. For each witness, a sworn or affirmed witness statement shall be submitted to the Tribunal in accordance with the schedule set out above. Testimony of fact and expert witnesses which is not produced with the relevant written submission shall not be admissible absent a showing of reasonable cause for the omission, as determined by the Tribunal.
>
> 13.2 By 28 February 2013, each Party shall provide the opposing Party, with a copy to the Tribunal: (a) the names of the witnesses whose statement or report has been submitted by the other Party with the request that they be available for cross-examination at the hearing; and (b) as the case may be, a request for the Tribunal to permit the appearance at the hearing of witnesses whose statement or report has been submitted by that Party. The Tribunal shall rule on any outstanding issue in connection with the appearance of witnesses by, at or soon after the pre-hearing conference call.
>
> 13.3 Failure to make a witness available for cross-examination without good cause shall result in the witness statement or expert report being struck from the record. If a witness is unable to appear personally at the final hearing for reasons of health or force majeure, the Tribunal may permit alternative arrangements (such as videoconference facilities).
>
> 13.4 Witnesses shall be heard on affirmation.
>
> 13.5 Witnesses giving oral evidence shall first be asked to confirm their statement or report. Subject to limited examination-in-chief, each witness shall then be examined by counsel for the opposing Party ("cross-examination"), and subsequently by counsel for the Party offering the witness, with respect to matters that arose during cross-examination ("re-direct examination"). The Tribunal shall have the right to pose questions during or after the examination of any witness.

13.6 The Tribunal shall at all times have control over the oral proceedings, including the right to limit or deny the right of a Party to examine a witness when it appears to the Tribunal that such evidence is not likely to serve any further relevant purpose.

13.7 A fact witness, even if also a representative of a Party, shall not be present in a hearing room during opening statements and the hearing of oral testimony, discuss the testimony of any other witness who has already testified prior to giving his/her examination, except with the express permission of the Tribunal upon request from a Party. The Parties' representatives that are also witnesses will be cross-examined before all other witnesses. These conditions do not apply to expert witnesses.

13.8 Counsel may meet witnesses and potential witnesses to establish the facts, assist with the preparation of witness statements and oral examinations.

(2) Hearings held in camera

Methanex Corp and *United States of America*, Decision on Petitions from Third Persons to Intervene as "*Amici Curiae*" (January 15, 2001) (ICSID administered, 1976 UNCITRAL Rules, NAFTA Chapter Eleven), at 19:

> 41. ... Article 25(4) [of the 1976 UNCITRAL Rules] provides that: *"[Oral] Hearings shall be held in camera unless the parties agree otherwise... "*. The phrase "*in camera*" is clearly intended to exclude members of the public, i.e. non-party third persons such as the Petitioners. As the *travaux préparatoires* disclose, the UNCITRAL drafting committee deleted a different provision in an earlier draft which could have allowed the arbitration tribunal to admit into an oral hearing persons other than the parties. However, as discussed further below, Article 25(4) relates to the privacy of the oral hearings of the arbitration; and it does not in like terms address the confidentiality of the arbitration.

Chevron Corp, et al and *Republic of Ecuador*, Procedural Order No 8 (April 18, 2011) (PCA administered, 1976 UNCITRAL Rules, US-Ecuador BIT), at 5:

> 17. The Tribunal recalls once again the communication by the PCA on behalf of the Tribunal, by which the Tribunal has already declined the Petitioners' second order sought, relating to "[p]ermission to attend and present the Petitioners' submission at the oral hearings when they take place, or in the alternative, attend the oral hearings as observers", in light of Article 25(4) of the [1976] UNCITRAL Arbitration Rules.

Jan Oostergetel, et al and *Slovak Republic*, Final Award (April 23, 2012) (*Ad Hoc* Proceeding, 1976 UNCITRAL Rules, Netherlands-Slovak Republic BIT), at 14:

> 57. Following Respondent's objections (about the presence at the hearing on jurisdiction of certain persons on behalf of the Claimants), on 13 November 2009, the Tribunal ruled that such persons could only attend the hearing if they were designated as party representatives, because, under the [1976] UNCITRAL Rules, hearings are held in *camera*.

D. Extracts from the Practice of the Iran–US Claims Tribunal

(1) Tribunal Rules (1983), Article 25(1)

Chas T Main Intl, Inc and *Khuzestan Water & Power Authority*, Case No 120, Chamber Two, Order of February 14, 1986:

> With respect to the organization of the Hearing, the Tribunal tentatively establishes the following schedule for the conduct of the Hearing:
>
> 7 April 1986 morning: the Claimant's presentation
> Questions by the Arbitrators
> afternoon: the Respondent's presentation
> Questions by the Arbitrators

8 April 1986 morning: Questioning of Experts
afternoon: Rebuttals

Rockwell Intl Systems, Inc and *Islamic Republic of Iran (The Ministry of National Defence)*, Case No 430, Chamber One, Order of September 18, 1986:

> The Parties are requested to appear before Chamber One of the Tribunal for a Hearing which is scheduled to take place on 15 and 16 April 1987 at Parkweg 13, The Hague, starting on 1 April 1987 at 9.30 a.m.
>
> ...
>
> c. With respect to witnesses, the Tribunal reminds the Parties of the requirements of Article 25 of the Tribunal Rules.

Plicoflex, Inc and *Islamic Republic of Iran*, Case No 354, Chamber One, Award No 535-354-1 (October 16, 1992), reprinted in 28 Iran-US CTR 309, 312 (1992):

> 10. ... Having regard to its Order of 19 February 1992 by which the Parties were notified of the Hearing, see *supra*, para 8, and to the fact that Plicoflex itself did not show sufficient cause for its failure to appear at the Hearing, the Tribunal decided pursuant to Article 28 [of the 1983 Tribunal Rules], ... to proceed with the arbitration in the absence of Plicoflex.

Thomas K Khosravi and *Government of the Islamic Republic of Iran*, Case No 146, Chamber Three, Order of March 2, 1995:

> 1. The Chamber is considering whether the pleadings in this Case are such that it may decide the question of nationality on the documents submitted to date, or whether a Hearing is necessary. Since the Respondent has not commented upon Claimant's submission of January 26, 1995, it is invited to do so by March 15, 1995.
> 2. In addition, both Parties are kindly invited to comment on further procedural steps in general, and in particular, if the Chamber were to decide that nationality cannot be determined on the documents submitted to date, whether a Hearing should be convened to deal solely with the nationality question or whether a Hearing could be held, after pleadings on the merits have been completed, to cover both nationality and the merits. Such comments should also be submitted by March 15, 1995.

Frederica Lincoln Riahi and *Government of the Islamic Republic of Iran*, Case No 485, Chamber One, Order of October 26, 1998:

> The Parties are requested to appear before Chamber One of the Tribunal for a Hearing which is scheduled to take place on 24–28 May 1999 at Parkweg 13, The Hague, starting on 24 May 1999 at 9.30 a.m. In case of need and due to the Tribunal's official holiday on 31 May 1999, Memorial Day, Tuesday 1 June 1999 and Wednesday 2 June 1999 are reserved for further proceedings.
>
> ...
>
> (c) With respect to witnesses, the Tribunal reminds the Parties of the requirements of Article 25 of the Tribunal Rules. The Tribunal emphasizes that the particulars of the witnesses should be filed in accordance with Article 25, paragraph 2 of the [1983] Tribunal Rules.

Islamic Republic of Iran and *United States of America*, Case Nos A3, A8, A9, A14 and B16, Full Tribunal, Order of June 15, 2004:

> In light of the Parties' submissions (Docs. 451–455) as well as of the consultations between the Agents of the two Governments and the President of the Tribunal, the Tribunal takes the following decision concerning the holding of a Hearing in these Cases.
> (a) The Tribunal will begin by hearing the general issues raised by the Parties in these Cases. This part of the Hearing is scheduled to take place on 2–6 and 9–May 13, 2005 at Parkweg 13, The Hague, starting each day at 9:30 a.m. If required, this part of the Hearing will continue on May 17–18, 2005.

(b) Subsequently, the Tribunal will hear the individual claims in these Cases. This part of the Hearing is scheduled to take place during the periods September 12–October 4, 2005 and November 7–December 16, 2005 (with a brief suspension for the Thanksgiving holiday) at Parkweg 13, The Hague. The Tribunal expects in most instances that there will be four working days during each week of the Hearing, starting each day at 9:30 a.m. The Hearing will resume in February 2006; the specific dates will be set at a later time.

(c) In any event, the Tribunal plans to terminate the Hearing in these Cases no later than mid-March 2006.

(d) The Tribunal requests the Parties to submit by November 18, 2004 their proposals concerning (1) the groupings of the individual claims; (2) their sequence during the Hearing; and (3) the maximum number of days required for each grouping. If necessary, the President will thereafter convene a meeting with the Agents of the two Governments to work out a detailed schedule for hearing the individual claims within the framework indicated *supra*, in subparagraph (b).

(2) Tribunal Rules (1983), Article 25(2)

See *Rockwell Intl Systems* (1983 Tribunal Rules), quoted above in Section D(1).

Economy Forms Corp and *Islamic Republic of Iran*, Award No 55–161–1 at 30, reprinted in 3 Iran-US CTR 42 (1983–II), Dissenting Opinion of Mahmoud K Kashani (December 8, 1983), reprinted in 5 Iran-US CTR 1, 23 (1984–I):

> This occurred under circumstances in which the Claimant's request at the Hearing to be permitted to appear as a witness was refused. Due to the sensitivity of the matter, the minutes of this portion of the Hearing are here quoted verbatim:
>
> It was so decided that Mr. Jennings would not be heard as a witness, because he is the chairman of the board of directors of the Company and is therefore considered to be an interested party.

William J Levitt and *Islamic Republic of Iran*, Award No 297–207–1 (April 22, 1987), reprinted in 14 Iran-US CTR 91, 197–98 (1987–I):

> (ii) admissibility of rebuttal evidence
>
> 22. On 24 October 1985, the Respondents filed a notification purporting to designate a "rebuttal witness" they intended to present at the hearing in this Case pursuant to Note 2 to Article 25 of the [1983] Tribunal Rules. The person so named, Mr. Ahmed Zahedi Kermani, was present at the hearing, held four days later on 28 and 29 October 1985, and made statements which principally concerned the course of dealings leading to the Contract.
>
> 23. Article 25, paragraph 2, [of the 1983 Tribunal Rules] requires each party to communicate at least thirty days before the hearing the names and addresses of any witnesses it will call and the subject on and language in which the witnesses will testify. Note 2 to the same Article subjects this rule to an exception, however, in the case of rebuttal witnesses:
>
>> The information [otherwise required] is not required with respect to any witnesses which an arbitrating party may later decide to present to rebut evidence presented by the other arbitrating party. However, such information concerning any rebuttal witness shall be communicated . . . as far in advance of hearing the witness as is reasonably possible.
>
> In light of the general notice requirement of Article 25, paragraph 2, and the provisions of the second sentence of Note 2, it is clear that the exception for rebuttal witnesses created by the first sentence of Note 2 applies only to witnesses who are called to rebut evidence presented at the hearing or so soon before it as to render the normal period of notice impossible. To construe this limited derogation to encompass witnesses whose testimony would address matters raised earlier in the proceedings would be effectively to exclude from the scope of the general rule a large class of witnesses which it was clearly intended to cover.
>
> 24. Mr. Kermani's statements did not address matters recently raised and hence there was no reason why the Respondents could not have communicated their intention to call him

by means of the ordinary Article 25 procedure. Accordingly, his statements are not admissible as rebuttal within the meaning of Note 2 to Article 25 of the [1983] Tribunal Rules.

Harris Intl Telecommunications, Inc and *Islamic Republic of Iran*, Award No 323–409–1 (November 2, 1987), reprinted in 17 Iran-US CTR 31, 62–63 (1987–II) (other footnotes omitted):

f) Witnesses

102. The Tribunal next addresses an objection raised by the Respondents to the Claimant's witness list. The Tribunal received an English version of the witness list on 11 August 1986. The Registry notified the Claimant that, absent agreement of the arbitrating Parties, Article 17, Note 3, of the [1983] Tribunal Rules requires that witness list be submitted in both Farsi and English. The witness list was submitted in both languages on 20 August 1986 (Doc. 165). This was only 20 days before the Hearing as originally scheduled. Because this was less than 30 days before the Hearing, the Respondents objected to the witness list.

103. The general rule regarding witness lists is stated by Article 25, paragraph 2 [of the 1983 Tribunal Rules], which provides that

> If witnesses are to be heard, at least [thirty days] before the hearing each party shall communicate to the arbitral tribunal and to the other party the names and addresses of the witnesses he intends to present, the subject upon and the languages in which such witnesses will give their testimony.

104. There are special provisions in the [1983] Tribunal Rules, however, with respect to rebuttal witnesses. Article 25, Note 2, provides that

> The information concerning witnesses which an arbitrating party must communicate pursuant to paragraph 2 of Article 25 of the [1983 Tribunal] Rules is not required with respect to any witnesses which an arbitrating party may later decide to present to rebut evidence presented by the other arbitrating party. However, such information concerning any rebuttal witness shall be communicated to the arbitral tribunal and the other arbitrating parties as far in advance of hearing the witness as is reasonably possible.

105. As noted in *William J. Levitt* and *Government of the Islamic Republic of Iran*, Award No 297–2091, pp. 9–10 (22 Apr 1987), Note 2 contains a limited derogation from the general notice requirement of Article 25, paragraph 2, in favor of rebuttal witnesses called upon to rebut evidence presented at the Hearing or so soon before it that it is impossible to observe the normal period of notice. It cannot be construed to encompass witnesses addressing matters raised earlier in the proceedings. Indeed, such a construction would create an exception so large as to swallow the rule.[19]

106. Because the witnesses offered by the Claimant in the present case were not rebuttal witnesses, the witness list filed on 20 August 1986 was clearly late-filed. Any relaxation of this standard is likely to prejudice the Respondents and thus cannot be condoned. Consequently, the Tribunal held at the Hearing, and confirms in this Award, that it cannot accept the proffered witnesses.

107. Although refusing to admit the persons named by the Claimant in its late filing as witnesses, the Tribunal noted at the Hearing that any Party is free to choose the persons it wishes to present its case, including those not accepted by the Tribunal as witnesses and may receive information from them. *See Economy Forms Corp.* and *Government of the Islamic Republic of Iran*, Award No 55–165–1 (14 June 1983). Such persons do not make the declaration that witnesses are required to make in accordance with Note 6(a) to Article 25 of the [1983] Tribunal Rules. The Tribunal, of course, may attach a different "weight" (Article 25, paragraph 6) to information provided by such persons as compared to the testimony of witnesses.

108. For the foregoing reasons, in assessing the evidence before it, the Tribunal does not consider the statements made at the Hearing on behalf of the Claimant by Mr. Stitt and Mr. Scott, who were both on the witness list, as those of witnesses, but does consider them as part of the presentation of the Case by the Claimant in the Hearing.

[Footnote] 19. However, it should be noted that in *Otis Elevator Company* and *The Islamic Republic of Iran et al.* Award No 304–284–2, para 21 (29 Apr. 1987), 14 Iran-US CTR 283 at 291 (1987–I), the Tribunal permitted two witnesses, both officers of the Claimant at the relevant times, to give evidence although the notification was filed only eighteen days before the Hearing. It did not accept the presentation of a third witness who had prepared a valuation report "except to the extent, if any, justified in rebuttal to the presentations made by the Respondents at the Hearing."

Uiterwyk Corp and *Islamic Republic of Iran*, Award No 375–381–1 (July 6, 1988), reprinted in 19 Iran-US CTR 107, 113–116 (1988–II):

28. Absent any convincing explanation by the Respondents, the Tribunal cannot accept a tactic that unveils previously-existing evidence at literally the last moments of the hearing, without prior notice having been given that the witness would testify, without showing that the evidence is presented in rebuttal, and when the documents the witness proffered had not been included with—or even referred to in—the Respondents' various prior submissions. For procedural reasons the documents cannot therefore be accepted. It might be added, however, that, given the nature of the issue and the conflicting evidence of the Parties with respect to it, it is far from certain that the matter would be clarified by further briefing or an additional hearing. Moreover, even if the evidence sought to be offered by Mr. Paksima were admitted and believed, its principal consequence would be to reflect adversely upon the credibility of various members of the Uiterwyk family. The tribunal need not resolve this thorny issue because, as shown below, it has adequate evidence upon which to determine the issue in this Case without relying upon the affidavits or testimony of the members of the Uiterwyk family. Accordingly, the Tribunal does not consider it procedurally sound or substantively necessary to admit the late proffered evidence by both sides, or to prolong the proceedings by further briefing or an additional hearing.
29. The Tribunal therefore declines to accept the documents offered by Mr. Ali Paksima at the end of the hearing, as well as the document offered by the Claimants in response. No further briefings or oral hearings are found to be necessary.

Dadras Intl and *Islamic Republic of Iran*, Case Nos 213, 214, 215, Chamber Three, Order of January 13, 1993:

3. By telefax received 7 January 1993 the Claimants advised the Tribunal that "Mr. Osborn may not be able to be present in person" at the Hearing. In the same fax the Claimants substituted Mr. Theodore Liebman, architect, as a witness, for Mr. Osborn. According to the Claimants' "Mr. Liebman [would] testify concerning the signature of Mr. Golzar, the experience which Mr. Liebman had with Tehran Redevelopment Corporation ("TRC") and the apparent authority which Mr. Golzar had to make binding decisions for TRC."
4. Considering that the replacement of Mr. Osborn by Mr. Liebman, whose subject of testimony is broader than that of Mr. Osborn, does not comply with Article 25, Paragraph 2 of the [1983] Tribunal Rules, the Tribunal does not permit the substitution under that Rule.

Dadras Intl and *Islamic Republic of Iran*, Case Nos 213, 214, 215, Chamber Three, Order of January 22, 1993:

3. Mr. Theodore Liebman shall be allowed to present evidence as a rebuttal witness to the extent, if any justified in rebuttal to the presentations made by the Respondents.

Dadras Intl, et al and *Islamic Republic of Iran*, et al, Award No 567–213/215–3 (November 7, 1995), reprinted in 31 Iran-US CTR 127, 133–34 (1995):

   15. Witness lists were filed by the Respondents on 30 November 1992 and by the Claimants on 30 December 1992. A facsimile from the Claimants listing their witnesses had, however, been received by the Tribunal on 24 December 1992.

   ...

   17. By facsimile of 7 January 1993 (subsequently filed on 11 January 1993) the Claimants informed the Tribunal that one of their designated witnesses, Mr. John Paul Osborn, would not be able to testify at the Hearing, although he would provide an affidavit. The Claimants further notified the Tribunal of a substitute witness, Mr. Theodore Liebman, and submitted an affidavit by him. On 8 January 1993 the Respondents objected to the Claimants' original list of witnesses on the ground that it had not been filed thirty days before the Hearing, as required by the Tribunal Rules; to the substitution of Mr. Liebman for Mr. Osborn; and to the late filing of the affidavit by Mr. Liebman.

   18. By Order of 13 January 1993, the Tribunal denied the Respondents' request that the Claimants' original list of witnesses be rejected. Noting that the English version of the Claimants' list of witnesses had been received by the Tribunal in facsimile form and communicated to the Respondents on 24 December 1992, and that the same list was subsequently filed in both English and Persian on 30 December 1992, the Tribunal decided that the witnesses identified on that list should not be barred from testifying at the Hearing.

   19. A separate Order of the same date informed the Parties that the substitution of Mr. Liebman for Mr. Osborn as a witness did not comply with Article 25, paragraph 2 of the [1983] Tribunal Rules, because Mr. Liebman's testimony appeared to cover a broader range of subjects than Mr. Osborn's would have. The Tribunal further determined that the Liebman affidavit could not be admitted into evidence at that late stage of the proceedings.

   20. By facsimile dated 14 January 1993, the Claimants objected to the Tribunal's ruling denying permission to substitute Mr. Liebman for Mr. Osborn and gave notice under Article 25, note 2 of the [1983] Tribunal Rules that to the extent matters were placed in issue by the Respondents to which Mr. Liebman could provide relevant rebuttal testimony, he would present such testimony at the Hearing.

   21. On 19 January 1993 the Respondents noted that the Claimants had designated Messrs. Duve and Perry as witnesses and that these individuals had not previously presented affidavits to the Tribunal. They therefore designated Mr. Hashem Atifeh Rad as a potential rebuttal witness.

   22. By Order of 22 January 1993 the Tribunal informed the Parties that Prof. Dadras would be allowed to present evidence as a Party witness, and that both Mr. Liebman and Mr. Rad would be allowed to present evidence as rebuttal witnesses to the extent justified by the Respondents' and Claimants' presentations.

Frederica Lincoln Riahi and *Government of the Islamic Republic of Iran*, Case No 485, Chamber One, Order of May 4, 2000:

   b. According to Article 25(2) of the [1983] Tribunal Rules, the names and addresses of the witnesses shall be communicated to the Tribunal and the other party at least thirty days before the hearing. The Respondent has notified the Tribunal and the other party of Mrs. Nabavi's name on 24 April 2000, when the deadline for submitting names of witnesses was on 18 April 2000. The Tribunal cannot accept Mrs. Nabavi as a witness because of the Respondent's untimely communication. Nevertheless, the Respondent is free to call Mrs. Nabavi as a rebuttal witness, if it wishes, in the manner explained in Note 2 to Article 25.

(3) Tribunal Rules (1983), Article 25(3)

Sedco Inc and *National Iranian Oil Co* and *Islamic Republic of Iran*, Award No ITL 55–129–3 (October 28, 1985) at 6, reprinted in 9 Iran-US CTR 248, 252 (1985–II):

> ...With the agreement of the Parties the hearing to be held on 11 and 12 March 1985 was rescheduled for 14 and 15 May 1985 and the Final Hearing was set for 18 and 19 June 1985. On 14 and 15 May 1985 Respondents Iran and NIOC did not appear for the scheduled Hearing. Moreover, the Iran-appointed Member of Chamber Three was not present. The Tribunal proceeded on 15 May 1985 for the limited purpose of hearing Claimant's expert witness Mr. Whitney. The testimony and the simultaneous translation of such testimony, including all questions and answers, was tape-recorded for use by the Tribunal and the Parties in this Case. At that Hearing Claimant requested that it receive in an Interlocutory Award its unnecessary costs of attending the 14 and 15 May 1985 Hearing. All remaining issues in the Case were scheduled for a Final Hearing to be held on 18 and 19 June 1985 with a possible continuation on 21 June 1985. The Final Hearing actually was held on 21, 22 and 23 June 1985 in the presence of all members of Chamber Three. All Parties appeared and presented oral argument.

Flexi-Van Leasing, Inc and *Islamic Republic of Iran*, Decision No DEC 54–36–1 (December 18, 1986) at 4, reprinted in 13 Iran-US CTR 324, 324–27 (1986–IV):

> 1. This Decision resolves the request of the Claimant Flexi-Van Leasing, Inc. ("Flexi-Van") for an additional award in its Case against the Respondent the Government of the Islamic Republic of Iran (the "Government").
>
> ...
>
> 3. Flexi-Van argues that while the Tribunal has dismissed the claims against the "Government of the Islamic Republic of Iran" in the Award, it has not made any award as to Flexi-Van's claims against the "Islamic Republic of Iran," the Respondent named in the caption of Flexi-Van's Statement of Claim. Accordingly, Flexi-Van requests that the Tribunal render an additional award as to claims presented against the "Islamic Republic of Iran."
>
> ...
>
> 8. Further clarification as to who Flexi-Van considered the Respondent came at the Hearing, at which only the Government appeared as Respondent, when, according to the Minutes, Flexi-Van confirmed that [it] was asserting its claim solely against the Government of Iran.[2] Significantly, at the Hearing Flexi-Van submitted a document entitled "Basis of claim" in which it summarized the bases of its claim. *See* Award, p. 16. Flexi-Van stated that this document should be regarded as a clarification, not an amendment, of its claim. This document described four bases which allegedly supported Flexi-Van's claim. As to each of these four bases, Flexi-Van explicitly named only the Government as the responsible party. In particular, Flexi-Van alleged that the "Government of Iran" (i) had expropriated Flexi-Van's contractual rights by causing Star Line and Iran Express to breach the lease agreements; (ii) had interfered with Flexi-Van's contractual relations by preventing payments of amounts due under the lease agreement and return of equipment; (iii) is liable for the breach and repudiation of the lease agreements by Star Line and Iran Express; and (iv) was unjustly enriched through the retention and use of Flexi-Van's equipment. Thus, it is clear that these four bases constituted Flexi-Van's "claims presented in the arbitral proceedings" as referred to in Article 37, paragraph 1, of the [1983] Tribunal Rules and that the Government was the sole Respondent as to each of those four bases of claim.

[Footnote] 2. Note 7 to Article 25 of the [1983] Tribunal [Rules] provides that the Tribunal "shall draft minutes of each hearing... The arbitrating parties in the case, or their authorized representatives, shall be permitted to read such minutes." The Minutes were filed on 16 July 1984. Flexi-Van has not commented on them.

Aram Sabet, et al and *Islamic Republic of Iran,* et al, Case Nos 815, 816, and 817, Chamber Two, Order of November 19, 1996:

> 5. The Tribunal informs the Parties that it does not deem it necessary to make any arrangements for a tape-recording of the hearing. Any Party can make a stenographic record of the hearing in accordance with Article 25, paragraph 3, of the [1983] Tribunal Rules of Procedure and Note 4 to that Article.

(4) Tribunal Rules (1983), Article 25(4)

United States of America and *Islamic Republic of Iran* (Case No A/16), *Bank Mellat* and *United States of America* (Case Nos 582 and 591), Award No 108-A-16/582/591-FT (January 25, 1984) at 3, n 1, reprinted in 5 Iran-US CTR 57, 59 (1984–I):

> On 2 December 1983, counsel for Ford Aerospace and Communication Corporation filed a request to participate in case A-16. In view of the fact that the same counsel had been permitted to participate in this case in accordance with Note 5 to Article 25 of the [1983] Tribunal Rules for GTE International Inc., one of the Respondents in case No 582, the Tribunal did not deem it necessary to permit Ford Aerospace & Communication Corporation to participate in Case A-16.

Dadras Intl, et al and *Islamic Republic of Iran,* et al, Award No 567–213/215–3 (November 7, 1995), reprinted in 31 Iran-US CTR 127, 133 (1995):

> 16. On 11 December 1992 the Claimants objected to the inclusion in TRC's rebuttal brief of an extract from the testimony of a Mr. Rahman Golzar Shabestari at the hearing held before the Tribunal in Case No 812. The Claimants requested that they be furnished with a copy of the complete testimony of Mr. Golzar in Case No 812 in order to refute the conclusions drawn by the Respondents from the extract. By Order of 15 December 1992, the Tribunal decided that, in view of the confidential nature of the Tribunal's hearings, the transcript excerpt in question would not be admitted into evidence unless the Respondents submitted to the Tribunal no later than 30 December 1992 a written declaration by the Claimant in Case No 812 agreeing to the release of Mr. Golzar's entire hearing testimony. No such declaration was filed by the Respondents, and the extract was not admitted into evidence.

3. Closure of the Hearing—Article 31

A. Text of the 2010 UNCITRAL Rule[78]

Article 31 of the 2010 UNCITRAL Rules provides:

1. The arbitral tribunal may inquire of the parties if they have any further proof to offer or witnesses to be heard or submissions to make and, if there are none, it may declare the hearings closed.
2. The arbitral tribunal may, if it considers it necessary owing to exceptional circumstances, decide, on its own initiative or upon application of a party, to reopen the hearings at any time before the award is made.

---

[78] Corresponding Article 29 of the 1976 UNCITRAL Rules provides:

1. The arbitral tribunal may inquire of the parties if they have any further proof to offer or witnesses to be heard or submissions to make and, if there are none, it may declare the hearings closed.
2. The arbitral tribunal may, if it considers it necessary owing to exceptional circumstances, decide, on its own motion or upon application of a party, to reopen the hearings at any time before the award is made.

B. Commentary

(1) Closure of the hearing—Article 31(1)

Pursuant to Article 31(1), when the arbitral tribunal is satisfied that no additional proof, witnesses, or submissions are necessary in preparation for deliberations, it may "declare the hearings closed." Use of the term "hearings" in this context is something of a misnomer. At this point in the proceedings, in the absence of legitimate party objections, the tribunal will very likely be in a position to declare the entire proceedings closed and turn its attention to deliberations.[79] In light of this fact, the Working Group responsible for revising the UNCITRAL Rules considered a proposal to replace the word "hearings" with "proceedings," because Article 31, in fact, referred to the "closing of the arguments," as opposed to the closing of only the hearing phase of the proceedings.[80] This proposal was rejected, however, out of concerns that it might cause confusion in relation to other articles of the Rules. For example, because Article 43(2) empowers the arbitral tribunal to request supplementary deposits from the parties "during the course of the arbitral proceedings," the change in terms might raise doubts as to whether deposits could be requested after the hearing phase had passed.[81]

In practice, arbitral tribunals have construed their ability to close the proceedings broadly and have exercised it at different stages in the arbitration. In *CME Czech Republic*, for example, the arbitral tribunal "declared the arbitration formally closed" at the end of the hearing, in light of the fact that all final pleadings from the parties had been submitted.[82] In *White Industries Australia*, the arbitral tribunal "declared the proceedings closed as regards the filing by the parties of further evidence or submissions" sometime after the hearing had concluded.[83]

Before a declaration of closure, the provision encourages the arbitral tribunal to inquire whether any party has additional evidence, oral or written, to present in support of its case. If a party responds positively, the arbitral tribunal must determine whether the request reflects a legitimate need to further develop a material aspect of the party's case or merely an attempt to prevent the conclusion of the proceedings.[84]

In the event that post-hearing submissions are required, Articles 17, 24, 25, 27(4) and 30 govern the admissibility of all documentary evidence.[85] (As noted by one arbitral

---

[79] The closure of the hearing typically marks the end of the evidentiary phase of the arbitration and the beginning of the deliberative process by which the arbitrators formulate their final decision on the case. See VS Mani, *International Adjudication: Procedural Aspects*, n 55, 245. See also T Webster, *Handbook of UNCITRAL Arbitration: Commentary, Precedents and Material for UNCITRAL Based Arbitration Rules* (2010) 437 ("Art. 31 is not limited to closing oral hearings but rather to closing the proceedings by which parties make submissions and provide evidence. It is intended to cover the period between the time when the Tribunal believes that the parties have had an opportunity to present their case and the date on which the Award is rendered."); see also J van Hof, "UNCITRAL Arbitration Rules, Section III, Article 29 [Closure of hearings]" in L Mistelis (ed) *Concise International Arbitration* (2010) 214 ("it is likely that [former article 29] was intended to have the same effect as art. 22 of the ICC Rules of Arbitration, which provides a mechanism for the closure of the overall proceedings (rather than just the hearing phase)").

[80] *Report of Working Group II (Arbitration and Conciliation) on the Work of its Fifty-First Session* (Vienna, September 14–18, 2009), UNCITRAL, 43rd Session, UN Doc A/CN.9/684, at 10, para 36–37 (2009).

[81] UNCITRAL, 43rd Session, UN Doc A/CN.9/684, n 80, at 10–11, para 38.

[82] See *CME Czech Republic BV* (1976 Rules), reprinted in section 3(C)(1).

[83] See *White Industries Australia Ltd* (1976 Rules), reprinted in section 3(C)(1).

[84] One of the Commission's aims in drafting Article 31(1) was to prevent unreasonable delay of the arbitral proceedings "by repeated requests for hearings and the taking of further evidence." See *Report of the UNCITRAL on the Work of its Ninth Session*, UN GAOR, 31st Session, Supp No 17, UN Doc A/31/17, para 149 (1976), reprinted in (1976) VII UNCITRAL Ybk 66, 77. See also P Sanders, *The Work of UNCITRAL on Arbitration and Conciliation* (2001) 14.

[85] See *Vera-Jo Miller Aryeh* (1983 Tribunal Rules), para 48 (citing *Harris Intl Telecommunications*), reprinted in section 3(D)(1). See also J van Hof, *Commentary on the UNCITRAL Arbitration Rules*, n 14, 296.

tribunal, the admission of post-hearing submissions "does not lead to a reopening of the hearing, but only to a decision on the admissibility of the late-filed documents."[86]

The decision to close the proceedings is a discretionary matter for the arbitral tribunal.[87] In cases in which a party appears to be abusing the hearing process, it may be especially useful for the arbitral tribunal to establish a formal endpoint to the proceedings in order to preclude frivolous requests for additional hearings.[88] It is arguable that in other cases the need for formal application of Article 31(1) may be less pressing and the arbitral tribunal may decide to conclude the proceedings without formal closure.[89] This approach injects flexibility into the arbitral process, thereby reserving as a formal matter the possibility for the tribunal to call for additional pleadings or hearings, should the need arise during the deliberations.[90] In general, however, the proceedings should end with a formal closure.

(2) Reopening of the hearing—Article 31(2)

Article 31(2) confers authority upon the arbitral tribunal to reopen a hearing. This provision was included in the UNCITRAL Rules with an eye towards enforcement of the arbitral award. The Committee expressed concern that the enforceability of awards under the New York Convention might be jeopardized in cases where a fair resolution of an arbitral dispute required an additional hearing but none was provided.[91]

The reopening of a hearing may occur only if the arbitral tribunal finds that such action is warranted by "exceptional circumstances."[92] The UNCITRAL Rules provide no definition of the meaning of this phrase. However, it is submitted that a reopening may be appropriate in at least two scenarios. First, the arbitrators may realize during post-hearing deliberations that a certain point of law or fact has not been developed sufficiently in either the submissions or the hearing and thus requires further clarification through an additional hearing.[93] Second, newly discovered evidence might emerge which has a material impact on the case and which requires further exposition in an additional hearing. Under both scenarios, a reopening of the hearing may be necessary to ensure fairness and equality in the arbitral process, consistent with the arbitral tribunal's obligations under Article 17(1) of the Rules.[94] It should be noted that while the authority to reopen a hearing extends through the deliberative phase of the arbitration, it ceases simultaneously with the making of the

---

[86] *Vera-Jo Miller Aryeh* (1983 Tribunal Rules), para 24, n 11, reprinted in section 3(D)(1).

[87] It is interesting to note that the drafters of the Model Law did not feel the provision was so crucial that it could not be excluded. Indeed, there is no provision for closure of the hearing in the Model Law.

[88] During discussions to revise the UNCITRAL Rules, some delegates had concerns that Article 31(1) might be misconstrued as allowing the parties to dictate when the hearing could be closed simply by deciding to present additional proof, witnesses, or submissions. *Report of Working Group II (Arbitration and Conciliation) on the Work of its Fifty-First Session* (Vienna, September 14–18, 2009), UNCITRAL, 43rd Session, UN Doc A/CN.9/684, at 10, para 34 (2009). The Working Group clarified that this was "not the intention of the provision as otherwise parties could delay the proceedings by unnecessary offers of proof or submissions." Para 34. See also discussion in n 87.

[89] In the practice of the Iran–US Claims Tribunal, "the Chairman sometimes asked each party if it wished to make an additional statement, but this invitation was largely ceremonial, and the Tribunal normally adhered closely to the hearing's scheduled ending time." S Baker and M Davis, *The UNCITRAL Arbitration Rules in Practice: The Experience of the Iran-United States Claims Tribunal* (1992) 131.

[90] See generally V S Mani, *International Adjudication: Procedural Aspects*, n 55, 246 (describing the practice of the ICJ).

[91] See *Report of the UNCITRAL on the Work of its Ninth Session*, UN GAOR, 31st Session, Supp No 17, UN Doc A/31/17, para 149 (1976), reprinted in (1976) VII UNCITRAL Ybk 66, 77.

[92] 2010 UNCITRAL Rules, art 31(2).

[93] See P Sanders, *The Work of UNCITRAL on Arbitration and Conciliation*, n 84, 14; P Sanders, "Commentary on UNCITRAL Arbitration Rules," n 28, 207. See also *Vera-Jo Miller Aryeh* (1983 Tribunal Rules); *Dadras Intl* (1983 Tribunal Rules), Order, reprinted in section 3(D)(2).

[94] See Chapter 2, section 3(B)(1) on Article 17(1).

award.⁹⁵ Thus, Article 31(2) provides a narrow procedural mechanism for reopening the hearing phase of an arbitration.⁹⁶

Of the handful of requests to reopen hearings made during the long history of the Iran–US Claims Tribunal, only a fraction have been granted and only for very limited purposes.⁹⁷ In the most significant case of this kind, *Dadras International*, the Tribunal granted a request to reopen a hearing under what it deemed an "unprecedented situation."⁹⁸ The Tribunal applied Article 29(2) of the Tribunal Rules, which is virtually identical to Article 31(2) of the 2010 UNCITRAL Rules. The primary dispute in the case centered on whether a contract had been formed between Mr Dadras, the claimants' representative, and Mr Golzar, then managing director of the respondent company. Very early in the case, the respondents challenged the validity of the contract, claiming that Mr Golzar's signature on it was a forgery, but failed to present Mr Golzar's testimony at the hearing. Many months into deliberations, and over a year and a half after the hearing took place, the respondents filed a letter by the Iranian Agent, including an affidavit by Mr Golzar, in which he attested that the signature on the contract was not his. The admission of the new evidence was followed by post-hearing pleadings on the forgery issue and a request by the Iranian Agent to reopen the hearings.

For the first time in thirteen years, the Tribunal granted the request and reopened the hearings for the limited purpose of obtaining testimony and cross-examination of Mr Golzar and Mr Dadras.⁹⁹ The "exceptional circumstances" on which the decision rested were three-fold. First, the Tribunal believed that if Mr Golzar's statement were true, it would result in dismissal of the claim. Second, as Mr Golzar was the alleged signatory to the contract, the Tribunal maintained that he had direct knowledge of the crucial transaction at issue. Third, the Tribunal found that the disposition of the dispute turned primarily on the credibility of the main players, Mr Golzar and Mr Dadras. These reasons, the Tribunal explained, underscored the need to submit the two key players to examination before the Tribunal.¹⁰⁰

The American arbitrator, Judge Allison, objected strongly to the decision. He argued that a reopening was not justified in light of the three factors that the Tribunal traditionally had considered in evaluating such requests: the justification for the delay in presenting the evidence at issue, the need for orderly proceedings, and the likelihood of prejudice to the other party.¹⁰¹ As

---

⁹⁵ See 2010 UNCITRAL Rules, art 31(2); *Dames & Moore* and *Islamic Republic of Iran*, Decision No DEC 36–54–3 (April 23, 1985), reprinted in 8 Iran-US CTR 107, 115 (1985–I).

⁹⁶ The provision is of very limited application and should not be interpreted as providing the parties the opportunity to rehash their case.

⁹⁷ The Tribunal reopened hearings in only two cases. See excerpts from *Dadras Intl* (1983 Tribunal Rules), reprinted in section 3(D)(2); and *Vera-Jo Miller Aryeh* (1983 Tribunal Rules), reprinted in section 3(D)(1). However, the Tribunal rejected a number of such requests. See *Dames & Moore* and *Islamic Republic of Iran*, Decision No DEC 36–54–3 (April 23, 1985), reprinted in 8 Iran-US CTR 107 (1985–I); *Touche Ross and Company* and *Islamic Republic of Iran*, Award No 197–480–1 (October 30, 1985), reprinted in 9 Iran-US CTR 284 (1985–II); *Development and Resources Corp* and *Government of the Islamic Republic of Iran*, Award No 485–60–3 (June 25, 1990), reprinted in 25 Iran-US CTR 20 (1990–II); *Vernie Rodney Pointon* and *Government of the Islamic Republic of Iran*, Award No 516–322–1 (July 23, 1991), reprinted in 27 Iran-US CTR 49 (1991–II); *General Petrochemicals Corp* and *Islamic Republic of Iran*, Award No 522–828–1 (October 21, 1991), reprinted in 27 Iran-US CTR 196 (1991–II).

⁹⁸ *Dadras Intl* (1983 Tribunal Rules), Award, para 53, reprinted in section 3(D)(2).

⁹⁹ *Dadras Intl* (1983 Tribunal Rules), Order, reprinted in section 3(D)(2).

¹⁰⁰ *Dadras Intl* (1983 Tribunal Rules), Award, para 53, reprinted in section 3(D)(2).

¹⁰¹ *Dadras Intl* (1983 Tribunal Rules), Order, Dissenting Opinion of Richard C Allison, reprinted in section 3(D)(2).

to the first factor, Judge Allison asserted that because the respondents had been on notice of the relevance of Mr Golzar's testimony since the inception of the case and had access to him during much of that time, the respondents' delay in producing Mr Golzar's affidavit was inexcusable at this very late stage in the proceedings. Second, Judge Allison claimed that the reopening of the hearing disrupted the orderliness and efficiency of arbitral procedures, especially where claimants before the Tribunal traditionally had been afforded prompt and fair treatment of their claims.[102] Third, Judge Allison insisted that the reopening of the hearing would prejudice the claimant by causing substantial additional expense and delay.[103]

As the above exchange of views demonstrates, the decision to reopen the hearings in *Dadras International* was not without controversy. While the potential impact of Mr Golzar's affidavit on the outcome of the case was quite clear, the circumstances under which this statement arose, at a very late stage in the proceedings, called into doubt the freshness of the evidence. Without a detailed and convincing explanation as to why certain evidence could not have been presented in the pleadings or during the main hearing in the case, a request for reopening should be approached skeptically. In the end, the Tribunal found Mr Golzar's testimony at the second hearing unpersuasive and determined that his signature on the contract bound the respondent to its terms.[104]

Further, the proceedings in *Dadras* clarified the relationship between Article 31(2) and Article 17(3) of the UNCITRAL Rules, as adopted by the Tribunal, in the context of the reopening of a hearing. During the proceedings, both the Iranian Agent and Judge Aghahosseini took the position that in addition to Article 31(2), Article 17(3)—which provides the parties the full opportunity to present their case at a hearing—provided an independent basis for reopening the hearings in the case.[105] Accordingly, the Iranian camp proposed that by admitting Mr Golzar's affidavit as evidence, the Tribunal had reopened the case and thus revived the respondents' automatic right to a hearing under Article 17(3), which had been extinguished upon closure of the hearings. The Tribunal disagreed with this argument, finding that Article 17(3) did not apply to the reopening of the hearing.[106] This is indeed the only correct response, as a ruling otherwise would permit Article 17(3)'s general guarantee of a hearing to swallow the requirement in Article 31(2) that "exceptional circumstances" be present before reopening the hearing.

(3) Comparison to the 1976 UNCITRAL Rules

Article 31 of the 2010 UNCITRAL Rules is virtually identical to corresponding Article 29 of the 1976 UNCITRAL Rules, with one minor difference. Article 31(2) grants the arbitral tribunal authority to reopen the hearings "on its own initiative," whereas original Article

---

[102] *Dadras Intl* (1983 Tribunal Rules), para 29 (citing the Concurring Opinion of Richard M Mosk in *Ultrasystems Inc*).

[103] *Dadras Intl* (1983 Tribunal Rules), paras 30–31.

[104] For subjecting the claimant to costly proceedings that failed to be determinative, the Tribunal awarded the claimant compensation for a substantial portion of the costs incurred in defending this aspect of the respondent's charges. *Dadras Intl* and *Government of the Islamic Republic of Iran*, Award No 567–213/215–3 (November 7, 1995), reprinted in 31 Iran-US CTR 127, 204–5 (1995). See also below Chapter 27, section 4(B) on awarding and apportioning the costs of arbitration.

[105] *Dadras Intl* and *Government of the Islamic Republic of Iran*, Case Nos 213 and 215, Chamber Three, Order of July 22, 1994, Concurring Opinion of Mohsen Aghahosseini (August 12, 1994), reprinted in 30 Iran-US CTR 105, 109–12 (1994); *Dadras Intl* and *Government of the Islamic Republic of Iran*, Case Nos 213 and 215, Chamber Three, Letter from the Agent of the Islamic Republic of Iran, (May 27, 1994) at 1–2. The Iranian Agent also argued, rather unpersuasively, that Articles 15(1) and 25(6) of the 1983 Tribunal Rules provided the Tribunal an additional basis of authority for reopening the case. See Letter, 1–2.

[106] *Dadras Intl* (1983 Tribunal Rules), Award, paras 56–57, reprinted in section 3(D)(2).

29(2) used the phrase "on its own motion." This revision has no effect on the meaning or operation of Article 31.

C. Extracts from the Practice of Investment Tribunals

CME Czech Republic BV (The Netherlands) and *Czech Republic*, Final Award (March 14, 2003) (*Ad Hoc* Proceeding, 1976 UNCITRAL Rules, Netherlands–Czech Republic BIT), reprinted in (2003) 15(4) World Trade & Arb Materials 83, 114:

> 95. The parties after having submitted their skeleton closing arguments on November 4, 2002 submitted their final pleadings at the hearing in London November 11–November 14, 2002. At the end of the hearing the Tribunal declared the arbitration formally closed (Art. 29(1) [1976] UNCITRAL Rules.)

Methanex Corp and *United States of America*, Award (August 3, 2005) (ICSID administered, 1976 UNCITRAL Rules, NAFTA Chapter Eleven), (Part II, Chapter C), at 22:

> 39. At the end of the main hearing on 17th June 2004, subject to Article 29(2) of the [1976] UNCITRAL Rules and the receipt of specified written materials from the Disputing Parties and Canada and Mexico, the Tribunal closed the hearings pursuant to Article 29(1) of the [1976] UNCITRAL Rules.

White Industries Australia Ltd and *Republic of India*, Final Award (November 30, 2011) (*Ad Hoc* Proceeding, 1976 UNCITRAL Rules, Australia–India BIT), at 11:

> 2.3.6 On 4 November 2011, pursuant to Article 29 of the [1976] UNCITRAL Rules, the Tribunal notified the parties that it had that day declared the proceedings closed as regards the filing by the parties of further evidence or submissions.

D. Extracts from the Practice of the Iran–US Claims Tribunal

(1) Tribunal Rules (1983), Article 29(1)

Vera-Jo Miller Aryeh, et al and *Islamic Republic of Iran*, Award No 581–842/843/844–1 (May 22, 1997), reprinted in 33 Iran-US CTR 272, 282, 287 (1997):

> 24. At the end of the Hearing, the Chairman, following the adopted practice of the Chamber and in accordance with Article 29, paragraph 1, of the [1983] Tribunal Rules, closed the proceedings in these Cases.[11]
>
> 2.1 Admissibility of Late-Filed Documents: Documents Submitted at the Hearings and Post-Hearing Submissions
>
> ...
>
> 48. The Tribunal notes that, according to its practice reflected in *Harris International Telecommunications, Inc. and The Islamic Republic of Iran, et al.*, Partial Award No 323–409–1, paras 57–75 (2 Nov 1987), *reprinted in* 17 Iran-U.S. C.T.R. 31, 45–52, Articles 15, 22, 23, and 28 of the [1983] Tribunal Rules are the primary rules regulating the status of late-filed documents. Generally, based upon Article 22, the Tribunal considers and decides which further submissions in addition to the statement of claim and the statement of defence, are to be required from the parties in each case and sets forth the schedule for communicating such statements. Moreover, Article 28 gives the Tribunal the authority to make an award based on the evidence before it, if a party that has had the opportunity to file documentary evidence fails to file within the established period of time, and fails to show sufficient reason for its nonconformity. This rule equally applies to the situation in which a party has properly filed its documents, but subsequently tries to submit additional, unauthorized material for inclusion in the record of the case.

49. Furthermore, on the basis of Article 15, both parties to the case have to be treated equally. This means that both parties to the case are entitled to have an equal opportunity to present written submissions and to respond to each other's submissions. This also means that the parties must have an equal opportunity to go through the evidence and the arguments submitted by the other party, and to prepare their own position and arguments in advance of the hearing.

50. Chamber One has taken a strict stance on these matters: no new evidence is permitted prior to the hearing unless the Tribunal finds that it is justified by exceptional circumstances and is filed no later than two months before the hearing in the case. Moreover, as a matter of routine in its orders scheduling a hearing the Chamber advises the parties that any party is free to make whatever arguments it wishes at the hearing; however, parties may not introduce new documents into evidence absent the Tribunal's permission. Such permission normally is not granted except for rebuttal evidence introduced to rebut evidence produced at the hearing.

[Footnote] 11. The general practice of the Tribunal is that the Chambers do not formally or explicitly declare that they apply Article 29, paragraph 1, of the [1983] Tribunal Rules; but, this fact automatically follows from the scheduled termination of a hearing. Accordingly, the Tribunal views additional evidence submitted after a hearing as post-hearing submissions. Given the foregoing, it stands to reason that the filing of documents after the closure of a hearing does not lead to a reopening of the hearing, but only to a decision on the admissibility of the late-filed documents.

(2) Tribunal Rules (1983), Article 29(2)

Dadras Intl and *Islamic Republic of Iran*, Case Nos 213 and 215, Order of July 22, 1994, reprinted in 30 Iran-US CTR 104, 104–05 (1994):

1. Reference is made to the Request by the Agent of the Islamic Republic of Iran filed on May 27, 1994 for the reopening of the Hearing in these Cases and to the objection of the Claimants filed on June 10, 1994.
2. The Tribunal notes that the post-Hearing submission of an affidavit by Mr. Golzar and the subsequent acceptance of that affidavit into the record, as well as the evidence which was admitted by order of February 23, 1994 and through the submission scheduled by the Tribunal, has introduced new material into the record.
3. The Tribunal notes further that it is now confronted with directly conflicting and irreconcilable statements from the two alleged signatories to the contract. The Tribunal considers that its task to determine which version of events is more accurate can better be accomplished by observing and examining Messrs. Golzar and Dadras in each other's presence at a hearing.
4. The Tribunal hereby determines that exceptional circumstances exist such that the Hearing in these Cases should be reopened in accordance with Article 29, paragraph 2, of the [1983] Tribunal Rules, for the sole and limited purpose of hearing the testimony of Messrs. Rahman Golzar Shabestari and Aly Shahidzadeh Dadras. Because of the advanced stage of deliberations and the procedural history of these Cases, in the interests of procedural orderliness the Tribunal will not reopen the Hearing for any other than this very limited purpose.
5. A Hearing is scheduled to take place on October 20, 1994 at 9:30 a.m. at Parkweg 13, The Hague, The Netherlands.
6. The Parties are hereby informed that in the interests of orderliness and fairness to both Parties, the following conditions will apply at the Hearing:
    (i) The object of inquiry by the Tribunal will be the authenticity of Mr. Golzar's signatures on the Contract dated September 9, 1978 and the letter dated 27 August 1978. Questions and answers are to be confined to that subject.
    (ii) The proceedings will be confined to the subject outlined in para 6(i) above and will be limited to:
    - testimony by Mr. Golzar and Mr. Dadras;
    - cross-examination of Mr. Golzar by the Claimants and Mr. Dadras by the Respondent;

- examination of Mr. Golzar and Mr. Dadras by the Tribunal;
- opening and closing remarks by Counsel for Claimants and Respondents.

(iii) No additional witnesses, rebuttal witnesses or interested parties will be permitted to testify.

(iv) The Parties will not be required or permitted to file additional pleadings either before or after the Hearing.

The Tribunal will consider inadmissible any document or testimony containing new material.

Dadras Intl and *Islamic Republic of Iran*, Case Nos 213 and 215, Order of July 22, 1994, Dissenting Opinion of Richard C Allison (July 25, 1994), reprinted in 30 Iran-US CTR 112, 118–20 (1994):

27. In short, the Tribunal consistently has denied requests to reopen in the few prior cases in which such requests have been made. In each instance, the Tribunal looked primarily to three factors—the justification for the delay in presenting the evidence at issue, the need for orderly proceedings, and the likelihood of prejudice to the other party—to decide whether reopening was appropriate. Applying these three considerations to the facts of the instant matter, it seems to me obvious that Respondents' request should be denied. First, the justification advanced by Respondents for the delay in proffering Mr. Golzar's testimony is entirely unpersuasive. Respondents have been on notice of the possible relevance of Mr. Golzar's testimony since the earliest days of these Cases and have had knowledge of his whereabouts, and access to him, for much of the period that these Cases have been pending. Moreover, the Government of Iran had Mr. Golzar under oath, and subject to cross-examination on the very matters relevant to their forgery defence in these Cases, during the *Golshani* Hearing. Inexplicably, its counsel failed to ask him the key question.

28. The only purported justification for the delay offered in Mr. Nobari's letter is that Mr. Golzar "was Iran's adversary" in *Golshani* and that therefore "Iran had reasons to believe that he would not cooperate with it." This explanation is patently inadequate for at least two reasons. First, all that is required by Article 15(1) [of the 1983 Tribunal Rules] and the Tribunal's precedents is that a party have a meaningful opportunity to present its case, not that it be assured of a particular result. Respondents had ample opportunity to solicit Mr. Golzar's testimony during the twelve-year period between 1982 and 1993, and the fact that they may have refrained from doing so out of concern as to his "cooperation" cannot relieve them of the burden of trying. Second, even under Respondent's theory Mr. Golzar ceased to be an "adversary" in *Golshani* on 2 March 1993, the day that the Award in that case was issued; yet Respondents nonetheless did not contact Mr. Golzar until nearly a year later and even then, according to Respondents, the encounter arose purely by chance and not through the efforts of their own. Thus, the excuse that Mr. Golzar was "Iran's adversary" simply does not hold up under scrutiny.

29. Another factor identified in the Tribunal's precedents as relevant to requests to reopen is the orderliness of the Tribunal's proceedings. This body's precedents rightly recognize that the parties that appear before it are entitled to a fair and adequate opportunity to present their cases, a dictate that was fully satisfied in the pleading and Hearing phases of these Cases. However, there is a further interest that must also be observed—namely, the protection of the procedures and efficiency of the Tribunal itself—if justice is to be served.... Indeed, the latter precept is inherent in the fundamental principle of equality of treatment embodied in Article 15(1) of the Tribunal's [1983] Rules. As explained by Judge Mosk more than a decade ago,

> A Tribunal having thousands of cases is far different than an international arbitration involving only one case. The claimants and respondents before this Tribunal are entitled to have cases heard and decided in a prompt, efficient, and fair manner, in accordance with Tribunal rules and the law. Long delayed and expensive proceedings in which parties are not accorded equal treatment create much greater injustice than the failure to permit unlimited means and time to establish every fact in a particular case.

Concurring Opinion of Richard M Mosk in *Ultrasystems Inc.* and *The Islamic Republic of Iran*, Partial Award No 27–84-3 (4 March 1983), reprinted in 2 Iran-U.S. C.T.R. 114, 123. The need for orderliness and efficiency in this Chamber's proceedings weighs heavily against the granting of Respondents' belated request to reopen.

30. A further factor identified in the cases—prejudice to the other party—likewise speaks strongly against granting Respondents' request to reopen. The Claimants in these Cases stated in their objection to Respondents' request that the reopening of the Hearing will cause Claimants to incur "substantial further expense and delay." The element of delay is already obvious. To substantiate their contention as to expense, Claimants submitted on 26 May 1994 a "Bill of Costs" showing that the proceedings related to the Golzar affidavit had, as of that date, cost the Claimants more than $94,000 in legal fees and expenses.

31. Even more fundamentally, the Claimants in these Cases, like all parties who appear before this Tribunal, have a right to expect the opposing party to present its case in the pleadings and at the Hearing, where it can be subjected to effective challenge, and not at some later time of its own choosing. Today's Order frustrates that proper expectation, and in the process creates a perverse incentive for future parties who may perceive delay as being to their strategic advantage.

Dadras Intl and *Islamic Republic of Iran*, Award No 567–213/215-3 (November 7, 1995), reprinted in 31 Iran-US CTR 127, 142–43, 145 (1995):

53. The key criterion in deciding whether to reopen a hearing under Article 29, paragraph 2 [of the 1983 Tribunal Rules] is whether the Tribunal finds "exceptional circumstances" to be present—a finding that had never before been made by the Tribunal in any case in its 13-year history. However, the Tribunal in the present Cases considered that it faced an unprecedented situation, and one unlikely to recur. The Tribunal believed that this derived from three factors. The first factor was the nature of the allegations made by Mr. Golzar, allegations that directly contradicted the Claimants' case and—if found to be true by the Tribunal—would lead to the dismissal of the claim and the characterization of Prof. Dadras as the perpetrator of an attempted fraud upon an international tribunal. The second factor was the identity of Mr. Golzar as the alleged signatory to the Contract, and therefore as the one person, besides Prof. Dadras, who could be expected to hold direct knowledge of and who was most intimately involved with the transaction in question. The third factor was that the disposition of these Cases rested heavily on the credibility of the main players. Therefore, the Tribunal considered it crucial to submit the two key players to cross-examination in each other's presence. For these reasons, the Tribunal decided to reopen the Hearing in these Cases under Article 29, paragraph 2 of the [1983] Tribunal Rules.

...

56. The Tribunal concludes that Article 15, paragraph 2 [of the 1983 Tribunal Rules] is primarily applicable to the situation where there has not yet been a hearing and one of the parties requests one. The right of the parties to request a hearing under Article 15, paragraph 2 is not, however, an absolute right. For example, in *World Farmers Trading, Inc. v. Government Trading Corporation, et al.*, Award No, 428–764-1 (7 July 1989), *reprinted in* 22 Iran-U.S. C.T.R. 204, 209, the Tribunal held that although Article 15, paragraph 2 of the [1983] Tribunal Rules states that a party may request a hearing "at any stage of the proceedings," "[t]his provision should be interpreted, in light of the particular circumstances of each case, to mean that Hearings are to be held upon the reasonable request of a party made at an appropriate stage of the proceedings." This interpretation of Article 15, paragraph 2 was followed in *Tchacosh Company, Inc., et al.* and *The Government of the Islamic Republic of Iran, et al.*, Award No 540–192–1, para 21 (9 December 1992), *reprinted in* 28 Iran-U.S. C.T.R. 37, 380, in which the Tribunal refused to grant the claimant's request for a hearing, saying that the request had not been made at an "appropriate time" because it was made more than one year after the Tribunal had informed the Parties of its intention to take a decision on jurisdiction on the basis of the written evidence before it.

57. Thus even where no hearing has been held, Article 15, paragraph 2 does not oblige the Tribunal to accede to any request by a party for a hearing. The applicable criteria in evaluating each request are whether the request is both reasonable and made at an appropriate stage of the proceedings. In a context such as the present, where a Hearing has already been held, the reasonableness of the request and the appropriateness of the timing become even more important because the disruption of the arbitral process is that much greater and because the parties have already had an extensive opportunity to present their cases.

64. For the foregoing reasons, the Tribunal is of the opinion that the only Article of the [1983] Tribunal Rules applicable to the present circumstances is Article 29, paragraph 2, which it invoked in its Order dated 22 July 1994 reopening the Hearing in these Cases.

20
Tribunal-Appointed Experts

1. Introduction	635
2. Tribunal-Appointed Experts—Article 29	636
A. Text of the 2010 UNCITRAL Rule	636
B. Commentary	637
(1) General comments	637
(2) Appointment by the tribunal and terms of reference—Article 29(1)–(2)	638
(a) Appointment	638
(b) Terms of reference	640
(3) Objections to the qualifications or the impartiality and independence of the tribunal-appointed expert—Article 29(2)	642
(4) The provision of relevant information to the tribunal-appointed expert—Article 29(3)	644
(5) The tribunal-appointed expert's report—Article 29(4)	645
(6) Expert hearings—Article 29(5)	646
(7) A note on party-appointed "expert witnesses"	647
(8) Comparison to the 1976 UNCITRAL Rules	648
C. Extracts from the Practice of Investment Tribunals	648
D. Extracts from the Practice of the Iran–US Claims Tribunal	650
(1) Tribunal Rules (1983), Article 27(1)—appointment and terms of reference	650
(a) The *Shahin Shaine Ebrahimi* case	650
(b) The *Arco Exploration* case	653
(c) The *Starrett Housing* case	655
(d) The *Richard D Harza* case	656
(e) The *Behring International* case	660
(2) Tribunal Rules (1983), Article 27(2)—provision of relevant information	662
(3) Tribunal Rules (1983), Article 27(3)—expert report	663
(a) The *Shahin Shaine Ebrahimi* case	663
(b) The *Arco Exploration* case	664
(c) The *Behring International* case	665
(d) The *Richard D Harza* case	665
(e) The *Starrett Housing* case	665
(4) Tribunal Rules (1983), Article 27(4)—expert hearing	667

1. Introduction

International arbitration allows the parties to choose an arbitrator whose specialized skill or knowledge regarding a particular legal, financial, or technical field can aid in resolving the dispute most accurately and efficiently. At times, however, complicated questions arise the answers to which, while essential for resolving the dispute, are beyond the expertise of the arbitral tribunal. On these occasions, the tribunal may wish to seek the advice of one or more experts who possess this critical knowledge. The UNCITRAL Rules envision the use of two kinds of experts: tribunal-appointed experts and party-appointed experts. Article 29 applies only to tribunal-appointed experts and establishes a set of procedures that allow considerable involvement by the parties in the tribunal's dealings with the expert. Article 29 addresses the appointment of the expert by the tribunal and the expert's terms of reference (29(1)), the impartiality and independence of the tribunal-appointed expert (29(2)), the provision of relevant information to the expert (29(3)), the tribunal-appointed expert's report (29(4)), and the expert hearing (29(5)). The use of party-appointed experts is governed by Article 17(3), Article 27, and Article 28, which apply to witnesses generally.[1]

2. Tribunal-Appointed Experts—Article 29

A. Text of the 2010 UNCITRAL Rule[2]

Article 29 of the 2010 UNCITRAL Rules provides:

Experts appointed by the arbitral tribunal

1. After consultation with the parties, the arbitral tribunal may appoint one or more independent experts to report to it, in writing, on specific issues to be determined by the tribunal. A copy of the expert's terms of reference, established by the arbitral tribunal, shall be communicated to the parties.
2. The expert shall, in principle before accepting appointment, submit to the arbitral tribunal and to the parties a description of his or her qualifications and a statement of his or her impartiality and independence. Within the time ordered by the arbitral tribunal, the parties shall inform the arbitral tribunal whether they have any objections as to the expert's qualifications, impartiality or independence. The arbitral tribunal shall decide promptly whether to accept any such objections. After an expert's appointment, a party may object to the expert's qualifications, impartiality or independence only if the objection is for reasons of which the party becomes aware after the appointment has been made. The arbitral tribunal shall decide promptly what, if any, action to take.
3. The parties shall give the expert any relevant information or produce for his or her inspection any relevant documents or goods that he or she may require of them. Any dispute between a party and such expert as to the relevance of the required information or production shall be referred to the arbitral tribunal for decision.
4. Upon receipt of the expert's report, the arbitral tribunal shall communicate a copy of the report to the parties, which shall be given the opportunity to express, in writing, their opinion on the report. A party shall be entitled to examine any document on which the expert has relied in his or her report.

---

[1] These articles are discussed, respectively in chapters 2, 18, and 19.
[2] Corresponding Article 27 of the 1976 UNCITRAL Rules provides:

1. The arbitral tribunal may appoint one or more experts to report to it, in writing, on specific issues to be determined by the tribunal. A copy of the expert's terms of reference, established by the arbitral tribunal, shall be communicated to the parties.
2. The parties shall give the expert any relevant information or produce for his inspection any relevant documents or goods that he may require of them. Any dispute between a party and such expert as to the relevance of the required information or production shall be referred to the arbitral tribunal for decision.
3. Upon receipt of the expert's report, the arbitral tribunal shall communicate a copy of the report to the parties who shall be given the opportunity to express, in writing, their opinion on the report. A party shall be entitled to examine any document on which the expert has relied in his report.
4. At the request of either party the expert, after delivery of the report, may be heard at a hearing where the parties shall have the opportunity to be present and to interrogate the expert. At this hearing either party may present expert witnesses in order to testify on the points at issue. The provisions of article 25 shall be applicable to such proceedings.

5. At the request of any party, the expert, after delivery of the report, may be heard at a hearing where the parties shall have the opportunity to be present and to interrogate the expert. At this hearing, any party may present expert witnesses in order to testify on the points at issue. The provisions of article 28 shall be applicable to such proceedings.

B. Commentary

(1) General comments

In an ideal world, an arbitral tribunal would be composed of arbitrators who not only possess the skills and disposition necessary for adjudicating legal matters, but also the requisite expertise in the substantive or technical issues that the parties dispute. According to Berger, such expertise may be required for the resolution of "complicated problems of accounting or high-technology," the evaluation of "the quality and condition of goods," or the application of "complex accounting principles to determine the quantum of damages to be awarded."[3] Expertise of this kind ensures that the arbitral tribunal has a proper understanding of the facts and their relation to the applicable law, and increases the prospects that decisions regarding liability and damages will be fully informed, accurate, and, most of all, just.[4] In practice, however, the arbitral tribunal's level of expertise often does not exactly match that required to resolve the dispute before it. Where this divide is significant—ie, where expertise is lacking to an extent capable of compromising the quality of a resulting

---

[3] K Berger, *International Economic Arbitration* (1993) 435. See also H van Houtte, "Conduct of Arbitral Proceedings," in P Šarčević (ed), *Essays on International Commercial Arbitration* (1989) 123. Leading commentators add the following examples:

[E]xpertise in cryogenics may be required to determine why a metal storage tank cracked; or civil engineering experience may be required to determine why an airport runway became unusable. Expert help may be needed to investigate the quantification of a claim. The arbitral tribunal may, for example, need quantity surveyors to assist in evaluating claims for measured work under a civil engineering contract; or accountants, to assist in determining the value to be put on a company's balance sheet.

N Blackaby and C Partasides with A Redfern and M Hunter, *Redfern and Hunter on International Arbitration*, (5th edn 2009) 306–7. Further, the original commentary to the 1976 UNCITRAL Rules provides that expert advice may be required in determining "the existence of particular commercial usages" or answering "questions of law." See *Report of the Secretary-General on the Preliminary Draft Set of Arbitration Rules*, UNCITRAL, 8th Session, UN Doc A/CN.9/97 (1974), reprinted in (1975) VI UNCITRAL Ybk 163, 176.

The Iran–US Claims Tribunal has appointed experts to provide advice on a wide range of questions. See *Richard D Harza* and *Islamic Republic of Iran* (1983 Tribunal Rules), Award No ITL 14–97–2 (February 17, 1983) (geology and hydraulics), reprinted in 2 Iran-US CTR 68 (1983-I); *Chas T Main Intl Inc* and *Khuzestan Water and Power Authority* (1983 Tribunal Rules), Award No ITL 23–120–2 (July 27, 1983) (hydro-electric engineering), reprinted in 3 Iran-US CTR 156, 164–66 (1983-II); *Behring Intl Inc* and *Islamic Republic of Iran*, Case No 382 (1983 Tribunal Rules), Chamber Three, Decision of December 19, 1983 (inventory), reprinted in 4 Iran-US CTR 89, 92 (1983-III); *Starrett Housing Corp* and *Government of the Islamic Republic of Iran* (1983 Tribunal Rules), Award No ITL 32–24–1 (December 19, 1983) (accounting and valuation), reprinted in 4 Iran-US CTR 122 (1983-III); *Intl Technical Products Corp* and *Government of the Islamic Republic of Iran* (1983 Tribunal Rules), Partial Award No 186–302–3 (August 19, 1985) (linguistics), reprinted in 9 Iran-US CTR 10, 32–5 (1985-II); *Paul Donin de Rosiere* and *Islamic Republic of Iran* (1983 Tribunal Rules), Case No 498, Chamber One, Order of 6 Sep 1985, at 3 (property evaluation); *Arco Exploration, Inc*, et al and *National Iranian Oil Co* (1983 Tribunal Rules), Case Nos 20 & 21, Chamber One, Order of June 13, 1990, at 4 (petroleum engineering); *Shahin Shaine Ebrahimi* and *Government of the Islamic Republic of Iran* (1983 Tribunal Rules), Case Nos 44, 46 & 47, Chamber Three Order of February 4, 1993, (accounting and valuation), reprinted in 30 Iran-US CTR 170, 204–5 n 21 (1994). See also *SD Myers* (1976 Rules); and *Wintershall AG* (1976 Rules), both reprinted in section 2(C), for additional examples of the use of experts in investor–state arbitration.

[4] As the ICJ observed, expert advice assists the international tribunal in obtaining "any technical information that might guide it in the search for the truth." *Corfu Channel Case* (UK v Alb), 1949 ICJ 4, 20.

award—the arbitral tribunal may consider enlisting the help of experts with specialized knowledge of the particular matters in question.[5]

Two primary methods exist in international arbitration for employing the assistance of experts: (1) the arbitral tribunal may appoint an expert to provide advice on a particular matter of interest; or (2) a party may appoint an expert as a witness in support of its case.[6] The chief distinction in methods is the respective level of neutrality expected of the two kinds of experts. Tribunal-appointed experts report only to the arbitral tribunal and, as discussed below, are expected to be completely unbiased in formulating their opinions. Party-appointed experts, by contrast, are enlisted (usually for remuneration) by a disputing party and present at least a superficial conflict of interest that arguably undermines their value to a tribunal.[7] Both methods are permissible under the Rules, but only the former method is the primary focus of Article 29.[8]

When seeking expert advice, the tribunal should always keep in mind that the tribunal-appointed expert is not an additional member of the tribunal, but merely an adviser.[9] While he or she may assist the arbitrators in their fact-finding duties, a role which may often require drawing conclusions based on an analysis of the facts, "the expert cannot usurp the judicial function of the tribunal."[10] According to White: "It is not for [the expert] to 'identify' which facts are 'relevant and significant,' nor to examine and weigh them 'for the purpose of determining liability and assessing damages.'"[11] These are the sole and non-delegable responsibilities of the arbitral tribunal.

Finally, who pays for services rendered by a tribunal-appointed expert? Pursuant to Article 43 of the Rules, the tribunal is empowered to demand monetary deposits from the parties to cover the anticipated costs of the tribunal-appointed expert. This subject is discussed in greater detail in Chapter 27 on the costs of arbitration.

(2) Appointment by the tribunal and terms of reference—Article 29(1)–(2)

Article 29(1) addresses two important steps in the enlistment of a tribunal-appointed expert: (a) the appointment of the expert by the tribunal, and (b) the establishment of the expert's terms of reference.

(a) Appointment

Three fundamental questions surround an expert's appointment: who has discretion to appoint; is appointment appropriate; and by what procedures should appointment occur? Article 29 answers the first question straightforwardly by vesting the arbitral tribunal with

---

[5] Professor Mani states: "Expert evidence is presented before a tribunal in cases involving complicated facts that require elucidation or solution by persons having, by virtue of their specialization, training, vocation or experience, a special and intimate knowledge of these or similar facts." V S Mani, *International Adjudication: Procedural Aspects* (1980) 234. On the use of experts generally, see *Arbitration and Expertise*, ICC Publication No 480/7 (EF) (1994).

[6] In one arbitration under the 1976 UNCITRAL Rules, the possibility of using both types of experts was considered. See *Chevron Corp* (1976 Rules), reprinted in section 2(C). In another case, both party-appointed and tribunal-appointed experts were employed, with the latter in part reviewing the work of the former. See *National Grid PLC* (1976 Rules), reprinted in section 2(C).

[7] See A Faurè, "Improving Procedures for Expert Testimony," in A van den Berg (ed), *ICCA Congress Series No 7, Planning Efficient Arbitration Proceedings* (1993) 156.

[8] The use of party-appointed experts is governed by Article 17(3), which applies to witnesses generally. See generally Chapter 2, section 3(B)(3).

[9] G White, *The Use of Experts by International Tribunal* (1965) 164.

[10] G White, *The Use of Experts*, n 9, 165.

[11] G White, *The Use of Experts*, n 9, 165.

ultimate authority to decide whether or not to appoint an expert.[12] The arbitral tribunal may exercise this power to appoint an expert either *sua sponte* or in response to requests for appointment submitted by the parties.[13] In cases in which both parties present a united position concerning appointment, either for or against, the tribunal's discretion in this regard is more attenuated, and any decision regarding appointment must take into consideration the will of the parties.[14]

The second question of whether appointment is appropriate is more variable and subjective. After reviewing all relevant submissions, including the opinions of any expert witnesses supplied on behalf of the respective parties, the arbitral tribunal must determine whether appointment is necessary for adjudication of the case.[15] Allison and Holtzmann, former judges at the Iran–US Claims Tribunal, propose two factors for consideration: (1) the complexity of the issue before the arbitral tribunal, including the complexity arising from differing opinions of any expert witnesses; and (2) the expediency of appointment of an expert under the circumstances of the case.[16]

The first factor speaks to the arbitral tribunal's inherent ability to comprehend and evaluate the crucial points of the parties' arguments. The inability to complete this basic task stands strongly in favor of seeking expert advice.[17] Yet even if the arbitrators are in favor of appointment, the expediency of appointment, including cost considerations, will enter the calculus.[18] For example, in small cases, a simple cost-benefit analysis may quickly rule out the hiring of an expert, ie, where the size of the amount at stake does not exceed the projected costs of an expert, making appointment impractical.[19] Even in bigger, more complex cases, an arbitral tribunal should also consider the real possibility that the appointment of a tribunal expert—especially one who is not mutually agreeable to the parties—may invite a costly "battle of experts" in which each party feels compelled to seek expert advice for purposes of evaluating and possibly challenging the conclusions of the tribunal-appointed expert.[20]

---

[12] Note that Article 26 of the Model Law, as amended, in contrast, grants the arbitrators a mere conditional power to appoint experts subject to the overriding will of the parties. For commentary, see H Holtzmann and J Neuhaus, *A Guide to the UNCITRAL Model Law on Commercial Arbitration: Legislative History and Commentary* (1989) 153–3.

[13] See *SD Myers, Inc* (1976 Rules), reprinted in section 2(C). See also *McCollough & Co* and *Ministry of Post, Telegraph and Telephone* (1983 Tribunal Rules), Award No 225–89–3 (April 22, 1986) (dismissing respondents' request for appointment of experts), reprinted in 11 Iran-US CTR 3, 5 (1986-II).

[14] The Iran–US Claims Tribunal, for example, has implemented various procedures that enable the parties to participate in the decision to appoint experts. See M Straus, "The Practice of the Iran-U.S. Claims Tribunal in Receiving Evidence from Parties and from Experts," (1986) 3 J Intl Arb 57, 63–9.

[15] As a threshold matter, the arbitral tribunal should decide whether the parties' cases are sufficiently developed to warrant the assistance of an expert. H Holtzmann, "Fact-Finding by the Iran-US Claims Tribunal," in R Lillich (ed), *Fact-Finding Before International Tribunals* (1991) 123.

[16] See R Allison and H Holtzmann, "The Tribunal's Use of Experts," in D Caron and J Crook (eds), *The Iran-United States Claims Tribunal and the Process of International Claims Resolution* (2000) 271.

[17] It perhaps goes without saying that the arbitral tribunal must guarantee that the expert whom it wishes to appoint is indeed capable of completing the task. See *Behring Intl Inc* (1983 Tribunal Rules), Dissenting Opinion of Richard Mosk, reprinted in section 2(D)(1)(e).

[18] According to Article 43 of the UNCITRAL Rules, the parties must make deposits with the arbitral tribunal to cover any expenses relating to the appointment of experts. See Chapter 27, section 5.

[19] See *Gruen Associates, Inc* and *Iran Housing Co* (1983 Tribunal Rules), Award No 61–188–2 (July 27, 1983), reprinted in 3 Iran-US CTR 97, 107 (1983-II) (finding appointment of expert too expensive in light of type and magnitude of case). The Tribunal has been reluctant to appoint in other cases as well, such as where "any possible benefits to be derived from the appointment of an expert were not in proportion to the delays and consequential prejudice to all parties which would ensue." See *American Bell Intl Inc* and *Islamic Republic of Iran* (1983 Tribunal Rules), Award No 255–48–3 (September 19, 1986), reprinted in 12 Iran-US CTR 170, 228 (1986-III).

[20] For Professor Sanders' cost-saving proposal, see section 2(B)(7).

The third question concerns the appropriate process for selecting an expert. Article 29(1) requires the arbitral tribunal to consult with the parties before appointing an expert.[21] Consultation ensures not only that the arbitral tribunal has obtained maximum input from critical sources before appointing an expert, but also that the parties are solidly invested in the selection process. Confident in the abilities of the expert, the parties may be less likely to raise disputes over matters relating to the expert's work.[22] The practice of the Iran–US Claims Tribunal serves as a useful model in this regard.[23] There, the selection process has involved an initial request by the Tribunal to the parties to select a mutually agreeable expert by themselves.[24] In some cases, if this first step fails, the Tribunal has asked the parties to submit a list of three acceptable expert candidates in a sealed envelope, which the Tribunal keeps in confidence. If a match emerges upon comparison of the parties' lists, the Tribunal adheres to the parties' wishes and appoints the candidate as the Tribunal expert. In the absence of a match, the Tribunal assumes responsibility for choosing the expert.[25]

Pursuant to Article 29(2), the expert is required in connection with his or her appointment to submit both to the arbitral tribunal and the parties "a description of his or her qualifications and a statement of his or her impartiality and independence." The timing for the submission of these materials is flexible; the expert must submit them "in principle before accepting appointment." Inclusion of the words "in principle" was meant to "accommodate situations in which the arbitral tribunal found urgent need of an expert, such as to evaluate perishable evidence" and thus could not submit the description in advance of appointment.[26] As explained in Section 3 below, Article 29(2) establishes a mechanism that allows a party to challenge the qualifications or impartiality and independence of the tribunal-appointed expert.

(b) Terms of reference

An important task for an arbitral tribunal in relation to the use of an expert is the establishment of the expert's terms of reference. The terms of reference are a written set of instructions that contain the parameters by which the expert must conduct his investigation.[27] The ultimate responsibility for the drafting and interpretation of the terms of reference lies with the tribunal. This fact is crucial if the terms of reference are to serve their dual purpose effectively. First, they contain the expert's mandate, telling him not only what to do, but

---

[21] This requirement is new to the 2010 UNCITRAL Rules and was added to fill a procedural gap in the Rules. However, some Working Group delegates believed the change was unnecessary because either the obligation to consult was implied or inclusion of such an obligation would expressly create a negative inference that consultation with the parties was not necessary with respect to other matters, such as the content of an expert report. *Report of the Working Group on Arbitration and Conciliation on the Work of its Forty-Fifth Session* (Vienna, September 11–15, 2006), UNCITRAL, 40th Session, UN Doc A/CN.9/614, at 22, para 106 (2007).

[22] See generally M Straus, "The Practice of the Iran-U.S. Claims Tribunal," n 14, 65–7 (observing the benefits of the tribunal's full consideration of the parties' views on the number and kind of experts to be appointed).

[23] See generally M Straus, "The Practice of the Iran-U.S. Claims Tribunal," n 14, 63–9.

[24] This procedure was successful in at least one case. See *Shahin Shaine Ebrahimi* (1983 Tribunal Rules), Order of October 5, 1992, reprinted in section 2(D)(1)(a) (given the opportunity to choose a mutually agreeable expert, claimants agreed to use one of the experts proposed by the respondent).

[25] R Allison and H Holtzmann suggest four essential qualifications for a tribunal-appointed expert: (1) requisite level of expertise in the relevant field, (2) independence and impartiality, (3) availability, and (4) an ability to perform their function within the financial constraints imposed by the arbitral tribunal. See Allison and Holtzmann, "The Tribunal's Use of Experts," n 16, 275–7.

[26] *Report of Working Group II (Arbitration and Conciliation) on the Work of its Fifty-Second Session* (New York, February 1–5, 2010), UNCITRAL, 43rd Session, UN Doc A/CN.9/688, at 13, para 54 (2010).

[27] For examples of terms of reference, see extracts in section 2(D)(1).

also on what information to base his investigation and report.[28] Second, the terms of reference should "guarantee against any delegation of the tribunal's judicial function to a non-member against the original collective will of the parties."[29]

Once the terms of reference are drafted, Article 29(1) requires only that the arbitral tribunal communicate a copy to the parties. In practice, however, the involvement of the parties and possibly the expert in establishing and shaping the terms of reference may be beneficial in certain circumstances.[30] The Iran–US Claims Tribunal, for example, has been receptive to input from these sources when it enhances the quality and clarity of the terms of reference.[31] In some cases, the Tribunal has circulated draft terms of reference for review and comment by the parties.[32] The Tribunal also has responded to suggestions by the parties by amending the terms of reference.[33] In addition, the Tribunal has looked to the tribunal-appointed expert on whether modification of the terms of reference is necessary for completion of his task.[34]

Finally, one should note that the tribunal's authority and responsibility over the terms of reference do not end after their drafting is complete but also continue with respect to their interpretation. The power to interpret becomes relevant when one party claims that the tribunal-appointed expert has exceeded the terms of reference in reaching a certain conclusion contained in the expert report.[35]

---

[28] The arbitral tribunal may adjust the expert's range of operation as it deems appropriate. See R Allison and H Holtzmann, "The Tribunal's Use of Experts," n 16, 274. For a discussion of what issues should be covered in the terms of reference see T Webster, *Handbook of UNCITRAL Arbitration: Commentary, Precedents and Materials for UNCITRAL Based Arbitration Rules* (2010) 415–16.

[29] V S Mani, *International Adjudication: Procedural Aspects*, n 5, 235. Similarly, Berger provides:

As experts frequently tend to enter into the determination of purely legal issues which are reserved to the competence of the tribunal ("run-away expert"), the arbitrators have to fix exactly the terms of reference of the expert, i.e., through posing precise questions to the expert in order to ensure that he confines his duties to the finding and evaluation of facts and submits a report which covers the points at issue and is readily understandable for the arbitrators and the parties.

K Berger, *International Economic Arbitration*, n 3, 437.

[30] The Rules leave open the possibility that the arbitral tribunal might consult with the parties before determining the substance of the terms of reference. P Sanders, "Commentary on UNCITRAL Arbitration Rules," (1977) II Ybk Commercial Arb 172, 203.

[31] See generally N Blackaby and C Partasides, *Redfern and Hunter on International Arbitration*, n 3, 408. Allison and Holtzmann believe that such early involvement in the process minimizes the risk that the parties will later object to the expert's investigation. R Allison and H Holtzmann, "The Tribunal's Use of Experts," n 16, 274. In some cases, for example, the Tribunal even considered nominating an expert adviser to provide assistance in determining the scope and content of the terms of reference for a yet-to-be-appointed expert. See *Starrett Housing Corp* (1983 Tribunal Rules), Order of December 8, 1982, reprinted in section 2(D)(1)(c); *Richard D Harza* (1983 Tribunal Rules), Order of November 4, 1982, reprinted in section 2(D)(1)(d).

[32] See *Shahin Shaine Ebrahimi* (1983 Tribunal Rules), Order of October 5, 1992, para 5 (comments requested), and Order of December 14, 1992, para 3 (revisions made and more comments requested), reprinted in section 2(D)(1)(a).

[33] See, eg, *Arco Exploration, Inc* (1983 Tribunal Rules), Order of November 20, 1990, reprinted in section 2(D)(1)(b). See also *Behring Intl Inc* and *Islamic Republic Iranian Air Force*, Case No 382, Chamber Three, Amendment to Decision (May 3, 1984), reprinted in 6 Iran-US CTR 30 (1984-II).

[34] In the *Arco Exploration* case (1983 Tribunal Rules), for example, the following clause appeared in the expert's terms of reference:

In the event the expert in the course of its investigation forms the opinion that modification of the foregoing terms of reference would be necessary to permit the preparation of a proper report, or if any other difficulty arises, the expert may request from the Tribunal a modification, clarification or resolution.

Paragraph (e), Terms of Reference, in Order of June 13, 1990, reprinted in section 2(D)(1)(b).

[35] See, eg, *Richard D Harza* and *Islamic Republic of Iran* (1983 Tribunal Rules), Award No 232-97-2 (May 2, 1986) (finding that the expert did not exceed his terms of reference), reprinted in 11 Iran-US CTR 76, 124–5 (1986-II).

The significant orders and decisions regarding the appointment of experts and the establishment of the terms of reference in five cases before the Iran–US Claims Tribunal are reproduced below in section 2(D)(1).

(3) Objections to the qualifications or the impartiality and independence of the tribunal-appointed expert—Article 29(2)

Article 29(2), a provision new to the 2010 UNCITRAL Rules, permits a party to raise an objection to the qualifications or impartiality and independence of an expert chosen by the arbitral tribunal. The new procedure draws on Article 6 of the International Bar Association (IBA) Rules on the Taking of Evidence in International Commercial Arbitration[36] and envisions two possible phases (pre- and post-appointment), with all objections to be decided by the arbitral tribunal.

Typically objections to a proposed expert occur early in the process, soon after the parties have had a chance to review relevant materials about a candidate's background. Article 29(2) envisions that, as a general rule, a proposed expert submit a description of qualifications and a statement of impartiality and independence *before* an appointment is made. This requirement ensures that the parties have the necessary information before them to provide informed input in advance of the appointment. In this pre-appointment phase, any party may raise objections to a proposed appointment "[w]ithin the time ordered by the arbitral tribunal." No precise time limit is specified in the Rules. However, in striking the balance between fairness to the parties and avoidance of delay, the arbitral tribunal may find that the 15-day time period for submitting a challenge of an arbitrator[37] is a useful model for modifying the Rules to address the timing for raising similar objections to a proposed expert.[38] Once objections have been raised, the arbitral tribunal must decide them promptly.

A second phase for raising objections occurs "[a]fter an expert's appointment"[39] and allows for objections to be made on a more limited basis. During this time, a party may only object "for reasons of which the party becomes aware after the appointment has been made." The "reasons" justifying a challenge may include, among other things, a significant conflict of interest or a serious question concerning an expert's credentials that has come to light only after his or her appointment, as well as any conduct during the arbitration that unjustifiably favors one party over another. Objections raised post-appointment are not subject to any time limitations and thus can be brought at any time, a fact that raised some concerns about the potential for invoking the process as a dilatory tactic.[40] Again, the

---

[36] See *Settlement of Commercial Disputes: Revision of the UNCITRAL Arbitration Rules, Note by the Secretariat*, UNCITRAL, UN Doc A/CN.9/WG.II/WP.157/Add.1 at 13, para 37 (2009). Article 6.2 of the 1999 IBA Rules requires submission of a statement of independence before appointment, whereas the 2010 version adds to the requirement submission of a description of qualifications. Neither version contains a process for challenging a tribunal-appointed expert post-appointment.

[37] See 2010 UNCITRAL Arbitration Rules, art 13(1).

[38] One commentator agrees. T Webster, *Handbook of UNCITRAL Arbitration*, n 28, 416. Note also one proposal by the Bolivian delegation, which was not adopted by the Working Group, to include a 10-day time limit for challenging tribunal-appointed experts that could be extended for good reason. UNCITRAL, 43rd Session, UN Doc A/CN.9/688, n 26, at 12, para 49. See also *Settlement of Commercial Disputes: Revision of the UNCITRAL Arbitration Rules, Proposal by the Government of the Plurinational State of Bolivia*, UNCITRAL, 52nd Session, UN Doc A/CN.9/WG.II/LII/CRP.2 (2010).

[39] The *travaux préparatoires* are unfortunately scant on the rationale for including new provisions which are not found in the IBA Rules. See UNCITRAL, 43rd Session, UN Doc A/CN.9/688, n 26, at 13–14, para 56.

[40] See UNCITRAL, 43rd Session, UN Doc A/CN.9/688, n 26, at 13, para 55.

15-day time limit for challenging an arbitrator may provide a useful structure that may reasonably limit a party's ability to raise objections.[41]

One unique situation may arise from the deviation of Article 29(2) from the approach of the IBA Rules. Unlike Article 6 of the IBA Rules, Article 29(2) provides that "in principle" the description of qualifications and statement of impartiality and independence must be submitted before appointment of the expert. Though rare, it is thus possible that an expert could be appointed before he or she submits the information necessary for the parties to complete their evaluation. The Rules do not expressly account for this situation, though presumably any objections to the expert's qualifications or impartiality and independence could be viewed as constituting "reasons of which the party becomes aware" after the appointment was made.

The basis on which a party may object to a person chosen by the tribunal to be an expert is broader than that for challenging an arbitrator. Both procedures permit objections based on an alleged lack of impartiality and independence. While the Rules do not expressly state a tribunal-appointed expert's continuous duty of impartiality or independence, this is expected.[42] In addition to a lack of impartiality and independence, a party may also attack an expert's qualifications (or lack of qualifications). This is a reasonable condition of the expert's appointment since his or her services are being enlisted on the basis of offering expertise that the tribunal is lacking. This situation does not generally arise in the context of the appointment of arbitrators.

Finally, while Article 29(1) requires the prospective expert to provide a statement of his or her impartiality or independence, the Rules do not offer a model template for this purpose. The model statements of impartiality and independence for arbitrators that are annexed to the Rules could be easily modified to serve this purpose. In addition, the Rules contain no provisions regarding the expert's customary oath of sincerity and confidentiality, which serves the important purpose of reinforcing the expert's neutrality.[43] The parties therefore may wish to fill this procedural gap, if permitted under applicable law,[44] by modifying the Rules to include an oath, which the tribunal would administer to the expert before he or she begins his investigation, and perhaps again before he or she testifies at the expert hearing. The content of the oath may be similar to that utilized by ICSID:

I solemnly declare upon my honour and conscience that my statement will be in accordance with my sincere belief.[45]

---

[41] See discussion of time limits in Chapter 5, section 4.

[42] At least some Working Group delegates did not consider an express rule to be necessary because any potential for bias on the part of the tribunal-appointed expert could be addressed through the tribunal's discretion in weighing the relevance and weight of the expert's report and could be checked by the parties' own expert reports. UNCITRAL, 43rd Session, UN Doc A/CN.9/688, n 26, at 13, para 55.

[43] Other arbitration rules, such as Article 35(3) of the ICSID Arbitration Rules, require such an oath. Requiring such an oath is generally advisable. See Faurè, "Improving Procedures for Expert Testimony," n 7, 158.

[44] Articles 1042(6) and 1041(1) of the Netherlands Arbitration Act, for example, expressly grant a tribunal authority to examine experts under oath. For further discussion on oaths, see Chapter 19 on Hearings, section 2(B)(2)(a).

[45] ICSID Arbitration Rules, art 35(3). See also Article 27, Note 2 of the 1983 Rules of Procedure of the Iran–US Claims Tribunal (reprinted in Appendix 5), which provides the following oath: "I solemnly declare upon my honour and conscience that I will perform my duties in accordance with my sincere belief and will keep confidential all matters relating to the performance of my task." The Tribunal decided that this declaration could be made orally before the Tribunal or in writing. See *Starrett Housing Corp* (1983 Tribunal Rules), Interlocutory Award of December 19, 1983, reprinted in section 2(D)(1)(c). It should be noted that the expert's declaration is distinguishable from that made by a witness testifying before the Tribunal in that a witness must "speak the truth,

(4) The provision of relevant information to the tribunal-appointed expert—Article 29(3)

As the work of the expert often requires information in the possession of one or both of the parties, their cooperation with the expert investigation is crucial. Article 29(3) establishes a general obligation of the parties to furnish the expert any "relevant information," and a more specific obligation to supply him with "any relevant documents or goods" that he or she may require. These obligations are sufficiently broad to cover a wide range of information requests, including site inspections of relevant documents, goods, or other information.[46] The expert's authority to hear any person with relevant knowledge or obtain any relevant information or materials from the parties is often spelled out in the terms of reference.[47]

Although the expert may request information from the parties, only the tribunal possesses the right to enforce such demands for the provision of information. This may not be entirely clear from the plain terms of the first sentence of Article 29(3), which is drafted from the perspective of a party's obligation to the arbitral process in general. Nevertheless, Article 29(3) provides the tribunal with authority to enforce violations with respect to expert demands on the parties. Although a request for production may come from either an expert or the arbitral tribunal, only the latter is empowered to sanction non-compliance by applying the default procedures of Article 30 or by drawing adverse inferences against the delinquent party.[48] As stressed at the outset of this chapter, the expert is merely an adviser to the tribunal.

The second sentence of Article 29(3) specifically requires the arbitral tribunal to resolve any disputes between a party and the expert regarding the relevance of requested information or the need for production.[49] The tribunal's reviewing authority serves to safeguard the

---

the whole truth and nothing but the truth," while an expert must perform his duties according to his "sincere belief." Compare Article 27, Note 2 of the 1983 Tribunal Rules with Article 25, Note 6(a) of the 1983 Tribunal Rules.

[46] The Iran–US Claims Tribunal has modified the UNCITRAL Rules to expressly permit site inspections, see Appendix 5, which have occurred from time to time as necessary. See *Richard D Harza* (1983 Tribunal Rules), Order, reprinted in section 2(D)(2). Site inspections were addressed in a number of other cases. See *Starrett Housing Corp* and *Government of the Islamic Republic of Iran* (1983 Tribunal Rules), Award No 314–24–1 (August 14, 1987), reprinted in 16 Iran-US CTR 112, 192 (1987-III) (denial of second trip of expert to Iran to inspect original sales contracts); *Chas T Main International Inc* and *Khuzestan Water and Power Authority* (1983 Tribunal Rules), Award No ITL 23–120–2 (July 27, 1983), reprinted in 3 Iran-US CTR 156, 166 (1983-II) (possibility of site inspection included in terms of reference). The use of site inspections may be particularly important in boundary arbitrations. See D Sandifer, *Evidence Before International Tribunals* (1975) 344–5.

[47] See, eg, *Starrett Housing* (1983 Tribunal Rules); *Richard D Harza*, Interlocutory Award (1983 Tribunal Rules); and *Arco Exploration, Inc* (1983 Tribunal Rules), reprinted in section 2(D)(2).

[48] With respect to the Model Law, H Holtzmann and J Neuhaus have explained:

[A]lthough the expert can no doubt request the parties to provide relevant evidence or information, only the arbitral tribunal can actually order production and sanction noncompliance. In practice, though, this procedure is probably little different from the dispute-resolution role assigned to the arbitral tribunal by the UNCITRAL Arbitration Rules.

H Holtzmann and J Neuhaus, *A Guide to the UNCITRAL Model Law on Commercial Arbitration*, n 12, 720.

[49] The tribunal's authority to oversee and regulate the expert's demands on the parties for information is often spelled out in the terms of reference themselves. See, eg, *Chas T Main Intl, Inc* and *Khuzestan Water and Power Authority* (1983 Tribunal Rules), Award No ITL 23–120–2 (July 27, 1983), reprinted in 3 Iran-US CTR 156, 166 (1983-II); *Starrett Housing Corp* and *Government of the Islamic Republic of Iran* (1983 Tribunal Rules), Award No ITL 32–24–1 (December 19, 1983), reprinted in 4 Iran-US CTR 122, 158 (1983-III); *Behring Intl, Inc* and *Islamic Republic Iranian Air Force* (1983 Tribunal Rules), Case No 382, Chamber Three, Decision of December 19, 1983, reprinted in 4 Iran-US CTR 89, 92 (1983-III).

parties' interests in the face of excessive or unreasonable demands by experts for information.[50] Article 29(3) arguably authorizes the arbitral tribunal to impose additional requirements regarding the information production process, subject to the requirements of Article 17(1) to treat the parties fairly and equally. For example, it may be reasonable for a tribunal to require each party to provide the other with copies of any documents given to the expert,[51] and to grant the parties the right to attend any meetings between the expert and persons invited by the expert to provide information relating to an investigation.[52] The arbitral tribunal also may be called upon to determine the reasonableness of the expert's requests to produce documents that are claimed to be privileged or held by individuals claiming immunity from process.[53]

(5) The tribunal-appointed expert's report—Article 29(4)

The main task of the expert is to produce a report containing opinions that may guide the arbitral tribunal's decision-making.[54] In fulfilling this task, the expert must conduct his investigation in strict accordance with his terms of reference, without treading on the adjudicatory functions of the tribunal.[55] The chief role of the tribunal is to determine the proper weight to assign the information contained in the expert report. As a general rule, this task is accomplished by reading the expert's report carefully and critically and adopting the expert's opinions only after the reasoning on which they rest has been rigorously tested in light of all the evidence in the case. In the *Starrett* case, the Iran–US Claims Tribunal determined that the weight of an expert's opinions may depend upon a number of factors. These factors include: the expert's qualifications; the procedure that he has followed in developing his opinions, including his consideration of the parties' comments; the thoroughness of the process by which the expert sought to verify all information presented to him by the parties; and the thoroughness of the report, including citation to evidentiary support.[56]

---

[50] See *Behring Intl, Inc* and *Islamic Republic of Iran* (1983 Tribunal Rules), Case No 382, Chamber Three, Decision of December 19, 1983, Dissent of Richard Mosk (December 19, 1983), reprinted in 4 Iran-US CTR 93, 95 (1983-III). Conversely, the arbitral tribunal may also shield the expert from the unwarranted demands of a party on the expert. In one case, for example, an arbitral tribunal dismissed a party's request that the tribunal-appointed expert be urged to examine new submissions of evidence which "were filed too late, were impossible to verify reliably, and not in accordance with the Expert's valuation premises." *Starrett Housing Corp* and *Government of the Islamic Republic of Iran* (1983 Tribunal Rules), Award No 314–21–1 (August 14, 1987), reprinted in 16 Iran-US CTR 112, 119 (1987-III).

[51] *Richard D Harza* and *Islamic Republic of Iran* (1983 Tribunal Rules), Award No ITL 14–97–2 (February 17, 1983), reprinted in 2 Iran-US CTR 68, 75 (1983-I); *Chas T Main Intl Inc* and *Khuzestan Water and Power Authority*, Award No ITL 23–120–2 (July 27, 1983), reprinted in 3 Iran-US CTR 156, 166 (1983-II).

[52] *Richard D Harza* (1983 Tribunal Rules), reprinted in section 2(D)(2) (permitting the parties to attend a site inspection by the expert). See also *Behring Intl, Inc* and *Islamic Republic Iranian Air Force* (1983 Tribunal Rules), Case No 382, Chamber Three, Amendment to Decision of December 19, 1983, reprinted in 6 Iran-US CTR 30, 31 (1984-II) (approving attendance of non-party, US Government, at expert inventory "in order to ensure compliance with United States laws and regulations and to safeguard U.S. security interests.").

[53] See *Behring Intl, Inc* and *Islamic Republic of Iran* (1983 Tribunal Rules), Case No 382, Chamber Three, Dissent of Richard M Mosk to Decision of December 19, 1983, reprinted in 4 Iran-US CTR 93, 95 (1983-III). See generally, G White, *The Use of Experts*, n 9, 183–96. For a discussion of privileges in international arbitration, see R Mosk and T Ginsberg, "Evidentiary Privileges in International Arbitration," (2001) 50 ICLQ 345.

[54] A reasonable interpretation of Article 29(4) is that the expert's report must be in writing, although in urgent situations an oral report may suffice.

[55] *Starrett Housing Corp* and *Government of the Islamic Republic of Iran* (1983 Tribunal Rules), Award No 314–24–1 (August 14, 1987), reprinted in 16 Iran-US CTR 112, 197 (1987-III) ("[I]t is fundamental that an arbitral tribunal cannot delegate to [the expert] the duty of deciding the case.").

[56] *Starrett Housing Corp* (1983 Tribunal Rules) at 196–9, reprinted in relevant part in section 2(D)(3)(e).

The expert's report is but one factor that the tribunal considers in light of the totality of circumstances of the case.[57] The report is not legally binding on the arbitrators, who may pick and choose from its content as they deem appropriate. However, an award may become vulnerable to subsequent challenge proceedings if it appears that the arbitral tribunal has simply incorporated the expert's views wholesale, without subjecting them to an appropriate level of intellectual scrutiny. To safeguard the validity of the award, the prudent arbitral tribunal, when relying on some or all of the contents of an expert report, will be sure to explain in the award its reasons for doing so in sufficient detail.[58]

Article 29(4) provides yet another mechanism for involving the parties in the arbitral tribunal's dealings with an expert. The parties are entitled to provide comments, in writing, on the expert's report.[59] In practice, these comments may be useful not only to the arbitrators for purposes of deciding the case, but also to the expert for identifying any flaws or gaps in his work.[60] The invitation for comments, however, is not an opportunity for a party to introduce new evidence or argue new aspects of the case. Any attempts to do so should be dismissed promptly to avoid prejudicing the other party.[61] Finally, Article 29(4) entitles the parties to examine all documents on which the expert bases his report, though most responsible experts, in any event, will file their reports with attachments containing all supporting evidence.

(6) Expert hearings—Article 29(5)

After the tribunal-appointed expert's report is completed and the parties have had the opportunity to provide their comments, points still in dispute or unresolved questions regarding analysis and methodology may require further elucidation. Article 29(5) provides the parties yet another vehicle for involvement in the expert process: the expert hearing.[62] Upon either party's request, the arbitral tribunal must hold a hearing in which both parties have the opportunity to interrogate the expert. The expert hearing is not limited to an examination of the tribunal-appointed expert only. Article 29(5) expressly provides that the parties may present their own expert witnesses to challenge or to bolster the testimony of the tribunal-appointed expert.[63] In fact, the testimony of expert witnesses at the hearing

---

[57] *Starrett Housing Corp* (1983 Tribunal Rules) at 197. See also *Chas T Main Intl, Inc* (1983 Tribunal Rules) and *Khuzestan Water and Power Authority* (1983 Tribunal Rules), Case No 120, Chamber Two, Order of November 23, 1983, reprinted in 4 Iran-US CTR 60, 60 (1983-III) ("[T]he reports of the experts do not bind the Tribunal but only assist it in making its decision."). See also 2010 UNCITRAL Arbitration Rules, art 27(4).

[58] See, eg, *Shahin Shaine Ebrahimi* (1983 Tribunal Rules), Award of October 12, 1994, reprinted in section 2(D)(3)(a) (explanation of reasons for adopting expert's conclusion).

[59] These comments may include the observations of the parties' expert witnesses. It should also be noted that any such comments are written statements within the meaning of Article 24 and must be filed within 45 days, pursuant to Article 25. See P Sanders, "Commentary on UNCITRAL Arbitration Rules," n 30, 203.

[60] Often an expert will submit a preliminary or draft report for comments by the parties. For this reason, Article 29(4)'s reference to "the report" should not be construed so narrowly as to preclude the provision of commentary on any preliminary or draft reports of the expert. The Iran–US Claims Tribunal has interpreted Article 29(4) liberally in this regard. See *Behring Intl, Inc* and *Islamic Republic Iranian Air Force* (1983 Tribunal Rules), Award No ITM/ITL 52–382–3 (June 21, 1985), reprinted in 8 Iran-US CTR 238, 276, n 51 (1987-I); *Starrett Housing Corp* and *Government of the Islamic Republic of Iran* (1983 Tribunal Rules), Award No 314–21–1 (August 14, 1987), reprinted in 16 Iran-US CTR 112, 192 (1987-III).

[61] See *Starrett Housing Corp* (1983 Tribunal Rules), at 190–1 (finding documents containing new evidence inadmissible in order to shield the other party from prejudice).

[62] For examples of orders for expert hearings, see section 2(D)(4). Like any other hearing instituted under the UNCITRAL Rules, Article 28 would govern. See Chapter 19, on hearings.

[63] See, eg, *Starrett Housing Corp* and *Government of the Islamic Republic of Iran* (1983 Tribunal Rules), Award No 314–24–1, reprinted in 16 Iran-US CTR 112, 198 (1987-III) (parties' expert witnesses involved in hearing).

may provide the arbitral tribunal with a useful basis for evaluating the merits of the advice offered by the tribunal-appointed expert.[64] During the hearing, the arbitral tribunal is also entitled to put questions to the tribunal-appointed expert, the party-appointed expert witnesses, and the parties themselves.

(7) A note on party-appointed "expert witnesses"

The Rules contain several references to party-appointed experts, but only in the context of their use as "expert witnesses" during the hearing phase of the arbitration. The second sentence of Article 29(5), for example, permits the parties to present expert witness testimony at the expert hearing after delivery of the expert report.[65] If construed literally, these references would limit the use of party-appointed experts in UNCITRAL arbitration until a rather advanced stage of the proceedings, namely the hearings. The *travaux préparatoires* of the 1976 UNCITRAL Rules, however, confirm that this was not the intention of the original drafters who supported the use of party-appointed experts at any stage of the arbitral proceedings.[66] In fact, during discussions on the Revised Draft of the 1976 Rules, the Commission seriously debated whether to qualify the rights and duties regarding tribunal-appointed experts with the phrase "[w]ithout prejudice to the expert proof provided *by the parties*."[67] Whether or not expressly stated in the Rules, UNCITRAL's support for the use of party-appointed experts at any time and in any manner necessary is unambiguous.[68]

While it is clear that party-appointed experts may play a useful role, it is less certain how a tribunal chooses between relying on the parties' experts and appointing its own.[69] In all cases, the arbitral tribunal must balance the interests carefully. On the one side are the

---

Note that this express invitation should not be read as barring the parties' use of expert witnesses in other stages of the proceedings. See section 2(B)(7).

[64] See *Starrett Housing Corp* and *Government of the Islamic Republic of Iran* (1983 Tribunal Rules), Award No 314–24–1 (August 14, 1987), reprinted in 16 Iran-US CTR 112, 198 (1987-III) ("[T]he Tribunal was able to test the Expert's views in the light of testimony of expert witnesses"). The expert hearing may also provide the arbitral tribunal with another opportunity to question the experts and the parties. See *Starrett Housing Corp* and *Government of the Islamic Republic of Iran* (1983 Tribunal Rules), Award No 314–24–1 (August 14, 1987), reprinted in 16 Iran-US CTR 112, 120 (1987-III) (arbitral tribunal may question the experts); *Richard D Harza* and *Islamic Republic of Iran* (1983 Tribunal Rules), Case No 97, Chamber Two, Order of July 24, 1985, at 2 (arbitral tribunal may question the parties).

[65] See 2010 UNCITRAL Rules, art 17(3), art 27(2), art 28(2)–(4), and art 29(5).

[66] See *Summary Record of the 9th Meeting of the Committee of the Whole (II)*, UNCITRAL, 9th Session, UN Doc A/CN.9/9/C.2/SR.9, at 7, paras 60–62 (1976). See also *Report of the UNCITRAL on the Work of its Ninth Session*, UN GAOR, 31st Session, Supp No 17, UN Doc A/31/17, para 134 (1976), reprinted in (1976) VII UNCITRAL Ybk 66, 76 (1976).

[67] UN GAOR, 31st Session, Supp No 17, UN Doc A/31/17, n 66, para 134 (emphasis added). Subsequently, one of the principal drafters of the 1976 Rules proposed to "add a provision in the UNCITRAL Rules on Party-Appointed Experts based on art. 5(3) of the IBA Rules." See P Sanders, "Has the Moment Come to Revise the Arbitration Rules of UNCITRAL?," (2004) 20(3) Arb Intl 243, 263.

[68] Professor Sanders supports this view, stating that "the parties may bring expert witnesses not only to hearings at which an expert appointed by the arbitrators will testify, but they may also bring expert witnesses to a hearing when no such expert witnesses have been appointed previously by the arbitrators." P Sanders, "Commentary on UNCITRAL Arbitration Rules," n 30, 204. Some commentators have suggested that the possibility of using both kinds of expert witnesses "reflects an accommodation between the civil law and common law approaches." C Brower and J Brueschke, *The Iran-United States Claims Tribunal* (1998) 200. See also R Allison and H Holtzmann, "The Tribunal's Use of Experts," n 16, 270.

[69] When raised by the International Council for Commercial Arbitration, this question received varied responses. See P Sanders (ed), *ICCA Congress Series No 3, Comparative Arbitration Practice and Public Policy in Arbitration* (1987) 108–10.

potentially high costs of using tribunal-appointed experts.[70] On the other side is the benefit of avoiding partiality and dependence. Unlike party-appointed witnesses, whose interests can be aligned with those of the party that hired them, the tribunal-appointed expert by definition is impartial and independent from the parties, their legal counsel, and the arbitral tribunal. To any arbitrator who has attempted to assess the often complicated and inevitably conflicting opinions of party-appointed experts, impartiality and independence may be worth the steep price in some cases.

In choosing between the two kinds of expert advice, Professor Sanders makes the following useful suggestion: The tribunal should adopt a policy in regard to expert advice of first encouraging the parties to present their own experts, and then, if necessary after reviewing the experts' opinions, enlisting the assistance of a tribunal-appointed expert for further advice.[71]

(8) Comparison to the 1976 UNCITRAL Rules

Article 29 is very similar to corresponding Article 27 of the 1976 UNCITRAL Rules in its object and purpose, with two noteworthy differences.

First, Article 29(1) contains an express obligation that the arbitral tribunal consult with the parties before appointing experts. While original Article 27(1) lacks a comparable provision, it is nevertheless good practice for the tribunal to consult with the parties, where possible, in order to make the most informed decision regarding the appointment of an expert.

Second, as discussed above, Article 29(2) not only requires an expert to provide a description of his or her qualifications and a statement of his or her impartiality, but also creates a procedure for party evaluation of the qualifications and impartiality and independence of an expert, both before and after appointment. Though Article 29(2) is new to the 2010 Rules, it should be noted that the Iran–US Claims Tribunal, which uses a modified version of the 1976 Rules, has subjected tribunal-appointed experts to the same general challenge procedures for arbitrators set forth in Articles 10 and 11 of the 1983 Tribunal Rules of Procedure—with the important distinction that the Tribunal, not the appointing authority, has authority to decide a challenge.[72] Parties using the 1976 UNCITRAL Rules thus may wish to incorporate the text of Article 29(2) into their version of the Rules, or at least modify the 1976 Rules to provide disclosure statements concerning possible conflicts of interest and, if possible, take an oath before conducting their work and testifying.

C. Extracts from the Practice of Investment Tribunals

Wintershall AG, et al and *Government of Qatar,* Partial Award on Liability, para B.VIII (February 5, 1988) (*Ad Hoc* Proceeding, 1976 UNCITRAL Rules, Concession Agreement), reprinted in (1989) 28 ILM 798, 803:

---

[70] See S Baker and M Davis, *The UNCITRAL Arbitration Rules in Practice: The Experience of the Iran-United States Claims Tribunal* (1992) 128; J Selby and D Stewart, "Practical Aspects of Arbitrating Claims Before the Iran-United States Claims Tribunal," (1984) 18(2) Intl Lawyer 211, 226 (recommending that parties supply their own experts); G Aldrich, *The Jurisprudence of the Iran-United States Claims Tribunal* (1996) 347. See also D Stewart, "The Iran-United States Claims Tribunal: A Review of Developments 1983–84," (1984) 16 Law and Policy in Intl Business 677, 744.

[71] P Sanders, "Commentary on UNCITRAL Arbitration Rules," n 30, 204. See also H van Houtte, "Conduct of Arbitral Proceedings," n 3, 123. The Iran–US Claims Tribunal has followed this approach in at least one case. See *Shahin Shaine Ebrahimi* and *Government of the Islamic Republic of Iran* (1983 Tribunal Rules), Award No 560–44/46/47–3 (October 12, 1994), reprinted in 30 Iran-US CTR 170, 181–3 (1994).

[72] See *Shahin Shaine Ebrahimi* (1983 Tribunal Rules), Order of July 20, 1992, reprinted in section 2(D)(1)(a).

On Monday, March 23, 1987, Weldon T. Kruger was advised of his appointment as an expert of the Tribunal pursuant to Article 27(1) of the [1976] UNCITRAL Arbitration Rules, as modified by paragraph (3) of the Agreement of October 22, 1986. On June 9, 1987, a copy of the Tribunal's technical expert's Terms of Reference was communicated to the Parties pursuant to Article 27(1) of the [1976] UNCITRAL Arbitration Rules. An amendment to these Terms of Reference was communicated to the Parties on June 15, 1987.

SD Myers, Inc and *Government of Canada*, Second Partial Award, (October 21, 2002) (*Ad Hoc* Proceeding, 1976 UNCITRAL Rules, NAFTA Chapter Eleven), reprinted in (2001) 40 ILM 1408, 1411, 1443:

23. By a letter dated 13 February 2001, the Tribunal directed that a case management meeting take place in Toronto on 21 February 2001 to consider:

...

- Whether or not the Tribunal should appoint its own forensic accountancy expert pursuant to Article 27 of the [1976] UNCITRAL Rules.

...

308. If the Disputing Parties are unable to agree on the relevant calculations they may place the issue before the Tribunal as a matter to be determined, together with the question of the allocation of costs, in the Final Award. In that event the Tribunal will consider appointing an accountancy expert, in accordance with Article 27 of the [1976] UNCITRAL Arbitration Rules, to review the Disputing Parties' respective positions and to report to the Tribunal.

National Grid PLC and *Argentine Republic,* Award (November 3, 2008) (*Ad Hoc* Proceeding, 1976 UNCITRAL Rules, UK-Argentina BIT), at 11–13:

7. Appointment of Professor Calvet as the Tribunal-Appointed Expert and the Filing of his Report
44. On November 2, 2007, the Tribunal informed the Parties that, in accordance with Article 27 of the [1976 UNCITRAL] Arbitration Rules, the appointment of one or more experts might be of assistance to the Tribunal to review the expert report of Mr. Wood-Collins and the critical valuation of it done by experts Bello and Molina, inviting the Parties to attempt to reach an agreement on the selection of one or more independent experts. On November 30, 2007, the Claimant (i) informed the Tribunal that the Parties had been unable to reach an agreement in such regard, and (ii) proposed certain criteria to the Tribunal for the selection and procedure for the appointment of the expert.
45. By letter of December 5, 2007, the Respondent commented on the selection criteria proposed by the Claimant, and proposed the consideration of additional criteria. Further letters were filed by the Parties in this regard between December 7 and 12, 2007.
46. Having considered the views and proposals of the Parties, on December 20, 2007, the Tribunal issued Procedural Order No 20 concerning the criteria, terms of reference, and procedure to be followed with regard to the selection of an independent expert. By letter of December 28, 2007, the Parties were informed of the Tribunal's intent to appoint Professor Louis Calvet, unless the Parties raised compelling objections to his appointment. None having been raised, on February 1, 2008, the Parties were informed of the appointment by the Tribunal of Professor Louis Calvet as an independent expert.
47. In accordance with Procedural Order No 20, on February 6, 2008, Professor Calvet's Draft Report dated February 3, 2008 (the "Draft Report") was submitted for the consideration of the Parties. On March 3, 2008, the Claimant filed its comments on the Draft Report, and so did the Respondent on March 4, 2008. Further communications were made in such regard by the Respondent on March 6, 2008 and by the Claimant on March 12, 2008, the latter attaching the views of its own expert, Mr. Wood-Collins. Having been authorized by the Tribunal, on March 25, 2008, the Respondent filed Messrs. Bello and Molina's views on the Independent Expert's Draft Report.

...

49. On April 29, 2008, the Centre notified the Parties of the Independent Expert's Final Report (the "Final Report") dated April 28, 2008. On May 12, 2008, in accordance with Procedural Order No 20 of December 20, 2007, as amended by the Tribunal on April 25, 2008, each party submitted its corrections to any manifest errors in the Final Report, adding its respective comments on the Final Report. On May 15 and 19, 2008, the Claimant and the Respondent filed further communications in this regard.
50. On May 23, 2008, the Tribunal, referring to the Parties' various communications related to the Final Report of Professor Calvet, informed the Parties that it had taken note of the Parties' submissions to the extent they purported to identify manifest errors in the Final Report. The Tribunal also informed the Parties that it considered that Professor Calvet had completed his assignment as described in his terms of reference and that should the Tribunal decide that it needed further assistance, it would consult with the Parties.

Chevron Corp, et al and *Republic of Ecuador*, Procedural Order No 8, (March 31, 2010) (PCA administered, 1976 UNCITRAL Rules, US-Ecuador BIT), at 2–3:

3.1 Should not agreement be reached according to section 2 above, [regarding the amount of taxes owed by the claimant], between Claimants and Respondent, each side will appoint an expert on Ecuadorian tax laws by June 30, 2010.
3.2 The Tribunal may consider appointing an expert on its behalf, whose terms of reference will be determined at the time of such appointment in accordance with the purpose of this procedure and Article 27 of the [1976] UNCITRAL Rules.
3.3 The party-appointed experts and the Tribunal-appointed expert, if any has been appointed, will cooperate and attempt to present a joint proposal to the Tribunal as to the amount, if any to be deducted from the total set forth in the Table at paragraph 549 of its Partial Award on account of any applicable Ecuadorian tax laws.
3.4 Should the experts above be unable to form a joint proposal to the Tribunal by August 30, 2010, the Tribunal may ask for individual submissions from each expert or from any of them in accordance with instructions to be set out by the Tribunal at that time.

D. Extracts from the Practice of the Iran–US Claims Tribunal

(1) Tribunal Rules (1983), Article 27(1)—appointment and terms of reference

(a) The *Shahin Shaine Ebrahimi* case

Shahin Shaine Ebrahimi and *Government of the Islamic Republic of Iran*, Case Nos 44, 46 & 47, Chamber Three, Order of July 20, 1992, at 1–3:

1. The Tribunal has decided to appoint an expert in accordance with Article 27 of the [1983] Tribunal Rules to render a report as to certain matters relating to the valuation of Gostaresh Maskan Company as of November 13, 1979. In order to facilitate the procedure described in paragraph 2, the Draft Order concerning the expert's terms of reference is attached hereto.
2. The Tribunal intends to give the Parties the opportunity to agree on the selection of the expert, which shall be a firm of independent public accountants or appraisers. The expert will therefore be appointed by a further Order after the following procedure has been carried out:
    (a) Each of the Parties is requested to file by August 20, 1992 a list of names and addresses of three experts in a sealed envelope marked "confidential" with the Registry of the Tribunal, which will be instructed not to open the envelopes. The Tribunal will then determine whether one or more experts appear on both lists and, if so, will then attempt to make the appointment accordingly.
    (b) If the lists do not contain a common name, the Tribunal will, by further Order, ask the Parties to attempt to agree on an expert within a further period of four weeks.
    (c) If the Parties fail to reach agreement on an expert, the Tribunal will proceed to appoint an expert.

(d) No extension of any of the aforementioned time limits will be granted unless an extension is requested by both Parties.
3. Before making the appointment the Tribunal will consult the prospective expert with regard to the terms of reference and thereafter submit a draft to the Parties for comments, which comments shall be filed within six weeks. The Tribunal intends to instruct the expert to take as a basis those issues upon which the Parties or the experts that have been presented by the Parties or the experts that have been presented by the Parties are in agreement and, as far as possible, to limit its analysis to those issues which are in dispute.
4. The Tribunal intends to discuss with the expert prior to its appointment the question of costs....

...

6. Finally, the Tribunal notes that prior to its appointment the expert shall make a disclosure statement in the same form as required of a Tribunal arbitrator pursuant to Article 9 of the [1983] Tribunal Rules and that the expert can only be challenged as provided for in Article 10 and Article 11, paragraph 1, in the case of a challenge of an arbitrator. If such challenge is made, the validity thereof will be decided by the Chamber.

Shahin Shaine Ebrahimi and *Government of the Islamic Republic of Iran*, Case Nos 44, 46 & 47, Chamber Three, Order of October 5, 1992, at 1–2:

2. The Tribunal takes note of the Claimants' agreement to the use of one of the experts proposed by the Respondent, Professor Richard Brealey.
3. The Tribunal therefore has contacted Professor Brealey to solicit his views, based on the documents listed in item 6 of the draft terms of reference, on the preliminary matters mentioned in items 4 and 6 of the Tribunal's Order filed 20 July 1992.
4. In accordance with the procedure outlined in item 3 of the Tribunal's Order filed 20 July 1992, the Tribunal also is consulting Professor Brealey with regard to the use of the terms of reference, following which the Tribunal intends to submit a draft to the Parties for comments.
5. Without prejudice to the procedure outlined in item 3 of the Tribunal's Order filed 20 July 1992, each Party is free, if it so wishes, to file comments on the draft terms of reference as appended to the Tribunal's Order filed 20 July 1992.
6. The Tribunal reminds the Parties of item 6 of the draft terms of reference. Additional documents shall not be filed unless the Tribunal has specifically invited or requested the Parties to do so.

Shahin Shaine Ebrahimi and *Government of the Islamic Republic of Iran*, Case Nos 44, 46 & 47, Chamber Three, Order of December 14, 1992, at 1–2:

1. (a) Further to paragraph 2 of the Tribunal's Order filed October 5, 1992, the Tribunal appointed Professor Richard Brealey as the expert in these Cases.
   (b) The Parties are informed that the expert on October 20, 1992 provided the following disclosure statement: "I am not aware of any circumstances that would affect my impartiality or independence in this case. In particular, I have not worked for, nor am I in any way indebted to, any member of the [Claimant] Ebrahimi family, the [Respondent] Islamic Republic of Iran, the Gostaresh Maskan Company or any of its affiliated companies. I have in the past acted as an expert witness for the United States Department in a case that has no connection with the Iran-United States Claims Tribunal."
   (c) The Parties shall not communicate with the expert without specific prior authorization from the Tribunal.

...

3. (a) As indicated in paragraph 4 of the Tribunal's Order filed October 5, 1992, the Tribunal has consulted the expert with regard to the draft terms of reference. It has also received comments from each of the Parties in response to paragraph 5 of the said Order. Copies of these comments, including their enclosures, are appended for the Parties' information.

(b) These comments so received have led the Tribunal to revise the draft terms of reference where deemed appropriate. A copy of the terms so revised, marked for the Parties' convenience, is appended.

(c) In accordance with paragraph 3 of the Tribunal's Order filed July 20, 1992, the Parties shall file any remaining comments they may have on the revised draft terms of reference by January 26, 1993. The Tribunal does not intend to grant any extension of this period. Comments filed by a Party pursuant to this paragraph shall be distributed to the other Party only after the latter has filed its comments or has lost its right to do so.

Shahin Shaine Ebrahimi and *Government of the Islamic Republic of Iran*, Case Nos 44, 46 & 47, Chamber Three, Order of February 4, 1993, 1–3, reprinted in 30 Iran-US CTR 170, 204–205 n 21 (1994) (citations omitted):

Terms of Reference

1. The Tribunal requires the assistance of the expert in determining the fair market value, as of November 13, 1979, of Gostaresh Maskan Company ("GMC"). The expert's valuation shall be made on the basis of fair market value, taking into account the tangible physical and financial assets of the undertaking and other elements, if any, including but not limited to, contractual and intellectual property rights, commercial prospects, goodwill, and likely future profitability. The effects of the very act of nationalization or effects of events that occurred subsequent to nationalization shall be excluded; however, prior changes in the general political, social, and economic conditions which might have affected GMC's business prospects as of the date it was taken shall be taken into account.

...

2. For the purpose set forth above, the expert, after familiarizing itself with the documents filed by the Parties which the Tribunal, in consultation with the expert, has selected as necessary to the performance of its task, shall give its opinion as to such fair market value including:

   A. Value of fixed assets applying the appropriate index[es] and deducting actual depreciation, making such adjustments, if any, as may be appropriate in respect of (i) project expenses (vs. plant and equipment account) and (ii) allegedly fictitious transactions;
   B. Value of current assets, including but not limited to those set out below;
   C. Value of GMC's letters of credit;
   D. Value of:
      (1) accounts receivable, assuming (i) that price adjustments are applicable and, alternatively, (ii) that price adjustments are not applicable
      (2) progress payments not yet posted, including *inter alia* progress payments with respect to (i) New Town and (ii) NIOC;
   E. Value of other assets including, *inter alia*:
      (1) GE license
      (2) rights to Gypsum Mine
      (3) shares in Palayeshgar
      (4) shares in Gostaresh Blount;
   F. Value of GMC's contract backlog, taking into consideration *inter alia*:
      (1) assumptions regarding contract performance (GMC's capability, government payments)
      (2) applicability of price adjustments
      (3) status of contracts, i.e., were they cancelled by November 13, 1979 or not?
   G. Value, if any, of GMC's goodwill;
   H. Effects, if any, of
      (1) doubtful debt provision
      (2) whether purchases of equipment and supplies by GMC pursuant to letters of credit were properly debited to its account by issuing banks

(3) whether NIOC (employer supplied) materials were properly credited to NIOC
(4) taxes applicable under Iranian law to GMC's income.
  I. Possible effect, if any such effect were deemed relevant by the Tribunal, of the Claimants' shares representing a minority interest in GMC, or the Respondent's acquisition of a controlling interest in GMC.
3. In the event the expert, in the course of its investigation, forms the opinion that modification of the foregoing terms of reference would be necessary to permit the preparation of a proper report, or if any other difficulty arises, the expert may request from the Tribunal a modification, clarification, or resolution.
...
6. The expert shall make its investigation and report on the basis of the following documents: [Names of documents omitted]...

(b) The *Arco Exploration* case

Arco Exploration, Inc and *National Iranian Oil Co*, Case No 21, Chamber One, Order of December 7, 1989, at 1–3:

1. The Tribunal has decided to appoint an expert in accordance with Article 27 of the [1983] Tribunal Rules of Procedure to render a report as to the annual production of crude oil that could reasonably have been expected from LAPCO's Sassan and Bahram Fields from April 1, 1979 through November 16, 1998.
2. The Tribunal intends to give the Parties the opportunity to agree on the selection of the expert which should be a firm and not a person in individual capacity. The expert will therefore be appointed by a further Order after the following procedure has been carried out:
   (a) Each of the Parties is requested to file by January 8, 1990 a list of names and addresses of three experts in a sealed envelope marked "confidential" with the Registry of the Tribunal, which will be instructed not to open the envelopes. The Tribunal will then determine whether one or more experts appear on both lists and, if so, will then attempt to make the appointment accordingly.
   (b) If the lists do not contain a common name, the Tribunal will, by a further Order, ask the Parties to attempt to agree on an expert within a further period of four weeks.
   (c) If the Parties fail to reach agreement on an expert, the Tribunal will proceed to appoint an expert.
   (d) No extension of any of the aforementioned time limits will be granted unless an extension is requested by both Parties.
3. Before making the appointment the Tribunal will consult the prospective expert with regard to the terms of reference and thereafter submit a draft to the Parties for comments, which comments shall be filed within four weeks. The Tribunal intends to instruct the expert to take as a basis those issues upon which the Parties or experts presented by the Parties are in agreement and, as far as possible, to limit its analysis to those issues which are in dispute.
4. The Tribunal intends to discuss with the expert prior to its appointment the question of costs....
...
6. Finally, the Tribunal notes that prior to its appointment the expert shall make a disclosure statement in the same form as required of a Tribunal arbitrator pursuant to Article 9 of the [1983] Tribunal Rules and that the expert can only be challenged as provided for in Article 10 and Article 11, paragraph 1, in the case of a challenge of an arbitrator. If such a challenge is made, the validity thereof will be decided by the Chamber.

Arco Exploration, Inc and *National Iranian Oil Co*, Case Nos 20 & 21, Chamber One, Order of June 13, 1990, at 2–4:

Terms of Reference

(a) After familiarizing itself with the documents filed by the parties which the Tribunal, in consultation with the expert, has selected as necessary to the performance of its task, the expert shall give its opinion as to the annual production of crude oil that could, in December 1979, have reasonably been expected from LAPCO's Sassan and Bahram Fields for the entire period from April 1, 1979 through November 16, 1998.

(b) The expert is instructed to assume, in preparing its report, that the Parties would have fully complied with their obligations throughout the term of the Joint Structure Agreement, in particular, but not limited to, Article 13, paragraphs 1 and 7, and Article 21, paragraph 1, thereof, requiring the Parties

"[t]o exert their utmost efforts to develop any discovered fields to the maximum extent consistent with good petroleum industry practice and having due regard at all times to the market availability to extract such Petroleum as shall be discovered at a rate ensuring that such part of the discovered reserves as may be economically extracted and sold by the utilization of the most up-to-date methods and practices of the petroleum industry shall be fully extracted during the term of the Agreement; and in particular to observe sound technical and engineering principles in conserving the deposits of hydrocarbons and in general in carrying out the operations authorized under this Agreement;" (Article 13, paragraph 1)

"[t]o be always mindful, in the conduct of their operations, of the rights and interests of Iran;" (Article 13, paragraph 7)

And each Party to "exercise its utmost efforts in order to ensure the sale of the maximum possible quantity of Petroleum economically justified." (Article 21, paragraph 1)

On the basis of these assumptions the expert is instructed:

(i) to express an opinion as to whether it would have been the proper, customary and preferred practice in the international petroleum industry for LAPCO to have produced Sassan Field at its capacity in order to prevent migration to Abu Dhabi, even if Iran and NIOC were otherwise implementing a policy of curtailment of production in Iran generally.

(ii) to provide in its report two alternative forecasts as follows:
  (a) full production on the basis that there would be no curtailment on LAPCO's production, and
  (b) full production less such percentage of curtailment as, in the expert's opinion, would have reasonably been expected in December 1979 to be imposed, from time to time, upon LAPCO's production, taking into consideration the possibility of migration of oil to Abu Dhabi.

  . . .

  (e) In the event the expert in the course of its investigation forms the opinion that modification of the foregoing terms of reference would be necessary to permit the preparation of a proper report, or if any other difficulty arises, the expert may request from the Tribunal a modification, clarification or resolution.

Arco Exploration, Inc and *National Iranian Oil Co*, Case Nos 20 & 21, Chamber One, Order of November 20, 1990, at 1:

In view of the recent submission by the Parties, and after consulting with the expert, the Tribunal make the following clarifications concerning the expert's terms of reference:

1. Recoverable reserves from the Buwaib reservoir should not be included in the estimate of total production to be assessed by the expert.
2. Further studies and concepts submitted by the Parties to the expert (such as the "prudent operator" concept, the Gaffney Cline and Associates report, etc.) can be taken into account by the expert only in so far as they contain information available already as of December 1979, but irrespective of whether that information was known to or used by the Parties or not.

3. With regard to circumstances such as those mentioned in the Respondents' "Reply pursuant to the Tribunal's Order dated September 5, 1990" (Doc. 397) section C, pp. 24 and 25, the expert should only take into consideration the possible effect of OPEC ceilings on production quantities and present alternative calculations with and without such consideration. This is without prejudice to whether and in which way the Tribunal may decide on the relevance of other circumstances.

(c) The *Starrett Housing* case

Starrett Housing Corp and *Government of the Islamic Republic of Iran*, Award No ITL 32–24–1 (December 19, 1983), reprinted in 4 Iran-US CTR 122, 157–58 (1983-III):

The Tribunal sets forth the following as the terms of reference for the expert:

1. The expert shall give his opinion on the value of Shah Goli as of January 31, 1980, including the value of the Project in Shah Goli's hands, considering as he deems appropriate the discounted cash flow method of valuation.

   The expert shall mention in his report as he deems appropriate the items, if any, referred to in the counter-claims which his investigation shows are liabilities of Shah Goli or the Project.

   Any substantial items relating to the claims or counter-claims which require further substantiation or determination by the Tribunal of legal issues shall be noted in the report by footnote or other suitable means.

   The expert shall examine the counter-claims with a view to including in his valuation such liabilities mentioned therein which are related to Shah Goli or the Project, recognizing that the Tribunal has not yet made any legal determinations concerning the counter-claims.

2. The expert shall also give his opinion as of January 31, 1980 on the net profit of the Project, if any, Starrett Housing would reasonably have received through the management fees paid to Starrett Construction.

3. The expert shall give his opinion as to how the amount of compensation, if any, to which the Claimants are entitled shall be reduced to accurately reflect the 20.3 percent interest in Shah Goli not owned by the Claimants.

4. The expert shall also give his opinion as of January 31, 1980 on the proper method for taking into account loans made to Shah Goli for the purposes of the Project, as defined in the Basic Project Agreement. In this connection, his report shall include:
   (a) The amount of principal and accrued interest of each such loan, identifying as to each the lender and the borrower;
   (b) The extent to which the proceeds of each such loan were expended for the purposes of the Project.

5. The expert shall investigate to which corporation the heavy duty construction equipment, which is referred to in Claimants' Exhibit 34, belonged, and to make an estimation as to the value of that equipment as of January 31, 1980.

...

Before beginning the performance of his duties, the expert shall make the declaration required by Note 2 to Article 27 of the [1983] Tribunal Rules. The Declaration may be made orally before the Tribunal or may be submitted in writing signed by the expert.

In the event the expert in the course of his investigation forms the opinion that modification of the foregoing terms of reference would be necessary to permit a proper valuation, or if any other difficulty arises, the expert shall be allowed to refer to the Tribunal for modification, clarification or resolution.

Starrett Housing Corp and *Government of the Islamic Republic of Iran*, Award No ITL 32–24–1 (December 19, 1983), Concurring Opinion of Howard M Holtzmann (December 20, 1983), reprinted in 4 Iran-US CTR 159, 176 (1983-III):

When one analyzes these interrelated provisions of the terms of reference, it becomes apparent that the entire Project and all the Starrett companies involved in it are to be taken into account in arriving at the value of the property rights which were expropriated. Although I would have preferred to state that in a simpler and more concise way, the terms of reference will, I believe, provide sufficient guidance for the expert. There remains the potential problem that, because of the way the terms of reference are structured, some gap may exist. This is possible because the Starrett companies, following generally accepted accounting practice, report their financial results on a consolidated basis and, in consequence, some of the evidence focuses on the whole, and does not always identify the particular parts. As a result, the terms of reference may have omitted some element which the expert may discover in his detailed studies, and which should be taken into account in order to achieve a fair valuation of the expropriated property. The terms of reference are, however, sufficiently flexible to deal with that contingency. They provide that the expert may refer to the Tribunal for modification of the terms of the reference if "in the course of his investigation [he] forms the opinion that modification... would be necessary to permit a proper valuation."

(d) The *Richard D Harza* case

Richard D Harza and *Islamic Republic of Iran*, Case No 97, Chamber Two, Order of November 4, 1982, reprinted in 1 Iran-US CTR 234, 235 (1981–82):

> The Tribunal is considering the appointment of one or more technical experts pursuant to Article 27 of the Provisionally Adopted [1983] Rules of the Tribunal. The Tribunal has requested a preliminary consultation with Mr. S. Thouvenot of Paris in the terms of the attached copy letter. A résumé of Mr. Thouvenot's qualifications is also attached.
>
> The hearing scheduled for 30 November 1982 will not take place. The Parties are instead invited to attend a meeting with Chamber Two of the Tribunal at 9.30 a.m. on that date, at Parkweg 13, The Hague, at which Mr. Thouvenot will be invited to submit his proposals for the terms of reference of the expert advice to be sought and a schedule will be discussed for any necessary site inspections and the submission of any reports. The Tribunal expects to take a final decision on expert advice shortly after the meeting on 30 November if the Parties have not agreed on the subject. A new hearing date will be notified to the Parties as soon as the timing of the expert assistance is determined.

Richard D Harza and *Islamic Republic of Iran*, Case No 97, Chamber Two, Order of December 6, 1982, at 1:

> The Parties are hereby invited to file with the Tribunal by 1 January 1983 their proposals as to the expert advice to be sought by the Tribunal in the light of the Preliminary Report of Mr. S. Thouvenot, in particular as to:
>
> 1) the number of experts, their fields of expertise and terms of reference.
> 2) the method of selection to be adopted.
> ...
> 4) payment of the fees and expenses of the experts.

Richard D Harza and *Islamic Republic of Iran*, Award No ITL 14–97–2 (February 17, 1983), reprinted in 2 Iran-US CTR 68, 69 (1983-I):

> From the pleadings, the voluminous documentary evidence and the written or oral explanations submitted by the Parties, it appears that the case raises certain complex factual and technical issues which require either clarification or a technical opinion in order to allow the Tribunal properly to adjudicate this case.

Richard D Harza and *Islamic Republic of Iran*, Award No ITL 14–97–2 (February 17, 1983), reprinted in 2 Iran-US CTR 68, 70–71 (1983-I):

> The Claimant and Respondent agree that the Tribunal should appoint experts but they disagree both as to the desirable number of experts and the scope of their tasks.

The Claimant contends that the expertise should be limited to the hydraulics and geology questions raised by the counterclaim, and that there is no need for experts' opinions concerning the claim and concerning all aspects of the counterclaim which do not raise technical issues of hydraulics or of geology. Further, the Claimant contends that the counterclaim based on the alleged disregard by Harza of the seismological constraints of the country made on 21 October 1982 was late and should be dismissed pursuant to Article 19(3) of the Provisionally Adopted [1983] Tribunal Rules.

The Respondent stated at and subsequent to the conference held on 30 November 1982 that the opinion of experts should be sought on all aspects of the claim and of the counterclaim. It has suggested a panel of six experts to cover all factual and technical aspects of its defence and of its counterclaim.

From the pleadings, the voluminous documentary evidence and the written or oral explanations submitted by the Parties, it appears that the case raises certain complex factual and technical issues which require either clarification or a technical opinion in order to allow the Tribunal properly to adjudicate this case.

Despite the fact, stressed by the Claimant, that the claim for payment of fees due does not raise strictly technical issues, it appears from the pleadings and the substantiating evidence submitted by both Parties that the reasons for the disagreement between the Parties need to be clarified to the Tribunal by an expert familiar with the business practices and administration of important consulting engineering contracts such as the 1965 contract concluded between Harza International and the Ministry of Energy.

Concerning the counterclaim the Tribunal cannot decide the liability issues raised by the various alleged defects of site selection, engineers' drawings, and actual construction of major dams and related irrigation networks without a proper technical description of the alleged defects and of the causes from which they arose. This will require opinions to be sought at least from two experts, one experienced in the field of geology and rock mechanics and the other in hydraulics, both of whom are also experienced in the building of major dams.

No experts will be appointed to study the counterclaims relating to seismology, insofar as those counterclaims were presented too late within the terms of Article 19(3), and our own Order of June, 1982 scheduling the proceedings. The use of our discretion under 19(3) to admit the late filing would be inappropriate in view of the uncertain and speculative nature of the alleged damages.

Moreover, it does not appear at this stage of the proceedings that the appointed experts should address the issue of evaluation of damages. Such investigation should be made later and only insofar as liability is found by the Tribunal.

Richard D Harza and *Islamic Republic of Iran*, Award No ITL 14–97–2 (February 17, 1983), reprinted in 2 Iran-US CTR 68, 71–75 (1983-I):

III. Terms of Reference and Appointment of Experts

The Tribunal accordingly sets forth the following as the terms of reference of three experts:

Expert No 1

After familiarizing himself with the Preliminary Report of 23 November 1982 submitted by Mr. Thouvenot and with the documents filed by the Parties and necessary to the performance of his task, shall give his opinion on the following:

(1) which services performed by Harza International were to be compensated on the basis of the contract's lump-sum payment schedule and which services were to be compensated on the basis of the man-month formula provided in the 1971 amendment?

(2) which items of expense incurred by Harza International were to be reimbursed by KWPA in addition to the lump-sum and man-month payments provided in the contract?

(3) whether taxes and social security contributions paid by Harza International in Iran were to be reimbursed by KWPA?

(4) what documentation Harza International was required to submit to KWPA to support its billings?

(5) whether KWPA was obligated under the contract to pay interest for late payments, and at what rate?
(6) whether Harza International's invoices were accurately computed?
(7) whether the written observations made by KWPA, about certain of the invoices on the basis of which payment of these invoices was refused, were justified?
(8) whether Harza International's invoices include items which KWPA is not required to pay?
(9) whether the invoices were supported by the required documentation?
(10) whether Harza International carried out its duties with respect to the estimation of the cost of the Gotvand Irrigation Project and the alleged transmission by Harza International to KWPA of irregular invoices for payment using its best technical knowledge and according to the best accepted professional standards?
(11) in liaison with Expert No 3, whether Harza International submitted the computation documents and final reports of the Behbehan irrigation network, and whether the preliminary report on Phase I of the Jayzan and Khalajabad irrigation projects submitted by Harza was adequate and in conformity with its best technical knowledge and the best accepted professional standards?

The Tribunal appoints Mr. S. Thouvenot, 74, Rue Raynouard, 75016 Paris to act as Expert No 1. In the course of performing his duties, Mr. Thouvenot may seek permission from the Tribunal to call upon the services of an accountant, or an irrigation expert giving specific reference to those portions of his task which are unable to be resolved without such expertise.

Expert No 2

After familiarizing himself with the Preliminary Report of 23 November 1982 submitted by Mr. Thouvenot and with the documents provided by the Parties and necessary to the performance of his task, shall give his opinion on the following:

(1) whether the information available to Harza International prior to commencement of construction of the Karun Dam revealed the presence of a large clay seam in the right abutment of the Dam?
(2) whether Harza International's program for foundation investigation at the Karun Dam site, (including, but not limited to, core borings, soil samplings, soil analysis, geological surveys, assistance to the Ministry in connection with the surveys and tests to be carried out by the Ministry, and supervision of the carrying out of such surveys and tests), was carried out using its best technical knowledge and according to the best accepted professional standards as they existed at the time of that investigation?
(3) whether and to what extent the geological discoveries made in the course of construction of the Karun Dam made necessary the works undertaken in order to ensure the stability and the security of the dam, and especially of its right abutment?
(4) whether Harza International was responsible for undue delays, if any, in the design and the execution of the works made necessary by the composition of the soil?
(5) whether Harza International's design of the Marun Dam drainage system was carried out using its best technical knowledge and according to the best accepted professional standards as they existed at the time when the design was completed?
(6) whether Harza International carried out its duties using its best technical knowledge and according to the best professional standards with respect to the submission of properly executed detailed drawings and to the completion and supervision of the works of the Gotvand Irrigation Project, especially concerning the alleged disregard by contractors of the technical specifications, which allegedly resulted in the inadequate thickness of the linings of the canals, the existence of deep pits of stagnant water close to the canals and roadways and the endangering of various constructions (bridge 16 + 052 and culverts).

The Tribunal appoints Mr. Jean Lehuerou Kerisel, 28 avenue d'Eylau, 75016 Paris, France, to act as Expert No 2.

Expert No 3
After familiarizing himself with the Preliminary Report of 23 November 1982 submitted by Mr. Thouvenot and with the documents provided by the Parties and necessary to the performance of his task, shall give his opinion on the following:

(1) whether the cavitation phenomenon in the Karun Dam Spillway was caused by the design of the spillway or by deficiencies in the construction work?
(2) whether Harza International's design of the Karun Dam spillway and its provision of engineering services during the construction were carried out using its best technical knowledge and according to the best accepted professional standards as they existed at the time the design was completed and the supervision carried out and, if not, whether any such design or supervision defects contributed to the damage which occurred to the spillway in late 1977?
(3) whether Harza International's responsibilities with respect to remedying the damages which occurred to the spillway in late 1977 were carried out using its best technical knowledge and according to the best accepted professional standards?
(4) whether Harza International's design of the valves in Tunnel No 1 at the Karun Dam and its provision of engineering services during construction were carried out using its best technical knowledge and according to the best accepted professional standards as they existed at the time the design was completed and the supervision carried out and, if not, whether any such design or supervision defects contributed to the leakage of one of these valves?
(5) whether Harza International's design of the Marun Dam spillway and the later proposed modification to that design were carried out using its best technical knowledge and according to the best accepted professional standards as they existed at the times the design was completed and the modification proposed?
(6) whether Harza International's design of the Marun Dam diversion tunnel gate was carried out using its best technical knowledge and according to the best accepted professional standards as they existed at the time the design was completed;
(7) what were the causes of the excessive retention of water which in 1980 led to the flooding of the Gotvand irrigation system?
(8) whether Harza International carried out its duties with respect to the design of the Gotvand Irrigation Dam, the supervision of its construction and the transmission of instructions concerning its operation, using its best technical knowledge and according to the best accepted professional standards?
(9) in liaison with Expert No 1, whether Harza International submitted the computation documents and final reports of the Behbehan irrigation network, and whether the preliminary report on Phase I of the Jayzan and Khalajabad irrigation projects submitted by Harza was adequate and in conformity with its best technical knowledge and the best professional standards?

The Tribunal appoints Prof. Knauss, Dr. Ingen. Vorsuchanstalt für Wasserbau der Technische Universität, 8111 Obernach Walchensee, Federal Republic of Germany, to act as Expert No 3. In the course of performing his duties, Prof. Knauss may seek permission from the Tribunal to call upon the services of Expert No 2 identifying specifically those portions of his mandate which are incapable of resolution without such expertise.
...
In case of any difficulty arising in the course of their investigation, the Experts shall be allowed to refer to the Tribunal for clarification or resolution.
...
In order to ensure coordination and eliminate duplication of investigations, the Experts shall carry out their work in liaison with Mr. Thouvenot, who shall have the freedom for that purpose to meet with the other Experts individually or together, and to organize any general meeting with the Parties.

The Tribunal further decides, in accordance with Provisionally Adopted [1983] Tribunal Rule 41(2), that Harza International and Khuzestan Water & Power Authority shall each deposit within two months from the date of this Award the sum of Twenty-Five Thousand United States Dollars (US $25,000) into account number 24.58.28.583 at Pierson, Heldring and Pierson, Korte Vijverberg 2, 2513 AB The Hague, in the name of the Secretary-General of the Iran-United States Claims Tribunal (Account No II), as advances for the costs of expert advice. The account shall be administered by the Secretary-General of the Tribunal, who shall consult with the Tribunal. The Tribunal further retains jurisdiction to request from the arbitrating parties such other amounts as may be required from time to time in connection with the expert's work, or to decide any disputes which may arise in connection with that work.

(e) The *Behring International* case

Behring Intl, Inc and *Islamic Republic Iranian Air Force*, Case No 382, Chamber Three, Decision of December 19, 1983, reprinted in 4 Iran-US CTR 89, 92–93 (1983-III):

The Tribunal sets forth the following as the terms of reference for the expert:

1. The expert shall inventory the items of property belonging to the Air Force of the Islamic Republic of Iran and being stored in Behring's warehouse, indicating the following particulars, as may be applicable to each specific item:
   a. nomenclature (name of the item)
   b. unit of issue (number of items)
   c. part number
   d. stock number
   e. serial number
   f. date of arrival at the warehouse
   g. consignor
   h. consignee
   i. shelf life time.
2. The expert shall determine the condition of the above items through visual inspection or through any kind of required tests, including electronic or hydrolytic tests, as may reasonably be warranted by the nature of the equipment. If an item is found to be faulty or damaged, the expert should, if possible, give his opinion as to whether the fault or damage is likely to have occurred during the time before January 19, 1981 in which it was in Behring's custody.
3. The expert shall submit to the Tribunal a copy of the inventory taken in accordance with point 1. and a report on his findings with regard to the items in accordance with point 2. above.
4. The expert shall be entitled to obtain from any party inventories or other documents which he deems necessary for the performance of his work under these terms of reference.
5. The expert may be assisted in performing his work under these terms of reference by another person of his own choice.
6. The cost of the expert's work (including any assistance as mentioned under 5.) must not exceed the sum of US $30,000. If the expert finds that this amount is not sufficient to cover all the costs, he shall refer to the Tribunal for further directives.
7. In case of any difficulty in the course of performing his work under these terms of reference, the expert may refer to the Tribunal for clarification or resolution, as may any party.
8. The Tribunal decides, in accordance with Article 41, paragraph 2, of the [1983] Tribunal Rules that the Respondents shall deposit the sum of Thirty Thousand United States Dollars (US $30,000) as advances for the costs of expert advice, to be deposited within 20 days from the date of this Decision. This amount shall be remitted to account number 24.58.28.583 (Dollar Account) at Pierson, Heldring and Pierson, Korte Vijverberg 2, 2513 AB The Hague, in the name of the Secretary-General of the Iran-United States Claims Tribunal (Account NoII). The account shall be administered by the Secretary-General of the Tribunal, who shall consult with the Tribunal. The Tribunal further retains jurisdiction to request from arbitrating parties such other amounts as may be required from time to time in connection with the expert's work, or to decide any disputes which may arise in connection with that work.

The Tribunal shall later determine as to which party shall ultimately bear the cost of the expert's work (including any assistance as mentioned under 5. above).

Behring Intl, Inc and *Islamic Republic Iranian Air Force* et al, Case No 382, Chamber Three, Decision of December 19, 1983, Dissenting Decision of Richard M Mosk (December 19, 1983), reprinted in 4 Iran-US CTR 93, 93–95 (1983-III) (footnotes omitted):

Dissent to Decision

The appointment of an expert in this case has simply provided a Tribunal-created mechanism to assist one of the parties to obtain evidence in support of unsubstantiated allegations. The appointment of an expert is supposed to be for the benefit of the Tribunal. By appointing an expert at this stage of the proceedings, the Tribunal is in reality aiding one Party to engage in what amounts to a "fishing expedition". In this case, the Respondents have been represented by counsel in the United States. They have access to their property and information in the United States....

In the instant case Claimant Behring International Inc. ("Behring") alleged that it stored goods for Respondent Iranian Air Force ("Air Force") without receiving required compensation. What obligations Behring may have with respect to the Air Force's property has not been alleged specifically, much less established, and there has been no showing that, under the circumstances, Behring would have any legal obligation to the Air Force even if any of the property has deteriorated. Moreover, Behring's allegation of non-payment of storage charges is relevant to the issue of Behring's responsibility with respect to the goods in question.

...

By appointing an expert, the Tribunal is ignoring a number of prerequisites. In order to obtain an expert, the Air Force, which has already been accorded full access to the goods by Behring, should at least have been required to make a *prima facie* showing of the following: that there are problems with respect to the goods; that Behring caused the problems; that Behring is legally responsible for the problems; that Behring has proximately caused the Air Force to suffer damages; that the claims are within the Tribunal's jurisdiction; that there is a dispute over a fact; and that the resolution of the fact can be facilitated by the use of one or more experts. Then, the Air Force should have been required to identify with specificity the exact type of expert that should be utilized and the expert's task. Finally, the Parties should have been given an opportunity to reach agreement on the expert or experts to be appointed.

The Tribunal simply avoids these obvious prerequisites. In reality, the Tribunal is using its facilities to assist the Air Force in taking possession and making an inventory of the goods—something the Air Force could do without an "expert"—and to find and discover facts upon which the Air Force can base a claim.

...

The defects in the Tribunal's decision are further disclosed by the fact that the Tribunal is unable to specify exactly what kind of expert or experts are necessary and precisely what peculiar expertise is required. In other words, the terms of reference are far too indefinite.

Indeed, one may wonder how the appointed expert will be able to determine the origin and time of the emergence of any defects—i.e. whether the goods were defective when shipped to Behring or whether the goods deteriorated before January 19, 1981 or after that date. Before retaining an expert, the Tribunal should ascertain whether the task assigned to him is possible. The Tribunal has selected an "expert" of Swedish nationality who provided only the minimum amount of information about himself. There is no indication of the university degrees he holds, if any, or of the nature of his past work experience. Indeed, he states that he needs to hire someone else "to get a wider technical background." We have virtually no information on the additional person he intends to hire. The parties have had no input in the selection of the "expert".

The Tribunal provided that the expert is entitled to obtain from the parties documents "he deems necessary", without any restriction. I assume this provision does not permit requests for documents that would be privileged or requests which would be burdensome and oppressive.

Compliance with the decision may entail expenses to the Claimant, but the Tribunal has made no effort to determine the nature, extent and ultimate responsibility for such expenses. Moreover, the Tribunal's $30,000 figure for an advance of costs is not based on any information or investigation.

In sum, it was premature to appoint an expert; the task for which the expert was appointed is inappropriate; the terms of the appointment and the type of expertise required are too indefinite; the method of selection of the expert is questionable; and the decision provides assistance to one of the parties unnecessarily and in violation of [1983] Tribunal Rule 15 requiring equal treatment of the parties. Accordingly, I dissent to the decision.

(2) Tribunal rules (1983), Article 27(2)—provision of relevant information

Richard D Harza and *Islamic Republic of Iran*, Award No ITLt 14–97–2 (February 17, 1983), reprinted in 2 Iran-US CTR 68, 75 (1983-I):

> III. Terms of Reference and Appointment of Experts
>
> ...
>
> The appointed Experts shall be entitled to hear any person with knowledge of the Karun and Marun Projects, in the presence of the Parties or the Parties having been duly invited to attend such meeting.
>
> The appointed experts shall also be entitled to obtain from any Party all documents which they deem necessary for their investigations. Each Party shall without delay provide the other Party with a copy of any documents which it communicates to the Experts.
>
> ...
>
> In the event that it should prove necessary, the Experts shall be allowed to visit the site if circumstances permit.

Richard D Harza and *Islamic Republic of Iran*, Case No 97, Chamber Two, Order of September 13, 1983, at 1:

> One of the Experts appointed in this case by the Interlocutory Award of 23 February, Mr. S. Thouvenot, has requested and obtained authorisation from the Tribunal to go to Chicago, United States of America, in order to make investigations in the framework of his mission (copies of the letters are attached). Mr. Thouvenot will be in Chicago from 16 to 21 October 1983.
>
> The Parties are hereby informed that, pursuant to Article 27(2), final sentence, of the [1983] Tribunal Rules, the Tribunal has decided that they are entitled to send a representative to attend this inspection.
>
> Should the Parties wish to make use of this right, they are advised to take up contact with Mr. Thouvenot at his address in Paris, France, which is given in the Interlocutory Award of 23 February 1983.

Starrett Housing Corp and *Government of the Islamic Republic of Iran*, Award No ITL 32–24–1 (December 19, 1983), reprinted in 4 Iran-US CTR 122, 157–58 (1983-III):

> The expert shall be entitled to hear any person with knowledge of the Project, if he deems it appropriate and if the Parties have been duly invited to attend such meeting.
>
> The expert shall also be entitled to obtain from any Party all documents which he deems necessary for his investigation. Each Party shall without delay give the other Party a copy of any documents which it gives to the expert; if a Party arranges for the expert to inspect documents without giving him a copy, the other Party shall be invited to inspect such documents.

Chas T Main Intl, Inc and *Khuzestan Water and Power Authority*, Case No 120, Chamber Two, Order of February 14, 1986, at 1–2:

> 1. The Tribunal confirms that documents and other material submitted by the Claimant to the Experts are not filed with the Registry and therefore are not in evidence before the Tribunal,

except to the extent incorporated in the Experts' final report. As copies of these materials have been submitted to the experts, the Respondents would not be prejudiced if they were now to be accepted for filing by the Tribunal. Accordingly, the Claimant may file the documents specified in paragraph 1 of their letter of February 5, 1986, not later than March 7, 1986....

...

3. Claimant's request to submit minutes of witness testimony heard by the Experts in Boston and/or statements of these witnesses is denied. The Tribunal decides that notes taken by assistant clerks of testimony given by witnesses before the Experts cannot be considered appropriate evidence. As to the submission of statements by the witnesses themselves, Claimant has offered no justification or excuse for its delay in submitting such statements. In view of the potential prejudice to the Respondents, the Tribunal cannot accept them at this late stage in the proceedings without such justification.

Arco Exploration, Inc and *National Iranian Oil Co*, Case Nos 20 & 21, Chamber One, Order of June 13, 1990, at 3–4:

Terms of Reference

...

(c) The expert shall be entitled to hear any person with knowledge of the LAPCO project, if it deems it appropriate and if the Parties have been duly invited to attend such meeting. In such a case it shall inform the Tribunal and the Parties in advance and shall indicate the nature of the meeting and in general terms the subject matter or matters which the expert proposes to be discussed. At any such meeting the procedure shall be determined by the expert.

(d) Each Party shall without delay give the expert all documents which the expert deems necessary for its investigation. By July 16, 1990 either Party may submit any additional information to the expert which the Party deems necessary for the expert's review. One copy of all written communications and documents exchanged between a Party and the expert shall be sent to the other Party and the Tribunal. If a Party arranges for the expert to inspect the documents without giving it a copy, the other Parties shall be invited to inspect such documents.

(3) Tribunal rules (1983), Article 27(3)—expert report

(a) The *Shahin Shaine Ebrahimi* case

Shahin Shaine Ebrahimi and *Government of the Islamic Republic of Iran*, Case Nos 44, 46 & 47, Chamber Three, Order of July 20, 1992, at 2:

4. The Tribunal intends to discuss with the expert prior to its appointment...the time required for the presentation of a draft report and a final report.
5. The report of the expert will be sent to the Parties for comments to be filed within a period of eight weeks.

Shahin Shaine Ebrahimi and *Government of the Islamic Republic of Iran*, Case Nos 44, 46 & 47, Chamber Three, Order of February 4, 1993, at 1–3 (citations omitted):

Terms of Reference

...

6. The expert shall submit its report to the Tribunal by 15 March 1993. The expert may request from the Tribunal an extension, which will be granted to the extent it is deemed reasonable. The Parties may make any comments in writing on the report, which comments shall be transmitted in writing to the Tribunal within a period of eight weeks from the filing of the report. The Tribunal does not intend to grant any extension of this period.

Shahin Shaine Ebrahimi and *Government of the Islamic Republic of Iran*, Award No 560–44/46/47–3 (October 12, 1994), reprinted in 30 Iran-US CTR 170, 212–13 (1994):

> 123. The Tribunal finds, in agreement with the Expert, that the available information suggests that Gostaresh Maskan was indeed entitled to the payment of these PARs. In reaching its conclusions, the Tribunal has given particular weight to the uncontested fact that Gostaresh Maskan received Rls 673 million (i.e., almost U.S. $10 million) in PARs payments before taking, i.e. in tempore non suspecto. This practice, in addition to Mr. Towfighi's explicit request to the Plan & Budget Organization to pay Gostaresh Maskan's PARs without further delay, would seem to corroborate Mr. Ali Ebrahimi's testimony on the existence of an understanding (possibly instrumented by the type of protocol which he described) entitling Gostaresh Maskan to price adjustments from its employer under the New Town contract. On the other hand, the Tribunal is not persuaded by the Respondent's argument that the term "*maghtoo*" (which it first construed to mean that "the contract value is final" and later in the proceedings explained to mean that such value was "fixed") offers conclusive evidence that the signatory to the New Town contract explicitly agreed to exclude any indexation of the contract price. The Tribunal understands that the price for the New Town project quoted by Gostaresh Maskan (and subsequently accepted by KUDO) was an "all-in" price for the whole project. Accordingly, in the Tribunal's view, the term "maghtoo" is more likely to have been added to emphasize the parties' mutual agreement that any changes in labor costs, material costs, etc. would not affect the "all-in" price for this project. The Tribunal believes that such a price arrangement does not in and of itself exclude any adjustment for inflation of the nominal amount of the all-in price. In view of the above, the Tribunal shares the view of the Expert that it was likely that there was authority for the payment of the PARs.

(b) The *Arco Exploration* case

Arco Exploration, Inc and *National Iranian Oil Co*, Case No 21, Chamber One, Order of December 7, 1989, at 2:

> 4. The Tribunal intends to discuss with the expert prior to its appointment . . . the time required for the presentation of a draft report and a final report.
> 5. The draft report of the expert will be sent to the Parties for comments to be filed within a period of six weeks. The expert will be instructed to consider the Parties' comments in preparing its final report.

Arco Exploration, Inc and *National Iranian Oil Co*, Case Nos 20 & 21, Chamber One, Order of June 13, 1990, at 4:

> Terms of Reference
>
> (f) The expert shall file its draft report with the Tribunal by 21 November 1990. The expert may request from the Tribunal an extension, which will be granted to the extent it is deemed reasonable. The Parties may make any comments on the draft report within a period of six weeks. The expert is instructed to consider the Parties' comments in preparing its final report, which shall incorporate the expert's observations on these comments.
> (g) The expert shall file its final report with the Tribunal not later than three months after the filing of the draft report.
> (h) The Tribunal does not intend to grant any extensions of the time periods for the Parties set forth above.
>   (i) The expert's attention is drawn to Article 27 of the [1983] Tribunal Rules and the Order filed on 7 December 1989.

Arco Exploration, Inc and *National Iranian Oil Co*, Case Nos 20 & 21, Chamber One, Order of February 5, 1991, at 2:

> 2. On 28 January 1991, the expert filed a request for advice on whether it could use the raw well log data of wells AK41 and AK61 in its study of the Sassan field. In this respect the Tribunal notes the general instruction contained in paragraph 2 of the Order filed on 20 November 1990 to the effect that documents or data "can be taken into account by the expert only is so far as they contain information available already as of December 1979, but irrespective of whether that information was known to or used by the Parties or not." The expert is thus instructed not to take into consideration in preparing its report the data referred to in the expert's request of 28 January 1991.

Arco Exploration, Inc and *National Iranian Oil Co*, Case Nos 20 & 21, Chamber One, Order of June 2, 1992, at 1:

> 1. The draft report having now been filed by the expert, the Tribunal invites the Parties to make any comments on the draft report within a period of 6 weeks, to be filed at the latest on July 13, 1992.
> 2. These comments may only be submitted in writing and must be filed with the Tribunal, which will provide copies to the expert. Further submissions or communications to the expert by the Parties are not permitted.

(c) The *Behring International* case

Behring Intl, Inc and *Islamic Republic Iranian Air Force*, Case No 382, Chamber Three, Amendment to Decision of December 19, 1983, reprinted in 6 Iran-US CTR 30, 32 (1984-II):

> Before finalization and submittal of his report to the Tribunal, the expert should send a preliminary report to the Parties for their possible comments.

(d) The *Richard D Harza* case

Richard D Harza and *Islamic Republic of Iran*, Award No ITL 14–97–2 (February 17, 1983), reprinted in 2 Iran-US CTR 68, 75 (1983-I):

> III. Terms of Reference and Appointment of Experts
>
> ...
>
> Not later than 6 months after deposit by the Parties of the advances for the costs of expert advice, the Experts shall distribute their proposed reports to the Parties and allow them to make any comments within one month. The final reports may incorporate the Experts' observations on these comments.
>
> The final reports shall be submitted to the Tribunal by the Experts individually not later than 2 months after the proposed reports have been distributed to the Parties.

(e) The *Starrett Housing* case

Starrett Housing Corp and *Government of the Islamic Republic of Iran*, Award No 314–21–1 (August 14, 1987), reprinted in 16 Iran-US CTR 112, 196–99 (1987-III)(citations omitted):

> 265. In determining the weight to be given to the Expert's Report, the Tribunal must first consider his qualifications. It is noteworthy that no issue arose between the Parties on this point. While the Respondents contested a number of aspects of the Expert's investigation and Report, none of the Parties questioned his qualifications. The Tribunal, which had reviewed the Expert's background and experience before appointing him, finds that its initial impressions have been fully confirmed by the high professional quality and impartiality evident in his work.
>
> ...

267. The Tribunal has considered a number of factors in determining the weight to be given to the Report. First, the Tribunal has observed the painstaking procedures that the Expert followed. The Tribunal finds that the Expert's procedures were, on the whole, meticulous and comprehensive. These qualities have led to the substantial value of the Report. Although the specific steps that the Expert took are described in some detail in paras. 6–10, supra, it is worthwhile to recall his overall approach as described in his own words. He explained that his basic principle was to give "the Parties an opportunity to put forward their opinions within all crucial sectors of the valuation." To accomplish this, at various stages "of the valuation process both Parties have been given a fair opportunity of presenting their views." The Expert affirmed that he "has given careful consideration" to the suggestions of the Parties and has reflected in his Report those suggestions that he "found to be motivated on the basis of relevant and factual arguments." Where his opinions differed from the views of a Party he "sought to account for the Parties' opinions and motivations therefore as correctly as possible." He noted, particularly, that both Parties had access to "qualified advisors of different disciplines and fields of expertise" and that he "examined" their views and "attempted to clarify the reasons for the identified differences of opinion." He submitted a draft of his Report to the Parties and received and reflected their comments before submitting his Report to the Tribunal. The Tribunal finds that the written evidence in the record confirms that the Expert fully carried out the procedures that he described.

268. The substantial weight that the Tribunal gives to the Report is also influenced by the thoroughness of the process by which the Expert sought to verify all information presented to him by the Parties. Members of his staff visited Tehran twice, and he and his staff visited New York once for inspections and auditing of records, a process which representatives of both Parties were invited to observe. He reviewed a huge amount of material which the Parties submitted to him, and held three meetings with them. The only data submitted to him by a Party that he did not consider is discussed above at paras. 139 and 249, and the Tribunal finds that he acted correctly in rejecting that material. Additionally, the Expert consulted other experts in specialized fields and carefully identified and reflected their views in his Report.

269. The material submitted by the Expert to the Tribunal is literally "weighty." It consists of 12 volumes, together with a descriptive transmittal letter summarizing his views. In this massive submission, the Expert set forth not only his conclusions but also cited the evidentiary support for them and described the positions of the Parties on each significant issue. He included full texts or quotations of relevant portions of the documents upon which he relied. His credibility is enhanced by his candor. Thus, where he drew inferences or made subjective judgments, he pointed them out and explained his reasons. Where he considered that he may have made a judicial interpretation, he identified the point and referred it to the Tribunal for final decision. Where he considered a matter beyond his terms of reference, he specifically called attention to it.

270. Moreover, the Tribunal had the opportunity to question the Expert and receive clarifications from him at the Hearing held pursuant to Article 27, paragraph 4, of the [1983] Tribunal Rules. At the same time, the Tribunal was able to test the Expert's views in the light of testimony of expert witnesses presented by the Respondents on various points at issue.

...

273. ... Thus, the Tribunal adopts as its own the conclusions of the Expert on matters within his area of expertise when it is satisfied that sufficient reasons have not been shown that the Expert's view is contrary to the evidence, the governing law, or common sense. On the other hand, the Tribunal does not hesitate to substitute its own judgment of what is reasonable with respect to matters that do not require expertise as to accounting or valuation methodology.

(4) Tribunal rules (1983), Article 27(4)—expert hearing

Richard D Harza and *Islamic Republic of Iran*, Case No 97, Chamber Two, Order of July 24, 1985, at 1–2:

> Tribunal has considered the proposals regarding the conduct of the Hearing in this case filed by the Claimant on 2 May 1985 and those filed by the Respondent on 11 July 1985 and decides as follows:
>
> ...
>
> 7. While the deadline for submission of documentary evidence and written comments on the Experts' final reports expired on 15 June 1984, in view of the year's postponement in the Hearing and the Respondent's request, the Tribunal is willing to accept further such evidence and comments provided that they are filed not later than 13 September 1985. No extension of that date can be granted.
> 8. The Tribunal has invited two of the experts, Mr. Thouvenot and Mr. Kerisel, to be present during the Hearing, and they have agreed to attend. The Tribunal considers the presence of the third expert, Mr. Pinto, to be unnecessary.
>
> ...
>
> 9. With respect to the organization of the Hearing, the Tribunal will ensure that each Party has equal time.... [T]he Tribunal envisages the following program: On 15 October the two experts will be interrogated by the Parties and by the Tribunal and thereafter the Tribunal will put questions to the Parties. 16 October is reserved for rebuttal and summing up by the Parties.

Chas T Main Intl Inc and *Khuzestan Water & Power Authority*, Case No 120, Chamber Two, Order of January 14, 1986, at 1:

> The Tribunal hereby informs the Parties that the Experts appointed in this Case have been invited to be present at the Hearing scheduled for April 7 and 8, 1986 and the Parties will have the opportunity to interrogate them.

Starrett Housing Corp and *Government of the Islamic Republic of Iran*, Case No 24, Chamber One, Order of July 30, 1986, at 1–2:

> 2. A five-day Hearing will be held for the purposes set forth in Article 27, Paragraph 4 of the Tribunal Rules commencing at 9.30 a.m. on 19 January 1987. The Hearing will take place at Parkweg 13, The Hague.
> 3. The Tribunal notes the statement by the Respondents in their "Request for Extension of Time Limit For Respondents' Comments on the Expert's Report and Suggestion For the Hearing", filed on 7 July 1986, that "time will have to be allowed for the questions to be put to the expert by the Parties and the Tribunal". The Tribunal considers that this constitutes a request to interrogate the expert as provided for in Article 27, Paragraph 4 of the [1983] Tribunal Rules. Accordingly, the Tribunal has arranged for the expert appointed by it to be present at the Hearing for that purpose.
>
> ...
>
> 6. The Parties are invited to consider whether they are able to agree upon or settle all, or part, of the facts or other matters covered by the expert's submissions, so as to simplify the forthcoming Hearing or eliminate the need for it. The facilities of the Tribunal are available to the Parties for any meetings they may desire to hold in this connection.

Arco Exploration, Inc and *National Iranian Oil Co*, Case Nos 20 & 21, Chamber One, Order of July 17, 1992, at 1:

> 1. In response to the request filed by the Respondents on 30 June 1992 (Doc. 625) the Tribunal requests the Parties to appear before Chamber One of the Tribunal for a Hearing on the expert's Final Report which is scheduled to take place on 15 through 17 December 1992 at the Peace Palace, Carnegieplein 2, The Hague, starting on 15 December 1992 at 09.30.

PART V

DEFAULT AND WAIVER

Introduction

When arbitrating under the 2010 UNCITRAL Rules, the parties are entitled to the litany of procedural rights enumerated therein. These rights aim to protect the intentions of the parties, ensure the efficiency of the proceedings and, more importantly, the fairness of the arbitral process. The parties are generally secure in all these rights, unless they forfeit them under one of two situations identified in the Rules. First, pursuant to Article 30, a party may be deprived of certain rights if it defaults on its general obligation to participate in the proceedings. Second, pursuant to Article 32, a party may waive certain procedural rights when it knowingly fails to assert them after an instance of non-compliance with the Rules. As a general rule, any time the arbitral tribunal contemplates denying a party a procedural right, it should proceed with extreme caution to avoid compromising the fairness of the process and, in turn, the validity of any subsequently rendered award.

The topics of default and waiver are dealt with in Chapters 21 and 22, respectively.

21
Default

1. Introduction	671
2. Default—Article 30	671
A. Text of the 2010 UNCITRAL Rule	671
B. Commentary	672
(1) General comments	672
(2) Failure to file early written submissions—Article 30(1)	675
(3) Failure to appear at a hearing—Article 30(2)	677
(4) Failure to produce documentary evidence—Article 30(3)	677
(5) Comparison to the 1976 UNCITRAL Rules	678
C. Extracts from the Practice of Investment Tribunals	679
D. Extracts from the Practice of the Iran–US Claims Tribunal	683
(1) General and Tribunal Rules (1983), Article 28	683
(2) Tribunal Rules (1983), Article 28(2)	685
(3) Tribunal Rules (1983), Article 28(3)	687

1. Introduction

There are few more disruptive forces in arbitration than a party's unwillingness to engage in the proceedings.[1] Party recalcitrance can impose unexpected costs on the arbitral process by dragging out the proceedings unnecessarily or, in a worse-case scenario, by holding up the proceedings indefinitely. The UNCITRAL Rules would have little utility if they did not include a provision for combating this problem. Accordingly, Article 30 authorizes the arbitral tribunal to advance its work in the face of a party's default on its obligation to participate in the arbitration.

2. Default—Article 30

A. Text of the 2010 UNCITRAL Rule[2]

Article 30 of the 2010 UNCITRAL Rules provides:

1. If, within the period of time fixed by these Rules or the arbitral tribunal, without showing sufficient cause:

---

[1] See generally "Preventing Delay and Disruption in Arbitration," in A J van den Berg (ed) *ICCA Congress Series No 5* (1990) 197.

[2] Corresponding Article 28 of the 1976 UNCITRAL Rules provides:

1. If, within the period of time fixed by the arbitral tribunal, the claimant has failed to communicate his claim without showing sufficient cause for such failure, the arbitral tribunal shall issue an order for the termination of the arbitral proceedings. If, within the period of time fixed by the arbitral tribunal, the respondent has failed to communicate his statement of defence without showing sufficient cause for such failure, the arbitral tribunal shall order that the proceedings continue.

(a) The claimant has failed to communicate its statement of claim, the arbitral tribunal shall issue an order for the termination of the arbitral proceedings, unless there are remaining matters that may need to be decided and the arbitral tribunal considers it appropriate to do so;
(b) The respondent has failed to communicate its response to the notice of arbitration or its statement of defence, the arbitral tribunal shall order that the proceedings continue, without treating such failure in itself as an admission of the claimant's allegations; the provisions of this subparagraph also apply to a claimant's failure to submit a defence to a counterclaim or to a claim for the purpose of a set-off.
2. If a party, duly notified under these Rules, fails to appear at a hearing, without showing sufficient cause for such failure, the arbitral tribunal may proceed with the arbitration.
3. If a party, duly invited by the arbitral tribunal to produce documents, exhibits or other evidence, fails to do so within the established period of time, without showing sufficient cause for such failure, the arbitral tribunal may make the award on the evidence before it.

B. Commentary

(1) General comments

As a general matter, once the arbitral proceedings are initiated and the jurisdiction of the arbitral tribunal is established, the parties are bound by the final outcome—whether or not they participate.[3] Still, a party may delay or disrupt the arbitration by failing to participate in the proceedings. To minimize the effect of a party's default, Article 30 empowers the arbitral tribunal to terminate the proceedings in one situation, where the claimant fails to submit a statement of claim (and there are no remaining matters to be decided), and to advance the proceedings, despite such default, in three other situations. The feature common to all of these situations is non-participation in some form. Generally, there is no summary procedure resulting in a default decision (as in some national legal systems). Rather, the proceedings "continue" despite the absence or non-participation of a party. The four situations include: where a claimant has failed to submit its statement of claim, but other matters remain to be decided by the tribunal; where the respondent fails to submit a statement of defence; where a party fails to appear for a hearing; and where a party fails to produce documentary evidence as requested by the arbitral tribunal.[4]

Whether a party's conduct amounts to default in these situations is left to the tribunal's discretion.[5] Some cases are obvious, eg where a party explicitly communicates its intended

---

2. If one of the parties, duly notified under these Rules, fails to appear at a hearing, without showing sufficient cause for such failure, the arbitral tribunal may proceed with the arbitration.
3. If one of the parties, duly invited to produce documentary evidence, fails to do so within the established period of time, without showing sufficient cause for such failure, the arbitral tribunal may make the award on the evidence before it.

[3] See J L Simpson and H Fox, *International Arbitration: Law and Practice* (1959) 283.
[4] Article 30(1)–(3), UNCITRAL Arbitration Rules. The enumeration of these specific circumstances is without prejudice to the tribunal's inherent authority to advance the proceedings by fixing time limits and by defining the stages of arbitration. See JL Simpson and H Fox, *International Arbitration*, n 3, 283. Thus, in the *Avco* case, the Iran–US Claims Tribunal proceeded with a pre-hearing conference in the face of the unexplained absence of the respondent and its counsel, even though such a default did not fall into one of the four categories enumerated in Article 28 [of the 1976 UNCITRAL Rules]. See *Avco Corp* and *Iran Aircraft Industries,* et al, Award No 377–261–3 (July 18, 1988), Concurring and Dissenting Opinion of Charles N Brower (July 18, 1988), reprinted in 19 Iran-US CTR 231, 235 (1988-II) (referencing the Tribunal's Order of June 6, 1985).
[5] Along with the power to advance the proceedings, the tribunal may also award and apportion costs against the defaulting party in accordance with Article 42. See Chapter 27, section 4.

default to the arbitral tribunal. Others are more ambiguous, eg where a party files repeated extension requests for the filing of a submission, which result in a delay of the proceedings. In the gray areas, the arbitral tribunal must ascertain default on the basis of whether the conduct in question is unreasonable or prone to threaten the integrity of the arbitral process.

As the American judges at the Iran–US Claims Tribunal have observed about corresponding Article 28 of the 1976 UNCITRAL Rules, termination or continuation as a form of sanction under that provision are "virtually the sole means available to the Tribunal to enforce its Orders and to ensure that it, rather than a party, is in charge of the proceedings."[6] However, the scope of the arbitral tribunal's power to sanction a defaulting party is limited to measures that reasonably advance the proceedings beyond the procedural step at issue. For example, in response to a party's failure to attend a hearing, the arbitral tribunal may only sanction the defaulting party with respect to the hearing phase of the arbitration, ie, by denying its requests to reschedule the hearing.[7] However, the arbitral tribunal may not prevent the defaulting party from participating in the subsequent phases of the proceedings, such as post-hearing submissions.[8] Even with this limitation on the scope of the tribunal's powers, Article 30 can produce harsh results if applied too strictly. Depending on the circumstances of the case, the arbitral tribunal may wish to temper the rule by relaxing filing deadlines through the extension request process.[9]

Application of Article 30 has no effect on the parties' evidentiary burdens, although it may alter the arbitral tribunal's general approach to gathering evidence. The non-defaulting party may not profit from a lighter evidentiary standard simply because its adversary is absent from some or all of the proceedings. Rather, that party must prove its case to the satisfaction of the arbitral tribunal as it normally would pursuant to the evidentiary requirements of the UNCITRAL Rules.[10] In international arbitration, the arbitral tribunal does not have the same powers as a court to issue what is known in some legal systems as a "default judgment"; the arbitrators must render any award or decision on the basis of the arguments and evidence proffered by the non-defaulting party.[11] According to Redfern and Hunter, when the proceedings are ex parte:

> [t]he arbitral tribunal is compelled to take a more positive role. In effect, the tribunal takes on itself the burden of testing the assertions made by the active party; and it must call for such evidence and legal argument as it may require to this end. The task of an arbitral tribunal is not to 'rubber stamp' claims that are presented to it. It must make a *determination* of these claims.[12]

---

[6] Dissent by Judges Holtzmann, Aldrich, and Mosk from the Procedural Decisions in Nine Forum Selection Clause Cases (1983 Tribunal Rules), reprinted in section 2(D)(1). See also Dissent by Judge Mosk from Orders Granting Further Extensions of Time to File Statements of Defence (1983 Tribunal Rules), reprinted in section 2(D)(1).

[7] See, eg, the *George J Meyer* case (1983 Tribunal Rules) discussed in section 2(D)(2).

[8] Accord J van Hof, "UNCITRAL Arbitration Rules, Section III, Article 28 [Default]," in L Mistelis (ed) *Concise International Arbitration* (2010) 212.

[9] See, eg, *Gordon Williams* (1983 Tribunal Rules); and *Thomas Khoshravi* (1983 Tribunal Rules); both reprinted in section 2(D)(1). This is particularly necessary where the claimant fails to submit its statement of claim. See *Report of the Secretary-General on the Revised Draft Set of Arbitration Rules*, UNCITRAL, 9th Session, Addendum 1 (Commentary), UN Doc A/CN.9/112/Add.1 (1975), reprinted in (1976) VII UNCITRAL Ybk 166, 176–7 (Commentary on Draft Article 25 of the 1976 UNCITRAL Rules).

[10] See Chapter 18.

[11] See N Blackaby and C Partasides with A Redfern and M Hunter, *Redfern and Hunter on International Arbitration* (5th edn 2009) 427.

[12] N Blackaby and C Partasides, *Redfern and Hunter on International Arbitration*, n 11, 524. See also T Esko, "The Arbitral Proceedings," in M Savola (ed), *Law and Practice of Arbitration in Finland* (2004) 45 ("However,

While challenges to awards rendered despite procedural default by a party are typically rejected by the courts,[13] there are nevertheless pitfalls associated with the enforcement of such awards. Under the New York Convention, a national court may refuse to recognize or enforce an award that has been rendered without permitting a party a full and fair opportunity to present its arguments and evidence.[14] Consequently, in the event of ex parte proceedings, a tribunal is well-advised to apprise the defaulting party of all developments in the proceedings and to transmit to the defaulting party all submissions by the non-defaulting party and communications by the arbitral tribunal. This approach is designed to provide the defaulting party with every opportunity to join in the proceedings and to ensure the fairest process possible under the circumstances. Further, when drafting the award, the arbitral tribunal should set forth in detail the reasons for applying Article 30, along with the tribunal's efforts to include the defaulting party in the proceedings, in the event such information is required by a reviewing court.

Finally, Article 30 contains two prominent safeguards in each of its three paragraphs, which prevent an abuse of authority by the arbitral tribunal. The first is a notice requirement. Before invoking Article 30, the tribunal must ensure that the defaulting party has received sufficient notice of its duties to the arbitral process. To that end, Article 30 makes reference to the filing deadlines for the claimant's and respondent's early written submissions, the requirement of advance notification of scheduled hearings, and the filing deadlines for the production of evidentiary documents.[15] The second safeguard requires that a defaulting party should have the opportunity to make a "showing of sufficient cause" before Article 30 is invoked. Whether such cause is "sufficient" to avert ex parte proceedings is determined at the discretion of the arbitral tribunal.

The meaning of "sufficient cause" under the nearly identical Article 28 of the 1976 UNCITRAL Rules was addressed in the *Himpurna* arbitrations. In an initial arbitration, Indonesia's state-run electricity corporation, PT (Persero) Perusahaan Listuik Negara ("PLN"), was ordered to pay damages to Himpurna California Ltd ("Himpurna") for the government's failure to purchase energy under energy sales contracts concluded with Himpurna.[16] PLN refused to pay the required damages and a second arbitration ensued against the Republic of Indonesia, in which Himpurna claimed that Indonesia had breached its promise to ensure PLN's performance under the contracts, including its obligation to pay damages under the initial award. Shortly after Himpurna initiated the second arbitration, Pertamina, Indonesia's state-run oil company, sought to enjoin the proceedings in the Central District Court of Jakarta. The Jakarta Court issued an injunction ordering the suspension of the arbitral proceedings and indicating that a fine of US $1 million per day would be imposed against any party for breaching the order.

---

the arbitrators have no authority to render an award comparable to a default judgment issued by a state court. The arbitrators will ensure that the respondent's submissions and evidence are, as far as possible, placed before the tribunal in written form.").

[13] See H van Houtte, "Conduct of Arbitral Proceedings," in P Šarčević (ed), *Essays on International Commercial Arbitration* (1989) 123. See generally B Hanotiau, "Default Procedure," in *International Commercial Arbitration, Procedure and Evidence* (1985).

[14] Article V(1)(b), 1958 New York Convention on the Recognition and Enforcement of Arbitral Awards.

[15] Implicit in these references are the requirements of Articles 20, 21 and 25 (filing of statements of claim and defence), Article 28(1) (notification of oral hearing), and Article 27(3) (notification of request for document production).

[16] *Himpurna California Energy Ltd* and *Republic of Indonesia*, Final Award (May 4, 1999) (*Ad Hoc* Proceeding, 1976 UNCITRAL Rules, Concession Agreement), reprinted in (2000) XXV Ybk Commercial Arb 13.

Citing the Jakarta Court injunction as an impediment, Indonesia failed to submit its case-in-chief in the second arbitration. In response, Himpurna asserted that Indonesia was in default pursuant to original Article 28 of the 1976 UNCITRAL Rules.[17] The tribunal agreed. It noted that Indonesia had the "burden of proof" in establishing "sufficient cause" for its failure to submit its case-in-chief. It was also skeptical that Indonesia could not have controlled the actions of Pertamina, "deem[ing] Pertamina's initiatives not to be independent of the Republic of Indonesia's will." The tribunal observed that "the Republic of Indonesia has offered no proof of the slightest attempt to reign in Pertamina." Because Indonesia failed to rebut that it could have and should have prevented the injunction, the tribunal found that Indonesia had not proven "sufficient cause" for its failure to produce its case-in-chief. Accordingly, Tribunal proceeded with the arbitration ex parte pursuant to Article 28(3) of the 1976 UNCITRAL Rules.[18]

(2) Failure to file early written submissions—Article 30(1)

Article 30(1) covers the situations in which a claimant or respondent fails to submit the statement of claim or statement of defence, respectively, within the time period established by the tribunal. Different consequences befall a defaulting claimant and respondent.

Under paragraph (a) of Article 30(1), if a claimant communicates its intent to arbitrate but does not submit a statement of claim, the tribunal is not only empowered, but rather required to terminate the proceedings, unless it chooses to decide "remaining matters."[19] Because at this stage of the arbitration the tribunal has not assessed the merits of the case, the termination order itself does not necessarily prejudice the claimant against re-filing its claim at a later date.[20] However, as discussed below, Article 30(1)(a) may allow the arbitral tribunal, in appropriate circumstances, to continue the proceedings and issue an award with some preclusive effect against a claimant's future claim. In principle, any costs incurred by a non-defaulting party as a result of a claimant's default could be apportioned against the claimant.[21]

Even where the claimant has failed to submit a statement of claim, the arbitral tribunal may continue with the proceedings under Article 30(1)(a), if it determines that there are "remaining matters" that should be decided. Inclusion of the word "remaining" before "matters" clarifies that the qualification gives the arbitral tribunal discretion to decide matters previously raised in either the notice of arbitration or the response to the notice of arbitration.[22] The arbitral tribunal's discretion thus tempers the general requirement to terminate the proceedings, which may be overly strict in some circumstances. For example, if the claimant fails to submit a statement of claim, but the respondent has raised a counterclaim in its response to the notice of arbitration, the arbitral tribunal may choose to

---

[17] *Himpurna California Energy Ltd* (1976 Rules), Interim Award, para 59, reprinted in section 2(C).
[18] *Himpurna California Energy Ltd* (1976 Rules), n 17, para 198.
[19] As mentioned, the potential harshness of this mandatory rule can be tempered by the granting of extensions of time to meet filing deadlines. See section 1.
[20] See *Report of the UNCITRAL on the Work of its Ninth Session*, UN GAOR, 31st Session, Supp No 17, UN Doc A/31/17, para 136 (1976), reprinted in (1976) VII UNCITRAL Ybk 66, 76. Whether other grounds arise so as to bar a claimant's re-filing is, of course, a different matter.
[21] UN GAOR, 31st Session, Supp No 17, UN Doc A/31/17, n 20, para 137. See *Oil Cases* (1983 Tribunal Rules), reprinted in section 2(D)(1). For a discussion of the apportionment of costs, see Chapter 27, section 4.
[22] *Report of Working Group II (Arbitration and Conciliation) on the Work of its Fifty-First Session* (Vienna, September 14–18, 2009), UNCITRAL, 43rd Session, UN Doc A/CN.9/684, at 8, para 25 (2009).

continue the proceedings in order to resolve the counterclaim.[23] Exercising its discretion in this manner may foster efficiency in arbitration under the Rules.[24] The scope of the arbitral tribunal's authority is not necessarily limited to treatment of counterclaims, however.[25]

Other situations might arise where even in the absence of a statement of claim, the arbitral tribunal might still decide to render an award in relation to the principal claim, for example, to decide issues of jurisdiction or costs.[26] An award of this nature may be useful in addressing claims filed for purposes of harassing the respondent.[27] However, the tribunal should bear two important considerations in mind, if it chooses to render an award of this type: (1) there must be sufficient evidence in the record (from either the notice of arbitration or the response to the notice) to justify such an award,[28] and (2) in some jurisdictions, an award dismissing a claim with prejudice in the absence of a statement of claim may not be valid and enforceable.[29] In exercising its authority to decide any "remaining matters," the arbitral tribunal is well advised to consider the interests not only of the respondent or respondents, but also of co-claimants, if there are any, and other interested parties.[30]

In contrast, the respondent's failure to file a response to the notice of arbitration or a statement of defence results in the imposed continuation of the arbitral proceedings under Article 30(1)(b).[31] What this means in practical terms is that the proceedings will advance to the next stage (in most cases the pre-hearing conference) and beyond until the parties' dispute is resolved. The absence of a statement of defence does not prevent the respondent from responding to the claimant's allegations at any stage in the proceedings, but may prejudice the respondent's ability to raise new claims or counter-claims.[32] Finally, when the respondent fails to produce a statement of defence—and thus to deny the claimant's assertions formally—the arbitral tribunal shall order the proceeding to continue, but "without treating such failure as an admission of the claimant's allegations."[33] However, in this

---

[23] For discussion by the Working Group, see *Report of the Working Group on Arbitration and Conciliation on the Work of its Forty-Seventh Session* (Vienna, September 10–14, 2007), UNCITRAL, 41st Session, UN Doc A/CN.9/641, at 13, para 62 (2007); and UNCITRAL, 43rd Session, UN Doc A/CN.9/684, n 22, at 7–8, paras 22, 25.
Settlement of Commercial Disputes: Revision of the UNCITRAL Arbitration Rules, Note by the Secretariat, UNCITRAL, UN Doc A/CN.9/WG.II/WP.149 at 10–11, para 35–36 (2007) (Draft Article 28).

[24] UNCITRAL, 41st Session, UN Doc A/CN.9/641, n 23, at 13, para 62. ("[I]t was widely considered that, if the counterclaim met the jurisdictional requirements…there was no reason to prevent it from being entertained by the arbitral tribunal in the interest of efficiency.")

[25] According to the *travaux préparatoires*, a prior formulation of the qualification that focused only on counterclaims ("unless the respondent has submitted a counterclaim") was considered "too limited, as it failed to cover situations where, despite the failure to submit a statement of claim, the issues in dispute might still require a decision to be made by the arbitral tribunal, in particular in view of the interests of the other parties involved." UNCITRAL, 43rd Session, UN Doc A/CN.9/684, n 22, at 7, para 22. Before adopting the final text, the Working Group considered various other proposals: "unless there remain other issues to be decided," "unless the respondent needs other issues to be considered," "unless the respondent needs matters to be decided." UNCITRAL, 43rd Session, UN Doc A/CN.9/684, at 7–8, para 24.

[26] UNCITRAL, 43rd Session, UN Doc A/CN.9/684, n 22, at 7, para 22–23.

[27] UNCITRAL, 43rd Session, UN Doc A/CN.9/684, n 22, at 7, para 22.

[28] As explained, Article 30 does not permit an arbitral tribunal to render a "default" award based solely on a party's failure to participate in the proceedings.

[29] UNCITRAL, 43rd Session, UN Doc A/CN.9/684, n 22, at 7, para 23.

[30] UNCITRAL, 43rd Session, UN Doc A/CN.9/684, n 22, at 7–8, para 24.

[31] According to Article 30(1), the arbitral tribunal "shall" order a continuation of the proceedings. See *Phillips Petroleum Co Iran* (1983 Tribunal Rules); and *Marine Midland Bank* (1983 Tribunal Rules); both reprinted in section 2(D)(1).

[32] See *Amoco Intl Finance Corp* (1983 Tribunal Rules), reprinted in section 2(D)(1).

[33] In revising the UNCITRAL Rules, the Working Group added this clause to bring the 2010 Rules in line with Article 25(b) of the UNCITRAL Model Law, as amended, which contains identical language.

situation the arbitral tribunal is left to interpret the respondent's silence in the manner most reasonable in light of the claimant's evidence and arguments. Article 30(1)(b) also provides that the rule of continuation applies *mutatis mutandis* for a claimant's failure to submit a defence to a counterclaim or to a claim for the purpose of a set-off.

(3) Failure to appear at a hearing—Article 30(2)

Article 30(2) allows the tribunal to move the arbitral proceedings forward in the event one of the parties fails to appear at a hearing.[34] In the unlikely event that both parties fail to appear at the hearing, the arbitral tribunal may wish to call a second hearing and, if the parties again fail to appear, to consider terminating the proceedings.[35]

A prototypical example of failure to appear at a hearing is found in the *Meyer* case decided under Article 28(2) of the 1983 Rules of the Iran–US Claims Tribunal, which is substantially similar to Article 30(2) of the 2010 UNCITRAL Rules.[36] There, neither the respondent company nor its counsel appeared for a scheduled hearing and so the hearing took place in their absence. Responding to the Tribunal's inquiry into the matter, the Iranian Agent explained that the respondent believed that its status as a private company (not subject to the Tribunal's jurisdiction), made its presence at the hearing unnecessary. Three weeks after the hearing, the respondent provided a different explanation for its absence from the hearing, namely that its legal counsel had fallen ill. The respondent sought not only admission of the memorial, which addressed various issues in the case, but also requested that a new hearing be scheduled. The Tribunal denied the respondent's request and proceeded with the arbitration pursuant to Article 28(2). In support of its ruling, the Tribunal noted that the respondent had failed to communicate its inability to appear either before or on the date of the hearing, to substantiate the asserted cause of its absence, or to explain the differences in explanations offered by the respondent and the Iranian Agent for its absence.

The *Meyer* case demonstrates the limited punitive effect of Article 30. A party's failure to cooperate in the arbitral proceedings may result in the loss of a specific opportunity to present its case, eg presenting arguments and witnesses at a hearing. However, in *Meyer*, the Tribunal nevertheless granted the respondent's request to submit a memorial into the arbitration record subsequent to the respondent's default. Thus, while the respondent was barred from participating in the hearing, its broader involvement in the arbitral proceedings was not foreclosed.

(4) Failure to produce documentary evidence—Article 30(3)

At times during the arbitration, a party may request or the arbitral tribunal may order the other party to produce documentary evidence in accordance with Article 27(3) of the Rules. When a party fails to produce such evidence, Article 30(3) provides that the tribunal "may make the award on the evidence before it." The provision does not require that the

---

UNCITRAL, 41st Session, UN Doc A/CN.9/641, n 23, at 13, para 63. For a discussion of the original provision, see H Holtzmann and J Neuhaus, *A Guide to the UNCITRAL Model Law on International Commercial Arbitration: Legislative History and Commentary* (1989) 700.

[34] For a general discussion on ex parte hearings, see N Blackaby and C Partasides, *Redfern and Hunter on International Arbitration*, n 11, 425–8; "Preventing Delay and Disruption in Arbitration," in A J van den Berg (ed), *ICCA Congress Series No 5* (1990) 225–39.

[35] See *Report of the UNCITRAL*, 8th Session, Summary of Discussion of the Preliminary Draft, UN Doc A/10017, paras 171–72 (1975), reprinted in (1975) VI UNCITRAL Ybk 24, 40.

[36] See *George J Meyer* (1983 Tribunal Rules), reprinted in section 2(D)(2). For other examples, see *Sedco, Inc* (1983 Tribunal Rules); and *Plicoflex, Inc* (1983 Tribunal Rules); both reprinted in section 2(D)(2).

arbitral tribunal immediately wrap up the proceedings and render the award when a party fails to produce requested documents, exhibits or other evidence. Indeed, where further pleadings or a hearing is required, doing so would be inappropriate and may run afoul of the principles of fairness and equality embodied in Article 17(1).[37] Rather, Article 30(3) is meant to ensure that the non-production of evidence by a defaulting party does not sabotage the proceedings and prevent the tribunal from fulfilling its mandate.[38]

Although not expressly provided therein, Article 30(3) can be construed as empowering a tribunal to sanction a party who fails to produce requested documentary evidence,[39] for example, by possibly disregarding new evidence that the defaulting party files after the scheduled submission deadline.[40] The preferable and more reasonable approach, in our view, however, is for the tribunal to weigh the utility of sanctions against the value of late-filed evidence to the resolution of the dispute. For example, in a series of cases before the Iran–US Claims Tribunal, the Tribunal applied Article 28(3) of the Tribunal Rules (nearly identical to Article 30(3)) after the respondent failed to produce evidence regarding the dominant and effective nationality of various claimants. Still, the Tribunal received and evaluated evidence that the respondent submitted, sometimes months later.[41] Another possible sanction mechanism is for the tribunal to draw a negative inference against the defaulting party for its failure to provide the requested evidence, although this may not always be possible.[42]

(5) Comparison to the 1976 UNCITRAL Rules

Despite some minor restructuring of paragraphs,[43] Article 30 is substantially similar to corresponding Article 28 of the 1976 UNCITRAL Rules in content and approach, save for four differences.

One difference significantly changes the scope of the arbitral tribunal's powers under the article. Unlike Article 30(1), original Article 28(1) does not qualify the arbitral tribunal's duty to terminate the proceedings, where the claimant has failed to file a statement of claim, with the phrase "unless there are remaining matters that may need to be decided and the arbitral tribunal considers it appropriate to do so." The addition of this clause to revised Article 30(1) reflects a clear intent to "no longer limit the power of the arbitral tribunal in case the claimant failed to submit its statement of claim to a dismissal order for

---

[37] See, eg, *Component Builders, Inc* (1983 Tribunal Rules), reprinted in section 2(D)(3).

[38] See, eg, *Norman Gabay* (1983 Tribunal Rules); *Karim Sabet* (1983 Tribunal Rules); *John Francis Cummins* (1983 Tribunal Rules); *Juliette Allen* (1983 Tribunal Rules); and *Behring Intl Inc* (1983 Tribunal Rules); all reprinted in section 2(D)(3).

[39] During discussion to revise the Rules, the Working Group considered proposals to include express guidance in Article 30(3) on the consequences of a party's failure to comply with production requests. These proposals did not gain support out of concerns that they would complicate the provision. UNCITRAL, 43rd Session, UN Doc A/CN.9/684, n 22, at 9, para 32.

[40] See H Holtzmann and J Neuhaus, *A Guide to the UNCITRAL Model Law*, n 33, 701.

[41] See, eg, *Reza Said Malek* and *Government of the Islamic Republic of Iran*, Award No ITL 68–193–3 (June 23, 1988), reprinted in 19 Iran-US CTR 48 (1988-II); *Katrin Zohrabegian Abrahamian* and *Government of the Islamic Republic of Iran*, Award No ITL 74–377–3 (December 1, 1989), reprinted in 23 Iran-US CTR 285 (1989-II); *Kianoosh Jafari* and *Islamic Republic of Iran*, Award No 349–420–3 (February 29, 1988), reprinted in 18 Iran-US CTR 90 (1988-I); *Richard Nourafchan* and *Islamic Republic of Iran*, Award No 348–414–3 (February 29, 1988), reprinted in 18 Iran-US CTR 88 (1988-I).

[42] See H Holtzmann and J Neuhaus, *A Guide to the UNCITRAL Model Law*, n 33, 700–1.

[43] Article 30(1) was reorganized to parallel the structure of Article 25 of the Model Law. *Settlement of Commercial Disputes: Revision of the UNCITRAL Arbitration Rules, Note by the Secretariat*, UNCITRAL, UN Doc A/CN.9/WG.II/WP.151/Add.1 at 11, para 18 (2008).

termination."[44] Given the significance of this change, parties arbitrating under the 1976 Arbitration Rules may wish to modify them accordingly.

Article 30 includes other revisions that are less significant. Consistent with the introduction of the response to the notice of arbitration as a new procedural step under the 2010 UNCITRAL Rules, Article 30(1)(b) now references the respondent's failure to submit a response, in addition to a statement of defence. In addition, Article 30(1)(b) now clarifies that when an arbitral tribunal must order the proceedings to continue—because the respondent has failed to submit a response or a statement of defence, or the claimant has failed to submit a defence to a counterclaim or to a set-off claim—"without treating such failure in itself as an admission of the claimant's allegations." Revised Article 30(1) also expressly covers situations in which a claimant has failed to submit a defence to a counterclaim or to a set-off claim, whereas original Article 28(1) is silent in these areas, leaving it to the arbitral tribunal to address under its general authority to conduct the proceedings in such manner as it deems appropriate.

Finally, Article 30(3) addresses a party's failure to comply with an arbitral tribunal's invitation to produce "documents, exhibits or other evidence," whereas original Article 28(3) used the more generic term "documentary evidence" in this context. The revision contained in Article 30(3) reflects a technical change aimed at aligning the terminology of Article 30(3) with that of Article 27(3), which provides: "At any time during the arbitral proceedings the arbitral tribunal may require the parties to produce documents, exhibits or other evidence within such a period of time as the arbitral tribunal shall determine."[45]

C. Extracts from the Practice of Investment Tribunals

Himpurna California Energy Ltd and *Republic of Indonesia*, Interim Award (September 26, 1999) (*Ad Hoc* Proceeding, 1976 UNCITRAL Rules, Concession Agreement), reprinted in (2000) XXV Ybk Commercial Arb 109, 132–35, 167–69, 171–76, 185:

[52] On 5 August 1999, Karim Sani [Counsel for Respondent] communicated to the Arbitral Tribunal a copy of the injunction issued by the Jakarta Court on 22 July, as well as a "rough translation of the relevant part", which made clear that the Court had indeed ordered:
(1) suspension of the execution of the PLN Awards until the merits of Pertamina's suit have been decided by the Court,
(2) suspension of the present proceedings, likewise until the merits of Pertamina's suit have been decided by the Court,
(3) that a breach of the Court's second order would result in a daily fine (known as *dwangsam*) of US$ 1 million.

[53] Karim Sani's covering letter stated:

> ... It is, however, now very clear that were the Tribunal to order submission of our evidence at any time before the injunction is lifted, such order would indeed constitute such violation. Furthermore, should the Tribunal thereafter declare us in default for obeying an order of the court with authority over this matter, in particular where we have not had the benefit to know what is the case against us, and issue a default award against us, not only would such an award constitute a violation of the injunction, but could hardly be expected to be enforceable, seeing that it was illegally issued.

---

[44] UNCITRAL, 43rd Session, UN Doc A/CN.9/684, n 22, at 8, para 26.
[45] See UNCITRAL, 41st Session, UN Doc A/CN.9/641, n 23, at 13, para 64.

...

[59] Latham & Watkins followed up with another letter on 10 August 1999:

> Under the Terms of Appointment, respondent's case-in-chief was due today. Respondent did not serve its case-in-chief. In light of the fact that respondent's failure to serve its evidence was without sufficient cause, as argued in claimants' 5 August 1999 letter, claimants request that the Tribunal proceed with the arbitration pursuant to Art. 28 of the [1976] UNCITRAL Rules.

...

V. Default

1. Overview

[107] The Republic of Indonesia undertook to participate in these proceedings on the contractual foundation of two documents: the MoF Letter and the detailed Terms of Appointment. It now asserts that it is prevented from doing so by reason of the Jakarta Court injunction of 22 July 1999. The central issue is whether that injunction provided a valid excuse. The Arbitral Tribunal here accepts the view of Professor Rogers, expressed on page 14 of his Opinion, that the Terms of Appointment constitute

> a contractual agreement binding all parties which can be departed from only in accordance with appropriate principles of contract law.

[108] Art. 1245 of the Indonesian Civil Code excuses non-performance in the event of force majeure.... Alleged impediments do not excuse a non-performing party unless they are *insurmountable, irresistible*, and *external* to the will of the defendant. ...

[109] The Arbitral Tribunal has not the slightest hesitation in holding that the Republic of Indonesia had the power to overcome to avoid the impediment which it now invokes to excuse its default. The Arbitral Tribunal also deems Pertamina's initiatives not to be independent of the Republic of Indonesia's will. The consequence of these findings is that the proceedings have gone forward. Under Art. 28 of the [1976] UNCITRAL Rules, the Arbitral Tribunal has the authority to do so whenever the defaulting party has not shown "sufficient cause" for its failure to produce documentary evidence and to appear at a hearing.

[110] The relevant portions of Art. 28 read as follows:

> If one of the parties, duly notified under these Rules, fails to appear at a hearing, *without showing sufficient cause for such failure*, the arbitral tribunal may proceed with the arbitration.
>
> If one of the parties, duly invited to produce documentary evidence, fails to do so within the established period of time, *without showing sufficient cause for* such failure, the arbitral tribunal may make the award on the evidence before it. (Emphasis added.)

[111] The position of the Arbitral Tribunal is thus based on its appreciation of the facts of this case, and founded on the authority granted by the Parties when they agreed to arbitrate under the [1976] UNCITRAL Rules.

[112] The issue of respect for the Jakarta Court does not enter into the picture. The Court's order of 22 July 1999 is not addressed to the Arbitral Tribunal, but to the claimant and to the Republic of Indonesia. (See the more detailed analysis in Sect. V.*4*) of this Interim Award). The claimant, which is professionally advised and assumes its own responsibilities, has chosen not to consider the injunction to be an impediment to its participation. The Republic of Indonesia has claimed that the injunction is an impediment. As described in further detail in Sect. V.*2*, however, it has not discharged its burden under Art. 28 of the [1976] UNCITRAL Rules of so proving to the satisfaction of the Arbitral Tribunal.

[113] The Arbitral Tribunal therefore has no choice but to fulfil its mandate.

...

2. The Republic of Indonesia's Ability to Avoid or Overcome the Injunction

[118] Pertamina's petition to the Jakarta Court squarely contradicted the Terms of Appointment not only in that it called for a halt to proceedings which under point 5(h) of the Terms of Appointment were to be concluded "as expeditiously as possible", but also in its request that the Jakarta Court declare that the MoF Letter did not create enforceable rights—the very merits of the dispute to be resolved by arbitration pursuant to the Terms of Appointment.

[119] The Republic of Indonesia has argued that it was powerless to prevent Pertamina from instituting and maintaining this action. Under Art. 28 of the [1976] UNCITRAL Rules, the Republic of Indonesia has the burden of proving that this proposition is correct, for if the Republic of Indonesia could have prevented Pertamina's initiative before the Jakarta Court the injunction would not have eventuated.

[120] The Arbitral Tribunal holds that the Republic of Indonesia has failed to discharge this burden of proof. It submitted no credible evidence to support its assertions. This conclusion suffices to establish the Republic of Indonesia's default under the Terms of Appointment.

[121] The Arbitral Tribunal's decision is based on its factual findings with respect to both Pertamina's juridical subservience to the Republic of Indonesia, and the Republic of Indonesia's actual conduct in the course of these proceedings.

...

[129] The Arbitral Tribunal is impressed by the claimant's argument, in its letter of 31 August 1999, that the recognition of Government control implicit in the MoF Letter should bar the Republic of Indonesia "from asserting a defence that contradicts it to claimants' detriment". This estoppel-based argument is supported, in the claimant's submission, by a number of familiar and well-recognised authorities. The Arbitral Tribunal considers, however, that its decision rests on even firmer ground.

[130] In the first place, the Republic of Indonesia cannot be excused for an alleged inability to exercise its powers effectively. Thus, a government does not escape liability for the actions of its armed forces because it claims that rogue elements are not following orders. See, e.g. *Asian Agricultural Products v. Republic of Sri Lanka*, ICSID Case 87/3, Award of 27 June 1990, 6 ICSID Review—Foreign Investment Law Journal 526 (1991), noting with approval at page 557 Professor Ian Brownlie's "categorical" statement that: "There is general agreement that the rule of non-responsibility cannot apply where the Government concerned has failed to show due diligence."

[131] Secondly, the Republic of Indonesia has offered no proof of the slightest attempt to reign in Pertamina. This failure is all the more remarkable in that it was preceded by explicit admonitions from the Arbitral Tribunal, which wrote on 28 July 1999 "arbitrators are most certainly not bound by a disputant's *ipse dixit* founded on unverifiable ex parte communications" (see Paragraph [47]) and on 11 August 1999:

> The Republic of Indonesia has not shown any evidence of its having instructed (or even sought to persuade) Pertamina to act in a manner that would ensure compliance with the Terms of Appointment signed by the Republic of Indonesia. Most of all, the Republic of Indonesia has not even attempted to demonstrate that it used its legal dominion to prevent Pertamina from pursuing a judicial initiative which is fundamentally at variance with the Republic of Indonesia's undertakings. In other words, the Republic of Indonesia seems to excuse its failure by invoking an event which it could have prevented. Such an excuse has, prima facie, little chance of being accepted. The respondent is formally put on notice that unless it forthwith makes a compelling demonstration to the Arbitral Tribunal that it is powerless to influence the actions of Pertamina, it will be held to be in breach of the Terms of Appointment and will have to face the full consequences of that breach. The Arbitral Tribunal will not be satisfied with formalistic assertions. (See Paragraph [60].)

[132] There is no doubt that the Republic of Indonesia, having signed the Terms of Appointment, had the duty to do what was in its power to ensure its performance. The record is conspicuously

devoid of any evidence that the Republic of Indonesia sought to direct, or even persuade, Pertamina to refrain from pursuing its application for the injunction from the Jakarta Court.

[133] The various representations made by counsel to the Republic of Indonesia to the effect that it was seeking to comply with the Terms of Appointment, and indeed to resist the issuance of the injunction (see, e.g. Paragraphs [36], [37] and [42]), are contradicted by its actual conduct.

[134] Even before the injunction was issued on 22 July 1999, the Republic of Indonesia repeatedly warned the claimant, and indeed the Arbitral Tribunal, that any party participating in the arbitration in the face of an injunction would be subject to criminal prosecution; thus, in paragraph 30 of its Statement of Defence (see Paragraph [30]), the Republic of Indonesia, rather than indicating how it would resist the issuance of the injunction, "reserved" the right to apply to the Indonesian courts for "sequestration of the claimant's assets" if such an injunction were to be granted. What interest it could have in seeking financial relief for itself on account of the prospective violation of an injunction sought by an alleged third party, and allegedly resisted by the Republic of Indonesia, was never explained. (The Statement of Defence, it will be recalled, was submitted 17 days before the injunction was issued.)

[135] Nor did the Republic of Indonesia seek to have Pertamina's claim dismissed, whether by reference to its own undertaking to arbitrate, or to Pertamina's similar undertaking pursuant to the JOC.

[136] Moreover, when responding to Pertamina's application to the Jakarta Court, the Republic of Indonesia readily assented to Pertamina's request for a declaration that the MoF Letter did not constitute a legal obligation....

. . .

[141] The Republic of Indonesia has put considerable stress on its arguments to the effect that Pertamina had a legitimate interest in seeking the injunction. (The Arbitral Tribunal notes in passing the contrast between this approval of Pertamina's initiative before the Jakarta Court and the contextually unmistakable accusations of corruption levelled at Pertamina on page 8 of counsel's memorandum entitled "Can the Government Control Pertamina?" submitted with their letter of 26 August 1999.) The Arbitral Tribunal has already rejected the argument that Pertamina is an autonomous third party for the purposes of assessing the Republic of Indonesia's actions in the light of Art. 28 of the [1976] UNCITRAL Rules. As shall now be demonstrated the Arbitral Tribunal's analysis is that Pertamina did not in any event have a cognisable interest in seeking the injunction. This conclusion confirms beyond redemption the default of the Republic of Indonesia.

[142] The focus of this part of the discussion is the Opinion of Professor Rogers, upon which the Republic of Indonesia has placed comprehensive reliance and which indeed is predominantly focused on this topic.

[143] One of the great difficulties the Arbitral Tribunal has with the Rogers Opinion transpires from the very first words of the learned author's text, where he says that the way the arbitration provisions in the ESC were framed placed the arbitrators in the PLN proceedings "in an impossible position" to go forward in the absence of other proceedings being instituted under another contract, namely the JOC. The Arbitral Tribunal is unwilling to accept that the claimant was encouraged to make large investments in Indonesia on the basis of contractual provisions later revealed to be impossible to apply. Such a conclusion would suggest a *culpa in contratendo* on the part of the Indonesian authorities of which the Arbitral Tribunal has seen no evidence, and is unwilling to presume. At any rate, the matter was dealt with in Sect. V.3 of the PLN Award, and this Arbitral Tribunal obviously cannot be called upon to reconsider the *res judicata*.

[144] The Rogers Opinion is devoted principally to identifying perceived defects in the PLN Award, and elaborating on their ramifications. The Arbitral Tribunal fully understands that the purpose is not to invite the arbitrators to correct the PLN Award. That they are powerless to do. Rather, Professor Rogers suggests that Pertamina's interests were adversely affected

by the PLN Award, and that this adverse effect may be aggravated by an award in the present arbitration. Accordingly, the purpose of the Arbitral Tribunal's consideration of the PLN arbitrators' findings is to examine whether they give rise to a legitimate reason *for Pertamina* to seek the interruption of these proceedings.

[145] The Arbitral Tribunal immediately notes that both of these propositions, although *indispensable*, are not *sufficient* to establish Pertamina's legitimate intent in seeking the injunction. It must also be shown that there is some compelling reason (not just an *arguable* reason, since the Republic of Indonesia bears the burden of proof under Art. 28 of the [1976] UNCITRAL Rules) why Pertamina's alleged interest could not abide the end of these proceedings—if indeed it transpired that the Award here affected Pertamina's interest in some actionably adverse manner. It would have to be shown that the proper course for Pertamina would not be to initiate arbitral proceedings at its own behest, and at a time of its choosing.

[146] The Rogers Opinion suggests that if an award is made against the Republic of Indonesia under the MoF Letter, the Government could look to Pertamina for reimbursement. The Arbitral Tribunal sees no need to evaluate the degree of realism inherent in the notion of the Government seeking to recover monies from a wholly-owned entity. Nor need it consider the plausibility of Indonesian Directors of Pertamina clinging—as Professor Rogers considers they should—to the *Salomon v. Salomon* principle, established over a century ago in England (!), to the effect that Pertamina is a separate legal entity to which they owe fiduciary duties notwithstanding that Pertamina's capital—which is undivided into shares—is a state asset and that they are subject to statutory grounds of dismissal if they fail to act in the interest of the Republic of Indonesia. The arbitrators simply do not accept Professor Rogers' theory per se. (. . . .)

[147] Pertamina's "only recourse," *pace* Rogers, was not the Jakarta Court. And Pertamina not only did not *need* injunctive relief, but had promised not to seek it.

[148] In sum, the Arbitral Tribunal is compelled to conclude that the injunction of the Jakarta Court is the consequence of the refusal of the Republic of Indonesia to submit to an arbitration to which it has previously consented. The injunction therefore does not, under Art. 28 of the [1976] UNCITRAL Rules, excuse the Republic of Indonesia's default.

. . .

[198] For the reasons stated above, and rejecting all contentions to the contrary, the Arbitral Tribunal holds with definitive effect that:
 (i) the Republic of Indonesia has defaulted under the Terms of Appointment by failing to submit its documentary evidence, as required under paragraph 5(f) of the Terms of Appointment, by August 10, 1999;
 (ii) the Republic of Indonesia has failed to show "sufficient cause for such failure" for purposes of Article 28(3) of the [1976] UNCITRAL Rules, with the result that the Arbitral Tribunal "may make the award on the evidence before it."

D. Extracts from the Practice of the Iran–US Claims Tribunal

(1) General and Tribunal Rules (1983), Article 28

Phillips Petroleum Co Iran and *Iran NIOC*, Case No 39, Chamber Two, Communication to the Claimant of June 29, 1982, at 1:

Chamber Two is in receipt of your "Request for Order that Proceedings Continue in the Absence of Statement of Defence (Including Request for Pre-Hearing Conference)," dated June 18, 1982.

We expect that at the close of the Preliminary Hearing scheduled for September 13, 1982 in the above referenced case, time will be afforded to the arbitrating parties to discuss with the Chamber other matters, including clarification of the issues in the case and a schedule for further proceedings.

> The Chamber has noted the Respondent's failure to file the Statement of Defence when due on June 15. The Chamber hopes that such a Statement will be forthcoming from the Respondents. In any event, the proceeding will continue.

Dissent of Howard M Holtzmann, George H Aldrich, and Richard M Mosk from the Procedural Decisions in Nine Forum Selection Clause Cases, Case Nos 6, 51, 68, 121, 140, 159, 254, 293 and 466 (July 6, 1982), reprinted in 1 Iran-US CTR 320, 320, 324 (1981–82):

> We dissent from the decision of the Tribunal permitting the Islamic Republic of Iran and the other Respondents in these cases, who failed to file any Memorial within the period established by Order of the Tribunal and who refused even to appear at the hearing, to file a Memorial more than six weeks after the hearing. The prejudice to orderly process is manifest, and we fear that respect for the Orders of the Tribunal will suffer if the Tribunal shows itself so irresolute.
>
> ...
>
> Under Article 28 of the [1983] Tribunal Rules, if a party fails to produce documents ordered by the Tribunal within the established time or fails to appear at a hearing, without a sufficient showing of cause, the Tribunal may proceed with the arbitration. That is a fair and necessary rule and one typically found in international arbitral rules. This sanction is virtually the sole means available to the Tribunal to enforce its Orders and to ensure that it, rather than a party, is in charge of the proceedings. In our view, the Tribunal erred in not applying the rules in these circumstances.

Dissent of Howard M Holtzmann from Orders Granting Further Extensions of Time to File Statements of Defence, Case Nos 452 and 926, Chamber One (June 20, 1983), reprinted in 3 Iran-US CTR 84, 85–86 (1983-II):

> For Article 28 to be effective it must be enforced by setting a hearing date within a very short time. In Case No 452 a Pre-Hearing Conference has been scheduled on 19 December 1983—a move I consider too little and too late. In Case No 926, a Hearing has been scheduled on 10 April 1984—much too far in the future to send a message to all parties that the Tribunal intends to enforce its Orders. I appreciate that the Tribunal's docket is crowded for many months ahead and that the summer recess is about to begin; but just as calls for interim measures of relief demand our prompt attention, so must we find time to act swiftly and decisively when our Orders are ignored.

Marine Midland Bank, NA and *Bank Tejarat*, Case No 163, Chamber Two, Order of July 14, 1983, at 1:

> The Tribunal notes that the time fixed for the filing of a Statement of Defence has expired and that no agreement exists between the Parties as to further extension of that time.
> In these circumstances, the Tribunal has decided, pursuant to Article 28,1 of the [1983] Tribunal Rules, that the arbitral proceedings shall continue.
> The Parties are hereby notified that a Pre-hearing Conference will take place on 26 October 1983 at 9:30 a.m. at Parkweg 13, The Hague. The Parties should be prepared to discuss the matters indicated in the schedule annexed.
> Date and time of this meeting will be confirmed at a later stage.

Amoco Intl Finance Corp and *National Iranian Oil Co*, Case No 56, Chamber Three, Order of February 22, 1984, at 1–2:

> The Agent of the Islamic Republic of Iran in his letter filed on 23 January 1984 has requested that the date for filing of its Statement of Defence and Counterclaim be extended until 15 May 1984.
> Considering fully the procedural history of this case, the Tribunal orders the following schedule of proceedings:

1. By no later than 15 May 1984, the Respondents shall file the Statements of Defence including any counter-claims or claims made for the purpose of set-off. This new date follows numerous extensions and grants Respondents the entire period requested for the filing of their Statements of Defence and Counter-claim. Against this background the Tribunal wishes to emphasize that if any such filing is not made by 15 May 1984, the Tribunal must seriously consider under [1983] Tribunal Rules 28, to order the proceedings to continue in this case; and as a result of such an order Respondents would be barred from filing any further counterclaims or claims for the purpose of set off.

Oil Cases, Case Nos 72–76, 78–81 and 150, Chamber Three, Order of February 22, 1984, at 3:

Claimants in their letter filed on 27 January 1984 have requested that monetary sanctions be imposed upon the Respondents if the date for the filing of the Statements of Defence and Counterclaims is ignored. This request will be considered when and if such a default occurs.

Gordon Williams and *Islamic Republic of Iran*, Case No 187, Chamber Three, Order of April 5, 1984, at 1:

The Pre-Hearing Conference in this case was held on 27 September 1982. By an Order of 5 October 1982 the Claimant was requested to submit no later than 26 November 1982 a Memorial including any and all written evidence he wants to rely on and a brief addressing the legal issues. Since then the relevant time limit has been extended four times, the latest extension having expired on 3 April 1984.

On request made by the Claimant on 2 April 1984 the time limit for submitting the Memorial referred to above is hereby extended until 4 May 1984.

If the Claimant fails to observe the last-mentioned time limit without showing sufficient cause for such failure, the Tribunal, on the basis of Article 28 of the [1983] Tribunal Rules, will terminate the proceedings in this case.

The question of costs shall be decided at a later date.

Thomas K Khoshravi and *Government of the Islamic Republic of Iran*, Case No 146, Chamber Three, Order of October 18, 1985, at 1:

Reference is made to the Tribunal's Order filed on 28 June 1985.

The Tribunal notes that the Claimant has neither filed the required submission nor any extension request.

The time limit for the Claimant to file the submission described in the Order of 28 June 1985 is hereby extended until 20 December 1985.

If the Claimant fails to observe this filing date without showing sufficient cause for such failure, the Tribunal shall consider taking action in accordance with Article 28 of the [1983] Tribunal Rules.

(2) Tribunal Rules (1983), Article 28(2)

George J Meyer Manufacturing Division of Figgie Intl, Inc and *Zamzam Bottling Company*, Case No 299, Chamber One, Order of March 22, 1984, at 1–3:

Pursuant to the schedule set forth in the Tribunal's Order of 26 September 1983, the Hearing in this case was held on 15 November 1983. The Respondent did not appear in person, nor was it represented by counsel. In answer to an inquiry by the Tribunal, the Agent of the Government of Iran stated that the Respondent maintained that it was a private company not subject to the jurisdiction of the Tribunal, and therefore the Respondent was of the opinion that the Hearing did not require the presence of the Respondent or its representatives.

Following deliberation, the Tribunal decided, with Mr. Kashani dissenting, to continue with the Hearing in accordance with Article 28, paragraph 2 of the [1983] Tribunal Rules . . .

On 9 December 1983, more than three weeks after the Hearing, the Respondent filed a Memorial in which it asserted that its absence at the Hearing has been "owing to the severe illness of its legal advisor in the case." Because of this, Respondent sought to submit its Memorial, addressing various issues in the case, and also requested the Tribunal to schedule a new Hearing.

On 22 December 1983 the Claimant filed a letter objecting to the admission of the Respondent's Memorial and opposing the Respondent's request for a new Hearing. In the event that the Tribunal should accept the Respondent's Memorial, the Claimant in its letter addressed an alleged misrepresentation of its position in that Memorial. The Claimant also requested that an additional document, a newspaper report of an interview with the Supervisor of the Foundation for the Oppressed which had not been available to it at the time of the Hearing, be accepted in evidence.

The Tribunal notes that the Respondent did not communicate to the Tribunal, through letter, telex or telephone prior to or on the date of the Hearing, its asserted inability to attend. The Tribunal also notes that the Respondent has not offered any substantiation of the asserted clause of its inability to attend. The Tribunal further notes that the explanation offered by the Respondent three weeks after the Hearing—i.e., the illness of its representative—differs from the explanation given by the Agent of the Government of Iran at the Hearing.

For these reasons, the Tribunal deems it appropriate, pursuant to Article 28, paragraph 2, to deny the Respondent's request for a new Hearing and to proceed with the arbitration. However, the Tribunal also deems it appropriate to accept the Respondent's Memorial filed on 9 December 1983, and the letter filed by the Claimant on 22 December 1983, together with the document attached thereto.....

Sedco, Inc and *National Iranian Oil Co*, Case No 129, Chamber Three, Order of May 17, 1985, at 5–8:

On 14 and 15 May 1985 Respondents, the Islamic Republic of Iran and the National Iranian Oil Company, did not appear for the scheduled Hearing. In this regard the Tribunal notes that the Islamic Republic of Iran has never stated that it would be unable to attend the Hearing. Moreover, inasmuch as the Agent for Iran or his representatives are located in The Hague as required by Article VI(2) of the Claims Settlement Agreement, the Tribunal can conceive of no justification for the absence of the Respondent Iran and none has been tendered. The Tribunal also notes that Claimant's counsel stated at the session held on 14 May 1985 that he had on Thursday, 10 May 1985, and Friday, 11 May 1985, from New York talked via telephone to the principal counsel in this case (and others) for the National Iranian Oil Company ("NIOC"), said NIOC representative being in The Hague at that time. In addition, the same principal counsel appeared with other representatives of said Respondent on 16 and 17 May 1985 in Chamber One for Pre-Hearing Conferences in Cases 258 and 259.

On 14 and 15 May 1985, the Iran-Appointed Member of Chamber Three, Judge Parviz Ansari Moin, also was not present at the scheduled Hearing. This absence occurred without notification and without any expressly official explanation to date. Dr. Niaki, who from time to time substitutes for the Agent for the Islamic Republic of Iran, visited Chairman Mangård and Judge Brower on the morning of 14 May 1985 to state (assertedly not as a representative of the Iranian Members of the Tribunal or the Iranian Government) that the Iranian Members had been recalled the previous evening to Iran by the Iranian Government and that it was his understanding that they were enroute to Iran. Dr. Niaki was officially requested to present this statement at the 14 May session in this case, but he declined, stating that he had no authority to act officially in this case.

In the 14 May 1985 session, Claimant argued that the absence of Respondents and Judge Ansari was unjustified. In particular, it argued that Judge Ansari's compliance with the reported instruction of the Government of Iran allegedly leading to his absence was contrary to the "independence" required of a Tribunal Member as set forth particularly in Articles 9 and 10 of the [1983] Tribunal Rules. Claimant requested that the scheduled Hearing proceed without Respondents before the two remaining Members of the Chamber. Claimant requested particularly that

Claimant's expert witness present in The Hague be heard because this witness would not be available for the June Hearing. Claimant also requested that it receive in an Interlocutory Award any unnecessary costs of attending the 14 and 15 May Hearing.

The Tribunal decided to proceed and to hear Claimant's expert witness, Mr. Whitney, and did so on 15 May 1985 because he would be unable to attend the final Hearing in June. The testimony and the simultaneous translation of such testimony, including all questions and answers, was tape recorded for use by the Tribunal and the Parties in this case. The Tribunal also requested Claimant to submit within 10 days an itemized request for any unnecessary costs of attending this Hearing.

...

Given the history of this case, the Tribunal wishes to emphasize that in the event of any failure to appear 18 and 19 June 1985 such as occurred 14 and 15 May 1985 as set forth above, the Tribunal will then seriously consider, including under [1983] Tribunal Rule 28(2), to proceed with the arbitration in this case at that time.

Plicoflex, Inc and *Islamic Republic of Iran*, Award No 535–354–1 (October 16, 1992), reprinted in 28 Iran-US CTR 309, 312 (1992):

10. The Hearing concerning the NIGC's Counterclaim was held on 15 June 1992. At the Hearing, representatives of the Respondents and the Deputy Agent of the United States were present. No representatives for Plicoflex appeared. Nor did the Tribunal receive any communication by Plicoflex explaining its failure to appear at the Hearing... Having regard to its Order of 19 February 1992 by which the Parties were notified of the Hearing... and to the fact that Plicoflex itself did not show sufficient cause for its failure to appear at the Hearing, the Tribunal decided pursuant to Article 28, paragraph 2, of the [1983] Tribunal Rules to proceed with the arbitration in the absence of Plicoflex.

(3) *Tribunal Rules (1983), Article 28(3)*

Konstantine A Gianoplus and *Islamic Republic of Iran*, Case No 314, Chamber One, Order of March 29, 1984, at 1:

The Tribunal, by its Order of 19 October 1983, ordered the Claimant to file certain documentary evidence by 1 December 1983. The Claimant has failed to do so within the established period of time, has not responded in any way to the Order, and has not made any showing of cause for its failure to comply with the Order.

Accordingly, the Tribunal intends to proceed under Article 28, paragraph 3, of the [1983] Tribunal Rules and to decide the case on the basis of the pleadings and documents submitted.

Component Builders, Inc and *Islamic Republic of Iran*, Case No 395, Chamber Three, Order of November 22, 1985, at 1–2:

On 16 September 1985 Claimants filed a "Request that the Tribunal Make an Award on the Evidence and Record before it." Referring to an extension request, filed by the Agent of the Government of the Islamic Republic of Iran on 10 September 1985, concerning Respondents' Memorials which were due to be filed on the same day, Claimants stated that "[t]his request is without any pretense of showing 'sufficient cause' for Respondents' failure to produce their Memorials and written evidence. Claimant' [sic], therefore, respectfully urge the Tribunal to act in accordance with its [1983] Rules Article 28 (3) and to make an award on the evidence before it."

On 19 September 1985 the Agent of the Government of the Islamic Republic of Iran filed a letter objecting to Claimants' above-mentioned request. In the letter it was stated, *inter alia*, that in this Case "the convening of a Hearing is... essential."

Noting that by Orders filed on 1 October 1985 and 24 October 1985, Respondents have been granted an extension until 20 December 1985 to file their Memorials and any written evidence upon which they intend to rely, and also taking into account the provisions of Article

15, paragraph 2 of the [1983] Tribunal Rules, the Tribunal rejects the request. The matter may be reconsidered, should conditions for the application of Article 28, paragraph 3 of the [1983] Tribunal Rules arise at a later stage of the proceedings.

Norman Gabay and *Islamic Republic of Iran*, Case No 771, Chamber Two, Order of December 5, 1986, at 1–2:

1. By its Order of October 4, 1984, the Tribunal instructed the Parties to submit all documentary evidence they wished the Tribunal to consider in determining whether the Claimant is a national of the United States of America or of the Islamic Republic of Iran, or of both, and, in case the Claimant is a national of both, the Claimant's dominant and effective nationality.
2. The Claimant submitted his evidence on December 18, 1984 but no evidence was submitted by the Respondent. After numerous extensions granted to the Respondent, the Tribunal informed the Parties in its Order of November 8, 1985 that it would take its decision on the basis of the documents before it.
3. The evidence indicates that the Claimant was born a national of Iran on June 26, 1929. He emigrated to the United States with his family on July 30, 1971, where he lived as a resident alien until he was naturalized as a United States citizen on April 25, 1980. On May 1983, the High Islamic Revolutionary Court issued a judgment confirming a previous decision of the Central Islamic Revolutionary Court which, *inter alia*, apparently determined that the Iranian citizenship of the Claimant had been effectively withdrawn. A copy of the previous decision of the Revolutionary Court was not submitted in evidence at this stage of the proceedings and it is not clear to the Tribunal whether this is the same judgment whereby the Claimant's property was allegedly confiscated and which was stated to have been issued on November 8, 1980.
4. On the basis of the evidence presently before it, it appears to the Tribunal that the Claimant is a national of the United States of America only. In these circumstances, all jurisdictional questions can be joined to the consideration of the merits of the Case.

John Francis Cummins and *Islamic Republic of Iran (a claim of less than US $250,000 presented by the United States of America)*, Case No 11723, Chamber One, Order of January 21, 1987, at 1, reprinted in 14 Iran-US CTR 21, 21 (1987-I):

Reference is made to the Order of 7 November 1986 and the extension request filed by the Agent of the Government of the Islamic Republic of Iran on 22 January 1987.

Since the Respondent was already granted five extensions of time, the Tribunal hereby denies the Agent's request and intends to proceed under Article 28 of the [1983] Tribunal Rules and may make an Award on the evidence before it.

Karim Sabet and *Islamic Republic of Iran*, Case No 816, Chamber Three, Order of February 20, 1987, at 1–2:

The Tribunal recalls that in its Order of 27 January 1987 it stated that in view of the previous extensions granted in this Case no further extension would be granted save for strong and compelling reasons.

...

In view of the present stage of proceedings, the Tribunal intends, pursuant to Article 28, paragraph 3 of the [1983] Tribunal Rules and as soon as its working schedule permits, to proceed with its deliberations on the issues of jurisdiction in this Case on the basis of the evidence then before the Tribunal.

The Tribunal will defer this course of action only if it is informed that ongoing settlement negotiations have reached a stage which would justify a postponement of the proceedings.

Juliette Allen and *Government of the Islamic Republic of Iran*, Case No 930, Chamber Three, Order of May 14, 1991, at 1–2:

> Reference is made to the Tribunal's Order filed 30 November 1990 in which the Claimant was ordered to submit by 28 December 1990 full English and Persian translations of her submissions filed 6 August and 11 September 1990.
>
> Reference is also made to the Tribunal's Order filed 5 March 1991 in which it was noted that none of the required translations had been filed within the time limit set by the Order of 30 November 1990 and whereby the Parties were informed that the Tribunal would consider application of Article 28(3) of the [1983] Tribunal Rules, if the Claimant, without showing sufficient cause failed to submit by 28 March 1991 the said translations.
>
> The Tribunal notes that the Claimant has not filed the required translations within the extended time limit set by the Order filed 5 March 1991 and that she has not provided any explanation for her failure to do so.
>
> The Tribunal therefore intends, pursuant to Article 28(3) of the [1983] Tribunal Rules, to proceed with its deliberations on the issue of jurisdiction in this Case on the basis of evidence properly filed in both Persian and English as of 28 March 1991.

Behring Intl, Inc and *Islamic Republic of Iran Air Force*, Award No 523–382–3 (October 29, 1991), reprinted in 27 Iran-US CTR 218, 221 (1991-II):

> 10. In its Order of 17 February 1988 the Tribunal noted that none of the above required submissions were filed within the time limits and informed the Parties that it would consider application of Article 28, paragraph 3 of the [1983] Tribunal Rules if the Claimant, without showing sufficient cause, failed to submit by 16 March 1988 its formal notice of withdrawal of the Claim or its Memorial and evidence.
> 11. In their submission dated 12 September 1989 the Respondents requested the Tribunal to "apply paragraph 3, Article 28 of the [1983] Tribunal Rules to the case, and to declare the Claimant's Claims as extinguished". It was also requested that the Tribunal set a Hearing for deciding the Counterclaims. The Respondents argued that the Claimant withdrew all the Claims brought in Case No 382 and that the Claimant consistently ignored the Tribunal's Orders for the filing of its Memorial and evidence.
> 12. In its Order dated 14 December 1989 the Tribunal noted that, since it had not received any formal request from the Claimant for withdrawal or termination of the proceedings, it was still seized of both the Claims and Counterclaims in the Case. Further, because none of the documents requested of the Claimant had been received by the Tribunal, it decided to apply Article 28, paragraph 3 of the [1983] Tribunal Rules and accordingly "make an award [on the Claim] on the evidence before it".

22
Waiver

1. Introduction	691
2. Waiver—Article 32	691
A. Text of the 2010 UNCITRAL Rule	691
B. Commentary	692
(1) General comments	692
(2) The level of knowledge required	693
(3) Comparison to the 1976 UNCITRAL Rules	695
C. Extracts from the Practice of Investment Tribunals	695
D. Extracts from the Practice of the Iran–US Claims Tribunal	696

1. Introduction

The UNCITRAL Rules secure the parties a host of procedural rights ranging from the right to file submissions and comments, to the right to a hearing, to the right to challenge an arbitrator. At times, the arbitral proceedings may deviate from the procedural track laid down by the UNCITRAL Rules or procedural requirements contained in the arbitration agreement. Such deviations may occur unintentionally when the arbitral tribunal misses a step in procedure, or intentionally when the parties choose to modify the Rules or the terms of the arbitration agreement during the proceedings to suit their changing needs. Under Article 32, if a party does not object promptly to any instance of non-compliance its rights are waived, unless it can prove that its failure to object was justified under the circumstances. The rule generally ensures that the arbitral proceedings will not be disrupted by late complaints submitted by an inattentive or tardy party.

2. Waiver—Article 32

A. Text of the 2010 UNCITRAL Rule[1]

Article 32 of the 2010 UNCITRAL Rules provides:
A failure by any party to object promptly to any non-compliance with these Rules or with any requirement of the arbitration agreement shall be deemed to be a waiver of the right of such a party to make such an objection, unless such party can show that, under the circumstances, its failure to object was justified.

---

[1] Corresponding Article 30 of the 1976 UNCITRAL Rules provides:

A party who knows that any provision of, or requirement under, these Rules has not been complied with and yet proceeds with the arbitration without promptly stating his objection to such non-compliance, shall be deemed to have waived his right to object.

B. Commentary

(1) General comments

Article 32 addresses the consequences of a party's failure to object promptly to an instance of procedural non-compliance of the UNCITRAL Rules or any requirements set forth in the arbitration agreement, such as regarding the constitution of the arbitral tribunal. Procedural non-compliance may occur when either the arbitral tribunal or the parties deviate from the course of procedure agreed upon by the parties. Under Article 32, a party loses its right to object to any non-compliance if it fails to object promptly and cannot establish that its failure to object was justified. The waiver of rights therefore seeks to minimize disruption of the proceedings by a late objection[2] and to protect the award from challenges by disgruntled parties against claims that, for example, their due process rights have been violated or that the tribunal exceeded its authority when the deviation from agreed-upon procedures occurred.[3]

Although Article 32, by its own terms, calls for waiver by automatic application under certain conditions,[4] its scope of application in practice may depend upon the importance of the procedural right at stake. Where fundamental procedural rights are concerned,[5] it is unlikely that Article 32 alone could extinguish a party's ability to challenge the award in collateral proceedings.[6] However, if there is evidence in the record that the parties intended to deviate from the Rules, a stronger case may exist for waiver. Indeed, these concerns about waiving fundamental procedural rights are clear from the *travaux préparatoires* of the 1976 UNCITRAL Rules, which caution against the application of corresponding Article 30 of the 1976 Rules in situations outside "minor violations" of the Rules.[7] The same policy should apply with respect to Article 32.

Good practice dictates that a tribunal should sufficiently document its determinations in all known cases of waiver or the absence of any objections by the disputing parties.[8] Such a record may take the form of a description of the nature of the procedural objection and the reasoning for its resolution.[9]

---

[2] Article 39 of the 2012 ICC Rules of Arbitration contains a waiver provision that serves the same goal. On the comparable rule under 1998 ICC Rules, see Y Derains and E Schwartz, *A Guide to the New ICC Rules of Arbitration* (2nd edn 2005) 379–81.

[3] In drafting the 1976 UNCITRAL Rules, the Committee raised concerns, in particular, about challenges brought under Article V, paragraph 1(D) of the New York Convention, which provides that "the arbitral procedure was not in accordance with the agreement of the parties." See *Report of the Secretary-General on the Revised Draft Set of Arbitration Rules*, UNCITRAL, 9th Session, Addendum 1 (Commentary), UN Doc A/CN.9/112/Add.1 (1975), reprinted in (1976) VII UNCITRAL Ybk 166, 177 (Commentary on Draft Article 26). Similarly Article 34(2)(ii) of the Model Law provides grounds for setting aside an award where "the party...was otherwise unable to present his case." See also N Blackaby and C Partasides with A Redfern and M Hunter, *Redfern and Hunter on International Arbitration* (5th edn 2009) 595.

[4] The Article directs that the right to object "shall be deemed" waived.

[5] Professor Mani, for example, identifies six fundamental procedural rights: the right to composition of the tribunal; the right to be heard; the right to due deliberation by a duly constituted tribunal; the right to reasoned judgment; the right to a tribunal free from corruption; and the right to proceedings free of fraud. See V S Mani, *International Adjudication: Procedural Aspects* (1980) 25–36. See also K Carlston, *The Process of International Arbitration* (1946) 36–9. Born notes some procedural protections that can be considered to be non-waivable, G Born, *International Commercial Arbitration Volume II* (2009) 1775–6.

[6] See N Blackaby and C Partasides, *Redfern and Hunter on International Arbitration*, n 3, 597. They use the example of the arbitral tribunal lacking jurisdiction and, as a result, exceeding its terms of reference.

[7] *Report of the UNCITRAL on the Work of its Ninth Session*, UN GAOR, 31st Session, Supp No 17, UN Doc A/31/17, para 146 (1976), reprinted in (1976) VII UNCITRAL Ybk 66, 77.

[8] For an example of the latter, see *Romak SA* (1976 Rules), reprinted in section 2(C).

[9] Substantial disputes may require explication in an interlocutory award. Minor disputes may be resolved orally or by a basic communication to the parties, so long as sufficient details of the dispute appear in the text of the award.

The arbitral tribunal should also be aware of any provisions of the governing arbitration law that may supersede the provisions of Article 32.[10]

(2) The level of knowledge required

One question that has long challenged UNCITRAL drafters is the extent to which a party must know about an instance of procedural non-compliance before its rights to object are waived. In drafting the 1976 UNCITRAL Rules, the members of the Committee agreed that a knowledge requirement was necessary, though they were divided as to its nature and scope. Some members argued that a waiver should occur not only when a party actually knew about a deviation from the Rules, but also when the party "should have known" about it.[11] The Committee maintained that a constructive knowledge requirement would simplify the task of "proving the time when a party first 'knew' that a provision of the Rules was violated."[12] This view did not prevail and, in the end, the 1976 Rules endorsed only the concept of actual knowledge, ie, a party must "know" of the procedural deviation, before it waives its rights.[13] Under this standard, a waiver arguably cannot occur unless it is proven that a party was aware of a deviation from the Rules.[14]

The drafters of the 2010 UNCITRAL Rules revisited the topic of a knowledge requirement. Some delegates supported inclusion of a constructive waiver requirement and proposed adding the words "ought to have known" to the text of the original rule.[15] Their position was driven primarily by concerns that actual knowledge was difficult to prove, particularly in jurisdictions requiring proof of positive knowledge, and might therefore allow for "mischief" or "procedural manoeuvres" by a party seeking to shield itself from waiver behind the high standard.[16]

To critics of a constructive knowledge requirement, the standard was prone to subjective application and might therefore produce "different standards for parties in the same proceedings, depending upon the level of arbitration experience of parties or their counsel."[17] According to them, this inherent subjectivity might result in increased litigation at the enforcement stage of an award.[18] Further, critics noted that adding a constructive

---

[10] For a discussion of related national law issues, see T Webster, *Handbook of UNCITRAL Arbitration: Commentary, Precedents and Materials for UNCITRAL Based Arbitration Rules* (2010) 445–55.

[11] See, eg, *Summary Record of the 10th Meeting of the Committee of the Whole (II)*, UNCITRAL, 9th Session, UN Doc A/CN.9/C.2/SR.10, at 6, para 43 (1976) (Comment by Mr St John, Australia).

[12] *Report of the UNCITRAL on the Work of its Ninth Session*, UN GAOR, 31st Session, Supp No 17, UN Doc A/31/17, para 144 (1976), reprinted in (1976) VII UNCITRAL Ybk 66, 77.

[13] Thus, actual knowledge is the standard of scienter. See S Baker and M Davis, *The UNCITRAL Arbitration Rules in Practice: The Experience of the Iran-United States Claims Tribunal* (1992) 147.

[14] It should be noted, however, that the drafters of the 1976 UNCITRAL Rules were not sympathetic to the argument that a party was not aware of an instance of procedural non-compliance because it was not aware of the provisions in the Rules:

[W]here a party has submitted to arbitration under [the] Rules, it will be very difficult for him to allege during the arbitral proceedings that he lacks knowledge of the contents of one or more of the provisions of these Rules. Such an allegation would be even more difficult to sustain if the parties had adopted the text of the model arbitration clause or separate arbitration agreement recommended in the introduction to these Rules …, since the text contains an express declaration by the parties that the Rules are known to them.

Report of the Secretary-General on the Revised Draft Set of Arbitration Rules, UNCITRAL, 9th Session, Addendum 1 (Commentary), UN Doc A/CN.9/112/Add.1 (1975), reprinted in (1976) VII UNCITRAL Ybk 166, 177.

[15] *Report of Working Group II (Arbitration and Conciliation) on the Work of its Fifty-First Session* (Vienna, September 14–18, 2009), UNCITRAL, 43rd Session, UN Doc A/CN.9/684, at 12, para 44 (2009).

[16] UNCITRAL, 43rd Session, UN Doc A/CN.9/684, n 15, at 12, para 44, 46.

[17] UNCITRAL, 43rd Session, UN Doc A/CN.9/684, n 15, at 12, para 45.

[18] UNCITRAL, 43rd Session, UN Doc A/CN.9/684, n 15, at 12, para 45.

knowledge requirement to the Rules might create confusion in countries that had adopted the UNCITRAL Model Law, which did not embrace the concept.[19]

The difficulties in applying both the actual knowledge and constructive knowledge standards prompted the Working Group to search for new solutions. One group of proposals, aimed at moderating the actual knowledge requirement, added language allowing for consideration of the "circumstances," "legitimate grounds," or "valid reasons" for a party's failure to raise an objection.[20] Another proposal, inspired by Article 33 of the ICC Arbitration Rules, sought to avoid any express reference to knowledge: "Any failure to comply with any provision of these Rules or any requirement under the arbitration agreement shall be objected to by the other party without undue delay."[21] That proposal, however, was criticized for "unfairly exclud[ing] any extenuating circumstances explaining the failure to object."[22]

Another approach, and the solution that was ultimately adopted by the Working Group, was to shift to the party who failed to object the burden of proving whether its failure was justified. The original 1976 rule required proof that the party failing to object had actual knowledge of the procedural non-compliance. One proposal to reverse the burden provided that procedural non-compliance "may not be invoked by a party that has failed to object without undue delay" and added: "This provision does not apply if the party invoking the failure had no knowledge of it."[23] Another proposal along these lines, but with a broader exception, provided that a failure to object constitutes a waiver, "unless such party can prove that, under the circumstances, its failure to object was [justified][excusable]." The last proposal was modified slightly (including by including the word "justified") and adopted by the Working Group.

Though Article 32 no longer contains an express knowledge requirement, a party's knowledge of the instance of procedural non-compliance in question is often still relevant. Though the rule begins from the premise that a party's right to object late is waived, that party is still free to argue that its tardiness in objecting was justified because it was unaware that the procedural non-compliance had occurred. Article 32 then leaves it to the arbitral tribunal, or possibly a reviewing court, to determine whether the objecting party has met its burden of proving that the "circumstances" surrounding the failure to object, ie, its lack of knowledge, to justify the alleged excuse.

A waiver under Article 32 is triggered when a party fails to object "promptly," though that critical term is not defined in the Rules. Thus, the arbitral tribunal, or perhaps a reviewing court, must assess on an incident-by-incident basis whether the extent of delay justifies the denial of a party's right to object to procedural non-compliance.[24] The authors

---

[19] UNCITRAL, 43rd Session, UN Doc A/CN.9/684, n 15, at 12, para 45 (citing Article 4 of the Model Law.).

[20] UNCITRAL, 43rd Session, UN Doc A/CN.9/684, n 15, at 12, para 47.

[21] UNCITRAL, 43rd Session, UN Doc A/CN.9/684, n 15, at 13, para 48.

[22] UNCITRAL, 43rd Session, UN Doc A/CN.9/684, n 15, at 13, para 48.

[23] UNCITRAL, 43rd Session, UN Doc A/CN.9/684, n 15, at 13, para 49 (drawing on Article 1027 of the German Code of Civil Procedure).

[24] The Iran–US Claims Tribunal has dealt with the issue of promptness on two documented occasions. See *Varo Intl Corp* (1983 Tribunal Rules) (claimant waived its right to object to the admission of respondent's documentary submissions because the Tribunal granted respondent's extension requests relating to the same submissions without a prompt objection by the claimant); and *Cook Industries, Inc* (1983 Tribunal Rules) (respondent waived its right to object to the improper translation of claimant's submissions filed nearly eighteen months earlier); both reprinted in section 2(D).

favor a flexible approach in applying the temporal element of Article 32 in order to ensure that a fundamental right of a party is not dispensed with too hastily. Though the drafters of the 2010 UNCITRAL Rules did not appear to question the use of the term "promptly" in Article 32 (perhaps because it already appeared in corresponding Article 30 of the 1976 UNCITRAL Rules), it should be noted that the drafters the UNCITRAL Model Law[25] chose instead to include the phrase "without undue delay" as a way of "softening" the more restrictive approach of the 1976 Rules.[26]

(3) Comparison to the 1976 UNCITRAL Rules

Article 32 represents a significant overhaul of corresponding Article 30 of the 1976 UNCITRAL Rules, though both versions of the rule serve the same general objective: to avoid disruptions in the proceedings and challenges to the award based on objections filed unjustifiably late. Both revised Article 32 and original Article 30 require that objections be raised "promptly." Beyond this similarity, the two versions of the rule differ significantly in their basic approaches.

As discussed above, Article 32 eliminates the requirement in original Article 30 that the waiving party have actual knowledge of the incidence of procedural non-compliance at issue.[27] Rather, Article 32 places the burden on the waiving party to prove its failure to object promptly was justified under the circumstances.

Article 32 also drops the requirement that the waiving party "proceed with the arbitration" after failing to object promptly.[28] Under the 1976 Rules, in contrast, in addition to having knowledge of the non-compliance, a waiving party is required to have advanced to the next stage of the arbitral proceedings. Appearing at a hearing or offering submissions to the arbitral tribunal or another party, for instance, are clear examples of a party's continuation.[29] This is not to say, however, that original Article 30 should be read so strictly as to permit a party to avoid the effect of a waiver through deliberate and calculated efforts *not* to continue with the proceedings. Where a party fails to continue with the proceedings, the tribunal is obligated to investigate any dilatory motive and is entitled, should any such motive exist, to apply Article 28 of the 1976 Rules to address the party's misconduct.[30]

C. Extracts from the Practice of Investment Tribunals

Himpurna California Energy Ltd and *Republic of Indonesia*, Interim Award (September 26, 1999) (*Ad Hoc* Proceedings, 1976 UNCITRAL Rules, Concession Agreement), reprinted in (2000) XXV Ybk Commercial Arb 109, 147–48:

> [75]. ...A number of important issues have been dealt with by the Arbitral Tribunal under my sole signature without demur. Taking the month of June alone, I refer you to letters signed

---

[25] See Article 4 of the UNCITRAL Model Law for its waiver provision.

[26] *Report of the Working Group on the Work of its Sixth Session* (Vienna, August 29–September 9, 1983), UNCITRAL Model Law, 14th Session, UN Doc A/CN.9/245, reprinted in (1984) XV UNCITRAL Ybk 155, 174 at para 178.

[27] In one case decided under the 1976 UNCITRAL Rules, the respondent waived its right to object to the issuing of an order under sole signature of the presiding arbitrator because it had not done so with respect to numerous previous orders. See *Himpurna California Ltd* (1976 Rules), reprinted in section 2(C).

[28] Accord J Castello, "UNCITRAL Rules," in F Weigand (ed) *Practitioner's Handbook on International Arbitration* (2nd edn 2009) 1507.

[29] H Holtzmann and J Neuhaus, *A Guide to the UNCITRAL Model Law on International Arbitration: Legislative History and Commentary* (1989) 200. (citing these examples in the context of the UNCITRAL Model Law).

[30] See Chapter 19.

by myself, announcing decisions of the Arbitral Tribunal, on the 9th, 15th, 16th, 18th, 24th, and 25th. For you to affirm at this late date that you find the procedural order of 7 September to be unacceptable [for failure to contain the signatures of all three members of the tribunal] is difficult to square with Art. 30 of the [1976] UNCITRAL Rules.

Romak SA and *Republic of Uzbekistan*, Award (November 26, 2009) (PCA administered, 1976 UNCITRAL Rules, Switzerland-Uzbekistan BIT), at 21:

> 88. Prior to the closing of the Hearing, with express reference to Article 30 of the [1976] UNCITRAL Rules, the Arbitral Tribunal asked counsel for the Parties whether they had any objections regarding the manner in which the arbitration proceedings had been conducted. Counsel for the Parties each stated that they had no such objections.

D. Extracts from the Practice of the Iran-US Claims Tribunal

Cook Industries, Inc and *Foreign Transactions Co,* et al, Case No 393, Chamber Two, Order of September 6, 1985, at 1:

> The Tribunal has taken note of the Respondents' requests filed on 9 August 1985 and 15 August 1985. The request of 15 August 1985 is untimely and is therefore denied in accordance with Article 30 of the [1983] Tribunal Rules.

Varo Intl Corp and *Government of the Islamic Republic of Iran*, Award No 482–275–1 (June 21, 1990), reprinted in 25 Iran-US CTR 3, 6 (1990-II):

> 11. This procedural history shows that the Claimant's request for a decision on its 6 August 1987 application to close the record is unfounded, as the Tribunal has already ruled on it by issuing its Order of 21 September 1987, extending the time limit for IEI to submit its Rebuttal Evidence. By so doing, the Tribunal manifested that the documentary record was not closed. Therefore, the Claimant's application obviously had been denied. If the Claimant had doubts whether the Tribunal had acted on its application, or on the admissibility of the Respondent's Rebuttal Evidence, it could have promptly informed the Tribunal of its doubts, or objected to these submissions. Article 30 of the [1983] Tribunal Rules requires that any objection to the conduct of the Arbitration be stated promptly, or else be deemed to have been waived. By failing promptly to react, in any way, to the Tribunal's grant of extensions or to the Respondents' filings, the Claimant waived its right to object.

PART VI

THE AWARD

Introduction

A final, but no less important, aspect of arbitration is the manner in which the arbitral tribunal brings the parties' dispute to a close. Whether conclusion is reached through an adjudication of the merits or a settlement by the parties, the main goal in arbitration is typically to produce a final and binding award, valid and enforceable both at the place of arbitration and in foreign jurisdictions. A number of important provisions in the 2010 UNCITRAL Rules assist in this regard.

Article 33, discussed in Chapter 23, guides the arbitral tribunal in matters of official decision-making, both with respect to substantive and procedural issues. Article 34, discussed in Chapter 24, establishes a number of technical criteria that govern the award-making process, with the aim of ensuring the general validity and enforceability of the award. Article 36, discussed in Chapter 25, sets forth procedures for concluding the parties' dispute in the event that a settlement is reached or conditions otherwise necessitate the termination of the arbitral proceedings. Articles 37, 38, and 39, discussed in Chapter 26, establish narrow exceptions to the basic rule of finality of the award, permitting, where necessary, that the award be interpreted, corrected or supplemented with an additional award.

On a separate, but related subject, the Rules include provisions concerning the costs of arbitration, the subject of Chapter 27. The parties' involvement in the arbitral proceedings typically gives rise to litigation costs, which in turn may give rise to derivative claims for reimbursement of those costs. Articles 40 and 42 permit the arbitral tribunal to apportion and award costs. Articles 41 and 43 deal with ancillary issues, such as the arbitrators' fees and the payment of monetary deposits by the parties to cover the costs of arbitration.

23
Deliberations and Decisions

1. Introduction		699
2. Decisions—Article 33		700
A. Text of the 2010 UNCITRAL Rule		700
B. Commentary		700
(1) Awards and other Decisions by Majority Vote—Article 33(1)		700
(a) General comments		700
(b) Majority decision-making by the Iran–US Claims Tribunal		704
(1) The dynamics of deliberations		704
(2) The practice of deliberating and drafting awards		705
(2) Decision-Making on Procedural Questions—Article 33(2)		706
(a) The meaning of "questions of procedure"		709
(b) Revision		710
(3) Confidentiality of deliberations—Article 31, Note 2 of the 1983 Tribunal Rules		711
(a) The scope of the rule of confidentiality		712
(b) Enforcing the rule of confidentiality		715
(1) Censure of written statements		715
(2) Statements of disapproval by fellow arbitrators		716
(3) Challenge proceedings		716
(4) Comparison to the 1976 UNCITRAL Rules		716
C. Extracts from the Practice of Investment and other Tribunals		717
D. Extracts from the Practice of the Iran–US Claims Tribunal		719
(1) Tribunal Rules (1983), Article 31(1)		719
(2) Tribunal Rules (1983), Article 31(2)		722
(3) Tribunal Rules (1983), Article 31, Note 2—Confidentiality of deliberations		723

1. Introduction

One of the most important aspects of the arbitral process is how a tribunal's decision is made. Article 33 of the UNCITRAL Rules sets forth the basic rules as to the degree of consensus required for its decisions. Article 33(1) establishes the general principle that "any award or other decision" is subject to the rule of majority voting. Article 33(2) provides that the presiding arbitrator may decide procedural matters alone where a majority opinion cannot be formed or where authorized by the other arbitrators to act on the entire tribunal's behalf. Procedural decisions, however, are subject to revision by the arbitral tribunal. Although not governed expressly by any provision of the UNCITRAL Rules, it is a generally accepted principle of international arbitration that the deliberations of the tribunal are to be kept confidential by the tribunal, save for extreme circumstance where disclosure is compelled in the interest of justice.

2. Decisions—Article 33

A. Text of the 2010 UNCITRAL Rule[1]

Article 33 of the 2010 UNCITRAL Rules provides:

Decisions

1. When there is more than one arbitrator, any award or other decision of the arbitral tribunal shall be made by a majority of the arbitrators.
2. In the case of questions of procedure, when there is no majority or when the arbitral tribunal so authorizes, the presiding arbitrator may decide alone, subject to revision, if any, by the arbitral tribunal.

B. Commentary

(1) Awards and other decisions by majority vote—Article 33(1)

(a) **General comments**

Article 33 does not address decision-making by a sole arbitrator, as that task is straightforward and simple enough.[2] Reaching agreement among three members of an arbitral tribunal may be decidedly more complicated, however.[3]

Article 33(1) requires an arbitral tribunal comprised of more than one member to decide by majority rule. If there are three arbitrators, this means that at least two out of the three arbitrators must agree on an award or decision.[4] The majority voting requirement applies broadly. By adding the words "or other decision" to the Final Draft of the 1976 UNCITRAL Rules, the drafters made clear that a voting majority is required not only in determining the outcome of a proceeding (the award), but also as to *all* matters relating to the tribunal's official functions.[5] This broad scope, however, must be viewed simultaneously as somewhat limited by the scope of Article 33(2), which authorizes the presiding arbitrator, under certain circumstances, to decide procedural matters subject to the tribunal's revision.

---

[1] Corresponding Article 31 of the 1976 UNCITRAL Rules provides:

1. When there are three arbitrators, any award or other decision of the arbitral tribunal shall be made by a majority of the arbitrators.
2. In the case of questions of procedure, when there is no majority or when the arbitral tribunal so authorizes, the presiding arbitrator may decide on his own, subject to revision, if any, by the arbitral tribunal.

[2] The appointment of a sole arbitrator under Article 8 of the UNCITRAL Rules is discussed in Chapter 4, section 4.

[3] The provision is easily adaptable to situations where more than three arbitrators comprise the arbitral tribunal. The Iran–US Tribunal, for example, adhered to the principle of majority rule when making decisions as a Full Tribunal of nine members. See Note 1 to Article 31 of the 1983 Rules of Procedure of the Iran–US Claims Tribunal, reprinted in Appendix 5.

[4] The principle of majority rule obviously also encompasses cases of unanimity among the arbitrators. As Sanders explained, the provision accounts for "different customs in various parts of the world," such as Asia, where there is "a marked preference for unanimity in making arbitral awards and conciliation was generally preferred to arbitration." *Summary Record of the 11th Meeting of the Committee of the Whole (II)*, UNCITRAL, 9th Session, UN Doc A/CN.9/9/C.2/SR.11, at 2, para 3 (1976).

[5] It is unclear from the available *travaux préparatoires* when the additional text ("or other decision") was added, although it appears to have occurred sometime after the Commission's discussion of the Revised Draft, which did not include the phrase. See *Report of the Secretary-General on the Revised Draft Set of Arbitration Rules*, UNCITRAL, 9th Session, UN Doc A/CN.9/112 (1975), reprinted in (1976) VII UNCITRAL Ybk 157, 165 (Draft Article 27(3)).

The rule in Article 33(1) allows a majority to be formed by any combination of tribunal members; the agreement of the presiding arbitrator is not required.[6]

What happens when the arbitrators are unable to form a majority was a question debated extensively by the negotiators of the 1976 Rules. One delegate proposed that when the arbitrators fail to make an award by majority decision, "they should communicate that fact to the appointing authority which would then appoint new arbitrators."[7] Other delegates quickly rejected this proposal as rendering the Rules "too cumbersome" for the parties and redundant in light of other provisions of the Rules covering an arbitrator's failure to act.[8] Rather, the main debate focused on whether the presiding arbitrator should be given a decisive role in ending a stalemate among the arbitrators. Some delegates proposed that the UNCITRAL Rules, like the ICC Arbitration Rules and other arbitration rules, should empower the presiding arbitrator of the tribunal to cast the deciding vote.[9] Other members rejected this proposal, arguing that such authority would create an all-powerful chairman capable of rendering "extreme awards."[10] Still others expressed concerns that investing the presiding arbitrator with deadlock-breaking authority would reduce the party-appointed arbitrators to "mere assessors," thus degrading the consultative process.[11]

The negotiators of the 1976 Rules ultimately agreed that the resolution of a decision-making impasse would depend on the *type* of issue presented to the arbitral tribunal. Article 33 of the 2010 Rules, which is virtually identical to corresponding Article 31 of the 1976 Rules, continues to reflect this decision. As discussed below, in limited situations, Article 33(2) permits the presiding arbitrator to act unilaterally with respect to questions of procedure.[12] With respect to all other situations, Article 33(1) requires, subject to any mandatory provisions of the governing arbitration law, that the arbitrators engage in deliberations until a majority is formed.[13]

On the practicalities of applying the majority rule, Professor Sanders has observed that arbitrators are "forced to continue their deliberations until a majority, and probably a compromise solution, has been reached."[14] This observation suggests not only a possible

---

[6] *Report of the Secretary-General on the Revised Draft Set of Arbitration Rules*, UNCITRAL, 9th Session, Addendum 1 (Commentary), UN Doc. A/CN.9/112/Add.1 (1975), reprinted in (1976) VII UNCITRAL Ybk 166, 178 ("[I]t is not required that the presiding arbitrator be one of the two arbitrators who agree on the award."). One example of such an award, though not rendered under the UNCITRAL Rules, is *Tokios Tokelés* and *Ukraine*, ICSID Case No ARB/02/18, Decision on Jurisdiction (April 29, 2004) (Prosper Weil, President of the Tribunal, dissenting).

[7] *Summary Record of the 11th Meeting of the Committee of the Whole (II)*, UNCITRAL, 9th Session, UN Doc A/CN.9/9/C.2/SR.11, at 2, para 6 (1976) (Comments by Mr Mantilla-Molina, Mexico).

[8] See respectively UNCITRAL, 9th Session, UN Doc A/CN.9/9/C.2/SR.11, n 7, at 2, para 9 (Comment by Ms Oyekunle, Nigeria) and para 10 (Comments by Mr Holtzmann, United States).

[9] *Summary Record of the 10th Meeting of the Committee of the Whole (II)*, UNCITRAL, 9th Session, UN Doc A/CN.9/9/C.2/SR.10, at 10, paras 78, 81 (1976) (Comments by Mr Szasz, Hungary, and Mr Melis, Austria).

[10] See UNCITRAL, 9th Session, UN Doc A/CN.9/9/C.2/SR.10, n 9, at 10, para 79 (Comment by Mr Holtzmann, United States). Mr Melis of Austria, however, raised the counter-argument that, as the ICC's deadlock-breaking provision, in his understanding, had only been invoked once in 50 years, the danger of abuse was outweighed by the advantage of avoiding a deadlock among arbitrators. See para 81.

[11] UNCITRAL, 9th Session, UN Doc A/CN.9/9/C.2/SR.11, n 7, at 3, para 7 (Comments by Mr Boston, Sierra Leone).

[12] See section 2(B)(2).

[13] According to the commentary to the Revised Draft, "[i]f a majority of the arbitrators fail to agree on an award, the arbitral tribunal must resolve the deadlock in accordance with the relevant law and practice at the place of arbitration," which in many jurisdictions require arbitrators to "continue their deliberations until they arrive at a majority decision." *Report of the Secretary-General on the Revised Draft Set of Arbitration Rules*, UNCITRAL, 9th Session, Addendum 1 (Commentary), UN Doc A/CN.9/112/Add.1 (1975), reprinted in (1976) VII UNCITRAL Ybk 166, 178. See also Model Law, as amended, Article 29 (requiring decisions by a majority of the arbitrators).

[14] P Sanders, "Commentary on UNCITRAL Arbitration Rules," (1977) II Ybk Commercial Arb 172, 208.

continuation of deliberations in some cases in order to reach agreement as to the proper award, but also that in the process the arbitrators may have to compromise their positions. The notion of a compromise between arbitrators may imply for some that something irregular in the decision-making process has occurred. If by "compromise," Professor Sanders meant that one arbitrator ultimately agrees with the reasoning offered by one or other arbitrators in order to form a majority (even though it is not his or her preferred reasoning), that is not, in our opinion, a tainted form of compromise. Rather, it is part and parcel of reasoned deliberations. Indeed, an arbitrator can concur in an award in order to form a majority, while doing so on the basis of different reasoning.

The validity of the practice of concurring in an arbitral award so as to form the necessary majority has been confirmed by the International Court of Justice. In *Case Concerning the Arbitral Award of July 31, 1989*, the International Court of Justice ruled:

As the practice of international tribunals shows, it sometimes happens that a member of a tribunal votes in favor of a decision of the tribunal even though he might individually have been inclined to prefer another solution. The validity of his vote remains unaffected by the expression of any such differences in a declaration or separate opinion of the member concerned, which are therefore without consequence for the decision of the Tribunal.[15]

As Judge Schwebel, former ICJ President, has pointed out, the "practice of international tribunals" to which the ICJ refers is readily found in the awards of the Iran–US Claims Tribunal made pursuant to a rule identical to Article 33(1) of the 2010 UNCITRAL Rules.[16]

If by "compromise," however, it is meant that the arbitrators are deliberating not upon different visions of the proper award under the applicable law but rather negotiating acceptable outcomes for the dispute, then in our opinion such "compromise" is inappropriate given that it does not reflect a reasoned award under the applicable law. It has been observed that, for example, where compensation is to be awarded, the final amount in practice may be varied so as to gain the concurrence of one of the party-appointed arbitrators.[17] Indeed, it is likely the case that it is the amount of damages, rather than the legal questions of jurisdiction or liability, that require accommodation to form a majority. However, in our opinion, such practice is not appropriate or authorized implicitly by Article 33, if it involves a departure from the general duty to apply the governing law to resolve the dispute in good faith.

While Article 33(1) contains no fall-back mechanism to break a stalemate,[18] the requirement of majority rule in Article 33(1) nevertheless presents important advantages. First, majority rule protects the parties against the extreme views of a presiding arbitrator by

---

[15] *Case Concerning the Arbitral Award of July 31, 1989 (Guinea-Bissau v. Senegal)*, ICJ Rep 1991, 40.
[16] "The Majority Vote of an International Arbitral Tribunal," in S Schwebel, *Justice in International Law: Selected Readings* (1994) 213. For another example from the practice of *ad hoc* tribunals, see Professor Brownlie's concurring opinion in *Wintershall AG* (1976 Rules), reprinted in section 2(C).
[17] See N Blackaby and C Partasides with A Redfern and M Hunter, *Redfern and Hunter on International Arbitration* (5th edn 2009) 572 (noting that the "award of monetary compensation arrived at by a majority vote is sometimes the result of a bargaining process").
[18] This arrangement has drawn criticism. See N Blackaby and C Partasides, *Redfern and Hunter on International Arbitration*, n 17, 570 (commenting on the possibility that "there will be no award at all if a majority cannot be achieved"); see also Y Derains and E Schwartz, *A Guide to the ICC Rules of Arbitration* (2nd edn 2005) 306 (stating that without allowing the chairman to act alone in cases of no majority, it requires the "chairman to obtain the agreement of at least one of the co-arbitrators, which can force compromises that may be neither legitimate nor reasonable"). However, in practice, cases of deadlock are "extremely rare" (307); see also H Holtzmann and J Neuhaus, *A Guide to the UNCITRAL Model Law on International Commercial Arbitration: Legislative History and Commentary* (1989) 809.

requiring the majority to reach common, and perhaps more reasonable, ground. Second, a majority award is arguably more legitimate and thus more authoritative than one made unilaterally by the presiding arbitrator.[19] When an extreme case of party discord can be foreseen, however, modifications to the majority rule may be necessary.[20]

The issue of arbitrator deadlock was revisited with equal vigor in Working Group discussions to revise the Rules,[21] though without resulting in any change to the UNCITRAL Rules. Some delegates favored the "presiding arbitrator solution" because the majority rule could obligate the presiding arbitrator to compromise his or her views "to join with the least unreasonable of the co-arbitrators in order to form a majority."[22] Others saw no compelling reason to change the rule given the rarity of deadlocks in practice.[23] Some also feared placing ultimate decision-making power in the hands of one arbitrator, particularly in the case of "an authoritarian presiding arbitrator."[24] Finally, it was also noted that the "presiding arbitrator solution" might be less acceptable to the disputing parties, particularly to sovereign parties in investor–state arbitration.[25]

The Working Group considered various proposals to revise the majority rule. These either endorsed wholesale adoption of the "presiding arbitrator solution" or allowed the parties by agreement either to opt out of the majority rule[26] or opt into the "presiding arbitrator solution."[27] Article 29 of the Model Law, for example, requires majority voting "unless otherwise agreed by the parties." Unable to reach consensus on a revised rule,

---

[19] This attribute of a majority award may be more attractive in the context of politically sensitive disputes, such as arbitration involving one or more sovereign parties. See M Pellonpää, "The Process of Decision-Making," in D Caron and J Crook (eds), *The Iran-United States Claims Tribunal and the Process of International Claims Resolution* (2000) 238.

[20] See, eg, *Republika Srpska* (1976 Rules), reprinted in section 2(C) (noting that the polar opposite positions of the parties caused them in advance of arbitration to abandon the majority rule in favor of allowing the decision of the presiding arbitrator to be final and binding).

[21] Paulsson and Petrochilos's report to UNCITRAL began the discussion by proposing to add a provision to the rule on majority voting, modeled after the ICC and LCIA Rules, that would provide: "If no majority is formed, any award or other decision shall be made by the presiding arbitrator alone." See J Paulsson and G Petrochilos, *Revision of the UNCITRAL Arbitration Rules*, Report to UNCITRAL Secretariat, at 5, para 12(a) (2006).

[22] *Report of the Working Group on Arbitration and Conciliation on the Work of its Forty-Fifth Session* (Vienna, September 11–15, 2006), UNCITRAL, 40th Session, UN Doc A/CN.9/614, at 23, para 109 (2007); *Report of the Working Group on Arbitration and Conciliation on the Work of its Forty-Seventh Session* (Vienna, September 10–14, 2007), UNCITRAL, 41st Session, UN Doc A/CN.9/641, at 14, para 69 (2007).

[23] UNCITRAL, 41st Session, UN Doc A/CN.9/641, n 22, at 14–15, para 70 .

[24] *Report of Working Group II (Arbitration and Conciliation) on the Work of its Fifty-First Session* (Vienna, September 14–18, 2009), UNCITRAL, 43rd Session, UN Doc A/CN.9/684, at 14 para 57 (2009). See also UNCITRAL, 41st Session, UN Doc A/CN.9/641, n 22, at 15, para 72; UNCITRAL, 40th Session, UN Doc A/CN.9/614, n 22, at 23, para 109. Along similar lines, some delegates maintained that abandoning the majority rule could alter the "the internal dynamics of the deliberations, weakening the resolve to achieve a majority." UNCITRAL, 41st Session, UN Doc A/CN.9/641, n 22, at 14–15, para 70. See also UNCITRAL, 43rd Session, UN Doc A/CN.9/684, n 24, at 14, para 55.

[25] UNCITRAL, 41st Session, UN Doc A/CN.9/641, n 22, at 14–15, para 70; UNCITRAL, 43rd Session, UN Doc A/CN.9/684, n 24, at 14, para 57.

[26] This proposal tracks the approach of Article 29 of the Model Law, which provides, in relevant part: "In arbitral proceedings with more than one arbitrator, any decision of the arbitral tribunal shall be made, *unless otherwise agreed by the parties*, by a majority of all its members." Emphasis added.

[27] The precise language of the proposals provide:

1. *Option 1*: When there is more than one arbitrator, any award or other decision of the arbitral tribunal shall be made, unless otherwise agreed by the parties, by a majority of the arbitrators.

    Option 2, Variant 1: When there is more than one arbitrator and the arbitrators are not able to reach a majority on the substance of the dispute, any award or other decision shall be made by the presiding arbitrator alone.

however, the Working Group agreed not to unsettle the approach of the 1976 Rules.[28] Thus, Article 33(1) of the 2010 UNCITRAL Rules retains what has been described as a "tried and tested feature of the Rules," the majority rule on decision-making.[29]

(b) Majority decision-making by the Iran–US Claims Tribunal

(1) The dynamics of deliberations

The Iran–US Claims Tribunal has served as a unique laboratory for studying the majority vote rule.[30] Early in the Tribunal's history during the adoption of the 1983 Tribunal Rules, Iran expressed concerns about the possible inflation of amounts awarded against Iran given that the majority forming the award necessarily consisted of the chair and the arbitrator appointed by the United States. The Iranian arbitrators proposed modifying Article 31 of the 1976 UNCITRAL Rules to permit the presiding arbitrator to determine the amount of compensation sought in the event of a dispute.[31]

The proposal was rejected by the Full Tribunal. In practice there was a dynamic inclining toward compromise in some cases. As two well informed observers noted, the respective chairmen of the Tribunal's Chambers "usually strove in deliberations to reach decisions agreeable to at least one of the two arbitrators, and judges did indeed compromise and modify their positions in order to form a majority."[32]

As to the possibility that the amounts of awards against Iran were inflated, the Iranian-appointed arbitrators were arguably responsible in part for the situation that concerned them. In virtually every case that resulted in an award against Iran, it was clear that the Iranian arbitrator would not take a position adverse to his country, a decision which effectively removed him from the process of forming a majority. In these circumstances, the chairman and the American arbitrator were left as the "majority," responsible for hammering out the details of an award.

> *Variant 2*: When there is more than one arbitrator and the arbitrators are not able to reach a majority on the substance of the dispute, any award or other decision shall be made, if previously agreed by the parties, by the presiding arbitrator alone.
> 2. In the case of questions of procedure, when there is no majority or when the arbitral tribunal so authorizes, the presiding arbitrator may decide alone, subject to revision, if any, by the arbitral tribunal.

Settlement of Commercial Disputes: Revision of the UNCITRAL Arbitration Rules, Note by the Secretariat, UNCITRAL, UN Doc A/CN.9/WG.II/WP.151/Add.1 at 12, para 22 (2008). For the Working Group's discussion on these proposals, see UNCITRAL, 43rd Session, UN Doc A/CN.9/684, n 24, at 13–15, para 52–62.

[28] UNCITRAL, 43rd Session, UN Doc A/CN.9/684, n 24, at 15, para 61. The sole technical change to the general rule on decision-making in paragraph 1 was to replace the word "three" with "more than one."

[29] UNCITRAL, 41st Session, UN Doc A/CN.9/641, n 22, at 14–15, para 70. It was also noted at para 70, "in a recent review of the International Arbitration Rules of the American Arbitration Association ('AAA Rules'), a proposal to modify the majority requirement had been rejected."

[30] For an overview of decision-making at the Tribunal, see Pellonpää, "The Process of Decision-Making," n 19. For enlightening discussions on the interpersonal dynamics of Tribunal decision-making by Judge Charles Brower (US), Judge Nils Mangård (Swedish), and Judge Ansari Moin (Iran), see Pellonpää, 249, 253, 263.

[31] "Tribunal Approves Settlement from Security Account," Iranian Assets Litigation Rep 4562, 4563 (May 7, 1982). See also Minutes of the 71st Meeting of the Full Tribunal, January 7, 1983.

[32] S Baker and M Davis, *The UNCITRAL Arbitration Rules in Practice: The Experience of the Iran-United States Claims Tribunal* (1992) 154. It is virtually impossible to deduce the level of bargaining, if any, from the awards or decisions in which no separate opinion was filed by the second arbitrator joining in the majority. Further, Article 31, Note 2, of the [1983] Tribunal Rules of Procedure, requiring that deliberations must remain secret, prohibits any additional revelations regarding the process of deliberation. See below, section 2(B)(3) regarding the rule of confidentiality of deliberations.

It is also noteworthy that one member of the Tribunal expressed concerns that the majority vote requirement could be undermined by the chair if he or she cast the decision in the case as a series of votes. See separate opinions of Judge Mosk in *Ultrasystems Inc* (1983 Tribunal Rules) and Case No A/11 (1983 Tribunal Rules), reprinted in section 2(D)(1).

In a number of cases the deliberations between the chairman and American arbitrator appeared, as can be best gleaned from the public record, to break down. The chairman and the American arbitrator still managed to form a majority for an award. Even in the absence of the Iranian arbitrator, the chairman and the American arbitrator would be unable to agree on a majority decision and, eventually, the American arbitrator yielded, feeling compelled to concur in the award to form the necessary majority, while opining separately on the alleged errors in the award.[33] The rationale for this unique practice, as Judge Holtzmann frankly explained, was that "something is better than nothing" in light of "the prospect of indefinite postponement" of the award.[34] Thus, it seems that in the Tribunal's quasi-permanent setting, where an award could be sidelined in the face of a voluminous docket, the credible threat of delay in some cases leveled the bargaining field and deprived the party-appointed arbitrator of some leverage in the process of forming a majority.

(2) The practice of deliberating and drafting awards

After the hearings and the evidentiary records are closed, the Iran–US Claims Tribunal turns to the task of deliberation. As the UNCITRAL Rules provide no guidance regarding the deliberative process, the practice of the Tribunal, recognizing that variations existed between chambers and over time, may provide useful insights.[35] The process officially begins shortly after the final hearing has concluded (usually within a few days) when the presiding arbitrator provides the schedule for the deliberative session. Even before this session takes place, the arbitrators often prepare and circulate memoranda amongst themselves, either *sua sponte* or at the presiding arbitrator's request, on issues of particular concern that might require more treatment in deliberations. The arbitrators then convene at the deliberative session to air their views on the issues and to formulate the majority position on the terms of the award or decision. The session may last days or weeks depending on the complexity of the issues or the amount of disagreement on how they are to be resolved. As discussed below in section 3, the deliberations take place in secret. It is the practice of the Tribunal to invite only the Members of the Tribunal (and their legal assistants) and, in some instances, the Secretary-General or other members of the Secretariat to attend deliberations.

Soon after the closure of deliberations, the presiding arbitrator prepares a draft of the award or decision, which, upon completion, is circulated among the arbitrators for review and comment. It is often the practice of the Tribunal for the arbitrators to provide their comments to the presiding arbitrator in two forms: a memorandum detailing issues of particular interest and a line-by-line edit of the award or decision offering both substantive and stylistic comments. On the basis of these comments, the presiding arbitrator will often produce a second draft of the award or decision and present it again to the party-appointed arbitrators for review and comment. The process of drafting and providing commentary repeats as many times as necessary, but typically does not exceed two or three rounds. Additional deliberative sessions may be scheduled if requested and if deemed necessary. Throughout the entire process up until the filing of the award or decision with the Registry, the

---

[33] See G Aldrich, *The Jurisprudence of the Iran-United States Claims Tribunal* (1996) 43. For extracts of concurring opinions by American arbitrators (1983 Tribunal Rules), reprinted in section 2(D)(1).

[34] *Economy Forms Corp* (1983 Tribunal Rules), Concurring Opinion of Howard M Holtzmann, reprinted in section 2(D)(1).

[35] For a general discussion on the process of deliberations, see G Born, *International Commercial Arbitration* (2009) 1868–71; see also L Fortier, "Chapter 22: The Tribunal's Deliberations" in L Newman and R Hill (eds), *The Leading Arbitrators' Guide to International Arbitration* (2nd edn 2008) 477.

arbitrators are continuously communicating their views both orally and in writing to the presiding arbitrator and to one another, making suggestions as to how the award or decision can be improved.[36]

Although the Tribunal's practice has evolved into an effective method of deliberation, it is not entirely consistent with the Tribunal Rules and guidelines established to regulate the process. Note 2 to Article 31 of the 1983 Tribunal Rules requires that "[a]ny question which is to be voted upon shall be formulated in precise terms in English and Farsi and the text shall, if a member so requests, be distributed before the vote is taken." This procedure is rarely followed. Further, while the deliberations normally do commence soon after the hearing, as required by the Tribunal's Internal Guidelines, thereafter the Tribunal rarely meets the suggested 90-day deadline for issuing an award.[37] The Tribunal's variation from its own rules and guidelines on the way toward developing an effective deliberation process proves only that strict regulation of this important area may be impossible.[38]

(2) Decision-making on procedural questions—Article 33(2)

Article 33(2) represents a compromise between the rule of majority voting, which could lead to a "compromise solution," and the "presiding arbitrator solution," which affords the presiding arbitrator unilateral decision-making powers.[39] With respect to questions of procedure only, Article 33(2) invests the presiding arbitrator with authority to end a stalemate among the arbitrators in two instances.[40] First, if a majority fails to form regarding a procedural matter, then the presiding arbitrator is empowered to resolve the matter on his own. Second, the presiding arbitrator may decide matters of procedure alone where the arbitral tribunal "so authorizes."[41] In both cases, the unilateral powers of the presiding arbitrator are subject to revision by the arbitral tribunal.[42] Article 33(2) is intended to make the arbitration "quicker and more efficient" by permitting the presiding arbitrator to advance the arbitral proceedings decisively in the face of disagreement.[43]

Article 29 of the Model Law sets forth a slightly different rule for decision-making on procedural questions; it provides that "questions of procedure may be decided by a presiding arbitrator, if so authorized by the parties or all members of the arbitral tribunal."[44] Thus, Article 29 of the Model Law, in contrast to Article 33 of the 2010 UNCITRAL Rules, contains no default rule of unilateral decision-making where a majority cannot be

---

[36] See Statement of the President, *Iran* and *United States*, Case No A/28 (December 21, 2000) at 1–2 (describing the process of deliberation).
[37] Texts Adopted as Internal Guidelines of the Tribunal (Rev 1), 3(a)–(b).
[38] See M Pellonpää, "The Process of Decision-Making," n 19, 235. Establishing certain basic parameters for deliberating is, of course, useful. See *International Thunderbird Gaming Corp* (1976 Rules), reprinted in section 2(C).
[39] See UNCITRAL, 9th Session, UN Doc A/CN.9/9/C.2/SR.10, n 9, at 10, para 79 (Comment by Mr Holtzmann, US); and at para 80 (Comment by Mr St John, Australia). According to Baker and Davis, an early draft of this exception covered "procedural or interim matters," but "interim matters" was deleted to avoid confusion. S Baker and M Davis, *The UNCITRAL Arbitration Rules in Practice*, n 32, 155.
[40] See *International Systems & Controls* (1983 Tribunal Rules), Dissenting Opinion of Judge Brower, reprinted in section 2(D)(2).
[41] For an example of the disputing parties' agreement to authorization, see *International Thunderbird Gaming Corp* (1976 Rules), reprinted in section 2(C). *See also Vito Gallo* (1976 Rules); *William Ralph Clayton* (1976 Rules), both reprinted in section 2(C).
[42] See section B(2)(b).
[43] *Summary Record of the 6th Meeting of the Committee of the Whole (II)*, UNCITRAL, 9th Session, UN Doc A/CN.9/9/C.2/SR.6, at 11, para 97 (1976) (Comment by Mr Strauss, Observer).
[44] For an explanation of the differences between the Model Law and the 1976 Rules with respect to procedural decisions, see H Holtzmann and J Neuhaus, *A Guide to the UNCITRAL Model Law*, n 18, 809–10.

formed.⁴⁵ Rather, the presiding arbitrator's unilateral powers with respect to procedure arise only by virtue of an "authorization" by either the parties or all members of the arbitral tribunal. In practice, however, there is no genuine conflict between the Rules and the Model Law since by adopting Article 33, the parties may be viewed as exercising their rights under Article 29 of the Model Law to opt out of majority voting in any manner they choose.⁴⁶

Procedural questions facing the Iran–US Claims Tribunal have typically been resolved by majority rule, with unilateral decision-making occurring infrequently. The Tribunal applied Article 31(2) of the 1983 Tribunal Rules, which is identical to Article 33(2) of the 2010 UNCITRAL Rules. Whether acting as Chairman of a Chamber or President of the Tribunal, the presiding arbitrator generally begins deliberations on procedural questions by conferring with his colleagues. These deliberations have ranged from informal meetings in the chairman's office in Chamber cases to formal sittings in Full Tribunal cases that include an official vote of the members conducted and recorded by the President. Both methods permit the presiding arbitrator to solicit the views of the arbitrators and identify the majority position, which is then memorialized in a written action statement—almost always in the form of a draft Tribunal order.⁴⁷

To ensure maximum input, a second round of deliberation typically occurs. The presiding arbitrator will circulate the draft order for review by the other arbitrators, with a request that any comments be made promptly, usually within a few days. Comments generated during this second round—often recommending the use of alternative language or the omission of language—guide the presiding arbitrator in making any necessary adjustments to the text of the order. Where the suggested modifications are significant, additional rounds of feedback may be conducted before the order is finalized and issued to the parties.

Consistent with the rule that orders (in contrast to awards) need not be signed by all the arbitrators, procedural orders generally are issued only under the name of the Chairman or the President.⁴⁸ That practice does not imply, however, that the decision as to the content of the order was not reached other than in consultation with all members of the tribunal, nor should it be taken as authorization for such unilateral action.

The right of the presiding arbitrator to act alone has rarely been documented in Tribunal case law. In *American Bell International*, an exceptional case, the Full Tribunal considered whether Judge Mångard should continue to serve as Chairman of Chamber Three with respect to the remainder of Case No 48, following Judge Mångard's resignation and replacement by Judge Virally, pursuant to Article 13(5) of the Tribunal Rules.⁴⁹ Judge Virally abstained from voting on the question, appropriately in our view, leaving the remaining eight members to resolve the dispute.⁵⁰ The vote split four to four. Accordingly, Judge

---

⁴⁵ H Holtzmann and J Neuhaus, *A Guide to the UNCITRAL Model Law*, n 18, at 808.
⁴⁶ H Holtzmann and J Neuhaus, *A Guide to the UNCITRAL Model Law*, n 18, at 810 (noting that the drafters specified that Article 29 was "non-mandatory, the parties may lay down different requirements").
⁴⁷ See Communication to the Parties, *Fereydoon Ghaffari* and *The Islamic Republic of Iran*, Case No 968 at 1 (February 10, 1988) (indicating that the practice of Chamber Two is to communicate questions of procedure to the parties by an order).
⁴⁸ For a discussion of the signature requirement, see Chapter 24, section 2(B)(4).
⁴⁹ Specifically, the provision provides: "After the effective date of a member's resignation he shall continue to serve as a member of the Tribunal with respect to all cases in which he had participated in a hearing on the merits, and for that purpose shall be considered a member of the Tribunal instead of the person who replaces him."
⁵⁰ For purposes of all matters other than Case No 48, Judge Virally had replaced Judge Mångard.

Böckstiegel decided that because "no majority could be found either for or against the applicability of Article 13, paragraph 5, to Mr. Mångard in Case No 48, it appears to me that Article 13, paragraph 1, should be considered to prevail and that Chamber Three in its present composition with Mr. Virally as Chairman should further deal with this case."[51] Judge Böckstiegel thus directed the composition of Chamber Three with Judge Virally as Chairman.[52]

Judge Böckstiegel interestingly qualified his order as "without prejudice to the President's power to act pursuant to Article 31 [of the 1983 Tribunal Rules], paragraph 2."[53] In a dissenting opinion, Judge Brower criticized the logic of the order.[54] In light of Chamber Three's practice of adhering to Article 13(5), Judge Brower questioned how "an even division of opinion" in the Full Tribunal could lead to a decision to curtail Judge Mångard's further participation in Chamber Three rather than to confirm it. Accordingly, Judge Brower concluded that "[i]n these circumstances the President perforce dissembles when he attempts to *direct* that the proceedings in this case shall continue in Chamber Three" without Judge Mångard and at the same time to imply that such direction does not constitute a positive exercise of his Presidential authority under Article 31(2) of the [1983] Tribunal Rules."[55]

In other cases, arbitrators cited Article 31(2) when they believed they or their colleagues had been unduly marginalized from the decision-making process.[56] A notable example arose in Case No B1 when the Tribunal issued a procedural order that required the production of documents from both government parties.[57] The order was issued under the name of the Tribunal President, Judge Böckstiegel, and appears to have been the work of a drafting committee comprised of Judges Ameli, Aldrich, and Böckstiegel, which the Full Tribunal formed to offer advice on handling Case No B1. Judge Ameli dissented from the order, claiming that neither the Full Tribunal nor the drafting committed had deliberated on the order, that Judge Böckstiegel had never been authorized to act unilaterally, and that he lacked delegated authority to act on behalf of the Full Tribunal.[58] In particular, he accused Judge Böckstiegel of deciding questions "unilaterally, without proper deliberations or appropriate authorization from other Tribunal members."[59]

---

[51] Memorandum from the President Regarding the Question of Whether Article 13, paragraph 5, of the Tribunal Rules Applies to Mr. Mångard, *American Bell Intl Inc* and *Government of the Islamic Republic of Iran*, Case No 48 (September 12, 1985), reprinted in 9 Iran-US CTR 409 (1985-II). Whether or not Judge Böckstiegel exercised his rights pursuant to Article 31(2) [of the 1983 Tribunal Rules] is disputed. While Judge Böckstiegel specified that the order was made "without prejudice to the President's power to act pursuant to Article 31, paragraph 2," 9 Iran-US CTR at 410, Judge Brower concluded that "[t]he only course open to the President that would not have impaired our institutional integrity would have been … in the exercise of his powers under Article 31(2) to confirm such application." *American Bell Intl Inc* and *Government of the Islamic Republic of Iran,* et al, Case No 48, Memorandum from the President of the Tribunal (September 12, 1985), Dissent by Charles N Brower (September 20, 1985), reprinted in 9 Iran-US CTR 410, 413 (1985-II).

[52] 9 Iran-US CTR at 410.

[53] 9 Iran-US CTR at 410.

[54] 9 Iran-US CTR at 410.

[55] 9 Iran-US CTR at 412.

[56] See, eg, Case No B1 (1983 Tribunal Rules), Dissenting Opinion of Mr Ameli; *International Systems & Controls Corp* (1983 Tribunal Rules), Dissenting Opinion of Judge Brower; *American Bell Intl, Inc* (1983 Tribunal Rules), Dissent by Charles Brower; all reprinted in section 2(D)(2).

[57] *Iran* and *United States*, Case No B1, Full Tribunal, Order of July 2, 1987, reprinted in 18 Iran-US CTR 45 (1987).

[58] Dissenting Opinion of Mr Ameli, reprinted in 18 Iran-US CTR 47, 47–8 (1988-I).

[59] 18 Iran-US CTR at 47.

(a) The meaning of "questions of procedure"

As a presiding arbitrator's power to act alone, either for deadlock-breaking purposes or by authorization, is limited to the realm of procedural matters, perhaps the most important question arising under Article 33(2) is the meaning of the phrase "questions of procedure."[60] The Rules make no attempt to define this term or to distinguish between procedural and substantive questions.[61] This task would appear to fall upon the arbitral tribunal to resolve at its own discretion.[62] On an abstract level, the answer to the question might seem obvious. Substantive questions should involve matters affecting the creation, definition, and regulation of the rights of the parties to the dispute. Procedural questions, on the other hand, should relate to the technical steps of the arbitral process through which the substantive rights of the parties are ultimately determined. Not surprisingly, this distinction quickly blurs, upon real-life application of the Rules.[63]

For example, is the determination of the place of arbitration, in accordance with Article 18 of the Rules, a procedural or substantive question? Professor Sanders believes that this question should not be deemed procedural in nature because the determination of the place of arbitration will necessarily define the applicable law governing the arbitration, or *lexi fori*, which, in turn, could have significant consequences for the substantive rights of one or both of the parties.[64] Procedural questions for Professor Sanders, on the other hand, would include more "technical regulations" such as determining the language of the tribunal,[65] making arrangements for translation or records of a hearing,[66] and resolving a dispute between an expert and a party concerning the relevance of information required by the expert.[67]

Even the most mundane procedural decisions, however, have the potential to affect the course of the arbitration and ultimately the rights of the parties.[68] As a result, the test for defining "questions of procedure" as a practical matter should involve consideration of whether the decision could have a measurable impact on the rights of one or both of the parties, which could result in unfair advantage or prejudice. An identifiable significant

---

[60] An early draft of the Rules made reference to "procedural questions and interim matters," but the latter term was deleted on grounds that it might be confused with "interim awards." See *Summary Record of the 17th Meeting of the Committee of the Whole (II)*, UNCITRAL, 9th Session, UN Doc A/CN.9/9/C.2/SR.17, at 2, para 1 (1976) (Comment by Mr Lebedev, USSR); See also S Baker and M Davis, *The UNCITRAL Arbitration Rules in Practice*, n 32, 155.

[61] Difficulties with respect to the distinction also arise in the context of award making. See Chapter 24, section 2(B)(1).

[62] With regard to the Model Law, there is general consensus that since the arbitral tribunal has the power to decide questions of procedure and substance, it is entitled to define the differences between these questions. See UN Doc A/CN.9/SR.327, para 44 (Comments of the Secretary of the Working Group); F Knoepfler and P Scweizer, "Making of Awards and Termination of Proceedings," in P Šarčević (ed), *Essays on International Commercial Arbitration* (1989) 163. But see F Davidson, *International Commercial Arbitration: Scotland and the UNCITRAL Model Law* (1991) 157 (questioning whether the law of the forum confers this power on the arbitral tribunal).

[63] See N Blackaby and C Partasides, *Redfern and Hunter on International Arbitration*, n 17, 570.

[64] P Sanders, "Commentary on UNCITRAL Arbitration Rules," n 14, 194.

[65] P Sanders, "Commentary on UNCITRAL Arbitration Rules," n 14, 194–5.

[66] P Sanders, "Commentary on UNCITRAL Arbitration Rules," n 14, 201–2.

[67] P Sanders, "Commentary on UNCITRAL Arbitration Rules," n 14, 203.

[68] As Judge Brower has noted, even the treatment of procedural questions by a tribunal can affect the substantive rights of a party. See Brower, n 30, 251. See also Case No B1 (1983 Tribunal Rules), Dissenting Opinion of Mr Ameli, reprinted in section 2(D)(2) ("Although the questions involved in this Order are procedural, they are nevertheless highly significant and any attempt to change the course of the proceedings may eventually change the fate of this multibillion dollar Claim.").

impact should give an arbitral tribunal pause to treat a decision as purely procedural.[69] As a rule, an arbitral tribunal may wish to err on the side of caution when addressing borderline cases and render the decision by majority rule pursuant to Article 33(1).[70] Of course, if the tribunal has any intention that its decision have legal effect, for example under the New York Convention, then the decision should take the form of an award.[71]

(b) Revision

Any decision made unilaterally by a presiding arbitrator, pursuant to his deadlock-breaking or authorized powers under Article 33(2), is subject to revision by the arbitral tribunal.[72] A reasonable interpretation of the revision power is that it serves to check the presiding arbitrator's unilateral authority in the area of procedure.[73] If the presiding arbitrator's unilateral decision on procedure is sufficiently offensive to the other members of the tribunal, they may collectively overrule it. The usefulness of revision in practice is questionable, however. As Professor Sanders explained, it is difficult to imagine "that procedural decisions which would have already taken effect should be reversed by the tribunal."[74] Nonetheless, the fact that the presiding arbitrator's unilateral decisions on procedure are subject to challenge cannot be entirely minimized, especially in cases where the decision in question affects the outcome of the arbitration.[75]

On occasion, requests for revision of a procedural order have been filed with the Iran–US Claims Tribunal by a party government.[76] This is not a situation under Article 33(2) as revision under the Article is to be undertaken by the tribunal, not the parties. However, a statement of a party may serve to trigger action by a tribunal.

---

[69] In Case No B1, Judge Ameli suggested that the degree to which a procedural decision is outcome-determinative should affect the presiding arbitrator's authority to act on his own. Dissenting Opinion of Judge Ameli to the Order of July 2, 1987, *Islamic Republic of Iran* and *United States*, Case No B1 (July 17, 1987), reprinted in 18 Iran-US CTR 47, 48 (1988-I). While this factor may affect the manner in which the presiding arbitrator exercises his unilateral powers, it should not be deemed as circumscribing those powers. See J van Hof, *Commentary on the UNCITRAL Arbitration Rules: The Application by the Iran-U.S. Claims Tribunal* (1991) 214 (indicating that Judge Ameli would have been more persuasive if he had argued that "the consequences of the procedural decisions would have a direct and inevitable impact on substantive questions.").

[70] F Knoepfler and P Scweizer, "Making of Awards and Termination of Proceedings," n 62, 163 (favoring a restrictive interpretation of the term "questions of procedure").

[71] On the final and binding effect of awards, see Chapter 24, section 2(B)(2).

[72] The power to revise a procedural decision was introduced late in Committee negotiations as part of a revised draft of what ultimately became Article 31(2) of the 1976 UNCITRAL Rules. See *Summary Record of the 17th Meeting of the Committee of the Whole (II)*, UNCITRAL, 9th Session, UN Doc A/CN.9/9/C.2/SR.17, at 2 (1976) (referring to *Report of the Drafting Group on a new Article 26 bis in section IV (France and Federal Republic of Germany)*, UN Doc A/CN.9/IX/C.2/CRP.27 (restricted circulation)).

[73] The little recorded discussion on revision by the UNCITRAL drafters only confuses the matter. The delegate from the Federal Republic of Germany, whose working draft introduced the revision power to the Rules, explained that revision might be useful where a presiding arbitrator initially has acted on his own in opposition to his colleagues, but comes to "accept the view of the other two arbitrators." UNCITRAL, 9th Session, UN Doc A/CN.9/9/C.2/SR.17, n 72, at 2, para 5. Such an example, however, reduces revision to a mere consultative power, something that the arbitrators already possess without Article 33(2). Thus, to be efficacious at all, revision must empower the party-appointed arbitrators effectively to challenge the presiding arbitrator on matters of procedure.

[74] UNCITRAL, 9th Session, UN Doc A/CN.9/9/C.2/SR.17, n 72, at 2, para 6.

[75] UNCITRAL, 9th Session, UN Doc A/CN.9/9/C.2/SR.17, n 72, at 2, para 7 (Comments by Mr Roehrich, France).

[76] See, eg, Request for Revision by the Iranian Agent, *Islamic Republic of Iran* and *United States of America*, Case No B1 (December 12, 1986) (requesting revision of Tribunal order requiring US comments on Iran's request for document production); Letter from the US Agent, *United States* and *Iran*, Case No A/33 (March 26, 2002) (requesting reconsideration of Tribunal order scheduling hearings in Case No B1 (Counterclaim) before those in Case No A/33). Neither request was granted.

(3) Confidentiality of deliberations—Article 31, Note 2 of the 1983 Tribunal Rules

It is a well established principle of international adjudication that the "deliberations" of an arbitral tribunal must "remain confidential in perpetuity unless the parties release the arbitrators from this obligation."[77] Article 31, Note 2 of the 1983 Rules of Procedure of the Iran–US Claims Tribunal enshrines this principle by providing that the "deliberations" of the Tribunal "shall be secret and remain secret."[78] As stated by Sir Robert Jennings in his capacity as Appointing Authority for the Tribunal, the *raison d'être* of a rule of confidentiality:

is the practical consideration that secrecy of deliberations is essential if the deliberation is to produce a true discussion and argument and not become a mere exchange of cautiously expressed and selected views.[79]

His successor, Judge W E Haak, similarly observed that the purpose of secrecy of the deliberations is:

to protect the members of the Tribunal from outside influence and to enable them to freely exchange their views and arguments to reach a decision. Departing from the rule of confidentiality... would prevent a true discussion between the arbitrators, undermine the principle of arbitral collegiality, and jeopardize the independence of the arbitrators.[80]

Absent a rule of confidentiality, a party arbitrator would run the risk of being called upon by his or her appointing party to justify positions taken and concessions made during deliberations that are adverse to that party's interests.[81] This danger is particularly relevant to deliberations under the UNCITRAL Rules where an arbitrator may need to concur with his or her colleagues, despite favoring different reasoning, in order to form a majority.[82] Of equal, if not

---

[77] Paragraph 9, Code of Ethics for International Arbitrators, IBA (1987). See also R Bernhardt (ed), 1 *Encyclopedia of Public International Law* (1981) 185 ("Art. 54(3) of the ICJ Statute, which provides that 'the deliberations of the Court shall take place in private and remain secret,' represents a practice of such widespread application as to be arguably a general principle of law"); *Unidyne Corp* (1983 Tribunal Rules), Supplemental Opinion of Arangio-Ruiz and Allison, reprinted in section 2(D)(3) (commenting on the rule of confidentiality "so widely accepted in international dispute settlement").

[78] In addition, Note 2 to Article 31, reprinted in Appendix 5, provides that Tribunal deliberations are restricted to the Members of the Tribunal and the Secretary-General, although in practice the Members' legal assistants are regularly in attendance. The provision requiring, if requested, formulation and distribution of a question for deliberation in Farsi (in addition to English) before a vote is taken has rarely been utilized.

[79] Decision of the Appointing Authority, Sir Robert Jennings, on the challenge of Judge Bengt Broms (May 7, 2001), at 5. See also *Himpurna California Energy Ltd*, para 87 (1976 Rules), reprinted in section 2(C) ("confidentiality, a fundamental element of the arbitral process, is intended to ensure that each arbitrator is able to exercise his or her independent judgment in a collegial context free of any outside influence.").

[80] Joint Decision of the Appointing Authority, Judge W E Haak, on the challenges of Judge Krzysztof Skubiszewski and Judge Hamid Reza Oloumi Yazdi, April 2, 2008, at 15 (1983 Tribunal Rules), reprinted in section 2(D)(3).

[81] See Decision of Justice Ch M J A Moons, Appointing Authority (September 19, 1989) (1983 Tribunal Rules), reprinted in section 2(D)(3). Baker and Davis rightly observe that such pressure from the parties would produce a "chilling effect" on the openness and frankness of deliberative debate. S Baker and M Davis, *The UNCITRAL Arbitration Rules in Practice*, n 32, 157. The Iran–US Claims Tribunal has maintained that even inquiries as to the status of deliberations runs foul of Article 31, Note 2 of the Tribunal Rules. See *Uiterwyk Corp* (1983 Tribunal Rules), reprinted in section 2(D)(3).

[82] See P Sanders, "Commentary on UNCITRAL Arbitration Rules," n 14, 208; *Raygo Wagner Equipment Co* (1983 Tribunal Rules), Comments of Richard M Mosk with Respect to Mr Jahangir Sani's Reasons For Not Signing The Decision in Case No 17; *Granite State Machine Co, Inc* (1983 Tribunal Rules), Concurring Opinion of Richard M Mosk; both reprinted in section 2(D)(3).

greater, concern are breaches of the confidentiality rule when an arbitrator leaks information about the status of discussions in a deliberation to the party that appointed him or her, thus unfairly benefiting that party in any outside settlement talks with the other party.[83]

The UNCITRAL Rules, unlike many other procedural rules, do not contain an express rule on confidentiality of deliberations,[84] though one is implied in light of the well established practice of international tribunals.[85] The practice of the Iran–US Claims Tribunal, discussed below, is therefore instructive even if the parties choose not to modify the Rules to include an express provision on the subject.

(a) The scope of the rule of confidentiality

Because Article 31, Note 2 of the 1983 Tribunal Rules applies only to the arbitral tribunal's "deliberations," the meaning of that term has been the subject of considerable debate before the Iran–US Claims Tribunal. On three occasions, in the context of challenge proceedings, Iran has taken the position that only the formally scheduled deliberative meetings of the Tribunal are "deliberations." In the first instance, Iran challenged Judge Briner based on allegedly inappropriate informal discussions between Judge Khalilian and Judge Briner. Iran argued that these discussions regarding the method of calculating the amount of the award and a memorandum from Judge Aldrich to Judge Briner allegedly containing evidence of such calculations were not part of the "deliberations" of the Tribunal.[86] Thus, Iran maintained, the rule of confidentiality did not bar the appointing authority from considering this information, as the United States claimed.[87] The second instance involved the US challenge of Judge Broms. Similarly, Iran argued that Judge Broms's statements in his separate opinion in Case No A/28 regarding the alleged absence of formal deliberations on the operative terms of the award was not a breach of secrecy, as the United States asserted, since such comments merely stated the absence, not the contents, of Tribunal deliberations.[88] Lastly, in

---

[83] See, eg, *Rexnord, Inc* (1983 Tribunal Rules), Concurring Opinion of Richard M Mosk, reprinted in section 2(D)(3); *ITT Industries, Inc* and *Islamic Republic of Iran,* et al, Award No 47–156–2 (May 26, 1983), Note by Dr Shafie Shafeiei Regarding the "Concurring Opinion of George H Aldrich," (August 19, 1983), reprinted in 2 Iran-US CTR 356, 356–8 (1983–I). See also S Baker and M Davis, *The UNCITRAL Arbitration Rules in Practice*, n 32, 37–9, 159.

[84] Paulsson and Petrochilos proposed inclusion of a secrecy rule in the UNCITRAL Rules. See J Paulsson and G Petrochilos, *Revision of the UNCITRAL Arbitration Rules*, n 21, 126, paras 230–233. However, the Working Group that revised the Rules did not take up the matter.

[85] See E Gaillard and J Savage (eds), *Fouchard Gaillard Goldman on International Commercial Arbitration* (1999) 750 ("[a]lthough, again, most laws do not explicitly require deliberations in international arbitration to be secret, such secrecy is generally considered to be the rule."); see also G Born, *International Commercial Arbitration*, n 35, 2269–70 (stating that arbitrators' deliberations are treated as confidential under "most national laws and institutional rules... by ethical and professional guidelines for the conduct of international arbitrators, and are universally recognized by commentators").

[86] See [Iran's] Response to the Few Technical Points on Which the Appointing Authority Invited Comments, Challenge to Judge Briner (Undated), reprinted in 21 Iran-US CTR 360, 364–6 (1989–I). For a description of controversial comments made by Judge Khalilian, see Supplemental to the Statement by Judge Khalilian, *Phillips Petroleum Co Iran* and *Islamic Republic of Iran*, Case No 39 (June 29, 1989), reprinted in 21 Iran-US CTR 245 (1989–I).

[87] [Iran's] Response to the Few Technical Points on Which the Appointing Authority Invited Comments (Undated), reprinted in 21 Iran-US CTR 360, 366 (1989–I). For the US Response, see Letter, The Agent of the United States to the Appointing Authority (August 8, 1989), reprinted in 21 Iran-US CTR 349, 349 (1989–I) (maintaining that "it is inappropriate to consider a challenge based on material provided in violation of the Tribunal Rules, for this could encourage such violations in the future").

[88] Letter regarding Iran's Response to United States' Notice of Challenge of Honourable Judge Broms, The Agent of the Islamic Republic of Iran (February 15, 2001), at 10–12. For the US position, see US Notice of Challenge of Arbitrator Bengt Broms from the Agent of the United States to the Appointing Authority (January 4,

the challenge of Judge Krzysztof Skubiszewski, Iran argued that Judge Oloumi's disclosures regarding the Tribunal's decision to reject his request for postponement of deliberations in Case No B61 were not confidential because they related to "a purely administrative issue."[89]

On each occasion, Iran's restrictive view of the meaning of "deliberations" failed to persuade the appointing authority. As to Briner's challenge, the Appointing Authority, Judge Moon, decided "[i]n the interest of a proper functioning of the Tribunal" not to consider any information revealed in violation of the rule of confidentiality, including discussions among arbitrators taking place outside formal Chamber meetings.[90] In the challenge of Judge Broms, the Appointing Authority, Sir Robert Jennings, reached a similar conclusion:

> A rule of confidentiality of the deliberations must, if it is to be effective, apply generally to the deliberation stage of tribunal's proceedings and cannot realistically be confined to what is said in a formal meeting of all the members in the deliberation room. The form or forms the deliberation takes varies greatly from one tribunal to another. Anybody who has had experience of courts and tribunals knows perfectly well that much of the deliberation work, even in courts like the ICJ which have formal rules governing the deliberation, is done less formally. In particular the task of drafting is better done in small groups rather than by the whole court attempting to draft round the table. Revelations of such informal discussion and of suggestions made could be very damaging and seriously threaten the whole deliberation process.[91]

Finally, in addressing the challenge of Judge Skubiszewski, the Appointing Authority, Judge W E Haak, found that Judge Oloumi's request for a postponement of deliberations, the related discussions among Tribunal members, and the decision rejecting it fell squarely within the scope of deliberations:

> Internal discussions and decisions with respect to the organisation of deliberation work, during and for the purposes of the deliberations, are part of the deliberations and, as such, confidential. Arbitrators may disagree as to how the deliberation work should be organized (e.g. when and in what order the relevant issues should be addressed) and the reasons underlying their respective preferences may vary from one arbitrator to another. The purpose of the confidentiality rule would be entirely defeated if individual arbitrators could be open to attack for the views or the reactions that they express in relation to such issues in the deliberations.[92]

Accordingly, the Appointing Authority found that "the internal debates between Tribunal Members regarding the merits of [Judge Oloumi's] request" were subject to the rule of confidentiality.[93]

2001), at 5–6. For another earlier instance in which Iran made the same argument, see also Mr Jahangir Sani's Reply to Mr Mosk's "Comments" of March 3, 1983 Concerning Case No 17, *Raygo Wagner Equipment* and *Star Line Iran Co*, Case No 17, Chamber Three (April 7, 1983).

[89] Joint Decision of the Appointing Authority, Judge W E Haak, on the challenges of Judge Krzysztof Skubiszewski and Judge Hamid Reza Oloumi Yazdi, April 2, 2008, at 15 (1983 Tribunal Rules), reprinted in section 2(D)(3).

[90] Decision of Justice Moons, Appointing Authority (September 19, 1989) (1983 Tribunal Rules), reprinted in section 2(D)(3).

[91] Decision of Sir Robert Jennings, Appointing Authority (May 7, 2001) (1983 Tribunal Rules), reprinted in section 2(D)(3). Interestingly, the Appointing Authority drew a distinction in propriety between the disclosure of an arbitrator's own comments and those of another. While the former may be in some cases merely a "venial breach of the confidentiality rule," opined the Appointing Authority, Judge Broms's revelation of his belief that three other members of the Tribunal shared his position was "a step too far" resulting in an undisputed violation of confidentiality. As to Judge Broms's comments regarding the conduct of deliberations in respect of the drafting of Paragraph 95, the appointing authority also found that a serious breach of confidentiality had occurred.

[92] Joint Decision of the Appointing Authority, Judge W E Haak, on the challenges of Judge Krzysztof Skubiszewski and Judge Hamid Reza Oloumi Yazdi, April 2, 2008, at 16 (1983 Tribunal Rules), reprinted in section 2(D)(3).

[93] Joint Decision, n 92, at 16.

The aforementioned decisions indicate that the deliberations of a tribunal extend well beyond the formal meetings of the tribunal as a whole; it extends to the informal communications undertaken (either orally or in writing) by arbitrators, which may occur anytime up until the moment the award is rendered.[94]

Is the rule of confidentiality absolute and, if not, under what circumstances can it be abrogated? This issue has arisen at the Tribunal on two occasions. On the first occasion, in the *Raygo Wagner Equipment* case, Judge Sani provided a statement of his reasons for failing to sign the award because he charged that crucial deliberations had taken place in his absence.[95] When accused by Judge Mosk of breaching the confidentiality of deliberations, Judge Sani defended his statement on the theory that Article 32(4) of the 1983 Tribunal Rules, requiring disclosure of his reasons, took precedence over the rule of confidentiality.[96]

In terms of the Rules, Judge Sani's argument is misplaced. As described below, under Article 34(4) of the UNCITRAL Rules, it is the *signing* arbitrators, not the *abstaining* arbitrator, who are responsible for providing the statement of reasons for an arbitrator's failure to sign the award.[97] Thus, there was in fact no conflict between the UNCITRAL Rules and the rule of confidentiality of deliberations. However, Judge Sani's argument, even if not correct as a technical matter, raises the interesting question of whether, in the event of a true conflict of norms, the rule of confidentiality of deliberations would prevail. The UNCITRAL Rules do not present such a conflict in their unmodified form. The parties are, however, at liberty to modify the Rules pursuant to Article 1(1), and may wish to formally limit the rule of confidentiality. In such a situation, the specific will of the parties would offset the general presumption of confidentiality of deliberations. When carving out exceptions to the rule of confidentiality of deliberations, the parties, wary of potentially competing norms, should endeavour to draft as precisely as possible to minimize subsequent disputes over the scope of the exception.

On a second occasion, the Tribunal debated whether the rule of confidentiality may be abrogated to vindicate higher interests of justice. In the *Unidyne Corporation* case, Judge Aghahosseini disclosed in his dissenting opinion certain procedural aspects of the Tribunal's deliberations in an attempt to demonstrate that the claimant was wrongly awarded compensation for a claim that was never formally raised.[98] When criticized by his colleagues for these revelations,[99] Judge Aghahosseini argued that "not everything can be done under the protective shield of the sanctity of deliberations." He further stated: "[w]here a correct reflection of facts demands, all other considerations must give way: *Necessitas vincet legem; legum vincula irridet.*"[100] While the need to disclose in the *Unidyne Corporation* case,

---

[94] See section 2(B)(1)(b) on the practice of deliberating and drafting awards by the Iran–US Claims Tribunal. See also Statement of the President, *The United States of America* and *The Islamic Republic of Iran*, Case No A/28 (December 21, 2000) (1983 Tribunal Rules), reprinted in section 2(D)(3) (questioning Judge Broms's use of the term "final deliberations," the President noted that "[d]eliberations may, and in fact do, continue until the last moment before the filing of a Decision or Award," taking place through "formal meetings" and "less formal exchanges (whether written or oral or both)" among the arbitrators).

[95] Mr Jahangir Sani's Reasons for Not Signing the Decision Made by Mr Mangård and Mr Mosk in Case No 17 (*Raygo Wagner Equipment*), reprinted in 1 Iran-US CTR 415, 415–16 (1981–82).

[96] Mr Jahangir Sani's Reply to Mr Mosk's "Comments" of March 3, 1983 Concerning Case No 17 (*Raygo Wagner Equipment*), reprinted in 1 Iran-US CTR 428, 430 (1981–82).

[97] For more discussion on this obligation, see Chapter 24, section 2(B)(4).

[98] *Unidyne Corp* (1983 Tribunal Rules), Dissenting Opinion of Mohsen Aghahosseini, reprinted in section 2(D)(3).

[99] *Unidyne Corp* (1983 Tribunal Rules), Supplemental Opinion of Judge Arangio-Ruiz and Judge Allison, reprinted in section 2(D)(3) (criticizing Judge Aghahosseini).

[100] *Unidyne Corp* (1983 Tribunal Rules), A Statement in Case No 368 by Mohsen Aghahosseini, reprinted in section 2(D)(3).

in particular, was debatable, the principle of disclosure where justice requires it is sound. Just what conditions would compel disclosure is an area for development in future cases. The Appointing Authority, Judge W E Haak, has noted that "the obvious exclusion of an arbitrator by his co-arbitrators might justify abrogation of the rule of confidentiality."[101]

(b) Enforcing the rule of confidentiality

Enforcing the rule of confidentiality poses a significant challenge to the arbitrators. Unlike the ICC Arbitration Rules, which require that all awards be submitted to the International Court of Arbitration for review before being signed by the arbitrator, the UNCITRAL Rules offer no institutional control over the content of a tribunal's written work product.[102] Thus, if an arbitrator includes secret information about tribunal deliberations in his separate or dissenting opinion, even if unwittingly, such information generally will be passed unfiltered onto the parties and possibly to the general public, if the award is published.[103] As discussed below, the Iran–US Claims Tribunal has attempted to enforce the rule of confidentiality in a variety of ways, but with only limited success.

(1) Censure of written statements

The issue of censure arose early in the Tribunal's life after Judge Sani filed several statements explaining his refusals to sign a number of awards.[104] Believing that Judge Sani's submissions divulged chamber secrets and thus contravened Article 31, Note 2 of the Tribunal Rules, Judge Mosk expressed regret that they were not withheld from the parties.[105] Notably, for a brief period at the start of the Tribunal's work, the Tribunal's Registry refused to accept and transmit certain types of documents. However, such a policing role for the Registry did not have the political support of a majority of the Full Tribunal. Thus, despite Judge Mosk's concerns, the Tribunal was unable to censure any of the arbitrators' statements. Rather, the Tribunal has continued to release to the parties dissenting opinions believed by some arbitrators to contain confidential information regarding Tribunal deliberations.[106] One may attribute the Tribunal's unfortunate inability to police the rule of secrecy to its politically charged working environment in which review, let alone the redaction, of a party-appointed arbitrator's opinions could not gain the support of a majority of the Full Tribunal.[107]

---

[101] Joint Decision of the Appointing Authority, Judge W E Haak, on the challenges of Judge Krzysztof Skubiszewski and Judge Hamid Reza Oloumi Yazdi, April 2, 2008, at 15 (1983 Tribunal Rules), reprinted in section 2(D)(3). One former Tribunal arbitrator has proposed the general rule that "if there are allegations that the deliberation process wrongfully excluded an arbitrator or that another arbitrator otherwise acted in an improper manner, then such allegations can be disclosed." R Mosk and T Ginsberg, "Dissenting Opinions in International Arbitration," in M Tupamäki (ed), *Liber Amicorum Bengt Broms* (1999) 5.

[102] See Article 33 of the 2012 ICC Rules of Arbitration entitled "Scrutiny of the Award by the Court."

[103] See Chapter 24 section (2)(B)(5) on the potential drawbacks of dissenting and separate opinions.

[104] See, eg, Mr Jahangir Sani's Reasons for Not Signing the Decision Made by Mr Mangård and Mr Mosk in Case No 17 (*Raygo Wagner Equipment*), reprinted in 1 Iran-US CTR 415 (1981–82).

[105] Comments of Richard M Mosk with respect to Mr Jahangir Sani's Reasons for not Signing the Decision Made by Mr Mangård and Mr Mosk in Case No 17 (*Raygo Wagner Equipment*) (arguing that Judge Sani's statement was not part of the award and thus was subject to the rule of confidentiality); Further Comments of Richard M Mosk (*Raygo Wagner Equipment*) (1983 Tribunal Rules), reprinted in section 2(D)(3). *Rexnord, Inc* and *Islamic Republic of Iran*, et al, Award No 21–132–3 (January 10, 1983), Concurring Opinion of Richard M Mosk (April 13, 1983), reprinted in 2 Iran-US CTR 27, 29 (1983–I).

[106] Statement by the President, Case No A/28 (1983 Tribunal Rules), reprinted in section 2(D)(3). See also Supplemental Statement of George H Aldrich (*Phillips Petroleum Co Iran* (1983 Tribunal Rules)), reprinted in section 2(D)(3).

[107] Indeed, arbitrators always have been entitled to file their submissions directly with the Tribunal Registry for transmission to the parties without any circulation to other members for review.

(2) Statements of disapproval by fellow arbitrators

On two occasions, the Tribunal has issued statements disapproving of a colleague's disclosure of allegedly confidential information. Following the filing of Judge Broms's separate opinion in Case No A/28, which revealed the substance of confidential deliberations of the Tribunal, the President issued a stern statement of criticism on behalf of the Full Tribunal and noted with regret that Judge Broms had violated Article 31, Note 2 of the Tribunal Rules.[108] In Chamber Three, Judges Arangio-Ruiz and Allison reprimanded Judge Aghahoseini for divulging in his dissenting opinion the particulars of the majority's award-drafting procedures.[109] While such statements of disapproval are unquestionably appropriate, their punitive effect is dubious, especially since the targeted arbitrator will likely deny that a breach of confidentiality has occurred.[110]

(3) Challenge proceedings

In extreme cases, a breach of confidentiality may provoke a challenge of the alleged offending arbitrator.[111] Judge Broms's revelations of deliberations in his separate opinion in Case No A/28 prompted the US Government to initiate a multifaceted challenge. In challenging Judge Broms's impartiality and independence, the US raised several arguments with respect to his disclosure of deliberation comments, including: that Judge Broms's allegation that the Tribunal did not formally deliberate upon portions of the *dispositif* was meant to "undermine the remedy afforded the United States";[112] that his revelation that he favored a position favorable to Iran was an "attempt to demonstrate publicly his efforts on behalf" of Iran;[113] and that his disclosure raised doubts as to impartiality in future matters before the Tribunal.[114] While cautioning that it was not for him as appointing authority to monitor and discipline alleged breaches of confidentiality, Sir Robert Jennings found that the appointing authority may examine such breaches "as a factor in a decision on the 'justifiable doubt' question."[115] After reviewing the US Government's claims against the backdrop of the objectionable disclosures, Sir Robert concluded that no grounds existed for the removal of Judge Broms from his position. He did note, however, that further breaches might "change the balance of a decision in respect of any further challenge."[116]

(4) Comparison to the 1976 UNCITRAL Rules

Only a few minor differences separate Article 33 from corresponding Article 31 of the 1976 UNCITRAL Rules. The phrase "When there is more than one arbitrator" replaces the phrase "When there are three arbitrators" to account for the possibility of an arbitral tribunal

---

[108] Statement by the President, Case No A/28 (1983 Tribunal Rules), reprinted in section 2(D)(3). In the subsequent challenge of Judge Broms, Sir Robert Jennings, acting as Appointing Authority, stated that the President's statement correctly handled Judge Broms's breach of the rule of confidentiality. Decision of Sir Robert Jennings, Appointing Authority (1983 Tribunal Rules), reprinted in section 2(D)(3).

[109] *Unidyne Corp* (1983 Tribunal Rules), Supplemental Opinion of Arangio-Ruiz and Allison, reprinted in section 2(D)(3).

[110] A Statement in Case No 368 (*Unidyne Corp* (1983 Tribunal Rules)) by Mohsen Aghahosseini; Letter from Judge Bengt Broms to the Appointing Authority, reprinted in section 2(D)(3).

[111] The same risk exists when an arbitrator divulges his views in the course of assisting in the settlement of a case. See Chapter 25, section 2(B)(1)(a).

[112] Memorandum in Support of the Challenge by the United States of Mr Bengt Broms (January 4, 2001) at 5, n 88.

[113] Memorandum, n 112, at 6.

[114] Memorandum, n 112, at 13–15.

[115] Decision of Sir Robert Jennings, Appointing Authority, reprinted in section 2(D)(3).

[116] Decision, n 115, at 11.

with two or more than three arbitrators.[117] In addition, the phrase "may decide alone" supplants the phrase "may decide on his own" to ensure the gender neutrality of the Rules.

C. Extracts from the Practice of Investment and other Tribunals

Wintershall AG, et al and *Government of Qatar*, Partial Award on Liability (January 29, 1988), Separate Opinion of Professor Ian Brownlie (January 29, 1988) (*Ad Hoc* Proceeding, 1976 UNCITRAL Rules, Concession Agreement), at 1, reprinted in (1989) 28 ILM 827, 827:

> This Opinion is confined to the findings of the Tribunal concerning Structure A, and addresses two distinct issues.
>
> The first issue relates to the finding of the Tribunal (Section 3 of C.II at p.37) "that, in order for the Claimants to exercise their rights under the EPSA in respect of this area, the relinquishment provisions under Article XI apply to such Structure A only from the date the Claimants are permitted to exploit this area under the EPSA provisions". On this question, I agree with the conclusion of the Tribunal on the precise point of principle involved, but with respect am unable to agree with the reasoning which lies behind the conclusion.

The Republika Srpska and *Federation of Bosnia and Herzegovina* (Control Over the Brcko Corridor), Award (February 14, 1997) (*Ad Hoc* Proceeding, 1976 UNCITRAL Rules, Special Agreement), reprinted in (1997) 26 ILM 396, 401 (footnote omitted):

> 5. Although Article 31 of the [1976] UNCITRAL Rules contemplates that in normal circumstances "any award or other decision of the arbitral tribunal shall be made by a majority of the arbitrators," the parties can always agree on a different procedure, and in this case they have so agreed. It was understood at Dayton, as subsequently confirmed in writing, that if a majority decision of the Tribunal is not reached, "the decision of the presiding arbitrator will be final and binding upon both parties." It may be observed that such an agreement was in fact a virtual necessity in this particular case: from the outset the positions of the two parties on the merits have been polar opposites and each party has explicitly refused to compromise. These polar positions and accompanying intense animosities, consistently in evidence from the opening of the Dayton conference onward, made clear from the outset that any party-appointed arbitrator would encounter significant difficulties in conducting himself with the usual degree of detachment and independence. The parties therefore decided to change the rule on decision-making in view of the substantial likelihood that an arbitral resolution could be achieved only by the two parties' agreeing that the rulings of the Presiding Arbitrator will be treated as decisive.

Himpurna California Energy Ltd and *Republic of Indonesia*, Interim Award (September 26, 1999) (*Ad Hoc* Proceeding, 1976 UNCITRAL Rules, Concession Agreement), reprinted in (2000) XXV Ybk Commercial Arb 109, 146–47, 152:

> [74] On 9 September 1999, Karim Sani [Counsel for Respondent] wrote to the following effect:
>
> > We cannot accept this order, not only on account of its content but also its form. This order purports to emanate from the full Tribunal, yet it has been signed only by the Chairman, and it contains no indication as to the disposition of the other arbitrators on the matter. We are not prepared to accept that this is a reasoned decision of all three arbitrators and, in accordance with Art. 32(4) of the [1976] UNCITRAL Rules, require that the order be signed by all arbitrators or, if not agreed by all, that the reasons of the dissenting arbitrator be clearly stated in writing....

---

[117] UNCITRAL, 41st Session, UN Doc A/CN.9/641, n 22, at 16, para 76.

[75] On 13 September 1999, the Arbitral Tribunal answered:

> Your letter of 9 September 1999 purports to "require" that the Arbitral Tribunal's Procedural Order of 7 September 1999 be signed in accordance with Art. 32(4) of the [1976] UNCITRAL Rules.
>
> No Procedural Orders in these proceedings have been rendered under Art. 32 of the [1976] UNCITRAL Rules, which concerns *awards*. Your "requirement" is therefore not accepted by the Arbitral Tribunal. All Procedural Orders, including that of 7 September 1999, were rendered pursuant to paragraph 3(b) of the Terms of Appointment, and in conformity with Art. 31 of the [1976] UNCITRAL Rules. The Procedural Order of 7 September 1999 self-evidently has the further specific basis of Art. 28 of the [1976] UNCITRAL Rules.
>
> A number of important issues have been dealt with by the Arbitral Tribunal under my sole signature without demur. Taking the month of June alone, I refer you to letters signed by myself, announcing decisions of the Arbitral Tribunal, on the 9th, 15th, 16th, 18th, 24th, and 25th. For you to affirm at this late date that you find the procedural order of 7 September to be unacceptable is difficult to square with Art. 30 of the [1976] UNCITRAL Rules.

...

[87] On 17 September 1999, the Arbitral Tribunal wrote to Karim Sani:

> With reference to comments made in your letter dated 9 September 1999, and considering your failure to avail yourself of the opportunity given to the Republic of Indonesia by the Arbitral Tribunal to reverse its default posture by 17 September (as I write it is midnight in Jakarta and the end of the business day in Paris), I view it as appropriate to record that your speculation about Procedural Orders reflecting the President's "personal opinion" or the possibility that there might be a "dissenting arbitrator", are quite unfounded. All submissions of the Parties have been considered and discussed by all three arbitrators. Although it would be entirely inappropriate to reveal the inner workings of the Arbitral Tribunal, I can inform you that the Procedural Orders of 11 August and 7 September 1999 were the fruit of extensive discussion, and even in-person deliberations, of all three arbitrators. The text of this letter itself has been reviewed by, and discussed with, both of my co-arbitrators.
>
> It is improper for any party to probe the secrecy of deliberations. That confidentiality, a fundamental element of the arbitral process, is intended to ensure that each arbitrator is able to exercise his or her independent judgment in a collegial context free of any outside influence. I shall not comment on any criticisms of my personal conduct, but as President of the Arbitral Tribunal I find it disturbing that your letter pervasively focuses on what you imagine to be individual positions of the arbitrators. My co-arbitrators are to be treated as persons of independent mind, and your statement that "as we suspected, ... at least two members of the tribunal are biased" is quite unacceptable.

...

International Thunderbird Gaming Corp and *United Mexican States*, Procedural Order No 1 (June 27, 2003) (ICSID administered, 1976 UNCITRAL Rules, NAFTA Chapter Eleven), at 6:

18. Presiding Arbitrator

18.1 As provided in Article 31(2) of the [1976] UNCITRAL Arbitration Rules, the Presiding Arbitrator is authorized to decide questions of procedure alone, subject to revision, if any, by the Tribunal.

18.2 The Presiding Arbitrator is authorized to sign Procedural Orders on behalf of the Tribunal.

18.3 All members of the Tribunal shall physically participate in deliberations amongst themselves (whether in person, by telephone or otherwise) as well as in hearings and meetings with the parties, save for telephone conferences on procedural matters between the Presiding Arbitrator and counsel to the parties unless a party specifically requests that all members of the Tribunal participate in the telephone conference. The Presiding Arbitrator shall ensure that the co-arbitrators are timely and adequately appraised of such conferences.

Vito G Gallo and *Government of Canada*, Procedural Order No 1 (June 4, 2008) (PCA administered, 1976 UNCITRAL Rules, NAFTA Chapter Eleven), at 4:

> 19. In cases of urgency, the presiding arbitration may decide procedural matters along, upon reasonable consultation with the remaining members of the Arbitral Tribunal.

William Ralph Clayton, et al and *Government of Canada*, Procedural Order No 1 (April 9, 2009) (PCA administered, 1976 UNCITRAL Rules, NAFTA Chapter Eleven), at 7:

> 25. The President of the Tribunal may decide procedural matters alone, upon reasonable consultation with the other members of the Arbitral Tribunal.

D. Extracts from the Practice of the Iran–US Claims Tribunal

(1) Tribunal Rules (1983), Article 31(1)

Iran and *United States*, Case A/1 (Issues I, III and IV), Decision No DEC 12-A1-FT (August 3, 1982), Separate Opinion of Members Aldrich, Holtzmann, and Mosk (August 3, 1982), reprinted in 1 Iran-US CTR 200, 200 (1981–82):

> We concur in the majority decision of the Tribunal on the disposition of interest accruing on the Security Account because it is a fair, if conservative, interpretation of the text of paragraph 7 of the Declaration. While we consider that crediting the interest directly to the Security Account rather than placing it in a separate account would have been more consistent with the language, object and purpose of the Algiers Declarations and more in keeping with banking practice, we nevertheless join the majority in order to enable this question to be resolved In an acceptable manner.[2]
>
> ...
>
> [Footnote] 2. Such a majority is required by Article 31, paragraph 1 of the [1983] Tribunal Rules. *See* Sanders, Commentary on UNCITRAL Arbitration Rules, II [1977] Yearbook Commercial Arbitration 172, 208.

Ultrasystems Inc and *Islamic Republic of Iran*, Partial Award No 27–84–3 (March 4, 1983), Concurring Opinion of Richard M Mosk (March 4, 1983), reprinted in 2 Iran-US CTR 114, 114–15, 123 (1983–I):

> I concur in the Tribunal's Partial Award. I do so in order to form a majority so that an award can be rendered.[1] Although, as I discuss below, my analysis varies from that set forth in the Reasons for Award, I recognize that in view of the circumstances of this case, other points of view on the merits are not unreasonable. As I explain below, however, I believe that the decision to leave some issues presently unresolved was inappropriate.
>
> ...
>
> As I noted at the outset, despite my view that I would have preferred different reasoning on the merits and despite my dismay over certain procedures and events associated with this case, I do join in the result of the Partial Award, which I deem tenable, in order to form a majority for it.
>
> [Footnote] 1. As Professor Pieter Sanders has written, arbitrators are "forced to continue their deliberations until a majority, and probably a compromise solution, has been reached." Sanders, Commentary on UNCITRAL Arbitration Rules, 1977 II Yearbook Commercial Arbitration 172, 208. If no majority can be reached, no award can be rendered, thus creating a great injustice to the parties.

Economy Forms Corp and *Government of the Islamic Republic of Iran*, Award No 55–165–1 (June 20, 1983), Concurring Opinion of Howard M Holtzmann (June 20, 1983), reprinted in 3 Iran-US CTR 55, 55 (1983–II) (footnote omitted):

> I concur in the Award in this Case. The Award correctly holds that contracts of sale were formed, that the Respondents breached those contracts and that they are liable to pay damages. Unfortunately, however, the damages awarded are only about half of what the governing law requires.

Why then do I concur in this inadequate Award, rather than dissenting from it? The answer is based on the realistic old saying that there are circumstances in which "something is better than nothing." The operative circumstances here are that under Article 31, paragraph 1 of the [1983] Tribunal Rules (as well as under the [1976] UNCITRAL Arbitration Rules), "when there are three arbitrators, any award or other decision of the arbitral tribunal shall be made by a majority of the arbitrators." Thus, in a three-member Chamber a majority of two members must join, or there can be no Award. My colleague Dr. Kashani having dissented, I am faced with the choice of either joining in the present Award or accepting the prospect of an indefinite postponement of any Award in this Case. For, as Professor Sanders has explained in his Commentary on [1976] UNCITRAL Arbitration Rules, arbitrators must continue their deliberations until a majority has been reached. II Yearbook Commercial Arbitration [1977] 208. The deliberations in this Case have continued long enough; the hearing was closed on February 15, 1983, four months ago. Neither the parties nor the Tribunal will, in my view, benefit from further delay.

Alan Craig and *Ministry of Energy of Iran*, Award No 71–346–3 (September 2, 1983), Concurring Opinion of Richard M Mosk (September 2, 1983), reprinted in 3 Iran-US CTR 293, 293 (1983–II):

I concur in the Award in order to form a majority for it.

Ultrasystems Inc and *Islamic Republic of Iran*, Award No 89–84–3 (December 7, 1983), Dissenting Opinion of Richard M Mosk to Final Award (December 7, 1983), reprinted in 4 Iran-US CTR 80, 80 (1983–III):

I am also disturbed by the potential consequences of unnecessarily separating a case into segments and then deciding it piecemeal at different times and with different majorities. The procedure gives the Chairman the ability to divide a case into a number of issues and thereby to dictate the final result without there being any majority for the award. Such a practice, especially if misused, conflicts with the spirit, if not the letter, of the rule requiring an award to be made by a majority of the arbitrators. [1983] Tribunal Rule 31, paragraph 1. In the instant case, the Chairman, having obtained my reluctant compromise vote in order to form a majority for the Partial Award (see my Concurring Opinion to Partial Award No 27–84–3), has now taken a portion of that award away with a different majority. Such actions are not conducive to the formation of majorities.

Starrett Housing Corp and *Government of the Islamic Republic of Iran*, Interlocutory Award No ITL 32–24–1 (December 20, 1983), Concurring Opinion of Howard M Holtzmann (December 20, 1983), reprinted in 4 Iran-US CTR 159, 159 (1983–III):

I concur with reluctance in the Interlocutory Award in this case. I do so in order to form a majority for the key finding that the Government of the Islamic Republic of Iran has expropriated property of the Claimants in Iran. My concurrence is reluctant because the Interlocutory Award sets the date of the taking far later than when it actually occurred. The Interlocutory Award also includes a number of errors, and contains needlessly muddled terms of reference for the accounting expert who is appointed to give an opinion concerning the value of the expropriated property.

In view of the many errors in the Interlocutory Award, it would be easier to dissent from it than to concur in it. The Tribunal Rules provide, however, that awards can only be made by a majority vote. Thus, in a three-member Chamber, at least two members must join or there can be no decision. My colleague, Judge Kashani, having dissented, I am faced with the choice of joining the President in the present Interlocutory Award despite its faults, or accepting the prospect of an indefinite delay in progress toward final decision of this case. *See*, [1983] Tribunal Rules, Article 31, paragraph 1. *See also* Sanders, Commentary on UNCITRAL Arbitration Rules, II *Yearbook of*

Commercial Arbitration 172, 208 (1977). The Hearing in this case closed more than ten months ago; now that an Award has at last been prepared, no one would benefit from further delay.

American Intl Group Inc and *Islamic Republic of Iran*, Award No 93–2–3 (December 30, 1983), Concurring Opinion of Richard M Mosk (December 30, 1983), reprinted in 4 Iran-US CTR 111, 111–12 (1983–III):

> I concur in the Tribunal's Award in order that a majority can be formed. As one authority has written, if there is no majority, the "arbitrators are therefore forced to continue their deliberations until a majority, and probably a compromise solution, has been reached." Sanders, Commentary on UNCITRAL Arbitration Rules, II *Yearbook of Commercial Arbitration* 172, 208 (1977). This Award represents a "compromise solution" in which I have joined so that some award could be issued. Otherwise, this case heard almost a year ago, would remain undecided.
>
> I recognize that the value of Claimant's nationalized interest in Iran America cannot be established with precision. I believe, however, that there are justifications for an award of damages higher than that provided by the Tribunal in this case.

Questech, Inc and *Ministry of National Defence of the Islamic Republic of Iran*, Award No 191–59–1 (September 25, 1985), Separate Opinion of Howard M Holtzmann (September 25, 1985), reprinted in 9 Iran-US CTR 138, 138 (1985–II):

> I agree with the amount of damages awarded in this case, but I disagree quite sharply with a key element of the reasoning by which the Award reaches that result.
>
> I join fully in all other aspects of the Award, except that I vote for the unrealistically low amount of costs awarded only because that is necessary in order to form a majority on this question.

Starrett Housing Corp and *Government of the Islamic Republic of Iran*, Award No 314–24–1 (August 14, 1987), Concurring Opinion of Judge Holtzmann (August 14, 1987), reprinted in 16 Iran-US CTR 237, 238 (footnote omitted):

> I have serious questions, however, concerning the correctness of several findings in the Final Award that lower the valuation below the amount that was carefully and cogently determined by the Tribunal's expert. I also question the award of interest at the rate of only 8.5 percent....
>
> I also write to discuss the points in the Final Award that I would prefer to be decided differently, and to comment on the failure to award Starrett any of its costs of arbitration. Notwithstanding these misgivings, I join in the Final Award in order to form a majority, for otherwise no award can be issued.

Shahin Shaine Ebrahimi and *Government of the Islamic Republic of Iran*, Award No 560–44/46/47–3 (October 12, 1994), Separate Opinion of Richard C Allison (October 12, 1994), reprinted in 30 Iran-US CTR 236, 236 (1994):

> 1. I concur in the result reached in the Award in these Cases in order to form the requisite majority. As set forth herein, however, there are elements of the Award's reasoning with which I cannot agree.
>
> ...
>
> 3. I must respectfully, but profoundly, disagree with this interpretation of the law...

Islamic Republic of Iran and *United States of America*, Case No A/11, Award No 597-A11-FT (April 7, 2000), Separate Opinion of Richard M Mosk (April 7, 2000), at 1–2:

> I concur in the Tribunal's Partial Award in order to form a majority so that an Award can be rendered. Consistent with Tribunal practice, I discuss below my analysis of certain issues that differs from the reasoning expressed in the Partial Award. My points have been raised by at least one

of the parties, but inexplicably, receive little, if any, discussion by the Tribunal in its lengthy opinion. Although I have a different point of view on certain issues, do not join in some of the reasoning, and regret the form of the award, under the circumstances, I join in the Partial Award as set forth in the dispositif in order to form a majority. There is one Partial Award that requires a majority of the members of the Tribunal.... Four Members purport to dissent from, and concur with, the Partial Award. I do not believe that there can be different majorities for the different issues that comprise this Partial Award, especially when there was no actual division of the issues into segments. I have noted at one time that I was disturbed "by the potential consequences of unnecessarily separating a case into segments and then deciding it piecemeal at different times and with different majorities."... Here the issues were not even separated into segments. To have separate majorities for various issues in a case "conflicts with the spirit, if not the letter, of the rule requiring an award to be made by a majority of the arbitrators."... Such a practice is inconsistent with the development of a consensus in decision-making. The majority requirement in the [1976] UNCITRAL Tribunal Rules has a long history in intergovernmental dispute resolution and has received widespread support. Accordingly, notwithstanding any Tribunal practice to the contrary, I believe that my concurrence is necessary for a true majority for this Partial Award.

(2) Tribunal Rules (1983), Article 31(2)

American Bell Intl, Inc and *Government of the Islamic Republic of Iran*, et al, Memorandum from the President regarding the Question of whether Article 13, paragraph 5, of the Tribunal Rules applies to Mr Mangård (September 12, 1985), Dissent by Charles N Brower (September 20, 1985), reprinted in 9 Iran-US CTR 410, 412–413 (1985–II) (citations omitted):

> In these circumstances the President perforce dissembles when he attempts to "*direct* that the proceedings in this case shall continue in Chamber Three" without Judge Mangård and at the same time to imply that such direction does not constitute a positive exercise of his Presidential authority under Article 31(2) of the [1983] Tribunal Rules. (Emphasis added.) Merely denying that he has acted under Article 31(2) does not make it so. The President has performed a dispositive act for which he cannot credibly disclaim responsibility.
>
> It is regrettable that this exercise of authority inevitably compromises in some measure the integrity of the Tribunal's processes. The exclusion of Judge Mangård from completing this Case can mean only one of two things: either it constitutes an interpretation of Article 15(5) at variance with that previously made by Chamber Three, in which case the previous Award would be called into question; or it means that Article 13(5) thereby is changed, presumably to make its application discretionary (which was not the Tribunal's intention in adopting it). The latter possibility would have the additional problem that a change of Article 13(5) was never discussed in the Full Tribunal, a fact which in turn would cast doubt on the character of the Tribunal deliberations if not on the validity of the amendment itself. Either result would leave the Tribunal undeservedly blemished.
>
> The only course open to the President that would not have impaired our institutional integrity would have been (1) either to note officially that the Tribunal had failed to disaffirm the application of Article 14(5) to Case No 48 by Chamber Three or (2) in the exercise of his powers under Article 31(2) to confirm such application.

International Systems & Controls Corp and *Industrial Development and Renovation Organization, et al*, Award No 256–439–2 (September 26, 1986), Dissenting Opinion of Judge Brower (September 26, 1986), reprinted in 12 Iran-US CTR 265, 268 note 9 (1986–III):

> As I did not concur in this Order or in authorizing the Chairman of Chamber Two to "decide on his own" the Chairman necessarily signed this Order either with the concurrence of Judge Bahrami or after determining that "no majority" existed either supporting or opposing it.

Ministry of Defence of the Islamic Republic of Iran and *Dept of Defense of the United States of America*, Case No B1, Order of July 2, 1987, Dissenting Opinion of Mr Ameli (July 2, 1987), reprinted in 18 Iran-US CTR 47, 47–48 (1988–I):

1. It is highly regrettable that the present President of the Tribunal has made a habit of disregarding the Tribunal Rules by deciding matters, whether procedural or substantive, unilaterally, without proper deliberations or appropriate authorization from other Tribunal members.
2. Article 31 of the [1983] Tribunal Rules on Decisions provides:
   1. When there are three arbitrators, any award or other decision of the arbitral tribunal shall be made by a majority of the arbitrators.
   2. In the case of questions of procedure, when there is no majority or when the arbitral tribunal so authorizes, the presiding arbitrator may decide on his own, subject to revision, if any, by the arbitral tribunal.
3. The present Case is before the Full Tribunal of nine members, requiring decision by all of them on the questions at hand. Although the questions involved in this Order are procedural, they are nevertheless highly significant and any attempt to change the course of the proceedings may eventually change the fate of this multibillion dollar Claim.

(3) *Tribunal Rules (1983), Article 31, Note 2—Confidentiality of deliberations*

Granite State Machine Co Inc and *Islamic Republic of Iran*, Award No 18–30–3 (December 15, 1982), Concurring Opinion of Richard M Mosk (January 25, 1983), reprinted in 1 Iran-US CTR 449, 449 (1981–82) (footnotes omitted):

I am restrained by Tribunal Rules and other considerations[2] from commenting fully on the accuracy of the description of the deliberations in this case in the "opinion" of Judge Jahangir Sani, who did not sign the award. If I were free at this time to discuss these deliberations, I would be able to set forth a true, accurate and complete statement of events.

...

It should be noted that confidentiality of deliberations is widely recognized as desirable and was supported by both the Government of the Islamic Republic of Iran and the United States of America. Such confidentiality is particularly essential in arbitration proceedings such as these in which arbitrators may, as Professor Sanders wrote, be "forced to continue their deliberation until a majority, and probably a compromise solution, has been reached."...

In the event that the Tribunal remains unwilling or unable to enforce its own rules and other generally recognized rules of conduct, such rules may no longer be of any effect.

[Footnote] 2. Canon VI of the American Arbitration Association Code of Ethics for Arbitrators in Commercial Disputes; Rule 2(2) of the Internal Rules of the Court of Arbitration of the International Chamber of Commerce; *Nuclear Test Case* (Australia v. France) 1973 I.C.J. 99; 1974 I.C.J. 253, 273 (declaration of Lachs, J.) and 293–296 (separate opinion of Gros, J.).

Raygo Wagner Equipment Co and *Star Line Iran Co*, Award No 20–17–3 (December 15, 1982), Comments of Richard M Mosk with Respect to "Mr. Jahangir Sani's Reasons For Not Signing The Decision Made by Mr. Mangard and Mr. Mosk in Case No 17" (March 3, 1983), reprinted in 1 Iran-US CTR 424, 424–27 (1981–82):

The document entitled "Mr. Jahangir Sani's Reasons for Not Signing the Decision Made by Mr. Mangard and Mr. Mosk In Case No 17" ("document") is both inappropriate and inaccurate. See Concurring Opinion of Richard M Mosk in Case No 30.

First, it is a violation of Tribunal Rules and generally accepted ethical standards to attempt to divulge the deliberations of an arbitral tribunal. Article 31, Note 2, [1983] provisionally Adopted Tribunal Rules. As one authority has written,

Art. 54(3) of the ICJ Statute, which provides that "the deliberations of the Court shall take place in private and secret", represents a practice of such widespread application as to be arguably a general principle of law. 1 *Encyc. of Pub. Int. Law* 185 (1981).

Such confidentiality is particularly essential in arbitration proceedings such as these in which arbitrators may, as the eminent Dutch arbitration expert, Professor Sanders has written, be "forced to continue their deliberations until a majority, and probably a compromise solution, has been reached." (citation omitted).

...

I do not feel it necessary at this time to give a point by point rebuttal to every assertion of Judge Sani. But other facts and representations by him are incorrect. The fact that this dialogue is taking place demonstrates the wisdom of rules of confidentiality of proceedings and the custom that legal opinion should be restricted to legal and factual issues on the merits of the case. Moreover, everything that Judge Sani says is irrelevant to his conclusion as to the validity of the award. The fact is that all applicable procedural rules were complied with. There was a majority in favor of the award and it was properly prepared and filed. Judge Sani is unable to point to any rule or law which would affect the validity of the award or suggest any impropriety. *What is important is that all members of the Tribunal be immune, and appear to be immune, from unfounded accusations and that they decide cases impartially, on the merits, in accordance with the evidence before them and on the basis of respect for law as required by the Claims Settlement Declaration.*

Raygo Wagner Equipment Co and *Star Line Iran Co*, Award No 20–17–3 (December 15, 1982), Further Comments of Richard M Mosk (April 13, 1983), reprinted in 1 Iran-US CTR 441, 441 (1981–82) (footnote omitted):

My colleague, Judge Jahangir Sani, has filed a document entitled "Mr. Jahangir Sani's reply to Mr. Mosk's 'Comments' of 3 March 1983 Concerning Case No 17." Such a document contains unfair complaints about the Chairman's internal administration of the Chamber and reflects bickering among members of the Tribunal which does little more than detract from the decorum of the Tribunal. As I have noted before, ... it is unfortunate that [in allowing the release of such comments] the Tribunal has not enforced its own rules and traditional standards of propriety. The failure to do so can be particularly serious in government established international tribunals which, throughout history, have been particularly fragile.

...

I again must state that I hope that the members of the Tribunal will not be affected by unfounded accusations and will decide cases impartially and on the basis of respect for law as required by the Claims Settlement Declaration.

Rexnord, Inc and *Islamic Republic of Iran*, Award No 21–132–3 (January 10, 1983), Concurring Opinion of Richard M Mosk (April 13, 1983), reprinted in 2 Iran-US CTR 27, 27–29 and n 3 (1983–I):

Once again Judge Sani inaccurately describes procedures adopted and implemented by the experienced Chairman of this Chamber who was selected by mutual agreement of the members appointed by Iran and the United States.

...

Judge Sani's complaint seems to be that after the draft opinion was prepared,[3] he wanted more deliberations, despite the fact that he would not attend them and would not sign any award in any event.

...

Regrettably, the Tribunal has permitted the release of Judge Sani's statements, which include material in violation of the Tribunal rule providing for confidentiality of deliberations (Article 31, Note 2 of the [1983] Provisionally Adopted Tribunal Rules). Although other members of the Tribunal undoubtedly disapprove of such violations of the rules, it is unfortunate that the Tribunal has been unwilling to take appropriate steps to enforce its rules. Moreover, the dialogue itself constitutes an unnecessary diversion from the task of the Tribunal.

[Footnote] 3. After the award was prepared, but before its release, the Chamber was informed that the Respondents in the instant case initiated settlement negotiations....

Uiterwyk Corp and *Government of the Islamic Republic of Iran*, Order of December 4, 1987, Chamber One, at 1:

> [O]n 24 November 1987 the Agent of the Islamic Republic of Iran filed a letter concerning the present state of proceedings in this Case. In response to that letter, the Tribunal makes the following observations:
>
> ...
>
> 3. The Agent's request for information also relates to matters presently under deliberation in this Case. Note 2 to Article 31 of the [1983] Tribunal Rules requires that deliberations be kept secret and, accordingly, it is the Tribunal's practice not to divulge any information concerning them.

Text of Memorandum from Mr Briner to Mr Khalilian dated July 14, 1989 attached to the Letter from Mr Briner to the Appointing Authority dated August 10, 1989, reprinted in 21 Iran-US CTR 354, 354 (1989–I):

> Your note of 28 June 1989 regarding the Draft Award in Case No 39...as well as certain remarks you made on 29 June 1989 indicate that you are labouring under a misconceived idea regarding the deliberation process, as you state that "memoranda exchanged between the Members are also regarded as part of the deliberation process and should be fully communicated to all the Members concerned."
>
> I should first of all like to point out that it has always been the practice of Chamber Two, once a draft had been issued, to discuss and exchange views on the legal and factual issues involved. Such discussions have frequently taken place between myself as Chairman and you or Mr. Aldrich alone. I also understand that at certain occasions discussions have taken place between you and Mr. Aldrich without my being present. When written comments are made with regard to a draft deliberated by me, it is up to the author of such comments to decide to whom to address them. In this context I only take note of the long-standing practice, also in the Full Tribunal and of Chambers One and Three, to address comments on the Presiding Arbitrator's draft directly to the Presiding Arbitrator without communicating them to the respective other Members of Members. It is then up to the Presiding Arbitrator to take into account or not such comments when issuing the subsequent draft.
>
> I should therefore make it very clear that there exists no obligation whatsoever on a Presiding Arbitrator to always make the other Member(s) aware of such communications addressed to him. On the other hand, it is equally clear that a draft of an award prepared by the Presiding Arbitrator has to be submitted to all other Members for comments before signature.

Phillips Petroleum Co Iran and *Islamic Republic of Iran*, Award No 425–39–2 (June 29, 1989), Supplemental Statement of George H Aldrich (August 30, 1989), reprinted in 21 Iran-US CTR 256, 256, 258–59 (1989–I):

> 1. I write this statement with regret, for I believe that the Award in this Case and my Concurring Opinion adequately express my views, and I find post-award exchanges among the Members of the Tribunal unseemly, particularly when they violate, as do Judge Khalilian's comments, Article 31, Note 2 of the [1983] Tribunal Rules which requires all Tribunal Members and Staff to maintain the privacy of deliberations. Nevertheless, in light of Judge Khalilian's comments and in view of the importance of this Case, I feel compelled to set the record straight on several of his assertions.
>
> ...

5. Judge Khalilian asserts that the calculations were attached to a memorandum that I communicated to the President, which he says he obtained "from a source which [he] do[es] not feel obliged to disclose." Judge Khalilian is misinformed. There never was a memorandum from me to the President on this subject; there were merely my legal assistant's hand-written calculations made in the circumstances described and a one-sentence transmittal memo from him to the President. I might add that even if I had written that memorandum to the President—which I did not—it would not have been improper. Thus it is not uncommon, or incorrect, for a judge, or a member of his staff, to communicate comments and information, orally or in writing, to the President or one or more other judges, without making a general distribution to all judges. I understand that such practices have been followed within the Tribunal, including by Judge Khalilian, as they have been among the judges of the International Court of Justice.

Decision of Justice Ch M J A Moons, Appointing Authority for the Iran–US Claims Tribunal, (Challenge of Judge Briner) (September 19, 1989), reprinted in 21 Iran-US CTR 384, 387 (1989–I):

Article 31 of the [1983] Tribunal Rules—as it is to be understood and applied according to Note 2 of this article—prescribes that deliberations in camera are confidential and must remain so. In the interest of proper functioning of the Tribunal this rule should be strictly observed, so that every Arbitrator may put forward his opinions and arguments in camera in full freedom, without fear of being called upon by the parties to account for them.

To my mind it would not be consonant with this interest if an appointing authority, as provided for by the [1983] Tribunal Rules, were to consider, in deciding a challenge, also information which should have remained confidential pursuant to the said Article 31.

Unidyne Corp and *Islamic Republic of Iran*, Case No 368, Award No 551–368–3 (November 10, 1993), Dissenting Opinion of Mohsen Aghahosseini (November 12, 1993), reprinted in 29 Iran-US CTR 349, 355–56 (1993):

This was immediately followed by the Chamber's oral deliberations. Still no suggestion, from any corner, that any such claim was before the Tribunal for decision.[6] ...

The deliberations on the Case were followed, on 27 December 1991, by a Draft Award prepared by a Member on facts and contentions. No reference was there made to the existence of a claim on the Shipyard work before the Chamber. A second suggested Draft, this time on the merits of the Parties' contentions, was distributed on 27 March 1992. Still, no allusion to such a claim. Finally, the Chamber's First Draft Award was prepared and submitted to the Members on 19 May 1993. Once again, no trace of such a claim being before the Chamber for determination. By then, of course, some three years had passed since the Hearing. ...

Such was the case before the Chamber, and these were the reasons why the Chamber in its oral deliberations, which immediately followed the Hearing, and in its preparation of the earlier Draft Awards, which lasted for over three years, did not as much as refer to a possible claim on the work performed at the Shipyard.

[Footnote] 6. I am well aware of, and intend to observe, the rule on the confidentiality of deliberations. It is for that reason that references in that regard will be made in most general terms, and only when they are absolutely necessary for the present purposes.

Unidyne Corp and *Islamic Republic of Iran*, Award No 551–368–3 (November 10, 1993), Supplemental Opinion of Judge Arangio-Ruiz and Judge Allison (November 17, 1993), reprinted in 29 Iran-US CTR 364, 364–65 (1993):

1. The Members of the Tribunal rarely respond to Dissenting Opinions, and, accordingly, we do not comment on Judge Aghahosseini's Dissenting Opinion in Case No 368 insofar as it relates

Deliberations and Decisions 727

to the Tribunal's procedure in arriving at the Award in this Case. However, in his Dissenting Opinion Judge Aghahosseini has chosen to enter into a discussion of the substance of the Chamber's deliberations in this Case as he claims to perceive them.[1]

2. In entering into the said discussion the Judge violates the Rules of this Tribunal as well as the generally observed principle of the confidentiality of arbitral deliberations.... It is not sufficient that his breach of confidence is, in his opinion, "absolutely necessary for the present purposes" (whatever those may be). The salutory effect of a rule so widely accepted in international dispute settlement cannot be well served if it is to be subject to the opinion, however strongly held, of individual arbitrators. We deeply regret the course taken by Judge Aghahosseini.

[Footnote] 1. Judge Aghahosseini does not mention that he absented himself from the Chamber's oral deliberations immediately after the hearing; declared his unwillingness to participate therein; and refused in writing to resume his participation despite repeated written invitations to do so. The Chamber thereafter continued deliberations by trilateral written exchanges.

Unidyne Corp and *Islamic Republic of Iran*, Award No 551–368–3 (November 10, 1993), A Statement in Case No 368 by Mohsen Aghahosseini (November 19, 1993), reprinted in 29 Iran-US CTR 365, 365–66 (1993):

2. ... They are wrong factually, because the Dissent simply does not disclose the substance of any deliberation. All that it does say in this respect—and this is in order to demonstrate that the assumed claim had never been before the Chamber—is that neither in the oral deliberations nor in the three Draft Awards which were subsequently prepared, had there been any trace of such a claim. A reference to what had not been before the Chamber—and hence had not formed part of the deliberations—cannot, by any stretch of imagination, be taken as constituting a disclosure of the substance of what was deliberated.

> They are wrong legally, because not everything can be done under the protective shield of the sanctity of deliberations. This procedural rule, like any other rule of law, is to protect what is just and nothing else: *Lex est sanctio sancta, jubens honesta, et prohibens contraria*. One cannot simply fashion a claim, of which there has been no trace either in the pleadings or in three years of oral and written exchanges after the Hearing, and then seek to bury this irregularity under the rubble of the "salutory effect" of the rule of confidentiality. Where a correct reflection of facts demands, all other consideration must give away: *Necessitas vincet legem; legum vincula irridet*.

3. A glance at the Dissenting Opinion will readily show that what has troubled the Majority in there is not a general reference to what has not been deliberated upon, "..." but a reasoned demonstration of how an assumed claim, of which there has been no trace in the pleadings, has been fully granted. That is a fact which no arbitrator, faithful to his mandate can possibly fail to mention in his version of the events; and that is a fact in respect of which the majority, continuing their intimate joint efforts, have failed to challenge.

Statement by the President, Krzysztof Skubiszewski, Case No A/28, Full Tribunal (December 21, 2000), at 1–2:

1. Although it is not customary for a Member of the Tribunal to comment on another Member's individual opinion filed in a case, the nature of some of the statements made by Mr. Broms in his Concurring and Dissenting Opinion of December 19, 2000, appended to the Tribunal's Decision No DEC 130-A28-FT (December 19, 2000), warrants the present remarks on my part.

2. In para 1 of his Opinion, Mr. Broms states that "[a]s Paragraph 95 in its present form was proposed by the President after the final deliberations had ended, and as the President did not call the members to open further deliberations, the purpose of the two sentences remains unclear."

To the extent that this statement is suggesting that the Members were not given full opportunity to offer their views in the deliberative process leading to the Decision in this Case, the statement is wrong. It is unclear what Mr. Broms means by "final" deliberations. Deliberations may, and in fact do, continute until the last moment before the filing of a Decision or Award. Deliberations take place during formal meetings of Members of the Tribunal; and, in addition, they take place through less formal exchanges (whether written or oral or both) among Members. This is also what took place in the present Case. At all stages of the Tribunal's work on the Decision, all Members were given ample opportunity to present their views, either orally or in writing, on each and every issue that arose in this Case—including Paragraph 95 of the Decision.

3. Furthermore, I note with regret that Mr. Broms' Opinion in a number of instances contravenes the rule of confidentiality of the Tribunal's deliberations, as set forth in Note 2 to Article 31 of the [1983] Tribunal Rules (see, in particular, paras 1 and 5 of Mr. Broms's Opinion).

Letter from Judge Bengt Broms to the Appointing Authority, Sir Robert Jennings, dated February 22, 2001, at 1–2:

In the same context, I want to underline that the Challenge should have respected my right to give my Opinion so as to explain my legal understanding of the Decision without breaching the [1983] Rules of the Tribunal. Article 32(3) provides as follows:

Any Arbitrator may request that his dissenting vote or his dissenting vote and the reasons therefore be recorded.

That right belongs to all members of the Tribunal and the United States should respect. The United States cannot expect that I have to agree with the views of the United States. Such an attitude is totally against the principles of the impartiality and independence of the arbitrators, and, at the same time, it is also against the basic principles of the whole institute of arbitration.

Decision of Sir Robert Jennings, Appointing Authority, on the Challenge of Judge Broms (May 7, 2001), at 7:

I am, however, reluctant to endorse any purported general rule of thumb test in this matter of confidentiality. Each case should be judged on the merits. No doubt a revelation limited to a judge's own view may in certain cases be a relatively venial breach of the confidentiality rule. But Judge Broms' statement of his own view that three other Members appeared to agree with one of his views was in any event a step too far.

...

A rule of confidentiality of the deliberations must, if it is to be effective, apply generally to the deliberation stage of tribunal's proceedings and cannot realistically be confined to what is said in a formal meeting of all the members in the deliberation room. The form or forms the deliberation takes varies greatly from one tribunal to another. Anybody who has had experience of courts and tribunals knows perfectly well that much of the deliberation work, even in courts like the ICJ which have formal rules governing the deliberation, is done less formally. In particular the task of drafting is better done in small groups rather than by the whole court attempting to draft round the table. Revelations of such informal discussion and of suggestions made, could be very damaging and seriously threaten the whole deliberation process. There is no doubt then that the quoted passage in paragraph 1 of Judge Broms' Opinion was a breach. This, as well as the breaches in his paragraphs 2 and 5, were serious breaches of the confidentiality rule.

Dealing with this confidentiality breach as such is not, however, a matter for the Appointing Authority. The breach of confidence in the present case was viewed by the President as a matter calling for his immediate action, and resulted in the Statement of the President of 21 December 2000. In my view these instances of a breach of the rule of confidentiality in the present case have by this statement from the President already been properly and correctly dealt with by the President. My only concern, as the Appointing Authority, is what is the effect of the terms of Judge Broms' "concurring and dissenting Opinion" on the question of his impartiality and his independence. A judge may be strictly and correctly impartial and independent though massively indiscreet and forgetful of the rules.

The attention of the Appointing Authority is therefore to be paid to these breaches solely as a factor in a decision on the "justifiable doubt" question....

Joint Decision of the Appointing Authority, Judge W E Haak, on the Challenges of Judge Krzysztof Skubiszewski and Judge Hamid Reza Oloumi Yazdi, April 2, 2008, at 15–16:

It is widely accepted that the raison d'être of the secrecy of deliberations is to protect the members of the Tribunal from outside influence and enable them to freely exchange their views and arguments to reach a decision, Departing from the confidentiality rule laid down in Article 31, note 2 of the Tribunal Rules would prevent a true discussion between the arbitrators, undermine the principle of arbitral collegiality, and jeopardize the independence of the arbitrators.

It is therefore of the utmost importance that this rule be strictly complied with as soon as the Tribunal has reached the deliberation stage. In this particular case, the hearings were concluded several months before Judge Olourni made his disclosures. It is clear that the deliberative stage had been reached when Judge Oloumi's memorandum was communicated to the parties.

Judge Oloumi's disclosure in his memorandum of November 23, 2007 refers to a request to postpone the entire deliberations, the reaction of an individual arbitrator (the President) and the decision regarding that request. This all happened during and for the purposes of the deliberations,

Iran, however, has argued that the rule of confidentiality of deliberations does not apply in the present case. The reason that Iran has ultimately advanced is that Judge Oloumi's disclosures relate to a "purely administrative issue" and do not fall within the scope of deliberations as contemplated in Article 31 note 2 of the Rules. According to Iran, such issues as that raised by Judge Oloumi are usually "handled" by the President of the Tribunal and "openly communicated about" and yet Judge Skubiszewski failed to notify, the decision to the parties. Iran has further argued that in this case, Judge Oloumi had a duty to communicate the contents of his memorandum to the parties because the decision made with respect to his request reversed the "final and binding" May 1, 2007 decision and resulted in the exclusion of an arbitrator from the deliberations.

As further explained below, I find it difficult to agree with several aspects of Iran's reasoning. It is clear to me that Judge Olourni has disclosed confidential information in his memorandum of November 23, 2007, As such, this information cannot be taken into consideration by the Appointing Authority for the purposes of the challenge. Iran, however, has argued that Judge Oloumi was "virtually eliminated" from the deliberations. While the obvious exclusion of an arbitrator by his co-arbitrators might justify the abrogation of the rule of confidentiality, I fail to see how Judge Oloumi could be held to have been excluded from the deliberations in this particular case.

In order for the confidentiality rule to serve its purpose, the notion of "deliberation" has to be understood broadly, both in its form and content, The definition provided for in Black's Law Dictionary and relied upon by Iran reflects this concern. Indeed, as pointed out by Iran, "deliberations" are defined as "[t]he weighing and examining the reasons for and against a contemplated act or course of conduct or a choice of act or means" (Iran's submission of January 2, 2008, paragraph 17 in the challenge to Judge Oloumi). Yet, despite the breadth of this definition, Iran has argued that "by no stretch of imagination can Judge Oloumi's submission, though selectively viewed and quoted by the United States, he characterized as an exchange of views and opinions to reach a conclusion" (Iran's submission of January 2, 2008, paragraph 17 in the challenge to Judge Olourni). I must say that I am of a different view. Judge Oloumi's memorandum does refer, though in vague terms, to an exchange of views (the request of Judge Oloumi and the President's questioning of the merits of that request) and to the weighing and examining of reasons for and against a choice of act (the President "dealt" with the request for the postponement of deliberations "in a way that it met with a negative outcome").

Whether they be labelled procedural or administrative—the meaning of the latter term being left undefined by Iran—the request, the discussions thereon and the decision made upon it fall without any doubt within the scope of the deliberations. Internal discussions and decisions with respect to the organisation of deliberation work, during and for the purposes of the deliberations, are part of the deliberations and, as such, confidential. Arbitrators may disagree as to how the deliberation work should be organized (e.g. when and in what order the relevant issues should be addressed) and the reasons underlying their respective preferences may vary from one arbitrator to another. The purpose of the confidentiality rule would be entirely defeated if individual arbitrators could be open to attack for the views or the reactions that they express in relation to such issues in the deliberations. Thus, the internal debates between Tribunal Members regarding the merits of a request from a fellow arbitrator for delaying the deliberations must remain confidential.

In this challenge, I note that the challenging party has not provided any explanation with respect to the alleged criticism and denial of the request for the postponement of deliberations, although that would have been necessary to properly understand what happened and "the negative outcome" of the request. I further observe that, while Judge Oloumi could have taken the opportunity to file documents, in the challenge against him, in support of what he considers not a breach of confidentiality but his legitimate and even necessary reaction to the alleged deprivation of his right to "meaningfully participate" in the deliberations, he did not. I should state, further, that the timing and sequence of deliberations are intimately connected to the substance of deliberations. Fully discussing the request for the postponement of the entire deliberations and how it was decided upon and why would lead to further and perhaps more serious disclosures of confidential information, once again in violation of article 31 note 2 of the Rules.

With this risk in mind, it appears that Judge Aghahosseini's definition of deliberations as "a process through which judges mutually discuss and weigh the factual assertions and legal arguments of the opposing parties, with a view to a choice or a determination", is unnecessarily narrow (Judge Aghahosseini's letter to the President and the other Members of the Tribunal of December 4, 2007). This definition does not sufficiently protect the arbitrators; their internal discussions and decisions with respect to the organization of the deliberations, and many other procedural issues, would not be covered. The present case is, in my view, an illustration of the necessity not to restrict unduly the scope of deliberations.

24

Form and Effect

1. Introduction	732
2. Form and Effect—Article 34	732
A. Text of the 2010 UNCITRAL Rules	732
B. Commentary	733
(1) Discretion to make separate awards—Article 34(1)	733
(2) The award is "final and binding" and the parties must "carry out the award without delay"—Article 34(2)	738
(a) General commentary on "final and binding"	738
(1) "Final"	738
(2) "Binding"	741
(b) Waiver of recourse against the award—optional provision	742
(3) Written award and designation of the date and place of the award's making—Article 34(2) and (4)	745
(4) Obligation to sign and failure to sign the award—Article 34(4)	746
(a) General comments on the *travaux préparatoires*	746
(b) Practical matters regarding the statement of reasons for the absence of an arbitrator's signature	749
(5) Statement of reasons for the award and dissenting opinions—Article 34(3)	750
(a) Statement of reasons for the award	750
(b) Dissenting and separate opinions	752
(6) Publication of the award—Article 34(5)	755
(7) Copies of the award to the parties—Article 34(6)	757
(8) Filing and registration of the award	759
(9) Comparison to the 1976 UNCITRAL Rules	759
C. Extracts from the Practice of Investment and other Tribunals	761
(1) Article 32(1) (1976 Rules)—Types of award	761
(2) Article 32(2) (1976 Rules)—Final and binding	762
(3) Article 32(2) and (4) (1976 Rules)—Date, place, and signature	763
(4) Article 32(4) (1976 Rules)—Failure to sign the award	764
(5) Article 32(7) (1976 Rules)—Filing and registration of an award	765
D. Extracts from the Practice of the Iran–US Claims Tribunal	766
(1) Tribunal Rules (1983), Article 32(1)—Types of award	766
(2) Tribunal Rules (1983), Article 32(2)—Final and binding award	767
(3) Tribunal Rules (1983), Article 32(3) and (4)—Date, place, and signature	767
(4) Tribunal Rules (1983), Article 32(3)—Reasons for the award	768
(5) Tribunal Rules (1983), Article 32(4)—Failure to sign the award	769
(a) Statements of reasons for failure to sign the award	769
(b) Improper statements of reasons and post-award exchanges	773
(6) Tribunal Rules (1983), Article 32(5)—Publication of the award	776

1. Introduction

A decision of the arbitral tribunal can have binding legal effect, both domestically and internationally, if formalized properly. Article 34 addresses the technical requirements regarding the form and content of the award. In particular, the award: must be made in writing; must be signed by all the arbitrators or explain the failure of an arbitrator to sign; must include the reasons for the decision, unless otherwise agreed; must be dated and indicate the place where the award was made; and must be transmitted to the parties. Article 34 also identifies the types of awards that the arbitral tribunal may issue, allows the award to be made public, if the parties so desire, and states the rule that the award is final and binding.

The technical requirements contained in Article 34 are "subject to the mandatory provisions of the applicable national law," which may impose conflicting or additional requirements.[1] The arbitral tribunal's failure to adhere to these mandatory requirements may jeopardize the validity and enforceability of the award. Take, for example, the case where a majority award is rendered, but a dissenting arbitrator has refused to sign the award. The majority includes a statement of reasons for the dissenter's failure to sign in accordance with Rule 34(4), but the law governing the arbitration requires, without exception, the signatures of all three arbitrators. Consider further that the losing party could move to set aside the award in local courts, the award could be nullified, and the parties might have to arbitrate again from the start.[2] To avoid such severe consequences, it is thus paramount that the arbitral tribunal consider carefully any external legal requirements governing the award-making process.

2. Form and Effect—Article 34

A. Text of the 2010 UNCITRAL Rule[3]

Article 34 of the 2010 UNCITRAL Rules provides:

Form and effect of the award

1. The arbitral tribunal may make separate awards on different issues at different times.

---

[1] See *Report of the Secretary-General on the Revised Draft Set of Arbitration Rules*, UNCITRAL, 9th Session, Addendum 1 (Commentary), UN Doc A/CN.9/112/Add.1 (1975), reprinted in (1976) VII UNCITRAL Ybk 166, 177. Similarly, Article 1(2) of the Rules provides when the Rules are "in conflict with a provision of the law applicable to the arbitration from which the parties cannot derogate" the mandatory provisions of law prevail.

[2] This hypothetical scenario is modified from an example presented in J Paulson, "Delocalisation of International Commercial Arbitration: When and Why It Matters," (1983) 32 ICLQ 52, 58.

[3] Corresponding Article 32 of the 1976 UNCITRAL Rules provides:

1. In addition to making a final award, the arbitral tribunal shall be entitled to make interim, interlocutory, or partial awards.
2. The award shall be made in writing and shall be final and binding on the parties. The parties undertake to carry out the award without delay.
3. The arbitral tribunal shall state the reasons upon which the award is based, unless the parties have agreed that no reasons are to be given.
4. An award shall be signed by the arbitrators and it shall contain the date on which and the place where the award was made. Where there are three arbitrators and one of them fails to sign, the award shall state the reason for the absence of the signature.
5. The award may be made public only with consent of both parties.
6. Copies of the award signed by the arbitrators shall be communicated to the parties by the arbitral tribunal.
7. If the arbitration law of the country where the award is made requires that the award be filed or registered by the arbitral tribunal, the tribunal shall comply with this requirement within the period of time required by law.

2. All awards shall be made in writing and shall be final and binding on the parties. The parties shall carry out all awards without delay.
3. The arbitral tribunal shall state the reasons upon which the award is based, unless the parties have agreed that no reasons are to be given.
4. An award shall be signed by the arbitrators and it shall contain the date on which the award was made and indicate the place of arbitration. Where there is more than one arbitrator and any of them fails to sign, the award shall state the reason for the absence of the signature.
5. An award may be made public with the consent of all parties or where and to the extent disclosure is required of a party by legal duty, to protect or pursue a legal right or in relation to legal proceedings before a court or other competent authority.
6. Copies of the award signed by the arbitrators shall be communicated to the parties by the arbitral tribunal.

Possible waiver statement (contained in Annex to 2010 UNCITRAL Rules)

Note—If the parties wish to exclude recourse against the arbitral award that may be available under the applicable law, they may consider adding a provision to that effect as suggested below, considering, however, that the effectiveness and conditions of such an exclusion depend on the applicable law.

Waiver: The parties hereby waive their right to any form of recourse against an award to any court or other competent authority, insofar as such waiver can validly be made under the applicable law.

B. Commentary

(1) Discretion to make separate awards—Article 34(1)

Article 34(1), modeled exactly on the first sentence of Article 26.7 of the LCIA Arbitration Rules, recognizes the arbitral tribunal's inherent authority to make "separate awards on different issues at different times." The discretion to render separate awards serves the interests of organization and efficiency of the arbitral process. If, for example, it is most logical and appropriate to address issues of jurisdiction, liability, or damages separately, Article 34(1) recognizes the tribunal's authority to render individual awards with respect to each of these issues whenever appropriate in the arbitration.

Article 34(1) clarifies the emphasis under the Rules of substance over form in award-making. Whereas under the 1976 Rules potential types of awards were enumerated eg, "interim," "interlocutory," or "partial," the Working Group that revised the Rules concluded that such enumeration was unnecessary, even potentially misleading.[4] Some delegations noted that varying labels could create confusion as they may not be recognized or may be attributed different meanings across domestic legal systems.[5] Others raised questions about the term "final award," which could be subject to different interpretations, such as that the award was not appealable, was the last in a series of awards rendered by the tribunal,

---

[4] *Report of the Working Group on Arbitration and Conciliation on the Work of its Forty-Fifth Session* (Vienna, September 11–15, 2006), UNCITRAL, 40th Session, UN Doc A/CN.9/614, at 23, para 113 (2007) (preference against term "partial"); *Report of the Working Group on Arbitration and Conciliation on the Work of its Forty-Seventh Session* (Vienna, September 10–14, 2007), UNCITRAL, 41st Session, UN Doc A/CN.9/641, at 16, para 80 (2007) (preference against terms ("final," "interim," and "interlocutory"); *Report of Working Group II (Arbitration and Conciliation) on the Work of its Fifty-First Session* (Vienna, September 14–18, 2009), UNCITRAL, 43rd Session, UN Doc A/CN.9/684, at 16, para 63 (2009) (same).

[5] UNCITRAL, 41st Session, UN Doc A/CN.9/641, n 4, at 16, para 79.

or could not be modified by the arbitral tribunal.[6] By avoiding labels altogether, Article 34(1) does not even suggest appropriate appellations for different types of awards. In short, under the Rules, the same award could just as easily be called an "award on jurisdiction" as a "partial award."

The clarifying revisions to Article 34(1), in practice, should have little practical effect on the arbitral tribunal's inherent ability to render different types of awards.[7] Even the express enumeration of types of awards under the 1976 UNCITRAL Rules was not meant to limit the arbitral tribunal's award-making discretion in any way. To the contrary, as the *travaux préparatoires* indicate, the terms "interim award," "interlocutory award," and "partial award" were meant to be used broadly and even interchangeably.[8] In Committee discussions, Sanders clarified that in practice whether the arbitrators used, for example, the name "interim" or "interlocutory" was really of "no importance," since they are entitled to make "any kind of award they deem appropriate for the conduct of the arbitration."[9] Thus, Article 32(1) of the 1976 Rules was designed "to give the arbitrators as much freedom as possible in order to ensure maximum efficiency" in case management.[10]

Thus, despite their slightly varying approaches, Article 34(1) and Article 32(1) of the 1976 Rules serve the identical purpose. Whether by avoiding enumeration of the types of awards altogether or by recommending flexible nomenclature, both versions of the rule eschew overly technical and unnecessarily time-consuming disputes about the appellation of a particular decision.[11] Regardless of what label is attached to an award, if the arbitral tribunal intends for its decision to be embodied in an "award" within the meaning of the Rules, it must be made in accordance with applicable procedural and technical requirements. As described in the following sections of this Chapter, awards must be in writing; be signed by the arbitrators or, if one or more arbitrators fails to sign, include an explanation for the absence of the signature; contain reasons for the award, unless otherwise agreed; and include the date and place where the award was made.

While all awards made pursuant to the Rules share the same attributes of being final and binding with respect to the parties,[12] they may differ in terms of their specific legal consequences. The Working Group noted, for example, that "an award terminating the

---

[6] UNCITRAL, 41st Session, UN Doc A/CN.9/641, n 4, at 16, para 79. In addition, concerns were expressed that the term "partial award" was misleading because it should still be considered a "final award" with respect to the issues which it addressed. UNCITRAL, 40th Session, UN Doc A/CN.9/614, n 4, at 23, para 113.

[7] The arbitral tribunal generally has full discretion in this area. See *Lance Paul Larsen* (1976 Rules), para 6.5, reprinted in section 2(C)(1) ("[I]t is for the Tribunal to determine which issues need to be dealt with and in what order.") The commentary on the Preliminary Draft of the 1976 UNCITRAL Rules noted that the arbitrators were free to make interim, interlocutory, or partial awards before rendering the final award. *Report of the Secretary-General on the Preliminary Draft Set of Arbitration Rules*, UNCITRAL, 8th Session, UN Doc A/CN.9/97 (1974), reprinted in (1975) VI UNCITRAL Ybk 163, 178 (Commentary on Draft Article 26).

[8] All of these terms denote the fact that such an award, as a general rule, precedes the last award to be rendered in the arbitration. See UNCITRAL, 8th Session, UN Doc A/CN.9/97, n 7, (characterizing the three additional types of awards generally as "interim awards"). See also, J L Simpson and H Fox, *International Arbitration: Law and Practice* (1959) 234 ("[T]he decisions preceding that in the final phase may be described as 'interim.' ").

[9] P Sanders, "Commentary on UNCITRAL Arbitration Rules," (1977) II Ybk Commercial Arb 172, 210.

[10] See *Summary Record of the 10th Meeting of the Committee of the Whole (II)*, UNCITRAL, 9th Session, UN Doc A/CN.9/9/C.2/SR.10, at 7–8, para 59 (1976).

[11] On the 1976 UNCITRAL Rules in this regard, see S Baker and M Davis, *The UNCITRAL Arbitration Rules in Practice: The Experience of the Iran-United States Claims Tribunal* (1992) 163, 165.

[12] See *Methanex*, (1976 Rules) para 31, reprinted in section 2(C)(2). See also *Iran* and *United States* (Case Nos A3/A8/A9/A14/B61-FT), reprinted in section 2(D)(1).

proceedings would not have the same effect as an award on interim measures."[13] It appears that for this reason Article 34(1), which imports the first sentence of Article 26.7 of the LCIA Rules verbatim, does not adopt the second sentence providing "[s]uch [separate] awards shall have the same status and effect as any other award made by the arbitral tribunal."[14] To the Working Group, the second sentence was unnecessary because Article 34(2) provides that "all" awards are final and binding and must be carried out without delay.[15]

Compliance with the requirements for making an award under Article 34 cannot alone guarantee the external validity and enforceability of a decision by the arbitral tribunal, even if termed an "award." In most cases, the legal effect of such a decision depends on the requirements of the applicable arbitration law, which may stipulate specific criteria for constituting an "award." While an extensive examination of this subject is beyond the scope of this Commentary, it suffices to note the work of UNCITRAL in the context of Model Law negotiations. The Commission considered, but never adopted, the following proposed definition of the term "award":

An award means a final award which disposes of all issues submitted to the arbitral tribunal and any other decision of the tribunal which finally determine[s] any question of substance or the question of its competence or any other question of procedure but, in the latter case, only if the arbitral tribunal terms its decision an award.[16]

The first portion of the text, including the phrase "questions of substance," drew wide support from Model Law negotiators; the remainder was seriously criticized, particularly with respect to the inclusion of questions of procedure in the definition of award.[17] The work of the Commission on the Model Law, albeit incomplete, highlights areas of consensus regarding the meaning of the term "award." It appears namely that an "award" covers decisions on substantive issues of fact or law that are material to the resolution of the arbitral dispute.[18] Nevertheless, there may be disagreement as to whether decisions on procedural matters, such as those relating to case management, constitute "awards."[19] Consequently, some decisions by the arbitral tribunal—even if labeled as an "award"—ultimately may not be treated as such upon enforcement in some jurisdictions.[20]

---

[13] UNCITRAL, 43rd Session, UN Doc A/CN.9/684, n 4, at 16, para 65.

[14] Note that an earlier version of the rule included the text of Article 26.7 of the 1998 LCIA Rules in its entirety. See *Settlement of Commercial Disputes: Revision of the UNCITRAL Arbitration Rules, Note by the Secretariat*, UNCITRAL, UN Doc A/CN.9/WG.II/WP.149 at 13–14, para 51 (2007) (Draft Article 32).

[15] UNCITRAL, 43rd Session, UN Doc A/CN.9/684, n 4, at 16, para 65. Castello agrees, noting that "neither the wording of [the 1976] Art 32(1) nor the drafting history gives any reason to believe that partial, interlocutory and interim awards were to be distinguished from final awards as somehow not final and not binding." J Castello, "UNCITRAL Rules" in F Weigand (ed), *Practitioner's Handbook on International Commercial Arbitration* (2nd edn 2009) 1511.

[16] See H Holtzmann and J Neuhaus, *A Guide to the UNCITRAL Model Law on International Commercial Arbitration: Legislative History and Commentary* (1989) 154.

[17] H Holtzmann and J Neuhaus, *A Guide to the UNCITRAL Model Law*, n 16, 154.

[18] This definition would seem to apply even to decisions that are not labeled awards. In one case concerning the decision of an arbitral tribunal constituted under the UNCITRAL Rules, the reviewing court recognized that the decision, which was fashioned as a procedural order not an award, nevertheless had the effect of an award because it resolved the central dispute between the parties. See *Publicis Communication v True North Communications, Inc*, 206 F 3d 725 (7th Cir 2000).

[19] See N Blackaby and C Partasides with A Redfern and M Hunter, *Redfern and Hunter on International Arbitration* (5th edn 2009) 515 et seq; E Gaillard and J Savage (eds), *Fouchard, Gaillard, Goldman on International Commercial Arbitration* (1999) 737; K Berger, *International Economic Arbitration* (1993) 590–1.

[20] Moreover, certain awards, for example those that decide an issue rather than a claim, are not amenable to enforcement in any case, but rather serve primarily to finalize a specific point within the arbitration.

To avoid undermining the legal effect of its decisions, especially when rendering separate awards, it is incumbent upon the arbitral tribunal to investigate carefully the relevant provisions of the governing arbitration law. When in doubt as to how to categorize a decision, an arbitral tribunal is well advised to err on the side of caution and issue the decision in accordance with all the technical requirements associated with an award.[21] It is better to have created some false expectations among the parties, than to ignore a key criterion of the governing arbitration law, such as decision-making by majority rule, which may render the decision invalid.

Although Article 34(1) deliberately avoids terms like "partial," "interim," and "interlocutory" awards, arbitral tribunals do utilize these labels in a varied and flexible manner to facilitate and improve case management. The Iran–US Claims Tribunal came to develop its own practice under corresponding Article 32(1) of the 1983 Tribunal Rules as to when each appellation was to be used, which may serve as a general guide to tribunals when rendering separate awards under Article 34(1). Partial awards, for example, were employed by the Tribunal when one claim or a group of claims could be separated out for early resolution, while the development of the remainder of the case required additional time and resources.[22] Partial awards, however, have also been employed by the Tribunal and other tribunals in order to separate large or complex cases into discrete phases, such as jurisdiction,[23] liability,[24] damages,[25] and costs.[26] Another suggested use for partial awards is to decide specific legal questions such as the law applicable to the merits.[27] In one arbitration,

---

UNCITRAL, 43rd Session, UN Doc A/CN.9/684, n 4, at 16, para 64: "A concern was expressed that the word 'issues' in the first sentence of paragraph (1) might not properly convey the idea that the arbitral tribunal might render partial awards dealing only with certain aspects of an issue....".

[21] See, eg, *Himpurna California Ltd* (1976 Rules), reprinted in section 2(C)(1).

[22] See, eg, *Ultrasystems, Inc* (1983 Tribunal Rules); *Harnischfeger* (1983 Tribunal Rules); and *RJ Reynolds Tobacco Co* (1983 Tribunal Rules); all reprinted in section 2(D)(1). See also P Sanders "Commentary on UNCITRAL Arbitration Rules," n 9, 210; S Baker and M Davis, *The UNCITRAL Arbitration Rules in Practice*, n 11, 164.

[23] See, eg, *Continental Grain Export Corp* and *Government Trading Corp,* et al, Award No 75–112–1 (September 5, 1983), reprinted in 3 Iran-US CTR 319 (1983-II). Although not designated a "partial award," the issue of jurisdiction was treated separately in *Methanex Corp* and *United States of America*, Preliminary Award on Jurisdiction (August 7, 2002) (ICSID administered, 1976 UNCITRAL Rules, NAFTA Chapter Eleven), and *Ethyl Corp* and *The Government of Canada*, Award on Jurisdiction (June 24, 1998), (*Ad Hoc* Proceeding, 1976 UNCITRAL Rules, NAFTA Chapter Eleven), reprinted in (1999) 38 ILM 708. See also P Sanders, "Commentary on UNCITRAL Arbitration Rules," n 9, 210.

[24] See, eg, *Granite States Machine Co, Inc.* (1983 Tribunal Rules), reprinted below section 2(D)(1). See also *CME Czech Republic BV* and *Czech Republic*, Partial Award (September 13, 2001), (*Ad Hoc* Proceedings, 1976 UNCITRAL Rules, Netherlands-Czech Republic BIT), reprinted in (2003) 14(3) World Trade & Arb Materials 109; *Aram Sabet,* et al and *Islamic Republic of Iran*, Partial Award No 593–815/816/817–2 (June 30, 1999); *Antione Biloune (Syria)* and *Marine Drive Complex Ltd (Ghana)* and *Ghana Investment Centre* and *Government of Ghana*, Award on Liability (October 27, 1989), reprinted in (1994) XIX Ybk Commercial Arb 11; *Wintershall AG,* et al and *International Ocean Resources, Inc*, Partial Award on Liability (February 5, 1988) (*Ad Hoc* Proceeding, 1976 UNCITRAL Rules, Germany-Argentina BIT), reprinted in (1989) 28 ILM798.

[25] *SD Myers, Inc* and *Canada*, Second Partial Award on Damages (October 21, 2002), (*Ad Hoc* Proceeding, 1976 UNCITRAL Rules, NAFTA Chapter Eleven), reprinted in (2003) 15(1) World Trade & Arb Materials 103.

[26] See, eg, *Granite States Machine Co, Inc* (1983 Tribunal Rules), reprinted in section 2(D)(1). Although not designated as "partial awards," two NAFTA awards rendered under the UNCITRAL Rules served a similar function. *SD Myers, Inc* and *Government of Canada*, Final Award on Costs (December 30, 2002) (*Ad Hoc* Proceeding, 1976 UNCITRAL Rules, NAFTA Chapter Eleven); *Pope & Talbot, Inc* and *Government of Canada*, Award on Costs (November 26, 2002) (*Ad Hoc* Proceeding, 1976 UNCITRAL Rules, NAFTA Chapter Eleven).

[27] See, eg, P Sanders, *The Work of UNCITRAL on Arbitration and Conciliation* (2001) 15.

for example, the tribunal rendered a partial award which decided issues of liability and damages, but not costs or the taxes owed by the Claimant company that would determine the final figure to be awarded the company.[28]

Other tribunals similarly have issued "interim" awards for piecemeal resolution of separable issues.[29] For example, in the *Himpurna* arbitration, the tribunal set forth its decision on whether the respondent party had defaulted on its obligation to submit a statement of defence in a document entitled an "interim award."[30] The Iran–US Claims Tribunal tended to limit the use of the phrase "interim award" to awards issued in connection with a party's request for interim measures of relief pursuant to Article 26 of the 1983 Tribunal Rules. A number of such awards issued by the Tribunal addressed either a party's claims that its rights in property were in imminent danger and thus required immediate protection,[31] or a party's request for a stay of proceedings in a forum other than the Tribunal, ie, Iranian courts or another arbitral forum, pending the Tribunal's determination of its own jurisdiction.[32]

Interlocutory awards have been useful in resolving preliminary or threshold legal questions bearing on the overall direction of the arbitration. The Iran–US Claims Tribunal has issued interlocutory awards on many occasions to determine whether a party is properly before the Tribunal,[33] or whether a party's claim or counterclaim falls within the Tribunal's jurisdiction under the Algiers Accords.[34] Thus, in the practice of the Tribunal, the term "partial award" was assigned to an award that was final as to a distinct claim, while the "interlocutory award" was used to decide a substantive or procedural issue bearing on a claim. These preliminary rulings have no doubt saved the parties substantial time and money by narrowing the scope of the dispute at an early stage of arbitration. In other cases, the Tribunal has used the interlocutory award to deal with procedural matters, such as

---

[28] *Chevron Corp*, et al and *Republic of Ecuador*, Partial Award (March 30, 2010), (PCA administered, 1976 UNCITRAL Rules, US-Ecuador BIT), at 249–50.

[29] See, eg, *Pope & Talbot, Inc* and *Government of Canada*, Interim Award (June 26, 2000), (*Ad Hoc* Proceeding, 1976 UNCITRAL Rules, NAFTA Chapter Eleven) (2000) 13(4) World Trade & Arb Materials 19 (separating out issues of liability).

[30] *Himpurna California Energy, Ltd* and *Republic of Indonesia*, Interim Award (September 26, 1999), (*Ad Hoc* Proceeding, 1976 UNCITRAL Rules, Concession Agreement), reprinted in (2000) XXV Ybk Commercial Arb 11.

[31] See, eg, *Behring Intl, Inc* and *Islamic Republic Iranian Air Force*, et al, Award No ITM 46–382–3 (February 22, 1985), reprinted in 8 Iran-US CTR 44 (1985-I); *Government of the United States of America (on behalf and for the benefit of Shipside Packing Co, Inc)* and *Islamic Republic of Iran*, Award No ITM 27–11875–1 (September 6, 1983), reprinted in 3 Iran-US CTR 331 (1983-II).

[32] See, eg, *Panacaviar, SA* and *Islamic Republic of Iran*, Award No ITM 64–498–1 (December 4, 1986), reprinted in 13 Iran-US CTR 193 (1986-IV); *Fluor Corp* and *Government of the Islamic Republic of Iran*, Award No ITM 62–333–1 (August 6, 1986), reprinted in 11 Iran-US CTR 296 (1986-II); *Government of the United States of America (on behalf of and for the benefit of Linen, Fortinberry and Associates, Inc)* and *Islamic Republic of Iran*, Award No ITM 48–10513–2 (April 10, 1985), reprinted in 8 Iran-US CTR 85 (1985-I); *QuesTech, Inc* and *Islamic Republic of Iran*, Award No ITM 15–59–1 (March 1, 1983), reprinted in 2 Iran-US CTR 96 (1983-I).

[33] See, eg, *James M Saghi*, et al and *Government of the Islamic Republic of Iran*, Award No ITL 66–298–2 (January 12, 1987), reprinted in 14 Iran-US CTR 3 (1987-I); *International Schools Services, Inc* and *National Iranian Copper Industries Co*, Award No ITL 37–111-FT (April 6, 1984), reprinted in 5 Iran-US CTR 338 (1984-I).

[34] See, eg, *Westinghouse Electric Corp* and *Islamic Republic of Iran*, et al, Award No ITL 67–389–2 (February 15, 1987), reprinted in 14 Iran-US CTR 105 (1987-I); *SeaCo, Inc* and *Islamic Republic of Iran*, et al, Award No ITL 61–260–2 (June 20, 1986), reprinted in 11 Iran-US CTR 210 (1986-II); *ITEL Intl Corp* and *Social Security Organization of Iran*, et al, Award No ITL 43–476–2 (June 22, 1984), reprinted in 7 Iran-US CTR 31 (1984-III); *Gibbs & Hill, Inc* and *Iran Power Generation and Transmission Co*, et al, Award No ITL 1–6-FT (November 5, 1982), reprinted in 1 Iran-US CTR 236 (1981–82).

evidentiary matters,[35] the appointment of experts,[36] requests to amend a party's claims,[37] and issues of general case management.[38]

(2) The award is "final and binding" and the parties must "carry out the award without delay"—Article 34(2)

(a) General commentary on "final and binding"

The available *travaux préparatoires* for corresponding Article 32(2) of the 1976 UNCITRAL Rules are virtually devoid of commentary on the meaning of the phrase "final and binding."[39] The Committee did not appear initially to favor inclusion of both aspects of the principle of *res judicata*. Early drafts of the Rules provided only that an award was "binding" on the parties.[40] However, at the urging of the US representative,[41] the Committee agreed to insert the word "final" into the text of the rule.[42] Thus, at a minimum one can reasonably conclude that inclusion of the word "final" in Article 32(2) denotes that the terms "final" and "binding" should have separate meaning. In revising the Rules, the Working Group addressed the meaning of "final and binding" only generally and decided to adopt the text of the original provision verbatim as Article 34(2) of the 2010 UNCITRAL Rules.[43] This Section seeks to clarify the meaning of the terms "final" and "binding" as they relate to the UNCITRAL arbitration process.

(1) "Final"

Finality exists when the ability of the parties to bring direct and collateral challenges against the award ceases. The specifics of finality arise in two distinct contexts. Within the internal

---

[35] See, eg, *Islamic Republic of Iran* and *United States of America* (Case No B1), Award No ITL 60-B1-FT (April 4, 1986), reprinted in 10 Iran-US CTR 207 (1986-I); *Hyatt Intl Corp*, et al, and *Government of the Islamic Republic of Iran*, et al, Award No ITL 54–134–1 (September 17, 1985), reprinted in 9 Iran-US CTR 72 (1985-II).

[36] See, eg, *Chas T Main Intl, Inc* and *Khuzestan Water & Power Authority*, et al, Award No 45–120–2 (February 8, 1985), reprinted in 11 Iran-US CTR 41 (1986-II); *Chas T Main Intl, Inc* and *Khusestan Water & Power Authority*, et al, Award No ITL 35–120–2 (March 16, 1984), reprinted in 5 Iran-US CTR 185 (1984-I); *Richard D Harza*, et al and *Islamic Republic of Iran*, et al, Award No ITL 14–97–2 (February 17, 1983), reprinted in 2 Iran-US CTR 68 (1983-I).

[37] See, eg, *International School Services, Inc* and *Islamic Republic of Iran*, et al, Award No ITL 57–123–1 (January 30, 1986), reprinted in 10 Iran-US CTR 6 (1986-I); *Burton Marks*, et al and *Islamic Republic of Iran*, Award No ITL 53–458–3 (June 26, 1985), reprinted in 8 Iran-US CTR 290 (1985-I).

[38] See, eg, *Islamic Republic of Iran* and *United States of America* (Case No A15), Award No ITL 63-A15-FT (August 20, 1986), reprinted in 12 Iran-US CTR 40 (1986-III); *Computer Sciences Corp* and *Government of the Islamic Republic of Iran*, et al, Award No ITL 49–65–1 (April 18, 1985), reprinted in 8 Iran-US CTR 99 (1985-I).

[39] Circulation of the Working Group discussions on this provision were recorded in document with restricted circulation, UN Doc A/CN.9/IX/C.2/CRP.24 & CRP.29.

[40] Draft Article 26(1) of the Preliminary Draft and Draft Article 27(2) of the Revised Draft provide that "[t]he award shall be binding upon the parties."

[41] UNCITRAL, 9th Session, UN Doc A/CN.9/9/C.2/SR.10, n 10, at 9, para 77 (Comment by Mr Holtzmann, United States).

[42] There were no recorded objections to the US proposal. See *Summary Record of the 151st Meeting of the UNCITRAL*, 8th Session, UN Doc A/CN.9/SR.166, at 190 (1975) (Comment by the Chairman).

[43] The Working Group recognized the basic role these two concepts play in relation to both the internal and external processes that regulate arbitration:

The "final and binding" character of the award should be envisaged at three levels: in respect of the arbitral tribunal, which could not modify the award after it was rendered; in respect of the parties, who were bound by the findings of the award; and in respect of the courts, which were under a duty not to entertain any recourse against the award, save in the exceptional circumstances that justified the setting aside of the award.

UNCITRAL, 41st Session, UN Doc A/CN.9/641, n 4, at 17, para 81.

process of arbitration, an award is final when it is no longer capable of revision by the arbitral tribunal.[44] With respect to the external regulation of the arbitral process, such as under national arbitration regimes, finality typically results when the arbitral award is no longer susceptible to invalidation by a reviewing court.

Within the process of arbitration under the UNCITRAL Rules, finality attaches when the arbitral tribunal's decision becomes irrevocable. A strong indication of finality is that all the technical requirements for making an award have been satisfied, ie, the award is made in writing by a majority of the tribunal's members; includes reasons, unless otherwise agreed, and the date and place where the award was made; and is signed by at least two of the three arbitrators.[45] Upon satisfaction of these requirements, the tribunal's decision is locked in and the opportunity for further modification no longer exists.[46] Practically speaking, at this point in time the award is all but final. However, most agree that the parties are entitled to know the terms of the award before permanently losing their right to influence the arbitral tribunal. Principles of fairness therefore dictate that an award is not final under the Rules until its transmission to the parties pursuant to Article 34(6).[47]

The significance of satisfying all technical requirements is that the award is then final in the sense that the Rules themselves provide no mechanism to appeal or take recourse against an award on the merits, either before the presiding tribunal or a second-tier tribunal.[48] This fact has been confirmed frequently at the Iran–US Claims Tribunal, where Iran, when unhappy with the outcome of a case, has requested revision of the award in its favor. In most instances, Iran has sought to reopen a case by requesting correction, interpretation, or amendment of the award, pursuant to Articles 35, 36, and 37 of the 1983 Tribunal Rules, respectively, or by invoking a tribunal's inherent limited power of revision. In virtually every case, however, Iran's request has been rejected because it not only fell outside the limited scope of the Rules or the Tribunal's inherent revision power, but also because it violated the rule of finality contained in Article 32(2) of the 1983 Tribunal Rules.[49]

While the rule of finality in Article 34(2) of the 2010 UNCITRAL Rules does not expressly distinguish between the various types of award, eg, final or partial awards in practice, the effect of finality for different types of awards may vary.[50] To be sure, a final award, in the sense that it is the last award to be rendered by the tribunal, is definitive not only because it disposes of all of the parties' claims, but also because it terminates the tribunal's mandate under many national arbitration laws.[51] What are sometimes called "partial awards"

---

[44] This is more apparent from the French version of original Article 32(2), a translation of which provides that the award "is not susceptible to appeal before an arbitral authority" ("Elle n'est pas susceptible d'appel devant une instance arbitrale").

[45] See Articles 33(2), 34(3), and 34(4), respectively, of the UNCITRAL Rules.

[46] Theoretically, the voting majority could still fine tune the text of a signed award (and re-sign it if necessary), so long as any dissenting arbitrator had an opportunity to address the substance of any changes in tribunal deliberations.

[47] For a discussion on transmission of the award, see section 2(B)(7).

[48] See *CME Czech Republic BV* (1976 Rules), reprinted in section 2(C)(2).

[49] For a more detailed discussion of this subject, see Chapter 26 on post-award proceedings. See also *CME Czech Republic BV* (1976 Rules), reprinted in section 2(C)(2).

[50] For a detailed discussion on the *res judicata* effect on various types of awards, see E Jaramillo, "The Relationship Between Interim and Final Awards – Res Judicata Concerns" in A van den Berg (ed) *Arbitration Advocacy in Changing Times* (2011) 15 ICCA Congress Series 231.

[51] See, eg, Article 32 of the Model Law, as amended ("The arbitral proceedings are terminated by the final award..."); see also H Holtzmann and J Neuhaus, *A Guide to the UNCITRAL Model Law*, n16, 868; N Blackaby and C Partasides, *Redfern and Hunter on International Arbitration*, n 19, 514–15.

also possess finality in that they resolve discrete claims or issues, though they do so without severing the tribunal's powers over the dispute submitted to it. The Iran–US Claims Tribunal, for example, has consistently ruled that "partial awards" were final and could not be reopened.[52] The *Methanex* Tribunal, constituted pursuant to NAFTA Chapter Eleven, reached the same conclusion with respect to a previously rendered partial award.[53]

In contrast, interim awards on interim measures of relief are made in response to a set of contemporaneous circumstances, and while such rulings may not be revisited, they may be replaced by subsequent interim awards issued in response to a new request for interim measures made on the basis of changed circumstances.[54]

With respect to the external rules that govern the UNCITRAL arbitration process, finality means more broadly that the award is no longer capable of being overturned under the national arbitration law. In most jurisdictions, an arbitral party is entitled to challenge the award in "set aside" proceedings.[55] The most common grounds for setting aside an award are that the arbitration agreement was invalid; a party received improper notice of an arbitrator's appointment or was unable to present its case fully; the award exceeded the scope of the arbitral mandate; the tribunal was improperly composed; or the dispute was not arbitrable under the public policy of the forum state.[56] If a party's set aside action prevails, the award is rendered invalid and, in some cases, the arbitral proceedings must start anew.[57] An award therefore may not be "final" under the national arbitration law until the exhaustion of all available judicial recourse or the expiration of the statute of limitations for such challenges.[58] This broader sense of finality arises in the national law, while the narrower sense of "finality" arises within the arbitration by virtue of the Rules.

During discussions to revise the Rules, some Working Group delegations argued that the word "final" was subject to various meanings and thus should be clarified.[59] Others maintained that the word "final" did not accurately characterize an award on interim measures, which could be modified, suspended, or terminated under Article 26 of the Rules.[60] Although various proposals were made to address these concerns,[61] no revisions to the

---

[52] In some cases, the Iran–US Claims Tribunal stated in a partial award that it retained jurisdiction over the parties' remaining claims. See case extracts, reprinted in section 2(D)(1).

[53] See *Methanex Corp* (1976 Rules), reprinted in section 2(C)(2).

[54] For discussion of interim measures, see Chapter 17.

[55] See P Sanders, "Commentary on UNCITRAL Arbitration Rules," n 9, 209; G Born, *International Commercial Arbitration: Commentary and Materials* (2001) 497–8.

[56] See Article 34 of the Model Law, as amended. In less typical cases, the national law may permit a local court to undertake a more extensive review of the legal and factual conclusion contained in the arbitral award.

[57] Article 34(4) of the Model law, as amended, in contrast, empowers a reviewing court that sets aside the award to remit the case back to the arbitral tribunal in order to give the arbitrators "an opportunity to resume the arbitral proceedings or to take such other action as in the arbitral tribunal's opinion will eliminate the grounds for setting aside."

[58] Article 1(2)(d) of the 1927 Geneva Convention defined an award as "final in the country in which it has been made, in that it will not be considered as such if it is open to *opposition, appel* or *pourvoi en cassation* (in the countries where such forms of procedure exist) or if it is proved that any proceedings for the purpose of contesting the validity of the award are pending." As discussed below, the Geneva Convention's approach to determining enforceability based on finality has been superseded by that of the 1958 New York Convention, which links enforceability to whether the award is "binding."

[59] The Working Group considered the following possible meanings of the term "final": "that the award finally disposed of some, but not all, claims, that the award terminated the proceedings, or that the arbitral tribunal was no longer entitled to revise it." UNCITRAL, 43rd Session, UN Doc A/CN.9/684, n 4, at 16–17, para 67.

[60] UNCITRAL, 41st Session, UN Doc A/CN.9/641, n 4, at 17, para 82.

[61] UNCITRAL, 43rd Session, UN Doc A/CN.9/684, n 4, at 19–20, para 82–83. The text of one proposal provided: "An award shall be made in writing and shall be binding on the parties. Once rendered, an award shall

original rule were made, in large part, out of concerns that omitting or modifying the oft-used phrase "final and binding" might confuse users of the Rules.[62]

(2) "Binding"

The notion that an award is "binding," as opposed to "final," relates to the legal force of an award that obliges the parties to execute its terms domestically or internationally. Whether an award is binding is of particular importance with respect to the enforcement of the award in a foreign jurisdiction.[63] Under the 1927 Geneva Convention, since superseded by the 1958 New York Convention, an award was "final" and thus enforceable abroad when all available post-award judicial proceedings were exhausted.[64] This requirement, however, gave rise to the cumbersome system of "double *exequatur*," whereby a winning party was often required to move successfully to enforce the award in the awarding jurisdiction and then again in the foreign jurisdiction.[65] Thus, as a prerequisite, the New York Convention requires that the award be "binding,"[66] instead of "final," in order to clarify that "no leave for enforcement from the court of the country in which the award was made was needed."[67] An award therefore can be enforceable under the New York Convention *before* all challenges to the award have been resolved in the awarding jurisdiction.

The criteria for a "binding" award are often determined by the arbitration law of the awarding jurisdiction, which may set forth specific temporal or procedural requirements.[68] As to temporal requirements, the Commission's negotiations on the Model Law illustrate the wide divergence in state practice as to when an award binds the parties. The Commission entertained three different proposed dates: the date when the tribunal makes the

---

not be susceptible to revision by the arbitral tribunal, except as provided in Article 26(6) for interim measures rendered in the form of an award, article 35 and article 36." UNCITRAL, UN Doc A/CN.9/WG.II/WP.149, n 14, at 14–15, para 53.

[62] UNCITRAL, 43rd Session, UN Doc A/CN.9/684, n 4, at 17, para 68; UNCITRAL, 41st Session, UN Doc A/CN.9/641, n 4, at 17, para 82.

[63] Note also that the law of the awarding jurisdiction may contain procedural conditions, such as filing or registration of the award, which must be satisfied before an award becomes "binding."

[64] Article 1(2)(d) of the Geneva Convention. See n 58 for the full text of the provision. Note that Article 2(g) of the Inter-American Convention on Extraterritorial Validity of Foreign Judgments and Arbitral Awards similarly provides that awards are enforceable if "[t]hey are final or, where appropriate have the force of *res judicata* in the State in which they were rendered."

[65] As Professor van den Berg explains, "[S]ince according to Article 4(2) of the Geneva Convention the party seeking enforcement of the award had the burden of proving that the award had become final in the country in which it was made, in practice it meant that he could prove this only by submitting a leave for enforcement (exequatur or the like) issued by the court of the latter country. As an exequatur was also required in the country where the enforcement was sought, this amounted to the system of the so-called 'double exequatur.'" A van den Berg, *The New York Arbitration Convention of 1958: Towards a Uniform Judicial Interpretation* (1981) 333. The term "*exequatur*" refers to court-granted leave to enforce an arbitral award.

[66] See Articles III and VI(1)(e) of the New York Convention.

[67] See A van den Berg, *The New York Arbitration Convention of 1958*, n 65, 336.

[68] The meaning of "binding" as used in the New York Convention is a matter of some debate. The Convention itself offers no guidance in this regard. The prevailing approach is for a court reviewing a foreign arbitral award to determine the binding character of the award by reference to the arbitration law under which the award was made. See A Van den Berg, *The New York Arbitration Convention of 1958*, n 65, 339–41; H Holtzmann and J Neuhaus, *A Guide to the UNCITRAL Model Law*, n 16, 1010; see also E Gaillard and J Savage, *Fouchard, Gaillard, Goldman on International Commercial Arbitration*, n 19, 975–6 (citing the practice of French, Swiss and Italian tribunals); M Rubino-Sammartano, *International Arbitration Law and Practice* (2001) 791. Another position is that the term "binding" is subject to an autonomous interpretation to be undertaken without regard to the law of the awarding jurisdiction. See E Gaillard and J Savage, *Fouchard, Gaillard, Goldman on International Commercial Arbitration*, n 19, 975 (citing the practice of Italian, Swedish, Dutch, and Belgian tribunals).

award, the date when the parties receive the award,[69] and the date when the period for setting aside the award expires.[70] Unable to reach consensus, the Commission was forced to defer the matter for resolution by the courts of the jurisdiction where the award is made.[71] Consequently, seeking enforcement of an award under the New York Convention requires careful consideration of the meaning of the term "binding" under the arbitration law of the awarding jurisdiction.

The statement that the award is "binding on the parties" has an obvious connection to the exhortation on the parties "to carry out the award without delay."[72] As some Committee negotiators maintained, the latter is simply a restatement of the former and thus need not be included in the text of the Rules on grounds of redundancy.[73] Other delegates, however, were in favor of a provision that introduced an express note of urgency ("without delay") with respect to the execution of the award.[74] The Working Group that revised the Rules considered, but did not reach a conclusion, with respect to the meaning of the term "binding," particularly whether it refers to the obligation on the parties to comply with the award.[75]

In addition to obliging compliance with the terms of the award, Article 34(2) arguably imposes a separate duty on the arbitral tribunal to ensure that any award rendered is valid and enforceable. Although the UNCITRAL Rules contain no express provision to this effect,[76] the rule that the award is "final and binding on the parties" arguably requires that the arbitrators apply their best efforts to produce a valid and enforceable award. The scope of the arbitrators' duty will depend on the specific circumstances of the arbitration. At a minimum, however, this duty would encompass the making of an award that is legally effective in the awarding jurisdiction and in any foreign jurisdiction where a party most likely would seek additional enforcement.

(b) Waiver of recourse against the award—optional provision

The Working Group that revised the UNCITRAL Rules considered, but could not agree on, adding a new provision for waiver of recourse against the award in Article 34. Instead, it settled for including an optional provision in the annex to the Rules. If the parties agree to incorporate the optional provision into their arbitration agreement, they waive their rights to "any form of recourse" against the arbitral award "insofar as such waiver can validly

---

[69] A further distinction was made between the date of receipt of the party against whom the award was invoked or the last party to receive notification. See H Holtzmann and J Neuhaus, *A Guide to the UNCITRAL Model Law*, n 16, 842.

[70] H Holtzmann and J Neuhaus, *A Guide to the UNCITRAL Model Law*, n 16, 842.

[71] H Holtzmann and J Neuhaus, *A Guide to the UNCITRAL Model Law*, n 16, 843.

[72] Indeed, a distinguishing aspect of arbitration is that the compliance with an award of the tribunal is mandatory. See N Blackaby and C Partasides, *Redfern and Hunter on International Arbitration*, n 19, 32–3.

[73] See *Summary Record of the 17th Meeting of the Committee of the Whole (II)*, UNCITRAL, 9th Session, UN Doc A/CN.9/9/C.2/SR.17 at 3, paras 12–14 (1976) (Comments by Mr Jenard, Belgium, Mr Guevara, Philippines, and Mr Mantilla-Molina, Mexico).

[74] UNCITRAL, 9th Session, UN Doc A/CN.9/9/C.2/SR.17, n 73, at 4, para 16 (Comments by Mr Boston, Sierra Leone); para 15 (Comment by Mr Guest, United Kingdom) (noting the importance in determining the date from which interest was payable on the amount of the award); para 17 (Comment by Mr Roehrich, France).

[75] *Settlement of Commercial Disputes: Revision of the UNCITRAL Arbitration Rules, Note by the Secretariat*, UNCITRAL, UN Doc A/CN.9/WG.II/WP.151/Add.1 at 12, para 24 (2008); UNCITRAL, UN Doc A/CN.9/WG.II/WP.149, n 14, at 14–15, para 53.

[76] In contrast, Rule 41 of the 2012 ICC Arbitration Rules requires that the arbitral tribunal "make every effort to make sure that the Award is enforceable at law."

be made under the applicable law." The Working Group's recommendation was based on similar provisions that appear in the procedural rules of some of the leading arbitral institutions.[77]

In seeking to create a new rule, the Working Group agreed on a general approach of apportioning the parties' waiver of recourse. On the one hand, a waiver *should* prevent the parties from exercising any rights they have "to appeal against the award or to use any other recourse to courts on the merits of the case or on any point of fact or law."[78] On the other hand, it *should not* extend to grounds for non-recognition of awards[79] nor to traditional grounds for setting aside an award, such as those contained in Article 34 of the UNCITRAL Model Law.[80] These include: incapacity of a party to the arbitration agreement, invalidity of the arbitral agreement, improper notice of an arbitrator's appointment or of the proceedings, a party's inability to present its case, the arbitral tribunal's lack of jurisdiction, improper constitution of the arbitral tribunal, non-arbitrability of the dispute, or conflict between the award and public policy. The *travaux préparatoires* indicate the Working Group's intent to ensure, even if a waiver of set-aside rights were possible under domestic law, that the Rules themselves "should not result in such waiver being given automatically or merely (and possibly inadvertently) through the submission of a dispute to the Rules."[81]

Despite general agreement on the approach to delineating a waiver of recourse, drafting a new rule proved to be difficult. An early version of the rule proposed that a waiver cover any form of "appeal, review, or recourse" against an award, while excluding applications for "setting aside the award."[82] Many Working Group delegates expressed concern, however, that these terms could be subject to various meanings in different legal systems.[83] In some jurisdictions, for example, the term "setting aside" encompassed a challenge of an award on the merits.[84] The terms "appeal" and "review," it was also noted, varied in meaning under different national laws and, further, might be too specific to cover a sufficiently broad category of possible recourse.[85]

---

[77] Article 26.9 of the 1998 LCIA Rules provides that "the parties also waive irrevocably their right to any form of appeal, review or recourse to any State court or other judicial authority, insofar as such waiver may be validly made"; Article 34(6) of the 2012 ICC Rules states that "the parties undertake to carry out any Award without delay and shall be deemed to have waived their right to any form of recourse insofar as such waiver can validly be made." See J Castello, "UNCITRAL Rules," n 15, 1513.

[78] UNCITRAL, 41st Session, UN Doc A/CN.9/641, n 4, at 18, para 86.

[79] J Castello, "UNCITRAL Rules," n 15, 1513.

[80] It was widely agreed that any new rule "should preserve the parties' rights as set forth under Article 34 of the UNCITRAL Model Law." UNCITRAL, 41st Session, UN Doc A/CN.9/641, n 4, at 18, para 87. It should be noted, however, that some Working Group delegations believed even a party's right to seek to set aside an award should be waivable. Para 87.

[81] UNCITRAL, 41st Session, UN Doc A/CN.9/641, n 4, at 18–19, para 90.

[82] The phrase "appeal, review, or recourse" was used up until the very last discussion of the Working Group. See *Settlement of Commercial Disputes: Revision of the UNCITRAL Arbitration Rules, Note by the Secretariat*, UNCITRAL, UN Doc A/CN.9/WG.II/WP.145/Add.1 at 15–16, (2006) (Draft Article 32). Various formulations for excluding set-aside actions were explored. See UNCITRAL, UN Doc A/CN.9/WG.II/WP.149, n 14, at 13–14, para 51 (Draft Article 32(2))("save for their right to apply for setting aside an award, which may be waived only if the parties so agree"); UNCITRAL, UN Doc A/CN.9/WG.II/WP.151/Add.1, n 75, at 12–13, para 23 (Article 32(2)) ("The right to apply for setting aside an award may be waived only if the parties expressly agree."); *Settlement of Commercial Disputes: Revision of the UNCITRAL Arbitration Rules, Note by the Secretariat*, UNCITRAL, UN Doc A/CN.9/WG.II/WP.157/Add.2 at 3, para 5 (2009) (Draft Article 34(2)) ("except for an application for setting aside an award").

[83] UNCITRAL, 43rd Session, UN Doc A/CN.9/684, n 4, at 19–21, paras 79, 82.

[84] UNCITRAL, 43rd Session, UN Doc A/CN.9/684, n 4, at 19–21, para 79.

[85] UNCITRAL, 43rd Session, UN Doc A/CN.9/684, n 4, at 20, para 83; UNCITRAL, 41st Session, UN Doc A/CN.9/641, n 4, at 18, para 88.

While the term "recourse" appeared to be more palatable to the Working Group, its broader meaning warranted clarification. According to the *travaux préparatoires*, the Working Group agreed that the use of the term "recourse" should not bar a party from resisting enforcement of an award, such as pursuant to Article V of the New York Convention or Article 36 of the Model Law.[86] Nor should the term be understood as preventing a party from resisting execution of the award, such as on the basis of sovereign immunity.[87] Still, concerns about the vagaries of the term "recourse" lingered. Some delegations also believed its inclusion in the Rules would be inconsistent with its use in Article 34 of the Model Law, which refers to set aside as the "exclusive recourse" against an award.[88]

The Working Group's struggle with terminology also led it to abandon an express carve out for set-aside actions in favor of a more generalized and flexible approach. Under the optional provision, the parties can waive rights of recourse against the award "insofar as such waiver can validly be made under the applicable law."[89] This approach may produce results of varying consistency with the UNCITRAL drafters' original aim of allowing waiver of appeals on the merits, but not traditional set-aside actions. Under UK law, for example, appeals on points of law are possible, but waivable, whereas actions based on violations of due process or the competency of the arbitral tribunal are mandatory.[90] In other jurisdictions, however, the parties may not be barred from waiving their set-aside rights. The Model Law is silent on the matter, though Sanders has argued that set-aside rights should not be waivable absent express authority under the law.[91]

With little guarantee of uniform application across the world's legal systems, it is perhaps not surprising that the rule on waiver of recourse was relegated to an annex of the Rules as an optional provision. Parties considering incorporation of the optional provision into the Rules to exclude recourse against an award are wise to heed UNCITRAL's caution that "the effectiveness and conditions of such an exclusion depend on the applicable law."[92] It thus behoves them to carefully study the governing arbitration law in relation to the text of the optional provision to determine which rights of recourse can and cannot be waived and whether the rights the parties wish to waive—and only those rights—will be waived by application of the optional provision.[93] It may in fact be the case in many jurisdictions that

---

[86] UNCITRAL, 43rd Session, UN Doc A/CN.9/684, n 4, at 18, para 73.

[87] UNCITRAL, 43rd Session, UN Doc A/CN.9/684, n 4, at 18, para 74.

[88] UNCITRAL, 41st Session, UN Doc A/CN.9/641, n 4, at 18, para 89.

[89] Another version of the approach proposed limiting a waiver to any recourse "that may be waived and the waiver of which does not require express agreement." UNCITRAL, 43rd Session, UN Doc A/CN.9/684, n 4, at 20, para 84. Yet another proposal was to exclude expressly jurisdictional challenges from the scope of the waiver. Para 79.

[90] Compare Section 69 with Sections 67 and 68 of the UK Arbitration Act, see discussion in Turner and Mohtashami, *A Guide to the LCIA Arbitration Rules* (2009) 191. Compare French Code of Civil Procedure – Arbitration Article 1482 which allows parties to waive appeals, and Article 1484 which retains the ability to set aside on specific grounds despite a waiver under Article 1482, see E Gaillard and J Savage, *Fouchard, Gaillard, Goldman on International Commercial Arbitration*, n 19, Annex I, 8–9. Under US law, it is unclear whether the US Supreme Court's disfavor towards allowing the parties in domestic cases to contractually modify provisions for the recognition and enforcement of arbitral awards would extend to international cases, see G Born, *International Commercial Arbitration*, n 55, 2736.

[91] P Sanders, "Unity and Diversity in the Adoption of the Model Law," (1995) 11(1) Arb Intl 23 (arguing that the parties' right to exclude set-aside rights must be expressly provided for by law, lest a waiver exclude court control in violation of public policy).

[92] 2010 UNCITRAL Rules, Annex, introductory language.

[93] Note that in *Creighton v Qatar*, the French Cour de Cassation ruled that a waiver under the ICC Arbitration Rules waived Qatar's immunity from execution in France. Cour de Cassation, Appeal No A98019.068

a waiver is not necessary because the governing arbitration law already strikes the appropriate balance.

(3) Written award and designation of the date and place of the award's making—Article 34(2) and (4)

The UNCITRAL Rules require that: the award must be in writing and must include the date on which the award was made and indicate the place of arbitration. The requirement of a written award contained in Article 34(2) is an obvious necessity. No doubt the arbitrators will express the terms of the award and their underlying reasoning more clearly and precisely in written form, especially where the dispute involves complex issues. Likewise, the parties will better understand their rights and obligations under the award when they are memorialized in a written product. Moreover, a written award is a common prerequisite for enforcement of the award in court proceedings, where it serves as the primary record of the arbitral proceedings.[94] Because of the obvious practical need for a written award, there was little discussion of this during negotiation of the 1976 UNCITRAL Rules. Article 34(2) incorporates the text of Article 32(2) of the 1976 UNCITRAL Rules without modification.

Article 34(4), which is virtually identical to Article 32(4) of the 1976 UNCITRAL Rules,[95] requires that the date and place of the award appear in the text of the award as these are "matters of great importance for the enforcement of the award."[96] In some jurisdictions, the limitations period for filing or registration of the award or for challenge of the award runs from the date of the award.[97] As discussed above, the "binding" effect of an award, that is, whether an award is enforceable domestically or internationally, also may be determined by the date of the award in some jurisdictions.[98] The significance of the place of arbitration is discussed in detail in Chapter 2.[99] Suffice it to say here that inclusion in the award of the place where the award was made, for example, London, Paris, New York, etc, is an important indicator that the arbitral proceedings were "conducted in conformity with the mandatory rules of the law applicable at the place of arbitration" and that the award was "made at the place of arbitration" in accordance with Article 16(4) of the 1976 UNCITRAL Rules, now Article 18(4) of the 2010 UNCITRAL Rules.[100]

(Hearing on July 6, 2000), reproduced in English in (October 2000) 15(10) Mealey's Intl Arb Rep(s) A-1. In *Creighton*, the court interpreted the meaning of the Government of Qatar's agreement to Article 24 of the 1975 ICC Arbitration Rules, which provided in relevant part: "By submitting the dispute to arbitration by the International Chamber of Commerce, the parties shall be deemed to have undertaken to carry out the resulting award without delay and to have waived their right to any form of appeal insofar as such waiver can validly be made." The court ruled that by consenting to Article 24 of the ICC Rules, Qatar waived its right of sovereign immunity from jurisdiction and enforcement. For further discussion of *Creighton*, see Y Derains and E Schwartz, *A Guide to the New ICC Rules of Arbitration* (2nd edn 2005) 321.

[94] See Article IV(1)(a) of the New York Convention, which requires a "duly authenticated original award or a duly certified copy thereof" for recognition or enforcement of the award.

[95] The minor revisions that were made are discussed in section 2(B)(9).

[96] The requirements of Article 32(4) of the 1976 UNCITRAL Rules were a late addition to the Rules, but drew little objection. For comments in support of the provision, see *Summary Record of the 11th Meeting of the Committee of the Whole (II)*, UNCITRAL, 9th Session, UN Doc A/CN.9/9/C.2/SR.11 at 5, paras 28, 30–33, 35, 36 (1976). The only notable objection was that the question of the place of the award had already been addressed in Article 16(4) of the 1976 Rules. Para 34.

[97] *Report of the Secretary-General on the Revised Draft Set of Arbitration Rules*, UNCITRAL, 9th Session, Addendum 1 (Commentary), UN Doc A/CN.9/112/Add.1 (1975), reprinted in (1976) VII UNCITRAL Ybk 166, 178 (Commentary on Draft Article 27(4)).

[98] See section 2(B)(2). Note, however, that this is not the rule in every jurisdiction.

[99] See Chapter 2, section 4.

[100] UNCITRAL, 9th Session, Addendum 1 (Commentary), UN Doc A/CN.9/112/Add.1, n 97.

The arbitral tribunal is free to include information regarding the date and place of the award in any manner it chooses. It has been the practice of the Iran–US Claims Tribunal to include the words "Dated, The Hague" followed by the date of the award immediately before the signatures of the arbitrators. For examples of how awards may be formatted from the practice of international tribunals, see below sections 2(C)(2), 2(D)(2) and 2(D)(3).

(4) Obligation to sign and failure to sign the award—Article 34(4)

The first sentence of Article 34(4) provides that the award "shall be signed by the arbitrators." This requirement applies regardless of how many arbitrators comprise its membership. The second sentence provides that "[w]here there is more than one arbitrator and any one of them fails to sign, the award shall state the reason for the absence of the signature." The two sentences do not function as rule and exception. The use of the word "shall" in the first sentence clearly imposes on all members of the arbitral tribunal a mandatory obligation to sign the award. In fact, failure to sign the award, where signing is possible, arguably constitutes a breach of the arbitrator's duties.[101] The second sentence accordingly acts as a contingency plan, creating a mechanism for the two signing arbitrators to indicate the circumstances for the third arbitrator's failure to sign. The statement of reasons will be of particular interest to a reviewing court in understanding the circumstances surrounding the absence of a signature, particularly in a jurisdiction where the arbitration law requires that the award contain the signatures of all the arbitrators.

For examples of signature blocks from the practice of investment and other tribunals, see section 2(C)(3).[102]

(a) General comments on the *travaux préparatoires*

Article 34(4) is virtually identical to Article 32(4) of the 1976 Rules. The original *travaux préparatoires* thus remain relevant and instructive with respect to the revised rule. The requirement that all arbitrators sign the award remained unchanged throughout the Committee's negotiations and provoked no significant discussion among the delegates. Indeed, it was widely agreed that "in order to make clear that all the arbitrators participated in the arbitral proceedings and in the making of the award," they must sign the award.[103] The real controversy concerned portions of the draft text that ultimately were not adopted by the Commission.

The Preliminary Draft contained the following provision under the heading "Form and Effect of the Award":

> The award shall be signed by the arbitrators. Where there are three arbitrators, the failure of one arbitrator to sign the award *shall not impair the enforceability of the award*. The award shall state the reason for the absence of an arbitrator's signature, *but shall not include any dissenting opinion*.[104]

The first and second sentences of the draft text were modified and regrouped under Article 32(4) of the 1976 UNCITRAL Rules. The third sentence, with modifications, became

---

[101] See "Preventing Delay and Disruption in Arbitration," in A van den Berg (ed), ICCA Congress Series No 5 (1991) 317.
[102] See *Karaha Bodas Co LLC* (1976 Rules) and *SD Myers, Inc* (1976 Rules); both reprinted in section 2(C)(3).
[103] UNCITRAL, 9th Session, Addendum 1 (Commentary), UN Doc A/CN.9/112/Add.1, n 97. In effect, the arbitrators sign the award as a notary. UN Doc A/CN.9/SR.166, n 42, at 188 (Comment by the Chairman).
[104] *Report of the Secretary-General on the Preliminary Draft Set of Arbitration Rules*, UNCITRAL, 8th Session, UN Doc A/CN.9/97 (1974), reprinted in (1975) VI UNCITRAL Ybk 163, 177 (emphasis added).

Article 32(3) of the 1976 UNCITRAL Rules. The two highlighted portions of the above draft text sparked a heated debate among Committee negotiators.

A number of negotiators strongly objected to the phrase "shall not impair the enforceability of the award." The representative of Belgium pointed out that in some jurisdictions an award only became enforceable by court order pursuant to the national arbitration law.[105] The representative of the Federal Republic of Germany stressed that the national arbitration laws in some countries required all three arbitrators to sign the award before it became valid.[106] Minor revisions to the sentence in the Revised Draft (the word "validity" replaced the word "enforceability") did not appease the opposition.[107] The representative of the Federal Republic of Germany proposed that the text be deleted for fear that it would "mislead the parties into thinking that an award signed by at least two arbitrators would be valid in all cases irrespective of the requirements of the national laws applicable."[108]

The representative of the United Kingdom interpreted the phrase quite differently. He argued for retaining the text because, if removed, the Rules would imply that the failure of all three arbitrators to sign the award invalidated the award unless the national arbitration law expressly provided otherwise.[109] While the UK proposal persuaded a number of negotiators,[110] at the end of the day, the German proposal prevailed and the controversial text was removed.[111] The commentary to the Revised Draft explains the rationale for the decision: "[I]n some jurisdictions the applicable arbitration law may require that an arbitral award be signed by all the arbitrators before it becomes valid and enforceable; in such a case the applicable national law would prevail over the provision."[112] Accordingly, the Commission decided that the Rules "should be silent on this point."[113]

Several negotiators also took issue with the last clause in the final sentence of the initial text: "but shall not include any dissenting opinion."[114] This language ignited a general debate over the use of dissenting opinions in UNCITRAL arbitration, which is described in detail in section 5.[115] The apparent connection (at least grammatically) between the text

---

[105] See UN Doc A/CN.9/SR.166, n 42, at 190 (Comment by Mr Jenard, Belgium) and Comment by the Chairman noting that "in many cases an award was made enforceable through an act by the appropriate authority".

[106] UN Doc A/CN.9/SR.166, at 189 (Comment by Mr Pirrung, Federal Republic of Germany). The representative of Austria reiterated this point in later discussions. See UNCITRAL, 9th Session, UN Doc A/CN.9/9/C.2/SR.11, n 96, at 5, para 27 (Comment by Mr Melis, Austria).

[107] The proposal, see *Report of the UNCITRAL*, 8th Session, Summary of Discussion of the Preliminary Draft, UN Doc A/10017, para 180 (1975), reprinted in (1975) VI UNCITRAL Ybk 24, 41, was incorporated into Draft Article 27(4) of the Revised Draft.

[108] See UNCITRAL, 9th Session, UN Doc A/CN.9/9/C.2/SR.11, n 96, at 5, para 29. The US representative agreed, stating that "the language of the second sentence was more appropriate to a convention than to a private agreement between two parties and felt that it would be more satisfactory if the commentary accompanying the Rules were to point out the need to take account of national legislation." 5, para 30. The Belgian representative concurred. 6, para 32.

[109] See UNCITRAL, 9th Session, UN Doc A/CN.9/9/C.2/SR.11, n 96, at 6, para 33.

[110] The representatives from the United States and Japan concurred. See UNCITRAL, 9th Session, UN Doc A/CN.9/9/C.2/SR.11, n 96, at 6, paras 37–38.

[111] UNCITRAL, 9th Session, UN Doc A/CN.9/9/C.2/SR.11, n 96, at 6, para 40. An additional proposal by the German representative to specify that all three arbitrators must sign the award was not adopted, however. See 5, para 28 (Comment by Mr Pirrung, Federal Republic of Germany).

[112] UNCITRAL, 9th Session, Addendum 1 (Commentary), UN Doc A/CN.9/112/Add.1, n 97.

[113] *Report of the UNCITRAL on the Work of its Ninth Session*, UN GAOR, 31st Session, Supp No 17, UN Doc A/31/17, para 165 (1976), reprinted in (1976) VII UNCITRAL Ybk 66, 78.

[114] *Report of the Secretary-General on the Preliminary Draft Set of Arbitration Rules*, UNCITRAL, 8th Session, UN Doc A/CN.9/97 (1974), reprinted in (1975) VI UNCITRAL Ybk 163, 177.

[115] See section 2(B)(5).

and the requirement to explain an absent signature also raised questions regarding the proper motivation for not signing the award. As the Chairman pointed out in discussions, dissenting from and failing to sign the award are concepts that need not be linked; the arbitrator signed the award in essence as a notary and his dissent from the terms of the award did not require him to refuse to sign.[116] In addition, various other reasons existed for an arbitrator's failure to sign, such as his illness, death, or other unavoidable absence from the place of arbitration.[117] The Polish delegate was also critical, observing astutely that the draft text appeared to leave a dissenting arbitrator no choice but to refrain from signing the award, since he or she could not express disagreement in the form of a dissenting opinion.[118] Ultimately, the prohibition against dissenting opinions was removed from later drafts of the Rules.[119]

The *travaux préparatoires* explain the Committee's decision to uncouple the concepts of dissenting opinions and refusals to sign the award. Indeed, the commentary on the Revised Draft admonishes arbitrators against withholding their signature for divisive purposes: "where two of the three arbitrators agree on an award, the third arbitrator cannot prevent the making of the award by a refusal to sign the award."[120] Thus, even when an arbitrator disagrees with the terms of the award, he may not, by refusing to sign the award, thwart its enforcement in a jurisdiction that requires the signatures of all three arbitrators. In addition, the Report of the Committee of the Whole II states unequivocally "that all the arbitrators, including an arbitrator who dissented from the award should be required to sign the award."[121]

At the end of the day, the representative of France provided an apt summary of the Committee's position: "There was no reason for an arbitrator who disagreed with the majority decision not to sign the award; his signature would not signify his agreement with the majority decision but would simply render the award valid. If, however, an arbitrator was physically unable to sign the award, his failure to sign should not invalidate the award."[122]

The phrase "fails to sign" in the second sentence of Article 32(4) of the 1976 UNCITRAL Rules, as adopted, should not be read as weakening the above conclusions. That phrase arguably is susceptible to a broader interpretation than the phrase "cannot sign," which the representative from the Federal Republic of Germany proposed.[123] "Fails to sign" implies that an arbitrator was negligent in his duty, while "cannot sign" connotes the inability or lack of choice to perform the function. The German representative believed, quite correctly, that the latter formulation would better ensure that an arbitrator had "good

---

[116] UN Doc A/CN.9/SR.166, n 42, at 188 (Comment by the Chairman); see also UNCITRAL, 9th Session, UN Doc A/CN.9/9/C.2/SR.11, n 96, at 5, para 27 (Comment by Mr Melis, Austria: "[T]he Committee should distinguish between the two issues that had been raised, namely, whether a dissenting opinion should be attached to the award and whether a dissenting arbitrator should sign the award."); 6–7, para 41 (Comment by Mr Roehrich, France).

[117] UN Doc A/CN.9/SR.166, n 42, at 188 (Comment by the Chairman); see also UNCITRAL, 9th Session, UN Doc A/CN.9/9/C.2/SR.11, n 96, at 7, para 40 (Comment by Mr Roehrich, France: "If, however, an arbitrator was physically unable to sign the award, his failure to sign should not invalidate the award.").

[118] UN Doc A/CN.9/SR.166, n 42, at 188 (Comment by Mr Jakubowski, Poland).

[119] *Report of the Secretary-General on the Revised Draft Set of Arbitration Rules*, UNCITRAL, 9th Session, UN Doc A/CN.9/112 (1975), reprinted in (1976) VII UNCITRAL Ybk 1, 165.

[120] UNCITRAL, 9th Session, Addendum 1 (Commentary), UN Doc A/CN.9/112/Add.1, n 97 (Commentary on Draft Article 27(4)).

[121] UN GAOR, 31st Session, Supp No 17, UN Doc A/31/17, n 113, para 163.

[122] UNCITRAL, 9th Session, UN Doc A/CN.9/9/C.2/SR.11, n 96, at 6–7, para 41.

[123] UNCITRAL, 9th Session, UN Doc A/CN.9/9/C.2/SR.11, n 96, at 6–7, paras 39, 45.

reasons" for not signing and would prevent him from "simply refusing to sign for relatively insignificant reasons."[124] The Committee rejected the German proposal, but only for purposes of maintaining textual uniformity with other provisions in the Rules.[125]

(b) Practical matters regarding the statement of reasons for the absence of an arbitrator's signature

The statement of reasons for the absence of an arbitrator's signature may be of great practical value if a party seeks to challenge or enforce an award in a national court, especially in a jurisdiction favoring the signatures of all three arbitrators. With respect to the practicalities of the statement of reasons, the Rules leave several important questions unanswered: what are the appropriate contents of the statement, who should formulate it, and in what form should it be presented? A few basic guidelines on these matters are outlined below.

First, Article 34(4) requires all the arbitrators to sign the award "to make clear that [they] participated in the arbitral proceedings and in the making of the award."[126] The absence of an arbitrator's signature thus raises questions regarding the extent to which this duty has been neglected. Was the arbitrator merely unable to attend the final step of signing of the award or was his absence from the proceedings more pervasive, preventing him from participating in other phases of the arbitral process, such as the hearing or the deliberations?[127] The statement of reasons should answer these questions so a reviewing court can assess whether, under the applicable law, the arbitrator's failure to sign affects the validity of the award. Accordingly, a statement of reasons should convey the circumstances under which an arbitrator has not signed the award and his degree of involvement in other aspects of the arbitration. When drafting the statement of reasons, the signing arbitrators should adhere to the rules of confidentiality,[128] especially those governing the secrecy of the deliberations. Examples of statements of reasons for an arbitrator's failure to sign appear below in sections 2(C)(4) and 2(D)(5)(a).

Second, the arbitrators who sign the award—not the one who does not—have the duty to formulate the statement of reasons on behalf of their non-signing colleague.[129] This duty extends logically from Article 34(4), which contemplates a statement only when an arbitrator is *unable* to sign the award, not when he is *unwilling* to do so.[130] The Iran–US Claims Tribunal has seen numerous attempts by Iranian judges to turn this rule on its head. In many cases, the Iranian judges insisted on supplying their own statement of reasons for why they refused to sign an award, with the apparent aim of invalidating the award and

---

[124] UNCITRAL, 9th Session, UN Doc A/CN.9/9/C.2/SR.11, n 96, at 6–7, para 45.

[125] See UNCITRAL, 9th Session, UN Doc A/CN.9/9/C.2/SR.11, n 96, at 7, para 42 (Comment by Mr Holtzmann, United States).

[126] See also UNCITRAL, 9th Session, Addendum 1 (Commentary), UN Doc A/CN.9/112/Add.1, n 97, (Commentary on Draft Article 27(4)).

[127] On the related topic of truncated tribunals, see Chapter 6, section 2B(3)(b). See also S Schwebel, *International Arbitration: Three Salient Problems* (1987) 251–81.

[128] The rules of confidentiality are addressed in Chapter 2, section 3(B)(1)(b) on confidentiality generally, in Chapter 19, section 2(B)(2)(b) on hearings (Article 28(3)), in Chapter 23, section 2(B)(3) on deliberations, and in section 2(B)(6) of this chapter on publication of awards (Article 34(5)).

[129] UNCITRAL, 9th Session, UN Doc A/CN.9/9/C.2/SR.11, n 96, at 7, para 44 (Comment by Mr Sanders, Special Consultant); see also P Sanders, "Commentary on UNCITRAL Arbitration Rules," n 9, 208; Comments of Judge Mosk on Judge Sani's Reasons for not Signing Award No 20–1–3 (*Raygo Wagner Equipment* (1983 Tribunal Rules)) (March 3, 1983), reprinted in 1 Iran-US CTR 425 (1981–82) ("It is for the signing members to provide the reasons for the absence of Judge Sani's signature, not Judge Sani.").

[130] See section 2(B)(4)(a).

undermining the Tribunal's legitimacy.[131] This practice was not only improper under the Rules, as explained above,[132] but also inappropriately stymied the Tribunal's work. The statements of Iranian arbitrators often contained serious allegations of procedural misconduct by members of the voting majority. In order to respond in their defence, the members of the voting majority would often add a post-award statement, a practice that diverted time and energy away from other cases on the Tribunal's busy docket.[133]

Third, the statement of reasons forms part of the award and thus should reflect the endorsement of the two signing arbitrators, whether they comprise the voting majority or simply a numerical majority.[134] In some jurisdictions, for example, the failure to obtain the signatures of the two available arbitrators on the statement of reasons may expose the award to the risk of collateral challenge.[135] There is no required format for the statement of reasons, but two approaches have emerged in the practice of international tribunals. The statement may appear directly above or below the final signatures on the award (usually directly following the *dispositif*), provided the placement of the statement leaves no doubt that the final signatures apply to both the award and the statement.[136] The statement of reasons also may be separately attached to the award, so long as the statement contains a second set of signatures by the arbitrators who signed the award.[137]

(5) Statement of reasons for the award and dissenting opinions—Article 34(3)

(a) Statement of reasons for the award

Article 34(3) starts from the mandatory premise that the arbitral tribunal "shall" include reasons in the award.[138] When the Rules were drafted, this approach "reflect[ed] the law in many jurisdictions, particularly countries with a civil law system, to require that arbitral awards incorporate the reasons for the decision reached by the arbitrators."[139] It is thus not surprising that many Committee negotiators from the civil law countries supported the rule as drafted.[140] The representatives from the United Kingdom and the United States, two common law nations, were of a different view, however.[141] At the time, the prevailing

---

[131] Examples of improper statements of reasons for failure to sign submitted by the non-signing Iranian arbitrator are reprinted below, section 2(D)(5).

[132] See section 2(B)(4)(a).

[133] Extracts from post-award correspondence by American Judges Aldrich and Mosk are reprinted in section 2(D)(5)(b).

[134] See P Sanders, "Commentary on UNCITRAL Arbitration Rules," n 9, 208.

[135] This was the situation in a case before the *Hoge Raad*, which upheld a lower Dutch court's decision to invalidate an award because two arbitrators had signed the award but failed to sign a separate statement explaining the absence of the third arbitrator's signature on the award. *Hoge Raad* of January 21, 1966 NJ 1966, No 214.

[136] P Sanders, *Het Nieuwe Arbitragerecht* at 195, with reference to section 592, section 2 of the Austrian Code of Civil Procedure; K Berger, *International Economic Arbitration*, n 19, 602; see also K Rauh, *Die Schieds- und Schlichtungsordnung der UNCITRAL* (1983) 133. Note that Article 1057, s 3 of the Dutch Act requires this statement be made "beneath" the award signed by the arbitrators, and be signed by the arbitrators. See also Article 48, section 2 NAI-ArbR. For examples in the practice of arbitral tribunals, see *Republika Srpska (Boundary in Brcko Area)*; *CME Czech Republic BV* (1976 Rules), reprinted in section 2(C)(4).

[137] This has been the practice of the Iran–US Claims Tribunal. See section 2(D)(5)(a).

[138] This condition appeared consistently in all drafts of the 1976 UNCITRAL Rules. Compare Draft Article 26(1) of the Preliminary Draft ("shall contain reasons") with Draft Article 27(2) of the Revised Draft ("shall state the reasons upon which it is based").

[139] UNCITRAL, 9th Session, Addendum 1 (Commentary), UN Doc A/CN.9/112/Add.1, n 97.

[140] See UNCITRAL, 9th Session, UN Doc A/CN.9/9/C.2/SR.10, n 10, at 8, paras 65–68 (Comment by Mr Pirrung, Federal Republic of Germany, Mr Jenard, Belgium, Mr Dzikiewicz, Poland, and Mr Melis, Austria).

[141] UNCITRAL, 9th Session, UN Doc A/CN.9/9/C.2/SR.10, n 10, at 8, paras 62, 64 (Comments by Mr Guest, United Kingdom, and Mr Holtzmann, United States).

practice in those countries did not require a statement of reasons in the award; a tribunal's reasons typically were stated separately in an attachment that did not form part of the award or were not stated at all.[142] Consequently, the British representative proposed that the rule be made permissive rather than mandatory ("may" instead of "shall"), leaving the arbitrators "free to incorporate the reasons in the award or to state them separately, depending on the traditions in their country."[143] The British proposal did not prevail ultimately,[144] but prompted discussions that led the Commission to alter the rule to accommodate other practices.

Every draft of the original rule had contained a narrow exception to stating the reasons for the award when "both parties have expressly agreed that no reasons are to be given."[145] Some negotiators doubted the necessity of such an exception given that the parties could modify any rule pursuant to Article 1 of the Rules.[146] There appeared, however, to be consensus on the point that "[r]ules that are destined for world-wide use, like the UNCITRAL Arbitration Rules, must contain the possibility of an exception to the general principle that reasons should be given."[147] The exception, particularly the word "expressly" became a focal point for compromise between the civil law and common law positions.

To alleviate the concerns of the common law negotiators, the Commission adopted a proposal to broaden the exception by omitting the word "expressly" from its text.[148] According to the *travaux préparatoires*, the deletion permits the parties to agree not to include reasons in the award either expressly in writing or "by implication," for example, when the parties have "selected as the place of arbitration a country under whose national law reasons were not generally given in arbitral awards."[149] If the parties wish that the award contain reasons, but if the arbitration is in a "no-reasons" jurisdiction, then they may wish

---

[142] UNCITRAL, 9th Session, UN Doc A/CN.9/9/C.2/SR.10, n 10, at 8, paras 62, 64. See also P Sanders, "Commentary on UNCITRAL Arbitration Rules," n 9, 209 (describing the "Anglo-Saxon system of arbitration under which, as a rule, no reasons need be given.").

[143] See UNCITRAL, 9th Session, UN Doc A/CN.9/9/C.2/SR.10, n 10, at 8, para 62 (Comment by Mr Guest, United Kingdom, proposing that the arbitrators "may" state the reasons in the award). The United States supported the proposal. Para 64.

[144] This is clear from the final text of Article 32(3) of the 1976 UNCITRAL Rules. It appears, however, that the proposal was seriously considered. See UN GAOR, 31st Session, Supp No 17, UN Doc A/31/17, n 113, para 157 ("The Committee decided to restructure [the provision] to the effect that arbitrators would not be required to include in the award itself the reasons upon which it was based, but could elect to give reasons in a statement accompanying, but not forming part of, the award."). Concerns regarding the enforceability of an award lacking reasons may have kept the Commission from modifying the orientation of the rule in the end. See UNCITRAL, 9th Session, UN Doc A/CN.9/9/C.2/SR.10, n 10, at 10, para 69 (Comment by Mr Melis, Austria).

[145] Draft Article 26(1) of the Preliminary Draft and Draft Article 27(2) of the Revised Draft contained identical language. However, national law may require a reasoned award despite the parties' agreement otherwise. G Born, *International Commercial Arbitration*, n 55, 2452–3.

[146] See UNCITRAL, 9th Session, UN Doc A/CN.9/9/C.2/SR.10, n 10, at 9, paras 70–71 (Comments by Mr Mantilla-Molina, Mexico, and Mr Lebedev, Soviet Union). See also UN GAOR, 31st Session, Supp No 17, UN Doc A/31/17, n 113, para 156.

[147] See P Sanders, "Commentary on UNCITRAL Arbitration Rules," n 9, 208–9. See UNCITRAL, 9th Session, Addendum 1 (Commentary), UN Doc A/CN.9/112/Add.1, n 97 (Commentary on Draft Article 27(2)) (The exception "permits the parties to agree that the award should not contain reasons in cases where the place of arbitration is in a jurisdiction in which an award need not contain reasons in order to be valid."). Redfern and Hunter note that in practice, these agreements between parties "rarely happen." N Blackaby and C Partasides, *Redfern and Hunter on International Arbitration*, n 19, 555.

[148] The suggestion was made by Mr Pirrung of the Federal Republic of Germany, accepted by Mr Guest of the United Kingdom, and endorsed by the Chairman. See UNCITRAL, 9th Session, UN Doc A/CN.9/9/C.2/SR.10, n 10, at 8–9, paras 65, 73, 75.

[149] UN GAOR, 31st Session, Supp No 17, UN Doc A/31/17, n 113, para 157.

to inform the arbitral tribunal of their preferences regarding reasons expressly in writing.[150] Although the possibility of such an implied authorization remains in the 2010 Rules, the global tendency and convergence on giving reasons since the drafting of the 1976 Rules, suggests, in our opinion, that the national law or practice would need to be quite clear to justify such an implication.

The Rules provide no direction regarding the substance and form of the arbitral tribunal's statement of reasons for the award.[151] Obviously, the arbitral tribunal should craft the reasons for an award as carefully and precisely as possible,[152] not only to inform the disputing parties of their rights and obligations, but also, if the award is published, to offer possibly useful precedent for future tribunals.[153] The form of the reasons is not set in stone.[154] While it is common practice that the statement of reasons precedes the *dispositif* of the award, it may also be appended to the award as a separate attachment immediately following the *dispositif*.[155] In the case of administered arbitration, the arbitral institution may require adherence to additional criteria with respect to form or style.

(b) Dissenting and separate opinions

The Preliminary Draft of the 1976 UNCITRAL Rules provided that the award "shall not include any dissenting opinion."[156] This prohibition was ultimately removed from the text of the Rules for two reasons. As explained above, Committee negotiators expressed concern that disallowing dissenting opinions would leave an arbitrator who disagreed with the majority opinion no choice but to express his dissent by refusing to sign the award.[157] The other reason was the plain fact that the majority of negotiators favored dissenting opinions.[158] Thus, the Rule implicitly allows dissenting opinions,[159] and "the question of

---

[150] One commentator has suggested that the parties can approach the tribunal regarding these types of matters up until the final deliberations of the tribunal. See P Sanders, "Commentary on UNCITRAL Arbitration Rules," n 9, 208.

[151] For a general discussion of the key substantive components of an arbitral award, see B Cremades, "Chapter 23: The Arbitral Award" in L Newman and H Hill (eds) *The Leading Arbitrators' Guide to International Arbitration* (2nd edn 2008) 487–9.

[152] See F Knoepfler and P Scweizer, "Making of Awards and Termination of Proceedings, in P Šarčević (ed), *Essays on International Commercial Arbitration* (1989) 166 ("Reasons should be comprehensible to the parties"). In the event the reasons are not comprehensible, the parties may request an interpretation of the award pursuant to Article 35 of the Rules.

[153] For criticism of excessively lengthy awards that obscure the arbitral tribunal's reasons, see separate opinions by Howard M Holtzmann in *Starrett Housing Corporation* (1983 Tribunal Rules) and *Mohsen Asgari Nazari* (1983 Tribunal Rules), reprinted in section 2(D)(4). On publication of the award, see section 2(B)(6). For a discussion on different ways to give "reasons," see N Blackaby and C Partasides, *Redfern and Hunter on International Arbitration*, n 19, 556.

[154] Leading commentators note that the "general practice of arbitral tribunals in international cases is to devote more time and space in the award to giving reasons for its determination of the legal arguments than it devotes to a review of the factual issues." N Blackaby and C Partasides, *Redfern and Hunter on International Arbitration*, n 19, 556.

[155] See P Sanders, "Commentary on UNCITRAL Arbitration Rules," n 9, 209.

[156] *Report of the Secretary-General on the Preliminary Draft Set of Arbitration Rules*, UNCITRAL, 8th Session, UN Doc A/CN.9/97 (1974), reprinted in (1975) VI UNCITRAL Ybk 163, 177 (1975). The commentary to the Draft Article 26(3) of the Preliminary Draft added: "Dissenting opinions are generally unknown in arbitration practice outside of the socialist countries. If the award is published..., it will not contain any dissenting opinion."

[157] See discussion in section 2(B)(4).

[158] UN Doc A/CN.9/SR.166, n 42, at 189 (Comment by the Chairman). Those in favor of dissents included Mr Jakubowski of Poland, Mr Kearney of the United States, Mr Pirrung of the Federal Republic of Germany, Mr Krispis of Greece, Mr Gueiros of Brazil, and Mr Gorbanov of Bulgaria. See 188–9. Those against dissenting opinions included Mr Guest of the United Kingdom, Mr Jenard of Belgium and Mr Chafik of Egypt. See 189.

[159] J Castello, "UNCITRAL Rules," n 15, 1512 ("[t]he Rule's silence on the question of including dissents in awards must be read as permissive.").

whether an arbitrator may add his dissenting opinion to the award is left for decision to the law applicable at the place of arbitration."[160] The Iran–US Claims Tribunal modified the 1976 UNCITRAL Rules to authorize dissenting opinions.[161]

Even if entitled to dissent, an arbitrator may wish to consider the benefits and drawbacks of exercising that right. On the one hand, a dissenting opinion can enhance the award-making process in two important ways. First, "[b]y raising the most difficult problems with the majority's reasoning, dissent can ensure that the arbitral award is well-reasoned."[162] Of course, to achieve this important benefit, the dissenting member must circulate the dissenting opinion for review by the majority before the award is rendered.[163] Second, "[t]he dissenting opinion can enhance the legitimacy of the process by showing the losing party that alternative arguments were considered, even if ultimately rejected."[164] Indeed, if a losing party knows that its position was presented and debated fully and fairly, it arguably may be more inclined to carry out the terms of the award voluntarily.[165]

Dissenting opinions also have potential drawbacks. Just as a dissenting opinion may improve the quality of the award by providing critical feedback, it also may expose fatal flaws in the award. This was the case in the *Avco* arbitration before the Iran–US Claims Tribunal.[166] There, in an effort to minimize excessive documentation, the Tribunal granted Avco permission to summarize, with the assistance of a certified accountant, the numerous and voluminous invoices on which a portion of its case relied. After the presiding Chairman resigned and was replaced, the Tribunal rendered its award, which held both parties liable for damages. Notably, the award rejected the claims by Avco based on the summarized evidence, finding that "the Tribunal cannot grant Avco's claim solely on the basis of an affidavit and a list of invoices, even if the existence of the invoices was certified by an independent audit."[167] Judge Brower wrote a concurring and dissenting opinion in which he outlined in detail the Tribunal's reversal in position. He concluded:

---

[160] UNCITRAL, 9th Session, Addendum 1 (Commentary), UN Doc A/CN.9/112/Add.1, n 97. See also UNCITRAL, 9th Session, UN Doc A/CN.9/9/C.2/SR.11, n 96, at 5, para 30 (Comment by Mr Holtzmann, United States, noting that the issue of dissenting opinions "should be left to the arbitrators and the appropriate national legislation").

[161] Article 32(3) of the 1983 Rules of Procedure of the Iran–US Claims Tribunal, reprinted in Appendix 5, provides: "Any arbitrator may request that his dissenting vote or his dissenting vote and the reasons therefor be recorded." See n 3. According to Baker and Davis, in negotiating this modification, "[t]he third-country members of the Tribunal expressed a distaste for separate opinions and suggested that they not be permitted in Tribunal practice. But the six party-appointed arbitrators united to outvote the three third-country arbitrators—one of the very few times this has happened." S Baker and M Davis, *The UNCITRAL Arbitration Rules in Practice*, n 11, 167.

[162] R Mosk and T Ginsburg, "Dissenting Opinions in International Arbitration," in M Tupamäki (ed), *Liber Amicorum Bengt Broms* (1999) 271. See also S Baker and M Davis, *The UNCITRAL Arbitration Rules in Practice*, n 11, 167 (noting that a carefully crafted dissent "can have a sobering effect on the majority" and put "pressure on the author of the award to be sure that his reasoning is as thorough and persuasive as possible."). See also G Born, *International Commercial Arbitration*, n 55, 2469.

[163] See Final Report on Dissenting and Separate Opinions, (1991) 2(1) *ICC International Court of Arbitration Bulletin* 32, 35. In many cases before the Iran–US Claims Tribunal, the dissenting opinion of the Iranian arbitrator was filed months after the award was rendered with no impact on the majority award. See Case No A/18, Decision No DEC 32-A18-FT (April 6, 1984), Dissenting Opinion of the Iranian Arbitrators (September 10, 1984), reprinted in 5 Iran-US CTR 275 (1984-I) (filed five months after filing of the award).

[164] R Mosk and T Ginsburg, "Dissenting Opinions in International Arbitration," n 162, 272.

[165] R Mosk and T Ginsburg, "Dissenting Opinions in International Arbitration," n 162, 272.

[166] *Avco Corp* and *Iran Aircraft Industries*, et al, Award No 377–261–3 (July 18, 1988), reprinted in 19 Iran-US CTR 200 (1988-II).

[167] *Avco Corp* (1983 Tribunal Rules), at 211.

[T]he Tribunal has misled the Claimant, however unwittingly, regarding the evidence it was required to submit, thereby depriving the Claimant, to that extent, of the ability to present its case.... Since Claimant did exactly what it previously was told to do by the Tribunal the denial in the present Award of any of those invoice claims on the ground that more evidence should have been submitted constitutes a denial to Claimant of the ability to present its case to the Tribunal.[168]

Attempts by Iran Aircraft Industries to enforce the portion of the award in its favor were denied in a US district court. Citing heavily from Judge Brower's opinion, the US Court of Appeals for the Second Circuit affirmed on the basis that Avco was "unable to present [its] case."[169]

A dissenting opinion also may inappropriately disclose the secret deliberations of the arbitral tribunal. Demonstrating a difference of opinion is the very reason an arbitrator dissents and in itself is not cause for alarm. However, when a dissent reveals the substance of the arbitral tribunal's deliberations, eg who said what and for what reason, the rule of confidentiality is compromised.[170] This was the case in Case A/28 before the Iran–US Claims Tribunal in which Judge Broms filed a concurring and dissenting opinion that was said to reveal the views expressed in deliberations by some of his colleagues.[171]

Finally, dissenting opinions increase the costs of arbitration both in terms of time and money. In most cases, the dissenting arbitrator will bill for his additional services. In addition, dissenting opinions drag out the arbitral proceedings, sometimes unnecessarily. In *Granger Associates*, to cite an extreme example, the Iranian judge's dissenting opinion, which alleged procedural misconduct by the majority, was delivered after the award was rendered and resulted in several rounds of rancorous correspondence by the arbitrators.[172]

In addition to dissenting opinions, the arbitrators on the Iran–US Claims Tribunal have made extensive use of separate opinions. As discussed earlier, separate opinions have facilitated Tribunal decision-making pursuant to Article 31 of the 1983 Tribunal Rules, which requires the arbitrators to negotiate the terms of the award until a majority opinion is formed.[173] By rendering a separate opinion an arbitrator is able to consent to the award,

---

[168] Concurring and Dissenting Opinion of Judge Brower (July 18, 1988), reprinted in 19 Iran-US CTR 231, 238 (1988-II).

[169] The Court ruled that "by so misleading Avco, however unwittingly, the Tribunal denied Avco the opportunity to present its claim in a meaningful manner." *Iran Aircraft Industries v Avco Corp*, 980 F 2d 141, 146 (2d Cir 1992). *Avco* illustrates a case in which the dissenting arbitrator has a duty to reveal serious procedural irregularities in the decision-making process. While it is natural for an arbitrator to feel pressure to dissent when the party that has appointed him loses, see R Mosk and T Ginsburg, "Dissenting Opinions in International Arbitration," n 162, 275, the arbitrator should never commit an abuse of process by revealing weaknesses in the majority's award solely for purposes of assisting the losing party in bringing a subsequent challenge. Accord, N Blackaby and C Partasides, *Redfern and Hunter on International Arbitration*, n 19, 577. See also, G Born, *International Commercial Arbitration*, n 55, 2469 ("dissenting and separate opinions must be directed only towards explaining the reasons for the arbitrator's conclusions, and not towards obstructing recognition and enforcement of the award.").

For another example of a dissenting opinion's potential post-award effect, see *Dallal* and *Islamic Republic of Iran*, et al, Award No 53–149–1, reprinted in 3 Iran-US CTR 10 (1983-II), discussed in S Baker and M Davis, *The UNCITRAL Arbitration Rules in Practice*, n 11, 168.

[170] Born is in accord and further notes that the arbitrator in a dissenting or separate opinion still has the duty to "respect the secrecy of the arbitral deliberations... respect the collegiality of the arbitral tribunal... and respect the arbitrator's duties of impartiality." G Born, *International Commercial Arbitration*, n 55, 2467–8.

[171] See *United States of America*, et al and *Islamic Republic of Iran*, et al, Decision No DEC 130-A28-FT, Concurring and Dissenting Opinion of Bengt Broms (December 19, 2000), at 1–2. For discussion of the rule of confidentiality of deliberations, see Chapter 23, section 2(B)(3).

[172] *Granger Associates* and *Islamic Republic of Iran*, et al, Award No 320–184–1 (October 20, 1987), reprinted in 16 Iran-US CTR 317–34 (1987-III).

[173] See Chapter 23 on decisions by the arbitral tribunal.

thus forming the necessary majority, while distancing himself or herself, if desired, from the award's reasoning or determination of damages.[174]

Dissents and separate opinions in investor–state arbitration cases under the UNCITRAL Rules occur less frequently.

(6) Publication of the award—Article 34(5)

Article 34(5) establishes the presumption that the award is confidential, unless all the parties agree to make it public.[175] This presumption comes as no surprise since it is widely recognized that confidentiality is often what makes international arbitration preferable to litigation in a public forum—especially where the parties' dispute involves business, trade, military secrets, or other sensitive information.[176] The rule of confidentiality contained in Article 34(5) applies only to the publication of the award and not to any other aspect of the arbitral proceedings, although a duty of confidentiality also applies to the hearing and the deliberations of the arbitral tribunal.

Notwithstanding the benefits of secrecy, there are compelling reasons to publish an award.[177] Publication enhances transparency in international arbitration with great benefit to practitioners and scholars. Publication offers important historical information regarding the identity, expertise, and views of arbitrators and experts, as well as the comparative utility of arbitral forms (for example, *ad hoc* versus administered arbitration) and institutions (eg ICC versus AAA). Publication develops a corpus of arbitration case law, which provides invaluable examples on substantive and procedural matters. Publication also fosters critical feedback by scholars and commentators on all aspects of the field, which serves to improve the system of international arbitration generally.

---

[174] Born notes instances where a party challenged based on a lack of a majority award when "one arbitrator in the 'majority' appended a separate or concurring opinion to the award, stating that he or she believed that the correct result should have been different from that of the final award." G Born, *International Commercial Arbitration*, n 55, 2461–2.

[175] This approach to confidentiality of the award is consistent with the majority of leading arbitration rules. See 1998 LCIA Rules, art 30; 2010 AAA Rules, art 34; ICSID Convention, art 48(5) and 2006 ICSID Arbitration Rules, art 48(4).

[176] Expert Report of Stephen Bond in *Esso/BHP v Plowman*, reprinted in (1995) 11(3) Arb Intl 273, 273–4 ("When enquiring as to the features of international commercial arbitration which attracted parties to it as opposed to litigation, confidentiality of the proceedings and the fact that these proceedings and the resulting award would not enter the public domain was almost inevitably mentioned."); N Blackaby and C Partasides, *Redfern and Hunter on International Arbitration*, n 19, 33–4 ("[t]he confidentiality of arbitral proceedings, which was at one time general, has been eroded in recent years, but it still remains a key attraction to many participants."); see also Pierre Lalive, "Problèmes Relatif à l'Arbitrage International," (1976) 140 Recueil des Cours de l'Académie de Droit International 573 ("It would appear that among [its] advantages, the *confidential* nature of arbitration must be one of the most important. It is unnecessary to stress the interest that parties with international commercial connections have in maintaining business secrets and in not alerting the competition… or the tax authorities!") (emphasis in original).

[177] The overwhelming majority of commentators encourage publication of the award, where possible. See J Lew, "The Case for the Publication of Arbitration Awards," In J Schutsz and A van den Berg (eds), *The Art of Arbitration: Essays on International Arbitration* (1982) 223; P Sanders, "Commentary on UNCITRAL Arbitration Rules," n 9, 209 ("Insofar as international commercial arbitration can be helpful in establishing a new *lex mercatoria*, the publication of awards, or at least the essential parts thereof, should in my opinion be favourably regarded."); P Fouchard, *L'Arbitrage Commercial International* (1996) 451 ("If the international community of merchants aspires to give itself an autonomous system of law, this law has to be made known to all those who have interest in it: the arbitrators should not resemble the ancient pontifex of antique Rome, who, jealously, kept the knowledge of the law for themselves, and with it the religious and political power."). K Berger, *International Economic Arbitration*, n 19, 606.

The jurisprudence of most awards, even those containing sensitive information, can be made public, often with the approval of the parties, by applying simple precautionary measures. Specific information, such as the names of the parties or the amount of the award, can be redacted from the text of the award before publication.[178] In addition, the publication of extracts from the award can avoid revealing the parts of the award that are case specific or too sensitive in the view of the parties.[179]

Article 34(5) recognizes that rule of confidentiality may have to yield to disclosure in certain circumstances. These circumstances may include disclosure "by legal duty," "to protect or pursue a legal right," or "in relation to legal proceedings before a court or other competent authority."[180] For example, a corporate party may be required to share information in the award with its shareholders,[181] or a party seeking to enforce an award against another party may be required to enter the award into the public docket of a reviewing court.[182] Article 34(5) constitutes an agreement by the parties that in these types of situation confidentiality does not apply and, thus, the provision seeks to minimize unfounded challenges to disclosure by an opposing party.[183] At the same time, disclosure is permissible only if "required of a party." Thus, in the absence of a bone fide "legal duty," "legal right," or "legal proceeding," the rule of confidentiality should prevail.

When international arbitration involves a party that is a state, and thus potentially touches on issues of public interest, there has been a trend away from confidentiality in favor of publication of the award.[184] The Iran–US Claims Tribunal, for example, modified Article 32(5) of the 1976 UNCITRAL Rules to provide:

> All awards and other decisions shall be made public, except that upon the request of one or more arbitrating parties, the arbitral tribunal may determine that it will not make the entire award or other decision public, but will make public only portions thereof from which the identity of the parties, other identifying facts and trade or military secrets have been deleted.[185]

---

[178] See UNCITRAL, 9th Session, Addendum 1 (Commentary), UN Doc A/CN.9/112/Add.1, n 97 (Commentary on Draft Article 27(5)) ("When publication of an award does take place, the names of the parties are usually omitted and other measures are also taken to avoid disclosure of their identity."). See also P Sanders, "Commentary on UNCITRAL Arbitration Rules," n 9, 209.

[179] P Sanders, "Commentary on UNCITRAL Arbitration Rules," n 9, 209.

[180] The provision is new to the Rules and is modeled after Article 30.1 of the LCIA Arbitration Rules, which provides: "[D]isclosure may be required of a party by legal duty, to protect or pursue a legal right or to enforce or challenge an award in bone fide legal proceedings before a state court or other judicial authority." A minority of UNCITRAL delegations opposed the new provision, noting that it imported "questions that were not appropriate in the context of the Rules given that they related to matters already covered by national laws" and that the new provision "might not cover all situations where disclosure might be required and that, for that reason, it would be better to leave that matter to national laws." UNCITRAL, 41st Session, UN Doc A/CN.9/641, n 4, at 19, para 96.

[181] See N Blackaby and C Partasides, *Redfern and Hunter on International Arbitration*, n 19, 583 (referring to the obligation of a publicly traded corporation "to disclose in its published accounts material information relating to its liability").

[182] Even under the 1976 UNCITRAL Rules, which did not contain such a provision on required disclosure, the Commission was well aware of this possibility. See UN GAOR, 31st Session, Supp No 17, UN Doc A/31/17, n 113, para 167; see also J Paulsson and N Rawding, "The Trouble with Confidentiality," (1995) 11(3) Arb Intl 303, 306.

[183] In revising the Rules, the Working Group noted that the language of Article 32(5) of the 1976 UNCITRAL Rules, which did not recognize exceptions to confidentiality, "had been known to create practical difficulties as it might make it difficult for a party to use the award for the protection of its rights." UNCITRAL, 41st Session, UN Doc A/CN.9/641, n 4, at 19, para 96. See also para 97 (noting that an additional provision on required disclosure would provide "greater protection to parties who might need to disclose an award in court or other proceedings, and greater clarity as to the extent of their rights.")

[184] C Schreuer, *The ICSID Convention: A Commentary* (2nd ed 2009) 835.

[185] For examples of the Tribunal's variable treatment of requests made pursuant to this provision, see section 2(D)(6). As van Hof correctly notes, "[t]he cases in which the Tribunal rejected the requests for confidentiality

Similarly, the NAFTA and subsequent investment treaties by the NAFTA Parties have included provisions on publication of awards.[186] In addition, at the time of this writing, UNCITRAL was developing rules of transparency in investor–State arbitration, including with respect to publication of awards.[187] At the fifty-fifth session of the Working Group, broad support was expressed for a provision requiring that all awards be made available to the public, subject to exceptions for the protection of confidential information and the integrity of the process.[188]

(7) Copies of the award to the parties—Article 34(6)

Once the award is rendered, the arbitral tribunal must transmit a final, signed copy to the parties. This communication serves three primary purposes. First, it notifies the parties of their rights and obligations under the award, enabling them to "carry out the award without delay."[189] Second, it initiates the 30-day period for requesting post-award proceedings under Articles 37 (interpretation), 38 (correction), and 39 (additional award).[190] Third, it furnishes to the parties the requisite documentation for enforcement of the award in national court proceedings.[191] As a matter of practice, transmission of a copy of the award should be via a delivery method that guarantees receipt.

The duty to transmit a copy of the award to the parties ultimately falls upon the presiding arbitrator. This rule is clear from the *travaux préparatoires* for Article 32(6) of the 1976 Rules, which was reproduced without modification as Article 34(6) of the 2010 Rules. Early drafts of Article 32(6) of the 1976 Rules required that the award be communicated by the "arbitrators."[192] The representative of Belgium commented that "the award should be communicated to the parties only by the presiding arbitrator, since the parties would not need three copies of the award."[193] The representative of Nigeria agreed and proposed replacing the word "arbitrators" with the word "arbitral tribunal."[194] The proposal was adopted in order to clarify that the presiding arbitrator is responsible for distributing at least one copy of the award to each party.[195]

---

are not very consistent and provide little guidance about applicable standards." J van Hof, *Commentary on the UNCITRAL Arbitration Rules: The Application by the Iran-U.S. Claims Tribunal* (1991) 224.

[186] See, eg, Dominican Republic–Central America–United States Free Trade Agreement (CAFTA-DR), Article 10.21. See also Interpretation of the Free Trade Commission on Certain Chapter Eleven Provisions (July 31, 2001), para 2(a):

That nothing in the relevant arbitral rules imposes a general duty of confidentiality or precludes the Parties from providing public access to documents submitted to, or issued by, Chapter Eleven tribunals, apart from the limited specific exceptions set forth expressly in those rules.

[187] For a general discussion of UNCITRAL's work in this area, see Chapter 1, section 3(G).

[188] *Report of the Working Group on Arbitration and Conciliation on the Work of its Fifty-Fifth Session* (Vienna, October 3–7, 2011), UNCITRAL, 45th Session, UN Doc A/CN.9/736, at 15, para 67 (2011).

[189] 2010 UNCITRAL Arbitration Rules, art 34(2).

[190] See Chapter 26 on post-award proceedings.

[191] For example, Article IV(1)(a) of the New York Convention requires the presentation of a "duly authenticated original award or a duly certified copy thereof" for recognition or enforcement of the award. Note that the "time limit within which a party may apply to the appropriate court for recourse against the award often runs from the date of communication of the award." N Blackaby and C Partasides, *Redfern and Hunter on International Arbitration*, n 19, 560.

[192] See Draft Article 26(5) of the Preliminary Draft and Draft Article 27(6) of the Revised Draft.

[193] UNCITRAL, 9th Session, UN Doc A/CN.9/9/C.2/SR.11, n 96, at 8, para 51 (Comment by Mr Jenard, Belgium).

[194] UNCITRAL, 9th Session, UN Doc A/CN.9/9/C.2/SR.11, n 96, para 52 (Comment by Ms Oyekunle, Nigeria).

[195] UNCITRAL, 9th Session, UN Doc A/CN.9/9/C.2/SR.11, n 96, paras 53–54.

The Committee negotiators of the 1976 Rules also considered designating a time period for communication of the award. A number of delegates believed that an express time limit of a given number of days would bring certainty to the rule.[196] Others felt that an express time limit was too rigid and proposed alternatively to qualify the duty to communicate the award with phrases like "without delay"[197] or "without unnecessary delay."[198] The Soviet delegate opposed these proposals, arguing that such language might cause the award to be invalidated solely on grounds that the arbitrators failed to act in a timely fashion.[199] In the end, it was decided that the rule should not contain temporal qualifications on the duty to communicate the award, although it is clear that the rule is "designed to ensure that both parties will promptly receive copies of the award."[200] In some jurisdictions, the national arbitration law may establish the time limit for communication of the award.[201]

Can an arbitral tribunal withhold the award in the event the parties have failed to provide adequate monetary deposits to cover the fees and expenses of arbitration?[202] Such a practice appears to be accepted in a system of dispute resolution that typically is funded solely by the parties. In the absence of an express prohibition against such measures in the Rules and in light of the prevailing practice of international tribunals, arbitrators likely will continue, subject to any restrictions under the governing arbitration law, to postpone communication of the award until the parties satisfy their financial obligations.[203]

Perhaps even more important than the time it takes the arbitral tribunal to *communicate* the award is the time it takes to *make* the award—that is, the period from closure of the hearing until communication of the award.[204] Unlike most arbitral rules, the UNCITRAL Rules do not establish a time limit for the latter task.[205] In revising the UNCITRAL Rules,

---

[196] Mr Dey of India made the initial proposal, which drew support from Mr Roehrich of France and Mr Mantilla-Molina of Mexico, among others. UNCITRAL, 9th Session, UN Doc A/CN.9/9/C.2/SR.11, n 96, paras 55–58, 62, 64.

[197] UNCITRAL, 9th Session, UN Doc A/CN.9/9/C.2/SR.11, n 96, para 59 (Comment by Mr St. John, Australia).

[198] UNCITRAL, 9th Session, UN Doc A/CN.9/9/C.2/SR.11, n 96, para 60 (Comment by Mr Guevara, Philippines).

[199] UNCITRAL, 9th Session, UN Doc A/CN.9/9/C.2/SR.11, n 96, para 65. The Soviet representative also argued that phrases such as "without delay" were too uncertain. The Soviet proposal received the support of Mr Guest of the United Kingdom and the Chairman. Paras 66–67.

[200] UNCITRAL, 9th Session, Addendum 1 (Commentary), UN Doc A/CN.9/112/Add.1, n 97 (Commentary on Draft Article 27(6)).

[201] See *UNCITRAL Notes on Organizing Arbitral Proceedings*, UNCITRAL, UN GAOR, 51st Session, para 89, UN Doc A/51/17 (1996), reprinted in (1996) XXVII UNCITRAL Ybk 45, 56 [hereinafter "*UNCITRAL Notes*"]. For discussion of time limits under the arbitration laws of Brazil and Italy, see S Kroll, L Mistelis, and J Lew, *Comparative International Commercial Arbitration* (2003) 638, n 51.

[202] The *travaux préparatoires* indicate only that the French representative opposed such a practice. See UNCITRAL, 9th Session, UN Doc A/CN.9/9/C.2/SR.11, n 96, at 8, para 56.

[203] In the context of drafting the Model Law, the Commission observed that "arbitrators sometimes withheld their award until the parties had paid the fees and expenses for the arbitration and that this practice should not be precluded by the model law." *Second Working Group Report*, UN Doc A/CN.9/232, para 185 (1982), discussed in H Holtzmann and J Neuhaus, *A Guide to the UNCITRAL Model Law*, n 16, 841. See also Article 26.5 of the 1998 LCIA Arbitration Rules (transmission of copies of award to party "provided that the costs of arbitration have been paid to the LCIA in accordance with Article 28").

[204] This point was raised by an UNCITRAL observer during Committee negotiations. See UNCITRAL, 9th Session, UN Doc A/CN.9/9/C.2/SR.11, n 96, at 8, para 61 (Comment by Mr Strauss, Observer). In response, one delegate proposed to no avail that the Rules specify that the award should be handed down "without unnecessary delay." Para 62 (comments of Mr Guevara, Philippines). On the criteria for award making, see section 2(B)(2).

[205] Most of the major arbitration rules contain such a time limit. See 2012 ICC Arbitration Rules, art 30(1) (6 months); 2006 ICSID Arbitration Rules, Rule 46 (120 days, with possible 60-day extension); 2001 WIPO

the Working Group considered, but did not accept, a proposal to include a time period for rendering an award with the possibility of extending that time period.[206] To ensure that the award is timely rendered, the parties may wish to consider modifying the Rules to establish a reasonable time limit that, depending on the difficulty and complexity of the arbitration, is in the range of three to six months after closure of the hearing.

(8) Filing and registration of the award

Filing or registration of the award (also referred to as the deposit of the award) with local authorities is required in some jurisdictions.[207] In some cases, the obligation to do so may rest with the arbitral tribunal. The 2010 UNCITRAL Rules omit the obligation previously contained in Article 32(7) of the 1976 UNCITRAL Rules that the arbitral tribunal file or register the award where required by the law of the place of arbitration.[208] The Working Group found the original provision to be unnecessarily redundant.[209] Nevertheless, it is incumbent upon the arbitral tribunal to determine whether it is subject to domestic filing or registration requirements and, if so, to comply with these requirements. Further, the arbitral tribunal has a general duty to ensure that the award is "final and binding." Thus, it is not unusual for the tribunal to assist the parties, to the extent practicable, in meeting any filing or registration requirements.

(9) Comparison to the 1976 UNCITRAL Rules

In structure and purpose, Article 34 is substantially similar to corresponding Article 32 of the 1976 UNCITRAL Rules in many respects, though some revisions and one significant omission are noteworthy.

Article 34(1) clarifies that the arbitral tribunal may make "separate awards," whereas Article 32(1) of the 1976 UNCITRAL Rules entitles to make not only a final award, but also "interim, interlocutory, or partial awards." Despite these drafting differences, both provisions share the same goal of providing the arbitral tribunal the flexibility it may need to resolve discrete issues at different times during the arbitration. Like separate awards under Article 34(1), the various types of award enumerated in Article 32(1) of the 1976 UNCITRAL Rules could be made "whenever justified under the circumstances of the particular dispute" and "at any time during the arbitral proceedings."[210] Even under the 2010 Rules it is expected that arbitral tribunals will use such labels as "partial award" and "interim award" in the event they are required to render separate awards.

Arbitration Rules, art 63 (3 months); 2010 AAA Rules, art 27(1) (requiring that the award be made "promptly").

[206] While the Working Group recognized the existence of time limits for rendering an award, and the practice of systematically extending such time limits, the majority view was that time limits would be difficult to apply in non-administered arbitration. Further, practical problems were noted where a domestic arbitration law contained specific time limits. UNCITRAL, 40th Session, UN Doc A/CN.9/614, n 4, at 24, para 118–119.

[207] See *UNCITRAL Notes*, n 201, at para 89. Note, however, that the Model Law contains no such requirement. See Article 31 of the Model Law, as amended.

[208] For a discussion of Article 32(7) of the 1976 UNCITRAL Rules, see section 2(B)(9).

[209] UNCITRAL, 41st Session, UN Doc A/CN.9/641, n 4, at 21, para 105. For a discussion of various proposals to modify Article 32(7) of the 1976 UNCITRAL Rules, see paras 101–104.

[210] UNCITRAL, 9th Session, Addendum 1 (Commentary), UN Doc A/CN.9/112/Add.1, n 97 (emphasis added). In Committee discussions, Sanders spoke in general terms regarding the meaning of interim and partial awards. The former "helped to bring a case closer to a solution," while the latter "related to part of a case which could be settled immediately." See UNCITRAL, 9th Session, UN Doc A/CN.9/9/C.2/SR.10, n 10, at 8, para 59.

Article 34(2) incorporates Article 32(2) of the 1976 UNCITRAL Rules with two minor revisions. First, Article 34(2) states that "[a]ll awards," in contrast to "[t]he award" as in Article 32(2) of the 1976 UNCITRAL Rules, shall be final and binding. This change is merely stylistic to highlight the fact that a "separate award" rendered pursuant to the 2010 Rules is subject to the same technical requirements and has the same legal force as a final award. Awards rendered pursuant to the 1976 UNCITRAL Rules should be treated no differently. Second, the obligation to carry out all awards without delay is formulated using the word "shall" in the 2010 Rules and "undertake" in the 1976 UNCITRAL Rules. The obligation is mandatory under both formulations. However, the Working Group preferred the word "shall" over "undertake" because some delegations raised concerns that the meaning of the word "undertake" may not be clear in all countries.[211]

Article 34(3) is identical to Article 32(3) of the 1976 UNCITRAL Rules.

Article 34(4) is virtually identical to Article 32(4) of the 1976 UNCITRAL Rules, save for two minor revisions. First, the first sentence of Article 34(4) requires that the award "contain the date on which the award was made and indicate the place of arbitration," as opposed to "the date on which and the place where the award was made" under the original rule. The revision was made "for the sake of consistency with the modification under article 16, paragraph (4) [of the 1976 UNCITRAL Rules], which deals with the place where the award is deemed to be made."[212] Second, the second sentence of Article 34(4) addresses a failure to sign an award "[w]here there is more than one arbitrator," whereas the original rule uses the phrase "[w]here there are three arbitrators." The revision takes into account the situation permitted under Article 10(2) where parties may decide that the arbitral tribunal is to be composed of a number of arbitrators other than one or three.[213]

Article 34(5) contains revisions to the rule of confidentiality of the award. Both Article 34(5) and Article 32(5) of the 1976 UNCITRAL Rules state the basic rule that an award may be made public with the consent of the parties. However, only Article 34(5) recognizes expressly the exception that disclosure of an award may be required "by legal duty, to protect or pursue a legal right or in relation to legal proceedings before a court or other competent authority." To the extent that a party's obligation or right to disclose the award is addressed by the governing law and cannot be waived, the new text in Article 34(5) merely restates the fundamental rule of pre-emption contained in Article 1(3). However, where a party's obligation or right of disclosure is not clearly defined in the governing law, the revision in Article 34(5) may help avoid costly and time-consuming disputes.

Article 34(6) is identical to Article 32(6) of the 1976 UNCITRAL Rules.

The 2010 UNCITRAL Rules omit the provision on filing or registering an award previously contained in Article 32(7) of the 1976 UNCITRAL Rules. As explained above, the Working Group found the provision to be unnecessarily redundant as it merely restates the requirement that an arbitral tribunal is bound to follow the local law with respect to filing or registering the award.

---

[211] *Report of Working Group II (Arbitration and Conciliation) on the Work of its Fifty-Second Session* (New York, February 1–5, 2010), UNCITRAL, 43rd Session, UN Doc A/CN.9/688, at 21, para 103 (2009).

[212] UNCITRAL, UN Doc A/CN.9/WG.II/WP.145/Add.1, n 82, at 16, para 34.

[213] UNCITRAL, 41st Session, UN Doc A/CN.9/641, n 4, at 19, para 94; UNCITRAL, UN Doc A/CN.9/WG.II/WP.149, n 14, at 15, para 56.

C. Extracts from the Practice of Investment and other Tribunals

(1) Article 32(1) (1976 Rules)—Types of awards

Himpurna California Energy Ltd and *Republic of Indonesia*, Interim Award (September 26, 1999) (*Ad Hoc* Proceeding, 1976 UNCITRAL Rules, Concession Agreement), reprinted in (2000) XXV Ybk Commercial Arb 109, 154, 157:

> [95] The President of the Arbitral Tribunal made the following self-explanatory statement:
>
> ... The Arbitral Tribunal announced its fully-deliberated decision to the effect that the Republic of Indonesia is in default by its letter of 7 September 1999. Under the [1976] UNCITRAL Rules, a decision under Art. 28 does not require articulation in a formal award. Nevertheless, the Republic of Indonesia, in its letter dated 20 September 1999 to the Secretary-General of ICSID, has taken the view that this decision is "more in the nature of an interim award than a mere procedural order, and, as such, requires signatures or indications of dissent of the entire tribunal." The allegation that an indication of dissent is required is profoundly mistaken; it has no place in the [1976] UNCITRAL Rules. Nevertheless, the Arbitral Tribunal shall, *ex abundante cautela*, render an Interim Award on the subject of default, so that the Parties may satisfy themselves that their submissions were indeed taken into account.

Lance Paul Larsen and *Hawaiian Kingdom*, Award (February 5, 2001) (PCA administered, 1976 UNCITRAL Rules, Special Agreement), reprinted in (2001) 119 ILR 566, 579–80:

> 6.4. Following the delivery of the Tribunal's Procedural Order No 3 the parties entered into Special Agreement No 2 of 2 August 2000 and sought to raise a preliminary issue to be determined by the Tribunal in the following terms:
>
> > Pursuant to Article 32(1) of the [1976] UNCITRAL Rules, the Parties request the Arbitral Tribunal to issue an Interlocutory Award, on the basis of the 1843 Anglo-Franco Proclamation of 28 November 1843 and the rules and principles of international law, verifying the continued existence of Hawaiian Statehood with the Hawaiian Kingdom as its government.
>
> 6.5. The Tribunal responded to the making of Special Agreement No 2 with its Procedural Order No 4 of 5 September 2000, which read as follows:
>
> > ...
> >
> > 3. The Tribunal set out in its Order No 3 the questions which, in its view, are raised before it can proceed to the merits of the dispute. The issue identified in Article 1 of Special Agreement No 2 is not one of these. Rather it appears to be a reformulation of the first substantive issue identified as being in dispute.
> > 4. It is not open to the parties by way of an amendment to the Special Agreement to seek to redefine the essential issues, so as to convert them into "interim" or "interlocutory" issues. In accordance with article 32 of the [1976] UNCITRAL Rules, and with the general principles of arbitral procedure, it is for the Tribunal to determine which issues need to be dealt with and in what order. For the reasons already given, the Tribunal cannot at this stage proceed to the merits of the dispute; these merits include the question sought to be raised as a preliminary issue by Article I. If the arbitration is to proceed it is first necessary that the preliminary issues identified in its Order No 3 should have been dealt with.
> > 5. If the parties are not content with the submission of the dispute to arbitration under the [1976] UNCITRAL Rules and under the auspices of the Permanent Court of Arbitration, they may no doubt, by agreement notified to the Permanent Court, terminate the arbitration. What they cannot do, in the Tribunal's view, is by agreement to change the essential basis on which the Tribunal itself is constituted, or require the Tribunal to act other than in accordance with the applicable law.

(2) Article 32(2) (1976 Rules)—Final and binding

CME Czech Republic BV and *The Czech Republic*, Final Award (March 14, 2003) (*Ad Hoc* Proceeding, 1976 UNCITRAL Rules, Netherlands-Czech Republic BIT), at 98–99, reprinted in (2003) 15(4) World Trade & Arb Materials 83, 180–181:425.

> The Tribunal takes note of the Tribunal's explicit decision in para 624(4) of the Partial Award. This "*Partial Award is final and binding in respect to the issues decided herein.*" Further the Tribunal recalls to the terms of Art. 8(7) of the Treaty, according to which the Arbitral Award "shall be final and binding." The [1976] UNCITRAL Rules, Art. 32(2)). Consistently with this rule, no provision of the Treaty or the [1976] UNCITRAL Rules provides any mechanism for appeal, re-hearing or revision of an arbitral award unless by way of interpretation or correction within a time period of 30 days or by appeal to the Swedish Courts within the bounds of the New York Convention on the Recognition and Enforcement of Foreign Arbitral Awards. The Tribunal itself is not authorized to reconsider its Partial Award and, in any event, the Tribunal finds no good reason for doing so.

Methanex Corp and *United States of America*, Award (August 3, 2005) (*Ad Hoc* Proceeding, 1976 UNCITRAL Rules, NAFTA Chapter Eleven), Part II, Chapter E, at 16–19:

> 27. In the Tribunal's view, the first issue is whether, once a partial award is made by a tribunal, it is final and binding within Article 32(2) of the [1976] UNCITRAL Rules and, if so, whether the tribunal has any jurisdiction to re-consider such an award at a later stage of the same arbitration proceedings. As explained below, the Tribunal decides that its Partial Award was an award which was final and binding upon the Disputing Parties; and that, as such, the Tribunal has no jurisdiction to reconsider the Partial Award in the form sought by Methanex in its Second Request made in January 2004, i.e. admittedly more than thirty days after Methanex's receipt of the Partial Award in August 2002.
> 28. The Tribunal does not accept Methanex's contention that, in seeking reconsideration by its Second Request, it is seeking something other than a reversal of a significant decision in the Partial Award, namely that "certain allegations relating to the 'intent' underlying the US measures could potentially meet the requirements of Article 1101(1) NAFTA, thereby allowing part of Methanex's case to fall within the jurisdiction of the Tribunal" but that otherwise the Tribunal lacked jurisdiction over Methanex's claim. Methanex's Second Request seeks to reverse the core of the Partial Award.
> 29. The Tribunal's decision is not based on a mere technicality or semantic point under the [1976] UNCITRAL Rules. The application of these arbitration rules was triggered by Methanex's own choice in its 1999 Notice of Arbitration; and it should also be noted that, at the end of the jurisdictional hearing in July 2001, the Tribunal expressly asked the Disputing Parties whether the award that the Tribunal was intending to make should have any particular form, bearing in mind that the award might be subjected to challenge in a court of competent jurisdiction. It was then agreed by both Methanex and the USA that the award would be called a partial award (as, on any reading, it could not dispose of all matters potentially arising for decision by the Tribunal) and that the partial award would be final and enforceable. In the Tribunal's view, there was a common intention, expressly shared by Methanex at that time, that the partial award would be final and binding, within the meaning of Article 32 of the [1976] UNCITRAL Rules. It will be recalled that under Articles 32(1) and (2) of the [1976] UNCITRAL Rules, a "partial" award is expressly "final and binding on the parties".
> 30. Further, it appears to have been Methanex's position subsequent to the making of the Partial Award that this award was indeed "final and binding". In Methanex's first Request for Interpretation dated 28th August 2002, Methanex's "request that the arbitral tribunal give an interpretation of the award" was made pursuant to Article 35(1) of the [1976] UNCITRAL Rules. This request necessarily recognised the existence of an award that was final and binding on Methanex pursuant to Article 32(2) of the [1976] UNCITRAL Rules. Otherwise, Methanex could not have invoked Article 35 of the [1976] UNCITRAL Rules which applies only to an "award". (As expressed in its letter of 25th September 2002, the Tribunal considered that Methanex's Request did not fall within the scope of Article 35 of the Rules because the

Tribunal considered that what Methanex sought was not an interpretation, i.e. not because the Tribunal had not made an "award" within Article 32(2) of the [1976] Rules).

31. The Tribunal also rejects, for present purposes, any distinction between a partial award and a final award which leaves the arbitration tribunal functus officio. A partial award is a final and binding award within Article 32(2) of the [1976] UNCITRAL Rules in regard to the matter it decides, although it does not leave the tribunal functus officio. It is presented as an award; and as an award it disposes finally of certain issues in the arbitration proceedings. No question here arises as to the distinction between a tribunal's decision, ruling or order and an award (whether partial or final), such as confronted the French Court in *Brasoil* (1999) or the US Court in *Publicis* (2000)17: Methanex's arguments rest only upon the difference between a "partial" award and a "final" award.

32. The Tribunal therefore rejects Methanex's contention that the Partial Award is not a final and binding award under Article 32(2) of the [1976] UNCITRAL Rules and the contention that Article 32(2) concerns only final awards, not partial awards. That contention runs counter to the ordinary meaning of the Articles 32(1) and (2) as a matter of the English language. In the Tribunal's view, no weight is to be placed on the fact that "award" is not further defined in Article 32(2) expressly to include (inter alia) a partial award. It follows that, where reference is made to an award under Article 32(2), that is intended to include a partial award made under Article 32(1) of the [1976] UNCITRAL Rules.

[Footnote] 17. *Braspetro Oil Services Co. v. Great Man-Made River Project* (1999) XXIVa *ICCA YBCA* 296; *Publicis Communications v. True North Communications Inc.* 203 F.3d 725 (7th Cir. 2000); (2000) XXV *ICCA YBCA* 1152.

(3) Article 32(2) and (4) (1976 Rules)—Date, place, and signature

Karaha Bodas Co LLC and *Perusahaan Pertabangan Minyak Dan Gas Bumi Negara and PT PLN (Persero)*, Final Award (December 18, 2000) (*Ad Hoc* Proceeding, 1976 UNCITRAL Rules, Concession Agreement):

ON THE BASIS OF THE FOREGOING,
THE ARBITRAL TRIBUNAL FINDS AND DECIDES AS FOLLOWS:
[Text of *dispositif* omitted]
Made in Geneva, on September 30, 1999
[signed]   [signed]
Prof. Piero   Prof. Ahmed S El
BERNARDINI   KOSHERI

                 [signed]
                 Me Yves
                 DERAINS

SD Myers, Inc and *Government of Canada*, Partial Award (November 13, 2000) (*Ad Hoc* Proceeding, 1976 UNCITRAL Rules, NAFTA Chapter Eleven), reprinted in (2003) 15(1) World Trade & Arb Materials 184, 266:

CHAPTER XII

CONCLUSIONS AND DISPOSITIVE PROVISIONS OF THE AWARD

[Text of *dispositif* omitted]
Made at the City of Toronto, Ontario, Canada.
SIGNED:
[signed]   [signed]
Brian P. Schwartz   Edward C Chiasson, Q.C.
                      [signed]
                      J. Martin Hunter
                      November 13, 2000

(4) Article 32(4) (1976 Rules)—Failure to sign the award

Republika Srpska and *Federation of Bosnia and Herzegovina* (Control Over the Brcko Corridor), Award (February 14, 1997) (*Ad Hoc* Proceeding, 1976 UNCITRAL Rules, Special Agreement), reprinted in (1997) 26 ILM 396, 406, 437:

> 27. Following the Rome hearing, the Tribunal conducted its deliberations in Washington, D.C. All three arbitrators were present and fully participated in the deliberations. However, during the last day of deliberations both Professor Sadikovic and Dr. Popovic refused to sign the Award.
>
> ...
>
> [signed]
>
> Cazim Sadikovic   Roberts B. Owen   Vitomir Popovic
> Arbitrator   Presiding Arbitrator   Arbitrator
>
>
> Rome, 14 February 1997
> Reasons for the Absence of Signatures
> Pursuant to Article 32(4) of the [1976] UNCITRAL Rules, the Tribunal notes that, for the reasons stated Paragraph 27 of this Award, the party-appointed arbitrators have failed to sign the Award.

CME Czech Republic BV and *Czech Republic*, Partial Award (September 13, 2001) (*Ad Hoc* Proceeding, 1976 UNCITRAL Rules, Netherlands-Czech Republic BIT), reprinted in (2003) 14(3) World Trade & Arb Materials 109, 287:

> J. Decision
> 624. The Tribunal decides as follows:
> [text of *dispositif* omitted]
> K. Statement in accordance with Article 32(4) [1976] UNCITRAL Arbitration Rules related to Dr. Hándl's failure to sign the Partial Award
>
> 625. By letter dated September 11, 2001, Dr. Hándl requested the Chairman to attach to the Award (whose issuance he delayed) an explanation of his failure to sign the Award, as well as a dissenting opinion. Dr. Hándl refused to sign the Award with the following remark:
>
>> "Partial Award not signed by Dr. Hándl as expression of his protest and dissenting from this Award—dissenting opinion enclosed, date: 11.9.2001, signature Dr. Hándl"
>
> The Chairman of the Tribunal, on his behalf and that of Judge Schwebel, pointed out to Dr. Hándl that his failure to sign would be in breach of his obligations as arbitrator. In the event, it is also a breach of his repeated recent assurances to the Chairman, in writing, that he "will sign" the Award.
> The [1976] UNCITRAL Rules that govern this arbitration provide, in Article 32 (4), that: *"An award shall be signed by the arbitrators…"* (emphasis supplied). The Tribunal is confirmed in the conclusion that an arbitrator's failure to sign the award is a violation of the arbitrator's professional responsibilities by its examination of the rules and practice of the principal arbitral institutions as well as the papers and proceedings of the Stockholm and Paris Congresses of the International Council on Commercial Arbitration. Dr. Hándl's failure to perform his responsibilities as arbitrator is matched by the intemperance and inaccuracy of his dissent. He makes charges about the conduct of the hearings and the deliberations that are groundless. His position on the merits of the dispute speaks for itself.
>
> Stockholm, 13 September 2001

Mytilineos Holdings SA and *State Union of Serbia & Montenegro,* et al, Partial Award on Jurisdiction (September 8, 2006) (*Ad Hoc* Proceeding, 1976 UNCITRAL Rules, Greece-Former Yugoslavia BIT), at 57:

[signed]	[signed]	
(Dr. Wolfgang Kühn)	(Judge Stephen M Schwebel)	(JUDr. Jaroslav Hándl)
Chairman of the Arbitral Tribunal	Arbitrator	Arbitrator

Done in Zurich, Switzerland, being the place of arbitration, on 8 September 2006.
[signed]
Professor Dr. August Reinisch

[signed]
Professor Dr. Stelios Koussoulis

[unsigned]
Professor Dr. Dobrosav Mitrović
Reason for absence of signature (Article 32(4) of the [1976] UNCITRAL Arbitration Rules: In a letter to the Presiding Arbitrator dated 6 September 2006, Professor Mitrović indicated that he would not sign this Partial Award as he did not agree with the majority on the jurisdiction of the Arbitral Tribunal. Professor Mitrović participated in all aspects of the deliberated process.

(5) Article 32(7) (1976 Rules)—Filing and registration of an award

Patuha Power Ltd and *PT (Persero) Perusahaan Listruik Negara (Indonesia)*, Final Award (May 4, 1999) (*Ad Hoc* Proceeding, 1976 UNCITRAL Rules, Concession Agreement, reprinted in (1999) 14(12) Mealey's Intl Arb Rep B-12, B41:

102. Article 634 of the Indonesian Code of Civil Procedure provides that the award shall be deposited by the arbitrators at the Registry of the District Court in the District where it was rendered within 14 days. Although the applicability of this Article, or indeed of the other provisions of the Code of Civil Procedure concerning arbitration, appears to be uncertain (such codifications inherited from the Netherlands are often referred to as *pedoman,* or "guidelines," rather than as positive and binding law), the Parties have agreed that the Award shall be registered in the manner indicated in paragraph 505.

103. In light of the above, it is clear that the registration of the Award is in compliance with Article 32(7) of the [1976] UNCITRAL Rules and the agreement of the Parties....

...

504. The Arbitral Tribunal makes an original version of this Final Award, certified as such below by a manuscript notation of the President, available this day in Jakarta to Dr. Adnan Buyung Nasution SH and Ms Pia Akbar Nasution SH, on behalf of PLN, and to Mr. Andy Kelana SH or Mr. Joni Aries Bangun SH, on behalf of the Claimant.

505. In the course of the hearings on the merits, the Parties agreed that the Arbitral Tribunal would authorize counsel to one of them, in place of the Arbitral Tribunal, to deposit the Final Award at the office of the Registrar of the District Court of Jakarta, pursuant to Article 32(7) of the

Himpurna California Energy Ltd and *Republic of Indonesia*, Interim Award (September 26, 1999) (*Ad Hoc* Proceeding, 1976 UNCITRAL Rules, Concession Agreement), reprinted in (2000) XXV Ybk Commercial Arb 109, 185–86:

VII. Deposit of the Award

[201] The Arbitral Tribunal communicates an original version of this Interim Award, certified as such below by a manuscript notation of its President, to Messrs Latham & Watkins and Karim Sani.

[202] As indicated under point 3 of its Procedural Order of 7 September 1999, the Arbitral Tribunal has rejected the claimant's request to change the legal seat of the arbitration, which accordingly remains Jakarta.

[203] Paragraph 5(h) of the Terms of Appointment contemplates that the Arbitral Tribunal "shall deposit the award with the Central District Court of Jakarta." The Parties have not agreed how this deposit should be effected. The claimant has indicated that it wishes to preserve the option of depositing the award by means of an authorisation to that effect from the Arbitral Tribunal; the Republic of Indonesia in default has contributed nothing to the Arbitral Tribunal's understanding of how this step might be achieved.

[204] Authorisation to deposit the Interim Award is therefore given by letters from the President dated this day to counsel for both Parties.

D. Extracts from the Practice of the Iran–US Claims Tribunal

(1) Tribunal Rules (1983), Article 32(1)—Types of awards

Granite States Machine Co, Inc and *Islamic Republic of Iran,* et al, Partial Award No 9–30–3 (July 29, 1982), reprinted in 1 Iran-US CTR 185, 187–88 (1981–82):

The Tribunal has, by virtue of Article 32, Paragraph 1, of the [1983] Tribunal Rules, decided to issue a Partial Award on the sole question of liability for the draft amounts claimed, and retains jurisdiction to resolve the issues of interest and costs.

Ultrasystems Inc and *Islamic Republic of Iran,* et al, Partial Award No 27–84–3 (March 4, 1983), reprinted in 2 Iran-US CTR 100, 101 (1983-I):

The Tribunal has, by virtue of Article 32, paragraph 1, of the [1983] Tribunal Rules, decided to issue a partial award covering Ultrasystems' claims with the exceptions indicated at III B 1 and 2 below, and also covering the Respondents' counterclaims.

Harnischfeger Corp and *Ministry of Roads and Transportation,* et al, Partial Award No 144–180–3 (July 31, 1984), reprinted in 7 Iran-US CTR 90, 97–98 (1984-III):

With regard to the acceptance of the Claimant's Second Amendment to Statement of Claim filed on 2 May 1983 and naming MSA as a Respondent in the Sixth and Seventh Claims, the Tribunal, having reviewed the parties' evidence and arguments on this issue, has determined that further deliberation is required on that issue as well as on other jurisdictional and substantive issues relating to those claims. Pending such deliberation the Tribunal will issue a Partial Award on Claims One to Five and Claim Eight. An Award on Claims Six and Seven shall be rendered subsequently.

RJ Reynolds Tobacco Co and *Iranian Tobacco Co*, Partial Award No 145-35-3 (July 31, 1984), reprinted in 7 Iran-US CTR 181, 183 (1984-III):

> No majority has yet been formed within the Tribunal on the question of whether interest on any principal amount awarded Claimant should be calculated from a date prior to the filing of the Statement of Claim. This issue, which may involve a considerable amount of money, needs further research and consideration, *inter alia*, on points of law. The Tribunal, therefore, by virtue of Article 32, paragraph 1 of the [1983] Tribunal Rules, decides to render a Partial Award on all other issues raised in this case, and to retain jurisdiction over a portion of Claimant's claim for interest. A related issue also to be resolved in the final award will be the allocation between the Parties of arbitration costs relating to the interest issue over which jurisdiction is retained.

117. Turning now to the application of the doctrine of *res judicata* to the facts of this Case, the Tribunal does not agree with the United States' assertion that the Tribunal's finding of an implicit obligation in Case No A15(II:A) could not have the effect of *res judicata* because it was contained in a Partial Award rather than a Final Award. The Tribunal considers the fact that the Tribunal's ruling in Case No A15(II:A) was rendered in a Partial Award does not preclude a finding of *res judicata*. What matters is whether the Tribunal's finding of an implicit obligation finally disposed of this issue between Iran and the United States, and not whether the Tribunal's decision was rendered in a Partial Award or a preliminary judgment. A Partial Award may not decide all the issues in a case, but those issues it does decide, are decided with finality and not on a provisional basis. A Partial Award is, though partial, still an "award" for the purposes of Article IV, paragraph 1, of the Claims Settlement Declaration and Article 32, paragraph 2, of the Tribunal Rules of Procedure; hence, it is final and binding on the parties.

(2) *Tribunal Rules (1983), Article 32(2)—Final and binding award*

United States of America et al and *Islamic Republic of Iran*, et al, Case No A/28, Order of August 5, 1998, at 2:

> b ....Award No 586-A27-FT... is a "final and binding" Award of the Tribunal, pursuant to Article IV, paragraph 1, of the Claims Settlement Declaration, and must be carried out "without delay," in accordance with Article 32, paragraph 2, of the [1983] Tribunal Rules. While the United States asserts that payment of the amount awarded by that Award into the Security Account would constitute compliance with the Award because Iran is "obviously and clearly in breach of its own obligation under the [Algiers] Declarations to replenish the Security Account," that is, of course, the principal legal issue in Case No A28, and the Tribunal cannot properly prejudge its future decisions in that Case. Consequently, the Tribunal cannot accept the Claimants' request that the United States be allowed to satisfy its obligations pursuant to Award No 586-A27-FT by payment of the amount awarded in para 83(b) thereof into the Security Account. The Tribunal expects that the United States will pay that amount promptly and directly to Iran....

(3) *Tribunal Rules (1983), Article 32(3) and (4)—Date, place, and signature*

Aram Sabet, et al and *Islamic Republic of Iran*, et al, Partial Award, Award No 593-815/816/817-2 (June 30, 1999):

> VI. AWARD
> 130. For the foregoing reasons,
> THE TRIBUNAL DETERMINES AS FOLLOWS:
> [Text of *dispositif* omitted]
> Dated, The Hague
> 29 June 1999

                          [signed]
                          Krzysztof Skubiszewski
                          Chairman
                          Chamber Two
                          In the Name of God
[signed]   [signed]
George H Aldrich   *Koorosh H Ameli*
                          Concurring as to the *dispositif,* para 130,
                          except that dissenting as to its subparas.
                          (A) and (D)
                          (CTR, TRR and ICC). (Separate Opinion)

(4) *Tribunal Rules (1983), Article 32(3)—Reasons for the award*

Starrett Housing Corp, et al and *Government of the Islamic Republic of Iran,* Award No ITL 32–24–1 (December 19, 1983), Concurring Opinion of Howard M Holtzmann (December 20, 1983), reprinted in 4 Iran-US CTR 159, 179–80 (1983-III):

> Unnecessarily large parts of the Interlocutory Award are devoted to descriptions of the contentions of the parties. These are flawed in ways which reflect adversely on the quality of the work of the Tribunal.
>
> One problem is that it is difficult to identify which statements are findings of the Tribunal and which are only contentions of a party. Many statements which might appear to be findings of the Tribunal are identified as party contentions only in short prefatory clauses which sometimes appear several sentences, paragraphs—or even pages—earlier. Adding to the confusion, not all such contentions are confined to the section headed "Facts and Contentions"; many appear elsewhere in the text.
>
> The Interlocutory Award often fails to indicate which contentions are supported by evidence and which are not. Further, certain statements presented as contentions are, in my view, amendations of, or additions to, the record before us.
>
> The [1983] Tribunal Rules require that the Tribunal "state the reasons upon which the award is based." Article 32, paragraph 3. That calls for an explanation of the Tribunal's views, but it is not a requirement that an award regurgitate every unsupported allegation in every pleading and argument. The purpose of an award is to express and explain the decision of the Tribunal, not to serve as a vehicle for the polemics of any party.

Mohsen Asgari Nazari and *Islamic Republic of Iran,* Award No559–221–1 (August 24, 1994), Dissenting and Concurring Opinion of Howard M Holtzmann (August 24, 1994), reprinted in 30 Iran-US CTR 163, 163, 168–69 (1994) (footnotes omitted):

> I also write separately to call attention to the Tribunal's growing tendency to write Awards that are overly long and excessively detailed—a tendency that, regrettably, this Award exemplifies.
>
> …
>
> A plea for brevity must, in principle, be brief.
>
> The lengthy Award in this Case invites reconsideration of the Tribunal's practices in preparing its decisions. I write not in criticism of the draftsmen of this particular Award, but rather to point out a tendency that is growing throughout the Tribunal to prepare Awards that are overly long and unnecessarily detailed.
>
> The issue is not a choice of literary style. At stake is the efficient use of the Tribunal's limited time, funds and facilities—resources which are, in my view, endangered by present practices in drafting awards. Also at stake is the usefulness of the Tribunal's Awards to readers generally, for too often the main points are obscured by a mass of needless detail. The Tribunal Rules—which in this respect are identical to the [1976] UNCITRAL Arbitration Rules—require only that "[t]he arbitral tribunal shall state the reasons upon which the award is based…." Article 32, para 3. There is no requirement in the Rules, or elsewhere, that Awards include a description of every step in the arbitral proceedings. Nor is there any requirement to summarize virtually every submission of the parties on issues of fact and law. Although I am aware that judicial practice in some fora favors such practices, I find no need for a profusion of detail in the arbitral process of a tribunal such as this.

I respectfully suggest that it is entirely possible—and preferable—in most Tribunal Awards to (i) shorten the description of the procedural history of the Case to include only the key events, and (ii) concentrate the description of the facts and contentions on matters that form the basis of the reasons for the decision. These steps would not only conserve the resources of the Tribunal, but also would help readers to focus on the essential elements of the case.

(5) Tribunal Rules (1983), Article 32(4)—Failure to sign the award

(a) Statements of reasons for failure to sign the award

Statement of Reasons for Judges Kashani, Shafeiei, and Sani's Failure to Sign Award No FT-A1 (Case A/1 (I, III and IV)) (July 30, 1982), reprinted in 1 Iran-US CTR 197, 197 (1981–82):

> Having been informed of the time when the decision would be signed at the Headquarters of the Tribunal, Mr. Kashani, Mr. Shafeiei and Mr. Jahangir Sani failed to be present.
> The Hague, 30 July 1982

Statement of Reasons for Judge Sani's Failure to Sign Award No 20–17–3 (*Raygo Wagner Equipment Co*) (December 15, 1982), reprinted in 1 Iran-US CTR 411, 415 (1981–82):

> Judge Jahangir Sani took part in the hearing and deliberations in this case. The Tribunal was informed that he in effect would not sign the award, and he was not present or available at the signing.

Statement of Reasons for Judge Shafeiei's Failure to Sign Award No 31–157–2 (*Esphanian*) (March 29, 1983), reprinted in 2 Iran-US CTR 170, 170 (1983-I):

> Mr. Shafeiei took part in the hearing and deliberation of this case. He signed the English text of the Award. Having been invited by letter dated 25 March 1983 to sign the Farsi text on 28 March 1983, he attended the meeting, but refused to sign.

Statement of Reasons for Judge Shafeiei's Failure to Sign Award No 32–211–2 (*Golpira*) (March 29, 1983), reprinted in 2 Iran-US CTR 177, 177 (1983-I):

> Mr. Shafeiei took part in the hearing and deliberation of this case. He signed the English text of the Award. Having been invited by letter dated 25 March 1983 to sign the Farsi text on 28 March 1983, he attended the meeting, but refused to sign.

Statement of Reasons for Judge Shafeiei's Failure to Sign Award No 46–57–2 (*Kimberly-Clark Corp.*) (May 25, 1983), reprinted in 2 Iran-US CTR 343, 343 (1983-I):

> Mr. Shafeiei did not appear to sign the Award, though invited to come by the attached letter of 16 May 1983. Several hours before the signature, Mr. Shafeiei gave me a written request to postpone the signature.

Statement of Reasons for Judge Shafeiei's Failure to Sign Award No 61–188–2 (*National Airmotive Corp*) (July 14, 1983), reprinted in 3 Iran-US CTR 92, 92 (1983-II):

> Having been notified to be available to participate in Chamber deliberations and proceedings during the period from 6 July to 31 July 1983, Mr. Shafeiei has absented himself and has failed to inform the Chamber of any address or telephone number where he can be reached. The Chairman of the Chamber has delivered to Mr. Shafeiei's office on 13 July a letter enclosing the draft award, informing Mr. Shafeiei of the place and time of signature and inviting him to attend. Mr. Shafeiei failed to attend the signing.

Statement of Reasons for Judge Shafeiei's Failure to Sign Award No 61–188–2 (*Gruen Associates, Inc*) (July 27, 1983), reprinted in 3 Iran-US CTR 97, 108–09 (1983-II):

> After the Hearing in this case on 26 May 1983 the three arbitrators agreed to begin deliberations at the end of June. Throughout the period from February to late June the three arbitrators had been in agreement that July would be fully dedicated to the final deliberations in this and the other pending cases, in view of the 1 August effective date of Chairman Bellet's resignation from the Tribunal.
> On 23 June 1983, however, Mr. Shafeiei sent Chairman Bellet a note informing him that he intended to be absent from the Tribunal on vacation until the end of July. The Chairman responded by a note dated 29 June saying that, while a brief vacation was acceptable, Mr. Shafeiei was expected

after 5 July. Nevertheless, after a further exchange of notes, Mr. Shafeiei has absented himself until the present and has given no address or telephone number where he could be reached. Only yesterday afternoon, too late to be of any use, did Mr. Shafeiei's legal assistant give the Tribunal a telephone number in another country where Mr. Shafeiei might be reached. The Chairman has had all the successive drafts of this award since Mr. Shafeiei's departure deposited in his office in due time so that, if he had been present, he could have read and commented upon them, but no comments have been received. The Chairman also deposited in Mr. Shafeiei's office on 20 July 1983 a letter informing him of the place and time of signature. Mr. Shafeiei failed to attend the signing. In these circumstances, an arbitral tribunal cannot permit its work to be frustrated. This statement is made pursuant to Article 32, paragraph 4 of the [1983] Tribunal Rules of Procedure.

Statement of Reasons for Judge Shafeiei's Failure to Sign Award No 59–220–2 (*Intrend International, Inc*) (July 27, 1983), reprinted in 3 Iran-US CTR 117, 117–18 (1983-II):

> Deliberations in this case began soon after the Hearing on 19 April 1983. All three arbitrators participated fully in these deliberations, which continued until the end of May. Throughout the period from February to late June the three arbitrators had been in agreement that July would be fully dedicated to the final deliberations in this and the other pending cases, in view of the 1 August effective date of Chairman Bellet's resignation from the Tribunal.
>
> On 23 June 1983, however, Mr. Shafeiei sent Chairman Bellet a note informing him that he intended to be absent from the Tribunal on vacation until the end of July. The Chairman responded by a note dated 29 June saying that, while a brief vacation was acceptable, Mr. Shafeiei was expected after 5 July. Nevertheless, after a further exchange of notes, Mr. Shafeiei has absented himself until the present and has given no address or telephone number where he could be reached. Only yesterday afternoon, too late to be of any use, did Mr. Shafeiei's legal assistant give the Tribunal a telephone number in another country where Mr. Shafeiei might be reached.
>
> The Chairman has had all the successive drafts of this award since Mr. Shafeiei's departure deposited in his office in due time so that, if he had been present, he could have read and commented upon them, but no comments have been received. The Chairman also deposited in Mr. Shafeiei's office on 20 July 1983 a letter informing him of the place and time of signature. Mr. Shafeiei failed to attend the signing. In these circumstances, an arbitral tribunal cannot permit its work to be frustrated. This statement is made pursuant to Article 32, paragraph 4 of the [1983] Tribunal Rules of Procedure.

Statement of Reasons for Judge Shafeiei's Failure to Sign Award No 60–83–2 (*Reynolds Metals Co*) (July 27, 1983), reprinted in 3 Iran-US CTR 120, 120 (1983-II):

> Having been notified to be available to participate in Chamber deliberations and proceedings during the period from 6 July to 31 July 1983, Mr. Shafeiei has absented himself and failed to inform the Chamber of any address or telephone number where he can be reached.
>
> Only yesterday afternoon, too late to be of any use, did Mr. Shafeiei's legal assistant give the Tribunal a telephone number in another country where Mr. Shafeiei might be reached.
>
> The Chairman of the Chamber had a letter delivered to Mr. Shafeiei's office on 20 July enclosing a draft of the present award, informing Mr. Shafeiei of the place and time of signature and inviting him to attend the signing.
>
> [Author's note: For other similar statements of reasons for Judge Shafeiei's failure to sign awards dated 27 July 1983, see Statement of Reasons for Judge Shafeiei's Failure to Sign Award No ITL 24–49–23 (*Gould Marketing, Inc*) (July 27,1983), reprinted in 3 Iran-US CTR 155, 155 (1983-II); Statement of Reasons for Judge Shafeiei's Failure to Sign Award No ITL 23–120–2 (*Chas T Main International, Inc*) (July 27, 1983), reprinted in 3 Iran-US CTR 168, 168 (1983-II).]

Statement of Reasons for Judge Sani's Failure to Sign Award Nos 74–62–3 (*Blount Bros*), 73–67–3 (*Woodward-Clyde Consultants*), 72–124–3 (*Warnecke & Associates*), 70–185–3 (*Chas T Main*), 71–346–3 (*Alan Craig*) (September 2, 1983), reprinted in 3 Iran-US CTR 237–38, 254–55, 268–69, 276–77, 291–93 (1983-II):

The deliberations in this case were held, with members Mångard, Jahangir Sani and Mosk present, after the Hearing which was held on 5 April 1983 and before the Tribunal's summer recess, which began on 11 June 1983. During the Chamber's final meeting prior to the recess, it was determined that the Chamber would reconvene in early August 1983. In conformity with this determination, the Chairman issued a memorandum on 13 June 1983, requesting the arbitrators to reserve 8, 10 and 12 August 1983 for deliberations. Presidential Order No 10, dated 15 June 1983, provided that, in cases involving requests for interim relief or other urgent matters, Chamber Two was authorized to act in lieu of Chamber Three until 31 July 1983. Furthermore, the Tribunal's official schedule of proceedings, dated 6 June 1983, indicated that a meeting of the Full Tribunal was scheduled for 15–17 August 1983, that Hearings before Chamber Three were scheduled for 18, 19, 25 and 30 August, and that a Pre-Hearing Conference before Chamber Three was scheduled on 1 September 1983.

On 6 August 1983, the Chairman of Chamber Three issued a schedule of meetings under which the finalization of awards was to take place in Case Nos 84, 124, 185 and 346 on 11 and 12 August 1983, and further deliberations were to be held in Case Nos 35, 62, 67 and 127 on 13 August 1983.

By a letter dated 10 August 1983, the Agent of the Islamic Republic of Iran stated to the Tribunal, that Judge Mostafa Jahangir Sani the Iranian Arbitrator of Chamber Three of the Tribunal has submitted his resignation to the Government of the Islamic Republic of Iran. His resignation has been accepted by the Government and will be effective as of 10 August 1983. His successor will be introduced to the Tribunal in due course.

No reasons were cited for the purported resignation.

The President of the Tribunal ordered that certain Hearings before the Full Tribunal, which were scheduled to take place during its 15–17 August 1983 meetings, be postponed. In addition, the Chairman of Chamber Three cancelled the meetings set for the finalization of awards and further deliberations during the week of 8 August 1983.

Judge Jahangir Sani did not appear at the Full Tribunal meeting held on 15 August 1983. At the 17 August 1983 Full Tribunal meeting, the President stated that the Tribunal had as yet received no valid reasons for Judge Jahangir Sani's absence and had not authorized that absence. The President also declared that it would be for Chamber Three and the Full Tribunal to determine the legal consequences of that absence in the individual cases pending before them. Thereafter, the Chairman of Chamber Three ordered that the Hearings scheduled for 18, 19 and 25 August and the Pre-Hearing Conference scheduled for 1 September be postponed.

By a letter dated 18 August 1983 and conveyed by post and telex, the Chairman of Chamber Three informed Judge Jahangir Sani of the President's declarations and notified him that a new schedule had been set under which, inter alia, the finalization and signing of the award in this case would take place on 2 September 1983.

In a telex dated 24 August 1983 to the Chairman of Chamber Three, Judge Jahangir Sani acknowledged receipt of the letter of 18 August 1983 and informed the Chairman that he considered his resignation to the Islamic Republic of Iran to be effective upon the Tribunal and that he was no longer legally authorized or empowered to participate in the taking of decisions or the issuance of awards except for "the preparing and drafting, or drawing up and elaborating, of a judicial opinion or award which has previously been communicated or announced."

Neither in this telex nor in a telex received on the following day, addressed to the Full Tribunal, did Judge Jahangir Sani state that it would be physically impossible for him to take part in the meeting of 2 September.

Judge Jahangir Sani was not present for the signing of the Award in this case at the 2 September Chamber meeting.

Under the above circumstances, the Tribunal has determined that it may proceed with the signing of the Award in the absence of Judge Jahangir Sani pursuant to Article 32, paragraph 4, of the Tribunal Rules.

Statement of Reasons for Judge Ansari's Failure to Sign Award No 93–2–3 (*American Intl Group, Inc*) (December 19, 1983), reprinted in 4 Iran-US CTR 111, 111 (1983-III):

> The arbitrators in Chamber Three of the Tribunal having been invited to sign the Award on 19 December 1983 at 12 noon, Judge Ansari Moin appeared and stated that he would not sign the Award.

Statement of Reasons for Judge Shafeiei's Failure to Sign Award No 147–7–2 (*Tippetts, Abbett, McCarthy, Stratton*) (June 22, 1984), reprinted in 6 Iran-US CTR 229, 229 (1984-II):

> Mr. Shafeiei took part in the hearing and deliberation of this case. Having been invited to sign the Award, he refused to do so.

Statement of Reasons for Judge Ansari's Failure to Sign Award No 309–129–3 (*Sedco, Inc*) (July 2, 1987), reprinted in 15 Iran-US CTR 187, 187 (1987-II):

> The Chairman in a memorandum to the Chamber Members of 11 June 1987 declared that the Award in this Case would be signed during the week of 29 June 1987. On Thursday, 2 July 1987, the last working day of that week, the Arbitrators met on the Tribunal's premises at which time the completed Award was presented for signature. The Chairman and Judge Brower signed the Award at that time, and it was agreed that Judge Ansari would sign an explanatory statement to be appended to the Award so that it might be filed no later than 5 p.m. on Monday, 6 July 1987, thereby satisfying the requirement of Article 32, paragraph 4, of the [1983] Tribunal Rules that the Award be signed by all three Arbitrators.
>
> The Tribunal notes with regret that by the agreed deadline on 6 July Judge Ansari had not presented the statement and consequently, although Judge Ansari participated fully in the deliberations, the Award does not bear his signature.

Statement of Reasons for Judge Ameli's Failure to Sign Award No 314–24–1 (*Starrett Housing Corp*) (August 14, 1987), reprinted in 16 Iran-US CTR 237, 237 (1987-III):

> After the Hearing in this Case on 16–24 January 1987, all three arbitrators met for deliberations at the following times: 24 January, 9–13 March, 29 June–3 July, 20–23 July and 11–14 August 1987. Copies of successive drafts of the Final Award were circulated among all of the arbitrators, and were discussed in detail. The changes in the last draft that resulted in the text of the Final Award, as signed, were also reviewed and discussed by all of the arbitrators.
>
> During the deliberation meetings held on 20–24 July 1987, the time for signing the Final Award was scheduled for 5 p.m. 13 August 1987. The last week of deliberations began on 11 August 1987. During these meetings the time for signing the Final Award was re-scheduled to 4 p.m. on 14 August 1987 in order to permit further time for deliberations. All arbitrators were invited to attend and sign at that time. On the afternoon of 14 August all three arbitrators met and reviewed a few final proposed changes in the last draft. At the conclusion of that meeting Judge Ameli stated that he refused to sign the Final Award.

Statement of Reasons for Judge Mostafavi's Failure to Sign Partial Award No 375–381–1 (*Uiterwyk Corp*) (January 8, 1991), reprinted in 19 Iran-US CTR 169, 169–70 (1988-II):

> Mr. Mostavi, who is a Member of the Tribunal for this Case pursuant to Article 13, paragraph 5 of the Tribunal Rules, was invited to sign the Partial Award and to indicate whether he joins in it or disagrees. In response to that invitation, Mr. Mostafavi addressed a letter dated 3 June 1988 to the President ("the letter") in which he stated that he refused to sign and requested that the President "incorporate this response in its present form in the [Partial] Award, as constituting my reason for refusing to sign."…
>
> …

As Mr. Mostafavi's letter also confirms, he has at no time indicated that he wished to rejoin the deliberations—which he was, of course, free to do. In those circumstances, as Mr. Mostafavi had expressly refused to continue participating in any deliberations, had been informed by the Chairman that deliberations would nevertheless continue, and then actually withdrawn from deliberations, the working draft of the Partial Award which was part of the deliberations was not sent to him. But the text agreed to by the majority was mailed to him well in advance of its issuance. This text was received by him and he has had the opportunity to indicate his agreement or disagreement and to file a separate opinion, which he has done, in effect, by submitting his letter dated 3 June 1988.

Statement of Reasons for Judge Khalilian's Failure to Sign Award No 452–39–2 (*Phillips Petroleum Co Iran*) (June 29, 1989), reprinted in 21 Iran-US CTR 79 (1989-I):

Having fully participated in the deliberation of the Case and having been informed of the time when the Final Award would be signed at the Tribunal, Mr. Khalilian was present but declined to sign. In these circumstances we conclude that the Tribunal is justified, and in fact obligated, by international law and precedent to proceed with the signature of the Award. Any other conclusion, in a continuing tribunal of this type with many cases on its docket, would permit the Tribunal's work to be sabotaged. This statement is made pursuant to Article 32, paragraph 4, of the [1983] Tribunal Rules.

(b) Improper statements of reasons and post-award exchanges

Judge Sani's Reasons for Not Signing Award No 20–17–3 (*Raygo Wagner Equipment Co*) (February 3, 1983), reprinted in 1 Iran-US CTR 415–17 (1981–82):

I was not notified of the deliberative session which resulted in the issuance of an Award in the present case; nor did I happen to be present on the Tribunal premises and, consequently, at the meeting itself, when it was held.

In my "opinion" related to case No 30, a copy of which I annex hereto, I have already elucidated some elements of the events which resulted in the issuance of the present Award in my absence. In the present "opinion," I shall first relate the remaining events concerning case No 17, following which I shall discuss the major deficiencies in the Award issued.

The fact that said Award was rendered without consultation with, and in the absence of, one arbitrator—together with the deficiencies which I shall elaborate upon below—constitute in my view so serious a violation of recognized legal principles as to necessitate that I not take part in the signing of the issued Award.

...

The first part of this "Opinion," which reveal[s] the fact that I was neither aware of nor present at the deliberative session, is intended to show that what has been signed and published by Mr. Mångard and Mr. Mosk with respect to Case No 17 cannot be considered as a legally valid award.

Judge Mosk's Comments on Judge Sani's Reasons for not Signing Award No 20–17–3 (*Raygo Wagner Equipment Co*) (March 3, 1983), reprinted in 1 Iran-US CTR 424–28 (1981–82) (footnotes omitted):

The document entitled "Mr. Jahangir Sani's Reasons For Not Signing The Decision Made By Mr. Mångard and Mr. Mosk In Case No 17" ("document") is both inappropriate and inaccurate. *See* Concurring Opinion of Richard M Mosk in Case No 30.

...

Second, an arbitrator should not participate in or aid efforts to attack Tribunal awards, because to do so may cast doubt on that arbitrator's impartiality.

Third, Judge Sani refused to participate in some of the deliberations in Case No 72 and did not sign the Award. As Professor Sanders notes: "Refusal to sign is not looked upon favourably in arbitration practice." Sanders, *supra* at 208. It is for the signing members to provide the reasons for the absence of Judge Sani's signature, not Judge Sani.

Fourth, under international law, Judge Sani cannot frustrate the work of the Chamber or the Tribunal by wilfully absenting himself and refusing to sign an award....

Judge Shafeiei's Reasons for Not Signing Award No 31–157–2 (*Esphanian*) (March 29, 1983), reprinted in 2 Iran-US CTR 170, 170 (1983-I):

> I refuse to take part in the making of a decision which cannot be legally justified, but tainted with improper motives....

Judge Shafeiei's Reasons for Not Signing Award No 32–211–2 (*Golpira*) (March 29, 1983), reprinted in 2 Iran-US CTR 177, 177 (1983-I):

> I refuse to take part in the making of a decision which, in the part dealing with jurisdiction, cannot be legally justified, but tainted with improper motives....

Judge Shafeiei's Reasons for Not Signing Award No 46–57–2 (*Kimberly-Clark Corp*) (May 27, 1983), reprinted in 2 Iran-US CTR 343, 344 (1983-I):

> There had been no understanding therefore, that the draft Award would necessarily be signed on 25 May 1983. Deliberations of the case were in no way completed as must be in arbitral proceedings whose awards are not appealable to the same body and where there are serious probabilities for error and destruction of the Parties' rights.
>
> I was convinced in all sincerity that further deliberations were called for, and hoped that the issues I had raised would at least be discussed. On 25 May I attended the Tribunal with a short delay, but my colleagues signed the draft Award in my absence.
>
> The final deliberations and signing of the Award in the present case have been conducted in my absence and without my participation. I have played no role in those respects and therefore bear no responsibility.

Judge Shafeiei's Reasons for Not Signing Award Nos 58–449–3 (*National Airmotive*), 59–220–2 (*Intrend*), 60–83–2 (*Reynolds*), and 61–188–2 (*Gruen*) (August 9, 1983), reprinted in 3 Iran-US CTR 124, 124–25 (1983-II):

> The recording of the name of an arbitrator at the bottom of an award signifies that he participated in the making of that award—that is, that he participated in the Chamber hearings and in completely democratic discussions and deliberations, in taking a decision, in preparing the draft award, in studying it and, finally, in preparing the final award and signing it. I have had absolutely no part or role in the formulation of the present Awards, nor have I been present therein. Everything has been carried out in my absence and even without my knowledge. Therefore, it would have been appropriate for Mr. George Aldrich and Mr. Bellet to explain just why they have recorded my name. Throughout the month of July, I availed myself of my annual leave in order to take a much needed rest and to complete some backlogged Chamber work; and this was entirely permissible and justified. But meanwhile, Mr. Bellet and Mr. Aldrich held formal Chamber meetings on a two-member basis and rendered the present Awards.
>
> If these gentlemen had refrained from recording my name at the end of those Awards, I could at least have praised their frankness. However, these gentlemen wrote my name, along with making certain presentations. I call this action by Mr. Bellet, the former Chief Justice of the Supreme Court of France, and Mr. George Aldrich, the American arbitrator, as prevarication, duplicity, and hypocrisy.

Judge Aldrich's Comments on Judge Shafeiei's Reasons for Not Signing Award Nos 58–449–3 (*National Airmotive*), 59–220–2 (*Intrend*), 60–83–2 (*Reynolds*), and 61–188–2 (*Gruen*) (October 13, 1983), reprinted in 3 Iran-US CTR 145, 145–46 (1983-II):

> I have hesitated to respond to this document by Judge Shafeiei on 9 August 1983, as I do not wish to prolong this unfortunate public airing of our internal differences. However, I have concluded that there is one point to which I must respond in view of attacks on the awards in question. Judge Shafeiei says his absence for the month of July was permissible and justified and was for the

purposes of rest and completing some backlogged Chamber work. The facts, however, force me to the conclusion that his absence was impermissible and that it was intended: (a) to avoid any further deliberations with Judge Bellet; (b) to attempt thereby to prevent Chamber 2 from rendering awards in the pending cases prior to the 31 July effective date of Judge Bellet's resignation; and (c) to provide grounds for attacks on any awards issued issued during that absence.

Judge Mosk's Additional Comments on Judge Sani's Failure to Sign Award Nos 74–62–3 (*Blount Bros*), 73–67–3 (*Woodward-Clyde Consultants*), 72–124–3 (*Warnecke & Associates*), 70–185–3 (*Chas T Main*), 71–346–3 (*Alan Craig*) (September 2, 1983), reprinted in 3 Iran-US CTR 294, 294–96 (1983-II):

> I have concurred in the statement concerning the absence of a signature of one of the members of the Tribunal. Article 32, paragraph 4, of [1983] Tribunal Rules.
>
> There is ample authority for the proposition that the Tribunal may proceed with its work despite the circumstances concerning Judge Mostafa Jahangir Sani's purported departure. *See Sabotage Claims* (U.S. v. Ger.) 8 *R. Intl Arb. Awards* 458 (Decision of Roberts, Umpire) and 238–41 (Opinion of Garnett, Commissioner) (1939); Decisions 21 and 22, French-Mexican Claims Commission, 5 *R. Intl Arb. Awards* 510–14 (1936); *Columbia v. Cauca Co.*, 190 U.S. 524, 47 L. Ed. 1159 (1902); *Interpretation of Peace Treaties with Bulgaria, Hungary and Romania (Second Phase), Advisory Opinion* [1950] I.C.J. Repts. 221, 229; *see also Lena Goldfields Ltd v. Union of Soviet Socialist Republics*, reprinted at 36 *Cornell L.Q.* 42 (1930). Legal scholars have also suggested that the Tribunal can proceed under circumstances similar to those present in the instant case. *See* 2 Hyde *International Law* 1629 (1945); 1 J Voet, *The Selective Voet* 749 (Gane ed. and trans. 1955); 3 Phillimore, *Commentaries on International Law* 4 (1885); A Merignhac, *Traité theorique et pratique de l'Arbitrage International* 276–77 (1895).
>
> ...
>
> The Claims Settlement Declaration to which Iran and the United States of America adhered suggests that the Tribunal "conduct its business expeditiously" (Article III, paragraph 1) in order "to ensure that [the] Agreement can be carried out" (Article III, paragraph 2). Delays in deciding cases are inconsistent with the spirit of the Claims Settlement Declaration and with the sound administration of the Tribunal.
>
> Finally it should be noted that another Chamber of the Tribunal has proceeded to issue awards in the absence of one of its members. See, eg Award Nos 59–220–2 (*Intrend*); ITL 24–49–2 (*Gould*); ITL 23–120–2 (*Chas T Main*); 61–188–2 (*Gruen*).

Judge Kashani's Reasons for Not Signing Award No 127–257–1 (*Dow Chemical Co*) (undated), reprinted in 6 Iran-US CTR 39, 40 (1984-II):

> ... I refuse to accept and to sign the present Award on Agreed Terms and consider unlawful the payment on it.

Judge Shafeiei's Reasons for Not Signing Award No 141–7–2 (*Tippets, Abbet, McCarthy, Stratton*) (undated), reprinted in 6 Iran-US CTR 230, 252 (1984-II):

> Because I am entirely convinced that the deliberations and adjudication in connection with the present case were neither just nor impartial, and that the transfer of these millions of dollars to the United States from the account of the Iranian nation is taking place in an illegal and illegitimate manner, I have refused to sign the present award.

Judge Bahrami-Ahmadi's Reasons for Not Signing Award No ITL 66–298–2 (*Saghi*) (January 19, 1987), reprinted in 14 Iran-US CTR 8, 8 (1987-I):

> I take note of the legal opinion rendered by two members of Chamber Two, in connection with determination of the nationality of the Claimants in the above-referenced case. I have neither participated in the deliberations in that case nor signed the legal opinion relating thereto....

Judge Ansari's Reasons for Not Signing Award No 309–129–3 (*Sedco, Inc*) (July 7, 1987), reprinted in 15 Iran-US CTR 187, 187–88 (1987-II):

> The present document, which the former Chairman of this Chamber has issued as an "arbitral award" for the purpose of paying millions of dollars to the Claimant, is based on numerous incorrect premises. These incorrect premises, which include diverse substantive and fundamental errors, totally divest this "award" of value and validity. I repeatedly directed the attention of the former Chairman to various instances of these incorrect premises and substantive and fundamental errors but he unfortunately refused, on specious grounds, to accept these views and to correct the errors.... It would be improper to sign such an "award"...

Judge Ameli's Reasons for Not Signing Award No 314–24–1 (*Starrett Housing Corp*) (August 21, 1987), reprinted in 16 Iran-US CTR 255, 255–56 (1987-III):

> I did not sign the Final Award in this Case mainly for the following reasons:
> 1. The Award did not decide many disputed issues crucial to the outcome of the Case, although those issues were reflected in the Facts and Contentions of the Award itself.
> 2. As to the issues the Award has decided it has given no reasons for many of them, without agreement or authorization of the Parties to do so contrary to the clear requirements of Article 32(3) and 33(2) of the [1983] Tribunal Rules.
>
> [Other reasons omitted]
> ...
>
> In my view, each of these reasons is sufficient to set aside the Final Award in this Case, although proper decision rests with others....

(6) *Tribunal Rules (1983), Article 32(5)—Publication of the award*

Chevron Research Co and *National Iranian Oil Co*, Award on Agreed Terms No 48–18–1 (June 1, 1983), reprinted in 2 Iran-US CTR 364, 364–65 (1983-I):

> In the joint request the Parties have requested that the Settlement Agreement shall be kept confidential and not published as a part of the Award.
> ...
> The Tribunal determines in accordance with the request of the Parties and pursuant to Article 32, paragraph 5, of the [1983] Tribunal Rules that the Settlement Agreement shall not be made public.

Concurring Opinions in Case Nos 19 (*Chevron*) and 387 (*Carrier Corp*) and Dissenting Opinion in Case No 15 (*VSI*), attached to *Chevron Research Company* and *National Iranian Oil Co*, Award on Agreed Terms No 48–18–1 (June 1, 1983), reprinted in 3 Iran-US CTR 78, 79–80 (1983-II) (some footnotes omitted):

> I write separately in this case in order to call attention to what I consider to be a disturbing tendency of the Chamber routinely to grant requests that Settlement Agreements annexed to Awards be kept secret. In this case, such secrecy has been permitted by the Award, which states:
>> The Tribunal determines in accordance with the request of the Parties and pursuant to Article 32, paragraph 5, of the [1983] Tribunal Rules that the Settlement Agreement shall not be made public.
>
> Article 32, paragraph 5 does not permit indiscriminate grants of secrecy. Quite to the contrary, this provision expresses the vital principle that "[a]*ll awards and other decisions shall be made available to the public*," subject only to one sharply limited proviso. (Emphasis added). The proviso states that
>> Upon the request of one or more arbitrating parties, the arbitral tribunal may determine that it will not make the entire award or other decision public, but will make public only portions thereof from which *the identity of the parties, other identifying facts and trade or military secrets have been deleted*. (Emphasis added).

Two points are to be observed with respect to this exception to the general rule that all awards are to be made public. First, the arbitral tribunal has full discretion to determine whether or not to grant secrecy. Second, if secret treatment is permitted it is only by way of deletion of "the identity of the parties, other identifying facts and trade or military secrets." Thus, the arbitral tribunal is only authorized to delete certain carefully defined information; it is not authorized to suppress the entire text.

It must also be emphasized that Article 32, paragraph 5 relates to "all awards and decisions." It covers Awards on Agreed Terms and the annexes which are an indispensable part of such awards just as much as it relates to any other award or decision. That is a wise and proper policy. A primary purpose of Settlement Agreements is to provide for payment of settlements from the Security Account established by the Algiers Declarations. Any withdrawals from the Security Account affect the interest of parties in all cases. It is therefore highly inappropriate that a Settlement Agreement annexed to an Award which triggers such a withdrawal of funds should be cloaked in secrecy. At most, any military and trade secrets can be deleted from the text made public.[1]

In this case, the Tribunal has granted secrecy to a very simple Settlement Agreement which contains nothing which even remotely resembles a trade or military secret. I regret that the decision of the Tribunal to grant secrecy to the entire text prevents my illustrating that fact further.

[Footnote] 1. The identity of the parties or facts which would lead to their identification can hardly be kept secret, since the Award on Agreed terms must include the names of the parties and, in order for payment to be made, must be notified to the central banks which act as the Escrow Agent and Depository of the Security Account, respectively, as well as to the Agents of the two Governments and eventually to the Federal Reserve Bank of New York. In such a process, granting secrecy for the identity of parties would be entirely unworkable.

E-Systems, Inc and *Islamic Republic of Iran*, Award on Agreed Terms 94–388–1 (December 19, 1983), reprinted in 4 Iran-US CTR 197, 197–98 (1983-III):

> In the Joint Request the Parties request that the Settlement be kept confidential until the obligations contained in the Settlement Agreement have been fulfilled.
>
> ...
>
> The Tribunal determines in accordance with the request of the Parties and pursuant to Article 32, paragraph 5 of the [1983] Tribunal Rules that the Settlement Agreement shall not be made public until the obligations contained in the Settlement Agreement have been fulfilled.

Pan American World Airways, Inc, et al and *Government of the Islamic Republic of Iran,* et al, Award on Agreed Terms No 96–488–1 (December 19, 1983), reprinted in 4 Iran-US CTR 205, 205–06 (1983-II):

> The Parties to the Joint Motion request that the contents of the Settlement Agreement and the Memorandum of Understanding be kept strictly confidential.
>
> ...
>
> The Tribunal determines in accordance with the request of the Parties and pursuant to Article 32, paragraph 5 of the [1983] Tribunal Rules that the Settlement Agreement and Memorandum of Understanding shall not be made public.

Pan American World Airways, Inc, et al and *Government of the Islamic Republic of Iran,* et al, Award on Agreed Terms No 96–488–1 (December 19, 1983), Dissenting Opinion of Howard M Holtzmann (February 9, 1984), reprinted in 4 Iran-US CTR 206, 209 (1983-III):

> As I have written in an earlier opinion, the requirement of the Tribunal Rules that Awards on Agreed Terms, together with all annexed documents which are integral parts of them, be made public "is a wise and proper policy":

> A primary purpose of Settlement Agreements is to provide for payment of settlements from the Security Account established by the Algiers Declarations. Any withdrawals from the Security Account affect the interest of parties in all cases. It is therefore highly inappropriate that a Settlement Agreement annexed to an Award which triggers such a withdrawal of funds should be cloaked in secrecy. Opinions of Howard M Holtzmann re Three Awards on Agreed Terms; Concurring as to Case Nos 19 and 387; Dissenting as to Case No 15 (part I) (filed 20 June 1983).
>
> For the reasons explained above, I am disappointed that the parties have presented to us a settlement in this form. I am dismayed that the Tribunal has approved it, and that the settlement has been shrouded in secrecy. Therefore, I dissent from the Award on Agreed Terms.

Government of the United States of America, on behalf and for the benefit of *Shipside Packing Co, Inc* and *Islamic Republic of Iran*, Award on Agreed Terms No 102–11875–1 (January 12, 1984), reprinted in 5 Iran-US CTR 80, 80–81 (1984-I):

> In the Joint Request the Parties request that the terms of the Settlement Agreement and its exhibits be kept confidential. The Deputy Agent of The Government of the United States reserved its position as to this request.
>
> ...
>
> The Tribunal determines pursuant to Article 32, paragraph of the [1983] Tribunal Rules, that the Settlement Agreement and its Exhibits shall not be made public.

Government of the United States of America, on behalf and for the benefit of Shipside Packing Co, Inc and *Islamic Republic of Iran*, Award on Agreed Terms No 102–11875–1 (January 12, 1984), Separate Opinion of Howard M Holtzmann (February 9, 1984), reprinted in 5 Iran-US CTR 82, 84 (1984-I) (footnotes omitted):

> I must dissent from the action of the majority of the Chamber in granting a request of the parties that the Award on Agreed Terms be kept secret. As I have pointed out in other cases, the Tribunal Rules permit confidential treatment only for military and trade secrets. Article 32, paragraph 5 [of the 1983 Tribunal Rules].
>
> In this case, the Tribunal has mistakenly granted secrecy to a Settlement Agreement which contains nothing even remotely resembling a trade or military secret—and the parties have not pointed to any confidential material or otherwise offered any reason for secrecy.
>
> Sound considerations of policy point to the desirability of making public this entire Award on Agreed Terms, including the Settlement Agreement which is included by reference as part of it. The example of the mechanisms agreed to by the parties might be helpful in structuring settlements in other cases. Here secrecy hides a good example, as it hides a bad one in the Pan American Award on Agreed Terms. I therefore dissent from the portion of the Award which provides that the Settlement Agreement be kept secret.

United Technologies Intl, Inc, et al and *Iranian Air Force*, Award on Agreed Terms No 146–42–3 (August 8, 1984), reprinted in 7 Iran-US CTR 209, 210 (1984-III):

> The Parties in their Joint Request ask that the Tribunal treat the Settlement Agreement as confidential until the obligations of the Agreement have been completed. Since the Parties, however, have not invoked any special reasons which, in the light of Article 32, paragraph 5 of the [1983] Tribunal Rules, would justify the grant of such a request, the request is denied. Consequently, copies of the Joint Request, the MOU and the Escrow Agreement are attached hereto.

General Motors Corp, et al and *Government of the Islamic Republic of Iran,* et al, Partial Award on Agreed Terms No 147–94–1 (August 28, 1984), reprinted in 7 Iran-US CTR 220, 221–22 (1984-III):

> The Joint Request contains a request that the contents of Appendices A and B to the Settlement Agreement be kept confidential on the grounds that they contain sensitive commercial information.

...
The Tribunal determines in accordance with the request of the Parties and pursuant to Article 32, paragraph 5 of the [1983] Tribunal Rules that Appendices A and B to the Settlement Agreement shall not be made public.

Dora Sholeh Elghanayan, et al and *Islamic Republic of Iran*, Award on Agreed Terms No 576–800/801/802/803/804–3 (December 10, 1996), reprinted in 32 Iran-US CTR 221, 222 (1996) (citations omitted):

4. In the Joint Request the Parties ask the Tribunal to provide that this Award, the Joint Request and the Settlement Agreement remain confidential. However, pursuant to Article 32, paragraph 5, of the [1983] Tribunal Rules, it is within the discretion of the Tribunal to decide whether it will grant such request and delete portions of the Award from which the identity of the Parties, other identifying facts and trade or military secrets appear.... The Parties have not indicated any portions of the Settlement Agreement as containing sensitive information justifying confidentiality, and the Tribunal does not find any such sensitive information. Therefore, the request is denied. A copy of the Joint Request and the Settlement Agreement is annexed hereto.

25
Settlement and other Grounds for Termination

1. Introduction	781
2. **Settlement and other Termination—Article 36**	781
A. Text of the 2010 UNCITRAL Rule	781
B. Commentary	782
(1) Settlement—Article 36(1)	782
(a) Types of settlement agreement and the practice of awards on agreed terms	782
(b) Discretion to record a settlement agreement	784
(c) Pre-settlement negotiations	786
(2) Other grounds for termination—Article 36(2)	788
(a) Continuation of the arbitration is "unnecessary" or "impossible"	788
(b) The existence of "remaining matters"	790
(3) Technical requirements for awards on agreed terms—Article 36(3)	790
(4) Comparison to the 1976 UNCITRAL Rules	790
C. Extracts from the Practice of Investment Tribunals	792
D. Extracts from the Practice of the Iran–US Claims Tribunal	793
(1) Tribunal Rules (1983), Article 34(1)	793
(2) Tribunal Rules (1983), Article 34(2)	798

1. Introduction

In some cases, the parties may resolve their dispute during the course of the arbitration through a negotiated settlement. In other cases, the arbitration may become unnecessary or may be impossible to continue, for reasons such as the claimant's failure to pursue its claim, the resolution of the arbitral dispute in another forum, or the parties' failure to fund the arbitral tribunal through required deposits of money. In these circumstances, and possibly others, the arbitration will not end with an award that reflects a full adjudication of the issues, but rather with an award on agreed terms or a termination order. Article 36 guides the conduct of the arbitral tribunal in these circumstances.

2. Settlement and other Termination—Article 36

A. Text of the 2010 UNCITRAL Rule

Article 36 of the 2010 UNCITRAL Rules provides:[1]

1. If, before the award is made, the parties agree on a settlement of the dispute, the arbitral tribunal shall either issue an order for the termination of the arbitral proceedings or, if

---

[1] Corresponding Article 34 of the 1976 UNCITRAL Rules provides:

1. If, before the award is made, the parties agree on a settlement of the dispute, the arbitral tribunal shall either issue an order for the termination of the arbitral proceedings or, if requested by both parties and accepted by the tribunal, record the settlement in the form of an arbitral award on agreed terms. The arbitral tribunal is not obliged to give reasons for such an award.

requested by the parties and accepted by the arbitral tribunal, record the settlement in the form of an arbitral award on agreed terms. The arbitral tribunal is not obliged to give reasons for such an award.

2. If, before the award is made, the continuation of the arbitral proceedings becomes unnecessary or impossible for any reason not mentioned in paragraph 1, the arbitral tribunal shall inform the parties of its intention to issue an order for the termination of the proceedings. The arbitral tribunal shall have the power to issue such an order unless there are remaining matters that may need to be decided and the arbitral tribunal considers it appropriate to do so.

3. Copies of the order for termination of the arbitral proceedings or of the arbitral award on agreed terms, signed by the arbitrators, shall be communicated by the arbitral tribunal to the parties. Where an arbitral award on agreed terms is made, the provisions of article 34, paragraphs 2, 4 and 5, shall apply.

B. Commentary

(1) Settlement—Article 36(1)

(a) Types of settlement agreement and the practice of awards on agreed terms

Article 36(1) contemplates two situations for settlement by agreement by the parties depending on whether or not the parties wish to have their settlement recorded as an award on agreed terms.

In the first situation, where the parties choose not to have the arbitral tribunal record their settlement, their settlement agreement is not an award, but rather an agreement between the parties, enforceable to the extent that the governing law permits. Because no award is rendered in this situation to mark the conclusion of the arbitration, Article 36(1) requires the arbitral tribunal to issue an order for the termination of the arbitral proceedings. Article 36(1) imposes no deadline on the parties for informing the arbitral tribunal of a settlement. However, the parties should endeavor to state their intentions promptly to avoid incurring additional costs and to allow the arbitrators time to adjust their work schedules accordingly.[2]

Parties to a dispute may choose not to record a settlement in the form of an award on agreed terms because the terms of settlement are simple and easily enforceable without an award or the settlement is outside the scope of the tribunal's power. Case No B-25 before the Iran–US Claims Tribunal presents such an example. In that case, the United States

---

2. If, before the award is made, the continuation of the arbitral proceedings becomes unnecessary or impossible for any reason not mentioned in paragraph 1, the arbitral tribunal shall inform the parties of its intention to issue an order for the termination of the proceedings. The arbitral tribunal shall have the power to issue such an order unless a party raises justifiable grounds for objection.

3. Copies of the order for termination of the arbitral proceedings or of the arbitral award on agreed terms, signed by the arbitrators, shall be communicated by the arbitral tribunal to the parties. Where an arbitral award on agreed terms is made, the provisions of article 32, paragraph 2 and 4 to 7, shall apply.

[2] According to Berger, the parties are under a "procedural obligation" to inform the arbitral tribunal of the settlement so it may dispense with the arbitration. See K Berger, *International Economic Arbitration* (1993) 590–1; S Baker and M Davis, *The UNCITRAL Arbitration Rules in Practice: The Experience of the Iran-United States Claims Tribunal* (1992) 183. But see N Blackaby and C Partasides with A Redfern and M Hunter, *Redfern and Hunter on International Arbitration* (5th edn 2009) 526 (maintaining there is no such obligation, although it would be "a normal act of courtesy" to inform the tribunal of any settlement).

agreed to withdraw its claim that Iran had expropriated US government funds held in an Iranian bank, once the Tribunal received notification that these funds had been transferred into the US Government's possession.[3] Upon receipt of the funds by the US Government, the enforcement of the parties' agreement was no longer an issue and thus an award on agreed terms was not necessary.

In the second situation, the parties have their settlement agreement recorded as an award on agreed terms, resulting in several important benefits. First and foremost, a recorded settlement becomes an "award" within the meaning of the Rules[4] and is generally considered to be enforceable domestically and internationally.[5] In addition, when a party invokes the recording procedure, the arbitrators have an opportunity to review the settlement agreement and, if necessary, offer suggestions to improve the parties' final product.[6] Such oversight is particularly useful in situations where the parties have agreed orally or only generally to settle the dispute and subsequently seek the tribunal's assistance in memorializing the agreement in precise terms.[7]

The process of recording the award under the Rules occurs in two steps. First, pursuant to Article 36(2), the parties *jointly* petition the arbitral tribunal to record the settlement agreement. Although not required by the Rules, it is preferable that the request be in writing and signed by both parties.[8] The settlement agreement is typically attached to the joint request for the arbitral tribunal's review.[9] Second, the tribunal renders the award on agreed

---

[3] In a letter dated April 27, 1987, the US Agent made a conditional request that the Tribunal not withdraw the US claim until it received confirmation that payment had been made. Upon receipt of the confirmation, the Tribunal terminated the proceedings in accordance with Article 34(1) of the Tribunal Rules. See *Government of the United States* and *Islamic Republic of Iran*, Case No B-25, Chamber One, Order of November 17, 1987.

[4] See *Report of the Secretary-General on the Revised Draft Set of Arbitration Rules*, UNCITRAL, 9th Session, Addendum 1 (Commentary), UN Doc A/CN.9/112/Add.1 (1975), reprinted in (1976) VII UNCITRAL Ybk 166, 179 (Commentary on Draft Article 29) ("A settlement recorded in the form of an award on agreed terms acquires the legal force of an award."); P Sanders, "Commentary on UNCITRAL Arbitration Rules," (1977) II Ybk Commercial Arb 172, 212 (noting award on agreed terms is "final and binding on the parties and will be carried out by them without delay").

[5] See Article 30(2) of the Model Law, as amended ("The award on agreed terms has the status of any other award on the merits."); A van den Berg, *The New York Arbitration Convention of 1958: Towards a Uniform Judicial Interpretation* (1981) 49–50 ("The award on agreed terms...can be deemed to come within the purview of the Convention, provided that in the country of origin such award is considered a genuine award, which is almost always the case.").

[6] The arbitral tribunal's discretion to record a settlement agreement is discussed below in section 2(B)(1)(b).

[7] UNCITRAL, 9th Session, Addendum 1 (Commentary), UN Doc A/CN.9/112/Add.1, n 4, (Commentary on Draft Article 29). Another reason for obtaining a recorded settlement is "the desirability (particularly where a state or state agency is involved) of having a definite and identifiable 'result' of the arbitral proceedings, in the form of an award which may be passed to the appropriate paying authority for implementation." N Blackaby and C Partasides, *Redfern and Hunter on International Arbitration*, n 2, 525.

[8] See K Berger, *International Economic Arbitration*, n 2, 583. In the context of the Model Law, it has been noted that a request may come from only one party if no doubt remains that the request was made on behalf of the other party with that party's full consent. H Holtzmann and J Neuhaus, *A Guide to the UNCITRAL Model Law on Commercial Arbitration: Legislative History and Commentary* (1989) 822–3

It is useful practice for all parties to the proposed settlement agreement to place their signatures on the joint request so that the tribunal has the appropriate contact information to confirm each party's consent, if necessary. The signatures of all the parties also informs the tribunal that, unless otherwise stated, the joint request is for an award on agreed terms that resolves all, not a part of, the arbitral claims. J Selby and D Stewart, "Practical Aspects of Arbitrating Claims Before the Iran-United States Claims Tribunal," (1984) 18(2) Intl Lawyer 211, 241.

[9] Although the contents of the settlement agreement will vary depending on the circumstances of the dispute, the parties may wish to consider the terms of the standard settlement agreement used by parties before the

terms in accordance with the applicable technical provisions of the Rules.[10] The award on agreed terms should incorporate the settlement agreement by reference, include statements that the arbitral tribunal has accepted and recorded the settlement agreement, and set forth the operative terms of the settlement in the *dispositif*.

Examples of settlement agreements and awards on agreed terms appear below in sections 2(C) and 2(D)(1).[11]

(b) Discretion to record a settlement agreement

According to Article 36(1), the parties' decision to record their settlement as an award on agreed terms must be "accepted by the tribunal." Whether the arbitral tribunal should have discretion to refuse to record an award on agreed terms was the subject of debate.[12] Some members maintained that the decision to record a settlement should be determined solely by the will of the parties.[13] The majority of representatives, however, believed that the arbitral tribunal should possess some measure of discretion to refuse an award on agreed terms, even if requested by the parties, in cases in which the settlement was deemed unlawful or against the *ordre public* at the place of the arbitration.[14] In its final form, Article 36(1) grants the arbitral tribunal discretion to record a settlement.

This discretion is circumscribed by the duty to record only those settlements that fall within the arbitral tribunal's jurisdiction, as established by the arbitration agreement.[15] If the parties' settlement involves new subject matter outside the scope of the original agreement, the arbitral tribunal may interpret the settlement agreement as an implied amendment of the arbitration agreement.[16] If the settlement includes third parties who are not original signatories to the arbitration agreement, however, then those new parties must accede to the arbitration agreement in order for the settlement agreement to be recorded as a valid award.[17]

Iran–US Claims Tribunal: "(1) termination of all pending litigation by both parties wherever filed; (2) mutual release and discharge of claims; (3) indemnity and hold harmless against future claims by related parties; (4) transfer of all rights of property; (5) waiver of claims of costs and attorneys; and (6) agreement to submit jointly to the arbitral tribunal a request for approval of the settlement agreement and requiring approval for the agreement to have legal effect provision that agreement would have no legal effect if not approved." See P Trooboff, "Settlements," in D Caron and J Crook (eds) *The Iran-United States Claims Tribunal and the Process of International Claims Resolution* (2000) 295.

[10] See section 2(B)(3).

[11] See *TCW Group, Inc* (1976 Rules), reprinted in section 2(C), and *Sun Co, Inc* (1983 Tribunal Rules), reprinted in section 2(D)(1).

[12] One commentator notes that "the parties are free to settle their claims as they wish, but they are not free to require that the tribunal exercise its own authority to approve that settlement" and to do so would "misconceiv[e] an arbitral tribunal's adjudicatory role" G Born, *International Commercial Arbitration* (2009) 2437.

[13] See *Report of the UNCITRAL*, 8th Session, Summary of Discussion of the Preliminary Draft, UN Doc A/10017, para 194 (1975), reprinted in (1975) VI UNCITRAL Ybk 24, 42–3. See *Summary Record of the 11th Meeting of the Committee of the Whole (II)*, UNCITRAL, 9th Session, UN Doc A/CN.9/9/C.2/SR.11, at 10, para 79 (1976) (Comment by Mr Melis, Austria).

[14] UNCITRAL, 9th Session, UN Doc A/CN.9/9/C.2/SR.11, n 13, at 10, para 195; UNCITRAL, 9th Session, Addendum 1 (Commentary), UN Doc A/CN.9/112/Add.1, n 4, (Commentary on Draft Article 29(1)). See also *Summary Record of the 151st Meeting of the UNCITRAL*, 8th Session, UN Doc A/CN.9/SR.167, at 203 (1975) (Comment by Mr Holtzmann, United States, stating that the "arbitrators should be left free to decide whether they agreed or refused to record a settlement in the form of an arbitral award" because without this discretion "arbitrators [would be] at the mercy of possible abuses by the parties").

[15] K Berger, *International Economic Arbitration*, n 2, 586.

[16] K Berger, *International Economic Arbitration*, n 2, 586.

[17] K Berger, *International Economic Arbitration*, n 2, 586.

The arbitral tribunal's power to refuse to record a settlement agreement is, in practice, limited.[18] Only a light standard of review is appropriate with the aim of proofing the terms of the settlement agreement for egregious violations of the law and clear violations of the *ordre public*.[19] It is not the task of the arbitrators to investigate the parties' *reasons* for settlement.[20] The arbitrators' concern is not *why* a party has agreed to a particular term as part of the settlement, but rather *whether* such terms are valid and enforceable under the applicable law and policy.[21] Suggestions by the arbitral tribunal regarding technical matters, such as with respect to the format or structure of the award, are of course helpful.

What are the circumstances under which refusal to record a settlement agreement is appropriate? Professor Sanders has suggested that a settlement agreement that violates foreign exchange controls should be refused.[22] In negotiations on the UNCITRAL Model Law, the Secretariat observed that refusal may be appropriate "in case of suspected fraud, [or] illicit or utterly unfair terms."[23] Commentators have proposed additional examples, including awards that encourage or facilitate the performance of an illegal act, such as the manufacture of an internationally banned drug or the smuggling of contraband.[24]

In the unique context of the Iran–US Claims Tribunal, the standard for refusing to record an award established by the Algiers Declarations was addressed in Case No A/1.[25] The case arose out of conflicting interpretations of the role of the Security Account in paying out settlements entered into by Iran and private claimants. While both the United States and Iran eventually agreed that the Security Account should serve this purpose, the governments' views on the standard to be applied in recording a settlement continued to differ. Iran argued that the Tribunal should make an award on agreed terms any time a claim was found to be *prima facie* within the Tribunal's jurisdiction. The United States took the position that the Tribunal's discretion to record should be broader. It argued that in addition to determining that the claim to be settled was within the Tribunal's jurisdiction, the Tribunal must review the settlement to ensure that it represents a "reasonable resolution" of the claim.[26]

---

[18] This accords with the drafters' likely intention of narrow discretion, J Castello, "UNCITRAL Rules," in F Weigand (ed) *Practitioner's Handbook on International Commercial Arbitration* (2nd edn 2009) 1516–17 (noting that the drafters "evidently expected the tribunal's discretion to be narrow, since they appeared to discuss only two grounds for refusing a request: 'the settlement agreed on by the parties might be unlawful or contrary to public policy'").

[19] P Sanders, "Commentary on UNCITRAL Arbitration Rules," n 4, 212 ("as a rule...the arbitrators will be prepared to incorporate the settlement into an award signed by them."). In the context of the Model Law, Holtzmann and Neuhaus believe that refusal should occur only in "exceptional cases," such as violations of law and policy, along with affronts to "fundamental notions of fairness and justice." H Holtzmann and J Neuhaus, *A Guide to the UNCITRAL Model Law*, n 8, 824–5 (citing *Commission Report*, UN Doc A/40/17, para 249 (August 21, 1985).

[20] H Holtzmann and J Neuhaus, *A Guide to the UNCITRAL Model Law*, n 8, 824–5.

[21] See J van Hof "UNCITRAL Arbitration Rules, Section IV, Article 34 [Settlement or other grounds for termination]" in L Mistelis (ed) *Concise International Arbitration* (2010) 220.

[22] See UNCITRAL, 9th Session, UN Doc A/CN.9/9/C.2/SR.11, n 13, at 10, para 82; P Sanders, "Commentary on UNCITRAL Arbitration Rules," n 4, 212. See also UN Doc A/CN.9/SR.167, n 14, at 202 (Comment by Mr Gueiros, Brazil, proposing language that provides: "If the arbitrators are of the opinion that the settlement would be against public policy or against the rights or interests governed by the statutes of mandatory trade rules, they should refuse to record the settlement in the form of an arbitral award....").

[23] *Seventh Secretariat Note, Analytical Commentary on Draft Text*, UN Doc A/CN.9/264, at para 2 (March 25, 1985), reprinted in H Holtzmann and J Neuhaus, *A Guide to the UNCITRAL Model Law*, n 8, 832.

[24] See N Blackaby and C Partasides, *Redfern and Hunter on International Arbitration*, n 2, 526–7.

[25] See *Iran* and *United States*, Case A/1 (Issue II), Decision (May 14, 1982), reprinted in 1 Iran-US CTR 144 (1981–1982).

[26] *Iran* and *United States*, Case A/1 (1983 Tribunal Rules), at 152.

Recognizing the limits on the Tribunal's jurisdiction established by Iran and the United States in the Algiers Declarations, the Tribunal found that it could have "no jurisdiction over any matter not conferred on it by these Declarations."[27] Thus, the Tribunal determined that it was incumbent upon the Tribunal to determine whether the claim on which a settlement rests is within its jurisdiction with respect to each request for an award on agreed terms.[28] However, given the complex nature of the Tribunal's jurisdiction, the Tribunal made no attempt to establish a standard for making such a determination. That task was left to the Tribunal to resolve in particular situations "as it deems necessary."

The Tribunal went on to reject the US claim that a settlement must be reviewed for "reasonableness" before it can be recorded as an award. Based on a review of the *travaux préparatoires* of the 1976 UNCITRAL Rules, it concluded that while no agreement was reached among the drafters as to the appropriate grounds for refusal to record, it was certain that "the power to refuse to record a settlement cannot be exercised in an arbitrary manner."[29] Thus, to avoid acting arbitrarily the Tribunal found that the arbitrators "should not attempt to review the reasonableness of the settlement in the place of the arbitrating parties."[30] Finally, the Tribunal condoned refusals to record on grounds of lack of jurisdiction "if the settlement does not appear to be appropriate in view of the framework provided by the Algiers Declarations."[31]

When a settlement agreement is recorded as an award on agreed terms, the arbitration comes to an end.[32] When a request for recording a settlement agreement is denied, the arbitral tribunal may issue an order to terminate the proceedings, unless the parties agree to continue with the arbitration.[33]

(c) Pre-settlement negotiations

A controversial topic in international arbitration is whether an arbitrator or arbitral panel should attempt to facilitate a settlement by the parties.[34] The UNCITRAL Rules do not address the participation of the arbitral tribunal in settlement negotiations. Although the arbitrators may assist the parties in reaching agreement on substantive matters and in drafting the terms of an award on agreed terms,[35] such negotiations can, and often do, fail.

---

[27] *Iran* and *United States*, Case A/1 (1983 Tribunal Rules), at 152.
[28] *Iran* and *United States*, Case A/1 (1983 Tribunal Rules), at 152.
[29] *Iran* and *United States*, Case A/1 (1983 Tribunal Rules), at 153.
[30] *Iran* and *United States*, Case A/1 (1983 Tribunal Rules), at 153.
[31] *Iran* and *United States*, Case A/1 (1983 Tribunal Rules), at 153. For an in depth discussion, see J Carter, "The Iran-United States Claims Tribunal: Observations on the First Year," (1982) 29 UCLA Law Review 1076, 1097–102; J Selby and D Stewart, "Practical Aspects of Arbitrating Claims," n 8, 241.
[32] In some cases before the Iran-US Claims Tribunal, the arbitral proceedings were not terminated until the parties fulfilled the conditions of the award on agreed terms. See, eg, *Iran Chevron Oil Co* (1983 Tribunal Rules), reprinted in section 2(D)(1). It is unlikely, as a practical matter, that this practice would extend to ad hoc commercial arbitration where the panel normally ceases to exist once the period for requesting correction, additional award, or interpretation has passed.
[33] See UNCITRAL, 9th Session, Addendum 1 (Commentary), UN Doc A/CN.9/112/Add.1, n 4 (Commentary on Draft Article 29(1)).
[34] For a continued discussion see H Raeschke-Kessler, "Making Arbitration More Efficient: Settlement Initiatives by the Arbitral Tribunal," (2002) 6 Vindobona J Intl Commercial L and Arb 245; see also M Schneider, "Combining Arbitration with Conciliation," in A van den Berg (ed) ICCA Congress Series No 8, *International Dispute Resolution: Towards an International Arbitration Culture* (1998) 57.
[35] In fact, the UNCITRAL drafters anticipated such conduct. See *Report of the Secretary-General on the Preliminary Draft Set of Arbitration Rules*, UNCITRAL, 8th Session, UN Doc A/CN.9/97 (1974), reprinted in (1975) VI UNCITRAL Ybk 163, 179 (noting that a settlement might be reached during a hearing with the arbitrators' assistance). According to Sanders, a settlement might also be facilitated after the hearing. P Sanders, "Commentary on UNCITRAL Arbitration Rules," n 4, 212.

Consequently, the parties may hesitate to (and many would argue the arbitral panel should not) enter into arbitrator-assisted negotiations out of fear that information offered during the negotiation process may complicate subsequent arbitral proceedings if agreement cannot be reached.[36] Arbitrators share a similar concern that by participating in settlement talks they might express a view on the merits that could serve as grounds for a party's future claim of bias or pre-judgment of the issues. Furthermore, ethical issues may arise as to the level of involvement that an arbitrator can engage in when encouraging or participating in settlement negotiations.[37] The parties can avoid some of these concerns through full disclosure of the Tribunal's role in the settlement process and a well drafted agreement regarding the roles of all involved.[38] Issues such as who the mediator will be, the Tribunal's authority during the settlement process, and how any disclosed evidence in the negotiations will affect the arbitration must be decided.[39] Specifically, there are two principal paths for protecting confidentiality during settlement negotiations.

The parties may enlist the services of a third-party conciliator who is capable of conducting settlement discussions under strict rules of confidentiality.[40] Articles 14, 19, and 20 of the UNCITRAL Conciliation Rules ("Conciliation Rules"), for example, prohibit the disclosure of the substance of the conciliation proceedings, including the settlement agreement, preclude the conciliator from acting as arbitrator, counsel, or witness in future proceedings, and prevent the use of evidence adduced in conciliation in future arbitral or judicial proceedings.[41] Third-party conciliation, while providing a more secure environment for settlement negotiations, may come at a high price. Conciliation is itself an expensive process and, if unable to yield a positive result, will very likely draw out the arbitral proceedings.

---

[36] One commentator notes that it is possible for the Tribunal to exclude any evidence not in the arbitral record, however, "many sceptics regard this requirement as impossible to satisfy." D Plant, "ADR and Arbitration," in L Newman and R Hill (eds) *The Leading Arbitrators' Guide to International Arbitration* (2nd edn 2008) 255; see also M Schneider, "Combining Arbitration with Conciliation," in A van den Berg (ed) ICCA Congress Series No 8, *International Dispute Resolution: Towards an International Arbitration Culture* (1998) 57, 94–5.

[37] See C Rogers, "The Ethics of International Arbitrators," in L Newman and R Hill (eds) *The Leading Arbitrators' Guide to International Arbitration* (2nd edn 2008) 647. For example, the IBA Rules of Ethics for International Arbitrators, Rule 8 allows for the arbitrator to be involved in settlement proposals if the parties consent, and notes that "the arbitral tribunal should point out to the parties that it is undesirable that any arbitrator should discuss settlement terms with a party in the absence of the other parties...."

[38] D Plant, "ADR and Arbitration," n 36, 253 et seq.

[39] D Plant, "ADR and Arbitration," n 36, 253 et seq.

[40] Conciliation offers a heightened standard of confidentiality in comparison to the UNCITRAL Rules and is increasingly recommended by experienced arbitrators. See P Sanders, *The Work of UNCITRAL on Arbitration and Conciliation* (2001) 18; K Berger, *International Economic Arbitration*, n 2, 581. However, at least one commentator is uncertain whether confidentiality applies when parties to an arbitration pursue conciliation unsuccessfully and then return to arbitration. See Berger, 450–1.

[41] In particular, Article 14 provides:

The conciliator and the parties must keep confidential all matters relating to the conciliation proceedings. Confidentiality extends also to the settlement agreement, except where its disclosure is necessary for purposes of implementation and enforcement.

Article 19 provides further:

The parties and the conciliator undertake that the conciliator will not act as an arbitrator or as a representative or counsel of a party in any arbitral or judicial proceedings in respect of a dispute that is the subject of the conciliation proceedings. The parties undertake that they will not present the conciliator as a witness in any such proceedings.

Finally, Article 20 provides:

The parties undertake not to rely on or introduce as evidence in arbitral or judicial proceedings, whether or not such proceedings relate to the dispute that is the subject of the conciliation proceedings;

Another possibility is the adoption of a rule of evidence similar to that in Article 20 of the Conciliation Rules, which at a minimum would ensure that evidence adduced in settlement talks will remain inadmissible in arbitration. The Iran–US Claims Tribunal, which did not itself actively promote third-party conciliation, has applied such a rule successfully on the basis of the following rationale:

> It is well settled that a Tribunal, which must decide a case subsequent to the failure of the parties to arrive at a settlement by way of negotiations, need not take into account the proposals and concessions that either party might have made in the course of such negotiations. The reason is obvious: such proposals and concessions have no purpose other than to allow an agreement to be attained and may well be very far from what each party legitimately considered to be its rights. Since such proposals were rejected, they have lost all validity and become meaningless.[42]

While a rule of evidentiary exclusion cannot protect the arbitration from all the pitfalls of settlement negotiations, it nevertheless offers a cost-effective alternative to conciliation.

(2) Other grounds for termination—Article 36(2)

(a) Continuation of the arbitration is "unnecessary" or "impossible"

Article 36(2) applies to all other circumstances in which continuation of the arbitral proceedings becomes "unnecessary" or "impossible." In early drafts of the 1976 UNCITRAL Rules (the final version of which contains provisions that are nearly identical to Article 36 of the 2010 Rules), the provisions pertaining to settlement and to "other grounds for termination" were grouped together in the same paragraph. At the urging of Committee members, this version of the Rules was amended to include a separate paragraph dedicated solely to the latter topic to underscore its distinct significance.[43] Unlike Article 36(1), which deals with the manner in which the arbitral tribunal gives effect to a settlement by the parties, Article 36(2) sets the parameters for termination of the arbitration in all cases, except settlement, in which the arbitral proceedings cannot or should not proceed to conclusion.

The most typical case to arise under Article 36(2) is the claimant's decision to withdraw its claim.[44] Withdrawal may occur when the claimant realizes, perhaps after reviewing the respondent's submissions, the relative weakness of his claims and the dim prospects for

---

a. Views expressed or suggestions made by the other party in respect of a possible settlement of the dispute;
b. Admissions made by the other party in the course of the conciliation proceedings;
c. Proposals made by the conciliator;
d. The fact that the other party had indicated his willingness to accept a proposal for settlement made by the conciliator.

In 2002, UNCITRAL adopted the Model Law on International Commercial Conciliation as a guide for establishing or improving national legislation governing the use of conciliation and mediation techniques.

[42] *Mobil Oil Iran, Inc,* et al and *Government of the Islamic Republic of Iran* et al, Award No 311–74/76/81/150–3 (July 14, 1987), reprinted in 16 Iran-US CTR 3, 55 (1987-III). See also *Iran* and *United States,* Decision No DEC A1(I, III & IV)-FT (August 3, 1982), reprinted in 1 Iran-US CTR 189, 190–1 (1981–1982).

[43] See UNCITRAL, 9th Session, UN Doc A/CN.9/9/C.2/SR.11, n 13, at 9, para 74 (Comments by Messrs Roehrich, France, and Mantilla-Molina, Mexico).

[44] Withdrawal may be unilateral, see, eg, *Seaboard Flour Corp* (1983 Tribunal Rules), *Union Special Corp* (1983 Tribunal Rules), and *Charles W Boyle* (1983 Tribunal Rules), mutual, see, eg, *Brown & Root* (1983 Tribunal Rules), or conditional, see, eg, *Xtra Inc* (1983 Tribunal Rules), all reprinted in section 2(D)(2).

Article 32(2)(a) of the Model Law explicitly establishes withdrawal as grounds for termination of the arbitral proceedings. For commentary, see H Holtzmann and J Neuhaus, *A Guide to the UNCITRAL Model Law,* n 8, 869.

success. Another reason for withdrawal is that the claimant cannot obtain the documents or locate the witnesses necessary for presenting its case. This problem has arisen, for example, in a number of cases before the Iran–US Claims Tribunal where the claimant was forced to abandon his claims because of his inability to gather documentary evidence located in Iran.[45]

In deciding whether to terminate the proceedings on the basis of a claimant's request for withdrawal, the arbitral tribunal may wish to consider two factors. The first is whether the respondent agrees or objects to the withdrawal. If the respondent agrees, termination is uncontroversial and the claimant's request may be granted after notice has been provided pursuant to Article 36(2). If the respondent objects to the proposed withdrawal, the arbitral tribunal must determine whether the respondent, or any other party, has a legitimate interest in the continuation of the proceedings. In arbitration that has proceeded at least as far as the filing of the statement of defence, the key issues will most likely be the resolution of any outstanding counterclaims. Second, before deciding a request for withdrawal, the arbitral tribunal should verify that the party petitioning for the withdrawal is in fact authorized to do so. This factor is most relevant in cases in which one claimant withdraws a claim on behalf of another.[46]

Another likely scenario covered by Article 36(2) is a claimant's failure to pursue its claim.[47] This may happen either when the claimant fails to submit a statement of claim, which results in procedural default pursuant to Article 30(1)(a), or when the claimant leaves its claim idle at a later stage of the proceedings.[48] Still other circumstances requiring application of Article 36(2) may include: when the parties resolve their dispute in another forum thus eliminating the need for or having preclusive effect on the UNCITRAL arbitration;[49] when the arbitral tribunal lacks jurisdiction because the dispute is determined to fall outside the scope of the arbitration agreement;[50] and when the arbitrators decide, after the parties fail to make required deposits, to terminate the proceedings pursuant to Article 43(4).[51]

Once an arbitral tribunal concludes that continuation of the arbitral proceedings is "unnecessary" or "impossible," Article 36(2) requires that it notify the parties of its

---

[45] See, eg, *W Jack Buckamier* and *Islamic Republic of Iran*, et al, Award No 528–941–3 (March 6, 1992), reprinted in 28 Iran-US CTR 53, 75–6 (1992).

[46] See *Tchacosh, Inc* and *Government of the Islamic Republic of Iran*, Award No 540–192–1 (December 9, 1992), reprinted in 28 Iran-US CTR 371, 376–7 (1992) (finding one claimant had authorization to withdraw the claims of two other claimants since those claimants had not submitted any documents since filing the statement of claim, and since all three claimants shared the same lawyer).

[47] *Mercantile Trust Co National Association* (1983 Tribunal Rules), reprinted in section 2(D)(2).

[48] For example, in the *Poura* case the claimant filed a statement of claim alleging he owned three parcels of land in Iran that were expropriated by the Iranian Government. The claimant, however, neither identified with particularity the location of the plots of land at issue nor provided the relevant land registration numbers. The claimant, a dual national, also failed to adduce evidence in support of the claim that his dominant and effective nationality was that of the United States. In light of the lack of evidence on which to rule, the Tribunal made repeated requests that the claimant provide evidence in support of his claims, to which the claimant failed to respond. Consequently, the Iranian Agent filed a letter with the Tribunal requesting that the Tribunal terminate the case since the claimant's failure to file any evidence signified his intention to withdraw his claim. Approximately one year later, on January 20, 1993, the Tribunal issued an order indicating that it assumed that the claimant did not intend to pursue his claim and requesting comments by the claimant to the contrary. Having received no comments, the Tribunal terminated the proceedings in accordance with Article 34(2) approximately five weeks later. *Isaac Poura* (1983 Tribunal Rules), reprinted in section 2(D)(2). See also P Sanders, "Commentary on UNCITRAL Arbitration Rules," n 4, 206.

[49] See UN Doc A/CN.9/SR.167, n 14, at 203 (Comment by Mr Krispis, Greece).

[50] *Bank Markazi Iran* (1983 Tribunal Rules), reprinted in section 2(D)(2).

[51] For a discussion of the consequences of the parties to make deposits, see Chapter 27, section 5.

"intention" to issue a termination order. As discussed in the following section, the arbitral tribunal has the power to terminate the proceedings, unless "there are remaining matters that need to be decided and the arbitral tribunal considers it appropriate to do so." Though the arbitral tribunal has ultimate discretion to determine the existence of "remaining matters," good practice nevertheless requires it to solicit the views of the parties on this question, in conjunction with its notification of its "intention" to end the proceedings.

(b) The existence of "remaining matters"

Before the arbitral tribunal is empowered to terminate the proceedings pursuant to Article 36(2), it must determine that there are no "remaining matters" to be decided. This condition on the tribunal's authority is new to the 2010 UNCITRAL Rules and appears to have been included primarily to ensure consistency with revisions made to the rule on a claimant's default, adopted as Article 30(1)(a) of the 2010 Rules.[52] The original 1976 rule, corresponding Article 28(1), required the tribunal to terminate the proceedings when a claimant failed to submit a statement of claim. As explained in Chapter 21, that rule was viewed by the Working Group charged with revising the Rules as too inflexible. It was thus changed so that even when a claimant defaults, a tribunal could retain jurisdiction to resolve any "remaining matters," namely any counterclaims raised by the respondent.

(3) Technical requirements for awards on agreed terms—Article 36(3)

The UNCITRAL drafters intended awards on agreed terms to be treated like any other award rendered under the Rules.[53] Consequently, an award on agreed terms must satisfy the technical requirements governing the form and effect of an award contained in Article 34(2), (4), and (5) of the Rules. Article 34(3) is expressly inapplicable pursuant to Article 36(1), which provides that "[t]he arbitral tribunal is not obliged to give reasons." This exemption is logical given that the parties, not the arbitrators, establish the terms of a settlement agreement. Article 34(1) regarding the types of permissible awards, ie, separate awards on different issues at different times, is also inapplicable, although in some cases it may be useful to record a separate award on agreed terms, such as where the parties resolve a discrete claim or group of claims but wish the tribunal to decide the remainder of the claims.[54] Finally, Article 36(3) requires the tribunal to communicate to the parties copies of the award on agreed terms or the order for termination of the arbitral proceedings.

(4) Comparison to the 1976 UNCITRAL Rules

Article 36 is nearly identical to corresponding Article 34 of the 1976 UNCITRAL Rules, save for the following differences.

---

[52] See *Settlement of Commercial Disputes: Revision of the UNCITRAL Arbitration Rules, Note by the Secretariat*, UNCITRAL, UN Doc A/CN.9/WG.II/WP.157/Add.2 at 4–5, para 10 (2009). Accord J Castello, "UNCITRAL Rules," n 18, 1518.

[53] UNCITRAL, 9th Session, Addendum 1 (Commentary), UN Doc A/CN.9/112/Add.1, n 4, (Commentary on Draft Article 29(1)) ("[a] settlement recorded in the form of an award on agreed terms acquires the legal force of an award.").

[54] See, eg, *Frederica Lincoln Riahi* and *Government of the Islamic Republic of Iran*, Partial Award on Agreed Terms No 596–485–1 (February 24, 2000); Partial Award on Agreed Terms No 568–A13/A15(I and IV:C)/A26(I, II, and III)-FT, para 9 (February 22, 1996), reprinted in 32 Iran-US CTR 207 (1996); *Westinghouse Electric Corp* and *Islamic Republic of Iran*, et al, Partial Award on Agreed Terms No 177–389–2 (May 10, 1985), reprinted in 8 Iran-US CTR 183 (1985–I).

In Article 36(1), the phrase "the parties" replaces the phrase "both parties" used in the 1976 version of the rule, reflecting UNCITRAL's decision to clarify that the Rules may be applied in cases of multi-party arbitration.[55]

Article 36(2), as explained above, conditions the arbitral tribunal's power to terminate the proceedings with the phrase "unless there are remaining matters that may need to be decided and the arbitral tribunal considers it appropriate to do so." In contrast, corresponding Article 34(2) of the 1976 UNCITRAL Rules used the phrase "unless a party raises justifiable grounds for objection."[56] The *travaux préparatoires* indicate only that the change was made to ensure consistency with other revisions to the Rules.

The Iran–US Claims Tribunal has addressed the meaning of the phrase "justifiable grounds for objection." In the *Cherafat* case, the claimants, Ms Gloria Jean Cherafat and her two daughters, sought compensation for the alleged expropriation by Iran of certain property that they claimed to own.[57] After the claim was filed, Mr Hossein Cherafat, Gloria Cherafat's ex-husband, filed a submission requesting termination of the proceedings. According to a divorce decree rendered under Kansas law, a separation agreement, and a power of attorney designating Mr Cherafat as Ms Cherafat's attorney (all of which were ultimately submitted to the Tribunal), Mr Cherafat asserted that he was the natural guardian of the two daughters and that all the claimed property in the case belonged to him. The Tribunal requested comments from the parties, which they did not provide. As a result, the Tribunal informed the parties of its intention to terminate the proceedings, unless justifiable grounds for objection were raised by a designated date. Neither party raised objections and the proceedings were terminated.

In an unusual move, three and a half years later, Mr Cherafat submitted a letter to the Tribunal requesting reinstatement of the claimants' case. The claimants, in support, argued *inter alia* that the Tribunal's decision to terminate the case was based on an "error of municipal law" because Kansas law, the alleged applicable law, did not authorize Mr Cherafat to withdraw his minor daughters' claims. The claimants also alleged that Mr Cherafat was coerced by "Iranian political figures" into engineering the termination of the claims in exchange for the return of expropriated family land in Iran. The Tribunal rejected the claimants' request for reinstatement, finding:

The fact remains that the [claimants] did not raise the error of law argument in 1985 when the Tribunal informed the Parties of its intention to terminate the proceedings in the Case, and they

---

[55] See *Settlement of Commercial Disputes: Revision of the UNCITRAL Arbitration Rules, Note by the Secretariat*, UNCITRAL, UN Doc A/CN.9/WG.II/WP.151/Add.1 at 15, para 33 (2008).

[56] In a preliminary draft of the 1976 Rules, the arbitral tribunal was permitted to terminate the proceedings "unless a party objects," which effectively granted each party a veto power. See Draft Article 29(1) of the Revised Draft. As adopted under the 1976 UNCITRAL Rules, the substance of Article 36(2) provides that a party's grounds for objections are only cognizable insofar as they are determined to be "justifiable" by the arbitral tribunal. UNCITRAL, 9th Session, UN Doc A/CN.9/9/C.2/SR.11, n 13, at 11, para 89 (Comment by Mr Dey, India, noting that the inconsistency in the provision since first sentence granted the arbitrators discretion while the second granted the parties the right to object).

Note in many cases, the request for justifiable objections may represent the parties' last formal opportunity to communicate with the arbitral tribunal. This is by no means an open invitation for the parties to rehash the merits, but may provide a vehicle for bringing legitimate concerns to the arbitral tribunal's attention. For example, in *Islamic Republic of Iran* and *United States of America* (Case Nos A/3 and A/8), the United States objected to termination of the arbitration unless it received an award of costs. The objection prompted the Tribunal to undertake a full assessment of the matter. See *Ministry of National Defence of the Islamic Republic of Iran* and *United States of America*, et al, Decision No DEC 100-A3/A8-FT (November 22, 1991), reprinted in 27 Iran-US CTR 256 (1991-II).

[57] *Gloria Jean Cherafat*, et al and *Islamic Republic of Iran*, Decision No DEC 106–277–2 (June 25, 1992), reprinted in 28 Iran-US CTR 216 (1992).

can justifiably raise this argument now only if the reason for the failure to object in 1985 was the fact that Mr. Cherafat was under duress and the [claimants] refrained from objecting for this reason.[58]

From the Tribunal's reasoning, one can easily infer that the withdrawal of a claim under duress would constitute justifiable grounds for objection and that an error in law may be justifiable grounds if raised in a timely manner.

Finally, Article 36(3) provides that an award on agreed terms must satisfy the technical requirements of Articles 34(4) through 34(6), whereas the 1976 version of the rule required satisfaction of corresponding Articles 32(4) through 32(7).[59] The change results from UNCITRAL's decision, discussed in Chapter 24, to delete the text of Article 32(7) of the 1976 Rules from the 2010 Rules.[60]

C. Extracts from the Practice of Investment Tribunals

TCW Group, Inc, et al and *Dominican Republic,* Consent Award (July 16, 2009) (PCA administered, 1976 UNCITRAL Rules, CAFTA-DR Chapter 10), at 2:

> After reviewing the Settlement, Transfer and Mutual Release Agreement dated May 26, 2009 (the "Agreement") between Claimants and Respondent (each, a "Party" and collectively, the "Parties"), the Tribunal records by consent the irrevocable statements made to the Tribunal by the Parties in their letter dated June 30, 2009 (the "Joint Letter") that:
>
> 1. This arbitral proceeding and the disputes and differences over which this Tribunal possesses jurisdiction have been fully and finally settled in accordance with and pursuant to the terms of the Agreement.
> 2. Claimants and Respondent submit themselves to the jurisdiction of the Tribunal for the purposes of making this Consent Award.
> 3. Claimants and Respondent jointly agree that no Party has admitted any liability by entering into the Agreement, and that neither the Agreement nor this Consent Award shall be construed or deemed to be evidence of a presumption, concession or admission of any liability or wrongdoing on the part of either Party.
>
> Pursuant to Article 34(1) of the [1976] UNCITRAL Arbitration Rules, the Tribunal makes this Consent Award as follows:
>
> 1. In accordance with and pursuant to the terms of the full and final settlement agreed between Claimants and Respondent, the arbitral proceedings are hereby terminated.
> 2. Claimants on the one hand, and Respondent on the other, shall bear equally the Tribunal's fees and expenses.
> 3. Claimants on the one hand, and Respondent on the other, shall bear equally the fees and expenses of the Permanent Court of Arbitration incurred in connection with this arbitration.
> 4. Each Party shall bear its own attorneys' fees, expenses and other costs with respect to these arbitral proceedings.
>
> The Tribunal records that it has made this Consent Award in accordance with the Parties' request in their Joint Letter.
>
> MADE at the place of arbitration, New York, this 16th day of July 2009.

---

[58] *Gloria Jean Cherafat* (1983 Tribunal Rules) at 222.
[59] *Settlement of Commercial Disputes: Revision of the UNCITRAL Arbitration Rules, Note by the Secretariat,* UNCITRAL, UN Doc A/CN.9/WG.II/WP.149 at 18, para 69 (2007).
[60] UNCITRAL, UN Doc A/CN.9/WG.II/WP.149, n 59, at 18, para 69.

[signed]
Prof. Dr. Karl-Heinz Böckstiegel
Chairman of the Tribunal

[signed]
Prof. Dr. Juan Fernández Armesto
Arbitrator

[signed]
Mr. Mark Kantor, Esq.
Arbitrator

D. Extracts from the Practice of the Iran–US Claims Tribunal

(1) Tribunal Rules (1983), Article 34(1)

Iran Chevron Oil Co and *Islamic Republic of Iran*, Case No 73, Chamber Three, Order of April 15, 1986:

> In Award No 208–73–3 filed on 13 January 1986 in this Case the Tribunal stated in paragraph 11:
>
> "The proceedings in this case shall be terminated when evidence, satisfactorily proving receipt of the payment provided for in the Claims Settlement Agreement, has been filed with the Tribunal."
>
> On April 8 1986 the Claimant submitted a letter with an enclosed copy of a National Westminster Bank (London) statement of account for Iran Chevron Oil Company which confirmed the receipt of funds specified in paragraph 1 of the Claims Settlement Agreement dated 18 December 1985 entered into between the Parties to this Case.
>
> The Tribunal accepts this confirmation as being according with the requirements of the paragraph 11 of the Tribunal's Award.
>
> In view of the foregoing, the Tribunal hereby terminates the arbitral proceedings in this Case pursuant to Article 34(1) of the [1983] Tribunal Rules.

Sun Co, Inc and *National Iranian Oil Co*, Joint Request for Arbitral Award on Agreed Terms (September 28, 1992), reprinted in 28 Iran-US CTR 395 (1992):

> JOINT REQUEST FOR ARBITRAL AWARD
> ON AGREED TERMS
>
> Pursuant to Article 34 of the Rules of Procedure of the Iran-United States Claims Tribunal (the "Tribunal"), Sun Company, Inc ("Claimant"), a Pennsylvania corporation, on one part, and National Iranian Oil Company ("NIOC") and the Government of the Islamic Republic of Iran ("Iran"), hereinafter collectively called "Respondents," on the other part, jointly request that the Tribunal issue an Arbitral Award on Agreed Terms that will record and give effect to the attached Settlement Agreement, which is incorporated herein by reference.
>
> The Settlement Agreement, which was entered into on 14th August 1992, provides that in consideration of the full and final settlement of all disputes, differences, claims, counterclaims, and matters directly or indirectly raised or capable of arising out of the relationships, transactions, contracts, and events related to the subject matter of Case No 21, the sum of one hundred thirty million, four hundred fifty thousand United States Dollars (U.S. $130,450,000) shall be paid to the Claimant.
>
> The representatives of the Parties expressly declare and warrant that they are duly empowered to sign this Joint Request, and the signing and submission of the Joint Request by the representatives of Iran, NIOC and Claimant shall signify that all necessary authorities have given their approval.
>
> Respectfully submitted,
> The Islamic Republic of Iran
> [signed]
> National Iranian Oil Company
> [signed]
> Sun Company, Inc.
> [signed]
> September 28, 1992

Sun Co, Inc and *National Iranian Oil Co*, Settlement Agreement (August 14, 1992), reprinted in 28 Iran-US CTR 396 (1992):

SETTLEMENT AGREEMENT

This Settlement Agreement is made and entered into this 14th day of August, 1992, by and between Sun Company, Inc ("Claimant"), a corporation organized and existing under the laws of the Commonwealth of Pennsylvania, Iranian Sun Oil Company, a corporation organized and existing under the laws of the State of Delaware, and Sun International Limited, a corporation organized and existing under the laws of Bermuda, on one part; and National Iranian Oil Company ("NIOC") and the Government of the Islamic Republic of Iran ("Iran"), hereinafter collectively called "Respondents," on the other part. Claimant and Respondents are hereinafter collectively referred to as the "Parties."

WHEREAS, Claimant, on behalf of its subsidiary, Sun International Limited, the assignee of the claim of Iranian Sun Oil Company as the successor to and transferee of rights, interests, benefits, obligations, and liabilities of Claimant pursuant to the Joint Structure Agreement ("JSA") of February 13, 1965, between NIOC, as the First Party, and Claimant and three other companies, as the Second Party, filed a Statement of Claim with the Iran-United States Claims Tribunal ("the Tribunal") raising certain claims against the Respondents relating to the JSA, which claim was docketed by the Tribunal as Case No 21;

WHEREAS, Respondents have asserted defences and filed counterclaims in Case No 21;

WHEREAS, the Parties desire to resolve and to make full, complete, and final settlement of all their claims and disputes existing or capable of arising between them related to Case No 21 and the claims and counterclaims filed therein;

NOW, THEREFORE, the Parties agree:

1. In consideration of the full and final settlement of all disputes, differences, claims, counterclaims, and matters directly or indirectly raised or capable of arising out of the relationships, transactions, contracts including but not limited to the JSA, and events in any manner related to the subject matter of the Statement of Claim, counterclaims, and other submissions by the Parties in Case No 21, and in consideration of the covenants and promises set forth herein, Claimant shall be paid the amount of One hundred thirty million, four hundred fifty thousand United States Dollars (U.S. $130,450,000) (the "Settlement Amount"). The Settlement Amount shall be paid out of the Security Account established pursuant to paragraph 7 of the Declaration of the Democratic and Popular Republic of Algeria of January 19, 1981. Payment shall be deemed to have occurred when the Settlement Amount is received by the Federal Reserve Bank of New York.

2. In consideration of the payment of the Settlement Amount, Claimant for itself and for its subsidiaries, affiliates, parents, predecessors, successors, and assigns hereby release, quitclaim, and forever discharge Respondents and their affiliates, subsidiaries, agencies, instrumentalities, predecessors, successors, and assigns, from and against any and all claims, demands, losses, damages, suits, actions and causes of action of any nature, whether in rem or in personam or otherwise, which they have ever had, now have or may have in the future arising out of or in connection with Case No 21 and related to the JSA.

3. In consideration of the covenants and promises set forth herein, the Respondents for themselves and for their affiliates, subsidiaries, agencies, instrumentalities, predecessors, successors, and assigns hereby release, quitclaim, and forever discharge Claimant and its subsidiaries, affiliates, parents, predecessors, successors, and assigns from and against any and all claims, demands, losses, damages, suits, actions and causes of action of any nature, whether in rem or in personam or otherwise, which they have ever had, now have or may have in the future arising out of or in connection with Case No 21, including, but not limited to, (a) the purchases of crude oil that are the subject matter of Counterclaim No Eight and (b) any Stated Payment, Additional Payment, or other financial imposition or tax of any kind by Iran or NIOC.

4. In consideration of the payment of the Settlement Amount, Claimant, its subsidiaries, affiliates, parents, predecessors, successors and assigns shall indemnify and hold harmless Respondents,

their affiliates, subsidiaries, agencies and instrumentalities, predecessors, successors, and assigns against any claim, counterclaim, action or proceeding that any or all of the Claimant, its subsidiaries, affiliates, parents, predecessors, successors, and assigns may raise, assert, initiate or take against any or all of the Respondents, their affiliates, subsidiaries, agencies, instrumentalities, predecessors, successors, and assigns relating to, or arising out of, or capable of arising out of, the contracts, transactions, relationships, rights, or occurrences including but not limited to the JSA and any matters that are the subject of the claims raised in Case No 21.

5. In consideration of the covenants and promises set forth herein, Respondents, their affiliates, subsidiaries, agencies, instrumentalities, predecessors, successors and assigns shall indemnify and hold harmless, Claimant, its subsidiaries, affiliates, parents, predecessors, successors and assigns against any claim, counterclaim, action or proceeding that any or all of the Respondents, their affiliates, subsidiaries, agencies, instrumentalities, predecessors, successors and assigns may raise, assert, initiate or take against any or all of the Claimant, its subsidiaries, affiliates, parents, predecessors, successors, and assigns relating to or arising out of, or capable of arising out of, the contracts, transactions, relationships, rights or occurrences including but not limited to the JSA and any matters that are the subject of the counterclaims raised in Case No 21.

6. Upon payment of the Settlement Amount, the Parties shall not directly, indirectly, individually, or in conjunction with others at any time thereafter take or pursue any legal action or initiate or pursue arbitral or court proceedings or otherwise make any claim whatsoever against each other or any of their respective subsidiaries, affiliates, parents, predecessors, successors, assigns, agencies, or instrumentalities with respect to the subject matter of the claims and counterclaims in Case No 21.

7. In consideration of the payment of the Settlement Amount, Claimant, Sun International Limited, and Iranian Sun Oil Company hereby transfer and assign to and vest in NIOC unconditionally, irrevocably, without any lien or encumbrance, and without the right to any recourse all of their rights, benefits, interests, shares, and titles in LAPCO and LAPCO's properties, assets, and accounts whatsoever, that were kept or held in Iran or outside of the United States of America or the United Kingdom of Great Britain and Northern Ireland, and account number 910–1–222025 at the Chase Manhattan Bank, New York, New York. In consideration of the covenants and promises set forth herein, Respondents, their affiliates, subsidiaries, agencies, instrumentalities, predecessors, successors and assigns hereby transfer and assign to and vest in Claimant unconditionally, irrevocably, without any lien or encumbrance, and without the right to any recourse all of their rights, benefits, interests, shares, and titles in LAPCO's properties, assets and accounts whatsoever that were kept or held in the United States of America or the United Kingdom of Great Britain and Northern Ireland, except account number 910–1–222025 at the Chase Manhattan Bank, New York, New York.

8. Upon payment of the Settlement Amount, the Parties shall waive any and all claims for costs, including attorneys' fees, arising out of or related in any way to the arbitration, prosecution, or defence of any claim before any forum including the Iran-United States Claims Tribunal with respect to Case No 21.

9. This Settlement Agreement is for the sole purpose of settling the disputes at issue in Case No 21. Nothing in this Settlement Agreement shall be relied upon or construed as relevant to or to affect in any way any argument or position that the Parties or their subsidiaries, affiliates, parents, predecessors, successors, assigns, agencies, or instrumentalities have raised or may raise concerning the jurisdiction or the merits of this case or other cases, whether before the Tribunal or any other forum or fora. This Settlement Agreement shall not constitute a legal precedent for any person or Party, and shall not be used except for the sole purpose of giving effect to its terms, and shall not prejudice or affect other rights of the Parties or the rights of any other person in other cases before the Tribunal or elsewhere.

10. The releases, waivers, transfers, undertakings, declarations, obligations, and agreements herein are self-executing upon payment of the Settlement Amount, and need not be authorized, evidenced, or signified by any additional document, agreement, or other writing.

11. By September 28, 1992, the Parties shall submit to the Tribunal a Joint Request for Arbitral Award on Agreed Terms in the form attached as Exhibit 1 ("Joint Request") asking the Tribunal to record this Settlement Agreement as an Arbitral Award on Agreed Terms giving effect to this Settlement Agreement. The Parties agree to take all reasonable steps necessary to file the Joint Request as soon hereafter as possible and to cooperate to effect the expeditious issuance by the Tribunal of an Arbitral Award on Agreed Terms. The Joint Request may be filed with the Tribunal by any Party on or after September 28, 1992, and such filing shall constitute the request of all Parties that the Tribunal record this Settlement Agreement as an Arbitral Award on Agreed Terms giving effect to this Settlement Agreement. Prior to September 28, 1992, Claimant may deliver written notice to any of the Respondents, or any Respondent may deliver written notice to the Claimant, at an address or in a manner designated by or acceptable to the Party receiving notice, that the Party receiving notice may file the Joint Request with the Tribunal. Such filing shall constitute the request of all Parties that the Tribunal record this Settlement Agreement as an Arbitral Award on Agreed Terms giving effect to this Settlement Agreement. Prior to October 28, 1992, neither Claimant nor Respondents shall request the Tribunal to amend, modify or change the terms of the Tribunal's scheduling Order in Cases 20 and 21 filed July 17, 1992, Tribunal document number 635. If the Joint Request is not submitted by October 28, 1992, this Settlement Agreement shall be null and void and of no effect whatsoever, unless otherwise agreed upon in writing by the Parties.

12. If for any reason the Arbitral Award on Agreed Terms is not issued, final, and binding, in accordance with the Tribunal Rules, within 30 days of the filing of the Joint Request, then, unless otherwise agreed in writing by the Parties, the Tribunal shall resume jurisdiction over all claims and counterclaims in Case No 21 and the Parties shall be placed in the same position as they had occupied prior to this Settlement Agreement as if it had not been entered into.

13. The representatives of the Parties expressly declare that they are duly empowered to sign this Settlement Agreement and that their signatures will commit their respective principals to fulfillment of their obligations under this Settlement Agreement without any limitations whatsoever, and the signing of this Settlement Agreement by the representatives of Iran, NIOC and Claimant shall signify that all such authorities have given their approval.

14. For the purpose of construction and interpretation of this Settlement Agreement the entire agreement shall be read and construed as a whole without giving any specific effect to any article separately.

15. This Settlement Agreement (in four originals in each language) has been written and signed in both English and Persian, and each text shall have equal validity.

IN WITNESS WHEREOF, the Parties have executed and delivered this Settlement Agreement this 14th day of August, 1992.

The Islamic Republic of Iran
[signed]
National Iranian Oil Company
[signed]
Sun Company, Inc
[signed]
Sun International Limited
[signed]

Sun Company, Inc and *National Iranian Oil Co*, Award on Agreed Terms No 537–21–1 (October 19, 1992), reprinted in 28 Iran-US CTR 394 (1992):

AWARD ON AGREED TERMS

1. SUN COMPANY, INC ("SUN" or the "Claimant"), on behalf of its subsidiary SUN INTERNATIONAL LIMITED ("Sun International"), the assignee of the claim of IRANIAN SUN OIL COMPANY ("Iranian Sun") as the successor to and transferee of rights,

interests, benefits, obligations, and liabilities of the Claimant pursuant to the Joint Structure Agreement ("JSA") of February 13, 1965, filed its Statement of Claim on November 9, 1981 against THE GOVERNMENT OF THE ISLAMIC REPUBLIC OF IRAN ("IRAN") and THE NATIONAL IRANIAN OIL COMPANY ("NIOC") (the "Respondents"). On May 24, 1982 and June 15, 1984, the Respondents filed Statements of Defense and Counterclaim.

2. On September 28, 1992, the Claimant and the Respondents (the "Parties") submitted a Joint Request for Arbitral Award on Agreed Terms (the "Joint Request"). Attached thereto the Parties submitted a Settlement Agreement dated August 14, 1992, signed by the Agent of IRAN and by representatives of NIOC, the Claimant, Sun International and Iranian Sun (the "Settlement Agreement"). The signatories to the Settlement Agreement stated their "desire to resolve and to make full, complete, and final settlement of all their claims and disputes existing or capable of arising between them related to Case No 21 and the claims and counterclaims filed therein."

3. The Joint Request states that "in consideration of the full and final settlement of all disputes, differences, claims, counterclaims, and matters directly or indirectly raised or capable of arising out of the relationships, transactions, contracts, and events related to the subject matter of Case No 21, the sum of One hundred thirty million, four hundred fifty thousand United States Dollars (U.S. $130,450,000) shall be paid to the Claimant." Furthermore, in the Joint Request the Parties requested that the Tribunal issue an Arbitral Award on Agreed Terms that will record and give effect to the Settlement Agreement. Copies of the Joint Request and Settlement Agreement are attached hereto and incorporated herein by reference.

4. The Tribunal accepts the Settlement Agreement in accordance with Article 34, paragraph 1, of the [1983] Tribunal Rules.

5. Finally, the Tribunal notes that as per its Order dated October 1, 1992, Judge Ansari's withdrawal as an arbitrator from Case No 21 was accepted by the Tribunal and Mr. Ahmed Sadek El-Kosheri was designated by Presidential Order No 79 (Rectified Version) dated October 6, 1992 to act as a Member of Chamber One in Case No 21 and accordingly signs this Arbitral Award on Agreed Terms.

6. Based on the foregoing,

THE TRIBUNAL AWARDS AS FOLLOWS:

(a) The Settlement Agreement is hereby recorded as an Award on Agreed Terms binding upon the Parties each of which is bound to fulfill the conditions set forth in the Settlement Agreement.

(b) The payment obligation specified in the Settlement Agreement in the amount of One hundred thirty million, four hundred and fifty thousand United States dollars (U.S. $130,450,000) shall be satisfied by payment to SUN COMPANY, INC. out of the Security Account established pursuant to Paragraph 7 of the Declaration of the Government of the Democratic and Popular Republic of Algeria dated January 19, 1981.

(c) This Award is hereby submitted to the President of the Tribunal for notification to the Escrow Agent.

Dated, The Hague
19 October 1992
   [signed]
   Karl-Heinz Böckstiegel
   Chairman
   Chamber One
               In the name of God
[signed]   [signed]
Richard C Allison   Ahmed Sadek El-Kosheri

(2) Tribunal Rules (1983), Article 34(2)

Seaboard Flour Corp and *Islamic Republic of Iran*, Case No 318, Chamber Three, Order of April 9, 1985:

> By its submission dated 30 May 1984 Claimant requested "that the Tribunal terminate this case with each party to bear its own costs and counsel fees."
>
> Commenting on this request, the Agent of the Islamic Republic of Iran, in a submission filed on 22 January 1985, informed the Tribunal that Respondent Morghe Kadkhoda Chicken Company agrees "with Claimant's request for termination provided that damages for costs and counsel fees be included in the award."
>
> By Order of 28 January 1985, the Tribunal notified the Parties "that it intends to terminate the proceedings in the Case, unless any of the Parties file with the Tribunal not later than 28 February 1985 objections in accordance with Article 34 of the [1983] Tribunal Rules."
>
> On 28 February 1985 Respondent Morghe Kadkhoda Chicken Company filed a submission in which it repeated the view point it had presented in its earlier submission. Other Parties did not file comments by the same date.
>
> The Agent of the Islamic Republic of Iran filed 11 March 1985 a letter stating that "...the Government of the Islamic Republic of Iran is in agreement with withdrawal of claim with prejudice."
>
> In view of the above, the Tribunal hereby terminates the proceedings in this case pursuant to Article 34 (2) of the [1983] Tribunal Rules. Each Party shall bear its costs of arbitration.

Brown & Root, Inc and *Islamic Republic of Iran*, Case No 432, Chamber One, Order of May 31, 1985:

> Each of the Parties has requested that this Case be dismissed on the basis of lack of jurisdiction. In view of the apparent desire of both Parties that the case be terminated, the Tribunal sees no need to reach or decide the issue of whether or not it has jurisdiction.
>
> Accordingly, it intends to terminate all proceedings in this case pursuant to Article 34, paragraph 2, of the [1983] Tribunal Rules unless either Party raises justifiable grounds for objection to this procedure to this procedure on or before 30 June 1985.

Bank Markazi Iran and *Rainier National Bank*, Case No 738, Chamber Two, Order of November 29, 1985:

> In its Order of 24 July 1985, the Tribunal advised the Parties of the Decision of the Full Tribunal in Case No A–17... in which the Tribunal held, *inter alia*, that:
>
> "Claims by Iranian banks against United States banking institutions are within the jurisdiction of the Tribunal only to the extent, if any, that they are disputes as to amounts owing from Dollar Account No 2 for the types of debts payable out of that account which have been referred to the Tribunal in accordance with Paragraph 2(b) of the undertakings."
>
> In view of the Claimant's letter of 1 October 1985 stating that the present Claim does not involve an amount or amounts owing and payable to it from Dollar Account No 2, the Tribunal decides that it lacks jurisdiction over the Claim filed in this Case.
>
> In view of the foregoing, the Tribunal hereby terminates the arbitral proceedings in this Case, pursuant to Article 34 of the [1983] Tribunal Rules. The Co-Registrars are instructed to strike the Case from the Register....

Union Special Corp (a claim of less than US $250,000 presented by the United States of America) and *Islamic Republic of Iran*, Case No 10863, Chamber One, Order of August 29, 1988:

> 1. By its submission filed on March 8, 1988, the Claimant sought to withdraw its Claim.
> 2. By Order filed on March 10, 1988, the Tribunal informed the Parties that it intended to terminate this Case unless the Respondent by May 9, 1988 raised justifiable grounds for objection

in accordance with Article 34 of the [1983] Tribunal Rules, which time limit was by Order filed on May 25, 1988 extended to July 8, 1988.

3. The Respondent has not filed any objection to date. Accordingly the Tribunal hereby terminates the proceedings in this Case pursuant to Article 34(2) of the [1983] Tribunal Rules.

Charles W Boyle (a claim of less than US $250,000 presented by the United States of America) and *Islamic Republic of Iran*, Case No 12129, Chamber Three, Order of September 13, 1990:

Reference is made to the submission of the Agent of the United States filed on 5 September 1990 in which he stated that the United States of America on behalf of the Claimant "hereby withdraws the... claim."

On 5 September 1990, the Respondent informed the Tribunal that it has no objection to the Claimant's withdrawal.

Accordingly, the Tribunal hereby terminates the proceedings in this Case pursuant to Article 34(2) of the [1983] Tribunal Rules.

Xtra, Inc and *Government of the Islamic Republic of Iran*, Case No 500, Chamber One, Order of January 8, 1991:

1. By a submission filed on May 29 1989, the Claimant informed the Tribunal that it had "reached agreement" with Uiterwyk Corporation, "Claimant in Case No 381,... with respect to the replacement value of [150] containers." The same submission identifies these 150 containers by number. The Claimant, by this submission, seeks to withdraw its entire claim against Respondent.
2. Claimant's withdrawal is made conditionally, so that it becomes effective only "at such time as th[e] Tribunal enters an award which will permit the release to Uiterwyk Corporation of that portion of the award which th[e] Tribunal set aside at paragraph 90 of *Uiterwyk Corporation,* et al. and *Government of the Islamic Republic of Iran,* et al., Partial Award No 375–381–1 (July 6, 1988)."
3. By Order filed on June 14, 1989, the Tribunal invited the Respondent to comment on this withdrawal. By a submission filed on December 27, 1989, Respondent the Islamic Republic of Iran objects to the withdrawal.
4. The Tribunal notes that a Final Award has been issued today in Case No 381 pursuant to the jurisdiction retained under Paragraph 98 of Partial Award No 381–375–1. The terms of the Final Award fulfill the conditions that Xtra has established for its withdrawal in the present Case. Therefore, pursuant to Article 34(2) of the [1983] Tribunal Rules, the Tribunal terminates the proceedings in this Case.

Isaac Poura and *Islamic Republic of Iran*, Case No 323, Chamber One, Order of March 3, 1993:

1. By Order filed on September 3, 1992, the Claimant was invited to file by November 22, 1992 copies of any documentary evidence on which he sought to rely in rebuttal of previously presented evidence. The Claimant neither filed any evidence nor any extension request.
2. On December 31, 1992, the Agent of the Government of the Islamic Republic of Iran filed a letter in which he construed the Claimant's failure to file any submission as an indication that the Claimant intended to withdraw his Case, and requested for that reason that the Tribunal terminate the Case by virtue of Article 34 of the [1983] Tribunal Rules.
3. In an Order of January 20, 1993 the Tribunal further took note of the Claimant's failure to provide any information pursuant to the Order of November 11, 1982 and in light of the procedural history of the Case assumed that the Claimant did not intend to pursue his Claim. By the same Order the Tribunal informed the Parties that it intended to terminate proceedings in the Case pursuant to Article 34 of the [1983] Tribunal Rules, unless the Claimant by February 18, 1993 raised justifiable grounds for objection.
4. The Claimant has not filed any objection to date. Accordingly, the Tribunal hereby terminates the proceedings in this Case pursuant to Article 34(2) of the [1983] Tribunal Rules.

Mercantile Trust Co National Association and *Islamic Republic of Iran*, Case No 351, Chamber Two, Order of April 23, 1993:

3. On 27 June 1990, the Tribunal issued an Order in which it noted that the arbitral proceedings in this Case had been suspended since the summer of 1984, and requested the Parties to inform the Tribunal by 15 August 1990 of the present status of the Case. The Tribunal also requested the Parties to identify the extent to which there remained a dispute between the Parties on the claims and counterclaims, if any, and to indicate whether the suspension should be continued and, if so, the reasons therefor.
4. The Respondents in their response filed on 15 August 1990 stated that the Claim in this Case had been entirely settled. There was no response from [Claimant] Mercantile.
5. The Tribunal in its Order of 10 September 1990 requested Mercantile to file its submission by 10 October 1990. Mercantile again having failed to respond, the Tribunal in its Order of 2 November 1990 requested Mercantile "to inform the Tribunal by 2 December 1990 whether it agrees that its Claim has been entirely settled, in which event the Tribunal intends to terminate the proceedings in this Case pursuant to Article 34 of the [1983] Tribunal Rules unless any Party raises justifiable grounds for objection by 2 January 1991."
6. Mercantile did not respond to the Tribunal's Order of 2 November 1990. After having granted the Respondents two extensions of time to respond, the Tribunal in its Order of 8 July 1991 ordered the Parties to file any submission they wished to make by 30 August 1991. The Tribunal indicated that after that date it would make a decision on the remaining issues in this Case on the basis of the documents before it.
7. The Tribunal noted that the Parties made no submissions in response to the Tribunal's Order of 8 July 1991. Consequently, no justifiable grounds for objections having been raised by any Party, the Tribunal hereby terminates the arbitral proceedings in this Case ... in accordance with Article 34, paragraph 2 of the [1983] Tribunal Rules....

26

Post-Award Proceedings

1. Introduction	801
2. Interpretation of the Award—Article 37	802
A. Text of the 2010 UNCITRAL Rule	802
B. Commentary	802
(1) General	802
(2) Comparison to the 1976 UNCITRAL Rules	806
C. Extracts from the Practice of Investment Tribunals	806
D. Extracts from the Practice of the Iran–US Claims Tribunal	808
3. Correction of the Award—Article 38	811
A. Text of the 2010 UNCITRAL Rule	811
B. Commentary	811
(1) General	811
(2) Comparison to the 1976 UNCITRAL Rules	814
C. Extracts from the Practice of Investment Tribunals	815
D. Extracts from the Practice of the Iran–US Claims Tribunal	815
(1) Request for correction granted	815
(2) Request for correction denied	817
4. Additional Award—Article 39	821
A. Text of the 2010 UNCITRAL Rule	821
B. Commentary	821
(1) General	821
(2) Comparison to the 1976 UNCITRAL Rules	824
C. Extracts from the Practice of Investment Tribunals	825
D. Extracts from the Practice of the Iran–US Claims Tribunal	825
(1) Request for additional award granted	825
(2) Request for additional award denied	825
5. The Finality of Awards and the Inherent Power to Reconsider	827
A. Commentary	827
B. Extracts from the Practice of Investment Tribunals	831
C. Extracts from the Practice of the Iran–US Claims Tribunal	832
(1) Limited power of review	832
(2) Revision to address fraud or corruption	836

1. Introduction

Among the most important obligations that the arbitral tribunal owes the parties is to render a coherent, accurate, and complete award.[1] Because international arbitration often involves complex claims adjudicated at a quick pace by arbitrators who may not be operating in their native language, ambiguities, mistakes, and omissions can taint the final

---

[1] One commentator contends that this obligation is part of the arbitrators' ethical and post-contractual duties towards the parties. See K Berger, *International Economic Arbitration* (1993) 637.

product—perhaps to the point of compromising the validity of the award. To allow the arbitrators to rectify these problems, Articles 37, 38 and 39 of the UNCITRAL Rules, respectively, grant the arbitral tribunal post-award authority to interpret, correct, and complete an award, if necessary.[2] In so doing, they provide a narrow exception to the basic rule of finality of awards.[3] Articles 37, 38, and 39, however, are not mechanisms by which a party may reargue its case or introduce new arguments or claims for resolution by the arbitral tribunal.

In addition to interpretation, correction and completion of an award, this chapter addresses the debatable subject of an arbitral tribunal's inherent power to revise an award in the event of fraud or corruption.

2. Interpretation of the Award—Article 37

A. Text of the 2010 UNCITRAL Rule[4]

Article 37 of the 2010 UNCITRAL Rules provides:

1. Within 30 days after the receipt of the award, a party, with notice to the other parties, may request that the arbitral tribunal give an interpretation of the award.
2. The interpretation shall be given in writing within 45 days after the receipt of the request. The interpretation shall form part of the award and the provisions of article 34, paragraphs 2 to 6, shall apply.

B. Commentary

(1) General

Unfortunately, in some cases, the terms of an award may be written unclearly, obscuring the arbitral tribunal's decision on the claims presented by the parties. Article 37 of the UNCITRAL Rules establishes a procedure whereby a disputing party may request the arbitral tribunal to provide an interpretation of a previously rendered award.

Interpretation, as distinguished from other post-award proceedings, provides a means of "clarification of the award" by resolving any ambiguity and vagueness in its terms.[5]

---

[2] In addressing "post-award proceedings" this chapter does not discuss proceedings relating to the recognition or enforcement of an award initiated under national arbitration laws and international conventions.

[3] See Chapter 24, section 2(B)(2).

[4] Corresponding Article 35 of the 1976 UNCITRAL Rules provides:

1. Within thirty days after the receipt of the award, either party, with notice to the other party, may request that the arbitral tribunal give an interpretation of the award.
2. The interpretation shall be given in writing within forty-five days after the receipt of the request. The interpretation shall form part of the award and the provisions of article 32, paragraphs 2 to 7, shall apply.

[5] *Report of the Secretary-General on the Revised Draft Set of Arbitration Rules*, UNCITRAL, 9th Session, Addendum 1 (Commentary), UN Doc A/CN.9/112/Add.1 (1975), reprinted in (1976) VII UNCITRAL Ybk 166, 180 (Commentary on Draft Article 30(2)). Committee representatives debated whether the term "interpretation" accurately reflected the meaning and purpose of what ultimately became Article 35. Many expressed a preference for the term "clarification" instead. *Summary Record of the 151st Meeting of the UNCITRAL*, 8th Session, UN Doc A/CN.9/SR.167, at 205–7 (1975). Representatives also offered their views on the meaning and purpose of interpretation. Mr Mantilla-Molina of Mexico stated that interpretation was the clarification of "the purport of the award and the resultant obligations and rights of the parties." 205. Mr Rèczei of Hungary observed that interpretation was useful in resolving confusion and ambiguity in the wording of the award arising in cases where the award was not rendered in the native language of the parties. 206.

Interpretation may be particularly useful in the context of a continuing business relationship, where because of the award's unclear terms the parties require further guidance from the arbitral tribunal on the meaning of their future obligations.[6]

Interpretation is not a mechanism for revisiting an issue or claim that the arbitral tribunal should have addressed in the award but did not.[7] Any such omission would have to be dealt with under Article 39 of the Rules, which grants the arbitral tribunal the authority to make an additional award.

Nor does the interpretation process provide grounds for review "when a party seeks to reargue the case or disagrees with the conclusions reached by the Tribunal."[8] Likewise, it does not allow a party to raise new arguments or introduce new evidence in the case. Numerous tribunals have confirmed this limited purpose of interpretation. Chief among them is the Iran–US Claims Tribunal which applied an earlier, but nearly identical, version of Article 37 to deny numerous attempts by Iran to invoke interpretation as a basis for the Tribunal to reconsider an adverse award.[9] In every case, the Tribunal rejected Iran's request as being both beyond the scope of interpretation and in violation of the rule of finality of awards.

Article 37 requires that, upon the request of a party, an interpretation "shall be given." This mandatory requirement naturally applies only to requests for interpretation that fall within the scope of Article 37, as determined by the arbitral tribunal. An arbitral tribunal is thus not required to render an interpretation in the absence of a real need to clarify the meaning of the award.[10] It is nevertheless good practice for the arbitral tribunal to set forth

---

For examples of interpretation from international jurisprudence, see S Rosenne, *Interpretation, Revision and Other Recourse from International Judgments and Awards* (2007) 91 et seq.

[6] See *Wintershall AG* (1976 Rules), Final Award and Interpretation, reprinted in section 2(C). This was generally not the case in arbitration before the Iran–United States Claims Tribunal where the Tribunal was addressing "commercial relations that had been broken off and frozen by decades long hostility." S Baker and M Davis, *The UNCITRAL Arbitration Rules in Practice: The Experience of the Iran-United States Claims Tribunal* (1992) 194.

[7] See N Blackaby and C Partasides with A Redfern and M Hunter, *Redfern and Hunter on International Arbitration*, (5th edn 2009) 590.

[8] See *Methanex Corp* (1976 Rules), para 2, reprinted in section 2(C); *Parviz Karim-Panahi* (1983 Tribunal Rules), reprinted in section 2(D). See also E Gaillard and J Savage (eds), *Fouchard, Gaillard, Goldman on International Commercial Arbitration* (1999) 776. Nor does the interpretation process permit a party to ask the arbitral tribunal *how* to meet the obligations set forth in the award. See *United States* and *Iran* (Case No B36), Decision No DEC 128-B36–2 (May 23, 1997), reprinted in 33 Iran-US CTR 346, 348 (1997) (finding Tribunal has no jurisdiction to order a refund by the United States to the Security Account of funds alleged by Iran to have been improperly withdrawn). Likewise, in *Haya de la Torre*, the ICJ refused a request from the Colombian Government to indicate whether it was bound "in execution of the...Judgment of November 20th 1950" to hand over Haya de la Torre to the Peruvian Government. *Haya de la Torre Case* (*Colom v Peru*) 1951 ICJ 79 (June 13). See also G Fitzmaurice, *The Law and Procedure of the International Court of Justice* (1986) 555–6.

[9] In these cases, the tribunal examined Article 35 (along with Articles 36 and 37 in some cases) of the 1976 UNCITRAL Rules, which is nearly identical to Article 37 of the 2010 UNCITRAL Rules. The inherent authority of an arbitral tribunal to re-open a case in exceptional circumstances, another argument raised by Iran, is discussed in detail in section 5.

[10] See, eg, *Methanex Corp* (1976 Rules), para 3, reprinted in section 2(C). See also *Ford Aerospace* (1983 Tribunal Rules); *Picker Intl Corp* (1983 Tribunal Rules); *Pepsico, Inc* (1983 Tribunal Rules); *Paul Donin de Rosiere* (1983 Tribunal Rules); *American Bell Intl* (1983 Tribunal Rules); *Endo Laboratories, Inc* (1983 Tribunal Rules); *Uiterwyk Corp* (1983 Tribunal Rules); *Phibro Corp* (1983 Tribunal Rules); and *Norman Gabay* (1983 Tribunal Rules); all reprinted in section 2(D). Born notes that a request for interpretation "will ordinarily only be successful if directed to specific portions of the dispositive part of the award." G Born, *International Commercial Arbitration* (2009) 2540–1.

its reasons for rejecting a request for interpretation in an explanatory decision. In the absence of a party's request, the arbitral tribunal has no authority to interpret an award *sua sponte*.

What legal effect does a post-award interpretation have on the parties, when under many national arbitration laws an arbitral tribunal's jurisdiction over a dispute terminates once the award is rendered?[11] UNCITRAL drafters addressed two specific questions in this regard: (1) how does an arbitral tribunal retain post-award authority to render an interpretation, especially in a jurisdiction where interpretation is not expressly permitted,[12] and (2) how does an interpretation become part of the award for purposes of domestic and international enforcement?[13] In answering these questions, drafters of the 1976 UNCITRAL Rules concluded that, upon adoption by the parties, the provision of the Rules on interpretation would serve as an express agreement to extend the arbitral tribunal's mandate solely for purposes of interpretation.[14] In addition, Article 37 of the 2010 UNCITRAL Rules states that an interpretation "form[s] part of the award," a phrase that was meant to underscore that an interpretation is "necessarily and authoritatively linked" to the underlying award.[15] To this same end, Article 37 requires that an interpretation must satisfy the same technical requirements for an award established in Article 34(2) through 34(6).[16] Although not expressly required in Article 37, an arbitral tribunal is advised to render an interpretation by a majority vote pursuant to Article 33.[17]

Whether an interpretation is enforceable as a part of the award is ultimately determined under the governing national arbitration law. The potential difficulty in ascertaining applicable national law standards is demonstrated by the *Wintershall* arbitration, conducted in The Hague under the Netherlands Arbitration Act 1986 ("Dutch Act").[18] The Dutch Act authorized the arbitral tribunal to make additional awards, but was silent as to interpretations.[19] After receiving the tribunal's partial award on liability, the claimants requested an interpretation or, in the alternative, an additional award to clarify the meaning of certain provisions of the underlying oil exploration agreement. Apparently unsure whether the Dutch Act barred interpretations, the tribunal decided that its interpretation could also

---

[11] K Carlston, *The Process of International Arbitration* (1946) 241; Hyde, *International Law Chiefly as Interpreted by the United States* (2d edn 1945) 1628–9; G Schwarzenberger, *International Law* (1945) 428–9.

[12] UN Doc A/CN.9/SR.167, n 5, at 207 (Comment by Mr Chafik, Egypt). Articles 1060 and 1061 of The Netherlands Arbitration Act 1986, for example, expressly permit rectification, correction, and additional awards, but not interpretation. For an additional discussion on different sources of power to interpret, see R Knutson, "The Interpretation of Arbitral Awards – When is a Final Award not Final?" (1994) 11(2) J Intl Arb 99.

[13] UN Doc A/CN.9/SR.167, n 5, at 206 (Comments by Mr Bennet, Australia, and Mr Takakuwa, Japan).

[14] UNCITRAL, 9th Session, Addendum 1 (Commentary), UN Doc A/CN.9/112/Add.1, n 5 (Commentary on Draft Article 30(2)). See also K Berger, *International Economic Arbitration*, n 1, 641; JL Simpson and H Fox, *International Arbitration: Law and Practice* (1959) 245. By way of contrast, Article 33(1)(b) of the Model Law, as amended, permits the arbitral tribunal to give an interpretation only if the parties have agreed to such action before or at the time of the request. For commentary, see H Holtzmann and J Neuhaus, *A Guide to the UNCITRAL Model Law on Commercial Arbitration: Legislative History and Commentary* (1989) 890.

[15] The same phrase was used in Article 35 of the 1976 UNCITRAL Rules and was meant to underscore that an interpretation was "necessarily and authoritatively linked" to the award to which it corresponds. *Report of the UNCITRAL on the Work of its Ninth Session*, UN GAOR, 31st Session, Supp No 17, UN Doc A/31/17, para 191 (1976), reprinted in (1976) VII UNCITRAL Ybk 66, 79.

[16] See Chapter 24 on the form and effect of the award.

[17] See P Sanders, "Commentary on UNCITRAL Arbitration Rules," (1977) II Ybk Commercial Arb 172, 213; S Baker and M Davis, *The UNCITRAL Arbitration Rules in Practice*, n 6, 193.

[18] For a summary of the case, see J Carver and K Hossain, "An Arbitration Case Study: The Dispute That Never Was," (1990) 5 ICSID Rev-Foreign Investment L J 311.

[19] Netherlands Arbitration Act of 1986, art 1061.

constitute an additional award, if necessary, pursuant to Article 37 of the 1976 UNCITRAL Rules and Article 1061(3) of the Dutch Act.[20]

The *Wintershall* tribunal's approach was perhaps most prudent in light of the uncertainty as to the Dutch law. Although the tribunal's analysis of Dutch Law is debatable,[21] an interpretation, even if not legally binding, nevertheless may usefully assist the parties in understanding and thus satisfying their obligations under the award.[22] Moreover, the problem with the *Wintershall* award appears to have been not its ambiguity, but rather its incompleteness, a deficiency best rectified through an additional award under Article 39.[23]

Article 37 includes two important time limits.[24] First, the parties have 30 days after receipt of the award to submit a request for interpretation. The original drafters of the UNCITRAL Rules debated the appropriate time period. The representative of the Federal Republic of Germany proposed a three-year period, arguing that the need for interpretation typically arises at the time of execution of the award, which can be much later than the date on which the award was rendered.[25] The representative of Mexico opposed a longer deadline on grounds that it would create a longer period of uncertainty for the parties.[26] In the end, the Committee retained the 30-day time limit to ensure that "the arbitrators would know reasonably quickly that some further action in respect of the award would be requested of them."[27] Implied in the 30-day requirement is the right of the non-requesting party to comment on or contest its opponent's request for interpretation. The Iran–US Claims Tribunal has adhered strictly to the thirty-day deadline.[28]

The second time limit in Article 37 requires the arbitral tribunal to render an interpretation within 45 days of receiving a request by one or more parties. The 45-day time limit was designed to give the arbitrators sufficient time to take the steps necessary to interpret the

---

[20] See *Wintershall AG* (1976 Rules), Final Award, para 5, reprinted in section 2(C).

[21] The tribunal placed significant weight on the fact that the Minister of Justice of The Netherlands "referred to the new [Dutch] Act duly taking into account the Model Law ... which expressly provides in Article 33 for an interpretation of an award, if so agreed by the parties." See *Wintershall AG* (1976 Rules), Final Award, para 4, reprinted in section 2(C). Other commentators, however, have maintained that a provision on interpretation was intentionally omitted from the Dutch Act due to the drafters' concerns that such a procedure might be abused by the parties. See J van den Berg, "National Reports (The Netherlands), (1987) 12 Ybk Commercial Arb 3, 27; H Duintjer Tebbens, "A Facelift for Dutch Arbitration Law", (1987) 34(2) Netherlands Intl L Rev 141, 155 n 60. For this reason, Article 1058, Section 2 of the new Dutch Act dealing with the termination of the arbitrators' mandate upon deposit of the last final award does not contain a provision allowing the parties to extend the mandate in cases other than those mentioned in Article 1060 et seq. of the new Act. Note that Berger takes the extreme position that providing an interpretation, where forbidden by the governing arbitration law, is a violation of Article 1(2) of the UNCITRAL Rules. See K Berger, *International Economic Arbitration*, n 1, 643, 644 n 433.

[22] See also *Methanex Corp* (1976 Rules), para 3, reprinted below, section 2(C). By way of contrast to the UNCITRAL Rules, the drafters of the ICSID Convention rejected a proposal providing that an interpretation would have the legal effect of being part of the award. See C Schreuer, *The ICSID Convention: A Commentary* (2nd edn 2009) 868.

[23] However, upon closer scrutiny, the real problem with the award was the tribunal's failure to undertake *any* assessment of the cited provisions of the Exploration Agreement in the Partial Award. See section 4.

[24] For a discussion of the time limits, see Chapter 16, section 3.

[25] See *Summary Record of the 12th Meeting of the Committee of the Whole (II)*, UNCITRAL, 9th Session, UN Doc A/CN.9/9/C.2/SR.12, at 2, para 3 (1976) (Comment by Mr Pirrung, Federal Republic of Germany).

[26] UNCITRAL, 9th Session, UN Doc A/CN.9/9/C.2/SR.12, n 25, at 2, para 4 (Comment by Mr Mantilla-Molina, Mexico).

[27] UN GAOR, 31st Session, Supp No 17, UN Doc A/31/17, n 15, para 190.

[28] If a request was dismissed for lack of timeliness, the Tribunal did not feel it necessary or appropriate to address the substantive question of whether the rendering of an interpretation would have been required. See, eg, *Intl Technical Products Corp* and *Islamic Republic of Iran*, Decision No DEC 41–302–3 (June 16, 1986), reprinted in 11 Iran-US CTR 182, 183 (1986-II).

award, including the commencement of new deliberations, if necessary.[29] The time limit also brings finality to the award within a short period of time, by ensuring that the entire process of interpretation is concluded within approximately six weeks from the time the award was rendered. In practice, many arbitral tribunals have adhered rather strictly to the 45-day time limit. A notable exception is the Iran–US Claims Tribunal, whose flexibility is perhaps attributable to its unique institutional setting in which most awards do not require international enforcement but rather are paid out of the Security Account funded by Iran.[30]

(2) Comparison to the 1976 UNCITRAL Rules

Article 37 differs from corresponding Article 35 of the 1976 UNCITRAL Rules in only two technical respects.[31] First, references to "either party" and "other party" used in the original rule have been replaced, respectively, by "a party" and "other parties."[32] These revisions clarify that the Rules are applicable to multi-party arbitrations. Second, Article 37(2) provides that an interpretation must satisfy the technical requirements of Article 34(4) through (6), thus omitting the requirement in the 1976 Rules that the tribunal file or register the arbitral award.[33] This change is consistent with the Working Group's decision to omit the filing/registration requirement from the 2010 Rules.[34]

C. Extracts from the Practice of Investment Tribunals

Wintershall AG, et al and *Government of Qatar*, Final Award (May 31, 1988) (*Ad Hoc* Proceeding, 1976 UNCITRAL Rules, Concession Agreement), reprinted in (1989) 28 ILM 834, 834–36:

> 4. The Tribunal recognizes, as pointed out in Clifford Chance's Further Observations (the "Further Observations") of May 16, 1988 that the Netherlands Arbitration Act 1986 does not provide for an interpretation of an award and that the Minister of Justice's report referred to in paragraph 11 of the Further Observations indicates that the Minister of Justice does not propose to insert in the Act the possibility of an interpretation of an award by the Tribunal. However, the Parties by their agreement of October 22, 1986, signed by duly authorized representatives of the Parties, adopted as procedural rules the [1976] UNCITRAL Rules adopted by the United Nations General Assembly on 15 December 1976, and Article 35 of these Rules provides for an interpretation of the award and Article 37 for an additional award, subject to certain notice provisions which have been fully satisfied in this case. It is the Tribunal's view that this agreement governs the arbitration since the [1976] UNCITRAL Arbitration Rules are not in conflict with any provision of the Netherlands law from which the Parties cannot derogate (Article 1–2. of the [1976] UNCITRAL Arbitration Rules) and Article 1036 of the Netherlands Arbitration Act 1986, providing that "Subject to the provisions of this Title,

---

[29] P Sanders, "Commentary on UNCITRAL Arbitration Rules," n 17, 213.

[30] See, eg, *Phibro Corp* (1983 Tribunal Rules) (interpretation provided almost 10 weeks after request); and *Ford Aerospace & Communications Corp* (1983 Tribunal Rules) (interpretation provided almost nine weeks after request); both reprinted in section 2(D).

[31] The discussion in the Working Group was minimal. Two proposals that failed to gain traction were for the parties to request an interpretation jointly and for the power to interpret to apply only "where there was a need to interpret what the award ordered the parties to do." *Report of the Working Group on Arbitration and Conciliation on the Work of its Forty-Fifth Session* (Vienna, September 11–15, 2006), UNCITRAL, 40th Session, UN Doc A/CN.9/614, at 25, paras 125–26 (2007).

[32] See *Settlement of Commercial Disputes: Revision of the UNCITRAL Arbitration Rules, Note by the Secretariat*, UNCITRAL, UN Doc A/CN.9/WG.II/WP.149 at 18, paras 70–71 (2007).

[33] See UNCITRAL, UN Doc A/CN.9/WG.II/WP.149, n 32, at 18, paras 70, 72.

[34] UNCITRAL, UN Doc A/CN.9/WG.II/WP.149, n 32, at 18, paras 70, 72.

the arbitral proceedings shall be conducted in such manner as agreed between the parties…". There is no provision in the Netherlands Arbitration Act 1986 expressly excluding the Parties from agreeing to an interpretation and their agreement under [1976] UNCITRAL Article 35 is, in the Tribunal's opinion, controlling.

It is further the view of the Tribunal that Article 1059 of the Netherlands Arbitration Act 1986 providing for the *res judicata* effect of a partial award in no sense deprives the Parties of the ability to agree to an interpretation of a partial award under Article 35 of the [1976] UNCITRAL Rules. The Tribunal agrees with the Claimants that the "principle of *res judicata* prevents the re-opening of necessarily decided points. It does not prevent the clarification of a decision nor the giving of a decision on points which an award has left undecided."

The Tribunal has also noted that in his preface to the Netherlands Arbitration Act 1986, the Minister of Justice of The Netherlands, F Korthals Altes, referred to the new Act duly taking into account the Model Law on International Commercial Arbitration, adopted in 1985 by the United Nations Commission on International Trade Law (UNCITRAL), which expressly provides in Article 33 for an interpretation of an award if so agreed by the parties [Article 33(1)(b)]. Finally, while in no sense controlling, the Respondent by recognizing in its letter of April 28, penultimate paragraph, that Article 40–4. of the [1976] UNCITRAL Rules prohibits the charging of additional fees in respect of an interpretation, in effect, recognizes that Article 35 is applicable.

5. Nonetheless, in view of the contention by the Respondent that the Tribunal is without authority under Netherlands law to interpret its award, the Tribunal has determined whether the substance of the attached interpretation could be included in an additional award under Article 37 of the [1976] UNCITRAL and Article 1061 of the Netherlands Arbitration Act 1986, and, as required by Article 1061(3) of the Netherlands Arbitration Act 1986, the Tribunal has given to the Parties an opportunity to be heard on this question, in particular, the view of the Claimants as set forth in paragraph 14 of the Claimants' submissions of April 14, 1988 that "the inevitable and logical consequence of the Respondent's counterclaim is that claims and matters related to Article XV.3, Third Alternative, were before the Tribunal for decision." These included clarification of how the cost recovery and production sharing principles of Article XIII of the EPSA apply to a non-associated Natural Gas project under the third paragraph of Article XV.3.

It is the determination of the Tribunal that the substance of the attached interpretation could be included in an additional award under Article 37 of the [1976] UNCITRAL rules and/or Article 1061 of the Netherlands Arbitration Act 1986.

6. The Tribunal hereby incorporates into and makes a party of this Final Award its interpretation of the Partial Award and/or additional award, issued today's date.

Wintershall AG, et al and *Government of Qatar*, Interpretation of Partial Award on Liability (May 31, 1988) (*Ad Hoc* Proceeding, 1976 UNCITRAL Rules, Concession Agreement), reprinted in (1989) 28 ILM 837, 838:

6. In summary, the Tribunal is of the view that the Claimants' application for interpretation is a request that the Tribunal should decide matters falling within the scope of the existing reference to arbitration and has determined that under Article XXXIV of EPSA a "difference or dispute" between the Respondent and Claimants arose during the hearings and exchange of submissions by the Parties concerning the interpretation of EPSA and, accordingly, it is within the Tribunal's jurisdiction to resolve this difference or dispute.

Methanex Corp and *United States of America*, Letter from the Tribunal to the Parties (September 25, 2002) (*Ad Hoc* Proceeding, 1976 UNCITRAL Rules, NAFTA Chapter Eleven), paras 1–3:

1. By its Request for Interpretation, Methanex seeks from the Tribunal an interpretation of the Tribunal's Partial Award in respect of four matters:

(i) The definition of "Legally Significant Connection," cited from Paragraph 147 of the Partial Award (page 62);
(ii) The contents and scope of the "Fresh Pleading" ordered by the Tribunal, cited from Paragraph 172(5) of the Partial Award (page 74);
(iii) The requirements of the Tribunal as to the "Evidence" to be submitted by Methanex, cited from Paragraphs 163, 164 & 165 of the Partial Award (pages 70–71); and
(iv) The nature and timetable of the "Future Proceedings," cited from Paragraph 168 of the Partial Award (page 70).

We shall consider each of these matters in turn, subject to a general preliminary comment.
...

2. ...It is well settled that such a request [under Article 35 of the 1976 UNCITRAL Rules] is limited to an interpretation of the award in the form of clarification; and that it cannot extend to a request to modify or annul the award or take the form of an appeal or review of the award. Indeed, Methanex disclaims expressly any intention of "relitigating any issue the Tribunal has already decided": see pages 1–2 of Methanex's letter.

3. In our view, Methanex's Request does not fall within the scope of Article 35. Accordingly, we decline to treat it as such; and this response does not form part of the Partial Award. Nonetheless, it can do no harm and possibly some good if we were to address certain of the points raised by Methanex, albeit outwith Article 35 of the [1976] UNCITRAL Rules.

D. Extracts from the Practice of the Iran-US Claims Tribunal

Ford Aerospace & Communications Corp, et al and *Air Force of the Islamic Republic of Iran,* Decision No DEC 47–159–3 (October 2, 1986), reprinted in 12 Iran-US CTR 304, 305 (1986-III):

[T]he Tribunal finds that the Request does not identify any ambiguity in the Award or other basis upon which an interpretation within the meaning of Article 35 [of the 1983 Tribunal Rules] can be based.

Picker Intl Corp and *Islamic Republic of Iran,* Decision No DEC 48–10173–3 (October 7, 1986), reprinted in 12 Iran-US CTR 306, 307 (1986-II):

The Tribunal finds that the wording used in the Award No 229–10173–3 exactly reproduces the language of Article III, paragraph 3 of the Claims Settlement Declaration and therefore is more appropriate than the formulation proposed by the Agent. For this reason the Tribunal cannot accept the opinion expressed by the Agent that the wording adopted would have the effect of altering the identity of the Claimant in Case No 10173 which was presented pursuant to Article III, paragraph 3, of the Claims Settlement Declaration.

For the foregoing reasons, the Tribunal determines that no correction or interpretation of the Award is warranted and denies the Request.

In light of this conclusion, the Tribunal need not determine whether the Request for Correction and Interpretation is of the nature specified in Article 35 and Article 36 of the [1983] Tribunal Rules.

Pepsico, Inc and *Islamic Republic of Iran,* Decision No DEC 55–18–1 (December 19, 1986), reprinted in 13 Iran-US CTR 328, 329–30 (1986-IV):

The Tribunal finds that while the Respondents' submission reargues certain aspects of the Case and disagrees with various conclusions of the Tribunal, it fails to point to any element of the Award that is ambiguous. The *dispositif* of the Award is specific and detailed. Moreover, examination of the text of the Award shows that there is no ambiguity with respect to any of the four items mentioned in the Respondents' submission. In particular, (i) the Award is clear on its face as to the denial of the Respondents' request for appointment of an expert to determine the value of the shares of the Zamzam Companies and as to the reasons for that denial...; (ii) the Award is unambiguous in determining that the Claimant was in the circumstances entitled to accelerate the Promissory Notes and quotes the explicitly interrelated provisions of paragraphs 3(f) and 4 of the Main Agreement which established that right...; (iii) the Award plainly notes that New York law governs the Loan Agreements...; and (iv) the Award sets forth the factors the Tribunal considered in determining that amount.... Thus, there is nothing in the Award that requires interpretation within the meaning of Article 35, paragraph 1, of the [1983] Tribunal Rules.

Paul Donin de Rosiere, et al and *Islamic Republic of Iran,* Decision No DEC 57–498–1 (February 10, 1987), reprinted in 14 Iran-US CTR 100, 101–02 (1987-I):

[T]he legislative history of Article 35, paragraph 1 of the [1976] UNCITRAL Arbitration Rules, to which the present Article is identical, indicates that the term "interpretation of the award" was intended to mean "clarification of the award". Thus Article 35, paragraph 1, was intended to apply only where an award contains language which is ambiguous. The dispositif of the Interim Award is specific and unambiguous. Moreover, the Tribunal finds no ambiguity with respect to its use of the term "status quo." Thus, there is nothing in the Interim Award that requires interpretation within the meaning of Article 35, paragraph 1, of the [1983] Tribunal Rules.

American Bell Intl, Inc and *Islamic Republic of Iran,* Decision No DEC 58–48–3 (March 19, 1987), reprinted in 14 Iran-US CTR 173, 174 (1987-I):

Insofar as the Request allegedly seeks an interpretation of the Award, the Tribunal finds that it does not identify any aspect of the Award where the Tribunal's interpretation is necessary.... These requested interpretations largely parallel the alleged computational errors, and... would require the Tribunal to review or revise its Award. Consequently the requested interpretations fall outside the scope of Article 35 [of the 1983 Tribunal Rules].

Endo Laboratories, Inc and *Islamic Republic of Iran,* Decision No DEC 74–366–3, (February 25, 1988), reprinted in 18 Iran-US CTR 113, 113–14 (1988-I):

The Respondents contend that the Award requires interpretation "because it does not specify whether the parties' relationship was based on the purchase or sale of goods or whether it was based on the distributorship and commission." The Respondents refer to and rely on para 21 of the Award, in which the Tribunal, *inter alia,* describes the Parties' relationship until 1978. The Tribunal notes, however, that the claim at issue does not pertain to any agreement prior to 1978. As specified in para 21 it arises out of "an agreement for the sale and purchase of certain pharmaceutical products" entered into in 1978. The sale and purchase at issue is pursuant to "Order No 81" detailed in para 25 of the Award. The Tribunal therefore concludes that the Award does not require interpretation in this respect.

Uiterwyk Corp and *Islamic Republic of Iran,* Decision and Correction to Partial Award (November 22, 1988), reprinted in 19 Iran-US CTR 171, 172–73 (1988-II):

The Claimants' request seeks an "interpretation and correction" of paragraphs 98 and 177 of the Partial Award.... [P]aragraphs 98 and 177 are clear as to the granting of interest on the $2,948,619.50 that the Tribunal awards in the Partial Award. It is also self-evident that the jurisdiction that the Tribunal retains "over $1,564,537.36 of Uiterwyk's claim" includes jurisdiction to grant interest on that amount, in accordance with the Tribunal's practice of granting interest on claims and consistent with the awarding of interest on the other claims granted in this Case.

The Tribunal has held that Article 35, paragraph 1 [of the 1983 Tribunal Rules] was intended to apply only when an award contains ambiguous language.... Paragraphs 98 and 177 are specific and unambiguous. Accordingly, the Tribunal finds that paragraphs 98 and 177 do not require interpretation within the meaning of Article 35, paragraph 1.

Phibro Corp and *Ministry of War-Etka Co Ltd*, Decision No DEC 97–474–3 (May 17, 1991), reprinted in 26 Iran-US CTR 254, 254–55 (1991-I):

> Article 35 [of the 1983 Tribunal Rules] permits a party to request an explanation of ambiguous language contained in an Award.... Iran has pointed to no ambiguity in the Award. Moreover, its request merely repeats an argument previously made before the Tribunal. As such, the request constitutes an impermissible attempt to reargue an aspect of the Case....
>
> The Tribunal therefore determines that no interpretation of the Award is warranted.

Norman Gabay and *Islamic Republic of Iran*, Decision No DEC 99–77–2 (September 24, 1991), reprinted in 27 Iran-US CTR 194, 195 (1991-II) (citations omitted):

> 1. On 12 August 1991, the Claimant, Norman Gabay, also known as Nourollah Armanfar, timely filed a letter requesting an "interpretation" of Award No 515–771–2 (the "Award"), filed on 10 July 1991. In the Award, the Tribunal found that the Claimant had failed to prove that his claims for the expropriation of his properties by the Respondent were outstanding on the date of the Algiers Declarations, 19 January 1981. Accordingly, the Tribunal dismissed the claims for lack of jurisdiction.
> 2. In his letter, the Claimant states that
>
>> ... the most important aspect of the Award is the date of expropriation. I feel ... that several key points regarding the date of expropriation and the evidence relating to those points have been overlooked in reaching the decisions on which the Award [i]s based.
>
> The Claimant goes on to evaluate evidence in the record that, in his opinion, would point to a finding that the taking of his properties by the Respondent occurred before 19 January 1981.
> 3. The Claimant concludes by stating that "[t]his letter is not intended as a retrial, and it is solely for purposes of clarification."
>
> ...
>
> 6. Nothing in the Claimant's request falls within the scope of Articles 35, 36, or 37 of the [1983] Tribunal Rules. Article 35 permits a party to request from the Tribunal an explanation of ambiguous language contained in an Award.... The Tribunal cannot identify any ambiguous language in the Award, and the Claimant has pointed to none. Accordingly, there is nothing to interpret.

Parviz Karim-Panahi and *Government of the United States of America*, Decision No DEC 108–182–2 (October 27, 1992), reprinted in 28 Iran-US CTR 318, 318 (1992):

> 2. The Tribunal finds that neither the [1983] Tribunal Rules nor its practice contemplate post-award proceedings over the merits of an award. According to the [1983] Tribunal Rules, after a final Award has been rendered, the Tribunal may only "give an interpretation of the award" (Article 35), correct "any errors in computation, any clerical or typographical errors, or any errors of similar nature" (Article 36), or "make an additional award as to claims presented in the arbitral proceedings but omitted from the award" (Article 37).
> 3. Nothing in the Claimant's request falls within the scope of Articles 35, 36, or 37 of the [1983] Tribunal Rules. Indeed, the Tribunal has consistently held that there is no basis in the [1983] Tribunal Rules, or elsewhere, for the Tribunal to review its own awards when a party seeks to reargue the case or disagrees with the conclusions reached by the Tribunal....

Islamic Republic of Iran and *United States of America*, Case No A/27, Full Tribunal, Order of August 5, 1998, at 1:

> 1. The Tribunal notes the Islamic Republic of Iran's "Request to Order the United States to Comply with Award No 586-A/27-FT dated 5 June 1998," filed on 24 July 1998 (Doc. 40) ("Request").
> 2. According to the [1983] Tribunal Rules, after a final award has been rendered, the Tribunal may "give an interpretation of the award" (Article 35), correct "any errors in computation, any

clerical or typographical errors, or any errors of similar nature" (Article 36), or "make an additional award as to claims presented in the arbitral proceedings by omitted from the award" (Article 37). *Westinghouse Electric Corporation* and *Islamic Republic of Iran*, Decision No DEC 127–389-2 (23 Apr. 1997). Iran's Request does not fall within the scope of Articles 35, 36, or 37 of the [1983] Tribunal Rules. Nothing in the Tribunal Rules provides a basis for granting the Request, which is therefore denied.

3. Correction of the Award—Article 38

A. Text of the 2010 UNCITRAL Rule[35]

Article 38 of the 2010 UNCITRAL Rules provides:

1. Within 30 days after the receipt of the award, a party, with notice to the other parties, may request the arbitral tribunal to correct in the award any error in computation, any clerical or typographical error, or any error or omission of a similar nature. If the arbitral tribunal considers that the request is justified, it shall make the correction within 45 days of receipt of the request.
2. The arbitral tribunal may within 30 days after the communication of the award make such corrections on its own initiative.
3. Such corrections shall be in writing and shall form part of the award. The provisions of article 34, paragraphs 2 to 6, shall apply.

B. Commentary

(1) General

Unintentional errors or omissions in an award, such as a misplaced decimal point or a neglected signature, may distort the intended outcome of an arbitral dispute or undermine the validity of the award. Article 38 allows the arbitral tribunal to correct computational, clerical, typographical or similar errors or omissions in an award, where necessary.[36]

Correction is meant to "restor[e] the award's proper contents as adopted by the [arbitral tribunal]."[37] Thus, Article 38 permits correction of errors in the award that the arbitral tribunal made unintentionally or heedlessly.[38] When the Iran–US Claims Tribunal granted

---

[35] Corresponding Article 36 of the 1976 UNCITRAL Rules provides:

1. Within thirty days after receipt of the award, either party, with notice to the other party, may request the arbitral tribunal to correct in the award any errors in computation, any clerical or typographical errors, or any errors of similar nature. The arbitral tribunal may within thirty days after the communication of the award make such corrections on its own initiative.
2. Such corrections shall be in writing, and the provisions of article 32, paragraphs 2 to 7, shall apply.

[36] In addition, national arbitration laws may grant a tribunal the authority to correct minor clerical errors. See N Blackaby and C Partasides, *Redfern and Hunter on International Arbitration*, n 7, 578; G Born, *International Commercial Arbitration* (2009) 2522–31. For a comparative discussion on US national law and arbitral rules see C Ció, "Dealing with Mistakes Contained in Arbitral Awards" (2001) 12 American Rev Intl Arb 121.

[37] *Harold Birnbaum* (1983 Tribunal Rules), reprinted in section 3(D)(2).

[38] One commentator notes that correction, as opposed to clarification, addresses self-evident errors that the tribunal incorrectly expressed in its decision. L Baptista, "Correction and Clarification of Arbitral Awards," in A J van den Berg (ed) *Arbitration Advocacy in Changing Times*, ICCA Congress Series Volume 15 (2010) 275, 280 (providing a detailed discussion on clarification versus correction of awards).

requests for correction, for example, it was in large measure to correct for faulty mathematical calculations[39] and typographical errors.[40] Other correctable errors of a similar nature may consist of a misspelled party's name, inaccurate dates, or mistranslations.[41]

Correction may also address certain types of omissions in the award. In 2004, Professor Sanders argued that the phrase "errors of a similar nature," contained in the 1976 Rules,[42] would not address, for example, an arbitrator's failure to sign an award or to state in the award the date or place of the award, omissions which might invalidate the award.[43] Upon revising the UNCITRAL Rules, the Working Group agreed it was necessary to broaden the scope of correction and, accordingly, revised Article 38 to include the phrase "errors *or omissions* of a similar nature."[44] The word "omissions" (like "errors") in this context is qualified by the phrase "of a similar nature," leaving no doubt that correctable omissions are those of a technical, not substantive, nature.[45]

Article 38(3) provides that a correction "shall form part of the award." Thus, for reasons similar to those discussed above with regard to interpretation, the provision serves as an agreement between the parties to extend the arbitral tribunal's authority beyond the date of the award, solely for purposes of correction. As part of the award, the Rule requires that any correction by the arbitral tribunal comply with the technical requirements for awards set forth in Article 34(2) to (6) and the rule on majority voting contained in Article 33.[46] However, the ultimate status of a correction to an award will depend on the terms of the applicable national arbitration law.[47]

The arbitral tribunal's power of correction applies to "awards." Thus, any award, including "separate awards on different issues at different times," as described in Article 34(1), may be corrected.[48] In one case, the Iran–US Claims Tribunal applied Article 36 of the 1983 Tribunal Rules (nearly identical to Article 38) to correct not an award, but an order. The Tribunal had issued an order erroneously terminating the proceedings with respect to a certain group of claims. Without an express procedural mechanism to address its mistake, the Tribunal, "using by analogy its power under Article 36 of the Tribunal Rules," corrected

---

[39] See, eg, *Uiterwyk Corp* (1983 Tribunal Rules); and *Vivian May Tavakoli* (1983 Tribunal Rules); both reprinted in section 3(D)(1); and *Avco Corp* (1983 Tribunal Rules), para 5, reprinted in section 3(D)(2).

[40] See, eg, *American Intl Group, Inc* (1983 Tribunal Rules); *Uiterwyk Corp* (1983 Tribunal Rules); and *Control Data Corp* (1983 Tribunal Rules); all reprinted in section 3(D)(1).

[41] In one case decided under the nearly identical correction provision of the 1976 UNCITRAL Rules, the Iran–US Claims Tribunal "corrected" an award by deleting the description of a letter as "undated." See, eg, *Component Builders Inc* (1983 Tribunal Rules), reprinted in section 3(D)(1).

[42] See corresponding Article 36(1) of the 1976 UNCITRAL Rules, reprinted in n 35.

[43] See P Sanders, *The Work of UNCITRAL on Arbitration and Conciliation* (2nd edn 2004) 40.

[44] *Settlement of Commercial Disputes: Revision of the UNCITRAL Arbitration Rules, Note by the Secretariat*, UNCITRAL, UN Doc A/CN.9/WG.II/WP.145/Add.1 at 19, para 41 (2006).

[45] *Report of Working Group II (Arbitration and Conciliation) on the Work of its Fifty-First Session* (Vienna, September 14–18, 2009), UNCITRAL, 43rd Session, UN Doc A/CN.9/684, at 25, para 110 (2009).

[46] Although mandatory, the drafters of the 1976 UNCITRAL Rules seemed less concerned about compliance with original Articles 32(3) and 32(6) because Article 36 of the 1976 UNCITRAL Rules on correction was meant to address only small changes in the text of the award. See UNCITRAL, 9th Session, UN Doc A/CN.9/9/C.2/SR.12, n 25, at 3, para 18 (Comment by Mr Sanders, Special Consultant).

[47] For this reason some UNCITRAL delegates did not support inclusion of the phrase "shall form part of the award." UNCITRAL, 43rd Session, UN Doc A/CN.9/684, n 45, at 25, para 111. Still others believed that "such a provision would create difficulty, in particular with deadlines for recourse, depending on the date of the corrected award." Para 111. According to Born, "[t]he dominant view... is that the decision correcting the initial award cannot be recognized or enforced separately, but instead forms part of the award." See G Born, *International Commercial Arbitration* (2009) 2535.

[48] See, eg, *Paul Donin De Rosiere* (1983 Tribunal Rules), reprinted in section 3(D)(2) (correcting an interim award).

the error and nullified the termination.⁴⁹ The arbitral tribunal in the *Howard* arbitration also corrected an order for the termination of the proceedings but appears to have concluded it could derive its authority directly from corresponding Article 36 of the 1976 UNCITRAL Rules.⁵⁰

Like other post-award mechanisms under the Rules, the correction process is not a means for revisiting the substance of the award or for reconsidering the arbitral tribunal's reasoning.⁵¹

The Iran–US Claims Tribunal, for example, found that Article 36 of the Tribunal Rules did not contemplate correction for alleged errors regarding "the standard of evidence applied by the Tribunal,"⁵² "the Tribunal's evaluation of the evidence,"⁵³ or the Tribunal's characterization of the underlying dispute in an award of interim measures of protection.⁵⁴

Three technical rules regulate the correction process. First, the party that requests correction must do so within 30 days of receiving the award and must notify all other disputing parties of the request.⁵⁵ Implied in this requirement is the right of the non-requesting party to comment on or contest his opponent's request for correction. Second, if an arbitral tribunal considers a request for correction to be justified, it must make the correction within 45 days of receipt of the request.⁵⁶ Third, the arbitrators may decide *sua sponte* to correct the award within 30 days of its communication to the parties.⁵⁷ In most cases, the

---

⁴⁹ *Bank Markazi Iran* (1983 Tribunal Rules), reprinted in section 3(D)(2).

⁵⁰ See *Melvin J Howard* (1976 Rules), reprinted in section 3(C).

⁵¹ The line between correction of a computational or clerical error or technical omission and revision of a reasoned conclusion is seen in the *Picker* and *Petrolane* awards. *Picker Intl Corp* (1983 Tribunal Rules); *Petrolane Inc* (1983 Tribunal Rules); both reprinted in section 3(D)(2). In *Picker*, the respondent sought a correction of the wording used by the Tribunal to identify the claimant. In *Petrolane*, the Respondent sought a correction of the Tribunal's characterization of an earlier decision of the Tribunal as an "award." In these cases, the request for correction did not involve an unintended calculation, mistake or typographical error on the part of the Tribunal. In both cases, the Tribunal understood full well the choice it had made and thus the requests were outside the scope of Article 36. See also *American Bell Intl, Inc* (1983 Tribunal Rules); *Harris Intl Telecommunications* (1983 Tribunal Rules); and *United States* and *Iran*, Case No B36 (1983 Tribunal Rules); all reprinted in section 3(D)(2); JL Simpson and H Fox, *International Arbitration: Law and Practice*, n 14, 241; T Webster, *Handbook of UNCITRAL Arbitration: Commentary, Precedents and Materials for UNCITRAL Based Arbitration Rules* (2010) 554 ("The scope of the Tribunal's ability to correct an Award is limited to issues of misinterpretation of intent, typographical errors and similar corrections. The correction does not reach the level of changing the outcome of the Award.").

⁵² See, eg, *Component Builders Inc* (1983 Tribunal Rules), reprinted in section 3(D)(2).

⁵³ *Component Builders Inc* (1983 Tribunals Rules), n 52.

⁵⁴ See, eg, *Paul Donin de Rosiere* (1983 Tribunal Rules), reprinted in section 3(D)(2).

⁵⁵ Note that tardiness has been a leading basis for rejection of a correction request before the Iran–US Claims Tribunal. See, eg, *Component Builders Inc* (1983 Tribunal Rules), reprinted in section 3(D)(2).

⁵⁶ This requirement, found in the last sentence of Article 38(1), is new to the article on corrections, though a similar provision existed in Article 37 of the 1976 UNCITRAL Rules on additional awards. UNCITRAL, 43rd Session, UN Doc A/CN.9/684, n 45, at 24, para 106–07. For a discussion of the discretion afforded to the arbitral tribunal to determine whether a request is "justified," see section 4(B)(1).

⁵⁷ The only significant dispute to arise during the drafting of Article 36 of the 1976 UNCITRAL Rules was in regard to the parties' 30-day time limit for making a request for correction. Some representatives spoke in favor of no time limit. UN Doc A/CN.9/SR.167, n 5, at 207 (Comments by Mr Ganske, Federal Republic of Germany, Mr Melis, Australia, and Mr Eyzaguirre, Chile). See also UNCITRAL, 9th Session, UN Doc A/CN.9/9/C.2/SR.12, n 25, at 3, para 15 (Comment by Mr Guevara, Philippines). One delegate suggested that the proposed time limit for requesting corrections to an award run, not from the date of the award, but from the time the parties were required to discharge their obligations. See UN Doc A/CN.9/SR.167, n 5, at 208 (Comment by Mr Réczei, Hungary). Another representative argued that when it came to dealing with requests for correction the window of opportunity "could not be left open indefinitely." UNCITRAL, 9th Session, UN Doc A/CN.9/9/C.2/SR.12, n 25, at 3, para 16 (Comment by Mr Mantilla-Molina, Mexico).

task of assessing and correcting any technical errors in the award can be accomplished in this time frame.

In unfortunate circumstances, a party might attempt to abuse the correction process for purposes of delaying or disrupting the arbitral proceedings. The time limits established in Article 38 provide ways of minimizing the potential for dilatory tactics.[58] Another perhaps more effective safeguard is the arbitrators' inherent discretion to determine whether to apply the correction process. As the commentary on the Revised Draft of the 1976 UNCITRAL Rules explains:

> Even in cases where the arbitrators receive a timely request from one or both of the parties that an error in the award is corrected, the arbitrators have *full discretion* to decide whether or not they wish to issue such a correction (e.g. the arbitrators may decide that the alleged error whose correction was requested was not an error at all).[59]

Similarly, the arbitral tribunal has authority to decide against correction if an error is genuine but has no material impact on the validity of the award.

The Iran–US Claims Tribunal has established a useful practice for correcting an award. When applying corresponding Article 36 of the 1983 Tribunal Rules, the Tribunal typically issues a "Correction to Award," which sets forth its decision on each of the alleged errors at issue. Appended to the "Correction to Award" are the corrected pages of the award for the parties' files and a signature page that includes the signatures of at least a majority of the arbitrators in favor of the correction.[60] The "Correction to Award" is dated, but that date is not intended under the Rules to have any legal effect on the original date of the award, a question that ultimately is determined by the law governing the award.

(2) Comparison to the 1976 UNCITRAL Rules

Article 38 is substantially similar to corresponding Article 36 of the 1976 UNCITRAL Rules, though with some changes in addition to a minor restructuring of the text.

Article 38(1) grants the arbitral tribunal the power to address, in addition to computation, clerical or typographical errors, "any errors *or omissions* of a similar nature." As explained above, the words "or omissions" were added to the 2010 Rules to ensure that omissions that were relatively minor, but could have negative consequences for the validity of an award, eg, an arbitrator's failure to sign an award or to indicate the date and place of the award, could be corrected.

Article 38(1) expresses the arbitral tribunal's discretion to correct an award in slightly different terms than Article 36 of the 1976 UNCITRAL Rules. Whereas under the old rule a tribunal "may" make a correction to an award, the new rule states that if a tribunal considers a request for correction to be "justified," it "shall" make the correction. Although the second formulation is more detailed, both statements provide discretion to decide whether making a correction is appropriate.

The last sentence of Article 38(1) adds a new time limit to the Rules, requiring the tribunal to respond to a valid request for correction within 45 days of receiving it.

---

[58] A Vollmer and A Bedford, "Post-Award Arbitral Proceedings," (1998) 15(1) J Intl Arb 37, 49, warn that "a party could delay finality for substantial periods by filing request after request." We do not agree. The 30-day time limit does not reset each time corrections to the award are made. It is possible, however, that an additional 30-day period would exist for a valid request to correct a previously corrected award.

[59] UN Doc A/CN.9/112/Add.1, n 5, reprinted in (1976) VII UNCITRAL Ybk 166, 180 (Commentary on Draft Article 32(2)).

[60] See, eg, *Harold Birnbaum* (1983 Tribunal Rules), reprinted in section 3(D)(1).

Article 38(3) now clarifies expressly what was previously implied in Article 36(2) of the 1976 Rules: that a correction "shall form part of the award."

C. Extracts from the Practice of Investment Tribunals

Melvin J Howard, et al and *Government of Canada*, Correction of Order for the Termination of the Proceedings and Award on Costs (August 9, 2010) (PCA administered, 1976 UNCITRAL Rules, NAFTA Chapter Eleven), at 1:

3. In exercise of its powers under Article 36(1) [of the 1976 UNCITRAL Rules], the Tribunal hereby corrects the Order for the Termination of the Proceedings and Award on Costs rendered on August 2, 2010.
4. Paragraph 83 of the Order for the Termination of the Proceedings and Award on Costs shall be amended as follows:
   – the phrase "considering the Disputing Parties' agreement that the first procedural meeting be held at the premises of the PCA in The Hague" shall be struck and replaced with the phrase "taking note of the absence of an agreement between the Parties as to the place of arbitration";
   – the words "The Hague, the Netherlands" shall be struck and replaced with the words "Toronto, Canada."
5. On the final page of the Order for the Termination of the Proceedings and Award on Costs, the words "The Hague" shall be struck and replaced with the word "Toronto."
6. All other decisions remain as stated in the Order for the Termination of the Proceedings and Award on Costs dated August 2, 2010.

D. Extracts from the Practice of the Iran–US Claims Tribunal

(1) Request for correction granted

American Intl Group, Inc and *Islamic Republic of Iran*, Award No 93–2–3 (December 19, 1983), reprinted in 4 Iran-US CTR 96, 111 (1983-II):

> Pursuant to Article 36 of the [1983] Tribunal Rules, the Tribunal hereby corrects Award No 93–2–3 as follows:
> The Terms "Two Million Eight Hundred and Fifty Seven Thousand One Hundred and Fifty Three United States Dollars (U.S. $2,857, 153)" appearing on page 23 of the Award are corrected to read "Two Million Eight Hundred and Fifty Seven Thousand One Hundred and Forty Three United States Dollars (U.S. $2,857, 143)".

Uiterwyk Corp and *Islamic Republic of Iran*, Decision No DEC 96–381–1 (November 22, 1988), reprinted in 19 Iran-US CTR 171, 173–74 (1988-II):

> The Respondents first note that there is a discrepancy between the amount awarded for "per diem rental" in paragraphs 101 and 102 of the Partial Award and the figure in paragraphs 189 and IV(i). The Tribunal determines that this is due to a typographical error. The amount awarded for "per diem rental" should be corrected, pursuant to Article 36, paragraph 1 of the [1983] Tribunal Rules.
>
> Second, the Respondents note that in paragraph 189 the total amount awarded the Claimant does not correspond to the sum of the amounts referred to in earlier paragraphs of the Partial Award. The Tribunal determines that this is the result of an error in computation that should be corrected pursuant to Article 36, paragraph 1 of the [1983] Tribunal Rules.
>
> Third, the Respondents point out that the amount due Uiterwyk with respect to Sea-Man-Pak bonds was included in the Award against Iran Express Lines as well as in the Award against Sea-Man-Pak. The Tribunal determines that this is due to an error in computation and should be corrected pursuant to Article 36, paragraph 1 of the [1983] Tribunal Rules....

Taking into account the cumulative effect of the corrections referred to [in] this Decision, Iran Express Lines is obligated to pay Uiterwyk U.S. $16,244,770.23, plus interest....

Control Data Corp and *Islamic Republic of Iran*, Decision No DEC 86–88–3 (June 30, 1989), reprinted in 22 Iran-US CTR 151, 153 (1989-II):

> As to the request for correction of allegedly inconsistent dates of Persian and English versions of the Award, the Tribunal notes that there is no such inconsistency. The Gregorian and Persian dates in line 3 of page 7 of the Persian version of the Award have been inadvertently switched. The Tribunal notes that Article 36, paragraph 1, of the [1983] Tribunal Rules provides for the correction of "errors in computation, any clerical or typographical errors, or any errors of similar nature." The Tribunal further notes that the request for correction of the error in the Persian version of the Award falls within the scope of Article 36, paragraph 1, of the [1983] Tribunal Rules.

Component Builders, Inc and *Islamic Republic of Iran*, Correction to Award No 431–395–3 (February 2, 1990), reprinted in 23 Iran-US CTR 122, 123, 125 (1989-III):

> 4. ...As to Dr. Rassekh's letter, described by the Award as "undated," the Tribunal notes that in the English translation submitted by the Respondents the letter is undated, and that the date provided in the Persian text is not legible. In response to Bimeh Iran's request, the Tribunal deems it proper to delete the term "undated" from the letter's description provided in paragraph 175 of the Award. To this extent, therefore, the Tribunal grants Bimeh Iran's request in accordance with Article 36 of the [1983] Tribunal Rules.

Harold Birnbaum and *Islamic Republic of Iran*, Correction to Award No 549–967–2 (July 19, 1993) (footnote omitted):

> The Tribunal has come across a mathematical error in paragraph 97 of the Award in this Case filed on 6 July 1993. The error in question is the following.
>
> The amount stated in paragraph 97 of the Award as the value of those AFFA assets discussed in paragraphs 53 through 96 of the Award was 1,084,175,345 rials. It should have read 1,100,253,669 rials.
>
> The correction of this error affects a number of figures used in the computation of the amount awarded. Consequently, in accordance with Article 36, paragraph 1, of the [1983] Tribunal Rules, the Tribunal makes the following corrections to its Award No 549–967–2. Copies of the corrected pages are attached.
>
> 1. *Paragraph 97*
>
>   In the second line of paragraph 97, the figure "1,084,175,345 rials" is replaced with "1,100,253,669 rials."
>
>   In the sixth line of paragraph 97, the figure "1,241,675, 122 rials" is replaced by "1,257,753,446 rials."
>
>   [Other corrections omitted]

Vivian May Tavakoli and *Islamic Republic of Iran*, Correction to Award No 580–832–3 (June 16, 1997):

> The following corrections of a typographical nature are hereby made to the English version of Award No 580–832–3, filed on 23 April 1997.
>
> On page 5, in the Table of Contents, the paragraph number for the commencement of the section on "Interest" is "250", not "225."
>
> In paragraph 192, line 8, the figure "U.S. $200,000" is deleted and is replaced by the figure "U.S. $2,000,000."
>
> A copy of the corrected page is attached.

(2) Request for correction denied

Component Builders, Inc and *Islamic Republic of Iran*, Decision No DEC 40-395-3 (December 18, 1985), reprinted in 9 Iran-US CTR 404, 404–05 (1985-II):

> ...Respondent Bank Maskan filed a document...in which the said Respondent asked that the Award be corrected in so far as regards its section on "Procedural History" and the Tribunal's findings concerning Claimant's nationality....
>
> Decisive in the counting as to when a party shall be deemed to have received the Award pursuant to the above-quoted rules is the date on which the Agent of the Government of that party has received the Award. The English text of the Award was received by the Agent of the Government of the Islamic Republic of Iran on 27 May 1985. The Farsi text of the Award was received by the Agent of the Government of the Islamic Republic of Iran on 8 August 1985. It shall be deemed to have been received also by Bank Mashan on 8 August 1985. The request for interpretation and correction filed on 13 September 1985 was thus not made within "thirty days after the receipt of the award," as required by Articles 35 and 36 [of the 1983 Tribunal Rules]. The Tribunal therefore dismisses the request for having been filed too late.

Bank Markazi Iran and *European American Banking Corp*, Case No 679, Chamber Two, Order of January 22, 1986:

> By Order of 24 July 1985, the Tribunal advised the Parties that it intended to terminate this Case pursuant to its Decision in Case No A/17 unless the Claimant, by 2 September 1985, informed the Tribunal that the Claim involved amounts owing and payable from Dollar Account No 2. This deadline was subsequently extended to 1 October 1985.
>
> On 1 October 1985 Claimant filed two letters. In one, Claimant requested a further two month extension of time to submit its response to the Tribunal's Order of 24 July 1985; in the other, Claimant responded to that Order, stating that the Claim did not involve amounts owing and payable to it from the Dollar Account No 2.
>
> The Tribunal notes its Orders filed on 9 October 1985 and 26 November 1985, respectively granting the extension requested in the one letter and terminating the Case in response to the other letter.
>
> The Tribunal also notes the letter filed on 29 November 1985 by the Agent of the Islamic Republic of Iran, requesting correction of the Tribunal's Order of 26 November 1985 terminating the arbitral proceedings in this Case, on the ground that such termination was erroneous in view of the Tribunal's Order of 9 October 1985 granting an extension and requesting a further extension of three months to answer the Tribunal's Order of 24 July 1985. The Tribunal also notes Respondent's letters of 14 January 1986 urging the Chamber to adhere to that Order.
>
> The Tribunal further notes the letter filed on 30 December 1985 by the Agent of the Islamic Republic of Iran, apparently reversing one of Claimant's 1 October 1985 letters, stating that the claims set forth in schedule B to Claimant's Statement of Claim and denominated "Interest Only Claims" are payable out of Dollar Account No 2 and urging that the Tribunal has jurisdiction regarding that portion of this Case.
>
> In view of the above-mentioned circumstances and in order to avoid any prejudice to the Claimant, the Tribunal using by analogy its power under Article 36 of the [1983] Tribunal Rules, hereby corrects its order of 26 November 1985 so as to reinstate that portion of this Case which is related to schedule B entitled "Interest Only Claims," attached to Claimant's Statement of Claim. Such reimbursement will enable the Tribunal to clarify whether it has jurisdiction over the schedule B "Interest Only Claims."
>
> The Claimant is hereby instructed to file a supplemental brief not later than 20 April 1986, detailing its schedule "Interest Only Claims" and explaining why it believes such Claims are payable from Dollar Account No 2. The Respondent shall file its comments thereto by 20 July 1986.

Picker Intl Corp and *Islamic Republic of Iran*, Decision No DEC 48–10173–3 (October 7, 1986), reprinted in 12 Iran-US CTR 306, 307 (1986-II):

> The Tribunal finds that the wording used in the Award No 229–10173–3 exactly reproduces the language of Article III, paragraph 3 of the Claims Settlement Declaration and therefore is more appropriate than the formulation proposed by the Agent. For this reason the Tribunal cannot accept the opinion expressed by the Agent that the wording adopted would have the effect of altering the identity of the Claimant in Case No 10173 which was presented pursuant to Article III, paragraph 3, of the Claims Settlement Declaration.
>
> For the foregoing reasons, the Tribunal determines that no correction or interpretation of the Award is warranted and denies the Request.
>
> In light of this conclusion, the Tribunal need not determine whether the Request for Correction and Interpretation is of the nature specified in Article 35 and Article 36 of the [1983] Tribunal Rules.

Paul Donin de Rosiere and *Islamic Republic of Iran*, Decision No DEC 57–498–1 (February 10, 1987), reprinted in 14 Iran-US CTR 100, 101 (1987-I):

> First, the Request argues that the Tribunal in paragraph 9 of its Interim Award mischaracterized the nature of the underlying dispute between the Parties and seeks a "correction" of this alleged mischaracterization....
>
> As to the request for a "correction" of paragraph 9 of the Interim Award, the Tribunal notes that the Interim Award contains no finding by the Tribunal as to the actual nature of the underlying dispute. Further, Article 36, paragraph 1, of the [1983] Tribunal Rules provides only for the correction of "errors in computation, any clerical or typographical errors, or any errors of a similar nature". The Tribunal finds that the present request for a "correction" does not fall within the scope of Article 36, paragraph 1, of the [1983] Tribunal Rules, and therefore denies this request.

American Bell Intl Inc and *Islamic Republic of Iran*, Decision No DEC 58–48–3 (March 19, 1987), reprinted in 14 Iran-US CTR 173, 173–74 (1987-I):

> Insofar as the Request allegedly seeks the correction of computational errors in the provisions of the Award, the Tribunal finds that Respondents have identified no such errors. Rather they have submitted an elaborate reargumentation based on the evidentiary record aiming at the reconsideration and revision of some of the findings on the basis of which computations are made in the Award. Such a request does not fall within the scope of Article 36 [of the 1983 Tribunal Rules].

Harris Intl Telecommunications, Inc and *Islamic Republic of Iran*, Decision No DEC 73–409–1 (January 26, 1988), reprinted in 18 Iran-US CTR 76, 76 (1988-I):

> 2. The Request for a "review and correction" concerns "certain of the calculations" in the Award. Article 36 [of the 1983 Tribunal Rules] permits corrections only of "any errors in computations, any clerical or typographical errors, or any errors of similar nature." The basis of the Claimant's request is its disagreement with the Tribunal's approach to determining certain elements of the Claimant's claim for performance. The Award states that the Tribunal adopted its approach "[a]fter careful consideration of various options"... and then explains its reasoning in considerable detail. The Claimant here seeks a revision of the Tribunal's reasoned findings, not a mere correction of an arithmetic error. The provisions of Article 36 do not apply in such a circumstance.

Endo Laboratories, Inc and *Islamic Republic of Iran*, Decision No DEC 74–366–3 (February 25, 1988), reprinted in 18 Iran-US CTR 113, 114 (1988-I):

> The Respondents also take issue with the Award on several matters of substance and base thereon several requests for correction. These include a) a request for the Tribunal to correct its alleged failure to take into account in the Respondents' favor gratis samples amounting to 10% of the

ordered amount; b) a request for the Tribunal to correct its findings in paragraph 57(b) for which, according to the Respondents, no evidentiary basis exists; c) a request for the Tribunal to apply a 30% credit due the Respondents on account of commission, as opposed to a 25% credit, on the grounds that the Claimant had applied a 30% credit throughout the course of the relationship; d) a request that the Tribunal decrease the total sum awarded by the amount of the clearance charges; and finally e) a request that the Tribunal not award interest in this Case.

The Tribunal notes that Article 36 of the [1983] Tribunal Rules authorizes the Tribunal solely to correct "any errors in computation, any clerical or typographical errors or any errors of similar nature". The Tribunal finds that none of the Respondents' requested corrections falls within the parameters of Article 36.

Avco Corp and *Iran Aircraft Industries*, Decision and Correction to Partial Award, Award No 377–261–3 (January 13, 1989), reprinted in 19 Iran-US CTR 253, 254–55 (1988-II):

4. IACA's requests... relate to the dates selected in paragraphs 135, 136 and 139 of the Partial Award for calculating interest on various elements of the award made to both the Claimant and the Respondents. The rationale for choosing the relevant dates is explained fully in the Partial Award and the Tribunal note that there is no inaccuracy in any of paragraphs 135, 136 and 139.... The Tribunal finds that the request to change the dates from which interest is awarded does not fall within the scope of Article 36, paragraph 1 [of the 1983 Tribunal Rules]. The Tribunal therefore denies this portion of the Request.

5. Although IACI has not specified clearly the nature of the alleged errors in the figures in paragraph 2 of the Partial Award, the Tribunal notes certain inconsistencies in the figures recited in this paragraph with those elsewhere in the Partial Award. The Tribunal determines that paragraph 2 of the Partial Award contains a clerical error which should be corrected, pursuant to Article 36, paragraph 1 of the [1983] Tribunal Rules.

Component Builders, Inc, et al and *Islamic Republic of Iran,* et al, Correction to Award 431–395–3 (February 2, 1990), reprinted in 23 Iran-US CTR 122, 122–23 (1989-III):

3. [Respondent] Bimeh Iran first points out that it was entitled to rely on Article 36 of the Iranian Insurance Law relating to the statute of limitations, and that the Tribunal should have requested the text of this Article if required for its decision. On this issue, the Award states, *inter alia*, that "Bimeh Iran has not submitted in evidence the text of the Iranian Insurance Law upon which it bases its defence. Accordingly, this defence is dismissed for lack of evidence and so the Tribunal need not consider whether such limitation was subsequently nullified." Bimeh Iran's request, while taking issue with the standard of evidence applied by the Tribunal fails to identify an error of the kind contemplated by Article 36 of the [1983] Tribunal Rules. Consequently, this part of Bimeh Iran's request does not fall within the scope of this Article.

4. Bimeh Iran's second comment is that "Claimants' assertion that Dr. Rasekh re-inspected the workshop on 5 December 1978 (14 Azar 1357) is not true and not supported by evidence...." As to the re-inspection, this is a matter of the Tribunal's evalution of the evidence.... This part of Bimeh Iran's request is therefore outside the scope of Article 36 of the [1983] Tribunal Rules....

Petrolane, Inc and *Islamic Republic of Iran*, Decision No DEC 101–131–2 (November 25, 1991), reprinted in 27 Iran-US CTR 264, 264–65 (1991-II):

In his letter, the Agent asserts that a citation in paragraph 50 of the Award to *Phillips Petroleum Company Iran v. Islamic Republic of Iran,* et al., Award No 425–39–2 (29 June 1989), is an incorrect citation because the parties in the Phillips Case had agreed in their subsequent Settlement Agreement that the English version of that Award... shall "be deemed by the Parties as null and void and of no effect whatsoever". The Agent submits that this request should be dealt with as a request to correct a clerical error pursuant to Article 36 of the [1983] Tribunal Rules of Procedure....

The objection to a citation of an Award on the grounds raised by the Agent's letter does not, in the view of the Tribunal, constitute a request for correction of an error within the meaning of Article 36 of the [1983] Tribunal Rules. The citation was correct and was to an Award rendered by the Tribunal, albeit one rendered in English only. While the parties in their subsequent settlement agreed that they would deem that Award null and void upon the issuance of an Award on Agreed Terms giving effect to their Settlement Agreement, that cannot alter the fact that Award 425 was rendered in English and stated the conclusions and reasoning of the Tribunal. As such, the subsequent citation of that Award cannot be considered erroneous.

Harold Birnbaum and *Islamic Republic of Iran*, Decision No DEC 124–967–2 (December 14, 1995), reprinted in 31 Iran-US CTR 286, 288 (1995):

10. The correction in an award of "any errors in computation, any clerical or typographical errors, or any errors of similar nature," provided for by Article 36 of the [1983] Tribunal Rules, does not constitute any revision of the award, in the sense of a change in a substantive holding. The correction under Article 36 is simply an elimination of what in law does not form part of the award; it is a restoration of the award's proper contents as adopted by the Tribunal. The deadlines are tight: thirty days after the receipt of the award for a correction request by a Party and, equally, thirty days after the communication of the award for a correction of the award by the Tribunal on its own initiative.

Fereydoon Ghaffari and *Islamic Republic of Iran*, Decision No DEC 123–968–2 (October 30, 1995), reprinted in 31 Iran-US CTR 124, 124–25 (1995):

2. On 4 August 1995, the Claimant submitted a request for correction (the "request") of the Award pursuant to Article 36, paragraph 1, of the [1983] Tribunal Rules. In the request, the Claimant contends that the 8 percent interest rate used by the Tribunal, in paragraph 112 of the Award, "must be the result of a calculation, typographical or similar error."

...

10. Were the 8 percent rate employed by the Tribunal in paragraph 112 of the Award the result of an error envisioned by Article 36, paragraph 1, of the [1983] Tribunal Rules, the Tribunal would not hesitate to correct the error. See *Birnbaum*, Correction to Award No 549–967–2 (19 July 1993). Such a computational error, however, did not occur in this Case.

11. The Tribunal was fully aware of the consequences of its choice, and, considering the evidence and arguments submitted in the present claim, determined that an 8 percent rate of interest fairly compensated the Claimant for damages suffered due to delayed payment. The difference from the rate of interest awarded by the Tribunal in *Birnbaum* did not result from an error in calculation or otherwise and is consequently not subject to correction pursuant to Article 36 of the [1983] Tribunal Rules.

United States and *Islamic Republic of Iran*, Decision No DEC 126-B36–2 (March 17, 1997), reprinted in 33 Iran-US CTR 56, 58 (1997):

Article 36 of the [1983] Tribunal Rules allows the correction in an award of "any errors in computation, any clerical or typographical errors, or any errors of similar nature." The Tribunal has previously held that the type of correction envisaged by this provision "does not constitute any revision of the award, in the sense of a change in a substantive holding" and that it simply provides for "an elimination of what in law does not form part of the award; it is a restoration of the award's proper contents as adopted by the Tribunal."... Efforts to reargue certain aspects of a case or to review conclusions in awards rendered by the Tribunal find no basis in the [1983] Tribunal Rules....

The Tribunal has examined the Award, in particular, the figures and calculations used to compute the amount payable to the United States. No error in computation or error of a similar nature has been detected. For this reason, the Tribunal denies the request in so far as it is based on Article 36 of the [1983] Tribunal Rules.

Islamic Republic of Iran and *United States of America*, Case No A27, Full Tribunal, Order of August 5, 1998, at 1:

1. The Tribunal notes the Islamic Republic of Iran's "Request to Order the United States to Comply with Award No 586-A/27-FT dated 5 June 1998," filed on 24 July 1998 (Doc. 40) ("Request").
2. According to the [1983] Tribunal Rules, after a final award has been rendered, the Tribunal may "give an interpretation of the award" (Article 35), correct "any errors in computation, any clerical or typographical errors, or any errors of similar nature" (Article 36), or "make an additional award as to claims presented in the arbitral proceedings but omitted from the award" (Article 37). *Westinghouse Electric Corporation* and *Islamic Republic of Iran*, Decision No DEC 127–389–2 (23 Apr. 1997). Iran's Request does not fall within the scope of Articles 35, 36, or 37 of the [1983] Tribunal Rules. Nothing in the Tribunal Rules provides a basis for granting the Request, which is therefore denied.

4. Additional Award—Article 39

A. Text of the 2010 UNCITRAL Rule[61]

Article 39 of the 2010 UNCITRAL Rules provides:

1. Within 30 days after the receipt of the termination order or the award, a party, with notice to the other parties, may request the arbitral tribunal to make an award or an additional award as to claims presented in the arbitral proceedings but not decided by the arbitral tribunal.
2. If the arbitral tribunal considers the request for an award or additional award to be justified, it shall render or complete its award within 60 days after the receipt of the request. The arbitral tribunal may extend, if necessary, the period of time within which it shall make the award.
3. When such an award or additional award is made, the provisions of article 34, paragraphs 2 to 6, shall apply.

B Commentary

(1) General

Article 39 authorizes the arbitral tribunal to make an award "as to claims presented in the arbitral proceedings but not decided by the arbitral tribunal." The provision reflects a concern that in most jurisdictions an award that fails to address all claims raised in arbitration will not be recognized or enforced.[62] Article 39 thus provides the arbitrators a

---

[61] Corresponding Article 37 of the 1976 UNCITRAL Rules provides:
1. Within thirty days after the receipt of the award, either party, with notice to the other party, may request the arbitral tribunal to make an additional award as to claims presented in the arbitral proceedings but omitted from the award.
2. If the arbitral tribunal considers the request for an additional award to be justified and considers that the omission can be rectified without any further hearings or evidence, it shall complete its award within sixty days after the receipt of the request.
3. When an additional award is made, the provisions of article 32, paragraphs 2 to 7, shall apply.

[62] UNCITRAL, 9th Session, Addendum 1 (Commentary), UN Doc A/CN.9/112/Add.1, n 5, reprinted in (1976) VII UNCITRAL Ybk 166, 180 (Commentary on Draft Article 32).

mechanism for completing their mandate, when necessary, by making an award that resolves all remaining claims.[63] As the *travaux préparatoires* note, in the absence of such a provision, "a lengthy, costly arbitration might be totally invalidated because the arbitrators inadvertently failed to rule in their award on each part of every claim raised during the arbitral proceedings."[64]

Article 39 potentially applies in two scenarios in which the arbitral tribunal has failed to address claims presented in the arbitral proceedings. First, where any existing award or awards are incomplete, Article 39 allows the arbitral tribunal to make an "additional award." Second, where the arbitral proceedings are concluded by a "termination order" that fails to resolve all matters in the arbitration, the arbitral tribunal may render an "award" with respect to all remaining claims. In the latter situation, the term "additional award" is not necessarily applicable since it is very possible that during the arbitration no previous award has been made. The terms "termination order" and "award" (as opposed to "additional award") are new to the 2010 UNCITRAL Rules. They were included to ensure that arbitral tribunals would have the requisite authority to fulfil their duties in the event it neglected to resolves claims, regardless of what mechanism was used to conclude the proceedings.[65]

Article 39 serves as an express agreement by the parties to extend the arbitrators' jurisdiction over the dispute to make an additional award.[66] Such agreement may or may not be necessary in practice depending on the requirements of the applicable national arbitration law. In some jurisdictions, an award that fails to address all claims is not a final award; thus the arbitral tribunal's jurisdiction over the dispute remains in force until all outstanding claims are resolved.[67] Nevertheless, an additional award is an "award" within the meaning of the Rules and thus should comply with Article 34(2) through 34(6), as required by Article 39, and the rule on majority voting contained in Article 31.[68]

Professor Sanders observed during the original Committee discussions that corresponding Article 37 of the 1976 UNCITRAL Rules was intended to cover "obvious cases of omission" in which the arbitrators failed to render a complete award.[69] Article 39 should be similarly understood. Examples of obvious cases of omission may include when the arbitrators have failed to fix or apportion the costs of arbitration,[70] rule on a claim for

---

[63] UNCITRAL, 9th Session, Addendum 1 (Commentary), UN Doc A/CN.9/112/Add.1, n 5, reprinted in (1976) VII UNCITRAL Ybk 166, 180.

[64] UNCITRAL, 9th Session, Addendum 1 (Commentary), UN Doc A/CN.9/112/Add.1, n 5, reprinted in (1976) VII UNCITRAL Ybk 166, 180.

[65] UNCITRAL, 43rd Session, UN Doc A/CN.9/684, n 45, at 25, para 115 (describing a proposal for the revision as "a solution for parties in case the arbitral tribunal failed to address all issues in a termination order). Another proposal, which received support but was ultimately not adopted, called for revising the Rules to ensure that a termination order has "the legal effect or character of an award." Para 115 (proposing to insert in the Rules: "For purposes of Article 37 [on settlement and other grounds for termination], a termination order should be treated as an award"). Accord J Castello, "UNCITRAL Rules," in F Weigand (ed) *Practitioner's Handbook on International Commercial Arbitration* (2nd edn 2009) 1523.

[66] J Castello, "UNCITRAL Rules," n 65, 1523.

[67] See K Berger, *International Economic Arbitration*, n 1, 637. Article 32(1) of the Model Law, as amended, provides: "The arbitral proceedings are terminated by the final award...."

[68] An additional award, like all awards rendered under the Rules, is subject to the rule of majority voting, pursuant to Article 33.

[69] Professor Sanders observed that corresponding Article 37 of the 1976 UNCITRAL Rules "was intended to cover obvious cases of omission on the part of the arbitrators, in other words cases in which, although all the elements necessary for an award had been submitted, the arbitrators had not rendered a complete award." UNCITRAL, 9th Session, UN Doc A/CN.9/9/C.2/SR.12, n 25, at 4, para 22. See also P Sanders, "Commentary on UNCITRAL Arbitration Rules," n 17, 214.

[70] See, eg, *Assistance in Developing Educational System, Inc* (1983 Tribunal Rules), reprinted in section 4(D)(1).

interest payments, or adjudicate in the award a counterclaim that was asserted without substantial supporting evidence.[71] Article 39 obviously has no effect in cases of deliberate omission where an arbitral tribunal has for specific reasons intentionally chosen not to address a claim or issue in the award.[72] Nevertheless, to avoid any misunderstandings, it is good practice for an arbitral tribunal to document in the award the disposition of each of the parties' respective claims, no matter how small or inconsequential their bearing is on the outcome of the case.

Article 39(2) grants the arbitral tribunal wide discretion to determine if a request for an additional award is "justified."[73] The arbitrators, for example, may reject a request on grounds that there was no omission of claims,[74] that the award sufficiently addressed the alleged omissions,[75] and that the party's request generally falls outside the scope of Article 39.[76] The arbitrators have no express authority to make additional awards *sua sponte*, although arguably they must inform the parties of the discovery of any important omissions as part of their general duty to ensure the validity and enforceability of the award.[77]

Article 39 permits an arbitral tribunal to conduct further hearings or gather additional evidence, if necessary, in order to address claims that it neglected to decide. In so doing, the Working Group that revised the Rules broke from the approach of corresponding Article 37 of the 1976 UNCITRAL Rules, which expressly prohibited further hearings and evidence.[78] Rather, Article 39 follows the approach of Article 33(3)–(4) of the UNCITRAL Model Law. In drafting that instrument, the Working Group recognized that denying the arbitral tribunal these procedures could place the entire award in jeopardy of being set aside.[79] In discussions to revise the Rules, some delegates expressed concerns that the possibility of further hearings and evidence might encourage dilatory tactics,[80] though the general consensus appears to have been that the authority to conduct further hearings and gather additional evidence may be crucial to ensuring the validity of an award. Article 39 thus omits the prohibition against further hearings and evidence found in the 1976 UNCITRAL Rules.[81]

---

[71] UNCITRAL, 9th Session, Addendum 1 (Commentary), UN Doc A/CN.9/112/Add.1, n 5, reprinted in (1976) VII UNCITRAL Ybk 166, 180 (Commentary on Draft Article 32(1)).

[72] UN Doc A/CN.9/SR.167, n 5, at 208 (Comment by Mr Krispis, Greece). See also UNCITRAL, 9th Session, UN Doc A/CN.9/9/C.2/SR.12, n 25, at 4, para 25. See *Islamic Republic of Iran* and *United States* (Case B61), reprinted in section 4(D)(2).

[73] The commentary on the Revised Draft explains that the arbitrators have "full discretion, upon receipt of the request of a party for an additional award, to decide whether or not to make such an award." UNCITRAL, 9th Session, Addendum 1 (Commentary), UN Doc A/CN.9/112/Add.1, n 5, reprinted in (1976) VII UNCITRAL Ybk 166, 181 (Commentary on Draft Article 32(2)).

[74] *Woodward-Clyde Consultants* (1983 Tribunal Rules); *Flexi-Van Leasing* (1983 Tribunal Rules); *Intl Schools Services, Inc* (1983 Tribunal Rules); *Exxon Research and Engineering Co* (1983 Tribunal Rules); *Reza and Shahnaz Mohajer-Shojaee* (1983 Tribunal Rules); and *Esahak Saboonchian* (1983 Tribunal Rules); all reprinted in section 4(D)(2).

[75] *Harris Intl Communications, Inc* (1983 Tribunal Rules), reprinted in section 4(D)(2).

[76] *Iran* and *United States*, Case No A/27 (1983 Tribunal Rules), reprinted in section (D)(2).

[77] See also Chapter 24, section 2(B)(2).

[78] Article 37 of the 1976 UNCITRAL Rules is reprinted in n 61. Note that in revising the Rules some delegates argued that Article 37(2) could be read as allowing further hearings and evidence. UNCITRAL, 40th Session, UN Doc A/CN.9/614, n 31, at 26, para 129.

[79] See H Holtzmann and J Neuhaus, *A Guide to the UNCITRAL Model Law*, n 14, 891 (commenting on Article 33(3) of the Model Law).

[80] UNCITRAL, 40th Session, UN Doc A/CN.9/614, n 31, at 26, para 128.

[81] See Article 37, 1976 UNCITRAL Rules. Note that proposals were considered by the Working Group to include express language in the Rules to define the conditions required for further hearings or evidence, but these

Article 39 imposes a notable limitation on the arbitral tribunal's power to address omissions in the award or termination order. An additional award may address only "claims presented in the arbitral proceedings." Thus, the arbitrators are not authorized to make an award or additional award to address a claim that was not legitimately raised in the parties' written submissions or at the hearing, even if the parties jointly request such action.[82] If further arbitration is required on new or related issues, the parties must initiate a new arbitration.

The process for completing an award or termination order under Article 39 is subject to two time limits.[83] First, a party has 30 days after receipt of the award or termination order to submit a request for an additional award. Implied in this requirement is the right of the non-requesting party to comment on or contest its opponent's request for an additional award. Second, if the arbitral tribunal chooses to grant a party's request, it has 60 days from the date of receipt of the request to render the additional award. However, pursuant to the second sentence of Article 39(2), the arbitral tribunal may extend the 60-day period, if necessary.[84] The *travaux préparatoires* suggest that an extension beyond 60 days may be appropriate when the arbitral tribunal requires additional time to consider further hearings or evidence.[85]

(2) Comparison to the 1976 UNCITRAL Rules

Article 39 is similar to corresponding Article 37 of the 1976 UNCITRAL Rules, though with certain significant exceptions.

First, Article 39 broadens the scope of the original rule, which expressly granted the arbitral tribunal to complete a previously rendered award. In addition, Article 39 now allows the tribunal to address claims that were not dealt with in a prior termination order. To encompass both situations, Article 39 uses the general phrase "claims presented in the arbitral proceedings but not decided by the arbitral tribunal" and includes a reference to the "termination order." In contrast, corresponding Article 37 of the 1976 UNCITRAL Rules contains the narrower formulation: "claims presented in the arbitral proceedings but omitted from the award."

Second, Article 39 omits the requirement that an additional award be made if it "can be rectified without any further hearings or evidence." This limitation, found in Article 37(2) of the 1976 UNCITRAL Rules, was the subject of intense debate in Committee negotiations. The representative of the Soviet Union opposed the clause. He argued that if the arbitrators were to blame for not addressing the omitted claim or taking the necessary evidence, it would be unfair to require the parties to initiate a new arbitration to resolve the remaining claims.[86] On the other side, the representative of the Federal Republic of

---

did not receive significant support. *Report of the Working Group on Arbitration and Conciliation on the Work of its Forty-Seventh Session* (Vienna, September 10–14, 2007), UNCITRAL, 41st Session, UN Doc A/CN.9/641, at 22–23, para 19 (2007).

[82] UNCITRAL, 41st Session, UN Doc A/CN.9/641, n 81, at 22, para 118 ("The Working Group agreed that paragraph (2) was intended to be limited to claims presented during the course of the arbitral proceedings.").

[83] For a discussion regarding the timing of submissions, see Chapter 12.

[84] This provision tracks Article 33(4) of the Model Law, as amended, though, unlike the Rules, the Model Law provision applies not only to additional awards, but also to corrections and interpretations. For discussion of the provision, see H Holtzmann and J Neuhaus, *A Guide to the UNCITRAL Model Law*, n 14, 891–2.

[85] See UNCITRAL, UN Doc A/CN.9/WG.II/WP.149, n 32, at 20, para 79 (Secretariat's commentary on Draft Article 37(2)).

[86] UNCITRAL, 9th Session, UN Doc A/CN.9/9/C.2/SR.12, n 25, at 3–4, para 21 (1976) (Comment by Mr Lebedev, USSR).

Germany observed that without the clause parties might abuse the completion process by attempting to present new claims.[87] The Committee retained the clause, concluding that any downsides would be offset by the parties' right, pursuant to Article 29, to reopen the hearings in certain cases.[88]

As explained in the previous section, in drafting the Model Law, the Commission reversed its position in the 1976 UNCITRAL Rules and allowed further hearings and evidence in order for the arbitral tribunal to complete its work. Since original Article 37 could be interpreted as requiring that additional awards be rendered solely on the basis of "evidence that the arbitrators had before them at the time that they made they made their original, incomplete award,"[89] the parties to a dispute under the 1976 UNCITRAL Rules may wish to modify Article 37 by deleting the prohibition against further hearings and evidence.

Third, Article 39(2) grants the arbitral tribunal the authority to extend the 60-day time limitation on completing its work, if necessary, such as when further hearings and evidence require additional time.

Finally, any award or additional award rendered by the arbitral tribunal, pursuant to Article 30, must comply with the technical requirements for an award, as revised in the 2010 UNCITRAL Rules.[90]

C. Extracts from the Practice of Investment Tribunals

No practice is being extracted in this area.

D. Extracts from the Practice of the Iran–US Claims Tribunal

(1) Request for additional award granted

Assistance in Developing Educational System, Inc and *Islamic Republic of Iran*, Case No 218, Chamber One, Order of October 31, 1983:

> Applying the provisions set out in Article 37 of the [1983] Tribunal Rules and since the Tribunal has omitted to render a decision regarding the request for costs, the Tribunal decides that the Claimant, Assistance in Development Educational System, Inc., is obligated to pay costs to Respondent the National Defence Industries Organization in the sum of US $4,000.00.

(2) Request for additional award denied

Woodward-Clyde Consultants and *Islamic Republic of Iran*, Case No 67, Chamber Three, Order of December 30, 1983:

> The Tribunal has determined that no portion of the claim or counterclaim has been omitted from the above Award so as to warrant an additional award as requested by AEOI.

---

[87] UNCITRAL, 9th Session, UN Doc A/CN.9/9/C.2/SR.12, n 25, at 4, para 25 (Comments by Mr Pirrung, Federal Republic of Germany).
[88] See P Sanders, "Commentary on UNCITRAL Arbitration Rules," n 17, 214.
[89] UNCITRAL, 9th Session, Addendum 1 (Commentary), UN Doc A/CN.9/112/Add.1, n 5, reprinted in (1976) VII UNCITRAL Ybk 166, 181 (Commentary on Draft Article 32(2)).
[90] UNCITRAL, UN Doc A/CN.9/WG.II/WP.149, n 32, at 18, para 72. The revised technical requirements in Article 34(2)–(6) omit the requirement that the arbitral tribunal must file or register an award.

Flexi-Van Leasing, Inc and *Islamic Republic of Iran*, Decision No DEC 54–36–1 (December 18, 1986), reprinted in 13 Iran-US CTR 325, 327 (1986-IV):[91]

> As noted, Article 37, paragraph 1, of the [1983] Tribunal Rules permits an additional award only with respect to "claims presented in the arbitral proceeding but omitted from the award." The record in this Case, as described above, leaves no doubt that no claims were omitted from the Award, for all of the claims were directed solely against the Government and all were explicitly decided by the Tribunal. Accordingly, there is no basis for an additional award under the Tribunal Rules.

Exxon Research and Engineering Co and *Islamic Republic of Iran*, Decision No DEC 63–155–3 (July 29, 1987), reprinted in 16 Iran-US CTR 110, 111 (1987-III):

> The Agent of the Government of the Islamic Republic of Iran on behalf of the Respondent Bank Markazi Iran ("Bank Markazi"), stated in the Request that "legal damages, including, *inter alia*, damages arising out of preparing briefs and attending hearings which relief was sought ... should have been awarded to Bank Markazi Iran."
>
> The Tribunal notes that, pursuant to Article 38, paragraph 1 of the [1983] Tribunal Rules, Paragraph 71(g) of the Award disposes of the claim referred to by Bank Markazi.
>
> The Tribunal concludes that it did not omit in the Award any claims presented in the arbitral proceedings in this Case and therefore the Award does not warrant any additional consideration.

Harris Intl Telecommunications, Inc and *Islamic Republic of Iran*, Decision No DEC 73–409–1 (January 26, 1988), reprinted in 18 Iran-US CTR 76, 77 (1986-IV):

> [T]he Tribunal notes that Article 37 of the [1983] Tribunal Rules permits a party to make a request for an additional award only "as to claims presented in the arbitral proceedings but omitted from the award". The subject matter of this request was not omitted from the award, but is discussed in detail in paragraphs 177 through 181 and is also referred to in the dispositif.... The Tribunal, therefore, finds that there is no basis under the Tribunal Rules for making the additional award requested.

Reza and Shahnaz Mohajer-Shojaee and *Islamic Republic of Iran*, Decision No DEC 95–273–1 (December 26, 1990), reprinted in 25 Iran-US CTR 273, 274 (1990-II):

> [W]hile the Request falls, prima facie, within the scope of Article 37 [of the 1983 Tribunal Rules], the Tribunal cannot agree that a claim which was presented in the arbitral proceedings was omitted from the Award. The Award specifically addressed the Claimants' contention that their dominant and effective nationality during the relevant period from the date the Claim arose to 19 January 1981 was that of the United States; indeed, it was expressly restricted to that issue. Consequently, the Tribunal finds that there is no omission to be rectified in the Award.

Esahak Saboonchian and *Islamic Republic of Iran*, Decision No DEC 103–313–2 (February 13, 1992), reprinted in 28 Iran-US CTR 51, 51–52 (1992):

> In his letter the Claimant asserts that "[t]he Tribunal has not considered other claims of the Claimant, namely the ownership of his late father of the buildings and improvements up to the date of his death in 1979...."
>
> [T]he Tribunal cannot agree that the Claimant presented a claim which was omitted from the Award. The Award in its *dispositif*... dismissed all claims of the Claimant. It dismissed the claim based on the alleged expropriation of the buildings and improvements on the land after

---

[91] A substantially similar example of practice can be found at *International Schools Services, Inc* and *Islamic Republic of Iran*, Decision No DEC 61–123–1 (April 28, 1987), reprinted in 14 Iran-US CTR 279, 281 (1987-I).

determining that the Claimant did not have ownership interests in either the land or the buildings and improvements on the land after 1975, when both land and such fixtures had been transferred to NPIC, as stated in the parts dealing with Facts and Contentions and Reasons for the Award.... Moreover,... the Tribunal dismissed any claim for personal property left on the farm. Accordingly, in the present Case there is no basis for an additional Award under the [1983] Tribunal Rules.

Islamic Republic of Iran and *United States of America*, Case No A/27, Full Tribunal, Order of August 5, 1998, at 1:

1. The Tribunal notes the Islamic Republic of Iran's "Request to Order the United States to Comply with Award No 586-A/27-FT dated June 5, 1998," filed on 24 July 1998 (Doc. 40) ("Request").
2. According to the [1983] Tribunal Rules, after a final award has been rendered, the Tribunal may "give an interpretation of the award" (Article 35), correct "any errors in computation, any clerical or typographical errors, or any errors of similar nature" (Article 36), or "make an additional award as to claims presented in the arbitral proceedings but omitted from the award" (Article 37). *Westinghouse Electric Corporation* and *Islamic Republic of Iran*, Decision No DEC 127–389–2 (April 23, 1997). Iran's Request does not fall within the scope of Articles 35, 36, or 37 of the [1983] Tribunal Rules. Nothing in the [1983] Tribunal Rules provides a basis for granting the Request, which is therefore denied.

Islamic Republic of Iran and *United States of America*, Cases Nos A3, A8, A9, A14 and B61, Decision No DEC 135-A3/A8/A9/A14/B61-FT (July 1, 2011), at 6–7 (citations omitted):

21. Thus, Article 37 of the [1983] Tribunal Rules permits a party to make a request for an additional award only "as to claims presented in the arbitral proceedings but omitted from the award." Article 37 is not applicable in cases where the Tribunal has deliberately elected not to decide a certain claim or deal with a certain question in its award and has given reasons for not doing so.
22. The United States' Request for an Additional Award is premised on the contention that the Tribunal omitted from Partial Award No 601 Iran's claim for damages relating to the unlawful Treasury Regulations. The Tribunal cannot agree with this position. Partial Award No 601, which found that the unlawful Treasury Regulations also applied to Iranian export controlled properties, plainly determined (1) that during the proceedings in Case No B61 there had been limited discussion of the question of the unlawful Treasury Regulations, including the question whether they may have caused damages to Iran and (2) that therefore the Parties should be given an opportunity to submit briefs and evidence relevant to all issues relating to those Treasury Regulations: Hence, Partial Award No 601 expressly deferred the Tribunal's decision of the matter pending receipt of further briefing by the Parties. Accordingly, the "subject matter" of the United States' Request "was not omitted from the award" but rather "discussed in detail" in paragraphs 176 through 179 "and is also referred to in the dispositif." In these circumstances, there is no basis under the Tribunal Rules for making the additional award that the United States requests.

5. The Finality of Awards and the Inherent Power to Reconsider

A. Commentary

A debatable point with long lineage is an international arbitration panel's inherent power to reconsider its award in the face of alleged due process or public policy violations; typically fraud. The UNCITRAL Rules, like most arbitral rules, provide no explicit authority to the panel to reconsider its award.[92] Article 34(2) provides that an award is "final and binding" and "the parties undertake to carry out the award without delay."[93] Articles 37, 38, and 39, as discussed above, invest the panel with only limited jurisdiction to interpret, correct and supplement its decision. Therefore, absent inherent power for the panel to reconsider an award, an unhappy party must turn to a national court under the relevant arbitration laws.[94]

The key to approaching this debate is found in the nature of inherent powers. Articles 37, 38, and 39 are examples of *explicit powers* given to the Tribunal. *Implied powers* could be read into a certain set of arbitration rules, but also could be expressly denied the tribunal. *Inherent powers*, however, imply something more than implied powers. Something inherent is something necessarily a part of the object in question. Inherent powers in this sense are those powers that are not explicitly granted to the tribunal but must be seen as a necessary consequence of the parties' fundamental intent to create an institution with a judicial nature. Inherent powers may be limited or denied by the parties, but the more such powers are necessary to the judicial nature of the tribunal, then the more strictly the limitation or denial is construed so as to preserve the overall intention of the parties. The debate then becomes precisely what powers are necessary for an institution to possess a judicial nature.

Two further points must now be added. First, much of the long lineage of inherent powers comes from interstate arbitration. One should not simply assume that the interstate precedents are applicable to the international commercial arbitration context. As a process, interstate arbitration differs from international commercial arbitration in that it is not envisioned that interstate arbitration will be subject to review in national courts. The entire international commercial arbitration *process*, unless there is settlement, in contrast involves an arbitration followed by certain procedures before national courts. It is true that the lineage regarding inherent powers now extends into the international commercial arbitration field.[95] In an *ad hoc* arbitration under the UNCITRAL Rules, one distinguished panel (Judge Stephen M Schwebel, Professor Don Wallace, and Monroe Leigh, Esq) found:

> Nevertheless, a court or Tribunal, including this international arbitral Tribunal, has an inherent power to take cognizance of credible evidence, timely placed before it, that its previous determinations were the product of false testimony, forged documents or other egregious "fraud on the Tribunal." [Cites to interstate arbitrations decisions deleted.] Certainly if such corruption or fraud in the evidence would justify an international or a national court in voiding or refusing to enforce the award, this Tribunal also, so long as it still has jurisdiction over the dispute, can take necessary corrective action. See the Statute of the International Court of Justice, Art. 61 (permitting revision of an award upon the subsequent discovery of a new decisive fact); ICSID Convention Art. 51 (same); US Arbitration Act, 9 USC Sect. 10 (permitting judicial annulment of an arbitral award "procured by corruption, fraud or undue means").
>
> The present Tribunal would not hesitate to reconsider and modify its earlier award were it shown by credible evidence that it had been the victim of fraud and that its determinations in the previous

---

[92] Such authority cannot be derived from Article 17(1) of the UNCITRAL Rules. See *Methanex Corp* (1976 Rules), reprinted in section 5(B).

[93] See Chapter 24, section 2(B)(2).

[94] Under Article V(2)(b) of the New York Convention, recognition and enforcement of an arbitral award may be refused if the competent authority in the country where recognition and enforcement is sought finds that recognition and enforcement would be contrary to the public policy of that country. The US Federal Arbitration Act allows for the setting aside of an award procured by corruption, fraud, or undue means. 9 US Code § 10. For further discussion, see N Blackaby and C Partasides with A Redfern and M Hunter, *Redfern and Hunter on International Arbitration*, (5th edn 2009) 591.

[95] Born comments that a "number of arbitral awards have discussed the possibility that the arbitrators have 'inherent powers,' under exceptional circumstances involving corruption, fraud, forgery, or false testimony" G Born, *International Commercial Arbitration* (2009) 2547.

award were the product of false testimony. However, no such evidence has been adduced. As in many complex cases, this Tribunal has been required to weigh and resolve occasional inconsistencies in the evidence of both sides in this arbitration, and to come to its best determination of the relevant facts. Nevertheless, the Tribunal is satisfied that the material facts on which it based its previous award on jurisdiction and liability, as well as the present award on damages and costs, are sufficiently explained and proved by credible evidence.[96]

As appears almost always to be the case, the arbitrators acknowledge an abstract authority to reopen awards in the face of severe misconduct by the winning party, but do not do so in cases where such misconduct does not exist.

One must ask, however, why the existence of a power in national courts to void or to refuse to enforce an award "certainly" means that the arbitral panel also has that power. Indeed, the opposite conclusion is suggested by the second point to be made: The notion of inherent powers could be easily abused. It is a sense of necessity that justifies a tribunal invoking inherent powers; it is the sense of necessity that allows the acceptance of such powers by the parties. Together these two points suggest that it may not be necessary for an international commercial arbitration panel to invoke an inherent power if that necessary part of the whole process is available in either the courts of the place of arbitration or the place where enforcement is sought.[97]

The Iran-US Claims Tribunal, sometimes viewed as interstate arbitration and sometimes viewed as international commercial arbitration,[98] followed the general tendency of suggesting, while not in fact needing to wield, an inherent power to reconsider its awards in certain extreme circumstances. The Tribunal was faced with repeated requests for reconsideration, fashioned more or less ingeniously under Articles 35–37 of the 1983 Tribunal Rules, but steadfastly defended the finality of awards issued under Article 32(2).[99] The Tribunal seemed to endorse the existence of inherent authority to reopen, but never faced a fact situation sufficiently severe to warrant exercising it.

The only extreme circumstances mentioned specifically by the Tribunal were fraud, forgery or false testimony.[100] In the 1983 *Morris* decision, Chamber One stated:

> Whether a Chamber or the Full Tribunal, despite the absence of any express provision, has inherent power to review and revise an Award under exceptional circumstances—e.g. when an Award was based on forged documents or perjury—is a question which the Tribunal does not need to reach in this decision.[101]

In the oft-quoted *Dames & Moore* decision denying Iran's request for reconsideration, based in part on Articles 35 and 37, on the grounds that Dames & Moore had obtained its award through fraud and forgery, Chamber Three of the Tribunal stated:

> The implied or inherent power of an international claims tribunal in this area is an issue which has been subjected to learned analysis, and limited judicial scrutiny, with wholly inconsistent results. The

---

[96] *Antoine Biloune* (1976 Rules), para 34, reprinted in section 5(B).
[97] As to "inherent powers," see generally D Caron, "Interim Measures of Protection: Theory and Practice in Light of the Iran-United States Claims Tribunal," (1986) 46 Zeitschrift für ausländisches öffenliches Recht und Volkerrecht 465, 473–80.
[98] See generally D Caron, "The Nature of the Iran-United States Claims Tribunal and the Evolving Structure of International Dispute Resolution," (1990) 84 AJIL 104–56.
[99] For discussion of the issue by the Tribunal, see section 5(C)(1). See also G Aldrich, *The Jurisprudence of the Iran-United States Claims Tribunal* (1996) 452.
[100] See section 5(C)(2).
[101] *Henry Morris* and *Government of the Islamic Republic of Iran* et al, Dec No DEC 26–200–1 (September 16, 1983), reprinted in 3 Iran-US CTR 364, 364–5 (1983-II).

instant request for reopening and reconsideration, however, falls well short of justifying any such effort to ascertain the precise balance struck between finality of Tribunal dispositions, on the one hand, and the integrity of its processes on the other.[102]

Although fraud was thus referred to as a circumstance perhaps addressed by an inherent power to reconsider, other circumstances, given the Tribunal's silence, apparently did not rise to that level of concern. In *Eastman Kodak*, "the Respondent describe[d] the legal basis of its objection as 'the failure to observe the Tribunal's findings in the [earlier] Partial Award, ... and the conflict and inconsistency between the Tribunal's findings in the Partial and Final Awards.'"[103] In other words, it was alleged that the Tribunal's Final Award was inconsistent with, and therefore breached the finality of, the Partial Award. The Tribunal disposed of the request simply noting that this objection did not fall within the scope of Article 35, 36, or 37 of the 1983 Tribunal Rules. The Tribunal did not consider whether an inherent power exists in such a case:

... Insofar as the Respondent's request constitutes an attempt to reargue certain aspects of the Case on which the Respondent disagrees with the Tribunal's conclusions in the Final Award, there is no basis in the Tribunal Rules or elsewhere for review of an award on such grounds.[104]

Iran's request for reconsideration and revision of the Tribunal's partial award in Case B61 was also rejected. In that case, Iran alleged that the majority in support of the partial award in that case committed fundamental errors of procedure when, among other things, they ruled on the basis of a legal argument that was never raised by the Parties.[105] The Full Tribunal rejected Iran's request, emphasizing that the lack of express authority in the Claims Settlement Declaration and the 1976 UNCITRAL Rules, as modified (despite opportunities for the Parties to establish such powers), and the importance of ensuring finality in the context of the Tribunal's mandate.[106] The Tribunal thus was "not prepared to hold that it has an inherent power to revise a final and binding award," while at the same time recognizing in a footnote that "[n]either fraud nor perjury are alleged in the present case" and thus the Tribunal "need not address the matter for present purposes."[107]

Interestingly, the Tribunal did not have to reopen the one award known to have been based on fraud, the now infamous *Gordon Williams* case.[108] In that case, the Tribunal awarded "Mr. Williams" an award of approximately US $300,000. In the course of attempting to pay "Mr. Williams" his award, the New York Federal Reserve Bank received payment instructions from six different "Mr. Williams" and representatives. A New York court ultimately determined that an Iranian national had impersonated a dead US national to pursue the claim. Because the Tribunal unequivocally lacked jurisdiction over claims by Iranian nationals against Iran, the court ordered the New York Fed to return the funds to the Tribunal Security Account. Therefore justice was done without the need for the Tribunal to

---

[102] *Dames and Moore* and *Islamic Republic of Iran*, Dec No DEC 36–54–3 (April 23, 1985), reprinted in 8 Iran-US CTR 107, 117 (1985-I) (footnotes omitted).
[103] *Eastman Kodak Co* and *Islamic Republic of Iran*, Dec No DEC 102–227–3 (December 30, 1991), reprinted in 27 Iran-US CTR 269, 269 (1991-II).
[104] *Eastman Kodak Co* (1983 Tribunal Rules), at 271.
[105] *Islamic Republic of Iran* and *United States of America*, Cases Nos A3, A8, A9, A14 and B61, Decision No DEC 134-A3/A8/A9/A14/B61-FT (July 1, 2011), at 5–13.
[106] See *Islamic Republic of Iran* and *United States*, Case B61, reprinted in section 5(C)(1).
[107] *Islamic Republic of Iran*, Case B61 (1983 Tribunal Rules), n 105.
[108] *Gordon Williams* and *Islamic Republic of Iran,* et al, Award No 342–187–3 (December 18, 1987), reprinted in 17 Iran-US CTR 269 (1987-IV).

reopen and nullify its award. The *Gordon Williams* case demonstrates that there are dramatically real instances of fraud in international commercial arbitration, but that they also are not likely to go unnoticed or unremedied.[109]

B. Extracts from the Practice of Investment Tribunals

Antoine Biloune, et al and *Ghana Investments Centre,* et al, Award on Damages and Costs (June 30, 1990) (*Ad Hoc* Proceedings, 1976 UNCITRAL Rules, Contract), reprinted in XIX Ybk Commercial Arb 11, 22–23 (1994):

> [32] As provided in Art. 32(2) of the [1976] UNCITRAL Rules, the award on jurisdiction and liability which this Tribunal issued on 27 October 1989 was and is "final and binding on the parties." The [1976] UNCITRAL Rules make no provision for reconsidering an award. Arts. 35, 36 and 37 provide that within thirty days of an award a party may request "interpretation" of an award, may request correction of clerical or typographical errors, or may request an additional award covering issues omitted from the award. The present request for reconsideration was not made pursuant to any of these articles, and (apart from the fact that the request was first made more than thirty days after the original award) none of these articles would seem to support the kind of reconsideration that has been requested.
>
> [33] Nevertheless, a court or Tribunal, including this international arbitral Tribunal, has an inherent power to take cognizance of credible evidence, timely placed before it, that its previous determinations were the product of false testimony, forged documents or other egregious "fraud on the Tribunal." See *United States on behalf of Lehigh Valley Ry. v. Germany, (Sabotage Claims),* Mixed Claims Commission, United States and Germany, Opinions and Decisions from 1 October 1926 to 31 December 1932 (1933) at 967; *id.,* Report of the American Commissioner (30 December 1933) at 7–8; *id.,* Opinions and Decisions in the *Sabotage Claims* (15 June 1939 and 30 October 1939). Certainly if such corruption or fraud in the evidence would justify an international or a national court in voiding or refusing to enforce the award, this Tribunal also, so long as it still has jurisdiction over the dispute, can take necessary corrective action. See the Statute of the International Court of Justice, Art. 61 (permitting revision of an award upon the subsequent discovery of a new decisive fact); ICSID Convention Art. 51 (same); U.S. Arbitration Act, 9 U.S.C. Sect. 10 (permitting judicial annulment of an arbitral award "procured by corruption, fraud or undue means").
>
> [34] The present Tribunal would not hesitate to reconsider and modify its earlier award were it shown by credible evidence that it had been the victim of fraud and that its determinations in the previous award were the product of false testimony. However, no such evidence has been adduced. As in many complex cases, this Tribunal has been required to weigh and resolve occasional inconsistencies in the evidence of both sides in this arbitration, and to come to its best determination of the relevant facts. Nevertheless, the Tribunal is satisfied that the material facts on which it based its previous award on jurisdiction and liability, as well as the present award on damages and costs, are sufficiently explained and proved by credible evidence

---

Methanex Corp and *United States of America,* Award (August 3, 2005) (*Ad Hoc* Proceeding, 1976 UNCITRAL Rules, NAFTA Chapter Eleven), Part II, Chapter E, at 19 (some footnotes omitted):

> 33. Turning to the issue under Article 15(1) of the [1976] UNCITRAL Rules, there is nothing there to suggest that an arbitration tribunal has a broad jurisdiction to reconsider a final and

---

[109] See Remarks by Jacomijn Van Haersolte-van Hof on the topic of a tribunal's inherent authority to reconsider awards in the *Contemporary International Law Issues: Opportunities at a Time of Momentous Change: Proceedings of the ASIL/NVIR Second Joint Conference held in The Hague, July 22-24, 1993,* (1993) 9–13. Ms van Hof suggests that the Tribunal can and should address the issue of fraud in the *Gordon Williams* case in the course of conducting the final reconciliation of the Security Account.

binding award that it has already made. (The possible exception for fraud by a party is here irrelevant). To the contrary, both the ordinary meaning and the context of Article 15(1) lead to the opposite conclusion. Article 15(1) is located in Section III of the Rules, "Arbitral Proceedings"; and it is a general provision that regulates the conduct of the arbitral proceedings. By contrast, Article 32 is to be found in Section IV, "The Award"; and it is concerned with the form and effect of an award. Article 15(1) cannot be read as creating such a huge derogation from Article 32; it has a significantly different subject-matter. Moreover, Article 15(1) requires that a party be given a full opportunity of presenting its case *"at any stage of the proceedings"*. This accepts that arbitral proceedings may comprise differing stages, as also appears from Article 15(2), and a given stage in the proceedings may of course be brought to an end by a final and binding award. It would both undermine Article 32 and lead to an inequality between the parties if at any time the losing party could seek to re-litigate matters contained in an award simply by invoking Article 15(1) of the [1976] UNCITRAL Rules.

C. Extracts from the Practice of the Iran–US Claims Tribunal

(1) Limited power of review

Islamic Republic of Iran and *United States of America*, Case No A/20, Decision No DEC 45-A20-FT (June 26, 1986), reprinted in 11 Iran-US CTR 271, 274 (1986-II):

> It is obvious, and both Parties are in full agreement, that neither Article VI, paragraph 4 [of the Claims Settlement Agreement] nor the Tribunal Rules provide for any kind of review by the Full Tribunal of Orders or Awards made by the Chambers. To the Contrary, Article IV, paragraph 1, which applies equally to actions by the Full Tribunal and the Chambers, states that "[a]ll decisions and Awards of the Tribunal shall be final and binding". The only exceptions to this rule of finality are those contained in Articles 35 and 36 of the [1983] Tribunal Rules, dealing with interpretation and correction, which clearly do not apply here.

International Schools Services, Inc and *Islamic Republic of Iran*, Award No 290–123–1 (January 29, 1987), reprinted in 14 Iran-US CTR 65, 70–71 (1987-I):

> The request does not rely on, or fall within, any of the relevant provisions of the [1983] Tribunal Rules, and it is questionable whether, even in exceptional circumstances, the Tribunal would have authority to act outside those Rules to revise or correct an award. It is even more questionable whether the Tribunal would have authority to do so where, as here, the Party seeking revision does not complain of any irregularities in the procedure, but merely asserts the existence of legal error in the decision itself.

Sedco, Inc and *National Iranian Oil Co*, Decision No DEC 64–129–3 (September 18, 1987), reprinted in 16 Iran-US CTR 282, 283–84 (1987-III):

> [T]he Tribunal is unable to grant the relief sought in the Requests. The Requests allege several procedural and legal errors which the Respondents assert were committed by the Tribunal in the Award, and urge the Tribunal to reconsider its decisions. The Tribunal is without power to entertain the Requests, however, which amount in effect to a request for appeal or review of the Award by the Tribunal.

Letter, the US Agent to the Appointing Authority (August 8, 1989), reprinted in 21 Iran-US CTR 349 (1989-I):

> The [1983] Rules do not provide for review or appeals. No party should be permitted to relitigate Tribunal awards in the guise of a challenge, no matter how unhappy it may be about the results of the award.

Development and Resources Corp and *Islamic Republic of Iran*, Decision No DEC 98–60–3 (May 30, 1991), reprinted in 26 Iran-US CTR 256, 261 (1991-I):

> MOA states that its request is based on Articles 36 and 37 of the [1983] Tribunal Rules. MOA does not, however, make a request for correction of the award, as provided for in Article 36, nor does it make a request for an additional award, as provided for in Article 37 of the [1983] Tribunal Rules. Instead, MOA seeks to reargue certain aspects of the case and to submit additional evidence, in the form of an alleged Settlement Agreement, dated 18 December 1981. The Tribunal finds that MOA has had ample opportunity to present all arguments and submit all evidence it considered relevant. The [1983] Tribunal Rules do not provide for additional arguments and evidence after a case has been concluded by Award.

Unidyne Corp and *Islamic Republic of Iran*, Decision No DEC 122–368–3 (March 9, 1994), reprinted in 30 Iran-US CTR 19, 20 (1994):

> With regard to the request for a correction to the award concerning the amount of $176,304.02 awarded for work performed for the PMS Development at Bandar Abbas, Tribunal precedent is clear. Insofar as the request constitutes an attempt to reargue certain aspects of the Case, to disagree with the conclusions of the Tribunal in its Award, or to request the Tribunal either to review its Award or further to explain its reasons for the Award, there is no basis in the [1983] Tribunal Rules for a request of this kind on such grounds.

Harold Birnbaum and *Islamic Republic of Iran*, Decision No DEC 124–967–2 (December 14, 1995), reprinted in 31 Iran-US CTR 286, 289–90 (1995) (footnotes omitted):

> There are both national and international jurisdictions which, while recognizing the final and binding nature of judgments, do not exclude revision thereof.
>
> Where revisions are permitted, they are normally provided for in an express rule of procedure. Decisions by international tribunals which, in the absence of such express provisions, admitted the existence of the inherent power of an international tribunal to revise, under extraordinary circumstances, its own awards, are rather rare and exceptional. There is not much room for reading implied powers into a contemporary bilateral arrangement; for its authors are aware of past experience. It is to be expected that today, two States that intended to allow the revision of awards rendered by a tribunal established pursuant to a treaty between them would do so by unequivocal expression of their common will. Clearly Iran and the United States did not so provide in the Algiers Declarations.
>
> The Tribunal has recognized that it has inherent power to issue certain interim orders.... The revision of a final award, however, belongs to a different category
>
> ...
>
> [T]he final and binding force of an award does not necessarily exclude the possibility of a revision thereof. But the existence of express rules providing that the award is "final and binding," coupled with the silence of the contracting Parties concerning the possibility of revision, makes it difficult to conclude that any inherent power to revise a final award exists.

Frederica Lincoln Riahi and *Islamic Republic of Iran*, Decision No DEC 133–485–1 (November 17, 2004), at 13–14, reprinted in (2004) 19(12) Mealey's Intl Arb Rep C–1, C–3:

> 32. ... Clearly, there is nothing in the Claimant's applications which would fall within the ambit of Articles 35–37 of the [1983] Tribunal Rules. The Claimant herself does not suggest this. She is instead urging the Chamber to reconsider its Final Award and to arrange a new legal procedure including the possibility of presenting additional documents and statements by witnesses and eventually a new hearing, too. In other words, the Claimant is making an appeal for a total review of the Award.

33. The legal difference between an appeal for a total review of a Final Award and a revision based on Articles 35–37 of the [1983] Tribunal Rules is remarkable. While the latter type of request is admissible by definition if it is so based, these Rules do not contain any provision for the admissibility of an appeal for a total or even partial review of a final award....

Islamic Republic of Iran and *United States of America*, Cases Nos A3, A8, A9, A14 and B61, Decision No DEC 134-A3/A8/A9/A14/B61-FT (July 1, 2011), at 18–25 (citations omitted):

51. In its practice thus far in Tribunal Chambers, the Tribunal has raised but left open the question whether, given the absence of an express grant of authority to the Tribunal to reopen and reconsider cases on the merits after the issuance of an award, it possesses the inherent power to do so "under exceptional circumstances." The Tribunal examined that question at some length in the following two cases.
[Discussion of *Ram International Industries, Inc* and *Harold Birnbaum* omitted.]
54. Indeed, in Article IV, paragraph 1, of the Claims Settlement Declaration, which commands that "[a]ll decisions and awards of the Tribunal shall be final and binding," the State Parties gave expression to the principle of finality of international arbitral awards. This fundamental principle "serves the purpose of efficiency in terms of an expeditious and economical settlement of disputes." The desire for finality is a significant factor in international arbitration.
56. ...the Tribunal carefully reviewed and modified the UNCITRAL Arbitration Rules after giving the two State Parties full opportunity to express their views. The Tribunal finally adopted the Tribunal Rules in May 1983.
58. During the process of modification of the UNCITRAL Arbitration Rules neither the Tribunal nor the State Parties concluded that, in order for the Tribunal to carry out its functions under the Claims Settlement Declaration – 'to ensure that [the Claims Settlement Declaration] can be carried out' – any exceptions to the fundamental rule of finality of awards were required other than the narrow exceptions provided in Articles 35, 36, and 37 of the Tribunal Rules (respectively, interpretation of the award, correction of the award, and making of an additional award). In particular, neither the Tribunal nor the State Parties deemed it necessary to include a provision permitting the revision of an otherwise final and binding award, even though they were "aware of past experience." In connection with the latter, it should be noted that contemporary dispute-settlement instruments that were in force on the date of the Algiers Declarations, such as the Statute of the International Court of Justice and the ICSID Convention, expressly provide for the revision of final and binding judgments and awards. Notably, further, the 1899 Hague Convention for the Pacific Settlement of International Disputes, to which both Iran and the United States have been parties since 4 September 1900, provides that "[t]he parties can reserve in the 'Compromis' the right to demand the revision of the Award." As Chamber Two stated in *Harold Birnbaum,* '[i]t is to be expected that today, two States that intended to allow the revision of awards rendered by a tribunal established pursuant to a treaty between them would do so by an unequivocal expression of their common will.'
59. The Tribunal now turns to the question of inherent powers of international courts and tribunals. As a general matter, the Tribunal accepts that an international arbitral tribunal, such as the present one, possesses certain inherent powers. Inherent powers "are those powers that are not explicitly granted to the tribunal but must be seen as a necessary consequence of the parties' fundamental intent to create an institution with a judicial nature." It has been suggested that "the source of the inherent powers of international courts is their need to ensure the fulfilment of their functions." Thus, for example, the Tribunal has held that it has "an inherent power to issue such orders as may be necessary to conserve the respective rights of the Parties and to ensure that this Tribunal's jurisdiction and authority are made fully effective."
60. With respect to the existence of an international tribunal's inherent power to revise a final and binding award, opinions of legal scholars diverge, and the practice of international courts and tribunals is inconsistent....

61. In the Tribunal's view, in order to determine which powers international courts and tribunals may exercise as inherent powers one must take into account the particular features of each specific court or tribunal, including the circumstances surrounding its establishment, the object and purpose of its constitutive instrument, and the consent of the parties as expressed in that and related instruments. This principle will guide the Tribunal in determining whether it possesses the inherent power to revise its awards.

62. On 19 January 1981, after protracted and difficult negotiations conducted through the Government of Algeria acting as the official intermediary, Iran and the United States entered into the Algiers Declarations, which consist of a General Declaration and a Claims Settlement Declaration. The Algiers Declarations ended a long and acute political crisis between two Governments that had essentially severed all diplomatic relations and that regarded each other with extreme distrust. This Tribunal, which was one of the measures intended to defuse that crisis, was established through the Claims Settlement Declaration for the purpose of deciding certain claims by nationals of one State against the Government of the other and certain claims between the two Governments. The final settlement of such claims was one of the crucial features of the bargain struck by the two Governments to end the crisis; this aspect is also reflected in Article I of the Claims Settlement Declaration, which provides that "Iran and the United States will promote the settlement of the claims described in Article II by the parties directly concerned.,,101 Against this backdrop, the State Parties' agreement, in Article IV, paragraph 1, of the Claims Settlement Declaration, that "[a]ll decisions and awards of the Tribunal shall be final and binding" acquires particular significance.

63. In the Tribunal's view, to avoid upsetting the strict and careful construction and application of the politically sensitive Algiers Declarations, the Tribunal must be especially cautious in finding that it possesses inherent powers.

64. In light of the above and considering (i) that, when the Tribunal, in consultation with the two State Parties to the Claims Settlement Declaration, modified the UNCITRAL Arbitration Rules, neither the Tribunal nor the two State Parties considered the remedy of revision of a final and binding award necessary "to ensure that [the Claims Settlement Declaration] can be carried out" and (ii) that a mechanism is available under the Claims Settlement Declaration and Article 1, paragraph 1, of the Tribunal Rules to modify those Rules should the Tribunal or the two State Parties to the Claims Settlement Declaration at any point in time deem it necessary and appropriate to provide the remedy of revision, the Tribunal is not prepared to hold that it has an inherent power to revise a final and binding award.[105] Equally crucial, the Tribunal believes that it is, not in the context of a Tribunal decision in a particular case, but rather in the context of a formal modification of the Tribunal Rules that essential features and modalities relating to a remedy of revision – such as its scope, the time limits within which an application for revision may be submitted, and the structure of the revision proceeding – can be established with the proper degree of rigor.

65. Additionally, the Tribunal notes that, to its knowledge, the statutes and rules of procedure of modem international courts and tribunals expressly providing the remedy of revision do not provide for "manifest errors of law" or "fundamental errors of procedure" as grounds for revising a final and binding decision. Rather, they typically provide that an application for revision of such a decision may be made only if it is based upon the discovery of some new and decisive fact; they also specify the time limits within which any such application may be submitted.

Fn 105 It has been suggested that, because a decision proven to have been induced by fraud or perjury does not constitute a "decision in law, ... the right and indeed the duty to render a valid judgment or award must be seen to continue;" and that the "argument that, in such circumstances, the reopening of the case can hardly be described as revision in the normal understanding of the notion is clearly a strong one." [Citations omitted] Neither fraud nor perjury are alleged in the present case. Consequently, the Tribunal need not address the matter for present purposes.

(2) Revision to address fraud or corruption

Mark Dallal and *Islamic Republic of Iran*, Decision No DEC 30–149–1 (January 10, 1984), reprinted in 5 Iran-US CTR 74, 75 (1984-I):

> The request made by Mr. Dallal is not based on any of the circumstances covered by Articles 35, 36 or 37 [of the 1983 Tribunal Rules]. Nor is there any provision for the rescission of, or appeal from, an Award of the Tribunal, or for the re-hearing of a case in which an Award has been rendered.
>
> Whether, in the absence of any express provision, the Tribunal has inherent power to review and revise an Award under exceptional circumstances—e.g. when it subsequently transpires that an Award was based on forged documents or perjury—is a question which the Tribunal does not need to reach in this decision.

Dames and Moore and *Islamic Republic of Iran*, Decision No DEC 36–54–3 (April 17, 1985), reprinted in 8 Iran-US CTR 107, 117 (1985-I) (footnotes omitted):

> In the absence of an express grant of authority to the Tribunal to reopen and consider cases on the merits after issuance of an award, the question has been posed as to whether an "inherent power" to do so may exist "under exceptional circumstances," at least where an award "was based on forged documents or perjury." ... The implied or inherent power of an international claims tribunal in this area is an area which has been subjected to learned analysis and limited judicial scrutiny with wholly inconsistent results. The instant request for reopening and reconsideration, however, falls well short of justifying any such effort to ascertain the precise balance struck between finality of Tribunal dispositions, on the one hand, and the integrity of its processes on the other.
>
> ... The Tribunal states no opinion as to the existence of the hypothesized power, but rather expressly reserves such questions for future decision should the same be required.

RAM Intl Industries, Inc and *Air Force of The Islamic Republic of Iran*, Decision No DEC 118–148–1 (December 28, 1993), reprinted in 29 Iran-US CTR 383, 390 (1993):

> On the basis of the foregoing review, it might possibly be concluded that a tribunal, like the present one, which is to adjudicate a large group of cases and for a protracted period of time would by implication, until the adjournment and dissolution of the tribunal, have the authority to revise decisions induced by fraud. However, in view of what follows, this case does not need to be fully pursued and decided for the purposes of the present Case. On the other hand, one requirement, namely, that an application for revision of an award "may be made only when it is based upon the discovery of some fact of such a nature as to be a decisive factor" follows closely the language of all reviewed legal provisions, judicial decisions and views of learned writers. Therefore, the Tribunal holds that for the purpose of a revision the new fact has to be decisive, in the sense that when placed alongside the other facts of the case, earlier assessed, it seriously upsets the balance, and consequently the conclusions drawn by the tribunal.

United States of America and *Islamic Republic of Iran*, Case No B36, Decision No DEC 126-B36–2 (March 17, 1997), reprinted in 33 Iran-US CTR 56, 59 (1997):

> In its present request, Iran does not allege fraud or perjury or submit decisive new *evidence*. Iran's submissions are far removed from such instances which might possibly give rise to the revision of an award. Iran contests the reasoning by which the Tribunal arrived at its conclusions. The Tribunal is not persuaded by Iran's assertions. Moreover, the request fails to cite any evidence which was not on the record at the time the Tribunal deliberated this Case. Absent any exceptional ground upon which the request is made, the Tribunal need not decide whether it has an inherent or implied power to revise its Award in the present Case.

Islamic Republic of Iran and *United States of America*, Case No A/27, Award No 586-A/27-FT (June 5, 1998), reprinted in 31 Iran-US CTR 39, 58 n 11 (1998):

> [N]o tribunal can declare itself immune from procedural error or the possibility of fraud, forgery, or perjury that it may not detect. In such hypothetical cases, however, revision of the award could be done only by the Tribunal, if it concluded that it had authority to do so, not by any other court.

Frederica Lincoln Riahi and *Islamic Republic of Iran*, Decision No DEC 133–485–1 (November 17, 2004), at 17, 20, reprinted in (2004) 19(12) Mealey's Intl Arb Rep C-1, C-6–C-7 (footnote omitted):

> 38. ... So far, neither the Full Tribunal nor any of the Chambers of the Tribunal have been prepared or even willing to formulate any definition of what is meant by the term "inherent power." This is due to the generally accepted interpretation that is based on the Algiers Declarations (Article IV, paragraphs 1 and 3, in particular, which gives a final and binding nature to the Tribunal's awards and decisions) and on the clear terms adopted by the [1983] Tribunal Rules in Article 32(2)....
>
> ...
>
> 43. ... [O]n the basis of the Tribunal's jurisprudence, and in the circumstances of this Case, the Tribunal concludes that there is no need to define the inherent power of the Tribunal, if any, or to delineate under what particular circumstances such a power might be invoked. So far, this issue has been discussed especially in relation to possible cases of fraud and perjury and not as a general problem related to reconsideration. Even in that context, the Tribunal has not reached a single decision confirming the existence and the need to apply its "inherent power," whatever that may be. In the present Case, there has been no mention of any aspect of fraud or perjury, and the Tribunal need not investigate any further the possibility of applying the theory of inherent power insofar as the request for reconsideration of the Award is concerned.

Frederica Lincoln Riahi and *Islamic Republic of Iran*, Decision No DEC 133–485–1 (November 17, 2004), Dissenting Opinion of Judge Brower (November 17, 2004), at 21–22, reprinted in (2004) 19(12) Mealey's Intl Arb Rep D-1, D-7–D-8 (footnote omitted):

> 40. It is clear that the question as to whether or not the Tribunal has an inherent authority to reconsider an Award under certain circumstances has not been decided and therefore has not been foreclosed. While the majority states that the Tribunal has "turned down" the "notion of [such] inherent power," the cases it cites for this proposition merely held that it was unnecessary on the facts thereof to decide whether or not such authority existed, not that it does not exist. On the contrary, the Tribunal has in many cases in fact *expressly reserved* the question of whether such inherent authority exists, including those cases cited by the majority, as the majority itself acknowledges....

Chapter 27
The Costs of Arbitration

1. Introduction	840
2. The Costs of Arbitration—Article 40	841
A. Text of the 2010 UNCITRAL Rule	841
B. Commentary	841
(1) The duty to fix the costs of arbitration	841
(2) Costs defined	843
(a) Subparagraph (a)	843
(b) Subparagraphs (b) and (c)	844
(c) Subparagraph (d)	844
(d) Subparagraph (e)	845
(e) Subparagraph (f)	846
(3) The costs of interpretation, correction and completion of an award—Article 40(3)	847
(4) Note on the costs of the Iran–US Claims Tribunal	848
(5) Comparison to the 1976 UNCITRAL Rules	848
C. Extracts from the Practice of Investment and other Tribunals	849
3. Arbitrators' Fees—Article 41	852
A. Text of the 2010 UNCITRAL Rule	852
B. Commentary	853
(1) Regulation of the arbitrators' fees and expenses under the Rules—general background, Article 41(1) and (2)	853
(2) Determining the fees and expenses of the arbitral tribunal and potential review by a neutral arbiter—Article 41(3)–(6)	855
(a) The manner in which fees and expenses will be determined—Article 41(3) and (5)	856
(1) Transparency	857
(2) Neutral Mechanism	858
(3) Efficiency	859
(b) The computation of the arbitral tribunal's fees and expenses—Article 41(4)–(6)	860
(1) Transparency	860
(2) Neutral mechanism	860
(3) Efficiency	861
(3) Comparison to the 1976 UNCITRAL Rules	862
C. Extracts from the Practice of Investment Tribunals	863
4. Apportionment of Costs—Article 42	865
A. Text of the 2010 UNCITRAL Rule	865
B. Commentary	865
(1) Apportioning and awarding costs	865
(2) "The circumstances of the case"	870
(a) The degree of success of the parties	870
(b) The conduct of the parties	871

(c) The nature of the parties		873
(d) The nature of the dispute resolution mechanism		874
(3) Requirements for making a claim for costs		875
(a) Documentation		875
(b) Timing of requests		875
(c) Proof of reasonable legal costs		876
(4) Comparison to the 1976 UNCITRAL Rules		877
C. Extracts from the Practice of Investment Tribunals		877
(1) Article 40(1) and (2) (1976 Rules)—General		877
(2) Article 40(1) and (2) (1976 Rules)—"Circumstances of the case"		879
(a) The success of the parties		879
(b) The conduct of the parties		882
(c) The nature of the dispute resolution mechanism		887
D. Extracts from the Practice of the Iran–US Claims Tribunal		891
(1) Tribunal Rules (1983), Article 40(1) and (2)—General		891
(2) Tribunal Rules (1983), Article 40(1) and (2)—"Circumstances of the case"		892
(a) The success of the parties		892
(b) The conduct of the parties		894
5. Deposit of Costs—Article 43		**896**
A. Text of the 2010 UNCITRAL Rule		896
B. Commentary		897
(1) The request for deposits		897
(2) Consultation with the appointing authority		899
(3) Failure to make requested deposits		899
(4) The right to an accounting and the return of unexpended deposits		900
(5) Comparison to the 1976 UNCITRAL Rules		901
C. Extracts from the Practice of Investment Tribunals		901
D. Extracts from the Practice of the Iran–US Claims Tribunal		903

1. Introduction

International arbitration may be quite costly because, unlike litigation, the parties pay not only for the costs of presenting their case, but also for the costs of the arbitral tribunal, including the arbitrators' remuneration and expenses and any administrative fees.[1] Further, the parties must typically pay upfront for the costs of the arbitral tribunal through advance monetary deposits. Unlike litigation in some countries, the prevailing party may be reimbursed for its costs at the end of arbitration through an award by the arbitral tribunal. The UNCITRAL Rules devote four articles to the costs of arbitration, Articles 40 through 43, which address the definition of "costs" (Article 40), guidelines for establishing arbitrators' fees (Article 41), the award and apportionment of costs (Article 42), and the deposit of costs (Article 43).

---

[1] For a discussion on methods of reducing the costs of arbitration, see M Schneider, "Arbitration, Cost Control and Efficiency Through Progressive Identification of Issues and Separate Pricing of Arbitration Services," (1985) 1 Arb Intl 2, 119; J Coe, "Pre-hearing techniques to promote speed and cost-effectiveness—some thoughts concerning arbitral process design," (2002) 2 Pepperdine Disp Resolution L J 53. On cost reduction in the context of investor–state arbitration, see L Caplan, "A Proposed Set of Arbitration Rules for Weaker Players in Investor-State Arbitration" in (2010) Ybk Intl Investment L and Policy 2009–2010 333, 353.

2. The Costs of Arbitration—Article 40

A. Text of the 2010 UNCITRAL Rule[2]

Article 40 of the 2010 UNCITRAL Rules provides:

Definition of costs

1. The arbitral tribunal shall fix the costs of arbitration in the final award and, if it deems appropriate, in another decision.
2. The term "costs" includes only:
   (a) The fees of the arbitral tribunal to be stated separately as to each arbitrator and to be fixed by the tribunal itself in accordance with article 41;
   (b) The reasonable travel and other expenses incurred by the arbitrators;
   (c) The reasonable costs of expert advice and of other assistance required by the arbitral tribunal;
   (d) The reasonable travel and other expenses of witnesses to the extent such expenses are approved by the arbitral tribunal;
   (e) The legal and other costs incurred by the parties in relation to the arbitration to the extent that the arbitral tribunal determines that the amount of such costs is reasonable;
   (f) Any fees and expenses of the appointing authority as well as the fees and expenses of the Secretary-General of the PCA.
3. In relation to interpretation, correction or completion of any award under articles 37 to 39, the arbitral tribunal may charge the costs referred to in paragraphs 2 (b) to (f), but no additional fees.

B. Commentary

(1) The duty to fix the costs of arbitration

Article 40(1) requires the arbitral tribunal to fix the costs of arbitration "in the final award and, if it deems appropriate, in another decision."[3] This requirement does not mean that the arbitral tribunal must list *each and every* cost incurred in the course of arbitration, but

---

[2] Corresponding Article 38 of the 1976 UNCITRAL Rules provides:
The arbitral tribunal shall fix the costs of arbitration in its award. The term "costs" includes only:

(a) The fees of the arbitral tribunal to be stated separately as to each arbitrator and to be fixed by the tribunal itself in accordance with article 39;
(b) The travel and other expenses incurred by the arbitrators;
(c) The costs of expert advice and of other assistance required by the arbitral tribunal;
(d) The travel and other expenses of witnesses to the extent such expenses are approved by the arbitral tribunal;
(e) The costs for legal representation and assistance of the successful party if such costs were claimed during the arbitral proceedings, and only to the extent that the arbitral tribunal determines that the amount of such costs is reasonable;
(f) Any fees and expenses of the appointing authority as well as the expenses of the Secretary-General of the Permanent Court of Arbitration at The Hague.

[3] See section 2(C) for extracts from the practice of investment and other tribunals under the 1976 UNCITRAL Rules specifically *Antoine Biloune* (1976 Rules); *Karaha Bodas Co LLC* (1976 Rules) (Preliminary and Final awards); *Pope & Talbot, Inc* (1976 Rules); *BG Group plc* (1976 Rules); *Chemtura Corp* (1976 Rules); *ICS Inspection and Control Services Ltd* (1976 Rules); all reprinted in section 2(C). Note that the practice of the Iran–US Claims Tribunal is far from exemplary, as the Tribunal often fixes the costs of arbitration with little or no explanation in a one-sentence statement awarding a lump sum amount. See S Baker and M Davis, *The UNCITRAL Arbitration Rules in Practice: The Experience of the Iran-United States Claims Tribunal* (1992) 208.

rather those costs owed to the arbitral tribunal in exchange for its services or awarded to a party as compensation in accordance with Article 42(2). What constitutes "costs" under the UNCITRAL Rules is discussed in the following section.

Typically, the arbitral tribunal fixes the costs in the final award after assessing the disputing parties' request for costs. However, the arbitral tribunal may deem it appropriate under the circumstances to issue a separate award on costs.[4] It may also be necessary to fix costs in a termination order, such as where the arbitration is terminated pursuant to Article 36 without issuing an award.[5] The reference to "another decision" in Article 40(1) recognizes the need for such flexibility. Where possible, a judgment for costs should be stated in the form of an award rather than an order, as typically only an award is enforceable in foreign jurisdictions under international conventions.[6] A decision in the form of an award protects not only the parties, but also the arbitrators, where enforcement of the award may be the only means of recouping unpaid fees.[7]

Article 40(2)(a) establishes a specific rule on fixing the arbitrators' fees, a topic discussed in detail below in the context of Article 41.[8] The amount of the arbitrators' remuneration must be stated in the final award or other decision "as to each arbitrator."[9] By requiring an itemized disclosure of the arbitral tribunal's billable work, the drafters of the 1976 UNCITRAL Rules meant to "check the ability of both the arbitrators and the arbitrating parties to run up the costs of arbitral proceedings."[10] In Working Group discussions to revise the Rules, it was noted that this obligation had proven useful "in disciplining arbitrators and avoiding exaggerated costs."[11] The 1976 UNCITRAL Rules were revised by including the word "reasonable" before the items of expenditure described in Article 40(2)(b), (c), and

---

Note also that in controversies where the tribunal finds that it lacks jurisdiction, there is some debate whether the tribunal has authority to award costs. In our opinion, the power of the tribunal to rule on its own jurisdiction implicitly carries within it the power to award costs for that determination. For a general discussion see G Born, *International Commercial Arbitration II* (2009) 2501–2; M Bühler "Awarding Costs in International Commercial Arbitration: an Overview" 22(2) ASA Bulletin 249, 257–8. See also *Econet Wireless Ltd* and *First Bank of Nigeria*, et al, Award (June 2, 2005) (*Ad Hoc* Proceeding, 1976 UNCITRAL Rules, Contract), excerpt reprinted in (2006) XXXI Ybk Commercial Arb 49, 64–5.

[4] See, eg, *SD Myers, Inc* and *Government of Canada*, Final Award on Costs (December 30, 2002) (*Ad Hoc* Proceeding, 1976 UNCITRAL Rules, NAFTA Chapter Eleven); *Pope & Talbot, Inc* and *Government of Canada*, Award on Costs (November 26, 2002) (*Ad Hoc* Proceeding, 1976 UNCITRAL Rules, NAFTA Chapter Eleven).

[5] See, eg, *Canfor Corp*, et al and *United States of America*, (*Softwood Lumber Cases*), Joint Order on the Costs of Arbitration and for the Termination of Certain Arbitral Proceedings (July 19, 2007) (ICSID administered, 1976 UNCITRAL Rules, NAFTA Chapter Eleven) (terminating the arbitration in accordance with Article 34(2) of the 1976 UNCITRAL Rules).

[6] According to Berger, "[t]he parties' intention to receive an enforceable award on the costs of the arbitration must therefore be regarded as an implied condition of their arbitration agreement." K Berger, *International Economic Arbitration* (1993) 616. In addition, domestic laws applicable to the arbitration can alter the Tribunal's authority to award costs. For a discussion see G Born, *International Commercial Arbitration*, n 3, 2489 et seq; see also M Bühler "Awarding Costs in International Commercial Arbitration," n 3, 249, 252–5.

[7] An obviously more favorable approach is for the arbitral tribunal to demand at the outset of arbitration sufficient deposits, pursuant to Article 43, to cover its fees. See P Sanders, *The Work of UNCITRAL on Arbitration and Conciliation* (2001) 17.

[8] See section 3(B).

[9] According to Article 41, the arbitrators establish their fees themselves, subject to certain restrictions. See section 3(B).

[10] "As the length and detail of the cost-related rules suggest, the UNCITRAL Drafters hoped to check the ability of both the arbitrators and the arbitrating parties to run up the costs of arbitral proceedings." See S Baker and M Davis, *The UNCITRAL Arbitration Rules in Practice*, n 3, 208.

[11] *Report of Working Group II (Arbitration and Conciliation) on the Work of its Fifty-First Session* (Vienna, September 14–18, 2009), UNCITRAL, 43rd Session, UN Doc A/CN.9/684, at 26, para 121 (2009).

(d) as a "useful reminder to arbitrators that they must act efficiently in all respects in the conduct of the arbitration."[12] Apart from the arbitrators' fees, all other costs of arbitration, such as legal expenses or witness expenditures, are often stated with minimal itemization, as a simple lump sum figure.[13]

(2) Costs defined

Article 40(2) enumerates a list of expenditures incurred by either the parties or the arbitral tribunal in the course of arbitration that constitute "costs."[14] The list is exhaustive.[15] As indicated in the chapeau, it includes "only" certain expenditures.[16] The classification of certain expenditures as "costs" gives rise to important rights and obligations under the UNCITRAL Rules. For example, pursuant to Articles 40 and 42, the arbitral tribunal may award the parties compensation for certain arbitral expenses deemed to be "costs."[17] Pursuant to Article 43, the parties may be required to make advance deposits of money with the arbitral tribunal to cover certain enumerated "costs."[18] Accordingly, determining what items of expenditures are "costs" within the meaning of Article 40 is a key initial inquiry.[19]

(a) Subparagraph (a)

There was little dispute among the drafters of the Rules that the fees of the arbitral tribunal, ie, the remuneration for the arbitrators' services in resolving the parties' dispute, were a part of the "costs" of arbitration. Nor was there any resistance to the requirement that the arbitrators' fees be stated separately in the award.[20] The real controversy with respect to the

---

[12] The UNCITRAL Secretariat suggested that such a change might constitute "a useful reminder to arbitrators that they must act efficiently in all respects in the conduct of the arbitration." *Settlement of Commercial Disputes: Revision of the UNCITRAL Arbitration Rules, Note by the Secretariat*, UN Doc. A/CN.9/WGII/WP.143/Add.1 at 11, para 36, (2006).

[13] *Report of the Secretary-General on the Revised Draft Set of Arbitration Rules*, UNCITRAL, 9th Session, Addendum 1 (Commentary), UN Doc A/CN.9/112/Add.1 (1975), reprinted in (1976) VII UNCITRAL Ybk 166, 181 (Commentary on Draft Article 33(1)).

The Tribunal Rules include the following note to Article 38: "As used in Article 38 of the [1976] UNCITRAL Rules, the term 'party' means the arbitrating party."

[14] See *Report of the UNCITRAL on the Work of its Ninth Session*, UN GAOR, 31st Session, Supp No 17, UN Doc A/31/17, para 205 (1976), reprinted in (1976) VII UNCITRAL Ybk 66, 80 (Commentary on Draft Article 33(1)). The parties, of course, can supplement or replace the UNCITRAL cost regime as they wish. See, eg, *Association of Service Industry Firms* and *Service Industry Firm*, Award (May 27, 1991) (*Ad Hoc* Proceeding, 1976 UNCITRAL Rules, Contract), reprinted in (1992) XVII Ybk Commercial Arb 11, 26–7 (honoring the parties' contractual agreement that the costs of arbitration be borne equally, save for instances of wilful default on the part of a party); *Banque Arabe et Internationale D'Investissement*, et al and *Inter-Arab Investment Guarantee Corporation*, Award (November 17, 1994) (*Ad Hoc* Proceeding, 1976 UNCITRAL Rules, Contract), reprinted in (1996) XXI Ybk Commercial Arb 13, 38–9.

[15] See UN GAOR, 31st Session, Supp No 17, UN Doc A/31/17, n 14, para 205, reprinted in (1976) VII UNCITRAL Ybk 66, 80. This was not the case with earlier versions of the 1976 UNCITRAL Rules, however. See Commentary to Draft Article 31(1) of the Preliminary Draft, reprinted in (1975) VI UNCITRAL Ybk 180.

[16] See *Report of the Working Group on Arbitration and Conciliation on the Work of its Forty-Fifth Session (Vienna, September 11–15, 2006)*, UN Doc. A/CN.9/614 at 26, para 130 (2006). Of course, the parties may be entitled to claim for additional costs if provided for in their arbitration agreement or under the governing arbitration law.

[17] See section 4(B).

[18] See section 5(B).

[19] The use of an exhaustive list of "costs" under the Rules is in accord with the general approach taken to costs in international arbitration, see N Blackaby and C Partasides with A Redfern and M Hunter, *Redfern and Hunter on International Arbitration* (5th edn 2009) 545–6.

[20] For a detailed discussion of the regulation of the fees and expenses of arbitrators, see Section 3(B).

arbitrators' fees was whether the arbitral tribunal's power to set its own fees should be circumscribed in some way, such as through a standard schedule of fees or consultations with the appointing authority, to avoid the potential for abuse.[21] The arbitral tribunal's proposal as to how it will determine its fees and its actual determination of those fees is more rigorously regulated under the 2010 UNCITRAL Rules than the 1976 UNCITRAL Rules.[22]

(b) Subparagraphs (b) and (c)

There was also wide agreement among the drafters that "costs" included the arbitrators' travel and other incidental expenses, as well as the costs of "expert advice" and "other assistance required by the tribunal." The term "expert advice" covers situations when a party hires an expert witness to support his case and when the arbitral tribunal enlists a third-party expert witness for guidance.[23] The arbitral tribunal may demand deposits from the parties only in the latter situation.[24] The term "other assistance" includes expenditures for administrative support for the arbitral tribunal, such as the provision of secretarial support, stenographic services, and language translation,[25] or for services requested of the appointing authority, if one has been appointed.[26]

In Working Group discussions to revise the Rules, the question arose whether subparagraph (c) of Article 40 should include an express reference to the fees and expenses of a secretary appointed by the arbitral tribunal. The Working Group agreed that a revision along these lines was unnecessary, as it was clear from the text that the cost of a secretary was already covered in paragraph (c) by the phrase "other assistance required by the arbitral tribunal."[27]

(c) Subparagraph (d)

A number of UNCITRAL drafters wanted to exclude travel and other expenses of witnesses from the definition of "costs." Worried that the parties might run up the costs of arbitration by calling witnesses without regard to expense,[28] they proposed deleting the relevant provision from the Rules or limiting its scope to the expenses of witnesses "who were called by the arbitrators."[29] Other delegates noted, however, that a

---

[21] See section 2(B)(5).
[22] See section 3(B)(2).
[23] See Chapter 20 on experts.
[24] See section 5(B) on deposit of costs.
[25] Examples of where the Iran–US Claims Tribunal interpreted the slightly modified term "other special assistance" are instructive: *Gulf Associates,* et al and *Islamic Republic of Iran,* et al, Case No 385, Chamber Two, Order of December 11, 1997 (requiring equal deposits from the parties for stenographic costs associated with a hearing); see *Starrett Housing Corp,* et al and *Government of the Islamic Republic of Iran,* et al, Case No 24, Chamber One, Order of December 18, 1986 (ordering that deposits be made as an advance for Swedish language interpretation costs); Separate Opinion of Judge Holtzmann, *Sylvania Technical Systems, Inc,* et al and *Government of the Islamic Republic of Iran,* Award No 180–64–1 (June 27, 1985), reprinted in 8 Iran-US CTR 329, 331 (1985-I) ("The phrase 'other special assistance' is comprehensive and includes, *inter alia,* the assistance of those who make the translations required by the Tribunal.").
[26] P Sanders, "Commentary on UNCITRAL Arbitration Rules," (1977) II Ybk Commercial Arb 172, 218.
[27] See UN Doc. A/CN.9/614, n 16, at 26, para 131.
[28] One delegate reported, "[i]t was possible for a party to produce so many witnesses that the costs of arbitration became an unbearable burden." *Summary Record of the 12th Meeting of the Committee of the Whole (II),* UNCITRAL, 9th Session, UN Doc A/CN.9/9/C.2/SR.12, at 10, para 71 (1976) (Comment by Mr Guevara, Philippines). For other comments against inclusion of witness expenses, see paras 63, 69, 71 (Comments by Mr Melis, Austria, and Mr Roehrich, France).
[29] UN GAOR, 31st Session, Supp No 17, UN Doc A/31/17, n 14, para 213, reprinted in (1976) VII UNCITRAL Ybk 66, 81 (Commentary on Draft Article 33(1)(d)).

prevailing party should receive compensation for the expense, even if considerable, of putting on the witnesses that were "instrumental in establishing the correctness of his position."[30] In the end, the Committee retained the provision on witness expenses, noting that the arbitral tribunal has the power both to approve and to apportion such expenses.[31] Whereas the meaning of travel expenses of witnesses is clear, the term "other expenses" is less so, but has been read to include the subsistence costs of witnesses[32] and the "costs in connection with witnesses whose testimony is presented in the form of affidavits."[33]

(d) Subparagraph (e)

The expenses associated with a party's "legal and other costs" incurred "in relation to the arbitration" are included in the definition of the costs of arbitration. The phrase "legal and other costs" is broad,[34] covering the cost not only of legal representation,[35] but also of non-legal assistance, such as expert advice on the calculation of damages or scientific or other technical matters.[36] That such costs must be "incurred...in relation to the arbitration" ensures that only expenditures with a reasonable nexus to the preparation

---

[30] UN GAOR, 31st Session, Supp No 17, UN Doc A/31/17, n 14, para 214. See also UNCITRAL, 9th Session, UN Doc A/CN.9/9/C.2/SR.12, n 28, at 9–10, paras 67, 68, 70 (Comments by Mr Guest, UK, Mr Holtzmann, United States, and Mr Dey, India).

[31] UN GAOR, 31st Session, Supp No 17, UN Doc A/31/17, n 14, para 215, reprinted in (1976) VII UNCITRAL Ybk 66, 81. The Rules say nothing about the time or manner of such approval, but presumably the tribunal would focus on the matter in the course of assessing a party's demand for costs. Such approval or disapproval has never occurred in the practice of the Iran–US Claims Tribunal. See G Aldrich, *The Jurisprudence of the Iran-United States Claims Tribunal* (1996) 479.

[32] UNCITRAL, 9th Session, UN Doc A/CN.9/9/C.2/SR.12, n 28, at 10, para 77 (Comment by Mr Sanders, Special Consultant).

[33] *Sylvania Technical Systems, Inc* (1983 Tribunal Rules), Separate Opinion by Judge Holtzmann, n 25, at 331. In particular, the "other expenses" of witnesses may include the cost of subsistence.

[34] This phrase evolved during Working Group discussions to revise the 1976 UNCITRAL Rules from "legal representation and assistance," as used in the 1976 Rules, to "representation and assistance," *Settlement of Commercial Disputes: Revision of the UNCITRAL Arbitration Rules, Note by the Secretariat*, UNCITRAL, UN Doc A/CN.9/WG.II/WP.151/Add.1 at 16–17, para 37 (2008) (Draft Article 38), and ultimately to "legal and other costs." While the *travaux préparatoires* are scant on the meaning of "legal and other costs," *Report of the Working Group on Arbitration and Conciliation on the Work of its Forty-Eighth Session* (New York, February 4–8, 2008), UNCITRAL, 41st Session, UN Doc A/CN.9/646, at 6, para 19 (2008), there is no indication that the drafters meant to limit the meaning of this item of expenditure in any way.

[35] This provision places no restrictions on a party's right to choose its own legal counsel. In early drafts of the 1976 UNCITRAL Rules, it was proposed to limit compensation for legal costs to circumstances in which "the arbitrators deem that legal assistance was necessary under the circumstances of the case." *Report of the Secretary-General on the Preliminary Draft Set of Arbitration Rules*, UNCITRAL, 8th Session, UN Doc A/CN.9/97 (1974), reprinted in (1975) VI UNCITRAL Ybk 163, 180 (Commentary on Draft Article 31(1)(e)). This provision was deleted after being severely criticized on grounds that it unduly prejudiced the parties' right to choose their own legal representation. See *Summary Record of the 151st Meeting of the UNCITRAL*, 8th Session, UN Doc A/CN.9/SR.168, at 210 (1975) (Comment by Mr Holtzmann, United States). See also *Report of the UNCITRAL*, 8th Session, Summary of Discussion of the Preliminary Draft, UN Doc A/10017, para 217 (1975), reprinted in (1975) VI UNCITRAL Ybk 24, 44. See also 210–12 (Comments by Mr Gueiros, Brazil, Mr Eyzaguirre, Chile, and Mr Sam, Ghana). Other attempts to limit which legal expenses were included in the costs of arbitration also failed. For example, one delegate felt that no compensation for legal assistance should be permitted. UN Doc A/CN.9/SR.168, at 209 (Comments by Mr Jakubowski, Poland). Another proposed that compensation should be awarded only in the face of frivolous claims or dilatory tactics. See 211 (Comment by Mr Sumulong, Philippines). See also UN Doc A/10017, para 218.

[36] The Working Group noted that representation and assistance can be performed by non-lawyers as well, J Castello, "UNCITRAL Rules" in F Weigand (ed) *Practitioner's Handbook on International Commercial Arbitration* (2nd edn 2009) 1525.

and presentation of a party's case in the arbitration at hand will meet the definition of "costs."[37]

This conclusion is consistent with the practice of the Iran–US Claims Tribunal under the 1976 UNCITRAL Rules, as modified, even though they did not include the phrase "in relation to the arbitration." For example, the Tribunal has refused to award costs for a claimant's expenditures to collect on claims against Iran prior to its preparation of an arbitral statement of claim.[38] The Tribunal has also found that expenses incurred in litigation against Iran in US courts prior to the establishment of the Tribunal were not legitimate costs of arbitration.[39] The same may be said about expenditures incurred in connection with the challenge or enforcement of an award.[40] However, an exception to this general rule may be appropriate where the litigation and arbitration expenses of the parties are so intricately entwined—such as when expenses are incurred in obtaining court-ordered provisional measures—that fairness requires that they be deemed "costs," provided a court has not already addressed them.[41]

"[L]egal and other costs" are considered costs under Article 40 only if the arbitral tribunal determines that the amount of such costs is "reasonable." The significance of this qualification in the context of the arbitral tribunal's power of apportionment and the requirements for a request for costs is discussed in section 4.[42]

(e) Subparagraph (f)

The UNCITRAL drafters agreed that the fees and expenses of the appointing authority, along with those charged by the Secretary General of the Permanent Court of Arbitration (PCA) in designating the appointing authority or appointing an arbitrator,[43] were included in the costs of arbitration.[44] With regard to the latter costs, for example, the PCA's Procedure for Requesting the Designation of an Appointing Authority requires an "administration fee for the analysis of a request for the designation of an appointing authority... to be paid in advance."[45] Other costs might include the administrative services of the PCA in reviewing an arbitral tribunal's determination of its fees and expenses, pursuant to Article

---

[37] One commentator notes several factors to consider for reasonableness: "[c]osts incurred in comparison with those of the opposing party; [c]omplexity of the case; [u]se of experts and whether experts were requested by the Tribunal; [u]se of in-house counsel and effect on overall cost and whether internal work is clearly distinguishable from other work." T Webster, *Handbook of UNCITRAL Arbitration: Commentary, Precedents and Materials for UNCITRAL Based Arbitration Rules* (2010) 574.

[38] See *Granite State Machine Co, Inc and Islamic Republic of Iran,* et al, Award No 18–30–3 (December 15, 1982), reprinted in 1 Iran-US CTR 442, 447 (1981–82); Concurring and Dissenting Opinion of Judge Brower, *McCollough & Co, Inc and The Ministry of Post, Telegraph and Telephone,* et al, Award No 225–89–3 (April 22, 1986), reprinted in 11 Iran-US CTR 44 n 19 (1986-II).

[39] See *Sylvania Technical Systems, Inc,* et al and *Government of the Islamic Republic of Iran,* Award No 180–64–1 (June 27, 1985), reprinted in 8 Iran-US CTR 329, 24 (1985-I), and Separate Opinion of Judge Holtzmann, n 25, at 334–5; *Computer Sciences Corp and Government of the Islamic Republic of Iran,* et al, Award No 221–65–1 (April 16, 1986), reprinted in 10 Iran-US CTR 269, 316 (1986-I).

[40] See *Sylvania Technical Systems, Inc* (1983 Rules), Separate Opinion of Judge Holtzmann, n 25, 334 n 7.

[41] J van Hof, *Commentary on the UNCITRAL Arbitration Rules: The Application by the Iran-U.S. Claims Tribunal* (1991) 296.

[42] See section 4(B)(2).

[43] See Articles 8 and 9 of the 2010 UNCITRAL Rules.

[44] See UN GAOR, 31st Session, Supp No 17, UN Doc A/31/17, n 14, para 220, reprinted in (1976) VII UNCITRAL Ybk 66, 81.

[45] "Procedure for Requesting the Designation of an Appointing Authority" in UNCITRAL cases reprinted on PCA website available at <http://www.pca-cpa.org/showpage.asp?pag_id=1062> (accessed on October 24, 2012).

41(4)(b), in resolving a challenge to an arbitrator, if acting as appointing authority, or in administering the arbitration, such as the provision of translation services.[46]

(3) The costs of interpretation, correction and completion of an award—Article 40(3)

Article 40(4) of the 1976 UNCITRAL Rules expressly banned the tribunal from charging additional "fees" for work related to a request to interpret, correct or complete the award. In revising the UNCITRAL Rules, the drafters debated whether or not to retain the ban. Supporters reiterated the original rationale for the ban—that the tribunal should not benefit from additional remuneration when its own errors in making the award are to blame.[47] Other delegates believed that the prospect of uncompensated post-award work would encourage the tribunal to draft its award with "optimal clarity" and to deal expeditiously with any frivolous requests for interpretation, correction or completion of the award.[48] Critics of the ban, however, believed it was overly broad and failed to account for cases in which legitimate work on an unmeritorious request or in completing the award had to be performed.[49]

Compromise solutions were proposed to bridge the gap between proponents and critics of the ban on fees. One solution, inspired by Article 33(1)(b) of the UNCITRAL Model Law, drew the line between requests for interpretation, correction and completion of the award that were unanimous and those that were unilateral.[50] The ban applied to the former, which suggested a deficiency in the award caused by tribunal error, but not to the latter, which likely involved a frivolous attempt to delay the proceedings.[51] Another proposal aimed to grant the arbitral tribunal limited discretion to determine whether the ban on fees should be lifted in exceptional circumstances, such as in addressing a frivolous request. To this end, it was proposed to add a phrase to the rule, such as: "unless there are compelling reasons to charge such fees."[52] The ensuing debate over whether affording such discretion to the arbitral tribunal raised ethical concerns appears to have ended in a stalemate. While some feared that the arbitral tribunal might abuse its discretion, others believed the line between ordinary requests, such as to correct errors or omissions in the award, and exceptional requests was clear enough to guard against such misconduct.[53]

The divergent views expressed in the Working Group resulted in an outcome that softens the original ban on fees, but only modestly. Article 40(3) still prohibits charging additional arbitrator fees in connection with the interpretation, correction or completion of an award.

---

[46] On the provision of translation services, see *Summary Record of the 13th Meeting of the Committee of the Whole (II)*, UNCITRAL, 9th Session, UN Doc A/CN.9/9/C.2/SR.13, at 5, para 26 (1976) (Comment by the Chairman).

[47] UNCITRAL, 41st Session, UN Doc A/CN.9/646, n 34, at 8, para 31. As to the 1976 UNCITRAL Rules, see UN GAOR, 31st Session, Supp No 17, UN Doc A/31/17, n 14, para 192, reprinted in (1976) VII UNCITRAL Ybk 66, 79 ("[T]he arbitrators should not be entitled to extra remuneration for issuing an interpretation of their award, since it was the vagueness of their award that gave rise to the request for its interpretation.").

[48] UNCITRAL, 41st Session, UN Doc A/CN.9/646, n 34, at 8, para 32.

[49] UNCITRAL, 41st Session, UN Doc A/CN.9/646, n 34, at 8, para 31.

[50] Article 33(1)(b) of the Model Law, in relevant part, provides that a party may request the arbitral tribunal to provide an interpretation "if so agreed by the parties... ."

[51] UNCITRAL, 41st Session, UN Doc A/CN.9/646, n 34, at 8, para 33.

[52] UNCITRAL, 41st Session, UN Doc A/CN.9/646, n 34, at 8–9, para 34 (other proposed language included: "unless the request is unfounded" and "[o]nly in exceptional circumstances may additional fees be charged by an arbitral tribunal for interpretation or correction or completion of its award under articles 35 to 37.").

[53] UNCITRAL, 41st Session, UN Doc A/CN.9/646, n 34, at 8–9, para 34.

However, whereas the 1976 rule was silent on the arbitral tribunal's ability to bill the parties for other arbitration costs, Article 40(3) expressly adds: "the arbitral tribunal may charge the costs referred to in paragraphs 2(b) to (f)." The provision thus eliminates any ambiguity under the original rule as to whether the ban on fees extended to other costs of arbitration.

(4) Note on the costs of the Iran–US Claims Tribunal

In adopting its rules of procedure, the Iran–US Claims Tribunal modified Article 38 of the 1976 UNCITRAL Rules in certain respects to account for the fact that most of the Tribunal's costs, ie, its operating cost, as well as the salaries of the arbitrators, the Secretary General, the legal assistants, and other administrative personnel, were to be satisfied in equal monetary contributions by the two governments.[54] In implementing this obligation, the Tribunal Rules allocate responsibility for establishing the Tribunal's costs to the Full Tribunal,[55] and, in accordance with that responsibility, the Full Tribunal has worked in cooperation with the governments to ensure that the financial needs of the Tribunal are met.[56]

Because the party governments fund the Tribunal, many of the provisions of Article 38 of the 1976 UNCITRAL Rules relating to the fees, travel expenses, or other expenses of the arbitrators, or fees for the appointing authority and the Secretary General of the Permanent Court of Arbitration, were deleted.[57] However, because many private litigants before the Tribunal have had to finance certain aspects of their particular cases, including the costs of legal representation and assistance and of putting on witnesses and experts, the Tribunal Rules retain the substance of Articles 38(c), (d), and (e) of the 1976 UNCITRAL Rules.[58]

(5) Comparison to the 1976 UNCITRAL Rules

Article 40 is similar to corresponding Article 38 of the 1976 UNCITRAL Rules in most respects, though some clarifying revisions have been made.

Article 40(1) requires the arbitral tribunal to fix the costs of arbitration "in the final award and, if it deems appropriate, in another decision," whereas the chapeau of Article 38

---

[54] Article VI(3) of the Claims Settlement Declaration provides that "[t]he expenses of the Tribunal shall be borne equally by the two governments." This is in line with the general practice of sharing costs equally in arbitrations between states. According to Redfern and Hunter, "There are considerable advantages in dealing with costs in this way. Not the least of them is that it saves the parties from having to deliver to the arbitral tribunal (and to the opposing party) accounts showing how much each of them has spent on the case. It is a practice that also tends to be followed in large *ad hoc* arbitrations, particularly where the costs of the case are relatively unimportant in relation to the sums involved or the issues of principle at stake." A Redfern and M Hunter, *Law and Practice of International Commercial Arbitration* (3rd edn 1999) 406. See J Castello, "UNCITRAL Rules," n 36, 1529–30 (noting that in arbitrations where both parties are state governments "normally each such party should bear its own costs").

[55] Article 38(2) of the 1983 Rules of Procedure of the Iran-US Claims Tribunal, reprinted in Appendix 5.

[56] Early in its history, the Full Tribunal established the Committee on Administrative and Financial Questions (CAFQ), whose membership includes one American arbitrator, one Iranian arbitrator, one non-party-appointed arbitrator, and the respective agents and deputy agents of the party governments. Since its inception, the CAFQ has held regular meetings and has made recommendations to the Full Tribunal regarding the Tribunal's budget, employee salaries and benefits, and a host of other administrative and operational matters.

[57] When presenting the claims of Americans or dual nationals in amounts less than US $250,000, Article III(3) of the Claims Settlement Declaration, however, the US Government retained 1 percent or 1.5 percent of the total amount awarded to the private litigant to cover its expenses. See Iran Claims Settlement Act, USC § 1701 (1985); *United States v Sperry Corp*, 387 US 52 (1989) (upholding the constitutionality of the legislation). Still, private litigants before the Tribunal enjoyed a considerable windfall in terms of litigation expenses as compared to typical parties to an international arbitration.

[58] See 1983 Rules of Procedure of the Iran–US Claims Tribunal, reprinted in Appendix 5.

of the 1976 UNCITRAL Rules indicates that the arbitral tribunal must do this "in its award." The 2010 Rules thus accommodate the fact that costs may be fixed in a separate award or in a termination order, although the 1976 Rules allow for similar practices.

The enumeration of items of expenditure constituting "costs" under the 2010 Rules differs in certain marginal respects from the 1976 Rules. Inclusion of the word "reasonable" in Article 40(2)(b), (c), and (d) expressly conveys what was already implied under Article 38 and other provisions of the 1976 Rules: that the arbitral tribunal should conduct the arbitral proceedings as efficiently as practicable so as not to cause the parties to incur unnecessary costs.[59]

Article 40(2)(e) deviates from Article 38(e) of the 1976 UNCITRAL Rules in its formulation, but has little, if any, substantive difference. Though the phrase "legal and other costs" replaces the phrase "legal representation and assistance," both may be read as similarly broad in scope. Moreover, the important qualifier—that the arbitral tribunal must determine that the amount of these costs is reasonable—is identical in both versions of the rule. More significantly, the word "successful" appearing before the word "party" in Article 38(e) of the 1976 UNCITRAL Rules has been deleted. However, that decision was made only to clarify that Article 38 of the 1976 UNCITRAL Rules, later renumbered as Article 40 of the 2010 UNCITRAL Rules, was not meant to address the criteria for apportioning costs, ie, whether only the expenditures of a "successful" party constitute costs capable of apportionment by the tribunal.[60] Such determinations were to be made pursuant to the separate provision on the allocation of costs, Article 42 of the 2010 UNCITRAL Rules.

Two additional clarifying changes to Article 40 are noteworthy. First, the provision qualifies the meaning of "legal and other costs" as only costs "in relation to the arbitration." This qualification is implied under the 1976 Rules, as demonstrated by the practice of arbitral tribunals described earlier.[61] The omission of the phrase "if such costs were claimed during the arbitral proceedings" from Article 40(2)(e) is also not significant. The condition is implied since the arbitral tribunal would not be able to determine whether to award a party "legal and other costs," unless the party identifies those costs to the tribunal.[62]

Article 40(3) represents a modification of a rule previously located in Article 40(4) of the 1976 UNCITRAL Rules. The previous rule provided: "No additional fees may be charged by an arbitral tribunal for interpretation or correction or completion of its award... ." As explained,[63] Article 40(3) retains the basic rule, but clarifies that "the arbitral tribunal may charge the costs referred to in paragraphs 2(b) to (f) ... ."

C. Extracts from the Practice of Investment and other Tribunals

Antoine Biloune, et al and *Ghana Investments Centre,* et al, Award on Damages and Costs (June 30, 1990) (*Ad Hoc* Proceeding, 1976 UNCITRAL Rules, Contract) reprinted in (1994) XIX Ybk Commercial Arb 11, 30–31:

---

[59] For a further discussion on "reasonableness" see N Blackaby and C Partasides, *Redfern and Hunter on International Arbitration,* n 19, 548.

[60] See UN Doc. A/CN.9/646, n 34, at 6, para 19.

[61] See section 2(B)(2)(d).

[62] Note that one tribunal did not award the claimant costs for legal representation when the claimant took the position that each party should bear its own legal costs. See *White Industries Australia Ltd* and *Republic of India,* Final Award (November 30, 2011) (*Ad Hoc* Proceeding, 1976 UNCITRAL Rules, Australia-India BIT), at 138–9.

[63] See section 2(B)(3).

Under the [1976] UNCITRAL Rules, Art. 38, the fees and costs of the arbitration are to be separately stated in the award. The total costs of this arbitration are $84,781.14. This figure has been calculated as follows: The arbitrators have been compensated at a rate based on the current rate applied by the International Centre for Settlement of Investment Disputes (ICSID). This rate was chosen as appropriate for a case with a modest amount at stake. It is the more appropriate in light of the designation of Mr. Ibrahim Shihata, Secretary-General of ICSID, as the appointing authority in this arbitration. On an actual hourly basis, the fee of each of the three arbitrators totals $15,610.00. The President of the Tribunal has not found it appropriate to accept fees higher than those of the other arbitrators.

In addition, other costs of the arbitration, including out-of-pocket expenses, secretarial and office expenses, hearing expenses, and the time of the registrar total $37,951.14.

The Tribunal has assessed and received $20,000 from each side as a deposit against the costs of arbitration. The difference between the deposit of $20,000 already made by the respondents and the costs and fees of the arbitration is $64,781.14. This amount is assessed against the respondents, to be paid directly to the Tribunal's registrar. Upon receipt of this payment, the Tribunal will transmit the deposit of $20,000 advanced by the claimants to their counsel.

Karaha Bodas Co LLC and *Perusahaan Pertambangan Minyak Dan Gas Bumi Negara*, Preliminary Award (September 30, 1999) (*Ad Hoc* Proceeding, 1976 UNCITRAL Rules, Concession Agreement), at 32–33:

The costs of arbitration for this phase of the procedure, including the arbitrators fees and expenses are fixed as follows:

Yves DERAINS:	US$ 35.500
Piero BERNARDINI:	US$ 26.300
Ahmed S EL KOSHERI:	US$ 26.300
Total:	US$ 88.100

The expenses of the Arbitral Tribunal amounts to US$11.900. Thus, the costs of the arbitration amounts to US$ 100.000. This amount is covered by the initial deposit made by the parties.

Thus, the portion of the costs of the arbitration to be borne by PERTAMINA and PLN amounts to US$ 66.666 and the portion to be borne by KBC amounts to US$ 33.333.

As far as the proceedings relating to the preliminary issues decided in this award are concerned, PERTAMINA, PLN and the GOI have jointly made a deposit of US$ 50.000 and KBC has made a deposit of the same amount.

Consequently, PERTAMINA and PLN are jointly and severally condemned to pay an amount of US$ 16.666 to KBC.

The amount of the costs of legal representation and assistance claimed by KBC is US$ 525.624,86. The amount of the costs of legal representation and assistance claimed by the Respondents is US$ 611.499,14. The Arbitral Tribunal considers that these amounts are reasonable.

Consequently, PERTAMINA and PLN are jointly and severally condemned to pay US$ 350.416.56 to KBC and KBC is condemned to pay US$ 203.833,04 to the GOI.

Karaha Bodas Co LLC and *Perusahaan Pertambangan Minyak Dan Gas Bumi Negara*, Final Award (December 18, 2000) (*Ad Hoc* Proceeding, 1976 UNCITRAL Rules, Concession Agreement), at 45–46:

141. The costs and expenses of the arbitration for this second and final phase of the arbitration are fixed as follows:

Arbitrators Fees

Yves DERAINS:	US$ 146.337,00
Piero BERNARDINI:	US$ 109.752,69
Ahmed S EL KOSHERI:	US$ 109.752,69

The expenses of the Arbitral Tribunal amounts to US$34.140,00. Thus, the costs and expenses of this second phase of the arbitration amount to US$399.982,38. This amount is covered by the deposit made by the parties, the Claimant having paid US$199.982,38 and the Respondent US$200.000. Since the Claimant has only to pay one third of the amount of US$399.982,38, the Respondents are condemned to refund it US$66.654,92 for the costs and expenses of the arbitration.

Pope & Talbot, Inc and *Government of Canada*, Award on Costs (November 26, 2002) (*Ad Hoc* Proceeding, 1976 UNCITRAL Rules, NAFTA Chapter Eleven), at 2:

2. In accordance with Article 38 of the [1976] UNCITRAL Arbitration Rules which apply to this arbitration the arbitral tribunal is required to fix the costs of arbitration. In the present case the relevant items constituting the costs include (a) the fees of the arbitral tribunal, (b) the travel and other expenses incurred by the arbitrators and (c) the costs of expert advice and of other assistance required by the arbitral tribunal. At the date of this award each party has advanced US $750,000, i.e. a total of $1,500,000. The fees of the members of the Tribunal were fixed at the outset of the arbitration as to daily and hourly rates, and the entire sum advanced subject to certain bank deductions but together with interest earned thereon has been expended thereon, taking into account the expenses incurred by each arbitrator and the costs of assistance from Mr. Michael Miller, advocate, except for the sum of US $39,571.30.

BG Group plc and *Republic of Argentina*, Final Award (December 24, 2007) (*Ad Hoc* Proceeding, 1976 UNCITRAL Rules, UK-Argentina BIT), at 136:

462. ... the expenses of the Arbitral Tribunal amount to US$261,907.82. This sum includes the fees and expenses of the Administrative Secretary, the costs of translating the award, and the administrative fee of $59,312.50 paid to ICSID as custodian of the funds deposited by the Parties pursuant to Article 41 of the [1976] UNCITRAL Rules (Section 16 of Procedural Order No 2). Moreover, the costs of the Preliminary Conference and of the evidentiary hearing are US$126,020.74. This yields a total for the costs of the arbitration, including Tribunal fees and expenses, and costs of the Preliminary Conference and evidentiary hearing, of US$1,236,500.00.

Chemtura Corp and *Government of Canada*, Award (August 2, 2010) (PCA administered, 1976 UNCITRAL Rules, NAFTA Chapter Eleven), at 79:

269. The members of the Tribunal have spent on this matter, as follows: The Honorable Charles Brower 30 days; Prof. James Crawford 25.5 days; and Prof. Gabrielle Kaufman-Kohler 66.5 days. The Secretary of the Tribunal has spent 356 hours. The rates for time spent by the Tribunal and Secretary on this case were set in section C of PO 1 (USD 4,000 per day or 8 hours of work for the Arbitrators and USD 280 per hour for the Secretary). Accordingly, the total fees accrued for the Tribunal and the Secretary amount to USD 587,680.
270. The PCA's fees amount to USD 2,286 and the Tribunal's expenses to USD 98,253 (including in particular costs for the various hearings and deliberations).
271. Adding up expenses, PCA and Arbitrators' fees, the total costs of the arbitration amount to USD 688,219, with an unused remainder of the advance of USD 131,781.

ICS Inspection and Control Services Ltd and *Argentine Republic*, Award on Jurisdiction (February 10, 2012) (PCA administered, 1976 UNCITRAL Rules, UK-Argentina BIT), at 111–112:

331. The fees of the Hon. Marc Lalonde, the arbitrator appointed by the Claimant, amount to EUR 74,000.00. The fees of Dr. Santiago Torres Bernárdez, the arbitrator appointed by the Respondent, amount to EUR 72,500.00. The fees and expenses of Professor Pierre-Marie Dupuy, the Presiding Arbitrator, amount to EUR 88,000.00.

332. Pursuant to Procedural Order No 1, the International Bureau of the PCA was designated to act as Registry in this arbitration. The PCA's fees for registry services amount to EUR 64,135.00.
333. All other tribunal expenses, including travel, transcription, translation, interpretation, courier deliveries, conference calling, catering, bank charges, and all other costs relating to the arbitration proceedings, amount to EUR 62,852.22.
334. Based on the above figures, the combined tribunal costs, comprising the items covered in Articles 38(a) to (c) of the [1976] UNCITRAL Arbitration Rules, total EUR 361,487.22.

3. Arbitrators' Fees—Article 41

A. Text of the 2010 UNCITRAL Rule[64]

Article 41 of the 2010 UNCITRAL Rules provides:

1. The fees and expenses of the arbitrators shall be reasonable in amount, taking into account the amount in dispute, the complexity of the subject matter, the time spent by the arbitrators and any other relevant circumstances of the case.
2. If there is an appointing authority and it applies or has stated that it will apply a schedule or particular method for determining the fees for arbitrators in international cases, the arbitral tribunal in fixing its fees shall take that schedule or method into account to the extent that it considers appropriate in the circumstances of the case.
3. Promptly after its constitution, the arbitral tribunal shall inform the parties as to how it proposes to determine its fees and expenses, including any rates it intends to apply. Within 15 days of receiving that proposal, any party may refer the proposal to the appointing authority for review. If, within 45 days of receipt of such a referral, the appointing authority finds that the proposal of the arbitral tribunal is inconsistent with paragraph 1, it shall make any necessary adjustments thereto, which shall be binding upon the arbitral tribunal.
4. (a) When informing the parties of the arbitrators' fees and expenses that have been fixed pursuant to article 40, paragraphs 2 (a) and (b), the arbitral tribunal shall also explain the manner in which the corresponding amounts have been calculated;
   (b) Within 15 days of receiving the arbitral tribunal's determination of fees and expenses, any party may refer for review such determination to the appointing

---

[64] Corresponding Article 39 of the 1976 UNCITRAL Rules provides:
1. The fees of the arbitral tribunal shall be reasonable in amount, taking into account the amount in dispute, the complexity of the subject-matter, the time spent by the arbitrators and any other relevant circumstances of the case.
2. If an appointing authority has been agreed upon by the parties or designated by the Secretary-General of the Permanent Court of Arbitration at The Hague, and if that authority has issued a schedule of fees for arbitrators in international cases which it administers, the arbitral tribunal in fixing its fees shall take that schedule of fees into account to the extent that it considers appropriate in the circumstances of the case.
3. If such appointing authority has not issued a schedule of fees for arbitrators in international cases, any party may at any time request the appointing authority to furnish a statement setting forth the basis for establishing fees which is customarily followed in international cases in which the authority appoints arbitrators. If the appointing authority consents to provide such a statement, the arbitral tribunal in fixing its fees shall take such information into account to the extent that it considers appropriate in the circumstances of that case.
4. In cases referred to in paragraphs 2 and 3, when a party so requests and the appointing authority consents to perform the function, the arbitral tribunal shall fix its fees only after consultation with the appointing authority which may make any comment it deems appropriate to the arbitral tribunal concerning the fees.

authority. If no appointing authority has been agreed upon or designated, or if the appointing authority fails to act within the time specified in these Rules, then the review shall be made by the Secretary-General of the PCA;

(c) If the appointing authority or the Secretary-General of the PCA finds that the arbitral tribunal's determination is inconsistent with the arbitral tribunal's proposal (and any adjustment thereto) under paragraph 3 or is otherwise manifestly excessive, it shall, within 45 days of receiving such a referral, make any adjustments to the arbitral tribunal's determination that are necessary to satisfy the criteria in paragraph 1. Any such adjustments shall be binding upon the arbitral tribunal;

(d) Any such adjustments shall either be included by the arbitral tribunal in its award or, if the award has already been issued, be implemented in a correction to the award, to which the procedure of article 38, paragraph 3 shall apply.

5. Throughout the procedure under paragraphs 3 and 4, the arbitral tribunal shall proceed with the arbitration, in accordance with article 17, paragraph 1.

6. A referral under paragraph 4 shall not affect any determination in the award other than the arbitral tribunal's fees and expenses; nor shall it delay the recognition and enforcement of all parts of the award other than those relating to the determination of the arbitral tribunal's fees and expenses.

B. Commentary

(1) Regulation of the arbitrators' fees and expenses under the Rules—general background, Article 41(1) and (2)

Early drafts of the 1976 UNCITRAL Rules did not include a separate article that specifically addressed arbitrators' fees. Originally, the only reference to such fees appeared in Article 38(a) of those Rules, which provided that the arbitrators may fix their own fees, but must state them separately in the award.[65] According to the *travaux préparatoires*, most representatives agreed that to avoid abuse by the arbitrators there should be some additional limitation on the arbitrators' power to fix their own fees.[66] In the first UNCITRAL meetings, two proposals to regulate fee-setting were made. The Egyptian representative spearheaded a proposal for establishing a schedule of arbitrators' fees, possibly based on a percentage of the amount claimed or the length of the proceedings.[67] The US representative proposed that where the parties had designated an appointing authority, it would be appropriate to include a rule that the appointing authority would consult with the arbitrators on the subject of fees.[68] Both proposals were seriously considered by the Committee, although only the latter was ultimately incorporated in the 1976 UNCITRAL Rules.

To determine the feasibility of developing a schedule of fees for the Rules, the Commission established a working group. The working group noted that arbitration rules that establish a schedule of fees usually also provide for an administrative body with discretion

---

[65] See section 2(B)(1).
[66] UN Doc A/10017, n 35, para 214, reprinted in (1975) VI UNCITRAL Ybk 24, 44. See also UN GAOR, 31st Session, Supp No 17, UN Doc A/31/17, n 14, para 207, reprinted in (1976) VII UNCITRAL Ybk 66, 80.
[67] UN Doc A/CN.9/SR.168, n 35, at 209. He was supported by Mr Gokhale, India, Mr Jenard, Belgium, Mr Eyzaguirre, Chile, Mr Mantilla-Molina, Mexico, and the Chairman. See 210–11.
[68] UN Doc A/CN.9/SR.168, n 35, at 209–10 (Comments by Mr Holtzmann, United States, Mr Khoo, Singapore, Mr Gueiros, Brazil).

to fix the fees in accordance with the schedule.[69] The working group also observed that since the aim of the Rules was to facilitate worldwide arbitration of all kinds of cases, a fee schedule would have to establish a wide margin between minimum and maximum rates.[70] This wide margin would hamper the parties' ability to predict the costs of arbitration and would fail to safeguard against abusive charges by the arbitrators.[71] The working group thus concluded that the effectiveness of a schedule of fees depended on the involvement of an independent body, such as the appointing authority, which could be given discretion to set the arbitrators' fees or at least consult with the arbitrators before fees are fixed.[72]

According to the Commentary to the Revised Draft of the 1976 UNCITRAL Rules, ultimately "it was not believed possible to develop a uniform schedule of fees for arbitrators."[73] Instead, the negotiators concluded that arbitrators who were selected "based on faith in their expertise and in their readiness to adjudicate the dispute with impartiality and fairness, [should] be expected to act reasonably in setting their own fees."[74] This expectation is still reflected in Article 41(1) of the 2010 UNCITRAL Rules, which, like the 1976 Rules, requires that the arbitral tribunal's fees and expenses be "reasonable in amount."[75] The Rules do not establish or incorporate a schedule of fees, although the parties are, of course, free to do so, either on their own or by consulting with an arbitral institution.[76] In lieu of a fee schedule, Article 41(1) requires the consideration of four criteria in determining the appropriate amount of remuneration: the amount in dispute, the complexity of the

---

[69] *Note by the Secretariat on a Schedule of Fees of Arbitrators*, UNCITRAL, 9th Session, UN Doc A/CN.9/114 (1976), reprinted in (1976) VII UNCITRAL Ybk 190, 191.
[70] UNCITRAL, 9th Session, UN Doc A/CN.9/114, n 69.
[71] UNCITRAL, 9th Session, UN Doc A/CN.9/114, n 69.
[72] UNCITRAL, 9th Session, UN Doc A/CN.9/114, n 69.
[73] UNCITRAL, 9th Session, Addendum 1 (Commentary), UN Doc A/CN.9/112/Add.1, n 13, reprinted in (1976) VII UNCITRAL Ybk 166, 181 (Commentary on Draft Article 33(1)). Mr Holtzmann of the United States was reported as stating:

[I]t would be impractical and inappropriate to include a schedule of fees in the Rules because of the difficulty of applying such a schedule uniformly on a world-wide basis and because the establishment of such a schedule was an economic task outside the competence of the Committee. Once such a schedule had been devised, it would be necessary to update it continually, since arbitrators would not accept appointments under a schedule which was out of date. Furthermore, whereas most sets of rules made provision for the administering authority to decide at which point in the schedule fees were to be fixed, under the UNCITRAL Rules there might be no appointing authority. Moreover, a schedule of fees would be inappropriate in rules designed for ad hoc arbitration.

UNCITRAL, 9th Session, UN Doc A/CN.9/9/C.2/SR.12, n 12, at 7, para 50.

[74] UNCITRAL, 9th Session, UN Doc A/CN.9/9/C.2/SR.12, n 12, at 7, para 50. This was not the last word from the Committee negotiators, however. See n 78.
[75] Born notes that in letting the arbitrators choose their own fee schedule, the UNCITRAL Rules adopted "a relatively unusual approach to establishing the arbitrators' fees" as compared to other arbitral rules. G Born *International Commercial Arbitration*, n 3, 1647.
[76] See *Guaracachi America Inc* (2010 Rules); and *Glamis Gold Ltd* (1976 Rules); both reprinted in section 3(C) (incorporating ICSID Schedule of Fees). Note that the Permanent Court of Arbitration provides limited assistance with regard to arbitrators' fees:

Upon Request, the International Bureau [of the Permanent Court of Arbitration] will make all arrangements concerning the amounts of the arbitrator's fees, and advance deposits to be made on account of such fees in consultation with the parties and the arbitrators. The International Bureau does not fix the amount of fees of arbitrators and has no fee schedule for arbitrators. Upon request, the International Bureau will hold deposits from the parties and account for the same.

Permanent Court of Arbitration: Services under the UNCITRAL Arbitration Rules: Guide for Practitioners (2000) 13.

subject matter, the time spent by the arbitrators, and any other relevant circumstances of the case.[77]

Uncertain as to the feasibility of establishing a schedule of fees for the arbitrators,[78] the drafters focused on involving the appointing authority in the process of fixing the arbitrators' fees. Article 41(2), like corresponding Article 39(2) of the 1976 UNCITRAL Rules, instructs the arbitrators to take into account any schedules of fees that the appointing authority, presumably an institution, applies or has stated that it will apply in international cases.[79] The appointing authority's schedule of fees may provide a useful point of reference, especially if the appointing arbitrator is a less familiar or regional institution. However, the arbitral tribunal must take this schedule into account only "to the extent that it considers appropriate in the circumstances of the case."

Article 39(3) and (4) of the 1976 UNCITRAL Rules also allowed the parties to request from the appointing authority, in the event it had not issued a schedule of fees, a statement setting forth the basis for establishing fees which is customarily followed in international cases. It also required the arbitral tribunal, upon the request of a party, to consult with the appointing authority before fixing its fees. These provisions were again premised on the expectation that the arbitrators would set their fees reasonably, but they did not require the arbitrators to abide by the appointing authority's advice.

The 2010 UNCITRAL Rules replace these voluntary procedures with a more robust and effective mechanism for addressing the rare cases in which an arbitrator's conscience alone is not enough to deter unreasonable fee setting.[80] Article 41(3) through (6), described in the following section, empower the appointing authority or in some cases the PCA Secretary-General to review and adjust, if necessary, the arbitral tribunal's proposal for establishing its fees and expenses as well as its actual calculation of fees and expenses.

(2) Determining the fees and expenses of the arbitral tribunal and potential review by a neutral arbiter—Article 41(3)–(6)

The problem of excessive fees and expenses can manifest itself in various ways in international arbitration. For example, an arbitrator who has negotiated a particular fee rate with the party that appointed him or her may decide to increase that rate upon learning later that his or her co-arbitrators are charging higher rates. Or an arbitrator, who has agreed to fix his or her fees at a certain rate, may nevertheless bill the parties for an unreasonably high number of work hours. Because the parties may be ordered to bear the costs of the arbitral

---

[77] See, eg, *Canfor Corp* (1976 Rules), reprinted in section 3(C).
[78] The debate on the subject continued. See UNCITRAL, 9th Session, UN Doc A/CN.9/9/C.2/SR.12, n 12, at 6–8. Another proposal was introduced to incorporate the rules of existing arbitral institutions into the UNCITRAL Rules at the parties' choosing. 6, para 42 (Comment by Mr Guevara, Philippines).
[79] See, eg, *Zeevi Holdings* (1976 Rules), reprinted in section 3(C) (referring to ICC cost rules). The fee schedules of the major arbitral institutions, such as ICSID, LCIA and WIPO, even if not serving as appointing authority, may be useful.
[80] UNCITRAL, 41st Session, UN Doc A/CN.9/646, n 34, at 6, para 20 ("It was observed that article 39 had been the source of difficulties in practice when exaggerated fees were charged by arbitral tribunals, leaving parties without practical solutions other than perhaps resorting to a State court."). See also See J Paulsson and G Petrochilos, *Revision of the UNCITRAL Arbitration Rules*, Report to UNCITRAL Secretariat (2006) at 8, para 12(k) (noting "there has been disturbing instances of 'negotiations' regarding fees between arbitrators and parties, especially where one party finds it tactically appealing to accept anything the arbitrators say"). Castello notes, "[r]forming the mechanism for setting arbitrators' fees was one of the 'main lines of revision' in the Rules recommended in the report commissioned by UNCITRAL's Secretariat when the Working Group began its current revision project" J Castello, "UNCITRAL Rules," n 36, 1527.

tribunal equally or pay some portion of the other party's costs, abuse by even one arbitrator in determining his or her fees and expenses can adversely affect all the parties. Without an effective mechanism for regulating the fees and expenses of the arbitral tribunal in the procedural rules of arbitration, the parties may be left without a remedy, save for suing the arbitrators in local courts, if possible.

When revising the UNCITRAL Rules, the Working Group agreed more regulation was necessary with respect to how the arbitral tribunal sets its fees and expenses. The benefits of stricter regulation were clear to many Working Group members. It could enhance the legitimacy and integrity of the arbitral process and avoid resort to local courts, which under some legal systems might lead to review of the merits of the award.[81] In fact, many delegations believed that without stricter regulation the Rules might become less attractive to users, particularly since they are often used in *ad hoc* arbitration where a pre-existing fee structure is lacking.[82]

In developing new rules on setting the arbitral tribunal's fees and expenses, three basic principles guided the work of the Working Group. First, the process of determining fees and expenses should be made more transparent.[83] Second, a neutral arbiter, such as the appointing authority or the Secretary-General of the Permanent Court of Arbitration (PCA), should have the power to resolve definitively disputes concerning fees and expenses.[84] Third, the process of dispute settlement should delay the arbitral proceedings as little as possible.[85]

Consistent with these principles, Article 41 regulates the determination of the arbitral tribunal's fees and expenses at two critical junctures in the arbitration: (1) at the outset when the tribunal proposes the manner in which it will determine its fees and expenses, eg, pursuant to an hourly rate (the manner of determination); and (2) at the conclusion of the arbitration after the tribunal has determined the total amount of its fees and expenses (the calculation).[86] The procedures associated with each juncture are discussed in the following sections.

(a) The manner in which fees and expenses will be determined—Article 41(3) and (5)

Paragraphs (3) and (5) of Article 41 afford the parties an opportunity to influence the determination of the arbitrators' fees and expenses at an early stage of the proceedings.

---

[81] UNCITRAL, 41st Session, UN Doc A/CN.9/646, n 34, at 6, para 20.
[82] UNCITRAL, 40th Session, UN Doc A/CN.9/614, n 16, at 26, para 133.
[83] See, eg, *Settlement of Commercial Disputes: Revision of the UNCITRAL Arbitration Rules, Note by the Secretariat*, UNCITRAL, UN Doc A/CN.9/WG.II/WP.157/Add.2 at 9, para 24 (2009) (explaining that the obligation to explain the calculation of the fees "in the interest of transparency").
[84] UNCITRAL, 41st Session, UN Doc A/CN.9/646, n 34, at 6, para 21. The Working Group generally favored providing for a "general supervisory power...over the methodology and the final computation of the fees." Para 26. While some delegates worried that giving appointing authorities such a role might "extend beyond their experience," it was noted that a number of appointing authorities were well versed in arbitration, including the setting of costs. UNCITRAL, 40th Session, UN Doc A/CN.9/614, n 16, at 26, para 134. Another proposal, which did not receive support, was including a provision in the Rules that would encourage the parties "to agree on the method of calculating the arbitral tribunal's fees from the outset, at a consultation or preparatory meeting." UNCITRAL, UN Doc A/CN.9/WG.II/WP.143/Add.1, n 12, at 12, para 37.
[85] See, eg, UNCITRAL, 41st Session, UN Doc A/CN.9/646, n 34, at 7, paras 24–26 (emphasizing early resolution of open issues regarding methodology of fees).
[86] *Report of Working Group II (Arbitration and Conciliation) on the Work of its Fifty-Second Session* (New York, February 1–5, 2010), UNCITRAL, 43rd Session, UN Doc A/CN.9/688, at 8–9. 25, paras 31–33, 120 (2010) ("The Working Group reaffirmed its decision...that the review mechanism by the appointing authority should apply to both the fees and expenses of the arbitrator....").

Article 41(3) requires the arbitral tribunal, once constituted, "to inform the parties as to how it *proposes* to determine its fees and expenses, including any rates it intends to apply."[87] Any arrangement with a party concerning an arbitrator's fees and expenses made prior to the tribunal's required disclosure thus can be no more than a proposal. As such, any prior arrangement may be subsequently adjusted, if necessary, either voluntarily through the tribunal's agreement with all the parties or involuntarily by the appointing authority through the process of review and adjustment established in Article 41(3).

The arbitral tribunal may propose any manner in which to determine its fees and expenses, including not only "any rates [the arbitral tribunal] intends to apply," but also other methodologies. These may include *ad valorem*, time-based, or fixed-fee methods, as well as cancellation or commitment fees, so long as they result in reasonable fees and expenses.[88] Further, nothing in Article 41(3) prevents individual arbitrators sitting on the same tribunal from being compensated or reimbursed according to different methodologies, though such situations are uncommon. In practice, all arbitrators are usually compensated under the same methodology, though it may also be the case that the presiding arbitrator receives a slightly higher remuneration to compensate for his or her increased responsibilities, from producing the first draft of awards, decisions, and orders to handling the administrative affairs of the arbitral tribunal.[89] Where remuneration is based on an hourly rate, however, the presiding arbitrator's higher remuneration typically flows from the greater number of hours worked, not a higher rate per hour.

(1) Transparency

The arbitral tribunal's obligation to inform the parties as to the proposed manner in which it will determine its fees and expenses also serves the goal of transparency.[90] Notably, the obligation falls to the "arbitral tribunal" as a whole, not individually to each arbitrator, and must be discharged in relation to "the parties," meaning all the parties. The provision therefore demands full disclosure to all relevant actors of the manner in which the tribunal proposes to determine its fees and expenses. Private arrangements among a subgroup of actors are thus unacceptable. Full disclosure has the benefit of clearly establishing the expectations of both the arbitrators and the parties up front, thus avoiding surprises at the end of the process with respect to how the arbitral tribunal has fixed costs. There is no requirement that the arbitral tribunal make its proposal in writing, though a written record of some kind, even if only the agreed minutes of a preliminary conference, is advisable. In *Guaracachi*, for example, an arbitral tribunal applying the 2010 Rules memorialized its

---

[87] (Emphasis added.)

[88] UNCITRAL, 41st Session, UN Doc A/CN.9/646, n 34, at 7, para 25. For a general discussion of fee arrangements, see N Blackaby and C Partasides, *Redfern and Hunter on International Arbitration*, n 19, 304 et seq. For examples of postponement and cancellation fee arrangements, see *Guaracachi America Inc* (2010 Rules); and *Chemtura Corp* (1976 Rules), both reprinted in section 3(C).

[89] See P Sanders, *The Work of UNCITRAL on Arbitration and Conciliation*, n 7, 20 (explaining that a 40–30–30 split, in favor of the chairman, is typical practice); G Born, *International Commercial Arbitration*, n 3, 1649.

[90] "The Working Group agreed on the principle of providing a more transparent procedure for the determination of the arbitral tribunal's fees and expenses from the outset." *Settlement of Commercial Disputes: Revision of the UNCITRAL Arbitration Rules, Note by the Secretariat*, UNCITRAL, UN Doc A/CN.9/703/Add.1 at 13, para 25 (2010).

agreement with the parties on fees in a procedural order providing for remuneration in accordance with the ICSID schedule of fees.[91]

(2) Neutral Mechanism

Article 41(3) creates a neutral mechanism for resolving disputes concerning whether the arbitral tribunal's fees and expenses are "reasonable in amount." Pursuant to that provision, where a party believes the arbitral tribunal's proposal on fees and expenses is unreasonable, it may seek review by the appointing authority within the 15-day specified time period. If an appointing authority has not already been designated, the time period begins to run only after the parties have agreed on an appointing authority or, if no agreement can be reached, after the Secretary-General of the PCA makes the designation, pursuant to Article 6.[92]

When reviewing an arbitral tribunal's proposal, the appointing authority must determine whether the proposal is "inconsistent" with the requirement in Article 41(1) that the fees and expenses of the arbitrators be "reasonable in amount, taking into account the amount in dispute, the complexity of the subject matter, the time spent by the arbitrators and any other relevant circumstances of the case." Earlier drafts of Article 41(3) proposed that the standard of review be "manifestly inconsistent," as opposed to merely "inconsistent."[93] However, the Working Group concluded that inclusion of the word "manifestly" would create an unacceptably high standard of review.[94] Consequently, Article 41(3) may be reasonably construed as affording the appointing authority significant discretion to make any necessary adjustments to the arbitral tribunal's proposal on fees and expenses.

The appointing authority may apply an Article 41(3) remedy directly. Where the appointing authority determines that the arbitral tribunal's proposal on fees and expenses is inconsistent with Article 41(1), it may make "any necessary adjustments thereto," which are "binding upon the arbitral tribunal." Pursuant to Article 41(4), the tribunal must incorporate the appointing authority's determination into its award on costs.

Article 41(3), unlike Article 41(4) discussed in section 3(B)(2)(b), does not address the situation in which an appointing authority fails to act on a request for review. Pursuant to

---

[91] *Guaracachi America Inc* (2010 Rules), reprinted in section 3(C). Though corresponding Article 39 of the 1976 UNCITRAL Rules contains no provision on transparency, some tribunals constituted under those Rules have approached fee setting in a transparent manner, setting forth the hourly rate of the arbitrators in the first procedural order. See *Canadian Cattlemen* (1976 Rules); *Canfor Corp* (1976 Rules); and *ICS Inspection and Controls Services, Inc* (1976 Rules); all reprinted in section 3(C).

[92] An earlier version of Article 41(3) was more express on this point:

"Within 15 days of receiving that proposal, any party, which considers that the proposal does not satisfy the criteria in paragraph 1 may either refer the proposal to the appointing authority for review or, if no appointing authority has been agreed upon or designated, *initiate the procedure for agreeing on, or designating an appointing authority and then, within 15 days of such agreement or designation,* refer the proposal of the arbitral tribunal for review."

UNCITRAL, UN Doc A/CN.9/WG.II/WP.157/Add.2, n 83, at 7–8, para 19 (Draft Article 41(3) (emphasis added). The emphasized text appears to have been dropped for simplicity's sake—having an appointing authority in place is a prerequisite for the review process to function.

[93] UNCITRAL, 43rd Session, UN Doc A/CN.9/688, n 86, at 23–24, para 115. Furthermore, earlier drafts included a provision stating that the "methodology" used to compute fees and a computation of the fees incurred using that "methodology" must be communicated to the parties. However, there were objections to the term "methodology" in the article because the term "methodology" is not clear—it could give rise to challenges and the computation of fees may be changed by the appointing authority's decision. UNCITRAL, 43rd Session, UN Doc A/CN.9/684, n 11, at 27, para 124. This phrase was ultimately replaced by "how it has computed its fees." 27, para 124.

[94] UNCITRAL, 43rd Session, UN Doc A/CN.9/688, n 86, at 25, para 120.

Article 41(4), in such a situation, the PCA Secretary-General may conduct the review. However, this is not the case under Article 41(3). Thus, the only remedy available for addressing an appointing authority's failure to act on a request for review within the 45-day time period established under the Rules is for the parties to follow the procedures for appointing a substitute appointing authority.[95] According to the *travaux préparatoires*:

> In case the appointing authority does not reply to the parties within a period of 45 days, the parties may consider that it constitutes a failure to act and, under draft article 6, either agree on the appointment of a substitute appointing authority or request the Secretary-General of the PCA to make that designation.[96]

The differences in approach between Article 41(3) and Article 41(4) are logical.[97] At an early stage of the proceedings when Article 41(3) would apply, an appointing authority's failure to act can be resolved under the ordinary designation procedures of the Rules, without causing significant delay in the course of the overall proceedings. There is thus little justification at this preliminary stage for depriving the parties of their longstanding right under the Rules to choose an appointing authority jointly or have one designated for them by the PCA Secretary-General. As explained below, the circumstances are quite different at the end of the proceedings when Article 41(4) would apply.

(3) Efficiency

The time periods established in Article 41(3) contemplate the expeditious resolution of disputes regarding how the arbitral tribunal proposes to determine its fees and expenses. First, the arbitral tribunal shall make its proposal "promptly after its constitution." Second, the parties must refer the matter to the appointing authority "[w]ithin 15 days of receiving the proposal." Third, the appointing authority must make its determination "within 45 days of receipt of such a referral."[98] According to the *travaux préparatoires*, "[e]arly resolution of open issues [relating to the arbitral tribunal's fees and expenses] was desirable for the parties who typically were eager to obtain a predictable and fair basis for the determination of the fees, as well as for the persons who undertook to act as arbitrators."[99]

Article 41(5) reinforces the goal of efficiency by requiring the arbitral tribunal to proceed in accordance with Article 17(1), including the obligation to conduct the proceedings so as to avoid unnecessary delay and expense "[t]hroughout the procedure." While Article 17(1) is of general application and would in any event guide the process established in Article 41(3), Article 41(5) serves to emphasize the intent of the drafters to ensure that "issue[s] of fees do not delay the arbitral proceedings."[100]

---

[95] Some last-minute proposals to address an appointing authority's failure to act were considered, but ultimately not adopted by the Working Group. These included, among others, allowing the PCA Secretary-General to grant the appointing authority "a reasonable extension of time" to make its determination and omitting the 45-day time limit in which the appointing authority is required to make its determination. UNCITRAL, UN Doc A/CN.9/703/Add.1, n 90, at 13, para 25.

[96] UNCITRAL, UN Doc A/CN.9/703/Add.1, n 90, at 13, para 25. This approach resolved the question of whether an appointing authority's silence should be viewed as approval of the arbitral tribunal's proposal or determination on fees and expenses or a failure to act. For the Working Group's discussion, see UNCITRAL, 43rd Session, UN Doc A/CN.9/688, n 86, at 24, para 116.

[97] UNCITRAL, 43rd Session, UN Doc A/CN.9/688, n 86, at 24, paras 117–18 (rejection of proposal to apply SG process to 41(3)).

[98] Note that in Working Group discussions to revise the Rules, some delegates expressed the minority view that a 45-day time period was too long. UNCITRAL, 43rd Session, UN Doc A/CN.9/688, n 86, at 24, para 116.

[99] UNCITRAL, 41st Session, UN Doc A/CN.9/646, n 34, at 7, para 24.

[100] UNCITRAL, UN Doc A/CN.9/WG.II/WP.157/Add.2, n 83, at 8–9, para 23.

(b) The computation of the arbitral tribunal's fees and expenses—Article 41(4)–(6)

Even if the arbitral tribunal's methodology for calculating its fees and expenses is acceptable to the parties, its actual calculation may be unreasonable, eg, because one or more arbitrators has billed an unreasonably high number of work hours in relation to the amount or complexity of the work at hand. Consistent with the guiding principles of transparency, neutrality, and efficiency, Article 41(4) through (6) establishes a mechanism for regulating the amount of fees and expenses that an arbitral tribunal may charge at the conclusion of the arbitration.

(1) Transparency

In the interest of transparency, Article 41(4)(a) requires that when informing the parties of the fees it has fixed pursuant to Article 40(2)(a)–(b), the arbitral tribunal must "explain the manner in which the corresponding amounts have been calculated." The obligation to explain requires the tribunal to show more than a mere statement of the sum total of its fees and expenses, but rather *how* it arrived at that figure. Thus, the tribunal must provide adequate detail about its computation of fees and expenses so that the parties may understand what they are being asked to pay with reasonable certainty. In this sense, where the arbitral tribunal bills the parties at an hourly rate, it may be advisable to provide to the parties not only the number of total hours worked by each member of the arbitral tribunal, but also information concerning how many hours each arbitrator worked on the principal aspects of the arbitration, eg, review of written submissions, hearings, deliberations and drafting of the award.

(2) Neutral mechanism

Article 41(4) establishes a neutral procedure for review of the arbitral tribunal's determination of its fees and expenses. A party may refer such determination to the appointing authority, if one has been designated. If no appointing authority has been designated or the appointing authority fails to act within the 45-day time period specified under the Rules, a party may refer such determination to the PCA Secretary-General. Direct referral to the PCA Secretary-General is unique to Article 41(4).[101] If the parties were required to follow the ordinary procedure for designating an appointing authority under the Rules, the arbitral process would easily extend several more weeks. Thus, with respect to challenges to the tribunal's calculation of its fees and expenses, the Rules emphasize efficiency, though in doing so they sacrifice the parties' traditional right to designate an appointing authority or have the PCA Secretary-General designate one for them.

Article 41(4)(c) contains two distinct standards of review. Under the first standard, the appointing authority decides whether the arbitral tribunal's calculation of its fees and expenses is "inconsistent" with its original proposal or that original proposal as adjusted by the appointing authority pursuant to Article 41(3). This standard of review screens for any deviations from the agreed compensation methodology. It therefore differs from the broader review established under Article 41(3) that ensures consistency between the arbitral tribunal's proposal and the general reasonableness requirement established in Article 41(1). The first standard of review under Article 41(4)(c) is deliberately narrower so as to "avoid[] unnecessary duplication of reviews previously conducted" pursuant to Article 41(3).[102]

---

[101] Article 41(3), in contrast, requires the parties to follow the ordinary procedure for appointing a substitute appointing authority.

[102] UNCITRAL, 43rd Session, UN Doc A/CN.9/688, n 86, at 25, para 121.

The second standard requires a review of whether the arbitral tribunal's determination of its fees and expenses is "otherwise manifestly excessive." This standard does not screen for deviations in the arbitral tribunal's methodology, as proposed and applied. Rather, it is meant to cover more generic situations of abuse, such as where an arbitrator's fees are "based on a questionably high number of hours."[103] Inclusion of the word "manifestly" in the standard indicates that only significant instances of excess should be considered problematic.[104] In determining whether the arbitral tribunal's determination of its fees and expenses is "manifestly excessive," the factors enumerated in Article 41(1), including the amount in dispute, the complexity of the subject matter, and the time spent by the arbitrators, are natural reference points. For example, an excessively high number of hours billed for consideration of a factually and legally simple case could be manifestly excessive.

In the case of an inconsistent or manifestly excessive determination of fees and expenses, the remedy established by the Rules is binding revision. Pursuant to Article 41(4)(c), the appointing authority or PCA Secretary-General has authority to make "adjustments" to the arbitral tribunal's determination that are "binding upon the arbitral tribunal." Thus, for example, a "manifestly excessive" number of work hours may be decreased to a reasonable amount. Similarly, an "inconsistent" application of a fee rate may be rectified by recalculating fees according to the terms of the arbitral tribunal's original proposal, subject to any imposed adjustments thereto.

Article 41(4)(d) requires the arbitral tribunal to incorporate any imposed adjustments to the arbitral tribunal's determination of fees and expenses into its decision-making. If the award has not yet been rendered, adjustments must be "included by the arbitral tribunal in its award." If the award has already been issued, the arbitral tribunal must render a correction to the award, pursuant to Article 38, that incorporates any adjustment.[105] These options resolved concerns among Working Group delegations about how an award should reflect a binding adjustment of the appointing authority or PCA Secretary-General.[106]

(3) Efficiency

The time periods established by Article 41(4) encourage resolution of any concerns about the calculation of the arbitral tribunal's fees and expenses, without significantly delaying conclusion of the arbitral proceedings.[107] The parties must refer the matter to the appointing authority or the PCA Secretary-General "[w]ithin 15 days of receiving the arbitral tribunal's determination of fees and expenses" and the review must be completed "within 45 days of receiving such a referral."

Article 41(5) and (6) complement the goal of efficiency. Article 41(5) requires the arbitral tribunal to adhere to principles established in Article 17(1) "[t]hroughout the procedure"

---

[103] UNCITRAL, 43rd Session, UN Doc A/CN.9/688, n 86, at 25, para 121.

[104] Compare with the Working Group's decision to drop the word "manifestly" from the proposed phrase "manifestly inconsistent" because that term created a standard of review that was too high. See section 3(B)(2)(a).

[105] In the event a valid adjustment is ordered more than 30 days after the award has been rendered, and thus outside the limitations period for correcting an award, Article 41(4)(d) should be construed as an agreement between the parties to extend the time period in order for the tribunal to satisfy its obligation to adjust its cost determination.

[106] Earlier versions of the article provided that the decision to adjust the award "shall be deemed to be part of the award." UNCITRAL, UN Doc A/CN.9/WG.II/WP.151/Add.1, n 34, at 17–18, para 38 (Draft Article 39(4)). However, some Working Group delegates feared that this formulation would delay potential recognition and enforcement of the award. See UNCITRAL, 43rd Session, UN Doc A/CN.9/684, n 11, at 27, para 126.

[107] UNCITRAL, UN Doc A/CN.9/WG.II/WP.157/Add.2, n 83, at 9, para 24.

established under Article 41(4). While Article 17(1) applies generally to the management of the proceedings, Article 41(5) serves to underscore the desire to ensure that "the issue of fees do[es] not delay the arbitral proceedings."[108] Article 41(6) confirms the independence of the review process established in Article 41(4) from all other aspects of the arbitration. The review process may not address "any determination in the award" other than with respect to the arbitral tribunal's fees and expenses. Nor can it prevent the recognition and enforcement of "all parts of the award" other than those relating to a decision on fees and expenses.[109]

(3) Comparison to the 1976 UNCITRAL Rules

Article 41 is similar to corresponding Article 39 of the 1976 UNCITRAL Rules in certain important respects but differs substantially in others, namely the procedures for addressing disputes over the arbitral tribunal's fees and expenses.

Article 41(1) and Article 39(1) of the 1976 UNCITRAL Rules contain the same reasonableness standard. However, the 2010 Rule covers the "fees and expenses" of the arbitrators, whereas the 1976 Rule encompasses only "fees." The difference should not be construed as giving arbitrators subject to the 1976 Rules license to charge unreasonable expenses. The arbitral tribunal at a minimum has an ethical duty, if not an implied obligation under the 1976 Rules, not to do so. Rather, the addition of the words "and expenses" to the 2010 Rule merely clarifies what was already expected under the 1976 Rules.

Article 41(2) has been revised slightly, as compared to Article 39(2) of the 1976 UNCITRAL Rules, though both serve the same purpose of requiring the arbitral tribunal to take any schedule of fees—or in the case of Article 41(2) a "schedule of fees or method for determining fees"—into account to the extent it considers appropriate under the circumstances of the case. In Article 41(2), the phrase "applies or stated that it will apply" in relation to a schedule or method of determining fees replaces the words "has issued" in the 1976 Rule. The revision recognizes that in some cases the appointing authority, particularly if it is a person, will not have "issued" a schedule of fees, but may still endorse and apply "a schedule of fees defined by other authorities or rules."[110]

Articles 41(3) through (6) depart significantly from the approach of Article 39(3) and (4) of the 1976 UNCITRAL Rules. As compared to the binding dispute resolution procedures established by Article 41, discussed earlier, Article 39(3) and (4) of the 1976 UNCITRAL Rules relies primarily on guidance from and non-binding consultation with the appointing authority. If the appointing authority has not issued a schedule of fees, Article 39(3) allows any party to petition the appointing authority at any time, to furnish a statement which explains the customary practice in establishing fees in international arbitrations in which the authority appoints arbitrators.[111] Under this procedure, the parties may

---

[108] UNCITRAL, UN Doc A/CN.9/WG.II/WP.157/Add.2, n 83, at 8–9, para 23.

[109] Thus, a party could seek to recognize and enforce any aspect of an award on costs that is not pending resolution under Article 41(4).

[110] UNCITRAL, 43rd Session, UN Doc A/CN.9/684, n 11, at 26, para 122; UNCITRAL, UN Doc A/CN.9/WG.II/WP.151/Add.1, n 34, at 18, para 38.

[111] This provision may also apply if the appointing authority is an arbitral institution, such as the American Arbitration Association, which has not issued a schedule of fees. See Paragraph 5, Procedures for Cases under the UNCITRAL Arbitration Rules, as amended and effective on September 15, 2005, Introduction, Services as the Appointing Authority, American Arbitration Association ("The AAA has no schedule of fees for arbitrators, but

receive useful comparative fee information to assist them in aligning their expectations regarding the costs of the arbitral tribunal.[112] However, because the arbitral tribunal is bound to adhere to the appointing authority's statement only "to the extent that it considers appropriate in the circumstances of the case," the coercive value of the provision is minimal.[113]

Article 39(4) of the 1976 UNCITRAL Rules establishes a party's right in circumstances described in Articles 39(2) and 39(3) to request consultations between the arbitrators and the appointing authority regarding the tribunal's proposed fees.[114] If the appointing authority agrees to such a consultation, it is entitled to provide "any comment it deems appropriate... concerning the fees." This procedure is perhaps the most forceful of the three established under the 1976 UNCITRAL Rules, and in some cases may have the desired "sobering effect" on the arbitrators.[115] However, Article 39(4) does not require that the arbitral tribunal heed the suggestions made by the appointing authority. The tribunal's only obligation is to wait to fix its fees until after consultation with the appointing authority has taken place. Consequently, the efficacy of the consultative procedure in regard to arbitrators' fees is one of persuasion rather than binding decision. If Article 39(4) of the 1976 UNCITRAL Rules is to be at all effective, the parties should engage the arbitrators and the appointing authority at the earliest possible phase of arbitration.[116]

If users of the 1976 UNCITRAL Rules have concerns that the arbitral tribunal will charge excessive fees and expenses, they may wish to consider agreeing to the terms of the more robust dispute settlement procedures of the 2010 UNCITRAL Rules.

C. Extracts from the Practice of Investment Tribunals

Canfor Corp and *United States of America*, Procedural Order No 1 (November 3, 2003) (ICSID administered, 1976 UNCITRAL Rules, NAFTA Chapter Eleven), at 1:

7. Pursuant to paragraph 23 of the Terms of Agreement, the Arbitral Tribunal fixes the fees of each of the Arbitrators at an hourly rate of US$500 and the fees of the administrative secretary at an hourly rate of US$235, subject to future revision, if any. In so deciding, the Arbitral Tribunal has borne in mind its duty to keep the appropriate amount of its compensation at a reasonable level and has taken into account the complexity of the subject-matter of the dispute, the amount in dispute, and the relevant circumstances of the case that the Arbitral Tribunal has had the opportunity to assess at this time.

---

it will furnish a statement concerning customary fees based on its experience in administering large numbers of cases.")

[112] Professor Sanders doubts the usefulness of Article 39(3) of the 1976 Rules and believes it could be omitted from the Rules. He maintains that in most cases a private appointing authority will not possess this kind of information. He also finds it unlikely that a private appointing authority would be willing to share this kind of information. See P Sanders, *The Work of UNCITRAL on Arbitration and Conciliation*, n 7, 20. It is unclear to the authors why the second proposition would be the case.

[113] Articles 39(2) and 39(3) of the 1976 UNCITRAL Rules.

[114] According to Mr Strauss, the Observer for the International Council for Commercial Arbitration, the prospect of consultation with the appointing authority would have a "sobering effect" on the arbitrators. UNCITRAL, 9th Session, UN Doc A/CN.9/9/C.2/SR.12, n 28, at 6–7, para 47.

[115] UNCITRAL, 9th Session, UN Doc A/CN.9/9/C.2/SR.12, n 28, at 6–7, para 47.

[116] See P Sanders, *The Work of UNCITRAL on Arbitration and Conciliation*, n 7, 20–1; N Blackaby and C Partasides, *Redfern and Hunter on International Arbitration*, n 19, 304; J Gotanda, "Setting Arbitrator's Fees: An International Survey," (2000) 33 Vanderbilt J Transnatl L 779, 783 n 7.

Glamis Gold Ltd and *United States of America*, Agreement on Certain Procedural Matters (January 20, 2004) (ICSID administered, 1976 UNCITRAL Rules, NAFTA Chapter Eleven), at 1:

> 3. As contemplated by Article 1.1 of [the 1976] UNCITRAL Arbitration Rules, the dispute parties hereby agree to modify Article 39 of the [1976] UNCITRAL Arbitration Rules to provide as follows: "Compensation for the arbitration tribunal shall be at the rates specified in the International Centre for Settlement of Investment Disputes (ICSID) Schedule of Fees, and administered as provided in ICSID's Administrative and Financial Regulation 14."
> 4. ICSID shall administer the arbitration.

Canadian Cattlemen and *United States of America* (*Cases Regarding the Border Closure due to BSE Concerns*), Procedural Order No 1 (October 20, 2006) (*Ad hoc* Proceeding, 1976 UNCITRAL Rules, NAFTA Chapter Eleven), at 9:

> 12.2: In accordance with Article 39 [of the 1976 UNCITRAL Rules], after the consultation with the Parties during the Washington meeting, the Tribunal fixes the fees of the members of the Tribunal to be US-Dollars 500.00 per hour.

Zeevi Holdings and *Bulgaria* and *Privatization Agency of Bulgaria*, Final Award (October 25, 2006) (*Ad Hoc* Proceeding, 1976 UNCITRAL Rules, Contract), at 53:

> 41:... In application of Article 39.2. of the [1976] UNCITRAL Rules, the Tribunal had by analogy used the ICC cost rules to determine the advance payments, since the ICC was the appointing authority in this UNCITRAL case. Therefore, according to Article 30.5 of the ICC Rules the Tribunal requested Claimant to transfer the 2nd advance payment of USD 180,000.00 due under section 2 of PO No 12 no later than 1 March 2005.

Chemtura Corp and *Government of Canada*, Procedural Order No 1 (January 21, 2008) (PCA administered, 1976 UNCITRAL Rules, NAFTA Chapter Eleven), at 4:

> 9. Fees and Expenses of the Arbitral Tribunal
>   a) Each member of the Arbitral Tribunal shall be remunerated at a rate of USD 4,000 for each day of participation in meetings of the Arbitral Tribunal or 8 hours of other work performed in connection with the proceeding or pro rata; and
>   b) Each member of the Arbitral Tribunal shall receive a charge of 10 percent of the hearing time reserved but not used as a result of a postponement or cancellation of a hearing less than 60 but more than 30 days prior to the commencement of the hearing and a charge of 30 percent for postponement or cancellation less than 30 days before the hearing.

Guaracachi America, Inc, et al and *Plurinational State of Bolivia*, Terms of Appointment and Procedural Order No 1 (December 9, 2011) (PCA administered, 2010 UNCITRAL Rules, US-Bolivia BIT/UK-Bolivia BIT), at 7:

> 11.1 Each member of the Tribunal shall be remunerated at the rate specified in the current ICSID Schedule of Fees plus VAT, if applicable, for all time spent in connection with the arbitration. Time spent on travel will be charged at 50% of this rate.
> 11.2 The arbitrators shall be only remunerated in the amount of 50% of their fees, for each day reserved for a hearing or meeting, based on an eight hour day, in respect of any hearing or other meeting for which they had to reserve more than one day, whenever that hearing or meeting is cancelled or postponed by more than one week, at the request of either one or both Parties, without a previous four weeks notice from the day when such hearing or meeting was scheduled to start. If the cancellation or postponement materialized once an

arbitrator has already started his travelling, the rule set out in article 11.1 in regards of travels will also apply.

ICS Inspection and Control Services Ltd and *Argentine Republic*, Award on Jurisdiction (February 10, 2012) (PCA administered, 1976 UNCITRAL Rules, UK-Argentina BIT), at 13 (reprinting Procedural Order No 1 dated May 18, 2010):

> 5.1 Each member of the Tribunal shall be remunerated at the rate of €500 per hour for all time spent in connection with this arbitration.

4. Apportionment of Costs—Article 42

A. Text of the 2010 UNCITRAL Rule[117]

Article 42 of the 2010 UNCITRAL Rules provides:
Allocation of costs

1. The costs of the arbitration shall in principle be borne by the unsuccessful party or parties. However, the arbitral tribunal may apportion each of such costs between the parties if it determines that apportionment is reasonable, taking into account the circumstances of the case.
2. The arbitral tribunal shall in the final award or, if it deems appropriate, in any other award, determine any amount that a party may have to pay to another party as a result of the decision on allocation of costs.

B. Commentary

(1) Apportioning and awarding costs

Article 42(1) is the source of the arbitral tribunal's power to apportion and award compensation for the costs of arbitration.[118] Apportionment of costs occurs when the arbitral tribunal decides that one party must bear some or all of the costs of arbitration of another party. The rules for apportionment contained in Article 42(1) are, in accordance with

---

[117] Corresponding Article 40 of the 1976 UNCITRAL Rules provides:

1. Except as provided in paragraph 2, the costs of arbitration shall in principle be borne by the unsuccessful party. However, the arbitral tribunal may apportion each of such costs between the parties if it determines that apportionment is reasonable, taking into account the circumstances of the case.
2. With respect to the costs of legal representation and assistance referred to in article 38, paragraph (e), the arbitral tribunal, taking into account the circumstances of the case, shall be free to determine which party shall bear such costs or may apportion such costs between the parties if it determines that apportionment is reasonable.
3. When the arbitral tribunal issues an order for the termination of the arbitral proceedings or makes an award on agreed terms, it shall fix the costs of arbitration referred to in article 38 and article 39, paragraph 1, in the text of that order or award.
4. No additional fees may be charged by an arbitral tribunal for interpretation or correction or completion of its award under articles 35 to 37.

[118] The items of expenditure included in the definition of "costs" are discussed in section 2(B)(2). As the *HICEE* Tribunal rightly noted, costs that may be apportioned include "in addition to the arbitrators' fees, the fees, costs and other expenses of [any administering authority] and the appointing authority. *HICEE BV* and *Slovak Republic*, Supplementary and Final Award (October 17, 2011) (PCA administered, 1976 UNCITRAL Rules, Netherlands-Slovak Republic BIT), at 2, para 7.

Article 1(3), subject to any mandatory requirements with respect to cost apportionment established under the governing arbitration law.[119] Absent such restrictions, the arbitral tribunal enjoys substantial flexibility under the Rules in apportioning the costs of arbitration.[120]

Article 42(1) starts from the basic premise that the unsuccessful party shall bear all the costs of arbitration "in principle."[121] However, the provision simultaneously grants the arbitral tribunal authority to apportion any such costs among the parties, if, in light of the "circumstances of the case," it decides that apportionment is "reasonable."[122] Arbitral tribunals interpreting this provision have understood the relationship between the "loser pays" principle and the tribunal's general authority to order "reasonable" apportionment in different ways. Some arbitral tribunals have emphasized their "wide discretion" to apportion costs,[123] sometimes without any reference at all to the "loser pays" principle.[124] Others, in contrast, have found that they could not deviate from the "loser pays" principle without a "compelling reason"[125] or save in "exceptional circumstances."[126]

Although the formulation of Article 42(1) clearly provides the arbitral tribunal substantial flexibility in apportioning and awarding the costs of arbitration,[127] that provision also contains an unequivocal preference for application of the "loser pays" rule, a preference that many parties have come to expect. Thus, a tribunal's analysis should begin there. However, this preference is readily reversible when two conditions are met: (1) the arbitral tribunal has considered the "circumstances of the case"; and (2) based on that consideration has determined that apportionment is "reasonable." Because the Rules leave the phrase "circumstances of the case" undefined, the determination of whether apportionment is reasonable is subject to the arbitral tribunal's own judgment. Further, whether apportionment is reasonable is a subjective inquiry—"reasonable" in this context means what the arbitral tribunal finds to be reasonable, not what is necessarily objectively reasonable based

---

[119] See, eg, *Petrobart* (1976 Rules), reprinted in section 4(C)(1) (taking into account the Swedish Arbitration Act).

[120] Note that some tribunals have found that they have no authority to apportion costs upon finding that they lack jurisdiction to resolve the dispute. See, eg, *Econet Wireless Ltd* (1976 Rules), reprinted in section 4(C)(1).

[121] For a cost award emphasizing this premise, see *Methanex Corp* (1976 Rules), Award dated August 3, 2005, paras 5–6, reprinted in section 4(C)(2)(a). During discussions to revise the UNCITRAL Rules, a proposal was made to replace the phrase "successful party" with a more neutral formulation, like the one contained in Article 31(3) of the 1998 ICC Arbitration Rules ("which of the parties shall bear [the costs]"), since "it might not be easy in all instances to determine which party was to be considered the successful party." UNCITRAL, 41st Session, UN Doc A/CN.9/646, n 34, at 8, para 29. This proposal was not accepted. Many leading arbitral rules provide for the tribunal to award costs in favor of the prevailing party, see N Blackaby and C Partasides, *Redfern and Hunter on International Arbitration*, n 19, 546.

[122] These costs may be apportioned item-by-item if the arbitral tribunal so chooses. See P Sanders, "Commentary on UNCITRAL Arbitration Rules," n 26, 214.

[123] *Econet Wireless Ltd* and *First Bank of Nigeria,* et al *(Nigeria)*, Award (June 2, 2005) at para 44 *(Ad Hoc* Proceeding, 1976 UNCITRAL Rules, Contract), excerpt reprinted in (2006) XXXI Ybk Commercial Arb 49.

[124] *Chemtura Corp* and *Government of Canada*, Award (August 2, 2010) (PCA administered, 1976 UNCITRAL Rules, NAFTA Chapter Eleven), at 79, paras 272–73.

[125] *Methanex Corp* (1976 Rules), Part V, at para 5, reprinted in section 4(C)(2)(a).

[126] *Canfor Corp*, et al and *United States of America*, Joint Order on the Costs of Arbitration and for the Termination of Certain Arbitral Proceedings (July 19, 2007) (ICSID administered, 1976 UNCITRAL Rules, NAFTA Chapter Eleven), para 149.

[127] The drafters agreed that the Rules should be "neutral...leaving the apportionment of these costs fully to the discretion of the arbitral tribunal." See UN GAOR, 31st Session, Supp No 17, UN Doc A/31/17, n 14, para 222, reprinted in (1976) VII UNCITRAL Ybk 66, 81. This standard is in line with general international arbitration practice. See P Sanders, "Commentary on UNCITRAL Arbitration Rules," n 26, 214.

on, for example, the prevailing practice of other arbitral tribunals. This broad discretion is, of course, limited by the arbitral tribunal's responsibility to carry out its duties in good faith. Thus, it may not apportion costs on a basis that is unrelated to the arbitral proceedings.

Further, once the arbitral tribunal decides to apportion costs, it may apportion in any proportions that it deems reasonable under the circumstances. The only limitation imposed by Article 42(1) is that apportionment be "between the parties." Thus, an award of compensation for such costs may range anywhere from requiring the unsuccessful party to pay its own costs and those of the other parties to requiring each party to bear its own costs, effectively awarding no costs to the successful party.

Article 42 represents a unification of the two distinct standards of apportionment previously found in the 1976 UNCITRAL Rules. Article 40(1) of the 1976 UNCITRAL Rules contained the identical standard for apportionment of costs as Article 42(1), but its coverage excluded the costs of legal representation and assistance.[128] Article 40(2) of the 1976 UNCITRAL Rules addressed the "costs of legal representation and assistance,"[129] but did not incorporate the "loser pays" principle. With regard to legal costs, the drafters agreed that "no principle of compensation would be laid down."[130] Thus, by its own terms, Article 40(2) of the 1976 UNCITRAL Rules leaves the arbitral tribunal "free to determine which party shall bear [legal] costs," without any presumption of compensation for the successful party, and may apportion such costs if such action is "reasonable."[131] The only limitation on the arbitral tribunal's discretion is that it must in awarding costs consider "the circumstances of the case."[132]

The different standards for apportionment under the 1976 UNCITRAL Rules represented a compromise among the drafters.[133] Early drafts of the 1976 UNCITRAL Rules contained a general principle of compensation that the unsuccessful party must bear the costs of arbitration, but that the arbitrators may apportion the costs between the parties if circumstances warrant.[134] Some representatives criticized this approach, especially with respect to the costs of legal representation, as inconsistent with state practice and prejudicial to less affluent parties. They favored the rule that each party would bear its own expenses for legal representation, but that the arbitral tribunal was entitled to award such costs in appropriate cases.[135] This view persuaded the drafters to incorporate two approaches to

---

[128] Namely, the items of cost outlined in Article 40(2)(a)–(d) and 40(2)(f)).

[129] The drafters discussed the application of these standards not only to awards rendered by the arbitral tribunal after deliberations, but also to awards on agreed terms. The Preliminary Draft envisioned that upon settlement the costs of arbitration would be borne equally by the parties. See Draft Article 28(2) of the Preliminary Draft. However, later versions of the Rules dropped this requirement, providing the arbitral tribunal discretion in this area. See Draft Article 29(2) of the Revised Draft. Nevertheless, the arbitral tribunal, assuming no extraordinary circumstances exist, may wish to follow the not uncommon practice of equal apportionment of costs in arbitrations that end in settlement.

[130] UNCITRAL, 9th Session, UN Doc A/CN.9/9/C.2/SR.13, n 46, at 4, para 20. The varying practice in this area is discussed in *SD Myers Inc* (1976 Rules), para 33, reprinted in section 4(C)(2).

[131] See P Sanders, "Commentary on UNCITRAL Arbitration Rules," n 26, 217. See also UN GAOR, 31st Session, Supp No 17, UN Doc A/31/17, n 14, para 291, reprinted in (1976) VII UNCITRAL Ybk 66, 80.

[132] See section 4(B)(2).

[133] For the Committee's discussion, see UNCITRAL, 9th Session, UN Doc A/CN.9/9/C.2/SR.13, n 46, at 2–4.

[134] See, eg, Draft Article 33(2) of the Revised Draft.

[135] The representatives of the United States and India proposed the following amendment to the draft provision on legal costs:

cost apportionment set forth, respectively, in Articles 40(1) and 40(2) of the 1976 UNCITRAL Rules.

In revising the 1976 UNCITRAL Rules, the Working Group took note of the varying approaches to apportionment across legal systems, but nevertheless favored inclusion of a single standard for apportionment under the Rules.[136] Thus, the standard for apportioning the costs of legal representation and assistance contained in Article 40(2) of the 1976 UNCITRAL Rules was omitted, and the standard for apportioning all other costs of arbitration was expanded in scope to cover legal costs. As a result, the 2010 UNCITRAL Rules require that all of the costs of arbitration, including legal costs, in principle be borne by the unsuccessful party, unless the tribunal deems it reasonable to apportion them in a different manner, taking into account the circumstances of the case. How arbitral tribunals apply the revised rule remains to be seen. Differing national practices may cause some arbitrators to resist applying the "loser pays" principle to the apportionment of legal costs.[137] In addition, party expectations will likely influence how arbitrators use the broad discretion afforded the arbitral tribunal in the second sentence of Article 42(1). Because the single standard for apportionment contained in Article 42(1) is so flexible, a clear and consistent practice regarding cost recovery under the 2010 UNCITRAL Rules is unlikely to emerge for some time, if prior practice under the 1976 UNCITRAL Rules is any indication.[138] For example, each Chamber of the Iran–US Claims Tribunal developed its own approach to costs under a modified version of the 1976 UNCITRAL Rules.[139] Traditionally, Chamber Two never awarded legal costs to a successful party.[140] In contrast, Chambers One and Three awarded legal costs on many occasions, but with little explanation of their reasoning

---

(e) Each party shall bear its own expenses for legal assistance, provided, however, that the arbitrators may include such expenses as costs of the arbitration if they determine it is appropriate to do so under the circumstances of the case, and then only if such costs were claimed during the arbitral proceedings and to the extent that the amount is deemed reasonable by the arbitrators.

UNCITRAL, 9th Session, UN Doc A/CN.9/9/C.2/SR.13, n 46, at 2, para 1.

[136] UNCITRAL, 41st Session, UN Doc A/CN.9/646, n 34, at 7, para 28.

[137] The differences in practice have been recognized in *Methanex Corp* (1976 Rules), Award, Part V, paras 9–10 (noting that some international tribunals do not apportion the costs of legal representation "unless the successful party has prevailed over a manifestly spurious position taken by the unsuccessful party," whereas others do apportion so that "the successful party should not…be left out of pocket in respect of the legal costs reasonably incurred in enforcing or defending its rights."), *SD Myers* (1976 Rules), Final Award on Costs, para 33 (same), and *International Thunderbird* (1976 Rules), Dissent by Thomas Wälde to Award, para 124.

[138] According to Webster, a broad survey of arbitral practice, including UNCITRAL practice, reveals varying approaches to apportionment. See T Webster "Efficiency in Investment Arbitration: Recent Decisions on Preliminary and Costs Issues" (2009) 25(4) Arb Intl 469, 507 et seq.

[139] The subject of costs provoked much controversy at the Tribunal. The Iranian Government opposed any requirement for Iran to pay costs to successful parties in individual cases on grounds that the government funding of the Tribunal, along with the Security Account maintained by Iran, significantly reduced the costs of arbitration and enforcement of an award. The Iranian arbitrators frequently echoed this position. See, eg, *Watkins-Johnson Co and Islamic Republic of Iran*, Award No 429–370–1 (July 28, 1989), Dissenting Opinion of Judge Noori (January 8, 1990), reprinted in 22 Iran-US CTR 257, 336 (1989-II) (noting that "United States claimants can obtain judgment amounts from awards, to which they were never entitled in most cases, without having to bear the arbitration costs incurred by other litigants before other fora, and without having to get caught up in the numerous difficulties and labyrinthine processes normally required to enforce awards"). See also J Westberg, *International Transactions and Claims Involving Government Parties: Case Law of the Iran-United States Claims Tribunal* (1991) 265–7.

[140] Judge Aldrich, the American arbitrator in Chamber Two, provides the following commentary on that approach:

While the Chamber never explained its reasons for that position, I, as a member of the Chamber, can say that there were several relevant considerations, among which were the facts that the costs incurred by American parties

and usually in amounts that fell far short of full compensation.[141] In other areas, however, such as apportioning the costs of expert advice, the Chambers acted more consistently, generally requiring the parties to bear these costs in equal proportions.[142] Apportionment of costs in investor–state arbitration under the 1976 UNCITRAL Rules has also varied significantly in approach; some tribunals have apportioned the costs of the arbitral tribunal equally and required the parties to bear their own legal costs, whereas others have applied the "loser pays" principle.[143]

With few strict rules to guide apportionment of the costs of arbitration, an arbitral tribunal's approach under Article 42 of the 2010 UNCITRAL Rules should at least be transparent and logical. First and foremost, the arbitral tribunal must give effect to any express agreement by the parties to modify Article 42(1).[144] If modification has not occurred, the arbitral tribunal may wish at an early stage in the arbitration to solicit comments from the parties regarding their desired approach to costs.[145] Second, if the parties themselves cannot agree on a desired approach, then the arbitral tribunal must assume the task, taking into account, as much as possible, the expectations of the parties. If both parties originate from legal systems that require each party to bear its own legal expenses, for example, then a similar rule may be appropriately applied in arbitration.[146] If both parties are sufficiently sophisticated that it can be assumed that the preference for the "loser pays" principle was understood at the time the Rules were chosen, then application of the preference may be appropriate. Otherwise, a divided arbitral tribunal may wish to follow the local rule on awarding costs at the place of arbitration.

Article 42(2) requires the arbitral tribunal to "determine any amount that a party may have to pay to another party as a result of the decision on allocation of costs." According to the *travaux préparatoires*, it was noted:

that difficulties with the execution of the decision on costs had frequently arisen in certain jurisdictions, where the final order or award had not made specific reference to the amount that one party had to pay to the other party.[147]

---

were usually far higher than those incurred by Iranian parties, that successful American parties had the enormous benefit of the Security Account to guarantee prompt and full payment of all Awards against Iran, and that if the parties had been left to litigate their disputes in American courts, they generally would have had to bear their own costs.

G Aldrich, *The Jurisprudence of the Iran-United States Claims Tribunal*, n 31, 480.

[141] But see *Sedco, Inc* and *National Iranian Oil Co,* et al, Award No 309–129–3 (July 7, 1987), reprinted in 15 Iran-US CTR 23, 184 (1987-II) (awarding the claimant the full amount of non-legal costs requested, US $194,866, and US $100,000 of US $2,000,000 in legal costs requested). See also J Westberg, *International Transactions and Claims*, n 139, 267.

[142] But see *Richard D Harza,* et al and *Islamic Republic of Iran,* et al, Award No 232–97–2 (May 2, 1986), at para 175, reprinted in 11 Iran-US CTR 76, 136 (1986-II) (ordering the unsuccessful party to bear all the expenses of the tribunal-appointed expert).

[143] See section 4(B)(2)(c).

[144] See *Association of Service Industry Firms* (1976 Rules), reprinted in section 4(C)(1). Accord G Born, *International Commercial Arbitration*, n 3, 2499.

[145] This should be done as early in the arbitration as possible, lest the parties' views become influenced by their expectations of victory.

[146] See *Himpurna California Energy Ltd* and *PT (Persero) Perusahaan Listruik Negara*, Final Award (May 4, 1999) (*Ad Hoc* Proceeding, 1976 UNCITRAL Rules, Concession Agreement), reprinted in (2000) XXV Ybk Commercial Arb 13, 106, para 390 (refusing to award any costs of legal representation or assistance because "recovery of significant legal costs is foreign to the legal system of Indonesia, where the parties chose to hold the arbitration").

[147] UNCITRAL, 43rd Session, UN Doc A/CN.9/688, n 86, at 25–6, para 123.

Thus, rather than allowing apportionment of costs in general terms, eg, "the respondent shall bear two thirds of the costs of arbitration," Article 42(2) requires the arbitral tribunal to specify the precise amount that one party is required to pay another to satisfy the arbitral tribunal's ruling on cost apportionment.

The arbitral tribunal must make the determination required in Article 42(2) "in the final award or, if it deems appropriate, in any other award." This language does not jibe precisely with Article 40(1), which requires the tribunal to fix the costs of arbitration "in the final award and, if it deems appropriate, in another decision." While the words "another decision" clearly leaves open the possibility that costs may be fixed in a termination order, if necessary, the use of the narrower phrase "any other award" in Article 42(2) should not necessarily be construed as barring the tribunal from apportioning costs in a termination order. Rather, the formulation in Article 42(2) is better understood as promoting the sound practice of apportioning costs in an award in order to maximize the validity and enforceability of the tribunal's decision both domestically and internationally.

(2) "The circumstances of the case"

When deciding whether it is reasonable to apportion costs pursuant to Article 42(1), the arbitral tribunal must "tak[e] into account the circumstances of the case." Neither the Rules nor the *travaux préparatoires* provide guidance on the meaning of this important requirement. Although apportionment determinations are often highly fact-specific, some international tribunals applying the 1976 UNCITRAL Rules have considered one or more of the following factors in interpreting and applying the phrase "the circumstances of the case": the success of the parties on their claims, the conduct of the parties during the arbitral proceedings, the nature of the parties to the dispute, and the nature of the dispute resolution mechanism.

(a) The degree of success of the parties

In determining how to apportion costs, arbitral tribunals have considered the degree to which a party prevails on its claim—as opposed to simply whether or not the party has prevailed outright.[148] The rationale for this variation of the "loser pays" approach is that a "successful" claimant or respondent that has been "forced to go through the [arbitral] process in order to achieve success...should not be penalised by having to pay for the process itself."[149] "Success" in arbitration is typically not a zero-sum determination, however, as the parties may win on some issues but not others, and some issues may be of greater importance than others for the outcome of the arbitration. In the *Sylvania* case, Judge Holtzmann offered two examples of when the degree of the parties' relative success may determine a tribunal's level of apportionment.[150] First, apportionment may be appropriate in cases where the success of the parties is split, eg, the claimant prevails on the claim and the respondent prevails on the counterclaim.[151] Second, cases involving "quite separate and

---

[148] A less nuanced approach may be required in the case of a party's unilateral withdrawal of a claim, which one arbitral tribunal found to fall within the meaning of "unsuccessful party." *Canfor, Tembec & Terminal Forest* and *United States*, Joint Order on Costs and Termination (July 19, 2007) (ICSID administered, 1976 UNCITRAL Rules, NAFTA Chapter Eleven), at para 149.

[149] *SD Myers, Inc* and *Government of Canada*, Final Award on Costs (December 30, 2002) (*Ad Hoc* Proceeding, 1976 UNCITRAL Rules, NAFTA Chapter Eleven), at 7, para 15.

[150] *Sylvania Technical Systems, Inc* (1983 Tribunal Rules), Separate Opinion of Judge Holtzmann, n 25, at 329.

[151] *Sylvania Technical Systems, Inc* (1983 Tribunal Rules), Separate Opinion of Judge Holtzmann, n 25, at 331. See also P Sanders, "Commentary on UNCITRAL Arbitration Rules," n 26, 214–15. In cases of a draw, that

independent causes of action" may warrant apportionment if the claimant succeeds on one claim but not on the other.[152] Numerous arbitral tribunals have apportioned the costs of arbitration in proportion to a party's overall degree of success.[153]

Arbitral tribunals have determined the degree to which a party has prevailed in arbitration according to different methodologies. In *BG Group*, for example, success was measured in large part by comparing the amount of compensation sought by the claimant to the amount it was actually awarded. Finding a 78 percent success rate on the amounts claimed while factoring in the claimant's losses on certain jurisdictional issues, the arbitral tribunal apportioned 70 percent of the costs of arbitration against the respondent, after adjusting for additional factors.[154] The *International Thunderbird* tribunal was less mathematical. While it found that the respondent ultimately succeeded in the arbitration, it required the claimant to bear 75 percent of the costs of arbitration, because the respondent "did not prevail on all the issues."[155]

One factor that may mitigate against apportionment of costs based on a party's success in arbitration is the novelty of the issues being decided. This factor may be particularly relevant in the context of investor–state arbitration which may present new and unsettled questions of international law.[156] It may therefore not always be reasonable to require the losing party to pay costs when it was difficult, if not impossible, for that party to predict the potential success of a novel claim.

(b) The conduct of the parties

The conduct of a party during the arbitral proceedings is another potential factor for consideration when apportioning and awarding costs.[157] Tribunals, for example, have awarded

---

is, discontinuance or settlement, an equal sharing of the costs may be appropriate. See UNCITRAL, 9th Session, Addendum 1 (Commentary), UN Doc A/CN.9/112/Add.1, n 13, reprinted in (1976) VII UNCITRAL Ybk 166, 179–80 (Commentary on Draft Article 29(2)). See also n 129.

[152] Judge Holtzmann used the example of "where a contractor claims under two separate contracts involving different building projects." *Sylvania Technical Systems, Inc* (1983 Rules), Separate Opinion of Judge Holtzmann, n 25, at 331.

[153] For the practice of investment tribunals see, for example, *Karaha Bodas Co* (1976 Rules), at para 140; *SD Myers, Inc* (1976 Rules), paras 15–19; *Pope & Talbot, Inc* (1976 Rules), paras 8–11; *International Thunderbird Gaming Corp* (1976 Rules), paras 219–221; *Glamis Gold Ltd* (1976 Rules), para 833; *Ulysseas, Inc* (1976 Rules), paras 364–365; and *Chevron* (1976 Rules); all reprinted in section 4(C)(2)(a). For the practice of Chambers One and Three of the Iran–US Claims Tribunal, see, for example, *Agrostruct Intl, Inc* (1983 Tribunal Rules); *Electronic Systems Intl, Inc* (1983 Tribunal Rules); *General Electric Co* (1983 Tribunal Rules); *Development and Resources Corp* (1983 Tribunal Rules); all reprinted in section 4(D)(2)(a). See also *McCollough & Co, Inc*, Separate Opinion of Charles N Brower (1983 Tribunal Rules); *Rockwell Intl Systems, Inc* (1983 Tribunal Rules), Separate Opinion of Howard M Holtzmann; both reprinted in section 4(D)(2)(a).

[154] *BG Group Plc* (1976 Rules) paras 458–460; See also *Karaha Bodas* (1976 Rules); both reprinted in section 4(C)(2)(a).

[155] *International Thunderbird* (1976 Rules), para 219–221, reprinted in section 4(C)(2)(a).

[156] See *Robert Azinian* (1976 Rules) para 126; *Romak SA* (1976 Rules), para 250; and *ICS Inspection and Control Services, Inc* (1976 Rules), para 341; all reprinted in section 4(C)(2)(c). See also *Glamis Gold Ltd* (1976 Rules), para 833, reprinted in section 4(C)(2)(a). But see *International Thunderbird* (1976 Rules), para 218, reprinted in section 4(C)(2)(c) ("investment arbitration in general and NAFTA arbitration in particular have become so well known and established as to diminish their novelty as dispute resolution mechanisms.")

[157] Some members of the Committee suggested that costs should be awarded in response to a party's inappropriate conduct. See UNCITRAL, 9th Session, UN Doc A/CN.9/9/C.2/SR.13, n 46, at 2, para 4 (Comment by Mr Holtzmann, United States, indicating that delay tactics and bad faith might be grounds for awarding costs); See also 5, para 30 (Comment by Mr Pirrung, Federal Republic of Germany, suggesting that a party that fails to nominate an arbitrator should bear any costs as a result of its conduct.) One leading commentator on the ICSID Arbitration Rules is of a similar view, writing that: "[m]isconduct by a party during the proceedings such as non-cooperation with the tribunal, disregard for a recommendation of provisional measures, default in

costs to a party as "estimated compensation" for expenses incurred as a direct result of another party's conduct that was frivolous, in bad faith, or unnecessarily burdensome.[158] As described by one arbitral tribunal, this practice "serves the dual function of reparation and dissuasion."[159] Apportionment based on the conduct of the parties has occurred under a variety of circumstances: a respondent's repeated failure to file a required submission requested by the tribunal;[160] a claimant's late delivery of evidentiary materials requiring postponement of the hearing;[161] a respondent's failure to produce documents requested by the tribunal;[162] a respondent's failure without cause to attend a scheduled hearing;[163] a respondent's failure to finalize an award on agreed terms for unreasonable reasons;[164] a respondent's attempt to reargue a previously decided jurisdictional question;[165] a respondent's delay by making unfounded allegations of forgery;[166] a respondent's unnecessary use of tribunal resources by belatedly producing unpersuasive witness testimony;[167] a claimant's failure to address the respondent's repeated objections to the arbitral tribunal's jurisdiction;[168] a claimant's initiation of similar parallel proceedings;[169] a respondent's refusal to provide information about its legal status until a late stage of the proceedings;[170] and a claimant's unsolicited further submission.[171]

Similarly, the Iran–US Tribunal, on occasion, has awarded costs against a party whose conduct, while not necessarily inappropriate, directly and unnecessarily imposed additional costs on its adversary.[172] For example, the Tribunal ordered Iran to pay for the costs to the claimant, in one case, resulting from Iran's unsuccessful request for an additional award[173] and, in another case, for filing counterclaims that raised technical engineering

---

participating in the proceedings or violation of the Centre's exclusive jurisdiction should be reflected in the award on costs." C Schreuer, *The ICSID Convention: A Commentary* ((2nd edn 2009)) 1230–32,1239. See also K Berger, *International Economic Arbitration*, n 6, 617; *Dadras Intl* (1983 Tribunal Rules), reprinted in section 4(D)(2)(b).

[158] *Behring Intl, Inc* (1983 Tribunal Rules), reprinted in section 4(D)(2)(b). See also L Nurick, "Costs in International Arbitrations," (1992) 7 ICSID Rev—Foreign Investment L J 57, 58 (where one party "has acted frivolously, in bad faith or otherwise irresponsibly, arbitrators are likely to award addition, sometimes full, costs to the other party"). Accord M Smith "Costs in International Commercial Arbitration" (February/April 2001) 56 Disp Resolution J 30, 33.

[159] *Robert Azinian* (1976 Rules), para 125, reprinted in section 4(C)(2)(c).

[160] See *Behring International, Inc* (1983 Tribunal Rules), reprinted in section 4(D)(2)(b).

[161] See *SD Myers Inc* (1976 Rules), para 26, reprinted in section 4(C)(2)(b).

[162] See *Pope & Talbot, Inc* (1976 Rules), paras 13–14; See also *Ronald S Lauder* (1976 Rules), para 318; both reprinted in section 4(C)(2)(b).

[163] *Houston Contracting Co* (1983 Tribunal Rules); *Ronald E Chamness* (1983 Tribunal Rules); and *Sedco, Inc* (1983 Tribunal Rules); all reprinted in section 4(D)(2)(b).

[164] *International Schools Services, Inc* (1983 Tribunal Rules), reprinted in section 4(D)(2)(b). For details of the terms of the settlement agreement, see *International Schools Services, Inc and Islamic Republic of Iran*, et al, Award No ITL 57-123-1 (January 30, 1986), reprinted in 10 Iran-US CTR 6 (1986-I).

[165] *Ministry of National Defense and the United States* (1983 Tribunal Rules), Case No B59/B69, reprinted in section 4(D)(2)(b).

[166] *Dadras Intl* (1983 Tribunal Rules); and *Vera-Jo Miller Aryeh* (1983 Tribunal Rules), both reprinted in section 4(D)(2)(b).

[167] *Dadras Intl* (1983 Tribunal Rules), reprinted in section 4(D)(2)(b).

[168] *Ronald E Chamness* (1983 Tribunal Rules), reprinted in section 4(D)(2)(b).

[169] See *CME Czech Republic BV* (1976 Rules), para 621, reprinted in section 4(C)(2)(b).

[170] See *Ultrasystems Inc* (1983 Tribunal Rules), reprinted in section 4(D)(2)(b).

[171] See *Link-Trading Joint Stock Co* (1976 Rules), para 96, reprinted in section 4(C)(2)(b).

[172] ICSID has followed this practice as well. See C Schreuer, *The ICSID Convention*, n 157, 1232.

[173] See *International Schools Services, Inc and Islamic Republic of Iran*, et al, reprinted in 14 Iran-US CTR 279, 281–2 (1987-I).

questions that required the appointment of experts.[174] In one case, the Tribunal even required the claimant to pay Iran for costs because "the Respondent's task of preparing pleadings and evidence was made more difficult by the lack of coherence in the Claimant's written presentation of its case."[175]

While arbitral tribunals have typically focused on a party's conduct during the arbitration in assessing the "circumstances of the case," the Rules do not prevent consideration of a claimant's motivation for initiating arbitration in the first place. In *Himpurna*, for example, the arbitral tribunal concluded that the respondent's mismanagement of its contractual relationship with the claimant left the claimant no choice but to bring its claims to arbitration. Thus, the arbitral tribunal found no reason to deviate from the "loser pays" principle, which would require the unsuccessful respondent to pay all of the costs of the arbitral tribunal.[176]

Finally, in determining whether to apportion costs, some tribunals have considered the positive conduct of a party, such as the professionalism and competence of that party's legal counsel, as a mitigating factor.[177]

(c) The nature of the parties

A third potential factor relating to the apportionment of costs is the nature of the parties to the dispute, namely whether they are sovereign or private entities. Where the parties to an UNCITRAL arbitration are private or commercial, apportionment of costs, depending on the circumstances of the case, is the norm. With regard to arbitration between two sovereign states, the general practice is to require each party to bear its own costs.[178] The international agreements creating the Iran–US Claims Tribunal, for example, provide that "the expenses of the Tribunal shall be borne equally by the two governments."[179] In the mixed arbitrations involving sovereign and private parties held before that claims institution, it has been the practice of the Tribunal not to apply a rule of equal apportionment.[180]

On one occasion, the Tribunal diverged from this practice with arguably unfair consequences. Cases A/3 and A/8 were brought by Iran against the US and Bell Helicopter Textron Co ("Bell") to clarify certain provisions of the Algiers Accords.[181] Iran filed its statement of claim only days before the decision in Case A/2, which held that the Tribunal is without jurisdiction over claims by a government directly against a national of the other

---

[174] See *Richard D Harza*, et al and *Islamic Republic of Iran*, et al, Award No 232-97-2 (May 2, 1986), reprinted in 11 Iran-US CTR 76, 136 (1986-II).

[175] *Near East Technological Services USA, Inc* (1983 Tribunal Rules), reprinted in section 4(D)(2)(b). The same concern appears to have in part motivated an investment tribunal to apportion costs against a claimant. See *Jan Oostergetel* (1976 Rules), para 339, reprinted in section 4(C)(2)(b).

[176] See *Himpurna California Energy Ltd* (1976 Rules), reprinted in section 4(C)(2)(b). See also *Ronald S Lauder* (1976 Rules), reprinted in section 4(C)(2)(b).

[177] See *Merrill & Ring* (1976 Rules), para 270–72, reprinted in section 4(C)(2)(b). See also *Robert Azinian* (1976 Rules) and *International Thunderbird* (1976 Rules), both reprinted in section 4(C)(2)(c); *Glamis Gold Ltd* (1976 Rules), reprinted in section 4(C)(2)(a); *Econet Wireless Ltd* (1976 Rules) and *HICEE BV* (1976 Rules), both reprinted in section 4(C)(2)(b).

[178] Accord Castello, "UNCITRAL Rules," n 36, 1530.

[179] Article VI(3) of the Claims Settlement Declaration. The provisions on state–state arbitration contained in international investment agreements often contain the same rule, though under some agreements the arbitral tribunal has discretion to apportion costs. See, for example, US–Uruguay Bilateral Investment Treaty, Article 37(3).

[180] The practice of investor–State arbitral tribunals has varied more in this regard. See section 4(B)(2)(d).

[181] *Ministry of National Defence of Islamic Republic of Iran* and *United States of America*, et al, Decision Nos DEC-100-A3/A8-FT (November 22, 1991).

state party. As a result, Iran's claim against Bell was outside the Tribunal's jurisdiction.[182] Despite the ruling in Case A/2, Iran failed to withdraw its claim and Bell was forced to continue its participation in the proceedings.[183] Upon being released from the arbitration, Bell filed a request for compensation for its costs of arbitration, which was denied.

The decision drew dissent from the American arbitrators, including Judge Aldrich, who stated that he would have awarded Bell its costs of arbitration:

> Private parties have no place in "A Cases," which involve disputes between the Government of Iran and the United States concerning the interpretation and performance of the Algiers Declarations.... Consequently, when a private party, like Bell, is unjustifiably dragged into such a dispute by one of the Governments, it should not be responsible for its costs simply because the Tribunal—quite properly—has declined to charge to one Government the costs incurred by the other Government in disputes between them.[184]

(d) The nature of the dispute resolution mechanism

Investor–state arbitration is a unique form of dispute resolution, the nature of which may inform an arbitral tribunal's decision whether to apportion costs pursuant to Article 42(1). One current of thought among arbitrators is to require the parties to investor–state arbitration to divide the costs of the arbitral tribunal evenly and to bear their own costs of representation, save in cases of frivolous or bad faith claims.[185] One reason for this approach is that because investor–state arbitration presents novel issues of international law, the resolution of which cannot be easily predicted, it would be unfair to apportion costs based on a party's success in arbitration.[186] The late Professor Wälde, in his dissenting opinion in *International Thunderbird*, provided additional reasons. He argued that apportionment of costs was inconsistent with the aims of international investment agreements because it discourages investors, particularly smaller investors, from exercising their "unilateral right" to seek "judicial review of administrative conduct."[187]

Another current of thought among arbitrators places less emphasis on the nature of investment arbitration, approaching apportionment no differently for the most part than in commercial arbitration.[188] However, even within this camp, arbitral tribunals have

---

[182] *Islamic Republic of Iran* and *United States*, Decision No DEC–2-A2-FT (January 21, 1982), reprinted in 1 Iran-US CTR 101 (1981–1982).

[183] *Islamic Republic of Iran* and *United States*, n 182. Bell filed a 14-page brief, a motion to cancel the hearings, a letter responding to Iran's claims, and two responses to the Tribunal's orders.

[184] *Ministry of National Defence of Islamic Republic of Iran* and *United States of America* and *Bell Helicopter Textron Co*, Decision No 100-A3/A8-FT (November 22, 1991), Dissenting Opinion of George Aldrich (November 22, 1991). See also Dissenting Opinion of Howard M Holtzmann and Richard C Allison (November 25, 1991).

[185] See *ICS Inspection and Controls Services, Inc* (1976 Rules), reprinted in section 4(C)(2)(c) (noting, but not following, "[t]he traditional position in investment treaty arbitration, in contrast to commercial arbitration,... to follow the normal practice under public international law... that the parties shall bear their own costs of legal representation and assistance"). See also *Chevron* (1976 Rules), reprinted in section 4(C)(2)(a) (same). See also N Rubins, "The Allocation of Costs and Attorney's Fees in Investor-State Arbitration" (2003) 18(1) ICSID Rev–Foreign Investment L J 109, 126 (finding no clear practice of apportioning costs has emerged in investor–state arbitration); W Ben Hamida, "Cost Issue in Investor-State Arbitration Decisions Rendered Against the Investor: A Synthetic Table" (2005) 2 Transnatl Dispute Management 1 (same).

[186] *Robert Azinian* and *United Mexican States*, Award (November 1, 1999) (ICSID administered, 1976 UNCITRAL Rules, NAFTA Chapter Eleven), at para 126.

[187] *International Thunderbird* (1976 Rules), Separate Opinion of Thomas Wälde, para 139, reprinted in section 4(C)(2)(c).

[188] See, eg, *International Thunderbird* (1976 Rules); and *Canfor Corp* (1976 Rules); both reprinted in section 4(C)(2)(c).

recognized certain situations in which the arbitral tribunal's power of apportionment should be limited on account of the unique nature of international investment arbitration. For example, in *International Thunderbird*, despite apportioning costs against the claimant, the arbitral tribunal nevertheless acknowledged it may be inappropriate to do so "in the case of an investor with limited financial resources where considerations of access to justice may play a role."[189]

(3) Requirements for making a claim for costs

(a) Documentation

A request for costs, like any claim before the arbitral tribunal, must be supported by sufficient evidentiary documentation to satisfy the burden of proof.[190] Such documentation permits the arbitral tribunal to apportion and award costs meaningfully by establishing an accurate baseline of actual incurred costs. Sufficient proof of costs typically consists of copies of travel documentation and tickets, hotel, dining, phone and fax bills, credit card receipts, and bills for professional services and expenses rendered, which should include an adequate and itemized description of the tasks performed and the relevant billing rates.[191] Failure to document claims sufficiently may result in no award of compensation.[192] When complicated costs issues arise, a hearing may be appropriate in addition to party submissions.[193]

(b) Timing of requests

The Rules are silent as to the timing of a request for costs. In one case, the Iran–US Claims Tribunal held that "documents relating to the costs of the proceedings, which are submitted at or reasonably following the final hearing are not normally rejected as untimely filed, since costs cannot be assessed until a very late stage."[194] In a case before a NAFTA tribunal, the parties agreed at the final hearing "that the Tribunal would make a second Partial Award on the quantification of the compensation to be awarded and that the Disputing Parties would be given an opportunity to submit their claims in respect of

---

[189] *International Thunderbird* (1976), Separate Opinion of Thomas Wälde, reprinted in section 4(C)(2)(c). On the challenges facing smaller investors, see L Caplan "Making Investor-State Arbitration More Accessible to Small and Medium-Sized Enterprises" in C Rogers and R Alford (eds), *The Future of Investment Arbitration* (2009) 297.

[190] See Chapter 18 on evidence.

[191] Witness statements may also be useful.

[192] *Sylvania Technical Systems, Inc* (1983 Rules), n 25, at 323 ("The Claimant has not indicated the amount of such non-legal costs—such as translation or travel expenses of witnesses—and has not provided evidence as to them. Accordingly, the Tribunal makes no award for the Claimant's non-legal costs."). See also *Futura Trading Inc and Khuzestan Water and Power Authority*, Award No 187–325–3 (August 19, 1985), reprinted in 9 Iran-US CTR 46, 59–60 (1985-II) (deciding that each party shall bear its own costs of arbitration because "Claimant has not requested costs for legal representation and assistance at any time in these proceedings and has presented no evidence to this Tribunal concerning its other costs); *International Technical Products Corp, et al and Government of the Islamic Republic of Iran*, Award No 196–302–3 (October 24, 1985), reprinted in 9 Iran-US CTR 206, 242 (1985-II) (making no allowance for certain claimed costs "[a]s none of the claimed disbursements has been documented); *Blount Brothers Corp and Islamic Republic of Iran*, Award No 216–53–1 (March 6, 1986), reprinted in 10 Iran-US CTR 95, 102 (1986-I) (deciding not to make an award as to costs because the "request remains unsubstantiated by documentation").

[193] See, eg, *Canfor Corp, et al and United States*, Joint Order on the Costs of Arbitration and for the Termination of Certain Arbitral Proceedings (July 19, 2007) (ICSID administered, 1976 UNCITRAL Rules, NAFTA Chapter Eleven), para 3.

[194] See *Amoco Intl Finance Corp* (1983 Rules), reprinted in section 4(D)(1).

costs, together with any submissions they wish to make, after they have seen the Second Partial Award."[195]

(c) Proof of reasonable legal costs

As legal expenses typically are the largest cost of the arbitration, they often figure prominently in a party's request for compensation for costs. Unlike the costs of the arbitral tribunal which, pursuant to Article 41, the appointing authority or in some cases the PCA Secretary-General reviews for reasonableness, the arbitral tribunal determines the reasonableness of any claims for legal costs, pursuant to Article 40(2)(e), before deciding whether to apportion such costs. Judge Holtzmann has commented aptly on the reasonableness of legal costs:[196]

> A test of reasonableness is not... an invitation to mere subjectivity. Objective tests of reasonableness of lawyers' fees are well known. Such tests typically assign weight primarily to the time spent and complexity of the case. In modern practice, the amount of time required to be spent is often a gauge of the extent of the complexities involved. Where the Tribunal is presented with copies of bills for services, or other appropriate evidence, indicating the time spent, the hourly billing rates, and a general description of the professional services rendered, its task need be neither onerous nor mysterious. The range of typical hourly billing rates is generally known and, as evidence before the Tribunal in various cases including this one indicates, it does not greatly differ between the United States and countries of Western Europe, where both Claimants and Respondents before the Tribunal typically hire their outside counsel. Just how much time any lawyer reasonably needs to accomplish a task can be measured by the number of issues involved in a case and the amount of evidence requiring analysis and presentation. While legal fees are not to be calculated on the basis of the pounds of paper involved, the Tribunal by the end of a case is able to have a fair idea, on the basis of the submissions made by both sides, of the approximate extent of the effort that was reasonably required.[197]

Judge Holtzmann also noted that in cases in which the party requesting legal costs is a business entity, there is a *prima facie* indication that the reasonableness test has been satisfied. According to Judge Holtzmann, "The pragmatic fact that a businessman has agreed to pay a bill, not knowing whether or not the Tribunal would reimburse the expenses, is a strong indication that the amount billed was considered reasonable by a reasonable man spending his own money, or the money of the corporation he serves."[198]

The *SD Myers* tribunal distinguished its approach to determining reasonable costs from that of Judge Holtzmann in some respects, finding that:

> the test is not how much the "successful" party actually spent; and the fact that the client has initiated or approved that expenditure is a matter only between the client and his attorney. The actual amount spent may have been "reasonable" in that sense. The test of reasonableness in the context of recovery from an "unsuccessful" party does not seek to second-guess these decisions, but looks to what amount

---

[195] *SD Myers, Inc* and *Government of Canada*, Final Award on Cost (December 30, 2002) (*Ad Hoc* Proceeding, 1976 UNCITRAL Rules, NAFTA Chapter Eleven), para 4.

[196] Leading commentators note that in most international arbitrations, tribunals that award costs in favor of the prevailing party consciously or unconsciously adopt Judge Holtzman's approach. N Blackaby and C Partasides, *Redfern and Hunter on International Arbitration*, n 19, 548.

[197] Judge Holtzmann's opinion in *Sylvania Technical Systems, Inc* (1983 Tribunal Rules) on legal costs is reprinted in its entirety in section 4(D)(1). In many cases before the Tribunal, the complexity of the issues has affected the amount of compensation awarded for legal costs. See, eg, *General Electric Co* (1983 Tribunal Rules), reprinted in section 4(D)(2)(a).

[198] *Sylvania Technical Systems, Inc* (1983 Tribunal Rules), reprinted in section 4(D)(1).

it would be "reasonable" to require the unsuccessful party to pay... *taking into account the circumstances of the case*.[199]

In this vein, the *Link-Trading* tribunal, applying the 1976 UNCITRAL Rules, found it reasonable to award the prevailing respondent only a portion of its claimed legal expenses. Whereas the respondent claimed US $138,352 in legal fees, the arbitral tribunal awarded only $20,000 "[c]onsidering that th[e] arbitration did not involve any hearing and that Respondent's counsel appeared at a late date in the proceedings and was required to make only limited submissions."[200]

(4) Comparison to the 1976 UNCITRAL Rules

Article 42 is substantially similar to corresponding Article 40 of the 1976 UNCITRAL Rules in purpose and function, despite the omission, addition, and relocation of certain provisions.

As explained in detail above, Article 42 incorporates the general standard of apportionment for the costs of arbitration originally contained in Article 40(1) of the 1976 UNCITRAL Rules, but without excluding from its scope the costs of legal representation and assistance, which were addressed separately under Article 40(2) of the 1976 UNCITRAL Rules. This amalgamation of standards, however, has little substantive effect on the operation of Article 42. Though the general standard proceeds from the principle that the costs of arbitration shall be borne by the unsuccessful party (whereas the original standard on the costs of legal representation and assistance does not), both standards are sufficiently flexible so as to afford the arbitral tribunal wide discretion in apportioning costs in any reasonable manner it deems appropriate, in light of the circumstances of the case.[201]

Article 42 omits the text of Article 40(3) of the 1976 UNCITRAL Rules concerning the fixing of costs in an order or an award in the case of termination of the proceedings or an award on agreed terms. This provision was no longer deemed necessary in light of revisions included in Article 39 of the 2010 UNCITRAL Rules, which require the arbitral tribunal to fix the costs of arbitration "in the final award and, if it deems appropriate, in another decision."[202]

Article 42 also no longer contains the text of Article 40(4) of the 1976 UNCITRAL Rules, as that provision was relocated to Article 40(3) of the 2010 UNCITRAL Rules, after being modified to expressly permit the tribunal to charge the parties for certain expenses in relation to interpretation, correction or completion of an award. The rationale for this change is discussed in section 2(B)(3).

C. Extracts from the Practice of Investment Tribunals

(1) Article 40(1) and (2) (1976 Rules)—General

Association of Service Industry Firms and *Service Industry Firm*, Award (May 27, 1991) (*Ad Hoc* Proceeding, 1976 UNCITRAL Rules, Contract), at 26–27, reprinted in (1992) XVII Ybk Commercial Arb 11, 26–27:

---

[199] *SD Myers Inc* and *Government of Canada*, Final Award on Costs (December 30, 2002) (*Ad Hoc* Proceeding, 1976 UNCITRAL Rules, NAFTA Chapter Eleven), para 40.

[200] *Link-Trading Joint Stock Co* (1976 Rules), para 95, reprinted in section 4(C)(2)(b).

[201] In addition, the words "or parties" was added after the words "the unsuccessful party" to take into account the possibility of multi-party arbitration under the Rules. UNCITRAL, UN Doc A/CN.9/WG.II/WP.151/Add.1, n 34, at 18, para 40.

[202] UNCITRAL, UN Doc A/CN.9/WG.II/WP.157/Add.2, n 83, at 9, para 26; UNCITRAL, 43rd Session, UN Doc A/CN.9/684, n 11, at 26, paras 117–19.

[30] According to Art. 40 of the [1976] UNCITRAL Arbitration Rules, costs of the arbitration shall in principle be borne by the unsuccessful party. However, this principle is not binding on the Tribunal when the parties have agreed on another regime. In the present case, the agreement to arbitrate contained in the Articles and Supplemental Agreements of claimant, provides that "all costs that may be incurred in connection with any such arbitration, including attorney's fees, shall be borne equally by the parties involved," except if the arbitrator(s) find "willful default" on the part of one party (Arts. 24.01(c), S-15.01(c)). Though the Tribunal by majority vote finds the principal claim to be justified, it is unanimous in rejecting the claim of "willful default." Accordingly, the Tribunal applies the basic understanding of Arts. 24.01(c) and S-15.01(c). Rather than attempting to evaluate and apportion all of the separate items of costs, the Tribunal finds that an equal sharing of the costs will be achieved in this case by each party bearing its own costs for attorney's fees, travel, experts, and other expenses, and sharing equally the costs of the arbitration set forth in [1976] UNCITRAL Rules Art. 38(a) and (b). The Tribunal finds that the preparation of the stenographic transcript of the hearing was useful to the proceeding and the preparation of the Award, and that the costs of the transcript should be shared equally by the parties.

Petrobart and *Kyrgyz Republic*, Award (February 13, 2003) (*Ad Hoc* Proceeding, 1976 UNCITRAL Rules, Concession Agreement), at 51–52:

Given the Arbitral Tribunal's decision to decline jurisdiction, Section 37, first paragraph, of the Swedish Arbitration Act must also be taken into account. It reads:

The parties shall be jointly and severally liable to pay reasonable compensation to the arbitrators for work and expenses. However, where the arbitrators have stated in the arbitral award that they lack jurisdiction to try the dispute, the party that did not request arbitration shall be liable to pay only to the extent that special circumstances so require.

Consequently, as far as the compensation to the arbitrators is concerned, it follows from the second sentence that Petrobart only is liable therefor, unless special circumstances require otherwise. The Arbitral Tribunal finds that no such special circumstances exist. The arbitrators have, when fixing their fees, taken all relevant circumstances into account. Consequently, Petrobart must pay the compensation to the arbitrators which totals US $231,504, including fees and disbursement ....

...

As far as other arbitration costs are concerned, they must also be paid by Petrobart, since Petrobart must be deemed to be the losing party in this dispute. In the view of the Arbitral Tribunal there are no other circumstances in this case which warrant a different apportionment of the costs ....

Econet Wireless Ltd and *First Bank of Nigeria*, et al, Award (June 2, 2005) (*Ad Hoc* Proceeding, 1976 UNCITRAL Rules, Contract), excerpt reprinted in (2006) XXXI Ybk Commercial Arb 49, 64–65:

[45] "While the Respondent has succeeded in making out its case on jurisdiction, the Claimant has demonstrated the complexity of the issues at hand, and has comported itself in a professional and cooperative manner at all times. More fundamentally, it is questionable whether the Tribunal has any authority to render a decision on costs (particularly the apportionment of legal fees) in the absence of an agreement to arbitrate before it. This consideration has led a number of tribunals operating under the UNCITRAL Rules to decline to shift costs to the losing party where the result is based on a finding that jurisdiction is lacking."

[46] "As a result, the Tribunal is not in a position to issue an order that Claimant reimburse the Respondents' legal and other costs incurred in participating in this arbitration."

(2) Article 40(1) and (2) (1976 Rules)—"Circumstances of the case"

(a) The success of the parties

Karaha Bodas Co LLC and *Perusahaan Pertambangan Minyak Dan Gas Bumi Negara*, Final Award (December 18, 2000) (*Ad Hoc* Proceeding, 1976 UNCITRAL Rules, Concession Agreement), at 45–46:

> 140. According to Article 40(1) of the [1976] UNCITRAL Arbitration Rules, "*The costs of arbitration shall in principle be borne by the unsuccessful party. However, the Arbitral Tribunal may apportion each of such costs between the parties if it determines that apportionment is reasonable, taking into account the circumstances of the case.*" In this case, the Respondents have been unsuccessful on the principle but a significant part of the quantum requested by the Claimant as damages has been denied by the Arbitral Tribunal. In such circumstances, the Arbitral Tribunal considers that it is reasonable that the Respondents bear 2/3 (two thirds) of the costs and expenses of the arbitration and the Claimant 1/3 (one third).

Pope & Talbot Inc and *Government of Canada*, Award on Costs (November 26, 2002) (*Ad Hoc* Proceeding, 1976 UNCITRAL Rules, NAFTA Chapter Eleven), at 4–5:

> 8. While the Investor was successful in that it obtained an award of damages from the Tribunal, that success was limited to one Article only of those upon which claims were made, and the sum awarded was less than 1% of the sum claimed at earlier stages in the arbitration, and about 20% of the sum claimed at the damages phase. The claims presented by the Investor under Articles 1102, 1106 and 1110 failed. On the merits, so did the claims based on Article 1105 in all respects other than in relation to the Verification Review Episode, which occurred after the arbitration proceedings had been commenced. Upon that basis, in summary, Canada submits that although technically the Investor may have "won" the arbitration it was in effect unsuccessful in all the major issues raised and for that reason should be required to pay the legal costs incurred by Canada.
>
> 9. It appears to the Tribunal that it is over simplistic to treat this case as one where the Investor "won" and therefore should recover costs, or where Canada "really won" having regard to the very limited degree of success of the Investor and should therefore recover costs. Rather it is necessary to consider a variety of aspects in order to arrive at a reasonable result.
>
> 10. In the first place, many issues were raised by each party by way of incidental pleading. Canada sought to have the case dismissed for lack of jurisdiction on three different bases—that the claim was not an "investment dispute", that the measures challenged did not "relate" to investment and that the Softwood Lumber Agreement was not a "measure". These all failed after consideration by the Tribunal of written submissions. Similarly Canada's attempt to have paragraphs 34 and 103 of the Statement of Claim struck out (the "Harmac" matter) failed. Similarly the attempt by Canada to have the "Super Fee" issue excluded failed. It is thus clear that Canada failed on important legal aspects of the case.
>
> 11. The matter of documentary production requires special attention. Canada made documentary requests, and to the extent that the Investor objected to production, that objection was in large measure upheld. Similarly, the Investor made requests for documents and some of Canada's objections were upheld. However, particular difficulties were created by Canada's treatment of the issue of confidentiality in the arbitral process on the one hand and its reluctance to produce documents on the grounds of cabinet confidence on the other. The Tribunal does not consider it necessary to rehearse these matters in detail. It suffices to observe that Canada simply chose not to comply with the directions of the Tribunal in either respect.

SD Myers, Inc and *Government of Canada*, Final Award on Costs (December 30, 2002) (*Ad Hoc* Proceeding, 1976 UNCITRAL Rules, NAFTA Chapter Eleven), at 7–8:

15. … As stated above, Article 40.1 of the [1976] UNCITRAL Rules places emphasis on "success" as a significant element in an arbitral tribunal's consideration of the apportionment of the arbitration costs. The logical basis for this policy appears to be that a "successful" claimant has in effect been forced to go through the process in order to achieve success, and should not be penalised by having to pay for the process itself. The same logic holds good for a successful respondent, faced with an unmeritorious claim.
16. "Success" is rarely an absolute commodity. In the first ("liability") stage of the arbitration SDMI established CANADA's liability as a result of the Tribunal's findings of breach of certain provisions of the NAFTA, but in fact lost on a number of other issues (for example, its claim in respect of alleged expropriation under Article 1110) that occupied a good deal of the Tribunal's time and effort, as well as that of CANADA's legal team. In summary, SDMI "succeeded" on liability, but not as to the full extent of its pleaded case.
17. In the second ("quantum") stage of the proceedings it might fairly be considered that SDMI was the unsuccessful party. At the start of the second stage, SDMI quantified its claim at US$70,921,421.00 to US$80,002,421.00. By August 2001, about a month before the second stage hearing, SDMI had reduced its claim to "not less than US $53,000,000.00." The ultimate award was a little over CAN$6,000,000.00, which is only a small percentage of the amount claimed, particularly bearing in mind that SDMI presented its claims in US$, not CAN$.
18. …The only benchmarks, in terms of "success", are (a) the results on the various liability issues and (b) the difference between the amounts claimed by SDMI and the amount ultimately awarded.
19. The Majority considers that neither party has achieved absolute "success" in the sense used in Article 40.1 of the [1976] UNCITRAL Rules, and that there must be some apportionment as mandated by that Rule. Overall, taking into account "the circumstances of the case" as provided for in Article 40.1 of the [1976] UNCITRAL Rules, the Majority considers that SDMI is entitled to recover a significant portion of its arbitration costs, but not all of them. The amount of compensation awarded was very substantially less than the amount claims, but some compensation was awarded.

…

33. The practices of international arbitral tribunals in the exercise of their discretion vary widely, as may be seen from the English language literature on the recovery of the costs of legal representation. Some arbitral tribunals are reluctant to order the losing party to pay the winner's representation costs, unless the winner has prevailed over a manifestly spurious or unmeritorious position taken by the loser. Other arbitral tribunals evidently feel that the winning party should not normally be left out of pocket in respect of the expenses incurred in enforcing its legal rights. Some adopt a median position, based perhaps on the idea that further proceedings to quantify the winner's costs claims would be an expensive exercise, or because neither party can be said to have been wholly successful. In any event, it is clear that the costs claimed must be demonstrably "reasonable" in order to be awarded.

Methanex Corp and *United States of America*, Award (August 3, 2005) (*Ad Hoc* Proceeding, 1976 UNCITRAL Rules, NAFTA Chapter Eleven), Part V, at 2–4:

5. The Tribunal determines that there is no compelling reason not to apply the general approach required by the first sentence of Article 40(1) of the [1976] UNCITRAL Rules. Although over the last five years, Methanex has prevailed on certain arguments and other issues against the USA, Methanex is the unsuccessful party both as to jurisdiction and the merits of its Claim. There is no case here for any apportionment under Article 40(1) of the [1976] Rules or other departure from this general principle. Accordingly, the Tribunal decides that Methanex as the unsuccessful party shall bear the costs of the arbitration.

6. It follows that Methanex shall be responsible for reimbursing the USA for all sums which the USA has deposited successively with the LCIA and ICSID as deposit-holder in connection with the costs of the arbitration together with interest accruing thereon, in the total amount of US $1,071, 539.21 (comprising US $1,050,000 by way of interim deposits and US $21, 539.21 as interest).

...

11. In this case, the USA has emerged as the successful party, as regards both jurisdiction and the merits. The Tribunal has borne in mind that, at the time of the Partial Award, it could have been argued that the USA had lost several important arguments on the admissibility issues; but over time the Partial Award does not affect the end-result of the dispute overall, as decided by this Final Award. Likewise, the issues on which the USA did not prevail in this Award were of minor significance. The Tribunal does not consider any apportionment appropriate under Article 40(2) of the [1976] UNCITRAL Rules.

12. Accordingly, the Tribunal decides that Methanex shall pay to the USA the amount of its legal costs reasonably incurred in these arbitration proceedings. The Tribunal assesses that amount in the sum claimed by the USA, namely US $2,989,423.76, which the Tribunal deems to be reasonable in the circumstances within the meaning of Article 38(e) of the [1976] UNCITRAL Rules. It is also far inferior to the sum claimed by Methanex in respect of its own legal costs, namely US $11-12 million.

International Thunderbird Gaming Corp and *United Mexican States*, Award (January 26, 2006) (ICSID administered, 1976 UNCITRAL Rules, NAFTA Chapter Eleven), at 72:

219. In the present case, the Tribunal has found that Mexico is the successful party, except on issues of jurisdiction and/or admissibility.

220. Accordingly, the Tribunal finds that Mexico may in principle recover an appropriate portion of the costs of its legal representation and assistance. In this regard, the amount of US$1,502,065.84 claimed by Mexico appears to be reasonable in light of the scope and length of the present arbitral proceedings. Mexico did not however prevail on all issues. In consideration of this fact, the Tribunal shall exercise its discretion and allocate the costs on a ¾-¼ basis. Accordingly, the Tribunal hereby determines that Thunderbird shall reimburse Mexico in the amount of US$1,126,549.38 in respect of the costs of legal representation for this arbitration.

221. As regards the fees of the arbitrators, the Arbitral Tribunal has determined the fees of the Arbitrators to be US$405,620.... For the same reasons as expressed in the preceding paragraph, the costs referred to in this paragraph shall be allocated between Thunderbird and Mexico on a ¾-¼ basis. Accordingly, the Arbitral Tribunal hereby determines that Thunderbird shall reimburse Mexico in the amount of US$126,313.02 in respect of the afore-mentioned deposits made by Mexico.

BG Group PLC and *Republic of Argentina*, Award (December 27, 2007) (*Ad Hoc* Proceeding, 1976 UNCITRAL Rules, UK-Argentina BIT), at 136:

458. BG brought a claim for US$238.1 million plus interest. This award finds for BG in the amount of US$185.3 plus interest. BG therefore prevailed with respect to 78% of the amount it claimed.

459. As to jurisdiction and admissibility, while this Tribunal has entered an affirmative finding on jurisdiction, it also concluded that BG does not have standing to bring "claims to money" and "claims to performance", or to assert other rights, derived from the MetroGAS License....

460. Under the circumstances and pursuant to Article 40 of the [1976] UNCITRAL Rules, the Tribunal finds that it is reasonable for Argentina to bear 70% of: (i) the costs of the arbitration as fixed in paragraph 462 below; and (ii) BG's legal fees and expenses.

Glamis Gold Ltd and *United States of America*, Award (June 8, 2009) (ICSID administered, 1976 UNCITRAL Rules, NAFTA Chapter Eleven), at 354:

> 833. The Tribunal notes that, under the [1976] UNCITRAL Rules, the costs of the arbitration, if not those of representation, would shift to Claimant as it has indeed failed with respect to both of its claims. The Tribunal finds, however, that Claimant raised difficult and complicated claims based in at least one area of unsettled law, and both Parties well argued their positions with considerable legal talent and respect for one another, the process and the Tribunal. The Tribunal therefore determines that Claimant shall bear two-thirds of the arbitral costs and Respondent shall bear the remaining one-third. Each Party shall bear its own costs of representation.

Chevron, et al and *Republic of Ecuador*, Final Award (August 31, 2011) (PCA administered, 1976 UNCITRAL Rules, US-Ecuador BIT), at 139–40:

> 375. The Tribunal is aware of a certain practice in investment treaty arbitration that each party bears its own costs and that the parties divide tribunal costs equally. That practice is not binding on this Tribunal, which prefers the more recent practice in investment arbitration of applying the general principle of "costs follow the event," save for exceptional circumstances, such as when concerns regarding access to justice are raised. That approach is the more compelling one in the present case which is governed by the [1976] UNCITRAL Arbitration Rules that expressly contemplate the rule of "costs follow the event" in Article 40(1) by its emphasis on "success" or lack thereof. This conclusion is reinforced by the fact that both sides in this case indeed argue that the unsuccessful side in this arbitration should have to bear the full amount of tribunal costs as well as the other side's costs of legal representation.
>
> 376. Nonetheless, in the present case the Claimants have been largely successful on jurisdiction and liability, but the Respondent's have been mostly successful on damages. The Tribunal finds therefore that there is no clearly successful Party and consequently decides that each side shall bear its own costs of legal representation and assistance (as well as the expenses of witnesses referred to in Article 38(d)) and divide tribunal costs evenly.

Ulysseas, Inc and *Republic of Ecuador*, Final Award (June 12, 2012) (PCA administered, 1976 UNCITRAL Rules, US-Ecuador BIT), at 110 (citation omitted):

> 364. Among the circumstances of the case that the Tribunal has taken into account is its finding that Claimant has been successful as to the jurisdiction of the Tribunal while Respondent has been successful as to the merits of the case.
>
> 365. Taking all the circumstances of the case into account, the Tribunal decides as follows. Each Party shall pay one half of the fees and expenses of the Tribunal and of the PCA and that Claimant shall bear its own costs for legal representation and assistance. Having examined each Party's costs, the Tribunal has determined that the amount of Respondent's costs for legal representation and assistance is reasonable. Claimant shall reimburse Respondent's costs for legal representation and assistance in the amount of USD 2.000,000.00 (two million United States dollars). This amount shall be paid within 30 (thirty) days following receipt of the Award, failing which simple interest shall run on such amount at LIBOR (annual), as requested by Respondent.

(b) The conduct of the parties

Himpurna California Energy Ltd and *PT (Persero) Perusahaan Listruik Negara*, Final Award (May 4, 1999) (*Ad Hoc* Proceeding, 1976 UNCITRAL Rules, Concession Agreement), reprinted in (2000) XXV Ybk Commercial Arb 13, 106–07:

> [388] Under Art. 40(1) of the [1976] UNCITRAL Rules, the costs of arbitration "shall in principle be borne by the unsuccessful party." Although the same article goes on to specify that

the Arbitral Tribunal has discretion to apportion the costs, the arbitrators see no reason to do so in this case. PLN's management of its contractual relationship with the claimant was poor. No matter the gravity of PLN's overall financial plight, there is no excuse for its failure to articulate its position clearly to the claimant, which was kept in a state of uncertainty and did not even receive responses to its requests for meetings and its offers of substantive concessions to alleviate PLN's plight. It is unacceptable for PLN, a large State utility, to plead that it was too confused or overwhelmed to inform the claimant whether or when it was prepared to pay a certain proportion of the price, or a price reflecting a certain rate of currency conversion, or even to give some concrete indication of the time when it would be making a proposal for an adjustment of contractual terms it was no longer fulfilling. (This was of course a contract which on any analysis is of great magnitude, and should have been given the fullest attention.) To recover its claim, even in the limited amount upheld by the Arbitral Tribunal, the claimant had no choice but to bring these proceedings. There is no reason to deviate from the general principle that the unsuccessful party should bear the costs.

Ronald S Lauder and *Czech Republic*, Final Award (September 3, 2001) (*Ad Hoc* Proceeding, 1976 UNCITRAL Rules, US-Czech Republic BIT), reprinted in (2002) 14(3) World Trade & Arb Materials 35, 106–07:

318. Among the circumstances the Tribunal has taken into account is its finding that the Respondent, at the very beginning of the investment by the Claimant in the Czech Republic, breached its obligations not to subject the investment to discriminatory and arbitrary measures when it reneged on its original approval of a capital investment in the licence holder and insisted on the creation of a joint venture. Furthermore, various steps were taken by the Media Council, especially, but not only, the 15 March 1999 letter to CET 21. Although the Arbitral Tribunal came to the conclusion that such acts did not constitute a violation of the Treaty obligations of the Respondent, the Claimant bona fide could nevertheless feel that he had to commence these arbitration proceedings. Furthermore, the behaviour of the Respondent regarding the discovery of documents, which the Claimant could rightly feel might shed more light on the acts of the Respondent, needs to be mentioned in this context.

CME Czech Republic BV and *Czech Republic*, Partial Award (September 13, 2001) (*Ad Hoc* Proceeding, 1976 UNCITRAL Rules, Netherlands-Czech Republic BIT), reprinted in (2003) 14(3) World Trade & Arb Materials 109, 284–85:

620. In assessing what costs of the Claimant to be refunded by the Respondent are acceptable and reasonably incurred, the Tribunal further considered inter alia that the Claimant initiated these arbitration proceedings after having initiated and partly carried through the Lauder vs. The Czech Republic UNCITRAL Arbitration Proceedings which, in essence, deal with the same dispute. The parties used, as the Tribunal was informed, the work product of their advisors and the witness statements of these parallel UNCITRAL Arbitration Proceedings. The Respondent expressly stated in its Statement of Costs that the Respondent was able to use to a large extent the pleadings and witness statements originally drafted for the use by the Respondent in the Lauder vs. Czech Republic UNCITRAL Arbitration.
621. The Arbitral Tribunal took account of this situation and also the fact that the Claimant and its ultimate shareholder, by initiating two parallel UNCITRAL Treaty Proceedings had, as the Claimant expressed it, "*two bites of the apple*", and thereby enlarged costs and risks. It is, therefore, reasonable to decide that the Respondent, although this Partial Award is wholly unfavourable to it, shall be required to refund to Claimant only a portion of the Claimant's legal fees and disbursements, which portion is determined by the Arbitral Tribunal being US $750,000.
[For the remainder of the Tribunal's decision on costs, see above Section 2(D).]

Link-Trading Joint Stock Co and *Dept of Customs Control of the Republic of Moldova* (April 18, 2002) (*Ad Hoc* Proceeding, 1976 UNCITRAL Rules, US-Moldova BIT), at 29–30:

> 95. Considering that this arbitration did not involve any hearing and that Respondent's counsel appeared at a late date in the proceedings and was required to make only limited submissions, the Tribunal considers that it would be reasonable to award to Respondent an amount for its counsel fees and expenses of USD20,000. The fees of the legal expert appear to be reasonable at USD2,200. There is no substantiation for Respondent's other expenses, and these expenses are therefore denied. The total amount of party costs awarded to Respondent shall therefore be USD 22,200.
>
> 96. The Tribunal has received a total amount of USD120,000 solely from Claimant as a security for the Tribunal's fees and disbursements in the arbitration. At the time of the Award on Jurisdiction, the Tribunal had incurred fees and expenses in the amount of USD40,000, which was paid to the Tribunal by way of an advance. The time incurred by the Tribunal since then has significantly exceed what the Tribunal reasonably anticipated when the security deposit was set. This was due principally to the unsolicited further submission of Claimant on December 18, 2001 which necessarily required a further responsive pleading from Respondent. This being said, the Tribunal has decided not to award fees and expenses beyond the amount of the security deposit, but to allocate the deposit as follows in full satisfaction of its fees and expenses, to wit:
>
> | | Expenses | Fees | | Totals |
> | --- | --- | --- | --- | --- |
> | J.M. Hertzfeld, Esq. | USD 2,200 | USD 51,174 | (45%) | USD 53,374 |
> | Prof. I. V. Buruiana | USD 1,080 | USD 31,273 | (27.5%) | USD 32,353 |
> | Prof. I. S. Zykin | USD 3,000 | USD 31,273 | (27.5%) | USD 34,273 |
> | | USD 6,280 | USD 113,720 | | USD 120,000 |
>
> For these costs the parties are liable jointly and severally. As between the parties they shall ultimately be borne by Claimant. They will be covered out of the advance.

Pope & Talbot Inc and *Government of Canada*, Award on Costs (November 26, 2002) (*Ad Hoc* Proceeding, 1976 UNCITRAL Rules, NAFTA Chapter Eleven), at 5–6:

> 11. ... However, particular difficulties were created by Canada's treatment of the issue of confidentiality in the arbitral process on the one hand and its reluctance to produce documents on the grounds of cabinet confidence on the other. The Tribunal does not consider it necessary to rehearse these matters in detail. It suffices to observe that Canada simply chose not to comply with the directions of the Tribunal in either respect.
>
> ...
>
> 13. One other matter of concern to the Tribunal is that Canada, despite requests by the Investor and by the Tribunal, did not produce any Travaux Preparatoires in relation to the relevant Articles of NAFTA, in particular 1105, until virtually the end of the arbitration, having previously asserted they did not exist.
>
> 14. Of equal concern to the Tribunal is the fact that certain documents were withheld from the Investor and the Tribunal until the actual hearing on breach of Article 1105, which had a direct and material impact upon the matters in dispute (see Award on Merits Phase II paras 177–179).
>
> 15. The Investor made an application at the end of the damages hearing to change the place of arbitration. It was rejected because of the very late stage at which it was made. The issues raised were important and difficult.
>
> 16. The Investor put before the Tribunal certain letters passing between the parties with a view to arriving at a settlement. Canada objected to these having been produced but in the event produced some further material. The Tribunal has not found this material particularly helpful.

SD Myers, Inc and *Government of Canada*, Final Award on Costs (December 30, 2002) (*Ad Hoc* Proceeding, 1976 UNCITRAL Rules, NAFTA Chapter Eleven), at 9–10, 16–17:

> 20. ... The conduct of the Disputing Parties during the course of the proceedings is certainly a matter to be taken into account in assessing the apportionment to be made in respect of costs. Contrary to SDMI's assertion, the Majority does not consider it appropriate to take into account the conduct of CANADA that gave rise to the determination of liability for the purpose of the Tribunal's consideration of the apportionment of costs.... .
>
> [The Tribunal addressed SDMI's claims for compensation regarding expenses incurred for court reporting at the hearings, an on-site visit by party-appointed experts, and hotel cancellation charges for a postponed hearing.]
>
> ...
>
> 26. The postponement of the hearing scheduled for early September 2001 was the direct result of the late delivery by SDMI of a significant quantity of evidentiary material. This material should have been produced by SDMI at a much earlier stage, pursuant to the Tribunal's procedural order.... CANADA has not advanced a claim in respect of these costs, but submits that SDMI's portion should not be paid by CANADA. The Majority agrees.
>
> ...
>
> 46. So far as conduct of the parties may properly be taken into account, the Majority considers that this must be conduct in the initiation of the proceedings, or while they are in progress. Both sides contend that the conduct of the other during the arbitration added to their costs.
>
> 47. SDMI cannot fairly be criticised for starting the arbitration, as there was no evidence of any meaningful offer of compensation by CANADA prior to its commencement. SDMI was obliged to initiate the arbitration to obtain redress. It may be that SDMI "over-litigated" the case; but CANADA responded in kind, and in any event it would not be fair for the Tribunal (or the Majority) to reach such a conclusion for the purposes of apportionment of costs without an extensive enquiry into the relevant facts.... Success on contested procedural issues was divided, perhaps not equally, but at least not on a sufficiently one-sided basis to justify taking this factor into account in the award in respect of costs.

Econet Wireless Ltd and *First Bank of Nigeria*, et al, Award (June 2, 2005) (*Ad Hoc* Proceeding, 1976 UNCITRAL Rules, Contract), excerpt reprinted in (2006) XXXI Ybk Commercial Arb 49, 64–65:

> [45] "While the Respondent has succeeded in making out its case on jurisdiction, the Claimant has demonstrated the complexity of the issues at hand, and has comported itself in a professional and cooperative manner at all times. More fundamentally, it is questionable whether the Tribunal has any authority to render a decision on costs (particularly the apportionment of legal fees) in the absence of an agreement to arbitrate before it. This consideration has led a number of tribunals operating under the UNCITRAL Rules to decline to shift costs to the losing party where the result is based on a finding that jurisdiction is lacking."
>
> [46] "As a result, the Tribunal is not in a position to issue an order that Claimant reimburse the Respondents' legal and other costs incurred in participating in this arbitration."

Merrill & Ring Forestry LP and *Government of Canada*, Award (March 31, 2010) (ICSID administered, 1976 UNCITRAL Rules, NAFTA Chapter Eleven), at 106:

> 270. The parties have duly submitted their respective claims for costs. The Tribunal is of the view that the Investor had in some respect plausible arguments and indeed raised question of particular interest for the Tribunal to consider both under NAFTA and international law. Professional competence characterized the submissions, allegations and arguments of both parties at all times.

271. Because of this, the Tribunal concludes that each party should bear equally the costs of the arbitration and that each shall pay for its own costs....

HICEE BV and *Slovak Republic*, Partial Award (May 23, 2011) (PCA administered, 1976 UNCITRAL Rules, Netherlands-Slovak Republic BIT), at 56–57 (citation omitted):

> The criterion to be applied by the Tribunal [under Article 40 of the 1976 UNCITRAL Rules] is accordingly that of reasonableness, taking into account the circumstances of the case. Having considered those circumstances with care, the Tribunal finds that the issues raised in the present phase of this arbitration were difficult, and in some respects novel; that the Parties were animated by a sense of practicality and economy in agreeing to hive off the Treaty Interpretation Issue for preliminary decision, and that their sound judgement in that respect has been vindicated by events; that the Parties are particularly to be commended for their cooperation with the Tribunal and for the conciseness and precision of their written and oral arguments. That being so, the Tribunal sees no justification for the blanket application of a costs rule in favour of the successful Party, as in the first sentence of Article 40(1). Exercising its discretion under the Rule, it decides instead that the Claimant will meet 6/10 of the costs of the arbitration, which the Tribunal hereby certifies as amounting to €461,686.44, but that each Party will bear the costs of the preparation and presentation of its own case.

Jan Oostergetel, et al and *Slovak Republic*, Final Award (April 23, 2012) (*Ad Hoc* Proceeding, 1976 UNCITRAL Rules, Netherlands-Slovak Republic BIT), at 89 (citation omitted):

337. The UNCITRAL Rules thus adopt the rule "costs follow the event" with respect to the costs of the arbitration and confer broad powers to the Tribunal in connection with the Parties' costs.
338. With respect to the arbitration costs and VAT (as opposed to the Parties' legal and other costs), the Claimants did not succeed on their claims. Therefore, they shall bear the arbitration costs and VAT expenses advanced by the Respondent. As stated above, the arbitration costs advanced by the Respondent amount to EUR 422'396.46. The surplus of advances, i.e. EUR 37'767.53, will be returned to the Respondent Therefore, the Tribunal directs the Claimants to pay to the Respondent the balance, i.e., EUR 384'628.93 (EUR 422'396.46 less EUR 37'767.53). Additionally, the Tribunal directs the Claimants to reimburse the VAT expenses advanced by the Respondent, I.e. EUR 34'992.75.
339. On the other hand, the costs of legal representation and other costs incurred by the Parties call for a number of observations. First, the discrepancy between the amounts expended is striking. One party has invested a lot into this case, the other much less. Each one made its choices and bears the consequences. The Tribunal does not consider that one should necessarily pay for the choice of the other. Second, the deficiencies in the presentation of the Claimants' case have made the resolution of this dispute unusually burdensome for the Tribunal and presumably also for the Respondent. At the same time, the Tribunal stresses the Parties' cooperative attitude throughout the arbitration. Third, in the exercise of their discretion in cost matters, investment tribunals often rule that each party bears its own costs. Sometimes, more under ICSID than UNCITRAL Rules, they even decide that the arbitration costs should be borne equally, even where one party has undoubtedly prevailed. In light of Article 40(1) and of the clear outcome of this case, the Tribunal does not find this latter solution appropriate, which is the reason why it determined that the Claimants will bear the entirety of the arbitration costs.
340. The situation is different for the party costs for which the Tribunal enjoys wide discretion under Article 40(2). Having pondered all the elements set out in the preceding paragraph, the Tribunal considers it fair that the Claimants pay to the Respondent an amount of EUR 2'000'000 as contribution to party costs. This is in the range of the amount which the Claimants expended for the presentation of their own case.

(c) The nature of the dispute resolution mechanism

Robert Azinian, et al and *United Mexican States*, Award (November 1, 1999) (ICSID administered, 1976 UNCITRAL Rules, NAFTA Chapter Eleven), at 35:

125. The claim has failed in its entirety. The Respondent has been put to considerable inconvenience. In ordinary circumstances it is common in international arbitral proceedings that a losing claimant is ordered to bear the costs of the arbitration, as well as to contribute to the prevailing respondent's reasonable costs of representation. This practice serves the dual function of reparation and dissuasion.

126. In this case, however, four factors militate against an award of costs. First, this is a new and novel mechanism for the resolution of international investment disputes. Although the Claimants have failed to make their case under NAFTA, the Arbitral Tribunal accepts, by way of limitation, that the legal constraints on such causes of action were unfamiliar. Secondly, the Claimants presented their case in an efficient and professional manner. Thirdly, the Arbitral Tribunal considers that by raising issues of defective performance (as opposed to voidness ab initio) without regard to the notice provisions of the Concession Contract, the Naucalpan Ayuntamiento may be said to some extent to have invited litigation. Fourthly, it appears that the persons most accountable for the Claimants' wrongful behaviour would be the least likely to be affected by an award of costs; Mr. Goldenstein is beyond this Arbitral Tribunal's jurisdiction, while Ms. Baca—who might as a practical matter be the most solvent of the Claimants—had no active role at any stage.

127. Accordingly the Arbitral Tribunal makes no award of costs, with the result that each side bears its own expenditures, and the amounts paid to ICSID are allocated equally.

International Thunderbird Gaming Corp and *United Mexican States*, Separate Opinion to Award (December 2005) (ICSID administered, 1976 UNCITRAL Rules, NAFTA Chapter Eleven), at 108–11 (citations omitted):

139. ... The only concept under which this so far well-established rule has not been observed or a different treatment suggested is for "manifestly spurious or unmeritorious" positions taken by the loser, unprofessional conduct and significant breach of good-faith in arbitration. There are a good reasons for this approach which has so far been intuitively, but not yet explicitly appreciated by tribunals in thrall to the attitudes prevalent in commercial arbitration: Investment arbitration is not a reciprocally agreed and structured method of dispute resolution. It is a unilateral right of investors – not mirrored by a reciprocal government right – to claim against alleged misconduct by governments under an investment treaty. It is in substance comparable at most to national and international judicial review of administrative conduct – rather than to the reciprocal "contract" model of commercial arbitration. Governments can not sue investors because investors can not breach the treaty disciplines such as "expropriation", discrimination or fair and equitable treatment. They focus exclusively on governmental action targeting foreign investors. Governments have made this asymmetric right available because it helps them to attract capital and improves their internal governance, and the perception of their governance quality internationally.

140. This principle of cost allocation in international judicial review of government conduct is also applied in GATT litigation. There has been a formal proposal to award litigation costs to winning developing countries because of the prohibitively high costs of WTO litigation; one can see this as a similar concept to the idea that investors – in particularly smaller companies – should not be penalized for complaining about host state breach of treaty investment protection obligations; the common idea is that for under-resourced claimants access to justice is illusionary if the cost (and risk) of litigation is prohibitive....

142. Imposing the risk of government attorney costs on losing investors in effect undermines the very purpose of such treaties; it raises the litigation risk in factual situations which are as a rule ambiguous, confused and contradictory to a prohibitive level, in particularly for smaller

companies for whom litigation risk is high and where a government enjoys significant superiority in terms of expertise, experience and resources available for defense against NAFTA arbitration.... The approach to costs in this award suggests that investment arbitration is only for the very large companies, leaving out entrepreneurs with initiative, willingness to take (sometimes perhaps recklessly) risk and who may not have the same "international corporate style" appeal of the "men in dark suits". But there is no indication that this was the intention of the negotiators of such treaties. The highly unusual cost award thus casts a "chill" over attempts by junior companies to rely on the NAFTA's investment protection regime and makes that recourse – very high-risk anyway – doubly prohibitive because of the now added cost risk. In effect and in practice, it makes recourse to independent justice for smaller companies prohibitive.

International Thunderbird Gaming Corp and *United Mexican States*, Award (January 26, 2006) (ICSID administered, 1976 UNCITRAL Rules, NAFTA Chapter Eleven), at 70–71 (citation omitted):

214. It is also debated whether "the loser pays" (or "costs follow the event") rule should be applied in international investment arbitration. It is indeed true that in many cases, notwithstanding the fact that the investor is not the prevailing party, the investor is not condemned to pay the costs of the government. The Tribunal fails to grasp the rationale of this view, except in the case of an investor with limited financial resources where considerations of access to justice may play a role. Barring that, it appears to the Tribunal that the same rules should apply to international investment arbitration as apply in other international arbitration proceedings.

215. It may be added that Article 1135 of the NAFTA explicitly contemplates the possibility for a tribunal to award costs: "[a] tribunal may also award costs in accordance with the applicable arbitration rules." The treaty does not contain any limitation in regard of the award of costs.

216. The parties to the present case have themselves each claimed an award of costs (*see* Notice of Arbitration at ¶34 and SoD at ¶372). Although Thunderbird has contended that it is rarely appropriate for costs to be awarded to an unsuccessful NAFTA claimant, it has at the same time recognized: "[n]o Nafta provisions exist which would modify the application of [Articles 38 and 40 of the [1976] UNCITRAL] arbitration rules. Accordingly, it lies within the discretion of this Tribunal to award costs in the manner it determines to be the most appropriate and reasonable in the circumstances." (*see* PSoC at p.121)

217. The Tribunal is mindful of other NAFTA awards such as the decision in *Azinian v. Mexico*, in which the tribunal considered four factors for deciding that the losing investor need not pay the costs of the respondent (state party):

> The claim has failed in its entirety. The Respondent has been put to considerable inconvenience. In ordinary circumstances it is common in international arbitral proceedings that a losing claimant is ordered to bear the costs of the arbitration, as well as to contribute to the prevailing respondent's reasonable costs of representation. This practice serves the dual function of reparation and dissuasion.
>
> In this case, however, four factors militate against an award of costs. First, this is a new and novel mechanism for the resolution of international investment disputes. Although the Claimants have failed to make their case under the NAFTA, the Arbitral Tribunal accepts, by way of limitation, that the legal constraints on such causes of action were unfamiliar. Secondly, the Claimants presented their case in an efficient and professional manner. Thirdly, the Arbitral Tribunal considers that by raising issues of defective performance (as opposed to voidness *ab initio*) without regard to the notice provisions of the Concession Contract, the Naucalpan Ayuntamiento may be said to some extent to have invited litigation. Fourthly, it appears that the persons most accountable for the Claimants' wrongful behaviour would be the least likely to

be affected by an award of costs; Mr. Goldenstein is beyond this Arbitral Tribunal's jurisdiction, while Ms. Baca – who might as a practical matter be the most solvent of the Claimants – had no active role at any stage.

218. With respect to the first factor, investment arbitration in general and NAFTA arbitration in particular have become so well known and established as to diminish their novelty as dispute resolution mechanisms. Thus, this factor is no longer applicable when considering apportionment of costs in international investment disputes. As for the second factor, although it may be said that the Parties here presented their case in an efficient and professional manner, the Tribunal does not find it a decisive factor for awarding costs in deviation of the general principle. Finally, the third and fourth *Azinian* factors are not applicable in the present case.

Canfor, Tembec & Terminal Forest and *United States*, Joint Order on Costs and Termination (July 19, 2007) (ICSID administered, 1976 UNCITRAL Rules, NAFTA Chapter Eleven), at 66:

139. The tribunal is aware of a certain practice in investment arbitrations that each party bears its own costs and the parties bear the fees and costs of the tribunal and administering arbitral institution equally. That practice is not binding on this Tribunal, which prefers the more recent practice to apply also in investment arbitration the general principle of "costs follow the event," save for exceptional circumstances such as issues concerning access to justice.[144] That approach is the more compelling in the present case which is governed by the [1976] UNCITRAL Arbitration Rules that expressly contemplate the rule of "costs follow the event" in Article 40(1) by its emphasis on "success" or lack thereof.

...

144 *See Thunderbird*, n. 143 *supra*, at 214. *See also* U.S. District Court for the District of Columbia, *International Thunderbird Corporation v. Mexico*, Civil Action 06-00748, 14 February 2007, rejecting the petition to set aside the Award of 26 January 2006, at 3: "Undeterred by the rule's [i.e., Article 40(1)-(2) of the [1976] UNCITRAL Rules] plain language, Thunderbird cites prior NAFTA and UNCITRAL arbitrations for the proposition that precedent has narrowed the rule's wide scope. Nothing in those decisions, however, persuades the court that they have meaningfully narrowed the discretion granted in the rule. Even if Thunderbird had identified such precedent, its argument would still fail, as Thunderbird has not shown that the panel expressly recognized that precedent as controlling and nonetheless refused to apply it," available online at: http://ita.law.uvic.ca/documents/Thunderbird-setaside.pdf; *Generation Ukraine, Inc v. Ukraine*, ICSID Case No ARB/00/9, Award, 16 September 2003, at ¶ 24.8, available on line at: http://ita.law.uvic.ca/documents/GenerationUkraine_000.pdf; *Fireman's Fund Insurance Company v. Mexico*, ICSID Case No ARB(AF)/02/01, Final Award, 17 July 2006, at ¶ 221, available online at: http://ita.law.uvic.ca/documents/FiremansFinalAwardRedacted.pdf; *Telenor Mobile Communications AS v. Hungary*, ICSID Case No ARB/04/15, Award, 13 September 2006, at ¶ 107: "Though aware of a common practice in ICSID arbitrations for the parties to bear their own costs and bear the costs of ICSID and the tribunal equally regardless of the outcome of the case, this Tribunal is among those who favour the general principle that costs should follow the event," available online at: http://ita.law.uvic.ca/documents/Telenorv.HungaryAward_000.pdf.

Romak SA and *Republic of Uzbekistan*, Award, (November 26, 2009) (PCA administered, 1976 UNCITRAL Rules, Switzerland-Uzbekistan BIT), at 64–65 (citations omitted):

249. Firstly, it should be noted that the Respondent has prevailed entirely as a matter of jurisdiction. The question is whether, as a consequence, the Claimant should bear more than half of the arbitration costs and/or pay the Respondent's legal fees and expenses.

250. The Arbitral Tribunal has reviewed a number of arbitral awards in investment treaty disputes. These awards indicate that, in this field, a general trend has developed that arbitration

costs should be equally apportioned between the Parties, irrespective of the outcome of the dispute. One of the reasons for this, as stated in several awards, is that investment treaty tribunals are called upon to apply a novel mechanism and substantive law to the resolution of these disputes (see for example, *Azinian v. Mexico*, *Tradex v. Albania*, and *Berchader v. Russia*). Thus, the initiation of a claim that is ultimately unsuccessful is more understandable than would be the case in commercial arbitration, where municipal law applies. With respect to the present dispute, to the Tribunal's knowledge, there has never been an investment treaty claim decided outside the ICSID system in relation to the enforcement of an arbitral award. Other cases, such as *Saipem*, share similar factual elements with the present dispute, but offered no direct analogy.

251. Clearly, the general practice in investment treaty arbitration disfavoring the shifting of arbitration costs against the losing party does not always apply. In particular, deficiencies in the presentation of a case or obstructive behaviour, which leads to an unjustified increase of the costs of the proceedings, not infrequently justify apportioning the arbitration costs in another way.

252. In the present case, neither of the Parties has presented its case in a way justifying the shifting of arbitral costs against it. To the contrary, counsel for both Parties worked ably, diligently and efficiently in defense of their clients' respective interests. Nor are there any other reasons that support such apportionment. Each of the Parties shall therefore be liable to pay half of the arbitration costs. Each Party shall also bear its own costs for legal representation and other costs incurred in connection with presenting its case.

ICS Inspection and Control Services Ltd and *Argentine Republic*, Award on Jurisdiction (February 10, 2012) (PCA administered, 1976 UNCITRAL Rules, UK-Argentina BIT), at 112–113:

338. In light of the Tribunal's conclusion that it has no jurisdiction over any of the Claimant's claims, there is a clearly successful party, the Respondent, and a clearly unsuccessful party, the Claimant. Given this outcome, the Tribunal finds no reason to deviate from the presumption in Article 40(1) and consequently awards the costs of arbitration to the Respondent. The Claimant shall thus reimburse the Respondent the amount of EUR 180,743.61 in respect of the costs of arbitration.

339. With respect to the costs of legal representation and assistance as defined in Article 38(e), Article 40(2) of the UNCITRAL Arbitration Rules provides that the arbitral tribunal, taking into account the circumstances of the case, is free to determine which party shall bear such costs or may apportion such costs between the parties if it determines that apportionment is reasonable. Article 40(2) thus grants near total discretion to an arbitration tribunal.

340. The traditional position in investment treaty arbitration, in contrast to commercial arbitration, has been to follow the normal practice under public international law (as exemplified in Article 9(5) of the Treaty) that the parties shall bear their own costs of legal representation and assistance. The Tribunal is aware that a number of investment treaty tribunals have opted instead to apply the principle of awarding costs of legal representation and assistance to the prevailing party as with the costs of arbitration. The Tribunal accepts that this developing practice may be appropriate in some cases, but is not convinced that it should be adopted as a rule and prefers to follow the public international law practice unless a more holistic assessment of the circumstances of the case justifies a departure from that practice.

341. In this case, the Tribunal notes once again that the Respondent has been the prevailing party. Nonetheless, the Claimant's arguments can hardly be said to have been unreasonable, having been previously adopted by other tribunals even with respect to the Treaty at issue in this case. As such, while firmly convinced of its interpretation of Article 3 of the Treaty, the Tribunal is aware of the difficulty posed by the inconsistent jurisprudence on

the interpretation of MFN clauses in investment treaties and their application to jurisdictional issues.
342. The Tribunal further notes that it has found for the Respondent and against the Claimant on only one of the various objections to jurisdiction that were raised by the Respondent and argued by the Parties, albeit one that disposes of the entirety of the claims. The Tribunal has made no finding on these other issues and shall not presume that the Claimant's arguments were without merit and would not have succeeded. The Respondent's success is therefore not absolute.
343. The Tribunal thus, despite its finding against the Claimant, decides that the Parties shall bear their own costs of legal representation and assistance.

D. Extracts from the Practice of the Iran-US Claims Tribunal

(1) Tribunal Rules (1983), Article 40(1) and (2)—General

Sylvania Technical Systems, Inc and *Government of the Islamic Republic of Iran*, Award No 180–64–1 (June 27, 1985), Separate Opinion of Howard M Holtzmann (June 27, 1985), reprinted in 8 Iran-US CTR 329, 331–33 (1985-I):

Article 38, paragraph 1(c) [of the 1983 Tribunal Rules], quoted above, establishes two standards to be applied by the Tribunal with respect to the successful party's costs for legal representation and assistance. First, such costs must have been claimed during the arbitral proceedings. That, of course, means that the claim must have been timely made. Second, such costs are to be fixed "only to the extent that the arbitral tribunal determines that the amount of such costs is reasonable."

While Article 38, paragraph 1(c) thus points in the direction that the claimed, reasonable costs of the successful party for lawyers' fees will be borne by the losing party, Article 40, paragraph 2 introduces an element of discretion by providing that "the arbitral tribunal, taking into account the circumstances of the case, shall be free to determine which party shall bear such costs or may apportion such costs between the parties if it determines that apportionment is reasonable." Professor Sanders in his authoritative commentary on the [1976] UNCITRAL Rules contrasts this with the provisions governing other costs of arbitration and notes that "not only the reasonableness of the amount claimed is subject to the supervision and decision of the arbitrators, but also whether costs for legal representation or assistance will be awarded at all." P Sanders, Commentary on UNCITRAL Arbitration Rules, Yearbook Commercial Arbitration, Vol. II at 172, 216 (1977). In this respect, he observes that the rule as to lawyers' fees "deviat[es] from the general rule expressed in para 1" of Article 40, which provides that the costs of arbitration shall in principle be borne by the losing party. *Id.* at 217. Professor Sanders explains that this discretion was provided for in the [1976] UNCITRAL Rules because the drafters were preparing rules that could be used in a wide variety of disputes, including not only complex cases but also those involving very simple issues where no legal representation would be necessary. Thus, the circumstances in which that discretion was intended to be exercised are limited. Professor Sanders concludes that the question of whether the unsuccessful party should bear the winner's legal costs "depends on the decision of the arbitrators whether they deem legal assistance necessary under the circumstances of the case." *Id.* In this connection, he notes that services of lawyers are likely to be needed in complex international cases. *Id.*

In summary, the Tribunal Rules establish four tests to be applied by the Tribunal in determining the amount of costs for lawyers' fees and who should bear them:

1. Were such costs claimed in the arbitration?
2. Was employing lawyers necessary in this case?
3. Are the amounts of such costs reasonable?
4. Are there circumstances in this case that make it reasonable to apportion such costs?

Application of the first two tests is relatively simple. Whether costs were claimed, and, if so, which costs, can be readily determined from the record in each case. As to the second test, given the types of legal and factual issues that arise in the cases before this Tribunal, generally involving issues of both public and private international law, the necessity of employing lawyers is largely a foregone conclusion.

The third test—whether the amount of costs claimed is "reasonable"—imposes a more difficult task upon the Tribunal. A test of reasonableness is not, however, an invitation to mere subjectivity. Objective tests of reasonableness of lawyers' fees are well known. Such tests typically assign weight primarily to the time spent and complexity of the case. In modern practice, the amount of time required to be spent is often a gauge of the extent of the complexities involved. Where the Tribunal is presented with copies of bills for services, or other appropriate evidence, indicating the time spent, the hourly billing rate, and a general description of the professional services rendered, its task need be neither onerous nor mysterious. The range of typical hourly billing rates is generally known and, as evidence before the Tribunal in various cases including this one indicates, it does not greatly differ between the United States and countries of Western Europe, where both Claimants and Respondents before the Tribunal typically hire their outside counsel. Just how much time any lawyer reasonably needs to accomplish a task can be measured by the number of issues involved in a case and the amount of evidence requiring analysis and presentation. While legal fees are not to be calculated on the basis of the pounds of paper involved, the Tribunal by the end of a case is able to have a fair idea, on the basis of the submissions made by both sides, of the approximate extent of the effort that was reasonably required.

Nor should the Tribunal neglect to consider the reality that legal bills are usually first submitted to businessmen. The pragmatic fact that a businessman has agreed to pay a bill, not knowing whether or not the Tribunal would reimburse the expenses, is a strong indication that the amount billed was considered reasonable by a reasonable man spending his own money, or the money of the corporation he serves. That is a classic test of reasonableness.

The fourth test to be considered in awarding costs is whether circumstances exist that might make it appropriate to apportion costs. This test should be applied in a straightforward manner. As noted above, when one party wins a claim and another wins a counterclaim, apportionment is warranted. Similarly, some cases involve quite separate and independent causes of action, such as where a contractor claims under two separate contracts involving different building projects. If such a claimant were to be successful as to one project but lose as to the other, an apportionment of its total legal fees would be appropriate. Where no such circumstances exist the concept of apportionment is not applicable.

Amoco International Finance Corp and *Government of the Islamic Republic of Iran*, et al, Case No 56, Chamber Three, Order of October 8, 1986:

According to the general practice of the Tribunal, documents relating to the costs of the proceedings, which are submitted at or reasonably following the final Hearing are not normally rejected as untimely filed, since costs cannot be assessed until a very late stage.

Consequently, the Tribunal does not see any reason for rejection of the Claimant's affidavits.

(2) Tribunal Rules (1983), Article 40(1) and (2)—"Circumstances of the case"

(a) The success of the parties

McCollough & Co, Inc and *Ministry of Post, Telegraph and Telephone*, et al, Award No 225–89–3 (April 22, 1986), Separate Opinion of Charles N Brower (April 22, 1986), reprinted in 11 Iran-US CTR 35, 44 (1986-II):

30. I would have awarded all of these costs, which appear to be reasonable, against Respondents. Even accepting the Award's granting, albeit to a limited extent, of one of NIOC's counterclaims might justify no apportioning costs as regards NIOC claims and counterclaims, I feel strongly that PTT should be required at least to pay all of Claimant's costs related to it.

31. ...Claimant has prevailed one hundred percent against PTT.... All of PTT's counterclaims have been categorically and rather summarily rejected.

Agrostruct Intl, Inc and *Iran State Cereals Org*, et al, Award No 358–195–1 (April 15, 1988), reprinted in 18 Iran-US CTR 180, 197 (1988-I):

> 55. Agrostruct seeks legal and translation costs in the total amount of $72,798.87. In view of the general considerations outlined in *Sylvania*, ... at pp. 35–38, and taking into account that (1) Agrostruct was awarded approximately 25 percent of the amount claimed, (2) all Counterclaims were dismissed, and (3) the Respondents incurred translation costs for providing an English translation of the Contract in an estimated amount of $1,000, which Agrostruct must bear, the Tribunal determines that $9,000 is a reasonable amount of costs to be paid to Agrostruct.

Electronic Systems Intl, Inc and *Ministry of Defence of the Islamic Republic of Iran*, et al, Award No 430–814–1 (July 28, 1989), reprinted in 22 Iran-US CTR 339, 355 (1989-II):

> 63. In view of the fact that the Claimant has successfully discharged the burden of proving only approximately one eighteenth of its total Claim, and in view of the costs incurred by the Respondent in defending itself, the Tribunal considers that the Respondent should be granted U.S. $5000 as costs of arbitration, and that this amount should be deducted from the amount awarded to the Claimant.

Rockwell Intl Systems, Inc and *Government of the Islamic Republic of Iran*, Award No 438–430–1, (5 Sep 1989), Separate Opinion of Howard M Holtzmann, (September 5, 1989), reprinted in 23 Iran-US CTR 217, 229 (1989-III) (footnote omitted):

> 29. As indicated in my Separate Opinion in *Sylvania*, the Tribunal Rules should be applied to allocate legal costs of arbitration based on the degree of success that the prevailing party achieves. *See id.* In my view, the degree of Rockwell's success is most appropriately measured by reference to the fact that it was awarded approximately U.S.$12 million of the U.S.$19 million it sought for work performed under the Contracts—i.e. about 63%. Also, it prevailed 100% in defending against approximately U.S.$150 million of counterclaims. In addition, Rockwell unsuccessfully sought U.S.$17 million for lost profits. As noted above, decisions in prior IBEX cases had already made it clear since 1985 that lost profits were not payable under the IBEX contracts because of the particular provisions of the contracts. Accordingly, it appears that Rockwell's counsel realistically devoted only very limited time to this issue; for example, less than 3 pages of its 85 page Hearing Memorial were directed toward the lost profits claim. From this it is reasonable to infer that almost all of the time represented by the U.S.$928,036 which the Award finds that Rockwell incurred in legal fees and costs was spent on issues other than the lost profits issue. Somewhat similarly, the counterclaims that Rockwell successfully defended against involved largely issues for which Tribunal practice was already well-established in prior IBEX cases. Taking all of these factors into consideration, I believe Rockwell is entitled to legal costs of U.S.$555,000, i.e. approximately 60% of the legal costs it claims. Surely, the legal work performed, as well as the results achieved, warrant an award of at least that amount.

Development and Resources Corp and *Government of the Islamic Republic of Iran*, et al, Award No 485–60–3 (June 25, 1990), reprinted in 25 Iran-US CTR 20, 109–10 (1990 II):

> Taking into account that D&R prevailed in all claims, while none of the counterclaims was successful, the Tribunal finds that costs should be awarded to D & R in the amount of $45,000.

General Electric Co and *Government of the Islamic Republic of Iran*, et al, Award No 507–386–1 (March 15, 1991), reprinted in 26 Iran-US CTR 148, 183 (1991-I):

> In deciding the proper amount of such costs to be awarded the Tribunal has considered the nature and outcome of the proceedings including the complexity of the case and the extent to

which the prevailing party has been successful in its claims. *See Sylvania*, Award No 180–64–1 at pp. 35–38, *reprinted in* 8 Iran-U.S. C.T.R. at 323–24. In this Case, involving extensive legal and factual issues, the Claimant has prevailed on three of its four claims, but failed on its largest claim. All of the counterclaims have been dismissed. Applying these factors, the Tribunal determines that $40,000 is a reasonable amount of GE's costs to be paid by the Respondents.

(b) The conduct of the parties

Ultrasystems, Inc and *Islamic Republic of Iran*, Award No 27–84–3 (March 4, 1983), reprinted in 2 Iran-US CTR 100, 113 (1983-I):

> Ultrasystems has claimed its arbitration costs in the amount of $111,800. Although the amount lacks some specificity, it would appear that close to $30,000 were expended on non attorney fee costs (travel and translation costs) which are covered by Article 38 1(a) and (b) of the Tribunal Rules. In determining reasonable attorney's fees the Tribunal takes into account the fact that extra costs were incurred by the Claimant through Isiran's failure to provide information as to its status until a late stage of the proceedings.
>
> Applying Articles 38 and 40 of the [1983] Tribunal Rules, the Tribunal determines that the costs of arbitration shall be apportioned in such a way that Isiran shall bear Ultrasystems costs in the amount of $70,000.

Ministry of National Defence and *United States*, Award No 247-B59/B69–1 (August 15, 1986), reprinted in 12 Iran-US CTR 33, 36 (1986-III):

> In dismissing the claim against BMY, the Tribunal considers that an award of costs of arbitration in favour of BMY is appropriate in the circumstances. While it is not the Tribunal's practice to award costs in "official" claims as between the respective Governments, this particular Respondent is a United States national. MOD filed these claims after the rendering of the decision in Case No A-2, which conclusively disposed of the question whether jurisdiction existed over claims against such nationals. BMY has, nonetheless, been constrained to take part in the proceedings and to attend a pre-hearing conference. It has asked for costs in the amount of U.S. $55,153.04. In awarding costs in ordinary, as opposed to official claims, the Tribunal has been guided by the principles of reasonableness described in Sylvania Technical Systems, Inc and Islamic Republic of Iran, Award No 180–64–1 (27 June 1985). Since some of the same considerations apply with equal force to the present Case, the Tribunal makes an award of U.S. $25,000.

International Schools Services, Inc and *Islamic Republic of Iran,* et al, Award No 290–123–1 (January 29, 1987), reprinted in 14 Iran-US CTR 65, 80 (1987-I):

> 49. This Chamber has outlined its approach to costs in *Sylvania*.... There is an additional factor in the instant case, however. As the Interlocutory Award makes clear, ... there was no justification for NDIO's failure to join in the request filed by ISS for an Award on agreed terms in accord with the provisions of the 1981 MoU, an agreement which should have settled this Case some five years ago. Thus, the Respondent's failure to abide by the settlement agreement has caused the expenditure of far more costs of arbitration than would otherwise have been necessary.... Taking into account the history of the proceeding, ... the Tribunal awards $50,000 in costs.

Sedco, Inc and *National Iranian Oil Company,* et al, Award No 309–129–3 (July 7, 1987), reprinted in 15 Iran-US CTR 23, 185 (1987-II):

> 586. In addition, Claimant showed in its application of 21 May 1985 that it incurred $11,602 in unnecessary costs related to a Hearing scheduled for 14 and 15 May 1985 which Respondents failed without cause to attend and which therefore was rescheduled in June 1985. The Tribunal agrees that Claimant is entitled to reimbursement of extra costs which it was forced

to bear because of Respondents' actions. $9,567 of the amount requested is already reflected in the non-legal costs awarded above at para 585. The balance, $2,035 in legal fees, is therefore awarded as special costs.

Near East Technological Services USA, Inc and *Islamic Republic of Iran Air Force*, Award No 406–845–1 (January 9, 1988), reprinted in 21 Iran-US CTR 13, 19 (1989-I):

22. The Tribunal is mindful of the fact that the Respondent's task of preparing pleadings and evidence was made more difficult by the lack of coherence in the Claimant's written presentation of its case. This is reflected in the Tribunal's conclusions as to jurisdiction. It appears appropriate in the circumstances to award costs of $5,000 to the Respondent in accordance with Article 40 of the [1983] Tribunal Rules, and to make such award against the named United States legal entity, Near East Technological Services Ltd.

Houston Contracting Co and *National Iranian Oil Co*, et al, Award No 378–173–3 (July 22, 1988), reprinted in 20 Iran-US CTR 3, 128 (1988-III):

478. The Claimant and the Respondents also seek an award of costs. The Claimant has submitted evidence to show that it has incurred costs (other than legal fees) of U.S. $140,451.80 in connection with these proceedings, together with an element of U.S. $6,800 in respect of legal fees incurred as a direct result of the two-day postponement of the Hearing (see paragraph 7, above). The Claimant also requests that "a reasonable counsel fee...be assessed by the Tribunal" to recompense it for legal fees.
479. The Tribunal awards the Claimant U.S. $46,800 costs of arbitration.

Ronald E Chamness and *Government of the Islamic Republic of Iran*, et al, Award No 488–380–3 (August 9, 1990), reprinted in 25 Iran-US CTR 172, 176 (1990-II):

16. ... In the present Case, the Tribunal takes into consideration the Claimant's failure to address the Respondents' consistent objections to the Tribunal's jurisdiction. The Tribunal also notes the timing of the Claimant's request for a decision on the basis of the documents and the insufficient explanation of his failure to appear or to have himself represented at the Hearing. The Tribunal decides to award to IEI U.S. $8,000 in legal fees and U.S. $9,000 in costs incurred for attending the Hearing....

Behring Intl, Inc and *Islamic Republic of Iran Air Force*, et al, Award No 523–382–3 (29 Oct 1991), reprinted in 27 Iran-US CTR 218, 245–46 (1991-II):

72. Because of the Claimant's inappropriate conduct, particularly its failure to respond to the Tribunal's Orders of 30 April 1986, 13 August 1986, 24 January 1987 and 17 February 1988, the Respondents were forced to incur higher attorney's fees and costs than otherwise would have been necessary. The Tribunal, therefore, finds it reasonable to award the Respondents U.S. $60,000 as estimated compensation for such extra costs.

Dadras Intl, et al and *Islamic Republic of Iran*, et al, Award No 567–213/215–3 (November 7, 1995), reprinted in 31 Iran-US CTR 127, 205 (1995):

280. In determining the appropriate amount of costs to award, the Tribunal has on several occasions taken into account a party's conduct during the arbitral proceedings. Specifically, the Tribunal has held that a party is entitled to the reimbursement of extra costs that it was forced to bear because of the other party's inappropriate conduct.... .
281. The procedural history of these Cases shows that the Respondents have caused considerable disruption of the arbitral process and have unnecessarily occupied the resources of this Tribunal by pursuing their unfounded allegations of forgery and belatedly proffering the unconvincing testimony of Mr. Golzar. These actions have caused the Claimants to incur

substantial additional costs associated with obtaining legal advice on and responding to late-filed post-Hearing documents, as well as expenses associated with preparing for and attending a Second Hearing in these Cases. The Tribunal considers that these circumstances call for an award of costs against the Respondents more substantial than the amount customarily awarded by this Chamber of the Tribunal to a successful party.

282. Consequently, and bearing in mind that the Claimant in Case No 213 has ultimately been successful in its claim for work performed, the Tribunal determines that the Claimant in Case No 21 shall be awarded costs of arbitration from the Respondents in the amount of U.S. $75,000.00, and that the Respondents in that Case should bear their own costs.

Vera-Jo Miller Aryeh, et al and *Islamic Republic of Iran*, Award No 581–842/843/844–1 (May 22, 1997), reprinted in 33 Iran-US CTR 272, 342–43 (1997):

253. The Claimants claim fees and expenses for a total amount of $2,149,065.41. Of this amount, $252,769.81 and GBP £200,165.75 are for fees and costs which have been generated by the Respondent's forgery allegations. The Claimants argue that, in view of the nature of these allegations, the Tribunal should award the Claimants these fees and expenses in full.
254. Considering the outcome of these Cases, the Tribunal, referring to *Sylvania, supra*, pp. 35–36, 8 Iran-U.S. C.T.R. 323–324 and *Dadras, supra*, paras 280–282, determines that the Claimants shall be awarded costs of arbitration in the amount of $200,000.

5. Deposit of Costs—Article 43

A. Text of the 2010 UNCITRAL Rule[203]

Article 43 of the 2010 UNCITRAL Rules provides:

1. The arbitral tribunal, on its establishment, may request the parties to deposit an equal amount as an advance for the costs referred to in article 40, paragraphs 2 (a) to (c).
2. During the course of the arbitral proceedings the arbitral tribunal may request supplementary deposits from the parties.
3. If an appointing authority has been agreed upon or designated, and when a party so requests and the appointing authority consents to perform the function, the arbitral tribunal shall fix the amounts of any deposits or supplementary deposits only after

---

[203] Corresponding Article 41 of the 1976 UNCITRAL Rules provides:

1. The arbitral tribunal, on its establishment, may request each party to deposit an equal amount as an advance for the costs referred to in article 38, paragraphs (a), (b) and (c).
2. During the course of the arbitral proceedings the arbitral tribunal may request supplementary deposits from the parties.
3. If an appointing authority has been agreed upon by the parties or designated by the Secretary-General of the Permanent Court of Arbitration at The Hague, and when a party so requests and the appointing authority consents to perform the function, the arbitral tribunal shall fix the amounts of any deposits or supplementary deposits only after consultation with the appointing authority which may make any comments to the arbitral tribunal which it deems appropriate concerning the amount of such deposits and supplementary deposits.
4. If the required deposits are not paid in full within thirty days after the receipt of the request, the arbitral tribunal shall so inform the parties in order that one or another of them may make the required payment. If such payment is not made, the arbitral tribunal may order the suspension or termination of arbitral proceedings.
5. After the award has been made, the arbitral tribunal shall render an accounting to the parties of the deposits received and return any unexpended balance to the parties.

consultation with the appointing authority, which may make any comments to the arbitral tribunal that it deems appropriate concerning the amount of such deposits and supplementary deposits.

4. If the required deposits are not paid in full within 30 days after the receipt of the request, the arbitral tribunal shall so inform the parties in order that one or more of them may make the required payment. If such payment is not made, the arbitral tribunal may order the suspension or termination of the arbitral proceedings.

5. After a termination order or final award has been made, the arbitral tribunal shall render an accounting to the parties of the deposits received and return any unexpended balance to the parties.

B. Commentary

(1) The request for deposits

According to Article 43, the arbitral tribunal may request monetary deposits from the parties, as advances against those items of cost outlined in Article 40(2)(a), (b), and (c), respectively the fees of the arbitrators, their travel and other expenses, and the costs of expert advice and other assistance required by the tribunal.[204] The parties bear the financial burden of providing deposits equally, making proportional contributions based on the number of parties involved.[205] Where the arbitration is administered by an arbitral institution, the institution typically can provide useful information regarding the projected amount of deposits required.[206]

Article 43, subparagraphs (1) and (2) respectively envision possible payment of deposits at two stages in the arbitration: "on its establishment" and "[d]uring the course of the arbitral proceedings." At the inception of the arbitral process, deposits typically are necessary to make the arbitral tribunal operational.[207] Few arbitrators or appointing authorities will work without assurances that their fees and expenses will be paid.[208] Funds to cover

---

[204] The UNCITRAL drafters considered a proposal to add a provision to Article 41 of the 1976 UNCITRAL Rules that would authorize the appointing authority to request deposits to cover its fees and expenses. The proposal was rejected ultimately on grounds that the appointing authority could always condition its services on advance payment of anticipated fees and expenses. See UN GAOR, 31st Session, Supp No 17, UN Doc A/31/17, n 14, para 225, reprinted in (1976) VII UNCITRAL Ybk 66, 81.

[205] See, eg, *Guaracachi America Inc* (2010 Rules); *SD Myers, Inc* (1976 Rules); and *Chemtura Corp* (1976 Rules); all reprinted in section 5(C). See also *Shahin Shaine Ebrahimi*, (1983 Tribunal Rules), reprinted in section 5(D). This rule applies both to requests for initial deposits and supplementary deposits and does not limit the arbitral tribunal's power to apportion costs in an uneven manner, if necessary. See section 4.

In general, the Iran–US Claims Tribunal has followed the practice of requiring equal deposits from the parties. See, eg, *Richard D Harza* (1983 Tribunal Rules), Award dated February 17, 1983, reprinted in section 5(D). However, Article 41(2) of the 1983 Tribunal Rules of Procedure, reprinted in Appendix 5, does not require equal contributions with regard to "expert advice" and "other special assistance," as outlined in Article 38(1)(a). In some cases, the Tribunal has required only one party to cover these particular costs. See *Chas T Main Intl, Inc* and *Khuzestan Water and Power Authority*, et al, Award No ITL 23–120–2 (July 27, 1983), reprinted in 3 Iran-US CTR 156, 166–67 (1983-II) (claimant only); *Behring Intl, Inc* and *Iranian Air Force*, Decision No DEC 27–382–3 (December 19, 1983), reprinted in 4 Iran-US CTR 89, 92–3 (1983-III) (respondents only). Such a decision may be warranted when the party making the deposit was primarily responsible for or substantially benefited from the services for which the deposits were collected. See J van Hof, *Commentary on the UNCITRAL Arbitration Rules*, n 41, 317.

[206] See generally *UNCITRAL Notes on Organizing Arbitral Proceedings*, UNCITRAL, UN GAOR, 51st Session, para 29, UN Doc A/51/17 (1996), reprinted in (1996) XXVII UNCITRAL Ybk 45, 50.

[207] See P Sanders, "Commentary on UNCITRAL Arbitration Rules," n 26, 192–3.

[208] President William H Taft's participation as sole arbitrator in the *Tinoco Arbitration* is a notable exception:

administrative support, such as secretaries, stenographers, and interpreters, must also be secured.[209] If the parties' initial deposits prove to be insufficient or the circumstances of the arbitration impose new financial demands, Article 43(2) allows the arbitral tribunal to request supplemental deposits at any time during the arbitral proceedings. In this regard, the drafters of the Rules foresaw two situations in which the arbitral tribunal may require supplemental fees and expenses: first, where the arbitrators decide that they need "the testimony of experts reporting to them on particular issues" and, second, "where the proceedings take longer than expected."[210]

The degree to which the arbitral tribunal is involved in managing deposited funds may depend on whether the arbitration is administered by an arbitral institution. In administered arbitration, the institution typically offers services to assist in these areas. In unadministered arbitration, such services are not available. For this reason, the UNCITRAL Notes on Organizing Arbitral Proceedings caution that in cases of unadministered arbitration "matters such as the type and location of the account in which the [deposit] money will be kept and how the deposits will be managed" should be clarified.[211] Indeed, the parties have a right not only to a refund of any unused funds at the end of the arbitration, but also to any excess interest generated by their deposits. To avoid financial complications at the end of arbitration, good practice is for the arbitral tribunal to establish a new bank account (of a type agreed upon by the parties) for use exclusively in the particular dispute between the parties.[212]

It is common practice for investor–state tribunals applying the UNCITRAL Rules to demand significant deposits to cover an array of anticipated costs.[213] The Iran–US Claims Tribunal has requested deposits in only limited circumstances as the operation costs of the Tribunal, eg salaries and expenses of the Members and staff, are funded by annual contributions by the party governments.[214] The Tribunal has requested deposits to cover the costs of Tribunal-appointed experts[215] and "other special assistance" required by the Tribunal,

---

So far as the payment of the expenses of the arbitration is concerned, I know of none for me to fix. Personally, it gives me pleasure to contribute my service in the consideration, discussion and decision of the questions presented. I am glad to have the opportunity of manifesting my intense interest in the promotion of the judicial settlement of international disputes, and accept as full reward for any service I may have rendered, the honor of being chosen to decide these important issues between the high contracting parties.

Aguilar-Amory and Royal Bank of Canada Claims (*Tinoco Arbitration*) (*Great Britain* and *Costa Rica*) (October 18, 1923).

[209] See *Gulf Associates* (1983 Tribunal Rules), reprinted in section 5(D) (requiring equal deposits from the parties for stenographic costs prior to a hearing).

[210] UN Doc A/CN.9/112/Add.1, n 13,, reprinted in (1976) VII UNCITRAL Ybk 166, 181 (Commentary on Draft Article 34(2)). See also P Sanders, "Commentary on UNCITRAL Arbitration Rules," n 26, 193. For examples from the practice of the Iran–US Claims Tribunal, see *Starrett Housing Corp,* et al and *Government of the Islamic Republic of Iran,* et al, ITL Award No 32–24–1 (December 19, 1983), reprinted in 4 Iran-US CTR 122, 158 (1983-III).; *Chas T Main Intl, Inc* and *Khuzestan Water and Power Authority,* et al, Award No ITL 35–120–2 (March 16, 1984), reprinted in 5 Iran-US CTR 185, 185–6 (1984-I).

[211] See *UNCITRAL Notes*, n 206, at para 30.

[212] See, eg, *Guaracachi America, Inc* (2010 Rules); and *ICS Inspection and Control Services, Inc* (1976 Rules); both reprinted in section 5(C).

[213] See, eg, *Canfor Corp* (1976 Rules), reprinted in section 5(C) (ordering the payment of $300,000 in deposits "tak[ing] into consideration the significant amount in dispute, the complexity of the subject matter and the amount of time likely to be spent by the arbitrators"). See also *Guaracachi America, Inc* (2010 Rules) (ordering an initial deposit of EUR 100,000), reprinted in section 5(C).

[214] See section 2(B)(4).

[215] See, generally, Chapter 20 on experts.

namely language interpretation[216] and stenographic recording costs[217] at scheduled hearings.

(2) Consultation with the appointing authority

Pursuant to Article 43(3), the appointing authority serves a consultative function in order to protect the parties against unreasonable demands for deposits by the arbitral tribunal.[218] If the appointing authority agrees to a party's request for consultation, then the arbitral tribunal must confer with the appointing authority before fixing the amount of the deposit. Upon consultation, the appointing authority may provide the arbitral tribunal any comments "which it deems appropriate" concerning the pending request for a deposit. The practical utility of the consultative mechanism has been doubted. Professor Sanders, for example, questions whether the appointing authority would ever agree to provide comments on a matter that falls well within the arbitral tribunal's discretion.[219] He further doubts whether such comments would be disclosed to the parties to allow them any useful leverage against the arbitral tribunal.[220] There is no evidence that corresponding Article 41(3) of the 1976 UNCITRAL Rules has ever been applied. The Iran–US Claims Tribunal appears to have found little value in Article 41(3) of the 1983 Tribunal Rules, choosing not to adopt this provision, or any modification of it, in its Rules of Procedure.[221]

(3) Failure to make requested deposits

A party's refusal to make deposits threatens to derail the arbitral proceedings. Article 43(4) establishes a procedure to address this problem, if it arises. If one or both parties fail to make a deposit *en toto* within 30 days of receiving a formal request,[222] the arbitral tribunal must inform the parties of the deficiency and allow one of the parties to pay the outstanding balance.[223] Such a rule accounts for a party that has already made a deposit or believes it has "a strong interest in seeing that the arbitration proceeds to a conclusion."[224] The arbitral tribunal also benefits from a rule that denies a recalcitrant party the ability to scuttle the arbitration simply by refusing to make a deposit. If, however, neither party wishes to cover the unpaid portion of the deposit, the arbitral tribunal is empowered to suspend or terminate the arbitral proceedings.[225] In the event of termination or suspension lasting more

---

[216] See *Starrett Housing Corp* (1983 Tribunal Rules), Order of December 18, 1986, reprinted in section 5(D) (ordering deposits to be made as advance for Swedish language interpretation costs).

[217] See *Aram Sabet* (1983 Tribunal Rules); and *Gulf Associates, Inc* (1983 Tribunal Rules); both reprinted in section 5(D).

[218] This problem is less acute in administered arbitrations because the arbitral institution is typically responsible for requesting and collecting monetary deposits. UNCITRAL, 8th Session, UN Doc A/CN.9/97, n 35, reprinted in (1975) VI UNCITRAL Ybk 163, 180.

[219] See P Sanders, *The Work of UNCITRAL on Arbitration and Conciliation*, n 7, 22.

[220] P Sanders, *The Work of UNCITRAL on Arbitration and Conciliation*, n 7, 22.

[221] See Article 41 of the Tribunal Rules of Procedure.

[222] See Chapter 10 on notice and the calculation of time periods.

[223] See, eg, *Himpurna California Energy Ltd* (1976 Rules), reprinted in section 5(C). See also *Link-Trading Joint Stock Co* and *Dept of Customs Control of the Republic of Moldova*, Final Award (April 18, 2002) (Ad Hoc Proceeding, 1976 UNCITRAL Rules, US-Moldova BIT), at para 96 (recognizing that it has received funds solely from the claimant).

[224] UNCITRAL, 9th Session, Addendum 1 (Commentary), UN Doc A/CN.9/112/Add.1, n 13, reprinted in (1976) VII UNCITRAL Ybk 166, 181 (Commentary on Draft Article 34(3)); UNCITRAL, 9th Session, UN Doc A/CN.9/9/C.2/SR.13, n 46, at 7, para 46 (Comment by Mr Sanders, Special Consultant).

[225] One rationale that might support the provision is "that arbitrators [are] engaged under a contract of service, a term of which would be that the deposits in question were made. If such deposits [are] not forthcoming, the arbitrators would be entitled not to perform their contract." See UN Doc A/10017, n 35, para 225, reprinted in (1975) VI UNCITRAL Ybk 24, 45.

than a reasonable period of time, the arbitral tribunal must refund the balance of any unexpended deposits to the appropriate parties.[226]

The Iran–US Claims Tribunal modified corresponding Article 41(4) of the 1976 UNCITRAL Rules in two ways. Tribunal Rule 41(3) eliminates the 30-day time limit for acting against a delinquent party, permitting the Tribunal to proceed at its own pace "within the time fixed by the arbitral tribunal." In one of the few documented applications of Article 41(3) of the 1983 Tribunal Rules, the Tribunal granted the respondent, Iran, an additional month to comply with a request for deposit.[227] In addition to authorizing a suspension or termination of the arbitral proceedings in case of default, Article 41(3) of the 1983 Tribunal Rules permits the Tribunal to "take such action to permit continuation of the proceedings as is appropriate under the circumstances of the case." To our knowledge, the Tribunal has never resorted to such action.

(4) The right to an accounting and the return of unexpended deposits

The arbitral tribunal holds the parties' deposits of money in trust to satisfy certain costs of arbitration. The unexpended portions of these deposits, when no longer required, must be returned to the parties in amounts proportional to the relative percentage of contribution, plus interest. Article 43(5) requires the return of unexpended monies "[a]fter a termination order or final award has been made." The provision clarifies that unexpended monies should be returned any time the arbitration concludes with a remaining balance of deposits, even where the arbitration does not terminate with an award.[228] Namely, Article 43(5) applies with equal force to cases in which an arbitration is terminated by a tribunal order, in accordance with Articles 30(1)(a) (claimant's failure to file a statement of claim), 36(2) (other grounds for termination), and 43(4) (failure to make deposits). The arbitral tribunal is also required to render an accounting of all money received through deposits. Such an accounting may include: a statement of the amount of deposits obtained from a particular party; the portion of that deposit that was applied to the arbitral tribunal's work; the particular items on which the deposit, or a portion of the deposit, was spent; and any relevant account information, such as the name of the bank, the account number, and the average applicable rate of interest during the period of deposit.[229]

The Iran–US Claims Tribunal has modified corresponding Article 41 of the 1976 UNCITRAL Rules in a number of respects. These modifications include the establishment of a formal auditing program requiring the production and transmission of monthly, quarterly, and annual financial statements to the Full Tribunal and to the party governments, and annual audits of the Tribunal's books, conducted by outside certified accountants and reported to both the Full Tribunal and to the party governments.[230] Further, at the request of either of the governments' agents, the annual audit may be reviewed by an "Audit Committee" composed of "three professionally qualified persons," one appointed by each Agent and one by the President of the Tribunal.[231] Upon completion of its review, the Audit

---

[226] See discussion of Article 43(5) in section 5(B)(4).
[227] *Richard D Harza* (1983 Tribunal Rules), Award of November 21, 1983, reprinted in section 5(D).
[228] The arbitral tribunal may also wish to return unexpended deposits before making an award. See *Bechtel, Inc* (1983 Tribunal Rules), reprinted in section 5(D).
[229] See, eg, *Ulysseas, Inc* (1976 Rules); and *ICS Inspection and Control Services, Inc* (1976), para 335; both reprinted in section 5(C).
[230] See 1983 Rules of Procedure of the Iran–US Claims Tribunal, reprinted in Appendix 5.
[231] 1983 Rules of Procedure of the Iran–US Claims Tribunal.

Committee is required to submit a report containing its evaluation of the annual audit to the Full Tribunal, the Secretary-General of the Tribunal, and to the party governments.[232]

(5) Comparison to the 1976 UNCITRAL Rules

Article 43 is virtually identical to corresponding Article 41 of the 1976 UNCITRAL Rules. Minor revisions were made to better accommodate multi-party arbitration. Additionally, in clarifying the time frame of an accounting and return of unexpended deposits to the parties, Article 43(5) includes the phrase "[a]fter a termination order or final award has been made," whereas Article 41(5) of the 1976 UNCITRAL Rules contains the words "[a]fter the award has been made." This change merely clarifies that an accounting and return of unexpended deposits is also required in the event the arbitral tribunal terminates the arbitral proceedings, pursuant to Article 30(1)(a) or Article 36, without rendering a final award.

C. Extracts from the Practice of Investment Tribunals

Himpurna California Energy Ltd and *PT (Persero) Perusahaan Listruik Negara*, Final Award (May 4, 1999) (*Ad Hoc* Proceeding, 1976 UNCITRAL Rules, Concession Contract reprinted in (2000) XXV Ybk Commercial Arb 13, 107:

> PLN declined to pay its share of the deposit called for by the Arbitral Tribunal, which was therefor entirely funded by the claimant. Accordingly PLN is ordered to reimburse the claimant for the costs mentioned in [387] above, i.e. the sum of US$722,846. The amount of US$12,500, i.e. one half of the US$25,000 which PLN unnecessarily advanced on account of Dr. Sanyal's second appearance (which did not eventuate), is deducted from this sum, yielding a total amount of US$710,346....

SD Myers, Inc and *Government of Canada*, Final Award on Costs (December 30, 2002) (*Ad Hoc* Proceeding, 1976 UNCITRAL Rules, NAFTA Chapter Eleven), at 11:

> 28. The Disputing Parties paid the initial Article 41 deposits and the supplementary deposits in equal shares. SDMI claims that is had paid a total of CAN$647.666.60 by way of deposits to the account held by the Tribunal. Some interest has been earned on the deposit, for the benefit of the Disputing Parties, and this will be taken into account later when the Tribunal's final account is presented to the Disputing Parties.
>
> ...
>
> 30. In addition to the payments noted above, each Disputing Party has each given an undertaking to the Tribunal to pay its half share of the balance of amounts due to the Tribunal, the Tribunal having notified them that the amount remaining on deposit will not be sufficient to cover its unbilled fees and expenses.....

Canfor Corp and *United States of America*, Procedural Order No 3 (November 13, 2003) (ICSID administered, 1976 UNCITRAL Rules, NAFTA Chapter Eleven), at 1:

> 3. In accordance with Article 41 of the UNCITRAL Arbitration Rules and pursuant to paragraph 25 of the Terms of Agreement, the Arbitral Tribunal hereby sets the amount of the advance on costs of this arbitration at USD 300,000.
> 4. In determining this amount, the Arbitral Tribunal has taken into consideration the significant amount in dispute, the complexity of the subject matter and the amount of time likely to be spent by the arbitrators.
> 5. The above-mentioned amount shall be equally shared by the Parties, who shall pay an advance on costs of USD 150,000 to Shearman & Sterling LLP, Paris, Account No [account information omitted].

---

[232] 1983 Rules of Procedure of the Iran–US Claims Tribunal.

Chemtura Corp and *Government of Canada*, Procedural Order No 1 (January 21, 2008) (PCA administered, 1976 UNCITRAL Rules, NAFTA Chapter Eleven), at 5:

14. Without prejudice to the final decision of the Arbitral Tribunal regarding costs, the disputing parties agree to share equally advance payments to the Tribunal. Upon the issuance of an award, the Arbitral Tribunal may apportion the costs of the arbitration between the disputing parties if it determines apportionment is reasonable under the circumstances of the award.
15. Within 30 days from the issuance of this Order, each disputing party shall pay an initial advance for costs in the amount of USD 100,000 to be placed with the PCA in the following account: [Account information omitted.]
16. The PCA will review the adequacy of the deposit from time to time and, at the request of the Tribunal, may invite the disputing parties to make supplementary deposits in accordance with Article 41(2) of the [1976] UNCITRAL Arbitration Rules.

Guaracachi America, Inc, et al and *Plurinational State of Bolivia*, Terms of Appointment and Procedural Order No 1 (December 9, 2011) (PCA administered, 2010 UNCITRAL Rules, US-Bolivia BIT/UK-Bolivia BIT), at 7:

10.1 In order to assure sufficient funds for the Tribunal's fees and expenses, the Parties shall establish an initial deposit of EUR 100,000 (EUR 50,000 from each side), to be deposited, within the reasonable time (which will be determined by the Tribunal following consultation with the Parties) required for the State to dispatch funds according to procedure, by wire transfer to the following Administering Authority account:

Bank:	ING Bank N.V.
	Schenkkade 65
	2519 AS The Hague
	The Netherlands
Account number:	[Information omitted]
IBAN:	[Information omitted]
BIC:	[Information omitted]
Name of beneficiary:	Permanent Court of Arbitration
Reference:	GUA-BO

10.2 The Administering Authority will review the adequacy of the deposit from time to time and, at the request of the Tribunal, may invite the Parties to make supplementary deposits.
10.3 Any transfer fees or other bank charges will be charged by the Administering Authority to the deposit. No interest will be paid on the deposit.
10.4 The unused balance held on deposit at the end of the arbitration shall be returned to the Parties as directed by the Tribunal.

ICS Inspection and Control Services Ltd and *Argentine Republic*, Award on Jurisdiction (February 10, 2012) (PCA administered, 1976 UNCITRAL Rules, UK-Argentina BIT), at 14 (reprinting Procedural Order No 1 dated May 18, 2010):

6.1 In accordance with Article 41(1) of the UNCITRAL Rules, the Parties shall establish an initial deposit of €100,000 (€50,000 from each Party) within 30 days of the adoption of this order. The deposit shall be placed with the PCA by wire transfer to the following account:

Bank:	ING Bank N.V., The Hague, The Netherlands
Account number:	[Information omitted]
IBAN:	[Information omitted]
BIC:	[Information omitted]
Account name:	Permanent Court of Arbitration
Reference:	ICS-AR [name of Party]

6.2 The PCA will review the adequacy of the deposit from time to time and, at the request of the Tribunal, may invite the Parties to make supplementary deposits in accordance with Article 41(2) of the UNCITRAL Rules.

6.3 The unused balance held on deposit at the end of the arbitration shall be returned to the Parties as directed by the Tribunal.

6.4 Any transfer fees or other bank charges will be charged to the account. No interest will be paid on the deposit.

ICS Inspection and Control Services Ltd and *Argentine Republic*, Award on Jurisdiction (February 10, 2012) (PCA administered, 1976 UNCITRAL Rules, UK-Argentina BIT), at 111–112:

330. The Parties deposited a total of EUR 400,000 (EUR 200,000 by each of the Claimant and the Respondent) with the PCA to cover the costs of arbitration.

...

335. The Parties' respective portions of these tribunal costs [EUR 361,487.22], amounting to EUR 180,743.61 for each side, shall be deducted from the deposit and the PCA shall reimburse the amount of EUR 19,256.39 to each side in accordance with Article 41(5) of the UNCITRAL Arbitration Rules.

Ulysseas, Inc and *Republic of Ecuador*, Final Award (June 12, 2012) (PCA administered, 1976 UNCITRAL Rules, US-Ecuador BIT), at 110:

366. Under Article 41(5) of the UNCITRAL Arbitration Rules, the Tribunal has to render an accounting of the deposits received. The advances made by the Parties to cover the fees and expenses of the Tribunal and of the PCA are as follows:

Claimant: EUR 425,000.00
Respondent: EUR 425,000.00

367. The advances having being paid in equal shares, there shall be no settlement between the Parties in that regard.

368. The total costs for fees and expenses regarding the arbitrators and PCA are fixed at EUR 778,100.62, divided as follows:

Prof. Piero Bernardini: EUR 255,675.00 (fees), EUR 8,698.40 (expenses)
Prof. Michael Pryles: EUR 149,887.50 (fees), EUR 15,653.27 (expenses)
Prof. Brigitte Stern: EUR 125,475.00 (fees), EUR 32,425.19 (expenses/VAT)
PCA: EUR 76,353.69
Tribunal expenses: EUR 113,932.57

369. The Parties' respective portions of these tribunal costs, amounting to EUR 389,050.31 for each side, shall be deducted from the deposit and the PCA shall reimburse the amount of EUR 35,949.69 to each side in accordance with Article 41(5) of the [1976] UNCITRAL Arbitration Rules.

D. Extracts from the Practice of the Iran—US Claims Tribunal

Richard D Harza and *Islamic Republic of Iran*, Award No ITL 14–97–2 (February 17, 1983), reprinted in 2 Iran-US CTR 68, 71–75 (1983-I):[233]

The Tribunal further decides, in accordance with Provisionally Adopted Tribunal Rule 41(2) [1983], that Harza International and Khuzestan Water & Power Authority shall each deposit

---

[233] Substantially similar examples of practice before the Iran–US Claims Tribunal may be found at *Chas T Main Intl, Inc* and *Khuzestan Water and Power Authority* et al, Award No ITL 23–120–2 (July 27, 1983), reprinted

within two months from the date of this Award the sum of Twenty-Five Thousand United States Dollars (US $25,000) into account number 24.58.28.583 at Pierson, Heldring and Pierson, Korte Vijverberg 2, 2513 AB The Hague, in the name of the Secretary-General of the Iran-United States Claims Tribunal (Account No II), as advances for the costs of expert advice. The account shall be administered by the Secretary-General of the Tribunal, who shall consult with the Tribunal. The Tribunal further retains jurisdiction to request from the arbitrating parties such other amounts as may be required from time to time in connection with the expert's work, or to decide any disputes which may arise in connection with that work.

Richard D Harza, et al and *Islamic Republic of Iran*, et al, Award No ITL 14–97–2 (November 21, 1983), reprinted in 4 Iran-US CTR 59, 59 (1983-III):

> ... The Respondents are hereby reminded that the further advance of U.S. $60,000, to be paid, by them by 9 November 1983, for the costs of the expert advice, has not been received in the Tribunal's account. The Respondents shall make this payment not later than one month after the date of filing of this Amendment.

Bechtel, Inc, et al and *Government of the Islamic Republic of Iran,* et al, Case No 181, Chamber One, Order of February 17, 1986, at 1–2:

> By its Order filed on 17 April 1984, the Tribunal *inter alia* requested Peat Marwick Nederland to render a report on the ownership of the stock of several of the Claimants in this case. The Tribunal also requested the Claimants to deposit U.S. $10,000 as an advance for the costs of such report. The Claimant Bechtel Power Corporation deposited this advance on 16 May 1984. The report having been submitted by Peat Marwick Nederland, it is determined that Bechtel Power Corporation shall be refunded the remainder of the advance of U.S. $10,000 not expended as costs of this report.

Starrett Housing Corp, et al and *Government of the Islamic Republic of Iran,* et al, Case No 24, Chamber One, Order of December 18, 1986, at 1–2:

> In accordance with Article 41, paragraph 2, of the [1983] Tribunal Rules, and pursuant to the provision in the Interlocutory Award No ITL 32–24–1 that the Tribunal may request from the arbitrating parties such other amounts as may be necessary from time to time in connection with the expert's work, the Parties shall make further deposits of an aggregate amount of US $300,000 as further advances for the costs of expert advice, including the expert's preparation for and participation in the Hearing scheduled for 19–23 January 1987 as well as interpretation from Swedish at the Hearing.
>
> The Claimants are requested jointly to deposit US $150,000, and the Respondents are likewise requested jointly to deposit US $150,000. These amounts shall be deposited before 14 January 1987. These advances shall be remitted to account number 24.58.28.583, Pierson, Heldring and Pierson, Korte Vijverberg 2, 2513 AB The Hague, in the name of the Secretary-General of the Iran-United States Claims Tribunal (Account No 24.58.28.583; dollar account).

Shahin Shaine Ebrahimi, et al and *Government of the Islamic Republic of Iran*, Case Nos 44, 46, 47, Chamber Three, Order of December 14, 1992, at 2:

> 2. In accordance with Article 41, paragraph 2 of the [1983] Tribunal Rules, the Tribunal decides that the Parties shall deposit by [date] the aggregate amount of £55,000 in respect of the cost of the expert. Therefore, the Claimants are requested jointly to deposit £27,500 and the

---

in 3 Iran-US CTR 156, 166–7 (1983-II); *Behring Intl, Inc* and *Iranian Air Force*, Decision No DEC 27–382–3 (December 19, 1983), reprinted in 4 Iran-US CTR 89, 92–3 (1983-III); and *Starrett Housing Corp,* et al and *Government of the Islamic Republic of Iran,* et al, ITL Award No 32–24–1 (December 19, 1983), reprinted in 4 Iran-US CTR 122, 158 (1983-III).

Respondent is requested to deposit the same amount, to be remitted to pound sterling account no. 42.81.27.797 at ABN-AMRO Bank, Kneuterdijk 8, 2514 EN The Hague, The Netherlands, in the name of the Secretary-General of the Iran-United States Claims Tribunal. The Tribunal may request from the Parties such further amounts as may be necessary.

Aram Sabet, et al and *Islamic Republic of Iran,* et al, Case Nos 815, 816 and 817, Chamber Two, Order of September 10, 1997:

The Tribunal notes the letters from the Agent of the Islamic Republic of Iran and the Claimants' attorney, filed on 20 August (Doc. 279) and 1 September 1997 (Doc. 281), respectively.

In view of the Parties' requests in the above letters, the Tribunal has retained the services of Tennyson & Company, 5 The Old Stables, Merrow Way, Epsom Road, Merrow, Guilford, Surrey, GUI 2RF, United Kingdom, to make a stenographic record of the joint Hearing in Cases Nos 385, 815, 816 & 817. They have been instructed to produce a same-day transcript of all hearing days scheduled the period 7 to 28 October 1997.

To cover all costs incurred in the production of the above mentioned stenographic record, the Claimants and Respondents in Cases Nos 385, 815, 816 & 817 are both requested to deposit not later than 14 October 1977 twelve thousand five hundred Pounds Sterling into Account No II, Pounds Sterling A/C No 42.81.27.797 with ABN.AMRO at Kneuterdijk 1, The Hague, in the name of the Secretary-General of the Iran-United States Claims Tribunal. In the event that twenty five thousand Pounds Sterling would not be sufficient to cover the costs, both the Claimants and Respondents referred to in this paragraph will make up the difference in equal portions. Any excess payment will be refunded.

Gulf Associates, et al and *Islamic Republic of Iran,* et al, Case No 385, Chamber Two, Order of December 11, 1997, at 1:

1. The Tribunal acknowledges payment of 12,456.78 and 12,500.00 Pounds Sterling respectively by the Claimants and Respondents in Cases Nos 385, 815, 816 and 817 to cover stenographic recording costs.
2. The above payments have not been sufficient to cover all costs incurred in producing a stenographic record of the joint Hearing in Cases Nos 385, 815, 816 and 817. Consequently, the Claimants and Respondents referred to in paragraph 1 are both requested to deposit by Monday December 29, 1997 a further 2,500 Pounds Sterling A/c No 42.81.27.797 with ABN-AMRO at Kneuterdijk 1, The Hague, in the name of the Secretary-General of the Iran-United States Claims Tribunal. Any excess payment will be refunded.

APPENDIX 1

UNCITRAL Arbitration Rules (as revised in 2010)

General Assembly resolution 65/22	909
UNCITRAL Arbitration Rules as revised in 2010	909
Section I. Introductory rules	910
Scope of application (article 1)	910
Notice and calculation of periods of time (article 2)	910
Notice of arbitration (article 3)	911
Response to the notice of arbitration (article 4)	911
Representation and assistance (article 5)	912
Designating and appointing authorities (article 6)	912
Section II. Composition of the arbitral tribunal	912
Number of arbitrators (article 7)	912
Appointment of arbitrators (articles 8 to 10)	913
Disclosures by and challenge of arbitrators (articles 11 to 13)	914
Replacement of an arbitrator (article 14)	914
Repetition of hearings in the event of the replacement of an arbitrator (article 15)	915
Exclusion of liability (article 16)	915
Section III. Arbitral proceedings	915
General provisions (article 17)	915
Place of arbitration (article 18)	915
Language (article 19)	916
Statement of claim (article 20)	916
Statement of defence (article 21)	916
Amendments to the claim or defence (article 22)	916
Pleas as to the jurisdiction of the arbitral tribunal (article 23)	917
Further written statements (article 24)	917
Periods of time (article 25)	917
Interim measures (article 26)	917
Evidence (article 27)	918
Hearings (article 28)	918
Experts appointed by the arbitral tribunal (article 29)	919
Default (article 30)	919
Closure of hearings (article 31)	919
Waiver of right to object (article 32)	920
Section IV. The award	920
Decisions (article 33)	920
Form and effect of the award (article 34)	920
Applicable law, amiable compositeur (article 35)	920
Settlement or other grounds for termination (article 36)	920
Interpretation of the award (article 37)	921

Correction of the award (article 38)	921
Additional award (article 39)	921
Definition of costs (article 40)	921
Fees and expenses of arbitrators (article 41)	922
Allocation of costs (article 42)	923
Deposit of costs (article 43)	923
Annex	**923**
Model arbitration clause for contracts	923
Possible waiver statement	923
Model statements of independence pursuant to article 11 of the Rules	924

Resolution adopted by the General Assembly
[on the report of the Sixth Committee (A/65/465)]

65/22. UNCITRAL Arbitration Rules as revised in 2010

The General Assembly,

Recalling its resolution 2205 (XXI) of 17 December 1966, which established the United Nations Commission on International Trade Law with the purpose of furthering the progressive harmonization and unification of the law of international trade in the interests of all peoples, in particular those of developing countries,

Also recalling its resolution 31/98 of 15 December 1976 recommending the use of the Arbitration Rules of the United Nations Commission on International Trade Law,[1]

Recognizing the value of arbitration as a method of settling disputes that may arise in the context of international commercial relations,

Noting that the Arbitration Rules are recognized as a very successful text and are used in a wide variety of circumstances covering a broad range of disputes, including disputes between private commercial parties, investor-State disputes, State-to-State disputes and commercial disputes administered by arbitral institutions, in all parts of the world,

Recognizing the need for revising the Arbitration Rules to conform to current practices in international trade and to meet changes that have taken place over the last thirty years in arbitral practice,

Believing that the Arbitration Rules as revised in 2010 to reflect current practices will significantly enhance the efficiency of arbitration under the Rules,

Convinced that the revision of the Arbitration Rules in a manner that is acceptable to countries with different legal, social and economic systems can significantly contribute to the development of harmonious international economic relations and to the continuous strengthening of the rule of law,

Noting that the preparation of the Arbitration Rules as revised in 2010 was the subject of due deliberation and extensive consultations with Governments and interested circles and that the revised text can be expected to contribute significantly to the establishment of a harmonized legal framework for the fair and efficient settlement of international commercial disputes,

Also noting that the Arbitration Rules as revised in 2010 were adopted by the United Nations Commission on International Trade Law at its forty-third session after due deliberation,[2]

1. *Expresses its appreciation* to the United Nations Commission on International Trade Law for having formulated and adopted the revised provisions of the Arbitration Rules, the text of which is contained in an annex to the report of the United Nations Commission on International Trade Law on the work of its forty-third session;[3]
2. *Recommends* the use of the Arbitration Rules as revised in 2010 in the settlement of disputes arising in the context of international commercial relations;
3. *Requests* the Secretary-General to make all efforts to ensure that the Arbitration Rules as revised in 2010 become generally known and available.

57th plenary meeting
6 December 2010

---

[1] Official Records of the General Assembly, Thirty-first Session, Supplement No 17 (A/31/17), chap. V, sect. C.
[2] Ibid., Sixty-fifth Session, Supplement No 17 (A/65/17), chap. III.
[3] Ibid., annex I.

UNCITRAL Arbitration Rules
(as revised in 2010)

Section I. Introductory Rules

Scope of application*

Article 1

1. Where parties have agreed that disputes between them in respect of a defined legal relationship, whether contractual or not, shall be referred to arbitration under the UNCITRAL Arbitration Rules, then such disputes shall be settled in accordance with these Rules subject to such modification as the parties may agree.
2. The parties to an arbitration agreement concluded after 15 August 2010 shall be presumed to have referred to the Rules in effect on the date of commencement of the arbitration, unless the parties have agreed to apply a particular version of the Rules. That presumption does not apply where the arbitration agreement has been concluded by accepting after 15 August 2010 an offer made before that date.
3. These Rules shall govern the arbitration except that where any of these Rules is in conflict with a provision of the law applicable to the arbitration from which the parties cannot derogate, that provision shall prevail.

Notice and calculation of periods of time

Article 2

1. A notice, including a notification, communication or proposal, may be transmitted by any means of communication that provides or allows for a record of its transmission.
2. If an address has been designated by a party specifically for this purpose or authorized by the arbitral tribunal, any notice shall be delivered to that party at that address, and if so delivered shall be deemed to have been received. Delivery by electronic means such as facsimile or e-mail may only be made to an address so designated or authorized.
3. In the absence of such designation or authorization, a notice is:
   (a) Received if it is physically delivered to the addressee; or
   (b) Deemed to have been received if it is delivered at the place of business, habitual residence or mailing address of the addressee.
4. If, after reasonable efforts, delivery cannot be effected in accordance with paragraphs 2 or 3, a notice is deemed to have been received if it is sent to the addressee's last-known place of business, habitual residence or mailing address by registered letter or any other means that provides a record of delivery or of attempted delivery.
5. A notice shall be deemed to have been received on the day it is delivered in accordance with paragraphs 2, 3 or 4, or attempted to be delivered in accordance with paragraph 4. A notice transmitted by electronic means is deemed to have been received on the day it is sent, except that a notice of arbitration so transmitted is only deemed to have been received on the day when it reaches the addressee's electronic address.
6. For the purpose of calculating a period of time under these Rules, such period shall begin to run on the day following the day when a notice is received. If the last day of such period is an official holiday or a non-business day at the residence or place of business of the addressee, the period is

---

* A model arbitration clause for contracts can be found in the annex to the Rules.

Notice of arbitration

Article 3

1. The party or parties initiating recourse to arbitration (hereinafter called the "claimant") shall communicate to the other party or parties (hereinafter called the "respondent") a notice of arbitration.
2. Arbitral proceedings shall be deemed to commence on the date on which the notice of arbitration is received by the respondent.
3. The notice of arbitration shall include the following:
    (a) A demand that the dispute be referred to arbitration;
    (b) The names and contact details of the parties;
    (c) Identification of the arbitration agreement that is invoked;
    (d) Identification of any contract or other legal instrument out of or in relation to which the dispute arises or, in the absence of such contract or instrument, a brief description of the relevant relationship;
    (e) A brief description of the claim and an indication of the amount involved, if any;
    (f) The relief or remedy sought;
    (g) A proposal as to the number of arbitrators, language and place of arbitration, if the parties have not previously agreed thereon.
4. The notice of arbitration may also include:
    (a) A proposal for the designation of an appointing authority referred to in article 6, paragraph 1;
    (b) A proposal for the appointment of a sole arbitrator referred to in article 8, paragraph 1;
    (c) Notification of the appointment of an arbitrator referred to in article 9 or 10.
5. The constitution of the arbitral tribunal shall not be hindered by any controversy with respect to the sufficiency of the notice of arbitration, which shall be finally resolved by the arbitral tribunal.

Response to the notice of arbitration

Article 4

1. Within 30 days of the receipt of the notice of arbitration, the respondent shall communicate to the claimant a response to the notice of arbitration, which shall include:
    (a) The name and contact details of each respondent;
    (b) A response to the information set forth in the notice of arbitration, pursuant to article 3, paragraphs 3 (c) to (g).
2. The response to the notice of arbitration may also include:
    (a) Any plea that an arbitral tribunal to be constituted under these Rules lacks jurisdiction;
    (b) A proposal for the designation of an appointing authority referred to in article 6, paragraph 1;
    (c) A proposal for the appointment of a sole arbitrator referred to in article 8, paragraph 1;
    (d) Notification of the appointment of an arbitrator referred to in article 9 or 10;
    (e) A brief description of counterclaims or claims for the purpose of a set-off, if any, including where relevant, an indication of the amounts involved, and the relief or remedy sought;
    (f) A notice of arbitration in accordance with article 3 in case the respondent formulates a claim against a party to the arbitration agreement other than the claimant.
3. The constitution of the arbitral tribunal shall not be hindered by any controversy with respect to the respondent's failure to communicate a response to the notice of arbitration, or an incomplete or late response to the notice of arbitration, which shall be finally resolved by the arbitral tribunal.

Representation and assistance

Article 5

Each party may be represented or assisted by persons chosen by it. The names and addresses of such persons must be communicated to all parties and to the arbitral tribunal. Such communication must specify whether the appointment is being made for purposes of representation or assistance. Where a person is to act as a representative of a party, the arbitral tribunal, on its own initiative or at the request of any party, may at any time require proof of authority granted to the representative in such a form as the arbitral tribunal may determine.

Designating and appointing authorities

Article 6

1. Unless the parties have already agreed on the choice of an appointing authority, a party may at any time propose the name or names of one or more institutions or persons, including the Secretary-General of the Permanent Court of Arbitration at The Hague (hereinafter called the "PCA"), one of whom would serve as appointing authority.
2. If all parties have not agreed on the choice of an appointing authority within 30 days after a proposal made in accordance with paragraph 1 has been received by all other parties, any party may request the Secretary-General of the PCA to designate the appointing authority.
3. Where these Rules provide for a period of time within which a party must refer a matter to an appointing authority and no appointing authority has been agreed on or designated, the period is suspended from the date on which a party initiates the procedure for agreeing on or designating an appointing authority until the date of such agreement or designation.
4. Except as referred to in article 41, paragraph 4, if the appointing authority refuses to act, or if it fails to appoint an arbitrator within 30 days after it receives a party's request to do so, fails to act within any other period provided by these Rules, or fails to decide on a challenge to an arbitrator within a reasonable time after receiving a party's request to do so, any party may request the Secretary-General of the PCA to designate a substitute appointing authority.
5. In exercising their functions under these Rules, the appointing authority and the Secretary-General of the PCA may require from any party and the arbitrators the information they deem necessary and they shall give the parties and, where appropriate, the arbitrators, an opportunity to present their views in any manner they consider appropriate. All such communications to and from the appointing authority and the Secretary-General of the PCA shall also be provided by the sender to all other parties.
6. When the appointing authority is requested to appoint an arbitrator pursuant to articles 8, 9, 10 or 14, the party making the request shall send to the appointing authority copies of the notice of arbitration and, if it exists, any response to the notice of arbitration.
7. The appointing authority shall have regard to such considerations as are likely to secure the appointment of an independent and impartial arbitrator and shall take into account the advisability of appointing an arbitrator of a nationality other than the nationalities of the parties.

Section II. Composition of the Arbitral Tribunal

Number of arbitrators

Article 7

1. If the parties have not previously agreed on the number of arbitrators, and if within 30 days after the receipt by the respondent of the notice of arbitration the parties have not agreed that there shall be only one arbitrator, three arbitrators shall be appointed.
2. Notwithstanding paragraph 1, if no other parties have responded to a party's proposal to appoint a sole arbitrator within the time limit provided for in paragraph 1 and the party or parties concerned have failed to appoint a second arbitrator in accordance with article 9 or 10,

the appointing authority may, at the request of a party, appoint a sole arbitrator pursuant to the procedure provided for in article 8, paragraph 2, if it determines that, in view of the circumstances of the case, this is more appropriate.

Appointment of arbitrators (articles 8 to 10)

Article 8

1. If the parties have agreed that a sole arbitrator is to be appointed and if within 30 days after receipt by all other parties of a proposal for the appointment of a sole arbitrator the parties have not reached agreement thereon, a sole arbitrator shall, at the request of a party, be appointed by the appointing authority.
2. The appointing authority shall appoint the sole arbitrator as promptly as possible. In making the appointment, the appointing authority shall use the following list-procedure, unless the parties agree that the list-procedure should not be used or unless the appointing authority determines in its discretion that the use of the list-procedure is not appropriate for the case:
   (a) The appointing authority shall communicate to each of the parties an identical list containing at least three names;
   (b) Within 15 days after the receipt of this list, each party may return the list to the appointing authority after having deleted the name or names to which it objects and numbered the remaining names on the list in the order of its preference;
   (c) After the expiration of the above period of time the appointing authority shall appoint the sole arbitrator from among the names approved on the lists returned to it and in accordance with the order of preference indicated by the parties;
   (d) If for any reason the appointment cannot be made according to this procedure, the appointing authority may exercise its discretion in appointing the sole arbitrator.

Article 9

1. If three arbitrators are to be appointed, each party shall appoint one arbitrator. The two arbitrators thus appointed shall choose the third arbitrator who will act as the presiding arbitrator of the arbitral tribunal.
2. If within 30 days after the receipt of a party's notification of the appointment of an arbitrator the other party has not notified the first party of the arbitrator it has appointed, the first party may request the appointing authority to appoint the second arbitrator.
3. If within 30 days after the appointment of the second arbitrator the two arbitrators have not agreed on the choice of the presiding arbitrator, the presiding arbitrator shall be appointed by the appointing authority in the same way as a sole arbitrator would be appointed under article 8.

Article 10

1. For the purposes of article 9, paragraph 1, where three arbitrators are to be appointed and there are multiple parties as claimant or as respondent, unless the parties have agreed to another method of appointment of arbitrators, the multiple parties jointly, whether as claimant or as respondent, shall appoint an arbitrator.
2. If the parties have agreed that the arbitral tribunal is to be composed of a number of arbitrators other than one or three, the arbitrators shall be appointed according to the method agreed upon by the parties.
3. In the event of any failure to constitute the arbitral tribunal under these Rules, the appointing authority shall, at the request of any party, constitute the arbitral tribunal and, in doing so, may revoke any appointment already made and appoint or reappoint each of the arbitrators and designate one of them as the presiding arbitrator.

Disclosures by and challenge of arbitrators** (articles 11 to 13)

Article 11

When a person is approached in connection with his or her possible appointment as an arbitrator, he or she shall disclose any circumstances likely to give rise to justifiable doubts as to his or her impartiality or independence. An arbitrator, from the time of his or her appointment and throughout the arbitral proceedings, shall without delay disclose any such circumstances to the parties and the other arbitrators unless they have already been informed by him or her of these circumstances.

Article 12

1. Any arbitrator may be challenged if circumstances exist that give rise to justifiable doubts as to the arbitrator's impartiality or independence.
2. A party may challenge the arbitrator appointed by it only for reasons of which it becomes aware after the appointment has been made.
3. In the event that an arbitrator fails to act or in the event of the de jure or de facto impossibility of his or her performing his or her functions, the procedure in respect of the challenge of an arbitrator as provided in article 13 shall apply.

Article 13

1. A party that intends to challenge an arbitrator shall send notice of its challenge within 15 days after it has been notified of the appointment of the challenged arbitrator, or within 15 days after the circumstances mentioned in articles 11 and 12 became known to that party.
2. The notice of challenge shall be communicated to all other parties, to the arbitrator who is challenged and to the other arbitrators. The notice of challenge shall state the reasons for the challenge.
3. When an arbitrator has been challenged by a party, all parties may agree to the challenge. The arbitrator may also, after the challenge, withdraw from his or her office. In neither case does this imply acceptance of the validity of the grounds for the challenge.
4. If, within 15 days from the date of the notice of challenge, all parties do not agree to the challenge or the challenged arbitrator does not withdraw, the party making the challenge may elect to pursue it. In that case, within 30 days from the date of the notice of challenge, it shall seek a decision on the challenge by the appointing authority.

Replacement of an arbitrator

Article 14

1. Subject to paragraph 2, in any event where an arbitrator has to be replaced during the course of the arbitral proceedings, a substitute arbitrator shall be appointed or chosen pursuant to the procedure provided for in articles 8 to 11 that was applicable to the appointment or choice of the arbitrator being replaced. This procedure shall apply even if during the process of appointing the arbitrator to be replaced, a party had failed to exercise its right to appoint or to participate in the appointment.
2. If, at the request of a party, the appointing authority determines that, in view of the exceptional circumstances of the case, it would be justified for a party to be deprived of its right to appoint a substitute arbitrator, the appointing authority may, after giving an opportunity to the parties and the remaining arbitrators to express their views: *(a)* appoint the substitute arbitrator; or *(b)* after the closure of the hearings, authorize the other arbitrators to proceed with the arbitration and make any decision or award.

** Model statements of independence pursuant to article 11 can be found in the annex to the Rules.

Repetition of hearings in the event of the replacement of an arbitrator

Article 15

If an arbitrator is replaced, the proceedings shall resume at the stage where the arbitrator who was replaced ceased to perform his or her functions, unless the arbitral tribunal decides otherwise.

Exclusion of liability

Article 16

Save for intentional wrongdoing, the parties waive, to the fullest extent permitted under the applicable law, any claim against the arbitrators, the appointing authority and any person appointed by the arbitral tribunal based on any act or omission in connection with the arbitration.

Section III. Arbitral Proceedings

General provisions

Article 17

1. Subject to these Rules, the arbitral tribunal may conduct the arbitration in such manner as it considers appropriate, provided that the parties are treated with equality and that at an appropriate stage of the proceedings each party is given a reasonable opportunity of presenting its case. The arbitral tribunal, in exercising its discretion, shall conduct the proceedings so as to avoid unnecessary delay and expense and to provide a fair and efficient process for resolving the parties' dispute.
2. As soon as practicable after its constitution and after inviting the parties to express their views, the arbitral tribunal shall establish the provisional timetable of the arbitration. The arbitral tribunal may, at any time, after inviting the parties to express their views, extend or abridge any period of time prescribed under these Rules or agreed by the parties.
3. If at an appropriate stage of the proceedings any party so requests, the arbitral tribunal shall hold hearings for the presentation of evidence by witnesses, including expert witnesses, or for oral argument. In the absence of such a request, the arbitral tribunal shall decide whether to hold such hearings or whether the proceedings shall be conducted on the basis of documents and other materials.
4. All communications to the arbitral tribunal by one party shall be communicated by that party to all other parties. Such communications shall be made at the same time, except as otherwise permitted by the arbitral tribunal if it may do so under applicable law.
5. The arbitral tribunal may, at the request of any party, allow one or more third persons to be joined in the arbitration as a party provided such person is a party to the arbitration agreement, unless the arbitral tribunal finds, after giving all parties, including the person or persons to be joined, the opportunity to be heard, that joinder should not be permitted because of prejudice to any of those parties. The arbitral tribunal may make a single award or several awards in respect of all parties so involved in the arbitration.

Place of arbitration

Article 18

1. If the parties have not previously agreed on the place of arbitration, the place of arbitration shall be determined by the arbitral tribunal having regard to the circumstances of the case. The award shall be deemed to have been made at the place of arbitration.
2. The arbitral tribunal may meet at any location it considers appropriate for deliberations. Unless otherwise agreed by the parties, the arbitral tribunal may also meet at any location it considers appropriate for any other purpose, including hearings.

Language

Article 19

1. Subject to an agreement by the parties, the arbitral tribunal shall, promptly after its appointment, determine the language or languages to be used in the proceedings. This determination shall apply to the statement of claim, the statement of defence, and any further written statements and, if oral hearings take place, to the language or languages to be used in such hearings.
2. The arbitral tribunal may order that any documents annexed to the statement of claim or statement of defence, and any supplementary documents or exhibits submitted in the course of the proceedings, delivered in their original language, shall be accompanied by a translation into the language or languages agreed upon by the parties or determined by the arbitral tribunal.

Statement of claim

Article 20

1. The claimant shall communicate its statement of claim in writing to the respondent and to each of the arbitrators within a period of time to be determined by the arbitral tribunal. The claimant may elect to treat its notice of arbitration referred to in article 3 as a statement of claim, provided that the notice of arbitration also complies with the requirements of paragraphs 2 to 4 of this article.
2. The statement of claim shall include the following particulars:
    (a) The names and contact details of the parties;
    (b) A statement of the facts supporting the claim;
    (c) The points at issue;
    (d) The relief or remedy sought;
    (e) The legal grounds or arguments supporting the claim.
3. A copy of any contract or other legal instrument out of or in relation to which the dispute arises and of the arbitration agreement shall be annexed to the statement of claim.
4. The statement of claim should, as far as possible, be accompanied by all documents and other evidence relied upon by the claimant, or contain references to them.

Statement of defence

Article 21

1. The respondent shall communicate its statement of defence in writing to the claimant and to each of the arbitrators within a period of time to be determined by the arbitral tribunal. The respondent may elect to treat its response to the notice of arbitration referred to in article 4 as a statement of defence, provided that the response to the notice of arbitration also complies with the requirements of paragraph 2 of this article.
2. The statement of defence shall reply to the particulars *(b)* to *(e)* of the statement of claim (art. 20, para. 2). The statement of defence should, as far as possible, be accompanied by all documents and other evidence relied upon by the respondent, or contain references to them.
3. In its statement of defence, or at a later stage in the arbitral proceedings if the arbitral tribunal decides that the delay was justified under the circumstances, the respondent may make a counterclaim or rely on a claim for the purpose of a set-off provided that the arbitral tribunal has jurisdiction over it.
4. The provisions of article 20, paragraphs 2 to 4, shall apply to a counterclaim, a claim under article 4, paragraph 2 *(f)*, and a claim relied on for the purpose of a set-off.

Amendments to the claim or defence

Article 22

During the course of the arbitral proceedings, a party may amend or supplement its claim or defence, including a counterclaim or a claim for the purpose of a set-off, unless the arbitral tribunal considers it inappropriate to allow such amendment or supplement having regard to the delay in making it or prejudice to other parties or any other circumstances. However, a claim or defence, including a counterclaim or a claim for the purpose of a set-off, may not be amended or supplemented in such a manner that the amended or supplemented claim or defence falls outside the jurisdiction of the arbitral tribunal.

Pleas as to the jurisdiction of the arbitral tribunal

Article 23

1. The arbitral tribunal shall have the power to rule on its own jurisdiction, including any objections with respect to the existence or validity of the arbitration agreement. For that purpose, an arbitration clause that forms part of a contract shall be treated as an agreement independent of the other terms of the contract. A decision by the arbitral tribunal that the contract is null shall not entail automatically the invalidity of the arbitration clause.
2. A plea that the arbitral tribunal does not have jurisdiction shall be raised no later than in the statement of defence or, with respect to a counterclaim or a claim for the purpose of a set-off, in the reply to the counterclaim or to the claim for the purpose of a set-off. A party is not precluded from raising such a plea by the fact that it has appointed, or participated in the appointment of, an arbitrator. A plea that the arbitral tribunal is exceeding the scope of its authority shall be raised as soon as the matter alleged to be beyond the scope of its authority is raised during the arbitral proceedings. The arbitral tribunal may, in either case, admit a later plea if it considers the delay justified.
3. The arbitral tribunal may rule on a plea referred to in paragraph 2 either as a preliminary question or in an award on the merits. The arbitral tribunal may continue the arbitral proceedings and make an award, notwithstanding any pending challenge to its jurisdiction before a court.

Further written statements

Article 24

The arbitral tribunal shall decide which further written statements, in addition to the statement of claim and the statement of defence, shall be required from the parties or may be presented by them and shall fix the periods of time for communicating such statements.

Periods of time

Article 25

The periods of time fixed by the arbitral tribunal for the communication of written statements (including the statement of claim and statement of defence) should not exceed 45 days. However, the arbitral tribunal may extend the time limits if it concludes that an extension is justified.

Interim measures

Article 26

1. The arbitral tribunal may, at the request of a party, grant interim measures.
2. An interim measure is any temporary measure by which, at any time prior to the issuance of the award by which the dispute is finally decided, the arbitral tribunal orders a party, for example and without limitation, to:
   (a) Maintain or restore the status quo pending determination of the dispute;
   (b) Take action that would prevent, or refrain from taking action that is likely to cause, (i) current or imminent harm or (ii) prejudice to the arbitral process itself;
   (c) Provide a means of preserving assets out of which a subsequent award may be satisfied; or
   (d) Preserve evidence that may be relevant and material to the resolution of the dispute.
3. The party requesting an interim measure under paragraphs 2 *(a)* to *(c)* shall satisfy the arbitral tribunal that:

(a) Harm not adequately reparable by an award of damages is likely to result if the measure is not ordered, and such harm substantially outweighs the harm that is likely to result to the party against whom the measure is directed if the measure is granted; and

(b) There is a reasonable possibility that the requesting party will succeed on the merits of the claim. The determination on this possibility shall not affect the discretion of the arbitral tribunal in making any subsequent determination.

4. With regard to a request for an interim measure under paragraph 2 *(d)*, the requirements in paragraphs 3 *(a)* and *(b)* shall apply only to the extent the arbitral tribunal considers appropriate.
5. The arbitral tribunal may modify, suspend or terminate an interim measure it has granted, upon application of any party or, in exceptional circumstances and upon prior notice to the parties, on the arbitral tribunal's own initiative.
6. The arbitral tribunal may require the party requesting an interim measure to provide appropriate security in connection with the measure.
7. The arbitral tribunal may require any party promptly to disclose any material change in the circumstances on the basis of which the interim measure was requested or granted.
8. The party requesting an interim measure may be liable for any costs and damages caused by the measure to any party if the arbitral tribunal later determines that, in the circumstances then prevailing, the measure should not have been granted. The arbitral tribunal may award such costs and damages at any point during the proceedings.
9. A request for interim measures addressed by any party to a judicial authority shall not be deemed incompatible with the agreement to arbitrate, or as a waiver of that agreement.

Evidence

Article 27

1. Each party shall have the burden of proving the facts relied on to support its claim or defence.
2. Witnesses, including expert witnesses, who are presented by the parties to testify to the arbitral tribunal on any issue of fact or expertise may be any individual, notwithstanding that the individual is a party to the arbitration or in any way related to a party. Unless otherwise directed by the arbitral tribunal, statements by witnesses, including expert witnesses, may be presented in writing and signed by them.
3. At any time during the arbitral proceedings the arbitral tribunal may require the parties to produce documents, exhibits or other evidence within such a period of time as the arbitral tribunal shall determine.
4. The arbitral tribunal shall determine the admissibility, relevance, materiality and weight of the evidence offered.

Hearings

Article 28

1. In the event of an oral hearing, the arbitral tribunal shall give the parties adequate advance notice of the date, time and place thereof.
2. Witnesses, including expert witnesses, may be heard under the conditions and examined in the manner set by the arbitral tribunal.
3. Hearings shall be held in camera unless the parties agree otherwise. The arbitral tribunal may require the retirement of any witness or witnesses, including expert witnesses, during the testimony of such other witnesses, except that a witness, including an expert witness, who is a party to the arbitration shall not, in principle, be asked to retire.
4. The arbitral tribunal may direct that witnesses, including expert witnesses, be examined through means of telecommunication that do not require their physical presence at the hearing (such as videoconference).

Experts appointed by the arbitral tribunal

Article 29

1. After consultation with the parties, the arbitral tribunal may appoint one or more independent experts to report to it, in writing, on specific issues to be determined by the arbitral tribunal. A copy of the expert's terms of reference, established by the arbitral tribunal, shall be communicated to the parties.
2. The expert shall, in principle before accepting appointment, submit to the arbitral tribunal and to the parties a description of his or her qualifications and a statement of his or her impartiality and independence. Within the time ordered by the arbitral tribunal, the parties shall inform the arbitral tribunal whether they have any objections as to the expert's qualifications, impartiality or independence. The arbitral tribunal shall decide promptly whether to accept any such objections. After an expert's appointment, a party may object to the expert's qualifications, impartiality or independence only if the objection is for reasons of which the party becomes aware after the appointment has been made. The arbitral tribunal shall decide promptly what, if any, action to take.
3. The parties shall give the expert any relevant information or produce for his or her inspection any relevant documents or goods that he or she may require of them. Any dispute between a party and such expert as to the relevance of the required information or production shall be referred to the arbitral tribunal for decision.
4. Upon receipt of the expert's report, the arbitral tribunal shall communicate a copy of the report to the parties, which shall be given the opportunity to express, in writing, their opinion on the report. A party shall be entitled to examine any document on which the expert has relied in his or her report.
5. At the request of any party, the expert, after delivery of the report, may be heard at a hearing where the parties shall have the opportunity to be present and to interrogate the expert. At this hearing, any party may present expert witnesses in order to testify on the points at issue. The provisions of article 28 shall be applicable to such proceedings.

Default

Article 30

1. If, within the period of time fixed by these Rules or the arbitral tribunal, without showing sufficient cause:
    (a) The claimant has failed to communicate its statement of claim, the arbitral tribunal shall issue an order for the termination of the arbitral proceedings, unless there are remaining matters that may need to be decided and the arbitral tribunal considers it appropriate to do so;
    (b) The respondent has failed to communicate its response to the notice of arbitration or its statement of defence, the arbitral tribunal shall order that the proceedings continue, without treating such failure in itself as an admission of the claimant's allegations; the provisions of this subparagraph also apply to a claimant's failure to submit a defence to a counterclaim or to a claim for the purpose of a set-off.
2. If a party, duly notified under these Rules, fails to appear at a hearing, without showing sufficient cause for such failure, the arbitral tribunal may proceed with the arbitration.
3. If a party, duly invited by the arbitral tribunal to produce documents, exhibits or other evidence, fails to do so within the established period of time, without showing sufficient cause for such failure, the arbitral tribunal may make the award on the evidence before it.

Closure of hearings

Article 31

1. The arbitral tribunal may inquire of the parties if they have any further proof to offer or witnesses to be heard or submissions to make and, if there are none, it may declare the hearings closed.
2. The arbitral tribunal may, if it considers it necessary owing to exceptional circumstances, decide,

on its own initiative or upon application of a party, to reopen the hearings at any time before the award is made.

Waiver of right to object

Article 32

A failure by any party to object promptly to any non-compliance with these Rules or with any requirement of the arbitration agreement shall be deemed to be a waiver of the right of such party to make such an objection, unless such party can show that, under the circumstances, its failure to object was justified.

Section IV. The Award

Decisions

Article 33

1. When there is more than one arbitrator, any award or other decision of the arbitral tribunal shall be made by a majority of the arbitrators.
2. In the case of questions of procedure, when there is no majority or when the arbitral tribunal so authorizes, the presiding arbitrator may decide alone, subject to revision, if any, by the arbitral tribunal.

Form and effect of the award

Article 34

1. The arbitral tribunal may make separate awards on different issues at different times.
2. All awards shall be made in writing and shall be final and binding on the parties. The parties shall carry out all awards without delay.
3. The arbitral tribunal shall state the reasons upon which the award is based, unless the parties have agreed that no reasons are to be given.
4. An award shall be signed by the arbitrators and it shall contain the date on which the award was made and indicate the place of arbitration. Where there is more than one arbitrator and any of them fails to sign, the award shall state the reason for the absence of the signature.
5. An award may be made public with the consent of all parties or where and to the extent disclosure is required of a party by legal duty, to protect or pursue a legal right or in relation to legal proceedings before a court or other competent authority.
6. Copies of the award signed by the arbitrators shall be communicated to the parties by the arbitral tribunal.

Applicable law, amiable compositeur

Article 35

1. The arbitral tribunal shall apply the rules of law designated by the parties as applicable to the substance of the dispute. Failing such designation by the parties, the arbitral tribunal shall apply the law which it determines to be appropriate.
2. The arbitral tribunal shall decide as *amiable compositeur* or *ex aequo et bono* only if the parties have expressly authorized the arbitral tribunal to do so.
3. In all cases, the arbitral tribunal shall decide in accordance with the terms of the contract, if any, and shall take into account any usage of trade applicable to the transaction.

Settlement or other grounds for termination

Article 36

1. If, before the award is made, the parties agree on a settlement of the dispute, the arbitral tribunal shall either issue an order for the termination of the arbitral proceedings or, if requested by the parties and accepted by the arbitral tribunal, record the settlement in the form of an arbitral award on agreed terms. The arbitral tribunal is not obliged to give reasons for such an award.

2. If, before the award is made, the continuation of the arbitral proceedings becomes unnecessary or impossible for any reason not mentioned in paragraph 1, the arbitral tribunal shall inform the parties of its intention to issue an order for the termination of the proceedings. The arbitral tribunal shall have the power to issue such an order unless there are remaining matters that may need to be decided and the arbitral tribunal considers it appropriate to do so.
3. Copies of the order for termination of the arbitral proceedings or of the arbitral award on agreed terms, signed by the arbitrators, shall be communicated by the arbitral tribunal to the parties. Where an arbitral award on agreed terms is made, the provisions of article 34, paragraphs 2, 4 and 5, shall apply.

Interpretation of the award

Article 37

1. Within 30 days after the receipt of the award, a party, with notice to the other parties, may request that the arbitral tribunal give an interpretation of the award.
2. The interpretation shall be given in writing within 45 days after the receipt of the request. The interpretation shall form part of the award and the provisions of article 34, paragraphs 2 to 6, shall apply.

Correction of the award

Article 38

1. Within 30 days after the receipt of the award, a party, with notice to the other parties, may request the arbitral tribunal to correct in the award any error in computation, any clerical or typographical error, or any error or omission of a similar nature. If the arbitral tribunal considers that the request is justified, it shall make the correction within 45 days of receipt of the request.
2. The arbitral tribunal may within 30 days after the communication of the award make such corrections on its own initiative.
3. Such corrections shall be in writing and shall form part of the award. The provisions of article 34, paragraphs 2 to 6, shall apply.

Additional award

Article 39

1. Within 30 days after the receipt of the termination order or the award, a party, with notice to the other parties, may request the arbitral tribunal to make an award or an additional award as to claims presented in the arbitral proceedings but not decided by the arbitral tribunal.
2. If the arbitral tribunal considers the request for an award or additional award to be justified, it shall render or complete its award within 60 days after the receipt of the request. The arbitral tribunal may extend, if necessary, the period of time within which it shall make the award.
3. When such an award or additional award is made, the provisions of article 34, paragraphs 2 to 6, shall apply.

Definition of costs

Article 40

1. The arbitral tribunal shall fix the costs of arbitration in the final award and, if it deems appropriate, in another decision.
2. The term "costs" includes only:
   (a) The fees of the arbitral tribunal to be stated separately as to each arbitrator and to be fixed by the tribunal itself in accordance with article 41;
   (b) The reasonable travel and other expenses incurred by the arbitrators;

(c) The reasonable costs of expert advice and of other assistance required by the arbitral tribunal;

(d) The reasonable travel and other expenses of witnesses to the extent such expenses are approved by the arbitral tribunal;

(e) The legal and other costs incurred by the parties in relation to the arbitration to the extent that the arbitral tribunal determines that the amount of such costs is reasonable;

(f) Any fees and expenses of the appointing authority as well as the fees and expenses of the Secretary-General of the PCA.

3. In relation to interpretation, correction or completion of any award under articles 37 to 39, the arbitral tribunal may charge the costs referred to in paragraphs 2 *(b)* to *(f)*, but no additional fees.

Fees and expenses of arbitrators

Article 41

1. The fees and expenses of the arbitrators shall be reasonable in amount, taking into account the amount in dispute, the complexity of the subject matter, the time spent by the arbitrators and any other relevant circumstances of the case.

2. If there is an appointing authority and it applies or has stated that it will apply a schedule or particular method for determining the fees for arbitrators in international cases, the arbitral tribunal in fixing its fees shall take that schedule or method into account to the extent that it considers appropriate in the circumstances of the case.

3. Promptly after its constitution, the arbitral tribunal shall inform the parties as to how it proposes to determine its fees and expenses, including any rates it intends to apply. Within 15 days of receiving that proposal, any party may refer the proposal to the appointing authority for review. If, within 45 days of receipt of such a referral, the appointing authority finds that the proposal of the arbitral tribunal is inconsistent with paragraph 1, it shall make any necessary adjustments thereto, which shall be binding upon the arbitral tribunal.

4. *(a)* When informing the parties of the arbitrators' fees and expenses that have been fixed pursuant to article 40, paragraphs 2 *(a)* and *(b)*, the arbitral tribunal shall also explain the manner in which the corresponding amounts have been calculated;

(b) Within 15 days of receiving the arbitral tribunal's determination of fees and expenses, any party may refer for review such determination to the appointing authority. If no appointing authority has been agreed upon or designated, or if the appointing authority fails to act within the time specified in these Rules, then the review shall be made by the Secretary-General of the PCA;

(c) If the appointing authority or the Secretary-General of the PCA finds that the arbitral tribunal's determination is inconsistent with the arbitral tribunal's proposal (and any adjustment thereto) under paragraph 3 or is otherwise manifestly excessive, it shall, within 45 days of receiving such a referral, make any adjustments to the arbitral tribunal's determination that are necessary to satisfy the criteria in paragraph 1. Any such adjustments shall be binding upon the arbitral tribunal;

(d) Any such adjustments shall either be included by the arbitral tribunal in its award or, if the award has already been issued, be implemented in a correction to the award, to which the procedure of article 38, paragraph 3, shall apply.

5. Throughout the procedure under paragraphs 3 and 4, the arbitral tribunal shall proceed with the arbitration, in accordance with article 17, paragraph 1.

6. A referral under paragraph 4 shall not affect any determination in the award other than the arbitral tribunal's fees and expenses; nor shall it delay the recognition and enforcement of all parts of the award other than those relating to the determination of the arbitral tribunal's fees and expenses.

Allocation of costs

Article 42

1. The costs of the arbitration shall in principle be borne by the unsuccessful party or parties. However, the arbitral tribunal may apportion each of such costs between the parties if it determines that apportionment is reasonable, taking into account the circumstances of the case.
2. The arbitral tribunal shall in the final award or, if it deems appropriate, in any other award, determine any amount that a party may have to pay to another party as a result of the decision on allocation of costs.

Deposit of costs

Article 43

1. The arbitral tribunal, on its establishment, may request the parties to deposit an equal amount as an advance for the costs referred to in article 40, paragraphs 2 *(a)* to *(c)*.
2. During the course of the arbitral proceedings the arbitral tribunal may request supplementary deposits from the parties.
3. If an appointing authority has been agreed upon or designated, and when a party so requests and the appointing authority consents to perform the function, the arbitral tribunal shall fix the amounts of any deposits or supplementary deposits only after consultation with the appointing authority, which may make any comments to the arbitral tribunal that it deems appropriate concerning the amount of such deposits and supplementary deposits.
4. If the required deposits are not paid in full within 30 days after the receipt of the request, the arbitral tribunal shall so inform the parties in order that one or more of them may make the required payment. If such payment is not made, the arbitral tribunal may order the suspension or termination of the arbitral proceedings.
5. After a termination order or final award has been made, the arbitral tribunal shall render an accounting to the parties of the deposits received and return any unexpended balance to the parties.

ANNEX

Model arbitration clause for contracts

Any dispute, controversy or claim arising out of or relating to this contract, or the breach, termination or invalidity thereof, shall be settled by arbitration in accordance with the UNCITRAL Arbitration Rules.

Note. Parties should consider adding:

(a) The appointing authority shall be... [name of institution or person];
(b) The number of arbitrators shall be... [one or three];
(c) The place of arbitration shall be... [town and country];
(d) The language to be used in the arbitral proceedings shall be...

Possible waiver statement

Note. If the parties wish to exclude recourse against the arbitral award that may be available under the applicable law, they may consider adding a provision to that effect as suggested below, considering, however, that the effectiveness and conditions of such an exclusion depend on the applicable law.

Waiver

The parties hereby waive their right to any form of recourse against an award to any court or other competent authority, insofar as such waiver can validly be made under the applicable law.

Model statements of independence pursuant to article 11 of the Rules

No circumstances to disclose

I am impartial and independent of each of the parties and intend to remain so. To the best of my knowledge, there are no circumstances, past or present, likely to give rise to justifiable doubts as to my impartiality or independence. I shall promptly notify the parties and the other arbitrators of any such circumstances that may subsequently come to my attention during this arbitration.

Circumstances to disclose

I am impartial and independent of each of the parties and intend to remain so. Attached is a statement made pursuant to article 11 of the UNCITRAL Arbitration Rules of *(a)* my past and present professional, business and other relationships with the parties and *(b)* any other relevant circumstances. [Include statement.] I confirm that those circumstances do not affect my independence and impartiality. I shall promptly notify the parties and the other arbitrators of any such further relationships or circumstances that may subsequently come to my attention during this arbitration.

Note. Any party may consider requesting from the arbitrator the following addition to the statement of independence:

I confirm, on the basis of the information presently available to me, that I can devote the time necessary to conduct this arbitration diligently, efficiently and in accordance with the time limits in the Rules.

APPENDIX 2

UNCITRAL Arbitration Rules (1976)

General Assembly resolution 31/98	926
UNCITRAL Arbitration Rules as adopted in 1976	927
Section I. Introductory rules	927
Scope of application (article 1)	927
Notice, calculation of periods of time (article 2)	927
Notice of arbitration (article 3)	927
Representation and assistance (article 4)	928
Section II. Composition of the arbitral tribunal	928
Number of arbitrators (article 5)	928
Appointment of arbitrators (articles 6 to 8)	928
Challenge of arbitrators (articles 9 to 12)	929
Replacement of an arbitrator (article 13)	930
Repetition of hearings in the event of the replacement of an arbitrator (article 14)	930
Section III. Arbitral proceedings	930
General provisions (article 15)	930
Place of arbitration (article 16)	931
Language (article 17)	931
Statement of claim (article 18)	931
Statement of defence (article 19)	931
Amendments to the claim or defence (article 20)	932
Pleas as to the jurisdiction of the arbitral tribunal (article 21)	932
Further written statements (article 22)	932
Periods of time (article 23)	932
Evidence and hearings (articles 24 to 25)	932
Interim measures of protection (article 26)	933
Experts (article 27)	933
Default (article 28)	933
Closure of hearings (article 29)	934
Waiver of rules (article 30)	934
Section IV. The award	934
Decisions (article 31)	934
Form and effect of the award (article 32)	934
Applicable law, *amiable compositeur* (article 33)	935
Settlement or other grounds for termination (article 34)	935
Interpretation of the award (article 35)	935
Correction of the award (article 36)	935
Additional award (article 37)	935
Costs (articles 38 to 40)	936
Deposit of costs (article 41)	937

General Assembly Resolution 31/98

The General Assembly

Recognizing the value of arbitration as a method of setting disputes arising in the context of international commercial relations,

Being convinced that the establishment of rules for ad hoc arbitration that are acceptable in countries with different legal, social and economic systems would significantly contribute to the development of harmonious international economic relations,

Bearing in mind that the Arbitration Rules of the United Nations Commission on International Trade Law have been prepared after extensive consultation with arbitral institutions and centres of international commercial arbitration,

Noting that the Arbitration Rules were adopted by the United Nations Commission on International Trade Law at its ninth session, after due deliberation,[1]

1. *Recommends* the use of the Arbitration Rules of the United Nations Commission on International Trade Law in the settlement of disputes arising in the context of international commercial relations, particularly by reference to the Arbitration Rules in commercial contracts;
2. *Requests* the Secretary-General to arrange for the widest possible distribution of the Arbitration Rules.

[1] Official Records of the General Assembly, Thirty-first Session, Supplement No 17 (1/31/17), chap.V, sect. C.

1976 UNCITRAL Arbitration Rules
(adopted December 15, 1976)

Section I. Introductory rules

Scope of application

Article 1

1. Where the parties to a contract have agreed in writing* that disputes in relation to that contract shall be referred to arbitration under the UNCITRAL Arbitration Rules, then such disputes shall be settled in accordance with these Rules subject to such modification as the parties may agree in writing.
2. These Rules shall govern the arbitration except that where any of these Rules is in conflict with a provision of the law applicable to the arbitration from which the parties cannot derogate, that provision shall prevail.

* Model Arbitration Clause
Any dispute, controversy or claim arising out of or relating to this contract, or the breach, termination or invalidity thereof, shall be settled by arbitration in accordance with the UNCITRAL Arbitration Rules as at present in force.
Note—Parties may wish to consider adding:
  (a) The appointing authority shall be . . . (name of institution or person);
  (b) The number of arbitrators shall be . . . (one or three);
  (c) The place of arbitration shall be . . . (town or country);
  (d) The language(s) to be used in the arbitral proceedings shall be . . .

Notice, calculation of periods of time

Article 2

1. For the purposes of these Rules, any notice, including a notification, communication or proposal, is deemed to have been received if it is physically delivered to the addressee or if it is delivered at his habitual residence, place of business or mailing address, or, if none of these can be found after making reasonable inquiry, then at the addressees last known residence or place of business. Notice shall be deemed to have been received on the day it is so delivered.
2. For the purposes of calculating a period of time under these Rules, such period shall begin to run on the day following the day when a notice, notification, communication or proposal is received. If the last day of such period is an official holiday or a non-business day at the residence or place of business of the addressee, the period is extended until the first business day which follows. Official holidays or non-business days occurring during the running of the period of time are included in calculating the period.

Notice of arbitration

Article 3

1. The party initiating recourse to arbitration (hereinafter called the claimant) shall give to the other party (hereinafter called the respondent) a notice of arbitration.
2. Arbitral proceedings shall be deemed to commence on the date on which the notice of arbitration is received by the respondent.
3. The notice of arbitration shall include the following:
   (a) A demand that the dispute be referred to arbitration;
   (b) The names and addresses of the parties;
   (c) A reference to the arbitration clause or the separate arbitration agreement that is invoked;

(d) A reference to the contract out of or in relation to which the dispute arises;
   (e) The general nature of the claim and an indication of the amount involved, if any;
   (f) The relief or remedy sought;
   (g) A proposal as to the number of arbitrators (i.e. one or three), if the parties have not previously agreed thereon.
4. The notice of arbitration may also include:
   (a) The proposals for the appointments of a sole arbitrator and an appointing authority referred to in article 6, paragraph 1;
   (b) The notification of the appointment of an arbitrator referred to in article 7;
   (c) The statement of claim referred to in article 18.

Representation and assistance

Article 4

The parties may be represented or assisted by persons of their choice. The names and addresses of such persons must be communicated in writing to the other party; such communication must specify whether the appointment is being made for purposes of representation or assistance.

Section II. Composition of the arbitral tribunal

Number of arbitrators

Article 5

If the parties have not previously agreed on the number of arbitrators (i.e. one or three), and if within 15 days after the receipt by the respondent of the notice of arbitration the parties have not agreed that there shall be only one arbitrator, three arbitrators shall be appointed.

Appointment of arbitrators

Article 6

1. If a sole arbitrator is to be appointed, either party may propose to the other:
   (a) The names of one or more persons, one of whom would serve as the sole arbitrator; and
   (b) If no appointing authority has been agreed upon by the parties, the name or names of one or more institutions or persons, one of whom would serve as appointing authority.
2. If within 30 days after receipt by a party of a proposal made in accordance with paragraph 1 the parties have not reached agreement on the choice of a sole arbitrator, the sole arbitrator shall be appointed by the appointing authority agreed upon by the parties. If no appointing authority has been agreed upon by the parties, or if the appointing authority agreed upon refuses to act or fails to appoint the arbitrator within 60 days of the receipt of a party's request therefor, either party may request the Secretary-General of the Permanent Court of Arbitration at The Hague to designate an appointing authority.
3. The appointing authority shall, at the request of one of the parties, appoint the sole arbitrator as promptly as possible. In making the appointment the appointing authority shall use the following list-procedure, unless both parties agree that the list procedure should not be used or unless the appointing authority determines in its discretion that the use of the list-procedure is not appropriate for the case:
   (a) At the request of one of the parties the appointing authority shall communicate to both parties an identical list containing at least three names;
   (b) Within 15 days after the receipt of his list, each party may return the list to the appointing authority after having deleted the name or names to which he objects and numbered the remaining names on the list in the order of his preference;
   (c) After the expiration of the above period of time the appointing authority shall appoint the sole arbitrator from among the names approved on the lists returned to it and in accordance with the order of preference indicated by the parties;

(d) If for any reason the appointment cannot be made according to this procedure, the appointing authority may exercise its discretion in appointing the sole arbitrator.
4. In making the appointment, the appointing authority shall have regard to such considerations as are likely to secure the appointment of an independent and impartial arbitrator and shall take into account as well the advisability of appointing an arbitrator of a nationality other than the nationalities of the parties.

Appointment of arbitrators

Article 7

1. If three arbitrators are to be appointed, each party shall appoint one arbitrator. The two arbitrators thus appointed shall choose the third arbitrator who will act as the presiding arbitrator of the tribunal.
2. If within 30 days after the receipt of a party's notification of the appointment of an arbitrator the other party has not notified the first party of the arbitrator he has appointed:
   (a) The first party may request the appointing authority previously designated by the parties to appoint the second arbitrator; or
   (b) If no such authority has been previously designated by the parties, or if the appointing authority previously designated refuses to act or fails to appoint the arbitrator within 30 days after receipt of a partys request therefor, the first party may request the Secretary-General of the Permanent Court of Arbitration at The Hague to designate the appointing authority. The first party may then request the appointing authority so designated to appoint the second arbitrator. In either case, the appointing authority may exercise its discretion in appointing the arbitrator.
3. If within 30 days after the appointment of the second arbitrator the two arbitrators have not agreed on the choice of the presiding arbitrator, the presiding arbitrator shall be appointed by an appointing authority in the same way as a sole arbitrator would be appointed under article 6.

Appointment of arbitrators

Article 8

1. When an appointing authority is requested to appoint an arbitrator pursuant to article 6 or article 7, the party which makes the request shall send to the appointing authority a copy of the notice of arbitration, a copy of the contract out of or in relation to which the dispute has arisen and a copy of the arbitration agreement if it is not contained in the contract. The appointing authority may require from either party such information as it deems necessary to fulfil its function.
2. Where the names of one or more persons are proposed for appointment as arbitrators, their full names, addresses and nationalities shall be indicated, together with a description of their qualifications.

Challenge of arbitrators

Article 9

A prospective arbitrator shall disclose to those who approach him in connexion with his possible appointment any circumstances likely to give rise to justifiable doubts as to his impartiality or independence. An arbitrator, once appointed or chosen, shall disclose such circumstance to the parties unless they have already been informed by him of these circumstances.

Challenge of arbitrators

Article 10

1. Any arbitrator may be challenged if circumstances exist that give rise to justifiable doubts as to the arbitrator's impartiality or independence.
2. A party may challenge the arbitrator appointed by him only for reasons of which he becomes aware after the appointment has been made.

Challenge of arbitrators

Article 11

1. A party who intends to challenge an arbitrator shall send notice of his challenge within 15 days after the appointment of the challenged arbitrator has been notified to the challenging party or within 15 days after the circumstances mentioned in articles 9 and 10 became known to that party.
2. The challenge shall be notified to the other party, to the arbitrator who is challenged and to the other members of the arbitral tribunal. The notification shall be in writing and shall state the reason for the challenge.
3. When an arbitrator has been challenged by one party, the other party may agree to the challenge. The arbitrator may also, after the challenge, withdraw from his office. In neither case does this imply acceptance of the validity of the grounds for the challenge. In both cases the procedure provided in article 6 or 7 shall be used in full for the appointment of the substitute arbitrator, even if during the process of appointing the challenged arbitrator a party had failed to exercise his right to appoint or to participate in the appointment.

Challenge of arbitrators

Article 12

1. If the other party does not agree to the challenge and the challenged arbitrator does not withdraw, the decision on the challenge will be made:
   (a) When the initial appointment was made by an appointing authority, by that authority;
   (b) When the initial appointment was not made by an appointing authority, but an appointing authority has been previously designated, by that authority;
   (c) In all other cases, by the appointing authority to be designated in accordance with the procedure for designating an appointing authority as provided for in article 6.
2. If the appointing authority sustains the challenge, a substitute arbitrator shall be appointed or chosen pursuant to the procedure applicable to the appointment or choice of an arbitrator as provided in articles 6 to 9 except that, when this procedure would call for the designation of an appointing authority, the appointment of the arbitrator shall be made by the appointing authority which decided on the challenge.

Replacement of an arbitrator

Article 13

1. In the event of the death or resignation of an arbitrator during the course of the arbitral proceedings, a substitute arbitrator shall be appointed or chosen pursuant to the procedure provided for in articles 6 to 9 that was applicable to the appointment or choice of the arbitrator being replaced.
2. In the event that an arbitrator fails to act or in the event of the *de jure* or *de facto* impossibility of his performing his functions, the procedure in respect of the challenge and replacement of an arbitrator as provided in the preceding articles shall apply.

Repetition of hearings in the event of the replacement of an arbitrator

Article 14

If under articles 11 to 13 the sole or presiding arbitrator is replaced, any hearings held previously shall be repeated; if any other arbitrator is replaced, such prior hearings may be repeated at the discretion of the arbitral tribunal.

Section III. Arbitral proceedings

General provisions

Article 15

1. Subject to these Rules, the arbitral tribunal may conduct the arbitration in such manner as it considers appropriate, provided that the parties are treated with equality and that at any stage of the proceedings each party is given a full opportunity of presenting his case.

2. If either party so requests at any stage of the proceedings, the arbitral tribunal shall hold hearings for the presentation of evidence by witnesses, including expert witnesses, or for oral argument. In the absence of such a request, the arbitral tribunal shall decide whether to hold such hearings or whether the proceedings shall be conducted on the basis of documents and other materials.
3. All documents or information supplied to the arbitral tribunal by one party shall at the same time be communicated by that party to the other party.

Place of arbitration

Article 16

1. Unless the parties have agreed upon the place where the arbitration is to be held, such place shall be determined by the arbitral tribunal, having regard to the circumstances of the arbitration.
2. The arbitral tribunal may determine the locale of the arbitration within the country agreed upon by the parties. It may hear witnesses and hold meetings for consultation among its members at any place it deems appropriate, having regard to the circumstances of the arbitration.
3. The arbitral tribunal may meet at any place it deems appropriate for the inspection of goods, other property or documents. The parties shall be given sufficient notice to enable them to be present at such inspection.

Language

Article 17

1. Subject to an agreement by the parties, the arbitral tribunal shall, promptly after its appointment, determine the language or languages to be used in the proceedings. This determination shall apply to the statement of claim, the statement of defence, and any further written statements and, if oral hearings take place, to the language or languages to be used in such hearings.
2. The arbitral tribunal may order that any documents annexed to the statement of claim or statement of defence, and any supplementary documents or exhibits submitted in the course of the proceedings, delivered in their original language, shall be accompanied by a translation into the language or languages agreed upon by the parties or determined by the arbitral tribunal.

Statement of claim

Article 18

1. Unless the statement of claim was contained in the notice of arbitration, within a period of time to be determined by the arbitral tribunal, the claimant shall communicate his statement of claim in writing to the respondent and to each of the arbitrators. A copy of the contract, and of the arbitration agreement if not contained in the contract, shall be annexed thereto.
2. The statement of claim shall include the following particulars:
   (a) The names and addresses of the parties;
   (b) A statement of the facts supporting the claim;
   (c) The points at issue;
   (d) The relief or remedy sought.

The claimant may annex to his statement of claim all documents he deems relevant or may add a reference to the documents or other evidence he will submit.

Statement of defence

Article 19

1. Within a period of time to be determined by the arbitral tribunal, the respondent shall communicate his statement of defence in writing to the claimant and to each of the arbitrators.
2. The statement of defence shall reply to the particulars (b), (c) and (d) of the statement of claim (article 18, para. 2). The respondent may annex to his statement the documents on which he relies for his defence or may add a reference to the documents or other evidence he will submit.
3. In his statement of defence, or at a later stage in the arbitral proceedings if the arbitral tribunal decides that the delay was justified under the circumstances the respondent may make a counter-

claim arising out of the same contract or rely on a claim arising out of the same contract for the purpose of a set-off.
4. The provisions of article 18, paragraph 2, shall apply to a counter-claim and a claim relied on for the purpose of a set-off.

Amendments to the claim or defence

Article 20

During the course of the arbitral proceedings either party may amend or supplement his claim or defence unless the arbitral tribunal considers it inappropriate to allow such amendment having regard to the delay in making it or prejudice to the other party or any other circumstances. However, a claim may not be amended in such a manner that the amended claim falls outside the scope of the arbitration clause or separate arbitration agreement.

Pleas as to the jurisdiction of the arbitral tribunal

Article 21

1. The arbitral tribunal shall have the power to rule on objections that it has no jurisdiction, including any objections with respect to the existence or validity of the arbitration clause or of the separate arbitration agreement.
2. The arbitral tribunal shall have the power to determine the existence or the validity of the contract of which an arbitration clause forms a part. For the purposes of article 21, an arbitration clause which forms part of a contract and which provides for arbitration under these Rules shall be treated as an agreement independent of the other terms of the contract. A decision by the arbitral tribunal that the contract is null and void shall not entail ipso jure the invalidity of the arbitration clause.
3. A plea that the arbitral tribunal does not have jurisdiction shall be raised not later than in the statement of defence or, with respect to a counter-claim, in the reply to the counter-claim.
4. In general, the arbitral tribunal should rule on a plea concerning its jurisdiction as a preliminary question. However, the arbitral tribunal may proceed with the arbitration and rule on such a plea in their final award.

Further written statements

Article 22

The arbitral tribunal shall decide which further written statements, in addition to the statement of claim and the statement of defence, shall be required from the parties or may be presented by them and shall fix the periods of time for communicating such statements.

Periods of time

Article 23

The periods of time fixed by the arbitral tribunal for the communication of written statements (including the statement of claim and statement of defence) should not exceed 45 days. However, the arbitral tribunal may extend the time-limits if it concludes that an extension is justified.

Evidence and hearings

Article 24

1. Each party shall have the burden of proving the facts relied on to support his claim or defence.
2. The arbitral tribunal may, if it considers it appropriate, require a party to deliver to the tribunal and to the other party, within such a period of time as the arbitral tribunal shall decide, a summary of the documents and other evidence which that party intends to present in support of the facts in issue set out in his statement of claim or statement of defence.
3. At any time during the arbitral proceedings the arbitral tribunal may require the parties to produce documents, exhibits or other evidence within such a period of time as the tribunal shall determine.

Evidence and hearings

Article 25

1. In the event of an oral hearing, the arbitral tribunal shall give the parties adequate advance notice of the date, time and place thereof.
2. If witnesses are to be heard, at least 15 days before the hearing each party shall communicate to the arbitral tribunal and to the other party the names and addresses of the witnesses he intends to present, the subject upon and the languages in which such witnesses will give their testimony.
3. The arbitral tribunal shall make arrangements for the translation of oral statements made at a hearing and for a record of the hearing if either is deemed necessary by the tribunal under the circumstances of the case, or if the parties have agreed thereto and have communicated such agreement to the tribunal at least 15 days before the hearing.
4. Hearings shall be held *in camera* unless the parties agree otherwise. The arbitral tribunal may require the retirement of any witness or witnesses during the testimony of other witnesses. The arbitral tribunal is free to determine the manner in which witnesses are examined.
5. Evidence of witnesses may also be presented in the form of written statements signed by them.
6. The arbitral tribunal shall determine the admissibility, relevance, materiality and weight of the evidence offered.

Interim measures of protection

Article 26

1. At the request of either party, the arbitral tribunal may take any interim measures it deems necessary in respect of the subject-matter of the dispute, including measures for the conservation of the goods forming the subject-matter in dispute, such as ordering their deposit with a third person or the sale of perishable goods.
2. Such interim measures may be established in the form of an interim award. The arbitral tribunal shall be entitled to require security for the costs of such measures.
3. A request for interim measures addressed by any party to a judicial authority shall not be deemed incompatible with the agreement to arbitrate, or as a waiver of that agreement.

Experts

Article 27

1. The arbitral tribunal may appoint one or more experts to report to it, in writing, on specific issues to be determined by the tribunal. A copy of the experts terms of reference, established by the arbitral tribunal, shall be communicated to the parties.
2. The parties shall give the expert any relevant information or produce for his inspection any relevant documents or goods that he may require of them. Any dispute between a party and such expert as to the relevance of the required information or production shall be referred to the arbitral tribunal for decision.
3. Upon receipt of the experts report, the arbitral tribunal shall communicate a copy of the report to the parties who shall be given the opportunity to express, in writing, their opinion on the report. A party shall be entitled to examine any document on which the expert has relied in his report.
4. At the request of either party the expert, after delivery of the report, may be heard at a hearing where the parties shall have the opportunity to be present and to interrogate the expert. At this hearing either party may present expert witnesses in order to testify on the points at issue. The provisions of article 25 shall be applicable to such proceedings.

Default

Article 28

1. If, within the period of time fixed by the arbitral tribunal, the claimant has failed to communicate his claim without showing sufficient cause for such failure, the arbitral tribunal shall issue an order for the termination of the arbitral proceedings. If, within the period of time fixed by the

arbitral tribunal, the respondent has failed to communicate his statement of defence without showing sufficient cause for such failure, the arbitral tribunal shall order that the proceedings continue.
2. If one of the parties, duly notified under these Rules, fails to appear at a hearing, with showing sufficient cause for such failure, the arbitral tribunal may proceed with the arbitration.
3. If one of the parties, duly invited to produce documentary evidence, fails to do so within the established period of time, without showing sufficient cause for such failure, the arbitral tribunal may make the award on the evidence before it.

Closure of hearings

Article 29

1. The arbitral tribunal may inquire of the parties if they have any further proof to offer or witnesses to be heard or submissions to make and, if there are none, it may declare the hearings closed.
2. The arbitral tribunal may, if it considers it necessary owing to exceptional circumstances, decide, on its own motion or upon application of a party, to reopen the hearings at any time before the award is made.

Waiver of rules

Article 30

A party who knows that any provision of, or requirement under, these Rules has not been complied with and yet proceeds with the arbitration without promptly stating his objection to such non-compliance, shall be deemed to have waived his right to object.

Section IV. The award

Decisions

Article 31

1. When there are three arbitrators, any award or other decision of the arbitral tribunal shall be made by a majority of the arbitrators.
2. In the case of questions of procedure, when there is no majority or when the arbitral tribunal so authorizes, the presiding arbitrator may decide on his own, subject to revision, if any, by the arbitral tribunal.

Form and effect of the award

Article 32

1. In addition to making a final award, the arbitral tribunal shall be entitled to make interim, interlocutory, or partial awards.
2. The award shall be made in writing and shall be final and binding on the parties. The parties undertake to carry out the award without delay.
3. The arbitral tribunal shall state the reasons upon which the award is based, unless the parties have agreed that no reasons are to be given.
4. An award shall be signed by the arbitrators and it shall contain the date on which and the place where the award was made. Where there are three arbitrators and one of them fails to sign, the award shall state the reason for the absence of the signature.
5. The award may be made public only with the consent of both parties.
6. Copies of the award signed by the arbitrators shall be communicated to the parties by the arbitral tribunal.
7. If the arbitration law of the country where the award is made requires that the award be filed or registered by the arbitral tribunal, the tribunal shall comply with this requirement within the period of time required by law.

Applicable law, amiable compositeur

Article 33

1. The arbitral tribunal shall apply the law designated by the parties as applicable to the substance of the dispute. Failing such designation by the parties, the arbitral tribunal shall apply the law determined by the conflict of laws rules which it considers applicable.
2. The arbitral tribunal shall decide as *amiable compositeur* or *ex aequo et bono* only if the parties have expressly authorized the arbitral tribunal to do so and if the law applicable to the arbitral procedure permits such arbitration.
3. In all cases, the arbitral tribunal shall decide in accordance with the terms of the contract and shall take into account the usages of the trade applicable to the transaction.

Settlement or other grounds for termination

Article 34

1. If, before the award is made, the parties agree on a settlement of the dispute, the arbitral tribunal shall either issue an order for the termination of the arbitral proceedings or, if requested by both parties and accepted by the tribunal, record the settlement in the form of an arbitral award on agreed terms. The arbitral tribunal is not obliged to give reasons for such an award.
2. If, before the award is made, the continuation of the arbitral proceedings becomes unnecessary or impossible for any reason not mentioned in paragraph 1, the arbitral tribunal shall inform the parties of its intention to issue an order for the termination of the proceedings. The arbitral tribunal shall have the power to issue such an order unless a party raises justifiable grounds for objection.
3. Copies of the order for termination of the arbitral proceedings or of the arbitral award on agreed terms, signed by the arbitrators, shall be communicated by the arbitral tribunal to the parties. Where an arbitral award on agreed terms is made, the provisions of article 32, paragraphs 2 and 4 to 7, shall apply.

Interpretation of the award

Article 35

1. Within 30 days after the receipt of the award, either party, with notice to the other party, may request that the arbitral tribunal give an interpretation of the award.
2. The interpretation shall be given in writing within 45 days after the receipt of the request. The interpretation shall form part of the award and the provisions of article 32, paragraphs 2 to 7, shall apply.

Correction of the award

Article 36

1. Within 30 days after the receipt of the award, either party, with notice to the other party, may request the arbitral tribunal to correct in the award any errors in computation, any clerical or typographical errors, or any errors of similar nature. The arbitral tribunal may within 30 days after the communication of the award make such corrections on its own initiative.
2. Such corrections shall be in writing, and the provisions of article 32, paragraphs 2 to 7, shall apply.

Additional award

Article 37

1. Within 30 days after the receipt of the award, either party, with notice to the other party, may request the arbitral tribunal to make an additional award as to claims presented in the arbitral proceedings but omitted from the award.
2. If the arbitral tribunal considers the request for an additional award to be justified and considers that the omission can be rectified without any further hearings or evidence, it shall complete its award within 60 days after the receipt of the request.
3. When an additional award is made, the provisions of article 32, paragraphs 2 to 7, shall apply.

Costs

Article 38

The arbitral tribunal shall fix the costs of arbitration in its award. The term costs includes only:
   (a) The fees of the arbitral tribunal to be stated separately as to each arbitrator and to be fixed by the tribunal itself in accordance with article 39;
   (b) The travel and other expenses incurred by the arbitrators;
   (c) The costs of expert advice and of other assistance required by the arbitral tribunal;
   (d) The travel and other expenses of witnesses to the extent such expenses are approved by the arbitral tribunal;
   (e) The costs for legal representation and assistance of the successful party if such costs were claimed during the arbitral proceedings, and only to the extent that the arbitral tribunal determines that the amount of such costs in reasonable;
   (f) Any fees and expenses of the appointing authority as well as the expenses of the Secretary-General of the Permanent Court of Arbitration at The Hague.

Costs

Article 39

1. The fees of the arbitral tribunal shall be reasonable in amount, taking into account the amount in dispute, the complexity of the subject-matter, the time spent by the arbitrators and any other relevant circumstances of the case.
2. If an appointing authority has been agreed upon by the parties or designated by the Secretary-General of the Permanent Court of Arbitration at The Hague, and if that authority has issued a schedule of fees for arbitrators in international cases which it administers, the arbitral tribunal in fixing its fees shall take that schedule of fees into account to the extent that it considers appropriate in the circumstances of the case.
3. If such appointing authority has not issued a schedule of fees for arbitrators in international cases, any party may at any time request the appointing authority to furnish a statement setting forth the basis for establishing fees which is customarily followed in international cases in which the authority appoints arbitrators. If the appointing authority consents to provide such a statement, the arbitral tribunal in fixing its fees shall take such information into account to the extent that it considers appropriate in the circumstances of the case.
4. In cases referred to in paragraphs 2 and 3, when a party so requests and the appointing authority consents to perform the function, the arbitral tribunal shall fix its fees only after consultation with the appointing authority, which may make any comment it deems appropriate to the arbitral tribunal concerning the fees.

Costs

Article 40

1. Except as provided in paragraph 2, the costs of arbitration shall in principle be borne by the unsuccessful party. However, the arbitral tribunal may apportion each of such costs between the parties if it determines that apportionment is reasonable, taking into account the circumstances of the case.
2. With respect to the costs of legal representation and assistance referred to in article 38, paragraph (e), the arbitral tribunal, taking into account the circumstances of the case, shall be free to determine which party shall bear such costs or may apportion such costs between the parties if it determines that apportionment is reasonable.
3. When the arbitral tribunal issues an order for the termination of the arbitral proceedings or makes an award on agreed terms it shall fix the costs of arbitration referred to in article 38 and article 39, paragraph 1, in the text of that order or award.
4. No additional fees may be charged by an arbitral tribunal for interpretation or correction or completion of its award under articles 35 to 37.

Deposit of costs

Article 41

1. The arbitral tribunal, on its establishment, may request each party to deposit an equal amount as an advance for the costs referred to in article 38, paragraphs (a), (b) and (c).
2. During the course of the arbitral proceedings the arbitral tribunal may request supplementary deposits from the parties.
3. If an appointing authority has been agreed upon by the parties or designated by the Secretary-General of the Permanent Court of Arbitration at The Hague, and when a party so requests and the appointing authority consents to perform the function, the arbitral tribunal shall fix the amount of any deposits or supplementary deposits only after consultation with the appointing authority which may make any comments to the arbitral tribunal which it deems appropriate concerning the amount of such deposits and supplementary deposits.
4. If the required deposits are not paid in full within 30 days after the receipt of the request, the arbitral tribunal shall so inform the parties in order that one or another of them may make the required payment. If such payment is not made, the arbitral tribunal may order the suspension or termination of the arbitral proceedings.
5. After the award has been made, the arbitral tribunal shall render an accounting to the parties of the deposits received and return any unexpended balance to the parties.

APPENDIX 3

A Tabular Comparison of the 1976–2010 UNCITRAL Arbitration Rules

Note: Under '2010 Rules', the underlined text indicates newly-added text in the 2010 Rules; the text in strikethrough font indicates text that has been excluded in the 2010 Rules, from the 1976 Rules.

2010 Rules	1976 Rules
Section I: Introductory Rules	
Article 1 Scope of application	Article 1 Scope of application
1. Where ~~the~~ parties ~~to a contract~~ have agreed ~~in writing*~~ that disputes ~~in relation to that contract~~ between them in respect of a defined legal relationship, whether contractual or not, shall be referred to arbitration under the UNCITRAL Arbitration Rules, then such disputes shall be settled in accordance with these Rules subject to such modification as the parties may agree ~~in writing~~.	1. Where the parties to a contract have agreed in writing* that disputes in relation to that contract shall be referred to arbitration under the UNCITRAL Arbitration Rules, then such disputes shall be settled in accordance with these Rules subject to such modification as the parties may agree in writing.
2. The parties to an arbitration agreement concluded after 15 August 2010 shall be presumed to have referred to the Rules in effect on the date of commencement of the arbitration, unless the parties have agreed to apply a particular version of the Rules. That presumption does not apply where the arbitration agreement has been concluded by accepting after 15 August 2010 an offer made before that date.	2. These Rules shall govern the arbitration except that where any of these Rules is in conflict with a provision of the law applicable to the arbitration from which the parties cannot derogate, that provision shall prevail.
~~2~~ 3. These Rules shall govern the arbitration except that where any of these Rules is in conflict with a provision of the law applicable to the arbitration from which the parties cannot derogate, that provision shall prevail.	
Article 2 Notice~~s~~, and calculation of periods of time	Article 2 Notices, calculation of periods of time
1. A notice, including a notification, communication or proposal, may be transmitted by any means of communication that provides or allows for a record of its transmission.	1. For the purposes of these Rules, any notice, including a notification, communication or proposal, is deemed to have been received if it is physically delivered to the addressee or if it is delivered at his habitual residence, place of business or mailing address, or, if none of these can be found after making reasonable inquiry, then at the addressee's last-known residence or place of business. Notice shall be deemed to have been received on the day it is so delivered.

2010 Rules	1976 Rules
Section I: Introductory Rules	

2. If an address has been designated by a party specifically for this purpose or authorized by the arbitral tribunal, any notice shall be delivered to that party at that address, and if so delivered shall be deemed to have been received. Delivery by electronic means such as facsimile or e-mail may only be made to an address so designated or authorized.

3. In the absence of such designation or authorization, a notice is:

(a) Received if it is physically delivered to the addressee; or

(b) Deemed to have been received if it is delivered at the place of business, habitual residence or mailing address of the addressee.

4. If, after reasonable efforts, delivery cannot be effected in accordance with paragraphs 2 or 3, a notice is deemed to have been received if it is sent to the addressee's last-known place of business, habitual residence or mailing address by registered letter or any other means that provides a record of delivery or of attempted delivery..

~~1~~5. ~~For the purposes of these Rules,~~ A any notice, ~~including a notification, communication or proposal, is~~ shall be deemed to have been received ~~if~~ on the day it is ~~physically~~ delivered in accordance with paragraph 4. A notice transmitted by electronic means is deemed to have been received on the day it is sent, except that a notice of arbitration so transmitted is only deemed to have been received on the day when it reaches the addressee's electronic address. ~~to the addressee or if it is delivered at its habitual residence, place of business or mailing address, or, if none of these can be found after making reasonable inquiry, then at the addressee's last-known residence or place of business. Notice shall be deemed to have been received on the day it is so delivered.~~

~~2~~6. For the purposes of calculating a period of time under these Rules, such period shall begin to run on the day following the day when a notice, notification, communication or proposal is received. If the last day of such period is an official holiday or a non-business day at the residence or place of business of the addressee, the period is extended until the first business day which follows. Official holidays or non-business days occurring during the running of the period of time are included in calculating the period

2. For the purposes of calculating a period of time under these Rules, such period shall begin to run on the day following the day when a notice, notification, communication or proposal is received. If the last day of such period is an official holiday or a non-business day at the residence or place of business of the addressee, the period is extended until the first business day which follows. Official holidays or non-business days occurring during the running of the period of time are included in calculating the period.

Article 3 Notice of arbitration	Article 3 Notice of arbitration
1. The party <u>or parties</u> initiating recourse to arbitration (hereinafter called the "claimant") shall give to the other party <u>or parties</u> (hereinafter called the "respondent") a notice of arbitration.	1. The party initiating recourse to arbitration (hereinafter called the "claimant") shall give to the other party (hereinafter called the "respondent") a notice of arbitration.
2. Arbitral proceedings shall be deemed to commence on the date on which the notice of arbitration is received by the respondent.	2. Arbitral proceedings shall be deemed to commence on the date on which the notice of arbitration is received by the respondent.
3. The notice of arbitration shall include the following:	3. The notice of arbitration shall include the following:
(a) A demand that the dispute be referred to arbitration;	(a) A demand that the dispute be referred to arbitration;
(b) The names and ~~addresses~~ <u>contact details</u> of the parties;	(b) The names and addresses of the parties;
(c) ~~A reference to the arbitration clause or the separate~~ <u>Identification of the</u> arbitration agreement that is invoked;	(c) A reference to the arbitration clause or the separate arbitration agreement that is invoked;
(d) ~~A reference to the~~<u>Identification of any</u> contract <u>or other legal instrument</u> out of or in relation to which the dispute arises <u>or, in the absence of such contract or instrument, a brief description of the relevant relationship</u>;	(d) A reference to the contract out of or in relation to which the dispute arises;
(e) ~~The general nature~~ <u>A brief description</u> of the claim and an indication of the amount involved, if any;	(e) The general nature of the claim and an indication of the amount involved, if any;
(f) The relief or remedy sought;	(f) The relief or remedy sought;
(g) A proposal as to the number of arbitrators, ~~(i.e. one or three)~~, <u>language and place of arbitration</u>, if the parties have not previously agreed thereon.	(g) A proposal as to the number of arbitrators (i.e. one or three), if the parties have not previously agreed thereon.
4. The notice of arbitration may also include:	4. The notice of arbitration may also include:
(a) ~~The~~ <u>A</u> proposals for the ~~appointments~~ <u>designation</u> of ~~a sole arbitrator and~~ an appointing authority referred to in article 6, paragraph 1;	(a) The proposals for the appointments of a sole arbitrator and an appointing authority referred to in article 6, paragraph 1;
(b) A proposal for the appointment of a sole arbitrator referred to in article 8, paragraph 1;	(b) The notification of the appointment of an arbitrator referred to in article 7;
(<del>b</del><u>c</u>) ~~The~~<u>N</u>otification of the appointment of an arbitrator referred to in article ~~7~~ <u>9 or article 10</u>.	(c) The statement of claim referred to in article 18.
~~(c) The statement of claim referred to in article 18.~~	
5. The constitution of the arbitral tribunal shall not be hindered by any controversy with respect to the sufficiency of the notice of arbitration, which shall be finally resolved by the arbitral tribunal.	

Article 4 Response to the notice of arbitration	
1. Within 30 days of the receipt of the notice of arbitration, the respondent shall communicate to the claimant a response to the notice of arbitration, which shall include: (a) The name and contact details of each respondent; (b) A response to the information set forth in the notice of arbitration, pursuant to article 3, paragraph 3 (c) to (g);	

2. The response to the notice of arbitration may also include:
(a) Any plea that an arbitral tribunal constituted under these Rules lacks jurisdiction;
(b) A proposal for the designation of an appointing authority referred to in article 6, paragraph 1;
(c) A proposal for the appointment of a sole arbitrator referred to in article 8, paragraph 1;
(d) Notification of the appointment of an arbitrator referred to in article 9 or article 10;
(e) A brief description of counterclaims or claims for the purpose of a set-off, if any, including where relevant, an indication of the amounts involved, and the relief or remedy sought.
3. The constitution of the arbitral tribunal shall not be hindered by any controversy with respect to the respondent's failure to communicate a response to the notice of arbitration, or an incomplete or late response to the notice of arbitration, which shall be finally resolved by the arbitral tribunal.

Article 4 5 Representation and assistance	Article 4 Representation and assistance
The parties Each party may be represented or assisted by persons chosen by it of their choice. The names and addresses of such persons must be communicated in writing to the other party all parties and to the arbitral tribunal;. Such communication must specify whether the appointment is being made for purposes of representation or assistance. Where a person is to act as a representative of a party, the arbitral tribunal, on its own initiative or at the request of any party, may at any time require proof of authority granted to the representative in such a form as the arbitral tribunal may determine.	The parties may be represented or assisted by persons of their choice. The names and addresses of such persons must be communicated in writing to the other party; such communication must specify whether the appointment is being made for purposes of representation or assistance.

Article 6 Designating and appointing authorities

1. Unless the parties have already agreed on the choice of an appointing authority, a party may at any time propose the name or names of one or more institutions or persons, including the Secretary-General of the Permanent Court of Arbitration at the Hague (hereinafter called the "PCA"), one of whom would serve as appointing authority.
2. If all parties have not agreed on the choice of an appointing authority within 30 days after a proposal made in accordance with paragraph 1 has been received by all other parties, any party may request the Secretary-General of the PCA to designate the appointing authority.
3. Where these Rules provide for a period of time within which a party must refer a matter to an appointing authority and no appointing authority has been agreed on or designated, the period is suspended from the date on which a party initiates the procedure for agreeing on or designating an appointing authority until the date of such agreement or designation.

4. Except as referred to in article 41, paragraph 4, if the appointing authority refuses to act, or if it fails to appoint an arbitrator within 30 days after it receives a party's request to do so, fails to act within any other period provided by these Rules, or fails to decide on a challenge to an arbitrator within a reasonable time after receiving a party's request to do so, any party may request the Secretary-General of the PCA to designate a substitute appointing authority.

5. In exercising their functions under these Rules, the appointing authority and the Secretary-General of the PCA may require from any party and the arbitrators the information they deem necessary and they shall give the parties and, where appropriate, the arbitrators, an opportunity to present their views in any manner they consider appropriate. All such communications to and from the appointing authority and the Secretary-General of the PCA shall also be provided by the sender to all other parties.

6. When the appointing authority is requested to appoint an arbitrator pursuant to articles 8, 9, 10 or 14, the party making the request shall send to the appointing authority copies of the notice of arbitration and, if it exists, any response to the notice of arbitration.

7. The appointing authority shall have regard to such considerations as are likely to secure the appointment of an independent and impartial arbitrator and shall take into account the advisability of appointing an arbitrator of a nationality other than the nationalities of the parties.

Section II: Composition of the arbitral tribunal

Article 5 7 Number of arbitrators	Article 5 Number of arbitrators
1. If the parties have not previously agreed on the number of arbitrators (i.e. one or three), and if within fifteen 30 days after the receipt by the respondent of the notice of arbitration the parties have not agreed that there shall be only one arbitrator, three arbitrators shall be appointed.	If the parties have not previously agreed on the number of arbitrators (i.e. one or three), and if within fifteen days after the receipt by the respondent of the notice of arbitration the parties have not agreed that there shall be only one arbitrator, three arbitrators shall be appointed.
2. Notwithstanding paragraph 1, if no other parties have responded to a proposal to appoint a sole arbitrator within the time limit provided for in paragraph 1 and the party or parties concerned have failed to appoint a second arbitrator in accordance with article 9 or article 10, the appointing authority may, at the request of a party, appoint a sole arbitrator pursuant to the procedure provided for in article 8, paragraph 2 if it determines that, in view of the circumstances of the case, this is more appropriate.	

Article 6 8	Article 6
Appointment of arbitrators (articles 8 to 10)	Appointment of arbitrators

~~1. If a sole arbitrator is to be appointed, either party may propose to the other:~~

~~(a) The names of one or more persons, one of whom would serve as the sole arbitrator; and~~

~~(b) If no appointing authority has been agreed upon by the parties, the name or names of one or more institutions or persons, one of whom would serve as appointing authority.~~

~~2. If within thirty days after receipt by a party of a proposal made in accordance with paragraph 1 the parties have not reached agreement on the choice of a sole arbitrator, the sole arbitrator shall be appointed by the appointing authority agreed upon by the parties. If no appointing authority has been agreed upon by the parties, or if the appointing authority agreed upon refuses to act or fails to appoint the arbitrator within 60~~ days of the receipt of a ~~party's request therefor, either party may request the Secretary-General of the Permanent Court of Arbitration at The Hague to designate an appointing authority.~~

<u>1. If the parties have agreed that a sole arbitrator is to be appointed, and if within 30 days after the receipt by all other parties of the proposal for the appointment of a sole arbitrator, the parties have not reached agreement thereon, a sole arbitrator shall, at the request of a party, be appointed by the appointing authority.</u>

3<u>2</u>. The appointing authority shall~~, at the request of one of the parties,~~ appoint the sole arbitrator as promptly as possible. In making the appointment, the appointing authority shall use the following list-procedure, unless the parties agree that the list-procedure should not be used or unless the appointing authority determines in its discretion that the use of the list-procedure is not appropriate for the case:

(a) ~~At the request of one of the parties~~ The appointing authority shall communicate to ~~both~~ <u>each of the</u> parties an identical list containing at least three names;

(b) Within 15 days after the receipt of this list, each party may return the list to the appointing authority after having deleted the name or names to which ~~he~~ <u>it</u> objects and numbered the remaining names on the list in the order of ~~his~~ <u>its</u> preference;

(c) After the expiration of the above period of time the appointing authority shall appoint the sole arbitrator from among the names approved on the lists returned to it and in accordance with the order of preference indicated by the parties;

---

1. If a sole arbitrator is to be appointed, either party may propose to the other:

(a) The names of one or more persons, one of whom would serve as the sole arbitrator; and

(b) If no appointing authority has been agreed upon by the parties, the name or names of one or more institutions or persons, one of whom would serve as appointing authority.

2. If within thirty days after receipt by a party of a proposal made in accordance with paragraph 1 the parties have not reached agreement on the choice of a sole arbitrator, the sole arbitrator shall be appointed by the appointing authority agreed upon by the parties. If no appointing authority has been agreed upon by the parties, or if the appointing authority agreed upon refuses to act or fails to appoint the arbitrator within sixty days of the receipt of a party's request therefor, either party may request the Secretary-General of the Permanent Court of Arbitration at The Hague to designate an appointing authority.

3. The appointing authority shall, at the request of one of the parties, appoint the sole arbitrator as promptly as possible. In making the appointment the appointing authority shall use the following list-procedure, unless both parties agree that the list-procedure should not be used or unless the appointing authority determines in its discretion that the use of the list-procedure is not appropriate for the case:

(a) At the request of one of the parties the appointing authority shall communicate to both parties an identical list containing at least three names;

(b) Within fifteen days after the receipt of this list, each party may return the list to the appointing authority after having deleted the name or names to which he objects and numbered the remaining names on the list in the order of his preference;

(c) After the expiration of the above period of time the appointing authority shall appoint the sole arbitrator from among the names approved on the lists returned to it and in accordance with the order of preference indicated by the parties;

(d) If for any reason the appointment cannot be made according to this procedure, the appointing authority may exercise its discretion in appointing the sole arbitrator.	(d) If for any reason the appointment cannot be made according to this procedure, the appointing authority may exercise its discretion in appointing the sole arbitrator.
~~4. In making the appointment, the appointing authority shall have regard to such considerations as are likely to secure the appointment of an independent and impartial arbitrator and shall take into account as well the advisability of appointing an arbitrator of a nationality other than the nationalities of the parties.~~	4. In making the appointment, the appointing authority shall have regard to such considerations as are likely to secure the appointment of an independent and impartial arbitrator and shall take into account as well the advisability of appointing an arbitrator of a nationality other than the nationalities of the parties.
Article ~~7~~ 9	**Article 7** **Appointment of arbitrators**
1. If three arbitrators are to be appointed, each party shall appoint one arbitrator. The two arbitrators thus appointed shall choose the third arbitrator who will act as the presiding arbitrator of the <u>arbitral</u> tribunal.	1. If three arbitrators are to be appointed, each party shall appoint one arbitrator. The two arbitrators thus appointed shall choose the third arbitrator who will act as the presiding arbitrator of the tribunal.
2. If within 30 days after the receipt of a party's notification of the appointment of an arbitrator the other party has not notified the first party of the arbitrator ~~he~~<u>it</u> has appointed~~:~~<u>,</u>	2. If within thirty days after the receipt of a party's notification of the appointment of an arbitrator the other party has not notified the first party of the arbitrator he has appointed:
~~(a)~~ the first party may request the appointing authority ~~previously designated by the parties~~ to appoint the second arbitrator~~.; or~~ ~~(b) If no such authority has been previously designated by the parties, or if the appointing authority previously designated refuses to act or fails to appoint the arbitrator within thirty days after receipt of a party's request therefor, the first party may request the Secretary General of the Permanent Court of Arbitration at The Hague to designate the appointing authority. The first party may then request the appointing authority so designated to appoint the second arbitrator. In either case, the appointing authority may exercise its discretion in appointing the arbitrator.~~	(a) The first party may request the appointing authority previously designated by the parties to appoint the second arbitrator; or (b) If no such authority has been previously designated by the parties, or if the appointing authority previously designated refuses to act or fails to appoint the arbitrator within thirty days after receipt of a party's request therefor, the first party may request the Secretary-General of the Permanent Court of Arbitration at The Hague to designate the appointing authority. The first party may then request the appointing authority so designated to appoint the second arbitrator. In either case, the appointing authority may exercise its discretion in appointing the arbitrator.
3. If within 30 days after the appointment of the second arbitrator the two arbitrators have not agreed on the choice of the presiding arbitrator, the presiding arbitrator shall be appointed by an appointing authority in the same way as a sole arbitrator would be appointed under article ~~6~~ <u>8</u>.	3. If within thirty days after the appointment of the second arbitrator the two arbitrators have not agreed on the choice of the presiding arbitrator, the presiding arbitrator shall be appointed by an appointing authority in the same way as a sole arbitrator would be appointed under article 6.
Article 10	
<u>1. For the purposes of article 9, paragraph 1, where three arbitrators are to be appointed and there are multiple parties as claimant or as respondent, unless the parties have agreed to another method of appointment of arbitrators, the multiple parties jointly, whether as claimant or as respondent, shall appoint an arbitrator.</u>	

2. If the parties have agreed that the arbitral tribunal is to be composed of a number of arbitrators other than one or three, the arbitrators shall be appointed according to the method agreed upon by the parties.

3. In the event of any failure to constitute the arbitral tribunal under these Rules, the appointing authority shall, at the request of any party, constitute the arbitral tribunal, and in doing so, may revoke any appointment already made, and appoint or reappoint each of the arbitrators and designate one of them as the presiding arbitrator.

~~Article 8~~ ~~Appointment of Arbitrators~~	Article 8 Appointment of arbitrators
~~1. When an appointing authority is requested to appoint an arbitrator pursuant to article 6 or article 7, the party which makes the request shall send to the appointing authority a copy of the notice of arbitration, a copy of the contract out of or in relation to which the dispute has arisen and a copy of the arbitration agreement if it is not contained in the contract. The appointing authority may require from either party such information as it deems necessary to fulfil its function.~~	1. When an appointing authority is requested to appoint an arbitrator pursuant to article 6 or article 7, the party which makes the request shall send to the appointing authority a copy of the notice of arbitration, a copy of the contract out of or in relation to which the dispute has arisen and a copy of the arbitration agreement if it is not contained in the contract. The appointing authority may require from either party such information as it deems necessary to fulfil its function.
~~2. Where the names of one or more persons are proposed for appointment as arbitrators, their full names, addresses and nationalities shall be indicated, together with a description of their qualifications.~~	2. Where the names of one or more persons are proposed for appointment as arbitrators, their full names, addresses and nationalities shall be indicated, together with a description of their qualifications.

Article ~~9~~ <u>11</u> <u>Disclosures by and</u> ~~C~~<u>c</u>hallenge of arbitrators <u>(articles 11 to 13)</u>	Article 9 Challenge of arbitrators
~~A prospective arbitrator shall disclose to those who approach him~~<u>When a person is approached</u> in connection with his or her possible appointment <u>as an arbitrator, he or she shall disclose</u> any circumstances likely to give rise to justifiable doubts as to his <u>or her</u> impartiality or independence. An arbitrator, ~~once appointed or chosen~~ <u>from the time of his or her appointment and throughout the arbitral proceedings</u>, shall <u>without delay</u> disclose <u>any</u> such circumstances to the parties <u>and the other arbitrators</u> unless they have already been informed by him <u>or her</u> of these circumstances.	A prospective arbitrator shall disclose to those who approach him in connexion with his possible appointment any circumstances likely to give rise to justifiable doubts as to his impartiality or independence. An arbitrator, once appointed or chosen, shall disclose such circumstances to the parties unless they have already been informed by him of these circumstances.

Article ~~10~~ <u>12</u>	Article 10 Challenge of arbitrators
1. Any arbitrator may be challenged if circumstances exist that give rise to justifiable doubts as to the arbitrator's impartiality or independence.	1. Any arbitrator may be challenged if circumstances exist that give rise to justifiable doubts as to the arbitrator's impartiality or independence.

Comparison of the 1976–2010 UNCITRAL Arbitration Rules 947

2. A party may challenge the arbitrator appointed by ~~him~~it only for reasons of which ~~he~~it becomes aware after the appointment has been made.	2. A party may challenge the arbitrator appointed by him only for reasons of which he becomes aware after the appointment has been made.
3. In the event that an arbitrator fails to act or in the event of de jure or de facto impossibility of his or her performing his or her functions, the procedure in respect of the challenge of an arbitrator as provided in article 13 shall apply.	

Article ~~11~~ 13	Article 11 Challenge of arbitrators
1. A party ~~who~~ that intends to challenge an arbitrator shall send notice of ~~his~~its challenge within 15 days after it has been notified of the appointment of the challenged arbitrator, ~~has been notified to the challenging party~~or within 15 days after the circumstances mentioned in articles 9<u>11</u> and ~~10~~12 became known to that party.	1. A party who intends to challenge an arbitrator shall send notice of his challenge within fifteen days after the appointment of the challenged arbitrator has been notified to the challenging party or within fifteen days after the circumstances mentioned in articles 9 and 10 became known to that party.
2. The notice of the challenge shall be ~~notified~~ communicated to ~~the~~all other ~~party~~ parties, to the arbitrator who is challenged and to the other arbitrators ~~members of the arbitral tribunal~~. The notice of challenge ~~notification shall be in writing and~~ shall state the reasons for the challenge.	2. The challenge shall be notified to the other party, to the arbitrator who is challenged and to the other members of the arbitral tribunal. The notification shall be in writing and shall state the reasons for the challenge.
3. When an arbitrator has been challenged by ~~one~~a party, ~~the~~ all ~~other party~~ parties may agree to the challenge. The arbitrator may also, after the challenge, withdraw from his or her office. In neither case does this imply acceptance of the validity of the grounds for the challenge. ~~In both cases the procedure provided in article 6 or 7 shall be used in full for the appointment of the substitute arbitrator, even if during the process of appointing the challenged arbitrator a party had failed to exercise his right to appoint or to participate in the appointment.~~	3. When an arbitrator has been challenged by one party, the other party may agree to the challenge. The arbitrator may also, after the challenge, withdraw from his office. In neither case does this imply acceptance of the validity of the grounds for the challenge. In both cases the procedure provided in article 6 or 7 shall be used in full for the appointment of the substitute arbitrator, even if during the process of appointing the challenged arbitrator a party had failed to exercise his right to appoint or to participate in the appointment.
4. If, within 15 days from the date of the notice of challenge, all parties do not agree to the challenge or the challenged arbitrator does not withdraw, the party making the challenge may elect to pursue it. In that case, within 30 days from the date of the notice of challenge, it shall seek a decision on the challenge by the appointing authority.	

~~Article 12~~ Challenge of arbitrators	Article 12 Challenge of arbitrators
~~1. If the other party does not agree to the challenge and the challenged arbitrator does not withdraw, the decision on the challenge will be made:~~	1. If the other party does not agree to the challenge and the challenged arbitrator does not withdraw, the decision on the challenge will be made:
~~(a) When the initial appointment was made by an appointing authority, by that authority;~~	*(a)* When the initial appointment was made by an appointing authority, by that authority;

~~(b) When the initial appointment was not made by an appointing authority, but an appointing authority has been previously designated, by that authority;~~

~~(c) In all other cases, by the appointing authority to be designated in accordance with the procedure for designating an appointing authority as provided for in article 6.~~

~~2. If the appointing authority sustains the challenge, a substitute arbitrator shall be appointed or chosen pursuant to the procedure applicable to the appointment or choice of an arbitrator as provided in articles 6 to 9 except that, when this procedure would call for the designation of an appointing authority, the appointment of the arbitrator shall be made by the appointing authority which decided on the challenge.~~

(b) When the initial appointment was not made by an appointing authority, but an appointing authority has been previously designated, by that authority;

(c) In all other cases, by the appointing authority to be designated in accordance with the procedure for designating an appointing authority as provided for in article 6.

2. If the appointing authority sustains the challenge, a substitute arbitrator shall be appointed or chosen pursuant to the procedure applicable to the appointment or choice of an arbitrator as provided in articles 6 to 9 except that, when this procedure would call for the designation of an appointing authority, the appointment of the arbitrator shall be made by the appointing authority which decided on the challenge.

Article ~~13~~ 14
Replacement of an arbitrator

1. Subject to paragraph (2), in any ~~In the~~ event ~~of the death or resignation of~~ where an arbitrator has to be replaced during the course of the arbitral proceedings, a substitute arbitrator shall be appointed or chosen pursuant to the procedure provided for in articles ~~6~~8 to ~~9~~11 that was applicable to the appointment or choice of the arbitrator being replaced. This procedure shall apply even if during the process of appointing the arbitrator to be replaced, a party had failed to exercise its right to appoint or to participate in the appointment.

~~2. In the event that an arbitrator refuses or fails to act or in the event of the *de jure* or *de facto* impossibility of his or her performing his or her functions, the procedure in respect of the challenge and replacement of an arbitrator as provided in the preceding articles shall apply.~~

2. If, at the request of a party, the appointing authority determines that, in view of the exceptional circumstances of the case, it would be justified for a party to be deprived of its right to appoint a substitute arbitrator, the appointing authority may, after giving an opportunity to the parties and the remaining arbitrators to express their views: (a) appoint the substitute arbitrator; or (b) if the same occurs after the closure of the hearings, authorize the other arbitrators to proceed with the arbitration and make any decision or award.

Article 13
Replacement of an arbitrator

1. In the event of the death or resignation of an arbitrator during the course of the arbitral proceedings, a substitute arbitrator shall be appointed or chosen pursuant to the procedure provided for in articles 6 to 9 that was applicable to the appointment or choice of the arbitrator being replaced.

2. In the event that an arbitrator fails to act or in the event of the *de jure* or *de facto* impossibility of his performing his functions, the procedure in respect of the challenge and replacement of an arbitrator as provided in the preceding articles shall apply.

Comparison of the 1976–2010 UNCITRAL Arbitration Rules

Article ~~14~~ 15 Repetition of hearings in the event of the replacement of an arbitrator	Article 14 Repetition of hearings in the event of the replacement of an arbitrator
If ~~under articles 11 to 13 the sole~~ an arbitrator ~~or presiding arbitrator~~ is replaced, ~~any hearings held previously shall be repeated; if any other arbitrator is replaced, such prior hearings may be repeated at the discretion of the arbitral tribunal~~ the proceedings shall resume at the stage where the arbitrator who was replaced ceased to perform his or her functions, unless the arbitral tribunal decides otherwise.	If under articles 11 to 13 the sole or presiding arbitrator is replaced, any hearings held previously shall be repeated; if any other arbitrator is replaced, such prior hearings may be repeated at the discretion of the arbitral tribunal.
Article 16 Liability	
Save for intentional wrongdoing, the parties waive, to the fullest extent permitted under the applicable law, any claim against the arbitrators, the appointing authority, and any person appointed by the arbitral tribunal based on any act or omission in connection with the arbitration.	

Section III: Arbitral Proceedings

Article ~~15~~ 17 General provisions	Article 15 General provisions
1. Subject to these Rules, the arbitral tribunal may conduct the arbitration in such manner as it considers appropriate, provided that the parties are treated with equality and that at ~~any~~ appropriate stage of the proceedings each party is given a reasonable ~~full~~ opportunity of presenting ~~his~~ its case. The arbitral tribunal, in exercising its discretion, shall conduct the proceedings so as to avoid unnecessary delay and expense and to provide a fair and efficient process for resolving the parties' dispute.	1. Subject to these Rules, the arbitral tribunal may conduct the arbitration in such manner as it considers appropriate, provided that the parties are treated with equality and that at any stage of the proceedings each party is given a full opportunity of presenting his case.
2. As soon as practicable after its constitution and after inviting the parties to express their views, the arbitral tribunal shall establish the provisional timetable of the arbitration. The arbitral tribunal may, at any time, after inviting the parties to express their views, extend or abridge any period of time prescribed under these Rules or agreed by the parties.	
~~2~~ 3. If ~~at any appropriate stage of the proceedings,~~ ~~either~~ any party so requests ~~at any stage of the proceedings~~, the arbitral tribunal shall hold hearings for the presentation of evidence by witnesses, including expert witnesses, or for oral argument. In the absence of such a request, the arbitral tribunal shall decide whether to hold such hearings or whether the proceedings shall be conducted on the basis of documents and other materials.	2. If either party so requests at any stage of the proceedings, the arbitral tribunal shall hold hearings for the presentation of evidence by witnesses, including expert witnesses, or for oral argument. In the absence of such a request, the arbitral tribunal shall decide whether to hold such hearings or whether the proceedings shall be conducted on the basis of documents and other materials.

Section III: Arbitral Proceedings

3<s>4</s>. All <s>documents or information supplied</s> communications to the arbitral tribunal by one party shall at the same time be communicated by that party to <s>the</s> all other <s>party</s> parties. Such communications shall be made at the same time, except as otherwise permitted by the arbitral tribunal if it may do so under applicable law.	3. All documents or information supplied to the arbitral tribunal by one party shall at the same time be communicated by that party to the other party.
5. The arbitral tribunal may, at the request of any party, allow one or more third persons to be joined in the arbitration as a party provided such person is a party to the arbitration agreement, unless the arbitral tribunal finds, after giving all parties, including the person or persons to be joined, the opportunity to be heard, that joinder should not be permitted because of prejudice to any of those parties. The arbitral tribunal may make a single award or several awards in respect of all parties so involved in the arbitration.	

Article <s>16</s> 18
Place of arbitration

Article 16
Place of arbitration

1. <s>Unless</s> If the parties have not previously agreed upon the place <s>where the</s> of arbitration, <s>the</s> <s>is to be held, such</s> place of arbitration shall be determined by the arbitral tribunal<s>,</s> having regard to the circumstances of the <s>arbitration</s> case. The award shall be deemed to be made at the place of arbitration.	1. Unless the parties have agreed upon the place where the arbitration is to be held, such place shall be determined by the arbitral tribunal, having regard to the circumstances of the arbitration.
<s>2. The arbitral tribunal may determine the locale of the arbitration within the country agreed upon by the parties. It may hear witnesses and hold meetings for consultation among its members at any place it deems appropriate, having regard to the circumstances of the arbitration.</s>	2. The arbitral tribunal may determine the locale of the arbitration within the country agreed upon by the parties. It may hear witnesses and hold meetings for consultation among its members at any place it deems appropriate, having regard to the circumstances of the arbitration.
3<s>2</s>. The arbitral tribunal may meet at any <s>place</s> location it <s>deems</s> considers appropriate for deliberations. Unless otherwise agreed by the parties, the arbitral tribunal may also meet at any location it considers appropriate for any other purpose, including hearings. <s>the inspection of goods, other property or documents. The parties shall be given sufficient notice to enable them to be present at such inspection.</s>	3. The arbitral tribunal may meet at any place it deems appropriate for the inspection of goods, other property or documents. The parties shall be given sufficient notice to enable them to be present at such inspection.
<s>4. The award shall be made at the place of arbitration.</s>	4. The award shall be made at the place of arbitration.

Article <s>17</s> 19
Language

Article 17
Language

1. Subject to an agreement by the parties, the arbitral tribunal shall, promptly after its appointment, determine the language or languages	1. Subject to an agreement by the parties, the arbitral tribunal shall, promptly after its appointment, determine the language or languages to be used in the

to be used in the proceedings. This determination shall apply to the statement of claim, the statement of defence, and any further written statements and, if oral hearings take place, to the language or languages to be used in such hearings.

2. The arbitral tribunal may order that any documents annexed to the statement of claim or statement of defence, and any supplementary documents or exhibits submitted in the course of the proceedings, delivered in their original language, shall be accompanied by a translation into the language or languages agreed upon by the parties or determined by the arbitral tribunal.

Article ~~18~~ 20
Statement of claim

1. ~~Unless the statement of claim was contained in the notice of arbitration, within a period of time to be determined by the arbitral tribunal,~~ The claimant shall communicate ~~his or her~~ its statement of claim in writing to the respondent and to each of the arbitrators within a period of time to be determined by the arbitral tribunal. The claimant may elect to treat its notice of arbitration in article 3 as a statement of claim, provided that the notice of arbitration also complies with the requirements of paragraphs 2 to 4 of this article. ~~A copy of the contract, and of the arbitration agreement if not contained in the contract, shall be annexed thereto.~~

2. The statement of claim shall include the following particulars:

(a) The names and ~~addresses~~ contact details of the parties;
(b) A statement of the facts supporting the claim;
(c) The points at issue;
(d) The relief or remedy sought~~.~~;
(e) The legal grounds or arguments supporting the claim.

~~The claimant may annex to his statement of claim all documents he deems relevant or may add a reference to the documents or other evidence he will submit.~~

3. A copy of any contract or other legal instrument out of or in relation to which the dispute arises and of the arbitration agreement shall be annexed to the statement of claim.

4. The statement of claim should, as far as possible, be accompanied by all documents and other evidence relied upon by the claimant, or contain references to them.

proceedings. This determination shall apply to the statement of claim, the statement of defence, and any further written statements and, if oral hearings take place, to the language or languages to be used in such hearings.

2. The arbitral tribunal may order that any documents annexed to the statement of claim or statement of defence, and any supplementary documents or exhibits submitted in the course of the proceedings, delivered in their original language, shall be accompanied by a translation into the language or languages agreed upon by the parties or determined by the arbitral tribunal.

Article 18
Statement of claim

1. Unless the statement of claim was contained in the notice of arbitration, within a period of time to be determined by the arbitral tribunal, the claimant shall communicate his statement of claim in writing to the respondent and to each of the arbitrators. A copy of the contract, and of the arbitration agreement if not contained in the contract, shall be annexed thereto.

2. The statement of claim shall include the following particulars:

(a) The names and addresses of the parties;
(b) A statement of the facts supporting the claim;
(c) The points at issue;
(d) The relief or remedy sought.

The claimant may annex to his statement of claim all documents he deems relevant or may add a reference to the documents or other evidence he will submit.

Article <s>19</s> 21 Statement of defence	Article 19 Statement of defence
1. <s>Within a period of time to be determined by the arbitral tribunal, t</s>The respondent shall communicate <s>his</s>its statement of defence in writing to the claimant and to each of the arbitrators within a period of time to be determined by the arbitral tribunal. The respondent may elect to treat its response to the notice of arbitration in article 4 as a statement of defence, provided that the response to the notice of arbitration also complies with the requirements of paragraph 2 of this article.	1. Within a period of time to be determined by the arbitral tribunal, the respondent shall communicate his statement of defence in writing to the claimant and to each of the arbitrators.
2. The statement of defence shall reply to the particulars (b), <s>(c) and (d)</s> to (e) of the statement of claim (art.<s>icle</s> <s>18</s> 20, para. 2). <s>The respondent may annex to his statement the documents on which he relies for his defence or may add a reference to the documents or other evidence he will submit.</s> The statement of defence should, as far as possible, be accompanied by all documents and other evidence relied upon by the respondent, or contain references to them.	2. The statement of defence shall reply to the particulars (b), (c) and (d) of the statement of claim (article 18, para. 2). The respondent may annex to his statement the documents on which he relies for his defence or may add a reference to the documents or other evidence he will submit.
3. In <s>his</s> its statement of defence, or at a later stage in the arbitral proceedings if the arbitral tribunal decides that the delay was justified under the circumstances, the respondent may make a counterclaim or <s>arising out of the same contract</s> or rely on a claim <s>arising out of the same contract</s> for the purpose of a set-off provided that the arbitral tribunal has jurisdiction over it.	3. In his statement of defence, or at a later stage in the arbitral proceedings if the arbitral tribunal decides that the delay was justified under the circumstances, the respondent may make a counter-claim arising out of the same contract or rely on a claim arising out of the same contract for the purpose of a set-off.
4. The provisions of article 20, paragraphs 2 and 4 shall apply to a counterclaim, a claim under article 4, paragraph 2 (f), and a claim relied on for the purpose of a set-off.	

Article <s>20</s> 22 Amendments to the claim or defence	Article 20 Amendments to the claim or defence
During the course of the arbitral proceedings, <s>either</s> a party may amend or supplement <s>his</s> its claim or defence, including a counterclaim or a claim for the purpose of a set-off, unless the arbitral tribunal considers it inappropriate to allow such amendment or supplement having regard to the delay in making it or prejudice to <s>the</s> other <s>party</s> parties or any other circumstances. However, a claim or defence, including a counterclaim or a claim for the purpose of a set off, may not be amended or supplemented in such a manner that the amended or supplemented claim or defence falls outside the <s>scope</s> jurisdiction of the arbitral tribunal <s>arbitration clause or separate arbitration agreement</s>.	During the course of the arbitral proceedings either party may amend or supplement his claim or defence unless the arbitral tribunal considers it inappropriate to allow such amendment having regard to the delay in making it or prejudice to the other party or any other circumstances. However, a claim may not be amended in such a manner that the amended claim falls outside the scope of the arbitration clause or separate arbitration agreement.

Article ~~21~~ 23 Pleas as to the jurisdiction of the arbitral tribunal	Article 21 Pleas as to the jurisdiction of the arbitral tribunal
1. The arbitral tribunal shall have the power to rule on <u>its own</u> ~~objections that it has no~~ jurisdiction, including any objections with respect to the existence or validity of the arbitration ~~clause or of the separate arbitration~~ agreement<u>. For that purpose, an arbitration clause which forms part of a contract shall be treated as an agreement independent of the other terms of the contract. A decision by the arbitral tribunal that the contract is null shall not entail automatically the invalidity of the arbitration clause.</u>	1. The arbitral tribunal shall have the power to rule on objections that it has no jurisdiction, including any objections with respect to the existence or validity of the arbitration clause or of the separate arbitration agreement.
~~2. The arbitral tribunal shall have the power to determine the existence or the validity of the contract of which an arbitration clause forms a part. For the purposes of article 21, an arbitration clause which forms part of a contract and which provides for arbitration under these Rules shall be treated as an agreement independent of the other terms of the contract. A decision by the arbitral tribunal that the contract is null and void shall not entail *ipso jure* the invalidity of the arbitration clause.~~	2. The arbitral tribunal shall have the power to determine the existence or the validity of the contract of which an arbitration clause forms a part. For the purposes of article 21, an arbitration clause which forms part of a contract and which provides for arbitration under these Rules shall be treated as an agreement independent of the other terms of the contract. A decision by the arbitral tribunal that the contract is null and void shall not entail *ipso jure* the invalidity of the arbitration clause.
<u>3</u>~~2~~. A plea that the arbitral tribunal does not have jurisdiction shall be raised ~~not~~ later than in the statement of defence or, with respect to a counterclaim <u>or a claim for the purpose of a set-off</u>, in the reply to the counterclaim <u>or to the claim for the purpose of a set-off. A party is not precluded from raising such a plea by the fact that it has appointed, or participated in the appointment of, an arbitrator. A plea that the arbitral tribunal is exceeding the scope of its authority shall be raised as soon as the matter alleged to be beyond the scope of its authority is raised during the arbitral proceedings. The arbitral</u> tribunal may<u>, in either case, admit a later plea if it considers the delay justified</u>.	3. A plea that the arbitral tribunal does not have jurisdiction shall be raised not later than in the statement of defence or, with respect to a counterclaim, in the reply to the counterclaim.
~~4. In general, the arbitral tribunal should rule on a plea concerning its jurisdiction as a preliminary question. However, the arbitral tribunal may proceed with the arbitration and rule on such a plea in their final award.~~	4. In general, the arbitral tribunal should rule on a plea concerning its jurisdiction as a preliminary question. However, the arbitral tribunal may proceed with the arbitration and rule on such a plea in their final award.
<u>3. The arbitral tribunal may rule on a plea referred to in paragraph 2 either as a preliminary question or in an award on the merits. The arbitral tribunal may continue the arbitral proceedings and make an award, notwithstanding any pending challenge to its jurisdiction before a court.</u>	

Article <s>22</s> 24 **Further written statements**	**Article 22** **Further written statements**
The arbitral tribunal shall decide which further written statements, in addition to the statement of claim and the statement of defence, shall be required from the parties or may be presented by them and shall fix the periods of time for communicating such statements.	The arbitral tribunal shall decide which further written statements, in addition to the statement of claim and the statement of defence, shall be required from the parties or may be presented by them and shall fix the periods of time for communicating such statements.
Article <s>23</s> 25 **Periods of time**	**Article 23** **Periods of time**
The periods of time fixed by the arbitral tribunal for the communication of written statements (including the statement of claim and statement of defence) should not exceed <s>forty-five</s> 45 days. However, the arbitral tribunal may extend the time-limits if it concludes that an extension is justified.	The periods of time fixed by the arbitral tribunal for the communication of written statements (including the statement of claim and statement of defence) should not exceed forty-five days. However, the arbitral tribunal may extend the time-limits if it concludes that an extension is justified.
Article 26 **Interim measures <s>of Protection</s>**	**Article 26** **Interim measures of protection**
<s>1. At the request of either party, the arbitral tribunal may take any interim measures it deems necessary in respect of the subject matter of the dispute, including measures for the conservation of the goods forming the subject matter in dispute, such as ordering their deposit with a third person or the sale of perishable goods.</s> <s>2. Such interim measures may be established in the form of an interim award. The arbitral tribunal shall be entitled to require security for the costs of such measures.</s> 1. The arbitral tribunal may, at the request of a party, grant interim measures. 2. An interim measure is any temporary measure by which, at any time prior to the issuance of the award by which the dispute is finally decided, the arbitral tribunal orders a party, for example and without limitation, to: (a) Maintain or restore the status quo pending determination of the dispute; (b) Take action that would prevent, or refrain from taking action that is likely to cause, (i) current or imminent harm or (ii) prejudice to the arbitral process itself; (c) Provide a means of preserving assets out of which a subsequent award may be satisfied; or (d) Preserve evidence that may be relevant and material to the resolution of the dispute.	1. At the request of either party, the arbitral tribunal may take any interim measures it deems necessary in respect of the subject-matter of the dispute, including measures for the conservation of the goods forming the subject-matter in dispute, such as ordering their deposit with a third person or the sale of perishable goods. 2. Such interim measures may be established in the form of an interim award. The arbitral tribunal shall be entitled to require security for the costs of such measures.

3. The party requesting an interim measure under paragraph 2 (a), (b) and (c) shall satisfy the arbitral tribunal that:

(a) Harm not adequately reparable by an award of damages is likely to result if the measure is not ordered, and such harm substantially outweighs the harm that is likely to result to the party against whom the measure is directed if the measure is granted; and

(b) There is a reasonable possibility that the requesting party will succeed on the merits of the claim. The determination on this possibility shall not affect the discretion of the arbitral tribunal in making any subsequent determination.

4. With regard to a request for an interim measure under paragraph 2 (d), the requirements in paragraph 3 (a) and (b) shall apply only to the extent the arbitral tribunal considers appropriate.

5. The arbitral tribunal may modify, suspend or terminate an interim measure it has granted, upon application of any party or, in exceptional circumstances and upon prior notice to the parties, on the arbitral tribunal's own initiative.

6. The arbitral tribunal may require the party requesting an interim measure to provide appropriate security in connection with the measure.

7. The arbitral tribunal may require any party promptly to disclose any material change in the circumstances on the basis of which the interim measure was requested or granted.

8. The party requesting an interim measure may be liable for any costs and damages caused by the measure to any party if the arbitral tribunal later determines that, in the circumstances then prevailing, the measure should not have been granted. The arbitral tribunal may award such costs and damages at any point during the proceedings.

3<s>3</s>9. A request for interim measures addressed by any party to a judicial authority shall not be deemed incompatible with the agreement to arbitrate, or as a waiver of that agreement.	3. A request for interim measures addressed by any party to a judicial authority shall not be deemed incompatible with the agreement to arbitrate, or as a waiver of that agreement.
Article <s>24</s> 27 Evidence <s>and Hearings</s>	Article 24 Evidence and hearings
1. Each party shall have the burden of proving the facts relied on to support <s>his</s> its claim or defence.	1. Each party shall have the burden of proving the facts relied on to support his claim or defence.
<s>2. The arbitral tribunal may, if it considers it appropriate, require a party to deliver to the tribunal and to the other party, within such a period of time as the arbitral tribunal shall decide, a summary of the documents and other evidence which that party intends to present in support of the facts in issue set out in his statement of claim or statement of defence.</s>	2. The arbitral tribunal may, if it considers it appropriate, require a party to deliver to the tribunal and to the other party, within such a period of time as the arbitral tribunal shall decide, a summary of the documents and other evidence which that party intends to present in support of the facts in issue set out in his statement of claim or statement of defence.

2. Witnesses, including expert witnesses, who are presented by the parties to testify to the arbitral tribunal on any issue of fact or expertise may be any individual, notwithstanding that the individual is a party to the arbitration or in any way related to a party. Unless otherwise directed by the arbitral tribunal, statements by witnesses, including expert witnesses, may be presented in writing and signed by them.

3. At any time during the arbitral proceedings the arbitral tribunal may require the parties to produce documents, exhibits or other evidence within such a period of time as the tribunal shall determine.

4. The arbitral tribunal shall determine the admissibility, relevance, materiality and weight of the evidence offered.

| Article 25 28 | Article 25 |
| Evidence and Hearings | Evidence and hearings |

3. At any time during the arbitral proceedings the arbitral tribunal may require the parties to produce documents, exhibits or other evidence within such a period of time as the tribunal shall determine.

1. In the event of an oral hearing, the arbitral tribunal shall give the parties adequate advance notice of the date, time and place thereof.

2. Witnesses, including expert witnesses, may be heard under the conditions and examined in the manner set by the arbitral tribunal.

2. If witnesses are to be heard, at least fifteen days before the hearing each party shall communicate to the arbitral tribunal and to the other party the names and addresses of the witnesses he intends to present, the subject upon and the languages in which such witnesses will give their testimony.

3. The arbitral tribunal shall make arrangements for the translation of oral statements made at a hearing and for a record of the hearing if either is deemed necessary by the tribunal under the circumstances of the case, or if the parties have agreed thereto and have communicated such agreement to the tribunal at least 15 days before the hearing.

4 3. Hearings shall be held in camera unless the parties agree otherwise. The arbitral tribunal may require the retirement of any witness or witnesses, including expert witnesses, during the testimony of other witnesses, except that a witness, including an expert witness, who is a party to the arbitration shall not, in principle, be asked to retire. The arbitral tribunal is free to determine the manner in which witnesses are examined.

4. The arbitral tribunal may direct that witnesses, including expert witnesses, be examined through means of telecommunication that do not require their physical presence at the hearing (such as videoconference).

1. In the event of an oral hearing, the arbitral tribunal shall give the parties adequate advance notice of the date, time and place thereof.

2. If witnesses are to be heard, at least fifteen days before the hearing each party shall communicate to the arbitral tribunal and to the other party the names and addresses of the witnesses he intends to present, the subject upon and the languages in which such witnesses will give their testimony.

3. The arbitral tribunal shall make arrangements for the translation of oral statements made at a hearing and for a record of the hearing if either is deemed necessary by the tribunal under the circumstances of the case, or if the parties have agreed thereto and have communicated such agreement to the tribunal at least fifteen days before the hearing.

4. Hearings shall be held *in camera* unless the parties agree otherwise. The arbitral tribunal may require the retirement of any witness or witnesses during the testimony of other witnesses. The arbitral tribunal is free to determine the manner in which witnesses are examined.

5. Evidence of witnesses may also be presented in the form of written statements signed by them.	5. Evidence of witnesses may also be presented in the form of written statements signed by them.
6. The arbitral tribunal shall determine the admissibility, relevance, materiality and weight of the evidence offered.	6. The arbitral tribunal shall determine the admissibility, relevance, materiality and weight of the evidence offered.

Article ~~27~~ 29 Experts <u>appointed by the arbitral tribunal</u>	Article 27 Experts
1. <u>After consultation with the parties, T</u>the arbitral tribunal may appoint one or more <u>independent</u> experts to report to it, in writing, on specific issues to be determined by the tribunal. A copy of the expert's terms of reference, established by the arbitral tribunal, shall be communicated to the parties.	1. The arbitral tribunal may appoint one or more experts to report to it, in writing, on specific issues to be determined by the tribunal. A copy of the expert's terms of reference, established by the arbitral tribunal, shall be communicated to the parties.
2. <u>The expert shall, in principle before accepting appointment, submit to the arbitral tribunal and to the parties a description of his or her qualifications and a statement of his or her impartiality and independence. Within the time ordered by the arbitral tribunal, the parties shall inform the arbitral tribunal whether they have any objections as to the expert's qualifications, impartiality or independence. The arbitral tribunal shall decide promptly whether to accept any such objections. After an expert's appointment, a party may object to the expert's qualifications, impartiality or independence only if the objection is for reasons of which the party becomes aware after the appointment has been made. The arbitral tribunal shall decide promptly what, if any, action to take.</u>	
3~~2~~. The parties shall give the expert any relevant information or produce for his <u>or her</u> inspection any relevant documents or goods that he <u>or she</u> may require of them. Any dispute between a party and such expert as to the relevance of the required information or production shall be referred to the arbitral tribunal for decision.	2. The parties shall give the expert any relevant information or produce for his inspection any relevant documents or goods that he may require of them. Any dispute between a party and such expert as to the relevance of the required information or production shall be referred to the arbitral tribunal for decision.
4~~3~~. Upon receipt of the expert's report, the arbitral tribunal shall communicate a copy of the report to the parties, <u>which</u> ~~who~~ shall be given the opportunity to express, in writing, their opinion on the report. A party shall be entitled to examine any document on which the expert has relied in his <u>or her</u> report.	3. Upon receipt of the expert's report, the arbitral tribunal shall communicate a copy of the report to the parties who shall be given the opportunity to express, in writing, their opinion on the report. A party shall be entitled to examine any document on which the expert has relied in his report.
5~~4~~. At the request of ~~either~~ <u>any</u> party<u>,</u> the expert, after delivery of the report, may be heard at a hearing where the parties shall have the opportunity to be present and to interrogate the expert. At this hearing, ~~either~~ <u>any</u> party may present expert witnesses in order to testify on the points at issue. The provisions of article ~~25~~ <u>28</u> shall be applicable to such proceedings.	4. At the request of either party the expert, after delivery of the report, may be heard at a hearing where the parties shall have the opportunity to be present and to interrogate the expert. At this hearing either party may present expert witnesses in order to testify on the points at issue. The provisions of article 25 shall be applicable to such proceedings.

Article 28 30 Default	Article 28 Default
1. If, within the period of time fixed by <u>these Rules or</u> the arbitral tribunal, <u>without showing sufficient cause:</u> <u>(a)</u> The claimant has failed to communicate ~~his~~ <u>its statement of</u> claim ~~without showing sufficient cause for such failure~~, the arbitral tribunal shall issue an order for the termination of the arbitral proceedings, <u>unless there are remaining matters that may need to be decided and the arbitral tribunal considers it appropriate to do so</u>; <u>(b)</u> ~~If, within the period of time fixed by the arbitral tribunal,~~ The respondent has failed to communicate ~~his~~ <u>its response to the notice of arbitration or its</u> statement of defence ~~without showing sufficient cause for such failure~~, the arbitral tribunal shall order that the proceedings continue, <u>without treating such failure in itself as an admission of the claimant's allegations; the provisions of this subparagraph also apply to a claimant's failure to submit a defence to a counterclaim or to a claim for the purpose of a set-off.</u>	1. If, within the period of time fixed by the arbitral tribunal, the claimant has failed to communicate his claim without showing sufficient cause for such failure, the arbitral tribunal shall issue an order for the termination of the arbitral proceedings. If, within the period of time fixed by the arbitral tribunal, the respondent has failed to communicate his statement of defence without showing sufficient cause for such failure, the arbitral tribunal shall order that the proceedings continue.
2. If ~~one of the parties~~ <u>a party</u>, duly notified under these Rules, fails to appear at a hearing, without showing sufficient cause for such failure, the arbitral tribunal may proceed with the arbitration.	2. If one of the parties, duly notified under these Rules, fails to appear at a hearing, without showing sufficient cause for such failure, the arbitral tribunal may proceed with the arbitration.
3. If ~~one of the parties~~ <u>a party</u>, duly invited <u>by the arbitral tribunal</u> to produce <u>documents, exhibits or other</u> ~~documentary~~ evidence, fails to do so within the established period of time, without showing sufficient cause for such failure, the arbitral tribunal may make the award on the evidence before it.	3. If one of the parties, duly invited to produce documentary evidence, fails to do so within the established period of time, without showing sufficient cause for such failure, the arbitral tribunal may make the award on the evidence before it.

Article 29 31 Closure of hearings	Article 29 Closure of hearings
1. The arbitral tribunal may inquire of the parties if they have any further proof to offer or witnesses to be heard or submissions to make and, if there are none, it may declare the hearings closed.	1. The arbitral tribunal may inquire of the parties if they have any further proof to offer or witnesses to be heard or submissions to make and, if there are none, it may declare the hearings closed.
2. The arbitral tribunal may, if it considers it necessary owing to exceptional circumstances, decide, on its own ~~motion~~ <u>initiative</u> or upon application of a party, to reopen the hearings at any time before the award is made.	2. The arbitral tribunal may, if it considers it necessary owing to exceptional circumstances, decide, on its own motion or upon application of a party, to reopen the hearings at any time before the award is made.

Article <s>30</s> 32 Waiver of <s>rules</s> right to object	Article 30 Waiver of rules
A failure by any party to object promptly to any non-compliance with these Rules or with any requirement of the arbitration agreement <s>who knows that any provision of, or requirement under, these Rules has not been complied with and yet proceeds with the arbitration without promptly stating his objection to such non-compliance,</s> shall be deemed to be a waiver of the right of such party to make such an objection, unless such party can show that, under the circumstances, its failure to object was justified <s>have waived his right to object</s>.	A party who knows that any provision of, or requirement under, these Rules has not been complied with and yet proceeds with the arbitration without promptly stating his objection to such non-compliance, shall be deemed to have waived his right to object.

Section IV: The Award	
Article <s>31</s> 33 Decisions	Article 31 Decisions
1. When there <s>are three arbitrators</s> is more than one arbitrator, any award or other decision of the arbitral tribunal shall be made by a majority of the arbitrators.	1. When there are three arbitrators, any award or other decision of the arbitral tribunal shall be made by a majority of the arbitrators.
2. In the case of questions of procedure, when there is no majority or when the arbitral tribunal so authorizes, the presiding arbitrator may decide <s>on his own</s> alone, subject to revision, if any, by the arbitral tribunal.	2. In the case of questions of procedure, when there is no majority or when the arbitral tribunal so authorizes, the presiding arbitrator may decide on his own, subject to revision, if any, by the arbitral tribunal.
Article <s>32</s> 34 Form and effect of the award	Article 32 Form and effect of the award
<s>1. In addition to making a final award, the arbitral tribunal shall be entitled to make interim, interlocutory, or partial awards.</s> 1. The arbitral tribunal may make separate awards on different issues at different times.	1. In addition to making a final award, the arbitral tribunal shall be entitled to make interim, interlocutory, or partial awards.
2. <s>The</s> All awards shall be made in writing and shall be final and binding on the parties. The parties undertake to carry out <s>the</s> all awards without delay.	2. The award shall be made in writing and shall be final and binding on the parties. The parties undertake to carry out the award without delay.
3. The arbitral tribunal shall state the reasons upon which the award is based, unless the parties have agreed that no reasons are to be given.	3. The arbitral tribunal shall state the reasons upon which the award is based, unless the parties have agreed that no reasons are to be given.
4. An award shall be signed by the arbitrators and it shall contain the date on which the award was made and indicate the place of arbitration. Where there <s>are three arbitrators</s> is more than one arbitrator and any one of them fails to sign, the award shall state the reason for the absence of the signature.	4. An award shall be signed by the arbitrators and it shall contain the date on which and the place where the award was made. Where there are three arbitrators and one of them fails to sign, the award shall state the reason for the absence of the signature.

Section IV: The Award	
5. ~~The~~ An award may be made public ~~only~~ with the consent of ~~both~~ all parties or where and to the extent disclosure is required of a party by legal duty, to protect or pursue a legal right or in relation to legal proceedings before a court or other competent authority.	5. The award may be made public only with the consent of both parties.
6. Copies of the award signed by the arbitrators shall be communicated to the parties by the arbitral tribunal.	6. Copies of the award signed by the arbitrators shall be communicated to the parties by the arbitral tribunal.
~~7. If the arbitration law of the country where the award is made requires that the award be filed or registered by the arbitral tribunal, the tribunal shall comply with this requirement within the period of time required by law.~~	7. If the arbitration law of the country where the award is made requires that the award be filed or registered by the arbitral tribunal, the tribunal shall comply with this requirement within the period of time required by law.
Article ~~33~~ 35 Applicable law, *amiable compositeur*	**Article 33** Applicable law, *amiable compositeur*
1. The arbitral tribunal shall apply the rules of law designated by the parties as applicable to the substance of the dispute. Failing such designation by the parties, the arbitral tribunal shall apply the law ~~determined by the conflict of laws rules which it considers applicable~~ which it determines to be appropriate.	1. The arbitral tribunal shall apply the law designated by the parties as applicable to the substance of the dispute. Failing such designation by the parties, the arbitral tribunal shall apply the law determined by the conflict of laws rules which it considers applicable.
2. The arbitral tribunal shall decide as *amiable compositeur* or *ex aequo et bono* only if the parties have expressly authorized the arbitral tribunal to do so ~~and if the law applicable to the arbitral procedure permits such arbitration.~~	2. The arbitral tribunal shall decide as *amiable compositeur* or *ex aequo et bono* only if the parties have expressly authorized the arbitral tribunal to do so and if the law applicable to the arbitral procedure permits such arbitration.
3. In all cases, the arbitral tribunal shall decide in accordance with the terms of the contract, if any, and shall take into account ~~the~~ any usages of ~~the~~ trade applicable to the transaction.	3. In all cases, the arbitral tribunal shall decide in accordance with the terms of the contract and shall take into account the usages of the trade applicable to the transaction.
Article ~~34~~ 36 Settlement or other grounds for termination	**Article 34** Settlement or other grounds for termination
1. If, before the award is made, the parties agree on a settlement of the dispute, the arbitral tribunal shall either issue an order for the termination of the arbitral proceedings or, if requested by ~~both~~ the parties and accepted by the tribunal, record the settlement in the form of an arbitral award on agreed terms. The arbitral tribunal is not obliged to give reasons for such an award.	1. If, before the award is made, the parties agree on a settlement of the dispute, the arbitral tribunal shall either issue an order for the termination of the arbitral proceedings or, if requested by both parties and accepted by the tribunal, record the settlement in the form of an arbitral award on agreed terms. The arbitral tribunal is not obliged to give reasons for such an award.
2. If, before the award is made, the continuation of the arbitral proceedings becomes unnecessary or impossible for any reason not mentioned in paragraph 1, the arbitral tribunal shall inform the parties of its intention to issue an order for the termination of the proceedings. The arbitral	2. If, before the award is made, the continuation of the arbitral proceedings becomes unnecessary or impossible for any reason not mentioned in paragraph 1, the arbitral tribunal shall inform the parties of its intention to issue an order for the termination of the proceedings. The arbitral tribunal

tribunal shall have the power to issue such an order unless ~~a party raises justifiable grounds for objection~~ there are remaining matters that need to be decided and the arbitral tribunal considers it appropriate to do so.

3. Copies of the order for termination of the arbitral proceedings or of the arbitral award on agreed terms, signed by the arbitrators, shall be communicated by the arbitral tribunal to the parties. Where an arbitral award on agreed terms is made, the provisions of article ~~32~~ 34, paragraphs 2, 4 and 5 ~~and 4 to 6~~ 7, shall apply.

shall have the power to issue such an order unless a party raises justifiable grounds for objection.

3. Copies of the order for termination of the arbitral proceedings or of the arbitral award on agreed terms, signed by the arbitrators, shall be communicated by the arbitral tribunal to the parties. Where an arbitral award on agreed terms is made, the provisions of article 32, paragraphs 2 and 4 to 7, shall apply.

Article ~~35~~ 37
Interpretation of the award

1. Within 30 days after the receipt of the award, ~~either~~ a party, with notice to the other ~~party~~ parties, may request that the arbitral tribunal give an interpretation of the award.

2. The interpretation shall be given in writing within 45 days after the receipt of the request. The interpretation shall form part of the award and the provisions of article ~~32~~ 34, paragraphs 2 to 6 ~~7~~, shall apply.

Article 35
Interpretation of the award

1. Within thirty days after the receipt of the award, either party, with notice to the other party, may request that the arbitral tribunal give an interpretation of the award.

2. The interpretation shall be given in writing within forty-five days after the receipt of the request. The interpretation shall form part of the award and the provisions of article 32, paragraphs 2 to 7, shall apply.

Article ~~36~~ 38
Correction of the award

1. Within 30 days after the receipt of the award, ~~either~~ a party, with notice to the other ~~party~~ parties, may request the arbitral tribunal to correct in the award any errors in computation, any clerical or typographical ~~errors~~, or any ~~errors~~ or omission of a similar nature. If the arbitral tribunal considers that the request is justified, it shall make the correction within 45 days of the receipt of the request.

2. The arbitral tribunal may within 30 days after the communication of the award make such corrections on its own initiative.

~~2~~3. Such corrections shall be in writing, and shall form part of the award. The provisions of article ~~32~~ 34, paragraphs 2 to 6 ~~7~~, shall apply.

Article 36
Correction of the award

1. Within thirty days after the receipt of the award, either party, with notice to the other party, may request the arbitral tribunal to correct in the award any errors in computation, any clerical or typographical errors, or any errors of similar nature. The arbitral tribunal may within thirty days after the communication of the award make such corrections on its own initiative.

2. Such corrections shall be in writing, and the provisions of article 32, paragraphs 2 to 7, shall apply.

Article ~~37~~ 39
Additional award

1. Within 30 days after the receipt of the termination order or the award, ~~either~~ a party, with notice to the other ~~party~~ parties, may request the arbitral tribunal to make an award or an additional award as to claims presented in the arbitral proceedings but not decided by the arbitral tribunal ~~omitted from the award~~.

Article 37
Additional award

1. Within thirty days after the receipt of the award, either party, with notice to the other party, may request the arbitral tribunal to make an additional award as to claims presented in the arbitral proceedings but omitted from the award.

2. If the arbitral tribunal considers the request for an <u>award or</u> additional award to be justified ~~and considers that the omission can be rectified without any further hearings or evidence~~, it shall <u>render or</u> complete its award within 60 days after the receipt of the request. <u>The arbitral tribunal may extend, if necessary, the period of time within which it shall</u> make <u>the award.</u>	2. If the arbitral tribunal considers the request for an additional award to be justified and considers that the omission can be rectified without any further hearings or evidence, it shall complete its award within sixty days after the receipt of the request.
3. When <u>such</u> an <u>award or</u> additional award is made, the provisions of article ~~32~~ <u>34</u>, paragraphs 2 to <u>6</u> ~~7~~, shall apply.	3. When an additional award is made, the provisions of article 32, paragraphs 2 to 7, shall apply.
Article ~~38~~ <u>40</u> **Definition of costs**	**Article 38** **Costs**
<u>1.</u> The arbitral tribunal shall fix the costs of arbitration in ~~it's~~ <u>the final</u> award<u>, and, if it deems it appropriate, in another decision.</u> <u>2.</u> The term "costs" includes only: (a) The fees of the arbitral tribunal to be stated separately as to each arbitrator and to be fixed by the tribunal itself in accordance with article ~~39~~ <u>41</u>; (b) The <u>reasonable</u> travel and other expenses incurred by the arbitrators; (c) The <u>reasonable</u> costs of expert advice and of other assistance required by the arbitral tribunal; (d) The <u>reasonable</u> travel and other expenses of witnesses to the extent such expenses are approved by the arbitral tribunal; (e) The <u>legal and other costs incurred by the parties in relation to the arbitration</u> ~~costs for legal representation and assistance of the successful party if such costs were claimed during the arbitral proceedings, and only~~ to the extent that the arbitral tribunal determines that the amount of such costs is reasonable; (f) Any fees and expenses of the appointing authority as well as the expenses of the Secretary-General of the ~~Permanent Court of Arbitration at The Hague~~ <u>PCA</u>. <u>3. In relation to interpretation, correction or completion of any award under articles 37 to 39, the arbitral tribunal may charge the costs referred to in paragraphs 2 (b) to (f), but no additional fees.</u>	The arbitral tribunal shall fix the costs of arbitration in its award. The term "costs" includes only: *(a)* The fees of the arbitral tribunal to be stated separately as to each arbitrator and to be fixed by the tribunal itself in accordance with article 39; *(b)* The travel and other expenses incurred by the arbitrators; *(c)* The costs of expert advice and of other assistance required by the arbitral tribunal; *(d)* The travel and other expenses of witnesses to the extent such expenses are approved by the arbitral tribunal; *(e)* The costs for legal representation and assistance of the successful party if such costs were claimed during the arbitral proceedings, and only to the extent that the arbitral tribunal determines that the amount of such costs is reasonable; *(f)* Any fees and expenses of the appointing authority as well as the expenses of the Secretary-General of the Permanent Court of Arbitration at The Hague.
Article ~~39~~ <u>41</u> **~~Costs~~ <u>Fees and expenses of arbitrators</u>**	**Article 39** **Costs**
1. The fees of the ~~arbitral tribunal~~ <u>arbitrators</u> shall be reasonable in amount, taking into account the amount in dispute, the complexity of the subject matter, the time spent by the arbitrators and any other relevant circumstances of the case.	1. The fees of the arbitral tribunal shall be reasonable in amount, taking into account the amount in dispute, the complexity of the subject matter, the time spent by the arbitrators and any other relevant circumstances of the case.

2. If there is an appointing authority has been agreed upon by the parties or designated by the Secretary-General of the Permanent Court of Arbitration at The Hague, and if that authority has issued it applies or has stated that it will apply a schedule or particular method for determining the of fees for arbitrators in international cases which it administers, the arbitral tribunal in fixing its fees shall take that schedule of fees or method into account to the extent that it considers appropriate in the circumstances of the case.

3. If such appointing authority has not issued a schedule of fees for arbitrators in international cases, any party may at any time request the appointing authority to furnish a statement setting forth the basis for establishing fees which is customarily followed in international cases in which the authority appoints arbitrators. If the appointing authority consents to provide such a statement, the arbitral tribunal in fixing its fees shall take such information into account to the extent that it considers appropriate in the circumstances of the case.

4. In cases referred to in paragraphs 2 and 3, when a party so requests and the appointing authority consents to perform the function, the arbitral tribunal shall fix its fees only after consultation with the appointing authority which may make any comment it deems appropriate to the arbitral tribunal concerning the fees.

3. Promptly after its constitution, the arbitral tribunal shall inform the parties as to how it proposes to determine its fees, including any rates it intends to apply. Within 15 days of receiving that proposal, any party may refer the proposal to the appointing authority for review. If, within 45 days of receipt of such a referral, the appointing authority finds that the proposal of the arbitral tribunal is inconsistent with in paragraph 1, it shall make any necessary adjustments thereto, which shall be binding upon the arbitral tribunal.

4. (a) When informing the parties of the arbitrators' fees and expenses that have been fixed pursuant to article 40, paragraphs 2 (a) and (b), the arbitral tribunal shall also explain the manner in which the corresponding amounts have been calculated;

(b) Within 15 days of receiving the arbitral tribunal's determination of fees and expenses, any party may refer for review such determination to the appointing authority. If no appointing authority has been agreed upon or designated, or if the appointing authority fails to act within the time specified in these Rules, then the review shall be made by the Secretary-General of the PCA;

2. If an appointing authority has been agreed upon by the parties or designated by the Secretary-General of the Permanent Court of Arbitration at The Hague, and if that authority has issued a schedule of fees for arbitrators in international cases which it administers, the arbitral tribunal in fixing its fees shall take that schedule of fees into account to the extent that it considers appropriate in the circumstances of the case.

3. If such appointing authority has not issued a schedule of fees for arbitrators in international cases, any party may at any time request the appointing authority to furnish a statement setting forth the basis for establishing fees which is customarily followed in international cases in which the authority appoints arbitrators. If the appointing authority consents to provide such a statement, the arbitral tribunal in fixing its fees shall take such information into account to the extent that it considers appropriate in the circumstances of the case.

4. In cases referred to in paragraphs 2 and 3, when a party so requests and the appointing authority consents to perform the function, the arbitral tribunal shall fix its fees only after consultation with the appointing authority which may make any comment it deems appropriate to the arbitral tribunal concerning the fees.

(c) If the appointing authority or the Secretary-General of the PCA finds that the arbitral tribunal's determination is inconsistent with the arbitral tribunal's proposal (and any adjustment thereto) under paragraph 3 or is otherwise manifestly excessive, it shall, within 45 days of receiving such a referral, make any adjustments to the arbitral tribunal's determination that are necessary to satisfy the criteria in paragraph 1. Any such adjustments shall be binding upon the arbitral tribunal;

(d) Any such adjustments shall either be included by the arbitral tribunal in its award or, if the award has already been issued, be implemented in a correction to the award, to which the procedure of article 38, paragraph 3, shall apply.

5. Throughout the procedure under paragraphs 3 and 4, the arbitral tribunal shall proceed with the arbitration, in accordance with article 17, paragraph 1.

6. A referral under paragraph 4 shall not affect any determination in the award other than the arbitral tribunal's fees and expenses; nor shall it delay the recognition and enforcement of all parts of the award other than those relating to the determination of the arbitral tribunal's fees and expenses.

Article 40 42 Allocation of costs	Article 40 Costs
1. Except as provided in paragraph 2, tThe costs of arbitration shall in principle be borne by the unsuccessful party or parties. However, the arbitral tribunal may apportion each of such costs between the parties if it determines that apportionment is reasonable, taking into account the circumstances of the case.	1. Except as provided in paragraph 2, the costs of arbitration shall in principle be borne by the unsuccessful party. However, the arbitral tribunal may apportion each of such costs between the parties if it determines that apportionment is reasonable, taking into account the circumstances of the case.
2. The arbitral tribunal shall in the final award or, if it deems appropriate, in any other award, determine any amount that a party may have to pay to another party as a result of the decision on allocation of costs.	
2. With respect to the costs of legal representation and assistance referred to in article 38, paragraph (e), the arbitral tribunal, taking into account the circumstances of the case, shall be free to determine which party shall bear such costs or may apportion such costs between the parties if it determines that apportionment is reasonable.	2. With respect to the costs of legal representation and assistance referred to in article 38, paragraph (e), the arbitral tribunal, taking into account the circumstances of the case, shall be free to determine which party shall bear such costs or may apportion such costs between the parties if it determines that apportionment is reasonable.
3. When the arbitral tribunal issues an order for the termination of the arbitral proceedings or makes an award on agreed terms, it shall fix the costs of arbitration referred to in article 38 and article 39, paragraph 1, in the text of that order or award.	3. When the arbitral tribunal issues an order for the termination of the arbitral proceedings or makes an award on agreed terms, it shall fix the costs of arbitration referred to in article 38 and article 39, paragraph 1, in the text of that order or award.

Comparison of the 1976–2010 UNCITRAL Arbitration Rules

4. ~~No additional fees may be charged by an arbitral tribunal for interpretation or correction or completion of its award under articles 35 to 37.~~

4. No additional fees may be charged by an arbitral tribunal for interpretation or correction or completion of its award under articles 35 to 37.

Article ~~41~~ 43
Deposit of costs

Article 41
Deposit of costs

1. The arbitral tribunal, on its establishment, may request ~~each~~ the part~~y~~ies to deposit an equal amount as an advance for the costs referred to in article ~~38~~ 40, paragraphs 2 (a)~~, (b) and~~ to (c).

1. The arbitral tribunal, on its establishment, may request each party to deposit an equal amount as an advance for the costs referred to in article 38, paragraphs *(a), (b)* and *(c)*.

2. During the course of the arbitral proceedings the arbitral tribunal may request supplementary deposits from the parties.

2. During the course of the arbitral proceedings the arbitral tribunal may request supplementary deposits from the parties.

3. If an appointing authority has been agreed upon ~~by the parties~~ or designated ~~by the Secretary-General of the Permanent Court of Arbitration at The Hague~~, and when a party so requests and the appointing authority consents to perform the function, the arbitral tribunal shall fix the amounts of any deposits or supplementary deposits only after consultation with the appointing authority, which may make any comments to the arbitral tribunal which it deems appropriate concerning the amount of such deposits and supplementary deposits.

3. If an appointing authority has been agreed upon by the parties or designated by the Secretary-General of the Permanent Court of Arbitration at The Hague, and when a party so requests and the appointing authority consents to perform the function, the arbitral tribunal shall fix the amounts of any deposits or supplementary deposits only after consultation with the appointing authority which may make any comments to the arbitral tribunal which it deems appropriate concerning the amount of such deposits and supplementary deposits

4. If the required deposits are not paid in full within 30 days after the receipt of the request, the arbitral tribunal shall so inform the parties in order that one or ~~another~~ more of them may make the required payment. If such payment is not made, the arbitral tribunal may order the suspension or termination of the arbitral proceedings.

4. If the required deposits are not paid in full within thirty days after the receipt of the request, the arbitral tribunal shall so inform the parties in order that one or another of them may make the required payment. If such payment is not made, the arbitral tribunal may order the suspension or termination of the arbitral proceedings.

5. After ~~the~~ a termination order or final award has been made, the arbitral tribunal shall render an accounting to the parties of the deposits received and return any unexpended balance to the parties.

5. After the award has been made, the arbitral tribunal shall render an accounting to the parties of the deposits received and return any unexpended balance to the parties.

Annex: Model arbitration clause for contracts

* Model arbitration clause

Any dispute, controversy or claim arising out of or relating to this contract, or the breach, termination or invalidity thereof, shall be settled by arbitration in accordance with the UNCITRAL Arbitration Rules ~~as at present in force.~~

Any dispute, controversy or claim arising out of or relating to this contract, or the breach, termination or invalidity thereof, shall be settled by arbitration in accordance with the UNCITRAL Arbitration Rules as at present in force.

Note – Parties ~~may wish to~~ should *consider adding:*

Note - *Parties may wish to consider adding:*

(a) The appointing authority shall be ... (name of institution or person);

(a) The appointing authority shall be ... (name of institution or person);

(b) The number of arbitrators shall be ... (one or three);

(b) The number of arbitrators shall be ... (one or three);

(c) The place of arbitration shall be ... (town ~~or~~ and country);

(c) The place of arbitration shall be ... (town or country);

(d) The language~~(s)~~ to be used in the arbitral proceedings shall be ...

(d) The language(s) to be used in the arbitral proceedings shall be ...

Possible waiver statement

Note. If the parties wish to exclude recourse against the arbitral award that may be available under the applicable law, they may consider adding a provision to that effect as suggested below, considering, however, that the effectiveness and conditions of such an exclusion depend on the applicable law. Waiver

The parties hereby waive their right to any form of recourse against an award to any court or other competent authority, insofar as such waiver can validly be made under the applicable law.

Model statements of independence pursuant to article 11 of the Rules

No circumstances to disclose:

I am impartial and independent of each of the parties and intend to remain so. To the best of my knowledge, there are no circumstances, past or present, likely to give rise to justifiable doubts as to my impartiality or independence. I hereby undertake promptly to notify the parties and the other arbitrators of any such circumstances that may subsequently come to my attention during this arbitration.

Circumstances to disclose:

I am impartial and independent of each of the parties and intend to remain so. Attached is a statement made pursuant to article 11 of the UNCITRAL Arbitration Rules of (a) my past and present professional, business and other relationships with the parties and (b) any other relevant circumstances. [Include statement] I confirm that those circumstances do not affect my independence and impartiality. I hereby undertake promptly to notify the parties and the other arbitrators of any such further relationships or circumstances that may subsequently come to my attention during this arbitration.

Note. Any party may consider requesting from the arbitrator the following addition to the statement of independence:

I confirm, on the basis of the information presently available to me, that I can devote the time necessary to conduct this arbitration diligently, efficiently and in accordance with the time limits in the Rules.

Additional provision

[Questions concerning matters governed by these Rules which are not expressly settled in them are to be settled in conformity with the general principles on which these Rules are based].

APPENDIX 4

UNCITRAL Notes on Organizing Arbitral Proceedings
(May 28–June 14, 1996)

Preface	968
Introduction	968
Purpose of the Notes	968
Non-binding character of the Notes	968
Discretion in conduct of proceedings and usefulness of timely decisions on organizing proceedings	968
Multi-party arbitration	969
Process of making decisions on organizing arbitral proceedings	969
List of matters for possible consideration in organizing arbitral proceedings	969
List of Matters for Possible Consideration in Organizing Arbitral Proceedings—Annotations	969
1. Set of arbitration rules	969
2. Language of proceedings	970
3. Place of arbitration	970
4. Administrative services that may be needed for the arbitral tribunal to carry out its functions	971
5. Deposits in respect of costs	971
6. Confidentiality of information relating to the arbitration; possible agreement thereon	972
7. Routing of written communications among the parties and the arbitrators	972
8. Telefax and other electronic means of sending documents	973
9. Arrangements for the exchange of written submissions	973
10. Practical details concerning written submissions and evidence (e. g. method of submission, copies, numbering, references)	974
11. Defining points at issue; order of deciding issues; defining relief or remedy sought	974
12. Possible settlement negotiations and their effect on scheduling proceedings	975
13. Documentary evidence	975
14. Physical evidence other than documents	976
15. Witnesses	977
16. Experts and expert witnesses	978
17. Hearings	979
18. Multi-party arbitration	981
19. Possible requirements concerning filing or delivering the award	981

Preface

The United Nations Commission on International Trade Law (UNCITRAL) finalized the Notes at its twenty-ninth session (New York, 28 May–14 June 1996). In addition to the 36 member States of the Commission, representatives of many other States and of a number of international organizations had participated in the deliberations. In preparing the draft materials, the Secretariat consulted with experts from various legal systems, national arbitration bodies, as well as international professional associations.

The Commission, after an initial discussion on the project in 1993,[1] considered in 1994 a draft entitled "Draft Guidelines for Preparatory Conferences in Arbitral Proceedings".[2] That draft was also discussed at several meetings of arbitration practitioners, including the XIIth International Arbitration Congress, held by the International Council for Commercial Arbitration (ICCA) at Vienna from 3 to 6 November 1994.[3] On the basis of those discussions in the Commission and elsewhere, the Secretariat prepared "draft Notes on Organizing Arbitral Proceedings".[4] The Commission considered the draft Notes in 1995,[5] and a revised draft in 1996,[6] when the Notes were finalized.[7]

UNCITRAL
Vienna International Centre
P.O. Box 500
A-1400 Vienna, Austria
Telex: 135612 Telephone: (43-1) 21345-4060/61 Telefax: (43-1) 21345-5813
E-mail: uncitral@unov.un.or.at

Introduction

Purpose of the Notes

1. The purpose of the Notes is to assist arbitration practitioners by listing and briefly describing questions on which appropriately timed decisions on organizing arbitral proceedings may be useful. The text, prepared with a particular view to international arbitrations, may be used whether or not the arbitration is administered by an arbitral institution.

Non-binding character of the Notes

2. No legal requirement binding on the arbitrators or the parties is imposed by the Notes. The arbitral tribunal remains free to use the Notes as it sees fit and is not required to give reasons for disregarding them.

3. The Notes are not suitable to be used as arbitration rules, since they do not establish any obligation of the arbitral tribunal or the parties to act in a particular way. Accordingly, the use of the Notes cannot imply any modification of the arbitration rules that the parties may have agreed upon.

Discretion in conduct of proceedings and usefulness of timely decisions on organizing proceedings

4. Laws governing the arbitral procedure and arbitration rules that parties may agree upon typically allow the arbitral tribunal broad discretion and flexibility in the conduct of arbitral proceedings.[8] This is useful in that it enables the arbitral tribunal to take decisions on the organization of proceedings that take into account the circumstances of the case, the expectations of the parties and of the members of the arbitral tribunal, and the need for a just and cost-efficient resolution of the dispute.

5. Such discretion may make it desirable for the arbitral tribunal to give the parties a timely indication as to the organization of the proceedings and the manner in which the tribunal intends to proceed. This is particularly desirable in international arbitrations, where the participants may be accustomed to differing styles of conducting arbitrations. Without such guidance, a party may

find aspects of the proceedings unpredictable and difficult to prepare for. That may lead to misunderstandings, delays and increased costs.

Multi-party arbitration

6. These Notes are intended for use not only in arbitrations with two parties but also in arbitrations with three or more parties. Use of the Notes in multi-party arbitration is referred to below in paragraphs 86–88 (item 18).

Process of making decisions on organizing arbitral proceedings

7. Decisions by the arbitral tribunal on organizing arbitral proceedings may be taken with or without previous consultations with the parties. The method chosen depends on whether, in view of the type of the question to be decided, the arbitral tribunal considers that consultations are not necessary or that hearing the views of the parties would be beneficial for increasing the predictability of the proceedings or improving the procedural atmosphere.

8. The consultations, whether they involve only the arbitrators or also the parties, can be held in one or more meetings, or can be carried out by correspondence or telecommunications such as telefax or conference telephone calls or other electronic means. Meetings may be held at the venue of arbitration or at some other appropriate location.

9. In some arbitrations a special meeting may be devoted exclusively to such procedural consultations; alternatively, the consultations may be held in conjunction with a hearing on the substance of the dispute. Practices differ as to whether such special meetings should be held and how they should be organized. Special procedural meetings of the arbitrators and the parties separate from hearings are in practice referred to by expressions such as "preliminary meeting", "pre-hearing conference", "preparatory conference", "pre-hearing review", or terms of similar meaning. The terms used partly depend on the stage of the proceedings at which the meeting is taking place.

List of matters for possible consideration in organizing arbitral proceedings

10. The Notes provide a list, followed by annotations, of matters on which the arbitral tribunal may wish to formulate decisions on organizing arbitral proceedings.

11. Given that procedural styles and practices in arbitration vary widely, that the purpose of the Notes is not to promote any practice as best practice, and that the Notes are designed for universal use, it is not attempted in the Notes to describe in detail different arbitral practices or express a preference for any of them.

12. The list, while not exhaustive, covers a broad range of situations that may arise in an arbitration. In many arbitrations, however, only a limited number of the matters mentioned in the list need to be considered. It also depends on the circumstances of the case at which stage or stages of the proceedings it would be useful to consider matters concerning the organization of the proceedings. Generally, in order not to create opportunities for unnecessary discussions and delay, it is advisable not to raise a matter prematurely, i.e. before it is clear that a decision is needed.

13. When the Notes are used, it should be borne in mind that the discretion of the arbitral tribunal in organizing the proceedings may be limited by arbitration rules, by other provisions agreed to by the parties and by the law applicable to the arbitral procedure. When an arbitration is administered by an arbitral institution, various matters discussed in the Notes may be covered by the rules and practices of that institution.

LIST OF MATTERS FOR POSSIBLE CONSIDERATION IN
ORGANIZING ARBITRAL PROCEEDINGS—ANNOTATIONS

1. Set of arbitration rules

If the parties have not agreed on a set of arbitration rules, would they wish to do so

14. Sometimes parties who have not included in their arbitration agreement a stipulation that a set of arbitration rules will govern their arbitral proceedings might wish to do so after the arbitration

has begun. If that occurs, the UNCITRAL Arbitration Rules may be used either without modification or with such modifications as the parties might wish to agree upon. In the alternative, the parties might wish to adopt the rules of an arbitral institution; in that case, it may be necessary to secure the agreement of that institution and to stipulate the terms under which the arbitration could be carried out in accordance with the rules of that institution.

15. However, caution is advised as consideration of a set of arbitration rules might delay the proceedings or give rise to unnecessary controversy.
16. It should be noted that agreement on arbitration rules is not a necessity and that, if the parties do not agree on a set of arbitration rules, the arbitral tribunal has the power to continue the proceedings and determine how the case will be conducted.

2. Language of proceedings

17. Many rules and laws on arbitral procedure empower the arbitral tribunal to determine the language or languages to be used in the proceedings, if the parties have not reached an agreement thereon.

(a) Possible need for translation of documents, in full or in part

18. Some documents annexed to the statements of claim and defence or submitted later may not be in the language of the proceedings. Bearing in mind the needs of the proceedings and economy, it may be considered whether the arbitral tribunal should order that any of those documents or parts thereof should be accompanied by a translation into the language of the proceedings.

(b) Possible need for interpretation of oral presentations

19. If interpretation will be necessary during oral hearings, it is advisable to consider whether the interpretation will be simultaneous or consecutive and whether the arrangements should be the responsibility of a party or the arbitral tribunal. In an arbitration administered by an institution, interpretation as well as translation services are often arranged by the arbitral institution.

(c) Cost of translation and interpretation

20. In taking decisions about translation or interpretation, it is advisable to decide whether any or all of the costs are to be paid directly by a party or whether they will be paid out of the deposits and apportioned between the parties along with the other arbitration costs.

3. Place of arbitration

(a) Determination of the place of arbitration, if not already agreed upon by the parties

21. Arbitration rules usually allow the parties to agree on the place of arbitration, subject to the requirement of some arbitral institutions that arbitrations under their rules be conducted at a particular place, usually the location of the institution. If the place has not been so agreed upon, the rules governing the arbitration typically provide that it is in the power of the arbitral tribunal or the institution administering the arbitration to determine the place. If the arbitral tribunal is to make that determination, it may wish to hear the views of the parties before doing so.
22. Various factual and legal factors influence the choice of the place of arbitration, and their relative importance varies from case to case. Among the more prominent factors are: (a) suitability of the law on arbitral procedure of the place of arbitration; (b) whether there is a multilateral or bilateral treaty on enforcement of arbitral awards between the State where the arbitration takes place and the State or States where the award may have to be enforced; (c) convenience of the parties and the arbitrators, including the travel distances; (d) availability and cost of support services needed; and (e) location of the subject-matter in dispute and proximity of evidence.

(b) Possibility of meetings outside the place of arbitration

23. Many sets of arbitration rules and laws on arbitral procedure expressly allow the arbitral tribunal to hold meetings elsewhere than at the place of arbitration. For example, under the UNCITRAL

Model Law on International Commercial Arbitration "the arbitral tribunal may, unless otherwise agreed by the parties, meet at any place it considers appropriate for consultation among its members, for hearing witnesses, experts or the parties, or for inspection of goods, other property or documents" (article 20(2)). The purpose of this discretion is to permit arbitral proceedings to be carried out in a manner that is most efficient and economical.

4. Administrative services that may be needed for the arbitral tribunal to carry out its functions

24. Various administrative services (e. g. hearing rooms or secretarial services) may need to be procured for the arbitral tribunal to be able to carry out its functions. When the arbitration is administered by an arbitral institution, the institution will usually provide all or a good part of the required administrative support to the arbitral tribunal. When an arbitration administered by an arbitral institution takes place away from the seat of the institution, the institution may be able to arrange for administrative services to be obtained from another source, often an arbitral institution; some arbitral institutions have entered into cooperation agreements with a view to providing mutual assistance in servicing arbitral proceedings.

25. When the case is not administered by an institution, or the involvement of the institution does not include providing administrative support, usually the administrative arrangements for the proceedings will be made by the arbitral tribunal or the presiding arbitrator; it may also be acceptable to leave some of the arrangements to the parties, or to one of the parties subject to agreement of the other party or parties. Even in such cases, a convenient source of administrative support might be found in arbitral institutions, which often offer their facilities to arbitrations not governed by the rules of the institution. Otherwise, some services could be procured from entities such as chambers of commerce, hotels or specialized firms providing secretarial or other support services.

26. Administrative services might be secured by engaging a secretary of the arbitral tribunal (also referred to as registrar, clerk, administrator or rapporteur), who carries out the tasks under the direction of the arbitral tribunal. Some arbitral institutions routinely assign such persons to the cases administered by them. In arbitrations not administered by an institution or where the arbitral institution does not appoint a secretary, some arbitrators frequently engage such persons, at least in certain types of cases, whereas many others normally conduct the proceedings without them.

27. To the extent the tasks of the secretary are purely organizational (e. g. obtaining meeting rooms and providing or coordinating secretarial services), this is usually not controversial. Differences in views, however, may arise if the tasks include legal research and other professional assistance to the arbitral tribunal (e. g. collecting case law or published commentaries on legal issues defined by the arbitral tribunal, preparing summaries from case law and publications, and sometimes also preparing drafts of procedural decisions or drafts of certain parts of the award, in particular those concerning the facts of the case). Views or expectations may differ especially where a task of the secretary is similar to professional functions of the arbitrators. Such a role of the secretary is in the view of some commentators inappropriate or is appropriate only under certain conditions, such as that the parties agree thereto. However, it is typically recognized that it is important to ensure that the secretary does not perform any decision-making function of the arbitral tribunal.

5. Deposits in respect of costs

(a) Amount to be deposited

28. In an arbitration administered by an institution, the institution often sets, on the basis of an estimate of the costs of the proceedings, the amount to be deposited as an advance for the costs of the arbitration. In other cases it is customary for the arbitral tribunal to make such an estimate and request a deposit. The estimate typically includes travel and other expenses by the arbitrators, expenditures for administrative assistance required by the arbitral tribunal, costs of any

expert advice required by the arbitral tribunal, and the fees for the arbitrators. Many arbitration rules have provisions on this matter, including on whether the deposit should be made by the two parties (or all parties in a multi-party case) or only by the claimant.

(b) Management of deposits

29. When the arbitration is administered by an institution, the institution's services may include managing and accounting for the deposited money. Where that is not the case, it might be useful to clarify matters such as the type and location of the account in which the money will be kept and how the deposits will be managed.

(c) Supplementary deposits

30. If during the course of proceedings it emerges that the costs will be higher than anticipated, supplementary deposits may be required (e. g. because the arbitral tribunal decides pursuant to the arbitration rules to appoint an expert).

6. Confidentiality of information relating to the arbitration; possible agreement thereon

31. It is widely viewed that confidentiality is one of the advantageous and helpful features of arbitration. Nevertheless, there is no uniform answer in national laws as to the extent to which the participants in an arbitration are under the duty to observe the confidentiality of information relating to the case. Moreover, parties that have agreed on arbitration rules or other provisions that do not expressly address the issue of confidentiality cannot assume that all jurisdictions would recognize an implied commitment to confidentiality. Furthermore, the participants in an arbitration might not have the same understanding as regards the extent of confidentiality that is expected. Therefore, the arbitral tribunal might wish to discuss that with the parties and, if considered appropriate, record any agreed principles on the duty of confidentiality.
32. An agreement on confidentiality might cover, for example, one or more of the following matters: the material or information that is to be kept confidential (e. g. pieces of evidence, written and oral arguments, the fact that the arbitration is taking place, identity of the arbitrators, content of the award); measures for maintaining confidentiality of such information and hearings; whether any special procedures should be employed for maintaining the confidentiality of information transmitted by electronic means (e. g. because communication equipment is shared by several users, or because electronic mail over public networks is considered not sufficiently protected against unauthorized access); circumstances in which confidential information may be disclosed in part or in whole (e. g. in the context of disclosures of information in the public domain, or if required by law or a regulatory body).

7. Routing of written communications among the parties and the arbitrators

33. To the extent the question how documents and other written communications should be routed among the parties and the arbitrators is not settled by the agreed rules, or, if an institution administers the case, by the practices of the institution, it is useful for the arbitral tribunal to clarify the question suitably early so as to avoid misunderstandings and delays.
34. Among various possible patterns of routing, one example is that a party transmits the appropriate number of copies to the arbitral tribunal, or to the arbitral institution, if one is involved, which then forwards them as appropriate. Another example is that a party is to send copies simultaneously to the arbitrators and the other party or parties. Documents and other written communications directed by the arbitral tribunal or the presiding arbitrator to one or more parties may also follow a determined pattern, such as through the arbitral institution or by direct transmission. For some communications, in particular those on organizational matters (e. g. dates for hearings), more direct routes of communication may be agreed, even if, for example, the arbitral institution acts as an intermediary for documents such as the statements of claim and defence, evidence or written arguments.

8. Telefax and other electronic means of sending documents

(a) Telefax

35. Telefax, which offers many advantages over traditional means of communication, is widely used in arbitral proceedings. Nevertheless, should it be thought that, because of the characteristics of the equipment used, it would be preferable not to rely only on a telefacsimile of a document, special arrangements may be considered, such as that a particular piece of written evidence should be mailed or otherwise physically delivered, or that certain telefax messages should be confirmed by mailing or otherwise delivering documents whose facsimile were transmitted by electronic means. When a document should not be sent by telefax, it may, however, be appropriate, in order to avoid an unnecessarily rigid procedure, for the arbitral tribunal to retain discretion to accept an advance copy of a document by telefax for the purposes of meeting a deadline, provided that the document itself is received within a reasonable time thereafter.

(b) Other electronic means (e. g. electronic mail and magnetic or optical disk)

36. It might be agreed that documents, or some of them, will be exchanged not only in paper-based form, but in addition also in an electronic form other than telefax (e. g. as electronic mail, or on a magnetic or optical disk), or only in electronic form. Since the use of electronic means depends on the aptitude of the persons involved and the availability of equipment and computer programs, agreement is necessary for such means to be used. If both paper-based and electronic means are to be used, it is advisable to decide which one is controlling and, if there is a time-limit for submitting a document, which act constitutes submission.

37. When the exchange of documents in electronic form is planned, it is useful, in order to avoid technical difficulties, to agree on matters such as: data carriers (e. g. electronic mail or computer disks) and their technical characteristics; computer programs to be used in preparing the electronic records; instructions for transforming the electronic records into human-readable form; keeping of logs and back-up records of communications sent and received; information in human-readable form that should accompany the disks (e. g. the names of the originator and recipient, computer program, titles of the electronic files and the back-up methods used); procedures when a message is lost or the communication system otherwise fails; and identification of persons who can be contacted if a problem occurs.

9. Arrangements for the exchange of written submissions

38. After the parties have initially stated their claims and defences, they may wish, or the arbitral tribunal might request them, to present further written submissions so as to prepare for the hearings or to provide the basis for a decision without hearings. In such submissions, the parties, for example, present or comment on allegations and evidence, cite or explain law, or make or react to proposals. In practice such submissions are referred to variously as, for example, statement, memorial, counter-memorial, brief, counter-brief, reply, réplique, duplique, rebuttal or rejoinder; the terminology is a matter of linguistic usage and the scope or sequence of the submission.

(a) Scheduling of written submissions

39. It is advisable that the arbitral tribunal set time-limits for written submissions. In enforcing the time-limits, the arbitral tribunal may wish, on the one hand, to make sure that the case is not unduly protracted and, on the other hand, to reserve a degree of discretion and allow late submissions if appropriate under the circumstances. In some cases the arbitral tribunal might prefer not to plan the written submissions in advance, thus leaving such matters, including time-limits, to be decided in light of the developments in the proceedings. In other cases, the arbitral tribunal may wish to determine, when scheduling the first written submissions, the number of subsequent submissions.

40. Practices differ as to whether, after the hearings have been held, written submissions are still acceptable. While some arbitral tribunals consider post-hearing submissions unacceptable,

others might request or allow them on a particular issue. Some arbitral tribunals follow the procedure according to which the parties are not requested to present written evidence and legal arguments to the arbitral tribunal before the hearings; in such a case, the arbitral tribunal may regard it as appropriate that written submissions be made after the hearings.

(b) Consecutive or simultaneous submissions

41. Written submissions on an issue may be made consecutively, i.e. the party who receives a submission is given a period of time to react with its counter-submission. Another possibility is to request each party to make the submission within the same time period to the arbitral tribunal or the institution administering the case; the received submissions are then forwarded simultaneously to the respective other party or parties. The approach used may depend on the type of issues to be commented upon and the time in which the views should be clarified. With consecutive submissions, it may take longer than with simultaneous ones to obtain views of the parties on a given issue. Consecutive submissions, however, allow the reacting party to comment on all points raised by the other party or parties, which simultaneous submissions do not; thus, simultaneous submissions might possibly necessitate further submissions.

10. Practical details concerning written submissions and evidence (e. g. method of submission, copies, numbering, references)

42. Depending on the volume and kind of documents to be handled, it might be considered whether practical arrangements on details such as the following would be helpful:

- Whether the submissions will be made as paper documents or by electronic means, or both (see paragraphs 35–37);
- The number of copies in which each document is to be submitted;
- A system for numbering documents and items of evidence, and a method for marking them, including by tabs;
- The form of references to documents (e. g. by the heading and the number assigned to the document or its date);
- Paragraph numbering in written submissions, in order to facilitate precise references to parts of a text;
- When translations are to be submitted as paper documents, whether the translations are to be contained in the same volume as the original texts or included in separate volumes.

11. Defining points at issue; order of deciding issues; defining relief or remedy sought

(a) Should a list of points at issue be prepared

43. In considering the parties' allegations and arguments, the arbitral tribunal may come to the conclusion that it would be useful for it or for the parties to prepare, for analytical purposes and for ease of discussion, a list of the points at issue, as opposed to those that are undisputed. If the arbitral tribunal determines that the advantages of working on the basis of such a list outweigh the disadvantages, it chooses the appropriate stage of the proceedings for preparing a list, bearing in mind also that subsequent developments in the proceedings may require a revision of the points at issue. Such an identification of points at issue might help to concentrate on the essential matters, to reduce the number of points at issue by agreement of the parties, and to select the best and most economical process for resolving the dispute. However, possible disadvantages of preparing such a list include delay, adverse effect on the flexibility of the proceedings, or unnecessary disagreements about whether the arbitral tribunal has decided all issues submitted to it or whether the award contains decisions on matters beyond the scope of the submission to arbitration. The terms of reference required under some arbitration rules, or in agreements of parties, may serve the same purpose as the above-described list of points at issue.

(b) In which order should the points at issue be decided

44. While it is often appropriate to deal with all the points at issue collectively, the arbitral tribunal might decide to take them up during the proceedings in a particular order. The order may be due to a point being preliminary relative to another (e. g. a decision on the jurisdiction of the arbitral tribunal is preliminary to consideration of substantive issues, or the issue of responsibility for a breach of contract is preliminary to the issue of the resulting damages). A particular order may be decided also when the breach of various contracts is in dispute or when damages arising from various events are claimed.

45. If the arbitral tribunal has adopted a particular order of deciding points at issue, it might consider it appropriate to issue a decision on one of the points earlier than on the other ones. This might be done, for example, when a discrete part of a claim is ready for decision while the other parts still require extensive consideration, or when it is expected that after deciding certain issues the parties might be more inclined to settle the remaining ones. Such earlier decisions are referred to by expressions such as "partial", "interlocutory" or "interim" awards or decisions, depending on the type of issue dealt with and on whether the decision is final with respect to the issue it resolves. Questions that might be the subject of such decisions are, for example, jurisdiction of the arbitral tribunal, interim measures of protection, or the liability of a party.

(c) Is there a need to define more precisely the relief or remedy sought

46. If the arbitral tribunal considers that the relief or remedy sought is insufficiently definite, it may wish to explain to the parties the degree of definiteness with which their claims should be formulated. Such an explanation may be useful since criteria are not uniform as to how specific the claimant must be in formulating a relief or remedy.

12. Possible settlement negotiations and their effect on scheduling proceedings

47. Attitudes differ as to whether it is appropriate for the arbitral tribunal to bring up the possibility of settlement. Given the divergence of practices in this regard, the arbitral tribunal should only suggest settlement negotiations with caution. However, it may be opportune for the arbitral tribunal to schedule the proceedings in a way that might facilitate the continuation or initiation of settlement negotiations.

13. Documentary evidence

(a) Time-limits for submission of documentary evidence intended to be submitted by the parties; consequences of late submission

48. Often the written submissions of the parties contain sufficient information for the arbitral tribunal to fix the time-limit for submitting evidence. Otherwise, in order to set realistic time periods, the arbitral tribunal may wish to consult with the parties about the time that they would reasonably need.

49. The arbitral tribunal may wish to clarify that evidence submitted late will as a rule not be accepted. It may wish not to preclude itself from accepting a late submission of evidence if the party shows sufficient cause for the delay.

(b) Whether the arbitral tribunal intends to require a party to produce documentary evidence

50. Procedures and practices differ widely as to the conditions under which the arbitral tribunal may require a party to produce documents. Therefore, the arbitral tribunal might consider it useful, when the agreed arbitration rules do not provide specific conditions, to clarify to the parties the manner in which it intends to proceed.

51. The arbitral tribunal may wish to establish time-limits for the production of documents. The parties might be reminded that, if the requested party duly invited to produce documentary evidence fails to do so within the established period of time, without showing sufficient cause for such failure, the arbitral tribunal is free to draw its conclusions from the failure and may make the award on the evidence before it.

(c) Should assertions about the origin and receipt of documents and about the correctness of photocopies be assumed as accurate

52. It may be helpful for the arbitral tribunal to inform the parties that it intends to conduct the proceedings on the basis that, unless a party raises an objection to any of the following conclusions within a specified period of time: (a) a document is accepted as having originated from the source indicated in the document; (b) a copy of a dispatched communication (e.g. letter, telex, telefax or other electronic message) is accepted without further proof as having been received by the addressee; and (c) a copy is accepted as correct. A statement by the arbitral tribunal to that effect can simplify the introduction of documentary evidence and discourage unfounded and dilatory objections, at a late stage of the proceedings, to the probative value of documents. It is advisable to provide that the time-limit for objections will not be enforced if the arbitral tribunal considers the delay justified.

(d) Are the parties willing to submit jointly a single set of documentary evidence

53. The parties may consider submitting jointly a single set of documentary evidence whose authenticity is not disputed. The purpose would be to avoid duplicate submissions and unnecessary discussions concerning the authenticity of documents, without prejudicing the position of the parties concerning the content of the documents. Additional documents may be inserted later if the parties agree. When a single set of documents would be too voluminous to be easily manageable, it might be practical to select a number of frequently used documents and establish a set of "working" documents. A convenient arrangement of documents in the set may be according to chronological order or subject-matter. It is useful to keep a table of contents of the documents, for example, by their short headings and dates, and to provide that the parties will refer to documents by those headings and dates.

(e) Should voluminous and complicated documentary evidence be presented through summaries, tabulations, charts, extracts or samples

54. When documentary evidence is voluminous and complicated, it may save time and costs if such evidence is presented by a report of a person competent in the relevant field (e. g. public accountant or consulting engineer). The report may present the information in the form of summaries, tabulations, charts, extracts or samples. Such presentation of evidence should be combined with arrangements that give the interested party the opportunity to review the underlying data and the methodology of preparing the report.

14. Physical evidence other than documents

55. In some arbitrations the arbitral tribunal is called upon to assess physical evidence other than documents, for example, by inspecting samples of goods, viewing a video recording or observing the functioning of a machine.

(a) What arrangements should be made if physical evidence will be submitted

56. If physical evidence will be submitted, the arbitral tribunal may wish to fix the time schedule for presenting the evidence, make arrangements for the other party or parties to have a suitable opportunity to prepare itself for the presentation of the evidence, and possibly take measures for safekeeping the items of evidence.

(b) What arrangements should be made if an on-site inspection is necessary

57. If an on-site inspection of property or goods will take place, the arbitral tribunal may consider matters such as timing, meeting places, other arrangements to provide the opportunity for all parties to be present, and the need to avoid communications between arbitrators and a party about points at issue without the presence of the other party or parties.

58. The site to be inspected is often under the control of one of the parties, which typically means that employees or representatives of that party will be present to give guidance and explanations.

It should be borne in mind that statements of those representatives or employees made during an on-site inspection, as contrasted with statements those persons might make as witnesses in a hearing, should not be treated as evidence in the proceedings.

15. Witnesses

59. While laws and rules on arbitral procedure typically leave broad freedom concerning the manner of taking evidence of witnesses, practices on procedural points are varied. In order to facilitate the preparations of the parties for the hearings, the arbitral tribunal may consider it appropriate to clarify, in advance of the hearings, some or all of the following issues.

(a) Advance notice about a witness whom a party intends to present; written witnesses' statements

60. To the extent the applicable arbitration rules do not deal with the matter, the arbitral tribunal may wish to require that each party give advance notice to the arbitral tribunal and the other party or parties of any witness it intends to present. As to the content of the notice, the following is an example of what might be required, in addition to the names and addresses of the witnesses: (a) the subject upon which the witnesses will testify; (b) the language in which the witnesses will testify; and (c) the nature of the relationship with any of the parties, qualifications and experience of the witnesses if and to the extent these are relevant to the dispute or the testimony, and how the witnesses learned about the facts on which they will testify. However, it may not be necessary to require such a notice, in particular if the thrust of the testimony can be clearly ascertained from the party's allegations.

61. Some practitioners favour the procedure according to which the party presenting witness evidence submits a signed witness's statement containing testimony itself. It should be noted, however, that such practice, which implies interviewing the witness by the party presenting the testimony, is not known in all parts of the world and, moreover, that some practitioners disapprove of it on the ground that such contacts between the party and the witness may compromise the credibility of the testimony and are therefore improper (see paragraph 67). Notwithstanding these reservations, signed witness's testimony has advantages in that it may expedite the proceedings by making it easier for the other party or parties to prepare for the hearings or for the parties to identify uncontested matters. However, those advantages might be outweighed by the time and expense involved in obtaining the written testimony.

62. If a signed witness's statement should be made under oath or similar affirmation of truthfulness, it may be necessary to clarify by whom the oath or affirmation should be administered and whether any formal authentication will be required by the arbitral tribunal.

(b) Manner of taking oral evidence of witnesses

(i) Order in which questions will be asked and the manner in which the hearing of witnesses will be conducted

63. To the extent that the applicable rules do not provide an answer, it may be useful for the arbitral tribunal to clarify how witnesses will be heard. One of the various possibilities is that a witness is first questioned by the arbitral tribunal, whereupon questions are asked by the parties, first by the party who called the witness. Another possibility is for the witness to be questioned by the party presenting the witness and then by the other party or parties, while the arbitral tribunal might pose questions during the questioning or after the parties on points that in the tribunal's view have not been sufficiently clarified. Differences exist also as to the degree of control the arbitral tribunal exercises over the hearing of witnesses. For example, some arbitrators prefer to permit the parties to pose questions freely and directly to the witness, but may disallow a question if a party objects; other arbitrators tend to exercise more control and may disallow a question on their initiative or even require that questions from the parties be asked through the arbitral tribunal.

(ii) Whether oral testimony will be given under oath or affirmation and, if so, in what form an oath or affirmation should be made

64. Practices and laws differ as to whether or not oral testimony is to be given under oath or affirmation. In some legal systems, the arbitrators are empowered to put witnesses on oath, but it is usually in their discretion whether they want to do so. In other systems, oral testimony under oath is either unknown or may even be considered improper as only an official such as a judge or notary may have the authority to administer oaths.

(iii) May witnesses be in the hearing room when they are not testifying

65. Some arbitrators favour the procedure that, except if the circumstances suggest otherwise, the presence of a witness in the hearing room is limited to the time the witness is testifying; the purpose is to prevent the witness from being influenced by what is said in the hearing room, or to prevent that the presence of the witness would influence another witness. Other arbitrators consider that the presence of a witness during the testimony of other witnesses may be beneficial in that possible contradictions may be readily clarified or that their presence may act as a deterrent against untrue statements. Other possible approaches may be that witnesses are not present in the hearing room before their testimony, but stay in the room after they have testified, or that the arbitral tribunal decides the question for each witness individually depending on what the arbitral tribunal considers most appropriate. The arbitral tribunal may leave the procedure to be decided during the hearings, or may give guidance on the question in advance of the hearings.

(c) The order in which the witnesses will be called

66. When several witnesses are to be heard and longer testimony is expected, it is likely to reduce costs if the order in which they will be called is known in advance and their presence can be scheduled accordingly. Each party might be invited to suggest the order in which it intends to present the witnesses, while it would be up to the arbitral tribunal to approve the scheduling and to make departures from it.

(d) Interviewing witnesses prior to their appearance at a hearing

67. In some legal systems, parties or their representatives are permitted to interview witnesses, prior to their appearance at the hearing, as to such matters as their recollection of the relevant events, their experience, qualifications or relation with a participant in the proceedings. In those legal systems such contacts are usually not permitted once the witness's oral testimony has begun. In other systems such contacts with witnesses are considered improper. In order to avoid misunderstandings, the arbitral tribunal may consider it useful to clarify what kind of contacts a party is permitted to have with a witness in the preparations for the hearings.

(e) Hearing representatives of a party

68. According to some legal systems, certain persons affiliated with a party may only be heard as representatives of the party but not as witnesses. In such a case, it may be necessary to consider ground rules for determining which persons may not testify as witnesses (e. g. certain executives, employees or agents) and for hearing statements of those persons and for questioning them.

16. Experts and expert witnesses

69. Many arbitration rules and laws on arbitral procedure address the participation of experts in arbitral proceedings. A frequent solution is that the arbitral tribunal has the power to appoint an expert to report on issues determined by the tribunal; in addition, the parties may be permitted to present expert witnesses on points at issue. In other cases, it is for the parties to present expert testimony, and it is not expected that the arbitral tribunal will appoint an expert.

(a) Expert appointed by the arbitral tribunal

70. If the arbitral tribunal is empowered to appoint an expert, one possible approach is for the tribunal to proceed directly to selecting the expert. Another possibility is to consult the parties as

to who should be the expert; this may be done, for example, without mentioning a candidate, by presenting to the parties a list of candidates, soliciting proposals from the parties, or by discussing with the parties the "profile" of the expert the arbitral tribunal intends to appoint, i.e. the qualifications, experience and abilities of the expert.

(i) The expert's terms of reference

71. The purpose of the expert's terms of reference is to indicate the questions on which the expert is to provide clarification, to avoid opinions on points that are not for the expert to assess and to commit the expert to a time schedule. While the discretion to appoint an expert normally includes the determination of the expert's terms of reference, the arbitral tribunal may decide to consult the parties before finalizing the terms. It might also be useful to determine details about how the expert will receive from the parties any relevant information or have access to any relevant documents, goods or other property, so as to enable the expert to prepare the report. In order to facilitate the evaluation of the expert's report, it is advisable to require the expert to include in the report information on the method used in arriving at the conclusions and the evidence and information used in preparing the report.

(ii) The opportunity of the parties to comment on the expert's report, including by presenting expert testimony

72. Arbitration rules that contain provisions on experts usually also have provisions on the right of a party to comment on the report of the expert appointed by the arbitral tribunal. If no such provisions apply or more specific procedures than those prescribed are deemed necessary, the arbitral tribunal may, in light of those provisions, consider it opportune to determine, for example, the time period for presenting written comments of the parties, or, if hearings are to be held for the purpose of hearing the expert, the procedures for interrogating the expert by the parties or for the participation of any expert witnesses presented by the parties.

(b) Expert opinion presented by a party (expert witness)

73. If a party presents an expert opinion, the arbitral tribunal might consider requiring, for example, that the opinion be in writing, that the expert should be available to answer questions at hearings, and that, if a party will present an expert witness at a hearing, advance notice must be given or that the written opinion must be presented in advance, as in the case of other witnesses (see paragraphs 60–62).

17. Hearings

(a) Decision whether to hold hearings

74. Laws on arbitral procedure and arbitration rules often have provisions as to the cases in which oral hearings must be held and as to when the arbitral tribunal has discretion to decide whether to hold hearings.

75. If it is up to the arbitral tribunal to decide whether to hold hearings, the decision is likely to be influenced by factors such as, on the one hand, that it is usually quicker and easier to clarify points at issue pursuant to a direct confrontation of arguments than on the basis of correspondence and, on the other hand, the travel and other cost of holding hearings, and that the need of finding acceptable dates for the hearings might delay the proceedings. The arbitral tribunal may wish to consult the parties on this matter.

(b) Whether one period of hearings should be held or separate periods of hearings

76. Attitudes vary as to whether hearings should be held in a single period of hearings or in separate periods, especially when more than a few days are needed to complete the hearings. According to some arbitrators, the entire hearings should normally be held in a single period, even if the hearings are to last for more than a week. Other arbitrators in such cases tend to schedule separate periods of hearings. In some cases issues to be decided are separated, and separate hearings set for those issues, with the aim that oral presentation on those issues will be completed within

the allotted time. Among the advantages of one period of hearings are that it involves less travel costs, memory will not fade, and it is unlikely that people representing a party will change. On the other hand, the longer the hearings, the more difficult it may be to find early dates acceptable to all participants. Furthermore, separate periods of hearings may be easier to schedule, the subsequent hearings may be tailored to the development of the case, and the period between the hearings leaves time for analysing the records and negotiations between the parties aimed at narrowing the points at issue by agreement.

(c) Setting dates for hearings

77. Typically, firm dates will be fixed for hearings. Exceptionally, the arbitral tribunal may initially wish to set only "target dates" as opposed to definitive dates. This may be done at a stage of the proceedings when not all information necessary to schedule hearings is yet available, with the understanding that the target dates will either be confirmed or rescheduled within a reasonably short period. Such provisional planning can be useful to participants who are generally not available on short notice.

(d) Whether there should be a limit on the aggregate amount of time each party will have for oral arguments and questioning witnesses

78. Some arbitrators consider it useful to limit the aggregate amount of time each party has for any of the following: (a) making oral statements; (b) questioning its witnesses; and (c) questioning the witnesses of the other party or parties. In general, the same aggregate amount of time is considered appropriate for each party, unless the arbitral tribunal considers that a different allocation is justified. Before deciding, the arbitral tribunal may wish to consult the parties as to how much time they think they will need.

79. Such planning of time, provided it is realistic, fair and subject to judiciously firm control by the arbitral tribunal, will make it easier for the parties to plan the presentation of the various items of evidence and arguments, reduce the likelihood of running out of time towards the end of the hearings and avoid that one party would unfairly use up a disproportionate amount of time.

(e) The order in which the parties will present their arguments and evidence

80. Arbitration rules typically give broad latitude to the arbitral tribunal to determine the order of presentations at the hearings. Within that latitude, practices differ, for example, as to whether opening or closing statements are heard and their level of detail; the sequence in which the claimant and the respondent present their opening statements, arguments, witnesses and other evidence; and whether the respondent or the claimant has the last word. In view of such differences, or when no arbitration rules apply, it may foster efficiency of the proceedings if the arbitral tribunal clarifies to the parties, in advance of the hearings, the manner in which it will conduct the hearings, at least in broad lines.

(f) Length of hearings

81. The length of a hearing primarily depends on the complexity of the issues to be argued and the amount of witness evidence to be presented. The length also depends on the procedural style used in the arbitration. Some practitioners prefer to have written evidence and written arguments presented before the hearings, which thus can focus on the issues that have not been sufficiently clarified. Those practitioners generally tend to plan shorter hearings than those practitioners who prefer that most if not all evidence and arguments are presented to the arbitral tribunal orally and in full detail. In order to facilitate the parties' preparations and avoid misunderstandings, the arbitral tribunal may wish to clarify to the parties, in advance of the hearings, the intended use of time and style of work at the hearings.

(g) Arrangements for a record of the hearings

82. The arbitral tribunal should decide, possibly after consulting with the parties, on the method of preparing a record of oral statements and testimony during hearings. Among different

possibilities, one method is that the members of the arbitral tribunal take personal notes. Another is that the presiding arbitrator during the hearing dictates to a typist a summary of oral statements and testimony. A further method, possible when a secretary of the arbitral tribunal has been appointed, may be to leave to that person the preparation of a summary record. A useful, though costly, method is for professional stenographers to prepare verbatim transcripts, often within the next day or a similarly short time period. A written record may be combined with tape-recording, so as to enable reference to the tape in case of a disagreement over the written record.

83. If transcripts are to be produced, it may be considered how the persons who made the statements will be given an opportunity to check the transcripts. For example, it may be determined that the changes to the record would be approved by the parties or, failing their agreement, would be referred for decision to the arbitral tribunal.

(h) Whether and when the parties are permitted to submit notes summarizing their oral arguments

84. Some legal counsel are accustomed to giving notes summarizing their oral arguments to the arbitral tribunal and to the other party or parties. If such notes are presented, this is usually done during the hearings or shortly thereafter; in some cases, the notes are sent before the hearing. In order to avoid surprise, foster equal treatment of the parties and facilitate preparations for the hearings, advance clarification is advisable as to whether submitting such notes is acceptable and the time for doing so.

85. In closing the hearings, the arbitral tribunal will normally assume that no further proof is to be offered or submission to be made. Therefore, if notes are to be presented to be read after the closure of the hearings, the arbitral tribunal may find it worthwhile to stress that the notes should be limited to summarizing what was said orally and in particular should not refer to new evidence or new argument.

18. Multi-party arbitration

86. When a single arbitration involves more than two parties (multi-party arbitration), considerations regarding the need to organize arbitral proceedings, and matters that may be considered in that connection, are generally not different from two-party arbitrations. A possible difference may be that, because of the need to deal with more than two parties, multi-party proceedings can be more complicated to manage than bilateral proceedings. The Notes, notwithstanding a possible greater complexity of multi-party arbitration, can be used in multi-party as well as in two-party proceedings.

87. The areas of possibly increased complexity in multi-party arbitration are, for example, the flow of communications among the parties and the arbitral tribunal (see paragraphs 33, 34 and 38–41); if points at issue are to be decided at different points in time, the order of deciding them (paragraphs 44–45); the manner in which the parties will participate in hearing witnesses (paragraph 63); the appointment of experts and the participation of the parties in considering their reports (paragraphs 70–72); the scheduling of hearings (paragraph 76); the order in which the parties will present their arguments and evidence at hearings (paragraph 80).

88. The Notes, which are limited to pointing out matters that may be considered in organizing arbitral proceedings in general, do not cover the drafting of the arbitration agreement or the constitution of the arbitral tribunal, both issues that give rise to special questions in multi-party arbitration as compared to two-party arbitration.

19. Possible requirements concerning filing or delivering the award

89. Some national laws require that arbitral awards be filed or registered with a court or similar authority, or that they be delivered in a particular manner or through a particular authority. Those laws differ with respect to, for example, the type of award to which the requirement applies (e.g. to all awards or only to awards not rendered under the auspices of an arbitral institution); time periods for filing, registering or delivering the award (in some cases those time

periods may be rather short); or consequences for failing to comply with the requirement (which might be, for example, invalidity of the award or inability to enforce it in a particular manner).

Who should take steps to fulfil any requirement

90. If such a requirement exists, it is useful, some time before the award is to be issued, to plan who should take the necessary steps to meet the requirement and how the costs are to be borne.

Endnotes

[1] Report of the United Nations Commission on International Trade Law on the work of its twenty-sixth session, Official Records of the General Assembly, Forty-eighth Session, Supplement No 17 (A/48/17) (reproduced in UNCITRAL Yearbook, vol. XXIV: 1993, part one), paras. 291–296.

[2] The draft Guidelines have been published as document A/CN.9/396/Add. 1 (reproduced in UNCITRAL Yearbook, vol. XXV: 1994, part two, IV); the considerations of the Commission are reflected in the report of the United Nations Commission on International Trade Law on the work of its twenty-seventh session, Official Records of the General Assembly, Forty-ninth Session Supplement No 17 (A/49/17) (reproduced in UNCITRAL Yearbook, Vol. XXV: 1994, part two, IV), paras. 111–195.

[3] The proceedings of the Congress are published in Planning Efficient Arbitration Proceedings/The Law Applicable in International Arbitration, ICCA Congress Series No 7, Kluwer Law International, The Hague, 1996.

[4] The draft Notes have been published as document A/CN. 9/410 (and will be reproduced in UNCITRAL Yearbook, vol. XXVI: 1995, part two, III).

[5] Report of the United Nations Commission on International Trade Law on the work of its twenty-eighth session, Official Records of the General Assembly, Fiftieth Session, Supplement No 17 (A/50/17) (and will be reproduced in UNCITRAL Yearbook, vol. XXVI: 1995, part one), paras. 314–373.

[6] The revised draft Notes have been published as document A/CN. 9/423 (and will be reproduced in UNCITRAL Yearbook, vol. XXVII: 1996, part two).

[7] Report of the United Nations Commission on International Trade Law on the work of its twenty-ninth session, Official Records of the General Assembly, Fifty-first Session, Supplement No 17 (A/51/17) (and will be reproduced in UNCITRAL Yearbook, vol. XXVII: 1996, part one), paras. 11 to 54.

[8] A prominent example of such rules are the UNCITRAL Arbitration Rules, which provide in article 15(1): "Subject to these Rules, the arbitral tribunal may conduct the arbitration in such manner as it considers appropriate, provided that the parties are treated with equality and that at any stage of the proceedings each party is given a full opportunity of presenting his case."

APPENDIX 5

The Tribunal Rules of Procedure
Provisionally adopted May 3, 1983, as amended May 27, 1997

Introductions and Definitions		984
Section I.	*Introductory Rules*	985
Article 1	Scope of Application	985
Article 2	Notice, Calculation of Periods of Time	985
Article 3	Notice of Arbitration	987
Article 4	Representation and Assistance	987
Section II.	*Composition of the Arbitral Tribunal*	988
Article 5	Number of Members	988
Articles 6–8	Appointment of Members	988
Articles 9–12	Challenge of Members	989
Article 13	Replacement of a Member	991
Article 14	Repetition of Hearings in the Event of Replacement or Substitution of a Member	992
Section III	*Arbitral Proceedings*	992
Article 15	General Provisions	992
Article 16	Place of Arbitration	993
Article 17	Language	993
Article 18	Statement of Claim	994
Article 19	Statement of Defence	995
Article 20	Amendments to the Claim or Defence	996
Article 21	Pleas as to the Jurisdiction of the Arbitral Tribunal	996
Article 22	Further Written Statements	997
Article 23	Periods of Time	997
Article 24	Evidence and Hearings	997
Article 25	Evidence and Hearings	998
Article 26	Interim Measures of Protection	999
Article 27	Experts	999
Article 28	Default	1000
Article 29	Closure of Hearings	1000
Article 30	Waiver of Rules	1000
Article 31	Decisions	1001
Article 32	Form and Effect of Award	1001
Article 33	Applicable Law	1002
Article 34	Settlement or Other Grounds for Termination	1002
Article 35	Interpretation of the Award	1003
Article 36	Correction of the Award	1003
Article 37	Additional Award	1003
Article 38	Costs	1003
Article 39	Costs	1004
Article 40	Costs	1005
Article 41	Deposit of Costs	1005

Introduction and Definitions

1. The Tribunal Rules which follow are organized in the following manner:
   — First, as to each Article, the text of the UNCITRAL Arbitration Rules is set forth.
   — Second, as to each Article, the text of any modifications to the UNCITRAL Rules made by the Tribunal is set forth. Such modifications have been made within the framework of the Algiers Declarations and specifically pursuant to Article III, paragraph 2 of the Claims Settlement Declaration.
   — Third, various Articles include notes to indicate how the Tribunal will implement or interpret the UNCITRAL Arbitration Rules, as modified.
2. The Tribunal Rules incorporate the UNCITRAL Rules and Administrative Directives 1, 2, 3 and 4 previously issued by the Tribunal, with certain modifications to each.
3. The following definitions apply for the purpose of the Tribunal Rules:
   (a) "Algiers Declarations" means the two Declarations of the Government of the Democratic and Popular Republic of Algeria, dated 19 January 1981.
   (b) "Arbitral tribunal" means either the Full Tribunal or a Chamber, depending on whichever is seised of a particular case or issue.
   (c) "Arbitrating party" means, in a particular case, the party or parties initiating recourse to arbitration (the claimant), or the other party or parties (the respondent). The term "arbitrating party" also means one of the two Governments when, in a particular case, it is a claimant or respondent, or when it refers a dispute or question to the Tribunal pursuant to the Algiers Declarations.
   (d) "Chamber" means a panel of three members composed by the President of the Tribunal from among the nine members of the Full Tribunal, pursuant to his powers under Article III, paragraph 1 of the Claims Settlement Declaration.
   (e) "Claims Settlement Declaration" means the "Declaration of the Democratic and Popular Republic of Algeria Concerning the Settlement of Claims by the Government of the United States and the Government of the Islamic Republic of Iran", dated 19 January 1981.
   (f) "Full Tribunal" means the nine member Tribunal.
   (g) "Member" as used in the Tribunal Rules shall have the same meaning as "arbitrator" where used in the UNCITRAL Rules.
   (h) "National", "Iran", and the "United States" shall have the same meanings as defined in Article VII of the Claims Settlement Declaration.
   (i) "President" means the President of the Tribunal.
   (j) "Presiding arbitrator" or "presiding member" means the President of the Tribunal or the Chairman of a Chamber, as the case may be.
   (k) "Registrar" means the Registrar of the Tribunal and includes any deputy of, or other person authorized by, the Registrar, the President, or the Full Tribunal to perform a function for which the Registrar is responsible.
   (l) "Secretary-General" means the Secretary-General of the Tribunal and includes any deputy of, or other person authorized by, the Secretary-General, the President, or the Full Tribunal to perform a function for which the Secretary-General is responsible.
   (m) "Tribunal" means the Iran-United States Claims Tribunal established within the framework of and pursuant to the Algiers Declarations.
   (n) "Tribunal Rules" means these Rules, as they may from time to time be modified or supplemented by the Full Tribunal or the two Governments.
   (o) "The two Governments" means the Government of the Islamic Republic of Iran and the Government of the United States of America.
   (p) "UNCITRAL Arbitration Rules" and "UNCITRAL Rules" means the Arbitration Rules of the United Nations Commission on International Trade Law which are the subject of Resolution 31/98 adopted by the General Assembly of the United Nations on 15 December 1976.

Section I: Introductory Rules

Article 1 Scope of Application

Text of UNCITRAL Rule

Article 1

1. Where the parties to a contract have agreed in writing that disputes in relation to that contract shall be referred to arbitration under the UNCITRAL Arbitration Rules, then such disputes shall be settled in accordance with these Rules subject to such modification as the parties may agree in writing.
2. These Rules shall govern the arbitration except that where any of these Rules is in conflict with a provision of the law applicable to the arbitration from which the parties cannot derogate, that provision shall prevail.

Modification of UNCITRAL Rule

1. Paragraph 1 of Article 1 of the UNCITRAL Rule is modified to read as follows:

    1. Within the framework of the Algiers Declarations, the initiation and conduct of proceedings before the arbitral tribunal shall be subject to the following Tribunal Rules which may be modified by the Full Tribunal or the two Governments.

2. Paragraph 2 of Article 1 of the UNCITRAL Rules is maintained unchanged.
3. The following is added to Article 1 of the UNCITRAL Rules as paragraph 3:

    3. The Claims Settlement Declaration constitutes an agreement in writing by Iran and the United States, on their own behalfs and on behalf of their nationals submitting to arbitration within the framework of the Algiers Declarations and in accordance with the Tribunal Rules.

Article 2 Notice, Calculation of Periods of Time

Text of UNCITRAL Rule

Article 2

1. For the purposes of these Rules, any notice, including a notification, communication or proposal, is deemed to have been received if it is physically delivered to the addressee or if it is delivered at his habitual residence, place of business or mailing address, or, if none of these can be found after making reasonable inquiry, then at the addressee's last-known residence or place of business. Notice shall be deemed to have been received on the day it is so delivered.
2. For the purposes of calculating a period of time under these Rules, such period shall begin to run on the day following the day when a notice, notification, communication or proposal is received. If the last day of such period is an official holiday or a non-business day at the residence or place of business of the addressee, the period is extended until the first business day which follows. Official holidays or non-business days occurring during the running of the period of time are included in calculating the period.

Modification of UNCITRAL Rule

Article 2 of the UNCITRAL Rules is modified to read as follows:

1. All documents must be filed with the Tribunal. Filing of a document with the Tribunal shall be deemed to have been made when it is physically received by the Registrar.
2. All documents filed in a particular case shall be served upon all arbitrating parties in that case through the Agents. The Registrar shall promptly deliver copies to the offices of each of the two Agents in The Hague, except for a filing Agent. Each Agent shall be responsible for

transmitting one copy to each concerned arbitrating party in his country or to the representative designated by each such arbitrating party to receive documents on its behalf.
3. The filing of documents with the Tribunal shall constitute service on all of the other arbitrating parties in the case and shall be deemed to have been received by said arbitrating parties when it is received by the Agent of their Government.
4. Notwithstanding the provisions of paragraphs 1-3 of Article 2, when the arbitral tribunal has so permitted in a particular case, service of written evidence may be effected by actual delivery to the representative of an arbitrating party during a hearing or a pre-hearing conference in that case. The Secretary-General shall make a record of such service which shall be signed by him. A copy of each document so served, together with such record of service, shall be delivered by the Secretary-General to the Registrar after the hearing or pre-hearing conference at which service was so made.
5. The Registrar may refuse to accept any document which is not received within the required time period or which does not comply with the Algiers Declarations or with the Tribunal Rules. Any such refusal by the Registrar is, upon objection by an arbitrating party concerned within thirty days of notification of refusal, subject to review by the arbitral tribunal.

Notes to Article 2
1. For the purposes of calculating a period of time under these Rules, such period shall begin to run on the day following the day when the document is received. If the last day of such period is an official holiday or a non-business day at the seat of the arbitral tribunal, the period is extended until the first business day which follows. Official holidays and non-business days occurring during the running of the period of time are included in calculating the period. The Secretary-General will issue a list of such days.
2. Twenty copies of all documents shall be filed with the Registrar, unless a smaller number is determined by the arbitral tribunal. In the event that there are more than two arbitrating parties in a case, a sufficient number of additional copies shall be filed to permit service on all arbitrating parties in the case. Also, the arbitral tribunal, or the Registrar, may at any time require a party which files a document to submit additional copies.
3. Exhibits and written evidence, other than those annexed to the Statement of Claim or Statement of Defence, shall be submitted in such manner and number of copies as the arbitral tribunal may determine in each case based on the nature and volume of the particular exhibit or written evidence and any other relevant circumstances.
4. Upon the filing of a document, the Registrar shall note on all copies the date received. The Registrar shall issue a receipt to the arbitrating party which filed the document. In all instances in which the Registrar is required to deliver copies to the Agents, he will secure a written receipt of such delivery, which will be kept in the case file and be available for inspection or copying by any arbitrating party in that case.
5. All documents filed with the Registrar are to be submitted on paper 8½ inches x 11 inches or on A-4 size paper (21 cm x 29.5 cm), or on paper no larger than A-4. If a document, exhibit or other written evidence cannot conveniently be reproduced on paper no larger than A-4, it is be folded to A-4 size, unless the Registrar permits otherwise in special circumstances.
6. Upon filing a Statement of Claim, the Registrar shall assign an identifying number to the claim, and the case shall be assigned to the Full Tribunal, or by lot to a Chamber. Thereafter, all documents filed in the case, including the award, shall have a caption stating:
   (i) the names of the parties,
   (ii) the case number assigned by the Registrar, and
   (iii) the number of the Chamber seised of the case;
        otherwise the caption shall state "Full Tribunal."
7. At least two copies in English and two copies in Farsi of all documents mentioned in Article 17, Note 3 and filed with the Tribunal shall be manually signed by the arbitrating party submitting

them or by its representative. Exhibits and annexes to documents need not be signed. If a document is presented without such signatures, it shall be accepted for filing, but the filing party shall be notified and required promptly to submit two manually signed copies in each language.

Article 3 Notice of Arbitration

Text of UNCITRAL Rule

Article 3

1. The party initiating recourse to arbitration (hereinafter called the "claimant") shall give to the other party (hereinafter called the "respondent") a notice of arbitration.
2. Arbitral proceedings shall be deemed to commence on the date on which the notice of arbitration is received by the respondent.
3. The notice of arbitration shall include the following:
    (a) A demand that the dispute be referred to arbitration;
    (b) The names and addresses of the parties;
    (c) A reference to the arbitration clause or the separate arbitration agreement that is invoked;
    (d) A reference to the contract out of or in relation to which the dispute arises;
    (e) The general nature of the claim and an indication of the amount involved, if any;
    (f) The relief or remedy sought;
    (g) A proposal as to the number of arbitrators (i.e. one or three), if the parties have not previously agreed thereon;
4. The notice of arbitration may also include:
    (a) The proposals for the appointments of a sole arbitrator and an appointing authority referred to in Article 6, paragraph 1;
    (b) The notification of the appointment of an arbitrator referred to in article 7;
    (c) The statement of claim referred to in article 18.

Modification of UNCITRAL Rule

No Notice of Arbitration pursuant to Article 3 of the UNCITRAL Rules is to be given.

Article 4 Representation and Assistance

Text of UNCITRAL Rule

Article 4

The Parties may be represented or assisted by persons of their choice. The names and addresses of such persons must be communicated in writing to the other party; such communication must specify whether the appointment is being made for purposes of representation or assistance.

Article 4 of the UNCITRAL Rules is maintained unchanged.

Notes to Article 4

1. As used in Article 4 of the UNCITRAL Rules, the term "parties" means the arbitrating parties.
2. For the purpose of a particular case, the two Governments may each appoint representatives in addition to their Agents and each of the other arbitrating parties may appoint representatives. An appointed representative shall be deemed to be authorized to act before the arbitral tribunal on behalf of the appointing party for all purposes of the case and the acts of the representative shall be binding upon the appointing party. A representative is not required to be licensed to practice law. Parties who appoint a representative shall file with the Registrar notice of appointment in such form as the Registrar may require.
3. Arbitrating parties may also be assisted in proceedings before the arbitral tribunal by one or more persons of their choice. Persons chosen to assist who are not also appointed as representatives are not deemed to be authorized to act before the arbitral tribunal on behalf of the appointing party, to bind the appointing party or to receive notices, communications or documents on behalf of the appointing party. Any such assistant is not required to be licensed to practice law.

Section II: Composition of the Arbitral Tribunal

Article 5 Number of Members

Text of UNCITRAL Rule

Article 5

If the parties have not previously agreed on the number of arbitrators (i.e. one or three), and if within fifteen days after the receipt by the respondent of the notice of arbitration the parties have not agreed that there shall be only one arbitrator, three arbitrators shall be appointed.

Modification of UNCITRAL Rule

Article 5 of the UNCITRAL Rules is replaced by the following:

> The composition of Chambers, the assignment of cases to various Chambers, the transfer of cases among Chambers and the relinquishment by Chambers of certain cases to the Full Tribunal will be provided for in orders issued by the President pursuant to his powers under Article III, paragraph 1 of the Claims Settlement Declaration.

Articles 6–8 Appointment of Members

Text of UNCITRAL Rules

Article 6

1. If a sole arbitrator is to be appointed, either party may propose to the other:
    (a) The names of one or more persons, one of whom would serve as the sole arbitrator; and
    (b) If no appointing authority has been agreed upon by the parties, the name or names of one or more institutions or persons, one of whom would serve as appointing authority.
2. If within thirty days after receipt by a party of a proposal made in accordance with paragraph 1 the parties have not reached agreement on the choice of a sole arbitrator, the sole arbitrator shall be appointed by the appointing authority agreed upon by the parties. If no appointing authority has been agreed upon by the parties, or if the appointing authority agreed upon refuses to act or fails to appoint the arbitrator within sixty days of the receipt of a party's request therefor, either party may request the Secretary-General of the Permanent Court of Arbitration at The Hague to designate an appointing authority.
3. The appointing authority shall, at the request of one of the parties, appoint the sole arbitrator as promptly as possible. In making the appointment the appointing authority shall use the following list-procedure, unless both parties agree that the list-procedure should not be used or unless the appointing authority determines in its discretion that the use of the list-procedure is not appropriate for the case:
    (a) At the request of one of the parties the appointing authority shall communicate to both parties an identical list containing at least three names;
    (b) Within fifteen days after the receipt of this list, each party may return the list to the appointing authority after having deleted the name or names to which he objects and numbered the remaining names on the list in the order of his preference;
    (c) After the expiration of the above period of time the appointing authority shall appoint the sole arbitrator from among the names approved on the lists returned to it and in accordance with the order of preference indicated by the parties;
    (d) If for any reason the appointment cannot be made according to this procedure, the appointing authority may exercise its discretion in appointing the sole arbitrator.
4. In making the appointment, the appointing authority shall have regard to such considerations as are likely to secure the appointment of an independent and impartial arbitrator and shall take into account as well the advisability of appointing an arbitrator of a nationality other than the nationalities of the parties.

Article 7

1. If three arbitrators are to be appointed, each party shall appoint one arbitrator. The two arbitrators thus appointed shall choose the third arbitrator who will act as the presiding arbitrator of the tribunal.
2. If within thirty days after the receipt of a party's notification of the appointment of an arbitrator the other party has not notified the first party of the arbitrator he has appointed:
   (a) The first party may request the appointing authority previously designated by the parties to appoint the second arbitrator; or
   (b) If no such authority has been previously designated by the parties, or if the appointing authority previously designated refuses to act or fails to appoint the arbitrator within thirty days after receipt of a party's request therefor, the first party may request the Secretary-General of the Permanent Court of Arbitration at The Hague to designate the appointing authority. The first party may then request the appointing authority so designated to appoint the second arbitrator. In either case, the appointing authority may exercise its discretion in appointing the arbitrator.
3. If within thirty days after the appointment of the second arbitrator the two arbitrators have not agreed on the choice of the presiding arbitrator, the presiding arbitrator shall be appointed by an appointing authority in the same way as a sole arbitrator would be appointed under article 6.

Article 8

1. When an appointing authority is requested to appoint an arbitrator pursuant to article 6 or article 7, the party which makes the request shall send to the appointing authority a copy of the notice of arbitration, a copy of the contract out of or in relation to which the dispute has arisen and a copy of the arbitration agreement if it is not contained in the contract. The appointing authority may require from either party such information as it deems necessary to fulfil its function.
2. Where the names of one or more persons are proposed for appointment as arbitrators, their full names, addresses and nationalities shall be indicated, together with a description of their qualifications.

Articles 6–8 of the UNCITRAL Rules are maintained unchanged.

Note to Articles 6–8

As used in Articles 6, 7 and 8 of the UNCITRAL Rules the terms "party" and "parties" refer to the one or both of the two Governments, as the case may be.

Articles 9–12 Challenge of Members

Text of UNCITRAL Rules

Article 9

A prospective arbitrator shall disclose to those who approach him in connexion with his possible appointment any circumstances likely to give rise to justifiable doubts as to his impartiality or independence. An arbitrator, once appointed or chosen, shall disclose such circumstances to the parties unless they have already been informed by him of these circumstances.

Article 10

1. Any arbitrator may be challenged if circumstances exist that give rise to justifiable doubts as to the arbitrator's impartiality or independence.
2. A party may challenge the arbitrator appointed by him only for reasons of which he becomes aware after the appointment has been made.

Article 11

1. A party who intends to challenge an arbitrator shall send notice of his challenge within fifteen days after the appointment of the challenged arbitrator has been notified to the challenging party or within fifteen days after the circumstances mentioned in articles 9 and 10 became known to that party.
2. The challenge shall be notified to the other party, to the arbitrator who is challenged and to the other members of the arbitral tribunal. The notification shall be in writing and shall state the reasons for the challenge.
3. When an arbitrator has been challenged by one party, the other party may agree to the challenge. The arbitrator may also, after the challenge, withdraw from his office. In neither case does this imply acceptance of the validity of the grounds for the challenge. In both cases the procedure provided in article 6 or 7 shall be used in full for the appointment of the substitute arbitrator, even if during the process of appointing the challenged arbitrator a party had failed to exercise his right to appoint or to participate in the appointment.

Article 12

1. If the other party does not agree to the challenge and the challenged arbitrator does not withdraw, the decision on the challenge will be made:
    (a) When the initial appointment was made by an appointing authority, by that authority;
    (b) When the initial appointment was not made by an appointing authority, but an appointing authority has been previously designated, by that authority;
    (c) In all other cases, by the appointing authority to be designated in accordance with the procedure for designating an appointing authority as provided for in article 6.
2. If the appointing authority sustains the challenge, a substitute arbitrator shall be appointed or chosen pursuant to the procedure applicable to the appointment or choice of an arbitrator as provided in articles 6 to 9 except that, when this procedure would call for the designation of an appointing authority, the appointment of the arbitrator shall be made by the appointing authority which decided on the challenge.

Modification of UNCITRAL Rules

1. Article 9 of the UNCITRAL Rules is maintained unchanged with the following addition:

    When any member of the arbitral tribunal obtains knowledge that any particular case before the arbitral tribunal involves circumstances likely to give rise to justifiable doubts as to his impartiality or independence with respect to that case, he shall disclose such circumstances to the President and, if the President so determines, to the arbitrating parties in the case and, if appropriate, shall disqualify himself as to that case.

2. Articles 10, 11 and 12 of the UNCITRAL Rules are maintained unchanged.

Notes to Articles 9–12

1. As used in Articles 9, 10, 11 and 12 of the UNCITRAL Rules, with respect to the initial appointment of a member the terms "party" and "parties" mean one or both of the two Governments, as the case may be. After the initial appointment, the terms "party" and "parties" mean the arbitrating party or parties, as the case may be. Arbitrating parties may challenge a member only on the basis of the existence of circumstances which give rise to justifiable doubts as to the member's impartiality or independence with respect to the particular case involved, and not upon any general grounds which also relate to other cases. Challenges on such general grounds may only be made by one of the two Governments.
2. In applying paragraph 1 of Article 11 of the UNCITRAL Rules, the period for making a challenge to a member of a Chamber to which a case has been assigned shall be fifteen days after the challenging party is given notice of the Chamber to which the case has been assigned, or

after the circumstances mentioned in Articles 9 and 10 of UNCITRAL Rules became known to that party. In the event the case is relinquished by the Chamber to the Full Tribunal, the period for challenging a member who is not a member of the relinquishing Chamber shall be fifteen days after the challenging party is given notice of the relinquishment, or after the circumstances mentioned in Articles 9 and 10 of the UNCITRAL Rules became known to that party.
3. In the event a member withdraws with respect to a particular case or if the challenge is sustained, he shall continue to exercise his functions as a member for all other cases and purposes except in respect of that particular case.
4. In the event that a member of a Chamber is challenged with respect to a particular case and withdraws, or if the challenge is sustained, the President will order the transfer of the case to another Chamber.
5. In the event the Full Tribunal is seised of a particular case and a member is challenged with respect to that case and withdraws, or if the challenge is sustained, a substitute member shall be appointed to the Full Tribunal for the purposes of that case in accordance with the procedure set forth in Article III of the Claims Settlement Declaration as was used in appointing the member being substituted. An appointing authority, if needed, shall be designated as provided in Article 12 of the UNCITRAL Rules.
6. Disclosure statements filed as to each member shall be made available by the Registrar to each arbitrating party in each case.

Article 13 Replacement of a Member

Text of UNCITRAL Rule

Article 13

1. In the event of the death or resignation of an arbitrator during the course of the arbitral proceedings, a substitute arbitrator shall be appointed or chosen pursuant to the procedure provided for in articles 6 to 9 that was applicable to the appointment or choice of the arbitrator being replaced.
2. In the event that an arbitrator fails to act or in the event of the *de jure* or *de facto* impossibility of his performing his functions, the procedure in respect of the challenge and replacement of an arbitrator as provided in the preceding articles shall apply.

Modification of UNCITRAL Rule

Article 13 of the UNCITRAL Rules is maintained unchanged with the following additions:
1. The following is added as the last sentence of paragraph 2:

   In applying the provisions of this paragraph, if the President, after consultation with the other members of the Full Tribunal, determines that the failure of a member to act or his impossibility to perform his functions is due to a temporary illness or other circumstances expected to be of relatively short duration, the member shall not be replaced but a substitute member shall be appointed for the temporary period in accordance with the same procedures as are described in Note 5 to Articles 9–12.

2. The following are added as paragraphs 3 and 4:
3. In the event of the temporary absence of the President, the senior other member of the Tribunal not appointed by either of the two Governments shall act as President of the Tribunal and as Chairman at the meetings of the Full Tribunal. Seniority shall be based on the date of appointment, or for members appointed on the same date shall be based on age.
4. A substitute member appointed for a temporary period shall continue to serve with respect to any case in which he has participated in the hearing, notwithstanding the member for whom he is a substitute is again available and may work on other Tribunal cases and matters.

Note to Article 13

Iran may, in advance, appoint up to three persons, to be available to act as a substitute member for a temporary period for a specified member, or members, of the Tribunal appointed by Iran; and the United States may, in advance, appoint up to three persons, to be available to act as a substitute member for a temporary period for a specified member, or members, of the Tribunal appointed by the United States. The members of the Tribunal appointed by Iran and the United States may select, in advance, by mutual agreement, a person to act as substitute for a temporary period for any of the remaining one third of the members of the Tribunal.

Amendment to Tribunal Rules, Article 13

Provisionally applied by decision of the Tribunal on 7 October 1983 at its 86th meeting (FTM 86, paragraph 9) and definitively adopted as an amendment to the Tribunal Rules by decision of the Tribunal on 7 March 1984 at its 90th meeting (FTM 90, paragraph 14).

The following is the text as issued by the Tribunal:

Article 13 of the Tribunal Rules is amended by the addition of a new paragraph (paragraph 5) as follows:

5. After the effective date of a member's resignation he shall continue to serve as a member of the Tribunal with respect to all cases in which he had participated in a hearing on the merits, and for that purpose shall be considered a member of the Tribunal instead of the person who replaces him.

Article 14 Repetition of Hearings in the Event of Replacement or Substitution of a Member

Text of UNCITRAL Rule

Article 14

If under articles 11 to 13 the sole or presiding arbitrator is replaced, any hearings held previously shall be repeated; if any other arbitrator is replaced, such prior hearings may be repeated at the discretion of the arbitral tribunal.

Modification of UNCITRAL Rule

Article 14 of the UNCITRAL Rules is modified to read as follows:

> If a member of the Full Tribunal or of a Chamber is replaced or if a substitute is appointed for him, the arbitral tribunal shall determine whether all, any part or none of any previous hearings shall be repeated.

Section III: Arbitral Proceedings

Article 15 General Provisions

Text of UNCITRAL Rule

Article 15

1. Subject to these Rules, the arbitral tribunal may conduct the arbitration in such manner as it considers appropriate, provided that the parties are treated with equality and that at any stage of the proceedings each party is given a full opportunity of presenting his case.
2. If either party so requests at any stage of the proceedings, the arbitral tribunal shall hold hearings for the presentation of evidence by witnesses, including expert witnesses, or for oral argument. In the absence of such a request, the arbitral tribunal shall decide whether to hold such hearings or whether the proceedings shall be conducted on the basis of documents and other materials.
3. All documents or information supplied to the arbitral tribunal by one party shall at the same time be communicated by that party to the other party.

> Article 15 of the UNCITRAL Rules is maintained unchanged.

Notes to Article 15

1. As used in Article 15 of the UNCITRAL Rules, the terms "party" and "parties" mean the arbitrating party or parties, as the case may be.
2. In applying paragraph 2 of Article 15, the arbitral tribunal shall determine without hearing any written requests or objections of the concerned arbitrating parties with respect to procedural matters unless it grants or invites oral argument in special circumstances.
3. In complying with paragraph 3 of Article 15, an arbitrating party shall follow the procedures set forth in Article 2 of the Tribunal Rules.
4. The arbitral tribunal may make an order directing the arbitrating parties to appear for a pre-hearing conference. The pre-hearing conference will normally be held only after the Statement of Defence in the case has been received. The order will state the matters to be considered at the pre-hearing conference.
5. The arbitral tribunal may, having satisfied itself that the statement of one of the two Governments—or, under special circumstances, any other person—who is not an arbitrating party in a particular case is likely to assist the tribunal in carrying out its task, permit such Government or person to assist the tribunal by presenting oral or written statements.

Article 16 Place of Arbitration

Text of UNCITRAL Rule

Article 16

1. Unless the parties have agreed upon the place where the arbitration is to be held, such place shall be determined by the arbitral tribunal, having regard to the circumstances of the arbitration.
2. The arbitral tribunal may determine the locale of the arbitration within the country agreed upon by the parties. It may hear witnesses and hold meetings for consultation among its members at any place it deems appropriate, having regard to the circumstances of the arbitration.
3. The arbitral tribunal may meet at any place it deems appropriate for the inspection of goods, other property or documents. The parties shall be given sufficient notice to enable them to be present at such inspection.
4. The award shall be made at the place of arbitration.

Article 16 of the UNCITRAL Rules is maintained unchanged.

Note to Article 16

As used in Article 16, paragraphs 1 and 2 of the UNCITRAL Rules, the term "parties" means the two Governments. As used in Article 16, paragraph 3 of the UNCITRAL Rules, the term "parties" means the arbitrating parties.

Article 17 Language

Text of UNCITRAL Rule

Article 17

1. Subject to an agreement by the parties, the arbitral tribunal shall, promptly after its appointment, determine the language or languages to be used in the proceedings. This determination shall apply to the statement of claim, the statement of defence, and any further written statements and, if oral hearings take place, to the language or languages to be used in such hearings.
2. The arbitral tribunal may order that any documents annexed to the statement of claim or statement of defence, and any supplementary documents or exhibits submitted in the course of the proceedings, delivered in their original language, shall be accompanied by a translation into the language or languages agreed upon by the parties or determined by the arbitral tribunal.

Article 17 of the UNCITRAL Rules is maintained unchanged.

Notes to Article 17

1. As used in Article 17 of the UNCITRAL Rules, the term "parties" means the two Governments.
2. In accordance with an agreement of the Agents, English and Farsi shall be the official languages to be used in the arbitration proceedings, and these languages shall be used for all oral hearings, decisions and awards.
3. In accordance with the provisions of Article 17 of the UNCITRAL Rules, the following documents filed with the Tribunal shall be submitted in both English and Farsi, unless otherwise agreed by the arbitrating parties:
    (a) The Statement of Claim and its annexes.
    (b) The Statement of Defence, and any counter-claim, including any annexes.
    (c) The reply (including any annexes) to any counter-claim.
    (d) Any further written statement (e.g. reply, rejoinder, brief), including any annexes, which the arbitral tribunal may require or permit an arbitrating party to present.
    (e) Any written request to the arbitral tribunal to take action or any objection thereto.
    (f) Any Challenge to a member.
4. The arbitral tribunal shall determine in each particular case what other documents, documentary exhibits and written evidence, or what parts thereof, shall be submitted in both English and Farsi.
5. Any disputes or difficulties regarding translations shall be resolved by the arbitral tribunal.

Article 18 Statement of Claim

Text of UNCITRAL Rule

Article 18

1. Unless the statement of claim was contained in the notice of arbitration, within a period of time to be determined by the arbitral tribunal, the claimant shall communicate his statement of claim in writing to the respondent and to each of the arbitrators. A copy of the contract, and of the arbitration agreement if not contained in the contract, shall be annexed thereto.
2. The statement of claim shall include the following particulars:
    (a) The names and addresses of the parties;
    (b) A statement of the facts supporting the claim;
    (c) The points at issue;
    (d) The relief or remedy sought.
   The claimant may annex to his statement of claim all documents he deems relevant or may add a reference to the documents or other evidence he will submit.

Modification of UNCITRAL Rule

Article 18 of the UNCITRAL Rules is modified to read as follows:

1. A party initiating recourse to arbitration before the Tribunal (the "claimant") shall do so by filing a Statement of Claim. Each Statement of Claim shall contain the following particulars:
    (a) A demand that the dispute be referred to arbitration by the Tribunal;
    (b) The names, nationalities and last known addresses of the parties;
    (c) A reference to the debt, contract (including transactions which are the subject of letters of credit or bank guarantees), expropriations or other measures affecting property rights out of or in relation to which the dispute arises and as to which the Tribunal has jurisdiction pursuant to Article II, paragraphs 1 and 2 of the Claims Settlement Declaration;
    (d) The general nature of the claim and an indication of the amount involved, if any;
    (e) A statement of the facts supporting the claim;
    (f) The points at issue;
    (g) The relief or remedy sought;

(h) If the claimant has appointed a lawyer or other person for purposes of representation or assistance in connection with the claim, the name and address of such person and an indication whether the appointment is for purposes of representation or assistance;
   (i) The name and address of the person to whom communications should be sent on behalf of the claimant (only one such person shall be entitled to be sent communications).
2. It is advisable that claimants (i) annex to their Statements of Claim such documents as will serve clearly to establish the basis of the claim, and/or (ii) add a reference and summary of relevant portions of such documents, and/or (iii) include in the Statement of Claim quotations of relevant portions of such documents.
3. No priority for the scheduling of hearings or the making of awards shall be based on the date of filing the Statement of Claim.

Notes to Article 18

1. No claims with respect to which the Tribunal has jurisdiction within the framework of the Algiers Declarations and pursuant to paragraphs 1 and 2 of Article II of the Claims Settlement Declaration may be filed before October 20, 1981.
2. All Statements of Claim with respect to matters as to which the Tribunal has jurisdiction pursuant to paragraphs 1 and 2 of Article II of the Claims Settlement Declaration which are filed between October 20, 1981 and November 19, 1981 will be deemed to have been filed simultaneously as of October 20, 1981. All such claims filed between November 20, 1981 and December 19, 1981 will be deemed to have been filed simultaneously as of November 20, 1981. All such claims filed between December 20, 1981 and January 19, 1982 will be deemed to have been filed simultaneously as of December 20, 1981.

Article 19 Statement of Defence

Text of UNCITRAL Rule

Article 19

1. Within a period of time to be determined by the arbitral tribunal, the respondent shall communicate his statement of defence in writing to the claimant and to each of the arbitrators.
2. The statement of defence shall reply to the particulars (b), (c), and (d) of the statement of claim (article 18, para. 2). The respondent may annex to his statement the documents on which he relies for his defence or may add a reference to the documents or other evidence he will submit.
3. In his statement of defence, or at a later stage in the arbitral proceedings if the arbitral tribunal decides that the delay was justified under the circumstances, the respondent may make a counter-claim arising out of the same contract or rely on a claim arising out of the same contract for the purpose of a set-off.
4. The provisions of article 18, paragraph 2, shall apply to a counter-claim and a claim relied on for the purpose of a set-off.

Modification of UNCITRAL Rule

Article 19 of the UNCITRAL Rules is modified to read as follows:

1. Within a period of time to be determined by the arbitral tribunal with respect to each case, which should not exceed 135 days, the respondent shall file its Statement of Defence. However, the arbitral tribunal may extend the time-limits if it concludes that such an extension is justified.
2. The Statement of Defence shall reply to the particulars (e), (f) and (g) and include the information required in (h) and (i) of the Statement of Claim (see Article 18, paragraph 1 of the Tribunal Rules). It is advisable that Respondents (i) annex to their Statement of Defence such documents as will clearly serve to establish the basis of the defence, and/or (ii) add a reference and summary of relevant portions of such documents, and/or (iii) include in the Statement of Defence quotations of relevant portions of such documents.

3. In the Statement of Defence, or at a later stage in the arbitral proceedings if the arbitral tribunal decides that the delay was justified under the circumstances, the respondent may make a counter-claim or rely on a claim for the purpose of a set-off, if such counter-claim or set-off is allowed under the Claims Settlement Declaration.

4. The provisions of Article 18, paragraph 1 shall apply to a counter-claim or claim relied on for purpose of a set-off.

Notes to Article 19

1. In determining and extending periods of time pursuant to this Article, the arbitral tribunal will take into account
   (i) the complexity of the case,
   (ii) any special circumstances, including demonstrated hardship to a claimant or respondent, and
   (iii) such other circumstances as it considers appropriate.

   In the event that the arbitral tribunal determines that a requirement to file a large number of Statements of Defence in any particular period would impose an unfair burden on a respondent to a claim or counter-claim, it will in some cases extend the time periods based on the above-mentioned factors or by lot.

2. In the event of a counter-claim or claim relied on for the purpose of a set-off, the claimant against whom it is made will be given the right of reply, and the provisions of paragraph 2 of Article 19 of the Tribunal Rules shall apply.

Article 20 Amendments to the Claim or Defence

Text of UNCITRAL Rule

Article 20

During the course of the arbitral proceedings either party may amend or supplement his claim or defence unless the arbitral tribunal considers it inappropriate to allow such amendment having regard to the delay in making it or prejudice to the other party or any other circumstances. However, a claim may not be amended in such a manner that the amended claim falls outside the scope of the arbitration clause or separate arbitration agreement.

Modification of UNCITRAL Rule

The last sentence of Article 20 of the UNCITRAL Rules is modified to read as follows:

> However, a claim may not be amended in such a manner that it falls outside the jurisdiction of the arbitral tribunal.

Note to Article 20

As used in Article 20 of the UNCITRAL Rules, the term "party" means the arbitrating party.

Article 21 Pleas as to the Jurisdiction of the Arbitral Tribunal

Text of UNCITRAL Rule

Article 21

1. The arbitral tribunal shall have the power to rule on objections that it has no jurisdiction, including any objections with respect to the existence or validity of the arbitration clause or of the separate arbitration agreement.

2. The arbitral tribunal shall have the power to determine the existence or the validity of the contract of which an arbitration clause forms a part. For the purposes of article 21, an arbitration clause which forms part of a contract and which provides for arbitration under these Rules shall be treated as an agreement independent of the other terms of the contract. A decision by the arbitral

tribunal that the contract is null and void shall not entail *ipso jure* the invalidity of the arbitration clause.
3. A plea that the arbitral tribunal does not have jurisdiction shall be raised not later than in the statement of defence or, with respect to a counter-claim, in the reply to the counter-claim.
4. In general, the arbitral tribunal should rule on a plea concerning its jurisdiction as a preliminary question. However, the arbitral tribunal may proceed with the arbitration and rule on such a plea in their final award.

Article 21 of the UNCITRAL Rules is maintained unchanged

Article 22 Further Written Statements
Text of UNCITRAL Rule
Article 22

The arbitral tribunal shall decide which further written statements, in addition to the statement of claim and the statement of defence, shall be required from the parties or may be presented by them and shall fix the periods of time for communicating such statements.

Article 22 of the UNCITRAL Rules is maintained unchanged.

Note to Article 22

As used in Article 22 of the UNCITRAL Rules, the term "parties" means the arbitrating parties.

Article 23 Periods of Time
Text of UNCITRAL Rule
Article 23

The periods of time fixed by the arbitral tribunal for the communication of written statements (including the statement of claim and statement of defence) should not exceed forty-five days. However, the arbitral tribunal may extend the time-limits if it concludes that an extension is justified.

Modification of UNCITRAL Rule

Article 23 of the UNCITRAL Rules is modified to read as follows:

The periods of time fixed by the arbitral tribunal for the communication of written statements (excluding the Statement of Defence) should not exceed 90 days. However, the arbitral tribunal may extend the time-limits if it concludes that an extension is justified.

Article 24 Evidence and Hearings
Text of UNCITRAL Rule
Article 24

1. Each party shall have the burden of proving the facts relied on to support his claim or defence.
2. The arbitral tribunal may, if it considers it appropriate, require a party to deliver to the tribunal and to the other party, within such a period of time as the arbitral tribunal shall decide, a summary of the documents and other evidence which that party intends to present in support of the facts in issue set out in his statement of claim or statement of defence.
3. At any time during the arbitral proceedings the arbitral tribunal may require the parties to produce documents, exhibits or other evidence within such a period of time as the tribunal shall determine.

Article 24 of the UNCITRAL Rules is maintained unchanged.

Note to Article 24

As used in Article 24 of the UNCITRAL Rules, the terms "party" and "parties" mean the arbitrating party or parties, as the case may be.

Article 25 Evidence and Hearings

Text of UNCITRAL Rule

Article 25

1. In the event of an oral hearing, the arbitral tribunal shall give the parties adequate advance notice of the date, time and place thereof.
2. If witnesses are to be heard, at least fifteen days before the hearing each party shall communicate to the arbitral tribunal and to the other party the names and addresses of the witnesses he intends to present, the subject upon and the languages in which such witnesses will give their testimony.
3. The arbitral tribunal shall make arrangements for the translation of oral statements made at a hearing and for a record of the hearing if either is deemed necessary by the tribunal under the circumstances of the case, or if the parties have agreed thereto and have communicated such agreement to the tribunal at least fifteen days before the hearing.
4. Hearings shall be held *in camera* unless the parties agree otherwise. The arbitral tribunal may require the retirement of any witness or witnesses during the testimony of other witnesses. The arbitral tribunal is free to determine the manner in which witnesses are examined.
5. Evidence of witnesses may also be presented in the form of written statements signed by them.
6. The arbitral tribunal shall determine the admissibility, relevance, materiality and weight of the evidence offered.

Modification of UNCITRAL Rule

Article 25 of the UNCITRAL Rules is maintained unchanged, except the period referred to in paragraph 2 shall be at least thirty days.

Notes to Article 25

1. As used in Article 25 of the UNCITRAL Rules, the terms "party" and "parties" mean the arbitrating party or parties, as the case may be, except that, as used in paragraph 4 of Article 25, the term "parties" means the two Governments and the arbitrating parties.
2. The information concerning witnesses which an arbitrating party must communicate pursuant to paragraph 2 of Article 25 of the UNCITRAL Rules is not required with respect to any witnesses which an arbitrating party may later decide to present to rebut evidence presented by the other arbitrating party. However, such information concerning any rebuttal witness shall be communicated to the arbitral tribunal and the other arbitrating parties as far in advance of hearing the witness as is reasonably possible.
3. With respect to paragraph 3 of Article 25 of the UNCITRAL Rules, the Secretary-General shall make arrangements for a tape-recording or stenographic record of hearings or parts of hearings if the arbitral tribunal so determines. If the arbitral tribunal determines that a transcript shall be made of any such tape-recording or stenographic record, the arbitrating parties in that case, or their authorized representatives, shall be permitted to read the transcript.
4. Any arbitrating party in the case may make a stenographic record of the hearings, or parts of the hearings, and, in that event, shall make a transcript thereof available to the arbitral tribunal without charge. Arbitrating parties are not permitted to make tape-recordings of hearings or other proceedings.
5. Notwithstanding the provisions of paragraph 4 of Article 25, the arbitral tribunal may at its discretion permit representatives of arbitrating parties in other cases which present similar issues of fact or law to the present to observe all or part of the hearing in a particular case, subject to the prior approval of the arbitrating parties in the particular case. The Agents of the two Governments are permitted to be present at pre-hearing conferences and hearings.
6. In applying paragraph 4 of Article 25 of the UNCITRAL Rules, the following provisions shall determine the manner in which witnesses are examined:
    (a) Before giving any evidence each witness shall make the following declaration: "I solemnly declare upon my honour and conscience that I will speak the truth, the whole truth and nothing but the truth."

(b) Witnesses may be examined by the presiding member and the other members of the arbitral tribunal. Also, when permitted by the arbitral tribunal, the representatives of the arbitrating parties in the case may ask questions, subject to the control of the presiding member.

7. The Secretary-General shall draft minutes of each hearing. After each member of the arbitral tribunal present at the hearing has been given the opportunity to comment on the draft minutes, the minutes, with any corrections approved by a majority of members who were present, shall be signed by the presiding member and the Secretary-General. The arbitrating parties in the case, or their representatives, shall be permitted to read such minutes.

Article 26 Interim Measures of Protection

Text of UNCITRAL Rule

Article 26

1. At the request of either party, the arbitral tribunal may take any interim measures it deems necessary in respect of the subject-matter of the dispute, including measures for the conservation of the goods forming the subject-matter in dispute, such as ordering their deposit with a third person or the sale of perishable goods.
2. Such interim measures may be established in the form of an interim award. The arbitral tribunal shall be entitled to require security for the costs of such measures.
3. A request for interim measures addressed by any party to a judicial authority shall not be deemed incompatible with the agreement to arbitrate, or as a waiver of that agreement.

Article 26 of the UNCITRAL Rules is maintained unchanged.

Note to Article 26

As used in Article 26 of the UNCITRAL Rules, the term "party" means the arbitrating party.

Article 27 Experts

Text of UNCITRAL Rule

Article 27

1. The arbitral tribunal may appoint one or more experts to report to it, in writing, on specific issues to be determined by the tribunal. A copy of the expert's terms of reference, established by the arbitral tribunal, shall be communicated to the parties.
2. The parties shall give the expert any relevant information or produce for his inspection any relevant documents or goods that he may require of them. Any dispute between a party and such expert as to the relevance of the required information or production shall be referred to the arbitral tribunal for decision.
3. Upon receipt of the expert's report, the arbitral tribunal shall communicate a copy of the report to the parties who shall be given the opportunity to express, in writing, their opinion on the report. A party shall be entitled to examine any document on which the expert has relied in his report.
4. At the request of either party the expert, after delivery of the report, may be heard at a hearing where the parties shall have the opportunity to be present and to interrogate the expert. At this hearing either party may present expert witnesses in order to testify on the points at issue. The provisions of article 25 shall be applicable to such proceedings.

Modification of UNCITRAL Rule

Article 27 of the UNCITRAL Rules is maintained unchanged, except that the following is added at the end of paragraph 2:

The expert shall invite a representative of each arbitrating party to attend any site inspection, and, when the arbitral tribunal so determines, a representative of each arbitrating party shall be invited to attend other inspections made by the expert.

Notes to Article 27

1. As used in Article 27 of the UNCITRAL Rules, the terms "party" and "parties" mean the arbitrating party or parties, as the case may be.
2. Every expert, before beginning the performance of his duties, shall make the following declaration:

"I solemnly declare upon my honour and conscience that I will perform my duties in accordance with my sincere belief and will keep confidential all matters relating to the performance of my task."

Article 28 Default

Text of UNCITRAL Rule

Article 28

1. If, within the period of time fixed by the arbitral tribunal, the claimant has failed to communicate his claim without showing sufficient cause for such failure, the arbitral tribunal shall issue an order for the termination of the arbitral proceedings. If, within the period of time fixed by the arbitral tribunal, the respondent has failed to communicate his statement of defence without showing sufficient cause for such failure, the arbitral tribunal shall order that the proceedings continue.
2. If one of the parties, duly notified under these Rules, fails to appear at a hearing, without showing sufficient cause for such failure, the arbitral tribunal may proceed with the arbitration.
3. If one of the parties, duly invited to produce documentary evidence, fails to do so within the established period of time, without showing sufficient cause for such failure, the arbitral tribunal may make the award on the evidence before it.

Article 28 of the UNCITRAL Rules is maintained unchanged.

Note to Article 28

As used in Article 28 of the UNCITRAL Rules, the term "parties" means the arbitrating parties.

Article 29 Closure of Hearings

Text of UNCITRAL Rule

Article 29

1. The arbitral tribunal may inquire of the parties if they have any further proof to offer or witnesses to be heard or submissions to make and, if there are none, it may declare the hearings closed.
2. The arbitral tribunal may, if it considers it necessary owing to exceptional circumstances, decide, on its own motion or upon application of a party, to reopen the hearings at any time before the award in made.

Article 29 of the UNCITRAL Rules is maintained unchanged.

Note to Article 29

As used in Article 29 of the UNCITRAL Rules, the terms "party" and "parties" mean the arbitrating party or parties, as the case may be.

Article 30 Waiver of Rules

Text of UNCITRAL Rule

Article 30

A party who knows that any provision of, or requirement under, these Rules has not been complied with and yet proceeds with the arbitration without promptly stating his objection to such non-compliance, shall be deemed to have waived his right to object.

Article 30 of the UNCITRAL Rules is maintained unchanged.

Note to Article 30

As used in Article 30 of the UNCITRAL Rules, the term "party" means the arbitrating party.

Article 31 Decisions

Text of UNCITRAL Rule

Article 31

1. When there are three arbitrators, any award or other decision of the arbitral tribunal shall be made by a majority of the arbitrators.
2. In the case of questions of procedure, when there is no majority or when the arbitral tribunal so authorizes, the presiding arbitrator may decide on his own, subject to revision, if any, by the arbitral tribunal.

Article 31 of the UNCITRAL Rules is maintained unchanged.

Notes to Article 31

1. Any award or other decision of the arbitral tribunal pursuant to paragraph 1 of Article 31 shall be made by a majority of its members.
2. The arbitral tribunal shall deliberate in private. Its deliberations shall be and remain secret. Only the members of the arbitral tribunal shall take part in the deliberations. The Secretary-General may be present. No other person may be admitted except by special decision of the arbitral tribunal. Any question which is to be voted upon shall be formulated in precise terms in English and Farsi and the text shall, if a member so requests, be distributed before the vote is taken. The minutes of the private sittings of the arbitral tribunal shall be secret.

Article 32 Form and Effect of Award

Text of UNCITRAL Rule

Article 32

1. In addition to making a final award, the arbitral tribunal shall be entitled to make interim, interlocutory, or partial awards.
2. The award shall be made in writing and shall be final and binding on the parties. The parties undertake to carry out the award without delay.
3. The arbitral tribunal shall state the reasons upon which the award is based, unless the parties have agreed that no reasons are to be given.
4. An award shall be signed by the arbitrators and it shall contain the date on which and the place where the award was made. When there are three arbitrators and one of them fails to sign, the award shall state the reason for the absence of the signature.
5. The award may be made public only with consent of both parties.
6. Copies of the award signed by the arbitrators shall be communicated to the parties by the arbitral tribunal.
7. If the arbitration law of the country where the award is made requires that the award be filed or registered by the arbitral tribunal, the tribunal shall comply with this requirement within the period of time required by law.

Modification of UNCITRAL Rule

Article 32 of the UNCITRAL Rules is maintained unchanged, except for the following:
1. The following is added as the last sentence of paragraph 3:

Any arbitrator may request that his dissenting vote or his dissenting vote and the reasons therefor be recorded.

2. Paragraph 5 is modified to read as follows:

5. All awards and other decisions shall be made available to the public, except that upon the request of one or more arbitrating parties, the arbitral tribunal may determine that it will not make the entire award or other decision public, but will make public only portions thereof from which the identity of the parties, other identifying facts and trade or military secrets have been deleted.

Note to Article 32

As used in Article 32 of the UNCITRAL Rules, the term "parties" means the arbitrating parties.

Article 33 Applicable Law

Text of UNCITRAL Rule

Article 33

1. The arbitral tribunal shall apply the law designated by the parties as applicable to the substance of the dispute. Failing such designation by the parties, the arbitral tribunal shall apply the law determined by the conflict of laws rules which it considers applicable.
2. The arbitral tribunal shall decide as *amiable compositeur* or *ex aequo et bono* only if the parties have expressly authorized the arbitral tribunal to do so and if the law applicable to the arbitral procedure permits such arbitration.
3. In all cases, the arbitral tribunal shall decide in accordance with the terms of the contract and shall take into account the usages of the trade applicable to the transaction.

Modification of the UNCITRAL Rule

Article 33 of the UNCITRAL is modified to read as follows:

1. The arbitral tribunal shall decide all cases on the basis of respect for law, applying such choice of law rules and principles of commercial and international law as the arbitral tribunal determines to be applicable, taking into account relevant usages of the trade, contract provisions and changed circumstances.
2. The arbitral tribunal shall decide *ex aequo et bono* only if the arbitrating parties have expressly and in writing authorized it to do so.

Note to Article 33

Paragraph 1 of the modified text of Article 33 corresponds to Article V of the Claims Settlement Declaration.

Article 34 Settlement or Other Grounds for Termination

Text of UNCITRAL Rule

Article 34

1. If, before the award is made, the parties agree on a settlement of the dispute, the arbitral tribunal shall either issue an order for the termination of the arbitral proceedings or, if requested by both parties and accepted by the tribunal, record the settlement in the form of an arbitral award on agreed terms. The arbitral tribunal is not obliged to give reasons for such an award.
2. If, before the award is made, the continuation of the arbitral proceedings becomes unnecessary or impossible for any reason not mentioned in paragraph 1, the arbitral tribunal shall inform the parties of its intention to issue an order for the termination of the proceedings. The arbitral tribunal shall have the power to issue such an order unless a party raises justifiable grounds for objection.
3. Copies of the order for termination of the arbitral proceedings or of the arbitral award on agreed terms, signed by the arbitrators, shall be communicated by the arbitral tribunal to the parties. Where an arbitral award on agreed terms is made, the provisions of article 32, paragraph 2 and 4 to 7, shall apply.

Article 34 of the UNCITRAL Rules is maintained unchanged.

Note to Article 34

As used in Article 34 of the UNCITRAL Rules, the terms "party" and "parties" mean the arbitrating party or parties, as the case may be.

Article 35 Interpretation of the Award

Text of UNCITRAL Rule

Article 35

1. Within thirty days after the receipt of the award, either party, with notice to the other party, may request that the arbitral tribunal give an interpretation of the award.
2. The interpretation shall be given in writing within forty-five days after the receipt of the request. The interpretation shall form part of the award and the provisions of article 32, paragraphs 2 to 7, shall apply.

Article 35 of the UNCITRAL Rules is maintained unchanged.

Note to Article 35

As used in Article 35 of the UNCITRAL Rules, the term "party" means the arbitrating party.

Article 36 Correction of the Award

Text of UNCITRAL Rule

Article 36

1. Within thirty days after the receipt of the award, either party, with notice to the other party, may request the arbitral tribunal to correct in the award any errors in computation, any clerical or typographical errors, or any errors of similar nature. The arbitral tribunal may within thirty days after the communication of the award make such corrections on its own initiative.
2. Such corrections shall be in writing, and the provisions of article 32, paragraphs 2 to 7, shall apply.

Article 36 of the UNCITRAL Rules is maintained unchanged.

Note to Article 36

As used in Article 36 of the UNCITRAL Rules, the term "party" means the arbitrating party.

Article 37 Additional Award

Text of UNCITRAL Rule

Article 37

1. Within thirty days after the receipt of the award, either party, with notice to the other party, may request the arbitral tribunal to make an additional award as to claims presented in the arbitral proceedings but omitted from the award.
2. If the arbitral tribunal considers the request for an additional award to be justified and considers that the omission can be rectified without any further hearings or evidence, it shall complete its award within sixty days after the receipt of the request.
3. When an additional award is made, the provisions of article 32, paragraphs 2 to 7, shall apply.

Article 37 of the UNCITRAL Rules is maintained unchanged.

Note to Article 37

As used in Article 37 of the UNCITRAL Rules, the term "party" means the arbitrating party.

Article 38 Costs

Text of UNCITRAL Rule

Article 38

The arbitral tribunal shall fix the costs of arbitration in its award. The term "costs" includes only:

(a) The fees of the arbitral tribunal to be stated separately as to each arbitrator and to be fixed by the tribunal itself in accordance with article 39;

(b) The travel and other expenses incurred by the arbitrators;
(c) The costs of expert advice and of other assistance required by the arbitral tribunal;
(d) The travel and other expenses of witnesses to the extent such expenses are approved by the arbitral tribunal;
(e) The costs for legal representation and assistance of the successful party if such costs were claimed during the arbitral proceedings, and only to the extent that the arbitral tribunal determines that the amount of such costs is reasonable;
(f) Any fees and expenses of the appointing authority as well as the expenses of the Secretary-General of the Permanent Court of Arbitration at The Hague.

Modification of UNCITRAL Rule

Article 38 of the UNCITRAL Rules is modified to read as follows:
1. The arbitral tribunal shall fix the costs of arbitration in its award. The term "costs" includes only:
   (a) The costs of expert advice and of other special assistance required for a particular case by the arbitral tribunal;
   (b) The travel and other expenses of witnesses to the extent such expenses are approved by the arbitral tribunal;
   (c) The costs for legal representation and assistance of the successful party if such costs were claimed during the arbitral proceedings, and only to the extent that the arbitral tribunal determines that the amount of such costs is reasonable.
2. The Full Tribunal shall fix the fees and expenses of the Tribunal which, in accordance with Article VI, paragraph 3 of the Claims Settlement Declaration, shall be borne equally by the two Governments.

Note to Article 38

As used in Article 38 of the UNCITRAL Rules, the term "party" means the arbitrating party.

Article 39 Costs

Text of UNCITRAL Rule

Article 39

1. The fees of the arbitral tribunal shall be reasonable in amount, taking into account the amount in dispute, the complexity of the subject-matter, the time spent by the arbitrators and any other relevant circumstances of the case.
2. If an appointing authority has been agreed upon by the parties or designated by the Secretary-General of the Permanent Court of Arbitration at The Hague, and if that authority has issued a schedule of fees for arbitrators in international cases which it administers, the arbitral tribunal in fixing its fees shall take that schedule of fees into account to the extent that it considers appropriate in the circumstances of the case.
3. If such appointing authority has not issued a schedule of fees for arbitration in international cases, any party may at any time request the appointing authority to furnish a statement setting forth the basis for establishing fees which is customarily followed in international cases in which the authority appoints arbitrators. If the appointing authority consents to provide such a statement, the arbitral tribunal in fixing its fees shall take such information into account to the extent that it considers appropriate in the circumstances of that case.
4. In cases referred to in paragraphs 2 and 3, when a party so requests and the appointing authority consents to perform the function, the arbitral tribunal shall fix its fees only after consultation with the appointing authority which may make any comment it deems appropriate to the arbitral tribunal concerning the fees.

Article 39 of the UNCITRAL Rules is maintained unchanged.

Note to Article 39

As used in Article 39 of the UNCITRAL Rules, the terms "party" and "parties" mean one or both of the two Governments, as the case may be.

Article 40 Costs

Text of UNCITRAL Rule

Article 40

1. Except as provided in paragraph 2, the costs of arbitration shall in principle be borne by the unsuccessful party. However, the arbitral tribunal may apportion each of such costs between the parties if it determines that apportionment is reasonable, taking into account the circumstances of the case.
2. With respect to the costs of legal representation and assistance referred to in article 38, paragraph (e) the arbitral tribunal, taking into account the circumstances of the case, shall be free to determine which party shall bear such costs or may apportion such costs between the parties if it determines that apportionment is reasonable.
3. When the arbitral tribunal issues an order for the termination of the arbitral proceedings or makes an award on agreed terms, it shall fix the costs of arbitration referred to in article 38 and article 39, paragraph 1, in the text of that order or award.
4. No additional fees may be charged by an arbitral tribunal for interpretation or correction or completion of its award under articles 35 to 37.

Modification of UNCITRAL Rule

Article 40 of the UNCITRAL Rules is maintained unchanged, except for the following:
1. The first sentence of paragraph 1 of Article 40 of the UNCITRAL Rules is modified as follows:

Except as provided in paragraph 2, the costs of arbitration referred to in paragraphs 1(a) and 1(b) of Article 38 shall in principle be borne by the unsuccessful party

2. The reference in paragraph 2 of Article 40 of the UNCITRAL Rules to "Article 38, paragraph (e)" is modified to read "Article 38, paragraph 1(c)."
3. Paragraph 3 is changed to read as follows:

    3. When the arbitral tribunal issues an order for the termination of the arbitral proceedings, it shall fix the costs of arbitration referred to in article 38 in the text of that order.

Note to Article 40

As used in Article 40 of the UNCITRAL Rules, the terms "party" and "parties" mean the arbitrating party or parties, as the case may be.

Article 41 Deposit of Costs

Text of UNCITRAL Rule

Article 41

1. The arbitral tribunal, on its establishment, may request each party to deposit an equal amount as an advance for the costs referred to in article 38, paragraphs (a), (b) and (c).
2. During the course of the arbitral proceedings the arbitral tribunal may request supplementary deposits from the parties.
3. If an appointing authority has been agreed upon by the parties or designated by the Secretary-General of the Permanent Court of Arbitration at The Hague, and when a party so requests and the appointing authority consents to perform the function, the arbitral tribunal shall fix the amounts of any deposits or supplementary deposits only after consultation with the appointing authority which may make any comments to the arbitral tribunal which it deems appropriate concerning the amount of such deposits and supplementary deposits.
4. If the required deposits are not paid in full within thirty days after the receipt of the request, the arbitral tribunal shall so inform the parties in order that one or another of them may make the required payment. If such payment is not made, the arbitral tribunal may order the suspension or termination of arbitral proceedings.

5. After the award has been made, the arbitral tribunal shall render an accounting to the parties of the deposits received and return any unexpended balance to the parties.

Modification of UNCITRAL Rule

Article 41 of the UNCITRAL Rules is modified to read as follows:
1. During the course of its proceedings the Full Tribunal may from time to time determine the costs referred to in paragraph 2 of Article 38 and may request each of the two Governments to deposit equal amounts as advances for such costs.
2. The arbitral tribunal may request each arbitrating party to deposit an amount determined by it as advances for the costs referred to in paragraph 1(a) of Article 38.
3. If the required deposits are not paid in full within the time fixed by the arbitral tribunal, the arbitral tribunal shall so inform the parties in order that one or another of them may make the required payment. If such payment is not made, the arbitral tribunal may order the suspension or termination of the arbitral proceedings or may take such action to permit continuation of the proceedings as is appropriate under the circumstances of the case.
4. The Secretary-General shall transmit monthly, quarterly and annual financial statements to the Full Tribunal and to the Agents. The accounts of the Tribunal shall be audited annually by an independent qualified accountant approved by the Full Tribunal. The Secretary-General shall transmit copies of the audit report to the Full Tribunal and to the Agents. At the request of either Agent, the annual audit shall be reviewed by an Audit Committee composed of three professionally qualified persons, one appointed by each Agent and one by the President. The Audit Committee shall submit its report to the Full Tribunal, to the Agents, and to the Secretary-General.
5. After the termination of the work of the Tribunal, it shall, after a final audit render an accounting to the two Governments of the deposits received and return any unexpended balance to the two Governments.

Note to Article 41

1. As used in paragraph 3, insofar as it refers to deposits made pursuant to paragraph 1 of Article 41 of the UNCITRAL Rules, the term "parties" means the two Governments; insofar as it refers to deposits made pursuant to paragraph 2 that term means the arbitrating parties.

APPENDIX 6
UNCITRAL

Recommendations to assist arbitral institutions and other interested bodies with regard to arbitration under the UNCITRAL Arbitration Rules as revised in 2010

A. Introduction	1007
B. Adoption of the UNCITRAL Arbitration Rules as the institutional rules of arbitral institutions or other interested bodies	1008
C. Arbitral institutions and other interested bodies administering arbitration under the UNCITRAL Arbitration Rules or providing some administrative services	1011
D. Arbitral institution acting as appointing authority	1014

A. Introduction

1. The UNCITRAL Arbitration Rules as revised in 2010

1. The UNCITRAL Arbitration Rules were originally adopted in 1976[1] and have been used for the settlement of a broad range of disputes, including disputes between private commercial parties where no arbitral institution is involved, commercial disputes administered by arbitral institutions, investor-State disputes and State-to-State disputes. The Rules are recognized as one of the most successful international instruments of a contractual nature in the field of arbitration. They have also strongly contributed to the development of the arbitration activities of many arbitral institutions in all parts of the world.

2. The 1976 UNCITRAL Arbitration Rules were revised in 2010[2] to better conform to current practices in international trade and to account for changes in arbitral practice over the past 30 years. The revision was aimed at enhancing the efficiency of arbitration under the 1976 UNCITRAL Arbitration Rules and did not alter the original structure of the text, its spirit or its drafting style. The UNCITRAL Arbitration Rules as revised in 2010 have been in effect since 15 August 2010.

2. General Assembly resolution 65/22

3. In 2010, the General Assembly, by its resolution 65/22, recommended the use of the UNCITRAL Arbitration Rules as revised in 2010 in the settlement of disputes arising in the context of international commercial relations. That recommendation was based on the conviction that "the revision of the Arbitration Rules in a manner that is acceptable to countries with

---

[1] *Official Records of the General Assembly, Thirty-first Session, Supplement No 17* (A/31/17), para. 57.
[2] Ibid., *Sixty-fifth Session, Supplement No 17* (A/65/17), paras. 13-187 and annex I.

different legal, social and economic systems can significantly contribute to the development of harmonious international economic relations and to the continuous strengthening of the rule of law".

4. In that resolution, the General Assembly noted that "the revised text can be expected to contribute significantly to the establishment of a harmonized legal framework for the fair and efficient settlement of international commercial disputes".

3. Purpose of the recommendations

5 The present recommendations are made with regard to the use of the UNCITRAL Arbitration Rules. (For recommendations on the use of the 1976 UNCITRAL Arbitration Rules, see the "Recommendations to assist arbitral institutions and other interested bodies with regard to arbitrations under the UNCITRAL Arbitration Rules",[3] adopted at the fifteenth session of UNCITRAL, in 1982.) Their purpose is to inform and assist arbitral institutions and other interested bodies that envisage using the UNCITRAL Arbitration Rules as described in paragraph 6 below.

4. Different usages by arbitral institutions and other interested bodies

6 The UNCITRAL Arbitration Rules have been used in the following different ways by arbitral institutions and other interested bodies, including chambers of commerce and trade associations:
  (a). They have served as a model for institutions drafting their own arbitration rules. The degree to which the UNCITRAL Arbitration Rules have been used as a drafting model ranges from inspiration to full adoption of the Rules (see section B below);
  (b). Institutions have offered to administer disputes under the UNCITRAL Arbitration Rules or to render administrative services in ad hoc arbitrations under the Rules (see section C below);
  (c). An institution (or a person) may be requested to act as appointing authority, as provided for under the UNCITRAL Arbitration Rules (see section D below).

B. Adoption of the UNCITRAL Arbitration Rules as the institutional rules of arbitral institutions or other interested bodies

1. Appeal to leave the substance of the UNCITRAL Arbitration Rules unchanged

7. Institutions, when preparing or revising their institutional rules, may wish to consider adopting the UNCITRAL Arbitration Rules as a model.[4] An institution that intends to do so should take into account the expectations of the parties that the rules of the institution will then faithfully follow the text of the UNCITRAL Arbitration Rules.

8. This appeal to follow closely the substance of the UNCITRAL Arbitration Rules does not mean that the particular organizational structure and needs of a given institution should be neglected. Institutions adopting the UNCITRAL Arbitration Rules as their institutional rules will certainly need to add provisions, for instance on administrative services or fee schedules. In addition, formal modifications, affecting very few provisions of the UNCITRAL Arbitration Rules, as indicated below in paragraphs 9-17, should be taken into account.

2. Presentation of modifications

(a) A short explanation

9 If an institution uses the UNCITRAL Arbitration Rules as a model for drafting its own institutional rules, it may be useful for the institution to consider indicating where those rules diverge from the UNCITRAL Arbitration Rules. Such indication may be helpful to the readers and potential users

---

[3] Ibid., *Thirty-seventh Session, Supplement No 17* and corrigenda (A/37/17 and Corr.I and 2), annex I.
[4] See, for example, the Arbitration Rules of the Cairo Regional Centre for International Commercial Arbitration in force as from 1 March 2011 (available from <www.crcica.org.eg>) or the Arbitration Rules (as revised in 2010) of the Kuala Lumpur Regional Centre for Arbitration (available from <www.klrca.org.my>).

who would otherwise have to embark on a comparative analysis to identify any disparity.
10 The institution may wish to include a text, for example a foreword, which refers to the specific modifications included in the institutional rules as compared with the UNCITRAL Arbitration Rules.[5] The indication of the modifications could also come at the end of the text of the institutional rules.[6] Further, it might be advisable to accompany the institutional rules with a short explanation of the reasons for the modifications.[7]

(b) Effective date

11 Article 1, paragraph 2, of the UNCITRAL Arbitration Rules defines an effective date for those Rules. Obviously, the institutional rules based on the UNCITRAL Arbitration Rules will have their own specific date of application. In the interest of legal certainty, it is recommended to refer in the arbitration rules to the effective date of application of the rules so that the parties know which version is applicable.

(c) Communication channel

12 Usually, when an institution administers a case, communications between the parties before the constitution of the arbitral tribunal would be carried out through the institution. Therefore, it is recommended to adapt articles 3 and 4 of the UNCITRAL Arbitration Rules relating to communication before the constitution of the arbitral tribunal. For example, in relation to article 3, paragraph 1:
   (a) If the communications take place through the institution, article 3, paragraph 1, could be amended as follows:
      1 The party or parties initiating recourse to arbitration (hereinafter called the "claimant") shall communicate to [name of the institution] a notice of arbitration. [Name of the institution] shall communicate the notice of arbitration to the other party or parties (hereinafter called the "respondent") [without undue delay] [immediately].
Or as follows:
      1. The party or parties initiating recourse to arbitration (hereinafter called the "claimant") shall file with [name of the institution] a notice of arbitration and [name of the institution] shall communicate it to the other party or parties (hereinafter called the "respondent").[8]
   (b) If the institution receives copies of the communications, article 3, paragraph 1, would remain unchanged, and the following provision could be added:
      All documents transmitted pursuant to articles 3 and 4 of the UNCITRAL Arbitration Rules shall be served on [name of the institution] at the time of such transmission to the

---

[5] For example, in the introduction to the Arbitration Rules of the Cairo Regional Centre for International Commercial Arbitration in force as from 1 March 2011, it is provided that those rules "are based upon the new UNCITRAL Arbitration Rules, as revised in 2010, with minor modifications emanating mainly from the Centre's role as an arbitral institution and an appointing authority". The Arbitration Rules (as revised in 2010) of the Kuala Lumpur Regional Centre of Arbitration provide that the rules for arbitration of the institution shall be the "UNCITRAL Arbitration Rules as modified in accordance with the rules set out below".

[6] See, for example, the Permanent Court of Arbitration Optional Rules for Arbitration between International Organizations and Private Parties, effective 1 July 1996 (based on the 1976 version of the UNCITRAL Arbitration Rules); available from <www.pca-cpa.org/showfile.asp?fil_id=201>.

[7] For example, in the text of the Permanent Court of Arbitration Optional Rules for Arbitrating Disputes between Two Parties of Which Only One Is a State, effective 6 July 1993 (available from <www.pcacpa.org/showfile.asp?fil_id=194>), the following note is inserted: "These Rules are based on the [1976] UNCITRAL Arbitration Rules, with the following modifications: ... Modifications to indicate the functions of the Secretary-General and the International Bureau of the Permanent Court of Arbitration: Article 1, para. 4 (added) ...".

[8] For example, this is the approach adopted in the Arbitration Rules of the Cairo Regional Centre for International Commercial Arbitration in force as from 1 March 2011.

[9] For example, a similar approach can be found in Rule 2, paragraph 1, of the Arbitration Rules (as revised in 2010) of the Kuala Lumpur Regional Centre for Arbitration.

other party or parties or immediately thereafter.[9]

13 To address the matter of communications after the constitution of the arbitral tribunal, the institution may either:

(a) Modify each article in the UNCITRAL Arbitration Rules referring to communications, namely: article 5; article 11; article 13, paragraph 2; article 17, paragraph 4; article 20, paragraph 1; article 21, paragraph 1; article 29, paragraphs 1, 3 and 4; article 34, paragraph 6; article 36, paragraph 3; article 37, paragraph 1; article 38, paragraphs 1 and 2; article 39, paragraph 1; article 41, paragraphs 3 and 4; or

(b) Include in article 17 of the UNCITRAL Arbitration Rules a provision along the lines of:

(i) If the institution decides to receive all communications for the purpose of notification:

"Except as otherwise permitted by the arbitral tribunal, all communications addressed to the arbitral tribunal by a party shall be filed with the [name of the institution] for notification to the arbitral tribunal and the other party or parties. All communications addressed from the arbitral tribunal to a party shall be filed with the [name of the institution] for notification to the other party or parties.";[10] or

(ii) If the institution decides to receive copies of all communications for the purpose of information:

"Except as otherwise permitted by the arbitral tribunal, all communications between the arbitral tribunal and any party shall also be sent to [name of the institution]."

14 In the interest of procedural efficiency, it might be appropriate for an institution to consider whether to require receiving copies of communications only after the constitution of the arbitral tribunal. If such requirement is adopted by the institution, it would be advisable to refer to the receipt of the copies in a manner that is technology- neutral, in order not to exclude new and evolving technologies. To receive copies of communications through new technologies could also result in a desirable reduction of costs for the institution.

(d) Substitution of the reference to the "appointing authority" by the name of the institution

15 Where an institution uses the UNCITRAL Arbitration Rules as a model for its institutional rules, the institution typically carries out the functions attributed to the appointing authority under the Rules; it therefore should amend the corresponding provisions of the Rules as follows:

(a) Article 3, paragraph 4 (a); article 4, paragraph 2 (b); article 6, paragraphs 1-4; and the reference to the designating authority in article 6, paragraph 5, should be deleted;

(b) The term "appointing authority" could be replaced by the name of the institution in the following provisions: article 6, paragraphs 5-7; article 7, paragraph 2; article 8, paragraphs 1 and 2; article 9, paragraphs 2 and 3; article 10, paragraph 3; article 13, paragraph 4; article 14, paragraph 2; article 16; article 43, paragraph 3; and, if the arbitral institution adopts the review mechanism to the extent compatible with its own institutional rules, article 41, paragraphs 2-4. As an alternative, a rule clarifying that reference to the appointing authority shall be understood as a reference to the institution could be added, along the following lines: "The functions of the appointing authority under the UNCITRAL Arbitration Rules are fulfilled by [name of the institution]."

16. If the functions of an appointing authority are fulfilled by an organ of the institution, it is advisable to explain the composition of that organ and, if appropriate, the nomination process of its members, in an annex, for example. In the interest of certainty, it may be advisable for an institution to clarify whether the reference to the organ is meant to be to the function and not to the person as such (i.e. in case the person is not available, the function could be fulfilled by his or her deputy).

---

[10] For example, a similar provision is included in article 17, paragraph 5, of the Arbitration Rules of the Cairo Regional Centre for International Commercial Arbitration in force as from 1 March 2011.

(e) Fees and schedule of fees

17. Where an institution adopts the UNCITRAL Arbitration Rules as its own institutional rules:
    (a) The provisions of article 40, paragraph 2 (f), would not apply;[11]
    (b) The institution may include the fee review mechanism as set out in article 41 of the Rules (as adjusted to the needs of the institution).[12]

C. **Arbitral institutions and other interested bodies administering arbitration under the UNCITRAL Arbitration Rules or providing some administrative services**

18. One measure of the success of the UNCITRAL Arbitration Rules in achieving broad applicability and in demonstrating their ability to meet the needs of parties in a wide range of legal cultures and types of disputes has been the significant number of independent institutions that have declared themselves willing to administer (and that do administer) arbitrations under the UNCITRAL Arbitration Rules, in addition to proceedings under their own rules. Some arbitral institutions have adopted procedural rules for offering to administer arbitrations under the UNCITRAL Arbitration Rules.[13] Further, parties have also turned to institutions in order to receive some administrative services, in contrast to having the arbitral proceedings fully administered by the arbitral institution.[14]

19. The following remarks and suggestions are intended to assist any interested institutions in taking the necessary organizational measures and in devising appropriate administrative procedures in conformity with the UNCITRAL Arbitration Rules when they either fully administer a case under the Rules or only provide certain administrative services in relation to arbitration under the Rules. It may be noted that institutions, while offering services under the UNCITRAL

---

[11] An arbitral institution, may, however, retain article 40, paragraph 2 (f), for cases in which the arbitral institution would not act as appointing authority. For example, the Qatar International Center for Conciliation and Arbitration states in article 43, paragraph 2 (h), of its Rules of Arbitration 2012 (effective 1 May 2012), which are based on the UNCITRAL Arbitration Rules as revised in 2010: "Any fees and expenses of the appointing authority in case the Center is not designated as the appointing authority."

[12] Such an approach has been adopted by the Cyprus Arbitration and Mediation Centre, which based its Arbitration Rules on the UNCITRAL Arbitration Rules.

[13] For example, the Permanent Court of Arbitration (PCA) indicates on its website (<www.pca-cpa.org>) that "in addition to the role of designating appointing authorities, the Secretary-General of the PCA will act as the appointing authority under the UNCITRAL Arbitration Rules when the parties so agree. The PCA also frequently provides full administrative support in arbitrations under the UNCITRAL Arbitration Rules." The London Court of International Arbitration (LCIA) indicates on its website (<www.lcia.org>) that "the LCIA regularly acts both as appointing authority and as administrator in arbitrations conducted pursuant to the UNCITRAL arbitration rules. Further information: Recommended clauses for adoption by the parties for these purposes; the range of administrative services offered; and details of the LCIA charges for these services are available on request from the Secretariat". See also the UNCITRAL Arbitration Rules Administered by the German Institution of Arbitration (available from <www.dis-arb.de>); the Administrative and Procedural Rules for Arbitration under the UNCITRAL Arbitration Rules as amended and effective on 1 July 2009 of the Japan Commercial Arbitration Association (JCAA) (available from <www.jcaa.or.jp>); and the Hong Kong International Arbitration Centre (HKIAC) Procedures for the Administration of International Arbitration, adopted to take effect from 31 May 2005 (available from <www.hkiac.org>). (The Administrative and Procedural Rules for Arbitration under the UNCITRAL Arbitration Rules of JCAA and the HKIAC Procedures for the Administration of International Arbitration are both, at the date of the present recommendations, based on the 1976 UNCITRAL Arbitration Rules.)

[14] For example, the HKIAC Procedures for the Administration of International Arbitration state in their introduction: "Nothing in these Procedures shall prevent parties to a dispute under the UNCITRAL Rules from naming the HKIAC as appointing authority, nor from requesting certain administrative services from the HKIAC without subjecting the arbitration to the provisions contained in the Procedures. Neither the designation of the HKIAC as appointing authority under the Rules nor a request by the parties or the tribunal for specific and discrete administrative assistance from the HKIAC shall be construed as a designation of the HKIAC as administrator of the arbitration as described in these Procedures. Conversely, unless otherwise stated, a request for administration by the HKIAC will be construed as a designation of the HKIAC as appointing authority and administrator pursuant to these Procedures."

Arbitration Rules as revised in 2010, are continuing to also offer services under the 1976 UNCITRAL Arbitration Rules.[15]

1. *Administrative procedures in conformity with the UNCITRAL Arbitration Rules*

20. In devising administrative procedures or rules, the institutions should have due regard to the interests of the parties. Since the parties in these cases have agreed that the arbitration is to be conducted under the UNCITRAL Arbitration Rules, their expectations should not be frustrated by administrative rules that would conflict with the UNCITRAL Arbitration Rules. The modifications that the UNCITRAL Arbitration Rules would need to undergo to be administered by an institution are minimal and similar to those mentioned above in paragraphs 9–17. It is advisable that the institution clarify the administrative services it would render by either:
    (a) Listing them; or
    (b) Proposing to the parties a text of the UNCITRAL Arbitration Rules highlighting the modifications made to the Rules for the sole purpose of the administration of the arbitral proceedings; in the latter case, it is recommended to indicate that the UNCITRAL Arbitration Rules are "as administered by [name of the institution]" so that the user is notified that there is a difference from the original UNCITRAL Arbitration Rules.[16]

21 It is further recommended that:
    (a) The administrative procedures of the institution distinguish clearly between the functions of an appointing authority as envisaged under the UNCITRAL Arbitration Rules (see section D below) and other full or partial administrative assistance, and the institution should declare whether it is offering both or only one of these types of services;
    (b) An institution which is prepared either to fully administer a case under the UNCITRAL Arbitration Rules or to provide certain administrative services of a technical and secretarial nature describe in its administrative procedures the services offered; such services may be rendered upon request of the parties or the arbitral tribunal.

22 In describing the administrative services, it is recommended that the institution indicate:
    (a) Which services would be covered by its general administrative fee and which would not (i.e. which would be billed separately);[17]
    (b) The services provided within its own facilities and those arranged to be rendered by others;
    (c) That parties could also choose to have only a particular service (or services) rendered by the institution without having the arbitral proceedings fully administered by the institution (see para. 18 above and paras. 23-25 below).

2. *Offer of administrative services*

23. The following list of possible administrative services, which is not intended to be exhaustive, may assist institutions in considering and publicizing the services they may offer:
    (a) Maintenance of a file of written communications;[18]
    (b) Facilitating communication;[19]

---

[15] For an illustration, see the services offered under both versions of the UNCITRAL Arbitration Rules by the Arbitration Institute of the Stockholm Chamber of Commerce (<www.sccinstitute.com>).

[16] See, as an illustration of such an approach, the UNCITRAL Arbitration Rules Administered by the German Institution of Arbitration.

[17] For example, in the Bahrain Chamber for Dispute Resolution (BCDR) Arbitration Rules, it is stated: "The fees described above do not cover the cost of hearing rooms, which are available on a rental basis. Check with the BCDR for availability and rates." The BCDR Arbitration Rules are from 2009 and based on the 1976 UNCITRAL Arbitration Rules.

[18] The maintenance of a file of written communications could include a full file of written correspondence and submissions to facilitate any inquiry that arises and to prepare such copies as the parties or the tribunal may require at any time during the arbitral proceedings. In addition, the maintenance of such a file could include, automatically or only upon request by the parties, the forwarding of the written communications of a party or the arbitrators.

[19] Facilitating communication could include ensuring that communications among parties, attorneys and the tribunal are kept open and up to date, and may also consist in merely forwarding written communications.

(c) Providing necessary practical arrangements for meetings and hearings, including:
    (i) Assisting the arbitral tribunal in establishing the date, time and place of hearings;
    (ii) Meeting rooms for hearings or deliberations of the arbitral tribunal;
    (iii) Telephone conference and videoconference facilities;
    (iv) Stenographic transcripts of hearings;
    (v) Live streaming of hearings;
    (vi) Secretarial or clerical assistance;
    (vii) Making available or arranging for interpretation services;
    (viii) Facilitating entry visas for the purposes of hearings when required;
    (ix) Arranging accommodation for parties and arbitrators;
(d) Providing fund-holding services;[20]
(e) Ensuring that procedurally important dates are followed and advising the arbitral tribunal and the parties when not adhered to;
(f) Providing procedural directions on behalf of the tribunal, if and when required;[21]
(g) Providing secretarial or clerical assistance in other respects;[22]
(h) Providing assistance for obtaining certified copies of any award, including notarized copies, where required;
(i) Providing assistance for the translation of arbitral awards;
(j) Providing services with respect to the storage of arbitral awards and files relating to the arbitral proceedings.[23]

3. Administrative fee schedule

24 The institution, when indicating the fee it charges for its services, may reproduce its administrative fee schedule or, in the absence thereof, indicate the basis for calculating it.[24]

25 In view of the possible categories of services an institution may offer, such as functioning as an appointing authority and/or providing administrative services (see para. 21 above), it is recommended that the fee for each category be stated separately (see para. 22 above). Thus, an institution may indicate its fees for:
(a) Acting as an appointing authority only;
(b) Providing administrative services without acting as an appointing authority;
(c) Acting as an appointing authority and providing administrative services.

---

[20] Fund-holding services usually consist of the receipt and the disbursement of funds received from the parties. They include the setting up of a dedicated bank account, into which sums are paid by the parties, as directed by the tribunal. The institution typically disburses funds from that account to cover costs, accounting periodically to the parties and to the tribunal for funds lodged and disbursed. The institution usually credits the interests on the funds to the party that has lodged the funds at the prevailing rate of the bank where the account is kept. Fund-holding services could also include more broadly the calculation and collection of a deposit as security for the estimated costs of arbitration. If the institution is fully administering the arbitral proceedings, then the fund-holding services may extend to more closely monitoring the costs of the arbitration, in particular ensuring that fees-and-costs notes are regularly submitted and the level of further advances calculated, in consultation with the tribunal, and by reference to the established procedural timetable.

[21] Providing procedural directions on behalf of the tribunal, if and when required, relates most typically to directions for advances on costs.

[22] The provision of secretarial or clerical assistance could include proofreading draft awards to correct typographical and clerical errors.

[23] Storage of documents relating to the arbitral proceedings might be an obligation under the applicable law.

[24] See, for example, article 42, paragraph 4, on definition of costs, of the Arbitration Rules of the Cairo Regional Centre for International Commercial Arbitration, which entered into force on 1 March 2011, according to which the provisions of its section on the costs of arbitration shall apply by default in case the parties to ad hoc arbitrations agree that the Centre will provide its administrative services to such arbitrations.

4. Draft model clauses

26. In the interest of procedural efficiency, institutions may wish to set forth in their administrative procedures model arbitration clauses covering the above services. It is recommended that:

    (a) Where the institution fully administers arbitration under the UNCITRAL Arbitration Rules, the model clause should read as follows:

    "Any dispute, controversy or claim arising out of or relating to this contract, or the breach, termination or invalidity thereof, shall be settled by arbitration in accordance with the UNCITRAL Arbitration Rules administered by [name of the institution]. [Name of the institution] shall act as appointing authority."

    (b) Where the institution provides certain services only, the agreement as to the services that are requested should be indicated:

    "Any dispute, controversy or claim arising out of or relating to this contract, or the breach, termination or invalidity thereof, shall be settled by arbitration in accordance with the UNCITRAL Arbitration Rules. [Name of the institution] shall act as appointing authority and provide administrative services in accordance with its administrative procedures for cases under the UNCITRAL Arbitration Rules."

    (c) In both cases, as suggested in the model arbitration clause in the annex to the UNCITRAL Arbitration Rules, parties should consider adding the following note:

    (a) "The number of arbitrators shall be [one or three];
    (b) "The place of arbitration shall be [city and country];
    (c) "The language to be used in the arbitral proceedings shall be [language]".

D. Arbitral institution acting as appointing authority

27. An institution (or a person) may act as appointing authority under the UNCITRAL Arbitration Rules. It is noteworthy that article 6 of the Rules highlights the importance of the role of the appointing authority. Parties are invited to agree on an appointing authority at the time that they conclude the arbitration agreement, if possible. Alternatively, the appointing authority could be appointed by the parties at any time during the arbitration proceedings.

28. Arbitral institutions are usually experienced with fulfilling functions similar to those required from an appointing authority under the Rules. For an individual who takes on that responsibility for the first time, it is important to note that, once designated as appointed authority, he or she must be and must remain independent and be prepared to act promptly for all purposes under the Rules.

29. An institution that is willing to act as appointing authority under the UNCITRAL Arbitration Rules may indicate in its administrative procedures the various functions of an appointing authority envisaged by the Rules. It may also describe the manner in which it intends to perform these functions.

30. The UNCITRAL Arbitration Rules foresee six main functions for the appointing authority: (a) appointment of arbitrators; (b) decisions on the challenge of arbitrators; (c) replacement of arbitrators; (d) assistance in fixing the fees of arbitrators; (e) participation in the review mechanism on the costs and fees; and (f) advisory comments regarding deposits. The paragraphs that follow are intended to provide some guidance on the role of the appointing authority under the UNCITRAL Arbitration Rules based on the *travaux preparatoires*.

1. Designating and appointing authorities (article 6)

31. Article 6 was included as a new provision in the UNCITRAL Arbitration Rules as revised in 2010 to clarify for the users of the Rules the importance of the role of the appointing authority, particularly in the context of non-administered arbitration.[25]

---

[25] *Official Records of the General Assembly, Sixty-fifth Session, Supplement No 17* (A/65/17), para. 42, and A/CN.9/619, para. 69.

(a) Procedure for choosing or designating an appointing authority (article 6, paragraphs 1-3)

32. Article 6, paragraphs 1-3, determines the procedure to be followed by the parties in order to choose an appointing authority, or to have one designated in case of disagreement. Paragraph 1 expresses the principle that the appointing authority can be appointed by the parties at any time during the arbitration proceedings, not only in some limited circumstances.[26]

(b) Failure to act: substitute appointing authority (article 6, paragraph 4)

33. Article 6, paragraph 4, addresses the situation where an appointing authority refuses or fails to act within a time period provided by the Rules or fails to decide on a challenge to an arbitrator within a reasonable time after receiving a party's request to do so. Then, any party may request the Secretary-General of the Permanent Court of Arbitration to designate a substitute appointing authority. The failure to act of the appointing authority in the context of the fee review mechanism under article 41, paragraph 4, of the Rules, does not fall under article 6, paragraph 4 ("except as referred to in article 41, paragraph 4") but is dealt with directly in article 41, paragraph 4 (see para. 58 below).[27]

(c) Discretion in the exercise of its functions (article 6, paragraph 5)

34. Article 6, paragraph 5, provides that, in exercising its functions under the Rules, the appointing authority may require from any party and the arbitrators the information it deems necessary. That provision was included in the UNCITRAL Arbitration Rules to explicitly provide the appointing authority with the power to require information not only from the parties, but also from the arbitrators. The arbitrators are explicitly mentioned in the provision, as there are instances, such as a challenge procedure, in which the appointing authority, in exercising its functions, may require information from the arbitrators.[28]

35. In addition, article 6, paragraph 5, provides that the appointing authority shall give the parties and, where appropriate, the arbitrators, an opportunity to present their views in any manner the appointing authority considers appropriate. During the deliberations on the revisions to the Rules, it was agreed that the general principle should be included that the parties should be given an opportunity to be heard by the appointing authority.[29] That opportunity should be given "in any manner" the appointing authority "considers appropriate", in order to better reflect the discretion of the appointing authority in obtaining views from the parties.[30]

36. Article 6, paragraph 5, determines that all such communications to and from the appointing authority shall be provided by the sender to all other parties. That provision is consistent with article 17, paragraph 4, of the Rules.

(d) General provision on appointment of arbitrators (article 6, paragraphs 6 and 7)

37. Article 6, paragraph 6, provides that, when the appointing authority is requested to appoint an arbitrator pursuant to articles 8, 9, 10 or 14, the party making the request shall send to the appointing authority copies of the notice of arbitration and, if it exists, any response to the notice of arbitration.

38. Article 6, paragraph 7, provides that the appointing authority shall have regard to such considerations as are likely to secure the appointment of an independent and impartial arbitrator. To that end, paragraph 7 states that the appointing authority shall take into account the advisability of appointing an arbitrator of a nationality other than the nationalities of the parties (see also para. 44 below).

---

[26] A/CN.9/619, para. 69.
[27] *Official Records of the General Assembly, Sixty-fifth Session, Supplement No 17* (A/65/17), para. 49.
[28] A/CN.9/WG.II/WP.157, para. 22.
[29] A/CN.9/619, para. 76.
[30] A/CN.9/665, para. 54.

2. Appointment of arbitrators

(a) Appointment of a sole arbitrator (article 7, paragraph 2, and article 8)

39. The UNCITRAL Arbitration Rules envisage various possibilities concerning the appointment of an arbitrator by an appointing authority. Under article 8, paragraph 1, the appointing authority may be requested to appoint a sole arbitrator, in accordance with the procedures and criteria set forth in article 8, paragraph 2. The appointing authority shall appoint the sole arbitrator as promptly as possible and shall intervene only at the request of a party. The appointing authority may use the list-procedure as defined in article 8, paragraph 2. It should be noted that the appointing authority has discretion pursuant to article 8, paragraph 2, to determine that the use of the list-procedure is not appropriate for the case.

40. Article 7, dealing with the number of arbitrators, provides as a default rule that, in case parties do not agree on the number of arbitrators, three arbitrators should be appointed. However, article 7, paragraph 2, includes a corrective mechanism so that, if no other parties have responded to a party's proposal to appoint a sole arbitrator and the party (or parties) concerned have failed to appoint a second arbitrator, the appointing authority may, at the request of a party, appoint a sole arbitrator if it determines that, in view of the circumstances of the case, this is more appropriate. That provision has been included in the Rules to avoid situations where, despite the claimant's proposal in its notice of arbitration to appoint a sole arbitrator, a three-member arbitral tribunal has to be constituted owing to the respondent's failure to react to that proposal. It provides a useful corrective mechanism in case the respondent does not participate in the process and the arbitration case does not warrant the appointment of a three-member arbitral tribunal. That mechanism is not supposed to create delays, as the appointing authority will in any event have to intervene in the appointment process. The appointing authority should have all relevant information or require information under article 6, paragraph 5, to make its decision on the number of arbitrators.[31] Such information would include, in accordance with article 6, paragraph 6, copies of the notice of arbitration and any response thereto.

41. When an appointing authority is requested under article 7, paragraph 2, to determine whether a sole arbitrator is more appropriate for the case, circumstances to be taken into consideration include the amount in dispute and the complexity of the case (including the number of parties involved),[32] as well as the nature of the transaction and of the dispute.

42. In some cases, the respondent might not take part in the constitution of the arbitral tribunal, so that the appointing authority has before it the information received from the claimant only. Then, the appointing authority can make its assessment only on the basis of that information, being aware that it might not reflect all aspects of the proceedings to come.

(b) Appointment of a three member arbitral tribunal (article 9)

43. The appointing authority may be requested by a party, under article 9, paragraph 2, to appoint the second of three arbitrators in case a three-arbitrator panel is to be appointed. If the two arbitrators cannot agree on the choice of the third (presiding) arbitrator, the appointing authority can be called upon to appoint the third arbitrator under article 9, paragraph 3. That appointment would take place in the same manner that a sole arbitrator would be appointed under article 8. In accordance with article 8, paragraph 1, the appointing authority should act only at the request of a party.[33]

44. When an appointing authority is asked to appoint the presiding arbitrator pursuant to article 9, paragraph 3, factors that might be taken into consideration include the experience of the arbitrator and the advisability of appointing an arbitrator of a nationality other than the nationalities of the parties (see para. 38 above, on article 6, paragraph 7).

---

[31] Ibid., paras. 62-63.

[32] For example, if one party is a State, whether there are (or will potentially be) counterclaims or set-off claims.

[33] *Official Records of the General Assembly, Sixty-fifth Session, Supplement No 17* (A/65/17), para. 59.

(c) Multiple claimants or respondents (article 10)

45. Article 10, paragraph 1, provides that, in case of multiple claimants or respondents and unless otherwise agreed, the multiple claimants, jointly, and the multiple respondents, jointly, shall appoint an arbitrator. In the absence of such a joint nomination and if all parties are unable to otherwise agree on a method for the constitution of the arbitral tribunal, the appointing authority shall, upon the request of any party pursuant to article 10, paragraph 3, constitute the arbitral tribunal and designate one of the arbitrators to act as the presiding arbitrator.[34] An illustration of a case in which parties on either side could be unable to make such an appointment is if the number of either claimants or respondents is very large or if they not form a single group with common rights and obligations (for instance, cases involving a large number of shareholders).[35]

46. The power of the appointing authority to constitute the arbitral tribunal is broadly formulated in article 10, paragraph 3, in order to cover all possible failures to constitute the arbitral tribunal under the Rules and is not limited to multiparty cases. Also, it is noteworthy that the appointing authority has the discretion to revoke any appointment already made and to appoint or reappoint each of the arbitrators.[36] The principle in paragraph 3 that the appointing authority shall appoint the entire arbitral tribunal when parties on the same side in a multiparty arbitration are unable to jointly agree on an arbitrator was included in the Rules as an important principle, in particular in situations like the one that gave rise to the case *BKMI and Siemens v. Dutco*.[37] The decision in the *Dutco* case was based on the requirement that parties receive equal treatment, which paragraph 3 addresses by shifting the appointment power to the appointing authority.[38] The *travaux preparatoires* of the UNCITRAL Arbitration Rules show that emphasis was given to maintaining a flexible approach, granting discretionary powers to the appointing authority, in article 10, paragraph 3, in order to accommodate the wide variety of situations arising in practice.[39]

(d) Successful challenge and other reasons for replacement of an arbitrator (articles 12 and 13)

47. The appointing authority may be called upon to appoint a substitute arbitrator under article 12, paragraph 3, or article 13 or 14 of the UNCITRAL Arbitration Rules (failure or impossibility to act, successful challenge and other reasons for replacement; see paras. 4954 below).

(e) Note for institutions acting as an appointing authority

48. For each of these instances where an institution may be called upon under the UNCITRAL Arbitration Rules to appoint an arbitrator, the institution may provide details as to how it would select the arbitrator. In particular, it may state whether it maintains a list of arbitrators, from which it would select appropriate candidates, and may provide information on the composition of any such list. It may also indicate which person or organ within the institution would make the appointment (for example, the president, a board of directors, the secretary-general or a committee) and, in the case of a board or committee, how that organ is composed and/or its members would be elected.

3. Decision on challenge of arbitrator

(a) Articles 12 and 13

49. Under article 12 of the UNCITRAL Arbitration Rules, an arbitrator may be challenged if circumstances exist that give rise to justifiable doubts as to his or her impartiality or

---

[34] A/CN.9/614, paras. 62-63, and A/CN.9/619, para. 86.
[35] A/CN.9/614, para. 63.
[36] A/CN.9/619, paras. 88 and 90.
[37] *BKMI and Siemens v. Dutco*, French Court of Cassation, 7 January 1992 (see *Revue de l'Arbitrage*, No 3 (1992), pp. 470-472).
[38] *Official Records of the General Assembly, Sixty-fifth Session, Supplement No 17* (A/65/17), para. 60.
[39] A/CN.9/619, para. 90.

independence. When such a challenge is contested (i.e. if the other party does not agree to the challenge or the challenged arbitrator does not withdraw within 15 days of the notice of the challenge), the party making the challenge may seek a decision on the challenge by the appointing authority pursuant to article 13, paragraph 4. If the appointing authority sustains the challenge, it may also be called upon to appoint the substitute arbitrator.

(b) Note for institution acting as an appointing authority

50. The institution may indicate details as to how it would make the decision on such a challenge in accordance with the UNCITRAL Arbitration Rules. In that regard, the institution may wish to identify any code of ethics of its institution or other written principles which it would apply in ascertaining the independence and impartiality of arbitrators.

4. Replacement of an arbitrator (article 14)

51. Under article 14, paragraph 1, of the UNCITRAL Arbitration Rules, in the event that an arbitrator has to be replaced in the course of the arbitral proceedings, a substitute arbitrator shall normally be appointed or chosen pursuant to the procedure provided for in articles 8-11 of the Rules that was applicable to the appointment or choice of the arbitrator being replaced. That procedure shall apply even if, during the process of appointing the arbitrator to be replaced, a party failed to exercise its right to appoint or to participate in the appointment.

52. This procedure is subject to an exception pursuant to article 14, paragraph 2, of the Rules, which provides the appointing authority with the power to determine, at the request of a party, whether it would be justified for a party to be deprived of its right to appoint a substitute arbitrator. If the appointing authority makes such a determination, it may, after giving an opportunity to the parties and the remaining arbitrators to express their views: (a) appoint the substitute arbitrator; or (b) after the closure of the hearings, authorize the other arbitrators to proceed with the arbitration and make any decision or award.

53. It is noteworthy that the appointing authority should deprive a party of its right to appoint a substitute arbitrator only in exceptional circumstances. To that end, the wording "the exceptional circumstances of the case" in article 14, paragraph 2, was chosen to allow the appointing authority to take account of all circumstances or incidents that might have occurred during the proceedings. The *travaux préparatoires* of the UNCITRAL Arbitration Rules show that depriving a party of its right to appoint an arbitrator is a serious decision, one which should be taken based on the faulty behaviour of a party to the arbitration and on the basis of a fact-specific inquiry and which should not be subject to defined criteria. Rather, the appointing authority should determine, in its discretion, whether the party has the right to appoint another arbitrator.[40]

54. In determining whether to permit a truncated tribunal to proceed with the arbitration under article 14, paragraph 2 (b), the appointing authority must take into consideration the stage of the proceedings. Bearing in mind that the hearings are already closed, it might be more appropriate, for the sake of efficiency, to allow a truncated tribunal to make any decision or final award than to proceed with the appointment of a substitute arbitrator. Other factors that might be taken into consideration, to the extent feasible, in deciding whether to allow a truncated tribunal to proceed include the relevant laws (i.e. whether the laws would permit or restrict such a procedure) and relevant case law on truncated tribunals.

5. Assistance in fixing fees of arbitrators

(a) Articles 40 and 41

55. Pursuant to article 40, paragraphs 1 and 2, of the UNCITRAL Arbitration Rules, the arbitral tribunal fixes the costs of arbitration. Pursuant to article 41, paragraph 1, the fees and expenses of the arbitrators shall be reasonable in amount, taking into account the amount in dispute, the

---

[40] A/CN.9/688, para. 78, and A/CN.9/614, para. 71.

complexity of the subject matter, the time spent by the arbitrators and any other relevant circumstances of the case. In this task, the arbitral tribunal may be assisted by an appointing authority: if the appointing authority applies or has stated that it will apply a schedule or particular method for determining the fees of arbitrators in international cases, the arbitral tribunal, in fixing its fees, shall take that schedule or method into account to the extent that it considers appropriate in the circumstances of the case (article 41, paragraph 2).

(b) Note for institutions acting as an appointing authority

56. An institution willing to act as appointing authority may indicate, in its administrative procedures, any relevant details in respect of assistance in fixing the fees. In particular, it may state whether it has issued a schedule or defined a particular method for determining the fees for arbitrators in international cases as envisaged in article 41, paragraph 2 (see para. 17 above).

6. Review mechanism (article 41)

57. Article 41 of the UNCITRAL Arbitration Rules addresses the fees and expenses of arbitrators and foresees a review mechanism for such fees that involves a neutral body, the appointing authority. Notwithstanding that an institution may have its own rules on fees, it is recommended that the institution acting as appointing authority should follow the rules set out in article 41.

58. The review mechanism consists of two stages. At the first stage, article 41, paragraph 3, requires the arbitral tribunal to inform the parties promptly after its constitution of how it proposes to determine its fees and expenses. Any party then has 15 days to request the appointing authority to review that proposal. If the appointing authority considers the proposal of the arbitral tribunal to be inconsistent with the requirement of reasonableness in article 41, paragraph 1, it shall within 45 days make any necessary adjustments, which are binding upon the arbitral tribunal. At the second stage, article 41, paragraph 4, provides that, after being informed of the determination of the arbitrators' fees and expenses, any party has the right to request the appointing authority to review that determination. If no appointing authority has been agreed upon or designated, or if the appointing authority fails to act within the time specified in the Rules, the review shall be made by the Secretary-General of the Permanent Court of Arbitration. Within 45 days of the receipt of such referral, the reviewing authority shall make any adjustments to the arbitral tribunal's determination that are necessary to meet the criteria in article 41, paragraph 1, if the tribunal's determination is inconsistent with its proposal (and any adjustment thereto) under paragraph 3 of that article or is otherwise manifestly excessive.

59. The *travaux préparatoires* of the UNCITRAL Arbitration Rules show that the process for establishing the arbitrators' fees was regarded as crucial for the legitimacy and integrity of the arbitral process itself.[41]

60. The criteria and mechanism set out in article 41, paragraphs 1-4, was chosen to provide sufficient guidance to an appointing authority and to avoid time-consuming scrutiny of fee determinations.[42] Article 41, paragraph 4 (c), by cross-referring to paragraph 1 of that article, refers to the notion of reasonableness of the amount of arbitrators' fees, an element to be taken into account by the appointing authority if the adjustment of fees and expenses is necessary. In order to clarify that the review process should not be too intrusive, the words "manifestly excessive" were included in article 41, paragraph 4 (c).[43]

7. Advisory comments regarding deposits

61. Under article 43, paragraph 3, of the UNCITRAL Arbitration Rules, the arbitral tribunal shall fix the amounts of any initial or supplementary deposits only after consultation with

---

[41] A/CN.9/646, para. 20.
[42] A/CN.9/688, para. 23.
[43] *Official Records of the General Assembly, Sixty-fifth Session, Supplement No 17* (A/65/17), para. 172.

the appointing authority, which may make any comments to the arbitral tribunal it deems appropriate concerning the amount of such deposits and supplementary deposits, if a party so requests and the appointing authority consents to perform this function. The institution may wish to indicate in its administrative procedures its willingness to do so. Supplementary deposits may be required if, in the course of proceedings, it appears that the costs will be higher than anticipated, for instance if the arbitral tribunal decides pursuant to the Rules to appoint an expert. Although not explicitly mentioned in the Rules, appointing authorities have in practice also commented and advised on interim payments.

62. It should be noted that, under the Rules, this kind of advice is the only task relating to deposits that an appointing authority may be requested to fulfil. Thus, if an institution offers to perform any other functions (such as holding deposits or rendering an accounting thereof), it should be pointed out that this would constitute additional administrative services not included in the functions of an appointing authority (see para. 30 above).

Note: In addition to the information and suggestions set forth herein, assistance may be obtained from the secretariat of UNCITRAL:

International Trade Law Division
Office of Legal Affairs
United Nations
Vienna International Centre
P.O. Box 500
1400 Vienna
Austria
E-mail: uncitral@uncitral.org

The secretariat could, for example, if so requested, assist in the drafting of institutional rules or administrative provisions, or it could make suggestions in this regard.

Select Bibliography

Reports

Iran–United States Claims Tribunal Reports (Grotius Publications).
Iranian Assets Litigation Reporter. Published twice monthly by Andrews Publications, PO Box 200, Edgemont, Pennsylvania 19028, (215) 353–3565. The first issue was released February 8, 1980.
Law Review of the Bureau for International Legal Services of the Islamic Republic of Iran.
Mealy Litigation Reports: Iranian Claims. Published twice monthly by Mealy Publications, PO Box 446, Wayne, Pennsylvania 19087, (215) 688–6566. The first issue was released February 3, 1984.
Paulsson, Jan and Petrochilos, Georgios, "Revision of the UNCITRAL Arbitration Rules," Report to UNCITRAL Secretariat, (2006).
Selected decisions of the Iran–US Claims Tribunal are also published in: Arbitration Materials (Werner Publishing Company, Geneva, beginning with Volume 1 (1989); International Legal Materials [ILM] (Oceana Publications, Inc.); Yearbook Commercial Arbitration [YCA] (Kluwer, The Netherlands, beginning with Volume VII (1982)).
The workings of UNCITRAL are covered in: United Nations Commission on International Trade Law: Yearbook (in the text referred to as UNCITRAL Yearbook), beginning with Volume 1 (1968–1970).

Books

Aden, Menno, *Internationale Handelsschiedsgerichtsbarkeit* (1988).
Aldrich, George, *The Jurisprudence of the Iran-United States Claims Tribunal* (1996).
Arfazadeh, Homayoon, *Ordre public et arbitrage international à l'épreuve de la mondialisation* (2005).
Avanessian, Aida, *Iran-United States Claims Tribunal in Action* (1993).
Baker, Stewart A and Davis, Mark D, *The UNCITRAL Arbitration Rules in Practice: The Experience of the Iran-United States Claims Tribunal* (1992).
Berger, Klaus Peter, *International Economic Arbitration* (1993).
Binder, Peter, *International Commercial Arbitration and Conciliation in UNCITRAL Model Law Jurisdictions* (3rd edn 2010).
Bishop, Doak and Kehoe, Edward G (eds), *The Art of Advocacy in International Arbitration* (2010).
Blackaby, Nigel and Partasides, Constantine with Redfern, Alan and Hunter, Martin, *Redfern and Hunter on International Arbitration*, (5th edn 2009).
Born, Gary B, *International Commercial Arbitration* (2009).
Brower, Charles and Brueschke, J, *The Iran-United States Claims Tribunal* (1998).
Carbonneau, Thomas E, *Lex Mercatoria and Arbitration* (1990).
Carlston, Kenneth, *The Process of International Arbitration* (1946).
Cheng, Bin, *General Principles of Law as Applied by International Courts and Tribunals* (1987).
Craig, W Laurence, Park, William and Paulsson, Jan, *International Chamber of Commerce Arbitration* (3rd edn 2000).
Dasser, Feloc, *Internationale Schiedsgerichte und Lex Mercatoria* (1989).
David, Rene, *Arbitration in International Trade* (1985).
Delaume, Georges, *Law and Practice of Transnational Contracts* (1988).
Derains, Yves and Schwartz, Eric A, *A Guide to the New ICC Rules of Arbitration* (2nd edn 2005).
Dore, Isaak, *Arbitration and Conciliation under the UNCITRAL Rules: A Textual Analysis* (1986).
El-Ahdab, Abdul Hamid, *Arbitration with the Arab Countries* (1990).
Elkind, Jerome, *Interim Protection: A Functional Approach* (1981).
Fitzmaurice, Gerald, *The Law and Procedure of the International Court of Justice* (1986).

Fouchard, Philippe, *L'Arbitrage Commercial International* (1996).
Gaillard, E and Savage, J (eds), *Fouchard, Gaillard, Goldman on International Commercial Arbitration* (1999).
Gentinetta, Jorg, *Die Lex Fori Internationaler Handelsschiedsgerichte* (1973).
Goldberg, John C P and Zipursky, Benjamin C, *The Oxford Introductions to U.S Law Torts* (2010).
Holtzmann, Howard M and Neuhaus, Joseph E, *A Guide to the UNCITRAL Model Law on International Commercial Arbitration: Legislative History and Commentary* (1989).
Kaufman-Kohler, Gabrielle and Stucki, Blaise, *Arbitration in Switzerland—A Handbook for Practitioners* (2004).
Kazazi, Mojtaba, *Burden of Proof and Related Issues* (1996).
Khan, Rahmatullah, *The Iran-United States Claims Tribunal: Controversies, Cases and Contribution* (1990).
Kurkela, Matti and Uoti, Petteri, *Arbitration in Finland* (1994).
Lew, Julian, *Applicable Law in International Commercial Arbitration* (1978).
Madsen, Finn, *Commercial Arbitration in Sweden: A Commentary on the Arbitration Act (1999: 16) and the Rules of the Arbitration Institute of the Stockholm Chamber of Commerce* (2004).
Manciaux, Sebastien, *Investissements étrangers et arbitrage entre États et ressortissants d'autres États: Trente années d'activité du CIRDI* (2004).
Mani, VS, *International Adjudication: Procedural Aspects* (1980).
Mapp, Wayne, *The Iran-United States Claims Tribunal: The First Ten Years, 1981–1991* (1993).
Mohebi, Mohsen, *The International Law Character of the Iran-United States Claims Tribunal* (1999).
Moses, Margaret, *The Principles and Practice of International Commercial Arbitration* (2008).
Mouri, Allahyar, *The International Law of Expropriation as Reflected in the Work of the Iran-US Claims Tribunal* (1994).
Nappert, Sophie, *Commentary on the UNCITRAL Arbitration Rules 2010: A Practitioner's Guide* (2010).
Newman, Lawrence W, and Hill, Richard D, *The Leading Arbitrators' Guide to International Arbitration* (2008).
Oellers-Frahm, Karin, *Die einstweilige Anordnung in der internationalen Gerichtsbarkeit* (1975).
Paasivirta, Esa, *Participation of States in International Contracts and Arbitral Settlement of Disputes* (1990).
Peter, Wolfgang, *Arbitration and Renegotiation of International Investment Agreements* (1988).
Rauh, Karlheinz, *Die Schieds- und Schlichtungsordnungen der UNCITRAL* (1983).
Raymond, Gregory, *Conflict Resolution and the Structure of the State System—An Analysis of Arbitrative Settlements* (1980).
Redfern, Alan and Hunter, Martin, *Law and Practice of International Commercial Arbitration* (2nd edn 1991).
Redfern, Alan and Hunter, Martin, *Law and Practice of International Commercial Arbitration* (3rd edn 1999).
Redfern, Alan and Hunter, Martin, with Blackaby, Nigel and Partasides, Constantine, *Law and Practice of International Commercial Arbitration* (4th edn 2004).
Regli, Jean-Pierre, *Contrats d'Etat et arbitrage entre Etats et personnes privées* (1983).
Rivkin, David and Platto, Charles (eds), *Litigation and Arbitration in Central and Eastern Europe* (1998).
Rubino-Sammartano, Mauro, *International Arbitration Law and Practice* (2001).
Saleh, Sarim, *Commercial Arbitration in the Arab Middle East: Shari'a, Syria, Lebanon and Egypt* (2nd edn 2005).
Sanders, Pieter, *Commentary on* UNCITRAL *Arbitration Rules*, II Yearbook Commercial Arbitration 172 (1977).
Sanders, Pieter, *The Work of* UNCITRAL *on Arbitration and Conciliation* (2nd edn 2004).
Sandifer, Kenneth, *Evidence Before International Tribunals* (rev edn 1975).
Savola, Mika (ed), *Law and Practice of Arbitration in Finland* (2004).

Schreuer, Christoph, *The ICSID Convention: A Commentary* (2nd edn 2009).
Schutze, Rolf, Tscherning, D and Wais, W, *Handbuch des Schiedsverfahrens* (1985).
Schwebel, Stephen, *International Arbitration: Three Saliant Problems* (1987).
Seidl-Hohenveldern, Ignaz, *Corporations in and under International Law* (1987).
Shihata, I, *The Power of the International Court to Determine Its Own Jurisdiction: competence de la competence (1965).*
Simpson, J L and Fox, H, *International Arbitration:Law and Practice* (1959).
St. John Sutton, David and Gill, Judith, *Russell on Abitration* (22nd edn 2003).
Stockholm Chamber of Commerce, *Arbitration in Sweden* (2nd rev edn 1984).
Sztucki, Jerzy, *Interim Measures in the Hague Court* (1983).
Toope, Stephen I, *Mixed International Arbitration: Studies in Arbitration between States and Private Persons* (1990).
Van den Berg, Albert Jan, *The New York Arbitration Convention of 1958: Towards a Uniform Judicial Interpretation* (1981).
Van Hof, Jacomijn J, *Commentary on the UNCITRAL Arbitration Rules: The Application by the Iran-U.S. Claims Tribunal* (1991).
Várady, Tibor, *Language and Translation in International Commercial Arbitration: From the Constitution of the Arbitral Tribunal through Recognition and Enforcement Proceedings* (2006).
Webster, Thomas, *Handbook of UNCITRAL Arbitration: Commentary, Precedents and Materials for UNCITRAL Based Arbitration Rules* (2010).
Westberg, John A, *International Transactions and Claims Involving Government Parties: Case Law of the Iran-United States Claims Tribunal* (1991).

Monographs/Theses

Caron, David D, "The Iran-United States Claims Tribunal and the International Arbitral Process," (Dr Jur Dissertation, University of Leiden, 1990).
Maiwald, Beate, "Das Iran-United States Claim Tribunal: Seine Rechtsgrundlagen und seine völkerrechtliche, prozessrechtliche und wirtschaftsrechtliche Rechtsprechungspraxis," (Inaugural—Dissertation der Rechtswissenschaftlichen Fakultät der Universität zu Köln, 1987).

Articles

A. Collections of Articles

Caron, David D and Crook, John (eds), *The Iran-United States Claims Tribunal and the Process of International Claims Resolution* (2000).
Lillich, Richard B (ed), *The Iran-United States Claims Tribunal 1981–1983* (1984).
Lillich, Richard B, Magraw, Daniel and Bederman, David (eds), *The Iran-United States Claims Tribunal: Its Contribution to the Law of State Responsibility* (1998).

B. Symposia/Proceedings

Symposium, "Iran-United States Claims Tribunal," (1984) 16 Law & Policy International Business 667–962.

C. Journal Articles and Chapters in Books

Aksen, Gerald, "The Iran-United States Claims Tribunal and the UNCITRAL Arbitration Rules, an Early Comment," in J C Schultsz and A J van den Berg (eds), *The Art of Arbitration I* (1982).
Amin, Sayid Hassan, "Iran-United States Claims Settlement," (1983) 32 International & Comparative Law Quarterly 750.
Ashman, Vivienne M, "The UNCITRAL Arbitration Rules and A Review of Certain Practices and Procedures," (2001) 1 International Business Litigation & Arbitration 765.
Audit, Bernard, "Les 'Accords' d'Alger du 19 janvier 1981 tendant au règlement des différends entre les Etats-Units et l'Iran," (1981) 108 Journal du Droit International 713.
Audit, Bernard, "Le tribunal des differends Irano-Américains' (1981–1984)," (1985) 112 Journal du Droit International 791.

Avanessian, Aida, "The New York Convention and Denationalized Arbitral Awards (with Emphasis on the Iran-United States Claims Tribunal)," (1991) 8(1) Journal of International Arbitration 5.

Bagner, Hans, "Enforcement of International Commercial Contract by Arbitration: Recent Developments," (1982) 14 Case Western Reserve Journal of International Law 573.

Baker, Stewart A and Davis, Mark D, "Establishment of an Arbitral Tribunal under the UNCITRAL Rules: The Experience of the Iran-United States Claims Tribunal," (1989) 23 International Lawyer 81.

Baker, Stewart A and Davis, Mark D, "Arbitral Proceedings Under the UNCITRAL Rules—The Experience of the Iran-US Claims Tribunal," (1989) 23 George Washington Journal of International Law & Economics 267.

Barcelo, John, "Who Decides the Arbitrators' Jurisdiction? Separability and Competence-Competence in Transnational Perspective," (2003) 36 Vanderbilt Journal of Transnational Law 1115.

Bederman, David, "Nationality of Individual Claimants before the Iran-United States Claims Tribunal," (1993) 42 International and Comparative Law Quarterly 119.

Belland, Stanton P, "The Iran-US Claims Tribunal: A Reassuring Exposure to International Arbitration," (1986) 9(1) Middle East Executive Reports 14 (January 1986).

Belland, Stanton P, "International Arbitration under Civil Law Concepts," (1986) Communication to the VIII International Congress for the International Council for Commercial Arbitration (New York).

Bellet, Pierre, "Foreword," (1984) 16 Law & Policy in International Business 677–5 (see "Symposium").

Bělohlávek, Alexander J, "Service in International Arbitration in Light of Articles 2 and 23 of the UNCITRAL Rules and International Practice," (2006) 24(4) ASA Bulletin (La Haye) 678.

Berger, Klaus P, "Art. 15 UNCITRAL Arbitration Rules: The Eternal Conflict Between Arbitral Discretion and the Parties Due Process Rights" (2006) 21(4) Mealey's International Arbitration Report 29.

Bergsten, Eric E, "The Interest of Developing Countries in the Work of UNCITRAL," in *Essays on International Law: Thirtieth Anniversary Commemorative Volume*, Asian-African Legal Consultative Committee (1987) 28.

Blessing, Marc, "The New International Arbitration Law in Switzerland," (1988) 5(2) Journal of International Arbitration 9.

Blessing, Marc, "The Major Western and Soviet Arbitration Rules: A Comparison of the Rules of UNCITRAL, UNCITRAL MODEL LAW, LCIA, ICC, AAA, and the Rules of the USSR Chamber of Commerce and Industry," (1989) 6(3) Journal of International Arbitration 7.

Böckstiegel, Karl-Heinz, "The Relevance of National Arbitration Law for Arbitrations under the UNCITRAL Rules," (1984) 1(3) Journal of International Arbitration 223.

Böckstiegel, Karl-Heinz, "Applying the UNCITRAL Rules: The Experience of the Iran-United States Claims Tribunal," (1986) 4 International Tax & Business Lawyer 266.

Böckstiegel, Karl-Heinz, "A Special Arbitration Convention: The Algiers Declaration Creating the Iran-United States Claims Tribunal and Their Application," in F Kemicha (ed), Proceedings of the First Euro-Arab Chambers of Commerce Conference on International Arbitration (1986) 78.

Böckstiegel, Karl-Heinz, "Zur Auslegung völkerrechtlicher Verträge durch das Iran-United States Claims Tribunal in Staat- und Völkerrechtsordnung," in K Hailbronner, G Ress, and T Stein, (eds), *Festschrift für Karl Doehring* (1989).

Böckstiegel, Karl-Heinz, "Zur Bedeutung des Iran-United States Claims Tribunal für die Entwicklüng des internationalen Rechts," in *Festschrift der Rechtswissenschaftlichen Fakultät zur 600-Jahr-Feier der Universität zu Köln* (1988).

Borris, Christian, "Die UNCITRAL-Schiedsregeln in der Praxis des Iran-United States Claims Tribunal," (1988) 2 Jahrbuch für die Praxis der Schiedsgerichtsbarkeit 3.

Brandon, Michael, "Hague Tribunal Recognized," (1986) 5(6) International Finance Law Review, 39.

Branson, David J and Tupman, W Michael, "Selecting an Arbitral Forum: A Guide to Cost-Effective International Arbitration," (1984) 24 Virginia Journal of International Law 917.

Brower, Charles N, "Recent Developments at the Iran-United States Claims Tribunal," (Summer 1984) 13 International Law News 4.

Brower, Charles N, "The Iran-United States Claims Tribunal," (1990-V) 224 Recueil des Cours 123.

Brower, Charles N, "The Anatomy of Fact-Finding before International Tribunals: An Analysis and a Proposal Concerning the Evaluation of Evidence," in Richard Lillich (ed), *Fact-Finding Before International Tribunals* (1992) 147.

Brower, Charles N, "Evidence before International Tribunals: The Need for Some Standard Rules," (1994) 28(I) The International Lawyer 47.

Brower, Charles N and Davis, Mark D, "The Iran-United States Claims Tribunal after Seven Years: A Retrospective View from the Inside," (December 1988) 43 Arbitration Journal 16.

Brunetti, Maurizio, "The *Lex Mercatoria* in Practice: The Experience of the Iran-United States Claims Tribunal," (2002) 18 Arbitration International 355.

Buxton, Richard, "The Rules of Evidence as Applied to Arbitrations," (2004) 58(4) Journal of the Chartered Institute of Arbitrators 229 (1992).

Carbonneau, Thomas E, "The Elaboration of Substantive Legal Norms and Arbitral Adjudication: The Case of The Iran-United States Claims Tribunal" in Richard Lillich (ed), *The Iran-United States Claims Tribunal 1981–1983* (1984) 104.

Caron, David D, "Interim Measures of Protection: Theory and Practice in Light of the Iran-United States Claims Tribunal," (1986) 46 Zeitschrift für ausländisches öffentliches Recht und Völkerrecht 466.

Caron, David D, "The Nature of the Iran-United States Claims Tribunal and the Evolving Structure of International Dispute Resolution," (1990) 84 American Journal of International Law 104.

Carter, James H, "The Iran-United States Claims Tribunal: Observations on the First Year," (1982) 29 UCLA Law Review 1076.

Carver, Jeremy, and Hossain, Kamal, "An Arbitration Case Study: The Dispute That Never Was," (1990) 5 ICSID Review-Foreign Investment Law Journal 311.

Castello, James E, "UNCITRAL Rules," in Frank-Bernd Weigand (ed), *Practitioner's Handbook on International Commercial Arbitration* (2nd edn 2009).

Castello, James E, "Unveiling the 2010 UNCITRAL Arbitration Rules," (May/October 2010) 65 Dispute Resolution Journal 21, 147–54.

Chen, Frederick Tse-shyang, "The Iran-US Claim Tribunal's Application of Commercial Law in the Economy Forms Award," (1984) 4 Chinese Yearbook of International Affairs 137.

Clagett, Brice M, "The Iran-United States Claims Tribunal: A Practitioner's Perspective" in Richard Lillich (ed), *The Iran-United States Claims Tribunal 1981–1983* (1984).

Cordero Moss, G, "Revision of the UNCITRAL Arbitration Rules: Further Steps," (2010) 13 Intl Arb L Rev 96.

Cremades, Bernardo M, "The Arbitral Award," in L Newman and H Hill (eds) *The Leading Arbitrators' Guide to International Arbitration* (2004).

Croff, Carlo, "The Applicable Law in International Commercial Arbitration: Is it Still a Conflict of Laws Problem?" (1982) 16 International Lawyer 631.

Crook, John, "Applicable Law in International Arbitration: The Iran-United States Claims Tribunal Experience," (1989) 83 American Journal of International Law 278.

Damrosch, Lori Fisler, Crook, John R, Lloyd Jones, David, Stein, Ted L and Clagett, Brice M, "Decisions of the Iran-United States Claims Tribunal," (1984) 78 American Society of International Law Proceedings 221.

Delaume, Georges, "ICSID Arbitration: Practical Distinctions," (1984) 1(2) Journal of International Arbitration 101.

de Vries, Henry P, "International Commercial Arbitration: A Contractual Substitute for National Courts," (1982) 57 Tulane Law Review 42.

Dietz, John P, "Introduction: Development of the UNCITRAL Arbitration Rules," (1979) 27 American Journal of Comparative Law 449.

Domke, Martin, "The Arbitrator's Immunity from Liability: A Comparative Survey," (1971) 3 University of Toledo Law Review 99.

Eliasoph, Ian, "A Missing Link: International Arbitration and the Ability of Private Actors to Enforce Human Rights Norms," (2004) 10 New England Journal of International and Comparative Law 83.

Feldman, Mark, "Implementation of the Iranian Claims Settlement Agreement—Status, Issues and Lessons: View from Government's Perspective," in Martha L Landwehr (ed), *Private Investors Abroad—Problems and Solutions in International Business* (1981) 75.

Ferrante, Mauro, "About the Nature of ICC Awards under the New York Convention," in Jan C Schultsz and Albert Jan van den Berg (eds), *The Art of Arbitration: Essays on International Arbitration* (1982) 129.

Fleischhauer, Carl-August, "The Contribution of UNCITRAL in the Field of Commercial Arbitration," in *Essays on International Law: Thirtieth Anniversary Commemorative Volume,* Asian-African Legal Consultative Committee (1987) 16.

Fouchard, Philippe, "Les travaux de la CNUDCI: Le règlement d'arbitrage," (1979) 106 Journal du Droit International 816.

Furnish, Dale, "Commercial Arbitration Agreements and the Uniform Commercial Code, (1979) 67 California Law Review 317.

Glossner, Ottoarndt, "Die UNCITRAL—Schiedsordnung in der Praxis," (1978) 24 Recht der Internationalen Wirtschaft: Aussenwirtshaftsdienst des Betriebs-Beraters 151.

Goldman, Bertold, "Lex Mercatoria," in *Forum Internationale* No 3 (November 1983).

Graig, William L, "Use and Abuses of Appeal from Awards," 4 Arbitration International 174 (1988).

Guo, Huacheng, "Arbitration in the People's Republic of China," (1992) 14 Comparative Law Yearbook on International Business 187.

Hanessian, Grant, "'General Principles of Law' in the Iran-United States Claims Tribunal," (1989) 27 Columbia Journal of Transnational Law 309.

Hardenberg, L, "De uitspraken van het Iran-United States Claims tribunal—naar Nederlands recht bezien," (February 11, 1984) 57 Nederlands Juristenblad 167, reprinted in English, "The Awards of the Iran-U.S. Claims Tribunal, seen in connection with the Law of the Netherlands," in International Business Law (September 1984) 337.

Heiskanen, Veijo, "Theory and Meaning of the Law Applicable in International Commercial Arbitration," (1993) IV Finnish Yearbook of International Law 98.

Herzfeld, Jeffrey F, "Applicable Law and Dispute Settlement in Soviet Joint Ventures," (1988) 31 ICSID Review—Foreign Investment Law Journal 249.

Holtzmann, Howard M, "Some Lessons of the Iran-United States Claims Tribunal, in Martha L Landwehr (ed), *Private Investors Abroad—Problems and Solutions in International Business* (1987) 1.

Holtzmann, Howard M, "Fact-Finding by the Iran-United States Claims Tribunal," in Richard Lillich (ed), *Fact-Finding By International Tribunals* (1991) 101.

Jarvin, Sigvard, "Is Exclusion of Concurrent Courts' Jurisdiction over Conservatory Measures to be Introduced by a Revision of the Convention?" (1989) 6(1) Journal of International Arbitration 171.

Jenard, Paul M, "Le règlement d'arbitrage de la commission des Nations Unies pour le droit commercial international," (1977) 54 Revue de Droit International et de Droit Comparé 201.

Johnson, Douglas, "The Constitution of an Arbitral Tribunal," (1953) 30 British Yearbook of International Law 152.

Jolowicz, John Anthony, "Procedural Questions," in *II International Encyclopedia of Comparative Law*, Chapter 4, 34.

Jones, David L, "The Iran-United States Claims Tribunal: Private Rights and State Responsibility," (1984) 24 Virginia Journal of International Law 259 (1984), reprinted in Richard Lillich (ed), *The Iran-United States Claims Tribunal 1981–1983* (1984) 261.

Jones, Doug, "Competence-Competence," (2009) 75 Arbitration 1, 56–64.

Kaye, Peter, "The EEC and Arbitration: The Unsettled Wake of the 'Atlantic Emperor'," (1993) 9 Arbitration International 27.

Khan, Muhammad Z, "The Appointment of Arbitrators by the President of the International Court of Justice," (1975) 14 Comunicazioni e Studi 1021.

Knoepfler, François and Schweizer, Philippe, "Making of Awards and Termination of Proceedings," in Petar Šarčević (ed), *Essays on International Commercial Arbitration* (1989) 163.

Kopelmanas, Lazare, "Le role des règlements d'arbitrage dans le développement des procedures arbitrales applicables au règlement de litiges commerciaux á caractère international (A propos de quelques règlements et projets de règlements d'arbitrage récents)," (1975) 21 Annuaire Français de Droit International 294.

Kozlowska, Daria, "The Revised UNCITRAL Arbitration Rules Seen Through the Prism of Electronic Disclosure" (2011) 28(1) Journal of International Arbitration 51.

Kunzlik, Peter F, "Public International Law Cannot Govern a Contract, Can Authorize an Arbitration," (1986) 45 Cambridge Law Journal 377.

Kuokkanen, Tuomas, "Todistelusta kaksoiskansalaisjutuissa Iranin Yhdysvaltain välitystuomioistuimessa," ("Evidence in Dual Nationality Cases before the Iran-United States Claims Tribunal") (1993) 91 Lakirnies 811.

Lagergren, Gunnar, "Iran-United States Claims Tribunal" in Adriaan Bos and Hugo Siblesz (eds), *Realism in Law-Making—Essays on International Law in Honor of Willem Riphagen* (1986) 113.

Lagergren, Gunnar, "Iran-United States Claims Tribunal," (1990) 13 Dalhousie Law Journal 505.

Lake, William T and Dana, Jane T, "Judicial Review of Awards of the Iran-United States Claims Tribunal: Are the Tribunal Awards Dutch?" (1984) 16 Law & Policy in International Business 755.

Lalive, Pierre, "Problèmes Relatif à l'Arbitrage International," 140 Recueil des Cours de l'Académie de Droit International (1976) 573.

Lando, Ole, "The *Lex Mercatoria* in International Commercial Arbitration," (1985) 34 International & Comparative Law Quarterly 747.

Lando, Ole, "The Law Applicable to the Merits of the Dispute," (1986) 2 Arbitration International 104.

Lando, Ole, "The 1986 Hague Convention on the Law Applicable to Sales," (1987) 51 Rabels Zeitschriftfiir ausländisches und internationales Privatrecht 60.

Lauterpacht, Elihu, "The Iran-United State Claims Tribunal—An Assessment," in Martha L Landwehr (ed), *Private Investors Abroad—Problems and Solutions in International Business* (1983) 213.

Leahy, Edward R, "Claims Tribunal for Iranian/American Disputes Requires Changes in Litigating Style," (Fall 1984) 10 Litigation News 3.

Levine, Judith, "Current Trends in International Arbitral Practice as Reflected in the Revision of the UNCITRAL Arbitration Rules" (2009) 31(1) University of New South Wales Law Journal 266.

Lew, Julian, "The Case for the Publication of Arbitration Awards," in Jan Schutsz and Albert Jan van den Berg (eds), *The Art of Arbitration: Essays on International Arbitration* (1982) 223.

Lewis, Robert P, "What Goes Around Comes Around: Can Iran Enforce Awards of the Iran-U.S. Claims Tribunal in the United States?" (1988) 26 Columbia Journal of Transnational Law 515.

Liew, Song Kun, "Commercial Arbitration in Korea with Special Reference to the UNCITRAL Rules," (1977) 5 Korean Journal of Comparative Law 79.

Lowenfeld, Andreas F, "The US-Iranian Dispute Settlement Accord: An Arbitrator Looks at the Prospects for Arbitration," (1981) 36 Arbitration Journal 3.

Lowenfeld, Andreas F, "The Iran-U.S. Claims Tribunal: An Interim Appraisal," (1983) 38 Arbitration Journal 14, reprinted in Richard Lillich (ed), *The Iran-United States Claims Tribunal 1981–1983* (1984) 77.

Mangärd, Nils, "The Hostage Crisis, the Algiers Accords and the Iran-United States Claims Tribunal," in *Festskrift till Lars Hjerner: Studies in International Law* (1990) 363.

Mann, FA, "*Lex Facit Arbitrum*," in Pieter Sanders (ed), *International Arbitration:* Liber Amicorum *for Martin Domke* (1967) 157.

Marriot, Arthur L, "Evidence in International Arbitration," (1989) 5 Arbitration International 280.
McCabe, Monica P, "Arbitral Discovery and the Iran-United States Claims Tribunal Experience," (1986) 20 International Lawyer 499.
McClellan, Anthony, "Commercial Arbitration and European Community Law," (1989) 5 Arbitration International 68.
McDonnell, Neil, "The Availability of Provisional Relief in International Commercial Arbitration," (1984) 22 Columbia Journal of Transnational Law 273.
Mistelis, Loukas, "Reality Test: Current State of Affairs in Theory and Practice Relating to 'Lex Arbitri'" (2006) 17 The American Review of International Arbitration 155.
Mohajer, Mahmoud S, "A Report on Awards Issued by the Iran-United States Claims Tribunal," (translation from the Persian original) in *Legal Bulletin for the International Legal Services of the Islamic Republic of Iran* (1984–1985).
Mohajer, Mahmoud S, "Withdrawal of Claims," (translation from the Persian original) in *Legal Bulletin for the International Legal Services of the Islamic Republic of Iran* (1984–1985).
Morgan, W G O, "Discovery in Arbitration," (1986) 3(3) Journal of International Arbitration 23.
Mosk, Richard M, "Lessons from The Hague—An Update on the Iran-United States Claims Tribunal," (1987) 144 Pepperdine Law Review 819.
Mosk, Richard M, "The Role of Party-Appointed Arbitrators in International Arbitration: The Experience of the Iran-United States Claims Tribunal," (1988) 1 Transnational Law 253.
Mosk, Richard M, "The Role of Facts in International Dispute Resolution," (2003) 203 Recueil des Cours—Collected Courses at the Hague Academy of International Law 11.
Mosk, Richard and Ginsberg, Tom, "Dissenting Opinions in International Arbitration," in Matti Tupamäki (ed), *Liber Amicorum Bengt Broms* (1999) 5.
Mouri, Allahyar, "Striking a Balance between the Finality of Award and the Right to a Fair Judgment: What is the Contribution of the Iran-United States Claims Tribunal?" (1993) IV Finnish Yearbook of International Law 1.
Mustill, Michael, "The New *Lex Mercatoria*: The First Twenty-Five Years," in Ian Brownlie and Maarten Bos (eds), *Liber Amicorum for the Rt. Hon. Lord Wilberforce* (1987) 149.
Newman, Lawrence and Castilla, Rafael, "Production of Evidence through US Courts for Use in International Arbitration," (1992) 9(2) Journal of International Arbitration 61.
Olesen, Elvi J, "*Baar v. Tigerman*: An Attack on Absolute Immunity for Arbitrators!" (1985) 21 California Western Law Review 564.
Özsunay, Murat, "The Arbitration Procedure – Principles and Rules of the UNCITRAL Model Law as Essentially Adopted by the Turkish Act on International Arbitration," in Christian Klausegger et al (eds), *Austrian Arbitration Yearbook* (2008) 343–368.
Park, William, "The *Lex Loci Arbitri* and International Commercial Arbitration," (1983) 32 International and Comparative Law Quarterly 21.
Park, William, "Judicial Controls in the Arbitral Process," (1991) 3 Arbitration International 230.
Paulsson, Jan, and Rawding, Nigel, "The Trouble with Confidentiality," (1995) 11(3) Arbitration International 303.
Pellonpaä, Matti and Fitzmaurice, Malgosia, "Taking of Property in the Practice of the Iran-United States Claims Tribunal," (1988) 19 Netherlands Yearbook of International Law 53.
Pirrung, Jorg, "Die Schiedsverfahrensordnung der UNCITRAL," (1977) 23 Recht der Internationalen Wirtschaft: Aussenwirtschaftsdienst des BetriebsBeraters 513.
Popper, Lewis M, "Conflict Between Tribunal Arbitrators," (November 1984) 3(11) International Finance Law Review 45.
Popper, Lewis M, "Resumption of Proceedings Expected," (January 1985) 4(1) International Finance Law Review 39.
Popper, Lewis M, "Bockstiegel Lifts Suspension Order," (February 1985) 4(2) International Finance Law Review 46.

Popper, Lewis M, "Judge Mangärd Resigns," (March 1985) 4(3) International Finance Law Review 46.

Pryles, Michael, "Application of the Lex Mercatoria in International Commercial Arbitration," (2004) 78 Australian Law Journal 396.

Reichert, Douglas "Issues of Language and Translation," in D Caron and J Crook (eds), *The Iran-United States Claims Tribunal and The Process of International Claims Resolution* (2000) 313.

Rivkin, David, "Enforceability of Arbitral Awards Based on *Lex Mercatoria*," (1993) 9(1) Arbitration International 67.

Robert, Jean, "Administration of Evidence in International Commercial Arbitration," (1976) I Yearbook Commercial Arbitration 221.

Rubino-Sammartano, Mauro, "Rules of Evidence in International Arbitration, A Need for Discipline and Harmonization," 1986 3(2) Journal of International Arbitration 87.

Rubino-Sammartano, Mauro "Arbitration under the Algiers Declarations," in Rubino-Sammartano, Mauro, (ed), *International Arbitration: Law and Practice* (2nd rev edn 2001) 107.

Saario, Voitto, "Asianosaisautonomia kansainvälisessa kauppaan liittyvassa välimiesmenettelyssä" ("Party Autonomy in International Commercial Arbitration"), Juhlajulkaisu Matti Ylöstalo (1987) 341.

Sacerdoti, Giorgio, "Il diritto dell'arbitrato commerciale internazionale nei nuovi regolamenti della Cameradi commercio internazionale e dell'UNCITRAL," (1976) 12 Rivista di Diritto Internazionale Privato e Processuale 22.

Sacerdoti, Giorgio, "The New Arbitration Rules of ICC and UNCITRAL," (1977) 11 Journal World Trade Law 248.

Sanders, Pieter, "Aspects de l'arbitrage international," (1976) 53 Revue de Droit International et de Droit Comparé 129.

Sanders, Pieter, "Commentary on UNCITRAL Arbitration Rules," (1977) 2 Yearbook Commercial Arbitration 172.

Sanders, Pieter, "Règlement d'arbitrage de la CNUDCI," (1978) 4 Droit et Pratique du Commerce International 269.

Sanders, Pieter, "La separabilité la clause compromissoire," in *Hommage à Frédéric Eisemann, Liber Amicorum* (1978)

Sanders, Pieter, "Procedures and Practices under the UNCITRAL Rules," (1979) 27 American Journal of Comparative Law 453.

Sanders, Pieter, "Has the Moment Come to Revise the Arbitration Rules of UNCITRAL?" (No. 3, 2004) 20 Arbitration International 243.

Schultsz, Jan C, "Ein neues Schiedsgerichtsgesetz für die Niederlande" (1987), Praxis des Internationalen Privat- und Verfahrensrechts (IPRax), 7 Jahrgang 383.

Schwebel, Stephen, "The Majority Vote of an International Arbitral Tribunal," in Stephen Schwebel, *Justice in International Law: Selected Readings* (1994) 213.

Seifi, Jamal, "Procedural Remedies Against Awards of Iran-United States Claims Tribunal," (1992) 8 Arbitration International 41.

Selby, Jamison M, "Fact-Finding Before the Iran-United States Claims Tribunal: The View from the Trenches," in Richard Lillich (ed), *Fact-Finding Before International Tribunals* (1992) 135.

Selby, Jamison M and Stewart, David P, "Practical Aspects of Arbitrating Claims Before the Iran-United States Claims Tribunal," (1984) 18 International Lawyer 211, reprinted in Iranian Assets Litigation Reporter 9483 (October 12, 1984).

Sen, Berry, "AALCC Dispute Settlement and the UNCITRAL Arbitration Rules," (1986) 4 International Tax & Business Lawyer 247.

Sevón, Leit, "UNCITRAL—UN's Kommission for Internationell Handelsrätt," ("UNCITRAL—UN's Commission on International Trade Law"), (1977) 113 Tidskrift utgiven av juridiska foreningen i Finland 216.

Shenton, David, "An Introduction to the IBA Rules of Evidence," (1985) 1 Arbitration International 118.

Skinner, Matthew et al (eds) "The UNCITRAL Arbitration Rules 2010" (2011) 7(1) Asian International Arbitration Journal 76.

Stein, Ted L, "Tribunal Decisions: The Reason for Reasons," Proceedings American Society of International Law (1984), reprinted in (May 4, 1984) Mealey Litigation Reports: Iranian Claims 547.

Stein, Ted L and Wotman, David, "International Commercial Arbitration in the 1980s: A Comparison of the Major Arbitral Systems and Rules," (1983) 38 Business Lawyer 1685.

Stewart, David P, "The Iran-United States Claims Tribunal: Accomplishments and Prospects" in Martha Landwehr (ed), *Private Investors Abroad—Problems and Solutions in International Business* (1983) 525.

Stewart, David P, "The Iran-United States Claims Tribunal: A Review of Developments 1983–84," (1984) 16 Law and Policy in International Business 677.

Stoecker, Christoph, "The *Lex-Mercatoria*: To What Extent Does it Exist?" (1990) 7(1) Journal of International Arbitration 101.

Straus, Michael, "A Communication on Certain Comparative Arbitration Practices of the Iran-United States Claims Tribunal," Communication to VIIIth International Congress for the International Council for Commercial Arbitration, New York (1986).

Straus, Michael, "The Practice of the Iran-U.S. Claims Tribunal in Receiving Evidence from Parties and from Experts," (1986) 3(3) Journal of International Arbitration 57.

Suy, Erik, "Settling U.S. Claims Against Iran Through Arbitration," (1981) 29 American Journal of Comparative Law 523.

Tackaberry, John, "Selection of Evidence for the Hearing," in John Tackaberry, Arthur Marriot, and Ronald Bernstein, *Bernstein's Handbook of Arbitration and Dispute Resolution Practice* (Rev 4th edn 2003).

Thieffry, Patrick, "The Finality of Awards in International Arbitration," (1985) 2(3) Journal of International Arbitration 27.

Thirlway, Hugh, "Dilemma or Chimera?—Admissibility of Illegally Obtained Evidence in International Adjudication," (1984) 78 American Journal of International Law 622.

Thompson, Terence W, "The UNCITRAL Arbitration Rules," (1976) 17 Harvard International Law Journal 141.

Trakman, Leon, "Confidentiality in International Commercial Arbitration," (2002) 18(1) Arbitration International 1.

Tuck, Andrew, "Investor-State Arbitration Revised: A Critical Analysis of the Revisions and Proposed Reforms to the ICSID and UNCITRAL Arbitration Rules" (2007) 13 Law and Business Review of the Americas 885.

Ugarte, Ricardo and Bevilacqua, Thomas, "Ensuring Party Equality in the Process of Designating Arbitrators in Multiparty Arbitration: An Update on the Governing Provisions," (2010) 27 Journal of International Arbitration 1.

Van den Berg, Albert J, "Proposed Dutch Law on the Iran-United States Claims Settlement Declaration, A Reaction to Mr. Hardenberg's Article," (September 1984) International Business Law 341, originally published in Dutch as "Wetsontwerp Iran-United States Claims Tribunal, Een reactie," (February 11, 1984) Nederlands Juristenblad 170.

Van Hof, Jacomijn, "UNCITRAL Arbitration Rules" in Loukas A Mistelis (ed), *Concise International Arbitration* (2010) 171.

Van Houtte, Hans, "Conduct of Arbitral Proceedings," in Petar Šarčević (ed), *Essays on International Commercial Arbitration* (1989) 113.

Viscasillas, Pilar P, "Place of Arbitration (Article 16) and Language of Proceedings (Article 17) in the UNCITRAL Arbitration Rules: Some Proposals for a Revision" (2006) 13 Croatian Arbitration Yearbook 205.

Von Hoffmann, Bernd, "UNCITRAL Rules für internationales Schiedsverfahren," (1976) 22 Recht der Internationalen Wirtschaft: Aussenwirtschaftdienst des Betriebs-Beraters 1.

Waincymer, Jeff, "The New UNCITRAL Arbitration Rules: An Introduction and Evaluation" (2010) 14 Vindobona Journal of International Commercial Law & Arbitration 223.

Wallgren, Carita, "Valet av tillämplig materiell rätt i ett till Finlandlokaliserat skiljemannaförfarande," ("The Law Applicable to the Merits of an International Dispute Arbitrated in Finland") (1984) 120 Tidskrift utgiven av juridiska föreningen i Finland 350.

Westberg, John A, "The Applicable Law Issue in International Business Transactions with Government Parties—Rulings of the Iran-United States Claims Tribunal," (1987) 2 ICSID Review—Foreign Investment Law Journal 473, reprinted in (1987) 14 Pepperdine Law Review 819.

Index

Algiers Accords
  application of 143
  interim measures 530
  interpretative disputes concerning 5
  Iran–United States arbitration 41, 206, 342, 366, 444, 552, 737
  provisions of 34, 137, 873
  Security Account 186
  'self-executing' nature of 43
Algiers Declarations 205–6, 223, 259, 300, 304, 367, 401–2, 407–8, 453, 543–5, 548–9, 719, 767, 777–8, 785–6, 794, 797, 810, 833–5, 837, 874
amendments to claim or defence 467–89
  see also initiation of arbitration; statement of claim; statement of defence
  arbitral tribunal, jurisdiction of 469–70
  comparison of 1976/2010 Rules 475
  general commentary on 468–9
  grounds for rejecting 471–4
    appropriateness 471
    delay 471–4
    'discovery' procedure 471
    other circumstances 473–4
    prejudice 471–4
    unjust enrichment 472
  investment tribunals, extracts from 475–9
  Iran-US Claims Tribunal, extracts from 474, 479–89
  liberal approach to 468–9
  procedural questions 474
  procedure of 467–8
American Arbitration Association (AAA)
  Code of Ethics for Arbitrators 209, 723
  Commercial Rules 209
  fee schedule 862
  International Arbitration Rules of 2, 7, 34, 37, 120, 215, 313, 327, 361, 377, 704, 759
  Panel of Arbitrators 206
  practice of 225
  publication of awards 755
American Bar Association (ABA) 205

amiable compositeur, *see* applicable law of the UNCITRAL Rules
amicus curiae submissions 31–2, 36, 39–41
  1976 UNCITRAL Rules, and 31
  Iran–US Claims Tribunal, and 46
applicable law of the UNCITRAL Rules 111–44
  applicable law, *amiable compositeur* 112, 119–21
  choice of applicable law, not designated by parties 118–19
  comparison of 1976/2010 Rules 123–7
  contract, significance of 121–3
  ex aequo et bono 119–21
  investment tribunals, extracts from 129–30
  Iran-US Claims Tribunal 128–9
    choice of law 142–4
    extracts from the practice of 131–42
    other practice of 142–4
  meanings of 'applicable law' 111
  party autonomy 112–17
    application of 112–17
  trade usages, significance of 121–3
  travaux préparatoires 118–19
appointing authority
  challenge process 339
  composition of 338–40
  designation of 340–1
  evolution of 337
  functions of 341
  impartiality and independence 340, 342
  Iran-US Claims Tribunal, lessons from 340–3
  selection criteria 341
apportionment of costs 865–96
  see also costs of arbitration
  allocation of costs 865
  apportioning and awarding costs 865–70
  'circumstances of the case' 870–5, 879–96
    conduct of the parties 871–3
    degree of success of the parties 870–1
    dispute resolution mechanism, nature of 874–5, 887–91
    nature of the parties 873–4

apportionment of costs (*cont.*)
  claim for costs, requirements for
      making 875–7
    documentation 875
    reasonable legal costs, proof of 876–7
    timing of requests 875–6
  comparison of 1976/2010 Rules 877
  conduct of the parties 882–6, 894–6
  investment tribunals, extracts from 877–91
  Iran-US Claims Tribunal, extracts
      from 891–6
  success of the parties 879–82, 892–4
arbitral tribunal
  see also applicable law of the UNCITRAL
      Rules; general provisions of the
      UNCITRAL Rules; initiation of
      arbitration; place of arbitration of the
      UNCITRAL Rules; scope of
      application of the UNCITRAL Rules
  fundamental principles of 13–143
  legal framework, operation of 13–143
  objections to the jurisdiction of 449–66, 917
    comparison of 1976/2010 Rules 458–9
    contract, objections to existence or
        validity of 453–5
    counterclaims 455
    doctrine of separability 453–5
    investment tribunals, extracts from
        459–63
    Iran-US Claims Tribunal, extracts
        from 463–6
    Kompetenz-Kompetenz, principle
        of 450–1
    necessity of two-stage proceedings,
        principle of 465
    objections 451
    power to determine jurisdiction 450–2
    procedure of 450
    raising objections, circumstances
        for 455–6
    ruling upon objections, circumstances
        for 457–8
    set-off, claim for the purpose of 455
    three Chambers, policy of 465–6
    travaux préparatoires 452
  a-national arbitration 36, 45
  autonomy, arbitral 13
    limitations of 30–6
  confidentiality, and 37
  definition 17
  domestic 18, 25

electronic commerce, and 26
International Investment Agreements (IIAs)
    and 20
investor–state arbitration 7
  future transparency rules 23–4
  opt-in approach 23
  opt-out approach 23
  UNCITRAL Rules, and 7–8
limitations of 25
NAFTA Chapter Eleven tribunal 31, 33,
    35
oral or tacit conduct, and 26
third party participation 36
tribunal
  delay, duty to avoid unnecessary 34
  expense, duty to avoid unnecessary 34
UNCITRAL, and 3
arbitral procedures to control 145–343
challenge of 175–275
  acceptance by all other parties 253–5
  actual prior knowledge 245–8
  appointing authority, decisions of 271–2
  appointing authority, limitations of
      power 272
  burden of proof 243–5
  challenge decision (April 15, 1993)
      178–9
  challenge decision (January 11,
      1995) 179
  circumstances 'became known' to
      challenging party 243–8
  circumstances for 230
  comparison of 1976/2010 Rules 274–5
  exclusive grounds for 228–30
  form of notice 248–53
  grounds for 207–41
  impartiality or independence, justifiable
      doubts as to 208–28
  initiation of 241–68
  investment (and other) tribunals, extracts
      from 231–5
  investment (and other) tribunals,
      overview of 178–83
  investment tribunals, extracts from
      256, 272
  Iran-US Claims Tribunal, extracts
      from 235–41, 257–67, 273–4
  Iran-US Claims Tribunal, overview
      of 183–91
  Judge Arangio-Ruiz, Iranian Govt.
      challenge of (1991) 186

Judge Bengt Broms, US Claimant's
    challenge of (2004) 187
Judge Bengt Broms, US Govt. challenge
    of (2001) 187
Judge Briner, Iranian Govt. challenge of
    (1988) 184
Judge Briner, Iranian Govt. challenges of
    (1989) 184–5
Judge Charles Brower, Iranian Govt.
    challenge of (2010) 190–1
Judge Hamid Reza Oloumi Yazdi, US
    Govt. challenge of (2007) 188–9
Judge Krzysztof Skubiszewski, Iranian
    Govt. challenge of (2007) 188–9
Judge Krzysztof Skubiszewski, Iranian
    Govt. challenges of (1999) 186
Judge Krzysztof Skubiszewski and Judge
    Gaetano Arangio-Ruiz, Iranian
    Govt. challenge of (2009) 189–90
Judge Noori, US Claimant's challenge of
    (1990) 186
Judge Seyed Jamal Seifi, US Govt.
    challenge of (2010) 190
Judges Assadollah Noori, Koorosh Ameli,
    and Mohsen Aghahosseini, US
    Govt. challenge of (2005–
    2006) 188
Judges Kashani and Shafeiei, US Govt.
    challenge of 184
LCIA, challenge decision by (Oct–Dec
    2005) 179
mechanism of 177
Mr J Christopher Thomas, claimant's
    challenge to (2009) 182–3
Mr Judd L. Kessler, Argentine Govt.
    challenge of (2007) 180–1
Mr Stanimir Alexandrov, Argentine Govt.
    challenge of (2009) 182
Nils Mangård, Iranian Govt. challenge of
    (1982) 183–4
notice of challenge 241–53
potential for agreement to 241–68
Prof. Gabrielle Kaufmann-Kohler,
    Argentine Govt. challenges of
    (2007–2008) 181–2
Prof. James Anaya, US Govt challenge of
    (2007) 180
recipient of notice 248–53
resolution of 268–74
Secretary General of the PCA, assistance
    of 270–1

sender of notice 248–53
sufficiency of notice 248–53
timeline for seeking a decision on 256
travaux préparatoires, general comments
    on 241–3
Judge Krzysztof Skubiszewski and Judge
    Gaetano Arangio-Ruiz, Iranian
    Govt. challenge of (2009)
    189–90
UNCITRAL challenge procedure,
    exclusivity of 191–3
withdrawal of challenged arbitrator
    253–5, 268–70
comparison of 1976/2010 Rules 172–3
declaration of acceptance 202
designating and appointing
    authorities 148–56
  agreement, opportunities for 149–51
  appointing authority, role of 153–5
  designating authority, role of 151–3
  importance of 149
  independent and impartial
    arbitrator 149
  Iran-US Claims Tribunal, extracts
    from 155–6
  Secretary-General of the PCA 148
  time periods, suspension of 153
disclosures by 914
duty to disclose 194–207
  circumstances to disclose 194
  failure to disclose 198
  investment tribunals, extracts from
    201–2
  Iran-US Claims Tribunal:
    disclosure guidelines of 200–3
    extracts from 202–5
  model statements of independence
    198–200
  no circumstances to disclose 194
  stages of 195–8
  statement of independence 194
  US arbitrators, disclosure by 205–7
exclusion of liability for 325–35, 915
  comparison of 1976/2010 rules 330
  immunity protection 326–8
  investment tribunals, extracts from 330
  Iran-US Claims Tribunal:
    extracts from 331–5
    practice of 330
  negligence, concept of 327
  procedure 325

arbitral tribunal (cont.)
    qualified immunity 328
    wrongdoing 326–7, 329
  failure to act and other disruptions
        278–305
    absence of Judge Mostafavi, Spring
        (1988) 284–5
    absence of Mr Sani, Fall (1983) 284
    comparison of 1976/2010 rules 289
    drafting history of the rule 278–80
    general commentary 278–80
    investment tribunals, extracts from
        289–90
    Iran-US Claims Tribunal practice:
        extracts from 290–304
      with respect to failure to act 280–1
      with respect to other disruptions 282–9
    pre-hearing conferences 286
    procedure 278
    rendering awards 286
    replacement of an arbitrator 305–23
    resignation of an arbitrator 286–9
    substitute arbitrators 282–3
    truncated proceedings 283–6
  fees of 852–65
    arbitral tribunal, computation of fees and
        expenses 860–2
    arbitral tribunal, fees and expenses
        of 855–62
    comparison of 1976/2010 Rules 862–3
    efficiency 859, 861–2
    expenses under the rules 853–5
    fees and expenses of arbitrators
        852–3, 922
    investment tribunals, extracts from 863–5
    manner of determining fees and
        expenses 856–9
    neutral arbiter, potential review by
        855–62
    neutral mechanism 858–60
    regulation of arbitrator's fees 853–5
    transparency 857–8, 860
  impartiality and independence
    confidentiality of deliberations, breach
        of 223–4
    decision-making 222–3
    failure to disclose 226–7
    handling of proceedings 220–2
    impartiality, meaning of 213
    independence, meaning of 213
    justifiable doubts:
      circumstances of 213–15
      criteria and examples of 211–12
      limitations on 228–30
    non-party-appointed arbitrators
        209–11
    objective standards 208
    parent corporation of a party, previous
        employment by 217
    party (salary), financial relationship
        with 217
    party (shareholding), financial
        relationship with 216–17
    party-appointed arbitrators 209–11
    physical assault of a fellow arbitrator 225
    previous advocacy 218–19
    representation in another forum 218
    stage of proceedings 225–6
    standard of 225–6
    statement regarding party or dispute 222
    third-party representation 219–20
    witnesses, relationship with 215–16
  multi-party arbitration, appointment of
    appoint and reappoint, power to 170–1
    challenges 169
    procedure 166–8
    requirements for appointment 169
  number of 157–61
    agreement on 157
    default rule on 157–9
    one or three, other than 161
    three arbitrators, exception to the default
        rule of 160–1
  replacement of 305–23
    agreement between disputing parties 313
    appointing authority, exclusivity of
        discretion 312
    comparison of 1976/2010 rules 314–18,
        320–2
    'exceptional circumstances' in 308–13
    express power to proceed 315–17
    'has to be replaced', procedures of 307–8
    inherent power to proceed 317–18
    Iran-US Claims Tribunal, extracts
        from 322–3
    necessary replacement 305
    procedural appointment 311–12
    procedure 305
    repetition of hearings in the event
        of 318–23, 915
    right to appoint, depriving a party
        of 308–11

spurious resignations 305–7
sole arbitrator, appointment of 162–4
  implications of 164
    list-procedure 163
    nationality of 163–4
    procedure 162
  statement of impartiality and independence 202
  three-person panel, appointment of
    investment tribunals, extracts from 166–8
    presiding arbitrator, appointment of 165–6
    procedure 164
    right of each party to appoint an arbitrator 164–5
ASEAN, *see* Association of Southeast Asian Nations
Association of Southeast Asian Nations (ASEAN)
  Regional Investment Agreement 8
Australian Centre for International Commercial Arbitration (ACICA) 17–18, 365
autonomy, party 19–20
award, the 697–905
  see also costs of arbitration; decisions; deliberations; form and effect; settlement and other termination; post-award proceedings

burden of proof *see* evidence

CAFTA-DR (Dominican Republic–Central America–United States Free Trade Agreement) 22, 58, 365
  Chapter Ten 385, 792
Cairo International Commercial Arbitration Centre 6, 18
calculation of periods of time *see* notice and calculation of periods of time
CERD, *see* Committee on the Elimination of Racial Discrimination
challenge, *see* arbitrators: challenge of
choice of language, *see* language, choice of
Civil Aviation Organization 405
claim, *see* amendments to claim or defence; statement of claim
Claims Settlement Declaration
  see under Iran–US Claims Tribunal
Committee on the Elimination of Racial Discrimination (CERD) 180, 218

comparative approach to UNCITRAL Rules (1976/2010)
  amendments to claim or defence 475
  applicable law of the UNCITRAL Rules 123–7
  apportionment of costs 877
  arbitral tribunal, objections to the jurisdiction of 458–9
  arbitrators 172–3
    challenge of 274–5
    exclusion of liability 330
    failure to act and other disruptions 289
    fees of 862–3
    replacement of 314–18, 320–2
  costs of arbitration 848–9
  default 678–9
  deposit of costs 900–1
  evidence 574–6
  form and effect 759–60
  further written statements 496
  general provisions 58–9
  hearings 611–13
    closure of 628–9
  interim measures 532–3
  language, choice of 384
  notice and calculation of periods of time 403–4
  notice initiating arbitration 368–9
    response to 373
  place of arbitration 95–6
  post-award proceedings:
    additional award 824–5
    correction of the award 814–15
    interpretation of the award 806
  representation and assistance 354–5
  scope of application 24–6
  settlement and other termination 790–2
  statement of claim 416–17
  statement of defence 429–31
  time limits on submission 508
  tribunal-appointed experts 648
competence-competence doctrine 450–3, 458
contractual relationship 16, 18, 24–5
Convention on the Limitation Period in the International Sale of Goods 363, 402
costs of arbitration 839–905
  see also apportionment of costs; arbitrators: fees of; deposit of costs
  background 840
  comparison of 1976/2010 Rules 848–9
  costs defined 843–7

costs of arbitration (*cont.*)
   costs of completion of an award 847–8
   costs of correction of an award 847–8
   costs of interpretation of an award 847–8
   definition of 'costs' 841
   duty to fix 841–3
   investment and other tribunals, extracts from 849–52
   Iran-US Claims Tribunal, costs of 848

decisions 699–730
   see also deliberations
default 671–89
   see also default and waiver
   background 671
   comparison of 1976/2010 Rules 678–9
   counterclaims 677, 679
   default judgment 673
   documentary evidence, failure to produce 677–9
   equality 678
   evidence 673
   ex parte proceedings 674
   extension request process 673
   fairness 678
   general comments on 672–5
   hearing, failure to appear at a 677
   investment tribunals, extracts from 679–83
   Iran-US Claims Tribunal 683–9
   notice requirement 674
   procedure 671–2
   'remaining matters' 675
   sanction mechanisms 678
   set-off, claim for the purpose of 677, 679
   statement of claim 676
   'sufficient cause', meaning of 674–5
   written submissions, failure to file early 675–7
default and waiver 669–96
   see also default; waiver
defence, *see* amendments to claim or defence; statement of defence
defined legal relationship 16, 18, 24
deliberations, *see* decisions
deposit of costs 896–905
   see also costs of arbitration
   accountant, right to 900–1
   appointing authority, consultation with 899
   comparison of 1976/2010 Rules 900–1
   investment tribunals, extracts from 901–3
   Iran-US Claims Tribunal, extracts from 903–5
   procedure of 896–7
   request for deposits 897–9
   requested deposits, failure to make 899–900
   unexpended deposits, return of 900–1
dispute resolution 13
   arbitration, and 17
doctrine of *quantum meruit* 133
doctrine of separability 453–5, 458

equality 32–4
   1976 UNCITRAL Rules, and 32
   Iran–US Claims Tribunal, and 33
EC Convention on the law applicable to contractual relations 115
European Commission of Human Rights (ECHR) 213
European Convention on International Commercial Arbitration 123, 529
European Convention on the Protection of Human Rights and Fundamental Freedoms 171, 213
evidence 555–600
   see also evidence and hearings; hearings
   admissibility of 571–4, 579–80, 594–600
   affidavit testimony 565–6, 574
   burden of proof 557–61, 576–7, 580–7
   common law/civil law systems 556, 563, 566
   comparison of 1976/2010 Rules 574–6
   confidential negotiations, information concerning 572
   context 555–7
   'discovery' procedure 566–7
   documentary, submission of 575–6
   documents, production of 565–71, 577, 588–93
      general comments 565–7
      production orders, 'enforcement' of 570–1
      request of a party, at the 567–70
   electronic evidence 47
   'fishing expeditions' 567
   hearsay evidence 573
   IBA Rules on the Taking of Evidence 556–7, 569–70
   inquisitorial civil law system 555–6
   interim measures 571

investment tribunals, extracts from 576–80
Iran-US Claims Tribunal, extracts from 580–600
materiality of 571–4, 579–80, 594–600
non-compliance 570
prima facie proof 559–61, 574
procedure 557
reasonable doubt standard 559–60
rebuttal evidence 564
relevance of 571–4, 579–80, 594–600
summary of 587–8
weight of 571–4, 579–80, 594–600
  categories of individuals 562
  company witnesses 573
  definition of 561–4, 576–7
  fact and expert witnesses 563
  general comments on 561–3
  Iran-US Claims Tribunal, practice of 563–4
  party witnesses 562–3, 576
  written witness statements 564–5, 577, 593, 938–9, 987
evidence and hearings 553–667
  see also evidence; hearings; tribunal-appointed experts
ex aequo et bono, see applicable law of the UNCITRAL Rules
expropriation 25

Foreign Claims Settlement Commission of the United States 581
form and effect 731–79
  absence of arbitrator's signature, reasons for 749–50
  'award on jurisidiction' 734
  award's making, date, and place of 745–6
  civil law 750
  comparison of 1976/2010 Rules 759–60
  confidentiality 749, 755–6, 760
  copies of award to parties 757–9
  date, place, and signature 763, 767–8
  definition of 'award' 735
  dispositif 750, 752
  dissenting and separate opinions 752–5
  failure to sign award 746–50, 764–5, 769–76
    improper statements of reasons 773–6
    post-award exchanges 773–6
    statement of reasons for 769–73

fairness 739
filing of award 759–60, 765–6
'final and binding' award 738–42, 759, 762–3, 767
  binding 741–2
  final 738–41
'final award' 733
interim award 734, 736–7, 759
interlocutory award 734, 736–8, 759
investment and other tribunals, extracts from 761–6
Iran-US Claims Tribunal, extracts from 766–79
'legal duty' 756
'legal proceeding' 756
'legal right' 756
Model Law negotiations 735, 744
obligation to sign award 746–50
'partial award' 734, 736–7, 739–40, 759
place of arbitration 745–6, 759–60
possible waiver statement 733
procedure 732–3
publication of award 755–7, 776–9
reasons for award 768
'recourse' 743–4
registration of award 759–60, 765–6
separate awards, discretion to make 733–8
'set aside' proceedings 740, 743
statement of reasons for award 750–2
time limits 758–9
transparency 757
travaux préparatoires, general comments on 746–9, 751, 757
types of awards 734, 761, 766–7
waiver of recourse against award 742–5, 920
'without delay' 742, 758
written award 745–6
background 491
comparison of 1976/2010 Rules 496
counter-memorial (respondent) statements 492–4
dilatory pleas 493
documentary evidence 493, 495
final rebuttal submission 495
general comments on 492–6
investment tribunals, extracts from 496–8
Iran-US Claims Tribunal, extracts from 498–505
legal argumentation 494

form and effect (*cont.*)
  memorial (claimant) statements 492–4
  Memorials in Rebuttal 493
  procedure 491
  rejoinder (*duplique*) 492
  reply (*réplique*) 492
  simultaneous pleadings 495
  submission of 492
  written pleadings 493–4
  written statements 493–4

general provisions of UNCITRAL Rules
      29–77
  arbitral autonomy 30–6
  communication of documents 53–4
  comparison of 1976/2010 Rules 58–9
  confidentiality 36–9
  consolidation of claims 57–8
  general application, issues of 49
  general provisions 30
  hearing, right to a 49–53
    preliminary meetings 52–3
    scope of hearings 49–51
    timing of hearing requests 51–2
  investment (and other) tribunals, extracts
      from 59–69
    amicus submissions 65–9
    equal treatment, safeguarding 66
    equality, requirement of 68–9
    NAFTA, relevant provisions of 68
    parties' right to present their case 68–9
  Iran-US Claims Tribunal 41–5
    extracts from the practice of 69–77
    general and tribunal rules (1983)
        69–73
    tribunal rules (1983) 74–7
  joinder of third persons 54–7
  lex loci arbitri 45–6
  non-disputing party (*amicus*) submissions
      39–41
  provisional timetable 46–7
  time periods, modifications of 47–8
Geneva Convention (1927) 740–1

Hague Convention on the Law Applicable to
    International Sale of Goods 115
Hague Convention on the Law Applicable to
    Matrimonial Property Regimes 139
hearings 601–33, 918
  see also evidence and hearings
  ad hoc arbitration 604

additional information 605, 626
closure of the hearing 624–33
  additional hearings 626
  comparison of 1976/2010 Rules 628–9
  exceptional circumstances 626–8
  hearings vs proceedings 624–5
  investment tribunals, extracts from 629
  Iran-US Claims Tribunal 629–33
  late-filed documents 625
  post-hearing submissions 625
  procedure 624
  proceedings 624–6
  reopening of the hearing 626–8
comparison of 1976/2010 Rules 611–13
conduct of the hearing 604–11
  cross-examination 605–6
  declarations 606–7
  hearing, record of the 610–11
  hearings held in camera 607–8, 617
  investment tribunals, practice of 607–8
  Iran-US Claims Tribunal 608
  notice of hearing and witness
      testimony 605
  oral statements, translation of 610–11
  witness examination:
    conditions for 604–7, 613–17
    manner of 604–7, 613–17
    without physical presence of 609–10
  witnesses, retirement of 608–9
efficiency 604
equal treatment 604, 626
fair trial, notion of 601
fairness 604, 626
IBA Rules on the Taking of Evidence 602
investment tribunals, extracts from 613–17
Iran-US Claims Tribunal, extracts
    from 617–24
  Language Services 611
language of arbitration 610
legal assistants in attendance 608
notice of hearing 602–4
oaths 606–7
observation of hearings 608
overregulation 605
place of arbitration 603
prior notice 603
procedure 602
questioning witnesses, aggregate amount of
    time for 941–2
rebuttal evidence 612–3
stenographic transcripts 611

telecommunication 602, 609–10
  videoconferencing 609
  testimony 608–9
  time, indication of 603
  travel requirements 603
Hong Kong International Arbitration Centre (HKIAC) 6

ICSID, *see* International Centre for the Settlement of Investment Disputes
implied consent, theory of 22, 55–7
initiation of arbitration
  see also arbitral tribunal: objections to the jurisdiction of; language, choice of; notice and calculation of periods of time; notice initiating arbitration; representation and assistance; statement of claim; statement of defence
  issues, identification and clarification of 345–549
Inter-American Panama Convention 86
Inter-American Commercial Arbitration Commission 6, 194, 361
Inter-American Commission on Human Rights 180, 218
Inter-American Convention on Extraterritorial Validity of Foreign Judgments and Arbitral Awards 741
Inter-American Panama Convention 86
interim measures 513–52, 917–18
  see also initiation of arbitration
  assets 519
  awards vs orders 525
  background 513–4
  categories of 518
  comparison of 1976/2010 Rules 532–3
  conditions for the ordering of 520–4
    agreement of the parties, conditions imposed by 524
    'harm not adequately reparable by an award of damages' 521–2
    likely harms, appropriate balance of 522
    success on the merits, reasonable possibility of 522–4
  conditions on the awarding of 524
  costs and damages, liability for 528–9
  costs of, security for 526–7
  criteria/guidelines 536
  decisions regarding 530
  definition of 517
  detail of 515–16
  disclosure of material change 527–8
  duplicative proceedings 518
  enforcement and recognition 519
  form (award or order) for granting 524–5
  function and scope 516
  investment tribunals, extracts from 533–43
  Iran-US Claims Tribunal 518, 530, 543–52
  issuance of:
    by arbitral tribunals 529–30
    by municipal courts 529–30
  modify, Tribunal's power to 525–6
  precondition of a request by a party 516–17
  preliminary orders, issuance of 530–2
  preservation of evidence, conditions relaxed for 524
  prima facie test 523, 536
  procedure for granting 514–15
  protective measures 530
  sale or transfer of goods 518
  securing funds 519
  security, ordering of 526–7
  suspend, Tribunal's power to 525–6
  terminate, Tribunal's power to 525–6
  types of 517–20
    arbitral process, prevent prejudice to 518–19
    preserve assets for possible satisfaction of award 519
    preserve evidence 519–20
    status quo, maintain or restore 518
  urgency 536
International Bar Association (IBA)
  Code of Ethics 213, 711, 787
  Rules on the Taking of Evidence 556, 578, 602, 642–3, 647
International Centre for Dispute Resolution (ICDR) 6
  International Arbitration Rules 6, 194, 196, 397, 449
International Centre for the Settlement of Investment Disputes (ICSID)
  additional awards 872
  Additional Facility Rules 89, 109, 449, 517
  administrative and financial regulation 27, 90, 108, 850, 864
  Arbitration Rules 7, 9, 41, 181, 192, 269, 367, 607, 615, 758, 871, 886

International Centre for the Settlement of
    Investment Disputes (*cont.*)
  case administration 27, 61, 63–5, 67, 78,
      89, 90, 100, 105, 107, 109, 120,
      129, 178, 181, 201, 209, 220,
      232–3, 246, 256, 271–2, 290, 350,
      384, 417–18, 432–3, 459–62, 469,
      470, 476–8, 496–7, 558, 566, 569,
      570, 577–9, 614, 616–17, 629,
      718, 736, 842, 851, 863, 866, 870,
      874–5, 881–2, 885, 887–90, 901
  confidentiality of awards 37
  costs of arbitration 881
  Convention 89, 181, 350, 451, 755, 805,
      828, 831, 834
  headquarters 101–2, 108–9
  investment treaty claim 890
  location of 89
  oath of sincerity 643
  offer of World Bank's facilities 107
  Schedule of Fees 854, 855, 858, 864
  Secretariat of 181
  Secretary-General of 166, 180, 183, 218,
      272, 365, 761, 850
    Deputy 183, 220, 244, 246–7
  tribunals 181, 606
International Chamber of Commerce (ICC)
  arbitral institution, as an 4, 7, 365, 755
  arbitration disputes 745
  arbitral tribunals 115, 205, 266
  Arbitration Rules 2, 7, 57, 58, 80, 94, 112,
      119 120, 122, 125, 129, 170, 194,
      196, 199, 259, 319, 329, 352, 365,
      371, 397, 399, 449, 625, 692, 694,
      701, 703, 715, 742–5, 758, 866
  awards of 127, 190, 470, 563
  consolidation, practice on 57
  cost rules 855, 864
  deadlock-breaking provision 701
  General Counsel of the 259
  International Court of Arbitration 54,
      171, 723
  party-appointed arbitrators, disapproval
      of 191
  practice of 191
  supervisory function 337
  terms of reference 376
  texts adopted by 118
International Court of Justice (ICJ)
  contentious cases 68
  deliberation 713, 728
  expert advice, on 637
  international authority 285, 292
  Judges of 726
  practice of 40, 66, 536, 545, 573, 626,
      702, 803
  President of 153, 341–2, 702
  Reports 165
  Statute of 711, 723, 828, 831, 834
international investment agreements (IIAs)
  arbitration arising under 20, 22
  consolidation provisions 58
  cost of arbitration 874
  non-contractual disputes 416
  number of 7–8
  proliferation of 7
  state–state arbitration 873
  types of 8
International Trade Commission (ITC) 103
Iran–US Claims Tribunal
  amicus curiae submissions 46
  applicable law 128–9
  appointing authority, lessons from 340–3
  Arco Exploration case 653–5, 664–5
  Behring International case 660–3, 665
  choice of law 142–4
  costs of 848
  default 683–9
  disclosure guidelines 200–3
  disruptions 280–1
  equality 33
  extracts from the practice of:
    amendments to claim or defence 474,
        479–89
    applicable law 131–42
    apportionment of costs 891–6
    arbitral tribunal 463–6
    arbitrators, challenge of 235–41,
        257–67, 273–4
    deposit of costs 903–5
    designating and appointing
        authorities 155–6
    duty to disclose 202–5
    evidence 580–600
    exclusion of liability 330–5
    failure to act and other disruptions
        290–304
    form and effect 766–79
    further written statements 498–505
    general provisions 41–5, 69–77
    notice and calculation of periods of
        time 404–8

post-award proceedings 825–7, 815–21, 832–7, 832–7, 808–11
replacement of arbitrators 322–3
representation and assistance 356–7
settlement and other termination 793–800
statement of claim 419–21
statement of defence 434–47
time limits on submission 508–12
tribunal-appointed experts 650–67
failure to act 280–1
general and tribunal rules (1983) 69–73
government challenges, *see* arbitrators: challenges of
hearings 617–24
closure of 629–33
conduct of 608
language services 611
interim measures 518, 530, 543–52
language, choice of 375, 377, 379–80
annexes 384
communications 383
contracts 383
correspondence 383
decrees 383
extracts from 385–92
invoices 383
place of arbitration 109
portions of laws 383
shipping documents 383
technical reports 383
translation criteria 382–3
tribunal guidelines 383
nature of proceedings before 41–5
notice and calculation of periods of time 401–2
notice initiating arbitration 366–8
other practice of 142–4
overview of 183–91
representation and assistance 353–4
Richard D Harza case 656–60, 665
Shahin Shaine Ebrahimi case 650–3, 663–4
Starrett Housing case 655–6, 665–6
statement of claim 415–16
statement of defence 426
tribunal rules (1983) 74–7
waiver 696
witnesses, practice of 563–4
Iranian Centre for International Legal Affairs 239

Iranian Social Insurance Organization 594

Kuala Lumpur Regional Centre for Arbitration 6, 18

language, choice of 375–92
see also initiation of arbitration
annexes 382
arbitrators and experts, linguistic backgrounds of 375
award, language of the 375
bilingualism 378–82
bills of lading 382
business correspondence 382
comparison of 1996/2010 Rules 384
costs of translation and interpretation 384
documents and exhibits, translation of 382–4
English 378–9
investment tribunals, extracts from 384–5
investor-state arbitration 377
invoices 382
Iran-US Claims Tribunal, at the 375, 377, 379–80
annexes 384
communications 383
contracts 383
correspondence 383
decrees 383
extracts from 385–92
invoices 383
portions of laws 383
shipping documents 383
technical reports 383
translation criteria 382–3
tribunal guidelines 383
language ability 378
language of arbitration, determination of 376–82
language of proceedings 931
oral presentations, possible need for interpretation of 931
translation and interpretation, cost of 931
translation of documents, possible need for 931
national languages, equality of 378
oral proceedings 375, 379
promptness 377
provisions for 376
Spanish 379
written statements 375, 379

London Court of International
    Arbitration (LCIA) 7, 150, 337
  Arbitration Rules 34, 37, 55–6, 79, 94,
      120, 313, 327, 329, 365, 371, 377,
      397, 414, 449, 563, 703, 733, 735,
      743, 755–6, 758
    case administration 62, 232, 271, 272,
      450, 477, 533
    costs of arbitration 881
    division of, challenge decision by a 179–80,
      221–2
    fee schedule of 855
    practice of 54, 365
    supervisory function 337

member
  definition of 994
Mexican-United States General Claims
    Commission 581
model arbitration clause for contracts 17
multi-party arbitration 943, 991

NAFTA (North American Free Trade
    Agreement) 166
  awards 736, 889
  breach of obligations 419
  Chapter 11: 6, 19, 20, 22, 26, 27, 31, 32,
      33, 35, 38, 60–1, 63–8, 78, 80–1,
      87–90, 92, 100–1, 103–9, 112,
      129–30, 159, 178, 180, 183, 209,
      218–20, 233–4, 244, 246–7, 256,
      271–2, 290, 330, 352, 355, 361,
      369, 384–5, 417–18, 432–3, 457,
      459–63, 469–70, 476–9, 496–8,
      558, 566, 569–70, 572, 577–9,
      614–17, 629, 649, 718–19, 736–7,
      740, 762–3, 807, 815, 831, 842,
      851, 863–6, 870, 874–7, 880–2,
      884–5, 887–9, 901–2
    Notes of Interpretation 37
  disclosure 39
  Free Trade Commission 37, 41
  interpretation of 493
  provisions of 8, 183
  publication of awards 756–7
  status of 871
  tribunals 415, 492, 875
national
  definition of 994
National Defence Industries Organization
    825

National Industries Organization of Iran
    (NIOI) 262
New York Convention (Convention on the
    Recognition and Enforcement of
    Foreign Arbitral Awards)
  a-national awards under 43, 45, 86
  applicability of 43
  arbitration system 1, 3, 26, 428, 762
  articles of 56, 84, 87, 117, 125, 376, 393,
      692, 741, 744–5, 757, 828
  'awards' 524, 540, 710, 741
  'binding', meaning of 741
  enforceability of an award 32, 42, 84,
      86–7, 115, 306, 381, 626, 740, 742
  estoppel 367
  'in writing' requirement 366
  NAFTA parties 89
  national law 44, 674
  non-commercial disputes 18
  non-contractual disputes 25
  'null and void', use of the phrase in 454
  parties to 102, 105, 107
  recognition and enforcement 381
  scope of application 18–19
  standards adopted in 35
  UNCITRAL Rules, consistency with 515
notice and calculation of periods of time
    393–408
  see also initiation of arbitration
  background 393–4
  comparison of 1976/2010 Rules 403–4
  deadlines 403
  deemed receipt 399, 403
  delivery 394
  designated/authorized addresses 399–400, 403
  Drafting Committee 398
  electronic communication 395–7, 400–1
  forms a notice may take 395–7
  investment tribunals, extracts from 404
  Iran-US Claims Tribunal, application
      by 401–2
    extracts from the practice of 404–8
  means of communication 397
  method of calculating time periods 402–3
  place of business 397
  procedure 394
  receipt of notice 397
  record of transmission 396, 400
  when notice become effective 397–402
    electronic communication 400–1
    means of delivery 399–401

notice 'deemed to have been
        received' 397–9
notice initiating arbitration
    see also initiation of arbitration
    additional information 364
    arbitration proceedings, date of
        commencement of 362–3
    comparison of 1976/2010 Rules 368–9
    date of receipt of notice 359
    Dutch legal system 366–7
    insufficiency of 364–5
    international investment agreements
        and 365–6
    investment tribunals, extracts from 369–70
    Iran-US Claims Tribunal, at the 366–8
    mandatory information 363
    multi-party arbitration 368
    notice requirement 359
    procedure 360
    provisions of the Rules 369
    requirement to communicate 361–2
    response to 370–3
        absence 373
        comparison of 1976/2010 Rules 373
        insufficiency of 373
        lateness 373
        mandatory contents of 372
        optional contents of 373
        procedure 370
        requirement to respond 370–2
    statement of claim vs 361, 366
    statements of claim and 410
    sufficiency of 364–5
    two-tiered approach 361–2, 371–2
    wording of the Rules 369

Permanent Court of Arbitration (PCA)
    appointing authority 152–3
    arbitration under 61, 100, 542, 761
    Arbitrator's Declaration of Acceptance 202
    arbitrator's fees 854
    case administration 26, 38, 50, 59–60, 64,
        69, 167–8, 330, 352, 355, 361,
        385, 425, 434, 451, 474, 539, 541,
        569, 576, 616–17, 650, 696, 719,
        737, 761, 792, 815, 851–2, 864–6,
        882, 886, 889–90, 902–3
    designation, process for requesting 153,
        270–1, 339
    disputes under UNCITRAL Rules 158
    fees and expenses of 792
    independence, model statements of 198
    International Bureau of 854
    Optional Rules for Arbitrating Disputes
        between two States 7
    representation on 152
    role of 153
    selection by 28
    Secretary-General of 90, 148, 150–3,
        155–6, 162, 164, 167, 172, 178,
        219, 273, 275, 339–41, 841, 846,
        848, 852–6, 858–61, 876, 896
    assistance from 270–1
    wrongdoing 327
place of arbitration of UNCITRAL rules
        77–109
    comparison of 1976/2010 Rules 95–6
    'deemed to have been made' 92–3
    investment tribunals, extracts from
        96–109
    cost and support services, availability
        of 102, 108
    law on arbitral procedure, suitability
        of 102
    multilateral treaties 102
    neutrality factor 101–2
    parties and arbitrators, convenience
        of 102, 107
    proximity of evidence 103, 108
    subject matter in dispute, location
        of 103, 108
    Iran-US Claims Tribunal:
        extracts from the practice of 109
    location of meetings 93–5
    meaning of 'place of arbitration' 78–9
    selection of place of arbitration 80–92
        considerations 80–91
        enforcement of the award 85–7
        legal significance of 91–2
        local law, nature, and suitability of
            80–5
        neutrality 87–9
        practical considerations 89–91
post-award proceedings 801–37
    see also award, the
    additional award 821–7
        comparison of 1976/2010 Rules
            824–5
        general comments on 821–4
        investment tribunals, extracts from 825
        Iran-US Claims Tribunal, extracts
            from 825–7

post-award proceedings (*cont.*)
    procedure 821
        request denied 825
        request granted 825
    background 801–2
    correction of the award 811–21
        comparison of 1976/2010 Rules 814–15
        correction process 811–14
        investment tribunals, extracts from 815
        Iran-US Claims Tribunal, extracts from 815–21
        procedure 811
    finality of awards 827–37
        general comments on 827–31
        investment tribunals, extracts from 831–2
        Iran-US Claims Tribunal, extracts from 832–7
        fraud or corruption, revision to address 836–7
        inherent power to reconsider 827–37
    general comments on 827–31
        investment tribunals, extracts from 831–2
        Iran-US Claims Tribunal, extracts from 832–7
    interpretation of the award 802–11
        comparison of 1976/2010 Rules 806
        interpretation process 802–6
        investment tribunals, extracts from 806–8
        Iran-US Claims Tribunal, extracts from 808–11
        procedure 802
    limited power of review 832–5
procedural conference
    discretion to schedule 47
property rights 25

representation and assistance
    see also initiation of arbitration
    changes in representation 350
    comparison of 1976/2010 Rules 354–5
    identity and role of advisors, communication of 351–2
    identity and role of representatives, communication of 351–2
    investment tribunals, extracts from 355–6
    Iran-US Claims Tribunal, practice of 353–4
    extracts from the practice of 356–7
    late appointments 350
    procedure of 347–8
    proof of authority 350, 352–3
    right to 347
    right to, by persons chosen 348–50
res judicata, doctrine of 190, 222–3, 682, 738–9, 741, 767, 807

scope of application of UNCITRAL Rules 16–29
    arbitration, general comments on 17
    comparison of 1976/2010 rules 24–6
    defined legal relationship 18
    investor-state arbitration:
        future transparency rules for 23–4
    model arbitration clause 24
    model arbitration clause for contracts 17
    modification of the Rules 19–20
    non-derogation from mandatory law (Article 1(2) 1976 Rules) 28–9
    parties to an arbitration agreement 16–17
    party autonomy 19–20
    presumptive scope of application 20–2
    scope and modification (Article 1(1) 1976 Rules) 26–8
    scope of the rules 18
    writing requirement, elimination of 18–19
Secretary-General
    definition of 98, 294
settlement and other termination 781–800, 920–1
    awards on agreed terms, technical requirements for 790
    background 781
    comparison of 1976/2010 Rules 790–2
    grounds for termination, other 788–90
        'impossible' continuation of arbitration 788–90
        'remaining matters,' existence of 790
        'unnecessary' continuation of arbitration 788–90
    investment tribunals, extracts from 792–3
    Iran-US Claims Tribunal, extracts from 793–800
    procedure 781–2
    settlement 782–8
        practice of award on agreed terms 782–4
        pre-settlement negotiations 786–8
        settlement agreement, discretion to record 784–6

settlement agreement, types of 782–4
settlement negotiations, possible 936–7, 985
statement of claim 916
   see also amendments to claim or defence; initiation of arbitration; statement of defence
   comparison of 1976/2010 Rules 416–17
   contents of 412–14
   investment tribunals, extracts from 417–19
   Iran-US Claims Tribunal 415–16
      extracts from 419–21
   notice of arbitration and 410
   procedure of 410–11
   sanctions for an inadequate 414–15
   submission of 411–12
statement of defence
   see also amendments to claim or defence; initiation of arbitration; statement of claim
   comparison of 1976/2010 Rules 429–31
   contents of 423–4
   counterclaims 421–2
      arbitral tribunal, jurisdiction of 426–8
      Counter-claim Memorial 426
      general issues with 424–6
      Iran-US Claims Tribunal 426
      late 442–4
      submission of 424–8
      supplementary provisions on 428–9
   investment tribunals, extracts from 432–4
   Iran-US Claims Tribunal, extracts from 434–47
   'out of the same contract' 430
   prejudice, concept of 425
   procedure of 422
   set-off, claims for the purpose of 424–9
   social security 431
   submission of 422–3
      time limit 422
   taxation 431
statements of claim and defence 409–47
   see also amendments to claim or defence; statement of claim; statement of defence
   written pleadings 409–10
Stockholm Chamber of Commerce (SCC) 7, 556
   case administration 451
   Rules 34, 371

Swiss Arbitration Association (SAA) 54

termination, *see* settlement and other termination
third parties 31
   1976 UNCITRAL Rules and 31
   arbitral process, participation in the 36, 39–41
time limits on submission 505–12
   see also further written statements; initiation of arbitration
   comparison of 1976/2010 Rules 508
   deliberations 508
   equality and fairness 508
   general comments on 505–8
   investment tribunals, extracts from 508
   Iran-US Claims Tribunal, extracts from 508–12
   late-filed documents 508
   linguistic modality, use of 506
   procedure 505
   'showing of sufficient cause' 507
time, calculation of periods of, *see* notice and calculation of periods of time
tribunal-appointed experts 635–67
   see also evidence and hearings
   appointment 638–40, 650–62
      complexity of 639
      cost-benefit analysis 639
      expediency of 639
      selection process 640
   background 635–6
   comparison of 1976/2010 Rules 648
   decision-making process of 645
   expert hearings 646–7, 667
   expert report 640, 645–6, 663–6
   expertise of 637
   fact-finding duties 638
   general comments on 637–8
   IBA Rules on the Taking of Evidence 642–3
   ICSID and 643
   impartiality and independence of, objections to 640, 642–3, 648
   investment tribunals, extracts from 648–50
   Iran-US Claims Tribunal, extracts from 650–67
      Arco Exploration case 653–5, 664–5
      Behring International case 660–3, 665
      Richard D Harza case 656–60, 665

tribunal-appointed experts (*cont.*)
  Shahin Shaine Ebrahimi case 650–3, 663–4
  Starrett Housing case 655–6, 665–6
  methods for employing assistance of 638
  neutrality of 643
  non-compliance 644
  oath of sincerity and confidentiality 643
  party-appointed 'expert witnesses' 647–8
  party-appointed experts 636
  pre- and post-appointment 642
  procedure 636–7
  qualifications of, objections to 640, 642–3, 645
  relevant information, provision of 644–5, 662–3
  terms of reference 640–2, 650–62

unjust enrichment, doctrine of 141, 472, 482
United Nations Convention on Contracts for the International Sale of Goods 118, 122
United Nations Convention on Independent Guarantees and Stand-by Letters of Credit 396
United Nations Convention on the Law of the Sea (UNCLOS) 7
United Nations Convention on the Use of Electronic Communications in International Contracts 395, 397

Vienna Convention on the Law of Treaties (VCLT) 21

waiver 691–6
  see also default and waiver
  automatic application, by 692
  background 691
  comparison of 1976/2010 Rules 695
  failure to object 694–5
  general comments on 692–3
  investment tribunals, extracts from 695–6
  Iran-US Claims Tribunal, extracts from 696
  level of knowledge required 693–5
    arbitration experience of parties 693
    failure to raise an objection 694
    mischief 693
    procedural manoeuvres 693
  procedural non-compliance 692, 694–5
  procedural rights 692
  procedure 691
  'without undue delay' 695
Washington Convention, on the Settlement of Investment Disputes Between States and Nationals of Other States 101, 229, 450
witness statements, *see* evidence
witnesses, *see* evidence
World Trade Organisation 66
written statements, *see* evidence; further written statements; statement of claim and defence

Printed and bound by CPI Group (UK) Ltd, Croydon, CR0 4YY